FINANCIAL MANAGEMENT
1880–1934

Volume 1

Edited and Introduced by
Morgen Witzel

THOEMMES

Financial Management, 1880–1934

Edited and Introduced by **Morgen Witzel**

Volume 1
Twenty Years of Inside Life in Wall Street, or Revelations of the Personal Experiences of a Speculator ... Illustrated (1880)
W. W. Fowler

Volume 2
Trusts, Pools and Corporations (1905)
William Z. Ripley

Volume 3
Corporation Finance (1910)
Edward S. Meade

Volume 4
Corporation Finance. An Exposition of the Principles and Methods governing the Promotion, Organization and Management of Modern Corporations (1909)
William H. Lough

Volume 5
Concentration and Control: A Solution of the Trust Problem in the United States (1914)
Charles R. van Hise

Credit and International Trade: How they Work in Practice (1934)
Barnard Ellinger

Volume 6
Problems in Business Finance (1921)
Edmund E. Lincoln

Volumes 7 and 8
Collected Articles and Chapters

Printed in England by Antony Rowe Ltd, Chippenham

TWENTY YEARS OF INSIDE LIFE IN WALL STREET

William W. Fowler

With an Introduction by
Morgen Witzel

THOEMMES PRESS

This edition published by Thoemmes Press, 2001

Thoemmes Press
11 Great George Street
Bristol BS1 5RR, England

http://www.thoemmes.com

Financial Management, 1880–1934
8 Volumes : ISBN 1 85506 633 5

British Library Cataloguing-in-Publication Data
A CIP record of this title is available from the British Library

Publisher's Note

The Publisher has gone to great lengths to ensure the quality of this reprint but points out that some imperfections in the original book may be apparent.

This book is printed on acid-free paper, sewn, and cased in a durable buckram cloth.

INTRODUCTION

Of all the disciplines of modern management, financial management is one which can perhaps lay the greatest claim to antiquity. Since classical times, large business empires have been built around a solid financial core, usually a bank or similar concern. The great international trading concerns of Tyre and Carthage were built around the financial strengths of the temples of those cities. In Athens, successful bankers like Pasion invested their profits in trading and manufacturing businesses, as did their successors in Rome.[1] Two thousand years later in the European Renaissance, we find the Medici family building up a large and diversified international business in textiles manufacturing, wholesaling and carrying trades centred on what was then Europe's largest bank. A century after the Medici rose to power, Jakob Fugger of Augsburg used the profits of his silver mining concessions in the Tyrol to found first a bank and then a whole series of manufacturing and trading enterprises across Europe and into Asia, moving into businesses as diverse as horse-breeding and wine-making. In these latter two cases in particular, it is notable how control of the financial apparatus was closely equated with control of the whole enterprise; in the case of the Medici, the owning family often surrendered managerial control of the diversified enterprises, usually through a series of partnerships with managers and agents, but always remain closely involved with the management of the bank.

It is no coincidence that the rise of these two organizations, the largest privately-owned businesses the world had yet seem, came at a time and place when financial instruments and markets were undergoing rapid change and development. Max Weber, in his classic *The Protestant Ethic and the Spirit of Capitalism*, published in 1904–05, dates the rise of the modern business

[1] See Karl Moore and David Lewis (2000) *Foundations of Corporate Empire*, London: FT-Prentice Hall, for a more detailed account of financial activity in these times.

organization to the Protestant reformation to the sixteenth century; but many of the changes Weber described date in fact to the later Middle Ages, and the impetus behind them was Catholic rather than Protestant. In the thirteenth century the Italian-born theologian Thomas Aquinas concluded that money and trade were important elements of society, as they provided necessary goods for the welfare of the people as a whole, implying that material and spiritual welfare were in some way connected. The same ideas were elucidated much more powerfully by his fifteenth-century successors, Antonio of Florence and Bernardino of Siena. Partly as a result of this new social acceptability of trade and commerce, and partly as a result of the fortunes being made – and lost – in the Oriental spice trade, financial instruments developed and proliferated. This was the age of the commoditization of money, when the bill of exchange – ancestor to the modern banknote – became the main medium of exchange for all but the smallest and simplest transactions. Usury, the lending of money for profit, was still officially prohibited, but a variety of other debt instruments such as bonds emerged, in which the lender shared in the risk and was allowed to retain a profit accordingly. Maritime insurance, developed in the Italian port cities in the twelfth century, evolved into a variety of other forms of insurance and investment. This was a era when, in 1340, the English government attempted to raise a new tax by creating a futures market in agricultural commodities and taxing the proceeds; it was an era when the government of the same country, two centuries later, sold bonds and bought money on the Antwerp money market to finance its foreign wars and internal debt. (Sir Thomas Gresham, founder of the Royal Exchange, first came to prominence as the brilliant financial agent who manipulated the Antwerp money market so successfully that he was able to clear the English crown's overseas debts in under twenty years.)

Enterprises like the Medici and Fugger organizations were complex and took years, sometimes generations, to build up, and most smaller firms, even those trading internationally, preferred to externalize their financial management to some degree. That is, rather than relying on purely internal financial resources, they sought financial backing from other institutions and investors. This could be done privately, as in the case of the many 'venture capital' projects in which Richard Arkwright engaged in the early years of the Industrial Revolution, but increasingly too they were done formally on the capital markets in major financial centres. These centres evolved and died organically over the centuries; Florence, built around the economic power of the Medici, was the financial capital of the fifteenth-century Western world until the eclipse of the Medici brought down much of the financial edifice. Florence was briefly succeeded by Genoa, but was overtaken by Antwerp in the north. By the end of the sixteenth century, however, London, newly rich on the back of international trade, was challenging Antwerp; there ensued a two-centuries long struggle between the two, which ended finally when Napoleon's Continental System bankrupted Antwerp and the leading London bankers, men like Thomas Coutts and Nathan Mayer Rothschild, moved London into a new era of international and intercontinental banking.

The variety of debt instruments which had emerged in the later Middle Ages remained the common method of raising money in the financial markets until the early eighteenth century. Again not by coincidence, the practice of issuing stocks and shares accompanies the transfer of power to London. This development was not without pain; the South Sea Bubble of the second decade of the century was just one of a series of financial scandals that rocked the European financial world. These scandals came about as a result of a credulous public seeking what appeared to be easy riches and the activities of dishonest promoters selling valueless or fraudulent securities. This was not the last time such things would happen but, aware of the dangers of such manias, the financial institutions of London such as Lloyds, the Royal Exchange and the newly-established Bank of England moved to become more regulated, stable and secure.

For all this, the London financial markets remained fairly small, and only comparatively few companies used them. There were some, such as the East India Company, which had a close relationship with the financial markets: the full history of the financial management of the Company has never been written, but is sure to be a fascinating story when it finally is. Most businesses, even large ones, preferred to avoid the speculative markets and develop longer and more enduring relationships, either with venture capital providers or with banks. Security rather than efficiency was the watchword in financial management, in a world where political and economic volatility was a major feature.

For British firms, this began to change in the late nineteenth century, when a period of prolonged peace and prosperity, excepting occasional crises such as the depression of the 1880s, began prompting businessmen to be more venturous. Here it was not the financial markets but a 'new' profession, that of accountancy, which showed the way. The development of this profession from that of book-keepers to fully-fledged accountants/consultants in the modern sense had been led by men like William Deloitte, who brought auditing to a high art and initiated the practice of companies appointing external auditors, and Edwin Waterhouse, who specialized in helping businesses convert from partnerships to share-holding corporations.[2] Between 1880 and 1914 the London Stock Exchange grew enormously in size, with hundreds of new share-trading firms emerging. At the same time, the British banking industry was going through a period of huge consolidation, led by men like the dynamic Edward Holden at the Midland bank. By 1914, London's position as the world's leading financial centre seemed to many observers unchallengeable.

In fact, of course, London's position was already being challenged by New York, where financial markets had developed under the pressure of imperatives that were often rather different.[3] In particular, the relationship between supply and demand as a financial commodity had developed under different circumstances and had different characteristics. London's markets had matured slowly, and for both investors seeking opportunities to use their capital and entrepreneurs seeking backing there were other channels. The American financial system, up to at least the American Civil War (1861–65) and really for some years after, was highly immature. A number of factors had contributed to this problem, not least of which was a stifling regulatory regime which prohibited large banks and discouraged the formation of large capital markets. An attempt in the early nineteenth century to set up large banks, led by Stephen Girard of the Philadelphia-based Bank of the United States had collapsed under government pressure. John Jacob Astor is probably the only notable American venture capitalist to

2 The modern firms of Deloitte Touche Ross and PricewaterhouseCoopers are descended from the accounting practices of these two men.

3 See the articles by E. M. Patterson and E .L. S. Patterson (no relation) in Volume 7.

emerge before the Civil War; thanks to American official distrust of big banks and big business, much of America's banking business was actually handled by British concerns.

This changed after the Civil War, and as is so often the case when examining aspects of late nineteenth-century American history, the railroads were the catalyst. The great long-distance railroads that connected America's cities and then opened up the West were highly risky ventures but they also promised enormous profits; further, they demanded very high levels of capital investment for both construction and operation. In order both to share risk and to raise capital, many of the early railroad promoters sold shares, and these were the first important share-owning corporations in America. So strong was the influence of the management practices of the railroad corporations in other business sectors that it was only a matter of time before other sectors began to follow suit. Stock markets emerged in Chicago, Philadelphia, Boston and San Francisco, but the largest and most important was that which developed along Wall Street in lower Manhattan, New York.

From Main Street to Wall Street

Wall Street in 1880 was a village, in which not only the share dealers and brokers but also many of the major investors knew each other personally. W.W. Fowler, in his classic *Twenty Years of Life on Wall Street*,[4] describes this milieu and its operating practices in detail. With fewer than a hundred companies listed on the exchange and a total issued share capital of around $300 million, this was a relatively cosy financial community in which comparatively few Americans participated. Many quoted companies had a few score shareholders at most, shareholders who often represented larger communities of interest and who had a strong and active interest in the management of the companies they owned. Many shareholders were also directors, and observing the behaviour of others it can be said that they often functioned as kind of non-executive board. J. P. Morgan, for example, did not take directorships in many of the companies in which he invested, but this did not stop him from making known his views on how those companies should be managed.

[4] See Volume 1.

From 1880 this began to change, slowly at first and then more rapidly. The number of shareholders rose from a few hundred thousand to 7 million by 1900, and then doubled to 14 million in 1924. By the latter date, more than one thousand companies were listed with the New York Stock Exchange. Even more astonishing is the growth in share capital, from $300 million in 1880 to $70 *trillion* by 1925.[5]

The structure of shareholding had also changed. In 1880, and even more so in 1900, the bulk of shares in most large businesses were held by a small number of shareholders. These men were mostly value investors, seeking long-term increase in share value over profits. The remainder were marginal shareholdings held by small speculators riding on the coat-tails of the big investors – Morgan, Vanderbilt, Rockefeller, Gould, Fisk and the like – and these were for the most part income investors, seeking either dividends or a quick profit through buying and selling a rapidly appreciating stock. A third class of small investor, those who put their money into investment trusts, can be identified closely with the value investors, as the trusts were dominated by the major shareholders.

Between 1880 and 1900 big business organizations increased greatly in power. This was a period of consolidation in American industry, and especially in financial markets. The prime mover in this trend was the banker J. P. Morgan, who with a coterie of like-minded bankers and financiers sought to amalgamate companies in key industries and consolidate shareholdings. Giant monopolies or near-monopolies such as United States Steel, Standard Oil, United States Shipbuilding, International Mercantile Marine, American Telephone & Telegraph (AT&T, later IT&T) and the mining and smelting giant ASARCO were created with Morgan's guidance and backing. Other leading industrialists of the day either sold out their interests and retired (like Andrew Carnegie), or joined forces and became heads of the new combines (like John D. Rockefeller at Standard Oil and Daniel Guggenheim at ASARCO). Rare was the industrialist such as Charles M. Schwab, who rejected an offer to join United States Steel and pursued his own path of dogged independence at Bethlehem Steel.

[5] These figures come from William Zebina Ripley's *Main Street and Wall Street*; see Volume 8.

Strange to relate today, Morgan's motives in creating these monopolies were, by his own lights at least, philanthropic. Like many leading businessmen and economists of his day, he watched the growth of the American free market economy and the 'Wild West' chaos of its virtually unrestrained competition with concern. In the competitive environment of the day he saw much waste and disorganization. Consumers were paying high prices for goods and services of low quality; at the other end of the value chain, investors were being repeatedly cheated by unscrupulous promoters. When government showed no sign of regulating the markets, Morgan used his massive financial clout to consolidate entire industry sectors, first in trusts and then, when these were outlawed and broken up in the 1890s, through massive holding corporations.[6]

In this hope, Morgan was largely disappointed. Some of the giant trusts were undoubted managerial and financial successes. The journalist Ida Tarbell, no friend to the trusts, concluded in her detailed study of Standard Oil[7] that the company was well-managed and efficient in its organization and methods. But others were failures, or at least failed to perform up to expectations. The weaknesses in the corporate system were quickly spotted, and attacks followed rapidly. But journalists were not the only ones to fear and dislike the trusts. Many of the leading academic figures in the study of finance and economics, like Edward S. Meade – one of the first professors of finance at the Wharton School and the man who gave the inaugural lectures on finance at Harvard Business School – Edmund Lincoln, William Lough, W. J. Jackman, Charles Gerstenberg and especially the vigorous and dogmatic William Z. Ripley from Harvard criticized the trusts and their corporate successors as undemocratic, lacking in transparency and against the best interests of the consumer and the shareholder alike.

The rise of corporation finance

It was against this background that the modern discipline of corporate finance (originally known as corporation finance)

[6] The edited collection by Ripley, *Trusts, Pools and Corporation*, gives details on the different forms; see Volume 2.

[7] Ida M. Tarbell (1904), *The History of Standard Oil Company*, New York: McLure & Philips.

emerged. Although Britain and the USA were both going through a period of great change at this time, the observer cannot help but feel that in the British case, before the First World War the change was more measured and managed, while after the war the main issue was not so much growth as simple financial survival in the face of the catastrophic wartime losses. Thus it is that the main writings from Britain of this period focus on issues such as international trade and on economics and money supply, and that the leading British financiers of this period were men like Edward Holden and Montagu Norman, the great postwar governor of the Bank of England, whose attention was focused as much on the macroeconomy as on individual micro-level economic and financial markets and practices. Following the war, led by Norman at the Bank of England, British banks became experts in rescue and turnaround practices, but this was a development of necessity rather than strategic policy.

British thinking on international trade is more interesting, and was considerably in advance of American thought on the subject where the concentration was, for reasons we shall come on to, still largely focused on the domestic scene. *Credit and International Trade* by Barnard Ellinger, a lecturer at the London School of Economics,[8] is an interesting example of this kind of work, especially in that it prefigures modern ideas on globalization. Ellinger uses the device of a case study, in which he follows a single set of financial transactions beginning with the growing and selling of cotton by a sharecropper in Mississippi to a buyer in New Orleans. From there the cotton is shipped to Liverpool, spun into a garment in Manchester, and exported again to China. But this is only part of the chain. The Chinese farmer who bought the garment grows and sells tea, which is sent to Manchuria. Soya beans grown in Manchuria are exported to Denmark, and butter from Denmark goes to England; meanwhile, pigs' bristles are exported from China to America, and so on. The global economy, says Ellinger, is a vast series of interconnecting chains, in which individual firms and banks each make up one link.

The linkages in these chains of transactions are, however, fragile. Ellinger considers five types of failure:

[8] See Volume 5.

1. Failure or alteration in consumptive demand
2. Failure of production, or alteration in the nature of production
3. Failure to release or acquire stocks of commodities
4. Failure to lend or borrow the money to finance the moving of the stocks of commodities
5. Government interference with the normal flow of trade through the imposition of tariffs, exchange restrictions, quotas, subsidies and other hindrances to trade.

It is interesting to note that although point 5 is important, the removal of government interference is not a guarantee to international trade growth, as the other 4 points may still obtain. An economic downturn in China can lead to a slackening of demand for cotton in the USA. The international financial manager, says Ellinger, needs to be aware of these linkages and the complex, ever-changing pattern of international finance.

We noted that the American system evolved in a different way, and a reading of the volumes and articles in this series shows just what those differences were. Briefly, we can categorize the specifics of the American problem into five categories:

1. the urgent need for rapid growth, and the development of financial institutions as engines for these;
2. a lax regulatory system which left companies, investors and markets open to fraud and deception and deprived shareholders of their rights;
3. a lack of transparency due to the domination of the financial markets by a few large vested interests;
4. a steady stream of criticism from government, the press and academia;
5. the need for a balance between the financial power of the investors and the management abilities of the entrepreneurs.

Engines of growth

Unlike the British economy, which by 1890 was mature and perhaps even in decline, the American economy had reached a state where rapid growth was a dominating feature. Often wild and uncontained, often punctuated by short sharp depressions which in turn led to bank failures, misery and strikes, the American economy with all its imperfections nonetheless succeeded in transforming itself into a second-rank producer of agricultural commodities in the mid-nineteenth century into a world-class industrial power by the early twentieth century. To do this, it needed money. Debt instruments could not raise the capital required, and the only way forward was through the sale of equity; hence the amazing growth of Wall Street alluded to above.

The rapid proliferation of companies requiring to raise capital in this way meant a corresponding demand for managers who were familiar with the workings of financial markets and the techniques of financial management. With the disappearance of the Wall Street village and its replacement with a larger and more impersonal market, deals could not longer be done on the basis of relationships. The more complex economics of shareholder capitalism brought concepts like shareholder value into focus. How much dividend should companies pay, and when? How much equity should a company issue, and in what kinds of shares? These and other technical issues became the central focus of financial management.

It also became apparent that without an understanding of the engines of finance, a manager could not be effective. The case of William C. Durant is instructive. The founder of General Motors, Durant was a talented engineer, designer and salesman, but he never mastered the arts of finance. His company was constantly in financial difficulties and his directors, who were usually also major shareholders, eventually deposed him. The same fate befell other car-makers, notably John North Willys at Willys Overland. Understanding finance equated with understanding and maintaining control.

Beginning with T. L. Greene's *Corporation Finance* in 1897,[9] textbooks on the subject intended for the instruction of managers began to proliferate. The Wharton School at the University of Pennsylvania was the first university institution to offer degree courses in financial management, but Harvard and others soon followed. By 1914 it was recognized that financial management occupied a central place in the set of managerial skills.

Shareholders and their rights

If some managers were financial naive, others understood the system and how to play it so well that they could capitalize on

[9] See Volume 7.

the naivete of others. The history of American finance from 1880 to the First World War is at times an unedifying one. Fraud was a constant problem, yet the total losses from fraud were probably only a very small percentage of total profits and gains from financial investment at the time. Although some newspapers fulminated against it, a much more serious problem was the use of financial instruments to deprive shareholders of their rights.

William Ripley, whose particular bugbear this was, documents instances of practice in his famous *Main Street and Wall Street*.[10] His particular target was the then common practice of creating two classes of stock, Class A or non-voting stocks, and Class B or voting stocks. He documented some abuses of the system: Industrial Rayon Corporation, for example, issued 598,000 Class A non-voting shares for distribution to the public, with just 2,000 voting or B shares reserved for the management. Hires Root Beer issued 180,000 Class A shares, with 3,872 Class B shares reserved to a trust owned by the Hires family. Other, less blatant examples could be found in plenty. Particularly objectionable was the practice, when merging two companies, of exchanging voting stock in the old companies for non-voting stock in the new entity. Ripley attacked this system as depriving stockholders, the owners of capital, of their rights of ownership; in a famous essay entitled 'A Mess of Pottage', he attacked both corporate management for deliberately hoodwinking shareholders and shareholders for tamely surrendering their rights in exchange for dividends.

Lack of transparency

In part, the problem was caused by a lack of transparency whereby companies were often neither required to make their accounts public nor did so voluntarily. Strange though it may seem, as late as 1920 many states did not require corporations registered there to make public their accounts. This practice had been attacked as early as the 1860s by the journalist and business writer Henry Varnum Poor when discussing the management of the railroads, who argued that transparency was essential if companies were to have the long-term support not only of shareholders but of society at large. The need for

[10] See Volume 8.

transparency is argued by academics like Lincoln and Meade in these volumes, and also notably by Charles Van Hise in his book *Concentration and Control*.[11] Van Hise accepts that business concentration and the growth of large corporations is necessary and essential, but like Ripley is alive to the potential abuses. He sees transparency as a necessity in checking abuses and ensuring shareholder rights are respected.

But how much transparency is enough? It was argued, with some cogency, that absolute commercial transparency would result in rivals gaining access to sensitive commercial information. Also, even if all information were made available to shareholders, would they bother to read it and act upon it? As a number of the authors in this collection note, shareholders themselves are not homogenous, and they have different motives; even then it was recognized that some shareholders were investing in order to receive dividend income and others to increase the value of their portfolio. The interests of these two groups could be and often were in direct conflict. If shareholders disagreed over the direction management should take, where did this leave management?

It was also argued that financial information was none of the shareholders' business; if the separation between ownership and control were to be maintained, management needed to be given absolute authority to make the right decisions. This view was held strongly by many directors, and was opposed with equal fervour by the journalists, academics and politicians who opposed them. To the former party, centralized control was essential for efficiency management; to the latter, it was anti-democratic and dangerous to America's social and economic interests.

Public criticism

In maintaining their views that concentration of control and authority in the hands of a few was the best way to manage efficiently, the financiers came under attack from two fronts. First, there were the journalists and public opinion, led by the 'muck-raking' journalists such as Ida Tarbell at *McLure's* and *Collier's*, who argued that no matter how efficient the big companies were, they were harming America's interests. Second,

[11] See Volume 5.

there were the academics, ranging from Edward Meade to William Ripley, who believed that centralized control was creating not efficiency, but its opposite. For them, and likewise for writers like Van Hise and William Lough, transparency which would allow scrutiny of the actions of management was the key balancing measure which would allow the system to work. Successive governments, notably those of Woodrow Wilson and the two Roosevelts, listened to the journalists and the academics, and gradually a system of nationwide regulation developed which forced companies to open up their accounts for scrutiny. Today, we take much of this legislation for granted, even though high-profile anti-trusts suits continue to be launched (IT&T in the 1970s, Microsoft in the 1990s). But for several decades, this issue was the touchstone on which most financial legislation and financial practice depended.

Ownership and control

The thesis of the separation of ownership and control is usually attributed to Adolph Berle and Gardiner Means in their famous book *The Modern Corporation* in 1932, but the first American writer to use the phrase was probably William Ripley (who taught Berle at Harvard), and he was only articulating a concept which had been discussed as early as before the First World War. If professional management was essential to run a company, and if those managers should be persons other than those who owned the company's capital, then how did the latter maintain control over their property? The answer, for Ripley as for Berle and Means, was that they did not (the ultimate extension of this thesis can be found in James Burnham's *The Management Revolution*, published a decade later, in which he foresaw managers seizing control of companies from their owners and actually displacing the capitalists as society's ruling class).

The problem, as Ripley saw it, was that most shareowners were quite happy to surrender control in exchange for dividends. He quotes the great Supreme Court Justice Louis Brandeis on this point: 'There is no such thing to my mind...as an *innocent* stockholder. He may be innocent in fact, but socially he cannot be held innocent. He accepts the benefits of the system. It is his business and his obligation to see that those who represent him carry out a policy which is consistent with public welfare.' Comments

Ripley: 'This accountability for wealth underlies and justifies the whole institution of private property on which the government of our great country is founded.'[12]

Yet it is precisely this accountability, he believed, which was being denied within the framework of the modern business corporation and the system of shareholder capitalism. The shareholder system has thus brought about a separation of ownership and control. The owners of capital and the managers have become separate people and, in many cases, the links between them have become deliberately severed. The concept of the corporation as an artificial person, Ripley believed, simply did not reflect the real situation. Instead, corporations resembled either battlegrounds between warring tribes as shareholders and managers struggled for control, or – more commonly – they had developed into semi-feudal relationships in which shareholders were no more than passive suppliers of capital and managers exercised almost unfettered control. Managers could and did dispose of assets or even of entire companies – assets and companies which belonged to the shareholders – without having to consult the majority of the shareholders themselves.

Two factors, Ripley believed, had led to the present situation. The first was that the increasing size of corporations was leading to financial experts taking an overly prominent role. Many businesses, he comments, 'have outgrown the financial capacity of the purely operating men'; in other words, the emphasis in terms of managerial control was shifting from the production and design function to the corporate finance function. This was not without its dangers: neither production managers nor financial managers were equipped to lead a modern large national or multi-national business. A partnership between the two was required, with each party contributing their requisite strengths and knowledge to the mix. Yet that partnership seldom materialized. Instead, the financial managers through their control of capital flows usually got their way and held sway over the production managers, dictating policy and strategy throughout the company. And, through that same control over capital flows, the financial managers could also control the shareholders. Ripley, somewhat savagely, puts it thus:

[12] See Volume 8.

> But inherently it is more often the banker, the financial man, who in the struggle for survival comes out on top. This it is which creates the situation wherein the power of the banker...is first applied to the subjugation of the operating group; and then, to cap the climax, seeks to reduce the great body of shareholders to subjection. This is the situation we find confronting the United States in 1925.[13]

The shape of corporate finance

The nature of modern corporate finance, then, whether the company operates locally or globally, has been influenced by four primary needs:

1. the need for capital resources to fund expansion
2. the need for professional management
3. the need for accountability and openness
4. the need for a balance between technical and financial management

It is against this background that most of our later practice has developed. Current views on financial instruments, efficiency of financial management and accounting, accountability, shareholder value and integration between the finance function and other departments still hark back to these early twentieth century debates. Indeed, many of these have not been resolved today. The issue of accountability, for example, still rears its head from time to time. Who really owns the company? The shareholders own its capital, but does this give them the right to dictate to management how the latter should perform their functions? The same applies to shareholder value. Which shareholders should take priority, those who seek to earn profits from dividends or those who seek to build the value of their portfolios? Even today, few companies know their shareholders well and few make the latters' needs a central priority in management decision-making, unless a number of large shareholders are themselves present on the board.

If corporate finance is the oldest management discipline, it is also the one that has changed the greatest. The advent of new communications technology and real-time information has

[13] See Volume 8.

changed the nature of analysis and decision-making. Increasing market size and sophistication has led to a proliferation of new financial instruments and new forms of investment (there have been at least two major new forms every decade since the Second World War). De-regulation has led to a proliferation of new players in most of the major financial markets. Although the world remains a dangerous place and economic cycles have by no means gone away, there is generally more stability and companies can accept levels of risk that their nineteenth-century predecessors could not. And, last but not least, the gross quantity of available wealth has increased to a level almost unimaginable to previous generations, meaning that companies can diversify their financial structures to a previously unheard-of extent.

Yet there is also much the remains the same. We are still concerned about accountability and control, and we still face the problem of how to ensure shareholder value and commitment. The argument that big business and especially big finance is not responsible to the needs of society continues to resonate. Corporate finance is still, in essence, about acquiring capital, managing it efficiently and responsibly, and ensuring a return on investment for all parties. Most of all, for all its technical sophistication, corporate finance is still a human activity. As Thomas Greene commented in 1897 in the first professional finance textbook published in the USA: 'Practised experience, as well as the best economic theory, lays emphasis upon the importance of an able manager. Nothing can take his place; and his rewards in the shape of salary or returns upon his shares, must be commensurate with his importance.'

Morgen Witzel
2001

VIEW OF THE STOCK EXCHANGE DURING A PANIC.

TWENTY YEARS

OF

INSIDE LIFE

IN

WALL STREET.

OR REVELATIONS OF THE

PERSONAL EXPERIENCE OF A SPECULATOR,

INCLUDING

SKETCHES OF THE LEADING OPERATORS AND MONEY KINGS, THE GREAT RISES AND PANICS, THE MYSTERIES OF THE RINGS, POOLS, AND CORNERS, AND HOW FORTUNES ARE MADE AND LOST ON 'CHANGE.

BY

WILLIAM WORTHINGTON FOWLER.

FULLY ILLUSTRATED.

NEW YORK:
ORANGE JUDD COMPANY,
245 BROADWAY.
1880.

LIST OF ILLUSTRATIONS.

PUBLISHERS' ANNOUNCEMENT.

HON. WILLIAM WORTHINGTON FOWLER, the author of this work, is a grandson of Noah Webster, and the author of several other volumes. He has been a member of the Connecticut Senate and House of Representatives, and held numerous other prominent positions. He is now Chairman of the Commission appointed by the Governor of Connecticut to examine and report as to the expediency of adopting an amended orthography of the Public Documents. This Commission embraces some of the most eminent scholars in the country.

In addition to his public and literary labors, Mr. Fowler has had long and varied experiences in financial matters. Ten years since he embodied these experiences in a volume which was so well received that forty thousand copies were sold in a short period, though the price of the work was fixed at three dollars. John G. Whittier wrote to the author, "Thy book is full of interest. Its descriptions of the tremendous games of speculation, the rise and fall of fortune, the reckless regard and desperate adventure which shocked and disturbed the world are exceedingly graphic and spirited." Charles Sumner, Salmon P. Chase, George S. Boutwell, Benson J. Lossing, John G. Saxe, and very many other individuals of prominence wrote in similarly complimentary terms to the author regarding his entertaining work. Nearly one hundred and fifty newspapers, including all the leading journals of New York, Boston, Philadelphia, Washington, Chicago, and other cities, gave most flattering notices of the volume, and it was everywhere read with avidity.

Mr. Fowler has now recast his original book of ten years ago and brought it up to date, including the colossal stock movements of the latter half of 1879, and given us twenty instead of ten years of his individual experiences and observations in the great maelstrom of speculation. The work is valuable, if for nothing more, as showing to the uninitiated how unsatisfactory are the efforts to acquire fortunes by speculation, and warning them against the dangerous pitfalls in which Wall street abounds. But the writer in graphically describing his own financial vicissitudes, running through twenty years, conveys at the same time a vast amount of entertaining and valuable information regarding the financial operators and operations of that period.

CONTENTS.

CHAPTER I.

WALL STREET.

CHAPTER II.

THE STOCK EXCHANGE AND GOLD ROOM.

CHAPTER III.

THE FIRST VENTURE.

CHAPTER IV.

PROFIT AND LOSS.

CHAPTER V.

PORTRAITS OF CORNELIUS VANDERBILT AND DANIEL DREW AS THEY WERE IN 1869.

CHAPTER VI.

JOTTINGS ON THE "STREET;" DREW ON THE WAR-PATH.

CHAPTER VII.

WAR TIMES AND GREENBACKS.

CHAPTER VIII.

BULL-LEADERS.

CHAPTER IX.

PACIFIC MAIL AND LEONARD W. JEROME.

CHAPTER X.

"GOLD, GOLD, GOLD, GOLD,—HOARDED, BARTERED, BOUGHT AND SOLD."

CHAPTER XI.

THE FIRST GREAT HARLEM RISE.

CHAPTER XII.

THE BRIGADE OF BEARS.

CHAPTER XIII.

ANTHONY W. MORSE AND THE CHANCELLORSVILLE RISE.

CHAPTER XIV.

"WHAT WILL HE DO WITH IT!"

CHAPTER XV.

WHAT BECAME OF IT—HENRY KEEP AND OLD SOUTHERN.

CHAPTER XVIII.

BUBBLE COMPANIES.

CHAPTER XIX.

PANIC—FALL OF A. W. MORSE—CLEARING AWAY THE WRECK.

CHAPTER XX.

MARGINS, POOLS, CORNERS, RUSSELL SAGE AND HIS PRIVILEGES.

CHAPTER XXIII.

DULL TIMES—AVERAGING ON "POINTS."

CHAPTER XXIV.

THE BREAK IN GOLD—PANIC-BIRDS.

CHAPTER XXV.

PIGS OF GOLD IN A CORNER.

CHAPTER XXVI.

THE WORSHIPERS OF THE GOLDEN CALF.

CHAPTER XXVII.

ASTRAND AND AFLOAT AGAIN.

CHAPTER XXVIII.

DREW PLAYS ON HIS ONE-STRINGED LYRE—ERIE.

CHAPTER XXXI.

WOODWARD, FISK, Jr., GOULD.

CHAPTER XXXII.

THE BATTLE OF THE GIANTS.

CHAPTER XXXIII.

THE GREAT GOLD CONSPIRACY OF 1869.

CHAPTER XXXIV.

CHAPTER XXXV.

THE PANIC OF 1873 AND AFTER.

CHAPTER XXXVI.

OPERATORS OF THE NEW ERA—CAMMACK, KEENE, AND WM. H. VANDERBILT.

CHAPTER XXXVII.

THE SPECULATION OF '77, '78, AND '79.

CHAPTER I.

TWENTY YEARS OF INSIDE LIFE IN WALL STREET.

Twenty years of Financial History—Popular Ideas of Wall Street—A Dutch Stockade—The Money forces—Winged Riches—Bulls and Bears—The "Longs" and the "Shorts"—A Ring, and how it is made—The Kings of the Market—"Puts" and "Calls"—The Ghosts of the Street.

FROM 1860 to 1880. Twenty years of financial history! Twenty years of vibrations in market values over a scale of five hundred degrees; vibrations over so long an arc that vast fortunes were piled up and swept away, as the gigantic pendulum moved to and fro, slower or faster, impelled by forces of nature—by forces of men—an era never before known. War and labor! The earth pouring forth its increase—solid wealth; the government pouring forth greenbacks—fictitious wealth. A thousand millions of paper money as representing value flowing like a broad river into or towards one great reservoir—Wall street. And what is Wall street? A thoroughfare in name, but something more. To the banker and the stock broker it is a financial center, collecting and distributing money, regulating the exchanges of a continent and striking balances of trade with London and Frankfort. To the outside observer and novice it is a kind of work-shop thronged by cunning artisans who work in precious metals, where vessels of gold and vessels of silver are wrought or made to shine with fresh lustre, and where old china is fire-gilt as good as new. The moralist and philosopher look upon it as a gambling-den,—a cage of unclean birds, an abomination where men drive a horrible trade, fattening and battening on the substance of their friends and neighbors,—or perhaps as a kind of modern coliseum where gladiatorial combats are joined, and bulls, bears and other ferocious beasts gore and tear each other for the public amusement. The brokers regard it as a place of business where, in mercantile parlance, they may ply a legitimate trade, buying and selling for others on commission. To the speculators it is a caravansera where they may load or unload their camels and drive them away betimes to some pleasant oasis. To the financial commanders it is an arsenal in which their arms and chariots are stored, the stronghold to be defended or besieged, the field for strategy, battles and plunder. All these ideas and a multitude of others, more or less true, rise up at the mention of Wall Street.

It has its memories, too. Bright as it is with glass and gilding, and festooned with column, capital and cornice of granite, freestone and marble, clean cut and fresh as of yesterday, still it has a color of gray antiquity. More than two centuries of years have come and gone and "changed the blood and made the frame" of seven generations of Aryan men who have trod this street. It dates back, the antiquarians tell us, to the year 1653, for its first survey was in the palmy days of Petrus Stuyvesant when Schouts Burgomasters and Schepens lorded it over the little colony of New Amsterdam. Its name (one of the few remaining landmarks of the early Dutch possession,) was derived from the wall or *cingle* built of palisades and earth on the northern line of the street to ward off the aborigines, and also possibly the aggressive Yankee from the east. This fortified wall extended on the northerly side of the street, from Broadway to Pearl Street, which was then washed by the tides of Oost or East River. It had its dry ditches, and its embrasures; its lower end was terminated by a half circular redoubt, and through its land-gate on Broadway, and its water-gate by the river, herds of cattle were driven every night from the woods and pastures to the north, in which we are informed by the same veracious antiquarians, *bears* and other wild beasts abounded. On this same street, when the Salt-mountain or some other broad-beamed ship came in from the Scheldt—the Holland merchants drove a lively trade with the red man, bartering beads and cloth of Leyden for peltries of the beaver and otter.

But what contrasts has the light of two hundred years painted between the mimic life of New Amsterdam and this great roaring, serious, tragic Babylon of to-day. No sign now of the quaint, peaked roofs covered with Dutch tiles, the fort flying the blue lions of Holland, the old stockade and half moon embankment at its lower end. No trace now of the sturdy Netherland soldier with pike or musquetoon. But the ancient name of Wall Street still remains. That name is something more than a shadow, too, for it is in fact *Wall* Street, still lined with a succession of fortresses, behind whose bastions are garrisons well disciplined and alert, guarding the treasures, if not the lives of a nation. Within its casemates and vaults lie piles of coin, enough to excite the cupidity of ten West India companies, or to lade a hundred Spanish galleons. Here the forces of commerce silently gather and equip themselves for distant expeditions, from which they return again with the spoils of "Ormus and of Ind." In these strongholds terms are dictated to the vanquished, and treaties made. Here in niches, and on many a buttress and "coigne of vantage," the fledglings of finance make "their pendent bed and procreant cradle." Towering over all stands old Trinity, like a giant sentry, day and night, clashing out in peals and chimes of bells from his watch-tower, "all's well."

Speaking financially, the annals of Wall Street are brief; but brief though they be, they are crowded with forms and faces, full of notable incidents and varied with all the lights and shadows that flare and disappear in the passing careers of a thousand eager money-getters. As through one camera, they concentrate a picture of the material progress of the nation towards wealth, its daring enterprises, its steady industries, its wild speculations, its sharp commercial crises, and all the myriad transformations of financial life. Of its story early in the present century, only faint echoes come back to us. The names of the old merchants who went down to the sea in ships, and of the money changers and high treasurers who, in those days, were wont to come into the street to draw from or deposit in the United States Bank, the Manhattan Company, or Bank of New York, to inquire for the quotations or exchange views on the state of the market, are almost forgotten, but moving about among these phantom groups, we recognize the stateliest figure of all—that of Alexander Hamilton. Then we see new banks set up and operations slowly widening through the terms of five Presidents.

But it is only within the past forty-five years that *Wall Street* has got to have a special significance as the centre, not only of money but of speculation. From 1835 to 1880 a series of great inflations and correspondent depressions occurring there, furnish a most protracted, singular and striking chapter in the annals of finance.

The history of nations is a history of wars of conquest. The temple of Janus in old Rome was shut but twice in a thousand years. The history of finance is a history of the rise and fall of values, in other words, of speculations and panics. Wall Street is our temple of Janus. The lust of money is as strong as the lust of dominion, and avarice, like its nobler brother, ambition, "scorns delights and lives laborious days."

Other analogies exist between wars and speculation. Campaigns are planned, and strategy displayed on 'change as well as on the tented field. Wall Street has its plots and counterplots, its dashing assaults, and stout defences. He who enters that arena must be armed cap-a-pie, and cunning in all the tricks of fence. The bank account of the stock operator is his martello tower, to be defended against all kind of attacks, secret as well as open, mine, storming and escalade. He must look well to his out-works, man his parapet by day and night for the besiegers will surely press him hard. His bank account must furnish him also with weapons of offense and defense, for money is the sinews of speculation as well as of war.

The strength of Wall Street then may be said to lie in a figure three with eight ciphers after it, for this is the money balance of the banks and other depositories. Three hundred million dollars.

That massive pile of light freestone, with fluted doric columns, abutting on three streets and overlooking the American Bourse, where the strong and nimble athletes of the Stock Exchange exercise their muscles and air their lungs, that is the Sub-Treasury so famous in the story of American Finance. It is the fly-wheel in the engine of trade accumulating and regulating the money forces. Its vaults hold ninety millions of specie and a sum in currency varying at different times from ten to thirty millions. Within rifle shot of this building are five-sixths of the banking institutions of New York City, whose daily deposits rise in flush times to one hundred and ninety millions. But these latter are overshadowed and dominated by the Sub-Treasury, the monster depository on which only the treasurer of the nation is permitted to draw. Through its gates, streams flow in and out, to deepen and broaden the river of commerce, or heighten the torrent of speculation.

In noting the prominent features of Wall Street, it will be remarked how strongly the idea of *negotiability* is there brought out. All the principal values of commerce are in this mart represented by so many paper certificates. The goods and credit of the merchant are represented by promissory notes, which are bought and sold, and pass from hand to hand, almost like bank-bills. Cotton, pork, grain, sugar, tobacco, and a thousand other bulky and gross products are represented under the form of warehouse certificates. The wealth of banks, of railway corporations, and of many other stock companies, are floating about under the guise of certificates, and to the very gold in the vaults of the Treasury, wings are given, and coin and bullion fly in notes of yellow and green.

What is the easiest mode of exchange and barter? this is the first inquiry in the operations of trade, and Wall Street has answered it. Those diaphanous slips of paper representing untold riches, pass from hand to hand, as fast as words can utter their value. The money lender can count his millions on a table three feet square, or inclose them in a bank-box not much larger than a family Bible or a Webster's Unabridged.

It is difficult to conceive of Wall Street values apart from the idea of their negotiability. Will a piece of property pass current at a market price? will it be transferred with little trouble? then is it a suitable object of purchase and sale.

The ease and swiftness with which securities change owners produce, of course, a vast volume of business, and profits or losses are duplicated with corresponding swiftness and ease.

Money and values represented on paper, are the passive forces; men who buy and sell or "operate," are the active forces of trade.

What constitutes a State? inquires the poet:

> "Not high raised battlement or labored mound,
> Thick wall or moated gate * * * *
> No! *Men.*" * * *

So we might inquire what constitutes a street?—certainly Wall Street—not the granite pavements nor the long piles of masonry covering stores of uncounted wealth, but the *men* who throng this thoroughfare and keep the machinery of commerce and speculation in motion.

Wall Street, viewed as an aggregation of trading humanity, may be divided into two great classes. First, the *speculators*, or as they are pleased to term themselves, *operators*, who buy or sell stocks at their own risk of loss or expectation of profit. Second, the *brokers*, who buy and sell for others in consideration of a fixed commission. All those who deal in the street, may be said to belong to the first class; for there is hardly one of the brokers who does not speculate, directly or indirectly, but there are many of the speculators who, themselves, never buy or sell, but employ the brokers to do it for them. A broker is almost necessarily a speculator, but a speculator is not necessarily a broker. We shall at present describe only the speculators, reserving the brokers for a separate chapter.

A speculator is called a "bull" or a "bear," according to his interest in the market. A bull buys stock for a rise, and the term may be derived from his likeness to the animal of the bovine genus who tosses upwards with his horns. He is said to be "long" of stocks, because he is presumed to always hold his stock ready for their delivery on sale.

A "bear" is one who sells stocks for future delivery, which he does not own at the time of sale. In other words, he contracts to deliver stocks at a fixed price and within a fixed time. If stocks should fall during the continuance of the contract, he buys them in the market at the reduced prices, and delivers them to the party to whom he agreed to sell them at the contract price. The difference between the two prices is his profit. To illustrate this operation, suppose A agree to sell to B one hundred shares of New York Central at 118, deliverable at any time at the option of A, within thirty days, A not having the one hundred shares at the time the contract is made. If the price of the stock falls to 108, A buys it at that price in the open market, and delivers it to B, who pays him 118, the contract price, at a *profit* to A of 10 per cent. on the shares, *i. e.*, $1,000. But if the price rises to 128, and A is obliged to complete his contract, he buys it at that figure and delivers it to B, who pays him 118, entailing in this manner a *loss* of $1,000 on A.

The name "bear" is said to have been first given, at the time of the South Sea Bubble, to such persons as were operating to depress stocks, because they were acting the part of a man who would kill a bear for the sake of his skin. As a bull is said to be "long" of stocks, so a bear is said to be "short" of stocks, just as a person who has no money is said to be "short of funds." The bear has no stock when he offers to sell, but merely contracts to deliver what he does not possess, and is of course interested in depressing the market so that he may fill his contracts at lower prices, just as the bull is interested in raising stocks, so that he may profit by the increased market value of the stocks which he holds.

Two forces, it should be noted, are all the while acting in the commercial world growing out of a great variety of causes which we will not now pause to enumerate. One is a projectile force, sending values upward; the other, a kind of financial gravitation, carrying values downwards. The effect of these forces respectively, the bulls and bears, seek to heighten and turn to their own profit. A community of interest begets a community of action, and so the bulls often unite to raise the value of particular stocks, and form those combinations known in the "Street" as "cliques," "rings" or "pools,"—terms nearly synonymous,—their object being to elevate the price of stocks by owning a controlling interest and *making a market price* so that they can unload at a large advance on the price at which they bought.

These cliques, rings and pools in stocks answer to the combinations which are termed monopolies in the staple articles of commerce, such as grain, rice, sugar and tobacco. They buy up the floating supply and then satisfy the demand at the price which they choose to impose. Suppose A, B and C have contracted to deliver five thousand shares of a certain stock which they do not hold, and D, E and F hold all the stock in question, obviously, A, B and C must, in order to fulfill their contracts, buy the five thousand shares of D, E and F at whatever price they choose to sell it. In this case A, B and C, who are "bears," are "cornered" by D, E and F, who make up, we will suppose, the "bull ring."

A ring is formed thus: When money is easy, and

the financial future bright, some shrewd operator casts about for a stock, (generally railway,) which is selling at a fair, or still better, a low price in the market. The whole amount of stock issued is, we will say, fifty thousand shares of one hundred dollars each, that is, five million dollars at par. But half of this amount is held abroad or in the hands of investors at home, and will not therefore be likely to come on the market. This leaves two millions and a half, or twenty-five thousand shares of stock floating about the market, and this is the amount which must be bought by the proposed ring if it would be thoroughly successful in its results. After consultation with some other noted operator or operators, the scheme is framed and a paper drawn up which will read something like this, viz.:

We, the subscribers, in consideration of our mutual promises, hereby agree to buy the number of shares of stock of the —— Railroad Company set opposite to our names, respectively. That we authorize Smith & Co. to buy said stock, and we promise to pay to Smith & Co., in order to secure them against loss which may arise in carrying said stock, ten per cent. of the market value of the shares which said firm are to buy for our account respectively, and they are authorized to sell and re-purchase the same to the best of their judgment, and to receive one eighth per cent. commission on all purchases, sales and re-purchases. We, the subscribers, agreeing to use our best efforts to aid in raising the price of said stock, and not to deal therein on our account, until said joint account is closed (or we are to be at liberty to deal in said stock at our option).

Signed	C. J. OSBORN,	5,000 shares.
	D P. MORGAN,	5,000 shares.
	S. M. MILLS,	5,000 shares.
	W. L. SCOTT,	5,000 shares.
	H. KENNEDY,	5,000 shares.
	etc., etc.	

The ring, or, as it is sometimes called, the *party*, having been made up, they proceed to buy the stock. Two pre-requisites are necessary to every successful ring; first, secrecy, second, simulation. The buying of the stock must be done under cover, and often occupies several months. Every possible method is taken to deceive those who are outside the ring, and prevent them from supposing that the stock is passing under the control of the party who are manipulating it. Sometimes the stock is made to assume a weakness, as though it would drop several per cent., and all sorts of reports are set afloat to depreciate its value. This is done to induce sales. As it slowly rises, more stock is brought out for sale, by holders who are tempted by the enhanced price, all of which is quietly bought by the party and laid away. The bears are meanwhile making contracts for the future delivery of the stock to the "ring." Some of these contracts are in the form of sellers' options for thirty and sixty days, during which period the bear or seller has the privilege of delivering a certain amount of stock at a fixed price. But most of these "short contracts" are made as follows, viz.: A sells a lot of stock, which he does not possess, to B, and borrows it from C, for delivery to B. A will then owe the stock to C, who can call for it at any time, and A is thus "short" of the stock to the amount which he has agreed to deliver. The ring will gladly buy the stock of the bears, and loan it to them for delivery, because in this way they create a demand for the stock, which they alone can supply. It will be readily seen that if the bears have contracted to deliver a large number of shares, so that the market is in the condition termed "over sold," a firmness is, created in the price, owing to the constant demand on the part of the bears, for stock to complete their contracts.

This state of affairs is heightened as the ring goes on getting a firmer grip of the stock, and as the bears become more courageous in putting out their contracts, owing to the opportunities for making money by a fall, which the higher price of the stock naturally suggests to them.

Many devices are resorted to by the ring to induce short sales by the bears. The stock held by them is offered to the bears as a loan on easy terms, and when they sell the borrowed stock, the ring buy the very stock they have just loaned. When the stock price has risen from 20 to 40 per cent. it suddenly grows scarce. The bears find themselves troubled to make their deliveries. Now the ring prepare to "twist" their antagonists. A favorable day is selected when everything looks bright and sunny in the financial world, a plausible report, relative to the prospects of the Railroad Company, whose stock is under the control of the ring, is noised abroad, and different brokers are employed to bid up the price in the market in order to frighten the bears, and at the same time they are notified to deliver the stock which they have borrowed of the ring. Thus, the bears are compelled to "cover," that is, to close their contracts by buying and delivering the stock, which the ring alone can sell them. Sometimes, instead of buying the stock, the bears "settle" with the ring by paying them the difference between the market price and the lower price, at which they contracted to deliver it.

In that case, the ring find themselves saddled with a large amount of stock, for which there is little demand. And now the problem is to unload. Accordingly, they sell enough stock to "break" the market 4 or 5 per cent. downwards. The bears rush in and sell at the lowered price. When the ring have taken a sufficient number of their contracts, they bid the stock up again, and compel the bears again to cover. Every time the stock rises sharply, it has such an appearance of strength on the rising slide, that many of the outside bulls are tempted into buying, and then sell out at a loss, when the stock declines. The ring, to use a Wall Street phrase in this way, "milk the street," taking money out of the bears, who sell at a low price, and out of the bulls, who buy at a high price. This game is played for many weeks, and sometimes months, until the ring have disposed of their stock, and can reckon their profits.

The culmination in the operations of a ring, such as we have been describing, is technically called a "corner," because the bears are unable to deliver the stock they owe, and are so said to be driven into a "corner." The history of the "street," for the past thirty-five years, is one constant succession of these "corners," in which great fortunes have risen and fallen, like the waves on a stormy sea. Among the more remarkable of these corners, may be mentioned that in Canton, 1834 and 1835, when it sold up, from 60, its par value, to 300; that in Harlem, in 1864, which carried the price to 285; also that in Prairie du Chien, in 1865, which sold in three months, from 40 to 250, and that in Northwest, which (1872) sold at 230.

Nearly all those prodigious oscillations in the stock market, which have startled the public for the past thirty years, have been due to the influence of those powerful combinations, which have obtained control of certain stocks, and made them dance up in long erratic jumps, or have hurled them down still more swiftly and strangely. Hardly a year goes by without a recurrence of these singular phenomena. Sometimes it has been Pacific Mail, sometimes Erie, or St. Paul, or D., L. & W., or W. Union. In these traps the bears are continually caught by the same devices, and not seldom the bulls fall into the very pits which they dig so industriously for their adversaries.

The army of speculators who form their battalions, and charge up and down the field of the stock market, is a motley crowd, and like the army of Xerxes, includes representatives from many nations,—Americans from all sections of the Republic, Englishmen, Scotchmen, Welshmen, Irishmen, Germans, Frenchmen, Spaniards, Italians, Russians, Norwegians, Danes, Hungarians, Hebrews, Greeks and Ethiopians, masquerading under the guise of bulls and bears, swell the host, and rush together in hostile combat.

The generations of professional speculators are short to a proverb, but after allowing for a floating population of occasional operators, and of those who make or lose fortunes and then disappear from the scene, there is still another portion which is a constant quantity in the estimate. These are the men whose sole business is stock speculation. When they have once entered the street, they never leave it except in a pine box or a rosewood case, according to circumstances. If they lose money, they stay there to regain it, and if they make money, they stay there to make more. Constitutionally, and by temperament, they are speculators. Hear them talk, and you would suppose they lived on hope, rather than on those delicious ragouts and choice wines which Lorenzo Delmonico, or some of the other famed restaurateurs furnish them. Those saddest words of tongue or pen, "it might have been," enter largely into the thoughts and conversation of the thoroughbred speculator. *If* and *but* are the most frequent conjunctions in his vocabulary. His whole life is a series of regrets, and strange to say, these regrets are more often for what he might have made, but did not, than for what he has actually lost.

According to the proverb of the race-course, everybody on the turf or under it, is equal, and the same is true of the field of stock speculation, in which a common interest on one side or the other, seems, for the time being, to level all social distinctions. All classes and grades are represented here—rich and poor, gentle and simple, learned and illiterate. Not unfrequently these noisy groups contain more than one white cravat, on divines who have left their lambs to graze at large, while they, the shepherds, wander among a herd of another complexion, clad in bull's or bear's clothing. A certain harmony reigns among these discordant elements, although not quite equal to that which prevails in the happy family of the menagerie, in which lambs and lions, doves, eagles and monkeys, dogs and cats, dwell together in peace and amity. The bankrupt elbows the millionaire, and asks of him the price of Northwest, and the millionaire replies with the utmost suavity, "eighty-five, sir, at the last quotation;" the broken operator takes whiskey "straight" with the wealthy capitalist, and the puritan and blackleg exhange a sympathetic smile, when they see the stocks advancing in which they are interested.

This social phenomenon is due not merely to the influence of a common interest, and a common hope of gain, but to a common apprehension of possible loss. Dickens, in one of his novels, has ludicrously described how polite men are to each other in the presence of a danger which all feel, but the fear of which none express. In seasons of earthquake and flood, wolves herd amicably with sheep, and the boa-constrictor twines his scaly length harmlessly beside the plumpest of does.

Besides, amid the wonderful metamorphoses of the stock market, it behooves all to be courteous to their fellows, for the Lazarus who picks up the crumbs that fall from the rich man's table to-day, may himself dispense liberal charities to-morrow; the bankrupt of yesterday may, in the circle of a single sun, become a power on change.

Notwithstanding this apparent leveling of the social conventionalities in the domain of speculation, still it is in other respects no republic, for it has its sovereigns and satraps, who often hold its tribes in captivity and subject to an iron yoke.

Charles Darwin, the English naturalist, in his great and fascinating work on the "Origin of Species," explains in part, the existence of so many different species in the animal kingdom, by the doctrine of what he terms *Natural Selection,* i. e., the weak and unfortunate becoming extinct, the strong and favored living and mating with their peers, and in this way particular species being perpetuated. There is always this struggle going on everywhere; and among men, as among animals, weak races become extinct, and the subjects of stronger races. In the battle of life, it is the few strong, determined and favored men who win the prizes. Pre-eminently is this true of Wall Street. Ever since 1862, when began the greatest era of speculation the world has ever seen, faces have been appearing and disappearing there as in a whirling stereoscope; but in all those shifting groups, certain massive faces are always seen—faces graven with the wrinkles of a purpose that never failed them. These men have "clutched the golden keys." Their names are the talismans which unveil many a dark financial secret, unlock vaults of untold treasure, and set the genii of panic at work. The world of change pays them tribute, not of applause merely, but of hard cash, with scarcely a murmur of rebellion against their sovereignty.

In the last decade among a host of lesser operators, Cornelius Vanderbilt and Jay Gould were central Titanic figures. Such men are the Nimrods, the mighty hunters of the stock market; they are the large pike in a pond peopled by a smaller finny tribe. They are the holders of those vast blocks of stock, the cubical contents whereof can be measured by an arithmetic peculiar to themselves; they are the makers of pools large enough to swallow up a thousand individual fortunes. Sooner or later, the money of the smaller tribe of speculators finds its way into the pockets of these financial giants.

Daniel Drew, from the year 1855 till the great panic of 1873, when he became bankrupt, was another large pike in the pool, and for nearly a quarter of a century amused himself with bolting the small fry, just as Wm. H. Vanderbilt, Russell Sage, James R. Keene, and Jay Gould do to-day. Youthful speculator! a word in your ear. Go straight to one of these magnates, and make them a free gift of all the money you are willing to risk, (for into their strong boxes it will come at last,) and thus you will be saved a world of wrong and trouble, entailed by that mysterious, protracted, and to you, painful process, which will surely end, finally, in the transfer of your money into the strong boxes aforesaid.

Next after these high princes and potentates comes another grade of operators,—men of great financial ability and resources, hard-headed, and strong of nerve, viz.: Wm. R. Travers, a wonderfully shrewd and successful speculator of twenty-five years standing; Addison G. Cammack, who came into the street in 1865, and has made two or three millions by shrewd operations on both the bull and the bear side; Charles J. Osborne, one of Gould's brokers; Henry N. Smith; H. Kennedy; Augustus Schell; D. P. Morgan; and many others who have taken an active part in the bull speculations of 1879. Other famous operators, who have passed to the silent land or retired from the street, such as Jacob Little, Leonard W. and Addison G. Jerome, Henry Keep, Horace F. Clark, James Fisk, Jr., W. S. Woodward, etc., etc., will be mentioned as we record the annals of the street since 1857. As for the smaller class of operators, who do business on capitals of from three hundred dollars to fifty thousand, their name is legion.

Many of the operators of small means, as well as the wealthier class, drive a smart trade in "puts" and "calls." These are contracts giving the holder the privilege, in consideration of a trifling sum, (rarely over one per cent. on the market value of a stock) of calling on the contracting party, or delivering to him, as the case may be, a certain amount of stock within a fixed time, at a price above the then market value in a "call," and below it in a "put."

The following is a copy of a "call:"

New York, September 1st, 1879.

For Value Received, the Bearer may CALL ON ME *for One Hundred Shares of the Preferred Stock of the* Chicago and North-Western Railroad Company, *at* 97 *per cent., any time in thirty days from date. The bearer is entitled to all the dividends or extra dividends declared during the time.*

Signed, *RUSSELL SAGE.*

Witness, *P. WILKINS.*

The market price of the stock at the date of the call is, we will suppose, 95. Now if the price rises to 99 in the course of the thirty days during which the "call" runs, the bearer can sell one hundred shares at 99, i. e., for 9,900, and call upon Russell Sage for one hundred shares at 97, i. e., 9,700, and deliver it to the party to whom he has just sold the same amount, netting, (after deducting the one hundred dollars which he paid for the privilege,) one hundred dollars by this operation.

The following is a copy of a "put:"

New York, September 1st, 1879.

For Value Received, the Bearer may DELIVER ME *One Hundred Shares of the Preferred Stock of the* Chicago and North-Western Railroad Company, *at 95 per cent., any time in thirty days from date. The undersigned is entitled to all the dividends or extra dividends declared during the time.*

Signed, *RUSSELL SAGE.*

Witness, *P. WILKINS.*

If we suppose the stock falls to 90 during the pendency of the "put," the bearer makes four hundred dollars net out of this operation.

The holder of a call, it will be seen, is a "bull," and the holder of a put is a "bear" on the market. But these contracts are often used, like so much money, to buy or sell stock, thus, viz.: Russell Sage's call being considered "as good as wheat," it may be deposited with some broker as security for a "short sale" of one hundred shares of Chicago and Northwestern at 85. If the price falls to 75, the holder makes ten hundred dollars, less the brokerage. If it rises to 95, the broker is secure by the privilege of calling on Russell Sage for a hundred shares at 85, which he delivers to the party to whom the short sale was made, and here the holder loses nothing, though he makes nothing. The "put," on the other hand, is used as security to *buy* stocks, in this manner, viz.: if the stock fall to 80, the putting price, the holder can buy one hundred shares at that price, through some broker who is fortified against loss in case the price falls, by having the privilege of delivering the one hundred shares he buys, to Russell Sage, at 80, while if the price rises above 80, he can sell it and take for the holder of the put, a profit on this operation. In an active market, the holders of puts and calls, after making several profits in the way we have described, are sometimes able to fall back on the original contract of their puts or calls, and close them up at a handsome figure.

Daniel Drew and the late Henry Keep were very active dealers in this kind of contract, with what singular effects upon the market, will be hereafter described.

No one who has entered the precincts of the stock exchange, will have failed to notice certain nondescripts, who constantly frequent the market. They are men who have seen better days, but having dropt their money in the street, come there every day as if they hoped to find it in the same place. These characters are the ghosts of the market, fixing their lack-lustre eyes upon it, and pointing their skinny fingers at it, as if they would say "thou hast done this!" They flit about the door-ways, and haunt the vestibules of the exchange, seedy of coat, blackingless of boot, unkempt, unwashed, unshorn, wearing on their worn and haggard faces a smile more melancholy than tears. They "put up" never a penny, and yet they are perpetually asking the prices of stocks which they never buy or sell. They have their life's history—it is that of many of "Les Miserables,"—stranger than fiction, more doleful than a funeral dirge,—a spring time of hope, health, love, prosperity and the amenities of social life, then a brief season of wild, reckless speculation, a brief revelry of smoke, splendor, champagne—then what? penury, darkness, despair!

We have thus far only indicated a few of the different classes which make up the *genus* speculator. It would require a volume to describe, in detail, the numerous *species*, the strong individuality of the men who compose them, the fortunes they roll up from nothing, or fling to the winds in a day, the thousand shifts to which they resort, to earn an honest or dishonest living, and the tricks they play which so often make the outsiders, if not the angels, weep. The stories to be told of some of them are worthy to be embalmed in another "thousand and one nights," pointed with morals, and teaching lessons, while they appeal to the love of the marvellous, like the tales by which the Princess Scheherezade held the ear of the Sultan, and redeemed her life from forfeit.

It is a popular fallacy that pronounces the life of the Wall Street man, as anything rather than laborious. They say he dresses in purple and fine linen, and fares sumptuously every day, though, like the Solomon lilies of Scripture, he toils not, neither does he spin. Let not the hard-working lawyer, the burdened and anxious merchant, or the hardy sons of manual labor, envy the gilded speculator, though he recline on silken couches, and dally with the daintiest of viands, and sip wines of the vintage of Waterloo, out of Bohemian glass. True, to the casual observer, his life seems easy enough. He produces nothing, he drives no plough, plies no hammer, sends no "shuttle flashing through the loom." In political economy he would be properly classed among the strictest order of *consumers*. His airy existence seems to be passed in chasing the flying fractions up and down the market, or in making the values which pass through his hands perspire golden drops, just as the Jews clip and sweat the coin they handle. And yet what life is more trying than his? Beneath his frontal sinuses, amid the convolutions of his brain, a silent, invisible struggle is going on, which if put into bodily shape, would startle the beholder. There the vulture passions are at work, led on by their generals, ambition and avarice. Pining envy, fear of an evil which always impends, rage over injuries inflicted by others, or by his own weakness and incapacity, jealousy and hatred of successful rivals, all hold carnival in the space of an hour, and are kept active and sleepless by hope which quickens them with her enchanted wings. Above him hovers, day and night, a vast, dark, formless shape, threatening ruin and penury. This is the spectre of panic. One day he is lifted to dizzy heights, the next, plunged into black depths. He is hurried through dark labyrinths through paths where a single step is destruction. He climbs on the edge of a sword to a fool's paradise, where he tastes joys brief as a dream, and in an hour is abased to the earth where he drinks the full cup of humiliation and want. Meanwhile nature is holding out strange signals of alarm. His lips and cheeks blanch without any assignable cause. Blacksmiths' sparks flicker before his eyes. His blood regurgitates to his heart, which seems to swell to the size of a bullock's, and beats on his ribs like a trip-hammer. Paralysis, apoplexy and aneurism are watching for their prey.

Not long since, a great man of the "street" lay

for weeks in the clutches of this last disease, and the muffled door-bell told the result of this harrowing career of a speculator. When he died, they said he left four millions. But he had paid for this colossal fortune with a life worn out in middle age by the weary burdens and sharp vicissitudes of the stock market.

The "fierce extremes" of Wall Street, may be best illustrated by the experience of W——. He came into the market, in 1862, with six hundred dollars, bought gold at 110, and sold it at 135; bought again three times as much, sold it for 160, went into Erie at 39, sold it for 80, bought Pacific Mail at 120, sold it for 165. In March, 1863, he had $49,000 at his bankers. But this was only the beginning. Something was going on, in Harlem, so he bought 2,000 Harlem; Morse was at work at Pittsburg, so he bought 2,000 Pittsburg; Erie was feverishly moving towards 90, he bought 1,000 Erie. Meanwhile, Hooker was moving on Chancellorsville, and there was silence in the stock market, for the space of a day. Now the news came, of a retrograde movement, in plain English, a repulse. The army was this side the Rappahannock, the signal was given, and the cohort of bulls moved on their enemy's works. Erie sold up to 110, Pittsburg 105 and Harlem in its proportion. He pocketed $90,000 more by this venture, and in March, 1867, he stood $250,000 ahead of the market. Then for twelve years he had a charming life. A pair of spanking bays, tandem, whirled him to the Park in a tall Belmont, with a flunkey in livery, on the back seat with a bug on his hat. Over his morning repast floated the aromatic steam of

Mocha, and the flavors of exotic fruits. He lunched off partridge, stuffed with truffles, washed down by a bottle of Chateau d'Yqem or the liquid pellucid gold of the vintage of Xeres, and his dinner was nine courses of fish, flesh and fowl at Delmonico's, flanked by the most toothsome of *entremets*, and wines that would make a Mussulman foreswear his creed.

In 1879 W—— suffered a change—"a sea-change" into something not "rich but strange." He had seen prices go down in the panic of April and May, 1877, and vowed that when they rose again he would "sell stocks short." Such an opportunity was soon afforded. When prices had risen fifteen per cent., in June, 1877, he proceeded to carry out his program boldly, by going short of Northwest Common, St. Paul, Del., Lack. & Western, and other active stocks. Prices rose upon him and he kept his position on the short side. In two years he had lost everything, and owed his brokers $5,000 besides.

We met W—— six days ago. He informed us that he had just breakfasted on a modest plate of hash and a cup of something called coffee, but in which the strongest imagination could not detect a drop of the infusion of the Arabian berry. His coat was foxey, his hat had a suspicious shine and he was generally run down at the heel. Such is the present condition of this individual, but the future may have great things in store for him. Let us hope it may.

Gambling in stocks, after following a legitimate business, is like quaffing brandy after sipping claret. When once a man has fairly committed himself to speculation, his imagination soon grows to lend a hideous fascination to the objects of his pursuit. An evil genius seems to hold possession of him. He takes no note of time, save as an interval between his gains and losses; the thrill of the one and the pain of the other, grow duller as the years wear away, until at length he becomes the opium eater of finance, living in a world peopled by phantoms which haunt his waking hours, and flit through his dreams. The unsubstantial pageant vanishes as the alarm bell of his ruin peals out, and he awakes to the desolation of reality.

How few of these men retire with fortunes approximate to their hopes, let the chronicles of the Stock Exchange tell. The number during the past ten years, might be almost told upon the digits. The few successful ones, are continually emerging from the intolerable repose of their retirement, and even in their dotage, coming back to the scene of their old intoxications mumbling old wives' tales of what they might have done thus and thus, and burning their fingers after a fashion, as ancient as Crœsus.

As for the rabble of the unsuccessful, they cling to their illusions, till want or decrepitude, or both, drive them into obscurity, to ruminate over a misspent life, and be laid finally in nameless graves, by the hand of charity.

CHAPTER II.

THE STOCK EXCHANGE AND GOLD ROOM.

The Focus of Speculation—The "Long Room" on a Field Day—Portraits of Operators—History of the Board of Brokers—The Public Board—Queer Characters—Volume of Business—How it is Done—Brokers' Vocabulary—Margins, Differences and Options—Machinery of Business—A Broker's Buckler—The Gold Room in New Street—Rise of the Gold Board—The Firm of We, Us & Co.—The Gold Bank, and its former Operations.

THE tide of humanity that pours down Broadway, is dashed against the bulwarks of Wall Street, and whirled to the eastward, between the mighty walls of granite and sandstone, which line that renowned thoroughfare. Through two mouths, New Street and Broad Street, it is sucked into that seething, whirling, roaring maelstrom—the stock-market. Speaking in the language of the common-place, these two streets are merely avenues in the lower part of the city for the passage of men and loaded wains, and for the transaction of business; but these streets also form the environs of the Stock Exchange, which, as from the focus of a gigantic parabolic reflector, throws a light, more or less lurid, over the whole financial community. That lofty façade on Broad Street, builded as of snowy marble of Paros, "of kingliest masonry," sinks into a modest, two-story brick rear on New Street, emblematical of the stately

CELEBRITIES OF WALL STREET.

fortunes which enter that stately front, and issue diminished from that diminished rear.

This is our palace of Aladdin. Here may be found that wonderful lamp which gives speedy and fabulous wealth to him who grasps it. Here also is stabled that remarkable horse, which, on being mounted, often flies away and leaves its rider on a certain desolate island, called Ruin.

The edifice is built to defy the powers of the air and fire—massively, of stone, iron, brick and glass, with thin veneerings of wooden floorings; its ruins ages hence may for aught we know be among those which the coming New Zealander may gaze upon as he sits on a mound of dust which was once old Trinity and moralizes on the fall of nations.

Some years ago the ground floor of this building was occupied by the "Long Room," so called, the hall of the Stock Exchange being on the second floor, facing New street. In the Long Room were witnessed, between the years 1865 and 1870, some of the most famous battles of that period, when Vanderbilt and Drew were pitted against each other, and when Leonard W. Jerome, Henry Keep, and James Fisk, Jr., were at their zenith. At present the members of the Board hold their sessions in a lofty apartment formed from their old hall and part of the "Long Room." This apartment, sixty by seventy feet, is surrounded by pilasters, and frescoed in blue and yellow. The rostrum of the chairman is at the northern end; an enclosure, fenced off by an iron railing at the southern end, is occupied by outsiders, who pay for the privilege of being near the scene of operations. Directly above this inclosure is the visitors' gallery, which is generally pretty well filled by such as are curious to see the brokers at work.

Leaning on the railing which surrounds this gallery, and looking down fifty feet below us, we see a crowd of men, some moving to and fro, others brandishing their arms and shouting their bids or offers. Most of the assemblage is made up of knots of from three to a dozen, or crowds of from twenty to fifty, each clique representing the dealers in some one of the active stocks, e. g., Lake Shore, Northwest, St. Paul, D., L. & W., &c.

It is a field day on 'Change. Stocks which for weeks have been slowly rising are now jumping upwards three per cent. in an hour. The Exchange is like Bedlam broke loose. The hall is jammed with buyers and sellers, brandishing their arms, shrieking with every variety of tone, from the booming basso to the shrill tenore. Wall Street is fully represented this morning. The great Banking and Brokerage firms are on the ground, executing their orders and reaping a golden harvest of commissions. Files of sharp-looking, smug fellows are rushing in and out, on the double-quick, holding in their hands pads of paper, on which the latest quotations are recorded; while the telegraph with ceaseless click is flashing the prices to every commercial city in the Union. The speculators both inside and outside are all here. The cunning artificers of "rings" and diggers of "pools" are either among the crowd watching the effect of their schemes, and quietly giving orders to their agents, or in offices within easy reach of the scene of operations. The great leaders in the game of speculation are not often seen on the street, or around the Stock Exchange. William H. Vanderbilt is at his office at the Grand Central Depot; Gould, Sage, Dillon, and other leaders of the Union Pacific and Southwestern rings are ensconced in dusky apartments at No. 80 Broadway; Travers & Cammack are at their up-town office, and James R. Keene is at the Windsor Hotel. But the telegraph wires annihilate space, and these operators, as well as their confidential agents, are to all intents and purposes on the field of action, watching the progress of events, giving or countermanding orders, and directing the course of prices up or down. One thousand telegraphic instruments in brokers' offices and hotels, all over the city, reel off, with ceaseless tick, from ten o'clock A.M. till three o'clock P.M., the prices of stocks, inscribed on paper ribbons. This invention has saved time to the brokers and their customers.

Nearly all the outsiders have a greater or lesser interest in the course of the market. Some of them stand by the railing, others watch the battle afar off, standing in New street. These outside operators have faces strongly marked by the exciting life they lead. Their features often become set into a fixed expression of anxiety. They gaze at the scale of prices with an apparent apathy, disturbed by the pain of loss or lighted up by the pleasure of gain only for an instant. Some of them seem to wear the waxen mask which grows on the faces of gamblers covering every emotion and rarely dropped except when some keener pang or more intense thrill startles them off their guard.

The combat between the bulls and bears commences with light skirmishing. As the day wears away, the solid columns move against each other, under a fire of heavy artillery. The bears begin to give ground and their banners wander in disarray. Suddenly a deafening hubbub breaks out from the hall. Kansas Pacific has risen ten per cent. in as many minutes. Some great bear is buying stock to cover his contracts, his followers rush after him and the whole army of bears are soon at work buying in or settling up. The bulls have won the day, and after counting the dead, wounded and missing, and reckoning the spoils and losses, respectively, the armies retreat to their camps, and prepare for new campaigns.

The association known as the New York Stock Exchange, was formed early in the present century. It germinated eighty years ago, in a little clique of stock dealers numbering scarcely a round dozen, who were wont to meet under a sycamore tree, which stood in Wall Street, opposite to the present banking house of Brown, Bros. & Co., and job off small lots of governments or stock in the Manhattan Company, and Bank of New York. In 1816, a permanent organization existed, consisting of twenty-eight members. The names of most of the men composing this coterie linger now only in the memory of the old New Yorkers, or are written on the "dull cold marble" which records in the conventional phrase of olden times, the virtues of these men of 'Change. One of them—a nonogenarian—Warren Lawton, veteran of a hundred campaigns, and survivor of fifty years of the sharp vicissitudes of Wall Street, is, or lately was, still wearing out a green old age.

As early as 1837, the organization had grown to be a power, but a power for evil rather than good, since it stimulated in the community a thirst for speculation. In that year, too, fell the great banking and brokerage firm of J. L. and S. Josephs, agents of the

Rothschilds, and rated at $5,000,000, involving multitudes in a wide-spread ruin. The successors and assigns of the twenty-eight brokers of 1816, have, indeed, fed on strong food, and waxed exceeding great. They number, in 1879, between ten and eleven hundred, and own, or control wealth which is counted by the ten million. The old sycamore has decayed, and fallen beneath the storm, and they meet no longer under the "greenwood tree," though there is a poetic fitness in such a place of meeting for the taurine and ursine herd; but in a marble temple dedicated to Mammon, the God of riches, the ponderous iron doors whereof turn like the Miltonic gates of the celestial city on golden hinges.

The Stock Exchange, as might be expected, was and is a highly exclusive body. Formerly three black balls were sufficient to bar out any applicant. To-day the question of membership is decided by a governing committee, which must be satisfied as to the age, health, moral character, and financial standing of the applicant for membership. The initiation fee of members in 1879 is $10,000. The number of members is limited to one thousand and sixty.

They were and are equally remarkable for their conservative views in respect to moneyed operations. In former years a few rich, grey-headed old fogies frowned down the more enterprising, but less wealthy "Young America" element, which went in for bold, dashing moves, cliques, corners, and the like. Hence it happened that an outsider, who had distinguished himself by some brilliant coup in finance, often found the doors barred against him, when he wished to enter the legitimate circle of this close corporation, partly, perhaps, from the jealousy awakened by a skill which threatened to surpass the trained financiers in their own arena.

Of course this exclusiveness produced a reaction among the speculative public, and rival organizations were formed, according as the volume of business tempted men to share in the heavy commissions earned thereby. Prior to 1836, a new board was formed, which, after maintaining a precarious existence for a few years, became extinct. In 1862, the same causes led to the formation of another association, known first as the Public Board, and afterwards as the Open Board of Brokers. Everything was favorable to such an organization. Uncle Sam's presses were printing greenbacks by the million. A large proportion of our mercantile population were thrown out of business by the depression of 1861, and ready to embark in anything which promised the improvement of their shattered fortunes; the ebbing and flowing tide of the war itself, distorted or exaggerated by manipulations of the telegraph, also multiplied the fluctuations; these were mighty conditions precedent to such a movement. Accordingly, men of all shades and classes flocked to the "coal-hole," as the subterranean apartment in William Street was called, where this Public Board first held its sessions. Lawyers, whose tastes were speculative rather than litigious, more than one clergyman, whose pastoral labors were unremunerative, broken down operators, merchants out of business, clerks out of situations, Jews, "native, and to the manner born," as well as the greenest and most unsophisticated parties from the rural districts, swelled the motley throng.

Most of these men had some capital, more or less—

principally less. Strange stories are told of some of them. One pawned his watch, paid his hundred dollars admission dues, and had ninety cents left in his pocket. This he expended in a sumptuous lunch, and a "quencher," on the strength of which he bought ten gold, made five hundred dollars in an hour, and closed the month with five thousand six hundred and fifty dollars profits. Another mortgaged his poultry stand in one of the markets, and made, in six months, seventy-five thousand on Harlem.

The Old Board looked with great disfavor on its young rival; a bitter contest arose, in which, the former had the advantage in wealth and established position, the latter in fire, energy and numbers. The New Board offered to do business for 1-32 brokerage, *i. e.*, three dollars and twelve cents on a hundred shares; the Old Board responded by lowering their commission rates from one-quarter per cent. to one-eighth per cent., and passed a resolution of expulsion against any one of its members who had any dealings with any member of the former organization.

Meanwhile, the tide of speculation kept rising higher, and both parties had all the business they could do. The denizens of the street will recollect the singular phenomena presented by this locality in 1862 and 1863. The basements of William, Wall and Broad Streets, and of Exchange Place, seemed to have been suddenly penetrated with innumerable burrows, inhabited by new and singular animals—mostly rodents—gnawing at the vast cheese of speculation. Among these, too, were the "woodchucks" of the class, sitting in their holes, and anon appearing, frisking about, picking up a few choice bits and disappearing like prairie dogs at stated intervals, or upon the least alarm. Every inch of space was occupied. Queer little niches in walls were scooped out or enlarged, so as to admit a desk, and over the door in flaming characters was the imposing sign, Sloper & Co., or Lunkhead & Bro., Bankers and Brokers. It is a surprising circumstance how many bankers were, just at this time, suddenly spawned in the most gorgeous panoply from the head of our financial Minerva. Some were infant prodigies, boys of twenty summers, reared in that sharpest of schools, a broker's office, whose financial ideas were founded on first principles. They seemed to have resolved society into its original elements, and gone back in their notions respecting the sacredness of other men's property to what ethnologists call the stone period, when men lived in caves, and appropriated to themselves all kinds of property, irrespective of those rights so studiously inculcated by Blackstone and Kent. They had heads of sixty, rolling the coldest and keenest of eyes, on shoulders in which the deltoid muscle had been hardly yet developed. Then, too, there were in more ostentatious offices, glittering with plate glass, and garnished with the most arabesque of black walnut furniture, the Oily Gammons of a more mature age, versed in the business wiles begotten of twenty-five years' experience. They offered the public schemes by which wealth could be amassed in the simplest of possible ways,—a few hundred or thousand dollars subscribed and paid down with the almost impossible contingency of future assessments. But, mysteriously enough, most of these schemes were founded on proper franchises, etc., which were situated hundreds and thousands of miles away. On Deadman's Ledge, near No Man's Peak, in Colorado, were claims yielding gold sulphurets, which assayed two thousand dollars to the ton. Near I-Euchre Lake, in Wisconsin, were ingots of virgin copper to be had for the asking. And the bituminous coal, at an easy distance from tide-water, knocked the spots out of Scotch bog and cannel. The street was fairly flooded (on paper) with flowing wells, and all these schemes were backed up by all sorts of certificates and affidavits. Swindling and imposition put on the cloak of Religion. Deacons and elders, vestrymen and church-wardens, lent their names, and too often shared in the plunder.

All these miscellaneous enterprises served to deepen and give new volume to the waves that bore upon their topmost crest, the bark which carried the Public Board and its fortunes. At the close of January, 1863, it found itself stronger in crew, better organized, with plenty of shot in the locker, and an experience won in the most perilous navigation through rough seas, and in treacherous squalls. In the spring of 1863, this organization transferred its sessions from the basement at No. 17 William Street, to which the plebeian name of the "coal-hole" had been given, and held them in a more commodious apartment on the first floor on the opposite side of the street. In 1864, they moved into their new hall, at No. 16 Broad Street, and were known thereafter as the "Open Board of Brokers." The warfare so long carried on between the rival Boards was gradually discontinued, and at last, in the spring of 1869, as consolidation eemed to be the order of the day, the two bodies joined forces, and united under the name of the New York Stock and Exchange Board, which meets in the building already described. The board organized some years ago for the purpose of buying and selling Government Bonds, was also, at the same time, incorporated with the Stock Board, forming, altogether, a monster association of men, who devote their lives, and their fortunes, if not their sacred honor, to the business of buying and selling stocks and bonds, etc., etc.

The Board of Brokers is a wheel within a wheel, an imperium in imperio—a government in itself. It makes laws and regulations which bear upon its members as strongly as the laws of the land. It has a presiding officer to compel order, to impose fines and to announce decisions and decrees; a judiciary in the shape of an arbitration committee, which passes upon disputes involving the contracts of members and its adjudications are final. It has a code in its constitution and by-laws. When a member fails to pay up he is expelled. When a bull or bear is unable to meet his contracts, the stock which he fails to deliver is "bought in" or "sold out," at the Board, "under the rule" which so provides, and the difference between the prices at which it is "bought in" or "sold out," and the contract price, is the measure of damages for the breach of contract. This expedient, by a rapid process, dispenses with the aid of the courts of law where causes drag their slow length along through weary years, in defiance of the Bill of Rights, which declares, that every man shall have justice speedily and without delay.

The room where this trading body-politic hold their regular daily sessions, is a magnificent hall, which we have already described. Here stocks are bought and sold from ten o'clock in the morning till the gong sounds at three P. M. Except between those hours all dealings are strictly prohibited. This rule was made some years since. Before it went into operation stocks and gold were bought and sold very largely in the street, and in the up-town hotels, both in the morning and after the board in the afternoon and evening.

Upon the first stroke of the clock at ten A.M., the hubbub begins. The regular call is at half past ten, when Chairman Mitchell, in a stentorian voice, calls off the bonds and stocks on the list. This call is repeated in the afternoon, and the prices of stocks and bonds are thus officially established. The Stock and Gold Telegraph Company, which sends the prices as they are made to a thousand offices, where they are ticked off on ribbons, saves a world of time and trouble to both brokers and speculators. All the business and organization of the Stock Exchange is conducted strictly in accordance with an elaborate constitution and by-laws, and members infringing the rules are punished by fine, suspension, or expulsion.

Two things will especially strike an observer on 'Change: First, The apparent looseness and recklessness with which business is done there. Second, The immense volume of business done. These facts may be explained by the rapidity necessitated by the shortness of business hours in the day, and by the range of speculation through the securities dealt in—securities representing an aggregate market value of nearly $6,000,000,000, and including Government, State, and Municipal bonds, and Railway, Bank, Insurance, and miscellaneous stocks.

It would seem at those seasons when speculation is rife, as if every one had a larger or smaller pecuniary interest in stocks. Not only the bankers, brokers and money-men, who are constantly in the circle, but the staid merchant, the retired capitalist, the trustee of estates, the manufacturer, mechanic, farmer, miner, the student, lawyer, doctor and clergyman, are drawn into the vortex. A large portion of these men are not seen in Wall Street, but are "operating" by telegraph and letter, putting up their margins and buying or selling with characteristic ardor and boldness, which has often been acquired in other lines of business, for there are many fields of speculation besides the Stock Exchange.

"You Americans. Ah! you are, in fact, a people reckless," says Myer, late of the Paris Bourse, "we do these things better in the beautiful France." You are wrong, Myer. More safely, perhaps, but not better. If a venture is safe, it is not a speculation. Safety is hardly an element in the calculation. It is the *risk*, after all. The greater the risk, the greater the profit seems like a paradox, but it is generally true. Boldness, shrewdness and nerve, pluck the flower fortune out of the nettle danger, and boldness, shrewdness and nerve are, at least, American traits. No doubt the volume of business on the Bourse is very great, but after all, how paltry seems the individual enterprise of the French speculator, compared to the magnificent daring of the American. Enter the Bourse from the east, on the Rue Notre Dame des Victoires, place yourself in one of those high, arched windows, which surround the interior, and beneath that vaulted and frescoed dome, you will see a tumultuous, vociferating crowd of buyers and sellers. It would seem as if the end of all things was come, and that the Frenchmen had forgotten their reliance on the Goddess of Reason and were clamoring for absolution from Saint Peter. But all this gesticulation, fuss and fury is little but "the wild hysteric of the Celt." Most of these men are buying small lots of the Rentes, or five hundred francs in the Chemin de fér du Nord, or the Crédit Mobilier. Pshaw! so the old women in the Rue St. Honoré sell you a plate of fried potatoes—price one sou. A few francs profit gives our old ally his café and omelet, and his modest diner and vin at the Palais Royal with the inevitable eau sucré, whereof he pockets the spare lumps.

How about London? There is our friend Bullwinkle,—he of the weeping-willow whiskers and fine Saxon color, true born Briton and agent of the great English house of Bearem & Bros., who lately observed that "really you know, my dear fellow, you are a young people, do ye see, and should'nt mention old England and this blasted country, in the same breath, when you talk of money." Quite true, we reply, but those ten share lots of stock dealt in at the Royal Stock Exchange, and those fortnightly settlements seem rather small and slow affairs, compared to the vast bargains and sales made in a breath in the New York Stock Exchange.

The aggregate volume of business in an active year has been estimated at $8,000,000,000. This does not include the principal part of the dealing in Government Bonds, (the amount of which is enormous, though difficult to be guessed, even approximately,) or the dealings in gold, which, though small now, amounted, ten years ago, to nearly $30,000,000,000, and in those famous two days, the 24th and 25th of September, 1869, ran up to $800,000,000, forty millions changing hands in five minutes. In 1863, Addison G. Jerome bid for six millions of old Southern, and was ready to take it. Anthony W. Morse was in habit of bidding for five or ten millions of stock in one block; but some of these were bluff bids, you will say. True, but they were bids in open market, nevertheless, and illustrate our proposition equally well. Transfers of a million in stocks from A to B, on a single bid, are of almost daily occurrence. The weekly clearings of the Gold Bank, in flush times, used to exceed a thousand millions of dollars.

We are informed that Gould's brokers have made as much as one hundred thousand dollars in one month, in commissions on the orders given them by that noted speculator. The stock deliveries of several firms have been known to reach as high as one hundred millions of dollars in a month. When we remember that the Union Pacific and Southwestern pool hold 300,000 shares of stock, we can understand the enormous business done by their brokers, and that such large deliveries should be made by the agents they employ. In the third week of September, 1879, more than two million shares of stocks changed hands, and a daily business of four hundred thousand shares is often done.

More than one leading operator may be found nearly any day who is long or short of five millions of stocks, *on his own account*, and these are mere flea-bites compared to the great Hudson, Harlem, and Central Pool of 1879, which, it is said, hold directly or by proxy from fifty to sixty millions in these stocks, besides a controlling interest of twenty or thirty millions more in the Lake Shore and Michigan Central lines.

How can such immense business be transacted? A large part of it is done by the payment of the *differences* between the buying and selling price, the securities bought and sold not being actually delivered. The remaining portion of the business is done by means of *certified checks*, a convenient device of the credit system. Suppose B, a broker, has bought of C, another broker, five thousand shares of Lake Shore, at 90, for which, he has to pay $450,000. B having a capital of only $50,000, but being of good standing and credit, the bank where he keeps his account will certify his check as good for $450,000, though he may then have only $10,000 on deposit. Before three o'clock, P. M., B will have obtained a loan on the five thousand shares, or have delivered the stock to other parties, who will pay him for it in certified checks, which he will deposit in his bank, and thus make good his over-draft.

These brokers' accounts are not taken by some of the banks, being founded as they are, entirely on confidence in the broker, and involving a certain amount of risk. When money is easy, and everything is bright in the financial world, all may go on well, but in times of stringency and panic, a bank is occasionally the loser by this accommodation. A notable instance occurred five years since, when a certain Wall Street bank was saddled with a loss of nearly a quarter of a million by an over-draft of a prominent broker, who failed the day after.

The business of a stock-broker may be classed among those professions which have a language of their own in which their mysteries are veiled. This lingo consists of a variety of single words, or concise expressions, which convey to the initiated alone, an idea of the operations of the trade, while to the uninitiated, they are almost as meaningless as the cabala of the old Jewish Rabbins.

The word *margin* is perhaps the most conspicuous in the Wall Street vocabulary. As everybody knows this word in its ordinary sense, signifies a *narrow strip of land*, an edge or border, as the margin of a lake, etc. In the stock-business it is, if we may use the phrase, a *narrow strip of money*, which *preserves* the broker from loss, and on which, the speculator may be supposed to stand before he has definitely ascertained the profit or loss of an operation. Suppose A, the speculator, gives B, the broker, one thousand dollars, and order him, B, to buy for his, A's, account, one hundred shares of N. W. Pref., at par; this one thousand dollars is the *margin*. Now, supposing B to have bought the stock at par, or 100; he pays $10,000 for it. $1,000 of this sum is represented by the margin, and $9,000 is paid by B. If the price falls to 93, B calls on A for more *margin*, to secure him against loss if the price should fall below 90. If A fails to respond, and the stock is sold at 93, A's loss is $700 besides the brokerage for buying and selling 100 shares, and interest on the $10,000, which the stock cost. The interest paid ranges from five to seven per cent. per annum, but when money is dear the interest rises sometimes to a fearful rate, running sometimes to 300 per cent. per annum; indeed, the rate of 1200 per cent. was paid for *carrying* stocks during the month of September, 1873.

The margin exacted for carrying stocks, is from three to twenty per cent., on the par value of the stock dealt in, and depends partly also on the kind of stock bought or sold; Western Union Tel., a high priced security liable to wide fluctuation, called for more ample margins than others which are lower priced, and which vibrate less frequently and swiftly. Governments are dealt in on much smaller margins, which run from one to five per cent. of the par value of the bonds.

The brokerage paid is from three dollars and twelve cents, *i. e.*, one thirty-second of one per cent. to twelve dollars and fifty cents, *i. e.*, one-eighth of one per cent. on one hundred shares, which is always reckoned at par, no matter what the market value of the stock may be; one hundred shares, at the price of ten (10), will cost $1,000, and the brokerage on the purchase or sale of this lot will be the same as on one hundred shares of Fort Wayne at 110, or one hundred shares of Delaware & Hudson at 50.

A broker is said to *carry* stock for his customer when he has bought and is holding it for his account. This *carrying* of stock is done in various ways. Sometimes the broker pays for the stock with his own money, or with the money he has on deposit from others; sometimes he borrows money on the stock from banks or private bankers. When his capital is small, he carries his customer's stock by *turning* it.

A broker is said to *turn* stock when he sells it out for *cash*, i. e., deliverable and payable the same day, and buys it back *regular*, i. e., deliverable and payable the next day. Under certain circumstances, *cash stock* and *regular stock* bear the same price in the market. But generally there is a difference of from one thirty-second to one eighth in favor of the seller of the *regular* stock. This difference is, of course, paid by the seller of the cash stock in lieu of interest for *carrying* it. When cash stock is very scarce, a difference of from one-quarter of one per cent. to four per cent. exists in favor of the cash stock. This scarcity of stock is produced by the action of rings, (as already described), for the purpose of compelling the bears to fulfil their contracts. Thus occasionally certain stocks, when cornered, will sell *regular* at 94, and cash 96.

Again, when money is very dear and in seasons of panic, a stock will sell for cash, one, two or three per cent. lower than the price *regular*. On the 29th of September, 1873, certain stocks sold at a difference of four per cent. between cash and regular, reflecting thereby the great apprehension and stringency that reigned in the market.

When stocks are *carried*, by raising a loan upon them, a stock note is sometimes given to the lender, which will read as follows, viz.:

$70,000. *New York, Oct. 26th, 1879.*

On Demand, we promise to pay to Brown Brothers, or Order, Seventy Thousand Dollars, for value received, with interest at the rate of 7 *per cent. per annum, having deposited with them as collateral security, with authority to sell the same at the* BROKER'S BOARD, or at public or private sale, *at their option, on the non-performance of this promise, and without notice, One. Thousand Shares of* Lake Shore Railroad Company.

JOHN DOE & CO.

But loans are generally negotiated without this formality, by simply depositing with the lender the stocks as collateral security, and receiving from him a check to the amount of 80 per cent. of their market value. Nearly all these loans are payable on demand, and are termed in Wall Street, *call loans*.

When stocks are in demand by the bears to fill their contracts, they are often carried by *loaning* them to the bears, who pay the holders the market price in currency. When the borrowed stock is returned, the sum paid the holders is returned to the bear borrower.

The following statement will show the prices at which stocks are bought and sold, and the interest and commissions paid for carrying stocks, viz.:

100 shares of Pittsburg, at $100 per share, will cost $10,000 at par. The market price of the same being 102 (i. e., 2 per cent. above par), 100 shares bought on the 8th of August, 1879, will cost	$10,200 00
The brokerage for buying ($\frac{1}{8}$ per cent. on $10,000), .	12 50
Interest 30 days, carrying same at 7 per cent., . .	57 87
Commissions, turning same (when money is tight), $\frac{1}{4}$ $25, again $\frac{1}{4}$ $25, two turns, $50, ...	50 00
Brokerage, selling same, ($\frac{1}{8}$ per cent. on $10,000), . .	12 50
	$10,332 87
Sold same September 8th, at 108 (market price) $10,400.	
Balance of profit due buyer, ...	67 13
	$10,400 00

(Or, if the price falls to par), sold same at 100, $10,000	
Balance loss of buyer, ...	332 87
	$10,332 87

Sometimes stocks are bought and sold on buyer's

or seller's option, as already mentioned. The following are copies of a buyer's and seller's option, viz.:

BUYER'S OPTION.

500 Shares.

New York, Sept. 11th, 1879.

I have PURCHASED *of John Q. Brown, Five Hundred Shares of the Stock of* Pittsburg Railroad Company, *at* 98 *per cent., payable and deliverable at his option, with interest at the rate of* 6 *per cent per annum.*

JAMES HOWARD.

SELLER'S OPTION.

500 Shares.

New York, Sept. 11th, 1879.

I have SOLD *to Solomon Stoddard, Five Hundred Shares of the Stock of the* Lake Shore Railroad Company, *at* 88 *per cent., payable and deliverable at my option, with interest at the rate of* 6 *per cent. per annum.*

HENRY E. WILSON.

Either party to one of these contracts has the privilege of calling, within a certain time, upon the other, for a margin of ten or twenty per cent. on the amount of the contract. The sum, or margin so called for, is deposited in one of the Trust Companies, to secure the party calling for it against loss on the contract. Parties who owe stocks on buyer's or seller's option, or who have borrowed stocks must be *notified* to deliver such stocks before and not after twelve o'clock, meridian, and all stocks are required to be delivered before quarter-past two in the afternoon.

The seller, in each of these cases, is supposed to *carry* the stock, and receive interest, and the buyer to pay interest on the contract price, until the contract is closed, either by the lapse of the time named, or by the buyer at his option, in the one case, or by the seller at his option in the other. The buyer is operating for a rise, and will call upon the seller, if the stock goes up above the contract price; while the seller is operating for a fall, and if the stock goes down, will buy it at the reduced price, and deliver it to the buyer at the higher contract price, as we have described in the preceding chapter.

Most of the stocks bought in the market are carried in other ways than by these options.

A large portion of the business is transacted, as already mentioned, by paying *differences* instead of actually delivering the stock called for. Suppose A sells to B 100 shares of Chicago and Northwestern at 75, A not having the stock to deliver; if the price falls to 70, B pays A $500, and if the price rises to 80, A pays B $500 *difference* between the present market price and the contract price. This will explain how it is that so many do an immense business on a moderate capital, for if all the stocks bought and sold in Wall Street were actually delivered, it would require thrice the number of hands, and ten times the capital, to do the business.

The object of the Bankers and Brokers' Association, which the defaulting Bonner ruined, was to help dealers to complete their contracts by paying differences. This was done on the Clearing House method, as in the case of the Gold Bank, which will be hereafter described; but only a small portion of the stocks bought and sold were sent through the Bankers and Brokers' Association.

The verdicts of juries, and the decisions of the courts, during the past twenty years, have in the litigation between brokers and their customers made the contract to carry stocks, a hard one for the brokers. Under these decisions, brokers have been held liable to carry stocks, even after the margin deposited with them has become exhausted, and notwithstanding the customer has been notified of the fact, and more margin demanded. In this way, brokers have sometimes found themselves incurring a heavy loss, after their customer's stock has been bought in or sold out in default of margin. A customer is thus enabled to fasten himself on his broker, as the old man did on the shoulders of Sinbad, the sailor, and may compel him to carry the stock held for his (the customer's) account through all manner of panics and corners, till a profit can be shown on the transaction.

To meet this difficulty, the customer is asked, by many of the brokerage houses, to sign some such memorandum as the following, to wit:—

Agreement, made this 20th day of September, 1879.

FOR VALUE RECEIVED, I hereby agree with JONES & CO., BANKERS AND BROKERS, of the city, county and State of New York, that in case I shall be or become indebted to them at any time during the existence of this contract, for money lent or paid to me or for my account or use, or for any overdraft, or for any deficiency arising out of contracts or transactions in or relating to Stock Securities or Bonds, the said

JONES & CO. may, in their discretion, sell at either of the Brokers' Boards, or wherever they deem advisable, or at public auction or private sale, with or without advertising the same, and with or without notice to me, all or any property, things in action, or collateral securities held by them belonging to me, or in which I am interested, or may hypothecate or otherwise use the same, and may apply the proceeds towards any such indebtedness and the interest thereon, and expenses of sale, or negotiation, holding me responsible and liable for payment of any deficiency existing after such application.

And in case of short sales, so called, or time contracts on my behalf, for sale or delivery of Stocks or Bonds, they may protect themselves by prompt purchase in manner and place as above provided in case of sales, whenever they may deem it necessary, and without prior call on me, holding me liable in like manner, for any deficiency.

And this AGREEMENT shall never be altered or annulled by any verbal agreement, it being the intention that this contract alone shall control all business transactions for my account by said JONES & CO. from this 20th day of September until this contract is surrendered to me, and the possession of this agreement by said JONES & CO. shall be conclusive evidence that it is in full force and effect.

Internal Revenue Stamp.

JOHN LEICESTER.

In presence of WILLIAM BROWN. (Customer.)

The speculation in gold had its focus so near that of stocks that they were almost one. The walls of the gold exchange were one with those of the stock exchange in a physical as well as a moral sense. A dingy room, fifty by seventy, painted in sombre fresco, on the shady side of New Street, hardly lighted by ten narrow windows, through which the golden sunlight flickered briefly of an afternoon, and then vanished over the tall blocks of brick and mortar along Broadway. Here was the Gold Room. Its style of architecture reminded one of the shanties erected for the temporary accommodation of miners, working some auriferous vein, which may any hour be cut off by a fault, and cease to be remunerative; and long before gold fell to par, this frail building, containing the busy bees in the honied cells of the eighths and quarters of the gold speculation, was swept and garnished, and divided into offices, which were occupied by the devotees of a more permanent speculation. Inside this shell of a building were numerous catty-corners and nooks, fenced off by iron railings or diaphanous pine planks. Into these recesses the weary operators were wont to retire and wait for prices to move, and then sally forth and catch the halves and units "living as they rise." Queer-looking little boys, whose knowing eyes belied the general vacuity of their faces, appeared and disappeared through side doors and gateways. Voices rose and fell in discordant chorus, and in the pauses a dull burr and rapid clicking, as of a small cotton factory, told that the telegraph was spinning out long rolls of paper ribbons marked with quotations from the marts of London, Frankfort, and Paris. The cast-iron figure in the centre of the hall (which ought to have been, but was not, a statue of Dame Fortune, standing by her wheel), threw up a shower of spray which fell into a basin, tinkling and clinking like coin of gold. The operators grouped around it, hurling phantom ten thousand dollar gold bricks, or staring at each other through the drops, looked as if they were interrogating the fountain respecting the success of their ventures; but like the enchanted fountain in Moore's song, it (generally) "answered no!" A gallery and a space, fenced off below, was lined with the anxious, haggard faces of speculative outsiders.

What was that sound. Music? Yes; and strange

music it was. Beside the president's rostrum there was a man sitting before a small piano, which communicated by electricity with an indicator on the wall, and marked the ruling price of the moment. The tunes played by this piano entered through the eye; both the air and the words were expressed by figures that rung on a scale of prices which ran from 120 to 130 years ago. On dull days the tune was *lento ralantando,* slow and moderate, but on a rampant, or a panic-market, the strain swelled to an awful diapason, through which was heard by some the pæans of victory, by others the dirges of ruin.

The nucleus of that financial comet, the gold speculation, distinctly displayed itself first in 1862, amid the darkness of the "coal hole," No. 17 William Street, a place to which reference has already been made, in connection with the public board. It rose slowly up, drawing after it a portentous train. In two years it reached its zenith, and covered half the sky of speculation with its baleful light.

The magnitude of the operations in the precious metal, rendered a separate room necessary. In the summer of 1864, Gilpin's reading-room, on the ground floor of the southeast corner of William Street and Exchange Place, was first used as the stamping ground of the bellowing herd which made gold speculation their chief end and aim. Any subscriber to the privileges of this reading-room, (the yearly dues being twenty-five dollars), could enter and bet his pile on the oscillations.

Speculators are like jealousy, "they make the meat they feed on." The volume of business kept rolling up in a geometrical ratio, and the limits of Gilpin's room soon became too "cabined, cribbed and confined" for the expansive genius of the gold men. A cry went up, "room for the leper! room!" (I mean the leper of modern finance, the gold speculator. This species of leprosy at that time seemed to have broken out in great yellow blotches over a goodly proportion of society here in Gotham.) Happy thought, No. 1. Let us resolve ourselves into the firm of We, Us & Co! Happy thought, No. 2. Let us raise the admission dues to $100, then to $250, then to $500, and thereby put money into our associate purse.

These happy thoughts occurred to certain veteran operators, and were acted upon instanter. One of these individuals was W. G. R., once of the firm of V. V., R. & D., a wiry, stocky little man, standing as firm on his pins as if he could whip his weight in wild cats, and looking as though he were constantly rolling several hundred thousand in certificates of his favorite metal, as a sweet morsel under his tongue.

A long, deep, low room, (the same where the public board once held its sessions), was soon fitted up on the southeast corner of William and Beaver Streets, and the multitudinous firm of W. U. & Co., rushed in and commenced business.

In the latter part of the summer of 1865, the members of this gold exchange moved into new quarters on New street (which we have already described). The admission dues of members were raised to $1,000, then to $2,000, then to $5,000, and finally to $10,000, the last sum being in the nature of a prohibitory tariff on the vessels which sought to enter the quiet haven of fortune through this stormy golden gate.

The Gold Bank was organized and went into operation in December, 1866. The object of this institution was by adopting a system of clearance on the plan of the Bank Clearing House, to simplify and facilitate the business arising out of the buying, selling, and delivering gold. The delivering and receiving from office to office of such vast sums of gold as were daily bought and sold at the Gold Room entailed not only great manual labor, but the risk of loss and theft. This trouble and expense was saved. The Gold Bank received and delivered the gold, and took the differences which were due from or to the operators, or, in other words, it *cleared* gold, just as the Clearing House clears the bank exchanges.

The Gold Bank was a very profitable enterprise to its projectors and stockholders. It charged ten cents on every ten thousand gold cleared, and as for many years it cleared from $20,000,000 to $50,000,000 daily, it accumulated profits, and up to September, 1869, paid sixteen per cent. dividends annually. In the course of its short history, it had, like many other Wall street institutions, its ups and downs. The clearances demanded by the extraordinary operations of Black Friday week in September, 1869, were too large for the machinery of the bank, and it was forced into the hands of a receiver by the brokers of Fisk and Gould. After its reorganization in 1870, it paid from ten to twenty-eight per cent. in yearly dividends till its dissolution, in December, 1877. The Gold Exchange went out of existence in 1878, the speculation in gold no longer furnishing a remunerative business. To-day, with gold at par, and imported from Europe at the rate of millions every week, then passing in the vaults of the Sub-Treasury, to lie there almost uncalled for, the great gold speculation of the eighteen years from 1863 to 1878 seems like a wild dream or a disordered imagination.

The decline of the Gold Exchange no doubt served to increase the speculation in stocks, by liberating millions of capital and hundreds of brokers once employed in that now defunct institution.

The growth of speculation in stocks may be best illustrated by a comparison of the stock exchange in 1860 with the same institution in 1880. In the former year the membership was four hundred; to-day it is more than one thousand.

Then the fee for admission was $500, now it is $10,000. The recent rise in the price of seats is, however, partly due to the admission of members residing in other cities.

When a member dies, the sum of $10,000 is paid by the insurance fund of the Stock Exchange, for the benefit of the family of the deceased.

In 1860, the list of stocks and bonds dealt in represented a par value of about $2,000,000,000. To-day it represents a par value of nearly $8,000,000.

Then the amount of daily dealings averaged $2,000,000. To-day the average is about $20,000,000.

The number of those who speculated on a grand scale in 1860 was very few. In 1879-80 there are twenty men whom we might name who speculate in stocks, and whose aggregate wealth, mostly invested in stocks and bonds, might be fairly set down as representing two hundred million dollars.

The foregoing is only a brief and very imperfect outline of Wall street and of the Stock and Gold Exchange. Institutions can be best illustrated by their moral workings on individuals. History by tragedy, comedy, and the limner's art. Wall street, too, shows clearest by the portraits, the moving tales and comic situations, the personal aspects and experiences, of the men who have given themselves up to the chances, changes and struggles of a speculator's life.

CHAPTER III.

THE FIRST VENTURE.

A New York Boarding-house in Perspective—Wall Street Patter—Curbstone Brokers "At Home"—A Flyer on Old Southern—A Bird of Omen—The Regular Brokers in Their Work-shop—Jacob Little—His Career—The Napoleon of the Bears—A Shrewd Move—He Scatters the Bulls—His Character and Peculiarities—Old Southern "Firm at the Close."

IN the year 1857, there stood a three story and attic mansion in the lower part of the City of New York, not many miles, or even yards, from College Place. It was the last of a row of similar domiciles which had been shoved from their foundations, and their place occupied by a tier of heavy built stores, which now reared themselves aloft, and looked down like so many tall bullies with beetling brows upon the solitary dwelling-house, hustled and crowded between them.

It was easy to guess its history from its appearance. In its first years it had been the abode of an opulent merchant. But what had once been a private use was now a public convenience. It was now fulfilling the destiny to which every house in the city would seem to be finally allotted; it was a boarding-house.

A roomy habitation cut up into chambers, windowed or windowless and pigeon-holed like a lawyer's desk with cells and dormitories, resonant through the watches of the night with the stertorous breathing of hard-worked dry-goods drummers or the night-mare cries of dyspeptic law-clerks.

The dining-room was a little Babel in respect of tongues, a miniature New York in respect of callings. Square merchants, angular lawyers and rotund doctors loudly bandying the bye-words and slang of their different professions. Mysterious men, cormorants of "Queer Street," who seemed to extract a rich sustenance out of the viewless air, like the chameleon changing their color with the objects of their pursuit, haunting hall-ways and dusky basements, or on elevated perches with winking eyes and darting viscid tongues, ensnaring the tiny insects of the hour. Old buffers, narrators of the commercial legends of Pearl Street and studiously marking with intermittent glance in the columns of the Journal of Commerce, the hoistings and tumblings of cotton and the ebbings and flowings of tea. Young lads, tyros in the great school of trade, to whose ears the peals from the cupola of old St. Paul might be supposed to ring out in prophetic tones as Bow bells did to Dick Whittington: "Turn again Dick Johnson, or Jones, or Smith! Mayor of New York!"

In this dining-room in the month of June, in the year aforesaid, seated at a side table, were five persons of the masculine gender, swiftly consuming, after the fashion of their country, their six o'clock dinner. An indescribable something about their air and manner, would have subtly but surely told to the thorough-bred New Yorker what their occupation might be, though a new comer would have not so readily guessed it. All were nattily dressed, but three of them sat self-absorbed, silently attending to the important, rather than (to them) agreeable business in which they were just then engaged. The two others, however, amply made up for the taciturnity of their companions. One of these two was a gentleman moulded on the cycloidal pattern. His body, which was as nearly circular as was consistent with the vital economy, was firmly set on a pair of columnar legs. His head and face was an oblate spheroid, hair curled like a Bacchanal, eyes twin orbs, wide open and staring, eyebrows well defined and semi-circular, as if drawn by compasses, his nose the segment of a circle, and his mouth a large, red dot; in fact, the two features last named, seemed to form a perpetual interrogation point, expressive of wondering inquiry.

The other was built on precisely the opposite plan. Tall of stature, and slender of limb, a long face, with lantern-jaws, a lengthy nose and straight hair, he might be imagined to represent linear measurement as his fellow did, spherical and cubical contents. A young lady, who sat at the large table, had given this couple the sobriquet of O. and I. from their resemblance to those letters of the alphabet, and a young gentleman, fresh from the classic shades of Yale, was wont to hail their entrance with the words, Io! triumphe!

Sitting directly opposite to this couple at table, my attention was attracted by the strange jargon in which they conversed in jerky staccato tones.

"Anything doing in Nicaragua?" inquired letter O. of letter I. "Nothing said at the close," replied letter I. From which I inferred they might have some connection with the fillibustering in that country. "What's the price of Cumberland coal?" asked O. From which immediately a surmise arose that O. and I. were in the coal business.

"How is old Southern," inquired O. again. These men must be in the theatrical line, from their inquiring so familiarly after Sothern, the actor.

"Not much margin on that," said O, holding a strip of leathery steak on a fork. "A good sale," retorted letter I.

"Seller three," rejoined O, "or regular?"

"Nothing up! and buyer three."

"No commish," &c.

These observations, uttered in a jocose tone, seemed to give exquisite gratification to the whole five, and strongly excited the risibles of O.

Just then, a grave gentleman addressed him, inquiring the news from Wall Street. This cleared up the mystery. These men were dealers in the stock market. They soon rose from the table and left the room, and the grave gentleman then informed me they were Wall Street brokers. "Curb-stone brokers," said Mrs. S., correcting him. "Gutter-snipes," mamma, added the young lady.

The tribe of curb-stone brokers, which in the greenback era swarmed like locusts and filled the air with their importunate chirk, in 1857 was comparatively few in number. Their offices when they have offices are merely desk-rooms in upper lofts or murky basements. More generally the flooring of their offices is the sidewalk and its ceiling the firmament "fretted with golden fire," perhaps we should say with golden fractions—the eighths and quarters of the market price which it is their business to catch. On a busy day they are all eyes and ears, scud and scamper, their fingers quivering like aspen leaves, their mouths pouring out a stream of bids and offers disencumbered of all the spare syllables, while they telegraph signals with the ten digits, and with nods and winks.

The curb-stone broker is the financial bud which if not nipped by some untimely frost, often blossoms into the flower which blooms in the garden of the regular board. He works for smaller wages than his regularly initiated brother of the Stock Exchange. In 1879 his brokerage is only 1-32, or three dollars and twelve cents for buying or selling one hundred shares, in 1857 it was 1-8, or twelve dollars and a half, and sometimes only half that amount. This brokerage is only for *buying and selling*, for the *delivering and carrying* of stocks is done mostly by the more wealthy brokers of the regular board. The curb-stone broker is the scullion in the brokerage kitchen, feasting on remnants and odds and ends, and is obliged to serve his time there before he can be admitted to the banquets and privileges of the parlor. His favorite stamping-ground in 1857, and as late as 1864, was in William Street; in 1879 his species is nearly extinct.

A few days after this, as I was passing down William Street, about ten o'clock in the morning, I ran against O. (by which name he will be designated in these pages), on the edge of a crowd of thirty or forty men who were standing on the sidewalk. He saluted me with all the familiarity of an old acquaintance, and offered with the greatest cheerfulness to show me the lions, or rather the bulls and bears of

CURBSTONE BROKERS.

the street, fairly deluging my ears with his lingo. "How is it done? Easiest thing in the world, put up your margin, say five hundred on a hundred shares, then keep margined up or they'll sell you out. Buy your stock any way you like. Buyer 30, or cash, or regular and carry it. Don't let 'em bluff you. Never sold short? No? Then sell on a seller thirty, put up your margin same as before, or, if you'd rather, sell it regular and borrow next day for delivery—interest runs in your favor on sellers' option, six per cent. Keep your eye peeled for corners. Brokerage? One quarter per cent. each way. I'll do your business for an eighth. Take one of my cards (handing me a card), good references you see. Office up three flights."

THE CARD.

WILLIAM L. P——,

BROKER IN STOCKS AND BONDS,

Refers by Permission to

NO. 49 WALL STREET,

W—— & B——,
J—— L—— & Co.,
F——, D—— & Co.

All this was rolled off as glibly as the patter of a mountebank, and as he paused I detected him in the act of winking to a short man on the other side of the crowd, who looked very much as if he might be the half-brother of Socrates, and who a moment after came round and joined us. He hailed my friend O. by the name of Little Bitters, which was the name under which he was known among his Wall Street associates, though why he should have borne this name it is hard to say; it was certainly not from any proclivity to the beverage, and his disposition and manners were of the blandest.

Socrates was duly introduced as Mr. D. A silent man with a high forehead and a face plowed into furrows by a ten years' experience in Wall Street, where, as I afterwards learned, he had been playing a game of see-saw, making and losing alternately, and paying every year a small fortune in the shape of commissions to his brokers.

His lofty brow and general appearance of owlish wisdom, led me to expect that this man could give me the entire philosophy of speculation in a few words, and I was not deceived, for on asking him his opinion of the market, and whether it would answer to take a chance in, he uttered the following somewhat turfy apothegm: "You can't tell till you bet." Quite true, Mr. D. You never *can* tell till you put up your margin, in other words, till you *bet* in Wall Street.

But all this time, while we stood there, the knot of brokers and speculators on the side-walk were as busy as bees over a honey-pot, coming and going, brandishing their arms and vociferating, making notes in little books, now buying stock, and running back to their offices, and reporting what they had done, and anon returning with fresh orders to buy or sell.

And now a slender young man, of twenty-five summers, came bounding into the crowd. It was R. He was be-ringed and be-jewelled like a Rajah, hatted, gloved, shod, coated and pantalooned, in all the glory of Broadway art. He seemed to know every one, and every one seemed to hail him with empressment, mingled with respect, for he had gone short of Old Southern a few weeks before, and had just bought in at a profit of twenty-five thousand.

Michigan Southern and Northern Indiana Railroad Stock, more familiarly known as Old Southern, or afterwards as Lake Shore, is one of the old historical stocks of Wall Street. The name calls up memories of great fortunes, won and lost in its mighty vibrations. The magic of its rings, the unfathomable depth of its pools, are known to many a speculator, to his joy or sorrow, and most of the great operators of the street, for the past eighteen years, have been mixed up with it for the weal or woe of themselves and the public. Little, the Litchfields, Travers and two of the Jeromes, Henry Keep, Daniel Drew and Cornelius Vanderbilt, used to toss it up and down, like a gigantic shuttlecock, from 8 to 140.

Old Southern was the card to-day. It had lately been taken hold of by a ring known as the Litchfield party, and hoisted to 55, from which point, it had dropped, and was selling that morning for 38. Nothing was heard on the street but Old Southern, Buyer ten, Seller ten, cash or regular. They who had gone short of it at a higher figure, were buying in and covering their shorts, and bagging their profits; they who had gone long of it at a higher figure, were selling it and ascertaining their losses. Some were buying for a future profit (or loss); the ring were busily crying down the stock, and all the while quietly buying it for another twist upwards.

"I can guarantee you a handsome profit on Old Southern," remarked O; "you see the time to buy stocks is when they are down." This familiar truism, together with the fact, that R, the lucky bear above mentioned, was in the crowd, buying like smoke, decided me. An order was forthwith made out, signed, and handed to O, as follows, to wit.: "Buy for my account and risk, 100 shares of Old Southern at the market; Buyer 30." Signed, etc.

O. then elbowed his way into the crowd with the air of a man who had important business to transact, and bought in a trice the 100 shares, giving me a memorandum which read thus: "N. Y., June —, 1857, I have to-day bought of W. B. C. & Co., for your account, 100 shares of Old So. Buyer 30 at 38⅝." Signed, etc.

Having handed O. five hundred dollars as a margin on this venture, my frail bark may be considered to have been duly launched on the stormy waters of Wall Street.

It is the first venture in speculation which costs, as many a man has found to his sorrow. Lucky is he whose first flyer of one hundred shares shows a loss, for this is a lesson and a warning sufficient often to turn him from the career of a stock-operator. But when the first flyer shows a profit, ah! that first profit! The first sip of the cup, this is delight, then comes rapture, frenzy, stupor and the dreary wakening, in quick succession.

The sound of the half hour stroke after ten, from the belfry of Trinity, had hardly died away, when looking towards Wall Street, I saw approaching, a quaint figure, holding in its hand a roll of stock certificates. It disappeared down a basement office at the corner of William Street and Exchange Place, but was up again on the sidewalk in a twinkling. A tall, slight figure, with a stoop, a black alpaca coat hanging loosely about it, walking towards the crowd at a rapid pace. What a strange face! The coloring a vivid darkness, a clear-obscure, like a tropical night. The eyes dark, with a dreamy, introverted look—the eyes of a philosopher or poet, the drooping, sagacious nose of a financier, and the flexible mouth of an orator. The expression mobile, changing not only emotionally, but in the shape of the features. As he paused on the fringes of the crowd, his lips were suddenly protruded, as if the market were something to be tested by the sense of taste, and then as suddenly withdrawn to their natural position. Again they were puckered up, and protruded as if he were preparing to kiss something, perhaps a plump profit. Every motion and look spoke the Wall Street man, and something more. For during the ten seconds that he stood on the edge of the walk, balancing himself on his toes, now dropping his head on his breast, now raising it and looking over the crowd, and turning it from one side to the other with fitful glances, he seemed something uncanny—a raven or other bird of omen, hovering over the market, and preparing to croak the warning of panic. Suddenly he wheeled about, and flitted through a door opposite the crowd, on the west side of William Street. Who could he be? Gazing so intently upon him during the brief interval between his coming and going, I had till now neglected to ask O., my coryphœus, the name of this strange looking personage. "I don't know whom you mean. Let's visit the Board," replied he, "and we will find out who he is."

The Board of Brokers, in 1857, and as late as the Fall of 1865, (when they moved into their new building in Broad Street,) held their sessions in a room which overlooked Lord's Court, which formed the center of a block, bounded on the north by Exchange Place, on the east by William Street, on the south by Beaver Street, and on the west by Broad Street. "All roads lead to Rome;" the Stock Exchange Room was approached by many entrances, or rather tunnels, from different streets and quarters of the compass. These tunnels led across corridors, up stairs and down stairs, now dark, now light, and then dark again, and all converged into the central mine, echoing with the hoarse cries of the workmen in stocks as they wielded the monetary pickaxe and spade, or with words like hammers, smote the drill preparatory to some explosion which was to shake the rooted pillars of finance.

O. stuck closer to me than a brother, and by the favor of one of his broker friends, we were soon ushered into a room thronged by one or two hundred men, some moving about in circles as in a voluntary tread-mill, others in little knots, holding a discussion or retailing gossip of the market, others gathered in the pit, apparently waiting for the president to call the stock which they had orders to buy or sell. The market was at that time full of cliques and corners. Erie, New York Central, Old Southern, La Crosse, and many other stocks were under manipulation.

The call that morning had run through Governments, State Stocks and miscellaneous securities, and now ERIE rang out from the rostrum.

The whole body of dealers rushed to the front, red-faced old gentlemen, with frosty heads, left their seats, and their huge quotation books, portly men "sleek headed and such as sleep o' nights" undisturbed by dreams of panics and ruined customers, lean and hungry-looking men of sallow complexion, youths with shining morning faces, and promenade attire, all skated across the floor with a ravenous eagerness, and yelled out bids and offers, poking their quivering forefingers almost into the eyes of their competitors. In two minutes, the sharp fire of voices died away into a few dropping shots, and again the president shouted NEW YORK CENTRAL. The hubbub rose again, and swelled still louder, and then died away as before. Swiftly the call proceeded. The name of stock after stock, fell from the president's lips, caught up by the crowd, and tossed about from mouth to mouth, echoed from the lofty ceiling, but falling dead upon the cloth-lined walls.

Here was a new form of the Wall Street lingo—a mathematical form. These men spoke in figures, instead of words, and figures uttered so quickly, and poured out in such numbers, that the spectator was fairly dizzied: $36\frac{1}{4}$, $\frac{1}{8}$, $\frac{3}{8}$, $11\frac{1}{2}$, $\frac{5}{8}$, $\frac{3}{4}$, 22, 300, 500. Only the clear voice of the presiding officer, announcing the closing bids, gives any idea to an outside observer, of the real price of the stock, and as to what has been actually bought and sold by any broker, that is only known to themselves. A single word—bought or sold—lost in the din, a crook of the finger, a slight nod of the head, or a wink of the eye, all unnoticed by the spectator, settles the business done between the buyer and seller. This language of signs, is as distinct and definite a part of the Wall Street lingo, as that of words and figures. The eye is the interpreter here instead of the ear, while the body, and, fingers, and features, are the speaking organs.

But all the time we had been gazing on this curious spectacle from behind the scenes, the same strange figure I had noticed in William Street, was moving restlessly about, now standing on the uppermost step, which descended into the crowded pit, and buying a sellers' option, now sitting down in a fidgety uncertain way for a moment, and then rising and bidding where he stood, for various stocks, as they were called.

When old Southern was reached, he moved quickly to the centre of the room, and bought five hundred shares, sellers' option, and sold five hundred shares, buyers' option, while the crowd paused and turned their eyes upon him.

"Who is that man?" inquired I. "That man," replied O, "that man is *Jacob Little*."

The portrait of this noted financier, which accompanies these pages, is only the faithful representation of that face in repose, the forceful will, the keen strong intellect, the swift play of the feelings, which lighten up that face, and shaped it into changeful successive expressions, could never have been brought out by art. Jacob Little! A great name for twenty years in Wall Street! Banker, broker, operator in stocks, exchanges and cotton, he ran through the whole scale, sounding all the heavy notes, from high to low. He would reign the king of the market, fight a dozen pitched battles, suffer defeat, abdicate, and then once more ascend the throne, all in the space of six months. Master of every kind of game played in stocks, rings, corners, sleight-of-hand, beggar your neighbor, bluff, lock-up and bar-out, straddling two horses going different ways, he had the skill as well as the nerve to play them all, and for the most part came out the winner.

Born in Newburyport, Massachusetts, the son of a ship-builder in that town, he came to New York when a boy, and entered the office of Jacob Barker, another celebrated financier, and soon showed himself by his diligence and shrewdness, to be a worthy pupil of his master, from whom also he may have derived those brusque and almost rough manners, for which he was afterwards so remarkable. Circumstances decided his future career and policy, as they have that of so many other men of mark. If he had commenced his life as a stock operator in 1861, instead of 1835, he might have been a great "Bull," and have shared with Cornelius Vanderbilt, the spoils and honors of his campaigns. But soon after he started in business, the financial omens all portended the great revulsion of 1837; this fact, and the failure of several banks, organized by Jacob Barker, his former employer, inspired him with distrust as to the future value of stock-securities, and so he became a "Bear." When the severe panic of that era ensued, he was heavily short of stocks, and made enormous profits by selling short, for several years afterwards. He used to sell Vicksburg Bank Stock, and other Southern securities on sellers' options, of one, two, and three years, and as those stocks fell almost to zero, his profits were correspondingly large. From 1838, to 1845–6, he was the leading man of the street, and was rated at two millions, a great fortune in those days.

It was in 1846, if we are rightly informed, that his first failure occurred, about the time of the corner in Norwich and Worcester Railroad Stock. In this operation he was contrary to his wont, a bull, and attempted to control this stock, and entrap his old companions in arms, the bears, by compelling them to buy in the stock, and fill their contracts at 95, or thereabouts. Among his associates in this enterprise, were certain wealthy Bostonians, who, in order to secure themselves against any sales of the stock below 90, had got Mr. Little to sign a bond in the penal sum of $25,000, by which, he agreed not to sell any of the stock below that price. But after the corner had been pushed to about 90, he found that the undertaking would be impracticable, and that he would be plunged into irretrievable ruin by proceeding in it. Accordingly, he sent a large amount of the stock to Rawdon & Groesbeck, who had been old clerks of his, with directions to send it to Boston, and sell it there. The Bostonians bought the stock, in order to sustain the market, and not knowing how to account for so much stock coming on the market, wrote to Mr. Little, who replied, that he had been compelled to sell the stock, and that he was ready to settle up on the bond, and a few days after sent them a check for $25,000, which relieved him from all legal liability thereupon.

Mr. Little's losses on this Norwich and Worcester attempted corner were $1,000,000, but his foresight had prevented a worse catastrophe, and he soon paid up in full and resumed.

Of course his numerous bear operations made him fair game for a corner, and sometimes he found himself surrounded by an army of bulls, whereupon he would retreat to his last fortress, and after making terms with his besiegers would surrender, and then proceed to re-organize his shattered forces. But he was generally a hard man to corner, and occasionally, when his antagonists thought they had accomplished their purpose, he would turn on them and rout them with great slaughter. Once he sold an enormous quantity of Erie Stock on sellers' options; the bulls quietly took it, and having bought up the loose stock floating in the market, proceeded to put on the screws, bidding the stock up, and holding it for the day when Mr. Little would have to deliver the stock which he owed. No flaw could be seen in the scheme. The stock was held in a firm grip—the great bear *must* come to the conspirators and beg for mercy. The eventful day for the completion of his contracts was now come. Before twelve a notification was sent to the parties to whom the stock was due, that the stock would be delivered immediately, and a few moments after, in marched Mr. Little himself, bearing a huge bundle of *fresh certificates of Erie Railroad Stock*. The bull party were in consternation. They found themselves loaded with a burden on which they had not calculated. A panic took place, the market fell twenty per cent., and Mr. Little had won the day. How was this? It appears that the Erie Railroad Company had sometime previously issued a large number of certificates of indebtedness, *convertible into stock*, (a fact unknown to the bull party,)—these certificates had been bought up by Mr. Little, and converted into stock the morning of the day when they were delivered.

The financial star of Mr. Little had, in 1857, long ceased to be in the ascendant, but its influence was still felt on the opinions, operations and fortunes of the frequenters of the stock-market. His qualities of head, heart and character were such as had always won the respect and confidence of the stock-dealing public. Not the least remarkable among these qualities, was his intense devotion to his life-work—the buying and selling of stocks. Action to him was happiness, and in his own experience he seemed to prove the truth of the poet's lines:

> "Even when the wished end's denied,
> Yet while the busy means are plied
> They bring their own reward."

Though he were buying or selling millions, he thought no detail of business beneath his notice. He overlooked his clerks in his office, and no one could enter or leave it without his knowledge, and any day he might have been seen hurrying through the streets, diving into basements and delivering his stocks like an errand boy. Sunday brought that busy brain and hand little rest, for while the bells were pealing the hour of worship, he could often be seen wending his way to *his* sanctum in William Street. His amusement, his pleasure, his life, was business, business, still business. The story of operations so wide-embracing, close, swift and daring, is among the best-kept traditions of the street. What a record of the thousands of millions bought and sold! What a tale of marvellous diligence could be unfolded, if that huge pile of stock registers and ledgers, now amid the forgotten lumber of a garret, could be opened! To make or lose an immense fortune was, to him, what a game of chess is to others, a pastime. More than once he failed, owing a million beyond what he could pay, and in twelve months resumed business with a capital of a half million, after paying his entire indebtedness.

But saturated as he was with the spirit of Wall Street, and breathing as he had done from early youth that moral atmosphere so deadening and blighting to the noblest natures, he preserved not only an unspotted commercial reputation, but all his native kindliness and magnanimity. Beneath his blunt words and ungracious ways there was a warm and generous heart, often too proud to accept favors, but always ready to bestow them. He would compromise the claims which he held against others for what they chose to offer, but constantly insisted upon paying his own debts in full. In the latter years of his life he failed for a large amount, and, as usual in such cases, gave his notes to settle the indebtedness. Certain friends of his held some of these notes, and not expecting ever to call on Mr. Little for payment, or that he would ever be able to pay them, had cancelled them, and wiped the indebtedness from their books. But the maker of the notes one day put in an appearance for the purpose of taking them up, having just made one of his great hits. He expressed the greatest indignation on finding the notes had been cancelled, and insisted on paying their amount, which he accordingly did.

If all the claims which he had compromised during his active business life, and every other debt which was due him could have been collected, the sum it is said would have amounted to several millions. As it was, after his death, out of his old accounts, his friends collected $150,000 as a provision for his family.

For some weeks previous to the morning referred to in the fore part of this chapter, Mr. Little had been operating for a decline in Old Southern. But in what way he was operating that particular morning was not patent, at least to the eyes of a novice. The price of Old Southern was firm at 38½, and was apparently tending upwards.

CHAPTER IV.

PROFIT AND LOSS.

Brokers Adjourn!—Machinery of Business—A Gutter-snipe's Cock-loft—"A Man may Smile, and Smile, and be a"—— Broker—An Operator's Day-Dream—The Old Bear Growls in his Den—The Ring Hoisting a Bale of Stock—The First Profit—A Broker's Account—Fingering the Cash—Out of the Woods into Wall Street—Flyer No. 2—The First Loss—A Short Sale and the Result—A Wild-cat Bank—Philosophy of Speculation—Beware, Greenhorns!

IT was twelve o'clock, meridian. The call of stocks was over, and the brokers, with their quotation books under their arms, were hurrying out of the door through the tunnel-hall into William Street, by one exit, and into Exchange Place by another, but a goodly number descended the staircase into Beaver Street, and bent their course to lower Delmonico, which stands hard by, to refresh themselves with those dainty viands and beverages so delectable to the palate of the regular Wall Street broker, who is almost invariably a delicate feeder, and a cautious drinker, if he would be successful.

While sitting in that resounding boudoir of finance —the broker's board—O. squatted on a chair by my side, was pouring into my ear his explanations of the mysteries of the trade in stocks, retailing the gossip of the market, and pointing out the notable dealers, and recounting their profits and losses. When the session broke up, he rose, remarking that he must go to his office and *report* what he had done, and asked me to accompany him thither.

A broker *reports* his purchases and sales to his office, so that they may be *compared,* in order to prevent misunderstandings and mistakes. A clerk, or office boy of the buyer, goes to the office of the seller, and announces to the stock-clerk there, that the firm or individual who employs him have bought 100 shares of Northwest or Lake Shore, buyer 30, cash or regular, as the case may be, and the stock-clerk, if the comparison is found correct, thereupon bawls out "all right." The same form of comparison is gone through with by a clerk of the seller, who visits the office of the buyer for that purpose. Slips of paper containing memoranda of the purchases and sales, and signed by the respective brokers, are also exchanged. This report and comparison of purchases and sales clenches the bargain, and is of course a very necessary part of the business.

O. gripping my arm affectionately, trundled along through the devious passage into William Street, and so on, up to the Sun building, on the corner of Wall Street; then ascending three flights of stairs, puffing and sweating, he burst into a small room where a tall man was sitting before a solitary desk adding up columns of figures. He turned, and I recognized my table acquaintance known to the reader as letter I. His true name was Lansing. He was man-of-all-work in the office of O. his functions being those of confidential clerk, book-keeper, stock-clerk, cashier, errand-boy, and quasi-partner withal.

VIEW OF THE SUB-TREASURY.

He gave me a subdued greeting, but when O. informed him that I had just taken a flyer on 100 Old Southern, the commissions whereon redounded to the profit of their office, his face became instantly wreathed in wooden smiles, and dotted with dimples like a figure-head of curled maple. That broker's smile with which he greets a new customer, who could describe it but a Hogarth or a Dantin? How indifferent, or serious, or glum the expression of his face to the outsider, from whom he expects nothing! How cold and repellant to the customer who is "cleaned out" and marginless! But when the young operator approaches him with his pockets stuffed with greenbacks, his nerves unbruised by the shocks and thrills of the market, ready to encounter risks without a thought of the danger, and buying and selling with all the vivacity of youth, then how the face of his broker expands, brightens and warms. The corners of his mouth curve upwards, the muscles of his cheeks are hollowed into cavities in which the very sylphs of mirth seem to lurk, his eyes twinkle out of semi-circles of crows' feet, and his whole countenance appears to be under the inspiration of Momus, the God of laughter.

"Happy to see you at our office. Make it your headquarters. You've made a good a purchase this morning. Old Southern is sure to go up again; the ring are not through with it. Keep watch of it, however; don't let it run away from you, etc., etc." Under these cordial assurances of Lansing, everything looked rose-colored.

"What pleasant people these brokers are! What a charming prospect is opened to me! Let me see;

if Old Southern goes up ten per cent., I shall make a profit of $1,000. This sum I will draw out, and put $900 into a railroad bond for investment, and have $100 besides for pocket money, or I can put the $1,000 in the bank as the seed-corn for a future harvest. Suppose I add this $1,000 to my present margin and buy 300 shares in my next operation, make $3,000 out of this purchase and so on. In a year a fortune will have been piled up, etc.

These delicious reflections were interrupted by O., inquiring if I would like to accompany Lansing, his factotum, to the office of Jacob Little, to compare the 100 shares of Old Southern, (as I had seemed so much interested in his strange story,) or, as he rather disrespectfully phrased it, "stir up the Old Bear in his den."

We went. The office of Jacob Little & Co. was in the old Merchant's Exchange, and as we entered it, we saw Mr. Little vibrating between the desk where he generally stood and the desk occupied by his clerks, now snatching up a pile of stock certificates which lay before him, and fumbling them over, and now growling out something to the clerks. When he caught sight of us, he stood eyeing us with flickering and expectant glance.

"Mr. Little, we bought of your firm this morning, 100 Old Southern, at 38⅝. Buyer 30," said Lansing.

"Who's that! Who's that?"

"William L. P——," returned Lansing, giving O's. true name.

"Don't know anything about it; call again! call again! Go to Mr. P.; he will tell you all about it!"

"But, Mr. Little, I have just come from Mr. P. in order to compare this stock."

"Very well! Then go back to Mr. P. He knows all about it."

So saying, he resumed his vibrations and fumblings.

Fortunately, just then, the clerk, of whom the stock had been bought, entered the office, and the comparison was made before Mr. Little could interrupt him.

"He's a crusty, fidgetty old fellow," remarked L., as we walked up the street, "and always gives us a heap of trouble when we come to compare purchases and sales. Sometimes I slip into his office slyly, and try to compare with one of the clerks, but he generally sees me, and puts in his oar and makes a mess of it."

This peculiarity arising out of a temperament excessively nervous by nature, and made more so by the excitements of business, grew on Mr. Little, and in the last years of his life, became a source of great vexation to his brother dealers.

Old Father Time is no laggard in the stock-market. The sultry days of July flew away. Old Southern was all the while rising. During the week which followed June 28th, the day when my 100 shares were bought, it sold at 46. Why was this? The public had no confidence in the value of the stock. The financial condition of the company was known to be bad. Every morning, the New York Herald and other dailies were calling attention to the rottenness of its concerns, and yet, the stock kept rising. The speculating public had *been selling it short.* It was this that encouraged the bull party to push it up, because, sometime those who had been going short of it, would have to come into the market and buy it of them for delivery. As the whole amount of the stock was but $6,000,000, or thereabouts, of which, only a portion was floating around in the street, it would be readily handled by any party who saw fit to take hold of it. On the 28th of July, the last day of the option, the stock was sold at 53. The following account of O. will show with what result:

MR. ——— ——— IN ACCT. WITH WILLIAM L. P——, (OTHERWISE O.)

Dr.		Cr.	
To 100 shares Old So., bought at $38\frac{5}{8}$, -	$3,862 50	By 100 Old So., sold at 53, . .	$5,300 00
To brokerage, Buying $\frac{1}{8}$,	12 50	By cash, (margin,) .	500 00
			$5,800 00
To brokerage, Selling $\frac{1}{8}$,	12 50		
To interest, 30 days, 6 per cent., . .	19 05		
	$3,906 55		
Balance due ———	$1,893 45		
	$5,800 00		$5,800 00

The balance due me then upon this operation was $1,893.45, from which, after subtracting $500, the margin which I had given O., there remained $1,393.45, as the profits of my first flyer.

If there is any feeling natural to the novice in Wall Street, it is the desire to look at the cash results of his first profitable operation, to finger and crumple up the bank-bills, whether crisp from the press, or limp with the manipulations of a hundred different possessors, to gaze with rapture on the classical features of the Goddess of Liberty stamped on ten dollar coins, and chink the golden metal in the capacious pocket.

Yielding to this desire, I found courage to ask O. to draw his check for balance due. His round face lengthened into an oval, and a cloud of disappointment passed over it, for he had been feasting his imagination on visions of prospective commissions from his new customer. Slowly he filled out and signed an elegantly engraved check which he extended towards me between his fat thumb and forefinger, then drew it back, and gazing at the figures with pride and satisfaction, exclaimed, "You should thank me for that little profit! come in and see us soon now you know who your friends are," with which remark, he handed it over to me, his thumb and fingers seeming to nurse and fondle it till it was folded up, and passed into my vest pocket.

Never fear, O.! this is not the last time that you are destined to see "that little profit." Again you will hold it as a margin, and it will drop many a commission into the "itching palm" of that plump hand.

After the scuffles and heat and noisome odors of the city, how cool and calm and sweet the air of the pine and hemlock woods. Reclining beneath some monarch of the forest, gazing at the blue sky, or at the sunlight streaming in shafts of gold between the branches, and watching the wild and beautiful things flitting through the air, or bounding along through the vistas of gray old trunks, for two weeks, I forgot that such things as stocks and quotations ever existed.

Returning to the city, on taking my seat in the

cars, on one of the great lines of travel, I heard the familiar cry, "New York papers." Hastily securing one, I opened it, when my eye fell on the money article where the price of Old Southern was quoted at 36, a fall of seventeen per cent., from 53, the price at which I had sold, and two per cent. below the price at which I had bought my first 100 shares. Here was a chance for another "little profit." It fairly "stuck out" to use the street slang. It swelled and took definite shape the longer the mind dwelt upon it. The steam-fiend which was dragging the express train at the rate of forty miles an hour was too slow for eager fancy which was already in William Street, and had bought already another 100 shares of Old Southern at 36.

It was on a close, hot evening, on the 13th of August, that I stood on the door-steps of my boarding-house, where I found O. sitting ready to receive me, clad in the lightest summer costume, his face rubicund with the heat, and radiant with good omens for the morrow. "Lively times in the street since you left," remarked he, "the ring have been unloading Old Southern, and Jake Little has been selling it right and left. If you feel like taking a turn in it be on hand to-morrow." Bright and early the next morning, I handed $1,500 margin to O., and ordered him to buy 300 shares of Old Southern. This lot cost 34½. In a week, the price went down to 30, and on the advice of O. it was sold, netting me a loss of $1,400.

The market was reported as very weak and declining. "Try a short sale," said O. I put up more margin, and *tried* a short sale of, a hundred shares, at 29,

Seller 10. Jacob Little took the contract. Three days after, the Ohio Life and Trust Company failed, and the market went down with a jump. On the 26th of August, the stock was bought in for delivery to Jacob Little, but before it could be delivered, his failure was announced. His failure had occurred in this wise. All along back there had been a difference of from three to six per cent. between a buyer's option of thirty days, and a seller's option of thirty days, in Old Southern and other leading stocks. Taking advantage of this, Mr. Little had been selling stocks on buyers' options, and buying them back on sellers' options, making a profit on the difference. When stocks fell so heavily the latter part of August, the stock on the seller's options was delivered to him at a much higher price and while the buyer's options were still open. But a few days after, these latter contracts were closed, and Mr. Little resumed business, and thus I was saved by the skin of my teeth, and bagged another profit of $900 by my first short sale.

The day was now approaching when another cycle in the history of American credit was to be finished with the crash known as the panic of 1857. The causes which led to that panic are familiar to all. It was the discovery of gold in California which mainly produced the vast expansion of the Banking system. In little more than eight years, prior to 1857, the paper money circulation had nearly doubled, and as early as 1854, five hundred new banks were issuing their bills, and stimulating trade and speculation. The basis of these banks was the *idea* of an increased supply of the precious metals. But when that supply had been diminished by exportation to Europe, to pay debts incurred by overtrading, the stimulus was withdrawn, and trade and speculation alike collapsed. American credit in that era may be likened to a vessel ill-built, badly worked, and carrying too heavy press of canvass, launched upon a spring freshet which poured through the golden sluices of Eldorado. As the waters flowed on, they broadened and grew shallower. The vessel at last broke its rudder, and went aground, and there stuck fast till a refluent tide could set it afloat.

He would have been a bold operator, who, knowing the dangers, would have dared then to buy and sell in Wall Street. During the eight weeks which succeeded the failure of the Ohio Life and Trust Company, banks and brokerage firms were breaking by the score, and the supposed profits of the lucky speculator were liable to be swept away in a moment, or actually converted into losses as the following operation, which I next engaged in, will show.

The market, towards the middle of September, began to brighten, and stocks went up for the moment. This looked like a favorable opportunity to operate for a decline, or sell short. Accordingly, I sold 100 shares Old Southern at 20, seller 10, to an operator named Slocum, who had been acting as an agent for certain western banks. A few days after, the stock was bought at 17, for delivery to Slocum, who was, by his contract, bound to pay me 20, and in this way I should have made a profit of $300. But when the stock was carried to Slocum, instead of paying for it, he announced that he was "in deep waters," "no remittances from Chicago," etc., etc., but stated that he "would be all right in a few days," and would take the stock and pay for it then. Accordingly, the stock was retained, and every day was presented to Slocum, and every day the same story was told, "come in to-morrow," while day by day the price of the stock was falling from 17 to 16, from 16 to 14, and so on, till in ten days it was selling at 10. Slocum then settled the matter, by giving his note for $1,000, that being the difference between what he agreed to pay for stock, namely, 20, and the present market price of the stock. The stock was then sold at 10, thus netting me an actual loss of $700, against which, I held the *negotiable* promissory note of Slocum for $1,000, though it would be difficult to explain why such a note should be called negotiable, since I tried in vain to negotiate it at a fifty per cent. discount.

While sitting in my office, the morning before the panic of October 13th, a tall, lathy man, with a bilious smile, walked in, and said that he had been informed that I held $1,000 of Slocum's paper. I produced the note in question, when he remarked again that Slocum was "dead broke," and would never pay a cent, but he wished to use the note as an offset, and was willing to pay something for it, perhaps as much as five per cent.

After the due amount of haggling, the bargain was struck at ten per cent., and my visitor counted down one hundred dollars in five's and ten's, looking suspiciously new, on the Bentonville Bank, Illinois. To my remonstrances against the character of the money, he produced, out of his coat pocket, a Bank Note Reporter, published the day before, in which, the notes of that bank were quoted at only one per cent. discount. As this rate took off but one dollar from the hundred which lay upon the table before me, nothing more was said, and the tall, lathy man and note vanished through the door-way.

I hastened to the office of an acquaintance, who bought Western bank bills, and on whisking my hundred dollars over, and studying the vignettes, he gave a long, doubtful whistle, and said the bills were not salable in New York, but that he would forward them to his correspondent at Chicago for redemption, though his own private opinion was, the bank was a "wild-cat," and the currency was "stump-tail and red-dog." The bills went to Chicago by express, and in due time, something like the following letter came back in reply:

CHICAGO, *October 18th*, 1857.

To —— ——, No. —— Wall Street, New York.

My Dear Sir:—Your valued favor of date 12th inst., received, and also package of ($100) one hundred dollars, bills of the Bentonville Bank, per express. In reply, I visited Bentonville day before yesterday, and found it a small hamlet, consisting of three houses and a grocery store, situated on a prairie, about ten miles from the railroad. The back part of the grocery store was occupied by the bank, but as this institution has now suspended operations, the President and Cashier have gone to Chicago. I saw no safe or other evidences of cash, and so conclude the assets are now in the breeches pocket of the President and Cashier.

The bills have only a nominal value in our market of from 2 to 5 per cent. We cannot, to-day, pay you over 2 per cent., should you wish to sell them.

My expenses to and from Bentonville were fifteen dollars, which I have charged to you.

Yours Respectfully,

C. D. CULLENDER.

My supposed profit of $300 had thus resolved itself into thin air, and left only the residum of a little bill of expense.

On footing up the accounts of three months' operations, I found my net profits a trifle over one hundred and forty dollars. Rather a small compensation for two months' wear and tear in Wall Street, let alone the risk. And now to buy or not to buy, that's the question! The memory of that first profit was yet green and pleasing to dwell upon, but listening to financial explosions in quick succession, and gazing on tumbling banks and fortunes melting away, is not calculated to give assurance and nerve to the stock-operator, and accordingly, shutting the ear to the blandishments of hope and of O., the decision was not to buy or sell more for the present.

At this point of the narrative, the question naturally arises, why do most of the operators in Wall Street come out minus on the sum total of their operations? The answer to this question involves the whole philosophy of speculation. To the looker-on, it seems the easiest thing in the world to make money there, and so it would be if men only did the business on mercantile principles, and only took fair mercantile risks. But they rarely do. The margins on which stocks and gold are bought and sold, are too small. Any merchant doing business properly, will fortify himself with a margin of from thirty to ninety per cent. on the amount of business he does, while the ordinary stock operator buys and sells stocks on a margin of from three to twenty per cent. on stocks, and of from one to ten per cent. on gold. Add to this the fact, that most of the outside public buy stocks, when they are high and rampant, and sell short, when they are low and weak. Now suppose one thousand men, with an aggregate capital of $5,000,000, who have bought or sold stocks on the above insufficient margin, and ten men like Vanderbilt, Gould, etc., whose interest is opposed to that of the one thousand aforesaid, and whose capital is ten times as great. If these ten men wish to make stocks go down, they create a panic by locking up money or in some other way "clean out" the small holders, and then buy their stocks at low figures, make money easy, and up prices go again.

It will also be readily seen, by any one who reflects for an instant, how intimately time enters, as an element, into every stock operation. Time fights on the side of the man who buys a lot of stock at a fair price and pays for it, inasmuch as the material interests of our country are steadily advancing, *on the whole*, and the value of the stock becomes enhanced. Time, too, fights on the side of the man who speculates, when he is fortified by large margins, because he is protected by those margins from the losses incidental to the constant vibrations of the market. The man who can *keep* his position in spite of the temporary condition of prices, is the man who, in the end, wins.

The frequency of operations is another fruitful cause of losses. Of course, brokers desire their customers to buy and sell as often as possible, because they get a commission on every transaction made. But the chances are against any one who operates on margins, and therefore the oftener he operates, the more of these dangerous risks he takes. If, instead of buying and selling every day, and giving all his money to his broker in the shape of commissions, he would only buy three or four times a year, when stocks are low and after the panics which periodically occur, and then hold for a ten or fifteen per cent. rise, he would find himself ahead of the market when he came to make up his yearly accounts.

A most weighty maxim, verified by Wall Street experience, is this: "Cut short your losses and let your profits run." This has been the making of many a speculator, and yet how few have the nerve to practice it. Pat Hearne, the late noted sporting man, was wont to operate thus. He would buy 100 shares of some stock, and when it rose one per cent. he would buy another 100 shares, and so on. As soon as it fell one per cent. he sold the whole. This, everybody will say, is a sound plan of operating. In the rise of 1870, a well-known young operator made $80,000 in Reading, by operating on this principle, and lost it all by forsaking this principle and letting his *losses* run. Again, in 1875, he sold short 100 shares of L. S., on credit, having no money to use as a margin; as the price fell he kept selling. This was during the Travers break in August. In four days he made $12,000, but a few weeks afterwards he lost the whole by violating his principle of operation.

The practice of selling stocks short will be found, *in the end*, to be *invariably* a losing business. For while the *buying of* stocks, under fair mercantile conditions, is perfectly legitimate and regulated by rules of finance, which in the long run bring the holder out "whole" or with a profit, operations on the "*short side*" are always nearly akin to gambling, in which the "Bank" has a percentage in its favor and on the doctrine of chances is at least the winner against the gamester who bets his money on the cards. If A contracts to deliver 100 shares of a certain stock in 30 days, and if B has the whole of the stock in his hands, how can A close his contract without paying B his price? A history of the fortunes of the leading bears of Wall Street, for the past twenty-five years, illustrates our proposition. Two examples will "point our moral" if not "adorn our tale," viz.: Daniel Drew and Jacob Little.

The losses which the former encountered on the short side for the twenty years before 1875, have been estimated at near, if not quite $7,000,000. It would not be an exaggeration to say that if he had operated on the long side with the same boldness, craft, and resources which he employed in his short operations, he would have become possessed of a fortune approaching in amplitude to that of his great rival, Vanderbilt, who never went short of stocks. No doubt Drew now and then made a great hit, as for instance in the winter of 1867, during the Erie break; but his successes in this line more often served to diminish the grand total of his losses than to build up a fortune on the plus-column. The traps which were prepared for him would have been the death of a man of smaller means and less resolution. But Daniel always made terms, if worsted, and used diplomacy as skillfully as he swung that large hammer of his with which he depressed the price of stocks.

The closing years of Jacob Little convey to all who would sell stocks short a still more instructive lesson.

Still clinging to the objects of a pursuit which was to

him a passion, his face bearing the marks of the fierce struggles of his life, a broken weird looking old man, he haunted the Board Room like a spectre where he had once reigned as a king, offering small lots of five shares of the same stock, the whole capital whereof he had once controlled. Where then were the piled millions which that cunning hand and scheming brain had rolled up? where the prestige of his victories on 'Change? Gone, scattered, lost. Poor and unnoticed, he passed away from the scene, and left nothing behind him but the shadow of what was once a great Wall Street reputation.

Men and women of America who, making haste to be rich, and taking evil counsel would enter Wall Street and put your money on the hazard of a die, give heed to the following maxims, the fruit of a dearly bought experience:

Buy only on the amplest margins.

Be an occasional and not a constant operator.

Cut short your losses, and let your profits run.

Never sell what you have not got.

CHAPTER V.

PORTRAITS OF CORNELIUS VANDERBILT AND DANIEL DREW AS THEY WERE IN 1869

A Panic in Stocks, and Where is the Commodore?—Driving in Central Park—Training for Wall Street—Maxims of the Vanderbilt Code, "never sell what you haven't got," etc.—Anecdotes—Vanderbilt the Bull and Drew the Bear—A Parallel between the Two—"Uncle Daniel's" Portrait and Ways—The "Merry Old Gentleman"—The Wisdom of the Serpent, but not the Harmlessness of the Dove—Daniel Drew as an Acrobat—The end of two Money Kings.

WEDNESDAY, September 30th, 1869! Ten years ago as we pen these lines! The sequel of Black Friday. There is a panic in the market. Prices of stocks, which have been sink-sinking, for a week, are now dropping, with a heavy thump. Values have shrunk $100,000,000. These, are the losses of stockholders. The tallest column, of all—New York Central— which stands under the dome of the stock market, has broken at the top, and is crumbling off, in sections, which shake the foundation, as they fall.

Among all the crowd, which that day thronged hall and stairway, of the stock exchange, struggling vainly to arrest the panic, or, standing and gazing, upon the full extent and hopelessness, of their losses, where was he, whose stake in that perilous game, was the largest, and who was liable now to pay a forfeit of millions?

Sun and sky mock with their brightness, the gloom which hangs over the market place. It is a day for the velvet turf, and not for the stony pavement. Passing from Wall street, into Central Park, on such a day, is like going from Tartarus, into the fields of Elysium. The distorted and forbidding faces, have disappeared, the hoarse cries died away, and everything is peace and beauty. The very air seems larger here, and in the wide, smooth, winding drives, grim-visaged business, puts on a holiday smile. Standing on a slope, covered with a verdure, not yet tinged with the sober coloring, of autumn, we see approaching, a light wagon, bowling along, at an eight mile gait, drawn by two blood trotters; gazelle-eyed, and slender of limb, as if desert-born, they tread the earth daintily, and their hoofs hardly dint the ground. Behind them, holding the reins, with a light and yet firm hand, is seated an old man, with a face like a Roman senator. This is Cornelius Vanderbilt, the greatest railroad capitalist, of the age. Forgetful, apparently, of his vast interests, that day imperiled, and of great losses, actually suffered, he rides along cool, thought-free, chatting with the blooming lady, his bride of six weeks, who sits by his side. This speaks the man.

From 1817, when Thomas Gibbons, the great steamboat man of that period, recognized the promise of the youth, till 1875, when in the lusty winter of his old age he dominated with such ease the largest consolidated railway interest in the world, there has been no more remarkable figure on the horizon of commerce, than Cornelius Vanderbilt.

Steam locomotion on water and land, this had been

his specialty, the trade to which he had given the energies of an entire life. In this trade he became more than an expert—he displayed genius. The two-oared skiff plied in the bays of his native island, grew into a steamboat, the steamboat multiplied into a fleet which plowed river, inland sea and ocean, and the young water-man was graduated as a commodore of the commercial marine, a rank to which he was raised by the spontaneous voices of his countrymen, and a title as worthily earned as if won upon the gun-deck.

He was born on Staten Island in the State of New York, in the year 1794. His ancestry was of the low Dutch stock, and he himself a worthy representative of the Holland sailors of the seventeenth century, who lashed a broom to the mast-head and boasted that they swept the seas. At the age of fourteen, he was master of a sail boat. When he was eighteen, he was captain and part owner of the largest periauger which plied in the harbor of New York. When he was twenty-three, he was captain of a steamboat, and within forty years from that time he had built and owned twenty steamships and forty steamboats.

We are, however, not to speak of him now as connected with the industrial interests of the country on the water, but as a Wall Street man, a railroad king, a stockholder and operator.

Picture to yourself, reader, a man of great natural powers of mind and body, strengthened by training in one of the roughest of commercial schools—the running of lines of steamboats—who for nearly thirty years had concentrated his faculties upon one object, viz.: the playing of games of rivalry and competition as they are played in such a business—games requiring nerve to encounter emergencies and risks and skill as against strong antagonists—and played with heavy stakes on a broad field. Then imagine that such a man in possession of vast winnings from these games, with all the ripeness of his wisdom and experience, and with even the native force of his mind and will unabated, enters Wall Street, and devotes all these various and large resources to the buying, holding and controlling of stocks, the forming of combinations and the holding of them together against all opposition, and you will have an outline sketch of what Vanderbilt for ten years was in his Wall Street operations. Intellect, resolution, foresight, the ability to measure and proportion means to ends, wealth, knowledge of men and things, all conjoined in one man,—one Will furnished a panoply of proof and weapons of attack to Vanderbilt, with which, like the Homeric hero, he generally defeated and scattered the opposing hosts of the market.

Like all great generals, he knew who should be his agents and coadjutors; but he bore "like a Turk, no brother near the throne," and when an agent or coadjutor became too powerful, or puffed up with a sense of his own importance, he "took him down a peg," and then after he had humbled him sufficiently, raised him again. Strange stories have been told of him in this respect, how he had degraded men, his associates, even those of his own family, to the ranks, when guilty of insubordination, and then promoted them again, when they had been sufficiently humbled.

His operations were only for a rise and never for a fall; he was a bull and never a bear in stocks.

Two facts appear to have led him to invest so largely in railroad stocks; first, the rapidly increasing carrying trade of the country; second, the gross mismanagement and peculation which prevailed among railroad corporations. The obvious corollary from these facts is this, viz., secure a controlling interest in a railroad stock at a reasonable price, manage it with economy, stopping all leaks and peculations, and then *hold it and wait.* This is precisely what Vanderbilt achieved, first in Harlem, next in Hudson, and finally in New York Central, and with what marvelous success, is known throughout the land.

If the experience of this man could be cast into the form of maxims, what a code it would furnish for the young merchant.

"I bide my time." was one of his maxims. Its truth every one can testify to, who has observed what strange transformations and revenges are brought about in the stock market, by the "whirligig of time."

"Never sell short,' was another.

In 1864, during the memorable rise in Harlem, so the story runs, a son of the late Dean Richmond, president of the New York Central Railroad, who had been selling Harlem at low figures, found himself likely to be several thousand dollars out of pocket, in consequence of the upward movement of the stock. In his extremity, he went to Vanderbilt, introduced himself as the son of his old friend, told him his situation, and asked his advice. "Never sell what you haven't got," grimly responded the Commodore. Upon this hint young Richmond covered his short contracts, and went long, *i. e.*, bought a considerable amount of the stock, and in a few weeks recovered what he had lost.

"Never tell any one what you are going to do till you've done it," said Vanderbilt, once, to a friend, who inquired of him what was the secret of success in business.

That he acted on this adage, which sounds something like a Hibernianism, will be proved by the following anecdote. In 1850, the Pacific Mail Steamship Company did the carrying trade between San Francisco and Panama, and an immensely lucrative trade it was. To establish some other line which would tap this trade would be, of course, a great object to accomplish. One day the Commodore was observed in his office, standing before a map of the western hemisphere, and placing his finger successively on three points. The first of these was San Juan de Nicaragua on the Atlantic shore, the second was the Lake of Nicaragua, the third was the port of San Juan del Sur, on the Pacific. Here was a route which, if feasible, would save nearly one thousand miles of travel, and put money in the purse of him who secured it. He silently investigated the practicability of the route, and made all his arrangements with a view to its establishment. A few days after, the new steamer Prometheus, owned by himself, lay at the dock, fired up, and furnished with coal and provisions for a cruise. He went on board, and telling a friend to give his good-bye to Mrs. V., that he was off for a trip, ordered the lines to be cast off and the prow to be turned southward. In due time he made his appearance in Nicaragua, where he lived for six weeks on toast and tea, took care of his health, and then returned to New York, and organized what was known as the Nicaragua Accessory Transit Company. In all his stock operations he used to proceed on the basis of intrinsic values, knowing that capital from all quarters will come in to aid him on that basis. As a bull, we may assert he traded on the hopes of men; and thus he differed from Daniel Drew, his rival in the market, who as a *bear* was wont to trade on financial fear and apprehension, for panics and general declines in stocks result from the timorousness of capital.

Cornelius Vanderbilt and Daniel Drew—how great each in his way, how similar, and yet how different they were! Both commenced without a penny. Drew, who was born in Putnam County, in the State of New York, in the latter part of the last century, commenced life as a cattle drover, then became the rival of Vanderbilt in the steamboat business, and finally was graduated as a stock operator.

Both of these men had the mind of crystal, the heart of adamant, the hand of steel, and the will of iron. Both too, unscrupulous, within the law, as to means to an end. But both have adorned their lives, by great charities, bestowed on their kind; Vanderbilt, by presenting to the Government, in its hour of need, one million of dollars, in the shape of the magnificent steamship, which bore his name, and Drew, by the gift of many hundred thousand dollars, to educational institutions.

Both, too, have identified themselves with the material progress of the country, by the great lines they have established, or held, on water and land. Put your ear to the ground, and you can hear the thunder of the trains, from Omaha to Manhattan, all day and all night long. As these words are penned, ten thousand brakemen, switchmen, firemen, and engineers, begrimed, wan, and haggard, are guiding and goading on those roaring, screaming steam-serfs, as they drag to tide water, across fat prairies, through black gorges, and over crazy trestle-work, and bridges, the treasures of our imperial valley, and gold-veined mountains, and the spices and lustrous fabrics of India.

Here the resemblance ceases. Both of these men, it is true, used to play a game on the same field, but in a very different way. Vanderbilt was the more daring of the two. His operations were through years of time, and through vast arcs of circles; the table on which he played was one hundred million acres, and the dice which he played loaded with ninety millions of the precious metal.

Vanderbilt's mind was the more comprehensive, Drew's the more subtle. The genius of the former a constructive, in building up values, that of the latter a destructive, in depressing them, for Drew was a diligent architect of panics. The one was the greater strategist, the other the greater tactician, his operations being rapid, compact, and local.

In personal appearance, how totally dissimilar. Vanderbilt looked an anax-andron, a king of men. Seventy-nine winters could not bow that stately form, or quench the light of that deep-set black eye.

Three-score years and ten, and more, engraved upon the figure of his rival some of the physical signs of decay, but through a wilderness of wrinkles his steel-gray eyes shone with all the vitality of one and twenty. His face, as it looked in the market to those who knew him, was indeed a study for a painter. An odd, grotesque face, with an air of self-communion brooding over it, and a pinched look, from the corrugated forehead down the rectangular jaw. His nose might form a separate study. It was surely the reverse of Roman, but to call it Grecian would be a slur upon Praxiteles. It might be termed *sagacious* in every line, and swelling, a nose to snuff a stratagem in the air, or scent in the "tainted gale" a tight money-market approaching.

No one would be apt to associate with Vanderbilt anything that savored of the jocose. We involuntarily think of him as striding along with a grim gigantesque dignity, buying with a large lordly manner, thousands and tens of thousands of shares, punishing his enemies with a remorseless hand, and placing his adversaries *hors du combat*, or as sitting like a generalissimo in his office, issuing his orders to his battallions. He was not known by any nick-name except "the Commodore," or the great consolidator, though his intimate friends sometimes spoke of him as "Cornele."

But Drew was called a variety of names—"the Old Man," "Uncle Daniel," "the Ursa Major," "the speculative director," "the Old Bear," etc.; these are a few of the designations which he bore. Well, too, did he deserve the title of the "merry old gentleman" of Wall Street. In his most earnest operations, he never once lost sight of "the fun of the thing." His most serious mood was easily broken in upon by ludicrous suggestions, and then he gave vent, every now and then, to short laughs, sounding like the cackle of a hen—thrown suddenly off from her propriety. He loved to rally "the boys," (as he used paternally to call his younger speculative acquaintance,) on their losses, or jest with them on their gains on occasions when, as he would say, they had "taken a slice out 'em." It was "good as nuts and cheese" to him when he had succeeded in getting up a corner, or when on a high market he had put out a heavy line of shorts. A mighty and versatile trapper. No game too small or too large for him. He laid his net for pigeons, set his springs for wood-cock, dug pit-falls for bears, and lassoed the bulls. What glee in that queer old face, as he drew the string to snare the game, and then bag them.

If a stranger had seen him driving down to his office of a morning, in his "one horse shay," he would at once pronounce him some hard headed old farmer, visiting Broad Street for the purpose of putting his savings into a small lot of government bonds. He who would learn the eccentric habits and odd ways of the man, had only to deposit a small margin with David Groesbeck, his partner, and one of his brokers, and then frequent the office and watch the old man as he went pottering about, talking little, but that little in homely phrase, and with a strong nasal twang.

We have said his intellect was subtle. The word *subtle* does not altogether express it. It should be *vulpine*. Yes! The intellect of a fox of the antediluvian period, gigantic of size and portentous of brush. He was fertile in shifts and ruses as Reynard himself. He hid his tracks, and took to the water, the underbrush or the open country as circumstances required. Traps innumerable were prepared for him, but he generally eluded them, or when caught broke away, though sometimes torn and bloody from jaws that thirsted for his blood (or, what is much the same, his money). The hounds of the street for twenty years followed hard on his track, now in silence, and now baying in deep-mouthed chorus when they had run him to earth, but his twistings and doublings, and countless devices have foiled them at last, and he sat in his stronghold with a grasp on his ten millions which only the last great panic could relax.

"Count no man fortunate before he dies," said the Grecian sage. Count no Wall Street speculator rich till his estate has been settled. Betting, as Daniel Drew did, against the material growth and progress of the country, and therefore against the enhancement of stock values, his ruin was only a question of time. That, in the course of a thirty years' career as a speculator and money-king, he displayed wonderful ability and resources, and performed numberless amazing feats of financial prestidigitation, no one can deny. In his palmy days his operations in steamboating, and afterwards in railroading, evinced great forecast and shrewdness. He competed with Vanderbilt on the water, and held the Erie Railroad Company completely in his hands. He was the legitimate successor of Jacob Little as a manipulator of values in the street, especially for a decline. He was a smasher of bull pools, an engineer of panics, and now and again an energetic hoister of prices.

All this force and cunning, all this fertility of resource was, however, expended for his own interest solely, and though occasionally he was generous to his brother speculators, that apparent generosity was often turned to his own advantage. The end of such a career may be foreseen. In his later years he encountered sharper intellects, bolder spirits, stronger nerves than his own. He could not match his younger rivals. They drove him to the wall, crippling him and leaving him in too feeble a pecuniary condition to resist the mighty rush of the panic of 1873. He succumbed, and though he patched up a settlement with his creditors and reappeared on the street as an operator, he failed again in 1875, and from that time till his death, on the 18th of September, 1879, was known no more on the street. Drew on the 30th of September, 1869, and Drew on the 18th of September, 1879! What a contrast is this! Then, rich, powerful, with troops of friends and retainers! Now, penniless, broken-hearted, and away from home, he dies in the arms of one of his few remaining friends.

Cornelius Vanderbilt was framed on a larger patten than Drew; his operations in stocks contemplated intrinsic and future values, rather than the prices of the day, from which the latter sought his profits.

He was a builder-up of great enterprises, and when it was known that he had embarked largely in the stock of any company, it was a guarantee that the value of the property would increase. He was all the while laying wagers in favor of the growth of the country; he was thus betting on a certainty, and was sure to win at last. Harlem, Hudson, N. Y. Central, Lake Shore, Western Union Telegraph Company, laid hold of successively, all appreciated largely in value under his management. He was a consolidator, a monopolist, and it is not strange that he should desire to see the immense railroad properties which he had so greatly enlarged, continue to be held after his death by one hand, and managed by one head.

The estimated wealth now in the hands of Wm. H. Vanderbilt, his son, is the enormous sum of $100,000,000. The successor to King Cornelius is all the time extending the empire and policy bequeathed to him by his father. Besides the railroads above named, the younger Vanderbilt has captured Michigan Central, Canada Southern, and, having gotten a foothold in the Chicago & Northwestern R. R. Company, is pushing for the control of Union Pacific. But we are anticipating. This brief sketch of the late Cornelius Vanderbilt and Daniel Drew will be filled in by the light and shade of coming chapters.

CHAPTER VI.

JOTTINGS ON THE "STREET;" DREW ON THE WAR-PATH.

More Philosophy of Wall Street—The Handwriting on the Wall—A Haunted Heart—The Panic Forgotten, and "Richard is Himself Again"—"Country Orders Executed with Promptness and Despatch!"—The Countrymen Respond to the Cry—A Rustic Bruiser on Change—My Little Commission Bill—The Devourers of Widows' Houses—What shall I buy, and How shall I buy it?—Notes on Erie—Views of the "General"—I buy One Hundred Erie, and pay for it, and what came of it—Drew the King of Erie—He Bulls Erie at 4, and sells it to "The Boys" at 40.

TO the man who looks from without upon Wall Street as the field of speculation, it seems a place of deep and dangerous mystery. A region of dens and caves and labyrinths full of perils which threaten loss and perhaps ruin to him who enters there.

When mustering up courage he ventures in, and standing in New Street, watches the success of his first purchase, all the stories he has ever heard about men who have been reduced from affluence to beggary by speculating in stocks, flash across his memory. He sees upon the very walls inscriptions of prediction, warning and despair, like the cells where the condemned have passed their last hours. Some of these inscriptions written with a lead pencil, vigorously anathematize Vanderbilt. Some are imprecations on Drew or Fisk. Some are apothegms expressing the very philosophy of desperation. All tell the same tale: "I came here, I speculated, I lost. Beware!"

But he heeds neither counsel nor warning for *the hope of gain* is a stronger principle in human nature, than *the fear of loss.* These two active principles underlie the whole practice of stock speculation. It is the hope of gain that induces a man to buy, and the fear of loss that induces him to sell, often precipitately. These are the two strings on which the merriest as well as the most doleful tunes are played by the cunning Paganini's of the stock market. Thus a thousand brokers gain large incomes from their customers, and great capitalists accumulate immense fortunes.

Those ceaseless vibrations of the prices in the stock market, what are they owing to except it be the same causes?

To and fro, up and down, backwards and forwards, the speculator moves with the market from the moment when that first profit slides into his fingers. Not always interested pecuniarily; absent, sometimes, hundreds of miles away, in gay society or alone, studying, walking, riding, sleeping, still is he haunted by the idea of fortunes made on 'Change swiftly, easily, by a lucky hit or a quick succession of happy strokes. The five fortunate speculators of the season, glitter in a false light which never discloses the hundreds of miserable losers.

M. made $200,000 in three months on Pacific mail, commencing only with $10,000. J. & T. made a million on Old Southern. B. went into the market with a paltry thousand and left it with a hundred thousand. S., a year ago, was a clerk in a bank on a salary of $600; to-day he draws a check with five figures on a deposit in the same bank.

What has been done may be done again. Such examples fortify the doubts and misgivings which possess the mind during the first stages of a speculative career, and stimulate the hardihood and pride that goeth before a fall.

The recollection of the panic of 1857, notwithstanding its severity, and long continuance, soon faded away from the Wall Street mind. The very next day, after the final crash, (October 14th,) stocks began to rise with a bound. Railways took the lead, and bank stocks followed. In twenty-four hours, American Exchange Bank stock rose fifty per cent.

But the outsiders were still wary. The mercantile community, especially, from whom the ranks of Wall Street operators are so largely recruited, now generally kept aloof. As the winter was wearing away, however, the old familiar faces of those who had been scared and driven out by the panic, came back one after one. Wizened bank cashiers, having recovered from their fright, sallied out from their fortresses, to take a turn in the street. Merchants, weary with brooding over piles of protested notes, came down to try and repair their losses, by taking a shy at Pacific Mail. They who had retired to the country for recuperation from the fatigues of the season, now came filing in, bringing with them others who had never tried their luck in the stock-market; confiding, genial-looking fellows, their countenances rotund with long sleeps, and sleek with the rustic cheer of the nitrogenous bean and cabbage, and the carbonaceous sausage; they brought their inviolate margins destined to furnish pocket money for a broker's holiday. The spring equinox found the street with very much the same appearance it had when the narrator first staked his modest five hundred dollars. The curb-stone brokers were not quite so clamorous, their brothers of the regular board not quite so bustling and important of manner, and the general movement of things not quite so impetuous as the year before; but the fever of speculation was still in the blood, and was kept alive by the fresh orders to buy and sell, which always come in after the smoke of a great financial conflict has cleared away.

What would become of the market if it were not for the countrymen? "Country orders solicited and executed with promptness and despatch!" This is the substance of the advertisement of Brokers and Bankers, we might almost say, the burden of their song. The country always responds to this solicitation. The four great monetary rivers that flow into the Wall Street reservoir from the four quarters of the compass, are fed by a thousand streamlets from city, town and village. The aggregate is a vast sum, a part of which goes into securities for a permanent investment, but perhaps a still greater part goes, as margins, into speculation. The countryman comes and takes a hand in the game which is all the while going on around the table of the stock market; he is like a young lion who has never known either sorrow or the lack of food. He is jovial, brave, active and sanguine. Untutored in guile, he has always heard that the Wall Street boys were a sharp set of fellows, but he cannot really understand why they are so much worse than other folks; and then the broker who takes charge of his pecuniary interests, is most agreeable and gentlemanly in his manners. In fact, the countryman reposes upon everything and everybody, with a confidence at once child-like and sublime.

How gallantly he enters the field, and storms the Malakoffs, where the emperors of the market lie entrenched. How incessantly he changes his position on the advice of his very dear friends, with whom he has met in the *street;* how obstinately he clings to a loss; how resentfully he "bucks" at the stock to which he owes his first or last loss, and oh! what a stream of commissions he pours into the pocket of his taciturn but absorbent broker!

From the history of one of these operators, you may learn the history of most of the others. They make money at the start, while their eyes are undazed by illusive lights, and their judgments unwarped by the influences to which they are unconsciously subjected; but in the end they almost invariably lose all their profits and their original margins besides.

Some few, very few there have been, however—hard-headed, determined men, who, after taking the first heavy knocks, have learned the art and mystery of the Wall Street trade and practiced it in a most slashing way upon the old bruisers of the market.

One of these is now in our mind's eye, a sturdy little fellow with thews and sinews like a champion of the light weights. He came from his native village into the street in 1877; was a bull, bought heavily and lost almost his all, in the fall which followed the J. R. Keene campaign of that year. Retiring for a while into the country, he thought out the matter, replenished his exchequer, came back, beat the trained speculators with their own weapons, and retired in six months with a princely fortune.

The year 1858 passed swiftly and in the stock market, uneventfully, away. Starting February with the old margin of five hundred dollars, I found that after twelve distinct purchases and sales, in which I had been playing the ancient Wall Street game of see-saw, up and down, making and losing alternately; upon looking over the account in December, my net profits were about $200. And now first occurred to me the fact which strikes every one after operating for a time in stocks, viz: how fast the interest and brokerage items run up. Against a profit of $200 there was interest paid $210, and brokerage $300. After all my trouble and worry, only $200, while my broker received $510. Deduction from this. The broker takes the money, *i. e.*, the profit. The customer takes the risk, of *almost certain loss in the end.* If the customer buys and sells 100 shares of stock every working day in the year, he will find by calculation, that he has paid his broker nearly $8,000 in the form of commissions, at the rate of one-eighth per cent. on each transaction. During a tight money market, he will have paid a large additional sum in the shape of turns or extra commissions, for carrying his stocks, and if he is cornered and unable to borrow stock for delivery, when short of it, he will have to pay fresh commissions for the use of stock.

During 1878 and 1879, an active operator using $20,000 as a margin, discovered on perusing his accounts, that he had paid his brokers $25,000 in the form of commissions, and as his capital of $20,000 was still unimpaired, this showed that he had made a profit of $25,000, all of which had thus gone into his broker's till.

Another who started with $10,000, and for four years operated heavily, making and losing hundreds of thousands, at the end of that time had less than eight hundred left out of his original capital, but estimated the interest and commissions he had paid his brokers at the large sum of $75,000, and these are only two out of hundreds of cases.

Nothing but *great* profits will save an operator from having his substance eventually devoured in brokerage and commissions, and great profits won by the Wall Street trader, are the rare exceptions. There are two remedies for this which are certain and speedy: *First,* Never speculate. *Second,* If you must speculate, *only buy what you can pay for and hold.* These remedies naturally occurred to me, January 1st, 1859, and as the first of the year is the time generally selected to adopt good resolutions, I resolved that whereas Wall Street was a delusion and a snare, I would thereafter cease from speculation.

Alas! for the good resolutions of the one who has felt the excitements of stock-speculation. In five months I was once more in the street, looking for something "good to buy," as the operator would say. But I had made a compromise with my first resolution, and now determined to buy only so much stock as I could pay for. What should it be? The market was full of low-priced stocks. There was Cumberland at 5,—"a worthless fancy;" Old Southern at 9,—my associations with Old Southern were, on the whole, disagreeable; Harlem at 11,—the burnt child dreads the fire, for I had lost $200 on Harlem in 1858. Erie at 5½. This looks cheap. Let me think.

This stock, so famous in the annals of Wall Street, was in a bad way in 1859. The company, for six years, had been going on from bad to worse. Financiering constantly to meet its temporary wants, it had been coming on the market periodically, to negotiate a new mortgage to fund its floating debt. One of these different classes of mortgages was now overdue, the road was in default, a foreclosure had taken place, the road was advertised for sale, and a receiver had been appointed. The sale would, of course, wipe out the stock, and the public generally, looking for this to take place any day, had marked the price already down to zero. A large proportion of the old investors had long since sold out, and most of the entire capital stock was floating in the street, at the nominal market value above indicated. The very idea of investing in Erie, and holding it any length of time for a rise, was sufficient to provoke a smile from any broker who thought he understood the financial situation of things in general, and of Erie in particular.

But week after week rolled by while I was hesitating what to do, and still no sale of the road took place. In September it fell to 4, and stacks of it could be bought at that price.

It was one pleasant day in the month last mentioned, while standing in a doorway in William Street, near where the brokers used to hold their street meetings, that I saw a stout old gentleman with a white head and a merry eye, whose full name has now escaped my memory, but who in the market was known as the "General." He lived in one of the river towns, where it was said he had "done the State some service" in connection with the train bands of militia, and had the reputation of being well to do and "awful cunning" in his speculations. He was full of crotchets and hobbies, and was never weary of talking upon them so long as he could find a listener. One of these was a strong prejudice against brokers as a class. He was in the habit of standing near the street crowd and venting his spite against them by calling them hard names. The brokers not being ever very sensitive to abuse or ridicule, seemed rather amused than otherwise by these little eccentricities of the old veteran.

But his great hobby was Erie. He stood in the center of a little knot of listeners, and was holding forth on his favorite topic, looking very red and determined, and emphasized each sentence by bringing his cane down with both hands upon the pavement. "Are you buying Erie, General?" inquired one of his auditors.

"Of course I am buying Erie, and paying for it, too. No margin business for me. You brokers would eat a man up in twenty-four hours, with your commission, and interest, and infernal turns. I bought a thousand shares for four thousand dollars, this morning, and here it is. [Producing the certificates.] That stock I intend to sell at par."

"At 0, more likely," remarked a bystander.

"Why don't you sell the road out under the decree of the court, then? you've been threatening to for six months. Why don't you do it? What's Vanderbilt doing now? Buying Erie. What's Drew doing?

Buying Erie, and keeping the price down till he can get all he wants. You wont hear anything more about decrees of the court, and foreclosures of chattel mortgages, or sales of the road at auction, when Drew gets all the stock he wants."

"You'd better sell the stock short, General," said a young broker, who had just entered the circle of auditors.

"Sell short!" retorted the General, "you boys would sell the shirt off your back. Look at Jake Little,—there he goes across the street,—he'll scratch a poor man's head before he dies, and you'll have to bury him by subscription."

"Isn't Drew selling it?" inquired a subdued looking operator, who had listened with a sickly smile to the whole conversation.

"Drew selling Erie at 4?" almost shrieked the General. "Daniel Drew doesn't sell stocks when they are low; he sells 'em when they are way up, and you boys are crazy to buy 'em *then*, and he sells 'em to you when you cry for 'em. That thousand shares you see in these ten certificates, I'm going to sell 'em at par, not one cent short of 100," reiterated he, "and when it sells at par you'll see me back here—not before," and he turned on his heel and walked up the street. Different opinions were now expressed by his late audience as to the soundness of these views, but the majority concurred in pronouncing the General a little "touched" on the subject of Erie.

But the more I thought about these views, the more correct they appeared. Here is a veteran in the market, who is willing to buy Erie at 4, and hold it. If it goes down to zero, a man can only lose four per cent., which he may lose any time by speculation. I invested in a few days, $400 in 100 shares of Erie at 4, laid it away in a snug place and watched for the tide to turn. Slowly it rose, but it *rose!* In thirty days it sold at 8; in sixty days it sold at 10.

Daniel Drew, in 1859, and for eight years afterwards, was chief director, high comptroller and purveyor, and head broker of the Erie Railway Company. Nothing in the conduct of the road escaped his surveillance. Every increase or diminution in the monthly earnings was known to him beforehand. He knew exactly where to place his finger on the stock circulating in the market, and how much to a share was held abroad. Every movement in the price of the stock produced by any operator or combination of operators, he watched with a jealous eye and often thwarted it. Knowledge is power. But his power over Erie was not derived simply from knowledge. The Erie Railway Company was poor, it must have money, or go into bankruptcy. Drew advanced them money. He cashed their drafts and indorsed their acceptances, *but* he always took security, sometimes in the form of bonds, convertible into stock, sometimes in the form, more useful to him, of a chattel mortgage on their rolling-stock. The borrower is the servant of the lender. Drew, during these years, held the Erie Railway Company in the hollow of his hand.

When it was for his interest that the price of the stock should decline, he closed his hand and it fell. When it was for his interest that the price should rise, he opened his hand and it rose. If the company failed to meet their obligations to him, straightway a report was spread through the market that Drew was about to foreclose the chattel mortgage, and then came a depression, but mysteriously enough, these depressions occurred when Drew was short of the stock, and the corresponding rises took place when he had bought the stock at the depressed price.

His power over the stock-price was almost unaccountable even in view of these causes. It rose and fell as if upon the waving of a wizard's wand. "Daniel says up!" and up it rose. "Daniel says down!" and down it was. "Daniel says wiggle-waggle!" and it bobbed to and fro in a small arc of two per cent.

From December, 1859, till March, 1860, Erie vibrated languidly between 8 and 10. Then it started up in good earnest. "What's going on in the stock?" was the inquiry around the board. The public ridiculed the movement. "A perfect bubble!" cried some. "Not worth the paper its written on," asserted others. "Sell it short, and you'll make your fortune!" and they did sell it short with a right good will. Panic-bitten bankers, incredulous merchants, conservative stockdealers, all took a flyer, large or small, on the short side. Month after month, the stock kept rising 15, 25, 30. Drew, and his associates, held a vast block of it, counting the number of shares, and the short contracts, and when it became generally known, that Erie's financial troubles were over, that the lawsuits were settled, and the earnings increasing, their grip tightened. Still the price kept rising, 32, 35, 38, 40, and on the 2d of October, it reached its culmination, $42\frac{3}{4}$. The majority of the bears having covered their contracts, the corner collapsed, the price fell back to 25, and dullness resumed her "ancient melancholy reign" over the market. My 100 shares bought at 4, were sold at 40½, showing a profit of $3,600.

This buying of stocks, and paying for them, is the true policy to be pursued by an outsider, and believe me, ye novices, if you wish to elude the traps, bid defiance to the corners, and gaze serenely on the panics of Wall Street, then buy only what you can pay for, and afford to keep, and expect in due time your increase.

CHAPTER VII.

WAR TIMES AND GREENBACKS.

One Little Cloud in a Fair Sky—Business Lively, and Crops coming in while a Thunder-storm is Brewing—The Cloud Gathers and Bursts—Stocks Fall Down and "Take a Nap."—New Fields for the Speculator—The Fortune of a Chemist, and How he Transmuted Saltpetre into Gold—The Parentage of the Greenback Currency—Wake Up, Wall Street!—The Stimulant Begins to Work—Music by the Whole Band!—Stocks on the Rampage—The Under-ground Telegraph Clicking—News from the Front—The Bulls Fall Back, but Reorganize and Prepare to Charge Again—An Army Without a Leader.

EARLY in 1860, arose in the political sky a cloud, at first, no larger than a man's hand. Every one saw it, but not so many looked at it with apprehension.

The financial prospect had never been so bright. The country had fairly recovered from the revulsion of '57. The banking system reorganized and strengthened, gave every facility to the expansion of legitimate enterprise. Commerce was widening, and manufactures were multiplying. The largest crops ever known before were that year gathered. Four million bales of cotton were piled in the warehouses, and more than fifteen hundred millions of bushels of wheat, corn, oats, rye and other cereals had been garnered from the harvest. All the remaining products were in similar proportions.

Here was solid wealth. Here was the means to pay our foreign debt, and the material for an immense carrying-trade on the ocean between America and other countries, and for a transportation still more immense on the *railways*.

The speculative public were looking forward to another era of inflation and of corresponding opportunities for profit in the stock market. And with reason. The amount of business done on the railways reflects the industrial activities of the country. The rises of stock which take place in Wall Street are not all the result of mere speculation. Behind all these movements lies the fact of intrinsic values always operating with a silent but mighty force. "Freight is the mother of wages." This maxim of admiralty law is as true of railroad trains as it is of sea-going vessels. The balance sheet of the earnings of railways is a mirror of the industries and products of the land. In it we can seem to see reflected, piles of cotton bales and stacks of corn and wheat, hogsheads of sugar and tobacco, herds of cattle, flocks of sheep and droves of swine, and a busy host of men working in mine and mill, for the scream of the locomotive is ever the shrillest and most frequent when the furnace, forge and factory roar the loudest.

But the hopes of the speculators were not yet to be realized. The little cloud within sixty days after the election of Abraham Lincoln was announced, had gathered blackness and swelled into a thunder-cumulus which overspread the southern sky and threw its gigantic shadow as far north as the St. Lawrence. Such a season as this had never been known before. Panics of every description had occurred, except that growing out of a political complication so embarrassing and aggravated as this. And yet, dark as the prospect was, the stock-operators, always sanguine of temperament, after a few weeks began to gather courage, and many capitalists were found, particularly in New England, who, tempted by the low prices, were bold enough to put their money in cash stock, for permanent investment. A long continued dull spell in Wall Street is the particular abhorrence of the broker, and if any one who was afflicted by the prevailing gloom, wished to derive comfort for the future, he had only to visit the Stock Exchange and listen to the hopeful prognostications which he would be sure to hear on every side.

The roar of the cannonade at Fort Sumter speedily dispelled these illusions. In three days thirteen of the leading stocks dropped an average of twenty per cent. Government Fives fell to 75, Sixes to 84, and the bonds of the seceded States slumped thirty per cent. After panic came dullness.

The few outsiders, who had for months been fluttering around the stock exchange, now took wing, and the brokers were left for a time to their own devices. The market was suffering under that condition known as the "dry rot." Money was abundant, but there was little "disposish," to use the Wall Street slang, to buy or sell. Months rolled by, and this condition seemed to have become chronic. It was part and parcel of the condition, which affected the entire country.

The same cannonade, "that deep and dreadful organ-pipe of war," which had reverberated through the Stock Exchange, and stunned its inmates into a lethargy, seemed to have lulled into a fitful slumber, a large portion of the commercial and other business enterprises of the republic. Looms and anvils were still, wharves were silent, and vessels lay rotting at anchor, on sea, river, and lake.

But, while legitimate trade seemed almost dead, new and abnormal forms of traffic arose. Army-uniforms, shoes, bunting, haversacks, arms, munitions, and deep-throated engines of war, were suddenly in demand. Cotton-mills were turned into rifle-factories. The steam-derrick hoisted rifled-cannon, the trip-hammer forged the shaft of the war-steamer, and the peaceful foundry poured forth shot and shell in pyramids.

War had thus opened new fields for the energies of the stock-operators. A few of them enlisted, and went to the front, to engage in struggles and stratagems, for which they had been educated, by their campaigns in Wall Street. Some became sutlers. Some bought old hulks, and sold them to the Government, and some haggled in army contracts. Most of them made money, with which they returned in 1862, to ply their ancient trade, in the stock-market.

One of these speculators, in munitions of war, was B., a chemist, who had a small laboratory, in Jersey City. He experimented in the reduction of metals, and furnished certificates of the richness of the specimens of the ores submitted to him by mining companies. Why is it that so many chemists are found among the buyers and sellers of stocks? Perhaps it is because the followers of the science of chemistry are naturally given to the speculative pursuit of gold under difficulties. Witness the old alchemists, who sought to transmute baser into precious metals; or, it may be they are brought into the stock-market, by their connection with mining companies, whose ores they assay and certify to. Certain it is, they may be frequently seen among the busy crowd in Broad Street.

B., had for many years supported himself, and earned something more by his profession; but all his surplus income went to pay his losses and commissions, in the purchase and sale of stocks. He could have been seen almost every day, from twelve to two, standing in the tunnel-entrance to the regular board, bearded like a dervish, his countenance "sicklied o'er with the pale cast of thought," or with the unwholesome fumes of his trade, waiting for the tide to turn in his favor. The tide never did turn, but kept ebbing, and finally left him high and dry on the beach.

Just before the panic which followed the bombardment and fall of Sumter, he had mortgaged his laboratory, chemicals and retorts to his broker and staked the proceeds in a margin on Border State Bonds. In less than two weeks his money was gone, and his broker's account showed him in debt $2,500, besides the mortgage of $1,000 which he owed. He therefore went back to his profession, and in six months had cleared $1,200. This sum would pay off the mortgage which fell due on the 1st of January, 1862, and save him from absolute ruin.

About the first of December he received proposals to go into the manufacture of saltpetre for making gunpowder, in partnership with a wealthy capitalist. The basis on which the expectation of great profits was founded, was the low price of nitrate of soda, which is one of the principal materials out of which saltpetre is made. This fact was enlarged upon, and also that nearly the whole stock of nitrate of soda (four million pounds), then on hand, was held by two firms, and had been bespoken by the capitalist who furnished this information.

B. suddenly recollected that a friend in the business of manufacturing chemicals, had bought some months before, four hundred thousand pounds of nitrate of soda, with the view to make it into saltpetre, but had given up the purpose and had offered to sell it to him, B., for two and a half cents a pound.

"What is the price of nitrate of soda?" inquired B. of the capitalist with whom he was negotiating.

"Three cents a pound," replied he.

No conclusion was arrived at respecting the proposed business, but that afternoon B. called on the chemical manufacturer, who sold him the lot (400,000 pounds), at two and a half cents per pound, ten per cent. of the purchase money payable cash down, the balance in thirty days. This operation stood thus:

400,000 lbs. nitrate of soda at two and a half cts. per lb., .	$10,000
Paid cash on acc., ...	1,000
Due from B., payable in 30 days, ...	$9,000

The next week was spent by B. in trying to work off his purchase at an advance over what he gave, but dealers would only buy at 2½. B. began to feel blue.

The news now came of the seizure of Mason and Slidell. The fear of trouble with England followed, and "villainous saltpetre," otherwise nitrate of soda, began to look up in the market.

Two or three weeks after this, while B. was sitting in his laboratory, one of the parties to whom he had offered the nitrate of soda at three cents, came in and offered three and a half cents a pound, and when his offer was refused, advanced it to four and then to five cents.

"What's got into the market?" inquired B.

"Haven't you seen Queen Victoria's proclamation just received, prohibiting the exportation of arms, saltpetre, nitrate of soda, etc.?" replied his customer. "Now then, B., talk business, at what price will you sell your nitrate of soda?"

"Six cents a pound, nothing less," returned B.

"I'll take it at six cents, and send you a check to-morrow, or as soon as we receive the stuff."

The bargain thus struck, netted B. a profit of $14,000. This sum he used as a five per cent. margin, to purchase U. S. Sixes, of which, he bought $252,000 at 90, and in six months sold them out at a net profit of $30,000. Six months after this he was at work at his old profession, with nothing left but his laboratory with which to win his bread. Such are the vicissitudes of a speculator's life.

A new cycle was soon to commence in American finance, and a new chapter to be written in the history of speculation. The people had pledged their sons to the Government, and five hundred thousand soldiers were in arms; the Government must pledge its credit to the people, to raise money to sustain that army. The money must be in the form of *promises to pay*, for hard currency was not to be had, the faith of the Government must be pledged upon the face of it, and it must have the chief attribute

CELEBRITIES OF WALL STREET.

of gold, viz: the power of extinguishing debts. Thus arose the Legal Tenders.

The credit, (or as some would say, the discredit,) of originating the Legal Tender, or as it is generally called the greenback currency, is usually given to Salmon P. Chase; but the parentage of this ingenious monetary device, is also claimed by a tall man, named P., with an eye like a squab, and a pendulous nether lip, not unknown to the purlieus of the lobby. It has been asserted, that he first suggested the plan to President Lincoln, some time in the summer of 1861. However, this may be the plan was agitated in financial councils, during the last two months of 1861. In February, 1862, after due deliberation, Congress passed the Legal Tender Act, authorizing the issue by the Government, of $150,000,000, in United States notes, thus, nearly doubling at one stroke, the money circulation of the country.

Strange to relate, Wall Street failed to appreciate, with its usual quickness, the significance of this Legislative enactment. During the past twelve months, there had been, with few exceptions, no lack of money for speculative purposes in the stock-market. What was lacking then? Confidence in the future.

During all that chronic dullness on the street, whereof we have spoken, there hardly occurred one notable movement, excepting an occasional sharp rise or decline in Border State Bonds. Brokers and operators, alike, had become so habituated to this lethargic condition of things, that, for more than two months after the passage of the bill, they seemed to desire or strive after no other.

The new currency began to be seen in the Exchange brokers' offices, early in April, first in large notes of $1,000, then of $500. In a fortnight, it was coming on in sums counted by the million. The American and National Bank-Note Companies, who did the engraving and printing for the Government, in New York, sent the notes on to Washington. From Washington, they came back to the sub-treasury, in New York, by the express-wagon load, in boxes, and in bags, but generally done up in packages, the size of small bricks, in brown paper, tied with red tape, sealed with the treasury seal, and numbered and marked; at the sub-treasury, they were paid out by Mr. John J. Cisco, the sub-treasurer. Still, the stock-market was as sluggish as ever. The enormous issue of paper-money inspired alarm, instead of stimulating speculation; and large sums, instead of going into stocks, were deposited with the sub-treasurer, at five per cent interest.

Suddenly, as if by magic, on the closing days of April, the feeling changed. The stimulant, whose virtues the drowsy brokers refused to believe in, began to work most potently. The stocks which had so long lain still, now like so many puppets strung on a wire, pulled by an unseen hand, danced upwards, according to their kind. First came Government Sixes, which had stood at about 93 for many months; on the third of May they touched par, amid loud cheers in the broker's board. Bank stocks, the value of which was interlaced with that of Governments, which the banks held so largely, rose next. Then came the soundest dividend paying securities among railway bonds and stocks. After which the doubtful stocks came limping and halting upwards. But all moved up in steps, measured some by five, and others by one per cent.

In most of the great rises in Wall Street, this order is maintained. The stocks most highly esteemed lead off in the rise, and the others follow in the rank of estimation in which they are held by the brokers or the public, the worthless fancies bringing up the rear like the rag-tag and bobtail of an army. This order, however, is often varied by the artificial movements produced by combinations which take hold of these same worthless fancies and make one or more of them the most remarkable features in a general rise.

The speculation promised in 1860, and postponed till now, had commenced; and it was sustained by something more than merely the abundance of money offered at a low rate in the market place. The same mighty force of intrinsic values, of which we have already spoken, lay behind it. The new circulating notes passing through the country, seemed like the kiss of the prince on the cheek of the sleep-enchanted lady in the fairy tale, to awaken to newness of life the myriad shapes of industry. The music of rewarded labor was heard in fuller tones through the land. Spindles hummed, wheels buzzed, hammers clanged, and the giant brood of agriculture and the useful arts awoke from their slumber.

The earnings of the railways were discovered to be larger than ever before. The volume of business which they did, kept pace with the increased production, stimulated by the enhanced value of the raw material, so wonderfully do the subtle fluids which stimulate the limbs of industry, gather new force, acting and reacting on each other, like positive and negative electricity. It should not be forgotten, also, that this general increase in values, together with the stoppage of the Mississippi artery, justified higher rates of transportation.

The peninsular campaign was progressing favorably, and this gave courage to the Wall Street men. Here it should be noted that early in the war, Union *successes* were used as arguments in favor of a rise in stocks, but as the war went on, Union *defeats* were used as arguments in favor of a rise. This was correct reasoning in both cases, for up to a certain point of time the cessation of hostilities would have enabled the country to recover the old channels of business, but after that point of time the continuance of the war produced permanent devastation and derangement, and became associated with the idea of increased issues of paper money to be redeemed only at the end of the war.

While McClellan and his grand army was pushing past Yorktown and Williamsburg, and enveloping Richmond between his right and left wings, stocks kept advancing, and the speculators began to flock into the stock-market from all quarters. Rings were formed which purposed to send stocks up with a rush when the grand army should march into Richmond.

In the latter part of June, while, to the general public, everything seemed bright and promising at the front, stocks, to the astonishment of the uninitiated, suddenly dropped heavily. Why was this? We may explain it thus:

Early in May, 1862, a plan had been devised by leading brokers and operators, by which, the earliest information could be obtained from the front. Often, before it was known to the Government, a fact would be communicated to the Wall Street magnate, and acted upon. By watching the financial mercury tube on the Stock Exchange, a shrewd observer could not unfrequently predict the news of a victory or a defeat, simply by noticing the rise and fall of stocks. The system consisted in giving those at the front, who gathered and transmitted the information, a certain interest in stocks, and thus stimulating them to every exertion to forward early news. Sometimes the telegraph lines were subsidized, and the most liberal sums were paid for reliable intelligence in advance. Officers, soldiers, sutlers, politicians, lobbymen, and high officials of the Government were employed to keep the Wall Street operators thoroughly posted, as to when to buy and when to sell. This system was afterwards still more completely organized by the gold speculators, as we shall hereafter see.

News had been received through the medium above mentioned, which justified the belief that the McClellan campaign would fail to accomplish its object, then that it had fallen back, and finally that the President was about to call for three hundred thousand more men to prosecute the war. This news was interpreted to be unfavorable to the upward movement in the price of stocks, and so prices fell, and drooped for thirty days.

In July, an increase of the greenback issue was authorized to the extent of $300,000,000. The notes of this new issue soon appeared in their freshest gloss in the sub-treasury, in brokers' windows, in the merchants' petty cash-box, and in farmers' greasy old wallets. The stream taking its rise in the treasury building, flowed on, widening to a mighty river, and like the flood of Old Nile, overflowing, if not fertilizing the country.

Money could soon be had at three per cent., on call, in the market. Once more the watchful operators loaded up. In September there again occurred the same quivering, saltatory, upward movement, that had taken place early in May. "Courage, Bulls!" passed from rank to rank. "Load up! load up!" was the cry. And for the first time, those stocks which were then called the "fancies," began to move. Erie and Harlem were looking up.

Something was still wanting to the market. Stocks were cheap, money plentiful, and hope buoyant. What, then, was lacking? Some one bold enough to bid stocks up. The market demanded leaders, and straightway leaders came forth.

CHAPTER VIII.

BULL-LEADERS.

"Circumstances Make Men"—Addison G. Jerome—The Napoleon of the Public Board—His Appearance, Character and Fortunes—His Fall from Power—John M. Tobin, the Wall Street Sea-rover—Style and Policy of his Operations—Vanderbilt's Lieutenant—New School of Tactics in the Stock-market—Composition of the Public Board—Fortunes of some of its Members—A Bankrupt turns Banker—The Luck of a "Bummer and Dead Beat"—The Story of D——y—Forward Bulls!—Stocks on the March—My First Visit to the Public Board, and what came of it.

WARS bring forth generals; and revolutions, statesmen. Times of financial excitement in the stock-market develop skill and ability in that field, and bring forth what are termed *Bull-leaders.* Wall Street, considered as an aggregation of human-forces and money-forces, without bull-leaders, would be like a flock of sheep without a bell-wether, a mob without a spokesman, an army without a commander. It is the bull-leader who organizes and compacts those forces, brings them under his banner and leads them to victory or—ruin.

He must, of course, have or control large sums of money, and be distinguished for clearness of perception and promptness of decision, but above all, he must have more *nerve,* than falls to the lot of common humanity.

This word *nerve,* in Wall Street, covers and includes

much. By it is signified courage as an active quality, and fortitude as a passive quality, a firmness of bodily fibre and an equal firmness of will, a capability for enduring "punishment," as is said of some pugilists, and the strength to inflict it. It is the same quality that enables the gambler to "bluff" the table and take the "pool" of money though some of the other players may hold a better hand than he, and what, after all, is the game of speculation, but a big game of bluff in which Vanderbilt, Keene and the other heavy-weighted players take the whole pot of money staked by a hundred less skillful and nervy.

Such a man as we have described, was Addison G. Jerome, during his brief reign of nine months, as the "Napoleon of the Public Board." He was formerly of Rochester, N. Y., and previous to going into Wall Street, had been a dry goods merchant in the city of New York, and we believe successful in that vocation. Merchandising and broking, are contiguous professions; the latter being an extension and intensification of the idea of traffic, for the broker buys and sells, both much oftener and much more heavily than the merchant, of the same grade.

He was a middle-sized, quiet-looking man, with a bluish gray eye, and a slight stoop. When he rose to bid for a stock in the Public Board, every eye was fixed upon him, and his gestures, and the expression of his face were studied, even while he was sitting down, during the call of stocks. The spring of 1863, found him master of a large personal fortune, and his prestige in the market, brought to his banking-house, immense deposits, from those who believed in his financial star. He organized, and carried through, some of the most successful corners of the year.

Mr. Jerome's associates in the Board followed his lead, with a blind confidence, that savored of infatuation, and too often with disastrous results to themselves, for he used his power most skillfully, when necessary for the success of some pet scheme, to mislead or hoodwink the uninitiated. We remember hearing him remark to a friend, "now see me fool the boys," (this was in the street after the expiration of the session.) He thereupon, offered to sell any part of fifteen thousand shares of Galena; the brokers around him thinking this only a bluff offer to depress the stock, eagerly caught him up, and in fifteen minutes he sold the whole fifteen thousand shares to different parties. Next morning the stock fell ten per cent. and he re-purchased, before night, the entire lot, bagging something like one hundred and twenty-five thousand by the operation.

Unlike many large operators, whose hearts are like the nether millstone, knowing neither "ruth nor pity," he was open to generosity, and the softer emotions. His treatment of fallen antagonists was liberal, and even magnanimous. Not unfrequently he allowed some of his outside friends to participate in the profits of some one of the numerous rings he controlled. In 1863, he called on H. L. D——, a large and successful operator, but whose painful lameness prevented him from being in the market, and told him to take a few thousand shares of a certain stock, in which he had a controlling interest. He did so, and in three days he drew out of Jerome's hands, a profit of sixty thousand dollars. Nearly every stock on the list (including gold,) first or last during his nine months reign, responded to his touch.

When he formed a ring, he was in the habit of assigning a certain interest to Mrs. Jerome, his wife, doubtless in view of the uncertainties of Wall Street. He always seems to have inspired his associates in these rings, with the same confidence which he himself felt, or seemed to feel, and if a disaster occurred, he was wont to keep up their courage, by pointing to the ease with which stocks could be manipulated, and the great profits to be earned thereby.

But nearly all our Wall Street necromancers meet, at last, some master spirit, before whom, their strongest spells become powerless, and their magic arts fail them. Mr. Jerome, with all his shrewdness and daring, formed no exception to this rule. He met his fate in Old Southern, at the hands of Henry Keep, in August, 1863, in the manner to be hereafter described. His personal losses in this stock on that occasion are said to have reached $800,000, and after that, he ceased to be a power in the street.

He died in 1864, of one of those obscure diseases of the heart, superinduced, probably, by the excitements and pressures of Wall Street life, and left no personal or real estate, unless he may be said to have had an interest in the estate of several hundred thousand dollars which he had settled upon his wife in the days of his affluence.

One of the contemporaries of A. G. Jerome, who first came out prominently as a member of the Public Board, in 1862, and as a general stock-operator, was John M. Tobin.

Tobin is an Anglo-Norman name. It is a corruption of St. Aubin. Some seven hundred years ago, St. Aubin was a Norman Baron, who accompanied Strongbow to Ireland, and assisted in the subjugation of that country. In John M. Tobin's veins doubtless runs, then, the blood of Norman Barons, and of Irish kernes. He has a spice of the old Norse Vikings about him, and has been a kind of freebooter on a large scale. He and Leonard W. Jerome have together plowed the main in Wall Street, and rifled and scuttled many a stately argosy, and taken for toll many good ducats out of Uncle Daniel Drew's strong box. All sorts of stories used to float about among the gossips of the market, respecting his antecedents. He had been a liquor dealer in Water Street; he had been employed on a ferry-boat; he was a returned Californian, etc., etc., etc. And then as to how he started in the street, some said he put up a horse and wagon as a margin, others that he came in with a capital of $500, and "bluffed the boys." The fact seems to be, that he commenced speculations some time before the war, lost heavily in the fall of stocks which followed the McClellan-Richmond-campaign, borrowed fresh capital, made heaps of money, and early in 1863, had become a power in the market. He was known to be somehow mysteriously connected with Vanderbilt. He was the principal agent of the Commodore in engineering the great rise in Harlem, during the spring and summer of 1864. This added to his prestige won in former operations. His style of operating, too, was so bold and so dashing and even reckless, and yet withal there was such method in his madness, that it quite captivated "the boys," and they were all agog when Tobin got on his pins and commenced bidding. Tall, lithe and straight as an Iroquois, his eyes flaming like two opals, he would charge up under Drew's heavy batteries and take all the big wads of certificates the old man would fire at him. Unlike most of the noted operators, whose faces are seamed and creased as if some ravenous bird had clawed them, he has a face which, though somewhat worn and haggard, is finely chiseled and lit up now and then by a smile which is of the most un-Wall Street geniality.

His policy in operations, as he, himself, lately informed a friend, has always been to select some stock which promised gain, find out all he could about it, and then concentrate his energies and capital in promoting its rise. When it had risen high enough to insure to him a sufficiently large profit, he would sell out, and turn his attention to some other single stock, and treat it in the same way.

Like his associate, and sometime colleague in rings, A. G. Jerome, his portfolio has contained at different times, very large amounts of stocks, now of Old Southern, now of Hudson, or Pacific Mail, or Erie, or Rock Island.

At the close of 1864, he was rated on the street, at five millions. But within four months after, he was rumored to have lost nearly two millions, chiefly by bulling gold at 200, in the teeth of Union victories, and while the shattered hulk of the Southern Confederacy was going down, head foremost. After this he is reported to have made and lost largely in New York Central. To-day he is poor.

These two men were the bull-leaders of the Public Board during the first few months of its existence.

They inaugurated a system of tactics in stocks, like that by which the "little corporal" defeated and scattered the Prussian and Austrian armies. This system consisted in rapid movements, and the concentration of their forces at the critical moment upon one point —a single stock. They soon found apt pupils and imitators in the market.

That energetic, but motley crowd, which composed the Public Board, in the latter part of 1862, was made up, as already remarked, of heterogeneous elements. It had more enterprise and talent than money. Many of its members had, previous to the war, carried on various lines of business extensively, but had lost their all in 1861, and owed hundreds of thousands besides. Though they had little money, they had what in Wall Street supplies its place, viz: confidence in the upward tendency of values. They had seen men almost as poor as themselves, become affluent in a few months, and the heavy operators about them were making or losing a hundred thousand in a single day. A volume might be filled with the marvelous stories of the waxing and waning fortunes of these men. One of them owed in December, 1862, one hundred and eighty thousand dollars, and in eight months after, had compromised his debts at fifty cents on the dollar, and was worth clear of the world, three hundred thousand dollars.

In 1861, I had often noticed a singular looking man standing in front of one of the billiard saloons in the upper part of Nassau Street. He bore all the marks which characterize the bar-room loafer or "bummer," seedy, bloated, he was apparently doomed to a speedy and miserable end, and a grave in the potter's field.

In one year from that time I saw him driving a pair of ponies in Central Park, and on inquiring his name, learned that he was C., a Wall Street man, who had made $80,000 on gold. He is now keeping a hotel, and to see him looking after the comfort of his guests in the lordly self-sacrificing way common to hotel proprietors, no one would imagine that this was the desolate "bummer" of Nassau Street.

Such was not the luck of D——y. He was a young man of New England extraction. In 1862, he was a salesman in a Broadway dry goods jobbing house, on a salary of $800 per annum. Having made $600, by buying a few cases of cotton goods on credit, he brought this sum to a friend who had been long engaged in speculation, requesting him to take it and use it as a margin to buy stock for his, D——y's, benefit. He received in reply, the usual good and disinterested advice, not always, however, in such cases given, viz: "Keep out of the street, or if you *will* speculate, do it on your own hook." He embraced the latter alternative, and joined the Public Board. His personal appearance and manners made an odd impression on 'Change. Tall, bulky and ungainly, his face and voice reminded one of a gigantic bull-frog, when in one of its happiest moods of a May evening, and the way in which he bellowed out on the call, set the whole room in hysterics. In an evil hour, he caught a virulent epidemic, which prevailed extensively in the market about that time. The name of this disease was *Harlem on the brain.* He bought and sold nothing but Harlem; he talked and thought of nothing but Harlem. "It was bound to go to two hundred, of course, and no one could stop it. The Commodore was bulling it, Jerome was bulling it, the 'street' was all bulling it." So he always was saying and acting conformably—buying it. In four months he made, out of his $600 margin, $40,000 on his pet stock during its rise from 30 to 181. In the course of sixty days from the time when he might, by selling, have realized his profit to that amount, the stock had dropped to 90. During this decline he clung obstinately to his stock, and borrowed largely from his friends to keep his margins good, but long before the price had touched 90, he was obliged to succumb, with the loss of all he had, besides $30,000 of borrowed money. Within a week he sailed for California, and was last heard from while keeping sheep on the hills of one of the grazing counties of that State, calculating the amount of the next wool crop, as he watched his nibbling flock.

To return to the point in the preceding chapter, from which we have digressed. The eager cohort which had been waiting for orders, now commenced moving under the commands of their Generals, Jerome and Tobin. The battle of Antietam, and the retreat of Lee to the other side of the Potomac gave the bulls courage. Illinois Central opened the ball by a rise of ten per cent., Pacific Mail danced behind it almost as fast. Hudson, Old Southern, Panama, Reading, Rock Island and Pittsburg stepped blithely up, while Erie, that Rip Van Winkle of stocks, astonished the market by its nimble bounds, rising in a few weeks thirty per cent., and selling at 67. This campaign lasted about thirty days. Then stocks fell back a little and paused.

According to the traditions of the street, certain

seasons used to be assigned in which stocks were active, and certain others in which they were dull and depressed. December is usually set down as a dull month, while after the new year, stocks pick up and become more active. So it was in 1862. For six weeks prices remained firm, but comparatively dull.

My first visit to the Public Board was early in January 1863. The room in which they then held their sessions, it will be remembered, was the basement of No. 17 William Street. It was under the auspices of my old broker, O., that I obtained access to this grotto. The day was a nipping one. The hangers-on about the door had retreated to some of the neighboring restaurants. The winter rise had already commenced. The dense, black-coated mass of humanity swayed to and fro, while the room rang with the dissonance of bids and offers. No stock without some advance, but Hudson was the favorite that day. It opened at 77 and rose to 80 on the call, then fell back, or, as they say in Wall Street *reacted* to 78.

"Hudson is the card to-day," remarked O.

As he uttered these words, a broker came up, and asked if he was buying Hudson.

"At what price?"

"Seventy-eight and a quarter, five hundred shares, at that price?" holding up his finger, interrogatively.

"No, unless my friend," turning to me, "wishes to buy," and at the same time he nudged me and whispered: "Buy it, Buy it."

Before I knew it, the words came out from my lips, "I'll take it." "I'll take your stock," repeated O., to broker, "put it down to me." In sixty seconds by the clock, 80 was bid for the stock, and by the close of the day, it stood at 84.

Before narrating the issue of this unexpected enterprise, let us go back and follow the history of that $3,600 profit on Erie, which accrued to me in the fall of 1860.

A series of careful purchases in which the whole stock thus bought was always paid for and held till it showed a profit, had swelled the $3,600 by December 1861 to $5,000. This, and the original margin of $500 constituted all the capital that I purposed sinking in stocks.

Of this sum $5,300 was then invested in two hundred shares of Erie, at 26½. In April, 1862, 100 of these shares were sold at 37, and the proceeds, $3,700, invested in (600) six hundred shares of Harlem, at 12¼. Harlem, it should be stated, is half stock, *i. e.*, fifty dollars, instead of one hundred dollars, per share, at par; so that these six hundred shares were only equal to three hundred shares of full stock, and stood me in $3,675. (In two years and three months from the day when it was purchased, that pitiful lot of Harlem, costing only $3,675, could have been sold for $85,000. Why don't men hold on to good things when they have them? Wall Street men never do.) In November, the remaining one hundred shares of Erie, had been sold at 64. This, with the old margin of five hundred dollars, made nearly $7,000 cash on hand, besides the 300 shares of Harlem, which showed a considerable profit. *But I had broken my rule, never to operate on margins. Here was danger ahead.*

Hudson had risen fifty per cent, during the past

six or eight months. Supposing it should "break," and fall twenty-five per cent. Let me see; twenty-five per cent. on five hundred shares, would be $12,500, whew! Nearly all my profits scraped together by so much pains, swept away in an instant. These thoughts occurred as swift as lightning, the moment after the stock had been so rashly bought. My reverie was interrupted by O., reminding me, that I had no cash in his hands, and that he should want ten per cent. margin, *i. e.*, $5,000. Having been satisfied on this point, he parted from me, urging me to watch the market very closely, and not let my profit run away from me.

Hudson was passing into strong hands. A great financial doctor was paying it daily visits. Dr. C. Vanderbilt had it under his special care. Every day it grew better, stronger. It jumped about like a gymnast preparing for the prize leaps; then it took its first leap to 94. Its second leap was to be to the hight of 112. Its third was to carry it to 180.

I took my profit on 400 shares at 94, and kept 100 shares out of pure curiosity, to see where the price would finally land me.

Ten thousand dollars in cash is a very restless thing in a speculator's hands. A little waif picked up in the street, you can only keep it by griping it fast; relax your fingers for an instant and it is gone to wander among the other waifs and strays until some one else picks it up. My ten thousand dollar waif stayed with me until I saw something which attracted my attention in the steamship line, as will appear more fully in the following chapter.

CHAPTER IX.

PACIFIC MAIL AND LEONARD W. JEROME.

Creative Genius in America—The Opening of the Golden Gate—The Battles of the Steamship Kings—The Commodore Makes a Hearty Lunch off Accessary Transit Company—Features of Pacific Mail as a Wall Street Stock—It Oscillates like the Waves of the Sea—"Unstable as Water Thou *Shalt* Excel"—A Grave-yard for the Bears—A New Ring on the Changes of P. M.—L. W. Jerome's Portrait—The Sultan in Wall Street—"I Never Speculate, Sir, but I *will* Take a Little Pacific Mail"—A Secesher gives me "*Point*"—The Stock on its Upward March—Bulls Charge with Flying Artillery in Front.

WHO says the American people have no creative genius? True, they have never sung of an "Achilles' wrath," or of "Archangel fallen;" they have never painted a "Transfiguration," nor composed a "Seventh Symphony," nor constructed a "Novum Organum," nor written a tragedy like that of Hamlet. They have had no Homer nor Milton, no Raphael nor Beethoven, no Bacon nor Shakspeare to fill the untenanted niches in their temple of fame with the grander shapes of Poetry, Philosophy and Art. Imagination, in this country, lives in the future rather than in the past. It is the prophet of great industrial enterprises, the framer of inventions, and subordinates itself to the spirit of the practical, everywhere. The American people, we may say, are continually groaning and in travail with such strong conceptions as were brought forth, embodied in the steamboat, sewing-machine and telegraph. To this mighty brood, also, belong the schemes like the Pacific Railroad which spans a continent with a thousand leagues of iron band, and like the Pacific Mail Steamship Company which plows the waves of the peaceful sea with keels which bear almost to our doors the tea plant and the cinnamon plant before they can shed their flowers which bloomed under the sky of Cathay.

Of American enterprises embracing the great lines of travel, steering their course by the westward star of empire, and moving with it farthest and fastest, the Pacific Mail Steamship Company was the pioneer. Its originators were three men of mark in the mercantile world—Gardner G. Howland and William H. Aspinwall, of the firm of Howland & Aspinwall, and Henry Chauncey, of the firm of Alsop & Chauncey. These men had the eyes of prophets, ranging widely over the land of promise which stretched out towards the setting sun. The accession of California to our national domain was the immediate occasion of the incorporation, in 1848, of this company. The discovery of gold in that region secured its speedy success. For twenty years it was a veritable Pactolus, through whose channel were rolled to the marts of commerce, the golden sands whirled down by the mountain torrents from the scarped cliffs of the Sierra Nevada, or crushed by the more impetuous and eager hand of man, out of quartz and the sulphurets. The yearly income which the company derived from the freights of gold were from the start, considerable, and the aggregate foots up something enormous. But its great source of revenue, till 1869, was the carriage of passengers. From 1848 to 1852, the whole world seemed to be packing its trunks, and ho! for Eldorado! Down through the Gulf, across the Isthmus, northward to the Golden Gate they hurried, and a refluent tide of the successful or disappointed, swept back again by the same route. All this swelled the profits of Pacific Mail. In 1850, it doubled its original capital of one million, and in 1853, increased its capital to four millions to meet the necessities of travel.

Meanwhile, the same three men, Howland, Aspinwall and Chauncey had, by the aid of foreign capital, carried through another great enterprise, the Panama Railroad. Though only forty-seven miles in length, from Aspinwall to Panama, the completion of this road involved difficulties and disasters which would have appalled men less rich and resolute. No white man could long breathe the miasma of those dank swamps and jungles, and live. Commerce seemed to have become a Moloch, before whose grim shrine, thousands of Irish laborers were sacrificed. But the work must go on—means were soon devised. Some one proposed our kinky-haired friends, and a few ship-loads of Jamaica negroes accordingly supplied the waste and finished the line.

But the Pacific Mail Company were not long permitted to reap the fruits of their enterprise, undisturbed. The carrying trade from New York to Aspinwall had been taken by those modern sea-kings, C. K. Garrison, Charles Morgan and Marshall O. Roberts, and above these, loomed the figure of the irrepressible "Commodore," whose march (then) "was over the mountain wave," and not yet over the iron rail.

One of the rival enterprises in which he engaged, was the Nicaragua Accessary Transit Company, which has been heretofore mentioned.

In the history of steamship navigation, no more interesting passage could be written than that relating to the rivalries in the California trade during the first twelve years after the accession of that State to the Union. Morgan, Garrison, Roberts, Vanderbilt, the Accessary Transit Company and the Pacific Mail Company, all fighting for the largest share in that lucrative trade, and with fortunes that shifted from each to the other by turns. In some of the ancient naval battles, we read that the ships were armed with *gilded* beaks, for the purpose of running down and sinking the vessels opposed to them. In the emulous warfare of which we are speaking, the steamships may be said to have been armed with golden beaks, for the contest was to be decided by the force of hard money,—by the superior weight of the precious metal. After numerous collisions and a severe cannonade of ruinously low fares, it was found at the end of the conflict, that the eagle beak of C. K. Garrison was disfigured, Marshall O. Roberts lay crippled and helpless, and even the Commodore was not unscathed.

But, while this new edition of the old sea-rovers were fighting among themselves, the traveling public, upon whom they were wont to levy toll, were benefited. The prices of passage to California ran down to a low rate, and the hearts of the way-farers were gladdened.

In 1856, the affairs of the Nicaragua Accessary Transit Company were found to be in a bad way. C. Vanderbilt, the individual, had advanced to C. Vanderbilt, President, large sums, and was preparing to bolt without gagging the whole assets of the company which he held as collateral. This process was, as usual, speedily and (for C. V.) happily accomplished. The Pacific Mail Company deemed this a favorable opportunity to get rid of so formidable a competitor, paid King Cornelius an annual tribute of $480,000, per annum, for a fixed period, on condition that he would run no other competing line on the Pacific side, and once more, all was quiet on the San Juan. Out of these transactions, grew the famous suit brought by the receiver of the Nicaragua Accessary Transit Company, by John Sherwood, his attorney, *vs.* C. Vanderbilt, involving claims to the amount of $2,000,000, which dragged its slow length along through the courts for so many years. Pending this suit, the stock of the N. A. T. Co., oscillated for a season, between twelve and a-half cents, and nine dollars a share in the stock-market, and finally disappeared into that limbo of nothingness, to which the defunct stocks of Wall Street are consigned.

Of all the historical stocks of Wall Street, considering its vast arcs of vibration, its sudden fluctuations, its enormous dividends, the fortunes it has made and marred, its growth, and its far-reaching and accomplished aims, Pacific Mail is the most remarkable. In 1857 it sold for 50, in 1867 it sold for what was equivalent to 700, on the basis of the increased stock; in 1849 it had two second-class and frail steamships, plying between San Francisco and Panama; in 1876 it had thirty-two steamships, each one of which was a floating palace of a grandeur and beauty passing the common show of naval architecture, and plying between New York and Aspinwall, between Panama and "Frisco," and between "Frisco" and Yokohama, Nagasaki, Shanghai and Hong-Kong. He who visits the office of the company in the banking house of Brown Brothers, and in which marble, iron, plate glass, black walnut and fresco, form a pleasing combination of solidity and beauty, will be reminded that he may here shake hands with China for a small consideration.

But we are to speak of the stock as a market value, on 'Change, and of its singular fluctuations since 1861. It may be viewed as a type-stock of the street. The very fact that its value is contingent on so many circumstances arising out of the business of the Company, gives it that character. It has been associated with the water, that very unstable element; exposed to storms and marine disasters; to pirates; to the revolutions in Central America; to wars, and rumors of wars with foreign powers; to the ebbing of the tides of transmigration; to the completion of the Pacific Railroad; to competing lines on the ocean, and to mutations of business in that most speculative and ultra-enterprising of states, California. These are the variable quantities that have always entered into the calculations of the bears of Wall Street in depressing the stock. Then on the other side there are the vast assets and profits of the Company, the growth of the country in general, and of the mining interest, and latterly of the China trade in particular. These are constant quantities that have always entered into the calculations of the bulls in elevating the stock. Accordingly, long before the great speculation which commenced in 1862, it was one of the great balloons to be inflated or depressed according to the wishes of stock leaders. Jacob Little and Daniel Drew many a time made great sums by depressing it, but the stock has generally been a cemetery for the bears. The operator who deals in Pacific Mail, is like the mariner who embarks on a treacherous sea. He can look down through its depths and see the bleaching skeletons of bears who in their day made Wall Street resound with their growlings. Who could safely sell short a stock which rose by the hundred per cent.

More rarely this stock has proved the ruin of the bulls, not a few of whom, since 1867, have met their fate by operating in it for a rise. The smash-up of the great house of Lockwood & Co. is a noteworthy example. They owed their disasters mainly to the heavy fall in the price of stock which they had bought at a high rate.

In the year 1861, Pacific Mail was greatly depressed. The fear of complications with foreign powers kept down its market price, and at the time of the Trent affair in December of that year, it fell to 69. But the earnings of the succeeding year were enormous, and in the latter part of 1862, a "ring" of a new and singular character was formed in it. The whole stock was $4,000,000, divided into forty thousand shares. Twenty-six thousand shares of this amount were bought by a combination of such men as W. H. Aspinwall, and Brown Brothers, the Anglo-American Banking House, etc. This stock was transferred to Brown Brothers, by an irrevocable stock power, as trustees to hold it *five years* for the joint benefit of members of the ring. This left fourteen thousand shares, which was in the hands of private investors.

Who was to be the Wall Street representative of the ring—the manipulators of this stock—who would lead the upward dance of the price?

No one who traversed Central Park in 1867 failed to remark four bay horses, standing at least seventeen and a half hands high, bowling along on an easy trot, and drawing after them a huge "drag." Sitting on the box, holding the reins, was a man, fashionably, but somewhat carelessly attired, having a slight stoop, a clear olive complexion, a tigerish moustache, and a cerulean eye. This was Leonard W. Jerome, a leader of the fashion, a prince of the turf, and lately, a potentate in the stock-market. Some men are born speculators, some achieve it, and some have speculation thrust upon them. All these conditions may be predicated of L. W. Jerome, and when he left Rochester, and came into Wall Street, he found his proper niche. The head to conceive, the daring to undertake, and the nerve to persist, were his, and his confidence and buoyancy under disaster was remarkable. Like all men of his class, he was not infrequently temporarily prostrated by some one of those singular hurricanes in finance, which come and pass over as suddenly as a white squall in the Southern Pacific. But no matter how swift or low the fall, he has invariably kept up good heart, and hailed his surviving comrades with the words, "I am all right, boys; I'll be with you again in a jiffy." Under such circumstances, he invariably met every dollar of his obligations. Once he found himself saddled with half a million of bogus Indiana bonds. He paid up in full. Another time, in the years 1867–8, he found himself out of pocket on Pacific Mail nearly one million dollars. Then the carpers and malignants of the street were crying out—"Jerome has found his Waterloo!" but in six months he picked up half of his lost million, and made his adversaries pine with envy.

He was bred to the law, and this may account for a certain conservatism which seems to have led him to operate, for the most part, in dividend-paying securities, calling attention to the rule that intrinsic values will in the end bring profit, while the inflated "fancies" and mere market values, as surely in the long run bring loss. Like his brother Addison G. Jerome, he has generally been a bull in stocks.

A mortal feud long existed between him and Daniel Drew, in which they mutually gave and took wounds. In 1864 he took a slice out of Uncle Daniel, on Harlem, of the size of a quarter of a million. In 1865 his opponent retaliated by scooping out of him a couple of hundred thousands on Erie. There was a poetic fitness that such a man should be the bull-leader in Pacific Mail—a stock reminding us by its very name of the treasures of Eldorado, and of the "barbaric pearl and gold," which the Orient is said to "shower on its kings." In his tastes and his munificence he has been a kind of Sultan of India or Rajah of Benares. Stables rose at his bidding fit for the horses of Caligula. A race-course was laid, which bears his name, worthy of the plains of Elis, and his garlanded Apician banquets rivaled those of Lucullus. All that he did was on such a princely scale as to show that he knew how to spend as well as to make money. Under the heavy purchases which he made, Pacific Mail rose rapidly from par to one hundred and sixty.

The whole pack of Bandogs of the street sat on their haunches with mouths that watered and uttered feeble yelps of hungry excitement as they wistfully watched its upward progress, yearning to snatch at the tempting feast, but held in the leash, some by impecuniosity, and some by irresolution or prudence.

It seemed like madness to buy Pacific Mail, now that it had risen 100 per cent. in thirteen months. A few outsiders ventured in.

"What's the matter with P. M.?" inquired C., a well-known merchant, of G., a leading operator, whom he met on the street cars one morning, just as the stock had reached 145.

"Going up! Going up!" replied G., "you'd better take a little."

"I'd as soon think of opening a dress-goods store over a volcano!" rejoined C., "I never buy P. M. above 75."

"You'll never see it at 75, again," and G. whispered something in his ear, whereat C. looked astounded.

Whether C. ever bought any Pacific Mail, we cannot affirm, but this we know, that two or three weeks after, when the price was thirty per cent. higher, C. was seen emerging from G's. office, holding in his cherishing fingers, a plump check, which he regarded with a paternal smile.

In the spring of that year, and while Pacific Mail was being manipulated as above described, I became acquainted with a certain mysterious individual (a secret agent of the Southern Confederacy, as I afterwards learned), who was boarding at the same hotel, and was in the habit of taking "flyers" in the stock-market. He informed me that something very startling would soon occur in Pacific Mail, that the stock would inevitably depreciate 50 or even 100 per cent He spoke with all the confidence of certainty; he asseverated it with as much solemnity as if he were taking his oath on the holy Evangels. On my asking for the grounds of his assertions, he replied in the soft Tuscan accent of his native State: "Dog gone it! do you doubt the word of a southern gentleman? I tell you it's dead shore." I sold short 200 shares of P. M. at 160, and 100 shares more at 162.

The stock-market in January, 1863, was like an army moving up a steep declivity. The old guard, Erie, Harlem, etc., were still skulking in the rear, but Pacific Mail was leading the van upon the double-quick. The bears sat upon different peaks of this declivity, watching the upward movement and licking their lips over the rich opportunities which would soon be offered them for attack and plunder, "for," said they, "whatever goes up much, must come down much." When the price reached 160, they began to hurl down blocks of shares to drive P. M. back. It still rose, staggering to 164, then turned and slowly fell back to 160. The bears now threw a perfect shower of missiles. It quivered a moment, and then dropped heavily to 155, rested there for one short breathing space, then darted up in a few hours to 165. In a week it sold at 178. The bears gave way with dreadful losses. Many of the oldest heads had been caught. The stock never halted till it touched 200. The rumor went round the street, that Vanderbilt was buying it. The spectacle of Tobin, bidding fiercely for the stock at 190, with the aureola of the Commodore's prestige surrounding his blonde brow, disenchanted the bears from their illusions. Some of the more deeply initiated were now warned by their friends, with dark hints of what was going on in the Jerome pool. They covered their contracts, and the stock fell back to 180.

During this rise, and after I had closed my 400 shares, short stock, at a loss of $10,000, news came that the Joseph Chapman, an armed schooner, had been seized in the harbor of San Francisco. She was a letter-of-marque of the Southern Confederacy. The plan proposed was, to capture one of the Pacific Mail Steamers, arm her, and cruise for the others. This was the secret, which my Southern acquaintance was building his hopes upon. If the Joseph Chapman programme had been carried out successfully, no doubt the stock would have fallen heavily to my individual profit, but to the damage of the Union cause. Here it might be appropriate to indulge in a little burst of patriotic enthusiasm, but oh! the memory of that $10,000!

At this point, we must take leave of Pacific Mail, for several chapters, and turn our eyes upon another form of speculation, which had, in the autumn of 1862, assumed a definite shape, and in February, 1863, first rose into huge proportions.

VIEW OF THE GOLD ROOM ON "BLACK FRIDAY."

CHAPTER X.

"GOLD, GOLD, GOLD, GOLD,—HOARDED, BARTERED, BOUGHT AND SOLD."

"Fresh Fields and Pastures New" for "The Boys"—The Gold Genii—The Lobbymen and Politicians Take a Turn—Where all the Gold Was—Secesh at the Front—A Petroleum Maniac—I Take a Flyer in Oil, and Find it "Oil of Joy"—I Go "Down to the Sea in a Ship," and What my Ship Brought when it Came in—New Recruits in William Street—Things are Working—Gold "Breaks" for 200 and then "Breaks" to 156—Raking in the Profits—A Sum in Algebra, $73,000 + $20,000—The Bear-leader in Distress—The Gold Dreamer, and how His Dream Came out—Men and Money in Wall Street—The Autobiography of $500.

DURING the year 1861, gold ceased, generally, to circulate, as money, throughout the Republic. Early in 1862, and soon after the passage of the Legal Tender Act, it began to be dealt in as merchandise. It was bought in the market at varying prices, and then having been bought as merchandise, it was used as money to pay Government duties on the debts due abroad. From legitimate traffic it is an easy step to *speculation* which we have already termed the abuse of trade. And now commenced the most baleful form of speculation, that which made it for the interest of the parties engaged in it that the national currency should depreciate, for as every one knows a rise in gold is nothing but another name for a fall in the value of currency.

Thus, when gold sells for two hundred, a dollar in currency is worth only fifty cents in gold; when gold sells for five hundred, a dollar in currency is worth only twenty cents in gold.

I will not here and now reiterate the hackneyed arguments against the morality of trafficking on the rise and fall of greenbacks, and the embarrassments caused in the commercial world, by the unsettling of the standards of value. No doubt, every one but the gold gamblers, and their friends and dependents would be better off if they were swallowed up in the ocean. I speak now as a scribe, not as a moralist. The *fact* is before us, gross and palpable and thus we are to deal with it. The precious metal prior to the year 1861, acted its part in the operations of commerce, like the beneficent Afrite, in Arabian story, obeying the behests of its master, with commendable fidelity, but the breaking out of our civil war seemed to have driven it into its casket, where it lay for a year, and then issued forth under the guise of a malevolent genié. This genié took the form of a cloud-statue, not "moulded in colossal calm," but changing its shape according to the financial weather; now looming up to a portentous size, and anon dwarfing and dwindling under all kinds of influences. Like similar malign agencies, it had its chief abiding place in Wall Street.

The daring speculators, who had by the assistance of causes already mentioned, so successfully forced up the price of stocks, now flushed with their good fortune, and comprehending the situation, turned their attention to gold. The dealings in it at the coal hole, which at first were limited, soon came to rival the transactions in stocks. In September, 1862, under the combined influence of Union disasters, and heavy purchases, it shot up to 135. Early in February following, it had risen to 150.

Now was formed the first notable combination to put up gold. The state of affairs which led to that sharp and sudden rise to 173, which was to prepare the public mind for the wild and reckless speculations, extending already through seven years, and still hardly diminished, may be described as follows, viz:

The sum total of gold and silver, estimated to be then in the country, was upwards of $250,000,000; rather a big pile to get into a "corner," you will say. But only little over one-quarter of this was in the banks, and no inconsiderable portion of that was held on special deposit. The balance was scattered throughout the country, much of it in the South. The private bankers held several millions. Several millions were in the form of plate. Much was buried in the earth and hoarded up in chimneys and garrets. How much the industrious farmers and raven-like crones of the rural districts had hidden away in old stockings, between mattresses and in cupboards, secret drawers and hollow trees, no one can imagine, but probably enough to pay a year's interest on a $1,000,000,000 of debt. Apart from the idea of speculation, multitudes laid away sums, larger or smaller, against that very wet day, when a bushel of currency might not buy more than a peck of meal. Some of the large, but timorous capitalists, also put much of their property into exchange on London. In this way the floating supply of gold could be readily absorbed by any strong ring which might be organized. Bills of exchange drawn on the commercial cities of Europe, it should be here remarked, are payable in gold, and therefore rise and fall in price with gold.

During the preceding year, the already large army which was "fighting the tiger" on 'Change, received a re-inforcement. It came from the South, and having had ocular proof of the depreciation of the currency in that section, had fixed its eyes on the course of gold in the Union States, and looked for a corresponding rise here. Most of these men had brought with them sums, larger or smaller, principally the latter, in bills of exchange on London, the aggregate amount whereof was great, and was deposited as margins, in the hands of Wall Street brokers, for the purpose of buying gold. These exiles, or rather emigrants from the Sunny South, were a motley crowd. Some of them tall, gentlemanly-looking men; others swarthy, lank-haired, tobacco-ruminant individuals from the Gulf States. They haunted William Street, birds of ill-omen, croaking all manner of disaster to the Federal arms, and predicting gold at 500. Many made fortunes by being always consistent bulls, but lost them again, by the tumble of 1865. Such was the situation, when I made my first venture, and bagged my first profit in gold. In order to tell the whole story, I must go back, and trace that profit to its doubtful beginnings.

In the month of October, 1861, two gentlemen sat in a private parlor of the Grammercy Park House. The one was a well-known pioneer in the petroleum enterprise, wearing a face of perennial redness and gold-bowed spectacles; the other was the narrator of these scenes. The ruddy gentleman was holding forth with great volume and fluency upon the subject of petroleum, his favorite theme. If he was to be believed, besides the illuminating and lubricating properties of this article, it had a great variety of other uses. It was death to vermin, a capital disinfectant, and a gorgeous colorizer. As boot grease, and as hair oil, it was unequaled. The most delicious perfumes might be manufactured from it. It was a panacea for most of the "ills that flesh is heir to." It was a liniment for rheumatism, a lotion for wounds, and a "sovereign remedy for an inward bruise." In token of which last he produced a small vial from his vest pocket, and swallowed a part of its contents, declaring that he took it for an affection of the kidneys, and had derived great benefit from the medicine.

"This article," added he, "is now selling at five cents a gallon (including barrel,) at the wells, and will be a great speculation for any one who buys it."

"What will you sell me fifteen hundred barrels at?" inquired I.

"Fifteen hundred barrels, crude petroleum—I will sell at—two dollars, per barrel."

"To be paid on delivery, in New York?"

"To be paid, on delivery—at—the wharf, in New York."

This bargain was nailed by a small memorandum in writing, signed by the parties, to be charged according to the statute, so made and provided.

Six weeks after this, the barrels were duly delivered, per Camden and Amboy Railroad, and were sold on the wharf, at a net profit of $3,500, and some odd cents, petroleum having advanced largely meanwhile.

The proceeds of this lucky stroke were a few weeks subsequently, invested in refined petroleum, packed in cans and cases and shipped to Australia. The figures in this venture stood thus, viz: $9,700, of which, $6,200 was an advance on the bills of lading; the ballance, $3,500, was the actual cash embarked. The vessel which carried this merchandise, was an old tub, warranted not to make over six knots, even with "a wet sheet and a flowing sea." She reached her destination after a voyage of one hundred and twenty-five days, just after a "spirt" in the prices of the articles shipped, so that the consignees were enabled to close the shipment at a net profit of $6,500, after deducting freight, commissions, brokerage, etc., etc., etc. Several other delays now occurred, all very much to my benefit, such, for instance, as disputes over samples, references, making up the account sales, and finally, when the return bills of exchange were forwarded, the steamer which conveyed them was wrecked in the Indian Ocean. All this time, gold, and therefore exchange, was steadily rising. When the slow old ship left New York, gold was 101½; when the gold bill on the Union Bank of London for return sales, reached New York, gold was 153. Here was a new profit. Without stopping to sell my draft, amounting to $10,000, I promptly invested it as a ten per cent. margin on $100,000 gold, bought at 153. This was late in January, 1863.

In that month, a combination had been formed, known as the "Washington party," which bought up several millions for a rise, on the grounds that Congress would authorize the issue of three or four hundred millions more currency.

This movement soon became known to the leading operators on the street. They relaxed their hold of stocks, which paused in their course upwards, and increased their line in gold.

The rise appeared so reasonable, and so inevitable, that men who had never speculated, began to make their first essay, we might say *assay*, in the precious metal. Strange faces were seen in the vicinity of the "coal-hole." Financial oracles of the rural districts, were heard on the corners uttering their predictions, as to the future price of gold. Quiet old bachelors, living on their dividends, were seen emerging from their up-town snuggeries, prepared to renew their youth, like young eagles, in the courts of the Stock Exchange. Some of the novices could be observed, hovering on the edges of the battle, or gazing with gloating eyes, on the ascending price, but hardly daring to venture in.

Meanwhile, gold kept rising. It touched 160. Now the bull machinery was put in motion. The telegraph between William Street and Washington, went click-a-ty-click. The crowd buzzed, the workmen were hard at work, lubricating the steam-presses, preparatory to another edition of greenbacks, containing all the modern emendations.

George Francis Train was seen daily leaning gracefully on the iron railing near the coal-hole, engaged in perusing telegraph literature. Beside him, stood Pepoon, looking like a Dutch Burgomaster of the olden time. George Francis said gold would sell at

200. Pepoon repeated after him, 200; Addison G. Jerome said 200; the coal-hole echoed the words.

I bought $100,000 more at 160. In a week the price rose to 173, and looked for the moment as if it were really booked for 200. It began to sink.

The $200,000 I held, was dumped overboard, and left me with a profit of $28,000, to which add $10,000 in the gold bill, sold at 170, and making $17,000 in currency, footing up as a sum total of profit, $45,000.

But gold now commenced falling. Large amounts were forced on the market, according to rumor, by the Washington party. In a day or two, the secret came out. The Government had imposed a tax of one-quarter per cent. on all sales. I thereupon sold short, $200,000 at 169⅞ to 170½. Down it went by the run, and in three days, sold for 156. Profits on this transaction, $28,700.

In two years and upwards, with hardly more than the scratch of a pen, the fifteen hundred barrels of petroleum bought at a venture on credit, and without the ultimate expenditure of a penny, thus rolled up for the lucky buyer, $73,700!

During the rise of gold, from 130 to 173, most of the outside public, and the younger and bolder operators in the street favored a rise, and were active bulls; a few inveterate bears like Drew, etc., true to their instincts, still sold short, but were severely punished, and after the rise of gold to 170, covered their contracts and stood aloof. Drew, however, whose losses on the rise were said to have been half a million, is said to have persisted in his programme, and when it fell, recovered a good portion of his losses. The decline, which was steadily going on for the next six months, after February 26th, 1863, quite upset the calculations of those enthusiastic operators, who looked for 200, as a limit for the realization of their profits. Many of these individuals held manfully to their position, fortified by the enormous profits of their operations for a rise. Among this class were the young and inexperienced operators, who in the spring, thought themselves possessors of ample fortunes, and in the succeeding fall, found themselves either worse off, or in very much the same position, as when they commenced.

The speculation of which we have been speaking, brought out in strong relief, that which we may call the monomania of Wall Street. Men who pass all their time there, are often afflicted with this form of the speculative disease. A Wall Street monomaniac is one, who, devoting himself exclusively to some one stock, by thinking long and deeply upon it, and continually operating in it, comes at last to think and talk of little else. He clings to it, through good report and evil report, and through actual losses. The gains he makes in it, strengthen his mania. It is only by absolute ruin that he can be cured, and even then, often not permanently. He still babbles of it in the social circle, and when he revisits the street, always inquires with solicitude, the price of his old favorite, and if it has eventually risen very greatly, appeals triumphantly to that fact, in justification of his course. This was the case with H——.

He was a German-American from one of the Western cities, and came into the street with $4,500 which he had scraped together, by buying and selling the "wild-cat" currency which flooded his native

State. His personal appearance was something of the oddest. The bumps on his head, which was sparingly thatched by a "plentiful lack" of the capillary substance, would have astonished a phrenologist. His face had the color and general shape of a half-boiled Indian pudding. His eyes, large and bleary, had a dreamy look, as though they were contemplating the phantom of a million dollars which haunted his imagination; and that feature which he dignified by the name of nose, was merely an excrescence expanded into two nostrils. The facilities furnished him by his gentlemanly broker, soon taught him to appreciate the beauties of the margin system, and he was afterwards heard to express the opinion, that the time would come when he would buy up the whole of New York on a margin. By two or three lucky operations he doubled his original capital of $4,500, and commenced buying gold in the summer of 1863, at 117 or thereabouts. His first purchase was $90,000, when it rose five per cent., *i. e.*, to 122, he bought $90,000 more. Following this programme and buying at every five per cent. advance, when gold touched 173, he found himself carrying $990,000, with a profit of nearly $300,000. During the five or six months in which he was making these purchases, he seemed to be laboring under a kind of nightmare, under the influence of which, he was unable to realize his profits, and was always compelled to buy. He thought of nothing, dreamed of nothing, and talked of nothing but gold; impalpable gold-dust seemed to float in the air he breathed, and every object to take on a yellow hue. He carried in his left breast pocket, a chunked little blank book, in which all his purchases were entered, and his time was about evenly divided between the study of this book and the perusal of the daily quotations of the price.

This delirium of speculation seemed to have somewhat shattered his nervous system, and he was wont to lie late in the morning, rarely making his appearance in the street before eleven A. M. I remember meeting him often in Broadway, making a bee-line for Wall Street, on that double-quick gait, known as the negro trot; when he would suddenly halt and cry out, interrogatively, "gold?" On hearing the price he would throw up his arms, utter a little ecstatic scream and resume his trot. He used to declare he would never sell for less than a thousand. This was the limit he gave his broker every day, and every successive rise fortified him in this resolve and made him more and more callous to the arguments and ridicule of his friends, who advised him to take his profits.

But H——'s greatness was soon to be nipped by an untimely frost. In the fall of gold, which commenced on the 26th of February and continued for the next few days thereafter, his profits were abridged to the amount of $200,000, and early in June following, he was called upon by his broker, for more margin. Not being able to respond to the call, he was sold out and presented with an account which showed a balance of only five hundred dollars to his credit. This fall from such a sunlit hight to such a dead level, almost drove H—— distracted, but failed to cure him of his monomania. He still kept his dreamy eyes fixed on gold. Its tendency was plainly downwards. Gettysburg was fought, and it sank lower. Vicksburg fell and gold dropped to 131. When the "swamp angel" sent its messages into Charleston, and Fort Wagner became a Union fortress, gold at 122 looked as if it would drop to par. But now it suddenly reversed its course and began to mount that lofty hight which it was destined to scale before ten months were gone. H—— jumped in and bought ten. (Wall Street lingo for ten thousand.) He moved on now, taking every step gingerly, and bought ten more at each fifteen per cent. rise. In one year from September, 1863, he owned three brown-stone fronts. He is still a flourishing operator, but only in gold, never buying more than he can take care of, and never letting a profit run away from him.

In Wall Street, the man is nothing; the money, everything. The first inquiry when a new operator enters the field, is, how much money does he carry? Not at all what kind of a man is he, what are his antecedents, etc. This inquiry having been answered, he is labeled with the sum for which he is good, and after that loses his personal identity in the money he possesses. While a cracksman, slave-trader or pirate might walk the street, not merely unimpeached, but saluted with respect, if covered with the broad label inscribed with $100,000 in front and indorsed with it behind, an archangel would be of little account, unless he brought with him a good store of shekels in a golden urn, for here

"Mammon wins his way where seraphs might despair."

Thus it happens that an autobiography of experiences in Wall Street might properly be entitled the history and growth of so much money, whatever sum the operator may have started with. Such an autobiography as this might be presumed to commence thus: My name is one thousand dollars, my surname greenbacks. I was begotten in an engraver's office, and born from a steam-press early in the year 1863. My general appearance was pleasing, my color was that "soft green on which the eye loves to repose." I circulated freely in society and was much courted. At an early age I took up my permanent abode in Wall Street, where I thrived and grew very large. At last, from my increased size, they called me one hundred thousand dollars, etc., etc., etc.

In the foregoing pages, I have given the history of $500 in Wall Street, which by April, 1863, had after numerous trials and vicissitudes of fortune, grown into $20,000, or was readily reducible to that sum, standing thus:

600 Shares Harlem, (half stock, $50 per share), selling in the market at $56, ...	$16,800 00
100 Hudson, which showed a profit of	2,200 00
Margin on same, ...	1,000 00
	$20,000 00
Profits on gold, etc., ...	73,700 00
	$93,700 00

I stood $93,700 ahead.

The sun never shines so brightly, and fiercely, as just before a thunder-storm, which gathers its own force from that same brightness and heat. Metaphorically speaking, there are vast caverns in Wall Street, where, as in the realms of Æolus, of classic myth, the winds are accumulated and pent up. They are let loose in panics, and panics occur when stocks that have been over-sold, rise enormously, as well as when they fall enormously.

The rise in Harlem which we shall describe in our next chapter was a case in point. Other illustrations of a bear-panic resulting from the overselling of a stock are furnished by the Prairie du Chien corner in the fall of 1865, when that stock rose 100 per cent. in an hour, by the Northwestern corner in 1872, Gould, Clark and Schell bidding up that stock in two days from 95 to 250.

In the years 1878 and 1879 the wisdom of the late Commodore Vanderbilt's advice "never sell what you havn't got," has been proved in many instances by the experience of a multitude of bears, who rashly went short of low priced stocks and suffered severe losses by so doing. The coal stocks, especially, have served as a bear cemetery ever since their fall to such low prices in 1877. In August, September, and October, 1879, it was partly the sharp bidding of the frightened "shorts" which sent Del. & Hudson flying up to 82, Del., Lack. & Western to 90, and Central of New Jersey to 81—a rise of nearly forty per cent. in sixty days.

CHAPTER XI.

THE FIRST GREAT HARLEM RISE.

The Tale of Three Men who met in a Doorway During a Storm—Shall We Sell Harlem Short?—The Brokers Say Yes—Investigations—What is a Broker's Opinion Good For?—The Decision is Made, and We "Sell 'em"—Vanderbilt in Search of Investments—"I Have a Few Millions Lying Idle, Sir, and I Wish to put it into Something that Will Pay"—The Patriots of the City Hall in the Field—A Large Donation to Harlem—The Commodore Gets His Dander Up—The Clown of the Stocks Plays His Antics—A Miss is as Good as a Mile—Legislative Tricks—The Stock Mounts, and the Bears are Slaughtered—Harlem the Double-edged Sword of the Stock-Market—How I Came Out—Incidents of the Rise.

THE market was taking a breathing spell. It was a complete April day. The sun had risen in an unclouded sky, and the breezes from the noble bay, blew their reveillé to the waking spring, when suddenly the heavens became overcast, the wind shifted to the north-east, and blew a gale, mixed with snow. There were three of us. We had taken refuge out of the storm, in one of the hallways, on William Street, near Exchange Place, and were discussing the all-absorbing topic.

"I sold out my business," said one, who was a retired baker, "and came into the stock-market a year ago. I've no reason to complain. I bought stocks right, and sold them right. I'm $100,000, clear of the world. I am going to get out of this business, it uses me up. Only one more operation for me, and then I shall pull up stakes, and decamp."

"And what may that 'one more operation' be?" inquired another, who was a burly railroad contractor and engineer.

"I'm only waiting for Harlem to rise to 60, and then I mean to give 'em some on the short tack." The railroad man smiled, and spoke thus: "I came into the market four months ago. They always told me I had a good eye for a country. When I came here I took my survey, and staked out my route, kept clear of steep grades, and have brought myself in on time, with one hundred and fifty thousand dollars in my baggage car. Now I am going to back train. I'm through with Wall Street, but I *do* want to make one more operation." "And what may that one more operation be?" inquired I.

"I'm bound *to sell Harlem short*, when it gets up a little higher," he replied.

"I have a little Harlem all paid for; if it wasn't for that circumstance, I should feel like selling it short," I exclaimed.

"You don't surely say that you have been buying Harlem!" exclaimed both my companions at once.

"I should as soon think of buying old newspapers," said the baker.

"Or that dust heap in the street," said the railroad man.

"I think I shall hold that Harlem just to see where it will go. But let's go round and talk with some of these brokers."

So we went out into the storm.

V——, into whose office we first entered, was a well-groomed, little man, with a bright, black eye. He sat behind a long desk, handling his papers nimbly with both hands, and looking very much as if he were playing exercises on a piano.

He saw business written on the faces of the trio, as we entered, and he stepped briskly forth from his musical exercises.

"What do you think of Harlem, V——?"

"Harlem 57½ at the close, gone up too much, must react."

"What do they say about it in the board?"

"Well! all sorts of opinions. Some say that Vanderbilt is buying it, and that it will go to par, but most of the board seem to think there's no reason in the movement. G——, B—— and L—— were selling it freely this morning."

"When it strikes 60, sell one thousand shares for my account," said the railroad man, "order good till countermanded."

Next, we went to G——'s office. He was a different type of a man from V——. Being rather heavily moulded, and still of his tongue, he had obtained the reputation of possessing great good sense.

He thought Harlem higher than it should be. A good sale undoubtedly. Its intrinsic value was about fifteen, instead of fifty-seven. "But," inquired he, "what *about the street franchise?* Hasn't Harlem got something of that kind?"

All the other brokers, whose offices we visited, were unanimous in the opinion that Harlem was a good short sale. Some said the certificates were only good for wrapping paper. Others said they would speculate in it at about 15. But all concurred in thinking its value more speculative than real.

Here let us stop a moment to remark that most men, at least novices, are wont to ask advice of their brokers, as to what stock they shall buy or sell. But is a broker's opinion worth anything? Not generally. "Never buy or sell on a broker's judgment," said a member of one of the oldest and safest firms in the street, lately to a customer, "if you do, you'll be sure to lose your money." This is a great truth. The brokers borrow their feelings from the market. If the market is depressed, they are affected accordingly; if the market is active and high, they are elated in a corresponding degree. In this way their advice to their customers is to sell when they ought to buy, and to buy when they ought to sell. Again, a broker's judgment is warped by being constantly in an atmosphere of mere market values, irrespective of real values. A broker will often laugh at a customer, who is figuring up the true value of a security by examining the condition of the railroad company which issues it. If a stock has been selling at a very low price for several years, it is consigned to the portfolio of worthless fancies by the broker, who never stops to inquire what its true value is. When one of this class of stocks goes up on its merits, he will be sure to pronounce it a good sale.

That street franchise! what could G—— mean by that? We visited a lawyer's office and called for the laws of the State of New York, hunted up the original charter of the Harlem Railroad Company, which was dated about forty years ago, but could find no street franchise granted by it. We went to the office of General S——, the counsel of the company, and inquired if he knew of any franchise granted to the Harlem Railroad Company. He knew no more about it than he did about Numa Pompilius.

"All right," said the railroad man. "All right," responded the other twain. Within three days we found ourselves jointly short of eight thousand shares of Harlem, of which lot I had three thousand at different prices, from 57 to 59. There was one man who did not share in the ephemeral opinions which prevailed in the stock-market respecting Harlem.

Vanderbilt always seems to have held faith in the ultimate value of the stock as a security, and had been for some years a director in the road. As he was selling out his steamboats and steamships, he began to look about him upon terra firma for investments, which would make him comfortable in his old age, and, singularly enough, he pitched upon Harlem, that fag end of all the railway fancies leading apparently a precarious existence, and only tolerated by their high-mightinesses, the Regular Board of Brokers.

Did he do this with the expectation of getting control of the stock so that he could use it as the rings of Wall Street do? Not at all. He bought it at a low price, in order that he might put into it some of his spare cash, as a permanent investment. In 1862, he was known to be buying a large amount of the stock.

One day a well-known retired merchant, an intimate acquaintance, met him and asked how it happened that he was buying so much Harlem. He replied that its sale at par was only a question of time, and as he had a few millions lying idle, he was putting some of it into Harlem,—his children would reap the benefit if he himself did not live to do so.

During the winter, the price had been slowly rising, bringing up the rear of all the principal railways. In April, it had jumped in a few days, with rapid leaps to 61, and then fell back to 58. Thus it stood, when the short sales above recorded, were made. Within a week after, the price slumped to 43. The three thousand shares were bought in at a profit of $13,000, and when the price rose to 52, four thousand shares were sold short, for my account. The price hung at from 50 to 54, for a few days, then sprang up to 58, then down to 55, then up again. It seemed to have quicksilver in it, and hobbled up and down without much apparent cause, as though some strange atmosphere was at work on it. The stock was the favorite one of the whole catalogue, and was operated in, boldly, both on the long and short side, in amounts so large that the whole capital stock sometimes changed hands in a single day. Vanderbilt was known to be buying it for investment, and some of the sharp ones were chuckling at the idea of "sticking" him with big "jags" of it at 58 and 60. The idea that he was buying it for *investment*, seemed intensely funny to the brokers. They sold it right and left, in the most dashing style, amid the laughter of their associates. Still he kept buying it. He appears to have been open and above board. In these transactions, he reminded one of the tintorea shark, of the tropical seas, which announces its presence by the phosphorescent atmosphere in which it is enveloped; its prey is first stifled, and then devoured at leisure. And so it was now. The Commodore moved about through the turbid waters of the street, making no secret of his doings, and quietly absorbing into his vast financial maw, the huge slices of Harlem fed out to him, by the frolicsome and infatuated bears. The singular oscillations of the stock, set some people to thinking there was something more in it than appeared on the surface. Queer-looking boys, with pug noses, and eyes that embraced you and the opposite lamp-post at the same glance, were seen carrying notes with the most outlandish orthography, from the City Hall to the offices of prominent brokers. Men with strongly Celtic faces were seen on Wall Street, answering to the names of O'Flyn and Mac Murphy, Sixth-warders by the cut of their jib, and said to belong to the Ancient and Honorable Board of Aldermen.

The 21st of April developed the game with sufficient certainty. On the evening of that day an ordinance was rushed through the Boards of Aldermen and Councilmen, authorizing the Harlem Railroad to lay a double track through Broadway from Fourteenth Street to the Battery. This was in accordance with the terms of their amended charter of 1832, which vested in them the right to lay rails in any street in the city, subject to the consent of the Mayor, Aldermen and Commonalty of the city of New York. When we reflect that from one to two hundred millions of people pass up and down that roaring thoroughfare every year, the value of this grant may be estimated. Successive generations of speculators and lobbymen had fought to obtain it from every legislature for the preceding twenty years, but in vain; and now by the stroke of a pen, the Harlem

Railroad held it. The stock rose in an hour from 60 to 75. The bears were filled with consternation; venerable men, the grey coyotes of the Stock Exchange, who had fattened on stock depressions and panics for a quarter of a century and were now heavily short, were seen wending their way to the offices of their counsel learned in the law, to devise legal means to extricate themselves from their dilemma. The courts of justice were invoked and a shower of injunctions discharged itself forthwith on the Mayor to forbid him from ratifying the ordinance and on the company to prevent their laying rails in Broadway. The Mayor disregarded the injunction under legal advice, and signed the ordinance, while the other processes wended their sinuous way through the courts.

But the furious opposition to the grant from so many quarters, had meanwhile got the Commodore's "dander up." He and his friends held most of the stock. They made ready to twist the bears. Many of this latter class were men of large means and strong will. They believed that the franchise scheme would somehow fail, whether in the courts or in the ensuing session of the Legislature; accordingly they kept borrowing the stock and averaging themselves with commendable resolution.

The upward movement was assisted by the large purchases made by Addison G. Jerome, who drew after him a long train of imitators. Other members of the Public Board sold it short furiously.

Now commenced a dance, such as was never known before in the stock-market—the rise in stocks known as the Chancellorsville rise—which will be hereafter described. Of all the list, Harlem moved the wildest and most oddly. It pranced and capered. It had wings and flew up thirty points, then dropped like a shot partridge to its starting-place. It never would rest. Bulls and bears blessed it and cursed it in fierce chorus alternately. It ruined the bulls, and drove the bears to suicide. The Harlem operator was rich in the morning and poor at night, or vice versa.

Once when it flew up to 117, I received a call from my brokers for $40,000 more margin, but almost before I had left their offices in despair, it was down again to 105, and I was saved. During the next break, which carried it to 90, the four thousand shares, of which I was short at 52—55, was bought, and my loss was finally settled at something like $75,000. Thus ended a weary campaign of six or eight weeks.

New views of life in Wall Street!

Oh! That infernal Harlem! That terrible old Commodore!

But this is not the end of Harlem, nor of the bears. Still up and down, as the summer waxed hotter. The bears encouraged by occasional successes, became bolder; then they became bolder still, even to recklessness. Something was in the wind. Again, the Celtic faces, from the City Hall, were seen on the street. Again, the queer-faced boys were seen bringing notes from the Assembly Chamber of the City Fathers. These notes were all orders to sell Harlem, "at any price, only sell it." The Aldermen and Councilmen of the city of New York *were selling Harlem*, the pet of the Commodore, the life of the street.

Now it sinks slowly, now drops swiftly, now it's up again, no! it has fallen to 72. Wherefore?

The Common Council had rescinded the ordinance granting the right to lay rails in the streets of New York! And the stock fell.

They had played Vanderbilt a trick.

This was late in June. In three days the price stood 105.

This action on the part of the Common Council, was believed by the prominent holders of the stock to be of no effect. But the bears undeterred by their losses, still kept selling the stock. It vibrated heavily between 90 and 105. But some one was always ready to buy it, particularly when the sellers wished to *go short* of it. A great hand was always extended to receive the stock and pass it away out of sight, in a deep, broad iron chest. The Commodore was *biding his time* to take revenge on the Legislative tricksters.

In the latter part of July, Judge Brady, of the Court of Common Pleas, dissolved the injunction, forbidding the Harlem Railroad to lay rails in Broadway. Then the price, which had been slowly heaving and collapsing for four weeks, all at once jumped to 115, amid the execrations of the whole ursine tribe. No mercy! Still up, 120, 125, 130, 140. The bears loosed their hold by dozens as it rose. At 150, most of them had covered. Some hard heads still kept their position. But when it touched 180, there was not a single man of them left. As for their losses, one circumstance will show them more clearly than any array of figures; for months after the event, when any one desired to say that an operator was irretrievably ruined, he expressed it in a single phrase, "he went short of Harlem." What made the matter worse for these gentlemen, many of them when they covered at 140 and 150, bought the stock to hold for 200, and failing that point, were caught by the rebound in another trap, when Harlem fell from 180, not a few of these bulls too late, were of the City Hall clique.

The ends of the ring were now substantially and for the time being accomplished. They had sold out the bulk of their stock at prices ranging from 140 to 175; the shorts were covered. It was decided, therefore, that the stock should be dropped. Here, again, the aid of the courts and the municipal legislative bodies were invoked as hammers to smite the still erect and swelling crest of Harlem, and reduce it to its old comatose and worthless condition. A decision of Judge Hogeboom, adverse to the franchise grant, was first promulgated; this was followed by legislation of the Common Council unfavorable to the railroad company; the price dropped to 75, ruining almost as many by its fall as it had by its rise. So suddenly did this take place, that it effectually finished the enthusiastic outside holders of the stock, nor were the bears, who were sullenly waiting for their revenge, able to put out any considerable line of shorts. A few of these latter, however, when the stock was selling from 135 to 140, had still sufficient nerve to sell a few thousand shares, three weeks after which they might have been observed leaning against the various lamp-posts, gorged and happy.

I had almost forgotten to say that the 600 shares of the stock which was bought at 12, seventeen months before, and which I had held to see what would come of it, was sold at 140, with a profit of $38,400. Buy a stock low, pay for it, hold it, and finally sell it high. 'Tis well!

Many amusing anecdotes are told of the singular fortunes of some of the smaller operators during this rise. Once a broken operator asked a broker acquaintance to buy him a couple of hundred shares, as they were standing in the crowd, just after the fall to 72, which followed the rescission of the grant by the Common Council. The broker wedged his way into the crowd and bought the stock, but when he came out he could not find his impecunious customer to report the purchase and procure his margin; during this time, scarcely sixty seconds, the stock had risen five per cent. When the customer made his appearance, he promptly gave the order to sell it. Before the sale could be effected, the stock had risen five per cent. higher, and the buyer had made a thousand dollars. This sum was the foundation of a fortune of $150,000.

Another of these strange pieces of luck, was that of a butcher boy named Devoe, (no connection of Thomas D., General Scott's old caterer, in Jefferson Market), who had earned $400 driving his furious chariot at day-break, from the First avenue abattoirs to Fulton Market. Overhearing Alderman Mullowney of his ward, extolling the Commodore and his pet stock, and predicting an extraordinary rise, he became inoculated with the prevailing epidemic, and paying a visit to Wall Street, "spouted" his $400 with a broker, as margin for a hundred full shares of Harlem at 124. In five minutes it fell three and one-half per cent.; $350 of the hard earned money gone! Devoe was in despair, which he vented in the most energetic expletives known to his trade and place of residence, which was, we need not add, not far from Mackerelville. Just as the order was going forth to sell him out, a messenger from the Board brought tidings that Harlem was selling for 127. Devoe straightened himself, smiled a sheepish smile, and doubled his interest in the market, by taking another hundred shares. In two weeks he drew out $21,000 profits, of this his first and last venture among the bulls of Wall Street. He is now a flourishing broker among the bulls and other cattle who graze amid the fertile bottoms of the Illinois.

To recount the losses of individuals in this campaign, would be a dreary catalogue. Those of two, only, need be mentioned. The baker instead of retiring from Wall Street with $100,000, left in the fall with only $2,500, and returned to his old trade. The railroad man was more fortunate; he saved $40,000, but he never sold short any more.

Let us now return from the tangent on which Harlem has carried us away, and see how the general market fared during the spring and summer of 1863.

Coming down from the past to the present we would call attention here to the equally singular vicissitudes that marked the great rise of 1879. Men who were poor in August of that year became by bold and persistent buying on slender margins rich in the following October. Some made handsome fortunes in a week, and even in a day on a sharp rise a competency was made by many an operator.

CHAPTER XII.

THE BRIGADE OF BEARS.

How Bulls are Changed into Bears—The Short Gentleman on the Anxious Seat.—A Bear-garden in William Street—Office of D. Groesbeck & Co.—David Groesbeck the Pupil of Jacob Little, and the Partner of Daniel Drew—Portraits of Other Bear-operators—Dr. Shelton—C——'s Fortunes—William R. Travers, the Partner of Leonard W. Jerome—A Lucky Hit on the Bear Side—Anecdotes — The Marshalling of the Clans—The Bull-battalion—Lockwood & Co., and LeGrand Lockwood—Another Bull-leader! Who is it?

WALL STREET operators commence their career as bulls, and finish it as bears. This is a general rule, to which, of course, there are many exceptions. When a man enters the stock-market, he almost invariably operates for a rise. But when he sees how long it takes for stocks to go up, and how swiftly they sometimes fall, and moreover, when in one of those falls, he finds all the profits of months previous swept away in a day, he naturally reasons that if, instead of operating for a rise, he had waited and sold short, or operated for a fall, he would have acquired wealth with a haste commensurate with his desires. Besides this, he sees that interest always runs in favor of the bear, while it forms one of the heaviest items in the bull's account, for it will not have been forgotten that the buyer pays and the seller receives interest on all stock contracts. It is easier for a broker to sell stocks short than to carry them, and so he is prone to operate on the bear side, and is apt to encourage his customer to act on that side.

During the year ending April 1st, 1863, a numerous retinue of gentlemen with strong bear proclivities had been waiting for the tide to turn. They had had a "hard road to travel" for the twelve months then last past. One stock after another had been tried but only with ever increasing loss. The general rise had cost them money. Hudson had drawn heavily upon their purses. Gold had lowered them still more, and Pacific Mail had almost completed the drain.

Many of these gentlemen had been in the street, speculating for years, and had built up great fortunes out of the wrecks of panics, just as Christian churches in Rome have been built out of the ruins of Pagan temples. A large number of the members of the regular board of brokers, especially of the older members, were bearishly inclined, considering the enormous and unprecedent rise of stocks, and reasoning from past experience rather than from the present situation of financial affairs. Some of these brokerage houses thus affected, served as rallying points for those who thought they could make money now by selling short.

One of these rallying points was the house of D. Groesbeck & Co., of which, Daniel Drew, as already mentioned, was the chief operator and a partner. Here Uncle Daniel, for six or eight years conducted his numerous and extensive operations. Here was his head-quarters and strong-hold. Figuratively speaking, it might be supposed that it had underground passages, by which mines were dug beneath the enemies' works, when he was preparing for an explosion, which should hoist the bulls on some fine day when they least expected it, or that it had parapets, from which, a plunging fire of blocks of stock could be directed on the besiegers, or secret doors which could be suddenly thrown open, so that the delighted eyes of the ursine garrison could gaze on the pleasing spectacle of a panic. On the contrary the office of this firm, which, in 1863 and 1864, was at No. 15 William Street, was a very peaceful-looking place. Four little rooms, all so snug and cosy. In one sat a half dozen clerks behind a railing, figuring or drawing checks and paying for stocks, or sending them out by two or three mealy-faced boys. In the little room at the side, customers were wont to be consoled when luck was against them, or congratulated when the little joker was jumping to their satisfaction. A short, ruddy young man (one of the firm) was strolling about, and "talking horse." In the next room, were most of the customers of the house, some engaged in financial contemplation, others in a trance, wherein they seemed to see panics approaching with a beatific vision, or perhaps brooding over their losses; on the whole they were just then (in 1863 and 1864) rather a melancholy-looking crew. On the sofa in the rear room, seated cross-legged, was a not very handsome, but a harmless-looking old gentleman, in close confab with some one of the lights of the market; perhaps with Dick Schell, or it might be Charles Gould, or one of the directors of the Erie Railway Company. Was that Uncle Daniel the Great Bear? Yes. Who was that tall man with a cassimere sack coat on, who looked so saturnine and gloomy, as though he was haunted by the spectre of an adverse market? That was David Groesbeck, familiarly known among his numerous customers, as Grosy, and the head of the firm. A graduate from the office of Jacob Little, from whom he learned the art and mystery of the stock-trade, and inheriting his traditions, it was fitting that he should be the partner of the great bear of the last decade, and the head of the great bear house of 1863 and 1864. For many years, after starting in business on the street, he speculated on his own account, and like others, who, before or since, have followed his example in that respect, failed several times. But for the past eight years, he has given up legitimate commission business, in which he has rolled up a large fortune. This man is probably the repository of more financial secrets, than most men in the street. He could tell, if he chose, how it was that Jacob Little made and lost such vast sums, and by what legerdemain Daniel Drew has so often transferred to his own roomy pockets, the cash once in the pockets of a hundred different men.

Personally, Mr. Groesbeck is a man of a kind heart and quick sympathies. He does not forget the friends of his early years, and after the death of his old principal, Jacob Little, he was one of those who aided in collecting out of the debris of a great fortune, a sufficient sum to provide for the family of the deceased financier.

We would not be understood to assert that the customers of this house were necessarily, or all of them, operators for a decline, or bears. Both sides of the market were represented, and great fortunes have been made, as well as lost, in the house of D. G. & Co., on the bull side. Nor would we say that the firm were given to the practice of advising their customers to sell short. Still there *was* an influence there all the time, working to induce short sales, not by persuasion, advice or argument, it was something more subtle than these—an atmosphere of bearishness which each one breathed, until he took on the shape and action thereof. Uncle Daniel, the bear, was the great Panjandrum of the house of D. G. & Co., and all the little Joblillies and Piccalillies patterned their operations after his.

This office was the rallying point of the bears in 1863. Some of the dealers there, afterwards became noted during the great decline and subsequent rise of 1865. One of these was Dr. S——, sometimes known as Ursa Minor, and sometimes known as the "Retired Physician," the golden sands of whose life are not yet by any means run out. He was then and still is a veteran, and a daring speculator, whose fortunes swung between zero and a million, almost in the course of one revolving moon. During 1863, and the first three months of 1864, he sat watching his pile as it dwindled away under that process of attrition peculiar to the stock-market, until it only contained $20,000. But that oaken and smileless face and still tongue told no tales of waxing or waning fortune, but in grim silence waited for the wheel to come round full circle. It came in good time. In the spring of 1865, he rose the master of three-quarters of a million.

Since that year Dr. Shelton has had a checquered

experience, making and losing large sums, and has at last retired on a competence.

Another of the famous bears of the greenback era was Corey, a tall, dark, silent man, who ruminated deeply on the instability of all sublunary things, and particularly of market-values in Wall Street. He was, of course, a heavy loser by selling short, but was put on his financial legs by Drew, whose bowels warmed towards a brother bear.

A majority of the older members of the Stock Exchange were believers in lower prices during the great rises of sixteen and seventeen, and were severe sufferers in consequence of acting on their convictions. Here we may remark generally that as the bear side requires less capital to operate on than the bull side, a large number of the smaller speculators of the board of brokers are constantly taking turns on that side. After the grand break in 1877, the number of such operators was legion, and during the rises in the summer of 1877, and the spring and summer of 1878, and again in the winter and summer of 1879, they materially aided the engineers of these rises by often overselling certain of the pool stocks. In the fall of 1879 the numbers of this class of dealers has been greatly reduced, in consequence of their losses in "bucking" against the market; but even now there are not a few resolute operators who persist in believing that a great break is coming in 1880, and are unwilling to enter into the feeling that has carried the Granger stocks Wabash, Kansas Pacific, and various of the fancies to such a high point. The persistence of these individuals will doubtless be rewarded, but let us return to the thread of our narrative.

Daniel Drew indoctrinated many of his young associates in the art of selling short, and after the panic of 1864 the office where he did business was full of customers, who operated mainly on the short side. Many of these operators, like Dr. S——, had been pretty much cleaned out in the rises of 1863 and 1864, but retrieved themselves in 1865.

Joseph G. M——s, a tall, burly man, with a small, unwinking eye, early connected with the Public Board, was another bold bear in 1863, though he occasionally went in strong as a bull. He, too, retrieved his fortunes during the gold panic of 1865, and has since been a prominent operator of the Stock Board, oftener on the bear side.

Up to the passage of the Legal Tender Act, William R. Travers, another leading operator, known among his friends as Bill Travers, was to be counted among the bear brigade. He was formerly one of the firm of Jerome & Travers, Leonard W. Jerome, who has already been described, being his partner, and a likely span of bold, shrewd financiers they made.

Some years before the commencement of the war, this firm made a great hit in Old Southern, at the time when it was selling at from 120 to 140. It was done in this wise: The stock was a favorite one then, and was viewed as safe as a government bond. Nearly everybody in the street had a little, and the outside public speculators, as well as investors, were long of it. This created a favorable condition for the formation of a ring to depress the stock. Just now, Jerome & Travers discovered, either by their native shrewdness or by accident, that there had been a considerable over-issue, fraudulently, or at least irregularly. Acting on this, with the utmost secrecy and dispatch, they put out all the short contracts they could arrange for, and then sprung the mine. When the news of the over-issue had been communicated to the street, the stock fell heavily, from fifty to sixty per cent., and the profits of the sharp operators were enormous—rated by some as high as a million and a half.

The portrait of Travers is familiar to the stock-dealing public. A tall, slender man, with a rubicund face and a jolly nose, never smiles, and speaks with a pronounced stutter. Long since, I saw him while standing on the curb-stone, buying some stock of a dealer whose countenance bespoke his descent from Shem. "What is your n-n-name?" inquired T., of the Hebrew. "Jacobs," replied the seller. "But what is your c-c-christian name?" asked T., whereat the crowd was convulsed. But T's head is as clear as a crystal. From 1854, when he and his L. W. Jerome made their famous bear raid on Old Southern till the great speculation season in 1879, his operations have been almost always successful, because he better than others has understood the financial situation in each particular case. His reputation stands deservedly high as a business man and a sagacious operator. His fortune is estimated at three millions.

Previous to his entrance into the street, he resided and did business in Baltimore, where he married a daughter of Reverdy Johnson. His Southern affiliations, as well as his own judgment, taught him that the war between the sections was to be long and bloody, and he was among the first to understand its effect in Wall Street. At least, as early as the first months of 1862, he predicted the future course of the market, and a vast enhancement of values. About that time he met an acquaintance, on a ferry-boat, and the conversation turning on stocks, then very much depressed, asked what he was doing, and how much money he had to speculate with. He replied that he had about six thousand dollars unemployed, but dared not invest it, in those uncertain times. "Then," said Travers, "buy Governments, Erie, or anything else you please. When they advance, sell them, and buy as much more as you can, and don't, above all things, go short of a share." Acting on this advice, he bought and is now a rich and flourishing broker.

Occasionally, however, during the rises of 1863 and 1864, Travers would take a turn on the bear side, and often showed great judgment and skill in these operations, running against the general upward tide.

Before the panic of 1873 he went short of the market on a large scale, and bought in his shorts at very low prices, making an immense profit. His operations since that panic have been large, judicious, and very successful. He often operates now jointly with Addison G. Cammack, another famous speculator, whom we shall hereafter speak of.

The "bears" of the street had been dreadful sufferers in the rises of 1862, 1863, and 1864. Travers had, as we have said, confined his operations during these years to the "long" side, working with Leonard W. Jerome to make his profits by buying stocks. He saw that the time to sell stocks had not yet come, and that the strength of the street in money, numbers, talent and enthusiasm was in great majority on the side of the bulls.

No one who has operated in Wall Street, will have failed to remark how wonderfully the spirits and force of the market are stimulated by the rise of one or two leading stocks, when the rest of the market is halting and uncertain in its movements. So it was in the early part of 1863, when Pacific Mail jumped sixty per cent. upwards; the courage of the bulls was fortified by this to an amazing extent. The bears, however, in April, stood sulky and obstinate, rather strengthened in their resolution, by what to them, savored of insanity. This was only the beginning. They were soon to "blench and grow pale" at the very name of Harlem, and a new general rise was already being engineered, before which all former rises in Wall Street should sink into insignificance.

Outside of the two rival boards of brokers, stood Commodore Vanderbilt, Henry Keep, Leonard W. Jerome, etc., and backed up by a long file of capitalists who followed their lead, and believed in their policy. The Public Board led on by A. G. Jerome and John M. Tobin, focalized into one burning center the scattered rays of speculation from every quarter, while in the more conservative regular board, there were enterprising and sagacious firms who were considered the exponents of the bull feeling, as strongly as the house of D. Groesbeck & Co., were of the bear feeling, in the market.

Among these was the firm of Lockwood & Co., which, from its wealth, its long and high standing, and its business affiliations, stood from 1863 till 1869, not only as the rival of D. Groesbeck & Co., in competing for the business of the street, but as being almost as pronounced in its bull proclivity as the latter was in its bearish policy. Its business, of course, was large and various on both sides, but more on the bull side.

Le Grand Lockwood, the head and founder of the house, was in personal appearance the antipodes of D. Groesbeck. A short, rather stout gentleman, with a face unworn and almost youthful, after twenty-five or thirty years of that wearing, tearing, terrible Wall Street life. He was a native of Connecticut and brought into his business all the thrift and keenness of that most thrifty and shrewd of States. His financial views were generally large and sound. The commission business done by his firm during the war, was something unprecedented in the annals of the street.

But it was reserved for another man to earn the title of the bull-leader in the regular board, during 1863 and part of 1864.

His operations constitute a distinct and memorable chapter in the stock speculation of those two years.

CHAPTER XIII.

ANTHONY W. MORSE AND THE CHANCELLORSVILLE RISE.

The First Game of "Brag" in the Village of Hanover—"The Boy 's the Father of the Man"—First Appearance of Morse—Wall Street Men's Wives—Getting Ready for a Twist—The Ursine Vocabulary—A Vindictive Bear Going Short of Pittsburg—Waiting for News from the Front—Chasing a Telegram—The Hook-nosed Man Nursing the Market—Sounding the Charge Along the Whole Line—The Second Game of "Brag"—Raking in the Profits—$113,500 in My Right Boot-leg, and No Money to Pay for My Dinner.

ONE summer's day, about thirty-five years since, in the pleasant village of Hanover, in the old Granite State, celebrated for its seat of learning—Dartmouth College—and for its placid scenery of mountain, vale and river, four boys in their teens, were squatted on the green sward behind a tree in the outskirts, playing a game of cards. It was the game of "brag," so called, which some graceless collegian from the West had taught them in an hour of idleness. The young scape-graces had each contributed a copper penny, and thus made up a "pool," the stake they were playing for. One of these boys had a face somewhat besmirched by recent fistic combats, but his eyes and nose were like those of a hawk. He far surpassed his companions in that boldness and address requisite to a successful playing of the game. He won the stake every time. "The boy's the father of the man." Fifteen years later, that boy, then a man, made his appearance in Wall Street, where the game of "brag" is played all the time on a great scale and around a crowded table. His name was Anthony W. Morse. He came into the market as an adventurer, like so many of his fellows. He had little money or credit, but (which was as good as either), he was a member of the board of brokers in 1862, when the inflation began to take place. The name of the firm which he represented, was Morse & Co. Who were the separate members of this firm? What were their names? It appeared, on investigation, that the only person composing the firm, bore the Christian name of a woman instead of a man. It was the wife of A. W. Morse, who was buying and selling stocks; her husband was her agent and broker. This drew forth severe criticism from his associates. The making of a financial convenience of a wife is an old device of the stock-market. The Wall Street man's wife is often a lady of substance. She carries bags of gold coin under her crinoline; certified checks are quilted into her skirts. She hides notes of hand and stock certificates in her bosom, and sails down Fifth Avenue with gems worthy of a duchess, entangled in her hair, while her husband, panic-smitten and moneyless, limps up and down Wall Street.

Who would have picked out from among the brawny shoulder-hitters of the market, that slight, boyish figure, as the bull-leader of the regular board? This man, the casual observer would say, is an English Jew, who has gone into the business of a note broker. He always reminded us of a man who was playing a part, and rather a farcical part at that, as he came jauntily out into the crowd to take a survey of the market. But he had not forgotten the game of brag which he had played when a boy, and he was making ready to play it with a vengeance.

A few bold operations on the bull side had put two hundred and fifty thousand dollars into his pocket, and in the spring of 1863 he cast about him for something to make a good stroke in, after the Wall Street cornering fashion. Nothing offered better than Pittsburg. It was a small stock, only $4,000,000, and could be readily handled; its earnings were such as to justify the expectation of a speedy dividend, and less than half of the stock was floating about the street. The market price ranged from 65 to 70. He commenced to buy it. The act to increase the legal tenders, by a new issue of four hundred millions, passed. He bought more. Money grew easier, first 6, then 5, then 4 per cent. He borrowed money on the stock he had already bought, and with this money bought more largely. Stocks moved languidly upwards.

Suddenly the money rate tightened to 7 per cent. and stocks dropped to their old place. General Hooker had been lying for months, with the "finest army on the planet," watching the heights of Fredericksburg, the slaughter-ground of the December preceding. A dark rumor, hardly yet breathed, but believed in, told every one that another great military movement would soon be made. Capital grew timorous, and called in its forces. Money was scarce, but only for a brief season.

The greenbacks, which poured by the hundred million into the sub-treasury, were poured out again, to pay the government creditors. Money flowed into the stock-market, in a full steady stream. The interest rate fell once more. Stocks moved upwards in earnest.

Wall Street had already decided in its mind, that the spring campaign on the Rappahannock, would be disastrous. The sequence to this would be a great rise in values.

Stocks were moving up, one by one, after their ancient custom, but slowly as yet when I met J. F—— It was about the middle of April, on the brink of the coal-hole, while the market was lagging, and the doubtful condition of things looked just then doubly uncertain. J. F—— was the most plantigrade of bears. The panic of 1857, had changed him from an operator for a rise, into an operator for a fall. For six years he had kept his eyes fixed on the rises and falls of stocks, and now they haunted him. He presented a singular psychological phenomenon—a distinct phase of the mania for speculation. He had got to look upon the market as a live thing—a fantastic monster. He spoke of it as of the feminine gender. "She rises." "She falls." He seemed to think of it as a debtér which owed him money. It was a question of revenge, however, with him, more than money. He hungered for revenge for his losses. His operations were undertaken in a spirit of vindictiveness against every stock in which he had lost. When he made a lucky hit, he would flourish certified checks, and boast like an Indian brave over the scalps which he had taken from an enemy.

For nearly a year he had hardly kept himself from ruin, but when gold lurched and went down in March, he went down with it and came again to the surface with $30,000 in his hand, which he waved aloft in triumph, and now stood ready for another plunge into the vortex of a stock-panic.

"How's the market, F——?"

"Barely, steady!"

Somehow, the market is never more than "barely steady" to the constitutional bear. When it is dull, he quotes it "soft," which, in his vocabulary, means declining, or in a condition suitable to be depressed. When it is rampant, then it is "just on the verge of a severe break," and when its tendency is upwards, it is only "barely steady."

"How is money, to-day?"

"Easy enough, but what's money got to do with it?" "I've known many a panic on an easy money market." This is a favorite saying among the bears.

"Yes, and I've known stocks go up on a tight money market," said an old gentlemen who just that minute joined us, and was evidently operating on the bull side.

"This market must go down," said F——.

"Why?"

"Because stocks are selling too high."

"D'ye think so, for money?" inquired the old gentleman.

"I'll bet a hundred that Cleveland and Pittsburg sells at 50 before it sells for par," replied F——.

"Put up your money, then."

This having been done, F—— proceeded to hold forth at length on the subject of the inflated condition of the market.

"Has Daniel Drew made any money lately, selling short?" asked the old gentleman, banteringly.

"Never mind Daniel Drew," retorted F——, "he'll eat you all up yet."

"Now you've been talking about this Pittsburg stock, I'll take a thousand shares at 75, buyer thirty," quietly remarked the old gentleman.

F——'s face writhed and curled like a dog about to nip the leg of a beggar. "I'll sell it to you," snarled he.

"Sell me a thousand shares, buyer thirty, F——?" inquired I.

He wheeled around, and shaking his fist in my face as if he had some special grudge against me, which he wished to indulge by selling me a thousand Pittsburg, thundered "yes!"

"Thirty per cent. up, in the Trust Company?"

"Thirty per cent. up in the Trust Company, by both parties," he screamed, "and right away, too."

The buyer and the seller have the right to demand from each other a sum ranging from ten per cent. upwards, to secure the bargain. This sum or margin is generally deposited in the hands of some corporation or responsible firm, who thus become the stakeholders and pay over the money to the party who wins.

Two thousand shares of Pittsburg at 75, is $75,000, for this stock is like Harlem, only $50 per share at par.

We went together to the Trust Company. J. F—— put up in the Trust Company, $30,000. The old gentleman put up $15,000, and I put up $15,000, all in certified checks. Then we parted. The old gentleman took an omnibus up town, with a serene smile playing on his venerable features at the thought of his Pittsburg. J. F—— passed down William Street with the air of a man who had inflicted, or was about to inflict, a terrible revenge on his old enemy Pittsburg, and joined a group of sad but determined looking men, who belonged to the bear brigade and used to stand in front of the office of D. Groesbeck & Co.

During the two weeks then next ensuing, it was amusing to watch the goings, comings and general looks of the bear brigade. Every pleasant morning they could be seen roosting on the iron railings in William Street, and sunning themselves, or standing like lay figures around the inside entrance to the regular board. First they were loud-mouthed in their predictions that the market was just on the eve of panic. Then, as the prices rose, they grew stiller, and finally subsided into a sulky silence.

May was now come. Hooker and the grand army were across the Rappahannock. Stocks were up ten per cent., but were just then halting, as if waiting for something. What was it? News from the front.

Passing down Wall Street, about noon, one day, I saw a well-known operator named L——, rush out of the telegraph office, holding a paper ribbon which he gathered up into a wad as he ran. I plucked him by the sleeve as he flew past me, and asked what's the row? He mumbled something, broke away from me, jumped down into a broker's office in the basement corner of William Street, reappeared in an instant, and darted off the street into the tunnel which led to the regular board.

What news could he have?

I followed him closely and came up with him as he was giving an order to his broker, whom he had called out from the board which was then in session.

"What's up, L——?"

He drummed against the wall with his boot-heel and looked knowing, but kept his mouth shut.

His broker shortly made his appearance and handed L—— a memorandum, telling him that he had bought for his account, one thousand Erie and five hundred Hudson.

L—— now informed me that he had news from the front. Hooker was this side the Rappahannock. The campaign was over. Stocks must go up. "If you buy anything," added he, "let it be Erie and Hudson."

"How about Pittsburg?"

"Good! You can't help making money, only buy, buy! buy! go it blind. Pitch in your greenbacks and pick up gold."

I bought straightway three hundred Erie and five hundred Hudson.

The news from the front was already known to others, and they were acting on it. The market hummed like a bee-hive. Erie rumbled along up the declivity. Hudson flew up. Harlem tumbled up. Pittsburg skipped up gaily. My profits were rolling up at the rate of $1,000 an hour. But my losses on Harlem, of which I was short, as already told, swallowed up my profits. I kept buying Erie, Pittsburg, Hudson.

The neglected stocks which had lain lifeless at the foot of the list, now began to show life and dance

HALL OF THE OLD BROKERS' BOARD.

about like Fantocinni in a showman's box. Terre Haute "was a good thing to buy, cheap as dirt!" so said my broker. I bought four hundred shares, and before night it danced up ten points.

Meanwhile, one hooked-nosed man was observed to be very busy. In his office, he was packing away certificates of Pittsburg stock in a little black box, or inclosing them in portly brown envelopes. He was closeted with attenuated cashiers in bank parlors looking after his loans. He was nursing the general market, hovering over it broodingly, inquiring with solicitude after its welfare. But Pittsburg was his pet, and he had gathered it under his wing. When it was weak, he stimulated it. When it was halting and hesitating he coaxed it and drove it alternately.

Many of those who had bought stocks at a lower figure, now sold out, and realized their profits. The market yielded gracefully to this pressure; paused for a day ready to absorb anything in the way of a short sale or any small favors from those who thought of taking their profits. Then its ranks were re-formed; the hook-nosed man waved his baton, and sounded the charge. The whole line moved up in a twinkling to the top of the declivity. Erie from 70, had touched 110. Hudson from 105, had touched 142; and Pittsburg from 68, had touched 108.

It is one thing to "get stocks up," as they say, but quite another to sell them at the high price.

"Now, who is going to buy your high-priced stocks?" shouted the bear brigade.

This inquiry seemed very pertinent. Upon that hint I acted, giving orders to sell everything I held at the market price, and notifying J. F—— that I was about to sell the Pittsburg (I had bought of him at 75), and thus transfer $12,000 of his money into my pocket.

But how did the hooked-nosed man, alias A. W. Morse, succeed in working off his Pittsburg? He played the old game of brag. Everything assisted him in this. Money easy as an old shoe, the bears tremblingly eager to cover, the men who had sold out at a lower figure now crazy to buy back their stocks at a higher figure, the whole market looking as if it never would break again.

The prices which had been galloping up for ten days now closed the heat with a rush. When Pittsburg was struck on the morning call, Morse jumped into the center of the crowd and yelled at the top of his voice, "I'll give 105 for the whole capital stock (about $4,000,000), or any part. I'll give 100, seller one year, for the whole capital stock or any part." He bluffed the whole board. No one took him up on his liberal offers. But while he was holding up the market price by making these magnanimous propositions, his agents were busily at work selling Pittsburg quietly on every side. The bears bought it to cover their contracts, the bulls bought it for a new profit; in twenty-four hours the bulk of what he held had been worked off at from 97 to 105. He had raked in as his winnings about half a million.

The movement having culminated, and the heavy holders having sold out, the market, as usual, took a turn now in the other direction. There are always pretexts offered, for any course which stocks may take. They had just *risen,* because Hooker's campaign had been a failure, just as they had *fallen* when the McClellan campaign, the year before, had been a failure. Now they fell again, on the news that Grant had achieved some successes on the Mississippi. Such are the sapient reasonings of Wall Street. The bankers called in their loans, money became scarce, the weak holders were weeded out, and everybody was figuring up the column of profit and loss.

This was our pecuniary situation, in round numbers, on the 15th of June, 1863, after deducting all losses on Pacific Mail, Harlem, etc.

Profits on Hudson, including the 100 shares bought at 78,	$38,000
Terre Haute,	3,500
Pittsburg, bought at 75, of J. F.,	12,000
Erie,	11,000
Sundries, including Harlem, bought at 12,	49,000
	$113,500

This sum came into my hands in the form of checks, all elegantly lithographed, signed by different brokers with whom I had kept accounts, and duly certified as good by the banks on which they were drawn. These pleasing evidences of property were forthwith rolled into a wad, and consigned to an inner pocket.

I stood in a delicious reverie on the steps of the Bank of America.

"Have a hack?" said an insinuating voice at my elbow.

"I *will* have a hack."

The hackman held open the door of a dilapidated looking vehicle. I stepped in and lay back on the cushions.

"Where to?" said the Jehu, touching his hat in military style.

"Drive me —— up town."

Taking the checks out of my pocket, I contemplated them first sideways, then front, then upside down. Was it a dream? $113,500! there it was, in real green and black letters and figures! It ought to have been $200,000, and would have been but for those confounded losses on Harlem and Pacific Mail. Still, here was wealth, and what was better, freedom; freedom from the life of a speculator—freedom to do what I pleased, and to go where I pleased. Ah! there is ——.

These contemplations were rudely broken in upon by my Jehu, who had stopped in front of Delmonico, corner of Fourteenth Street and Fifth Avenue.

"Beg pardon; but I thought as you'd been making some money off 'em, you'd like to stop here, sir." How did he know I'd been "making some money off 'em?" He must have seen me handling my checks. Hide your money, said caution. I took it out and tucked it in my right boot-leg. It began to worry me, already. Not that I had the sum of $113,500 on my person, because it was in unendorsed checks, which if lost or stolen, would do nobody any good but myself. No, it was the mere fact that I possessed so much money, that began now to oppress me like a burden which a man has suddenly shouldered.

I entered the saloon, and sat down at a table. The walls seemed to be all written over with figures, 113,500! 113,500! on every side. I thought I saw a label before me with 113,500 written on it. It was the paper placed before me by the waiter on which to write my dinner order. I muttered "113,500." I looked up; the waiter was smiling as hard as is consistent with the gravity of a servitor.

I recollected myself and put my hand in my pocket to present him with fifty cents, as a *pour boire,* when it flashed across me that I hadn't a cent of money—nothing but certified checks! No money to pay my hack-hire or buy my dinner, or even to fee the waiter. Nothing but $113,500 in certified checks. I had to get the hack-man to trust me, and "ran my face" for a dinner that day; but this is not very difficult in New York at any time, especially when a man is backed by that peculiar moral force produced by the proud consciousness that he has carefully tucked away the sum of $113,500 in certified checks in his right boot-leg.

CHAPTER XIV.

"WHAT WILL HE DO WITH IT?"

The Life of an Operator; Excitement and Repose—In Pursuit of Happiness Furiously—The Terrestrial Paradise of a Money Winner—The Delights of the Eye and the Pride of Life—Two Comrades in Luck—"Is this Happiness?"—Birds of Passage on the Wing to Long Branch—Wall Street at the Watering Places—Dowagers, Damsels and Dunderheads—Saratoga the "Sweet Boon" to the Broker—The Congress and Court of Vanderbilt, and the Other Money Kings—They Spell S–t–o–c–k–s, and then They Buy Them—A Good Resolution in Danger of Being Broken—Operating by Telegraph—"Once More Upon the Waters, yet Once More and the *Stocks* Bound Beneath us like a Steed that Knows its Rider"—Grasp the Substance ere the Shadow Fade.

THE life of the Wall Street man is like that of savage races—a life of fierce extremes. One day he is in the hottest and busiest of all market-places—the stock-market-place—agitated by all the hopes and fears, and torn by all the emotions and passions, engendered by the thirst for speedy riches; the next day the struggle is over, and he is plunged, at once, into the opposite extreme of stillness and repose. This stillness and repose is bred sometimes of utter and irretrievable ruin, it is then the calmness of despair; sometimes it is derived from that serene sense of satisfaction, which the successful speculator feels when he has made a hit. This feeling is a negative one. He has *not* lost his money, he has *not* failed in his pursuit of money. The fact that he has great riches won against so much odds, gives him little pleasure. He undervalues it. It seems of little account, until he thinks what it will procure. It will buy such pleasures as money can buy—*material pleasures*.

The Wall Street operator is a materialist logically, and in the strictest consistence with his earnest pursuits. After his toils and anxieties he craves enjoyments. He would repay with prodigality these toils and anxieties to which he has been subjected in the pursuit of his gains. The captors of a fortress which has been obstinately defended, sometimes put the garrison to the sword. The hunter joyfully spears the wild animal which has led him a long chase. The successful Wall Street man takes *his* revenge on the money which has cost him dearly—he spends it on himself and his friends—he pours it out as though it were common and cheap as the water he drinks or the air he breathes.

He proposes to himself a terrestrial paradise, not like that of the Mahometan, however, who proscribes wine. He would "suck the subtle blood of the grape till the high fever seethe his blood to froth." Retinues of lackeys, studs of horses, banquetings, garlands, singing men and singing women, spectacles in the theatre shall be his, amid which, he shall walk as a literal cloud-compeller, while the partaga or the miraculously carved roseate foam-tinted meerschaum distills its fragrance under the quiet pressure of his lips.

The paths in this paradise are all circuitous; one eternal round of enjoyments which become at last tasteless. Then comes restlessness, a craving for change of scene. He becomes first a perambulator, then a pedestrian, then a tourist—the nomad of the watering places.

E—— was a "red check man," in other words he had made $100,000 in stocks.

Two men of about the same age, temperament and tastes may see each other every day for twenty-five years, and yet they may never come together; though their paths be ever so near, they are in parallel lines, which never meet. Now magnetize them by giving them a hundred thousand dollars apiece, and they fly together like the iron and the lodestone. This means conviviality, fraternity, sympathy.

E—— and I were Damon and Pythias, over again, like Juno's swans, we went always "coupled and inseparable." We had made our money in the same stocks and now we spent it in company—a partnership in the business of pleasure-seeking. We dined together, rode together, slept together. When we quarreled with each other we had never "let the sun in Capricorn go down on our anger."

We were both engaged in pondering the same important question: what shall we do with *it?* the $100,000. The answer to the question was partly contained in what we had just been doing, viz., dining at Delmonico's—innocent, but expensive amusement. We were spending it as fast as horses, banquets, and the etceteras would permit.

One thing, however, had been resolved upon, we would never, no, never, any more speculate in Wall Street, at least by buying and selling upon a margin, *except*, (ah! that unfortunate word) except in Government Bonds, of which we severally held $175,000 worth bought on a margin of $8,000, and paid for by loans obtained from Savings Banks.

Two men in their golden prime, both worthy to receive a first-class diploma from a Life Insurance Company, with $100,000 at their bankers, sitting before an open window, on the "avenue" in the twilight of a glorious July evening, after a sumptuous dinner, would, in the popular use of the term, be called *happy*. We tried to believe ourselves so. But there was something wanting. Somehow, that day, the soup *a la reine* was a trifle worse flavored than it was a month before. The filet of sole was not done to the proper turn, the game-bird was a "little too high." The Roederer champagne was flat, and suggested sugar of lead, to the already squeamish palate.

Restlessness again! Where can we go? not to ride, for our horses have the ring-bone, or quarter-crack, or some one of the other ills that horse-flesh is heir to. Ah! a happy thought—a watering-place.

"Garçon."

The waiter stood by us, looking fractional currency out of his eyes. "Bring us a Herald." "Oui, oui!" The newspaper was handed to us, and carefully conned, in search of new places of summer resort. We found nothing new that was tempting, so we made a trip to Long Branch; two days was enough for us there. Sachem's Head, then; after this, the Pequot House, from which we hurried to Newport.

One of these watering-places was a type of all the others. Of course, the beauty and fashion was there! it always is. There were the Smitthes, and the Taylourres, the De Bylkes, the Van Ohnehosens.

and other lights of the gay world. Scandal and flirtation hunted in couples. Argus-eyed dowagers watched Hesperidean damsels, and at the same time tore reputations to tatters. Damsels made dangerous play of eyes, fans and handkerchiefs. Fat babies stared very hard at the ocean. Stout, single old gentlemen sported like dolphins in the surf, or rolled ten-pins, and imagined they were young again. Of course, everybody was bound to consider himself happy, or act as if he did.

But Wall Street cropped out everywhere. The husbands of the matrons, the fathers of the damsels, the brothers of the dowagers and the single old gentlemen, all appeared to have made money in stocks, or if they had lost it no one heard anything about it there. The operators and brokers were on hand in force. It was stocks on the piazzas, stocks in the parlor, stocks at breakfast, dinner, tea. The bevy of dames in the drawing-rooms would listen with breathless interest to tales of hair-breadth escapes in the Harlem fight, or fortunes won "in the imminent deadly breach" in Pacific Mail or Hudson, all which tales were broken in upon after the usual style by such hen-words as "Oh, that's so nice," "perfectly splendid," "heavenly," etc., "to make a hundred thousand in a month, just think of it!" "Well I never," "no, I *never* did see," etc., etc., etc.

After this we went to Saratoga. If there is any one place for which the Wall Street man has a predilection in his days of relaxation, that place is Saratoga. King Cornelius held his court there. The other monarchs of the stock-market make royal progresses thither. Their lieutenants go there. The rank and file go there. The gay Spa, to borrow a phrase from Artemus, is a "sweet boon" to the whole tribe of stock-jobbers and operators, as a head-clearer, blood-cooler and general renovator of a biliary system too often disordered by deep potations of the Versenary brand—"the foaming grape of eastern France," or of that tutelar alcoholic genius of bibulous Columbia—corn juice.

Of course, E—— and I made the rounds at Saratoga after the usual fashion, drinking 'High Rock' in the morning, driving to the lake and eating the celebrated potatoes prepared there with the deftest manipulation of culinary fingers. Then we 'plied the cranks of the hand-cars on the circular railway, always selecting the stoutest young ladies for our companions with a sharp eye to the development of biceps, pectoral and deltoid muscles. The stout young ladies sat up very straight in the hand-cars, and smiled very sweetly upon E—— and me, while we toiled at the winch, and made the vehicle spin round the iron groove. We also didn't forget the bowling-alley, or the pistol gallery, or the Indian encampment. We made ten-strikes, and blazed away at the bull's-eye, and after we had made the rounds we came back and smoked very large and full-flavored regalias.

At other watering places, they *talked* stocks; at Saratoga they *bought* and *sold* them. Little knots of dealers stood in the piazzas of the United States Hotel, the Union and the Congress, and traded in Erie and Harlem. The great pulsations of the heart-financial, one hundred and eighty miles away, throbbed here through the telegraphic wires.

Another great rise in stocks began to be predicted.

Speculation is a contagious disease. In Saratoga it is generally more or less an epidemic.

E—— and I found ourselves discussing the point whether we might not reconsider our resolution and make just one more operation on a margin. Everything looked bright. It could do us no harm to buy a thousand shares or so of some good dividend paying stock.

Even deliberation is dangerous upon such points. The woman who hesitates is lost. The retired Wall Street man, who asks himself whether he may not buy stocks on a margin, just once more, is as good as committed again to his old vice—speculation.

One evening, early in August, just as the male animals were about to prance in the parlors of Union, at the bidding of the queens of society, E—— and I retired to a seat in the rear-grounds, for a quiet smoke, when looking towards the back piazza, we saw emerge from one of the parlor doors, somebody we had seen before. It was a tall man, all shaven and shorn, in a spotless evening costume, brisk and debonair, who seemed as if he were looking for some "party," he didn't know exactly whom.

We recognized him quickly, as L—— the operator, who had given me telegraphic news of the retreat of Hooker, the week before the Chancellorsville rise, and who had just arrived by the evening train.

L—— belonged to the unnoted branch of the Q—— family, which had established a kind of title by adverse possession to certain government offices, which they had held from Washington's administration, down to Lincoln's. At present, he had a brother in the treasury department, an uncle in the war office, a cousin was a brigadier-general, and his brother's wife's father was mixed up with telegraph companies. Hence, it was that L—— had organized a system of early telegraphic information, and had thereby, got admitted into some of the "rings" in the street. In this way he had made $300,000, and having sweltered in the stock-market all summer, now that he was in Saratoga, he was naturally in fine spirits.

He saw us, moulded his hands into the telescopic shape and took a squint at us. Then advanced towards us, pointing with his dexter forefinger as if to some planet then faintly twinkling in the zenith, put his left hand to one side of his mouth and whispered something as though he expected it to be conveyed to us by some unseen medium; all of which pantomime we interpreted to mean that he had sold his stocks at a high figure.

First, salutations, then "how are stocks, L——?" Stocks were firm with an upward tendency. He had sold everything he had, except Erie. That he was going to hold for 125. The pool in Hudson had carried the price to 180. He did not think they would be able to unload. He had sold his Hudson at 175, etc., etc. Did he know of anything good to buy? Yes. Erie was good. Daniel Drew had been going short of it, but he would lose money by it. There's another stock that's going up, sure. Old Southern; A. G. Jerome had taken hold of it, it was good for 120. Lots of shorts. Had left word with his broker to buy a thousand shares any where under 94. Thus L—— talked. He further added that he was going to stay at the Springs the rest of the month, and thought he could make more money by *keeping away from the market and operating by telegraph.*

That night E—— and I each telegraphed to our brokers thus: "Buy 500 Old Southern and 500 Erie at the market price. Have mailed $10,000, margin."

The following afternoon came the answer. "Have bought 500 Old Southern, 92; 500 Erie, 103." We had broken our resolution to buy no more stocks. We had once more embarked on the stormy sea, out of our haven of rest.

After this, our walks lay between Union Hall and the telegraph office, where we received the stock quotations two or three times daily, from our respective brokers in Wall Street. The telegraph commenced to prick off as the price of old Southern, 92; next day 88; then 96. Again the message was sent down: "Buy 1000 Old Southern, market price." Before that lot was bought, the price had risen to 104. Then whish! it went to 111. Old Southern was doing well. Erie rose more gradually. Heavy bodies move slowly. When Old Southern darted to 111, a rise of 19 per cent., Erie stood at 110. "Buy 1,000 more Erie," said greed. "Don't," whispered caution. Greed was stronger than caution. I telegraphed "Buy 1,000 Erie, market price." That lot cost 114. The regret that I had not bought sooner and before the price was lower, began to work in the mind. Its fruit was anger, rashness. I bought 1,000 more Erie at 115½. Then I sat down and figured up first what my profits would be on the supposition that I sold at the ruling prices, viz., Erie, 120, and Old

Southern at 108½; for Erie had risen, and Old Southern had fallen meanwhile.

Thirty-one thousand, six hundred and twenty-five dollars! Now, I had put my selling price at 125 for Erie, and 120 for Old Southern. If the 2,500 Erie, and the 1,500 Old Southern were disposed of at those prices, the profits would foot up fifty-nine thousand eight hundred and seventy-two dollars! I decided to hold for the higher price. Greed of gain like the horse-leeches daughters, which cry give, give! Was I grasping at the *shadow*, while I let the substance fade? Was I to furnish another example to point the moral of the fable of the dog, who dropped the bone to catch at the image reflected in the water? Time will show. Of this one thing be assured, reader, the Wall Street man lives in the midst of shadows.

Phantasies of what might be, memories of what has been, regrets for what might have been. His mind feeds upon these figments of the brain. They become to him the same as a living active reality, which soothes and pains alternately.

> "For like the bat of Indian brakes,
> Its pinions fan the wound it makes,
> And soothing thus the victim's pains,
> It drinks the life-blood from his veins."

CHAPTER XV.

WHAT BECAME OF IT. HENRY KEEP AND OLD SOUTHERN.

Our Financial Oracle gives us General Views on Stocks—News of Panic in the Woods—The Nightmare Ride in Sleeping-Cars—I Learn my Fate—The History of the Mystery—The P—— Pool in Erie—Cornering Uncle Daniel with $300,000—A. G. Jerome Playing with Old Southern, and Working the Bears—The Final Grip—A Gray-eyed Man Reading a Telegram at Saratoga, "Come on to New York Without Delay, the Fruit is Ripe"—Henry Keep, His Antecedents, Character and Operations—A Pauper's Son Dies Worth $4,000,000—The Plot—Money Tightens, and the Trap is Sprung—Jerome Laid Out Cold—A Meditated Scolding Terminates in a Dinner at Delmonico's—What Came of the Dinner—A Flyer in Harlem—The Last Resort—Almost Cleaned Out—An Operation in Seven-thirties—I Play my Last Card; Is it a Trump?

L—— was the oracle of our particular coterie at Saratoga. All knotty questions, having reference to finance and the mysteries of stocks, were referred to him, and his answers were received without demurrer. Any one who had snatched $300,000 out of the ravenous jaws of Hudson and Harlem, deserved to be called an oracle. Moreover, this oracle was somewhat given to voluntary expositions of the all-absorbing topic.

L—— had "views" of stocks and speculation in general. "Nothing can be easier than to make money in Wall Street," said he.

This, spoken in the tone of one having authority, caught our attentive ear.

"First, buy your stocks *low*. *Low* is of course a relative term, but any man who can tell B from a bull's foot can decide when stocks are *low*."

"Aye, aye," say we.

"Second, put up a large margin; by the term large I mean at least twenty per cent."

"Very well, what next?"

"Third, get out of the "street," leave the city, go away from hotels, railroads, telegraphs, out of the ken of brokers, into the woods, where the word *stocks* is never sounded."

"But why go away after you have bought stocks?"

"Because a man is befooled, bewitched and bedeviled by what he hears in the market. He is sure to sell out just when he ought to hold on, or do some other foolish thing."

"Now," continued he, "I'm off to the woods for a couple of weeks or so, and if you'll go along you'll make more money than you will here, listening to that buzzing telegraph."

That afternoon we bought rifles, fishing tackle, etc., etc., and in sixty hours were lying under a big hemlock, forty miles from a railroad or telegraph, smoking and laying out for a murderous campaign against the trout.

Two weeks sped away before we saw a daily paper —the New York Tribune. We laid it out on the grass and three heads bumped against each other, while three pair of eyes riveted on the financial column, saw the following announcement, viz.:

"Thursday, September 4th. *The panic which commenced in stocks yesterday, has been of greater magnitude and of a more excited character to-day!*" etc.

"Old Southern, 88!"

"Erie, 104½!"

"I'm out $80,000," said L——.

"I'm out $40,000," said E——.

"And I $40,000,"——

That ride, forty miles in a country wagon over a rough road, was a little the slowest and longest ever taken by Wall Street men. When we struck the railroad we made a general rush for the telegraph office. L—— wrote three separate telegrams to our three several brokers, "Don't sell our stocks. Have sent more margin." Then three separate checks were drawn and mailed. L——'s check was for sixty thousand dollars; E——'s and mine for thirty thousand, each. We reached Troy in time to take the ten o'clock night train.

"Sleeping cars!" "Ha! ha!" said E——, "a queer idea that. They are called sleeping cars, I suppose, because people never sleep in them." We certainly never slept a wink of genuine sleep that night. True, now and then, we sunk into a kind of doze, crowded with dreams—nightmares, in which we seemed to be falling from vast heights, amid screamings and the roaring of many waters. Men with lanterns came and shook us, when the train stopped, and said we were making too much noise, moaning and muttering, and disturbing the other passengers.

When the train started, we commenced falling again down the heights, amid the same unearthly noises, and the roar of the wheels sufficed again to drown our gurgling cries. Three pallid, hollow-eyed men, we rose betimes, as the cars thundered past Manhattanville, and watched for the first newspaper boy. It was in the gray of the dawn, that we read the gratifying announcement, that "there was an active speculative demand for stocks, etc."

Old Southern closed at 95.

Erie stood at 107.

We were saved! When we reached the station, we got into a hack, and drove down town. Breakfast at lower Delmonico's. While discussing our *dejeuner a la fourchette*, of which we stood greatly in need, after our nightmare journey, a dapper little man, with eyes that resembled black glass beads, fixed firmly in his head, entered the lower room where we were sitting, and proceeded to imbibe something which had a greenish hue, suspiciously reminding us of that demoniac drink absinthe, with which it seems he was in the habit of refreshing himself before his daily toil. This dapper little man did the outside buying and selling for my broker. He saluted us with a sedate smile, judiciously tinged with suggestions of panic, and a deprecating look withal, which augured ill as it appeared to my apprehensive sense.

"Did you get my telegram, and the margin I sent you?"

"Oh, yes. But too late."

"Too late! What do you mean?"

"Why, too late to apply on your stocks. We had to sell them."

"You had to sell them?"

"Yes. You see the market was panicky. There was only one per cent. of your margin left. You were away; we had to look out for ourselves. If you'll go to our office you can find out all about it. I'm in a hurry, the market is brisk to-day. Bye, bye."

On going to my broker's office, the account of my stock transactions for the past month was duly rendered.

The Erie had been sold at 100.

The Old Southern, at 82.

I had lost $60,000, my original margin, and found myself indebted to my broker in the sum of $1,000 and more! This is the custom of Wall Street. When an operator's margin runs low he is promptly sold out, if on notice he fails to furnish more margin.

At the time these sales were made, I had $40,000 in the bank to my credit. The thirty thousand dollar check, fresh margin, which I had forwarded after coming out of the woods, reached my broker three or four days after the stock had been sold. Of course I could not complain, it was my misfortune.

How happened it that it should come up to blow so quickly out of a sky, which looked as though it promised every one a long season of bright sunshine?

Hardly any two stocks could have been selected, which would have inflicted more serious damage upon a buyer than Erie and Old Southern. Erie and Old Southern had both been in the hands of cliques. The movement in the former stock commenced late in July. The leader in this movement was P——, a young operator who had, or controlled about $300,000. He is said to have been a Californian, and now came down like a lusty bullock from the Sierra, prepared to attack the king of all the Bears in his fortress. He and his coadjutors proposed to themselves the Herculean feat of cornering Daniel Drew! Corner Uncle Daniel with $300,000! "Canst thou draw out leviathan with a hook? Canst thou put a hook into his nose, or bore his jaw through with a thorn?" Quixotic as the enterprise appeared, it is said to have been very nearly successful.

Drew commenced selling Erie for future delivery, when it was in the neighborhood of 100. The stock amounted then to about $11,000,000. At least half this amount was on the street. The rest was held abroad, or in the hands of permanent investors at home, outside of Wall Street. As the price rose, Drew kept selling, and the clique kept buying. Everything seemed to assist them. Erie was earning dividends. The money market was easy at five per cent. Large blocks of the stock were taken by various outside bull operators, who vowed to hold it for 150. The borrowing demand created by the heavy short sales of Drew and his brother bears, helped to keep the price firm at 120. The stock rose to 123, and now the bulls were rampant. Bets were offered that Drew would have to settle within a week. Such was the situation of Erie during the latter part of August, 1863. The party which had the control of Old Southern then, was a much stronger one.

A. G. Jerome, the Napoleon of the Public Board in 1863, was then in the height of his power. A long series of dashing operations on the bull side had brought him a million or two in money on his own account, but what was more, had raised his prestige to such a point that he could command an almost unlimited credit, while a crowd of depositors brought money to his banking-house, bidding him use as he thought best. A dangerous point for a financier to reach, especially if he accepts the trusts thus forced upon him. His position in August seemed impregnable. The stocks in which he was most deeply interested showed him an enormous profit. One of these stocks was Harlem, so famed in financial story. Its wonderful vibrations for three months were due largely to him.

But Old Southern was his pet.

He commenced paying it attention early in July. He played with it, fondled it, tossed its bulk up and down, tantalizing the bears and bulls alternately. All the while he was apparently playing in this way, serious business was going on. He was weeding out the weak holders when he dropped the price, and quietly taking every short contract. Then he gripped it fast and pushed it steadily up, dropping it now and then, however, to encourage the short-sellers.

Torrid August came, but brought no rest or vacation for those who held Old Southern. Jerome had promised his customers and the street that he would make Old Southern a second Harlem. His grip tightened. On the 14th Old Southern jumped 16 per cent., from 92 to 108. The next day it rose to 113, *but fell suddenly back to 108*. Some undaunted bear was selling it. It was dropped from 113 to 107, in order to take these sales. The stock came on the market by the ten thousand shares. The greater part of these sales were made in the public board. The market was staggered, but only for a moment. Jerome, armed with a twenty per cent. profit, which the price of the stock then showed him, stepped into the breach, and held up the market price on his Atlantean shoulders. The stock at last was no longer offered, except in hundred share lots. Now he had the bears in his power.

We shall see.

Who was the undaunted bear who sold thirty thousand shares of Old Southern in August, 1863, and so would place his head between the upper and lower jaw of the lion of the Public Board?

Three weeks before the panic, by which we suffered as already described, and while we were still at Saratoga, feasting our imaginations with the prospect of the profits which we were going to finger when Old Southern should touch 120, something occurred, which, could we have guessed its full significance, would have made us fly to New York instead of going to the woods.

A middle-aged, thick-set man, with a round, smooth face, and a deep gray eye, stood on the piazza of Congress Hall, reading a telegram, the very morning we started on our sylvan excursion. We saw him fold it up and consign it to his pocket, just as we entered the 'bus which was to take us to the cars.

That telegram of a dozen words cost us an aggregate loss of $79,000. The middle-aged, thick-set man was Henry Keep. This noted operator and money king, was about to do several things, when he stood on the piazza of Congress Hall that morning. He was about to break the Old Southern corner, and ruin Jerome. He was about to make a million dollars for himself, and in doing this, he was about to take away from L——, E—— and myself, the sum of $79,000, as already stated.

For the past twelve years, Henry Keep had slowly, but surely been advancing his fortunes in the stock-market. Like most other very wealthy and successful Wall Street men, he commenced without a penny, and although he died when hardly past the meridian of life; he was then worth $4,000,000! He used to boast that he graduated in poverty-school, where he finished his academical education, and this was literallv true, for it is said his father was a poor man somewhere in the interior of the State of New York. He learned lessons in that iron school of poverty, which stood him in good stead. An open countenance, but thoughts concealed, a still tongue, but a busy brain and quick hand. He once told a gentleman, after his fortune was counted by the million, that the idea of money haunted him day and night, during all his boyhood. It stood before him as a visible presence, during his maturer years. His first operations were in money. He bought paper money at a discount, made a few thousand dollars by these operations, and then, about twenty years ago, came to the money seat —Wall Street.

Here he soon linked his fortunes with the stock market. Old Southern Railroad Company became his favorite stock. No clause in its charter, no railroad law having relation to it, no by-law of the Company, that he did not know by heart. In 1862, and in the early part of 1863, he had made large sums by buying it. I remember, in the spring of 1863, seeing him stand behind his broker in the street-crowd and pull his coat-tail, as a signal to buy. His broker after buying one thousand shares of Old Southern stopped, when he felt his coat-tail jerked again, violently, and he commenced buying until after seven successive jerks he had bought eight thousand shares, all for the account of the quiet man in the rear, who thereupon relaxed his grasp, and retired to his office without saying a word. He believed in the proverb,

HOW A FORTUNATE OPERATOR SPENDS HIS MONEY.

"Speech is silver; silence is golden." His reticence about everything relating to stocks was one of the strong points in his character as a financier, for certainly if there is one thing needful in stock operations, it is reticence, first, last and always.

This trait became, in his later years, somewhat less marked at least in matters relating to himself. I recollect seeing him show to a prominent broker, whom he met in the office of Lockwood & Co., a certificate for ten thousand shares of North Western stock, then selling for 60, which he held as an investment, and remarking that he should never sell that stock till it brought him one million dollars. A few months after, the price rose to par, and he could then have realized his profit. Whether he did so, I cannot say.

In 1863, Henry Keep was a director of the Michigan Southern and Northern Indiana Railroad Company, commonly nicknamed Old Southern.

The telegram before mentioned, was from another high official of the company, informing him that the stock was selling for 107, and requesting him to come to New York without delay!

Why was this message sent to him?

The next morning, he was seen in the office of the company. He was generally a bull; now he was preparing to play the part of a bear.

"The best laid schemes o' *mice* an' *men* gang aft agleg."

In the iron links of the Jerome ring there was one flaw which had escaped the eyes of the shrewd leader. The charter, or the by-laws of the Old Southern Company *permitted an increase in the amount of the capital stock by vote of the directors.*

Within a few hours after the return of Keep from Saratoga, a further issue of fourteen thousand shares was authorized by the directors in secret session. The new stock certificates were made out and everything was ready. But it would never answer to send out these *new* stock certificates without disguise. In that case the market would know of it too soon. The price would fall and the Old Southern Company would fail to derive the full benefit which they hoped would accrue from the selling the new stock at so high a price, and the great bear movement of Keep would be a failure. Accordingly the necessary amount of stock was borrowed from the ring and sold. This created the impression that a heavy short interest was being developed and completely blinded the ring. In addition to the shares of the new issue, Keep went short of the stock on his own account to an enormous amount, and then stood and watched the market. Not long, however.

September drew near and a delicate pressure began to be felt in the money market. Many of the heavy holders began to talk about realizing their profits, but as the prices began to yield they waited for them to rise again.

Such is the custom of operators who cannot bear to face a loss, however small. They waited too long, for stocks, instead of regaining the summit price, sagged down lower. To Secretary Chase has been attributed two great panics, that of September, 1863, and that of April, 1864. Whether or not with reason, we will not say. But certain it is, that he came into the market in Wall Street in August, 1863, for a loan, and early in September he secured from the banks a loan of $35,000,000, and now the Old Southern trap was sprung. The entire lot of fourteen thousand shares, was used to repay the borrowed stocks. The money-lenders tightened their hold of their cash-boxes; the interest ran up three per cent. In one day, stocks fell from ten to twenty per cent. The next day they fell ten per cent. lower. Harlem and Hudson came toppling down from Alpine heights. Erie fell down with a rush, and struck 99. But Old Southern came down like an avalanche. Jerome's personal losses were said to have been nearly one million dollars, his prestige was destroyed and after that his power ceased to be felt in the market. As for the P—— Pool which hoped to swallow Uncle Daniel and his strong box, it was utterly annihilated. Some of the members of that combination still haunt the market, mere shadows of operators, without money, or credit or even decent habiliments. Daniel Drew covered his shorts with an immense profit.

The first thing a loser in Wall Street does, after a heavy stroke of bad luck is, to find fault with his broker. The second thing he does is, to curse his luck. The third thing he does is, to gather together the wreck, and get ready for another venture on the treacherous waves.

In accordance with this programme, I held a conference with my broker, in his private room, out of ear-shot of his clerks, for I wished to spare his feelings, so far as a broker may be said to have feelings. He was a big man. His personal presence was overpowering. He was seated in a large chair. The province of big men like him seems to be to sit in large chairs, and take change, as one of the editors of a New York newspaper once remarked to me. His face was that of a globose Jupiter Tonans. Every wrinkle seemed large enough to form the grave of a small margin, all in the way of legitimate commission business. His principal occupation appeared to be smoking monstrous regalias, and signing checks.

When a broker reaches the dignity of a daily check signer for a million dollars, he may be said to have drunk the full cup of such bliss as Wall Street life can give. The mere fact that a man is daily signing his name to twenty or thirty bits of paper, all of which are certified as good by his bank, and each one of which can, on presentment at the counter, be exchanged for forty thousand dollars in crisp greenbacks, conveys to an observer's mind, an idea of mysterious power. My broker sat in his private room that day, signing checks for untold amounts, as coolly as though he were scribbling his name in pure chirographical wantonness. I waited for him to finish his task before I opened my broadside. Just as he was putting the final flourish on the last check, he opened his lips and let drop one word, "well!" This was to let me know that he had the floor, and was about to speak. Then he laid the pen down, removed the huge cigar from between his lips, blew an immense volume of smoke from his mouth, looked at me through it as it circled to the ceiling, rose from his seat and continued:

"I am going out to get something to eat, come along."

This "getting something to eat," after the heavy

labors of the day, means in Wall Street parlance, an elaborate dinner with all the etceteras, or at least an elaborate lunch.

My guns were spiked by this hospitable invitation, but were still loaded and threatening. I held my peace, and without more ado we wended our way to the neighboring chateau of Delmonico. My heavy-set broker had probed my wound, and now proceeded to apply healing lotions. Twice I began a sentence, half expostulatory, half indignant; and twice I was interrupted by his stopping business acquaintances and addressing them in a jocular strain.

We reached the saloon, and elbowing our way through a group of florid, coraline-nosed individuals, whose principal occupation between the hours of ten A. M. and four P. M., seems to be standing very erect in the lower room of that far famed restaurant, looking very jolly, and taking brandy straight at regular intervals. We sat down at one of the little tables. A waiter flew to us, as waiters always do at such places, when well known heavy feeders and sippers make their appearance. He chattered like a monkey in a southern forest, seized our plates and polished them with his napkin till they shone again, then fairly bewildered our ears with the names of a host of dishes, all smoking hot, and waiting the pleasure of Messieurs, beneath as many smoking tins.

"We will take soup a la Julien."

"Oui! oui!"

"Then a little fish—Spanish mackerel."

"Oui! oui!"

"A bottle of *haut sauterne* with the fish. After that we will take a filet of beef with mushrooms; then game, the half of a grouse. Vegetables, of course; potatoes lyonaise, French peas, and a bottle of Cliquot, with the meats. Then ice-cream meringues. *Café noir and petit verre.*"

In three minutes we were under full headway. The soup silenced me with its trickling juices. The *sauterne* mollified me. The filet and game equilibrized me, and when the Cliquot had diffused its genial glow, I took new views of Wall Street life. The broker had done nothing but what was right in selling my stock, after my margin had run down so low. The loss could easily be made up. I had $40,000 to do it with; it should be done! We lay back in our chairs and puffed at our cigars. We exchanged views. We both concurred in thinking that stocks were cheap, particularly *Harlem*. This last named stock had fallen sixty per cent. from 181. The Commodore had not got through with it, that was plain. He was an all-day man, and he would send Harlem up kiting yet.

We talked so long about it, and fortified each other with such potential reasons for believing that this stock must rise, that at last we considered it a foregone conclusion. Then we rose from the table, and passed out into the street. The Boards had both adjourned. The crowd was buzzing as usual on the sidewalk. Stocks were quoted firm, with an upward tendency. The votaries of Harlem began to recover faith in their Magnus, Apollo—the Commodore, and once more filled the street with rumors of another great rise in the stock.

"You see," remarked one enthusiast, "A. G. Jerome had to pitch overboard all the Harlem he was carrying, when Old Southern broke. The Commodore hasn't sold any stock. They (the ring,) are picking up all the loose stock. There is one of Vanderbilt's brokers now buying everything offered under 120. The next hitch will be 200."

A part of these remarks were whispered in the ear of my broker, who immediately bought two thousand shares, on his own account. This amount he generously offered to share with me, and his offer was accepted promptly.

One thousand shares of Harlem at 120, cost sixty thousand dollars, for as already noted, this stock is only fifty dollars per share, at par. This amount of stock was placed to my account on the broker's books.

"This Harlem," said my broker, "I shall consider as a kind of permanent investment, at all events, I shall not sell it for less than 198."

One thousand shares of Harlem, bought at 120, and sold at 198, (for it is never best to wait for the highest point, which was agreed to be 200) would show a profit of $39,000. This would go towards wiping out that loss of $61,000.

The position of this notorious stock was, in the fall of 1863, very peculiar. It had been, the past six months, the double-edged sword of the market, held in the hands of the Commodore. The bears had first been cut down like grass, then the legs of the bulls were hewn in two. What was singular, the men who had gone short of the stock during the spring and summer were now buying it for a rise while many of those, who, during the same period, had operated in it for a rise, were selling it now in expectation of a further decline. Its future depended on two things, viz.: a decision of one of the judges of the Supreme Court and the action of the Common Council of the city of New York, respecting the street franchise grant. After a few rapid vibrations, it fell to 110. The stock looked weak. I wished I was out of it. But I dared not face a loss of $5,000 which had already accrued. One desperate expedient remained. I could buy one thousand shares more at 110 and then as soon as it rose to 115, sell out the two thousand shares without any loss except two or three hundred dollars brokerage and interest, for carrying the stock.

I bought one thousand shares more at 110!

The price sunk lower and lower.

One morning, soon after this, a stout red-haired man, a stranger to every one, made his appearance on the street, and offered five hundred shares of Harlem at the ruling price. No one took him up, but some one on the other side of the crowd, bid one per cent. below the market price, and the red-haired man cried out, "sold," and gave up the name of a well-known broker. In a moment, every eye in the crowd was fastened on the stranger.

It might be laid down as a general proposition that in certain conditions of the market, any stout, red-haired man, (who is a stranger to the crowd of operators), appearing on the street and offering to sell five hundred shares of a certain stock one per cent. below the market, would occasion a panic.

The stranger in this case proved to be a lawyer from one of the river counties, who was believed to have obtained early information in some way, that the decision of Judge Hogeboom was adverse to Har lem. As soon as this fact became known to the street, Harlem dropped like lead, to 90. On the heels of this decision, came adverse legislation by the Common Council, and before my two thousand shares could be disposed of, the price had reached 81. Out of $113,500, I had remaining, five thousand and some odd in cash on hand, and the $9,000 invested on a margin in the 7 3-10 bonds, bought as mentioned in the last chapter. Should I sell the bonds and put the proceeds into stock margins? No! This eight thousand dollars was turning out to be one of the snuggest financial snow-balls that was ever rolled, as will appear to the reader, if he will examine the following account, the figures being approximate, and made up from memory:

175,000 worth of 7 $\frac{3}{10}$ per cent. Government Bonds, at 104, bought July, 1863, ...		$182,000
Interest accrued on same, at 7-$\frac{3}{10}$ per cent., (say three months,) in currency, ...		2,235
		$184,235
Which Bonds were paid for by a loan from Savings' Banks, at par, ...		$175,000
Margin, ...		9,235
		$184,235
Interest on loan, for four months, at $5\frac{1}{2}$ per cent., in currency, on $175,000, . . .	$5,616	
Interest on bonds, 7-$\frac{3}{10}$ in gold, for four months, ...	$8,036	
Premium on $8,036 gold, sold at 140, . . .	3,214	
	$11,250	
Add 2 per cent., rise in bonds, ...	3,500	
	$14,750	

My net profits was the difference between $14,750

and the sum of $5,616 interest paid the savings banks which showed the sum of $9,134 in which, however, was included the entire interest paid in gold, viz.: $2,235. Now, if gold rose to 200, my interest on this operation which I regarded in the light of a permanent investment would be nearly 150 per cent. on my margin, to say nothing of any rise which might take place in the price of the bonds. On looking at these figures my resolution was confirmed to keep my bonds. But what should be done to retrieve my losses? I would make one last venture. In what? Did the fickle goddess relent and whisper something in my ear when one day after taking a survey of the market, I gave an order to buy five hundred shares of Rock Island, at par. However this may be, the stock was bought and $5,000 margin delivered to my broker, with instructions to sell the stock if it fell to 91, but if it went up, to let my profit run. Then I took a week's rest, expecting every day the worst, and hardly daring to hope for the better.

CHAPTER XVI.

OPENING THE BALL ON ROCK ISLAND.

Bulls, Bears and Changelings—How Bears Make Stocks go Up—Dull Seasons, Rises and Panics—Dark Times for Bulls—A Rocket Shoots Up in the Darkness—More about A. W. Morse—How He Came to be a Broker—The Rock Island Pool Taking in the Shorts—Undercurrents—The Financial Outlook; Is it to be Up or Down with Stocks?—Loans and Taxation *vs.* Fresh Currency—Two Bears try to Cover their Shorts but Can't—A Tantalizing Stock—The Story of My Five Hundred Shares—A Bone-boiler's Opinion about Rock Island—"Boiling Down the Gristle of the Bears"—The Final Twist—A Big Profit, and a Smile all Round.

THE operators in Wall Street may be divided into three grand classes. First, those who are by constitution and temperament, operators for a rise, *i. e.*, bulls. Second, those who are by constitution, temperament and education, operators for a fall, *i. e.* bears. Third, those who are bulls or bears by turns. This last class is by far the largest.

As we have before remarked, they who commence by operating for a rise often end by operating for a fall.

A. G. Jerome was an example of these converts. The Napoleon of the Public Board, after a career of unparalleled success, found his Waterloo in Old Southern. Henry Keep was the Iron Duke who defeated him as we have already shown. When Old Southern fell to 77, Jerome, who had been operating for a rise with such success up to the time of that disaster, now became a bold operator for a fall. He and his associates in the clique, turned about and sold Old Southern short. Their losses on both these operations were rated at $2,500,000. But Jerome was only one of a host of men who, having lost heavily on the bull side, by the panic of September 3d and 4th, now changed their policy, and prepared hereafter to act as bears. It should be remembered, that *bears play an important part in assisting every great rise*, by creating a demand for the stocks which they have sold for future delivery. This fact should be noted in connection with what we have to describe hereafter.

In accordance with the traditions of Wall Street, the fall of the year is the dull season in stocks. The reason for this may be stated thus: the money which flows into the banks of New York City, from all parts of the country, at other seasons of the year, is withdrawn largely in the fall by its owners, for the purpose of using it in different ways. One of these ways is the moving to market of the crops of the West and South. In a few weeks, or at most, months, the money begins to flow back, and seek employment and investment in New York. The banks and other money-lending institutions, also call in their loans late in the fall or early in the winter, preparatory to making their January dividends. Hence it is, that operators generally shorten sail in the autumn, during which season the stock market is dull. These dull seasons are the breathing spells of the market between its great rises and corresponding falls, which might be illustrated by a diagram as follows, viz.:

From September 4th till December 16th, nothing occurred that was noteworthy in the course of prices, except the break in Harlem. But Harlem was looked upon now as a specialty quite unconnected with the general market. During all this period, the bear party were daily growing stronger and more clamorous. Everything seemed to work in their favor. The banks, alarmed by the wild speculations in stocks and gold, and noting the periodical panics which had occurred, were all this time contracting their loans and discouraging stock operations. The financial movements of the government in the direction of fresh loans to be negotiated in New York, were held in dread by the operators. The press thundered forth in its money articles, denunciations of the *stock bubble* and its engineers, accompanied with words of prediction of and warning against the speedy collapse. Under these circumstances, the bulls found it difficult to lift prices. In November, and early in December, they made a feeble effort which failed, and left them in a worse condition. The confidence of the public in the upward tendency of values was more than impaired.

The five hundred shares of Rock Island, mentioned in the last chapter, was bought on its intrinsic *merits*, after a break in the market, on the 9th of December. How dark and cheerless everything looked that day! The sun hardly shone through the leaden sky upon the stagnant market. For a week, Wall Street speculation looked like a dead sea, and the financial air grew closer and darker. Suddenly, out of this level waste, something shot up like a rocket with a bengal light fastened to its tail! The bull carnival had been ushered in by the rise of Rock Island! This movement startled men by its brilliancy, but inspired fresh confidence. It was the harbinger of another great rise. Its leader was hailed by the bulls with acclamation. The name of A. W. Morse rang through the street.

After an interregnum of seven months, he again took the throne, as king of the Regular Board, and of the street, to maintain his blazing reign till the following April. Now the outside public began to inquire who he was. It appears that in 1860, he was a clerk in a mercantile house, and was employed by them to go down into Wall Street, to negotiate their paper, and look after their money matters there.

One day a gentleman connected with a large firm in the street, noticing the rapidity with which he ran up columns of figures, and the general sharpness and accuracy of his mental operations, views on stock, etc., asked him why he did not come into Wall Street, and commence business on his own account. Morse replied that he had no capital. The gentleman told him, that with talents like his, he could go on without capital, and that most of the successful brokers commenced with little or no money. "Money," said he, "will flow into the hands of the Wall Street man, who has the qualities of shrewdness, activity, and boldness. Don't wait another day, but take a little office near the Stock Exchange, and get admitted into the board as soon as you can." On this advice, Morse acted without delay. In three years he had

VAULTS OF THE STOCK EXCHANGE.

risen to be the leader of the board, during the Chancellorsville rise, and he was now the fugleman, who formed the bulls into one compact and obedient phalanx, moving up the heights of the market in 1864.

He was the most dashing operator ever known in Wall Street. In buying stocks he rarely seemed to cover his hand. The heavy dealers held him at first in low estimation. His bodily appearance was so slight and frail, his air so jaunty and holiday-like, his money resources seemed so inadequate to what he undertook, that when after buying quietly as much Rock Island as he could pick up, he came out boldly, bid for heavy blocks of the stock at 107–109, the old money kings of the board sold him all he bid for, laughing in their sleeves at the "blind confidence" of this wild speculator, and when the price fell back to 105, cries of derision were heard all through the street. From this point it rushed to 114, with enormous transactions. The whole capital stock, $6,000,000, is said to have been bought and sold twice over in a week. Neither buyers nor sellers abated their confidence, the former in the continued upward movement, the latter in the ultimate downcome, coupled with a firm belief in the insanity of their rivals. Morse kept buying it by the thousand shares, buyer thirty, seller thirty, cash, regular or in any way he could get it best. The more conservative members of the board prognosticated his speedy downfall.

"Morse will get bit;" "Morse will be saddled with the whole capital stock;" "Morse will break;" "Morse is crazy;" these remarks passed around the bear conclave.

But the pool in Rock Island was stronger than these confident and prophetic gentlemen dreamed. It comprised, besides the brave leader and manipulator, a Washington banker, an eminent railroad capitalist and financier, and a wealthy retired California merchant, besides ten or twelve other operators. There was money enough pledged to carry the entire stock on a twenty per cent. margin, *i. e.*, $1,200,000. When the price struck 116, the pool is said to have held, in actual stock or contracts, thirty-nine thousand shares. These contracts were buyers' and sellers' options, for three, five, ten, fifteen, thirty and sixty days. As fast as they fell due they were renewed by the still confident bears.

A little lull now took place in the price, which languidly moved between 114 and 118. But though Morse no longer bid personally for the stock, he was not idle. In the nobbiest of sack-coats, his face a little thinner, and his nose a little more hooked than usual, he could have been seen flying from bank to bank, or standing behind his desk, adding up figures like the lightning calculator, or making playful bids for one or two hundred shares of Rock Island, or offering to sell ten thousand shares in one lot, at two per cent. below the market. All this time his agents were at work, taking every new contract offered, now bidding up the price, and now dropping it to entice more shorts.

The members of the Pool began to find fault with Morse, and ask why he did not put up the price. "Leave that to me," he would reply, "and I will make all your fortunes." When they importuned him to know what he was doing, he would laugh and tell them to be patient, and ask them what they thought of 175 for Rock Island. Here it should be noted that in the Rock Island Pool, nick-named by the bears, the "Blind Confidence Pool," Morse was the sole manager. All his associates did was to sign the Pool contract and pay the money which represented their interest. After that they knew little or nothing of what was going on in the stock. This was a shrewd policy for the Pool manager, for it deterred his associates from operating on the stock outside, to the prejudice of the combination. They dared not buy the stock, for fear of a break, and still less dared they to go short of it.

The money-market, during the month of December, had been by fits and starts, cheap and dear; capitalists were timorous. But when January came, there was for a while a *steady* stringency, and still stocks stood firm.

It was Morse standing on the "perilous edge" of the battle in December, that held the market up, by the moral effort of his thus far successful move.

One fear hung over the bears like a thunder-cloud. It was the fear of the new issue of $400,000,000 legal tenders, authorized in March, but a small part of which had yet been set afloat. The Government had shrunk from doing this as long as possible. Now it looked as if it must be done. The currency of the country would in that case be $1,000,000,000. This, to the Wall Street man, would signify a new and unparalleled era in speculation.

The panic of the preceding September had been precipitated by a loan made by the banks to the government on $50,000,000 of the new legal tender five per cent. notes, and as the policy which had been pursued by Secretary Chase for the past four months was that which contemplated the raising of money by loans and taxation, rather than by the issue of fresh currency, the bears had been flattering themselves on the prospect of a continued tightness in the money market from the absorption of the floating currency in the five-twenties and other government loans. The result of this state of affairs would finally be, lower prices in the stock market. Such were the grounds on which a host of bears had been resting ever since September.

But a new loan at a lower rate of interest (the ten forties) would have to be soon placed upon the market. Would the public subscribe to it if money were not made easier, *i. e.*, if new currency were not issued? The financial policy of the Secretary may be best described by a simile. The government loans may be likened to so many different vessels, large and small. The legal tenders may be likened to the waters in which those vessels were to be floated. The lower the interest of the bonds the more difficult to get them taken by the people, just as the lower the vessel's keel sinks the more depth of water required to float her.

This was the question about which the bulls and bears differed. The bulls had decided already that $1,000,000,000 millions of notes would soon be afloat. Morse foresaw it clearly when he made his apparently desperate venture in Rock Island. The shrewdest of those men, who had been selling stocks, began to take the same views and would have acted upon them by turning right about face and buying for a rise, but for one little circumstance. *If they bought in their shorts they would have to do so at a heavy loss.* They dared not look their losses boldly in the face; they dared not confess they were in the wrong. Avarice and vanity made cowards of them.

Here let us note, that as long as his contracts remain open, the Wall Street man is buoyed up by what is so often his evil genius, viz.: Hope—hope, either that his gains will be greater, or his losses less. He cannot bear to fix his eyes on those terrible accounts, rendered to him by his broker, with the long columns of interest, commissions and margins, all swallowed up in that voracious stock-market. When his account is handed to him, if it shows a loss, he will fold it, and thrust it into his most secret pocket, without even looking at the "demnition total." Successive accounts, each showing losses, are like successive blows of some demon-hammer, upon his sensitive nervous system. Even the iron nerves of Daniel Drew shook under it. It seemed that he kept several different accounts at his brokers, entitled thus, viz.: "Erie account," "North-west account," etc., etc. When he made a loss on one account, he used to put it down on some one of the other accounts, which made a profit, as if he would juggle himself out of the idea that he had made any loss.

On the 5th of January, 1864, the long pending question between the bulls and bears, was decided in favor of the former. $20,000,000 of the new interest bearing, five per cent. legal tender notes, were received by the banks of Philadelphia, New York and Boston.

Two days before this, and while Rock Island was selling at 123, two prominent bears, who were short of the stock fifteen per cent. below that figure, received a telegram from Washington, informing them that several millions of the new notes were to be sent to New York on the next day. They promptly gave orders to their brokers, to cover at 123¼. This was their limit, and but for an unfortunate accident, their order might have been executed. *The message was intercepted by the enemy.* It had been carried by a small boy, one of those rattle-pated little urchins, too often entrusted with important messages in Wall Street. While on his way to the brokers, he was seen by an agent of Morse, scuffling with one of his mates. A moment after, he dropped a slip of paper, which Morse's agent picked up, read, and handed it back to the boy, who thereupon, scuttled away to do his errand. In sixty seconds from that moment, Morse knew that two prominent bears had given an order to cover several thousand shares of Rock Island at 123¼. In sixty seconds more, two brief notes had been dispatched; one to his agent who bought and sold for him in the street, the other to his agent representing him in the Public Board. The purport of these notes was, not to let Rock Island go below 124, and if any one came in to buy at the market price, to bid the price up all the time, and buy everything that was offered. He himself attended to matters in the Regular Board. The two bears finding themselves unable to cover, kept giving fresh orders, one quarter per cent. above the market, 124¼, 125¼, 126¼. But just as they were going to lay their hands on the stock as they fondly hoped, it danced away from them, till it reached 129. These orders in accordance with a Wall Street custom, were only in force during the particular session of the board, held immediately after they were given. When they ceased giving orders, the stock price remained quiet, or fell off a trifle.

Let us leave, for a while, these brothers in misfortune, cutting their financial throats by the penny-wise and pound-foolish policy, of limiting their broker in the price at which he was to buy, blissfully unconscious of the hawk-eyes which watched their every motion, and return to the story of the five hundred shares of Rock Island, bought by me on the 9th of December, at 101.

Morse's office in 1864, was in William Street, nearly opposite to one of the entrances to the Regular Board. It was a small room, more like a niche in the wall than a banking office, in which operations were soon to be carried on, the results whereof were destined to shake the stock market to its very center. As there was little space inside to accommodate the numerous customers which began to flock thither, attracted by the fame of the bull leader, and hoping to build their fortunes upon it, these gentry were wont to stand outside upon the flag-stones which descended into the street, and a singular looking group they were. Among them I had often noticed a man with a carbuncular nose who was continually standing sentry at that particular spot, and seemed to act as if he knew something about what was going on.

One morning after Rock Island had risen to 129, and deeming now that my profits had been let run so long that this was the hour to embrace them, by fingering a check for $14,000 or thereabouts, I was on my way to my brokers, to give the necessary order to sell, when a friend introduced me to the carbuncular nose, as it glowed like a beacon in front of Morse's office. The owner of the nose, it appears, was also the proprietor of a small, but extremely vigorous bone-boiling establishment, somewhere up town. In this legitimate, but disagreeably odoriferous business, he had amassed the sum of five thousand dollars, which as luck would have it, had been recently staked as a ten per cent. margin, on five hundred shares of Rock Island. The first question I put to him involved his opinion of Rock Island. As this was his first appearance in the street as an operator, and not having yet acquired the Wall Street habit of reticence, he was free to say that he thought well of it, he had made a little money on it and was going to make more.

"Will she go up? She hasn't *begun* to bile yet. When she *does* bile, she won't leave a gristle or a jynt of them air bears. Morse is agoing to pile on the fire and melt 'em all into soup."

This forcible expression of his opinion, savoring so strongly of the bone-boiling trade, had its due effect. I decided to let my profits run.

She *did* "begin to bile." The following Saturday, Rock Island sold at 133. The two bears thought of the matter over Sunday. *Their* decision was made. Early Monday morning they gave the order which they ought to have given two weeks before. "Buy our Rock Island at the *market price!*"

That was a blue Monday for the ursine tribe. It was "twisting day." The pass-word was "excelsior." At half-past nine o'clock, I saw Morse standing on his office steps, a strange smile distorting his face as he looked at the curb-stone crowd, yelling for Rock Island at 140. Before night it touched 149. The two bears settled up their shorts at 145. The bone-boiler took his profits at 145. The writer, the next day, was perusing a deeply interesting volume of stock literature, by which it appeared he had to his credit on the books of his broker, a net profit of $21,546.45, derived from the sale of five hundred shares of Rock Island at 145.

Never sell stocks short!

Always be a bull! *Verb. Sap.*

Twenty-one thousand, five hundred and forty-six dollars and forty-five cents!

Here were the pin-feathers of a rich plumage for a bird so lately plucked! Everybody smiled in my broker's office that morning. The little errand boy grinned and winked as he darted past me. The clerks beamed with smiles. The book-keeper simpered, as he graciously allowed me to feast my eyes on my account in his ledger, which expanded before me. I thought I could perceive a slight contortion on the stony face of the cashier, as he passed me a check for $500 pocket money. And when I handed to my broker a series of orders to buy three hundred Michigan Central, five hundred Illinois Central, four hundred Old Southern, all at the market price, his countenance was one conglomeration of smiles as he looked down the vista of my future commissions. He punched me in the ribs, joked me about Old Southern and Harlem, vowed that I would have revenge on them yet, and finished by inviting me to go with him to dinner at 4 P. M. sharp, to take soup and wet my profit.

CHAPTER XVII.

THE GREAT RISE OF 1864.

A Drop in the Market, in Consequence whereof I Seek for advice and Sympathy from a Broker—Tricks of Wall Street Trade—He " Can't Stand the Press "—Forming Cliques and Pools—The Bull-leader Tries to Break the Market—Bulling Erie and Catching Uncle Daniel in the same old Trap—Morse on the War-path—A Quartette of Operators Plan a Campaign—Getting into Pools and Collecting Information—The Press Puts the Fact Before the People—The Countrymen in Wall Street—Scenes on 'Change—Our Little Excursion " Up in a Balloon, Boys "—Hauling in the Profits—Flyers in General, and *Our* Flyers in Particular—The Canton Pool—Visiting Our Property in East Baltimore—E—— Makes an Address to the Committee on Canton Stock.

THE general market, awakened from its long lethargy in December, by Morse's Rock Island pyrotechnics, began in January to throb and stir with a strange, feverish life.

The next stage was to be frenzy.

The three hundred shares of Michigan Central, cost me 132½. The five hundred shares of Illinois Central, cost me 125. The four hundred shares of Old Southern, cost me 87½. In one week, the first named of these stocks was selling at 139, the second, at 132 and, the third, at 90. I could, by selling, have realized a profit of $6,450; instead of which, I bought twice the amount of my first purchase. All at once, money tightened up to ten per cent., and in a few hours Michigan Central had fallen to 126, Illinois Central to 124, and Old Southern to 86. If I sold my stocks now, my loss would be $20,900, besides interest and brokerage.

When a heavy loss stares him in the face, a man is apt to seek advice and sympathy from his broker. Seeking advice and sympathy from brokers, when margins are diminishing, is like gathering grapes from thorns, and figs from thistles. Instead of smiles, I now saw only dark looks in my broker's office. The market was panicky; a further decline of 4½ per cent., and I should be laid on my back once more.

That globose face, which, ten days before, was radiant with smiles, was now overcast and lowering.

Why do brokers' faces look black when their customers' margins have nearly run out?

Tricks of the trade!

When stocks begin to break, they often quietly sell their customers' stocks. Then, after prices have declined so far as to leave little *apparent* margin on the account, the customer, quite unconscious that his stocks have been sold at a much higher price, finds himself subjected to various influences to induce him to give the order to sell. His broker looks glum, and talks of tight money, and the dangerous condition of the market. If the customer gives the order to sell, of course the broker puts into his own pocket, the difference between the higher price at which he sold his customer's stock, and the order to sell, given under the pressure of those glum looks and bear talk. This trick may be better illustrated by the following little account:

Customer buys one hundred Erie at 120, ...	$12,000
Market begins to fall, and broker sells the stock (without telling customer) at 119.	
Stock price falls to 105, ...	10,500

Then come the black looks and talk of bad market. The customer gets frightened and says sell. The stock has already been sold at 119, but the broker returns on the account, 100 Erie sold at 105, and pockets the difference between 119 and 105, *i. e.*, $1,400, which sum comes out of his customer's margin. We do not allege that *all* brokers are in the habit of doing this, but it is certainly one of the ways by which the public are fleeced.

I was unable to stand the pressure of that lowering face, and the doleful tale he told, respecting the market; I lightened ship by throwing overboard the nine hundred shares of Michigan Central at a loss of over $9,000, but still kept fifteen hundred shares of Illinois Central, and the twelve hundred shares of Old Southern though under the greatest trepidation lest the market, by a further decline, might clear away my remaining margin. Of course this sale was made at the lowest cash price, and as usual, in ten minutes afterwards, stocks began to rise again.

Two weeks passed away—two busy fervid weeks. Money was pouring into Wall Street now like the cataract of the great lakes. One after one, stocks had risen higher than the bulls would have dared to hope in bleak December. Even the colossal bulk of Erie was moving upwards with slow elephantine strides. Then stocks paused. Many holders thinking that prices had culminated, sold out. The market took all their stocks without budging, and still it did not advance much. Why? Pools were forming; powerful combinations on the pattern of the Rock Island pool. They were keeping down the prices till they had loaded up. Morse and his associates still kept their grip of Rock Island and were taking hold of Pittsburg, of Erie and of Fort Wayne. A pool in Old Southern made its head-quarters in the office of L—— & Co. The Commodore and his friends had Harlem and Hudson in hand. Illinois Central, Galena, in fact nearly every stock on the catalogue was passing into the hands of pools. The market was agitated for the moment by a great downward movement in Rock Island. In three days, Morse sold the bulk of his Rock Island between 140 and 118. He wished to break down the entire market, so that he could buy other stocks. He was preparing to concentrate his best energies on Fort Wayne and Erie. The chasm made by Rock Island closed up, and everything grew smooth again. Fort Wayne looked heavy for the moment. Its leader was taking a flyer on Erie! This movement in Erie, had, under the quiet purchase of Morse, advanced the price to 112. Then he tried to break the market down by hurling huge blocks of Rock Island and Erie upon it. But Erie stood firm.

It was time now to play the bold game. The first move in this game commenced at the *Evening Exchange.*

The Evening Exchange was one of the institutions of the stock market during the years 1864 and 1865. Some enterprising dealer hired a room in the basement of the Fifth Avenue Hotel. Any one could have access to it by paying fifty cents. In February of the former year, this room was jammed with buyers and sellers, from seven till nine P. M., after which hour they adjourned to the halls and bar-room above, and plied their vocation till midnight.

Morse jumped on a bench in this basement one night, dressed in a light blue beaver overcoat, and gracefully waving his potent hand, bid for ten thousand shares of Erie, or any part. No one "took him up." While he stood there, still holding open his bid, a slim young man with dark eyes, darted up the steep staircase, rushed into the hotel, and whispered to Daniel Drew's broker, who stood in the hall apparently waiting for something. "Sell him the ten thousand shares," said he "and give up my name."

The young man darted down into the basement, rushed up and shook his finger in the face of Morse, yelling out, "I'll sell you that ten thousand Erie."

Morse nodded his head, and then stretching out his hand, bid for twenty thousand shares more. The crowd knew that Daniel Drew was selling the stock, and shrunk back at the boldness of the man who dared to meet the old man "on his native heath," Erie.

In two days the whole capital stock of $11,000,-000 changed hands. The price ran up ten per cent. Morse had hoisted the huge load to 122, and the "Old Man's" account on that little operation was out $100,000.

Men began to count on their fingers, the successful operations of Morse. Pittsburg, Rock Island, Erie; and to enquire what stock this bold leader would take hold of next. I had not yet sold the fifteen hundred Illinois Central, nor the twelve hundred Old Southern, which at present prices, showed me a profit of something like $14,800. I bought one thousand more shares of Old Southern at 95, and five hundred Illinois Central at 134.

Then I was joined by allies. The Saratoga trio came together again. E——, who had retired from the market in disgust after his losses in September, now came into the market again, rejuvenated by his long rest, and bellowed like a bull of Bashan. L——, after being hit heavily on his long stocks, had been converted to the bear creed, and having covered his shorts at a further loss of $75,000, had determined hereafter never to go short, but always operate for a rise.

Our little coterie received an accession in the person of W. B. C——, a Westerner, with a heart as big as a bullock. Poor fellow! he sleeps now the sleep that knell of panic will never disturb. We laid out our campaign on the following plan: Each one was to keep an account in the office of a prominent broker, but no two in the same office. Each one was to get admitted to a different pool, and then we were mutually pledged to furnish each other with all the information we could obtain from these different sources. L—— opened an account with Morse, E—— with L—— & Co., W. B. C—— with M—— & B——. I kept one account with my old broker, and opened another with B—— & Co. L—— joined the Fort Wayne ring. E—— cast his bread upon the Old Southern Pool. W. B. C—— entered the Galena combination, and I took five hundred shares in the Canton pool at 38. Then we exchanged "views," the result of which was that each one made outside purchases of the different pool-stocks, inside of which his mates had embarked. I sold my two thousand Illinois Central at 135 and bought one thousand Fort Wayne, five hundred Galena, and five hundred Old Southern.

Then our quartette lay back, and went "up in a balloon."

What a tremendous moral engine, is the New York press. Every day this engine spreads before a million readers, and a thousand minor journals, a record of facts. To say that the money articles of the Daily Journal of Traffic, the Daily Harbinger, the Daily Rostrum, the Daily Age, the Daily Orb, the Daily Letter, the Daily Messenger, etc., etc., are written with great ability, would be but simple justice. If they sometimes make mistakes in their views of money matters, still, it cannot be denied, that they see as far into the financial grindstone as any one. Every day, during the great rise of 1864, this moral engine was laying before the people these facts, viz.: A thousand millions of currency will soon be circulating through the country; railroads are earning enormous sums; an unprecedented inflation is taking place in values; a certain daring speculator, named Morse, is setting Wall Street in a blaze; speculation is rampant, and no one can predict when this speculation will cease. The whole country was startled by this record of facts. The large ear of the confiding public was caught. The speculative element rushed into Wall Street, in one compact body. Countrymen rarely go short of stocks; they are generally bulls. Buy! buy! anything, no matter what! put in your greenbacks, and and pick up gold!

The whole street was lined with rustics. They marched in files, stood in groups, discussed matters and then formed in battalions and gave their orders to buy. Lank, sun-burned men, stout men, with husky voices, tall short and middle-sized men, with country-cut coats, entered the city in the morning, with nothing but a paper collar and a comb in their carpet bag and a small check on some city bank, and left town the next day with a bundle of greenbacks larger than a small sized encyclopedia! These were the lucky ones. Others staid there for three months and then left with very large fleas in their ears. Morse's office was besieged. Strangers came to him and thrust portly wallets into his hand. Shrewd financiers almost went down on their knees, begging him to tell them what to buy, and forcing upon him checks for hundreds of thousands of dollars. He was watched as closely as if he were some great criminal under the surveillance of detectives. In the board or on the curbstone, every shade of expression in his face was scrutinized by hundreds of sharp eyes.

The other bull leaders were ably seconding the great upward movement. Tobin had Harlem in hand for the Commodore. Every brokerage firm that had charge of any particular stock for a pool, became a General, urging on the bull movement. L. W. Jerome, though little seen in the street, was operating enormously for a rise and making millions. A well-known clergyman laid down a check for three thousand dollars on the desk of this noted financier. He didn't tell him to buy stocks, oh! no! That would be gambling. But mysteriously enough, in the course of a couple months after, the same clergyman was seen to deposit in his bank, a check for $80,000, signed by L. W. Jerome.

During the two months from the 18th of February till the 18th of April, there was no form of humanity, no profession, age, sex or condition, that might not have been seen in Wall Street. Even decrepitude and disease seemed for the time being, to have lost their power. The corridors of the Stock Exchange and the cushioned sofas of the brokers' offices looked like the wards of a hospital, filled with limbs palsied and swollen, and eyes purblind, while the hectic coughs of consumptives were echoing the robust shouts and yells of the surging crowd in William Street. Glittering coupés drove up to the doors of the great banking and brokerage houses, with fair dames veiled and loaded with jewels, who leaned back upon the satin-covered cushions and waited to learn the prices of stocks.

Three weeks after we had started on our balloon excursion, we pulled the valve and let out a little gas, in other words, we realized a part of our profits by selling everything except our interest in Fort Wayne and in our individual pools. The Fort Wayne we had decided, must be held for 150, and as for the pool interests, they could not be sold, because we had, on the blind confidence principle, surrendered the control of them to the rings which managed the different stocks which they undertook to hoist. L——, who was the boldest of the quartette, had realized $89,000. E—— $27,000, and W. B. C—— $22,000; while my net profits in hand, since the 9th of December, were $42,000.

Then we said we would go up town, and rest for a week. But we could not sever ourselves long from stocks. Our vacation was only for a day. We all met in the street the next morning, which was Monday. We only came in to take a look at the market.

We did not "mean business." L—— went into Morse's office, came out smiling, and said he had a point. Fort Wayne was to be jumped in a day or two!

By eleven A. M., we held two thousand shares apiece, which cost us from 116 to 118. The next day, just as twelve o'clock was hammered from the belfry of Old Trinity, I had sold all my Fort Wayne, at a profit of $57,000!

"This is the end. No more speculation for me, *except now and then a little flyer.*" Such was my mental resolution, as I deposited $100,000 in my bank, intending to use that sum for permanent investments. I still had $20,000 in my broker's hands. This sum was to furnish me my diversion, which was to consist in *taking flyers.* How many men can trace their ruin to that first or last flyer! There is nothing delusive and dangerous, to which they may not be likened. That flyer, in the shape of one hundred shares of stock, is the maggot in the brain; the springe set for the woodcock; the gilded butterfly, which leads its pursuer over the precipice; the bladders on which "little wanton boys" swim over the treacherous depths of a pool; the rainbow which hangs over the roar of the cataract.

The same afternoon that the little fortune had been snugly laid away in the burglar proof vaults of the —— Bank, L—— brought me another "point" out of Morse's office. *A great many Ohio and Mississippi certificates had lately been going into that office.* The par value of an Ohio and Mississippi certificate was $1,000. Ten of them were equal to one hundred shares of stock. I bought ten Ohio and Mississippi certificates at 49. They rose to 50; I bought fifty more. They rose to 53; I bought one hundred and forty more. Then I gave my broker orders to "sell them at 65—order good till countermanded." Thereupon I went into the country to buy a span of horses. Not that I had a passion for horses. On the contrary, I considered them very perishable property; delicate in health, and like a lady of fashionable circles, rather ornamental than useful. I had sold my horses the preceding fall, and was glad to dispose of them at forty per cent. below what they cost me. Still it is the thing for successful Wall Street men to own horses with ranging necks and long stride, Hambletonian trotters descended from the Godolphin Arabian, or connected by some dark affinity of lineage with Bucephalus or Pegasus. Brown, and other Wall Street men had horses, and why shouldn't I.

That trip to the country was not an agreeable one. My heart was not "in the Highlands;" it was in Wall Street. At the first railroad station I came to, on my way home, with my span of equine elephants, I bought a newspaper, and saw Ohio and Mississippi certificates 69! I telegraphed to my brokers and received answer: "Your certificates sold at 67!" My profits on this *flyer* were $29,100, less interest and brokerage.

The five hundred shares in the Canton pool, had always seemed a mere trifle. I paid very little attention to it, except to buy the stock outside the pool, and make fifteen or twenty thousand dollars. The party that held Canton under their control was not a strong one. There were three rings in it in 1864. The first ring was formed on the basis of 32–33. In February, a new ring was formed on the basis of 38.

This was the ring in which I had an interest. As I had only ten per cent. margin, *i. e.* five thousand dollars, I was perfectly willing to let the brokers, O——, S——, G—— & Co., take the entire control of the matter. But now that it had risen to 60, it began to look enticing, and I commenced to take flyers freely in it, especially when one of the daily papers had stated that the property of the company was marked down on its books as being worth par, and the manipulators of the stocks asked me what I thought of 150 as the future price. When Canton reached 66, a third ring was formed. This was to be a sweetener. The heavy capitalists were going into it now, and the price was to be carried up to par. "Would I go into it, and take a thousand shares? No additional margin would be required. I had a large profit on their books now." "Yes, I would." This thousand shares of Canton would give me diversion, something to think about and talk about. I was member of the new pool to the extent of one thousand shares.

Canton is one of the few stocks on the list, which has a history of thirty years. It was based upon property in Baltimore; lands, wharves, warehouses, etc., etc. To be sure, it was not dividend paying. That circumstance was of little weight, however. Erie had just paid a dividend, and why not Canton? The suggestion that it might be used as a government navy-yard, was a good one; so was the idea that Baltimore was a growing city, and that a railroad ran through the property. In 1835 this stock sold for three hundred. This was a pleasing fact to remember. F. B——, a wealthy merchant, had loaned the ring a large sum, not to be called for in several months, the interest on which was payable in gold; the shorts were in it heavily. I bought one thousand shares at 65. The price dropped back to 60, then rose to 70. E—— and I thought we would go in now and buy five thousand shares of this stock. But before doing so, we took a trip to Baltimore for the purpose of examining the Canton property, which as we held an undivided interest ot three-twentieths, we thought ourselves justified in calling *our* property. We stopped at East Baltimore, and after making the proper inquiries, succeeded in *locating* the property in question. E—— took his position on a pile of rubbish, and waving his hand to southward and westward over a dreary waste of vacant lots, thinly besprinkled with mouldy looking brick and wooden buildings, delivered a brief oration as if he were addressing the entire executive committee of the Canton Company. He commenced by alluding to the fact that appearances were deceitful, that this celebrated property—our property—had a great future before it; that at some time, it might be only a few years, and it would certainly be within the next century, this property was destined to have value. He pointed to the various heaps of rubbish in evidence of the activity of business thereupon, alluded to the memories of Canton, and closed by inviting the committee to his hotel (a small shanty), in the city of Canton, where they might refresh themselves after their arduous labors, with the wine of hops and malt, otherwise lager beer.

It need hardly be stated that when we got back to New York *we sold our* outside interest in the Canton

Company, and I wished I had never gone into the last ring at 66.

And now, while in search of "flyers," in which to employ profitably my loose cash, and of investments for my $100,000, I found something which seemed, at once a most tempting flyer and a most permanent investment.

CHAPTER XVIII.

BUBBLE COMPANIES.

Ripples, Oscillations and Tide Waves in Speculation—New Enterprises on the Crest of the Wave—Wall Street Men Become Miners and Mineralogists — Mining-patter and Wealth Going a Begging — How They Blow the Bubbles—"A Limited Number of Shares" Offered to the Public—The Bubble Full Blown; it Glitters Like the Rainbow—Ropers-in Pulling in Victims—The Corpulent Gentleman in Gold-bowed Spectacles—What's in a Name?—Very Much in the Case of a Mining Company—We Go In on the "Hard-pan" Basis—Chasing Bubbles Through the Market—We Catch Them Without Difficulty—Fighting for Subscriptions—"Gregory Consolidated," and "Gunnell Gold" Books Open—A General Bursting.

ALL former speculations in Wall Street had been merely ripples, or at most; waves of oscillation on the ocean of finance. This was a great tide wave, let us say rather an earthquake wave of the tropics, embracing in its huge semicircle, every form of hazardous venture. Its crest was already whitening with foam, but few, very few, caught the low, dull roar, which was soon to swell into thunder, as it broke on the beach—Ruin.

"The earth hath bubbles, as the water has."

These bubbles are stock companies, formed on the basis of property, the value of which, sometimes, bears to the nominal capital of the company, no more than the ratio of 1 to 1,000. The actual cost of the property of the Titan Ledge, and Back Mountain

Gold, Silver and Copper Company, for example, was $1,000. Its actual paid in capital, was $1,000,000. The Grand Junction Gold Mining Company's property cost $40,000. The subscribers to this stock, had to pay only $30 per share, and as there were 60,000 shares, they paid $1,800,000 for their interest. This was generous on the part of the projectors of the enterprise. They only made $1,760,000, when they might have made $3,000,000.

The flood of paper money poured from the steam presses, working day and night, sufficed now to float all kinds of speculative enterprises.

March, and the first days of April, 1864, were palmy days for the bubble blowers of Wall Street. Having inflated railroad-stocks to a profitable altitude, they proceeded to organize companies in all manner of those useful, costly, and beautiful things, which bountiful mother earth pours out of her lap in the rough. Samples of these things could be seen in Wall Street; brokers and bankers appeared to have been suddenly smitten with a passion for mineralogy. Their offices were transformed into cabinets of minerals, containing very fine specimens of sulphuret of lead, carbonate of copper, and oxide of iron, besides blocks of quartz bespangled with virgin gold, and lumps of coal which burned like a candle. Their talk was in mining slang, and "pockets," "fissure veins," "faults," "spurs," "lodes," "pyrites," "chimneys," ran all through their vocabulary. They had a deal to say about "Comstock Ledge," producing at that time, $1,000,000 per month, not to particularize respecting "Gould & Curry," "Ophir," "Yellow Jacket," "Crown Point," and a host of other successful claims.

They appeared to have transferred their speculative affections from Rock Island, Fort Wayne, and the railways generally, to "The Alligator Bayou Salt Company," "The Big Mountain Iron Company," "The Black Valley Coal Company," and "The Angels' Rest Quicksilver Company."

The press teemed with advertisements of these various enterprises, and some of the daily journals devoted columns to the record of what had been done, was doing, or was about to be done, in this new field of speculation. There were unsuspected gulches, where the precious metals were a drug. There were mountains of silver and copper, where junks could be had as a gift. Gold ready to be torn from the loose embrace of the maternal quartz. In fine, far off in the wilderness, as well as close to the fringes of civilization, there were hidden treasures without number, materials for wealth without stint, ungarnered, unminted, unmoulded, almost unwatched. These companies were organized in the following manner:

Mr. A——, a gentleman having some connection with the mining interests of the country, and owning a claim which had been staked out on some auriferous ledge in Colorado, being naturally desirous of disposing of his property to advantage, would go to some prominent banker, for the purpose of negotiating a sale. But prominent bankers are not in the habit of paying cash for property two thousand miles away. Accordingly, this particular banker would propose that the claim be made the basis of a stock company, and that the owner convey his property in it to the company, and receive therefor a certain sum in cash, say $10,000, to be paid out of the first subscriptions, and also a certain number of shares of the stock. The nominal capital of the company to be, say $2,000,000, represented by forty thousand shares of $50 each, and the subscription price at which it was to be offered to the public to be $25 per share. This proposition being acceded to, specimens of the gold ore perhaps in the form of sulphurets would be submitted to some well-known chemist and mineralogist, who subjected them to an *assay*, and in due time gave his certificate that these specimens furnish by assay, $1,000 in gold to the ton of ore. (The amount of gold extracted by an *assay* is, be it remembered, vastly greater than what is actually taken out in the practical working of a mine.) The banker would then approach some wealthy merchant and hold out an inducement for him to lend his name as one of the directors of the company. This inducement might be the gift of one or two thousand shares, or the subscription price might be lowered from $25 to $12.50 in some cases, for the merchant, of course, would wish to "go in" on "hard-pan," as it is called, *i. e.*, the lowest subscription price. The merchant's name having been secured, it was an easy matter to get other names which would add strength to the company in the public estimation, among which generally were, a well known retired capitalist, a heavy manufacturer, and perhaps a philanthropist, who desire to have the riches of the country developed.

Thereupon the company would be duly organized under the general mining and manufacturing law of the State of New York. A president, secretary and treasurer would be chosen, the last of which offices would be filled by the banker aforesaid. A name would then be selected which would be likely to strike the eye of the public. This name might be suggestive of what is at once rich, barbaric and inaccessible. Something lone, far off and guarded like the diamond of the desert, *e. g.*, the "Arizona Metaliferous and Scalping Ledge Gold and Silver Mining Company," or the "Mount St. Elias Silver Lode and Gold Vein Mining Company." Perhaps it might suggest birds, beasts or fishes of prey, *e. g.*, "The Vulture's Nest, or the Wolf's Peak, or the Pickerel Lake Nugget and Virgin Gold Pocket Company." All this gave play to the fancy of the future subscribers.

Then came the flaming prospectus, setting forth all the richness, activity and certain success of the enterprise, got up in the greatest splendor of typographical art, and worded cunningly with a view to any possible future legal liability of the projectors. The advertisement in the daily journals, set forth that the subscription books were open for a *limited number* of shares of the company (no personal liability of the stock-holders), at the office of the banker aforesaid, at the low price of $25 per share.

"Don't all speak at once, gentlemen! The shares are going off very rapidly; only one thousand are left, but we have reserved a few shares of treasury stock for our friends, which can be had by *immediately* applying to the office of ——, the banker, as the books are to be closed irrevocably on the 10th instant."

Somehow there always is a large reserve of treasury stock for the friends of the projectors in all these cases.

On the first of April, the whole market hummed

and rang again, with the most tempting solicitations to subscribe and make a fortune. The bubbles swelled, and shone with all the colors of the rainbow, while each investor gazed upon them through the prism of hope and fancy, which lent new glories to the iridescent, but, alas! unsubstantial orbs.

Bubble companies have their scouts and whippers-in. Outside machinery. These gentry are on the look-out for one hundred thousand dollar men. They scrutinize the bank accounts of operators, and track their profits. They point their detecting fingers at columns of figures, and then make the acquaintance of the man who piles up the money represented by the figures, to the ultimate end of making themselves familiar even to the handling of the piler's money.

The scout who tracked the profits of the quartette, named in our last chapter, was a corpulent gentleman, who wore gold-bowed spectacles. E—— tells me, that ever since March, 1864, he can never see a pair of gold-bowed spectacles, without a sense of goneness in the region of his pantaloon right pocket. He was presented to us, by his request, one day just after dinner. He saw us go to a restaurant, and waited for us to come out. A kitten might play with a Wall Street financier, after dinner *a la mode*, particularly when he had that day bagged a profit of $29,000 on Ohio and Mississippi certificates. He invited us to his office, which was round the corner, on the first floor. The bubble-blower's office is often on the first floor, for he knows that the successful operator dislikes to exercise his gastrocuemius by climbing stairs.

In a twinkling we found ourselves in the spider's

parlor. It was a complete curiosity-shop. Models of petroleum barrels, made by a new machine, which took a log of wood into its jaws, chewed it for five minutes, and then threw it out again, a perfect barrel, statuettes of nymphs, made out of cannel-coal, small hydrostatic presses, etc. The walls of the parlor were papered with prospectuses of companies. The mantle-piece and tables spread with specimens of ore. Specks of gold winked out of masses of quartz. Crystals of lead, shone like candelabra. Virgin copper blushed by the side of its green-eyed sister, the carbonate of the same metal. On the wall, above the chimney-piece, was a section of a quartz ledge in profile, which resembled a rocky giant, with his face carved as if into a fixed chuckle, over the nuggets buried in his capacious pockets. The corpulent gentleman produced a box of Partaga firsts, out of a drawer in his desk, and furtively drew forth from the recesses of a cupboard, a bottle which looked as though it might have been recently dusted, to give it the appearance of age. The liquid from this bottle, tasted of alum, burnt sugar, and bitter almonds, but the partagas were unimpeachable.

Then came business. Our host rattled away gaily, and at length remarked (quite incidentally) that he never speculated in railway-stocks. He thought that he was the true benefactor of the human race, who succeeded in developing the internal resources of his country. Then he took high patriotic grounds, and waxed eloquent. It was the bounden duty of every capitalist to take a pecuniary interest in the great work of bringing out the riches of that magnificent wilderness, stretching out from where the mighty

LOOKING FOR DIVIDENDS. BUBBLE COMPANIES. FIGHTING FOR STOCK.

father of waters rolled his torrent, to the shores of the Pacific, etc. At the conclusion of his oration, he exhibited his specimens. First, lead. We looked rather coldly on the fine crystals of this metal, as he turned them around and made them sparkle, for at that very moment, at least two of us had, folded up in very small compass in our pocket-books, several hundred shares of Buck's Lead Company, which the year before we had bought at the highest market price, and which was then selling at one dollar a share. He seemed quickly to discover the secret of our coldness on the subject of lead, and judiciously changed the subject, dropping his lead, and sounding us on the subject of gold. His free gold specimens were really splendid, but his sulphurets were his pride. They had been found to produce from five to twenty thousand dollars to the ton, by *assay*, and he showed us certificates of eminent chemists to that effect.

"Were these picked or only average specimens?"

"They were," he replied, "only average specimens, the run of the mine."

Next, he mentioned the names of leading public men associated with him in these laudable enterprises, and showed us their autographs on his books; and having at length exhausted his theme, concluded with a brief peroration, in which he did not fail delicately to hint at the immorality of stock-jobbing in Wall Street, and broadly express his conviction that every capitalist would do well to "salt down" a large proportion of his profits derived from stock-speculation, into something like a permanent investment in these mining enterprises, which could not fail to pay him a large return. He would only add, "that the demand for these shares was very great, and he could not say how long the opportunity would be open to subscribe for them." We had been inoculated and the virus worked.

In five days we were striking a bargain with the corpulent gentleman in gold-bowed spectacles, on the subscription price to four different gold mining companies, viz.: the Woolah-Woolah Gulch Gold Mining and Stamping Company. Capital, $3,000,000; shares numbering thirty thousand; par value, $100; subscription price, $60 per share. The Gulliver Canon Gold and Silver-Lead Mining and Water Sluice Company. Capital, $8,000,000; shares numbering one hundred and sixty thousand; par value, (we should not forget the par value,) $50; subscription price, $25 per share. The Federal Republic Gold Dust and Silver Dirt Mining Company. Capital, $2,500,000; shares numbering five hundred thousand; par value, $5; subscription price, $3 per share. (This was the biggest swindle of all). And, lastly, The Dry Digging and Gold Washing Company. Capital, $800,000; shares numbering twenty thousand; par value, $40; subscription price, $15 per share.

We objected to these subscription prices. We demanded to be let in, if at all, on the "hard-pan" price, and at length we thought we had carried our point, when twenty per cent. was knocked off from the subscription price, as a special favor, which fact, of course, we were never to mention to a living soul.

The mining-bubble fever rose higher as March rolled away. We began to look for other investments on the "hard-pan" basis. It was not difficult to find them. Opportunities presented themselves on the first story; and above us, on the second and third stories, below us in the basement, as well as in windows and hallways. The Newspapers teemed with them. Little boys stood on the corners and handed elegant prospectuses to the passers-by. Mineralogists and geologists were in clover.

We had commenced with gold and we ran down the scale according to value, through silver, copper, lead and graduated into iron. Then we commenced over again with the rocks, starting with marble, and ending in trap and sandstone. After that we got into fluids. This move carried us into petroleum, of which, more hereafter. E. O—— (a deacon) introduced us to iron and coal. The projector in this enterprise was another professional bubble-blower, who had an office not a thousand miles from Pine Street. He was a tall man, with a hang-dog look, a fringe of gray whiskers and a baritone voice, who delivered orations on the importance of getting ready to supply the South with iron and coal, as soon as the war was over. We took a few hundred shares of the Fallset Iron and Coal Company, against the happening of that much wished for and long expected event.

Late in March, the fever had risen to its height. One day about this time, E—— and I saw L—— issue from the swinging doors of a restaurant, looking very red and smiling. He hailed us beamingly, and announced to us the interesting fact, that on the morrow the books of the "Gregory Consolidated" would be opened at the office of J. R—— & Co. He had just spoken (he said) to three capitalists, who had told him (in confidence) that here was a great chance. "Don't fail to be on hand to-morrow," said he, "there is *only a limited* number of the shares to be had, and there will be a great rush to subscribe." Then jocularly bidding us to charge the next morning, where we saw his purple necktie wave, he disappeared through the door of the banking house of Morse & Co.

The next day, the 31st of March, was fine. The golden sun threw its golden rays on the curtains and carpets of our eastward-facing chamber, as E—— and I, rose bright and early, and throwing open the casement, like Parsees, paid it our adorations, as the tutelar genius, and fit symbol of Gregory Consolidated Gold Mining Company!

A crowd of expectant subscribers, were hovering about the office of J—— R—— & Co., at an early hour. Few of them were recognized as regular operators in the street. Most of them were outsiders who had come prepared to invest in something that *would pay*. One man, the proprietor of a millinery store, up town, pulled off his glove, and showed me four one thousand dollar bills, which he was about to cash down, in return for one hundred shares of G. C. Co. Another was a clergyman, from one of the river counties, who had taken the early train down to the city that morning, in order to secure fifty shares of the stock. Lawyers, doctors, mechanics, and retired capitalists were also fully represented As soon as the books were opened, L—— who was the tallest, and most robust of the quartette, succeeded in establishing himself in the line which extended from the counter, where the subscription book lay, to the street, not however without a brief, but severe struggle with a short resolute-looking countryman, who, after he had yielded his position, was heard stoutly affirming his right of precedence.

The capital stock of Gregory Consolidated was $5,000,000. Its shares numbered fifty thousand, at the par value of $100 each, and the subscription price was $40 per share. In one hour from the time when the books opened, the whole amount, $2,000,000, was subscribed!

A few tardy individuals now made their appearance, eager to subscribe, but too late. They bid two per cent. premium for four thousand shares, but in vain; the holders of the stock could not be induced to part with their precious investment. L—— divided his subscription of one thousand shares equally among the quartette. Then he led the way to the office of Morse & Co. We followed him, and here another scene took place. This time it was in Gunnell Gold Company, the subscription books of which were open at that office. The subscribers to this stock actually fought to get their subscriptions recorded. After a short struggle the whole capital was subscribed for, and $100,000 more. The subscribers to the overplus begged and importuned the projectors of the company to surrender to them the individual interest they had reserved for themselves. Their prayers were answered; the projectors generously waived their private interests and gave up their reserved stock to their petitioners.

During the six weeks which intervened between March 1st and April 10th, 1864, the nominal capital of the joint stock companies presented to the public in Wall Street, has been estimated at $300,000,000.

The nominal capital of mining enterprises organized since that time has reached the enormous sum of $5,000,000. The centre of speculation in gold and silver companies has for many years been in San Francisco. But after the exploitation of the big Bonanzas, the attention of New York capitalists was directed anew to speculation in mining stocks. The Mining Exchange was organized in the year 1877. San Francisco commission houses had their agents in New York, and operators made and lost fortunes in a day by buying and selling Consolidated Virginia, California, Belcher, Yellow Jacket, and the other famous mines of the Comstock Lode.

In the year 1879, just as the Nevada mines were giving out, new discoveries in Colorado furnished food for fresh speculation. The story of Leadville, and the wonders of those frozen ledges, reads more like a fairy tale than a statement of sober fact.

There are bubbles and bubbles, and then again there are solid nuggets, which will weigh heavy in the pocket, and will coin into eagles and stay by the lucky owner as long as he is content with his find, and does not pine for millions more and look for them by speculating in mining bubbles.

The Mining Board gave a new impetus to this form of speculation in 1877, '78, and '79. The new Open Board which went into operation in November, 1879, has added to the speculative furor and widened the circles of speculation still more.

CHAPTER XIX.

PANIC—FALL OF A. W. MORSE—CLEARING AWAY THE WRECK.

Going In for *Just One More Operation*—Standing on the Apex of a Fortune—The Bull-leader in His Glory—Helping the Unlucky Ones—Daniel Drew Selling Erie—A Constitutional Bull—The Last Spirt in Stocks—Signs and Auguries of the Disaster—Morse Trying to Sell Fort Wayne—Planning the Last Stroke—The Market Trembles, Totters and Falls—Panic All Day and All Night—The Evening Exchange Pandemonium—" 'Tis Done ; but Yesterday a King, and Now He is a Nameless Thing, so Abject yet Alive "—Morse After His Ruin—The Last Scene of all that " Strange Eventful Story "—The Fortunes of The Quartette—Meeting a Prophet of Evil—A Black Sunday and a Blue Monday—Bubble Company Stocks at a Discount.

WE may assert with confidence, that, granting these three things, viz.: that a man has become habituated to speculation in stocks; that he has $100,000 in the bank, and that he daily visits the stock-market; then, and in that case, he will be sure to make *just one more venture.*

The experience of hundreds and thousands of operators, will attest the truth of this proposition. Speculation, at first a sentiment, or if you please, a taste, passes next into a habit, then it grows into a passion, a master passion, which like Aaron's serpent, swallows up and strengthens itself with other passions. It becomes at last more fierce than anger, more gnawing than jealousy, more greedy than avarice, more absorbing than love. The stock-market may be likened to a withered old harridan, enameled, painted, and decked in the latest mode, which leers on the speculator, and points to golden prizes, that like the desert mirage, fades away and leaves him to his ruin. The chronicles of speculation are little else than a list of tornadoes and wrecks.

On the 10th of April I stood $160,000 ahead of the market, without counting the profits on Canton. One hundred thousand dollars of this amount was cash in bank, forty thousand was invested snugly and permanently in various enterprises, looking to the "development of the internal resources of the country," and twenty thousand was in the hands of brokers. Included in this amount, was the five thousand dollars margin on five hundred shares of Canton at 38. This was the apex of my fortunes, to which I had climbed, with the ladder of the five hundred dollars planted on Old Southern in 1857.

"*Facilis descensus Averni.*"

On the 1st of April, the bull-leader, Morse, was at the height of his glory. Every stock that he touched had turned into gold for the fortunate buyers. Rock Island, Erie, Fort Wayne, Pittsburg, Ohio and Mississippi certificates responded in succession to the wand of the great enchanter. Great fortunes had dropped from his hands into the pockets of his followers. Not content with making the rich richer, he had lifted many an unfortunate out of the slough of Wall Street poverty—the worse species of poverty—into affluence. One of these unfortunates was L. H——, who had lost everything—money, credit and friends. He went to Morse in the form of a mendicant, disclosing his forlorn condition and begging that he would assist him. Morse took him by the hand and told him to buy two hundred shares of Fort Wayne, and send it in to his (Morse's) office for his account. L. H——, instead of buying two hundred shares, bought seven hundred shares. Morse thought this a little cheeky, but took charge of the stock, and in six weeks, by this and other successful operations, under the wing of his generous banker, L. H—— made $50,000. Many such deeds as this marked the career of the great speculator, and should help to cover his after pecuniary short-comings.

During that brief, but brilliant campaign, he had fought the bears as one would his natural enemies, and now throughout the whole market, it was in vain to search for any of that tribe. Yes, there was one— an old veteran who did not fear to sell stocks. It could be no other than Daniel Drew. While Erie was selling from 128–130, every day a nimble young broker could have been seen reporting to him the price of Erie, whereat he would chuckle and give orders to sell by the thousand shares. He was converting his bonds into stock and delivering it to fill his contracts. He also obtained authority from the Legislature to increase the capital stock of Erie, and used ten thousand shares of the new stock to load up the bulls at these inflation prices.

Early in the month last named, there came a lull in the market. Then a sudden leap upwards, and the fire burned more fiercely than ever. It was like a tongue of flame, shooting from a palace, just before it falls in ruins; the funeral pyre of a thousand speculators. This spirt in the market, took place at the

Evening Exchange. It deceived many, and among them the writer of this narrative. Three times had the market been lulled into dullness, and each time the lull had been followed by a new burst upward. Then came regrets that I had ever sold out, and calculations of how much I would have made by holding my stocks.

W. B. C—— was a bull, from the crown of his head, to the sole of his foot. In all his veins there was never a drop of ursine blood. Consequently, he had not yet sold his stocks, which, for a man who started six months before, with only $6,000, showed him an enormous profit. "Let your profits run," was his constant cry. For two weeks he had fairly bristled with information, (commonly called "points,") respecting certain roads, especially Reading, Fort Wayne, and Galena. These stocks had hardly yet begun to rise. The names of the manipulators were a tower of strength. Money was so easy, and the bull-element was so powerful. The earnings of the roads, too, justified a further rise. Consolidation, Morse, W. B. Ogden, etc.,—these were the themes of his taurine dissertations.

On the morning after the last upward leap of stocks, I drew out sixty thousand dollars, distributed it among three different brokers and bought three thousand two hundred shares of railroad stocks of which one thousand was Galena, at 142; one thousand Fort Wayne, at 145; nine hundred (full shares) Reading, at 163, and three hundred Old Southern, at 117. Before night the market sagged and my stocks could not have been sold without a considerable loss. I was like a wild thing caught in a trap, not daring to break away with the loss of a limb, and waiting in terror the coming of the cruel hunter.

Miserable days passed away in agonies of doubt. There are seasons when Wall Street men are agitated by

"More pangs and fears than wars or women have."

when after fortune has smiled upon him, he suddenly sees her beginning to frown. He has incurred a small loss which he dares not accept, but fears every day a greater loss. If there is then any handwriting on the wall of the speculator's banqueting hall, he sees it, aye, and interprets it, perchance; and yet, though "the joints of his loins are loosed, and his knees smite one against another," he keeps his seat and flies not from the enemy as terrible to him as the Medes and Persians were to the king of Babylon.

Signs and portents of coming disaster multiplied, as that weary week drew to its close. Wise financial prophets like Jay Cooke, had been heard to predict an approaching evil. The Secretary of the Treasury had been selling millions of gold, and locking the proceeds in greenbacks, in the sub-treasury. Money was palpably tightening. Conservative banking-houses, such as Lockwood & Co., refused any longer to *buy* stocks on margins, or, except for cash; but offered to sell stocks short for their customers, on ten per cent. margins. Wild rumors were afloat, of how Morse had gone down on his knees to certain bank cashiers, and begged for a million dollars on Fort Wayne, as collateral, but without avail. At the Evening Exchange on Friday, the 15th of April, he mounted the rostrum beside the president, while one of his lieutenants stood beside him. In a husky voice, and with a feeble smile upon his haggard face, he offered to *sell* ten or twenty thousand shares of Fort Wayne. A shiver went through the hushed crowd, and low, ominous whispers were heard, "The bull leader isn't quite himself to-night." "What's the matter with Morse?" "Is he in liquor?" But all these signs of disaster failed to open the eyes of the deluded multitude, who still clung to their treacherous favorites.

Speculative fevers must run their course, before they turn the sharp corner which leads into the great darkness. Stocks had now reached this corner. Men's nerves are not of steel. Julius Cæsar had his Brutus, Anthony W. Morse had his Secretary Chase. The causes which were to precipitate ruin had been silently gathering force. The chain had been heated and welded, and rove into the huge block, which had been hoisted and suspended aloft. Its fall was to crush and pulverize the fabric of a thousand stately fortunes, and now the chain was to be severed by the hand of panic.

On Saturday the 16th, and Sunday the 17th, Morse took a survey of the market. He had six weeks before, pledged himself to a crowd of capitalists, who ranged under his banner, to lead them to victory and wealth. Now they crowded around him, and begged him to redeem his pledge. His resolution was soon taken. Like a commander-in-chief hard pressed by the enemy, he determined to abandon all his other fortresses, and concentrate his forces in one stronghold. Early on Monday morning he decided to sell all the other stocks he had, and then hold up Fort Wayne against all odds.

The 18th of April fell on Monday. The interval of Holy-day, had only strengthened the downward tendency. When he entered the regular board that morning, he found nearly every broker eager to sell at heavy concessions, before the call of stocks opened, and the feeling in the street was still worse. He turned and left the room. At half-past eleven o'clock, a broker rose in his seat, and announced the failure of Morse & Co. An appalling stillness, like that which precedes a tornado, followed the words, then the storm burst. The board-room seemed suddenly transformed into a Cyclopean work-shop, where a hundred great trip-hammers were being plied. Pillar after pillar toppled over, till the dome fell. The palace of enchantment, builded by a strong and cunning magician of so many golden hopes, passed away like a cloud-pageant.

A three months mad revelry of speculation, in which were concentrated all the emotions, all the incidents of a century of sober, legitimate traffic—then the dark dawn of another melancholy awakening!

All day long the panic raged, without pause or hindrance. The Evening Exchange was a Pandemonium. A crowd of ruined operators reeled and surged up to the rostrum, half crazed by their losses, and stupefied or maddened by drink, while the whole room rang with yells and curses. The space outside the railing was jammed with weary faces, on which was written only the word—ruin! Close to the door stood a figure in widow's weeds, wild eyed and shrinking. She had risked her last dollar on Fort Wayne, which was selling for 90. She stood there only for a moment, and then passed out into the damp, chilly night forever.

Above all the chorus of execrations was heard the word "Morse." Human nature now showed its basest side. No epithet too vile with which to couple the name of the prostrate financier. He had fallen like Lucifer in one day, from the zenith of his fame. The men who, but yesterday, extolled him to the skies, now vied with each other in cursing him. His failure was irreparable. He owed millions to his brother brokers, and to depositors, who had trusted him. The lion of the hour had become a dead jackass. The king of the market was a lurking fugitive. Men calling themselves gentlemen, met him in the street, and showered abuse upon him. Shoulder-hitters, who had lost some of their ill-gotten gains by his fall, sought him out, and struck him like a dog.

This was outrageous. Let us give Anthony W. Morse his due. He *was* a great arithmetician, a shrewd, far-seeing, bold financier. The subsequent history of some of the stocks in which he dealt with such recklessness, has justified his then apparently wild predictions. Fort Wayne, Rock Island, and Pittsburg have proved a mine of wealth to those who bought them in December, 1864, and have held them to the present day. He was a free-hearted generous man, and would if he could, have nullified the decrees of fate, and made the fortunes of his followers. But like most great speculators he got at last to believe in his star. Then he attempted impossibilities. A longer and more cautious training in the school of finance, and it might have been different. But it was not so ordained. The example of A. W. Morse, only serves as a moral to close the lesson taught by Wall Street speculation.

His end speaks to all like a warning voice. He departed from the arena, a stripped, penniless, heart-stricken man. Out of the troops of wealthy friends which but lately clustered about him, only one or two still clung to him. He had now only the shadow of a great name. He was pointed out in the streets as the man who had once set the market in a blaze, but capitalists shrunk from him as if he had the leprosy. His attenuated face now and then flitted past the streaming throng in Broadway. One day, more than a year after his failure, he was seen on the street, and Fort Wayne *rose five per cent.* His name still spread alarm among the bears, and inspired the bulls with new courage, like Ziska's drum beaten at the front of the battallions of the departed king. Then came disease gnawing at his nerves and heart-strings. He became a changed man. No longer blithe and gay of mien, but morose and irritable. The vast burden of his debts and losses wore upon him. He sought relief in gambling, his old excitement, but under a new form. A gentleman who had lost by Morse's failure, one evening visited, out of curiosity, a notorious gambling hell in Twenty-fourth Street. Sitting near the dealer was one whom he remembered having seen in happier days. A gaunt, pallid face, the features sharpened by the fell disease under which he was suffering, and wearing those death-like lines with which consumption marks its prey. Alas! how changed from that Morse, who but the year before, had led his dashing ranks to the summits of the market. A few months more and he lay upon his death-bed in a second-class boarding-house, and without means to pay for the common necessities of life.

Even when he died, his landlady held his body for the trifling debt which he owed her. It was only when some friend stepped forward and paid the sum, that the funeral rites could be performed over all that remained of what was once a king of Wall Street.

The feeling and condition of the stock-men, after the panic of April 18th, 1864, had subsided, can never be forgotten by the actors in those scenes. Wall Street was like a city of the dead, a kind of Pompeii or Herculaneum, when the volcanic fires were still seething, and the lava still hardly cooled, which had buried, in the course of one brief sun, the high raised hopes, the garnered fortunes, and the financial identity of thousands. Men hardly dared inquire what might be the status of their debtors, for fear they should know too clearly, the certainty and irreparableness of their own losses.

In the midst of this universal distrust, unfounded rumors were bruited abroad, concerning the solvency of wealthy houses. One report said that Lockwood & Co. had failed. Another, that D. Groesbeck & Co. had succumbed, but this latter story was promptly squelched, by the card of that firm, published in the daily journals, showing the snug amount of $1,300,000 to their credit in bank, and offering to carry stocks on a reasonable margin, and at six per cent. interest.

But how stood the quartette after the storm? During the week preceding the panic, we were engaged in bolstering each other up, not by money, for we thought ourselves impregnable in that respect, but with arguments in favor of another rise. We knew we were wrong, but tried to convince ovrselves that we were right. On Saturday, the pressure of our internal convictions became too strong to withstand. We decided to unload. And now we made the same mistake, made by so many others. We limited our brokers in the price at which they were to sell. I succeeded in getting rid of three hundred shares of Old Southern, at a loss of $2,800. The afternoon found me with two thousand nine hundred shares still on hand, on which there was by this time a heavy loss, of which I was reminded, in a disagreeable way, by a call from various brokers, *for more margin*. L—— thought there was a "better feeling," towards night. E—— said that he had resolved to hold his stocks through everything, and W. B. C—— said there would be a reaction next week, and hummed "rally round the flag boys, rally round the flag:" but this patriotic pæan sounded like a dirge, as he hummed it.

We started to go home early in the afternoon. At the corner of William Street and Exchange Place, we met S——. He was once a man of wealth, but he had left it all in that same unfathomable abyss on the brink of which we were just then standing. He was a harmless but very disagreeable lunatic, a Cassandra, who predicted nothing but evil. A horrible man to look upon. The skin on his face was like yellow wrinkled parchment, his mouth a chasm, his eyes a glassy blue, over all of which a ghastly smile constantly played. He had for six weeks been uttering his doleful prophecies. When he caught sight of us, he began to throw up his hands and give vent to hollow laughs, which grated very disagreeably on our keyed-up nerves. "I told you so! I told you so! Ha, ha, ha!" We tried to shake him off, but he stuck to us like a leech, hovered about us like an owl, and chuckled when he had wrenched out of us the reluctant acknowledgment that we had not yet sold our stocks. This conversation was unpleasant to men who had lost altogether during the past four days, one hundred thousand dollars. At last he left us, shaking his skinny fingers in our faces, and telling us to "look sharp at stocks on Monday, and see how we came out." S—— was only one of the prophets of evil who seemed to dog our steps during the next thirty-six hours. We met them at the Evening Exchange, in the Fifth Avenue Reading Room, on the street, everywhere. Just as E—— and I were doffing our unmentionables preparatory to seeking our couches in that room, which three weeks before had been illuminated by the sun of "Gregory Consolidated," but which now was barely lighted from the single gas jet, which burned blue on that moist spring evening, L—— made his appearance and said he had just heard P——, a wealthy operator offer a heavy bet that Morse would break before the next week was past.

The Sunday's rest and quiet weighed upon us like an incubus. On Monday, we screwed our courage to the sticking point, and gave the order to sell every thing at the market price. But this order was not given till after the failure of Morse had been announced. The quartette stood by the door of the Regular Board for one hour. E—— was looking pale, L—— scowling; W. B. C—— strove to look cheerful, and failed.

In three hours we knew the very worst. Out of

$120,000 cash in hand the week before, only about $20,000 was left to me. The Canton profits and margin were swept away, and I held only my mining stocks as the memento of my forty thousand loose cash. These stocks were neither saleable nor negotiable, of which fact I was disagreeably reminded by the sardonic smile of my bank cashier, when I applied to him the day after the panic, for a small loan of $1,000 on what had cost me $40,000.

CHAPTER XX.

MARGINS, POOLS, CORNERS, POINTS, AND OF HOW BROKERS MAKE THEIR MONEY.

Philosophy of Rises and Panics in Wall Street—Margins Before and Since 1862—Effect of Doing Business on Margins—Different Kinds of Pools—Percentages Paid by Bears for the Privilege of Selling Stocks—Do Pools Pay?—Instances of Unsuccessful or Successful Pools—Why They are Generally Unsuccessful—Trying to Unload Upon the Shoulders of the Outsiders—Points! What are They?—Engineering a Short Interest—How Brokers Make Money in Pools—The Time to Buy, and the Time to Sell Stocks—They Sell or Buy in the Stocks of their Customers—The Percentage Paid for Carrying and Turning Stocks—Jolly Old Boys Keeping Their Dimes Busy.

THE first thing a man does after he has recovered from the shock of a great and mysterious disaster, is to philosophize about the causes of that disaster in particular, and other disasters of a similar nature.

When do great rises and great panics in stocks take place? Rises take place when the majority of operators *desire* to buy and buy. Panics, when the majority of operators *desire* to sell and sell. By the term *majority* I mean the greater number of persons, and the larger amount of *money*.

This brings us to the matter of *margins*, a word which we have already defined. This word *margins* contains the *essence of stock-speculation*. Great fortunes are made and lost by speculating on margins.

It is the facility with which large amount of stocks can be bought with a small amount of money-margin, that stimulates great rises, and it is the facility with which those same money-margins are wiped out when stocks fall, that creates the fear which precipitates a panic.

As already described, the amount of the margin depends on circumstances. Before the late war, stocks could be bought generally on five per cent. of the par value of the stock; *e. g.*, a hundred shares of New York Central of the par value of $10,000 (market value 70) called for five hundred dollars margin.

But the heavy fluctuations in prices produced by the greenback inflation which commenced in 1862, rendered larger margins necessary to guard the broker against loss. Ten per cent., and by conservative brokerage houses, twenty per cent. was then generally exacted from their customers. But many of the new tribe of brokers who did business on the curb-stone or in the Public Board, were still willing to buy stocks on five and even three per cent, margin, protecting themselves against loss by continually watching the market and selling their customers' stocks on the least alarm.

It will be readily seen that as the fear of loss is stronger when a man has bought stocks on a small margin, he will be more likely to sell frequently and change his position continually, very much, of course, to the advantage of his broker. One brokerage firm, doing business on small margins, has derived an immense income in commissions from their customers in this way. When everything is bright and stocks are advancing, brokers are often very liberal in allowing their customers to buy, but when a panic comes, accompanied by a scarcity of money, they will refuse to carry stocks on any amount of margin. Their customer must then either pay for his stocks in cash, or *sell them*. The latter is generally the only practicable course The stocks are accordingly slaughtered, *i. e.*, sold out at low figures with loss, and even ruin to the customer. This was the case in the panic of April, 1873. Man, everywhere a gregarious animal, is never more so than when in Wall Street. A flock of sheep following the bell wether trotting up hill,—this is a picture of the stock market, during a rise. Now supposing that same flock sees, on the top of the hill, a scare-crow; it wheels about and rushes down hill twice as fast as it goes up. Lambkins are trampled under the feet of their maternal ewes, and the bell wether tumbles head over heels. When the flock reaches the bottom of the hill, it turns about and stares with innocent wonder, at the scare-crow on the top of the hill. This is a picture of the stock-market in a panic. Everybody seems crazy to sell. The customers dog their broker's footsteps, begging them, as a personal favor, to sell their stocks at any price, only to sell immediately. The brokers are apparently as eager to sell as their customers. Capitalists who might keep their stock, catch the infection and sell. To crown all, the bears emerge from their dens, swell the panic-chorus, and sell everything in expectation of lining their pockets by the decline.

Such are some of the beauties of the margin system. In fact a margin may be called a device contrived to create rises and panics, and to keep the market in a ferment, so that brokers may make, and their customers lose, money.

As for pools, cliques and rings; terms which are used synonymously in these pages, these combinations are traps in more senses than one, for they not only serve to ensnare the bears by cornering them, but generally to result in loss to the members of the combinations themselves.

Pools are of different kinds.

First, there is the secret pool, the operations whereof are carried on in darkness, until some fine day the bears find themselves unexpectedly in a tight place.

Second, the open and above-board pool, into which the bears walk, because the very frankness with which the combination talk of their plan, leads the bears to suppose that there is nothing in it, for who would suspect a poolist of frankness. This species of combination is of rare occurrence.

Third, the moderate pool, which is satisfied with five or ten per cent. advance in the stock under manipulation. Daniel Drew often engineered Erie on this plan, taking in as his associates, only one or two members, and holding only five, ten or twenty thousand shares of the floating stock in some favorable conjuncture of the market.

Fourth, the grasping and voracious pool, which aims at the entire control of a certain stock and the extermination of outside sellers.

Fifth, the vindictive pool, which aims to punish its opposers. Vanderbilt and Gould severally tried their hands at this game.

Pools may be also classified into two other forms.

First, those having for their object the raising of

stocks, artificially, irrespective of their intrinsic values. The more worthless the stock, the more men will go short of it. This better enables the combination to manipulate the stock, and finally to compel the short sellers to settle up on the terms which they may dictate, the Cumberland pool of 1866 and 1867, when that worthless fancy was raised from 35 to 90 is an example.

Second, those having for their object, the control of stocks possessing a high intrinsic value. The New York Central pool of 1868–9 is an instance of this second species.

By far the larger portion of the short sales now made in Wall Street, are transacted by selling the stock, and then borrowing it for delivery. Suppose B—— desires to go short of Erie, when all the floating stock is in the hands of a pool. B—— has no Erie stock, remember, but sells, that is agrees to deliver, one hundred Erie at 30, to C——. He then borrows the one hundred shares of the pool, and delivers it to C——, who pays for it by a certified check for $3,000. This certified check B—— passes over to the pool, and then owes it (the pool) one hundred shares of Erie, which is payable on demand. On returning them one hundred shares of Erie, the pool pays B—— his $3,000. If the stock should go up to 40, B—— in that case, if called upon for the stock, is obliged to go into the market and pay $4,000 for his Erie, thus losing $1,000 by the operation, which sum is presumed to go into the pockets of the combination. In some cases, when the pool has control of all, or nearly all the floating stock, they compel B—— to pay them a fixed sum, instead of calling upon him to return the stock. When a pool holds most of the floating stock of a railroad or other company, they are in a position to play the lock-up game, in other words to make the corner. They call upon the bears to whom they have loaned stock, to return it, and if they fail to do so, they buy them in under the rule as already described, or allow them to keep their contracts open by paying a fixed sum daily, for that privilege. As high as one per cent. per day, *i. e.*, one hundred dollars for each hundred shares of the stock due, has been sometimes exacted. The bear, it will be remembered, gets interest generally on his contract, but in this case, he is paying interest at the ruinous rate of over three hundred per cent. per annum, and may be in addition finally compelled to buy in his stock at a heavy loss.

The difference in price between *cash stock* which is deliverable and payable the same day it is bought, and regular stock which is deliverable and payable the next day, has occasionally run as high as five per cent., and in the case of stock sold, seller three, as high as ten per cent., and of a stock sold, seller thirty, as high as thirty per cent. Difference has been paid between the seller's option price and the cash price. But this occurs rarely, except when a general locking-up of the stock by a pool takes place, and is invariably when the pool is trying to unload, or to compel the bears to cover.

How many of these combinations make money out of their operations? Very few. A large number actually lose money. A bare list of those which have proved disastrous to their projectors, would fill the rest of this chapter. Among them, we may note the

Morris Canal and Banking Pool, of some thirty years since. In this case, the bears refused to settle their contracts, and the matter was left to the arbitration of the Board of Brokers, who decided that it was a conspiracy, and accordingly released the bears from their contracts. In the Norwich and Worcester Pool, Jacob Little lost $1,000,000, as related in our fourth chapter.

Since the year 1860–62, the successful pools may be almost numbered on one's fingers, while the names of those unsuccessful are legion. The Hudson combination, which carried that stock to 180, in the summer of 1863, is said to have divided 12 per cent. among its members.

Of all the pools formed during the great rise of 1864, there was scarcely one, if any, that did not finally end in heavy loss to its members. The Morse Rock Island pool of December, 1863, and January, 1864, is said to have netted a profit of only 4½ per cent. But all the members of this combination, we believe, without exception, allowed their profits to remain in the hands of the bull-leader, until the panic of April following, swept them away. The great Pacific Mail pool, already mentioned, and more fully to be described hereafter, could however, hardly have failed to show a handsome profit to each of its members. The Vanderbilt pools have been thoroughly successful, because they have continued to hold and control the stocks of the Harlem, Hudson, and New York Central. But, the pool in Erie which lasted a year from April, 1865, to the same month in 1866, under the direction of Daniel Drew, is said to have netted a heavy loss to all its members except the old man and one or two of his friends. The same is true of the Erie pool, which lasted five or six months, during the summer and fall of 1866. The Garner pool in St. Paul in 1868 was a failure. The Pacific Mail pools of 1872 netted a profit of a million dollars to Jay Gould, who retired from them in good season, while Alden B. Stockwell stayed in them too long and lost two millions dollars. Gould, Clark, and Schell are reported to have made nothing from the rise in Northwest to 230 in the same year, notwithstanding the large sums paid them by those who were short of the stock. Eugene N. Robinson suffered very severely from the losses entailed by his attempt to put Lake Shore from 51½ to 70 in the winter of 1876. The Sam. M. Mills Western Union pool, in 1876–7, lost largely in trying to put that stock to 80.

The Northwest and St. Paul rings, in the spring and summer of 1878, after putting up those stocks thirty per cent., were heavy losers by the break in July of that year. The pools of 1879 have been successful thus far, but may be losers in the end.

It will not be difficult to explain why it is that pools are so generally unsuccessful. Sometimes a powerful combination will lock up money and thus break down their rivals by compelling them to sell out their stocks. Sometimes the directors of a railroad will secretly issue a large amount of new stock, sell it to the pool at high prices, and then proclaim the fact of the new issue. This causes a panic in the stock and the pool is broken up.

One of the greatest obstacles to the success of a pool is the treachery of its members, who, knowing when the summit price is reached, sell out their interest, and perhaps go short of the stock besides. In this way, the pool find themselves saddled with a large amount of stock at high prices, since they are obliged to buy all the stock offered in the market, in order to keep up the price. Thereupon, after shouldering the weary weight for a season, they are forced at last to let it drop amid a hail-storm of anathemas from the poolists against their treacherous associates. Again, supposing a pool has raised the price of the stock thirty per cent. above its original value, it does not follow from that circumstance that a profit of thirty per cent. will accrue. The cost of the stock bought at different prices, may average within ten per cent. of the inflated price, and after the short contracts have all been closed, the pool may find itself unable to sell at even an average of twenty per cent. below the ruling price.

All sorts of inventions are resorted to in that case. Sometimes a new pool is organized on the basis of the then market price, golden hopes are held out of putting the stock very much higher; new members are brought in and urged to take a large interest, so that the old members may slip out. If this plan is not feasible, various influences are brought to bear on the outside buyers, to induce them to come in and take the load. In some cases, the stock is allowed to drop heavily, and a new crop of bear contracts are garnered up; then the price is run up again, and the bears cover their contracts at a loss to themselves and at a profit to the ring. This process is repeated several times, the price going lower at each successive drop, until the ring, or pool, can show a net profit, or what is more probable, a net loss, on all their operations.

Pools and points, the two P's of Wall Street, are inseparably connected. A "point," as the reader is doubtless well aware, is a piece of information furnished by one operator to another, respecting the upward or downward course of a stock. The operator who gives the point, is presumed to know what he is talking about. He may have intimate relations with the director of some railroad company, the stock of which is actively dealt in, or he may himself be a director. Perhaps he is known to do his business in the office of a prominent brokerage-house, where pools are organized, or, which is more probable, he may be a member of a pool.

No one who has speculated in stocks, will have failed to notice how eagerly information is sought for, by parties interested in stocks. When a man is writhing under the sense of expected loss, or wildly eager to grasp a profit, his mind is like a photographer's negative plate, ready to receive the subtlest impressions. The first question which an operator asks his fellow, on meeting him in the morning, or in fact at any time during the day, is, "What do you think?" If he is a German, he says, "Vot you dinks?" If a Frenchman, "Vich is dat of vich you teenks?" He wishes to get an opinion respecting stocks, and this question often leads him to "points." These points are often given as merely rumors floating in the market, which the informant does not vouch for; he merely gives them as he has heard them. Sometimes, they are breathed into the ear of the operator, as facts not generally known, but which are now communicated to him alone, under the pledge of the strictest secrecy. The susceptible mind of the recipient of the rumors or facts, promptly makes its decision, and then acts on it, buying or selling, as the case may be. Thereafter he imparts the "point" to his nearest friend, who does not fail to spread the information for the benefit of *his* nearest friend.

In this manner, pools are enabled to engineer a short interest in a stock, and when they are ready to unload, they also make free use of points, in order to get the public to take their stock off from their hands.

Short sales are indispensable to a pool. A large part of the stock which they buy, is not actual stock, but contracts for the future delivery of stock, *i. e.*, short sales. These short sales benefit them in several ways, especially by enabling them to *carry* the stock by lending it to the short sellers. When a stock is heavily oversold at a low price, it is almost certain to go up, just as when the majority of operators are long of stocks at a high price it is as certain to fall.

Various methods are adopted to entice operators to sell short the stock which a pool have under their manipulation. Sometimes the price is made to simulate a weakness which deceives the street by producing the false impression that the price will soon be lower. This is the partridge trick. That game bird, it will be remembered, flutters as if wounded, in order to draw the hunter away from her young. As soon as the price of a stock looks "weak," it becomes the mark for short sales. The bears rush in and sell it under the expectation of a further decline. After a sufficient number of the contracts of these gentlemen have been taken by the pool, the price is lifted again, and the short sellers find themselves in the trap. This in the slang of the street is known as the "scoop game."

Instances are not unfrequent where members of the pool are paid by their leaders to solicit and procure short sales. One quarter per cent. has been occasionally paid on the short sales influenced and procured in this way.

B——, a member of the pool goes to a friend or acquaintance and gives him a "point." The pool, he may say is short of money, and is paying heavy rates to have their stock carried, or he may simply decry the market value of the stock. If, on the faith of what he says, his friend should sell one hundred shares, the operator receives twenty-five dollars for his wages. This amounts to robbery, for it is nothing else than hiring a man to put his hand into his friend's pocket and taking one, two or three thousand dollars therefrom, and delivering it to the pool, since the short sale thus induced, is quite certain to be covered at a loss.

We have stated that scarcely any one ever makes any money in these stock pools. We should except from this statement the brokers, who, whether the pool ever divides a profit or not, are sure to receive their profit. If they are members of the pool, they know exactly when to slip out. If they are merely the manipulators of the stock, they know just when to buy and just when to realize their profit outside of the combination. Their surest source of profit, however, is from the enormous brokerages resulting from the purchases and sales which they make for the pool's account. During the three, six or nine months that the operations of one of these operators may continue, the whole capital stock of a railroad amounting, perhaps, to six or eight millions, may be bought and sold by the brokers of the combination, four or five times over, and the brokerage on these transactions often amounts to more than $50,000. Besides this brokerage, there are multitudes of pickings in the way of interest and profitable turns, which help out the sum total.

In general speculation, everything seems to work for the benefit of the broker. One of his principal sources of revenue which we have already alluded to, is the use he makes of his customer's stocks.

It is an adage in the stock-market, that the outside public, as it is called, buys stocks when they are high, and sells them when they are low. When a dull season has been succeeded by an active market, and stocks have risen very high, the entire speculative community seems to have emptied itself into the purlieus of the stock-market. From many a lonely hamlet, from many an inland city, as well as from the brown-stone fronts, and marble hotels of the great metropolis itself, they pour amain into Wall Street, to *buy high-priced stocks.* A few weeks before, the same stocks at a price twenty per cent. lower, failed to tempt them, but now, stocks have become suddenly valuable. "Points" are communicated on every side, with the greatest freedom. The prevailing feeling says *buy.* The broker says *buy.* The pools say *buy*, for this rampant market is their harvest time, in which they shuffle off their loads upon the shoulders of the new gangs of buyers.

The hour and the men for the brokers have now both

come. The public give orders to buy these high priced stocks. The brokers execute their orders, and buy. But speedily a cracking sound is heard. The market prices begin to break. The broker quietly throws his customer's stocks on the market. This helps on the decline. The customer, in sad unconsciousness that his stocks have been sold, clings to his supposed loss. Then he is called upon for more margin, but when stocks have fallen ten or fifteen per cent. from where he has bought, they no longer seem valuable, and at last he gives the order to sell, as eagerly as but lately he gave the order to buy. His margin has been transferred to the broker's pocket. This having been accomplished, the customer begins to regret that instead of buying, he did not sell short, and thus profit by the decline. Whereupon he studies the market. It has gone down, (reasons he) to be sure, but not so low as it might go. It is quoted now as "weak," and "heavy." The "points" now are in favor of selling. He sells short at the low price, but scarcely has he done so when the market suddenly stiffens, and he finds that he has made another mistake. Still he clings to his loss. The broker, on his part, seeing the market advancing, promptly buys in the stock of which his customer is short, and when the market has risen nearly to the limit of the customer's margin, he notifies him of this fact, and asks what shall be done. Ten chances to one that the customer thereupon orders him to buy in and cover the short contract, not knowing that it has been already covered at a much lower figure. Thus the broker makes another profit out of his customer. This process is kept up, the customer buying at high, and selling at low prices, till his money and patience alike are exhausted, and he retires from the scene of his labors, to renew his strength, and after a time returns refreshed and replenished, to repeat the same old moves, buying when everything is selling at summit prices, and selling when the market is depressed and weak.

One of the most attractive forms of speculation to operators of small means during the years 1877, 1878, and 1879 has been operating in "privileges," *i. e.*, "puts," "calls," "spreads," and "straddles," the two last named being combinations of a "put" and a "call." A shrewd and lucky operator will sometimes make, in a few days, one thousand per cent. on his capital invested. Of course it is absolutely essential that the capitalist who sells these privileges should be a "solid man," and it so happens that one of the wealthiest operators in the market sells every year from 500,000 to 1,000,000 shares in the shape of either "puts," "calls," "spreads," or "straddles." This operator is Russell Sage, who is reputed to be worth $10,000,000, and therefore his contract is A1. A fresh-complexioned, gray-bearded old gentleman, rising sixty years, he has his office at No. 80 Broadway, where Gould and several members of the Union Pacific and Southwest pool also have their headquarters; here he holds a *levee* daily, brokers and speculators flocking to his office by the hundred to buy his gilt-edged contracts.

There are two reasons, among others, why these privileges are so popular this year (1879): first, because the market has been a very fluctuating one, and second, because when an operator has bought one of these contracts he has limited his loss, and at the same time has the chance afforded, in a rapidly fluctuating market, of making something handsome.

Mr. Sage is said to derive an income of nearly one million dollars per annum from the sale of these privileges; other operators, E. G. Keene, Gould, Kennedy, etc., also sell them. The business done in them is so large that the stock commission house of Voorhees & Imbrie, members of the Stock Exchange, have made a specialty in operating for their customers in Sage's privileges.

Great profits are not infrequently made by those who buy these gilt-edged contracts. D. P. Morgan and Charles J. Osborn, both noted speculators, made one hundred thousand dollars apiece by buying "puts" of Jay Gould in Union Pacific just before the great rise in that stock early in 1875, and using the "puts" to buy stock against. The amount of cash embarked in this transaction was ten thousand dollars, and the profit was made inside of thirty days.

Russell Sage sells thirty day "straddles" for from $300 to $400, and thirty day "spreads," ten per cent. apart, for $100. This looks very attractive, but as a matter of fact the average operator can do little better than keep himself from losing while speculating in this way, although once and again he may make a monstrous profit.

Sometimes Sage is caught badly, being obliged to shoulder thousands of shares "put" to him at a high price after the market has gone through a panic, but as he can pay cash for tens of thousands of shares by drawing on his corpulent bank account, he has only to wait, and in a few weeks or months the market may rise and let him out without any loss.

As a general rule money begets money, and the money kings gather in profits from many sources in the course of stock dealings. Not the least of these sources of profit is the interest paid them for carrying stocks. In times of money stringency the wealthier class of brokers derive a large revenue by carrying stocks for their brethren whose waists are, pecuniarily speaking, slenderer.

These "common carriers" on the Wall Street road, are, many of them, capitalists who have retired from the active business of buying and selling, and are content to earn twenty or thirty per cent. on their money by carrying stocks. Sleek old boys, with blushing autumnal faces, surrounded by snowy December locks and beard, they keep their nimble sixpences always busy, and like the ivy-green which "creeps o'er ruins old," they fatten and flourish in times of panic, or when the interest rate is cent per cent.

Douglas Jerrold wittily defined marriage as the result of an insane desire on the part of a young man to pay a young woman's board. Speculation may be in like manner defined as an insane desire on the part of a stock operator to pay the board and make the fortune of a broker.

CHAPTER XXI.

THE SECOND HARLEM CORNER.

More Figuring on Balances—Gathering Up the Fragments—A Flyer on Five Hundred Fort Wayne for Cash—What Can I Sell Short?—One Solitary Column Standing Erect Among a Heap of Ruins—The Commodore Holds up Harlem and Waits for His Revenge—"Sell Harlem at 190, and now You're Right"—History and Causes of the Second Harlem Rise—The Plot to Break Harlem—The Counterplot—The Stock on the Rampage—The Biters Bit—The Greatest of All the Bears in the Trap—Daniel Drew Selling Calls—A Lobby-engineer with a Broken Wing—Bears Dancing on Red-hot Plates—The Commodore says, "Put Up the Price to One Thousand"—The *Coup de Grace* to All the Bears—How I Came Out on Selling Harlem Short—A Cotton Operation.

IN the Arabian Nights' Entertainments there is a story of an honest butcher, who sold meat to a magician, and received his pay in what he thought was money, which he carefully laid away, but when he went to count his hoard, he found instead of gold coin, nothing but withered leaves. This tale exactly illustrates the condition of stock-speculators, after the panic of April 18th, 1864. Instead of golden profits, they had only a beggarly account of minus balances. Many of them had simply lost their all. Others were largely indebted to their brokers. The sole assets of some, were debts due from their brokers, who had failed flat. He might be accounted fortunate, who had a few thousands left, with which to begin over again.

The quartette met by appointment, at the office

of L——, at eleven A. M., April 19th. Four weary leaden-eyed men, breathless and scathed, after a three months' storm, ending in thunder, lightning, and wreck. A dead silence, and then W. B. C—— took out his pencil gloomily, and commenced figuring on a sheet of paper. Poor fellow! He had been hit hard. His two brokers had failed, and out of what was worth $78,000 one short week before, he had only $500 in cash left. The rest of his assets were what his brokers owed him, (about $15,000,) the certificates of those confounded mining companies, and a *call* for two hundred shares of Harlem, at 175. E—— could muster only $8,000 in cash, and *his* mining company certificates. L——, out of $190,000, had $28,000 in cash, and *his* certificates.

I turned my pockets inside out, and took a new inventory of assets. Result: $20,000 cash, the bubble certificates of course, and a small paper, three inches by four, which declared me entitled to call on a well-known operator, for two hundred shares of Harlem at 200, any time within sixty days, from the fifth day of April.

By Plutus! Wait a bit! What is this? A memorandum of $175,000 at par in 7 3-10 bonds, with a margin of $8,000 and accumulated profits of at least twice as much more! I had forgotten all about this transaction during the fierce campaign just over. The bonds had all this time been snugly lying in the vaults of different savings banks, drawing interest, while I was sleeping or trying to "work the oracle" on 'Change. Then I commenced figuring in hot haste.

Ten months interest in gold on $175,000, 7 3/10, ...	$10,645 80
Premium on gold at 170—70, ...	7,452 06
	$18,097 86

The interest charged by the savings banks of 5½–6 per cent. in currency, had been paid for six months in advance, in January. The bonds were selling, even in that panicky season, at 109. This swelled my profits $8,000 more, for the bonds had only cost me 104–105. I had $46,000 to start the ball rolling once more. After our figuring had been thus completed, we held a council of war, and decided upon the following policy, viz: First, to buy only as much stock as we could pay for. Second, to look about, and see if there was any high-priced stock, which it would answer to sell short, for the late panic had taught us the bear-lesson, that money could be made by selling stocks at a high price.

I now leave L——, E—— and W. B. C——, to shift for themselves, for a season, and give my individual experience while endeavoring to construct a new edifice out of the debris of my late high-piled fortunes.

What could be bought for cash which would pay best? On taking a survey, I pitched upon Fort Wayne, my old favorite. It had fallen from 153 to 90. But after every severe panic there is always a sharp recovery of prices, or as it called, "the reaction." This is often produced by the fact that the bears sell largely of stocks which they do not actually hold, and when prices have reached the bottom of the hill, they rush in to cover their shorts by buying. Fort Wayne had already begun to feel this reaction, and was now selling for 101. I asked one of my brokers—the least shaky of them—if he would buy five hundred Fort Wayne, if I would give him $20,000 in cash and orders on three savings banks for $175,000, 7 3-10 bonds, which he might sell on the first of May, the margin and accumulations being $26,000. He hummed and hawed, looked distrustful (for money was five per cent. a month, and the whole street was ringing with reports of failures), and finally inquired if everything was right and regular about the bonds.

"Send your boy up and get the orders accepted, if you are not satisfied with what I tell you."

"All right, I'll take your word for it. You must excuse my suspicions, but the whole street just now is rotten, you know."

The five hundred Fort Wayne was bought at 102. This purchase was made in fear and trembling. We were not yet out of the jaws of the panic.

If we could judge from the doleful looks of bank cashiers and money-lenders, everything said *sell!* The whole street was in ruins. Of all the stately columns, one only, still stood erect. It was Harlem, which now loomed up like Pompey's pillar under a desert sky. It had reeled and quivered during the storm, but stood bravely at the height of 190. Beside this solitary column, like Marius among the ruins of Carthage, sat a grim old man, brooding over his wrongs, and preparing to revenge them. Our Marius was none other than Cornelius Vanderbilt. For thirty days his masons had been at work rearing the column of Harlem, while the Commodore propped and buttressed it with four millions of hard cash. It was to be the engine with which he would accomplish his revenge. To sell Harlem short at that time, would seem in the light of what afterwards happened, to be little less than madness.

But Harlem, selling at 190, nearly everybody said was more than one hundred per cent. higher than its true value. It was held up by artificial means. It would break down heavily at sometime, and if a man would sell it for future delivery, and *stay short of it*, he would make a great profit. So said they who understood not the true significance of the Harlem movement. My broker evidently thought it a great piece of folly to buy Fort Wayne at par, as I had done an hour before, but when I spoke of going short of Harlem at 190, his face lighted up as if he would say "Now you're right."

The order was given, "Sell two hundred Harlem at 190–195." In three minutes a tall, slender individual (one of the Commodore's men) had gobbled my two hundred shares, with an air and look that reminded us of young Oliver asking for more. I was short of Harlem at 190, and long of Fort Wayne at 101. My position was apparently in strict accordance with that great maxim, *sell stocks when they are high, and buy them when they are low*. This maxim was verified by the rapid upward movement in Fort Wayne. During the next four days it rose to 129. Profits on this operation, $12,000. The maxim, however, was utterly falsified by the rise of Harlem during the same period, to 230. When it reached 200, I sold two hundred shares more at that price, and gave my broker orders to sell two hundred shares more, when the price reached 210. It touched 210 almost as soon as I had given the order. My broker had just time to sell two hundred Harlem at 210, and then up it bounded to 220.

My profits on Fort Wayne were being swallowed up in the Harlem shorts. It was a race between a bull and a bear, between buying stocks for a rise and selling them for a fall. I bought Canton at 35, and sold it at 40, with a profit of $3,000, but my short Harlem eat up that profit, and stood me still $1,500 out of pocket. I bought other stocks and made profits every time on my purchases, but Harlem kept relentlessly moving up and the profits I made on my purchases were not sufficient to cancel the fresh losses which accrued from Harlem as it rose.

But before giving the result of this race, it may not be uninteresting to the reader to go back and give a brief history of the Harlem rise, with the causes which produced it.

As we remarked in a preceding chapter, the primary object which Vanderbilt had in view in buying so largely of Harlem in 1862 and 1863, was the investment of some of his spare millions, in order to make him snug and comfortable in his old age, for already he clearly foresaw that Harlem, under proper management, would soon pay dividends. When he found himself opposed and thwarted by his enemies, in the courts of law, in the Common Council and elsewhere, he turned upon and twisted Harlem up to 180, and in this way punished his enemies, who had sold it short in expectation that the measures they had taken would depress the stock to a very low point.

After that and in the fall of 1863, the price had fallen back to 75–90. The matter of the franchise grant now rested with the Legislature, and the new campaign in Harlem was to be fought in Albany. Soon after the opening of the session, a bill was reported favorable to the grant. In expectation of this move, many members of the Legislature and the lobby, and their friends, as well as the adherents and coadjutors of Vanderbilt, had bought the stock freely from 90 to 105.

When the favorable report was known to the general public, they rushed in and loaded themselves up with the stock, which now rose rapidly to 150. One of Vanderbilt's confidential agents at Albany, telegraphed repeatedly that the bill would surely pass. The Commodore and his associates largely increased their line of stock, and as high a figure as 200 was confidently predicted.

But while everything promised well, and already in imagination, the advocates of a Broadway railroad, saw that renowned thoroughfare lined with street cars under the management of the Harlem board, a sly game had been playing at Albany. The members of the Legislature, seeing the facility with which the price had been raised from par to 150, by a favorably reported bill, rightly concluded that an adverse report would depress the value of the stock to par. They accordingly sold to the Commodore's friends, at from 140 to 150, the stock which had cost them somewhere in the neighborhood of par, and then went heavily short of the stock. On the 25th of March, the conspirators sprung the trap on the unsuspecting old sea-faring man and his mates. The price fell in two days, amid the greatest excitement, to 101.

The short gentlemen thought they had feathered their nests nicely, beside giving the Commodore a bloody coxcomb in return for what he had given them, by twisting Harlem to 181 in the summer of 1863. They fluttered about the market uttering loud clucks of exultation.

One of these individuals was Y——s, a plump little man with an eye like a startled cock-partridge. He had affiliations with the lobby and also with the Common Council, and having been caught in the first Harlem corner, he looked upon that stock as something which owed him money, not to say revenge. Having been so fortunate as to put out shorts at 140, he might have been seen on that loud Saturday when Harlem sold down to 101, hovering about the market, beaming with smiles and hob-nobbing with his numerous bear friends. Of course he did not take his profit (bears often seem very reluctant to do this) for he thought Harlem would drop to 75. Towards night he became less gushing in his manifestations of delight, for Harlem had mysteriously risen to 110. In a few days he subsided into that state of financial incubation called "sitting on his shorts." When Harlem had risen to 190 he still sat there as "patient as the mourning dove." A week after he suddenly took flight with a brokers billet under his wing, showing him stripped of plumage and financial eggs broken to the amount of $40,000.

But let us return to the thread of our narrative. How happened it that the Harlem Broadway Franchise Bill was killed, when, as the Commodore supposed, a majority of both houses were pledged to its support?

Treachery in the camp! The Commodore's agent had deceived him. His friends in the Legislature had betrayed him, and were now adding injury and insult to their treachery.

That very day, while the whole market was a playground for the merry and exultant bears in Harlem, in the recesses of a mind capacious of such things,

Commodore Vanderbilt organized a scheme of revenge so "wide and ample" that it would embrace in one fall and tremendous circle, faithless adherents, enemies, both secret and open, as well as all others whom he regarded as hostile to his schemes, in consequence of their selling short his pet stock. Summoning around him his trusty lieutenants, he issued his orders that they should buy every share of the stock that might be offered whether on sellers' or buyers' options, or for cash or "regular."

The bears fortified with a margin of thirty or forty per cent. profit, were not displeased with the opportunity to put out more shorts at a higher price than 101, and the contest commenced. As the price rose, each party waxed furious.

Every day, at the Public Board or in the street, John M. Tobin could have been seen bidding for and buying thousands of shares, his face pale with excitement and his opalescent eyes blazing like a basilisk's. He grabbed at the stock with fury, for he had suffered by the decline.

"No feeling, John!" vociferated the crowd, as the stock rose with wild leaps to 127.

"I'll make you feel," retorted he.

In ten days, the stock, in the face of enormous sales, had risen to 150—the highest price at which the legislative bears had lately commenced their short sales. A week later and the price rose to 185, and then for ten days dully vibrated between 175 and 200. When the movement had carried the stock to 140, the bears, remembering the terrible trouncing they had received eight months before, and remembering also how sweet was revenge to their powerful and inflexible antagonist, began to reflect and inquire whether it might not be advisable to close up their contracts and pocket their loss. But while they were in this dubious state, a circumstance occurred which served to fortify them in their course, and thus to lead them to their destruction.

The hundreds of bears who had been already caught in the death-trap, Harlem, now saw approach the biggest, merriest, most cunning of all their tribe. He nosed the trap, then put his forepaws upon it, and finally put his whole body into it.

It was Uncle Daniel!

Who would suppose that *he* could have been deceived? But so it was. He had sold (rumor said) thirty thousand shares, one-third of the capital stock, in the form of "calls." He who sells calls in a stock, acts upon the supposition that the price will not rise higher than the price named in the calls; he is a bear, and the party who buys and holds the calls, is a bull in the stock. A call sold by an operator who is known to be wealthy and able to respond when called upon for the stock described in the call, is often as already mentioned, used as a margin by the holder to *sell short* that particular stock. Suppose, for example, that Russell Sage sell to John Smith, in consideration of one hundred dollars, the privilege of calling on him, Russell Sage, for two hundred shares of St. Paul at 68, at any time within thirty days. John Smith takes this contract to his own broker and orders him to sell short, two hundred shares of St. Paul, at 68. If the price of the stock goes down, John Smith buys it at the *reduced price*, delivers it to the party to whom he has contracted to deliver it at 68, and makes, as his profit, the difference. But if the price rises and shows

John Smith a loss, he then calls upon Russell Sage to deliver the stock at 68. This keeps John Smith whole in the transaction.

By selling thirty thousand shares in the form of calls, Daniel Drew had really loaned his credit to the amount of millions to the call-holders, to be used in the form of margins on which to sell Harlem, short. In this way, for the trifling consideration of $15,000, paid to him by the call-holders, he helped to forge the very chains in which he was soon to be led captive at the chariot wheels of the triumphant Harlem ring.

When it became noised abroad that Uncle Daniel stood ready to sell calls on Harlem, running for thirty or sixty days, the bears knew that a powerful and crafty ally had joined them. The calls were eagerly snatched by those who wished to hold them for a rise, as well as by those who used them as a margin to sell short. Members of the ring snapped them up greedily. L. W. Jerome and John M. Tobin, personally held calls, which a few weeks after showed Drew indebted to them $138,000.

The speculative public were selling Harlem all through the street. Conservative brokerage houses sold it slyly. The whilom bull, A. G. Jerome, although his brother Leonard was heavily embarked in the upward movement, was a large seller of the stock. Any broker who had Harlem in his office could lend it any moment of the day, to those who were selling short. One of the customers of L.—— & Co., had six hundred shares of the stock. These certificates were loaned to another customer, who sold it *short* to the ring, who then, after taking the numbers on the certificates, loaned it to another bear who sold it again, in open market, *to the ring.* This operation was repeated six times, by as many different men, who all went short of Harlem, using these identical certificates for that purpose.

As the price approached 200, through all the darkness which hung over the short sellers, only one ray of hope gleamed. They saw something drawing near; itself a gloomy and terrible shape, to them it had rather a semblance of brightness and deliverance. It was *Panic,* to which they looked for relief! Panic, which would be ruin to a thousand others, would be salvation to them, for it would throw Harlem down in its sweep, and help them to fill their contracts.

That panic was not wholly due to the action of Secretary Chase in selling gold and locking up greenbacks; it was heightened, beyond doubt, by firms who were short of Harlem, and were willing that the public should suffer frightful losses, provided only Harlem could be broken down, so that they could extricate themselves from their unfortunate position as short sellers.

The 18th of April came, but it brought no deliverance for them. In vain they strove to make money still tighter, and filled the whole market with their dismal auguries, though stocks were falling on every side, and the hammer blows rained on Harlem, it stood like a rock. Now that the panic was past, they could only stand and gaze stupidly at their enemy, and still hope for that which was never to come, a break in the corner.

The agony was soon to be over. One day in May, when Harlem was selling for upwards of 200, the manipulators of the stock called on the Commodore, and told him that they held stock, or contracts for stock, to the amount of twenty-seven thousand more shares, than the whole capital of the company, which was $4,500,000. Then, said Vanderbilt, put the price up to 1,000. The manipulators, including John Morrissey, demurred to this, on the plea that this proceeding would break every house in the street. Accordingly, it was decided that 300, or thereabouts, would be a more judicious figure. Straightway Harlem rose, in long leaps, until it reached 285. At that point it was firmly held. The very day it reached this price, contracts matured for the delivery of more than fifteen thousand shares of the stock. These were closed at a loss of over one million dollars to the short sellers.

The Commodore was taking his revenge. Five hundred strong men, hard of head and deep of coffer, lay at his mercy. Never telling their losses, one by one as "mute as fox mong'st mangling hounds," they walked up to the offices of the brokers of that terrible old man, and settled their differences. Each morning new wrinkles seemed to have been graven, and old lines hardened, in their faces. As for the smaller tribe of the entrapped ones, they were caught up and whirled away like chaff, never to show their faces in the street again. No one but they and their payers will ever know the amount paid by all these men who were short of Harlem, but the aggregate would foot up something frightful.

But how did the greatest bear of all, to wit, Uncle Daniel, succeed in extricating himself from the trap in which he found himself fast caught? His losses on Harlem at 285, would, it was said, amount to $1,-700,000. This would take a large slice out of his late profits on Erie. His first movement was to throw himself on the tender mercies of the Commodore, and plead old friendship, etc. Vain appeal! The bosom of the ancient steamboat mariner and rail-road king was steeled against the entreaties of the old bear, and he very pertinently inquired whether, if Harlem had fallen to 75, instead of rising to 285, he would in that case, have paid any portion of his (Vanderbilt's) losses. Failing in this appeal, his next movement was to set up the plea of conspiracy, and that he had been entrapped by false representations, etc.; "besides," said he, "these contracts merely say that you may *call* upon me for so much stock; they say nothing about my *delivering* the stock. *Call* then, and keep *calling*, I am not obliged to *deliver* any stock." So he stood at bay, telling his opponent to seek redress in the courts of law.

But as Wall Street abhors litigation, a compromise was at last talked of. Tobin and L. W. Jerome were now nearly every day closeted with him, in his den at No. 15 William Street, and a settlement was at last effected for about one million.

After the price of Harlem had been kept in the neighborhood of 280 long enough to close all the short contracts held by the ring, it fell like lead to 115, and not a single bear could be found with hardihood enough to sell it for future delivery during its downward course.

This Harlem rise is said to have crippled or ruined more men than any similar movement in the annals of Wall Street, while it enriched and gave new prestige to Vanderbilt, who in connection with his associates in the movement, is said to have netted money enough to buy the whole capital stock.

I now return to the story of the six hundred shares of Harlem, of which I was short, at an average of 200. Of course, as the price rose, I "sat on my shorts," clinging manfully to my loss after the most approved Wall Street plan. At 280 I had to close like my ursine brothers, and found my loss $24,000. I had hoped, however, that this would be diminished to the amount of $8,000, since the two hundred shares sold at 200 was secured by the call before mentioned, which a wealthy (?) operator had sold me a few weeks before for the trifling sum of $12.50. This occurred in a moment of badinage at a dinner, when the above wealthy (?) operator (while Harlem was selling at 130), offered me the privilege of calling on him at any time within sixty days, for two hundred shares at 200, in consideration of the trifling sum last named.

But an operator, wealthy on the first of April, is not necessarily so on the twenty-fifth of May following, at least in Wall Street. The operator in question had been laid low in the Morse panic, and when I *called* for two hundred shares at 200, the response was anything but satisfactory, in fact to the extent of $8,000 out of my little surplus.

As for W. B. C——, he kept his call, and when the price was 275, *he called* and was answered. He made exactly $10,000 out of what cost him only $50.

It was while smarting under the Harlem flagellation that I made my first operation in cotton, buying one hundred bales of that useful staple at 87½ cents per pound. The history and result of this speculative purchase will be given hereafter, under another head.

CHAPTER XXII.

IN SEARCH OF A BROKER—THE GOLD-BURST UPWARDS—DULL TIMES.

The Three Brokers; a Vulture, a Sparrow, and a Jolly Boy—Brokers' Safes are Like the Lion's Den—Lunching in the Office of N—— & Co.—We Find What We are Looking For, and Put Our Margins in the Lunch-Room—A Jag of $50,000 Gold and What Came of It—Beautiful June and Halcyon Days for the Quartette—A Financial Dissertation at an Inn on the Road—The Military Outlook—Grant's Hand on the Throat of the Rebellion—Congressional Folly and Its Consequences—The Gold Bill—We Take a Trip to Rockaway—Telegraphing in Cipher—Wherein of a Telegraphic Puzzle—The Gold Burst—A Mistake Which Gave Me a Profit of $85,000—Buying 50 Gold Instead of Selling 50.

THE customer, after every severe loss, is apt to cherish towards his natural enemy, the broker, a feeling of dissatisfaction, not to say mild indignation. Thereupon he casts about him for another broker, some paragon who may do his little business for him, and render him happy with a continuous series of the plumpest and most delicious of profits, over which the shadow of a loss may never come. He must be young and jolly, and honest of course. He must be ready to communicate the most reliable points, he must never be obstreperous on the subject of margins, and above all he must always, and under all circumstances, be buoyant.

L—— enjoyed an extensive acquaintance among those gentry who are popularly supposed to do a "strictly commission business in buying and selling stocks." On learning that I was in search of something new and improved in that line, he kindly offered to show me what I wanted, viz., a broker who was an "entire and perfect chrysolite." "The first man I shall introduce you to," remarked L—— after we had set out on our search for this paragon broker, "may not be a very prepossessing man at first sight, but I can indorse him as in every respect, the man for your money. I've just made ten thousand in his office!" This little profit had prejudiced L——, I think; for a moment after, on entering the office of the individual referred to, I saw a tall, heavily-beaked man, who was craning over a couple of customers with bony knees and wearing a flaccid drained look, and apparently impressing on them the necessity of handing over more margin, or of being sold out incontinently. Physiognomy has certainly something to do with the selection of an agent to buy and sell stocks, though it does not always follow that a man may not smile, and smile, and yet be a broker. As soon as introduced, I began to study the face of the tall man. The ruling expression suggested only one trait, and that conspicuously—cruelty—which wandered through and lurked in every line of his face, but took up its permanent abode in his eye—that cruel eye. The bony knees of the flaccid-looking customers and that cruel eye were enough. We hastened away to continue our search for the paragon aforesaid.

The next office we entered was that of W——, quite a different kind of man. If the tall, heavily beaked man from whom we had just parted brought to my mind the solitary vulture, W—— as strongly reminded me of a chirping sparrow constantly in pursuit of worms. He was a short man, with a magnificent chest and slender legs, dressed in a style of sombre gorgeousness. He never was quiet an instant. Now dancing up and down the street; now taking short flights to the Board; then back again, perching for a moment in his office and off once more. He seemed to be constantly in pursuit of worms—I mean orders. He had little time to talk English. His language was the Wall Street patter, clipping syllables audaciously. Commission, which seemed to be the most frequent word in his vocabulary, he called "commish," "Pittsburg," "Pitts," and so on.

Action is the essential of oratory, first, last, and always, said Demosthenes. Activity is the essential of the brokerage business. Activity means orders to buy and sell. Activity means commissions for the broker. But I had discovered some time before this, that activity on the part of the broker was productive of large brokerage bills, which his customer would have to pay. W—— was a trifle too active in the line of commissions, and so we looked farther.

"Now," said L—— "I've thought of *the* man to take care of your margins."

And while he was speaking, he opened the door which conducted into the banking and brokerage house of N—— & Co. The first feature that struck the eye, on entering this office, was the safes. In one corner stood a large salamander safe; sunk in the wall there was a burglar proof safe; under the cashier's desk, there was a small safe, which looked like a lineal descendant of the salamander, before named. All this conveyed the idea of security, at least, for the banking and brokerage firm. Experience has certainly taught us, at this date, however, that brokers' safes are like the lion's den, the tracks of the gentler beasts all lead in, and none lead out from it. A constant stream of checks pass away from the relaxed fingers of the customers, and flow into those chilled iron doors; but never again do they flow out to gladden *his* heart, or to be crumpled up in his "itching palm."

From the private office of this house, came a sound of mirth and revelry, mingled with the clinking of glasses and the clattering of knives and forks. A slim clerk, dressed in the height of the fashion, nodded gaily as we entered, and then jumped off the high stool, on which he was sitting before a desk, protected by a lofty barrier of black walnut, and walking rapidly to the private office, threw open the door, disclosing thereby a banqueting scene. Several men were sitting around a table loaded with the delicacies of the season, and surmounted with tall, slender flasks, bearing such labels as *haut sauterne*, *amontillado*, etc. Beside each chair was a champagne cooler, from out of which protruded the neck of a bottle swathed in ice. We thought at first sight that we had made a mistake, and were in a restaurant, where some board of a mining company was celebrating the anniversary of subscription day. But we were quickly undeceived, by the appearance of the senior member of the house, wiping a bit of lobster salad from his exuberant beard. He was a stout, well-fed man, with a dome of brow fit for the intellectual habitation of some illustrious statesman, and thinly adorned with blonde curls. After introductions had been exchanged, he led us, nothing loth, to two vacant seats, which, as he remarked, seemed to have been providentially reserved for us. As "swift as dreams," we found our plates heaped with good things, then was heard a gurgling sound, as of a hidden brook, and a moment after, every banqueter began to give his views on the condition and prospects of the railway stocks most actively dealt in.

N—— sat at the head of the table, uttering in a barytone voice between mouthfuls of salad, the most daring financial paradoxes interspersed with amusing anecdotes, in which he dwelt with much humor upon the singular facility with which the margins of speculators were disposed of. Then he passed into the prophetic vein and predicted future rises to empyrean heights. Gold and its future course seemed to be his pet theme. It was to rise to 300 within six months, and on this assertion he booked a little bet with a sallow complexioned gentleman on the opposite side of the table.

The genial glow diffused by the lunch, and the barytone buoyant predictions as to the course of gold, had their due effect. In fifteen minutes after the company rose from the table, I had deposited all my cash with N—— & Co., who then bought for me $50,000 in gold, which cost 179. Then I introduced E—— and W. B. C—— to the convivial man with the fine dome of brow and keen financial apprehension. They also took flyers in gold, and on the strength of this thought themselves entitled to the privileges of lunch which was spread every day in the most sumptuous style. It may be here related that E—— informed me several months after, that these lunches had cost him an average of $200 dollars each, a fact that he was reminded of on contemplating the last account which N—— & Co. had rendered him, on taking leave of their eminent banking and brokerage house.

After that we spent two or three weeks very pleasantly, exercising our steeds and airing our light wagons and phaetons in the park, breakfasting out on the road, dining at Delmonico's, and, of course, lunching at our broker's, where we "lay off" on ample sofas and dabbled in stocks, losing more than we made, but caring little for this, so long as gold kept us more than whole by rising to 198.

Beautiful June, queen of the months, was come. Perfect days, and nights more beloved than the days. South-west winds at evening, and bespangled skies of unfathomable blue.

It was on one of those matchless nights that we sat on the piazza of a suburban hotel, on the High Bridge road. We heeded not the "unutterable glory of the stars," nor the breath of "the sweet south," but were deep in the discussion of gold, its future course, etc., all the while sipping our Cliquot and puffing furiously at the finest regalias.

From August 1863, gold had been steadily rising from 122, the point it reached after a series of Union successes. This rise seemed to depend little upon those temporary and artificial causes which make stocks go up. The laws of commerce and of money were at work, steadily depreciating the value of paper currency, and so affecting the market price of the precious metal. *This* rise was founded on reason.

The amount of paper currency was already more than five times greater than before the war. That gold should have ever risen above 200, is not wonderful. The wonder is that it never rose to 500. The fact that it did not so rise, proves the confidence of the great body of the American people in the resources of their country and in the ultimate success of the Union army.

The tremendous panic of April 18th, produced little effect upon the price of gold. There was no combination in it like those which sent stocks so wildly upwards, nor did its movements depend upon the scarcity or abundance of money to be loaned in the market place. Upon the results of the summer campaign on the Potomac, depended its future course. Victory would bring down the price; defeat and even a doubtful issue would cut the cord, and away the price would fly into the clouds.

Twelve myriads—one hundred and twenty thousand good men and true, horse, foot, and artillery—were lying on their arms north of the Rapidan, waiting for the two words of command. One bright May morning those words passed through the ranks—"forward! march!" Corps after corps, division after division, brigade after brigade, regiment behind regiment, they swept across the stream, soon to be reddened with their blood; on, threading the death-labyrinths of the wilderness, piling great mounds of shroudless graves around Spotsylvania and Cold Harbor, and gathering at last in dusky circles about Richmond and Petersburg.

Of all the millions of eyes that watched the onward march of the Grand Army of the Potomac, none were riveted upon it so closely as the gold speculators. Every source of early information from the front was explored. It was not enough to scrutinize the columns of the daily press for every scrap of army news; the telegraph operators were subsidized, government officials were tampered with, and a more perfect system of couriers and messages adopted, in order to advise the speculators as to the exact condition of matters on the Rapidan, the Pamunkey, and the James River. If a great army movement was about to take place, the gold speculator in Wall Street would receive a message from his coadjutor at Washington, or at the front, something like this, "John is still here." If an engagement, disastrous to the Federal army, had taken place, word would come "Henry is worse." This meant, "buy gold." Or if a victory had been won, "John is sitting up to-day." This meant, "sell gold."

It would be safe to assert that there were only two classes of persons who always knew the exact status of the campaign. First, the government; second, the gold operators, for both these classes obtained the earliest information, not only from the Union, but from the Rebel army.

When, after a series of bloody battles and flanking movements, Grant was preparing to draw his lines around Richmond, it might have been expected that the price of gold would have declined. But these successes were interpreted by financiers, to be of a character not sufficiently decisive to affect the price, which stood firmly at 198.

Something new now entered into the calculations of the gold dealers. Congress had just passed a bill affixing severe penalties to the practice of dealing in gold by contract for future purchases and delivery, and that bill only lacked the President's signature to become a law. How would this affect the price of gold? The act intended to repress speculation in the metal, passed March, 1863, had been used as an argument to throw gold down from 172 to 156. This was the problem which puzzled us, as we discussed matters on that pleasant June evening. On the whole, we were inclined to sell, but came to no decision then, though we had dwelt upon the subject till the last light wagon had bowled past us in the direction of the city. Then we whistled for our team. It was sharp twelve, before we reined in our dapple grays in front of their stable door, and betook ourselves to our several hotels.

When we met the next morning, two things were settled upon. First, we would sell our gold at the market price. Second, we would unite in a trip to the sea-side. L—— was the arithmetician and telegraph operator of the party, and so to him was delegated the matter of giving the order to sell, which we were to send down to the office of N—— & Co. by the city telegraph.

Previously to this we had agreed with N—— & Co., upon a telegraphic cipher, as follows, viz.: "Ben" meant sell, "jag" meant our gold, "whirl" meant at the market price, and "Bob" meant buy. Our telegram read thus: "Ben, jag, whirl, answer to us at Rockaway, *signed*, etc., etc., etc."

In three hours after, we stood on the smooth, firm beach at Rockaway, listening to the breakers' roar. It was not till the next day, that we received from our buoyant and festive broker, the following telegram: "*Got,* jag, Wiggins, whirl, Morrissey, everything lovely, signed, etc., N—— & Co." Which being translated, signified: "Got your gold at 199⅛, market price strong and higher. Everything lovely."

This telegram bothered us. Instead of saying Benny, which meant sold, our broker had written *got.* On this fine old Anglo-Saxon word *got* we held a philological discussion. It seemed here to signify *bought.* But our order was to *sell.* L—— having sent the telegram giving the order to sell, defended the answer vigorously, and asserted that *got* was here applied to the *getting* of our profit, or it might mean a joke on the part of N—— to inform us that we were "got" by selling out just before the price rose. But what logical connection in that case between the fact that the price had risen after we had sold and the expression "everything is lovely?" The discussion was brought to an end, however, as soon as we recollected that *our* telegram was certainly correct; and if N—— & Co. had made a mistake we could hold them responsible for any consequences disastrous to ourselves arising therefrom.

The stock operator is rarely much of a society-man. It is never written on his tombstone, "sociability was his pride." At the watering-places, instead of passing his time with that portion of the fair sex, who there resort, forming what is usually known as society, he withdraws to quiet corners, calls around him his little clan of fellow-operators, and occupies and diverts himself with exchanging views, conning telegrams, rummaging in the money articles of New York dailies, and chewing the sweet and bitter cud of prospective profit and loss. While thus engaged for ten days, our coterie became, from time to time, apprised of the flutterings of the Volscians at Corioli, otherwise, the gold dealers of New York.

Great doings on 'Change!

The law of Congress, forbidding all time contracts in gold, under penalty of heavy fine and imprisonment, first took effect on the 21st of June.

This piece of legislative fatuity, was promptly interpreted by the financiers, as a confession of weakness on the part of the government, and of its conviction that the war was to be a protracted one. Its first effect was to compel all who were short of gold, to cover their contracts. The demand thus suddenly created, drove up the price in one day to 225. Its second effect was to throw out of gearing, the entire machinery of the banking, and of the importing mercantile business; for time contracts in gold, ever since 1862, have been employed in legitimate trade, as well as in speculation.

When an importer wishes to pay duties on his goods, or remit exchange to Europe, he borrows gold of his bank at the market price, provided he thinks gold is going down, and buys gold in the market for the same purpose, whenever he thinks that gold is going up. If gold should go down in the former case, then he repays the gold borrowed of the bank, buying it in the market at the lower price to which it may have fallen, thus making his profit; and if gold goes up in the latter case, his imported goods will feel the effect of the rise, and in this way he also makes a profit.

On the 23d of June, gold sold for 245, and during the week which ensued, it vibrated twenty and thirty

LOCKING UP GREENBACKS.

per cent. a day, throwing the commercial community into the greatest confusion. The price soon reached the highest point known during the war.

Meetings in the Chamber of Commerce were held, and petitions forwarded to Washington, praying for the repeal of the law. But though the repeal took place shortly after, it did not undo the mischief which had been wrought. Gold did not, for many months, fall back to 185, the point from which it started upwards, when the gold bill was first agitated in Congress.

We set out for New York, on the first of July, in consequence of receiving another mysterious telegram from our broker. This message read as follows, viz.: "Hannah is jumping now, what shall I do?" "Hannah" was gold. What did N—— & Co. mean? They seemed to be soliciting orders very strangely. The last train down from Jamaica, was delayed by an accident. We reached the Fifth Avenue Hotel just after the Evening Exchange had adjourned. As we entered the hall, a short, rubicund gentleman, whom we recognized as one of the customers of N—— & Co., hailed us as if we were so many rising suns, and grasping our several hands with fervor, congratulated us on our good luck.

"Good luck? Oh, in gold. Yes, we have done pretty well, about $10,000 apiece," was the response,

"About $10,000! Why, the book-keeper of N—— & Co. told me to-day that you could sell out for sixty-five thousand dollars apiece. Gold sold for 55 to-day, (*i. e.* 255,) you know."

A light broke in upon us at these words. The mysterious telegrams were now as clear as noon-day.

N—— & Co., instead of selling our gold at 199⅛, must have bought as much more. We exchanged significant glances, and received the congratulations of the rubicund gentleman quite as a matter of course. Just at this juncture, entered N——, looking, if that were possible, more exuberant than when I first saw him dispensing the favors of his lunch table. He also congratulated us on our good fortune. On the last lot of fifty gold, which cost 199⅛, there was a profit of about $28,000, and on the first lot of fifty, which cost me 179, there was a profit of $37,500, as N—— rapidly showed me by figures in his memorandum book. This profit was on the basis of gold at 255. "What would I do; sell out on the spot?" "No, wait till to-morrow." I waited, and sold out at 275 the next day, which was the 2d of July, when as every one will remember, gold sold up to 285. My profits were $85,000 net. It appears that N—— & Co. had made a mistake in reading L——'s telegram, instructing them to sell our gold, and had read "Ben," *i. e.* sell, as "Bob," *i. e.* buy, and so bought another lot at 199⅛, instead of selling what we had.

It would fill a volume to give an account of the fortunes made and lost during the eleven days from June 22d to July 2d. One bold broker, doing business on a capital of $9,000 bought $250,000 of gold at about 200 at the Evening Exchange on the 21st of June, and by a series of lucky operations, selling at higher rates and buying back at lower rates, as the price oscillated, found himself in forty-eight hours $140,000 richer. Another man who had on the 20th of June been obliged to cover his shorts with the loss of everything that could possibly be used as a margin, excepting three diamond studs, pawned these for $200, and in a week had made from this little capital, over $12,000.

Our quartette drew out all our profits from N—— & Co., got our several checks certified at the bank, and having carried them in our pocket for two days, then went back and deposited them with N—— & Co. as margin for a new campaign. L——, however, bought a brown stone front with part of his profits, and there every evening we held a council of four, deliberating how we might increase our pile.

Looking back to these campaigns in gold, from the equally remarkable campaigns in stocks, during the latter part of 1879, with the Gold Exchange a thing of the past, and the Gold Room dark and silent, the entire speculation in gold seems like some monstrous and uncanny dream. But we must remember that the madness which ruled the hour in October and November, 1879, and which seemed at the time so real in character, may before many months be regarded as equally the "baseless fabric of a vision," vanishing into "thin air," and leaving "not a rack behind." Such is the life of a speculator.

CHAPTER XXIII.

DULL TIMES—AVERAGING ON "POINTS."

A Retrospect of the Situation—An Army Without Leaders—Description of a Dull Market—"Playing With Stocks" to the Tune of $22,000—Buying on "Points"—A Disagreeable Looking Millionaire—A Wall Street Pointer; His Picture, Antecedents and Mystery—His Geese Always Lay Golden Eggs—We Buy Five Hundred Cumberland Joint Account on a "Point"—Averaging a Loss—How Men Save Themselves by Averaging—Advice Given to an Operator in a Tight Place—"Cumberland not Worth Ten Cents on the Dollar," and I am Long of it at 80—A Bad Show for a Profit—Keep up Your Averaging, My Dear Boy.

THE two great features of the market in Wall Street in the summer of 1864, were Harlem and gold, both of which, by a singular coincidence, rose to 285. The general stock market was lifeless, at least compared to the preceding spring and to the summer of 1863. The situation in respect to the conflicting parties, stood thus.

The bears, owing to their heavy losses during the Morse campaign and the Harlem rise, were too demoralized and impecunious to become the assailants and take advantage of the causes which tended to produce lower prices.

The panic of April 18th had given them moral encouragement, though they had derived little or no pecuniary advantage from it. But as they were gathering together their shattered forces, the gold-burst came and once more disconcerted them.

The bulls, on the other hand, who had been severely crippled by the same panic, had their courage and money forces bolstered up by Harlem and the gold rise. And yet they still lacked something always essential to an upward movement, viz.: bull-leaders. Their army had no general. A. G. Jerome had retired after the defeat which he suffered in August, 1863, on Old Southern, at the hands of Henry Keep. A. W. Morse had been blown skywards as he was scaling the ramparts of Fort Wayne. The Commodore was engaged in nursing his investments. Tobin was resting on his Harlem laurels. Of the other chieftains, not one advanced to cheer on their ranks to victory.

The strong upward movement which followed the April panic was the natural rebound after so heavy a fall, rather than any concerted scheme on the part of the bulls. In May, June and July, various stocks had been taken hold of in succession and lifted by main strength several per cent.; but somehow in all these cases, just as the lifters were preparing to reap the reward of their exertions, stocks would suddenly be depressed as if by some unseen power, and then all the bears would join hands and execute a *pas de fascination* around the venerable form of Uncle Daniel, who, as the master of the ballet, would thereupon gaze with an approving smile upon his nimble pupils.

The tendency of stocks was downward.

Sultry August brought with it the reign of *dullness*, that condition of things in the stock-market forcible but somewhat inelegantly styled the "dry rot," to which, allusion has been made in Chapter VII.

Imagine five hundred men all standing before the pendulum of a gigantic clock, and ejaculating with every tick, "Here she goes, and there she goes." This is the likeness of Wall Street in a dull season. Stocks move up one per cent., then down one per cent., and so on day after day, and week after week. No orders to buy or sell are given by the heavy operators; the outsiders stand listlessly by and wait for the moving of the waters. In the Board, feeble attempts are made to create an excitement in some old favorite stock, which responds lazily to sharp bidding and moves up a notch; but as soon as the bidding ceases, down it plumps again to the figure from which it started. Little knots of speculators are made in the Board, to talk stocks and book small bets on the course of the market. The song of the fraction pursuer becomes still and small. Ever and anon some spruce and agile clerk of one of the prominent commission houses worms his way into these Board knots and bids for one or two hundred shares, when deep voices immediately take up the note like the boom of the bittern in some lonely swamp. Then the throng of buyers and sellers roar out a stave of some popular song, such as "The Skidmore Guards," or perhaps "Sally Waters," some one cries out, "Shoo fly, don't bodder me," and the song ceases as suddenly as it began. "The boys" often amuse themselves by playing pranks. A newly arrived gentleman from the rural districts, who is a looker-on in the street, finds his hat suddenly tipped over his eyes, or his shoulder smartly tapped by one of the habitues, who immediately mingles with the crowd, while the butt of these little practical jokes is looking vigilantly on every side for his tormentor. A dignified old veteran stalks about with a placard, "*For sale at auction*," which some mischievous broker has fastened to his coat-tail.

In dull seasons, the only thing left to operators is, "playing with stocks." This, it need not be remarked, is very much like playing with fire, for the operator is almost sure to get burnt. However, as this is the sole remedy for that restlessness, which dogs and urges the speculator on from behind, like the iron goad of destiny, he gladly avails himself of it, even though he knows it may cost him a pretty penny in the way of losses.

In the course of this diversion, it would be hard to mention the name of a stock to which we did not pay our respects, as "the Cynthia of the minute." After fifty or sixty different operations, in which I had jumped in, and then jumped out again, I found my losses in these transitory enterprises, had amounted to $22,000.

Then we (the quartette aforesaid,) joined forces, and gave four separate orders to as many different brokers in the Public Board, to buy one thousand shares of North-western Preferred, at the market price. The stock rose three per cent. under our joint purchase of four thousand shares. Naturally it was very gratifying for us to know that we had sufficient influence to make North-west rise three per cent., but this feeling of gratification was somewhat marred, when the price fell back again, entailing upon us a loss of four hundred dollars apiece.

Then we tried our hands at making those "quick

turns," which brokers so delight in. "Quick turns" are buying or selling for a profit of a quarter per cent. or more. No returns were rendered to us on these operations, though our broker reaped a harvest of commissions.

All our little operations for two months during the summer were based upon the most reliable "points," which we gathered from every conceivable source, with the greatest assiduity. As the market was generally a declining one during this period, we had barely saved ourselves from being thoroughly impaled on these points, by "cutting short our losses," in every case, excepting one, and that was my private and individual case, as will be seen by the following statement.

While perambulating in Broad Street, in search of points, I met J——, a stock-market acquaintance. He had a most unprepossessing countenance, in fact quite disagreeable. Some would have called it sinister in its expression, but he was worth $500,000, and consequently Wall Street voted him as good looking and agreeable. In society he was set down as fascinating.

"Did he know of any stock to make a turn in? Just a flyer of a thousand shares, good for one or two per cent., enough to pay for a trip to Niagara?" I asked.

"Well, no! I'm only this morning in from the country, and a'nt posted; but here comes G——, he can tell you something worth knowing, I'll wager."

So saying, he introduced me to G——, and passed on. I had often seen G——, who haunted the market, and had wondered who he was. *He* also had a very unpleasing face, which always wore a fixed Mephistophelian smile, commonly known as the clam-shell smile. He vainly endeavored to hide the ravages inflicted by twenty-five years of a speculator's life, by dyeing his full beard a dead black. I had understood that he had affiliations with several leading railroad directors. A second cousin of his was said to be connected with the Erie direction, and his wife's brother had relations to the coal interests. His uncle was a permanent investor in New York Central. Then there was his grandfather, a venerable stock operator, who could have been seen toddling down two or three times a year, wearing the family smile. G—— was the image of his grandfather, only more so.

As he had dropped three or more fortunes in different convenient places around the street, he was, and had been for several months, living on very short commons, so much so that his most intimate acquaintances alleged that he never at this time was in the habit of taking more than one square meal in a day. As to costume, however, he could not be impeached, for he "traveled on his style," and always found it pay to dress. His toilet was an important part of his capital in the trade, which he worked at. *This trade was selling points.* Here was unfolded the mystery of his existence. He sold information; he jobbed off secrets; he dealt in "points" warranted not to cut in the eye, and thus extracted sustenance for himself and the young buzzards which fluttered in his domestic nest. He would put in his "point" against the capital of some wealthy friend, who, on the information thus furnished, would buy or sell one or more hundred shares of stock, G—— having a certain interest in the operation. If there was a profit growing out of it, G—— had a part of it, allotted to him as a remuneration for his point. If a loss occurred, G—— would give his note for his proportion, but owing to G——'s impecuniosity these notes, of course, were never paid.

It will be readily seen that G——'s geese generally laid golden eggs.

In some cases he was known to give contradictory points to different operators. He would tell one operator, for example, that Erie was about to be put up; on this point two hundred shares of Erie would be bought. Then he would go to another operator and inform him that Erie was about to be dropped; and on this point, two hundred shares of Erie would be sold short. Then G—— "had a sure thing;" out of one of these transactions a profit would certainly accrue.

G—— looked me steadily in the face as if he would take the latitude and longitude of my bank account. Then he seemed suddenly to grow to me like a limpet to a rock. He hooked his arm in mine, jerked his head in a southerly direction, and walking rapidly round the corner of Exchange Place, passed through several winding passages into the tunnel leading to the Regular Board, then halted to breathe something in a husky whisper into the ear of a small, but very well-groomed broker, passed down stairs into Beaver Street, stalked into a saloon and sat down opposite to me at a little table. Then calling for some rare, delicious dishes, such as can be got only by paying costly prices, he gazed at me, trying very hard to infuse into his smile, something at once plaintive and affectionate.

Mysterious silence! G—— was evidently pregnant and laboring with some momentous secret. Suddenly his left eyelid drooped, then closed very tight; he bent over and whispered in my ear:

"Do you want to make some money? Of course you do. I'll put up a job for you, if you say so."

"Yes. What's your job?" replied I.

"Buy five hundred shares of——. I'll tell you the stock if you say you'll do it. Joint account, profit and loss, you and I."

"All right! What's the stock?" rejoined I.

Thereupon he delivered a brief and impressive dissertation on the value of coal-stocks in general, and of this stock in particular; and, looking all around him, to assure himself that no listener was near, he pronounced the word "Cumberland!" Having paused for a moment, to see the effect produced by this communication, he winked again very hard and continued: "Saw a director this morning. Slope mine; sale soon to be consummated. Cash dividend, ten per cent. Bet you twenty-five dollars (taking out a very lean pocket-book as if he was eager to plank down his money) that Cumberland sells at par in thirty days. Don't wait, buy five hundred right away."

In fifteen minutes after this interview, five hundred shares of Cumberland were registered on the stock-book of N—— & Co., as held for the joint account of G—— and myself. It cost about 80. In the course of the next week it had fallen five per cent. The loss on it was twenty-five hundred dollars. The next best thing to cutting short a loss, is "averaging" it by buying more stock at a lower price.

G——, who turned up when Cumberland was selling at 74, reported that the sale of the Slope mine had been delayed, and that the stock had been dropped for the purpose of "Scooping a few more shorts." He advised that we keep our position, and "average," by buying more stock at the decline. We *averaged*, by buying five hundred more Cumberland at about 74.

This averaging or buying separate lots successively as the price declines, when an operator is saddled with stock at a high price, is all very well if stocks soon recover themselves, or if the buyer's margins are sufficiently ample to enable him to keep buying until the tide turns. Should the stock, however, fall fifty per cent., the operator who starts by buying five hundred shares, and repeats the purchase at every five per cent. decline, will find himself at last loaded with five thousand five hundred shares, at an average loss of twenty-five per cent., or about $125,000, rather a heavy burden for any one but a millionaire. Still, very many of the Wall Street men follow this plan with great success so long as they gauge it according to their means.

M——, a noted Wall Street man, has been heard to boast that he never sold a stock at a loss during the past ten years. He bought one hundred shares of Erie at 128, during the Morse rise, and bought another hundred at 95, and after that at every ten per cent. decline, repeated his purchase till April, 1865, when Erie after touching 42, rose again to 98.

His average was 79, and after nearly eighteen months, his stubbornness was rewarded with a profit. The same individual, in 1873, bought one hundred Erie at 65, and now holds five hundred shares which averages him 45. He has waited six years for the tide to turn, and we venture to predict that he will yet sell his Erie at a handsome profit.

To resume our story. Cumberland continued falling, and we (G—— and I,) continued averaging. G—— always had some plausible story to tell about the occasion of each five per cent. decline. When Cumberland reached 56, we held two thousand shares which brought us in for a loss of more than $30,000. By this time G——'s point had vanished, without leaving a residuum, and he about the same time was missed from Wall Street. Nothing was left to his partner but to keep averaging, or sell out, and pocket his loss.

When a man is in danger of heavy loss upon a purchase, it is remarkable how lavish his friends are of advice and information of a disagreeable nature. So it happened during the Cumberland drop to 56. One of the first men I met was a prominent broker of the "party," for there was a "party" in the stock. That mysterious word, "party." Somehow there always seems to be a "party" in every stock on the list. "Don't hold a share of it," said he, "the party are getting out of it as fast as they can, and in six weeks the whole capital stock will be knocking around the street dear at 40."

The next man I met was an old capitalist, who had been a dealer for twenty years in Cumberland. When I said "Cumberland" to him, he pranced and curvetted, metaphorically speaking, like an aged war-horse at the sound of a trumpet.

"Cumberland?" cried he.

"How much is it worth?" inquired I.

"Well, about ten cents on the dollar. Dividends! it never has and never will pay a dividend. We made up a party and bought nearly all of it at five cents on the dollar, five or six years ago, and then subscribed five per cent. as a working capital. We tried to work the mines, but it was no go. We lost the whole of our working capital, $250,000, and then sold out our stock at five, the price we paid for it."

The advice given by the prominent broker, and the information elicited from the capitalist, were not calculated to give nerve to a man who held Cumberland at 80.

And yet I stood up and prepared myself to continue my programme.

Dull seasons in the stock-market are always the precursors of some marked change one way or the other. If stocks have unduly risen, a dull time precedes a fall; if they have been unduly depressed, it precedes a rise. And so it fell out. As August drew near its close, there were signs and omens of approaching change.

Before telling how I came out of Cumberland, it will be proper here to switch off our stock train into the track of gold. As I have before mentioned, it was not till August, 1864, that a separate place was assigned to the dealings in this commodity.

Soon after the repressive Congressional act was repealed, Gilpin's reading room, on the corner of William Street and Exchange Place, was the place of meeting first selected by the gold crowd. Here commenced an era of speculation in the precious metal, which was to last ten months, and was marked by greater vicissitudes in fortune, than even the stock speculation, which was its forerunner.

It should be noticed here, that enormous transactions were privately made every day, during the operation of the act against dealing in gold on contracts, proving how little power legal enactments have over a trade which promises great profits.

The vibrations in gold have never been equaled in Wall Street except by the swift decline in stocks during the months of September and October, 1873, and by the almost equally swift rise in the autumn of 1879. In the two months last named the bulls fared as well as they did when they were pushing up the price of gold in the summer of 1864, and again in the autumn of the same year. The coal stocks, the Southwestern stocks, and the Grangers, were mines of gold to the daring manipulators of 1879, as was the precious metal in the sharp vibrations of 1864 and 5.

CHAPTER XXIV.

THE BREAK IN GOLD—PANIC-BIRDS.

The Gold Fire-balloon—Vibrations from the Cannon's Roar—The Gathering of the Clans in the Gold-room—Desperate Speculators at the Front—Portraits of Operators—N—— Bulls Gold, and We Bull It—A Loss, first on the Long and then on the Short Side—A Call for More Margin, and an Examination of our Bubble-company Assets—A Visit to the Den of the Bloated Spider—The Clergyman and Farmer Looking After Their Investment—They Find the House "Swept and Garnished"—We Meet the "Corpulent Gentleman" in a Picture Gallery—The Interview and its Result—The Fall of Atlanta, and Gold on the Rampage Downwards—Panic-birds at Their Feast—A Portrait of the "Stormy Petrels"—Buy Cumberland—I "Average" out of My Loss.

FROM July 2d till August 30th, 1864, gold hung from 250 to 280, like a monstrous fire-balloon by the side of a thunder-cloud. Not a few daring aeronauts sailed over the massed blackness, which darkened the financial sky, as if they would garner its thunder-bolts in sheaves.

Low mutterings already foreboded a storm which would either drive gold before it to 500 and depress greenbacks to twenty cents on the dollar, staggering if not prostrating the shaky system of Government credit, or which should hurl gold down to the neighborhood of par amid the ruin of American commerce and all its dependencies.

On the James River two hosts lay watching each other sullenly through the embrasures of mighty earth-moles, or behind sand bags, or couched in trenches through many a circling league; Sheridan and Early were playing a bloody game of tag, up and down the Shenandoah, while every one was listening to catch the sound of the cannon of the army of the Tennessee, as it swept up to the gates of the confederacy. Ever and anon the deep booming of the guns of Sherman as his long deep columns rolled past the blood-stained heights of Kenesaw, on! on! across the Chattahoochie, awoke dismal echoes in the hearts of the gold-bulls. And now Atlanta was beleaguered.

The dull season was over at last, and the carnival of speculation had commenced. Even on tame days the price vibrated two or three per cent. in an hour, and there were not many tame days. Here was the swiftest chance to make or lose a fortune in a day. Stocks were nothing to it. The wildest and most desperate speculators from every side flocked into the new gold room, a motley multitude of well dressed barbarians with seamed faces and cavernous eyes, screaming and brandishing their arms from morning till night. Their voices were like that of Stentor, their lungs like iron, their fingers seemed fairly electrified with charges from the ticking telegraph.

Many of the operators in the crowd went in for short turns, buying and selling millions in a day. Among these was a short thick-set Missourian, named C——. He stood on a chair in one corner, registering his purchases and sales in a little book which he constantly held in his hands. The heavy break three weeks after, clipped his audacious wings, and he disappeared from the scene. High above the din occasionally could be heard the hollow bull-bison roar of

D. H——, whose face wedged between the shoulders of the crowd, resembled that of a blonde and apoplectic bull-dog.

Another man who operated on short turns for enormous amounts, was S——, who might have been a member of the Lydia Thompson troupe, with his hair of pale tow, and his eyes of the hue and sharpness of a newly polished axe.

Later in the day, a conspicuously tall and ugly man might have been seen, generally holding in his hand a crumpled paper, containing the latest news from the Southern Confederacy. It was C——, and when he bid for $100,000 gold, the price always stiffened. Then the crowd would be crazy to buy. Lockwood's man would sell them half a million or so, and the excitement would subside.

Fresh news from the front. "Johnston driven back by Sherman." Now, everybody wanted to sell, and gold would drop off two or three per cent. These scenes were renewed at the Evening Exchange, and in the bar-room of the Fifth Avenue Hotel; telegrams flew around like snow-flakes, while gold changed hands by the million.

Late in August the bankers held gold in a firm grip at 260. Large sums had been locked up, and as enormous short sales had been made by the bears on the faith of better military prospects, gold could be readily carried by loaning it to the short sellers. A serious disaster to any one of the Union armies would have driven the price up to 300. And in the absence of any news, the fears of the bears would have induced them to bid it up to 275.

N——, our buoyant broker, had never abated one

jot of his confidence of the ultimate rise of gold to 300. He talked it up at lunch-time; he bought it in magnificent lots in the gold room, in fact he bulled it always and everywhere. Hence it was that in company with L—— I made a venture at that perilous height. I bought $100,000 at 260; in two days I cut short my loss by selling at 250. Ten thousand out on this flyer. The price stayed not long at 250. Suddenly on the last day of August, the grasp of the gold bulls was paralyzed, and the price fell with a dull thud to 233.

What was the matter?

Trouble in the Southern camp. The underground telegraph kept up a constant click. Little groups of still Confederates, scowling and glum, stood on the side-walk, while the looks of those who were long of gold disclosed their secret consternation.

If Sherman took Atlanta, gold would fall fifty per cent. L—— and myself reversed our engines and sold $100,000 gold at 235. This time we clung to our loss till the price had risen to 250. Then we covered. Twenty-five thousand dollars gone in two weeks! Besides these losses on gold, I stood minus $17,000 on Hudson and North-west Preferred, and $30,000 on Cumberland!

N——'s dome-like brow was over-clouded. He called us into his private office, and told us that we must margin up on our stocks, twenty per cent.

Things began to have a mixed look. We must examine our assets.

Most of our assets, outside of margins in our broker's hands, were in the compact and permanent shape of certificates of mining companies. What could they be sold for? We threw them upon the market. For Gregory Consolidated, we had never a bid. Gunnel Gold, we sold, wonderful to relate, for forty per cent. less than we had given for it.

As for "The Alligator Bayou Salt Company," "The Big Mountain Iron Company," "The Black Valley Coal Company," and "The Angels' Rest Quicksilver Company," there were no quotations.

We next sought out the corpulent gentleman, with gold-bowed spectacles, who had succeeded in placing our money, at least $25,000 of it, in the securities last named. His office was near by, just round the corner from the Regular Board of Brokers. As L—— and myself approached it, we saw a couple of countrymen deeply engaged in deciphering two placards, one of which hung in the window, and announced that these offices were *To Let!* The other placard informed anxious inquirers that the office of various mining companies, therein named, was removed to —— William Street, Room No. 28. A look of quizzical wonder sat on the faces of the two men, who were studying the placards. They had come to the city to see how their investments were doing, and to inquire for dividends. The taller of the two was evidently a clergyman. He seemed to take in the situation with remarkable rapidity, and after staring into the windows meekly, for a moment, turned up the street, and walked away as if he were shaking the dust off his feet. The other, who was apparently an agriculturist, had a weather-beaten face, a country made coat, and a blue cotton umbrella. After reading the placard on the door, he aired his eye at the keyhole, then went into the street, and gazed into the window, saw that the office was swept and garnished, cast a searching glance about him, as if he were hunting for specimens of gold quartz, and then, giving a prolonged whistle, ejaculated, "Sloped, my gosh!"

We left the rustic ruminating upon the uncertainty of mining investments, and wended our way to —— William Street, Room No. 28, fourth floor. We found this apartment locked and cob-webs over the key-hole. By removing these obstructions, and looking through the aperture, we could only discover a pile of dusty stock certificate books and a small heap of stones on the floor, which we recognized with some difficulty, as being those remarkably rich samples and specimens of quartz, sulphurets, etc.

We shed no tears, yet we had "thoughts too deep for tears," as we walked homeward that night. Nothing was left to us except to find the corpulent gentleman with gold-bowed spectacles, and see if he would take our certificates off our hands, even at ten cents on the dollar; "failing in that," remarked L—— "we can resort to arms and punch the head of the author of our woes."

On the way home, we happened to step into a picture sales-room on Broadway. The paintings in this establishment were advertised to be the collection of a gentleman just about to start for Europe, and some of his pictures were fondly supposed to be works of the old masters. They embraced the usual themes to which artists are prone to devote themselves, viz., a certain number of cherubs rather beef-faced, and run to fat; several portraits of women with very high color, staring eyes and Roman noses; two or three nude figures after Greuze, a historical picture, the battle of Brandywine, besides landscapes, etc., etc., all newly varnished and in bright gilt frames, made to order.

While contemplating the beauties, and endeavoring to penetrate the "clear obscurity" of these works of art, we became conscious that some one else had joined us, and on casting our eyes around, saw the very man we were in search of, breathing asthmatically, and standing like some gigantic owl directly in front of a very stout Magdalen, and feasting his eyes upon it.

Two hands clapped upon his fat shoulders and two pair of wrathful eyes startled him nearly out of his artistic trance. He stepped back an instant, then recovering himself, grasped our hands affectionately and inquired after our healths with truly paternal solicitude.

"A soft answer turneth away wrath." We were taken aback by so much courtesy, but regained ourselves and cross-examined him on the subject of our investments, and begged to know if he would take them off our hands at a discount.

"Well! no!" replied he, "I am not buying now."

"What's the matter with the securities?" inquired we.

"Antimony is the matter; sulphur is the matter," was his reply. "You see that our gold ores are very rich, but the gold is mixed up with antimony and sulphur, and it can't be extracted so as to pay. But this problem of separating the gold from the antimony and sulphur will be solved before long, then you'll wake up and find yourselves rich, etc., etc."

Although we thought it extremely improbable

that this problem would be solved in our day, yet the corpulent gentleman was so exquisitely bland, and ready with his explanations, that from indignation, we relapsed into uncomplaining sorrow, which in turn passed into forgetfulness, and in three days we had ceased to call to mind how much money we had sunk in bubble-companies.

It is a remarkable trait in human nature, this facility with which the outside public forget how they have been bamboozled by these bogus companies. Perhaps they do not really forget, but they certainly seem to forget how much money they have thrown away in these investments. It may be, that their vanity keeps them from disclosing how they have been taken in.

Meanwhile gold had risen to 254, and was scarce for delivery. It was the news that General Hood was sending his advance guard to Columbus, which had thrown gold to 233; it was the absence of any news, which had driven the price back to 254.

One hot afternoon, at four o'clock, early in September, the gold dealers emerged from their den, and stood on the sidewalk, in a compact and almost silent group. Something hung over the market. The operators stood staring at each other; not a bid or an offer was made. All at once a burly man appeared on the edge of the crowd, and bid for fifty thousand gold, in a loud voice. The price grew firmer when two or three men were observed selling quietly large amounts, and then the price sagged to 250.

There was news in the market! It must be from Atlanta!

That evening every gold-man was at his post, long

before the appointed hour. The bulls were prepared to bolster up the tottering column; and the bears, to make up some of their losses incurred during the past summer; for late that afternoon, the news had been flashed over the wires that Atlanta had fallen.

The Evening Exchange now was like a blacksmith's shop. Gold fell to 243, under the hammers of fifty operators, all striking at once. But just as this anvil chorus was swelling into the roar of a panic, the heavy holders of gold girded up their loins, and arrested, by sharp bids, the downward movement. Their only course now was to let the market down as easily as possible, and stave off a panic until they could unload.

This course they followed for two weeks, selling all they could secretly, and bidding up the market openly. Once or twice the price broke away from them, when gold would fall in a semi-panic, fifteen or twenty per cent. in an hour; but each time that it did so, they stepped into the gap, and ran up the price again, "scooping" many a bear just as he was stretching his paws for the profit, which he thought he had in his grasp. When at last they had sold out, though at a heavy loss, they let the price go, and down it dropped, amid the wildest excitement, to 187.

Our profits in the great gold break will be recounted in the following chapter.

We now return to our "averaged Cumberland."

While gold was flying wildly about, oscillating in long arcs towards 200, Cumberland all at once sprang in a day back to 68, and a great mass of stock was hurled upon the market. The ring had during the dull season taken a great number of short contracts and then twisted them by bidding up the stock. But the fifteen thousand shares which they sold upon the rise, soon carried the price back to 60. Here it stuck for two weeks. Stocks which had been tending downwards for five months had received a fresh impetus in the same direction, from gold as it fell.

The 6th of October following came a panic which carried Cumberland to 41. On that day I made the acquaintance of one of that class of stock-operators whom we shall designate as *panic-birds*. These men are the stormy petrels of Wall Street. They are never seen in the market when everything is bright and buoyant, but let a tempest breed there and when stocks are going down by the run, they flock to the scene of disaster, prepared to take advantage of it by *buying stocks* at low prices. Any one who has passed through panics will remember those strange faces standing near where the contest is raging, and quietly giving their orders.

Who are they, and where do they come from? All of them are veterans of the market, who have learned by sad experience, that the only way to make money in stocks is to buy when everybody else is selling, that is during panics. Some come from the country, stay over one train and then depart, loaded with securities bought at a low price, and all of them take their flight the moment stocks turn and react upwards. One of these veterans has seen twenty panics with his own eyes, and boasts that he has made his fortune of $200,000 by never buying except in those seasons.

F. S—— was a type of this class. I saw him for the first time, during the October panic of 1857.

Then he disappeared from view for more than three years, turning up again in April, 1861, after the bombardment of Fort Sumter. In July, 1862, in May and September, 1863, on April 18th, 1864, in the gold panic just described, and finally on October 6th, in 1873, he was always on the spot, not one minute too late to see prices reach the bottom of the grade.

A singular looking man. His mould was of the herculean pattern, and he turned the scale at sixteen stone two pounds. His face was like a tame eagle's, carved out of red oak; his hair was cut fighting fashion, as if he wished to keep himself in constant training, to cope with the bruisers of the stock-market, and while brokers were shrieking as the prices fell, he would stand very firm on his legs with his square solid set head cocked on one side, puffing firmly at a regalia as long as a small bowsprit.

I stood beside him on a mound of dust in Broad Street, and being in a fever of anxiety, such as is usually brought on by staring at a loss which threatens to fall on one, sought to relieve myself by asking his opinion about the market. He said nothing for a moment, then turning his head put his fat hand to his mouth and gurgled into my ear: "Buy Cumberland." Our account stood us out something over eighty thousand dollars, and now it was "play or pay."

Thanks to my short gold operations, to be hereafter described, I could buy one thousand Cumberland for cash, at from 42 to 45, and two thousand shares more on a margin at 46–47. In three days it rose to 59, and I was enabled to unload for a trifling loss.

A new campaign was now opening in gold, but before pursuing that jagged, serrated line of financial history, by which may be traced as on a many colored chart of alternate mountain peaks and lowland flats, the rising and sinking fortunes of the gold men, let us turn aside for a chapter to notice the speculation in something more substantial and staple than stocks; a speculation which sympathized with that in gold, moving up and down in lines parallel to it.

We give a brief account in our next chapter of the pork speculation, which, extraordinary as it was, becomes dwarfed in comparison with the grain speculation of 1879. In the spring of that year James R. Keene bought, according to common report, something like thirty million bushels of wheat in the Chicago market. He sold out in a few months at a large profit. In the autumn of 1879 the transactions in grain swelled to a huge volume, and had Keene held his grain longer he would have made millions. However, it is said his stock operations in the six months ending December, 1879, have netted him as much as if he had kept his wheat.

CHAPTER XXV.

PIGS OF GOLD IN A CORNER.

The Rise in New Mess—The Pork Trade—Its Magnitude and Seat—A Village Built of Hogs—The Movements of the Article—Cornering the Packed Pigs—I Make $10,000 in Cotton and then Slip into Pork Barrels—An Evening Lecture on Provisions, etc., at the Fifth Avenue Hotel—The Pork Corner of July 1864—Who Made It?—My First Visit to the Corn Exchange, and What I Saw There—A Crowd of Porkists—The Retired Pirate Buys a Thousand Barrels at 47—Panic on the Produce Exchange—I Sell a Call, Buy a Call, and Make $59,000 on One, and Lose $6,000 on the Other—Multiplying $500 by $100.

NO one connected with the agricultural interests, more especially with that branch which is concerned in the raising and fattening of swine, will fail to remember the great rise in pork which took place in 1864. This article in the provision line, so useful in regulating our foreign exchanges, and so sweet to the palate of those who delight in the dish popularly known as pork and beans, had risen from nine dollars per barrel in 1861, to fifty-three dollars per barrel in July 1864. If the deliciousness of a viand is proportioned to its price, then, indeed, was pork a delicious viand. Had one of the old Roman epicures survived till 1864, he would doubtless have mingled pork with the peacocks' brains, and ostriches' tongues, which gave zest to his banquets.

Few, who have not visited the Western States, will be able to estimate the extent of the business, which is larger now, in 1879, than ever.

"This is a great country," remarked H——, a New York merchant, one day as we were traveling together with our faces turned towards the setting sun.

The place where this trite observation was made, was a small town on the western bank of the Mississippi; the time was the dead of winter in 1863, and the occasion of it was simply pork, or as it is called among the killers and packers, *hog*. We walked up to the village hotel between *hog*, we stepped over *hog*. Hecatombs of hog were piled up on every side, in stacks, in pyramids, in mountains. It met us at breakfast, dinner and tea, fried, baked, boiled and stewed. From our chamber window we overlooked a wide expanse of country, dotted with droves of hogs, and in great pens in the village, thousands of hogs were squealing, grunting, piling on, and suffocating each other in search of warmth (for the mercury stood five degrees below zero) of which last fact, (the piling,) we were notified by a hoarse voice calling out in the hall of the floor where we were sleeping that night: "John Hackerberry, your hog are piling! Turn out and look arter 'em!"

In this way we got our first ideas respecting the magnitude of the pork trade, which is growing daily.

The harvest of the pork-raiser is in the winter. From December till April the carcasses are forwarded to the cities of Chicago, Cincinnati and New York etc., to be packed in barrels. The packed pork continues to come to New York from the West till July, after which there are small arrivals till the ensuing winter.

After July the regular cornering season commences, for corners are engineered in pork as well as in stocks. The number of barrels of pork on store in New York is accurately known. This is an important fact entering into the calculations of ambitious provision dealers, when they plan a corner in the article, since a new issue of pork cannot be made by those who are seeking to break down the corner, by throwing a fresh supply upon the market, as bearish railroad directors are wont to do in stocks, when they find themselves cornered.

A corner in pork is just as close, and the cornerers themselves just as remorseless, as those in stocks.

This was how I came to be caught short in one of these same corners. The five hundred bales of cotton bought in May, netted me $10,000, the price having risen, in ten days, no less than forty cents a pound.

This lucky operation at once brought me into the speculative mercantile circle. I began to take an interest in the price of produce and provisions, and to learn the A B C of operations in tobacco, sugar, grain, and PORK.

The Fifth Avenue Hotel has long been the financial up-town evening center, and in 1864, all who were interested in the rise and fall of merchandise, etc., as well as stocks and gold, flocked thither just as politicians now do for election news.

One evening, early in July, a few days after the gold-burst upwards, six men sat in a circle within the reading room of that huge marble tavern, exchanging views upon a great variety of subjects. Two of these men, L—— and myself, were stock operators, one was a noted gold broker, and the other three were in the dry goods and raw cotton line. What we didn't say on the subjects of stocks and general merchandise, would hardly be worth telling, for our session was a protracted one, and one or the other of us had taken flyers in almost every speculative direction. First it was stocks and gold, then cotton, iron, petroleum, turpentine, wheat, tea, molasses, butter, cheese, etc., etc., through the whole scale.

At length some one said "Pork!" and now all our tongues wagged merrily. "Pork was the thing to go into now, on the short side." Four of our circle had bought it a few weeks before, and sold out at a profit of ten dollars a barrel, and seemed thoroughly booked in the business; while L—— and myself had taken notes on it, for a month previous, and were watching the article in question, as it slipped upwards on its greasy trail.

Enter J. L—— at this moment.

He was a partner in the house of R——, H——, B—— & Co. He stared round the room, quickly espied our circle, and steered towards it, discharging volumes of cigar smoke as he drew near. He was an authority on the subject of pork, for his firm was in the provision business.

"How is pork?" chorused all.

"Strong! Fifty-three dollars bid for August deliveries," was the reply.

After that he gave us an account of the "corner," which had been engineered in the pork market.

The leader in the movement was C——, a wealthy packer, and storage man. With him were joined a number of other firms who had bought pork at various prices, from thirty dollars upwards. Three circumstances had assisted them in their scheme, viz., the great ease in money which had ruled in June at five or six per cent., the rise in gold with which pork as well as other exportable commodities sympathized, and the enormous short interest in pork. The more conservative firms, in consideration of its rise of four or five hundred per cent., had been selling it for future delivery, and the cornerers had taken their contracts for July and August. If money continued easy, and gold kept up for six weeks longer, pork would rise to seventy dollars per barrel, but if not, then it would drop back to thirty or forty dollars, and the corner would be broken up.

These were the questions to be answered.

But whereas after so protracted a season of easy money, it was likely to grow tight, and gold, after a rise of one hundred per cent., might naturally fall fifty per cent., (so we all reasoned,) pork was a better sale than purchase. We would sell short to-morrow. This was the decision of L—— and myself, when we parted that night.

The next morning we went to the office of R——, H——, B—— & Co., in Water Street. The senior member of this firm, a stout, cheery, wholesome looking gentleman, intimated that we were on the right track if we sold pork; "in fact," said he, "I should take a chance at it myself if I hadn't been heated up and cooled down so often;" meaning thereby that he was now on the shady side of fifty.

So we accompanied J. L—— to the *Corn Exchange*, or, as it is sometimes called, the Produce Exchange. This is one of the institutions of New York. A huge brick building on the corner of Whitehall and Pearl Streets, only the upper part of which however is used by the association of merchants who meet there from twelve to two o'clock daily. The hall in which they meet, occupies the whole of the second floor of the building. The clock struck twelve as we entered this room, which was already crowded with dealers. They were a very different looking set of men from those who congregate in and about the Stock Exchange. There was about them an air of solidity and of legitimate trade. As the hour flew by we waited for business to commence, but nothing seemed to be doing. There was no noise, and all the conversation was carried on in a low tone. They seemed to be waiting for something which never came, and reminded us very much of the visitors inspecting an agricultural fair. Some of them gathered round little pans of flour, and took pinches between their fingers and moistened them in saucers, as if they were making paste samples; others poked their fingers into lard tubs, or punched out small pieces of cheese, or spooned up little lumps of butter and tasted them, smacking their lips and holding their heads on one side, with the most knowing of looks upon their faces. One old gentleman in a black coat, black stock, and a wig of the jettiest hue, was peering into a barrel of beans, like a magpie squinting into a marrow-bone. The majority of the crowd, however, seemed to be engaged in pleasant, social conversation.

In the north-east corner of the room, stood a cluster of twenty or thirty men who were apparently more busy. Those of low stature were in the center, and the tall ones looked over their shoulders. They talked almost in a whisper and in a very few words, handling their memorandum books briskly and jotting down as they talked. What could they be doing? Buying and selling pork! We joined this coterie, and J. L—— informed us that if we wished to sell, he could dispose of two thousand barrels of new mess, deliverable in July or August, at forty-seven dollars per barrel, and ten dollars a barrel margin to be put up by both parties. We gave the order. Our two thousand barrels were immediately snapped up by a sallow little man in a green vest, yellow pants, red neck-tie, covered with a profusion of jewelry, and looking very much like a successful and retired pirate, who was hovering about the skirts of the crowd.

My proportion of this short sale was one thousand barrels. For the next two weeks we sought the fellowship of the pork men. Pork on the brain. We thought pork, talked pork, handled pork, dreamed of pork, and did everything with it except eat it, because it cost too much. The pork men are very much after the pattern of the Wall Street men. Jolly boys, astonished at nothing, much given to the eating and drinking of good things, fond of jokes, and of stories with a point, and always on the lookout for commissions, with a sharp eye to the margins of their customers.

Everything now "went merry as a marriage bell," for pork was falling, and we were preparing to put money in our purses. It was also gratifying to our vanity, when we reflected that we were right in the financial reasonings on which our sales of pork had been based. Money, we said, would tighten, and gold fall. Sure enough, gold did drop to 244, and as for money, it became suddenly as scarce as roses in December. This pressure, the pork men said, was a "squealer." There were palpitations and flutterings at the Corn Exchange that morning, and the stalwart cornerers shook in their well greased boots, for was not new mess pork down to thirty-eight dollars?

I could cover my short sale at $9,000 profit, not reckoning in the commission due to R——, H——, B—— & Co., which was two and one-half per cent. on $47,000, the contract price at which the pork was sold. But who ever heard of a man covering a short sale in a panic? Prices looked then as if they would never recover themselves. So it was now, instead of taking my profit I sold another thousand barrels at 37. In one week pork had risen to 42. Then I covered, and found, instead of a nice little profit, I had a nice little commission bill of $2,000, to pay R——, H——, B—— & Co. In fact, I found that pork owed me money, and was uneasy till pork paid me that money, or—owed me more. That money must be recovered. How could it be done? I dared not sell, for I was in the position of the burnt child, who dreads the fire. Ha! a thought! I would sell a call on favorable terms.

Calls and puts are sold in pork, just as they are in stocks.

I sold a call for one thousand barrels of pork, that very night at the Fifth Avenue Hotel, or rather J. L—— sold it for me. I thus became responsible to deliver to —— ——, any time within sixty days, at forty-three dollars and fifty cents per barrel, one thousand barrels of new mess, and in consideration thereof, I received one thousand dollars. This partly wiped out my loss, but there was the call still hanging over me.

"These calls are nasty things," observed Uncle Daniel, after his Harlem fight.

"So say we all of us." Especially a sixty day call. If pork should go to seventy dollars, I should stand out fifteen thousand besides commissions, which should never be forgotten in these little operations.

This was late in August, gold was tottering, but sixty days is a long time. There was one way in which I could save myself; I could hedge by buying a call for the same amount; let the one call offset the other.

I bought my call. Pork rose, and in two weeks it showed me a net profit of five hundred dollars. Atlanta had just fallen, and gold was on the down grade, but all my spare cash was locked up in margins. I yearned to sell, but could not.

But while dwelling on my uncomfortable position, I remembered the profit on my call. I took the contract to my broker, but he refused to accept it as a margin. As I was going out of the office, I met the Lobster, so called from his very red face and bulging eyes. He had recently gone into the business of buying and selling on commission, and so was willing to make concessions for the purpose of getting business. His eyes bulged still more, and his face grew a shade redder, as he listened to my proposals, then thrusting my call into his pocket, he rushed into the gold room, and in the twinkling of a star rushed out again and announced that he had sold ten thousand gold at 243. In twenty-four hours gold struck 230, but the Lobster had been meanwhile kept diligently at work selling for my behoof, and already I had $6,000 profits. In two weeks after, when gold reached 214, my profits had run up to $19,000. Now gold flew up to 228, and if my transactions had been closed at that figure, I should have stood just where I started. But the upward spasm soon passed, and gold resumed its downward course. When it touched 190 I gave the order to cover my shorts. This was done at a profit of $39,000. Then reversing my engine, I bought $200,000; when the price shot to 200 the next day, I sold and raked in $20,000. In one month I had made $59,000 out of a pitiful $500 on a pork call.

Now that pork owed me nothing, I closed my pork call without either profit or loss. Still there remained the thousand barrels, which I had agreed to deliver at forty-three fifty, with pork rising every day. It touched 43, and I bought one thousand barrels to hold ready for delivery, when a little speck appeared in the western sky, in the shape of a provision and produce panic, in Chicago and other western cities. Money grew tight, and the pork and grain men were in distress. They had stood up firmly under their loads, but contemplating the fall of gold, and its reduced price for ten days, was too much for their nerves, and they weakened.

The 7th of October was a lively day among the pork men of the New York Corn Exchange, as I afterwards learned from L——, (who had an interest of five hundred barrels in the pork market, and to whom I had delegated the task of looking after my thousand barrels that day, inasmuch as I was then busily engaged in taking care of Cumberland.) The first thing which caught his eye, on approaching the pork crowd, was the retired pirate to whom I had sold my first thousand barrels, flying about as if he were busily engaged in scuttling some merchant vessel. He came up to L——, and recognized him at once, as his legitimate prey. Unfortunately, our broker was late that day, and the pirate ascertaining that fact, from L——, promptly volunteered his services, which L—— as promptly accepted, for pork was dropping one dollar per barrel, every five minutes.

"Sell fifteen hundred barrels at 42," said L——.

"All right!" said the pirate, and he shuffled off to execute the commission; poking his head under the coat-tails of a tall, weary looking porkist, he came back speedily, and reported the best price as 41½.

"Then sell at 41½," said L——.

Again his volunteer agent insinuated himself into the crowd, and *stayed there.* The crowd kept up a perpetual whispering. L—— was in dismay, for pork was now reported as offered at 41, and weak at that; he poked his long arm between two heads, touched the pirate on the shoulder and nodded very hard to him to sell; he nodded back, and kept his place in the crowd.

L—— then made a feeble offer of fifteen hundred barrels of new mess, at 41. Several turned round and stared at him, and then resumed their whispering. L—— said he felt very bad.

The pirate here made his appearance, and taking L—— affectionately by the arm, led him aside, and informed him in confidence, that he knew a party, a friend of his, who would take that fifteen hundred barrels at 40¼. That was about the market price.

This offer was gladly embraced by L——, for the next day pork might go to 35. Such is the reasoning of one who is suffering from a panic. We surmised that the "party" in question was probably the pirate himself, for pork rose in a few days up again to 43, but there was no means of proving our suspicions, and so we pocketed our losses. I was nearly four thousand dollars out already on that call. The sixty days, during which the call ran, shortly after expired, and once more I breathed freely.

Space will not admit of our noticing at greater length, the various speculative operations carried on at the New York Corn Exchange, nor describe our further transactions in that field.

Suffice it to say that combinations are there organized and corners engineered, not only in pork, but in wheat, corn, beef, butter, cheese, and many other commodities, very much to the disadvantage of the public generally, to say nothing of the speculators who are caught thereby.

When we had made our first operation in pork, we went into grain. This article may be said to be in a state of chronic corner, as every housekeeper who has occasion to buy flour is well aware. We had the satisfaction of knowing that we sold grain to the corner-brigands at a very high price, which doubtless, in the end proved to them a losing purchase, although an unfortunate sale for us. After that, we sampled some butter, and thinking it too high considering its quality, we sold butter short, and as it melted down under the fierce rays of the sun of Atlanta, we coined its oily substance into double eagles. Then we thrust our speculative knives into cheese, and flattered ourselves that we had helped to puncture the caseous balloon, and contributed to the collapse of the aeronaut who had inflated it, to the sorrow of all lunchers and sandwich-eaters.

Finding, that after a campaign of three months on the Corn Exchange, we had come out nearly even, we bid adieu forever to pork, corn, wheat, butter, and cheese, except in a dietetic way, and in the future, concentrated ourselves upon gold and stocks, having discovered that we knew more about our own special trade than about cut meats and cereals.

CHAPTER XXVI.

THE WORSHIPERS OF THE GOLDEN CALF.

The Old Fogies Go In—The Cavern of the Gold Brigands—Fresh Levies From the Country—Margins on the Wing to Their Nests in the Gold-Room—The Bulls and Bears Marshal Their Forces for Another Engagement—The Bears Under the Yoke—Gold Once More on the Rampage—What Became of Our Quartette—I Sell "One Hoondret Tousand on a Dree per Shent. Marchin"—The Old Rat Nibbles at a Cheese—My Pile—A Jew Broker Extracts Many Shekels From a Gentile—The History of My Friend L—— —The Gold Carnival at its Height—Dancing in the Gold Room—A Riotous Market at the Fifth Avenue Hotel—A Message from the Death-bed of L———The Last Scene in the Career of a Great Speculator.

THE gold men moved into their new room on the corner of William and Beaver Streets, late in September.

The downward course of gold after the fall of Atlanta, seemed so reasonable, that a new element entered into the speculation, consisting of cooler and more cautious men. As the current rolled down from the mountain height of 254, they put their arms up to the elbows in the golden gravel, and in ten days became as mad as the maddest of the throng.

The gold room was like a cavern, full of dank and noisome vapors, and the deadly carbonic acid was blended with the fumes of stale smoke and vinous breaths. But the stifling gases engendered in that low-browed cave of evil enchanters, never seemed to depress the energies of the gold-dealers; from "morn to dewy eve" the drooping ceiling and bistre-colored walls reëchoed with the sounds of all kinds of voices, from the shrill, piping treble of the call boys, to the deep bass of R. H——, J. R——, L. J——, etc., etc., while an upreared forest of arms was swayed furiously by the storms of a swiftly rising and falling market.

When we consider the number of operators, the amount of capital employed, and the volume of business transacted, the wide and rapid fluctuations, and the frequency with which operations were repeated, it will be no exaggeration to say, that in that room from September, 1864, till July, 1865, more fortunes were made and lost, than in any space of the same size before or since. Here occurred most of the Atlanta tumble, the rocket-like movement from 187 to 260, the swift and countless vibrations between 260 and 200, the flying gallop, which carried the price from 200 to 128, and finally, the hoist to 146, all in the course of nine short months.

The story of great fortunes made in a day, drew thousands from all parts of the Republic. Solid men of Boston; spare men from Connecticut, whose sharpness, as regards money, might have enabled them to beguile St. Peter to swap his golden keys; logy men, with bovine eyes, from the state of Maine, stalwart Westerners, familiar with the game of bluff from their earliest boyhood; besides that numerous army of speculators from south of Mason and Dixon's line, already mentioned. These were only a squadron of the host.

Each broker and commission house seemed to have

been transformed into a human magnet, attracting to itself all the old and young "files" who thought their teeth sharp enough to bite into the golden pasty; while the wealthy banking houses, by their very name and reputed solvency, received by mail, by hand, and even by telegraph, in the form of credits, vast amounts to be used as margins, and passed them rapidly out of sight forever of the hopeful depositors. Those men who had money, and were known to be of a speculative turn of mind, were approached directly, by the nimble mercurial tribe of younger brokers, who solicited their business, painting in glowing hues the prospect of making speedy fortunes.

After gold dropped to 187, on the 26th of September, it reacted to 200, then fell back to 190–191, where it remained for ten days.

There were now, as there always are, in the stock market, two sets of opinions. One of these was loud-mouthed in the expression of the belief that gold was on the way to 150. The other as strongly held to the belief in another great rise. But this latter opinion was scarcely expressed. The party which looked for a further decline, was the more numerous and the more clamorous, besides being strengthened by the large profits on their short sales during the recent fall. The party which looked for another rise was by far the more wealthy, and numbered in its ranks most of the great banking houses. It was observed that they were continually crying down the price of gold and as continually buying it. The short sales were immense, and were as usual, quietly taken by the bull party. For a few days the market was in suspense.

One morning the roar of cannon was heard in the bay, and a report ran through the street, that Richmond had been captured. The bear cohort rushed in a body to the gold room and sold millions in expectation of a fresh break. The price never yielded under this tremendous pressure, and in twenty-four hours, gold was 203. The bear cohort never flinched, but kept selling. In three days, gold was 216. The faces of the short sellers here became elongated, when news came of cavalry Sheridan's victory, after his swift gallop up the valley of the Shenandoah, and down fell gold to 208. Now the bears commenced again their furious hammering, but only succeeded in knocking the price down one-half per cent., when whisk! it jumped to 220.

The crew of short sellers now sat like shipwrecked mariners upon a coral reef in mid ocean, watching with wild eyes for a sail, which was never to appear, while night and storm closes above them.

The tide rose rapidly, and the agony of the shipwrecked ones was soon over.

Gold, in ten days, was 246, then surging back to 230, it gathered itself, and poured in one great wave up to 260. The same men who had sold it at 190, and predicted its fall to 150, now bought it, and laid bets that it would be at 300 inside of thirty days. Frailty, thy name is the Wall Street bear!

Of all the exultant crowd, who bathed in Pactolian waters, and upon whom the golden rain had fallen in showers, six weeks before, who was the richer now? They had prayed for riches, "Let the stream of wealth be swift and violent." The golden torrent had come in answer to their prayers. On September 26th, they laved in it, rolled in and drank of it to intoxication. On November 9th, they woke as from a dream, and found, instead of a golden torrent, nothing but a bed of stones and sand. They who had engineered this enormous rise, and had wrought the ruin of so many, were blown up with wealth, and with the self-confidence that was, in four short months, to lead some of them to their ruin. But now they were triumphant, counting their gains, and planning new stratagems.

After every great rise and fall in stocks and gold, there comes the gazette, in which the names of the losers, and of the financially dead, are recorded. This gazette is not like that which follows a battle, published and spread abroad, but circulates only in the stock-market, or among the friends of the losing individuals.

Men drop out of the ranks, and their forms are seen, and their voices heard no more on 'Change. The word goes round, "Brown has gone up!" the next day he is forgotten. The rise of gold to 260 broke up our quartette. W. B. C—— left the street in despair at his losses, and never returned to it again. E——, my *alter ego*, lost all of his fortune except $5,000.

The writer was fortunate enough to receive a lesson early in the campaign, which taught him to stand clear of short sales.

It happened thus:

One day in October, just after gold had fallen to 208, on the news of the Sheridan victories, I met, in the doorway of the gold room, one L. O——, a German stock broker, who resembled, in his personal appearance, a huge wharf rat, smoothly shaved and dressed in the garb of a broker. Hailing me, he spoke, breaking English into the following pieces:

"Hein! Mishter ——, a vort mit you. Vy you not do your bishness mit me? I do your bishness sheap. I sharge you only dree per shent. marchin, dree tousand dollars on von hoondert tousand gold, and you bay me dree dollars and von shilling comeeshion, den I garry it eider way, long or short. Shell a hoondert dish minoot, you mak blanty moonish."

The bargain was clinched on the spot by my handing him a check for three thousand dollars, and ordering him to sell one hundred thousand gold at the market price. Whereupon he dove into the bowels of the crowd, waved his hand and screamed out something that sounded like von hoondert, and returned to me, reporting that he had sold $100,000 at 208½, though I am confident now, that the rascal never sold a dollar. Then he vanished up the street.

I thought that gold seemed a little stiffer that morning, and on coming back to the gold-room, after two hours' absence, gold stood at 210½.

L. O—— soon made his appearance with a woebegone look on his face, and asked me what he should do. While I was deliberating, he broke in upon me.

"Oh! Mishter ——, tish all right. You geep your poseetion; but I musht have more marchin; gif me dree tousand dollars more and I geep you short of gold, den you mak monish."

A second check for three thousand dollars was drawn and duly consigned to the pocket of L. O——, who just then seemed to recollect some important business which required his presence elsewhere, and vanished as before.

It need hardly be told that I kept my position in accordance with the advice of L. O——.

In forty-eight hours, gold was 215.

"Shoost von leetle sheck more for dree tousand dollars," said my Teuton.

He received it and vanished as usual.

It was growing interesting. Gold kept rising, and when it reached 217, "von leetle sheck more" was handed over.

On visiting the Evening Exchange that day, I learned from one of the door-keepers that some one had been bawling out my name a moment before, and on entering, I saw L. O—— jumping about like a chittagong rooster which had been feasting upon brandy-cherries, and bidding "two hoondert and seventy-one for von hoondert tousand gold." The moment he caught sight of his luckless customer, he ran towards him, vociferating, "von leetle sheck more for dree tousand dollars, or I buy in your gold. Tish shtrong, tish dretful shtrong;" (meaning the market was rampant and rising.)

He was quieted down by receiving his "last leetle sheck," together with an order to buy in my hundred thousand, short.

This transaction taught me at an expense of $12,500, not to go short of gold on *that* twist.

But L——, whom we called the richest, wisest and strongest of our quartette, was not so fortunate.

Poor L——, what fortunes and what a fate was his!

One evening in the month of August, while sitting on a balcony of his brown stone front, in —— Street, he told us the story of his Wall Street life.

He came into the market in 1862, with $10,000,

and in less than a year had $250,000 to his credit at his brokers. He resolved to retire when he had made $500,000, but having been caught short of Pacific Mail, found himself in four months, poorer by $100,000. Five months after this, his "pile" showed him $200,000; in two months it was only $50,000. The Morse rise had put $100,000 into his pocket, and the panic which followed it, had taken $90,000 out of his pocket.

In August, and while telling us his story, he had still $80,000 lying in a very exposed situation, being deposited as a margin at his broker's, besides owning the brown stone front house, in which we were then sitting, which had cost him $40,000.

"I am going to make it up to $150,000," said he, "and then, good-bye Wall Street."

The Atlanta tumble took place, but L—— did not profit by it.

When gold rose to 200, he sold $200,000 short, and made $20,000. Then he made a lucky turn on the short side, in Erie, when it dropped to 85 in the panic of October 6th. He lacked now, only $500 of the $150,000, on which he purposed to retire. Gold had soon after risen again to 200, and L—— sold $100,000 at that price, giving his broker orders to cover at 199⅜. This would have exactly made the $150,000, and L—— would have reached the golden climacteric of fortune and repose.

But alas! this was not to be.

Gold rose in less than a week to 210. L—— commenced "averaging."

He sold another $100,000 at that price. It rose to 216, and then gave him the shadow of a hope, by falling back to 207, which was quickly dispelled by its rise to 220. Again he sold $100,000. The price mounted to 230. Once more he sold the same amount, and repeated the sale at 240. He stood a loser in twenty-four hours, in the sum of $130,000. Still he kept his position manfully, strained his credit, borrowed $20,000 fresh margin, and sold another lot at 250. Three hours later, and his broker called for more margin, and L—— failing to respond, bought in, at 251, the whole $600,000 of which his unfortunate customer was short. L—— had lost everything, cash, margin, brown stone front, horses and furniture, and owed more than $30,000 borrowed money. But this was not his worst loss. He lost the one thing that sustains the ruined operator—Hope.

Three weeks he lingered, hopeless and haggard, on the fringes of the market, and then disappeared. After two days had gone by, and we had not seen him, I called with E—— at his boarding-house. He was no longer there, nor could the landlady give us a hint as to where he might be found. We saw him no more for six weeks.

Meanwhile the gold carnival was at its height. Each day the crowd grew denser, it packed the gold-room with fervid masses, it formed in a three-quarter segment of a circle at the corner of William and Beaver Streets, buried ankle deep in the muddy slush, watching the indicator, which recorded their gains and losses. The whole strength of the speculation was here. While stocks were halting and bobbing up and down in minute arcs of a circle, gold rose and fell in huge parabolic curves.

The stock-dealers poured into the crowd. They

who had got their hand in by dealing in New York Central, which moved in a stately promenade, generally closed up the ball by a frenzied galopade or a daring swing on the flying trapeze in the gold-room. As the winter wore away, the fun "grew fast and furious." No hour without some change in the scenes, fortunes vanished in a day, or rose like exhalations in a night. Fresh bands of revelers rushed in as the weary ones departed, and margins with long trains and ciphers, danced about and then disappeared, like Tam O'Shanter's witches. In the pauses between the mad cotillons, the well-known Wall Street game of "beggar your neighbor" was industriously played. Then suddenly would be heard the roar of Union and Southern guns at the front, calling off new figures in the dance, when the bulls and bears grinning at each other, *vis-a-vis,* started once more up and down, cross over, *dos-a-dos,* cutting all manner of capers, and each one "holding out to dance the other down."

From 9 A. M. till 12 P. M., fifteen hours every day, speculation knew no pause. All day long prices spouted up and then foamed themselves away, and when night came the whole body of speculators adjourned to the Fifth Avenue Hotel and kept it up till midnight.

Winter was rolling away, and the sun was climbing the sky towards Cancer. Night fell on one dark, stormy day in January. The "street" had been agitated by a thousand rumors of battles, and disasters to the Union armies. Gold was flying upwards. The crowd at the hotel was never madder than upon that evening. The market was riotous. We stood, wedged in the center of the circle, watching the fate of the

$100,000 we had just staked, when a face peered over the shoulders of the outside ring, and a long arm thrust a letter before our eyes. It was directed to E——, or to me. Opening it we read: "L—— is dangerously ill. He wishes to see you immediately. Come to —— —— Street." The letter was dated the evening before, and should have reached us that morning. We forced our way through the press, and hurried to the place indicated.

The storm had broken away; it was a wholesome night. The air was pure and still; the moon, in her first quarter, was sailing down the sky like a great birch bark canoe. Whether it was from distempered fancy, or the reflection of the rifted storm-clouds, we know not, but it looked as though it were made of gold. Hastening on through glimmer and gloom, in the direction indicated by the letter, we soon reached our destination. It was a miserable tenement house, only six blocks due east from the palaces of fashion. We climbed five flights of stairs, and found ourselves in a low attic, apparently untenanted. As we stood in the hall, our ears caught the sound of stifled sobs, which proceeded from a door which was half-way open. We approached, and gazed into the chamber. The dim light from a tallow candle would have failed to show us the interior, but the yellow moon-light, streaming through the attic window, fell upon a truckle-bed, where knelt the sobbing wife, and lit up the ghastly features of a dead man. We stepped softly in, and gazed upon all that remained of L——, our old friend, and late comrade in the battle of speculation. His losses had killed him. * * * * *

The clocks from a hundred belfries slowly hammered out twelve as we turned again into Fifth Avenue. The long lines of gas-lights winked at us like so many flaming cressets, all converging in the baleful focus of the Evening Exchange, and seeming to beacon us away. The moon was set, and the great constellations were marching up and down the sky. But the crowd of sodden-faced men who poured out from the front of the hotel, as we passed on our way, took no heed of Arcturus beaming in the northern sky, nor of the stars blazing in the belt of Orion. Their eyes were bent on each other in ravenous greed, or cast down upon the muddy pavement, while they marred the beauty of the night with their hoarsely screamed bids and offers.

Stories as sad as the above could be told every month of the fate of those who have tempted fortune and found her adverse. The sudden plunge from wealth to poverty in stock-speculation has broken the heart and shattered the reason of many an unfortunate speculator. Suicides like that of Dalton, in 1866, and of Le Roy Nichols, in 1879, are examples to warn against the "making haste to be rich." After the panic, which will follow the last great rise in stocks, we may look for another crop of suicides and sudden deaths.

THE END OF A GREAT SPECULATOR.

CHAPTER XXVII.

ASTRAND AND AFLOAT AGAIN.

The Gap Closes Up, and the Column Moves on as Before—Loss on Loss—Tobin Comes to the Front—Fifty Millions of Gold Sold—E—— makes a Little Mistake—A Dinner at Delmonico's—A Philharmonic Concert—Lengthened "Sweetness Long Drawn Out"—Golden Dreams—A Slight Misunderstanding Cleared Up in a very Disagreeable Manner—$45,000 Loss by a Slip of the Pen—Sunlight Again—The Bears Putting In Their Sickles to Reap a Harvest—Who Went Short of Gold?—A Bold Stroke for Fortune—On the Rack Once More—E—— and Myself Stand Guard Over $2,000,000—A Speculator's Dream—The Fatal Order Given and We are Astrand—The Final Break-up—Floating Away on a Pot of Money.

WE have said that a man without money was nothing in the calculations of the stock-market. Let us add that a man's *life* counts for little there. The beggared operator buffets the waves unregarded, and when he throws up his arms and sinks below the surface of the stormy sea, by which he has so long been tossed, not even a ripple marks the place where he went down. Even his friends, the companions of his voyage, soon forget his loss amid the din and whirl and absorbing anxieties of their daily life.

We had to fight the battle alone now—E—— and I. On the 15th of January our positions were reversed—E—— had made fifty thousand, and I had lost the same amount. Standing up, like a pugilist under punishment at the hands of some strong opponent, for five weeks, I had received more blows than I had given. Holding gold at 230, the victory of Nashville had shaken $10,000 worth of it out of my grasp. The capture of Savannah had torn away $20,000. The surrender of Fort Fisher had cost me $20,000 more.

These blows came heavy and fast. Gold dropped to 200, when nearly the whole force of the market seemed suddenly to change front. The great banking-houses who had been buying gold, now commenced selling it for a further decline. Vast sales were made between 200 and 205. When the price touched 198, it stood firm for two hours in spite of the most terrific hammering.

Some power behind the scenes was holding it up! It mounted to 201. Then the hidden cause revealed itself. During the preceding two months, John M. Tobin had been persistently selling gold short, at high prices, predicting that he would "take it in" at 200. His predictions proved true. He had "taken in" his short gold at 200, and then bought heavily for a rise. At four o'clock, P. M., he made his appearance on the street, just as the board adjourned, and commenced bidding for lots of from $100,000 to $1,000,000, while a little black-eyed, keen broker stood by his side and recorded his purchases. The price rose rapidly to 205. The bears, supposing he was making bluff bids for the purpose of selling through other brokers, at first sold him all he bid for, but at length they saw he was an actual buyer, and paused. The amount of short sales made in the course of the forty-eight hours previous, was estimated to have been fifty millions. There was not this amount of gold in New York. The market was "oversold." The short sellers at once saw their situation.

The crowd began to lift up their voices in supplication and astonishment. "Oh, let me off from that last half million I sold you, John!"

"What's your game, Tobin?"

"Boys, you've been selling more gold than you can deliver, and I've been buying some of it," replied Tobin.

Although many of the smaller and more timorous of the bear tribe, now covered their shorts, the stronger and thicker-waisted ones still kept their position, judging that Tobin would fail in carrying up the price, in the face of Union victories.

E—— and myself were each short of $50,000 gold, at 200½. When it rose to 206, under Tobin's bids, our mood of mind became highly reflective. The pressure at last became too great, when we remembered how neatly we had been caught in the October rise. We decided to cover our shorts, and buy for a rise; E—— filled out a joint order, by which the "Lobster" who was now our sole broker, was empowered to buy in, at the market price, the $100,000 of which we were short, and also buy another lot of $100,000 for the rise which seemed about to take place.

Without waiting to see at what price our gold was purchased, we took a hack and went up town to a saloon, where we partook of a sumptuous repast, with the concomitants; in fact, a dinner such as stock-speculators are able to indulge in when they are fortunate. The repast was, as might have been expected, somewhat disturbed by anxieties over our position on the gold market: they who in the summer of 1879 went short of the coal stock, or who in October of that year bought Wabash at 60, or some other fancy, may appreciate our feelings during that repast. We hurried to the dessert.

After that we dressed and went to the Philharmonic. The music there, of course, was very classical, and we tried to enjoy it; but at the conclusion of each piece we devoutly hoped that the musicians could not be prevailed upon to repeat the performance, for our thoughts were roving away from the concert hall to that garden of Gul(l), the Gold Exchange, where we had "garnered up our heart." At last, overhearing a gentleman, who had just come in as the last piece but one was being worked through slowly on the violoncellos, whisper to a friend that gold was 208½ at the Fifth Avenue, we broke away from the musical treat we were trying to enjoy, and hurried thither. The Lobster had gone home, but R. H—— reported to us that gold was "strong at 208⅝, with a mounting tendency." We were on the right track now. That night we dreamed that it rained double eagles and a variety of other golden coins. The next morning the idea struck us of remaining up town and operating by telegraph. We did so. At eleven, A. M., we telegraphed as follows, under a new system of cipher which we had lately agreed upon: "To ——— ——— (the Lobster), — Exchange Place. "How is Joker?" (Joker meant gold.) Signed, etc."

The answer received at three P. M., read thus: "Joker Sampson whacker, axed, signed, etc.," which was, being interpreted, "Gold very strong at 215, what shall we do?"

Our reply went back on the wings of the lightning thus: "Swallow Plum," (*i. e.* Sell $100,000.)

Then we went to a dinner, very much on the sample of the evening before, and after that strolled into the Fifth Avenue Hotel, prepared to receive the congratulations of our broker, on having bagged that day, a profit of between $8,000 and $9,000 apiece.

The first man we saw was the "Lobster," his face a shade less glowing than usual. He came towards us on the double quick, and stretched out his claws, as if he wanted something. This something was more margin.

"More margin!" cried E—— and I, in consternation, "how so?"

"Why, you're short $400,000, and your loss, with gold at 218, the price it has just sold for, is $45,000. You must give me more margin, or I shall have to buy it in and charge you with the difference."

"But, my dear fellow, didn't we give you an order to buy in our $100,000 short at 206, and buy one hundred thousand more for a rise?"

"Not a bit of it. Here is your order to *sell* 100,000 at the market price, and I sold it at 206¼. Then you telegraphed down to sell 100,000 more at 115, and I executed your order."

There was our order sure enough, in letters that seemed to our distorted optics, two feet long. Sell $200,000 at market price, (206.) E—— had written by mistake *sell* instead of *buy*.

We margined up, and waited in trepidation the result of the Tobin movement. Gold jumped to 221, and nine thousand more of our margin was gone.

And now, the nervy fingers of the arch-cornerer were extended to pluck the fruits of his venturesome enterprise, when the price collapsed to 218. The market was shuddering under the first breath of astounding news. The telegraph had just flashed over the wires, that the commissioners of the Southern Confederacy were treating for peace, with President Lincoln on board a gunboat on the James River, and once more gold dropped to 205.

Tobin's losses in this attempted corner were rumored to have been $1,500,000.

E—— and myself, instead of losing $45,000 now bagged a profit of $6,000 on the whole of our joint sales.

Sherman and Grant, that modern Thor, meanwhile, were raining blows with their ponderous hammers upon the shell of the Confederacy, which now showed to the whole country a yawning lateral fissure. A fierce and bitter contest was going on between those who still dared to hold gold for a rise and those who sold it for a fall. Every speculator from Maine to Minnesota, who knew what selling short signified, felt that this was the time to do it. The ranks of the bears were swelled by fresh accessions, daily. Telegrams kept flying in, "Sheridan has cleaned out Early;" "Sherman has sacked Columbia and is sweeping through the Carolinas;" "Grant has advanced his parallels and is shelling Petersburg;" yet still gold stood like a rock, near 200, in the strong grasp of Tobin and many other bull operators. E—— and myself, after a series of petty losses, still stood $40,000 ahead. Now we made a bold stroke for fortune by selling $1,000,000 apiece at 200. We were led to do this by joining the *Hotel Brigade.*

Among the thousands of mysterious indviduals with which the great metropolis abounds, there is a certain class which we cannot describe better than by calling them hotel men. They dress in "purple and fine linen, and fare sumptuously every day," but how they get their living is a problem to the casual observer. They may be seen loitering in the reading-rooms and halls of the different hotels throughout the day, and are always in their seats when the dinner hour comes. The problem of their existence is solved when we state that they almost invariably have small capitals of from $5,000 to $20,000, which they employ in Wall Street, when the market is in a favorable condition, buying after a panic or selling short when the market is higher than is reasonable. On every such occasion, these men who are generally stout, rubicund fellows, may be seen wending their way to Wall Street, as fast as their corpulency will permit, and walking from the same cause, somewhat wide between the legs, "as though they had gyves on." Their shrewdness and good judgment in stock operations is quite remarkable. Hence it was that E—— and myself joined this coterie, when they marched down in one solid column, to sell gold short in February, 1865.

We had now placed ourselves on the rack. Our margin of four per cent. was liable to be used up any hour. The "Lobster" had consented to keep us short till the price rose to 203; provided we would, for his protection, watch gold every moment from early morning till twelve o'clock, P. M. Then the torture commenced. The price rose to 202½. Only one-half per cent. more and we should be shut down upon with a loss of thirty thousand apiece, when we were relieved by the price falling to 201.

We stood guard thus for four days, now wrenched with agony by a slight rise, and now cheered up by as slight a decline. Sleepless nights and days of pain. To me sleep came at length; but such a sleep. It was after a day of more than usual suspense that I returned home at seven in the evening, leaving E—— to stand sentry, and, if necessary, give the order that sealed our fate, for gold stood again at 202½.

Dropping on a lounge in my chamber, I was in an instant lost in sleep, heavy and dreamless, as if struck by some unseen hand. It was four hours before the *brain awoke* and showed me dreams. I was wandering through splendid halls, listening to music; banquets and garlands were spread upon tables, around which forms flitted and faces lightened. Then the scene shifted to a wilderness of beauty, moonlit and lonely. Suddenly a sound of roaring waters broke in upon me, and looking up I saw the face of L—— stretched cold and stark in his miserable attic, far above me as if miles away; while a terrible figure stretched down its hands filled with treasure, just beyond my reach, and beckoned me to follow it. Then a bell tolled slowly, and finally rang quick peals. I awoke and saw E—— standing at the door.

The agony was over.

At eleven o'clock gold had risen to 203, and E——

THE DREAM OF A SPECULATOR.

had given the fatal order to cover. The Lobster wedged his way into the crowd, and bid 203 for fifty thousand, and bought it at that price. While he was bidding for $100,000 more, a well-known operator rushed in from the telegraph room, and bid 203¼ for five hundred thousand. In thirty seconds gold was 204. Our $1,950,000 was bought in at an average price of 203¾.

Out of forty thousand dollars, I had five hundred only remaining; exactly the amount which I had deposited eight years before, in the hands of O——, as a margin for my first venture in Old Southern.

Naturally enough, E—— fell sick on this result, and for four months the stock-market never saw his face. I was now alone.

If there is a blissful feeling, it is that experienced by the weary operator, when, after a long campaign, in which fortune has run against him, he rests from his toils, with the consciousness that all is not lost, so long as hope and a small margin still remain.

After such a rest for two weeks, I rejoined the ranks.

Meanwhile, the sword of Sherman, which scarred the fair bosom of the Carolinas, was cutting great slits in the balloon of the gold speculation, which was fast collapsing. Gold had broken to 187, and then, on the news of the repulse at Fayetteville, North Carolina, ran up to 194. That news came one morning at the Exchange, and I sold $5,000, on the pledge of my now modest margin of $500.

It has been already stated in these pages, that the amount of gold and silver in the United States, in 1863, was estimated at $250,000,000. But the amount floating about, outside of the banks, the sub-treasury, and the private hoardings, was comparatively small, and grew still smaller in the summer of 1864.

In February, 1865, immense sums in gold coin, which had been locked up, were suddenly brought out and thrown on the market, in view of the speedy termination of the war. Some of the New York banks sold all the gold they held. The merchants, also, wishing to hedge against the prospective loss on the large amounts of imported goods they held, and which they had paid for when gold was high, now borrowed large sums in coin from the banks, and sold it, expecting to repay it by buying gold at a much lower price, within sixty days.

The burden became too great for the gold bulls. They fought stubbornly against the decline, but all in vain. One after one relaxed their hold, and let their precious nuggets drop on the market. But some of the largest holders still kept their position, hoping that something would happen to turn the tide in their favor. Gold fell to 175. Then they became desperate. Something must be done to stem the downward current.

Which of these men it was who played the game I cannot say; but one evening, at the up-town exchange, a speculative broker of small means entered the crowd and bid for gold by the million. In a few minutes he had bought three millions. The next morning the price, instead of rising on these heavy purchases, fell three per cent. The failure of the buyer was announced; and though he claimed that the purchases were for his own account, it was understood by the street that it was an arranged plan between him and certain leading gold bulls for the purpose of arresting the decline; but finding this move failed to accomplish the object, they made their broker the scapegoat. This was the last card played by the desperate holders of high-priced gold.

Nothing was left for them now but to slide out as well as they could. The immense number of short sales which had been made during the preceding six weeks created a constant demand for gold, and helped the heavy holders to dispose of the vast amounts they held. But many a million, won upon the great upward movement, was swallowed up as gold fell with sharp spasms down, down, to 128.

When it reached 140 I figured up my profits. Fifteen thousand dollars, all made in four weeks out of $500 by putting out a series of short contracts as the price dropped. I had snatched treasure out of the wreck, and was now ready for a new voyage on the sea of speculation.

These rapid changes, from profit to loss, and from loss to profit, tend to make men reckless, as has been often shown in the street, and especially in the great bull movement of 1879, when money was made so fast by the holders of stocks that they seemed to be under a temporary insanity, which drove them into paying absurd prices for even the most worthless fancies. The Open Board, established in the heighth of the speculation of '79, has proved but an indifferent success; its organization, however, at that time, was an evidence of the rage for buying and selling stocks on margins.

CHAPTER XXVIII.

DREW PLAYS ON HIS ONE-STRINGED LYRE—ERIE.

Uncle Daniel in Clover—His Views Respecting "Them Erye Sheers" He Plays on His Musical Instrument, Erie—Buy! Oh, Buy! Sell! Oh, Sell!—He Pays Off Some of His Old Harlem Scores—He Slides Down Hill with no Erie in His Hand, Then Picks Up Erie and Travels Up Hill—D—— and S—— Form a Partnership—Setting and Baiting Traps for Shorts—Springing the Traps and Bagging the Game—The Old Man Soliloquizes—My Fortunes During the Erie Rise—A "Point," and Advice from R——, the Railroad Director—The Trick My Broker Played on Me—The Final Twist—A Big Gold Trade—The Ketchum Forgeries and Their Effect on the Stock-Market—The First Move for Another Corner.

WALL STREET, April 3d, 1865. The bears were on a "bender," that day; the market was full of honey-combs, on which they were feasting, for Erie had been hurled down from 90 to 42.

Then was Daniel Drew's hour of triumph. For nine months stocks had been on the downward track, and he had predicted it. In the summer of 1864, he showed by an ingenious argument, that Erie was selling too high; stated in his homely vernacular, it was as follows, viz.:

"Them Erye sheers are a sellin' naow for a leetle more'n they're wuth. It costs a heap naow to pay runnin' expenses. The Erye Railroad Company has to pay up'ards of $20,000 for an ingyne what cost only $10,000 afore the war. Coal and iron has riz, so has men. Whar are dividends a comin' from? You, boys, better not be too fond of your sheers."

The "old man" was right. Erie at par, was a capital short sale.

In the fall of 1864, he commenced a campaign in that stock, which was to last four years, a campaign in which he took revenge on old enemies, wiped out old losses, filled his treasury with plunder, until 1868, when he retired from the field a heavy loser, by the closing battle. During three years of that time, Erie was like a one-stringed Chinese lyre in his hands, on which he played two tunes; when its price was high, he sung "who'll buy my Erye? who'll buy my valuable Erye? buy it, oh buy!"

When it was low, he sung "who'll sell me Erye, who'll sell me worthless Erye? sell me Erye, sell, sell!"

And the "street" listening entranced to his mellifluous voice, bought it of him at a very high price, and sold it to him at a very low price. Every night Uncle Daniel dreamed of money-bags, and every day his dream turned out true. He coined money out of his musical performances on his one-stringed Chinese lyre—Erie.

In October, 1864, Erie fell with a crash to 85. This fall tempted two prominent members of the Harlem Combination, L. W. J——, and J. M. T——, to take up Erie and corner it. No corner could be engineered without the concurrence of the leading director, who was, of course, none other than Daniel Drew. Accordingly the would-be cornerers broached the matter to him. Nothing could have suited him better, for now he saw an opportunity offered to pay off old scores in Harlem. He loaned them a very large sum, and made an agreement with them not to sell any Erie above a certain price. The cornerers thereupon bought an immense block of Erie above 90. The price quickly rose to 105, and everything looked rose-colored, not only to them, but to Uncle Daniel. "Love laughs at locksmiths;" Daniel Drew smiled at contracts, for he generally saw a gap in them, through which, though it may not be "as wide as a church door," he managed to slip, when it was his interest to do so. The cornerers found themselves loaded with fresh stock at summit prices, and began to sag under their burden.

December passed into January, and Erie broke down to 80, then lurched heavily upward to 87.

Now was the hour for the "old man" to act. He arose and saddled his coal-black steed named Panic, and descended like Thalaba the destroyer into the Dom-Daniel caverns to evoke to his aid the spirits of financial fear and distrust. He sold a large amount of Erie, and thereupon made ready to depress the price. Having conveyed to one of his minions $20,000 worth of convertible bonds, he instigated the procuring of an injunction forbidding the payment of any dividends by the Erie company.

Then he constricted the money market, and called upon L. W. J—— and J. M. T—— for the money which he had loaned them. This demand compelled them to throw overboard their stock. The price fell twenty per cent. The would-be-cornerers had lost a million, and the Harlem "calls" were partially avenged.

Now Uncle Daniel prepared to reap a more substantial harvest. When Erie had reached the neighborhood of 50, he covered his shorts at an enormous profit.

Grant and Sheridan were pounding at the gates of Richmond, and another great stampede now took place. Wall Street then might have been taken for Landseer's picture of Highland bulls in a storm. They who had bought Erie at 80, and thought it cheap at that, now sold it at 45, and said it was not worth 20. It was offered and sold in blocks of five thousand and ten thousand shares. As fast as it reared itself upwards, fresh blows threw it back lower than before. It touched bottom at 42.

The two leading bears, Uncle Daniel and Dr. S——, (whom we have before described,) now became metamorphosed into bulls, and formed an alliance to lift Erie out of the slough into which it had fallen. Having bought all the stock they could buy under cover, when concealment was no longer possible they bought openly immense amounts. A rumor went through the street that all this stock, which daily was sent into G——, their broker, was merely to cover their shorts.

The fever for selling hardly flagged as Erie rose to 49, at which price E. B. K——, whose forgeries soon after startled the street, sold D—— & S—— ten thousand shares, seller 60. In three days the price of Erie was 63, when it broke and fell back to 54. Again the cry went up, "Sell! Sell!" on every side. The conspirators gathered from this a fresh supply of shorts. Then Erie rose to 65.

D—— and S—— were still gluttonous for shorts.

The whole street was full of traps, baited to catch short sales. All these traps were connected with the great slaughter-trap set by D—— & S——. The bears furnished their own bait, as follows: The price of Erie ought to go lower. First, because it has to borrow the money for its dividends. Second, because it has risen twenty-three per cent. in two weeks. Third, because it is not intrinsically worth 20. Fourth, because ten thousand shares are coming from Europe, etc., etc.

These baits were quickly swallowed, and in thirty days the traps were full of game—shorts.

All this time Erie had been rising with the usual downward spasms for the purpose of encouraging the ensnared ones. As it rose, D—— & S—— bagged the game, in other words, compelled the bears to cover. It touched 85 and the shorts were all taken in; then broke in a panic to 68. Tobin here stepped forward and arrested the fall by taking ten thousand shares on his sinewy shoulders. Dr. S—— now retired from the field with a profit of several hundred thousands, and Uncle Daniel "went it alone" on a new twist.

Once more the traps were set and baited as before. Once more the bears seeing the mistake they had made by closing their contracts, swallowed the bait in crowds. Erie, early in July, rose to 82, then dropped back to 76, and looked very weak. The bears were again jubilant. For three weeks, Erie vibrated dully between 76 and 80. Like some huge monster of the deep, its torpidity was feigned, for it was only waiting for more shorts. Many of the short sellers were pupils and imitators of Uncle Daniel in his old bearish policy, and they could hardly persuade themselves now, that the "old man" was not on their side instead of working against them.

He stood one day on the steps of his broker's office, and soliloquized thus, as he looked on the noisy crowd, where "his young barbarians were all at play," selling Erie:

"Happy creeturs! how merry they be. Wal, wal, I guess I must pinch 'em."

He did "pinch 'em." That very day Erie rose to 85. The market fairly smoked with excitement. There was no pause in the upward movement during the next forty-eight hours.

The 31st day of July was a scorcher. From the blistering pavements of Broad Street, wave after wave of heat rose and vibrated in mid-air, while the merciless sun kept radiating new volumes.

W. R. T——, wiping his flaming forehead with the finest of cambric, was overheard to whisper to a brother broker in his peculiar stutter, "B–B–Big th–th–thing in Erie."

The price rose to 92, fell back to 87, mounted to 95, fell back to 94, then galloped to 98⅞.

All the time from March till the middle of June, I had been patronizing the "Lobster" with orders on the most liberal scale, buying or selling on an average, two or three thousand shares per day. Twice my margin had been swelled to thirty thousand, and twice it had shrunk back to its original amount, fifteen thousand. I had paid my active broker nearly fifteen thousand dollars commissions by these quick turns.

Now this helping to support brokers is a weary business, unless one can make a little money by it.

It was this conviction that led me to sell two hundred Erie short at 76, with the intention of staying short, whatever might betide.

When Erie rose to 80, I also "averaged" by selling a second lot of two hundred shares. But when it jumped to 85, under the nipping fingers of Uncle Daniel, I thought the matter should be inquired into, and accordingly proceeded to consult R——. Some men are born poets, others are born railroad directors. R—— belonged to the latter class. For aught that may be said to the contrary, a railroad stock-certificate may have been the ominous plaything of his childhood, and he may have organized mimic boards of directors among his school-fellows. At all events, he was now a railroad director, and although we do not assert that he belonged to the Erie Direction, he was always presumed to know a thing or two about Erie. R——, it should be remembered, was the lucky speculator mentioned in our third chapter; but in 1865 he was very much changed from the slender youth of 1857. He was thick-set now, with jowls which hung down like the dewlaps of a prize ox. As for the color of his face, to say that it was red would feebly express it. It was not suffused by "the patriot's shame," nor by the celestial roseate tinge, which has been, with doubtful truth, at least in this age of brass, called "love's proper hue." It fairly glowed and blazed, on the morning when I consulted him. He lay in bed in his chamber, and the very sheets borrowed a ruddy tint from that burning, blood-red face.

He was a man of few words. Men of his kidney always are. But the substance of what he said was, "Keep your position, and let Daniel squeeze you."

Not doubting that this advice was given in good faith, I kept my position.

When Erie reached 94, it grew scarce for delivery. In fact my broker told me it could not be borrowed either for love or money, and that unless I could deliver it in fifteen minutes, he should be under the painful necessity of buying it in, and closing me out, with a loss of $6,400. In fifteen minutes the stock was bought in, and in an unguarded moment my broker entrusted me with the duty of reporting it at his office, whereby a very large cat jumped out of the bag. It appears that the faithless Lobster, not satisfied with the commissions to the amount of $15,000, which he had already extracted out of his customer, desired to make an additional sum by speculating on my margins. When I reported the four hundred shares of Erie to the Lobster's book-keeper, "This," said he, consulting his books, "makes you long of Erie, at 94."

"How so," replied I.

"Four hundred shares of Erie, bought at 81, appears on my books to your credit. That closed up your shorts. This last lot makes you long four hundred, at 94."

Sure enough, my shorts had been bought in without my knowledge, and the Lobster expected to put the difference between 81 and 94, or $5,200, into his own pocket. The ingenuousness of his book-keeper saved me this amount, and in one hour I made $800 on my four hundred shares by selling it at 96.

I need not add that my account was removed from the office of the Lobster as soon as his treachery had been discovered.

"New brooms sweep clean." At least I thought so, two hours later, when I raked in three thousand by selling Erie at $98\frac{1}{2}$ and taking it in at $92\frac{1}{4}$, in the office of my new broker. Suddenly Erie sprang up again to 96. Groesbeck, Drew's broker, had called upon the "short" gentlemen aforesaid, for thirty thousand shares. Then Uncle Daniel began to twang his Chinese lyre, "Buy my Erie, buy, oh buy!"

Never did the market so bristle with "points" as at four o'clock on the afternoon of that day. Fifty men could have been seen whispering in the ears of fifty other men, or grasping them affectionately by the arm and leading them apart from the roaring crowd, to tell them that Erie was the thing to buy. The jackals who hunt in the track of the lions of the market, were all 'loping about to induce the outsiders to relieve plethoric gentlemen of their heavy loads of stock.

At this juncture, R——, the railroad director, drew me aside and imparted "*his point.*" "Daniel Drew is going to put Erie up to 110 in less than twenty-four hours. Buy all you can swing." R——'s advice, respecting my short Erie, had somewhat impaired my confidence in his judgment, and yet still I believed him honest. I bought eight hundred shares at 97. That evening Erie broke, and the next day sold at 90, lessening my margin by $5,600. During the entire three months' campaign which we have been describing, something was going on below the surface which was shortly to disclose itself and rock Wall street to its foundations. We allude to the forgeries of E. B. Ketchum.

This operator, afterwards so notorious, had been speculating for more than a year, to an enormous amount. In 1864, he was reported to have made $1,500,000. The gold break in March, had made him the loser of millions. When Erie was hoisted by Uncle Daniel, he covered at 76, one lot of ten thousand shares, which he had sold for delivery, at 49. This transaction cost him $270,000, and was only one in a series of losses, which footed up an aggregate that made even the thorough-paced Wall Street man stand aghast.

For months the fatal drain had been going on. He lost money by selling short, and then he lost money by buying stocks. The capital of the banking-house to which he belonged was four millions, and still a large sum of money was lacking to meet his engagements. In an evil hour he forged gold certificates, to how large an amount will never be exactly known, for some of those who advanced money upon them refused to tell their losses; but these forgeries are known to have run up to several millions.

On the 15th of August, something was plainly brooding over the market. Mysterious whispers were afloat. That evening the same tall broker above-mentioned sold out for the account of E. B. K—— forty thousand shares of stock. The secret was known. K—— was a fugitive. Stocks fell in a fierce panic.

The next day Erie was driven back to 76. Uncle Daniel bought twelve thousand shares of the Ketchum Erie, and laid his plans for another corner.

CHAPTER XXIX.

FEMALE SPECULATORS.

Do Women Speculate?—Why Not?—Speculation Not Unsuited to the Female Character—A Question Answered—Ladies on 'Change, and Young Misses Receiving Billet Doux from Their Brokers, and Dreaming of Stocks—A Feminine Pool in Harlem—Notable Instances of Female Speculators—The Fortunes of Miss M——, a She-bear, in the Stock Market—The Gold Rise of 1866—Why a Panic in London Makes Gold Go Up—Women Who Keep Accounts in Their Own Names, and Women who Do Not—How Brokers Carry Their Fair Burdens—Beauty a Woman's Margin—Influence of Women upon Stock-panics,

DO Women speculate in stocks? This question is readily answered in the affirmative. More than this, they are not only frequent, but daring speculators. They encounter risks that would appall the stoutest Wall Street veteran, and rush boldly into places, where even a Vanderbilt would fear to tread. The female character is, in many respects, suited to a life of speculation. Speculation is founded on hope, and women are generally remarkably prone to hope. Speculation requires patience and fortitude, which are, or should be, both womanly virtues. Speculation derives its food from excitement, and women often feed on excitement. Speculation comes from fancy, and women are much given to fancy. Women of a certain type, are naturally, or by education, inclined to speculate in stocks. Perhaps they may catch the infection from their brothers, or uncles, who talk stocks while bolting their meals in haste, so that they may hurry down town, and buy a little more Wabash or cover their short Erie. Wealthy ladies, who are their own mistresses, and have plenty of leisure time, might be expected, as they sit embroidering golden bees and butterflies, on black velvet, to have their thoughts turned upon stock-flyers, and to dream of new equipages, jewels, and silks, won out of stocks or bonds. From whatever cause it may arise, there were no more eager and venturesome gamblers at Baden Baden, in Germany, than women, and there are no more eager and venturesome speculators in stocks, than women.

On almost any bright day, when stocks are rising, a dozen or more showy carriages may be seen drawn up in front of the offices of prominent brokerage houses, waiting for the gorgeous dames who ride in them to come out, when they have transacted their business with their brokers. Most of these speculative ladies are dowagers with large bank accounts, for which they, perhaps, thank their departed husbands, or fathers, or uncles, and which they are now using as margins in stock-speculation, almost always for a rise, for it seems to them an incomprehensible thing that any money can be made by a fall in stocks. Like so many Magdalens, they roll their fine eyes, not repentantly, but avariciously upwards, towards the towering heights of Rock Island, or Western Union, where they hope to make their profits.

Besides these middle-aged matrons, there are not

a few misses in their teens, whose faces are turned Wall Street-wards.

Imagine these sylph-like creatures ogling the elephantine bulk of Erie as it paces up with a dignified stride, or casting sheep's eyes at St. Paul as it dances on the tight-rope held by the hands of a clique.

One fair young creature, with a wealth of blonde hair, leans pensively on her hand, and indulges in pleasant thoughts of Wabash, or in her sleep has sweet dreams of Lake Shore. Another quick brunette opens with palpitating bosom a billet-doux from her broker, informing her of the closing prices, and enclosing a balance of profits which she devours with her eyes; or perhaps it is a more unpleasant missive, by which she learns that N. W., her first love, has proved treacherous, or Erie has ceased to respond to her vows.

At Saratoga, in Sept., 1873, three young ladies, possessed of a will and several thousand dollars of their own, made up a "pool" in Harlem on their individual account, and bought two thousand shares in the neighborhood of 100. Within four weeks the rise to 117 showed them to be winners to the amount of 25,000. This seemed to justify them in going into the wardrobe line. Consequently, they might have been seen every day sitting on cushioned stools at Stewart's and Arnold, Constable & Co.'s palaces, and making heavy investments in moire antique, Mechlin lace, and India shawls. But alas for the vanity of human expectations; they did not sell their Harlem, but bought more, and within a few weeks received, not a billet-doux, but a call for more margin, for Harlem had sold down to 99, and instead of making $25,000, they would, if they sold, now lose $25,000.

Fortunately all of these young ladies belonged to the heroic mould, and instead of going into hysterics or sitting down and having a good cry, they went manfully, or rather womanfully, to work and raised money, furnished the necessary margin to their broker and vowed by Nemesis that they would hold their Harlem till they could make their $25,000 once more.

Brave girls! Their heroism in six weeks was rewarded, for in the latter part of Nov., 1873, while the Commodore was hoisting Harlem, they drew $30,000 out of their broker's hands.

One of the notable female speculators in Wall Street is a maiden lady, who counts her property by the million. She is never seen there, however, except when stocks are falling, and properly belongs to the class of panic-birds before described. In these seasons she may be seen in her "customary suit of solemn black," tripping down to her broker's office, prepared to buy at the lowest prices, and when stocks go up she always sends word to her broker to sell out. Her profits from these investments have sometimes risen to more than one hundred thousand per annum.

The most remarkable case of all, is that of a lady whom we will call Miss M——. She belongs to the class of the strong-minded ones. Her face is that of a goshawk, and the white dove which she wears sometimes upon her jockey hat, seems constantly in the act of playfully swooping down upon the less amiable bird beneath. In her views on financial questions, she has always taken high moral ground, discountenancing all attempts to raise the price of gold. During her ten years' experience she has made and lost a fortune every year. In the great rise of 1878, she stood one hundred and thirty thousand dollars better than she was in 1877. Then, woman-like, her hopes rose to the ambitious height of half a million, which seems to be the goal which most speculators propose to themselves. But

> "When lovely woman stoops to folly,
> And finds, too late, that stocks betray,"

and brokers beguile! She awoke from her dream of fortune on the 29th of Jan. 1879, when panic was raging, with the residue of her fortune, about $4,000, fast locked up in the hands of her broker, who had failed, and was unable even to pay her this small balance.

But brokers are the most elastic of mortals, commercially speaking; their failures are generally only temporary, and in three weeks our heroine received from her supposed insolvent agent, $2,000 of her balance. With this she commenced to operate on the short side, for her losses in the panic had, as is usual in such cases, converted her into a bear—a she-bear, now mourning for her whelps, and on the third of April, 1879, she had recovered forty thousand dollars of her losses. What little bird now whispered in her ear, "buy K. P," cannot be told, but she bought it at 25, and flew up with it to 60, like a witch astride of a broomstick. Once more she had built up her fortune, but she did not snatch it out of the jaws of the market, always open and ravenous. The vision of a half million still haunted her. She caressed several of her stock-favorites, the coal stocks, etc., on a three per cent. margin, all of which conduct cost her dear. Her margin was gone in a month. Another lady nearly fourteen years ago was operating for a fall in gold.

Gold had dropped to 126. Everybody said gold would go down to 110. Her broker told her that Government was selling; and so she staked her remaining $60,000 on a short sale of $200,000 gold, at 130.

The gold-bulls celebrated their carnival, in May, 1866. When the price fell to 126, in April, nearly every banker, broker, and operator in the street stood short of it, for future delivery. This time the bears thought they were right. Some said the price would go to par, others to 110, but all concurred in believing that gold would never go up again. Three times more gold had been sold than could be borrowed for delivery.

A sound from across the Atlantic, like "a fire-bell in the night," awoke them suddenly from their dreams of fortune. A panic in London!

But how should a panic in London make gold go up in New York?

Let us explain.

All commercial transactions, it should be remembered, are conducted, in England, on a gold basis. When money is easy, and the Bank of England has a low rate of discount, an active business is often done in American securities, particularly in railway-bonds, and Governments. It was affirmed by Mr. David S. Wells, that one thousand millions of the latter were held abroad. When the rate of discount by the Bank of England is raised, and money becomes tight, many of these securities are sent to the United States to be sold, and the proceeds of these sales, in gold, is remitted to England, diminishing in this proportion, the amount of gold in this country.

Gold had risen to 130, and rumors of commercial distress in London were already forewarning the bears of their dangerous position, from which they saw only one means of relief, viz.: the *sales of gold by the Government.* These sales in a few days ran up to $30,000,000. The Government agent was beset by those who were short of gold. He was waited for, button-holed, and his coat-tails were almost torn off, by the eager buyers, when he entered the gold room. Still the price stood firm.

Late in May the storm broke. The arrival of the Cuba brought the news of the greatest financial panic which had ever occurred in England. The Government stopped selling, and gold jumped to 40. Erie certificates and Government bonds came pouring in by every steamer, and every outgoing steamer carried millions of gold. In six weeks, more than $40,000,000 had been sent out of the country.

On the 9th of June the price stood at 169. One of the largest holders of gold at 130 was the firm of M—— & D——, and this house was almost the only prominent one which bulled gold heavily. Their profits there, after the arrival of the Cuba could be counted by the million.

Many a shrewd merchant and operator found himself during the rise bound hand and foot.

J. M. T——, the great speculator, was caught short of a million or so, which he bought in at something over 150. This same individual then bought largely, and sold $700,000 of his purchases to the noted merchant, H. B. C——, at 169. As for the smaller tribe of operators, the field was strown with their financial corpses.

This "spirt" in gold, it should be noted, arose purely from commercial causes.

How fared it with our heroine meanwhile?

She "sat like patience on a monument" of short gold. When it touched 150, she descended from her pedestal, and gazing with tearless eyes upon her losses, ($50,000,) then proceeded coolly to gather up the wreck, and reconstruct her edifice.

Who will say, after hearing the story of these ladies, that women cannot speculate?

As already noted, the wife of the heavy stock-operator is quite certain to be provided for, and when her husband loses his all, he can fall back on his wife's money, and renew his fortune. Most of the women who speculate in stocks, conduct their speculations in the names of male friends and relatives. Hence it comes that they very often make money, for what broker would be so ungallant (and all brokers are gallant to the fair sex), as to suffer a lady to lose money in his office. Sometimes the broker, or operator, in whose name these accounts stands, puts his shoulder under the load, when a panic occurs, and saves his lady-customer at all hazards. Sometimes he introduces her to a magic ring, and she speedily becomes the bride of fortune. When her margin is exhausted, she may be said to travel on a margin of beauty, grace, and smiles, which, with a skillful tear now and then dropped, quickly subdue the hyenas of the street and supply her with the sinews of war on 'Change.

It is well, however, that women rarely come in person into the stock-market to look after their interests. One can easily imagine the effect produced by several hundred women interested in stocks, being present at a panic and giving way with feminine impulsiveness to the feelings of the hour. We might then expect some new and strange appearances in these disasters. A bevy of dames dissolved in tears, with hair disheveled, and giving way to hysterics, or screaming like "Pythoness possessed," and slaughtering stocks as eagerly as the veteran stock-butchers.

We have answered the inquiry, "do women speculate?" and now we ask, could, or would, or should, a woman be a broker? Could, or would, or should, she line her delicate throat with bell metal, put triple brass upon her face, change her tender heart into stone, crush out her human sympathies with the unfortunate and the distressed, and see men reduced from affluence to beggary, and profit by it as a broker?

This profession of a stock broker would seem to be almost the last one that woman would aspire to fill, or could fill successfully; the dissolution in 1871 of the feminine firm of Woodhull, Claflin & Co., which for two years or more did business as stock brokers at 44 Broad Street, is evidence how unsuited to woman's nature is such a field of enterprise. At the present time there are no female brokers, though during the advance of stocks, in the summer and autumn of 1879, many ladies made large sums of money.

A BROKER'S OFFICE ENTER VERDANT GREEN.

CHAPTER XXX.

THE FORTUNES OF A COUNTRYMAN.

A Scene in a Broker's Office—B——t Has the Petroleum Fever—Blowing Bubbles in Oil—A Masterpiece of the Engraver's Art—Ravages of the Petroleum Epidemic—The Mining Board and How They Make Corners There—The Bubble Breaks, and the "Lobster" is Busted—We Take a Nervine—B——t Buys a Call in "Prairie Dog"—H. G. Stimpson and Billy Marston Carry the Bears Up in a Balloon—Prairie du Chien in the Clouds—What Came out of B——t's Call—$20,000 Made from $200 in Forty-eight Hours—"Calls and Puts" on the Brain—Henry Keep Nursing His Pet Stock—"Buying In Under the Rule"—Uncle Daniel Says "We Must Ingine 'em"—The Story of Pacific Mail—L. W. Jerome Unloading His One Hundred Thousand Shares—B——t's Luck in Pacific Mail—He Takes a Flyer in Atlantic Mail and then Buys One Hundred Erie of *White* for Cash.

THE first scene in this chapter, is laid in the office of the "Lobster." The time is in January, 1865, while we, (E—— and I,) were sweating under heavy burdens of gold. We are sitting in the private office of the broker aforesaid, which we made our head-quarters, engaged in our usual occupation of figuring, and perusing the literature of the stock-market, *i. e.* quotations.

Enter a rustic, cut out on the usual stage pattern, viz.: tall, gawkey, and eccentric-looking.

"Ah!" quoth E——, "here comes more tribute to the Moloch of Wall Street."

As he approached us, smelling strongly of the pine

woods, a shade, either of surprise or regret, passed over the expressive features of E——, who recognized the rustic as one of his country relations. He rejoiced in the euphonious surname of B——. After the customary salutations had been exchanged, the countryman produced a portly wallet from his breast pocket, and proceeded to rummage in its recesses for certain documents. The first paper he produced was a certificate of good, moral character, from his school-master. The second was a certificate of the deposit of $2,300 in the bank of his native village. It need scarcely be remarked, that he found the latter certificate much more potent in Wall Street than the former. Then he produced half a column cut out of a newspaper, unfolded it, and spread it before our eyes. It was headed thus, in very large letters, PETROLEUM! and set forth substantially, that the books of the Sixtieth National Petroleum Company were still open for subscription. Capital, one million dollars, one hundred thousand shares at ten dollars par; that the company had (magnanimously) allowed the public to take an interest in the shares, by paying $3.00 per share; that the property consisted of thirty acres in fee simple, in the very center of the oil region, and only ten miles from the celebrated Buchanan Farm; that three wells were already sunk, and ready for tubing, another down below the first sandstone; room for more wells; every indication of oil. A dividend of two per cent. a month *guaranteed*. Books to be closed positively and irrevocably on the 21st instant. Then followed the names of the directors, all well known men of business.

"Them air Petrollum shares is what I've come for.

Two per cent. a month dividends is enough for me," remarked the rustic.

The glittering bubble of Petroleum Stock Companies had caught the eye of B——.

E—— and I had long prior to this time pricked our own bubbles, and thereafter had resolved ourselves into a vigilance committee of bubble-prickers for the benefit of other people.

But here was a very obstinate case. B—— had resolved *to invest,* and in that particular company. It was only after long argument, and by quoting to him the familiar agricultural proverb, "Never put your eggs all in one basket," that we prevailed upon him to invest only $1,300 in this company, and keep $1,000 for some of the other tempting opportunities which then abounded in the market. Then all three of us went to the office of the company, No. — Broadway, where B—— paid out his $1,300, and received in return certificates of four hundred and thirty-three shares. B—— thought the engraving on these certificates was really beautiful, and so it was. In the foreground was a flowing well, sending an oleaginous jet one hundred feet or so into the air, and falling in a graceful parabolic curve into a huge tank inscribed with the name of the company, near which was a pile of barrels apparently as large as the pyramid of Cheops. In the background were several vessels and railroad trains being loaded with petroleum. B—— feasted his eyes upon this work of the graver's art, and looked hopefully forward to his guaranteed dividend.

The Petroleum Stock Company fever raged for nine months, and culminated in February, 1865.

Companies with a nominal capital of $300,000,000, were organized during that period. All that has been said in our chapter on bubble-companies, applies with equal force to Petroleum. A volume might be written to describe how the English language was twisted and turned, to paint the prospect of fortunes and avoid the legal liabilities incident to false representations; how the bubbles shone as if colored with every brilliant dye that could be extracted out of Petroleum; what engines were set at work to bring in the public; what stool-pigeons were called from the solid and respectable circles, from the halls of legislation, from the learned professions, and from the church, to entice dupes, and feather the nests of needy adventurers; how the owners of lands that smelt of oil, the mineralogists, the geologists, and chemists were in clover, and then to tell how one by one the phantom-flowing wells dried up, the magnificent oil territory became abandoned to its original desolation, watched over only by skeleton derricks, while the thousands of victims came dropping in, file after file, to draw their dividends, as the bubbles were bursting. It would form a chapter in the history of speculation, at once interesting, instructive, amusing and sad.

The Petroleum fever gave rise in February, 1865, to the organization known as the Petroleum Stock Exchange, which however, died in a few months with the fever which produced it, and its remains were incorporated with what was known as the Mining Stock Board, another fragment hurled off from the meteoric speculation, in the unsubstantial properties incorporated in joint stock companies.

This Board was a miniature of the Stock Exchange, and consisted of upwards of seventy-six members. Here, on a smaller scale, corners were gotten up, and close pools organized, which made many an outsider weep tears of gold. Two circumstances united to make such pools highly successful. First, the general worthlessness of the stocks bought and sold there, which drew in short sellers. Second, the ease with which stocks were handled owing to the small amount of money required to carry them, and the fact that they were often held in a few hands after the original subscribers have sold out in disgust, over long delayed dividends. When three or four men hold all the stock of one of these companies, they can very readily "milk the street" by simulating a great activity in that particular stock. This is done by what is known as "wash sales," *i. e.*, sales in which no stock is actually delivered. A. pretending to sell, and B. pretending to buy, in the open market under a secret agreement. In this way a price is made, and often numerous transactions are reported which are never really carried out. Of course these fictitious sales are forbidden under penalty of expulsion, but are continually made without any fear of detection. As soon as a stock is thus made to assume an activity, the outside public pricks up its huge ears and listens to the disinterested suggestions of the whole tribe of "pointers," "singed cats," and "ropers-in," who ply their vocation in the stock-market. If inclined to buy, they take "jags" of the stock in question, whereupon the price suddenly breaks from under them and they "cut short" their losses by selling in pursuance often of the same disinterested suggestions. Or perhaps in view of the worthlessness of the stock, they make short sales, when up the price jumps and they have to "cover" at a heavy loss.

This Mining Stock Board has long since gone out of existence. The present mining exchange, organized in 1877 by H. Tracy Arnold and others, is the outgrowth of the legitimate demand for mining stocks by investors and speculators who have seen the vast fortunes made in Nevada, Colorado, Utah, and other sections that abound in mineral wealth. In 1875 the Big Bonanzas and in 1879 Leadville stimulated this form of speculation.

But to return to the fortunes of B——. His individual bubble, collapsed in less than five months, when he shook off the odor of petroleum from his skirts, by selling his stock for ten cents a share. Meanwhile, he had not lain upon his oars. His first operation was in gold, which he had sold short, or as he called it "bought short," and made $5,000. Then he mounted on the wave of Erie, which washed five thousand dollars more into his capacious wallet, when it broke at the height of 98. We tried to release him from the claws of the "Lobster," when we discovered his treachery, in buying in our shorts, but unfortunately B—— had bought Erie at 96, and now that it had fallen back to 90, he preferred keeping his position on the "Lobster's" books.

We lost sight of him for three months, until one day in November, when he rushed into our new headquarters, crying out, "The Lobster has busted, and I'm busted."

He had just $200 remaining out of his $11,000. It was a vile day in November, 1865. The air was chill and muggy, the pavement had broken out into a cold perspiration, and the buildings were covered with damp blotches. Everybody looked blue, and B——'s face was the longest and bluest of all. He looked as if a little stimulus would help him.

"Come and get a nervine, B——!"

"A nervine! what's a nervine?" said B——.

"Come and see."

We went to the neighboring chateau of famous reputation, sat down at one of the tables, hailed a sombre-looking Ganymede, who looked as if he might be the grandson of some old French soldier, who went through Napoleon's Russian campaign, and had his nose frozen therein, and requested him to bring three nervines. This singular beverage is, by a pleasing fiction, made out to be compounded of decoctions of roots and herbs, gathered by Indian squaws, in the vicinity of Baffin's Bay, when the moon is at the full, and blended "judgmatically" with the fluid known to chemists as $C^4 H^6 O^2$, but more generally recognized under the name of alcohol. During the percolations and genial glow diffused by this beverage, B—— opened his stiffly starched shirt-bosom, and showed us the fox gnawing at his financial entrails.

B—— *had borrowed money* from friends in his native village in order to meet the demands of the rapacious Lobster for more margin. This obligation weighed heavily upon his spirits, for he had not yet learned the Wall Street art of bearing with an air of graceful unconsciousness a vast burden of debt. While he was bewailing his sad condition, C——, a well-known operator, joined us in the most joyous of moods, inasmuch as he had made that morning $5,000 on Prairie du Chien, which, after rising to par, had fallen back to 91. C—— was a bear in Prairie du Chien. He predicted that it would sell at 50 inside of a week, and volunteered to sell calls in it at 110, and which should run deliverable at any time within thirty days.

B——'s face brightened. He plucked C—— by the sleeve, and told him he would give him two hundred dollars for a call of two hundred shares. C—— filled one out, signed it, sent it in to his broker, who guaranteed it, and handed it to B——, who completely emptied his pockets by giving C—— the $200 agreed upon. The precious little memorandum was folded by B—— into a wad small enough to be enclosed in a filbert and hidden in the most secret compartment of his wallet. Then he retired to his boarding-house to "recooperate," as he expressed it.

November, 1865, was made memorable in the history of Wall Street, as all my readers will recollect, by the Prairie du Chien combination. The leader in this enterprise was H. G. Stimpson, a tall, taciturn man, with a face as if cut out of yellow sandstone, and seeming to wear a look which says, "I am never to be bluffed." His lieutenant was William H. Marston, commonly known in the market as Billy Marston, a portly gentleman, with a twinkling eye and great fondness for bidding up stocks five per cent. at a leap.

These were the two conspirators, who in the summer and autumn of 1865, did with pecuniary intent, and contrary to the peace of Wall Street, and all the bears therein and thereunto appertaining, buy and take unto themselves, all, or nearly all, that certain stock, known as Prairie du Chien, otherwise Prairie Dog.

It was not a heavy burden, for there were only twenty-nine thousand and some odd shares of the stock to be handled. During the Ketchum break in August, its price was 33. Within less than three months, and on that Saturday, when B—— bought a call, it had risen to par. On the following Monday it sold from 125 to 250, in twenty minutes, amid the fiercest excitement ever known before in the Brokers' Board. On that day could have been seen, the singular spectacle of brokers shedding tears over their own losses, and strange to say, over those of their customers. Here, too, should be recorded, an instance of generosity on the part of Stimpson, the pool-leader. He gave to his customers who had been unfortunate in previous operations, an interest in the pool, and enabled them, in this way, to recover their losses. This is a bright example, shining out of that dreary waste of selfishness—Wall Street.

B——, worn out by his labors and losses, slept late on that black-bear Monday, and when he reached the lobby of the Brokers' Board, Prairie du Chien had just struck 200.

His face grew white with joy. With hands that trembled with eagerness, he fumbled once more in his wallet, brought forth his precious "call," sent it into the board to his broker, and in three minutes he had sold the two hundred shares at 210. In ten minutes more he "called" upon C——, who bought the stock at 225 and delivered to the party to whom B——'s two hundred shares had been sold.

B——'s \$200 had in forty-eight hours, swelled to \$20,000.

It was natural after this happy event, that "calls

and puts" should run like a silver thread through the tangled skein of B——'s existence. He wound his way through the mazes of the "street," hunting for them as if they were so much game, until one fine day in February he heard that Henry Keep, surnamed the "Silent," was selling calls in Old Southern on the most favorable terms. Our hero snatched at this opportunity as a pike bites at a shiner. In due time he had hidden in his wallet, calls for five hundred Old Southern, duly signed by Henry Keep.

This celebrated stock magnate had taken hold of his pet stock in January, and was brewing a cup of "cold poison" to put to the lips of the bears who were then dancing Juba in their Wall Street garden, for stocks were tumbling on every side.

When these ursine individuals heard that Keep was selling calls in Old Southern at a price slightly above the market, they reasoned that Keep was not such a fool as to sell calls on Old Southern, if it were going to rise. They accordingly bought the calls and used them as a margin to sell short. This was exactly what Keep desired, and he succeeded thus in procuring a large short interest in the market, while Old Southern danced swiftly upwards.

After a time and when the price had risen sufficiently, it was announced that Keep was selling "puts," also on the most favorable terms. Then the bulls bought these puts and used them as margins to buy Old Southern. In this way he stiffened the price in a double ratio, first, by inducing short sales at a low price, and second by inducing purchases at a high price.

Then he put on the screws. Two hatchet-faced

brokers in the regular board, and two bullet-headed brokers in the open board, to whom the task had been delegated, stood by the levers, turned the screws, and squeezed the bears as in a hydrostatic press. "Their silver skins were laced with their golden blood," while their growlings shook the massive walls of the new Stock Exchange. When they were obstinate, the order went forth to "buy them in under the rule." Whereupon the stentorian voice of the vice-president was heard proclaiming that he had been directed by the brokers of Keep to buy in for the account of John Doe, Richard Roe, etc., etc., so many shares of Old Southern to complete their contracts." "What is it offered at, gentlemen? I will give 98 for one thousand shares, 99, 100, 101," at which last named price he bought the stock, and thus compelled the recusant bears to cover their contracts. While the stock was thus selling for 101 cash, it was offered at 94 regular, *i. e.*, deliverable next day, and at 86, seller three, *i. e.*, deliverable at the option of the seller within three days. Such is the magic worked by rings.

Among the herd so neatly caught that day, there was no one who roared so loudly with pain as Uncle Daniel. He had agreed to deliver two thousand three hundred shares, at a price twenty-five per cent. lower than the then price, and now thought $50,000 "a good deal of money" to pay for the amusement of selling short. His broker, D. G—— came to inform him that the stock would be bought in, unless he "came to time." The old man sat in his easy chair, with a most lugubrious face. After ruminating upon the situation for a moment, he replied, "we must ingine 'em, we must ingine 'em." (Ingine, Drew-anglice injoin.) He did ingine 'em. A temporary injunction was granted by a justice of the Supreme Court, forbidding the president of the Board of Brokers from buying in two thousand three hundred shares of Old Southern, for S——, C—— & Co., the brokers from whom it had been borrowed. But this did not save Uncle Daniel, for his own broker took the responsibility of buying in, and delivering the stock, very much to the disgust of the old man.

"We must ingine 'em," has ever since been one of the jokes of the street. It was Uncle Daniel who inaugurated that system of injunctions, which has played so important a part in the tactics of the stock-market, for the past four years. As our hero had not yet learned the art of selling stock on calls, as a margin, he simply held his call for five hundred shares, and when it touched 98, he *called*, received the stock, sold it for cash at 100, and made a profit of $12,000.

"Bless thee, Bottom! thou art translated."

For the first time since his entrance into the stock-market, he burst through his outer integuments, shone forth in all the glory of the tailor's art, and sought the fellowship of capitalists. Good clothes, and $30,000 were all the passports needed, and he soon made the acquaintance of H——, who told him the wondrous story of Pacific Mail. Pacific Mail has been by turns, the great yellow Chinese dragon of the stock-market; now flying, with its courageous riders, to the highest peaks of fortune, and now, like the bears of the Himmalaya Mountains, rolling down from crag to crag, amid the consternation of its holders.

For fourteen years, from 1850 to 1864, it had been twisting and twirling, shooting upwards and flying downwards, dizzying the brain, piling up, or scattering riches, and driving to suicide the men who dealt in it. Then for two years it moved upwards, with periodic and tremendous strides. In 1865, its capital was increased from four to ten millions, and still the price stood at 240. In 1866, the capital was further increased to $20,000,000, an assessment of $3,000,000 was levied on the stock-holders, and dividends made in full paid scrip to the amount of $7,000,000. Even then, the price stood at 180, while the assets of the company were reported at $34,000,000. He who had bought at par in 1862, and had held his stock till the autumn of 1866, would have made, by selling his stock, including the regular yearly dividends of twenty per cent., a profit of over nine hundred per cent.

Brown Brothers & Co., the trustees of the pool described in our ninth chapter, held, in the autumn of 1866, one hundred and thirty thousand shares for the benefit of the combination.

L. W. Jerome, the "superb," now made one of his great operations. He contracted with the pool for the sale to him of one hundred thousand shares, at about twenty per cent. below the market price. This huge block amounting in its market value to nearly $20,000,000, Jerome proceeded to unload upon the shoulders of the "street," by selling it in the form of sellers' options, or borrowing other stock for delivery, in this way creating the impression that he was a short seller. The sharp ones thought they had caught him this time, and snapped greedily at the supposed short sales.

Now, in order to clear himself, Jerome would have to sell his stock at about 145. A large portion of it he actually succeeded in working off at higher figures. But the autumn report of the company marked down their assets to $22,000,000. This showed the intrinsic value of the stock to be 110.

The buyers of the Jerome stock at 170 now began to open their eyes. Just after this came the great depression of the winter of 1867, resulting from the contraction of the legal-tender currency to the extent of $28,000,000. The irrevocable stock-power held by Brown Bros. was released, and Pacific Mail stock came on the market in a deluge. The price fell in a few days from 163 to 115. Jerome's losses were estimated at $800,000. Subsequently, the pool released him from his contract to the extent of forty thousand shares, and once more he "came up to scratch smiling," as they would say in the language of the prize ring.

The same blow which felled Jerome, the financial giant, also struck hard upon B——, our bucolic pigmy.

Attracted by H——'s brilliant story of the fortunes won in Pacific Mail, he took four hundred shares at 175, and put up 60 per cent. margin. This time, as he expressed it, he had "a dead open and shut thing." "Sixty per cent.," said he, "is certainly a judicious and ample margin." And so it would have been on every stock *except* Pacific Mail.

In thirty days, B——'s "judicious and ample margin" was wiped out, and in order to prevent any further loss, he sold, at the suggestion of his panic-smitten broker, at the lowest cash price, his four hundred shares, with a loss of $24,000.

Why didn't B—— draw out his $30,000, invest it in Five-twenties, and retire to his native village content with his competency?

Operators never do draw out their money, at least novices do not, so far as we have heard. They come into the street with the intention of making five or ten or twenty thousand dollars, which having been done, they say they will draw out their profits and retire. But they don't. Their broker blandly hovers over and guards their precious little piles *for himself.* He inquires in an insinuating voice, just as he is going to the board, whether his customer "has anything to say." The customer generally has something to say in the shape of an order to buy or sell, and then in five minutes or thereabouts, he finds his pile is locked fast as a margin in the fond embrace of his broker, who sits over it and feeds upon it till what with interest, commissions, turns, losses, etc., the precious little pile dwindles, and finally either disappears into the broker's till, or is sprinkled upon the tails of innumerable "kites" and flyers.

B—— for a month was lost amid the "awful solitude" of his native forest, and then returned scintillating with speculative enthusiasm. *His* pile was only $5,000 now, but by a series of lucky turns, he had in eight months swelled it to $13,000. It was upon the very day that his broker's account-books disclosed to him this pleasing fact, that he run across H—— the veracious historian of Pacific Mail, who gave him a "point" smoking hot, from the forge of a ring. *This* "point" was respecting Atlantic Mail, another famous steamship stock. As its price had fallen twenty per cent., and now stood at 93, it looked to B—— reasonable to operate in it for a rise. He bought a hundred shares, and as he remarked at the time, "Success in Wall Street, is purely a question of stamps," he deposited seventy per cent. margin, *i. e.* $7,000 on this purchase.

But as ill-luck would have it, Atlantic Mail began to drop that very day; it hung at 87 for a few more days, and then broke in one hour sixty-four per cent. downwards till it struck 23. Of course B—— now sold his stock at the lowest price. Men always do under such circumstances.

Our unfortunate hero, after this last calamity, retired forever from the field of stock-speculation, with $2,500, just $200 more than he had brought down in his original certificate of deposit.

The wonderful gyrations of Pacific Mail, after the period of which we have just been speaking, will be described in some of our succeeding chapters. We should especially note that at last, having survived the buffets of fortune during the *regimes* of Stockwell, Gould, Hatch, and T. W. Park, and after this famous stock had sold down to 10, it was taken hold of by a new party, in 1879, and pushed to 39, at which price operators sought to buy it as eagerly as in its palmiest days.

CHAPTER XXXI.

WOODWARD, FISK JR, GOULD.

The New Race of Financiers—W. S. Woodward—His Portrait, Character and Fortunes—The Ulysses of the Stock-market—His Wealth—James Fisk, Jr.—A Theatrical Character—His History and Antecedents—His First Appearance in the Street—A Funny Man—Anecdotes—Scenes in His Life—Jay Gould's Portrait—Erie Under the Care of Drew—The Marston Pool—Uncle Daniel Cornered—He Makes Terms and Revenges Himself on the Cornerers—New Chapters of Erie—The Market Crowded with Losers—Drew and Vanderbilt Take all Their Money—An Original Opinion Respecting Vanderbilt and Drew—Drew Throws Dirt—Fortunes of M——.

FROM 1862 till 1866, the ground shook with the tread of the new race of financiers who came filing into the stock-market. As the foremost retired with the spoils of their campaigns, or routed and disheartened to sleep the last long sleep after their "life's fitful fever," fresh men stepped in and filled or more than filled their places.

W. S. Woodward was for eight years one of the most prominent of the class of stock speculators. It would be hard to mention a leading railroad stock that did not feel the effect of his strong manipulations. Erie, Pittsburg, Reading, New York Central, Old Southern, and more lately Rock Island, have been favorites in the repertoire of this noted operator, and an account of the cliques and corners he has organized would fill a volume, which could with truth be entitled "The

Speculator." A short, quiet-looking gentleman, with an assiduous air, a dark eye, a face moulded into a fixed expression of solicitude, he hardly looked the daring and incessant speculator that he was. His reputation and credit as a business man stood high on the books of the stock mart.

His career was, speaking commercially, a most chequered one. If any man deserve the epithet of the Ulysses—the much-enduring man of Wall Street, it is Woodward. He has wandered about that treacherous sea for many years, been shipwrecked on its desert islands, threaded the narrow channel between Scylla (panics) and Charybdis (corners), visited the cave of the Cyclops (Polyphemus Vanderbilt), heard the Sirens sing (Uncle Daniel and his Chinese Lyre), sojourned among the Lotus Eaters (in a dull market), and feasted in the gardens of Alcinous (Rock Island). Like the Homeric hero, however, he usually came out right. Mr. Drew hammered him upon his anvil, and the Commodore elevated him skyward with most Olympian kicks, but he used to have as many lives as a cat. When short of stocks, he has been twisted by the bulls up long spiral shafts, and flattened like a pancake against the iron dome of a rampant market; when long of stocks, he has (speaking in the same figurative manner), time and again been thrown by the bears out of six-story garret windows, with nothing to break his fall but an India rubber credit, but like his feline prototype, he generally alighted on his legs and "sailed in" once more, as if nothing killing had happened.

In the summer of 1863, his contract was said, in the street, not to be worth fifty dollars. In 1870, his exchequer was rated at from two to four millions. In 1871 he failed with liabilities of from one-and-a-half to two millions greater than his assets, and he has from that time ceased to be a power in the market.

"Look here upon this picture and on this."

What portraits could be more unlike than that of the dark, still, care-laden Woodward, and the blonde, bustling, unprincipled James Fisk, Jr., who, in 1865, came bounding into the Wall street circus, like a star-acrobat, fresh, exuberant, glittering with spangles, and turning double summersaults, apparently as much for his own amusement, as for that of a large circle of spectators. He was first, last, and always, a man of theatrical effects, of grand transformations, and blue fire. All the world was to him literally a stage, and he the best fellow who shifted the scenes the fastest, danced the longest, jumped the highest, and raked the biggest pile.

His whole business career was a series of scenic hits and stage metamorphoses. His first appearance was as the Prince of Peddlers in New England. His wagon was magnificent; his four horses sleek and mettlesome. At different points in his triumphal progress through the rural districts, he was met by a train of his subalterns, who filled the sheds of the country inns with their wagons, held audience with their chief, and obeyed his orders. His next appearance was as a dry goods merchant, a member of the well-known house of Jordan, Marsh & Co. Then quickly the scene changes once more, and he looms up as a stock-broker in New York, with a capital of $64,000, the profits of his season at merchandise. His office in Broad Street was a banqueting hall, in which he presided over tables which groaned daily with the most sumptuous lunches.

From this point of time (1865) there had always been in the turbulent stream of Erie an undercurrent and an upper whirl of James Fisk, Jr. Uncle Daniel welcomed him (or perhaps we should say his bank account), patted him upon the back, indoctrinated him into the mysteries of pools (of course always in Erie), gave him a paternal hug, during which James saw his pile growing small by degrees and beautifully less; and early in 1868, as he told a friend, he was not worth a dollar in the world.

Six months after this the scene changed again, with much rumbling and the shifting of blazing and many-colored lights, and he stood forth with a million dollars at his bankers, the high comptroller of Erie, a general theatrical manager, a steamboat potentate; in fact, Prince Erie James Jubilee Admiral James Fisk, Jr. Now the scenes shift swiftly—the eye can hardly follow them—first to Wall Street, where, to use his own words, "he made Rome howl" in the Erie ring of November, 1868; then to the courts; then to the office of the Union Pacific Railroad Company, amid the hammering in of great Salamander safes with ponderous sledges; then back to Wall Street, amid the growlings of a thousand bears and the bellowings of as many bulls, in the great gold ring of September, 1869; then in the courts once more, tampering with the Commodore's iron chest, all the while the voices of his enemies raining odium and curses upon him, which fell off like water from a duck's back as he drove on his dozen teams, railroads, steamboats, theaters, pools, contracts, political combinations, etc., etc., as imperturbable as a faro-croupier, and as "cool as a couple of summer mornings."

Boldness! boldness! twice, thrice, and four times. Impudence, cheek! brass! unparalleled, unapproachable. He demoralized and corrupted society.

Perhaps the strong point of this man was his physique, so robust, so hale, so free from the shadow of every peptic derangement. His boldness, *nerve*, and business capacity, were supplied by this physique, which also supplied him with animal spirits beyond measure. He was continually boiling over with jokes, good, bad and indifferent.

Once when he and his father were peddling goods in New Hampshire, an old woman charged Fisk, Senior, with having deceived her as to the value of a piece of calico worth twelve and one-half cents.

"Well, now," said Fisk, Jr., "I don't think father would tell a lie for twelve and one-half cents, though he might tell eight of 'em for a dollar."

He always seemed to look upon his operations in Wall Street, no matter how large they may have been, as a gigantic, side-splitting farce. After the great gold break of September, 1869, one B——, a broker, called upon him at the Erie railroad office, for the purpose of tendering to him $500,000 gold, which he claimed to have sold him. Now, as this amount of gold would weigh something like a ton, Fisk was well aware that B—— had not brought it with him, and therefore the tender could not be legal. So as soon as B—— stated what he came for, Fisk promptly replied, "Certainly, Mr. B——, we will take that gold. Here,

John (calling to an attendant), go down and help Mr. B—— to bring up his gold." Poor Mr. B——, not having brought his ton of gold with him, could only look sheepish and retire.

Jay Gould was the complement—the foil of James Fisk, Jr. He is a short, slight man, with a sable beard, a small, bright, introverted eye, and a cool, clear head. His forte is planning, and he represented the man of thought, as Fisk did the man of action, in the firm of Fisk & Gould. He was the engineer, with his hand on the engine-lever, while Fisk was the roar of the wheels, the volume of smoke from the stack, the glare of the head-light, and the screaming whistle of the locomotive. We shall have more to say hereafter respecting this extraordinary financier. But let us return to the stock-market in 1866 and 1867.

The block of twelve thousand shares of Erie, which Daniel Drew took off the hands of the luckless Ketchum, from 76 to 80, served partly to replace what he had sold at higher figures, when the price culminated in July 31, 1865, and again he proceeded to play his new role of bull, by hoisting Erie to 96, again he tortured the bears and bled them one per cent. a day for the use of Erie stock to complete their contracts. But it is one thing to bid up Erie to 96, and quite another to sell it at that price. To add to Drew's embarrassment an outside ring had bought 10,000 shares on their own account and were expecting to throw this lot upon the market after the old man had lifted the stock to the selling point, and they succeeded in selling it to D. D. at 95. The "street" would not buy it, the public would not buy it, and Drew and his associates held nearly all of the stock.

> "Ye know not of the ways I have,
> I turn, and pass, and come again."

This was his old song, and he sang it now in an under-tone, when he recommended a friend, Captain H——, to buy a few thousand shares of Erie on the point that the "pool" would put it higher. Captain H—— bought ten thousand shares, but discovered accidentally, that this lot of stock came from Drew's brokers, in fact, the old man was selling the very stock that he had recommended Captain H—— to buy. The victim stopped the payment of the check, kept the stock and compelled Drew to cancel the bargain. Uncle Daniel thus thwarted, gradually relaxed his hold on Erie, and it dropped to 56 with great loss to the pool, assisted in its downward course by the short sales made by D. D——, who once more resumed his old character of a bear.

It was in the spring of 1866, while the market was shuddering with the great London panic, the sound of which came rumbling along under the waters of the Atlantic, into Wall Street, that a new party took hold of Erie, the same that had so successfully cornered Prairie du Chien, in the preceding November. William H. Marston was the leader of this new ring. The enormous short sales of Daniel Drew, and those who sold under his inspiration, between 56 and 65, enabled Marston and his associates to obtain complete control of Erie, which by the middle of July, they had raised to 75, and once again Drew found himself cornered quite to his astonishment, since he thought himself thoroughly master of the situation in view of a little stroke of financiering, which he had plied with the Erie Railroad Company a short time before. The corporation being in urgent need of money, had borrowed of him $3,500,000, giving him twenty-eight thousand shares of new stock, and $3,000,000 in bonds convertible into stock, as collateral for the loan. A part of this collateral had been already disposed of at lower prices, when he found himself cornered as above mentioned. He now foresaw a way by which he could revenge himself on those who had conspired against him, and make up his losses. The first step to this way was through diplomacy. He made terms with the ring, and having compromised his back contracts, struck hands with them secretly in their scheme for putting Erie up. That same day the price was allowed to drop ten per cent., converting by these means hosts of jubilant bulls into bears; thereafter for two months the price was manipulated to work in a large short interest; then it was jumped in swift leaps to 97.

September was a halcyon month for all the bulls, great and small. Marston, the bull-leader, was a veritable tycoon for a few weeks. The crowd of those who had suffered in the spring tumble and during the summer, had haunted the purlieus of the Long Room in a variety of doubtful costumes, or "boozed" in the neighboring resorts, now skipped gleefully through the halls of the Fifth Avenue Hotel in gay attire, or sipped their champagne and Sauterne. Erie had shot up, and stood towering like some monarch of the forest; Billy Marston was seated in a crotch of the trunk, his eyes twinkling with delight, the bright plumaged broker-birds twittered on its branches, and many a hungry operator was plucking of its fruit.

And now the "old man" came in the darkness and cut down the tree, sent Billy Marston sprawling, and put to flight every bird and beast which sat on its limbs, then staggered away under the burden of his harvest. To return to the language of the matter of fact, Daniel Drew had sold twenty thousand shares, or thereabouts, at summit prices, and thus took his revenge by breaking the ring, besides pocketing $1,000,000 by the operation. Erie kept falling till it reached 52. This was in the spring of '67. Then commenced a new chapter in speculation, and covering thirty months of time, and marked by more singular events, perhaps, than ever occurred before in the financial history of this or any other country. Battles between the money kings; the Courts of Law and Legislatures of States ranging themselves for or against the rival factions; swift rises, ruinous panics, all ending in the aggrandizement of the few and the impoverishment of the many.

Daniel Drew, Cornelius Vanderbilt, and the other stock potentates, stood all the time in the market like so many mountains of magnet which drew to themselves all the metal out of the pockets of thousands of lesser operators. In 1868 and 1869 the street swarmed with men who came, staked their money, lost, and then vanished, or still haunted the vestibules of the Stock Exchange, possessed by the illusive hope of retrieving their fortunes. The tales that could be told of some of these unfortunates would be as marvelous, doleful and moving as any romance. How they enlisted in the ranks of the speculators, ran down through the whole sounding scale of wealth, joy, splendor, doubt, disaster, penury, misery, then up again, and so on to the end of their career. Such stories as these often contain dark secrets, and belong to the unwritten lives of those men, only to be told by their close-mouthed brokers and those mysterious stock-ledgers, which, like dead men, tell no tales of the customer, either how he made and lost, or from whence he obtained his fresh supplies of cash margin, whether from robbing banks or using the funds of widows and orphans.

It will be noticed by any one who visits the market how greatly the unhappy losers there are given to gossip, in which respect no tea-party of old women in a country village can surpass them. They collect in knots of three or more on the sidewalk and pick financial characters to pieces. They ventilate discreditable stories affecting the credit of noted operators; in fact they convert the stock-mart into a school for scandal.

Naturally the money kings come in for their full share of abusive gossip from these individuals. Vanderbilt, they called a brigand. Drew, a sneak. Fisk, a cut-throat, etc., etc.

In the summer of 1869, while E—— and I were standing in New Street, near the entrance to the Long Room, our attention was attracted by two singular looking men who belonged to the class above described, and were conversing in a style which drew about them a small group of amused listeners. They were giving their opinions respecting the Commodore and Uncle Daniel with more freedom than elegance.

One of them after asserting that it was easier to make money in every business than in stock-speculation, followed up this proposition by announcing his belief that the only way to win a fortune in stocks, was to tickle Vanderbilt and Drew, meaning thereby to make ones self agreeable or useful to the great bull and bear. The idea of Cornelius Vanderbilt and Daniel Drew writhing with inextinguishable laughter under the seedy operator's fingers, as they were poked in among the small ribs, was followed by a burst of merriment from the little audience who seemed to thoroughly appreciate the truth as well as the ludicrousness of the remark. No doubt any one who could tickle Vanderbilt and Drew could make a fortune by it, just as one can catch a bird if he can put salt on his tail.

The other of the two was a man, in whose face the comic and the sad were strangely mingled, though on the whole the comic predominated. He gave his views of the now deceased speculator thus:

"You see, boys, that Uncle Daniel, as you call him, (I wish he *was* my uncle,) is a dirt thrower. He spoils every stock he touches."

"How so?" inquired his auditors.

"Why! he started in life as a cattle drover, and when his cattle didn't drive to suit him, he used to pick up mud and throw at 'em until he'd plastered 'em all over, and so when he brought 'em to market they were just one mass of mud and filth. Now he treats stocks just as he used to treat cattle, he pens 'em, drives 'em up and down the market, corners 'em; in fact, Daniel Drew calls stocks his critters and abuses 'em accordingly. He waters 'em and plasters 'em all over with dirt till they are not worth shucks. He is not a very bad old man, however."

This original illustration of Drew's policy in depressing stocks, led me to inquire the name of this eccentric-looking individual.

"I know him," replied E——, "it is M——, one of that numerous class who have a regular business out of which they make a small fortune every year, and then lose it in stocks."

"He is a liquor dealer," continued E——. "I became acquainted with him in 1860. His store, or, as he was pleased to call it, his office, was in ——— street, close by the Stock Exchange. It consisted of two floors; the ground-floor was his sample-room, lined with bottles, having on them the newest possible of labels, bearing a variety of nectareous inscriptions, which were, however, open to question as to their precise truth and veracity.

The cases of claret on the floor, always looked as though they were fresh from the plane of some carpenter in Greenwich Street, or Manhattan Alley, and the corpulent casks ranged in dignified rows along the rear wall, reminded one of the Benzine Barrel Company, rather than of the French coopers of Bordeaux.

The other floor was the basement, and about this apartment always hung the odor of mystery, and of a druggist's shop, until one day, paying M—— a visit, and not finding him in the sample-room, I penetrated to the subterranean regions. There I found M——, as busy as a bee, distilling honey out of poisonous flowers. He wore a white apron, which bore a great variety of suspicious stains, and was engaged in filling bottles from a large tank. He hurried with me up stairs, as soon as he could doff his apron and wash his hands, but in the brief survey I took of his laboratory, I noticed several vials of oil of cognac for manufacturing brandy out of proof spirits, together with various other flavoring essences; a large bottle that looked like tincture of logwood; jars of alum, and sugar of lead; others which looked as if they might contain chrystallized strychnine; and still another labeled hydrocyan—which I interpreted to be prussic acid.

A flood of light suddenly burst upon me. I had often remarked diagnostically, singularly disagreeable sensations, not only in the head, but also in the stomach, in the morning after imbibing at M——'s restaurant. I now smelt the rat, I might almost say the ratsbane. M—— was a compounder as well as a seller of liquors. In the basement of his store, he mixed and manufactured cordials, and various other beverages, to suit the palate of his customers. As he informed me in a moment of confidence, "what people wanted was fuddle, and he accordingly mixed his beverages with a sharp eye on fuddle."

By diligence in business, and by the suavity with which he commended his doses to a bibulous and too confiding public, he succeeded in amassing about $20,000. This was in 1863. Then he looked about him for some judicious investment or other means for swelling the dimensions of his little pile. He did not have far or long to look. Money could be made (or lost) with wonderful speed in the neighboring stock-market. The speculative movements in Wall Street had long attracted his notice, which was kept alive by the numerous brokers and operators who took their arid lunch of crackers and cheese at noon-day in his sample-room. Some of them had been customers for years, and had doubtless consumed whole hogsheads of "Mountain Dew," "Milk of Kentucky," etc., and thus created a great activity in the trade of poisonous drugs used in the adulteration of liquors, besides paying M—— a pretty penny, to say nothing of doctors' bills. The talk of M——'s customers was of margins, profits, commissions, "puts and calls." As for the word "profits," they tossed it about in their conversation with the most enchanting freedom. Fifty thousand dollars was but a drop in the bucket, and their marginal notes and references put all the laws of legitimate profits at defiance. Five thousand could be made in an hour by one lucky turn, and a hundred thousand in a short campaign.

Is it any wonder that M—— should have caught the infection, or that the *feu de joie* fired daily in his presence should have "put his soul in arms and eager for the fray?" And so it did; for one fatal day he found the little fortune of $20,000, which he had scraped together, was too hot to hold in his pocket. A poetic and unconscious revenge was about to be taken on M—— by P——, a broker and his oldest customer, in return for the stupefying and stomach-deranging draughts which he had so often imbibed at M——'s sample-room.

The $20,000 was deposited in P——'s hands.

A few weeks passed in see-sawing up and down the market; then a bold dash at Harlem on the short side, accompanied with a little coquetting with gold, and M—— found his fortune had dwindled to $500.

P—— and his brother brokers, the customers of M——, had unconsciously taken a terrible revenge on the unfortunate sample-room proprietor, who thereupon returned immediately to his unhealthy laboratory, plied his trade with new vigor, and drew to his sample-room large accessions from his new acquaintances of the Stock Exchange. He talked glibly in the street, his nectar-fluids flowed in cataracts, his office clinked with glasses as of a chime of bells, and a perpetual shower of fractional currency and greenbacks, made his counters verdant as the herbage after a rain.

Time rolled on, and in twelve months he found himself in possession of $15,000. This pleasing fact came under his notice, when he was taking account of stock, April 1st, 1864, just when the bulls were enjoying their spring carnival, led gaily on by their dashing leader, A. W. Morse. He drew out all his money from his bank, emptied his till of its loose change, and in an hour was in the office of P——. M——'s customers welcomed him back to the market, and speedily stuck him so full of "points," that his head fairly bristled with them.

What it was that finished him this time, whether it was that treacherous lake, Erie, the tumbling ramparts of Fort Wayne, or the precipices and toppling crags of Galena, I cannot say, but on the 19th of April, the day after the great panic, he was seen scudding under bare poles, in the direction of his chemical haven.

"His present status in the stock-market," added E——, "rests upon a slender margin of four hundred dollars, no thanks to North West or Jay Gould."

CHAPTER XXXII.

THE BATTLES OF THE GIANTS.

Vanderbilt Obtains Control of Central and Erie—Drew to be Left Out in the Cold—The Commodore Warms a Viper—Drew at his Old Games—The Opening of the Battle—Injunction and Counter-Injunction—The Plot Thickens—Ten Millions of Fresh Erie Saddled upon the Commodore—Will he Break?—Stampede of the Conspirators—Thunder All Around—New York Central Hoisted into the Rain Clouds, and Why—A Compromise—The "Old Man" Weak in the Knees—A Treaty of Peace, its Terms, etc.—New Developments—Locking Up Greenbacks, and Punishing Drew.

THE wealth of the richest valley shone upon by the sun—the valley of the Mississippi and its tributaries—is poured into the lap of the Queen City of America, through three grand trunk railways—the Pennsylvania Central, the Erie, and the New York Central. The first of these lines long since passed under the control of a combination of wealthy capitalists. The second had been for ten years previous to 1867 a kind of stock ten-pin, set up and bowled down in Wall Street by Daniel Drew and his associates; while the third had for many years, prior to the year 1865, been supposed to be under the control of the Albany Regency as a part of their political machinery.

Cornelius Vanderbilt, in 1864, took possession of the Harlem & Hudson lines, two mouths of one of these trunks. The next step in his programme was to secure the control of the trunk fed by these mouths, viz.: the New York Central. But this could not be done without a struggle. His earliest attempt to obtain his object was a failure. Henry Keep, his antagonist in the first onset, triumphed, and in 1866 was chosen president of the company. But Henry Keep had merely certain ends of his own to subserve in becoming president of the New York Central; and when these ends had been subserved, he retired from the position. The way was then open for a new campaign, which Vanderbilt speedily undertook, and in 1867 he had secured the prize. He was master now of Hudson, Harlem and Central.

The next move was upon the works of Erie, the only other competing line which it was possible for him to obtain control of. In the summer of 1867, Vanderbilt and his friends had secured a majority of the Erie stock, and were about to elect a new board of directors, in which *Daniel Drew's name was not to appear*.

To throw Daniel Drew out of the Erie board would be like skinning the bear, or plucking the plumage from the peacock; it would strip the "old man" of his prestige, deprive him of his bread and butter, and send him forth to wander in desolation through the stock-market.

Daniel Drew felt the iron enter his soul at this prospect, and threw himself in supplication at the feet of Cornelius Vanderbilt, who was moved by the spectacle, and comforted the old bear. A compromise was made, and early in the fall of 1867, Daniel Drew was allowed to come into the combination as a director, and the treasurer of the Erie Railroad Company. Daniel Drew could no more refrain from playing his old games in Erie, than the veteran gamester can withold his hand from cards and dice. It was play to him, but death to others. He intrigued to enlist in his schemes, the most active and able of the board of directors, and in January, 1868, they were with him in furthering these schemes.

A pool in the Vanderbilt interest was then engaged in engineering a rise in Erie, and the street was full of rumors of something which was to carry Erie to par. It reached 79, when suddenly it fell back heavily to 71, to the astonishment of the bull faction. A great mass of stock had been quietly shuffled off by Daniel Drew, on the shoulders of the pool.

On the evening when Erie stood at 71, the whole strength of Wall Street seemed to have poured into the halls of the Fifth Avenue Hotel. Daniel Drew, with his face pucked into an expression more than usually sombre and solicitous, stood near the grand stairway, watching the writhings of his victims, the late exultant bulls. A prominent broker accosted him as follows, "Well, Mr. Drew, is Erie going down?"

"Other folks think it is," replied Daniel Drew, with an ill-suppressed chuckle, "though I can't give you any pynts in it."

"Other folks is fond of cats," remarked Mr. Brooks, the pieman in the Pickwick papers, when Samuel Weller of famous memory, observed the great number of those useful domestic animals frisking about the pie-shop.

The hollow truce patched up in the preceding summer, had been broken. Daniel Drew, true to his bitter instincts, had been undermining the Commodore and his friends who composed the pool be-before named, and now the Commodore fired the first gun which was to usher in the battle. This gun roared out on the 17th of February, in the form of an injunction obtained from the Supreme Court, forbidding Drew and his brother directors from the payment of the interest and principal of the $3,500,000 borrowed of Drew in 1866. This was followed up by another action petitioning for the removal from office of Mr. Treasurer Drew. On the 3d of March, another injunction was issued forbidding the Erie Board to issue any more new stock, by the conversion of bonds or otherwise, in addition to the two hundred and fifty-one thousand and fifty-eight shares appearing in the last report of the company.

Prior to this, and on the 19th of February, by a vote of the Erie Board, the stock of the road was increased to four hundred and fifty thousand shares ($45,000,-000 at par.) Five millions of convertible bonds were forthwith sold to Daniel Drew, who promptly converted them into stock, and on or about the 29th of February, those shares were disposed of in the market, carrying down the price of Erie to 65, to the delight of Drew, and the entire bear brigade, which fought under his banner. But just as these triumphant mercenaries were counting the hours when Erie should plunge down among the fifties, it wheeled and rose like lightning to seventy-three, under the enormous purchases of the Commodore, fortified as he now was, by the injunction forbidding the issue of any more stock. The smaller bear tribe were scooped up as in a net by the dozen, but the leaders in the downward movement preserved their serenity in the face of this sudden blow. Drew chuckled a little more often. Fisk, in his cataract of shirt-front, and enveloped in an atmosphere of patchouli, attended his Nourmahal to the opera as usual, and Gould glided with a sinuous grace, through the conclave of directors, who met just at this time, with remarkable frequency, at the office of the Erie Railroad Company.

The secret of this serenity was soon disclosed. The Erie conspirators prepared five thousand convertible bonds, and promptly converted them into fifty thousand shares of stock. Then they addressed themselves to strike the blow. They had been ordered to stand still, by the last Vanderbilt injunction granted by one judge, and now they applied for and obtained, an injunction in the name of a third party, from another judge, forbidding them to stand still.

The plot was ripe. It only remained to select the broker who should strike the blow. The broker selected was William Heath, the head of the prominent and favorably known firm of William Heath & Co. He was a Boston boy, and his career as a buyer and seller of stocks on commission, dates back only to the year 1864, when his fortune was swallowed up by the Morse failure, and he was thrown back on his oars to start life again as a broker. But in that brief period, by main strength exerted in the exercise of an unwearied industry, and by the display of fine business qualities, he built up an enormous business, and won for himself a worthy name and high credit on 'Change. He is said to have earned in ten years the gross sum of nearly two million dollars in commissions; and when it is remembered that a large portion of this sum was from buying and selling on a commission of one thirty-second, *i. e.*, three dollars and twelve cents on each hundred shares bought or sold, the extent of his business can be better appreciated.

The stock commission house of D. Groesbeck & Co., which we have already mentioned, was then, as for some years it had been, the confidential agent of Daniel Drew, the custodian of his secrets, and the head manager of the great speculative movements in which he embarked his ten or fifteen millions of hard cash. At the office of this firm, then in Broad Street, was the headquarters where was planned and carried forward to its execution the daring plot we are describing: William Heath was the sub-agent who struck the final blow.

On the 29th of February, Uncle Daniel might have been seen scuttling into the office of William Heath & Co., No. 19 Broad Street. A few moments later, that office was resonant with the rustling of fifty thousand shares of fresh, crisp, Erie certificates, like the chirping of locusts at noontide in July. On the 10th of March again, in the same office, was heard the rustling of fifty thousand fresh shares, as they dropped from the plump jeweled fingers of James Fisk, Jr.

The open board met as usual at ten o'clock in the morning. Erie stood firm as a pillar of granite at 79. The Vanderbilt cohort sat with grim smiles upon their faces; their glances and voices were level with assured triumph. The nods, becks, winks, and odd smiles exchanged between them, seemed to tell their adversaries that, struggle as they might, it was all in vain; that they would have to settle up, or pay the piper a swinging rate.

Most of the bear brigade who dared still to keep short of Erie, unconscious of the measures taken for their speedy release, were a pallid group endeavoring to hide their agony by looking straight before them, or conversing in short jerky whispers with those who sat next to them, or lolling back in their chairs, feigning indifference, with their eyes fixed upon the adipose cherubs frescoed upon the ceiling.

The whole market hung on one word—Erie. The strident voice of George Henriques, the Vice President of the Open Board, was heard calling off in quick succession, Government Bonds, State Bonds, Pacific Mail, New York Central, then a pause, a shadow rippled across his face and a shiver ran through the hall as he ejaculated in a tone still more strident—Erie! For ten minutes bedlam seemed to have broken loose. Every operator and broker was on his feet in an instant, screaming and gesticulating. The different Vanderbilt brokers stood each in the center of a circle, wheeling as on a pivot from right to left, brandishing their arms and snatching at all the stock offered them. As the presiding officer's hammer fell and his hoarse voice thundered out, "That will do, gentlemen, I shall fine any other offer," Erie stood at 80. The crowd leaving the other stocks not yet called, poured into the street, where nothing was heard but Erie. Vanderbilt's brokers had orders to buy every share offered, and under their enormous purchases the price rose, by twelve o'clock, to 83.

Meanwhile, William Heath had not been idle. The fifty thousand shares of stock which had been given him to sell, had been distributed in lots of five and ten thousand shares to his sub-agents, and by half-past one, they had all been disposed of.

In the very height of this battle between giant avarice, fighting like a demon with his fellow over the grave of all the passions, a whisper was heard which sent an electric thrill through the whole market. This whisper, breathed thus, was "thousands of shares of fresh certificates, dated three days back, and in the name of James Fisk, Jr., are on the street." The price dropped like lead to 71.

Vanderbilt had lost the day. The news of this disaster was carried to him by a friend, who asked if he would now sell his Erie? He roared a thundering No! His situation was indeed critical, loaded as he was with ten millions of fresh Erie stock, which marked down the intrinsic value of the stock to 50, to say nothing of the huge blocks of Central, Hudson, and Harlem, which he was carrying on his aged shoulders. Any lack of nerve would have produced a financial collapse, which would have involved himself and thousands of others in frightful loss, and perhaps ruin. But he never flinched.

His first move was to punish his adversaries, by bringing them under the process of the court, whose injunction they had disregarded.

The executive committee of the Erie Board were holding high festival over their triumph, at the offices of the company, at the foot of Duane Street, on the morning of the 11th of March. Uncle Daniel's corrugated visage was set into a chronic chuckle. Jay Gould's financial eye beamed and glittered, and the blonde bulk of James Fisk, Jr. was unctuous with jokes, when a messenger arrived, conveying to them the intelligence that process of the court had been issued, to punish them for contempt of its mandates, and would soon be placed for service in the hands of the high sheriff's spongy officers.

Then there were hurryings to and fro in the Erie Railroad Office. A few moments later, and the policeman on that beat observed a squad of respectably dressed, but terrified looking men, loaded down with packages of greenbacks, account books, bundles of papers tied up with red tape, emerge in haste and disorder from the Erie building. Thinking perhaps that something illicit had been taking place, and these individuals might be plunderers playing a bold game in open daylight, he approached them, but he soon found out his mistake, they were only the executive committee of the Erie Company, flying the wrath of the Commodore, and laden with the spoils of their recent campaign.

By three o'clock that afternoon the fugitives had established their headquarters at Taylor's Hotel, in Jersey City, and were sheltered from the process of the New York Courts under the broad ægis of the free and sovereign State of New Jersey. They were provided with ammunition in the shape of from six to ten millions of money, principally the proceeds from the sale of one hundred thousand shares of new Erie stock, which they had saddled upon Vanderbilt, and now were ready to open fire all around, though at long range.

The old proverb, that laws are cobwebs which catch only small flies, while the large flies break through and escape, was now fully illustrated.

The litigation which followed, was a carnival for

the legal fraternity. The fees of one of the lawyers amounted to $150,000. This was only one item in a bill of costs payable to an army of attorneys and counselors. The files of the courts were stacked with affidavits and counter affidavits, complaints, answers, replies, demurrers and orders. The Supreme Court rang with the criminations and recriminations of the rival factions, while reluctant witnesses were stretched upon the rack and badgered and threatened in order to elicit from them the dark secrets of the stock-trade. The gravest insinuations were made against the purity of the judicial ermine.

Outside the courts of law, the battle was renewed in other fields. The press, siding with one party or the other, teemed with articles and affidavits affecting the combatants by forestalling public opinion. In the Legislature of New Jersey, an act was passed making the Erie Railway Company a corporation of that State. In the Legislature of New York, a bill was introduced for the purpose of legalizing the new issue of Erie stock, providing for a broad gauge connection between New York and Chicago, and forbidding the consolidation of Erie with Central. The securing of the passage of this bill was entrusted to Jay Gould, a master of diplomacy, who, braving the process for contempt which was out against him, succeeded in establishing himself in Albany, fortified with a trunk full of greenbacks, and proceeded to lobby for its passage. The Erie Company leveled another blow at Vanderbilt, by lowering the tariff of freights and passengers on their road, to a ruinous rate.

Meanwhile the withdrawal of the vast sum carried

away by the conspirators into New Jersey, had created a stringency in the money market, and stocks declined in a semi-panic. New York Central fell from 132 to 108¾. The market was full of rumors affecting the solvency of Vanderbilt. He had declared his intention to hold up Erie, if he had to mortgage every dollar of property he possessed. But could he do it? He was exposed to fresh issues of Erie stock, which it was reported his opponents had threatened to make. Some of his associates, terrified at the prospect, threw their New York Central stock upon the market. Heavy bets were made, that the bill legalizing the new issue of Erie stock would pass the Legislature, and that New York Central would go down to par.

The whole street seemed to be selling Central. When it reached 108¾, it wheeled and shot back to 111, amid the consternation of the bears, who still persisted in selling.

Monday, April 20th, was a dark, cloudy day. The effect of the weather upon stocks is very apparent. That strange, and many-chorded instrument, the human nerve, is nowhere more delicately strung, or more responsive to the subtlest influences, than in the orchestra of stock-speculation. Eye, ear, touch, and all the ganglia, are morbidly alive. Sometimes a harmless piece of tissue-paper, thrown by one operator to another, or a half-uttered confidence, would seem to be enough to start a panic, or send the market "kiting" up among the tall figures. The outside atmosphere is one of these influences. Hence it is that the barometer of finance seems to respond to the atmospherical barometer, the nerve fluid seeming to be as susceptible as the mercury in the bulb. When cliques have control of a stock, they rarely select a wet, unpleasant day in which to run up the price.

But this rule did not hold good in the case of New York Central. On the Monday before mentioned, at twelve o'clock, meridian, the news reached the Long Room, that the Erie bill had passed by a large majority. The bears (who generally sympathized with the Erie faction), now sold Central short on every side. The skies grew black, and a pouring shower followed, amid which the strong hand of the Commodore, regardless of the elements which were against him, hoisted the enormous bulk of Central to 120.

How did it happen, that he had thus resumed his grip on Central? Had a settlement been made by the litigants?

Vanderbilt understood the character of Drew. He knew, and said that he had "no backbone," and would be inclined to compromise. The event proved that he knew his man. Hardly had the Erie confederates been installed in Taylor's Hotel, when his younger, and more robust associates, noticed the workings of his timid, vacillating nature. He had been borne along by their stronger wills, and now felt painfully his trying position. He missed his pleasant fireside, where had so often toasted his aged limbs, and dreamed of panics.

One evening he was missed from the conclave; where could he be? His associates distrusted him, and put detectives on his track. He was followed to Weehawken ferry, and it was ascertained, that he was making secret visits to New York. From that time, he was never free from the surveillance of detectives. He drew out the money, which had been brought over at the time of his flight, and carried it to New York. James Fisk, Jr., attached his securities in Jersey City, and compelled him to restore it.

Under the process of the court, Daniel Drew was liable to be immured in Ludlow Street jail. But Sunday brings, besides its other blessings, immunity from arrest. One Sunday in April saw the "old man" at the house of the Commodore. Once more he shed salt tears and supplicated for mercy. "The gentle dew of mercy" was dropped upon him, and a few days after that he was seen in Broad Street, on a week day. Rumors began to spread, but nothing definite was known for some weeks. The rise in Central, however, told the story to those who chose to put two and two together.

The terms of this settlement were subsequently made public in the most thorough manner, in the great suit of the Erie Railway Company *vs.* Cornelius Vanderbilt.

He was relieved of fifty thousand shares of Erie stock, and received therefor, $2,500,000 in cash, and $1,250,000 in bonds of the Boston, Hartford and Erie Company, at 80. He also received the further sum of $1,000,000 for the privilege given the Erie Company thus purchased, of calling upon him for his remaining fifty thousand shares at 70, any time within four months. This settlement was effected late in April. The day after it took place, Fisk, Jr. could have been seen on the street in a nobby velvet coat, whispering into the ears of his old comrades, "Erie is going down."

The next thing to be done was to sell the one hundred thousand shares of Erie. How could it be effected? for one hundred thousand shares is no flea bite. Very easily, thus: Orders were given every day to sell a certain amount of the stock and to hold the market steady meantime. The stock thus sold, was borrowed of different parties for delivery, and in this way the impression was created among those not in the secret, that a large short interest was being made; this induced the belief that Drew and Vanderbilt were working together to raise the price so as to sell their stock. In a few weeks, one hundred thousand shares were sold. Then the parties from whom the stock had been borrowed, were repaid with the hundred thousand shares held jointly by the Erie Company and by Vanderbilt.

Three months of comparative dullness in Erie passed away, and then Uncle Daniel took down his rusty and cobwebbed armor, donned his bear-skin cap, and prepared to enter a new campaign against all the bulls. Erie was to be depressed. The first step towards this depression had been already taken. The Erie Company was now under the control of Jay Gould, who had been chosen president, and James Fisk, Jr., who had been chosen comptroller of the company. The leaders of the Tammany ring, Peter B. Sweeney, and William M. Tweed, were added to the Board of Directors. During the four months prior to the 24th of October, 1868, fresh issues of Erie stock, had been forced upon the market. The capital stock had been increased by two hundred and thirty-five thousand shares, and now stood at $57,766,300. The stock-price ran down to 44.

The next step was to lock up greenbacks, and thus produce an artificial stringency in the money market.

It has been stated in these pages, that money in the fall season, flows westward and southward, away from New York. The money system is like the circulatory system in the human body. The sub-treasury in New York, is the financial heart of the nation. The money which flows in and out of that great depository, is the blood of commerce running through great arteries.

It was now proposed, that this circulatory system should be constricted, so that money could flow with less freedom, and stocks be depressed.

Three doctors, Daniel Drew, Jay Gould and James Fisk, Jr., now put their fingers on the financial pulse and then constricted the money arteries by *locking up greenbacks.* This is a device of comparatively recent invention. It is accomplished in this way. Checks for a large amount are drawn on various banks by some of the heavy depositors. Then these checks are certified as good by the banks, and greenbacks are borrowed upon them as collateral and locked up. A scarcity of money ensues and stocks fall.

The Erie conspirators had in their possession many millions, the proceeds from the sales of the new stock. Drew added four millions to the combination. Thereupon, $14,000,000 was withdrawn from the circulation. The money rate tightened fearfully, and the large holders of stocks saw ruin impending. Among the number was Henry Keep. He was loaded down enormously with North-west stock, and would break unless he could secure $2,000,000. In his extremity he applied to his old associate Drew, who saved him by loaning him the required sum.

Drew now retired from the "locking up" combination. This excited their ire. The old man was short of 70 thousand shares of Erie, and his associates resolved to punish his treachery. They bought an immense amount of Erie at low prices, and then "unlocking greenbacks," money became easy again. Erie was hoisted to 61. Drew was cornered, and tried to compromise his contracts, but his old associates refused to "let him up." He had to buy in his shorts with the loss of a million and a half of dollars.

It was plain that Drew had now seen his best days. A septuagenarian, he could not cope with the younger race of speculators. He himself felt this, and after 1869 diminished the size of his stock operations. But the old fever of speculation still lingered in his aged veins, and he kept dabbling in stocks till the panic of 1873, when he suspended. This lesson was not enough. Again embarking the remnant of his fortune he was at last, after a series of losses, completely ruined in 1875. His death, on the 18th day of September, 1879, sudden and in the night, closed his earthly account, and his name hereafter will be only one of those great shadows in the traditionary landscape of the street.

"Respecting the dead say nothing but what is good," says the proverb, and we are glad to brighten the darker side of the picture by calling to mind the invariable good temper and amiability of the deceased, his large benevolence, and a thousand good traits which will make him long remembered by a large circle of friends.

CHAPTER XXXIII.

THE GREAT GOLD CONSPIRACY OF 1869.

How Gold was Put Up and Down since 1865—Gold Looks Downwards in 1869, and Why—Jay Gould Organizes a Scheme—Amount of Gold to be Handled—The Complicity of Government Sought to be Obtained—Influences Brought to Bear—The Leaders of the Conspiracy —Everybody Selling Gold Short—The Vast Sums Bought by the Clique—Jay Gould on the Rack—Fisk Comes to the Front—A New Programme—The Conspiracy Draws to a Head—Dawning of Black Friday—Strategy Adopted—Actresses Gazing on the Drama—The Battle in the Gold-Room—Rout of the Conspirators—Speyers Bidding Up Gold—The Bears Triumph—Scenes in Broad Street—The Stock Panic.

ON the corner of Twenty-third Street and Eighth Avenue stands a white marble palace, adorned on the exterior with statues and elaborate cornices, and hollowed in the interior into a sumptous opera hall, surrounded by spacious and richly furnished rooms—at once a fortress and a temple. Here once were planned the fiercest campaigns in the stock market, and here, too, are still exhibited the most gorgeous scenes of the spectacular drama. Pike's Opera House, after 1868, became known as Erie Castle.

This now famous block of buildings passed, in that year, into the hands of the stock and theatrical impressario, James Fisk, Jr., by whom it was leased to the Erie Railway Company as their principal office.

PLOTTING THE GREAT GOLD RING OF '69.

Here, sitting at their ease, surrounded by luxury, in a magnificent apartment, with shrewd lawyers at their elbow, two confederates plotted the great gold conspiracy of 1869, and coolly organized the ruin of thousands.

From April, 1865, to September, 1869, a period of more than four years, the movements of gold had been brought about by artificial means, in conjunction with commercial causes, or rather pretexts. The price of Government Bonds abroad, wars or rumors of wars in Europe, disturbances of trade, the shipments of the precious metal in payment of our imports, sales of gold by our government; these and a thousand other strings were harped upon by the gold gamblers to produce those singular upward and downward oscillations in the price, which enriched the members of the Gold Board, while they disturbed the peace of commerce and beggared a host of infatuated outside dealers.

Wall Street, like history, repeats itself. Every summer, since 1865, there had been a rise in gold. In March, 1869, gold fell to 131. The astute intellect of Jay Gould now foresaw another opportunity to push up the price of gold, and having purchased $7,000,000 of it, by playing on the strings of the Cuban insurrection, the Alabama difficulties, the prospect of a war between France and Prussia, etc., terrified the bears and rushed up the price to 145. Emboldened by the success of this move, he formed a new and daring scheme.

We call it a daring scheme, for outside influences to help it there were none.

At home, the Republic was at peace; barns bursting with a garnered harvest, cattle on a thousand hills, cotton whitening innumerable fields. The government rapidly diminishing the debt, gave assurance of the speedy resumption of specie payments. The balance of trade necessitating the shipment of coin to foreign countries, was but slightly against the United States.

Abroad, the cloud of war between France and Prussia had faded to a mere speck. England was looking with equanimity upon the Alabama claims. The policy of our government toward Cuba was that of non-intervention.

It was to be a dead lift. Nothing but the shorts would help it. It could only be successful by a judicious application of the great law of supply and demand. The demand must be created, and then the supply must be shut down upon.

Jay Gould, the arch conspirator, calmly surveying the situation, and undeterred by the difficulties it presented, proceeded to organize in the most secret forges of Wall Street, a band of Vulcans, who should weld and rivet the chains by which all the bears on 'Change should be bound and made to dance as if on red-hot plates; first to slow, and then to quick music.

To accomplish the ends proposed, both the actual and the possible supply of gold in the city of New York must be provided for.

Gold coin in the city of New York is found under three conditions. In the first place, there is the floating gold, which is used by the speculators to make their deliveries, and for other commercial purposes. In August, 1869, the amount of this floating gold was estimated at from $15,000,000 to $20,000,000.

This was but a bagatelle for a ring to buy up. In the second place, there is the gold held by the banks, a part of which is loaned to the importing merchants, for the payment of duties to the Government. But little of this gold, held by the banks, comes upon the street. In the third place, there was the gold in the sub-treasury of the United States, amounting to a daily average of $80,000,000. The Government, in the summer of 1869, was selling one million of this amount every alternate week.

The pivot upon which the whole scheme would turn, was the policy of the Government in their sales of gold. The coin in the sub-treasury hung like an avalanche over any combination which should undertake to raise the price. The complicity of high officials would have to be secured, in order to keep down the sales to a limited amount.

In June of that year the planners of the gold scheme began to use all their influence in order to obtain a better control of the gold market.

The then President of the United States was approached directly, for the purpose of ascertaining what the future financial policy of the Government might be with respect to sales of gold, but without eliciting any information from the reticent chief magistrate.

A plausible theory respecting the necessity to commercial interests of high-priced gold, was suggested by James McHenry, a prominent English financier, and was ventilated freely by Jay Gould for the purpose of forestalling official action.

The medium selected by the conspirators for securing the complicity of the high officers of the

Government, was the then prominent Abel R. Corbin, who, by virtue of a marriage connection, claimed to be able to influence the chief executive of the nation in the matter of gold sales. Upon the promises and representations of this man, hung the whole success of the plot. The planners relied sufficiently upon him to proceed to organize their forces and enter upon the prosecution of their scheme.

The nucleus of the combination consisted of Jay Gould, James Fisk, Jr., W. S. Woodward, the veteran speculator, and Arthur Kimber, the youthful agent of a wealthy London banking house. Around this nucleus revolved a number of rich bankers, sly politicians, officials, and corporations made compact by the potentiality of a wealth beyond the dreams of avarice, and cohesive with the hope of plunder.

When gold fell, in August, to 131, it looked as if the finger of a child could have rolled it down to 120. Nearly everbody thought, and said, that the price was doomed to fall lower than at any time since 1862. All the world, in a commercial sense, stood ready to profit by the fall. The importing merchants borrowed it, and sold it, by the million. The foreign bankers sold it by the car load. The brokers sold it all around the board; the bond-holders, the administration politicians, and the outside public, all sold it for future delivery. They "stood on their shorts," or rather, sat incubating on them, as if they were golden eggs. The clique bought this gold.

About the middle of September, Woodward bought nine millions, at 133½ to 134, for the account of himself, Kimber and Gould. Prior to this, large amounts of gold had been bought.

The price rose heavily to 138, at which price Woodward and Kimber are said to have sold their interest, and retired from the combination. Their associates enlisted new coadjutors and still persisted in their scheme.

On the morning of Wednesday, the 22d of September, the conspirators held several millions more gold than was in the city of New York, outside of the sub-treasury, and yet the price had risen, in the face of these purchases, only to 141.

The price would soon have to be bid up to 150, at least, but the buying of high-priced gold in the form of contracts from those who were selling it for future delivery, is quite a different thing from buying the actual coin, which the Government might sell and deliver.

It was natural, in contemplation of the difficulty with which the price was raised, that Jay Gould should feel anxiety as to the ultimate success of the movement. He knew thoroughly well how much depended on the influence of Corbin, in retarding official sales, and already he more than distrusted him, with how much reason the event has shown. He well knew that if his suspicions were correct, and official sales of Government gold should not be withheld through Corbin's influence, the only thing to be relied upon, was a bold game, to terrify the shorts and compel them to cover their contracts at a high figure. The personal magnetism and brute pluck of James Fisk, Jr., were now brought to the front. Let this individual tell the story in his own characteristic manner.

"When Gould found himself loaded down to the gunnels and likely to go under, the cussed fellow never said a word—he's too proud for that—but I saw him tearing up bits of paper. When Gould snips off corners of newspapers and tears 'em up in bits, I know that there's trouble. Then I come in to help—he knows I'd go my bottom dollar on him,—and said to him, 'Look here, old fellow, when I was a boy, on a farm in Vermont, I've seen the old man go out to yoke up Buck and Brindle; he'd lift the heavy yoke on to Brindle's neck, key the bow, and then, holding up the other end, motion to old Buck to come under, and old Buck would back off and off, and sometimes, before he could persuade him under, the yoke would get too heavy for dad. And, Gould, old fellow, Wall Street won't be persuaded, and the yoke is getting ——— heavy—and here I am to give you a lift.'"

The time was rapidly approaching when the decisive blow must be struck. The vaults of every bank in the Union, in Montreal and the Bank of England had been called upon to disgorge, and the gates of the national treasury had been stormed with prayers to let loose the coin and save the country, or at least the bears.

On the evening of the 23d of September, the clique rushed in and took possession of the private office of William Heath & Co., after the firm had left for the day. A sumptuous banquet and wine were ordered in from a neighboring restaurant. Nothing definite seems to have been resolved on at this meeting, except that the bears must, within a day or two, be compelled to fulfill their contracts. It was at sometime on the same day, however, that a new programme was determined upon, for which purpose William Belden, a former partner of Fisk, was brought actively into the combination. He proceeded to buy that day not less than $8,000,000 for the account of the clique, and thus appeared prominently as their agent.

The question always to be asked in buying stocks, is for whom they are to be bought, who is responsible for them. By the rule of law, every agent dealing for an unknown principal, is personally liable for all the contracts he makes. The new programme decided upon, was the making of William Belden, a man of little means, the principal in immense contracts for purchases of high-priced gold, which were to be made through Fisk, who was to act merely as an agent, and would thus avoid all personal liability. A paper was given by Belden to Fisk, granting him unlimited power to buy gold for his (Belden's) account. The brokers employed by Fisk would buy on his orders, supposing that he was the principal. Belden was in this way to be the scape-goat on whose shoulders an immense burden of liability for purchases of high-priced gold would ultimately fall.

On Thursday, the 23d, Fisk made his personal magnetism felt by visiting the gold-room, where he struck terror into the hearts of the bears, by offering a bet of any part of $50,000, that gold would sell at 200. Wherever he went that day he bulled gold, predicted an enormous rise, and openly boasted of the complicity of the Government in the schemes of the conspirators. He proposed to his associates that a complete list of two hundred and fifty firms, known to be short of gold, should be published in the daily papers of the next day, stating the amount that each firm was short of; declaring how much gold the clique held; and informing the victims that if they did not settle at 145, by three o'clock, a higher rate would be demanded. But this proposition was rejected upon the advice of counsel.

The extent of the operations of the clique can be best understood by a few figures. The calls or options for the delivery of gold by other parties, and the cash gold which they held, was stated to be from $80,000,000 to $110,000,000. The amount of short interest is said to have been $250,000,000, the larger portion of which had been made under 144.

The plot was ripe on the evening of the 23d, when the conspirators held a meeting as already described. The cash gold bought had been loaned by the ring to the bears, who, to fulfill their contracts, were in this way carrying it for the clique in the manner described in our preceding chapters. This fact dispensed with the necessity, on the part of the clique, for any very large amount of money. One prominent brokerage firm held $10,000,000 and upwards, which had cost them an average of 138, and on which they had received no margin from the clique. They carried it by loaning it, and fortified by a rise of four or five per cent. advance in the price. Belden is said to have received no margin, and, having little money himself, provided in the same way for the cash gold which he bought.

Here it should be noticed that the Gold Bank gave the greatest facilities for speculation by the system it had adopted for paying differences, which dispensed with the cumbrous machinery of deliveries, and enabled men with a few thousand dollars capital to do a daily business of millions.

The problem now was how to compel the bears to

cover, for they were obstinate and refused to believe in the upward movement.

Beneath the Stock Exchange there are dungeons for the confinement, not of men, but of money. The resources of art have been exhausted to make these dungeons secure. Hundreds of safes, built of huge granite blocks, lined with chilled iron and tempered steel, closed with treble patent locks, are ranged in long rows in the dim gas-light, and guarded day and night by trusty watchmen sitting behind grated bars. Here is more wealth laid away than in any other depository on the hemisphere. In these vaults it was proposed that on the morning of the 24th, the gold that had been loaned should be called for, locked up, and then that the bears should be forced to settle by buying them in under the rule or otherwise.

To this end the Tenth National Bank, where the principal members of the clique owned a controlling interest, was instructed to certify the checks of their brokers to any amount which might be called for. This precaution was taken to provide for the large sums necessary in shifting the gold from the bears, who had borrowed it, and locking it up in the vaults of the Stock Exchange.

But this plan was disconcerted in the following manner. Some of the bears, noticing the extent to which checks were certified for the account of the clique, made representations at Washington to the effect that the bank was overstepping its legal powers. Accordingly, on the morning of the 24th, the bank examiners made their appearance for the purpose of investigating the books of the Tenth National Bank. Although the bank passed through the ordeal unscathed, there is no doubt that the operations of the clique were greatly hampered by this move.

The programme now was to put up gold swiftly, and terrify the bears into settlements. Albert Speyers, a wealthy German, who, after a life of chequered experience, had settled down into a gold-broker, was the agent selected to accomplish this, under the orders of Fisk and Gould. Speyers was a true type of the gold-dealer class. A slender, wiry man, with inflammable eyes, a face criss-crossed with wrinkles, and an impulsive, dashing style in making purchases and sales, he was a supple tool in the hands of his principals. The private office of William Heath & Co. was chosen as the head-quarters of the clique. The services of other brokers were retained to negotiate settlements with the bears. A brigade of other agents and sub-agents was marshalled, to help on the movement as they best might. Everything was now ready for the blow to be struck.

The sun rose up lightly and brightly on the morning of that black-Friday, September 24th, 1869, as though the day were to be a jocund one. To-day the play was to be played out; so it had been announced by the theatrical manager. The audience assembled early; every window on the west side of New Street had its spectators, the walks and roadway were jammed, the gold-room was packed to suffocation. A carriage wheeled into the street. On the back seat sat the actresses, Miss L. W—, and Miss P. M——, the latter the queen of the blonde troupe.

> "Her lips were red, her looks were free,
> Her locks were as yellow as gold."

A thick-set, blue-eyed man, dressed in magnificent

costume, and perfumed like a milliner, descended from the carriage, and entered the office of William Heath & Co. It was James Fisk, Jr., "the oiled and curled Assyrian Bull" of Wall Street. He came prepared to play a part, but in no mimic drama. The curtain rose with gold at 143½. Fifty men, the agents of the conspirators, put their shoulders under it, and held it like a rock, while a hundred bear-hammers rained blows upon it as if it were an anvil. The price rose swiftly, 145, 146, 147, 148, 149, and at eleven, gold stood at 150. The duo, James Fisk, Jr. and Jay Gould, sat in their head-quarters. The business of the former was to hold up the price on his broad back. The latter sat cool and silent, watching the battle, preparing new moves, and whispering low his orders to his lieutenant, the irrepressible Fisk.

Meanwhile the other agents were busily at work frightening the bears into settlements. The bears hurled defiance in their teeth. "Up she goes, then," cried Fisk, and in five minutes gold was selling for 160. Albert Speyers bought during the morning, $26,000,000.

William Heath, on the order of the duo, wedged his way through the throng and bid 160 for $1,000,000. The bid was followed by an appalling silence. The crowd saw Heath, the cautious, steady broker, rarely seen personally in the gold-room, now standing in the thickest of the throng, and heard him bidding for a million. No one was bold enough to meet the bid. He stood only for an instant, with his finger poised high in the air, and then, as if with some presentiment of the coming panic, he wheeled and fled from the room.

Many of the bears, terrified at last, were now pouring into the office of Smith, Gould, Martin & Co., of which firm Jay Gould was partner, and were settling up their contracts to the amount of millions. But the heavy foreign bankers still stood firm under the standard of Brown Bros., Duncan, Sherman & Co., Seligman, and others.

"Settle up!" shrieked the cornerers.

"Never! do your worst," was the retort.

Up it went, then, to 162½, while Speyers bid for any number of millions. The bear leaders wiped their brows, and prayed that Boutwell or night would come. High noon was "clashed and clamored from a hundred towers."

While Speyers was bidding furiously for gold at 160, Gould was selling all the gold he could through a dozen different brokers, at 135 to 140, and still Speyers, his black eye flaming, and his wrinkled face purple with excitement, kept up his bids, "160 for a million, 160 for any part of a million." He bought seven millions in two lots, when a shiver ran through the crowd as some one cried out, "the Government is selling." How much? "Thirteen millions!" rang out the voice of some bold bear. Down, down fell the price, twenty-five per cent. in two minutes, and then up again to 160, like a gigantic shuttlecock, as some one cried out, "the Government will only sell four millions." Speyers brandished his arms and shrieked only seven words, "160 for a million." Winged missiles, bids and offers hurtled through the dense air for an instant, and then the bear-hammers seemed to have been all welded into one great sledge, which fell upon the price like a forty-ton boulder, and smashed it down to 135, while Speyers fell back into the crowd, quivering like an aspen. Lights seemed to dance before the eyes of the multitude, and then go out in darkness, as they rushed tumultuously into Broad Street.

From Wall Street to Exchange Place there was a sea of bewildered, pallid faces. The wildest rumors were afloat, but none worse than the ruinous facts which stared all in the face. Frenzied operators hurled curses at the clique leaders, and battered at the offices of Smith, Gould, Martin & Co., which were closed and barred, while hard-featured men, deputy-sheriffs and shoulder-hitters, guarded the avenues which led to the head-quarters of the conspirators.

A. Speyers, looking like a goblin rather than a man, with dim eyes and face as pale as ashes, was vibrating between the offices of Smith, Gould, Martin & Co. and William Heath & Co. His limbs moved automatically. His fortune of one million dollars had been swept away in five minutes. In the Gold Bank, on Thursday, the 23d, $239,000,000 of clearances had dizzied the arithmetic of a hundred pallid accountants. On Friday, the 24th, $500,000,000 more paralyzed them. The Gold Bank tottered; its assets had been loaned to shaky firms; and this mighty foster-mother of speculation passed into the hands of a receiver.

The daring authors of all these calamities had slunk away on the first intelligence of the catastrophe, and were now buried in the recesses of Erie Castle in Twenty-third Street.

But ten days before, and Wall Street had been waving with banners of pride and fortune; on Saturday, the 25th, it was a Golgotha—a place of skulls. The celebrated firm of William Heath & Co., it was claimed, were responsible for millions of gold which Fisk, without any authority from them, had ordered to be delivered to them. In this supreme hour, they had nearly one million dollars locked up in the gold bank until clearances could be made. But the margins on the gold they were carrying, had been wiped out in an instant, and the clique owed them an immense sum. Thus, although they had no interest in the conspiracy, they were made to suffer by it. The situation of a firm standing so well, added to the general distrust. Fortunately the gold bank soon released the funds so locked up, and enabled the firm to resume payment.

Ten of the other principal gold dealers were known to have failed. Some of the great banking houses were reported as shaky. No one knew in whom to confide. Many whose assets were in the possession of the gold bank, suspended temporarily. Scarcely one was a gainer by the collapse. The street was full of the rueful faces of those who had settled their short contracts with the clique. They who had sold gold to Speyers for account of Belden, were little better off; their profits were in the form of lawsuits. One bold operator had gone short of gold at 160, to the amount of $7,000,000. When gold fell, he covered his contracts at from 135 to 140, but the parties to whom he had sold failed, and he found instead of making a profit of $2,000,000, that he was saddled with $7,000,000 of gold, which was selling five per cent. below the price at which he had bought. His losses were more than $300,000.

The liabilities of the clique were rated at $20,000,000, all incurred in the space of an hour. What their profits might be, was the cloudiest of problems.

Saturday dawned upon a market in ruins. The fires of yesterday, smouldering, showed the full extent of the disaster, to the crowd which once more packed the sidewalks of Broad Street. Half of the firms which did business in the gold-room were reported as having failed, and the rest were suspected. The street was full of lawyers. The gates of the ring in Broad Street and at Erie Castle were still guarded, while a host of creditors pressed forward, and asserted claims for millions against the chief conspirators. Two aged men could have been seen slowly making their way through the throng. They were Cornelius Vanderbilt, who came to lend courage to their stock cliques, by his presence, and Daniel Drew, who surveyed, with strange, puzzled look, the ruin just wrought by some of his youngest pupils.

But the worst was not yet. The darkness which had fallen upon the market about noon on Friday, that day of financial wrath and doom, still brooded over it—thunderings lightnings and thick darkness. Monday brought no relief. Firms failing by the score. The engine of the law was set at work. Equity!—Heaven save the mark!—put on the mask of injunctions, and came into court with unclean hands. The Gold Bank, the Gold Room, the Stock Exchange, and a dozen prominent firms were tied up with orders by the court.

And now money tightened, first to 100, then to 300 per cent. per annum; and four per cent. a day was charged for carrying New York Central.

A new disaster was soon to take place. The house of Lockwood & Co. had a capital of $5,000,000, and an unspotted credit of twenty-five years' standing. Who, on the first of September would have dared to predict the failure of this house? Their name was a tower of strength on 'Change. The senior member of the firm had expended nearly $1,000,000 on a private residence in his native village in Connecticut. Everything promised a lengthened career of wonderful prosperity.

But their time was come. They were loaded down with untold amounts of Pacific Mail, Lake Shore, and Chicago and North-western railroad stocks, on which the loss was millions, and with money at from 300 to 1200 per cent. per annum.

Wednesday, the market rallied, and everything looked bright, when a dreadful whisper was breathed, —"Lockwood & Co. have failed."

It was true. Then stocks came on the market like a landslide from the mountain tops. Down! down! New York Central fell to 145—seventy-three per cent. from the highest point. Sweeping away a hundred great fortunes as it fell, a hundred more rested on the ability of one man to withstand the pressure. The whole market trembled when a report ran through the street that the ring was now depressing stocks, and that Jim Fisk had sworn that he would break Vanderbilt. Vain boast!

Suddenly Lake Shore sprang up like magic. The Commodore raised millions and carried his point. He held the key to the gates of the West. He had Lake Shore in his grip. Then he snatched at Central. If that should break lower, no one could picture the ruin that would follow. He held it and then hoisted it.

From Black Friday dates a new era in speculation lasting four years, till the panic of 1873. Fisk and Gould were now a paramount influence in the market. By dint of bullying, coaxing, and by a variety of ingenious legal devices, they extricated themselves from their liabilities. They gathered around themselves an army of agents and retainers by liberal wages. Their brokers waxed rich on the commissions received from the millions of shares bought and sold by F. and G.

Charles J. Osborn, a shrewd, jovial operator, had made himself useful to the gold conspirators, and became one of their chief managers in the street. He is now a millionaire.

Samuel M. Mills, a famous manipulator, became wealthy from his operations for the Erie ring, and for Gould individually, but afterwards turned on his chief and attempted to corner him in Western Union. The issue was what might have been expected: Mills was caught in his own trap, and driven at last into insolvency. He is now, however, back in the Board and growing rich again.

Wm. Belden, the scapegoat of the Gold Ring, Washington Connor, Wm. Heath, and a dozen other brokers employed by Gould since the assassination of James Fisk, have earned large sums in brokerage from their principals.

Fisk and Gould had full control of Erie, and from July, 1868, till the death of Fisk in January, 1872, conducted a series of startling operations, mainly through the house of Smith, Gould, Martin & Co.

The failure of Lockwood & Co. was a disastrous one, involving the Lake Shore R. R. Co. and the estate of Henry Keep to the extent of a million or more. The house made an assignment and afterwards resumed, but never recovered its financial standing. LeGrand Lockwood, the senior partner, not long after died, and the palace he built in South Norwalk, at an expense of $800,000, passed into the hands of strangers.

The losses incurred by many Wall and Broad Street firms on Black Friday and during the stock-panic that followed were enormous on paper, but the apparent ease with which so many millions of liabilities were paid or compromised was due largely to the shrewdness of the chief plotters of the Gold conspiracy, whose interest it was to silence the complaints of their victims.

William Belden, who, as before stated, was one of the main tools of the gold ring, was a man of little ability and less conscience. He went through bankruptcy in 1870, but being possessed of dangerous power as the custodian of certain secrets of his principals he was afterwards, in 1877, made partner in a firm in which Gould had a special interest. In the following year Gould withdrew from this firm, and in 1879 Belden was arrested on a serious charge, and so he passes out of the ken of speculation.

CHAPTER XXXIV.

My Flyer in Gold—A Narrow Escape—What a Looker-on Saw—Pools and Pools—Henry N. Smith—Gould's Partner, and How He Made $4,000,000—Daring Exploits—Sketch of Jay Gould—The Magician of Values—Milking Erie—James Fisk, Jr.'s Exit—Collapse of the Erie Ring—Rise of Alden B. Stockwell—Another Red-Haired Operator—The Pacific Mail Ring—Going for Smith Vigorously.

IN the rush and din of past events we have just described, the story of a modest "flyer" in gold is like the hum of a musquito to the roar of a park of artillery—unheard except in the intervals between the broadsides. *Our* story is soon told. When, ten years ago last month (September, 1869) gold suddenly fell, I sold $50,000 at 135, and left with my broker a "stop order" to cover if it rose to 135¼. Down went the price to 133; up again to 135¼ in a trice; my gold was bought in, thanks to a little say, at 135; loss only $62.50, that being the amount of the brokerage.

Then, in spite of enormous sales, the price stood like a rock at 135. Rumors of large purchases by Fisk, and Gould, and Woodward were rife. At this junction I met Fisk. It was at the Grand Opera House; time twelve P.M., sharp; he was in full dress, and his diamond brooch blazed like an electric light. He had just handed a lady into a carriage, and as he turned away I spoke to him.

"Gold!" he cried echoing my words.

"Gold! sell it short, and invite me to your funeral."

On that hint the next morning I bought a jag of $50,000 at 135½. In an hour it was up to 138½, and I took my profits $1,500, less brokerage, and did not rest until my margin of $5,000 and my profit was turned into a certified cheek. In four days after the broker through whom I made this last purchase, and the broker to whom I sold the gold, vanished into the smoke of Black Friday, leaving behind a residuum of worthless claims, and never thereafter reappearing as financial entities.

The effort of such catastrophies as that of the gold conspiracy of September, 1869, upon the physical system of operators is akin to that of a sharp fever or a slight stroke of palsy. That wondrous battery plate, the brain, loses its sensitiveness under the shock of thousands of startling impressions received through the nerves. The only remedy then is rest.

My physician remarking my languid air, felt my pulse, which he pronounced feverish, and thereupon issued his fiat:

"Stop right here! Be a spectator of but not an

actor in this dangerous game! Amuse yourself in any way except taking flyers, or I won't answer for the consequences." This advice tallied with my own inclinations; I was tired, and more than ever before conscious of the utter uncertainty of Wall street speculation. I invested my little pile in Rock Island, and played the role of walking gentleman and "looker-on in Venice."

And this is what I saw.

A long lethargy in the stock market, during which the fluctuations seemed to be caused by the fluid of Galvani rather than by human energy.

An abortive attempt on the part of Woodward and S. V. White to corner Reading.

A sharp but temporary rise in gold in the summer and fall of 1870, known as the Franco-Prussian gold flurry.

Woodward "kiting" Rock Island in the summer of 1871 up to 130, and then falling from the giddy height, ruined beyond repair, and after that wandering through the market, a swarthy, bearded, but to the financial eye a very unsubstantial ghost. Then the Chicago Fire Panic, which brought to the front another famous speculator—Henry N. Smith. He was long the senior partner of the firm of Smith, Gould, Martin & Co., and intimately concerned in the great operations conducted by Fisk and Gould during his connection with that well-known firm. A short, dapper man with a blue eye, sandy complexion, and what Prof. Huxley would call xanthus (*i. e.* red) hair, a bustling gait, and an inexpressive face, there is little to distinguish him from the crowd of daring gamblers which daily fills the hall of the Stock Exchange. He made good use of his opportunities as a member of the Fisk-Gould ring, passed through the trying ordeal of Black Friday though not unscathed, absorbed a large line of profits from the manipulations of Erie stock, and in 1870 and '71 was rich enough to engage in vast speculations on his own account, which issued successfully with enormous profits to himself.

His heaviest stroke was in the fall of 1871. Stocks had been engineered into the tall figures, and in spite of the usual autumnal outflow of currency and the tendency towards a more stringent money market, they yielded but little to the hammering to which they were daily subjected by the more ardent of the bears.

Smith had a considerable line of shorts which he had for some weeks hoped to cover at a handsome profit; this he had failed to do prior to the 9th of October, when something happened which enabled him to effect his object.

It was early Monday morning, the 9th of October, 1871, that telegrams were received in New York that Chicago was in flames throughout its length and breadth, and that unless rain should fall nothing could save the Lake city from utter destruction. All the morning fresh telegrams came streaming in confirming the first news of the day and giving it a blacker coloring. Then one of those inspirations that possess men at times happened to the speculator of whom we are speaking. At the first moment that morning when stocks could be dealt in, Smith commenced selling every active stock on the list. The full extent of the disaster in its effects upon stocks was quickly seen; prices did not fall, they *plunged* downward; the soundest stocks on the list were hurled downward as if shot out of a rifled cannon; New York Central struck 80; the fancies, like North West common, seemed as if they were to be swallowed up in the limbo of nothingness; the feeling that if Chicago was destroyed the whole transcontinental system of railways would suffer damages almost irretrievable, was uncontrollable for a few days upon the Stock Exchange. When prices struck their lowest point, Smith covered his contracts and bought enormously for a rise.

Within a week the community were amazed at the swiftness with which the burned city was springing from its ashes; prices began to rally; the market had been oversold, and recovered itself with corresponding rapidity. Within four months Smith succeeded in disposing of the major part of his holdings; his profits were estimated at between two and three million. His success in speculation tempted him into operations on the turf; he bought Goldsmith's Maid, the trotting mare which rivalled Dexter; his stud containing several other trotters almost equally famous; he built a magnificent steam yacht at an expense of a quarter of a million.

Jay Gould and Henry N. Smith, partners in business and friends of each other, now were co-rulers of Wall street. It is rare that a man reaches and holds long a high position as a stock speculator without being soon reminded that riches have wings; Smith was destined to receive at this point in his career a number of serious checks, which damaged his prestige as an operator and made heavy inroads upon his huge bank account.

The first of these disasters was in the Hannibal and St. Joseph movement. This railroad company had been pooled up above par by a clique which comprised among its members the notorious Wm. M. Tweed, P. B. Sweeny, and other members of the Tammany ring, besides Gould, Fisk, and other desperate speculators. H. N. Smith was elected President of the Hannibal and St. Joseph road, and all would have gone well, but a rival line (the Burlington and Quincy railroad,) by building an extension postponed indefinitely the promised dividends of the Hannibal and St. Joseph company. The price fell 40 per cent. It was nevertheless still one of the favorite fancies, and was freely bought at from 60 to 70. The pool, headed by Smith, now sold short a large amount and then prepared to make its deliveries with 50,000 shares of new stock issued to order; these deliveries were refused by the Stock Exchange, and the pool would have been cornered but for an accidental decline in the price, which enabled Smith and his associates to fill their contracts without material loss.

Again in April 12, Smith having gone short of the market, he attempted to create an artificial tightness in money to depress the market; in order to carry out this scheme he sold a large amount of gold, and depositing $4,000,000 of greenbacks in the Tenth National Bank, drew them out and locked them up. A stroke so bold and undisguised at once filled the souls of those who held stocks with indignation. An investigation of the matter was set on foot simultaneously in the courts, in Congress, and in the associated banks. Although nothing came out of these investigations, they seemed to deter any one from repeating such an operation in the future, and the attempt to create a stringency in money to any marked degree was a failure.

In the years 1868–9, '70, '71, and '72, perhaps the most compact and powerful railway ring was that of which James Fisk, Jr., and Jay Gould were the chiefs: the former of these noted stock operators we have described in chapter thirty-first: the latter, who was the abler man of the two, and whose network of railroads to-day nearly span the continent, deserves a more extended notice than we have yet given him.

Born in Roxbury, a small village in Delaware county, New York, he early manifested those qualities of intellect which have since made him the controller of great railway lines and the acknowledged king of the stock market. Bold and yet not reckless, quick to acquire knowledge, resolute in purpose, patient of toil, acute in his judgment of men and things, rapid in his decisions, following a plan tenaciously as long as it promised well, but abandoning it whenever it seemed likely to fail and adopting something better—to these qualities he added a bodily organization remarkably enduring, wiry, and compact. Thus endowed, and without the taste for pleasure which sometimes besets and drags down noted financiers, he was well fitted by nature to play a prominent part in the great theatre of speculation.

He seems from the start to have been attracted to the profession of a railway man, a profession now distinct, and requiring to some extent a distinct education. We cannot, from want of space, describe his earliest essays in that field, which proved that though a boy in years, he even then possessed the mind of a man.

He made his appearance in Wall street, soon after the greenback speculation commenced, and as early as 1867 he had identified himself with it.

He is a theorist and at the same time a man of practice and affairs.

As a manipulator of market values on a gigantic scale, Wall street has never seen his equal. He reminds one of Rubinstein in the delicacy of his touch on the grand piano of finance. Values rise and fall under his cunning fingers. Nearly every active stock has felt the power of his strong and subtle intellect. Of course he is unscrupulous. He believes that as in love, war, or politics, so in the stock market everything is fair. At the same time he is a man of generous impulses, as is shown by his recent munificent gift to the yellow fever sufferers of Memphis.

His fortune was assured when, in 1868, he with Fisk stepped into the control of the Erie Railroad Company. This was an elephantine milch cow, and copiously did it give down the lacteal fluid under the grip of Jay and James. They "coralled the critter" by aid of legislative acts which they bought and judicial orders which they procured from a venal bench. From July, 1868, it seemed as though Erie was assured to them *en permanence.* Fisk had his harem, his opera troupes, his diamonds, his four in hands, and his crew of retainers; Gould was on a still hunt, and quickly accumulated in a hundred ways, from contracts, from new issues to break the market, from a game of loaded dice—in fact, until he could draw his check for $10,000,000.

The Erie ring seemed to be entrenched so strongly now that nothing could dislodge them. But in the fall of 1871 the Tweed clique was broken to atoms, and the sudden taking off of Fisk paved the way for the grand collapse of March, 1872.

The assassination of James Fisk, Jr., in January, 1872, was like a thunder clap to the Erie Ring. The Tammany explosion of the preceding fall was the first step towards their downfall, and now the removal of Fisk enabled them to see the handwriting on the wall. The murdered man always claimed that James Fisk, Jr., was an essential spoke in the Erie wheel, and was wont to slap Gould on the back after some successful stroke and say in his jocose way, "Jay, my boy, you fellows can't get on without J. F., Jr.;" no doubt there was more truth in this than perhaps Gould would even admit; at all events it is certain that Fisk's fate struck consternation into the hearts of his associates of the Erie ring. By means of what is known as the classification law, Fisk and Gould were assured of their continuance in the Erie Board for some years to come; the fall of Tammany and the impeachment of certain subservient judges, followed by the death of Fisk, showed them how insecure was their tenure of power.

For more than a year movements had been on foot among the English stockholders of Erie to dispossess Fisk and Gould of their hold on that railway company. These movements culminated in what is called the Erie *coup d' etat*, in March 1872, when after a sharp fight, Gould was ousted and the road passed into the hands of what was called the McHenry-Bischoffsheim party, whose headquarters are in London.

Notwithstanding this breaking up of the Erie Ring and the loss of the steady profits they had so long drawn from their milch cow Erie, both Gould and Smith are said to have profited enormously by it through the thirty per cent. rise which followed the success of the London party. Gould has since testified under oath that at the time of the *coup d' etat* 240,000 shares of Erie stood in the name of Smith, Gould, Martin & Co. The rise of thirty per cent. on a quarter of this amount of shares would have netted $1,800,000 to the holders. Gould's profits alone on this transaction are said to have been $1,500,000.

The collision of Smith with Stockwell during the summer of 1872 considerably depleted his exchequer.

Alden B. Stockwell rose like a meteor, reached the zenith and fell within the space of two years. He was a westerner, at least he was for some time settled in Cleveland, Ohio, but having married the daughter of Elias Howe, the sewing machine man, he became connected with the Howe Sewing Machine Company in Bridgeport, Ct., and finally its President. He is like Smith, a short, stocky, Xanthus-haired personage, of a sanguine temperament, and rather more than average business talents. He came into Wall street in 1868–9 with a few thousand dollars, and prepared quickly and systematically to grapple with "the tiger." His operations were for a season conducted with circumspection, judgment, and secrecy.

The low price to which Pacific Mail had fallen after the failure of Lockwood & Co., set him to thinking whether it would not pay to buy some of it. After studying over the matter he arrived at the very wise conclusion that two things were necessary before any operator should attempt to invest largely in Pacific Mail: First, he must control the Panama Railroad company; second, he must control the Pacific Mail company; thenceforward he bent his whole energies and "went his whole pile" in order to secure these two objects, and he was successful. He was chosen

President of both companies; he made an alliance with the Union Pacific Railroad Company which accrued to the advantage of his own line; he succeeded in securing a large subsidy from Congress; he procured the passage of a law by the legislature of New York which enabled the Pacific Mail Company to speculate in their own stock; he had the treasury of the Panama Railroad Company to resort to for loans on an emergency; the wealth of the Howe Sewing company, an immense concern, was at his back.

The effect of these various movements upon Panama showed itself by the rise in the stock of that company from 50 to 146.

The price of Pacific Mail stock rose more slowly. Some hidden obstacle seemed to block its upward path. It appears that one of the directors was a prominent member of the Jay Gould and Henry N. Smith clique; the same individual was also one of Stockwell's brokers. Whenever an order was given by Stockwell with a view to the manipulation of the price in either direction, its execution failed to accomplish the object intended, because Gould and Smith nullified it by some contrary movement for their own purposes. Stockwell, as soon as he discovered the cause of failure of these moves, dismissed the broker and ultimately defeated him in the next annual election of directors.

From the moment when this discovery was made, the Stockwell interest and the Gould-Smith interest were arrayed against each other. Each party tried to outwit the other. The Stockwell faction were bulls and the rival faction bears, and as Stockwell had the inside track he worsted his antagonists. While Smith was heavily short of the stock his rival jumped it swiftly up from 65 to 87; Smith took a loss of nearly $500,000 on the short side, and then buying at high prices for a rise, the stock broke 18 per cent. Once more Smith took his loss and went short of it again for a steady pull downwards.

Both Smith and Gould believed at this time that the true policy was to sell stocks for a decline; to this end they had invested largely in gold, by means of which they expected to control currency sufficiently to create a stringency in the market and help stocks downward. But the strong movement in Pacific Mail gave a general upward tendency to the market. The heats of of the summer were come, and Smith's magnificent steam yacht was fired up for a cruise, but Captain Smith was detained ashore by his embarrassing position on the market.

Both he and his partner had sold more Erie than they could deliver. Drew, who knew that the bulk of the stock was held abroad, had, assisted by certain German bankers, bought up the floating stock in the street, and when it became scarce for delivery, Smith and Gould had to go to their "Uncle," to borrow the stock, for which they had to pay an exorbitant commission. Daniel was of course reluctant to extort these commissions from his old associates, but he felt it to be a duty to himself and his family,—a duty from which he should not shrink. "I've known Jay and Henry," said the old man, to his broker, in a deprecatory tone, "goin' on seven year. They is good boys! Don't charge 'em three per cent. a day—charge 'em one and a half, and they'll give down freer, and more'n that, they'll feel better."

It was soon after this time that Gould made that

famous sudden change of front. Cutting loose from Smith, who still kept his position on the short side, he covered his contracts and bought enormously on the long side.

It was, from henceforth, war to the knife between Smith and Gould.

The former was reported to be short of Pacific Mail to the extent of fifty thousand shares, one fourth part of the whole capital stock of the company. He clung to his position with a tenacity that seemed under the circumstances like an infatuation.

Gould and Stockwell joined hands in bulling Pacific Mail, and one fine day in August, under the skilful manipulation of William Heath & Co., the pool brokers, the stock was seen to pass 103 in its upward course.

Smith again was forced to come to terms. His net losses on this transaction were half a million, and Stockwell's star was in the ascendant; two years before he had been addressed as plain Mister Stockwell; he was now given a title, he was called Commodore Stockwell.

CHAPTER XXXV.

THE PANIC OF 1873 AND AFTER.

The Northwest Corner.—Arrest of Jay Gould.—One hundred per cent. in an hour.—Tight money and dull days.—The Bull Rings.—The shadow of the panic.—The storm breaks.—Gould and Vanderbilt in a tight place.—Darker and darker.—Shrinkage in values.—Organizers of panic.—Sunshine and an eclipse.—The last grand collapse.—When bottom was touched.

THE rise of Pacific Mail was the most brilliant pool movement since the year 1869, when New York Central was lifted by the strong hands of Vanderbilt and his followers from 135 to 218. It was soon overshadowed, however, by another gigantic operation, which was unparalleled by any similar movement since the Prairie du Chien corner in 1865.

We allude to the corner in Chicago and Northwestern. The secret history of this wonderful rise will, perhaps, never be written, for it is known only to the leaders who engineered it.

The three men who achieved the startling result were Horace F. Clark, Augustus Schell, and Jay Gould. Clark, whom we have before alluded to, was a lawyer and prominent railroad man. Augustus Schell had also in former years been a leading lawyer and politician, and was for many years chairman of the National Democratic Committee. Both were able men, experienced financiers, and possessed of great wealth, chiefly acquired in the Vanderbilt movements.

Several months were consumed in 1872 in buying the common stock, which had been slowly rising, under this absorption. One great danger threatened the success of the movement, and that was the possibility that the directors of the company would issue a batch of convertible bonds, and, exchanging them for stock, load down the ring with this new stock at high prices. In fact some of the directors were heavily short of the stock, believing that it was much higher than it was worth. This circumstance became known in the street, and several of the largest operators had followed their example, believing that the directors knew what they were about. Henry N. Smith was said to have sold short 40,000 shares. Daniel Drew nearly as much more. John L. Tracy, the President of the Company, was also on the short side, and a host of smaller operators followed the example of these leaders.

The pool had by the first of October bought the whole capital stock, $11,000,000, either for cash or in the form of "calls" and contracts. The directors suspecting the danger they were in, met and authorized the issue of $11,000,000 of convertible bonds; the pool took the whole issue off the hands of the company; Tracy covered his shorts, and joined the trio in pushing the stock upwards; for a few weeks the price stood firm, at from 80 to 85; but early in

November, while the eyes of the "street" were daily watching the long vibrations of Pacific Mail, suddenly Northwest bounded up to par, dropped back to 90, and then rushed to 105.

Smith and Drew both knew that they were trapped; the latter had already relieved himself by borrowing 10,000 shares of Mrs. Keep, widow of the late Henry Keep, and filling his contracts to that extent; Smith, unable to make his deliveries, bought largely of the preferred stock of the same company, and tendered it in lieu of the common stock, but the tender was refused. He had one last card to play—a desperate measure, but one that he hoped would bring Gould to terms; he was cognizant of certain old transactions in Erie which would enable the Erie Company to demand of Gould an immense sum,—about $6,000,000. He disclosed these matters to the President of the Erie Railway Company; a warrant was issued for Gould's arrest, and this operator was taken by the sheriff soon after the price had risen above par, as already mentioned. Clarke and Schell promptly gave bail, and Gould was soon back in the street, burning for revenge. Meanwhile, and during his temporary absence, the stock rose like lightning to 200, and all who were responsible to deliver saw themselves in the abyss of ruin. The next day it rose to 230. The smaller tribe of bears were let off at from 150 to 160. Drew and Smith alone were denied any compromise. But at last they were allowed to settle at a considerable discount from the summit price; still the losses of both were enormous—millions would not have covered them. The price then sank back to 75, and the pool were still holders of most of the capital stock, their situation under the burden being somewhat relieved by the large sums paid them by the bears in order to be let off from their contracts.

The sequel to the arrest of Jay Gould was an extraordinary one.

It was believed that a hard fight would be made by Jay Gould over the Erie claim, on account of which, at the instance of H. N. Smith, he had been subjected to arrest. But very much to the astonishment of everybody he promptly made restitution to the Erie Railway—*nominally*—$6,000,000, excusing himself from personal liability in the matter by the plea that he was merely holding the property of the company in trust, and had always been ready to surrender it upon demand. To this plea some color of reason was given by the fact that a considerable number of the legal instruments under which he held the property expressed upon their face that he held it in trust.

Before making this restitution, he bought 200,000 shares of Erie in the neighborhood of 50; the price soon rose to 69; a dividend of one per cent. was declared, and Gould, under the firmness of the price thus created, succeeded in disposing of his 200,000 shares; and selling short 100,000 shares more for a turn on the other side.

These vast operations which we have just described gave a new activity to the market, and the public were drawn into the vortex of speculation by the thousand. An interval of some weeks passed away, and everything was quiet on the American bourse. The pools were inactive; the outside battalions were lying on their arms; after the fever of the past three months, Wall street and its purlieus fell into a great lethargy which lasted from the culmination of the Northwestern corner in November, 1872, till the 5th day of September, 1873. Deep down below the sluggish outside current of daily fluctuations, there was all this time growing a feeling of distrust. The great monetary stringency of the winter of 1873 was one of the symptoms of this feeling. The powerful bull party groaned under their load of stocks. Weaker holders paid from one-sixteenth to one per cent. a day to have their stocks carried. Some, like Frank Baker, died; others lost all the profits of the year; others were tired out and sold their stocks. Stockwell succumbed at last and let go of his Pacific Mail, which plunged down to 60, rallied, and then "gave a lurch and then a heel to port, and going down headforemost sunk in short" to 45. Stockwell, no longer "Commodore" or even "Captain," was now known "as that red-headed cuss from Cleveland." *Sic transit!*

March, April, May, June, July, August, and still the great rings held their own.

The Jay Cook-Fisk & Hatch-Clews' U. S. Bond party were apparently as solid as adamant.

The Vanderbilt, N. Y. C., Harlem, Lake Shore and Western Union clique looked impregnable.

The Dows-Tracy pool held Rock Island in a strong grip.

The Gould-Clark side show put away their surplus Northwest for the next season.

The William Street party were happy, and so was the venerable Daniel, who had very large jags of Canada Southern, Canton, Quicksilver, etc.

The Coal Barons bore aloft Del., Lack. and Western, Del. and Hudson, Central of New Jersey, Reading and Lehigh Valley, and the huge bulk of these stocks seemed to them light as a flower.

In the summer of 1873 it seemed as if neither money stringencies nor panics could shake the power of these combinations. Under the shelter of an irredeemable paper currency, and strengthened continually by our growing internal and foreign commerce, and the increasing population of the country, the position they held seemed to be impregnable.

In the light of succeeding events, the confidence of these moneyed combinations seems like infatuation. Only one man thoroughly understood the financial situation, and dared to act on his convictions. Jay Gould saw that there had been too many railroads built, too many watered stocks, and too great an expansion of both currency and credit. During the summer of 1873 he was heavily short of stocks and at the same time held upwards of $30,000,000 of gold in the form of either cash or options.

In August the mutterings of the coming tornado were first distinctly audible, and Wm. R. Travers, quick to snuff panic in the air, came down from Newport and put out a large line of shorts.

On the 5th of September, Gould struck his first blow. The little man stands only five feet four in his stockings, but as he stood in the vestibule of the Stock Exchange, poising his $30,000,000 of gold, he loomed up like a giant. The transactions in gold that day were $200,000,000. Within three days the price fell seven per cent., and his entire holdings had been disposed of. He drew in the proceeds and locked them up. The plot thickened. By the 10th of September the fancies had shrunk from five to fifteen per cent. Daniel Drew had failed, and a half dozen railway companies were reported in trouble.

Step by step, terrace after terrace, we were approaching the brink of the precipice. On the 18th of September we took the plunge.

Western Union, of which Gould was short to the amount of 40,000 shares, led the way into the abyss, falling ten per cent. in one hour.

Soon after twelve o'clock the great house of Jay Cooke & Co. was gone. A quiet run was taking place on nearly every banking house in the street. The day closed amid the deepest depression of feeling. Everyone feared the worst was yet to come.

Sept. 19. Worse and worse: the Vanderbilt stocks dropped like lead in a vacuum. Harlem down thirty per cent. Fisk & Hatch and a score of brokerage houses succumbed to the pressure. By three o'clock P. M. values had shrunk $100,000,000, and greenbacks were worth five per cent. a day.

Sept. 20. The Union Trust company, the National Trust company, the Bank of the Commonwealth, and twelve more brokerage houses suspended, and Western Union was down forty per cent. from the prices of three days before. At noon the doors of the Stock Exchange closed, slam, bang! not to be re-opened till the 30th of September.

This stopping of the machinery of stock-business was the means of saving hundreds of operators from ruin. Gould's position was nevertheless a ticklish one; he had covered his immense line of shorts too soon, and was now loaded down with stock which he could not get the cash for.

Vanderbilt was unable to raise money enough to hold his stocks up.

The banks paid out currency only in small amounts. Business was done by checks, for there was no money to be had. The banks were in fact suspended, and refused to certify brokers' checks without the money on deposit. Grant and Secretary Richardson had come on to New York and gone, without doing anything for the relief of the street. The air was thick with rumors of fresh disasters.

For a day or two after the re-opening of the Stock Exchange the skies brightened, but darkened again almost immediately. Geo. Bird, Grinnell & Co., the brokers of the Vanderbilt party, suspended, and the area of desolation began to stretch outward from Wall street. The great house of A. & W. Sprague crashed down, and terrifying rumors came over the water from London.

Topple! topple! crash! crash! Stocks went down lower than ever. But Vanderbilt's house still was only shaken, and Gould had cleared his stocks and was out of danger; still the genius of panic, as if unsated with the destruction it had wrought, stalked through the darkness seeking for fresh victims.

The great American panic of 1873 had passed over the street in successive waves, each one of which broke, whelming multitudes. Three of these waves had broken on Friday, three black Fridays,—one on the 19th of September, one on the 31st of October, and one on the 7th of November, the blackest Friday of all, darkened as it was by the great cloud that hung over London.

But behind all this blackness, was not the sun of

future commercial prosperity? Four million bales of cotton were on the plantations of the South; one thousand millions bushels of cereals were in the granaries of the West; the currency of the country, secured by the pledge of the National faith, was all here; gold was pouring in from Europe; gold had fallen to 106½; specie payments and a sound basis for commerce were near at hand; the government had reissued $30,000,000 of greenbacks, which were flowing into the banks by the million; the banks had been paying out currency more freely; the merchants had borne the pressure with wonderful firmness, and but few had succumbed; some who had suspended were resuming business; some of the great Wall Street houses were making full settlements with their creditors; Daniel Drew had extricated himself from the meshes of bankruptcy; the Union Trust Company would soon pay in full, and start with a doubled capital; Vanderbilt, the Colossus of modern Roads, was known to be buying stocks. Nevertheless, one thing was still lacking—confidence! confidence! without which commercial values are but as useless paper!

On Saturday, the 8th of November, came the change in the sky, the turn in the tide. No more bad news from London! and Erie flew up to 40, while the whole market steadied itself, and seemed to tremble on the rise. Monday, Tuesday, Wednesday, Thursday, better and better! The four Vanderbilt stocks, the old guard, New York Central, Lake Shore, Harlem, and Western Union mounted in a strong, steady flight towards their old perches; the other stocks, each in their order and after their sort, followed the vanguard, while the throng of buyers and sellers, crying out "the panic is over," tossed hither and thither the millions of the market, as if panics would be no more.

Not yet! not yet! If prices rose like a rocket, they soon began to settle again. There was to be a lower range of values before there could be any steady, permanent improvement. For three years and six months the tendency was downward. If prices went up in sharp paroxysms, they fell again on the reaction to a lower depth than ever. Ten, twenty, thirty, forty, fifty per cent. up; but ten, twenty, forty, sixty, eighty, one hundred per cent. down!

A coterie of powerful operators saw the tendency, and set themselves to guide and further that tendency for their own benefit. Gould, Travers, Addison G. Cammack, and others, organized panic after panic. A huge weight was ever hanging on the market, and once the forlorn hope of bulls relaxed their efforts, away things went to the bad again.

As long as Cornelius Vanderbilt lived, a staying force was ever present to partially arrest the tendency downward. But when he crossed the Styx and bequeathed his vast interests to his son, the tendency exerted itself with almost full sway. Slowly at first, but swifter and swifter, for a twelvemonth the dead weight of five thousand millions of paper values shrank and dwindled, till the grand collapse in the spring of 1877.

Wm. H. Vanderbilt, the granger lords, and the coal barons relaxed their grasp at last, and the lowest prices seen for many a long year were made in Lake Shore, Western Union, Northwest, St. Paul, the coal, and all other stocks.

The shrinkage in the stock-values most known on

'change had now reached nearly $200,000,000. One thousand millions of railway values had apparently been wiped out forever by receiverships. Other general commercial values had shrunk thousands of millions. This was in April and May, 1877.

We had, it appears, reached bed rock, and from that point the era of improvement must date.

CHAPTER XXXVI.

OPERATORS OF THE NEW ERA.—CAMMACK, KEENE, AND WM. H. VANDERBILT.

The Union Pacific rise.—Gould as an Architect, and as a Depressor of Values.—Three Noted Speculators.—Sketch of Addison G. Cammack.—A Great Shortist.—James R. Keene and his Antecedents.—Fighting the Bonanza Kings.—Coming into Wall Street.—Matching Gould.—A Lucky Hit.—Wm. H. Vanderbilt.—The Commodore's Successor.—One Hundred Millions in one Hand.—A Big Stake in Western Union.—A Grand *Coup*.—How the Street fared in the New Deal.—Working up from Hard Pan.

THREE years and six months of sharp and long fluctuations, with a law of gravitation operating to draw prices to zero! It seemed at times as if the colossal fortunes piled up during the greenback era would without an exception be swept away. During all that period of depression there was really but one genuine upward movement, and that was engineered by an operator who had been a most energetic depressor of values.

The failure of the Northern Pacific, and of the Southern Pacific enterprises in 1873, left to the Union Pacific and the Central Pacific lines a monopoly of the trans-continental business. One noted operator saw this clearly and acted on it. Union Pacific stock was knocked around among the wild-cats in September and October, 1873, at 16 or thereabouts. But even then some one was quietly buying all that was offered, and these purchases continued to be made on a large scale until, early in the following February, it was announced that the unknown buyer was none other than Jay Gould, who had already acquired a controlling interest in the company, and in March following stepped into the board of direction.

Union Pacific had now risen to 38, and the same operator having gained his point marketed his holdings, and the price dropped to 25.

It was summer now, and Gould accompanied by one of his brokers started for the White Mountains. "The boys" thought it safe to sell Union Pacific in his absence, and sold it freely. Gould meanwhile was buying the stock on telegraphic orders in cipher despatched from the Crawford and other mountain resorts. In this way he was able to buy forty thousand shares, and still for months after his return to the street he kept on buying till he had over one hundred thousand shares. Then for two months or more the price vibrated between 32 and 37, and at last in Febuary, 1875, it rose in long leaps till it touched 80.

Gould, heretofore a depressor or at most only a temporary advancer of market values, now appeared for the first time as a builder up of a great business enterprise. He bought more Union Pacific, doubled the freight-rates, and assiduously nursed the Company in Congress, and in the courts.

Dividends were soon declared, and with a single exception have ever since been paid.

This was a marvelous exploit of railway financiering, and did not a little to restore confidence in the street. But while Gould was a bull in Union Pacific, he was in other stocks the grizzliest of bears. He knocked to pieces, in the spring of 1876, the Eugene Robinson combination in Lake Shore; hammered New York Central; ran a muck against the holders of Pacific Mail, colliding thereby with Trenor W. Park, a noted operator in both Panama and Pacific Mail, and early in 1876 commenced a fierce attack on the coal stocks and on Western Union.

In operating for a fall in the prices of stocks during the year 1876 and 1877, Gould was seconded by three celebrated operators, viz.: W. R. Travers, Addison G. Cammack, and James R. Keene. Travers we have already described; Cammack and Keene deserve more than a passing notice.

Any one who chooses to pass through the lower hall of the Fifth Avenue Hotel of an evening will not fail to remark a tall, brawny man, with an impassive, colorless face, lounging on one of the settees or strolling through the halls of that famous caravansera. This is Addison G. Cammack, one of the most fortunate speculators of the past decade. He was a New Orleans man, and came into the street in 1865, bringing with him something like a quarter of a million. Here he formed a partnership with Charles J. Osborn, the operator who, as already described, first came into notice through his connection with the gold speculations of Fisk and Gould.

Retiring from this firm he has since played in the Wall street game a lone hand, though sometimes in association with W. R. Travers, these two forming the head and front of what is known as the Twenty-third street party, their principal and most successful operations being on the bear side.

Longheaded, daring, and persistent, it is not wonderful that Cammack should during the panic era have immensely increased his bank account. He commenced selling the coal stocks in 1876, and in fifteen months by their decline made, it is said, nearly a million dollars.

His attack on the grangers in the summer of 1878 was the most brilliant and successful bear exploit of the year. He has also taken no inconsiderable share, though in a quiet way, in the great upward movement of 1879, occasionally turning about and raiding the market when he thought it too high.

James R. Keene has during the past two years attracted more attention than any one of the great stock speculators, unless we except Jay Gould. He is an Englishman by birth, and first came to the surface of events in the San Francisco Bourse—a severe training school for a young speculator considering how wildly prices fluctuate there, one hundred per cent. rises or falls in a day piling up or sweeping away great fortunes. Operations in such a field call for sagacity, nerve, daring resolution of the first class, and Keene showed in many a hot fight that he had in a large measure all the qualities. Soon after the advent of the Bonanza stocks, he guessed the secret of the manipulators and quietly acted on it. This secret was to water those stocks, sell out, and having hurled the price down two or three hundred per cent. to buy in and engineer a new rise. Thus following in the boiling wake of Mackey, Flood, and O'Brien he made millions out of the stupendous rises and falls of Virginia Consolidated, and the other stocks thumbed by the Bonanza kings.

It was in the latter part of 1876 that he made his

appearance in Wall street, with the reputation of being able to check for five million dollars. The money kings and speculators welcomed him with open arms. Such a man is looked upon by these gentlemen very much as a cow like the renowned Filbert is regarded by stock-raisers—useful for the money they can draw from him.

It was soon known that he was hand and glove with Jay Gould. Now the late James Fisk, Jr., was wont to say in his sportive way, "If you sleep in the same bed with Jay and take the inside, you will be sure to wake up and find him next the wall, and no matter how cold the night he will plant his clammy feet in the small of your back and land you on the floor." To average operators it was a foregone conclusion that Keene's fate was now sealed. But they reckoned without their host. He held his own against Gould and every other man-eater.

His first operations on entering the street were in bearing the coal stocks, Lake Shore, and various other shaky commodities. From January, 1876, to May, 1877, New Jersey Central and Delaware & Hudson fell 100 per cent. and Del., Lack. & West. only little less. Keene and the other great "shorts" rolled up their profits by the million as they slid down the precipice of the market during those darkest days of the panic-era.

Jas. R. Keene's portrait is not very familiar to the habitues of the street. He does not court notoriety. A slender, middle sized man, with a sedate expression, his sallow face fringed with a brown beard, and possessing the quietest of manners, he would never be taken for the reckless, daring speculator that he has proved himself to be. His character as a keeper of his word and his contracts stands high, and his friends idolize him as one of the kindest hearted and most generous of men.

The death of Cornelius Vanderbilt in the spring of 1876 had been awaited for months with feverish expectancy by every operator who thought New York Central was selling for more than its value. But it was not immediately followed by any break in the so-called Vanderbilt stocks. He had taken precautions against any such disaster by bequeathing these investments in a block to his son Wm. H. Vanderbilt, together with the policy of absorption and consolidation of railway properties so long pursued by the deceased.

Wm. H. Vanderbilt thus became, by a stroke of the pen in the presence of witnesses, the richest railway capitalist in the world, owning as he now does stocks and bonds amounting in market value to the round sum of $100,000,000. A stupendous trust! but one that he has thus far shown the ability to hold and exercise.

Photograph and engraving have made the portrait of this railroad king familiar to the general eye—a heavily set man, with flowing side whiskers and a "stay put" look. His railroad education was in his father's private school, and there he must have become indoctrinated with the C. V. policy. While his father lived he was only a wheel in the large and elaborate system of railway mechanism. But the moment the testament of his father was read he became an organic form, clothed with wealth and sovereignty. The year that followed his accession to

WM. H. VANDERBILT

power was a trying time for the Vanderbilt party. In the spring of 1877 occurred the break of New York Central to 87, of Western Union to 56, and of Lake Shore to 47, all of these stocks being held and controlled by the Vanderbilt influence. It is said that the Commodore's son shared in the panic feeling that affected Lake Shore so disastrously, and threw over large blocks of that stock. His grip was strong enough, however, to lift New York Central to par in the course of a few weeks; but Western Union for many weeks remained below 60. There were peculiar reasons why Western Union should be and remain depressed. It was the hand of Gould that heavily rested on it. For years he had kept short of it, and in 1874 he had acquired control of the Atlantic & Pacific Telegraph Company, which he used as a sledge hammer to smash down the price of Western Union by the force of competition. It was blow after blow repeated for months and years, aided by the falling tendency of the market, that at last enabled him to carry his point and beat down the price of Western Union to 56. The object and end of this contest on his part was not merely to make profits on his shorts, but to effect a sale of A. & P. T. Co. to its rival. Keene and Sage now formed an alliance with Gould. Then the latter covered his shorts, and bought 40,000 shares of Western Union below 60.

Everything was ripe for the stroke. After several secret negotiations with the Vanderbilt party, a sale was effected. The Western Union company took 71,000 shares of A. & P. T. stock from Gould, Sage, and Keene at 25, and having thus disposed of a dangerous competitor put up their rates, and away flew

Western Union to 84. This was a brilliant *coup* for the triumvirate. It gave them a triple profit, but it was a fine stroke, too, for the holders of Western Union. That company had now a clear field. The price rose to par, and in the summer of 1879 a scrip dividend of 17 per cent. was declared out of the stock owned by the company.

Gould, it appears, is now playing another hand in the same game against Western Union. A new company styled the American Union has been formed under his auspices, and has already laid its wires over the cream of the territory occupied by Western Union. Before the year 1880 closes another telegraph war will rage, and the price of Western Union will likely enough have some fluctuations as remarkable as any it has ever experienced.

The last grand crash in stocks came, it will be remembered, in the spring of 1877. This was the last long pang—the finishing stroke which ended the protracted agony of hundreds of such as had for more than three years clung with desperate tenacity to their shares. It needed only this to break to pieces the enfeebled remnants of every bull pool in the street, with two notable exceptions, viz., the Union Pacific and the N. Y. Central-Harlem parties. The coal barons were routed, the William street party disorganized: the Tracy-Dows combination scattered, Harvey Kennedy their burly manipulator, suspended, and the stocks held by half a score other cliques were turned over for distribution to all who cared to cover their shorts, or who as buyers had cash to pay for low-priced stocks to be laid away for better times.

Terrified by this last disaster and disheartened by

repeated losses the few outsiders left in the street disappeared, and the speculation was left to the professionals; hundreds of inveterate speculators quit buying and selling stocks on margins, and took to privileges as the only safe mode of dealing. Russell Sage, the principal seller of such contracts, was often saddled with great blocks of stock put to him by those who bought his privileges, but his immense wealth enabled him to meet every engagement. Other sellers of puts, calls, spreads, and straddles were not so fortunate and went under.

In these unsettled times arose and flourished a new form of speculation. We allude to what is known in broker's slang as "bucket shops."

Imagine a roomy apartment, often in the basement, one side almost covered by a large black board; a partition of black walnut and glass fencing off a space sufficient to accommodate the proprietor and his clerks; the body of the room full of chairs for the convenience of customers. From ten A.M. till three P.M. any active day in these retreats the broken down or impecunious speculator, held in the grip of the gambling demon, slakes his thirst for the game by staking one per cent. on as trifling an amount as five shares.

The prices are ticked out on telegraphic ribbon and set down on the black board. The bettor knows his gain or loss in a twinkling; the proprietor subtracts his diminutive commission, and the game goes on.

Some fine day a great rise or a bad break comes, the proprietor with the slinking eye and the hatchet nose fails to respond to his customers' demand, and the "bucket shop" is to let. But another adventurer soon comes in. Advertisements and circulars draw in a fresh crowd of bettors, and the game is as brisk as ever. Black sheep are in every trade; black sheep of the bucket shops and of the pool advertisers, aye, black sheep in the heart of that generally respectable flock, the members of the Stock Exchange, fleece the public at their will. But this is saying nothing against the large majority of the Board of Brokers.

The speculator who loses is pretty sure to curse his broker, no matter how unjustly, and thus obloquy has been poured on as honorable and "square" a body of men as exist in any business interest in the United States.

The cards are true, the dealer is true here as a general rule; it is only the speculator himself that is false—false by his lack of nerve, false by his lack of judgment, false and utterly reckless too often by his mode of dealing. Scores and scores of trustworthy commission houses, such as Kennedy, Hutchinson & Co., Voorhees & Imbrie, Allen & Stead, H. L. Johnson, etc., etc., might be named, in whose hands the interests of their customers may be safely trusted. The history of the panics during the past forty-five years proves how worthy of confidence are a majority of the members of the New York Stock Exchange. We might almost state, in the light of past experience, that the money of an outside speculator is as secure in the hands of many of the commission houses as if it were in a double chilled iron chronometer safe—that is to say, secure from loss in consequence of the failure of its custodian.

CHAPTER XXXVII.

THE SPECULATION OF '77, '78, AND '79.

Going Down with the Ebb, and Up again with the Flood.—Keene in a Tight Place.—A Friendly Lift.—Gould in his Old Role.—Hammering the Market.—A Season of Fingering and Thumbing.—The Crop question, and the Granger roads.—New Pools at Work.—Northwest and St. Paul on the Rise.—Cammack and his Bear Raid.—Collision of Gould and the Northwest Ring.—Caught in a Trap.—Trembling on the Rise.—The Southwest Pool and Wabash.—The Great Speculation of 1879.—The Grangers and the Coal Stocks.—Wm. H. Vanderbilt's Operations.—The Coal Barons in Alliance.—The Erie Rise.—Grand Finale.

THE law of change which acts on all sublunary things operates fast and far in the domain of speculation. From riches to penury and from penury to riches is but a step; darkness follows light and light darkness swiftly as day dawns or night falls in the tropics. This swinging to and fro between "fierce extremes;" these fitful pulses of trade beating off hour by hour and day by day the record of values, are the evidence and effect of purely human sentiment in action; of hope and fear, the greed of gain, the spirit of emulation, or the apprehension of loss. Speculators feel, see, and act with electric rapidity, and he whose feeling, perception, and action are at once the most correct and the most rapid wins the prize.

Thus just as prices were lowest and the stock market was about the gloomiest place on the hemisphere, in the spring of 1877, there came to the great operators a feeling, an inspiration, or perhaps a conviction of the judgment that the worst was over, and that now was the hour to turn right about and catch the refluent surge and push of the tide which was then on the turn, and would soon bear prices up to at least their proper level.

Travers, Cammack, Keene, and Gould saw it, though the pressure still seemed to urge them downward to gather more profits on the short side. Wm. H. Vanderbilt saw it as he braced himself to keep his immense legacy of stocks from being disintegrated and torn into fragments by the rush of the panic; Sage saw it, and breathed easier under the ponderous load of privileges which he had taken upon himself. To feel, to see, and to act on a feeling and perception is almost instantaneous with these veteran speculators. If they had short contracts unclosed they closed them, and then loaded their galleons with all manner of cheap commodities hawked about the street for a song.

St. Paul Common had touched 11; Northwest Common, 18; Delaware & Hudson, 25; Michigan Central, 35; these, and a score of other low priced stocks, were caught up, and as they gripped them the tide fairly turned and bore them upwards. Still day after day the chiefs bought stocks as they rose, and meantime new combinations were formed which scooped up old "shorts" who refused to believe the panic was over, and new "shorts" who looked for another break.

The grangers were rushed up fifteen per cent.; Delaware & Hudson was put to 57, and nearly every active stock on the market rose as fast it had fallen. The apprehensions of the street as usual had carried it too far, and the reaction was correspondingly great, aided as it was by favorable crop reports and by the condition of our foreign trade.

But so tremendous was the weight and drag that was pulling at values all through the American commercial world, that the natural reaction and the enormous purchases, both for the long and short account, availed not immediately to carry up certain stocks, notably Central of New Jersey, which by vices of management had been brought to the verge of bankruptcy. At a meeting of the stockholders to consider the condition of the company, a resolution introduced by Wm. M. Imbrie calling for a thorough investigation into the books of the company was vigorously opposed by several managers, and the result was a series of breaks which carried the price down to six!

Another important incident was the relation of Jay Gould to the market. He had no doubt aided in lifting prices after the panic of 1877, but when the force of the immediate reaction had spent itself he was again found on the short side. The game he was playing against Western Union at that time has been described in the preceding chapter. He wished to keep down the price of the stock of that company, and he was also working to depress Lake Shore. The weight of his millions and his prestige as a depressor of values rested on the whole market.

In July an ominous rumor went through the street. Values shrank in an instant, and with reason, for if it were true that a railroad strike was spreading through the country, the companies would lose in the aggregate untold sums. Prices fell heavily, and the whole street was on the verge of a panic. More than one of the great operators was in peril.

James R. Keene with his usual daring had loaded himself down heavily with stocks, and now found his margins melting away. In his extremity he applied for relief to Gould and Sage. The former advanced the necessary means to tide his brother speculator through the crisis, but he also exacted terms. In a few days the dangers from the railway strike were averted, and soon after Gould, Sage, and Keene made their grand *coup* on the Western Union as we have already detailed.

The eight months following the first of September, 1877, was remarkable only for the manipulations of the leading operators who "milked the street" in a very thorough and systematic way. To drop prices and sicken the whole market; to trap little shorts and then to spirt prices up and skin the tribe of small bears; to entice the little "longs" to buy, and then having sold them a few thousand shares, to drop prices and repeat the same operation day after day—this was the history of the stock market until April, 1878, when events were shaped, or shaped themselves for a notable rise in what are styled the Granger stocks, *i. e.*, Chicago and Northwestern, and Chicago, Milwaukee & St. Paul.

These are great wheat carrying roads. The vast and fertile States of Wisconsin and Minnesota, the northwest peninsula of Michigan, and now the virgin soil of Dakota are among the granaries of the west. Let us suppose the cities of Milwaukee and Chicago are the palms of two open hands, then are the Northwest and the St. Paul lines the long spider fingers with iron tendons which pick up and convey the millions of bushels of wheat and corn to those huge palms, by which they are distributed to other and longer and more nimble spider fingers, which convey the grain to other and larger open palms—the great cities of the Atlantic coast.

The earnings of those two roads are therefore largely dependent on the amount of cereals to be carried each year. A good crop in the northwest means dividends, and so the prospects of the crops in that region are every spring watched and reported with great minuteness of detail. The crops of 1877 were good; the foreign demands consequent upon the Russo-Turkish war had been large. Would the crops of 1878 be abundant? Some of the largest speculators in the street said yes, and bought great blocks of both St. Paul and Northwest. Gould was a buyer because he wished to secure another link in the through line from San Francisco to New York; the crops promised famously, and by the 10th of June, Northwest common stock had risen to 55. Gould stepped into the Board of Direction, and shortly after a dividend of three per cent. was declared, the first paid for many years on the common stock.

The success of the Northwest clique gave courage to the large holders of St. Paul Common, and in a few weeks this stock also reached 55—a rise of forty-four per cent. from the panic price of 1877.

This is what is called a street rise; outsiders had little to do with it; the bulk of the three hundred thousand shares of the common stock of the two companies was held in the hands of the large speculators and their followers. Such was the confidence of some of the heaviest holders in their power to maintain prices above 50, that Russell Sage sold thousands of shares in sixty-day puts at four or five per cent. below the market for one-half per cent., *i. e.*, fifty dollars on each one hundred shares.

Rumors of damage to the wheat crop were circulated early in July, but made little impression on the prices. One sharp-eyed operator—Addison G. Cammack—saw the opportunity afforded to make a bear raid, and lost no time in embracing it. He commenced selling Northwest and St. Paul when they were above 50, and as they slumped followed his programme till he brought about a panic, which Gould, Sage, and all their clique confederates were powerless to resist.

In a few days Northwest Common touched 32 and St. Paul Common struck 30. It was a brilliant exploit—one man single handed against the Goliaths of the Rings, and putting them all to flight. Usually panics make victims of the small operators: this time the large ones suffered most.

Hardly had the force of the panic spent itself, when a new combination was formed in Northwestern. But after they had loaded up with it, buying, it is said, some 70,000 shares, they found it a dead lift. Some unseen weight lay upon it, and when it rose four or five per cent. it would slip back in spite of all the pool could do to hold it. The mysterious weight was Gould. The great depressor, through William Belden, W. E. Connor, and his other brokers, was trying to keep down the price. Against such a resistance it was slow work lifting Northwest, but the bull party succeeded at last in putting it to 65. This was late in January, 1879. Then Gould, by a violent attack on both St. Paul and Northwest, succeeded in breaking the latter to 56, but the pool soon put it up to 64.

It was about this time that Gould made terms with his antagonists, utilizing a large block of his Union Pacific stock for that purpose. This was judicious. A continuation of the contest would have cost him dear. The settlement left him "solid," though a little less colossal than before his last heavy venture on the bear side.

A falling out among the members of the Northwest ring, a tightening in the money rate, and a fall in every active stock was the sequel to the Northwest campaign. The bull combinations were disconcerted, and those who operated for a decline seemed to have the upper hand. The shifting of the loan from the six per cents. to the four per cents., and the failure in March of a New Orleans bank, communicated a somber tinge to the market. But through this rather dark veil there came a subdued light, the harbinger of another sunburst of commercial prosperity.

The first broadside that hailed this near dawn was fired by the late raging bear Jay Gould. He appeared once more in the role of a builder up of values. The rise in Kansas Pacific from 20 to 50, and that in Wabash from 18 to 36 in April, 1879, were pregnant with meaning. They signified the establishment of a great southwest through line, an attack in the flank on the Vanderbilt railway system, but above all a confidence that the dark days of railroads were over.

One by one the active stocks dealt in at the New York Stock Exchange wheeled into line, and took their course up the long slope to the heights of the great rise of 1879. Every capitalist in the country was the advocate and worker for a rise. Every one of the great Wall Street speculators was a holder of stocks, expecting the rise and working to that end. The Vanderbilt party had coined millions out of the rise of Michigan Central to 90, of Western Union to 100, and having secured a large interest in Northwestern as another link in the through line from New York to San Francisco, were waiting to move Lake Shore and Western Union to higher points than these stocks had ever yet reached.

In May the march of the grangers and of the coal stocks commenced. The combinations that controlled St. Paul, Northwest, Del., Lack. & Western, Del. & Hudson, and New Jersey Central embraced nearly every one of the street operators. Besides Vanderbilt, Sage, and Keene there were Harvey Kennedy, Charles G. Osborn, David Dows, W. L. Scott, Frank Work (one of the Vanderbilt party), D. P. Morgan, Moses Taylor, H. N. Smith, and a score of other noted stock speculators, who had a larger or smaller interest in some one or more of these stocks.

In the Southwest combination were Gould, Sage, Keene, Cammack, Cyrus W. Field, and several other capitalists having close affiliations with railroads. A large majority of the brokers were also believers in much higher prices, and every outside operator either was or wished to be long of stocks. But with all this weight of money and influence, all this dexterity of market-manipulation and awakening anew of commercial business, the progress of the bull movement in the most active stocks was rather unsatisfactory. The army of brokers and speculators were like men who had been waiting long for the arrival of a train; the train had come, and they had bought their tickets and gone aboard, when, instead of starting off at a speed of a mile a minute, the train after a long start commenced backing, and anon came to a standstill. But the dull season was soon over.

Vanderbilt had gone to Europe and returned and "cut the melon" of Western Union, which, after rising to 118 upon the stock dividend, had again dropped to 95; but Erie refused to move above 29. Gould went abroad for some Erie or Kansas Pacific or American Union Telegraph company account: but Erie and Wabash did not rise, nor did Western Union break. The coal barons bestirred themselves to lift the prices of the coal stocks, but the "lift" was neither large nor well maintained. The tendency, however, towards higher prices was shown conspicuously in other directions: there was all the time an astonishing buoyancy shown by the stocks of many roads which had gone into the hands of receivers since 1873 and been reorganized. Stocks representing in the eyes of the street a value of zero, 1, 2, and 3, suddenly shot up ten, fifteen, twenty, and even thirty per cent., and what was equally strange did not go down again. The buoyancy of all classes of railway bonds was equally remarkable. At last the Grangers commenced again to move up, but the coal stocks and Lake Shore and Michigan Central and Erie & Ohios still lagged.

Suddenly out of a dull market Michigan Central, about the middle of July, sprang from 73 to 84. Hardly had this feat been executed by the Vanderbilt party, when St. Paul and Northwest showed an advance of eight per cent., and then Lake Shore, which had been slowly moving up from 73 to 76, began to lift its vast mass and bound up like an enraged elephant. It reached 80, paused an hour, and then resumed its lumbering bounds till, on the 12th of August, it touched 93. A plausible story to the effect that Lake Shore was or soon would be leased to the New York Central Company made the entire street wild to buy the stock above 90. Telegraphic orders to buy from the speculator-clique, of which Vanderbilt was the center, came from Saratoga, and nearly every operator thought it would go to 100, when all at once it turned and dropped 10 per cent. to 83, carrying down the whole market with it, and for a few hours producing something very like a panic.

This was a severe check to the upward movement, and it took four weeks to recover from its effects.

The fitful and rather unsatisfactory character of the market late in August was due also partly to the condition of the coal carriers. Del., Lack. & Western, Delaware & Hudson, and Central of New Jersey, the three coal stocks most actively dealt in on the New York Stock Exchange, were confessedly in a desperate condition. On the 30th of August the prices of these stocks had dropped away with a facility that argued intrinsic weakness. Alden B. Stockwell, of Pacific Mail memory, and other noted speculators, were short of them in the confident expectation of a further break. It was a plausible theory that as there had been an immense increase in the production of coal since the first of January, 1879, with a small corresponding increase in the demand, and as the coal mining and carrying companies were in anything but accord, and running behind hand in their net earnings every day, therefore the price of the stocks would fall. But this theory was between two suns proved to be utterly baseless. A letter recommending an alliance, from Mr. Gowen, the President of the Reading R. R. Company and hitherto an apparently irreconcilable advocate of independent action, was addressed to F. S. Lathrop, the Receiver of the Central R. R. Company of New Jersey, and published in the morning papers of August 31st. The next day Del. & Hudson, Del., Lack. & Western, and Central of New Jersey rose five per cent. Soon after the iron forges and furnaces were reported as busier than they had been for six years. The price of coal was put up; a quasi-combination was formed among the great companies, and in eight weeks an advance of from 30 to 35 per cent. was established in the price of Del. & Hudson, Del., Lack. & Western, and Central of New Jersey. This new movement in the coal stocks gave a prodigious impetus to the advance of the general list. The Grangers were pushed to higher points than they had been for many years: the Southwest Pool bid up the price of Wabash, Kansas Northern, and Kansas Pacific to unexpected figures; Lake Shore & Western Union and New York Central, were advanced ten per cent.; the fancies sailed aloft to dizzy heights; but the most astonishing movement of all was that in Erie, which commenced late in September, and progressed amid an excitement rarely felt even in Wall street.

The position of this stock in relation to the rest of the market has for many years been rather anomalous. Within ten years from the spring of 1868, when it fell into the hands of the Drew-Fisk-Gould party, to the spring of 1878, when it was reorganized, the capital stock and bonds had been increased from something over $50,000,000, to $152,000,000. From 1864 to 1878, the common stock had swelled from 110,000 shares to 780,000 shares. What hope of a speculative advance, and still less of a dividend on such a mass of shares as this! By liberal assessments, however, and by deferring the payment of interest on a large portion of the bonds of the company, the basis was established on a fair scale of earnings for not only the prompt payment of all fixed charges in the future, but also of the payment of a dividend on the preferred, to say nothing of the common stock.

The street was quick to discount these favorable expectations, and in the winter and spring of 1879 nearly every operator, large or small, bought Erie freely.

The large holders of the stock, however, did nothing to promote the rise of Erie. Indeed, Keene and Gould, and Hugh J. Jewett, the receiver of the company, seemed to exert themselves to keep down the price whenever marked buoyancy in the price was manifested. After the break in Lake Shore from 93 to 83, Erie was attacked with vigor by the very men whose interest it was to lift the price, and it was hammered down to 23. This was of course a ruse to enable the large holders and dextrous manipulators to buy more stock. From that point it began slowly to rise. The street guessed that something was going on in the stock, but dealt in it warily. Heavily and with a lumbering motion the huge bulk trundled up till it passed 30; then lurched back as if it would break to 25, paused for a few hours and at last moved, as if with its whole mass, at one bound to 34.

The excitement now rose to fever heat; the brokers

of nearly every great speculator seemed to be bidding for Erie; the Gould interest and the Vanderbilt interest seemed to be bidding against each other; the street followed in the wake of the large operators; the transactions were unprecedented; more than the whole capital stock of 780,000 shares changed hands every week; a rise to 43 followed, and still, though Osborn, Keene, and other magnates were reported to be selling out, the excitement abated not a jot, and vibrations of six per cent. daily furnished a tempting field for the fraction-pursuers and "scalpers" of the Board to exercise their mercurial energies upon.

The market was fast approaching the stage which usually precedes a panic, but there was not the remotest dread of any such disaster in the minds of the majority of dealers. Every stock on the list shared in the stimulus given to Erie. Stocks long since buried and forgotten were exhumed by parties of bull resurrectionists, divested of their cerements, and galvanized into a life which sufficed to carry them up the slope which the batallions of the market were ascending. After eight weeks of the most extraordinary activity and buoyancy ever known in the history of the New York Stock Exchange, it was not wonderful that prices should pause for a while, and that a certain hesitation should have been seen in the daily vibrations. A new and powerful bear party of such as had taken their profits was formed, which attempted to break down prices by manipulating the rates for loans made to the holders of stock. But their efforts were not rewarded with success to any extent. The pools generally kept their positions, and the outside public picked up floating stock almost as greedily as ever. Higher and still higher prices were predicted, and the new rise in New York Central, Rock Island, the coal stocks, and Western Union, the firmness in all the dividend paying stocks, and the buoyancy of the fancies, gave earnest of another outburst of speculation before the new year.

The most active stage of the long talked of rise of 1879 extended from the third week of September to the end of the fourth week of October, and during that period fifteen million shares of stock changed hands. There was a sound basis for just such an immense rise as that which occurred in September and October, 1879. One thousand million of gold and of paper dollars equal to gold! Coin received from Europe at the rate of nearly $1,000,000 per day! Furnaces smoking, forges clanging, looms rattling, and spindles humming all over the land! A thousand million bushels of cereals garnered from the fields! Five million bales of cotton to be gathered, and pressed, and strapped! And above these material resources and forces of industry there was confidence blossoming broadly and swiftly all through our western commercial world!

The great rise of stock values from the low grade of 1877, and the wonderful steadiness of prices, week after week without the sign of a severe break, still less of panic, were, in the autumn of 1879, the exponents, intense and brilliant, like an electric light, though over a narrow field, of a prosperity such as was never known before in the commercial history of this hemisphere.

The long-headed capitalists and railway kings who engineered the movement in railways stocks, from the panic in the spring of 1877 to their altitude in

1879, have been at once prophets to foretell and architects to plan and build, and so long as these restless financial giants devote their vast wealth and energies to the task of construction, let us forgive them for breaking down in the past what they are seeking to rebuild in the present.

In the first days of November there occured a sudden tightening in the money rate. The upward movement halted for a week. But $10,000,000 in currency was then poured out of the U. S. Treasury for bonds bought to be canceled; money was easy again and the bull movement received a new impetus.

The report that Vanderbilt, Gould, and Sage had formed a railroad alliance furnished fresh stimulation to the rage to buy, and every thing was once more on the rise.

The coal stocks and Erie were run up 10 per cent. higher. The fancies again soared aloft, and by the 15th of November the bull movement was at its height.

For six months the number of outside speculators had been daily increasing until it was estimated that upwards of thirty thousand of this class were actively engaged in stock operations.

Taking advantage of this circumstance some of the large operators had for some days been quietly selling out. Jas. R. Keene took his immense profits on coal stocks and Pacific Mail and Erie; Wm. R. Travers and Addison G. Cammack sold out their line of stocks; other shrewd operators followed the lead of these veterans. On Monday, the 17th of November, a poverful bear party made its appearance and proceeded to demonstrate against the market. The bull battalion made a strong resistance for forty-eight hours, but when it became known that Jay Gould and Russell Sage were sellers on a large scale, the spirit of Panic once more stalked abroad. On Wednesday and Thursday, holders of stocks were ruled by a new madness. One and a half million shares changed hands. Delaware & Hudson fell 20 per cent. in twenty minutes. Every other stock shared in the decline, the shrinkage in those two memorable days ranging from 2 to 28 per cent. The market was a boiling surge in which the waves of value rose and fell not by units but by tens. The reaction so long talked of had come at last. The wealthy speculators who, aided by commercial influences, had ever since the panic in the spring of 1877 toiled to lift values to the figures of October and November, 1879, now yielded to the storm and sacrificed some of their profits on paper.

It was a break on a colossal scale, not a panic; a prodigious rally and then another break followed in succession. On the 26th of November came the astonishing announcement of the sale of 250,000 shares of New York Central by Wm. H. Vanderbilt to a syndicate of bankers and of the alliance of the Gould-Sage with the Vanderbilt railroad combination. A series of wild fluctuations followed: the market at length settling down to the usual Decemberdullness in which we begin to see the first motions of the campaign of 1880.

THE END.

FINANCIAL MANAGEMENT
1880–1934

Volume 2

Edited and Introduced by
Morgen Witzel

THOEMMES

Financial Management, 1880–1934

Edited and Introduced by **Morgen Witzel**

Volume 1
Twenty Years of Inside Life in Wall Street, or Revelations of the Personal Experiences of a Speculator ... Illustrated (1880)
W. W. Fowler

Volume 2
Trusts, Pools and Corporations (1905)
William Z. Ripley

Volume 3
Corporation Finance (1910)
Edward S. Meade

Volume 4
Corporation Finance. An Exposition of the Principles and Methods governing the Promotion, Organization and Management of Modern Corporations (1909)
William H. Lough

Volume 5
Concentration and Control: A Solution of the Trust Problem in the United States (1914)
Charles R. van Hise

Credit and International Trade: How they Work in Practice (1934)
Barnard Ellinger

Volume 6
Problems in Business Finance (1921)
Edmund E. Lincoln

Volumes 7 and 8
Collected Articles and Chapters

Printed in England by Antony Rowe Ltd, Chippenham

TRUSTS, POOLS AND CORPORATIONS

William Z. Ripley

THOEMMES PRESS

This edition published by Thoemmes Press, 2001

Thoemmes Press
11 Great George Street
Bristol BS1 5RR, England

http://www.thoemmes.com

Financial Management, 1880–1934
8 Volumes : ISBN 1 85506 633 5

British Library Cataloguing-in-Publication Data
A CIP record of this title is available from the British Library

Publisher's Note

The Publisher has gone to great lengths to ensure the quality of this reprint but points out that some imperfections in the original book may be apparent.

This book is printed on acid-free paper, sewn, and cased in a durable buckram cloth.

TRUSTS, POOLS AND CORPORATIONS

EDITED

WITH AN INTRODUCTION

BY

WILLIAM Z. RIPLEY, Ph.D.
PROFESSOR OF ECONOMICS, HARVARD UNIVERSITY

GINN & COMPANY
BOSTON · NEW YORK · CHICAGO · LONDON

PREFACE

THIS volume is intended to be more than a mere collection of economic reprints. Such compilations have often been made; as for example in Dunbar's "Laws relating to Currency, Finance and Banking"; Rand's "Economic History"; and in the Reports of the United States Industrial Commission. This collection is planned for use specifically as a text-book; not merely as a handy volume for reference, or as a collection of original documents. It is not intended, however, to supplant, but rather to supplement, the standard treatises on the trust problem; and may readily be used in connection with Jenks's "Trust Problem," Ely's "Monopolies and Trusts," or Meade's "Trust Finance." It denotes a deliberate attempt at the application to the teaching of economics of the *case system*, so long successful in our law schools. With this end in view, each chapter is intended to illustrate a single, definite, typical phase of the general subject. The primary motive is to further the interests of sound economic teaching, with especial reference to the study of concrete problems of great public and private interest. A difficulty in the substitution of present-day social and economic studies for the good, old-fashioned, linguistic ones, or for the modern sciences, — a difficulty especially peculiar to descriptive economics as differentiated from economic theory, — has always been to secure data sufficiently concrete, definite and convenient to form a basis for analysis, discussion and criticism. The lecture system has its advantages in stimulating interest and — it is to be hoped — arousing enthusiasm among students. But lectures alone entirely fail to do justice to the possibilities inherent in economic science for rigorously training the mind in habits of close and consecutive thought. The law has always enjoyed a peculiar and well-merited prominence among other studies for this reason.

The first requisite, therefore, for the successful conduct of economic instruction in the descriptive field is to provide raw material; which in discussion, supplementary to the general lectures, may be worked over in detail in the class room. Such material, by reason of the great increase in economic periodical literature since 1890, is now rapidly augmenting. Yet with classes, as at Harvard University, often aggregating in such economic courses from one to two hundred men, resort by each student to the files of such periodical literature is out of the question. Public documents are also impossible for reference reading with a class of considerable size. And finally, in my judgment, a generally neglected and amazingly rich find lies embedded in the mass of factual evidence accumulated in the course of legal proceedings in our courts. The mere decisions, as long currently used, are of course well known. But it is not the *legal* pronouncement in the case, infrequently interlarded with brief statements of fact; but the actual testimony adduced — "The Record" of evidence submitted — which has rarely been utilized. Such matter must be painstakingly uncovered, abridged, even digested, and made more conveniently accessible to serve its due end for the teacher. To direct attention to this material by a few concrete illustrations from such sources, reprinted in this volume, is not an unimportant motive in its production.

A second, and by no means inconsiderable, motive in the preparation of this volume has been the hope that it might contribute toward a crystallization of public opinion favoring a reasonable policy of public control over monopolistic and corporate enterprises. The general reader and the legislator, in the mass of loose generalizations upon this topic, can scarcely be expected to follow publications in the technical economic journals. Such articles, unswayed as they should be by selfish interest and personal prejudice, nevertheless, are the main ones which may safely be relied upon in the formation of a final judgment. By gathering together in convenient form this series of papers and documents, it is confidently hoped that progress toward the solution of one of our most troublesome public questions may be in some slight degree facilitated.

Most cordial acknowledgment is due to the Editorial Boards of the *Political Science Quarterly*, the *Economic Journal*, the *Yale Review* and the *Quarterly Journal of Economics*, and in even greater measure to the authors of the several papers herein reprinted, for permission to make use of their material in this enterprise. In every instance a most hearty acquiescence in the project has been expressed, for the which I cannot be too grateful. Without such assent the meagre original contributions of the editor would have made but a sorry show. Nor can I refrain in this instance from an expression of my peculiar obligation to Professor J. W. Jenks of Cornell University, my former colleague in the work of the United States Industrial Commission, who has been long and deservedly recognized as a pioneer in this field of economic study. To my former teacher, Professor Goodnow of Columbia; to my colleague, Professor Bullock; and to Dr. E. S. Meade of the University of Pennsylvania, I am also more than ordinarily indebted. Hon. E. B. Whitney, former Assistant Attorney-General of the United States, now of the New York bar, has also been of great service in awakening my interest in the legal sources of economic information, to which reference has been made. This volume, as it appears, is largely the work of my professional colleagues and friends. It is earnestly to be desired that my editorial endeavors may serve to direct attention anew to the value and interest of their contributions.

WILLIAM Z. RIPLEY.

CONTENTS

INTRODUCTION

The historical development of the so-called Trust Problem in the United States naturally falls into four more or less clearly defined periods. The revival of industry following the long depression of 1873–79 began the modern development of large-scale production. Corporations embodying the principles of limited liability, delegated management and indirect ownership became increasingly prominent after 1880. The first period in our trust history may be said, therefore, to extend from about this time until 1887. It was characterized by a steady increase in the size and number of large-scale industrial units. Various pools and the Standard Oil Trust foreshadowed the future. The decade from 1887 to 1897 forms the second period. It was the time of the trust in the strict legal sense. Standard Oil Trust success since 1882 invited imitation in the two important industries of distilling and sugar refining. The progress of monopoly was such that an outbreak of state anti-trust laws from 1889 to 1893 indicated how fully public interest had turned from the regulation of railroads to that of industrial monopoly. It was assumed, in fact, that the railroad question had been in a large measure settled by the enactment of the Interstate Commerce Act in 1887. As instanced later in this brief review, the entire failure of the trust expedient, however, in furnishing a legal basis for monopoly led to various other devices, notably pooling. And the continuation of industrial depression, during the four years to 1897, rendered constructive development unlikely. The third period from 1897 until the Northern Securities decision in the spring of 1904 was largely influenced by the phenomenal prosperity which began in the former year and culminated in 1902. The formation of combinations in various branches of iron and steel manufacture, followed by the great outbreak of corporate promotion in 1899, led up to the formation of the United States Steel Corporation in 1901. And the prominence of holding corporations, organized under the laws of New Jersey, seemed to offer a convenient substitute for the old and discredited trust.

The latest period in the development of the problem begins with the year 1904. Speculative scandals hereafter mentioned; the great decline of stock market quotations in 1903; the failure of bright promises made by promoters; a reviving interest in railroad regulation and the tariff; and an increasing demand for publicity, have successively made their appearance. More important concretely than all of these, however, was the influence of the Northern Securities decision in the spring of 1904, which determined the legal instability of the holding corporation. The present seems, then, to be a period of uncertainty in the minds of organizers and directors of large-scale production. Having tasted the advantages of monopoly, they are not content to relapse into a régime of competition. Publicity through the newly organized Bureau of Corporations in the United States Department of Commerce has become possible. Faint suggestions of additional repressive legislation appear in spite of increasing proof that the Common Law, even in the absence of statutory enactment, is sufficient, if manfully invoked, to protect the rights of the individual. It remains now to be seen whether new legal expedients in organization will be sought, in the attempt to settle the great controversy between large-scale industry which seeks the advantages of monopoly, and the individual producer and the public who demand the benefits of competition.

Monopoly has been sought under four distinct forms of organization, which may be briefly considered in turn. These are the pool, the trust, the simple corporation and the finance company or holding corporation.

The *pool* is perhaps the oldest, commonest and, at the same time, most recently popular mode of obviating the evils of competition. Industrial pools, in fact, appear at every stage of our economic development since the Civil War. They are not even eliminated from the situation by gigantic mergers, so long as the latter are not absolutely monopolistic. Thus even the most powerful present-day combinations, such as the United States Steel Corporation, find it necessary to become parties to pooling arrangements with independent producers. The secrecy of these agreements, owing to a wholesome fear of the law, renders them apparently less widespread and effective than they perhaps are in fact. Such agreements may even be international in their scope, as shown by the recent allotment of the European export trade in steel rails in 1904 between the great German Steel Corporation, known as the Stahlwerkverband, and the English rolling mills. A seemingly undue amount of attention has been devoted to the subject of pools in this volume, because of their persistency and evidently increasing adoption in these various ways.

A type of the earliest form of pool is afforded by the Michigan Salt Association, dating practically from 1868. As described hereinafter in detail,[1] this was an agreement for the purchase of the entire output of all the important producers in a certain field. Similar agreements were certainly operative in the decade 1880–90, as in the manufacture and sale of cotton bagging, wherein was controlled perhaps two-thirds of the output of the country. The most notable pools twenty years ago, however, arousing widespread attention, were in the distilling industry. In 1882 and probably even earlier, until the formation of the trust, a limitation of output and allotment of sales was certainly relied upon to prevent undue competition.[2] The well-known pools in the cordage manufacture dating from 1860 are also cases in point. A far less defensible scheme from a moral point of view, revealing the possible evils inherent in pooling, is revealed by the case of the Addyston Pipe Co. Our record of this combination[3] shows it to have consisted of an agreement among competing producers to fix a monopolistic price by means of fictitious bids, with a division of the field to insure complete local monopoly for each plant. More recently still, and developing a peculiar vigor since the failure of other attempts at monopolization, either by outright purchase or a holding company, are the existing pools in the iron and steel industry. These, as described in Chapter IV,

[1] Chapter I, p. 1. [2] See pp. 22 *et seq.* [3] pp. 86 *et seq.*

are acquiring increased importance in the attempt to secure stability of price in a field peculiarly subject to violent fluctuations between prosperity and depression. When reasonably and fairly administered, having due regard, that is to say, to the welfare and patience of the consuming public, they promise some measure of success; otherwise managed, when rapacious in unduly forcing up prices, such pools have generally resulted in collapse; with greater evils both to the public and their own members than those whose cure was attempted. This is clearly exemplified in our reprinted outline of the history of the Wire Nail Association of 1895–96.[1] A still more complicated arrangement, of special interest as throwing light upon the difficult question of public control in our own anthracite coal field, is afforded by the German Coal Cartell, which at the present time completely dominates the situation in that country.[2]

Patent as are the advantages to producers of pooling contracts, they suffer from two inherent defects. Of these the first is that they are at variance with the underlying principles both of common and statute law, and hence are not enforceable in the courts. No effective guarantee for good faith is afforded other than the creation of deposits, the imposition of fines and other more or less mechanical devices. And a second objection lies in the fact that pools are necessarily but temporary expedients after all, affording no certainty for stability of price or of industrial policy for any extended period. It was undoubtedly an appreciation of these facts which led to the attempts in the late '80's to remodel industrial combinations on the pattern of the Standard Oil Trust of 1882. On the other hand, it may perhaps be affirmed truly that the very indefiniteness and elasticity of such agreements has often rendered them successful at times like the present, when more rigid devices are proving somewhat ineffective in controlling prices in the face of a rising tide of independent production.

A *trust* may be defined as an organization managed by a board of trustees to whom all the capital stock of the constitu-

[1] pp. 46 *et seq.*

[2] Publications American Economic Association, 3d ser., Vol. V, 1904, contains an excellent and elaborate study by Dr. Francis Walker.

ent companies is irrevocably assigned; in other words, the original shareholders accept the trustees' certificates in lieu of former evidences of ownership. The outline of a typical trust hereinafter printed will serve as an illustration.[1] As a legal expedient for obviating competition such a trust is usually discussed as if it were now obsolete, possessing historic interest alone. This is only in part true. As an improvement upon the pool, both as regards stability and effectiveness, certainly it merits the importance ascribed to it during the decade following 1887. The first appearance of this legal expedient dates, of course, from the formation of the Standard Oil Trust in 1882.[2] It derived added prominence through the formation of the Distillers and Cattle Feeders' Trust (Whiskey) and the Sugar Trust, both in 1887. It disappeared with the final judicial condemnation under adverse state and Federal legislation in the years 1891–92. The adverse decision in the case of the North River Sugar Refining Co. and the Standard Oil Co., in Ohio, finally proved the impossibility of this legal basis for effecting combinations.[3] Recourse was necessarily had, therefore, to novel expedients, such as corporate organization under the newly revised laws of New Jersey and other charter-bartering states.

It is an odd coincidence, that organization under a board of trustees issuing certificates representative of ownership of property, although condemned by the courts and obsolete as a resource for the great industrial combinations of the country at large, should still flourish under the laws of Massachusetts. This commonwealth has, in the main, steadfastly resisted pressure for a loose, or even for a liberal, policy in corporate legislation; yet it is notable among the other states to-day as permitting the trust form of organization to flourish as an expedient for consolidation. This is perhaps indirectly an outcome of the consistent policy of the state not to permit the holding of real estate for investment by corporations organized

[1] Consult Chapter II, pp. 22 *et seq.*

[2] Miss Ida M. Tarbell's monumental study of the Standard Oil Co. gives full details concerning both the form and dissolution of this trusteeship.

[3] *Vide* pp. 244 and 265 *infra.*

under its general laws. Moreover, this latter practice would be difficult under the common law rule against perpetuities. For about half a century, therefore, real estate in Boston, if held for permanent investment by a number of people jointly, must have its ownership vested in voluntary associations, managed by trustees. An important ruling of the Massachusetts supreme court in 1899, upholding the validity of such associations, has greatly enhanced their prestige. A recent compilation includes no fewer than sixty real estate trusts in the city of Boston alone, holding upwards of $60,000,000 of property.

The immunity from governmental supervision of voluntary associations under trusteeship especially in the issue of capital stock, under the strict Massachusetts anti-stock-watering laws applicable to corporations, has recently invited an extension of the principles of trusteeship into the fields both of transportation and industry. Thus the Massachusetts Electric Companies, controlling the stock of several hundred miles of street railways throughout the eastern part of the state, is managed through a board of trustees. This board issues certificates representing the equity interest of the original stockholders of the constituent companies included in the combination in the enterprise. This, it will be observed, is quite analogous to the devices originally adopted by the Sugar and Standard Oil Trusts. The Massachusetts Gas Companies, in the industrial field, have likewise, as the virtual successors of the New England Gas & Coke Co., acquired control of illuminating plants in and about Boston.[1] Still another form analogous to these is found in the voting trusts until recently so common among American railways. These forms of control as vested in a board of trustees represent, not ownership of stock, but merely a unified voting power during a specified term of years. As applied in the cases of a number of industrial combinations, such as the American Bicycle Co. since reorganization, and the International Mercantile Marine Co. at its inception, these voting trusts vir-

[1] Professor John H. Gray has recently published a considerable series of articles on the Massachusetts gas situation in the *Quarterly Journal of Economics*. Consult the same author's address in *Publications American Academy Political Science*, 1900, and also *Journal of Political Economy*, 1903, pp. 257–272.

tually perpetuate monopoly. Although their primary object purports to be protection against rude disturbance of continuity in financial policy, their utility for the purposes of combination is quite evident. It thus appears that the principle of trusteeship in industrial management is by no means obsolete; although the statement is perhaps true as applicable to consolidation in the great staple interstate industries of the country.

The failure of the Trust form of combination under adverse legislation and judicial decisions[1] came at a time when the industry of the country was languishing. The period from 1893 to 1897 being one of prolonged and acute industrial depression, the tendency toward consolidation made little headway. Sporadic attempts at pooling in the iron and steel industry were made in 1895 and 1896 as herein described.[2] But the resumption of trade activity after this prolonged depression promptly brought the combination question to the fore. At the same time the revival of confidence among investors following a protracted period of speculative dulness opened new channels of activity for the financial agent. Meade, in his Trust Finance, has ably described the work of the industrial promoter at this time. The phenomenal outburst of industrial consolidation in 1899 made necessary a resort to a new legal expedient, that of the *holding corporation.* Prior to the enactment of the revised General Corporation Act of New Jersey in 1899, the uniform practice both in this country and abroad had been to prohibit by law the holding of the stock of one corporation by another. Vast possibilities were involved in the amendment of this clause in a code of American corporation law. Corporate organization could henceforth be promoted, not to serve the ends of industrial management, but solely in order that financial combinations might indirectly control operating companies through ownership of their capital stock. This practice had already been tested in isolated cases among railroads; as, for instance, in the organization of the Pennsylvania Co in 1870 to hold and control the stocks of subsidiary corporations owned by the Pennsylvania Railroad Co. west of Pittsburg. In 1880 the American Bell Telephone Co. was organized under

[1] Consult pp. 244 *et seq.*

[2] pp. 46 and 78 *supra.*

Massachusetts law practically as a holding company. Four years later the Southern Pacific Co. was chartered by the state of Kentucky to hold the stocks of parts of a great railway system in other and remote states. These were, however, all organized under special laws; while the General Corporation Act of New Jersey of 1899 made it possible to organize a pure finance company under a general statute. No operating duties at all were involved other than to hold the stock, elect officers, receive dividends from constituent companies and turn them over to their own shareholders. At the same time it was necessary merely to maintain a nominal connection with the authorities in the chartering state by renting desk room, displaying a sign and making a meagre and non-committal annual report.

Relatively few companies seem to have taken advantage of the New Jersey legislation at once. Among those which have been tested by extended experience is the United States Rubber Co., dating from 1893. Certain decisions of the United States Supreme Court, notably those touching the sugar combination in 1894,[1] manifested an indisposition on the part of the Federal courts to interfere. The prospect was inviting also in many cases because of the elasticity of the arrangement. It enabled promoters to purchase the stock control of companies in the open market rather than at private sale. Less capital would be tied up in effecting a combination; inasmuch as ownership, not of all, but merely of a bare majority of the capital stock of companies absorbed, was necessary. Legal experts, moreover, hoped the scheme would prove invulnerable. Consequently, for a brief period the holding company suddenly assumed a noteworthy prominence in every branch of American business life. The Federal Steel Co., with a capital of about $100,000,000, later absorbed by the United States Steel Corporation, was chartered by New Jersey in 1898. Ownership by stock control was extended over a considerable range of interlocking properties such as ore bodies, steel works and railways. The following year witnessed the incorporation of the Amalgamated Copper Co., capitalized at $75,000,000, as a holding corporation to acquire and control the stocks of copper-mining companies. The year

[1] *U. S.* v. *E. C. Knight Co.* See pp. 255 and 265 *infra*.

1900 was one of pause in the consolidation movement following the craze for company promotion in the preceding year. The gigantic United States Steel Corporation with stocks and bonds aggregating $1,400,000,000 speedily followed.[1] In the railway field the Northern Securities Co. with $400,000,000 of authorized stock was to acquire and control the northern transcontinental railway corporations.[2] Then came the so-called Whiskey Trust, previously transmuted into the Distilling Co. of America, an actual merger of four constituent corporations, taken over by a pure finance company, the Distillers' Security Corporation, capitalized at $32,000,000. The movement invaded the field of commercial distribution in the Associated Merchants Co., a holding corporation organized this time under the laws of Connecticut, to hold the stocks of retail dry goods establishments and incidentally to transact such business on its own account. The Rock Island Co., with a capital of $115,000,000, again of New Jersey, was in 1902 patterned after the Northern Securities Co. As a holding corporation it has formed the basis of wholesale consolidation of railway lines west and south of Chicago. It was even rumored that a Southern Securities Co. would ultimately take over the control of the great transportation systems south of Mason and Dixon's line. In the field of electric transportation, also, the holding company has become exceedingly popular since 1902–03; as witness the prominent instances of the Metropolitan Securities Co. of New York; the Rhode Island Securities Co., owning street railways throughout that commonwealth; and the Public Service Corporation of New Jersey, aiming at consolidation of electric carriage and lighting in an important field.[3]

Owing to the uncertain legal status of the pure finance company or holding corporation since the Northern Securities decision,[4] the tendency at the present time seems to be in favor of an actual merger of constituent corporations in a single company. This form of organization involves an actual exchange, in some agreed ratio, of the securities of the constituent com-

[1] Meade's Trust Finance, Wilgus's United States Steel Corporation and Moody's Truth about the Trusts are perhaps the best references on this company.

[2] *Vide* pp. 322 *et seq.* [3] *Vide* pp. 146 *infra.* [4] *Vide* pp. 322 *et seq.*

panies for those of the absorbing concern. It is what would seem to have been done in the case of the Distilling Co. of America in 1899, afterward replaced by a holding corporation. An earlier example is that of the Trenton Potteries Co., composed of eight factories which united in 1892. It has been frequently stated that the United States Steel Corporation has been strengthening its position, under possible adverse judicial decisions following the line of the Northern Securities case, by likewise eliminating some of its constituent concerns and acquiring a direct ownership.[1] The practical difference between this form of merger and a holding company appears principally in those cases where the holding company owns not all but only a part of the capital stock of its constituent corporations. Where, as in the case of the United States Steel Corporation or the American Agricultural Chemical Company, the entire ownership of the stock of the constituent companies occurs, the holding company becomes truly a legal fiction. There is no legitimate excuse for its existence. The Distillers' Security Corporation, on the other hand, owns only about ninety per cent of the preferred and common stock of its predecessor, the Distilling Co. of America. In the case of railroad holding companies the general rule seems to be that all, or nearly all, of the stock of the operating companies is controlled. The Northern Securities Co. absorbed all of the Northern Pacific stock, although it held merely a controlling interest in the Great Northern Railroad. The Rock Island Co. owns all of the stock of the C., R. I. & P. Railroad Co., which in turn holds nearly all the stock of the C., R. I. & P. Railway Co., which last is the real operating concern. The additional difficulty in the case of the intervention of a holding company which has not absorbed all the securities of its constituent parts is, of course, the existence of a minority interest. Great and growing importance is thereby placed upon the final determination of the rights of minority holders where the majority is not a merely temporary body, but a definite and permanent corporation.

[1] The "community of interest" basis of consolidation so widely heralded among railways has not been industrially applied, except possibly in the Standard Oil Co. after the dissolution of its Trust in 1892.

Another peculiar feature of modern corporate finance which is seemingly an outgrowth of the holding companies is the ever increasing complexity of corporate organization. This evil, for so it must be denominated, is peculiarly apparent in the case of companies controlling municipal franchises. Wheels within wheels multiply until it becomes practically impossible to fix responsibility either in the courts or by way of public control administratively. The Brooklyn Rapid Transit Co.[1] and the Metropolitan Securities Co., controlling the street railways of New York city, have most complicated relations. One of the best illustrations is, however, afforded in the control of the street railways of the city of Providence. The original concern is the Union Railway Co., a Rhode Island corporation. Its stock was purchased by the United Traction and Electric Co. of New Jersey, which company has since leased it again to another Rhode Island corporation, known as the Rhode Island Company. The stock of this corporation is in turn owned by the Rhode Island Securities Co., which is a New Jersey corporation. All the stock of this organization is finally owned by the United Gas and Improvement Co., which is a Pennsylvania corporation. The infinite possibilities in cases of this kind for obscuring profits or losses and minimizing public accountability are too apparent to need elaboration. And where, as sometimes happens, a small number of minority stockholders in each company exists, the confusion is greatly accentuated.

The trust movement has brought to light a number of peculiar *evils in corporate finance*, or rather it has magnified preëxisting tendencies which have long been apparent in the case of smaller organizations. The principal ones may perhaps be classified as fraudulent promotion and speculative management. It is difficult, however, to draw the line clearly between recklessness and downright dishonesty. A vast increase in irresponsible direction has paved the way to financial practice which, according to the point of view, may be denominated as extravagance or fraud.

Many of the *promotions* described in the evidence before the United States Industrial Commission in 1900 impress the conser-

[1] p. 146 *infra.*

vative financier as extravagant. The returns of both organizers and banking syndicates seem to be excessive. Meade, in his able chapters in Trust Finance, has analyzed many of these in detail, showing a certain justification for large profits because of the risk involved. But later developments have brought to light practices in promotion which are more certainly reprehensible, and which merit the name of theft. Two notable instances are described in the official reports of receivers in the cases of the Asphalt and Shipbuilding Companies, reprinted in this volume.[1] Similar practices have also been proven in the organization of the International Salt Co.; wherein, apparently, a syndicate received upward of $6,000,000 worth of stock out of a total of $18,750,000 issued. The scandal of the padded balance sheet of an important combination is too recent to be overlooked; and, despite the secrecy of its promoters, there appears to be every probability that enormous profits were made in the organization of the Amalgamated Copper Co. The most obvious method of stopping these nefarious practices is undoubtedly to have them condemned by the courts. This has been done in several notable instances of late.[2] It would seem to involve less economic loss to remove the incentive to such reckless promotion at the outset, by regulation of the conditions of flotation, as is done in the excellent German law described herein.[3] The Massachusetts policy of restriction has also undoubtedly worked well.[4]

The *payment of unearned dividends* is another evil which in the past has not been curbed by a series of decisions in our American courts attempting to distinguish clearly between capital and income accounts. Nice questions of policy are involved in the determination of net profits. Meade, in his Trust Finance, again has clearly set forth the unwise policy of many industrial combinations in failing to provide a sufficient surplus reserve before beginning the payment of dividends. Unfortunately, instances of downright deception often merging into fraud, have

[1] pp. 182 and 218 *infra*.

[2] On the liability of promoters for unrevealed profits consult the review of cases by the present writer in the *Journal of Political Economy*, Vol. VIII, 1900, pp. 535 *et seq.*

[3] Chapter XVI, p. 393.

[4] Chapter XV, and also p. 126.

made their appearance in the last few years. The Asphalt Companies clearly exemplify the lack of a conservative policy in accounting; as when, for instance, the Audit Co. of New York changed an apparent surplus of $758,000 to a deficit of $541,000. The United States Realty Co. is another case in point. Dividends were here paid on the basis of profits on uncompleted contracts, recalling the similar policy in the case of the U. S. Shipbuilding Co.[1] Numerous other concerns have since been shown to have followed the same practice, notably the New England Cotton Yarn and the Virginia-Carolina Chemical Co. Perhaps the worst offender was the American Malting Co., in a case so extreme and so clearly fraudulent that the courts have held the directors liable both to creditors and stockholders to the full amount of the unearned dividends declared.[2] It is earnestly to be hoped that a few more judgments of this kind will serve to restrain the directorates of other great corporations.

The evil of *speculative management* falls into several distinct parts. The earliest form which it took was the buying and selling by its own officers of the securities of a corporation for speculative purposes. Of this sort are the events in the history of the Whiskey Trust, and a few scattered instances such as the manipulation of Diamond Match funds in 1896. American corporations, unlike those of England and Germany, fail in too many instances to prohibit dealings in the securities of a company by its own officers. The best of them certainly do so, and the scandals of a decade ago probably emphasized the desirability of preventing this evil. An unlimited power to contract loans without the approval of the directors or stockholders, as in the case of the American Ice Co., is also a constant menace to conservative management. Another phase of this matter concerns the temptation to industrial management with a view to its effect upon the stock market rather than upon the permanent welfare of the company. A classic example is afforded

[1] pp. 190 *et seq.*

[2] The first decision before the New Jersey Court of Errors and Appeals held the directors liable; but before the appeal was heard the state legislature so amended the law as to render the final decision of little value. The case was then taken to the Supreme Court of New York, and a decision for damages amounting to over $1,000,000 was obtained in December, 1904.

by the episode of the American Steel & Wire Co. in 1900. Secrecy is a constant invitation to the insider to take advantage of forthcoming events at the expense of the stockholders. It is undeniable also that such speculative management greatly encourages speculative ownership on the part of stockholders. The old-fashioned investor, secure in his belief in the stability of his company, is replaced by a body of temporary holders who look for the returns upon their investment, more in the chances of buying and selling and manipulation, than to permanent and regular dividends. That this kind of ownership is greatly encouraged by the very low quotations of the stocks of overcapitalized companies cannot be doubted.

The spread of the practice of indirect ownership through the mediation of holding or finance companies has also produced a peculiar set of abuses. These are all dependent in the main upon the preservation of secrecy as to the exact status of the operating concern. Dividends or deficits may be shifted at the will of the directors from one to another company of the hierarchy. Only when disclosure is forced by financial stress or judicial proceedings is the real state of affairs revealed. Our reprint of the Receiver's report of the United States Shipbuilding Co. serves to illustrate this evil.[1] Other instances of the creation of large floating debts by constituent companies, which debts are not apparent in the reports of the parent concern, are familiar in the case of the United States Rubber Co. and the New England Cotton Yarn Co. The failure to disclose may, however, at times operate in the other direction. Stockholders are induced to sell because of failure on the part of the management to make clear the accumulated profits of constituent companies. This would seem to be exemplified in the recent history of the companies which constitute the so-called Tobacco Trust. On the formation of the Consolidated Company in 1901, the majority of the common stocks of the American and Continental Tobacco companies were taken over in exchange for four per cent collateral bonds. The holders of the non-dividend Continental stock parted with their property without any knowledge whatever of the profits which it had been earning. Only after

[1] pp. 182 *et seq.*

they had been given in exchange a security with a fixed return, did it appear that very large profits had accrued. In fact, the dividends of the Continental Co. were soon increased to ten and afterward to sixteen per cent. The profits to those who had assumed control of the Consolidated Company were correspondingly great; inasmuch as they received all the surplus income over the fixed returns given in exchange for the old securities. It is the possibility of such shuffling as this which has rendered the bonds of the Consolidated Company so unpopular that recent plans for their retirement have been consummated.

Excessive profits to the management or to banking syndicates from the manipulation or exchange of one security for another are exemplified in still another way in the notable case of the United States Steel bond conversion scheme. This complicated affair is sufficiently described in our reprint, so that further comment upon it is perhaps unnecessary.[1]

Overcapitalization is one of the most frequent, time-honored and persistent charges brought against industrial combinations and against corporations particularly as distinct from other forms of business organization.[2] The general public avers, in behalf of its interest as consumer, that while of course there is no direct relation between capitalization and prices, an excess of securities craving dividends is in itself an indirect incentive to unreasonable charges. An even more cogent objection than this is that the absence of any direct relation between investment value and the volume of stocks and bonds confuses all parties concerned. This was an underlying motive in the enactment of the Massachusetts Anti-Stock-Watering Laws of 1894. For a divergence between the actual property value and capitalization may lead to exorbitant prices and dividends at the expense of the public.[3] It invites unearned profits on the part of promoters leading to corporate organization or financial readjustment in unnecessary or unmerited instances. It stimulates extravagance on the part of banking syndicates in the prices

[1] Chapter VIII, pp. 149 *et seq.*

[2] On this topic see Chapters VI, VII, XV, XVI and XVII.

[3] For recent state legislation along this theory consult E. D. Durand in *Yale Review*, Vol. XII, p. 412.

offered or paid for constituent companies. It facilitates internal mismanagement, even promotes actual fraud, by the ease with which the most alert stockholders may be confused as to the real standing of their own company. And finally, it invites speculation and stock market jobbery among the public by the relatively small capital necessary to deal in, or acquire control of, considerable blocks of stock. It is certainly difficult to trace a direct relation between capitalization and prices. In most cases, probably, the evils ascribed to overcapitalization are merely concomitant rather than resultant. In other words, overcapitalization is often merely an indication of financial recklessness, which makes itself known coincidently in other phases of corporate conduct. There can be no doubt that most of the industrial combinations launched in 1899–1901 were seriously open to most of these criticisms. The belated experiment of the International Mercantile Marine Co., hereafter described in these pages, serves as a good illustration of such reckless financiering in recent years. Later developments, however, are tending to show that the lessons of overcapitalization are being impressed upon both promoters and the investing classes. Experience is proving that in the long run the conservatively capitalized companies alone can command banker's credit, weather periods of fiscal strain and hold the allegiance of investors. Consequently a number of large companies have voluntarily, or in the process of reorganization, reduced the volume of their outstanding securities. The National Lead Co. in 1891 reduced its capitalization from ninety to thirty million dollars. The Distillers' Securities Corporation now has less than half the amount outstanding against its predecessors. Only recently the New England Cotton Yarn Co. has eliminated the good-will item from its accounts, thereby reducing the totals on its balance sheet by about five million dollars. The American Ice Co. represents its condition in the following words of its own president: "It is clear that the capitalization is excessive; that the common stock represents no earning capacity even under normal business conditions." Other recklessly promoted companies now find themselves similarly placed. Such elements in this evil as are not self-remedying through bitter experience may be most successfully treated by means of laws insuring full publicity and accountability on the part of promoters.

What is the effect of industrial combination upon *prices?* No candid observer can deny that monopoly price where possible is much higher than the price level under competition. The price of sugar, for instance, as Jenks has pretty conclusively proven, has been effectively maintained at a high level, despite improvements in manufacture in which the public would probably share through declining prices, with the market an open one. In the same way the price of petroleum products has been successfully upheld by the Standard Oil Co. in the face of declining costs of manufacture. Miss Tarbell has shown in a convincing way how the market has been controlled at the expense of the consumer. In addition to such facts as these, it is unquestionable also that the producer of raw materials has likewise suffered under the industrial tyranny of the Standard Oil Co. Both markets, alike for the raw and finished product, have been absolutely controlled. The tendency is for the margin between crude and refined oil to increase steadily — wherefrom, of course, arises the enormous profits of the company. In the coal famine of 1902–03 the price of crude oil advanced as a natural response to the situation; but the price of the refined product was arbitrarily raised, not proportionately, but to a point which demonstrates clearly the menace to public welfare which the continued existence of the monopoly involves. The same allegations seem to hold true also of the great monopoly which controls the beef and meat packing interests of the country. There again an augmentation of price to the consumer appears to be joined with a relative depression of price to the cattle raiser. Other instances of the maleficent influence of monopoly in thus controlling staple industries are less rare than they should be.

This extremely evil condition of affairs is fortunately not characteristic of all the lines of industry wherein industrial combination has been attempted. Perhaps this is because the monopoly is less complete, competition having arisen under the prevalence of abnormal prices; or it may be due to the fact that other commodities, not being staple and necessary to life, are exposed to the dangers of substitution of some other commodity produced in a more open market. The most serious evil in respect of monopoly price is often not its high level absolutely, but its arbitrary inequality as between both persons and places. Absolute control also implies possibility of manipulation. It has frequently been maintained by advocates of combination that a far greater steadiness of price will usually result. This plea has been exhaustively analyzed in a number of instances. Miss Tarbell discusses it in respect to petroleum products, and Jenks has investigated the course of prices in sugar, whiskey and other commodities produced under monopolistic control. In all of these cases it has been proven that sudden and violent changes of price are no less apt to occur than in an open market. The cause in such a case is, of course, often different from that which obtains under free competition. But the fact is that prices may be suddenly lowered in a locality in order to destroy independent local production; or that discrimination between persons is made to effect the same end; whereas, formerly, prices rose and fell because of a fluctuation in the general relations of demand and supply. On the other hand, certain combinations, like the United States Steel Corporation, seem effectively to have withstood an undue depression of prices during the industrial relapse of 1903–04. Whether they could have done this without the intervention of pooling agreements, which enabled them to include independent producers in their general programme, is not as yet clear. Perhaps, also, the monopoly prevented an abnormally high price level in the "boom" which preceded this collapse. That the general level of prices in iron and steel products — steel rails, for example — has been artificially supported during 1904–05, scarcely admits of reasonable doubt.

A brief outline of *possible remedies* for the present evils of the industrial situation may properly begin with the assumption that so far as individual repressive action by the separate states is concerned, the limit of legislative activity has about been reached. State anti-trust laws have been enacted everywhere and in all degrees of severity. The utmost that the separate states can do is perhaps indicated by the laws of Massachusetts, making provision for publicity and general supervision.[1] The charter-bartering abuses rife in New Jersey, Delaware, Maine and West Virginia, by which states confer rights upon corporations to do things in other states, forbidden by the laws of those states, can be abated only by Federal decisions like the Northern Securities case.[2] Even under them, the most that could be accomplished would be for each state to purge its own territory of the nuisances committed by its neighbors, through taxation, licenses or other means. It becomes increasingly apparent that all effective remedies must be applied by the Federal government. As commerce becomes ever wider in its range, so must legislation proceed from a source of authority equally great and comprehensive. A delegation of greater powers to the states from the central government would only increase the present complexity of the situation.

The discussion of feasible remedies may also be facilitated by eliminating those measures which would require an amendment of the Constitution of the United States.[3] Simpler means should be first tested as to their efficacy. The Northern Securities decision has cleared the way for a trial of several of these. Another elimination may also be made of projects for merely strengthening the present prohibitory features of the Sherman Act. It is now good legal opinion that the English Common Law is almost as effective as that or any other similar statute against the evils of unfair competition and conspiracy in restraint of trade.[4] Reduction of some of our absurdly prohibitory tariff duties would surely accomplish much in abating monopolistic prices, either under permanent combinations or temporary pooling agreements.[5] But that question is so compli-

[1] Consult Chapter XV, pp. 382 *et seq.*, also p. 121. E. D. Durand, in *Yale Review*, Vol. XII, pp. 409–428, outlines new legislation since 1901.

[2] Chapter XIV, pp. 322 *et seq.*

[3] Compare 56th Cong., 1st Sess., H. R. 1501. Report of the House Committee on Judiciary on proposed amendment to the Constitution.

[4] Hon. E. B. Whitney, in the *Yale Review*, May, 1904; compare also pp. 230 *et seq. infra.* Bruce Wyman of the Harvard Law School proposes an application of the Law of the Public Callings in *Harvard Law Review*, Vol. XVII, pp. 156 and 217.

[5] *Vide* pp. 289 *et seq.;* and also p. 54, and Jenks, Trust Problem, p. 44; and *Political Science Quarterly*, September, 1904.

cated by other issues and interests that effective action will require a profound modification of present public opinion. Hopeful signs that some relief in this direction may be soon granted are not wanting; although one may doubt whether anything very radical in tariff revision will be accomplished in the near future.

The most direct lines for remedial legislation are indicated by the proposals of the former Attorney-General of the United States as herein reprinted.[1] His drastic suggestion of a prohibition of interstate transport of commodities produced by monopolistic combinations was embodied in the Littlefield bill which passed the House of Representatives in February, 1903. And the prohibition of use of the mails would seem to be rendered more practicable since the recent Supreme Court decisions in the Lottery cases.[2] Certainly the necessity for amendment of the Interstate Commerce Act to prevent a continuance of the evils of secret rebates and preferential tariffs is well recognized. The Elkins amendments of 1903 have accomplished some good, but much yet remains to be done. Several bills are now prominently before Congress for action, being manfully supported by President Roosevelt. The field of possible legislative action is thus narrowed to three distinct proportions. Of these, the first is incorporation under Federal law. This plan, originally proposed by Mr. James B. Dill of the New York bar, has the approval of eminent corporation lawyers both in and out of Congress.[3] Such a law must needs be permissive, not mandatory; but it is urged that sufficient legal privileges and immunities could be offered, to induce large corporations to accept charters directly from the Federal government. The second of our remaining remedies is somewhat analogous. This is the recent proposition by Hon. James R. Garfield, Commissioner of Corporations in the newly organized United States Bureau of Corporations in his annual report for 1904. He suggests the granting of a Federal franchise or license for permission to engage in interstate commerce; prohibition of all such

[1] pp. 280 *et seq.* [2] *Vide* p. 274 *infra.*

[3] Consult especially the discussion and proposed bill of Professor H. L. Wilgus in the *Michigan Law Review*, Vol. II, 1904, at pp. 358 and 501. Also opinion of Counsel of the U. S. Industrial Commission, Vol. XIX, pp. 686–722.

commerce to unauthorized corporations; full protection of the grantees of such licenses; and the requirement of such administrative supervision and publicity as may be reasonable. This last provision immediately brings us to our third remaining proposition for remedial legislation, underlying in principle all the others, — publicity.

Reasonable publicity should constitute an important feature in any well-ordered scheme of legislation. Its importance has never been duly recognized in any of the drastic state anti-trust laws thus far. The aim in such laws has been to prevent the occurrence of monopoly by prohibiting it under severe penalties. But the difficulty in the application of such laws has always been to prove the existence of the monopoly. The laws have fallen short in this regard. They have aimed to perform a work of supererogation. For, proof being given, any conspiracy in restraint of trade could in large measure have been condemned under the established rules of the English Common Law. Publicity enters at this point to supply the deficiency in the remedy, as well as to render the growth of the evil more difficult in first instance. For a proper degree of publicity as to the conduct of large businesses will speedily reveal the existence of abnormal sources of income. It will protect the consuming public and individual rivals in this way; and at the same time it will afford some guarantee of security for the investing public against internal financial rottenness. The dishonest promoter, director or banking syndicate flourish only in the secret recesses of corporate finance. For these reasons the successful establishment of the United States Bureau of Corporations in 1903 marks a long step in advance. Much yet remains to be done. Information gathered by this bureau ought within reasonable limits to be open to the public, and especially to stockholders; instead of being as at present reserved to the administrative use of the President of the United States. And action looking to the same end should be taken also by the separate states.[1] The goal is certainly not yet reached; but no

[1] F. E. Horack, The Organization and Control of Industrial Corporations, gives a most elaborate *résumé* of the provisions for securing publicity in the different states of the United States.

one can doubt that a reasonable publicity and administrative supervision for railroads and great industrial monopolies, akin to that now applied to National Banks, will be realized in due time. No other single remedy for the evils of monopoly can hope to accomplish results of equal importance.

Three steps have already been taken in the path of reform. The Elkins amendments to prevent secret discrimination in freight rates, the law facilitating the progress of anti-trust suits in the Federal courts, and the establishment of the Bureau of Corporations have all been secured within two years. With a revised tariff and an amended Interstate Commerce Act in 1905 the present administration would justly have reason to be proud of its services to the nation.

WILLIAM Z. RIPLEY.

TRUSTS, POOLS AND CORPORATIONS

I

THE MICHIGAN SALT ASSOCIATION[1]

WITHIN the last half-century, the amazing comparative growth of capital as a factor in production; the combinations of workingmen arising from their forced association in manufacture according to modern methods, and the ensuing discontent — or rather, the frequent and increasingly emphatic expression of discontent — with their lot on the part of the workingmen, as combination has increased their sense of strength; the combinations of capitalists and the startling revelations of power afforded by such organizations as the Standard Oil Company and the coal syndicates of Pennsylvania, — all these things have lent to the study of combinations among either capitalists or workingmen, or of coöperative unions of the two, an especial interest. More frequently the subject has been studied with reference to workingmen, the advantages and disadvantages to them; but it seems no less desirable, from the standpoint of the economist at least, that combinations among capitalists, either for purposes of protection against unreasonable demands of workingmen or for their own interests as producers, should be studied; and that the investigation should cover the influence of such combinations on the consumers as well as upon the capitalists themselves.

The story of the Standard Oil Company has been told more than once, in words eloquent with the conviction of the danger threatening our government and civilization from the growth of such corporations. The consumers of anthracite coal throughout the United States during the past two years, have needed

[1] From the *Political Science Quarterly*, Vol. III, 1888, pp. 78–98.

no publicist to tell them that some powerful influence has been brought to bear upon the price of this product. Although far less in power than either of the combinations mentioned, the Michigan Salt Association, from the extent of its influence over the price of an article of food so common and so necessary as salt, as well as from the magnitude of its operations and its great and apparently increasing power, seems to be a fit subject for a study of this kind. The extent of the influence of the association may be noted, when we consider that Michigan produces more than 40 per cent of all the salt manufactured in the United States, and that, of the Michigan product, not far from 95 per cent will be sold by the association during the coming year. In short, speaking generally, the price of the salt consumed in all the Northern states west of Pennsylvania and New York, until we approach those bordering on the Pacific ocean, is the price set by the managers of this association. It is the purpose of this article to give a short sketch of the history of this combination of manufacturers, with that of others which preceded it; to describe its plan of organization and its work, and to estimate the influence which it has exerted and that which it can exert on the price of salt.

The early settlers of Michigan had learned from the Indians of the existence of many salt "licks," or springs, in different parts of the state, and it was thought even by them that there was an opportunity for the growth of a great industry in its manufacture. In 1838 Dr. Houghton, the state geologist, called the attention of the legislature to these facts, and suggested that an appropriation be made for the sinking of test wells. The time was propitious for such a request. The newly adopted constitution had declared: "Internal improvements shall be encouraged by the government of this state;" and the governor had been authorized by the ambitious first legislature to borrow on the credit of the state the sum of $5,000,000, to constitute an internal improvement fund.[1] From this fund $3000 were at once appropriated; the next year $15,000 more, and small sums in succeeding years. While salt was found, the wells were not sunk deep enough to yield brine in paying quantities.

[1] Cooley, Michigan, ch. xiv. [American Commonwealth Series.]

In 1859, an act was passed exempting from taxation all property used in the manufacture of salt and offering a bounty of ten cents per bushel on all salt made in the state. A corporation, the Saginaw Salt Manufacturing Company, was formed the same year in East Saginaw to put down a well and engage in the manufacture of salt. So little was known, even by the board of directors and officers of the company, regarding the character of the work, that it was necessary for a committee to visit the Onondaga salt works to learn what buildings, machinery, and tools were necessary for boring the well. But by February 7, 1860, the directors felt warranted in making a report to stockholders, declaring the work a success. In March the well was completed; another one was immediately put down; and manufacture began in July. The works were thrown open for inspection July 4. In this first year, 1860, about 4000 barrels of salt were manufactured.[1]

As soon as it became known that brine of paying quality and quantity was to be found in the valley, capital was rapidly invested. In 1862, 243,000 barrels were made, and in six years there were engaged in the manufacture of salt in the Saginaw valley, sixty-six different companies with an investment of nearly $2,000,000.

TABLE I

ANNUAL SALT PRODUCT OF MICHIGAN, 1860–1886

YEAR	BARRELS	YEAR	BARRELS
1860	4,000	1874	1,028,979
1861	125,000	1875	1,081,865
1862	243,000	1876	1,462,729
1863	466,356	1877	1,960,997
1864	529,073	1878	1,855,884
1865	477,200	1879	2,058,040
1866	407,077	1880	2,676,588
1867	474,721	1881	2,750,299
1868	555,690	1882	3,037,317
1869	560,818	1883	2,894,672
1870	621,350	1884	3,161,806
1871	728,175	1885	3,297,403
1872	724,481	1886	3,677,257
1873	823,346		

[1] Statistics relating to the Saline Interests of Michigan, by S. S. Garrigues, Ph.D., State Salt Inspector; Lansing, 1881.

This table shows, in the falling off of the yearly product, 1865–1867, the result of the rapid and in many instances ill-advised investment of capital. Under the conditions obtaining at the time, unrestricted competition soon drove the weaker companies to the wall. In those days, the extent of the salt-producing territory and the methods of manufacture were less well known, and the business was much more of a natural monopoly than now. Under these circumstances, the solution of the difficulty was evident: combination was indicated and combination soon appeared. In a statistical summary of the leading products of the Saginaw valley, published by *The Saginaw Daily Enterprise* in 1867, we read: "This interest [salt] is somewhat under a cloud at present through the evil influence of speculation and inconsiderate management." Then, farther down the page come, as one might expect, the words: "At least two-thirds of those [blocks] now running turn in their production to the Saginaw Salt Company." Thus, as early as 1866, six years only after the industry was started, we find that many of the manufacturers were uniting their interests so far as the sale of the product was concerned.

Soon, from individual agreements the leading firms came to something more stable and far-reaching in its influence. On the 16th of April, 1868, the articles of association of the Saginaw and Bay Salt Company were adopted. The first year of its existence, this association handled four-fifths of all the salt shipped from the Saginaw valley. Its benefits to the manufacturers, as well as to the consumers, — so far, at least, as the quality of salt is concerned, — were at once recognized, and are clearly set forth in the *Statistics of the Saginaw Valley* for 1868:

The operations of this company have been completely satisfactory, and the organization is unquestionably of great benefit to the salt manufacturers who have availed themselves of the advantages it offers. It has, so far as its line of operations has extended, brought about the one thing needful, a uniform system of inspection, and introduced system, order and reliability into a business, which, without such general regulations, has in no quarter ever proved remunerative.

In spite of the competition of New York and the Ohio river (relieved in part by an agreement with the Onondaga Salt Company which will be considered later), the business grew with remarkable rapidity, and the association ran smoothly till 1871, when the vigorous efforts of some of the members opposed to the management became of serious moment. The real merits of the controversy, which became bitterly personal, several letters of a violently abusive character being published, it is hard to determine. On the one side, charges of mismanagement, even of dishonest practices, were made against the officers of the association by Duncan Stewart, president of a salt manufacturing company; on the other, Stewart's dissatisfaction was said to have been caused by the refusal of the managers to ship salt by a line of boats in which he was interested, at rates above those offered them elsewhere. For our purpose it is enough to know the result. In the *Annual Statement* of the business of the Saginaw valley for 1871, we find it in compact form:

> In salt, the season of '71 may be quoted as of extra activity both in manufacture and sale. Early in the season it became evident that a commercial rivalry had been excited which could not end but by the going to the wall of one of the parties engaged in it. Assuming the shape of individual antagonism to a corporate company, it became at an early day evident that many of the manufacturers who are members of the Salt association, would take sides with the opponents of the association, and as a result fully one-fifth of the entire salt product of the valley, which under ordinary circumstances would have been handled by the association, was purchased by the firm of J. L. Hurd & Co., of Detroit, at prices in advance of those realized by those who remained in the association. Since the close of navigation, the association has resolved to suspend operations for the present, and each manufacturer will, during the season, be left free to realize as best he may on his products.

It is significant, and somewhat surprising to note that by the determined efforts of one man, the association was forced to suspend operations, even though, as has been reported, this man was compelled to destroy his own financial standing to bring about such a result. Table I, again, furnishes us with an interesting comment upon this financial battle. For 1872 the production of salt in the state is more than 3600 barrels less than that of the year preceding; whereas both 1871 and 1873 show a gain of about 100,000 barrels.

Five years passed before a thoroughly effective union could again be made. Smaller organizations were formed to sell salt for groups of manufacturers, notably the Saginaw Salt Association and the Michigan Salt Association; but the competition was fierce, prices went steadily down, and the weaker companies found themselves in need. At length, after low and declining prices throughout the year 1875, the time seemed ripe for another organization which could control the sale of a large proportion of the Michigan salt, and through this added power of union both secure a saving in the expenses of sale and transportation, and either compete more effectively with the New York and Ohio river manufacturers or force them into a union which should control the whole American product. January 8, 1876, J. E. Shaw, president of the Michigan Salt Association (a smaller combination of manufacturers), issued a circular address to the salt manufacturers of Michigan, calling a meeting to be held at Bay City, January 20, to effect such an organization, if it should be possible. The address exhibits in an almost pitiable light the situation of the manufacturers, and urges strongly the need of organization. Mr. Shaw declared:

The old adage, "in union there is strength," is true wherever you apply it, and in manufacture of salt there is no exception. To secure this *union* with its attendant *strength* is the object of the Michigan association. This is the object it had in view when it was organized, and this is the object it has in view to-day. That the organization has remained inactive, is attributable to the fact that it could not secure control of a sufficiently large *percentage* of the state product to warrant [aggressive action], a few manufacturers declining, for reasons best known to themselves, to enter the association. And what was the result? Salt has depreciated in value, dropped steadily down, until to-day it has no market price on the Saginaw river, and is quoted at only $1.27 in Chicago, and $1.00 in Toledo. That the experience of '75 will be that of each succeeding year, unless something is done to check the general demoralization, cannot be gainsaid. The oldest manufacturers of the Syracuse, Kanawha, and Ohio districts, tell us that their experience, dating back forty years in some cases, has *always* been this: "*Organized we have prospered. Unorganized we have not.*" This is the experience which we have been buying and paying dearly for. . . . The trouble lies in the *marketing* of the product. Each man has taken care of (or attempted to) his own product. . . . The other salt districts of the United States are now organized, and are ready to treat with us (as soon as we have an association) relative to fixing and maintaining prices, dividing the territory, and making other arrangements which will inure to the advantage of the trade. But we must first be organized. They cannot treat with individuals.

The appeal was successful. The meeting was held; others followed; and in April the Saginaw Salt Company and the Michigan Salt Association were consolidated and other outside firms were taken in, so that from the beginning more than 85 per cent of the product of the state was controlled. The new association took the name of The Michigan Salt Association.

When in 1881 the association expired by limitation, it was immediately reorganized under the name of The Salt Association of Michigan; and, in 1886, again expiring by limitation, it was again organized under its former name. The three associations have been, in fact, the same association under different names; the president and secretary elected in 1876 still hold their offices, and the business is conducted on the same principles, slight changes only having been made in the articles of association and by-laws.

The organization of the association, effective as it is, is very simple. Less than a page contains the articles of association, which declare that the purpose of the association is "the manufacture and dealing in salt," and the "transportation of its products to market"; that the amount of capital stock shall be $200,000, divided into $25 shares, of which the amount actually paid in is two dollars per share; that its affairs shall be managed by a board of nineteen directors (of whom not more than one shall be from the same firm or company of manufacturers) chosen by the stockholders; that the offices for transaction of business shall be in East Saginaw and Bay City, and that the business shall be carried on in the salt-manufacturing counties; and, finally, that the association shall exist as a corporation for the period of five years.

From the by-laws, we learn that the stockholders shall be manufacturers of salt, and that the number of shares taken by any one "shall not exceed one share of the capital stock for every barrel of the average daily capacity of his manufactory on a fair estimate" — an excellent provision to prevent manipulation of stock to the detriment of the real business.

An annual dividend of seven per cent payable semi-annually on the amount of stock actually paid in, together with the losses, costs and expenses incurred in handling and selling, including the state inspection fees, is deducted from the proceeds of sales before division is made.

That the business management of the association may be as personal and direct as possible, the president is given the general supervision of the entire business, subject to the general rules laid down by the board and the executive committee. A secretary and a treasurer with the usual duties of such officers are appointed by the board, and also an executive committee, which has general control and is charged with the duty of auditing all accounts, inspecting all books, etc., at least once a month. The officers receive a stipulated salary. The organization, it will be seen, is such that the executive efficiency of a single head is combined with all proper checks to guard against any abuse of trust on the part of any of the officers. The fact that the chief officers of the association have held their positions since its organization, and the continued prosperity of the association, never greater than now, reflect the greatest credit on the management as well as on the authors of the plan.

The relations of the association with the members, however, constitute the main point of interest. A contract is made *every year* with each manufacturer who wishes to become a member, in accordance with Article vii of the by-laws, which reads as follows:

Every manufacturer, in becoming a member of this association, shall execute and deliver to it a contract for all salt manufactured by him or them, or a lease of his salt-manufacturing property, including all apparatus and appurtenances thereunto belonging, for the purpose of manufacturing. Such contract or lease shall be for the term of one year, or until the dissolution of the association, and shall not impose any restriction that will prevent the manufacture of salt at any and all times.

Each and every contractor shall manufacture salt for this association on the terms and conditions as follows:

That he will make salt solely on the association's account, of the best quality of the kind manufactured by him, according to the conditions of his contract or lease.

The contracts provide, further, that in case the manufacturer sells salt on private account, he shall pay to the association ten cents for every barrel so sold; that the contract, however, is not thereby forfeited, but remains in force throughout the stipulated time.

While this gives full control of the product to the association, and effectually prevents all competition among the manufacturers, the provision that no restriction shall be imposed which will prevent the manufacture of salt at any and all times, operates powerfully against any raising of prices to exorbitant rates such as might perhaps be secured otherwise, if combination with the New York and Ohio river manufacturers could be effected. The reason that this clause stands in the by-laws, and that the practice of the association differs so entirely, on this point, from that of the anthracite coal syndicate and other combinations of like character, is found in the peculiarity of the manufacture. A great part of the larger salt blocks are run in connection with saw-mills; and the slabs, sawdust, etc., from the mills are used for barrels and fuel. Not only would this material, if not so used, be a dead loss, but its removal would be a source of expense. Manufacturers so situated could never expect a rise in the price of salt sufficient to compensate them for the loss that would be incurred in stopping their works; and consequently they will not join the association unless assured that they will not be subjected to such a loss and inconvenience in their more important business.

Another provision of great advantage, especially to the manufacturer of comparatively small capital, is that which provides for an advance of money on all the salt inspected each month, whether the salt is taken from the bins and sold or not, if the manufacturer wishes such advance and is willing to pay interest on it. The rate of advance and the rate of interest are fixed by the board and may be changed from time to time; but liberality is always shown both in the amount advanced and in the rate of interest. The advance has been lately 25 cents per barrel in the bins, or 45 cents per barrel if packed, with interest at 7 per cent. Money may be loaned in the state at 10 per cent, and this rate is often obtained on small sums for short periods of time.

The salt becomes the property of the association as soon as inspected; but the manufacturer is still bound to deliver it free of charge on the wharf or on the cars, as the association shall direct, and to sustain all losses by fire or otherwise, if they occur before such delivery. The association agrees on its part to remove within a reasonable time all the salt manufactured.

Reports are rendered every month to each member of the association, giving not merely his own special account, but all the sales, with the average price both gross and net, and all the necessary expenses with principal items — average freight, commission, home and storage charges, etc. All the members receive credit at the same average rate, and for an amount proportioned to their manufacture as shown by the inspection — a provision greatly to the advantage of the poorly situated companies. The receipts of salt for each month are sold and accounted for separately.

The association keeps its agents — most of them selling on commission, but some on salaries — in Chicago, St. Louis, Cincinnati, Cleveland, Columbus, Duluth, Detroit, Milwaukee and other places, wherever this is warranted by the amount taken.

It will perhaps be well, further, to notice some attempts that have been made, since the manufacture of salt in Michigan became a leading industry, to form combinations of all the leading manufacturers in the country, and thereby to secure from consumers a price limited only by the competition of foreign salt and the lessened demand consequent on the rise in price.

Not many months after the Saginaw and Bay association was formed (April, 1868), the managers began negotiations with the manufacturers in New York and in the Ohio river district. This first attempt, instead of resulting as had been hoped, led, from a rather peculiar combination of circumstances, to an even fiercer competition than had existed before.

The president of the association gives the facts in his report of 1870 to the board of directors. The association in Michigan succeeded in making terms with the Onondaga Salt Company, but failed with the Ohio river association, because the latter could not control the product of their district either as to quantity or price. Some new works at Pomeroy, it seemed, had refused to join the Ohio river association. The other manufacturers of that district, having sold *all their product* to the association *at a fixed price*, increased their output and flooded the market. As the association could not control the works at Pomeroy, there was a general cutting of prices in which, of course, Michigan and New York were compelled to join. As the eloquent writer puts it: "It was a Donnybrook Fair in the salt market. When you saw a head, you hit it." The immediate result was, naturally, detrimental to all the works. The final outcome was that the outsiders on the Ohio river joined the association, and a change in the character of the contract with the former members enabled that association to control the *quantity* as well as the price in that quarter. This being done, it became an easy matter to make the combination general. The Washington correspondent of *The Chicago Tribune* gave an account of the pool which is corroborated by other papers and by officers of the present Michigan association. The Syracuse, the Ohio, and the Saginaw and Bay companies entered into an agreement at Detroit, March 22, 1871,

> To make a pool of all the salt in the market in the territory bounded by the lakes on the North and East and by the Ohio river on the South, the western and southwestern boundary to be entirely discretionary, according to the prices of freights to places whence orders for this article might be sent. This discretion was confided in a board, there appointed, which consisted of one representative from each of the three salt corporations, who are also empowered to fill orders and forward all supplies, to advance or reduce prices as occasion may require. The percentage of the pool, and all future supplies and profits under existing arrangements, were agreed to as follows: Syracuse, 40 per cent; Ohio river, 32 per cent; Saginaw, 28 per cent.[1]

The prices fixed were $2.00 per barrel for Chicago, Cincinnati, Cleveland and Detroit; $2.10 for Toledo; and $2.40 for St. Louis.

[1] *The Chicago Tribune*, April 4, 1871.

Reference to Table II (see page 15) will show the effect of the "Donnybrook Fair" period, as well as the rise in price consequent on the pool in 1871. The Chicago prices of the first of January show the effects of both movements, as do also the average prices at Saginaw. Gold prices show a less decrease, but emphasize the rise in 1871–2. At the close of 1871, as we have seen, the Saginaw and Bay association, having lost control of a large proportion of the Michigan men, could not uphold their end of the bargain. As they were not bound, however, to take *at a fixed price* any large product, no such immediate cutting of prices followed as had been seen the year before.

A somewhat more firmly controlled pool was made ten years later to cover about the same territory. A special arrangement was made with the Ohio river manufacturers, the exact terms of which cannot be given; but they are of little consequence, since by far the larger part of the amount was sold by the other companies.

The territory covered was bounded on the east by a line drawn north and south through Buffalo, and on the south by the Ohio river, as before. The importance of the Michigan product, relatively speaking, is worthy of special notice. In 1871, as we have seen, Michigan put in 28 per cent; Ohio river, 32 per cent; and New York, 40 per cent. In 1881, Michigan put in $\frac{15}{17}$ and New York $\frac{2}{17}$, while some special arrangement regarding a small fixed number of barrels, or a fixed rate, was made with the Ohio company. The management of the pool, as before, was confided to a committee selected from both companies. The contract went into effect May 1, 1881, and was terminated March 1, 1882, a month's notice having been given by the Michigan association in accordance with the terms of the contract. The effect of the pool on prices is shown in Table III (page 16). The cause for the breaking of the pool, and the following sudden lowering of prices, is stated by the managers of the association to be simply that the markets, especially Chicago, had become overstocked with salt, and the Michigan association felt the need of having full control there. They broke the pool, and "slaughtered the market."

Though other combinations have been talked of at times, no other has been made.

Such, in brief, is the history and the plan of organization of The Michigan Salt Association. It remains to consider somewhat more fully its economic effects.

First, much credit must be given the association for the improvement of the quality of the salt manufactured in the state. The necessity for a rigid system of inspection to keep up the quality of the product and prevent injury to the reputation of Saginaw salt in the market, led the old Saginaw and Bay Salt association to appoint a committee in 1868 to draft a law meeting the wants of the salt manufacturers. As early as 1865 a system of local inspection had been adopted by a number of manufacturers,[1] but something more rigid was required; and this bill, which became a law in March, 1869, was the result. As amended in 1875, it remains to-day in the statute book, and to it is doubtless due in large measure the superior quality of the Michigan salt.

The inspector is appointed by the governor and senate, is paid a stated salary by the state, and is, of course, entirely independent of the manufacturers. The state is divided into as many districts as seem to him practicable for the thorough carrying-out of the work, and all salt made is carefully inspected, a deputy inspector visiting each block *every day* for this purpose. The early association deserves the credit of securing this effective law. Some manufacturers, it is true, attempt at times to evade the law and to pass off an inferior grade of salt for the best; but the larger manufacturers, and of course the Salt association, are interested in having the grade of salt kept up, and therefore assist the work of inspection as much as possible.

The question which next suggests itself — that of the influence of the association upon prices and profits — cannot be answered so briefly. In many of the markets it is clear that the association is really without competition as long as it keeps its prices reasonably low, or perhaps we had better say, only moderately high. The effective competition of New York — or even that of any Michigan manufacturers who are "running

[1] S. S. Garrigues, Saline Interests of Michigan, p. 32.

wild" — is practically out of the question. It must not be forgotten that the average cost of manufacture in Michigan is considerably less than in New York; and though westward-bound freights are low, they are still worthy of consideration. Of course no single manufacturer could escape competition to so great an extent, since his neighbors would be his strongest competitors. Again, by means of its thorough organization and the daily reports sent to the home office by agents in all important markets, the association is able to make sales not merely more advantageously as regards price, but also with a much less expense in the way of commissions, travel, number of agents, etc. Besides this, the freedom from care and responsibility and the certainty that the product is in hands that will make the most of it, is worth not a little to the average manufacturer. The last-named item alone, that of greater intelligence and knowledge of the market, should receive more consideration than the manufacturer usually gives it.

Another point of advantage is this: by means of its large sales and long experience, the association can reduce losses from bad debts to a lower figure than could individual manufacturers.

Further, when the sales are all made from a central point, with a right to deliver from any of the manufactories at will, it is clear that a large saving in transportation can be made. Contracts will be filled always from the works most favorably situated. Vessels and cars can be secured at such times and places as will enable them to carry at the lowest rates. The average rate of freight is thereby much lessened.

The plan of advancing a large part of the value of the salt to the manufacturer before the salt is sold, enables him to carry on his business with less capital than would be required if he were not a member of the association.

The first consideration, the abolition of competition, comes solely to the benefit of the manufacturer; the others mentioned are advantages from organization which lessen the cost of production, — including sales and transportation, — and may benefit either the manufacturer, through greater profits, or the consumer, through lower prices, or the benefit may be divided.

A study of prices before the formation of the association, and after, would seem to show that while the saving had chiefly benefited the manufacturer, as was to be expected, the consumer had not suffered seriously.

TABLE II

PRICE OF SALT PER BARREL IN SAGINAW AND CHICAGO

YEAR	SAGINAW	CHICAGO	YEAR	SAGINAW	CHICAGO
1860, January 1,		$1.50	1875, average,	$1.10	
1861, Jan. 1,		1.75 @ 2.00	1876, Jan. 1,		$1.35
1862, Jan. 1,		2.25	1876, average,	1.05	
1863, Jan. 1,		2.25	1877, Jan. 1,		1.40
1864, Jan. 1,		2.10 @ 2.15	1877, average,	.85	
1865, Jan. 1,		2.75	1878, Jan. 1,		1.10
1866, Jan. 1,		2.35 @ 2.40	1878, average,	.84	
1866, average,	$1.80		1879, Jan. 1,		1.10
1867, Jan. 1,		2.40 @ 2.45	1879, average,	1.02	
1867, average,	1.77		1880, Jan. 1,		1.45
1868, Jan. 1,		3.25	1880, average,	.75	
1868, average,	1.85		1881, Jan. 1,		1.05
1869, Jan. 1,		2.60	1881, average,	.83⅔	
1869, average,	1.58		1882, Jan. 1,		1.35
1870, Jan. 1,		2.25 @ 2.30	1882, average,	.70	
1870, average,	1.32		1883, Jan. 1,		1.00
1871, Jan. 1,		2.05 @ 2.10	1883, average,	.81	
1871, average,	1.46		1884, Jan. 1,		1.15
1872, Jan. 1,		2.35 @ 2.40	1884, average,	.75⅔	
1872, average,	1.46		1885, Jan. 1,		.95
1873, Jan. 1,		2.40	1885, average,	.70	
1873, average,	1.37		1886, Jan. 1,		.95
1874, Jan. 1,		1.90	1886, average,	.66	
1874, average,	1.19		1887, Jan. 1,		.80
1875, Jan. 1,		1.65	1887, average,	.57½	

Table II shows that, while the prices have on the whole tended downward since 1876, the time of the formation of the association, the rate of decrease has been somewhat less rapid. On the other hand it must be noted that the prices in the earlier years are reckoned in legal tender notes. This causes the prices during the sixties, and the rate of decrease during the years preceding resumption, to appear greater than they really were, though a slight check in the rate of decrease can be seen even when prices are reckoned in gold. The influence of the war, too, in pushing the price to what was really an abnormal height, must not be overlooked. The improved methods of manufacture would naturally cause a lowering of price, and it is impossible to accurately judge the influence of all the factors. The earlier prices, of course, were not determined to any marked extent by the Michigan product, as the manufacture in the state began in 1860, and was not really on an even footing with New York for several years. It seems probable, however, that the association checked somewhat the tendency toward a lower price, and, if so, the consumer is so much the worse off. This difference in price cannot on the whole have been much, the chief advantage to the manufacturer coming, probably, from the lessened cost of putting his product on the market.

It is, again, quite probable that without the association, the larger dealers would take part of the profit which now goes to the manufacturer, and that the consumer would be forced to pay as much as now, and even more. Certain it is that large dealers in Chicago, Toledo, Cleveland and Sandusky express themselves generally as opposed to any association, even when they have been appointed agents. At present they receive a low commission per barrel of salt sold; whereas, before the formation of the association, they could buy salt in the summer months when it was very plentiful, and store it till after the close of navigation, and then the few larger dealers in such an important market as Chicago, by uniting, could advance the price enough to reap a handsome profit. This practice, which was common, came to the benefit of the few dealers, while neither the manufacturer nor the consumer received any share.

TABLE III

ASSOCIATION PRICE OF SALT EACH MONTH, FROM JUNE, 1877, TO NOVEMBER, 1887[1]

June 1877	$0.80¼	Feb. 1878	.70	Oct. 1878	.70
July "	.79	March "	.71	Nov. "	.70
Aug. "	.72½	April "	.76	Dec. "	.70
Sept. "	.74½	May "	.75	Jan. 1879	.72
Oct. "	.74	June "	.77	Feb. "	.80
Nov. "	.75	July "	.77	March "	.83
Dec. "	.80	Aug. "	.76	April "	.82
Jan. 1878	.73	Sept. "	.70	May "	.80

[1] Prices given are for the sales of the preceding month.

TABLE III — *Continued*

June 1879	.80	April 1882	.71	Feb. 1885	.69
July "	.86	May "	.72	March "	.68
Aug. "	.88	June "	.70	April "	.66
Sept. "	.90	July "	.70	May "	.63
Oct. "	.94	Aug. "	.70	June "	.62
Nov. "	1.02	Sept. "	.69	July "	.60
Dec. "	1.05	Oct. "	.69	Aug. "	.60
Jan. 1880	1.05	Nov. "	.69	Sept. "	.65
Feb. "	1.08	Dec. "	.70	Oct. "	.70
March "	1.09	Jan. 1883	.70	Nov. "	.72
April "	1.05	Feb. "	.70	Dec. "	.73
May "	.85	March "	.70	Jan. 1886	.71
June "	.72	April "	.70	Feb. "	.72
July "	.72	May "	.75	March "	.71
Aug. "	.72	June "	.80	April "	.70
Sept. "	.72	July "	.80	May "	.69
Oct. "	.72	Aug. "	.80	June "	.68
Nov. "	.72	Sept. "	.80	July "	.66
Dec. "	.72	Oct. "	.81	Aug. "	.65
Jan. 1881	.74	Nov. "	.83	Sept. "	.65
Feb. "	.77	Dec. "	.83	Oct. "	.63
March "	.77	Jan. 1884	.83	Nov. "	.60
April "	.76	Feb. "	.83	Dec. "	.60
May "	.76	March "	.83	Jan. 1887	.60
June "	.76½	April "	.83	Feb. "	.60
July "	.81½	May "	.80	March "	.57
Aug. "	.88⅓	June "	.74	April "	.55
Sept. "	.92½	July "	.72	May "	.55
Oct. "	.94	Aug. "	.71	June "	.53
Nov. "	.95	Sept. "	.70	July "	.51
Dec. "	.95	Oct. "	.70	Aug. "	.57
Jan. 1882	.94	Nov. "	.70	Sept. "	.58
Feb. "	.99	Dec. "	.69	Oct. "	.60
March "	.99	Jan. 1885	.68	Nov. "	.62

Table III, giving the average monthly prices of the association (the net prices paid to manufacturers), shows, on the whole, a decline; but one not so great after all, when one considers the general tendency of prices of all manufactured products. Moreover, there are several times when the price has gone up enough to counterbalance in great part the decline.

Besides the statements of reliable manufacturers regarding their profits, a comparison of the table of prices with the table showing the amount produced in different years in Michigan gives us still further reason for the belief that the association cannot secure prices which make the profits at all extraordinary. A distinctly marked rate of increase (not absolute increase) or falling off in production usually follows, especially in later years, like changes in the average yearly price. One should not lay too much stress, however, upon such similarities, as there are many other determining factors.

Many of the advantages to manufacturers of such an association, especially the freedom from competition with one's neighbors, cannot be secured unless a very large proportion of the manufacturers of the state are united. The association aims, of course, to have as many join as possible; and in case of necessity it does not hesitate to "squeeze" a manufacturer whose block is so situated that he has no need of the association, and whose competition is troublesome. This brings to our notice the disadvantage it might be to some manufacturers to become members. As the prices, freight charges, etc., are arranged for the whole association, the manufacturer who has a ready market near at hand could oftentimes realize somewhat more by remaining outside.

In the year 1886, about 600,000 barrels of Michigan salt were sold by outsiders. The amount was large enough to make a real competition that could be severely felt by the association. At length, the managers issued the order to their agents to meet any rates, however low they might run. Table III shows the gradual decrease, as the fight went on. In August, 1887, the unprecedentedly low price of 50 cents per barrel was reached. In the same month manufacturers representing some 350,000 to 400,000 barrels, yearly product, joined the association; and we note the consequence in the rise of price to 57 cents for that month's product, while the prices for the following three months (58, 60, and 62 cents) still show the upward tendency.

It has been impossible to obtain with any degree of accuracy the data which would indicate the influence of the competition within the state; namely, the times of the accession of different manufacturers to the association and of their withdrawal from it. As the contracts are made yearly, some enter the association and others leave it every year. In one or two instances, however, the effect of such changes is marked. Reference to Table III shows, in 1880, a sudden decline in price from $1.09 to 72 cents within three months. This is probably to be explained by the fact that "a large number of the manufacturers went out March 1, and that they commenced cutting prices, and we [the association] concluded to more than meet them." [1] The sudden drop in prices in the early part of 1882 followed the breaking of the pool with New York. The rise in August, 1887, is due, as noted above, to the accession of a number of manufacturers. It should rather be called the setting back of the price toward that obtained before the cutting to force the manufacturers in. Doubtless, too, many of the other changes noticed are to be ascribed to the same causes.

When a barrel containing 280 lbs. of fine salt of the first quality can be bought in the Chicago market at a price ranging from 75 to 85 cents, there is not likely to be very much complaint on the part of consumers, nor much talk about "monopolies," "coalitions for robbing the people," etc.; and yet the Michigan Salt Association is sometimes attacked as a monopoly, and it doubtless has some of the features of one. Adolph Wagner is strongly inclined to recommend the manufacture of salt by the state, on account of the danger of so common an article of consumption being monopolized by the manufacturers and dealers.[2] The advisability of state control seems to him, on the whole, greater than in the case of the coal industry. Our experience with anthracite coal companies within the past few years has been such that we may well note the circumstances of our salt industry in this regard. Is it likely or even possible that a really oppressive monopoly in this article can be made?

The salt-producing territory of the United States, while widespread, is nevertheless so limited that competition in manufacture is by no means so free as in other lines where the raw material may be shipped in at low rates; *e.g.* cotton, or shoes. This makes it much easier for two or three combinations to unite

[1] Letter from the secretary of the association.

[2] Wagner, Finanzwissenschaft, Bd. I, §§ 251, 254.

and control the whole product; and we have seen that in two instances, at least, for short times, such a union was made to control "disputed territory"—an expression, by the way, which in itself emphasizes the limited nature of the competition.

The coal and petroleum industries have been able to secure complete control by the aid of the railways. Aside from the fact that the capital invested in salt is much smaller, it would be much more difficult for the associations to control the means of transportation. The territory is more widely scattered, and is, besides, much of it adjacent to the great lakes. Such a control as the coal syndicates exercise, would require a controlling influence over all the larger railways east of the Mississippi, and over the boats on lakes Huron, Michigan and Erie, as well.

A further matter to be noted is the large import of salt. In 1880 some 38 per cent of all the salt used in the United States came from abroad. Though part of this is of a different quality and does not enter into competition with the American product, yet a large part of the sea-board traffic in salt, and the larger part of the salt used in the South, is controlled by the importers. The salt is brought as ballast, so that the cost of transportation to our coast is practically nothing. It is the cost of transportation from the sea-board that keeps it out of the territory now controlled by the Michigan association. It may be readily seen that our protective tariff on salt would need to be far higher than at present, before our manufacturers, even if all in the United States were united, could command prices comparable, when considered with reference to the cost of production, to those obtained on anthracite coal. The character of the combinations, too, would need to be much stricter.

Without such combinations, considering the Michigan association as it is, the New York competition is enough to keep the price from becoming exorbitant. Add to this the above-mentioned fact that the association has no power to limit production, and the fact that new wells are being sunk continually, whose owners can be forced to join the association, if inclined to remain outside, only by a tedious and expensive fight on prices, and the dangers to consumers from the association seem slight. Doubtless, the manufacturers who have been in effect forced into it, and who feel that without an association in the state more profit could be made, are inclined to think that such a combination is oppressive. These manufacturers, however, form but a small proportion of those in the state.

The conclusion to which one must come, then, regarding the influence of the association is this: it is probable that the average consumer is but slightly affected, though it is possible that he has to pay a little more for his salt than would otherwise be the case; it is certain that, with the exception of a few who are uncommonly well situated, the manufacturers are decidedly benefited by the association. Certain it is that most of them are well content, and that the association never stood firmer than it does to-day.

J. W. JENKS.

The subsequent history of combination in this industry has been unfortunate. The National Salt Company was organized in New Jersey in 1899, acquiring the business of a company of the same name chartered by West Virginia. Most of its properties were in New York, but the company purchased the best plants in Ohio and Michigan, claiming in 1900 to include 94 per cent of the evaporated salt of the entire country excepting the Pacific coast. In 1900 plans for controlling salt works in Spain and Italy were inaugurated.

The next step was the formation of a New Jersey company in 1901, known as the International Salt Company, which absorbed the National by interchange of securities. This operation was financially tainted by the enormous compensation, amounting to about one-third of the stock of the new company, issued to the promoters. By 1902 also it became clear that the National Salt Company, which had been paying dividends at 8 per cent on the common stock, was practically insolvent, not even having earned interest on its bonds. It was officially stated that this embarrassment was due more to extravagant purchases of plants than to losses in operation. Meanwhile disorganization and losses of property under receivership has greatly reduced the proportion of the entire industry controlled. In so far as the possession of natural salt deposits constitutes a basis for monopoly, a foundation for successful combination would seem to be present; but failure has evidently resulted hitherto from a combination of extravagance, mismanagement and perhaps even downright fraud. — ED.

II

THE DEVELOPMENT OF THE WHISKEY TRUST[1]

It is probably too soon to tell with even a reasonable degree of certainty what the outcome of the present tendency towards combination among producers is to be. So far there have been not a few egregious failures, the most noteworthy being the collapse of the copper syndicate — though that was hardly a trust, technically speaking; but there have been also a few apparently noteworthy successes. It seems clear, at any rate, that we have still some time to wait before we can say what the resulting normal is to be; and in the meantime it seems best not to be too hasty in exterminatory legislation, in sweeping denunciation nor in unqualified praise, but to study as accurately as is possible the history, management and tendency of the individual organizations, that when the time for action comes we may act with knowledge. The present article is an attempt to describe, as accurately and fully as the information that can be secured will permit, one of the (apparently, at least) most successful of these organizations: "The Whiskey Trust"; more accurately: "The Distillers' and Cattle-Feeders' Trust." The significance and tendency of such an organization as this cannot be understood without a knowledge of the circumstances leading to its formation. In this case, interest is added by the fact that legislation by the United States and by some European nations is, doubtless, indirectly responsible in good part for the condition of business that led to the formation of the trust.

It is well known that, from the establishment of our government till the outbreak of the Civil war, distilled spirits were for the most part comparatively free from taxation by the United States. The tax levied by the recommendation of Alexander

[1] Abridged from the *Political Science Quarterly*, Vol. IV, 1889, pp. 296–319.

Hamilton, which led to the Whiskey insurrection in Western Pennsylvania, was comparatively very light (only 9 to 11 cents per proof gallon, as compared with 90 cents at present), and even this was repealed soon after the accession of Jefferson to the presidency. From that time, with the exception of four years (from 1813, when an increase of revenue was necessary to carry on the war, till 1817), spirits were free until the outbreak of the Rebellion. As a consequence, they were sold at a very low price, — 24 cents on the average in New York for the five years preceding 1862, with a minimum price of 14 cents per proof gallon, — and there was little temptation to overproduction for either the home or foreign market.

At the outbreak of the Rebellion the necessity for increased revenue that led to the imposition of internal taxes wherever it was thought that a revenue could be raised, "without much regard to acknowledged politico-economic laws or precedents,"[1] resulted, of course very properly, in the taxation of distilled spirits. The first tax of 20 cents a proof gallon (July 1, 1862) was followed, March 7, 1864, by an act raising the tax to 60 cents per gallon. July 1 of the same year the rate went to $1.50; and January 1, 1865, to $2.00 per gallon.

At each increase of the tax, considerable time intervened before the highest rate was imposed. As a natural consequence, distilleries were run to their utmost capacity, and even new distilleries were built to get a stock on hand.[2] As Mr. H. B. Miller, the president of the whiskey pools, writes:

> Some time intervened before the various amounts were collected, and during this time the distiller and speculator had nearly the whole benefit of the tax without paying it. The speculation in whiskey during this time was tremendous. Editors, ministers, statesmen, — all took a hand. Distilleries were erected all over the country, and at the end of the war there was three times the capacity that could be utilized.

[1] Reports of United States Revenue Commission, 1865–66, p. 2.

[2] *Ibid.* p. 6: "Thus, for example, the commission estimate that on the 1st of July, 1864, the date when the advance in the tax on distilled spirits of from 60 cents to $1.50 per gallon took effect, there *were made and stored*, in anticipation of this advance, at least forty millions of gallons, or a quantity sufficient to supply the wants of the country for at least a year in advance."

To the same effect David A. Wells, in the article on "Distilled Spirits" in Lalor's *Cyclopedia of Political Science*, writes:

> The immediate effect of the enactment of the first three and successive rates of excise was to cause an almost entire suspension of the business of distilling, which was resumed again with great activity as soon as an advance in the rate of tax in each instance became probable. The stock of whiskey and high wines accumulated in the country under this course of procedure was without precedent; and Congress, by its refusal to make the advance in taxation, in any instance, retroactive, virtually legislated for the benefit of distillers and speculators rather than for the treasury and the government. The profits realized by the holders of stocks, thus made in anticipation of the advance in taxation, has probably no parallel in the history of any similar speculation or commercial transactions in this country, and cannot be estimated at less than $50,000,000.

When the period of speculation was over, the great amount of surplus capacity for manufacture and the large amounts of stored products on hand made it, of course, almost or quite impossible for distillers who did not practise frauds on the revenue to continue in business. The high taxes, however, led to such frauds that whiskey often sold in the market for less than the amount of the tax.

Another factor that contributed to the general depression was the lessened demand for alcohol for use in the arts and manufacture. With alcohol at 30 or 40 cents a gallon, it was used in large quantities for the manufacture of burning fluid, varnishes, furniture polish, perfumeries, patent medicines, even as fuel for cooking, etc.; the United States revenue commission estimating that in 1860 not less than 25,000,000 gallons of proof spirits were so used. When the tax was $1.50 and $2.00, or even 50 cents, as it was from 1868 to 1872, spirits, of course, became too expensive for such purposes. As the tax has been still higher since that date (70 cents till 1875, and 90 cents since that time), no increased demand for such purposes has been felt.

These causes, including the large amounts fraudulently manufactured in the earlier years of the high taxes, had tended to keep the distilling business in a comparatively depressed condition after the speculative period following the war had passed. Even as early as 1870 or 1871 the distillers felt themselves compelled to enter into an agreement to limit their distilleries to two-fifths production; and all north of the Ohio, with two or three exceptions, made such an agreement. No very decisive effect, however, was produced by this arrangement. The facilities for manufacturing adapted themselves gradually to the demand; and, on account of our cheap grain, a fair export trade was growing up that relieved the situation somewhat. But in the years from 1878 to 1882, on account of successive crop failures in Europe, a very heavy export demand at paying prices sprang up. In 1879, 1880, and 1881, nearly 16,000,000 gallons a year were exported.

TABLE I

SPIRITS REMOVED IN BOND FOR EXPORT[1]

Year	Taxable (proof) gallons exported	Percentage of production	Year	Taxable (proof) gallons exported	Percentage of production
1873 . . .	2,358,630	3.45+	1881 . . .	15,921,482	13.52+
1874 . . .	4,060,160	5.90+	1882 . . .	8,092,725	7.64+
1875 . . .	587,413	0.96+	1883 . . .	5,326,427	7.19+
1876 . . .	1,308,900	2.25+	1884 . . .	9,586,738	12.70+
1877 . . .	2,529,528	4.22+	1885 . . .	10,671,118	14.24+
1878 . . .	5,499,252	9.80+	1886 . . .	5,646,656	7.02+
1879 . . .	14,837,581	20.63+	1887 . . .	2,223,913	2.85+
1880 . . .	16,765,666	18.55+	1888 . . .	1,514,205	2.15+

To meet this demand many new distilleries, including some of the largest in the country, were built, while the old ones, of course, were run at full capacity. After 1880, good crops in Europe, poor crops at home, with some changes in the tariff laws[2] of leading European countries, especially discriminating duties against the United States, cut off this demand, and left

[1] Report of the Commissioner of Internal Revenue, 1888.

[2] René Stourm, L'Impot sur l'alcool dans les principaux pays, p. 48.

the distilleries of this country with a capacity sufficient to produce four times what the home market needed.[1]

Of course, there was, at first, great over-production, and consequent distress among distillers. They could not export except at a loss; their cattle were in the barns (the feeding of cattle on the slop from the distilleries is one important adjunct to the distilling business), so that it was difficult to close the distilleries; their warehouses were filled with goods, and the market was broken. Something must be done.

> Some said: Let this go on and let the fittest survive. Our experience was that a distiller would keep on until all his own money and all he could borrow was gone, and when he was used up there was another man ready to step in his shoes.[2]

In November, 1881, a general meeting was called to form a pool. Prices were really below the cost of manufacture in many places, and the only remedy seemed to be to limit the output, and to export the surplus, even at losing prices. The "Western Export Association" was formed, the officers of which were authorized to levy a monthly assessment on each distiller running his distillery. This assessment was to be proportionate to the amount of grain used in manufacture, and high enough to pay the losses arising from the exportation of a quantity of spirits sufficient to relieve the home market.

An appeal was made to Congress, asking that an export bounty be given equal to that granted by Germany; or, if a bounty for export should not be given for fear of lessening the revenue, that the internal revenue tax be raised to $1.00 and then a bounty of 10 cents for export be granted. Congress and

[1] In the references to the trade, especially the exports, all the manufacturers of whiskey have so far been considered. As the whiskey pools have mostly concerned only one branch of the business, and as the trust is limited to this branch, *i.e.* the manufacturers of a product for immediate use, it is worth while to call attention to the distinction. One class of producers, especially those in Kentucky, manufacture "Kentucky whiskey," technically so called, *i.e.* a product that needs to be stored for some time (from two to five or more years) before it is in good condition for use (J. M. Atherton: Testimony before Committee on Manufacture, p. 3); the other class of distillers, located mostly north of the Ohio river, manufacture alcohol, pure neutral or cologne spirits, etc., a product that is fit for immediate use.

[2] Letter from H. B. Miller, former president of the pool.

the people, however, had not forgotten the whiskey-ring scandal, and consequently Congress did not dare legislate in favor of distillers, even if such legislation should injure no one.

This first pool lasted till May, 1882; then, some members refusing to pay their assessments, it broke up. The distillers had been able to keep prices somewhat higher by its means; but after the breaking of the pool, they ran at low profits, many of them at a loss, or else shut down during the summer — a proceeding which in itself involved of course a decided loss. In September, 1882, they organized again for one year on a similar plan; but it was found necessary to make an attempt to limit the output of the distilleries to a small percentage of their capacity, in addition to the relief of the market by exporting.

It soon became evident that it was cheaper to limit production by paying some distilleries to suspend production entirely, permitting the others to work at more nearly their full capacity, than to limit all to a fixed percentage of their normal production.

Though the Kentucky product is of a different kind from that manufactured by members of the pool, it of course came into competition with the latter when it had aged enough to be put upon the market. The law allowing distillers to keep their product in bond for three years before paying the tax had led to a heavy overstocking in Kentucky, and when this stored product first began to come upon the market, the situation became still more trying.

From 1883 till 1887 the pool continued for a year at a time, with a suspension as often as once each year. Sometimes the better plan seemed to be to limit the output of the distilleries, leaving each distiller to attend to the marketing of the product himself; sometimes for the officers of the pool themselves to provide for the export of any surplus, assessing the individual distillers the amount required to pay any loss on the export. In the articles of organization of the pool of 1884, we read:

> Only 28 per cent of the full capacity shall be operated, and no stocking up beyond this amount allowed under any circumstances. Any member operating his house and producing any kind of distilled spirits

must take care of them himself. The association is debarred from paying any member for maintaining any market, exporting goods, or warehouseing them.

In spite of the small percentage of capacity run during this year, the pool suspended in the spring of 1885, though it reorganized again in October of the same year. At the organization of this pool (in 1885) a committee reported:

It is the sense of this committee that no distillery shall be allowed to run beyond 40 per cent. The basis for market price should be fixed at the lowest possible figure, it being recognized by all that high prices are detrimental and difficult to maintain.

Section 12 of their articles of agreement, differing from those of the preceding year, provides for exportation as follows:

To maintain prices at all times, the officers shall cause to be exported at any time without the United States any surplus that may at any time appear, allowing and paying therefor [such] a bonus as will equal the quotation prices, and [shall] report all such exports, the quantity shipped, the bonus paid, etc.

Section 13 further provided that the president should cause a suspension of the association for the following causes:

If a distiller runs more than he is entitled to run; if a distiller refuses to exhibit his government book to an authorized agent; if a distiller refuses or neglects to make his monthly report or refuses to accept his draft or pay his monthly assessments; if a distiller resumes his capacity and operates his distillery having once sold it; in case exported goods are re-imported and placed upon the domestic market; in case closed houses are not paid in full, and in one payment, for each month, before the close of said month.

A resolution was also passed providing that the association be suspended when any new distillery should be built and start to run. Provisions were also made for the examination of the government books of each distiller by the officers of the pool, in order to prevent deception and cutting of rates on the part of any distiller; but in spite of these precautions, and in spite of the high prices they were able to maintain for their goods in the pool, it was found that the temptations to secure sales by the cutting of prices were so great that members would violate the terms of the agreement. Within two months after its formation, in calling a meeting of the distillers whose houses were running, in order to determine the amount of assessments, prices of goods, etc., the president of the pool expresses clearly the state of the trade. It should be remembered, in considering his words, that they were written not to influence legislation or public opinion, but that they were addressed to men directly concerned, who knew the circumstances. Among other things, he says with reference to over-production and the proper policy of the pool:

That we shall over-produce after the holidays we all know — we knew it when we organized in Chicago and for that very reason made the assessment 12 cents on 40 per cent to create an export fund.[1] That we have already over-produced, figures will show. . . . A few more days running without a pool would have wound you up, and this over-production we are not trying to get rid of by exportation. You want to look these figures square in the face; and if it takes more money to do our exporting than you thought, it is occasioned by your own folly in over-producing so heavily in September and October. As long as we have funds to export the surplus there will be no difficulty in maintaining prices. When goods accumulate without any outlet, then is the time when cutting commences. . . . It will not do to make the price of goods too high, for as we raise the price we must raise the bonus on exports correspondingly. . . . There are but two things left for us to do; either provide sufficient means to keep our warehouses clear of the surplus by exportation, or let the market go to pieces of its own weight. I am well convinced there is cutting going on secretly now, and unless provision is made at once to arrest it, it will be done openly, until there is nothing left of the market. Situated as we are, the question is no longer as to making a great amount of money, but to prevent our suffering great losses. This is the problem for you to solve, and the meeting is called thus early as an imperative necessity, and all running houses should be present. Distillers, when they have an accumulation of goods on hand, will not hesitate to cut prices *one cent* a gallon to make a sale, when they will hesitate to pay one-half cent a gallon to make cutting *unnecessary*, even if double the amount is placed in their hands. Right

[1] That is to say, 12 cents for each bushel of capacity run, when the houses were running at 40 per cent of their full capacity. The capacity of a distillery is measured by the number of bushels of grain consumed per day.

here I will repeat what I have so often stated before, that the amount of the assessment does not come out of the distiller, but out of the consumer, the same as the government tax, and he [the distiller] is merely the agent to collect and pay it over, of course with the qualification that prices are maintained.

He closes a series of statistics (regarding the output in competing states) with the words:

I have been particular in giving you all the information possible, so you can act intelligently at the next meeting. The only way to maintain prices is to get rid of the surplus by exportation. You can fly in the face of Providence if you see fit, but it will bring its own punishment with it.

TABLE II

POOL ASSESSMENTS, SEPTEMBER, 1884, TO APRIL, 1887, INCLUSIVE

	1884 Cents per bushel mashed	1885 Cents per bushel mashed	1886 Cents per bushel mashed	1887 Cents per gallon
January		8	16	3
February		8	9	3
March		8	10	4
April		8	10 (Extra assessment for 1 day: 35 cents.)	4
May		7	10	
June		9	8	
July		9	4	
August		9	6	
September[1]	6		per bush. 2; per gal. 2	
October	6		per gal. 3	
November	8	12	" 3	
December	8	12 (Also extra assessment for 1 day: $1.50 per bushel.)	" 3	

[1] Assessment for September, 1886, was 2 cents per gallon produced (equal to 9 cents per bushel), and also an assessment of 2 cents per bushel; making a total of 11 cents per bushel. By multiplying the assessment per gallon by 4½, the amount per bushel will be obtained nearly. About 4½ gallons of spirits are made per bushel corn.

A pool seemed a necessity; but the experience of this and of the following year seemed to show that a pool could not be maintained. The competition, there can be no doubt, was for many ruinous, though those best situated could live and make profits. The difficulty in maintaining the pool, together with the effect of the pool on prices, may be seen in the fluctuating figures of Table III (page 37). The same movements are illustrated graphically in the Diagram (pages 42, 43), and there the changes may be more readily noted. Table II shows the extent of the assessments from September, 1884, to the time of the formation of the trust. It has not been possible to obtain the earlier assessments.

In consequence of the competition, and in order that a closer organization might be established, it was determined by the leading distillers, in the spring of 1887, to organize a trust, formed upon the model of the Standard Oil Trust. The "trust agreement," published in the examination of the president of the trust before the congressional committee in 1888, provides that the trust created shall be vested in nine trustees; that these trustees, under bonds of $100,000 each, shall, in accordance with section 11:

. . . exercise supervision, so far as their ownership of stocks enables them to do, over the several corporations or associations whose stock is held by said trustees. As stockholders of said corporations they shall elect or endeavor to elect honest and competent men as directors and officers thereof, who shall be paid a reasonable compensation for their services. They may elect themselves as such directors and officers, and shall endeavor to secure such judicious and efficient management of such corporations as shall be most conducive to the interests of the holders of trust certificates.

No distillery was to be allowed to join this trust except the members of the former pool; but any member of the former pool, if a corporation, might join upon the assignment of a majority of stock by the individual stockholders to these trustees. For the stock thus assigned, the trustees prepared stock certificates, which showed the interests of each beneficiary in said trust. The certificates were divided into shares of the par value of $100 each, and were known as the "Distillers' and Cattle-feeders' Trust certificates." Any distillery not owned by a corporation might be re-organized in corporate form in order, by the aforesaid assignment of stock, to join the trust. In accordance with section 4 of the trust agreement, no certificates could be issued except for stock, and the par value of the certificates issued were to represent as nearly as possible the actual cash value of the stock held by the trustees in trust. In estimating the value of the plants owned by the different corporations, the following elements were considered: (1) the cost of the construction of the plant; (2) the amount of working capital required for its management, and (3) its earning power. This last element, of course, depends upon various factors, and of necessity was left largely to the judgment of the committee appointed. The location of the distillery, the skill of its former managers, their ability to secure a sale for their product, and other factors would all need to be considered. Furthermore, the earning capacity of the distillery under the management of the trustees, if it should be allowed to run, might vary quite materially from its former earning power. These different considerations led the committee to issue certificates for from two to three times the cash value of the plants. This has led some of the critics to state that the trust certificates were about two-thirds water. A careful consideration of the factors involved will enable the reader to judge how far this is true.[1] That jealousy among the different corporations might be avoided, the value placed upon the stock of each corporation was not made known except to the corporation immediately interested and to the trustees.

The trust was to continue for twenty-five years from the date of its organization, and thereafter until terminated by a vote of sixty-six and two-thirds per cent in value of the holders of certificates, at a meeting called for that purpose.

At the first annual election three trustees were to be elected to hold their office for one year; three to hold their office for two years, and three for three years. Thereafter three trustees were to be elected annually to take the place of those retiring, each to hold his office for three years, except in case of those

[1] See Testimony of J. B. Greenhut before Committee of Manufactures, pp. 73 *et seq.*

elected to fill a vacancy, who should hold until the expiration of the term. A person to hold the office of trustee must be the actual owner of at least 500 shares of trust certificates.

The meetings of the certificate holders take place annually, and may be called oftener at the request of thirty-three and one-third per cent of value of the trust certificates.

It is to be noted that this trust agreement expressly provides that the trustees are not limited in their duties, as has been often suggested, to the receipt of dividends or interests upon the stocks or moneys held in trust, and to the division of such dividends to the holders of trust certificates; but they are also to elect competent men as directors and officers of said corporations represented, and are to exercise supervision over the several corporations whose stock is held by them as trustees. Furthermore, it is to be noted that these trustees in every case hold a majority of the stock in each corporation, so that their control over each distillery is absolute. A manager is appointed by the trustees for each distillery, whose salary is paid out of the trust funds. This manager is, of course, usually one of the leading original stockholders and managers in that distillery.

In order that the business may be kept well in hand, reports are required daily from each distillery engaged in manufacture; and each distillery that is running sends in a detailed report every month, showing the exact cost of manufacture of the product and all other details regarding the management of the business. Again, by these monthly reports the trustees are able, if they wish to lessen or to increase the amount produced, to close the distilleries that are working least successfully or to open those that furnish the best opportunity to supply any special market. The trustees are also at liberty to purchase distilleries that are running outside of the trust, and to lease distilleries managed by the trust, whenever in their opinion this plan seems more profitable than to operate them by trust officers. In the latter case, of course, the profits are still held under the control of the trust.

This firm control over the different distilleries enables the trustees to control the market by limiting the output of the product to the amount demanded rather than by exporting the surplus at a loss, as was done under the old pools. Almost no attempt has been made by the trust to gain control of the foreign market, and none of the product has been exported at a loss since the formation of the trust. Their comparatively small exports (see Table I, page 25) have been at paying prices. A brief examination of Table II (page 30), which gives the monthly assessments levied upon the members of the old pool (from 6 cents to 18 cents per bushel) from September, 1884, to the formation of the trust in May, 1887, will show how great a saving has thus been effected.

Another saving is that which comes from the lessened expenses of management, resulting from the closing of so many distilleries. Nearly all the distilleries in the former pool, to the number of more than eighty, have become members of the trust. In order to limit the output to the demands of the market, these distilleries, if running when they joined, have been from time to time closed, until at the present time twelve distilleries supply the total amount that is placed by the trust upon the market. One or two others are running, but for the production of yeast, or some other product than spirits. It is by no means to be assumed that the decrease in the output corresponds in any manner with the number of distilleries closed. When it is taken into consideration that for several years the output of the distilleries had been often limited to from 25 to 50 per cent of their capacity, many of them even closing for portions of the year, it will be seen that an equal output might be produced by a much less number of distilleries. That there has been a smaller aggregate output is doubtless true, and that to an extent more than enough to balance the lessened amount exported. The amount is held in hand well enough, so that the trust can manage to control the market.

An examination of Table III (page 37), which gives the market prices of corn and whiskey from the time of the formation of the first pool, in 1881, to March, 1889, will show that the price of alcohol has not been to any noticeable extent raised by this closing of the distilleries. For some six or eight months after the formation of the trust the prices were lowered eight or nine cents per gallon, although the prices of corn ruled somewhat higher than before. Presumably the purpose of this lowering of the prices at first was to bring pressure to bear upon the distilleries yet remaining outside of the trust in order to force them to join the trust, or else because in the beginning the trust did not yet have strength to force the market. After all or nearly all of the members of the former pool had joined the trust, so that its membership was practically complete, and it became evident that a contest with the distillers yet remaining outside was at hand, the managers of the trust raised the price. The new members would need dividends to keep them contented, and there was also a necessity of accumulating a fund upon which to enter upon this contest with their rivals.

A comparison of the prices of corn and alcohol for the year preceding the formation of the trust with the prices from May, 1888, to January, 1889 (see Table III, or Diagram), will show that the profits made by the trust have not been greater than those made by the old pool, unless the cost of management of the distilleries has been much decreased; and yet, during this period from May, 1888, to January, 1889, the trust had put the price high enough to enable them to pay good dividends to members that might otherwise have become dissatisfied and to accumulate a surplus for the purpose of a contest with outsiders. It is from this very evident that the saving in cost of management and manufacture has been very great. It must also be kept in mind that from twelve to twenty distilleries have been earning these dividends on stock that represents some eighty-three distilleries. This emphasizes still more the great saving effected in expenses.

The immediate result of this increase in price (from $1.05 to $1.09 per gallon, and then to $1.14) was the building of new distilleries, notably the large distillery at St. Paul; the opening of many small distilleries, and the manufacture of spirits by the smaller distilleries in Kentucky, whose normal product was whiskey for aging. When at length it became evident that the distilleries outside of the trust were also making a large product and the output from these distilleries was beginning to have its effect upon the market, the trustees, on the 1st day of January, 1889, again cut the price of the product to $1.04 per gallon, in order to crush their opponents. The smaller distilleries in Kentucky and elsewhere of course closed promptly, or changed the character of their product. The most formidable rivals of the trust, Shufeldt & Co. of Chicago, who had doubtless also made large gains from the increase in price and who had run their distillery at even more than its normal capacity, at once cut down their output, though they have not closed and are even building a new house of 3000 bushels capacity.

What the next move will be, remains to be seen. It is said by the managers of the trust that their best policy is to hold the price of the product below the cost of manufacture by most of the rival distilleries and thus keep the market steady. They claim that they are able to do this from the saving in management and from the fact that they run only the distilleries most favorably located. For local trade they can run those that will save freight; and, in fact, they run one in Cincinnati, one in St. Louis, one in Kansas City, etc. The figures of the trust, gathered from the various distilleries under their control, show that the distilleries at Peoria have an advantage of from 14 to 15 per cent over most of the distilleries located elsewhere, so that here some six are running. It is the belief of distillers not members of the trust, as well as of the trustees, that a Peoria distillery has at least 10 per cent advantage over a distillery located at Chicago, and nearly 20 per cent over one located at St. Paul. This claim seems to be substantiated by the statement of Charles Clark, for many years past a prominent distiller at Peoria, though not now in the business himself. He says that at times of great depression in the business, during the existence of the former pools and earlier, his distillery made regularly 10 per cent on the running capital and 25 per cent on the plant, besides good salaries for the managing members of the firm. With the exception of one year this rate of profit was made for many years prior to the formation of the trust, and in that unfortunate year there was a clear profit of $12,000. During this very time the complaints of distillers in other parts of the country that money was being lost and that no interest could be made on their investments were doubtless often true. On the other hand, in estimating the ability of the trust to com-

TABLE III

MARKET PRICES AT PEORIA FOR WHISKEY AND CORN FROM 1881 TO 1888 INCLUSIVE

Month	1881		1882		1883		1884	
	Whiskey	Corn	Whiskey	Corn	Whiskey	Corn	Whiskey	Corn
January			1.15-1.16	62-59	1.13-1.14	44½-50½	1.15-1.16	41½-47
February			1.16-1.17	58½-54	1.14-1.15	48-55½	1.16-1.17	47-42
March			1.16	58¾-66½	1.15	56¼-49	1.17	41½-48
April			1.17	66¾-75½	1.15	47½-52½	1.17-1.12	43½-50½
May			1.13-1.17	75-70½	1.15	50-53	1.12	48-54½
June			1.11-1.15	72-69¼	1.15	53-47½	1.08	50-45½
July			1.11-1.14	73-75½	1.15	48-45	1.08-1.07	44-49
August			1.14-1.16	74½-77	1.15	45-51	1.05	47½-50½
September			1.16-1.18	75-59½	1.15	49½-46	1.10-1.11	51-45
October			1.16-1.18	61-70¼	1.15	45-47¾	1.11	40-53
November	1.11-1.15	62½-58	1.14-1.15	70½-67	1.15	46½-49	1.11-1.12	42-30
December	1.15	58½-62	1.13-1.15	55½-45	1 15	52-45	1.12	30½-35

Month	1885		1886		1887		1888		1888	
	Whiskey	Corn	Whiskey	Corn	Whiskey	Corn	Whiskey	Corn	Whiskey	Corn
January	1.12-1.14	34½-40	1.10	33-35	1.14	33¾-35½	1.09	48¼-47	1.04	30
February	1.14	38½-36½	1.10	34-32¾	1.14	35¼-33¾	1.09	47-45¼	1.04	29½
March	1.14	37¼-40½	1.10	33-34¼	1.14	33¾-38	1.09	45¾-49	1.04	30
April	1.14	39¾-47½	1.10	33¾-32½	1.14	37¼-36	1.09	47¼-53¼		
May	1.14	50-45	1.10	33-29½	1.14-1.05	37-38½	1.09-1.13	52½-57½		
June	1.14	44-47½	1.10	29-31	1.05-1.09	38¾-36	1.13-1.14	53¼-46½		
July	1.14	47-43¾	1.10-1.07	28¼-41½	1.05	38¼-34¼	1.14	49-43½		
August	1.14	45¼-42½	1.09-1.11	40½-39	1.05	38¾-42¼	1.14	45¾-40		
September	1.05	43½-40½	1.11-1.13	38¾-36	1.05	41½-39¼	1.14	44-40½		
October	1.04-1.09	42½-38½	1.13-1.14	35½-32½	1.05	39½-41¾	1.14	39¼-44		
November	1.09	44½-32	1.14	33¾-36½	1.05	39½-46	1.14	42½-38		
December	1.09-1.10	33½-31½	1.14	35½-33½	1.05	44¾-49½	1.14	33½-29½		

AVERAGE YIELD PER BUSHEL[1]

Year	Yield	Year	Yield	Year	Yield	Year	Yield
1881	3.694	1883	3.874	1885	4.076	1887	4.62
1882	3.792	1884	3.895	1886	4.55	1888	4.53½

[1] The average yield for the last three years is for the Trust or Peoria distilleries. The government report, including all distilleries, gives for the years 1886, '87, '88, respectively, the yield 4.09+, 4.23+, 4.24+.

pete with its rivals, it must be remembered that fourteen distilleries must make profit enough to pay dividends on the capital invested in more than eighty distilleries, a drawback amply sufficient to offset any slight benefit in the cost of manufacture. A distiller who has no closed houses to carry, no dividends to pay on capital that is inactive, has certainly something of an advantage. If the trust holds its own firmly, however, this advantage will soon to a great extent disappear, as the trust will doubtless, as opportunity offers, dispose of the useless closed distilleries and turn the dead capital into profitable channels.

The trust has, doubtless, had some benefit from the fact that dealers would fear to incur the hostility of so powerful an organization by purchasing from its rivals. This is again offset in part, by the popularity of certain brands of whiskey (though this would apply especially to the Kentucky product) the manufacturer of which can always be sure of his market. It is probable, at any rate, that the advantage is not so decidedly with the trust that it can totally crush out all competition, though this can be determined more certainly after a year or two. At present it manufactures only from 80 to 85 per cent of the total product in the market, and its rivals are preparing to compete still more vigorously. Shufeldt & Co. of Chicago, as has been said, are building a new distillery, and there are reports that others in Illinois are soon to be built. The trust cannot afford to buy out all distilleries that may be built. If it is to succeed, it must keep its prices so low that new distilleries will not be built. Its action in pushing up the price last year, if a merely temporary expedient to accumulate a fund, was perhaps a wise move from the standpoint of the trust; but such prices, quoted too often, would not be of advantage. The trust must succeed by underselling its rivals, not by buying them out. This is evidently, too, the policy of the organization; for it is a rule that no distilling company not in the old pool can join the trust. Even those companies have not been coaxed in by too large offers, as is sometimes asserted. The assertion made in the New York *Evening Post* of January 2, 1889, by the agent of Shufeldt & Co., that the trust had tried in many ways to force that firm into union, and had even offered it $1,000,000 in cash to join the organization is, even if correctly reported, not true. Both the trust officers and Shufeldt & Co. deny it. Doubtless the trust would be glad to be joined by so important a rival; and it is conceded by members of the trust that, had the company joined them when the trust was organized, its managers could have had much influence in the new organization. The implication is that they might have had a trustee. It is worth while to give this much of the case, because it shows the position the trust has taken regarding perhaps its most formidable rival, and the course it must pursue if it is to succeed. It must meet its competitors in fair business rivalry and be able to control by low prices the larger part of the sales.

As much is said regarding the influence of trusts and combinations of all kinds on wages and prices of materials, it may be worth while to mention the statements on this subject furnished by the president of the trust to the congressional committee. The coopers that manufacture barrels for the distilleries and the miners that furnish coal both testify that the distilleries connected with the trust voluntarily raised the prices for barrels and coal so that fair wages could be paid. Before the organization of the trust such a rise in prices could not be given on account of the fierce competition, and even after its formation distilleries not connected with the trust held the miners to their former oppressively low contracts, instead of following the example of the trust. The president of the trust adds that while they "do not wish to take the position as posing before the public as benefactors to any extent," yet they do believe in "the principle of intelligent coöperation," and as they can afford to pay good wages they are willing in justice and fairness so to do.

Most of the advocates of trusts and pools claim that one of the chief advantages to come from them is *stability* of prices. An examination of Table III, or better, of the Diagram, will show that while the fluctuations are somewhat less frequent under such a régime, yet, when a fall or rise in price does come, it is sudden, and is apt to be a change of considerable extent. It is very questionable if there is any gain from such a policy. The lack of stability under the old pool was due, it was claimed, to the instability of the pool itself; but so far matters have been little better in this respect under the trust. One thing seems better under the trust: the trust itself has stability, and seems to have power; it may steady prices if it will put them somewhat low and be satisfied with moderate steady returns, instead of striving for great gains interspersed with very small ones. The future will determine what is to be its policy. The managers of the trust say that the policy of the trust is to secure steady, moderate gains; others who are interested question this. The system of high gains alternating with low ones, if pursued as a regular policy, would do much to justify the distrust of the public and would take away the only ground on which such combinations can fairly be justified: low, steady prices.

A sufficiently accurate estimate of the real benefits accruing to the various distilleries from their association in the trust may be obtained from an examination of the dividends paid by the trust since its formation, and from the value of the trust certificates. Although the trust was organized in June, 1887, many of the distillers belonging to the old pool had not been received into the trust until about the beginning of the following year; so that any dividends paid before January, 1888, cannot be considered fair tests of the management or of the success of the trust. From January, 1888, to July, 1888, inclusive, a dividend of one-half of one per cent per month was paid; for August the dividend decreased to one-fourth of one per cent; and from September till January, 1889, inclusive, dividends of one-third of one per cent per month were declared. The dividend for February, 1889, again decreased to one-fourth of one per cent, owing doubtless to the late cut in price. It must be borne in mind, also, that in addition to the dividends throughout the year 1888, a surplus was being accumulated to carry on the contest with outside distillers. It was said by some members of the trust, when the trust certificates were valued at 30, that they then represented about the actual cash value of the plant. If this be accepted as an accurate estimate, and it is doubtless not far from the truth, we can readily see that the trust has paid dividends, during somewhat more than one year of active existence, of more than 12 per cent per annum.

TABLE IV

QUOTATIONS OF MARKET VALUE OF DISTILLERS' AND CATTLE-FEEDERS' TRUST CERTIFICATES

1888.	March	1.	50.	1888.	Aug.	28.	43.	1889.	Jan.	15.	30.
		14.	48.		Sept.	7.	40.			31.	31.
	April	1.	45½.			19.	39½.		Feb.	9.	32.
		20.	42½.		Oct.	10.	36½.			18.	33.
	May	11.	45½.			20.	35½.		March	4.	34.
	June	4.	43.		Nov.	13.	39.			7.	35.
		18.	40.			21.	39.			13.	36½.
	July	2.	41.		Dec.	12.	35.			20.	35½.
		7.	44.			21.	33.		April	1.	34.
		24.	45.	1889.	Jan.	4.	33.			6.	34.
	Aug.	13.	42.								

An examination of Table IV, which gives the value of trust certificates for each month from March, 1888, to the present time, will lead us to about the same conclusion. As soon as it became evident that the trust was firmly established and bade fair to be a success, some small sales of certificates were made to enthusiastic buyers as high as 65; others among distillers at 55; but no real market for trust certificates was established above 50. With some slight variations the value has slowly decreased, until in January, 1889, the lowest value (30) was reached, since which time a slight increase in value is to be noted. The figures in this table are based upon actual sales, and there can be no doubt as to their accuracy. It is, however, to be remarked that the certificates are held mainly by the large distillers as investments (though the number of individual certificate holders has largely increased), and that comparatively few transfers of trust certificates have been made. The prices quoted of course depend, too, to some extent, upon the amount invested at the time. The certificates are not listed in any stock exchange, and there cannot be said to be any regular market for them, though they can be obtained through brokers in four of the principal cities: Peoria, Chicago, Cincinnati and New York. The figures given represent, then, almost with perfect accuracy, the value placed by the distillers and the liquor dealers upon the certificates.

The facts given with reference to the working of the trust

seem to show that it has been beneficial to the greater portion of the manufacturers of alcohol and spirits in the United States, although individual distillers have perhaps made no more, and some, it may be, have made even less profit than they could have made acting independently; while, so far at least, the prices to consumers have not been on the whole increased, and the tendency seems to be towards lower and steadier prices for the future. As has been said, however, only the future can

Diagram illustrating the History

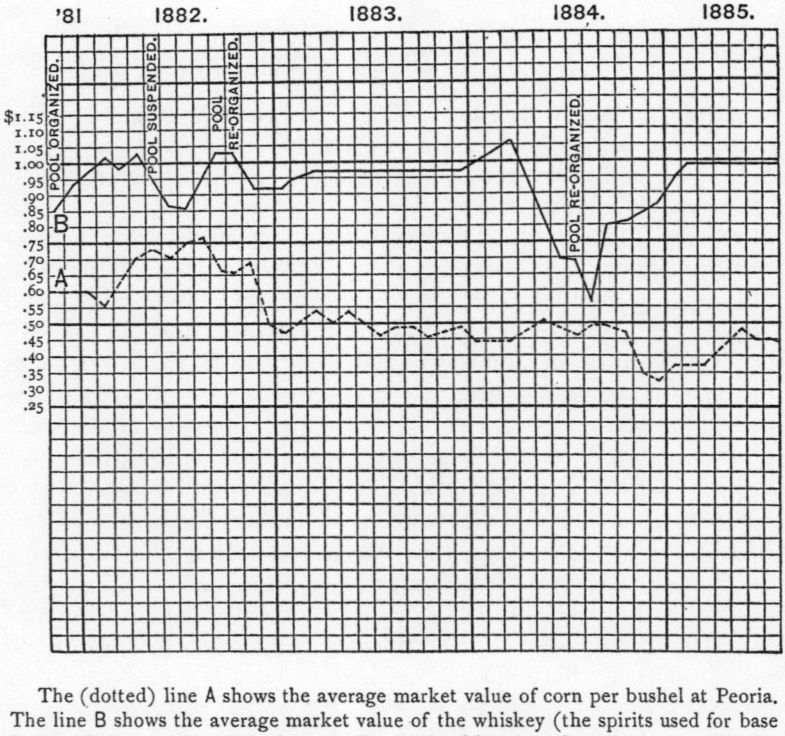

The (dotted) line A shows the average market value of corn per bushel at Peoria. The line B shows the average market value of the whiskey (the spirits used for base in prices) from one bushel of corn. To obtain this value, the revenue tax was deducted from the market value of one gallon, and the difference multiplied by the average yield per bushel of corn. — The space between the lines A and B represents, of course, the cost of production plus the profits. During the greater part of the pool's existence, assessments for export expenses must be deducted from the profits. (See Table II.)

determine what the policy of the trust is to be. The facts seem to show that it is within the power of the trust to bring about this result; and it seems to be for its interest so to do. As regards the stronger rivals of the trust, the prices have so far been so high that they have not suffered materially. The next year or two will show whether they can endure the competition. Even if they should be forced to close, the question is still an open one whether more distilleries would have not been closed

OF THE WHISKEY POOLS AND TRUST.[1]

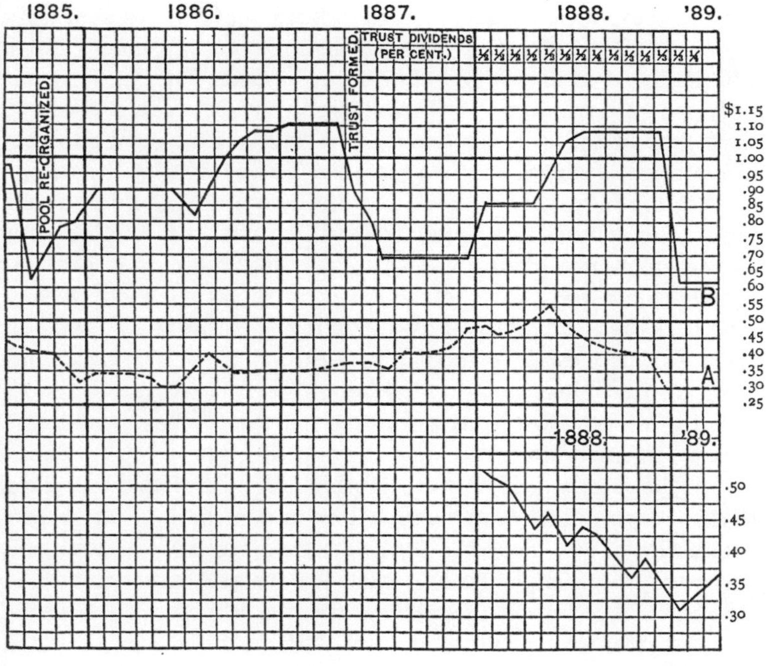

The line in the lower right-hand corner shows the fluctuations in the value of the trust certificates: par value, 100; cash value of plant estimated at about 30.

[1] Professor Jenks, in his *Trust Problem*, N.Y., 1902, p. 146, continues this price diagram to 1900. Much other information is in the Reports United States Industrial Commission, Vol. I, 1900. — ED.

under free competition. Many stockholders are now drawing dividends from the trust who, without the trust, would doubtless have lost much of their capital.

At the time of the formation of the trust, it was thought by some of the distillers living at Peoria that, on account of their unusual facilities for manufacture, the trust should be limited to Peoria distilleries and a few others favorably located. The experience of the trust seems to show that, had this plan been followed, the trust might have paid higher dividends to its members and might also have held the price of alcohol so low that outside competition would not have been much more successful than it has been under the present arrangement. Some distillers who believed in this latter plan — presumably for the most part Peoria manufacturers — still think it would have been better to have limited the organization to five years with the option then to continue, suspend, or reorganize. They feel that the owners of the less favorably situated distilleries have an undue advantage. Of course, this depends mainly upon the relative value placed upon the plants when they entered; but it is probable that it would have been cheaper to crush some of the weaker members than to buy them by admitting them to draw dividends. Against this view is, of course, the fact that such action would have aroused bitter hostility that might well have resulted in the building of new distilleries in locations where they would have become formidable rivals.

On the whole, while there is this slight tendency to think that matters might have been better under some other form of organization, or even, for a few, with no organization; and while there may be a slight feeling that the trustees are not entirely free from nepotism in their appointments, any more than are our highly esteemed executive officers of the United States; yet, as was shown a year ago by the unanimous reëlection of all the trustees at a meeting in which ninety-nine and one-half per cent of all the certified holders were represented, as well as by the general expression of satisfaction on the part of the distillers one meets, the trustees are thought to have performed their responsible duties with descretion, and the trust is considered by its members a success.

J. W. JENKS.

The later history of this combination has been checkered. In 1890, it was reorganized as a corporation, as the Distilling and Cattle Feeding Co. Its ownership of distilleries was extended to practically all important competitors. In 1893, failure impending because of the accumulation of floating debts for unpaid rebates, bonds were issued. For two years various scandals, mainly speculative, developed under its control by receivers; and the Supreme Court of Illinois in 1896 ousted it from its franchises (156 Ill. 448). Meanwhile in 1895 it had been again reorganized as the American Spirits Manufacturing Co., incorporated in New York. This company took over all the best distilleries in the field. Other plants and branches of the business were independently incorporated under the laws of New Jersey during the next four years in three principal companies. These were again united to the main stem in 1899, as The Distilling Co. of America, capitalized at $125,000,000. Over ninety per cent of the securities of this company in 1902 were in turn acquired by a holding or finance company, the Distillers' Security Corporation of New Jersey, which has issued about $50,000,000 of capital stock. — Ed.

III

THE WIRE-NAIL ASSOCIATION OF 1895-96[1]

SO lately as 1888 *The American Architect* began an article on nails in this way: "The nails commonly used in connection with building operations are too well known to require any description. They are specifically designated as plate nails."[2] That year, 1888, was almost the first in which plate or cut nails felt a real competition from wire nails. In that year the latter formed less than a fifth of the total product;[3] in 1895 they constituted nearly three-fourths. The idea of making nails of wire did not arise in America; in fact, our people were even somewhat slow to adopt it. The first wire nails — headed by hand and ground to a point — appear to have been made in France early in this century.[4] Mr. M. Baackes, an old wire-nail manufacturer of Cleveland, says that the first machine for forming the heads was made in France about 1850.[5] According to Mr. John Hassall, who is still engaged in making wire-nail machinery in New York city, his father was active in making and running the first wire-nail machines used in this country, early in the fifties.[6] The business seems to have extended itself only modestly, for Mr. Baackes regards the factory which he helped to start at Covington, Ky., in 1875, as "the first mill for the manufacture of wire nails on this side of the Atlantic."[7] The production rose from 20,000 kegs in 1880, according to Mr. Baackes's estimate, to 125,000 in 1887; and the average price fell from $20.00 per keg in 1875 and

[1] From the *Political Science Quarterly*, Vol. XII, 1897, pp. 246–272.
[2] *American Architect*, Aug. 18, 1888, p. 73.
[3] Report of American Iron and Steel Association, 1889, p. 45.
[4] M. Baackes, in *Iron Age*, Jan. 2, 1896, p. 106.
[5] *Ibid.* [6] *Iron Age*, April 23, 1896, p. 997.
[7] M. Baackes, in *Iron Age*, Jan. 2, 1896, p. 106.

$10.00 in 1880 to $4.81 in 1887. At the end of 1887 a manufacturer wrote: "Wire nails are now quoted at less than actual cost, as results will in time demonstrate."[1] About the same time the *Iron Age*, the leading paper of the hardware trade, said editorially: "It is evident that the business is now greatly overdone."[2] The production increased, however, to more than 300,000 kegs in 1890, and to nearly 600,000 kegs in 1895; and the average price fell to $2.85 in 1890, according to the estimate of Mr. Baackes, and to $1.60 in 1894. At present, April 1, 1897, it is about $1.50. These facts show how recently and how rapidly the business has attained importance, and how fast the price of wire nails has fallen.

The profits of the early wire-nail men, as first comers in the field, were doubtless good; but the cost of production at that time must not be gauged by the later selling prices. At the outset their machinery was imperfect. Then, the first nails were of small sizes, for special purposes, such as use in cigar boxes, furniture, mouldings, and wagons; and small nails are relatively costly. It was not till 1886 that a list of regular or "penny" nails was published, and a serious effort was made to compete with cut nails in the general market. The wire of the first makers, too, was all of Norway iron; for they could not get any other material on which they could form a head that would not break off in driving. The H. P. Nail Co., established in 1879, is said to have been the first to succeed in using Bessemer steel wire. Finally, the price of Bessemer steel itself was at first much higher than now. Although quotations on steel billets earlier than 1887 are not available, their fall in price may be gauged by that of steel rails, which dropped from an average of $48.25 per ton in 1879 and $67.50 in 1880 to $37.08 in 1887. Billets were $32.55 on the average in 1887 and $16.58 in 1894,[3] while they are now quoted at about $15.00. It was the removal of these early limitations that made possible the great expansion of the industry.

As the business is now carried on, regular nails are sold with reference to a "base price" and a uniform schedule, or "card,"

[1] *Iron Age*, Jan. 5, 1888, p. 22. [2] *Ibid.*

[3] Report of American Iron and Steel Association, 1896, p. 26.

of "extras." Excepting under the card made in 1895, the base has always been the same as the price of the largest nails. It is the base only that is named in market reports and in quotations. The extras, which are added to the base to determine the prices of the smaller sizes, are fixed by agreement of the manufacturers, and are likely to remain unchanged for several years together. From April 11, 1892, to July 19, 1895, the card was as follows:

60-d.	base (no extra)
50-d.	$.10 extra
30-d. and 40-d.	.25 "
20-d.	.35 "
12-d. " 16-d.	.45 "
10-d.	.50 "
8-d. " 9-d.	.60 "
6-d. " 7-d.	.75 "
4-d. " 5-d.	.90 "
3-d.	1.20 "
2-d.	1.60 "

When 60-d. nails were quoted at $.85, put up in a keg which I am assured by a manufacturer cost at least $.09, the wire from which they were made was quoted at $1.15. Every nail-maker who bought his wire in the market lost the whole cost of handling and manufacture, and nearly four-tenths of a cent besides, on every pound of 60-d. nails he sold. The explanation of his apparent willingness to sell below cost is found in the character of the list of extras, and in the manner in which all orders were required to be assorted. The extras on all the smaller nails were far greater than the differences in cost between them and the largest. Indeed, the wire for a keg of 12-d. nails cost no more than that for a keg of 60-d. No manufacturer would sell 60-d. alone at the market price. All orders had to be so assorted that the average of the extras on the whole should be at least $.60 per keg: that is, if a dealer gave an order for a hundred kegs, at a base price of $.85, he had to make it up in such a way that the average price of the whole, by the schedule, would be not less than $1.45. So the loss on the larger and cheaper sizes was covered by the gain on the smaller and dearer. Some small manufacturers took advantage of this artificial adjustment of prices, by making only the smaller sizes, and leaving the losing end of the schedule to the great establishments.

I. History of the Association

Iron and steel products have been particularly fruitful of combinations; but before 1895 circumstances had not been favorable to bringing wire nails into the list. The manufacturers had been fairly contented, making the comfortable profits of a new and rapidly growing business. It is probable that combinations are not easily formed in any industry so long as the average man of those concerned, with average advantages, can make such a profit as the general opinion of business men pronounces fair; and that consolidation generally results from a strong sense of pressure. In this business, by the beginning of 1895, the necessary pressure had developed. The manufacturers cried out with one voice that they were ruined by competition. It must be noted, however, that most men do not consider it good policy, under any circumstances, to magnify their profits before the world; that men who have been accustomed to large profits do really imagine themselves ruined when they are reduced to not much more than ordinary interest on their capital; and that lugubrious statements, made in general terms and without figures, ought not to be taken without salt. The bulk of the wire-nail business was in the hands of six or eight great companies, which had their own wire mills and rod mills, and put the material through all the processes from the form of the steel billet. So long as smaller concerns, buying their wire in the market, continued to do business, it strains credulity somewhat to believe that the great establishments did not make moderate profits. The curious arrangement of the schedule of extras does seem to have given a certain opportunity to small makers; but the matter was in the hands of the great companies, and they would have changed the schedule if they had found it to work strongly against them. The strict requirement of assorted orders made it impossible for any maker of small nails only to do more than a very restricted business. If any dealer bought many nails of such a maker, he could not buy his large nails at the market price.

The days of good profit to the average man with average advantages were, however, gone by; and the manufacturers — large and small alike — were in a state of mind to yield themselves plastic to the hand that could organize the machinery for increasing profits. This hand belonged to Mr. John H. Parks of Boston, who had been a member of the old firm of Loring & Parks, long well known as manufacturers of tacks. That firm combined with their principal competitors, some six years ago, in forming the Atlas Tack Corporation, which is still the giant of the tack trade; though the leading men connected with it have thought it well during the last few months to put it through a receivership and a reorganization, with the usual absorption of the interests of the smaller investors. For several years past, Mr. Parks has confined his personal attention to the promotion of combinations in various lines of hardware. Bolts and shovels, as well as tacks and nails, have known his supple hand. From a time early in the spring of 1895, he seems to have been busy in working up an agreement among the manufacturers of nails. The approaching consummation of this enterprise was announced on May 2, through the *Iron Age*, in the following words:

> With a view to securing a better condition of things and correcting influences which hitherto have tended toward irregularity in prices and the unsettling of the market, the manufacturers have been conferring with a view to concerted action in this direction.

The combination began its activity with the customary declaration as to its moderate purposes with respect to price. In the article from which I have quoted, this vital matter is thus dealt with: "The manufacturers directly concerned in the movement disclaim any intention of advancing prices unreasonably, their purpose being to market their goods at a reasonable profit."

The first effect of the rise of the combination was a press of orders. Many jobbers bought all the nails that they expected to need for six months or more. From about May 1 the manufacturers refused to accept any orders for shipment later than May 30. By May 15 the base price had risen to $.95; and by the 20th it had become so difficult to place large orders that there was no quotable price. Some sales were, however, reported about this time at $1.15 to $1.20. The combination was formally completed in the last week of May, and the base price for June was fixed at $1.20, for car lots, f. o. b. Pittsburg. All nails, no matter from what mill, were to be sold, freight paid, on the basis of the Pittsburg price, plus the rate of freight from Pittsburg to the point of destination. For instance, a customer at Anderson, Ind., would have to pay a base price, consisting of $1.20 plus the rate of freight from Pittsburg to Anderson, whether he bought in Pittsburg, or in Cleveland, or from the mill in his own town. Jobbers were allowed a discount of five cents per keg on purchases of a thousand kegs from one mill within one calendar month; and the minimum was soon reduced to five hundred kegs. In addition, a rebate of ten cents per keg, payable after six months, was offered to jobbers who should neither buy any nails from outside makers nor sell below the association price.

The form of the association was that of a simple pool. Prices and output were always fixed for a month in advance. The agreed production was apportioned to the companies on a basis depending partly on sales for three months before the pool was formed, partly on production in one of those three months, and partly on capacity as indicated by the number of machines. Any mill could sell its privilege of production, or any part of it; but every mill was rigidly restricted to its allotment during each calendar month, unless it bought the allotment of another. A cost price was assumed, which was supposed to represent the cost of production at Pittsburg; and the cost at every other point was assumed to be equivalent to the Pittsburg cost with freight from Pittsburg added. This was because the raw material comes chiefly from the Pittsburg region. So the selling price, including delivery at the buyer's railroad station, and the assumed cost price were harmonized by the use of the Pittsburg base. All the profits, above the cost prices so arrived at, were paid into the pool; and the amount in the pool, after paying all expenses, was divided monthly. The basis of division was the same as the basis for the allotment of production.

An inspector, hired by the association, was placed at each association mill, with the most sweeping powers of investigation. Every part of the mill, every book, every letter written or received, was open to him. So far as possible, outside owners of nail machines were hired to keep them idle, and makers of machines were hired to refuse orders for them from persons outside the association. For a year it was very difficult to buy a machine, and while the association lasted it was never easy. A company which went into the business in the autumn of 1896 writes:

> We found the market in which we could buy machines was very limited, most of the machine manufacturers having entered into an arrangement with the combination to stop making them for outside parties. We were unable to obtain what we wanted, and consequently our production of nails was much below what we intended it to be when we started.

With a similar combination of Canadian nail manufacturers, the association made an agreement by which each bound itself not to offer goods in the territory of the other. Efforts were also made to induce the European manufacturers to agree to let none of their nails come to America. Although it is said that they did not meet with much success, only one large lot of nails and a few small lots were actually imported during the existence of the pool.

The agreement of the wire-nail men was accompanied by a similar agreement of the cut-nail men. Although separate in form, these two organizations acted as one. The price of cut nails was accordingly advanced with that of wire nails, at first 20 cents below, and afterwards uniformly 25 cents below — a difference not relatively greater than that which had existed before the pool was formed. Wire nails were so far preferred that, in spite of the difference in price, their competition had reduced the trade in cut nails to a fraction of its former size, and had thrown hundreds of cut-nail machines out of use. The existence of these machines was one of the chief sources of embarrassment to the two associations. The wire-nail pool had to turn over large sums to its weaker associate, to be used in paying the owners of these old cut-nail machines to keep them idle.

The demand for nails continued very strong through June. The production for the month had been restricted somewhat, in order to insure control of the market. Before the 12th the mills had sold their entire allotments for the month and were refusing all orders.[1] Yet, at their meeting held the week following, they made a further restriction of their output for July, reducing it to about half the average monthly product for the previous year,[2] and fixing the price for July at $1.55. Dealers anticipated a further advance, and in their desire to protect themselves clamored for nails. Before July 4 some manufacturers had sold their entire allotment for the month and were again refusing orders. By the 10th, few nails could be bought from manufacturers.[3] On July 18 a new "card," or schedule of extras, was adopted. The extras on 10-d. and smaller nails were not changed; but all larger sizes were put on an equality with 10-d., with an extra of 50 cents. The requirement of assorted orders, or a minimum average of extras, was abolished; but the lowest extra was now almost up to the old required average. The base price for August was made $2.05.

The success of the nail combination had been followed by a sharp and general advance in the prices of iron and steel products, and had doubtless contributed to cause it. A market report of May 30 said: "Billets are $17.50 and will likely be higher, and the agreement reached by the wire-nail mills is also having its effect on rods, and prices are very much higher."[4] Between May 1 and August 1 plain wire, from which nails are made, rose from a base price of $1.10 per cwt. to $1.50; wire rods, from which wire is drawn, from $21.00 per gross ton to $29.00; steel billets, from which rods are rolled, from $15.50 per gross ton to $21.50. There seems to have been what is called a good understanding between the producers in these lines, but no formal combination. On August 22, however, this announcement appeared: "The barb-wire trade has been organized on the same lines as the wire-nail trade. A sharp

[1] *Iron Age*, June 13, 1895, p. 1248.
[2] *Ibid.*, July 11, 1895, p. 85.
[3] *Ibid.*
[4] *Ibid.*, May 30, 1895, p. 1143.

advance in prices has been made. Plain wire will likely advance in sympathy with barb wire."[1] On September 5 it was announced that prices of plain wire had been advanced, "as the result of an understanding arrived at by the manufacturers." The base price of wire nails was advanced to $2.25 on September 1, "in view of the increased cost of raw material." The demand had continued good during August. In the latter part of the month, in consequence of the restriction of output, there had been some scarcity. In September the demand began to fall off notably, but the mills disposed of their allotments for the month. Trade was poor in October, and in November it was very light. The manufacturers complained particularly of the large stocks which the jobbers had on hand, and which some of them were offering rather under the combination price. The pool was strengthened in November, however, by the accession of several companies which had been operating outside.

About November 25 the only large lot of nails which has been imported into this country in many years was received by the Bigelow & Dowse Co., of Boston. Rumor puts the amount at about 5000 kegs, or 20 carloads. Several small lots were received at New York during the next year, but the largest is not believed to have exceeded 500 kegs. It is not known by what means the Bigelow & Dowse Co. were convinced that it would be better not to repeat their operation; but apparently they did not cut the association price, and they brought in no more nails. Jobbers, who investigated the matter with a view to importing, say that English nails could not at any time have been imported with profit, but that German and Belgian nails could have been laid down in Boston or New York at from 50 to 70 cents below the highest price reached by the pool, even after paying the duty of 25 per cent. It required more courage than appears at first sight, however, to venture on placing foreign orders. The German and Belgian nails are shipped in bags, and to make them salable in the American market they must be kegged after receipt, at an expense of from 10 to 20 cents a keg. The head is formed a little differently from that of the American nail, and the tendency of human nature to

[1] *Iron Age*, Aug. 22, 1895, p. 404.

reject the unaccustomed might cause some objection to it. But the chief deterrent of imports, aside from the tariff, was the power of the pool to drop the price at any time to a point that would cause the importer a very serious loss. Nothing would have been so likely to cause a drop as the fact that large foreign orders were being placed.

The duty on nails does not now serve any purpose except to increase the power of combinations. Nails are produced here as cheaply as anywhere in the world, and are regularly exported. The duty does not protect the industry, and under full competition does not affect the price. But if there had been no duty when the pool was organized, either it would not have been organized, or it would have had to content itself with a much more moderate advance. An excessive advance would have caused the other obstacles to importation to be overcome, and would have led to free purchases abroad.

In December the manufacturers gave jobbers a guaranty on their December purchases against decline in January: that is, they agreed that, if they made a reduction of price in January, they would give jobbers a corresponding rebate on such nails bought in December as they had still on hand. This policy was thereafter followed from month to month till near the breaking up of the association. It was meant to induce freer buying by the jobbers; but its success was slight. The demand for nails was exceedingly light during the winter, and the stagnation propagated itself back to the market for raw material. In a market report of January 2, 1896, is this remark: "Until there is an improvement in the wire and wire-nail trades, it is not likely there will be any demand for rods." On January 16 it was stated from Pittsburg that no sales of rods had been reported in that market for some time. Early in February the nail association announced an advance of 15 cents, to take effect March 1. This galvanized the market into a mild, convulsive movement. The operation was repeated in April, with an announcement of an advance of 15 cents to take effect May 1. Trade was very dull, however, and the manufacturers admitted that the market was a good deal disturbed by outside nails and by the offerings of jobbers. High prices had so curtailed consumption that a considerable quantity of nails, bought before the pool was formed or in its early days, was probably still in the jobbers' hands. These formed a disturbing element, in addition to the growing production of outside factories.

About April 1, 1896, the makers of steel billets formed a pool. The amount of billets in the hands of middlemen, or contracted for by them, was so great, however, that the attempt of the pool to raise prices $3 or more per ton was only partially successful. The wire-rod makers also tried to form a pool, but after much negotiation were unable to agree. Their good understanding, however, seems to have continued.

Early in June the nail association succeeded in coming to terms with the Pittsburg Wire Co. and Baackes & Co., of Pittsburg, by which these companies agreed to stop making wire nails. Their nail mills were by no means of the first rank; but they were large enough to make a considerable figure in the market under the existing circumstances of very small consumption, and they had been selling somewhat below the association price.

If the statements of the manufacturers could be accepted freely, we should need to explain to ourselves the rather curious phenomenon of producers keeping the price of their product abnormally high, contrary to their own desires, in deference to the wishes of their customers. It was semi-officially announced that while the manufacturers came to their meeting on June 3

> with the general expectation that some action would be taken looking toward a reduction in price, they were confronted with many letters from jobbers emphasizing the injury that would be done to the market by the reduction in the price of so staple a commodity as nails, and urging the manufacturers to maintain existing prices.[1]

Such a phenomenon would not have been inexplicable if it had existed; but an examination of twenty-nine letters of jobbers on the situation, published about that time, indicates that it was essentially a myth. Two of these regarded the price as a matter which concerned no one except the manufacturers, and which no one else ought to trouble himself about. Only seven could be counted against an instant reduction, on any construction of their words. Nineteen either were opposed

[1] *Iron Age*, June 11, 1896, p. 1384.

to the existing high prices or at least went so far as to say that, if a reduction were to come before January 1 (a matter on which they expressed no opinion), it had better come at once. The retailers were unanimous for reduction, complaining of a great falling off in their sales, which some put as high as fifty per cent. They reported that building and repairing were much interfered with.

Meantime a growing number of small mills gave the association increasing annoyance. By July 1 it was estimated that 25,000 kegs a month were made by outside mills. The total sales for June, by the association and outsiders, were estimated at 90,000 kegs;[1] while it was said that the allotment for July was 65,000 kegs,[2] and that the associated manufacturers did not sell so many.[3] These statements were made by the Pittsburg office of the *Iron Age*, which was at the centre of the movement, and which ought not, it would seem, to have sent out any but well-founded statements — at least about matters so definitely fixed as the monthly allotment. There is reason, however, for supposing that these figures were too low. A man who knows the innermost history of the combination has said that he does not think there was any month in which the manufacturers in the pool did not sell 150,000 kegs. This statement seems modest enough, considering that the average monthly production for 1895 was nearly 500,000 kegs.

Rumors of concessions and irregularities in price increased. On September 1 the guaranty to jobbers on each month's purchases against decline in the succeeding month was discontinued. It was noted with satisfaction that, in spite of the low prices which had to be made to meet foreign competition, the export trade was assuming relatively large proportions.[4] Early in September several outside manufacturers were induced, on expensive terms, to withdraw from the market. It was claimed that the production of those still outside was insignificant; but, in spite of this claim, the association lost its grip on prices to an extent far greater than at any earlier time. Chicago was the centre of greatest disturbance. Nails were openly offered there by jobbers

1 *Iron Age*, July 23, 1896, p. 186.

2 *Ibid.*, July 30, 1896, p. 236.

3 *Ibid.*, Aug. 13, 1896, p. 334.

4 *Ibid.*, Sept. 10, p. 512.

at $2.50, and finally at $2.25, for small lots from store, for which the association price was $2.80. The demand, however, showed a great improvement in September, and it continued good in October. It was estimated that the total output for October would be about 250,000 kegs,[1] or about half the average monthly output for 1895. Soon after October 1, the manufacturers succeeded in patching up the trouble at Chicago; and about the 15th the market reports said that there was "not a suspicion of weakness in any direction," and that the association had "demonstrated its ability to control the situation." It was, nevertheless, hardly two weeks before the final break appeared. About November 1 Chicago jobbers began to offer nails from store at $2.40. The break spread rapidly, and by the 10th the association price was merely nominal. Demand continued light. No one bought more nails than he had to have, because to-day's price was always likely to be bettered to-morrow. About November 20 nails were openly offered at Chicago at $1.50 by representatives of association mills. On December 1 the association held its last meeting, adopted a new card of extras, and formally dissolved. The new extras on common nails are as follows:

20-d. to 60-d.	base
10-d. " 16-d.	$.05
8-d. and 9-d.	.10
6-d. " 7-d.	.20
4-d. " 5-d.	.30
3-d.	.45
2-d.	.70

This schedule makes a large reduction in the relative price of small nails, which was undoubtedly intended to shut out the small manufacturers who had been making small nails only. The new card, however, comes much nearer than any previous one to representing the relative cost of large and small nails, under present conditions of manufacture.

II. The Course of Prices

When it is said that nails were selling on May 1, 1895, at $.85, and that on May 1, 1896, the association made the price

[1] *Iron Age*, Oct. 29, 1896, p. 837.

$2.55, the price appears to have been multiplied within a year exactly by three. The case looks still worse when it is said that 60-d. nails sold in 1895 for $.85 a keg, and in 1896 for $3.05. In reality, while an ordinary bill of nails would have cost on May 1, 1896, at least $1.70 per keg more than a year earlier, it would not have cost three times as much. No nails were sold at the nominal base price in 1896; and though 60-d. nails were nominally sold at the base rate before the change of card in 1895, the statement that the price of 60-d. nails was at one time $.85 gives a false impression, for reasons which I have explained. A comparison of base prices after December 1, 1896, with earlier ones is altogether misleading, because the present extras are much smaller. It has been estimated that a well-assorted order of nails would carry an average extra of about $.62 on the old card, $.70 on that of July 19, 1895, and $.12 on that of December 1, 1896.[1] Perhaps there is no better simple measure of the actual course of the market than the change in the price of 8-d. nails. This size is used in large quantities; and when assorted orders were required, the extra on it was the same as the required average of extras. But this does not give a perfectly true idea of the changes of price. It is necessary to remember that during the life of the association the prices of the larger nails were increased even more by the increase of the extras on them.

The diagram printed below shows the movement during 1895 and 1896 of the prices of 8-d. wire nails, of No. 11 wire, from which these nails are made, of wire rods and of steel billets. It is based upon the Pittsburg quotations, as published from week to week in the *Iron Age*. No. 11 wire costs about $.10 per cwt. more than the base sizes quoted in the market reports.

Iron and steel went through a notable boom and collapse in 1895. Without any marked change in the general condition of the country, without any corresponding change in general prices, without any strong parallel movement in other countries, the prices of crude iron and steel, and other prices directly dependent on them, rose fast and steadily for some five months, and fell even faster in the next three. Between April 1 and September

[1] *Iron Age*, Dec. 10, 1896, p. 1161.

15 steel billets rose more than sixty per cent, while by December 15 they were within ten per cent of the old level. It is not easy

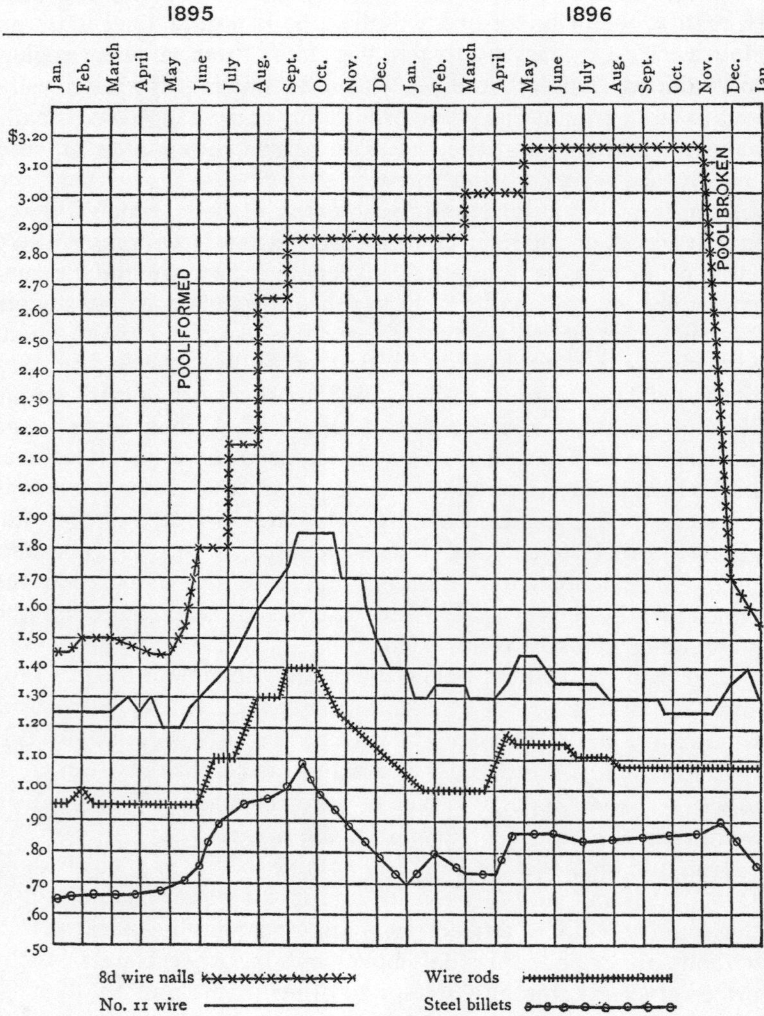

to get a fully satisfactory explanation of the rise. Near the end of March the Carnegie interests contributed to start it by very large purchases of iron. About the same time the H. C. Frick Coke Company announced an advance of fifteen per cent in wages, and an advance of more than thirty per cent in the price of coke, to take effect April 1;[1] and other coke shippers followed their lead. This made a great increase in the cost of producing and working iron and steel. A little later labor disputes threatened to stop production; and when they were settled, it was by an advance of wages. Other advances were announced by the great steel companies during May and June. These increases seemed to justify and to fasten the higher prices. Men gathered confidence that good times were coming, and that prices were not only to stay up, but to go higher. This confidence, reacting, bred demand; and renewed demand pushed prices higher and higher. The success of the nail combination, and the temporary activity which the advance in nails and the expectation of advance occasioned in the market, were among the causes which contributed to these phenomena. It is doubtful whether the rise of raw material had the slightest influence upon the price of nails; for the rise of nails began before that of steel, was eminently artificial, and was continued after the raw material had sunk nearly to its former price.

III. The Interests of Dealers and Laborers

The undesirability, from the standpoint of those who want to use nails, of any restriction upon the use of them and of having to pay high prices to get them, is too obvious to be insisted on. The retail hardware dealers suffered with the consumers. Their sales were curtailed, without a proportionate increase in their profit per pound. They had to bear the brunt of their customers' complaints about the price of nails. They complained, also, of the annoyance which was caused by the new card of extras, under which the cheapest nails cost fifty cents per keg more than the nominal base price. When their customers saw nails quoted in the papers at $2.25, it was hard to convince them that the actual wholesale price of 60-d. spikes

[1] *Iron Age*, March 21, 1895, p. 607.

was $2.75. The jobbers, on the other hand, made large profits on the stocks which they bought before the pool was formed, or soon after; and they were enabled, by the system of discounts and rebates, which the manufacturers maintained, to make at least their usual profit on current purchases. This policy was meant to make the jobbers friendly to the association; and it seems to have been largely successful.

Some of the mills showed a disposition to raise wages as they advanced their prices, and so to make some little division of profits with their men. It was reported that one of the great companies gave its men an advance of ten per cent in June, 1895,[1] and ten per cent more about March 1, 1896;[2] that another raised wages ten per cent in July, 1895;[3] and that a third, after a strike, in September, 1895, advanced its wire-drawers ten per cent and fifteen per cent, and its nail-makers five per cent.[4] But the last-mentioned company, which at its full capacity employs about one thousand hands, at one time cut down its force to about three hundred. This reduction is proportional to the reduction of total sales from 500,000 kegs a month to 150,000. It seems safe to assume that the other companies must have made similar reductions. If half or two-thirds of the laborers were thus thrown out of work, they were not much helped by a small increase in the rate of wages paid to the rest.

The restriction of the employment of labor did not stop at the nail mills; there was a diffused effect which was probably greater, though it is less traceable. There is reason to believe that building, and especially repairing, were perceptibly retarded.[5] To raise the retail price of a keg of nails, say from two dollars to four, must under any circumstances diminish purchases to some extent. The effect will be greater if the circumstances make it seem likely that the rise is temporary. In the present case, there was the added influence of a lively conviction of the buyers that the manufacturers were trying to rob them. If a man thinks that an effort is made to impose upon him, he

[1] *Iron Age*, June 20, 1895, p. 1288.
[2] *Ibid.*, March 12, 1896, p. 656.
[3] *Ibid.*, July 18, 1895, p. 129.
[4] *Ibid.*, Sept. 5, 1895, p. 496.
[5] *Ibid.*, June 25, 1896, pp. 1490–1493.

will often subject himself to a good deal of inconvenience, for the satisfaction of thinking that he has not been imposed on. It is likely that thousands of men did without improvements which they could not afford to do without, because they would not submit to what they regarded as the arbitrary demands of the nail combination. It was, perhaps, in part because the manufacturers left this moral effect out of their reckoning, that the extent of the diminution of demand took them by surprise. Their calculations doubtless accorded with the view recently expressed by a small manufacturer, who experienced a strong demand while the association lasted, because he sold nails a little under the association price. He said:

I do not think that the high price of nails restricted consumption to any perceptible extent. The item of nails in the cost of building is a very small one, and it was not over five or six years ago that the price was about the same as that fixed by the recent combination.

Consumption was not so small as production during the last months of 1895, or perhaps during the early months of 1896, while the jobbers still had some part of the stocks which they had laid in about the time the pool was formed. But the best information obtainable makes it appear that, during 1896, consumption as well as production must have been small beyond any possible expectation.

IV. The Interest of the Manufacturers

It is apparently the general opinion that, quite aside from any consideration of the public welfare, and looking only to the pecuniary interest of the manufacturers, the combination carried the policy of high prices too far. The association went to pieces after eighteen months, and prices went down to their former level; therefore it is assumed that the combination failed or, at least, that it would have accomplished its purpose more fully by a more moderate policy. The matter does not seem to me so simple. Mr. Parks, who was undoubtedly the guiding spirit in the whole transaction, went into it with eyes very wide open. He had already been connected with several tack combinations managed on the same principles. Of course they came to a rather speedy end; but Mr. Parks seems to have counted their experience as favorable, on the whole, to the policy of a short life and a merry one for pools. Moreover, he still maintains the wisdom of the course that he counselled. When the association collapsed, he said that it had lived longer than its most sanguine promoters expected, and as a financial undertaking had been an unprecedented success.[1] The manner of argument of a man who was connected with the association throughout its existence is as follows:

> Suppose we had put up the price $.15 a keg. A great many men who had had their eye on the nail business, would have said: "Those men have put up the price $.15, and they will probably make it $.25. There is going to be money in the nail business. I will go in." But when we put up the price $1.50, they said: "Those fellows are lunatics. They can't hold together. There will be a smash before they get fairly started. I will keep out of that business." As a matter of fact, we had hardly any new competition during the first year of the association. The new competition came mostly after the beginning of the second year. Then men began to say: "Those fellows have kept together twelve months, and they will probably do it a while longer. They are making a lot of money. I will try to get a slice of it." I am sure we kept the association going longer with a high price than we could have kept it going with a low price. I don't believe it would have lasted six months with a raise of $.25. The high price frightened off some people, and gave us plenty of money to buy off the rest.

It is hardly possible to over-emphasize the distinction between the great consolidations of which the so-called sugar trust may be taken as a type—consolidations which it may not be improper to distinguish specifically as trusts, because the typical examples were first united under the proper trust form of organization—and pools like the nail association. The broad differences of organization have their root partly in the conditions of the businesses concerned, and partly, it may be, in the mental characteristics of the managers; and they issue in great differences of policy and power. It would probably not be impossible to bring the making of wire nails under the control of one great company; but it would be much more difficult than it was to do the like

[1] *Iron Age*, Dec. 3, 1896, p. 1108.

with the refining of sugar. To refine sugar by methods commercially practicable to-day, a man must have hundreds of thousands of dollars to put at the risk of the business. With ten thousand dollars and six weeks' time, however, any man who likes can become a manufacturer of wire nails. A little factory can make them, not quite so cheaply as the great establishments which make their own wire, but at no very great disadvantage. It needs only a small rise above the lowest price at which the best mills can pay interest on the cost of their plants, to enable an indefinite number of small mills to start, making each its twenty-five or fifty kegs per day. This is the weakness of any form of combination in a business of this character — the possibility of a new factory in every thriving town.

No limit can be named to the success of skilful and determined managers of a centralized combination or trust, in any line, in crushing competition. An abnormal lowering of price in the local field of a small competitor is a weapon which needs nothing but persistence to make it inevitably fatal to him; and the revenues which the trust draws constantly from other fields, even if it loses in the region of cut prices, give it an unlimited power of persistence. There is no doubt of the trust's ability to destroy any competitor of a size which does not approach its own. This process is troublesome, however, and somewhat expensive; and in a case in which new competitors can spring up with so little money and in so short a time, the query is whether the situation of the trust would not be unpleasantly like that of a man fighting with mosquitoes.

It probably would be so, unless the trust should be content with a policy of greater moderation in its profits than any trust has yet had the self-denial to adopt. Any trust, having once got control of the market, could make it impossible for any competitor to establish a business which would pay a profit for a day, or would need any attention from the trust to make it disappear. This possibility depends upon the power of the trust to do for society such service as no competitor could do. The representatives of the trusts have not been negligent in setting forth the economies which they are able to effect: the production of all goods by the most efficient plants; the universal use of all improvements, patented or not; the economizing and full use of expert knowledge; the incorporation of subsidiary industries, like the making of packages; the saving of transportation by shipping from the factory nearest the consumer. Greatest of all, perhaps, and most decisive, because it is the economy that is absolutely out of the reach of a competitor, is the commercial economy that depends upon the control of the market — the saving of the expense of inducing customers to buy of this concern and not of that. A trust which should make over the greater part of these savings to its customers, and should content itself with prices which would give it only fifteen or twenty per cent per annum on the value of its productive property, as measured by the cost of replacing it, would probably never be troubled with any shadow of competition. But the general conclusion of competent and disinterested investigators seems to be that, up to the present time, every trust, when its control of the market has been established, has not only kept the whole of the savings of consolidation to itself, but has taken from the public something besides, making prices somewhat higher than they would have been under full competition.

The form of organization of a pool is less unattractive than that of a full consolidation, to a man who values his independent position and dislikes to become an employee; but there is in it as much less power as there is less unity. Under a pool, the economy of closing some establishments may be effected by paying them a bonus, as was done for years by the steel-rail pool. The nail men dealt with outside mills by this plan, but under circumstances and in a way which hardly permit it to be regarded as an economy. It is probable that a pool, with production strictly limited to what the market will easily absorb at the prices fixed, might make some saving in the commercial expenses of advertising and selling, particularly if the circumstances and the policy of the pool were such as to give it a character of comparative permanence. The nail men were probably not able to make any savings of this class. The other economies which are possible to a trust seem to be out of the reach of a pool, while the central organization and the system of mutual watching seem even to add something to the cost of superintendence. It is probably safe to say that nearly all the gain which any manufacturers may make through a pool is made by raising their selling prices.

It can be maintained with a good show of reason that the nail men would have got more profit in the course of years from the policy of full consolidation, with prices permanently fixed low enough to make competition impossible. But experience has not yet shown this policy to be practically attainable in our present stage of civilization. Between that extreme and the other, which the nail men chose, it is doubtful whether there is any mean which they would have found golden. The choice practically open to them appears to have lain between a tolerably large profit, which might possibly last two or three years, and a very large one, which might be expected to last six months or a year. They chose the very large one; and they kept it, or at least kept the price up, for eighteen months. It is true that a very large part of the profits, especially in the later months, was consumed in subsidies and other expenses of the association. Some well-informed men, intimately connected with the trade and friendly to the manufacturers, think that their policy was short-sighted. The question has more sides than one, however, and it seems possible to make out a very good case for the view that the manufacturers did not choose the least profitable course.

V. The Interest of the Public

It may not make much difference to the manufacturer whether he reduces his costs or raises his selling price; but it makes a great difference to the consumer. Aside from any lowering of prices, it is to the public interest that economies be made — that a given product be obtained with less cost and less exertion. If a consolidated trust would sell as cheaply as competing producers would have to sell, keeping to itself the whole of its economies but taking nothing more, the economies would benefit the public somewhat in the end. The production of wealth and the sum of capital are certainly increased by them; and such increase of capital and of production tends in itself to the general good. The actual policy of the trusts, in taking from the public something in higher prices besides their gain through saving, complicates the question; but there is a very considerable gulf between the effects of a trust, like the American Sugar Refining Co., and the effects of a pool, like the Nail association. The actual lessening of the human effort that is required for a given result does accompany the trust, and we all are privileged at least to cherish the pious hope that some small fraction of the gain may ultimately work its way around to us. The pool, on the other hand, does not effect any saving of human effort. Its avowed purpose is to increase its members' share of the products of such effort. Its form of organization is probably incapable of producing the greater part of the social benefits which the trusts lay claim to; and it does not make much pretence of trying to produce them.

The claim of the trusts to a socially desirable effect on price takes two forms — that they make prices lower and that they make them steadier. The former effect has probably not appeared permanently in any instance; and the latter does not seem to have appeared generally. Both effects are, however, within their power. Unsteadiness of price, so far as it results from the action of trusts which have once established their control of the market, is generally the result of high prices. The raising of prices above the competitive level causes competition to develop; and competition can be dislodged only by buying it out or by sinking prices below the competitive level. The trusts are regarded by their managers as permanent institutions, and they tend toward the policy which the managers think likely to bring the greatest net revenue in the long run. They tend toward a comparatively moderate forcing of present profits, with a fair degree of attention to the future. In consequence, if the prices of their goods are not steadier than they would be under full competition, they are probably not much less steady. The nail pool, on the other hand, was an ephemeral thing, designed for a quick rush into the market, a grasping of whatever gains might be within reach, and then — collapse. Its purpose was that of a corner — to get the greatest possible amount of profit out of those who had to have nails within a limited time. Its effect, therefore, was a great exaggeration of the normal unsteadiness of prices.

Too great productive capacity is one of the reasons which are regularly given for forming combinations. The providing of machinery for making far more goods than are demanded at the necessary prices is one of the wastes of competition. Of course it would not be practicable, with the completest centralization, to keep the nominal capacity of machinery down to the actual demand; for variations in the quantities demanded, variations in the kinds demanded, the necessity of being able to make many kinds at each of several places — all forbid an exact adjustment. There is no doubt, however, that here a trust can effect a saving over competitive methods, though it may nullify this benefit more or less completely by stimulating new competition through too high prices. The policy of the nail pool, on the other hand, greatly stimulated the tendency to the overproduction of machinery. The association tried to check it by subsidies to machinery-makers, but with only partial success. Such makers of nail machinery as would accept orders were overwhelmed with them. It was said that persons anxious to get into the nail business "overbid each other, and lucky buyers of machines were offered premiums for their bargains."[1] When the pool collapsed, the machines which the artificially stimulated demand had called forth became, for the most part, dead property. Both to the owners and to society, they are an almost entire waste of capital.

In this way the pool aggravated one of the fundamental difficulties of the situation which it was formed to change. This is, perhaps, its most visibly lasting effect, and from it a serious obstacle arises in the way of renewing the pool. So far as their current business is concerned, the manufacturers might have been in no very different position if the pool had not been formed. The price of nails is now about the same, allowing for the change of extras, as in the spring of 1895. Of the hundreds of new machines which were set up during the eighteen months of fever, a large part have ceased to turn out nails, and as the months go by, others will cease. Some of the older

[1] *Iron Age*, Dec. 10, 1896, p. 1147.

and less efficient will go, one by one, to the scrap pile, and some of the newer may replace them. With the continued progress of invention the rest will doubtless grow relatively less and less efficient. The growth of the country, too, will make a fixed number of machines continually less important as a possible factor in the market. These, however, are processes of years. For a long time to come the hundreds of machines which stand ready to start at a week's notice must be reckoned with by any new combination. A small manufacturer, who was not in the pool, wrote in February, 1897: "I doubt if there will be another combine for a year, but I think it will ultimately come." It will come, as surely as seedtime and harvest; but not in one year, nor, in all probability, in two. It will probably not be possible, until several years have gone by, to form another association which shall effectively control the market.

VI. Conclusions

Only two rather small classes are probably ready to give thanks for the concentrations of industrial and social power which are loosely covered by the name of trusts — those who draw wealth and power from them, and those who, desiring a general absorption of the control of production by society, think that the trusts are forwarding their aim; and some of the former class perhaps would not give thanks without certain haltings of conscience, while many of the latter account the case as one of those in which God makes the wrath of man to praise him. But an unfavorable judgment of the economic and social effects of an institution does not at all involve an unfavorable ethical judgment of the men who visibly represent it — at least in comparison with the rest of the community. The members of the Nail association did what the rest of us would have done in their places. One who was active in forming the association gives this statement of their point of view:

> There is nail machinery enough in this country to produce four times as many nails as can be sold. When there is no pool the makers simply cut each other's throats. Some people think there is something wicked

about pools. When we were trying to get up the nail pool, I talked with directors of companies who held up their hands against going into any sort of combination. I said to them, "How much did you make last year?" "Not a cent." "Are you making anything now?" "No." "Well, what do you propose to do? Sit here and lose what capital you have got in the business?" Some of them thought they could run along until some of the weak concerns died off. But I tell you plants don't die. If a concern fails, they reorganize it. They buy in the plant cheap, they have got rid of the old debts, and they are in better shape to compete than ever. There is only one way to make any money in a business like the nail business, and that is to have a pool.

This is the aspect that things would wear to us if we were in the position of the manufacturers. Some of us are perhaps opposed to combinations; but so were some that went into the nail pool. In weighing any man's opposition to combinations, it may be doubted whether it is of the sort to keep him out of them, till he has sailed the strait between failing profits and the trust, and has passed the siren voice.

The trusts simply do, with larger resources and higher organization, the things that every manager of a competitive business is trying to do. It is possible that we see the character of such things better when they are done on the larger scale; it may be one of the missions of the trusts to give us clearer and higher notions of ethics. But it seems probable that, if we begin to cast stones, the houses of the trusts will not be the only ones to suffer. If it is asserted to be wrong to crowd up the prices of the things we sell and to crowd down the prices of things we buy, wrong to make our business large by the destruction of our neighbor's, a good deal may be said for the ethical superiority of the altruistic man who should refuse to do these things; but no ethical distinction can be drawn between the man who does them strongly and successfully and the man who is only able to do them with less strength and less success.

The mechanism of the trust, properly so called, is perhaps not unworthy to be ranked among the greatest inventions of this century, either as a monument of intellectual acuteness or as an engine of momentous social effects. Like most of those other inventions which are more unanimously classed as useful, and for which individuals get credit, the invention of the trust did not really depend on the activity of any particular men. If neither Bell, nor Reis, nor McDonough, nor Edison had lived, a score of other men were looking for the telephone, and would soon have discovered it. Scientific and technical knowledge had reached a point from which it could not but be discovered; and no man could do more than hasten the discovery by a little. Just so, the development of the pool, the trust, and the giant consolidated corporation was inevitable in the social and economic conditions of our age. If the world had lacked Mr. Rockefeller and his associates, it had other men of business and other lawyers; and it would not long have lacked the trust.

CHARLES E. EDGERTON.

IV

INDUSTRIAL POOLING AGREEMENTS[1]

POOLING agreements are occasionally brought to light by the courts; but a large number live and die in obscurity, without interference, and without attracting attention from the general public. This form of combination has been strengthened and extended simultaneously with the growth in size of our manufacturing companies. The present industrial combinations, which succeeded the downfall of the trust organizations condemned by the courts more than a decade ago, have not obviated the necessity for these pooling agreements. As a matter of fact they seem at the present time rather to have stimulated a revival; for a considerable number of combinations are now parties to the very form of agreement which they were expected to supersede. For this reason, as an important factor in the determination of prices, especially at this present time of low ebb in the fortunes of the combinations formed in 1899–1900, the character and power of these agreements deserve study.

Certain features are common to nearly all forms of pooling. Manufacturers desiring to form a pool usually create an unincorporated organization, such as the Bessemer Steel Association, the Merchants' Ore Association, or the Steel Rail Association. All agree to maintain a schedule of prices fixed by the association, and to limit their production accordingly. Each manufacturer is allowed to produce (or sell) only a certain percentage of the whole output, depending upon the capacity and advantages of his plant. To prevent violation of the agreement, a money deposit is often required from each, forfeitable to the association. In many of the more intricate cases, the

[1] From the *Quarterly Journal of Economics*, Vol. XIX, 1904, pp. 111–123. The History of a Pool, a pamphlet (pages 109) reprinted from the *Iron Age*, N. Y., 1898, is an interesting description of the inside working of these organizations. — ED.

agreement is drawn up by counsel in New York, Pittsburg, or Chicago, the lawyers' offices being used as headquarters for the association. The duties of the legal firm often include, at the same time, the auditing and verification of reports from the various companies. To do this work, a large force of expert accountants may be employed. A fine is imposed where these reports show a production greater than the allotted percentage, and a corresponding bonus is given to plants producing less than their allotment.

The regular meetings of the representatives of the constituent companies are held usually in November or December, in order to adjust prices and allotments for the ensuing year. On account of the non-enforceability of the agreement the minority must be treated fairly. Their withdrawal would mean the breaking up of the association. The money deposit restrains the members from withdrawal only when under slight provocation. The affairs of the pool are handled by the united action of the ablest men in the business. Each owner can manage and develop his own plant, with every inducement to reduce expenses. He knows very closely the amount of his annual output, so that the most economical production would seem possible under such an arrangement.

Territorial division of the market was a feature of the railroad pools, but has not been adopted by many industrial associations. This end is sometimes loosely accomplished by making all factory prices uniform, and adding the freight from factory to selling place to obtain the price at that point. Thus, in the iron and steel associations, prices are usually figured from a base price at Pittsburg. The amount of the freight from this base to the selling point must be added to the base price, to obtain the selling price. For example, if the Pittsburg base price of steel plates is $1.40 per hundred pounds, and the freight from Pittsburg to Iowa is 35 cents, the price in Iowa is $1.75, whether a Chicago or a Philadelphia concern does the selling. This operates to prevent waste in transportation by keeping shipments moving in directions away from the base point. Shipments made toward it suffer a loss in selling value as well as by reason of the expense for freight. Only very strong local interest can secure such a schedule, increasing still further the strength of its position.

Several pools have omitted the feature of percentage allotment, and have placed a tax upon all manufacturing. These are familiar, as they have come before the courts. In the case of the Candle Manufacturers' Association,[1] formed in Ohio in 1880, the members were required to pay into the treasury 2½ cents for every pound of candles sold. A more modern pool, the Addyston Pipe and Steel Company, had an elaborate system by which it fixed the price that a city should pay for pipe, and then gave the contract to the member offering to pay to the pool the highest amount for it. The others put in bids to cover appearances, but took care to name a higher price than that agreed upon. Certain companies were permitted to take all the contracts let by large cities near them, called "reserve" cities. In 1899 the Sherman Act was successfully invoked to terminate this arrangement.[2]

An entirely different form of avoiding competition is through the adoption of a joint sales agent. The various firms agree to sell only through a certain agent or selling corporation. This agent contracts with each firm separately, but guarantees a uniform selling price. He also disposes of the goods from different firms in a given ratio. This ratio may be fixed or may vary with agreed conditions. An exported article would be advantageously controlled in this way. An arrangement of the same sort is most common in the case of articles not patented, and of long established use and approximately standard design. The Union Blue Stone Company[3] in this way effected all the sales for the Blue Stone Association, fixing the price to be charged and the quota to be furnished by each member.

Still another form of pool is based upon patents essential to the manufacture of the article. The patentee sells the rights of use, for a uniform royalty, to all who apply. He also limits the quota to be produced by each firm, above which amount the royalty increases rapidly. Various ways by which patents may be used to control production have been adopted. Thus, for example, the United States Consolidated Seedless Raisin Com-

[1] 47 Ohio State, 320. [2] 20 U. S. 97. [3] 164 N. Y. 401.

pany was an association of nine California firms, owning all the patented raisin-seeding machinery. Members of the company paid a royalty of $\frac{1}{8}$ cent per pound, but outside firms were to pay $\frac{1}{2}$ cent. This form of agreement the courts have upheld as legal.[1] In another case — that of the National Harrow Company — the manufacturers agreed to pay to the owner of the patents, $1 royalty on each harrow sold, and $4 additional on every harrow sold for less than a stipulated price. This form of agreement, unlike the preceding one, was held to be unenforceable at law.[2]

It is common knowledge that pooling agreements of one sort or another are numerous at the present time, but the secrecy with which they are guarded makes it difficult to discover their real extent and character. A single New York law firm, a few months ago, making a specialty of these associations, superintended no less than thirty-nine, each covering some manufactured product in the metal trades. But pools are not restricted to the iron and steel business. They cover a wide range of industry. A part of Mr. C. M. Schwab's testimony before the Industrial Commission bears upon this point.[3]

In the iron and steel trade, however, there would seem to be the majority of these pooling associations and price agreements in operation. As soon as the ore is dug, it is regulated by an association. The "independent" ore producers have organized the Merchants' Ore Association of Cleveland, which adjusts their relations with each other and with other ore producers, such as the United States Steel Corporation. The association attempts to establish the price of the various grades of iron ore and to state to each "independent" the maximum amount of ore that it may produce. The price must be satisfactory to the

[1] 126 Fed. Rep. 364.

[2] 76 Fed. Rep. 667.

[3] Industrial Commission Report, Vol. XIII, p. 474: "The steel rail pools were simple price agreements between the managers of the various works, to sell rails at the same price at the same point.

"*Q.* For manufacturers before the organization of the United States Steel Corporation were similar arrangements existing?

"*A.* Yes: in all lines of business, not only in steel, but in everything else. There were similar agreements, known as joint agreements, to maintain prices. They have existed in all lines of business as long as I can remember."

Steel corporation. The Merchants' Ore Association naturally desires low prices to enable it to sell the largest possible amount of product. With the steel makers owning ore deposits, the price is largely a matter of bookkeeping; but the endeavor is, nevertheless, to keep it high, in order to raise the cost of production for rival steel mills not owning mines. The price of Bessemer ore for 1903 was $4.50 per ton.[1] For 1904 the association wished it to be between $3.25 and $3.80, while the Steel corporation demanded that $4 be the price, threatening to sell ore itself. The Ore association was, however, allowed to fix it at $3.50, although several of its members made long-term contracts to deliver at a sliding scale price, fluctuating with the price of pig iron. This made it impossible for the association to adjust the allotments satisfactorily, and its continued existence was threatened.[2]

Concerning the next stage of manufacture above mining, — namely, of pig iron, — there are also price agreements among the furnace men, who have formed the Bessemer Pig Iron Association. A pool based on steel ingot production was attempted unsuccessfully. Steel billets, however, we find pooled in 1896, and again since 1900. The heavier materials — steel rails, beams, channels, angles, bars, plates of all kinds, shafting axles and rods, wire and wire fencing — are likewise all priced by pools. Among the lighter forms covered by such agreements are chains, nuts, bolts, steel hoops, and bands, pipes and tubing, and hardware. A prominent retail hardware firm stated to the writer that the hardware manufacturers had agreements as to prices covering practically everything in the store, "all shelf hardware" in fact. Judging from the iron business, we may expect to find pooling agreements developed up to the point where trade-marks, style, or individual reputation, become predominant considerations in making a market for the goods.

Four of the most important steel products — billets, rails, beams, and plates — have been specially selected in this study for more detailed analysis as to the effect of pooling upon prices.

[1] *New York Journal of Commerce*, April 22, 1904.
[2] *Iron Age*, May 5, 1904.

The appended diagram has been prepared to show the range of prices since 1890. Only a very brief review of the pools that existed during these years can be given. Were a detailed history of their operations available, the problem presented by their existence might be dealt with more intelligently.

The first billet pool was formed in April, 1896, as an attempt to remedy the extreme fluctuations in price of the year 1895. The Bessemer Steel Association, as it was called, allowed to each firm a percentage of the billet business of the country, estimated at 4,500,000 tons, and imposed a fine of $2 per ton for any excess produced. The association immediately fixed the selling price considerably higher than demand justified, at $21.50. Outside firms promptly took orders at $19.50; and there was also much selling contrary to the agreement by insiders, thereby weakening the pool from the beginning. Moreover, it was possible for the larger firms to avoid the fines for over-production by converting the steel billets into finished shapes before selling. The pool was so very ineffective that a reorganization followed; but even then the agreement could not maintain prices against a demand refusing to accede to the high figure. As the agreement applied only to Bessemer steel, the open hearth steel production was greatly stimulated. An additional open hearth capacity of 500,000 tons and a score of new outside converters helped break up the pool. The guarantee fund of $5,000 failed to prevent its collapse in December, prices falling to $15. The pool had sacrificed what business there was, and had brought out an array of new competitors.[1]

In 1899 the price of billets rose wildly from $16 to $38 per ton, and in 1900 fell no less abruptly to $16. The billet makers decided that they must attempt another agreement.[2] A base price of $19.40 was established, which was easily held, as prices began to rise. But the sliding scale device for fixing the price of billets became an important factor in 1901, the price being

[1] *Iron Age*, 1896, Vol. I, p. 875, gives the original price agreement adopted; Vol. II, p. 223, gives the difficulties encountered; Vol. II, p. 967, describes the billet market, names the leading producers, and the chances of the pool.

[2] *Ibid.*, Jan. 3, 1901, gives a summary of the billet business of 1900, and conditions leading to the pool of Nov. 8, 1900.

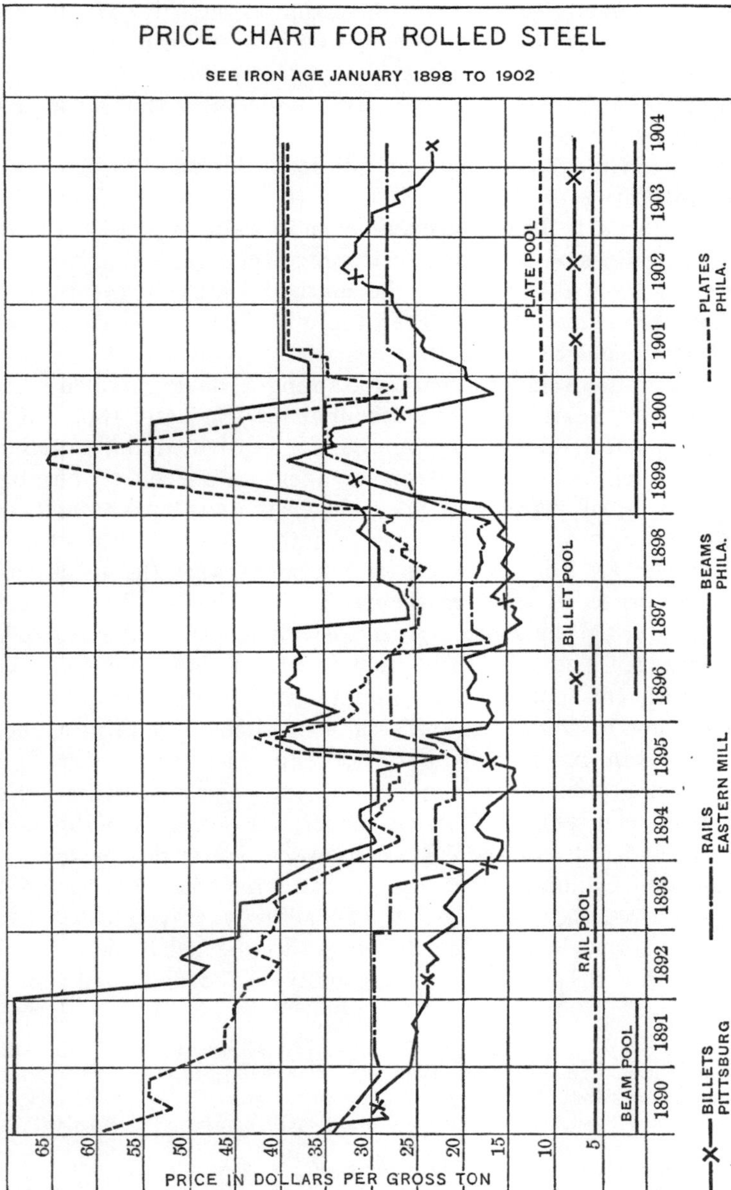
PRICE CHART FOR ROLLED STEEL
SEE IRON AGE JANUARY 1898 TO 1902
PRICE IN DOLLARS PER GROSS TON
65
60
55
50
45
40
35
30
25
20
15
10
5
1890
1891
1892
1893
1894
1895
1896
1897
1898
1899
1900
1901
1902
1903
1904
BEAM POOL
RAIL POOL
BILLET POOL
PLATE POOL
BILLETS PITTSBURG
RAILS EASTERN MILL
BEAMS PHILA.
PLATES PHILA.

found by adding the cost of conversion to the price of pig iron. For instance, if the price of pig iron lies between $16 and $17 per ton, the price of billets is found by adding $6.50. The larger manufacturers adopted this scale, and the subsequent existence of the billet pool has been nominal. Price agreements have been made, and hold or fail as the demand varies. The nominal price of $28, agreed upon by the pool in July, 1903, was reduced to $24 in November, and then to $23.[1] The descending lines of the price curve since 1902 show that the pool has not been able to name the market price. It seems to be shown that the outside billet supply is always very elastic, rendering the billet manufacture essentially competitive.

The rail pool shows remarkable strength, having named prices for sixteen years, with the exception of 1897 and 1898. This pool was formed in August, 1887.[2] It divided the estimated rail demand among the fifteen members, in agreed proportions. The fixing of prices was not part of the written contract, but informal agreements were entered into. A penalty of $1.50 to $2.50 per ton for all excess of allotment kept the firms from cutting prices in order to secure more business. In regard to prices during the existence of this combination the *Iron Age* remarks: "The price that was asked for rails by the mills was decidedly reasonable. Manufacturers whose demand varies ought not to starve the mills in poor times." The agreement came to an end in 1893, but was renewed after a sharp fight. Increasing difficulty was met in adjusting the allotments during the following years. Outside concerns had to be bought off or subsidized until, in 1896, $1,000,000 was spent in this way. It had been estimated that the demand for that year would be about 2,200,000 tons, but it was actually only 800,000 tons. Concerns that had produced little, and expected heavy bonuses, found that they had to pay a penalty. The dissatisfaction re-

[1] The *Journal of Commerce*, April 8, 1904, reports a meeting of the pool, naming the members. The present agreement includes the United States Steel Corporation, Jones & Laughlin's, Wheeling Steel and Iron Company, Cambria Steel Company, Lackawanna Steel Company, Pennsylvania Steel Company, and Maryland Steel Company.

[2] *Iron Age* of Nov. 16, 1893, gives full details.

sulted in secret cutting of prices and the breaking up of the pool.[1] There was immediate talk of renewal; but it was not attempted until prices began to rise in 1899, when the present pool was formed.[2] *

The contrast between the billet and the rail price curves is very striking. The former is irregular, showing constant fluctuations; while the latter is made up of long horizontal lines, with abrupt changes, showing that the effect of the pool was to steady prices for considerable periods. In justice to the rail pool it should be noted that in 1901 and 1902, when billets rose from $20 to $32, the price of rails remained $28. The price of beams was also held, but the plate pool raised the price $4. Agreements hold well in the rail business, because it is confined to less than a dozen firms, and is comparatively easy to control.[3] Rails are sold direct to the consumer; and, moreover, special freight rates may have helped to keep up the market price of this product.

The beam pool was organized soon after the rail pool by the mills rolling structural steel shapes, such as I-beams and channels. The $70 figure of 1890 was a pool price, maintained under small demand, by eleven firms producing nine-tenths of the supply. Foreign beams began to be imported in 1891 at $46; and, to stop this, the pool agreed to lower the price to $56. But the Carnegie company had just finished a beam mill large enough to supply the whole demand of the country, and was not satisfied with the allotment given by the pool. This company seems to have been constantly on the alert, when pooling

[1] *Iron Age*, Feb. 11, 1897, reviews the pool's history.

[2] *Ibid.*, Jan. 1, 1901, describes the agreement made.

* In June, 1904, an international pool between the German and English manufacturers was attempted. It is too early to determine its effect upon the export trade of the two countries. — Ed.

[3] *Iron Age* of Feb. 11, 1897, gives the 1897 allotment thus:

Carnegie	53.50 per cent.
Lackawanna	19.00 " "
Cambria	8.25 " "
Bethlehem	8.25 " "
Maryland	2.75 " "
Pennsylvania	8.25 " "
	100.00 " "

agreements were weakening, to gather in orders at lower figures. Prices fell $22 at once. Boston merchants had a stock of 2500 tons of imported beams left on their hands to dispose of at a loss, and many manufacturers suffered heavily.

An agreement made in 1896 held for a short time, but was broken in the attempt to keep prices stationary in a declining market. Even when the rail pool broke, the beam makers do not seem to have realized that it may be expedient for pools to lower prices as well as to raise them. When the break occurred, in May, 1897, the price of beams fell $12 a ton.[1]

The present pool was formed in 1898 by six leading firms.[2] The agreement since then has been renewed annually. The price has been kept at $1.60 per hundred pounds, Pittsburg, since 1901. Foreign beams came in during 1902–03 on account of the overcrowding of our mills, being able to command a premium by quick delivery. The steadiness of the price of steel beams during 1901–02, as shown by the chart, when billets rose rapidly, is in marked contrast with the fluctuations of 1899, when, as billet prices rose, the beam makers advanced prices with leaps and bounds. This change of policy was partly due to the influence of the Steel corporation. More than any other steel company it must maintain a large volume of business without interruption in order to meet heavy charges. The price of beams in this case was already sufficient to give a reasonable profit. Moreover, a large demand indirectly increased the corporation's profits by reason of its ownership of other subsidiary companies.

The plate pool is a recent development, having existed since 1900 only. The line on the diagram, showing the course of prices of steel plates, is remarkable, inasmuch as it shows a far more violent fluctuation during 1899–1900 than in the case of the other pooled products — rails and beams. In February, 1899, the price of plates was $1.30 per hundred pounds at Pittsburg. Buyers who anticipated high prices bought until in

[1] *Iron Age* of May 20, 1897, describes this pool.

[2] *Ibid.*, Jan. 12, 1902. The firms are the Carnegie Steel Company, Jones & Laughlin's, Cambria Steel Company, Pennsylvania Steel Company, Passaic Iron Works, Pencoyd Iron Works.

August the price had reached $3. As the turning-point was seen, buyers, becoming frightened, withdrew; and the rolling mills fought to secure business, until a price of 95 cents was reached in July, 1900. This ruinous condition was the cause of several meetings, resulting in an agreement between the plate mills in October. Orders came in as soon as the stability of the pool seemed assured, and the year closed with 400,000 tons of orders on hand. Prices were fixed as usual, with a Pittsburg base, freight being added to this base for prices at other points.

An enormous demand for steel plates developed during 1901–1902, due largely to the steel car and steel ship industries. The price was raised to $1.60 in April, 1901, at which it has now stood for three years. The growth of new rivals was checked, and the maintenance of the price during the present slackness was made easier, by the policy of reasonable prices in good times. The pool prevented buyers from competing and pushing up prices in 1901–02, although small mills at one time secured 65 cents excess, for immediate delivery. This excess disappeared in July, 1903, when mills began to close down for lack of orders. The old price was renewed, however, in December.[1] It was thought that the small demand could not be increased by a slight reduction in price. This, however, would seem to be dangerous reasoning, judging by the failures of other pools under similar circumstances.

General conclusions are apt to be misleading on a subject such as this, where full information is carefully withheld; but from the available history of these pools, as outlined, certain facts seem to be fairly well established. It is not possible by law to prevent all price agreements, nor is such a policy desirable. For in such an event, with quick transportation at low rates, competitors are free to fight each other until the more powerful firms drive the weaker ones to the wall. The victors are then free to recoup their losses as quickly as possible at the public expense. Both very low prices and exceptionally high ones are harmful to business in general, and to the public. The manufacturers would seem to be justified in making some

[1] *Journal of Commerce*, Dec. 19, 1903.

agreement, and in allowing one another to continue to share in the business in definite proportions, in order to prevent this destructive warfare.

Two remedial policies are open to competitors in such an event. Either an industrial combination may be effected; or refuge may be sought in one of these price agreements or pools. The railroads were driven to adopt the policy of buying up competitors, — a policy resulting, for a time at least, in embarrassments and receiverships. They have found it necessary to come to some agreement on reasonable and equal rates. The industrial companies, following them some years later, have attempted gigantic consolidations, the result of which is at present doubtful. Most manufacturers would prefer to own their own plants, making whatever arrangements were necessary for continued existence, rather than to lose their identity by selling to a corporation. And direct management by a manufacturing owner may be expected to be more efficient than management by distant financiers representing stockholders.

The second remedy for ruinous competition lies in industrial pools, such as were constantly formed, broken up, and re-formed, until about 1900. This instability seems to have resulted from the fact that no pool or price agreement can continue where the price has not been fixed at a reasonable figure; for new capital is always ready to seek investment where profits are known to be ample. However widely the pool may extend, it cannot absorb all of this idle capital. Only when the pool price is too low unduly to tempt the outsider to build or enlarge his plant is its position at all secure. Another factor of note is that pools are always most favorable to the outside plants, which can enjoy the advantages of the pool price without feeling the restrictions.[1]

Inherent weakness breaks up many, from dissatisfaction with the allotment and the constant temptation to shade the price or

[1] See the Industrial Commission Report, Vol. XIII, p. 492. Mr. Butler says: "I would state as a general law that combinations are always to the advantage of the small concern, . . . that a combination was always to the advantage of the little fellow, whose growth is at the expense of the large concern."

to conceal sales. The pools are in several instances being supplanted by the sliding scale adjustment of prices, based upon the price of the raw material. The effect of the temporary pools is thoroughly bad. Their false profits lead to a misdirected investment of capital, as in the case of the nail pool, where plants sprang up during high prices, so that two months' full operation would have supplied the market for a year. The inevitable price variations are greatly exaggerated, because purchasers refrain from buying when the market is falling, sending prices to the very bottom. Mr. Meade's statement, that the prices which follow the dissolution of a pool are lower than those that brought the producers together,[1] has been frequently illustrated.

These powerful associations exist without supervision of any kind, our knowledge of them being gained chiefly as they fail. Although, since the Trans-Missouri Freight Association, and other anti-combination decisions, all such arrangements have been carried on in secret, it is doubtful if their scope has been appreciably diminished. During the last four years they seem to be on the increase, as a matter of fact. Having been denied recognition by law, they have necessarily devised methods of their own, to preserve their agreement by fines and bribes. Their existence and effectiveness at present would seem to indicate reasonable prices as well as reasonable use of their inherent power in other ways. Experience shows that, were their policy otherwise, the pool would be in danger of breaking suddenly at any time. In any event, a more satisfactory arrangement is certainly desirable. In Germany, pooling agreements have been made enforceable by the courts, and their affairs are subject to government supervision. The evils caused by pools with the "get-rich-quick motive" might, perhaps, in the United States be avoided by a similar legal recognition of the economic justification for associations among independent manufacturers, with agreements both reasonable and enforceable.

WALLACE E. BELCHER.

[1] Trust Finance, p. 28.

V

THE ADDYSTON PIPE COMPANY[1]

THE relevant facts may be classified under the following headings: first, the terms of the trust agreement; second, its purposes; third, its practical construction and operation; fourth, its effects upon the public.

I. Terms of the Agreement

The six companies are located as follows:

Addyston Co.	Cincinnati, Ohio.
Dennis Long & Co.	Louisville, Ky.
South Pittsburg Co.	South Pittsburg, Tenn.
Chattanooga Co.	Chattanooga, Tenn.
Anniston Co.	Anniston, Ala.
Howard Harrison Co.	Bessemer, Ala.

It is to be borne in mind in understanding this agreement that the greater part of the business consists in taking contracts for municipal corporations, gas or water companies, and other large institutions which usually invite bids from various competitors.

The earlier agreement of December 28, 1894, is of present importance only in so far as its provisions have been continued in effect, namely, in respect to the "reserved cities" and to the extent of the "pay territory." The main agreement was proposed by John W. Harrison, President of the Howard Harrison Co., on May 16, 1895, and adopted on May 27, 1895, in the form of a resolution entered upon the minutes of the association. It is as follows (page 83):

[1] From argument of Hon. E. B. Whitney, U. S. Assistant Attorney-General, in *U. S.* v. *Addyston Pipe and Steel Co.*, U. S. Circuit Court of Appeals, Sixth Circuit. Appeal Case No. 498. Page references run to the testimony in the official court record.

That from and after the first day of June that all competition on the pipe lettings shall take place among the various pipe shops prior to the said letting. To accomplish this purpose it is proposed that the six competitive shops have a "representative board" located at some central city to whom all inquiries for pipe shall be referred, and said board shall fix the price at which said pipe shall be sold, and bids taken from the respective shops for the privilege of handling the order, and the party securing the order shall have the protection of all the other shops. . . . All division of bonuses to remain as now established during the year 1895.

This system of bidding is known as "buying a job" (page 89). One exception to the general rule is that of the "reserved cities" which remain tacitly under the resolution of December 28, 1894, as follows (pages 77–78):

Third. The Addyston Pipe and Steel Company shall handle the business of the Gas and Water companies of Cincinnati, Ohio, Covington and Newport, Ky., and pay the bonus hereafter mentioned, and the balance of the parties to this agreement shall bid on such work such reasonable prices as they shall dictate.

Fourth. Dennis Long and Company of Louisville, Ky., shall handle Louisville, Ky., Jeffersonville, Ind., and New Albany, Ind., furnishing all the pipe for Gas and Water works in above named cities.

Fifth. The Anniston Pipe and Foundry Company shall handle Anniston, Ala., and Atlanta, Ga., furnishing all pipe for Gas and Water companies in above named cities.

Sixth. The Chattanooga Foundry and Pipe Works shall handle Chattanooga, Tenn., and New Orleans, La., furnishing all gas and water pipe in the above named cities.

Seventh. The Howard Harrison Iron Company shall handle Bessemer and Birmingham, Ala., and St. Louis, Mo., furnishing all pipe for Gas and Water companies in the above named cities; extra bonus to be put on East St. Louis and Madison, Ill., so as to protect the prices named for St. Louis, Mo.

Eighth. South Pittsburg Pipe Works shall handle Omaha, Neb., on all sizes required by that city during the year of 1895, conferring with the other companies and coöperating with them; thereafter they shall handle the Gas and Water companies of Omaha, Neb., on such sizes as they make.

NOTE.—It is understood that all the shops who are members of this association shall handle the business of the gas and water companies of the cities set apart for them including all sizes of pipe made by them.

A modification was made, however, on December 19, 1895, as follows (page 84):

That upon all inquiries from prices from "reserved cities" for pipe required during the year of 1896, that prices and bonus shall be fixed at a regular or called meeting of the principals.

Another exception recognized was that of "special customers" of the different concerns. As to these it was resolved on May 27, 1895 (page 84):

That when an inquiry is reported to which a member can properly establish a claim as a special customer, such inquiry should not be disposed of by the "auction basis," but shall be handled by such member, the committee fixing the price and bonus, such price and bonus to be commensurate with prices and bonuses at the time such inquiry shall be reported.

It was further resolved on the same day (page 84):

That all parties to this association having quotations out shall notify their customers that the same will be withdrawn by June 1, 1895, if not previously accepted, and upon all business accepted on or after June 1st, bonuses shall be fixed by the committee.

The provisions of this agreement operated only in what was called the "pay territory" or "bonus territory." This territory is described in the pleadings, the opinion of Judge Clark, and the resolution at page 78 of the record. It includes the whole of the United States except Virginia and the States north and east thereof, and except the Territory of Alaska.

The bonuses, when not fixed on the "auction basis," are fixed by a schedule shown on page 78, by such modifications as have since been made therein, or by special order of the committee.

To carry out the objects of the association, headquarters were established at Cincinnati, Ohio, with an office force and a committee of representatives from the various shops (pages 83–84). The bonuses, after December 20, 1895, were divided according to a schedule based on the following estimated tonnage of the various shops (page 86):

	Tons
South Pittsburg	15,000
Anniston	30,000
Chattanooga	40,000
Bessemer	45,000
Louisville	45,000
Cincinnati	45,000

The bonuses were not paid upon the acceptance of the bid or even upon the successful closing of the contract with the purchaser, but only upon the actual shipment of the pipe. Thus the schedule last quoted reads as follows (page 86):

1st. On the first 90,000 tons of pipe *shipped* into "pay territory" 16" and smaller sizes shall be divided among the six shops [etc.].

In order to insure the proper working of the combination, an auditor's office was established and regular reports required. Thus (pages 80–82):

Third, Sec. 1st. Each shop shall report daily to the auditor all orders secured in bonus or free territory, giving the shop number [etc.].

Sec. 2d. On the 1st and 16th of each month they shall report to the auditor all *shipments* made in all territory, giving shop number [etc.]; showing the amount of bonus and tonnage, of the bonus as well as free territory.

Sec. 4th. The auditor shall make carbon copies daily of all reports received, and send one to each shop, and to such others as may be designated.

* * * * * * * *

Sec. 3d. He shall on the 1st and 16th of each month, or as soon as practicable, send to each shop a statement of all shipments reported in the previous half months, with a balance sheet showing the total amount of the premiums on *shipments*, the division of the same, and a debit credit balance of each company; also a statement of free orders secured during the same period; and a memorandum of balance payable from one to another.

* * * * * * * *

Whoever has a representative at any public letting shall instruct him to send to the auditor a full list of the bids and bidders on same; also that all information in regard to work taken in pay territory by the shops outside of this association shall be reported to the auditor, who shall keep a proper record of such information and send carbon copies of same to all of the members of this association.

* * * * * * * *

That whenever an order is reported by any shop, and a doubt exists as to the proper bonus to be paid, that it be reported with the facts in the case, to be acted upon at the next meeting of the executive committee.

The combination also kept a "black list" for some boycotting purpose not explained (page 90).

* * * * * * * *

2. Purposes of the Agreement

The agreement of May 27, 1895, contains the following recital of its purpose (pages 82–83):

Whereas, the system now in operation in this association of having a "fixed bonus on the several States" has not in its operation resulted in the *advancement in the prices of pipe* as was anticipated, *except in "reserved cities,"* and some further action is imperatively necessary in order to accomplish *the ends for which this association was formed:* Therefore [etc.]

Mr. Bowron of the South Pittsburg company says that the association was established "to maintain fair prices and a just distribution of work" — "to maintain fair prices and secure for each a fair proportion of the work in a certain territory, by restraining in a certain measure competition as among themselves only" — "to restrain competition as among defendants and allow to each a profitable division of work according to its relative capacity, and thereby maintain fair prices to all" (pages 194–195).

Mr. C. W. Harrison of the same company says that it was "on the theory that destructive competition results in monopoly," and that it "was the purpose of this association to maintain fair prices and secure for each of its members a fair proportion of the work in a certain territory by restraining in a reasonable measure competition as among themselves only" (page 216).

Mr. Callahan of the Louisville company says that it was "to maintain fair prices, to regulate credits, and to accomplish an equitable distribution of such orders as the six defendants could secure in competition with the other manufacturers of cast iron pipe" — "by regulating to a certain extent the competition among the defendants only, to endeavor to maintain fair prices, and to secure to each of the defendants a fair proportion of the orders in a certain territory" (pages 263–264).

In describing the auction system, Mr. Callahan clearly states what "fair prices" mean as understood by such combinations: "These voluntary offers from defendants were each based upon such prices for the respective orders as these defendants considered would be fair and reasonable prices" (page 264).

That fairness and reasonableness from the consumers' point of view was not at all taken into consideration is shown by the prices actually charged in "pay territory" as set forth in the record, and by a letter of Mr. Thomasson of the Chattanooga company (pages 102–103):

> We believe that as a general thing we have had our prices entirely too high, and especially do we believe this has been the case as to prices in "reserved cities." The prices made at St. Louis and Atlanta are entirely out of all reason, and the result has been and always will be, when high prices are named, to create a bad feeling and an agitation against the "Combination." There is no reason why Atlanta, New Orleans, St. Louis, or Omaha should be made to pay higher prices for their pipe than any other places near them who do not use anything like the amount of pipe and whose trade is not as desirable for many other reasons.

The affidavits of defendants show how in some respects this combination works beneficially by distributing orders in such a manner that a greater regularity of employment is obtained at the different shops. This is immaterial. Probably few unlawful combinations would fail to secure economy of service to some considerable extent. The element of evil does not fail to vitiate the agreement because it contains likewise an element of good. A most interesting letter of Mr. Thomasson (pages 110–112) shows that the bonus system was not intended to work, and did not actually work, simply as a distributor of employment, leaving the price charged to the consumer merely the actual cost with a fair business profit. While some proportion of the bonus may represent economy in production, a part of it is shown to represent an extra profit divided up among the different companies. Mr. Thomasson points out how the Bessemer company is going too far in speculating on this extra profit, and how his own company is secretly taking advantage of this error of its associate (page 111):

If they should continue to buy all the pipe that goes up to such figures as they have paid for Jacksonville and other points, they would wreck their shop in a few months. However, they of course calculate this bonus *will be returned to them on work taken by other shops*. We are very much pleased with the bonus that has been paid, and we only hope they will keep it up as it is only money in our pockets. . . . We note Mr. Thornton's report of average premiums from June 1 to December that the average was $3.63. The average bonuses that are prevailing to-day are $7 to $8. We cannot expect this to continue. . . . If we cannot secure business in "pay territory" at paying prices, we think we will be able to dispose of our output in "free territory," and of course make some profit on that. At the prices that Howard Harrison people paid for Jacksonville, Des Plaines, and one or two other points, they are losing from $2.50 to $3 per ton, that is, provided "bonuses" would not be returned to them. Therefore when business goes at a loss we are willing that the other shops make it. . . .

P.S. — Do not leave this letter on your desk, where it might fall into the hands of others. Make a memorandum and tear the letter up. Above all things make a confidant of no one in business matters.

I shall comment again later on this letter.

3. Practical Construction and Operation

The record gives some interesting information about the working of this agreement in different cities.

Chicago. — At a meeting of the associates on February 14, 1896, it was decided that an order of the Chicago Gas Company should be filled at $22 and $21.50 with a bonus of $5 (page 88), and (apparently on some other Chicago advertisement, page 89):

On motion of A. F. Callahan, it was agreed on the dates of the Chicago letting at least five of the shops should be represented and a majority of them should decide what bid should be made. The job to be regularly disposed of by the committee before the letting.

The presence of five shops at the letting was in pursuance of the system of "protecting bids," by slightly higher false bids on the part of the companies which had agreed with the combination not genuinely to compete for the order. This system has been consistently maintained by the associates. Its advantages for purposes of concealment are obvious.

Louisville. — The record of December 28, 1895, contains the following (page 85):

F. B. Nichols moved that Dennis Long & Company be *allowed* to close contract for the year of 1896, with the Louisville Water Company at the best price they can obtain for same, and after securing contract refer the same to the meeting of the principals to fix bonus.

Seconded by A. F. Callahan. Carried.

St. Louis. — Mr. Nichols of the Bessemer company writes to the other companies on January 24, 1896, as follows (page 94):

I prefer that if any of you find it necessary to put in a bid without going to St. Louis, please bid not less than $27.00 for the pipe, and 2¾ cents per pound for the specials. I would also like to know as to which of you would find it convenient to have a representative at the letting. It will be necessary to have two outside bidders.

St. Louis was a "reserved city" belonging to the Bessemer company (page 77), and paying a bonus of $2 per ton (page 78). The amount shipped from April 1, to December 31, 1895, was 10,970 tons, giving a bonus of about $22,000 to the combination (pages 94–95).

Knoxville. — The Knoxville Woollen mills on April 25, 1896, wrote to Chattanooga and Bessemer for quotations of cast iron pipe (page 62). This contract seems to have been bid in by Chattanooga, which telegraphed the other companies on April 29: "We will advance price Knoxville Woollen mills dollar and half; please protect" (page 96), at the same time bidding $22 per ton (page 63). Bessemer accordingly, through Mr. Nichols, bid $22.24 per ton on April 30, with the hypocritical comment, "Trusting that we will be favored with your order, we are yours truly" (pages 63–64).

Omaha. — The working of the agreement is well shown by the bidding for Omaha on December 20, 1895 (page 87):

W. L. Davis moved to sell the 519 pieces of 20″ pipe for Omaha, Neb., for $23.40 delivered.

Seconded by D. R. P. Dimmick. Carried.

F. B. Nichols moved that Anniston participate in this bonus and the job be sold over the table.

Seconded by W. L. Davis. Carried.

Pursuant to the motion the 519 pieces of 20″ pipe for Omaha was sold to Bessemer at a premium of $8.

The water companies of Omaha belong to South Pittsburg (page 77). The receiver of one of them called for bids in April, 1896, under competitive circumstances which the company's agent evidently thought "will make him some trouble, especially if we try to obtain too high a price" (pages 120–121). In response to a call upon Chattanooga for "protection" Mr. Thomasson wrote as follows on April 28 (page 121):

Please advise us at once as to what figure we shall make on this work. Please do not ask us to make a price of two or three dollars per ton higher than yours, but give us a reasonable price to name.

The Pittsburg company responded (page 122):

We request that you please quote the American Water Works Company of Omaha price of $24.80 per ton of 2000 pounds f. o. b. Omaha.

Accordingly Chattanooga wrote the following candid letter to the Receiver at Omaha (page 122):

DEAR SIR: Replying to your favor of the 25th instant, we propose to furnish cast iron pipe as per specifications for $24.80 per ton two thousand pounds, and will furnish special castings from our regular patterns for two and one-fourth cents per pound, all delivered on board cars Omaha, Neb. We are in a position to give you prompt shipment on this pipe *and trust this time we will be favored with your order.*

Very truly, yours,
CHATTA. FDY. & PIPE WORKS,
By E. B. THOMASSON.

Such letters may afford the court some hint as to the amount of weight which can be placed upon the testimony of the gentlemen who manage this honest combination.

Atlanta. — This city was the property of the Anniston company (page 77), which paid a bonus of $2 per ton as the rent of the property (page 78), until it was provided that such bonuses should be fixed at a meeting of the principals (page 84). On February 15, 1896, the Chattanooga company had an inquiry from the Atlanta Water Works for 1500 feet of 12″ pipe, and about 12,000 feet of pipe varying from 6″ to 10″ with a lot of special castings. The company, through Mr. Thomasson, at once asked Anniston "As to what price you desire us to protect on this contract" (page 97). Anniston answered through Mr. Dimmick (page 97):

> Please protect $24 on approximately 375 tons of cast-iron pipe for the city of Atlanta, Ga., on which we are asked to-day for prices. We have sent a man over to Atlanta and will get as much more as possible.

This price was nearly $10 per ton (less cost of transportation) over what would be a paying profit at Chattanooga (page 111). Chattanooga, however, bid $24.50 per ton delivered on board cars at Atlanta, adding with its usual ingenuousness: "We can give you a prompt delivery on above pipe and would be pleased to receive your order" (page 98). A lower bid had been received from R. D. Wood & Co., of Philadelphia, but all bids were rejected by the Atlanta people, as they "were extremely high" (page 98). The bids thus rejected give a good example of the method by which these companies "protected" each other, and incidentally led the consumer to suppose the prices reasonable. They were: Anniston, $24; Bessemer, $24.25; South Pittsburg, $24.25; Chattanooga, $24.50 (page 53).

Anniston at once telegraphed Chattanooga: "Stand pat on your price" (page 99), and in response to complaints about the high price replied: "We believe we made a mistake in trying to get $24 for pipe and 2½ cents for specials, but there would have been no difficulty in this respect had we not run up against R. D. Wood & Co.'s man there putting in his bid for hydrants, and he also put in a bid for the pipe and specials at the last moment;" that "they [the Atlanta authorities] stated it was their belief that the four southern shops have an arrangement by which Anniston is to get the work; in other words, that we had a combination between us, and if they can find it out positively, they will never receive a bid from any of us again;" and recommended that all four southern shops have representatives on the ground at the next letting on March 4 (pages 99–100). The Anniston company's report from its agent at Atlanta is given in full at pages 100–101. Besides the Philadelphia man he met Mr. Torbett, Secretary of the Water board, Mr. Erwin, one of the Water Commissioners, and Colonel Woodward, Superintendent of the Water Works. He told the city council that "the ruling market price" would be about $24, and got a favorable resolution through the council without a dissenting vote. The Philadelphia man, however, at the last moment put in a bid of $23. The threat against the four southern shops came from Mr. Erwin, and Colonel Woodward also advised the rejection of all bids. The colonel's advice may have been on the ground that "he promised me when there last he would give us another chance in the event we were not the lowest bidders." In other words, he knew that the Anniston company could afford to furnish the pipe at a lower price than what they were passing off as the "ruling market price." It is not surprising that the colonel appears as an affiant on behalf of the Anniston company, maintaining that its prices were "fair, reasonable, and moderate" (pages 200–202), though perhaps it may be surprising that Mr. Erwin fell in line with him (page 202).

Negotiations were opened with the Philadelphia concern to prevent its appearance at the second bidding (page 103). On April 10 (page 59) the contract was made with the Anniston company at $22.75 for the year's supply, and $22 for some "special shipments." Assuming the cost with a fair profit at Anniston to be substantially the same as at Chattanooga, and assuming the freight from Anniston to Atlanta to be $1.60 per ton (page 90), this made a price of about $6.75 per ton over and above a fair and reasonable profit. This seems to be an underestimate, because we find the following entry in the minutes of the Associated Pipe Works for March 13, 1896 (page 90):

Moved that "bonus" on Anniston's Atlanta Water Works contract be fixed at $7.10, provided freight is $1.60 a ton. Carried.

Before payment was made by the Atlanta Water Works, an investigation was had, based upon charges by the same man whose information led to the present suit. The charges were referred to a special committee, consisting of Messrs. Erwin and Torbett and one Hass, on May 18, 1896 (page 203). The city's attorneys had advised that the city could recover in a suit against the Anniston Works (pages 207–210). The committee, however, unanimously overruled the attorneys after hearing the officers of the Anniston company (pages 203–210).

4. The Effects upon the Public

It is not essential to show deleterious effects upon the public, but the subject is an interesting one, and the gleams of light from this record are also interesting.

The defendants have repeated *ad nauseam* affidavits tending to show that there were other large works — larger perhaps than their own — in the United States. A tonnage statement, for instance, is given (by an interested witness and annexed to an evasive affidavit) of factories through the country, including some very large ones in Pennsylvania and New Jersey (page 270).

It also appears, however, that the rates of freight are very high. For instance, pipe which is worth from $13 to $14.75 at the shop in Chattanooga (page 111) pays $6 to Peabody, Mass., and $5.55 to Lockhaven, Pa. (page 104); $5.60 to Clifton, N. Y. (page 105), $4.80 to Wytheville, Va., $5.40 to Troy, N. Y., $3.90 to Allegheny, Pa., and $4.95 to Syracuse, N. Y. (page 106). The effect of these high rates, together with the location of these factories on or near the west slope of the Appalachian mountain range, gives to them (and to the few other western works) a practical monopoly of nearly all the "pay territory"— in other words, of everything but the Northern and the Middle states. To this general statement there must be, of course, an exception as to localities on the coast line and elsewhere within the "pay territory" that are within the reach of northeastern factories. The small importance of these exceptions, however, may be gathered from the affidavits submitted by defendants themselves. They have undertaken to show the actual origin of the pipe used in large portions of the "pay territory," and have only succeeded in identifying the great Pennsylvania and New Jersey factories with two small lots of unspecified amount (pages 213, 271). They content themselves with such evasive statements as those of Mr. Callahan at page 265 of the record, specifying neither the size of the orders nor the portions of the "pay territory" where they are found.

It is clear that as to the bulk of the "pay territory" — that is, as to the bulk of the United States — their competition comes from but few rivals. In main it seems to be confined to the works at Cleveland, Columbus, and Newcomerstown, Ohio, and Detroit, Mich., whose capacity is 200, 100, 75, and 75 tons per day, respectively (pages 197, 250, 181, 188). A concern is indeed mentioned as competing at St. Louis, but it is suspected to be identical with the Bessemer concern (pages 61–62), with which it is almost identical in name. The factories in Colorado and Oregon are small and seem to cut only a local figure. The same may be said of the Texas penitentiary.

Such information as is given us leads to the conclusion that the Ohio and Michigan concerns have the smaller end of the business, even in territory for which transportation rates permit them to compete. Mr. Hallett, a general contractor in Aurora, Ill., gives the precise figures for his purchases in 1895 and 1896. He purchased 514 tons from the combination, 25 tons from the Newcomerstown concern (J. B. Clow & Son), and 50 tons from jobbers (pages 123–124). Mr. W. H. Garrett, of Batavia, Ill., gives the purchases of the Water Works Department of Fairbanks, Morse & Co. for the same period. They included 1023 tons from the combination, 690 tons from Columbus, 79 tons from Cleveland, and 35 tons from the Glamorgan Pipe and Foundry Co. of Lynchburg, Va. These purchases were "in the business of contracting water works for municipalities *throughout the United States*" (pages 129–130).

We could judge more accurately of the strength of the Associated Pipe Works if we were definitely informed as to their capacity *per diem*. They have been so careful to produce testimony as to the *perdiem* capacity of other companies (pages 178–179, 180–181, 187–189, 196–198, 198–200, 249–250) that we may infer that there was good reason for their failing to be specific as to their own. The only specific testimony bearing on the point is that of Mr. Llewellyn as to his Chattanooga company. He gives its capacity at "about 40,000 tons of cast iron pipe and special castings annually" (page 243). This figure, however, is evidently taken from the minutes of the combination at page 86, which is shown by Mr. Thomasson of his own company not to represent the actual capacity of the various works, but their usual output (page 111). The 40,000 tons ascribed to Chattanooga represent its proportion of the 220,000 which are assumed, not as the full capacity of the works, but as their probable annual shipments into pay territory. The total of these shipments is estimated at 220,000 for the six companies, but Mr. Thomasson says:

> We think a very conservative estimate of shipments into this territory will amount to fully 200,000 this year; more than that — probably overrun 240,000 tons.

The same estimate which gives Chattanooga 40,000 gives South Pittsburg and Anniston 45,000 combined (page 86); but the officers of these companies join with Mr. Llewellyn himself in verifying the answer (pages 43–44), which contains the following statement as to the "pay territory" (page 36):

> They, however, deny that the shipments of pipe for 1896 amount to more than 100,000 tons in said territory, which they aver could have been supplied by any two of defendants so as to deprive all others of any share thereof.

In ascertaining the actual capacity we may therefore pretty safely double the estimate at page 86, and assume it to be 440,000 tons a year, or nearly 1,500 tons per day, as against the 450 tons per day of their four principal rivals.

As confirmatory of the position that no reliance is to be placed upon the statements of these defendants as to the relative working capacity of the different shops (except when their statements are not made for use in the present suit), we may compare the answer which they all join in verifying with the testimony of their own witnesses concerning the capacity of other works. Thus, the answer states the capacity of Scottdale as 200 tons instead of 100; of Columbus as 150 tons instead of 100; and of Detroit as 100 tons instead of 75 (pages 44, 179, 188, 250).

Another example of the misleading character of this testimony is in the statement of Mr. Callahan at page 265 as to the actual clearance settlements amounting in 1895 to only 38 cents per ton, when compared with Mr. Thomasson's letter of January 2, 1896, showing that the average premiums from June 1 to December 31, 1895, were $3.63 (page 111).

Besides the partial monopoly which they were enabled to maintain through the high transportation rates and the limited output of their western rivals, they doubtless resorted to special means for diverting rivalry, such as the negotiation for the withdrawal of the Philadelphia company from competition at Atlanta (page 103), and the plan to prevent one Drummond "from invading our western territory" (page 113).

Reasonableness of prices. — It will be borne in mind that, even under the common law doctrine permitting reasonable restraints of trade, the burden of proof as to reasonableness is on the defendant.

"Wherever such contract *stat indifferenter*, and, for aught appears, may be either good or bad, the law presumes it *prima facie* to be bad" (Lord Macclesfield in *Mitchel* v. *Reynolds*, *supra*, at page 701). "In all restraints of trade, where nothing more appears, the law presumes them bad" (id., at page 704). "The general rule is that all restraints of trade which the law so much favors, if nothing more appear, are bad" (Willes, C. J., in *Master of Gunmakers* v. *Fell*, Willes, 388). "Contracts in restraint of trade are in themselves, if nothing more appears to shew them reasonable, bad in the eye of the law" (Tindal, C. J., in *Horner* v. *Graves*, 7 Bing., 735, 744; S. P. Patterson on "Contracts in Restraint of Trade," page 5; *Pierce* v. *Fuller*, 8 Mass., 223; *Chappell* v. *Brockway*, 21 Wend., 157, 159; Addison on "Contracts," page 1154).

We have in this record, however, affirmative evidence of the unreasonableness of the profits obtained by these corporations. Their unreasonableness is shown in various ways, such as by adding the price at the factory (page 111) to the transportation rate (page 90), and comparing this with the prices actually obtained, which usually range from about $22 to $25 per ton. It is also shown by the actual bonuses paid to the combination for the privilege of getting a contract, these bonuses running up to such figures as $7.10 (page 90), $7.50 (page 88), and $8.00 (page 87) — averaging from $7.00 to $8.00 in January, 1896 (page 111). It is also shown by the large amounts of the aggregate bonuses which were divided up among these companies (pages 116–117). It is confirmed by the statement of the Chattanooga company itself that the prices were "entirely too high," especially in the "reserved cities"; that "the prices made at St. Louis and Atlanta are entirely out of all reason;" and that "there is no reason why Atlanta, New Orleans, St. Louis, or Omaha should be made to pay a higher price for their pipe than other places near them" (page 103). No objection was made to this statement on the score of competency; nor can its competency be doubted (*Wiborg* v. *United States*, 163 U. S. at pages 657–658).

By unduly and vastly raising the normal price of cast iron pipe among communities which, by their geographical position, should have enjoyed special advantages, the combination has the indirect result of increasing competition in the northeastern or "free territory." This is shown by Thomasson's letter (pages 110–112), stating the policy of the Chattanooga company in view of the high bonusus paid by the Bessemer company for southern contracts. He figures out an advantage to the Chattanooga company in refraining from bids and taking its share of the bonus without contributing to the fund, and adds:

> If we cannot secure business in "pay territory" at paying prices, we think we will be able to dispose of our output in "free territory" and of course make some profit on that.

$13.00 to $14.75 per ton is stated in the same letter to be a profitable figure, and the Chattanooga company's propositions to northeastern cities after this letter (pages 104–107) show how the theory is carried into practice by giving those cities an advantage of several dollars per ton in price over the naturally better situated cities immediately adjacent to the works of these defendants. Mr. Llewellyn of Chattanooga, the chairman of the combination and one of its principal witnesses, was thus secretly inimical to its interests.

The letter announcing this scheme is dated January 2, 1896. We are furnished with the balance sheet showing payments and divisions of bonus for the ensuing four and a half months (page 117). We find that Chattanooga during those months paid in $2016.25, and drew out $15,077.99—truly a vindication of the wisdom, if not of the candidness, of this valuable witness.

Cast iron pipe, if we may believe Mr. Harrison of South Pittsburg, "has no market value" (page 214). "On account of the manner in which these contracts are let, the customer prevented the establishment of any market price" (page 216). We are therefore without any standard of reasonableness derivable from market quotations. The evidence, however, is overwhelming that in large portions of the country the price is half as much again what it ought to be.

There is, indeed, a large collection of affidavits stating that these prices are reasonable in the opinion of the affiants. Some of the affidavits are by interested parties, more or less discredited as above shown. Most of the rest are by persons who have no real expert knowledge. It will be remembered that cast iron pipe, on account of the peculiarities of its use, and on account of the high transportation rates, has no general market price throughout the country. Each local witness knows only that the combination gives him as low prices as any one else, knowing nothing of the conditions governing the price as it would be if the combination should dissolve.

Moreover the opinions are not accompanied by facts to back them, further than the single fact that the combination is able to underbid its competitors in certain localities. Such unsupported opinions have no weight under the rules governing expert evidence, as set forth in *The Conqueror*, 166 U. S. 110, 130–134, and cases cited.

Conclusion

Enough certainly has been said to show that this secret and hypocritical combination is in violation of the anti-trust law.

If necessary, it could easily be established that it is unlawful also at common law, so that the only question that the Attorney General would have had to consider, had the anti-trust law never been enacted, would have been whether the injury to the public was sufficient to justify his filing a bill upon general principles of equity, as in the Debs case.

These water pipes and gas pipes belong to the class of articles, monopolies in which are especially disfavored by the law. (*Gamewell Fire Alarm Co.* v. *Crane*, 160 Mass., 50, 57.) Every combination tending to prevent competition for public contracts is absolutely void. (*Atcheson* v. *Mallon*, 43 N. Y., 147; *Whalen* v. *Brennan*, 34 Neb., 129, 153.) Combinations to divide up territory, and thereby maintain rates free from influence of competition, are void *per se* at common law, and their validity does not depend upon the result of any inquiry as to the percentage of profits actually obtained. (*Hooker* v. *Vandewater*, 4 Denio, 349; *Stanton* v. *Allen*, 5 Denio, 434; *Salt Co.* v. *Guthrie*, 35 Oh. St., 672; *Craft* v. *McConnoughy*, 79 Ill., 346; *Vulcan Powder Co.* v. *Hercules Powder Co.*, 96 Cal., 510; *Hoffman* v. *Waters*, 11 Weekly Law Bulletin, 358; *More* v. *Bennett*, 140 Ill., 69; *Bishop* v. *American Preservers' Co.*, 157 Ill., 284; *Nester* v. *Continental Brewing Co.*, 161 Pa. St., 473; *Oliver* v. *Gilmore*, 52 Fed. Rep., 562; *Anderson* v. *Jett*, 89 Ky., 375; *Urmston* v. *Whitlegge*, 63 L. T. N. S., 455; *Chapin* v. *Brown*, 83 Ia., 156; *Emery* v. *Ohio Candle Co.*, 47 Oh. St., 320; *Pacific Factor Co.* v. *Adler*, 90 Cal., 110; see also *Hilton* v. *Eckersley*, 6 E. and B., 47; *Ford* v. *Chicago Milk Shippers' Association*, 155 Ill., 166; *Railway Co.* v. *Railway Co.*, 61 Fed. Rep., 993; *Pittsburg Carbon Co.* v. *McMillan*, 119 N. Y., 46; *Santa Clara Co.* v. *Hayes*, 76 Cal., 387.)

Milwaukee Masons' and Builders' Asso. v. *Niezerowski*, 70 N. W. Rep., 166, was decided by the supreme court of Wisconsin on February 2, 1897. Sixty out of seventy or seventy-five mason contractors of Milwaukee made an association, paying into its treasury six per cent on all contracts taken by them, first submitting all bids for work to the association and raising the lowest bid six per cent before submitting it to the owner or architect. This was held an unlawful restraint of trade at common law, without the aid of any statute.

In the famous case of *People* v. *North River Sugar Refining Co.*, 54 Hun, 354, Judge Charles P. Daly, the distinguished counsel for the sugar trust, conceded "that combinations are unlawful the design and effect of which necessarily is . . . to regulate and control the price of a commodity"; and Judge Barrett, referring to this concession, said that "all the cases, ancient and modern, agree that a combination, the tendency of which is to prevent competition and to control prices, is detrimental to the public, and consequently unlawful" (page 370, note).

It is therefore respectfully submitted that this judgment should be reversed, and a decree entered in favor of the plaintiff.

EDWARD B. WHITNEY,
Assistant Attorney-General.

VI

THE CAPITALIZATION OF THE INTERNATIONAL MERCANTILE MARINE COMPANY[1]

THE International Mercantile Marine Company completed, on December 31, 1903, its first year of life as a going concern. Up to the date of this writing, if stock quotations are any indication of its financial condition, the success of the company, from a market standpoint, is problematical. Its preferred stock is quoted at 18 and its common stock at 5, prices which indicate a general conviction that the equity in the company is worth little.

There is, however, a possibility that the stock market may be mistaken in its estimate of Mercantile Marine. In a declining market, stock values are influenced more strongly by the financial necessities of holders than by the earning power of the companies whose ownership they represent. This is especially true of the stocks of corporations launched on a declining market where the influence of every adverse factor is exaggerated. International Mercantile Marine has, in this respect, been peculiarly unfortunate. It was brought out during the fall of 1902, when the decline in the market was in full swing, and after the public buying power had been exhausted. Under the circumstances, these securities had no chance of a favorable reception. Moreover, almost from the start they were subject to inside pressure. The English vendors, stimulated by some natural distrust of the unknown economies of combination, and strenuously exhorted thereto by the financial press of Great Britain, which has been

[1] From the *Political Science Quarterly*, Vol. XIX, 1904, pp. 50–65. Compare also the same author on Capitalization of the United States Steel Corporation in the *Quarterly Journal of Economics*, Vol. XVI, 1902, pp. 214–232; afterward reprinted in his able Trust Finance.

from the outset hostile to the combination,[1] sold the stock which they received in payment for their interest, and the members of the American underwriting syndicate, as well as the American vendors, hard pressed by the continued stringency in the money market, have contributed to the selling pressure.

The proposition should be considered on its merits, without special reference to the market price of the company's securities.

The outstanding capital of the Mercantile Marine Company is divided as follows:

Underlying bonds	$16,000,000
20-year collateral debenture bonds (4½ per cent)	52,000,000
Preferred stock, cumulative (6 per cent)	54,600,000
Common stock	48,000,000
Total	$170,600,000

To pay interest and preferred dividends — common dividends, at least for some years to come, are hardly to be expected — will require the following amounts:

Interest on underlying bonds, taken at 5 per cent	$ 800,000
Interest on debentures	2,340,000
Dividends on preferred stock	3,276,000
Total	$6,416,000

Following the practice of the older German and English companies and allowing 60 per cent of net earnings for depreciation, insurance, and renewals, the total requirements, letting these funds include the sinking fund, are $16,000,000.[2]

[1] For example, the *Economist* on Nov. 29, 1902, referring to the report that certain English vendors had expressed a desire to receive bonds in lieu of cash, remarked as follows: "They (J. S. Morgan and Co.) also state that the offer was made on the expressed desire of some shareholders, who wished to invest in the bonds. If that be the case, it seems to imply a singular lack of business capacity on the part of the vendor shareholders, since they need not seek far to find securities with a much greater margin of security than these bonds to return a higher rate of interest. All they do know is that its capitalization will be enormously in excess of that of the undertakings that have been absorbed in it, and none should be better aware than themselves of the difficulty that will be met with in earning dividends on such a large sum, since they have had the experience of the same difficulty with a much smaller capitalization."

[2] The bonds of the International Navigation Company, of which $13,686,000 are outstanding, call for a sinking fund of $250,000 to $500,000 annually, beginning May 1, 1905, which will retire the bonds at maturity in 1929. No sinking fund is

Shortly after the Mercantile Marine Company was organized, the statement was made, unofficially, but apparently on good authority, by the Wall Street *Journal*, that the average net earnings of the different fleets for four years were $6,107,675. The same authority stated that the estimated savings in the cost of operation for the year were $10,000,000. Adding these to the average profits above mentioned, the earnings of 1903 should have amounted to a sum sufficient to pay dividends on the preferred stock, although it was not expected that any disbursement would be made. In other words, accepting the corporation's own estimate of the economies which can be secured by its changes in administration, the amount of its earnings falls short of the amount necessary to pay dividends on the common stock.

Before proceeding further in the analysis, let us test the accuracy of this conjectural estimate by comparing these figures with the amount actually earned by other companies during 1902, a year which was more favorable for the shipping industry than 1903. Such a comparison is presented in the following table:

	Tonnage	Net Earnings	Net Earnings per Ton
Cunard Company	114,410	$ 1,235,750	$10.80
North German Lloyd	583,042	4,392,500	7.53
Hamburg-American	651,151	4,458,198	6.85
International Mercantile Marine	1,034,884	16,107,000 (est.)	15.57

It thus appears that the estimated tonnage earnings of the Shipping trust for 1903 are nearly twice the average amount—$8.39—which was earned during the preceding year by its leading competitors. Moreover, the German companies have for many years operated under a close pool which secures them all of the economies which the Shipping trust was organized to obtain. Unless some other factors shall be discovered by the combination to increase its earnings, these preliminary estimates will eventually require some revision.

provided for the bonds of the International Mercantile Marine Company, but they are subject to call at 105 after five years. If an adequate reserve is provided, the necessity of a sinking fund on bonds secured by shipping property does not appear.

Accepting the same figure of tonnage earnings for the Shipping trust which was attained in 1902 by its competitors, namely $8.39 per ton, we have next to inquire how the combination measures up to its interest and dividend requirements. The net earnings of the company, on this basis, would stand at $8,941,398, leaving $5,801,398 over fixed charges, for depreciation, renewals, and replacements. This amounts to about $5.60 per ton as compared with $4.30 per ton for the Hamburg-American line in 1902, $6.19 for the North German Lloyd, and $8.04 for the Cunard line. If we debit the earnings of the International Mercantile Company with $5.00 per ton for these various necessary expenses, an amount which, considering the age of their fleet and the necessity of providing for the redemption of their bonds, would seem to be no more than is required, and if we assume, as before, their tonnage earnings at $8.39 per ton, the Trust has only $606,978 remaining for its preferred stockholders. That this supposition is not wide of the truth, may be seen from the experience of the North German Lloyd Company in 1902, which earned, over interest, 14,770,000 marks, and credited to renewals and insurance all but 212,477 marks of this amount, reducing their dividend payments from 5,278,131 to 210,623 marks. Taking a three years' average of the earnings of the Cunard, Hamburg-American, and North German Lloyd companies, we find that their combined depreciation and insurance charges amount to $24,719,112 out of $37,976,794 of net earnings, or about 65 per cent. It is impossible to escape the conclusion that the Shipping trust must appropriate a similar proportion of its profits for the service of the company, if the first care of its management is for the property of the company. If this is done, however, a readjustment of the capital of the company is among the probabilities.

We have not reached the end of the chapter. The Shipping trust was organized during a period of great prosperity, when the earnings of ocean transportation, although depressed somewhat below the abnormal figures of 1900, were still large. To pass final judgment upon its financial future, it is necessary that we cast backward and discover, if possible, from the history of other shipping companies, what may be expected if earnings follow the course of former years.

In the accompanying table appears the income account of the Cunard Company for a period of twenty years, including 1883 and 1902.

CUNARD STEAMSHIP LINE

YEAR	PROFITS, INCLUDING BALANCE FORWARD	RESERVED FOR DEPRECIATION	RESERVED FOR INSURANCE	TOTAL BALANCE	DIVIDENDS	FORWARD	INSURANCE FUND STANDS AT
	£	£	£	£	£	£	£, Often Written lb.
1902	263,617	158,722	24,686	68,808	64,000 (4 %)	4,807	357,000
1901	226,022	167,900	5,766	65,984	64,000 (4 %)	1,984	350,000
1900	553,241	284,488	119,037	143,434	128,000 (8 %)	15,434	350,000
1899	294,856	173,223	34,247	83,527	80,000 (5 %)	3,527	260,000
1898	261,691	172,169	29,496	57,663	56,000 (3½ %)	1,663	235,000
1897	222,475	166,938	27,999	41,691	40,000 (2½ %)	1,691	212,000
1896	249,788	184,822	32,417	42,181	40,000 (2½ %)	2,181	202,000
1895	144,305	180,325	. . .	183,731[1]	. . .	deb. int. 1,466	187,000
1894	94,953	177,104	. . .	183,020[2]	. . .	2,072	230,000
1893	200,091	154,419	39,966	35,868[3]	32,000 (2 %)	3,868	322,000
1892	174,607	125,856	33,496	36,296[4]	32,000 (2 %)	4,296	317,500
1891	220,991	125,426	38,407	52,382	48,000 (3 %)	4,382	315,000
1890[5]	246,601	125,840	43,144	72,838	64,000 (4 %)	8,838	280,000
1889	350,203	130,573	41,918 54,480	175,469	96,000 (6 %)	4,988	240,000
1888[6]	314,736	135,327 23,000	46,815 40,472	130,172	64,000 (4 %)	2,700	. . .
1887	254,482	135,500	77,839	41,143	40,000 (2½ %)	1,143	Debenture debt reduced from £450,000 to £96,000
1886	160,910	137,721	23,189	nothing left	nothing left	. . .	Loss of *Oregon* costs £113,241
1885	165,943	141,506	24,437	nothing left	nothing left	. . .	140,000
1884[7]	103,948	87,018 23,000	nothing left	nothing left	. . .	. . .	117,000
1883	146,920	93,134[8]	50,094	. . .	none	1,270	150,094

[1] £39,426 from insurance fund.
[2] £88,067 from insurance fund.
[3] £30,000 from insurance fund.
[4] £25,000 from insurance fund.
[5] The company had on hand at the end of 1890 in investments, bills, and cash, £559,922.
[6] £96,000 debentures paid off July 1st. Balance of cash and investments, £205,804.
[7] £23,000 taken from insurance fund and added to sum reserved for depreciation.
[8] Depreciation fund stands at £302,000.

The feature of the movement which will immediately impress the reader is the extraordinary fluctuations of net earnings. From a minimum of £103,948 in 1884, they rose to a maximum of £350,203 in 1889, an increase of 237 per cent. From that point, although fairly maintained until 1893, they fell in 1894 to £94,953, the smallest figure ever reached. The depression continued during 1895, but in 1896 began the great upward swing which carried earnings up more than 550 per cent, to the enormous total of £553,241 in 1900. From this maximum, the decline was rapid, profits standing at £226,022 in 1901, and £263,617 in 1902. Passing over, for the time being, the explanation of these remarkable fluctuations, let us examine the disposition of profits which this company employed. We note at once that the reserves for depreciation took up a large share: £3,104,011 out of a total of £4,650,380. Another large amount, £787,905, or $16\frac{2}{3}$ per cent of the total, went to the insurance fund, which the company has always maintained at a high figure. Out of the surplus remaining, to which was added £182,493 from the insurance fund, bringing the total amount available for distribution up to £940,957, £848,000 was paid in dividends, leaving £93,957 to be carried forward, an amount successively included in the annual profits. In other words, out of £4,650,380 of profits earned in 20 years, the Cunard Company paid out £848,000, or 18.8 per cent to its owners, and kept 81.2 per cent in the business. We note, moreover, that the disbursement of dividends was by no means regular. In six years out of the twenty, nothing was paid on the stock. In five other years, less than 3 per cent was paid, and in only one year, 1900, was as much as 8 per cent distributed to stockholders.

We note also with what extreme care the directors guarded their insurance and depreciation funds, taking every occasion of large earnings to build up these safety deposits, and refusing to sacrifice to the temporary advantage of the owners the permanent welfare of the company. In thirteen years out of the twenty, the profits of the company exceeded £200,000, aggregating £3,658,794. Of this amount only £816,000 was paid in dividends, £2,842,794 being carried to reserve. The shareholders reaped no small benefits, however, from their enforced self-denial. In four years of the period 1892–95, the insurance fund, which is held in cash and securities, was drawn upon for dividends or to maintain the depreciation fund. Of the £64,000 paid out to stockholders during these four years, £55,000 came from the reserves.

In short, it was only by the most careful economy, by the utmost prudence and conservatism in the distribution of profits, that the Cunard Company was able, over a twenty-year period, to average 2.6 per cent to its stockholders and, during the past ten years, to earn 3.1 per cent on a capital which at no time exceeded the book value of its ships.

For an explanation of the irregularity of these profits, we turn to the nature of the industry. The shipping business is, of all industries, the most irregular. It is liable not merely to the usual alternations of prosperity and depression, but to sudden fluctuations of rates and traffic which are entirely without parallel in any other branch of trade.

To begin with, the industry is strictly competitive. The high seas can never be monopolized. Dockage facilities in the leading countries are open to the ships of all the world, and shipyards will furnish a cargo steamer at a moderate price. Under these conditions, a permanent control of the shipping industry, sufficient to maintain rates or to control traffic, is out of the question. Agreements among the regular lines may introduce a certain degree of stability into passenger rates, and into the freight charges on the higher classes of commodities, but for the great mass of traffic, the raw materials and rough and half-finished products of commerce, carriers and shippers will continue, as they have from time immemorial, to make their individual bargains, and the rates of charge will continue to be fixed by the higgling of the market.

This situation has two consequences. If at any port the supply of shipping waiting for cargoes exceeds the amount of business offered, the competition between owners will force rates down sometimes to the smallest admissible margin above operating expenses. The amount asked by the marginal ship will fix the rate for the time being for all vessels leaving the port. On the other hand, a small excess of tonnage offered will have an equal effect in raising the rate. Some classes of commodities can be delayed in shipment longer than others, and some vessel owners can afford to lay up a portion of their tonnage rather than accept unremunerative rates. Generally speaking, however, the rule holds good. From every port and on every line of traffic, the rates are constantly changing in a way which would stagger a railway traffic manager, although he was deeply versed in the theory and practice of rebates and special concessions.

For example, take the following table of outward rates on coal from Wales to various ports in 1899:

	s. d.		s. d.	Per Cent of Variation
Port Said	7 9	to	13 6	74
Genoa	7 6	to	11	47
Aden	11 6	to	16 6	43
Bombay	12	to	18 6	54
Colombo	12	to	19	59
Cape Town	19	to	30	58
Rio Janeiro	11 6	to	16	39

The movement of grain rates from the United States, while less irregular than the figures quoted above, is also subject to wide variations.

Examples of more extreme fluctuations are easy to find. The course of rates in the British market in 1896 offers a typical illustration of the extreme instability of ocean rates. The *Economist*, in its annual review of the shipping industry for 1895, reported, at the close of that year: "The tonnage afloat is enormously in excess of the world's requirements, and so long as this continues we cannot see that there will be an improvement." During the early part of 1896, this condition of extreme depression continued. Only in outbound rates to the East, where the China-Japan troubles made a brisk demand for shipping, was any profit presented. These rates advanced, and remained on a high level throughout the year. A large number of ships, finding no profitable employment at home, went out to the East. Once there, however, and the war ended, they could not get back again, for return freights were not to be had, and it was impossible to return such a long distance in ballast without the prospect of remunerative employment. This situation left a large number of cargo vessels stranded in eastern ports, unable to get back to western waters. A large part of the world's carrying trade was thus locked up. The available supply of shipping was suddenly diminished. The tonnage afloat accessible to English shippers was no longer as in 1895, "enormously in excess of the world's requirements."

Upon a straitened supply was now precipitated an avalanche of orders. Says the *Economist:*

> The corn trade in the past year assumed a novel and unexpected position; the production of the world was slightly short of the consumptive requirements, . . . two of the large producing and exporting countries (India and Australia) being actually converted into considerable importers, and several hitherto small importers making largely increased demands.

The general trade of the country, as the *Economist* notes, maintained the improvement and expansion awakened and started more than twelve months earlier.

> These combined influences came to bear on the freight market almost simultaneously; shippers of nearly every description, all wanting the same thing at the same moment, with a rather short supply of the article; result, blind competition sending up the price of tonnage by leaps and bounds, in many cases 200 to 300 per cent, from the end of September to the end of November. . . . By so much as the rise was rapid, by so much was the decline equally rapid, and at the close of the year we find freights all around, in every trade, worse if anything than at the commencement.[1]

This experience has been repeatedly duplicated in every market. It is true that the total supply of ocean shipping will in time become available to relieve any congestion; but much time must often elapse before relief can be extended, the tonnage must be moved at once, and the ship-owners who are fortunate in being on the spot reap a rich harvest. On the other hand, vessels which have gone out in ballast to Argentine or the United States, expecting full cargoes of grain, or which have made the long voyage to Australia, expecting a large movement of wool, suffer the full effects of a crop failure or a small wool clip.

The following table shows the fluctuations over a ten-year period in four of the leading items in the world's export trade.

[1] Commercial History and Review of 1896. *Economist*, Vol. LV, supplement, p. 25.

Year	Export of Wheat from U. S. Bushels	Per Cent of Change from Previous Year	Export of Cotton from U. S. Bales	Per Cent of Change from Previous Year	Export of Corn from U. S. Bushels	Per Cent of Change from Previous Year	Export of Wheat from Russia Thousand cwt.	Per Cent of Change from Previous Year
1892	225,665,812		5,858,000		76,602,285		26,297	
1893	191,912,635	− 15	4,390,000	− 27	47,121,894	− 39	50,351	+ 91
1894	164,283,129	− 14	5,232,000	+ 19	66,489,529	+ 48	65,966	+ 31
1895	144,812,718	− 12	6,726,000	+ 29	28,585,405	− 57	76,453	+ 16
1896	126,443,968	− 12	4,627,000	− 31	101,100,375	+243	70,774	− 6
1897	145,124,972	+ 15	5,979,000	+ 29	178,817,417	+ 77	68,670	− 2
1898	217,306,004	+ 49	7,540,000	+ 26	212,055,543	+ 19	57,047	− 15
1899	222,618,420	+ 2	7,313,000	− 3	177,255,046	− 17	34,466	− 40
1900	186,096,762	− 17	5,946,000	− 19	213,123,412	+ 20	37,627	+ 9
1901	215,990,073	+ 15	6,538,000	+ 9	181,403,473	− 20	44,626	+ 19

Many of these fluctuations took the shipping trade by surprise, and either too few or too many boats were available. In other cases, the supply of shipping the world over was either excessive or redundant, and freights fell or rose to correspond.

So much for the temporary fluctuations of ocean freight rates and tonnage. There are also movements of longer duration, corresponding to the ebb and flow of general business, but subject in peculiar measure to the influence of special forces. From 1893 to 1897, for example, the leading commercial countries were suffering from a commercial depression which caused a general decrease in the tonnage of international trade, and a still greater fall in the value of exports and imports. The effect of this situation upon the shipping industry has been already indicated. Tonnage could not be decreased, and, in fact, the tonnage of the world during these three years increased. The result was an unprecedented depression in the shipping industry. In 1893, the *Economist's* review reports a large number of steamers laid up and a number disposed of at forced sale. In 1894, the report was "low, unprofitable freights and declining values of property engaged; the whole of the enormous trade has brought little or no profit, and a very bare margin over working expenses, far from enough to cover depreciation." In 1895, came a year "which will not readily be forgotten by the ship-owners. . . .

Our anticipations have been to the full realized, and probably a worse year than the present has not been experienced by the very oldest in the business."[1] The condition of the trade, in 1896, as already remarked, was little better.

During the four succeeding years, the situation was entirely changed. The widespread industrial revival caused a large increase in the value of foreign trade; and the shipping trade, as illustrated by the rapid and extraordinary rise in the profits of the Cunard Company, became very profitable.[2] The main support of the market, during 1897 and 1898, was the American export trade, which was characterized in the *Economist's* annual review of 1897 as follows:

> It contributed largely toward sustaining rates in the early months, and causing a material advance during the autumn and late summer in all other rates by the ready absorption and continued demand for tonnage of all descriptions from the leviathan 8000 to 20,000 ton cargo boats, to small fruit steamers.[3]

In 1899 the advance continued. General trade, the world over, was active, and the South African war resulted in the largest withdrawal of shipping that had been known for more than a generation. An outbreak of hostilities, involving even a second-rate power, always demands the services of a large amount of shipping. Even the effect of the Greco-Turkish war was sensibly felt; the influence of the China-Japanese war has been already mentioned; and the Spanish-American war materially contributed to the prosperity of the trade in 1898. The shipping industry can, over a period of years, depend with reasonable certainty upon the assistance of several wars. If international disturbances occur during a period of depression, the freight and traffic situation is relieved, and if, as in the case of the Boer war, the outbreak of hostilities comes hard upon the heels of general and abounding prosperity, the result is enormous

[1] *Economist*, Vol. LIV, supplement, p. 26.

[2] The combined exports and imports of the United States, Germany, and Great Britain, in 1895 were valued at $6,323,207,441. In 1901, six years later, their value had risen to $8,635,362,581. A large portion of this increase was undoubtedly due to the rise of prices, but the gain in tonnage was chiefly responsible.

[3] *Economist*, Vol. LVI, supplement, p. 24.

profits for all ship-owners. Not only does war increase the demand for ships, usually on terms highly favorable to the owners, but it raises the level of freight the world over by reducing the supply of tonnage.

These results followed from the South African conflict. At the close of 1900, the British government had withdrawn some 2,000,000 tons of shipping, an amount nearly equal to the total steam tonnage of Germany, and nearly double that of France. In 1900, moreover, the troubles in China required the transportation of large numbers of troops to the East, and throughout the Boer war, a large coal tonnage was kept moving to the Cape. The result, as stated in the *Economist's* annual review, was that

> The tonnage taken on time charter for all trades during the past year has been unprecedented. The rates paid by our Government for transports were 20*s*. per gross register per month, and in some cases more. Many charters in ordinary trades were made for long periods at very remunerative rates. Modern boats have commanded from 7*s*. to 11*s*. 6*d*. per gross ton, according to the trade and length of charter.[1]

In 1901, however, the tide turned. During the preceding four years, the supply of tonnage had been increased 4,049,260 tons, and with the close of the war, the British government rapidly released the ships which it had employed. To make matters worse, the American corn crop was a failure, and the industrial depression on the continent reduced the amount of freight movement. Rates fell 30 per cent throughout the year, and have continued to fall during 1902 and 1903, the close of 1903 finding the trade extremely depressed, with little prospect of early improvement.

We find in this hasty review of the recent history of the shipping trade an explanation of the irregularity of the profits of the Cunard Company, and can understand why the directors have pursued such a niggardly policy in the disbursement of profits. The management of a shipping company lives in constant apprehension. Exposed to increasing competition on every hand; compelled every year to build new and larger boats to keep pace

[1] *Economist*, Vol. LX, supplement, p. 28.

with their rivals; anxiously scanning the commercial horizon for signs of business depression, crop failures, famines, or labor disturbances; hoping and scheming for a few crumbs of subsidy, to introduce a modicum of fixed income into their earnings; engaged in a business as shifting and unstable as the sea on which that business is conducted—is it any wonder that the experienced ship-owners hold fast to their profits and regard the results of a year like 1900 as a gift of Providence to be guarded with zealous care?

Into this peculiar business came the promoters of the International Mercantile Marine Company. Attempting to apply to the shipping industry, the same principles of consolidation and capitalization which had been superficially successful on land, they imposed upon the new corporation an unusually heavy burden of capitalization, and they so arranged the capitalization as to make conservative financial management of the new company very difficult. The purchase price of most of the subsidiary companies was based on the profits of 1900. In the vendors' agreement between the syndicate and the White Star line, for example, it was stated that

> the valuation of the said shares hereunder and under said principal contract shall, subject as hereafter provided, be a sum equal to ten times the net profits of the company of the year 1900, subject to the following exceptions . . . (*a*) a sum for depreciation equal to 6 per cent on the amounts at which the property of the company stood on its books on the first day of January, 1900, and a sum for insurance . . . equal to £3 10*s*. on the same amount . . .[1]

It was further stipulated that the earnings of steamships employed by the British government should "be credited . . . with net earnings of the same amount as were earned or would be earned by similar steamships of the company for the same periods in their ordinary trades."

The year 1900, as has been shown, was one of abnormal profits. The Cunard Company nearly doubled its net earnings, and it is reasonable to suppose that other companies were equally

[1] For the text of these vendors' agreements, see Report of the U.S. Commissioner of Navigation, 1902, Appendix T, pp. 380 *et seq.*

fortunate. A partial record of the prosperity of this year is furnished by the record of dividends. The average dividend of twenty-five leading companies in 1896 was 6 per cent; in 1898, 7.7 per cent; and in 1900, 9.4 per cent. In the extract from the vendors' agreement quoted above, we find a recognition of the fact that the profits of 1900 were exceptional, viz., the provision reducing the earnings of ships employed in the government service to the general average of private employment. This reservation, however, does not go far enough. The mere fact of a large government employment, as has been shown, was sufficient to heavily increase the earnings of ships in private employment, and in capitalizing the earnings of this single year, the promoters of the Shipping trust made a serious mistake.

Indeed, so apparent was the mistake, and so clearly did the trade foresee that reaction was impending, that this fact was openly urged upon the shareholders by the Leyland line as an inducement to fall in with Mr. Morgan's plans. Said Mr. Ellerman, in May, 1901, at the shareholders' meeting of Frederick Leyland and Company:

> The outlook for freights in the near future is, in my judgment, an uncertain one. We have had prosperous times, and I feel that the near future may bring, at all events for a time, a reflux of bad times, particularly when the tonnage which is usually employed in the North Atlantic trade, but which is now employed in government transport work, returns to normal employment; in addition to which a large amount of tonnage is building in America for employment in the Atlantic trade . . .[1]

Not only was the amount of capitalization excessive, but what was more important, the arrangement of the capital of the Shipping trust, taken in connection with the amount of the different issues, was open to serious criticism. In addition to an amount of bonds fully sufficient to absorb the maximum earnings of the company, a liability of $54,600,000 of cumulative preferred stock was assumed, all of whose passed dividends must be paid before the common stock receives anything. Our previous discussion has shown the shipping business to be so irregular that even with

[1] Report of Commissioner of Navigation, 1901, p. 321.

the most moderate capitalization, in some years dividends must be passed, and in other years paid out of reserve. At all times, the directors should have a free hand in determining whether profits shall be distributed to stockholders, used for replacements and depreciation, invested in securities, or held in cash. The irregularity of the business is so great, that a free disposition of profits to stockholders is out of the question. The policy of a well-managed shipping company is dominated by the necessity of reserving from two-thirds to three-fourths of the profits in order that one-fourth may be paid out in dividends. In view of this fact, the absolute amount of the Shipping trust's capitalization is of much less consequence than the nature of the liabilities which it includes. The fact that the company is excessively capitalized is of less consequence than the fact that the arrangement of this capitalization is such as to make prudent financial administration very unpopular with stockholders. In this arrangement, fixed charges and obligatory payments predominate. Of the $170,600,000 of capital, $122,600,000 consist of bonds and cumulative preferred stock. If the debenture interest is passed, while the form of the bonds puts foreclosure proceedings out of the question, the unpaid interest must be discharged before anything is paid on the preferred stock; and if the preferred stockholder is forced to await the convenience of the corporation, the hope of the common stockholder of receiving anything on his investment becomes remote. In other words, a conservative administration of the finances of the shipping consolidation involves a series of postponements, an accumulation of deferred claims. The collection of a reserve sufficient to pay dividends in years of depression, if we may judge from the experience of other companies capitalized on a basis similar to that of International Mercantile Marine, is likely to be seriously interfered with by the importunities of deferred claimants.

It would be going too far to say that the International Mercantile Marine Company is a failure. Its future lies in the hands of the stockholders. If they will sanction a policy of conservatism in the distribution of earnings there is no reason to suppose that the preferred stock of the company may not eventually be raised to the rank of an investment. The unfortunate experience of the corporation up to the present time, however, emphasizes the fact that it is necessary, in arranging the capitalization of a new company, to take into careful account the conditions of the business in which the new concern is to operate, and in every case to assume that industrial history is to be repeated. The "economies of combination" are no doubt considerable, but they are too problematical to be safely included in an estimate of earnings available for distribution to stockholders.

EDWARD SHERWOOD MEADE.

VII

THE CAPITALIZATION OF PUBLIC-SERVICE CORPORATIONS[1]

EXAMINATION of the statutes and the judicial decisions of our American commonwealths reveals, aside from those cases where no definite policy has ever been entertained, two distinct theories as to the proper basis for capitalization of corporations. One is that the total amount of stock and bonds issued should stand in a definite relation to the actual investment of capital in the enterprise.[2] The other is that capitalization should be based upon earning capacity alone, let the source of such revenue power be what it may, — property, patents, franchises, or mere good will. Under the first policy, an enterprise to be capitalized at $1,000,000 must represent that sum of money paid in at some time, either as cash or an equivalent in tangible property. This is the policy consistently followed in Massachusetts, and somewhat less stringently perhaps in Connecticut.[3] Five years ago a reform in this direction was seriously proposed for New York, although little seems to have been actually accomplished.[4]

The second policy presupposes that, at a market rate of 6 per cent, an earning capacity of $60,000 per year is properly capitalizable at $1,000,000, be the actual investment what it may. The franchise or the good will, it is contended, can be sold for valuable consideration. In the eyes of the law it is property

[1] From the *Quarterly Journal of Economics*, Vol. XV, 1900, pp. 106–137.

[2] For the purposes of this article both stock and bonds are alike classed as capital. Cf. the reasoning in Statistics of Railways in the United States, 1888, p. 13. The inclusion of floating debt is variously viewed in different states.

[3] In Connecticut, until recently, special legislation, especially in the case of street railway corporations, prevailed. For this reason the general laws mean but little, save for those traction companies organized since 1893.

[4] A special committee of the Assembly reported in favor of limiting capitalization to one and one-half times the cost of construction.

during the period of its life at all events.[1] Even in Massachusetts it is considered tangible enough to be attachable for debt.[2] This second policy allows the inclusion of the franchise value — that is to say, the *surplus* earning capacity over a normal return upon the investment — in the nominal capitalization. And the limit of issues of stock and bonds is fixed only by the amount of such actual or estimated earnings, as the case may be. Thus the State Commission in 1899 provided for allowance to the street railway company of Detroit of $8,000,000 for its plant and of $8,500,000 for its franchise, this latter being merely the capitalization of the surplus earnings.[3] Among our American commonwealths the most flagrant examples of unlimited capitalization occur under the laws of West Virginia, Delaware, and New Jersey. In the first of these, no limitation whatever is placed upon stock issues beyond payment of a small registration tax. The Delaware constitution follows the usual statutory enactment of other states, prohibiting all issues of stock except for money paid, labor done, or property actually received. The absence of all administrative control, and the apparent failure of the state courts to rule adversely, naturally renders this law of no effect. New Jersey has met the issue adroitly.[4] Its Corporation Act, as revised in 1896, recites that "nothing but money shall be considered as payment of any part of the capital stock"; except that any corporation may purchase property by the issue of securities, in which case "the judgment of the directors as to the value of the property purchased shall be conclusive." The status of Maine, formerly a refuge for over-capitalized companies, has been recently reversed without modification of its statutes through a decision of its Supreme Court. This has, in effect, held stockholders liable as against a judgment creditor to the

[1] Numerous decisions have established this clearly, among them primarily that of the Monongahela Bridge Company, 148 U. S. 312, and 144 Pa. St. 365, in case of the Mifflin Bridge Company; and recently in *Washburn* v. *National Wall Paper Company*, 81 Fed. Rep. 17.

[2] Public Statutes, chap. 105, 30–38. Cf. the case of Brokaw Brothers, establishing that in private business good will — that is to say, capitalized *future* prospects — is not taxable. *Financial Chronicle*, LXIX (1899), p. 1086.

[3] *Street Railway Journal*, 1899, pp. 477–483.

[4] *The Chicago Banker*, I, 1889, pp. 407–411, gives interesting data on the history of New Jersey legislation.

amount of the balance of the capital stock at par, over and above the value of the tangible property.[1] This decision, based upon the theory that such stock is not yet fully paid up, has already acted as a salutary deterrent in many cases.

The best examples of the effect of the unrestrictive policy is to be found in the industrial combinations organized in the United States during the last few years. Excluding some of the peculiarly speculative ones, thirty-nine of the trusts reporting to the expert of the Industrial Commission indicate that their property owned is worth, even at prevailing high market prices, but 64.42 per cent of their nominal capitalization.[2] It is rare that the preferred stock and bonds do not fully equal the value of the plant, stock, and cash on hand, leaving the huge mass of common stock to represent good will or estimated earning capacity. Under British company law much the same conditions are coming to prevail. Thus the English Sewing Cotton Company's capital is atmospheric to the extent of one-quarter, that of the Cotton and Wool Dyers' Association being more than half fictitious.[3] That similar inflation in the case of our railroads was formerly the rule is equally well known, honorable exception being made of a few companies, such as the Lake Shore, Chicago & Alton, and the Old Colony of Massachusetts.[4] It is probable, however, that in the case of many railroads these abuses have of late been somewhat mitigated.[5] Much of the water has been expunged from the poorer roads through rigid reorganization in periods of depression, such as 1893–98. And, in the case of the stronger ones, the properties have been improved from surplus earnings, so as to fill out their once too generous allotments of capital. This does not seem to be true to an equal degree in England, where over-capitalization of the railroads still seems to be on the increase, owing to their peculiar

[1] *Libby* v. *Tobey*, 19 Atl. Rep. 904.

[2] Bulletin United States Department of Labor, No. 29 (1900), p. 671. Cf. the cases of the United States Leather Company and the Federal Steel Company. In both the preferred stock bought the plants, while the remainder went mainly to commissions and promoters' profits. *Bradstreet's*, 1899, pp. 436 and 531.

[3] *Economist* (London), 1900, p. 532.

[4] *Financial Chronicle*, LVII, p. 203; LX, p. 352; and LXII, pp. 347 and 480.

[5] Cf. *The Chicago Banker*, V (1900), pp. 335–339.

methods of finance, of which we shall have occasion to speak later.[1]

Two arguments in favor of permission to capitalize earning capacity or future prospects, rather than mere investment, may justly be advanced. One is that in no other way can the risks incident to a novel enterprise, repelling timid capital, be overweighted by possible profits through premiums in the form of securities purchasable at a discount. This argument, however, presupposes risk, — a condition entirely absent from many of the public-service companies, even at the outset of their careers. It also assumes that the persons who take the risk are the ones who ultimately reap the rewards. This, also, is a fallacy in too many cases; since the capital really risked in the plant is often raised on bonds, which receive but a moderate return, keeping them near par at all times; while the speculative profits come to the shareholders who acquire the stock for little or who take it for nothing as a reward for promotion.[2] The second argument has somewhat more force. Mere plant or dead property becomes profitable only through operation. This requires a quick capital in the form of credit or of cash. Without such working capital, the plant not being a "going" concern loses much of its value.[3] Consequently, it is urged, capital in excess of the value of the plant may rightfully be created for this purpose, by the sale of stock or bonds. The importance of this argument in the case of private companies cannot be denied. Recent evidence tends to show that an amount varying from 15 to 175 per cent of the value of the plant is in most of the industrial organizations devoted to working capital.[4] In fact, one of the powerful incentives to the formation of trusts is the desire of the individual producers to be relieved from the strain

[1] Woodlock, in the *Engineering Magazine*, XI, p. 238. Cf. also *Financial Chronicle*, LV (1892), p. 1061, comparing the Pennsylvania Railroad and the Midland.

[2] On the promotion of companies, see a note by the present writer in *Journal of Political Economy*, VIII, p. 535.

[3] This point was covered in the recent Newburyport water-works award, to be discussed *infra*.

[4] Bulletin United States Department of Labor, No. 29 (1900), p. 672. *Bradstreet's*, 1899, p. 739, cites two trusts handicapped from failure to procure sufficient working capital in this way. See also Papers and Proceedings American Economic Association, 1900, p. 150.

of dependence upon the banks for their quick capital. A difference between the public-service company and a private corporation is, however, discoverable in this: that, as a rule, the possession of a valuable franchise, attachable for debt, as we have seen, is sufficient security to enable working capital to be raised by the ordinary means.

The evils incident to allowing a wide divergence in either direction between actual investment and nominal capitalization are quite apparent. Among these, as applied to public-service companies, the most important of course is that all relationship between the charges to the public for service and the net profits upon the real capital concerned is obscured. The actual return upon investment can never be precisely determined without an appraisal of the property. And, inasmuch as such an inventory subverts the primary purpose of over-capitalization, it is a difficult matter to have it authoritatively taken. The case of the Lynn and Boston Street Railway Company, now pending in Massachusetts, is in point. Having been manipulated under exemption from general statutes to a high degree of inflation through successive consolidations, its directorate now bitterly opposes the attempt of the Railroad Commissioners to ascertain the real basis upon which its securities rest. This suggests a second fundamental evil of over-capitalization, the absence of all adequate security, — first, for the creditor, and, secondly, for the shareholders, — especially in any terminable enterprise. As to the first of these, it is obvious that borrowing capacity, while dependent upon current revenue for its interest, must ultimately rest upon the attachable property for final security. And the maintenance intact of this capital — too often taken as synonymous with property — is one of the leading objects of the law regulating limited liability.[1] As for the possible losses of

[1] The inadequacy of the law to prevent dividends paid at the expense of capital, especially in England, is well described in the *Economic Journal*, X (1900), p. 9; and the *Economist*, 1888, p. 407, and 1890, p. 919. Dicksee, Auditing, is also very good. Where the law permits the bonding of an enterprise up to the full amount of the capital stock, security for this indebtedness can only be attained by keeping capitalization well within the value of tangible plant. The stricter Connecticut and Nebraska laws, limiting bonded debt to one-half and two-thirds of the capital stock respectively, would seem, from the creditor's view-point alone, to permit of a greater latitude in this respect.

shareholders in an over-capitalized concern at its dissolution, the danger in most of our public-service companies would seem to be remote. For the franchise grants to the older companies being perpetual, and the growth of population steadily enhancing profits, dissolution can never mean more than a resale at high prices or merger in a succeeding corporation. Only under the newer forms of terminable franchise may such loss probably occur to the shareholders. And it is to be presumed that they will safeguard their interests, or at least should be compelled to do so, by a policy of amortization and of writing off for depreciation.[1]

The rigid policy of Massachusetts respecting its public-service corporations is in large measure an outgrowth of its hereditary policy towards the domestic railroad companies, somewhat halting at first, but afterwards clearly defined by its eminent board of Railroad Commissioners. The corporate evil of railroad stock issued merely as a bonus to stimulate the sale of bonds which are in themselves sufficient to defray all expenses of construction has never been tolerated. Its railroads have, to a greater extent than in any other state, perhaps, been built by sales of stock rather than of bonds, such stock being marketed at a respectable percentage of its face value. The result has inevitably been that, with the assured success of the enterprise, the stock has risen far above par instead merely, as when issued as a bonus to bond purchasers, of rising towards par. The consequence has been that, with prosperous roads like the Boston & Albany, frequent applications arise for right to issue new stock to keep pace with growing value of the plant. And the resultant anti-stock-watering agitation has kept the matter before the public. The focus of attention of late years, however, has shifted to the gas, electric, and street railway companies. The most explicit statement of policy, crystallized into law, is found in the anti-stock-watering laws of 1894 and 1896.[2]

The effect of the conservative policy in Massachusetts appears in the accompanying table representing the capital stock

[1] On the practice of English companies, liable to purchase by the municipalities, see *Economist*, 1898, p. 349.

[2] Acts of 1894, chaps. 350, 450, 452, 472; and of 1896, chap. 473.

and funded debt of various street railway companies. In no type of public-service corporations have the evils of over-capitalization been pushed to greater excess than in the case of this class of corporations. Several causes seem to have coöperated to bring about this result. In almost all our cities, profits dependent upon gratuitous franchise grants have almost in a night become so large as to require concealment. Then again, the progress of the industry has been so rapid since the first electric street road was operated in Richmond, little more than a decade ago, that revolutionary changes in equipment have been necessary. These, in turn, have invited financial manipulation at each turn-over and replacement, just as we know that discoveries of new means of gas manufacture have opened the way to inflation.[1] And, finally, the rapid growth of urban centres has in itself compelled a great extension of track and of service leading to pooling and consolidation, with all their attendant opportunities. We may instance the Chicago street railways as a case in point, with their more than doubled mileage from 1886 to 1896, each mile of track having increased, moreover, in average capitalization from $66,000 to $126,000.[2]

CAPITALIZATION PER MILE OF TRACK, 1899

STOCK AND FUNDED DEBT

(*Street Railway Journal, October, 1899*)

London street railways	$79,632
New York street railways	201,381
New York elevated railways	662,520
Chicago street railways	118,334
Chicago elevated railways	873,231
Berlin street railways	74,708
Brooklyn street railways	119,072
Philadelphia street railways	265,510
Liverpool street railways	94,494
Eastern Massachusetts street railways	61,972
Boston street railways	100,615
Glasgow street railways	54,866
St. Louis street railways	306,644
Cleveland street railways	96,585

[1] *Quarterly Journal of Economics*, XIV (1900), pp. 509–536.
[2] Illinois Bureau of Labor Statistics, 1896, on Franchises and Taxation, p. 48.

(*Massachusetts Railroad Commissioners, 1898*)

Massachusetts street railways	$46,600
New England street railways	49,500
New York state street railways	177,800
Pennsylvania street railways	128,200
United States street railways	94,100
Great Britain street railways	47,000

(*Eleventh Report Statistics of Railways*)

United States steam railroads	$60,000
New England states steam railroads	60,000
Middle Atlantic states steam railroads	111,000
Southern states steam railroads	45,000

Scanning this table, the relatively low capitalization of the Massachusetts and New England companies stands forth clearly, especially in contrast with those of New York and Pennsylvania. St. Louis heads the list, with the extreme case of a capitalization averaging five times that of the steam railroads of the United States.[1] Philadelphia and New York are not far behind in this regard.[2] Nor can it be admitted that the service is less efficient in Massachusetts than in either of the other cases. Even for New York state as a whole, with a goodly proportion of suburban roads, which, of course, lower the average, the capitalization is three times that of the steam roads of the country at large, and 50 per cent greater than that of the railroads in the Middle Atlantic states.[3] It is probable that the average for Massachusetts and New England is somewhat depressed by a relatively greater proportion of purely suburban lines, built at minimum cost. The same factor of low cost also explains in some measure the relatively low capitalization of the European roads. Many are still operated by horse-power or by light electric service, so that comparison with our own country is largely vitiated thereby.

[1] See Report of the Missouri Commissioner of Labor, 1896, for history of this company.

[2] See the extended tables of financial characteristics in the *Street Railway Journal*, October, 1899, pp. 680–684, as also the Report of Special Committee of the New York Assembly upon Municipal Ownership of Railroads, 1896.

[3] Cf. Report of the Massachusetts Committee on Relations between Cities and Towns and Street Railway companies, 1898, p. 37.

That the policy of Massachusetts in attempting to keep capitalization down to actual investment has been fairly successful is attested also by a second table, which compares for Massachusetts the sworn returns of cost with those of capitalization.

COST AND CAPITAL INVESTMENT PER MILE

(*Massachusetts Railroad Commissioners, 1897*)

	Construction.	Equipment	Real Estate	Total	Capital
Massachusetts, 1887 . . .	$17,600	$8,300	$9,700	$35,600	$32,700
Massachusetts, 1893 . . .	26,800	11,700	15,500	54,000	53,400
Massachusetts, 1896 . . .	23,400	9,800	12,800	46,000	46,400
West End Co., 1896 . . .	$56,600		39,800	96,400	100,700
Worcester Co., 1896 . . .	41,500		6,500	48,000	45,000
Springfield	25,000		8,800	33,500	31,000
Holyoke	23,700		9,400	33,000	31,000

The agreement between the last two columns, for a few companies chosen from a long list, as typical of varying conditions of service, is as close as need be. Discrepancies, where they occur, tend rather to excess of tangible assets over capital liabilities than the reverse.[1] Assuming the maximum cost of a street railway adapted for heavy service, and exclusive of real estate holdings, to be not far from $65,000 per mile, the immense over-capitalization of surface roads in other parts of the country becomes at once apparent.

The regulation of the capitalization of gas and electric light companies in Massachusetts has not been less effective in this direction, dishonorable exception being made lately of the city of Boston. Judging by the latest returns, the majority of the larger companies show a surplus of tangible assets over stock and bonds of from one-third to one-half of their total capital. Thus the Cambridge company, capitalized at $700,000, has a surplus of $358,000; Fall River, capitalized at $450,000, surplus $160,000; Lowell, capital $500,000, surplus $334,000; and

[1] Certain cases occur, as of the West End Company, now leased to the Boston Elevated Railroad. Cf. Report Massachusetts Railroad Commissioners, 1898, pp. 140–155. The first lease proposition was revoked because the capitalization was $26,340,000, while the plant was worth but $25,600,000.

so on.[1] The old Boston Gas Company, capitalized at $2,500,000, actually paid taxes upon $4,129,000, so completely was it swamped by a huge surplus.[2] The aggregate balance sheets of all companies in the state in 1899 showed a total capital of $24,878,000, with a surplus of assets over and above this of $8,115,000, upwards of a million dollars being charged to reserves and depreciation at the same time.[3] In fact, exclusive of Boston, the main problem for the gas companies was as to the proper disposition to be made of these surpluses, as we shall see. The contrast with the situation in New York is adequately illustrated by the facts in that city in 1885, when, with a property worth not over $20,000,000, the Consolidated Gas Company was capitalized at $45,000,000.[4]

Assuming that the conservative policy of strict limitation of capitalization, as exemplified in Massachusetts, is the safer one in the case of public-service corporations, we are at once confronted by a perplexing question: What should be the standard by which the proper volume of stock and bonds is to be measured? A number of possible ones suggest themselves. Among these, we may profitably consider, in turn: first, the total original cost or actual investment from the outset; secondly, the reproduction cost of the plant under present conditions; thirdly, the "structural value,"—value, that is to say, for service and wear, irrespective always of earning capacity; and, in the fourth place, market value, or the price obtainable at open sale. To show how widely different these may be, we may cite the leading case of the Interstate Consolidated Railroad Company.[5] Operating both in Rhode Island and Massachusetts, it had obtained a charter from the former state, with the right to issue stock and bonds to the amount of $650,000. It then applied to the Railroad Commission for authority to issue this amount under the

[1] From Investigation of Boston Gas Companies, Committee on Manufactures, March, 1900, tables presented by G. W. Anderson. (Pamphlet.)

[2] *Supplement Annals of American Academy of Political Science*, May, 1900, p. 41.

[3] Fifteenth Report Gas and Electric Light Commissioners, 1900, p. 97.

[4] Report Special Senate Committee to investigate the Supply of Gas in New York, 1885, p. 12.

[5] Report Massachusetts Railroad Commission, 1896, pp. 165–172.

Massachusetts charter as well. The original capitalization of a defunct predecessor had been $875,000, of which only about $470,000 represented the actual investment, the remainder being water. Owing to the fall in prices of electrical equipment, it was established that the plant could be duplicated for about $400,000. Its present structural value was estimated to be not over $255,000, while the price paid for it at public auction by its then present holders was $152,000. Excluding the possible basis of capitalization upon earning capacity, which ranged upon estimate from nothing to $900,000, which of these other standards, between $470,000 and $152,000, ought rightly to be applied? This particular case happened to be simplified by a late change of ownership at forced sale, through which the actual capital invested in the enterprise by the petitioners was known. This being shown, with immediate improvements projected, to amount to $317,197, the board authorized a capitalization of $317,200 in conformity thereto. Had the case, as in ordinary practice, been one of petition for new capitalization by the original company, the decision would have been less easy.

It would seem as if, in an enterprise still in the hands of its projectors, *the original and total cost* might be a fair criterion for capitalization. Such would seem to have been the norm first adopted in Massachusetts. "As the established rule of our law, the capital stock of every business corporation must represent the cash actually contributed by its stockholders, — no more and no less."[1] Or, quoting from a private letter from one of the Railroad commissioners in Connecticut, "The capital in an enterprise is the amount put into it at the time when the enterprise was initiated; although it would cost less to embark in the same undertaking to-day." The latest revision of German company law follows this policy also, in allowing all property to be taken at cost price, minus depreciation, notwithstanding the fact that its actual value is less.[2] There are many valid objections to this rule. The state cannot permit the capitalization of dishonesty, of extravagance, or of incompetence; nor can it permit the burden of obsolete industrial pro-

[1] Report Massachusetts Railroad Commission, 1896, p. 171.

[2] *Economic Journal*, X, p. 13.

cesses or administration to be laid upon future generations. Capital may have been needlessly wasted, as in the case of many Western railroads, through construction companies,[1] or as in the recent scandalous electricalization of the Third Avenue Railroad in New York city. Legitimate expenses of incorporation may be very heavy, as in England; or large expenditures for entirely improper purposes, as in "kissing" bills through legislatures, may have been made. The money may have been actually expended by the promoters, as Jacob Sharp undoubtedly paid many hundred thousand dollars in 1883 for the franchise of the Broadway Surface Railroad Company.[2] This represents real capital invested. Had it been legitimately spent in openly bidding for a franchise, its capitalization might have ensued without question. Or, again, consolidation of various companies, necessary for unity and efficiency of service, may perhaps be attainable only through purchase or control of contributory or supplemental systems. These are to be had only at an exorbitant price. Such, for example, has been the case in most of our large cities, where fancy prices have been paid for local companies; such prices being far above any actual franchise value based upon future earnings. An earnest advocate of street railway interests naïvely observes in extenuation of the admitted fact of over-capitalization that the present high valuation is probably not in excess of the cost of equipment *plus* the cost at the present time of purchasing the rights of way.[3] Such expenditures may be the necessary forerunner of successful operation. Shall a return upon them as capital stock be denied? This cannot be done so long as the criterion of original investment obtains.

These fundamental objections against original investment as

[1] The device of the construction company is still utilized for evasion of strict capitalization laws. Two companies have been privately cited to me in which the actual cost of installation to the construction companies, which were identical in *personnel* with the parent corporation, were $62,000 and $211,000 respectively. The contracts for this work were let, however, at $100,000 and $500,000.

[2] An excellent account is given in *Municipal Affairs*, IV (1900), pp. 139 *et seq.*

[3] *Street Railway Journal*, 1897, p. 212. German company law applies well here in prohibiting the charge to assets of any item above cost price. Thus, if it cost nothing, it must not be allowed to swell the capital account.

a basis for capitalization have led to general acceptance of the *cost of present reproduction* in its place. This is the norm usually accepted by judicial appraisers, as in the recent case, still pending in the courts, concerning purchase by the city in 1895 of the Newburyport water-works.[1] It seems to have been adopted also in appraisal of the Milwaukee street railroads in 1898 as well as in Detroit.[2] It is the one recognized by the Massachusetts Railroad commissioners in their regulation of capitalization.[3] The Gas and Electric Light commissioners in the same state also adhere to it closely in fixing the price of product. This is plainly evidenced in the case of the Brockton Gas Company in 1895. The board ordered a reduction of price, maintaining that the company was justified in earning dividends only upon the cost of duplicating the plant. In the words of the decision, "The profits of companies supplying this kind of public service must compare favorably with those which a new company might need to pay a fair dividend when fully equipped to render the same service."[4] Such is the apparent intention of the laws in most states which make any attempt at regulation of this sort.[5]

It is apparent at once that this substitution of duplication price for original investment shifts the base entirely; inasmuch as prime cost bears no necessary relation whatever to present value, even supposing the investment to have been wisely and properly made. Recent as the trusts are, twenty-four of those reporting to the Industrial Commission state the original cost of their plants to amount to 73.22 per cent of their nominal capitalization, while the cost of reproduction amounted to only 64.42 per cent of the same.[6] The divergence between the two

[1] Bill of Complaint, in case of *Newburyport Water Co.* v. *Newburyport*, United States Circuit Court, District of Massachusetts, No. 924, p. 12. Also raised in the case of Mifflin Bridge Company, Pa. St. 144, p. 36, where, the bridge being swept away while the case was pending, the cost of its duplication became involved.

[2] *Street Railway Journal*, 1898, p. 397, and 1899, p. 480.

[3] Cf., for example, the West End Street railway lease in Boston. Massachusetts Railroad Commissioners, 1898, pp. 140–155.

[4] Eleventh Annual Report, p. 14, cited by J. H. Gray in *Quarterly Journal of Economics*, XIV, p. 531.

[5] Cf. Bulletin Department of Labor, No. 29 (1900), p. 670. [6] *Ibid.*, p. 671.

is, of course, most notable in the case of those businesses in which methods and processes are rapidly changing. The electrical industries, characterized by a rapid fall in the costs of equipment since 1893, will serve as examples. Electric motors, costing perhaps $2850 in 1891, may be replaced to-day in greatly improved type for perhaps one-third of that price. Instances may be cited where the entire cost of a suburban street railway has decreased from $35,500 in 1892 to $22,600 per mile in 1899.[1] Equally great have been the changes in cost of plant to the electric lighting companies, entailing serious problems of regulation of capitalization and of price for the Massachusetts Gas commissioners.[2] The steady fall in the duplication value of these plants has, on the strictest interpretation of the Massachusetts policy, amounted virtually to an impairment of capital, due, however, to no fault on the part of the companies themselves. And it has greatly hampered them in the acquisition of new capital for additions to the plant. The public convenience in the matter of extensions of electric lighting must have suffered severely, had not the companies been allowed greater latitude than the original statutes apparently contemplated in this regard. As a rule, they have been granted time in which, by retrenchment and reduction of dividends, this deficiency may be remedied. On the other hand, the movement of prices oftentimes becomes of advantage to companies desirous of swelling their capitalization. Thus a street railway equipped with steel rails during the industrial depression of 1893–98 at $22 a ton may now find this portion of its property appraisable at upwards of $35 per ton or presently dropping again to the new price for 1900 of $26 per ton. Here is a distinct fluctuation of more than a third in the value of tangible property upon which capitalization may be based, according to the law.[3] Nor does it seem to be possible for the Railroad com-

[1] *Street Railway Journal*, 1898, p. 381, and 1899, p. 402.

[2] See, for example, their Fifteenth Annual Report, 1900, pp. 22, 29, and 32.

[3] The analogy to the case of a trust company whose capital is invested in securities of fluctuating value is close. Cf. the English case of *Verner* v. *General and Commercial Investment Company*, cited in Dicksee, Auditing, p. 467. See also *Economist*, 1900, p. 147, and 1890, p. 1504.

missioners to deny the rightfulness of such a demand. Cases are on record, even, where changes of price between the time of purchase of equipment and of application for issues of stock with which to pay for it have been taken into account, so strictly is the statute interpreted.[1]

Corroborative proof of the strictness of the Massachusetts policy is shown in another way by the table on page 129. Comparing the returns as to tangible assets for Massachusetts as a whole, year by year, a steady increase in valuation is shown from 1887 to 1893, while thereafter an equally noticeable decline is apparent. The cause of this is obvious. The year 1887 marks the early stage of electrical operation, with a low average due to the inclusion of many horse roads and a light electrical equipment at best. Down to 1893 a phenomenal development of electricalization ensued, with high prices, due both to great demand and to costly and cumbrous modes of manufacture. Since 1893 the effects of industrial depression upon prices, the satiation of the demand for electrical transformation, and a notable economy in manufacturing processes have all combined to reduce the expenses of construction and equipment. Note, then, the close correspondence between this phenomenon and the average capitalization, as shown in the last column. The notable decrease is not due to the expulsion of water, but merely to a required conformity of capitalization to value. Such a showing, it is believed, would be impossible under the laws of most of our commonwealths.

Peculiar difficulty is presented in the case of systems transformed from horse to electric motive power. Almost none of the public-service corporations, until recent years, seem to have written off any annual amount for depreciation. Mere maintenance, entirely distinct from depreciation, has generally, though not always, been provided for out of current revenue; but nothing further has been covered. As a result, the suddenly imposed necessity of entirely transforming the old plant into scrap, and

[1] In Connecticut, where greater reliance upon original investment seems to be placed than in Massachusetts, the only case where cost of reproduction is taken into consideration is in case of petition for an issue of bonds, which under the law must never exceed one-half the cost of construction and equipment.

equipping the system anew, offered a great opportunity to the capitalist. To the original capital, now extinct as far as tangible plant is concerned, could be added the entire cost of electricalization. Such was, indeed, the common practice; and much of the flagrant over-capitalization of street railways can be ascribed to this fact. On any theory of original investment as a base of capital, it is at first sight not easy to contest the policy.[1]

The leading case of the so-called "Milwaukee four-cent fare" decision raised this issue.[2] The constitutionality of an ordinance reducing fares from five to four cents was in question, under the Fourteenth Amendment to the Constitution; and the court was called upon to decide as to the real value of the plant of the street railway company, irrespective of its fictitious capitalization of $15,000,000. Counsel for the city contended that the cost of reproduction at present prices, not the original investment, should be considered as a dividend base. To this objection was properly made that to disallow all costs of original installation, forcing thereby capital to attend upon industrial and price stability, would be to put a severe penalty upon enterprise. And in this particular case, to the reproduction value of the plant of $5,000,000 was allowed an addition of $2,000,000 for "costs of pioneering." Adding to this the capitalization of the *surplus* earnings as a measure of the purchase value, decision was rendered that a four-cent fare yielded an inadequate return; and the ordinance thereupon was set aside.

The practical rule of appraisal generally adopted is, as we have said, to estimate the value according to cost of reproduction. From this, however, in order to determine the *structural value*, — that is to say, the "fair value for the purposes of its use," — an allowance for depreciation must be made.[3] This

[1] Cf. Report of Bureau of Labor Statistics, Illinois, 1896, p. 54, on Chicago experience; as also New York Report on Municipal Ownership of Railroads, 1896, pp. 1851 and 1865.

[2] *Street Railway Journal*, 1898, p. 397. Cf. also *Municipal Affairs*, IV (1900), p. 212.

[3] Consult E. Mathieson, The Depreciation of Factories, third edition, London, 1893; and L. R. Dicksee, Auditing, third edition, London. The Massachusetts Municipal Ownership Act requires depreciation to be charged off at 5 per cent annually.

must be sharply distinguished from allowance for expenses of maintenance, — a distinction often lost sight of in practice. Depreciation is entirely different from loss through "wear and tear." No matter how thoroughly in repair a plant may be kept, under modern industrial conditions it is bound to require entire reconstruction within a calculable time. This time may vary from a very few years in the case of gas retorts, through ten or a dozen for street railway road-bed, and up to fifty years for buildings and permanent structures. The necessity of ultimate reconstruction or replacement is the same in any case.

The English courts have never recognized the economic law that capital must ultimately be replaced from profits.[1] Not until 1878 was the principle recognized in the assessment of the English income tax. Prior to that time the only deduction from gross income allowed was the average actual expenditure for repairs. A test case then showed the necessity of an additional "just and reasonable deduction" for depreciation. The gas companies in this country seem to have had the facts of depreciation, as distinct from maintenance expenses, impressed upon them by long experience; although in Massachusetts a plethora of reserve funds has been the rule by reason of the strict regulation of stock issues. From the statements of twelve of the largest gas-works in the United States, the charge to depreciation far outweighs that for maintenance and repairs.[2] On the other hand, it may be stated with certainty that until 1895 almost none of the electric surface roads set off any proportion of profits for this purpose.[3] The necessity for such a charge to "deferred operating expenses" formed an interesting element in the Milwaukee four-cent fare decision above men-

[1] Cf. article Capital in Palgrave's Dictionary of Political Economy. Many additional cases will be found in Dicksee's Auditing.

[2] Fourteenth Report United States Department of Labor, 1899, p. 387. Cf. the excellent paper on Depreciation in Gas Works, by H. S. Chase, in *The Public Accountant*, Philadelphia, 1900. (Reprint.)

[3] Ninth Report Bureau of Labor, Illinois, 1896, p. 56; and *Street Railway Journal*, 1899, p. 403. Consult How to determine the True Net Earning Power of Street Railway Properties in *Street Railway Journal*, XVI (1900), pp. 246–250, for an adequate discussion of this. As also on reserve and suspense accounts in *Ibid.*, 1898, p. 796.

tioned.[1] It appeared that the company until 1896 had made no deduction from gross income for depreciation of the plant. The city, therefore, seeking to establish the fact of exorbitant earnings at the former five-cent rate, sought to compel estimation of these net earnings strictly according to the company's books. The court, however, was constrained to admit the patent fact of depreciation, despite the absence of any writing-off for this purpose by the company; and it was allowed that operating expenses ought really to have been a quarter more than they had been made to appear.[2] Since this time the almost universal foreign practice of creating a special depreciation fund or of carrying reserve or suspense accounts, has been generally adopted.

It is difficult to excuse this haphazard sort of finance on the part of American street railways. Even in Massachusetts they have gone bravely on, reporting a steady decrease in the proportion of operating expenses to gross income, — from upwards of 81 per cent in 1888 to 68.2 per cent in 1899.[3] With sounder financial methods, this proportion of operating expenses to gross income, perhaps, ought to be now appreciably higher. Failure in earlier days to reckon with this factor is probably due to imitation of the financial methods of the steam roads. So long have these been in operation that American experience has accurately distributed the proper annual expenditure for repairs, maintenance, and reconstruction, necessary to perpetuate the plant in full efficiency upon a cost of reproduction basis. On European roads the accounts are differently kept. Betterment through reconstruction is more commonly charged to fresh capital account rather than to current operating expenses. Yet the practice of keeping distinct accounts with depreciation is said to be general.

[1] *Supra*, p. 123.

[2] The Milwaukee company's accounts are now models in this respect. *Street Railway Journal*, 1899, pp. 351 and 369. The experience of the West End railway (Boston) is a case in point. Within six years after the installation of an entirely new nine thousand horse-power electric plant, the entire station was remodelled at an expense of $500,000, merely to substitute direct driving engines for power transmission by belts.

[3] Report Massachusetts Railroad Commission, 1900, p. 75. Cf. *Street Railway Journal*, 1897, p. 214, commenting upon this.

Thus far we have spoken of depreciation as applied to deterioration or supersession of physical plant. Depreciation, or rather perhaps amortization, as it might more properly be called, due to a limited franchise life, is of a different sort. The Massachusetts policy, however, not permitting the capitalization to include any franchise valuation, avoids this difficulty altogether.

We may dismiss the final criterion of capitalization, according to *market value*, with a few words. In the first place, such market price bears no relation to the value of the plant "for the purposes of its use," so long as it is in successful operation. And, even in those cases where subsequent sale may have been contemplated, such a sale, in absence of a continuous open market, might take place at an absurdly low figure under pressure. Thus the Massachusetts Railroad commissioners refused in the case of the Interstate Railroad Company, above mentioned, to consider the auction price as any fair criterion even of structural value. And, on the other hand, such market price, if it be computed upon the price of securities, can never make distinction between the value of the plant and the worth of the franchise. This, in Massachusetts at least, where no value in the franchise is ever allowed to enter into capitalization, means that the franchise rights merely enhance the market price of the existing issues based upon real property. To allow this market price of securities to enter, even remotely, into any calculation of property value, would obviously be to overset the restrictive policy entirely.

The problem of legally restricting the capitalization of an old-established corporation is essentially different from that of controlling the organization of a new one. In order to elucidate this, we must consider separately some of the means by which the volume of corporate securities is increased during the life of the companies. Probably the commonest of these is by the payment to shareholders of so-called stock dividends. These consist either of an outright bonus of new shares of stock or bonds; or, in a mitigated form, as stock sold below par or at less than market quotations. Such "melon-cutting," in the parlance of Wall street, may range as high as 100 per cent, as in the Adams Express Company dividend of 1898. The notable

Boston & Albany distribution of state stock in 1882 is a familiar example. This crudest form of inflation of capital, whether up to or beyond the increasing value of the plant, is the easiest to control directly. And statutory prohibition of the issuance of stock at other than a price fixed at public sale would seem to be easily enforceable.

Another somewhat more subtle mode of accommodation of capitalization to enhanced revenue potential, since it may not really augment the volume of securities outstanding, is to substitute stock issues for funded debt. The tendency in this direction seems to be very marked at the present time among the strongest of the American railroads, such as the New York Central, the Pennsylvania, the Central of New Jersey, New York, New Haven & Hartford, and others.[1] In some of these, outside of Massachusetts, the primary motive would seem to be to take advantage of rights to issue securities at par, where market value is high. But in addition there would seem to be the advantage of great elasticity in future dividend possibilities, within the same limits of total capitalization. Thus a substitution of possible 8 per cent stock for present 4 per cent bonds clearly permits of the absorption of greater earnings to be derived in future. The advantages of stock issues over bonds in the way of elasticity downward, is, of course, always to be added; as they permit of a cessation of dividend burdens during periods of depression. Probably for this reason the tendency of most reorganization schemes seems to have been in the direction of retirement of bonds in favor of stocks. This mode of substitution is, however, clearly confined to those companies whose finances are in such excellent condition that their stocks will sell above par. To substitute stocks, which can only be placed on the market at ruinous discounts from par value, for bonds, — which, being well secured legally, are quoted much higher, — would seem to be bad finance. Ability to increase capitalization by stock issues to advantage may in general be taken as evidence of prosperity. The only efficient safeguard for public

[1] Cf. *Bradstreet's*, XIX, p. 356, and XXI, p. 163. The Delaware & Hudson controversy is interesting in this connection: *Ibid.*, XXII, p. 227. Cf., also, *Ibid.*, XV, p. 534, on reorganizations.

interests in such cases would seem to be through the right of approval exercised by an able administrative commission, where consent should be required prior to all such substitutions.

The gradual accumulation of a surplus, either by good management or by exceptional opportunities, followed by a petition for its capitalization into stocks or bonds, constitutes one of the most troublesome problems in any attempt at strict regulation. For, as will readily be observed, in so far as such a surplus — either in the form of cash, of securities of other companies, or of additions to the original plant — represents augmented investment, it would seem to offer a proper basis for addition to capitalization. It cannot be denied that in this case the property has enhanced in value. Unfortunately for the company, however, a surplus stands too often in the public eye as witness to abnormal and undeserved earnings in the past. In those commonwealths which once provided in their early railroad charters for escheat to the state of all earnings in excess of a certain amount, usually 10 per cent; or those, like Massachusetts, which under the recent law of 1898 provide for a special tax upon dividends of street railways in excess of 8 per cent, such a surplus may denote an actual evasion of legal liabilities.[1] To permit such deductions from dividends in earlier years to be capitalized at a later date would seem to be, indeed, a flagrant subversion of public policy. On the other hand, in many cases the surplus may not represent undeserved earnings or concealed profits. It may be due to enhanced values in right of way, or in investments, whether of real estate or in securities of other companies; thus in no wise indicating an excessive burden upon the consuming public. Even more difficult of just determination, such surplus may be entirely due to exceptionably able business management by which, even with low rates to the public, economy has come to its deserved fruition. To deny the right to capitalize such accumulated earnings is to penalize enterprise and to discourage economy; neither of which, certainly, is consonant with wise public policy.

As illustrative of the difficulties presented by the above-

[1] The pending suit of the state of New Hampshire against the Manchester & Lawrence railroad is a case in point.

described situation, we may instance the recent case of the Haverhill Gas Company in Massachusetts. The capitalization of this company — originally, in 1871, fixed at $75,000 — was not increased through years of prosperity, until a surplus amounting to nearly $300,000 had been accumulated. This existed, not as cash or securities, but in the form of plant; that is, in new buildings, enlarged retorts and reservoirs, extensions of mains, and the like. The surplus, moreover, far from being the result of extortionate rates for gas, was largely due to exceptional management. This point must be strongly emphasized; for it constitutes the novel element in the case. For years the rate of $1 or $1.10 per thousand cubic feet had prevailed, — a rate recently obtainable only in the metropolitan centre of Boston, and appreciably below that customary in other neighboring cities of equal size. The situation was complicated by the attempt of certain foreign capitalists to water its stock through a lease to a finance company. With this phase of the matter we shall have to do later. For the moment we have to discuss merely the justice of allowing the company directly to realize some return upon these accumulated earnings, through an increase of its capitalization, up to the structural value of the plant. The Gas commissioners ordered the price of gas reduced to 80 cents, upon petition of the mayor and others, who asked that it be fixed at 70 cents. This figure, it was estimated, would enable the company to pay 8 per cent dividends upon its original capital, carrying nothing further to surplus. Similar standards, according to the showing of the petitioners for reduction, would give prices per thousand in other cities as follows: Cambridge, $1.02; Fall River, 94 cents; Lowell, 87 cents; Springfield, $1.08; and Worcester, 91 cents.[1] All of these, as will be noted, are very much above the Haverhill rate.

The argument of the advocate of restriction is to the effect that, even granting the surplus to be a reward of economy and efficient management, and not of extortion, this surplus belongs to the public. It should be regarded merely as a deferred dividend, which reaches the people in instalments, through the low

[1] Investigation of Boston Gas Companies Committee on Manufactures, March, 1900, tables presented by G. W. Anderson, p. 10. (Pamphlet.)

price of gas which the greatly improved plant makes possible; in other words, that municipal ownership of the plant has really ensued, leaving it to be operated, however, by a private company for the fixed rental of 8 per cent. To this contention, answer is made that the argument fails, both theoretically and practically. From the former point of view alone, it is defective, in that it strikes at the root of all enterprise. It confounds this present case with those in which the surplus is a result of exorbitant charges or of deficient service. Its effect would inevitably be to give support to mediocrity of management alone. It is absolutely at variance with the theory that profits form no part of price. For although no direct condition of competition of plants may exist, there being municipal monopoly; yet, the purview of the public being made state-wide through public reports, competitive price conditions prevail, nevertheless. All reward beyond the normal return upon investment being denied to extraordinary economy and ability, no incentive to improvement of service would longer exist. Such extensions and improvements must, however, continually be made in the interest of the public. And herein the practical weakness of too restrictive a programme appears. Denied the incentive to accumulation of surplus through economy, — that is to say, discouraged from making additions to the plant necessary for improved service out of operating expenses, — the way is always open to acquire new capital for the same purpose, by an increased issue of stock or bonds. Is it not better that this new capital should be produced from within, allowing the company some participation in the profits through a moderate capitalization of its surplus, rather than that all expenditure for improvement should come from without, thereby saddling upon the consumers the additional interest or dividend charges? A tardy recognition of the cogency of this argument would seem to appear in the refusal of the Commission to order a reduction of the price of gas in Lynn to a strictly minimum profits level.[1] Whether similar reasoning in the parallel Haverhill case would have been followed, could the infamous stock-jobbing element have been eliminated, must remain in doubt.

[1] Decision rendered May 15, 1900. House Document No. 1351.

Next in importance to the conversion of a surplus into stock as a means of increasing capitalization is the expedient of funding contingent liabilities or a floating debt. These may exist in any of their common forms, as loans, bills payable, credited vouchers and accounts, wages and salaries due, or even in the mixed status of receiver's certificates. Such debts are generally indicative of reckless financiering. They may sometimes be necessary to the conduct of a growing business. Nevertheless, an abnormally large proportion of current liabilities, as a rule, is an unfavorable symptom. It implies, as in the familiar examples of the Erie and the Union Pacific railroads, an inability to raise additional capital as needed, by the sale of bonds. Such a condition is usually the accompaniment of a deficiency of current income, whereby maintenance has to be met in part by a charge to capital account; or, as in the sudden appearance of a gigantic floating debt of $12,000,000 in the case of the Third Avenue railroad in New York city, it may be a result of corruption or political "bleeding." But, on the other hand, the creation of such a floating debt may sometimes serve as a means to the enlargement of capitalization. This would seem to have been the case of late with public-service corporations in Massachusetts, particularly the electric light and power companies. Denied the expedient of surplus conversion into stock, both by the public policy already discussed and by the great depreciation in the cost of equipment, recourse has most naturally been made to the opposite expedient. Almost ten years ago[1] the Gas commissioners called attention to the desire on the part of companies managed by "men of a speculative turn of mind" to cover all expenditure for construction by issues of interest-bearing scrip. A striking example of such financiering occurred in 1894, in the attempt of the Boston Electric Light Company to fund some $240,000 of floating indebtedness.[2] It appeared that the tangible assets were not equal to the capitalization, presumably because too large a proportion of earnings had been distributed as dividends, leaving too little for maintenance of the plant and writing off for depreciation. "Floating debt, representing the

[1] Sixth Annual Report, 1901, p. 34.
[2] Tenth Annual Report of the Gas Commission, 1895, p. 42.

cost of new plant needed to take the place of that which had been worn out and useless, is essentially a part of the expense of carrying on the business, and should be provided for, if possible, out of the earnings. Capital stock has no claims upon the earnings precedent to those of creditors, and not to be governed by this fact is to endanger the well-being of the stock itself."[1] Oversight of the finances of each company year by year, especially in this matter of the proportion of current income applied to betterment, particularly in a field where falling costs of reproduction prevail, seems to be an essential part of any effective scheme.[2]

The consolidation of companies offers a convenient mode of surreptitiously adding to capitalization. This may take place in any one of three ways. In the first place, the merger may lead to reconstruction or replacement of operating plant, with its attendant devices of betterment entirely defrayed by means of new stock issues. This has already been described. Less common is the second method. This consists in gerrymandering the constituent companies, so that those strong ones oppressed with surplus earnings may have aggregated about them the roads which are less favorably situated. The claim is openly made[3] that the Massachusetts Electric Companies, composed of forty odd suburban traction lines, is having its membership so distributed in three main groups, each to be separately operated, as to effect this end. Thus the Lynn and Boston road, earning perhaps twice its legally allowed dividend of 8 per cent, is made to average up its earnings with a number of small roads which are scarcely meeting operating expenses. The result is a 6 per cent dividend upon their united capital, with a net yield to shareholders far in excess of that contemplated under the law of 1898. The third stock-watering device attendant upon consolidation consists merely in the substitution of a high-grade for a low-grade security. For example, a weak company, whose

1 Similar and more recent cases occurred in Malden and Waltham respectively. Fifteenth Annual Report Gas commissioners, 1900, pp. 22 and 39.

2 A case has been privately cited to me, where a street railway company, wishing to make a favorable exhibit of earnings, tore up its recently laid rails, providing for new ones by issue of stock; and then credited the large proceeds from sale of old equipment to current revenue.

3 Street Railway Items, Boston, Oct. 1, 1900.

stock is quoted at 50, is merged in a second operating corporation, with stock, bid, we will say, at 200. This latter company issues new stock worth $200, share for share, in exchange for the $50 stock, which is thereupon cancelled. The legality of such operations under Massachusetts law is open to question. But they would seem to have been not infrequently undertaken in recent years.

The final method of evasion of anti-stock-watering statutes is found in the creation of independent finance corporations, to which the operating company may be leased, sold, or trusteed. The practice may best be made clear by a few examples. In 1893 the Brooklyn City Railroad Company, operating with horse-power, was capitalized at $6,000,000. At that time its power was transformed to electricity; and, as has been customary in such cases, the opportunity was seized for an increase of stock and bonds to $18,000,000. Simultaneously the road was leased to the Brooklyn Heights Railroad Company, a tiny corporation operating only a mile of track and capitalized at $200,000. This company agreed to meet interest charges upon $6,000,000 of bonds and to pay 10 per cent upon the $12,000,000 of stock of the leased company. Finally, in the same year, the Long Island Traction Company, incorporated under the laws of West Virginia with $30,000,000 capital, purchased the stock of the intermediary, — the Brooklyn Heights Company, — in order to absorb such surplus revenue as might remain over and above its obligations to the primary and sole operating concern. Thus was a fivefold increase of capitalization up to the desired figure finally effected.[1]

The creation of such finance companies has not until recently occasioned much difficulty under the strict prohibitions of Massachusetts law. The Light, Heat, and Power corporation, organized under the laws of West Virginia, has been attempting since 1898 to operate the electric plants in Milford and Clinton, for example.[2] It would seem, however, that — legal quibbles aside — a clear case of violation of the statutes could be estab-

[1] From letter of Judge Gaynor of the Supreme Court, reprinted in Report of the Committee upon Municipal Ownership of Railroads (Albany, 1896), II, p. 1604.

[2] Report Massachusetts Gas and Electric Light commissioners, 1900, p. 33.

lished. Far more serious is the expedient adopted by the Haverhill Gas Securities Company.[1] This finance concern, by incorporating under the laws of Massachusetts, evaded the provisions of the law of 1894, which declared invalid alone all leases of a domestic to a *foreign* corporation. The new company issued stock to the amount of $500,000, in payment to the owners of the gas company for their original capital of $75,000 and their accumulated surplus of about $300,000. The money necessary for formal compliance with the Massachusetts law requiring all stock issues to be paid up in full was temporarily advanced by the promoters, and paid over to the owners of the gas company in exchange for their property. The next step was to issue and sell 5 per cent debentures to the amount of $500,000 to recoup themselves for their advance, depositing the original stock of the gas-light company with a trustee as collateral. Thus the bondholders of the Securities Company virtually paid for the gas works; while the control of its business remained in the promoters' hands, they retaining the Securities Company's stock of $500,000 as their share of the proceeds. As a net result, then, we find the capitalization of the operating plant, upon which the public are to pay charges, advanced from $75,000 to $1,000,000. Only two remedies were open. One was to annul the charter of the finance company; the other was to reduce the price of gas. This latter course was the one adopted by the Commission, as we have seen, they recommending, also, that the legislature dissolve the company's corporate existence.

Still a third similar mode of evasion, in addition to leases to foreign or domestic finance companies, is being tried in Massachusetts. This is to avoid the corporation laws altogether, by leasing the operating companies to mere business associations. These are, in practice, nothing more nor less than partnerships, with all the provisions of unlimited liability in force. In this respect they closely resemble the New England Gas and Coke Company,[2] or the real estate trusts, of which there are several

[1] Report Massachusetts Gas and Electric Light Commissioners, 1900, p. 6.

[2] See the excellent history of this organization in the *Quarterly Journal of Economics*, XIV, 1899, pp. 92–120.

in Boston. The leading example of these in the field of quasi-public corporations is the Massachusetts Electric Companies. This association now controls what were originally some forty distinct street railroad companies, forming an unbroken network throughout the eastern quarter of the state. These operating companies have an aggregate stock capitalization of about $9,000,000.[1] They seem to be slowly consolidating, it is said[2] with the end in view of merger in a single corporation, to be known as the Massachusetts Electric Company. The $10,000,000 of stock of this consolidation will then be entirely owned by the Massachusetts Electric Companies' Association, represented by securities outstanding to the amount of $24,000,000. The legal status of this latter organization is as yet undetermined by the courts. In any event, a prompt extension of the provisions of the anti-stock-watering acts to cover all such associations would surely act as a powerful deterrent in future.

Enough has been said to illustrate the extreme complexity of the problem of regulating capitalization, even in the limited class of public-service companies. The ultimate remedy, as applied to all classes of corporations, must come from the courts and the legislatures. But in either case the continued necessity of a strong and steady administrative control through some permanent board or commission, supplementing and giving due effect to the law, is apparent. Massachusetts has not, perhaps, accomplished all that could be desired as yet either in justice to the companies or to the public; but her experience should be of great value, in view of the honest purpose which seems to have inspired it throughout.

William Z. Ripley.

Massachusetts Institute
of Technology.

[1] The bonded indebtedness, amounting to approximately $10,000,000 (?), remains outside the control of the association, largely in the hands of the original purchasers.

[2] Street Railway Items, Sept. 15, 1900.

VIII

THE UNITED STATES STEEL CORPORATION'S BOND CONVERSION[1]

ON April 17, 1902, the president of the United States Steel Corporation issued a circular to the stockholders, which invited their coöperation in a plan to raise $50,000,000 of new capital. Half of this amount was to repay loans incurred by the constituent companies for construction work which was in part rendered unnecessary by the merger, but which, owing to advance commitments, could not be suspended. In addition, $25,000,000 was required for improvements, which, it was stated, would effect an annual saving of at least $10,000,000. The plan proposed to the stockholders for raising this money was "to rearrange your corporation's capitalization (which, in round numbers, now consists of $300,000,000 of bonds, $500,000,000 of preferred stock, and $500,000,000 of common stock) by substituting for $200,000,000 of the preferred stock, $200,000,000 of sinking fund sixty year 5 per cent mortgage gold bonds, and by selling $50,000,000 of additional bonds of such issue for cash. As the preferred stock carries 7 per cent dividends, while the bonds would bear but 5 per cent interest, the $50,000,000 desired could, in this way, be added to the corporate resources, and the aggregate of the annual charges for interest and dividends, instead of being increased $3,500,000, would be decreased $1,500,000 as compared with the present sum total of these two requirements."

The plan offered to each preferred stockholder the right to subscribe to the new bonds to the extent of one-half his holdings of preferred stock, 40 per cent of each subscription to be

[1] From the *Quarterly Journal of Economics*, Vol. XVIII, 1903, pp. 22–53, with certain minor editorial emendations approved by the author. The genesis of the Steel Corporation and its promotion, finance, and capitalization are described in *Ibid.*, Vol. XV, pp. 517–550, and Vol. XVI, pp. 214–233. Both chapters are incorporated in his Trust Finance. — ED.

payable in preferred stock, and 10 per cent in cash, or the subscription could be limited to 40 per cent, in which event no cash payment was required. The circular also stated that a syndicate had been formed, "including some directors," to further the success of the plan; and, in the call for a special meeting of stockholders to be held May 19, one of the purposes of the meeting was stated to be the ratification of an agreement between the United States Steel Corporation and J. P. Morgan and Company, acting for this syndicate.

This agreement is dated April 1, 1902, and contains the following provisions:

1. That the party of the second part, known as "the bankers," on or before the first day of July, 1902, should offer to the preferred stockholders the right to subscribe to the second mortgage bonds of the company, on the terms mentioned in the circular, for a period of thirty days;

2. That such part of the $250,000,000 of bonds as should not be taken by the preferred stockholders, should be issued to the bankers on their request for the syndicate, to be paid for in preferred stock, and in cash, on the same terms as those offered to the preferred stockholders, in such amounts and at such times as the bankers might request, up to October 1, 1903;

3. That the bankers guarantee to the Steel Corporation that subscriptions to the new bonds to the amount of $100,000,000 would be made, payable $20,000,000 in cash, and $80,000,000 in preferred stock;

4. That, as compensation for the risk, the guarantee, and the various obligations assumed by the syndicate, the Steel Corporation should pay to the bankers a cash compensation equal to 4 per cent upon the aggregate amount of the bonds which should be sold or delivered, either to the preferred stockholders or to the syndicate, until October 1, 1903.

The plan and the syndicate agreement were submitted to the stockholders, and both were approved by a vote of 7,704,288 shares to 12,540 shares out of a total number of 10,185; 811 shares outstanding.

Before the plan could be put into effect, an injunction was applied for on June 8, 1902, before the Chancellor of New

Jersey, against J. P. Morgan & Co. by Miriam Berger, a preferred stockholder, to forbid them to issue bonds for stock under the bankers' contract, and alleging that the plan of conversion was unlawful for the following reasons: (1) that the plan, if carried out, would impair the complainant's vested rights as a stockholder; (2) that the plan of issuing bonds to retire stock was void against any dissenting stockholder; (3) that the plan was ruinous and disastrous, and impaired the value of complainant's stock; (4) that four members of the bankers' firm were directors of the corporation; and (5) that the compensation which might be received by the bankers under their contract was without consideration and illegal, and that the scheme was devised to secure exorbitant commissions by this firm. An order restraining the bankers from issuing any bonds in exchange for preferred stock was granted by Vice-Chancellor Emery on the ground that the complainant's vested rights would be impaired by the exchange of bonds for preferred stock under the terms proposed.[1] The case was appealed, the appeal being argued on June 25.

Before the appeal was decided, on July 5, a second bill was filed by J. Aspinwall Hodge, Bernard Smith, and William H. Curtis against the corporation, the bankers, and the directors.[2] The grounds on which relief was asked for were as follows:

1. That the plan interfered with the vested rights of the complainants;

2. That it was *ultra vires* and void;

3. That the Steel Corporation, under the act of 1902, could not issue bonds for stock, because it had not paid dividends on the preferred stock for at least a year preceding the date of the

[1] The ground on which the injunction was granted was: "that it (the conversion plan) is a preferential distribution of capital among some of the shareholders to the exclusion of others, and not a plan for an equal distribution among all the preferred stockholders. That the capital represented by preferred stock up to a limit of $200,000,000 is to be reduced to the extent the holders agree to take bonds, and . . . the stock of those who decline to take bonds is thus made subject to the prior claim and lien of those who take bonds."

[2] Smith and Curtis, it being proven that they were not registered owners of stock at the time suit was brought, obtained no recognition in the litigation. The right of Hodge to petition for an injunction was recognized.

meeting, and because its assets, after deducting the amount of its bonded debt, were not equal in value to the par value of its preferred stock;

4. That the scheme was disadvantageous, and would seriously damage the corporation and its stockholders, and that the compensation to the bankers was exorbitant;

5. That the action of the directors in approving the plan and contract was void, because fifteen or more of the board of directors were interested in the underwriting syndicate;

6. That the plan was never legally ratified by the necessary two-thirds vote of the stockholders, because the votes upon the stock controlled by the bankers and members of the syndicate must be counted to make up the two-thirds vote required by law.

The injunction asked for was granted October 29, 1902, on a portion of the third item of the bill of complaint, on the ground that only four continuous payments of dividends on the preferred stock had been made, the duration of the period from the time of the first declaration of a dividend, July 2, 1901, to the date of the stockholders' special meeting, May 19, 1902, being forty-four days less than one year, while five continuous quarterly payments should have been made to fulfil the requirements of the law. An appeal was allowed to the Court of Errors and Appeals, where the case was re-argued in the November term. Decision was rendered on February 18, 1903, reversing the Vice-Chancellor, and deciding in favor of the defendants, on the ground that all the requirements of the law had been complied with, and that "there is no ground presented by the case or agitated in the briefs of counsel which will justify the interposition of a court of equity to arrest the proposed action of the defendants." A similar decision had been rendered by the Court of Appeals in the Berger case on October 11, 1902. The Steel Corporation at once put its plan into effect.

It is proposed, in the following pages, to outline the principal arguments in the Hodge suit as found in the affidavits, briefs, and arguments of counsel. Space does not, however, permit an extended analysis of these arguments; and, for the most part, the merits of the controversy will be determined by the decisions of the Vice-Chancellor and the Court of Appeals upon the different points presented. The complainants in the Hodge suit presented the most varied and forcible criticisms which have been made of the bond conversion plan. It may also be presumed that the defendants placed their side of the question in the most favorable light. With the opinions of two courts to assist him, the reader will have little difficulty in determining on which side lay the weight of the evidence.

Omitting the claim that the vested interests of the complaining stockholders would be impaired by the proposed conversion of preferred stock into bonds,—this point being decided in the Berger suit in favor of the corporation,[1]—and passing over, as being of merely technical interest, the ground on which the Vice-Chancellor granted the injunction, we find that the complainants rested their case upon the following principal arguments:

1. That the action of the directors in sanctioning the plan was illegal, by reason of the private interest of several of their number, while the stockholders, to whom the extent of the directors' interest had not been fully disclosed, could not validate their illegal action;

2. That the scheme was vitiated by actual fraud, being plainly designed to favor J. P. Morgan & Co. and their associates, at the expense of the corporation;

3. That the contract with the syndicate was unfair to the stockholders, both in the length of time given to them to subscribe for the bonds as compared with the time allotted to the syndicate, and the unreasonable options granted to the bankers;

4. That the Steel Corporation did not have assets of the value required by law.

In developing the alleged illegal private interest of the directors, the complainants began by claiming that fifteen of the directors of the Steel Corporation, including the six members of

[1] Opinion of the Court of Errors and Appeals, Van Syckel, J., (p. 11): "That this plan involves a reduction of capital stock is conceded: it is the very purpose of the plan to reduce it and to retire it; but to the assertion that it is preferential, I am unable to assent. The same opportunity is given to all to accept the offer, none are excluded, and the complainant who has declined the offer cannot say to the ninety and nine who have accepted it that they have been preferred. There has been no preference on the part of the corporation; the position occupied by the complainant is of her own option."

the Finance committee, were members of the underwriting syndicate whose agreement with the syndicate managers was dated March 12, twenty-eight days before the resolution of the directors approving the contract between the syndicate and the Steel Corporation. In other words, at the meeting on April 1, when the contract with the syndicate came up before the directors, a majority of the board were "personally and individually interested in the profits and advantages to be derived by Morgan & Co. and their associates." . . .

These benefits were considerable. If the stockholders subscribed to the full amount of $250,000,000 of bonds, the syndicate would receive $10,000,000 in cash from the corporation. In addition to this large commission, the syndicate had the privilege of exchanging preferred stock for all bonds which were not taken by the stockholders; and this option, it was claimed, presented the certainty of a large additional profit. It is the law of New Jersey that where the personal interest of a director is concerned in a contract with his corporation, that contract is voidable. On this ground, the complaints asserted that the action of the directors was illegal.

The answer to this argument, reserving to a later page a discussion of the benefits of the contract, was short and decisive. Such contracts as the one in question, said the defendants, while voidable at the option of the stockholders, can be validated either expressly by a vote of the stockholders, or by the stockholders not electing to take any action in the matter. In the present instance, since the stockholders, by an enormous majority, had sustained the directors in their approval of the plan of conversion, to say nothing of the fact that the by-laws of the corporation expressly provided that directors might be interested in contracts with the corporation, and, further, "that . . . any act or contract that shall be approved or ratified by the vote of the holders of a majority of the capital stock of the company . . . shall be as valid and binding upon the corporation and upon all the stockholders as though it had been approved or ratified by every stockholder of the corporation," the court held that the infirmity in the contract had been entirely eliminated, and that the ratification of the agreement and plan was complete.

The complainants then attempted to show that less than the necessary amount of stock was legally voted, by setting up the plea that the members of the syndicate had no right to vote for the ratification of a scheme in which they were personally interested as opposed to the interest of the corporation, thus affirming the doctrine that the rights of a stockholder, when he becomes a director, are limited by the director's obligation to the corporation, which, it was alleged, was violated in the present instance, and going so far as to impose a similar obligation upon a stockholder who was not a director. This argument was stated as follows: . . . "It is contended that where a large number of stockholders conspire to impose a burden upon a corporation for their own benefit, ignoring the interest of the corporation, they thereby become constructively trustees for their fellow-stockholders, assume the obligations of trustees toward their fellow-stockholders, and must deal with them accordingly."

The defendants replied, and the court agreed with them, that a stockholder can never be deprived of his right of ownership in a corporation and of the right to vote the number of shares which he holds upon any question affecting his interest. Judge Van Syckel remarked in his opinion:

> They [the directors] voted upon that resolution, not as directors, not in their fiduciary capacity, but solely in the right of the shares of stock held by them. A most valuable privilege, which attaches to the ownership of stock in a corporation, is the right to vote upon it at any meeting of stockholders. As to the resolution considered by itself, as stockholders, they owed no greater duty to their co-stockholders than those stockholders owed to them. Like other stockholders, they had a right to be influenced by what they conceived to be for their own interest, and they cannot lawfully be denied that right, nor can it be limited or circumscribed by the fact that they occupied the position of directors in the company.

But, continued the complainants, granted that the vote was legal on the assumption that the stockholders fully understood the nature of the resolutions upon which they were voting, that assumption was contrary to the facts. The stockholders were not aware of the nature of the contract already made with the syndicate, nor with the extent of the personal interest of the directors in this contract. The only information in regard to these matters contained in any of the documents sent to the stockholders, appears in the circular of April 17, and was as follows: "To further the success of the plan, there has been formed a syndicate, including some directors, which will receive four-fifths of the 4 per cent compensation to be paid under the contract with Messrs. J. P. Morgan & Co. mentioned in the notice of stockholders' meeting." It was further stated in the notice of the stockholders' special meeting, that copies of the directors' resolution, in which the nature of the contract was explained, and of the contract itself, could be obtained on application at Morgan & Co.'s office. This notice, the complainants asserted, was insufficient to acquaint the stockholders with the nature of these contracts which they were were asked to approve.

The defendants replied in the words of a decision upon another case cited in the brief of the defendants upon appeal:

> If the party notified make reasonable investigation, he obtains actual knowledge of these facts; if he choose not to make it, he is charged constructively with knowledge of them. . . . If he is unwilling to act upon the facts as the notice presents them, then the law demands that he shall make proper examination, and upon the result of that examination he may safely stand. . . . But, if he prefer not to examine, it must be because he is satisfied to act as if the matters disclosed in the notice were true, and he cannot afterward complain if his rights are made to rest upon them so far as they are true. The information given by the notice is equivalent to that obtained by the inquiry.[1]

This principle has been established in a number of cases. It was reaffirmed by the Court of Appeals in its decision that the information furnished to the stockholders of the Steel Corporation in regard to the various contracts and resolutions was sufficient to put them on inquiry. In fact, so little question was raised at the time concerning the expediency of the scheme that no stockholder applied to J. P. Morgan & Co. for a copy of the contract. The defendants were, therefore, apparently justified in their claim that the stockholders received all the information which they required.

[1] *Gale* v. *Morris*, 3 Stew. 285, 289, 290.

The Charge of Fraud

The evidence submitted by the complaining stockholders to substantiate their charge of fraud lay in the nature of the transactions in controversy. They claimed that the conversion scheme was bound up with the syndicate agreement; that it would not have been brought forward had it not been for the benefits which the syndicate was to derive; and that the compensation received by the syndicate, and the privileges allotted to it, were unreasonable and extortionate.

Here was a corporation, they said, in urgent need of at least $50,000,000 to complete improvements already begun, and to undertake further improvements whose completion would add at least $10,000,000 to its profits. This money was to be borrowed on the security of a second mortgage. The interest was to be provided by converting a 7 per cent dividend charge on $200,000,000 of preferred stock into a 5 per cent interest charge on the same amount of bonds. Ostensibly to insure the success of this plan, the aim and object of which was to raise a certain amount of cash, an underwriting scheme was devised, which, however, entirely subordinated the raising of cash to the conversion of stock into bonds. The underwriting plan devised by the directors undertook to guarantee, not the amount of cash required, but a plan of conversion whose complete success would not have increased the security of the proposed bond issue, nor have rendered the bonds more attractive in the eyes of investors, — a measure, moreover, which made inadequate provision for the real needs of the corporation. The syndicate, in other words, instead of guaranteeing to take $50,000,000 of bonds at par, and to pay for these bonds in cash, which the commonly understood principles of underwriting demanded, agreed to take only $20,000,000 of bonds at par, for which, after deducting their assured commission of $4,000,000 on the $100,000,000 of bonds whose purchase with cash and stock they had guaranteed, the corporation would receive only $16,000,000 of cash. Moreover, if the amount of bonds remaining should be taken by the stockholders, the additional commissions of the syndicate would reduce their actual cash guarantee to $11,200,000, or little more than one-fifth of the amount which the stockholders have been told was necessary. On the basis of the actual cash furnished, the commission to the syndicate, assuming that the plan was successfully carried out, would be 44 per cent, — an extraordinary and unreasonable compensation.[1]

Furthermore, in answer to the argument set forth in the affidavit of Mr. Perkins, in which he claimed that, in the opinion of the Finance Committee of the Steel Corporation, the immediate effect of the announcement of the contemplated withdrawal of 40 per cent of the preferred stock would be to send its price above par, and so make conversion unattractive, and that the necessity of segregating a large amount of preferred stock in order to make sure that at least $80,000,000 of stock would be exchanged, as provided by the syndicate agreement, involved great risk and the locking up of a large sum of money for a considerable time, the complainants urged that, in any event, the bonds, which were, on the admission of the Finance Committee of the Steel Corporation, a higher grade security than the preferred stock, — else why convert the stock into bonds? — would always sell at a higher price than the stock, and that, therefore, the necessity of guaranteeing the conversion did not appear. There could be no reasonable doubt that the corporation could sell $20,000,000 of its second mortgage bonds for more than $16,000,000, the maximum amount of cash which it stood to receive from the syndicate. The assurance given by the syndicate that the amount required for distribution to the security holders would be decreased $1,500,000 per year could have no effect upon the price of the bonds, and could therefore lend only indirect assistance to the conversion. Moreover, a large amount of this $80,000,000 preferred stock was already the syndicate's property at the time the contract was made; and, so far from locking up funds in fulfilling their agreement, the members of the syndicate were in reality increasing the value of their property. In short, it was claimed that the guarantee of the syndicate contained an inconsiderable benefit for the Steel Corporation, in return for which the syndicate was to receive a large cash commission.

[1] Argument of Edward B. Whitney for Appellees, p. 21.

The Charge of Discrimination

In support of the charge of discrimination, the complainants argued that the plan created two classes of subscribers to the new bonds: (1) the syndicate; (2) the other preferred stockholders. Class 1 were offered the bonds at 96; class 2, at 100. Class 1 had an option on part of the bonds for seven and one-half months, and an option on such portion of the remainder as were not taken by the preferred stockholders for sixteen and one-half months, which period could be extended by agreement between the syndicate and the directors. Class 2 had an option limited to fifty-eight days. Class 1 could exchange their holdings of preferred stock to any amount, while class 2 were limited to 40 per cent of their preferred stock holdings. "The syndicate," said the complainants, "after cutting off the preferred stockholders not in the syndicate by the thirty (or fifty-eight) days' notice, could, at any time before the first day of January, 1904 (and later by means of extending the time), purchase 1000 shares of preferred stock at the market price, — say 83, — paying therefor $83,000; then call upon the Steel Corporation under one of the options to deliver to them bonds to the amount of $100,000 in exchange for the 1000 shares of stock, and sell the bonds at the market price, — say 95, — thus making $12,000 without the slightest trouble or expense, except that which would attend a few minutes' clerical work. And this process could be repeated in larger or smaller amounts from time to time, whenever the relative market prices of the stock and bonds should make it profitable to do so. Would not this be a palpable injustice to stockholders of the corporation, and especially to the preferred stockholders, not members of the syndicate, who had exchanged 40 per cent of their preferred stock for bonds?"

The answer of Mr. Perkins to this charge has been already referred to. He asserted that, without the guarantee of the syndicate, the success of the conversion plan would have been endangered by the appreciation in the value of the preferred stock. He does not answer the argument that the compensation was excessive in consideration of the benefit received by the corporation, except so far as to assert that the syndicate agreement was "a most desirable one for the United States Steel Corporation," but rests the justification of the compensation almost entirely on the risk assumed by the syndicate.[1] In the Berger suit, where this point was more fully discussed, and to which constant reference was made in the Hodge litigation, the expediency of the contract with the syndicate was justified by the argument which Mr. Perkins employed, and the large risk incurred by the syndicate was thus explained in the brief of counsel for the corporation:

Is it reasonable to contend that the tying up of $100,000,000 of capital involves no risk or consideration and warrants no compensation? Can it be said that a syndicate, which undertakes an obligation of $100,000,000 and for the purpose of performing that obligation ties up by actual deposit $80,000,000 of property, is furnishing no consideration for an agreement to pay a commission? Suppose, pending action by the stockholders, the preferred stock of the syndicate had fallen in value from 94 to 87½ (as it actually did) or even lower, and there was a falling market occasioned by strikes or financial disaster, who would recompense the syndicate for the loss that it would sustain by the depreciation of its stock? . . . A variation of four points in the relative value of the seven per cent cumulative preferred stock and the new five per cent bonds would at once wipe out the profits of the syndicate and turn the venture into a loss. . . . For example, it may well be that the present market value of the proposed new five per cent bonds is 95, and that the present market value of the preferred stock is 88, a depreciation of 6 per cent since the syndicate deposited the $80,000,000 of stock. What, then, would be the outcome of the risk of the syndicate if the plan had been disapproved by the stockholders, or if it should now be set aside by the courts? The syndicate has tied up $80,000,000 of stock, which now shows a loss of 6 per cent, or $4,800,000, and this loss exceeds the promised commission, which they would not receive if the contract were not approved, and in addition the syndicate is

[1] The following quotation from Mr. Perkins's affidavit is of interest in this connection: "The largest participations in the syndicate were taken only after urgent solicitation by me and upon my agreeing that my firm would take an equal amount. The participation taken by Mr. Schwab and by some of the other directors was upon the understanding that, if we found other parties to take any part of such participations, we would do this, and thus release them. My firm considered, and I believe most of the directors believed, that the syndicate contract was not a particularly profitable one for the syndicate. In no instance did we find any stockholder willing to subscribe for the full amount of his holdings in preferred stock."

bound to take $20,000,000 of bonds, which bonds are only worth 95 in the market, showing an additional loss of $1,000,000. It is submitted that the mere statement of these facts must satisfy any court that the syndicate has since the first of April, 1902, run a very great risk, that it is still running a great risk, that in all fairness and propriety a reasonable compensation may be paid for that risk, and that the agreed compensation is not excessive.[1]

It is unfortunate that the defendants did not feel themselves compelled to legitimate the syndicate agreement, not merely by citing the risk undergone, but, as the complainants challenged them to do, by showing a corresponding benefit to the corporation. As complainants' counsel remarked:

> The directors of an industrial corporation would not be justified in paying a million dollars to a person who offered to swim the Atlantic, unless they could show that some benefit would be conferred upon the corporation by the accomplishment of that feat. The fact that the gentleman proposing the scheme insisted upon the enormous risk that he ran would not justify the directors in closing the contract.

It would have been better, we must admit, if only for the sake of gaining a larger measure of general approval for their project, if the defendants had presented this portion of their argument in a less general and sweeping manner.

For the immediate purpose of winning their case, however, it was merely necessary for the defendants to keep before the court the fact that the contract between the Steel Corporation and Messrs. J. P. Morgan & Co. was approved of by more than $99\frac{4}{5}$ per cent of the stockholders represented at the special meeting. Behind this fact, in passing upon the legitimacy of the transaction, in the absence of specific proof of fraud, the court could not go. As Vice-Chancellor Emery said in his opinion which was quoted in the decision of the appellate court:

> The reasonableness or judiciousness, in the business aspect, of a reduction of the preferred stock of the Steel Corporation, and the distribution of capital resulting therefrom, by the conversion of stock into bonds, is . . . altogether a matter of management of the affairs

1 Brief on Behalf of Defendants — appellants in *Miriam Berger* v. *United States Steel Corporation*, pp. 42, 43, 44.

of the corporation, upon which the decision of the directors and stockholders given in the manner required by law is final, so far as it relates to its business aspects.

And Judge Van Syckel, in the final decision, stated the same principle in more general terms, quoting from his opinion in the Berger case:

The manner in which a duly authorized plan is to be carried through is part of the business of the corporation, and, in the absence of fraud or bad faith, is not the subject of judicial control to any greater extent than any other business of the corporation. The court cannot substitute its judgment for that of the directors and majority stockholders, and say that a less expensive plan could be successfully adopted.

In short, so long as the directors acted in good faith and with entire frankness, they might, unless expressly forbidden by the law, have converted all their preferred stock into a 6 or 7 per cent bond; they might have incurred a floating debt equal to their mortgage indebtedness; they might have abolished the charge for depreciation; they might have paid their president a salary of $5,000,000 per year. In fact, they might have violated many rules of business prudence if only they could secure the approval of a majority of the stockholders. In New Jersey, a stockholder, generally speaking, is allowed to do what he will with his own.

That the court was convinced of the honesty and good faith of the transaction appears from the expression of Justice Van Syckel:

There is an entire absence in the case of anything to show a taint of fraud, or an attempt to conceal from the shareholders any fact which should have influenced their action. That the entire proceeding was conducted with good faith, without concealment, and with fairness to both parties, is evinced by the fact that during all the litigation which has ensued, under the promotion of a shareholder who did not attend the meeting, not one of the vast number of shareholders who were present in person or by proxy, comprising men of great business capacity, interested to the extent of millions of dollars in the conversion plan, has questioned its propriety, or expressed a desire, so far as appears, to recede from it.

The Valuation of the Assets

A New Jersey corporation cannot convert preferred stock into bonds unless its assets, after the deduction of all indebtedness, are equal to its preferred stock.[1] In their attempt to prevent the conversion of preferred stock into bonds, the complaining stockholders laid final emphasis upon the alleged fact that the assets of the Steel Corporation were not worth the necessary amount; namely, $880,024,900. In proof of this assertion, the complainants relied mainly upon the affidavits of one James H. Lancaster, who represented himself to be "a mechanical and mining engineer and expert on ores and steel and iron properties and their products." . . . Mr. Lancaster made two affidavits in the suit, — the first, a preliminary affidavit, on July 3, 1902, and the second, in more detail, on July 14.

In his first affidavit, Mr. Lancaster stated that he was "familiar with and had made a study of all the various properties and plants" of the Steel Corporation, that the plants and properties could be duplicated for about $300,000,000, and that the total value of all the properties, including good will and organization, was not worth $500,000,000.

Two weeks later, Mr. Lancaster, in his second affidavit, went into the subject of valuation in more detail, and presented the statement upon which this portion of the complainants' case was to depend. He stated, first, that the plants of the Carnegie company, representing 44 per cent of the productive capacity of the Steel Corporation, had been valued on March 12, 1900, by the partners of the Carnegie Steel Company at $75,600,000. This valuation was stated in the answer of the company to Mr. Frick's bill of complaint to be "a full, fair, and accurate valuation of these assets," and also that "the experience and judgment of business men justify us in saying (as we do) that such a method of valuation in large manufacturing companies, and especially of iron and steel in our country, as a rule, is more liberal to the seller than to the buyer; for experience has shown that partnership assets on a just appraisement seldom reach

[1] This was the act of March 28, 1902, under which provisions the plan of exchanging bonds for preferred stock was authorized.

the value at which they stand on the books of the concern." Mr. Lancaster, accepting this statement as accurate, estimated the total value of the Steel Corporation's properties, upon the basis of the 1900 valuation of the Carnegie properties, and including \$27,000,000 of Frick Coke Company assets subsequently added, at \$200,000,000.

He also presented a table showing the conversion value of the securities of the constituent companies in the securities of the United States Steel Corporation, as follows:

	Common Stock	Preferred Stock	Bonds
Constituent companies	\$300,000,000	\$247,000,000	\$219,000,000
United States Steel Corporation	508,000,000	510,000,000	362,000,000
Increase	\$208,000,000	\$263,000,000	\$143,000,000
Percentage of increase	69	106	65

The inference drawn from this comparison of capitalizations was that, unless the capital of the constituent companies was far below the value of their assets, the capitalization of the United States Steel Corporation greatly exceeded the value which supported its securities. Mr. Lancaster concluded his affidavit by expressing the opinion that the 1902 earnings of the United States Steel Corporation represented the results of an exceptionally prosperous condition of the market, and that many new plants were then building to compete with the corporation in all its departments.

The arguments of complainants' counsel in support of these affidavits were mainly taken up with showing that the iron and steel trade was subject to sudden and extreme reverses and to long periods of depression, and that these contingencies had not been allowed for in the capitalization of the Steel Corporation. They contended: (1) that the value of a group of assets was based on the selling price of those assets, which in turn depended solely upon their earning power, and that, while the Steel Corporation was then earning interest and dividends on all classes of its securities, there was no assurance that these earnings would be sufficiently permanent to warrant the belief that the selling value of the company's assets could properly be based upon a capitalization of their amount; (2) that the 1902 price of steel was an abnormal price, dependent on temporary conditions, and resulting in earnings which should be disregarded in making an estimate of the ability of the corporation to pay the large increase in interest charges which would result from the success of the conversion plan; (3) they asserted that the directors of the Steel Corporation were about to carry through a plan which was not merely unnecessary and expensive, but dangerous as well, — a plan which would increase its mortgage debt beyond what experience showed would be the minimum value of its assets, a plan whose success spelled bankruptcy, should the history of the steel trade be repeated. The argument of the complainants, in brief, was based entirely on considerations of business probability, and on the results of business experience. Affirming that the requirements of the New Jersey corporation law were designed for the protection of the investor, they asked the court to interpret the meaning of the statute in the light of business probability, and to refuse its sanction to a measure which conservative judgment would disapprove.[1]

This, however, as shown by its refusal to throw out the conversion plan because of its alleged expensiveness, the court was not prepared to do. So long as the requirements of the law were complied with, which in this case meant a certification by the officers of the corporation that its assets, after deducting all indebtedness, were equal in value to the amount of its preferred stock, and in the absence of fraud, the court had no right to interfere.

This certification was furnished in a series of affidavits remarkable because of their prodigal frankness and the varied standards of valuation which they set up. The subject-matter of these affidavits, so far as they relate to the question of assets, may be

[1] Argument of Edward B. Whitney (p. 41): "I submit that the sole object of the Legislature in establishing this restriction as to the amount of assets was to make the recapitalization entirely safe for at least the preferred stock, . . . to secure that in case of insolvency a foreclosure of the new bonds would result in the realization of the full value of the preferred stock if the latter were properly protected."

divided as follows: (1) valuations of property; and (2) estimates of future earnings. The leading affidavit for the defendants was made by Mr. Schwab, who swore to the statement that the total value of the corporation's assets, without making any allowance for good will and established business, patents, trade-marks, and processes, or for $150,000,000 of orders on hand, exceeded the total amount of its capitalization. This statement was not made in general terms, but was supported by a list of assets, giving the value assigned to each and the basis of valuation employed. For purposes of convenience, the material of this affidavit has been arranged in the following table:

Assets	Valuation	Principles governing Valuation
1. Iron and ore properties.	$700,000,000	1. Properties cannot be duplicated at any price. 2. Yield direct profit of $30,000,000 on present price of ore. 3. The Steel Corporation would be compelled to pay $700,000,000 in order to obtain these deposits.
2. Plants, mills, fixtures, machinery, equipment, tools, and real estate.	$300,000,000	1. Impossibility of duplicating these mills for a less amount. 2. The mills are necessary to make the profits of the corporation, stated to be at the rate of $140,000,000 per year.
3. Coal and coke fields (87,589 acres).	$100,000,000	1. Net profits to the corporation, based on the present prices of coal and coke, over $12,000,000.
4. Transportation properties.	$80,000,000 after deducting $40,340,000 of bonded debt.	1. Cost of duplication. 2. Profits of mills increased $10,000,000, because of possession of transportation facilities.
5. Blast furnaces.	$48,000,000	1. Cost of duplication.
6. Natural gas fields.	$20,000,000	1. Profit of $2,000,000.
7. Limestone properties.	$4,000,000	1. Cost of duplication. 2. Profit of $500,000.
8. Cash and cash assets.	$214,278,000	1. Cash assets valued at cost.

Mr. Schwab employs two leading principles in valuing these assets, — (1) cost of duplication and (2) profits derived from their possession. Of his estimate of $140,000,000 as the earnings of the corporation, $54,500,000 is directly accounted for by the savings on ore, coal and coke, transportation, limestone, and natural gas. The direct profits of the mills easily make up the remainder.

Mr. Schwab's affidavit was supplemented by the affidavits of other officials. Mr. Elbert H. Gary, chairman of the Finance Committee, testified that the "intrinsic value" of the properties, as set forth by Mr. Schwab, were true and conservative. Mr. James Gayley, first vice-president, and in general charge of the mining and transportation of raw material, stated in his affidavit that the ore properties of the corporation were not only the most extensive known, but were of such high grade and quality as to make them specially suited to the production of the best quality of iron and steel; and: "that investigations have demonstrated that the deposits of this region are practically circumscribed as to quality, and that, if any new deposits are to be found, it will undoubtedly be at points which are much further removed from sites suited to the economical manufacture and distribution of product," and, further, "that they could not be duplicated or reproduced at any price."

President Lynch, of the Frick Coke Company, supported Mr. Schwab's statement by the assertion that the 315,000,000 tons of coking coal still contained in the Connellsville basin were worth, on a profit of 50 cents per ton, — 75 cents below the profit then being made, — $157,500,000. President James H. Reed of the Pittsburg, Bessemer & Lake Erie Railroad Company, in perhaps the most carefully worded affidavit of the series, affirmed that the cost of the transportation properties of the corporation, after deducting the amount of their bonded debt, was approximately $50,000,000, and that their cost of duplication would be far in excess of this amount, since in many cases it would be impossible to duplicate these facilities. The final affidavit as to the value of the property was made by William J. Filbert, comptroller of the Steel Corporation, who stated that on the basis of the highest prices reached for the two stocks, the total market value of all the corporation's securities was $1,149,014,932.

The defendants were also at considerable pains to controvert the statements, sworn to in the Carnegie-Frick litigation of 1900, that $75,600,000 represented a "full, fair, and accurate valuation of the Carnegie Steel Company's assets." James J. Campbell, auditor and assistant secretary of the Carnegie company, in his affidavit demolished the truth of the statement made by the defendants in *Frick* v. *The Carnegie Steel Company*. He showed that all the properties of the Carnegie Steel Company had been carried on the books for many years at the original costs, and that no allowance had ever been made for the money expended on them for improvements, which in some instances far exceed the original outlay. The question at issue in the Frick-Carnegie litigation, said Mr. Campbell, did not concern the actual value of the Carnegie company's property, but merely involved the basis of settling for the interests of deceased or withdrawing partners. Mr. Schwab also took the same ground in his affidavit: "It was claimed in such litigation, and such was the fact, that the book value did not represent the actual value of the properties. Under the terms of the agreement to which Mr. Frick was a party, it was provided that the book value should determine the interests of the several associates, and the controversy between Mr. Frick, on the one hand, and Mr. Carnegie and his associates, on the other, was as to whether this nominal book value should control, or the actual value, which Mr. Frick alleged to be in excess of $250,000,000."

The defendants did not stop with estimates of present valuation. They accepted the standard of business probability which the complainants claimed should be applied to determine the value of the Steel Corporation's assets, and asserted that, in their judgment, the earnings of the Steel Corporation would never fall so low as to endanger the interest on the second mortgage bonds. As a matter of record, these predictions should be preserved.

Mr. Schwab stated that, if the conversion plan were carried through, the fixed charges of the corporation — he makes no allowance for depreciation — would be $31,737,850. The earnings of the corporation were then more than four and one-half times this amount, leaving a margin of 75 per cent above the danger of bankruptcy. "The most careful investigation," said Mr. Schwab, "was made at the time the board of directors voted to recommend the issue of $250,000,000 of second mortgage bonds, to determine whether, under any reasonable possible conditions, the earnings of the Steel Corporation would be reduced below the total fixed charges of $31,737,850. The unanimous opinion of the officers and directors who had a lifetime of experience in the business was that, under no conditions of the iron and steel trade or of business depression, was there any reasonable likelihood that the earning capacity of these vast properties would be reduced to any such extent." This part of Mr. Schwab's affidavit was repeated in almost identical terms by Mr. Gary, who stated that the board of directors was unanimously of this opinion. It is unfortunate that these vigorous statements do not start from an assumption of at least $60,000,000 of fixed charges, for, on Mr. Schwab's basis of valuation, a $30,000,000 charge for depreciation would be none too large.

Under the weight of this mountain of testimony, the arguments of the complainants, which they admitted were founded on "*ex-parte* and argumentative affidavits," were crushed to the ground. They were forced to admit that their part of the case was in a condition far from satisfactory, and, in fact, were unable to bring any rebuttal evidence or argument worthy of comment, contenting themselves with repeating their original contentions.[1]

Furthermore, the appearance of Mr. Lancaster in the case gave the defendants an opportunity to impeach the good faith of the suit, which they did not fail to improve. As an illustration of the motives which animate the movers in these so-called "strike suits," of which it was charged that this was an example,[2] a portion of

[1] Extract from Section VIII of Brief for Complainants on Appeal: "The complainants' papers at the commencement of this litigation were necessarily prepared hastily, and it is obvious that great labor and a long time would be required, especially for parties not having access to the books and papers of the corporation, to make an inventory of the property, even approximately accurate. . . . We frankly concede that the record on the question of value is not in a satisfactory condition from the complainants' point of view."

[2] See page 176 *infra.*

the affidavit of Joseph E. Corrigan, an attorney in the office of Guthrie, Cravath & Henderson, may be advantageously presented. Mr. Corrigan stated that on August 15 Mr. Lancaster, on his own initiative, made to him and Mr. Guthrie substantially the following statement:

"That on the third day of July, 1902, a young man named Preskauer handed them the business card of the law firm of James, Schell & Elkus, and told him that Mr. Elkus wanted to see him at his (Elkus') office. That he at once proceeded to said office, and there for the first time met Mr. Elkus whom he had never known before. That he was introduced by Mr. Elkus to David Lamar, that said Lamar thereupon talked to him in the presence of said Elkus about the United States Steel Corporation's properties and their values, and after some conversation said that he desired an affidavit as to the values; that said Lancaster did not know and was not told that the affidavit was to be used in litigation, and did not observe any title of a suit, to what at the time he swore to. That he protested that it was impossible for him in so short a time to make an affidavit; but that said Lamar said they would be satisfied with his present impressions, and what he knew generally about the steel business; and that they would give him $100 for the affidavit. Said Lancaster further stated that he needed the money, and that, as this was an easy way to make $100, he was willing to swear to the affidavit, although he did not know what it was to be used for, and supposed it was simply for said Lamar's information, or for some purpose said Lamar had in mind, and that he gathered from what Lamar said to him that it was to be a guide for investing in stocks. Said Lancaster further stated to Mr. Guthrie and myself that, a few days afterwards, he for the first time ascertained that his affidavit had been used in a suit against the United States Steel Corporation. That he went at once and protested to Mr. Lamar . . . that he had been deceived. Said Lamar thereupon agreed to pay him $250 a week and $10,000 when they succeeded in making a settlement, which he (Lamar) assured Lancaster would not be later than November 1. That he made a second affidavit in the suit, for which he was paid $400. That he then had a row with Lamar over the subject of his compensation, that he threatened to expose them all, and that finally Lamar agreed to pay him $500, making $1000 in all, provided said Lancaster would execute a general release and sign a letter to the effect that he would not disclose to any one what had occurred in Mr. Elkus' office — that he understood from what Mr. Lamar and others said in Mr. Elkus' office that they expected to make big money out of the suit, and that a number of the suits were in preparation and would be brought one after another until a settlement was forced."[1]

The weight of the argument as to the value of the Steel Corporation's assets was plainly with the defendants. Vice-Chancellor Emery supported their contention at every point. He stated in his opinion that the certificate of value required by the law had been filed by the proper officers, and that "upon the affidavits filed there can be no question whatever as to their honesty and good faith in making this certificate as to value." This certificate, it is true, was not conclusive evidence, but might be shown to be false. The proof of its falsity, however, in this case, had not been furnished. The affidavits filed by the defendant company, said the Vice-Chancellor, on this question of the value of the assets, are "full, complete, and detailed, and are made by persons entirely familiar with the property, or portions of the property, as to whose value they affirm. The affidavits as to value filed by complainant are, on the other hand, general, vague, and made without special knowledge or examination, and the credibility of the principal affiant on the part of the complainant is seriously impaired by his own admissions in his latest affidavit. Upon these affidavits as to value, I would not be justified in enjoining the issue of the bonds, pending the final hearing." The Court of Appeals, while passing upon the arguments of the complainant, apparently did not consider the discussion of the value of assets of sufficient importance to even refer to it.

The United States Steel Corporation, in the Hodge suit, won a complete victory. Its opponents were not merely routed, but

[1] Lancaster, in a supplementary affidavit, denied the correctness of some of Mr. Corrigan's statements, but admits their general correctness, and places himself in a generally unfavorable light.

the honesty of their motives was seriously impugned. The legality, and, so far as the court went in this direction, the wisdom of the plan for converting bonds into stock, were upheld. The vindication of the defendants could not have been more complete.

There is, however, another side to the question. Apart from the provisions of the New Jersey corporation act which the directors were careful to obey, the facts brought out by the Berger and Hodge suits constitute a serious indictment of the wisdom of the bond conversion plan. Surely, at this late day, few will be found to indorse a plan to change a dividend requirement on $200,000,000 of stock into an interest requirement on $200,000,000 of bonds, for no better reason than to save the interest and sinking fund charges on an additional $50,000,000 of bonds. The mere statement of the plan, which runs directly against every recognized canon of corporation finance, is sufficient to secure its condemnation. The proposal ignored the mortgage lien of the bonds which were to be substituted for stock, and the fact that with the issue of the new bonds the borrowing capacity of the corporation would be exhausted, for the sake of saving $4,000,000 in dividend payments, 2 per cent of the net profits of the company in 1902.

We have become familiar with plans for the conversion of bonds into stock where the purpose is to reduce fixed charges. Projects for purchasing stock with bonds secured by the stock — for example, the purchase of Burlington, Jersey Central, and Louisville & Nashville — are not uncommon. In such cases, the purchasing company can apply the dividends on the stock to the payment of interest on the new bonds; and the lien, aside from a guarantee which can be enforced only with great difficulty, is on the stock which the bonds were issued to purchase. Such projects have to commend them either the reduction of fixed charges, or the gaining control of companies where control means a large increase in the earnings of the parent corporation. But to propose a conversion scheme for no better reason than to reduce dividends in favor of interest, is a proposition which has little to commend it.

Then, too, can the syndicate agreement, when drawn from under the healing wings of the stockholders' approval, stand the test of critical examination? The theory advanced by defendants' counsel, that the amount of the syndicate's compensation should be determined, not by the benefit to the corporation, but by the risk of the syndicate, would seem to be untenable. Underwriting syndicates are usually supposed to guarantee cash. Their commission is based upon the amount of cash for which they are liable. The maximum commission in the case under consideration was 44 per cent of the cash guarantee, — an amount out of proportion to the benefit received. The argument that it was necessary to sequester a large amount of preferred stock in advance of the announcement of the conversion plan, because of the practical certainty that the announcement would raise the price of the preferred stock above par and make conversion undesirable, is singularly weak. In what manner the placing of $12,500,000 of interest charges ahead of the preferred stock dividends, would advance the value of the latter security, can better be imagined than described. The course of the preferred stock since the conversion plan was announced offers an interesting commentary upon the prescience of the Finance Committee.

Space does not permit an extended examination of the methods employed in valuing the assets of the Steel Corporation. At the time these affidavits were made, there can be no question that, as worded, they deserved the high praise awarded them by the Vice-Chancellor, of being full, complete, and detailed, and of being made in honesty and good faith. In July, 1902, the corporation was earning at the rate of $140,000,000 per year; and the "present worth" of its assets, which is the plain meaning of the law, was in excess of $1,400,000,000. If the argument of the complainants was to stand, the law should have read something as follows: "that no corporation shall be permitted to retire its preferred stock by the issue of bonds whose earnings, in the judgment of some competent tribunal, shall not at all times be adequate to pay dividends on the preferred stock." In such an event, however, the question would never have come before the court in the course of litigation.

It would have been definitely settled beforehand. As the law stands, and looking only to present value, the adequacy of Steel Corporation's assets in July, 1902, to conform to the requirements is evident.

But what shall be said of the wisdom of the policy which accepts such a valuation as a basis for incurring $10,000,000 additional of fixed charges without corresponding increase of assets? The fixed charges of the Steel Corporation, assuming that the conversion scheme had been a complete success, and making adequate allowance for depreciation, would have been at least $70,000,000 per year. As they now stand, with only $150,000,000 of preferred stock exchanged, they are not far from $65,000,000.[1] Here is a necessary reduction in earnings before the limit of fixed charges is reached, not of 75 per cent, as stated in the directors' affidavits, but of 50 per cent. There will be few persons found, who are in any way conversant with the history of the steel trade, to affirm that the earnings of any steel corporation could not be reduced one-half by a very moderate decline in prices. The Steel Corporation averaged a profit of $16 per ton during 1902. It may fairly be questioned whether the conditions of competition and demand warrant the proposition that a profit of $8 per ton can be secured when the trade is at its lowest ebb.

As above remarked, however, while the directors were ready to swear to the belief that the profits of the Steel Corporation would never be reduced as low as $31,000,000, they included no allowance for depreciation in their estimate of fixed charges. Their judgment would not, therefore, be impeached, should the earnings of the Steel Corporation fall below its fixed charges. If the rule be accepted, however, — that, in issuing bonds, a corporation should always maintain a wide margin between minimum net earnings and fixed charges, — it is impossible to approve a plan to add $12,500,000 to the interest charges of

[1] This statement is not based upon official announcements, but upon common report at the time the life of the syndicate was extended. If the gap between preferred stock and bonds is not closed, there is every reason to expect that the operations of the syndicate in purchasing preferred stock for retirement will insure the final success of the plan of commission.

the United States Steel Corporation. The fixed charges of the company were too high before for entire safety. The issue of $250,000,000 of bonds, or even $150,000,000, can be described by no other word than unwise.

The Hodge and Berger suits may have been inspired by improper motives, but they have served to call attention to certain glaring defects in American corporation law. The time has gone by when the determination of great questions of corporate policy, involving the welfare of the community as well as the interests of stockholders, can be safely left to their own judgment. The average stockholder in corporations such as the Steel Corporation is incapable of forming a judgment on questions such as those under discussion. He is one of a flock of sheep who follow first one false shepherd and then another, until, inverting the parable, for every sheep that is safely folded, ninety-and-nine are hopelessly led astray. He invests because he has confidence in some individual. Unfortunately, his confidence is frequently misplaced. The laws of those states, such as New Jersey, in which most large companies are incorporated, give the stockholders abundant protection against directors and officers who attempt, by concealment and fraud, to violate their trust. These laws, however, give no protection to the stockholder against his own ignorance and credulity. If the stockholder was the only one to suffer the consequences of his own simplicity, there might be no reason for advocating a plan of federal control which would compel directors to follow a conservative policy in the distribution of earnings and the readjustment of capital. But where the history of each day is furnishing new evidence that the prosperity of the community is jeopardized by reckless financiering, it is plain that the people should, for their own protection, take out of the hands of stockholders the control of matters with which they are incompetent to deal, and by the enactment of laws similar to those which regulate the conduct of national banks, compel directors to keep at all times within the limits of conservatism.

If the tremendous decline in the securities of the largest industrial corporation in the world — a decline which is almost without parallel, and which has inflicted heavy losses upon tens of thousands of stockholders — shall furnish the object-lesson necessary to bring the American people to their senses upon this question of the necessity of rigid federal control of large corporations, the United States Steel Corporation will not have lived in vain.

EDWARD SHERWOOD MEADE.

THE UNIVERSITY OF PENNSYLVANIA.

THE STEEL CORPORATION'S BOND CONVERSION: A CORRECTION[1]

In the preceding article Professor Meade gives prominence to the recent suit of Mr. Hodge against the Steel Corporation, referring to it as if it might have been a "strike suit." That the defendants in this suit could obtain a withdrawal without pecuniary outlay was well known to them. Mr. Hodge's offer of withdrawal, made through me in writing at an early stage of the litigation, asked simply a resubmission of the scheme to the stockholders with full information as to its main features, or else its modification by taking from the Morgan syndicate all advantage over the other preferred stockholders, giving it no longer option to subscribe for the bonds, no greater time to pay subscriptions, and no commission except upon the amount which the syndicate should absolutely bind itself to underwrite.

The point upon which the Vice-Chancellor decided the case in Mr. Hodge's favor, if sustained, would have forced a resubmission to the stockholders. It would probably then have been voted down. The notice upon which their proxies had been obtained had been so drawn as to give the impression that the whole bond issue had been underwritten; and the syndicate's extraordinary option was not apparent. The stockholders were indeed informed that by calling at the Morgan office they could secure complete copies of the proposed contract; but, as Professor Meade truly says, nobody called. Each assumed that he had enough information, and did not need to examine legal documents. The most interesting question to the public in the

[1] From the *Quarterly Journal of Economics*, Vol. XVIII, 1904, p. 303.

Hodge suit was whether this notice sufficiently discharged the duties of the directors. The New Jersey court held that it did. Other courts have set up a much higher standard, and required of interested directors the fullest disclosure. The standard set by the state which has fathered so large a proportion of the modern "trusts" has had no small influence upon public confidence in their securities.

Time has already vindicated Mr. Hodge. Public sentiment recognizes this, and has forced the surrender of the syndicate option. Mr. Schwab's valuations have been condemned by the market, and by the abandonment of dividends, to the loss of so many common stockholders. The principle of his valuation, that in bonding a company it should be capitalized on the basis of the profits of a year of prosperity, instead of upon the availability of its assets in a period of depression, was never indorsed by conservative men, although it passed muster with the New Jersey courts.

The fact that Mr. Hodge was publicly joined as complainant by no other stockholder of record was not due to lack of sympathy, — of that he received a plenty, — but to two conditions which are among those that most contribute to the success of the modern "trust" financier. Persons with large interests at stake cannot afford to join openly, because they are afraid that the dominant powers in Wall street may take revenge by attacking their financial credit and excluding them from profitable enterprises. Small stockholders have not sufficient interest pecuniarily to justify the annoyance and notoriety and the newspaper abuse to which they would be subjected. Even necessary expert testimony is difficult and expensive to obtain, through fear of boycott; and the swiftness with which the directors' plans are carried through after their announcement leaves stockholders but little time for consultation and none for deliberate action. It is only when the plans fail for other causes, as in the shipbuilding case, that the minority have time for investigation or combined action.

EDWARD B. WHITNEY.

NEW YORK.

THE LATER HISTORY OF THE UNITED STATES STEEL BOND CONVERSION[1]

THE underlying motives for this most extraordinary fiscal operation have been variously interpreted. It has been freely ascribed to the desire of important owners of the preferred stock to dispose of their unwieldy holdings to the public in the form of bonds. Others allege that participation in industrial investments by large life insurance companies would be less indefensible in the purchase of bonds than of preferred stock. Even among the large body of private investors, there are many who will purchase bonds, but will buy stocks only of the highest grade. The bond having a right of foreclosure cannot decline in value below a point determined by its equity interest in the property. Stocks are not thus limited as to their possible decline in value; but may fall to any degree. A double motive, in the judgment of authorities, existed. The bonds would naturally have a better market than the stock. The stock, also, if on a dividend basis would command a better price, if the supply of it in the market were thus reduced. This consideration, in days of "undigested securities," was an important one. That imperative need of cash for improvements was not the sole motive, as publicly alleged by the company, would seem to follow from a number of considerations. For, in the first place, cessation of dividends on common stock would speedily have supplied the necessary funds from current earnings, following the conservative policy of railway companies, without resort to conversion at all. This expedient was certainly possible under the conditions which prevailed when the plan was resumed in March, 1903. A year of litigation had resulted in a dissolution of the injunction granted by a lower court. Enormous earnings of the company meanwhile had resulted, in December, 1902, in "undivided earnings" of $33,841,565 upon the year's business. Under such circumstances the imperative need for cash urged on behalf of the original plan certainly did not exist. A second cogent criticism against this alleged motive is that the plan as

[1] From the *Quarterly Journal of Economics*, February, 1905.

approved, and afterwards as actually carried out, would result in entirely insignificant cash receipts as compared with the magnitude of the other operations involved. At the most, the only source of ready cash from the plan would be the sale of $20,000,000 of bonds at par, from which the commission of 4 per cent for the syndicate would be necessarily deducted. Yet the official statement given out on November 19, 1903, by the Executive Committee of the Board of Directors showed that only $2,902,000 of such bonds had been actually sold at par for cash, paid for in full October 1, and already issued. On the remainder of the minimum $20,000,000 of bonds guaranteed by the syndicate for cash on October 21, only 25 per cent had been called for and paid to the corporation. Had the real reason for this entire operation lain, as alleged, in the imperative need for cash, why was not the syndicate called upon promptly for the balance of its guarantee?

From the foregoing considerations it seems perfectly clear that an important motive for this transaction was to secure a large profit to prominent bankers who were represented at the same time on the Board of Directors of the Steel Corporation. This interpretation seems to flow from the original plan as proposed. It derives added force from the subsequent history of the enterprise. Stockholders were permitted until May 16, 1903, to take advantage of the conversion scheme. At that time the bonds were selling above 90 and the preferred stock was a few points lower. The exchange would therefore leave a profit probably less than 5 per cent. The syndicate, however, had not only *guaranteed* a conversion of $80,000,000 of this preferred stock; but its contract provided that it might, if so disposed, convert the balance of the $200,000,000 of preferred stock authorized for exchange into bonds. The life of the syndicate was to terminate October 1, 1903. Meanwhile the margin between the market price of the new bonds and the preferred stock had perceptibly widened. In other words, depression in the steel industry was becoming evident. Suddenly the financial community was startled by a circular notice announcing that the life of the syndicate had been extended from October 1, 1903, until the following July.[1] Obviously this cleared the way for a continued conversion of the preferred stock into bonds at a continually growing profit determined by the widening margin between the two classes of securities. This profit was not open to the general stockholders whose option had expired in the preceding May. November brought news of still further trade contraction, until the preferred stock was quoted at about 50, while the new 5 per cent bonds were selling some fifteen points higher. This meant a profit of about $150 per bond, exclusively reserved to the banking syndicate. Moreover, a cumulative process was evidently involved, inasmuch as the greater the amount of conversion, placing bonds ahead of stock, the less was the preferred stock on the market worth. This scandalous condition of affairs finally induced the company to terminate the contract and limit the amount of conversion to $150,000,000 in place of $200,000,000 as originally planned.[2]

The net results of the transaction would seem to be as follows. Of the $50,000,000 bonds originally to be sold for cash, none were taken by the public. The price never rose above 95, while they were offered at par. The syndicate assumed its guarantee of $20,000,000 at par, but only a small fraction of this offer of cash had been taken by the company when the contract was cancelled. As to the $200,000,000 of preferred stock to be converted (afterwards reduced to $150,000,000), outside shareholders whose rights expired in May availed themselves of the privilege to an amount variously estimated at from $35,000,000 to $50,000,000. The syndicate, compelled by its guarantee to convert $80,000,000, must therefore have taken care of the balance of $150,000,000. This last was the limit finally set by the company on terminating the contract upon completion in November, 1903. The results to the United States Steel Corporation of the entire transaction were then twofold. At best, an insignificant amount of cash was provided, not all of this being taken as offered. Secondly, an evident saving in the annual charges was made, determined by the difference between the dividends on old preferred stock at

[1] Official documents are reprinted in Moody, Truth about the Trusts, p. 185.

[2] A searching analysis of this phase of the matter is given by A. D. Noyes in *The Forum*, January, 1904, pp. 368 *et seq.*

7 per cent and the interest at 5 per cent on the new bonds. But as an offset to this, as previously shown, was the fact that the new bonds were a fixed charge with foreclosure rights, while the dividend payments were contingent upon earnings. There remains, then, for discussion only the amount of profit which must have accrued to the syndicate, many of whom were directors in the company; a profit which, had no options been given to the syndicate, could have been made by the Corporation itself. As a loss must be reckoned the sale of the bonds at figures ranging from 95 down to 75, such bonds having been taken at par. On the other hand, profits arose from two sources. The cash commission at 4 per cent on $170,000,000 of the new bonds was considerable and certain. In addition to this came the exclusive privilege after May, 1903, of converting the stock into bonds at a margin of difference vastly greater than could have been contemplated when the contract was drawn. Whatever, legally, the judgment of the courts may have been, as hereinbefore described, there can be no doubt that from a fiscal point of view the entire operation betrayed a disregard of the principles of sound finance and even of common honesty and fair dealing with the stockholders.

WILLIAM Z. RIPLEY.

IX

UNITED STATES SHIPBUILDING COMPANY[1]

Incorporation

THE United States Shipbuilding Company was incorporated on June 17, 1902, under the laws of the state of New Jersey. The incorporators were Howard K. Wood, Horace S. Gould, and Kenneth K. McLaren. . . . The incorporators collectively subscribed for fifteen shares of the preferred and fifteen shares of the common stock of the company.

On June 24, 1902, the incorporators above named, constituting the stockholders of the company, held their first meeting. . . . At this meeting Frederic K. Seward was elected a director for one year, Raymond Newman was elected a director for two years, and Louis B. Dailey was elected a director for three years, the minutes of the company reciting that Howard K. Wood, one of the incorporators and subscribers to the stock, had assigned his right to one share of common stock to each of the persons above named to qualify them as directors. No stock of the United States Shipbuilding Company, however, was issued to or placed in the name of these directors, so far as the records of the company disclose.

On the said 24th day of June, 1902, the first meeting of the directors of the United States Shipbuilding Company was held. At this meeting there were present Louis B. Dailey, Raymond Newman, and Frederic K. Seward, being all of the directors. The minutes recite that the Board proceeded to the election of officers for the ensuing year, and, ballots having been cast and counted, it was found that Raymond Newman had been elected

[1] From Report of James Smith, Jr., Receiver, filed Oct. 31, 1903; United States Circuit Court, District of New Jersey, *R. R. Conklin, et al* v. *United States Shipbuilding Co.* [Condensed by omission of immaterial parts and legal repetitions.]

president; Louis B. Dailey, vice-president; and Frederic K. Seward, secretary and treasurer. The persons above named as incorporators were . . . all connected with the Corporation Trust Company of New Jersey as officers or otherwise, and the place of residence above stated being the New Jersey office of said Trust Company. The directors were also employees of said company.

At this meeting of the directors an offer was received from one John W. Young, of which the following is a copy:

Offer of Promoters

New York, June 24, 1902.

To the Board of Directors, etc.,

I hereby offer to convey, sell, etc., . . . unto your Company for the consideration hereinafter stated, the following property, viz.:

(1) All of the capital stock of the Union Iron Works of San Francisco, Cal., . . . together with all of its property, real and personal, business and good will as a going concern, I hereby agreeing that this corporation has no bonds out and no indebtedness except current accounts, etc.

Messrs. Henry T. Scott and Irving M. Scott have agreed with me . . . to enter into the usual contract with your Company not to compete with it in its business, and not to employ their capital . . . for the period of ten years.

This offer of the stock and property of the Union Iron Works is made also upon the following express conditions, viz.: That your Company shall enter into a contract extending over a period of five years with Messrs. . . . , now connected with the management of the Union Iron Works, to act as officers or managers . . . for this period of five years at an annual salary to be paid to each of $10,000, etc.

(2) The entire capital stock of the Harlan & Hollingsworth Company of Wilmington, Del., etc.

(3) Also the entire capital stock of the Eastern Shipbuilding Company, etc.

(4) All of the real estate of the Canda Manufacturing Company, etc.

(5) Also the entire capital stock of the Crescent Shipyard Company . . . and the business of the Crescent shipyards heretofore conducted by Lewis Nixon.

* * * * * * * *

(6) Also the entire capital stock of the Samuel L. Moore & Sons' Company. . . .

(7) Also the entire capital stock of the Bath Iron Works . . . and of the Hyde Windlass Company. . . .

(8) Also 300,000 shares out of an entire issue of 300,000 shares of the capital stock of the Bethlehem Steel Company . . . engaged in the business of manufacturing and dealing in iron and steel and the products thereof.

I will also pay, or cause to be paid, to your Company $1,500,000 for working capital, and will also deliver, or cause to be paid and delivered to your Treasurer or other nominee, the following securities, viz.: $1,500,000 in par value 5 per cent, thirty-year gold bonds of United States Shipbuilding Company, the same to be held as Treasury assets and disposed of for working capital or other purposes of the Company as your Board of Directors shall hereafter determine.

It is a further condition of this offer that in cases where your Company shall acquire both capital stock and properties of any of the corporations included in this offer, you shall guarantee, or otherwise assume, any promissory notes or other obligations which it may be necessary or desirable to put into the treasuries of such corporation or corporations for the protection of their creditors, or to avoid violation of the statutes of any state or states.

I will accept in full consideration for the conveyances . . . above offered to be made $19,998,500 in par value of the full paid and non-assessable preferred stock of your Company, $24,998,500 in par value of the full paid and non-assessable common stock of your Company, $16,000,000 par value of the first mortgage five per cent sinking fund thirty-year gold bonds, Series A, of your Company secured by a mortgage which will be a first lien upon all the property and plants of the Union Iron Works, etc. (above named companies); also $10,000,000 par value of the 5 per cent twenty-year gold bonds to be made by your Company and to be secured by a mortgage upon the shares of stock of the Bethlehem Steel Company and otherwise, as hereinafter stated.

In case you accept the offer of the stock of the Bethlehem Steel Company the purchase must be made upon the following conditions:

(1) The stock . . . is to be deposited with the New York Security & Trust Company under a mortgage or deed of trust which shall be a first lien upon the stock so acquired, and, subject to the priority of the mortgage to secure said $16,000,000 of bonds, shall be a lien upon the property and plants covered by said $16,000,000 mortgage. . . . The holders of each $1,000 par value of said bonds to have the same voting power as the holders of each $1,000 par value of the stock of your Company.

(2) For the purpose of further securing said issue of $10,000,000 of bonds, your Company shall also procure to be executed and delivered to the New York Security & Trust Company, the single bond of the Bethlehem Steel Company payable to said Trust Company for the sum of $10,000,000 gold coin, with interest thereon at the rate of five per centum . . ., conditioned for the due payment of the principal and interest of said issue of $10,000,000 of bonds, etc.

(3) That an agreement shall be executed between the Bethlehem Steel Company and your Company, by which said agreement your company shall undertake to guarantee so long as any of said issue of $10,000,000 bonds are outstanding, that the Bethlehem Steel Company shall pay dividends upon its capital stock at the rate of Three Dollars per share per year, aggregating an annual dividend contribution of $900,000, and for that purpose that your Company will supply and furnish said Bethlehem Steel Company . . . business and . . . means of earning to enable it to pay said annual dividends . . . or advance sufficient money . . . to make such annual dividend payments which may be credited on any business or work which said Bethlehem Steel Company may thereafter have for or on account of your Company. Said agreement shall further provide that so long as any of said issue of $10,000,000 bonds remain outstanding, said Bethlehem Steel Company shall be protected in keeping on hand and maintaining cash or cash assets of not less than $4,000,000 cash value over and above its current business liabilities (not including its present and projected issue of bonds) as its working capital, no part of which shall at any time be used or applied towards the payments of dividends or for purposes other than the operation and conduct of the business of said Bethlehem Steel Company.

(4) That so long as any of said $10,000,000 bonds are outstanding said Bethlehem Steel Company shall always remain an independent and distinct corporation, and shall not be merged in or consolidated . . . unless . . . requested or consented to by the holders of not less than 75 per cent of said outstanding bonds.

(5) That your Company may at any time pay all of said outstanding bonds as an entirety by depositing a sum equal to the par value . . . with interest . . . to the New York Security & Trust Company as trustee.

I will cause to be delivered to your Company suitable deeds, bills of sale and transfers, etc.

* * * * * * * *

(Signed) JOHN W. YOUNG.

Upon the receipt of this offer the directors above named, holding no stock whatever in the Company, but at most a mere subscriptive right, by assignment, to one share each, adopted the following resolution:

ACCEPTANCE BY COMPANY

Whereas, John W. Young has offered to convey, sell, etc., . . .; and,

Whereas, In the judgment of this Board the value of the properties so offered . . . is at least the par value of the stocks and bonds of this Company proposed to be issued therefor, to wit, the sum of $70,997,000, and said properties are necessary for the business of this Company;

Resolved, That said offer be and the same is hereby accepted, etc., . . .

Further resolved, That for the purpose of enabling this Company to accept the foregoing offer, it shall as soon as practicable take the steps required by law for the increase of its authorized capital stock from thirty shares of $100 each . . . to four hundred and fifty thousand shares of $100 each, two hundred thousand shares of which shall be preferred stock, and two hundred and fifty thousand shares of which shall be common stock, making a total authorized capital stock of $45,000,000. . . .

Further resolved, That the officers of this Company be, and they hereby are authorized and directed to make . . . to the Mercantile Trust Company as Trustee, a mortgage or deed of trust upon the properties purchased pursuant to the offer of said John W. Young (exclusive of the shares of stock of the Bethlehem Steel Company), to secure the payment of $16,000,000 par value of first mortgage 5 per cent thirty-year sinking fund gold bonds, etc., . . .

Further resolved, That the proper officers of this Company be and they hereby are authorized and directed to make . . . a mortgage or deed of trust to the New York Security & Trust Company as Trustee, of the shares of the capital stock of the Bethlehem Steel Company . . . to secure the payment of $10,000,000 par value of the 5 per cent twenty-year gold bonds of this Company, which mortgage shall contain the provisions required under the terms of said offer, etc., . . .

Further resolved, That the officers of this Company are hereby authorized to execute, issue, and deliver to the said Young . . . the first mortgage . . . gold bonds of this Company of the aggregate par value of $16,000,000, . . . $10,000,000 and certificates for 199,985 shares of the preferred capital stock . . . and for 249,985 shares of the common capital stock, etc.

Increase of Capital Stock

On the same day, to wit, the twenty-fourth day of June, . . . a meeting of the stockholders of said Company was held for the purpose of authorizing and increasing the capital stock of the United States Shipbuilding Company and of considering and acting upon the offer of said John W. Young. There were present Frederic K. Seward, Louis B. Dailey, Kenneth K. McLaren, Horace S. Gould, Howard K. Wood, and Raymond Newman, claiming to be holders of fifteen shares of preferred and fifteen shares of common stock of the United States Shipbuilding Company, being all the capital stock of said Company. At this meeting the following resolution was adopted:

Resolved, That the action of the Board of Directors . . . be . . . approved, ratified, and confirmed, etc.

At a meeting of the Board of Directors of the United States Shipbuilding Company held on July 31, 1902, the following resolution was adopted:

The Board of Directors, etc., do hereby resolve and declare that it is advisable that the capital stock of this Company be changed from thirty shares . . . to four hundred and fifty thousand shares . . . of capital stock, etc.

* * * * * * * *

Purchase of Subsidiary Plants

Between the fifth day of August, 1902, and the twelfth day of August, 1902, in evident compliance with the offer of said John W. Young and the acceptance thereof . . . the companies . . . conveyed to the United States Shipbuilding Company all their real and personal property. . . .

* * * * * * * *

Leases to Subsidiary Companies

Your Receiver further reports that after the delivery of said deeds . . . leases were entered into between the United States Shipbuilding Company and the (various companies hereinbefore named). . . . By the terms of these leases "all the yards, docks, and plant," etc., were leased to the above named constituent companies "at the yearly rent or sum of the net profits of the said party of the second part in its business during the term of this lease." . . . In the Union Iron Works lease the entire plant and property were leased for one year to the Union Iron Works for the nominal rental of one dollar. All such leases were terminable on five days' notice.

Alleged Basis of Directors' Actions

The resolution of the Board of Directors of the United States Shipbuilding Company accepting the offer of John W. Young, above set forth, was stated by said Board in its minutes to be based upon a report in writing from Messrs. W. T. Simpson, Fellow Institute Accounts, New York, and Riddell and Common, Chartered Accountants, on the condition of the business of the several companies mentioned in said offer, excepting the Bethlehem Steel Company. This report is alleged to have certified, among other things, that the contracts of the constituent companies for construction then in hand amounted to over thirty-six millions of dollars. That the time necessary to complete the work contracted for averaged about eighteen months from January first, nineteen hundred and two, and that the estimated net profits thereon had been calculated at over five millions of dollars. That new work was being constantly offered, and this new work, replacing completed contracts from time to time, should result in the realization of an average annual profit on work in hand and in sight of two million two hundred and twenty-five thousand dollars.

With reference to the Bethlehem Steel Company, the minutes of the Board of Directors recite that Messrs. Jones, Cæsar & Company, chartered accountants, had been investigating the affairs of the Bethlehem Steel Company, and had made a report that the company was earning at the rate of one million eight hundred thousand dollars per year; that it had a working capital of over four millions of dollars, and that it had contracts in hand sufficient for its full running capacity for three years. In reliance upon these alleged reports, and without knowledge of, or investigation into, the merits of the properties, the resolution in question was adopted.

Acts of the Directors

A comparison of the figures alleged to have been relied upon by the Board of Directors in accepting the offer of John W. Young, with the true figures ascertained from an examination of the subsidiary companies subsequent to the purchase of said plants, discloses so great a variance as to impel the belief that the figures contained in the minutes were wilfully misstated. It is extremely doubtful whether any report was submitted by any accountants made as of that time, as the minutes recite. In a certain Prospectus marked "Private and Confidential," bearing date the 19th day of April, 1902, there is contained a letter purporting to be signed by Messrs. Simpson and Riddell and Common, under date of January 24th, 1902, which letter would seem to serve as a basis to a certain extent for the allegation in the minutes of the Board of Directors. If the examination of these accountants was made as of January 1st, 1902, as the letter would imply, it must have been of the most superficial kind. The letter in question makes such exaggerated representations with reference to the profits, present and prospective, as to make it absolutely worthless as a guide in ascertaining the real condition of the plants. It is entirely refuted by their later reports and detailed statements made as of June 30th and July 31st, 1902.

Your Receiver has seen and inspected the statements made by these accountants as of June thirtieth, nineteen hundred and two, and July thirty-first, nineteen hundred and two, and finds nothing therein to support the statements contained in the minutes of the Board of Directors.

The statement of Messrs. Simpson and Riddell and Common of the condition of the subsidiary plants as of June thirtieth, nineteen hundred and two, contains, among other things, the following figures:

1. Contract price	$34,377,408.70
2. Value of work done under said contracts up to June 30, 1902 .	13,771,768.96
3. Value of work to be done under said contracts subsequent to June 30, 1902	$20,605,639.74

The report of these accountants also contained a statement of the volume of business done by the constituent companies for the three years ending June thirtieth, nineteen hundred and two, on which the profit was shown to be about ten per cent. The report also shows that the contracts remaining unfinished on June thirtieth, nineteen hundred and two, would require three years for their completion.

From this report the following facts clearly appear:

1. That the amount of contracts on hand June thirtieth, nineteen hundred and two, instead of being Thirty-six Millions of Dollars, as recited in the minutes of the Board of Directors, was $15,394,360.26 less than the amount therein stated.

2. That it would take three years to earn whatever profit was involved in these contracts, instead of eighteen months, as alleged in the minutes.

3. That the profits on such contracts, instead of amounting to $5,000,000, as the minutes recite, basing the estimate upon the past earnings contained in the report, would be about two millions of dollars; and,

4. That the statement that the average annual profit on work in hand and in sight of the constituent companies, exclusive of the Bethlehem Steel Company, was $2,225,000, appears to have no more substantial basis than the wildest conjecture.

AMOUNT OF CONTRACTS, JULY 31, 1902

Your Receiver has caused to be prepared a statement showing the contracts in force on the 31st day of July, 1902, the portion thereof completed, the balance remaining uncompleted, and the estimated profit thereon, based upon the highest possible estimate of earnings, which is annexed hereto marked "Schedule No. 2," and made a part thereof. From this statement it appears that the face value of the contracts on hand, including extras, on July 31, 1902, was	$34,097,739.23
The value of work done on said contracts up to July 31, 1902, was .	14,295,195.15
Leaving the value of the uncompleted work on said contracts on July 31, 1902	$19,802,544.08

Estimated Earnings on Such Contracts

Adopting the figures of the accountants and estimating profit on the basis of percentage of completion reported by them and the actual cost of such percentage, the highest possible estimate of earnings on the balance of the contracts to be completed would be $2,203,269.83, as appears from said "Schedule No. 2."

An examination of the books of the Company, however, with care and the exercise of some intelligence, and adjusting the amount of the contracts at corrected figures, would have shown that there was no basis for the foregoing figures, but that there might be justification for an estimated profit of $1,660,021.59, as appears from the statement hereto annexed, made a part hereof and marked "Schedule No. 3."

An examination as of August 1, 1903, however, with the past year's work as a basis, and allowing for changes in extras, discloses another set of figures and shows that the profit on such uncompleted contracts cannot exceed the sum of $1,078,261.42, as appears from the statement hereto annexed, made a part hereof and marked "Schedule No. 4."

From this latter Schedule, which is based upon the actual cost of the work, so far as ascertainable, a situation is disclosed so much at variance with the figures alleged to have been relied upon by the Board of Directors as to lead to the belief that the minutes of the Board of Directors in this respect must have been wilfully falsified. The Five Millions of profits dwindle to about One Million; the contracts therein referred to will not be completed for upwards of three years, and, judging from past experiences, it is safe to say that this estimated profit will suffer great depreciation before the completion of the contracts.

Working Capacity of Plants in Relation to Earnings

So far as your Receiver is able to ascertain, the full capacity of the yards, exclusive of the Bethlehem Steel Company, is about fourteen million dollars of work annually, while twelve million dollars is an average volume of work. From the figures contained in the report of the Messrs. Simpson and Riddell and

Common, it appears that the average profit of the yards for the three years preceding their purchase by the United States Shipbuilding Company did not exceed ten per cent. Upon this basis the average annual profit derived from the yards, on the basis of the capacity above stated, would not exceed a million four hundred thousand dollars.

Earnings for the Year ending August 1, 1903

This basis, however, is no guide to the actual earnings of the constituent companies. After being in operation for one year under the control of the United States Shipbuilding Company, the earnings of the constituent companies, exclusive of the Bethlehem Steel Company, instead of being $2,225,000, as alleged by the Directors, or $1,400,000, as figured on the above basis of ten per cent, did not exceed $833,458.74, as appears from "Schedule 5," hereto annexed and made a part hereof.

It has been suggested that the poor showing in regard to earnings is due to the increased cost of labor and material during the past year. It is true that the cost of labor was greater during the past year than the previous years, and that there were some losses occasioned by strikes; but it is also true that, by reason of the combination of all the yards under one management and the attempted control thereof by the United States Shipbuilding Company, there should have been a great reduction in the management expenses. This reduction in expense, however, did not come to pass, and one reason for it may be found upon an examination of the offer of Young, above set forth. In this offer it will be found that in the case of the Union Iron Works, Eastern Shipbuilding Company, Samuel L. Moore & Sons' Company, Bath Iron Works, and the Hyde Windlass Company, it was provided that the United States Shipbuilding Company should enter into contracts with certain persons therein named for upwards of five years at salaries, in many instances, greater than the earnings of the subsidiary company would warrant. The acceptance of this offer, therefore, with these conditions imposed, not only reduced the earnings of the subsidiary companies, but left the officers in charge thereof practically free from interference by the Board of Directors of the United States Shipbuilding Company for a period of five years, a fact that must necessarily have had considerable influence upon the management and earnings of the individual plants. This fact, however, does not wholly explain the failure of the earnings of the constituent companies to reach the amount of earnings estimated in the preliminary reports. The real reason why the earnings fell below the anticipated profits was because previous alleged earnings had been figured upon a percentage of completion of contracts, which percentage in many instances was erroneous. For instance, in the case of the torpedo boats "Nicholson" and "O'Brien," it was stated that these boats were fully completed. As a matter of fact there was subsequently expended thereon the sum of $56,271.04, and it is estimated that upwards of $20,000 is still needed to complete these boats. Your Receiver, therefore, respectfully submits that the method of arriving at profits earned previous to the combination was practically worthless for the purpose of ascertaining accurate results, and led to the inaccuracies in the estimates for the future.

Bethlehem Steel Company

In regard to the Bethlehem Steel Company, the minutes of the Board of Directors with reference to the offer of the said Young, recite that an investigation of the affairs of that company discloses that it was earning at the rate of $1,800,000 a year, and that it had a working capital of over $4,000,000. For the two years preceding the adoption of the resolution in question by the directors the earnings of the Bethlehem Steel Company for the fiscal year ending the thirtieth day of April were as follows:

1900–1901	$381,403.83
1901–1902	978,743.81

From these figures, as to the earnings of the Bethlehem Steel Company, which are made up from the report submitted by the Bethlehem Steel Company, it appears that the earnings of that company at the time of the adoption of the resolution were much below the amount alleged in the minutes of the Board of

Directors of the United States Shipbuilding Company, and that there was then no justification for the use of such figures.

It also appears that the working capital of the Bethlehem Steel Company at the close of their fiscal year on the thirtieth day of April, nineteen hundred and two, was not over $4,000,000, but was at least $250,000 less than such amount, as hereinafter set forth.

Working Capital

From the report of Messrs. Simpson and Riddell and Common, as of July 31st, 1902, not made, however, until after the properties had been acquired and paid for, it appears that the working capital of the constituent companies, exclusive of the Bethlehem Steel Company, was $3,278,798.48. The figures making up this total were subsequently found to be excessive in the case of nearly every company, the shrinkage amounting to $1,450,367.41, so that the working capital of the constituent companies was but $1,828,431.07, as appears from the statement hereto annexed, marked "Schedule No. 6," and made a part hereof. From the statement hereto annexed, marked "Schedule No. 7," and made a part hereof, it appears that with the exception of the Union Iron Works, the subsidiary companies, taken together, had absolutely no working capital; but on the contrary their liabilities exceeded their resources in the sum of $294,719.33. By reference to this schedule it appears that the following was the condition of said companies at the time of their purchase:

DEFICIT		
Bath Iron Works	$3,518.74	
Crescent Shipyard Company	403,192.28	
Harlan & Hollingsworth Co.	73,813.44	
S. L. Moore & Sons' Company	5,039.27	
		$485,563.73
SURPLUS		
Eastern Shipbuilding Company	$1,391.34	
Hyde Windlass Company	189,453.06	
		$190,844.40
Net Deficit being excess of Liabilities over Assets		$294,719.33

From an examination of "Schedules 6 and 7," it will appear that the alleged working capital was provided largely by the

Union Iron Works, with slight help from the Hyde Windlass Company and the Eastern Shipbuilding Company.

The amount of Accounts Payable and Notes Payable of the different companies at the time of their purchase by the United States Shipbuilding Company was $2,334,987.64. Of this amount $2,192,145.98 was owing by the subsidiary shipbuilding companies other than the Union Iron Works, as appears from said "Schedule No. 7." As the principal part of the alleged working capital above mentioned was confined to Union Iron Works, it will appear that so far as the remaining companies are concerned, when taken over by the United States Shipbuilding Company, they not only had no working capital, taken collectively, but were in immediate need of financial assistance.

From the foregoing facts, viewed not only in the light of subsequent developments, but also from the figures obtainable at the time of the incorporation of the United States Shipbuilding Company, it appears to have been the intention of those responsible for the statements and figures alleged to have been relied upon to mislead and deceive the investing public and the then present and future creditors of the Company.

Prospectus

In this connection, your Receiver begs to refer to the prospectus issued to the public, with a view to inducing subscriptions for the bonds of the United States Shipbuilding Company, under date of June 14, 1902. This prospectus seeks to invite the public to subscribe for nine millions of dollars of the first mortgage 5 per cent sinking fund gold bonds of the United States Shipbuilding Company. It recites that the United States Shipbuilding Company "has been organized under the laws of the State of New Jersey." It implies that the total capital stock of the Company is twenty millions of dollars, $10,000,000 of which is preferred and $10,000,000 common. It sets out a list of the directors of the United States Shipbuilding Company, numbering ten in all. It recites that the subsidiary plants of the Company, exclusive of the Bethlehem Steel Company, have been appraised as going concerns at twenty millions of dollars; that these companies would have a combined working capital of more than five million of dollars; that they have on hand contracts for work amounting to more than $36,000,000, on which the profits were estimated at over $5,000,000.

Waiving for the present all discussion as to the value of the plants as going concerns, a comparison of this prospectus with the facts disclose the following false and misleading statements:

1. At the date of this prospectus the United States Shipbuilding Company had not been incorporated.

2. Its capital stock was never Twenty Millions. Originally it was Three Thousand Dollars; which amount was subsequently increased to Forty-five Millions.

3. Six of the ten persons mentioned as directors in the prospectus were not directors of the company, and never have been.

4. The amount of contracts on hand did not exceed $36,000,000, their face value being $34,182,861.94, but of this amount a profit was available only on the uncompleted portion of the contracts, which profit, as heretofore shown, will not exceed $1,078,261.42, and will take three years to earn.

5. These companies did not have a working capital of more than $5,000,000; the figures of the accountants show only a working capital of $3,278,798.48. This working capital, however, was almost obliterated by subsequent adjustment, as hereinbefore set forth.

6. The statement that the profits on contract work in hand would be $5,000,000 was undeniably false. If it is claimed that the profit was estimated on the entire amount of $36,000,000, the answer to this is that, admitting there was $36,000,000 worth of contracts (which was not true), the utmost profit that could be looked for, according to the figures of the accountants, was $3,600,000. When this prospectus was issued, the persons who were responsible for it must have deliberately disregarded figures which would have shown that the amount of work still to be done on the contracts was but $20,605,639.74, instead of $36,000,000, and that upon such uncompleted work a liberal estimate would have placed the earnings at only a trifle over $2,000,000.

Value of the Plants

The net surplus of the various constituent companies, including their plants, according to the statement of the accountants, as shown by the books of said companies, were on the 31st day of July, 1902, as follows:

Bath Iron Works	$827,316.19	
Hyde Windlass Co.	358,121.29	
Crescent Shipyard Co.	470,583.99	
Samuel L. Moore & Sons' Co.	404,788.88	
Eastern Shipbuilding Co.	237,278.53	
Harlan & Hollingsworth Co.	1,294,767.16	
Union Iron Works	4,303,378.97	
Total	$7,896,235.01	
Bethlehem Steel Co. (deducting underlying mortgages)	4,245,281.25	
Canda Manufacturing Co. (estimated)	300,000.00	
Total		$12,441,516.26

For this property the directors of the United States Shipbuilding Company parted with the following obligations of that company:

Preferred stock of the U. S. S. Co.	$19,998,500	
Common stock of the U. S. S. Co.	24,998,500	
First mortgage 5 per cent bonds	16,000,000	
Twenty-year gold bonds	10,000,000	
Total		$70,997,000.00

There was returned to the company, however, the following cash and securities:

Cash	$1,500,000	
First mortgage bonds	1,500,000	
Total		$3,000,000.00
Total bonds and stock paid by Shipbuilding company's directors for the subsidiary plants		$67,997,000.00

In connection with the purchase of the Canda Manufacturing Company, $1,100,000 of the cash and securities of the United States Shipbuilding Company were parted with. The Canda company gave up nothing except its lands and buildings, its good will, if any, and practically all of its machinery being retained by the vendors. The above estimated value of $300,000 is undoubtedly greatly in excess of its true value. No use has ever been made of this plant, and none was apparently contemplated when it was purchased. After its purchase the directors of the United States Shipbuilding Company caused an inquiry to be made with a view to ascertaining whether it could be put to any use, and an adverse report was made. (See minutes of the directors.) Why this property was purchased at all is not apparent.

Viewing the acquisition of the properties from the standpoint of the surplus and plant values, as disclosed by the books of the companies, the directors appear to have made a gift of upwards of $55,000,000 worth of stock and bonds of the United States Shipbuilding Company entrusted to their care.

It may be claimed, however, that the book values give no adequate idea of the real value of the plants as going concerns, and that the earnings of the plants should be taken into account in ascertaining such value. With reference to this matter, the minutes of the directors recite that the constituent companies, exclusive of the Bethlehem Steel Company, had an earning capacity annually of	$2,225,000.00
and that the Bethlehem Steel Company was earning . . .	1,800,000.00
Making a total earning capacity of	$4,025,000.00

This statement was false, and must have been known to be so at the time the plants above mentioned were taken over. It can serve no useful purpose, therefore, in establishing value from the standpoint of earning capacity. In this connection the earnings of the past year are presented for consideration:

The earnings of all the companies for the year ending July 31st, 1903, were as follows:

Constituent companies	$833,458.74
Bethlehem Steel Company (net earnings) after deducting interest on underlying mortgages, discounts, and depreciation . . .	1,662,530.80
Total	$2,495,989.54

A word of explanation with reference to the earnings of the subsidiary shipbuilding companies. These earnings, as to continuing contracts, are arrived at as follows: An estimate is made of the proportion of the contract completed. If this proportion should represent 50 per cent of the entire contract, and the actual cost of such percentage should be found to be 10 per cent less than the proportion of the entire contract price then earned, the profit, when such estimate is made, is put down at a figure which will represent 10 per cent of such earned proportion of the contract price. Frequently this method of arriving at profits is found to be erroneous. The percentage of completion is found to have been placed too high, and as a consequence, the profits on the entire contract are reduced much below the estimate, and, in many cases, entirely wiped out and a loss sustained.

With reference to the Bethlehem Steel Company, a different method prevails. The method of the latter company is to take profits only upon deliveries, and not to estimate earnings as the work progresses. By this method the actual profits may be arrived at.

Assuming, however, that the earnings of the constituent companies are correctly set forth above (and in the case of Bethlehem they are not understated), of what use are such earnings for the purpose of establishing values unless they are available by the United States Shipbuilding Company?

These companies claim to have earned $2,495,989.54, but the United States Shipbuilding Company has been benefited to the extent only of a trifle over twelve per cent of this amount. Of these alleged earnings the constituent companies have paid during the eleven months ending July 1, 1903, to the United States Shipbuilding Company	$60,754.23
The Bethlehem Steel Company, for the purpose of meeting the semi-annual interest on the $10,000,000 mortgage . . .	250,000.00
Making a total of	$310,754.23

Of the $833,458.74 alleged to have been earned by the Shipbuilding companies, there has been expended for new machinery . .	$165,066.38
Of the earnings of Bethlehem company there was expended for plant betterment	683,370.24
There was paid by all of the companies to the United States Shipbuilding Company, as above stated	310,754.23
Making a total of	$1,159,190.85

The balance of the earnings (considering the above amount as having been earned) amounting to the sum of $1,336,798.69, was retained by the companies. By reason of the unsafe method of ascertaining the profits of the shipbuilding companies, it is extremely doubtful whether they have earned any such amount as above set forth. It is true, however, assuming that their earnings have been as above mentioned, that their financial condition has not been such as to warrant them in withdrawing any considerable sum from their assets for payment to the United States Shipbuilding Company. The utmost that they could do during the past year was a trifle over seven per cent of the amount claimed by them to have been earned. The Bethlehem company, during the past year, insisted that no sum in excess of the $250,000 paid by them to meet the interest on the $10,000,000 instrument, known as the Schwab mortgage, could be withdrawn from their assets for payment to the United States Shipbuilding Company; or, in other words, that about fifteen per cent of their entire earnings was the best they could do for the United States Shipbuilding Company. Concerning the earnings of the Bethlehem, your Receiver will deal at length elsewhere in this report, but it may be said here that Bethlehem deliberately used up its earnings in making enormous purchases of material for its own benefit, and in extensions, improvements, and repairs, in order apparently to keep its earnings from the United States Shipbuilding Company.

On the basis of what the United States Shipbuilding Company received from all the companies last year, there would be sufficient income only to meet the interest, at five per cent, on an investment of a trifle over $6,000,000. It may be insisted that this is not the best the companies can do, and therefore this amount should not be taken as a guide in establishing the value of the plants. Your Receiver is satisfied that it is not the best the companies can do, especially in the case of Bethlehem. It is certain that better returns would have been received from the constituent companies if they had been brought within closer reach of the central company, and if officers had been placed in charge who had looked to the interests of the central organization and not wholly to the betterment of the constituent companies. It is undoubtedly true that the fastening upon the constituent companies of certain officials, at fixed salaries, and for a long term of years, practically beyond the reach of the central organization, has materially prevented the United States Shipbuilding Company from obtaining the best results from its properties. In the case of the Bethlehem, a Board of Directors having the welfare of the United States Shipbuilding Company at heart, rather than its destruction, would have conduced much to the gain of the latter company. With these defects in management removed, the earning capacity of all the companies, so far as the United States Shipbuilding Company is concerned, would be greatly enhanced.

At the end of eleven months of operation, the United States Shipbuilding Company was adjudged insolvent and a receiver appointed. This was due either to the fact that the earnings were insufficient to meet its obligations, or because those earnings were improperly diverted. Your Receiver will hereinafter discuss this matter, but under this head he respectfully submits that the earnings of the several companies during the past year may not safely be used for the purpose of establishing the value of the plants.

Excessive Price paid for Plants

Considering the value of the plants, therefore, either from the standpoint of the books, or the earning capacity of the companies, and allowing for an increase in earnings in the future, it is evident that the accommodating directors of the United States Shipbuilding Company, in acquiring these properties, deliberately gave away many million dollars in the stock and bonds of their Company.

Who participated in this wholesale plunder? The testimony now being taken in the above entitled proceedings will doubtless disclose the name of all the participants; but as such testimony will be submitted to this Court for action, your Receiver does not deem it proper to comment upon it here. Certain it is that much of this vast amount of stock and bonds was taken by persons and corporations who parted with little or no consideration in exchange therefor. Blocks of the stock went to the vendors of the constituent plants and to the purchasers of bonds, as bonus, absolutely without benefit to the Company; $20,000,000 of it admittedly went to Mr. Charles M. Schwab in addition to the agreed price for Bethlehem. Some of it went to the promoters of this artistic swindle; and when all had been provided for, what was left of the bonds, amounting to $1,500,000, was handed back to the Company ostensibly to supply it with "working capital."

From the foregoing statement as to values, it is apparent that the $24,500,000 of bonds given up by the directors was an excessive price for all the plants purchased. Your Receiver is advised that as to the $44,997,000 of the preferred and common stock handed over by the directors to the vendors and promoters of this scheme, it cannot successfully be maintained that any value was paid therefor. Treating the issue of bonds, therefore, as full payment for the properties (and in so doing the Shipbuilding company alone is being injured), it follows that the vendors and promoters and their associates in the transfer and conveyance of the various plants to the United States Shipbuilding Company, by the acceptance of this $44,997,000 of the capital stock of the Shipbuilding company, without paying value therefor, became liable thereon to said corporation, by virtue of the provisions of section 21 of an act of the Legislature of the State of New Jersey, entitled an act concerning corporations (Revision of 1896). The United States Shipbuilding Company was entitled to recover such indebtedness from the holders of such stock and your Receiver is advised that he is entitled to enforce the same. Accordingly, your Receiver has offset against the sum alleged to be due on the $10,000,000 mortgage to the New York Security and Trust Company as trustee, to protect the issue of bonds to Charles M. Schwab, the liability of the said Charles M. Schwab on the $20,000,000 of stock received by him as aforesaid, and has interposed an answer in the suit by said trustee to foreclose the mortgage given as security for said bonds, claiming that by virtue of said offset the total issue of said bonds has been fully paid and satisfied. As to the issue of the bonds under the mortgage for $16,000,000 made to the Mercantile Trust Company, your Receiver charges that many of said bonds were received by the vendors and promoters and their transferees, and were issued by said Mercantile Trust Company, with full knowledge of the right of the United States Shipbuilding Company to be paid for the common and preferred stock taken by said vendors and other holders of said bonds without value, and as to all bonds secured by said mortgage so received, your Receiver has offset against the amount alleged to be due thereon, the liability of the holders thereof on the common and preferred stock so received by them, or their transferrers, and has interposed an answer in the suit instituted by the Mercantile Trust Company to foreclose said mortgage, claiming that by virtue of such offset the total issue of said bonds, or the principal part thereof, has been fully paid and satisfied.

Culpability of the United States Shipbuilding Company's Directors and Others

Your Receiver has spoken of the directors of the United States Shipbuilding Company as if they were wholly responsible for parting with many million dollars in the stocks and bonds of the United States Shipbuilding Company without value. The directors who were guilty of this act are responsible and should be held accountable for their unlawful act; but they are not alone responsible. In the first place, they were not bona-fide holders of the stock of the United States Shipbuilding Company. They were clerks selected by the promoters of this scheme from the Corporation Trust Company. They took an assignment of a subscriptive right to a share of stock, and upon the strength of this alleged subscription they dealt with the property of the United States Shipbuilding Company in the manner above recited. These young men were mere figureheads, placed in this position in order that the scheme of others might be carried into effect. This scheme was placed before them by its instigators, through the medium of an alleged offer of John W. Young, and the so-called directors in conformity with their instructions, and, without the ability or the knowledge to pass upon the matters therein contained, proceeded to do as they were told. Your Receiver charges that the properties of the various constituent companies were sold to the United States Shipbuilding Company for an amount which the vendors of such properties, at the time of such sale, knew to be far in excess of the fair value of said plants; and that the plan to combine such properties was conceived by certain promoters and was consummated by them with full knowledge of its injustice to the United States Shipbuilding Company.

Your Receiver begs to direct the attention of the Court to the fact that in the purchase of the various constituent companies, the United States Shipbuilding Company was absolutely without independent and intelligent representation. No inspection of the properties was made on behalf of the Shipbuilding company. No independent appraisement was had. No steps seem to have been taken by any one with a view to protecting the interests of the United States Shipbuilding Company. The directors who purported to act for the Company were the tools of the promoters; the debts of the constituent companies, aggregating $2,334,987.64, seem to have been purposely withheld, and the bonds and stock of the United States Shipbuilding Company were placed wholly at the mercy of the vendors and promoters.

Operation of the United States Shipbuilding Company

Under such auspices the United States Shipbuilding Company began operations. On paper the constituent companies had a working capital in excess of $3,000,000, yet offices had hardly been secured by the United States Shipbuilding Company before the latter company was compelled to assist the constituent companies to pay their debts. The alleged working capital of the constituent companies existed on paper only. It was made to appear as available capital in order that the sale might be consummated. After such sale there was no longer any necessity for the continuance of this pretence, and accordingly demands for remittances began to pour into the central organization. During the eleven months ending July 1, 1903, the United States Shipbuilding Company was compelled to advance to the constituent companies the sum of $1,019,955.78. Of this amount $60,754.23 was returned to the Company, making the net amount advanced to the constituent companies $959,201.55. In addition to this sum it was compelled to part with $520,000 of the bonds which had been placed with it as working capital, for the purpose of securing indorsements on promissory notes which the United States Shipbuilding Company was required to make for the accommodation of the constituent companies.

The reason for this has been herein elsewhere suggested. When the various properties were purchased, the debts of such companies were not disclosed. Had there been independent, intelligent representation on the part of the United States Shipbuilding Company in connection with the acquisition of these properties, it would have been discovered that the new company was taking over $2,334,987.64 of debts, a considerable part of which called for immediate attention. Had there been such representation, it would have been disclosed that the companies had practically no working capital except such as they might receive from their vendee, and with this knowledge the wholesale delivery of bonds and stocks of the United States Shipbuilding Company would undoubtedly have been averted. But there was no one in that transaction to protect the interest of the new company, and as a consequence it was not only made to pay excessive prices for the property purchased, but obligations were assumed by reason of this vast amount of debt that practically exhausted the resources of its treasury.

While the bills of sale from the various constituent companies purported to transfer all the personal property of such companies to the United States Shipbuilding Company, including their cash, amounting to the sum of $389,317.57 (exclusive of Bethlehem), this amount was retained by the various companies when the leases above mentioned were made, and no benefit therefrom was ever received by the United States Shipbuilding Company, except the doubtful one of allowing this amount to help swell the alleged working capital of the constituent companies.

The United States Shipbuilding Company was not fairly organized until some time in September, 1902. On the 24th day of December, 1902, with a view to inducing the New York Stock Exchange to list the entire stock and bond issue of the Company, amounting to $69,500,000, a statement was made to such exchange, over the signature of A. C. Gary, treasurer of the United States Shipbuilding Company. This statement recites that the earnings of the subsidiary companies, exclusive of the Bethlehem Steel Company, for the year ending June 30, 1902, amounted to the sum of $1,942,522.03, and that the net earnings of the Bethlehem Steel Company for twelve months ending July 31, 1902, amounted to the sum of $1,441,208.03.

Without taking time to controvert this statement, which was clearly erroneous, and which, upon a proper examination, would have been shown to be so, an allegation appears in this statement of far more serious import. It is therein alleged that the net earnings of the United States Shipbuilding Company and the Bethlehem Steel Company for the three months ending November 30, 1902, amounted to the sum of $1,163,022.22. Of this amount the United States Shipbuilding Company was said to have earned up to that time $554,021.45, and the portion earned by the Bethlehem Steel Company was placed at $609,000.77. These earnings were said to be net; but in the case of the Bethlehem Steel Company no allowance was made therein for depreciation, and, furthermore, such earnings constituted no basis for averaging the annual profit, as the later report of the Bethlehem Steel Company shows. In the case of the United States Shipbuilding Company, the earnings existed on paper only, as appears from subsequent reports. Your Receiver believes that the officials of the United States Shipbuilding Company did not know that erroneous reports were being made to them by the constituent companies, but their action was at least injudicious in so wording the statement to the Stock Exchange as to impel the inference that the earnings of the United States Shipbuilding Company up to the 30th day of November, 1902, were available for the purpose of meeting the accrued interest and sinking fund payment on all bonds of the company for that quarter, for during the very time within which the alleged earnings of $554,021.45 had been made by the subsidiary companies, and which the statement infers were available for the payment of all accrued interest and sinking fund charges, they had been compelled to advance in cash to the constituent companies the sum of $424,467.59.

On this showing the application to list the securities was granted by the New York Stock Exchange on January 14th, 1903. A little over four months later, on the 25th day of May, 1903, a statement was issued to the public embodying a plan for the reorganization of the United States Shipbuilding Company upon a basis that would enable it to exist. This proposed plan of reorganization stated that "by reason of the excessive mortgage obligations of the United States Shipbuilding Company, its borrowing capacity and credit has become so seriously affected that outstanding notes are being pressed for payment and the making of further loans is rendered impossible," and recommended that the Company should be reorganized upon a basis of almost 40 per cent less than was originally considered the fair value of the plants. If other evidence than the figures above set forth be needed to prove that vendors and promoters of this scheme sought to secure stocks and bonds of the United States Shipbuilding Company without consideration, it is supplied by this proposed Plan of Reorganization, which practically states that the Company is unable to pay interest on a greater capitalization and bond issue than $43,000,000, an amount $1,487,000 less than the capital of the United States Shipbuilding Company distributed in connection with the purchase of the properties, to say nothing of the bond issues of $24,500,000.

Causes of Failure

What were the causes of failure of the United States Shipbuilding Company? One of such causes was the fact that the directors parted with bonds to an amount upon which it was impossible to meet the interest. The failure, however, was precipitated, if not directly brought about, by the fact that in the Bethlehem transaction the United States Shipbuilding Company officers had to deal with people who, while thoroughly understanding the intricacies of "higher finance," seemed to have overlooked the requirements of common fairness. In speaking of plant values elsewhere in this report, the Bethlehem property has been dealt with as though it had been purchased by the United States Shipbuilding Company, but an examination of the transaction will show that it was otherwise. While the agreed price for the Bethlehem company was $9,000,000, to be paid for by an issue of $10,000,000 of bonds at 90, the directors of the United States Shipbuilding company, upon request, handed over to Mr. Charles M. Schwab an additional amount of $20,000,000 in the common and preferred stock of the United States Shipbuilding Company. As this $20,000,000 of stock would not be sufficient to give Mr. Schwab the control of the United States

Shipbuilding Company, there was inserted in the mortgage given to secure his $10,000,000 of bonds, a provision that such bonds should have a voting power equal to $10,000,000 of stock. As the total issue of stock of the United States Shipbuilding Company was but $45,000,000, the $30,000,000 voting power thus given to Mr. Schwab was sufficient to justify him in saying that he did not sell the Bethlehem Steel Company, but took over the United States Shipbuilding Company, the directors of that Company giving him $30,000,000 in stock and bonds for taking it off their hands.

In this deal Mr. Schwab parted with nothing. In the sale of the other constituent companies, the real and personal property, as well as their capital stock, were transferred to the United States Shipbuilding Company by the necessary deeds, bills of sale, and assignments. But in the case of Bethlehem, Mr. Schwab permitted to be given up only its capital stock, and this he did in such manner as to place it beyond the control of the Shipbuilding company. If interests friendly to the United States Shipbuilding Company had controlled this stock, it would have been able to reach the earnings of the Bethlehem Steel Company through a friendly Board of Directors; but in the $10,000,000 mortgage it was provided that the Trustee should designate three of such directors, and the United States Shipbuilding Company should designate four. As Mr. Schwab controlled the United States Shipbuilding Company, by reason of his aforesaid majority of stock, and as the Trustee was of his own selection, the United States Shipbuilding Company was absolutely at the mercy of Mr. Schwab. His advisers, however, in evident fear that something had been overlooked, caused the United States Shipbuilding Company to execute a contract wherein it agreed and guaranteed that so long as any part of the $10,000,000 issue of bonds above referred to should be outstanding and unpaid, the Bethlehem company should pay dividends on its entire outstanding capital stock at the rate of not less than six per cent per annum, and for the purpose of making such payments the Shipbuilding company agreed that the Bethlehem company should earn, over and above its operating expenses and fixed charges (including interest on its bonds and taxes), and over and above the working capital of

$4,000,000 therein provided for, a sum sufficient to make such annual dividend disbursements; and, in the event of the failure of the Bethlehem company earning sufficient to pay such dividend at the rate of six per cent, then the United States Shipbuilding Company was to pay to the Bethlehem company, on demand, a sum sufficient to make such annual dividend disbursements. The Shipbuilding company further agreed to supply the Bethlehem company with all such orders, contracts, work and earning capacity as should be necessary to enable it to earn and pay the annual dividends above mentioned. Was ever such another agreement, so apparently harmless, yet so ruinous, conceived by the mind of man? On its face it was simply an agreement to the effect that if sufficient earnings were not made by the Bethlehem to pay a dividend of 6 per cent on its capital stock, the United States Shipbuilding Company would advance such sum. This agreement was an absurd arrangement, in view of the fact that the United States Shipbuilding Company was the nominal owner of this stock, and as such was entitled to its dividends; nevertheless the United States Shipbuilding Company was made to agree in effect that if it wanted dividends from Bethlehem it should contribute the means to enable the payment of such dividends. An excuse for the United States Shipbuilding Company officials entering into such an agreement might be found in the supposition that they may have believed that as they had the right to designate four of the seven directors of the Bethlehem Steel Company, they would be able to control the earnings of that company, and the agreement above mentioned might become inoperative. Such a belief, however, had no substantial foundation, for, as heretofore stated, the control both of the Bethlehem and the United States Shipbuilding Company was vested in Mr. Schwab. Your Receiver will not attempt to advance any reason why the latter thought it necessary to take any such agreement in view of the fact that he had previously thereto obtained a control of the Shipbuilding company that would enable him at any moment to throttle it. As if the foregoing provisions in said agreement were not sufficient, the United States Shipbuilding Company was further made to agree that in the event that the working capital of the Bethlehem Steel Company should at any time fall below $4,000,000, the United States Shipbuilding Company would, upon demand, make up such sum as might be necessary to bring the working capital up to that figure. The agreement contains other provisions, all operating against the United States Shipbuilding Company, but enough has been referred to to show that in signing it the United States Shipbuilding Company had lost all chance of ever reaching the earnings of the Bethlehem Steel Company. For, assuming that Mr. Schwab's directors of the United States Shipbuilding Company should demand of Mr. Schwab's directors of the Bethlehem Steel Company that a dividend be declared from the earnings of the latter company, Mr. Schwab's directors of the Bethlehem Steel Company could always reply (as they did when demand was made) that it was not considered wise to declare a dividend at that time.

In April, 1903, it became apparent that unless funds were advanced by the Bethlehem Steel Company for the purpose of meeting the semi-annual interest on the first mortgage bonds due July 1st, a default in the payment thereof would ensue. Notwithstanding the urgent need apparent at that time for retrenchment, and the necessity for requiring Bethlehem to set aside some of its large earnings for the purpose of meeting the coming interest, the Executive Committee of the United States Shipbuilding Company, on the 7th day of April, 1903, adopted a resolution approving a report of the president of the Bethlehem Steel Company with reference to certain improvements and extensions alleged to have been required at the works of the latter company, showing a total required expenditure of $2,802,000 (including $365,000 previously appropriated). On the 14th day of April, 1903, the directors of the United States Shipbuilding Company held a meeting, at which time it was sought to approve the minutes of the previous meeting of the Executive Committee. On a motion to approve such minutes, Mr. Lewis Nixon, the president of the company, stated that he desired to go on record concerning the resolution passed, to the effect that in providing for any such extensions and improvements it should be made a condition of any such expenditure that proper provision should be made to safeguard the amount of $900,000, which must be declared as a dividend by the Bethlehem company, and suggested that provision to that effect be added to the authority asked for. Notwithstanding this request of Mr. Nixon, the minutes of the Executive Committee were approved by the directors.

Your Receiver is informed, and believes it to be true, that thereafter Mr. Lewis Nixon repeatedly sought to induce the directors of the United States Shipbuilding Company to coöperate with him in compelling the Bethlehem company to pay over some of its earnings for the purpose of staving off the impending default of the United States Shipbuilding Company; but from the 14th day of April, 1903, until the 22d day of June, 1903, it was impossible to obtain a quorum either of the Executive Committee or of the directors of the United States Shipbuilding Company. Again, on the 27th of June, while the proceedings were pending in this court for the appointment of a Receiver, Mr. Nixon demanded the Bethlehem Steel Company's assistance for the purpose of averting the impending default, through the medium of the following letter:

NEW YORK, June 27th, 1903.

E. M. MCILVAIN, ESQ.,
President Bethlehem Steel Company,
South Bethlehem, Pa.:

DEAR SIR—The Bethlehem Steel Company, having earned during the year ending August 1st, 1903, over and above its operating expenses and fixed charges (including interest on its bonds and taxes), and without impairment of its working capital of $4,000,000, a sum sufficient to pay a dividend of 6 per cent on its entire present outstanding capital stock, I request and demand, in behalf of the United States Shipbuilding Company, as owner of all of said capital stock, that your company, on or before June 30, 1903, declare a dividend in an amount sufficient to pay a bond interest of $362,500, due July 1st, 1903, and pay the same as required by the terms of the agreement of August 12th, 1902, between your company and the United States Shipbuilding Company, and credit this upon the yearly dividend on the stock of the Bethlehem Steel Company, $250,000 of which has already been declared and paid in a similar manner to meet the interest on the twenty-year bonds.

Yours truly,
(Signed) LEWIS NIXON,
President.

No attention was paid to this demand, and the default followed. Had the efforts of Mr. Nixon been successful, the subsequent adjudication of insolvency and the appointment of a receiver would have been averted.

Your Receiver considers it his duty to bring to the attention of the Court the fact that while the Bethlehem company was earning upwards of $2,000,000 annually, these earnings were being placed beyond the reach of the United States Shipbuilding Company by the making of vast extensions and improvements in the Bethlehem company and the purchasing and ordering of enormous quantities of merchandise, with the apparent purpose of bringing about the destruction of the United States Shipbuilding Company.

Further proof in this behalf is supplied by Mr. E. M. McIlvain, President of the Bethlehem Steel Company, in his letter to Mr. George R. Sheldon, Chairman of the Reorganization Committee. In this letter, dated the 25th of May, 1903, Mr. McIlvain states that during the fiscal year of the Bethlehem Steel Company ending April 30th, 1903, the net earnings of his company were $2,518,264.58. In the third paragraph of this letter he states that for the year beginning May 1, 1903, a conservative estimate of the net earnings of the Bethlehem Steel Company would be about $2,250,000 after deducting $517,550 of earnings for the purpose of paying interest on the underlying mortgages. Of this amount of earnings, he states, in the fourth paragraph of his letter, that he feels confident that there could be withdrawn for distribution (for dividends) the sum of $1,200,000. During the year within which Mr. McIlvain says the net earnings of the Bethlehem Steel Company were $2,518,264.58, the utmost that the Bethlehem Steel Company could be induced to give up to the United States Shipbuilding Company was $250,000. But in presenting the matter to the public, through the medium of the Reorganization Committee, and with a view to inducing the acceptance of a plan that would further the interests of Mr. Schwab, he states that from the earnings which are not in excess of the fiscal year ending April 30, 1903, he would be able to withdraw and pay over to the reorganized company a sum almost five times as much as his company was able to do when there was the utmost need for its greatest contribution. Your Receiver is unwilling to believe that Mr. McIlvain would deliberately make a false statement in this connection. He is also willing to accept his statement that the Bethlehem company would be able to withdraw from its current assets the sum of $1,200,000 for distribution during the year beginning May 1, 1903, but in accepting this statement and considering it in connection with the fact that all Bethlehem would advance during the past year was $250,000, and bearing in mind that the major part of the improvements and extensions above authorized were to be completed in subsequent years, it is difficult to draw any other conclusion than that the earnings of Bethlehem company during the past year were deliberately withheld for the purpose of wrecking the United States Shipbuilding Company. During the year ending July 31, 1903, Bethlehem expended for additions to its plant the sum of $683,370.24. In addition to this amount it expended for extraordinary and general repairs, during the year ending April 30, 1903, according to the report of Price, Waterhouse & Co., the sum of $450,000. It increased its material (unfinished and finished product and stores) $687,149.16. Its notes payable, which amounted to $350,000 when the stock of this company was attempted to be purchased by the United States Shipbuilding Company, were reduced $200,000 up to August 1, 1903, and have since been entirely wiped out, and finally it reduced its accounts payable to the extent of $179,468.22. Why such enormous sums should be expended for additions, repairs, and material at a time when the United States Shipbuilding Company was in urgent need of financial aid can be reasonably accounted for only upon the theory that it was in conformity with a deliberate plan to provide a plausible excuse for having withheld all dividends when the crash should come in the affairs of the United States Shipbuilding Company. Some attempt has been made by Bethlehem to justify its retention of its earnings by the statement that its credit had become impaired, and it was therefore necessary to pay cash for supplies, as well as to reduce its accounts and bills payable in order to placate its creditors. The alleged cause of the impairment of credit was said to be a mortgage for $10,000,000 which the

Bethlehem company made to the Colonial Trust Company upon its plant and property at the time of the purchase of Bethlehem by the United States Shipbuilding Company. As further security to Mr. Schwab for the $10,000,000 of bonds delivered to him as the purchase price of Bethlehem, the Bethlehem Steel Company executed to the Colonial Trust Company the mortgage above referred to to secure a bond in the like amount. Your Receiver is advised that the execution and delivery of such bond and mortgage by Bethlehem to secure Mr. Schwab for the purchase price of the sale of the stock of the Bethlehem was a fraud upon the creditors of said company, and was otherwise void because of the control of the directors by Mr. Schwab. In addition thereto, it is evident that the impairment of credit, if any, which Bethlehem complains of, was the result of its own deliberate, unwarranted, and illegal act. Your Receiver submits, therefore, that there was no justification for withholding from the United States Shipbuilding Company the entire earnings of the Bethlehem company, and charges that the inability of the Shipbuilding company to continue its business was due in large part to the failure of the Bethlehem company to relinquish its earnings.

At this point your Receiver desires to call the attention of the Court to another matter somewhat small in comparison with the enormous and unlawful appropriation of stocks and bonds of the United States Shipbuilding Company above mentioned, but of some importance in showing the manner with which the Bethlehem company dealt with the United States Shipbuilding Company. At the time of the sale of the Bethlehem Steel Company to the United States Shipbuilding Company, a statement was made that the amount of inventory was a certain figure. After the sale of the Bethlehem company to the United States Shipbuilding Company, $250,000 of this amount was charged off by the Bethlehem company, for the purpose of adjusting the book value of the inventory with the actual value which had been placed thereon by the accountants after examination. This examination had been made in April, 1902, and the Bethlehem company had been instructed at that time to charge off, to adjustment of inventory, $609,541.95. Instead of complying with this request, they charged off only $359,541.95, and at the time of the sale of the plant to the United States Shipbuilding Company the statement submitted contained a surplus $250,000 in excess of what Bethlehem knew to be the actual amount.

Still another matter should be brought to the attention of the Court. On the 22d of June, 1903, while proceedings were pending for the appointment of a receiver of the Shipbuilding company, and, as it seems to your Receiver, with a view of forestalling the action of the Court, and in contempt thereof, the directors of said Company adopted a resolution, as provided for under Mr. Schwab's mortgage, requesting the New York Security Trust Company to vote the entire shares of the capital stock of the Bethlehem Steel Company in favor of and for the following persons, as directors of said Bethlehem Steel Company, namely, E. M. McIlvain, Archibald Johnson, Adolphe E. Borie, and Lewis Nixon. Mr. McIlvain was at that time and is now the President of the Bethlehem Steel Company; Mr. Borie was and is the Vice-President of the Bethlehem Steel Company, and Mr. Johnson was and is the General Superintendent of said Company. As the remaining directors were selected by Mr. Schwab's trustee, it is apparent that but one of the seven could be said to represent interests other than those of Mr. Schwab. By this means, if successful, Mr. Schwab was able to place the control of Bethlehem beyond the reach of the Court for at least another year.

Bethlehem Steel Company

From the reports submitted by the officials of this Company, it is evident that during the past year it earned far more money than the necessities of the plant required to be retained there. From what is hereinabove set forth, it is also evident that so long as the present Board of Directors, or a Board subject to present influences, shall retain office, no benefit shall ever be permitted to escape to the Receivership. Your Receiver is convinced that the present controlling influence at this plant is wholly hostile to the Shipbuilding company and its representatives, and your Receiver believes, in view of the excessive price paid for its plant, that the Shipbuilding company, or its representative, should be permitted to have at least some voice in its management. At present this is denied, but your Receiver hopes that such action may be taken as may result in the removal of the present Board of Directors, or a majority of them. Your Receiver believes that the meeting of the Board of Directors of the United States Shipbuilding Company, held on the 22d day of June, 1903, and hereinbefore referred to, at which four directors were designated to represent the United States Shipbuilding Company on the Board of the Bethlehem Steel Company, was solely for the purpose of circumventing any order of this Court which might be made in the proceedings then pending; that it was intended to hinder and delay the creditors of the United States Shipbuilding Company and to place this property beyond their control and the control of the Receiver to be appointed, and was otherwise illegal and void. Your Receiver believes such Board is deliberately furthering a course at once illegal and greatly injurious to the creditors represented by your Receiver, and accordingly he makes the recommendation concerning this Company hereinafter set forth.

Generally

Since the appointment of your Receiver the principal office has been engaged in legal matters rather than building ships. Accordingly your Receiver found the services of several of the officers and subordinates of the Shipbuilding company to be unnecessary, and in this connection has reduced expenses upwards of $55,000 a year.

Recommendations

Your Receiver respectfully submits the following recommendations:

1. That in order to avoid depreciation by disuse, and because of the existence of controversies as to the validity of the encumbrances upon the premises, the Crescent Shipyard be sold free and clear of all such encumbrances as soon as the work now in contemplation is completed.

2. That similar action be taken with reference to the plant

of the Harlan & Hollingsworth Company, Wilmington, Delaware.

3. That as soon as the debts of the Company shall have been ascertained suit be instituted against all persons who received the stock of this Company without paying full value therefor to recover from them such an amount as shall be necessary to pay said debts in full, under section 21 of an act of the Legislature of the State of New Jersey, entitled, An Act concerning Corporations (Revision of 1896).

4. That suit be instituted against the Bethlehem Steel Company to procure the appointment of a Receiver and to compel the appropriation of the earnings of that Company by way of dividends on the stock.

Respectfully submitted,

JAMES SMITH, JR.,

Receiver, United States Shipbuilding Company.

Dated October 31, 1903.

Certain other highly disreputable details of this affair, were concerned with the attempts to float the stock in Europe. Much of the correspondence, showing connivance with notorious parties in Paris, was published in the New York daily papers between December 22, 1903, and the first of January, 1904. Moody's Truth about the Trusts, pp. 366–369, gives many additional details. A paper by L. W. Sammis of the *New York Sun*, published in the Annals of the American Academy of Political Science, 1904, is also suggestive. After protracted controversy and litigation, a reorganization plan was agreed upon and published May 25, 1903; and a new company has just been formed to take over the wreck of the old one. — ED.

X

PROMOTERS' LIABILITY FOR UNREVEALED PROFITS[1]—THE ASPHALT COMPANIES

THE visible assets of Asphalt Company of America having been sold and their proceeds distributed, . . . it is proper that the Court should be informed of certain matters and things relating to the promotion of Asphalt Company of America, for such action thereupon as the Court may determine should be taken. The facts hereinafter set forth have been ascertained through investigations made by the Receivers continuing from immediately after their appointment up to the present time.

Asphalt Company of America was incorporated under the laws of the state of New Jersey, June 28, 1899, with an authorized capital stock of $30,000,000, divided into 600,000 shares of the par value of $50 each. The corporation was the outcome of plans previously arranged by and among some or all of the persons hereinafter mentioned as promoters, the essential features of which were (1) the transfer to the corporation of the shares of stock of certain other corporations engaged in the asphalt business and more or less competitive in character, and the issue to the owners of such shares, so transferring their holdings, of Collateral Gold Certificates, in the nature of bond obligations of the new corporation in exchange for said shares of stock, the terms of exchange being mutually arranged, the shares of stock so transferred then being deposited with a trust company (The Land Title and Trust Company being selected) as security for the payment of the interest and principal of the said certificates. (2) The providing of working capital

[1] From Transcript of Record, U. S. Circuit Court of Appeals for the Third Circuit, September Term, 1903. *The Land Title and Trust Co.* v. *Henry Tatnall* as Receiver of Asphalt Co. of America, etc., pp. 370–380. Receiver's Report on Promoters' Liability, etc.

for the new corporation by calls upon its capital stock. In the case of the transfer of the shares of stock by some of the said companies to the new corporation, it was stipulated that, in addition to the purchase price to be paid in Collateral Gold Certificates, the vendors should have the privilege of purchasing stock of Asphalt Company of America, without premium at par, to the amount of 50 per cent of the par value of the stock deposited by them. The following is a list of the corporations whose shares of stock to the amounts and on the terms therein stated were transferred to Asphalt Company, and Collateral Gold Certificates, to the amounts therein mentioned paid therefor:

Name of Company	Total No. of Shares	Par Value	Shares Purchased	Price Paid	Cost in Cash	Cost in Certificates
Barber Asphalt Paving Company	39,000	$100.00	38,993	$300.00	——	$11,697,900.00
The New Trinidad Lake Asphalt Company	50,000	48.50	49,550	100.00	——	4,955,000.00
			50	84.886	$4244.32	——
Alcatraz Company of West Virginia	800,000	5.00	799,900	6.00	——	4,799,400.00
United Asphalt Company	40,000	100.00	39,975	91.808	——	3,670,000.00
Atlantic Alcatraz Asphalt Company	1,000	100.00	995	1000.00	——	995,000.00
Southern Asphalt Paving Company	250	100.00	245	1020.00	——	249,900.00
Alcatraz Paving Company	1,000	50.00	995	500.00	——	497,500.00
Alcatraz Asphalt Paving Company	1,000	100.00	995	150.00	——	149,250.00
Warren-Scharf Asphalt Paving Company	9,500	100.00	9,483	240.00	5618.42	2,278,320.00
Utica Paving Company	250	100.00	245	510.21	——	125,001.45
Denver Paving Company	35,000	1.00	34,950	5.714	——	199,714.09
Southwestern Alcatraz Asphalt & Construction Company	2,000	100.00	1,995	64.16	——	127,999.20
Alcatraz Construction Company	1,500	100.00	1,495	104.31	——	155,943.45

The evidence in the possession of the Receiver shows that the persons who transferred to Asphalt Company of America the shares of stock in the above named corporations, receiving Collateral Gold Certificates of the former company therefor, had been holders of shares of stock of some of the companies prior to the inauguration of the plan which was subsequently consummated of transferring them to Asphalt Company of America. In the case of some of the companies, however, some of the vendors who were connected with the organization of Asphalt Company of America as promoters, purchased the whole or some part of the shares which they exchanged for Collateral Gold Certificates on the above terms, after they, with others, had determined upon such organization and either while it was in process of organization or after it was actually incorporated. The essential purpose of this report is to show to the Court the facts which have come to the Receiver's knowledge as to those purchases, and to recommend action thereon.

The organization of Asphalt Company of America appears to have been under consideration as early as March 6, 1899, and to have been entered upon very shortly thereafter. At that time the following persons appear to have been holders of record of shares of stock of some of the corporations which were subsequently combined in the manner above stated, to about the following amounts:

	Barber Asphalt Paving Company	The New Trinidad Lake Asphalt Company
	Shares	Shares
Amzi L. Barber held . . .	5507	4394
Francis V. Greene held . .	900	1822
George W. Elkins held . .	1831	1639
J. J. Albright held	2613	3050
Edmund Hayes held . . .	1264	2131
C. K. Robinson held . . .	281	997
E. Burgess Warren held . .	5164	4849
Wm. L. Elkins held . . .	500	—
Geo. D. Widener held . .	1091	1273

	Alcatraz Company of West Virginia	Denver Paving Company
	Shares	Shares
William H. Crocker held .	401,320	1863

	Alcatraz Paving Company	Southwestern Alcatraz & Construction Company
	Shares	Shares
William J. Latta held . .	30	—
Harry C. Spinks held . .	—	585

Some of the above named parties then acquired shares of stock of other companies subsequently turned into the combination, and they also acquired more shares of stock of some of the companies in which they already had interests. Some of the shares of stock so acquired were then transferred to Asphalt Company of America, when incorporated, at prices payable in Collateral Gold Certificates in excess of the prices at which they were respectively obtained by the purchasers, and the Receiver believes that further investigation will show that all of said shares were transferred by the said purchasers to Asphalt Company of America at a profit. So far as the Receiver knows, no disclosure to Asphalt Company of America was made by the persons who so transferred their shares of stock to it of the profits received by them. All of the above named parties, it is believed, were beneficially interested in the acquisition of some of said shares, and in their transfer to Asphalt Company of America.

The facts in detail for the consideration of the Court follow:

As to United Asphalt Company.

Amzi L. Barber, Francis V. Greene and George W. Elkins each transferred to Asphalt Company of America 13,325 shares of stock of this company, aggregating 39,975 shares. Amzi L. Barber and George W. Elkins each received therefor $1,223,300, and Francis V. Greene received $1,223,400, in Collateral Gold Certificates of Asphalt Company of America, the said three parties receiving as a whole $3,670,000 of said certificates. At the time of said transfers United Asphalt Company was the holder, either in its corporate name, or by its representatives, of practically the entire capital stock of four corporations known as Columbia Construction Company, of New York; Trinidad Bituminous

Asphalt Company, of New Jersey; Standard Asphalt Company, of New Jersey, and Rock Creek Natural Asphalt Company of Kansas. The shares of capital stock of these corporations constituted its entire assets. The evidence in the possession of the Receiver points to the fact that these shares of stock were bought by or under the direction of Amzi L. Barber, Francis V. Greene and George W. Elkins, with money or obligations furnished, or procured, by them to be furnished as follows:

For the stock of Columbia Construction Company . . .	$250,000
" " Trinidad Bituminous Asphalt Company . .	150,000
" " Standard Asphalt Company	200,000
" " Rock Creek Natural Asphalt Company . .	18,000
	$618,000

Said purchases were made between March 21 and August 4, 1899. In the meantime United Asphalt Company had been organized as a holding company, and on July 12, 1899, 13,325 shares of its capital stock were issued to Amzi L. Barber, Francis V. Greene and George W. Elkins each, making 39,975 shares in the aggregate, issued to them out of a total capital stock of 40,000 shares. The above 39,975 shares were subsequently, on July 15, 1899, transferred to Asphalt Company of America for $3,670,000 of its Collateral Gold Certificates. The first sales of the Temporary Certificates standing for said Collateral Gold Certificates were in August, 1899, in the neighborhood of 90 per cent of par. Taking the value of the Collateral Gold Certificates at 97 per cent of par, the highest price at which said certificates sold, the profit each of the said three parties to said transaction was about $980,601, and to all of them together was about $2,941,803. Taking the value of the said certificates at 89½ per cent of par, which was their lowest market price in August, 1899, the profit to each of said parties was about $888,853.50, and to all of them together was about $2,666,560.50.

As to Warren-Scharf Asphalt Paving Company.

Amzi L. Barber, Francis V. Greene and George W. Elkins each transferred to Asphalt Company of America 3164 shares (George W. Elkins transferring 3165 shares) of stock of Warren-Scharf Asphalt Paving Company, aggregating 9493 shares out of a total capital stock of 9500 shares. They each received therefor $759,360 (George W. Elkins receiving $759,600) in Collateral Gold Certificates. The said three persons received as a whole $2,278,320 par of said certificates.

The said three persons had previously purchased from the then owners the said shares of stock at an outlay to them of about $1,500,000, and the said shares were transferred into their names on July 27, 1899. The transfers of said shares by them to Asphalt Company of America were made on July 31, 1899, and the above mentioned temporary certificates of said company were issued to them therefor. Taking the value of the Collateral Gold Certificates at 97 per cent of par, the profit to each of the said three parties to said transaction was about $236,579, and to all of them together was $709,970. Taking the market value of the certificates at 89½ per cent of par, the profit to each of the said parties was about $179,627.20, and to all of them together about $539,096.

From certain papers in the possession of Receiver it would appear that the moneys necessary to purchase said shares of stock from the preceding holders were contributed by the following parties in the following proportions, and the Receiver believes that distribution of Collateral Gold Certificates was made to said parties in proportion to their contribution to purchase money as follows, and that they shared the profits proportionately:

	Payment of Purchase Money	Distribution of Collateral Gold Certificates
J. J. Albright	$115,875	$176,130
A. L. Barber	233,175	334,426
F. V. Greene	50,550	76,836
Edmund Hayes	64,950	98,724
C. K. Robinson	20,325	30,894
Geo. D. Widener	49,800	75,696
E. B. Warren	215,325	327,294
Geo. W. Elkins	250,000	380,000
Wm. L. Elkins	250,000	380,000
Sydney F. Tyler	250,000	380,000

As to The New Trinidad Lake Asphalt Company, Limited.

Shortly after the organization of Asphalt Company of America was projected, the Board of Directors of Barber Asphalt Company, which company owned 1718 shares of the capital stock of The New Trinidad Lake Asphalt Company, Limited, caused said shares to be offered for sale to its stockholders. This action was taken pursuant to the authorization of its Executive Committee, acting as a Board of Directors, on March 15, 1899, and was approved by the Board on March 29, 1899, the said Board of Directors being composed at the time of the following persons: J. J. Albright, Amzi L. Barber, Francis V. Greene, Edmund Hayes, C. K. Robinson, George D. Widener, George W. Elkins, E. Burgess Warren, and P. W. Henry. 1638 of the said shares of stock of The New Trinidad Lake Asphalt Company, Limited, were thereupon bought by the stockholders of Barber Asphalt Paving Company at the limit fixed by the Executive Committee in its resolution for their sale, to wit, $48.50 per share. 1515 of the said shares so bought were purchased and paid for by the following persons who were also Directors of Barber Asphalt Paving Company at the rate of $48.50 per share, to wit:

J. J. Albright	210	shares
Amzi L. Barber	206	"
Francis V. Greene	178	"
Edmund Hayes	209	"
C. K. Robinson	103	"
George D. Widener	207	"
George W. Elkins	211	"
E. Burgess Warren	211	"

After said purchases of said shares of stock at $48.50 per share, they were transferred to Asphalt Company of America at the valuation of $100 per share and Collateral Gold Certificates were received in exchange therefor to the amount in the aggregate at par of $151.500.

The Receiver believes it can be established that the said parties shared in the profits of said purchases and sales in proportion to their said holdings.

Taking the Collateral Gold Certificates at 97 per cent of par, the profit to said parties from the said purchases and transfers amounted to $73,477. Taking the value of the Collateral Gold Certificates at 89½ per cent of par, the profit to the said parties amounted to $62,515.

As to Alcatraz Company.

William H. Crocker transferred to Asphalt Company of America on or about August 3, 1899, 799,650 shares of the capital stock of Alcatraz Company of West Virginia. Prior to the formation of the plan of organization of the Asphalt Company of America the said Crocker was the holder of record of 401,320 shares of said company, the balance of the holdings transferred by him to Asphalt Company of America, to wit, 398,330 shares, having been acquired by him after March 8, 1899. The Receiver has not as yet been able to obtain information as to the amount paid by the said Crocker for said 398,330 shares transferred into his name after the organization of Asphalt Company of America was determined upon, nor what profit, if any, was made by him on the purchase or other acquisition by him of said shares and the sale thereof to Asphalt Company of America. The said shares, with the other shares previously held by him ($5 par value), were transferred to Asphalt Company of America at the rate of $6 per share, payable in Collateral Gold Certificates. The actual sum received by him in Collateral Gold Certificates for the shares obtained by him after the plan of organization of Asphalt Company of America was determined upon was at par $2,389,980. The Receiver has reason to believe that a substantial profit was made by the said Crocker in said transaction. He is advised that the relation of the said Crocker to the enterprise was that of a promoter, and that whatever profit was obtained by him he is in law obliged to pay to the Receiver of the Asphalt Company of America.

As to Denver Paving Company.

The said William H. Crocker transferred to Asphalt Company of America 28,725 shares of Denver Paving Company stock at the rate of $5.71 428/1000 per share (the shares being $1 par) and received in exchange therefor at par $164,142.69 in Collateral Gold Certificates. He was the holder of record prior to the formation of the plan of organization of Asphalt Company of America of only 1863 of said shares. The balance of his holdings transferred to Asphalt Company of America as aforesaid, 26,862 shares, appears to have been acquired by him after the plan of organization of Asphalt Company of America was entered upon. The actual sum received by him in Collateral Gold Certificates for said shares, so as aforesaid subsequently obtained, was at par $153,496.98. The Receiver has reason to believe that a substantial profit was made by the said Crocker in the said transaction. He is advised that the relation of the said Crocker to the enterprise was that of a promoter, and that whatever profit was obtained by him, he is in law obliged to pay to the Receiver of Asphalt Company of America.

As to Alcatraz Paving Company.

William J. Latta transferred to Asphalt Company of America, in July, 1899, 305 shares of Alcatraz Paving Company ($100 par) at the rate of $500 per share, payable in Collateral Gold Certificates of Asphalt Company of America. The actual sum received by him for the said shares, payable in Collateral Gold Certificates at par aforesaid, was $152,500. Prior to the formation of the plan of organization of Asphalt Company of America the said Latta was the holder of record of only 30 of said shares of stock. He appears to have acquired 275 of the shares transferred to Asphalt Company of America as aforesaid after said date. The actual sum received by him in Collateral Gold Certificates for said 275 shares was $137,500. The Receiver has reason to believe that a substantial profit was made by the said Latta in said transaction. He is advised that the relation of the said Latta to the enterprise was that of a promoter and that whatever profit was obtained by him he is in law obliged to pay to the Receiver of Asphalt Company of America.

As to Southwestern Alcatraz Asphalt & Construction Company.

Harry C. Spinks transferred to Asphalt Company of America on or about August 10, 1899, 1995 shares of the stock of the Southwestern Alcatraz Asphalt & Construction Company at the rate of $64.16 per share, payable in Collateral Gold Certificates of Asphalt Company of America. He received therefor in said certificates at par $127,999.20. The said Spinks actually held of record prior to the entry upon the plan of organization of Asphalt Company of America only 585 of said shares. The evidence in the Receiver's possession indicates that he obtained from various other persons after said date 1410 of said shares which he transferred to Asphalt Company of America upon the total consideration payable in Collateral Gold Certificates at par $90,465.60. The Receiver has not as yet been able to ascertain what profit the said Spinks made out of the purchase of said shares and the transfer thereof to Asphalt Company of America. He is advised, however, that the relations of the said Spinks to the organization of Asphalt Company of America were such that he is obliged to account for and pay over whatever profit he obtained in connection with the said transaction.

From the facts which have come to the knowledge of the Receiver he believes that some or all of the parties above named, to wit, Amzi L. Barber, Francis V. Greene, George W. Elkins, J. J. Albright, Edmund Hayes, C. K. Robinson, E. Burgess Warren, William L. Elkins, George D. Widener, Sydney F. Tyler, William H. Crocker, William J. Latta and Harry C. Spinks, can be established to have been promoters of Asphalt Company of America, and that they made profits in connection with its organization in the manner above stated, which they are obliged to account for, and that they can be compelled to account for and pay over the same. He therefore recommends, the premises considered, that he be authorized by the Court to take such proceedings against the said parties, or any of them, by suit or suits in law or equity, as he may be advised are proper, and as he may deem expedient under the facts as they exist and shall be made to appear upon further investigation, with a view to collecting all profits that were made by the said persons, or any of them, in connection with the organization of Asphalt Company of America and the transfer of securities to it. He also recommends that he be authorized to bring like proceedings against any other persons whom he may hereafter ascertain to have obtained such profits.

He respectfully calls attention of the Court to the fact that an Act of Limitation was passed by the Legislature of the state of New Jersey at the last session, approved the 8th day of April, 1903, which limits the period during which suits may be brought against directors, officers, promoters and other agents of corporations of the state to recover unlawful profits made by them, to the period of four years from and after the making or receipt of such profits. A saving clause being, however, incorporated in the said Act which permits such suits which otherwise would be barred to be brought within six months after the Act took effect. The result of the passage of the said Act is that proceedings against promoters in connection with Asphalt Company of America with a view to the recovery of unlawful profits obtained by them as the Receiver is advised, must be begun before October 8, 1903. He therefore respectfully urges upon the Court the desirability, if it should seem proper that the Court instruct that any suits of this kind be brought, that the authorization to him to so proceed be given forthwith.

Respectfully submitted,

HENRY TATNALL,

Receiver Asphalt Company of America.

July 6, 1903.

It is scarcely to be expected that a company launched under the conditions described in the foregoing report should have a successful career. Two reorganizations promptly followed in less than four years. The original Asphalt Company of America, organized in July, 1899, acquired the stocks of a large number of competing concerns, issuing in payment therefor $30,000,000 of collateral trust bonds. These bonds were issued on the security of the stock so acquired. The next step was to assure the control of the enterprise by the promoters through ownership of a majority of the capital stock. Accordingly practically all of the original stock subscriptions were taken in the name of two dummies. A large part of this issue of original stock was immediately turned over to the promoters, giving them virtual control of the enterprise. The stock was not paid for in full, but an amount equivalent to 20 per cent of the par value, which was $50 per share, was actually paid. The funds to meet this partial payment on the stock held by the promoters were raised by a sale of the balance of the stock not held by insiders to the public at prices ranging as high as $19 per share. Thus did the promoters acquire control of the holding company without any additional investment on their part; and at the same time possess themselves of a volume of bonds, which, on the basis of the excessive payments described in the preceding report, proved more than sufficient to absorb the entire earnings of the consolidation.

The existence of a stockholders' liability for the remaining four-fifths of the par value of the capital stock was the cause of the speedy reorganization of the company in May, 1900. By reason of fraudulent and reckless accounting, as partially indicated by our preceding reprint, the inevitable bankruptcy of the parent company was hidden from the public temporarily. In brief, the Asphalt Company of America was superseded in May, 1900, by a new company entitled the National Asphalt Company. This new corporation issued $6,000,000 of Collateral Gold Certificates which were used to take up the stock of the old corporation. In addition, its own capital, amounting to $22,000,000, was used in part to acquire control of formidable competitors who had invaded the field, and in part as a bonus to secure deposit of the old underlying bonds. In December, 1901, this company, in turn, went into the hands of a receiver. Then began a long series of suits and countersuits in connection with the activity of a reorganization committee; which, judged by results, seems to have been working in the interest of insiders. The outcome of the matter was the final organization in May, 1903, of the General Asphalt Company which acquired the properties of its predecessors, sold at auction for a trifle over $6,000,000. This General Asphalt Company was capitalized at $31,000,000, in place of $60,000,000 of stock and bonds issued by the original Asphalt Company of America. The troublesome underlying bonds of the first company were to be retired by exchange for preferred stock; and the common stock was issued in part to raise working capital.

A partial recovery of the enormous losses by innocent investors could be effected only in two ways. Successful suits against the promoters for unrevealed profits in the organization of the company might be hoped for, following precedents in a number of recent cases, notably that of the East Tennessee Land Company. In addition it was possible that the Receiver might be able to hold the original stockholders liable for the balance of their payments on the capital stock of the Asphalt Company of America. This latter should amount to about $24,000,000, while at the same time it was hoped that nearly $3,000,000 could be extorted from the promoters. The first of these remedies against the promoters, however, has now been closed through purchase by the promoters themselves of all the outstanding bonds. As representing all the creditors of the company, they have asked the Court to discontinue the suits. This has been done. Moreover, the Receiver has abandoned the attempt to assess the stockholders for their unpaid capital stock on the ground that such suits cannot be successfully prosecuted. Thus closes a story of fraud and financial rottenness not less enlightening than that of the United States Shipbuilding Company, as showing the necessity for provision by law to secure a reasonable amount of publicity in the finances of monopolistic combinations. — Ed.

XI

TRADE COMBINATIONS AT COMMON LAW[1]

THE rule that all contracts in restraint of trade were void, was early established in the English law. The first case in which this principle was announced is said to have been decided in the reign of Henry V.[2] In this case an action for debt was brought on a bond, conditioned that the defendant should not use his art of a dyer's craft within a certain city for six months. Judge Hall declared the bond void, and expressed his indignation at this attempt to restrain trade by exclaiming, "And, by God, if the plaintiff were here, he should go to prison till he paid a fine to the king." This refusal to recognize the validity of any contract in restraint of trade was for a long time characteristic of the English law; but gradually the rule was relaxed.

The modern application of this rule was very well expressed by Judge Christiancy in the case of *Hubbard* v. *Miller*.[3] Dissenting from the doctrine sometimes laid down, that all contracts in restraint of trade are *prima facie* or presumptively void, he said:

If, considered with reference to the situation, business and objects of the parties, and in the light of all the surrounding circumstances with reference to which the contract was made, the restraint contracted for appears to have been for a just and honest purpose, for the protection of the legitimate interests of the party in whose favor it is imposed, reasonable as between them, and not specially injurious to the public, the restraint will be held valid.[4]

[1] From the *Political Science Quarterly*, Vol. XII, 1897, pp. 212–245. [On decisions interpreting state anti-trust laws to 1900, consult the *Quarterly Journal of Economics*, Vol. XIV, 1900, pp. 416–424. — ED.]

[2] See Year Book, 2 Henry V, fol. 5, pl. 26.

[3] 27 Mich., 15.

[4] This statement was really nothing but an elaboration of the rule which had long before been laid down in the English courts by Chief Justice Tindal, in the case of *Horner* v. *Neves*, 7 Bing., 743.

Under this rule two interests are to be considered, those of the parties to the contract and those of the public. As to the former, the rule was laid down that no contract which did not benefit both parties to the contract should be regarded as reasonable; as to the latter, no contract in restraint of trade was to be regarded as lawful which was injurious to the public. As a matter of fact, most of the cases actually decided have turned exclusively on the interests of the parties, and the tendency of the courts has therefore been to relax very greatly the old rule of the common law. This tendency probably reached its culmination in a case decided in 1887, by the New York Court of Appeals, *Diamond Match Co.* v. *Roeber.*[1] Here the Court was called upon to construe a contract made by Roeber with the Swift, Courtney & Beecher Co., the grantor of the Diamond Match Co., in which he agreed that he would not within ninety-nine years, except in the capacity of agent or employee of the Swift, Courtney & Beecher Match Co., directly or indirectly engage in the manufacture or sale of friction matches in any part of the United States except Nevada and Montana. The Court held the contract to be valid, although practically in general restraint of trade, saying:

> When the restraint is general, but at the same time is coextensive only with the interest to be protected and with the benefit meant to be conferred, there seems to be no good reason why as between the parties the contract is not as reasonable as when the interest is partial and there is a corresponding partial restraint.

But the Court of Appeals, in making this decision, did not intend to depart from the old rule, so far as the maintenance of that old rule was necessary for the protection of the interest of the public. It said distinctly:

> Covenants of the character of the one now in question operate simply to prevent the covenanter from engaging in the business which he sells, so as to protect the purchaser in the enjoyment of what he has purchased. To the extent that the contract prevents the vendor from carrying on the particular trade, it deprives the community of any benefit it might

[1] 106 N. Y., 473.

derive from his entering into competition; but the business is open to all others, and there is little danger that the public will suffer harm from lack of persons to engage in a profitable industry. Such contracts do not create monopolies; they confer no special or exclusive privilege. If contracts in general restraint of trade where the trade is general are void as tending to monopolies, contracts in partial restraint where the trade is local are subject to the same objection, because they deprive the local community of the services of the covenanter in the particular trade or calling, and prevent his becoming a competitor with the covenantee.

And again:

Combinations between producers to limit production and to enhance prices are or may be unlawful, but they stand on a different footing.

This case has frequently been cited, as indicative of a change in the rule of the common law, and as establishing the proposition that in our present economic conditions the policy of the law is, in order to promote the greatest freedom of contract, not to declare void contracts even in total restraint of trade. But the Court of Appeals based its decision upon the express ground that the public interest was not involved. While holding valid the particular contract before it, although in general restraint of trade, the Court specifically declared that combinations to raise prices stood upon a different footing, and recognized the fact that where the public interest was involved, the rule might well be different. The common law has all along refused, and does now refuse, to recognize the validity of agreements made between individuals for the purpose of raising the prices of commodities, and has stamped any such attempt as a criminal conspiracy.

1. Agreements aiming to raise Prices are Invalid

That such agreements are invalid has always been the rule of both courts of equity and courts of law. Thus, take the case of *Craft* v. *McConoughy*.[1] This was a bill in equity brought for an accounting and distribution of the profits of an alleged partnership based upon a contract to the following effect: Several grain houses were put into the business upon a basis of distribut-

[1] 79 Ill., 346, decided in 1875.

ing shares to the signers of the agreement; each separate firm was to conduct its own business as if there were no partnership in existence. It was to be the duty of a general bookkeeper to make a record of all the grain bought by each party, to debit him with the amount of money paid for the same, and to credit him with all sales; and at the end of every month each individual account was to be balanced, showing the profit or loss, which amount was to be divided *pro rata*, according to the number of shares held by each party. It was further agreed that prices were to be fixed from time to time, and each party to the agreement was to abide by them. Soon after the agreement was made, one party to it died, and his son demanded an accounting. The Court held that the agreement was void, as contrary to public policy, and as being an attempt to foster a monopoly and to raise prices; and notwithstanding the fact that it had been partially executed, refused to require an accounting, saying: "The complainant and the defendants were equally involved in the unlawful combination; a court of equity will assist neither."

A similar and even stronger case, decided in Pennsylvania, is that of *Nester* v. *The Continental Brewing Co.*[1] Here an association had been formed in Philadelphia among the brewers, for the purpose of controlling the sale and fixing the price of beer in Philadelphia and in Camden and Camden County, New Jersey. It was shown that the plaintiff had for valuable consideration obtained from a member of the association an assignment of a claim due such member from the association, without knowledge that the claim was based upon an agreement to monopolize the sale of beer. Notwithstanding his *bona fides*, the Court refused to aid him, and denied his application for an accounting.

Not only courts of equity, but also courts of law, refuse to aid in the execution of such agreements. Thus, in the case of *Chapin* v. *Brown*,[2] the grocers engaged in business in the town of Storm Lake agreed in favor of a third person to quit the business of buying butter for two years, and such third person agreed to carry on that business exclusively for the same period

[1] 161 Pa. St., 473, decided in 1894.

[2] 83 Iowa, 156, decided in 1891.

of time. In pursuance of this agreement, the plaintiffs came to the town and engaged in the business of buying butter ; at the commencement of the suit they were so engaged, and had made arrangements to continue the business for the period of two years. The defendant, however, continued in the business of buying butter; and it was alleged that by so doing he had damaged the plaintiffs to the extent of one hundred and fifty dollars, for which judgment was asked. The court refused the application of the plaintiffs, on the ground that the agreement was against public policy, as tending to monopolize the butter trade at Storm Lake, and to destroy competition in that business. This case is particularly interesting because the agreement was as to purchase and not as to sale. It therefore did not result in disadvantage to the consuming public generally, but only in disadvantage to the producers of butter.[1]

A somewhat similar case, *More* v. *Bennett*, was decided in January, 1892, by the Supreme Court of Illinois.[2] Here the stenographers in the city of Chicago had formed an association, of which all the parties to the suit were members. The object of the association was to establish and maintain uniform rates. A schedule had been adopted, and it was alleged that the defendant, contrary to the rules of the association, had cut rates against the other members thereof, whereby the plaintiffs had been damaged. The Court refused to pass upon the question whether a contract could be found in such articles of association, and decided that, even if a contract could be found, the agreement was void on account of its attempt to regulate prices. The Court refused, therefore, to award damages to the plaintiff. The case is interesting as showing that the courts will apply the same rules to the attempt to regulate the price of labor as to the attempt to regulate the price of commodities.

Another good case is that of the *Texas Standard Oil Co.* v. *Adoue*, decided in Texas in 1892.[3] This suit was brought to recover guaranteed net prices for all the products of certain

[1] It is only fair to say that the contract was declared void, not only because it was contrary to public policy, but also because in the opinion of the Court it was not based upon a consideration.

[2] 140 Ill., 69.

[3] 83 Tex., 650.

mills, and for the costs and expenses of production, in consideration of the strict performance of all convenants in a contract. This contract, it was held by the Court, gave the defendant an almost unrestricted field to obtain the raw material for its mills, and the exclusive right to control, free from the competition of the plaintiffs and others, not only the sales and ruling prices of the product of its own mills, but also the entire yield of the mills of the other parties to the contract. The Court held that the manifest purpose and natural tendency of this agreement were to prevent competition in too many localities — upon the one hand, to reduce the price of the raw materials; and upon the other, to enhance that of the manufactured product by artificial means, to the disadvantage and detriment of the public. Therefore the complaint was dismissed.[1]

A similar case is *Arnott* v. *The Pittston and Elmira Coal Co.*[2] Here the plaintiff's assignor, the Butler Colliery Co., had made an agreement with the defendants that it would not send coal north to any point except to the defendants, the latter agreeing to take from the Butler Co. not exceeding 2000 tons of coal per month. In pursuance of this agreement, the Butler Colliery Co. shipped 2700 tons to The Pittston and Elmira Coal Co., and the plaintiff, to whom it had assigned its claim, brought suit for the price of the coal. The Court held that the contract was made by the defendants with the purpose of establishing a monopoly of coal in the city of Elmira, that this purpose was known to the plaintiff's assignor, the Butler Coal Co., that the contract was contrary to public policy, and therefore that suit might not be brought upon it. The Court said:

Every producer or vendor of coal or other commodity has the right to use all legitimate efforts to obtain the best price for the article in which he deals. But when he endeavors to artificially enhance prices by suppressing or keeping out of market the products of others, and to accomplish that purpose by means of contracts binding them to withhold

[1] This case, like *Chapin* v. *Brown*, noticed above, shows that the courts will take notice that the effect of a combination in restraint of trade is to reduce the prices of articles to be purchased, as well as to increase the price of articles to be sold by the combination.

[2] 68 N. Y., 558, decided in 1877.

their supplies, such arrangements are even more mischievous than combinations not to sell under an agreed price. Combinations of that character have been held to be against public policy and illegal. . . . The purpose of the vendee was against public policy, and the vendor knew it. This brings us straight to the question whether the vendor delivering goods under such a contract can recover for the price. I think that under the circumstances of the present case, as found by the referee, he cannot. . . . He had a right to dispose of his goods, and (under certain limitations) the vendor of goods may recover for their price, notwithstanding that he knows that the vendee intends an improper use of them, so long as he does nothing to aid in such improper use, or in the illegal plan of the purchaser. This doctrine is established by authority, and is sufficiently liberal to vendors. But — and this is a very important distinction — if the vendor does anything beyond making the sale to aid the illegal scheme of the vendee, he renders himself *particeps criminis* and cannot recover for the price.

So, also, it has been held that a loan made for the purpose of aiding in a combination to raise the price of a particular article, cannot be recovered. In the case of *Raymond* v. *Leavitt*,[1] plaintiff had loaned the sum of $10,000 to the defendant for the purpose of controlling the wheat market at Detroit, with a view of forcing up prices. The defendant, who was to give the plaintiff a third of the expected profits, was at all events to repay the $10,000, with or without profits. In rendering its decision, the Court said:

The object of the arrangement between these parties was to force a fictitious and unnatural rise in the wheat market, for the express purpose of getting the advantage of dealers and purchasers whose necessities compelled them to buy, and necessarily to create a similar difficulty as to all persons who had to obtain or use that commodity, which is an article indispensable to every family in the country. . . . We shall decline enforcing such contracts. If parties see fit to invest money in such ventures, they must get it back by some other than legal measures.

Probably the strongest case of all is that of *Morris Run Coal Co.* v. *Barclay Coal Co.*[2] This was an action upon an accepted draft of the defendants in favor of the plaintiffs. The draft was made in execution of a contract between five coal companies

[1] 46 Mich., 447, decided in 1881.
[2] 68 Pa. St., 173, decided in 1871.

for a sum found due in the equalization of prices under the contract. Provision was made in the contract for a committee of three to take charge of the business of all of these companies, to decide all questions and to appoint the general sales-agent. Provision was also made for the mining and delivery of coal, and for its sale through this agent, subject, however, to the restriction that each party should at its own cost deliver its proportion of the different kinds of coal in the different markets, at such times and to such parties as the committee should from time to time direct. The committee was authorized to adjust the price of coal in the different markets, and the rates of freight, and also to enter into such an agreement with the anthracite coal companies as should promote the interest of the parties. The companies were allowed to sell their coal themselves, but only to the extent of their proportion, and only at the prices adjusted by the committee. In answer to the claim that this agreement tended to establish a monopoly, the plaintiff replied that the true object of it was to lessen expenses, to improve the quality of the coal and to deliver it in the market in the best order to the consumer. These allegations the Court said were immaterial:

Admitting their correctness, it does not follow that these advantages redeem the contract from the obnoxious effects so strikingly presented by the referee. The important fact is that these companies control this immense coal-field; that it is the great source of supply of bituminous coal to the state of New York and large territories westward; that by this contract they control the price of coal in this extensive market, and make it bring sums it would not command if left to the natural laws of trade; that it concerns an article of prime necessity for many uses; that its operation is general in this large region, and affects all who use coal as a fuel; and this is accomplished by a combination of all of the companies engaged in this branch of business in the large region where they operate. The combination is wide in scope, general in its influence, and injurious in effects. These being its features, the contract is against public policy, illegal, and therefore void.

Further commenting upon the agreement, the Court said:

The effects produced on the public interest lead to the consideration of another feature of great weight in determining the illegality of the contract, to wit: the combination resorted to by these five companies. Singly, each might have suspended deliveries and sales of coal to suit its own interests, and might have raised the price, even though this might have been detrimental to the public interest. There is a certain freedom which must be allowed to every one in the management of his own affairs. When competition is left free, individual error or folly will generally find a correction in the conduct of others; but here is a combination of all the companies operating in the Blossburg and Barclay mining regions and controlling their entire productions. . . . This combination has a power in its confederative form which no individual action can confer. The public interest must succumb to it, for it has left no competition free to correct its baleful influence. When the supply of coal is suspended, the demand for it becomes importunate, and prices must rise. Or if the supply goes forward, the price fixed by the confederates must accompany it. . . . Such a combination is more than a contract; it is an offence. . . . The present case is free of difficulty, the money represented by the bill arising directly upon the contract to be paid by one party to another party to the contract in execution of its terms. The bill itself is therefore tainted by the illegality, and no recovery can be had upon it.

While the courts will not enforce an unlawful agreement or give damages for the non-execution of an unlawful agreement, it does not by any means follow that they will prevent the execution of an agreement which is in reasonable restraint of trade. A good case upon this point is that of the *Bohn Manufacturing Co.* v. *Hollis.*[1] The plaintiff was a manufacturer and vendor of lumber and other building material, a large and valuable part of his trade being with retail lumber dealers. The defendant, the Northwestern Lumbermen's Association, was a voluntary association of retail lumber dealers, formed to protect its members against sales by wholesale dealers and manufacturers to contractors and consumers. The method employed by the association was to demand of every wholesale dealer who sold directly to contractors and consumers 10 per cent of the amount of such sales, and to notify all the retail dealers to refrain from dealing with such wholesale dealer until the payment was made. The plaintiff in this suit, having sold

[1] 54 Minn., 223, decided in 1893.

directly to consumers, was requested to pay the 10 per cent to the association, failing which payment the secretary of the association threatened to send to the other retail dealers the notice provided for in the agreement of the association. Plaintiff demanded an injunction to restrain the issuing of these notices. The Court refused the injunction; it held that the agreement was not in unreasonable restraint of trade or unlawful, and recognized that it was a general rule of trade in every department that wholesale dealers should refrain from selling at retail within the territory from which their customers obtain their business.

What one man may lawfully do singly [says the Court], two or more may lawfully agree to do jointly; the number who unite to do the act cannot change its character from lawful to unlawful. The gist of a private action for the wrongful acts of many is not the combination or conspiracy, but the damage done or threatened to the plaintiff by the acts of the defendant. If the act be unlawful, the combination of many to permit it may aggravate the injury, but cannot change the character of the act. In a few cases there may be some loose remarks apparently to the contrary, but they evidently have their origin in a confused and inaccurate idea of the law of criminal conspiracy, and in failing to distinguish between an unlawful act and a criminal one. It can never be a crime to combine to commit a lawful act, but it may be a crime for several to conspire to commit an unlawful act which, if done by one individual alone, although unlawful, would not be criminal. Hence the fact that the defendants associated themselves to do the act complained of is wholly immaterial in this case.

A somewhat similar case is that of *Cote* v. *Murphy*.[1] In this case, workmen engaged in building trades had combined to advance wages by reducing the hours of labor; and associations of employers in such trades had combined and agreed not to sell materials to contractors who acceded to the demands of the workmen, and to induce other dealers by all lawful means not to furnish such materials. The Court held that such associations of employers were not liable in damages for conspiracy to contractors who, by reason of the combination, were not able to procure all the materials they could dispose of.

[1] 159 Pa. St., 420, decided in 1894.

2. Agreements aiming to raise Prices are Criminal

The early English and American cases, regarding labor as in the nature of a commodity, held very frequently that combinations among workingmen for the purpose of raising wages were, even if unaccompanied by any violence or other unlawful acts, criminal conspiracies. One of the earliest cases in this country was that of *People* v. *Fisher*.[1] In this case, certain journeymen shoemakers had combined for the purpose of fixing the wages of members of the combination. They were indicted under a provision of the New York Revised Statutes which declared that if two or more persons should conspire to commit any act injurious to trade or commerce, they should be deemed guilty of a misdemeanor. This provision is regarded as declaratory of the common law. The Court, in its opinion, declared that a combination to raise wages was injurious to trade or commerce, adding:

> It is important to the best interest of society that the price of labor be left to regulate itself, or rather be limited by the demand for it. Combinations and confederacies to enhance or reduce the prices of labor or of any articles of trade or commerce are injurious. They may be oppressive by compelling the public to give more for an article of necessity or of convenience than it is worth, or, on the other hand, by compelling the labor of the mechanic for less than its value.

It is only fair to say that the Court was influenced in its decision by the fact that the indicted shoemakers left the employment of a master workman, in order to force him to discharge one who had formerly been a member of the shoemakers' association, but who had refused to pay the penalty fixed by the association for violation of the agreement not to work for less than a certain sum. It will be seen, therefore, that in this particular case the conspiracy included not only the combination to raise prices, but also something in the nature of a boycott. The Court remarked:

> In the present case an industrious man was driven out of employment by the unlawful measures pursued by the defendants, and an injury done

[1] 14 Wendell, 9, decided in 1835.

to the community by diminishing the quantity of productive labor and of internal trade. . . . He had a right to work for what he pleased. His employer had a right to employ him for such price as they could agree upon. The interference of the defendants was unlawful; its tendency is not only to individual oppression, but to public inconvenience and embarrassment. I am of the opinion that the offence is indictable.

In commenting upon this general subject of labor combinations, the supreme court of Pennsylvania, in the case of *Cote* v. *Murphy*, already referred to, said:

The fixed theory of courts and legislators . . . was that the price of everything ought to be, and in the absence of combinations, necessarily would be, regulated by supply and demand. The first to deny the justice of this theory and to break away from it was labor; and this was soon followed by . . . legislation . . . relieving workmen of the penalties of what for more than a century had been declared unlawful combinations or conspiracies.[1] Wages, it was argued, should be fixed by the fair proportion labor had contributed in production. The market price determined by supply and demand might or might not be fair wages, often was not, and, as long as workmen were not free by combinations to insist upon their right to fair wages, oppression by capital, or which is the same thing, by their employers, followed. It is not our business to pass on the soundness of the theories which prompt the enactment of statutes. One thing, however, is clear: the moment the legislature relieved one and by far the larger number [*sic*] of the citizens of the commonwealth from the common-law prohibitions against combinations to raise the price of labor, and by a combination the price was raised, down went the foundation on which common-law conspiracy was based, as to that particular subject.

The logical consequence of this change in the law was, in the opinion of the Court, that, after employees had combined to raise wages, any combination made by employers against raising wages was not an unlawful conspiracy, inasmuch as the purpose of the employers was, not to interfere with the price of labor as determined by the common-law theory, but to defend themselves against a demand made altogether regardless of the price as regulated by the supply.

[1] Thus, in New York it is provided that it shall not be a criminal conspiracy for persons to combine for the purpose of advancing or maintaining wages. — Laws of 1870, c. 19.

A perusal of the later decisions upon this subject, sometimes made as a result of a change in the ideas of the judges, sometimes made as a result of specific statutes passed upon the subject, must lead to the conclusion that at the present time a combination of laborers for the purpose of raising wages, if unaccompanied by any unlawful act, — as, for example, a boycott or violence, — is not to be regarded as a criminal conspiracy. One of the latest cases upon the subject is *The Longshore Printing Co.* v. *Howell.*[1] In this case the Court held that it was not unlawful for a union to make provision in its by-laws for a scale of wages, or for limiting the number of apprentices; nor was it unlawful for several or many employees to agree among themselves to quit their employer, in order by so doing to induce him to confine his employment to certain kinds of labor.[2]

But while the law at the present time is that combinations of laborers to raise wages, when unaccompanied by any unlawful acts, are not criminal conspiracies, it cannot be said that the old common law generally has been thus changed. That is, notwithstanding the change made in favor of labor, it is still a crime to combine for the purpose of raising the price of commodities. One of the latest cases decided upon this point is *People* v. *Sheldon.*[3] In this case, certain coal dealers in the city of Lockport entered into an agreement to organize a coal exchange. The object of this exchange was to secure a general supervision and protection of the interests of retail dealers in coal and similar commodities. It was made the duty of members strictly to obey all the provisions of the constitution, by-laws and resolutions of the exchange. Any member guilty of violating any provision of the by-laws, or of conduct unbecoming a member, or of giving short weight or overweight, was liable to forfeit his membership. The agreement further declared that the retail price of coal should as far as practicable

[1] 26 Oregon, 527, decided in 1894.

[2] The common law was the same in the case of a combination of employers to reduce wages. Such a combination was a criminal conspiracy. *Com. ex rel. Chew* v. *Carlisle*, Brightley's Report, Pa., 36.

[3] 139 N. Y., 251, decided in 1893.

be kept uniform ; and that no price should be made at any time which should exceed a fair and reasonable advance over wholesale rates, or which should be higher than the current price at Rochester or Buffalo, figured upon corresponding freight tariffs ; and that at no time should the price of coal at retail exceed by more than one dollar the wholesale cost, except by the unanimous vote of all the members of the exchange. A certain member of the exchange was indicted, on the ground that this agreement constituted an unlawful conspiracy to increase the price of coal at retail in the city of Lockport, and that in pursuance of it the defendant and other members of the exchange elected officers and by resolution increased the price of coal seventy-five cents per ton. The indictment was found under section 168 of the Penal Code, which is a reënactment of the provision of the Revised Statutes, making it a misdemeanor for any two or more persons to conspire " to commit an act injurious to the public health, to public morals or to trade or commerce." The trial judge submitted the case to the jury upon the proposition that, if the defendants entered into the organization agreement for the purpose of controlling the price of coal and managing the business of the sale of coal so as to prevent competition in price between the members of the exchange, the agreement was illegal ; and that if the jury found that this was their intent, and that the price of coal was raised in pursuance of the agreement to effect this object, the crime of conspiracy was established.

The Court of Appeals, in deciding upon the propriety of this charge, said :

The question here does not, we think, turn on the point whether the agreement between the retail dealers in coal did, as a matter of fact, result in injury to the public, or to the community in Lockport. The question is : Was the agreement, in view of what might have been done under it, and the fact that it was an agreement the effect of which was to prevent competition among the coal dealers, one upon which the law affixes the brand of condemnation? It has hitherto been an accepted maxim in political economy that "competition is the life of trade." The courts have acted upon and adopted this maxim in passing upon the validity of agreements the design of which was to prevent competition in trade, and have held such agreements to be invalid. . . . The organization was a carefully devised scheme to prevent competition in the price of coal among the retail dealers; and the moral and material power of the combination afforded a reasonable guaranty that others would not engage in the business at Lockport except in conformity with the rules of the exchange. . . . The *gravamen* of the offence of conspiracy is the combination. Agreements to prevent competition in trade are in contemplation of law injurious to trade because they are liable to be injuriously used. . . . If agreements and combinations to prevent competition in prices are or may be hurtful to trade, the only sure remedy is to prohibit all agreements of that character. If the validity of such an agreement was made to depend upon actual proof of public prejudice or injury, it would be very difficult in any case to establish the invalidity, although the moral evidence might be very convincing. We are of opinion that the principle upon which the case was submitted to the jury is sanctioned by the decisions in this state, and that the jury were properly instructed that if the purpose of the agreement was to prevent competition in the price of coal between the retail dealers, it was illegal and justified the conviction of the defendant.

Finally, it has been held that corporations may be guilty of the crime of conspiracy, and that they are so guilty when they refuse to sell their products to dealers handling the products of rival companies.[1]

3. "Trust" Agreements justify Forfeiture of Corporate Charters

The impossibility, under the existing law, of making contracts in restraint of trade which would be enforced by the courts, and the danger that such agreements would be followed by punishment, led to the formation of agreements which took absolutely out of the power of the original owners of a business all control over it. These agreements, commonly known as trust agreements, provided for trustees who could operate a number

[1] *People* v. *Duke et al., N. Y. Law Journal,* Jan. 23, 1897. It would seem, however, that rebates given on condition that the person receiving the rebate shall deal exclusively with the person giving the rebate are perfectly legal. *Mogul Steamship Co.* v. *McGregor,* H. L. App. Cases, 1892, p. 25; *Nat. Distilling Co.* v. *Cream City Importing Co.,* 86 Wis., 352; *Olmstead* v. *Distilling and Cattle Feeding Co.,* 77 Fed. Rep., 265.

of different enterprises in accordance with their own ideas of what was proper, and who could thus absolutely prevent competition between the parties to the agreements. Such an agreement usually, but not universally, provided for the formation of a corporation out of a partnership wherever a business had been conducted under the latter form. In organizing the trust the stockholders in these corporations exchanged their stock for trust certificates issued by trustees, elected by the persons in interest. The trustees, it was believed, would thus become the only stockholders known to the law, and would therefore have the power of controlling the operations of the corporations whose stockholders had become parties to the trust agreement. In other words, the attempt was made to prevent competition by means of a federation of corporations.

This method was very commonly employed in this country for almost a quarter of a century without being opposed by the public authorities. In 1888, however, attention was directed to a trust agreement in the state of New York, and the attorney-general decided to bring an action in the nature of a *quo warranto* to forfeit the charter of a corporation whose stockholders had participated in its formation. The matter was decided in the case of *People* v. *The North River Sugar Refining Co.*,[1] and this decision was followed by the supreme court of Ohio in *State* v. *Standard Oil Co.*[2] In the New York case the action of the stockholders, even without any formal action upon the part of the corporation, was held to be corporate action, and to be contrary to public policy; the charter of the corporation itself was therefore forfeited. Judge Finch, who delivered the opinion of the Court, said:

I think there may be actual corporate conduct which is not formal corporate action; and where that conduct is directed or produced by the whole body both of officers and stockholders, by every living instrumentality which can possess and wield the corporate franchise, that conduct is of a corporate character, and if illegal and injurious may deserve and receive the penalty of dissolution. . . . The directors of a corporation, its authorized and active agency, may see the stockholders

[1] 121 N. Y., 582, decided in 1890.
[2] 49 Ohio St., 137, decided in 1892.

perverting its normal purposes by handing it over bound and helpless to an irresponsible and foreign authority, and omit all action which they ought to take, offer no resistance, make no protest, but apparently acquiesce as directors in the wrong which as stockholders they have themselves helped to commit. That is corporate conduct, though there may be utter absence of directors' resolutions. . . . The abstract idea of a corporation, the legal entity, the impalpable and intangible creation of human thought, is itself a fiction and has been appropriately described as a figure of speech. It serves very well to designate in our minds the collective action and agency of many individuals as permitted by the law, and the substantial inquiry always is: What, in a given case, has been that collective action and agency? As between the corporation and those with whom it deals, the manner of its exercise usually is material. But as between it and the state the substantial inquiry is only what that collective action and agency has done, and what it has in fact accomplished; what has seemed to be its effective work; what has been its conduct? It ought not to be otherwise. The state gave the franchise, the charter, not to the impalpable, intangible and almost nebulous fiction of our thoughts, but to the corporators, the individuals, the acting and living men, to be used by them, to redound to their benefit, to strengthen their hands and add energy to their capital. If it is taken away, it is taken from them as individuals and corporators, and the legal fiction disappears. The benefit is theirs; the punishment is theirs; and both must attend and depend upon their conduct. And when they all act collectively as an aggregate body without the least exception, and so acting reach results and accomplish purposes clearly corporate in their character, and affecting the vitality, the independence, the utility of the corporation itself, we cannot hesitate to conclude that there has been corporate conduct which the state may review and not be defeated by the assumed innocence of a convenient fiction.

In the Ohio case the reasoning on this head was very similar.[1] In both of these cases, however, the judges felt called upon to consider the further question whether the act which had thus

[1] Judge Marshall said: "The general proposition that a corporation is to be regarded as a legal entity existing separate and apart from the natural persons composing it is not disputed. But that the statement is a mere fiction existing only in idea is well understood and not controverted by any one who pretends to accurate knowledge on the subject. . . . Now, so long as a proper use is made of the fiction that a corporation is an entity apart from its shareholders, it is harmless, and, because convenient, should not be called in question; but where it is urged to an end subversive of its policy, or such is the issue, the fiction must be ignored and the question

taken the form of a corporate act was sufficiently injurious and contrary to public policy to justify the forfeiture of the charter. Here the decisions were somewhat divergent. In New York the Court held that the act of which the corporation had been guilty was in excess of its powers, and that the charter, therefore, was forfeited. The combination of sugar refineries was declared to partake of the nature of a partnership of corporations, and hence to be in violation of law. There was in the opinion a *dictum* as to the injurious effects of monopolies upon the public; but the Court in terms declined

> to advance into the wider discussion over monopolies and competition and restraint of trade, and the problems of political economy. . . . Without either approval or disapproval of the views expressed upon that branch of the case by the courts below, we are enabled to decide that in this state there can be no partnerships of separate and independent corporations, whether directly or indirectly, through the medium of the trust; no substantial consolidations which avoid and disregard the statutory permissions and restraints; but that manufacturing corporations must be and remain several, as they were created, or one under the statute.[1]

In the *dictum* with regard to monopolies, there were several very interesting statements, indicative of the opinion of the Court as to the public policy of permitting combinations whose

determined whether the act in question, though done by shareholders, that is to say, by the persons united in one body, was done simply as individuals and with respect to their individual interests as shareholders, or was done ostensibly as such but, as a matter of fact, to control the corporation and affect the transaction of its business in the same manner as if the act had been clothed with all the formalities of a corporate act. This must be so because, the stockholders having a dual capacity and capable of acting in either, and a possible interest to conceal their character when acting in their corporate capacity, the absence of the formal evidence of the character of the act cannot preclude judicial inquiry on the subject. If it were otherwise, then in one department of the law fraud would enjoy an immunity awarded to it in no other."

1 The statutes here referred to permitted the consolidation of manufacturing corporations, and the Court in a previous part of the opinion seemed to intimate that a consolidation under the statute would have been perfectly proper, inasmuch as "the resultant combination would itself be a corporation deriving its existence from the state, owing duties and obligations to the state, and subject to the control and supervision of the state, and not [as in the case presented] an unincorporated board, a colossal and gigantic partnership, having no corporate functions and owing no corporate allegiance."

purpose or effect is to promote monopolies. The public interest which corporate grants are always assumed to subserve is most unfavorably affected, said Judge Finch,

when beyond their own several aggregations of capital they compact them all into one combination which stands outside of the ward of the state, which dominates the range of an entire industry and puts upon the market a capital stock proudly defiant of actual values and capable of an unlimited expansion. It is not a sufficient answer to say that similar results may be lawfully accomplished; that an individual having the necessary wealth might have bought all of these refineries, manned them with his own chosen agents, and managed them as a group at his sovereign will; for it is one thing for the state to respect the rights of ownership and protect them out of regard to the business freedom of the citizen, and quite another thing to add to that possibility a further extension of those consequences by creating artificial persons to aid in producing such aggregations. The individuals are few who hold in possession such enormous wealth, and fewer still who peril it all in a manufacturing enterprise; but if corporations can combine and mass their forces in a solid trust or partnership with little added risk to the capital already embarked, without limit to the magnitude of the aggregation, a tempting and easy road is open to enormous combinations vastly exceeding in number and in strength and in their power over industry any possibilities of individual ownership; and the state, by the creation of the artificial persons constituting the elements of the combination and failing to limit and restrain their powers, becomes itself the responsible creator, the voluntary cause of an aggregation of capital which it simply endures in the individual as the product of his free agency. What it may bear is one thing; what it should cause and create is quite another.

In the Ohio case the Court declared the action of the corporations which formed the trust to be void, as contrary to public policy, on the ground that the attempt was made to form a monopoly. The judge said that the object of the agreement

was to establish a virtual monopoly of the business of producing petroleum and of manufacturing, refining and dealing in it and all its products throughout the entire country, and by which it might not merely control the production, but the price, at its pleasure. All such associations are contrary to the policy of our state and void. . . .

Much has been said in favor of the object of the Standard Oil Trust and what it has accomplished. It may be true that it has improved the quality and cheapened the cost of petroleum and its products to the consumer. But such is not one of the usual or general results of a monopoly, and it is the policy of the law to regard not what may, but what usually happens. Experience shows that it is not wise to trust human cupidity where it has the opportunity to aggrandize itself at the expense of others. . . . Monopolies have always been regarded as contrary to the spirit and policy of the law. The objections are stated in "The Case on Monopolies," *Darcy* v. *Allein*, Coke, Pt. XI, 84 b. They are these: (1) "That the price of the same commodity will be raised, for he who has the sole selling of any commodity may well make the price as he pleases"; (2) "The Incident to a monopoly is that after the monopoly is granted, the commodity is not so good and merchantable as it was before, for the patentee, having the sole trade, regards only his private benefit and not the commonwealth"; (3) "It tends to the impoverishment of divers artificers and others who before, by the labor of their hands in their art or trade, had maintained themselves and their families, who will now of necessity be constrained to live in idleness and beggary." The third objection, though frequently overlooked, is none the less important. A society in which a few men are the employers and a great body are merely employees or servants is not the most desirable in a republic; and it should be as much the policy of the laws to multiply the numbers engaged in independent pursuits, or in the profits of production, as to cheapen the price to the consumer. Such policy would tend to an equality of fortunes among its citizens, thought to be so desirable in a republic, and lessen the amount of pauperism and crime. It is true that in the case just cited the monopoly had been created by letters patent; but the objections lie not to the manner in which the monopoly is created. The effect on industrial liberty and the price of commodities will be the same, whether created by patent or by an extensive combination among those engaged in similar industries controlled by one management. By the invariable laws of human nature, competition will be excluded and prices controlled in the interest of those connected with the combination or trust.[1]

[1] A similar decision was made by the supreme court of Nebraska in *State* v. *Nebraska Distilling Co.*, 29 Neb., 700, decided in 1890. See also *Mallory* v. *Hananer Oil Works*, 8 S. W. Rep. (Tenn., 1888), where suit was brought against trustees of a trust agreement by a corporation which was a party to such agreement to recover possession of its property. Judgment was given in favor of the plaintiff on the ground that the corporation could not enter into such an agreement, which the Court considered to be a partnership of corporations.

4. Are Corporations for Purposes of Monopoly Illegal?

The effect of the foregoing and similar decisions was that any persons who intended to form a combination for the purpose of limiting competition were obliged to seek a substitute for the trust agreement. As a general thing they effected an organization in the shape of a large corporation, since, as has been shown, the New York Court of Appeals had appeared to regard this as a legal method of forming a combination. The courts were soon required to decide upon the legality of such action. The first case that came up was that of *People* v. *The Chicago Gas Trust Co.*[1] A gas trust company, as it was called, had been formed, in whose certificate of incorporation the purposes of the corporation were stated to be the manufacture of gas and the purchase, holding and selling of stocks in other gas and electric companies in Chicago or elsewhere in Illinois. *Quo warranto* was brought against the corporation to obtain judgment of ouster against its use of the franchise to purchase and hold or sell the capital stock of other companies. It was clearly admitted on both sides that the Court was not precluded from examining into the legality of the exercise of this franchise by the fact that the certificate of incorporation had been approved and filed with the proper executive officers of the state. The general incorporation act of the state permitted the formation of corporations in the manner provided by it for any lawful purpose. The question which arose was, therefore, whether the corporation in question had been formed for a lawful purpose.

In answering this question the Court found that one result of the exercise of this franchise by the Chicago Gas Trust Company would be that it could control the four other companies in Chicago. The control of these four companies, it was thought, would suppress competition among them, and thus build up a virtual monopoly in the manufacture and sale of gas. The Court said:

> Whatever tends to prevent competition between those engaged in a public employment or business impressed with a public character is

[1] 130 Ill., 268, decided in 1889.

opposed to public policy, and therefore unlawful. Whatever tends to create a monopoly is unlawful, as being contrary to public policy.

It therefore held that

if contracts and grants whose tendency is to create monopolies are void at common law, then where a corporation is organized under a general statute, a provision in the declaration of its corporate purposes, the necessary effect of which is the creation of a monopoly, will also be void.

Further on in the opinion it is stated:

To create one corporation for the express purpose of enabling it to control all the corporations engaged in a certain kind of business, and particularly a business of a public character, is not only opposed to the public policy of the state, but is in contravention of the spirit, if not the letter, of the constitution.

The Court also cited with approval the following views expressed by the supreme court of Georgia in the case of *Central Railroad Co.* v. *Collins.*[1]

All experience has shown that large accumulations of property in hands likely to keep it intact for a long period are dangerous to the public weal. Having perpetual succession, any kind of a corporation has peculiar facilities for such accumulations, and most governments have found it necessary to exercise great caution in their grants of corporate powers. Even religious corporations professing, and in the main truly, nothing but the general good, have proven obnoxious to this objection, so that in England it was long ago found necessary to restrict them in their powers of acquiring real estate. Freed as such bodies are from the sure bound to the schemes of individuals, the grave, they are able to add field to field and power to power until they become entirely too strong for that society which is made up of those whose plans are limited by a single life.

For these reasons judgment of ouster was issued against the Chicago Gas Trust Company, as to the exercise of the franchise of purchasing the stocks in other gas companies.

All the cases thus far considered certainly give evidence that the courts of this country regard any combination, whatever form it may take, whose tendency or whose purpose is to form a monopoly, as contrary to public policy and illegal at common

[1] 40 Ga., 582, decided in 1869.

law; but none of them, not even the last, distinctly declares unlawful the formation of a corporation whose purpose or whose effect is to promote monopoly. This question it remained for the supreme court of Illinois to consider in the case of the *Distilling & Cattle Feeding Co.* v. *The People.*[1]

In view of the decisions which the courts were almost universally rendering as to the illegality of trust agreements, the holders of trust certificates in the Distillers' & Cattle Feeders' Trust, commonly called The Whiskey Trust, had in February, 1890, adopted a recommendation of the trustees to form a corporation with a capital stock of $35,000,000. The corporation was thereafter organized. The trustees of the former trust subscribed for all the stock of the new corporation and elected themselves its first directors. They, or so many of them as were necessary to constitute a majority of the directors of each of the corporations composing the trust, also ordered a conveyance of all the property which those corporations held, to the newly formed corporation; and as directors of these corporations, they executed to the Distilling & Cattle Feeding Company a transfer of all of the property of these corporations, and surrendered to the holders of the trust certificates the shares of stock in the newly formed corporation in return for the trust certificates. The new corporation subsequently purchased the property and business of other corporations not parties to the former trust agreement. Suit was brought against the new corporation, and judgment of ouster from its franchise was demanded, on the ground that it had created a monopoly in the manufacture and output of distillery products, and secured such control over the consumers thereof as to destroy all competition in the manufacture and sale of such products throughout the United States.

The Court, in rendering its opinion, said:

There can be no doubt, we think, that the Distillers' & Cattle Feeders' Trust, which preceded the incorporation of the defendant, was an organization which contravened well-established principles of public policy, and that it was therefore illegal. [The new corporation succeeded] to the trust, and its operations are to be carried on in the same way, for the same purposes and by the same agencies as before. The trust then

[1] 156 Ill., 448, decided in 1895.

being repugnant to public policy and illegal, it is impossible to see why the same is not true of the corporation which succeeds to it and takes its place. The control exercised over the distillery business of the country — over production and prices — and the virtual monopoly formerly held by the trust are in no degree changed or relaxed, but the method and purposes of the trust are perpetuated and carried out with the same persistence and vigor as before the organization of the corporation. There is no magic in a corporate organization which can purge the trust scheme of its illegality, and it remains as essentially opposed to the principles of sound public policy as when the trust was in existence. It was illegal before and is illegal still, and for the same reasons.

In answer to the objection that the defendant corporation by its charter was authorized to purchase and own distillery property, and that there was no limit placed upon the amount of property which it might thus acquire, the Court said:

It should be remembered that grants of powers in corporate charters are to be construed strictly, and that what is not clearly given is by implication denied. The defendant is authorized to own such property as is necessary to carry on its distillery business, and no more. Its power to acquire and hold property is limited to that purpose, and it has no power by its charter to enter upon a scheme of getting into its hands and under its control all, or substantially all, the distillery plants and the distillery business of the country, for the purpose of controlling production and prices, of crushing out competition, and of establishing a virtual monopoly in that business. All such purposes are foreign to the powers granted by the charter. Acquisitions of property to such extent and for such purpose do not come within the authority to own the property necessary for the purpose of carrying on a general distillery business. In acquiring distillery properties in the manner and for the purposes shown by the information, the defendant has not only misused and abused the powers granted by its charter, but has usurped and exercised powers not conferred by, but which are wholly foreign to, that instrument. It has thus rendered itself liable to prosecution by the state by *quo warranto*. We are of the opinion that upon the facts shown by the information, the judgment of ouster is clearly warranted.

A case involving somewhat similar questions is that of *The People* v. *The Milk Exchange*, decided by the New York Court of Appeals.[1] The Milk Exchange had ninety-odd stockholders,

[1] 145 N. Y., 267, decided in 1895.

a large majority of whom were milk dealers in the city of New York, or creamery or milk-commission men doing business in that vicinity. At the first meeting of the exchange after its incorporation, the following among other by-laws was adopted: "The board of directors shall have the power to make and fix the standard or market price at which milk shall be purchased by the stockholders of this company." Acting upon this by-law, the board of directors from time to time fixed the price of milk to be paid by dealers, and the prices so fixed largely controlled the market in and about the city of New York.

The court, in deciding the case, declared its conviction that there was a combination on the part of milk dealers and creamery men in and about the city of New York to fix and control the price that they should pay for milk; and that a case was presented in which the jury might have found that the combination referred to was inimical to trade and commerce, and therefore unlawful. Accordingly, the charter was declared forfeited.

> It may be claimed [the Court said] that the purpose of the combination was to reduce the price of milk and, it being an article of food, such reduction was not against public policy. But the price was fixed for the benefit of the dealers, and not the consumers, and the logical effect upon the trade of so fixing the price by the combination was to paralyze the production and limit the supply, and thus leave the dealers in a position to control the market, and at their option to enhance the price to be paid by the consumers.

This case is interesting as showing that the courts will take cognizance of an attempt through a combination in the form of a corporation to lower the price of commodities to the detriment of the producer as well as of an attempt to enhance the price at the expense of the consumer.

5. Attitude of the United States Supreme Court

Notwithstanding the decisions thus far considered, persons who desired to form a trade combination were able to do so with impunity, on account of the fact that if their organization was declared illegal in one state, they could organize under the laws of another, provided the public opinion in the latter was not opposed to trade combinations. An attempt was therefore made in what is known as the Anti-Trust Law, passed by Congress in 1890, to give the national government the power, in addition to that which the states already possessed, to suppress trade combinations. But it was recognized by the promoters of this bill that Congress had no jurisdiction of specifically state industry and commerce. The act was, therefore, worded as follows: "Every contract, combination in the form of trust or otherwise, or conspiracy in restraint of trade or commerce among the several states or with foreign nations is hereby declared to be illegal." Every one participating in such a contract or engaging in such a combination was declared to be guilty of a misdemeanor, and made liable to severe punishment. It was provided that the circuit courts of the United States should have jurisdiction to restrain violations of the act, and that it should be the duty of the law officers of the United States to institute the proper proceedings. A suit was begun in Pennsylvania against certain sugar-refining corporations which had been absorbed by the American Sugar Refining Company. Evidence was taken before Judge Butler, of the Circuit Court, who said in his opinion: "The object in purchasing the Philadelphia refineries was to obtain a greater influence or more perfect control over the business of refining and selling sugar in this country." The opinion also showed that, after the purchase of these refineries by the American Sugar Refining Company, the latter corporation had obtained control of all refineries in the United States except one in Boston, whose output was about two per cent of the sugar refined in this country.

This case went on appeal to the Supreme Court of the United States.[1] Here, on the state of facts presented by Judge Butler, the Court held that the act of 1890 was framed in the light of well-settled principles; that

> Congress did not attempt thereby to assert the power to deal with monopoly directly as such, or to limit and restrict the rights of corporations created by the states or the citizens of the states in the acquisition,

[1] *United States* v. *E. C. Knight Co.*, 156 U. S., 1.

control or disposition of property, or to regulate or prescribe the price or prices at which such property or the products thereof should be sold, or to make criminal the acts of persons in the acquisition and control of property which the states of their residence or creation sanctioned or permitted. . . . The contracts and acts of the defendants related exclusively to the acquisition of the Philadelphia refineries and the business of sugar-refining in Pennsylvania, and bore no direct relation to commerce between the states or with foreign nations. . . . It is true that the bill alleged that the products of these refineries were sold and distributed among the several states, and that all the companies were engaged in trade or commerce with the several states and with foreign nations. But this was no more than to say that trade and commerce served manufacture to fulfil its functions. . . . It does not follow that an attempt to monopolize or the actual monopoly of the manufacture was an attempt, whether executory or consummated, to monopolize commerce, even though in order to dispose of the product the instrumentality of commerce was necessarily invoked. . . . There was nothing in the proofs to indicate any intention to put a restraint upon trade or commerce; and the fact, as we have seen, that trade or commerce might be indirectly affected was not enough to entitle the claimants to a decree. The subject-matter of the sale was shares of manufacturing stock, and the relief sought was the surrender of property which had already passed and the suppression of the alleged monopoly in manufacture by the restoration of the *status quo* before the transfers; yet the act of Congress only authorized the circuit courts to proceed by way of preventing and restraining violations of the act in respect of contracts, combinations or conspiracies in restraint of interstate or international trade or commerce.

It will be noticed that this decision was based upon three grounds: (1) that the proper remedy was not invoked, or at any rate was not invoked at the proper time; (2) that the combination did not disclose an attempt to monopolize; (3) that, even if it did so, it was not a combination in restraint of interstate or foreign commerce.

As to the first of these grounds, it may be said that the bill which was before the court asked that an injunction might issue to prevent and restrain the said defendants from further and continued violations of the act of Congress. This was in addition to the demand that the agreements between the defendants be cancelled and that the shares of stock transferred in performance of the contracts be restored to their original owners.[1] As to the second ground of the decision, the trial judge found, as has been stated, that the object in purchasing the Philadelphia refineries was to obtain a greater influence or more perfect control over the business of refining and selling sugar in this country. Moreover, the state courts, in the decisions heretofore cited, have declared that they will go back of any alleged purpose of an agreement or of a certificate of incorporation and will inquire what is its real purpose and effect; and that if the latter are to establish a monopoly unreasonably limiting competition, they will declare the agreement void.

But while these first two considerations undoubtedly influenced the Supreme Court somewhat, the main ground upon which the decision was based was that the manufacture and sale of sugar were not interstate or foreign commerce. In order to reach this decision, the Court laid little stress upon the purpose to monopolize the sale. The sale of sugar was declared to be merely an incident to the manufacture. As the Court said, "trade and commerce serve manufacture to fulfil its functions." Laying the weight which they did upon the manufacture, they considered that they were bound by the case of *Kidd* v. *Pearson.*[2] Here the

question was discussed whether the right of a state to enact a statute prohibiting within its limits the manufacture of intoxicating liquors, except for certain purposes, could be overthrown by the fact that the manufacturer intended to export the liquors when made; and it was held that the intent of the manufacturer did not determine the time when the article or product passed from the control of the state and belonged to commerce, and that therefore the prohibitory act was not in conflict with the constitutional provision giving the right to regulate interstate commerce to Congress.

[1] Judge Harlan, in his dissenting opinion, said on this point: "While a decree annulling the contracts under which the combination in question was formed may not in view of the facts disclosed be effectual to accomplish the object of the act of 1890, I perceive no difficulty in the way of the court passing a decree declaring that that combination imposes an unlawful restraint upon trade and commerce among the states and perpetually enjoining it from further prosecuting any business pursuant to the unlawful agreements under which it was formed or by which it was created."

[2] 128 U. S., 1.

Another case which seems to have influenced the Court was that of *Coe* v. *Erroll*.[1] Here the question was "whether certain logs cut at a place in New Hampshire and hauled to a river town for the purpose of transportation to the state of Maine were liable to be taxed like other property in the state of New Hampshire"; and it was held that they were liable to taxation just as much as any other property in the state, and that the owner's intention and his partial preparation to ship them out of the state would not exempt them from taxation as articles of interstate commerce.

Judge Harlan, in a dissenting opinion, pointed out, however, that, under previous decisions of the Supreme Court, interstate commerce embraced something more than the mere physical transportation of articles of property and the vehicles or vessels by which such transportation was effected. He referred in particular to the case of *Mobile County* v. *Kimball*,[2] where it was said that commerce with foreign countries and among the states, strictly considered, consists "in intercourse and traffic, including in these terms navigation and transportation and transit of persons or property, as well as the *purchase, sale and exchange* of commodities." Judge Harlan did not consider that these early statements and decisions had been modified by either of the cases referred to in the majority's opinion. As regards the question of monopoly, he said:

> A combination such as that organized under the name of the American Sugar Refining Company has been uniformly held by the courts of the states to be against public policy and illegal because of its necessary tendency to impose improper restraints upon trade.

And further:

> The object of this combination was to obtain control of the business of making and selling refined sugar throughout the entire country. Those interested in its operations will be satisfied with nothing less than to have the whole population of America pay tribute to them. That object is disclosed upon the very face of the transactions described in the bill, and it is proved — indeed conceded — that that object has been accomplished to the extent that the American Sugar Refining

[1] 116 U. S., 517. [2] 102 U. S., 691.

Company now controls 98 per cent of all the sugar-refining business in the country, and therefore controls the price of that article everywhere. Now the mere existence of a combination having such an object and possessing such extraordinary power is itself under settled principles of law — there being no adjudged case to the contrary in this country — a direct restraint of trade in the article for the control of the sales of which in this country that combination was organized. And that restraint is felt in all the states for the reason known to all, that the article in question goes, was intended to go and must always go into commerce among the several states and into the homes of people in every condition of life.

Finally, Judge Harlan argued for the public policy of the Anti-Trust Law in the following language:

We have before us the case of a combination which absolutely controls, or may at its discretion control, the price of all refined sugar in this country. Suppose another combination organized for private gain and to control prices should obtain possession of all the large flour mills in the United States; another of all the grain elevators; another of all the oil territory; another of all the salt-producing regions; another of all the cotton-mills; and another of all the great establishments for slaughtering animals and the preparation of meats. What power is competent to protect the people of the United States against such dangers except a national power — one that is capable of exerting its sovereign authority throughout every part of the territory and over all the people of the nation?

The decision of the United States Supreme Court, holding that the manufacture and sale of commodities were not, as not being objects of interstate commerce, subject to the regulation of Congress, was therefore not reached without protest; but the Court was so nearly unanimous in its decision as to justify the belief that the decision itself will not be reversed in the immediate future.[1] The experiences of the states and the arguments advanced by Judge Harlan in his dissenting opinion would lead also to the belief that the regulation of these trade combinations by the states is practically impossible. Any attempt at efficient regulation must come from the national government.

[1] The opinion of the majority in the recent case of the Trans-Missouri Freight Association seems, however, to render the future tendency somewhat uncertain.

In view of the fact that great insistence was laid in the last presidential campaign upon the necessity of some efficient regulation of combinations in restraint of trade, it may be well to summarize the views that the courts have expressed as to the impolicy of permitting these combinations to exist and of recognizing or enforcing in any way contracts for executing their purposes.

The reasons given by the courts for their attitude may be classified under three heads, — economic, social and political. The economic reasons are two in number. In the first place, it is believed by the courts that a combination in restraint of trade and tending to promote a monopoly will result either in the sale of a depreciated article to the public, or in an enhancement of the price of the article which is so controlled. This was the important economic reason at the basis of the decision in the time of Queen Elizabeth, relative to monopolies granted by the crown. This reason has had so much weight with the courts that they have refused to investigate the question whether such has been the effect of a combination. They have simply declared that the possession of monopoly powers by any combination must inevitably result in an enhancement of price or in a depreciation in the quality of the article sold. Their reasoning here, it will be noticed, is distinctly *a priori;* and so long as they adhere to this principle, it will be impossible to prove by reference to actual facts whether it is based upon the truth or not. The second economic argument advanced by the courts in support of their policy is that the fixing by any combination of the price of raw materials injures the producer of the raw material, and will ultimately result in disadvantage to the consumer.

The social argument against combinations also dates from the time of Elizabeth. A monopoly, the Court said,

> tends to the impoverishment of divers artificers and others who before by the labor of their hands in their art or trade have maintained themselves and their families, who will now of necessity be constrained to live in idleness and beggary.

In the form in which it is put, this argument would seem to rest on a misapprehension of the conditions caused by monopolies; and if applied in as broad a way as it is stated in this case, it would be available against the introduction of all labor-saving machinery. In the Ohio case of *The State* v. *The Standard Oil Co.*, already referred to, this argument was somewhat modified. The Court took the ground, not so much that the formation of the combination throws great numbers of individuals out of employment, as that the development of monopolies transforms great numbers of persons formerly independent into employees or servants. This argument, though treated by the Ohio court as a development of the view of the English court in the case of monopolies, is really quite different in character. A further argument of a social character is to be found in the opinion of Judge Finch in the Sugar Trust case. He based the right of the state to limit the activity of corporations, as distinct from that of individuals, on the ground that a direct grant of corporate powers would, if these powers were not limited, aid in the aggregation of wealth in a few hands. He did not desire to limit the right of individual action, but merely claimed that when specific powers which can only exist as a result of the grant of the state are exercised by individuals, they become rightly subject to regulation in the interest of the state as a whole. It is one thing, said he, for the state to respect the rights of ownership and protect them out of regard to the business freedom of the citizen; but it is quite another thing for the state positively to promote the aggregation of capital by creating artificial persons such as corporations, without limiting their powers.

The political reason advanced by the courts for their position with regard to trade combinations is perhaps as well stated as anywhere by the supreme court of Georgia. Here it is pointed out that all large accumulations of property in hands likely to keep it intact for a long period are dangerous to the public weal. In England it was found necessary to limit the amount of property which even religious corporations might possess, notwithstanding the fact that they, far more than trading bodies, might be expected to exercise their powers for the general good. Given the privilege of legal immortality, corporations, it was held, are apt to "become entirely too strong for that society which is made up of those whose plans are limited by a single life."

Such are the rules of law in the United States with regard to the legality of trade combinations, and such are the reasons which the courts have advanced for the adoption of these rules. If these reasons are not sound, if the conditions of society are not what they were when these rules were adopted and these reasons were first advanced, it would be well that the rules of law be changed. Changes may be made by legislation, as has very generally been done in the case of labor combinations. If, on the other hand, these reasons are now sound and the rules of law based thereon are at the present time in accordance with public policy, some method ought to be provided for their efficient enforcement. This, it has been pointed out, can in the cases of the largest combinations now in existence be done only through the modification of the present rule of the United States Supreme Court with regard to national regulation of monopolies; or, in case the Supreme Court shall not see fit to modify its rules, by the adoption of a constitutional provision giving the Congress of the United States the necessary powers.

FRANK J. GOODNOW.

XII

INTERPRETATION AND AMENDMENT OF THE SHERMAN ANTI-TRUST ACT[1]

I HAVE the honor to submit, in response to your request, the following statements under the three heads which you have indicated, namely: The questions which have been decided by the courts, the questions which are pending in the courts, and suggestions respecting further legislation.

I. QUESTIONS WHICH HAVE BEEN DECIDED BY THE COURTS

The act of July 2, 1890, entitled "An act to protect trade and commerce against unlawful restraints and monopolies," has been before the Supreme Court of the United States in the following cases:

United States v. *E. C. Knight Co.*, 156 U. S., 1;

United States v. *Trans-Missouri Freight Association*, 166 U. S., 290;

United States v. *Joint Traffic Association*, 171 U. S., 505;

United States v. *Hopkins*, 171 U. S., 578;

Anderson v. *United States*, 171 U. S., 604; and

Addyston Pipe and Steel Co. v. *United States*, 175 U. S., 211.

In the Knight case there was involved an alleged monopoly in the production of sugar, commonly known as the "sugar trust"; in the Freight Association, and Joint Traffic Association cases, agreements among interstate railways to fix and maintain rates and fares; in the Hopkins and Anderson cases, two live

[1] Reply of the Attorney-General to a communication from the Hon. George F. Hoar, Chairman of the Committee on the Judiciary of the United States Senate, Jan. 3, 1903.

stock exchanges located in Kansas City, and in the Addyston Pipe and Steel Company case, a combination among competing shops located in different states, and engaged in making cast-iron pipe for gas, water, and sewer purposes, to control prices by suppressing competition among themselves.

In the Knight case the Court held that the creation of a monopoly in production does not necessarily and directly restrain commerce among the states. The Court drew the line between production and interstate commerce, the former being subject to the regulation of the states, the latter alone to that of Congress.

In the Freight Association case the Court held that the Anti-Trust Law applies to railroads, and that it prohibits *all* agreements in restraint of interstate commerce, whether the restraint be reasonable or unreasonable.

This was followed by the Joint Traffic decision, the Court holding in addition that the Anti-Trust Law is valid and constitutional, and that Congress has the power to say that a contract shall not be lawful which restrains trade or commerce among the several states by stifling competition.

In the Hopkins case, it was held that the business of the members of the Kansas City Live Stock Exchange was not interstate commerce within the meaning of the Anti-Trust Law, and therefore the agreement creating that exchange did not operate to restrain trade or commerce among the several states.

In the Anderson case the Court took the view that whether the members of the Traders' Live Stock Exchange of Kansas City were or were not engaged in interstate commerce, the agreement creating the exchange was not one in restraint of such trade.

In the Addyston Pipe Company case the Court held that Congress may prohibit the performance of any contract between individuals or corporations where the natural and direct effect is to regulate or restrain interstate commerce, and that a combination among formerly competing shops, which directly restrained not simply the manufacture, but the sale of a commodity among the several states, comes within the Anti-Trust Law.

Stated in more detail the cases are as follows:

UNITED STATES *v.* E. C. KNIGHT COMPANY (Sugar Trust)

(60 Fed. Rep., 306; Pennsylvania.)
(60 Fed. Rep., 934; circuit court of appeals, third circuit.)
(156 U. S., 1; U. S. Supreme Court, March 26, 1894; Opin., Fuller, Ch. J. Harlan, J., dissenting.)

A bill in equity to enjoin the operation of the so-called "sugar trust." The bill was dismissed by the circuit court, its decree affirmed by the circuit court of appeals, and its judgment affirmed by the Supreme Court of the United States.

It appeared in this case that, by the purchase of the stock of four Philadelphia refineries, through the exchange of shares of its own stock, the American Sugar Refining Company acquired nearly a complete control of the manufacture of refined sugar in the United States. The Government charged that the contracts under which these purchases were made constituted combinations in restraint of trade or commerce in refined sugar among the several states and with foreign nations and asked the cancellation of the contracts and the redelivery of the stock.

The Government's contention was that the purpose of the purchase was to acquire a substantial monopoly of sugar refining, and as the product was a necessary of life, manufactured for sale and distribution among the several states and in foreign countries, that the effect of the arrangement was to restrain and monopolize interstate and foreign commerce.

But the Supreme Court held that, conceding a monopoly was created, it was a monopoly in the production of sugar and not in its sale or distribution among the several states. If a monopoly in interstate commerce followed a monopoly in production, it was but indirect and incidental and not within the prohibition of the Anti-Trust Law. It was for the states to regulate production; the authority of Congress was limited to commerce among the states.

Doubtless, said the Chief Justice (page 12), the power to control the manufacture of a given thing involves in a certain sense the control of its disposition, but this is a secondary and not the primary sense; and although the exercise of that power may result in bringing the operation of commerce into play, it does not control it, and affects it only incidentally and indirectly. Commerce succeeds to manufacture, and is not a part of it.

Again, page 16:

Contracts, combinations, or conspiracies to control domestic enterprise in manufacture, agriculture, mining, production in all its forms, or to raise or lower prices or wages, might unquestionably tend to restrain external as well as domestic trade, but the restraint would be an indirect result, however inevitable and whatever its extent, and such result would not necessarily determine the object of the contract, combination, or conspiracy.

* * * * * * * *

It was in the light of well-settled principles that the act of July 2, 1890, was framed. Congress did not attempt thereby to assert the power to deal with monopoly directly as such; or to limit and restrict the rights of corporations created by the states or the citizens of the states in the acquisition, control, or disposition of property; or to regulate or prescribe the price or prices at which such property or the products thereof shall be sold; or to make criminal the acts of persons in the acquisition and control of property which the states of their residence or creation sanctioned or permitted. Aside from the provisions applicable where Congress might exercise municipal power, what the law struck at was combinations, contracts, and conspiracies to monopolize trade and commerce among the several states or with foreign nations; but the contracts and acts of the defendants related exclusively to the acquisition of the Philadelphia refineries and the business of sugar refining in Pennsylvania, and bore no direct relation to commerce between the states or with foreign nations.

United States *v.* Trans-Missouri Freight Association

(53 Fed. Rep., 440 Kansas.)

(58 Fed. Rep., 58; circuit court of appeals, eighth circuit.)

(166 U. S., 290; Supreme Court, March 22, 1897; Opin., Peckham, J.)

The contract or combination assailed in this case was an agreement among a large number of interstate railways, creating an association and providing a method of fixing rates and fares on competitive interstate freight traffic south and west of the

Missouri River. The agreement expressly declared that the association was formed, among other things, "for the purpose of mutual protection, by establishing and maintaining *reasonable* rates," etc.

The questions vigorously discussed in the case were whether the Anti-Trust Law applies to railroads, and whether it declares illegal all contracts in restraint of trade, whether reasonable or unreasonable.

The Court held that the law does apply to railroads and that it prohibits all contracts in restraint of trade or commerce among the several states and with foreign nations, whether the restraint be reasonable or unreasonable.

Four of the justices — White, Field, Gray, and Shiras — dissented in an opinion delivered by Mr. Justice White, upon the ground that the restraint of trade condemned by the statute is an unreasonable restraint, such as was unlawful at common law.

UNITED STATES *v.* JOINT TRAFFIC ASSOCIATION

(76 Fed. Rep., 895; New York.)

(89 Fed. Rep., 1020; circuit court of appeals, second circuit.)

(171 U. S., 505; Supreme Court, October 24, 1898; Opin., Peckham, J.)

The Joint Traffic case grew out of an agreement, similar to that in the Trans-Missouri, creating an association to fix rates and fares on competitive interstate traffic east of Chicago. Nine trunk line systems — the Baltimore and Ohio, the Chesapeake and Ohio, the Erie, the Grand Trunk, the Lackawanna, the Lehigh, the Pennsylvania, the Vanderbilt, and the Wabash, — practically controlling the business of railroad transportation between Chicago and the Atlantic seaboard, were covered by the arrangement.

The agreement expressly declared that it was entered into only to establish and maintain "reasonable and just rates, fares," etc., and stated that the powers conferred upon the managers should be so construed and exercised as not to permit the violation of the interstate commerce act or any other applicable law.

In addition to the points discussed in the Trans-Missouri case, which counsel for the railroads attempted to re-argue, it was insisted that the Anti-Trust Law is unconstitutional.

The Court followed its decision in the Trans-Missouri case, holding that there was no substantial difference between the Trans-Missouri and the Joint Traffic agreements, and, upon the constitutional question, held that Congress has the power, in regulating interstate commerce carried on by railroad corporations, to say that no contract or combination shall be legal which restrains such trade or commerce by shutting out the operation of the general law of competition.

In this case, as in the Trans-Missouri, the Court considered it no defence that the rates established or to be established were reasonable. The fact that the creation of the association prevented any real competition between the railway systems involved was held to restrain the trade or commerce carried on by them.

> The natural, direct, and immediate effect of competition, said the Court (page 577), is, however, to lower rates, and to thereby increase the demand for commodities, the supplying of which increases commerce, and an agreement, whose first and direct effect is to prevent this play of competition, restrains instead of promoting trade and commerce.

Hopkins *v.* United States

(82 Fed. Rep., 529; Kansas.)

(84 Fed. Rep., 1018; circuit court of appeals, eighth circuit.)

(171 U. S., 578; Supreme Court, October 24, 1898; Opin., Peckham, J.)

This was a bill in equity, filed by direction of the Attorney-General, against Hopkins and other members of the Kansas City Live Stock Exchange, to secure a dissolution of the exchange on the ground that its members were in a combination in restraint of commerce among the several states.

It seems that this exchange was an association of men doing business at the stock yards in Kansas City, part of these yards being in Missouri and part in Kansas. The business of the members was to receive live stock shipped from other states, care for and sell the same, and account to the owners for the proceeds after deducting charges and expenses. Under the rules, members were prohibited from buying live stock from commission merchants in Kansas City not members of the exchange. The rules also fixed a commission, prohibited the employment of agents to solicit consignments except upon stipulated salary, and forbade the sending of prepaid telegrams or telephone messages with information as to the condition of the markets.

The Court held that the business conducted by the members of the exchange was not interstate, but local in character, and therefore decided the case against the government.

Page 588:

The sale or purchase of live stock as commission merchants at Kansas City is the business done, and its character is not altered because the larger proportion of the purchases and sales may be of live stock sent into the state from other states or from the territories. Where the stock came from or where it may ultimately go after a sale or purchase, procured through the services of one of the defendants at the Kansas City stock yards, is not the substantial factor in the case. The character of the business of defendants must, in this case, be determined by the facts occurring at that city.

If an owner of cattle in Nebraska accompanied them to Kansas City and there personally employed one of these defendants to sell the cattle at the stock yards for him on commission, could it be properly said that such defendant, in conducting the sale for his principal, was engaged in interstate commerce? Or that an agreement between himself and others not to render such services for less than a certain sum was a contract in restraint of interstate trade or commerce? We think not. On the contrary, we regard the services as collateral to such commerce and in the nature of a local aid or facility provided for the cattle owner toward the accomplishment of his purpose to sell them, and an agreement among those who render the services relating to the terms upon which they will render them is not a contract in restraint of interstate trade or commerce.

Page 590:

The selling of an article at its destination, which has been sent from another state, while it may be regarded as an interstate sale and one which the importer was entitled to make, yet the services of the individual employed at the place where the article is sold are not so connected with the subject sold as to make them a portion of interstate commerce, and a combination in regard to the amount to be charged for such service is not, therefore, a combination in restraint of that trade or commerce. Granting that the cattle themselves, because coming from another state, are articles of interstate commerce, yet it does not therefore follow that before their sale all persons performing services in any way connected with them are themselves engaged in that commerce, or that their agreements among each other relative to the compensation to be charged for their services are void as agreements made in restraint of interstate trade.

Page 592:

The contract condemned by the statute is one whose direct and immediate effect is a restraint upon that kind of trade or commerce which is interstate. Charges for such facilities as we have already mentioned are not a restraint upon that trade, although the total cost of marketing a subject thereof may be thereby increased. Charges for facilities furnished have been held not a regulation of commerce, even when made for services rendered or as compensation for benefits conferred.

Anderson *v.* United States

(82 Fed. Rep., 998; Kansas; circuit court of appeals, eighth circuit.)

(171 U. S., 604; Supreme Court, October 24, 1898; Opin., Peckham, J.)

This case was somewhat similar to the Hopkins case, being a bill in equity filed by direction of the Attorney-General against the members of the Traders' Live Stock Exchange of Kansas City to compel its dissolution. The main difference between this exchange and that involved in the Hopkins case was that while the members of the Traders' Exchange were purchasers of live stock on the market, the members of the Live Stock Exchange were only commission merchants who sold the live stock upon commission as a compensation for their services.

The rules of the exchange relied upon by the government as restraining interstate commerce were those which forbade the recognition of any yard trader unless he was a member of the exchange, which required all the members of a partnership to be members of the exchange, which provided that no member of the exchange should employ any person to buy or sell cattle unless such person was a member of the exchange, and which prohibited the payment of any fee to any buyer or salesman for buying cattle from or selling cattle to such party.

Without passing upon the question whether the members of this exchange were or were not engaged in interstate commerce, the Court held that the rules objected to were of a character to enforce the purpose and object of the exchange, and viewed in that light were reasonable and fair. They could affect interstate trade or commerce in but a remote way, and therefore could not be regarded as in restraint of such trade or commerce.

The Court (page 615) restated the rule that where the subject-matter of the agreement does not directly relate to and act upon and embrace interstate commerce, and where the undisputed facts clearly show that the purpose of the agreement was not to regulate, obstruct, or restrain that commerce, but that it was entered into with the object of properly and fairly regulating the transaction of the business in which the parties to the agreement were engaged, such agreement would be upheld as not within the statute.

ADDYSTON PIPE AND STEEL COMPANY *v.* UNITED STATES[1]

(78 Fed. Rep., 712; Tennessee.)
(85 Fed. Rep., 271; circuit court of appeals, sixth circuit.)
(175 U. S., 211; Supreme Court, December 4, 1899; Opin., Peckham, J.)

This case grew out of a combination of six shops, located, one in Ohio, one in Kentucky, two in Tennessee, and two in Alabama, which were engaged in making cast-iron pipe for gas, water, and sewer purposes. These shops controlled the market in that commodity in thirty-six states west of the Alleghany mountains and south of Virginia. They entered into an agreement to control prices by suppressing competition among themselves. This was done by appointing a representative board of

[1] See Chapter V, p. 86, *supra* for fuller details.

one from each shop, to which all inquiries for pipe were referred. The board fixed the price it thought the job would stand. The job was then sold over the table, the shop which bid the highest bonus for the benefit of the pool getting it. At the public letting, the shop that got the job bid the fixed price, and the other shops overbid in order to deceive the public.

On behalf of the combination it was contended that the power of Congress, under the interstate-commerce clause, does not extend to agreements among private corporations, but is limited to acts of interference by the states and by quasi-public corporations, such as railroads. Private manufacturing corporations, it was insisted, are not public agencies and cannot be compelled to keep their shops running or sell their goods to any person who applies. In the next place, it was urged that there was no restraint put upon interstate commerce, and that under the decision in the Knight case the creation of a monopoly in the manufacture of a commodity is not prohibited by the Anti-Trust Law.

The Supreme Court held, however, that Congress may prohibit the performance of any agreement between individuals or corporations where the natural and direct effect of it is to regulate or restrain interstate commerce. In other words, the Anti-Trust Law applies to every agreement in restraint of interstate trade, whether made by corporations or individuals.

In the next place the Court held that any agreement or combination which directly restrains not only the manufacture but the sale of a commodity among the several states comes within the Anti-Trust Law.

Commenting on the Knight case the Court said (page 240):

> The case was decided upon the principle that a combination simply to control manufacture was not a violation of the act of Congress, because such a contract or combination did not directly control or affect interstate commerce, but that contracts for the sale and transportation to other states of specific articles were proper subjects for regulation because they did form part of such commerce.

II. QUESTIONS WHICH ARE PENDING IN THE COURTS

CHAMPION *v.* AMES AND FRANCIS *v.* UNITED STATES (SUPREME COURT)

(The Lottery Cases)

These cases arose under the act of March 2, 1895 (28 Stat., 963), which makes it an offence to cause lottery tickets or matter "to be carried from one state to another." The Francis case grew out of the transit of a man carrying a lottery ticket from Newport, Ky., to Cincinnati, Ohio, across an interstate bridge; the Champion case from the carriage by an express company over a railroad, for hire, of a box of lottery tickets from one state to another.

The provision prohibiting the carriage of lottery tickets from one state to another by any instrumentality was designed to supplement the prohibition of the carriage of lottery matter through the mails, and thus make the law effective. Its constitutionality is assailed on the ground that while, under the power to establish post-offices and post-roads, Congress may exclude from the mails lottery matter, it has no authority, under the power to regulate commerce among the several states, to prohibit the carriage of lottery matter from one state to another.

The cases have been argued three times, and are now under advisement.

Those assailing the law insist that a lottery ticket is not an article of commerce, its carriage is not interstate commerce, and therefore Congress has not power to prohibit its carriage from one state to another. It is further contended that even if such carriage be commerce, the power to regulate does not include the power to prohibit.

On the other side, the Government insists that as lottery tickets are commonly bought and sold they are articles of commerce; but even if not, their carriage from state to state is commerce, inasmuch as transit or transportation is not merely a means of commerce, but is commerce itself.

With respect to the second point, the Government contends that the right to regulate includes the right to prohibit, where the character of the article warrants its exclusion from commerce.

The judgment and opinion of the Court may therefore more clearly define the nature of interstate commerce and the extent of the power of Congress to regulate it.

Since decided, Feb. 23, 1903, in favor of the United States. 188 U. S., 321, and 188 U. S., 375. — Ed.

United States *v.* Northern Securities Company et al.[1]

(United States circuit court, district of Minnesota.)

(Petition filed March 10, 1902.)

In the year 1901 the Northern Pacific Railway Company and the Great Northern Railway Company operated two parallel and competing transcontinental lines of railway, extending across the northern tier of states west of the Great Lakes, from the Great Lakes and the Mississippi River to the Pacific Ocean, each system connecting at its eastern terminals, not only with lines of railway, but with lake and river steamers to other states and to foreign countries, and at its western terminals with sea-going vessels to other states, territories, and possessions of the United States, and to foreign countries, and were then engaged in active competition with one another in freight and passenger traffic among the several states and with foreign countries.

Early in that year, these two railway companies, acting for the purpose of promoting their joint interests, and, as the Government claims, in contemplation of the ultimate placing of the Northern Pacific and Great Northern systems under a common source of control, united in the purchase of the total capital stock of the Chicago, Burlington, and Quincy Railway Company, issuing for that purpose about $200,000,000 of their joint bonds, at the rate of $200 in bonds for each $100 in stock. The Burlington system was about 8000 miles in length, covering the vast region between Chicago and St. Paul on the east, and Kansas City, Denver, Cheyenne, and Billings on the west, and was gradually pushing its rails northwesterly into the territory

[1] The final decision of March 14, 1904, is reprinted in full at p. 322, *infra*. — Ed.

occupied by the purchasers, and westerly toward the Pacific Ocean. It connected with the Great Northern and Northern Pacific systems at St. Paul and with the Northern Pacific system at Billings, Mont., and was in part parallel and competing with the Union Pacific system.

Shortly after the purchase of the Burlington system the controlling stockholders of the Northern Pacific and Great Northern companies organized, under the laws of New Jersey, the Northern Securities Company, with a capital stock of $400,000,000, for the purpose of exchanging its stock for the stock of the two railway companies, at the rate of exchange of $115 of the capital stock of the Northern Securities Company for each share of the capital stock of the Northern Pacific, and $180 of the capital stock of the Northern Securities Company for each share of the capital stock of the Great Northern. The subscribed capital of the Northern Securities was but $30,000 and its authorized capital of $400,000,000 was just sufficient, when all issued, to represent and cover the exchange value of the entire stock of the two railway companies, at the rate agreed upon, which was about $122,000,000 in excess of the combined capital stock of the two railroad companies taken at par.

The suit filed by the Government was against the Northern Securities Company, the two railway companies, and their controlling stockholders, for the purpose of dissolving the merger resulting from the creation of a holding corporation and the turning over to it of the stock of the railway companies.

It is the contention of the Government that, by the creation of the holding corporation and its taking over the stock of the competing railway companies, the individual stockholders of the formerly competing railway companies were to be eliminated and a single common stockholder, the holding company, was to be substituted; the interest of the individual stockholders in the property and franchises of the two railway companies was to terminate, being thus converted into an interest in the property and franchises of the Northern Securities Company. The individual stockholders of the Northern Pacific Company were no longer to hold an interest in the property or draw their dividends from the earnings of the Northern Pacific system, and the individual stockholders of the Great Northern were no longer to hold an interest in the property or draw their dividends from the earnings of the Great Northern system, but having ceased to be stockholders in the railway companies and having become stockholders in the holding corporation, both were to draw their dividends from the earnings of both systems, collected and distributed by the holding corporation. In this manner, by making the stockholders of each system jointly interested in both systems, and by practically pooling the earnings of both systems for the benefit of the former stockholders of each, and by vesting the selection of the directors and officers of each system in a common body, to wit, the holding corporation, with not only the power but the duty to pursue a policy which would promote the interests, not of one system at the expense of the other, but of both at the expense of the public, all inducement for competition between the two systems was to be removed, a virtual consolidation effected, and a monopoly of the interstate and foreign commerce formerly carried on by the two systems as independent competitors established.

It is further contended that the Northern Securities Company was not organized in good faith to purchase and pay for the stocks of the Great Northern and the Northern Pacific Railway companies. It was organized solely to incorporate the pooling of the stocks of said companies. It is a mere depositary, custodian, holder, and trustee of the stocks of the Great Northern and the Northern Pacific Railway companies, and its shares of stock are virtually but beneficial certificates issued against such railroad stocks to designate the interest of the holders in the pool.

At the time of the passage of the act of July 2, 1890, the method used to combine competing companies was by placing their stocks in the hands of trustees and issuing trust certificates in exchange therefor. The interesting question in this case is whether substantially the same result can be reached by creating a holding corporation to take over the stock of companies competing in interstate commerce, and thus pool their earnings, consolidate their control, and remove all inducement for effective competition between them.

UNITED STATES *v.* SWIFT & CO. ET AL. (THE BEEF TRUST CASE)

(United States circuit court, northern district of Illinois.)

(Petition filed May 10, 1902.)

This is a bill of complaint, brought by the direction of the Attorney-General, against seven corporations, one partnership and twenty-three persons, constituting what is commonly called "The Beef Trust," engaged in the business of purchasing live stock, converting the same into fresh and cured meats, and selling the products to dealers and consumers throughout the United States and in foreign countries. The bill charges the defendants with being engaged in a combination or conspiracy to restrain trade or commerce in the articles mentioned among the several states and with foreign countries, and to monopolize or attempt to monopolize, the same by a number of different methods which are set out in detail in the bill, to wit, by requiring their agents to refrain from bidding against each other in the purchase of live stock; by collusively bidding up the market price for a time in order to attract shipments of live stock to the yards and then refraining from bidding; by arbitrarily fixing uniform prices on interstate sales of meat, either directly or through their agents, and by lowering or raising such prices; by curtailing the quantity of meats shipped from one state to another; by fixing uniform terms of credit to dealers and uniform charges for cartage, for the purpose of preventing competition in the interstate sales of meat; and by combining to secure rebates on interstate shipments of meat products from the railway companies.

A demurrer, general and special, was filed by the defendants, which was argued on December 16, 1902, and is now under advisement by the court. The contention of the defendants is, that although the live stock may have been purchased in states other than where converted into fresh meats, and the fresh meats sold in states other than where prepared, nevertheless the shipments between these states were in no wise affected by the arrangement complained of, which only touched the live stock at the point of purchase and the meats at the point of sale, both local. Therefore they insist that no restraint of interstate commerce is shown.

Since decided April 18, 1903, in favor of the Government, holding that such a combination is in effect in restraint of trade. 122 Fed. Rep., 529. The case now awaits argument in the Supreme Court.— ED.

UNITED STATES *v.* RAILROADS (THE RAILROAD INJUNCTION SUITS)

These are bills in equity, filed by direction of the Attorney-General, against fourteen railroad companies, eight pending in the United States circuit court for the western district of Missouri, and six in the United States circuit court for the northern district of Illinois.

The bills allege that the railroad companies (acting separately) combined with certain favored shippers to grant the latter unlawful rebates or concessions from their published tariffs in rates on grain, carried from one state to another, notwithstanding they maintained their published rates as against all other grain dealers and the general public.

It appeared, from the investigation made, that on each of the principal grain-carrying railroads a different shipper enjoyed this preference. The discrimination was so great that the grain dealer denied the preference could not long continue in the business in competition with the favored one. The effect of the preference was to force those who conformed to the law out of the grain business, leaving the favored dealers to enjoy a practical monopoly of the purchase and shipment of grain on the railroads preferring them.

As the Federal courts have held that, under the interstate-commerce law, a corporation is not indictable, only its officers being answerable for violations, and that unjust discrimination does not exist where no other shipper pays the published rate at the same time the preferred shipper receives the concession, it will be observed that the penal provisions of the interstate-commerce act afford no practical remedy. Even if the act should be amended so as to make the corporation criminally liable, no adequate relief would be afforded to those who wish to engage in the grain business. To open the business to them, it is necessary to prevent the railroads from granting preferences in transportation rates or facilities.

This being the situation, the bills in equity were filed, in which, after reciting the facts, it is claimed that not only were the acts complained of in violation of the interstate-commerce act, but also were in restraint of trade or commerce among the several states, and constituted an attempt to monopolize such commerce in the grain business, in violation of the act of July 2, 1890.

Temporary injunctions were passed upon by Judge Grosscup in April, 1903, 122 Fed. Rep., 544. The Elkins amendment to the act to regulate commerce had meanwhile been enacted. The right of the Government to maintain a suit in equity was recognized. — Ed.

The railroad companies demurred to the bills, contending:

1. That the remedies provided in the act to regulate commerce are exclusive, and do not include a remedy by injunction at the suit of the Government.

2. That under the general jurisdiction in equity, injunction does not lie to restrain the violation of a law, even if the public is being injured by such violation.

3. That a combination between a railroad company and a shipper to grant the latter an unlawful rebate, which results in establishing a monopoly, is not covered or condemned by the provisions of the act of July 2, 1890; and therefore the remedy by injunction will not lie under the law.

The demurrers were argued December 15, 1902, before the judges (sitting together) of the two circuit courts, and are now held under advisement.

Montague & Company *v.* Lowry

(Error to the circuit court of appeals for the ninth circuit.)

(193 U.S. Rep., 38. Decided February 23, 1904.)

An association was formed in California by manufacturers of and dealers in tiles, mantels and grates; the dealers agreed not to purchase materials from manufacturers who were not members, and not to sell unset tiles for less than list prices, which were fifty per cent higher than to members. Manufacturers, resident in other states than California, agreed not to sell to any other than members. Membership was prescribed by rules, such as carrying $3000 worth of stock. A firm of outside dealers who were not members, and who did not carry $3000 worth of stock, brought action under § 7 of the Anti-Trust Act of 1890. It was held, that although sales within the state were but a small part of the total transactions involved, the general effect of the scheme was to enhance prices; and that it was impossible to separate intra-state from inter-state business; and that a combination in restraint of trade had been shown. The parties aggrieved were entitled to recover threefold damages as found by the jury. — Ed.

III. SUGGESTIONS RESPECTING LEGISLATION

I come now to your invitation to communicate to the committee "any suggestions that your reflection or experience shall suggest as to what may be desirable in the way of further legislation."

In view of the wide experience of the committee in dealing legislatively with legal and economic questions, I venture upon the line of suggestion with much hesitation and feeling that the utmost the committee desires in this respect is that some concrete thing be set down that may be considered, in connection with other views that may be presented, as to what might be done within the short period allowed for consideration during the life of this present Congress.

I think it proper enough to briefly premise such suggestions as I shall make for immediate action by a statement of some of the reasons upon which they are based.

The end desired by the overwhelming majority of the people of all sections of the country is that combinations of capital should be regulated and not destroyed, and that measures should be taken to correct the tendency toward monopolization of the industrial business of the country. I assume a thing to be avoided, even by suggestion, is legislation regulating the business interests of the country beyond such as will accomplish this end.

In my judgment, a monopoly in any industry would be impossible in this country, where money is abundant and cheap and in the hands or within the reach of keen and capable men, if competition were assured of a fair and open field and protected against unfair, artificial, and discriminating practices.

Two or more persons or corporations cannot by any combination or arrangement between themselves either contract or expand the rights of others to engage in a similar business. The utmost they can do is to discourage the disposition to do so by restricting the opportunities, or by securing to themselves some exclusive facilities or the enjoyment of some common facilities upon exclusive terms.

If the law will guarantee to the small producer protection against piratical methods in competition and keep the highways to the markets open and available to him for the same tolls charged to his powerful competitor, he will manage to live and thrive to an astonishing degree.

Individualism in production has its advantages as well as combination. Small individual enterprises not uncommonly spring up and thrive within the shadow of the larger ones, though enjoying none of their supposed advantages of control of sources of raw material, fuel, and transportation facilities, yet realizing large profit per ton of output because of the closer economies possible through direct, personal, interested management. Indeed, it is true that the great concerns whose stocks have been gathered in by the holding companies (the real trusts) are themselves largely but aggregations of successful smaller ones which, one by one, have made their competition so severely felt by an ambitious rival that he has absorbed them.

I believe the rebates and kindred advantages granted by carriers to large operators in the leading industries of the country, as against their competitors, in many years amounted to a sum that would represent fair interest upon the actual money invested in the business of such operators.

If substantially all of a given business is controlled by one company, the more threatening to potential competition does this iniquity become, and with greater timidity does such competition approach the field.

In some respects the holding company is weaker than its independent rivals. It pays as much, if not more, for labor. Advantage in the saving of an intermediate profit upon raw material and fuel is largely offset by the enormous cost of the sources of supply represented in high capitalization.

This capitalization, in almost every case of a holding company, represents far more than the aggregate intrinsic value of its constituent companies. The method of computing values for purpose of concentration has invariably been upon earning power, and rebates have frequently swelled earnings so that enormous volumes of capital stock represent nothing but unfair advantage obtained over rivals.

The situation is much improved in respect to transportation discriminations within the last two years. This is the result, first, of a determined effort upon the part of the Government to apply existing laws in an effective way against discrimination; and second, to the fact that some of the higher-minded railroad managers of the country have exerted their large influence in the direction of equitable dealing with the shippers of the territory which they serve. Whether it is a consequence of these influences or a mere coincidence, it is nevertheless stated on high authority to be a fact that the embarkation of new capital in enterprises in competition with the supposedly controlled industries within the period named probably equals the capital of the trusts. The effect of certainty of protection against predatory competition can be safely prophesied to increase this figure.

The country is filled with men whose lives have been devoted to industry, who have developed and made profitable the properties now possessed by the trusts at prices far in excess of the cost of modernized duplicates, who will not long remain idle when assured that their capital and experience can be securely employed in the business to which they were trained.

Too much has been conceded in public discussion to the trusts in this respect. Organizations in one state to control production in other states of commodities consumed in all the states are as a rule devices of shrewd men to capitalize for their own benefit the country's prosperity. They are begotten in prosperous times. Poor times offer no inducements. They are essentially different from the combinations effected by producers, of their own motion, for economic reasons. Those which have been recklessly conceived contain within themselves the germ of their own undoing. They have, as a rule, only acquired the ownership of the stocks of the industries of the country which had already attained their gigantic stature. Their existence does not increase the productive capacity of the country, except as high prices of products have stimulated competition, nor have they because of their existence increased demand, as the demand for products has never been thought to depend upon the title to capital stocks of producing companies.

My suggestion, therefore, is that as a first step in a policy to be persistently pursued until every industry, large and small, in the country can be assured of equal rights and opportunities, and until the tendency to monopolization of the important industries of the country is checked, that all discriminatory practices affecting interstate trade be made offences to be enjoined and punished. Such legislation to be directed alike against those who give and those who receive the advantages thereof and to cover discrimination in prices as against competitors in particular localities resorted to for the purpose of destroying competition in interstate and foreign trade, as well as discrimination by carriers.

Such practices are so obviously unreasonable that to inhibit them would be a measure of regulation of commerce to keep it free and unrestrained and not an attempt to exercise arbitrary power. Such legislation, to certainly reach producers guilty of practices injurious to national and international commerce, should, in my judgment, take the form of penalizing the transportation of the goods produced by the guilty parties, and the Federal courts should be given power to restrain such transportation at the suit of the Government.

It may be said that under the "act to regulate commerce," a shipper may be punished for receiving rebates or special rates less than the lawful published rates; and that it is unnecessary to provide additional legislation in this respect to curb trusts, monopolies, and combinations. This, however, is an erroneous statement.

Whatever the Congress may have designed in the act to regulate commerce regarding the punishment of shippers for participation in violation of that act, as construed by the courts, their punishable offences fall under two heads:

First. Where the shipper has solicited or participated in instances of unjust discrimination, and

Second. In cases of fraud perpetrated by him against the carrier, ex. gr., by false representation of the contents of a package.

As to the first, the courts have held that to constitute unjust discrimination it is necessary to prove that at the time the lower unlawful rate was being granted to the favored shipper, the higher lawful rate was imposed against another shipper on like commodities between the same points.

In many cases of departure by a carrier from its published tariffs, the favored shipper has enjoyed his advantage for so long a time that all rivals have disappeared. In such cases, and they are the most numerous, no illegal discrimination exists; consequently the recipient of the unlawful rebates escapes the penalties of the act to regulate commerce.

The act prohibits the carrier from charging any one a greater or less rate than the rates named in its schedules; but the penalties provided therefor have been held by the courts not to be applicable to any carrier that is an incorporated company.

The officers or agents of such incorporated company, who grant the rebate or make the unlawful concession in rates, are subject to indictment and punishment. That, however, is generally an impracticable remedy, because the agent who makes the concession is usually the only person by whom it can be ascertained that the rebate has been paid; and when he has testified in relation to the matter he has thereby obtained amnesty from prosecution.

Even if the corporation and its officers could be effectively reached by criminal proceedings, the law leaves unrestrained the persons, corporations, and combinations who are beneficiaries of the unlawful rebates.

This *casus omissus* of the act to regulate commerce should be supplied by imposing a penalty upon the incorporated carrier and beneficiary alike, and the right of courts to restrain such practices at the suit of the United States, a right not settled and now vigorously challenged, should be made certain.

I think the operation of such an act should be limited to the transportation by common carriers subject to the act to regulate commerce. This is necessary for the reason that there is no requirement of law that rates shall be published by common carriers, except by railroad, or railroad and water, carriers acting as one line. When the act to regulate commerce was under consideration it was deemed impracticable if not unwise to attempt to regulate the rates of water or other common carriers. It was understood that in the nature of things water rates could not be stable.

In addition to that it was believed that water competition must be unrestricted. As it is the least expensive means of transportation, it, wherever it could directly or indirectly compete with carriers by rail, would, approximately, furnish a basis for rates by railroad, and measurably keep such rates within the limits of extortion.

So that if provision is made by law to prevent rebates, a standard or established schedule must be referred to; and as the admitted abuse of magnitude has been in the favors granted by railroad companies, their rates, which the law requires shall be made public, should be taken as the rates which must be adhered to and made equal to all the people under similar conditions.

It should, therefore, be made unlawful to transport traffic by carriers subject to the "act to regulate commerce" at any rate less than such carriers' published rate, and all who participate in the violation of such law should be punished.

An additional provision should be made to reach corporations, combinations, and associations which produce and manufacture wholly within a state, but whose products or sales enter into interstate commerce. It should relate, first, to such concerns as fatten on rebates in transportation, and, second, to concerns which sell below the general price of a commodity in particular localities, or otherwise in particular localities wantonly seek to destroy competition. These could be excluded with their commodities, products, or manufactures from crossing state lines.

As the power of Congress over interstate commerce is plenary, excepting as it may be limited by the Constitution, it is believed that it may impose such a punishment for the violation of the public policy of the nation.

A comprehensive plan should be framed to enable the Government to get at all the facts bearing upon the organization and practices of concerns engaged in interstate and foreign commerce essential to a full understanding thereof and to compel the observance of the law. This should be framed upon tested lines.

A commission should be created to aid in carrying out the provisions of the act of July 2, 1890, and any further legislation relating to commerce. It should be the duty of such commission, among other things, to make diligent investigation into the operations and conduct of all corporations, combinations, and concerns engaged in interstate or foreign commerce, and to gather such information and data as would enable it to make specific recommendations for additional legislation for the regulation of commerce, and annually, and oftener if it shall seem needful, to make report thereon to the President.

Such a commission should have authority to inquire into the management of the business of such corporations and concerns, to keep itself informed as to the manner and method in which the same is conducted, and to obtain from such concerns full and complete information necessary to enable the commission to perform the duties and carry out the objects for which it is created; it should have the power, when in its judgment it is necessary, to require reports from them and to require from them and their officers, agents, and employees specific answers to all questions upon which the commission needs information. As there are no means now provided by law for compelling testimony, such a law should provide that no person should be excused from attending and testifying or from producing books, papers, contracts, and documents before such commission or the courts.

Of course, the general scheme of legislation to correct trust abuses should be developed with great care, for it is not nearly so important to act quickly as to act wisely. Primarily, the question of the power of Congress to reach what the Sherman Act seems to have missed should be authoritatively determined, as upon that proposition the whole structure of effective regulative legislation must rest. We should at once take the first steps by a law aimed at what we certainly know to be unreasonable practices directly restrictive of freedom of commerce upon which the fundamental question can be raised, and by a law conferring upon the Government a general supervisory power as above outlined.

Another step in legislation which I earnestly recommend, and which will, if enacted, greatly hasten a solution of the problem, is that an act be passed as soon as possible to speed the final decision of cases now pending and others that may be raised under the Anti-Trust Law. I refer to an act to enable the Attorney-General to secure the original hearing by a full bench of the circuit judges in the circuit wherein is pending any suit brought by the United States under the Anti-Trust Law which the Attorney-General certifies to the court to involve questions of great public importance, and giving an appeal from their decision directly to the Supreme Court of the United States in such cases, and also giving an appeal directly to the Supreme Court in all pending cases in which the United States is a party which have been heard and are as yet unappealed.

There are a number of cases now provided by statute where appeals may be made directly to the Supreme Court from the district and circuit courts, namely, in cases in which the jurisdiction of the court is in issue, from final sentences and decrees in prize cases, in cases of conviction of a capital or otherwise infamous crime, in cases that involve the construction or application of the Constitution of the United States, in cases in which the constitutionality of any law of the United States, or the validity or construction of any treaty is drawn in question, and in cases in which the constitution or law of a state is claimed to be in contravention of the Constitution of the United States.

The class of cases that I suggest should be brought within this rule, it seems to me, is of as great importance as any of those referred to. The suggested provision requiring a full bench of the circuit judges would insure the cases receiving as full consideration before presentation to the Supreme Court as if heard by the United States circuit court of appeals.

It is too much to say that with these gaps closed the scheme of governmental regulation will be complete; but it is clear that without some similar legislation it would continue to be inadequate. And such legislation will make a long, first stride in advance.

Very respectfully yours,

P. C. Knox,

Attorney-General.

XIII

THE TIN-PLATE INDUSTRY[1]

I

BY tin-plate is meant a sheet of iron or steel varying in thickness from 22 to 30 wire gauge coated with tin. In the language of the trade, plates before they are covered with tin are referred to as "black plates." These plates are made in several sizes, but the standard is a plate 14x20 inches and when coated with tin is placed in a box containing 225 sheets.[2] These boxes weigh 108 lbs. Besides the regular commercial tin-plate is another commodity made by the mills which is called "terne plate." A terne plate is an iron or steel sheet covered with an alloy of lead and tin, generally two-thirds lead and one-third tin. The terne plate is used very largely for roofing and cornice purposes.

The method of manufacturing tin and terne plates is rather simple so far as the process is concerned, but a great deal of skill is required to turn out good plates. The process begins with the rolling of thin sheets from billets of steel especially prepared for the industry. When the required thickness has been reached the plates are sheared to a size and made ready for pickling. A plate is pickled when placed in a bath of sulphuric acid and water. This process clears the sheets of scales. When taken out of the pickling bath the plates are rinsed free of the acid and packed in pans with layers of sawdust between the plates. The pans are then carefully sealed and put in an annealing furnace, where they are allowed to remain for ten hours. The heat of the furnace is gradually reduced and the plates allowed to cool slowly. A second rolling is now neces-

[1] From the *Yale Review*, November, 1898, and August, 1899.

[2] Called by the trade IC, 14x20, and weighing 50 lbs. or less per 100 sq. ft. Other grades are IX, weighing between 50 and 62½ lbs.; and IXX, weighing 63 lbs. per 100 sq. ft.

sary. This is done by passing them through three sets of cold steel rollers. Another sulphuric acid bath and annealing are undertaken and the plates are ready for tinning. In the tinning department the plates are first coated with grease, then dipped into the tinning pot, taken out and placed in a bath of molten tin. The plates are brushed, again greased and passed through melted tin for a third time. The plates are now allowed to cool, carefully wiped free of grease, assorted and packed in boxes according to quality. This is the process of tin-plate manufacture.[1]

The tin used in the process comes from several sources. The best of these is found in Australia and the Straits Settlements. The latter furnish the most desirable tin, known as Banca tin. This is regarded as the purest, and is in consequence more sought after by the manufacturers of tin-plate. The Cornwall mines were discovered about 55 B.C. and for twelve centuries were the one source of this mineral. In 1240 tin was found in Bohemia. Five hundred years later, in 1760, the Banca mines were opened. In the following century Australia became a producer of block tin on a large scale. From 1872 tin has been found in commercial quantities in New South Wales, Queensland, and Tasmania. The United States have not been so fortunate, although many attempts have been made from time to time to find tin. Tin was discovered in California as early as 1840, but there was no mining done until 1868. Only for a short time were the mines operated; they were then closed down, and remained so until 1888. In this year an American company bought the property with the intention of operating, but it was sold to an English syndicate before two years had passed.[2] Something like $800,000 were spent, but no special results were secured. The total product of the mine was 269,000 lbs. of tin valued at $56,000.[3] The Harney Peak mine is the story of another futile attempt to get tin in commercial quantities. The Harney Peak, as it is familiarly called, is situated near Custer City, S. D. A great deal of money has been spent in the development of this mine, but it is doubtful if

[1] Senate Ex. Doc., 52 Cong., 1 Sess., Vol. 6, No. 102, p. 11. J. D. Weeks in Tin-Plate Industry, Pittsburg, 1892.

[2] Senate Ex. Doc., 52 Cong., 1 Sess., Vol. 6, No. 102, p. 45.

[3] Mineral Industry, Vol. I, p. 542.

more than ten tons of metal have been taken out of the ground.[1] The English capitalists were also heavily interested in this attempt. In Alabama, North Carolina, and Virginia tin-bearing rock has been found. In no sense can the United States be regarded as a tin-producing country.[2]

The cost of mining tin varies with locality, kind of labor employed, and character of the ore. The average cost of breaking and selecting ores in the Cornish mines is from 4*s.* to 8*s.*, per ton of ore; the depreciation of machinery is estimated at 2*d.* The total mining charges average £12 to the ton of tin, the dressing costs £9, and management, expense of buildings, and wear and tear on machinery carry the amount to £35 per ton of tin. This statement of cost is not altogether accurate, but is probably very near the truth. Banca mines have the advantage of cheap labor. The price paid there for experienced labor is £1 per month. The workmen average twelve hundredweight of metallic tin per year.[3] The yield of the Cornwall mines is about 20 per cent of the tin ore or 45 lbs. of tin to the ton of ore.

Before the ore is ready for reduction to pig tin, the sulphur and arsenic must be driven off by roasting the ore. This requires from twelve to eighteen hours. The consumption of fuel for refining is thirty to thirty-five hundredweight per ton of metallic tin. The tin of the Banca mines is almost pure, so that it has a decided advantage in cost of production. Although England is so near to the Cornish mines the price of block tin in London is about the same as in New York. The prices given on March 4, 1898, at New York, per long ton of 2240 lbs., was $310.44. At London Straits tin (Banca) was sold for $311.10.[4] It will be seen from this statement that the manufacturers of tin-plate in England have no particular advantage over the American producers so far as the raw material is concerned. It might be

[1] *Supra, Ibid.*

[2] The total tin production of the world in 1895 was estimated at 186,786,880 lbs. Of this amount the United States imported 54,252,045 lbs., or 29 per cent, at a valuation of $7,405,619. See U. S. Geological Survey, 1895; Mineral Industry, Vol. I, p. 457.

[3] Tin and Terne Plate, J. D. Weeks, p. 13.

[4] The prices given above are taken from the Monthly Summary of Finance and Commerce of the U. S., Feb. 1, 1898, pp. 1207, 1218. The price in New York was 14.35c. per pound, and £64 16*s.* 3*d.* per ton in London.

urged that the Cornish mines undersell the Straits, but the fact is that Cornish mines are not able to supply all the English demand for tin. Naturally the price of tin is governed by the price of Straits tin.

II

The United States have always been a large consumer of tin-plate. In 1892 this country was taking 60 per cent of the English production of the commodity. A remarkable falling off in the imports occurred in 1898. This decline began with the tariff legislation of 1890. The table below tells the story more forcibly than words can.

Importations of English Tin-Plate

1893	628,425,902 lbs.
1894	454,160,826 "
1895	508,038,938 "
1896	385,138,983 "
1897	230,073,683 "

A similar decline has taken place in the imports of black plates not yet tinned, as indicated in the following table:

Importation of English Black Plates

Year	Long Tons	Pounds
1893	—	—
1894	—	—
1895	8914	19,967,560
1896	3128	7,006,720
1897	689	1,554,360
1898[1]	171	381,040

The demand as well as the consumption of tin and terne plates has not decreased in any way, so that the source of supply must be looked for elsewhere than in England. This demand is therefore largely supplied by the American industry. The statement here made is further upheld by the fact that in 1892 some 13,642,719 lbs. of tin-plate were made in the United States, 31 per cent of which was manufactured from foreign black plates. The amount had increased enormously in 1897, so that 446,982,063 lbs. were produced, and of this amount only

[1] January and February, 1898. Tin and Terne, March 24, 1898.

one per cent was made from foreign black plates.[1] These facts certainly indicate the existence of a rapidly growing industry.

Leaving the matter of the tariff out of consideration for the time being, the United States were handicapped in the early history of the industry by the high price of labor, the lack of technical knowledge concerning the industry, and the distance of iron ore from fuel. These difficulties have been overcome in some measure. The industrial depression from 1892–97 was a decided aid to the growing industry. The wages of labor fell about 15 per cent in this period, although there is a marked tendency at present to recover from the decline. The fall in the wages of labor placed the English and American makers more nearly on a basis of equality. As a general thing, American labor is quicker and works harder than even the English workingman. This does not hold true in the tin industry. The reduction in wages just referred to was not sufficient of itself to make up differences in cost. According to Sir R. Griffen, the Welsh laborer averages £1 *2s.* 5*d.* per week, equivalent to $5.46, while in Pennsylvania the wages average $10.68 per week.[2] The higher American wages are not accompanied by an increased efficiency of labor. Taken all in all, the Welsh producer makes tin-plate about 30 per cent cheaper than the American, but the latter when purchasing from the former has never got the benefit of the $2.20 per box cost. Tin can be delivered in New York, freight paid, for $2.49 per box[3] by the English merchant. Tin never reached this point until the Americans began to make it.

The knowledge of the method of manufacture had also to be acquired. This gave for a while an additional advantage to the English makers. The distance of ore from fuel was another question involving delay and expense. In this matter the last five years have seen a remarkable improvement. Ore is now mined by steam shovels and then conveyed in steel barges to the ports of Lake Erie, where it is sent by rail to the smelters. The old method of bringing fuel to the ore has been abandoned, the ore is now brought to the fuel. Lower freight

[1] Report of Special Agent Ayer, January, 1898, Treasury Department, p. 8.
[2] Eng. Foreign Office Report, Mis. No. 26, p. 10. [3] *Ibid.*, p. 11.

rates have made this possible. So cheap has steel become in this country through these various processes and changes that it is now exported to England.[1]

In the cost of steel bars (Bessemer) the tin-plate makers of the United States had an advantage over the English of about 20 per cent in April, 1896.[2] In March, 1897, the price ranged from $15.50 per ton to $16.00.[3] As the price has not materially changed the advantage still remains. Mr. J. D. Weeks, in an article on the Tin-Plate Industry, referred to above, gives four statements of cost of manufacture in Wales. An English correspondent gives one, placing the cost of making a box 14 x 20 I C tin-plates at 13*s.* 4*d.* The United States Consul gives another estimate, placing the cost at 11*s.* 9.6*d.* Still another statement is made in which 12*s.* 2½*d.* is regarded as the expense of production. The most conservative and reliable report, which proves to be that of a former manufacturer of tin-plate, fixes the cost at 12*s.* 6*d.* This last amount is equivalent in our money to $3.11. A deduction of 18 cents should be made from this amount for saving in waste, making the cost equivalent to $2.93.[4] This estimate is rather old. Since its

[1] Eng. Foreign Office, Mis. Rep. No. 426, p. 5.

[2] Price steel bars (Bessemer) U. S., $15.50 per ton = £3 2*s.*
" " " England, " £3 17*s.*

[3] Monthly Summary U. S. Commerce, p. 1212.

[4] J. D. Weeks, Tin-Plate Industry, 1892, p. 22.

Statement of Cost

Steel bars at works, 136 lbs. at £4 15*s.* per ton	$1.39
Block tin	.62
Sulphuric acid	.10
Flux for tinning	.01
Coal for steam and heating works	.16
Costing for general repairs	.04
Clay, brick, lumber for boxes	.08
Nails, hemp, skin brushes, bran	.01½
Palm oil	.06
Other items not enumerated	.04½
Material	$2.52
Labor	.58½
	$3.11
Credit for waste	.18
	$2.93

date, 1878, a great many improvements have been made in machinery, and the cost of steel has been reduced very materially. With the cost of steel just given the expense of production would be cut down to $2.56. The improved machinery will still further reduce this price to the one now ruling in England, $2.20. As will be remembered, the American wages averaged about twice those paid in Wales. This will materially increase the cost of the American product, so that it is not likely that American tin-plate is manufactured under a cost of $2.75 per box for first-class material. The present price of tin-plate in this country leaves a margin of 75 to 85 cents per box for our producers. When the commissions and profits of middle men are taken from this, it will be seen that tin-plate is being sold close to cost. If this is true, an adjustment of prices to the industry and the demand must follow which will again give the English industry some hope of entering our markets.

Properly equipped machinery was difficult to secure at first. This part of the problem has been met by inventions and improvements over the English machines. In this matter it is probable that the Americans have been most successful in reducing the expense. The preparation of steel is the best example. In tinning machinery the advance has been much slower and less satisfactory. Under the English system the mills are run by one central engine, while in this country the tendency has been to run an engine for each set of mills. This increases the expense for coal and adds to the cost of manufacture, but gives greater efficiency. The mills in the United States are better built and can do more work. It remains to be seen whether the industry will warrant the elaborate preparations which have been made.

III

The legislation for the establishment of the tin-plate industry rests upon three ideas: first, that seventy millions of people should not depend upon Welsh works for tin-plate; second, that the foreign tin-plate is poorly made and does not meet our particular wants; third, that the country needs a new industry in which more labor can be employed. In these three statements we have a blending of the commercial, the economic, and the political. So long as the foreign makers possessed a monopoly, they refused to listen to any suggestions from this side of the water concerning the improvement of their plate. There were also times when the foreign dealers took advantage of the scarcity of tin-plate in this country to force up the price. This attitude naturally influenced very considerably the American mind. Behind the scenes another class, the men who owned supposed tin mines, endeavored to secure the attention of Congress. They were anxious that the tin-plate industry should be encouraged, provided that block tin was put on the tariff list. Manufacturers of steel were ready to make tin-plates if adequate protection was given them. When the various elements, just mentioned, were coupled with public opinion, which after all was public indifference, and brought to bear upon Congress, the necessary legislation was forthcoming. The new industry having received these necessary conditions, it was considered that time alone was all that was needed to bring it into full fruitage.

Previous to 1890 block tin had been on the free list for twenty years, while tin-plate had been subject to a duty since 1864. Under the tariff of 1883, no tin-plate was produced in this country. The consumers of the article paid $35,000,000 in duties for the support of an industry that did not come into existence.[1] The probable reason for the failure to establish an industry was the lack of facilities for making steel plates. In addition to this the financial condition of the country hardly warranted any extension of enterprise. The tariff of 1864 placed a duty of 2½ cents per pound on "all imports of tin-plates and iron galvanized, or coated with any metal by electric batteries or otherwise." The Treasury Department so construed the law that a duty of 15 per cent "ad valorem" was substituted in the place of the original amount.[2] Although the protection thus given was low, nevertheless several plants were built in the hope that the high price then ruling would continue. It did not do so, and the plants were forced out of the business.[3]

[1] House Reports, 52 Cong., 1 Sess., Vol. 4, No. 1040. [2] *Ibid.*

[3] Plants were established at Wellsville, Ohio, 1872; Leechburg, Pa., 1873; Demmler, Pa., 1875.

There was no real effort to manufacture tin-plate until the McKinley Bill was adopted. This act received the sanction of Congress October 1, 1890. The clause relating to tin went into effect July 1, 1891. It was declared that after that date tin and terne plates should pay a duty of 2.2 cents per pound instead of one cent as before. The very significant addition was made that "after October 1, 1897, tin and terne plates lighter than 63 lbs. per one hundred square feet should be admitted free of duty, if it shall be made to appear to the satisfaction of the President that the aggregate quantity of such plates lighter than 63 lbs. per one hundred square feet, produced in the United States during either of the six years next preceding June 30, 1897, has equalled one-third the amount of such plates imported and entered for consumption during any fiscal year after the passage of this act and prior to October 1, 1897."[1] Several conditions were added to this part of the bill with the intention of making out the highest production and the smallest importations. Under the rule of the Treasury Department it was permissible to compare the highest production of any one year with the lowest importation of any single year. Imported plates upon which a drawback had been received, when exported in the form of manufactured articles, were not to be counted as importations. On the other hand, black plates when imported for tinning and coated in this country were to be regarded as part of the country's product. The miners of tin were not forgotten in the bill. A duty of four cents per pound was placed on pig tin. The provisions of this part of the act were to take effect July 1, 1893, and to continue in existence two years. If at this time it could be shown that the production of block tin had reached five thousand tons, the duty was to be continued.

Many protests were made against this legislation before and after the enactment of the bill. The Tin-Plate Consumers' League, consisting of the representatives of the canning, oil, and manufacturing interests, sent delegates to the House Committee of Ways and Means.[2] Soon after the passage of the McKinley Act the Republicans were defeated in the Congressional elec-

[1] McKinley Bill, Oct. 1, 1890.

[2] House Reports, 52 Cong., 1 Sess., Vol. 4, No. 1040.

tions. Naturally the opponents of the tinning classes hoped that some reactionary legislation would be brought about, and this change in the character of Congress encouraged the interests above mentioned to appear before the committee. Several attempts were made to alter the bill, and these furnished occasions for the appearance of various delegates before the Committee on Ways and Means. The introduction and the consideration of a bill to reduce the duty on tin-plate to one cent until October 1, 1894, after which date the articles should be admitted free, fairly represents the views held in Congress on the subject.[1] Two reports were presented by the House Committee. The majority report upheld the bill on the ground that little or no tin-plate had yet been produced, and that the legislation thus far resulted in the forestalling of the market and produced a speculation in prices ruinous to consumers. In support of these arguments the statements of companies and business firms were quoted in the majority report. These all showed higher prices and a very small manufacture. The minority report was a vindication of the tariff and the need of such an industry. It was shown that in the twenty years from 1871–91 the consumers of tin had paid foreigners $307,341,404, exclusive of freights and importer's profits, for tin and tin-plates. The bill finally reached the Senate Finance Committee, but was never acted upon.[2]

A similar attempt was made to reduce the tariff on block tin. On February 27, 1893, a bill was introduced by the House Committee of Ways and Means to admit free of duty on and after July 1, 1893, imports of bar, block, and pig tin, cassiterite or black oxide of tin.[3] The committee presented with the bill much evidence to show that the then existing price of raw tin was a hardship to consumers. The canning interests found that they were compelled to pay $1.15 per dozen of one quart cans in 1893 as against 70 cents in 1890. In this connection the statement of Mr. Schiver, president of a Baltimore canning company, was offered by the committee as evidence. Mr. Schiver stated that up to February, 1893, he was unable to secure any Ameri-

[1] House Reports, 52 Cong., 1 Sess., Vol. 4, No. 1040.
[2] *Nation*, March 16, 1893.
[3] House Reports, 52 Cong., 2 Sess., Vol. 3, No. 2583.

can plate, and that he was now paying 33 per cent more for tin goods than was asked in Europe.[1] The evidence of the committee, together with their favorable report, were not sufficient to persuade Congress to make the bill a law. The Senate as well as the House was besieged with memorials praying for the repeal of the duty on block tin.[2] But to no purpose. The McKinley Bill was not modified until the Republican Congress had been superseded by a Democratic majority. This change occurred in the fall of 1893.

The Wilson Bill of 1894 reduced the rate on tin and terne plates from 2.2 cents per pound to $1\frac{1}{5}$ cents per pound, and block tin was placed upon the free list. The Democratic Congress soon after gave place to a Republican one, and the Dingley Bill of 1897 again modified the tariff on tin so that the rate was placed at $1\frac{1}{2}$ cents and block tin allowed to remain on the free list.

The act of 1890 was the creator of the tin-plate industry. The incentive from it was sufficiently great to draw a good deal of capital into the field. Although the legislation since then has made a lower rate, nevertheless the industry was well enough established in the years intervening between 1890 and 1894 to retain its place and to grow. The elements of growth more powerful than legislation, in the opinion of the writer, were the low prices of steel and wages existing during this period.

It remains to test this industry on the following points: (1) growth of production, (2) reduction of imports, (3) number of plants, (4) comparison of prices, (5) effect on foreign manufactures, and (6) probability of continued growth. This will be done in the final section of our study.

IV

1. The special agent of the Treasury Department in a report of April 26, 1892, states that "the firms replying to his inquiry

[1] House Reports, 52 Cong., 2 Sess., Vol. 3, No. 2583.
[2] Senate Mis. Doc., 52 Cong., 2 Sess., Vol. 1, No. 55.

declared that they had manufactured no tin-plates as yet."[1] The report of the same agent gives for the year ending June 31, 1892, thirteen million pounds as the product of American tin-plate. The industry evidently did not get well started until the middle of the year, 1892, but from that time the output has steadily increased. The table given below indicates the rapid development of the industry. The yearly production of tin-plate now reaches nearly five hundred million pounds. The

PRODUCTION OF TIN-PLATE IN THE UNITED STATES

YEAR	POUNDS	PER CENT FROM FOREIGN PLATE
1892	13,646,719	31.88
1893	99,819,212	56.32
1894	139,223,467	38.26
1895	193,801,073	17.15
1896	307,228,621	1.38
1897	446,982,063	.01

— From Special Report to Treasury by Ira Ayer, Jan. 28, 1898.

decline in the importation of black plates shows the ability of manufacturers to furnish these for tinning purposes. In 1893 over half the black plates from which tin and terne plates are made were furnished by foreign mills. This ratio has so far declined that in 1897 almost none of the American tin-plate was made from imported plates.

2. The decline in the imports of tin and terne plates has been as rapid and as marked as the increase in the production. The people of the United States consume between six and seven hundred million pounds of tin and terne plates each year. At times the importations for a single year have gone above this mark. The fear of tariff legislation and the intention of avoiding any increase in the duty were the causes of such heavy shipments. Two years are particularly noticeable in this particular, 1890 and 1891.

[1] Senate Ex. Doc., 52 Cong., 2 Sess., Vol. 6, No. 102.

IMPORTS OF TIN AND TERNE PLATES

Year	Pounds
1890	737,935,079
1891	734,425,267
1892	600,819,566
1893	628,425,902
1894	454,160,826
1895	508,038,938
1896	385,138,983
1897	230,073,683

— United States Custom House Reports.

Of the six hundred and seventy-seven million pounds consumed in the United States in 1897 nearly two-thirds were manufactured within its borders. When this statement is compared with the fact that no tin and terne plates were made in this country in 1890, the growth of the industry seems almost marvellous.

3. March, 1898, saw forty-one plants operating 235 mills engaged in the industry.[1] The capital invested is variously estimated from three to five million of dollars. The number of persons employed has been placed as high as fifty thousand. The Congressional estimate at the time of the Wilson Bill was twenty-four thousand, but this is also too large.[2] It is not likely that over eighteen thousand persons are connected with the industry. But even this number is large when the short existence of the industry is taken into consideration.

4. During the last two years the price of Bessemer tin-plates IC 14 x 20, 100 lb. box, has been from $3.60 to $3.85 at New York.[3] In the period from 1880–90 the price for the same kind of tin varied from $5.37½ to $7.[4] During the same period the price at Liverpool ranged from 15*s*. 6*d*. to 34*s*.[5] The price in 1890 was much less than this last quotation. On the basis of our money the English price was $3.71 to $9.16. During the last eight years the price of tin-plate in this country has steadily declined. The tariff is $1.62 per box of 108 lbs., and

[1] *Tin and Terne*, March 24, 1898.
[2] House Reports, 52 Cong., 2 Sess., Vol. 3, No. 2583.
[3] Monthly Summary of Commerce of the U. S., February, 1898, p. 1215.
[4] Senate Ex. Doc., 52 Cong., 1 Sess., Vol. 6, No. 102, p. 38. [5] *Ibid.*

in consequence English plates are now delivered in New York at just this sum below the prices ruling in the United States. Although it is now possible to buy English plates at this very low rate, it is not at all certain that such would have been the case if the present industry had not come into existence. Comparison with prices previous to 1890 fully warrants this statement. Two dollars and thirty-seven cents are about the minimum price for plates delivered at Liverpool. The ocean freight will average 13 cents per one hundred pounds. Add to these items the tariff charge of one dollar and sixty-two cents and the price of English plates reaches $4.12 for the American consumer. Mr. Cronemeyer, the president of the American Tin-Plate Association, stated before the House Committee of Ways and Means that three dollars and forty-five cents left a moderate profit for first-class tin-plates.[1] On this basis the American consumer pays ninety-five cents more per box than he would for the English plate provided no tariff existed. At the same time it is true that the price of English plates would be higher than $3.75 per box if this industry had not come into existence.

The *Tin and Terne*,[2] commenting on the condition of the market, says, "The market has continued very unsettled and unsatisfactory to both buyer and seller alike. War and rumors of war, trusts and rumors of trusts, all have a disturbing influence, and in no branch of metal industry have prices been as unsettled and as confusing as in tin-plates. There is a wide range between the high seller and the low seller on spot goods to-day, and a wide difference of opinion in regard to the future market. The Indiana mills are fairly well sold up, and are rather firm in their views; while the Pittsburg mills, it is reported, are seeking business for delivery after July at prices lower than anything hitherto made. It is reported that some very large sales — 100,000 boxes — have been closed in the last few days at a basis below $2.70 per box."

The statement given above is a forecast of the future condition of the industry. The truth of the matter is that already there are more than enough mills to supply the market. Just how far the demoralization may extend is difficult to say, but it

[1] Eng. Foreign Office Report, Mis. No. 426, p. 9. [2] March 24, 1898.

is more than likely that American plate will fall below the three-dollar line. If this happens, we may look for repeated attempts to organize trusts and to close down some of the weaker plants. A period of readjustment will follow, and higher prices again prevail.

5. The establishment of the industry has had a marked effect upon foreign makers of tin-plate. This is well illustrated by the report of the American consul at Cardiff in which the following is given:[1] "The tin-plate trade of South Wales has persistently gone from bad to worse during the last few months." In a manifesto appearing in the *Industrial World*, the official organ of the Tin-Plate Worker's Union, are several interesting statements that corroborate the opinion of the American consul. The one now given sets forth the condition of the tin-plate business in a dismal picture. "At the beginning of the week 144 out of our 512 mills were idle. This can be contrasted with the state of affairs before the McKinley tariff came into operation. In January, 1889, there existed 482 mills, 17 of which were idle. . . . The Welsh mills, with the comparatively few mills on the continent of Europe, are capable of fully meeting the requirements of the world for plates; that being so, every box of plates made in America means a box less in Wales."[2] Many other statements of like character have appeared in the various English newspapers. The writers are perfectly aware of the decline of the English industry and are fearful that the American market will be forever lost to them.[3] Mr. John H. Rogers, a large manufacturer of tin-plate in England, and president of the Tin-Plate Makers' Association, in a letter to the Tin-Plate Makers' Union, predicts that many of the men will lose their positions and that the coating part of the business will leave the country.[4] Preparations have already been made by some of the plants to change their business into that of galvanizing. All these facts point to a demoralization of the Welsh trade due evidently to a falling off in the American demand.

6. One final question remains for our consideration: What is

[1] Consular Reports, May, 1896, p. 67.
[2] *Ibid.*, p. 68.
[3] Consular Report, November, 1897, p. 323.
[4] Consular Reports, May, 1898.

the probability of the continued existence of the industry? The elements of success in the trade are the tariff, the cheapened production of steel, and the low price of labor. These three things have made it possible for the industry to gain a foothold in this country. The tariff seems to have given the incentive and at the same time to have protected the business from excessive competition in the beginning. The fact, as shown by previous tariffs, that such protection alone was unable to create the industry, gives additional importance to the other elements. If steel had not been low in price at the time wages were falling, it is doubtful whether the McKinley Act would have created the industry. In regard to the future, the indications are that steel will continue low in price for some time to come. The exports of steel made in the last two years certainly point to a decided advantage in this material over the English industry. So long as the progress in mining machinery and rolling mills continues, we may expect to retain this advantage. Wages, however, are certain to rise, and it is more than likely that two years will see them restored to the old level. Unless this advance can be offset by improved machinery, which is more than probable, there must be a slight rise in the price of tin-plate and with it some encouragement to foreign makers to enter our markets.

About the only market now left to the English makers is that of the Pacific coast. The freight rate on one hundred pounds from Wales to San Francisco is 18 cents; the rate from Pittsburg to the same city is 61¼ cents.[1] The price of English plates, duty paid, at the latter port would be $4.17. If the price for American plates is $3.45, then two makes are about the same, $4.17 and $4.16 per boxes of 108 lbs. delivered. Even this market is likely to be closed to England if the price falls below $3.45 per box.

			Per 100 Lbs.
[1] South Wales	to	Atlantic ports	12c.
" "	"	Pacific "	18c.
" "	"	Gulf "	15c.
Pittsburg	"	Atlantic coast	15c.
"	"	Pacific "	61¼c.
Indiana	"	Gulf "	20c.
New York	"	Chicago	20c.

—From Eng. For. Office Report, Mis. No. 426, p. 13.

The American tin-plate industry will undoubtedly continue in existence. At the present, combinations and trusts threaten to control the industry. A short-sighted policy on the part of the managers may lead to higher prices and renewed competition with English makers. Such an organization is more likely to cut expenses and hold the price just below the point of foreign competition, so that the danger from foreign rivalry is not great. The industry is not so dependent upon the tariff as might be supposed, and the actual possession of the market, accompanied by good product and sensible management, will make it possible to meet the foreign competition as the tariff is lowered.

The American consumer now pays about ninety-five cents more for American tin than the price of English plate delivered at New York. This is really a premium for the maintenance of the American industry. If in the course of ten or fifteen years our manufacturers can meet the English price, the cost, expense, and trouble in creating the industry have been justified. As it now stands three things may endanger the industry: (1) rise in cost of steel, (2) in wages, (3) and in block tin. If this rise should occur in the three cases at the same time, the industry would hardly stand under the blow. As has already been pointed out, steel is not likely to increase in price, while the output of the Banca mines will protect us in some degree from any change in the price of Welsh block tin. At the same time American ingenuity will undoubtedly increase the efficiency of labor so that the disadvantages now labored under may gradually disappear. Taken all in all, the development of this industry is a remarkable example of timely legislation. The conditions were present, the tariff permitted their utilization, but in no sense must the importance of the conditions be underestimated.

The Tin-Plate Combination

I

The excessive competition of the many tin-plate plants established under the hot-house influences of the tariff of 1890, in company with rising prices of materials, has brought about the formation of a combination known as the American Tin-Plate Company. Three things — tariff, low price of steel, and low wages — fortunately meeting at the same time made possible the rapid growth of this industry. In 1890 there were two or three plants struggling under great difficulties, barely competing with foreign makers. The McKinley, Wilson, and Dingley bills restricted this competition to such an extent, and incited enterprise to such a degree, that 1898 saw forty-one plants engaged in the industry with every promise of prosperity.[1] The transformation, just spoken of, was almost marvellous. The tariff, checking foreign competition, made it possible for those engaged in the industry to construct their mills and at the same time secure the double advantage of cheap steel and low wages. The output increased rapidly from a few hundred thousand pounds to hundreds of millions of pounds,[2] while the great imports of early years fell rapidly to less than a third of what they had been in 1890. Meantime the English industry suffered greatly. The American market was the one great consumer of English tin. There had been some dissatisfaction with English methods and English manufacture, so that the American producers had no opposition to fight and overcome among the consumers of English tin in this country. In fact, the purchasers of the commodity seemed ready to welcome any movement likely to affect English prices.

The price during the period of English supply ranged above $5.00 per box IC 14 x 20 plates. Although the tariff added some $1.62 to the price of English tin-plate per box of 108 lbs., nevertheless so great was the influence of the loss of the American market that the price f.o.b. at Liverpool fell to about $2.40.[3] This in a way set a limit to the price of American tin-plate, so that the quotation in this country has remained below five dollars. Since 1893 the price was pushed, under the rivalry of the different tin-plate makers, lower and lower below this limit, until $2.70 was reached in December, 1898.[4] This was undoubtedly pretty near cost.

[1] *Yale Review*, VII, 302, November, 1898. The Tin-Plate Industry.

[2] *Ibid.*, p. 313.

[3] Eng. Foreign Office Report, No. 426, p. 9.

[4] *Tin and Terne*, Jan. 26, 1898.

This movement from the comparatively high prices of 1893 steadily downwards to a point so near cost was not a healthy one. It was indicative of excessive output and competition. One-half of the forty-one plants could easily have supplied the market. The fall in price alone was not sufficient to cause the failure of any of the plants, although new factories were erected during the year, increasing the competition. The industry would only be permanently[1] endangered by (1) a rise in the price of steel, (2) a rise in wages, (3) an increase in the cost of pig tin, or (4) the repeal of the tariff. Any one of these, with the exception of the last, was hardly sufficient to cause the continued embarrassment of the tin-plate companies, but two working together were sure to make the conditions of manufacture exceedingly hard, while a movement upward in the case of the first three threatened the renewal of foreign competition and the possible extinction of the business. Two at least of the above-mentioned possibilities have taken place; tin and steel have both risen in the last year and, in the case of steel, the chances are that the price will range high for some time to come. Block tin is now hard to get and is rising in price. In regard to labor, there is considerable question, but undoubtedly the tendency is in the direction of higher payment. The Amalgamated Association has constantly insisted that such should be the case in the iron and steel industries, and the tin-plate makers will be compelled to follow the example set by the kindred industries.

At the opening of the year pig tin was selling for 13¾ cents per pound in New York.[2] In January, 1899, the quotation had advanced eleven points, the market showing great firmness with every indication of going still higher and possibly equalling the price of 37½ cents of 1889. This increase added twenty-seven cents to the cost of producing a box of IC 14 x 20 tin-plates. During the same time the market price of steel billets rose two dollars per ton. By this change in the cost of material eleven cents more were added to the charge of making tin-plates. In a year's time the manufacturer found he was producing plates

[1] *Yale Review*, November, 1898, VII, p. 318.

[2] *Tin and Terne*, Jan. 26, 1898.

at an increased expense of thirty-eight cents per box, and the market price down to $2.70 at mill for first-class plates. The situation is indicated by the accompanying table:

WHOLESALE PRICE OF TIN-PLATE (BESSEMER STEEL IC 14 X 20, IN NEW YORK PER BOX OF 100 LBS.) AND OF STEEL BILLETS (PER LONG TON, AT PITTSBURG, PA.)[1]

1893	STEEL BILLETS	TIN-PLATES
July,	$21.50–22.00	$5.05
August,	21.00–21.25	5.00
September,	–20.50	4.85
October,	–18.50	5.00
November,	17.50–18.00	5.00
December,	17.00–17.50	4.90
1894		
January,	–15.90	4.87½
February,	16.00–16.25	4.85
March,	–15.50	4.85
April,	–15.75	4.80
May,	16.75–17.00	4.75
June,	19.00–19.50	4.75
July,	–18.50	4.72½
August,	17.00–17.25	4.72½
September,	–18.00	4.77½
October,	16.75–17.00	3.85
November,	–15.45	3.75
December,	15.25–15.50	3.65
1895		
January,	15.00–15.25	3.60
February,	15.00–15.25	3.57½
March,	15.00–15.25	3.50
April,	15.25–15.60	3.50
May,	15.50–15.75	3.52½
June,	17.75–18.00	3.52½
July,	20.50–20.75	3.65
August,	21.50–22.00	3.75
September,	–	3.65
October,	24.00–24.25	3.65
November,	21.00–21.50	3.65
December,	18.00–18.50	3.60
1896		
January,	16.00–16.25	3.60
February,	18.25–18.50	3.52½
March,	–17.00	3.45
April,	–20.00	3.42½
May,	–20.25	3.47½
June,	–20.25	3.47½

1896	STEEL BILLETS	TIN-PLATES
July,	$18.25–20.25	$3.47½
August,	–20.25	3.50
September,	–20.50	3.50
October,	–20.25	3.50
November,	–20.25	3.65
December,	–20.25	3.70
1897		
January,	–16.00	3.75
February,	–15.50	3.80
March,	18.00–20.00	3.75
April,	–15.25	3.60
May,	–14.75	3.70
June,	14.25–14.50	3.70
July,	14.00–14.25	3.70
August,	–14.25	3.70
September,	15.00–15.25	3.70
October,	–16.50	3.70
November,	16.25–16.50	3.90
December,	–15.00	3.70
1898		
January,	15.00–15.25	3.80
February,	–15.00	3.85
March,	15.25–15.50	3.85
April,	15.50–15.75	3.85
May,	15.00–15.25	3.85
June,	–15.00	3.85
July,	–14.75	3.85
August,	–14.75	3.85
September,	–16.25	3.95
October,	–16.00	3.95
November,	15.50	3.95
December,	15.75–16.00	3.95
1899		
January,	16.50–16.75	2.92½
February,	–17.25	3.25
March,	21.00–22.00	3.70
April,	25.00–26.00	3.91
May,	–26.50	3.97½

[1] Monthly Summary of Finance and Commerce of the United States, December, 1897, pp. 885, 889; April, 1899, pp. 2434, 2437, 2441, 2445. Quotations taken at the beginning of each month.

It is not difficult to understand why steel billets should increase in value. The great demand for rails and steel for bridges and buildings under the reviving industry of the year explains fairly well this rise, but pig tin does not come under the influence of American production. The probabilities are that the market in this material has been cornered. Such a feat would be by no means difficult. The output is comparatively small, and passes through but few hands. If such is the case, the next year will see an increased output and the correction of the present condition. In this relation *Tin and Terne*, commenting on the situation, says the advance is a most radical one, and it seems certain that if the tin-plate manufacturing business in the country had remained in control of the individual companies, many would have been forced to the wall in the effort to fill contracts.[1]

It will be seen from what has been already said that the tin-plate industry was in far from a healthy condition. Everything pointed to demoralization. It was very natural that, under these conditions, repeated attempts should be made to form a combination. The wasteful methods that had characterized the early industry had been largely corrected, and in their place had been substituted economies so sweeping that it was almost impossible for the companies to get to a lower cost basis without consolidation.[2]

II

Early in 1898 negotiations were begun by persons interested in the tin-plate industry to ascertain if it were possible to form a company that should control the plants of the country. A meeting of the most important manufacturers was held at Pittsburg in January of last year.[3] Many representatives of the different interests were there. An attempt was made to get options on the various plants engaged in this industry. A number of the concerns thinking the time opportune to place a high valuation on their properties did so, but in most instances,

[1] *Tin and Terne*, Jan. 26, 1899.
[2] *Ibid.*, Jan. 12, 1899.
[3] *Iron Age*, Jan. 20, 1898.

especially in those cases where plates had been sold below cost, the owners were willing to be a party to a reasonable agreement. The result of the meeting was undoubtedly a step toward further organization. Evidently there was a carefully arranged plan back of the whole movement which was to be carried out on well-determined lines. This conference was followed by a committee meeting in New York during the first week of February. Four of the tin-plate manufacturers present at Pittsburg had been appointed to confer with the jobbers in New York city. During the importing period the "Big Four," consisting of brokerage firms in the city just mentioned, dominated the business of tin-plate jobbing. The object of the committee was to deal with these firms, who were regarded as powerful factors in the business. It was expected that they would oppose consolidation, and it was therefore determined that firmness should be the tactics of the committee. The committee made the following proposition: that if the four merchant concerns wished to coöperate, they must furnish funds necessary to meet one-third of the expense of consolidation. To this proposition the merchants objected, but they were informed that the consolidation would go on even if they did not take advantage of the offer. It is quite evident, from the arrangements which have been made for the sale of tin-plates as well as the disappearance of these firms from the market, that the offer was not accepted. The attempt was to unite both mill owners and principal dealers, but in the event of failure to bring together the mill owners, at least. A great many in the trade were exceedingly sceptical in regard to the movement. So well, however, did the conditions in the market aid the promoters that 1899 saw the formation of the syndicate and the purchase of thirty-nine plants controlling 279 mills.

The final goal of the promoters of the syndicate (and it was constantly insisted that the movement was a syndicate movement rather than a combination) was to imitate the organization of the American Steel and Wire Company. This last concern completed its organization early in 1898, and furnished a practical example for the tin-plate promoters. A comparison of the two combinations is, therefore, more than usually interesting.

COMPARISON

AMERICAN STEEL AND WIRE CO.[1]

Stock

1. Capital stock of $90,000,000, of which $40,000,000 is 7 per cent cumulative preferred stock and $50,000,000 common stock.

Dividends

2. Dividends upon preferred stock shall be cumulative. In case of dissolution or liquidation the holders of preferred stock are to be paid in full both the principal and accrued dividend charges before any amount is paid to the holders of common stock.

Capital

3. The amount of capital stock with which it will commence business is $250,000.

Object

4. (*a*) To manufacture and trade in steel, iron and other metals; to make, purchase and sell manufactured articles made partly or wholly from metals of any kind and all like or kindred products; to acquire and dispose of rights to make and use the same; to make and purchase and sell such other products or merchandise as may be conveniently or advantageously used or sold in connection with said metals and business; and to apply for, purchase or otherwise acquire and hold, own, use, operate, sell, assign or otherwise dispose of patents, rights, and processes.

(*b*) The corporation shall have power to *purchase, hold, transfer, mortgage, pledge or otherwise dispose of the shares of the capital stock of, or any bonds, securities or evidences of indebtedness created by any other corporation or corporations of this or any other state, and while owner of such stock may exercise all*

AMERICAN TIN-PLATE CO.[2]

Stock

1. Capital stock, $50,000,000; $20,000,000 preferred and $30,000,000 common stock. The preference shares bear 7 per cent interest cumulative.

Dividends

2. In the event of liquidation or dissolution of the corporation the holders of the aforesaid cumulative preference shares shall be paid the full amount with accrued dividends. After such payments the remaining assets shall be divided among the holders of the other shares.

Capital

3. The amount of capital stock with which it will commence business is $10,000.

Object

4. (*a*) To manufacture and trade in tin, terne, block plates, steel sheets, and all like or kindred products, to mine, manufacture, prepare for market, market and sell the same, and any articles or product in the manufacture or composition of which metal is a factor; including the acquisition by purchase, mining, manufacture or otherwise of all materials, supplies and other articles necessary or convenient for use in connection with and in carrying on the business herein mentioned, or any part thereof.

(*b*) In addition to the general powers the company shall also have the following powers: To manufacture, deal, own, sell, transfer, etc., goods, wares and property of every description and to do mining of any kind. To also own and dispose of real estate in any part of the world to any amount. To acquire good will and rights and property of any kind *and to undertake the whole or any part*

[1] *Tin and Terne*, Jan. 26, 1899.

[2] Charter of American Tin-Plate Co.

NOTE.—Both companies are chartered under the laws of New Jersey.

AMERICAN STEEL AND WIRE CO.

Object

rights, powers and privileges of ownership including right to vote. The corporation shall have the power to establish offices in this and other states and may hold or transfer any real or personal property in this and other countries.

Directors

5. Directors shall be divided into three classes, equal in number, in respect to the time for which they shall severally hold office. The first for three years, the second two years, third one year. Office shall be for three years thereafter.

With the assent in writing or pursuant to the vote of holders of two-thirds of the capital stock, the directors shall have power to sell, assign or transfer, convey or otherwise dispose of the property and assets of this corporation as the directors may see fit.

The power to make and alter the by-laws shall remain with the directors. The directors shall have power to hold their meetings wherever may be designated by them. The accounts of the corporation are only open to stockholders upon conditions determined by the directors.

AMERICAN TIN-PLATE CO.

Object

of the assets and liabilities of any person, firm, association or corporation, and to pay for the same in cash, stocks of this corporation, bonds or otherwise. To also apply for, hold, own, dispose of patents, processes, licenses and trade marks, etc.

To make contracts with any individual firm, association, corporation, and with the government of the United States, state or colony. To do all and everything necessary to promote the interests of shareholders whether manufacturing, mining or otherwise.

Directors

5. *Directors* shall be divided into five classes. The first class being elected for five years, the second, four years, etc., so that the term of office shall be five years thereafter. The board shall fill vacancies in the board. Shall have the power to make and alter by-laws.

With the assent in writing and pursuant to the vote of holders of two-thirds of all stock irrespective of class, directors shall have the power to sell, assign and transfer, convey or otherwise dispose of the property and assets of this corporation as the directors may see fit.

An executive committee consisting of five members shall have the power to conduct the business when the directors are not in session. Officers of the committee shall be a chairman, vice-president and a secretary. They shall be elected by all the stockholders. The term of office shall be coextensive with the office of director. Members of the committee shall not be subject to removal for any cause by the board of directors, and shall hold office until their successors are elected. No stockholder shall have the right to inspect any account, book, or document of the corporation except as conferred by statutes of New Jersey or authorized by the directors.

The thing that impresses the reader of the comparison made above is similarity of organization, the broad features of the charters, and the general and undetailed character of the provisions. In section four it will be noticed that the intention of the framers is to give the corporations the power of control over all properties bought in any manner, whether from individual, firm, or corporation, and that in the case of the American Steel Wire and Rod Co. the right to vote acquired by the purchase of such properties remains with the board of directors. There is nothing in the provisions of the two charters which would make it impossible for either one to incorporate the other and form one great concern. Whether the logic of combination will lead to such a result is difficult to say.

Let us turn now to some of the more salient features of the American Tin-Plate Company's charter. First, the stock. The amount of this is fifty millions of dollars, twenty millions of which is preferred and thirty millions common. It has been determined that two millions of each are to remain in the treasury, while but eighteen millions of each are to be issued, leaving ten millions for the promoters.[1] There is a further provision that for each subscription of one hundred dollars of preferred stock one hundred dollars of common stock is given to the subscriber.[2] On March 27 the preferred stock of this company was selling for 95 and the common was quoted at 42. This means that the promoters have received something over four millions for their work. The total capitalization of all the tin-plate firms in the United States was estimated, before the formation of the company, at between three and five millions of dollars.[3] Even granting that it was ten millions, which is undoubtedly too high an estimate, the excessive capitalization of the syndicate means watered stock on the face of it. If it is possible for the syndicate to carry such a load, there is always the danger of competition, failure to pay dividends, especially on the common stock, and as a consequence great losses to the innocent purchasers of common stock. The syndicate thus

[1] *Iron Age*, Dec. 10, 1898.
[2] *Bradstreet's*, Nov. 26, 1898, p. 766.
[3] *Yale Review*, November, 1898, VII, p. 314.

begins its business operations hampered by excessive obligations and immediate prospect of competition, unless effective means are taken to prevent it.

In the organization of this company a distinction is to be made between it and the usual trust. The provisions of trusteeship are altogether absent, so that the legal restrictions upon trusts may be avoided. This is true so far as the letter of the law is concerned, but in the actual working of the company the executive committee provided for by the charter is in almost every sense the equivalent of the trustees in a trust. This body is elected by the stockholders and the members of it cannot be removed by the board of directors. It undoubtedly goes without saying that this committee will control the business of the company. The stockholders have no right "to examine or inspect the accounts, books, or documents of the corporation, except as conferred by the statutes of New Jersey or authorized by the directors." This, of course, means just as absolute a control of the affairs of the company as though the organization were a trust in letter as well as in actual fact. It is also to be noticed that the usual freedom of the directors is made a prominent part of the charter. It is only by a two-thirds vote that the stockholders can order the sale, assignment, or transfer of any of the assets of the company and then only as the directors see fit. The holders of the stock of the local companies have exchanged it, or sold it, and then bought the general shares of the American Tin-Plate Company. The promoters of the combination do not give the owners of the different plants any option in the disposition of their stock; it is sell or shut up your works. The movement is, therefore, in reality a complete trust in all respects, except the one which gives to the holders of stock the right to vote on the disposition of the stock by the directors.

We now turn to the policy of the company.

III

In considering the policy of the syndicate the following points suggest themselves for treatment: (1) relation to the tin-plate plants of the combination, (2) dividends, (3) attitude toward the trade, (4) machinery firms, (5) various economies, (6) wages. It is exceedingly difficult to get detailed information concerning the inner working of the combination, but sufficient is indicated here to show in a general way what the trend of the movement is.

1. At the present time a number of the plants have been closed down.[1] Among these are some of the largest and best equipped mills in the country. The company now owns every tin-plate plant in the United States making a product for the general trade. Just how long these establishments are to remain closed is impossible to say, but undoubtedly the company is trying to find out to just what extent it is necessary to operate the different plants to supply the demand. If it is discovered that all or nearly all are necessary, two lines of policy are open to the directors: first, to operate all the mills owned by the company; second, to close the more poorly equipped and badly situated mills and to increase the producing power of the better plants. It is more than likely that the second, or at least a modification of it, will be followed, as is indicated to some degree by the contracts of the syndicate with the equipment firms.

2. It is continually asserted that the American Tin-Plate Co. will[2] be able to pay dividends from the start not only on the preferred stock, but on the common stock as well. This dividend, it is said, will be declared on April 1 to at least 1½ per cent.[3] The company has only been in existence since December, 1898, and although large orders have undoubtedly been given to the company, nevertheless the prices of tin-plate have not advanced sufficiently to pay the increased cost of steel and tin in production.[4] If this is so, it is not likely that any dividends will be paid on common stock for some time, although in some instances the combine bought the material on hand at the

[1] *Tin and Terne*, Feb. 23, 1899.

[2] *Ibid.*, Feb. 9, 1899.

[3] Statement made in February, 1899.

[4] This means on $46,000,000 of capital $1,420,000, including preferred dividends. Add to this organization expenses, operation and material, and the difficulty of such a course is at once apparent.

various mills at cost.[1] This will give a larger margin. There is, of course, the temptation constantly before such a concern to pay dividends out of capital stock in order to push up the quotation of common stock. But the whole attitude of the company seems to be that of a legitimate manufacturing enterprise rather than a speculative movement. Taken all in all, the company is not likely to force the payment of dividends before it earns them.

3. In relation to the trade, a radical change has been instituted. The company has laid down the principle that it will not have any dealings with brokers in tin-plate.[2] The idea upon which this policy is based is that with but one producing company of tin-plate there is no need of a broker. The company makes no quotation except on request and in carload lots. The territory is divided into two districts: the eastern section with headquarters at New York, and the western division with headquarters at Chicago. The Alleghany Mountains are the dividing line. Two men have been appointed as general agents over these divisions. The sales part of the business will be independent of the other parts, the management of the mills having no jurisdiction over the general agents.[3] The price of $3.00 has been fixed for carload lots of 100 lb. boxes of coke plates at the mill. Business involving less than a carload is turned over to the jobber nearest to the customer. All quotations will be f. o. b., New York, Chicago, or destination, so that there will probably be some advance on the quotation given above. The increasing price of raw material will also change from time to time the quotation of $3.00 f. o. b. at mills.[4]

4. Arrangements have been made with nearly every firm in the land engaged in manufacturing machinery for tin-plate plants, to sell their entire product to the American Tin-Plate Co. Any combination always brings a lot of promoters into existence who expect to build plants and force the combination to buy them at a fancy price. This the new company expects to forestall by arranging with the equipment firms to take their entire output. It is said that an agreement

[1] *Tin and Terne*, Feb. 9, 1899.

[2] *Ibid.*, Jan. 26, 1899.

[3] *Iron Age*, Jan. 19, 1899.

[4] *Tin and Terne*, Feb. 9, 1899.

has been made between the two parties for five years ending January 1, 1904.[1] Just what and how much this product is to be is determined by the tin-plate company, and the managing committee distribute the machinery secured under this agreement among the different plants as it sees fit. The prices paid for machinery are lower than if equipments were bought in the open market. There will also be an attempt made to get the machinery firms to specialize, so that each will be a producer of a certain kind of machinery. It will thus be all but impossible to start a new mill to produce such machinery. If, however, there is any special demand because of the attitude of the company, it may be assumed that machine companies in other lines will enter the field as makers of tin-plate equipment. The whole arrangement, nevertheless, is indicative of the shrewd and not to be defeated attitude of this new combination.

5. In addition to the savings already pointed out the company has instituted various other economies of some importance. It is usually the custom upon the organization of a big concern like the tin-plate combination to give enormous salaries. This the directors and promoters have absolutely refused to do. The compensation will be fair, but not high. The *Tin and Terne* says in regard to this point, "We have it on good authority that the salaries paid the officers of the new concern will be very low."[2] The number of officers will also be cut down to the smallest number possible.

The company, in quoting prices f. o. b. from New York and Chicago, and shipping to the purchaser from the nearest mill, will be in a position to save some very considerable amounts in the course of a year on freight rates. Whether it will secure any concessions from the railroads in freight rates is not known. Until the rate between Pittsburg and Chicago is very considerably reduced, the company will have to face the English competition on the Pacific coast. The rate on one hundred pounds from Wales to San Francisco is 18 cents, from Pittsburg to the same city $61\frac{1}{4}$ cents.[3] The English tin-plates were

[1] *Tin and Terne*, Feb. 9, 1899. [2] *Ibid.*, Jan. 12, 1899.
[3] *Yale Review*, November, 1898, VII, p. 317.

selling in December at $2.30 per box of 100 lbs. at Liverpool.[1] It is therefore possible for the English companies to deliver plates at San Francisco, tariff paid, for $4.10. The present cost to the tin-plate company is some three or four cents above this when the price quoted is $3.50. This means that English and American plates will be somewhat on an equality in their competition on the Pacific coast. Undoubtedly, if there is a sufficient incentive, the railroads will reduce the rate, and make it possible to go under the English price.

The company is too new to show how much of a saving may be effected by the new management. Probably greater uniformity and closer attention to cutting and waste will produce some economies.

6. The question of wages is one of the difficult things with which the new company has to deal. The tendency is in the direction of a considerable increase in wages in all the steel industries. The advance in the selling price of tin-plate has stimulated the officers of the Amalgamated Association to ask for a higher scale of wages. "Previous to July 1, 1896, the base wages were to be paid as long as the selling price of tin-plate was not more than one-fourth the selling price of a ton of steel billets; since then the ratio has been one-fifth."[2] The company is in a peculiar position in the matter of wages. According to the agreement above, the company must pay higher wages if the ratio between steel and tin increased. This has changed. Tin-plates have increased in price on account of the added cost of pig tin, and because of this addition the market quotation has risen and the company must pay more wages. "With the rapidly advancing prices of sheet iron, there is a possibility that an advance may be called for in the wages of the sheet mill men also. The Amalgamated Association places an arbitrary limit upon the output, so that the increased machinery equipment does not bring a proportional benefit to the manufacturer.[3] The company is, therefore, encountering high prices in raw material (steel and pig tin) and in wages." It is questionable whether the economies spoken of above will

[1] Monthly Summary of Commerce and Finance, December, 1898, p. 1413.

[2] *Tin and Terne*, Feb. 23, 1899.

[3] *Iron Age*, March 31, 1898, p. 16.

any more than make up for these extra expenses. The economic strength of the company will enable it to meet these difficulties without any great trouble.

IV

The tin-plate combination is an arbitrary but natural attempt to raise the price of that product. It is interesting to note to just what extent the combination is due to the tariff. In the first section of our study reference was made to the repeal of the tariff as one of the possible ways of injuring the industry. Without the protection now afforded to tin-plate through the Dingley Bill it would be impossible for the industry to exist. The tariff, however, did not directly create the combination. Under the protection afforded since 1890 many plants came into existence, competing with one another until the price was unduly lowered. Then came efforts to organize a great syndicate, which were successful. In consequence of that organization, the price of tin-plate has been increased, and a monopoly over the production of it secured through the policy of the company in relation to dealers and machine makers. The consumer is thus forced to pay for not only the maintenance of the industry, but also the profits of the company. The English makers are shut out of the market and the combination thus completely controls the production of the commodity inside of the country. So long as the tariff remains at a protective figure, it is likely that the syndicate will be able to stop any effort to renew the competition.

Another factor bids well to enter the problem which has probably been overlooked in the calculations of the syndicate managers. That is the repeal of the tariff duties. In the last few months several of the more prominent papers representing the political party that established the tariff on tin-plate have commented editorially on the necessity of that party taking up the question of monopolies.[1] Severally these papers have reached a common solution. Their editors have come to regard the tariff as responsible for trusts and, therefore, the

[1] *Philadelphia Ledger, Chicago Times-Herald, St. Paul Pioneer Press.*

repeal of such legislation the direct and effective way of dealing with them. It is not necessary to consider any arguments for or against the above supposition. But any such attitude to the extent of legislation threatens the existence both of the tin-plate syndicate and the industry. It would be impossible for the American syndicate to withstand the renewal of English imports. Two movements might result from such a policy on the part of Congress: first, to break the syndicate into many parts, the individual companies claiming that they were no longer a party to the monopoly agreement, but were still in need of the protection; second, for the present company to unite with the English firms in an effort to form an international combination. This would be the more natural step to take, but at the same time the more difficult one to accomplish. The popular demand and the hostile attitude of the people toward large capitalistic concerns will undoubtedly cause the party to very seriously consider the movement spoken of above. The possibility of such an attitude will impress itself on all thinking men.

On the other hand, another movement, other than political, can be seen in the iron and steel industries. Within the last two years a number of concerns have entered combinations so that to-day instead of there being many companies engaged in allied lines of industry, there are several combinations corresponding to the several lines of production. A very large part of the iron and steel product is controlled by seven corporations.[1] A reference to the respective charters of the American Tin-Plate and American Steel and Wire companies, is sufficient to indicate that the union of combinations with combinations is by no means impossible. There is one limitation upon such a movement and that is the inability of men to manage a concern economically that has a capital and output beyond a certain amount. Until that point is reached, combination will probably continue, and it is possible that we may see an attempt to unite all of the iron and steel industries

[1] American Steel and Wire Co., American Tin-Plate Co., the Granite Ware Co., the Carnegie Co., Union Chain and Steel Co., the Illinois Steel Co. and Mesaba Range Mining Co.

under one management. As has already been pointed out, there is nothing in the charters of the two concerns compared in the second section of this article to prevent union. The provisions are so wide that the manufacture of steel wires and rods could be carried on by the tin-plate company or the production of tin-plate by the steel wire and rod company. It would be natural that the two should unite, or the entire steel industry might possibly come under the control of one gigantic combination.

The industry of our study thus stands in two dangers: first, of possibly placing prices so high that it will be impossible to maintain them, leading to a virtual revolt on the part of consumers; and second, the political movement culminating in the possible withdrawal of the tariff. If the consumers of tin become dissatisfied with the attitude of the company in the matter of prices, the political movement may be reënforced by their opposition to the combination.

The American Tin-Plate Company has existed less than six months, so that the developments possible to the future are necessarily conjectural. Strong as the company is in its organization, it is particularly vulnerable from the political movement mentioned above.

FRANK L. MCVEY.

UNIVERSITY OF MINNESOTA.

XIV

THE NORTHERN SECURITIES COMPANY[1]

MR. JUSTICE HARLAN announced the affirmance of the decree of the circuit court, and delivered the following opinion:

This suit was brought by the United States against the Northern Securities Company, a corporation of New Jersey; the Great Northern Railway Company, a corporation of Minnesota; the Northern Pacific Railway Company, a corporation of Wisconsin; James J. Hill, a citizen of Minnesota; and others.

Its general object was to enforce, as against the defendants, the provisions of the statute of July 2, 1890, commonly known as the Anti-Trust Act, and entitled "An Act to Protect Trade and Commerce Against Unlawful Restraints and Monopolies." 26 Stat. at L., 209, chap. 647, U. S. Comp. Stat. 1901, page 3200. By the decree below the United States was given substantially the relief asked by it in the bill.

As the act is not very long, and as the determination of the particular questions arising in this case may require a consideration of the scope and meaning of most of its provisions, it is here given in full:

§ 1. Every contract, combination in the form of trust or otherwise, or conspiracy, in restraint of trade or commerce among the several states, or with foreign nations, is hereby declared to be illegal. Every person who shall make any such contract, or engage in any such com-

[1] Abridged from the text of the decision. Supreme Court of the United States, No. 277, October Term, 1903, *Northern Securities Company, etc.*, v. *The United States*, March 14, 1903.

An excellent history of the case is given in outline by Professor B. H. Meyer, in the *Railway Age*, March 18, 1903, to be published in more extended monographic form shortly. A bibliography of the subject is also appended to A List of Books relating to Railroads, published by the Library of Congress, 1904. — ED.

bination or conspiracy, shall be deemed guilty of a misdemeanor, and, on conviction thereof, shall be punished by fine not exceeding five thousand dollars, or by imprisonment not exceeding one year, or by both said punishments, in the discretion of the court.

§ 2. Every person who shall monopolize, or attempt to monopolize, or combine or conspire with any other person or persons to monopolize, any part of the trade or commerce among the several states, or with foreign nations, shall be deemed guilty of a misdemeanor, and, on conviction thereof, shall be punished by fine not exceeding five thousand dollars, or by imprisonment not exceeding one year, or by both said punishments, in the discretion of the court.

§ 3. Every contract, combination in form of trust or otherwise, or conspiracy, in restraint of trade or commerce in any territory of the United States or of the District of Columbia, or in restraint of trade or commerce between any such territory and another, or between any such territory or territories and any state or states or the District of Columbia, or with foreign nations, or between the District of Columbia, and any state or states or foreign nations, is hereby declared illegal. Every person who shall make any such contract or engage in any such combination or conspiracy shall be deemed guilty of a misdemeanor, and, on conviction thereof, shall be punished by fine not exceeding five thousand dollars, or by imprisonment not exceeding one year, or by both said punishments, in the discretion of the court.

§ 4. The several circuit courts of the United States are hereby invested with jurisdiction to prevent and restrain violations of this act; and it shall be the duty of the several district attorneys of the United States, in their respective districts, under the direction of the Attorney-General, to institute proceedings in equity to prevent and restrain such violations. Such proceedings may be by way of petition setting forth the case and praying that such violation shall be enjoined or otherwise prohibited. When the parties complained of shall have been duly notified of such petition the court shall proceed, as soon as may be, to the hearing and determination of the case; and, pending such petition, and before final decree, the court may at any time make such temporary restraining order or prohibition as shall be deemed just in the premises.

§ 5. Whenever it shall appear to the court before which any proceeding under section four of this act may be pending, that the ends of justice require that other parties should be brought before the court, the court may cause them to be summoned, whether they reside in the district in which the court is held or not; and subpœnas to that end may be served in any district by the marshal thereof.

§ 6. Any property owned under any contract or by any combination, or pursuant to any conspiracy (and being the subject thereof) mentioned in section one of this act, and being in the course of transportation from one state to another, or to a foreign country, shall be forfeited to the United States, and may be seized and condemned by like proceedings as those provided by law for the forfeiture, seizure, and condemnation of property imported into the United States contrary to law.

§ 7. Any person who shall be injured in his business or property by any other person or corporation by reason of anything forbidden or declared to be unlawful by this act may sue therefor in any circuit court of the United States in the district in which the defendant resides or is found, without respect to the amount in controversy, and shall recover threefold the damages by him sustained, and the costs of suit, including a reasonable attorney's fee.

§ 8. That the word "person" or "persons," wherever used in this act, shall be deemed to include corporations and associations existing under or authorized by the laws of either the United States, the laws of any of the territories, the laws of any state, or the laws of any foreign country.

Is the case as presented by the pleadings and the evidence one of a combination or a conspiracy in restraint of trade or commerce among the states, or with foreign states? Is it one in which the defendants are properly chargeable with monopolizing or attempting to monopolize any part of such trade or commerce? Let us see what are the facts disclosed by the record.

The Great Northern Railway Company and the Northern Pacific Railway Company owned, controlled and operated separate lines of railway, — the former road extending from Superior, and from Duluth and St. Paul, to Everett, Seattle and Portland, with a branch line to Helena; the latter extending from Ashland, and from Duluth and St. Paul, to Helena, Spokane, Seattle, Tacoma and Portland. The two lines, main and branches, about 9000 miles in length, were and are parallel and competing lines across the continent through the northern tier of states between the Great Lakes and the Pacific, and the two companies were engaged in active competition for freight and passenger traffic, each road connecting at its respective terminals with lines of railway, or with lake and river steamers, or with sea-going vessels.

Prior to 1893 the Northern Pacific system was owned or controlled and operated by the Northern Pacific Railroad Company, a corporation organized under certain acts and resolutions of Congress. That company becoming insolvent, its road and property passed into the hands of receivers appointed by courts of the United States. In advance of foreclosure and sale a majority of its bondholders made an arrangement with the Great Northern Railway Company for a virtual consolidation of the two systems, and for giving the practical control of the Northern Pacific to the Great Northern. That was the arrangement declared in *Pearsall* v. *Great Northern R. Co.* 161 U. S., 646, 40 L. ed., 838, 16 Sup. Ct. Rep., 705, to be illegal under the statutes of Minnesota which forbade any railroad corporation, or the purchasers or managers of any corporation, to consolidate the stock, property or franchises of such corporation, or to lease or purchase the works or franchises of, or in any way control, other railroad corporations owning or having under their control parallel or competing lines. Minn. Gen. Laws, 1874, chap. 29, 1881, chap. 109.

Early in 1901 the Great Northern and Northern Pacific Railway Companies, having in view the ultimate placing of their two systems under a common control, united in the purchase of the capital stock of the Chicago, Burlington & Quincy Railway Company, giving in payment, upon an agreed basis of exchange, the joint bonds of the Great Northern and Northern Pacific Railway Companies, payable in twenty years from date, with interest at 4 per cent per annum. In this manner the two purchasing companies became the owners of $107,000,000 of the $112,000,000 total capital stock of the Chicago, Burlington and Quincy Railway Company, whose lines aggregated about 8000 miles, and extended from St. Paul to Chicago, and from St. Paul and Chicago to Quincy, Burlington, Des Moines, St. Louis, Kansas City, St. Joseph, Omaha, Lincoln, Denver, Cheyenne and Billings, where it connected with the Northern Pacific Railroad. By this purchase of stock the Great Northern and Northern Pacific acquired full control of the Chicago, Burlington & Quincy main line and branches.

Prior to November 13, 1901, defendant Hill and associate

stockholders of the Great Northern Railway Company, and defendant Morgan and associate stockholders of the Northern Pacific Railway Company, entered into a combination to form, under the laws of New Jersey, a *holding* corporation, to be called the Northern Securities Company, with a capital stock of $400,000,000, and to which company, in exchange for its own capital stock upon a certain basis and at a certain rate, was to be turned over the capital stock, or a controlling interest in the capital stock, of each of the constituent railway companies, with power in the holding corporation to vote such stock and in all respects to act as the owner thereof, and to do whatever it might deem necessary in aid of such railway companies or to enhance the value of their stocks. In this manner the interests of individual stockholders in the property and franchises of the two independent and competing railway companies were to be converted into an interest in the property and franchises of the holding corporation. Thus, "by making the stockholders of each system jointly interested in both systems, and by practically pooling the earnings of both for the benefit of the former stockholders of each, and by vesting the selection of the directors and officers of each system in a common body, to wit, the holding corporation, with not only the power, but the duty, to pursue a policy which would promote the interests, not of one system at the expense of the other, but of both at the expense of the public, all inducement for competition between the two systems was to be removed, a virtual consolidation effected, and a monopoly of the interstate and foreign commerce formerly carried on by the two systems as independent competitors established."

In pursuance of this combination, and to effect its objects, the defendant, the Northern Securities Company, was organized November 13, 1901, under the laws of New Jersey.

Its certificate of incorporation stated that the objects for which the company was formed were:

1. To acquire by purchase, subscription or otherwise, and to hold as investment, any bonds or other securities or evidences of indebtedness, or any shares of capital stock created or issued by any other corpo-

ration or corporations, association or associations, of the state of New Jersey, or of any other state, territory or country.

2. To purchase, hold, sell, assign, transfer, mortgage, pledge or otherwise dispose of any bonds or other securities or evidences of indebtedness created or issued by any other corporation or corporations, association or associations, of the state of New Jersey, or of any other state, territory or country, and while owner thereof to exercise all the rights, powers and privileges of ownership.

3. To purchase, hold, sell, assign, transfer, mortgage, pledge or otherwise dispose of shares of the capital stock of any other corporation or corporations, association or associations, of the state of New Jersey, or of any other state, territory or country, and while owner of such stock to exercise all the rights, powers and privileges of ownership, including the right to vote thereon.

4. To aid in any manner any corporation or association of which any bonds or other securities or evidences of indebtedness or stock are held by the corporation, and to do any acts or things designed to protect, preserve, improve or enhance the value of any such bonds or other securities or evidences of indebtedness or stock.

5. To acquire, own and hold such real and personal property as may be necessary or convenient for the transaction of its business.

It was declared in the certificate that the business or purpose of the corporation was from time to time to do any one or more of such acts and things, and that the corporation should have power to conduct its business in other states and in foreign countries, and to have one or more offices, and hold, purchase, mortgage and convey real and personal property out of New Jersey.

The total authorized capital stock of the corporation was fixed at $400,000,000, divided into 4,000,000 shares of the par value of $100 each. The amount of the capital stock with which the corporation should commence business was fixed at $30,000. The duration of the corporation was to be perpetual.

This charter having been obtained, Hill and his associate stockholders of the Great Northern Railway Company, and Morgan and associate stockholders of the Northern Pacific Railway Company, assigned to the Securities company a controlling amount of the capital stock of the respective constituent companies upon an agreed basis of exchange of the capital stock of the Securities company for each share of the capital stock of the other companies.

In further pursuance of the combination, the Securities company acquired additional stock of the defendant railway companies, issuing in lieu thereof its own stock upon the above basis, and, at the time of the bringing of this suit, held, as owner and proprietor, substantially all the capital stock of the Northern Pacific Railway Company, and, it is alleged, a controlling interest in the stock of the Great Northern Railway Company, "and is voting the same and is collecting the dividends thereon, and in all respects is acting as the owner thereof, in the organization, management and operation of said railway companies and in the receipt and control of their earnings."

No consideration whatever, the bill alleges, has existed or will exist, for the transfer of the stock of the defendant railway companies to the Northern Securities Company, other than the issue of the stock of the latter company for the purpose, after the manner, and upon the basis stated.

The Securities company, the bill also alleges, was not organized in good faith to purchase and pay for the stocks of the Great Northern and Northern Pacific Railway Companies, but solely "to incorporate the pooling of the stocks of said companies," and carry into effect the above combination; that it is a mere depositary, custodian, holder or trustee of the stocks of the Great Northern and Northern Pacific Railway Companies; that its shares of stock are but beneficial certificates against said railroad stocks to designate the interest of the holders in the pool; that it does not have and never had any capital to warrant such an operation; that its subscribed capital was but $30,000, and its authorized capital stock of $400,000,000 was just sufficient, when all issued, to represent and cover the exchange value of substantially the entire stock of the Great Northern and Northern Pacific Railway Companies, upon the basis and at the rate agreed upon, which was about $122,000,000 in excess of the combined capital stock of the two railway companies taken at par; and that, unless prevented, the Securities company would acquire, as owner and proprietor, substantially all the capital stock of the Great Northern and Northern Pacific Railway Companies, issuing in lieu thereof its own capital stock to the full extent of its authorized issue, of which, upon the agreed basis of exchange, the former stockholders of the Great Northern Railway Company have received or would receive and hold about 55 per cent, the balance going to the former stockholders of the Northern Pacific Railway Company.

The government charges that if the combination was held not to be in violation of the act of Congress, then all efforts of the national government to preserve to the people the benefits of free competition among carriers engaged in interstate commerce will be wholly unavailing, and all transcontinental lines, indeed, the entire railway systems of the country, may be absorbed, merged and consolidated, thus placing the public at the absolute mercy of the holding corporation.

The several defendants denied all the allegations of the bill imputing to them a purpose to evade the provisions of the act of Congress, or to form a combination or conspiracy having for its object either to restrain or to monopolize commerce or trade among the states or with foreign nations. They denied that any combination or conspiracy was formed in violation of the act.

In our judgment, the evidence fully sustains the material allegations of the bill, and shows a violation of the act of Congress, in so far as it declares illegal every combination or conspiracy in restraint of commerce among the several states and with foreign nations, and forbids attempts to monopolize such commerce or any part of it.

Summarizing the principal facts, it is indisputable upon this record that under the leadership of the defendants Hill and Morgan, the stockholders of the Great Northern and Northern Pacific Railway corporations, having competing and substantially parallel lines from the Great Lakes and the Mississippi River to the Pacific Ocean at Puget Sound, combined and conceived the scheme of organizing a corporation under the laws of New Jersey which should *hold* the shares of the stock of the constituent companies; such shareholders, in lieu of their shares in those companies, to receive, upon an agreed basis of value, shares in the holding corporation; that pursuant to such combination the Northern Securities Company was organized as the holding corporation through which the scheme should be executed; and under that scheme such holding corporation has become the holder — more properly speaking, the custodian — of more than nine-tenths of the stock of the Northern Pacific, and more than three-fourths of the stock of the Great Northern, the stockholders of the companies who delivered their stock receiving upon the agreed basis shares of stock in the holding corporation. The stockholders of these two competing companies disappeared, as such, for the moment, but immediately reappeared as stockholders of the holding company, which was thereafter to guard the interests of both sets of stockholders as a unit, and to manage, or cause to be managed, both lines of railroad as if held *in one ownership*. Necessarily by this combination or arrangement the holding company in the fullest sense dominates the situation in the interest of those who were stockholders of the constituent companies; as much so, for every practical purpose, as if it had been itself a railroad corporation which had built, owned and operated both lines for the exclusive benefit of its stockholders. Necessarily, also, the constituent companies ceased, under such a combination, to be in active competition for trade and commerce along their respective lines, and have become, practically, one powerful consolidated corporation, by the name of a holding corporation, the principal, if not the sole, object for the formation of which was to carry out the purpose of the original combination, under which competition between the constituent companies would cease. Those who were stockholders of the Great Northern and Northern Pacific and became stockholders in the holding company are now interested in preventing all competition between the two lines, and, as owners of stock or of certificates of stock in the holding company, they will see to it that no competition is tolerated. They will take care that no persons are chosen directors of the holding company who will permit competition between the constituent companies. The result of the combination is that all the earnings of the constituent companies make a common fund in the hands of the Northern Securities Company, to be distributed, not upon the basis of the earnings of the respective constituent companies, each acting exclusively in its own interests, but upon the basis of the certificates of stock issued by the holding company. No scheme or device could more certainly come within the words of the act, — "combination in the form of a trust or otherwise . . . in restraint of commerce among the several states or with foreign nations," — or could more effectively and certainly suppress free competition between the constituent companies. This combination is, within the meaning of the act, a "trust"; but if not, it is a *combination in restraint of interstate and international commerce;* and that is enough to bring it under the condemnation of the act. The mere existence of such a combination, and the power acquired by the holding company as its trustee, constitute a menace to, and a restraint upon, that freedom of commerce which Congress intended to recognize and protect, and which the public is entitled to have protected. If such combination be not destroyed, all the advantages that would naturally come to the public under the operation of the general laws of competition, as between the Great Northern and Northern Pacific Railway Companies, will be lost, and the entire commerce of the immense territory in the northern part of the United States between the Great Lakes and the Pacific at Puget Sound will be at the mercy of a single holding corporation, organized in a state distant from the people of that territory.

The circuit court was undoubtedly right when it said — all the judges of that court concurring — that the combination referred to "led inevitably to the following results: first, it placed the control of the two roads in the hands of a single person, to wit, the Securities Company, by virtue of its ownership of a large majority of the stock of both companies; second, it destroys every motive for competition between two roads engaged in interstate traffic, which were natural competitors for business, by pooling the earnings of the two roads for the common benefit of the stockholders of both companies." 120 Fed., 721, 724.

Such being the case made by the record, what are the principles that must control the decision of the present case? Do former adjudications determine the controlling questions raised by the pleadings and proofs?

The contention of the government is that, if regard be had to former adjudications, the present case must be determined in its favor. That view is contested and the defendants insist that a decision in their favor will not be inconsistent with anything heretofore decided and would be in harmony with the act of Congress.

Is the act to be construed as forbidding every combination or conspiracy in restraint of trade or commerce among the states or with foreign nations? Or, does it embrace only such restraints as are unreasonable in their nature? Is the motive with which a forbidden combination or conspiracy was formed at all material when it appears that the necessary tendency of the particular combination or conspiracy in question is to restrict or suppress free competition between competing railroads engaged in commerce among the states? Does the act of Congress prescribe, as a *rule* for *interstate* or *international* commerce, that the operation of the natural laws of competition between those engaged in *such* commerce shall not be restricted or interfered with by any contract, combination or conspiracy? How far may Congress go in regulating the affairs or conduct of state corporations engaged as carriers in commerce among the states or of state corporations which, although not directly engaged themselves in *such* commerce, yet have control of the business of interstate carriers? If state corporations, or their stockholders, are found to be parties to a combination in the form of a trust or otherwise, which restrains interstate or international commerce, may they not be compelled to respect any rule for such commerce that may be lawfully prescribed by Congress?

* * * * * * * *

We will not encumber this opinion by extended extracts from the former opinions of this court. It is sufficient to say that from the decisions in the above cases certain propositions are plainly deducible and embrace the present case. Those propositions are:

That although the act of Congress known as the Anti-Trust Act has no reference to the mere manufacture or production of articles or commodities within the limits of the several states, it does embrace and declare to be illegal every contract, combination or conspiracy, in whatever form, of whatever nature, and whoever may be parties to it, which directly or necessarily operates *in restraint* of trade or commerce *among the several states or with foreign nations;*

That the act is not limited to restraints of interstate and international trade or commerce that are unreasonable in their nature, but embraces *all* direct *restraints* imposed by any combination, conspiracy or monopoly upon such trade or commerce;

That railroad carriers engaged in interstate or international trade or commerce are embraced by the act;

That combinations, even among *private* manufacturers or dealers, whereby *interstate or international commerce* is restrained, are equally embraced by the act;

That Congress has the power to establish *rules* by which *interstate and international* commerce shall be governed, and, by the Anti-Trust Act, has prescribed the rule of free competition among those engaged in such commerce;

That *every* combination or conspiracy which would extinguish competition between otherwise competing railroads engaged in *interstate trade or commerce,* and which would *in that way* restrain *such* trade or commerce, is made illegal by the act;

That the natural effect of competition is to increase commerce, and an agreement whose direct effect is to prevent this play of competition restrains instead of promoting trade and commerce;

That to vitiate a combination such as the act of Congress condemns, it need not be shown that the combination, in fact, results or will result, in a total suppression of trade or in a complete monopoly, but it is only essential to show that, by its necessary operation, it tends to restrain interstate or international trade or commerce or tends to create a monopoly in such trade or commerce and to deprive the public of the advantages that flow from free competition;

That the constitutional guaranty of liberty of contract does not prevent Congress from prescribing the rule of free competition for those engaged in *interstate and international* commerce; and,

That under its power to regulate commerce among the several states and with foreign nations, Congress had authority to enact the statute in question.

No one, we assume, will deny that these propositions were distinctly announced in the former decisions of this court. They cannot be ignored or their effect avoided by the intimation that the court indulged in *obiter dicta*. What was said in those cases was within the limits of the issues made by the parties. In our opinion, the recognition of the principles announced in former cases must, under the conceded facts, lead to an affirmance of the decree below, unless the special objections, or some of them, which have been made to the application of the act of Congress to the present case, are of a substantial character. We will now consider those objections.

Underlying the argument in behalf of the defendants is the idea that, as the Northern Securities Company is a state corporation, and as its acquisition of the stock of the Great Northern and Northern Pacific Railway Companies is not inconsistent with the powers conferred by its charter, the enforcement of the act of Congress, as against those corporations, will be an unauthorized interference by the national government with the internal commerce of the states creating those corporations. This suggestion does not at all impress us. There is no reason to suppose that Congress had any purpose to interfere with the internal affairs of the states, nor, in our opinion, is there any ground whatever for the contention that the Anti-Trust Act regulates their domestic commerce. By its very terms the act regulates only commerce among the states and with foreign states. Viewed in that light, the act, if within the powers of Congress, must be respected; for, by the explicit words of the Constitution, that instrument and the laws enacted by Congress in pursuance of its provisions, are the supreme law of the land, "anything in the constitution or laws of any state to the contrary notwithstanding,"—supreme over the states, over the courts and even over the people of the United States,—the source of all power under our governmental system in respect of the objects for which the national government was ordained. An act of Congress constitutionally passed under its power to regulate commerce among the states and with foreign nations is binding upon all; as much so as if it were embodied, in terms, in the Constitution itself. Every judicial officer, whether of a national or a state court, is under the obligations of an oath so to regard a lawful enactment of Congress. Not even a state, still less one of its artificial creatures, can stand in the way of its enforcement. If it were otherwise, the government and its laws might be prostrated at the feet of local authority. *Cohen* v. *Virginia*, 6 Wheat., 264, 385, 414, 5 L. ed., 257, 286, 293. These views have been often expressed by this court.

It is said that whatever may be the power of a state over such subjects, Congress cannot forbid single individuals from disposing of their stock in a state corporation, even if such corporation be engaged in interstate and international commerce; that the holding or purchase by a state corporation, or the purchase by individuals, of the stock of another corporation, for whatever purpose, are matters in respect of which Congress has no authority under the Constitution; that, so far as the power of Congress is concerned, citizens, or state corporations, may dispose of their property and invest their money in any way they choose; and that in regard to all such matters, citizens and state corporations are subject, if to any authority, only to the lawful authority of the state in which such citizens reside or under whose laws such corporations are organized. It is unnecessary in this case to consider such abstract, general questions. The court need not now concern itself with them. They are not here to be examined and determined, and may well be left for consideration in some case necessarily involving their determination.

In this connection, it is suggested that the contention of the government is that the acquisition and *ownership* of stock in a state railroad corporation is itself interstate commerce if that corporation be engaged in interstate commerce. This suggestion is made in different ways; sometimes in express words, at other times by implication. For instance, it is said that the question here is whether the power of Congress over interstate commerce extends to the regulation of the ownership of the stock in state railroad companies, by reason of their being engaged in such commerce. Again, it is said that the only issue in this case is whether the Northern Securities Company can acquire and hold stock in other state corporations. Still further, it is asked, generally, whether the organization or ownership of railroads is not under the control of the states under whose laws they came into existence? Such statements as to the issues in this case are, we think, wholly unwarranted, and are very wide of the mark; it is the setting up of mere men of straw to be easily stricken down. We do not understand that the government makes any such contentions or takes any such positions as those statements imply. It does not contend that Congress may control the mere acquisition or the mere ownership of stock in a state corporation engaged in interstate commerce. Nor does it contend that Congress can control the organization of state corporations authorized by their charters to engage in interstate and international commerce. But it does contend that Congress may protect the freedom of interstate commerce by any means that are appropriate and that are lawful, and not prohibited by the Constitution. It does contend that no state corporation can stand in the way of the enforcement of the national will, legally expressed. What the government particularly complains of — indeed, all that it complains of here — is the existence of a combination among the stockholders of competing railroad companies which, in violation of the act of Congress, restrains interstate and international commerce through the agency of a common corporate trustee, designated to act for both companies in repressing free competition between them. Independently of any question of the mere ownership of stock or of the organization of a state corporation, can it in reason be said that such a combination is not embraced by the very terms of the Anti-Trust Act? May not Congress declare that *combination* to be illegal? If Congress legislates for the protection of the public, may it not proceed on the ground that wrongs, when effected by a powerful combination, are more dangerous and require more stringent supervision than when they are to be effected by a single person? *Callan* v. *Wilson*, 127 U. S., 540, 556, 32 L. ed., 223, 228, 8 Sup. Ct. Rep., 1301. How far may the courts go in order to give effect to the act of Congress, and remedy the evils it was designed by that act to suppress? These are confessedly questions of great moment, and they will now be considered.

By the express words of the Constitution, Congress has power to "regulate commerce with foreign nations and among the several states, and with the Indian tribes." In view of the numerous decisions of this court there ought not, at this day, to be any doubt as to the general scope of such power.

* * * * * * * *

As late as the case of *Re Debs*, 158 U. S., 564, 582, 39 L. ed., 1092, 1101, 15 Sup. Ct. Rep., 900, 905, this court, every member of it concurring, said: "The entire strength of the nation may be used to enforce in any part of the land the full and free exercise of all national powers and the security of all rights intrusted by the Constitution to its care. The strong arm of the national government may be put forth to brush away all obstructions to the freedom of interstate commerce or the transportation of the mails. If the emergency arises, the army of the nation, and all its militia, are at the service of the nation to compel obedience to its laws."

The means employed in respect of the combinations forbidden by the Anti-Trust Act, and which Congress deemed germane to the end to be accomplished, was to prescribe as *a rule* for *interstate and international* commerce (not for domestic commerce) that it should not be vexed by combinations, conspiracies or monopolies which restrain commerce by destroying or restricting competition. We say that Congress has prescribed such a rule, because, in all the prior cases in this court, the Anti-Trust Act has been construed as forbidding any combination which, by its necessary operation, destroys or restricts free competition among those engaged in interstate commerce; in other words, that to destroy or restrict free competition in interstate commerce was to restrain such commerce. Now, can this court say that such a rule is prohibited by the Constitution or is not one that Congress could appropriately prescribe when exerting its power under the commerce clause of the Constitution? Whether the free operation of the normal laws of competition is a wise and wholesome rule for trade and commerce is an economic question which this court need not consider or determine. Undoubtedly, there are those who think that the general business interests and prosperity of the country will be best promoted if the rule of competition is not applied. But there are others who believe that such a rule is more necessary in these days of enormous wealth than it ever was in any former period of our history. Be all this as it may, Congress has, in effect, recognized the rule of free competition by declaring illegal every combination or conspiracy in restraint of interstate and international commerce. As, in the judgment of Congress, the public convenience and the general welfare will be best subserved when the natural laws of competition are left undisturbed by those engaged in interstate commerce, and as Congress has embodied that rule in a statute, that must be, for all, the end of the matter, if this is to remain a government of laws, and not of men.

It is said that railroad corporations created under the laws of a state can only be consolidated with the authority of the state. Why that suggestion is made in this case we cannot understand, for there is no pretence that the combination here in question was under the authority of the states under whose laws these railroad corporations were created. But even if the state allowed consolidation, it would not follow that the stockholders of two or more state railroad corporations, having *competing lines and engaged in interstate commerce*, could lawfully combine and form a distinct corporation to hold the stock of the constituent corporations, and, by destroying competition between them, in violation of the act of Congress, restrain commerce among the states and with foreign nations.

The rule of competition, prescribed by Congress, was not at all new in trade and commerce. And we cannot be in any doubt as to the reason that moved Congress to the incorporation of that rule into a statute. That reason was thus stated in *United States* v. *Joint Traffic Asso.*: "Has not Congress, with regard to interstate commerce, and in the course of regulating it, in the case of railroad corporations, the power to say that no contract or combination shall be legal which shall restrain trade and commerce by shutting out the operation of the general law of competition? We think it has. . . . It is the combination of these large and powerful corporations, covering vast sections of territory and influencing trade throughout the whole extent thereof, and acting *as one body* in all the matters over which the combination extends, that constitutes the alleged evil, and in regard to which, *so far as the combination operates upon and restrains interstate commerce*, Congress has power to legislate and to prohibit." Pages 569, 571, L. ed., pages 287, 288, Sup. Ct. Rep., page 32. That such a rule was applied to interstate commerce should not have surprised any one. Indeed, when Congress declared contracts, combinations and conspiracies in restraint of trade or commerce to be illegal, it did nothing more than apply to interstate commerce a rule that had been long applied by the several states when dealing with combinations that were in restraint of their domestic commerce. The decisions in state courts upon this general subject are not only numerous and instructive, but they show the circumstances under which the Anti-Trust Act was passed. It may well be assumed that Congress, when enacting that statute, shared the general apprehension that a few powerful corporations or combinations sought to obtain, and, unless restrained, would obtain, such absolute control of the entire trade and commerce of the country as would be detrimental to the general welfare.

In *Morris Run Coal Co.* v. *Barclay Coal Co.*, 68 Pa., 173, 186, the supreme court of Pennsylvania dealt with a combination of coal companies seeking the control, within a large territory, of the entire market for bituminous coal. The court, observing that the combination was wide in its scope, general in its influence, and injurious in its effects, said: "When competition is left free, individual error or folly will generally find a correction in the conduct of others. But here is a combination of all the companies operating in the Blossburg and Barclay mining regions, and controlling their entire productions. They have combined together to govern the supply and the price of coal in all the markets from the Hudson to the Mississippi rivers, and from Pennsylvania to the Lakes. This combination has a power in its confederated form which no individual action can confer. The public interest must succumb to it, for it has left no competition free to correct its baleful influence. When the supply of coal is suspended the demand for it becomes importunate, and prices must rise. Or if the supply goes forward, the price fixed by the confederates must accompany it. The domestic hearth, the furnaces of the iron master and the fires of the manufacturer all feel the restraint, while many dependent hands are paralyzed and hungry mouths are stinted. The influence of a lack of supply or a rise in the price of an article of such prime necessity cannot be measured. It permeates the entire mass of the community, and leaves few of its members untouched by its withering blight. Such a combination is more than a contract; it is an offence. . . . In all such combinations where the purpose is injurious or unlawful, the gist of the offence is the conspiracy. Men can often do by the *combination* of many what, severally, no one could accomplish, and even what, when done by one, would be innocent. . . . *There is a potency in numbers when combined* which the law cannot overlook, where injury is the consequence." The same principles were applied in *Arnot* v. *Pittston & E. Coal Co.*, 68 N. Y., 558, 565, 23 Am. Rep., 190, 194, which was the case of a combination of two coal companies in order to give one of them a monopoly of coal in a particular region, the court of appeals of New York holding that "a combination to effect such a purpose is inimical to the interests of the public, and that all contracts designed to effect such an end are contrary to public policy, and therefore illegal." They were also applied by the supreme court of Ohio in *Central Ohio Salt Co.* v. *Guthrie*, 35 Ohio St., 666, 672, which was the case of a combination among manufacturers of salt in a large salt-producing territory, the court saying: "It is no answer to say that competition in the salt trade was not in fact destroyed, or that the price of the commodity was not unreasonably advanced. *Courts will not stop to inquire as to the degree of injury inflicted upon the public; it is enough to know that the inevitable tendency of such contracts is injurious to the public.*"

So, in *Craft* v. *McConoughy*, 79 Ill., 346, 350, 22 Am. Rep., 171, 174, which was the case of a combination among grain dealers by which competition was stifled, the court saying: "So long as competition was free, the interest of the public was safe. The laws of trade, in connection with the rigor of competition, was all the guaranty the public required; but the secret combination created by the contract destroyed all competition, and created a monopoly against which the public interest had no protection." Again, in *People ex rel. Peabody* v. *Chicago Gas Trust Co.*, 130 Ill., 269, 297, 8 L. R. A., 497, 506, 22 N. E., 798, 804, which involved the validity of the organization of a gas corporation which obtained a monopoly in the business of furnishing illuminating gas in the city of Chicago by buying the stock of four other gas companies, it was said: "Of what avail is it that any number of gas companies may be formed under the general incorporation law, if a giant trust company can be clothed with the power of buying up and holding the stock and property of such companies, and, through the control thereby attained, can direct all their operations and weld them into one huge combination?" To the same effect are cases almost too numerous to be cited. But among them we refer to *Richardson* v. *Buhl*, 77 Mich., 632, 6 L. R. A., 457, 43 N. W., 1102, which was the case of the organization of a corporation in Connecticut to unite in one corporation all the match manufacturers in the United States, and thus to obtain control of the business of manufacturing matches; *Santa Clara Valley Mill & Lumber Co.* v. *Hayes*, 76 Cal., 387, 390, 18 Pac., 391, which was the case of a combination among manufacturers of lumber, by which it could control the business in certain localities; and *India Bagging Asso.* v. *Kock*, 14 La. Ann., 164, which was the case of a combination among various commercial firms to control the prices of bagging used by cotton planters.

The cases just cited, it is true, relate to the domestic commerce of the states. But they serve to show the authority which the states possess to guard the public against *combinations* that repress individual enterprise and interfere with the operation of the natural laws of competition among those engaged in trade within its limits. They serve also to give point to the declaration of this court in *Gibbons* v. *Ogden*, 9 Wheat. 197, 6 L. ed., 70, — a principle never modified by any subsequent decision, — that, subject to the limitations imposed by the Constitution upon the exercise of the powers granted by that instrument, "the power over commerce with foreign nations and among the several states is vested in Congress as absolutely as it would be in a single government having in its constitution the same restrictions on the exercise of the power as are found in the Constitution of the United States." Is there, then, any escape from the conclusion that, subject only to such restrictions, the power of Congress over interstate and international commerce is as full and complete as is the power of any state over its domestic commerce? If a state may strike down combinations that restrain its domestic commerce by destroying free competition among those engaged in such commerce, what power, except that of Congress, is competent to protect the freedom of interstate and international commerce when assailed by a combination that restrains such commerce by stifling competition among those engaged in it?

Now, the court is asked to adjudge that, if held to embrace the case before us, the Anti-Trust Act is repugnant to the Constitution of the United States. In this view we are unable to concur. The contention of the defendants could not be sustained without, in effect, overruling the prior decisions of this court as to the scope and validity of the Anti-Trust Act. If, as the court has held, Congress can strike down a combination between private persons or private corporations that restrains trade among the states in iron pipe (as in *Addyston Pipe & Steel Co.* v. *United States*) or in tiles, grates and mantels (as in *W. W. Montague & Co.* v. *Lowry*), surely it ought not to be doubted that Congress has power to declare illegal a combination that restrains commerce among the states, and with foreign nations, as carried on over the lines of competing railroad companies exercising public franchises, and engaged in such commerce. We cannot agree that Congress may strike down combinations among manufacturers and dealers in iron pipe, tiles, grates and mantels that restrain commerce among the states in such articles, but may not strike down combinations among stockholders of competing railroad carriers, which restrain commerce as involved in the transportation of passengers and property among the several states. If private parties may not, by combination among themselves, restrain interstate and international commerce in violation of an act of Congress, much less can such restraint be tolerated when imposed, or attempted to be imposed, upon commerce as carried on over public highways. Indeed, if the contentions of the defendants are sound, why may not *all* the railway companies in the United States, that are engaged, under state charters, in interstate and international commerce, enter into a combination such as the one here in question, and, by the device of a holding corporation, obtain the absolute control throughout the entire country of rates for passengers and freight, beyond the power of Congress to protect the public against their exactions? The argument in behalf of the defendants necessarily leads to such results, and places Congress, although invested by the people of the United States with full authority to regulate interstate and international commerce, in a condition of utter helplessness, so far as the protection of the public against such combinations is concerned.

Will it be said that Congress can meet such emergencies by prescribing the rates by which interstate carriers shall be governed in the transportation of freight and passengers? If Congress has the power to fix such rates — and upon that question we express no opinion — it does not choose to exercise its power in that way or to that extent. It has, all will agree, a large discretion as to the means to be employed in the exercise of any power granted to it. For the present, it has determined to go no farther than to protect the freedom of commerce among the states and with foreign states by declaring illegal all contracts, combinations, conspiracies or monopolies in restraint of such commerce, and make it a public offence to violate the rule thus prescribed. How much further it may go, we do not now say. We need only at this time consider whether it has exceeded its powers in enacting the statute here in question.

Assuming, without further discussion, that the case before us is within the terms of the act, and that the act is not in excess of the powers of Congress, we recur to the question, How far may the courts go in reaching and suppressing the combination described in the bill? All will agree that if the Anti-Trust Act be constitutional, and if the combination in question be in violation of its provisions, the courts may enforce the provisions of the statute by such orders and decrees as are necessary or appropriate to that end and as may be consistent with the fundamental rules of legal procedure. And all, we take it, will agree, as established firmly by the decisions of this court, that the power of Congress over commerce extends to all the instrumentalities of such commerce, and to every device that many be employed to interfere with the freedom of commerce among the states and with foreign nations. Equally, we assume, all will agree that the Constitution and the legal enactments of Congress are, by express words of the Constitution, the supreme law of the land, anything in the constitution and laws of any state to the contrary notwithstanding. Nevertheless, the defendants, strangely enough, invoke in their behalf the 10th Amendment of the Constitution, which declares that "the powers not delegated to the United States by the Constitution, nor prohibited by it to the states, are reserved to the states respectively or to the people"; and we are confronted with the suggestion that any order or decree of the Federal court which will prevent the Northern Securities Company from exercising the power it acquired in becoming the holder of the stocks of the Great Northern and Northern Pacific Railway Companies will be an invasion of the rights of the state under which the Securities company was chartered, as well as of the rights of the states creating the other companies. In other words, if the state of New Jersey gives a charter to a corporation, and even if the obtaining of such charter is in fact pursuant to a *combination* under which it becomes the holder of the stocks of shareholders in two competing, parallel railroad companies engaged in interstate commerce in other states, whereby competition between the respective roads of those companies is to be destroyed and the enormous commerce carried on over them restrained by suppressing competition, Congress must stay its hands and allow such restraint to continue, to the detriment of the public, because, forsooth, the corporations concerned or some of them are state corporations. We cannot conceive how it is possible for any one to seriously contend for such a proposition. It means nothing less than that Congress, in regulating interstate commerce, must act in subordination to the will of the states when exerting their power to create corporations. No such view can be entertained for a moment.

It is proper to say in passing that nothing in the record tends to show that the state of New Jersey had any reason to suspect that those who took advantage of its liberal incorporation laws had in view, when organizing the Securities company, to destroy competition between two great railway carriers engaged in interstate commerce in distant states of the Union. The purpose of the combination was concealed under very general words that gave no clew whatever to the real purposes of those who brought about the organization of the Securities company. If the certificate of incorporation of that company had expressly stated that the object of the company was to destroy competition between competing, parallel lines of interstate carriers, all would have seen, at the outset, that the scheme was in hostility to the national authority, and that there was a purpose to violate or evade the act of Congress.

We reject any such view of the relations of the national government and the states composing the Union as that for which the defendants contend. Such a view cannot be maintained without destroying the just authority of the United States. It is inconsistent with all the decisions of this court as to the powers of the national government over matters committed to it. No state can, by merely creating a corporation, or in any other mode, project its authority into other states, and across the continent, so as to prevent Congress from exerting the power it possesses under the Constitution over interstate and international commerce, or so as to exempt its corporation engaged in interstate commerce from obedience to any rule lawfully established by Congress for such commerce. It cannot be said that any state may give a corporation, created under its laws, authority to restrain interstate or international commerce against the will of the nation as lawfully expressed by Congress. Every corporation created by a state is necessarily subject to the supreme law of the land. And yet the suggestion is made that to restrain a state corporation from interfering with the free course of trade and commerce among the states, in violation of an act of Congress, is hostile to the reserved rights of the states. The Federal court may not have power to forfeit the charter of the Securities company; it may not declare how its shares of stock may be transferred on its books, nor prohibit it from acquiring real estate, nor diminish or increase its capital stock. All these and like matters are to be regulated by the state which created the company. But to the end that effect be given to the national will, lawfully expressed, Congress may prevent that company, in its capacity as a holding corporation and trustee, from carrying out the purposes of a combination formed in restraint of interstate commerce. The Securities company is itself a part of the present combination; its head and front; its trustee. It would be extraordinary if the court, in executing the act of Congress, could not lay hands upon that company and prevent it from doing that which, if done, will defeat the act of Congress. Upon like grounds the court can, by appropriate orders, prevent the two competing railroad companies here involved from coöperating with the Securities company in restraining commerce among the states. In short, the court may make any order necessary to bring about the dissolution or suppression of an illegal combination that restrains interstate commerce. All this can be done without infringing in any degree upon the just authority of the states. The affirmance of the judgment below will only mean that no combination, however powerful, is stronger than the law, or will be permitted to avail itself of the pretext that to prevent it doing that which, if done, would defeat a legal enactment of Congress, is to attack the reserved right of the states. It would mean that the government which represents all, can, when acting within the limits of its powers, compel obedience to its authority. It would mean that no device in evasion of its provisions, however skilfully such device may have been contrived, and no combination, by whomsoever formed, is beyond the reach of the supreme law of the land, if such device or combination, by its operation, directly restrains commerce among the states or with foreign nations in violation of the act of Congress.

The defendants rely, with some confidence, upon the case of the *Baltimore & O. R. Co.* v. *Maryland*, 21 Wall., 456, 473, 22 L. ed., 678, 684. But nothing we have said is inconsistent with any principle announced in that case. The court there recognized the principle that a state has plenary powers "over its own territory, its highways, its franchises and its corporations," and observed that "we are bound to sustain the constitutional powers and prerogatives of the states, as well as those of the United States, whenever they are brought before us for adjudication, no matter what may be the consequences." Of course, every state has, in a general sense, plenary power over its corporations. But is it conceivable that a state, when exerting power over a corporation of its creation, may prevent or embarrass the exercise by Congress of any power with which it is invested by the Constitution? In the case just referred to the court does not say, and it is not to be supposed that it will ever say, that any power exists with a state to prevent the enforcement of a lawful enactment of Congress, or to invest any of its corporations, in whatever business engaged, with authority to disregard such enactment or defeat its legitimate operation. On the contrary, the court has steadily held to the doctrine, vital to the United States as well as to the states, that a state enactment, even if passed in the exercise of its acknowledged powers, must yield, in case of conflict, to the supremacy of the Constitution of the United States and the acts of Congress enacted in pursuance of its provisions. This results, the court has said, as well from the nature of the government as from the words of the Constitution. *Gibbons* v. *Ogden*, 9 Wheat., 1, 210, 6 L. ed., 23, 73; *Sinnot* v. *Davenport*, 22 How., 227, 243, 16 L. ed., 243, 247; *Re Debs*, 158 U. S., 564, 39 L. ed., 1092, 15 Sup. Ct. Rep., 900; *Missouri, K. & T. R. Co.* v. *Haber*, 169 U. S., 613, 626, 627, 42 L. ed., 878, 883, 18 Sup. Ct. Rep., 488. In *Texas* v. *White*, 7 Wall., 700, 725, 19 L. ed., 227, 237, the court remarked "that 'the people of each state compose a state, having its own government, and endowed with all the functions essential to separate and independent existence,' and that 'without the states in union, there could be no such political body as the United States.' *Lane County* v. *Oregon*, 7 Wall., 76, 19 L. ed., 104. Not only, therefore, can there be no loss of separate and independent autonomy to the states, through their union under the Constitution, but it may be not unreasonably said that the preservation of the states, and the maintenance of their governments, are as much within the design and care of the Constitution as the preservation of the Union and the maintenance of the national government." These doctrines are at the basis of our constitutional government, and cannot be disregarded with safety.

The defendants also rely on *Louisville & N. R. Co.* v. *Kentucky*, 161 U. S., 677, 702, 40 L. ed., 849, 859, 16 Sup. Ct. Rep., 714, 724. In that case it was contended by the railroad company that the assumption of the state to forbid the consolidation of parallel and competing lines was an interference with the power of Congress over interstate commerce. The court observed that but little need be said in answer to such a proposition, for "it has never been supposed that the dominant power of Congress over interstate commerce took from the states the power of legislation with respect to the instruments of such commerce, so far as the legislation was within its ordinary police powers." But that case distinctly recognized that there was a division of power between Congress and the states in respect to interstate railways, and that Congress had the superior right to control that commerce and forbid interference therewith, while to the states remained the power to create and to regulate the instruments of such commerce, so far as necessary to the conservation of the public interests. If there is anything in that case which even intimates that a state or a state corporation may in any way directly restrain interstate commerce, over which Congress has, by the Constitution, complete control, we have been unable to find it.

The question of the relations of the general government with the states is again presented by the specific contention of each defendant that Congress did not intend "to limit the power of the several states to create corporations, define their purposes, fix the amount of their capital, and determine who may buy, own and sell their stock." All that is true, generally speaking, but the contention falls far short of meeting the controlling questions in this case. To meet this contention we must repeat some things already said in this opinion. But if what we have said be sound, repetition will do no harm. So far as the Constitution of the United States is concerned, a state may, indeed, create a corporation, define its powers, prescribe the amount of its stock and the mode in which it may be transferred. It may even authorize one of its corporations to engage in commerce of every kind, — domestic, interstate and international. The regulation or control of purely domestic commerce of a state is, of course, with the state, and Congress has no direct power over it so long as what is done by the state does not interfere with the operations of the general government, or any legal enactment of Congress. A state, if it chooses so to do, may even submit to the existence of combinations within its limits that restrain its internal trade. But neither a state corporation nor its stockholders can, by reason of the nonaction of the state or by means of any combination among such stockholders, interfere with the complete enforcement of any rule lawfully devised by Congress for the conduct of commerce among the states or with foreign nations; for, as we have seen, interstate and international commerce is, by the Constitution, under the control of Congress, and it belongs to the legislative department of the government to prescribe rules for the conduct of that commerce. If it were otherwise, the declaration in the Constitution of its supremacy, and of the supremacy as well of the laws made in pursuance of its provisions, was a waste of words. Whilst every instrumentality of domestic commerce is subject to state control, every instrumentality of interstate commerce may be reached and controlled by national authority, *so far as to compel it to respect the rules for such commerce lawfully established by Congress*. No corporate person can excuse a departure from or violation of that rule under the plea that that which it has done or omitted to do is permitted, or not forbidden, by the state under whose authority it came into existence. We repeat that no state can endow any of its corporations, or any combination of its citizens, with authority to restrain interstate or international commerce, or to disobey the national will as manifested in legal enactments of Congress. So long as Congress keeps within the limits of its authority as defined by the Constitution, infringing no rights recognized or secured by that instrument, its regulations of interstate and international commerce, whether founded in wisdom or not, must be submitted to by all. Harm, and only harm, can come from the failure of the courts to recognize this fundamental principle of constitutional construction. To depart from it because of the circumstances of special cases, or because the rule, in its operation, may possibly affect the interests of business, is to endanger the safety and integrity of our institutions and make the Constitution mean not what it says, but what interested parties wish it to mean at a particular time and under particular circumstances. The supremacy of the law is the foundation rock upon which our institutions rest. The law, this court said in *United States* v. *Lee*, 106 U. S., 196, 220, 27 L. ed., 171, 181, 1 Sup. Ct. Rep., 240, is the only supreme power in our system of government. And no higher duty rests upon this court than to enforce, by its decrees, the will of the legislative department of the government, as expressed in a statute, unless such statute be plainly and unmistakably in violation of the Constitution. If the statute is beyond the constitutional power of Congress, the court would fail in the performance of a solemn duty if it did not so declare. But if nothing more can be said than that Congress has erred, — and the court must not be understood as saying that it has or has not erred,— the remedy for the error and the attendant mischief is the selection of new senators and representatives, who, by legislation, will make such changes in existing statutes, or adopt such new statutes, as may be demanded by their constituents and be consistent with law.

Many suggestions were made in argument based upon the thought that the Anti-Trust Act would, in the end, prove to be mischievous in its consequences. Disaster to business and widespread financial ruin, it has been intimated, will follow the execution of its provisions. Such predictions were made in all the cases heretofore arising under that act. But they have not been verified. It is the history of monopolies in this country and in England that predictions of ruin are habitually made by them when it is attempted, by legislation, to restrain their operations and to protect the public against their exactions. In this, as in former cases, they seek shelter behind the reserved rights of the states and even behind the constitutional guaranty of liberty of contract. But this court has heretofore adjudged that the act of Congress did not touch the rights of the states, and that liberty of contract did not involve a right to deprive the public of the advantages of free competition in trade and commerce. Liberty of contract does not imply liberty in a corporation or individuals to defy the national will, when legally expressed. Nor does the enforcement of a legal enactment of Congress infringe, in any proper sense, the general inherent right of every one to acquire and hold property. That right, like all other rights, must be exercised in subordination to the law.

But even if the court shared the gloomy forebodings in which the defendants indulge, it could not refuse to respect the action of the legislative branch of the government if what it has done is within the limits of its constitutional power. The suggestions of disaster to business have, we apprehend, their origin in the zeal of parties who are opposed to the policy underlying the act of Congress or are interested in the result of this particular case; at any rate, the suggestions imply that the court may and ought to refuse the enforcement of the provisions of the act if, in its judgment, Congress was not wise in prescribing as a rule by which the conduct of interstate and international commerce is to be governed, that every combination, whatever its form, in restraint of such commerce and the monopolizing or attempting to monopolize such commerce, shall be illegal. These, plainly, are questions as to the policy of legislation which belong to another department, and this court has no function to supervise such legislation from the standpoint of wisdom or policy. We need only say that Congress has authority to declare, and by the language of its act, as interpreted in prior cases, has, in effect, declared, that the freedom of interstate and international commerce shall not be obstructed or disturbed by any combination, conspiracy or monopoly that will restrain such commerce, by preventing the free operation of competition among interstate carriers engaged in the transportation of passengers and freight. This court cannot disregard that declaration unless Congress, in passing the statute in question, be held to have transgressed the limits prescribed for its action by the Constitution. But, as already indicated, it cannot be so held consistently with the provisions of that instrument.

The combination here in question may have been for the

pecuniary benefit of those who formed or caused it to be formed. But the interests of private persons and corporations cannot be made paramount to the interests of the general public. Under the Articles of Confederation commerce among the original states was subject to vexatious and local regulations that took no account of the general welfare. But it was for the protection of the general interests, as involved in interstate and international commerce, that Congress, representing the whole country, was given by the Constitution full power to regulate commerce among the states and with foreign nations. In *Brown* v. *Maryland*, 12 Wheat., 419, 446, 6 L. ed., 678, 688, it was said: "Those who felt the injury arising from this state of things, and those who were capable of estimating the influence of commerce on the prosperity of nations, perceived the necessity of giving the control over this important subject to a single government. It may be doubted whether any of the evils proceeding from the feebleness of the Federal government contributed more to that great revolution which introduced the present system than the deep and general conviction that commerce ought to be regulated by Congress." Railroad companies, we said in the Trans-Missouri Freight Asso. case, "are instruments of commerce, and their business is commerce itself." And such companies, it must be remembered, operate "public highways, established primarily for the convenience of the people, and therefore are subject to governmental control and regulation."

* * * * * * * *

When such carriers, in the exercise of public franchises, engage in the transportation of passengers and freight among the states, they become — even if they be state corporations — subject to such rules as Congress may lawfully establish for the conduct of interstate commerce.

It was said in argument that the circumstances under which the Northern Securities Company obtained the stock of the constituent companies imported simply an investment in the stock of other corporations, — a purchase of that stock; which investment or purchase, it is contended, was not forbidden by the charter of the company, and could not be made illegal by any act of Congress. This view is wholly fallacious, and does not comport with the actual transaction. There was no actual investment, in any substantial sense, by the Northern Securities Company in the stock of the two constituent companies. If it was, in form, such a transaction, it was not, in fact, one of that kind. However that company may have acquired for itself any stock in the Great Northern and Northern Pacific Railway Companies, no matter how it obtained the means to do so, all the stock it held or acquired in the constituent companies was acquired and held to be used in suppressing competition between those companies. It came into existence only for that purpose. If any one had full knowledge of what was designed to be accomplished, and as to what was actually accomplished, by the combination in question, it was the defendant Morgan. In his testimony he was asked, "Why put the stocks of *both* these [constituent companies] into one holding company?" He frankly answered, "In the first place, this holding company was simply a question of *custodian*, because it had no other alliances." That disclosed the actual nature of the transaction, which was only to organize the Northern Securities Company as a *holding* company, in whose hands, not as a real purchaser or absolute owner, but simply as custodian, were to be placed the stocks of the constituent companies, — such custodian to represent the combination formed between the shareholders of the constituent companies, the direct and necessary effect of such combination being, as already indicated, to restrain and monopolize interstate commerce by suppressing, or (to use the words of this court in *United States* v. *Joint Traffic Asso.*) "smothering" competition between the lines of two railway carriers.

We will now inquire as to the nature and extent of the relief granted to the government by the decree below.

* * * * * * * *

Guided by these long-established rules of construction, it is manifest that if the Anti-Trust Act is held not to embrace a case such as is now before us, the plain intention of the legislative branch of the government will be defeated. If Congress has not, by the words used in the act, described this and like cases, it would, we apprehend, be impossible to find words that would describe them. This, it must be remembered, is a suit in equity, instituted by authority of Congress "to prevent and restrain violations of the act," § 4; and the court, in virtue of a well-settled rule governing proceedings in equity, may mould its decree so as to accomplish practical results, — such results as law and justice demand. The defendants have no just cause to complain of the decree, in matter of law, and it should be affirmed.

The judgment of the court is that the decree below be and hereby is affirmed, with liberty to the circuit court to proceed in the execution of its decree as the circumstances may require.

Affirmed.

Mr. Justice Brewer, concurring:

I cannot assent to all that is said in the opinion just announced, and believe that the importance of the case and the questions involved justify a brief statement of my views.

First, let me say that while I was with the majority of the court in the decision in *United States* v. *Trans-Missouri Freight Asso., etc.*, . . . and while a further examination (which has been induced by the able and exhaustive arguments of counsel in the present case) has not disturbed the conviction that those cases were rightly decided, I think that in some respects the reasons given for the judgments cannot be sustained. Instead of holding that the Anti-Trust Act included all contracts, reasonable or unreasonable, in restraint of interstate trade, the ruling should have been that the contracts there presented were unreasonable restraints of interstate trade, and as such within the scope of the act. That act, as appears from its title, was levelled at only "unlawful restraints and monopolies." Congress did not intend to reach and destroy those minor contracts in partial restraint of trade which the long course of decisions at common law had affirmed were reasonable and ought to be upheld. The purpose rather was to place a statutory prohibition, with prescribed penalties and remedies, upon those contracts which were in direct restraint of trade, unreasonable, and against public policy. Whenever a departure from common-law rules and definitions is claimed, the purpose to make the departure should be clearly shown. Such a purpose does not appear, and such a departure was not intended.

Further, the general language of the act is also limited by the power which each individual has to manage his own property and determine the place and manner of its investment. Freedom of action in these respects is among the inalienable rights of every citizen. If, applying this thought to the present case, it appeared that Mr. Hill was the owner of a majority of the stock in the Great Northern Railway Company, he could not, by any act of Congress, be deprived of the right of investing his surplus means in the purchase of stock of the Northern Pacific Railway Company, although such purchase might tend to vest in him through that ownership a control over both companies. In other words, the right which all other citizens had, of purchasing Northern Pacific stock, could not be denied to him by Congress because of his ownership of stock in the Great Northern Company. Such was the ruling in *Pearsall* v. *Great Northern R. Co.*, 161 U. S., 646, 40 L. ed., 838, 16 Sup. Ct. Rep., 705, in which this court said (page 671, L. ed., page 847, Sup. Ct. Rep., 712), in reference to the right of the stockholders of the Great Northern Company to purchase the stock of the Northern Pacific Railway Company, "Doubtless these stockholders could lawfully acquire, by individual purchases, a majority or even the whole of the stock of the reorganized company, and thus possibly obtain its ultimate control; but the companies would still remain separate corporations, with no interests, as such, in common."

But no such investment by a single individual of his means is here presented. There was a combination by several individuals, separately owning stock in two competing railroad companies, to place the control of both in a single corporation. The purpose to combine, and by combination destroy competition, existed before the organization of the corporation, the Securities company. That corporation, though nominally having a capital stock of $400,000,000, had no means of its own; $30,000 in cash was put into its treasury, but simply for the expenses of organization. The organizers might just as well have made the nominal stock a thousand millions as four hundred, and the corporation would have been no richer or poorer. A corporation, while by fiction of law recognized for some purposes as a person, and, for purposes of jurisdiction, as a citizen, is not endowed with the inalienable rights of a natural person. It is an artificial person, created and existing only for the convenient transaction of business. In this case it was a mere instrumentality by which separate railroad properties were combined under one control. That combination is as direct a restraint of trade by destroying competition as the appointment of a committee to regulate rates. The prohibition of such a combination is not at all inconsistent with the right of an individual to purchase stock. The transfer of stock to the Securities company was a mere incident, the manner in which the combination to destroy competition, and thus unlawfully restrain trade, was carried out.

If the parties interested in these two railroad companies can, through the instrumentality of a holding corporation, place both under one control, then in like manner, as was conceded on the argument by one of the counsel for the appellants, could the control of all the railroad companies in the country be placed in a single corporation. Nor need this arrangement for control stop with what has already been done. The holders of $201,000,000 of stock in the Northern Securities Company might organize another corporation to hold their stock in that company, and the new corporation, holding the majority of the stock in the Northern Securities Company, and acting in obedience to the wishes of a majority of its stockholders, would control the action of the Securities company and through it the action of the two railroad companies; and this process might be extended until a single corporation whose stock was owned by three or four parties would be in practical control of both roads; or, having before us the possibilities of combination, the control of the whole transportation system of the country. I cannot believe that to be a reasonable or lawful restraint of trade.

*   *   *   *   *   *   *   *

I have felt constrained to make these observations for fear

that the broad and sweeping language of the opinion of the court might tend to unsettle legitimate business enterprises, stifle or retard wholesome business activities, encourage improper disregard of reasonable contracts, and invite unnecessary litigation.

Mr. Justice Holmes, with whom concurred the Chief Justice, Mr. Justice White, and Mr. Justice Peckham, dissenting:

I am unable to agree with the judgment of the majority of the court, and although I think it useless and undesirable, as a rule, to express dissent, I feel bound to do so in this case and to give my reasons for it.

Great cases, like hard cases, make bad law. For great cases are called great, not by reason of their real importance in shaping the law of the future, but because of some accident of immediate overwhelming interest which appeals to the feelings and distorts the judgment. These immediate interests exercise a kind of hydraulic pressure which makes what previously was clear seem doubtful, and before which even well-settled principles of law will bend. What we have to do in this case is to find the meaning of some not very difficult words. We must try, — I have tried, — to do it with the same freedom of natural and spontaneous interpretation that one would be sure of if the same question arose upon an indictment for a similar act which excited no public attention, and was of importance only to a prisoner before the court. Furthermore, while at times judges need for their work the training of economists or statesmen, and must act in view of their foresight of consequences, yet, when their task is to interpret and apply the words of a statute, their function is merely academic to begin with, — to read English intelligently, — and a consideration of consequences comes into play, if at all, only when the meaning of the words used is open to reasonable doubt.

The question to be decided is whether, under the act of July 2, 1890 (26 Stat. at L., 209, chap. 647, U. S. Comp. Stat., 1901, page 3200), it is unlawful, at any stage of the process, if several men unite to form a corporation for the purpose of buying more than half the stock of each of two competing interstate railroad companies, if they form the corporation, and the corporation buys the stock. I will suppose further that every step is taken, from the beginning, with the single intent of ending competition between the companies. I make this addition not because it may not be and is not disputed, but because, as I shall try to show, it is totally unimportant under any part of the statute with which we have to deal.

The statute of which we have to find the meaning is a criminal statute. The two sections on which the government relies both make certain acts crimes. That is their immediate purpose and that is what they say. It is vain to insist that this is not a criminal proceeding. The words cannot be read one way in a suit which is to end in fine and imprisonment and another way in one which seeks an injunction. The construction which is adopted in this case must be adopted in one of the other sort. I am no friend of artificial interpretations because a statute is of one kind rather than another, but all agree that before a statute is to be taken to punish that which always has been lawful, it must express its intent in clear words. So I say we must read the words before us as if the question were whether two small exporting grocers should go to jail.

Again, the statute is of a very sweeping and general character. It hits "every" contract or combination of the prohibited sort, great or small, and "every" person who shall monopolize or attempt to monopolize, in the sense of the act, "any part" of the trade or commerce among the several states. There is a natural inclination to assume that it was directed against certain great combinations, and to read it in that light. It does not say so. On the contrary, it says "every," and "any part." Still less was it directed specially against railroads. There even was a reasonable doubt whether it included railroads until the point was decided by this court.

Finally, the statute must be construed in such a way as not merely to save its constitutionality, but, so far as is consistent with a fair interpretation, not to raise grave doubts on that score. I assume, for the purposes of discussion, although it would be a great and serious step to take, that in some case that seemed to it to need heroic measures, Congress might regulate not only commerce, but instruments of commerce, or contracts the bearing of which upon commerce would be only indirect. But it is clear that the mere fact of an indirect effect upon commerce, not shown to be certain and very great, would not justify such a law. The point decided in *United States* v. *E. C. Knight Co.*, 156 U. S., 1, 17, 39 L. ed., 325, 331, 15 Sup. Ct. Rep., 249, 255, was that "the fact . . . that trade or commerce might be indirectly affected was not enough to entitle complainants to a decree." Commerce depends upon population, but Congress could not, on that ground, undertake to regulate marriage and divorce. If the act before us is to be carried out according to what seems to me the logic of the argument for the government, which I do not believe that it will be, I can see no part of the conduct of life with which, on similar principles, Congress might not interfere.

This act is construed by the government to affect the purchasers of shares in two railroad companies because of the effect it may have, or, if you like, is certain to have, upon the competition of these roads. If such a remote result of the exercise of an ordinary incident of property and personal freedom is enough to make that exercise unlawful, there is hardly any transaction concerning commerce between the states that may not be made a crime by the finding of a jury or a court. The personal ascendency of one man may be such that it would give to his advice the effect of a command, if he owned but a single share in each road. The tendency of his presence in the stockholders' meetings might be certain to prevent competition, and thus his advice, if not his mere existence, become a crime.

I state these general considerations as matters which I should have to take into account before I could agree to affirm the decree appealed from, but I do not need them for my own opinion, because, when I read the act I cannot feel sufficient doubt as to the meaning of the words to need to fortify my conclusion by any generalities. Their meaning seems to me plain on their face.

The first section makes "every contract, combination in the form of trust or otherwise, or conspiracy in restraint of trade or commerce among the several states, or with foreign nations" a misdemeanor, punishable by fine, imprisonment, or both. Much trouble is made by substituting other phrases assumed to be equivalent, which then are reasoned from as if they were in the act. The court below argued as if maintaining competition were the expressed object of the act. The act says nothing about competition. I stick to the exact words used. The words hit two classes of cases, and only two, — contracts in restraint of trade and combinations or conspiracies in restraint of trade, — and we have to consider what these respectively are. Contracts in restraint of trade are dealt with and defined by the common law. They are contracts with a stranger to the contractor's business (although, in some cases, carrying on a similar one), which wholly or partially restrict the freedom of the contractor in carrying on that business as otherwise he would. The objection of the common law to them was, primarily, on the contractor's own account. The notion of monopoly did not come in unless the contract covered the whole of England. *Mitchel* v. *Reynolds*, 1 P. Wms., 181. Of course, this objection did not apply to partnerships or other forms, if there were any, of substituting a community of interest where there had been competition. There was no objection to such combinations merely as in restraint of trade or otherwise unless they amounted to a monopoly. Contracts in restraint of trade, I repeat, were contracts with strangers to the contractor's business, and the trade restrained was the contractor's own.

Combinations or conspiracies in restraint of trade, on the other hand, were combinations to keep strangers to the agreement out of the business. The objection to them was not an objection to their effect upon the parties making the contract, the members of the combination or firm, but an objection to their intended effect upon strangers to the firm and their supposed consequent effect upon the public at large. In other words, they were regarded as contrary to public policy because they monopolized, or attempted to monopolize, some portion of the trade or commerce of the realm. See *United States* v. *E. C. Knight Co.* 156 U. S., 1, 39 L. ed., 325, 15 Sup. Ct. Rep., 249. All that is added to the first section by § 2 is that like penalties are imposed upon every single person who, without combination, monopolizes, or attempts to monopolize, commerce among the states; and that the liability is extended to attempting to monopolize any part of such trade or commerce. It is more important as an aid to the construction of § 1 than it is on its own account. It shows that whatever is criminal when done by way of combination is equally criminal if done by a single man. That I am right in my interpretation of the words of § 1 is shown by the words "in the form of trust or otherwise." The prohibition was suggested by the trusts, the objection to which, as every one knows, was not the union of former competitors, but the sinister power exercised or supposed to be exercised by the combination in keeping rivals out of the business and ruining those who already were in. It was the ferocious extreme of competition with others, not the cessation of competition among the partners, that was the evil feared. Further proof is to be found in § 7, giving an action to any person injured in his business or property by the forbidden conduct. This cannot refer to the parties to the agreement, and plainly means that outsiders who are injured in their attempt to compete with a trust or other similar combination may recover for it. *W. W. Montague & Co.* v. *Lowry*, 193 U. S., 38; 24 Sup. Ct. Rep., 307. How effective the section may be or how far it goes is not material to my point. My general summary of the two classes of cases which the act affects is confirmed by the title, which is "An Act to Protect Trade and Commerce Against Unlawful Restraints and Monopolies."

What I now ask is under which of the foregoing classes this case is supposed to come; and that question must be answered as definitely and precisely as if we were dealing with the indictments which logically ought to follow this decision. The provision of the statute against contracts in restraint of trade has been held to apply to contracts between railroads, otherwise remaining independent, by which they restricted their respective freedom as to rates. This restriction by contract with a stranger to the contractor's business is the ground of the decision in *United States* v. *Joint Traffic Asso.*, 171 U. S., 505, 43 L. ed., 259, 19 Sup. Ct. Rep., 25, following and affirming *United States* v. *Trans-Missouri Freight Asso.*, 166 U. S., 290, 41 L. ed., 1007, 17 Sup. Ct. Rep., 540. I accept those decisions absolutely, not only as binding upon me, but as decisions which I have no desire to criticise or abridge. But the provision has not been decided, and, it seems to me, could not be decided without a perversion of plain language, to apply to an arrangement by which competition is ended through community of interest, — an arrangement which leaves the parties without external restriction. That provision, taken alone, does not require that all existing competitions shall be maintained. It does not look primarily, if at all, to competition. It simply requires that a party's freedom in trade between the states shall not be cut down by contract with a stranger. So far as that phrase goes, it is lawful to abolish competition by any form of union. It would seem to me impossible to say that the words "every contract in restraint of trade is a crime, punishable with imprisonment," would send the members of a partnership between, or a consolidation of, two trading corporations to prison, — still more impossible to say that it forbade one man or corporation to purchase as much stock as he liked in both. Yet those words would have that effect if this clause of § 1 applies to the defendants here. For it cannot be too carefully remembered that that clause applies to "every" contract of the forbidden kind, — a consideration which was the turning point of the Trans-Missouri Freight Association's case.

If the statute applies to this case it must be because the parties, or some of them, have formed, or because the Northern Securities Company is, a combination in restraint of trade among the states, or, what comes to the same thing, in my opinion, because the defendants, or some or one of them, are monopolizing, or attempting to monopolize, some part of the commerce between the states. But the mere reading of those words shows that they are used in a limited and accurate sense. According to popular speech, every concern monopolizes whatever business it does, and if that business is trade between two states it monopolizes a part of the trade among the states. Of course, the statute does not forbid that. It does not mean that all business must cease. A single railroad down a narrow valley or through a mountain gorge monopolizes all the railroad transportation through that valley or gorge. Indeed, every railroad monopolizes, in a popular sense, the trade of some area. Yet I suppose no one would say that the statute forbids a combination of men into a corporation to build and run such a railroad between the states.

I assume that the Minnesota charter of the Great Northern, and the Wisconsin charter of the Northern Pacific, both are valid. Suppose that, before either road was built, Minnesota, as part of a system of transportation between the states, had created a railroad company authorized singly to build all the lines in the states now actually built, owned or controlled by either of the two existing companies. I take it that that charter would have been just as good as the present one, even if the statutes which we are considering had been in force. In whatever sense it would have created a monopoly, the present charter does. It would have been a large one, but the act of Congress makes no discrimination according to size. Size has nothing to do with the matter. A monopoly of "any part" of commerce among the states is unlawful. The supposed company would have owned lines that might have been competing; probably the present one does. But the act of Congress will not be construed to mean the universal disintegration of society into single men, each at war with all the rest, or even the prevention of all further combinations for a common end.

There is a natural feeling that somehow or other the statute meant to strike at combinations great enough to cause just anxiety on the part of those who love their country more than money, while it viewed such little ones as I have supposed with just indifference. This notion, it may be said, somehow breathes from the pores of the act, although it seems to be contradicted in every way by the words in detail. And it has occurred to me that it might be that when a combination reached a certain size it might have attributed to it more of the character of a monopoly merely by virtue of its size than would be attributed to a smaller one. I am quite clear that it is only in connection with monopolies that size could play any part. But my answer has been indicated already. In the first place, size, in the case of railroads, is an inevitable incident; and if it were an objection under the act, the Great Northern and the Northern Pacific already were too great and encountered the law. In the next place, in the case of railroads it is evident that the size of the combination is reached for other ends than those which would make them monopolies. The combinations are not formed for the purpose of excluding others from the field. Finally, even a small railroad will have the same tendency to exclude others from its narrow area that great ones have to exclude others from the greater one, and the statute attacks the small monopolies as well as the great. The very words of the act make such a distinction impossible in this case, and it has not been attempted in express terms.

If the charter which I have imagined above would have been good notwithstanding the monopoly, in a popular sense, which it created, one next is led to ask whether and why a combination or consolidation of existing roads, although in actual competition, into one company of exactly the same powers and extent, would be any more obnoxious to the law. Although it was decided in *Louisville & N. R. Co.* v. *Kentucky*, 161 U. S., 677, 701, 40 L. ed., 849, 859, 16 Sup. Ct. Rep., 714, that since the statute, as before, the states have the power to regulate the matter, it was said, in the argument, that such a consolidation would be unlawful, and it seems to me that the Attorney-General was compelled to say so in order to maintain his case. But I think that logic would not let him stop there, or short of denying the power of a state at the present time to authorize one company to construct and own two parallel lines that might compete. The monopoly would be the same as if the roads were consolidated after they had begun to compete; and it is on the footing of monopoly that I now am supposing the objection made. But to meet the objection to the prevention of competition at the same time, I will suppose that three parties apply to a state for charters; one for each of two new and possibly competing lines respectively, and one for both of these lines, and that the charter is granted to the last. I think that charter would be good, and I think the whole argument to the contrary rests on a popular instead of an accurate and legal conception of what the word "monopolize" in the statute means. I repeat, that in my opinion there is no attempt to monopolize, and what, as I have said, in my judgment amounts to the same thing, that there is no combination in restraint of trade until something is done with the intent to exclude strangers to the combination from competing with it in some part of the business which it carries on.

Unless I am entirely wrong in my understanding of what a "combination in restraint of trade" means, then the same monopoly may be attempted and effected by an individual, and is made equally illegal in that case by § 2. But I do not expect to hear it maintained that Mr. Morgan could be sent to prison for buying as many shares as he liked of the Great Northern and the Northern Pacific, even if he bought them both at the same time and got more than half the stock of each road.

* * * * * * * *

In view of my interpretation of the statute I do not go further into the question of the power of Congress. That has been dealt with by my brother White and I concur, in the main, with his views. I am happy to know that only a minority of my brethren adopt an interpretation of the law which, in my opinion, would make eternal the *bellum omnium contra omnes* and disintegrate society so far as it could into individual atoms. If that were its intent I should regard calling such a law a regulation of commerce as a mere pretence. It would be an attempt to reconstruct society. I am not concerned with the wisdom of such an attempt, but I believe that Congress was not intrusted by the Constitution with the power to make it, and I am deeply persuaded that it has not tried.

Mr. Justice White, with whom concur Mr. Chief Justice Fuller, Mr. Justice Peckham and Mr. Justice Holmes, dissenting:

The Northern Securities Company is a New Jersey corporation; the Great Northern Railway Company, a Minnesota one; and the Northern Pacific Railway Company, a Wisconsin corporation. Whilst in the argument at bar the government referred to the subject, nevertheless it expressly disclaimed predicating any claim for relief upon the fact that the predecessor in title of the Northern Pacific Railway Company was a corporation created by act of Congress. That fact, therefore, may be eliminated.

The facts essential to be borne in mind to understand my point of view, without going into details, are as follows: the lines of the Northern Pacific and the Great Northern Railway Companies are both transcontinental, that is, trunk lines to the Pacific Ocean, — and in some aspects are conceded to be competing. Mr. Morgan and Mr. Hill and a few persons immediately associated with them separately acquired and owned capital stock of the Northern Pacific Railway Company, aggregating a majority thereof. Mr. Hill and others associated with him owned, in the same manner, about one-third of the capital stock of the Great Northern Railway Company, the balance of the stock being distributed among about eighteen hundred stockholders. Although Mr. Hill and his immediate associates owned only one-third of the stock the confidence reposed in Mr. Hill was such that, through proxies, his influence was dominant in the affairs of that company. Under these circumstances Mr. Morgan and Mr. Hill organized under the laws of New Jersey the Northern Securities Company. The purpose was that the company should become the holder of the stock of the two railroads. This was to be effected by having the Northern Securities Company give its stock in exchange for that of the two railroad companies. Whilst the purpose of the promoters was mainly to exchange the stock held by them in the two railroads for the Northern Securities Company stock, nevertheless the right of stockholders generally in the two railroads to make a similar exchange or to sell their stock to the Securities Company was provided for. Under the arrangement the Northern Securities Company came to be the registered holder of a majority of the stock of both the railroads. It is not denied that the charter and the acts done under it, of the Northern Securities Company, were authorized by the laws of New Jersey, and, therefore, in so far as those laws were competent to sanction the transaction, the corporation held the stock in the two railroads secured by the law of the state of its domicil.

The government by its bill challenges the right of the Northern Securities Company to hold and own the stock in the two railroads. The grounds upon which the relief sought was based were, generally speaking, as follows: That, as the two railroads were competing lines engaged in part in interstate commerce, the creation of the Northern Securities Company and the acquisition by it of a majority of the stock of both roads was contrary to the act of Congress known as the Anti-Trust Act. 26 Stat. at L., 209, chap. 647, U. S. Comp. Stat. 1901, page 3200. The clauses of the act which it was charged were violated were the first section, declaring illegal "every contract, combination in the form of trust or otherwise, or conspiracy, in restraint of trade or commerce among the several states, or with foreign nations"; and the provisions of the second section, making it a misdemeanor for any person to "monopolize, or attempt to monopolize, or combine or conspire with any other person or persons to monopolize, any part of the trade or commerce among the several states or with foreign nations." The court below sustained the contentions of the government. It, therefore, enjoined the two railroad companies from allowing the Northern Securities Company to vote the stock standing in its name or to pay to that company any dividends upon the stock by it held. On the giving, however, of a bond fixed by the court below the decree relating to the payment of dividends was suspended pending the appeal to this court.

The court recognized, however, the right of the Northern Securities Company to re-transfer the stock in both railroads to the persons from whom it had been acquired. The correctness of the decree below is the question presented for decision.

Two questions arise. Does the Anti-Trust Act, when rightly interpreted, apply to the acquisition and ownership by the Northern Securities Company of the stock in the two railroads? and, second, If it does, had Congress the power to regulate or control such acquisition and ownership? As the question of power lies at the root of the case, I come at once to consider that subject. Before doing so, however, in order to avoid being misled by false or irrelevant issues, it is essential to briefly consider two questions of fact. It is said, first, that the mere exchange by the Northern Securities Company of its stock for stock in the railroads did not make the Northern Securities Company the real owner of the stock in the railroads, since the effect of the transaction was to cause the Securities company to become merely the custodian or trustee of the stock in the railroads; second, that as the two railroads were both overcapitalized, stock in them furnished no sufficient consideration for the issue of the stock of the Northern Securities Company. It would suffice to point out (*a*), that the proof shows that nearly nine million dollars was paid by the Securities company for a portion of the stock acquired by it, and that, moreover, nearly thirty-five million dollars was expended by the Securities company in the purchase of bonds of the Northern Pacific Company, which have been converted by the Securities company into the stock of that railroad, which the Securities company now holds; and (*b*), that the market value of the railroad stocks is, moreover, indisputably shown by the proof to have been equal to the value fixed on them for the purpose of the exchange or purchase of such stock by the Northern Securities Company. Be this as it may, it is manifest that these considerations can have no possible influence on the question of the power of Congress in the premises; and therefore the suggestions can serve only to obscure the controversy. If the power was in Congress to legislate on the subject it becomes wholly immaterial what was the nature of the consideration paid by the company for the stock by it acquired and held if such acquisition and ownership, even if real, violated the act of Congress. If, on the contrary, the authority of Congress could not embrace the right of the Northern Securities Company to acquire and own the stock, the question of what consideration the Northern Securities Company paid for the stock or the method by which it was transferred must necessarily be beyond the scope of the act of Congress.

In testing the power of Congress I shall proceed upon the assumption that the act of Congress forbids the acquisition of a majority of the stock of two competing railroads engaged in part in interstate commerce by a corporation or any combination of persons.

* * * * * * * *

The plenary authority of Congress over interstate commerce,

its right to regulate it to the fullest extent, to fix the rates to be charged for the movement of interstate commerce, to legislate concerning the ways and vehicles actually engaged in such traffic, and to exert any and every other power over such commerce which flows from the authority conferred by the Constitution, is thus conceded. But the concessions thus made do not concern the question in this case, which is not the scope of the power of Congress to regulate commerce, but whether the power extends to regulate the ownership of stock in railroads, which is not commerce at all. The confusion which results from failing to observe this distinction will appear from an accurate analysis of *Gibbons* v. *Ogden*, for in that case the great Chief Justice was careful to define the commerce the power to regulate which was conferred upon Congress, and in the passages which I have previously quoted, simply pointed out the rule by which it was to be determined in any case whether Congress, in acting upon the subject, had gone beyond the limits of the power to regulate commerce as it was defined in the opinion. Accepting the test announced in *Gibbons* v. *Ogden* for determining whether a given exercise of the power to regulate commerce has in effect transcended the limits of regulation, it is essential to accept also the luminous definition of commerce announced in that case and approved so many times since, and hence to test the question for decision by that definition. The definition is this: "Commerce undoubtedly is traffic, but it is something more, — it is intercourse. It describes the commercial intercourse between nations and parts of nations in all its branches, *and is regulated by prescribing rules for carrying on that intercourse.*" (Italics mine.)

Does the delegation of authority to Congress to regulate commerce among the states embrace the power to regulate the ownership of stock in state corporations, because such corporations may be in part engaged in interstate commerce? Certainly not, if such question is to be governed by the definition of commerce just quoted from *Gibbons* v. *Ogden*. Let me analyze the definition. "Commerce undoubtedly is traffic, but it is something more, — it is intercourse;" that is, traffic between the states and intercourse between the states. I think the ownership of stock in a state corporation cannot be said to be in any sense traffic between the states or intercourse between them. The definition continues, "It describes the commercial intercourse between nations and parts of nations." Can the ownership of stock in a state corporation, by the most latitudinarian construction, be embraced by the words "commercial intercourse between nations and parts of nations"? And to remove all doubt, the definition points out the meaning of the delegation of power to regulate, since it says that it is to be "regulated by prescribing rules for carrying on that intercourse." Can it in reason be maintained that to prescribe rules governing the ownership of stock within a state, in a corporation created by it, is within the power to prescribe rules for the regulation of intercourse between citizens of different states?

But if the question be looked at with reference to the powers of the Federal and state governments, — the general nature of the one and the local character of the other which it was the purpose of the Constitution to create and perpetuate, — it seems to me evident that the contention that the authority of the national government under the commerce clause gives the right to Congress to regulate the ownership of stock in railroads chartered by state authority is absolutely destructive of the 10th Amendment to the Constitution, which provides that "the powers not delegated to the United States by the Constitution, nor prohibited by it to the states, are reserved to the states respectively or to the people." This must follow, since the authority of Congress to regulate on the subject can, in reason, alone rest upon the proposition that its power over commerce embraces the right to control the ownership of railroads doing in part an interstate commerce business. But power to control the ownership of all such railroads would necessarily embrace their organization. Hence it would result that it would be in the power of Congress to abrogate every such railroad charter granted by the states from the beginning if Congress deemed that the rights conferred by such state charters tended to restrain commerce between the states or to create a monopoly concerning the same.

Besides, if the principle be acceded to it must in reason be held to embrace every consolidation of state railroads which may do in part an interstate commerce business, even although such consolidation may have been expressly authorized by the laws of the states creating the corporations.

It would likewise overthrow every state law forbidding such consolidations; for if the ownership of stock in state corporations be within the regulating power of Congress under the commerce clause, and can be prohibited by Congress, it would be within the power of that body to permit that which it had the right to prohibit.

But the principle that the ownership of property is embraced within the power of Congress to regulate commerce, whenever that body deems that a particular character of ownership, if allowed to continue, may restrain commerce between the states or create a monopoly thereof, is, in my opinion, in conflict with the most elementary conceptions of rights of property. For it would follow if Congress deemed that the acquisition by one or more individuals engaged in interstate commerce of more than a certain amount of property would be prejudicial to interstate commerce, the amount of property held or the amount which could be employed in interstate commerce could be regulated.

* * * * * * * *

It is said, moreover, that the decision of this case does not involve the consequences above pointed out since the only issue in this case is the right of the Northern Securities Company to acquire and own the stock. The right of that company to do so, it is argued, is one thing; the power of individuals or corporations, when not merely organized to hold stock, an entirely different thing. My mind fails to seize the distinction. The only premise by which the power of Congress can be extended to the subject-matter of the right of the Securities company to own the stock must be the proposition that such ownership is within the legislative power of Congress, and if that proposition be admitted it is not perceived by what process of reasoning power of Congress over the subject-matter of ownership is to be limited to ownership by particular classes of corporations or persons. If the power embraces ownership, then the authority of

Congress over all ownership which, in its judgment, may affect interstate commerce, necessarily exists. In other words, the logical result of the asserted distinction amounts to one of two things: Either that nothing is decided, or that a decree is to be entered having no foundation upon which to rest. This is said because, if the control of the ownership of stock in competing roads by one and the same corporation is within the power of Congress, and creates a restraint of trade or monopoly forbidden by Congress, it is not conceivable to me how exactly similar ownership by one or more individuals would not create the same restraint or monopoly, and be equally within the prohibition which it is decided Congress has imposed. Besides the incongruity of the conclusion, resulting from the alleged distinction, to admit it would do violence to both the letter and spirit of the Constitution; since it would in effect hold that, although a particular act was a burden upon interstate commerce or a monopoly thereof, that individuals could lawfully do the act, provided only they did not use the instrumentality of a corporation. But this court long since declared that the power to regulate commerce, conferred upon Congress, was "general and includes alike commerce by individuals, partnerships, associations and corporations." *Paul* v. *Virginia*, 8 Wall., 168, 183, 19 L. ed., 357, 361.

Indeed, the natural reluctance of the mind to follow an erroneous principle to its necessary conclusion, and thus to give effect to a grievous wrong arising from the erroneous principle, is an admonition that the principle itself is wrong. That admonition, I submit, is conclusively afforded by the decree which is now affirmed. Without stopping to point out what seems to me to be the confusion, contradiction and denial of rights of property which the decree exemplifies, let me see if, in effect, it is not at war with itself and in conflict with the principle upon which it is assumed to be based.

Fundamentally considered, the evil sought to be remedied is the restraint of interstate commerce and the monopoly thereof, alleged to have been brought about through the acquisition by Mr. Morgan and Mr. Hill and their friends and associates, of a controlling interest in the stock of both the roads. And yet the decree, whilst forbidding the use of the stock by the Northern

Securities Company, authorizes its return to the alleged conspirators, and does not restrain them from exercising the control resulting from the ownership. If the conspiracy and combination existed and was illegal, my mind fails to perceive why it should be left to produce its full force and effect in the hands of the individuals by whom it was charged the conspiracy was entered into.

It may, however, be said that even if the results which I have indicated be held necessarily to arise from the principles contended for by the government, it does not follow that such power would ever be exerted by Congress, or, if exerted, would be enforced to the detriment of charters granted by the states to railroads or consolidations thereof, effected under state authority, or the ownership of stock in such railroads by individuals, or the rights of individuals to acquire property by purchase, lease or otherwise, and to make any and all contracts concerning property which may thereafter become the subject-matter of interstate commerce. The first suggestion is at once met by the consideration that it has been decided by this court that, as the Anti-Trust Act forbids any restraint, it therefore embraces even reasonable contracts or agreements. If, then, the ownership of the stock of the two railroads by the Northern Securities Company is repugnant to the act, it follows that ownership, whether by the individual or another corporation, would be equally within the prohibitions of the act. As to the second, true it is that by the terms of the Anti-Trust Act the power to put its provisions in motion is, as to many particulars, confided to the highest law officer of the government; and if that officer did not invoke the aid of the courts to restrain the rights of the railroads previously chartered by the states to enjoy the benefits conferred upon them by state legislation, or to prevent individuals from exercising their right of ownership and contract, the law in these respects would remain a dead letter. But to indulge in this assumption would be but to say that the law would not be enforced by the highest law officer of the government, — a conclusion which, of course, could not be indulged in for a moment. In any view, such suggestion but involves the proposition that vast rights of property, instead of resting upon constitutional and legal sanction, must alone depend upon whether an executive officer might elect to enforce the law, — a conclusion repugnant to every principle of liberty and justice.

Having thus by the light of reason sought to show the unsoundness of the proposition that the power of Congress to regulate commerce extends to controlling the acquisition and ownership of stock in state corporations, railroad or otherwise, because they may be doing an interstate commerce business, or to the consolidation of such companies under the sanction of state legislation, or to the right of the citizen to enjoy his freedom of contract and ownership, let me now endeavor to show, by a review of the practices of the governments, both state and national, from the beginning, and the adjudications of this court, how wanting in merit is the proposition contended for. It may not be doubted that from the foundation of the government, at all events to the time of the adoption of the Anti-Trust Act in 1890, there was an entire absence of any legislation by Congress even suggesting that it was deemed by any one that power was possessed by Congress to control the ownership of stock in railroad or other corporations because such corporations engaged in interstate commerce. On the contrary, when Congress came to exert its authority to regulate interstate commerce as carried on by railroads, manifested by the adoption of the Interstate Commerce Act (24 Stat. at L., 379, chap. 104, U. S. Comp. Stat. 1901, page 3154), it sedulously confined the provisions of that act to the carrying on of interstate commerce itself, including the reasonableness of the rates to be charged for carrying on such commerce and other matters undeniably concerning the fact of interstate commerce. The same conception was manifested subsequently in legislation concerning safety appliances to be used by railroads, since the provisions of the act were confined to such appliances when actually employed in the business of interstate commerce. 27 Stat. at L., 531, chap. 196, U. S. Comp. Stat. 1901, page 3174. It also may not be doubted that from the beginning the various states of the Union have treated the incorporation and organization of railroad companies and the ownership of stock therein as matters within their exclusive authority. Under this conception of power in the states, universally prevailing and always acted upon, the entire railroad system of the United States has been built up. Charters, leases and consolidations under the sanction of state laws lie at the basis of that enormous sum of property and those vast interests represented by the railroads of the United States. Extracts from the reports of the Interstate Commerce Commission and from a standard authority on the subject, which were received in evidence, demonstrate that in effect nearly every great railroad system in the United States is the result of the consolidation and unification of various roads, often competitive, such consolidation or unification of management having been brought about in every conceivable form, sometimes by lease under state authority, sometimes by such leases made where there was no prohibition against them, and by stock acquisitions made by persons or corporations in order to acquire a controlling interest in both roads. Without stopping to recite details on the subject, I content myself with merely mentioning a few of the instances where great systems of railroad have been formed by the unification of the management of competitive roads, by consolidation or otherwise, often by statutory authority. These instances embrace the Boston & Maine system, the New York, New Haven & Hartford, the New York Central, the Reading and the Pennsylvania systems. One of the illustrations—as to the New York Central system — is the case of the Hudson River Railroad on one side of the Hudson River and the West Shore Railroad on the other, — both parallel roads and directly competitive, and both united in one management by authority of a legislative act. It is indeed remarkable, if the whole subject was within the paramount power of Congress, and not within the authority of the states, that there should have been a universal understanding to the contrary from the beginning. When it is borne in mind that such universal action related to interests of the most vital character, involving property of enormous amount, concerning the welfare of the whole people, it is impossible in reason to deny the soundness of the assumption that it was the universal conviction that the states, and not Congress, had control of the subject-matter of the organization and ownership of railroads created by the states. And the same inference is applicable to the condition of things which has existed since the adoption of the Anti-Trust Act in 1890. Who can deny that from that date to this, consolidations and unification of management, by means of leases, stock ownership by individuals or corporations, have been carried on, when not prohibited by state laws, to a vast extent and that during all this time, despite the energy of the government in invoking the anti-trust law, that no assertion of power in Congress under that act to control the ownership of stock was ever knowingly made until first asserted in this cause. Quite recently Congress has amended the Interstate Commerce Act by provisions deemed essential to make its prohibitions more practically operative, and yet no one of such provisions lend themselves even to the inference that it was deemed by any one that the power of Congress extended to the control of stock ownership. Certainly the states have not so considered it. As a matter of public history it is to be observed that not long since, by authority of the legislature of the state of Massachusetts, a controlling interest by lease of the Boston & Albany road passed to the New York Central system.

The decisions of this court to my mind leave no room for doubt on the subject. As I have already shown, the very definition of the power to regulate commerce, as announced in *Gibbons* v. *Ogden*, excludes the conception that it extends to stock ownership. I shall not stop to review a multitude of decisions of this court concerning interstate commerce, which, whilst upholding the paramount authority of Congress over that subject, at the same time treated it as elementary that the effect of the power over commerce between the states was not to deprive the states of their right to legislate concerning the ownership of property of every character or to create railroad corporations and to endow them with such powers as were deemed appropriate, or to deprive the individual of his freedom to acquire, own and enjoy property by descent, contract or otherwise, because railroads or other property might become the subject of interstate commerce.

* * * * * * * *

Now, it is submitted, that the decided cases just reviewed

demonstrate that the acquisition and ownership of stock in competing railroads, organized under state law, by several persons or by corporations, is not interstate commerce, and, therefore, not subject to the control of Congress. It is, indeed, suggested that the cases establish a contrary doctrine. This is sought to be demonstrated by quoting passages from the opinions separated from their context, apart from the questions which the cases involved. But as the issues which were decided in the Knight, in the Pearsall, in the Louisville & Nashville case and in the Hopkins case directly exclude the significance attributed to the passages from the opinions in those cases relied upon, it must follow that if such passages could, when separated from their context, have the meaning attributed to them the expressions would be mere *obiter*. And this consideration renders it unnecessary for me to analyze the passages to show that when they are read in connection with their context they have not the meaning now sought to be attached to them. But other considerations equally render it unnecessary to particularly review the sentences relied upon. There can be no doubt that it was expressly decided in the Knight case that the acquisition of stock by one corporation in other corporations so as to control them all was not interstate commerce, *although the goods of the manufacturing companies whose stock was acquired might become the subject of interstate commerce.* If, then, the passage from the Knight case could be given the meaning sought to be affixed to it, the result would be but to say that that case overruled itself. And this would be the result in the Pearsall case, since in that case it was decided that the states had the power to forbid the consolidation of competing railroads, even by means of the acquisition of stock. Besides, as in the Louisville & Nashville case, immediately following the Pearsall, it was expressly decided that the interstate commerce power of Congress did not embrace such consolidation, and Congress, therefore, could not restrain a state from either forbidding or permitting it to take place, it would follow that if the sentences in the Pearsall case had the import now applied to them, that that case not only overruled itself, but was besides overruled by the Louisville & Nashville case, and this although the two cases were decided on the same day, the opinions in both cases having been delivered by the same justice.

The same confusion and contradiction arises from separating from their context and citing as applicable to this case passages from the opinions in the Freight Association and Joint Traffic cases. Those cases, as I have previously stated, related exclusively to a contract admittedly involving interstate commerce, and it was decided that any restraint of such commerce was forbidden by the Anti-Trust Act. Now, in the Hopkins case, decided subsequent to the Freight Association and Joint Traffic cases, the contract considered unquestionably involved a restraint, but, as such restraint did not concern interstate commerce, it was held not to come within the power of Congress. It would follow then, if the sentences quoted from the opinions in the Freight Association and Joint Traffic cases, which cases concerned only that which was completely interstate commerce, applied to that which was not such commerce, that the Hopkins case overruled both these cases, although the opinions in all of the cases were delivered by the same justice, and no intimation was suggested of such overruling. It would also result that, after having overruled those cases in the Hopkins case, the court, in expressing its opinion through the same justice, proceeded in the Addyston Pipe case, which related only to interstate commerce, to overrule the Hopkins case and reaffirm the prior cases.

Of course, in my opinion, there is no ground for holding that the decided cases embody such extreme contradictions or produce such utter confusion. The cases are all consistent, if only the elementary distinction upon which they proceeded be not obscured, — that is, the difference which arises from the power of Congress to regulate interstate commerce, on the one hand, and its want of authority, on the other, to regulate that which is not interstate commerce. Indeed, the confounding and treating as one, things which are wholly different, is the error permeating all the contentions for the government.

* * * * * * * *

The fallacy of all the contentions of the government is, to my mind, illustrated by the summing up of the case for the government made in the argument at bar. The right to acquire and own the stock of competing railroads involves, says that summing up, the power of an individual "*to do*" (italics mine) absolutely as he pleases with his own, whilst the claim of the government is that the right of the owner of property "*to do*" (italics mine) as he pleases with his own may be controlled in the public interest by legitimate legislation. But the case involves the right to *acquire and own*, not the right "*to do*" (italics mine). Confusing the two gives rise to the errors which it has been my endeavor to point out. Undoubtedly the states possess power over corporations created by them, to permit or forbid consolidation, whether accomplished by stock ownership or otherwise, to forbid one corporation from holding stock in another, and to impose on this or other subjects such regulations as may be deemed best. Generally speaking, however, the right to do these things springs alone from the fact that the corporation is created by the state, and holds its rights subject to the conditions attached to the grant, or to such regulations as the creator, the state, may lawfully impose upon its creature, the corporation. Moreover, irrespective of the relation of creator and creature, it is, of course, true in a general sense that government possesses the authority to regulate, within certain just limits, what an owner *may do* with his property. But the first power which arises from the authority of a grantor to exact conditions in making a grant or to regulate the conduct of the grantee gives no sanction to the proposition that a government, irrespective of its power to grant, has the general authority to limit the character and quantity of property which may be acquired and owned. And the second power, the general governmental one, to reasonably control the *use* of property, affords no foundation for the proposition that there exists in government a power to limit the quantity and character of property which may be acquired and owned. The difference between the two is that which exists between a free and constitutional government, restrained by law, an absolute government, unrestrained by any of the principles which are necessary for the perpetuation of society, and the protection of life, liberty and property.

It cannot be denied that the sum of all just governmental

power was enjoyed by the states and the people before the Constitution of the United States was formed. None of that power was abridged by that instrument except as restrained by constitutional safeguards, and hence none was lost by the adoption of the Constitution. The Constitution, whilst distributing the preexisting authority, preserved it all. With the full power of the states over corporations created by them and with their authority in respect to local legislation, and with power in Congress over interstate commerce carried to its fullest degree, I cannot conceive that if these powers, admittedly possessed by both, be fully exerted, a remedy cannot be provided fully adequate to suppress evils which may arise from combinations deemed to be injurious. This must be true unless it be concluded that, by the effect of the mere distribution of power made by the Constitution, partial impotency of governmental authority has resulted. But if this be conceded, *arguendo*, the Constitution itself has pointed out the method by which, if changes are needed, they may be brought about. No remedy, in my opinion, for any supposed or real infirmity, can be afforded by disregarding the Constitution, by destroying the lines which separate state and Federal authority, and by implying the existence of a power which is repugnant to all those fundamental rights of life, liberty and property upon which just government must rest.

If, however, the question of the power of Congress be conceded, and the assumption as to the meaning of the Anti-Trust Act which has been indulged in for the purpose of considering that power be put out of view, it would yet remain to be determined whether the Anti-Trust Act embraced the acquisition and ownership of the stock in question by the Northern Securities Company. It is unnecessary for me, however, to state the reasons which have led me to the conclusion that the act, when properly interpreted, does not embrace the acquisition and ownership of such stock, since that subject is considered in an opinion of Mr. Justice Holmes, which explains the true interpretation of the statute, as it is understood by me, more clearly than I would be able to do.

Being of the opinion, for the reasons heretofore given, that Congress was without power to regulate the acquisition and ownership of the stock in question by the Northern Securities Company, and because I think even if there were such power in Congress, it has not been exercised by the Anti-Trust Act, as is shown in the opinion of Mr. Justice Holmes, I dissent.

I am authorized to say that the Chief Justice, Mr. Justice Peckham, and Mr. Justice Holmes concur in this dissent.

After this disapproval of the merger, by the Supreme Court, it became necessary to dissolve the company. The Morgan-Hill party in control proceeded to divide the assets of the company pro rata among the owners. The practical result would have been that a majority of the stock of the Northern Pacific Co. would have remained in the hands of the Great Northern's owners. To this plan the Harriman interests, representing the Union and Southern Pacific Companies, objected, demanding the return of the same securities, with control of the Northern Pacific, which they had turned in originally, after having secured such control in May, 1901. An injunction against the Morgan-Hill plan of dissolution was obtained on July 15, 1904. This injunction was dissolved in favor of the Hill party by the Federal Appellate Court, Jan. 4, 1905; and now goes to the Supreme Court for final decision. Upon this decision the question of final control of the Northern Pacific Railroad by its transcontinental rivals depends. — ED.

XV

THE MASSACHUSETTS BUSINESS CORPORATION LAW[1]

THE Massachusetts Business Corporation Law, enacted by the legislature of 1903, has been the subject of discussion and criticism by no means limited to the state. The charge has been made that in the enactment of this code the conservative state of Massachusetts has at last surrendered to the demands of promoters, and has joined the states which vie with each other in bidding for the privilege of giving charters to irresponsible corporations. It is the purpose of this article first very briefly to point out the causes leading to the enactment of a new corporation law in Massachusetts, and then to discuss those features of the law which distinguish it from the more recently enacted corporation laws of other states and to indicate its probable influence upon the organization and legislative regulation of industrial corporations.

The fundamental reason for the enactment of the new law is to be found in the defects of the previous legislation of the state relating to business corporations. The groundwork of this legislation had survived nearly a hundred years since the earliest legislative regulation of such forms of organization. Successive amendments permitting incorporation without special act of the legislature, the payment of stock in property as well as in cash, and finally, as to certain classes of corporations, an unlimited capitalization, were obvious concessions to the demands of developing business methods. These amendments left the law, however, in form a mere patchwork, and in substance neither a real protection to stockholders or investors nor sufficiently liberal in some respects to attract the incorporation

[1] From the *Quarterly Journal of Economics*, Vol. XVIII, 1904, pp. 269–280.

of business enterprises organized and financed in the state. During the past five years the advantages offered by the more liberal corporation laws of other states have been availed of to a constantly increasing extent until in the year 1901 two business corporations were organized under a foreign charter for the purpose of doing business in Massachusetts for every such corporation organized under the laws of the state.

Business men felt a certain degree of resentment in being advised to organize their corporations outside of their own state, and a movement was set on foot in the early months of 1902 to secure, if possible, some relief. Under a legislative resolve passed in that year, Governor Crane appointed a special committee on Corporation Laws, which, after many public hearings and a very careful investigation of the subject, reported to the legislature in January, 1903, the draft of a Business Corporation Law which was subsequently enacted without substantial amendment, with the exception of one provision relating to taxation.

It was the avowed purpose of the special committee, upon which much of the responsibility for this new law must rest, to draft a law which would permit, under conditions generally as favorable as could be secured under a foreign charter, the incorporation under Massachusetts laws of business enterprises financed by Massachusetts capital. The new law certainly was not designed to increase the revenues of the state. Under the old law Massachusetts collected from both business and public service corporations a larger franchise tax for the year 1901 than was collected in that year from the same source by any other state except New York and New Jersey.[1] It can be stated with

[1] The amounts received in 1901 from the taxation of corporate franchises of business and public service corporations, as reported by the Massachusetts Committee on Corporation Laws, Report, pp. 299–303, are the following:

New York	$4,966,680.93
New Jersey	1,633,074.19
Massachusetts *	1,271,316.23
Pennsylvania	1,005,184.23
West Virginia	322,078.50
Maine	39,225.00

* The receipts from business corporations reported by the Committee on Corporation Laws were $331,434.38. The balance represents receipts from public service and other corporations reported by the Tax Commissioner. Report, 1901, p. 8.

equal positiveness that it was not the intention of the framers of the new law to place Massachusetts in the position of being a competitive rival for the business of incorporating enterprises financed and doing business exclusively outside of the state, or of drafting a law "which will be favorable to the organization of large corporations popularly known as trusts." [1] How far Massachusetts has succeeded in adopting a corporation code which, on the one hand, will attract the incorporation of the legitimate business enterprises in which its citizens are interested, whether designed to do business within or without the state, and yet will discourage the organization of inflated promotion schemes and adequately protect both the stockholder and creditor, can best be determined after considering in some detail those provisions of the new law which are particularly designed to accomplish these ends.

Although the subject of the taxation of corporations occupied by far the largest share of the consideration of the special committee, the recommended changes in the existing law are few in number. The existing theory, of a tax levied by the state indirectly upon the stockholder on the market value of his stock, has been retained, not because the theory upon principle commended itself especially to the committee, but for the practical reason that any other rule which could logically be adopted would very largely increase the amount of taxes paid by more than half of the existing Massachusetts corporations. The committee so amended the former laws relating to taxation as to enable the organization of Massachusetts corporations for the purpose of doing business outside of the state without being subject to undue taxation, and also to make possible the organization of corporations to hold the securities of Massachusetts companies. The legislature added a limitation of the maximum value of the taxable corporate franchise to an amount not exceeding 120 per cent of the actual value of the tangible assets of the corporation. While this amendment will reduce somewhat in the first instance the revenue of the state from its corporations, it was believed to be necessary in order to retain in the state some of the most successful corporations, and to attract business

[1] Report of Committee on Corporation Laws, pp. 24 and 61.

enterprises which otherwise might hesitate to incorporate under a Massachusetts charter for fear of the operation of an unlimited tax upon that portion of the value of their capital stock representing intangible assets. The provisions of the new law relating to taxation are, therefore, a reënactment of the former laws, with amendments which will prevent double taxation and place Massachusetts as nearly as possible on a basis of equality with other states in this particular.

Corporations organized under the Business Corporation Law are permitted the largest degree of freedom in conducting their business consistent with a sufficient protection of the interests of minority stockholders. All corporate action can be taken upon the affirmative vote of a majority in interest of the stockholders, except such action as may affect the value of the stock. It should be noted, however, that the creation of a new class of stock, or the sale, lease or exchange of all of the property of the corporation, requires the concurrent vote of two-thirds of its stockholders. At organization almost any scheme regulating the classification, powers and voting rights of the stock of the company may be lawfully adopted. The stockholders' and directors' liabilities are reduced to correspond in the main with those prevailing in most of the other states. The requirements of the former law relating to the annual filing of certificates of condition by domestic and foreign corporations have been retained. The machinery by which stockholders may secure information as to the doings of the corporation has been made more effective. It was the purpose of the committee to draft a law in this particular which would enable any stockholder who, in good faith, desired information, to secure it without delay or unnecessary expense, while, on the other hand, the law would protect the corporation from inquisitive annoyance, instigated perhaps by hostile motives.

In relation to foreign corporations, Massachusetts has followed the lead of several of the Western states in attempting to place upon an equal basis, so far as possible, the corporations organized under its own laws and those organized under foreign charters. Rather as a means of demanding recognition than for the purpose of securing a larger amount of revenue, an excise tax has been imposed upon foreign corporations. As this tax amounts to only one-hundredth of one per cent upon the authorized capitalization, and as corporations are permitted to deduct from this amount whatever taxes are locally paid by them, the tax will practically affect those corporations only which under the old law conducted their business in whole or in part in the state without directly paying any tax whatever in return for the privilege which the state as a matter of comity extended to them. As the maximum tax to be paid is limited to two thousand dollars, it is not expected that even the larger industrial corporations will be deterred from doing business in the state. It is believed that with the imposition of this nominal excise tax will come an increased degree of responsibility from the state towards foreign corporations; and, inasmuch as no action can be maintained in its courts by foreign corporations until this tax is paid and the annual certificate of condition filed, it is hoped that the new law will inspire a greater respect for the legislative requirements of the state than has been evinced during the past few years by such corporations.

From an economic point of view these features of the Business Corporation Law are overshadowed in interest by its provisions relating to the issue and payment of capital stock. The attacks which have been made upon the new law have been focussed upon the fact that it permits the unlimited capitalization of intangible assets, — "wind and water" is the more popular expression among the critics of the law. It may, then, be profitable to consider this provision of the new law in some detail.

Logically there are the three following theories upon which statutory provisions relating to the payment of capital stock by property conveyed to the corporation can be based:

1. That the incorporators are the judges of the value of property to be conveyed to the corporation in payment of stock, and that the state has no interest or duty in the matter except to create a liability for fraudulent action. This is the most generally accepted theory of the more recently enacted corporation laws in this country.

On this theory, in the absence of actual fraud, the judgment of the directors is conclusive. Even if fraud can be proved, which has only rarely been accomplished, the title to the stock in question cannot be attacked; and the only remedy is a personal one against the fraudulent directors. The practice, so widely advertised in connection with the receivership proceedings of the United States Shipbuilding Company, of electing irresponsible dummies to protect the parties to fraudulent proceedings from any danger of personal liability, is by no means unusual. The most obvious defect in this legislation is that the facts concerning the issue of stock for property are hidden in the records of proceedings of the board of directors to which the stockholder or prospective investor has no access. He is unable to form an independent judgment as to the value of the property of which his stock represents a fractional interest. He is guided in making his investment solely by the more or less misleading statements contained in a prospectus and by the equally fictitious quotations which manipulation in the stock market can give to such securities when issued and listed on a stock exchange.

2. The second theory relating to the payment of capital stock in property is that the issue of stock so paid for must be controlled and limited by the state. This theory has been logically adopted in the existing legislation in Massachusetts, so generally and justly commended, relating to the issue of securities by public service corporations. It has been asserted that it governed also the issue of stock of business corporations under the law now repealed by the Business Corporation Law. But this assertion would not be made by any one familiar with its administration.

The earlier law provided that capital stock might be issued for property to the extent sanctioned by the Commissioner of Corporations. The commissioner soon found it necessary to establish certain rules in regard to this subject. One was that no stock could be issued for patent rights or other intangible interests. This rule was conservative, and worked substantial justice in a majority of cases. In some instances, however, patent rights have proved to be very substantial assets from the point of view of the investments which they represent and the dividends which they can earn. In at least one case a well-established business in Massachusetts was compelled to secure a special act of incorporation from the legislature in order to make possible a partial capitalization of its very valuable good will.

As the statute provided no machinery, and as no appropriation was allowed, for securing a fair appraisal of the tangible property to be conveyed to the corporation in payment of its stock, the Commissioner of Corporations has always required a sworn statement to be made as to the value of property for which it is proposed to issue stock. This statement has been accepted by the commissioner, in the absence of further information, as a basis of his appraisal. The practical effect of this practice has been to enable incorporators to fix their own valuation of property for which stock is issued, as is the almost universal rule in other states. That the former law was unsuccessful in guaranteeing the success of corporations organized under its provisions is well indicated by the fact, as the writer has been informed, that nearly 75 per cent of the corporations which have been reported insolvent to the United States courts for the district of Massachusetts during the past three years have been organized under laws of that state. It may fairly be said, therefore, that under the former law the state in attempting to be sponsor for the solvency of private corporations organized under its provisions failed signally to accomplish the intended results. There can be no middle way. The state must either undertake an examination by its own experts of the value of the prospective assets of the corporation or it must not pretend to do anything of the kind.

There is much to be said in favor of such an appraisal in the case of public service corporations. The state has granted valuable franchises, and in many cases protects the corporation from disastrous competition. It may well be argued that in return it is the duty of the state to see to it that these franchises are not sold to the investing public at an unfair valuation. There is no such reason for protecting the investors in business corporations where competition is unlimited and the only right given by the state is the right of existence. In this class of corporations the state cannot afford to undertake for the benefit of prospective investors — many of whom, perhaps, are not its citizens — an appraisal for which it will be held responsible. If all the facts necessary to enable individual investors to exercise their own judgment as to the value of the securities of private corporations are required and enforced by suitable legislation, the state has done all that can be required of it.

3. The third theory, and the one adopted in the new Massachusetts law in regard to the duties of the state in regulating the issue of stock for property, is that, so long as incorporators are not acting fraudulently, they may capitalize any property, tangible or intangible, at any amount they desire, provided that no stock may be issued at or after organization until a statement has been prepared and placed upon public record, showing the amount of stock which has been issued and the exact manner in which it is paid for. If the payment is in cash, the facts will be so stated; if in property, a description of the same must be included in the statement, which will be sufficient for purposes of identification; if stock is to be issued for services or expenses, their nature or extent must be set forth. On this theory prospective stockholders and creditors deal with the corporation at their own peril. The state does not assume either to give its sanction to a "blind pool," as it may be said to do under the first theory mentioned, or to guarantee, directly or indirectly, the value of the property for which capital stock is issued, as it may be said to have done under the former law.

Publicity,[1] therefore, and not paternalism, is now adopted in Massachusetts as its remedy for the evil of overcapitalization. A public statement sufficient to acquaint prospective stockholders with the facts concerning the property of which they may become part owners is, under the new law, a condition precedent to the legality of stock issued. Directors are liable, as in other states and as they were liable under the former law in Massachusetts, for making statements which they know to be false. This protection, however, is merely secondary. If investors and speculators purchase, or make advance payments on a speculative

[1] Concerning publicity as a remedy for these and other evils in the corporation problem, consult the provisions of the English and German statutes herein described. — ED.

purchase by a broker, of a fractional interest in property which is described to them with sufficient detail for purposes of identification, they have themselves to blame if they pay too high a price for it. And when the investor has thoroughly learned his lesson, which can only be taught by experience, he will be able, with the assistance of legislation based upon the theory now adopted by Massachusetts, to make a search of the facts relating to the value of stock in which he is interested, with much of the same thoroughness which he now shows in examining the title to real estate.

At least for the present, the affirmative requirements of the new law relating to publicity, both in regard to the payment of capital and in the matter of annual statements of financial condition, will probably deter the incorporation in Massachusetts of the larger industrial organizations. The practical prohibition against the organization of corporations to hold securities other than those of Massachusetts companies, while not primarily designed for this purpose, is another very practical reason why the very large industrial corporations will continue to organize outside of that state. Finally, the requirement of the minimum state corporate tax of one-tenth of one per cent of authorized capital, without allowing, as is the practice in many of the so-called "corporation states," very large deductions for enterprises of large capitalization, in itself is sufficient to discourage the organization of such corporations. It was estimated by the special committee[1] that the United States Steel Corporation would, under this provision of the Massachusetts law, pay an annual tax of over six hundred thousand dollars as compared with its present annual tax in New Jersey of less than sixty thousand dollars.

The effect of the new law in attracting the incorporation of new companies and upon the revenues of the state cannot be definitely determined until it has been in effect for at least a year. The results already shown are gratifying to its friends. The following table indicates the number and the total capitalization of corporations organized under the Business Corporation Law from August 1 to November 1, 1903, with the amount received

[1] Report of Committee on Corporation Laws, p. 63.

by the state for organization fees.[1] The figures for the corresponding period in 1902 are also given as a basis of comparison:

Year	Number of Corporations	Total Capitalization	Fees
1902	44	$1,015,800	$550.00
1903	200	$12,481,100	$3,953.73

Of the newly organized corporations, one is capitalized for $1,500,000, one for $800,000, four with a capital of $500,000, six with a capital of $250,000, and the remaining ranging down to the minimum of $1000. In November an industrial corporation was incorporated with a capitalization of $5,900,000 to take over, under a plan of reorganization, the assets of a large industrial business operating chiefly in Massachusetts, formerly incorporated with a larger capitalization under the laws of New Jersey.

These figures show that the new law has already become acceptable to the organizers of the smaller partnership corporations. That more corporations with a larger capitalization have not already been organized is not surprising in view of prevailing financial conditions and the probable unfamiliarity of the business interests of the state with all of the advantages of the new law.

It will probably never be possible to enact a corporation law which will entirely solve the problem of giving sufficient freedom to the promoters of the enterprise, adequate protection to its

[1] Later data are confirmatory as follows. — Ed.

	Number of Corporations	Capitalization of Corporations
Old Law. August 1, 1902, to August 1, 1903 . . .	257	$11,590,460
New Law. August 1, 1903, to August 1, 1904 . . .	1000	$66,623,610

stockholders, and an equitable tax to the state which is responsible for its creation. It certainly will not be possible to frame such a code in this country until a national law can constitutionally be enacted. In emphasizing the necessity of publicity in relation to the question of capitalization, and the opportunities of regulation by taxation, in the case of foreign corporations, Massachusetts has, by the enactment of its Business Corporation Law, at least pointed the way which must be followed in future legislation.

GROSVENOR CALKINS.

XVI

THE PROMOTION OF COMPANIES AND THE VALUATION OF ASSETS ACCORDING TO GERMAN LAW[1]

GERMAN Company Law was entirely changed and recast by a statute passed in 1884, which introduced a number of checks and restrictions of an entirely novel character. Many fears were expressed at the time. All enterprise was to be hampered in the future and driven to foreign countries. No persons of means and standing were to be found who would incur the liabilities and risks to which directors and promoters were to be subject under the new state of things. Sufficient time has now elapsed to show that the forecast of these prophets of evil was based on misapprehension. The statistics prove conclusively that the formation of new companies, far from being arrested by the greater stringency of the law, has been progressing in a most remarkable manner, and that the career of German companies has, on the whole, been most prosperous.[2] Some of the new

[1] From the *Economic Journal*, Vol. X, 1900, pp. 1–19. See Ring, Aktiengesetz, 2d ed., Berlin, 1892; Pinner, Das Deutsche Aktienrecht, Berlin, 1899; Esser, Die Aktiengesellschaft, Berlin, 1899; Riesser, Die Neuerungen im Deutschen Aktienrecht, Berlin, 1899.

[2] There were in Germany in 1896 according to Professor R. van der Borght's estimate (Conrad's Handwörterbuch, Vol. I, 2d ed., pp. 192–194) 3712 companies limited by shares with a total paid-up capital of over £340,000,000, and with reserve funds amounting all together to £58,000,000; the annual net earnings of 3249 companies amounted to about £32,400,000, or about 10 per cent of the paid-up capital. It is safe to assume from the figures given that not less than one-half of the total number of these companies were formed after the Act of 1884. In the blue book published by the departmental committee of the Board of Trade in 1895 (7779) a letter is quoted from Mr. Gerb of the British Consulate General at Berlin estimating the total paid-up capital at £200,000,000 (see p. 29). I showed at the time (see p. 30) that the capital must be at least £300,000,000, and the statistics given in the text prove conclusively that Mr. Gerb's estimate was still further from the truth than I suspected.

safeguards have not proved quite as efficient as was expected by the legislature, but the net result has been a clear gain. There are good grounds for saying that dishonest or even reckless company promotion is no longer known in Germany. No doubt commercial and industrious enterprise in that country has lately passed through a period of prosperity, which cannot be expected to continue unchecked; but times of prosperity, as a general rule, facilitate the task of unscrupulous financiers, and the absence of unsound company promotion in such times may be accepted as satisfactory proof of the efficiency of the law.

The statute on stock-exchange and produce-exchange transactions passed by the German Reichstag in 1896, though laying down certain restrictions as to dealings in shares on the stock exchanges, does not touch the law on the formation and management of companies. The imperial commission on whose recommendation that statute was prepared[1] accepted the testimony of experts on all sorts of matters, however remotely connected with the subject of their inquiry, and would no doubt have listened to any complaints that might have been made as to the efficiency of the law of 1884. The fact that no such criticism came forward is good negative evidence of the non-existence of any substantial grounds of dissatisfaction.

Another opportunity for complaints against the efficiency of the Act of 1884 was given by the inquiries of the committee appointed to assist in the revision of the German mercantile code, but in this case also the only points referred to were matters of detail not affecting the main principles of the law. The amendments which were introduced into the new mercantile code in connection with company law are not without importance, but they are all in the direction of strengthening the principles laid down in 1884.

Company law can be looked upon from three different points of view: the shareholders' point of view, the creditors' point of view, and the point of view of the general public. If the shareholders' point of view was the only one to be considered, much might be said in favor of abstention from legislative inter-

[1] The reports and minutes of the sittings of this commission have been published and contain much interesting information.

ference. There is no reason why persons who invest or speculate in the shares of companies incorporated in their own countries should enjoy better protection than those who invest or speculate in the shares of foreign companies, or in other stock-exchange securities. But the two other points of view are of much greater importance; all trading with unlimited liability offers certain safeguards to the creditors and to the general public, which are withdrawn in the case of trading with limited liability, and ought in that case to be replaced by corresponding safeguards of another kind. I mention the general public as distinguished from the creditors, because the dangers to which the general public is exposed by limited-liability trading are of a kind differing entirely from the risks incurred by creditors. Bad company law, as will be explained in the further course of this article, is a direct inducement to the parties concerned to trade in an unsound manner, and the effects of unsound trade, like those of bad sanitation, go very far beyond the area from which it proceeds. There is one principle which should never be disregarded, whenever the privilege of limited liability is conferred by law; the liability of a fund having a fixed and ascertainable value should be substituted for the unlimited liability of individuals. The value of this fund should on the formation of the company correspond with the amount of its nominal capital, and precautions should be taken to prevent, as much as possible, the diminution of this fund during the subsequent stages of the company's existence. Company law should, therefore, find means to assure (*a*) that the value of the property which represents the capital of a company on its formation shall correspond with the amount of the nominal paid-up capital of the company; (*b*) that property of the same value should continue to represent the paid-up capital of the company as long as it is not increased, and that on any increase of the paid-up capital the property representing the increase should be of a value at least equal to the nominal amount of the increase. I shall deal with each set of rules separately.

A. — Provisions as to Valuation of Assets on Formation of Company

The amount of the nominal capital with which a company is started in England is purely arbitrary, and need not stand in any relation to the value of the assets by which it is represented. A trader who converts his business into a company and keeps the shares himself has every inducement to fix the capital at a high figure, and as he is buyer and seller in one person, the price at which the business is sold — apart from the question of stamp duties — is absolutely immaterial.

If the shares are to be taken by the public the character which Company Promotion is apt to assume is shown by the following illustration. A trader wants to sell his business, which is worth £10,000, and approaches a financial agent conversant with such matters. The agent enters into a conditional contract whereby he agrees to buy the business in the event of his being able to form a company with a paid-up capital of £50,000. The price promised under the circumstances would probably be £10,000 in cash and the same amount in shares. The agent then tries to find some financiers willing to form a syndicate for the purpose; if these are found they are substituted as purchasers for the financial agent, who would probably be satisfied with £5000 for his profit on the transaction. These £5000 would probably be divided by him with some friends who helped to collect the members of the syndicate. The syndicate would subsequently sell the business to the newly formed company for the £50,000, and if they succeed in placing the whole of the shares they will, under the above-mentioned circumstances, obtain a gross profit of £25,000, but out of this sum some other intermediaries must be paid, legal expenses and stamp duties must be disbursed, and, to judge from recent revelations, the financial press must receive encouragement. The final result of all this is that the company acquires the property at a price representing five times its real value, the difference being divided by a number of people who have all in their way helped to float the company. It is well known that this rate of profit is by no means exceptional and is frequently exceeded.

Another circumstance has also to be taken into consideration in places in which British Company Law is applied.

Assuming in the case just mentioned, that the public do not take all the shares, the syndicate may consider it worth while to go to allotment on the amount subscribed, and to trust to chance as to placing the rest of the shares at a subsequent period. In the instance given above this would have no effect on the working of the company, as the company would not get any of the proceeds of the shares in any event, but in some cases the purchase price does not absorb the whole of the nominal capital, some portion of the latter being reserved as a working capital; in such a case the company has of course to suffer by the non-success of the issue.

Thus it will be seen that the principle of establishing a definite fund available for the payment of the company's debts, the value of which can easily be ascertained, is in this country departed from in two ways: (1) by the absence of provisions insuring that the property in which the capital is invested in the first instance is taken over at a price representing its true value; (2) by the absence of provisions preventing a company from starting business before the whole of its capital has been subscribed. As regards the second point, the bill which is now before Parliament provides a partial remedy by requiring a statement as to the minimum amount of subscriptions on which the company will proceed to allotment, but this mode of dealing with the matter, though affording a certain amount of protection to subscribers for shares, does not in any way benefit the interests of the creditors or of the general public.

In Germany the genuine nature of the valuation put on the original assets is secured by elaborate provisions which I shall deal with at length, and the starting of business with an insufficiently subscribed capital is prevented by the rules laid down in sections 195 and 200 of the new mercantile code, according to which the corporate existence of a company cannot possibly begin before its whole capital has been subscribed for, and before at least 25 per cent of the amount payable in cash is in the actual possession of the managers. There are two modes of formation permissible in Germany: (1) the *simultaneous* method, according to which the promoters take up the whole capital and offer it to the public after the formation of the company; (2) the *successive* method, which enables the promoters to offer the shares before the registration of the company; but in either case the subscription of the whole capital must be complete before the company can begin business.

These requirements as to the subscription of the capital would not be of much importance, if the first point to which I have called attention, namely, the adequacy of the value of the property in which the capital is invested, had not been properly attended to. This was done by provisions requiring the following things: (*a*) that certain matters relating to the history of the formation of the company should be inserted into the articles of the company; (*b*) that the promoters should make a report on the promotion transactions, for the accuracy and completeness of which they are civilly and criminally liable; (*c*) by provisions requiring the members of both boards of the company to examine into the circumstances of the formation of the company; (*d*) by provisions requiring an examination by independent auditors in certain cases.

(*a*) The articles have to state (among other things):

(1) The nature of any consideration not being cash against which any shares are issued.

(2) The names of any persons from whom the company on its formation is to acquire any property, and the prices at which any such property is to be acquired.

(3) The total amount of any payments to be made by the company for services rendered in connection with the promotion of the company.

(*b*) In all cases in which any shares are issued for any consideration not being cash, or in which any property is to be acquired on the formation of the company, the promoters have to prepare and sign a written report, in which they have to set out the circumstances from which it appears that the property to be taken over in lieu of cash or to be acquired by the company is worth the amount for which it is to be taken. In this report all transactions which led up to the ultimate sale of the property in question to the company must be mentioned, together with all prices paid within the preceding two years for the purchase or construction of any part of such property; in the case of a company taking over a whole undertaking the results of the trading of the two preceding years must also be set forth. The term "promoter," according to c. 187, includes all signatories of the articles of association, and also all persons whose shares are not paid up in cash, and section 202 provides that all such promoters are answerable to the company in damages in respect of any inaccuracy or incompleteness in the above-mentioned report; and also that they have to refund to the company any pecuniary benefit conferred by them to any person in connection with the purchase of the property of which no mention is made in the report. Promoters are released from these liabilities if they can prove that the inaccuracy or incompleteness of the report was neither known to them nor could have been known to them if they had applied the diligence of a prudent trader. Third parties who have received any benefit not disclosed in the report are also liable in damages, if the concealment was (or under the circumstances of the case ought to have been) known to them. Any promoter who knowingly makes any false statement in the report in question is also punishable with imprisonment and a maximum fine of 20,000 marks (section 313).

(*c*) Every German company has a supervising board and a managing board; in the case of a "simultaneous" formation the first boards are appointed when the articles of association are signed; in the rare case of a "successive" formation, the general meeting, which has to be held before the registration of the company, has to appoint them. Both these boards have to examine and report on all the circumstances of the formation of the company. They have in particular to inquire into the accuracy and completeness of the statements contained in the promoters' report, and this inquiry must also include the examination of the question, whether the prices at which any property to be taken over by the company are open to any objection (sections 192, 193).

(*d*) In any case in which one of the members of either board is a promoter or derives any pecuniary benefit from the promotion of the company, and also in any case in which any property is to be taken over by the company on its formation, independent auditors appointed by the local chamber of commerce have to examine and report as well as the two boards and in the same manner. The auditors' report under the law of 1884 had degenerated into a mere formality, but the new code has added some provisions which will make it much more effective in the future.

Under the new law the auditors may ask for any information in connection with the subject of their inquiry which appears relevant to them, and in case of any dispute with the promoters as to the necessity of any such information, the authority by whom the auditors were appointed is entitled to give a binding decision. As long as the promoters decline to give the information, the auditors' report is not issued and the incorporation of the company cannot take place. The remuneration payable to the auditors is not fixed by any person connected with the company, but by the authority by whom they are appointed (section 194). Any agreement to the contrary is void. (Esser, page 24.)

All the reports have to be filed in the registry and are open to public inspection (sections 195, 199). This right of inspection is not taken advantage of to a large extent, but if the reports contained any damaging facts their contents would soon be known to the public and prevent them from taking shares. As mentioned before, the simultaneous method of formation is almost universally applied, and under that method the promoters have to keep the shares and pay up in full, unless the public comes forward. This circumstance alone is a sufficient check against purchases of property at excessive prices.

It is no doubt true that most persons who take shares in new companies are not very watchful in reading reports or inspecting documents, but if there is only one watchful person any irregularity will soon be known in the circles in which shares are usually placed and will damp the enthusiasm, which might otherwise have been created in favor of the new issue.

It may of course still happen that the prices at which property is taken over on the formation of a new company are too high, but the unnatural increase of these prices caused by the commissions and profits of middlemen, which is such a characteristic feature of English company promoting, is a practical impossibility under the above-mentioned provisions.

The question naturally arises, How do people in Germany, who take trouble or risk in the formation of a new company, obtain the remuneration, without which they would hardly be inclined to enter into such transactions? The answer is that the profit is entirely derived from the premium at which the shares are sold to the public. It is clear that the profits obtained in this manner cannot be nearly as high as those which are frequently obtained by the English methods of company promotion, but large and adequate profits are frequently obtained, which nobody can object to, as they are perfectly open. The necessity of paying for the shares before they are issued to the public shuts out a certain class of professional company promoters, who may now be said to be non-existent in Germany, but the starving out of this class of men is an advantage from the moral as well as from the economic point of view.

The principal point is this: in England the promoters' and middlemen's profit is added to the nominal capital of a company, whilst in Germany it is added to the price of the shares. To the shareholder it may be a matter of indifference whether he buys shares from the promoters at 100 per cent premium, or whether the company buys its assets at twice their real value and sells him his shares at par, but a creditor is necessarily misled by being told that a company's paid-up capital is £100,000, when the real value of its property is £50,000, the rest consisting of promoters' profits. Moreover, the necessity of paying dividends on a capital swollen by such profits leads to the adoption of unsound methods of trading and bookkeeping.

It has been suggested that the provisions requiring the whole of a company's capital to be taken up before the registration of the company may be evaded by the employment of dummies, in whose names the shares are taken, the real promoters remaining in the background and only pocketing the profit on the sale of the shares in case of such a profit being realized; but such a course does not appear to be adopted in practice, and would, if adopted, in all probability defeat its own object; if the promoters' report was signed by persons willing and able to contemplate their liability with the indifference of the "*vacuus viator*," the public would not be tempted to take the shares, and the real promoters would lose their chance of a profit.

There are some other possible modes of evasion which have been specially guarded against by the German law.

It is enacted by section 207 that all contracts made within the first two years after the formation of the company for the purchase or construction of any buildings or plant intended to be used permanently for the purposes of the company's business, or of any land or other immovable property at a price exceeding one-tenth of the company's capital, are invalid unless confirmed at a general meeting in a special manner which enables shareholders holding only 26 per cent of the company's capital to defeat the scheme.

A report must be presented to the meeting by the supervising board, which, together with the contract, must, in case of adoption by the meeting, be filed in the mercantile registry. The members of the supervising board are, according to section 208, responsible for the contents of this report in the same way as they are responsible for the original report on the formation of the company.

In the case of an increase of capital, sections 278 and 279 provide for similar safeguards as those existing with regard to the original formation of a company.

B. — Provisions presenting a Diminution of the Property representing a Company's Capital

The measures which are taken for the purpose of assuring that the amount of the original capital of a company is truly represented by the value of its property are insufficient, unless they are accompanied by measures preventing, as far as possible, the diminution of the capital during the subsequent stages of the company's existence. In this respect also the provisions of English law are hopelessly inadequate. The courts have indeed frequently laid down the rule that dividends must not be paid out of capital, but the payment of dividends, notwithstanding the contemporaneous diminution or depreciation of that part of its property which is called "fixed capital" is considered legitimate and cannot be prevented.

A trust company holding stock, which during the last business year has paid 50 per cent dividend, but before the end of the year became utterly worthless, may include the 50 per cent in its yearly profit, without deducting a penny for the depreciation of the property from which this profit was derived. This is not called paying dividends out of capital.[1] A company, owning a mining lease, may include the proceeds of the minerals extracted in each year in the profit of that year and value the mine at cost price in its balance sheet, although in the course of a few years the mine will be worthless and the lease will have expired. This is not paying dividends out of capital.[2] A company having paid £100,000 for good will and earning an income of £1000 with every prospect of earning nothing, or less than nothing, in the following year, may divide the profit as dividend, whilst the good will is still valued at £100,000. This is not paying dividends out of capital.

The distinction between the depreciation of fixed and circulating capital, which is the basis of these decisions, is unsound from a mercantile point of view.

Income derived from any source, which by furnishing the income becomes gradually exhausted, cannot be wholly considered as income. It is partly income and partly re-payment of capital, like a terminable annuity. There is hardly any property, classed as fixed capital, which is not of a wasting nature. In some cases the wasting process is very slow, in some cases it is very fast, but the rate of waste can be generally calculated with sufficient accuracy to enable a trader to write off the proper amount for depreciation.

If it was really correct to disregard the depreciation of the fixed part of the capital in the calculation of the profits, the total disappearance of such property would not have to be considered either; new buildings and machines would have to be provided and their cost added to the "Buildings and Machinery

[1] *Verner* v. *General, &c., Investment Trust* (1894), 2 Ch. 239.

[2] *Lee* v. *Neuchatel Asphalte Company*, 41 Ch. D. 1.

Account," but the demolished buildings and the disused machinery could still be valued at cost price. In the case of a private partnership such a mode of trading would invariably lead those who adopt it into the bankruptcy court, if it were persisted in for any length of time, but in the case of a private partnership, the fact that retiring partners must from time to time be paid out on the basis of the balance sheet of the last year, acts as an effective check against the overvaluation of permanent investments.

In the case of companies omitting to provide for the waste, new capital must of course be required from time to time, and such new capital may up to a certain point be furnished by a confiding public on the strength of the forced dividends, but the crash will inevitably come some day.

Another objection against the distinction between the two kinds of capital is pointed out by Mr. Palmer (one of the most experienced company lawyers in this country): "It is extremely difficult to determine what is and what is not fixed capital. Thus shares or other assets are sometimes bought by a company without any distinct determination whether they shall be kept or resold . . . further intentions change. Supposing a company formed to buy, sell, hold by way of investment, and deal in shares and that it holds some shares intending at the time to sell, they are circulating capital, but if they happen to fall in price, the company may determine to keep them and thereupon they become fixed capital, and a few months afterwards the company may determine to sell them and thereupon they again become circulating capital." (Company Precedents, Part I, 7th ed., page 540.)

The distinction which the courts have made between circulating and fixed capital and the rule which they have laid down, according to which a company may continue paying dividends notwithstanding the gradual disappearance of its "fixed" capital, have had the further consequence, that the notion of a permanent fund on which the creditors of a limited company can rely, has been entirely abandoned. This was shown in a very recent case,[1] in which it was held that a loss shown on the working of a particular year, for which no reserve is available,

[1] *In re National Bank of Wales* (1899), 2 Ch. 629, 669.

need not be replaced from the profit of the following year. The result of this, translated into bookkeeping language, is, that a debit balance on the profit and loss account may be carried forward as an asset in the balance sheet, and that, whilst this is done, dividends may be divided among the shareholders. By judicious bookkeeping a company may easily arrange to have a profit in each alternate year and a loss in each following year. The loss diminishes the capital, and the profit goes to the shareholders until the capital is exhausted. A law which allows such a state of things turns limited liability into a source of serious public danger. From the point of view of common business prudence the following rules ought to be strictly maintained: a sum representing the depreciation of a company's property, whether acquired for permanent investment or for the purpose of resale, should be deducted from the profits in each year, and either credited to a depreciation account or deducted from the amount at which such property was previously valued. If on the working of a year a loss is shown which cannot be met out of any reserve fund, that loss must be carried forward on profit and loss account, but no dividends can be paid until such debit balance has disappeared from the books.

Some difficulty arises as to the question, What constitutes depreciation? Is it the natural wear and tear and the gradual disappearance of the object only, or is it also the diminution in market or selling value produced by other causes? In this respect the distinction between fixed and circulating capital offers some guidance.

As regards property, such as buildings and machinery, bought or constructed for the purpose of being retained and used for the permanent purposes of the company, the selling value is not really of importance; the durability or usefulness of any such property is not affected by the conditions which affect the price, at which it can be sold, and the company is not any poorer because it is unable to sell such property at cost price; as regards property bought or manufactured for the purpose of being sold or resold, it is of course necessary to consider the market price, which is the only tests of its value. The two classes of property just mentioned do not as a rule exhaust the whole of a company's property; book debts, which do not belong to either class, are frequently an important item. It is generally recognized in this country that a reduction ought to be made with reference to bad and doubtful debts, but great laxity prevails with reference to debts payable in a foreign paper currency or in a currency based on silver; it is customary for bookkeeping purposes to convert these debts into sterling currency at a fixed rate of exchange, and this fixed rate is sometimes called the "par value" — as if there could be a par value between a metallic currency and a paper currency, or between a gold currency and a silver currency. There is, then, in such cases a tendency to disregard all fluctuations and to retain the old rate of conversion, although it differs materially from the actual rate. In cases where such debts are only of occasional occurrence this is not so important, but in the case of companies whose principal outstandings remain permanently in foreign countries, the consequences may be very serious; an English company having outstandings of a permanent nature in Brazil and converting them into sterling money at the old rate of 24*d.*, whilst the present rate is about 8*d.*, is doing exactly the same thing as if they valued their outstanding debts at their full value, notwithstanding the fact that two-thirds of the same were known to be absolutely irrecoverable; yet English law seems to allow this system of bookkeeping, and the payment of dividends cannot be prevented, although the company's capital is dwindling away by the depreciation of the currency in which it is invested.

As regards stock-exchange securities bought for permanent investment, it may be somewhat inconsistent to prescribe deductions in respect of loss of market value, but such deductions are prudent, especially in cases where the fall in the market price is due to causes materially affecting their intrinsic value. When, *e.g.*, a stock-exchange security has ceased to pay dividends, it ceases to serve the purpose of investment.

The German law proceeds on the principles for which I have contended in the foregoing observations. Section 261 enacts that (subject to the modifications to which I shall have to refer) the provisions contained in the mercantile code as to the balance sheets of traders generally are to be observed; according to these provisions all assets and liabilities must be taken at the value, which they had on the date, as from which the balance sheet is made out; debts must be taken at their probable value and irrecoverable debts be written off entirely. The modifications in the case of the balance sheets of companies are the following:

(1) Stock-exchange securities and goods having a stock-exchange or market value must be taken at such stock-exchange or market price, if such stock-exchange or market price is below the cost price; in any other case they are to be taken at cost price.

(2) Other assets are to be taken at a price not exceeding the cost price.

(3) Buildings and plant and other property not intended to be sold or resold, and being used for the permanent purposes of the company's business, may, notwithstanding the fact that their actual value is smaller, be taken at cost price, provided a sufficient amount is written off or placed to a depreciation account, by which the loss by waste or wear and tear is provided for.

(4) Promotion or administration expenses may not be included among the assets.

(5) The amount of the capital and of all reserve and depreciation funds must be included among the liabilities.

(6) The profit or loss resulting from a comparison of the assets with the liabilities must be stated separately at the end of the balance sheet.

It will be noticed from these rules that no asset may be valued above cost price, even in a case where the actual value is above cost price; this provision does not appear very logical at first sight, and it may be urged that it is just as wrong to undervalue the assets as to overvalue them; as regards the latter observation it is obvious that the only persons damaged by an undervaluation are particular classes of shareholders or directors or managers, whose remunerations vary with the profits, whilst an overvaluation, as I have shown above, causes an injury, not only to the solidity of the company and to the interests of its creditors, but also to its competitors and the public generally, through the encouragement which it gives to unsound trading.

There is therefore much more inducement to provide against overvaluation and to disregard the risk of undervaluation which, considering the many temptations in favor of high dividends, operating on the directors and managers of a company, is really not very serious. The illogical nature of the provisions in question cannot be entirely denied, but it was thought prudent that a company should not pay dividends out of unrealized profits, having also regard to the fact that the stock-exchange price or market price is not always quite genuine, and may easily be sent up by fictitious transactions for the very purpose of enabling a company to value securities or goods at a price producing a profit available for the company's dividends.

One of the consequences of the rule, that no asset can be taken above cost price, is that assets which were acquired gratuitously cannot be valued at anything. Some writers have asked, why a company who had received any property by way of gift should not be able to include their value among its assets; but it is hardly worth while to consider this point, as generous benefactors, who give away their savings to trading companies, are freaks of nature which need not trouble the legislator's mind.

A company which acquires the good will of a business for valuable consideration, may value such good will for its balance sheet at cost price, subject to the proper deduction for depreciation, but it cannot value its own good will if nothing was paid for it. (See Ring, pages 46, 602, 613.)

The German code does not lay down any rule as to the manner in which depreciation by wear and tear and waste ought to be calculated. In some cases the natural depreciation is obvious, as in the cases of leases or patents expiring after a certain number of years. The rate of depreciation in the case of buildings, machinery, etc., can also be easily ascertained with the advice of experts; in other cases, common sense and prudence will usually find a way out of the difficulty. As regards good will, depending on personal efforts and qualities, a somewhat rapid rate of depreciation ought to be allowed for; where good will is attached to particular premises, as in the case of inns and hotels, its value is not generally taken as a separate item, but included in the value of the premises. For these reasons the item of good will is not frequently seen in the balance sheets of German companies.

Another rule of law, which tends to the preservation of the capital of German companies, is contained in section 262, which provides that a reserve is to be formed in the following way: (1) at least one-twentieth part of the net profit of each year is to be credited to this fund, until it shall have reached the tenth part of the company's capital, or such larger part of such capital, as shall be provided in the articles; (2) in addition to this, any net premium realized by the issue of any part of the company's capital must be placed to the reserve fund, as well as (3) any amounts paid by shareholders in consideration of any preferential rights accorded to their shares (unless such payments are used for the purpose of making good any special losses).

The statutory reserve fund cannot be used for the payment of dividends in bad years, but separate reserve funds may be formed for that purpose. (Esser, page 164; Ring, page 631.)

The provisions which I have hitherto discussed are intended to prevent the following mischiefs:

(1) The watering of the original capital.

(2) The dwindling away of the company's assets by the omission of any allowance for their depreciation in the balance sheets.

They cannot, of course, prevent the gradual disappearance of the company's capital by losses in business in cases in which profits cease altogether, but there are provisions which prevent a company from carrying on business after a considerable part of its assets have been lost.

It is provided by section 240:

(1) That if, on the drawing up of any yearly or intermediate balance sheet, it appears that one-half of the company's capital has been lost, the managing board must immediately convene a general meeting, to whom the state of facts has to be submitted.

(2) That in the case of the insolvency of the company, and also in the case of any yearly or intermediate balance sheet, disclosing the fact, that the liabilities of the company exceed its

assets, it is the duty of the managing board to initiate bankruptcy proceedings without delay. A disregard of this provision is punishable with three months' imprisonment and a fine (section 315–2).

There are no similar rules in English law; in the case of insolvency, winding-up proceedings are of course taken as a general rule, but the mere fact that the assets are insufficient to pay its debts, does not prevent a company from continuing business. As long as a company can pay its way by the use of credit or otherwise, so long it can continue to trade in this country; in some lucky cases, this may enable it to retrieve its losses and to start a more prosperous career, but in the larger number of instances, a company, having reached such a low condition, has to procure accommodation on terms so onerous that the chances of profitable trading are very much reduced. The German rule is therefore preferable in the interest of creditors and of the general public.

The German law on stock-exchange transactions passed in 1896 has no such wide purposes as the above-quoted sections of the mercantile code relating to companies; its only object was to hinder certain kinds of stock-exchange speculations; in so far as it deals with shares in companies, it refers not merely to shares in German companies, but to shares generally, nor does it refer to all dealings in such shares, but only to dealings on any authorized stock exchange. In England the stock exchanges can at their discretion make rules as to the conditions, under which a settlement or quotation is granted to any shares or debentures or other securities, and this was also the case in Germany prior to 1896, but since the statute of that date, the stock-exchange rules are partly fixed by law. The provisions in question have therefore no direct connection with company law, but as they have to be considered on the formation of a company, whose shares are to be dealt in on the stock exchanges, and also on any increase of its capital, some reference must be made to them.

The rules in question prescribe:

(1) The compulsory issue of a prospectus, the authors of which are under a specially stringent liability;

(2) The lapse of a space of time between the incorporation of the company and the public issue of its shares;

(3) The fixing of a minimum capital for companies whose shares are to be dealt in on any stock exchange.

As regards the issue of a prospectus, it is provided by section 38 of the statute, that before any security is admitted for the purpose of being dealt in and quoted on any stock exchange, a prospectus must be issued, containing all information, which is of any importance for the purpose of ascertaining its true value. German government securities are exempted, and other securities may be exempted by the government of the state in which the application is made, but all shares in companies, whether incorporated in Germany or elsewhere, are included in any case.

It was already provided by the mercantile code, that persons issuing a prospectus by which shares are offered within two years from the incorporation of a company, are liable in damages in respect of inaccuracies or omissions in such prospectus. This liability can be enforced by the company only, whilst the liability imposed by the stock-exchange statute in respect to misstatements in the prospectus can be enforced by any holder of the security to which the prospectus refers. According to section 43 of that statute all persons who have issued or directed the issue of any prospectus containing any inaccurate statement on any matter affecting the value of the security are jointly and separately liable for any loss caused thereby, in so far as they knew, or ought in the absence of gross carelessness to have known, that the statement was incorrect. In the same way they are liable in respect of omissions as to essential facts, if caused by them knowingly or recklessly. If the inaccuracy or incompleteness was known to the claimant at the time of the purchase, or ought to have been known to him, on the application of the care usually given to his own affairs, he loses his claim to damages or restitution.

As regards the interval of time which must elapse before a company's shares can be dealt in on a German stock exchange, it is provided by section 39 that the shares of any undertaking which has been converted into a company cannot be admitted among the securities negotiable on any German stock exchange, unless at least a year has elapsed from the date of the registration of the company, and unless the first yearly balance sheet of the company has been published together with the profit and loss account. Power is given to the state government of the place in which the shares are to be dealt in, to dispense from this rule in exceptional cases. It will be noticed that this close time is only prescribed in the case of companies taking over an existing business; the shares of a company starting a new business may be publicly dealt in at once. The wisdom of the rule is very doubtful. A company cannot be registered before its capital is fully subscribed. The promoters must therefore hold the whole of the shares for at least a year and probably some months longer, as in most cases some time will elapse after the end of the year before the balance sheet can be drawn up and published; some compensation must, of course, be sought for the prolongation of the risk and capital outlay, and this compensation has, of course, to be paid by the public. On the other hand the safeguard is purely imaginary. By judicious manipulation profits belonging to a former year or to the subsequent year may be squeezed into the critical twelve months, so as to produce a specially good profit and loss account, and the idea that the public in this way have an opportunity to see the working of the undertaking before they are asked to subscribe to it is therefore purely imaginary.

The third regulation introduced by the stock-exchange statute is intended to prevent stock-exchange transactions in the shares of companies having a small capital only. The fixing of the minimum capital for each stock exchange is left to the federal council by section 42, which section also gives power to the same body to make further regulation for the admission of securities to any stock exchange.

An order was issued by the federal council pursuant to this power, containing the following provisions:

(1) The minimum capital of companies whose shares are to be dealt in at Berlin, Hamburg or Frankfort must be £50,000, whilst for all other stock exchanges a minimum capital of £25,000 is fixed.

(2) The prospectus must state (*a*) the name of the company, (*b*) the clause in the articles or resolution authorizing the issue, (*c*) the purposes for which the proceeds of the issue are to be applied, (*d*) the amount of the total issue, the amount offered, and the amount retained, and the time during which the last-named amount is to be retained by the promoters.

The provisions about statements in prospectuses and dealings on the stock exchanges are of minor importance and affect a limited class only; those relating to the prevention of over-capitalization and the preservation of capital affect the whole trade of the country. It is stated on good authority that some branches of trade (such as the cycle industry) are rapidly going down in England owing to the fact that they are worked by overcapitalized companies. This will show that the reform of company law has other objects than the protection of careless persons against unsound investments. If this fact could be understood and realized by public opinion, it would be seen that measures like those proposed in the bill which is now before Parliament touch the real mischief as little as the previous voluminous legislation on the subject.

ERNEST SCHUSTER.

XVII

THE NEW COMPANIES ACT, 1900[1]

THE wickedness of the company promoter is no new thing: in the wild bubble craze of 1715 one gentleman proposed to float a bubble, or company, to import jackasses from Spain, and another a company for a purpose "to be disclosed hereafter," and decamped in the evening with his pocket full of guineas; but at the same time it is the adoption of the principle of limited liability which has given the company promoter his great opportunity. That principle is now so familiar that it is difficult to realize how modern it is — in fact, not yet fifty years old. Since 1862, when previous tentative experiments of Parliament were reconsidered and embodied in the Code Napoleon of the limited company, there have been numerous amending Acts, but it is only within the last six or seven years that public opinion, of the city prince no less than of the country parson, has demanded radical reform.

The late Lord Chief Justice brought before the public in 1898 some startling figures.[2] During the seven years from 1891 to 1897, 28 millions of money was lost, 20 odd to shareholders, and 7 to creditors. These figures, though much quoted, require very considerable correction, for they are at the same time too comprehensive, and not comprehensive enough; on the one hand Lord Russell took no account of the losses made by companies wound up voluntarily and not under the jurisdiction of the Court, and if these be added, the average *annual* loss for the five years ending December, 1897, works out at 12 millions of money at

[1] From the *Economic Journal*, Vol. XI, 1901, pp. 180–192. The substance of this paper was delivered as a lecture at the London Chamber of Commerce, the President, W. Sandeman, Esq., in the Chair, on Wednesday, Nov. 21, 1900.

[2] See *Times*, Nov. 10, 1898.

the least.[1] On the other hand, the whole basis on which these figures of assumed loss are calculated is unsound; for much of the apparent loss of capital on winding up is compensated by schemes of subsequent reconstruction or amalgamation.[2]

The law allows, no doubt, far greater freedom in England than is possible abroad; anything, for instance, like the "simultaneous formation" usually employed in Germany, where the promoters *must* themselves take all the shares, would not be tolerated here for a moment; and many have felt there is a grave danger in sacrificing any portion of this freedom.

"Restrictive provisions which may have the effect of either curtailing the facilities for the formation of companies which bring so much business to England, or of embarrassing the administration of companies, or deterring the best class of men from becoming Directors, are not to be lightly entertained."[3]

In 1894 a Department Committee presided over by Lord Davey was appointed and reported in 1895:[4] the Committee received memoranda from many Chambers of Commerce and other public bodies throughout the United Kingdom, and took evidence as to the law of companies in France, Germany and America, and may be said to have brought within the four corners of a blue book every suggestion that the wit of man has ever heard, thought or dreamt of in connection with Company Law Reform. The Committee at the end of their report submitted a draft bill of 49 clauses: this Bill was examined by a committee of the House of Lords in 1897, and two following years, and was finally introduced into Parliament by the Secre-

[1] Eighth General Annual Report by the Board of Trade in companies winding up in 1899, p. 6; see also return of Joint Stock Companies, August, 1899, pp. 326–329.

[2] This the Board of Trade officials are the first to admit; see Eighth General Annual Report, *sup. cit.*, p. 6. How much apparent loss is so made good the Board of Trade Report says it is impossible to estimate.

[3] Report of Lord Davey's Committee, 1895, p. vi. Evidence was produced before that committee that the paid-up capital of companies in England amounted in 1894 to 1035 millions sterling, of companies in France to 420 millions, and of German companies to 300 millions, giving a surplus to English companies over the other two countries of 315 millions.

[4] The committee consisted of thirteen names, all of the highest authority in the world of commerce and law, amongst them, Lord Justice Vaughan Williams, Mr. Justice Buckley, Mr. Palmer, Mr. John Hollams and Sir Albert Rollit.

tary to the Board of Trade last summer and passed into law: every clause in the Bill has been tossed to and fro a hundred times; outworks against roguery skilfully run up by Mr. Palmer one day were swept away by the flood of Mr. Justice Buckley's caustic criticisms the next: every line of the Bill has been swamped in a flood of discussion and printers' ink: it is sad that after such a lengthy period of incubation the legislative chicken has emerged so imperfectly shaped.

The result of all this discussion has of course been a compromise, and the original 49 sections have now shrunk to 36. The discussions on the Bill revealed general agreement as to the more serious mischief to be remedied, and it is worth while to enumerate the prominent ones.

1. *The One Man Company.* — In order to secure registration with limited liability the Act of 1862 requires the signatures of seven[1] persons to the original memorandum of incorporation, each taking one share in the company, but up to the present English law has taken no heed whether those seven signatories are dummies or no; that company may be really constituted by one man who pays the first subscription for each of the other six, and so secures their signatures.[2]

2. *Insufficient Subscription.* — Many companies proceed to

[1] In Germany, since 1892, limited liability partnerships — Gesellschaften mit beschrankter Haftung — may exist. American law, of course, varies: in the state of New Jersey "three or more persons may become a corporation" (*i.e.* a company), Revision of 1896, Sec. 6: three also are sufficient for incorporation in the state of New York, Law of 1890, Sec. 2: Lord Justice Lindley advocated that one person should be allowed the privileges of incorporation provided he wrote *Limited* after his name.

[2] This is the result of the decision of the House of Lords in Aron Solomon's case in 1896. Solomon floated off his business as a leather merchant into a company consisting of himself, and his wife and daughter and four sons, from whom he received in payment £20,000 in shares, and £10,000 in debentures, with a floating charge over the whole business; he was managing director and could outvote the other six signatories, and by means of his debentures come in with priority in a winding up over ordinary creditors; when the inevitable winding up came the liquidator tried to get the whole set aside as futile in law and fraudulent in fact, that it was no company, but one man attempting to evade the ordinary law of bankruptcy and trade with limited liability by means of six dummies. Mr. Justice Vaughan Williams and the Court of Appeal sympathized with the liquidator, but the House of Lords held that the Act was satisfied with actual signatories whatever their motives.

allotment, though totally insufficient capital has been subscribed. English law, from 1862 up till January 1, 1901, has required neither a minimum amount per each share nor a minimum amount of shares to be subscribed before the company can proceed with its business.[1]

The Registrar of joint stock companies quotes a curious case which illustrates the absolute absence of restraint in these respects prior to the present Act; in 1891 "The Ancient Gold Fields of Africa, Limited" was registered with a capital of £10,000, divided into 9,600,000 shares of one farthing each; the total subscribed capital according to the last return was 1¾*d.*, *i.e.* precisely one share for each of the original seven signatories. It is obvious that a company which starts on its career with too little working capital is as much foredoomed to failure as a school without scholars.

3. *Overloading the Purchase-price.*—The law regards directors and promoters as trustees for the shareholders of the property of the company, but the difficulties of securing disclosures have always made evasions easy, and of these overloading the purchase-price was one of the commonest: in the normal course a promoter finds a flourishing industrial concern worth, say, £10,000, and decides to float it as a company for as much more as he can get; he obtains from the proprietors a contract or option to sell for £10,000; he then forms a small syndicate which is registered as a company, and purports to sell to it the contract or option at an enhanced price, say, £50,000; the syndicate next sells to the person who is to appear before the public as the vendor of the business, again, of course, with an advance;

[1] Abroad limits are usually fixed in both cases. As to the amount of the share this was in France originally required to be at least 100 francs, but in 1893 this limit was reduced to 25 francs, so as to encourage the small investors; in Germany the lowest amount per share is usually £50, though £10 shares are allowed in exceptional cases (1895 Report, p. 15). In America, New York requires shares to be not less than five, or more than one hundred dollars (law of 1890, Sec. 2, 4). As to amount of capital subscribed, in France, by the law of 1893, the whole capital must be subscribed and one-quarter paid up, and the same rule holds good in Germany. New York requires at least five hundred dollars with which to begin business (Sec. 4), and one-half of the whole capital stock to be paid up within a year (Sec. 5). New Jersey requires a minimum of one thousand dollars with which to commence business (Sec. 8, iv).

probably by this time we have got to £100,000; and lastly, the nominal vendor purports to make what is called a provisional contract with another dummy called the trustee for the company, subject to adoption by the company; by this time we are in the region of high finance, and the price may be anything up to seven figures. The promoters thus keep piling up profits on each transaction, and the so-called contract with the syndicate, with the nominal vendor, and the provisional contract with the trustee for the company are obviously not real contracts, all these persons being the nominees of the promoters.

4. *The Prospectus.* — It was generally felt that much more might be legitimately required of the prospectus than was secured by the old law; that all the material facts connected with the promotion of the company should be stated, and the directors forced to sign, so as to pin them down to legal liability for all statements in the prospectus.

5. *Registration of Debentures.* —The whole machinery of debentures (*i.e.* generally mortgages issued by the company of all its property) is beset with difficulty; the common course nowadays is for the new-born company to issue both shares and debentures together, and for the vendor to take the debentures in payment and so keep his grip on the neck of the company. Take a case mentioned in the last Board of Trade Report in winding up, of the Savoy Press, Limited, where an undischarged bankrupt formed a company to purchase from himself a worthless publishing business which he had been carrying on for twelve months previously; the price was £1500 paid to him in cash, shares and debentures; the company ran for two and one-half years, incurred debts up to £600 to ordinary creditors, then the vendor came in, ousted the company, and resumed possession by his mortgage as debenture holder.

What makes a company debenture such a powerful instrument is that the law allows to the company what it does not to the private trader, viz., the power to mortgage the whole undertaking as a going concern, by what is known as a *floating charge* in the debenture. This does not affect the property of the company so long as the latter is solvent, and the company can freely deal with the property, sell, replace and even mortgage the stock-in-trade, and so on; but directly the debenture holder proceeds to realize his security, the charge floats no longer, but attaches with limpet-like tenacity to all the property the company has at the moment. The Courts have so favored the floating charge that they even allow it now to attach to uncalled capital, though this result was not arrived at without a struggle,[1] and Lord Justice Romer[2] and others expressed strong opinions in favor of restricting floating charges so as not to attach to uncalled capital.

The Act of 1862 required each company to keep a register of mortgages, to be open to creditors and shareholders, but not to the general public. This provision, however, has long been a dead letter, for the Courts held that a mortgage was equally valid between the parties whether registered in the company register or not.

Lord Davey's Committee decided that in view of the peculiar advantages enjoyed by companies the law demanded amendment, and that a public register should be required, open to inspection by every one, to contain those particular kinds of mortgages or charges, with regard to which companies enjoyed a privileged position.

6. Lastly, there was much discussion about the rights and duties of auditors. Auditors are not valuers,[3] and must take much information at second hand, but the shareholders are entitled to believe they have some assurance that the company is sound if the balance sheet is signed by a competent firm of auditors. Proposals were made that balance sheets should be filed annually, and be open to public inspection, but this was resisted in the interests of both public and private companies.

[1] In principle this extension appears to be wrong, as it may be in effect to issue shares at a discount, so often declared to be contrary to the principle of the Act: if a company's capital is £100,000 in £1 shares, that, as Mr. Justice Buckley and others were never tired of insisting, should be a reality; supposing all the shares are subscribed for, but only 10*s*. is called up on each share, *i.e.* £50,000 in all. There is then £50,000 still uncalled, and any creditor should be able to rely on that as an asset of the company; yet if debentures with a floating charge are issued, as is usual, at the same time as the shares, the £50,000 uncalled is not really an asset at all; it is mortgaged to the debenture holders and the real capital of the company is only £50,000.

[2] 1897 Committee Report, p. 19.

[3] See Lord Justice Lindley's evidence.

With the one man company, the new Act fails to deal directly, while indirectly the Act considerably strengthens its position. Doubts were suggested by a learned judge in a recent case,[1] whether the certificate of incorporation granted by the Registrar had really created the company, on the ground that some of the original seven signatures to the memorandum were not genuine. Section 1 of the new Act provides that the Registrar's certificate of incorporation shall be "conclusive evidence that all the requisitions of the Companies' Acts in respect of registration, and *of matters precedent and incidental thereto*, have been complied with," so that had Aron Solomon forged the other six signatures to his memorandum, his company would have been all the same duly constituted.[2] Nor does the new Act contain any clauses directly defining the powers and responsibilities of directors and promoters, the clauses in the draft bill on the point being erased,[3] on the ground that the existing law was probably sufficiently stringent to meet all cases of misconduct.[4] Further, some really useful clauses defining the nature of the balance sheet and what it should contain have also been dropped, and there is no doubt that the Act is the weaker for their omission.

The principle of the new Act may be described as "publicity rather than penalty"; to give the death-blow not so much to the fraudulent promoter, as to the ignorant shareholder, in this following the conception of the late Lord Chief Justice.[5]

[1] Mr. Justice Kekewich, in National Debenture Corporation, 1891, ch. 2, p. 37.

[2] A clause in the original draft bill providing that where the certificate of incorporation had been obtained by fraud, this should be a ground of winding up, was cut out in committee.

[3] The proposal was to require of all directors "*reasonable care and diligence*": Lord Justice Lindley was of opinion that these words only reënacted the existing law, Lord Justice Romer thought they went beyond it.

[4] The law, however, is undoubtedly defective in many points, *e.g.* a promoter must make full disclosure to the company of any profits made, that is clear; but what is to happen if he does not? The company can of course have rescission of the contract: but if this be impracticable, the company cannot recover from the promoters their illicit profit; see the very recent case of *In re The Lady Forrest (Murchison) Goldmine*, *Law Journal*, Feb. 2, 1901, p. 54.

[5] "When appeals are made to the public to subscribe to the capital of undertakings, everything ought to be aboveboard, no concealment, no secret profits."

It is of course obvious that the machinery of the Companies' Acts has been adopted by many entirely private concerns, the managers of which never intend to appeal to the public, or to let any shares go out of the hands of the very small circle of holders, but who for family or business reasons find the principle of limited liability very convenient. Such companies never *mean* to appeal to the public, and most of the evils which the Act was intended to deal with, consequently, cannot in such cases arise, while to impose hampering conditions as to publication of amount of capital or of the holdings of shares and so on, would only be to handicap them in competition with trade rivals. Many witnesses[1] were anxious to draw a hard and fast line between ordinary public companies and private or family concerns. The difficulty of definition, if nothing else, deterred the Committee from attempting such a division, which does to some extent exist on the Continent. But while refusing to draw any clear distinction directly, the Act does, in a half-hearted sort of way, mark a difference between the two classes. Most of the new stringent provisions are to apply only to companies "*which issue an invitation to the public to subscribe.*" These, in fact, are the key-words of the Act, and their definition and application are alike beset with difficulties. Take the definition alone. Must the invitation be a written or printed document, for it seems difficult to "issue" a verbal invitation? And what constitutes an invitation to the public? Would an invitation to all one's friends or to all the members of one's club come within the words? These are questions with which the Courts may be expected soon to be occupied, and the difficulty of applying the phrase will appear directly. Of the provisions of the act, some apply to all companies, whether incorporated before or since January 1, 1901, and some only to those which are incorporated since that date. To take first the chief provisions applicable:

A. To all companies.

1. In order to check the evils of proceeding to allotment with insufficient capital subscribed, which have already been alluded to, the act imposes two new restrictions: on every application for a share, the applicant must pay a sum not less than five

[1] *E.g.* Lord Justice Vaughan Williams and Mr. Sinclair.

per cent of the nominal amount of the share (Sec. 4 (3)); and further, on the occasion of the first allotment by a company, the act requires for the first time a definite amount of money to be paid into the company's coffers before allotment, viz. either the whole amount of the shares offered to the public; or else, if the company has definitely fixed in its memorandum or articles, a certain amount less than the whole issue on which the directors may proceed to allotment, then that amount. If the amount subscribed does not comply with one or other of these conditions then the directors will be personally liable, after forty-eight days, to see that the money is repaid to the applicant, and any waiver by the applicant of the rules is expressly forbidden.[1]

Section 4 generally deals only with share capital, and with such capital when "offered to the public for subscription." As a further precaution, every company limited by shares is within one month of allotment to file a return with the Registrar of Joint Stock Companies, stating the amount of shares allotted, and the names and addresses of the allottees (Sec. 7): if any of the shares are allotted for services rendered, *e.g.* to a solicitor or vendor, and not for cash, the contract under which such shares are allotted, stating their amount and the services or consideration for which they have been given, must also be filed;[2] this contract will then be open to inspection by intending shareholders: this clause is in substitution for a similar and much discussed provision of the Act of 1867,[3] and is meant to secure the shareholders full knowledge as to the terms on which all shares have been allotted. Curiously enough this Section 7 as to allotment returns, applies to all share companies, public or private, and whether they have issued an invitation to the public to subscribe or not.

2. The third and fourth evils to be dealt with were overloading the purchase-price and the prospectus; and it is mainly through alterations in the law as to the latter that full disclosure is secured as to the former. The prospectus is defined as any "notice, circular, advertisement or other invitation, offering to the public for subscription or purchase any shares or debentures of a company," — not a very satisfactory definition: it would be

[1] Section 4, (3), (4), (5). [2] Section 7, 1, b. [3] Section 25.

comparatively easy to frame a document which would secure all the purpose of a prospectus, *i.e.* advertise the company and the fact that it was doing business and prepared to sell its shares without definitely "offering" them to "the public for subscription." But assuming a document within that definition, then Sections 9 and 10 apply a great variety of new rules to it: it is to be dated, signed by each director and filed with the Registrar (Sec. 9). The prospectus must further contain a great many features, which it is impossible to set out in anything like detail; it must state the contents of the memorandum, the number of founder's shares, and of qualification shares for directors, the minimum subscription on which the directors may proceed to allotment, together with particulars as to shares or debentures issued for considerations other than money. Then come several provisions to prevent overloading the purchase-price: the names and addresses of all vendors of property purchased by that company must appear, together with the amount payable in cash or shares to the vendor, and where there have been a *succession of vendors, then the amount paid to each;* the amount payable for good will (a frequent excuse for concealed fraud) is to be set out particularly: the sum paid as commission for procuring subscriptions, for preliminary expenses, and generally anything paid to the promoter, must also be clearly specified, and finally the dates and parties to every material contract entered into during the previous three years, not being a contract made in the ordinary course of business, must be set out, together with the place where such contracts may be inspected. In the bill as originally drawn disclosure was required of "every material contract and every material fact," but on the energetic protest of Mr. Palmer and others in committee these very wide words were somewhat narrowed and defined. With regard to second or subsequent prospectuses, if issued to the outside public (and not to members only), these provisions apply with modifications. Where published in a newspaper, too, the act takes pity on the pockets of the company and permits the requirements to be somewhat reduced, *e.g.* the contents of the memorandum may be omitted (Sec. 10, § 6). The act is silent as to the penalty if these rules are disobeyed: for any one, *e.g.* a director, *wilfully* violating the act in this respect, the penalty is probably that of a misdemeanor, with two years' imprisonment under Section 28; and any purchaser of shares, injured by non-compliance, will have an action for damages against the person liable, though he probably will not be able to secure rescission of his contract with the company.[1] But it is specially provided that a director can escape liability by showing that he was not aware of the facts, which should have been disclosed and were not (Sec. 10, § 7). The act supplements, it does not abrogate, the liability of the company or directors under the old law. Owing to the definition of a prospectus the new rules can only apply to companies which appeal to the public.

3. The fifth difficulty mentioned above was the insufficient registration of debentures: and Section 14 provides that, without interfering with the old register (though that, as we saw, was practically disused), a new register is to be kept by the Registrar of Joint Stock Companies, open to public inspection (Sec. 14, § 8), and a copy of the new register is also to be kept at the companies' offices: in this register must be inserted (not all mortgages, note, nor even all debentures), but (a) *any mortgage or charge to secure debentures:* this refers to the usual covering deed to secure debentures, but would probably also include the registration of debentures containing charges in themselves and unaccompanied by any covering deed: (b) *a mortgage or charge on uncalled capital:* the act does not go so far as Lord Justice Romer proposed and abolish such mortgages altogether: (c) *a mortgage or charge created or evidenced by an instrument which if executed by an individual would be a bill of sale:* it is impossible here to venture into the quagmire of the Bills of Sale Acts, but the general result of this clause is that every mortgage or charge of "personal chattels" as defined by those acts must be registered, if the mortgage or charge is such as to give the mortgagee or chargee the power to take possession of the chattels: "personal chattels" under the Bills of Sale Acts do not include stocks and shares: this subsection will not therefore compel mortgages by deposit of shares with a bank to be registered: (d) *a floating charge on the whole undertaking or property of the company.*

[1] Cf., for similar difficulty, Companies' Act, 1837, Section 38, now repealed by Section 33 of the 1900 Act.

The old law, as we saw, rendered the old register useless by allowing validity to mortgages though not registered: the present act closes up this hole of escape by providing that in the above four cases the mortgage or charge unless registered within twenty-one days shall be void as against liquidators and creditors.

4. The last difficulty mentioned was the definition of the duties of the *auditor*. The provisions of the original bill on the subject have been much cut down, at the same time Sections 21, 22, 23 are useful, and a great improvement on the old law. Every company, whether public or private, whether appealing to the world for subscriptions or not, must have an auditor, properly remunerated: if an auditor is not appointed at the annual general meeting the Board of Trade may themselves appoint (Sec. 21): when appointed the auditors are to have full right of access to the company's books and the right to demand all necessary information; they are to sign the balance sheet and to add a certificate definitely stating whether their requirements as auditors have been complied with, and also whether in their view the balance sheet exhibits a true and correct view of the state of the company's affairs. It is curious to note that the act does not in terms say there is to be a balance sheet, only that the auditor is to sign it, presumably if there is one: it is very doubtful if the Courts will treat this as impliedly requiring a balance sheet in every case.

B. 1. With regard to regulations applicable only to companies incorporated since January 1, 1901, there are new rules laid down as to directors' qualification shares; the act does not insist on such a qualification, but says that, where the articles of the company require it, in order to avoid difficulties which arose, under the existing law, either the director must sign the memorandum for the amount of these shares or (if not an original director) sign and file with the Registrar a definite contract to take the proper number of shares from the company and pay for them (Sec. 2, ii); the section does not say explicitly with whom the contract is to be entered into, whether with the company or not. In any case these requirements are only necessary in the case of companies which "issue an invitation to the public to subscribe," a phrase which again causes difficulty. What is to happen if a company, established on a private basis, and so managed for two years, then requires more capital and appeals to the public? Will the original appointment of directors become void because these rules were not observed? The act gives no answer to the question though the Courts will probably soon be called on to do so.

2. As already mentioned, the idea of a double registration (preliminary and final), of a company, common on the Continent, has not met with favor here, and Lord Davey's Committee reported against it. At the same time the act indirectly does adopt something of the sort by enacting in Section 6, that no company shall in future "commence business" until certain things have been done. This requirement will in no way affect the registration, but, unless and until the requirements of the section are complied with, the company though registered and in existence will be in suspense; it cannot make binding contracts nor borrow money. The preliminaries which must be complied with before business may be commenced are: (i) the proper amount of shares must have been allotted (*i.e.* either the whole amount offered or the proportion required by the articles, Sec. 4); (ii) the directors must have paid a required proportion of their qualification shares; and (iii) the secretary must have filed a statutory declaration that these rules have been complied with. The Registrar will then issue a certificate allowing the company to commence its business. This section again only applies to companies which "issue an invitation to the public to subscribe." A private company need not get the certificate to commence; but how are people, who wish to contract with a company, to know whether it is within the terms of this section or not? Whether it has appealed to the public or not? The point is important, for if it is a private company which has not gone to the public, then any person contracting with the company will be safe and the company will be bound, but otherwise, if the company has appealed to the public and not got the Registrar's certificate the company will not be bound by the contract.

3. Though these many restrictions are imposed on those companies which appeal to the public to subscribe, they are allowed one compensating privilege, viz. that in their case under-

writing is in future to be legal, and the long recognized custom of the City at length receives the sanction of the Legislature, but only on these express terms, viz. that the payment of the commission and the amount of rate per cent are authorized by the articles and disclosed by the prospectus [1] (Section 8).

Finally comes the question: Will the act achieve its purpose and check fraud? That it will provide work for the courts for years to come is clear. The drafting is not good and the difficulties of interpretation, some of which have been pointed out, are numerous. But criticisms of the act go deeper than that: the provisions as to the register of mortgages, the prospectus and the duties of auditors are all useful and should give some protection to the public, but as it is proverbially easy to drive a coach and four through Acts of Parliament, it should be easy to drive one through or at any rate round some of the chief provisions of this act: there is more than one way of circumventing the "commencement of business" provision, of which much is clearly expected; for instance, the company may in its articles mention some merely trifling sum on which to proceed to allotment, or if the promoters shirk the publicity of this course, they can simply start in a very small way, with seven members, all directors, a small capital of perhaps £100, issue this all nominally to the public, and so secure the Registrar's certificate; they could then at once launch out, increase their capital, say to £500,000 and proceed as at present.

Again, all the restrictions on companies which issue an invitation to the public can at one stroke be rendered futile: many companies domiciled near the Stock Exchange never appeal directly to the public at all; they are "baby creations," owing their birth to strong promoting parents, their shares are dealt in more or less artificially by the parent company, public quotations of the shares appear, and eventually the public rush in and buy: the effect of these clauses will probably be largely to encourage this underground process.

In a word, considering all the time spent upon it it is a pity that the act achieves so little.

MONTAGUE BARLOW.

[1] This clause has already received judicial interpretation. See *Burrows* v. *Matabele Gold Reef, Ltd.*, *Sol. Jo.*, 1901, p. 378.

XVIII

TRUST LITERATURE: A SURVEY AND CRITICISM[1]

THE industrial changes in the United States during the last two or three years have called forth inevitably a multitude of writings dealing with the problem of trusts,[2] just as, in the earlier years of the present decade, the condition of our national finances stimulated the discussion of the tariff or the silver question. It is the purpose of this article to present a brief survey of the recent output of trust literature, and then to attempt a critical estimate of the views advanced concerning the most important theoretical problems involved in the study of industrial consolidation.

I

In mere volume, at least, the product of the last few years is noteworthy. Discussion of the monopoly question in the United States seems to have begun early in the seventies, when popular dissatisfaction arose concerning railroad rates and management. Then, for a time, an occasional article in some periodical indicated only a fitful interest in the subject, until early in the eighties the formation of the Diamond Match Company and the Standard Oil Trust caused a livelier discussion of the problem of monopoly. Later in the same decade the appearance of other combinations, as well as a growing interest in railroads and municipal monopolies, caused a marked increase of writings dealing with this subject. An incomplete bibliographical summary shows that fifteen treatises or reports of official investiga-

[1] From the *Quarterly Journal of Economics*, Vol. XV, 1901, pp. 167–216.

[2] By "trusts" the writer means those great combinations of capital in our manufacturing industries which are commonly called by this name. It is not the purpose of this paper to deal with the literature devoted primarily to the problems presented by the so-called natural monopolies.

tions and over thirty-five noticeable articles in the chief periodicals appeared between 1887 and 1890. For the next six years the output diminished, probably for the reason that the tariff and the money questions were uppermost in the public mind;[1] and only eight books or reports and hardly more than a score of articles were published during the period. In 1897 and 1898 at least six books or pamphlets and about thirty articles appeared, foreshadowing an increased interest in the problem of monopoly. And, finally, the last two years have given us not less than twenty-eight books, reports, and pamphlets, together with a flood of periodical articles that will reach probably one hundred and fifty titles when the returns for 1900 have all been received. While these figures can claim only substantial accuracy, they will suffice to show that the production of trust literature has kept pace with the process of industrial consolidation.

Any bibliography of these writings, like lists of recently formed trusts, becomes antiquated before it leaves the press, so rapid is the rate of increase. The only serious attempt in this direction is Mr. A. P. C. Griffin's List of Books relating to Trusts,[2] which appeared early last summer. This is of considerable value to the student, but professes to give "only the chief authorities." The list of books and pamphlets is nearly complete, but the reader is surprised to notice that the bibliography refers to Nicholson's short chapter on monopoly value, and does not include the valuable discussion of combinations of capital, contained in Hadley's Economics; while in the references to periodical literature he will often wonder what principles of selection could have been followed.

[1] That the small amount of trust literature that appeared between 1890 and 1896 was due to the predominance of other issues may be inferred from the fact that in 1892 and 1896, the two years when presidential elections occurred, our bibliography shows that no books, and only a few articles, appeared. During the period from 1886 to 1900 these (1892 and 1896) were the only years in which no books were published.

[2] A List of Books (with References to Periodicals) relating to Trusts. Washington, 1900. [A second edition with additions appeared in 1902. The *Quarterly Journal of Economics* also contains in its current bibliography a complete list with annotations of both books and periodical literature on this subject. — Ed.] The one other recent list of trust writings that deserves mention may be found in the *Chautauquan*, XXX, 237, 238. For an excellent bibliography of earlier works, see von Halle, Trusts, 338–350 (New York, 1895).

Since the present article must be confined to *recent* literature, it has seemed best to draw a line somewhat arbitrarily at the year 1897, and to exclude from consideration most of the writings that appeared before that date. Within these limits the author will aim to give detailed references to the books, reports and pamphlets that have come to his attention up to the time of writing. In some cases, however, it will be necessary to refer to works that appeared earlier than 1897. With periodical literature no extended bibliography is necessary in these days, when Poole's Index is available for every reader, so that the citations here given will be confined to the most valuable articles, and to some others that are significant as representing certain shades of opinion.

Passing over certain discussions of the monopoly problem that have appeared in some recent economic treatises and general works of reference,[1] which, by the way, may be recommended to those who are beginning the study of this subject, we may divide recent trust literature into eight classes. It is true that any such procedure will be open to the charge of arbitrariness at some points; but, on the other hand, it will avoid so much repetition and bring opposing theories into such clear relief that it may be trusted to commend itself to the reader.

(1) The first of our eight classes comprises the reports of official investigations[2] and the proceedings of conferences called

[1] W. P. D. Bliss, Encyclopædia of Social Reform, 888–894, 1346–1348 (New York, 1898); R. H. I. Palgrave, Dictionary of Political Economy, II, 802–807 (London, 1896); C. J. Bullock, Introduction to the Study of Economics, 309–335 (2d edition, New York and Boston, 1900); A. T. Hadley, Economics, 151–173 (New York, 1896).

[2] Report and Proceedings of the Joint Committee of the Senate and Assembly appointed to investigate Trusts, Senate Document 60 (Albany and New York, 1897); Industrial Commission, Preliminary Report on Trusts (Washington, 1900); Same, Trusts and Industrial Combinations, — Statutes, Decisions and Digest of Corporation Laws; Bulletin of the Department of Labor, No. 29, pp. 661–831, Trusts and Industrial Combinations (Washington, 1900).

The entire report of the United States Industrial Commission has since appeared. Vols. I and XIII are specifically devoted to testimony; Vol. II contains a digest of statutes and decisions; Vol. XVIII is devoted to industrial combinations in Europe; Vol. XIX, pp. 594–685, contains the final report of the commission, with an appended opinion by counsel as to legislation. The Appendix to Vol. XIX, pp. 1120–1128, gives statistics supplementing those in

under the auspices of various organizations.[1] The New York investigation of 1897 was mainly a shrewd political move, intended to prove the undying hostility of the Republican party to trusts; but it brought out some interesting information. The trust magnates summoned to testify before the legislative committee suffered from those attacks of loss of memory with which they are usually afflicted upon such occasions; but Mr. Theodore Havemeyer volunteered the statement that he would not care to engage in a business enterprise that did not promise a profit of 15 or 20 per cent. The Industrial Commission was more successful than any previous body of investigators in securing testimony from persons interested in trusts, and its Report contains a careful digest of evidence that adds greatly to its usefulness. The Standard Oil combination seems to have made a most careful and systematic endeavor to clear itself from the many damaging charges that have been brought against its methods;[2] and, if the public still remains unconvinced of the spotless purity of this organization, it will not be due to any lack of sweeping denial and stout asseveration in the testimony of the oil magnates. The most valuable feature of this Report is the investigation, conducted under the direction of Professor Jenks, into the effect of combinations upon prices. This gives us the best available data for a trustworthy conclusion upon a most fundamental question. Nearly as much can be said of the Digest of Corporation Laws contained in the second volume of the Commission's Report. The conclusions and recommendations

Vol. XIII. On the general work of the commission, cf. *Quarterly Journal of Economics*, XVI, pp. 564–586.

The Twelfth United States Census, Manufactures, Part I, pp. lxxv–lxxxi, specially reports statistics, which are supplemented by Pubs. Amer. Statistical Association, N. S., No. 53, for March, 1901, pp. 1–20. — ED.

[1] The Chicago Conference on Trusts (Chicago, 1900); Official Report of the National Anti-Trust Conference (Chicago, 1900); Corporations and Public Welfare, Addresses at the Annual Meeting of the American Academy of Political and Social Science (New York, 1900).

[2] This testimony of the oil magnates has been gathered together into a single volume, An Inside View of Trusts (New York, 1899), which has been distributed broadcast, probably for "educational purposes."

A carefully edited and annotated edition of this testimony has recently been issued by the *Oil City Derrick*. — ED.

advanced by the Commission will never be charged with radicalism, and are marked by extreme sensitiveness concerning the relation of trusts to the protective tariff. The Bulletin of the Department of Labor contains further data concerning the effect of trusts upon prices, and publishes the results of an independent investigation into the working of these combinations. This investigation was conducted by sending out schedules of questions to forty-one organizations; and the Bulletin presents the results in tabular form, whenever that is possible. The information thus gathered is of no little interest; but it must be accepted with certain reservations, since it was not to be expected that the companies answering the inquiries would give testimony adverse to their own interests. This would probably be conceded readily by Professor Jenks, who had charge of the investigation.

The proceedings of the Trust Conference, held under the auspices of the Civic Federation of Chicago, attracted such general attention[1] at the time that little space need be devoted to them in this review. It will suffice to say that, while only a few of the papers and addresses at the conference possess any considerable value in themselves, the proceedings as a whole should be read by every student who desires to form an estimate of the present condition of popular opinion upon trusts. All sorts and conditions of men were present at the conference, and their opinions may be taken as fairly representative of the classes for which they spoke. The Report of the National Anti-Trust Conference has a similar interest, as an expression of the sentiments of a very large class of persons who see little or nothing that is good in the process of industrial consolidation. Some of the addresses contained in the volume are of decided value in calling attention to the undoubted abuses and dangers that attend the movement. Corporations and Public Welfare is devoted largely to discussions of railroads and other public service companies, but contains articles upon industrial securities as investments and the influence of corporations upon political life.

[1] See *Harper's Weekly*, XLIII, 954, 975; *Outlook*, LXIII, 199; *Independent*, LI, 2602; *Review of Reviews*, XX, 457; *Journal of Political Economy*, VIII, 1; *Annals of the American Academy*, XV, 69.

(2) In our second class may be placed those writings in which the trust movement is accepted as inevitable, and its causes, advantages, dangers and proper regulation are discussed. No less than five recent books belong to this group.[1] Harper's Restraint of Trade is a mere collection of extracts from various works upon trusts; but the compiler's opinion is, evidently enough, that "modern industrial conditions have demanded" that the "principle of combination be generally accepted." The books of Baker, Collier, von Halle, and Jenks agree in finding the cause of trusts in the conditions of modern competition and the economies that arise from the combination of capital. These writers hold that the trusts represent a distinct economic gain in productive power, but recognize that these organizations have been attended with many abuses. Professor Jenks and Mr. Collier advocate no radical action to restrain the evils of trusts, but propose various moderate remedies, of which the chief is always publicity. Mr. Baker, however, believes that no efficient method of regulation can be found short of placing a representative of the government upon the board of directors of every combination. The main contention of these works — that trusts are a natural and inevitable outcome of modern conditions — we shall reserve for more extended discussion, in subsequent pages.[2]

A decided majority of the articles that have appeared recently in the periodicals, popular or scientific, should be included in this class.[3] President Hadley and Professor Kinley argue that

[1] C. W. Baker, Monopolies and the People (2d edition, New York and London, 1899); W. M. Collier, The Trusts (New York, 1900); E. L. von Halle, Trusts, or Industrial Combinations in the United States (New York, 1895); W. H. Harper, Restraint of Trade (Chicago, 1900); J. W. Jenks, The Trust Problem (New York, 1900).

[2] With these books should be mentioned the chapter on trusts contained in Professor Giddings's Democracy and Empire, 137–143 (New York, 1900). The author holds that the trust "could never have become the great factor in the commercial world that it is to-day" unless it had been "an efficient device for dealing with existing industrial conditions."

[3] See articles by Hadley, in *Scribner's Magazine*, XXVI, 604; Kinley, in *Progress*, V, 7; Sherwood, in *Yale Review*, VIII, 362; Coleman, in *Journal of Political Economy*, VIII, 19; Robinson, in *Conservative Review*, IV, 33; Jenks, in *Quarterly Journal of Economics*, XV, 46; Smith, in *Chautauquan*, XXIX, 347; Ashley, Surveys,

trusts are due to destructive competition and the superior economy of concentrated production; Professor Sherwood believes that these organizations are the agency through which the most skilful management is secured; Mr. Coleman and Mr. Robinson look upon such combinations as an inevitable product of industrial evolution; and Professor Jenks again presents the views advanced in The Trust Problem. In these articles the reader will find little that is new.

(3) Radically different views are advanced in works of a third class.[1] M. de Rousiers is too faithful to the tenets of the orthodox French school to abandon his belief in the efficacy of the competitive system. His interesting work contains the results of an investigation into the leading industries that have fallen into the hands of trusts. He finds almost everywhere a tendency towards production on a large scale, but thinks that this is not the cause of monopoly. The real cause, he contends, is control over limited supplies of raw material and facilities for transportation, or the special advantages conferred by tariff and patent laws. His remedy for the evils caused by trusts is to abolish all restrictions, and thus to leave competition free to do its perfect work. Professor Ely's recent book is a treatise on the subject of monopoly; and begins with a study of definitions, a classification of monopolies and a formulation of the law of monopoly price. It then proceeds to discuss the subjects of industrial consolidation, the limits of monopoly and the permanence of competition. While the author holds that competition is impossible in the field of the "natural monopolies," he believes that elsewhere the tendency towards consolidation is limited by virtue of the fact that, beyond a certain point, combination of capital is not economical. Our present trusts he believes to be

Historic and Economic, 378–391 (London, 1900). See also article by Carnegie in *Century Magazine*, LX, 145.

[1] P. de Rousiers, Les industries monopolisées aux États-Unis (Paris, 1898); R. T. Ely, Monopolies and Trusts (New York and London, 1900); A. B. Nettleton, Trusts or Competition (Chicago, 1900); H. Wallace, Trusts, and how to deal with them (Des Moines, 1899).

Other secondary treatises, based mainly on American experience, are Le Rossignol, Monopolies Past and Present, 1901; and St. Léon, Cartells et Trusts, Paris, 1903; besides a number of German treatises. — Ed.

the result of special privileges and corporate abuses, — a conclusion which is very much like that reached by M. de Rousiers. Mr. Nettleton's book is to a great extent a compilation of facts and opinions, but in the second chapter the author presents his own conclusions in a vigorous argument against the trust. He believes that the economies of consolidation cease before the point of monopoly is reached, and that existing combinations are the "result of monopoly hunger" and the product of railroad discriminations and other unfair privileges. For a remedy he advocates rigorous legal prohibitions, supplemented by a reform of existing abuses. Mr. Henry Wallace concedes that the disorders sometimes attending modern competition not unnaturally lead producers to take refuge in combination. He believes, however, that the trust is a vicious method of remedying the evils which competition sometimes produces, and that the consolidations of recent years have caused a speculative "boom" which is sure to be followed by a disastrous reaction.

To Professor J. B. Clark we owe a series of papers[1] in which the contention is made that, while large scale production is economical and giant industrial undertakings are to be the order of the day, competition is certain to continue, nevertheless. Professor Clark believes that monopoly is almost wholly bad, and that the most efficient management is found in independent establishments, not in monopolistic concerns that are removed from the stimulus of competition. His remedy for evils that attend the present trust movement is to take away from the combinations their favorite weapons, — price discriminations, factors' agreements and other questionable devices, — so that competition can operate without let or hindrance. With this accomplished, he believes that industrial consolidation can proceed to any extent that may be deemed advantageous, without producing the evil results inseparably connected with monopoly.

If a digression is permissible at this point, we may suggest that Ely's Monopolies and Trusts and Jenks's Trust Problem

[1] See Theory of Economic Progress in *Economic Studies*, I, 5 (New York, 1896); *Atlantic Monthly*, LXXXV, 47; *Political Science Quarterly*, XV, 181; *Gunton's Magazine*, XIX, 209. [More recently in his Cooper Union lectures. — Ed.]

are the works that will be found most useful for the general reader.[1] Both of these books are thoroughly readable, and they will be found to supplement each other in a most helpful manner. Ely discusses the definition and classification of monopolies; while Jenks explains the methods by which trusts are promoted, financed and floated. The one writer formulates the law of monopoly price; and the other furnishes statistics showing precisely what influence combinations have exerted upon prices. The first book presents the arguments of those who believe that the monopolistic features of trusts are due to special privileges and unlawful practices; the second contends that these industrial combinations have developed naturally out of the conditions of modern competition. Monopolies and Trusts advocates remedies that are designed to restore competition to its former position as the fundamental economic force; The Trust Problem accepts the principle of combination, and proposes conservative methods of regulating monopolistic enterprises. From the study of the two books the reader can gain a competent knowledge of the chief subjects that now interest students of this important question.

(4) In a fourth group we may place a number of articles which relate to various phases of the trust movement. Upon the financial aspects of consolidation three references may be commended to the reader.[2] Mr. Charles S. Fairchild has discussed, from the point of view of the practical banker, the financing of trusts. Mr. James B. Dill has called attention to the dangers that have attended the manufacture of industrial securities, often falsely so-called, and has insisted that the only safety for the trusts can be found in the complete abandonment

[1] A new edition of Jenks with additions appeared in 1902. E. S. Meade, Trust Finance, is by far the most comprehensive and convenient treatise in the special field indicated by its title. G. H. Montague, Trusts of To-day, 1904, is a readable and convenient manual of the general subject. Moody, Truth about the Trusts, 1904, is a convenient compilation of data from his annual Manual of Corporations. — Ed.

[2] See Fairchild and Dill, in Publications of the American Economic Association, Third Series, I, 149 and 177; Dill, in Corporations and Public Welfare, 107; Dill, The College Man and the Corporate Proposition, privately printed (New York, 1900); and Meade, in *Annals of the American Academy of Political Science*, XVI, 345. [More completely in his Trust Finance. — Ed.]

of speculative management; while Dr. E. S. Meade has written a most valuable survey of the financial aspects of the trust problem.

Comparatively little work has been done in recent years upon the history of individual trusts, probably because the consolidation movement has been so well-nigh universal as to draw attention away from the fortunes of particular enterprises. Yet special articles have been devoted to the wire nail association of 1895, the tin-plate combination and some others;[1] while the testimony taken by the Industrial Commission contains a large amount of material for the history of recent industrial changes. Finally, the phenomenal activity of trust promoters in 1898 and the earlier part of 1899 has been well described by Mr. Byron Holt.[2]

(5) A fifth class comprises those writings which relate primarily to the special favors and other abuses by which, undoubtedly, trusts have profited to a considerable extent. Most prominent among such evils has been discrimination in railway rates. Mr. Lloyd's Wealth against Commonwealth did good service in showing the potency of the "smokeless rebate" as a weapon for destroying competition, and few recent writers have failed to say something on this subject.[3] Of late the tendency has been to give too little weight to this factor in the trust problem; and it is well for us to be reminded by Mr. Aldace

[1] See Edgerton, in *Political Science Quarterly*, XII, 246; McVey, in *Yale Review*, VIII, 156; also *Harper's Weekly*, XLII, 202; *Independent*, XLIX, 273. [The United States Steel Corporation is described by H. L. Wilgus, 1901, and fully by Meade in his Trust Finance. Cf. also The Inside History of the Carnegie Steel Co., by J. H. Bridge. The *Century Magazine*, in 1902–03, devoted a number of articles to the more prominent combinations. — Ed.]

[2] *Review of Reviews*, XIX, 675.

[3] For writings dealing *primarily* with railroad discriminations, see H. D. Lloyd, Wealth against Commonwealth (New York, 1894); J. Hardesty, The Mother of Trusts, 185–208 (Kansas City, 1899); Prouty, in *Annals*, XV, 41; Walker, in *Forum*, XXVII, 256–257; Newcomb, in *Gunton's Magazine*, XVII, 347.

Miss Ida M. Tarbell's History of the Standard Oil Co., which appeared serially in 1902–04 in *McClure's Magazine*, and is about to appear in book form, is by far the most authoritative study which has been made. G. H. Montague's Rise and Progress of the Standard Oil Co., 1903, reprinted from the *Quarterly Journal of Economics*, is rather more favorable to the company in its interpretation of its history. — Ed.

F. Walker that "the trusts have the railroads by the throat," and to have Mr. Prouty, of the Interstate Commerce Commission, explain the precise methods by which the federal law against discriminations is constantly violated.

Naturally enough, the relations of trusts to the protective tariff have claimed the attention of many writers; but comparatively little work has been devoted primarily to this subject. Economists have been so much occupied with discussions of the advantages of large-scale production and the destructive character of competition that they have probably minimized unduly the importance of the tariff as a factor in the present situation. The Industrial Commission, in particular, has evinced such an anxiety that no harm to the cause of high protection shall come from its investigations as to lead the Philadelphia *Ledger* to remark, in a recent editorial, that, "if this be a sample of the character of the inquiry the Industrial Commission is pursuing, it might as well suspend its hearings, since it is plainly committed to the preservation of the trust-promoting and sustaining provisions of the existing tariff, no matter how glaring may be the abuses perpetrated under cover of its schedules." We hardly need to be informed that some trusts are independent of tariff protection, and that combinations of capital exist in England under free trade; since very few people imagine that protective duties are the sole cause of trusts, and we know that unrestricted foreign competition prevents most English combinations from abusing their powers. The chief questions worth discussing are whether, as Mr. Havemeyer alleges, the tariff causes over-investment in certain industries, thus producing a period of depression that results in consolidation; and to what extent the prices of tin-plate, steel rails, wire nails, window glass, paper, salt, sugar, and other articles controlled by trusts or pools, have been raised to exorbitant figures under the shelter of protective duties. In this direction the New England Free Trade League has rendered us a service by publishing a series of letters relating to the extortion practised by many of the trusts.[1]

[1] Twenty-four Letters relating to Trusts and the Tariff (Boston, 649 Tremont Building). See, also, Taussig, in *Quarterly Journal of Economics*, XIV, 500, 501, 503, 507. [Cf. Liefmann, Schutzzoll und Kartelle, Jena, 1903. — ED.]

(6) In the sixth class belong the writings of the panegyrists of the trust movement.[1] In these works, industrial combinations are represented as the greatest invention and benefaction of this age or almost any other; and those who hold opposing views are designated by such pleasing terms as socialists, demagogues, blackmailers and the like. Popular discontent against trusts is due to "hatred of wealth," hostility to capital or at least to the desire to stir up class feeling and organize a crusade against prosperity. Particular mention will be made only of Gunton's Trusts and the Public, which is an amorphous collection of papers written at various times during the last dozen years. The author is most outspoken in condemning anti-trust agitation, and loud in his praises of industrial combinations, especially the Standard Oil Company. A noticeable feature of the book is the effort made to refute all charges brought against this organization. In the earlier papers, written before 1899, the sugar combination figures as a second model trust; but upon this subject Mr. Gunton's views changed after Mr. Havemeyer went to Washington, and told the Industrial Commission that the tariff is "the mother of all trusts." Before that time Mr. Gunton had insisted that good trusts, like the sugar and oil combinations, formed for economic purposes, are not monopolies; but, after Mr. Havemeyer's fall from grace, we find this author denouncing him as "a cunning monopolist." In a paper written in 1888, which forms the first chapter of the book, Mr. Gunton had proved that fears of the political influence of trusts are unfounded; but in 1899 he wrote that the activity of the sugar magnates in Washington had become "a national scandal," as bad, in fact, as anything that had ever "occurred in

[1] Although works of this class have been distributed broadcast, the writer has not been able to secure copies of all of them. Those at hand are: H. Apthorp, Trusts and their Relation to Industrial Progress (Cleveland, 1899); C. R. Flint, Industrial Combinations (N. P., N. D.); G. Gunton, Trusts and the Public (New York, 1899); D. F. Kennedy, Trusts: An Argument from Labor's Standpoint (N. P., N. D.). Mr. S. C. T. Dodd has brought together a number of papers previously published, and they now appear under the title Trusts (New York, 1900). As representative of magazine articles of this class, see R. P. Flower, in *Gunton's Magazine*, XIII, 251; Gunton, in *Gunton's Magazine*, XIX, 344. [Cf. The Trust: Its Book. By C. R. Flint, J. J. Hill, S. C. T. Dodd and F. B. Thurber. New York, 1902. — Ed.]

the public affairs of the Republic." Mr. Gunton's own conclusion is that, "Tariffs and trusts should be discussed on their own merits, separately," — a method that certainly possesses the merit of convenience for those who entertain views similar to his own.

(7) Writings of the seventh class we will designate as radical, since they come from those who advocate most radical methods of reform.[1] Mr. Hugh Lusk devotes special attention to the legislation adopted in New Zealand to check the growth of monopoly. Most of the other works included in this group have much to say concerning the relation of the money question to the trust problem. Thus it is urged that the era of falling prices drove producers into consolidation;[2] and "Coin" holds that the "money trust" is the mother of all others, and will ultimately control all other combinations. Of more interest are the specific references to the consolidation now in progress in the world of banking.[3] Beyond all doubt a combination, represented by such institutions as the National City Bank, is now under way, the purpose of which is to dominate the banking business in our chief financial centres. The day may come when all economists will be obliged to give this movement their serious attention.

(8) Our eighth class includes literature on the legal aspects of trusts, of which naturally enough the output has not been small.[4]

[1] F. A. Adams, Who Rules America? (New York, 1899); H. L. Chaffee, Book of Trusts (Chicago, 1900); W. H. Harvey, Coin on Money, Trusts and Imperialism (Chicago, 1899); H. Lusk, Our Foes at Home (New York, 1899); G. H. Shibley, A Trust of Trusts (Chicago, 1898); The Monopoly Question (New York, 1900); Momentous Issues (Chicago, 1900).

[2] See also E. B. Andrews, in *International Journal of Ethics*, IV, 323, and Swain, in Chicago Conference on Trusts, 537–539.

[3] See facts presented in Report of the Anti-Trust Conference, 326–327; Shibley, Momentous Issues, 77–78; Harper, Restraint of Trade, 342–345.

[4] For books see C. F. Beach, Treatise on the Law of Monopolies and Industrial Trusts (St. Louis, 1898); F. H. Cooke, The Law of Trade and Labor Combinations (Chicago, 1898). For important periodical literature see *American Law Register*, XXX, 751; *American Law Review*, XXXIII, 63, 499, XXXIV, 186; *Harvard Law Review*, VII, 128, 157, 333; *American Journal of Sociology*, I, 411; *Political Science Quarterly*, XII, 212, 622; *Quarterly Journal of Economics*, XIV, 416; *Forum*, XXVI, 452, XXVIII, 732.

The best collection of edited cases will be found in Cases on Restraint of

It is not the purpose of this article to emphasize the legal side of the trust question, and a bare outline of the results of recent discussions will suffice. The advocates of trusts believe that the legal position of these corporations is now unassailable. It is conceded that old-fashioned "conspiracies to engross the necessaries of life" are unlawful, and that the early trust agreements or such contracts as that of the Addyston Pipe combination cannot be sustained. But the large corporations now known as trusts are deemed perfectly secure, since the powers of Congress to regulate interstate commerce do not, under the decision of the Supreme Court in the Knight case,[1] extend to manufacturing enterprises; while the states cannot prevent their citizens from selling their property to domestic corporations or restrain them from purchasing the products of foreign companies. Upon the other hand there are those who contend that the formation of a monopoly is illegal, whether this is done by means of a pool, a trust or an incorporated company;[2] and there are not wanting writers who declare that, although state corporations engaged in manufactures are not directly amenable to the power of Congress to control interstate commerce, nevertheless these companies can be reached indirectly by laws excluding the products of monopolistic combinations from interstate commerce, prohibiting such organizations from using the mails, and employing other drastic measures.[3]

Trade, by Professor Bruce Wyman of the Harvard Law School. See also Noyes on Intercorporate Relations and Dill on Corporations, both of 1902, the latter especially on New Jersey practice. F. E. Horack, Organization and Control of Industrial Corporations, Philadelphia, 1903, compiles the law as to publicity. — Ed.

[1] 156 U. S., 1.

[2] Thus it is pointed out that in the Knight case the court had no difficulty in recognizing that the sugar combination was a monopoly, although it declined to interfere on the ground that the manufacture of refined sugar was not interstate commerce.

[3] Besides these eight classes of writings, there remain three pamphlets, for which a single note will suffice. Two of these are by socialists: J. B. Smiley, To What are Trusts Leading? (Chicago, 1899); B. Bouroff, The Impending Crisis (Chicago, 1900). The third describes a farmers' trust, L. L. Hopkins, The Coming Trust (New York, 1900).

II

Of the many important questions involved in the study of trusts, the most fundamental concerns the alleged monopolistic character of these combinations; and, since diagnosis must precede the rational treatment of the disease, — if disease there be, — this aspect of the problem may be considered to possess the greatest theoretical and practical importance. What, then, do recent discussions have to say upon this subject?

From a number of writers we meet the contention that the trusts are not monopolies in any proper sense of the term.[1] Mr. Gunton argues that, whenever these combinations have secured control of their respective industries, this power has come from their ability to render cheaper and better service, and not from the possession of any exclusive privileges. So that potential competition always remains, and monopoly cannot be said to exist. Mr. Dodd says that, since "all are free to combine," competition is not destroyed, but is merely "moved to a higher plane." Mr. Robinson tells us that, while trusts may involve "the repression of competition," they are monopolies neither "in scope nor method"; and many similar citations might be given if space would permit. But some of those who entertain this view of the case have adopted a very different tone when discussing such unfortunate enterprises as the New York Ice combination, which, for some singular reason, was not considered an orthodox trust in good and regular standing.

Some legal writers are inclined to insist upon a narrow definition of monopoly, which would restrict it to those cases where a person or company enjoys an exclusive grant from the government.[2] Thus Mr. Knox declares: "Monopolies can only exist by grant from the sovereign. They cannot be created by contract between individuals." Mr. Dodd would define monop-

[1] For the references, in order, see Gunton, Trusts and the Public, 5, 7, 8, 36; *Gunton's Magazine*, XIX, 350, 351; Dodd, Trusts, 44; Robinson, in *Conservative Review*, IV, 50, 52. See also Chicago Conference, 476; Apthorp, Trusts, 11; *Journal of Political Economy*, VIII, 29; *Forum*, XXVII, 260.

[2] See *American Law Register*, XXXVI, 423; Dodd, Trusts, 36, 37; Chicago Conference, 86.

oly as "a grant by the government for the sole buying, working, making or using of anything"; and Mr. Weil adopts a similar definition. In further support of this view, a few decisions of our courts may be cited.[1] But the general trend of the decisions is overwhelmingly in the contrary direction;[2] and Mr. F. H. Cooke makes a correct statement of the present legal doctrine when he says,[3] "Within a comparatively recent period the conception of a monopoly has been extended from a right created by government to a condition produced by the acts of mere individuals; thus, where within a given area all sales of a given article are made by a single individual or set of individuals."[4]

The vast majority of writers recognize that the trusts generally attempt to secure a monopoly and actually possess monopolistic features,—a fact upon which it is unnecessary to dwell. But oftentimes the word "monopoly" is qualified by the use of such adjectives as "partial," "incomplete," "precarious" or "temporary."[5] It is clear, furthermore, that the meaning attached to the term[6] is such a degree of control over the supply of a commodity as enables the person or persons possessing it to control the price, and fix charges at something more than the normal competitive rate. In order to be complete, the monopoly must be able to maintain prices at the point of highest net returns.

[1] 52 Fed. Rep., 115, 567.

[2] 54 Hun, 354, 356, 376, 379; 30 N. E. R., 279, 290; 44 Fed. Rep., 721; 85 Fed. Rep., 271; 156 U. S., 16, 18; 166 U. S., 322; 175 U. S., 244. The following words of Chief Justice Fuller seem to settle the question: "Again, all the authorities agree that in order to vitiate a contract or combination it is not essential that its result should be a complete monopoly. It is sufficient if it really tends to that end and to deprive the public of the advantages which flow from free competition." 156 U. S., 16.

[3] Law of Trade and Labor Combinations, 94, 95.

[4] For other legal writers holding the same view, see Huffcut, in Industrial Commission, I, part 2, p. 1211; Gaither and Keasbey, in Chicago Conference, 286, 384, and *Harvard Law Review*, XIII, 199.

[5] Jenks, Trust Problem, 61; Sherwood, in *Yale Review*, VIII, 365; Collier, The Trusts, 302; Brooks, in Chicago Conference, 62; Forrest, in *American Journal of Sociology*, V, 241. On the other hand, Andrews says the trusts mean "absolute monopoly" of a permanent character. *International Journal of Ethics*, IV, 325, 326.

[6] *E.g.* see Ely, Monopolies and Trusts, 14; Jenks, Trust Problem, 64, 65.

The conclusion that the element of monopoly inheres in the trust movement is based, in the first place, upon evidence concerning the purposes for which combinations are formed. Prominent business men who have declined invitations to enter trusts, or have had knowledge of the circumstances attending the formation of such enterprises, state most explicitly that the main inducement held out to the owners of the plants which are to be combined is the prospect of controlling the market and exacting higher prices.[1] Then the prospectuses issued by many combinations tell the same story, and control over the greater part of the output must generally be secured before the promoter can make his proposition attractive to financiers and investors.[2] Such control must be obtained at all hazards, even at the expense of paying extortionate prices for efficient plants or buying worthless factories at substantial valuations.[3] Moreover, the tactics employed to stifle possible competition are decidedly unlovely, and are almost inexplicable upon any other assumption than that a desire exists to secure monopolistic powers.[4] Finally, several trust magnates have admitted that the purpose of their companies was to control output and prices, and have conceded that this had been accomplished.[5]

But the best evidence of the existence of such intent is the fact, which appealed so strongly to Judge Taft in the Addyston case,[6] that monopolistic powers have been exercised. Econo-

[1] See T. B. Walker, in Chicago Conference, 540, 541; J. S. Pillsbury, in Nettleton, 250, 251; Griffiths, in Report Industrial Commission, I, 176.

[2] See *Annals*, XVI, 358; *Commercial and Financial Chronicle*, July 23, 1898; Nettleton, Trusts, 52.

[3] Thus one concern held up the American Tobacco Company for $12,500,000 in cash. *Annals*, XVI, 364. See, further, Collier, 67, 68; von Halle, 61; Nettleton, 250; Carnegie, in *Century*, LX, 148.

[4] Passing over the more objectionable tactics, a single instance may be cited. The American Tin-Plate Company made contracts with manufacturers of machinery by which the combination was to purchase the entire output. *Yale Review*, VIII, 167; Industrial Commission, I, 179. Could evidence of monopolistic purpose be clearer?

[5] McNulta, Havemeyer and Gates. Industrial Commission, I, 60, 63, 81, part 2, 1009, 1010. Jenks says that in private conversation such persons will usually admit that the chief purpose "has been to check competition." *Quarterly Journal of Economics*, XV, 47.

[6] 175 U. S. R., 237.

mists do not need to be told that a combination that produces from 70 to 90 per cent of the supply can substantially control prices,[1] and this is admitted by such expert witnesses as Messrs. Havemeyer and Archbold.[2] It is well known that many trusts control from 65 to 95 per cent of the products of their respective industries,[3] and that some of them announce from day to day the prices that prevail in domestic markets.[4] Therefore, we are not surprised to learn that the most reliable investigation into prices[5] shows that, in almost every case, combinations have managed to increase the margin[6] between the cost of materials and the price of the finished product for considerable periods of time.[7] This fact establishes the existence of monopolistic intent and monopolistic power.

III

Since most writers recognize that the recent combinations of capital have developed monopolistic tendencies to a considerable extent, the outlook for the future becomes a most interesting and important problem. Under all the circumstances, it is not surprising that recent years have witnessed numerous attempts to bring the control of various industries into the hands of single corporations of colossal magnitude, which possess and exercise the power of monopoly. But the reader of recent trust literature finds that many writers of recognized authority contend

[1] Only Gunton denies this. See *Gunton's Magazine*, XVIII, 566.

[2] Industrial Commission, I, 60, 129.

[3] See Industrial Commissions, I, 18, 19; Bulletin of Department of Labor, No. 29, pp. 731, 735.

[4] Industrial Commission, I, 19; Bulletin, 708.

[5] Industrial Commission, I, 39–57; Bulletin, 708–765; Jenks, 130–170.

[6] On this method of procedure see Bulletin, 709, 710.

[7] Partisans of the trusts follow generally one of two methods when presenting statistics of prices. Sometimes they naïvely quote merely the prices of refined oil from 1872 to the present, and claim for the trust the credit of the reduction. See Dodd, Trusts, 25, 26, 56; Flower, in *Gunton's Magazine*, XIII, 254; Gunton, Trusts and the Public, 218. In other cases, they exhibit tables showing the margin between the prices of crude and refined oil from 1871 down to the time of writing, and claim for the trust the credit of the decline. Here they carefully avoid comparing the margin before the formation of the trust in 1882 with the margin since that date. See Dodd, 62, 93, 94; Gunton, 14. Comment upon any of these performances is needless.

that these conditions of centralized control are to be permanent in industries that require heavy investments of capital for their successful prosecution, and that competition is a thing of the past.

In considering this proposition, careful discrimination is necessary at the very outset. There are three possible conditions under which industries may be conducted, — production upon a small scale, production upon a large scale and centralized management by a single company or combination. Every student of economic history knows that production upon a small scale was long ago superseded in most important branches of manufactures by undertakings of a large size. The combinations of recent years have sought to replace these large establishments by single consolidated enterprises; and this is the real meaning of the trust movement and the arguments advanced to prove its natural and desirable character. No one wishes to revert to the stage when production was carried on by small establishments. Controversy exists only concerning the advantages of superseding large-scale production by combinations that include all important establishments in a single line of business. The "industrial combination," which those who take a generally favorable view of trusts are upholding, must mean the replacement of independent enterprises already conducted on a large scale by a single centralizad management. To combinations of this character writers may or may not apply the term "monopolies"; but the real issue, nevertheless, is the alleged superiority of a single body of producers over independent rival concerns. When it is contended that combination means not "necessarily one great trust, comprising one great industry," but merely "an enlargement of capital,"[1] we must insist that this is not what the arguments in favor of centralization are considered or designed to prove. When another writer tells us that combination may be contrasted not with competition, but with "isolation," — by which, probably, production in small establishments is to be understood, — we may properly remind him that in his own works combination is used as the opposite of competition, and that he says that sometimes "indus-

[1] Apthorp, Trusts, 25.

trial units which are necessary for proper utilization of labor become so large as to produce actual monopoly."[1] When others tell us that the trusts have seldom secured that immunity from competition which monopoly implies,[2] it must be replied that this fact serves merely to discredit some of the arguments intended to prove the superiority of consolidation, and does not alter the purpose for which these arguments are advanced. If the tendency towards combination means anything, it means the substitution of centralized and consolidated management for the rivalry of independent concerns; and this may fairly be termed monopoly. If, furthermore, the advocates of combinations intend to defend nothing more than production upon a large scale, they should revise their list of arguments designed to prove that competition is "wasteful," "destructive," "suicidal," and "a thing of the past"; and should make it clear that they do not uphold the action of most of our trusts in consolidating all establishments of a given class, in order to "regulate production" or to "remove the evils of competition." We may advise the reader, therefore, to grasp firmly the distinction between large-scale production and monopoly, and to note carefully whether the arguments advanced in favor of combination relate to the one thing or the other. Unless this is done, clearness of thought becomes impossible.

Does the trust movement, then, mean a permanent régime of monopoly in industries where large amounts of capital must be employed? Some writers who consider the movement to be, upon the whole, a desirable development in industry, answer clearly in the negative. Thus Professor Sherwood says[3] that the dominant position which trusts now enjoy depends mainly upon "monopoly of undertaking ability," and that this is "in its nature temporary and the result of a competitive process." The large gains that now accrue to these monopolistic enter-

[1] See Hadley, in *Atlantic Monthly*, LXXIX, 377, 378. With this compare Hadley's Economics, 153, 154. The passage quoted refers immediately to public service industries, but at the bottom of page 154 the author applies this and other arguments to other branches of business.

[2] Collier, 106; von Halle, 72; *Gunton's Magazine*, XIX, 350: Apthorp, 11.

[3] *Yale Review*, VIII, 365–368.

prises are merely a temporary reward for the development of a superior form of business organization. And Mr. Carnegie, Mr. Dill, Mr. Wanamaker, and others[1] insist that "every attempt to monopolize the manufacture of any staple article carries within its own bosom the seeds of failure," or that "no men, or body of men, have ever been able, or will be able, permanently to hold control of any one article of trade and commerce."

But the arguments of most of those who take a favorable view of trusts cannot be given such interpretation. Some writers state clearly and frankly[2] that "the competitive system of industry is fast passing away," and that all lines of business "are, or soon are to be, monopolized"; that "monopolies of every sort are an inevitable result from certain conditions of modern civilization"; "that experience seems to justify the belief that monopoly within certain limits . . . may be secured simply by the possession of large capital"; or that trusts represent "a vast accumulation of productive resources which renders the competition of small concerns hopeless." And this is the view, of course, which is entertained by persons of socialistic tendencies.[3] Sometimes it is attempted to add force to such arguments by calling combination the result of an evolutionary process of survival; and one writer remarks[4] that the trust is "an evolution from the *heterogeneous* to the *homogeneous*," — a statement which will interest those who happen to remember the Spencerian formula.

But other economists are less explicit. Writing of the trusts, von Halle says[5] that "in the manufacturing industries, the victory of production on a large scale seems assured"; and he

[1] *Century Magazine*, LX, 148; Dill, The Corporate Proposition, 18; Corporations and Public Welfare, 128; Chicago Conference, 576, 623.

[2] See, in order, Andrews, in *International Journal of Ethics*, IV, 321, 333; Baker, 159; Jenks, 64, 65; *American Journal of Sociology*, V, 232. With these see Kinley, in Progress, V, 18; Shaw, in Nettleton, 36, 41.

[3] See writer quoted by Ely, Monopolies, 146; J. A. Hobson, Evolution of Modern Capitalism, 126 (London, 1894).

[4] *Century Magazine*, LX, 144.

[5] Trusts, 63, 140, 149. For another failure to make clear the distinction between large-scale production and monopoly, and therefore a failure to convey a clear impression to the reader, see Holt, in *Review of Reviews*, XIX, 675.

concludes his work with the somewhat oracular remark that "the future belongs neither to the prophets of individualism, nor to the ideals of the social democrats." Mr. Brooks thinks that "practical monopolies" have been formed, but that they can be permanent only in case "they put some kind of economic superiority upon the market."[1] Mr. Collier, rather inconsistently, says that competition is "business committing suicide," and then thinks that the trusts will be controlled by potential competition.[2] Professor Bemis looks upon a trust as "virtually a monopoly of large capital," possessing "vast possibilities of social advantage"; but thinks that we cannot pronounce a final judgment "until we have first removed all special privileges."[3] And, finally, President Hadley believes that modern conditions "work in favor of those who advocate combination, and make it harder for independent competitors to resist it, or for the law to prohibit it on grounds of public policy"; yet he holds that, if prices are raised unduly, "new capital will come into the business."[4] But, if the advantages of industrial combinations, in both producing and marketing their products, are as great as most of these writers affirm, it is hard to see how unity of management can fail to secure ultimate control of most branches of manufactures. The lack of explicit forecasts of the future need not, therefore, prevent us from concluding that the general position of these economists is that a tendency to permanent monopoly may be clearly recognized.

But economists who think that, for the future, monopoly is to be the order of the day, generally consider that this control of industry will be limited by what is termed potential competition. Thus they do not affirm that absolute monopoly will prevail, but merely such a control of production and prices as will not tempt new capital into the field. To this subject we shall return in our later paragraphs.

Attention may now be directed to the reasons for this belief

[1] Chicago Conference, 62. [2] The Trusts, 53, 143, 106.

[3] Chicago Conference, 395, 399; Report of Anti-Trust Conference, 339, 342.

[4] Economics, 153, 161. In *Scribner's Magazine*, XXVI, 607, he is more explicit, — sufficiently so, perhaps, to justify our classing him with the writers mentioned in the previous paragraph.

in the tendency of large-scale production to pass over into monopoly, and to the criticism which such views evoke from writers who deny the existence of such a tendency. In favor of this proposition three general lines of arguments may be distinguished: (*a*) the contention that a consolidated enterprise possesses advantages over independent companies in producing and marketing its goods; (*b*) the claim that mere mass of capital confers powers of destructive warfare so great as to deter possible competitors from entering the field; (*c*) the belief that modern competition between large rival establishments, representing heavy investments of fixed capital, is injurious to the public, ruinous to the producers and in its final outcome self-destructive. As our discussion proceeds, it will become evident to the reader that all of these arguments can be employed, with consistency, only by those who believe that the competitive régime is to be replaced by an era of monopoly.

IV

First in this list is the contention that a consolidated concern is a more efficient agent of production and exchange. It is claimed that a combination can effect a saving in no less than twenty different directions;[1] and the economy arising from such sources is declared to be great enough to give the trust a control over the market based solely upon superior efficiency,[2] and to make competition "hopeless."[3] For this reason it is held that such combinations may confer "enormous" benefits upon society.[4] The critic may well entertain the suspicion, however, after reading what is said upon this subject, that these arguments prove almost too much; for, if in twenty directions substantial economies may be realized by a combination, it would seem that the utter futility of competition would have been recognized by the business world long ago. If these argu-

[1] For detailed lists of these economies see Baker, 9–14; Jenks, 21–43, 212–213; Gunton, 11, 12, 37, 38; Ely, 145–160; Collier, 61–77; *Quarterly Journal of Economics*, XV, 49; *Progress*, V, 23–25; Nettleton, 19, 20, 25–27.

[2] See Gunton, Trusts, 5, 36; *Gunton's Magazine*, XIX, 350, 351; Chicago Conference, 476, 477, 588.

[3] *American Journal of Sociology*, V. 232.

[4] Jenks, 213. See also Baker, 25; Collier, 37–39; *Progress*, V, 18.

ments be altogether true, how is it that the trusts find competition so troublesome, and consider it "good business" to resort to the most disagreeable means of driving "interlopers" out of the field? Such tactics are decidedly "bad business," if they are needless; and we can hardly think that the shrewd managers of the trusts would care to arouse public resentment by unnecessarily harsh methods.

To consider this line of argument in any complete manner would expand this article into a volume; and we can discuss, therefore, only some of the more important savings that trusts are believed to realize. Of the twenty specific economies that have been enumerated, we shall take no notice of five which may be considered either doubtful or of minor importance.[1] Six others will be relegated to a foot-note, since it may be denied emphatically that they represent any substantial advantages which large independent companies cannot secure.[2] Three more

[1] These alleged advantages are: (1) combinations will prevent adulteration and improve products; (2) they will reduce losses from unwise extension of credits; (3) they will not suffer from stoppage of work by accidents in any one locality, or by labor troubles; (4) they need to carry smaller stocks of goods to meet demands of the market; (5) they may eliminate needless middlemen.

[2] These six items illustrate the necessity of discriminating sharply between large-scale production and monopoly. (1) It is said that combinations can specialize the machinery of the separate plants, thus saving the loss resulting from changing from one kind of work to another. Jenks, 36, 37. But large independent concerns have often done the same thing. (2) Combinations can push trade in foreign markets. But large independent companies have been equally successful, or almost so. This claim provokes a smile from a Minneapolis miller. See Nettleton, 250. Such concerns as the Baldwin Locomotive Company deny that combination is necessary for this purpose. Rivals of the Standard Oil Company are now following the trust into European markets. Industrial Commission, I, 22. The Industrial Commission concluded that foreign trade does not need a monopoly. *Op. cit.*, 23. Wherever a combination, by keeping domestic prices at high figures, is able to sell a larger surplus abroad at low rates, we may deny the desirability of such extension of trade. On the general subject see Nettleton, 65–66. (3) Trusts can conduct auxiliary or subsidiary industries. So do many independent enterprises. Note Taussig's description of the extent of the activities of our large iron and steel companies. *Quarterly Journal of Economics*, XIV, 159, 160. (4) Trusts utilize by-products. So do large independent establishments, while small establishments sometimes coöperate for this purpose. (5) Trusts can employ chemists, inventors and other experts to improve methods. This has for years been done by many large companies not in combinations. (6) Trusts can insure their own plants. But independent concerns may coöperate in establishing factory insurance companies, and secure the lowest possible rates, as some of our textile trades have done.

may be set aside for incidental discussion[1] in connection with the views of those who deny the tendency to monopoly. Of the remainder, three items relate to advantages in the manufacture and three to economies in the exchange of products.

Thus it is claimed that trusts, by filling orders from the nearest plant, can effect a great saving in cross-freights. Data upon this question are available in the recent Bulletin of the Department of Labor.[2] Of the forty-one combinations reporting, twenty-seven failed to answer this question, nine claimed a saving from this source, and five stated that there was no gain. Of the nine reporting a saving, the Bulletin states the amount only in three cases; and in two of these the item of cross-freights was combined with other economies, the aggregate sums being $400,000 and "considerably over $500,000." This, be it remembered, is the trusts' own showing, and is certainly not an underestimate. The reason for these comparatively small results is not difficult to discover, and has been recently explained by a writer who has heretofore emphasized most strongly this particular economy of consolidation.[3] When the monopolized product is of a bulky sort, the industry is already localized pretty thoroughly before combination takes place; and, since most of the former independent establishments were producing chiefly for their natural local constituencies, the trust can save little in cross-freights. When, however, the product is light, transportation charges become a matter of small moment. In either case the room for saving in cross-freights is not nearly as large as has been represented, while often it does not exist.

Then it is urged that a trust can draw upon all the patented devices of the constituent companies, and employ only those that are most efficient. But advantages accruing from this fact will in most cases prove to be of a temporary nature, as trusts that have tried to base a monopoly upon the control of all available patents have learned in the past, and will learn in the future. Moreover, a simple reform in our patent laws will make

[1] These three advantages are: (1) combinations can specialize skill in management; (2) they can compare methods and costs of production in different plants; (3) fixed charges decrease as the size of the enterprise increases.

[2] Bulletin, No. 29, p. 673. [3] Jenks, in *Quarterly Journal of Economics*, XV, 49.

the best processes available for all producers[1] at any time that the public finds such a measure to be necessary for protection against monopoly. Here, then, we find no natural law working resistlessly towards combination, but a man-made device which can be regulated as public policy may dictate.

Again, we are told that a trust can produce more cheaply than separate concerns, because all the plants utilized can be run at their full capacity; whereas, under competition, many establishments can be kept in operation but a part of the time. Two observations may be made concerning this claim. First, the extent of the economies thus realized is grossly exaggerated. The whiskey combination furnishes the stock illustration employed to enforce this argument;[2] and we are told that this trust was able to close all but twelve out of the eighty constituent plants, and yet produce almost the same quantity of spirits that formerly had been put upon the market. But the distilling industry is a highly exceptional case. For twenty-five years prior to the formation of the trust the federal tax upon whiskey had been so manipulated by the distillers as to call into the industry enormously excessive investments of capital. Competition, of itself, would never have produced conditions even remotely resembling those that prevailed in this business from 1865 to 1887.[3] The sugar refining industry is another stock illustration, but here, it is conceded,[4] the tariff had given an undue stimulus to investments; and the same thing is true, probably, of many, if not most, of the trusts that have been able to close up a considerable number of plants.[5] In general,

[1] All writers recognize that patents have contributed materially to the establishment of certain monopolies. See the case of the American Steel and Wire Company. Industrial Commission, I, 18. Some measure of reform in our patent laws is favored by such a conservative writer as J. B. Clark and by some of those who uphold trusts. See Chicago Conference, 408; Jenks, 220, 221; Collier, 201.

[2] See Jenks, Trust Problem, 34; von Halle, Trusts, 59, 66.

[3] These facts are clearly stated by Jenks in *Political Science Quarterly*, IV, 297 *et seq.*

[4] Jenks, Trust Problem, 45. See Havemeyer's testimony, in Industrial Commission, I, 59.

[5] For other cases see *Yale Review*, VII, 315, VIII, 157, 170; Industrial Commission, I, 207. Other instances can be found without great difficulty.

it may be denied that, whenever governmental interference has not produced unhealthy and abnormal conditions, competition has led to such absurdly excessive investments as is commonly assumed. We must concede, however, that under normal conditions some reduction can be made in the number of plants required to supply the market at ordinary times; but this does not dispose of the matter. If a trust is to be prepared for supplying the market promptly in times of rapidly increasing demand, it is necessary that some surplus productive capacity must exist in periods of stationary or decreasing demand; for, as believers in the tendency to monopoly often remind us, many months, or even one or two years, are required for the construction of new plants. When this fact is taken into account, the case will stand as follows: except where the action of government has produced abnormal conditions, the capacity of competing establishments does not exceed the requirements of the market to any such degree as is commonly assumed; even a trust must provide for periods of expanding trade, and this fact diminishes materially the margin for saving by avoiding the burden of idle factories; even then, not all rival establishments suffer seriously from inability to find continuous employment for their plants, so that probably the advantages secured by the trust are of consequence only when the least fortunate or least efficient independent concerns are made the basis of comparison. In those cases, however, where abnormal conditions have been created by the operation of our tax laws, we need entertain no surprise at the appearance of consolidated companies. But in the future, it may be asserted, this particular force will not prevent rival companies from competing for a share of an increasing trade.

The last three economies relate to advantages in buying materials or selling products. It is urged that a combination can purchase its raw materials more cheaply than separate concerns. This would probably be interesting news to many large companies not connected with trusts, and Professor Ely is undoubtedly right in remarking that all ability in bargaining is not controlled by combinations.[1] No one doubts that a large

[1] Monopolies, 162, 163.

company can often secure better terms than a small establishment; but it is not so clear that every trust can secure supplies more cheaply than large independent enterprises, unless it is true that all combinations can arbitrarily depress the prices of the materials which they consume. Undoubtedly, this has been done by some of the trusts,[1] although their partisans deny it;[2] but such a saving represents no social gain, and sometimes it may be possible for would-be competitors to profit by the depressed condition of the market for raw materials. We do not need to deny that *any* combination can gain an advantage in the purchase of supplies,[3] in order to support the contention that no *general* advantage accrues to the trusts from this source. On this point the Bulletin of the Department of Labor shows that a majority of the forty-one combinations investigated "did not answer this question specifically," while the representations made by the minority claimed no great economy in purchases except in a few cases. Even when considerable savings are realized, it is always possible that these represent, chiefly or wholly, gains on that part of the aggregate purchases which was formerly made by the smaller and weaker establishments; so that the realizing of a net gain does not establish the existence of an advantage over the largest companies that entered the combination.

And, finally, we come to economies in advertising and in soliciting business, where the wastes of competition are certainly serious and the room for improvement correspondingly great. Those who deny the tendency to monopoly generally admit that a trust can have a material advantage here,[4] while those who affirm the existence of such a tendency evidently realize that their case is strongest at this point.[5] Yet an opportunity for saving in these departments does not always exist,[6] and the extent

[1] Industrial Commission, I, 17, 142; Jenks, 155, 156; von Halle, 70.

[2] See Gunton, 82–87; Dodd, 62, 76. Dodd claims that the oil combination has *raised* the price of crude oil.

[3] For an instance, see Jenks, 145, 146.

[4] Ely, 167; Nettleton, 64.

[5] Jenks, 67, 68; Collier, 37, 61. Both of these writers admit that the gains of combination are rather in marketing products than the work of manufacture.

[6] Bulletin of Department of Labor, No. 29, p. 673. Here it is stated that several trusts reported that there was no saving in advertising, while one combination reported that more was spent.

of the economy is easily exaggerated in other cases. Mr. Nettleton is right when he says:[1] "But to whatever extent the trust-organizers have counted on practically cancelling expenditure for these two items, on the ground that buyers will be obliged to come to the sole manufacturers, they are likely to be surprised. Those trusts that have tried this experiment have discovered that demand for commodities falls off with remarkable rapidity as soon as effort in pushing sales is materially reduced. To an extent which few appreciate, the buying public has become accustomed to being reminded of its needs before making purchases. The country merchant often has more inertia than enterprise, and, with the periodical visits of his favorite drummer discontinued, his orders dwindle or are delayed until unseasonable. Except in staple and absolutely necessary commodities, demand is largely created and maintained by advertising through periodicals, catalogues or travelling salesman. Hence, the trust that expects to save the bulk of this important item must also expect to lose through diminished sales more than the economy represents. This is not theory, but the testimony of leading dealers in many lines." Moreover, those who believe in the permanence of competition will not lose sight of another consideration which is advanced by Professor Marshall,[2] who writes concerning the economies accruing from these sources: "But its weakness in this regard lies in the fact that to keep its monopoly it must be always bargaining and manœuvring on a large scale. And if its monopoly is invaded, it must bargain and manœuvre widely in matters of detail as well as in larger affairs."

The result of our discussion up to this point would seem to be that any advantages of a monopoly over independent concerns of a large size are but slight, except in the single matter of effecting sales. We must now take into account certain counteracting forces, upon which some writers rest their belief that competition will ultimately prevail. These economists contend, in the first place, that, outside the field of the natural monopolies, the growth of a business enterprise is limited by the fact that companies of a certain size will secure "maximum

[1] Trusts, 64. [2] Marshall, Some Aspects of Competition, 24.

efficiency" of investment, and that beyond this point concentration brings no increase in productive capacity. Without introducing the arguments of professional economists upon the subject,[1] it may be pointed out that this view is entertained by many men who have a practical acquaintance with our large manufacturing industries.[2] This position is based upon the belief that a factory of a certain size will enable machinery to be employed in the most advantageous manner; that a reasonable number of such plants will make possible all needful specialization of production; that allied and subsidiary industries can be, and are, carried on by large independent concerns; and that the cost and difficulties of supervision increase rapidly after a business is enlarged beyond a certain size, especially when it is attempted to unite plants situated in different parts of the country. For this reason, increased output does not decrease the burden of fixed charges after a company attains a certain magnitude;[3] but, on the contrary, new charges arise. Among such new expenses, not the least important are the cost of employing the most skilled legal talent to steer the combination just close enough to the law, the expenses necessary for "legislative" and "educational" purposes, and the outlays for stifling competition or the continual "buying out" of would-be rivals.

Not only is it denied that consolidation secures no decrease of fixed charges over independent concerns possessing sufficient capital, but it is argued that an established monopoly will suffer actual loss from listless and unprogressive management. As the *New York Journal of Commerce* rightly insists, "it is not to be denied that such concentrations of management will be subject to countervailing offsets from the absence of the stimulus of competition; from the uncertainty about the management

[1] See Clark, in Chicago Conference, 405; Adams, *op. cit.*, 37; Ely, 165, 166; Rousiers, 281, 320; Meade, in *Annals*, XVI, 353. See also Chicago Conference, 620; Nettleton, 62, 63. Even Jenks wavers at this point, 68.

[2] See Studebaker, in Chicago Conference, 575; Mr. Converse, of Baldwin Locomotive Works, in *Springfield Republican*, Dec. 20, 1900; Messrs. Doscher, Post, Clarke, Griffiths and Taylor, in Industrial Commission, 68, 88, 185; Pillsbury, in Nettleton, 251.

[3] An alleged decrease is one of the twenty supposed economies of combination.

falling into the best possible hands; from the discouragement to invention which always attends monopoly; and from the possibility that the administration may be intrusted to 'friends' rather than to experts." And the existence of such drawbacks is admitted by many of those who believe combination to be desirable and inevitable.[1] As Professor Clark suggests, an established monopoly, secure in the possession of the markets of a large country, "would not need to be forever pulling out its machines and putting in better," so that, as compared with countries where industry is upon a competitive basis, such a combination would fall behind in the struggle for international trade.[2] In ruthlessly and unceasingly displacing the expensive machinery with newer and better appliances, American manufacturers have probably led the world; but monopolies will inevitably feel reluctant to continue such an energetic policy of improvement. As combinations obtain a greater age, they will persist in old and established methods;[3] while nepotism and favoritism, tending towards hereditary office-holding,[4] will replace the energetic management that some of the trusts now display. Andrews is correct in holding that the quest for able and progressive management, which often marks the efforts of existing trusts to make their dominating position secure, is no argument against the probability of future apathy when monopolies have been long established.[5]

Here we may refer to two of the alleged advantages of trusts. It is said that combinations develop abler management through the opportunity they afford for a specialization of skill upon the part of their officials,[6] and that efficiency is increased by a

[1] See Andrews, in *International Journal of Ethics*, IV, 327, 328; Hadley, 159; Collier, 124. Sherwood thinks a point may be reached where monopoly "tends to prevent improvement." *Yale Review*, VIII, 367. Gunton and von Halle admit that, if complete control of markets could be secured, this would be the result. *Gunton's Magazine*, XIX, 349; Trusts, 68. See references to Jenks and Hadley in subsequent notes.

[2] *Gunton's Magazine*, XIX, 210. Cf. *Political Science Quarterly*, XV, 184.

[3] See Ely, 167. Note Hadley, in *Atlantic Monthly*, LXXIX, 383.

[4] See admission of Jenks, in *Quarterly Journal of Economics*, XV, 51–53.

[5] *International Journal of Ethics*, IV, 327, 328.

[6] Jenks, Trust Problem, 36, 37; *Quarterly Journal of Economics*, XV, 51.

comparison of the methods and costs of production in the various plants.[1] The first of these advantages may be open to question, since it is not clear that large independent concerns do not afford sufficient room for specialization of talent; while it may be denied that, in the long run, any possible gain from this source will suffice to counterbalance the apathy begotten by monopoly. Concerning the second it may be remarked that, at the outset, this gain would accrue only to the least efficient plants, and would not make the combination superior to the best of the original establishments; while, after a time, although all the factories might be brought up to the same level, the lack of competition would retard the rate of future improvement.

When it is contended that the "strength of the trust is that it gives the opportunity for the exercise of these highest qualities of industrial leadership," and that it gives us "a process of natural selection of the very highest order,"[2] we may question whether stock speculation and other causes lying outside the sphere of mere productive efficiency have not had more to do with the formation of recent combinations than demonstrated superiority in business management. And, even if it be admitted that dominating powers of leadership have played their part in the movement, it may be asserted that the establishment of permanent monopoly[3] will interfere seriously with the future process of selection. Professor Lindsay has remarked very justly[4] that the "development of a high order of undertaking genius in the few seems . . . to depend upon a wide range of undertaking experience in the many," and that under a régime of trusts "we would in the course of a few generations have very little available material from which to make selections." It must be remembered that the able leaders now at the head of the successful trusts were developed out of a field which afforded the widest opportunity for creative ability and independent

[1] Bulletin of Department of Labor, No. 29, p. 675; Collier, 77.

[2] Sherwood, in *Yale Review*, VIII, 364.

[3] I am not unmindful of the fact that Professor Sherwood considers such monopoly to be in its very nature temporary. This part of the argument relates to the claims of many writers that monopoly is to be permanent.

[4] See *Publications of American Economic Association*, Third Series, I, 204.

initiative. These are the supreme qualities requisite for great industrial leadership; and they are not likely to be fostered by a régime which, if the believers in monopoly are to be taken at their word, closes each important branch of manufactures to new enterprise, and renders hopeless all competition with a single consolidated company. Will successive generations of bureau chiefs or heads of departments in long-established corporations be able to continue the race of masterful leaders, which freedom in originating and organizing independent industries has given us in the present age?

This leads to another consideration. In an industry organized upon a national scale, under the control of a single company, there must arise an "irrepressible conflict" between that central responsibility necessary for intelligent, unified management and that individual freedom and energy requisite for the healthful life of the separate members.[1] For centralized control, elaborate and costly administrative apparatus is absolutely essential; and this mechanism of superintendence soon becomes fixed and bureaucratic in its methods, so that it bears heavily upon the individual parts. President Hadley has said recently that, as trusts gain in age and experience, good private business will become so similar to good public business that it will make little difference whether an enterprise is carried on by the public or by individuals.[2] In one respect, at least, his argument is well founded. Governmental enterprises usually suffer, at least when conducted upon an extensive scale, from the lack of that stimulus which only competition can give and from the growth of fixed bureaucratic methods of control. A private monopoly that engrosses an entire branch of industry must develop inevitably, in the course of time, the very characteristics that impair the efficiency of a public undertaking.[3] Both will exhibit the tendency to unprogressive management which comes from the

[1] This has been pointed out by Professor Marshall, Some Aspects of Competition, 17.

[2] *Scribner's Magazine*, XXVI, 610.

[3] President Andrews confronts this question squarely when he says, "In this important regard the system of trusts is obnoxious to the same criticism nearly always made against socialism." *International Journal of Ethics*, IV, 328.

absence of competition[1] and the weight of centralized administrative machinery.

When all the arguments are sifted, and the balance of advantage or disadvantage is determined, there is reason for thinking that the losses due to monopoly will more than offset occasional slight gains in the work of manufacture and the more substantial savings in placing products upon the market. This conclusion is strengthened by the showing which most of the trusts have made in the payment of dividends upon their securities. As is well known, the preferred shares have usually represented the amount paid in cash or securities for the plants that have been purchased and for the working capital supplied by the financier. The common stock represented nothing more than "the substance of things hoped for" in the way of alleged economies of operation. Although times have been unusually prosperous, and prices, already high, have often been increased by the trusts, dividends on the common stock have almost universally disappointed the expectations of those who invested with the hope of securing a part of the "enormous" savings of combination.[2]

V

The second argument advanced to prove the tendency to monopoly is the claim that mere mass of capital confers such powers of destructive warfare as to deter possible competitors from entering the industry, at least until prices have long been held above the competitive rate. It is said that a large combination can lower prices below the cost of production in any

[1] The writer does not overlook the fact that believers in monopoly contend that potential competition survives the formation of trusts. But in subsequent paragraphs it will be shown that, if the arguments advanced to prove the superior efficiency of trusts are sound, competition cannot continue in any form.

[2] Another consideration bearing upon this question of the efficiency of trusts is the fact that they have, in order to obtain control of their industries, bought up large numbers of antiquated or badly situated plants which will be a permanent burden. See Collier, 67, 68; von Halle, 61; Jenks, 195–197; Trust Conference, 623; *Century Magazine*, LX, 148; Nettleton, 250. In cases where plants are paid for by issues of preferred stock, as has usually been the case, the sums paid for worthless factories will affect dividends, but not financial solvency. Where bonds have been issued, however, then the burden will become more serious.

locality where a small rival concern is established, thus driving it out of the field. If, on the other hand, a large rival company attempts to compete in all markets, this will mean an investment of capital in excess of the needs of trade, with a consequent depression of business and loss to all concerned.[1] Without doubt the destructive competition waged by combinations is an important consideration, and it may well enough reënforce monopoly where other attendant circumstances favor consolidation.[2] But a monopoly based solely upon this power would be, confessedly, a temporary affair; for probably no one would claim that all capitalists would be intimidated permanently by such circumstances. This argument, therefore, may be used properly enough to strengthen the conclusions drawn from the alleged economies in production; but it does not of itself establish the existence of a permanent tendency to monopoly. Of this truth, any one who observes the trouble which trusts are having with new enterprises at the present moment may obtain sufficient evidence.[3]

It should not be forgotten, furthermore, that this argument depends upon the fact that combinations at present are allowed to employ the weapons of discriminating prices and other tactics, which violate every one's sense of fair play although they may be difficult to suppress. If uniform price lists could be made obligatory, then this power of intimidating rivals would largely disappear; for, if a trust must give its products away in all markets in order to ruin a competitor who enters a portion of the field, then its losses would be proportionate to the mass of capital, and the advantage over the independent concern would disappear.[4] Without doubt the prevention of price discrimina-

[1] Jenks, 66, 67; Forrest, in *American Journal of Sociology*, V, 241; Collier, 129; Baker, 350, 351.

[2] This is admitted by Ely, 178.

[3] One illustration from an earlier period may be cited. At the opening of 1892 it is said that the lead trust owned all the establishments in the country except two. In 1894, however, there were in existence independent plants producing as large a product as the trust. The trust had a capitalization of $30,000,000, the independent companies employed a capital of $2,000,000. See *Popular Science Monthly*, XLIV, 741, 742. More recent illustrations will be presented later.

[4] This is urged by Clark in *Political Science Quarterly*, XV, 194.

tions would be a work of great difficulty; but, if this must be done in order to prevent the abuses of monopoly, then some way of accomplishing the result can and will be found. Such a remedy will be less difficult than the elaborate schemes which those who believe in trusts advocate in order to remove admitted abuses in other directions. The menace of mere mass of capital is at the most a cause of temporary monopoly, and its potency can be destroyed by depriving the trusts of their favorite method of "sand-bagging" competitors.

VI

The final reason for the belief that combinations must ultimately prevail is found in the character of modern competition in those industries which require heavy investments of fixed capital. Under such conditions the difficulty of withdrawing specialized investments and the losses that are entailed by a suspension of production make competition so intense that prices may be forced far below a profitable level without decreasing the output; and industrial depression inevitably follows.[1] For such constant fluctuations in prices, combination is considered the natural and inevitable remedy. Some writers allege, furthermore, that it "is not possible to have competition without competitors, and, if there be competitors, one must prevail," so that monopoly "is the inevitable fruit of competition."[2]

The socialist who reads some of these arguments must feel that at last many of the criticisms which he has long urged against competition have been accepted by economists of the orthodox type. Certainly, few stronger indictments of the competitive régime have been formulated by socialistic critics of the existing social order. Thus the believers in trusts tell us that "individ-

[1] Jenks, 16–20, 199, 200; *American Journal of Sociology*, V, 232, 233; *International Journal of Ethics*, IV, 322, 323; *Forum*, XXVIII, 414, 415; Hadley, 158, 159; *Progress*, V, 18; Collier, 43.

[2] Cochran, in Chicago Conference, 476; Collier, 40. Since the existence of absolutely unique undertaking ability may be safely denied, this particular allegation may be dismissed with the single comment that, while leaders of remarkable talents may temporarily secure a dominating position, permanent monopoly can never be established upon such a basis as this.

ualism and the competitive system have run their course"; that "the competitive system of industry is fast passing away"; that competition is "inadequate and wasteful," resulting in "general depression" and "industrial loss"; that the competitive régime leads to warfare that is first "intense," then "destructive," then "self-destructive"; that competition is not the "life," but "the death of trade" and "a destroying force to those engaged in it," so that it is termed "business committing suicide."[1] Professor Ely remarks, justly enough, that such contentions are "a virtual surrender to the theory of socialism."[2] In any event, the reader will perceive that it is idle for economists who hold these views to imagine that their theories do not lead to the conclusion that competition is impossible and permanent monopoly inevitable in the industries to which the discussion relates.

In continuation of this line of argument, it is said that trusts are beneficial, because they can "exercise a rational control over industry," and "adjust production to consumption."[3] Thus it is believed that commercial crises can be prevented, or, at least, that their worst effects can be avoided.[4] But such arguments overlook the facts that a restriction placed upon production by a trust, especially if this is sufficient to raise prices above the competitive rate, may react injuriously upon other trades;[5] and that monopoly profits, accruing to a small body of capitalists for a long period of time, must constitute a tax upon the body of the people that will affect the distribution of wealth in such a way as to reduce the consuming power of the masses.[6] A reduction

[1] For these references in order see *Independent*, XLIX, 273; *International Journal of Ethics*, iv, 321; Nettleton, 36; Jenks, 199, 212, 213; Collier, 43; *Progress*, V, 18; Chicago Conference, 288; Collier, 55.

[2] Monopolies, 168.

[3] Gunton, 77, 78, 254, 255; Chicago Conference, 58, 69, 550; Apthorp, 25; Collier, 73; *International Journal of Ethics*, IV, 331; Hadley, in *Scribner's*, XXVI, 606.

[4] I shall pass over without comment such statements as "With a consuming power of 75,000,000, we have a producing power of 150,000,000," and the like. Thurber, in *Arena*, XXII, 310. Cf. Collier, 71.

[5] Note Marshall, Some Aspects of Competition, 24; Adams, in Chicago Conference, 37; also Bemis, *op. cit.*, 398.

[6] Even if trusts do not reduce nominal rates of wages, — as we are told they will not, — such a tax would result from holding prices above the competitive rate; for this would diminish real wages and decrease purchasing power.

in purchasing power thus produced would render excessive the existing investments in staple industries, and produce crises in precisely the manner described by Rodbertus and Marx. It will probably be wise, in any case, to postpone a final conclusion upon this subject until we know the ultimate consequences of the present depression in Germany, — a country whose industries are to a large extent "regulated" by various combinations. And it remains to be seen how our own trusts will deal with the almost inevitable reaction from the intense speculative activity of recent years in the United States. If trusts are unable to destroy the competition that is now disturbing the serenity of their managers, and must meet with continual interference from "interlopers," it may turn out that combinations professing ability to secure large profits on excessive capitalization are such a tempting mark for rival capital that our new remedy for industrial depression will merely intensify the evils which it was designed to cure.

Not only is it doubtful whether monopoly is a wise method of regulating industry, but it is certain that the evils of competition are greatly exaggerated in some cases,[1] while in others they are due to unhealthful conditions for which an interference with industrial freedom is responsible. Mention has already been made of the distilling industry, which has served as a typical example of the evils of competition and the benefits of combination. Here all will admit that excessive investment was due to the unwise action of Congress in changing the rate of taxation in such a manner as to benefit the distillers, and to lax enforcement of the revenue laws, which enabled those who evaded the exciseman to realize a profit of several hundred per cent. In this case, depression was not due to mere competition; and,

[1] While business depression is commonly assigned as the cause of combination (see Industrial Commission, I, 214, part 2, 21, 109, 168, 169, 255, 811), especially by trust magnates, it is certain that the large majority of our present trusts were formed in a period of unusual prosperity, when the stock market offered an opportunity for large speculative gains. Even when depression is known to have been a cause of consolidation, sometimes not all the companies, but only the weaker ones, were losing money. See *Yale Review*, VIII, 157; *Annals*, XVI, 355; Industrial Commission, I, 176. It is notorious that it has been the weaker plants that were most anxious for combination, while the better concerns could be induced to join, in many cases, only by the offer of excessive prices for their factories. Note Collier, 208, 209.

moreover, the formation of pools, and finally a trust, served merely to call more capital into the industry and to intensify the evils.[1]

In many other industries where trusts have been formed, the excessive investment of which writers complain was caused by the undue stimulus given by high protective duties and by the restriction of foreign competition. Upon over-investments caused by increases in the tariff, enough has been said in a previous paragraph; but the second topic requires further explanation. The iron and steel industries are the best illustration of the periodic fluctuations of prices, of which the believers in trusts complain; and Professor Taussig has recently demonstrated that these phenomena are greatly intensified by the operation of our tariff.[2] He shows that in times of rising prices the restriction of importation has thrown upon domestic producers nearly the whole work of supplying the expanding market. Since new plants cannot be erected in a short time, prices increase enormously before domestic production equals the demand. These high prices cause excessive investment, and hasten a reaction which results in a consequent period of depression. During the recent "boom" in the iron markets of the world, English prices rose from $9.80 to $16.70 per ton for one grade of pig iron, and from $11.70 to $18.60 for another, an increase of 70 per cent for the first kind and 59 per cent for the second. At the same time American prices rose from $10.00 to $25.00 per ton, an increase of 150 per cent, so that the absence of foreign competition made the fluctuations more than twice as great as they were in the English market. This, he adds, "is but an illustration of the simple principle that, the wider the range of the sources of supply, the greater the steadiness of prices." When Mr. Carnegie complains,[3] therefore, of the alternating periods of expansion and depression that beset the iron industry, he merely emphasizes the connection between our protective tariff and the intensification of the causes that

[1] This is conceded by Jenks, Trust Problem, 149; *Political Science Quarterly*, IV, 314.

[2] *Quarterly Journal of Economics*, XIV, 479–484.

[3] *Century Magazine*, LX, 147.

are alleged to produce trusts. Since the range of our protected industries is so great, the importance of the considerations just presented can hardly be overestimated. Competition is restricted by protective duties in most of the industries where combinations are formed; these duties increase the severity, and perhaps the frequency, of the fluctuations from which business suffers; then trusts, a further restriction of freedom, are advocated as a remedy for the ills caused by the initial interference with individual enterprise; and, finally, in order to regulate the trusts, an elaborate system of public supervision is proposed. Would it not be well to make a genuine trial of competition before condemning it for producing evils which are greatly increased by governmental interference with industrial freedom?

Competition cannot be proved a failure until it is given a trial. The evils from which many economists would seek refuge in industrial combination are greatly increased by unwise laws which have now outlived any usefulness that originally they may have possessed. If unhealthful conditions produced by our own interference with the course of business are ever removed, competition will probably develop no evils which could not be borne, as vastly preferable to monopoly, public or private. Indeed, even as things are, the shortcomings of the competitive system are exaggerated; and attempted monopoly is more likely in the end to increase, rather than mitigate, those periodic fluctuations from which industry suffers.

VII

Monopoly is not a pleasant word, and believers in the wasteful and destructive character of competition prefer to speak of trusts as combinations; or, when they use the term "monopoly," hasten to explain that this does not imply the absence of all competition. Thus it is said[1] that either actual or potential competition will oblige the trusts to share with the public the savings arising from consolidation, and will protect the consumer

[1] See Hadley, 161–163; Jenks, 224; Apthorp, 11; Gunton, 24, 25, 193–196; *Gunton's Magazine*, XIX, 349–351; *Progress*, V. 59; Industrial Commission, I, 200. This list of citations could be extended almost indefinitely.

from serious injury. Since this argument has been allowed hitherto to pass without serious criticism, the reader is asked to give it a moment's consideration.

When Professor Clark says that the actual investment of new capital is not always necessary in order to restrain the power of a combination to raise prices, because the mere possibility of rivals entering the field may suffice,[1] his argument is not inconsistent or absurd, because he does not believe that a monopoly is a more efficient agent of production than a large independent concern, or that the competitive régime is necessarily destructive and suicidal. And, when he shows that this "potential" competition of new capital can be made more effective by abolishing railroad discriminations and discriminating prices, he makes a distinct contribution to the discussion of the trust problem. But no such argument can come, without manifest inconsistency, from economists who believe that a trust is superior to independent companies. The gulf between permanent monopoly and competition cannot be bridged, even by appealing to such a subtle agency as potential competition.

In the first place, competition, actual or potential, could not distribute among consumers more than the most infinitesimal share of the alleged economies of monopoly. The reader will remember that the advocates of combination consider that it is proved that a single company can produce and market commodities at a much lower cost than independent concerns. If this be true, we may assume that, if the lowest price at which an independent company can afford to sell a commodity be one dollar, a combination can afford to sell for still less, say eighty cents, and that the difference of twenty cents represents the savings effected by monopoly. Now it is evident that competition can never, except for relatively short periods when the market is overstocked, reduce the price below one dollar, and that producers will never enter the field unless they hope to be able to secure at least these figures. A monopoly, therefore, can maintain the price at ninety-nine and nine-tenths cents without inviting competition; and the public cannot hope to secure more than the most insignificant fraction of the savings due to

[1] Chicago Conference, 407–409; *Political Science Quarterly*, XV, 186.

consolidation. Competition, manifestly, can do no more than prevent prices from rising as high as one dollar. Competitors might, at the outset, enter the industry under a misapprehension of the situation; but it would soon be demonstrated that a price just under one dollar would make competition hopeless. If, moreover, as is alleged, mere mass of capital tends to deter competition until prices are raised somewhat above the competitive point,[1] this argument becomes still stronger; and it would seem that the monopoly might charge even one dollar without holding out sufficient inducements to possible rivals. Thus the whole saving, and possibly something more, would go to the combination.

Secondly, even if competition could hold monopolistic power in check, the remedy would be wasteful and uneconomic, and would mark a return to the very evils which combination is supposed to cure. The argument for monopoly is based upon the claim that competition is wasteful, destructive and productive of all the evils in the calendar. To remedy the evils of competition, it is proposed to resort to combination: then, to cure the wrongs of monopoly, it is argued that we can return to competition. Indeed, the evils of renewed competition after monopoly has once been established are more intense, since the chances are that the high profits of the combination will call too much capital into the field; so that the last state of the industry that has been regulated "rationally" and "scientifically" by a single company will be worse than the first. Moreover, if combination possesses all the advantages that are claimed for it, wise public policy would necessitate the adoption of some method of preventing waste from the useless duplication of manufacturing plants. In public service industries, where all people have become convinced that competition does result disastrously both to producer and consumer, such a restrictive policy has been followed. We no longer think of paralleling existing lines of railroad in order to remedy the evils of extortion, and few cities will in the future permit their streets to be torn up in order to install unnecessary gas or water mains. If, in manufacturing business, consolidation has all, or nearly all,

[1] This is argued by Jenks, 65–68; Collier, 126–128.

of the advantages which it possesses in the railway, gas or water industries, public policy will dictate that the evil results of competition be recognized and that future waste of capital in rival establishments be prevented. The arguments in favor of combination suffer from a superabundance of proof that monopoly is more efficient in production and more healthful and rational in seeking for public favor. Those who accept these arguments as correct should carry them to their logical conclusion, and admit that competition is an undesirable remedy for whatever evils monopoly may develop,[1] and that public regulation is the only available method of correction short of socialism.

Finally, it should be remarked that competition is not only an undesirable, but an impossible remedy, if the tendency to monopoly is as strong as represented. If competition with consolidated concerns is hopeless on account of advantages in producing and marketing goods, capital will soon find this out, and refrain from further meddling with enterprises that are foredoomed to failure. If the business world becomes convinced that competition inevitably leads to suicidal warfare when large investments of capital are involved, then public opinion or positive restraints of law will demand that further criminal waste of capital and energy shall cease. *Potential* competition will lose all of its virtue when the futility and folly of *actual* competition are once forced upon the convictions of those who possess capital; and, when this happens, the monopolist will soon forget that the danger of rivalry ever existed. If experience ever demonstrates that the arguments of many economists are correct, then we shall be confronted by the grim fact that competition is dead and that monopoly is inevitable in most important branches of manufacturing industry. Remedy there will be none, save public ownership or public regulation; and past experience raises uncomfortable doubts whether, under the second method, the government or the trusts would be the regulating power.

[1] So far as I am aware, Mr. Baker is the only writer who accepts the results of his own logic. Monopolies, 204, 205.

VIII

The reader will have observed that most of the questions raised by this survey of trust literature do not admit of the application of precise methods of determination, and that all that can be done is to weigh opposing forces and form a rough estimate, based upon general impressions oftener than exact measurement, of the relative strength of the advantages and disadvantages of consolidation. While conclusions thus reached fall far short of certainty, and prediction is dangerous, this is due to the fact that data for a more exact investigation are denied to economists, who can, at the best, secure but occasional glimpses into the inner workings of great business corporations or draw what inferences seem warranted by the facts that come to the attention of the public. This examination of the recent drift of opinion concerning trusts would seem to have established only two conclusions: first, it will be wise to maintain a position of scepticism concerning the alleged advantages of combinations; and, secondly, it is very important to notice that the alleged tendency to permanent monopoly is irreconcilable with the continuation of anything that properly can be called competition.

If we adopt the conclusion that it is improbable that trusts are caused by superior efficiency in production, we are not, of course, without assignable reasons adequate to explain the movement towards consolidation in the United States. Control over limited supplies of natural resources is the strength of some combinations; railway discriminations, patent rights, and the shelter of protective duties have given material comfort and support to others. The opportunity to secure fancy prices for manufacturing plants, which could then be capitalized at still higher figures for the profit of the promoter and financier, is another explanation of vast importance. With so many premiums offered for combinations, the only cause for wonder is that any industries have escaped consolidation. Finally, the losses that competition often entails, which have been made worse by unwise laws, have furnished a pretext of no little plausibility for attempts to form monopolies. It is at this point that the arguments in favor of trusts possess most weight.

Yet, with all the strength that the movement towards combination has acquired, competition has always vexed the would-be monopolist, and is especially active at the present moment. As this is written, one trust is already confronted by fourteen independent companies, while another rival enterprise with a capital of $1,000,000 is in process of formation. Another combination owning 290 mills was, in October, confronted by independent companies operating 74 mills; and in December a new concern with a capital of $5,000,000 was formed. Almost every day brings word of the appearance of new competitors for various trusts, and the *New York Journal of Commerce* says that the revival of competition may be considered a general movement. Some of the independent enterprises may have been started with the purpose of selling out to the trusts; but, if combinations have the superior efficiency that is claimed for them, they are under no obligation to purchase, and the investors in rival concerns would be taking inconceivable risks if competition were really useless. Trusts purchase rival concerns because competition from such companies is dangerous, and not hopeless; and the revival of independent enterprise is a reason for believing that the business world has not accepted the theory that a combination possesses material advantages over separate companies of a large size. Experience may yet demonstrate that the attempt to "regulate" industry by consolidated enterprise is the surest method of producing over-investment and depression.[1]

If one concedes that competition is attended with real evils, he is admitting nothing that economists have not known for a long time; and, if it is denied that combination is a good, or even possible, remedy for the ills from which we occasionally suffer, all hope of escape does not disappear. The growth of fixed capital has undoubtedly introduced into industry a disturbing element, productive sometimes of fluctuating prices and excessive investments of capital in certain directions. The situa-

[1] On the inevitable persistence of competition, even under a general attempt to establish monopolies, see Clark in *Economic Studies*, I, 13.

tion can be improved by the repeal of unwise laws that intensify whatever unhealthful tendencies competition may have; and, beyond that, relief can be found in measures that will raise business management to a higher plane. The moral and legal responsibility of our captains of industry must be made commensurate with the enormous powers that they wield; and the same moral restraints to which, in the last analysis, even believers in combination appeal,[1] would prove a solvent of the very ills which monopoly is supposed to remedy. Then sound judgment can be fostered by the further development of industrial statistics; and, finally, the substitution of a moderate policy in the place of monopoly-hunger would be more helpful than all else. It may be found, in the long run, that a willingness to allow one's neighbors to live not only possesses more solid advantages than the "economies of combination," but is the only basis upon which private ownership and control of industry can continue. As corporate enterprises in America grow older, each company may cease to be dominated by a few men; and the management may come to represent the average opinion of the stockholders.[2] Such conditions would probably favor the development of a "live and let live" policy. In any event, it will prove easier to impress upon independent business firms the saving grace of moderation than to persuade the monopolist to exercise his powers in a wise and benevolent manner. Good despots there have been, undoubtedly; but we have had no experience with human nature that goes to prove that autocratic control is generally safer in industry than in politics.

CHARLES J. BULLOCK.

HARVARD UNIVERSITY.

[1] See Hadley, 120; Andrews, in *International Journal of Ethics*, IV, 334.

[2] Note Marshall's comparison of English and American corporation methods, Some Aspects of Competition, 14.

INDEX

FINANCIAL MANAGEMENT
1880–1934

Volume 3

Edited and Introduced by
Morgen Witzel

THOEMMES

Financial Management, 1880–1934

Edited and Introduced by **Morgen Witzel**

Volume 1
Twenty Years of Inside Life in Wall Street, or Revelations of the Personal Experiences of a Speculator ... Illustrated (1880)
W. W. Fowler

Volume 2
Trusts, Pools and Corporations (1905)
William Z. Ripley

Volume 3
Corporation Finance (1910)
Edward S. Meade

Volume 4
Corporation Finance. An Exposition of the Principles and Methods governing the Promotion, Organization and Management of Modern Corporations (1909)
William H. Lough

Volume 5
Concentration and Control: A Solution of the Trust Problem in the United States (1914)
Charles R. van Hise

Credit and International Trade: How they Work in Practice (1934)
Barnard Ellinger

Volume 6
Problems in Business Finance (1921)
Edmund E. Lincoln

Volumes 7 and 8
Collected Articles and Chapters

Printed in England by Antony Rowe Ltd, Chippenham

CORPORATION FINANCE

Edward S. Meade

THOEMMES PRESS

This edition published by Thoemmes Press, 2001

Thoemmes Press
11 Great George Street
Bristol BS1 5RR, England

http://www.thoemmes.com

Financial Management, 1880–1934
8 Volumes : ISBN 1 85506 633 5

British Library Cataloguing-in-Publication Data
A CIP record of this title is available from the British Library

Publisher's Note

The Publisher has gone to great lengths to ensure the quality of this reprint but points out that some imperfections in the original book may be apparent.

This book is printed on acid-free paper, sewn, and cased in a durable buckram cloth.

CORPORATION FINANCE

BY

EDWARD SHERWOOD MEADE, PH.D.
WHARTON SCHOOL OF FINANCE AND COMMERCE,
UNIVERSITY OF PENNSYLVANIA
AUTHOR OF "TRUST FINANCE"

NEW YORK AND LONDON
D. APPLETON AND COMPANY
1910

TO

J. LAURENCE LAUGHLIN

PREFACE

A RECENT computation showed $34,763,000,000 par value of securities issued by American railway and industrial corporations and now outstanding. These securities have been originally employed in obtaining capital for enterprises organized under the corporate form, or in enabling the owners of properties, or the promoters and financiers of new projects to realize their profits, or to distribute to the owners of corporations the accumulated profits of the past, or in exchange for other securities which it was found necessary to retire. The amount of income which these corporations receive is estimated at $4,572,000,000. An increasing share of American property is represented by stocks and bonds. An increasing proportion of American income is taking the form of interest and dividends.

The enormous and increasing values and profits represented by American business corporations have attracted general attention to corporate activities. The problem of corporation regulation is perhaps the leading issue of the day. Each of the leading political parties is committed to programs of corporation control, particularly in the field of public-service corporations. Many laws have been passed to supervise the activities of corporations, to control the administration of corporate income and expenses, and to limit capitalization. One of the most important elements of our economic life, the business corporation, is being taken under the direct supervision of the Government.

As yet, however, this control, regulation, and direction has proceeded with only a partial understanding on the part of legislators and administrators of the constitution and operations of the institution with which they are dealing. The best and most recent evidence of the inadequacy of knowledge upon the subject of the financial methods of corporations is the authorization by Congress of a commission to inquire into the circumstances connected with the issue of securities by American railroad companies. It is the task and duty of the American college and university to do its part in disseminating among our people, through the students who pass under its direction, correct and comprehensive information concerning all phases of our economic life. To assist this work in the field of Finance this book has been prepared.

" Corporation Finance " is designed as a college text-book. It aims to explain and illustrate the methods employed in the promotion, capitalization, financial management, consolidation, and reorganization of business corporations. Of necessity, the treatment of this extensive subject can, in no part, be exhaustive. A volume as large as this could be, and I hope will be, written by investigators upon the subject outlined in each chapter. Neither have I attempted to deduce from the facts of Corporation Finance any new laws or principles. All that I have tried to do is to describe in as much detail as the subject permits, the methods employed in Corporation Finance, to indicate the working rules of procedure and management which govern these methods, and to show some of the dangers which lie in ignorant and careless financial management.

The treatment of the subject follows the natural line of corporation development. We begin with the investigation of a business proposition. Control of this proposition is secured by a promoter, a financial plan prepared, the coöperation of bankers secured, and the securities are sold. The next group of problems encountered relate to the management of the corporate income in order that a regular rate of distribution of profits may be made by the directors to the stockholders. The methods of obtaining new capital, directly by the sale of securities and indirectly by consolidation with other companies are then examined. The last part of the book deals with the procedure in corporation bankruptcy, and with the reorganization of the capital accounts of both solvent and insolvent corporations.

The material of the book has been mainly taken from the *Commercial and Financial Chronicle.* Much of the material has been included in the text in its original form. I have reproduced three chapters from my "Trust Finance" entire, and have made large use of the lectures on Corporation Finance delivered in the Harvard School of Business Administration in 1908–1909. I have to especially acknowledge my indebtedness to my friend Dr. Thomas Conway, Jr., of the Wharton School staff, who has rendered to me valuable assistance throughout the preparation of this book, of which I desire to record my grateful appreciation. I wish also to thank Mr. H. Edgar Barnes, of the Philadelphia Bar; Mr. Ben Loeb, of Sutro Brothers and Company, New York; Mr. Milton W. Lipper, of Arthur Lipper and Company, New York; Mr. Roland L. Taylor, of the Philadelphia Trust, Safe Deposit and Insurance Company; and Mr. George Stevenson, of Sailer and Stevenson, Philadelphia, for advice, suggestions, and assistance. I wish that space permitted me to record the names of a large number of my friends and acquaintances who have placed their time at my disposal. Mr. Albert Hill and Mr. A. W. Taylor have greatly helped me in the work of revision and proofreading.

I have inscribed this book to Professor J. Laurence Laughlin, of the University of Chicago, as a tribute of my appreciation of his work as a teacher.

E. S. M.

PHILADELPHIA, *September 22, 1910.*

CONTENTS

ERRATUM

Page 1, line 16: For "during this ten years," read "during the seven years from 1900 to 1907."

CORPORATION FINANCE

CHAPTER I

INTRODUCTION

Every day of the year numerous opportunities for the production of wealth are being brought forward, deposits of minerals are discovered, franchises obtained, patents granted. Railway extensions are constantly bringing new land, timber, and coal into the market. Increasing population offers a basis for water, light and transportation plants. New inventions stimulate new wants, and these wants in their turn produce new means of satisfaction. In 1900, the production of bituminous coal in the United States was 172,600,000 tons; in 1908, eight years later, this amount had more than doubled, rising to 352,500,000 tons. The production of pig iron, which accurately shows the increase in the construction of the "plant" of society, during the same period increased from 13,600,000 tons to 25,780,000 tons, and the production of steel increased in practically the same ratio. The production of lumber in thousand feet during this ten years rose from 34,800,000 to 40,300,000.

This enormous increase in the production of fuel and materials signifies not only rapid growth in every department of industry but also a multiplication of the opportunities for money making of which producers have taken advantage. In the railway field, for example, the mileage of nearly every important railroad has shown a large increase within the decade mentioned. The Baltimore & Ohio, a typical trunk line railroad, in 1899, reported 2,047 miles of line, 45,764 cars and 954 locomotives, operating in a territory already developed. In 1908, the mileage had increased to 3,992, the cars to 61,647 and the locomotives to 1,396. Ten years ago the Interurban Electric Railway was in its infancy; to-day, between seven and eight thousand miles of line are reported as in operation, a new industry having been created within the decade.

In every branch of industry the opportunities for making money are coming forward in endless variety. Take but one field, the production of power; we find here a vast range of opportunity for profitable investment. We have the mechanical forced draft and the mechanical stoker, the latter in a variety of types; the use of superheated steam to reduce condensation and increase the efficiency of the boiler; the steam turbine to utilize the direct pressure of the steam; and the various devices and compounds which are designed to purify the water before it goes into the boiler. In other divisions of the field of power we have the development of electric power transmission which enables electricity to be sent long distances at high tension with a comparatively small expenditure for copper wire, bringing into profitable operation a large number of water powers which, until recently, were wasted; and we have the use of the gas engine which is now being built in very large units. New inventions are also succeeding. The Thermos bottle, for example, supplies a definite want, and within one year it is reported that more than 700,000 of these were sold at high prices. In the department of building operation, the growing use of concrete for dwelling houses promises to revolutionize the industry. Everywhere, improvements, long since discovered, are now forcing themselves into general notice and use, and new improvements are attracting instant attention. Never before in the world's industrial history has man increased his conquest over nature at such a rapid rate and simultaneously in so many fields.

These opportunities for the production of wealth are opportunities for the investment of money, for the investment of money aids, either directly or indirectly, in the production of wealth. The investor buys $50,000 of railway bonds.

With the proceeds the railroad replaces a wooden trestle with a steel bridge. Over this bridge it can run a heavier train load, which it obtains by the lower rate which the decrease in operating cost resulting from the heavier train load makes possible. The lower rate enables the farmer to turn a part of his grazing land into wheat, and so eventually the $50,000 invested in the railway bonds has increased the supply of wheat on the world's market. This increased production of wealth was made possible by the purchase of the bonds which the investor bought because, out of their increased earnings, the railroad could pay him four per cent interest. Without investment increased production would be impossible. Upon the investor rests the responsibility of adding to the wealth of the world. As he directs his funds to railroads, cotton mills, irrigation, or shipbuilding, the productive energy of society is exerted in this or that field of enterprise.

This office of investment is variously performed. Men may invest or capitalize their own savings. The farmer devotes one thousand dollars, half the proceeds of his last wheat crop, to the purchase of nitrate fertilizer. The New England cotton manufacturer invests his surplus earnings in a South Carolina mill where cheap power, labor, and material invite development. The Bessemer steel maker adds an open hearth furnace to his equipment, and takes advantage of a local supply of scrap. The Pennsylvania coal operator or lumberman buys the cheap coal and timber land of the South. Every successful producer is continually devoting his surplus funds to enlarge his enterprise along lines with which he is familiar as competition compels or as opportunity presents for greater profits. The producer often branches out into other fields, as when the farmers of a locality erect a flour mill or a sawmill, or open a stone quarry, or a carriage maker engages in the manufacture of automobiles, or a railroad spends a portion of its surplus in purchasing a coal property on its line. By such investments producers extend their business out of their profits and with their own funds.

Every industry is constantly growing from within—as the biologists say, by intussusception—out of the profits of the past, and individual producers are making ventures of their money into untried fields in enterprises where they alone stand to win or to lose, and where they act from personal knowledge of the opportunity.

There is a second class of investors which may include some of the first class but whose members are actuated by different motives and who act in a different way. These persons are also in possession of surplus funds from the employment of which they wish to obtain a profit, and they are ready to buy the stock of any corporation which gives them the assurance of satisfactory returns. They are in the market for any securities which they consider to be safe and profitable investments. The members of this class are not, as a rule, in close touch with the industries whose securities they buy. A leather merchant invests in steel, a banker in railroads, a retail dealer in mining stock, not because he desires to identify himself with the business in which he invests, so far as to give it his close personal attention and to assist in its management, but solely that he may share in its profits. Included in this class are investment institutions and managers of trust funds, who take no active part in the numerous enterprises whose securities they hold and who may know, indeed, little or nothing about the business.

The importance of this vicarious interest in industry is steadily increasing. Production is each year being carried on on a larger scale, and it becomes increasingly difficult for a few men to combine a sufficient amount of capital for the inauguration of a new enterprise or the development of an enterprise already established. Twenty years ago a few thousand dollars would build a sawmill. A half dozen farmers, by combining their savings, could start in the lumber business. To-day a well-equipped sawmill may cost $100,000, and added to this may be the expense of perhaps twenty miles of railroad to reach the timber. The assistance of outside capital is becoming every year more essential to the development of any industry or the exploitation of any resource.

A very good example is the Pennsylvania Tunnel Extension under Manhattan Island connecting New Jersey with Long Island. The primary object of this tunnel is to bring Long Island into direct touch with the congested district of Manhattan. The plan is this: The Pennsylvania Railroad Company owns a majority of the stock of the Long Island Railroad Company which completely dominates Long Island. Long Island is largely vacant territory. If Long Island can be brought into direct contact with Manhattan, a large number of people will move from Manhattan into Long Island, they will increase the population of the towns of Long Island, manufacturing enterprises will spring up along the lines of the Long Island Railroad, and a dense population will at no distant date be settled in the eastern end of the Island. The Long Island Railroad will supply the means of transportation to this population, and the Pennsylvania will profit from the dividends on its interest in the Long Island Railroad Company, and also because to the Pennsylvania will come the transportation of most of the freight which that large population will use. Then there is some advantage, though very slight, from the passenger traffic west-bound from Long Island, and also a certain advertising value connected with the building of a beautiful terminal in the center of Manhattan. This is a very large enterprise. While its outlines are clear and its success is assured, it could not be carried through out of the profits of the Pennsylvania Railroad. For the completion of the work which will cost over one hundred million dollars, the Pennsylvania Railroad Company has raised a large amount of money through the sale of stocks and bonds. In order to get money together for large undertakings of this character, it is necessary to draw upon the funds of a large number of investors, and especially upon financial institutions: trust companies, insurance companies and savings banks, which are great reservoirs of investment funds.

The investor is appealed to to furnish funds for two classes of enterprises: those which are already in existence, and new enterprises which are to come into existence through the money he advances. The investor will not look up new schemes of investment for himself. He will, however, buy securities which are offered to him when they are properly presented to him, for the purpose of increasing his interest on his capital. The proprietors of this outside capital know little about the technical aspects of the industries into which they put their money. They are acquainted with these industries merely as sources of profit. If they can be given satisfactory assurances that profits will be forthcoming from a proposed development, they are willing to invest money to that end. They will not, however, devote themselves to searching out and preparing the propositions into which, when once discovered and prepared, they are willing to put their money.

This attitude of the general investor brings forward the promoter whose function in industry is that of discovering investment opportunities, forming companies to develop these opportunities, and selling the securities of those companies to obtain funds for development. The function of promotion involves three stages: first, the discovery of the proposition; second, the assembling of the proposition and third, the presentation of the proposition.

The work of the promoter may be explained by describing the promotion of two enterprises: a small coal company in Western Pennsylvania, and the industrial combinations, commonly known as "trusts," which have now absorbed a large portion of our productive industry.

Western Pennsylvania is underlaid with great sheets of bituminous coal. It contains one of the most important fuel reserves of the United States. The coal is generally of good quality, and it is accessible to the largest markets in the country. A large number of mining propositions, most of which have, since their inauguration, been consolidated under the ownership of a few corporations, have been developed in this region. The law gives the owner of land the right to all the minerals which may be found beneath its surface. The land under which this coal lies is poor farming land, situated usually in narrow valleys intersected by streams which have excavated deep channels offering easy access to coal seams whose outcroppings are exposed on the banks and hillsides. This land is owned in tracts varying from ten acres up to three hundred acres. Many of the farmers mine coal for their own use and for local sale. A large number of "country banks" are found where, with primitive appliances, a considerable amount of coal is extracted. The sale of this coal is restricted to the immediate neighborhood since, in the absence of a large mining development, railway facilities would not be provided.

Such a region may attract the attention of bankers or capitalists who are interested in the development of coal properties, and they will organize a syndicate for its development. The syndicate will be organized, in much the same manner as a partnership association, under the terms of a syndicate agreement, whereby the subscribers associate themselves into an organization which it is agreed shall be managed by one or more of their number known as "Syndicate Managers," and agree to pay into a common fund a certain amount of money to be used in the development of a certain enterprise. Some part of this money may be borrowed by the syndicate; a larger amount is usually borrowed by the members. We shall, in a later chapter, consider the organization and administration of syndicates in detail; for our present purpose, this brief description will suffice. The syndicate having been organized, a call is made upon the members for a small percentage of their subscriptions for preliminary expenses. The syndicate is now ready for operation.

Some of their number will have received a considerable amount of information concerning the possibilities of the coal mining development under consideration, either from a local promoter or from some other source. The local promoter is usually a small lawyer or rural capitalist whose ambition outruns his means, and who may have spent some money in preliminary surveys and examinations, the results of which are communicated to some banker or mining official who has command of the necessary capital, and who can, with his associates, develop the possibilities of the proposition. At this point, the promoter, usually so-called, namely the local man who has introduced the proposition to the capitalist, passes out of the narrative. He may be paid a certain amount of cash for the work he has done, or may be allotted a small interest in the syndicate, which secures him in the possession of a small amount of the stock which the company to be organized may issue. He is not apt to be a very important factor in the future development of the proposition.

Starting with this preliminary information, the syndicate now has a thorough examination made of the property which they propose to develop. Engineers are sent into the field to furnish the necessary technical information upon which the proposition must be based. From the reports of these engineers, it will be determined whether the coal seam is regular, or faulted and broken, requiring a large amount of expensive rock excavation for large development, also if the proposed mining operation will be self-draining, or if pumping machinery must be installed; the percentage of sulphur and silicon which the coal contains, its properties as a coking coal out of which a coke can be made which will stand up under heavy burdens in the blast furnace. Surveys will also be made of the proposed railroad without which commercial coal production is impossible. The cost of mining development and of railway construction will be determined as accurately as possible. At a cost of perhaps $5,000, the syndicate can gain approximately exact information concerning the physical features of the proposition.

In addition to the information received from technical experts, although engineers usually assume to work in this field also, the financial aspect of the proposition is carefully considered. In a thorough investigation of a coal mining proposition, the price per acre at which the land can be purchased, the rate of freight charged by the connecting railroads, and the prices which can be obtained for this grade of coal in the different markets must be determined. Other considerations to be taken account of include the labor situation of the region, especially the strength of labor organizations, the laws of the State regulating the company store; and the attitude of the railroads toward a new mining enterprise—whether they will be helpful or indifferent.

After all this data has been gathered and collated, a decision may be reached to go forward, or the proposition may be abandoned because of the disclosure of unfavorable factors not revealed by the preliminary investigation on the basis of which the syndicate was organized. This initial investigation of a proposition, the disclosure of all the factors, favorable and unfavorable, affecting its ultimate success, must be thoroughly carried through or the enterprise is doomed to failure.

The countless disappointments in the development of new enterprises of all kinds are due, not so much to abuses of management or mistakes in capitalization, as to imperfect investigation reaching wrong conclusions as to business possibilities. So-called investigations made by local promoters are in most cases worthless. Their interests are so deeply involved in putting the best face possible on a scheme that both their observations and their deductions are of little value. Even the investigations of so-called "experts" are open to serious question. The expert's views are also colored by his interests since he is often, apparently, employed not so much to keep his principal out of an investment as to confirm his principal's judgment that the enterprise will be successful.

There is in the neighborhood of a large Eastern city a suburban railroad running out about twelve miles from a terminal station at the end of a city transportation line through a number of fashionable suburban towns, paralleling throughout its entire distance the main line of a large and well managed steam railway company. The fate of the company which constructed this line furnishes an excellent illustration of the blunders into which supposedly competent investigators are likely to fall in examining a business proposition. The syndicate which promoted this enterprise and which completed it with its own money, no securities being offered to the public, employed engineers of high reputation to examine into the cost and traffic of the enterprise. The line was accurately surveyed, estimates were made of the cost of obtaining ground for a private right of way, and options were secured on a large amount of real estate for the development of suburban towns.

The engineers also addressed themselves to the possibilities of traffic for the new line based on the population then in existence. The experience of interurban railroads in the West, where the experience of these experts had been gained, has been that a high-speed interurban line divides traffic with the steam line. It is usually assumed that, from an estimate of the traffic on the steam line, it will be possible to approximate the number of passengers which will be drawn away to the electric road. The engineers in this case followed this method. They made careful computations of the traffic at each one of the stations on the line of railroad which their line was to parallel, and on the basis of this traffic they made an estimate of the traffic to be gained by the suburban line. Their estimates were accepted and the line was built, about three and a half million dollars being provided by the syndicate.

No sooner was the new line put into operation than it was discovered that the engineers had made serious blunders in their calculations. The people of the towns through which the new line ran were entirely satisfied with the service furnished them by the steam line which landed them in the heart of the city. The new suburban line, on the other hand, would only give them a connection with a city line, necessitating a change of cars at considerable inconvenience. The class of people who were expected to patronize the new road are well-to-do. To them, the advantages of saving a few cents in fare, and the more frequent service offered by the electric line were of no consequence. The traffic of the new road proved a sore disappointment to its promoters. It failed from the beginning to pay its fixed charges, and for a time even its operating expenses were not earned. In 1908 its net deficit was $176,194. It has since been sold at less than one third of the amount of money invested in its construction; an expensive extension must be built to make it profitable; and it stands as a monumental blunder of supposed experts.

The difficulty in obtaining accurate information concerning the merits of the propositions which are brought to the attention and which arouse the interest of active men of affairs, has led to the development of a new type of promoter whom we will call, for lack of a better term, the promoting engineer. The promoting engineer is a firm or corporation engaged in the business of building trolley roads, power plants, railroads; doing all kinds of engineering and construction work within a certain field. They have a certain capital—the capital of some engineering firms runs into the millions—and they can borrow several times the amount from banks. They build up a permanent organization of engineers, chemists, accountants, and, in some cases, lawyers.

The engineering concern wishes to keep its organization constantly employed. Among its clients are bankers and capitalists who seek their advice on the merits of propositions. If their opinion is favorable, they are likely to obtain the engineering work. Usually, in such a case, they include the fee for investigation in their engineering commission. As a result of these inquiries and employments, the engineering concern in time advances to the investigation and presentation of propositions of their own. They have no lack of opportunities for independent effort of this kind. Large numbers of propositions are thrust upon them from which they can choose those which seem promising. If, after a preliminary investigation of a project, the engineers consider it worth undertaking, they secure the necessary options, and present the scheme to bankers and capitalists with whom they are connected.

A proposition submitted by an engineering concern of repute and authority in their chosen field will receive respectful attention from the banker who recognizes that the engineer's interest is not primarily to take part in the promotion, but to secure employment for himself and his organization, and to make his regular engineering profits. The engineer may also, in order finally to convince the banker, take part in the financing of the enterprise. He may acquire an interest in the syndicate which he proposes should be organized for its development. This interest the engineer will dispose of, should opportunity offer, even if he has to sell it at cost, either to the members of the syndicate, or to outside interests with the consent of the members of the syndicate. The engineer is not in the banking business, save incidentally and to obtain new business for himself. A usual condition of his participation in the flotation is that he should be given the supervision of the construction. The engineer may go a step farther and supervise the operations of the electric railway or gas plant during its initial stages. He assumes these duties, as a rule, with the cordial approval of the bankers. They are glad to secure, in this manner, an assurance of responsibility and competent management which the engineer is qualified to furnish.

The promoting engineer possesses advantages over any other kind of investigator, from the standpoint of the banker who advances the funds to make new enterprises possible, in that the engineer's interest is on the side of thorough investigation, economical construction, and careful management. Especially when the engineer shares the risks of the undertaking, is the banker glad to defer to his judgment and to invest money in the projects which the engineer indorses. There are a large number of engineering concerns of this character in the United States. One of the largest, the Stone & Webster Corporation of Boston, has gone so far as to develop a banking department in connection with its engineering work, through which it sells the securities of its own enterprises. The importance of thorough investigation is now so generally recognized that alliances of this character between engineers and bankers may be expected to become general. They are usually found more satisfactory than when the engineer is employed by the banker in an expert capacity.

CHAPTER II

THE WORK OF THE PROMOTER

After the investigation is completed, if it is decided to proceed, the next step is to assemble the proposition. By assembling is meant the securing of control of the property or rights upon which the proposition must be based. There are two methods of getting a property under control. The first is to buy it and the second is to buy the right to buy it, in other words, to secure an option upon it. Outright purchase is for the promoter usually impossible, especially in the case of new enterprises which are to be financed by the sale of securities to investors. The money to develop the enterprise must first be obtained from bankers who will reimburse themselves by selling the securities to their customers. Bankers will not undertake to advance large amounts of money for the development of a scheme until there is a definite proposition put before them. They will not, for example, set aside $1,000,000 of their funds to develop a water power proposition until all the lands adjacent to the water power, and which are necessary for its development, have been secured. A part of this money the bankers may have to borrow. They will not undertake these responsibilities merely to encourage the promoters to make an earnest effort to get the proposition together. The promoters must give them definite assurances that all the property necessary is under their control before the bankers will tell them whether they are prepared to advance the necessary funds. As for the promoters themselves to purchase the property, even if they have the money, they cannot afford to risk it in the purchase of resources whose development they may not be able to finance.

For example, in the coal land proposition which we have considered, to buy the 5,000 acres which is necessary, at $20 an acre, would require $100,000. Suppose this initial outlay to be made, and that the promoters find that, owing to the adverse conditions of the money market, or to some hitherto undiscovered imperfection in the project, bankers refuse to advance the necessary funds. They have $100,000 locked up in undeveloped property, which represents $6,000 a year in interest, a large part of which may have been borrowed, and they may be seriously embarrassed before they succeed, if indeed they ever succeed, in securing the funds for its development. Outright purchase of properties for the development of business propositions is not merely undesirable but unnecessary. The same result as purchase, so far as the promoters are concerned, can be reached by buying the right to purchase, in other words, by obtaining an option on the property which they desire.

An option is a privilege existing in one person, for which he has paid, giving him the right to buy certain realty, merchandise, or securities from another person within a certain time at a fixed price, or to sell such property to such other person at an agreed price or time. An option is, therefore, an unaccepted offer which runs for a definite time. It states the terms and conditions on which the owner is willing to sell or lease his property if the offeree elects to accept them within the time named in the option. If the holder of the option, known as the optionee, elects to accept the offer of the optionor, he must give notice to the optionor and the accepted offer thereupon becomes a binding contract. If an acceptance is not given within the time specified, the owner is no longer bound by his offer and the option is at an end. In effect, a man who grants an option on his property binds himself to make a contract to sell that property at a future time and to convey a good title. An option contract, like any other contract, is based upon a consideration.

This may be small; one dollar is a binding consideration. It is usual, if a substantial payment is made, to apply this on the purchase price if the offer of the optionor is eventually accepted.

The rights of the optionee in the property are those expressly named in the contract of option, and those which are implied from the terms of the contract. It is usual to give the optionee some right to enter upon and examine and sometimes even to take temporary charge of the property which he proposes to purchase. For example, in 1905, the Southern Railway Company and the Illinois Central Railway Company entered into a contract by which they purchased the prior lien bonds of the Tennessee Central and obtained options for three years upon the general mortgage bonds of the Tennessee Central, the bonds of the National Terminal Company and practically all the capital stock of this company except that held by counties and municipalities. Pending the acceptance or surrender of the option, they paid interest on the securities and operated the company under an agreement to keep it free from debt. The option expired July 1, 1908. The operation of the property had not been profitable, and the railroads surrendered their rights.

A privilege commonly given to the optionee, in the case of purchase of a going concern, is to have an exhaustive audit made of the books of the company to determine its profits for a term of years. For the protection of the optionee, it may be provided that the owner of the property shall do nothing which might impair its value, for example, that he must keep up the insurance, discharge all taxes, interest and mechanics lien obligations, and, in general, maintain the property in the condition which would render it available for the uses to which the optionee intends to put it in case he decides to exercise his rights under the option.

A valuable right connected with an option contract, from the standpoint of the optionee, is the right to assign the option. This is not implied but must be set forth in the option contract. If the right to assign exists, then the promoter is in a position to deal to advantage with the proposed corporation. He can either obtain from the company the funds with which to purchase the property which he has under option, afterwards transferring it to the company in return for his agreed compensation, or he can assign his rights under the option contract to the company which can then take them up direct.

The remedy of the optionee, in case the optionor refuses to carry out his agreement to sell the property, on being notified by the optionee that he is prepared to take it, and after the purchase price has been tendered, varies according to the ownership of the property at the time. When the property remains in the possession of the optionor, the optionee's remedy is to go into a court of equity and ask for a bill of specific performance which the court, on proper showing being made, will issue, requiring the optionor to transfer the property. When the property has passed into the hands of an innocent third party, however, the only remedy of the optionee is a suit for damages. The measure of the damages may be the margin between the price named in the option and the present market value of the property. It is easy, however, to block such conversions by recording the option at the time it is created. The purchaser of the property is then chargeable with notice that certain rights against this property have been created in the option contract, and he takes it subject to a liability to have a bill for specific performance issued against him. The form of the option contract conforms with the requirements of any contract as to form and consideration; capacity of parties; and legality of object.

Having decided to option 5,000 acres of coal land owned by perhaps one hundred farmers, the syndicate sends an agent into the district, and visits these farmers at their homes. He explains his purpose to them, assures them that he will be able to raise the money to develop his proposition, and asks them, for the sake of their mutual interest, and for a nominal consideration in hand paid, to sell him an option to purchase their property at any time within six months, at a price of, say, $20 per acre.

Various arguments may be employed to influence a general assent to this proposition. The landowners may be shown that the value of the surface soil, which will remain in their possession after the transfer of the coal, will be increased by the demands which a coal mining community will make for the produce of their farms. They may be offered the advantage of a railway which the opening of coal mines will bring. The hopelessness of developing their own property may be pointed out to them, and, as a last resort, the promoter may threaten to "sew them up" by refusing to transport their coal over his road. By employing such arguments, the promoter persuades the farmers to option or "lease" their land.

As far as possible, he keeps each owner in ignorance of the terms offered to his neighbors, for a general diffusion of such information would cause a general raising of prices. In dealing with the well-to-do and intelligent farmers, he must often pay a high price for the option, and the price named in their instrument is also high. The promoter submits to these onerous terms not merely because he wants the land of these hard bargainers who know just how indispensable their coal is to him, but also, and chiefly, because he desires to use their names and influence with other owners. These higher prices are recovered in dealing with the more ignorant landowners, who are greatly impressed with the representations of the promoter, and also by the fact that their richer neighbors have joined the scheme. It may even be necessary for the promoter to employ coercion through an alliance with the general storekeeper who may hold chattel mortgages and judgment notes against the recalcitrants—powerful arguments when skillfully employed.

The proposition has now been assembled; the owners have obligated themselves to sell to the syndicate at a certain price until the expiration of the period named in the option. It is known how much the land and development will cost and the land is under the syndicate's control. The next step is to finance the enterprise. At this point, a corporation is usually formed to take over the options. The bonds or stock of this corporation are taken by the syndicate whose members are now called upon to pay a substantial portion of their subscriptions. A portion of the necessary funds may also be borrowed, the securities being deposited as collateral for loans. With the money raised in this manner, the corporation, all of whose stock is owned by the syndicate, purchases the coal land, makes the development necessary, and starts the company as a going concern. After a record of earnings has been established, the securities of the company are usually offered for sale. If the enterprise has been wisely planned and economically developed, these securities may be sold at prices which will restore the syndicate's original investment, and either leave them in control of the stock of the company or enable them to sell out all their holdings of its securities at a profit.

This represents a typical promotion. Similar enterprises are constantly being promoted throughout the country, not only on mines, but on real estate, manufacturing enterprises, railroads, water powers, irrigation and timber projects. The details of each may vary from the form presented, but the essential principles are the same: (1) The securing of a right to purchase an opportunity to make money; (2) the capitalization of that opportunity at a higher figure than the price to be paid the original owner plus the funds required for development; and (3) the sale of the certificates of this capitalization to the investor, either directly or through the agency of middlemen, for a sum of money exceeding the amount necessary to purchase and develop the resource which it is intended to exploit. The difference represents the promoter's profit, a characteristic feature of corporation financiering.

What have the promoters done to entitle them to this large profit? They have produced no coal; that is done by the company to which they turn over their options. Nor have they risked an amount of money in any way comparable to the profit which they have made. To obtain fifty options under the circumstances described may not have required an outlay of more than $5,000. Judged by the canons of what is generally considered to be legitimate money making, the promoters have done nothing to entitle them to the $70,000 profit which, out of a flotation of this importance, they frequently take. And yet the profits of the promoter are as legitimate as are the profits of any of the more familiar professions.

The promoter is a creator of value. He brings into existence a means of producing wealth which did not before exist. By combining the control of a number of separate pieces of coal property into a fully equipped coal-mining enterprise, he is able to offer to the investor an opportunity to earn say twenty per cent net on his money; in other words, to sell to the investor $500,000 worth of stock which can be depended on to pay dividends of ten per cent, for $250,000.

Without this combination, in the hands of individual owners, without transportation facilities, and without equipment, the value of this coal, based on its earning power from the small mines which produce for the local trade, did not exceed $20 per acre. Combined under one ownership, connected with a trunk line railroad, and equipped for large operations, a value of $100 per acre is not excessive. This increase in value of $80 per acre is the result of the investment of $35 per acre—$20 in the purchase of the coal and $15 in its development. Deducting the $35 which must be spent to put the coal on the market, there remains $65 per acre as the promoter's profit, which he may share with the banker and investor, a profit differing in no essential feature from the gains of the manufacturer who contracts ahead for his material and takes advantage of a rise in the market price of his product.

But, it may be objected, why should the promoter be allowed to make this large profit? Why should it not be divided between the farmer who owns the land and the investor who furnishes the money? What is the justification for the promoter's profit? The answer to these questions lies in the nature of the transaction. Neither the owner nor the investor can do the work of the promoter, and they have, therefore, no claim to his profits. The farmers, save in exceptional instances, could not even organize their own proposition, much less finance it. Mutual jealousies, local feuds, and overmuch information about the character and financial standing of local individuals who might undertake this work interfere with any general agreement. It would be found next to impossible to agree upon the proper price for different prices of coal land. Farmer A, whose land lies near the creek, would insist upon a higher value for his property than farmer B, whose coal is less accessible; while B on his part might cite as a reason for disputing the justice of A's claim, the fact that his coal had been opened in several places while nobody knew that A had any coal on his property. Farmer C, who owned land across the right of way of the proposed railroad, and who therefore considered his coöperation indispensable, might insist upon a price of $150 per acre, which would probably disgruntle his less favored and jealous neighbors, and so defeat the scheme. The Brown family might refuse to go into any agreement with the Jones family, with whom one of the chiefs of the Brown clan may have had a lawsuit of some years' standing. Any-one of a number of similar causes which might be cited would be sufficient to prevent the concentration of control of these separate properties, which are of small value unless combined.

Some one interest acting exclusively for its own advantage, and dealing independently with each owner, is essential to the assembling of such a proposition. This interest may be local, and, as already noted, by means of local alliances the task of the promoter is made easier; but in most cases, the successful assembler of a proposition is the outsider who can pose as the man of wealth and connection, and can reap his harvest of options during the pleasant weather of a first impression. It is the experience of promoters that an outsider of imposing personality, pleasing address, and experience in handling men has usually much greater success in securing options than even a local "squire" or other celebrity whose standing in the community may be of the best, but who is too well known to be allowed by his neighbors to make any large amount of money out of their property.

Even if the farmers succeeded in getting their proposition together in the control of a selected committee or individual, they would have great difficulty in securing a financial connection. They would have to provide for expert reports on the property, and then to open negotiations with some financial interests with whom none of their members would probably be personally acquainted. After securing an introduction, they would present their proposition, probably in a lame and halting manner, which would not show that they possessed a comprehensive knowledge of the importance of the property in question to the general coal market or of the cost and conditions of its development.

Since they would have no connection with the investing public, if the banker to whom they would naturally apply for the funds was sufficiently interested to examine the proposition and to determine its value, he might take one of two ways to further his own advantage. He would either prolong the negotiations until the local contingent lost heart and withdrew, trusting to his own ability to obtain the options for himself, or he would compel the representatives of the owners, if they desired his assistance, to accept a price not greatly exceeding the face of their options; in which event the financier would be the promoter one stage removed, and acting by deputy. It is evident, therefore, that the larger part of the promoters' profits on such propositions cannot ordinarily be saved by the original owners of the coal.

The proprietor of an undeveloped opportunity is seldom in a position to bargain to advantage for its sale. His best course is to put his property in the control of some promoter at a fixed price and for a definite time, contenting himself with effecting a sale, not at the price which he thinks the property is worth, but at a price which will represent a fair return on his investment of brains or money. Any attempt on his part to promote his own scheme is likely to end in failure. The failure of inventors to make more money out of the sale of patents which have merit is probably due, more than to any other cause, to the fact that they insist upon an excessive interest themselves, and are unwilling to offer sufficient inducements to those who might otherwise promote the scheme.

It is equally impossible for the investor to secure the promoters' profits. The investor is looking for a security which will produce as large an income as is consistent with the safety of his principal. He is not likely to concern himself with the active management of these industries into which he puts his money. How much less likely is he, therefore, to abandon his regular business or profession and roam about the country in search of resources to develop. The investor, of necessity, assumes a receptive attitude. He is the customer to whom the promoter and financier offer their wares. He buys on his judgment, not so much of the merits of the proposition, as of the reputation of those who offer it for sale.

We must conclude, therefore, that the promoter performs an indispensable function in the community by discovering, formulating, and assembling the business propositions by whose development the wealth of society is increased. He acts as the middleman or intermediary between the man with money to invest in securities and the man with undeveloped property to sell for money. In the present scheme of production, the resource and the money are useless apart. Let them be brought together and wealth is the result. The unassisted coincidence of investment funds with investment opportunities, however, is uncertain. The investor and the land or patent or mine owner have few things in common. Left to themselves they might never meet. But the promoter brings these necessary elements together, and in this way is the means of creating a value which did not before exist, and which is none the less a social gain because much of its is absorbed in the first instance by the promoter and the financier.

CHAPTER III

THE TRUST—ITS PROMOTION AND EVOLUTION

WE have next to examine the application of the principles of promotion in the formation of the industrial combinations. In the present form, companies such as the United States Steel Corporation, the American Locomotive Company, and the American Smelting & Refining Company, are corporations organized under the laws of the State of New Jersey, and authorized by their charters, among other powers, to hold the stocks and securities of certain corporations engaged in the same or kindred industries. These companies have either exchanged their stocks for the stocks and property of a large number of small concerns located in the various producing localities of their respective industries, or they have sold their own securities, and with the proceeds have purchased the stocks and property of the various concerns which they wish to acquire from those owners who were unwilling to receive their stocks and bonds in exchange for their property and who demanded cash. The result of the trust development has been the creation of a large number of huge corporations which control many of the largest industries of the United States. The methods by which these companies were brought together, capitalized, and financed constitute one of the most interesting chapters in American economic history. Since these operations were largely carried on in the open, they enable us to illustrate in detail the principles of the promotion of companies.

The proposition which the trust promoter attacked was the consolidation of a large number of competing plants in a particular industry. He proposed to form a corporation to purchase these plants, either directly or by acquiring the stock of the companies which owned them. Instead of fifteen, twenty, or thirty firms and companies engaged in competition, the promoter planned to substitute one large corporation which should include every plant of importance in the competing territory. There was to be but one corporation in each industry—one wire company, one bicycle company, one tube company, one company manufacturing tin plate.

The value of each of the plants which it was proposed to include in the new trust was based upon its earning power. That earning power was greatly reduced by competition. The promoter expected to option each plant at a figure which should represent its past earnings, organize a company with a capitalization which should represent the increased earning power of these plants when competition had been eliminated, and sell the stock of this corporation to the public.

The advantage promised by this operation was the same as that of the coal-land proposition. By combining a large number of small holdings under one ownership, and properly equipping the property for large operations, the value of coal land can be increased from \$20 to \$100 per acre. Out of the securities representing this valuation, the promoter can equip the property and have a large profit remaining. The average value of the thirty plants which the promoter desires to combine into a trust, when engaged in mutually reducing profits by competition, may be \$500,000. This figure is the capitalization of their average earning power at \$50,000 per year. Combine all these plants under one ownership, thus eliminating competition, and you have increased this average value from \$500,000 to perhaps \$750,000. The enterprise can, therefore, be capitalized at \$22,500,000 of stock, and this stock can be sold for a sum of money sufficient to take up the options, equip the corporation with working capital, and leave a substantial margin of profit to the promoter. This, then was the advantage which the trust promoter sought to obtain—to capitalize the economies of combination, sell the certificates of the capital, and obtain a share of the proceeds as his own profit.

His work was to assemble his proposition—to get the plants under option. To this end, he had to convince the manufacturers that his scheme would be successful, that its industrial basis was sound and its financial support assured, and he had further to offer to each owner and stockholder a sufficient inducement to sell. The first part of the promoter's task was less difficult than the second.

The desire to eliminate competition was the principal reason for the formation of the trusts. From the producer's standpoint, this was a convincing reason. The promoter could name several important advantages to result from the acceptance of his proposals. Most important was the control of prices. Combination secures more stable prices to the producers, and also enables them to accommodate their quotations to the state of trade. When business is brisk and the demand for their product increasing, they are not impelled by fear of competition to tie themselves to a low price level by contracting for a year ahead. Contracts can be readjusted by a combination at short intervals so as to compel the large consumer to pay an increasing price.

With competition eliminated, the manufacturer is able to charge what the traffic will bear, to get from the buyer all that the buyer can be induced to pay, and he is no longer compelled to divide his profits with middlemen and secondary producers. For the same reason, when prices are falling, a combination is less exposed to the reckless cuts and sacrifice sales with which hard pressed individual concerns at such a time are constantly threatening the market. It is true that if mills are to be kept in full operation prices must be lowered when demand declines, but the reductions can be made gradually and tentatively, so that the buyer is at all times made to pay all that he can afford to pay, and gains no unreasonable advantage.

Moreover, if the depression is temporary, due to special

and exceptional causes, such as a stock panic or a foreign war, while the industrial condition of the country is satisfactory, a combination in control of the market can sharply reduce production, and in this way sustain prices until confidence returns. Under competition, a large part of the advantage gained by the increased demands of prosperity has often been sacrificed by a temporary setback. The mutual distrust of producers at such a time stands in the way of any restriction of output, and prices are allowed to sag at the dictation of the buyer, until when the sky is again clear, the mills are committed to prices much lower than the circumstances of the buyer warrant.

Combination also enables the manufacturers to hold the buyers to their contracts. Mr. Gates discussed this advantage before the Industrial Commission. "Q. How is it that your power is greater under this (system)? A. Well, under the old system a merchant might quibble with half a dozen manufacturers, and there might be some one particular manufacturer that he would treat fairly, so that he would feel that he had a port in a storm. And in the commercial term men claim shortage, make unreasonable demands, and we do not find these demands to exist to any such extent as they did before. They claimed a shortage, for instance, of five kegs of nails or five spools of wire and if we accepted their statement we had to fight it out with the railroad company. We had a check, and we thought we knew we were correct, and now we are pretty apt to be firm. We will always consider their claims, but we will not allow them freely, perhaps, as we would before; they have to be very thoroughly well founded on fact for us to make allowance."

When competition has been supplanted by combination, the unruly buyer has no "port in a storm." Should he prove refractory, as Mr. Gates said, "the only pressure we could bring to bear would be to ask him to send a draft with the order," a "pressure" quite sufficient to suggest moderation in demands for readjustments of contracts. The same discipline was applied to correct the abuse of long delays in settling for orders. Another important advantage secured by centralized control is found in dealing with railroads and producers of materials. Many of the concerns which united to form the trusts, although their aggregate purchases and shipments ran up into the millions of tons, were individually too weak to secure the most favorable rates and prices. They were often subject to discriminations in favor of the large producers in the same trade. This is illustrated by the development of certain large coal mining concerns which have grown in former years, somewhat at the expense of their weaker competitors, by rebates received from the railroad, and the concessions in car supply, speedy delivery and free storage on track, all of which advantages enabled these specially favored companies not merely to underbid their competitors, but, what is often of more consequence, to execute orders with dispatch.

Vexatious delays are experienced by every small buyer in a time of active demand. He must wait until the wants of his more important rivals have been supplied, and waiting means a loss of valuable business which is pressing for execution. A large buyer, moreover, can make a large contract at low prices, while the small buyer is shifted about with every turn in the market. These disabilities under which the individual concerns labored, it was evident, could be largely removed by combining them into a single organization which could obtain in its negotiations all the advantages which had hitherto been enjoyed only by the largest manufacturers.

In their relations with the jobbing trade manufacturers are strengthened by combination. Two illustrations of this advantage may be given: Manufacturers of hardware, under competitive conditions, have always been greatly injured on every occasion of increasing demand by the practice of large jobbers who had purchased heavily before the advance in reselling to other jobbers at prices less than those charged by the manufacturers, and also demoralizing the retail trade and interfering with the free distribution of goods, by selling at cut prices to retailers, thus preventing less fortunate wholesalers from making their usual sales and lessening their demands upon the factory. The injury inflicted upon the manufacturer by the practice of contracting ahead is mainly due to the irregularity of prices which are made by belated buyers. The reselling and underselling of large jobbers was, in the lines of furnished hardware, an evil equally serious, and was directly due to the competitive struggle, which forced the manufacturer to take business no matter how unfavorable might be the terms on which it was offered.

This necessity of forced selling also enabled a class of jobbers to exist who secured trade by questionable methods —for example, by dividing their profits with the retailer, the result being that the best customers of the manufacturer had their profits greatly curtailed and were forced to reduce their demands, unless the manufacturer also descended to the lower level of prices and profits. On the other hand, manufacturers, in their anxiety to get business, often addressed the retailer direct. This method of distribution is expensive to the manufacturer. He must charge the cost of maintaining an extensive selling and collecting department, and of shipping in small lots, against a single line of goods, no great quantity of which can be sold to anyone dealer, while the jobber, handling hundreds of lines, can supply the retailer with a complete stock, charging the expenses of selling against a $500 order, although the manufacturer of axes, locks, or stoves could sell perhaps only one tenth or one twentieth as much. It is, therefore, to the manufacturer's interest that the jobber be protected against such irregular methods, for the jobber is his best customer. A half dozen jobbers will take the entire output of a nail mill, and thus relieve the manufacturer of all expense and risk of selling and collection.

By combining and eliminating competition these evils are abated. The jobbers can be held to small orders, and the resulting necessity of frequent purchase tends to deter them from cutting prices. They are forced to deal with the combination, and must obey the rules which it lays down to regulate their purchases. While the jobbers are held to stricter account, and prevented from competing with the manufacturer or by other methods demoralizing to trade, they are, on the other hand, favored and helped by the combination refusing to sell to retail dealers even when these order in jobbers' lots, and cutting off the supply of any jobber who is detected in dividing his profits with the retailers. By confining their sales to the jobbers, the combined manufacturers can sell at lower figures for large lots, and in this way can protect the jobber in a larger margin of profit than he could secure under competitive conditions when the retail trade was given such improper advantages in buying. The elimination of competition, then, improves the relations between buyer and seller, and secures the manufacturer in a larger and more regular demand for his product.

One final advantage secured by combination deserves special notice. This is the improved position of the manufacturer in dealing with labor. From the manufacturer's standpoint the insistent demand of organized labor for higher wages and shorter hours is equivalent to a demand that the manufacturer should submit to a reduction of his profit. These demands his business training teaches him to resist. Under the system of competition, however, in resisting the demands of his employees he is placed at a serious disadvantage. For these employees are organized into great unions containing 20,000, 40,000, 90,000 or even 250,000 men, under the control of a single executive board which secures a united action of the entire membership of the union upon any matter of common interest. Competition in the field of skilled labor has been largely eliminated and well organized combination has long since taken its place. These contests between employer and employees are unequal. The manufacturer has pressing obligations to meet by the sale of his product. In order to meet these obligations he must fill his contracts and hold his customers. His financial position is not strong enough to permit a long continued suspension of his plant.

He is hard pressed by competitors who are doing their utmost to persuade his customers away from him. He stands alone, struggling for business with concerns whose hands are against him as his hands are against all his rivals.

To the manufacturer in this situation comes an official of the International Association of Machinists, or of the Amalgamated Association of Machinists, or of the Amalgamated Association of Iron and Steel Workers, or the Iron Molders' Union of America, with a peremptory demand for a reduction of hours, or an increase in wages, or the admission of walking delegates to the shop, or the limitation of the number of apprentices, or the discharge of all nonunion men. All or any number of these demands may be made upon the manufacturer. If he refuses, a strike is the alternative. His men will walk out at a word from their general officers, and there will be none to take their places.

The business instincts of the manufacturer lead him to refuse an advance in wages as he would resist an increase in the appraisal of his plant for purpose of taxation. He may feel that his men are receiving high wages—perhaps the proposition is to raise them from $3.50 to $4 per day. He looks upon the proposed reduction in hours as equivalent to a reduction of output, opposed not merely to his own interests, but to those of his employees. A demand that outsiders should dictate the management of his business he regards as effrontery. His judgment is unalterably opposed to granting the demands of the union. Each one of his competitors may feel the same way. In the absence of competition they would unanimously refuse to make the concessions demanded. They would even welcome a strike as offering an opportunity to break the power of the union. They would concentrate their efforts on the plants in which the union was weakest, sending thither all nonunion men that could be secured, filling as many orders as possible from these plants, and appealing to the sympathy of their customers to induce them to be patient with the delay involved in breaking the strike. They would collect a large defense fund, scour the country for nonunion men, educate unskilled labor into a knowledge of machines and processes, secure the assistance of the courts in protecting nonunion men from interference, and by gradually increasing their working force they would reopen first one mill and then another. Finally, the reserve funds of the strikers would be exhausted, their courage weakened by such determined resistance, their confidence in their leaders impaired, and the solid wall of their resistance honeycombed with disaffection, until, first singly, and then by hundreds, they would resume work and the union officials, to save their organization, would concede their defeat and make an abject surrender. Such would be the usual result of general strikes were unanimous action among employers to be secured. Such was the result of the strike of the United States Steel Corporation employees in 1901.

Under competition, however, such unanimous action is next to impossible to attain. Few employers feel safe in standing out against the union and thus precipitating a strike, for fear lest some of their competitors should grant the demands, keep their mills running, get the orders which the strike prevented them from executing or accepting, and in the profits from which these suspected competitors might find ample compensation for the concessions in wages and hours which had been made to secure this increased business from less complaisant rivals. Especially with the owners of the weaker mills do such considerations have weight. They hasten to take advantage of an opportunity to secure the trade of the best mills, which are usually the last to grant the demands of the strikers. In the strike of the International Association of Machinists, in 1901, a large number of the strikers almost immediately obtained the nine-hour-day, but they were most of them employed in the smaller shops, which took this easy, if short-sighted, method to fill their books with orders.

Combination was, on the foregoing account, greatly desired by manufacturers in order that by its means the menacing growth of the power of organized labor might be checked, and the manufacturers, freed from restraints of mutual distrust and suspicion which competition had fastened upon them, might stand firmly together against what they believed to be the unreasonable demands of the unions.

Other advantages might be mentioned which influenced manufacturers toward combination: The concentration of office forces, distribution of special processes and patents, employment of the best talent to raise the standards of all plants up to the level of the best, savings in cross freights, alliances with banks and lower interest rates thus resulting, and savings in reducing the numbers and salaries of selling agents and the cost of advertising. A number of important functions can be centralized: auditing, finance, advertising, construction and engineering, purchasing, can all be carried on from a central office, at reduced expenses and with greater efficiency. Mills can be specialized to different products, unprofitable plants can be closed. The trust promoter, therefore, had at the outset a great advantage. Necessity had long been working in his behalf. The manufacturers with whom he dealt were convinced beforehand that his proposition, from the industrial standpoint, was fundamentally sound. Indeed, so general was the sentiment in favor of combination that leading manufacturers in every trade which it was desired to consolidate were prominent in urging upon their associates the merits of the scheme.

In some instances, indeed, the persuasive part of the promoter's task was performed for him. The American Tin Plate Company was organized, as the president of the company has been already quoted as saying, "for the purpose of getting together to do away with foolishness in making prices." The tin-plate manufacturers, convinced that they had much to gain from getting together, held a meeting and appointed a committee to wait upon Judge William H. Moore, who had attained a considerable reputation as a company promoter, and invited him to undertake the consolidation of the tin-plate mills. Judge Moore tells the story of the invitation as follows: "I had organized the National

Biscuit Company, or while I was organizing the National Biscuit Company, a committee of manufacturers called on me in New York and requested me very urgently to take hold of the organization. At that time (they stated afterwards) they thought I was not very enthusiastic about it. I was very busy, and I knew it was a difficult thing to do. The result was, it was delayed two or three months. As I learned, they had meetings in Pittsburg, and possibly other places, and they came to me again. So it ran over a period of a year or a year and a half from the time they first called on me until the final organization of the company." Here was a proposition already prepared for the promoter.

The consolidation of the American Sheet Steel Company by the same promoter was also undertaken at the instance of the owners, whose situation is thus described by the *Iron Age,* of February 22, 1900: " It was easy to see that the sheet trade was in a hopeless condition, and that something would have to be done and that very speedily. There was fear that sheets would be dumped on the market by some mills in order to realize money, and this aggravated the situation. Options were again renewed, and progress on the deal was rapid from the fact that the mills recognized the hopeless position they were in with high-priced sheet bars and very low-priced sheets."

The American Car & Foundry Company was promoted by men who were large owners of the stock of the Michigan Peninsular Car Company, a company organized in 1892, which had greatly disappointed its promoters and underwriters by failing to show the earnings which had been predicted. By uniting a number of competing plants with this company, it was thought that its position could be greatly improved.

The question now arises: why, if the advantages of combination were so well understood, did not the manufacturers form their own company without the assistance of an outsider? The answer is found in the reasons presented in the last chapter to show how difficult it was for individual landowners to assemble a coal mining proposition. The manufacturers could not agree as to the valuation to be placed upon their plants in the new combination. As Judge Moore described it: "Each manufacturer imagines his plant is better located, better than his neighbor's; he knows it is, he has no doubt about it."

One manufacturer has patents and special machinery which have cost him a great deal of money and by which he sets much store. He will not enter the proposed combination unless these costs are made up to him. Another manufacturer may have a large productive capacity, fifty nail machines, for example. He may have been unable to find a market for the output of more than half his machines, but in the combination, he contends, all this capacity will become available. He, therefore, insists that productive capacity should be the basis on which the allotment of shares in the trust should be made. A third man, by the excellence of his equipment and the energy of his methods, has been able to run his plant at its full capacity, while his competitor, with a larger productive capacity, but a less favorable location or a less capable body of subordinates, has operated only half time. The successful manufacturer contends that average sales should be the basis of allotment.

Here are three propositions for the apportionment of interest in the trust: money invested, productive capacity, and average sales. Each is entirely distinct. No one of the three can be accepted without, in the opinion of the authors of the rejected propositions, jeopardizing their interests. If money invested be accepted as the basis of apportionment, then producer *A* will receive $500,000 of stock out of say $10,000,000, or one twentieth of the property of the combination, when on the basis of his total sales he would be entitled to only half this interest, or $250,000. Producer *B*, on his part, demands that his idle capacity be considered, while *C* insists that although he may have put only $100,000 into his mill, yet since his sales amount to one tenth of the total, he should have $1,000,000 of stock. Each of the three knows the claims of the other two and considers them to be unreasonable. There is no common ground of agreement, no basis for compromise. Two of the three must abandon their positions if the combination is to be effected.

An illustration is in place. In the manufacture of stoves a great deal of money is annually invested in patterns. These patterns are used not longer than ten years. New designs are always being introduced, and if they prove popular the demand for the old designs of stoves and ranges and the value of the old patterns is correspondingly reduced. It is, however, customary to preserve these patterns, which are usually patented, in the expectation that old styles may be revived, and also to protect against infringement. A firm in Philadelphia has preserved all the patterns of forty years of manufacturing. Now it is plain that the amount of money invested in such an accumulation of out-of-date designs is no criterion of the value of these patterns to a stove trust. A plant which had been running only five years might have only $20,000 invested in patterns, while an old plant might have spent as much as $400,000 on its patterns, yet the sales of Plant No. 1 might exceed by $20,000 per year the sales of Plant No. 2. If the old plant insisted upon $400,000 of stock for its patterns because so much money had been invested in them, its demands could be granted only at the expense of the new plant, whose earning power is much greater. Yet such demands, it was stated, were made by more than one manufacturer during an attempt to consolidate this trade, and it was found impossible to persuade them to recede from their position.

It might appear to the outsider who looked at the question dispassionately, that the earning power of a plant furnished the only basis for determining its value. Earning power, however, is subordinated in the minds of many people to money invested, and there is usually enough obstinacy and jealousy in a group of competitors to prevent a solution of the question along rational lines. The scars of the competitive struggle are too deep and its feuds are too ancient to induce one manufacturer to allow his rivals to gain an advantage over him.

Moreover, earning power is a variable quantity. Here is a reckless competitor who has been demoralizing the trade in a certain section by selling to the retail trade, lowering the standard of his product, and undercutting his more public-spirited rival, who has preferred to let his mill be idle for a part of the year rather than to sacrifice his business principles. If this wrecker of trade can be eliminated, the earning power of the second plant may be increased fifty per cent. Is not the owner of that plant warranted in demanding that his mill will be worth more to the trust than its present earning power would indicate?

It is next to impossible to form a trust in a caucus of manufacturers. A pool can be arranged with less trouble. A pool is a temporary organization from which any member can secede at short notice. The ownership of each plant is in no way disturbed. When the manufacturer goes into a trust, however, his property passes out of his possession, he has sold his plant for cash or stock, and he scrutinizes with great care the terms of sale.

Out of this situation arises the necessity of the promoter. The promoter is the outsider who offers to purchase each plant in a separate deal without reference to the price paid for the other mills. By dealing separately with each group of owners he avoids the obstacles of a mutual comparison of valuations, and can attack the proposition with some hope of success. Mr. Flint, testifying before the Lexow Commission for the Investigation of Trusts, explained the necessity for the promoter as follows: "Q. How can you explain to the Committee the fact that combinations of legitimate business enterprises have to be made the subject of promoters' agreements—have to be placed through banking establishments in Wall Street—if they are the normal outcome of a demand of the businesses themselves to enter into combination with each other? A. For the same reason that men of high intelligence are needed to make treaties between the nations, particularly during periods of war. Q. You mean it is a delicate diplomatic situation that has to be met? A. It is one that requires the very highest intelligence, and, as a rule, neutral parties—parties not interested, men of the intelligence and reputations to inspire unlimited confidence on the part of manufacturers, are needed to bring manufacturers together in order that they may move with the current of natural laws. The advantage of a neutral party, of a banker, is that he is in a position unlike another in the same trade, to get at the facts . . . to reduce the pretensions —the exaggerated pretensions of the manufacturers, and bring their minds together upon a reasonable and proper basis."

Mr. Flint has here succinctly stated the function of the promoter in the organization of the trust. "Natural law," it is true, impels the manufacturers to unite—without the existence of a strong desire for combination the task of the promoter would be impossible—but individual jealousy, ignorance, prejudice, and inertia interfere with and impede the operation of the natural law of advantage; and coöperative methods must be abandoned in order that the benefits secured by combination may be brought home to each manufacturer without reference to the stock interest that his competitor may secure.

The promoter, being appealed to by the manufacturers who may have failed, as did the tin-plate manufacturers, to succeed by coöperative methods, addresses himself to the second part of his task—to secure options upon the separate plants at a figure less than the capitalized earning power of the combination he proposes to form, which difference will represent his profit. He does not work on commission; that would make him merely the agent of the manufacturers, and would be coöperation by deputy, a method as futile as coöperation direct, since each party to the agreement would wish to investigate the acts of his agent. As Judge Moore expressed it: "They (the tin-plate manufacturers) were talking originally about compensating me with a certain amount of stock, but I could not handle it that way. I had to buy the properties and own them, and handle it as I saw fit." In short, the promoter in organizing his $50,000,000 trust had to follow methods similar to those which were employed to organize the coal-mining proposition. He was obliged to work for his own advantage, to "fight for his own hand," throughout the transaction, associating members of the trade with himself only when their coöperation was necessary to his largest success. The work of the trust promoter, in short, was to buy plants from their owners at one price and sell them to the investor at a higher price.

His first step was to estimate the probable earning power of the combination. To ascertain this earning power, the promoter has to obtain an answer to two questions: (1) What have the individual plants earned for, say, the past three years? and (2) how much will those earnings be increased by combining them into a trust? The companies threw their books open for inspection, and expert accountants were put to work upon them.

The first question could be fully answered by taking the statements from the separate companies of gross receipts and expenses. Other factors, however, must be considered, most important of which are the reserve and depreciation accounts of the several mills. Here is one company which charges the cost of new machinery to capital account, and makes an assessment upon its stockholders to pay for all machinery purchased. Another company deducts the expense of machinery from its net receipts before dividends are declared. The earnings of the first company, judging from the sums dispersed to stockholders, are much larger than those of the second company, while in reality its earnings have been much smaller. Another company may be "skinning" its plant by paying large dividends, while neglecting to keep up repairs. In the promoter's estimates, all these considerations must be taken into account. He must reduce the earnings of all the plants to a common denominator of identical conditions.

The following quotation from the *Iron Age,* of March

10, 1898, illustrates the valuation methods of conservative promoters: "J. P. Morgan & Company, bankers, some time since secured options on the plants and properties of a number of iron and steel producing concerns identified with the wire rod and wire interests of this country in a prominent way. These options are open until the end of the current month. The bankers appointed accountants to go over the books of the different concerns during the last three years, to ascertain the profits in each year and the average profits of the past three years. Expert engineers were called upon to make an appraisal of the plants and properties, their reports having gone in some time since. It is understood that the accountants, pursuing methods of their own, reached valuations in some instances considerably below those established by the bookkeepers of the companies involved. In the majority of cases, however, the options were considered fair, and are reported to be the basis of the settlement on the part of the bankers. It is a fact, however, that no one concern knows the price to be paid for the business of any other company."

The second part of the promoter's problem—to estimate the increased earning power of the combination—is more difficult of solution. The probable increase in the earning power of the combined plants depends upon a number of factors, some of which are known, while others can only be guessed at. To begin with, there are the more familiar economies of combination: (1) The centralization of offices and the dismissal of a number of high-priced officials—for example, one engineer of tests was sufficient in the eight plants of the American Locomotive Company—and this enables a considerable reduction of general expenses; (2) the saving in cross freights—if enough trouble be taken by the accountants this can be estimated with a good deal of accuracy; (3) the lower rate of interest on discounts—the price of time money at New Castle, Pennsylvania, may be six per cent while New York is charging only four per cent on equal security; and (4) the lower prices on materials secured by ordering in larger quantities. These are the most important of the economies where the amount saved could be definitely ascertained.

Beyond this restricted field of certainty, however, lies a vast but ill-defined region of probability—the savings to be achieved by the centralization of management and the elimination of competition. How much can be gained by the regulation of prices, by the increase of monopoly power, the closer regulation of the middleman, the reduction in the amount of bad debts, the shortening of contracts and credits, and the withdrawal of special concessions? How much will be gained by the increased power of resistance to the labor unions, and by the improved position of the combination in dealing with railroads? How may the internal economy of the organization be strengthened by the continuous operation of the best plants during periods of slack demand, by the discharge of incompetent officials held in place by the influence of their "pull," by the thorough testing and inspection of all materials purchased, by the general distribution of the special knowledge and the patented processes of each plant, by the opening of a depreciation account on the books of mills to which it has been a stranger, by the displacement of old and worn-out machinery with the latest improvements, and by the inauguration of a system of promotion to stimulate the working force to their highest efficiency? What will be the profit from the broader policy of a new management; from the concentration of production at the points of largest advantage; from the acquisition of iron mines, coal lands, and blast furnaces so as to be independent of the fluctuations in the prices of materials; from the broader market for the securities of a large company and the resulting facility of obtaining capital on favorable terms? And, of especial importance in view of recent developments in international trade, what will be the profit from the development of the world's market?

These many questions could not be answered in even the roundest of numbers. The proposed combination, if it is managed with intelligence, would increase its profits by each one of the improvements and economies suggested; but how much is impossible to discover. The promoter, in his endeavor to estimate the economies of combination, was reduced to elastic approximations. He was not in the position of the coal promoter, the elements of whose problem lay in his hand, who worked with known conditions—the cost of mining, the profits on the company's store, the rates of freight, and the price of sale. The estimates of the trust promoter were in an unknown field. His calculations were at best inaccurate guesswork. He could be certain only of so much, that the profits of the trust would be much larger than the combined profits of the companies which were to compose it, and of this profit he meant to secure for himself the largest possible share.

The promoter, having estimated the profits of combination, must now assemble his proposition; he must acquire the right to purchase the plants which he desires that the new corporation should own. To this end, usually with the coöperation of manufacturers who were well known in the trade, and who could, if necessary, vouch for his responsibility, besides enforcing his arguments by their own representations, the promoter made the following proposition to the owners; that they should sell him the right to purchase their plants for a corporation which he proposes to organize, at an agreed price and for a definite time. The capitalization of the proposed company was to be fixed at the amount which it was believed will be warranted by its earnings, increased, as they would be, over the combined earnings of the individual plants by the economies of combination. By selling their plants to the new company, the owners could either (1) secure a sum of cash; or (2) become stockholders or bondholders in the new company by receiving its securities in exchange for their property; or (3) sell these securities and free their capital for other uses.

The next step in the negotiations, after the owners had consented to sell, was to determine the valuation to be placed upon the separate properties. It was here that the promoter must work for his profits. He had based the capitalization of the new corporation upon his estimate of the earnings of the combined plants. The securities which represented this capitalization he expected to sell. With the funds received, he would take up his options and equip the company with the necessary working capital. What remained out of the proceeds of the sale is the promoter's profit. Expressed in terms of securities, this was the difference between the total amount of the securities of the consolidated company and the amount of those securities given in exchange for the properties and the cash which make up the assets of the consolidated company. It was the promoter's interest, therefore, to bargain shrewdly with the owners of the plants which he wished to purchase in order to reduce the amount of the stock and bonds of the consolidation which he must surrender to acquire these plants. His situation was, in general outline, similar to the situation of the coal promoter, similar indeed to the situation of every promoter. He wished to buy something cheap and sell it dear. Keeping this principle in mind, it is unnecessary to do more than to sketch in outline the methods of higgling and bargaining which were followed.

The promoter usually found at the outset that he had to divide his expected gains with some of the owners who were already associated with him in the enterprise and without whose coöperation he could not hope to succeed. The bargains which he made with these men were not hard. They were usually large manufacturers, and their influence and example were potent in persuading others to enter the combination. The high figures at which their plants were put into the scheme were warranted, if not by the value of the plants themselves, at any rate by the advantage which the promoter gained from their coöperation. Another class of owners was also in a position to compel the promoter to give them a liberal share of the increased value of combination. These were the strong firms and companies who have been making money even under competition, and who, while perhaps appreciating to the fullest extent the many advantages of combination, realized also just what their position is in the trade, and how important it was to the success of the combination that their plants should be included in its list of assets. If strong competitors refuse to combine, the attractiveness of the proposition was much diminished, and unless the promoter was able to overcome their reluctance to sell, the flotation was likely to fail.

The organization of the Continental Tobacco Company, for example, was delayed several months until terms could be made with Liggett & Meyers, the large plug tobacco manufacturers of St. Louis, whose competition would make control of the trade very doubtful. During the progress of the negotiations, Liggett & Meyers gave the promoters, who also controlled the American Tobacco Company, a foretaste of what was in store for the Continental Company if organized without them, by vigorously fighting the American Tobacco Company, carrying their competition even to the point of attempting to buy all the best tobacco in Kentucky, and so threatening to deprive the trust of its advantages in purchasing raw material. The outcome of this struggle was that Liggett & Meyers sold out to the Continental Tobacco Company for $12,500,000, a figure representing one sixth of the total capitalization of the company. Mr. Carnegie's success in extorting an enormous price, estimated at over $500,000,000 for the securities of himself and his partners, is a more familiar illustration of the necessity often imposed upon the promoter of dividing his prospective profits with the men who alone can make those profits a reality. Every trust promoter has had similar experiences. These valuations were often far above what the plants were worth under competitive conditions, and they were secured only because their owners knew that the promoter must get them, no matter at what sacrifice.

If this scale of payment were to be kept up, the promoter, after the equipment of his company, would have nothing left of the securities with which he started. He must recover these losses, in part at least, from the owners who are anxious to sell. They had been hard pressed by the competitive struggle; they might be advancing in years; their plants were often under mortgage and in an inferior condition. It was impossible that they could find purchasers for these plants as separate concerns for more than a small fraction of the money which had been put into them. To men in such a situation, the trust offered a haven of refuge. They were glad and anxious to come in on any terms that would relieve them of their obligations, and leave them a sum of money larger than could be secured by an individual sale. It should be noted in this connection that the salability of a mill is much increased by combining it with twenty other mills in the same line of production and disposing of it through the stock market. Before consolidation, the demand for a small property was narrow and uncertain. As a part of the trust, however, the demand was furnished by the speculative public of the entire country. It is also to be observed that the prospect of being left outside the combination served to moderate the demands of those who distrusted their ability to resist such powerful competition. The promoter could, in a measure, recover from the majority of manufacturers who are in the position just described, the advantage which he was compelled to sacrifice to the more important members of the trade.

By one means and another, by alliance, persuasion, and coercion, the promoter had assembled his proposition. All the plants which he considers necessary to the trust were under his control. He had options upon an entire industry, which, when exercised, would place a single corporation in control of that industry, in this way eliminating competition and increasing earning power.

CHAPTER IV

MATERIALS OF THE FINANCIAL PLAN

Our promoter has now proceeded in the flotation of his enterprise as far as he can go without assistance. He must now obtain money to take up his options, build his factory or railroad, and inaugurate his enterprise. He may obtain this money from the investing public to whom his appeal may be made directly, by published advertising, circular letters and agents. If the nature of his proposition permits, he will present it to bankers and ask them to purchase, or to agree to purchase, a sufficient amount of the securities of his new company to provide it with the money which it requires. In the United States it is a safe conclusion that in nearly all cases where the character of the proposition is such as to appeal eventually to the conservative investor, the promoter will approach bankers and endeavor to secure from them the funds which the new company requires. The bankers will purchase the securities with the expectation of selling them to the public, but, for the time being, the dealings are between the promoter and the banker.

A company has been incorporated which will hold title to the property with whose acquisition the promoter has occupied himself. This corporation will issue certain securities. These securities will be sold to the investor who will, in this way, furnish the money for the development of the enterprise. The preparation of the financial plan is therefore the next step.

A corporation is an association of individuals authorized

by law to own property, to contract debt, to appoint officers and agents, and to manage its business within the limits of the formal grant of authority by the state, which is known as its charter, in all respects as though it were a natural person. The association, it will be remarked, owns the property. It is represented in its management of the business of the company by trustees called directors. These trustees, in turn, appoint officers who carry on most of the work of business management.

The ownership in the association is called the "stock" of the corporation and this stock is divided into shares. It is the custom to represent this stock ownership in a company by a certain arbitrarily assumed sum, such as $500,000 or $1,000,000, or, in the case of the original capitalization of the United States Steel Corporation, $1,100,000,000. This capitalization, as the expression of ownership in the company, is divided into shares, each of which, being a proportionate part of the total capitalization, represents an assumed sum of money. This assumed sum is known as their par value. If the capital of the company, for example, is $100,000 and is divided into 1,000 shares, then the assumed or par value of each share would be $100. Since it is in this form that the ownership of business corporations is expressed, the first step in the preparation of the financial plan is to fix upon a certain capitalization which shall represent the ownership in the company. The considerations affecting the amount of this capitalization will presently appear.

These shares of ownership may be sold to provide funds for the company. In private companies, such as manufacturing or trading companies, this is the usual method. The company is capitalized for the amount of money which is immediately required, and those who desire to participate in the enterprise purchase varying amounts of stock. The rights of the holders of these shares are: (1) to vote for directors of the company, and on all propositions which the charter provides shall be submitted to a vote of the stockholders—for example, the sale of the property of the company or its dissolution; (2) to be faithfully represented by these trustees or directors; (3) to participate in the profits of the company, when the directors decide that these profits have been earned, and that it is expedient to distribute them; and (4) to share in the proceeds of the assets of the company in case of dissolution or liquidation. These rights of the stockholder are set down in detail in the certificate of incorporation or charter. The incorporators themselves draw up this certificate under the general incorporation law of the State. When duly authenticated, recorded and filed with the proper official, it becomes the charter of the company, the evidence of its right to be a corporation, the fundamental contract between the State and the corporation, between the corporation and its stockholders, and between the stockholders themselves, a contract which cannot be changed without the unanimous consent of every stockholder.

In but few cases can a public business corporation be financed in such a simple manner. When the appeal is made to the public to supply the funds, a more elaborate financial plan must be devised. It is customary to divide the stock into two classes: preferred stock and common stock, or, as the English describe it, ordinary stock. Preferred stock has preference in the distribution of profits, and, if provided in the charter, preference in any distribution of the assets of the company to stockholders. If a company issues 50,000 shares, the owner of 5,000 shares is the proprietor of one tenth of the corporation. In the absence of some special provision to the contrary, he can exercise one tenth of the voting power. If the directors declare a dividend out of the profits of the company, this distribution is made to the stockholders on the basis of the number of shares held by each. For example, if the sum distributed is $50,000, the holder of 5,000 shares would receive $5,000. If the company is dissolved and its assets bring $500,000, the holder of 5,000 shares would receive $50,000. This would apply, no matter what the capitalization of the company might be, or into how many shares it might be divided. Whether the capitalization is $5,000,000, or $50,000, or the par value $100, or $1, the position of the stockholder in participating in dividends and in assets is the same.

This holds true if only one class of stock is issued. If preferred stock is issued, two classes of owners are created: First, preference shareholders, who receive a certain rate of dividends, usually seven per cent on the par value of their shares, which must be paid them out of any profits distributed before the holders of any of the common stock can receive anything; second, common stockholders, who take what is left after the claims of preferred stockholders have been satisfied. The advantage of the preferred stockholder is that he has a prior claim upon the profits of the company, a claim inferior, it is true, to that of the creditor, but which takes precedence of the common stockholder. If the profits of the company are only sufficient to pay seven per cent on the par value of the shares, if this amount is called for in his preferred stock contract with the corporation, and in case the directors decide to distribute these profits, the preferred stockholder will receive his seven per cent, while the common stockholder will receive nothing. It may also be provided in the contract between the corporation and the preferred stockholder that he shall participate equally with the common stockholder in any distribution of profits, until a certain additional amount of return on the preferred stock has been paid; or this participation with the common stock may begin after a certain dividend has been paid on the stock, after which both classes of stock share equally in profits; or the participation of the preferred stock may be unlimited from the beginning.

Preferred stock may be classified into cumulative and noncumulative preferred stock. In the charters of companies issuing preferred stock, the following provision is usually found: "The dividends upon the preferred stock shall be cumulative so that if, in any year, the dividends amounting to seven per cent per annum, are not paid on the preferred stock, the deficiency is payable subsequently before any dividends are set apart or paid on the common stock." If the earnings of a corporation in a certain year are only sufficient for the distribution of $1,500,000, while the dividend of seven per cent on the preferred stock calls for a distribution of $2,000,000, in the following year, the preferred stockholders, in addition to their regular dividends of $2,000,000, must receive the $500,000 of dividends which they failed to get in the preceding year before the common stock can receive any dividend. No matter to what sum these unpaid dividends on the preferred stock may amount, all these back dividends must be paid in some form to the preferred stockholder before the common stockholders receive anything.

Preferred stock may be divided into series according to the order of preference as first, second, and third preferred. This arrangement is, however, uncommon. Preference may be given the preferred stockholder in assets as well as earnings by providing that, in the event of a dissolution of the company, and a sale of its assets, the par value of the preferred stock shall first be paid to its stockholders before anything is paid on the common stock.

The final form of security, utilized, as a rule, wherever possible in the preparation of a financial plan, is the bond. Corporation bonds are promissory notes, usually in denominations of $500 or $1,000, and as evidences of the same debt, $1,000,000, $50,000,000, or $300,000,000, as the case may be. The evidences of these large debts are issued in a number of notes, in order that they may be readily marketed. A corporation wishing to borrow $1,000,000 for thirty years on the best security, would have great difficulty in placing the entire loan with a single investor. No matter how good may be the security, few investors have sufficient funds to make a loan of this amount, and the few whose resources are sufficient are likely to have other uses for their money. By issuing, instead of one note for $1,000,000, one thousand notes of $1,000 each, the corporation is able to draw upon the funds of a large number of investors, who may buy its thirty year notes, in lots of one, five or fifty.

These notes are usually secured as an entirety, by a mortgage, the relation of each to the security being the same as every other. A mortgage is a written instrument for the conveyance of real or personal property by a debtor to the creditor or his representative to insure the performance by the debtor of his promise to pay interest and principal. The possession of the property may remain with the debtor, and this is the rule when real property is pledged, or, as is usually done with personal property such as shares of stock pledged as security for a loan, the actual property may be turned over to the lender's representative or trustee, usually a trust company.

The form of a bond is as follows:

(FORM OF COUPON BOND.)

UNITED STATES OF AMERICA,

State of New York.

No. 100 $500.00

THE LONG ISLAND RAILROAD COMPANY.

Four Per Cent Refunding Mortgage Gold Bond,
Due March 1, 1949.

THE LONG ISLAND RAILROAD COMPANY, a corporation organized and existing under and pursuant to the laws of the State of New York, for value received, hereby promises to pay to the bearer, or, if this bond be registered, then to the registered owner hereof, at its financial agency in the Borough of Manhattan, in the City and State of New York, 500 dollars in gold coin of the United States of America, of or equal to the present standard of weight and fineness, on the first day of March in the year nineteen hundred and forty-nine, and to pay interest thereon at the rate of four per cent per annum, from the first day of September, nineteen hundred and three, in like gold coin, semi-annually, on the first days of March and September in each year, upon presentation and surrender at its agency aforesaid of the coupons hereto annexed as they severally become due and until said principal sum is paid. Both the principal and interest of this bond are payable without deduction for any tax or taxes which the Railroad Company may be required to pay or retain therefrom under any present or future law of the United States or of the State of New York.

This bond is one of a series of bonds of like date and tenor, of the denomination of five hundred dollars or multiples thereof, known as Four Per Cent Refunding Mortgage Gold Bonds, issued and to be issued to an amount not exceeding in the aggregate the principal sum of forty-five million dollars at any one time outstanding, all of which bonds are issued and to be issued under and equally secured by a mortgage and deed of trust dated September 1, 1903, executed by THE LONG ISLAND RAILROAD COMPANY to THE EQUITABLE TRUST COMPANY OF NEW YORK as Trustee, to which mortgage and deed of trust reference is made for a description of the properties and franchises mortgaged, the nature and extent of the security, the rights of the holders of bonds under the same, and the terms and conditions upon which the bonds are issued and secured.

IN WITNESS WHEREOF, The Long Island Railroad Company has caused its corporate seal to be hereunto affixed and attested by its Secretary or Assistant Secretary, and this bond to be signed in its corporate name by its President or Vice-President, and has also caused the signature of its Treasurer to be engraved upon the annexed coupons, as of the first day of September, in the year one thousand nine hundred and three.

THE LONG ISLAND RAILROAD COMPANY,
By

President.

Attest:

Secretary.

(FORM OF COUPON.)

No. 100 $10.00

THE LONG ISLAND RAILROAD COMPANY will pay to the bearer at its financial agency in the City of New York, on the first day of March, ten dollars ($10.00) in gold coin, being six months' interest then due on its Four Per Cent Refunding Mortgage Gold Bond Number 100.

Treasurer.

This bond or promissory note refers to a certain mortgage executed to the Equitable Trust Company of New York by the borrowing company, for the equal securing of all the bonds, ninety thousand in number, into which this loan is divided. This mortgage describes in detail the property of the company set aside for the securing of its bonds, and transfers it to the trustee, in the following granting clause: [1]

> That in order to secure the payment of the principal and interest of all said bonds at any time issued and outstanding under this indenture, according to their tenor, purport and effect, and to secure the performance and observance of all the covenants and conditions herein contained, and to declare the terms and conditions upon which said bonds are issued, received and held, and for and in consideration of the premises and of the acceptance or purchase of said bonds by the holders thereof, and of the sum of one hundred dollars, lawful money of the United States of America, to it fully paid by the Trustee on or before the ensealing and delivery of these presents, the receipt whereof is hereby acknowledged. The Long Island Railroad Company, the party of the first part, has *granted, bargained, sold, aliened, released, conveyed, assigned, transferred* and set over, and by these presents does *grant, bargain, sell, alien, release, convey, assign, transfer* and set over unto the said Trustee and its successors in the trust hereby created, *all and singular the railroad and ferry prop-*

[1] Detailed provisions for registration omitted.

> *erty, and other property,* real and personal, used in connection with such railroad and ferry property, and franchises of every kind relating thereto or exercisable in connection therewith, of the Railroad Company, including the following, to wit:[1]

(A detailed description of the property follows.)

This grant, however, is not absolute, but conditional. If the borrowing company performs its obligations to pay principal and interest, and, as we shall show hereafter, to conserve the security of the bonds, then the grant lapses. It is made for a specific purpose, namely the securing of the bonds, and when the bonds have been paid, the purpose has been accomplished, and the title to the pledged property reverts to its owner who is, moreover, so long as he lives up to his obligations, allowed to remain in undisturbed possession. The clauses of the mortgage governing these matters are as follows: First, the "Habendum" clause:

> TO HAVE AND TO HOLD all and singular the above mentioned and described railroads, railroad property, ferries, ferry property, franchises, real estate and personal property unto the said The Equitable Trust Company of New York, as Trustee, its successors and assigns forever.
>
> BUT IN TRUST, NEVERTHELESS, for the equal and proportionate benefit and security of all holders of the bonds and coupons issued and to be issued under and secured by this indenture, and for the enforcement of the payment of said bonds and interest, when payable, according to the tenor, purpose and effect of such bonds and coupons, and to secure the performance and observance of and compliance with the covenants and conditions of this indenture, without preference, priority or distinction, as to lien or otherwise, of one bond over any other bond by or by reason of the purpose of its issue, so that each and every bond issued or to be issued hereunder shall have the same right, lien and privilege

[1] Italics are the author's.

under and by virtue of this indenture, and so that the principal and interest of every such bond shall, subject to the terms hereof, be equally and proportionately secured hereby as if all had been duly issued, sold and negotiated simultaneously with the execution and delivery hereof.[1]

ARTICLE SEVENTEENTH.—If, when the bonds hereby secured shall have become due and payable, the Railroad Company shall well and truly pay or cause to be paid the whole amount of the principal and interest due upon all of the bonds hereby secured then outstanding, or shall provide for such payment by depositing with the Trustee hereunder, for the payment of such bonds and interest thereon, the entire amount due or to become due for principal and interest, and shall also pay or cause to be paid all other sums payable hereunder by the Railroad Company and shall well and truly keep, perform and observe all the things herein required to be kept, performed and observed by it according to the true intent and meaning of this indenture, then and in that case the premises and all properties, rights and interests hereby conveyed shall revert to the Railroad company, or to whoever may be entitled thereto, and the estate right, title and interest of the Trustee therein shall thereupon cease, determine and become void; and the Trustee shall, in such case, on demand of the Railroad Company and at its cost and expense, enter satisfaction and discharge of this indenture upon the records; otherwise, the same shall be, continue and remain in full force and virtue.

In addition to promising to pay the principal and interest, the railway company enters into a number of agreements which are designed to maintain the security of the bonds intact. Some of these covenants are as follows: to

---

[1] The right of the railway company to remain in possession of the property is not expressly stated in this mortgage but is implied from numerous clauses. This conveyance of its property by a company to the trustee is not in perpetuity. When the obligations of the bonds are discharged the property reverts to the company.

pay all taxes, to keep the property in repair, and to perform all the obligations of the franchises and leases under which the lines of the system are operated. Failure to perform any of these covenants would evidently impair the value of the security underlying the bonds.

In case the railway company defaults in the payment of principal or interest, or fails to perform any of the covenants into which it has entered for the protection of the bondholder, the mortgage provides that the Trustee may either enter upon the property and operate it for the benefit of creditors, or sell the property and apply the proceeds of the sale to the payment of the company's debts, returning any balance which may remain to the company. The company agrees not to interpose any obstacle or objection to the enforcement of the bondholders' rights by the Trustee.

The purpose and effect of this mortgage is to set apart certain property of the company for the protection of its creditors should it default on any of its obligations, and to provide a method by which the representatives of the creditors may take possession of this property when default occurs, and apply its income or the proceeds of its sale to the payment of the company's debts. The company, in effect, says to its creditors: "We appoint you or your representative, our trustee, to pay our debts in the event that we are unable to pay them. In order that you may discharge your trust, we place in your hands certain property with the stipulation that as long as we perform our obligations we may be allowed to use the property as our own. Should we fail, however, in the performance of any of these obligations, then you, our trustee, are to sell the property and so discharge the obligation of your trust."

These mortgages may be of various grades, first, second, and third mortgages, all resting upon the same property, differing from each other in the relative superiority of their liens. Thus the bonds secured by the lien of a second mortgage, if the company defaults on their interest, cannot enforce their claim by seizing and selling its property, until they have first satisfied the claim of the holders of the first mortgage bonds, or, if they sell the property, they must sell it subject to this first mortgage lien. Except during a receivership, as will be explained hereafter, as long as the bonds which the first mortgage secures are in existence, the property of the company can in no way be separated from the lien of the first mortgage. In the same way, the lien of a third mortgage is inferior to that of a second mortgage.

The nature of a mortgage as a conveyance of property appears more clearly in a collateral trust mortgage, where the security of the bonds consists of the stocks or bonds of other corporations. Under these mortgages, not merely the title, but the physical possession of the property passes to the Trustee. For example, the Trust Indenture securing the bonds issued jointly in 1901 by the Great Northern and the Northern Pacific Railroad Companies, secured by the stock of the Chicago, Burlington & Quincy, provides:

> That, in order to secure the payment of the principal and interest of all such bonds at any time issued and outstanding under this indenture, and the performance of all the covenants and conditions herein contained, and in consideration of the premises and of the purchase and acceptance of such bonds by the holders hereof, and of the sum of one dollar to each of them duly paid by the Trustee at the ensealing and delivery of these presents, the receipt whereof is hereby acknowledged, the Railway Companies, parties of the first part, have assigned and transferred, and by these presents do assign and transfer unto the Trustee, party of the second part, its successors and assigns, one million and sixty-six thousand and six hundred (1,066,600) shares of the capital stock of the Chicago, Burlington & Quincy Railroad Company the certificates for which have been delivered to the Trustee, and all additional shares of the capital stock of said Company in exchange for which bonds hereby secured shall be certified and delivered hereunder.

> TO HAVE AND TO HOLD the said shares of capital stock, and all additional property that hereafter shall become subject to this indenture unto the Trustee and its successors and assigns, in trust for the equal and proportionate security of all present and future holders of bonds and interest obligations issued, and to be issued, under and secured by this indenture, and for the enforcement of the payment of said bonds and interest obligations when payable, and the performance of and compliance with the covenants and conditions of this indenture, without preference, priority or distinction as to lien or otherwise of any one bond over any other bond by reason of priority in the issue or negotiation thereof.

If any default should occur on the part of the borrowing Companies, the Trustee is authorized to sell the shares of stock securing the bonds, and to proceed against the Great Northern and the Northern Pacific for the recovery of any balance which may remain after the Trustee applies the proceeds of the sale to the payment of the bonds. As long, however, as the borrowing companies carry out the conditions and covenants of the mortgage, the Trustee empowers the company issuing the stock which he holds in pledge, the Chicago, Burlington & Quincy, to pay to the owners of the stock, the Great Northern and the Northern Pacific, the dividends on the stock, and issues to them his power of attorney, or proxy, which will authorize them to vote the stock as though the certificates representing it were in their possession, and they appeared as the registered owners of the stock on the books of the Chicago, Burlington & Quincy. In case of any default, however, the Trustee immediately resumes these delegated rights of ownership, and the two borrowers lose their right to vote the Burlington stock and to receive dividends.

CHAPTER V

THE ISSUING OF SECURITIES

We have now described the ordinary securities which our new company may issue to obtain the money required to construct its plant. Our next topic is the methods by which these securities are prepared and included in a plan of capitalization, for sale to bankers or to the public.

In taking up the considerations which the banker and promoter must have in mind in preparing a financial plan, we note first that their chief concern is to obtain the necessary money on the easiest terms. Up to the point of providing the money, their interests are united. It is only when the division of the profits is reached that they part company. We have now to consider the choice of securities of which the capitalization of the new company is to consist. These are, as we have seen, stock of various kinds, and bonds with various kinds of security.

As a rule, whenever the enterprise admits, the financial plan will call for the issue of bonds, and if that fails, for the issue of preferred stock. The reason for preferring this method of borrowing lies in the nature of a bond. The purchaser of a corporation bond, in return for what he considers to be sufficient security of income and principal, surrenders his right to participate in the profits of the company above the moderate rate of interest named in his bond, four, five or six per cent. With the preferred stockholder, the situation is the same. In return for a preferred claim to a fixed rate of dividend, the preferred stockholder, unless his stock is participating, surrenders the remainder of the dividends to the common stock. If, therefore, in the financial plan, all, or a large part of the money necessary, can be secured by selling bonds, and if the expectations of the promoters that large profits will be earned are realized, it is more profitable to employ this method.

Suppose, for example, that $1,000,000 is required to carry through the consolidation, or build the plant, or construct the railroad, and that the earnings of the enterprise will be at the rate of twelve per cent or $120,000 annually. Suppose, further, that this money can be raised either by the sale of bonds, or by the sale of stock, or that both methods can be used in combination. If $1,000,000 can be provided by the sale of bonds bearing six per cent interest, the promoters and bankers will have common stock which can share earnings of $60,000 a year, after paying interest on the cost of the property, and for this stock they may have paid nothing, except the cost of securing the options and selling the securities. Their stock is all "velvet." Although they may have to surrender part of this common stock in connection with the sale of bonds, they can usually retain a sufficient amount to control the company. If, on the other hand, they are obliged to sell common stock to obtain this $1,000,000, they must admit each share of stock to participation in their earnings at a higher rate than that which bonds usually carry. Furthermore, when the security is good, bonds can be more readily sold, and at proportionately higher prices, than any kind of stock. For these reasons, from the standpoint of the banker and promoter, bonds are preferred whenever the nature of the business admits of their issue.

We now take up the classification of industries and enterprises into those which furnish satisfactory security for the issue of bonds and those which do not. In the discussion of the mortgage as security for a bond issue, we have seen what great attention is paid to the enumeration of the items of property of a corporation, how carefully this property is segregated to protect the holders of the bonds. When this property is nonspecialized, that is when it can be put to a variety of uses, so that it can readily find a purchaser, for example, real estate, or stocks of finished goods, or materials, then the property itself furnishes the security for the loan. When, however, the property of the company is specialized to the use of a particular business, such as a railroad or manufacturing plant, where the business must be carried on in a certain place and by people who are skilled in its management, and where the property, once devoted to a particular use, can be turned to no other use, the real security of the creditor is not the property but the earnings of the property. With a mortgage on centrally located real estate, the selling value of the real estate can be easily realized, and a loan can be made without reference to the profitableness of the business which is to be carried on in the property. One million dollars, however, may be invested in the property of a manufacturing company which could not be sold for any other use than the one to which it is specifically devoted, for less than $100,000. The security of the creditors is here the profitableness of the business which is carried on in the factory.

Furthermore, a business is not an aggregate of physical property but consists of physical property—buildings, boilers, machine tools—plus an industrial opportunity, plus the organization and ability to operate the business. The corporation owning this business borrows the money, and the value of the business is based upon its earnings. The physical property, which is set aside with such a profusion of formality in the mortgage, is merely the visible symbol of its earning capacity. Without the plant, it is true, earnings would be impossible, but the plant has little value unless the spirit of profitable life is breathed into it by an intelligently managed organization. In estimating the stability of different classes of enterprises to furnish security for bond issues, we must take account first of this factor of earnings.

Since the bondholder is solely interested in the security of his principal, and regular payment of his interest, and since both security and interest depend upon the permanence of income, other things being equal the companies with the most stable earnings or a market for their products at all times reasonably satisfactory furnish the best security for bonds. Stability of earnings depends upon (1) the possession of a monopoly; (2) good management; and (3) the character of the business.

Monopoly is exclusive or dominant control over a market. The more complete this control, the more valuable is the monopoly. The advantage of monopoly lies in the fact that the prices of services or commodities are controlled by the producer rather than by the consumer. In the long run, the returns in profits from monopoly are greater than when the consumer is able to play off one seller against another, and so secure concessions in prices. Monopolies are of various origins. The most familiar are (1) franchises, the right to use public property for private purposes, for example, the furnishing of light, water and transportation, (2) control of sources of raw material supply such, for example, as that which the United States Steel Corporation exercises over the Lake Superior ore deposits, (3) patents, which give the exclusive right to manufacture an article for seventeen years; and (4) high cost of duplicating plant, which secures the railroads in thickly settled territory, where land values are high, and where terminal sites are especially costly, against competition from the duplication of their facilities. Of these forms of monopoly, those conferred by franchises and by high costs of duplication are most valuable from the standpoint of bond security. Next comes possession of supplies of raw material, and last patent monopoly.

Stability of earnings also depends upon good management. This means not merely economical operation but cultivation of new business. Stability of earnings depends finally upon the breadth of the demand. In manufacturing industries, for example, those enterprises which produce raw materials and the necessities of life have a more stable demand than those which produce highly finished articles and luxuries.

We may classify enterprises according to the quality of

the security which they offer for an issue of bonds. Mining enterprises—coal, iron, copper, lead—furnish a basis for bond issues only when the extent of the resource is known. When a bed of coal or a deposit of ore has been surveyed and its contents estimated, it furnishes a basis for a bond issue up to a moderate percentage of its market value. Industrial enterprises are mortgaged, as a rule, only when possessed of mineral properties or real estate. The limit of bond issues in these cases is narrow, and it has a close relation to the selling value of the property. Public Service Corporations, operating under franchises liberal in terms, furnish excellent security for bond issues. The monopoly of street railway or gas companies, which may have the exclusive right to serve the consumer for a term of years at prices which leave a large margin over the cost of production, is so perfect that the bondholder runs little risk of lending to a high percentage of the cost of the property. Railroads furnish perhaps the best basis of bond issue because of the stability of the demand for the transportation service which is rendered to every industry, and because of the high cost of duplicating the railroad plant, which secures existing lines in the possession of valuable territories, and, within the limits imposed by law, enables them to fix their rates on freight and passenger traffic. Most of the bonds which are outstanding in the United States are based on railroad property.

We now take up the amount of bonds which can be issued. The amount of bonds should not be so great as to impose upon the corporation a burden of interest charges which is above, or even equal to, a conservative estimate of the earning power of the company under the worst conditions which it is likely to meet. If a corporation does not pay its interest, and is put into bankruptcy, its affairs are thrown into confusion. Even though it is relieved from bankruptcy without reorganization by an improvement in its business, serious damage will always be found to have resulted. In issuing bonds, therefore, conservative financiers keep in mind the danger of bankruptcy to result from business depression or other unforeseen contingencies, and regulate the amount of debt to guard against any such untoward event.

The considerations which relate to the stability of different enterprises as security for bonds can also be employed to determine the percentage of income which can safely be represented by interest on bonds. A railroad company can safely assume interest payments which bear a much higher proportion to its income than a manufacturing company whose earnings fluctuate within much wider limits. In most cases, no more than twenty per cent of the gross earnings of a railroad company should be represented by interest charges. This standard is established in one of the most stable of industries. It furnishes a limit above which, speaking generally, no company should go in pledging its earnings for the payment of interest charges.

In fixing the amount of bonds to be issued, provision should be made for future issues of capital. Under normal conditions, every corporation, if well managed, will expand its operations and will largely increase its initial capital in handling the increased volume of business which the growth of the country and the energy of its management will bring to it. If the capital of the company was originally obtained by an issue of bonds, it will again resort to its credit to provide funds for the enlargement of its plant. The corporate mortgage, however, is an obstacle to the subsequent sale of the bonds. When a mortgage authorizes $5,000,000, this indebtedness cannot be increased without the consent of the bondholder, which is seldom obtained. The corporation is not likely to be in a position to offer inducements sufficient to persuade the bondholder to relax the obligation of his mortgage, and permit an increase in the amount of debt which it secures. Failing this provision, the natural method for the company to adopt in raising money for extensions will be to mortgage these extensions, either directly, or by organizing separate companies to issue their mortgage bonds. When the company is very strong in earnings, and its first mortgage debt is small, it may also raise money by a second or general mortgage.

These methods, however, while available and desirable in some cases, are not so effective as a first mortgage on the entire property of the company in satisfying the demands of the investor that the bonds which he purchases should be properly secured. Take, for example, the case of a railroad building a line from Kansas City to Galveston. Upon this line is placed a first mortgage, securing an issue of bonds sufficient to pay the cost of construction. The railroad prospers, and, within a few years, the necessity arises for a large amount of branch line mileage. If the first mortgage does not contain the provision, which is usual in the older mortgages, that the lien of the indenture should include all property owned or thereafter acquired, it would be possible for the company to issue bonds secured by a first mortgage upon the branches and a second mortgage upon the main line. These bonds would be inferior to the bonds secured by the first mortgage upon the main line, because the branches are not indispensable to the main line, while the main line is indispensable to the branches. The holders of bonds secured by a first mortgage upon branch lines, in case of default and foreclosure proceedings, come into possession of property which depends upon other property for its value. On the other hand, foreclosure of a mortgage upon the main line would bring into the possession of the bondholders property which could stand upon its own feet, which would not depend wholly or mainly upon the branches for its traffic, and to whose earning power the possession of branches would not be essential.

The best security for bonds issued by such a corporation is the lien of a first mortgage upon the entire property of a company, a lien protecting not merely the bonds first issued, but all later issues, so that every bond may be secured by the lien upon the entire system. In case of default, holders of bonds secured by such a mortgage come into the possession of the property as a whole. Their owners need not make concessions to the holders of securities protected by first mortgages on certain parts of the system. Recent financial plans, recognizing the value of the best security in securing a ready market and a high price for bonds, authorize amounts of first mortgage bonds which shall be sufficient to provide, not merely for the original construction of the property, but for all additions and improvements. An example of such an issue is furnished by the Chicago Bell Telephone Company which, in 1908, authorized an issue of $50,000,000 of first mortgage bonds of which $3,000,000 were to be issued immediately, and the remainder over a period of years as required.

At this point, however, we meet an objection. One of the chief advantages, from the standpoint of security, of a mortgage bond over any kind of stock, is the limitation of its issue. The buyer of a mortgage bond knows exactly what his security is in relation to the obligations outstanding against it. If $5,000,000 of first mortgage bonds are sold the investor knows that this amount can never be increased without his consent. If, however, he bought preferred or common stock, in the absence of special restrictions, there would be no limit to the increase in the number of shares. It is necessary, therefore, in providing for a large bond reserve in a financial plan, to satisfy the investor that the large amount of bonds held in reserve to be issued from time to time as the company's business expands, does not weaken the security of the bonds which he is asked to purchase.

The bondholder should have no objection to the unlimited issue of bonds secured by the same mortgage which protects his own holdings, provided that the additional proceeds of the additional issues could be invested to produce an income as great or greater than that earned by the initial investment. Indeed, from one point of view, the sale of additional bonds and their investment to yield to the business more than their interest, strengthens the position of all the bonds, especially if any large part of these excess profits are left in the business. The earnings over interest charges are the protection of the bondholder's interest. The surplus of assets over bond liabilities may be considered as an insurance reserve against such an impairment of the assets of the business as might threaten the security of the bonds. If a company is well managed, and if its improvements and extensions are conservatively made, the bondholder should have no objection to an increase of the amount of the debt secured by the same mortgage which protects his own bonds. It is, however, difficult to give him such assurances, and to satisfy him that, without specific safeguards in the mortgage, his earnings will not be jeopardized by additional issues. A bond reserve is, therefore, usually included in the financial plan with such stipulations that the investor knows in advance the conditions under which the various installments of bonds authorized can be sold.

A company, arranging for a large bond reserve, must provide safeguards in the mortgage which will assure the investor that the proceeds of the issues of bonds which may follow those which he buys will be so invested as to strengthen his security. The first of these safeguards is a limitation on the amount of bonds to be issued in any one year. A company with $50,000,000 of bonds authorized, which proposes to issue $20,000,000 or $30,000,000 within a short time after the first issue of $5,000,000, might weaken the confidence of the investor in the security of his bonds. The investor could not be made to understand why such a large investment would be necessary. He is assured on this point by such a restriction on the amount to be annually issued as appears in the mortgage of the Bell Telephone Company already referred to, which provides that no bonds in addition to the $5,000,000 sold on that date, could be issued until after December 1, 1909, and, thereafter, the trustee is permitted to certify bonds not exceeding $5,000,000 per annum.

We have already seen that, if the same earnings are obtained on the investment of the proceeds of successive bond issues, as were shown on the first expenditure, the position of the bondholder would not be weakened. There is, however, always danger that this rate of earnings may not be realized. In order to insure the bondholder that there will always be a wide margin of safety in the cost of any property acquired with the proceeds of subsequent issues of bonds, provision is made, again quoting from the restrictions in the mortgage of the Chicago (Bell) Telephone Company, that the "total amount of bonds issued shall at no time exceed fifty per cent of the value of the property as represented by its total assets, nor more than sixty per cent of the real estate and construction account." This protects the bondholders against an overestimate by the directors of the earnings from the new property by providing an ample margin in the value of the property of the company above the mortgage obligations.

Such restrictions, however, are unusual. As a rule, the bondholder will be satisfied if a limitation is made similar to the following in the mortgage securing the bonds of the Pacific Telephone & Telegraph Company: "Of the first mortgage and collateral trust bonds authorized, $12,000,000 may be issued for extensions, additions, etc., but only up to 66⅔ per cent of the cost thereof." The Pacific Telephone & Telegraph Company is more liberal. The trust deed of this company provides that "of the remaining $25,000,000 bonds over the $3,000,000 first issued, $22,000,000 shall be issuable only to cover actual expenses on plant and improvements, but at no time shall the amount of bonds issued exceed an amount equal to eighty-five per cent of such expenditures, nor shall they be issued to provide for repairs."

Another form of restriction makes additional bond issues depend upon earnings. A common provision is that inserted in the mortgage of the Utica & Mohawk Valley Railroad Company where the bonds reserved "could be issued for seventy-five per cent of the actual cash cost of additions and improvements, but not until the net earnings for the preceding twelve months are equal to or exceed double the interest charge on the total amount of bonds outstanding, including those to be issued." It is better, from the standpoint of the

6

holder, to limit the issue of new bonds with reference to the amount of surplus earnings of the company than by any other standard, although the provision that bonds can be issued only up to a reasonable percentage of the cash cost of improvements is also desirable.

A common stipulation for the protection of the bondholder, whether bonds are reserved or not, with a company whose business is subject to wide fluctuations, provides that a certain surplus of quick assets over liabilities should be maintained at all times. A large amount of convertible assets in proportion to its liabilities insures a company against financial embarrassment. It was a lack of quick assets that carried down the Westinghouse Electric and Manufacturing Company in 1907. In the mortgage securing the $10,000,000 of five per cent gold bonds issued by the Republic Iron & Steel Company the following provision appears:

> The net cash and quick assets over and above liabilities, other than the $10,000,000 of bonds and the interest thereon, shall never be less than $6,500,000 while any of the said issue of bonds remains outstanding, until the total amount of such issue of $10,000,000 not canceled, shall be less than $6,500,000, and thereafter shall never be less than the amount of such $10,000,000 of bonds at any time uncanceled. By the phrase "cash and quick assets" is meant cash in bank, good accounts and bills and notes receivable, contract notes, or similar or other securities received on the sale of products of the Republic Company, raw material, manufactured products (it being understood that the material shall be figured at actual cost without interest if cost is below the market value thereof at the time of the valuation thereof hereunder, but at market value if at such time below cost thereof). It is expressly understood and agreed that in the term raw material no ore or coal shall be included except such as has actually been mined and is then on the surface at the mines available for shipment by rail or in transit or at upper or lower lake docks, or at works.

This requirement resulted, in 1907, in the suspension by the Republic Iron & Steel Company of dividends on its preferred stock, all the cash assets of the company being necessary to preserve the stipulated margin of quick assets above liabilities.

We may summarize the restrictions upon the issue of bonds reserved to be sold under first mortgage as follows:

(1) A limitation on the amount which can be sold in any one year;

(2) Each installment to be restricted to a certain percentage of the cost of additions or improvements upon which the proceeds of the bonds are expended, the percentage varying with the type of property and the permanence of the business.

(3) That the earnings of the company shall show a substantial margin over its interest or fixed charges, including the interest charges on the new bonds;

(4) In special cases, a provision that a surplus of quick assets shall always be maintained for the protection of the bondholder.

If these restrictions are included in the mortgage, the existence of a large bond reserve need cause no apprehension to the holders of bonds already issued under the same mortgage. The company, for its part, is enabled to raise money on the most favorable terms and each succeeding capital expenditure, on account of the margin required in the cost of the property, increases the security of the bonds already outstanding.

CHAPTER VI

STATE SUPERVISION OF SECURITY ISSUES

ANOTHER form of protection, available for the investor against the excessive or improper issue of bonds by corporations, is furnished by the State. In some States, the amount of debt which can be incurred by a company is limited by statute. This is, however, unusual. The stockholders are dealing with their own property. The creditor is supposed to be able to look after his own interests. Arbitrary restrictions on indebtedness are, furthermore, objectionable in that they may interfere with the development of a company's business. A better safeguard to the stockholder and investor against unwise issue of securities is furnished by the Public Service Commission. These commissions are found in almost every State. In only a few of the larger States, however, have the commissions been clothed with sufficient powers to make their work really effective. In Massachusetts, New York, Maryland, Wisconsin, and Kansas the powers of the Public Service Commission are sweeping. The New York Commissions, for example, are given supreme control over all kinds of public service corporations, including railroads, street railroads, lighting and gas and telephone and telegraph companies. The supervisory and regulative powers of the commissions extend to character of service, to rates and fares, and to the approval of the issue of stocks, bonds and other forms of indebtedness. In this last power, the investor finds a considerable safeguard against the improper issue of securities.

The nature of this power over security issues is indicated by the following extract from Section 55 of the Act Creating the Public Service Commissions of New York:

> Any common carrier, railroad corporation or street railroad corporation organized under the laws of the State of New York, may issue stocks, bonds, notes or other evidences of indebtedness payable at periods of more than twelve months after the date thereof, when necessary for the acquisition of property, the construction, completion, extension or improvement of its facilities, or for the improvement or maintenance of its service or for the discharge or lawful refunding of its obligations, provided and not otherwise that there shall have been secured from the proper commission an order authorizing such issue, and the amount thereof and stating that, in the opinion of the commission, the use of the capital to be secured by the issue of such stock, bonds, notes, or other evidences of indebtedness is reasonably required for the said purpose of the corporation. For the purpose of enabling it to determine whether it should issue such an order, the commission shall make such inquiry or investigation, hold such hearings and examine such witnesses, books, papers, documents or contracts as it may deem of importance in enabling it to reach a determination.

Under this power, every corporation proposing to issue or authorize new securities must apply to the Public Service Commission for authority, and the authority will not be given until a thorough investigation has been made into the security back of the bonds and the purposes for which the money is to be spent.

The primary purpose of giving the commissions power over issues of securities was to protect the public against excessive issues of capital by public service corporations on the ground that an excessive capitalization might be used to defend rates or prices which were excessive. In the exercise of this power, however, the commissions have gone much farther and have undertaken the task of protecting the investor against unwise capital expenditures. The Commission of the Second District of New York has outlined its method of procedure in cases involving the authorization of bond issues as follows: [1]

"In passing upon the application for leave to issue additional capital stock, the Commission will consider:

"Whether there is reasonable prospect of fair return upon the investment proposed, to the end that securities having apparent worth but actually little or no value may not be issued with our sanction.

"We think that to a reasonable extent the interests of the investing public should be considered by us in passing upon these applications.

"The Commission should satisfy itself that, in a general way, the venture will be likely to prove commercially feasible, but it should not undertake to reach and announce a definite conclusion that the new construction or improvement actually constitutes a safe or attractive basis for investment. Commercial enterprises depend for their success upon so many conditions which cannot be foreseen or reckoned with in advance, that the duty of the Commission is discharged as to applications of this character when it has satisfied itself that the contemplated purpose is a fair business proposition."

In practice, however, the commission has made such careful investigation as to warrant the inference which has been generally drawn by the investing public that for them to authorize a bond issue is equal to their guarantee that the issue is good. In the case of the Rochester, Corning, and Elmira Traction Company decided March 31, 1908, the commission outlined in detail the methods of investigation which it proposed to follow in determining the amount of bonds which could be safely issued by a newly organized enterprise as follows:

---

[1] "Second Annual Report of the Public Service Commission," p. 12.

> An estimate will be made from a consideration of the results of operation of existing roads of the probable gross earnings.
>
> An estimate will be made in like manner of the probable operating expenses, taxes, and depreciation charges.
>
> The excess of earnings over the disbursements which must be made before fixed charges can be met represents the sum which is applicable to fixed charges.
>
> The maximum bond issue which will be allowed must be determined by the sum thus ascertained to be applicable to the payment of the interest charge.
>
> No bond issue should be permitted creating an interest charge beyond an amount which it is reasonably certain can be met from the net earnings.
>
> Stock representing a cash investment should be required to an amount sufficient to afford a moral guarantee that in the judgment of those investing the enterprise is likely to prove commercially successful.
>
> The order authorizing such stock and bond issues will contain approximate provisions designed to secure the construction of the road in accordance with the plans and specifications upon which the authorization was made and not in excess of the actual requirements.
>
> If the allowance proves inadequate for the required purposes, an application for further capitalization may be made, upon which application the expenditure of the proceeds of stock and bonds already authorized must be shown in detail.

After an issue of bonds has passed this searching scrutiny, the investor need have little fear concerning the safety of his bonds, whether a bond reserve many times the amount of the initial issue has been created or not. Indeed, in one notable instance, the first mortgage bonds of the Chicago Railways Company, which are issued under restrictions similar to those which have been outlined, such confidence has been placed in the efficacy of the precautions taken to guard against overissue, that bonds may be issued without limit under a so-called "open-end mortgage," every bond, no matter to what amount these may be issued, being equally secured as every other bond, by a first lien upon the property of the company. There is no essential difference between a large bond reserve and an open-end mortgage. The open-end mortgage, however, on account of the uncertainty as to the amount of bonds which may, at some time in the future, be issued, is inferior, in the opinion of most investors, to a large bond reserve. It is, moreover, in practice, no more effective in providing for the future capital needs of the corporation.

When a Public Service Commission has authorized the issue of securities, it is by implication bound to protect the company whose application it has authorized, not merely against the ill-advised action of their directors in using the credit of the company for improper purposes, but also against competing enterprises for which there is no public necessity and which would not, therefore, prove profitable. The New York Public Service Commission for the Second District, for example, in 1908, refused the application of the Buffalo, Rochester & Eastern Railroad Company for authority to issue securities for the construction of a line of railroad from Buffalo to Albany, paralleling the line of the New York Central, on the ground that the new enterprise would not prove profitable, and that the New York Central would be injured without any public benefit resulting. The new line proposed to interchange traffic at Albany with lines traversing New England, but the commission pointed out that the New England lines were not able to handle the traffic already delivered to them at Albany. This was sufficient reason for refusing to authorize the construction of another line which would make the congestion at the Hudson River even more acute.

At the time the New York Public Service Commissions were instituted, serious apprehensions were expressed by financial interests lest the new laws, because they took away from the directors or stockholders of corporations so much of the control which they had previously exercised over the issues of new capital, would seriously interfere with the efforts of companies to provide funds for development. Indeed, the passage of the New York law produced a feeling of consternation among bankers and investors. As the commissions have progressed with their work, however, they have been forced into the position of virtually guaranteeing every security whose issue they approve. So well organized and so favorably regarded are the Public Service Commissions by the investor, as a result of the interpretation which they have placed upon their powers, that the bond salesman offering a security whose issue they have approved has his work of persuasion largely accomplished. In one case the issue of bonds by a Massachusetts company secured by the stocks of two other companies, and with its own stock owned by a fourth, presenting a situation almost incomprehensible, were readily sold, in the main for no other reason than that they were issued under the authority of the Massachusetts Commission. Bond dealers and large investors, with few exceptions, cordially indorse the control of security issues by public service commissions, because of the assurance which this control gives to the investor that his interest will be safeguarded.

We next inquire concerning the term of the bonds. A new company has usually to sell its bonds at lower prices than when it has become established. After the business has been established, the bonds of the company can be sold at higher prices or can be refunded at lower rates. Although, therefore, the investor usually prefers a long term bond of an established company, a new company usually issues a short-term bond, not exceeding twenty or thirty years, expecting that when it matures, instead of selling on a five or five and a half per cent basis, its bonds will sell to yield four or four and a half per cent. It can then sell a new issue at a higher price and retire the bonds originally issued. In order to provide for refunding the bonds at lower rates of interest, should the opportunity offer, provision is frequently made in recent mortgages for retiring the entire issue at a premium often of five per cent, a premium low enough not to prove burdensome to a company wishing to pay off a six-per-cent loan by making another loan at five per cent, and yet a premium which amply compensates the holder of the six-per-cent bonds for any inconvenience he may suffer because he is forced to change his investment.

Our next question concerns the rate of interest to be fixed on the bonds. Corporations engaged in different enterprises pay different rates of interest, depending upon what investors in that particular class of bonds are accustomed to receive. The rate of interest also varies, to some extent, with the location of the enterprise. Certain conventional rates of interest may be indicated, varying with the class of enterprise in which the corporation is engaged. Railroad companies can usually borrow on first mortgage security at four to four and one half per cent. Public service corporations pay four and a half to five per cent; bonds of manufacturing, mining, lumber companies, etc., six per cent.[1] The explanation of these differences we find in the varying demand for different classes of bonds. The investor prefers railroad bonds since, as a class, these give him the best security. When corporations engaged in enterprises which, from the standpoint of stability and security are, in the minds of the investor, inferior to the railway industry, apply for funds, the demand for their bonds is weaker than the demand for railroad bonds, and a higher rate of interest must be paid.

A new enterprise must, as a rule, either sell its bonds at a discount or give a bonus in stock. Take, for example, an industrial corporation which has excellent prospects, and to which the creditor is willing to lend money. The company wishes to borrow at six per cent, and approaches a representative of the investor for a loan. The answer is that money can be loaned on security of this class to established companies with a record of earnings, interest payments, and

[1] Many exceptions can be found to these percentages. They indicate, however, the approximate differences in interest rates on bonds issued by different classes of enterprises.

dividends, and that if the new company wishes funds it must offer suitable inducements. These inducements can take various forms. A higher interest rate might be suggested, but this would create an unfavorable impression as to the security which the company offered.

Another method is to offer the bonds at a discount, which is equivalent to placing a higher rate of interest upon them. A six-per-cent bond, for example, which might be sold at par by an established company, might be offered by a new company at 80. This is equivalent to paying a higher rate of interest than six per cent. The corporation sells to the investor for $800 the right to receive six per cent on $1,000, and the further right, at the end of thirty years, to be repaid $1,000. In selling bonds at a discount a corporation is not merely paying six per cent for the money which it receives, but is also obligating itself to pay back a larger amount than it received. The sale of bonds at a discount is, therefore, less advantageous from the standpoint of the company than to offer the investor a higher rate of interest, although in practice it is more often resorted to.

To illustrate, leaving out of consideration the question of compound interest, suppose a corporation has the alternative of selling its bonds bearing eight per cent interest at par or selling a six per cent at 80. The bond in each case is to be repaid at the end of twenty years. In the first case the corporation receives $1,000 down, makes twenty payments of $80 each and repays $1,000 to the creditor. The interest cost is therefore $1,600, or $1.60 in interest for every dollar received for the bond. If, however, the corporation sells the six-per-cent bond at 80, it receives $800 in return for a promise to pay back $1,000 at the end of twenty years, and the obligation to pay $60 a year during that time. The $800 will cost the corporation $1,200 in interest, and $200 at the end of the period, being the difference between the amount of money received for this bond and the amount which must be paid back for its redemption, a total of $1,400. If this plan is adopted, for each dollar the corporation receives, it will pay in interest on the bond $1.75, fifteen cents per dollar more than if the eight-per-cent interest had been paid.

It is unusual, however, to find corporations paying more than the conventional rates of interest. The sale of bonds at a discount is more common. The reason is that investors grow suspicious when unusual rates of interest are offered, while they will very gladly buy bonds at a discount which represent, on their face, a moderate rate to the corporation.

Another method, less frequently employed than before the days of careful regulation of capital issues, in selling the bonds of a new company, is to make the creditor, in a sense, a partner in the concern, by giving him with his bond one or more shares of stock, and selling him the bond at or near par. In this way, the corporation receives a larger amount of money, and the creditor is admitted to share in the profits of the concern, a fact which may reconcile him to advancing money to new enterprises at no greater rates of interest than he could obtain from established corporations. The estimates of the earning power of the new company are usually so liberal as to permit a sufficiently large issue of stock to pay the bonus on bond sales, and still leave an ample supply in the hands of the projectors of the enterprise. As we shall see, however, in a later chapter, stock so issued does not often represent much value to the ultimate owner, to whom the purchaser of the bonds usually makes haste to sell his stock bonus.

CHAPTER VII

PROVISION FOR THE REPAYMENT OF BONDS

THE corporation bond is a promissory note. It differs from a bank loan only in the fact that it matures in twenty, fifty, or one hundred years, instead of in three months. When a promissory note matures, it must be paid, either in money or by a new note. With short-time obligations, such as are given in exchange for bank loans, payment of a substantial part if not all the debt is expected. With corporation bonds, however, the custom is to continue the debt indefinitely, exchanging new bonds for maturing bonds, keeping the security intact, and if possible improving it. If any holder of a bond at its maturity wishes cash for his obligation, the money is obtained by selling new bonds to other investors.

The reasons for this practice of refunding instead of paying corporate debts, lie in the relation of the bondholder to the corporation. Bonds are sold to investors who wish to secure a return on their money, with the guarantee that the principal sum will also be secured. These investments are regarded as permanent. The investor does not often desire the return of his money. He wishes the continuance of interest payments. If the principal of his bond is paid at maturity, he is obliged to look about for some other equally satisfactory investment, and this, at the time, it may be hard to find. The investor may wish to convert his bonds into cash at any time. As long as the interest is paid and the security is maintained, he can easily find a market for his bond, usually at a price equal to or greater than the price he paid, with some other investor who is looking for a secured income. So, when its bonds mature, it is not difficult for the corporation to offer a new issue to take the place of maturing bonds, and secured by a first lien upon the same property. Those of the old holders who desire to continue the investment may take the new bonds, while the means of redeeming those bonds whose holders want their money can be obtained by selling the equivalent in the new bonds to new investors. While the conditions of security are met, the bondholder is indifferent to the repayment of his principal. At maturity, or before maturity if he desires, he can obtain his money. The bond investor is one who contributes capital to a company in return for a fixed and secured amount of its earnings. All that he asks of the corporation is that this income and the security of his principal shall not be jeopardized.

The repayment of bonds at maturity is also opposed to the interest of the corporation. The method by which provision for repayment can be made is to accumulate a fund against the date of maturity of the bonds. This fund must be in cash or securities. In either form the return to the corporation which has deposited money in the bank, or has purchased bonds to make provision for the repayment of its debt, is less than the company could earn on the same amount by investing it in its business. The argument against accumulating a fund for the repayment of debt is similar to the argument for incurring the debt in the first place. If a company can make ten per cent on its investment it can safely sell bonds bearing five per cent interest. If, therefore, it is wise to incur an obligation to pay $1,000 in interest on a twenty-year bond, and also to agree to repay the principal at maturity in return for $1,000 in cash paid to the corporation, because ten per cent can be earned on the $1,000, it is wise to invest $50 per year in the business of the company on which a return of ten per cent can be made, rather than to put this $50 in the bank or in securities yielding not more than five per cent, in order to accumulate $1,000 to take up the twenty-year bonds at maturity. If the corporation has money which it can set aside for the purpose of redeeming its debt, it should let the debt run and invest this money in extending its business. By taking the second course, it increases the value of its property and the security of its bonds, and when its bonds mature, it will have small difficulty in issuing a new set of bonds, either to exchange for the maturing bonds, or to sell for the amount necessary to redeem them.

While the building up of sinking funds is usually unwise, there are exceptions to the rule. The first class of companies which should maintain sinking funds are those whose bonds are secured by a mortgage on property which is exhausted by the operations of the business. A railroad property may be expected to last forever. It is true that repairs and replacements are always going on, paid for out of earnings, and charged to operating expenses or depreciation. The property is, however, preserved by these outlays. At the end of the term of the bonds, their security is generally much larger, as a result of the expenditures upon its replacement and repair. When, however, bonds are secured by a mortgage on seams of coal or on standing timber, or on land which is to be broken up into small tracts and sold, the security of the bonds is exhausted by the operations of the business. Every ton of coal mined and sold, every thousand feet of timber cut down and sent to market, lessens by just so much the security of the bonds which have been issued on this property. When bonds are issued by companies operating in such industries, special provision must be made out of earnings for paying the bonds, either by installments or when they mature. The company must preserve the relation between its debt and the security for that debt, either by reducing the amount of the debt, as the value of the security falls, or by replacing the coal or lumber sold, by other property purchased out of its income.

The nature of sinking funds against bonds secured by

so-called "wasting" assets is seen in the following statement of the safeguards of bonds offered by a lumber company:

> The mortgage requires the deposit with the trustee of $5 per 1,000 feet, mill run, on all timber cut. It also requires the company to cut and manufacture exclusively from 15,920 acres containing 146,000,000 feet of timber, holding the remaining 38,000 acres, containing 232,000,000 feet, as a reserve, which cannot be cut during the life of this mortgage. This sinking fund should retire over $500,000 of this loan before maturity; the unpaid balance $300,000 will then have for security the remaining 38,000 acres.

Similar plans of keeping up the sinking fund are usually followed by all companies of this character. A coal mining company will set aside three or five cents for each ton mined to make good the loss in its coal. A land company will make certain payments for each acre sold, into the hands of a trustee.

Sinking funds are also needful when bonds are issued by companies whose business is not plainly of an enduring character. Railroad bonds carry no sinking funds. The bonds secured by companies operating interurban electric lines, although shorter in term than steam railroad bonds, offer this safeguard in addition to the mortgage. Certain classes of power companies, real estate companies, and manufacturing companies can usually offer to the investor no positive assurance that thirty years from the time he buys their bonds the original value of his property will be intact, and their business will be prosperous. Such companies, in order to sell their bonds, must provide for payments to a trustee from their annual earnings of an amount sufficient to pay all or the greater part of their mortgage debts at maturity.

Sinking funds are divided into two classes: first, where the company makes annual payments to a trustee; and the second where the company issues its bonds under the serial plan so that a certain part of the principal matures each year until the entire amount is repaid within the term named in the mortgage. When the first plan is adopted the question arises, What shall the trustee do with the money which is paid to him? Several methods of disposing of these funds are available. The mortgage securing the bonds of the Cudahy Packing Company provides that an annual cash sinking fund of $200,000, beginning November 1, 1910, shall be paid to the trustee, and shall be applied to the purchase and cancellation of these bonds at a price not exceeding 102½ and accrued interest; or, if not so purchasable, by drawing by lot at that price. The mortgage securing the first mortgage bonds of the National Enameling and Stamping Company provides that the bonds will be redeemable at 105 by annual drawings by the trustee over a period of twenty years by means of an annual sinking fund of $100,000, to which will be added the interest to be paid from time to time on the redeemed bonds. We have here the two methods usually employed in the expenditure of the money paid into the sinking fund to reduce a company's debt: (1) A trustee can by previous arrangement select at intervals, usually by lot, a certain number of bonds and call these in at a fixed price, paying, for example, $1,050 for a $1,000 bond; (2) he can purchase bonds in the open market.

The method of drawing bonds by lot for retirement at a fixed price is objectionable to the investor because he must be on the lookout for the announcement of the drawing of bonds for retirement, and frequently be put to the trouble of finding another investment for the money which the corporation may at any time return to him. These drawings of bonds, however, are often for payment at a good premium over the price paid, and this premium offsets any trouble to which the investor may be put because a part of his bonds are paid to him before maturity.

The plan of purchasing bonds in the open market is, from the investor's standpoint, better than the method of drawing bonds. The bond market is less active than the stock market. Bonds are usually bought for permanent investment. They come on the market but seldom as compared with stocks, and in smaller amounts. The taking of this small floating supply, by the purchases of the sinking fund trustee, operates to maintain a market price higher than could be had without such a regular demand. From the standpoint of the corporation, however, aside from the fact that the buyers of these bonds are apt to be well satisfied with their investment, and open to new offerings of the same kind, if the company must retire a certain par value of the bonds in each year by purchasing at the market price, it may sometimes suffer a loss, because of the artificially high price resulting from the trustee's purchases.

This objection is met in the later mortgages by provisions similar to those given above, whereby the trustee is obliged to spend $200,000 or $300,000 each year in the purchase of bonds in the open market if these can be had at or below a certain price—say 105 or 106. If enough bonds are not forthcoming at this price, then the trustee may draw a sufficient number of bonds at the price stated in the mortgage to expend the money in the sinking fund. This provision tends to keep down the market price to the figure at which the bonds can be drawn.

A second alternative might be offered to the trustee in case he was not able to buy bonds at the price named in the mortgage. He might be allowed to buy other securities with the sinking fund. Some of the Burlington sinking fund mortgages contain this provision. This method, however, brings into the sinking fund an element of chance. The bonds bought for the sinking fund may rise in price, in which case the security of the bondholders will improve, or their price may fall, and the objects of the sinking fund, to the amount of the fall, will not be achieved. If bonds are bought at par for the sinking fund, to offset a debt when it comes due, and if in the meantime the price of the bonds falls to 90, the sinking fund lacks ten per cent of the sum needed to pay the bonds. It is better, if any bonds are to be bought for the sinking fund, that they should be the bonds of the company which is building up the fund, so that the reduction of its debt may be certain.

A better method of using money in the sinking fund has been provided in recent mortgages. This is to invest the fund, either by absolute arrangement, or in case the trustee fails to buy bonds at a reasonable price, in improvements and additions. An example of this method is furnished by the following extract from the trust indenture securing the first mortgage bonds of the San Diego Consolidated Gas and Electric Company:

> ARTICLE THREE. Section 1. The company covenants and agrees that it will deposit with the Harris Trust and Savings Bank, Trustee, in a Depreciation and Renewal Fund the following amounts annually: On the first day of June in each of the years 1910 to 1914, inclusive, a sum equal to three per cent (3%), and on the first day of June in each of the years 1915 to 1938, inclusive, a sum equal to five per cent (5%) of the amount, in par value, of bonds outstanding hereunder on the first day of October next preceding each such respective deposit.
>
> Section 2. The Depreciation and Renewal Fund shall be held by the Harris Trust and Savings Bank, Trustee, as a special trust fund, and the company shall be entitled to withdraw therefrom, upon certificates satisfactory to said Trustee, the aggregate amount of the actual and reasonable cash expenditures made by the company subsequent to April 1, 1909, for renewals and replacements of its plant, properties, and equipment now owned or hereafter acquired, exclusive of customary expenditures for current repairs and current maintenance ordinarily chargeable to operating expenses.
>
> Section 3. At the option of the company any part of said Depreciation and Renewal Fund may be withdrawn, upon certificates to the Harris Trust and Savings Bank, Trusteė, to reimburse the company (a) for its actual and reasonable cash expenditures for permanent extensions and additions of and to its plants, properties, and equipment . . . provided such expenditures shall not have been previously made

> the basis for the issuance of bonds hereby secured; or (b) for its expenditures made in the purchase or redemption of bonds hereby secured at a price not exceeding par, accrued interest, and a premium of five per cent upon the principal thereof.

Here is a sinking fund provision, under another name, which gives the company the option of either buying its bonds at 105 and accrued interest, or of spending a certain amount upon its plant. When the business of the borrowing company is secure, as in this case, and if the trustee is vigilant in supervising the expenditure of the sinking fund, the security of the bonds can be conserved by the investment of the sinking fund on the improvement of the property. The value of the security will be increased at a more rapid rate under this method than the rate at which the liabilities of the company will be decreased by its purchases of its own bonds. This method does not apply to companies with wasting assets or to those whose future is uncertain.

The methods of disposing of bonds bought by the trustee for the sinking fund are as follows: (1) they may be canceled as purchased and delivered by the trustee to the company—the usual plan; (2) they may be kept in the sinking fund as an obligation of the company, and the interest paid into the sinking fund as an addition to the regular sinking fund appropriations—the retirement of the bonds proceeding at an increasing rate because of the addition of the interest on the bonds in the sinking fund to the appropriations from income for the benefit of the fund; and (3) the bonds held in the sinking fund may be sold for the benefit of the company.

The use of the third method is shown by the trust indenture of the San Diego Consolidated Gas and Electric Company, already referred to, which states that "said trustee upon the written request of the company shall hold uncanceled in said Depreciation and Renewal Fund any bonds so purchased, and the company may with the approval of said trustee sell any or all such bonds so held, in which case the proceeds from the sale thereof shall be held and applied according to the provisions of this Article." This method of disposing of bonds in the sinking fund is available only for companies whose assets and business are permanent.

A method of managing sinking funds which is as yet little used is that of the serial bond. This plan has been followed by several leading bond houses who have sold large amounts of serial bonds, largely because they have been able, by employing the method of issuing bonds in series, to sell high interest bonds of mining, lumber, and manufacturing companies, where the security, without the protection of serial payment, would be too small. Friends of the serial bond plan claim that "a safe margin of security on a bond issue at the time of its sale is by no means a guaranty that the same margin will exist during the life of the bond. Physical depreciation, changes in industrial conditions, changes in tariff, and transportation rates—any one of a large number of causes may impair the security, and the chances of business may impair the security of the bonds. The serial plan protects the investor against these accidents. Under this plan, a portion of the principal is paid off each year and no portion of the security released. The payments are graded according to the net earnings of the property, but are considerably larger than ordinary sinking fund payments. At each anniversary, upon payment of this installment of principal, the margin of security automatically rises." It is also claimed that the borrowing company, by the operation of the plan, is encouraged to keep the income from the property in the business in order to meet the annual installments. "He also finds it to his own advantage to maintain his property at a high standard. As his own capital invested in the property increases, there is an unconscious influence which tends toward promptness in meeting interest payments, taxes, and other charges." [1]

[1] It is fair to Peabody, Houghteling & Co., from one of whose circulars this quotation is taken, to state that in offering so-called low-grade bonds, bearing high rates of interest, they not only insist upon

The serial bond plan has this advantage from the standpoint of the bond house, that it is able to sell the bonds maturing at an early date on much the same terms as commercial paper is sold, or short term notes of corporations, to financial institutions with surplus funds for short time investment. It is possible, in this way, it is claimed, to obtain a much broader market and readier sale for serial bonds than for long maturities. The objection to the serial bond plan from the company's standpoint is that its entire surplus income is likely to be absorbed in paying off its debt and the stockholder will receive nothing. It is evidently an exaggerated sinking fund which aims to absorb most of the available revenue of the property in the extinction of its debt.

---

the serial plan of issue but also require that the owners should have invested a substantial amount in the property, seldom undertaking to purchase a sufficient amount of bonds to provide for the entire construction of the property.

CHAPTER VIII

THE ISSUE OF STOCK

WHENEVER possible, for reasons which we have already given, the promoters of a new corporation will include a bond issue in their plan of capitalization in order to secure for themselves or their successors a larger dividend per share than could be received if stock were used to obtain the necessary funds. Certain kinds of industries, however, do not furnish a satisfactory basis for a bond issue, at least until their success has been well established, and then only to a moderate proportion of the value of their assets. The bonds of the class of companies known as industrials including manufacturing, mining, and trading companies and also, under some classifications, companies engaged in the sale of gas and electric power, are seriously restricted at the outset in their issue of bonds as a means of obtaining funds. The bond buyer surrenders all chance of participation in the increased earnings of a company in exchange for the guarantee of a fixed rate of return upon his investment. If this guarantee is doubtful, the security of the investment is discounted in the price of the bonds, if indeed these can be sold at any price. The bonds of industrial corporations, especially manufacturing companies, are unpopular with investors for reasons which have already been indicated in some detail. Companies operating in these industries can issue bonds to a limited amount, and under special safeguards, only after their business has been well established. At the outset, however, this form of security is not usually available to them.

The use of bonds in the plan of capitalizing a new company to be formed by the consolidation of previously existing corporations, is especially unpopular. The owners of these constituent companies are not likely to consent to have the properties which they turn in to the new company subjected to the lien of a mortgage to secure bonds to be sold to the general investor. They will insist that most of these bonds shall be directly issued in exchange for their property, leaving only a small amount to be sold. Furthermore, the issuing of bonds materially lessens the value of the stocks of the new company, out of which promoters and bankers are to get their profits. Especially do stock values suffer if bonds are issued to a substantial proportion of the value of the plants of the constituent companies. In the formation of the industrial combinations, bonds were very little employed. The chief exception was the United States Steel Corporation, where Mr. Andrew Carnegie was in a position to exact hard terms from the promoters, and received for himself and associates $300,000,000 of first mortgage bonds. In most cases the promoters of these enterprises went to considerable trouble to pay off all the debts, both funded and unsecured, for which the various constituent companies were responsible, because they considered it of the utmost importance, in view of the necessity of appealing to the public to buy the stocks of these companies, that the dividends on these stocks should not be jeopardized by the claims of bondholders.

When bonds cannot be issued, either because the industry does not furnish adequate security for a bond issue, or because of the necessity of presenting an attractive stock proposition to the investor, the promoter, in formulating his financial plan, falls back upon the issue of preferred stock. Most of the preferred stocks dealt in on the public exchanges, and now outstanding as original issues, were put out by the industrial combinations. There are numerous issues of preferred stocks by railroads but most of these were put out in connection with reorganizations, in exchange for bonds whose interest could not, at the time, be earned. Preferred stock has been little used as original issues by promoters of railroad companies. Preferred stock has been quite largely used by public service corporations, but most of these issues are not dealt in on the exchanges. We shall find the methods employed in the original issue of preferred stock best illustrated in the practice of the trusts.

The *Railway and Industrial Supplement* published quarterly by the *Commercial and Financial Chronicle* gives a total of 101 important issues of preferred stocks by industrial companies, most of them consolidations. Most of this stock was given in exchange for the stocks or property of enterprises which entered the consolidations. In nearly every case preferred stock was also sold for cash to equip the new company with working capital, or to provide funds for the payment of owners or stockholders who would not accept stock in the new company. An examination of the list of preferred stock issues shows certain salient facts which may be taken as typical of this kind of security.

In most cases preferred stock is made cumulative as to dividends. Cumulative preferred stock gives to its holders a claim on earnings which is, in some respects, similar to that conferred by the possession of mortgage bonds. All unpaid dividends on such stocks must be paid before the common stock can receive any share of profits. Just as unpaid interest accumulates to the disadvantage of junior securities, so the preferred stockholder can assert his prior claim to profits, as against the common stockholder, up to the amount represented by the rate of dividends on the number of shares which he holds, times the number of years the stock has been in existence. If the profits are only sufficient to pay seven per cent on the par value of the preferred stock, if that is the rate named in the contract between the stockholder and the corporation, and in case the directors decide to distribute these profits, the holder of cumulative preferred stock will receive seven per cent, while the common stockholder will receive nothing.

Unless the cumulative feature is inserted, however, the advantage of the preferred stockholder over the common stockholder is more apparent than real. If preferred stock is noncumulative, the finances of the company may be so administered as to place the preferred and the common stockholder on a footing of exact equality. The corporation always needs money for improvements and extensions, and the directors may find a variety of excellent reasons for refusing to pay dividends on the preferred stock until the company is strong enough to begin paying both preferred and common stock dividends at the same time. Any money which may be reserved for the preferred stockholder and invested in the business will accrue, in part at least, to the benefit of the common stockholder, and the temptation is strong under these circumstances to sacrifice the preferred stockholder. If, however, the preferred stock is made cumulative, and if the earnings permit, the preferred dividends must be paid. They would otherwise accumulate against the common stock whose value might be entirely extinguished because of the hopelessness that the company would ever be able to discharge the arrears of accumulated preferred dividends.

The existence of the cumulative feature in the preferred stocks of the industrial combinations explains the persistence with which their directors have adhered to a liberal dividend policy, even in the face of depression when prudent management would seem to demand that the resources of the company be conserved. Even with weak companies of this class, plainly in need of capital for improvements, the practice of paying preferred dividends has been almost universal. The directors might, to the great physical benefit of the corporations themselves, have allowed these preferred claims to accumulate to any extent. They might have invested the money in improvements, piling up a large surplus over their liabilities. Such a policy, if continued for a number of years, would have placed the preferred stocks of everyone of these companies in a position where their dividends could be paid without question, no matter what the condition of trade. The payment of dividends upon the common stock, under such a policy would, however, have been placed permanently out of the question. In five years, with seven per cent cumulative preferred ahead of it on which no dividends were paid, the common stock would have been buried under thirty-five per cent of unpaid preferred dividends. These back dividends, in most cases, even under the most favorable circumstances, with the liberal capitalization of the industrials, could not be paid off while, at the same time, the regular dividend on the preferred was being maintained, in less than five years more. A policy of investing profits in improvements at the expense of the cumulative preferred stockholder, means that the common stockholder must, in the usual run of events, be kept out of any dividends for a long time, perhaps until the par value of his stock is reduced.

Such a policy would make the common stock entirely unattractive as a purchase if it were announced at the outset, and after the common stock had once been purchased in good faith on the promise of dividends as soon as they were earned, the directors could not, in fairness, extinguish this value by allowing dividends to accumulate on the preferred stock, no matter how much this course might be demanded by considerations of conservative management. If the failure to pay dividends on the common stock resulted from causes outside of their control, an overestimate of profits or an underestimate of expenses, directors could not be blamed by the common stockholder, but the adoption of a policy of reserving profits for the benefit of the company, although it might be justifiable and even necessary, when only common stock had been issued, the effect of which would be to make the payment of dividends on the common stock only a remote possibility, would have subjected the directors to severe criticism. No matter how necessary the postponement of preferred dividends might be when judged by the standard of investment requirements, so far as concerns the dividends on cumulative preferred stock, this course is usually impossible. If dividends on cumulative preferred stock have been earned in any year, the practice is to pay them.

In a few flotations, an attempt has been made to reconcile the necessity of conservatism in the distribution of profits with the demands of the preferred stockholder that he be insured in a prior claim to dividends, by providing that the cumulative feature shall not begin at once, but that the stock shall be made noncumulative for perhaps three or five years, and that when accumulation begins in the case of a seven-per-cent preferred stock, for example, it shall start with two per cent and increase in an ascending scale. It is difficult to sell preferred stock with such provisions included in the contract with the corporation, since they amount to a plain declaration to whoever buys the stock that the company may not pay him any dividends for perhaps five years, and that, at the end of that time, they may pay him dividends only on the ascending scale of accumulation.

The difficulties in the administration of a company's income account which result from the existence of cumulative preferred stock can only be avoided by limiting the amount originally issued to the principal sum on which the surplus revenues of the company will be sufficient to pay a dividend, while at the same time leaving a balance sufficient for the current requirements of the business, and for a dividend on the common stock within a reasonable time. While this requirement is sound in theory, if we may judge from the practice of American corporations which include cumulative preferred stock as a part of their original plans of capitalization, it is found, in most cases, impracticable.

The rate of dividend established on preferred stocks is usually either six or seven per cent on industrials, and five per cent on public service corporations. Railroad preferred stocks, issued in reorganizations, usually pay four per cent. The varying rates of preference in stocks issued by these different classes of companies represent the relative standing of these investments. In only a few cases, do we find preferred dividends higher than seven per cent. The first preferred stock of the United States Rubber Company and the preferred stock of the Virginia-Carolina Chemical Company pay eight per cent. Out of 101 issues of preferred stocks only fourteen paid over seven per cent. With the scale of capitalization adopted by most companies, involving large issues of cumulative preferred stock, and basing our conclusions on the experience of these companies during the last ten years, a cumulative rate of dividend of seven per cent is, for the average company, too high for the security of common stock. In fixing the high rate of seven per cent, the effect has been in many cases to absorb the surplus earnings which, in reasonable certainty, would be available for the preferred stock, and to leave the common stock only the chances and uncertainties of profits.

Preferred stock may be cumulative not merely as to dividends, but also as to assets. Charters sometimes provide, as does the charter of the American Car & Foundry Company, that the board of directors shall have power, without the assenting vote of the stockholders, to sell, or otherwise dispose of, any or all of the property of the company. When these large powers are given to the board of directors, the following situation may, conceivably, arise: The company may be earning barely enough to pay dividends on the cumulative preferred stock. Perhaps preferred dividends may have been passed for several years, piling up against the common stock, which may, as a result, have but a nominal value. Some outside interest, seeing a chance for a speculative profit may buy up this low-priced common stock, elect a board of directors favorable to his plan, and sell the property of the company. In case such a sale is made, and unless the preferred stock is also given preference in the distribution of assets, the common stock will participate equally with the preferred in the proceeds of the sale, although its market value, based on its prospects of dividends, was small. In order to guard against such a contingency, which, it must be admitted, is somewhat remote, it is not unusual to find preferred stock made cumulative both as to assets as well as dividends. A provision in the certificate of incorporation which gives this preference is worded somewhat as follows: [1]

> In the event of any liquidation or dissolution or winding up (whether voluntary or otherwise) of the corporation, then, before any amount shall be paid to the holders of common stock, the holders of preferred stock shall be entitled to be paid in full for the par amount of their shares, and in addition thereto all arrears of dividends—that is to say, an amount sufficient, with the dividends actually paid, to make seven per cent for each year; and after the payment to the holders of the preferred stock of such par value and arrears of dividends, the remaining assets and funds shall be divided and paid to the holders of common stock, pro rata, according to their respective shares.

Out of the issues already referred to, thirty-seven have these provisions. The dissolution of corporations almost always follows bankruptcy proceedings which result in the sale of all the property for the benefit of creditors, and the preference as to assets given to the preferred stockholder can hardly be regarded as a practical safeguard. The end desired, namely, the protection of the preferred stockholder against speculative dissolution of the company can be as well attained by providing that the directors may not dispose of the property of the company without the consent of two thirds or three fourths of both classes of stock. Such a provision does not discredit the common stock, while the provision that the preferred stock shall be cumulative as to assets as well as to dividends is apt, if the common stockholder looks into it, to dishearten him.

It is the danger of bankruptcy against which the preferred stockholder is particularly interested to guard by limiting the ability of the directors to incur mortgage indebtedness. He accomplishes this by a provision, similar to the following, inserted in the certificate of incorporation where

---

[1] Extract from the Amended Certificate of the International Harvester Company.

preferred stock is issued, taken from the articles of incorporation of the Crucible Steel Company:

> The corporation shall not mortgage any property except by purchase-money mortgage, without the written assent, or pursuant to the affirmative vote in person or by proxy, at any meeting called in accordance with the by-laws, of the holders of at least two thirds of its preferred stock then issued and outstanding.

The preferred stockholder may not be satisfied with preference in dividends and assets. He may also demand the right to participate with the common stockholder in distributed profits after his preferred dividends have been paid. When such participation is allowed, it is usual to provide for a certain dividend upon the common stock, say six or seven per cent, and that the preferred stock shall thereafter share with the common on some agreed basis. The Associated Merchants Company, for example, agrees that for every one per cent dividend paid in excess of seven per cent one half of one per cent is to go to the preferred stock. Such a provision is unusual. Out of the list under examination we find only three preferred stocks which are made participating.

Another method of allowing preferred stock the benefit of cumulative preference in dividends, combined with a large share in contingent profits, is to make the preferred stock convertible into common stock on an agreed basis, usually at par. The Associated Merchants Company and the Domonion Coal Company are, however, the only examples in the list above referred to where this privilege has been given. The position of the holder of cumulative six- or seven-per-cent stock, issued on a liberal scale, is far superior to that of the common stock, and the chances that conversion would have proved advantageous are so remote as to render the inducement of the privilege of converting into common stock of little value to an intending purchaser of preferred stock. The inclusion of this feature, moreover, would make the common stock less attractive to the investor, since it is already subjected to the serious handicap of a high cumulative dividend.

In original issues of preferred stock, special voting powers may be given to this security. The first preferred stock of the Rock Island Company, for example, elects a majority of the board of directors. It is unusual to find this provision. The rule is that preferred and common stock, when both are issued at the same time, have equal voting power. A wholesome provision for the protection of the preferred stockholder is that the common stock shall forfeit its vote whenever preferred dividends remain unpaid for the space of a year. A variety of other safeguards and restrictions upon the corporation issuing preferred stock are used but not, as a rule, with original issues. They will be taken up in detail in a later chapter.

Common stock is a feature of every financial plan. When no public flotation is expected, the amount of common stock is a matter of no consequence. It usually represents the controlling interest, and is sometimes placed at a nominal figure. In public flotations, however, common stock is usually issued to capitalize anticipated earnings. It is supposed to represent the future profits of the property. The industrial trusts, for example, issued preferred stock for the value of the separate companies before consolidation. The common stock was supposed to express the economies and profits accomplished by the consolidation, as well as those arising out of the natural growth of the business. Common stock is usually sold at a low figure, liberal representations concerning anticipated earnings being made to influence its purchase. These representations are not often realized.

The practical limit of the amount of common stock issued by a majority of the companies has been the amount of stock from which the largest amount of net returns over expenses could be realized by those into whose hands the stock came in exchange for property sold to the company. For example, if \$5,000,000 could be sold at eighty, and \$15,000,000 could be sold at forty, the second figure will be the one selected. The money value of stock sold to the public increases at a more rapid rate than the increase in the amount of stock offered. It might seem that since the common stock represents the entire value of the company over the claims of the bondholders and the preferred stockholder, it would be a matter of indifference to the market value of the stock whether it be fixed at $5,000 or $5,000,000. Such, however, is not the case. To the mind of the average buyer of stock, the figures printed on the face of the certificate convey a pecuniary suggestion, an idea of actual value. The more of these certificates that are issued, up to the point where it becomes apparent that the company will never be able to pay dividends on its stock, the larger will be the amount of money for which they can be sold. This fact explains the excessive capitalization of corporations whose stock is to be offered to the public. Up to the present time, no effective means has been devised to check this practice, save in a few states which control the security issues of public service corporations.

In conservative flotations, where it is not intended to immediately dispose of the common stock, and where those who sell their property to the corporation expect to retain control for a considerable time, holding their stock as an investment, a different standard is adopted. By such companies, the amount of common stock is fixed at a figure on which dividends, after a few years of successful operation of the company, can probably be paid. Common stock is frequently given to engineers who may be put in charge of a property during its early stages, with a view to increasing their diligence. It may also be given to banks and trust companies as a bonus for the loans which they make a new company. If the amount of stock issued was excessive and out of all reason, as it has been in the case of many large public flotations, there would be no purpose in holding it. Indeed, the desire would be to dispose of it as soon as possible. With a conservative capitalization, however, it is frequently possible to make more money by retaining the stock than by immediately selling it. Corporations promoted by established banking houses are also conservative in their common stock capitalization. These bankers have a reputation to maintain which is indeed their chief asset. They cannot afford to risk a flotation with whose bad results they may at some future time be reproached by some of those whom they may have victimized.

As a general proposition, if a corporation pays four per cent on its common stock after five years' operation, its common stock capitalization must be regarded as conservative. It is unreasonable to expect common dividends at once or before an adequate reserve of earnings has been established, but within five years, if the business of the company is sound, if it is properly managed, and with normal conditions of demand, it should pay four per cent on its common stock.

NOTE—I have designedly omitted all discussion of the question of over-capitalization. This is a point still in controversy, and likely to be unsettled for several years. In a text book, its discussion would be unprofitable. In order to avoid the suspicion of shirking a vital issue, I may state, as my own opinion, that irrespective of the merits of this method of settlement, the final solution of the problem will be found in a limitation of security issues, especially by public service corporations, to the cash cost or fair value of property constructed or purchased. This fair value will be, moreover, determined not by the directors of the purchasing company but by some disinterested public authority. In my opinion, this method of restricting security issues which are to be sold to the public, would not interfere with the development of any legitimate enterprise, and would operate to increase the security of investments.

CHAPTER IX

METHODS OF PAYING FOR STOCK

WE take up next the methods of paying for stock. We shall first consider the cases in which the stock is paid for in whole or in part by cash. Stock sold bv the corporation for cash is of two classes, assessable or full paid, according as the payment is full or partial. Full paid stock may be paid for at one time or in installments. When stock is issued for work of construction, such as the building of a new line of railroad or the erection of a mill, the company's payments are protracted over a considerable period. There is no purpose, therefore, in securing the full amount of the subscription at one time. The money is arranged to be paid as it is needed, the payments sometimes being extended over a year or even longer. The practice in such cases is not to pay dividends on the new stock until the entire amount has been paid up, but to allow the subscribers interest on their installments as these are paid into the treasury of the corporation.

Assessable stock is of a different character. Here the payment is made in cash and in promises to pay cash. The subscription to $10,000 of stock, par value $100, "ten per cent paid," will be $1,000 in cash, and $9,000 in a promise to pay that amount when called for by the board of directors. The advantages of this form of stock, viewed from the standpoint of the corporation, are considerable. In the first place, the issue of assessable stock makes it possible for a company embarking in a new enterprise to guard against underestimates of the cost of construction. If, for example, an interurban railroad is estimated to cost $500,000, and subscriptions to

$500,000 are secured, and supposing, as frequently happens, that the cost is raised by unforeseen circumstances to $750,-000, it then becomes necessary for the officers of the company to apply to the stockholders for additional subscriptions which they can usually obtain only by issuing preferred stock which may not have been contemplated in the original plan. Under such circumstances, however, it is practically impossible to persuade stockholders to subscribe to an additional amount of common stock. They are apt to lose confidence in the managers of the enterprise whom they hold responsible for the mistakes in the estimates of construction cost, and may even oust the directors from office and put in a new control. The writer once heard a banker who had been interested in promoting an iron furnace enterprise in Eastern Pennsylvania, say that it was easier to procure $2,000,000 at the outset than to secure $200,000 after $1,000,000 had been represented as all that would be necessary. If the method of assessable stock is adopted, stock can be issued to the amount of $1,000,-000, with an understanding, which is not, of course, a part of the subscription contract, that only $500,000 need be called. If, then, it is found necessary to call $250,000 more, this can be secured without difficulty since the stockholders will not wish to see their original investment forfeited by a sale of their stock by the company to pay up the assessment.

Assessable stock can also be issued to capitalize future profits when it is not deemed prudent to pay too large a dividend. If a street railway consolidation requires $15,000,-000 cash, and if public sentiment will not tolerate more than six per cent in dividends on the stock of a public service corporation, it may be possible to capitalize the new enterprise at $45,000,000, calling one third of the amount and allowing the balance to stand as a liability of the stockholder. If the earnings of the company warrant, the six per cent dividend can be paid on $45,000,000 which in reality is eighteen per cent on the amount paid in. While this method has been occasionally employed, however, it cannot be considered as a general practice among public corporations.

Assessable stock is not a popular form of security. The unpaid portion of such stock operates to depress its value. Investors can never be certain when the directors will call assessments. When a call is made, those holders who are unable to respond must throw a portion of their stock on the market to obtain sufficient funds to pay the assessments on the remainder. These sales not only make the value of partly paid shares irregular, but open the way to unscrupulous directors to enrich themselves at the expense of the stockholders by buying the stock on the decline and selling at the advance which, since the real value of the stock has been increased by the assessment, is likely to follow its payment.

The investor has a rooted objection to purchasing assessable stock because of the uncertainty as to the amount he will be called upon to pay, and because of a well grounded distrust of the danger of manipulation by directors who are in a position to control the times and amounts of the calls. When stock, therefore, is to be sold to investors, it is necessary to make it full paid. This can be done, either by paying for the stock in cash, or by issuing it in exchange for property or services. The only way in which promoters can make a profit on stock which has been paid up in cash is to sell this stock at a premium. Since we are dealing here, it will be remembered, with new enterprises, whose earning power is yet to be demonstrated, and which must offer inducements to investors to secure funds, this method is impossible, at least in the United States. In Germany, where the law forbids the stock of any new enterprise to be listed for sale until the company has been in operation for a year, and where the amount of capital is strictly limited, it frequently happens that a large premium can be secured, and a considerable profit realized. In Great Britain, where founder's shares, entitling their holder to a disproportionately large share of profits are used to compensate promoters, these shares frequently sell at a high premium. In the United States, however, where the law allows listing at once, and founder's shares are not as yet employed, the risks of new enterprises are so great and the demand for banker's capital so heavy, that very little time is allowed to elapse between the completion of the construction or consolidation and the sale of its securities. This unwillingness of the investor to buy securities of new enterprises, except on very favorable terms, extends to its bonds. To sell bonds, it is sometimes necessary to give a bonus in stock from which the corporation will receive no cash whatever. This stock, to be attractive to the investor, must be full paid.

From these several considerations, it is evident that some method must be devised of making stock full paid, which will not require the payment of its par value in cash. This method is the issuing of stock for property or services. The laws of every State permit the directors of corporations to purchase such property as it may need by issuing its stock. Corporations are also allowed to make contracts for construction work, payment for which is to be made in bonds and stocks. One of the most liberal statutes permitting the purchase of property with stock is that of New Jersey. Section 49 of the General Corporation Act of New Jersey is as follows:

> Any corporation formed under this act may purchase mines, manufactories, or other property necessary for its business, or the stock of any company or companies owning, mining, manufacturing, or producing materials, or other property necessary for its business, and issue stock to the amount of the value thereof in payment therefor, and the stock so issued shall be full paid stock and not liable to any further call, neither shall the holder thereof be liable for any further payment under any of the provisions of this act; and in the absence of actual fraud in the transaction, the judgment of the directors as to the value of the property purchased shall be conclusive, and in all statements and reports of the corporation to be published or filed this stock shall not be stated or reported as being issued for cash paid to the corporation, but shall be reported in this respect according to the fact.

The New Jersey Corporation Law also authorizes the issuance of stock and bonds for services rendered in the following section:

> Corporations having for their object the building, constructing, or repairing of railroads, water, gas, or electric works, tunnels, bridges, viaducts, canals, hotels, wharves, piers, or any like works of internal improvement or public use or utility, may subscribe for, take, pay for, hold, use, and dispose of stock or bonds in any corporation formed for the purpose of constructing, maintaining, and operating any such public works, and the directors of any such corporation formed for the purpose of constructing, maintaining, and operating any public work of the description aforesaid, may accept in payment of any such subscription, or purchase, real or personal property, necessary for the purpose of such corporation, or work, labor, and services performed or materials furnished to or for such corporations to the amount of the value thereof, and from time to time issue upon any such subscription or purchase, in such installments or proportions as such directors may agree upon, full paid stock in full or partial performance of the whole or any part of such subscription or purchase, and the stock so issued shall be full paid and not liable to any further call.

The method described in this section is that usually followed for making stock full paid. After the corporation is organized, the first meeting of the stockholders held, and the directors elected, a proposition is made to the directors to sell to the corporation certain property—patents, mining property, factory property, railroads or stocks and bonds, for all or part of the securities of the new corporation. The only limit in most States to the amount of bonds which may be issued under these circumstances is the conclusion of the directors as to their need of capital and their ability to sell these bonds. The law does, however, limit the stock "to the judgment of the directors as to the value of the property purchased." As long as this judgment is an honest judgment, and there is no suspicion of fraud in the transaction, it will be held to be final, and cannot be questioned in subsequent proceedings against the corporation.

In fixing a value upon the property purchased, or upon work which is to be done for the company, the directors are not to be limited to the sum for which the property would sell for cash, or to the amount for which the services could be purchased for cash. The payments are not made in cash, but in evidences of debt, and in certificates of rights to participate in profits. The ability of the corporation to pay interest on these bonds is yet to be demonstrated. The profits, in which the holders of these shares of stock are to participate, are yet to be realized. Anyone who transfers property or contracts to perform services for a company, in exchange for securities, has a right to charge a much higher price than if he is to receive cash for his property or services. The corporation, for its part, is warranted in paying a much higher price for property or services expressed in terms of securities. When the vendors or contractors will agree to accept, instead of cash, which the corporation might have great difficulty in securing, its bonds and stock, making it unnecessary for the corporation itself to raise more than a moderate amount of money for working capital, they are entitled to liberal terms. The valuation placed upon property or services by directors is generally accepted by the courts. They will not question the amount of stock to be issued, either in behalf of disgruntled stockholders, or of creditors, unless it appears that the transaction is tainted with fraud.

Practically speaking, the only risk attaching to the overvaluation of property, when purchased with stock, arises in case of the subsequent bankruptcy of the company issuing the stock. If the creditors of the corporation can prove that stock was fraudulently issued, and if they can find this stock in the possession of the original incorporators, or those for whom these incorporators were acting, it has been established that the receiver of the corporation, acting for the creditors, can recover from the subscribers such part of the difference between the par value of the stock which they received for their property, and what the court will regard as a fair value for the property measured in stock, as will make up the difference between the realizable value of the company's assets, and the amount of the creditor's claims. Under these circumstances, the so-called full paid stock of the company, if it has been issued to an excessive amount, is held to be assessable stock, the corporation not having received full value, and those who have received the stock, if it is found in their hands, are liable for the difference between the selling price and the par value of the stock.

The theory of the law under which liability attaches, is that the capital of the corporation takes the place of the individual liability of the partners, so far as the creditors are concerned, and that creditors have the right to assume that the capital of the company has been paid up in full, either with cash, or with property and services taken at a fair value. When, therefore, the company fails, and the creditors are able to prove that the stock was issued for property and services at fictitious and excessive values, it is held that they can recover through the corporation from the original subscribers if they find the stock in their hands. This liability does not attach to innocent holders for value, and it is a question whether the original subscribers may not divest themselves of all liability by transferring their stock on the books of the company.

The purchase of property with stock of a corporation directly from the owner presents no difficulty. When services are to be performed for the company, however, in order to make the stock full paid, it is necessary to interpose between the final purchaser of the stock and the corporation an agency known as the Construction Company, which exchanges its contract for services to be performed for the stock and bonds of the company in whose interest the work is to be done. A construction company is not often what its name implies. As a rule, it does not expect to carry on any work of construction. It has no force of engineers at its disposal.

It expects to let the contracts connected with the work to others. It is merely a device to make stock full paid so that it can be sold to the investor without any liability attaching.

A typical construction company transaction is outlined in the following:

OFFERING OF BONDS AND STOCK
OF
THE DENVER NORTHWESTERN & PACIFIC RAILWAY COMPANY

Payments to be Made in Instalments or at Once at Subscriber's Option.

DENVER, Col., October 21, 1902.

The Colorado-Utah Construction Company has contracted with the Denver Northwestern & Pacific Railway Company to build and equip, approximately, 500 miles of its railroad between Denver, Col., and Salt Lake City, Utah. The contract provides for a substantial roadbed, steel rails eighty pounds per yard, and a modern standard passenger and freight rolling stock equipment. Payments under this contract are to be made in the bonds and stock of the Railway Company which are now offered for subscription.

Under the provisions of the construction contract, there will be issued by the Railway Company to the Construction Company $40,000, and no more, of the first mortgage four-per-cent bonds of the Railway Company and $20,000, par value, of its full paid preferred stock and $20,000, par value, of its full paid common stock for each mile of main track of railroad as it is built, equipped, and turned over to the Railway Company for operation.

The authorized capital stock of the Railway Company is $20,000,000, of which $10,000,000 is five-per-cent noncumulative preferred stock and $10,000,000 is common stock.

The first mortgage of the Railway Company to The Mercantile Trust Company, of New York, provides for an issue of not exceeding $22,500,000 of Fifty-

Year Four-Per-Cent Gold Bonds, of which issue the balance of $2,500,000, remaining after the payments to be made under the construction contract will be held in reserve by the Railway Company.

The Colorado-Utah Construction Company will receive, through its designated depositaries, applications for subscriptions in $1,000, and multiples of $1,000, to the bonds and stock of the Denver Northwestern & Pacific Railway Company above mentioned until November 16, 1902, after which no further applications will be received.

The Colorado-Utah Construction Company reserves the right to scale down or to reject any and all applications.

The terms of the subscription agreement, which is to be signed by the parties whose applications shall be accepted by the undersigned, provide that payment shall be called in as money is required by the Construction Company for the purpose of fulfilling its contract with the Railroad Company, but that in no event shall the subscribers be required to pay more than ten per cent of their subscriptions in any one month; but that each subscriber shall have the option to pay the whole amount subscribed at once. Each subscriber will receive, as provided in the subscription agreement, for each $950 paid:

$1,000 four-per-cent fifty-year First Mortgage Gold Bonds of the Railway Company,

$250 par value of the Non-Cumulative Preferred Stock, and

$250 par value of the Common Stock of the Railway Company.

Until the bonds and stock of the Railway Company are engraved, executed, and received by the Construction Company under the terms of its contract with the Railway Company, the Construction Company will issue to the subscribers, as any payment is made upon their subscriptions, its receipts providing for the payment of interest from the date of such payment at the rate of four per cent per annum until the bonds and stock subscribed for are ready for delivery to the subscribers, subject to adjustment to be made as to any interest then accrued upon such bonds.

The one half of the common and preferred stock of the Railway Company not offered for subscription will be owned by the Construction Company.

. . . . .

The above offer is made upon the terms above stated, subject to advance or withdrawal without notice, and the undersigned recommends the bonds and stock of the Denver Northwestern & Pacific Railway Company as a safe and profitable investment.

THE COLORADO-UTAH CONSTRUCTION COMPANY,
By SYLVESTER T. SMITH, *President.*

The foregoing shows very clearly the service which the construction company performs. The Denver Northwestern & Pacific Railway property, at the time this offer was made, was not yet built. The public was expected to furnish a large part of the funds necessary for the work. Since the enterprise was not yet in being, it was necessary to offer special inducements to the subscribers to the bonds in the shape of bonus in stock. This stock bonus could not be legally offered by the railway company. The construction company was therefore employed to contract with the railroad company to build its line in return for securities. These securities the construction company forthwith offered to the public on the terms set forth in the advertisement.

The above method is not often employed. As a general thing bankers profoundly dislike to handle any other securities than those issued by going concerns. It is usually necessary, therefore, for a considerable amount of capital to be raised by the construction company, with which it margins loans made with financial institutions on the security of the stock and bonds which it receives from the railway company as the work progresses. The following is a detailed description of a typical operation of this character:

A construction company is organized for the purpose of building a line of railroad. The shares of the construction company are offered for subscription to obtain working capital. Simultaneously with the organization of the construction company, a railroad company is incorporated. An agreement is now made between the railroad company and the construction company for the building of a railroad, and for supplying a certain amount of equipment for its operation after completion. The construction company agrees to secure the necessary rights of way, and to construct or procure for the railroad company, upon such routes as it may select for the purpose, a certain line of railroad. It is stipulated that the work to be performed by the construction company shall be in accordance with standard specifications, and under the supervision and control of the chief engineer of the railroad company. The track shall be laid with first quality steel rail, and adequate siding facilities provided for a certain stipulated sum. Mileage, depots, water stations, section houses and all other structures necessary for the proper handling of the business shall also be provided for at such points as the railroad company may designate. Telegraph lines shall be constructed, and the equipment shall be of such a character and capacity as shall be designated by the railroad company. All the contracts for the grading, rails, equipment, and all other necessary work for the completion of the railroad, will be let by the construction company.

For the service performed in constructing the railroad and furnishing a certain amount of equipment, the railroad company agrees to deliver to the construction company its full authorized capital stock at a certain rate per mile of railroad constructed, and also bonds for each mile so constructed. The bonds issued shall be a first lien on the property, and before any shall be delivered by the railroad company to the construction company, the trustee under the mortgage shall be furnished with a certificate certifying to the completed mileage by the chief engineer of the railroad company. The construction company, upon the completion of its contract, becomes the owner of all the stock and bonds of the railroad company, except that stock which was subscribed for at the time of the incorporation of the railroad company, and that necessary for the qualification of the directors.

"A construction company is formed with a capital of $2,500,000. Out of this capital, it purchased mining interests which cost $500,000. In order to develop this operation, a railroad company is formed, and on the strength of the balance of the capital of the construction company, contracts are let and work begins. The mileage to be constructed is 200 miles, on which stock at the rate of $16,500 per mile, and bonds at the same rate can be issued. Each mile of railroad constructed and with the equipment furnished, costs the construction company $18,000 per mile. On a mileage of 200 miles, the cost would be, approximately, $3,600,000.

"Under the terms of the agreement of the construction company with the railroad company, as the work progresses in sections of so many miles, the construction company would be entitled to bonds at $16,500 for each mile so constructed upon delivery of the certificates of the chief engineer of the railroad company certifying to such completed mileage, to the trustee under the mortgage.

"After paying for its coal estate, the construction company's available capital would be $2,000,000. Upon the basis of a cost of $18,000 per mile, with this capital, it can construct approximately 110 miles, under which it would be entitled to receive bonds to the amount of $1,815,000. This would use all the available funds of the construction company. With the bonds thus received (which would be in the form of temporary certificates) it would seek loans from financial sources, pledging these certificates as collateral, on the basis of sixty per cent of their face value. Assuming that the loan can be made with this collateral on this margin, the construction company would obtain funds for the further construction to the extent of $1,089,000, which would complete an additional sixty miles, upon completion of which the construction company would be entitled to receive bonds at the rate of $16,500 per mile, or $990,000 of bonds. To complete the remaining thirty miles under the contract, the construction company would need an additional loan of $540,000, and if the same method of borrowing on the pledged collateral is pursued, it would require $900,000 of the $990,000 bonds received for the former sixty miles completed, which would leave in the hands of the construction company $90,000 of bonds, plus those issued for the last thirty miles ($495,-000) or a total of $585,000 of bonds with all the capital stock, amounting to $3,300,000, and the coal estate costing $500,000, as assets, and with liabilities of loans to the amount of $1,629,000 and capital stock of $2,500,000.

"The property of the railroad is now put into operation. The receipts and expenses are such that its earning power will be sufficient to meet the interest on the bonds, which will tend to increase their value. A syndicate is now formed to take the bonds at ninety. The $2,715,000 of bonds held as collateral would be sold, realizing in cash $2,443,500. From this sum, the loans amounting to $1,629,000 with interest would be paid off, realizing approximately $800,000 in cash. The $585,000 bonds among the assets of the construction company would also probably be sold at ninety, realizing in cash $526,500 which, with the $800,000 remaining from the loans, would furnish cash to the amount of $1,326,500. With this cash the construction company's capital stock, amounting to $2,500,000, could be proportionately paid off, thus reducing it to $1,173,500 with the $3,300,000 capital stock of the railroad company and the coal estate of $500,000 as remaining assets.

"In order to wind up the affairs of the company, and to distribute the stock of the railroad company to the construction company stockholders, it may be estimated that the stock is worth $25 per share (par value $50). For the 66,000 shares, $1,650,000 could be realized, which would be distributed to the stockholders out of the capital stock of the construction company, amounting to $1,173,500, leaving a credit balance of $476,500, with the coal estate. It has been assumed that all the securities would be sold for cash. The various securities could be distributed among the stockholders of the construction company. The stockholders might also become members of the underwriting syndicate to take the bonds at ninety." [1]

One more problem arises in connection with the issuing of stock for property or services. Every new enterprise needs working capital, and the financial plan must provide for this. A portion of the proceeds of the securities of the new company must be put into the treasury to serve the current needs of the corporation. The stock of the new company cannot be sold at par. It must either be sold at a discount, or given away as a bonus with bonds sold. The latter method is generally forbidden the corporation by law. The stock can be made full paid by transferring it for property or services, and then can come into possession of the corporation by gift. The company can sell this stock or give it as a bonus with the sale of bonds as it sees fit. The ordinary method of accomplishing this result is for the vendors of property, or the construction company, after the stock has been made full paid, to donate to the company a certain portion of what they have received, to be placed in the treasury and sold to provide working capital.

It may be argued for the construction company that without this agency whose subscribed capital guarantees the loans made on the security of bonds, enterprises would have great difficulty in raising money for construction. Investors are wary of new concerns which are not on a going basis. Investment bankers usually demand a showing of earnings before risking any money in such securities. The construction company, in return for the opportunity of large profit which its dealings with the railroad company presents, is willing to take risks with new enterprises, and to coöperate with financial institutions in furnishing money for construction, on the security of the bonds of the new company.

---

[1] This account of the operations of a construction company was obtained from a confidential source, on the promise that no names were to be mentioned.

A potent reason for the use of the construction company, aside from the evident advantages to the corporation which have been enumerated, is the fact that this is the only way in which the promoters of an enterprise which does not require the purchase of property, but, instead, involves the building of a trolley line or railroad, to bring into existence property which did not exist before, can make any money for themselves out of the scheme. Even if the law permits the railroad company to sell its stock as a bonus with bonds, and supposing a railroad company sells these securities direct and the money is placed in its treasury, these funds must be spent for the benefit of the corporation. There is no way in which the promoters can make any profit from them except by subscribing to the stock and holding it for an indefinite period until it shows some value. By utilizing the construction company, however, they can make a contract with the railroad company, which will involve the payment to them of a sufficiently large amount of securities to reimburse their expenses, and, at the same time, give them an immediate profit in case their calculations have been wisely made.

The opportunities for making money out of construction companies at the expense of the corporation are very great. This necessary and useful financial agency has been sometimes abused by certain officials of established companies in high credit which did not need the assistance of the construction company to secure funds. Construction companies have also, in some instances, been organized by those interested in these companies to make for themselves large profits by bargaining with the corporation, whose interest they were supposed to safeguard, to do construction work and take payment at exorbitant figures in securities which, as they well knew, would have an immediate sale.

CHAPTER X

THE SALE OF SECURITIES

WE have now reached, in the development of our corporation, the time when it is necessary to arrange for its permanent financing. Up to this point, the money which has been put into the enterprise has been advanced by members of the promoting syndicate. These advances are intended to be temporary. Both the members of the syndicate and the banks from which they have borrowed expect to be repaid when the securities are finally sold. Although the construction period may be prolonged for several years, either because of unforeseen difficulties, or because it is deemed essential that the enterprise should make a fair showing of earnings before its securities are offered for sale, the promoters wish to make this period of development as brief as possible. As soon as the company is in a position to make an attractive offer of stocks or bonds, the securities are sold.

There are two methods of selling securities; either to the public direct or to investment bankers. The security business is organized along lines generally similar to the business of producing and selling commodities. The corporation corresponds to the manufacturer, the investor to the consumer. Between the manufacturer and the consumer, stands the distributer. The wholesaler, in the field of commodities, and the banker, in the field of securities, occupy similar positions. The business of the private banker has assumed great importance in recent years. At one time it was thought that the function of distributing securities to the public might be taken over by the commercial banker who would buy from the corporation and sell to his own depositors. A number of the larger banks and trust companies have gone so far as to establish bond departments. But while there is a certain amount sold by commercial banks to depositors, for the most part through their bond departments, as a rule banks dispose of such bonds as they may purchase, in the general investment market, making no special effort to interest their depositors, on whose funds they can make a larger profit by lending them in the ordinary course than by using them in the purchase of bonds. It is now admitted that the bond business, as a branch of mercantile industry, does not belong to the commercial bank, and it is properly left to a special kind of financial institution.

The investment banker on his part, however, may advantageously carry on certain departments of the business of the commercial bank. The investment banker offers investment securities suitable to the needs of various classes of investors, furnishes to investors free of charge accurate information on securities, receives accounts subject to check, and allows interest on daily balances, collects and remits dividends and interest; negotiates collateral loans for various classes of borrowers, executes orders for the purchase, sale, or exchange of securities on the stock exchanges; and, in some cases, carries on the business of foreign exchange. The investment business is, however, the primary function of the private banker. To this all his other activities are subordinated.

The private banker organizes his business on the lines of a jobbing house. He has a large number of present, prospective or potential customers on his list sometimes running into the thousands. He circularizes these customers at intervals with letters and circulars, follows up all inquiries with attractive prospectuses, and also brings the merits of his wares to the attention of the buyer by means of public advertisements. The investment banker enjoys special advantages for the financing of his business. So far as possible, he aims to make his sales and purchases coincide. In an active bond market, it is not unusual that a large issue should be sold before the banker is obliged to make his final payment. When a stock of securities is to be carried, however, the investment banker employs his established lines of credit with banks and trust companies, pledging the securities which he is holding as collateral for loans on various margins of security, depending on the quality of the bond or stock pledged and the conditions of the loan market. By the liberal employment of his credit, he is able to do a large business with a comparatively small capital. A bond house with a capital of $500,000 is a very substantial institution of its class.

These investment bankers stand ready to purchase the securities of corporations for cash. The prices which they will offer are, of course, below those which they expect to receive, the margin of profit demanded depending on the salability of the security, and the salability usually depending on the quality determined from an investment standpoint. The question now arises, shall the promoters of the new corporation sell the securities to bankers, or shall they offer them direct to the public? This question can be answered, without serious qualification, and with few exceptions, in favor of dealing with the banker.

There are great advantages to a corporation in placing its securities with investment bankers. The cost of obtaining the required capital is definitely determined in the banker's contract. If the bonds are to be sold at $85, or $90, or $92½, the exact amount of money which will be received from these bonds is known. The money, moreover, will be paid at a definite date, so that the syndicate need have no uncertainty about recovering their advances and repaying their loans. The cost to the corporation of selling securities to bankers is also much less than if sales are made direct to the public, and the certainty of return is far greater. The banker, as we have seen, has a permanent organization and an established clientele of customers. This organization is constantly employed in marketing securities. Established banking houses of good reputation have a large number of customers who will buy from no one else. They can count on a certain amount of money from these customers at regular intervals, which will be spent on the securities which they offer. They are also able to make a market for new securities, for which the demand may be weak at the outset, by exchanging these new bonds on a favorable basis for seasoned bonds of long standing, which its regular customers have purchased in the past, and for which a ready market exists. With a large number of satisfied customers with whom the banker is in constant touch, new issues of securities can be quickly sold by exchange, when direct sale would be impossible. Bankers, moreover, are not obliged to force a market for the securities which they purchase. They can utilize their credit to carry stocks and bonds until a favorable season arrives for selling them.

A corporation engaged in the mining of coal or the operation of an interurban electric railway has none of the equipment for selling securities. If it desires to sell bonds direct to the public, it will be necessary for the company to construct a selling machine for the express purpose, and since it cannot keep this organization together after the necessity out of which it originated has passed, its cost will be excessive. It must rely on newspaper advertising to discover its customers, and newspaper advertising is an expensive method of selling securities. The corporation, while it might have a good credit for the purposes of its own business, would have great difficulty in establishing a credit with which to finance its venture into the security business. The same banker might look with favor on a proposition coming from an investment banker to lend money on the securities of a corporation, which that investment banker had purchased for sale, and might look with extreme disfavor upon a proposition to lend on the same securities offered by the corporation direct.

There is no certainty, when the securities are offered direct to the corporation, as to the cost of selling. The usual method will be to turn the work over to some advertising agency which would undertake, without any guarantee of results, to sell the securities on the basis of a certain percentage of the proceeds. In some cases, this percentage would run as high as forty per cent, and the selling campaign might, at that, have to be abandoned before half of the securities were disposed of. From every standpoint, the attempt of a company to market its securities direct will be likely to prove unsatisfactory and unsuccessful. The cost will be excessive, the results uncertain, and the risks great.

But while sale to a banker is advantageous to the company, bankers will not purchase every kind of security. They sell to investors, and the securities which they offer must be such as will appeal to their customers. We may distinguish between investment securities and speculative securities. Both the investor and the speculator are so called because they buy stock or bonds of companies which are the owners of productive properties. By means of the corporation which divides its stock or debt into shares or notes of $50, $100, or $1,000 each, and which is managed by officers elected by trustees whom the stockholders select, an individual can become a part owner, or a part creditor, of as large a number of corporations as his capital will allow, without identifying himself in any way with the management of any of these corporations. He has no concern in their affairs, save to receive out of their earnings his dividends or interest, or to increase his capital by selling his stocks or bonds should their price be advanced. Broadly speaking, there are two kinds of enterprises, and two kinds of securities which these enterprises may issue: Those which have been in existence a sufficient time to enable their earning power to be conclusively demonstrated; and those which have not yet demonstrated their earning power, either because they exist only on paper, or because their operations have, as yet, been unsuccessful.

Examples of investment stocks are furnished by such companies as the Pennsylvania Railroad, the Chicago and Northwestern, the Chicago, Milwaukee & St. Paul, among railroads; the Cambria Steel Company, the Standard Oil Company and the General Electric Company, among industrials; the Union

Traction Company and the Chicago City Railway Company, among street railways; the Calumet and Heckla among mines. An examination of these stocks shows the following characteristics: Each of these companies operates an established business, supplying articles or service for which there is a steady demand, and where the processes of the industry are standardized and thoroughly understood. Each one of these companies is efficiently managed. Their costs of production are low, their selling methods are efficient, and their financial management conservative. Each one of these corporations has been profitable for many years. In good times, as well as in periods of depression, their net profits have been far more than sufficient to pay their operating expenses and their fixed charges. Each one of these companies has a record of dividend payments. The directors have dealt fairly with the stockholders in paying to them such part of the profits as could be safely distributed. Anyone who buys the stocks of these companies knows that profits will be earned, and that he will receive as large a part of these profits as can be prudently paid to him.

We have here the requisites of an investment security: an established business, efficient management, assured profits and a conservative distribution of profits to stockholders. If any of these characteristics are absent from a security, it is not entitled to be called an investment, because there is no guarantee to the investor that the income, on the basis of which he buys the stock or bond, will be permanent.

A speculation is illustrated by the stock of The Consolidated Oil Company. This company controls 120 acres of land in the Coalinga district of Southern California, touching so-called "proven land," that is land in which paying oil wells are in operation. This company offers a portion of its capital stock for sale at one third of its par value. "With the proceeds it is proposed to drill a well and it is practically a certainty that we will have at least a 500 barrel well within a few months. If you have carefully read this book you will understand that the profits from this one well should drill two more and leave some money over for dividends. Then these three should produce enough to drill six more, and so on up to about twenty wells, which the company should have in two years. These twenty wells, remember, will be drilled with profits after the first one, and should make the company over $1,000,000 profits per year." The directors and promoters of this company are not known as men who have been successful in the oil business, and no representations of their previous experience are made in the prospectus. That their means are limited, is shown by the fact that, instead of taking advantage of this golden opportunity themselves, they are forced to appeal to the public to supply the means of developing their proposition. Here are all the elements of a speculation, an enterprise which may or may not be successful. Oil is being produced in California at a profit. The property of this company, if its representations are to be believed, is near the oil reservoir. If oil is discovered, it is probable that it can be produced at a profit. So much can be said in favor of the proposition. On the other hand, there are several unfavorable considerations. Oil may not be found, or if it is discovered, the flow may cease after a short time. The company may not be able to store or transport this oil. The officers, even though honest, having had no previous experience, may prove incompetent. They may involve the company in obligations whose maturity may destroy the value of its stock, or they may fritter away its funds. The Consolidated Oil Company is an illustration of a type of speculation where the company has not yet come into existence, where its future is wholly problematical.

The Allis-Chalmers Company was incorporated in 1901, as a consolidation of companies manufacturing heavy engines, mining and other machinery. This company has outstanding $19,820,000 of common stock, $16,150,000 of preferred stock, and $10,325,000 of bonds. On the preferred stock seven per cent was paid from July, 1901 to February, 1904. Since that time, no dividends have been paid. No dividends have been paid on the common stock from the beginning. Here, the separate concerns which were merged into this company were profitable, and they have continued to be profitable. The anticipated increase in profits, as a result of the combination, was not, however, sufficient to pay dividends on the stock, which represented a large increase over the combined stock of the merged companies. The Allis-Chalmers Company may some time prove to be an investment, but the earnings up to the present time have not been sufficient to warrant the maintenance of dividends on its preferred stock, and the common stock is apparently a long way off from a dividend. Even the bonds are not considered to be especially safe. The stock of the Allis-Chalmers Company illustrates a type of security in which the business has not been as profitable as was anticipated, and where dividends could not, therefore, be maintained.

The stock of the Westinghouse Electric & Manufacturing Company is issued by a company which, while profitable, and while paying dividends for many years, was yet so badly managed as to be forced into bankruptcy. The stock of this company cannot, therefore, be considered as an investment. Although the management has changed, several years of successful and conservative operation must elapse before the company is completely reinstated in the confidence of the investor, when its securities will be fully acceptable.

The Amalgamated Copper Company and the American Smelting & Refining Company are corporations which have paid out the greater portion of their earnings to their stockholders. In times of prosperity, these stocks sell at high values because of this policy of liberal distribution. During a period of depression, however, dividend payments are greatly reduced. These stocks are, therefore, regarded as speculations.

We see from a comparison of these illustrations, that the characteristics of a speculative security are the exact opposites of the distinguishing features of an investment. If a company is a new enterprise, or if the efficiency of its management is doubtful, or if it has not yet come into a stage of profitable operation, or if, as happens in rare instances, it has made profits and has not distributed them to the stockholders, or finally, if it has paid out too large a percentage of profits so that it has been obliged to suspend dividends when earnings declined, its stock must be regarded as speculative.

Between the best class of stock investments, of which the stock of the Pennsylvania Railroad is an illustration, and the stock of The Consolidated Oil Company which stands at the bottom of the list, there are degrees of difference, and it is difficult to sharply divide the sheep from the goats. For our present purpose, however, which is to examine the different methods of selling investment and speculative securities, it is sufficient to characterize as investment those enterprises which have already succeeded, or whose success can be confidently predicted from the experiences of similar enterprises operating under conditions generally identical, as for example the introduction of a street railway in a town of 50,000 people, and to distinguish from these, as speculative securities, stocks and bonds of enterprises whose success lies in the future. The distinguishing characteristic of a speculation is the fact that its value depends upon circumstances which cannot be known because the future is intended to reveal them. An investment on the other hand contains no "ifs" or "provideds" or "believes," its value is founded upon certainty. The value of a speculative security is built upon the unstable foundations of probabilities and suppositions.

These two classes of securities correspond broadly to the characters of the people who buy them. The stocks and bonds of established companies, where success is certain, are purchased by investors, speculative securities by speculators. The investor will not buy a security whose value is in any way doubtful. He demands in a stock or bond, before anything else, the virtue of stable value. He must be reasonably certain that his principal is safe, that he can, at any time in the future, disregarding the occasional fluctuations of the market, sell his stocks or bonds at or near the price he paid for them. If this assurance of safety of principal and certainty of income can be given him, he is satisfied with a moderate return.

The most important investors in the United States are the financial institutions, insurance companies, trust companies, banks and large estates. These institutions demand safety before every other consideration. They are willing to pay high prices for stocks and bonds where the assurance of safety can be given. Besides these institutions, the character of whose investments is determined not merely by prudence but by law, there are a great majority of the wealthy and well-to-do people of the country in the investing class. Their chief concern is to keep what they have. They demand of the securities, into which they put their surplus income, the highest degree of safety and stability, the most complete guarantee of security.

The investor will buy government bonds, well-secured railroad bonds or guaranteed stocks of railroads, municipal bonds, bonds of street railways, electric light or gas companies in large cities, and the best grade of railroad, street railway or gas stocks. Of later years, with much diffidence and hesitation, he has gone into industrials. The preferred stocks of some of the large concerns are now extensively held by conservative investors. The stocks of new industrials, and of oil and mining companies he usually lets alone. This investment demand, concentrated upon a portion of the securities offered for sale, fixes the value of every investment, no matter how high may be the return upon its face value, at a figure which will allow to the purchaser only a small return upon the money invested. There are few safe investments offered for sale on the New York Stock Exchange whose price when compared with their yield in interest or dividends, shows a return of more than six per cent.

When the investment banker is approached by the promoters of a new enterprise, and asked to assist in the flotation, he examines carefully the character of the scheme. The first thing he demands of the securities which are offered to him, is that they shall be salable. Unless he can sell them at a profit, he will have nothing to do with the scheme. Assuming that the securities are salable, the next question is, can he recommend them to his own customers? It must be remembered that the relation of the investment banker to his customers is a fiduciary relation. He is a wholesaler of securities. By an extensive organization, covering sometimes many states, he keeps in touch with funds offered for investment. He has classified in his catalogues the names, sometimes, of many thousands of people who buy securities; he knows how much money they have to invest and when this money will be available. He has an organization of salesmen who make regular visits to his customers, and he carries on an extensive correspondence with them to influence their purchases. This business the investment banker expects to be permanent. If he sells a bond, maturing in ten years, he has a record of that sale, and when the bond is paid off, he expects to be on hand with a new bond to take the place of the old one. He aims to cultivate, therefore, by every means in his power, the good will of his customers. The basis of that good will, the foundation upon which his business must rest, is the investment quality of the securities which he offers for sale. In his literature and through his salesmen, the banker lays primary emphasis upon the safety of the securities which he offers. He recommends them to his customers, and ordinarily he has bought them himself, before he offers them for sale. His constant endeavor is to protect his customers against loss. He will carry these efforts, in some cases, so far as to repurchase bonds concerning whose security there may be a doubt, or to undertake at considerable expense and trouble, the work of reorganizing bankrupt companies whose bonds he has sold, so that they may again be put upon a solvent basis.

A man in such a business as this cannot recommend speculative bonds or stocks to his clients. He might indeed sell a large amount of doubtful securities during a period of good times which would be bought from him by his clients because of their confidence in him, but when depression overtook these shaky enterprises they would go down, and with them would go the good will of the banker's business. A long record of successful flotations is not sufficient to protect a banking house against the discredit of offering and recommending securities which are not good, and whose quality could have been revealed by an investigation.

An illustration of the caution displayed by reputable financial institutions in standing sponsor for new and untried companies, so far as to recommend their securities, is furnished by the following letter received in answer to an inquiry concerning the merits of a Mexican mining proposition which had announced that subscriptions to its bonds would be received at a prominent trust company, large use being made of the trust company's name in the advertisements. The inquiry addressed to the trust company was as follows:

> Dear Sirs: I have received certain information on the proposition offered by the ——— ———. These reports are extremely interesting, and I have given them careful attention. I should like, however, to have your own opinion of the merits of the debenture bonds as a safe investment.
>
> The Corporation ———, by its Vice-President, Mr. ——, has heartily recommended them, and I presume you will have no hesitation in confirming his statement that he believes them to be a safe and profitable investment.

The reply of the trust company is as follows:

> Dear Sir: We have your favor of the 18th inst. In reply thereto would say that following our invariable policy, we regret our inability to advise you in the matter of the investment referred to. Our duty is merely to receive such subscriptions as may be tendered on behalf of the ——— ——— ———, and we have been selected to countersign the bonds. The parties interested in the matter have come to us properly recommended.

The statements contained in the advertisement and circulars are the statements of the —— and not of this Company.

Yours very truly,
(Signed) —— ——,
Second Vice President.

If the securities of the new company are of a speculative character, it is evident that the banker cannot purchase them directly and offer them as his own property to his customers. He can, however, insure or guarantee their sale. The trust company just mentioned would have been interested in these bonds at its own risk, or by lending to officers and directors on the security of the bonds, without openly indorsing them, unless the use of its name as the depositary of the mining company may be regarded as an indorsement.

CHAPTER XI

THE SALE OF SPECULATIVE SECURITIES

If the securities of a new corporation cannot be sold to the banker for resale to the investor they must be sold direct to the speculative public. The most conspicuous illustration of the methods successfully employed to provide large sums of money within a short time by selling stocks and bonds of doubtful investment quality to the general public is furnished by the sale of industrial securities from 1898 to 1902. We have already considered the circumstances under which the so-called trusts were promoted and have examined into their organization and the advantages which their promoters claim for them. Chief among these advantages was the restriction of competition out of which it was expected that large profits would be earned.

In the formation of these consolidations a large amount of cash had to be provided for the purchase of properties whose owners would not accept stock in the consolidation and for working capital. This cash, moreover, had to be produced within a short time and it became necessary to dispose of several billions of dollars par value of stocks and bonds and its provision was essential to the launching of the new companies. In nearly every case, arrangements were made with banking houses who organized underwriting syndicates which guaranteed the sale of these issues of industrial stocks and bonds at prices sufficiently below the price which they expected would be realized, to leave them a large profit. These underwriting syndicates did not expect to be permanently interested in the new enterprise and had large blocks to dispose of. The promoters, whether individuals or syndicates, had large quantities of securities for sale. The owners of the companies which entered the consolidations had also large amounts of securities to sell, especially common stock. These owners were usually obliged to wait before offering their stock for sale until the syndicate manager had disposed of his holdings, or until the syndicate had been dissolved. As soon as their contracts with the syndicate manager permitted, a large amount of the stock issued for the stock of the constituent companies was offered for sale. It was, in short, necessary that several billions of dollars par value of industrial stocks should be sold within a comparatively short time. An examination of the stocks of the industrial trusts was sufficient to convince any intelligent investigator that at the time of their issue they were not entitled to rank as investments. In an editorial under date of August 15, 1900, the *Wall Street Journal* submits a list of questions from the answers to which the buyers of securities may form an opinion as to the investment standing of the trust stocks. The substance of these questions is as follows:

1. What were the plants able to earn on the average for the five years preceding the combination?

2. What would this amount have paid on the present amount of stock?

3. How much have expenses been reduced by consolidation?

4. How much have gross earnings been increased by consolidation?

5. What will the combination have to earn net in order to pay seven per cent on its preferred stock?

6. How much in excess of that amount is the company earning now?

7. What is the amount of the net floating debt?

8. How is this floating debt secured?

9. Is the corporation hampered by burdensome contracts?

10. Can it enforce its own contracts with buyers?

11. What is the extent of the competition encountered?

12. What is the possibility of reducing operating expenses?

13. Is the management in every way competent and satisfactory?

Here is presented an outline for an investment judgment. If these questions can be fully answered, the investor can determine with some accuracy whether the trust stocks can be safely purchased. If the trust has a large annual surplus of profits over its dividends, declared or reserved; if its unsecured debt is kept within manageable limits; if the reports of its physical condition, its earnings, its assets and liabilities are frequent and circumstantial, and if it has maintained by wise and energetic management a dominant position in the trade, the investor may safely put his money into its stocks. His security would not be as good as the security which a general mortgage bond would give him, but he would receive a higher return, probably 5½ or 6 per cent, and by carefully watching his investment, he would be tolerably safe against loss. If the syndicate manager would give the information asked for, and if the condition of the new corporation was shown to be satisfactory, an investment demand would spring up for its stocks.

But all of these questions could not, in the nature of the case, be answered. The trust had just come into being. If the promoter had been frank with the public, the net earnings of the plants for the preceding three years were given in his prospectus. It may appear that the amount of preferred stock issued is warranted by the net earnings, and this, be it noted to the credit of the promoters, had been usually true of their preferred stock issues. But this fact only answers two out of thirteen questions on which the investor must have information before making a conservative judgment. The remaining eleven could not be answered for perhaps five years, or until the trust, in a period of industrial depression, had proved the strength of its organization and the skill of its management. The trust, at the time its stocks are offered for sale, had no expenses to reduce; it had not attempted to increase its earnings; if it had a floating debt, this was composed of the unsecured debts of underlying companies—not usually published—in the new company there had been no occasion to incur debts; the value of its contracts and its power over buyers were to be determined by future experience; the strength of the competition was uncertain, and the quality of its management under these new conditions had not been determined. The prospective investor was left in the dark concerning these matters. There were great speculative possibilities in the trust proposition, but he could not make an investment judgment as to the probability of their realization.

The investor, moreover, when he looked into the merits of the trust stocks, was confronted with many doubts and fears. What would be the attitude of the public toward the trust? Would its management be left unhampered to work out the possibilities of reduced expenses and more stable prices, or would the cry of monopoly be raised and popular sentiment take hostile form in special taxes, reduced tariffs, or assaults upon the corporation's right to exist? Would the public pay higher prices, or would they purchase cheaper substitutes? Had not the corporation, in issuing cumulative preferred stock, endangered its future by the compelling necessity of paying dividends on the preferred in order to protect the common? These were some of the considerations, in addition to the lack of most of the information on which he had been accustomed to base his judgment, which warned the conservative investor not to buy the trust stocks.

Even the preferred stock, based, as its value was supposed to be, on past earning power was not assured of dividends in the future. A new management had been placed in control, and this past earning power might not be sustained. Bonds or floating debt might be placed ahead of the preferred stock to absorb the earnings which were to go to that security. The cumulative feature, for which so much has been claimed, might prove a source of weakness rather than strength. If unpaid dividends should accumulate, the value of the common stock might be obliterated, and this might seriously damage the financial standing of the company. It might even, at a critical moment, deprive the corporation of a loan which would save it from bankruptcy. As for the common stock, burdened as it was by the extraordinary advantages which are given to the senior security, it had nothing to commend it. If the investor could not safely invest in the preferred shares, he would certainly have nothing to do with the common.

The syndicate manager could not count upon selling his stocks to the investor who buys only on the satisfaction of an intelligent judgment, either his own judgment or that of his broker or banker, that the stocks into which he puts his money will yield a certain and stable return, and above all, that he can be certain of selling the stock for the price at which it was purchased. No such claims could properly be made for the trust stocks. Their dividends were uncertain, prospective, problematical. They started with bright prospects, it is true, but these prospects might never be realized. The conservative investor would have none of them.

Cut off from recourse to the investment demand, the syndicate manager made his appeal to the speculators. They are usually persons of moderate means who are willing to buy the shares of new companies at low prices, trusting in the representations of those who have stocks to sell, that these stocks will pay large dividends and eventually increase in value. The speculative buyer has usually no knowledge of finance. He does not understand the nature of an investment judgment. He thinks of a stock as $100 and regards its dividends as certain and permanent. He has no skill in offsetting advantages with disadvantages. With him a security is either good or bad. There is no halfway point. If the syndicate manager had set before him all the materials for an investment judgment of the trust proposition, he could not have made such a judgment. If, moreover, the difficulties and uncertainties which deter the investor from buying trust stocks had been presented to the speculative buyer, he would have been frightened away. If these negative considerations are not presented, however, he will not ask for them nor will he suspect their existence. Great care must therefore be taken to give him only the most simple and favorable information concerning the stock which it is designed that he should buy. The "public" asks few questions—save as to the standing of the officers and directors of the new company, for they naturally do not want to be robbed—and the amount of dividends which is promised to its stockholders. It is from this class of buyers that a portion of the funds which are to reimburse the advances of the underwriter are to come.

There is, it is true, another method which might be suggested in such cases, and which, if successful, would have enabled the trust stocks to be originally sold to the investor. The promoters and underwriters might have held their stock, foregoing their profits for three or five years, and might require the vendors to do the same. At the end of this period, if the calculations of the promoters to which the underwriter had fixed his indorsement proved to have been accurate, the securities which had been held off the market pending this verification could have been sold to the investor at good prices. The corporation law of Germany, as we have seen, attempts to secure this confirmatory delay by prohibiting the listing of shares on the exchanges until one year from the date of the organization of the company. A longer time was needed to establish a new form of industrial, such as the trust, in the confidence of the investor.

This delay, however, although desirable from the standpoint of conservative investment judgment, is not contemplated by financiers of new companies. Not only would it be unreasonable to demand of them such a degree of self-denial, but the enforcement of such a regulation, it is safe to say, would make impossible the financing of speculative projects on a large scale. The underwriter would demand a prohibitive commission, and the promoter would have little inducement to bring forward large projects, if both interests were obliged to wait for several years before selling their stocks. To require such a delay, moreover, would be to destroy the function of the underwriter as the retailer of speculative securities from the promoter to the public. It would compel the underwriter, if he put his money into any project, to regard it as a permanent investment; that is to say, to abandon his character of banker, and assume that of investor, whose profits, at least for several years, must come from interest or dividends. As an investor, however, the underwriter would demand the information necessary to an investment judgment, and this information the promoter of a new form of enterprise such as the trust, is usually unable to furnish.

We are brought, therefore, to the conclusion that the financing which was necessary in the formation of the industrial trusts could not have been secured if those who furnished the cash had been required to realize their profits from selling the securities which they received to the investor who demands the conviction of safety before parting with his money. Or, to put the matter in another way, underwriters, as prudent men would not put their money into the stocks of the industrials without a reasonable certainty that these funds could be recovered with a profit in addition by selling the stocks to the general public. In short, the underwriter of speculative stocks or bonds asks the public to buy stocks for investment which he would not buy for himself. Only in this way can money be raised for new and risky projects.

The main recourse of the syndicate manager of the trust was to the speculator, and he was fortunate that he could draw upon a reservoir of funds which was full to overflowing. The methods by which he exchanged his trust stocks for cash we have now to consider.

The first step in the process of selling stock to a speculative buyer is to excite his imagination. There must be placed before him a picture of enormous wealth in which he is invited to share. In actual existence as yet there is nothing save a flat plain, a precipitous mountain, or a prospect of monopoly profits. The speculator must furnish the money to ascertain what lies below the surface, and if there is anything found, to develop it. But in order that the speculator shall advance these funds, he must be made to disregard the present and project his gaze into the future. He must behold, as does one in a vision, a fully equipped mining property or oil well, and he must see himself as part owner of this valuable property. In view of this necessity, the general arrangement of a prospectus, no matter of what enterprise it treats, is always the same. The project contains some new feature —a new resource, a new invention, a new form of industrial organization, oil lands in California, copper land in Arizona, real estate on the frontier of Brooklyn, or options on competing plants. The development of these resources and opportunities is to be followed by large earnings.

The reasons for this belief are forcibly set forth in a prospectus. The mine is either directly adjoining a fully developed property which is paying large dividends, or the geological indications point unmistakably to the existence of a resource of great value. Similar enterprises in other parts of the country have proved enormously profitable. The present scheme is fundamentally identical with these enterprises. There the present scheme will be equally successful.

A mass of expert testimony of this or that "professor," whose wealth of technical detail is most convincing, is usually added. Note, for example, the following extract from an expert's opinion of the Monterey district: ". . . The geological formation of the oil-bearing strata and extensive surface indications of petroleum seem to indicate the certainty of there being productive resources of oil below. Sandstone and shale of a bituminous character seem to be the general surface indications of petroleum. There are apparently three anticlinal ridges extending through this range which the oil belts seem to follow. Judging from the croppings, the west side of the Salines Valley contains a vast oil reservoir. I have formed this conclusion on account of the immense depth and thickness of the oil-bearing sands and also the immense beds of bituminous shale." Perhaps the "professor" has a record of success to enforce his statements. He may "stake his reputation" on the success of this last project which he indorses, and which he believes to be "far richer than United Verde," a mine which paid $2,924,000 in dividends in one year.

Accompanying the expert's reports will be maps and charts showing the exact location of the property, if the proposition is for a mining or oil enterprise, in relation to producing mines or wells, these latter being always in the immediate neighborhood of the land of the new company or else "the geological formation on this claim is identical with that found on the largest dividend paying properties in the districts." The National and State Geographical Surveys are dragged in to support the expert testimony.

Newspaper accounts of the "fabulous richness of the Kootenay country," or "Wonderful Tonopah, a Desert Camp of Fabulous Richness," written for local newspapers, or the more sober narratives of the metropolitan journals, also excite the imagination of the speculator. Such news items as the following appear in metropolitan journals: "Nevada, January 27th—At the Tonopah camp the most impressive things are the huge stacks of ore awaiting shipment. Henry Cutting, who came into the camp early last year with only $2.50 in his pocket, has one stack which is estimated to be worth $500,000. Another man who has been very lucky is Frank Golden, who has a great stack of sacks of ore like a fort, which is worth $700,000."

Strongly worded testimonials may be added to the schedule of evidence. The project is backed by substantial business men, often by men of national reputation—won in some other field—who publicly advise their friends, as did an ex-governor of a Western State, to "provide for the children" by investing a few dollars in rubber certificates. The best of bank references are also given.

All this mass of skillfully arranged data leading the mind almost imperceptibly from the known to the unknown, emphasizing advantages to the point of exaggeration, glossing over difficulties or preferably remaining silent about them, marshaling history, science, and reputation to the support of prophecy—all these specious and forceful arguments are directed to the end of creating in the mind of the prospective buyer a vision of enormous wealth. It is but seldom that they fail to accomplish the result. If it were possible, a sympathetic examination of their literature would deceive the very elect.

Cupidity is the next passion to which the promoter appeals. The stock in these companies whose prospects of large profits are so well assured, is offered at a low price, 50 cents, $1 or $2.50, per share, some indeed as low as five cents a share. The company issuing the stock, it is stated, is in possession of a resource of enormous value. Only a small amount of money is needed to develop the mine or drill the well—" in order to facilitate the development of the valuable lands of this company, the directors have placed on the market a limited amount of its treasury stock to be sold at the special introductory price of twenty cents per share, and the company reserves"—mark this, opportunity only knocks once—" the right to advance the price of the same without notice." After the initial expenditure, it is claimed, the enterprise will grow out of its own earnings.

And its assured dividends. " Marvelous and monstrous " is the only phrase that adequately describes them. It is a poor company that cannot assure the investor twenty per cent on his money. Note, for example, the following: " The value of this stock as an investment may readily be seen when it is understood that one well producing 100 barrels of oil daily will earn four per cent on the entire capitalization, or twenty per cent on the present selling price of the stock." The company in question had room for 150 wells on its property and the inference of the prospectus is that dividends of 1,000 per cent on the investment are by no means out of the question.

If the speculator asks for conclusive evidence that these huge dividends will be paid—let him look to the record of other enterprises which had at the outset no better prospects than that into which he is asked to put his money. "In one instance, about one and one half years ago, $1,200 was invested in three sections of oil land in one oil district. To-day these same lands are worth $5,000,000. In another instance $3,200 was invested in two sections. To-day these two sections are worth $6,000,000." Specimen advances in oil stocks are given—for example: "The New York Oil Company sold at fifty cents per share, present market price $200"; or "the Home Oil Company sold at $10 per share, present market price $5,000." Or, if the proposition is in gold or copper mining, figures like this are given: "United Verde once sold for fifty cents a share and is now paying nearly 8,700 per cent on that price. The LeRoi Mine was sold entire in 1890 for $12.50; it now has a market value of $10,000,000—$100 invested in LeRoi a few years ago is now worth $250,000 and has paid $35,000 in dividends. Alaska Treadwell has paid $5,000,000 in dividends and its stock has advanced 3,200 per cent," etc., etc. Evidence of this character is abundant and effective.

If doubt is expressed as to the future demand for these products even should they be successfully produced, the prospectus is ready with assurance that "the development of California will demand all the oil that can be produced" or "the electrical industry will continue to exhaust the supply of copper." Nothing is left uncovered. Every detail is attended to. A chance to draw a valuable prize is offered at a low price.

The whole argument is summed up with convincing brevity by a copper prospectus. "Bell telephone was given away for board bills, yet has paid over $36,000,000 in dividends. Calumet and Heckla went begging not so many years ago; its total dividends to date are over $60,000,000. It would take a day to enumerate the instances where properties rich and great to-day were offered for a song. The people who did buy them are rich now, and why? Not because they were 'lucky,' but because they investigated promptly, judged the merit of the proposition, and acted while there was time. If they had waited until to-day to buy the shares of these enterprises they would get perhaps five per cent on their money, possibly eight, but no more. But buying when they did, they got all the way from fifty per cent up to 500 per cent because they had both the judgment to recognize the worth of the opportunity and the courage to seize it. A thorough examination of the details of the Arizona Copper Syndicate will satisfy any man of judgment as to its merits. It is one of the greatest opportunities ever given investors. Investigate it now while the price is low."

Here are the principal inducements offered to the speculator in every new enterprise. Other men have made money in similar enterprises. Why should not he be equally fortunate? He is not asked to gamble, but merely to investigate an industrial opportunity and act as his judgment directs. He is carried away by the prevailing optimism of the time, and he is ready to listen to the advocates of new schemes for getting rich. Other people are making money fast, and he is certain of his ability to do as well as they. The appeal to his "judgment" and his "courage" is the bit of flattery which is often decisive, and the final outcome is that the man of small means invests $100, $200, or $5,000 in the stock of a new company in the confident expectation that from this small investment he will one day reap a fortune.

When once embarked on a doubtful enterprise, the speculator is impelled by sentiment and interest to draw others along with him. The speculator is by instinct a promoter. He is zealous in advocacy of this project to which he has committed his money. He urges upon his friends the merits of the new scheme. His enthusiasm is infectious. Others are drawn into the net by his representations, and they in turn compass sea and land to make one proselyte. In this way the wave of speculation is set going and sweeps through all classes of society, turning the accumulations of years of effort into the treasuries of the new companies.

The situation is universally familiar. A minister or a physician has a few thousands laid by; a woman has either saved or inherited a small amount; a workman or a farmer has managed to scrape together something for a rainy day. Such people are found by the thousands in every part of the country. From their accumulations they draw a small rate of return, often so small that they are constrained to add it to the principal and do not venture to apply it to expenditures. Four or five per cent clear gain is about all that can be expected. Their lives are hard, monotonous, and barren. Before their eyes is constantly flaunted the luxurious extravagance of the wealthy leisure class. To such people the prospectus of a new enterprise is wonderfully attractive. In exchange for a few thousand it offers them a fortune. The offer dazzles them. Their desires benumb their judgment. The risk of the undertaking is forgotten. Few of those who put their money into a speculative scheme enter it with the thought of risk. The calm balancing of chances is the exercise of a superior order of mind. The speculator does not buy a chance, he buys what he thinks is a fortune. He has had a vision of a vein of ore or a great reservoir of oil. He has seen a populous town arise around the factory in which he has invested. He has forsaken the difficult paths of reason for the flowery fields of imagination and conjecture.

The line of speculators is very ancient. In 1720 there was printed for W. Bonham, in London, "an argument proving that the South Sea Company is able to make a dividend of thirty-eight per cent for twelve years, fitted to the meanest capacities." This was one of the first prospectuses ever issued, and the succession has been worthy of its ancestor; Spanish Jackass Company, Louisiana Bubble, South American Bonds, American Improvement Bonds, English Railways, American Railways, American Mines, South American Railways, Australian Railways, Band Mines, American Industrials—John Law, Hudson, Barnato, Hooley, Gates, and Lawson. The line runs true. The Jackass Company still lives.

CHAPTER XII

THE SALE OF SPECULATIVE SECURITIES—(*Continued*)

THE foregoing presents in brief outline the methods of selling stock in an enterprise which is on its face so dangerously risky as to require the most spectacular representations and the most flamboyant promises in order to work the speculator up to the point of shutting his eyes to the risk and going in on faith alone. Hundreds of these companies are floated every year, and their promoters often find good markets for their wares. Most of these promoters are honest. They expect to spend a large part of the funds intrusted to their care in the exploitation of the resource or opportunity which they control. A minority are fraudulent. But, one and all, they must, in order to float their schemes, appeal to the imagination and the cupidity, and blindfold the judgment of the people who buy their shares. All that they can properly offer is a chance in a lottery in which there are few prizes and many blanks.

But how do the foregoing statements apply to the question in hand? The industrial trust was a very different enterprise from the Arizona Copper Syndicate. There was apparently nothing in common between them. The syndicate manager of the trust was a great banker whose name is a certificate of reputability. He fathers no wildcat schemes. The man with "sixty acres of oil land adjoining the land of the Standard Oil Company" would get no recognition from the head of the underwriting syndicate. His appeal was made to the "investor" not to the oil or copper speculator. The trust promoters had organized the wire mills or the paper mills of the United States into great corporations whose constituent companies had already succeeded in their individual capacities and whose profits must be far greater now that competition had been eliminated. There was no manner of doubt about it. There were the properties; their value had been carefully investigated by expert accountants, and the economies of combination were known. The underwriters were men of the highest responsibility.

With such a proposition there was no need to beat the tomtoms. A brief official statement was sufficient. Here is the trust prospectus:

> The International Paper Company, of New York, was incorporated January 1, 1898. It at once took over by purchase twenty-five of the principal pulp and paper mills of the country, which produce from seventy-five to ninety per cent of all the newspaper manufactured east of Chicago. The average daily output of these mills is: Ground wood pulp, 1,050 tons per day; sulfite pulp, 256 tons per day; finished paper (nearly) 1,500 tons per day. The leading manufacturers retain their interest in the industry, and many of them are giving their time and energy to the promotion of the business of the new company.
>
> The company has issued the following securities, the large majority of which have been used in payment for the mills, water power, and woodlands acquired by the new corporation: first consolidated mortgage six-per-cent gold bonds, $10,000,000; preferred stock, cumulative six per cent, $25,000,000; common stock, $20,000,000. The appraised value of the property securing the above-named bonds is $40,000,000. Net earnings are now more than sufficient to pay the interest on the bonds, dividends on the preferred stock, and ten per cent on the common stock; while the indications fully sustain the belief that they will be even higher in the future. Regarding competition, it can hardly be expected to prove successful, if attempted, for the valuable water power and timber lands, 400,000 acres of the latter being held by the company, could not be easily duplicated or acquired.

Observe the modest confidence of this statement. Competition is destroyed. A great monopoly is instituted. This monopoly is secured by the possession of water power and timber lands. The leading manufacturers, men who have already succeeded in the paper business, bring to the company their skill and experience. Surely a company so organized has a bright future. And notice how certain are its dividends. Here is a statement made by responsible authority that the earnings, increased by the elimination of competition, would be sufficient to pay interest, preferred dividends, and ten per cent on the common stock "while indications fully sustain the belief that they will be even higher in the future."

The official statement often descends to circumstantial details of prophecy. Witness the savings which the International Silver Company was expected to realize:

SAVINGS BY CONSOLIDATION

	Present Expenses	Reduced to
Salesrooms and clerk hire	$375,000	$100,000
Travelers' salaries	350,000	125,000
Travelers' expenses	400,000	75,000
Clerk hire, etc	275,000	50,000
Designers, machinists, etc	225,000	75,000
Advertising	200,000	50,000
	$1,825,000	$475,000
	475,000	
Total saving	$1,350,000	

PAYMENTS

	Present Expenses	Receipts
6 per cent interest on $3,500,000 bonds	$210,000	$1,350,000 [1]
7 per cent dividend on $4,500,000 preferred	315,000	526,000 [2]
10 per cent dividend on $10,000,000 common	1,000,000	
	$1,525,000	$1,876,000 [3]
		1,525,000
		$351,000 [4]

[1] Savings. [2] Previous earnings before consolidation.
[3] Total profits. [4] Surplus.

These samples are typical of the entire list. In the majority of official statements, it was claimed that the earnings of the constituent companies before consolidation were sufficient to pay dividends on the preferred stock, and that the common stock represented the capitalized value of the economies of combination. All the savings from management, shipping, buying and selling, and all the increased profits of monopoly were to go to the common stock, which was therefore assured of large dividends.

And yet, in spite of these detailed and apparently authoritative statements of profits, there was no real difference between the argument of the syndicate manager of the trust and that of the oil or town-site "boomer." The first was more dignified, that is all. The method of the appeal and the class to whom the appeal was made are the same in the case of either proposition. For, notice what the syndicate manager offered. These common stocks, which were certain of such large dividends, were freely offered at such low prices as to stamp them at the outset with the bar sinister. The average prices of various common stocks during the first month of their listing on the exchange were as follows:

American Car and Foundry	$20\frac{15}{16}$	Continental Tobacco	$53\frac{3}{4}$
American Ice	$39\frac{3}{4}$	Federal Steel	$31\frac{1}{8}$
American Malting	$27\frac{1}{8}$	International Paper	$57\frac{1}{2}$
American Smelting and Refining	$54\frac{3}{4}$	International Silver	$33\frac{1}{8}$
American Steel Hoop	$39\frac{15}{16}$	National Biscuit	$33\frac{5}{16}$
American Steel and Wire	$40\frac{1}{4}$	National Steel	$52\frac{3}{8}$
American Tin Plate	$40\frac{13}{16}$	Republic Iron and Steel	$25\frac{1}{16}$

These prices, when measured by the yield on safe investments, represented extravagant returns. Take, for example, two of the trusts above mentioned—International Paper and International Silver—both professing ability to pay ten per cent on their common stocks. With International Paper, the offering price—that is to say, the price at which the stock should have been purchased during the first month of listing—represented a yield on the investment, granted that the representations of the promoters were correct, of 17.2 per cent, while the common stock of International Silver, selling around 32 represented a return of 31.2 per cent on its purchase at that price. Nearly every trust prospectus contained, however, adroitly worded, an express or implied promise of dividends on the common stock, and any dividends on the common stock at the prices at which it was offered on the exchanges meant an enormous rate of return.

With the preferred stocks it was a little better. These stocks had actual earning power back of them, while the common stocks had only prospective earning power. The preferred stocks of the trust were generally offered around 76–80 which, at the usual dividend rate of seven per cent yielded 8.7 per cent on their purchase, a yield too large for the investor and indicating an inferior class of buyers. Even the best of the preferred stocks could not claim to rank as safe investments, although they had a certain amount of reality to sustain their value.

As for the common stock, however, what was the difference between selling a man oil stock or mining stock of fifty cents par value at five cents per share on the prospect that a gusher or a bonanza will be struck and the stock go to par or above, and selling him paper, or steel, or tobacco at 35 or 40 or 50 for a $100 share on the prospect that all the expectations of the promoter will be realized, and the stock go to par on the certainty of large dividends? Both were speculative propositions. Both are based on unknown conditions. Neither had any positive assurance to rest upon. In the one case the mine "ought" to be rich, and in the other the earnings of the trust "are expected" to be large. The mine boomer points to the growing demand for copper, and the trust boomer talks about the "marvelous prosperity of the country." The one had his calculations of cost and profit and his township and section maps; the other his expert accountants' reports, his "beliefs," "expectations," and "estimates" of the savings by consolidation and his imposing list of properties, sometimes covering the entire country. With the mining company, it is the judge, the merchant, and the mining expert who give weight to the proposition. With the trust, it was the great bankers and manufacturers who lent their influence to insure the success of the flotation. At all points, the similarity between the two propositions is complete. The trust stocks could not be sold to the investor. The speculator would buy them only on the prospect of a rate of return so large as to prove that the success of the trust was at the best problematical.

On its face, however, the proposition offered by the common stock was certainly attractive. The syndicate manager would sell a stock at 40 or 50, which must pay at least six or even ten per cent on its par value. The common stock was the residual claimant. The preferred stockholder, it is claimed, is not better off than before; but the common stockholder was to reap the full fruition of the great step in industrial progress which the formation of the trust represented. Here was offered a double inducement; a high rate of dividend if the stock was held, or an opportunity to sell at an advance.

Moreover, the syndicate manager need not rely solely upon published statements. Competent and authoritative opinion was not lacking to influence the wavering and uncertain speculator. The underwriting privileges had been sold as Judge Moore expressed it, "all over the country." Financial houses and moneyed men everywhere had been let in for a share of the underwriting and had stock to sell. Besides this, there were a large number of manufacturers in all the industrial centers who wished to realize on their stock. These institutions and individuals have a large following, and their opinions upon financial matters are held to be very weighty. The promoters of American asphalt, for example, had a long record of success in gas and electric railway enterprises behind them, and their following in Philadelphia was enormous. A proposition which had their indorsement was by most people considered worth looking into. The

11

influence which could be exerted in this way in favor of the new securities was powerful.

There need be no direct solicitation. That would be undignified, and might make trouble between friends if anything went wrong. More than this, direct solicitation was unnecessary. As Bacon remarks in his essay on Cunning: "It works better when anything seemeth to be gotten from you by question than if you offer it of yourself." This advice to buy speculative stock is almost always "gotten by question" and is disinterestedly given. The news of the formation of the trusts is in everybody's mouth. Their prospectuses are in the newspapers. Imagination magnifies their really enormous extent and power and the profits which they will realize. Their stock is now offered to the public at a low price. What more natural than to consult with one's financial adviser, and what so conservative as his opinion? He advised no one to buy, or if he ventured so far, it is always with the caution that "something may go wrong, that bit of caution which establishes him firmly as a safe adviser. He lets it be understood that he thinks well of the proposition, that he is personally interested in it, and he merely suggests that it is "worth investigating." In such matters, he who investigates is lost. The advice is often taken and the stock sold. The underwriters and owners had only to let it be known that they considered the trust stock a good thing, to gather in a large amount of money from the speculators.

There is another class to whom stock can be sold. These are the margin speculators, the people who buy stocks not to hold but to sell, whose object is not income but increased capital. By depositing a small per cent, say ten per cent, of the market value of any security with a broker, he will borrow the remainder of the money and buy stock for them, loaning them the difference between their deposit and the value of the stock, and holding the stock in his vault. His customers pay him interest on the money borrowed to buy the stock, usually a higher interest than he himself pays to the bank, and in addition a one eighth per cent commission on the par value of the shares.

The broker will buy or sell the stock as his customers may direct. By depositing $100 and paying $12.50 commission and six per cent interest on $900 the amount borrowed for him by the broker for the time he holds the stock —the speculator can become the owner of twenty shares of stock which is selling around 50. Suppose the stock goes up ten points, he may sell and double his money, less the commission and interest. If the stock declines, however, the broker takes the loss out of his margin, and if the decline is excessive the trader may be called on for more margin, failing to produce which the broker sells the stock and repays the loan incurred to buy it, crediting the speculator with any of the margin which may remain. Any dividends which may be paid on the stock during the time it is being carried are credited to the buyer. It is this fact that distinguishes gambling with chips or cards from gambling with stocks. In the first case the gambling instrument is unproductive. The "rake-off" of the house is clear loss to the players. With stocks, however, the "rake-off" is offset by the dividends. The gambling implements are themselves productive.

The speculator may also purchase an option to deliver stock in the future at the price now ruling. In this case, the broker borrows the stock or loans it out of his own office and makes the delivery within twenty-four hours for his customer. In case the stock is borrowed from another office, the borrowing broker deposits as security with the lender a sum of money equal to the market value of the stock on the day of the loan, and for this money he receives a rate of interest, called the "loan rate" on stocks, which offsets his customer's interest and makes short selling cheaper than buying. The broker is protected by the usual margin against an advance in the price of the stock. If the price declines from 100 to 95 the short seller of 100 shares orders his broker to buy for $9,500 the stock against which $10,000 has been deposited. The broker then delivers the stock to the one who has loaned it to him, and receives back his $10,000, placing $500 to his customer's account and returning to him, if he desires it, his original margin of $1,000, plus the net profits. If the stock advances, however, the short seller may be called on to protect his margin, for if the price has risen from 100 to 105, $10,500 will be necessary to buy the stock with which to take up the loan and receive back the $10,000 deposited as security. In this case, the customer has lost half his margin.

This form of gambling is very attractive. It is so much like "business," so much apparently depends on the judgment of the buyer and so little on the turn of the wheel or the chance of the draw. The speculator's pulses quicken and slow with the good or bad fortune of the nation. He is interested in the crops, in the railroad earnings, in national elections, and in foreign wars. His profits depend apparently upon his own judgment. He is as confident of winning as the gambler with a "system" is confident of breaking the bank. Moreover, speculation is respectable. It is not by all persons considered reputable to play the races; but it is not often that one loses caste by playing the stock market. Every class of the population is represented among the margin speculators. Business men and professional men are found in the better offices; clerks, teachers, ministers and women frequent the intermediate grades and the bucket shops.

The promoter may reckon with this class. It is to his interest to impress them with the favorable outlook for his enterprise in order to persuade them to buy for a rise. The outside buyer is almost always a bull. The margin speculator does not want the stock and is apt to sell on an advance. He puts his money into margins in the belief that the stock will rise in value. The more seductive the representations of the promoters, enforced as they are by the "tips" and the market letters of the brokers, the larger will be the buying. As the stock goes up, the profits realized are turned back into new margins and the advance gathers strength as it proceeds. Indeed, it often happens that the value of a speculative stock may be carried high above its investment value as indicated by the earnings of the company. The buyer for investment is, however, the half seen goal of the speculator. The investment demand always looms ahead, and the speculator deposits his margins in the belief that the market value is still below the investment value.

A stock whose value is highly uncertain, fluctuating within wide and irregular limits, affected by every breeze of rumor, such a stock as Reading common or United States Steel common, for example, is also a favorite with the speculators. It is so attractively uncertain, and there is always the chance that when it falls it will rise again. The trust stocks have all been of fluctuating value and so have been popular with the margin speculators. The inducement to engage in these operations is the national desire to get something for nothing, or rather much for little. Stories of successful operation are widely heralded, and losses are generally kept secret. Stories of large profits, like the advertisements of the Louisiana lottery, point the way to a desirable addition to a limited income. The psychology of gambling, however, is a study by itself and need no longer detain us.

In what way does this gambling furnish capital to the new enterprises? Their securities are wanted for speculative material by the brokers. They are the "chips" with which the public play the great game of speculation. The operation is something as follows: The surplus cash of the country is sent to New York City. This money can be recalled at any time, and the greater part of it is, therefore, not available for time loans. It may, however, be loaned on call. The brokers borrow this money and buy stocks for their customers. They also borrow large sums on time loans to carry their larger clients. So far as the promoter and underwriter are concerned, it is the same thing as though the broker was an investor. Their only object is to make the enterprise as attractive as possible to the public, so that the demand for speculative material may be large. The brokers, on their part, use the stocks for collateral at the banks, mixing it with other securities to support its wavering value, and make up the difference between the market price and the value which the bank puts on the stock as collateral—often about twenty points below the market—by their own funds and the margins which they require from their customers. Thus a large part of the surplus funds of the country is turned over to the founders of new enterprises through the channels of speculation. The money which the syndicate managers receive for their stock is borrowed money, but that makes no difference to them; they do not borrow it. The larger the demand for their stocks from margin speculators, the larger is the amount of money which is borrowed by the brokers and turned over to the syndicate.

The amount of this demand is very large. On September 7, 1899, the demand loans of the national banks of New York City amounted to $228,081,518. A large part of this money was loaned to speculators, and much of it on industrials. This money was turned over and over, and constantly replenished by new margins so that it might pass more than one in original exchange for stocks. The total number of shares sold on the New York Stock Exchange in 1899, a year of most active speculation in industrials, was 176,421,135, although the total number listed did not exceed 60,000,000. On the basis of these figures, each stock was sold three times over.

Speculation in high-priced stocks is too expensive for the average trader. A share selling for 300 would require $30 margin. Three thousand dollars are necessary to purchase 100 shares. A ten point rise in this stock means only $1,000 profit. But for $3,000 the speculator can purchase 600 shares of an industrial selling around 50, and a five point rise in such a stock means $3,000 profit. The lower the price of the stock, the larger is the number of shares which $1,000 invested in margins will control, and the larger is the possible profit from fluctuations. On the other hand, with the high-priced stock, the risk of loss from fluctuations, contrary to the buyer's expectation, is as great as with low-priced stocks. It was inevitable that the general advance in railway securities should transfer the speculative interest to low-priced industrials.

The *Wall Street Journal,* in an editorial of March 3, 1901, expressed this conclusion as to the speculative value of industrial shares: "It is as certain as anything in the future that industrial securities will form the principal medium for speculation in this country. The field for the formation of industrial corporations is vast, and varying degrees of skill in management coupled with the succession of good times and bad times, will make constant changes in values which will be discounted by movements in the prices of stocks."

The syndicate manager counted upon this speculative demand. It is his principal resort during the early stages of the flotation. He advertises his stock in no way so effectively as by the record of the ticker tape. By "wash sales" —i. e., sales immediately covered by purchases between brokers acting for the same interest—he creates an excitement on the curb. The stock begins to attract attention. The newspapers take it up. This or that report is given currency: "Interests that know something about steel are buying"; "The earnings of International Paper are reported by high authority to be exceedingly expectatious"; "Something is likely to be doing soon in Rubber common."

More considerable articles help these stray notes. The reader of the financial column is told that "the dividends of the industrial stocks during the past six or seven years have been remarkable in amount, and the more remarkable in that these years have been those of extended commercial depression. Now if these various companies have been able to pay good dividends through times so unprosperous commercially, the prospect is that they will continue and increase them in the years before us, when the soundest financiers have predicted an era of industrial and commercial expansion such as this country has not witnessed for a generation," etc., etc. Every day the papers are full of such material.

Leading operators come out boldly and indorse the stock. It is admitted to the Exchange. Dealings rapidly increase, and a broad market is established by a steady advance. The higher the stock climbs, the more eager are the speculators to purchase. If the syndicate manager catches the flood tide of a bull market, he may dispose of his entire holdings, as the syndicate managers of the Steel Trust would probably have done had not the panic of May 9, 1901 interfered. The New York Stock Exchange is the place where large flotations can be most quickly made. It is here that the speculative interest of the country centers. The mining boomer peddles his stock about the street and advertises it in the newspapers. He is a retailer of securities. If he realizes $50,000 from the public, he may consider himself exceptionally fortunate. The syndicate manager places his interest in charge of an expert manipulator, a wholesaler—who may "clean up" several millions in a few months.

CHAPTER XIII

UNDERWRITING

NEARLY all public flotations require the aid of the underwriter. The underwriter, as his name implies, insures or guarantees the sale of securities within a certain time at a price sufficiently below the anticipated market price to insure a profit to the guarantor. It is a matter of indifference to the corporation whether its securities are sold outright or whether a responsible syndicate guarantees the sale. In either case, the money necessary is provided at once by the bankers, who must look to the sale of the securities which they have underwritten or purchased, for their reimbursement.

In underwriting the securities of a new company, or in purchasing them outright, the banker who undertakes the responsibility of the transaction usually associates with himself a number of other individuals and banking houses in an organization known as an underwriting or subscription syndicate. The difference between underwriting and subscription is that in underwriting the securities underwritten by the banker are offered for sale by the corporation through the banker, and in subscription, the securities are purchased by the banker and offered by him to his own customers as sound investments. In either case, the association which is formed to assist him in carrying out his contract with the corporation is substantially identical, and the two forms of syndicate underwriting and subscription can be considered together.

The underwriting syndicate is a voluntary and temporary association of individuals or firms or corporations which is formed by a syndicate manager, usually a banking firm, to assist them in guaranteeing the sale of, or in purchasing an issue of stocks or bonds. The steps in the organization of the syndicate are as follows:

The original contract is made between the banker and the corporation, by which the banker agrees to either purchase certain securities at a price, or to guarantee their sale within a certain time, at a certain price. The corporation usually knows no one but the syndicate manager in the transaction, and looks only to him for the fulfillment of the agreement. The fact that the banker associates others with himself in the transaction, in an underwriting syndicate, is a matter of no concern to the corporation, although the members of the syndicate may be asked, with the consent of the corporation, to directly assume a share of the syndicate manager's liabilities.

While the syndicate manager may be a very strong banking firm, such as J. P. Morgan & Company; Kuhn, Loeb & Company, and may be able to guarantee the flotation of a very large issue of securities, it is usually advantageous to organize a syndicate. Most banking houses have a definite policy which regulates the amount of capital which they will allot to a particular enterprise. The house, for example, with a capital of $10,000,000 may have a rule that it will not invest more than $1,000,000 in any one undertaking, so that any losses which it may sustain by unsuccessful investments may be offset by the profits of those which have been profitable. When, therefore, this banking house makes an agreement to underwrite $10,000,000 of bonds or preferred stock, unless it departs from its established policy of dividing its risks, it must add to its capital the capital of its friends.

By admitting other bankers with wide connections and large numbers of clients to share in the profits of its subscription, a banking house obtains a broad market for the securities which it has for sale and by adopting this policy in all its undertakings it makes sure of quicker returns. The necessity of securing a broad market for bonds or stocks is sometimes recognized in the original contract between the corporation and the bankers by a joint agreement between several banking houses so situated as to command investment funds in different parts of the country. A recent bond issue of the American Telephone Company, for example, was taken by J. P. Morgan & Company; Kuhn, Loeb & Company; Kidder, Peabody & Company, of New York, and Baring Brothers, of London. Ordinarily, the subscription would have been offered to a New England banking house, but the New England market was unable to absorb more telephone securities and a broader market was required, to obtain which the coöperation of New York and London houses was enlisted.

An Eastern house, undertaking the underwriting or purchase of bonds of a Western enterprise, associates with itself, if possible, Western bankers whose clients are likely to be familiar with the enterprise. The syndicate is organized as follows: A contract is made between the Pennsylvania Railroad Company and Speyer & Company. The head of the banking house communicates with a number of firms and individuals with whom they have coöperated in the past. If, as in the case cited, Speyer & Company have agreed to guarantee the sale of $75,000,000 of stock of the Pennsylvania Railroad Company at 120 in return for a commission of $2,250,000, they will recite these facts in their communications to those whom they wish to join in the syndicate, and they will ask each one to indicate by return mail or telegraph, the amount of participation in the syndicate, which Speyer & Company state they propose to form, which he desires. One house will ask for $1,000,000, another house for $5,000,000, another house for $500,000, and so on. Very few will decline because, to refuse to participate in a syndicate when requested by a house of the standing of Speyer & Company, may result in excluding the banker from participation in any new syndicate, and may also cost him the coöperation of Speyer & Company in his own undertakings. After the replies have all been received, the amounts are summed up and either one of two results may be disclosed. The applications for participation in the syndicate may exceed the amount of securities which have been underwritten or purchased, and they may be below the required amount. In the second place, unless the deficiency is considerable, the plans of the syndicate manager are not disarranged, since he expected to take a certain amount of participation in the syndicate himself. It may also be necessary, in case his request for applications does not meet with a cordial response, for him to assume a much larger part of the responsibility than he originally intended. For the most part, however, this contingency is guarded against by offering participations in the syndicate to such a large number of important houses and financiers as to make it unlikely that the combined subscriptions will be below the amount which the syndicate manager considers necessary. In most cases the amount will be largely oversubscribed. He may require only $75,-000,000, and the sum of his applications to participate in the syndicate may be $150,000,000.

It is now necessary for the syndicate manager to allot these subscriptions. Since this is an association somewhat resembling the corporation, in which the liability of the participants is limited to the amounts of their subscriptions, it might be supposed that everyone would stand on the same footing, just as when subscriptions to the stock of a corporation are made. In this case, if the subscriptions are twice the amount necessary, each subscriber will expect to receive one half of the amount subscribed for.

With the underwriting or subscription syndicate, however, the procedure is different. This voluntary association or temporary corporation, which is in process of organization by the syndicate manager, is for his individual benefit. It is a business enterprise which he is promoting. While he requires the members of his syndicate to indicate how much of a participation they desire, he does not guarantee to give them all they ask for. He makes his allotment according to his understanding of his own advantage, and he considers nothing but his own interest, and the interest of the corporation for whose financial affairs he is temporarily responsible. He may assign one applicant 100 per cent of his application, another fifty per cent, another ten per cent, and another five per cent. No member of the syndicate is likely to be informed by the syndicate manager, although he may easily learn from members direct, how much allotment another member has received.

The principles which govern this allotment, looking at it from the standpoint of the syndicate manager, are as follows: In the first place, he wishes the flotation to be a success, and he makes his allotment with this object principally in view. A particular kind of securities will, in his judgment, find a ready market in Cleveland. He will allot the full amount of their applications to Cleveland bankers. If a flotation of a similar character has failed in Baltimore, Baltimore bankers will have to be content with a small share of their applications.

On the other hand, individual financiers who were not able to assist in marketing the bonds, or applicants for small amounts may receive only small percentages of allotment. The syndicate manager expects to be in business for many years; he wishes to participate in underwriting syndicates managed by other bankers. When he receives an application from a banker who is himself a manager of syndicates, he will give that banker what he asks for, since otherwise he might himself be cut off from some profitable participation in the future. Participations in syndicates, in other words, are allotted for the sake of securing participations in other syndicates. A banker makes his allotments to cultivate business good-will with the banks and trust companies from which he may wish to borrow money, and in every way possible to strengthen his position and influence by the disposition of the allotments which are entirely in his hands.

After the syndicate manager has decided upon the allotments, he sends to each subscriber a copy of the syndicate agreement which the subscriber signs, and opposite to his name places the amount of his allotment. The subscriber is then bound by the conditions of the agreement, up to, but no further than the amount for which he has subscribed. Provisions usually found in underwriting agreements are as follows:

First, the subscriber agrees to take and pay for the amount of securities for which he has subscribed when called upon by the syndicate manager, and this agreement may be enforced against him in the usual manner by a suit at law.

Second, he agrees that the syndicate manager shall have entire charge of the marketing of the bonds or stock, that he may make any and all contracts and incur any expenses necessary to secure their sale, and that all these charges and expenses shall be a first claim upon the profits of the syndicate. An illustration of the large discretion given to the syndicate manager is taken from the agreement between Speyer & Company and the members of the syndicate which underwrote the $75,000,000 stock issue of the Pennsylvania. This agreement provided in part as follows:

> The managers may from time to time in their discretion purchase upon the markets shares of stock of the railroad, or rights to subscribe for stock, and in case of any such purchases the syndicate obligation shall be increased by the amount thereof, and the obligation of each subscriber shall be increased proportionately, provided, however, that the aggregate syndicate obligation shall not at any time be increased by such purchases by an amount exceeding ten per cent of the aggregate subscription price of the stock offered to the stockholders.
>
> The syndicate subscribers appoint the syndicate managers their agents and attorneys, with full power to do any and all acts expedient to perform the agreement, including the repurchase and resale from time to time for the account of the syndicate of any stock or rights which may have been sold for account of the syndicate, and generally such transactions in shares and rights as they may deem best.
>
> The syndicate is to continue in force until January

1, 1904, but the managers may terminate it at any time on notice.

Any shares or subscription rights received by the managers may from time to time be sold at public or private sale at such prices as the managers may deem proper.

In case the managers shall distribute among the subscribers any stock or rights during the existence of the syndicate, it shall be held by the respective subscribers subject to the delivery to the syndicate managers upon demand, and no subscriber shall prior to the termination of the syndicate sell or contract for the sale of any of the syndicate stock or rights.

Third, it is usually, although not invariably, agreed that the syndicate manager shall assign to the members of the syndicate a certain percentage of the profits on the transaction. The remainder, sometimes one fifth, sometimes a smaller amount, is reserved as his own profit.

Fourth, the syndicate manager also reserves the right to participate, up to the amount of his reservation for himself, as a regular member of the syndicate.

Fifth, any member of the syndicate may, at any time during its life, withdraw any of the securities at the price named in his subscription.

Sixth, it may be provided that he may assign a portion or all of his responsibility to the syndicate manager or others, and that, with the consent of the syndicate manager, he may, in this manner, be relieved of his responsibility.

Seventh, it may be provided that the members of the syndicate are to coöperate with the syndicate manager in borrowing a portion of the price of the securities underwritten or subscribed for, from banks, in which case their participation may be put in the form of a negotiable instrument so that the syndicate manager can assign it as additional security.

Eighth, the syndicate manager agrees to be responsible for good faith in the management of the syndicate, and in the distribution of profits, and for nothing else.

The terms of the underwriting agreement carry out the

idea that this is the private enterprise of the syndicate manager, which the members enter on the terms which he prescribes, and which leaves him absolute control of all the transactions necessary to carry out the purposes of the syndicate. His associates in the syndicate place the whole management in his hands. He may make or modify contracts in the interest of the syndicate; he may incur such expenses as he deems necessary; he may buy or sell the securities on the market, and he is frequently authorized to hypothecate the subscriptions of the members to provide the funds necessary for his advances to the company.

A common feature of large syndicate transactions is the organization of sub-syndicates. These differ in no essential respect from the ordinary syndicate. They are divisions of the responsibility apportioned by members of the syndicate among their own friends on much the same terms and conditions as those to which they have subscribed in the original syndicate agreement. It often happens that a man will request a larger amount of participation in a syndicate than he expects to carry, so that he may admit some of his friends to share in his expected profits, or he may become doubtful of the outcome of the syndicate, and may wish to dispose of a part or all of his responsibility to others. As a rule, the syndicate manager does not know the members of the sub-syndicate any more than the corporation knows the members of the original syndicate. The ramifications of these sub-syndicates may be very extensive. The first United States Steel Underwriting Syndicate, which involved $200,000,000, for example, it was understood, was shared in by almost every financier of any importance in the United States.

After the syndicate has been organized, the syndicate manager usually makes a call upon the members for a certain percentage, often twenty-five per cent of their subscriptions. This must be paid in cash. With these subscriptions as a basis, he borrows the balance of the amount necessary from banks and trust companies which may themselves be interested in the syndicate, and therefore disposed to assist him.

These loans he may make on his own security, with the pledge of the bonds or stocks which he has underwritten or purchased, on the certificates representing these securities, or he may, as above described, pledge in addition the responsibility of the members of his syndicate. He then sells the stocks or bonds by the ordinary methods employed in marketing securities, direct to the investor, indirectly through fiscal agents, and also by utilizing the various stock exchanges on which the securities are listed. The members of the syndicate may act as his agents and sell on commission.

The syndicate is organized for a certain term. At the end of that term, if the securities are not sold, two alternatives are open, either the syndicate can be extended, in which case the securities remain in the hands of the syndicate manager, and the loans which he has made to supply the cash to the corporation are renewed, or the syndicate is dissolved. The proceeds of the securities which have been sold are then applied to paying any loans which may have been incurred, and the unsold securities are distributed to the members of the syndicate, according to their several participations, payment being made in cash. It is customary to make at least one extension of a syndicate which has not been successful during its original term, and in some cases syndicates have been extended several times.

The method of dissolving a syndicate is illustrated by the following letter, addressed by J. P. Morgan & Company, managers of the syndicate which guaranteed the preferred stock conversion plan of the United States Steel Corporation, to the syndicate members.

PREFERRED STOCK RETIREMENT SYNDICATE—FINAL NOTICE

DEAR SIR: Referring to our circular letter of Sept. 14, 1903, we beg to inform you that we shall be prepared to close the syndicate account on May 17, 1904.

Your subscription to the syndicate was for $3,750 bonds, of which amount 80 per cent was payable in preferred stock and 20 per cent in cash at par and interest.

Having delivered to you on Oct. 1, 1903, a portion of the bonds payable in preferred stock, there remains still to be delivered to you the balance of such bonds, amounting to $1,000 bonds, ex-matured coupons, accounted for below:

On Oct. 1, 1903, we called from you 25 per cent of your cash subscription, leaving still due from you 75 per cent of such cash subscription, which, with accrued interest to May 17, amounts to..................		$564.18
Your share of the amount standing to the credit of the syndicate on May 17, 1904, including interest at 5 per cent per annum on the portion of cash subscription paid Oct. 1, 1903, will be	$325.50	
To which is added the amount of coupons due Nov. 1, 1903 (7 months), and May 1, 1904, on the undelivered portion of bonds payable in preferred stock mentioned above....	54.18	379.68
This leaves a balance due from you in final settlement of		$184.50

for which kindly hand us your check on Tuesday, May 17, 1904, upon receipt of which and upon surrender of your certificate of participation, properly indorsed, we shall be prepared to deliver to you all the bonds subscribed for by you in cash, together with the balance of the bonds payable in preferred stock, as stated above, making total delivery to you at that time of $1,750 bonds. Fractional amounts of bonds will be adjusted in cash.

(Signed) J. P. Morgan & Co.

The syndicate manager may not have chosen to carry on the operation with the proceeds of loans, and may have called upon the members of the syndicate to pay up the full amount of their participations before the term of the syndicate has expired. In this case, since they have all paid for the securities, the dissolution of the syndicate involves merely the distribution of the unsold securities among the members.

In settling the affairs of an underwriting syndicate, the syndicate manager renders no accounting to the members, nor is any accounting asked for. The transaction is based upon good faith, and legal guarantees are not required. There is no instance on record where a banking house of good reputation was sued for an accounting by members of a syndicate which it had organized. If crookedness or sharp dealing were attempted by a syndicate manager, even though he renders no accounting, the fact would soon become known, and would make it impossible for him to secure participation in future syndicates. Thus the accounting is really not necessary in order to insure fair dealing. Furthermore, if any member of a syndicate fails to pay for his bonds as requested, no proceedings are instituted against him by the syndicate manager. He is simply dropped from the manager's list, and it may be difficult for him to obtain financial assistance or an opportunity to participate in profitable financial operations in the future. Instances of such failure are, however, rare. The consequences to a man's reputation are serious, and syndicate members will strain every resource, and will dispose of their participations even at a heavy sacrifice, in order to make good their word to the syndicate manager.

Participations in underwriting and subscription syndicates are sometimes very profitable. If market conditions are auspicious, it frequently happens that the entire issue of securities may be sold to the public before any calls are made upon the subscriber. Usually, however, a portion of the subscription is called, but if the syndicate is successful, only one call is likely to be made. The syndicate which subscribed $200,000,000 to assist in the flotation of the United States Steel Corporation, paid in $25,000,000 and received back $65,000,000. On the other hand, the security markets may be unfavorable, owing to stringent money markets, or to distrust of some classes of investments, and syndicates may be left with large amounts on their hands which their members must carry, sometimes for years, before they can dispose of them at a profit. An example of this failure is furnished by the dissolution of the syndicate which underwrote the convertible bond issue of $12,000,000 for the Erie. The syndicate was dissolved in January, 1907, with three fourths of the bonds remaining on hand. The failure of the International Mercantile Marine bond syndicate whose members were forced to take practically all the bonds, also shows how uncertain are the profits in these ventures. Syndicate participations are frequently taken by investors and financial institutions in order to secure bonds at a lower price than could be had from any other source of supply. This practice gave rise to grave abuses, since participation for directors and officers of life insurance companies, for example, would be carried by the company, at the company's risk, with nothing but a general understanding that it would be indemnified by the beneficiary for any loss. Such participations are now illegal in New York for insurance companies.

CHAPTER XIV

THE DETERMINATION OF PROFITS

THE financing of the corporation has now been completed. The money for the construction of its plant and the inauguration of its business has been paid into its treasury; its construction work has been completed; it has been formally launched as a going concern. We have next to consider the determination of its profits in order to indicate the principles which govern their management and distribution.

The subject of corporation finance is not concerned with the methods by which profits are made. The principles of profit making are of general application, and are not affected by the form of organization under which a business is conducted. They are alike for the partnership and for the corporation. It is, however, of peculiar importance to a corporation, even more important than to a partnership, that its profits should be, at regular intervals, accurately determined. The partnership or the private corporation, whose owners are in close touch with its affairs, may tolerate a degree of laxity or inaccuracy in the determination of its profits. If too much is drawn from the business in one year, the drawing accounts of the partners may be reduced the year following. If profits are overestimated, and the business on that account is too rapidly expanding, it may be possible, by economizing and contracting the scale of operations, for the concern, without injury to its credit, to regain its former position. These private corporations, moreover, grow out of earnings. They do not so often appeal to the outside investor, as the public corporation is forced to do, for funds with which to enlarge their business. Their shares and evidences of debt are not dealt in on the public exchanges. Partnership interests are not expressed in negotiable form, and the shares of private corporations are to a less extent employed as collateral for loans. For these reasons, while it is essential for every business enterprise to ascertain its exact financial status at fixed intervals, the accurate determination of profits for the partnership or the private corporation is less essential than for the public corporation.

The stocks and bonds of public corporations which appeal to the investor to provide them capital, are widely held by individuals and institutions who draw income from these securities. This interest should be regularly paid, and dividends should be distributed without serious and sudden changes in their rates. These regular payments can only be counted on if the fund out of which they are to be made is exactly determined. The securities of public corporations, moreover, are usually listed on the exchanges and are bought and sold every day. A free market for their securities is of great importance to corporations. They are enabled, by this means, to obtain, from time to time, additional sums of money for the enlargement of their business. A primary essential to a free market is accurate information concerning the financial status of the companies issuing these securities. Corporation stocks and bonds are deposited in enormous amounts with banks and trust companies as collateral for loans, and the bank cannot lend intelligently, unless it is placed in the possession of all essential information concerning the affairs of the enterprise.

It is not merely necessary that their profits should be accurately determined by public corporations, but it is equally essential that they should be stated in simple and intelligible form, so that the investor and the banker can, without difficulty, reach an accurate conclusion as to their earning power and financial condition. For a long time, American railway companies did not recognize the necessity of making such statements of assets and earnings, and their stocks were the objects of speculation which always thrives upon uncertainty. This condition has long since passed away. The reports of our railroad companies, even before the law compelled them to make an accurate determination of their profits and a full statement of their financial condition, leave little to be desired. The industrial corporations are more remiss in making statements of their condition. Until the United States Steel Corporation set the example by publishing what is, probably, the most satisfactory report of any of the large industrials, officials of these corporations generally refused to give information, on the ground that disclosure of the condition of their business would give an advantage to their competitors. In time, however, this aversion to revealing the condition of their affairs was worn away by the necessity of obtaining a broad market for their securities, which could not be had without some information upon which the investor could base his judgment. The reports of industrial corporations are still, as a class, far from being as complete as the reports of the railroads. Street railway and public service corporations generally give even more meager information than do the industrials. Steady improvement in the direction of publicity is, however, everywhere evident. Even if the laws do not intervene to compel full statements of income and expenditures, assets and liabilities, the force of financial opinion may be relied upon to accomplish this result.

It is not necessary, as corporation officials have feared, that the amount of information which is necessary to acquaint the investor with the financial condition of the property in which he is interested should involve the disclosure of the secrets of the business. This may be illustrated by an instance related by a public accountant, which shows the possibility of harmonizing publicity for the investor with secrecy as to essential details with which the investor had no legitimate concern. The accountant was engaged to make a report on a newspaper property which was about to be sold by order of the court. The report was especially full and detailed, but not sufficiently explicit to suit certain persons, who requested information as to the returns from advertising and the amount paid for salaries. The Master in Chancery refused to allow this information to be given on the ground that the competitors would discover the secrets of the business. The accountant pointed out, however, that by presenting merely the totals, without mentioning individual items, this danger could be avoided, and at the same time the investor could be fully informed. The competitors of this paper could not have profited from information as to the aggregate salaries paid or the total amount of advertising receipts. What they were concerned to discover, was the amount paid to certain individuals on the staff, and the terms of particular advertising contracts. This information, however, would have been of no assistance to the investor, and could easily have been dispensed with.

Recognizing the necessity, from the standpoint of the public corporation, that its profits should be exactly ascertained, and that clear and intelligible statements of its condition should be made, we proceed to consider the methods by which the determination of profits is accomplished. The profits of a corporation may be defined as the increase in the net worth of a corporation over a given period. The net or present worth of a business consists of the difference between assets and liabilities. In a manufacturing concern, the statement of assets and liabilities of a given year might be as follows on January 1st:

Assets		Liabilities	
Plant	$1,000,000	Capital stock	$100,000
Accounts receivable	500,000	Bonds secured by mortgage	500,000
Materials and supplies	300,000	Pay-rolls, vouchers, etc	200,000
Cash	250,000	Surplus	1,250,000
	$2,050,000		$2,050,000

On December 31st of the same year, if the business had been prosperously conducted, and no withdrawals had been made, the statement might be as follows:

Assets		Liabilities	
Plant	$1,250,000	Capital stock	$200,000
Accounts receivable	600,000	Bonds	500,000
Materials and supplies	400,000	Pay-rolls, vouchers, etc	350,000
Cash	350,000	Net present worth	1,550,000
	$2,600,000		$2,600,000

The results of this comparison would show in the following table of differences:

Net present worth, January 1st	$1,250,000
" " " December 31st	1,550,000
Increase	$300,000

It appears that the net present worth, the difference between assets and liabilities, usually called the "surplus," has increased $300,000 during the year. The company has succeeded in increasing its assets over the increase in its liabilities by this amount. During the year, however, various payments will have usually been made on account of interest and dividends. The amount of these payments must be added to the increase in surplus in order to ascertain the profits of the year.

The profits of a business are expressed in the following form which is used by the International Harvester Company to express the results of its business during 1908:

	1908
Total sales	$72,541,771
Manufacturing and distributing cost	59,615,222
Net earnings from operation	$12,926,549
Miscellaneous income	524,598
Total income	$13,451,147
Administrative and general expenses	520,769
Net income	$12,930,378

CHARGES:	
Total deductions	$4,044,695
Net profits	$8,885,683
Dividends	4,200,000
Undivided profits	$4,685,683
Previous surplus	12,006,306

This form, with unimportant modifications, is used by every corporation which makes any report of its condition. We start with gross earnings, the product of sales or commodities, services or contracts, according as the business is a manufacturing or jobbing company or a bank or insurance company. From the gross earnings of the International Harvester Company for 1908 these sales were $72,541,771. From these gross earnings are deducted the cost of running the business, maintaining the plant, and selling the product. For the International Harvester Company, this amount was $59,615,222. The difference between the receipts and the payments represents the net earnings from operation, in the above statement, $12,926,549. To this amount must be added items grouped under the head of other income. For the International Harvester Company, this "other income" was comparatively small, only $524,598, leaving total income at $13,451,147. This company next deducts administrative and general expenses before arriving at the balance of net income. It is a common practice to include administrative and general expenses with operating expenses. Making this last deduction, we arrive at the total of net income of the International Harvester Company of $12,930,378. This represents the combined earnings and income of the business during the calendar year ending December 31, 1908.

Various claimants now appear to this income. First comes the state which receives taxes; then the creditor with his demand for interest and sinking funds; then the corporation demanding that its plant shall be fully maintained, and that provision shall be made against the day when it is worn out; also asking money for insurance and losses incident to the conduct of the business. There is also the claim of the owner of property which the corporation holds under lease, known as rentals. These deductions, added together, make the "total deductions" by the International Harvester Company from income, before the owners can draw anything from the business, $4,044,695. Deducting this amount from the net income, there is a balance available for distribution to stockholders of $8,885,683. This company has $120,000,000 of capital stock, equally divided between preferred and common stock. The preferred stock pays seven per cent dividends and the dividend is cumulative. It is necessary, if the profits permit, that dividends on the preferred stock should be paid. Seven per cent on $60,000,000 of preferred stock calls for a distribution of $4,200,000, leaving $4,685,683 for the common stock. The directors of the International Harvester Company have recently declared a dividend on the common stock. At the date of this report, however, the business needed money for its development; it was not deemed wise to pay any common dividend, and the undivided profits, amounting to $4,685,683, were retained in the business. This amount was now transferred from the income account to the balance sheet, increasing the excess of assets over liabilities from $12,600,307 to $16,691,989.

This addition to the surplus was accomplished by an increase in certain assets of the company and a decrease in certain liabilities which appear in the table on page 176. The balance sheet surplus represents the accumulations of undisturbed profits over a series of years. It may, in turn, be distributed by a readjustment of the capitalization according to methods which will be discussed in a later chapter.

Having now defined the surplus of a corporation, we have next to examine the sources from which these profits are derived. We find these to be as follows:

First, income arising directly from the company's business.

Second, premiums on the sale of stocks and bonds of the company.

Assets	1908	1907
Property account	$63,680,776	$62,844,136
Deferred charges to operations	189,683	285,288
Insurance fund assets	400,832	....
Finished products, raw material, etc	33,854,933	35,140,416
Material purchased for current season	13,832,123	15,147,210
Farmers' and agents' notes	25,471,132	26,583,001
Accounts receivable less contingent reserve	10,840,098	12,708,509
Cash	9,339,055	3,573,894
Total	$157,608,632	$156,282,454
Liabilities		
Preferred stock	$60,000,000	$60,000,000
Common stock	60,000,000	60,000,000
Purchase money obligations	....	3,450,195
Bills payable	8,286,664	10,465,775
Audited vouchers, accrued interest, taxes etc	4,729,387	4,543,443
Preferred dividend payable	1,050,000	1,050,000
Reserves	6,850,540	4,766,734
Surplus	16,692,041	12,006,307
Total	$157,608,632	$156,282,454

Third, profits arising from the sale of other assets of the company no longer needed for its business.

Fourth, profits arising from a revaluation of the company's property.

We have now to consider these sources of profits from the standpoint of an accurate determination of their several accounts. Gross earnings represent the receipts from the sale of services, contracts, or commodities. These receipts are in the form either of cash or of promises to pay cash. In ascertaining their amount, it is necessary to exclude all items such as rebates to customers and cash discounts. When the business is carried on among several departments or sub-companies, all sales between departments or subsidiary companies should also be excluded. It is also necessary to exclude all bad or doubtful debts and accounts.

Operating expenses are divided into two general classes: expenses incurred in operating the plant; and expenses incurred in keeping the plant in good condition. A railroad company divides its operating expenses into five classes, namely, maintenance of way and structures; maintenance of equipment; conducting transportation, traffic, and general expenses. The nature of these expenses may be understood from some of the items under each classification. The largest items under maintenance of way and structure are track maintenance, road cleaning and ballasting, rails, ties, buildings and grounds and track material. Under maintenance of equipment, the largest items are repairs of locomotives, repairs of passenger and freight cars, and repairs of tools and machinery. Under conducting transportation, we find the following principal items:

Station service,
Road men,
Road enginemen and firemen,
Fuel for locomotives,
Engine house men,
Trainmen,
Telephone and telegraph.

The general expenses and the traffic expenses consist mainly of salaries paid to employees and officials.

We have here illustrated the essential distinction between the cost of running the road and the cost of maintaining it. All those expenses involved in obtaining freight and passengers, in receiving and caring for them, in transporting and delivering them in safety to their destination, are classed under the head of traffic and conducting transportation. Those expenses, on the other hand, which result in keeping the plant of the railway, its track, bridges, stations, cars, locomotives, round houses, repair shops, in good condition and in efficient working order, are classed under maintenance expenses, and, for purposes of convenience in railway accounting, are divided into Maintenance of Way and Structure, and Maintenance of Equipment.

The cost of operation—in the railway field, the cost of conducting transportation—need not further concern us. Its principles vary with every industry, and have no special significance for the subject of corporation finance. The cost of maintenance, however, is a division of operating expenses in which rules and principles have been developed of general application, and of peculiar importance in interpreting the financial operations of public corporations.

The maintenance of physical property involves the following: First, the establishment of certain standards of physical condition which may be either printed in books of rules or may exist only in the minds of foremen and superintendents; second; the expenditure of money on labor, appliances and materials in order to keep the property in a condition corresponding to this standard. A standard, for example, for a railway track is a description of the track and roadway as it ought to be, in other words, an ideal which the Maintenance of Way Department is constantly striving to attain, but which, while they may never fall far below, they never quite reach. The accompanying diagram gives

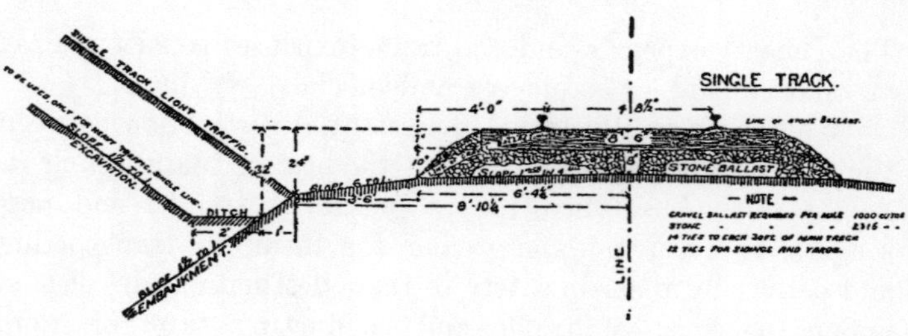

in cross section the standard roadbed adopted by the Pennsylvania Railroad. This diagram represents the condition of the roadbed as it should be if it is to be preserved at its highest efficiency. This diagram is supplemented and explained by specifications which furnish detailed direction to the Maintenance of Way Department as to the methods which must be followed in keeping the track in repair. Some of these specifications are as follows for the Pennsylvania Railroad Company:

1. *Roadbed.* The surface of the roadbed should be graded to a regular and uniform subgrade, sloping gradually from the centre toward the ditches.

2. *Ballast.* There shall be a uniform depth of six (6) to twelve (12) inches of well-broken stone, or gravel, cleaned from dust, by passing over a screen of one-quarter-inch mesh, spread over the roadbed, and surfaced to a true grade, upon which the ties are to be laid. After the ties and rails have been properly laid and surfaced, the ballast must be filled up as shown on standard plan; and also between the main tracks and sidings where stone ballast is used. All stone ballast to be of uniform size; the stone used must be of an approved quality, broken uniformly, not larger than a cube that will pass through a two-inch ring. On embankments that are not well settled, the surface of the roadbed shall be brought up with cinder, gravel, or some other suitable material.

3. *Cross-ties.* The ties are to be regularly placed upon the ballast. They must be properly and evenly placed, with ten (10) inches between the edges of bearing surface at joints, with intermediate ties evenly spaced; and the ends on the outside on double track, and on the right-hand side going north or west on single track, lined up parallel with the rails. The ties must not be notched under any circumstances; but, should they be twisted, they must be made true with the adze, that the rails may have an even bearing over the whole breadth of the tie. For all tracks on main line and branch roads, the rules governing the use of cross-ties shall be as follows:

a. First-class cross-ties shall be used in tracks where passenger and freight trains run at full speed.

b. For tracks where the trains run at slow speed, new second-class ties shall be used. For all tracks in yards, or temporary tracks laid for construction purposes or otherwise, second-class and cull ties, or good second-hand ties taken out of main track shall be used.

. . . . . .

Specifications for Cross-ties, Revised March 24, 1902.

Kind of Timber.—The approved timber for cross-ties shall be White Oak, Rock Oak, Burr Oak, Post Oak, Locust, Walnut, Yellow Pine or Chestnut. Other kinds of wood will not be accepted, unless regularly ordered and specified.

Quality and Manufacture.—The timber should be cut in the fall and winter, say from September 1st to March 1st. All ties must be cut from good sound living timber, well manufactured to size and length, straight, free from large, loose or decayed knots, splits, shakes or any other defects that may impair the strength and durability of the timber for the purpose intended; pole ties must have two parallel face sides, hewn or sawed with the grain of the wood out of wind or twist, and stripped of bark; square-sawed ties must be sawed with the grain of the wood; square-hewed ties may be made of split timber, but must be straight and out of wind or twist. Yellow pine must be long leaf, grown in the interior belt of Georgia, Florida, Alabama or Mississippi. Yellow pine ties must be square, and may be hewed or sawed; the heart should be in the center and not more than one inch of sap, measured on the face or side, will be allowed on each corner. All ties must be sawed off square at the ends.

Pole ties less than six inch face, square sawed or square-hewed ties less than seven inch face, and Yellow Pine ties less than eight inch face, will be classed as culls, and will not be accepted unless specially ordered.

Classes of Ties.—The following table [see page 181] shows the kind, size and permitted variation of crossties:

Kind of Ties	Size	Variations in Thickness	Variations in Width	Variations in Length
No. 1 Pole...........	7" thick x 7" face x 8' 6" long..	¼" under and ½" over 7"	7" over................	1" under and over
No. 2 Pole...........	Not less than 6" face.........	Not exceeding ¾" under 7"	....	1½" under and over
No. 1 Square Sawed...	7" thick x 9" face x 8' 6" long..	¼" under and ½" over 7"	1" under and 5" over......	1" under and over
No. 2 Square Sawed...	Not less than 7" face.........	Not exceeding ¾" under 7"	....	1½" under and over
No. 1 Square Hewed...	7" thick x 9" face x 8' 6" long..	¼" under and ½" over 7"	1" under and 5" over......	1" under and over
No. 2 Square Hewed...	Not less than 7" face.........	Not exceeding ¾" under 7"	....	1½" under and over
No. 1 Yellow Pine.....	7" thick x 9" face x 8' 6" long..	¼" under and ½" over 7"	Not over 5"............	1" under and over
No. 2 Yellow Pine.....	*Not less than 8" face, including sap allowance. If face is all heart, should be classed as No. 1	¼" under and ½" over 7"	....	1½" under and over

. . . .

c. On all running tracks where the weight of rail is seventy pounds per yard and over, fourteen ties shall be used to each thirty feet of track, and for all tracks in yards and for temporary use, *not more* than twelve ties shall be used for each thirty feet of track.

Line and Surface.—The track shall be laid in true line and surface; the rails are to be laid and spiked after the ties have been bedded in the ballast; and on curves, the proper elevation must be given to the outer rail and carried uniformly around the curve. This elevation should be commenced from fifty (50) to three hundred (300) feet back of the point of curvature, depending on the degree of the curve and speed of trains, and increased uniformly to the latter points where the full elevation is attained. The same method should be adopted in leaving the curve.

d. In removing cross-ties from the main tracks, they shall be taken out only as they become unfitted for service, in the manner generally known as "spotting ties," and not by entire renewals in continuous sections, and Subdivision Foremen will be held responsible for the proper observance of this rule. It shall be the duty of the Supervisor or his assistant to walk over the track with the Foreman and personally inspect the ties to be renewed before he authorizes the same to be taken out and replaced with the new ones.

. . . .

Ditches.—The cross-section of ditches at the highest point must be the width and depth as shown on the standard drawing, and graded parallel with the track, so as to pass water freely during heavy rains and thoroughly drain the ballast and roadbed. The line of the bottom of the ditch must be made parallel with the rails, and well and neatly defined, at the standard distance from the outside rail. All necessary cross drains must be put in at proper intervals. Earth taken from ditches or elsewhere must not be left at or near the ends of the ties, thrown up on the slopes of cuts, nor on the ballast, but must be deposited over the sides of embankments. Berm ditches

> shall be provided to protect the slopes of cuts, where necessary. The channels of streams for a considerable distance above the road should be examined, and brush, drift and other obstructions removed. Ditches, culverts and box drains should be cleared of all obstructions, and the outlets and inlets of the same kept open to allow a free flow of water at all times.

Similar standard specifications exist for every part of the railroad's property. It is the duty of the Maintenance Departments to see that the property is always kept in this condition. A variety of agencies are constantly at work to lower these standards. The pounding of heavy trains throws the track out of alignment, grinds the ballast to powder, wears the rails, especially on the curves, and loosens the spikes and fish plates. And while the locomotives and cars are destroying the track they are constantly destroying themselves. Wheels become worn, frames loose, paint wears off, glass is broken, boiler tubes are filled with scale, furniture and fittings become dirty and dingy.

While the running of the trains is doing all this damage, the agencies of nature are ceaselessly at work upon the roadway. Rain, sun, frost and running water are constantly wearing away the roadway. Water seeps into the ties around the spikes, carrying in bacteria and fungi, and in time the wood decays. In the spring, when the ground thaws, the track is lifted and wrenched out of line and surface; erosion is constantly filling up the ditches and damming up water which settles around the ballast and helps on the disintegration of the roadbed. The ballast, from its own weight and that of the track and trains, settles into the ground. Sunshine, wind and rain unite to destroy paint and timbers. Frost makes rails and fastenings brittle. All these manifold agencies of destruction are incessantly at work to pull down the road below its established standard.

The property of the railroad is also subjected to occasional accidents, sometimes rising to the dignity of catastrophes. Streams may flood and wash away large sections of track and numerous bridges, railway terminals may be destroyed by fire, numerous train wrecks from collisions or derailments are constantly occurring, destroying large amounts of property. It is the business of the Maintenance Department to combat these forces of destruction, and to repair the damage which is incessantly being inflicted upon the property of the company. The track and equipment of a railway are the subject of constant inspection and close scrutiny.

The work of the Maintenance Department of a corporation may be illustrated from the Maintenance and Repair Shop Practice of the Interborough Rapid Transit Company described in the *Street Railway Journal* for April 25th and May 23, 1908. This department has charge of keeping in good condition all the cars on the elevated and subway lines on Manhattan Island. The work is done in two shops, one at Ninety-eighth Street and Third Avenue, and the other at 148th Street and Lenox Avenue. These shops are equipped with machine tools, electric hoists and cranes, and the Ninety-eighth Street shop contains in addition a brass foundry and a paint shop. When a car needs any overhauling or repairs it is put into the shop, the elevated cars at Ninety-eighth Street and the subway cars at 148th Street. The selection of cars for overhauling is made on the basis of mileage. For the elevated roads, it is assumed that a car will run 65,000 miles before it needs attention. This standard has been modified for the subway cars so that each piece of equipment in the car, and the car itself, has a predetermined mileage which it is supposed to run before needing attention. As fast as this mileage is reached, the car is put into the shop and that particular part is overhauled. By this method the entire car does not need attention every time it reaches the shop. In the case of accidents to cars, general overhauling and complete repair may be necessary before the standard mileage has been reached.

The nature of the work done in these shops may be illustrated from the practice followed in painting the cars. Painting records and records of inspection for painting show the date the car was last in the shop, the date last inspected, the date it should be sent to the shop, and the class of painting for which it is due. The cars are graded in four classes with regard to the condition of the paint: Class A, to be burned off and repainted from the wood up. B, to be scraped thoroughly, cut in, lettering and striping touched up and varnished. C, sash to be removed, burned off and painted; otherwise same as Class B. D, car to be scrubbed and varnished.

Inspection of cars is made on the road from time to time, and the cars are brought in on predetermined dates as required. When they come into the shop they are classified; their trucks are taken off to be taken to the truck repair shop; any required carpenter work is done on the car, all trimmings are stripped off and the sash and doors are removed; sashes needing repairs are taken to the mill and afterwards painted. The cars are now hauled on the shop trucks to the paint shop. When the painting is completed they are returned to the repair shop and mounted on their regular trucks which, in the meantime, have been overhauled and repaired. Every large corporation follows some such system in maintaining its plant and equipment, although the system is not always so well worked out as by the Interborough. Every manufacturing business, no matter how small, would profit by an imitation of the practice adopted by these large companies in the up-keep of their plant and equipment.

It is the custom of those corporations, whose accounting methods are constructed along conservative lines, to charge to maintenance not merely the cost of repairing the property, but also the cost of all renewals due to breakages or failures in service, and of replacements due to the substitution of some improved appliance. If the maintenance account were strictly interpreted, the difference between the cost of new rails or ties substituted for rails or ties which are either worn out or inadequate to carry the strain of heavier cars or engines, might be a charge to capital account. The usual practice, however, is to call all such expenditures betterments, and either to charge them direct to maintenance or into some account, such as extraordinary expenditure, created for the purpose. Such expenditures should not be charged to capital.

A betterment expense is one which raises the standard of construction. Examples of such expenditures, taking our illustration from the railroads, are the substitution of stone for gravel ballast, and of masonry embankments or steel structures for wooden trestles, replacing light rail with heavy rail, lining tunnels with brick or concrete, substituting ties treated with some preservative to prolong life for untreated ties, fencing right of way, elevating tracks in cities, and such like expenditures whose object is to raise the physical standard of the property. When this new standard has been established, it is the duty of the Maintenance of Way Department to maintain it in the same manner as the lower standard which it succeeds.

These betterment expenses, although they represent an increase in the cost of the property, should not, in the opinion of most accounting officers of corporations, figure on the balance sheet as an addition to any asset account. It is true that they may reduce the cost of operation. They may even enable the company to handle a larger business, or to handle its existing business more expeditiously and economically. On the other hand, they may do no more than maintain the earnings of the company at their former level. A railroad company has always to meet competition which may force it to reduce its rates, or to improve the quality and cost of its service. The rates and prices of all public service corporations are also liable to reduction by action of the legislature or some public service commission, and the improvements and economies resulting from betterment expenses may be no more than sufficient to offset the increased cost in operation, due to higher prices or higher wages.

Former President Roberts, of the Pennsylvania Railroad Company, in his report of 1890, explained the betterment policy of the Pennsylvania Railroad which has always been to charge the cost of such expenditures to "Extraordinary Expenditures" as follows: "The next item is that of extraordinary expenditure not properly chargeable to capital account, and is one to which attention has been called by our English stockholders. They claim that this is a capital expenditure and should not be charged against the current income; it is made up largely of moneys expended in straightening the line, in improving the character of the stations, in providing additional track at various points, in changing iron bridges to stone, and wooden bridges to iron, and similar improvements that are necessary from time to time and that are not properly chargeable to capital account, because they do not actually increase the gross earnings of your property, but simply maintain it in a condition to effectively and economically handle the traffic at the low rates shown in the report, and enable it to earn the interest on the money previously invested."

President Roberts here shows why the Pennsylvania could not safely issue new capital for the betterments which he enumerates. In one period of five years, from 1898 to 1902, the Pennsylvania spent $33,804,000 out of earnings upon betterments, and yet the increase in the balance to the credit of profit and loss, representing the additions to the book value of assets resulting from these expenditures, was only $1,919,000. During this period of five years, $30,885,000 of earnings was apparently swallowed up in the property. The cost of these large additions to the value of productive assets was charged to capital account, but only in those cases where "they actually increased the earnings of the property." These betterment expenditures are only indirectly and remotely productive. They are demanded by the general advance in railway practice, and they may eventually become profitable. A conservative management, however, pays for them out of earnings and refuses to add their cost to the book value of the assets.

CHAPTER XV

THE DETERMINATION OF PROFITS—DEPRECIATION

WELL-MANAGED business enterprises, and especially public corporations to whose standing and reputation, as already explained, an accurate determination of their profits is essential, make provision out of their income for impairment in the value of their physical assets which is known as depreciation. The life of every tool, building, machine or structure which a company may own, with the possible exception of permanent structures, such as concrete bridges, wharves, permanent roadway, etc., is limited. No matter how carefully a machine may be repaired, no matter how attentive the Equipment Department may be to painting cars and rewinding armatures, the time finally comes when the machine, or car, or locomotive, or building is no longer fit for use. Every piece of productive property, like every normal individual, has a period of mature and vigorous life when repairs are at a minimum and work at a maximum, and a period of old age, finally ending in dissolution. This period of useful service, in a machine as in an individual, may be lengthened by proper care. If the individual does not observe the laws of health, if he works under unsanitary conditions, or is subjected to excessive labor, his working life is shortened. In the same way unless the machine is repaired when out of order, is sheltered from the weather, and is saved from undue stresses and strains, the term of its active life is reduced.

The termination of the active life of a machine may also be due to the discovery of some better machine for doing the same work. Competition forces progressive business concerns to keep their plants up to date so that they can produce articles of good quality at as low costs as their competitors. A good illustration of this class of depreciation which is called "Depreciation due to Obsolescence" is seen in the rapid increase in the size of railway cars. Within the last twenty years, these have increased from a capacity of from fifteen to twenty-five tons to a maximum load of fifty-five tons, due largely to the substitution of steel for wood in construction. This increase in the size of railway cars has rendered a large number of cars obsolete before the normal term of their working life has expired. The increase in the size and operative power of the locomotive has had the same result. Numbers of engines are now doing good service on logging railroads and local lines which, without the improvement in locomotive construction, would still be running on the leading trunk lines.

The third cause of depreciation is changes in business conditions which may seriously impair or entirely destroy the productive value of properties in perfect physical condition. A marked reduction in the tariff on the finer grades of textiles, for example, would throw out of use a large amount of perfectly good machinery, and a street railway operating under a limited term franchise which it carries on its balance sheet as an asset, may find, as in the cities of Cleveland and Chicago, that the value of this asset is destroyed or greatly impaired by a change in public sentiment imposing additional burdens and restrictions upon street-railway companies.

Understanding now the regular and inevitable, as well as the accidental and contingent reductions in the value of a company's productive property, we can recognize the necessity of providing in advance for its replacement. In so far as these losses can be estimated with approximate exactness, an accurate provision can be made. Contingent and extraordinary losses, however, can only be anticipated by providing such sums as experience shows will probably be sufficient to offset these losses, and there still remain the losses due to such causes as change in fashion or in the tariff, against which no foresight can provide because there is no method of predetermining the amount of the damage.

The losses due to depreciation, if provision is not made to apportion them over a series of years, may fall upon a business with such force as to annihilate it. When a plant is new, repairs are light and replacements are not necessary. This condition may persist for several years. In the meantime the management, not convinced of the necessity of making provision against the day when their plant shall be worn out, may have paid out all their earnings to their stockholders. At the end of the fifth or sixth year extensive renewals become necessary, machines are worn out or become obsolete; and a reconstruction, a rearrangement, or a relocation of the plant may be necessary. If money is not available for these purposes, all that the management can do is to issue stock or bonds and spend the proceeds, not in increasing the value of their property, but merely in maintaining it at its original figure.

An illustration on a small scale will serve: A man obtained a pumping contract from a railroad. The contract ran for ten years and called for a payment of $2,000 a year. The cost of the pump and other machinery was $5,000 and the operating expenses $1,000 each year. The owner gave but nominal supervision to the plant, which indeed was all that it required, and estimated his profits at $1,000 a year or $10,000 during the life of the contract. At the end of the time, however, when the contract came to be renewed, it was found that the pump was worn out, the $5,000 invested had been lost, and it was necessary for the contractor to raise another $5,000 for the purchase of new apparatus. Instead of a profit of $10,000 during the ten years, the actual profits of the business were only $5,000. A correct accounting system would have required the setting aside of $5,000 in such a form as to be available at the end of ten years for the purchase of a new pump.

The accounting for depreciation is managed by building up in the assets of the business an amount of value. Provision for depreciation is made as follows: A deduction is made from income of the amount estimated to be necessary in that year to provide for depreciation. This amount is kept in the business, either being held as a bank deposit, invested in securities, or spent in such a way as to increase the value of the company's property, for example, upon a new mill or a new piece of machinery. If an expenditure is made, cash is credited, and machinery or plant account, or the materials or securities purchased is debited. Then Profit and Loss is debited and depreciation reserve, appearing as a liability on the balance sheet, is credited. This plan is followed year by year, until a depreciation reserve of large amount may be built up as a liability to the business, balanced by various assets on which a certain amount of the income of the company has been spent.

Now suppose that, after a term of years, since depreciation does not usually count in the early stages of a company's operations, new equipment is necessary to replace that which is unfit for service, or that a complete overhauling, a relocation, or a reconstruction of the plant is necessary, including a general replacement of its machinery with machinery of new and improved design. The cost of the reconstruction or replacement is provided either out of the income of the company or by an increase of its bonds or stock. The entries are as follows: in case provision is made out of the current income of the year for necessary depreciation; cash is credited and the plant account concerned is debited; then depreciation reserve is debited and plant account is credited for the equipment thrown out. If the old machinery can be sold, cash is debited and the depreciation reserve is credited. If the cost of replacement is too large to be thrown upon the income of a single year, provision for the expense is made in the following manner: The company, we will suppose, presents the following balance sheet:

Assets		Liabilities	
Plant and equipment..	$2,000,000	Stock...............	$1,000,000
Cash and current assets..............	500,000	Bonds..............	500,000
		Depreciation reserve..	500,000
		Surplus.............	500,000
	$2,500,000		$2,500,000

Suppose that $500,000 is required for extensive replacements and reconstruction, and that only $200,000 of this amount can be provided out of the income of that year. Resort is now had to the depreciation reserve, the accumulations of past investments for the benefit of the depreciation fund. The company issued $300,000 of bonds, increasing its bonded debt to $800,000 and reducing the depreciation reserve by a corresponding amount. The proceeds of the bonds together with the $200,000 taken from income are spent in renewing the plant. After this operation is completed, the balance sheet is as follows:

Assets		Liabilities	
Plant...............	$2,000,000	Stock...............	$1,000,000
Cash and current assets..............	500,000	Bonds..............	800,000
		Depreciation reserve..	200,000
		Surplus.............	500,000
	$2,500,000		$2,500,000

What has been done is to substitute on the balance sheet one kind of liability for another, reducing the depreciation reserve and increasing the amount of bonds, leaving the surplus, the difference between assets and liabilities, at its former figure. Speaking in terms of capitalization, the company has capitalized a portion of its surplus assets for the sake of obtaining funds to renew its plant.

The accumulated reservations for depreciation may be disposed of in two ways: First, they may be handled as a fund and kept in assets which are either specifically set aside for the purpose of making renewals, when these shall become necessary, or kept in the current assets of the business immediately available for use. This is the method adopted by the United States Steel Corporation. The balances to the credit of sinking, depreciation and extraordinary replacement and improvement funds, which are all treated alike, on December 31, 1908, were included in the assets of the company in the following accounts:

Sundry securities at cost	$6,793,413.81
Cash	6,475,840.47
Invested in Tennessee coal, iron and railway company stock	4,222,537.11
In marketable securities at market value	723,380.34
In cash, special deposit	757,500.00
In current assets:	
Cash, loans, receivables, inventories, etc	23,573,641.94
	$42,546,313.67

This total was arrived at as follows: The balances to the credit of these various funds aggregated on December 31, 1907, $41,360,655.19. During the year 1908, there was set aside from income and by charges to current expenses $22,474,395.26, and other income and credits to the various funds brought up the total to $64,984,789.98. The amounts charged to the various funds during the year aggregate $22,438,476.31, leaving a balance as already stated, of $42,546,313.67. The United States Steel Corporation keeps its depreciation and other funds in a form readily available for use, invested in the current assets of its business as a part of its working capital. If the directors should conclude that a more definite separation of the assets representing these various funds should be made, they could make a special deposit of all the money, or invest it in securities which could be used for nothing else than to provide means for the replacement and renewals as required.

The International Harvester Company handles its depreciation account in a different manner. The accumulations in the plant depreciation and extinguishment funds of this company on December 31, 1908, amounted to $5,009,844. This amount appears on the balance sheet as a liability item under the head of "Provisional and Contingent Reserves." The total amount of these reserves at this date was $6,850,590.37.

In addition, the company had a surplus of $16,691,989.61; the two amounts together being $23,542,579.98. This sum represented the difference between assets and liabilities accumulated out of the profits of the business from the date of its organization. This accumulation was in part the result of increase in property account, in part the result of the payment of liabilities of which $3,173,398.21 under the head of "Purchase money obligations" were discharged in 1908, and in part of an increase in current assets. There is no attempt made by this company, so far as appears in its report, to keep its depreciation fund in any particular form of assets. As the money is reserved, it is apparently put to the most advantageous use, either in increasing the bank balances of the company or its stocks of railway materials, or in paying its debts, or in additions and improvements to its plant. The depreciation fund of the International Harvester Company is represented by amounts invested in different productive assets of the company without special segregation.

This method is the one ordinarily followed. Its general adoption by those companies which maintain depreciation funds has given rise to the statement often heard, that a depreciation reserve is only a bookkeeping item without special significance. There is no fundamental distinction between the surplus appearing on the balance sheet and the depreciation reserve also appearing as a liability. Added together, they represent the total accumulations out of income which are held in the business for the benefit of the business. The only difference between the surplus and the depreciation reserve lies in the fact that the former is usually regarded as the property of the stockholders to be distributed to them, from time to time, by various adjustments of capitalization, which will be considered in detail in a later chapter, while the depreciation reserve is regarded as something belonging to the business, which is to be withheld from the stockholders to make good any extraordinary replacements or renewals for which the current reservations from income for the purposes of depreciation will not prove adequate.

There is, of course, a limit beyond which it is unprofitable for a company to accumulate a fund of this character. When the amount of the depreciation reserve fund has reached beyond the figure which in the judgment of the directors is necessary to protect the business against extraordinary accidents, it can then be treated as a part of the surplus and distributed to the stockholders. As an example of such a distribution, the stock dividend of the Pullman Company, voted on February 10, 1910, was explained by the directors in part as follows: "There were certain reserve accounts in the manufacturing department which had hitherto been held in abeyance to meet contingencies which were possible to arise (fire insurance), but which present conditions render improbable. These items, together with the existing surplus as shown in the published statement of the last fiscal year and the current results of operation, are regarded by the board as a justification for making this recommendation." The Pullman Company, in making these dividends, transferred certain of its reserves to its surplus account, and then substituted for a portion of the surplus an equal amount of capital stock.

The balance sheets of conservatively managed companies may show reserves in addition to the depreciation reserve. Thus the International Harvester Company maintains a reserve for collection expenses and receivables to provide for losses which may ultimately be sustained in the realization of bills and accounts receivable, and a cash reserve when it is deemed wise for a company to carry its own insurance. A company may also maintain a dividend reserve fund to make good any temporary shortages in income available for distribution to stockholders. These reserves are built up out of the unexpended balances of the annual appropriations to these several purposes. For example, the International Harvester Company provided for contingent losses on receivables in 1908, $650,000. The debts which were charged off as uncollectable during 1908 amounted to only $228,048.15, so that there was an addition to the reserve for contingent losses on receivables during the year of $421,951,85. The efforts of this company are constantly directed toward reducing the losses against which these reserves are established to provide. It has spent large sums to equip its works and other buildings with automobile sprinkling systems and the latest devices for protection against fire, and it carries on continually a systematic investigation into the financial responsibility of prospective customers who give notes for purchases. This insures to the company a high grade of notes and accounts. These precautions, and the care taken to reduce losses, tend to increase the balances annually added to these various funds which may in time be carried to such a height that a portion of them can be distributed to stockholders.

These reserves are handled in the same manner as the reserve for plant depreciation, with the exception that the insurance reserves and the dividend reserves, in order to be immediately available for use, should be invested in good securities set aside for the purposes of these funds. As an illustration of this segregation, we find that the balance in the fire insurance reserve of the International Harvester Company of December 31, 1908, was $671,093.23, of which $400,832.20 had been invested in income-bearing securities on that date. Since that date the balance of the fund has also been invested in income-bearing securities.

In calculating depreciation, the first step is to determine the amount necessary. This is figured as a percentage of the cost of property to be depreciated. The percentage is obtained by estimating, sometimes in great detail, the active life of different kinds of equipment and dividing the result into 100 to obtain the annual rate of depreciation. By the method ordinarily followed, no account is taken of compound interest. If a business or property is estimated to last for twenty years, five per cent of this cost is assumed to be reserved out of income in each year in order to make good the annual depreciation. The Chicago Union Traction Company, for example, has adopted the following rates for its power-plant equipment:

	Life		Rate
Track, ties, bonding, etc.	12.85 years;		7.75%
Paving and grading:			
Granite block	16	"	6.6%
Cobblestone	25	"	4%
Electric equipment of cars	12–15	"	8.5% to 6⅔%
Iron poles	20	"	5%
Power-plant equipment	15	"	6.66%
Shop tools and machinery	20	"	5%
Buildings and improvements	50	"	2%

These various percentages are applied to the costs of the equipment, and the results added together are assumed to give the annual requirement for depreciation for that year.

These rates, however, are subject to wide variations under different conditions. Mr. C. I. Sturgis[1] explains these variations in relation to railway equipment as follows:

> On a railroad, the life of ties varies with soil and climate; the life of bridges depends on the weight of locomotives running over them; the life of locomotives depends on the quality of water and coal with which they are fed, and there is hardly a railroad tool or machine the life of which does not depend on local conditions, and even if, in determining depreciation, we could approximately estimate such variable factors as these, we would still have to consider what in the end will be the cost of the new articles to replace the old, and with markets ever fluctuating that is impossible definitely to determine. Furthermore, prosperous roads, in maintaining high standards, consider equipment is worn out when, on poorer roads, it would be considered still good for many years of service.

While admitting the influence of local conditions upon assumed rates of depreciation, it is possible to give proper weight to these influences on the basis of experience in that locality, and to ascertain, with a degree of accuracy, the life

[1] *Electric Railway Journal,* December 18, 1909.

of the company's property. It is also possible to ascertain, as we have explained in our discussion of maintenance, the effect of high and low standards of maintenance on depreciation. Property which is well maintained will last much longer, and give more effective service during its life, than where maintenance is neglected. We may conclude, therefore, that depreciation due to wear and tear and to natural decay can be closely approximated.

Depreciation due to obsolescence and extraordinary accidents involving extensive expenditures upon the plant cannot be estimated even approximately. A case came recently to the writer's notice where the owner of a textile mill had imported an expensive machine from England and estimated that it would last only five years. He therefore assigned to it a depreciation rate of twenty per cent. Within two years, however, this machine was displaced by a better one, so that the correct rate should have been fifty per cent. Other illustrations are the passage of city ordinances requiring large expenditures on track elevation or an electrification to abolish the smoke nuisance. Such changes as this cannot be foreseen. It is impossible to provide against them. Partial provision, it is true, may be made in the manner already indicated by establishing various rates of depreciation and, by improving the business methods of the concern, accumulating reserves against various contingencies. These reserves are available for emergencies. But even the most conservative company cannot make suitable provision out of its income accounts to protect it against any contingency which might arise. For example, depreciation on telephone equipment can be figured at ten per cent per annum. This will provide for the replacement of the plant at the end of ten years. But suppose the town is visited by a hurricane and most of the plant is destroyed. This would be a contingency against which no foresight consistent with ordinary business practice would provide. All that can be done in the event of such a catastrophe is for the owners of the business to take their loss and build anew, increasing their toll rates, if need be, in order to regain the money spent for the reconstruction of the plant.

As an offset to this sort of depreciation, several accountants and engineers have urged the natural appreciation in the value of the property due to the development of its business. This phase of depreciation accounting is discussed by Mr. Frederic A. Delano, president of the Wabash Railroad,[1] as follows:

> In most cases the depreciation due to the diminished value of equipment, track, bridges, structures of all kinds, shops and shop tools already referred to, is limited, as has been explained, and is, furthermore, a good deal more than counterbalanced by the appreciation due to the fact that the age of the railroad has given it an established business. This amounts to a good deal more in the case of a railroad than what is called "good will" in the case of a mercantile corporation. As a railroad is developed, industries, mines, factories, etc., are established along its tracks, with switches and side track facilities, towns grow up along it, and a certain amount of business becomes assured to it—business which it takes years and a large expenditure of money and energy to develop—all of which is charged into current operating expenses and should be considered as an offset to any depreciation of the property.
>
> Besides the appreciation due to this cause there is, of course, an actual physical enhancement of value due to the condition of the roadbed and embankments becoming better solidified, the water courses established and the original structures gradually replaced with others of a more permanent character, even without any addition to capital account; thus wooden trestles, bridges, culverts, etc., have been filled with earth or replaced by steel or iron, stone or concrete.
>
> No account is taken and no estimate can be made of the enhanced value of the railroad property (right of way and terminals) due to the enhanced value of the land, even though the existence of the railroad

[1] *Railway Age Gazette,* March 27, 1908.

> may have contributed largely to the development of the country through which it runs. The railroad corporation suffers by reason of this enhanced value which it has so largely contributed to create if it is compelled to purchase any additional property, as well as in the increased amount of the taxes it is called upon to pay each year as its contribution to the needs of the growing communities; but it has not been usual to make any allowance for this. Those who have had the greatest experience with railways generally believe that the enhancement in value or appreciation of the property in the direction already referred to far more than balances the depreciation, especially when it is remembered that the total physical depreciation, under proper maintenance rules, is, without doubt, limited to about half the first cost of the property subject to depreciation.

The considerations advanced by President Delano should be taken into account in estimating depreciation rates. In the writer's opinion, it is unsafe to go so far as he does in claiming that appreciation offsets all depreciation. This enhancement in the value of a business is dependent to a large extent upon the conditions of trade. Certainly, from 1892 to 1897, there was no appreciation in the value of railway property in the United States. At this time a large amount of railway mileage was in the hands of receivers, and railway earnings were greatly depressed. It is true, however, that under ordinary conditions the appreciation to which the president of the Wabash refers is present in every well-managed concern; and, while it does not seem wise to take it into account as offsetting depreciation due to use, it will go far to offset depreciation due to obsolescence and extraordinary accidents.

In final summary of the rules for establishing rates of depreciation, the following may be taken as conservative: First, charge to maintenance the cost of all replacements, even when the cost of the property substituted for that worn out or displaced by a better machine is greater than that originally purchased; second, maintain depreciation rates based on standards established by engineers familiar with the business in which the corporation is engaged, and after making due allowance for special and local conditions; third, provide additional reserves for special classes of losses not covered by outside insurance.

Our final topic for discussion under the head of depreciation concerns the comparison between sinking funds and depreciation. There is substantial identity between these two classes of deductions from income. The sinking fund, whether maintained against so-called "wasting" assets—that is, coal or ore—or against the plant of an electric railway, or the terminable franchise of a public service corporation, up to the percentage of the total cost of the company's assets which is represented by its bonds, and up to the percentage of the cost of the property which is represented by the annual appropriations for the sinking fund, is usually regarded as the identical equivalent of a depreciation charge. If the entire property of a company is represented by its bonds, which often happens, and if its life is twenty years, a sinking fund of five per cent on the bonds is the same as a depreciation of five per cent on the cost of the property. At the end of the twenty years, the plant is worn out, the bonds are paid, and the company is back where it started, with the addition of the good will and prestige which it has accumulated. It can then incur a new debt for the original amount, probably at a lower rate of interest, rebuild its plant, and maintain its surplus intact.

The identity of the sinking fund and the depreciation charge may be admitted, however, only with important qualifications. The depreciation fund should be available for replacements when these are required. When a sinking fund is invested in bonds, whether these are canceled or held, it is not available for current replacements, but only for extinguishment of the company's debt. The later forms of sinking fund, however, contain, as noted in a former chapter, certain provisions which remove the foregoing objection to identifying a sinking fund with a depreciation charge. If the bonds purchased for the sinking fund can be reissued to provide funds for improvements and extensions, or if the sinking fund can be invested in the plant at the option of the trustee, the sinking fund and the depreciation charges are in all particulars the same, and the amount of the sinking fund established should be deducted from the assumed rate of depreciation. If the company maintains a sinking fund against its debt, and also allows rates of depreciation on the cost of its physical property, it is, to the extent of the sinking fund, duplicating its depreciation charge, and accumulating reserves in its asset accounts which will eventually come to the stockholders, or which may be drawn out in case of emergency.

After ascertaining the total income of the company, consisting of net earnings from operation plus other income, certain deductions must be made known as fixed charges, which include taxes, interest, and rental. The only question which may arise concerning these payments is the treatment of interest paid on bonds during the construction period. It is customary to include this in the construction cost, issuing enough securities not only to provide for the cost of the plant, but to pay interest on the bonds while the plant is building. As long as no secret is made of the matter, and it is well understood, there can be no reasonable objection to the practice. All that could be required is for the stockholders to advance the money necessary to pay interest on bonds during the construction period.

The final item of charges consists of such miscellaneous items as commissions on sales of securities and other expenses which are chargeable against income, but which cannot properly be classified either as operating expenses or as fixed charges. Companies often include as "other charges" the cost of betterments and additions which, in the judgment of the directors, are not properly chargeable to capital account. This has been discussed in connection with depreciation. Such expenditures should be charged to operating expense rather than to fixed charges. The balance remaining after these charges have been paid is the surplus earned for the stock during the year, out of which dividends may be paid. Another source of surplus consists of profits from premiums on the sales of securities issued by the company. Discounts on all sales of securities are to be considered as losses and charged against the income of the year. For the same reason, premiums received are to be regarded as profit.

The next item in the income account is income from other sources. This is made as follows:

Interest received on bonds of others companies;
Dividends on stocks of other companies;
Rentals of property owned by the company and leased to outsiders;
Interest on the company's bank deposits or on any loans in which it may invest its cash balance.

These receipts are usually incidental to the main operations of the company.

Business corporations are not primarily investment companies. They are organized to transact a railroad or manufacturing or trading business; and, although they may acquire securities in the course of their regular business, these securities are usually acquired for other purposes than to obtain revenue. A railroad corporation, for example, may purchase an interest in the stock of another company with which it exchanges a large amount of traffic, and may receive a dividend on this stock. The principal advantage of the purchase is not, however, to receive the dividend, but to obtain a favorable traffic agreement.

Again, railroad companies may build new mileage through subsidiary companies to which they advance money, taking the bonds and stocks of the subsidiary companies as payment and holding these in their treasury. In this case, instead of treating the operations of all the companies under their control as a unit, we have the distinction between lines directly operated and lines controlled. In reality, however, the returns on the stocks and bonds of the subsidiary, while in the treasury of the parent company, represent merely a part of the operating income of the entire system.

The item of interest on bank deposits figures largely in the accounts of profitable corporations during periods when they are not expanding their operations, especially when their receipts are evenly distributed throughout the year, and their dividend and interest payments are made at periodical intervals. Under these circumstances, there is necessarily a considerable accumulation of money to the credit of the company, and this money they may either leave on deposit, receiving the bank rate of interest, or they may lend it out at a higher return than the banks will pay. During periods of great business activity, however, this source of income is ordinarily not available, since the corporation needs all of its money to conduct its regular operations, and is usually a heavy borrower besides.

Profits from premiums on securities sold are essentially different from profits or losses derived from income account. When securities of a company are sold at a premium, the usual practice is to show in the balance sheet as a capital liability only the par value of the security sold, and to credit to surplus, or profit and loss account, the premium received above the par value. Profits derived from the sale of capital obligations should be reserved as capital, unless the company is dissolved, and should be separately stated in the balance sheet.

In practice, this separate statement of premiums on sales of securities is rarely made. The consequence is that directors may get a wrong idea of the profits of the business, and may pay dividends which are not warranted by the earnings from operation. The practice of investing these premiums in productive assets is, however, so well established that the danger of basing dividends upon them is remote. A similar disposition is usually made of profits received from the sale of unpledged treasury assets, usually consisting of securities. Unless the total proceeds are distributed to stockholders as a special dividend, the practice is to invest the entire proceeds in the improvements in capital assets. Such a disposition was made by the Pennsylvania of the proceeds of the sale of the coal stocks following the passage of the Hepburn Law in 1906. A large profit was shown, but the entire proceeds were invested in the property.

Discounts on securities sold are treated as losses. If small in amount, they are charged against the income of the year. Discounts on bonds or stock sold at the outset for original construction are usually included in the cost of construction.

The third source of surplus is "profits and losses from the sale of assets." A company may have operated a factory situated in a large city where land values were steadily appreciating. In time, the growth of the company's operations make a country location desirable. The city real estate then comes up to be sold, and it is found that its value is greatly increased over its original cost. This increase in value is to be taken as a profit, but since the profit was not earned during a single year, but represented the appreciation in value over thirty years, it will be improper to count this in the surplus available for distribution to stockholders. It will be treated in the same manner as profits arising from premiums on the sale of securities. In cases, however, where the company purchases and sells property in the same year and shows a profit on the transaction, this profit may be included in the annual profits of the company upon which the distribution of profits is to be based.

Profits arising from the revaluation of assets are doubtful. It is frequently necessary, when the property of a business has been subjected to some unusual damage which is too great to be covered by the ordinary rate of depreciation, for example the discovery of new and richer deposits of iron ore which will reduce the valuation to be legitimately placed upon a company's iron-ore deposits, to write down the book value of assets in the form of a loss on the single year's operation, or, if the depreciation is excessive, to spread this loss over a series of years. On the other hand, it has been urged that the writing up of assets where property has appreciated in value is equally legitimate. This can be admitted only within narrow limits. It is entirely proper in the case of securities owned where the market value can be ascertained, and where the increased income corresponds to the increased price. Beyond this, however, the "writing up" of assets is of doubtful propriety. It is safer to maintain a book value of securities based upon cost, less depreciation, and to leave the surplus account undisturbed by any appreciation in their market value.

The danger of thus appreciating assets may be seen by an illustration. The property on which the Broad Street Terminal of the Pennsylvania Railroad Station stands has increased over 400 per cent since purchase. If this piece of real estate was to be revalued, its original cost to the company would be quadrupled. Broad Street Station is, however, not to be sold. It will for many years continue to be used for the purpose of the company. It is altogether probable that the contribution of this terminal location to the profits of the Pennsylvania Railroad has not increased as rapidly as its value as real estate. At the same time, it is impossible to ascertain how much is this increase in the contribution of Broad Street Station to the net profits of the Pennsylvania. The only basis on which its value could be written up upon the books of the company would be by comparing it with the value of real estate in the vicinity. This would result in an exaggeration of its value as a piece of property producing revenue for the Pennsylvania Railroad. The New York, New Haven & Hartford has a three fourths interest in the South Station, Boston, which cost $15,000,000 to build. The loss on the operation of this station, however, which is maintained largely for public convenience has been as high as $500,000 in a single year. As a piece of real estate this property is very valuable. As a piece of railroad property, however, it is a source of loss.

The only practical reason for increasing the value of railroad terminal property would be when it is desired to make this the basis for an issue of terminal bonds. In such a case, however, the lenders will make their own estimates as to the value of the real estate in question as security for the loan asked, and the corporation need not adopt the expedient of writing up the value of the property on its books. All things considered, the method of carrying the property of the company at its original cost, and maintaining that cost intact by proper rates of depreciation is best.

CHAPTER XVI

THE MANAGEMENT OF THE CORPORATE INCOME

CORPORATIONS exist and do business to produce dividends for their owners. A company which has no prospect of paying dividends should be either dissolved, or, according to methods which we shall have later occasion to explain, reorganized down to a dividend basis. After making the various deductions which have been indicated, the surplus profits belong to the stockholders, and if the company is successfully managed under conditions of ordinary good fortune, the stockholders will in time receive these surplus profits, directly or indirectly, either in the form of cash or dividends. A dividend is a payment of the profits of the company to its stockholders expressed in the form of a certain rate per cent on the par value of the stock. The dividend of the Pennsylvania Railroad Company is $3—six per cent on 8,021,296 shares, amount of capital stock $401,064,800; that of the United States Steel Corporation seven per cent on 3,602,811 shares of preferred stock, and $5 on 5,083,025 shares of common stock. The General Electric Company pays $8 per share on 651,674 shares; the Union Pacific Railroad Company pays $10 on 2,961,787 shares of common stock.

There are two steps in the process of distributing profits to stockholders: First, the directors by a formal resolution declare that profits have been earned. As a preliminary to the declaration of a dividend, the directors consider the following: (1) the cash or liquid assets of the company at that time from which the dividends must be taken; (2) the prospect of business for the early future; (3) the ability of the company to obtain any funds which may be necessary for new construction by the sale of new stock or bonds. A company may be exceptionally prosperous without being able, on account of the rapid growth in its business which has locked up its cash assets in the form of accounts receivable, materials, etc., to pay out any portion of these profits in dividends. A declaration of a dividend, under these circumstances, could be made only by selling stock or notes to obtain the money, and while this is sometimes done, as a common practice it is to be avoided. Again, the business of the company, at the time when the matter of paying a dividend is considered, may be exceptionally prosperous, but the outlook for the future may be in doubt. At a time, for example, when a revision of the tariff is in progress, the companies whose earnings will be affected by any changes under consideration are inclined to husband their resources and prepare for a possible shrinkage in earnings. A company whose business is rapidly expanding may require large amounts of new capital. It may not be desirable to raise this money by increasing capital stock. Any money required must come out of profits. The directors, under such conditions, would be cautious in paying dividends.

The law provides that the declaration of dividends is optional with the directors. They have authority to fix the amount of working capital which, in their judgment, the business of the corporation requires, and until they declare a dividend by resolution, there is no way in which the stockholder, except by his vote to displace one or more directors, can control their action. The directors are the trustees for the stockholders. They are given full power to dispose of the funds of the corporation as their best judgment may direct. No matter how large are the profits of the company, there is no way in which they can be compelled to declare a dividend. The stockholders can only participate in profits through the channel provided by law. Various attempts have been made to force a declaration of dividends, especially on preferred stock, on the ground that large profits had been earned, and that the stockholders were entitled to share in these profits. These attempts have been generally unsuccessful. The stockholder can invoke the aid of the courts to prevent the diversion of the company's funds to unlawful objects; he can restrain the officers and directors from paying to themselves exorbitant salaries; and he can prevent any improper use of the company's profits. As long, however, as the directors elect to leave the company's profits in the treasury, until they decide that a dividend shall be paid, the stockholder can obtain no share of these profits. His only remedy, in case he is dissatisfied with the management of the company, is to elect new directors or sell his stock and withdraw from the company. When a dividend has been declared, however, it becomes an obligation of the company, enforcable as any other debt.

The object which an honest and conservative board of directors set before them is to establish a dividend rate which can be maintained under all conditions of earnings. The interests of the stockholder and the corporation unite in the demand that a rate of dividend once established shall be maintained. The stockholder desires a stable dividend because the value of a stock whose dividends, for example, run six, six, two, two, and four, averaging four per cent for the five years, but irregularly distributed, will command a lower price than stock on which four per cent is paid every year. Investors, as distinct from speculators, although both elements are present in the minds of both purchasers of stock, desire stability in the income from their investments. The dividends which they receive go into their personal income accounts; their expenditures and appropriations are adjusted to these receipts; a reduction or the passing of a dividend disturbs their calculations and unsettles their confidence in the company. As a result of this preference of the investor for stocks with a regular rate of distribution, the payment of regular dividends produces a higher and more stable value for such stocks. Stocks with regular dividends are worth more to sell and are also more valuable as collateral security.

A stable rate of dividend with its resulting higher and more permanent value is of great advantage to the company. Many corporations, especially those whose receipts are not evenly distributed throughout the year, have occasion to borrow money in anticipation of income to meet obligations which mature before that income is received. Wages, interest, and taxes must be paid and supplies purchased often before the proceeds of sales are received. In order that a corporation should retain a strong position with the banks, it is important that its stock should be maintained at a good figure. A high and sustained value for the stock of a company is ordinarily taken by the bank as evidence of its high credit. Of course, if this value is merely a recent marking up of stock-exchange quotations, it may not have much weight with the bank officers, but if it is a steadily maintained quotation, and represents what investors really regard as the value of the stock, the banker considers it good evidence of the financial standing of the company applying for a loan. On the other hand, the fact that a stock sells at a low price is usually a warning to the banker to discriminate against the paper of the corporation issuing the stock, unless the notes are well secured by indorsement or collateral.

A settled investment value for its securities, which can be obtained only by the stability of its dividend rate, also benefits the corporation because it makes it possible for it to procure money for improvements and extensions on favorable terms. A prosperous company is a growing company, and is under frequent necessity of selling stock or bonds to obtain new capital. The prices obtained for the new securities will depend to a large extent upon the prices of those already outstanding. If the company issues bonds, a high value for the stock indicates that the interest on these bonds is amply secured by surplus earnings. If, however, the stock is selling at a low figure, the investor knows that the company which proposes to increase its debt has little security to offer its creditors aside from the property which the proceeds of the new bonds are to purchase. A low price of the stock indicates that the judgment of market observers is unfavorable to the company. The investor properly regards the past achievements of the corporation as the best assurances of its future prosperity. No matter how large the net earnings of a company may be at the time an increase of stock or bonds is made, the low market value of this stock resulting from an irregular dividend policy would be a warning to anyone investigating its credit that there was good reason for believing that these large earnings would not be permanent. Under these circumstances, it might be difficult to obtain high prices for these securities.

So important is an even distribution of corporate profits considered, that even when increasing earnings enable the corporation to raise the rate of dividend, care is usually taken to avoid any official statement, or even any implication from a statement, that the higher dividend rate is to be permanent. The method employed in such cases is to declare the "regular" dividend and then an "extra" dividend in addition. The increase is made in the form of the "extra" dividend as an intimation to the stockholder that the directors are not yet fully convinced that they can add the amount of the "extra" to the regular rate, and that they prefer to wait developments before establishing the regular rate at the higher figures. After the extra dividend has been paid for several years, and if profits are maintained, the rate will be made regular. In order to maintain an even rate of distribution on its stock, the directors of well-managed companies are governed by the following rules:

First, to pay no dividends for a considerable period after the company begins operation.

Second, to manage the expense accounts of the company in such a way as to reduce the fluctuations in surplus profits to the minimum.

Third, to pay out, in any one year, only a portion of these profits in dividends.

Every new corporation is, in some degree, an experiment. Even though it operates in an industry where the machinery, the methods of administration, and the product are standardized, and where the management have nothing more to do than to follow established models, the degree of its success cannot be accurately predicted. The number of unknown factors in every business situation is large; new laws to reduce profits, increases in taxation, unusual burdens imposed by the municipality in the way of public improvements, the incursions of competitors, changes in the tariff, dangers of industrial depression, encroachments of organized labor, substitutions of new products or the invention of machinery to produce at lower cost—these influences may enter to disappoint the calculations of the directors. Furthermore, in most public flotations, there is some overvaluation of the property purchased or constructed, and a corresponding element of inflation in the capitalization of the company. Even with the most painstaking care, mistakes of construction, location, or anticipation of demand may have been made. If the company is prosperous, these mistakes can be rectified, but the money with which these replacement and insurance funds are built up comes from the profits of the company. Conservative directors will, therefore, usually refuse to pay out profits until the company has demonstrated its ability to earn its fixed charges, and to produce a surplus out of which dividends can be paid.

The issue of cumulative preferred stock seriously interferes with a conservative management of the company's income. When dividends are carried over and accumulated to the prejudice of the common stockholder, fairness to him, as well as the usual necessity that a market should be made for new securities as quickly as possible, influences the directors to promptly begin the payment of dividends upon the preferred stock. In some cases, notably that of the United States Steel Corporation, the stock-market situation influenced the directors to immediately begin payment of dividends on the common stock as well as on the preferred. For this, however, they were severely criticised. The position of the company during the early period of its existence was weakened by a policy of dividend payment which was generally believed to be unduly liberal. In December, 1903, the depressed condition of the steel trade led to the suspension of dividends on the common stock of the United States Steel Corporation. The directors quickly took advantage of the opportunity to adopt a conservative dividend policy. Although the depression in the steel trade was only temporary, conditions approaching normal in the following year, the policy of investing large sums in plant and equipment which the directors would probably have been glad to follow from the first, had stock-market considerations not proved controlling, was steadily adherred to. No dividends were paid on steel common until 1906, when a two-per-cent rate was established, raised a year later first to three and then to four per cent. Not until the autumn of 1909, was the rate advanced to five per cent. During this period from 1903 to 1909, the company earned $300,044,000 on its common stock and paid only $63,537,813 in dividends, the balance being invested in various reserves, and in building up a surplus on the balance sheet which, at the date of the last annual report, stood at $151,354,528. As a result of this policy of investing profits in improvements, instead of paying them out in dividends, the United States Steel Corporation has eliminated much of the "water" in its original capitalization, and has placed itself in a strong position to continue the payment of the five-per-cent dividend—recently announced by the directors as the regular dividend on the common stock.

The later policy of the United States Steel Corporation in sacrificing its dividends to its surplus indicates the policy which every company whose financial situation permits should follow. In no other way can a corporation whose capital is excessive, and whose earning power is in any way doubtful, so certainly reach an investment position as by adherence to the policy of accumulating a large reserve out of income.

The more doubtful the success of the company, and the greater the number of dangers and risks to which it is subjected, the more important it is that dividends should be withheld until a strong financial position is attained.

Having fulfilled the initial requirement of accumulating an adequate reserve to offset the blunders of omission and commission which characterize the beginning of every new enterprise, the next problem confronting the directors of a company, anxious to place their stock upon a dividend paying basis, is the management of the expense accounts in such a manner as to reduce to a minimum the fluctuations in the income available for distribution to stockholders. A large part of the expense of operating any business varies with the volume of business done. An increase in the traffic of a railroad means more trains, and more employees to run the trains and to keep them in repair. A falling off in business results in a corresponding reduction in the cost of conducting transportation. The same is true of all other industries. The cost of operating the plant, as distinct from the cost of maintaining it, fluctuates with the amount of business done. There are, of course, in every business certain fixed expenses connected with the operation and selling which cannot be adjusted to changes in business, and which result in increased cost when earnings are reduced. Broadly speaking, however, the cost of running the plant, of manufacturing the goods, or transporting the freight and passengers, changes with the volume of business transacted. There is little opportunity, therefore, in the cost of operation, to adjust expenditure to fluctuations of income so as to minimize the changes in the balance of income available for distribution to stockholders.

In the maintenance and replacement items of operating expenses, however, a certain amount of adjustment and variation is possible. Maintenance charges, as we have seen, contain two items: the cost of up-keep and repairs, and the cost of betterments calculated to raise the standard of construction and decrease the cost of maintenance or operation. The rule which governs the management of the first class of maintenance expenses is that, so far as possible, without damaging the credit of the company, standards of maintenance once established should be rigidly adherred to. Maintenance, in other words, should be a comparatively fixed expense, varying only as the influences which affect the wear and destruction of the property are modified.

Rigid adherence to this rule admits of a considerable amount of fluctuation in the amount of annual appropriations for the up-keep of the property. The cost of railway maintenance of way, for example, is increased by an open winter, which results in greater damage to the track and roadway. It is increased by the high cost of labor and material incident to business prosperity, and also by the heavy traffic which results from large production. Maintenance cost, on the other hand, is naturally reduced, without injury to the property, during periods of depression. When traffic is light, the wear upon the track is reduced, the amount paid out in wages is lessened. The efficiency of labor is also increased at such a time, not merely because of the greater desirability of steady employment during a dull season, which can only be secured at such a time by diligence and faithful service, but also because track work is not so much interfered with by passing trains. The cost of materials is also reduced during periods of depression. The maintenance of plant or equipment not directly affected by weather conditions can also be reduced during the period of depression without injury to the property. The Pennsylvania railroad, for example, made a heavy reduction in the cost of maintaining equipment during 1908, amounting to $6,864,247. This was due to the fact that a large portion of its equipment was not in service, and consequently was not subjected to the wear and tear of operation. A large amount of substitution of parts, such as air-brake hose, belting, etc., can be made during a dull season, when only a portion of the plant or equipment is in operation, thus reducing the cost of maintenance. A case in point is a factory manufacturing leather goods which had four floors in operation during 1907. In 1908 business fell off so that only the machinery on the one floor was used. As fast as the belting wore out on the lower floor, belts were transferred from idle machines, where they would naturally deteriorate, and put into use. Such economies of maintenance do not involve any lowering of the standard of the plant, although the cost of maintenance may be greatly increased to restore the equipment used up in this manner when the entire plant again comes into operation.

With this exception, however, the safe rule to follow in maintaining the standard once established for a plant is that a "stitch in time saves nine." Neglect of maintenance, for any reason, is likely to be followed by the most serious consequences. The operating efficiency of a plant is so closely related to its physical condition, the success of its business is so dependent upon its efficiency of operation, that serious and permanent damage may be inflicted upon a company by failure to maintain the standards of its plant. A good illustration of the consequences of neglecting maintenance is furnished by the fifth annual report of the Kansas City Southern Railway Company for the fiscal year ending June 30, 1905. The capital stock of this company was originally vested in a voting trust for five years from April 1, 1900. This voting trust expired by limitation on April 1, 1905, when the stockholders came into possession of their property and elected a new board of directors.

They found the road in such a condition as to be practically unfit to carry on the business of transportation; twenty-five per cent of the engines were in bad order, sixty-five per cent of the freight equipment was unfit for use in the transportation of grain, merchandise and other freight demanding dry cars; fifty-five of the sixty-five per cent required heavy repairs, enough ties had not been renewed, ditches had not been cleaned, sufficient ballasting had not been done and sufficient rail had not been laid. The condition of the ties and wooden structures and track, as a result of the neglect of maintenance, was so bad that it was impossible to move trains at ordinary speed. During the six months from January 7th to June 30, 1905, as a result of the impaired condition of the property due to the neglect of its maintenance, there were 715 wrecks and derailments reported, "each of which was of sufficient magnitude to require a special report and therefore cause serious loss and delay. Such a great number of accidents could not fail to cause serious loss of confidence and good will of the public and consequent diversion of traffic, also destruction and damage to property, delay to trains, and resulting wasteful expense for extra fuel and overtime of employees."[1] During the month of May, 1905, overtime paid engine and train crews amounted to $8,311.28, although the average of overtime for the three years preceding, before the property had reached its worst condition, was $5,990.88. In addition large amounts were paid each month for labor in rerailing cars and engines, and for repairing track and equipment, as a result of derailment due to defective tracks. Large amounts were paid for loss and damage to freight due to such derailments. Finally, the company suffered severely in competition for business because of its inability to take all the traffic which might have been obtained, and also because the traffic which it did move was often seriously delayed in delivery and arrived in bad condition.

We see illustrated, in the case of the Kansas City Southern, the effect of the neglect of maintenance upon operating efficiency, and the effect of decreased operating efficiency upon traffic and earnings. While this is an extreme case, it illustrates a principle which is of invariable application. To allow a property to run down is to impair the property's efficiency and to inflict serious injury upon the operating company.

It is possible, however, and this is the practice of many corporations, especially those which have not yet reached a position where they can show large surpluses over the amount

---

[1] Fifth annual report of The Kansas City Southern Railway Company, fiscal year ended June 30, 1905.

required for their dividends, to vary their appropriations for maintenance according to their earnings, never allowing the condition of the property to deteriorate so far as to interfere with its efficiency, but postponing, on occasion, all but the most necessary replacements and repairs until earnings have improved. Such a policy may be justified by extreme financial necessity. When a reduction in the dividend of a company will impair the company's credit, or defeat the consummation of projects for raising large amounts of capital, the skimping of maintenance cost may be pardoned. A board of directors are always reluctant to reduce the dividend rate. Such action inflicts serious damage upon the stockholders, and is likely to lead to unforeseen criticisms. When companies are running on a narrow margin of earnings, their usual disposition, when conditions of reduced earnings are encountered, is to save at the expense of the plant. It is going too far to say that such a policy is never justifiable. Each case must be determined on its own merits, with reference to the peculiar circumstances in which the directors of the company find themselves. It is, however, well established that the policy of so-called "concentration" of maintenance expenses into years of large earnings is costly, in that it results in a higher average of expenses over a series of years in keeping the plant in condition, than would be necessary if fixed repairs were made.

This subject was investigated in 1908 by a committee of the American Street Railway Association. In their report they present the detailed figures of maintaining car bodies over ten years, first, when the car is put in the shop each year, and second, when it is shopped bi-yearly. The comparison of the cost of maintaining car bodies under the yearly and bi-yearly systems of shopping is shown in the table on the following page.

To the cost of the yearly maintenance over the ten years, should be added an estimated item of $44.40 on account of the additional equipment made necessary because of four days loss of time on each car while in the shop, and an item

Cost

Shopped Yearly		Shopped Bi-Yearly
1st year	$29.18	
2d "	61.49	$86.46
3d "	54.94	
4th "	60.99	97.46
5th "	60.44	
6th "	59.99	111.46
7th "	54.94	
8th "	67.74	115.96
9th "	55.44	
10th "	79.99	143.15
Total	$585.14	$554.45

of $10.40 on account of increased shoproom made necessary by the yearly maintenance, making a total of $639.85 as the cost of maintaining the cars when shopped yearly as compared with $554.45, the cost of bi-yearly repairs. This comparison, however, does not indicate the merits of the respective policies. The objects of car maintenance as stated by the committee are as follows:

First, to prevent accidents due to defective equipment.

Second, to prevent failure of service due to defective equipment.

Third, to prevent excessive depreciation of equipment.

Fourth, to maintain equipment comfortable and attractive to patrons and public.

The committee finds a marked saving under each one of these items as result of shopping the cars every year. First, less liability to accidents. "When a car is thoroughly overhauled each year, there is less liability of accidents due to defective flooring, straps, windows, door and seat mechanism than where such overhauling is done every second year. If such accident claims are made, the fact that the car had been carefully overhauled inside of a year would greatly improve the railway company's case in court, and it would seem that two cents per car per day would be a conservative estimate of its value." The liability to failure in service was also decreased by frequent overhauling. The life of the car body is also increased when the cars are put into the shop every year. "Very few electric car bodies have been abandoned on account of deterioration. Many have been retired on account of being obsolete and unprofitable to operate. Therefore, the proper value for ordinary depreciation is hard to determine, but it is a well-known fact that where wood is exposed to moisture it will deteriorate rapidly, that paint and varnish will crack at joints if they are not kept well covered and the varnish elastic, and that floors and sills will rot if they are not kept well painted. Therefore, it is safe to estimate that the life of a car body which has received proper attention each year will be ten per cent greater than one receiving attention every second year.

This conclusion of the committee is abundantly borne out by examination of the detailed figures of maintenance of cars under the two systems, which are given in the report. For example, the item of general woodwork repairs and tightening up frames, under the system of yearly shopping, cost the company in the eighth year $15 and in the tenth year $15.50. When the car has been shopped bi-yearly, however, this item cost $45 for the eighth year and $60 for the tenth year. The cost of varnishing and cleaning and renovating upholstery and curtains is also much greater for the later years of the period than on cars which have been shopped yearly. The committee estimates that the life of a car body which has received attention every year is ten per cent greater than one receiving attention every second year.

There is also a great advantage in yearly maintenance of equipment in reduced cost of car cleaning and in greater attractiveness leading to an increase in revenue. "It will also be conceded," says the committee, "that a car which is kept well varnished can be kept clean with less labor than is the case where the luster is gone and the paint exposed. This would amount to at least ten per cent of the cost of keeping the woodwork clean, but as it would not affect the sweeping, dusting and cleaning of glass, five per cent of the total car cleaning is taken as a fair value.

"A clean car excites pride in the car crews, tends to make them more attentive to their personal appearance, their work more pleasant, and, in consequence, they will render better service to the company. An attractive and comfortable car goes a long way toward making a satisfied passenger and a well-disposed public."

The committee estimates the gain under this head resulting from yearly maintenance at ten cents per car per day. The final comparison of the results of yearly and bi-yearly maintenance is presented in the following table of costs and credits:

Summary of Costs and Credits

	Cars Shopped Yearly		Cars Shopped Bi-yearly
	Costs	Credits	
Car body maintenance (for 10 years)	$585.14		
Interest, depreciation, taxes and insurance (for 10 years) on additional equipment on account of being in shops four days per year more than when shopped bi-yearly	44.40		
Interest, etc., on increased shop room	10.40		
Reduced liability of accidents for five years at two cents per day		$36.50	
Five per cent saving in cost of car cleaning for five years		84.65	
Value of car being more attractive and comfortable to passengers (at ten cents per day for five years)		182.50	
Decreased depreciation on longer life of car body (ten per cent.)		61.50	
Totals for ten years	$639.94	$365.15	$554.49
Average per year	63.99	36.51	55.44

The claim of regular maintenance could not be more clearly presented than in the final results of this comparison, showing an advantage of $27.96 for the method of yearly shopping. From every standpoint except that of immediate saving, the policy of postponing maintenance is to be condemned, not merely because of its effect upon the property maintained, but also because of the impaired operating efficiency which neglect of maintenance always brings in its train.

Having established our rules for the financing of maintenance, we have next to consider the financing of depreciation. Shall the depreciation charges be annually deducted from income as are maintenance charges and sinking funds, or shall the directors be given a certain amount of liberty in concentrating these charges upon years of large earnings? The various public service commissions which have passed rules on the subject and the Interstate Commerce Commission are inclined to the opinion that depreciation should be a fixed rule. The Wisconsin commission, for example, provides that:

> Every electric railway shall carry a proper and adequate depreciation reserve to cover the full replacement of all tangible capital in service. There shall be opened a depreciation account, to which shall be charged monthly, crediting the depreciation reserve, an amount equal to one twelfth of the estimated annual depreciation of the tangible capital in service of the railway, or as near that amount as the finances of the property will permit.

On the other hand, the practical view of this subject is expressed by Mr. Frank R. Ford, of Ford, Bacon & Davis, electrical railway engineers, in a paper presented at the mid-year meeting of the American Street & Interurban Railway Association on January 28, 1910:

> The depreciation fund is essentially a financial problem, the solution of which is apparently by law left to the directors of the corporation as they are em-

> powered to determine the amount of current income to be set aside for working capital and the amount of dividends to be declared. It is questionable if utilities commissions can lawfully impose rules for the charging of depreciation in cases where the physical property is fairly maintained and securities properly issued. I believe that no hard and fast rule can be laid down for charging a fixed amount to such a fund month by month or year by year; the proper amount to be charged should be known, and if in lean years this amount is not laid aside, in prosperous years the deficiency should be made up. It might even be necessary to use this fund for other purposes than renewal of physical property, due to business contingencies unforeseen.

Mr. Ford's view may be indorsed since it conforms to the practice of corporations noted for their conservatism. Depreciation differs radically from maintenance, interest, and sinking fund charges in that the losses to provide for which depreciation funds are built up, are not regularly recurring. For example, a power plant may be assumed to remain in active service for fifteen to twenty years, and provision should be made for its replacement at the end of that period. It is not necessary, therefore, although the necessary funds must be available at the end of twenty years, that one twentieth of the amount should be provided in each year. The company can take advantage of years of large earnings to increase its appropriation for depreciation, and can make corresponding reductions in these charges when earnings are small. By adopting this policy, the company can maintain an average rate sufficient to provide for the depreciation of its assets, while it can distribute the annual appropriations so that they fall lightly in years of small earnings. The fluctuations in the surplus available for dividends are thus reduced to the minimum. The practice of the United States Steel Corporation in managing its depreciation follows the rule laid down by Mr. Ford. The following table gives the net profits of the company, the amounts set aside for depreciation and extinguishment, the payments out of this fund, and the balance remaining, for the first seven years of the corporation's history:

UNITED STATES STEEL CORPORATION AND SUBSIDIARY COMPANY

Depreciation and Extinguishment, Extraordinary Replacement and Improvement

	Set Aside	Payment	Balances	Net Profits
1902	$24,150,325.04	$19,813,669.13	$18,273,801.49	$90,306,525
1903	23,897,353.36	24,937,033.95	17,568,222.39	55,416,653
1904	12,574,210.91	11,299,647.27	19,377,179.32	30,267,539
1905	21,665,063.04	16,109,701.72	26,792,216.37	68,585,492
1906	28,753,271.55	21,079,231.47	35,521,959.74	98,128,587
1907	28,025,124.41	26,995,540.51	38,038,842.56	104,565,564
1908	16,836,324.81	16,291,496.25	39,554,239.05	45,728,714
1909	24,447,673.00	14,739,939.79	50,630,279.45	79,073,695

An examination of this table shows that when the company's earnings are large, its appropriations for depreciation increase, and when earnings fall off, the depreciation allowances are reduced. The two years of smallest earnings for the corporation were 1904 and 1908. In 1904 the depreciation appropriations were reduced nearly fifty per cent, and in 1908 forty per cent. If the company had appropriated in 1904 and 1908 the average amount for the entire period, it could not have paid its full rates of dividend out of the surplus of these years. The table also shows how rapid is the accumulation in the depreciation reserve of the steel corporation owing to the fact that the payments out of these funds have as yet been small. In seven years the amount in these reserves has more than doubled. The company is accumulating large reserves against the day when it will be necessary for it to re-equip its plants.

CHAPTER XVII

FIXING THE PROPORTION OF PROFITS TO BE PAID OUT IN DIVIDENDS

THE third rule or principle which we find to govern the dividend policy of well-managed companies is to pay out in cash dividends only a portion of the balance of income remaining in any year available for distribution to stockholders. Even after a large surplus has been accumulated to safeguard the dividend rate, and with the most careful management of the depreciation and renewal accounts, the amount of this "balance for dividends" is subject to wide fluctuations, which, in view of the desirability of maintaining a fixed rate of dividend, makes the distribution of the entire amount in any year unwise.

The earnings of a corporation are the resultant of three factors: (1) The volume of traffic or sales; (2) the rate or price at which the business is done; (3) the cost of operation or production. A steel manufacturing company, for example, buys coke, pig iron and limestone and converts these products first into iron, and then into steel rails by purchasing the services of a number of employees, and finally sells the product to the consumer. The formula for calculating the profits of this company is as follows: (Receipts from sales) — (cost of materials) + (wages, salaries and general expenses) + (interest, rentals and taxes) + (cost of materials, machinery for replacements and new construction charged to depreciation). A variation in any of the items of expenses, unless accompanied by corresponding variation of receipts, will result in a fluctuation of profits.

Stability of profits, under these circumstances, is an impossibility. The price of the product changes with the periodical fluctuations of demand. The growing power of organized labor as well as the inefficiency of labor when employment is plentiful, makes labor cost uncertain. New inventions and improvements may require the company to discard large amounts of machinery. Only the items of general expense and interest charges can be regarded as factors of expense which can be reckoned with certainty. On the other hand, the receipts from sales are even more uncertain. In September, 1907, for example, few anticipated that within three months the leading manufacturing plants of the country would be operating at one half of their normal capacity. The regular alternations of prosperity and depreciation, to say nothing of general breakdowns, such as befell the steel industry in 1908, or difficulties with organized labor, or advances of freight rates or tariff changes, any one of these uncertainties may come in to make a marked change, both in prices and the volume of sales. Here are two sets of profit variables, one disturbing calculations of expense, the other calculations of income. As a result of their interaction, every industry is subject to excessive variations of profits.

We may illustrate from reports of the Baltimore & Ohio. The gross earnings of this company increased from 67.6 millions in 1905 to 82.2 millions in 1907. Then came the panic and the depression, which reduced gross earnings to 73.6 millions. Operating expenses, from 1905 to 1907, increased only ten millions. As a result, the net earnings of the company, the difference between gross earnings and operating expenses, increased nearly five million dollars. On the other hand, from 1907 to 1908, operating expenses were hardly reduced at all, standing at fifty-four millions each year. Net earnings from operation of the Baltimore & Ohio declined from twenty-seven millions to nineteen millions, the exact amount of the decrease in gross earnings, in consequence.

These fluctuations in profits are even more serious in the case of industrial corporations. For example, the American Smelting & Refining Company reported gross earnings of 13.2 millions in 1907, and 9.4 millions in 1908, and the net earnings from operation of the United States Steel Corporation which were 161 millions in 1907 to which figure they had increased from 119.7 millions in 1905, suffered a decline of approximately forty per cent during 1908, falling to 91.8 millions. This fluctuation of profits is not the same for all industries, nor is the rate of change the same for every corporation in each industry. The distinction between industries, in respect to the relative stability of their profits, we shall have present occasion to examine. For the time being, it is sufficient to note that these profit fluctuations do exist, and that they must be reconciled with the necessity of paying the regular dividend.

In view of these irregular earnings, it is impossible for corporation directors to pay out all their earnings to stockholders without making dividends unstable and damaging the financial standing of the company. To reconcile the necessity for stable dividends with the fact of unstable profits, the directors must pay out only such a percentage of profits as will leave a margin over the dividend requirements, assuming profits to fall to the lowest point which, in all reasonable probability, will be reached. A corporation should ascertain from its own experience, and from the experience of other companies similarly situated, what are likely to be the lowest earnings under the most unfavorable circumstances which it is likely to encounter, and then fix its dividend rate well below that point. In order to maintain a stable rate of dividend, a corporation should have its maximum dividend requirement always fall below its smallest earnings. If the opposite policy is adopted, large dividends will be paid out of large profits, small dividends out of small profits, and the value of the stock, as already explained, will be low and uncertain.

Our next question concerns the percentage of profits

which directors, having regard to the desirability of a stable dividend rate, can safely pay out to stockholders. The determination of this proportion is a matter for the judgment of directors in each case to determine, having regard to the peculiar circumstances of their own company. There are, however, certain broad considerations on the basis of which a classification of companies, with reference to the proportion of surplus earnings which should be paid to stockholders, can be made.

The percentage of average profits which can safely be paid out to stockholders varies with the regularity of its profits. To illustrate: a corporation, the difference between whose maximum and minimum profits over a period of years is fifty per cent, should pay out only half the proportion of annual earnings which can be safely distributed by another corporation whose earnings fluctuate only twenty-five per cent.

The stability of the earnings of a corporation depends primarily upon the demand for the product or service which it supplies. In manufacturing industry, this stability of demand is greatest in those corporations which produce the necessaries of life, such as sugar, oil and flour, and it declines as the article becomes less indispensable to the consumer. The percentage of average earnings which a lace or glove manufacturing company, for example, can safely pay to its stockholders is far less than that which a sugar or oil company produces. The fluctuations in the demand for all goods used in production, including machinery and materials, are also great. Iron and steel products, for example, are purchased that the buyer may make a profit by using these commodities in further production. Such articles as lathe, steel rails and structural steel are usually bought by producers who expect to make a profit by using them or reselling them. The strength of the demand for iron and steel depends, therefore, upon the movement of profits.

As a general principle, rising prices always mean advancing profits to the industries concerned, and falling prices mean declining profits. The reason for this is that costs of production move more slowly than prices of the product, since they contain certain elements such as wages and interest, which change very slowly. Industries are, moreover, so closely joined together in the relations of producer and consumer that an increase in the prices and profits of one industry is quickly passed to the others. When the price of wheat, for example, is rising, the farmer's profits go up, and with them his demand for agricultural implements, barbed wire, and nails. When the price of wheat falls, these purchases are postponed to a more convenient season. Rising prices increase the volume of traffic, the earnings of the railroads, and the prices of their securities, enabling them to raise money for extensions and improvements, which improves the demand for a great variety of articles entering into the construction and equipment of railroads. On the other hand, when prices are falling, and the volume of business shrinks, railway earnings decline, the security market will take only high-grade bonds, and these only at low prices, the railroads have no margin in their earnings to make improvements, and their securities cannot be sold to advantage. It is then necessary to stop their extension and improvement work, and to curtail their expenditures for materials. The same influence determines the demand for the products of all the metal industries, and also the demand for such articles as coal and lumber which are purchased for profit and not for the personal consumption of the buyer. The demand for these articles fluctuates widely and often wildly, corresponding to the alternations of business prosperity and business depression. Industries which produce production goods, therefore, if properly managed, will be very conservative in their distribution of profits to stockholders.

There is a wide difference between the profits of railway transportation companies and manufacturing companies, the instability of whose profits we have just been considering. The demand for the products of a single industry is limited to a small portion of the total number of commodities produced. The demand for railway transportation, on the other hand, is represented by every commodity of commerce. The demand for transportation corresponds to the supply of commodities. The broader is the demand for the products or service of an industry, the more stable are its earnings. A large and diversified demand is but slightly affected by any influence, but if this influence is left to operate by itself upon the price of a commodity or service, it produces wide fluctuations. The withdrawal of ten thousand gallons from a standpipe appreciably affects the level of water in the pipe. Withdraw the same amount from the reservoir, and the water level is scarcely affected. This analogy may be applied to explain the stability of the demand for railway transportation as compared with the demand for coal, sugar, or iron. The railroad company is patronized by the producers of every commodity. What it loses in freight earnings from a decline in price or supply of one group of products, is often more than regained by advances in others. The manufacturing company, on the other hand, by producing, at the most, only a small number of products, has usually less compensation for a decrease in demand. Its earnings usually, therefore, show a larger effect from a fall in prices.

The classified freight traffic of the Pennsylvania Railroad, for example, includes thirty-six general classes of freight, some of which comprise thousands of individual articles, and each one of which contributes to the $153,564,528 of gross earnings which the company earned in 1909. Each one of these commodities is acted on by a variety of influences which affect its demand or supply, and which, through these factors, influence the profits of its producers. The production of anthracite coal is reduced by a strike. As a result the demand for bituminous coal is increased. A failure of the corn crop reduces the profits of the farmer and rancher. A cut in duties decreases the profits of the manufacturer, and a change in internal revenue duties affects the profits of the grower and distiller. Prices and profits are in a state of constant change. No manufacturing industry can be certain of its earnings a year hence.

From these disturbing influences, however, the railway company is, to a large extent, protected. The great variety of its traffic prevents rapid changes in the gross amount. What is lost on one commodity is often regained on another, and the total tonnage is not reduced. This is well illustrated by a comparison of the gross earnings of the Pennsylvania Railroad with those of the United States Steel Corporation. The one is the largest railroad system in the United States and one of the best managed, and the other is the largest and one of the best-managed and best-organized industrials. The steel corporation, moreover, manufactures a great variety of products, so that its demand would naturally be more stable than those of steel manufacturing companies whose profits are more narrowly specialized. It has also been able to maintain for long periods stable prices for most of its products, and its supremacy in the steel trade since its organization has only recently been challenged. Competition, until the winter of 1909, has very slightly disturbed it, and yet the fluctuation of its gross earnings, compared with the Pennsylvania Railroad, which appears in the following table, where the figures are stated in millions of dollars, is extreme. The figures for the Pennsylvania Railroad are as follows, stated in millions of dollars:

1902	112
1903	122
1904	118
1905	133
1906	148
1907	164
1908	136

and for the United States Steel Corporation as follows:

1902	500
1903	536
1904	444
1905	585
1906	696
1907	757
1908	482

The percentages of fluctuation from one year to another in the two companies are as follows:

	Pennsylvania Railroad.	United States Steel Corporation.
1902	15.15	.....
1903	8.93	7.20
1904	3.28	17.16
1905	12.71	31.76
1906	11.28	18.97
1907	10.81	8.76
1908	17.08	36.33

Broadly speaking, the distinction which has been indicated between railway and manufacturing industries holds good wherever it is applied. The demand for the transportation services offered by some railways, especially those which depend exclusively upon iron and steel or kindred industries, is more irregular than those of some manufacturing companies—for example, gas or electric lighting companies or companies supplying certain food products which are regarded as necessaries of life. But as between the two classes of corporations, railroads and industrials, the comparison of stability of demand favors the railroad, primarily because of the breadth of the demand for its products.

The distinction between transportation and manufacturing industry, on the basis of the respective stability of their profits, is explained, not merely by varying conditions of demand, but by their respective liability to competition. A business in which competition prevails is certain to be a business of fluctuating prices. When demand is slack, the sellers, in their struggle to keep their plants in operation and their organizations employed, give the buyer concession after concession, which he very well knows how to extract by playing one seller against another. Then, when business revives, the producer, who has usually lost money during the depression, takes immediate and full advantage of the opportunity to charge the highest price which the traffic will bear. These high prices, as soon as the low-price contracts with which large consumers have protected themselves expire, lead to the curtailment of demand and to another outbreak of competition. When the steel industry, for example, was a competitive business, prices were highly irregular. In fact, for a long period there were no fixed prices on account of the rebates and discriminations; everything was uncertain, irregular, and unstable. Under such conditions profits were not only reduced in the aggregate, but their fluctuations were enormous. From 1901 to 1909, however, under the dominance of the United States Steel Corporation, which has controlled about sixty per cent of the production of finished material, and of whose power the smaller producers have stood in awe, stable prices have been maintained. The corporation has neither raised prices during periods of active demand—for example, in 1904, 1905, 1906, and 1907, when they could have materially advanced quotations—nor when business declined have they attempted the futile experiment of persuading the manufacturer half of whose plant is idle, or a railroad with one third of its equipment on the sidings, to invest large sums in steel products for extensions and improvements by making concessions in price. By maintaining prices they have earned a larger margin of profits on a reduced tonnage, and have protected their interest and preferred dividends.

From the influence of competition, the profits of the railway industry are almost fully protected. The railway company enjoys a natural monopoly. After the territory through which its lines pass has been fully settled, and the local donations of land and cash, upon which most American railways originally depended for their construction, have ceased, the building of competing lines becomes very difficult. An important deterrent to new railroad construction is the increasing cost of terminals. A recent illustration of this fact is the enormous expenditures of the Gould interests to put a line into Pittsburg, which it is claimed cost them $30,000,000, and which, because of their inability to connect with the leading industries of that city, and also because of the absence of an Eastern outlet which would enable them to compete for the bulk of the tonnage, has never been successful. Even where competition exists between the larger cities, the local traffic is generally free from this influence, and competition for through business, while effective in maintaining lower rates between competitive points, is nevertheless well regulated by uniform agreements, which are well observed, presumably because the decline of traffic during periods of depression is not so severe as to incite a struggle for existence between railroads, and also because all forms of secret rate cutting, rebating, and discriminations are now prohibited by a Federal criminal statute, which has been rigidly enforced in recent years.

A few years ago the attempt was made to permanently eliminate competition in the railway field by a system of community of interest by which one road purchased control, although not always a majority interest, in the stocks of its competitors. This system has been broken up by the enforcement of the Sherman Antitrust Law, but it lasted long enough to enforce upon the railroads the necessity of agreement upon rates. While railway competition, so far as it relates to speed and character of service, still exists, competition in rates has practically disappeared.

The elimination of competition from manufacturing industry, however, is exceedingly difficult. To return again to the United States Steel Corporation, which offered the best promise of accomplishing this result, we find that, during the winter of 1909, this attempt to control prices, although it was for the manifest interest of the trade, was completely broken down. The steel corporation at no time controlled two thirds of the steel production of the United States, but relied upon its control of raw materials and the influence which the dominant factor in the trade usually has upon the weaker members, to secure adherence to a policy of fixed prices. By uniting upon this policy, the small amount of business which was to be had was handled at remunerative prices, and the profits of all steel producers were much larger than they would have been had they surrendered to the consumer at the outset of the depression. Little by little, however, under the pressure of necessity, the independents broke away from the agreement, and cut prices in order to secure a larger share of the limited business available than they would have obtained had they followed the policy of the steel corporation in maintaining prices. At last this price cutting was seen to threaten the steel corporation with the loss of most of its business for the coming year. In self-defense it was compelled to announce an open market for steel. With this declaration, a portion of the benefits of combination, so far as these relate to the control of prices, were surrendered to the consumer.

The failure of the attempt of the United States Steel Corporation to control prices, an attempt made under the most favorable auspices, with the strongest leadership, and apparently with the cordial coöperation of all members of the trade, shows that the maintenance of stable prices in the field of production goods, unless the ownership of an entire industry can be secured by one producer, is difficult. Single ownership the Federal and State laws, as at present interpreted, will not permit.

In the field of consumption goods, where commodities are purchased directly by the consumer, monopoly is even more difficult to secure. The concentration of manufacture under the control of large corporations has worked for a larger measure of stability than was possible when an industry was carried on by a large number of productive units, but combination has thus far done no more than to mitigate the severity of competition. It has not been able to do away with competition.

These general differences between industries, however, do no more than furnish the starting point for the determination of the percentage of profits which a given corporation can carry. Within each industry, a great diversity of conditions as to the strength of demand, costs of production, control of raw materials, location in reference to markets, and a variety of other considerations are encountered. The existence of these differences in conditions makes it impossible, without reference to the circumstances of the corporation in question, to determine the proportion of average profits which can safely be distributed to stockholders.

Even within the industry whose profits are more stable than any other, the business of railway transportation, we find wide differences between the stability of profits of different railroads. The New England railroads—for example, the New York, New Haven & Hartford and the Boston & Maine—have a large percentage of passenger traffic which fluctuates little, and a high-class traffic of manufacturing goods and merchandise, which produces a stable revenue. Industrial conditions in this territory are very stable. The people, as a community, are well-to-do, and the New England States are affected in a much smaller degree by an industrial depression than are many other communities. As a result of these conditions, the traffic and earnings of the New York, New Haven & Hartford and the Boston & Maine are subject to relatively slight fluctuations. These companies can and do pay out a larger percentage of profits to stockholders than can be safely distributed by such companies as the Pennsylvania and the Baltimore & Ohio, both of which depend mainly on the coal and iron and steel traffic, or by the Granger lines, whose principal reliance is still on the products of agriculture.

But while it is impossible, for the reasons stated, to indicate, as between different industries, the percentages of profits which can be safely distributed in dividends, we may answer the question as to the proper amount of earnings which should be reserved for the protection of the dividend rate by reference to the practice of the most conservative railway and industrial companies. The Pennsylvania Railroad, for example, on an average of many years, has made it a rule that for every dollar paid out in dividends another dollar shall be put into the property. The Chicago & Northwestern has distributed about three fourths of its profits; the Great

Northern, a somewhat smaller percentage. The earnings of the railway business, with the possible exception of public service corporations located in a few of the larger cities, are, as we have seen, more permanent and stable than those of any other leading industry. In fixing the percentage of reserve required for corporations operating in industries where the stability of profits is less than in the railway industry, it is safe to require at least as large a proportion as that reserved by the strongest railway companies, since the nature of the railway business renders the earnings of long-established railway companies far more stable than the profits of even those manufacturing companies which are most firmly intrenched in the control of raw materials and in a stable demand for their product.

On the basis of this principle, we may assume that no railroad company, outside of corporations so exceptionally situated as are the railroads in Southern New England, can safely pay out in dividends, on an average of ten years, more than three fourths of its profits, and that the percentage of cash distributed by industrial corporations should not be more than fifty per cent of the average profits. The implication of this rule is, of course, that during periods of large profits a much higher percentage than fifty per cent must be reserved for the stock. As a general proposition, a corporation which follows the rule of a dollar for the company and a dollar for the stockholder is on the way to an investment position for its stock. In cases where the industry is exposed to exceptionally wide fluctuations of profits even a larger percentage must be reserved. The balance reserved for the company is invested for its benefit, the accumulation of this annual investment raising the earning capacity of the company so that a higher dividend rate can eventually be paid. As the dividends increase, however, the surplus should also increase, both dividends and surplus, with ordinary good management, moving upward, and the stockholders profiting, not merely from the increase in dividends, but from their greater security in any rate of dividend once attained.

CHAPTER XVIII

THE METHODS OF DISTRIBUTING THE SURPLUS

WHAT now is the relation of this surplus appearing on the balance sheet to the rate of dividend? May it be drawn upon in case of emergency to make up a deficit in income? May it be distributed in large amounts as special dividends to stockholders, or can the stockholders hope for no greater benefit from this accumulation out of profits than their proportion of the addition which will be made to the income of the company as a result of the investment of its profits? In the majority of companies the only service which the surplus accumulated out of profits renders to the dividend rate is to increase the amount of annual profits, which furnishes the basis for the amount of dividends declared. It may, however, in some cases serve as a fund out of which deficits in the amount necessary to pay the regular dividend may be made up, either by direct withdrawal or by borrowing. The surplus may also, from time to time, be directly distributed to stockholders, in a lump sum, as a special dividend. These various methods of utilizing the surplus we have now to examine.

The surplus of a corporation may be used as a source of dividends to its stockholders, aside from its service in increasing the net earnings of the business, in the following ways: The company may, during a season of depression, draw down its surplus by reducing its cash working capital for the purpose of making up a temporary deficiency in revenue. It may accomplish the same result by negotiating a temporary loan, which will be returned out of the income of a later period of the year. This method of borrowing money to meet dividends, when receipts are irregularly distributed throughout the year, is very common. It is a legitimate practice. If the revenues are in sight, a bank will lend money to a corporation to anticipate those revenues, no matter if the proceeds of the loan are to be immediately distributed to the stockholders in the form of a dividend.

The second method of distributing surplus directly to the stockholders is when a company may have acquired in the course of its business certain assets with which it can readily dispense, such, for example, as coal-mining or express companies, or land companies. The stocks representing these concerns may be held in the treasury of the parent company, and the dividends received on these stocks may be added to the other income of the parent company, and merged into its general surplus available for distribution. In case it is expedient or convenient for the corporation to divest itself of the control of these properties, the stocks or bonds issued by the subsidiary companies may be distributed to the stockholders of the parent company as a special dividend.

An illustration of this method is furnished by the distribution of the Great Northern Ore securities by the Great Northern Railway Company to its stockholders. Certain iron-ore lands in Minnesota had been acquired in the interest of the Great Northern Railway by Mr. James Hill, then its president, and his associates. These properties, aggregating about 60,000 acres, were located in the Missabe district of Minnesota. They were controlled by the corporation known as the Lake Superior Company, Ltd., controlled by the Great Northern Railway. The properties were transferred in the autumn of 1906 to Mr. James J. Hill, Louis W. Hill, and E. T. Nichols, as trustees, and 1,500,000 shares of permanent beneficial interest in the trust were issued in December, 1906, to the Great Northern stockholders. In August, 1906, a lease was executed to the Great Western Mining Company, guaranteed by the United States Steel Corporation, covering 39,295 acres of this land. The Great Western

Mining Company agreed to extract 750,000 tons of ore in 1907, with an increase of 750,000 tons annually, until a maximum annual extraction of 8,250,000 tons was reached in 1917. The lease fixes the royalty for each ton of ore delivered at the dock by the Great Northern at $1.65, and, after deducting eighty cents per ton as freight to the railroad company for transporting the ore, the balance is distributed to the holders of trust certificates at least once a year. These certificates were immediately distributed by the Great Northern to its stockholders as a special dividend.

It has long been the policy of the Great Northern to keep its dividend at seven per cent. Had it retained these ore certificates in its treasury and paid the rentals in the regular dividends, this rate would have been exceeded. The lease protected the railway company in the transportation of the ore to be mined under the lease. It could, therefore, without danger of losing control of this traffic, distribute the certificates of beneficial interest in the lease as a special dividend to the stockholders. This was a direct distribution of its surplus by the Great Northern Railroad Company.

A portion of the surplus may be annually set aside into a dividend reserve fund, withdrawn from the working capital of the business, and invested in a form in which it can be drawn upon without impairing the efficiency of the corporation. Unless the dividend reserve fund is built up in this manner, the assets of the company cannot be directly utilized to make up a deficiency in reserve. A railroad company, for example, has invested its surplus in equipment, or in improvements to its line, or in larger terminal facilities, or in securities of corporations. It also carries a certain cash balance. It cannot sell any of these properties or assets without impairing its efficiency. The investment of surplus funds in the business of the corporation merges and identifies them with the general assets of the company, which are used for its general corporate purposes, and which, unless the stockholder decides to wind up its affairs and to pay its debts and divide the balance, are not available for distribution. If, however, a company adopts the policy of maintaining a dividend reserve fund, it may utilize its surplus directly to make up deficiencies in revenue.

When a dividend reserve fund is established, an amount is withdrawn each year from the working capital of the business, and invested in securities which are held merely as investments, and which do not represent the control of the properties necessary to the business of the company. In a year of small profits, a portion of these securities can be sold, or they can be hypothecated for a loan, and the regular dividend can thus be paid. This plan is in effect the averaging of payments out of surplus over a period of years—the same principle as that followed by many companies in insuring their own plants.

An illustration is furnished by the Cunard Company, which, over the twenty years ending 1902, out of £4,650,380 of profits earned, paid only 18.8 per cent to the owners of the company and added 81.2 per cent to the various reserves which the company maintained. A large amount of this money withheld from the stockholders was invested in good securities, and during four bad years, from 1892 to 1895, these reserves were drawn upon for dividends. Of the £64,000 which was paid out to stockholders during these years, £55,000 came from the reserves. The maintenance of a dividend reserve fund is justifiable for corporations, such as ocean transportation companies, whose profits are subject to wide fluctuations. As a general proposition, however, the maintenance of these funds cannot be approved. The reason is the same as that which can be urged against maintenance of sinking funds—the fact that money invested in securities can earn at the best 4½ or 5 per cent, while if invested in the business its earnings are much larger. A growing company has always need of new capital to expand its business, and save in exceptional cases such as the one just described, it is bad policy to maintain any portion of its surplus in a form from which it can be directly distributed to the stockholders. It is better that the annual reservations from profits should be merged into the general assets of the company, since in this way they will contribute to the increase of its profits and property.

With the exception of the two methods described—temporary reduction of working capital or payment of dividends out of a dividend reserve fund—direct distribution of the accumulations of the profits of a corporation which have been invested in the enlargement of its business, is not possible. The surplus has become an integral part of the property of the company, merged into general assets, increasing in time the annual profits in which stockholders participate, but not available as a fund of assets for immediate distribution to stockholders. The company cannot sell any part of its plant to pay a dividend or dispose of any securities which it holds for the purpose of controlling corporations which these securities represent, or impair its working capital, in order to make a distribution to stockholders. The distribution of the surplus must be made, if at all, by increasing liabilities rather than reducing assets.

We have described the surplus as the difference between assets and liabilities, which appears on the liability side of the balance sheet. This surplus can be reduced either by reducing the assets or by increasing liabilities. In either case, the difference between assets and liabilities is reduced, and if the corporation issues stock or bonds directly to stockholders, or sells these securities and pays out the proceeds as special dividends, it may, without impairing its general assets or crippling in any way the efficiency of its plant, distribute its surplus to its stockholders.

An ordinary method of financing current requirements for new construction is to spend upon the property the amount available for a dividend, paying the dividend not in cash but in stock or scrip redeemable in stock. Cluett, Peabody & Company are carrying out an extensive plan of providing new capital by this method, which is merely a sale of stock to stockholders at par. No objection can be made to this practice so long as the amount of stock paid out does not exceed the cash dividend which could safely be paid at the time.

Corporations occasionally, however, go much further than this, and capitalize the accumulations of many years by a special dividend in stock or bonds, or in cash raised by the sale of securities. A celebrated illustration of this method of distributing surplus is furnished by the action of the Chicago & Alton Railroad Company in 1899 in paying out to its stockholders a portion of its surplus, amounting to $12,444,777, which during previous years, it was claimed, had been taken from earnings and expended for additions and permanent improvements, but in the first instance had been charged upon the books of the company to current expenditures. The funds for this payment were obtained by a sale of bonds. This transaction attracted little attention at the time, but some years later was subjected to severe criticism.

The explanation and justification of this transaction by Mr. Paul D. Cravath, of counsel for the company, is as follows:

> All agree that the expenditures in question were for capital account. That the Company had during the previous years devoted at least $12,444,177 of its profits to capital expenditures no one questions, and that these expenditures might have been charged from year to year to Capital Account and carried to Surplus is equally clear. The witness Hilliard, the present Comptroller of the Company, testified: "I have not any doubt that they might have been fairly so charged at the time." Mr. Blackstone, the President of the Company, in his annual report of 1894 stated that the capitalization of the Company, including its bonds and all obligations assumed by it, aggregated less than sixty per cent of the actual cost of the property in its present impaired condition, and that a dividend of eight per cent is, therefore, the equivalent of about $4\frac{3}{4}$ per cent upon such a number of shares as would, together with the funded debt, represent the actual cost of the property. The readjustment of accounts was entirely proper and is sustained by highest accounting

authority. After these expenditures for Capital Account had from year to year been charged to Current Expense, the Board of Directors could properly and lawfully readjust the accounts and transfer these expenditures to Capital Account, thus correspondingly increasing the Company's surplus. It is respectfully submitted that notwithstanding the opinion of the witness Hilliard to the contrary, there is not the slightest doubt about the legality and propriety of such procedure. This procedure is amply supported by the decisions of the courts. A case precisely in point is Mills vs. Northern Ry., &c., Co.[1] In that case a railroad company had for a considerable period pursued the practice of charging the cost of certain locomotives and other rolling stock to Revenue, but, finally, in order to increase the surplus available for distribution among the stockholders by way of dividends, the directors proposed to readjust the accounts and transfer these expenditures from Income Account to Capital Account, and to distribute by way of dividend among stockholders part of the surplus thus created. Against this procedure the plaintiff made precisely the objection which Mr. Hilliard has made against the similar procedure adopted by the Chicago & Alton Railroad Company, but the High Court of Appeal overruled the objection and said: "I have no hesitation in saying that the circumstance that they had been paying what ought to be charged to capital out of revenue does not prevent their right or their duty to the persons who are looking for their payment out of revenue to credit back to revenue those things which have been carried for the time to capital account." The use of $6,669,180 of the proceeds of the sale of the $32,000,000 of three per cent bonds to pay a dividend of thirty per cent upon the stock of the Chicago & Alton Railroad Company, against the Company's surplus, most of which was the result of the readjustment of accounts discussed in the preceding paragraph. A company having a surplus may lawfully use the proceeds of bonds as a dividend fund.

As a readjustment of accounts and the carrying of

[1] Chancery Appeals, 621 (1870).

past capital expenditures to surplus were lawful, so it was equally lawful to pay out $6,669,180 of that surplus by way of a thirty per cent dividend upon the stock. The proposition that money can be borrowed for the paying of dividends (assuming that the books of the corporation show a sufficient surplus) is amply supported by the authorities.

In 2 Cook on Corporations,[1] Section 546, it is said: "When the company has used profits for improvements, it may lawfully borrow an equivalent sum of money for the purpose of a dividend. And it may properly borrow money to pay a dividend if, upon a fair estimate of its assets and liabilities, it has assets in excess of its liabilities and capital stock equal to the amount of the proposed dividend." It is difficult to see how the legality of the dividend can be questioned. It is, therefore, only necessary to discuss its propriety. The propriety of a dividend to represent the earnings invested in permanent improvements is recognized by the Blackstone management.

In declaring this dividend the new management simply carried out the purpose of the old management as publicly declared in the circular quoted above, except that the dividend was paid in cash and represented only a part of the earnings invested in permanent improvements, while, apparently, the purpose of the prior management had been to issue a stock dividend to represent all the earnings theretofore invested in such improvements.

As President Blackstone pointed out in his annual report of 1894, such large amounts of earnings had been expended upon permanent improvements that the Company's securities outstanding, taken at their par value, represented "less than sixty per cent of the actual cost of the property . . ." and while dividends had been paid at the rate of eight per cent upon the par value of the stock, the rate upon the investment which the stock represented—that is, upon the actual cost of the property—was only $4\frac{3}{4}$ per cent. That, of course, is the chief reason why the common stock of the Company was worth the price of $175 a share

[1] Fifth Edition.

> which the Syndicate paid for it. What possible impropriety, therefore, could there be in the stockholders deciding that their investment in the stock should be reduced by the payment of a thirty per cent dividend, funds for that dividend to be furnished by the sale of low interest-bearing bonds? The distribution of a stock dividend under such circumstances is exceedingly common. It is equally proper to pay out a cash dividend and issue a reasonable amount of low interest-bearing bonds for the purpose of producing the cash for that dividend. This was not a case where a bare majority of the stockholders were forcing their will upon an unwilling majority, for practically all of the stockholders joined in the declaration of the dividend, and all of the stockholders without exception shared in the distribution of the dividend.

In the case which Mr. Cravath describes, the company issued bonds for cash and used a portion of the cash to pay the special dividend on the stock. The legality of this proceeding, unless specifically prohibited by statute, as it is in some States—for example, New York—is not to be questioned. The surplus could also be distributed by an issue of bonds direct to stockholders, or by an issue of stock, or a scrip dividend could be declared, redeemable either in cash or stock at some future time. All of these methods have been employed from time to time by various classes of corporations to distribute their surplus.

The expediency of this practice may be considered from two standpoints. The distribution of the surplus by some scheme of recapitalization involving an increase of liabilities without corresponding increase in assets, and the turning over to the stockholders of either bonds or stock or the proceeds of the sale of securities, as a special dividend, can be justified only if the surplus so distributed is a real surplus. It is not sufficient that the company should, from time to time, have reserved large sums out of earnings and invested these in the improvement of its property. These improvements should have actually added to the permanent earnings of the company. The issue of stock or bonds under these circumstances means an increase in the fixed charges of the company, or in its dividend requirements. Unless the investment of profits in improvements has produced the requisite increase in earnings, or unless the increase in earnings, no matter whence derived, has been actually accomplished, a capitalization of the surplus appearing on the balance sheet is without justification. Aside from financial expediency, it is wiser for a corporation which has no surplus, but whose earnings are large enough to pay dividends out of the proceeds of stock and bond sales to increase its interest or dividend payments, than for another corporation whose earnings are stationary or declining, but which has a large surplus accumulated out of earnings standing as a liability on its balance sheet. Instances abound where corporations have shown for many years large surplus accounts along with declining earnings. An excellent illustration of the disappearance of a book surplus is furnished by the history of the Baltimore & Ohio.

This company, under the administration of the Garretts, until 1880, had been extraordinarily prosperous. Its financial position was strong; it paid large dividends and earned a comfortable margin over these dividends. Its capital stock was small, under $20,000,000, and its funded debt was about $30,000,000, showing a total capitalization of only $35,400 a mile. Furthermore, this was always cited as the best evidence of its impregnable position that its books showed a surplus of $47,703,798, representing the accumulations of investment out of earnings, after paying ten per cent dividends for many years. The friends of the company claimed that, with a capitalization of only $50,000,000 and with a surplus of $47,000,000, the company really had no liabilities, and was at all times in a position to call in its bonds and stock. The Baltimore & Ohio, at this time, in the early eighties, was considered to be the strongest railway corporation in the United States. If the company had chosen to double its capital stock in order to capitalize a portion of its surplus, the transaction could not have been attacked either on the ground of expediency or legality.

Within ten years from 1886, however, the company was dragged into bankruptcy. It embarked in a policy of aggression directed against the Pennsylvania Railroad and the New York Central, and it incurred heavy liabilities for new construction. The result was that, while its fixed charges increased, its earnings were reduced. In 1883 and 1884, the Baltimore & Ohio had earned a surplus over dividends of $2,000,000. By 1887 this had fallen to less than $40,000, a large floating debt had been accumulated, and in 1888 a thorough reorganization was arranged for. In connection with this reorganization, the surplus appearing on the books of the company, and which was discovered to have been invested in forms which were no longer productive, was scaled down from $48,000,000 to $23,000,000. In reality, the surplus which the Baltimore & Ohio had been carrying for many years was no more than an accumulation in a depreciation account. The money had been spent upon the property, and the property had, notwithstanding, been allowed to fall below the standard of efficiency maintained by its rivals, the Pennsylvania Railroad and the New York Central. Within a few years after this reorganization, in 1896, the company went into the hands of a receiver. Its equipment was found to be in a wretched condition, the entire property needed reconstruction; the paper surplus had disappeared.

The same criticism can be directed against the directors of the Alton. The surplus which they capitalized and distributed was fictitious. This company connects Chicago, St. Louis, and Kansas City. In 1898 it had only a small capitalization, as indicated in the quotations from President Blackstone's reports. Its earnings for many years had been stationary, but it was regarded as a strong property. A syndicate, represented by Mr. Harriman, Mr. James Stillman, and Mr. Mortimer Schiff, set out to acquire the property for the purpose of recapitalizing it and making a quick profit. The method which they followed was to organize a competing company and to start the construction of a line paralleling the Alton from St. Louis to Chicago.

The Alton stockholders were greatly disturbed by these developments. The net earnings of the Alton were not increasing. The stockholders could gain no comfort from the large paper surplus which the books of the company showed, because the standard of efficiency of their property was not up to that of its competitors. The standards of construction were those of fifteen years before. The track was laid with steel rails, but those were only seventy pounds to the yard. The bridges were in good condition, but were too light for heavy engines. The capacity of the sidings and second tracks was inadequate to handle large increase in traffic. A circular sent out by a majority of the directors urging the sale of the stock to the syndicate at $175 a share contains the following statement: "The Chicago & Alton Railroad is without connections, either east or west, under its corporate control. At important points competition already existing and threatened, with the general tendency to reduced rates of transportation and to increased rates of taxation, it becomes more and more difficult for the road to continue the earnings of the past." It is evident that the directors had no confidence that the surplus accumulated out of earnings would be of any great service to the company in meeting competition.

The condition of the Alton was far below that of its competitors. This is proven by another quotation from the statement of Mr. Cravath explaining why the company failed to pay a dividend on the $20,000,000 of common stock, an issue which was made against an anticipated increase of earnings: "The failure of the Chicago & Alton Company to make the expected earnings for the common stock is due mainly to two causes: first, it took over $19,000,000 to modernize and fully equip the property, instead of about $6,000,000, as had been originally estimated; and, second, while the new management succeeded in promptly increasing the gross revenue of the company, the increase in net earnings was very slight, because of unexpected reductions in rates, which, in the case of freight rates, seem to have averaged about thirty per cent."

Here is a frank admission by counsel for the syndicate which conducted the reorganization of the Alton, that the company had not maintained a sufficient depreciation account, that its property had not been kept up to standard, and that it was necessary to borrow large sums of money to reconstruct it. Under the circumstances, the payment of this special dividend was wholly unwarranted, since it represented the capitalization of a surplus, which, if proper depreciation had been made, would have figured rather as a deficit.

We may conclude, therefore, upon this point, that great caution should be exercised in the recapitalization of a company for the purpose of distributing a surplus to stockholders. While such a distribution may not be prohibited by the laws of the state incorporating the company, and while it may be justified as a deferred payment of profits, unless the surplus has been correctly calculated by deducting the proper maintenance and depreciation charges, the company is very likely to find itself in the position of the Baltimore & Ohio, with a large paper surplus and a receiver in charge of the property.

The propriety of distributing a surplus by a process of capitalization may be also considered in comparison with the method which is followed by most corporations, and which has already been indicated, of investing profits in the business, increasing the earnings as a result of this investment of profits, and eventually adding to the dividend rate. If the stockholders are content to wait, and if the surplus earnings of the company have been wisely invested, they will in time receive the benefit of these dividends in the form of a larger return on their investment and a higher value of their stock. This method is far more conservative than that which was followed in the case of the Alton. In reality it makes little difference to the stockholder who holds the hundred shares of stock on which $5 a share is being paid, whether he receives from the company twenty shares of stock as a special dividend to capitalize surplus, or whether he receives out of the earnings of the company an extra dollar of dividend. In the first case, since the regular dividend is presumably to be maintained, he receives the existing rate of five per cent on 120 shares of stock, or $600 a year. In the second case he receives the same amount expressed as a six per cent dividend on 100 shares of stock, or $600 per year. In case he wishes to sell his new stock, he could probably take a larger profit in the appreciation of the market value of his holdings; the value of twenty shares of stock paying five per cent dividends would be greater than the addition to the value of his 100 shares by the increase of one per cent in the dividend rate. This consideration is, however, insufficient to outweigh the argument that the most conservative policy, in the majority of cases, is the wisest. The most conservative policy for a corporation, in distributing its surplus to stockholders, is to increase dividends whenever earnings warrant rather than to issue stocks or bonds for which no value is received. These may represent merely the capitalization of a surplus which is unlikely to be offset by assets producing a sufficient revenue to warrant the increase in capitalization.

CHAPTER XIX

THE PROVISION OF NEW CAPITAL

Every prosperous corporation is continually adding to its plant in order to increase its profits. The extent of these additions to plant may be seen by comparison of the item "cost of plant" in the case of a number of our leading corporations over a period of years. Such a comparison appears in the following table:

	1900	1907
Pennsylvania Railroad........	$125,789,918.95	$291,061,204.00
Baltimore & Ohio............	125,969,036.90	165,066,928.00
Chicago, Milwaukee & St. Paul.	218,302,680.50	259,148,727.00
Union Pacific...............	130,520,818.00	373,951,998.00
General Electric.............	3,400,002.00	9,000,000.00
United States Steel Corporation 1901......................	1,232,585,197.10	1,435,540,068.00
Republic Iron & Steel Co.......	41,142,251.00	53,592,166.00

Taking all the railroads of the United States, we find that their cost of road and equipment increased from 1900 to 1907, inclusive, $2,879,800,000. Every prosperous corporation, whether the fact appears in its balance sheet or not, has followed a similar line of development. Its productive assets are steadily growing, more rapidly during some periods than at others, but increasing to some extent in every year of its existence.

The distinction between an expenditure which should be charged to operating expense, and an expenditure which should be charged to capital and appear as an increase in some asset account, is found in the fact that an expenditure, to be properly capitalized, should result in a certain and approximately definite increase in the profits of the company, an increase which is more than sufficient to pay interest or dividends, at the rate paid by the company on its existing liabilities, on the amount necessary to make the improvement. From the class of expenditures which can be properly capitalized, on the basis of this definition, the so-called betterment expenditures should be excluded. While betterments may result in decreasing the operating expenses of a company, the amount of the increase is usually uncertain, and, as has already been shown, the necessities of competition and the demands of the public and of the consumer for improved service and better products, make it prudent and even necessary for a well-managed company to charge into their current operating expenses large amounts representing the cost of raising their property to higher standards. An expenditure is capitalized when it is added to some asset account, appearing also on the liability side of the balance sheet either as an addition to stocks, bonds, unfunded debt, surplus, or some one of the reserves which may be carried. Capitalized expenditures should result in positive additions to the business of the company. The construction, for example, of a new mill, or the purchase of railway equipment, or the construction of lines into new territory, are examples of expenditures which could be properly capitalized. On the other hand, under ordinary conditions, such expenditures as the substitution of heavy rail for light rail, the rebuilding of locomotives, the elevation of tracks to increase the speed and safety of passenger traffic, the improvement of passenger stations, the substitution for out-of-date machine tools of new shop equipment, are properly betterments, and their cost should not appear in any asset account.

The influence which is most effective in forcing a corporation into the policy of expanding its plant is the necessity of guarding against the encroachment of competitors by occupying the territory harboring the business on which these competitors would thrive. If the demand for its products or services increases, the corporation must enlarge its facilities to supply the demand; if it does not, and competitors are permitted to occupy the new territory without a struggle, there is danger that they may follow up this conquest by an approach to closer quarters. A forcible illustration of the reasons for providing additional capital funds is given in a circular letter of the president of the Central Union (Bell) Telephone Company to the stockholders in 1901, at the time when the Bell company was embarking on its policy of expansion:

"After two months' investigation I find it imperatively necessary that at least $3,000,000 be provided without delay. The people of the states of Illinois, Indiana, Ohio, and Iowa want telephone service. Will you supply it, or must some one else? Are you doing it with fewer than 70,000 stations? No. When you have 300,000 exchange stations, then you have a good start, not before. When you have 150,000 exchange stations, at proper rates, you will have a plant upon which you can earn something with which to build up the second 150,000. With your present 70,000 stations, you cannot build up anything except opposition. You are not satisfying the public, because your system does not reach far enough. There are scores of villages and small towns, taken as a whole, that should have 50,000 telephones, and in which the company has not one single instrument. What you want done must be done now. Later on, and a very little later at that, will be too late."

A recent illustration of the truth of the observations contained in this circular came under the writer's observation in Hammonton, N. J., a town of about 4,000 people. The Bell Telephone Company had exclusive possession of the field; there were only about twenty-five stations in the town; the instruments were antiquated, the service wretched, the rates high. Since the Bell company showed no disposition to improve matters, the citizens of the town organized a company, raised $20,000, and installed an exchange, which now serves 300 subscribers and which furnishes a considerable amount of long-distance business to the competitor of the Bell company. The Bell company could easily have had these 300 subscribers if they had shown proper enterprise. As it is, the business of this community is practically lost to them.

Closely allied to considerations of necessity are the considerations of financial advantage which are offered to every prosperous corporation in the enlargement of its plant or the extension of its control over other corporations. These advantages are as follows: First, the restriction or regulation of competition, by which rates or prices may be increased; second, the enlargement and improvement of the plant to handle increasing business at a lower cost; third, the expenditure of money to develop the territory and to enlarge the sales of the company. The policy of the Pennsylvania Railroad since 1900 furnishes illustrations of the realization of each of these advantages by a progressive corporation. In 1900 the capital liabilities of the Pennsylvania Railroad increased $72,838,475; in 1901, $31,379,637; in 1902, $52,829,-284; in 1903, $125,973,000—a total increase of $283,020,396 in the assets of the company within four years. This was followed in 1904, 1905, and 1906 by further increases of $136,-217,897. The money which the Pennsylvania Railroad received and spent from 1900 to 1906 was sufficient to build and fully equip, at $60,000 per mile, a trunk line railway of 6,987 miles in extent. It is an amount far greater than the capital liabilities of most of the larger railroad companies in the United States.

When this increase of the Pennsylvania's capital is analyzed, and when the purposes to which the funds were applied are understood, this large increase of capital is seen to have been not merely warranted by the earning power of the company's property, but imperatively demanded by the competitive situation in the trunk line territory and by the growth of the traffic which was pressing for immediate shipment.

The purposes for which the funds obtained by this increase of capital were devoted were three: (1) the purchase of a dominant interest in the stocks of the Baltimore & Ohio, the Norfolk & Western, the Chesapeake & Ohio, the Western New York & Pennsylvania, and the Long Island railroads; (2) the improvement and enlargement of the physical property of the Pennsylvania Railroad Company; (3) the building of extensive terminal improvements in New York City, involving the construction of a tunnel passing under Manhattan Island and connecting New Jersey with Long Island, and a large passenger station on Manhattan Island.

The inauguration of the policy of purchasing securities of competing lines was foreshadowed in the report of 1899:

"While the growth of your traffic and its successful movement are subjects for congratulation, your board has to report a further reduction in the average ton mile rate. For years, the compensation of the trunk lines for moving freight traffic has steadily decreased. As may be supposed, railway managers have not seen this reduction without serious concern, or without making strenuous efforts to check the downward movement. These efforts have met with but little success. Had the railway companies not been able to meet the diminution in the ton mile rate by a corresponding reduction in expenses, disastrous results must have followed. But there is a limit, and it cannot be far off, to the possible lessening of the cost of movement. The only alternative is to arrest the reduction in revenue, which has been largely brought about by apparently uncontrollable conflicts between the railway companies, and between rival communities. The problems involved are not incapable of solution, and it is believed that by earnest and united effort the difficulties in the way may be met and overcome. With this end in view, it has seemed wise to your board to acquire an interest in some of the railways reaching the seaboard and to unite with the other shareholders who control these properties in supporting a conservative policy. This will, it is hoped, result in securing reasonable and stable rates and do away with unjust discrimination."

These observations of President Cassatt referred to the inauguration of a program of purchasing stock interests in competing lines which was carried on until the Pennsylvania had acquired a dominant, although not a majority, stock interest in its three southern competitors in the soft coal traffic, and was able to influence their policy. Beneficial results were immediately apparent. Soft coal rates, which had been utterly demoralized, and in which the grossest and most burdensome discriminations had long existed, were immediately advanced to a profitable basis, and imposed upon all shippers alike. The most important item of the Pennsylvania traffic, in which there had hitherto been small profit, was turned into a valuable source of revenue. Although in the succeeding four years the freight traffic of the Pennsylvania increased only 9,625,000 tons, or 9.6 per cent, the gross earnings from freight traffic increased from $51,395,733 to $73,899,939, a conclusive proof of the beneficial results of the application of the principle of community of interest to the solution of the problem of soft coal rates with which the Pennsylvania was confronted in 1899. The profitableness of the freight traffic of the Pennsylvania during this period increased nearly five times as rapidly as the amount of the tonnage moved. These investments in the stocks of the bituminous coal carriers were profitable, not because of dividends received by the corporation which did not quite equal the interest paid on the purchase money obligations, but because of the higher rates on coal which these purchases, representing control of competing lines, made possible, and which amounted to considerably more than the interest on the bonds. Since the passage of the Hepburn Law in 1906, the Pennsylvania Railroad Company has disposed of a large part of these securities and has definitely abandoned the attempt to influence its competitors by a large representation on their directorates. The necessity for these holdings no longer existed owing to the disappearance of the distrust and uneasiness which formerly characterized the relations of the trunk line executives. Furthermore, the Interstate Commerce law has now been so strengthened that secret rate cutting is a thing of the past. It should be remarked that the Pennsylvania Railroad, in addition to the dividends which it received on the stocks of the soft coal carriers, made a profit of over thirteen million dollars on such of them as it sold.[1]

The second object of the Pennsylvania's expansion of its capital during this period was the improvement of its physical property. The equivalent of a double track railroad has been built from New York to Pittsburg and equipped with rolling stock and yard and terminal facilities. As a result of this expenditure the company now has a four-track road between Pittsburg and Philadelphia, and six tracks between Harrisburg and New York. By making large expenditures on equipment the company has also increased the tractive power of its locomotives and the capacity of its freight cars. Large sums have also been spent upon supplementary improvements, such as stations, expansion of yards and track elevation, all of which increased the capacity of the road.

In the face of enormous expenditures, and in spite of the notable gains in operating efficiency which they brought about, the facilities of the Pennsylvania proved inadequate to the demands of this period. As President Cassatt remarked in his report for 1902:

"The remarkable development of business, particularly in the sections served by your lines, created a demand for transportation which could not be supplied. For, although the traffic carried over the roads comprising your system east and west of Pittsburg aggregated nearly 270,000,000 tons, being an increase of 26,000,000 tons, or more than ten per cent over the previous year, the necessities of the industries dependent upon your lines demanded a much larger

[1] In 1909 a large interest in the Norfolk & Western was acquired by the Pennsylvania, whose control of the company is again effective.

movement. The inability to accommodate these industries was due mainly to lack of track and yard facilities. It has been the policy of your management for years past to continually increase these facilities so as to keep them up to the demands of the traffic; but although heavier expenditures have been made for this purpose since the beginning of the present period of business activity than ever before in the same time, the exceptional growth of the tonnage has outstripped the facilities that it was practicable to create."

Primarily as a result of these large expenditures, resulting in an increase of capacity of its plant, the tonnage carried by the Pennsylvania increased from 133,433,845 tons in 1902 to 223,810,040 tons in 1907, an increase of 90,376,195 tons, which represented the total tonnage of the entire system twenty-one years before. Without this expenditure, this traffic could not have been handled, and the increase in operating earnings from 1902 to 1907, which amounted to $32,051,552, could not have been realized.

The final field of the Pennsylvania Railroad's expansion policy was the New York terminal project. This will require, when completed, an expenditure of about $150,000,000. The traffic situation in New York is peculiar. The total area of Manhattan Island, excluding Central Park, is 20.6 square miles. Upon this small spot of ground is concentrated a population exceeding 2,000,000. In the census year of 1900, New York had a population of 89,805 to the square mile, as compared with 9,951 for Philadelphia, 13,044 for Boston, and 8,939 for Chicago. These figures indicate the extreme congestion of population which is due to the fact that the city is located upon an island. If communication with the surrounding country could be established, the population would spread into the suburbs, a movement similar to that which has followed the growth of other large cities. To the resident of New York, however, immigration to the suburbs is denied. East, on Long Island, are large territories, almost unoccupied, offering desirable places of residence, but from these opportunities of suburban residence the resident of Manhattan is cut off by the barrier of the East River. If easy communication with Long Island were to be established, there could be no doubt that a vast exodus of population from Manhattan would result. As the matter stood, however, the large number of hardy commuters who were willing to run chances of missed boats and trains is a small fraction of the number who will move into the suburbs when these obstacles are eliminated.

This task of eliminating the river problem from the transportation situation in New York has been left for the Pennsylvania Railroad to undertake. The Interborough Company and the Hudson companies, which have also carried tunnel projects to completion, followed the lead of the Pennsylvania. The Pennsylvania Railroad has completed two tunnels between New Jersey and its new terminal at Thirty-fourth Street and Seventh Avenue, and four tunnels from this point to its Long Island terminal at Long Island City. These tunnel improvements will bring Manhattan into immediate connection with the mainland and with Long Island, and will result in a large migration from Manhattan Island to places of more desirable residence. In Long Island particularly, the largest and most desirable residential territory which is tributary to any city in the United States, will be opened by these improvements, which will practically insure, within the next decade, an immense population throughout the eastern part of the island.

The advantages of these improvements to the Pennsylvania lies in the fact that this corporation owns a majority of the stock of the Long Island Railroad Company which controls the Long Island territory. It is true that the connection with the mainland will increase the share of the Pennsylvania in the competitive passenger business to the south and west, making the Pennsylvania route quite as convenient as the New York Central from its Forty-second Street terminal. It will also develop the passenger business between Washington and New York, already largely controlled by the Pennsylvania, and will throw to the Pennsylvania lines a large part of the through passenger business which originates in Brooklyn and along the lines of the Long Island Railroad.

These gains are, however, unimportant compared with the opportunities offered by the development of Long Island territory. In Long Island, the terminal improvements will build up a large and permanent suburban traffic for the Long Island Railroad. With the completion of the tunnel project, the Long Island Railroad Company will be able to carry passengers from Thirty-fourth Street thirty miles into the country in less time than the Manhattan Elevated Railroad now requires to take them from the Battery to 125th Street, offering them, moreover, not merely a quicker passage, but a more comfortable journey.

Of far greater importance, however, than the increase of passenger business which will follow the completion of the tunnel project, is the growth in the freight traffic. The receipts from freight traffic on the Long Island have been far below the returns from passenger traffic. This company has been mainly dependent upon summer resort travel. It usually fails to earn its interest charges during the winter months. On the New Haven & Hartford, on the other hand, the returns from freight and passenger traffic are about equal. The reason for this discrepancy in the division of receipts is that Long Island, up to the present time, has been practically vacant territory. Only in the summer is its population large. In 1900 its entire population, outside of Brooklyn, was only 286,000. With Long Island brought into communication with the mainland, the shifting of population, it is expected, will build up a large city in the eastern part of the island. This population will not only demand a large amount of merchandise for direct consumption, but the development of a variety of manufacturing interests will follow its growth. All these developments mean, moreover, a large amount of freight over the Long Island Railroad, and will give the Pennsylvania a long haul for a large amount of traffic.

New capital may also be required in the form of cash and cash assets as working funds to handle an increased amount of business. If a company makes large additions to its plant, or if the business of its existing plant shows a considerable increase, in case it does not make corresponding additions to its working capital, it is quickly forced to become a heavy borrower, and while this position causes little inconvenience when rates of interest are low and money easily obtained, should a financial stringency occur, bankruptcy may be the result. Even under ordinary conditions, an inadequate working capital may be the cause of heavy expense to the corporation. The experience of the Pressed Steel Car Company is in point. The report of the president for the year ending December 31, 1901, contains the following:

"Since the incorporation of the company the profits have aggregated $4,312,285. Out of these profits has been paid $2,625,000 in dividends. The McKees Rocks plant cost $1,581,580, and additions and improvements to original plants, amounting to $555,702, have been taken out of the initial working capital and earnings. From this it will be seen that the actual cash working capital has been somewhat encroached upon, but the plants and capacity have been more than doubled, and the monthly production increased from $1,000,000 to upward of $2,000,000, the full operation of the plants.

"It is necessary to carry between $4,000,000 and $5,000,000 worth of material on hand, and for this purpose the company has been compelled to be an extensive borrower. During the year it was thought prudent to fund this indebtedness. Therefore, a mortgage for $5,000,000 was made to secure five per cent notes maturing at the rate of $500,000 each year, with the right to anticipate payment of all or part. These notes have been disposed of on terms advantageous to the company. By this means the company secures extra working capital, and its interest charges are limited to not to exceed $250,000 the first year, and $25,000 less every year thereafter. There was disbursed last year for interest and borrowed money $215,821, which was charged off to operating expenses, and we believe that more than the difference appearing between this amount and $250,000 can be saved in extra discounts on materials purchased."

The Pressed Steel Car Company, in funding its large floating debt, not only made the economies indicated in the president's statement, but also removed a serious danger of financial embarrassment which might have resulted from failure to renew these loans. The receivership of the Westinghouse Electric & Manufacturing Company, in 1907, was due, in large part, to inadequate working capital, and to the efforts of the company to supply this deficiency by contracting heavy bank loans, and by piling up large obligations to merchandise creditors. Working capital is properly regarded, not merely as essential to the safety and prosperity of a company, but as perhaps the most profitable part of its equipment for business. It enables the company to carry large bank balances on the strength of which, with the company's good credit, heavy loans can be made on occasion, to take advantage of favorable opportunities for the purchase of materials and to discount bills, while, at the same time, it makes unnecessary the resort to the banks for more than temporary and occasional accommodation.

New capital may be finally required for the reconstruction of a plant where a profitable business has been sacrificed because the physical condition of the property has been neglected. A case in point is that of the Kansas City Southern Railway Company when taken over by the new management. Here was a road operating in a territory rich in traffic possibilities, and carrying a sufficient amount of traffic to pay its interest charges, in spite of its impaired physical condition. It was estimated that, to put the property in a suitable condition for handling present and prospective traffic, and to expand the business of the company to its proper proportions, the following expenditures would be necessary:

Repairs and improvements to track	$2,983,856.00
Reinforcements and reconstruction of bridges	510,000.00
Repairs and improvements to equipment	540,000.00
New tracks	388,000.00
New freight depot facilities	125,000.00
New water stations	65,000.00
New shop facilities	435,000.00
New telegraph	34,000.00
New fencing	180,000.00
Work at Port Arthur, Texas	50,000.00
New equipment	1,604,749.50
Total	$6,915,605.50

Practically all of these expenditures, with the exception of the equipment purchases, should have been spread over a period of years, and charged to operating expenses, not to capital. Over $5,000,000 of the amount which was deemed necessary to be spent on the property represented deferred charges to maintenance and betterments. The company should not, in a narrow view of the situation, have received any capital for the reconstruction of its plant, but should have devoted its surplus income to the purpose. Under the conditions confronting the management, however, there was no surplus income. At the same time, the expenditure of this large amount of money, no matter how provided, would put the company into position to make large earnings. Said President Edson:

"Your officers are convinced that with the improvements and additions which have been set forth, which will require two or three years to complete, and which will enable the road to handle expeditiously and economically all traffic which may be offered, the gross earnings will show an increase of from twenty to twenty-five per cent over the gross earnings for the year ending June 30, 1905, and that, with the economies which the additional facilities will make possible, the ratio of operating expenses, including taxes, to gross earnings, will not exceed seventy per cent.

"Taking as a basis the minimum of twenty per cent increase in gross earnings, the following results may be confidently expected under existing commercial conditions:

Gross earnings	$8,272,387.54
Operating expenses and taxes	5,790,671.28
Net earnings	2,481,716.26
Interest on bonds owned	32,501.00
Total income	$2,514,217.26
Interest on bonds	[1]900,000.00
Net annual surplus from income	$1,614,217.26

From which must be paid, of course, the interest on such funds as may be borrowed for improvement.

"From this it seems certain that, unless overtaken by some unforeseen and general commercial disaster, the earnings capacity of the property amply justified the capitalization of the amount necessary for improvements and extensions."

The surplus for the period to which this report refers was only $610,191.80. This income was in danger of disappearing, owing to the inability of the company to handle the business offered. The expenditure of approximately $7,000,000 would show earnings of 14.28 per cent on this amount. The conclusion that the cost of rehabilitating the Kansas City Southern Railway Company should be defrayed out of new capital provided for the purpose, and charged to the capital, instead of to operating expenses or depreciation, was evidently correct. Acting upon this advice, the stockholders authorized an issue of $10,000,000 4½ per cent second mortgage bonds, pledging as collateral $5,100,000 negotiable gold notes. Most of the proceeds were spent in making good the omissions of the past for the sake of obtaining the profits of the future.

[1]All deductions are not given.

CHAPTER XX

THE METHODS OF PROVIDING NEW CAPITAL

OUR next inquiry is concerning the methods by which the necessary extension of plant and enlargement of corporate power and influence is to be accomplished. A company may either raise money to be invested in the improvement and extension of its plant, or it may acquire interests in other corporations which possess the necessary assets. These interests it may acquire either directly by the exchange of securities, or through the medium of a holding company, or by selling its own securities to the investor, expending the proceeds upon the securities desired, or by some form of lease of the desired property, or by a working agreement by which the use of the desired facilities is obtained. The first plan is the direct method of providing capital out of income or by the sale of securities; and the second, the indirect provision of capital by various methods which come under the head of consolidation.

Capital funds may be directly provided for the corporation by one or more of the following methods: (1) The money required may be appropriated out of profits; (2) stock may be issued; (3) the corporation may borrow money either on short time notes or by the sale of long term bonds. In Chapter XVII we have discussed the necessity that a properly managed corporation should never pay out all its earnings to stockholders. Conservatism demands that a certain balance should be reserved and invested in the business. The purpose of this reservation is to make sure that a dividend rate, once established, may be maintained. The investment of these funds reserved from earnings, if wisely made, will increase the earnings of the company, and should appear as additions to its assets.

There is much to be said in favor of a policy of making extensions out of profits. A growth which is made out of earnings, without increase of stock or debt, is a natural growth; it is made gradually and cautiously, and therefore safely. The histories of the largest business concerns in the country show that even the largest possibilities can be reached by the investment of profits in the extension of plant. The growth of the Carnegie Steel Company from an insignificant beginning to the gigantic size it had attained when it was taken over by the United States Steel Corporation, is an illustration of the possibilities of the investment of profits. The growth of the Baldwin Locomotive Works, and of John Wanamaker's, and Marshall Field's retail establishments are familiar illustrations of the same fact. Indeed, most large business enterprises in this country which are still controlled by partnerships or private corporations, represent growth out of profits.

If directors follow a conservative policy in the administration of the income account of their company, they will make large investments out of revenues in working capital, plant and equipment. They will raise the standard of the property by betterment appropriations, charged either to additions or, preferably, to maintenance. They should also maintain a number of reserves for depreciation and renewal of plant, for bad debts, for insurance, for the extinguishment of the loss sustained by the sale of bonds at a discount, if this loss is not to be taken in the year in which it occurs. They may be required to set aside out of their income a sinking fund appropriation, and it may be provided that the amount of the sinking fund appropriation can be invested in the plant. Finally, in order to maintain an even rate of dividends, the directors are obliged to reserve a portion of each year's profits, which is also put into the business, and which, in time, may amount to a large sum. Shall the directors go farther than these requirements of safety and stability in reserving profits from stockholders? Shall they treat the profits as their first resource when in need of money, and comfort the stockholders, as did C. P. Huntington, who, on one occasion, remarked to the stockholders of the Pacific Mail Steamship Company, that it made no difference whether they received their dividends in money or in ships? Their dividends were only deferred.

It is improper for the directors of a public corporation to pursue this policy. The company has applied to the investor to furnish funds for their enterprise. The money has been contributed with the understanding that if profits were earned they would be distributed in dividends, so far as a distribution could safely be made. Beyond the maintenance of proper reserves, and the investment of surplus earnings over a conservative dividend rate, the directors of a public corporation cannot, as a rule, therefore, with entire good faith to their stockholders, withhold profits for investment in plant. If the business is profitable, and demands new capital, the stockholders have the right to demand that the capitalization of the company shall be increased in order to obtain this new capital, and that they shall not be kept out of their dividends for an indefinite period in order that a so-called conservative policy should be pursued. If the company needs new money, the stockholders are usually quite willing to furnish it, in case they have been liberally treated, and fairly dealt with.

There are other objections to the plan of exclusive dependence on profits as a source of capital funds. Profits are very irregular, and it is difficult to carry out a consistent plan of improvement while depending solely upon the business to furnish the funds for these improvements. Furthermore, the exigencies of the corporate situation sometimes demand that extensive schemes of improvement should be put through within a short time; for example, the extension of the Chicago, Milwaukee & St. Paul to the Pacific Coast; the construction of the Western Pacific from Salt Lake City to San Francisco; and the New York Terminal improvements of the Pennsylvania. Such gigantic works of construction may in some cases be provided out of earnings; for example, the new plant of the United States Steel Corporation at Gary has been built out of profits. As a rule, however, earnings are not sufficient for extensive additions.

Assuming a definite opportunity for the profitable investment of capital, it is to the interest of stockholders that this opportunity should be developed with the greatest expedition, and that the construction work should be carried through within the shortest possible time. If the improvement is to depend solely upon earnings for its completion, it may be unduly prolonged if the earnings are not forthcoming. The profits of the company over a period of years may be much less than if stock had been sold or money borrowed, and the work crowded through as rapidly as possible to the point of producing revenue.

The withholding of dividends from stockholders at the instance of the majority control also creates a bad impression, since it is often alleged, under these circumstances, that the majority interests who usually occupy important and lucrative positions in the service of the company, and who are not infrequently in the receipt of secondary and indirect emoluments as a result of their positions are unfairly discriminating against the minority stockholders. It may be charged that they are, in effect, pursuing a policy which, while increasing the value of the company's property, is depreciating the value of the stock which represents the ownership of the corporation owning the property. Such charges were forcibly made against the Southern Pacific management in 1903 by Mr. James R. Keene, who alleged that the Southern Pacific revenues were not only being withheld from the stockholders of that company, but that they were being devoted to improvements for the benefit of the Union Pacific which owned nearly half the stock of the Southern Pacific. Although the interests back of this attempt to force dividends on Southern Pacific stock were discredited because of their obvious connection with a large speculative pool operating for an advance in the stock, based on the alleged promise of a dividend, yet their contentions attracted wide attention, and brought out unfavorable criticism against the directors.

Especial conservatism in the distribution of profits is usually desirable during the early stages of an enterprise, a large part of whose stock, as we have already seen, is usually issued against anticipated earnings. With these exceptions, however, it seems best that a public corporation should not rely mainly upon its earnings to obtain funds for extensions and improvements, but when it has reached a position of assured strength and standing, it should take advantage of that position to provide funds for the enlargement of its plant by the expansion of its capital, allowing its stockholders to share in its profits, so far as the distribution of these profits is consistent with the maintenance of a regular rate of dividend.

In view of the rapidly increasing number of persons in the United States who rely upon dividends for a portion of their income, it will be profitable for us to examine in detail a case in which this policy of exclusive reliance upon income for betterments was followed for a number of years by a prominent and prosperous railroad, the Lehigh Valley Railroad Company.

A railroad balance sheet presents a statement of assets and liabilities. By comparing one balance sheet with another the progress of the road in assets and earning power can be noted. From the movement of the liabilities, the sources from which funds were obtained can be determined. A series of annual balance sheets, therefore, contains the record of progress or deterioration, the financial history of the corporation. When we examine the balance sheets of the Lehigh Valley from 1898 to 1902, however, we find, apparently, that for five years the company stood still. The principal items of the condensed balance sheet for the two years mentioned are as follows:

	Assets	
	1898	1902
Cost of road	$18,639,291.95	$18,639,291.95
Cost of equipment	19,018,419.98	19,018,419.98
Securities owned	32,949,322.14	39,300,209.80

The only change is an increase of $6,350,887.66 in the securities owned, accounted for by the acquisition of the stock of the Lehigh Valley Terminal Company. As might be expected, since the valuation of assets did not change, the liabilities remained unaltered. The stock remained at $40,441,100 and the bonds decreased from $45,642,000 to $41,900,000. A singular spectacle was presented by the balance sheets, a company whose accounts showed neither growth nor decline.

Turning from this spectacle of stagnation to examine the income account of the company, we find a record of growth and prosperity. Gross earnings from operation increased twenty-five per cent in five years. The revenue tonnage of the road gained 150 per cent, while the mileage remained at about 1,400 miles. Unless the rates received suffered a severe decline, or unless operating expenses considerably increased, the net income of the company over these five years should show a considerable increase. So far from decreasing, the ton mile revenue of the Lehigh Valley increased from 0.500 cents to 0.554 cents. Furthermore, not merely did the rate received for transporting each ton of freight increase, but the expense of moving the tonnage declined, and the total earnings per train mile increased from $1.58 in 1898 to $2.09 in 1902. From those figures of earnings and expenses, a considerable increase in income available for distribution to creditors and stockholders might be expected. On the contrary, the gross income of the Lehigh Valley, which in 1898, a year of depression in the traffic and earnings of this section, was $6,799,255, in 1900 was $3,939,-

155, and in 1901, when no strike was in progress, was only $6,871,010. In short, the stockholders, who had received no dividends since 1893, were puzzled to understand why their company could be at the same time prosperous and unfortunate, why it could be making so much money and have nothing left for dividend payments to its stockholders, many of whom were sorely distressed because of the suspension of dividends.

Reserving for the present the explanation of this anomaly, let us compare the results of 1903 with those of 1902, the last year of the administration which took over the management of the road in 1897, and resigned it in November, 1902. On June 30, 1903, the total income available for distribution was stated to be $8,279,248, an increase of $3,628,120 over the statement of the preceding year. Evidently, a sudden and radical change in accounting methods had taken place which, after allowing for a million and a quarter of dollars spent in improving the property, showed net income available for dividends of two million dollars, or five per cent on the stock. More strictly interpreted, the accounts of the Lehigh Valley for 1903 show a surplus available for distribution of 8.1 per cent on the stock, as compared with a deficit of more than a million and a quarter in 1902, an apparent gain of $4,606,485 in surplus, although gross earnings increased only $2,734,535.

We have here presented the outlines of a noteworthy chapter in railway financial history, which raises a question of deep interest to railway investors. How far should the cost of improvements which increase the earnings of a company be taken out of earnings, and how far should their cost be defrayed by the issue of new capital? In other words, how far can a corporation, in justice to its stockholders, by refusing to issue new capital, keep its stockholders out of their dividends?

Immediately after the retirement of Mr. Wilbur from the presidency and the election of Mr. Walter, the directors of the Lehigh Valley inaugurated a policy which, for conservatism and extreme caution in the disbursement of profits, has rarely been equaled. In his report for the following year the new president stated:

"The policy of the present management has been, and perhaps for some time to come must continue to be, in the line of liberal, and perhaps mutual expenditures on both roadbed and equipment, in order to adapt the property to the most economical operation. Substantially all the business of the company is competitive and rates are steadily and rapidly declining. To derive any profit from them the railway must be so improved in its characteristics as to be able to work much more cheaply than before. The companies with which the Lehigh Valley is in competition (New York Central and the Lackawanna) have been adapting themselves to like requirements for many years, but the Lehigh Valley, having done less in these respects until recently, must now proceed with greater activity."

In another report Mr. Walter explained the limited capital resources of the company, authority existing for the annual issue of only $1,000,000 of bonds. No application was made, however, for any increase of this authority.

The plant of the Lehigh Valley needed substantial improvement. There was no doubt of that. Both engines and cars were light and had to be replaced. Sidings had to be lengthened and bridges strengthened to admit of longer and heavier trains being handled. The repair shops had to be concentrated; the terminals enlarged and improved, and many additional replacements of way and structure were required.

The reconstruction of the system required a large amount of money and Mr. Walter proceeded to take this out of earnings and to charge it to operating expense. For many years the operating ratio of the road had been high, owing, in part at least, to inefficient management and inferior equipment. In 1894 the ratio was 76.86 per cent of gross earnings, from which it declined steadily to 70.16 per cent in 1898. From this point, the ratio advanced to 80.97, an enormous and almost unprecedented figure, in 1902. More significant than the increase in the general operation ratio, was the change in the relations between its component parts. In 1895, under the old régime, only 22.56 per cent of the total operating expense was represented by maintenance of way and structure. In 1902, this proportion had increased to 40.31 per cent. All this time the efficiency of the system, as represented in its average train load, was steadily increasing from 383.87 tons in 1898 to 466.83 tons in 1902, a larger train load than even the New York Central could show. This increased efficiency of operation was the result of the reconstruction of the property. The entire cost of these replacements and repairs was charged to operating expenses. From 1898 to 1902, if we allow sixty-five per cent as the normal operating ratio, the Lehigh Valley, under Mr. Walter's management, spent almost thirteen million dollars, which, under different circumstances, would have been available for interest and dividends.

We can now answer the question which was raised concerning the legitimacy of the policy pursued by the former management of the Lehigh Valley. Looking at the matter from the standpoint of the physical condition of the property, a very plausible defense can be made for charging the cost of its rehabilitation to operating expense. If all expenses which result in raising a railroad toward the standard set by its competitors are to be classed as operating expenses, no criticism can be made. The physical condition of the New York Central was apparently taken as the goal of the Lehigh Valley's ambition. Only when the Lehigh Valley had been rebuilt on the Central's model, were the stockholders to get anything. Looked at as a problem in comparative operating efficiency, Mr. Walter's method of solution can be approved, the more so because he succeeded in his attempt.

When we consider the matter from the standpoint of the

Lehigh Valley stockholders, however, the severe criticism to which the management was subjected is seen to be not without some measure of justification. There can be no question that if the difficulties in the way of issuing new capital had been got over, and these difficulties were by no means insuperable, the company could have borrowed far more than the amount which was reserved from earnings, and could have effected the necessary improvements within a short time, instead of protracting them over a series of years at the expense of their stockholders. It is equally certain that if this policy had been adopted, a substantial dividend could have been paid since 1899, while the physical efficiency of the property would have been fully as great as it is at present. Questions of railway policy, such as this, are not to be judged by reference to abstract canons of finance, but in the light of known conditions and with due reference to the rights of stockholders.

CHAPTER XXI

THE ISSUE OF STOCK

ASSUMING now that funds are to be raised for extensions by the sale of securities, the first question concerns the class of securities to be sold. Shall the corporation increase its stock or shall it borrow the money needed?

The capital stock of a company represents its ownership. This ownership is divided into shares. An increase of the amount of stock, therefore, increases the number of owners. If there is to be only one kind of stock, the shareholders have two alternatives when it is proposed to increase the capital. They may take the new stock themselves, in which case their respective shares of participation in the company's profits remain unchanged, or they may offer it for general subscription. If a corporation has $10,000,000 of capital and proposes to add $1,000,000, each stockholder of record would have the right, under the law, to participate in the increase, if the stock was to be sold for money, and not exchanged for some form of property. The holder of one hundred shares of stock, for example, would be allowed to subscribe to ten shares of the new stock, which would give him the same proportion of interest in the corporation that he had before. It frequently happens, however, that existing stockholders do not care to take the entire issue. Stock must then be sold to outsiders, who are admitted to participation in the earnings, and to share in the control of the company on equal terms with the existing stockholders.

To the controlling interest of the company, the admission of new stockholders is often a matter of great concern.

New stock coming upon the market may be absorbed by those who desire to wrest control from those who now hold it. And if, as usually happens, the control represents no more than a strong minority, this may be the outcome of an increase in the capital stock. A celebrated instance of this result is the ousting of Mr. August Belmont and his associates from the directorate of the Louisville & Nashville in 1902. Early in that year the directors of the Louisville & Nashville, in order to finance some extensions, authorized the sale of 50,000 shares of stock. Under the rule of the New York Stock Exchange, shares are not deliverable on contracts until thirty days after they have been issued. Funds were needed immediately, however, and in order to obtain them the chairman, Mr. Belmont, was instructed by the Board to sell 50,000 shares "short"—that is to say, he sold stock which he did not own, borrowed the stock to deliver what he had sold, and expected to take up the loan out of the new shares when these should have become deliverable. At the same time, however, unknown to the Belmont interests, a syndicate, headed by Mr. John W. Gates, was engaged in a campaign to purchase control of the company, and, in the course of their operations, they developed a short interest estimated at 120,000 shares, including the 50,000 shares sold by Mr. Belmont.

The directors of the Louisville & Nashville had, in other words, sold more shares than they owned, and they could obtain the stock to make their deliveries only from the syndicate whose advantage it was to bring about this situation. On April 14, 1902, it was discovered that a corner existed in Louisville & Nashville; the price of stock on this date touched 133 and a repetition of the May panic of 1901, which was brought about by a similar operation in Northern Pacific stock, seemed imminent. Serious trouble was averted, however, by the recognition that Mr. Gates controlled the Louisville & Nashville, and by the taking over of a majority interest in that company by the Atlantic Coast Line Railroad at a figure which rendered a large profit to the John W. Gates syndicate.

On account of the fear of such operations as that which has been described, every effort is made, when new stock is issued, to induce the existing stockholders to increase their holdings, or, failing in this, to obtain assurance that the new interest shall not only be such as will strengthen the position of the company, but will not be unfriendly to those in control. The strongest inducement which can be offered to the stockholders is to sell them a safe investment at a low price and the lowest price which the law allows is par, the figure at which stock is usually offered to stockholders. This prohibition against the sale of stock below par (unless such a step is necessary to save the company from embarrassment), limits the opportunity to raise capital by the sale of common stock to companies whose profits and dividends are so large that their stocks sell above par.

The common stock of prosperous companies frequently sells at a high premium. For example, the current price of the Canadian Pacific is $181\frac{7}{8}$; of the Great Northern, $131\frac{1}{2}$; of the General Electric, 146; of the Chicago & Northwestern, $147\frac{3}{4}$; and of the Union Pacific, $176\frac{7}{8}$.[1]

The existence of these premiums, which reflect high dividends and assured earning power, make possible the plan of financing the capital requirements of such strong companies by the issue of common stock on such terms as to induce stockholders to enlarge their holdings. This plan is known as the sale of privileged subscriptions. Under the law, the stock of a corporation, as already noted, must first be offered to the existing stockholders who have the right to participate in all new issues. Only in case they are unwilling to accept the terms offered, can stock be opened to general subscription. Stock can, of course, be issued in exchange for property.

Suppose that the stock sells at a premium. The new issues can then be either offered to the stockholders at a price above par, or an offer can be made on such a basis as to prefer the existing stockholders in the subscription. In case

[1] May 2, 1910.

the market value of the stock is realized by offering stock at a premium, a smaller number of shares need be sold to obtain a given amount of capital than if stock is sold at par. Suppose, for example, that $1,000,000 is required by a company whose stock can be sold at 150, paying eight per cent dividends. If the stock is sold at market value, 6,666 shares will be needed to obtain the $1,000,000 necessary. If it is sold at par, however, 10,000 shares will be required. The amount necessary to pay the eight per cent dividend on 6,666 shares is $53,328, while on 10,000 shares $80,000 would be required. If the stock is sold at a premium, $27,-672 of annual dividends, assuming that the eight-per-cent rate is continued, can be saved for the company, over the disbursements which must be made if the stock is sold at par. As a result, the rate of dividend can perhaps be increased, and the price of the stock advanced on the strength of its larger dividend returns.

In view of these facts, the directors may insist that they should make the best bargain possible for the company, that the stockholder shall derive no special or exceptional advantage from his position as part owner of the corporation; that he should be treated in the same way as any investor. Furthermore, under the plan of selling stock at a premium, the dividends paid by the company, and the price of the stock will show its true earning power. No more stock will have been issued than is necessary to provide the amount of money required for the desired improvements. The higher the price of the stock ascends, borne up on the rising tide of dividends, the smaller will be the number of shares to be sold to obtain the same amount of money. The Pennsylvania Railroad Company, for example, has received large sums as premiums on stocks sold. Without these premiums, which were invested in the business, the outstanding stock of the Pennsylvania might have been materially greater than it now is.

On the other hand. if stock is sold at par, or at less than market price, the corporation must issue a larger number of shares than may conceivably be required. It may be impossible, on account of the issue of this extra stock, to do more than maintain the regular dividend, and the price of the stock, therefore, may not advance to the point which it would reach did the directors refuse to sell more shares of ownership than are necessary to obtain the money required.

In the case of Public Service corporations, the principle has been conclusively established in most of the leading states that they shall not be allowed to earn more than a fair return on the value of their property, and it has also been considered important in some states that a corporation should not increase its capital stock beyond the amount actually necessary to secure funds for capital expenditures. In Massachusetts, for example, the issue of all bonds and of any increase of stock in excess of the original capital is limited to such amount as the railroad commissioners shall, after a public hearing, determine will realize the sum which has been properly expended, or will be reasonably required by the corporation for corporate purposes. As a rule, however, a company whose stock sells at a premium does not attempt to obtain any part of the premium by a public offering, but offers its stock to its owners at par. Such a sale is called the offer of a privileged subscription.

The stockholder receiving the privilege can avail himself of it either by selling his right to subscribe to the stock, which is made negotiable for the purpose, or by selling a certain portion of his existing holdings after he receives the evidence of his right to subscribe, at the existing market price, replacing these shares at par out of the new issue, or he can retain his stock and take the new shares as well. In the first two cases mentioned—namely, the sale of the negotiable right to subscribe, or the sale at the market price of an amount of stock equal to that to which the stockholder is entitled to subscribe at par—he makes a profit which approximates the market premium of the stock, times the number of shares which he sells. Since the right will only be purchased by some one desirous of becoming a subscriber to the stock, its price is usually less than the difference between par and market value. Unless the intending subscriber can obtain his new stock at a lower price by purchasing a right, he will prefer to buy the stock direct.

The value of some of these privileges has been very great. In an article in the *Quarterly Journal of Economics* for February, 1905, entitled "Stockholders' Profits from Privileged Subscriptions," Dr. T. W. Mitchell has computed the profits which could have been realized by stockholders of the leading railroad companies which have issued privileged subscriptions. Dr. Mitchell finds that if a stockholder of the Illinois Central had purchased 100 shares at a price of 135 per share in 1887, he would have received between that date and 1903 eight privileges. If he had sold the number of shares to which he was entitled to subscribe immediately after receiving his privilege and had invested the proceeds, Dr. Mitchell finds that, from 1887 to 1903, he would have received from all of his eight privileges a total, principal and interest, of $5,740. This is equivalent to a return of $222 a year during the seventeen years of his investment, or 1.64 per cent which would have been added to the regular dividends on this stock. A man making a similar purchase in 1895, would have received from his five privileges a total of $2,953, which is equivalent to $265, or 2.73 per cent, a year. Stockholders who made their investments in 1900, 1901 and 1902 respectively have made, according to Dr. Mitchell, from privileges alone, $4\frac{3}{4}$ to $5\frac{1}{4}$ per annum on their investment, and that, too, when their original purchases were made at high premiums. The Great Northern has also been very liberal to its stockholders. Since 1893 the stock of this company has sold above par. All the stock issues of the company after the first, with one exception, have been distributed, pro rata, among the stockholders of the road at par. The market value of the stock at the time these various issues were distributed ranged from $140 to $264 per share. The stockholder could, therefore, have paid $100 per share for his new stock, and could at once have sold it upon the market for a much higher price, realizing from the transaction from $40 to $164 per share.

If the stockholder does not care to sell his right to subscribe, or to part with any of his stock, the privilege gives him an opportunity to increase the return he receives on his investment. Suppose he has purchased the stock of a company paying six per cent dividends for $150. His return is four per cent. The company, within five years after he has purchased the stock, offers to stockholders the privilege of subscribing to new stock at par to an amount equal to eighty per cent of their holdings. This stockholder, instead of selling the right to the stock, prefers to increase his investment on the favorable terms offered. At the end of five years, he owns 180 shares on which the annual return is $6 per share, or $1,080, on an investment of $23,000, or 4.7 per cent. There is little doubt that this is the course followed by the majority of stockholders when privileges are offered to them. By the correct method of computing the yield on investments, the return on a stock should be obtained by dividing into the rate of dividends, not the cost price, but the market price. An investor who takes advantage of a privilege to buy a six per cent stock for $100 per share which is selling on the exchange at $150, has only a four per cent investment, since a share of stock represents to him $150 of capital and $6 of income. The investor, however, estimates the return by comparing the cost of the stock with the rate of dividend, and this belief influences him to hold fast to stock, new issues of which are occasionally sold at less than market value. In no other way could the failure of shares to show heavy declines after the announcement of privileges be explained. Some decline is usually experienced following the announcement of a privilege, but it is seldom sufficient to warrant the conclusion that a large number of stockholders are disposing of their shares. There is no reason for them to do so if they have confidence in the value of the stock, since they can take their profit at any time by selling at a premium stock which they purchased at par.

When a corporation increases its issue of stock, it must keep in mind not merely the amount of money which the new stock will bring, but the effect of the issue upon the composition of the stockholding constituency; the necessity that the subscription should be a success and that the money should be promptly forthcoming; the desirability of being able to receive new capital from the stockholders when required, no matter what the condition of the money market and to any amount that may be necessary; the justice and expediency of extending to stockholders more liberal treatment in the matter of subscription than they extend to outsiders; and, finally, the fact that the sale of a privilege is equivalent to an increase in the rate of dividends.

Let us take up these considerations in order. The sale of stock at a high premium means that new interests are brought into a company, and that its stockholders are continually changing. Existing stockholders, many of whom will have purchased the stock at much lower prices than those prevailing at the time an attempt is made to secure a premium from a new issue, will have no inducement, other than their general confidence in the company, to increase their holdings on less favorable terms than those which they previously secured. Under these circumstances, therefore, while a large amount of the new stock may be taken by existing stockholders, it is fairly certain that much of it will be sold to outsiders. These new interests may have their own preferences for directors and officers, and their influence may be sufficient to disturb the management and control. When, however, stock is sold at par with a valuable privilege attached, based on the existence of a high premium in the market, the stock is very closely held for investment. Little stock is offered for sale, since the stockholder of record knows that, from time to time, in addition to the yield on the stock represented by a comparison between the purchase price and the dividend paid, he will have an opportunity to increase his investment on more favorable terms than if he desires to gain an immediate profit in one of the ways described.

The election of such a course of action by the stockholder is the more certain when it is remembered that the values of stock privileges are not, as a rule, fully capitalized in the value of the stock. If a corporation would announce that on January 1st of each year its stock would be increased ten per cent, and that stockholders of record would have the privilege of subscribing to the new stock at par, then the value of the privilege would be expressed in the market value of the stock, which would be established on a permanently higher level. No such assurance can, however, be given to the stockholders. The directors will follow the policy which seems best at the time. They cannot limit themselves in the methods which they will employ for raising new capital. It is impossible, therefore, that these privileges should be counted upon at any particular time and to any particular amount. They are incidental and fortuitous gains to the stockholder, gains which he has every reason to believe he will receive in the future as he has received them in the past, but which will not be fully reflected in the higher market value of the stock. To gain these privileges, therefore, the stockholder must retain his shares. It is well known that those corporations, such as the Illinois Central; Chicago, Milwaukee & St. Paul; Great Northern; United Gas Improvement Company; and New York, New Haven & Hartford Company, which have granted valuable privileges, have a body of stockholders whose composition changes slowly.

Directors place a high value upon permanence in their stockholding body. Stockholders of long standing can be counted on to support the management. In the unlikely event of a contest for proxies, the limited supply of such a stock makes it very difficult and expensive for an outside interest to buy control. One of the most serious difficulties experienced by Mr. E. H. Harriman in his contest for the control of the Illinois Central in 1907, was the firmness with which most of the individual stockholders supported Mr. Stuyvesant Fish's administration.

Another argument in favor of selling stock at par is that

the securing of a premium on the sale of a large amount of stock is an uncertain matter, depending on the condition of the stock market, which may change overnight. In order to guarantee that a premium will be secured, unless the subscription price is placed so far below the market price that it amounts, in effect, to a privilege to stockholders of record, the services of an underwriting syndicate must be employed. The Pennsylvania Railroad, for example, in 1903 offered $75,000,000 of stock to holders of record at $120 a share. The stock was at that time selling above 150. No difficulty was anticipated in disposing of the stock as offered in the subscription. A general decline in stock values, however, set in which carried down the value of the Pennsylvania stock with it. It was feared that the stock might fall below the subscription price by the date when the subscriptions were to be made. In this event the credit of the company would have been seriously damaged, since the subscription offer would have to be withdrawn. To guard against such a contingency, an underwriting syndicate was formed, headed by Speyer & Company, which, in return for a commission of $2,250,000, agreed to take from the company any of the $75,000,000 of stock at the subscription price of 120 a share, which the stockholders should not take. The announcement of the formation of this syndicate steadied the price which had at one time fallen to 114½, and the syndicate had to assume only a small part of its obligation, making a large profit on the transaction. The Pennsylvania Railroad is probably the strongest railroad corporation in the world, and its stock is highly esteemed by investors. On this occasion the stock was offered far below the market price, and yet the securing of a premium was only made possible by the intervention of an underwriting syndicate.

On the other hand, a corporation whose stock sells at a high premium, and which offers new issues to stockholders at par, is never at a loss to obtain new capital funds. During 1906, when the bond market was seriously depressed, and when the strongest railroad and industrial corporations, rather-than sell long term bonds on a five per cent basis, were resorting to the expedient of short term notes paying five and six per cent interest, four of the largest railroad companies—the Great Northern, the Northern Pacific, the Chicago, Milwaukee & St. Paul, and the Chicago & Northwestern—raised, among them, about $300,000,000 from their stockholders, by the sale of stock at par. If they had gone into the bond market, it would have been difficult for them to obtain this amount of money. They might have had to pay for three years an interest rate of at least six per cent on notes issued in anticipation of the sale of the bonds.

There is this further to be said in favor of the sale of stock on a privileged basis to holders of record, that it is fair to the stockholder who does not care to increase his investment, and who would not be able to participate in any of the benefits of the new issue, if it were offered at a premium. Such stockholders receive their rights to subscribe which they can sell in the manner already explained, and in this way participate, although to a less extent than the stockholders who hold their stock, in the benefits of the new stock issue.

The issue of premium stock at par to stockholders is an indirect method of distributing the company's surplus in the sense that a larger disbursement must be made on the stock than if this has been sold at a premium. A corporation which obtains $1,000,000 by selling 10,000 shares of stock at par, when it could have obtained the same money by the sale of 6,666 shares at 150, is assuming a larger burden than is necessary to obtain the money. Its stock capital is 3,333 shares larger than it would have been had the full market price been obtained. The dividend rate cannot be increased so rapidly as though a smaller number of shares had been sold to obtain the amount required. For this reason, the sale of privileged subscriptions by public service corporations has been severely criticised. There is a strong tendency in public sentiment to compel these companies to sell their stock to realize the highest market price obtainable, and not to favor stockholders by the sale of stock on preferential terms.

The law usually does not take cognizance of the market value of stock. It merely requires that the par value should be paid in cash, and in the absence of a special statute or ruling to the contrary, the corporation has authority to sell its stock at par. Furthermore, market value, as already shown, is unstable and uncertain. The realization of a given profit by the sale of a privilege, which, as we have seen, is a course adopted by only a portion of the stockholders to whom privileges are offered, is a doubtful matter. The Interstate Commerce Commission in the case of the City of Spokane vs. Northern Pacific Railway Company, considered this question of the return from privileged subscriptions, in reaching a conclusion as to the earnings of the Northern Pacific. The complainants in this case asserted that the Great Northern, one of the defendants in the case, had distributed its stock, from time to time, in such a manner as to give its stockholders large profits in addition to their dividends, and insisted "that this manner of selling stock is vicious and unlawful, and that, in determining the return to these stockholders, we must have in mind the benefit conferred upon those stockholders by this operation."

The commission, however, rejected this view as follows:

"Assuming, without deciding, that the complainant is right in its position that this practice is both unlawful and unwise, how can we, in this proceeding, take any practical note of what has been done? This stock is selling to-day, January, 1908, upon the market at something less than $120 per share. If the original stockholder has retained and now owns his stock, he paid $100 in the beginning, has received a regular dividend, and now owns his stock at the above advance. While the profit to him has been a handsome one, there is certainly nothing here which would call for a penalizing of the stockholder. Suppose, now, that, instead of retaining the stock, the stockholder sold the same to some innocent purchaser who paid the market price, and who has continued to own the stock from then until now. This present stockholder paid perhaps $264 a share for his stock. He has lost $144 per share. Should we, for that reason, compel him to sustain a further loss? The manner in which this stock has been manipulated may furnish a strong argument against the propriety of permitting the sale of new stock in this manner, but so far as this particular company and the stock already issued are concerned, the transaction is ended, and can be given no practical consideration in determining what rates shall be charged by the Great Northern Railway Company."[3]

There is reason to believe that the practice of privileged subscriptions will not long be permitted without restrictions to public service corporations. They will probably be required, when selling new stock, to obtain the highest possible price. This does not, however, mean that stockholders will no longer be favored with opportunities to subscribe on preferential terms, but merely that the value of the preference may be reduced. If a public service commission is required to authorize an issue of stock selling at a premium, and to name a price at which the stock can be sold, unless they wish to take the responsibility for a possible failure of the subscription, they will not insist that the corporation should attempt to obtain the full premium ruling at the time the offer is made. Some lower figure will be named, and at this figure the stockholders of record, to whom the stock must first be offered, will usually take a considerable amount of the new issues, especially if the premium is guaranteed by an underwriting syndicate.

CHAPTER XXII

THE SALE OF PREFERRED STOCK

A CORPORATION desiring to provide new capital from the sale of stock seldom resorts to common stock unless this is selling at a high premium. The law usually requires that stock should not be sold at less than par value, unless it may be necessary to offer it at a discount in order to relieve the company from pressing financial embarrassment. When a company desires to offer stock at a discount, as did the Western Maryland recently in an offer of common stock at $50 a share, it is sometimes necessary to get permission from the Legislature to offer the stock at this low price. It is, moreover, usually difficult to find a purchaser for stock at a discount. A low price indicates the general lack of confidence in the ability of a company to pay reasonable dividends on the stock. Until, therefore, a company has reached an assured financial position, the sale of common stock is usually not available as a means of obtaining new capital. Failing common stock, there is left for the choice of the directors either preferred stock or bonds.

The bondholder has no voice in the management of the corporation. In return for its obligation to pay him a fixed sum at regular intervals, and to secure him in the return of his principal should he desire it, he is willing to forego participation in profits above the amount of his interest which, as a rule, does not exceed five per cent, and seldom goes above six per cent. The preferred stockholder, on the other hand, expects from six to eight per cent as a preferred charge in advance of dividends upon the common stock. He also demands a voice in the management of the company. So far as the common stockholder is concerned, an issue of bonds, if this can be safely made, is usually preferable to the sale of preferred stock. The common stockholder's share of the profits is larger if bonds are issued for new capital, and he is left undisturbed in the control of the company.

There are, however, opposing considerations. Dividends on the preferred stock, even if these dividends are made cumulative, although the investment standing of the corporation demands that they should be paid if earned, need not be paid. A company may pile up an unlimited amount of preferred dividends, while still remaining entirely solvent, and in a most flourishing condition. Interest, on the other hand, is an absolute charge against income. It must be paid, or the courts will seize the property of the company for the benefit of its creditors. When any doubt exists as to the ability of the corporation, in good years as well as bad years, to earn interest on the capital which it proposes to secure by the sale of bonds, and when the sale of common stock is not possible, then preferred stock, rather than bonds, should be sold. As between preferred stock and bonds, if safety is considered of primary importance, a conservative management will obtain funds by the issue of stock, and will limit its bond issues to the amount on which the smallest net earnings which the corporation is likely to secure, will be more than sufficient to pay the interest charges. If this minimum of net earnings will not pay interest on the amount of capital required, then preferred stock should be issued to obtain the amount on which interest cannot be assured.

In determining the expediency of a bond issue, moreover, the starting point should not be the earnings of the company, increased by the returns on the improvements in which it is proposed to invest the new capital funds, but the earnings of the company as they stand before the increase of its liabilities. The new capital will probably be productive, but there is no certainty that it will be immediately productive, and, in the meantime, bankruptcy might overtake the corporation if it relies upon the issue of bonds to provide the necessary funds for these improvements. Again, certain enterprises, as we have seen in a preceding chapter, do not furnish proper security for bond issues. The borrowing power of most industrial enterprises is limited to a small portion of their assets, in some cases, as we shall see later, to the amount of their current assets. If they wish to raise additional capital, it must be by the sale of preferred stock.

We have already discussed under the "Preparation of the Financial Plan" the conditions under which preferred stock can be issued, and the safeguards demanded by the purchasers of such stock when put out as a part of the original plan of capitalization. The precautions taken when preferred stock is issued after the organization of the company usually include both those safeguards already described, and also supplementary securities, which are intended to protect the preferred stockholder against any abuse of their power by the interests in control of the company. The purchaser of preferred stock put out by a going concern as the means of obtaining new capital occupies a different relation to the company from the holder of the stock as originally issued. In most of the consolidations, which have furnished nearly all the preferred stock now dealt in on the public exchanges, preferred stock was issued to the owners of plants which were put into the consolidation. The original holders of the preferred stock were, in a sense, partners in the enterprise, receiving common stock along with their preferred stock, and not exacting any unusual guarantees from the corporation. When preferred stock is issued by a going concern for cash, various precautions are taken to make the stock as safe an investment as possible; to give to the holder of preferred stock the nearest possible approach to the security of the bond.

Preferred stock issued to obtain new capital is, with few exceptions, made cumulative both as to dividends and to assets. The amount of the preferred stock issued under these circumstances cannot be increased without the consent of a large majority of the outstanding stock. Since the bonds of the company precede the preferred stock, precautions are taken to prevent any increase of debt without the consent of the preferred stockholder. Preferred stock, when issued to obtain new capital, is more likely to be made participating than when included in an original issue. The common stock originally issued has by this time been sold, no syndicate has any common stock which must be favored, and it may be necessary to give to the preferred stock the right to participate in dividends in order to make it attractive to the investor. Preferred stock issued to obtain new capital is also more likely to carry with it special voting powers.

An effort is sometimes made in preferred stock contracts to enforce conservative management upon the company. This is a new feature, but has been quite prominent in recent issues. The danger to the preferred stockholder is that the company shall make excessive disbursements in common stock dividends, so that the necessary surplus will not be accumulated. Every dollar which the preferred stockholder can withhold from common stock dividends is so much gained in the greater security of his stock. This reservation of profits may be made by including in the contract with the stockholder the obligation of the corporation to build up a reserve fund out of profits in advance of common stock dividends. A typical provision of this character appears in the recent issue of preferred stock by the Underwood Typewriter Company.

The charter of the company contains the following, among other provisions, for the protection of the preferred stock:

> There shall be set apart from the net profits of the Company at the rate of not less than $100,000 per annum, a fund to be known as "SPECIAL SURPLUS CAPITAL RESERVE ACCOUNT," which shall be

> made and kept good at the rate of $100,000 per annum for each year before any dividends shall be paid on the common stock, and after the expiration of three years from the date of incorporation of the Company said SPECIAL SURPLUS CAPITAL RESERVE ACCOUNT shall be used annually in the purchase and retirement of said preferred stock at the lowest price at which the same may be obtainable, but in no event exceeding a premium of twenty-five per cent over and above the par value thereof. Such purchases may be made at the option of the Company either at public or private sale, and all preferred stock so acquired shall be canceled.
>
> The Company shall, in no event, pay or declare any dividends on the common stock until the annual sum of $100,000 shall have been first set aside and paid into the SPECIAL SURPLUS CAPITAL RESERVE ACCOUNT for the purchase and retirement of preferred stock, nor as long as there shall be any arrears in respect of such SPECIAL SURPLUS CAPITAL RESERVE ACCOUNT, and no dividend in excess of four per cent shall be declared or paid on the common stock until and unless there shall first have been accumulated and set aside from and out of the net earnings of the corporation the sum of $1,000,000 by way of surplus to the credit of said SPECIAL SURPLUS CAPITAL RESERVE ACCOUNT, either in the form of cash or its equivalent or of retired and canceled preferred stock of the par value of $1,000,000. This SPECIAL SURPLUS CAPITAL RESERVE ACCOUNT may be used for the payment of dividends on the preferred stock provided there are no other funds applicable for that purpose, and provided further that all encroachments upon or arrears in said fund shall be made good out of future earnings before any dividends whatever shall at any time be paid or declared on the common stock.

The charter of the American Piano Company which recently offered preferred stock, provides that:

> No dividend on the common stock can at any time be paid either in cash or otherwise if such payment

> would reduce the actual surplus of the company to an amount less than ten per cent of the par value of the total amount of the issued and outstanding preferred stock; nor, when the actual surplus of the company is less than fifty per cent of the par value of the total issued and outstanding preferred stock, shall any dividend on the common stock be declared or paid unless, at the time of the declaration thereof, there shall be added to the surplus, out of the net profits, an amount equal to not less than one third of the total common stock dividend declared.

These provisions are included in the fundamental contract between the preferred stockholders and the corporation; they can be strictly enforced against the company; and they furnish a large measure of protection to the preferred stockholders against a too liberal management of income by the directors.

A feature which is usual in preferred stock contracts, when the issue is made to procure new capital, is the right of redemption. Ordinary issues of preferred stock do not often contain such a right. When the common stockholders have consented to placing six or seven per cent preferred stock ahead of their own right to participate in the profits of the company, it is fair to them, in case the earnings of the company improve to the point where a lower dividend preferred stock or some form of bond may be sold, that they should be allowed to retire the preferred stock. When a large part of the issue of preferred stock has been taken by the common stockholders who safeguard themselves by the preferred claim, these stockholders may wish to participate in the earnings of the company to a larger amount than that to which their preferred stock entitles them. If their contract allows them equal participation with the common stock in all dividends over the prescribed rate on the preferred stock, there is no advantage, from their point of view, in retiring the preferred. If, however, this right of equal participation has not been given, and it is unusual, they may desire to exchange their preferred stock for common stock, if the increasing earnings of the company make such a course attractive. It often happens, moreover, that the preferred stock has been given, as an extra measure of protection, the right to elect a majority of the board of directors. In such a case, the common stockholder is naturally anxious to regain control by retiring the preferred. For the protection of the preferred stockholder, however, and not to make his investment in this stock unattractive, the right of compulsory retirement or redemption is usually fixed at a point well above par, usually not less than 110. The right of redemption may terminate at the end of a given number of years, or may not begin until the expiration of a period.

When issued under proper safeguards, and by a prosperous company which is paying dividends on its common stock, cumulative preferred stock is coming to be regarded as an attractive investment, and is in increasing demand. While there is no reason to believe that companies will ever be able to obtain capital by the issue of such a security on as favorable terms as by issuing bonds, yet it is reasonably sure that preferred stock will be sold on terms more favorable to the corporation than those which now prevail.

CHAPTER XXIII

THE ISSUE OF EVIDENCES OF DEBT

THE method of providing new capital for corporations of established credit and assured earnings, which is steadily growing in popularity, is the method of borrowing. As between the issue of preferred stock and bonds, when the conditions of the company permit the issue of bonds, this method is usually selected. The bondholder, in return for a secured claim to a fixed return on the obligations which he buys, leaves the stockholder in possession of the property of the company, and in the enjoyment of all its profits over the amount necessary to pay interest, and, where this is provided, the appropriation to build up a sinking fund. Because of the security given, moreover, the rate of return which the bondholder exacts is much less than would be demanded by the holder of preferred stock. If the company can borrow money for extensions and improvements, therefore, the surplus remaining for the stockholders, after providing for a return on the new capital required, is usually two, and sometimes three per cent greater than if preferred stock is issued. These reasons for the issue of evidences of debt rather than preferred stock are, in almost all cases, controlling.

The evidences of debt which may be issued by a corporation seeking new capital may be divided into short term loans and long term bonds. The first class may be again divided into bank loans and short term notes. We shall consider these in their order.

Bank loans are made in anticipation of the proceeds of business transactions which will mature in the near future. It is unsafe for a bank to advance money to be put into any form of fixed capital which will do no more than return a safe margin over the interest on the loan. Bank loans must be either paid when due, principal and interest, or materially reduced. Experience shows that permanent capital cannot be obtained from the commercial bank. The business of the bank is to supply the temporary needs of business for working capital. Nearly every business is, to some extent, seasonal in its character. The agricultural implement dealer, who sells to the farmer, may deliver machinery in the spring and wait until after harvest for payment. In the fall, when he has collected for the season's sales, and has only begun to manufacture for next season, there will be no need for the implement manufacturer to borrow largely from the banks. The amount of capital locked up in machinery sold, will, however, steadily increase as the season advances, until, before harvest, he will have a large temporary investment in notes and accounts. It is not considered economical that the manufacturer should have invested sufficient capital to carry his business for the entire year without resort to the banks. If such a policy be decided on, for a part of the year, the manufacturer would have on hand a large amount of capital on which he might be paying six per cent dividends while receiving only three per cent for it from the banks.

The manufacturer of agricultural implements obtains notes from his customers, and these notes are used as collateral for his own notes, which are sold to banks. When the notes mature they are paid out of the proceeds of collections. This illustration shows the principal contribution of the banks to the working capital of industry. Banks sometimes extend permanent credit to concerns which are growing rapidly and require an increasing working capital, but the bank's contribution will be only a portion of the working capital of the business. It is better that a company should provide for the normal amount of working capital, resorting to the banks to supply the seasonal demands for capital, and any extraordinary demands to meet which permanent provision cannot be made.

Bank loans are not available as a source of permanent capital, although they may furnish a portion of the capital which a corporation requires. In some cases, however, a special form of obligation, either secured or unsecured, is favored by corporations, and largely sold to banks as well as to investors. This is known as the short term note. Such obligations run for one, two, or three years, and pay a high rate of interest—five or six per cent. This form of obligation is usually resorted to during periods of stringency in the money market, when long term bonds cannot be sold except on the basis of a high interest yield.

A first-class railroad corporation expects, under normal conditions of demand, to sell its first mortgage four per cent bonds at par. The money market may, however, get into such a condition that a four per cent bond of this class cannot be sold except at a price to yield five per cent to the investor. Suppose the corporation wishes to issue a thirty year bond. If it makes the issue at such a time, it will have to pay the one per cent extra for thirty years, or thirty per cent on the entire amount of the issue. Looking at the proposition solely from the standpoint of income, and assuming that an improvement in the bond market will, within two or three years, make it possible to again sell four per cent bonds at par, it is advantageous for a company, in the circumstances described, to borrow the amount required for, say, three years, paying six or seven per cent interest, and trusting to its ability to refund the obligation at maturity on a four per cent basis. Instead of paying thirty per cent premium, therefore, the company which makes an issue of two year six per cent notes, and refunds these on a four per cent basis, will only pay four per cent premium for the money over the entire period.

The conditions under which the issue of short term notes is advantageous are illustrated by the situation of the American money market in 1906. During this year, the bond market had been extremely dull. Prices generally declined; issues yielding less than four and a half per cent gained little attention. The explanation was found in the high rates for money. The largest bond buyers are the financial institutions, banks, savings banks, trust companies, and insurance companies. During 1906, these large bond buyers were able to lend their funds on call through the banks, or to purchase commercial paper at very high rates of interest, and with perfect security. As a result, they reduced their bond purchases. As an illustration of the stringency of money prevailing during this year, may be cited the case of one of the largest manufacturing concerns in Philadelphia, and one of the foremost enterprises in its field, which was obliged to sell its paper on an eight per cent basis. Individual bond buyers, large merchants and manufacturers who are, to an increasing extent, investing a portion of their profits in negotiable securities, had their funds so fully employed in their business that no surplus remained for investment. Railroad and industrial corporations were at this time heavily committed to new undertakings. To obtain the money for these extensions and improvements, rather than burden themselves with high rates of interest during the life of long term bonds, they preferred to sell short time notes, generally paying six per cent interest, which would be taken by banks and private investors on account of the security offered and the high rates of interest approximating those which could be obtained in the loan market. The amount of notes put out by the principal railroads and industrial corporations during this year was $136,000,000. The corporations making these issues preferred to pay higher rates for one, two, or three years in the belief that when the date of maturity arrived, the condition of the bond market would have so much improved as to permit the retirement of these short term obligations with bonds at lower rates of interest.

An illustration of the use of short term obligations was the $15,000,000 of six per cent gold notes issued by the Southern Railway on May 1, 1908. The bond market at this time was so greatly depressed that none but issues of the strongest corporations would be taken. The Southern Railway was not in this class. Its credit was considered so doubtful that it was not expedient to attempt to market its bonds. These notes were offered at 98½ and accrued interest and were payable on or before May 1, 1911.

Short term notes may be either secured or unsecured. If unsecured, their value rests upon the general credit of the company which depends primarily upon its surplus earnings over charges. The security of notes is also increased by the fact that, in most cases, their proceeds are invested in the improvement of the property. For example, in the case of the Southern Railway notes, it was proposed to apply the proceeds of the notes substantially as follows:

"First, to provide capital for obligations accrued and to accrue, representing generally the retirement of equipment obligations, the purchase of steel rails, construction now under contract, and additional betterments and improvements to the properties covered by the development and general mortgage, say $8,500,000; to provide for the redemption of the sterling notes which will mature on June 1st and July 2d next, say $3,000,000. The balance to be used to reimburse the treasury to that extent for moneys heretofore expended for construction and capital account, say $3,500,000."

Out of $15,000,000 of notes, the proceeds of $8,500,000 would go to improvements which might reasonably be supposed to produce revenue equal to the interest on the notes, and which increased, to that extent, the value of the property which secured the notes. Only $3,000,000 were provided to fund other notes. Short term notes are better secured when the proceeds of the sale are to be spent for the benefit of the company than when they merely take the place of other maturing obligations. The sale of these notes for refunding purposes is much more difficult than when at least the major portion of their proceeds is to be spent upon the property.

Short term notes are usually secured. In cases where they have been issued on account of the present unsalability at attractive prices of mortgage bonds already authorized, it is customary to pledge collateral as additional security for the notes. The $15,000,000 of Southern Railway notes, for example, were secured by $20,000,000 of Southern Railway development and general mortgage four per cent bonds, Series "A," by $2,500,000 of Tennessee Central Railroad prior lien mortgage four per cent bonds, and by $2,000,000 Virginia & Southwestern Railway first consolidated mortgage five per cent bonds. Earlier in 1908, the Hudson Company, of New York City, sold $15,000,000 of six per cent notes, secured by the deposit of $22,500,000 of the first mortgage 4½ per cent bonds of the Hudson & Manhattan Railroad Company which owns the tunnels between New York, Jersey City and Hoboken. Indeed, the securing of these short term obligations by collateral is so common that the giving of such security may now be considered obligatory. Even a strong company like the Pennsylvania Railroad Company, or its subsidiary, the Pennsylvania Company, secures its short term obligations by ample collateral.

Since these notes are sold on a banking basis, and are secured by collateral, it is fair to the company that they should have the same liberty of reducing their loans which is allowed to the ordinary borrower on collateral. This provision is usually made. The Hudson Company's notes, for example, were issued subject to the right of redemption on any interest date, upon thirty days' notice, at par and interest, plus a premium of one per cent per annum upon the principal from date of redemption to maturity.

If at any time during the life of the short term obligation, a favorable opportunity arises to sell the collateral, it is usual to provide that this can be done. Thus, in the issue above described it is provided that:

"The Southern Railway is to have the right at any time to withdraw by payment therefor in cash at the following prices: Development and general mortgage four per cent bonds, Series 'A,' at the same price and for the same periods as provided above for the conversion of the notes; Tennessee Central prior lien mortgage four per cent bonds at not less than 85 per cent; Virginia & Southwestern first consolidated mortgage five per cent bonds at not less than 90 per cent, with accrued interest in each case. Such cash is to be applied by the trustee to the purchase or redemption of the notes as provided in the trust indenture."

The use of notes is merely a temporary expedient to bridge over a period when bonds cannot be sold. Although they may be sometimes funded into other notes of the same kind, it is not possible for this process to be continued indefinitely, and refunding usually requires higher or better security on the new notes. These notes must, in other words, be paid, principal and interest, within a short time. On this account, large reliance upon this means of obtaining new capital is, for a weak corporation, considered unsafe. Although it is expected that the bond market may improve to admit of the collateral back of the notes being sold at good prices, yet this improvement cannot be guaranteed, and it has frequently happened that short term obligations came due at a time when it was most inconvenient for the company to pay them. With a strong corporation, in such an event, no difficulty is to be expected, but if the maturity of the notes coincides with a period of business depression, when the net earnings of the issuing company are below even their normal level, and when the bond buyer is unusually critical concerning the securities offered him, the company which, for the sake of saving interest, has burdened itself with the obligation to repay a large sum of money at such an inopportune time, may run great danger of bankruptcy. The difficulty experienced by the Wheeling & Lake Erie, and the Erie Railroad Companies in refunding their notes maturing in 1908, illustrates the danger of relying upon this method of procuring funds. The first of these companies was forced into bankruptcy by the maturity of a note issue, and the Erie was only saved from a like fate by the intervention of Mr. E. H. Harriman. For any but the strongest companies whose ability to take care of maturing obligations is undoubted, the provision of new capital by the issue of short term notes is to be entered upon with great caution.

CHAPTER XXIV

LONG TERM BONDS

Long term bonds are of two kinds—those without special security, known as debentures, and those with special security, such as mortgage bonds, collateral trust bonds, and car trust certificates.

A debenture is a certificate of debt issued by a corporation without mortgage or collateral security. An illustration of a debenture is an issue by the New York, New Haven & Hartford in 1904, which is, in substance, as follows:

> Fifty years after date, the New York, New Haven & Hartford Railroad Company promises to pay . . . . or order, $1,000 at the office of its Treasurer, in the city of New Haven, Connecticut, and to pay interest thereon from date at the rate of 3½ per cent per annum.

The security offered to the debenture holder is the right of action against the company in default of their payment of principal or interest. In this respect, debentures are superior to preferred stock which they resemble in having a prior claim to earnings, a claim, however, which is enforceable by legal action.

The measure of the value of the debenture bonds is the surplus earnings of the corporation over the prior fixed charges. They are, in no respect, save in name, different from junior mortgage bonds, and they usually bear a higher rate of interest than first mortgage bonds. Debentures differ radically from income bonds. An income bond is a bond whose interest is payable if, in the judgment of the directors, it has been earned, but whose principal, like that of any other bond, is payable at a definite date. So far as their interest is concerned, therefore, income bonds are in exactly the same position as preferred stock, and they are of inferior value to cumulative preferred stock in that the interest on incomes is not carried over to accumulate against future earnings. In so far, however, as the principal of income bonds must eventually be paid, they are superior to preferred stock. Income bonds have been but little used in recent years. They were extensively employed before 1890 in various railway reorganizations, the Wabash incomes being perhaps the most familiar instance, but they have fallen into disuse because they possess the virtues and the value neither of stock nor bonds.

Returning now to the consideration of debentures, we find that the contracts with the debenture holders may contain certain special securities which go far to compensate for the absence of mortgage security. It may be provided that no mortgage shall be placed upon the property unless the debentures are included in the lien of the mortgage. Thus, for example, in the offer of the debentures of the New York, New Haven & Hartford appears the following:

> These debentures will also provide, as far as lawfully may be, that if this company shall thereafter create any mortgage upon its now existing main line of railroad between Woodlawn in the City and State of New York, and Springfield in the Commonwealth of Massachusetts, or its now existing main line between New Haven in the State of Connecticut, and Providence in the State of Rhode Island, such debentures shall, without further act, be entitled to share in the security of such mortgage pro rata with any other obligations that may be secured thereby, and that any such mortgage shall expressly so provide.

It may be provided that, as long as the debentures are outstanding, the debt of the company shall not be increased. The agreement with the debenture bond-

> holders of the Colorado Fuel & Iron Company provides that "so long as any of said debentures or the interest warrants annexed thereto, shall be unpaid, no mortgage or other encumbrance shall be placed upon any of the property of the Iron Company, nor shall any other debentures be authorized or issued, nor any other bonds, except those provided for in the mortgages or deeds of trust outstanding July 1, 1901, and except bonds and mortgages to be authorized and issued to replace the bonds provided for in such mortgages or deeds of trust, in case the Iron Company may desire to refund the same or any of them, but in no event shall the par value of its said refunding bonds exceed the par value of the bonds which they shall be issued to replace, nor shall the rate of interest on any of such refunding bonds exceed the rate of interest upon the bonds which they shall be issued to replace, it being the meaning of this agreement that neither the total amount of bonds at any time outstanding nor the rate of interest thereon, so long as any of said debentures or the interest warrants annexed thereto shall be unpaid, shall be increased; nor shall any notes be issued or indebtedness authorized or created for any other purpose than the ordinary running expenses of the Iron Company.

The precautions indicated in the foregoing extract are highly desirable from the standpoint of the debenture bondholder.

A corporation which has issued debenture bonds may have retained the right to issue bonds under its various mortgages, by which the security of a debenture which can be satisfied only after the prior claims of mortgage bonds, would be seriously impaired. By inserting in the contract with the debenture bondholder such a provision as the foregoing, a corporation, so long as the debentures were outstanding, would be unable to issue any other form of debt than short term notes or an inferior grade of debentures.

It may also be provided for the protection of the debenture bondholders that the proceeds of these bonds shall be expended in a specified manner for the benefit of the property. To quote again from the agreement of the Colorado Fuel & Iron Company:

> The Iron Company agrees that the proceeds of the initial $10,000,000 of said debentures shall be used only for additions and improvements to the plant of the company, and for working capital and other corporate purposes, and that the proceeds of the remaining $5,000,000 of said debentures shall be used only for the acquisition of additional property.

It would be impossible, in view of this clause in the contract, for the proceeds of the debentures to be used to retire outstanding indebtedness of the company, or as a means of providing funds for the distribution of a portion of the company's surplus to stockholders. The provision stipulates that all the money which the purchasers of the debenture bonds pay into the treasury of the company shall be expended in such a manner as to increase the value of the company's property, and the net earnings upon which the debenture bondholders must rely for their interest. With these safeguards thrown about him, the position of the debenture bondholder is not greatly inferior to that of the holder of a second mortgage bond.

In order to make debenture bonds more attractive, and to sell them at higher prices, many corporations have adopted the plan of making these bonds convertible into stock at a certain figure. The issue of debentures with the convertible feature is rapidly growing in favor, and several of the strongest railroads in the country—the Union Pacific, the Atchison, and the New York, New Haven & Hartford—have adopted this plan of financing their capital requirements. These convertible debentures are direct obligations of the issuing company, although they are unsecured by mortgage. They carry a fixed rate of interest and are payable at a definite date. In addition, the holders of the bonds are given the privilege of converting them into stock, usually common stock, at a certain figure, either up to a certain date or after a certain date. For example, the ten-year five per cent convertible gold bonds of the Atchison, Topeka & Santa Fé are convertible into common stock prior to June 1, 1913, at the option of the holder, on the basis of ten shares of common stock, par value 100, for each $1,000 bond; and the Delaware & Hudson Company, in 1906, issued ten-year debenture four per cent convertible bonds, convertible into the common stock of the company prior to June 15, 1912, on the basis of five shares of stock for each $1,000 bond. The conversion privilege on some convertible bonds does not begin for a number of years, as, for example, the six per cent debenture bonds of the New York, New Haven & Hartford are convertible between 1923 and 1948, at par into the common stock of the company. As a rule, however, the conversion privilege is immediate. The conversion price is usually fixed at a figure considerably above the market price of the stock when the bonds are issued.

The advantages offered by these bonds to the investor are evident. Convertible bonds, considered as obligations of the company, rank with junior lien bonds. A company which has a long dividend record is reasonably certain to pay interest and principal of its junior mortgage bonds. The stock of the corporation represents the residuary claim to the increase in its profits and values. If the business of the company is well conducted, its stock may go to a high figure. The holder of the convertible bond can then make a large profit by exchanging his bonds for stock.

A feature connected with convertible bonds which makes them especially attractive to the speculative element always to be attentively considered in any sale of securities, is the movement of their value as compared with the movement of stock values. Since the convertible debenture is a bond, an unconditional obligation of the corporation to pay money, it will be valued as a bond by its holders, and there will be a certain point below which it will not fall. The purchaser of five per cent debenture bonds of a strong railroad company at, say, 96, can be reasonably certain that, no matter how unfavorable the financial situation may be, the price of his security will not fall much below 90. The stock of the same company, although it may pay a higher dividend than the rate of interest on the bond, may easily fall to 75. On the other hand, when the price of the stock advances, the convertible bonds, since they are exchangeable for the stock, also rise more rapidly than other junior lien bonds which do not have the conversion privilege. The Atchison, Topeka & Santa Fé has outstanding a large issue of convertible four per cent bonds as well as a second mortgage four per cent bond, known as Adjustment Mortgage four per cent. During the panic of 1907, the adjustment mortgage 4s fell to 77½ and the convertible 4s to 80. With the revival of business, the stock of the Atchison rapidly advanced, and the convertible bonds rose. On November 24, 1909, the convertible 4s sold at 119½ while the adjustment mortgage 4s had only recovered to 94½.

Up to and beyond the conversion figure, as long as any of the convertible bonds remain outstanding, the price of the stock and of the bonds into which the stock is convertible will move together. The price of the convertible bond will usually be lower than the price of the stock for which it is exchangeable, since a large part of the demand for convertible bonds, which have risen to high figures because of this exchange privilege, will come from investors who choose this method to acquire the stock at less than market figures. Convertibles sell at a lower price than the stock for which they are exchangeable, for the same reason that rights to subscribe to stock at par sell for smaller sums than the amounts represented by the differences between par and market price on any given date. The correspondence, however, between the price movements of convertible bonds and stock is sufficiently close to make these bonds very attractive to a large class of investors who are not averse to taking a speculative profit if this can be done with moderate risk.

Convertible bonds are also bought largely by speculators as a protection against short sales. Suppose, for example, a speculator desires to sell Atchison stock short around par. He begins his operations by buying ten of the convertible bonds which will be selling around 96. He then sells 100 shares of Atchison short, borrows the stock from some one who has it to lend, and deposits his bonds as the principal security for the loan, receiving $10,000 for the stock, less his commissions, with which he can pay for his bonds and have a small profit remaining, subject to the risks of his contract to deliver 100 shares of stock whenever called upon by the lender. Suppose, now, that his calculations are correct, and that Atchison falls to 90. His convertible bonds may decline, although this is not necessarily involved in a situation which would produce a fall in the price of the stock. He might, however, lose three points on his bonds. At the same time, however, he would make $10 a share on his transaction in the stock, since he could purchase 100 shares for $9,000, and deliver the stock to the one from whom he borrowed it, receiving back his convertible bonds. In the event of the speculator's calculations proving erroneous, and if Atchison stock advanced ten points to 110, he would lose $10 a share on his stock, or $1,000. His convertible bonds, however, would probably advance to 105, so that his net loss would be only $100. Furthermore, in the unlikely event of the stock being cornered, the holder of convertible debentures can protect himself by exchanging his bonds for stock which the company holds in its treasury available for the conversion from the date the bonds are issued. Owing in part to these speculative advantages possessed by convertible debenture bonds, they are in large demand, and their prices are often far above their investment values.

Whatever may be said of the debenture bond from the standpoint of the investor—and it must be admitted that the position of most debenture bondholders as unsecured creditors is, from an investor's standpoint, not especially attractive—there can be no question that they offer to a corporation whose stock is selling so close to par that it cannot count on disposing any large amount at that figure, and which is not in a position to issue first mortgage bonds, an opportunity to obtain money on favorable terms by combining the doubtful investment quality of debentures with the speculative possibilities involved in the conversion privilege. From the company's standpoint, the sale of convertible debentures is merely a deferred sale of the stock for which the convertibles are to be exchanged. This deferred sale of stock is often made, through conversion, at a high premium, a much higher premium than could be obtained by selling the stock direct. The use of convertible debentures has been criticised on the ground that a company by resorting to this form of security will spoil the market for its prior lien bonds. As a rule, however, debentures are not resorted to as long as first-class bonds under prior lien mortgages are available for sale.

CHAPTER XXV

MORTGAGE BONDS

We next take up long term obligations with mortgage, collateral, or lease security. American financiers are committed to the idea of specific security. Until recent years, it has been very difficult to sell debenture bonds at values commensurate with their real security. Laws regulating the investment of the funds of savings banks and trust funds usually stipulate first mortgage bonds. In Great Britain, on the other hand, mortgage bonds are rare; there the debenture is the usual form of security.

Recognizing the preference of the American investor for mortgage bonds, corporation directors, in formulating a plan for provision of new capital, must keep in view, in selecting a type of obligation, the following objects: First, they must secure for the corporation the money required; second, they must procure this money at a reasonable cost; third, they should provide, if possible, in a mortgage whose bonds are readily taken by investors, for subsequent issues of bonds. The directors come next to the consideration that the investor will pay a higher price for first mortgage bonds than for any junior security. Of two bonds of equal security, so far as earnings are concerned, one secured by a first and the other by a second mortgage on the same property, the first mortgage bond will always be preferred. This preference is easily explained. In case of bankruptcy and reorganization, the first mortgage bonds are in a position of great advantage. Up to the earning power of the property set aside to secure them, they must be protected. Before the holder of second mortgage bonds can enforce the lien of their security, they must satisfy all the claims of the first mortgage. The investor's first concern is the safety of his principal. He wishes the utmost protection. This protection the first mortgage, as distinct from any junior lien, gives him.[1]

Next in order to first mortgage bonds, in grading secured issues, the investor will rank collateral trust bonds where the security consists of other bonds or dividend-paying stock, and where the borrowing company can pay the interest, if need be, without depending upon the income produced by the collateral. Finally, he will put bonds secured by leases, such as car trust certificates. Two problems then confront the directors of corporations proposing to issue bonds. They must give the bonds, if possible, the security of a first mortgage, and, if this cannot be done, they must adopt some form of obligation which will give the bonds issued a first lien on either securities owned or on rights under leases. In case neither method is available, and also as additional security in all cases, the corporation may assume the indirect or conditional obligation of a guarantor or indorser of bonds which are sold for its benefit.

In giving bonds first mortgage security, it is necessary to deal with two types of existing mortgages. First, those which stipulate that all property subsequently acquired by the corporation shall come under the existing mortgages, and second, those which set aside specific property as security, leaving subsequently acquired property to be pledged as security for additional loans. Under the first classification we

---

[1] Many exceptions can be cited to this rule. Some of the best bonds are secured by general mortgages—that is, second and third mortgages. The Erie prior lien bonds, for example, are secured by a sixth mortgage on its main line. In these cases, however, the first mortgages are usually for small amounts calling for such moderate payments in relation to the surplus earnings of the company that the investor disregards the prior liens. A tendency is visible, however, in recent years, among railroad financiers, to retire, as far as possible, these underlying liens in order to bring the mortgages securing the large issues of general mortgage bonds nearer the property.

find two types of mortgages—the open-end mortgage, and the closed mortgage. Under the open-end mortgage bonds may either be issued to any amount without limit, or a bond reserve large enough to provide for all future needs of the company is authorized,[1] the bonds being protected, however, by the requirement that the money shall be invested in a specified way for the benefit of the company, or that their issue shall be controlled and approved by some disinterested authority.

Bonds are issued under a closed mortgage when the amount of bonds to be issued under the mortgage is limited. Closed mortgages are of two kinds: First, where the property subsequently acquired by the corporation is included under the lien of the mortgage; and second, where the lien is limited to the property enumerated in the instrument. The first may be called an *inclusive* and the second an *exclusive* closed mortgage. Closed mortgages have the following form of enumeration of property transferred:

> Together with all the branches, extensions and sidings thereof and therefrom, and all the lands and rights of way used and occupied, or surveyed, laid out, or intended to be used and occupied for the said railroads, branches, extensions and sidings, with all the railroad tracks, buildings and improvements thereon, and all and singular the lands, bridges, trestle works, wharves, shops, stations, depots, engine houses, engines, cars, rolling stock, furniture, equipments, and generally all and singular the estate, real and personal, of the said . . . Railway Company, *whatsoever and wheresoever, now owned or hereafter to be acquired by it.*[2]

An illustration of the exclusive closed mortgage where the lien of the mortgage is limited to specified property, and does not include any property which may be hereafter acquired, is furnished by the mortgage securing the first lien

[1] The true open-end mortgage is rare. For practical purposes a bond reserve several times the amount of the initial issue is equivalent to the authorization of unlimited issue.

[2] Italics are the author's.

convertible four per cent gold bonds of the Union Pacific Railroad Company, due May 1, 1911, which assigns to the trustee:

> All and singular the several lines of railroad, property, and premises belonging to the Railroad Company which are particularly described as follows. . . . Together with all additions, lands, terminals, yards, bridges, tracks, rights of way, trackage rights, buildings, telegraphs, shops, elevators, and other structures and fixtures, easements and leaseholds, corporate rights and franchises, now held or acquired or *hereafter held or acquired* for use in connection with the said lines of railroad, *specifically above described;* and also the earnings and profits thereof, also the following described bonds and stocks, namely: . . . Together with any and all shares of stock or bonds of any other corporation which the Railroad Company may hereafter deposit and pledge hereunder by way of substitution or otherwise.[1]

Under this mortgage, the security of the bonds is specifically restricted to the property enumerated in the mortgage, and there is no obligation on the part of the company, although it may do so, if it desires, to add to this security.

First mortgage bonds can be issued under inclusive closed mortgages only if a portion of the bonds authorized has been reserved to provide for the future needs of the company. Under most of the closed mortgages issued by the large railroad companies, only small amounts can still be issued. For example, the offering by the Guarantee Trust Company of $2,072,000 prior lien $3\frac{1}{2}$ per cent gold bonds of the Baltimore & Ohio Railroad Company in July, 1908, contained the following:

> With the above offering the mortgage is closed, and in consequence this is probably the last opportunity to obtain a round amount of these bonds at a satisfactory price. The general inability of the railroads

[1] Italics are the author's.

> to create in the future new bonds which will compare in point of security with first mortgages of this class renders this an opportunity which should be embraced.

If the authorization of bonds under a closed first mortgage has been exhausted by issue, the only recourse of the directors desiring to give to the investor bonds secured by a prior lien, is to the issue of bonds by a subsidiary company organized for that purpose, and guaranteed by the parent company; or to a collateral trust issue, if the first mortgage of the parent company does not include all securities owned in its schedule of property "to be hereafter acquired"; or to a combination of the two methods. These methods of raising capital we shall take up in detail in their proper places. If the closed mortgage does not include "all property to be hereafter acquired," so that the company can subject some of its property to the lien of a first mortgage, then it is usual to execute a general refunding first mortgage, or a consolidated first mortgage which will become a first mortgage on all the property of the company when the underlying bonds mature. Provision is made for a sufficient issue of bonds under the consolidated mortgage to retire the prior lien bonds, and the general effect and impression is that of a first mortgage bond. Referring again for illustration to the issue of bonds by the Union Pacific above noted, we find the following description of the security in a letter from President E. H. Harriman, under date of June 8, 1908:

"Referring to the 'first lien and refunding mortgage four per cent bonds' of this company, I beg to state that these bonds are to be secured by a first mortgage on 1,177.71 miles main track and 146.63 miles other track of owned railroad lines. The lines mortgaged are valuable and important parts of this company's system. . . . The amount of bonds which may be issued at present on the security above stated is $50,000,000, and no further amount can be issued in addition thereto until the security of the mortgage be extended to cover (subject only to the first mortgage of this company, dated July 1, 1897) all the lines covered by said first mortgage . . . the entire railroad mileage of the Union Pacific Railroad Company. When the lien of this mortgage is extended to cover all of the present railroad mileage of the Union Pacific Railroad Company, the total authorized amount of bonds which may be issued thereunder, including the above $50,000,000, will be $200,000,000, of which $100,000,000 are to be reserved to refund the first mortgage four per cent bonds, due July 1, 1947, for a like face amount, which first mortgage bonds shall not be extended when due, *so that the 'first lien and refunding mortgage shall ultimately become the sole first mortgage upon the entire present railroad property of the company, and upon any additional property hereafter acquired or constructed with the proceeds of bonds of this issue.'*[1] The remaining $50,000,000 bonds are to be reserved to be issued only for the construction or acquisition of additional lines of railroad, connecting with the lines then subject to the mortgage, and for the acquisition of other property for use on or in connection with the mortgaged lines and for improvements thereon, as specified in the mortgage, and all of which shall then pass under the lien securing the entire issue of these bonds."

The Union Pacific, it appears from this statement, took advantage of the fact that its first mortgage is not inclusive of all property which it may hereafter acquire, to pledge certain lines which had been built or purchased since the first mortgage was executed, under the lien of this first consolidated mortgage. This is, therefore, a first mortgage on some lines, and a second mortgage on others. It is also here provided, which is usual in this type of security, that eventually this first and refunding mortgage shall become an absolute first mortgage on all the property of the system.

Here again we find the precaution taken that the company should have available first mortgage bonds, in the pro-

[1] The italics are the author's.

vision that $50,000,000 are to be reserved for subsequent issue. Great care is taken in drawing refunding mortgages to provide that the maturing bonds should be retired, either by payment or conversion, as fast as they mature, so that the priority of the lien of the refunding mortgage shall be extended as rapidly as possible.

Bonds are not often issued under second and third mortgages except in reorganizations. So strong is the prejudice against them, that even here they have fallen into disuse. There are exceptions to this rule, but, generally speaking, second mortgage bonds cannot be sold to advantage.

CORPORATE INDORSEMENTS AND GUARANTEES

When first mortgage bonds cannot be sold, resort may be had to several methods of securing the obligations with which the desired capital is to be obtained. The purpose of each of these methods is to approximate as closely as possible the security of a first mortgage. The first of these methods is to organize subsidiary companies in the interest of the company which desires to provide the new capital. These companies issue to the parent company their bonds secured by a first lien on the property purchased or constructed, and also secured by the indorsement of the parent company. The parent company can either sell the subsidiary company's bonds direct, or can deposit them as collateral security for an issue of its debentures, unless compelled by the terms of its prior lien mortgages to deliver them to the trustees of its existing obligations. A large amount of railway mileage has been built in this manner through subsidiary companies, either because the parent company was limited in its borrowing by the terms of its mortgages, or because the laws of the State where the new lines were located required ownership by a local company. This form of financing new construction is not so common as formerly.

The use of the indorsement is still general. One of the most common uses of this method in recent years is the indorsement of bonds of terminal companies by the various railway corporations which make use of the facilities thus provided. A number of issues of bonds have been made by new or weak companies in recent years secured by the indorsement of certain prominent and wealthy individuals or firms. The most conspicuous illustration of this use of individual credit to bolster up the credit of weak companies was furnished by Mr. H. H. Rogers in his guarantee of the bonds of the Virginian Railway, and by Mr. Henry M. Flagler, on the strength of whose personal guarantee a large amount of notes were sold by the Florida & East Coast Railway Company. Another use of the guarantee is the sale of equipment notes given to such companies as the American Locomotive Company or the American Car & Foundry Company by weak railway companies, and which are sold with the indorsement of the equipment companies.

An indorsement of a corporate bond has, of course, the same form and significance as an indorsement on a promissory note. By indorsing a note, a person or corporation alike agree that in case the maker does not pay the note at maturity the indorser will pay it. Corporate guarantees are of two kinds: First, strong guarantees, and second, weak guarantees. An example of a weak guarantee is as follows:

> For value received the Great Western Power Co. hereby guarantees to the holder of the within bond the prompt and punctual payment, according to the terms thereof, of the principal of, and interest upon, the within bond, and further guarantees to the said holder that the sinking fund installments in respect to Series "A" bonds provided in the mortgage and deed of trust and in said bond referred to *shall be made in*[1] the manner and to the extent therein provided.

This guarantee is weak in the sense that it merely stipulates that the holders of the bonds of the California Electric Generating Company to which the guarantee referred, will

[1] Italics are the author's.

receive their interest and principal and will be protected in accordance with the terms of the mortgage. The Great Western Power Company does not itself formally assume the obligation, but merely agrees to assume it in case the California Electric Generating Company, which issues the bonds, fails to carry out its agreement. An example of a strong guarantee is as follows:

> For value received the St. Louis Southwestern Railway Company hereby unconditionally guarantees to the owner of the within bond the payment of the principal thereof and the interest thereon as the same matures and falls due, and hereby agrees itself to pay the said principal and interest if default in the payment thereof be made by the Terminal Company.

Here is an unconditional assumption of debt by the guarantor, and this form is preferred to that first given. An even stronger form is the following guarantee indorsed upon bonds of the New York & Westchester Lighting Company, a subsidiary of the Consolidated Gas Company of New York:

> For value received, the Consolidated Gas Co. of New York hereby assumes and agrees to pay the principal and interest of the within bond as the same shall respectively become payable.

Here is the strongest form of guarantee, the assumption by the guarantor of the obligation of paying interest and principal, assuming itself the risk of reimbursement from the treasury of the subsidiary company. Another form of guarantee provides that the guarantor shall deposit within a certain time before each interest date, with the trustee of the bonds, the amount required for the payment of that installment of interest. As a rule, the guarantee is preferred in proportion as the guarantor assumes an unconditional obligation under his indorsement. Another common form of guaranteed security is stock on which a certain rate of dividend has been guaranteed by another company. This method is mainly employed in connection with leases.

The remedy of the holders of guaranteed bonds or stock is the same as the remedy of the holder of an indorsed note, namely, a suit against the indorser for the amount remaining unpaid. The objections to this form of security are, therefore, the ordinary objections to indorsement security, namely, the necessity of suing the indorser, unless it is to his interest to protect his obligations, and the fact that there may be no limit to the amount of contingent liability which may be assumed. In case of strong companies, which have guaranteed bonds secured by mortgages on integral portions of their system, covering property which is essential to their business, guarantees are regarded as of great value. Such bonds are often sold on no other security than the indorsement, no attention being paid to the earnings of the company actually issuing the bonds.

The second objection to the guarantee as compared with the mortgage security, is more serious. When bonds are issued, secured by a mortgage, certain property is conveyed to the trustee. The purchaser of the bonds knows that when the issue authorized by that mortgage has been exhausted, no further bonds can be issued on the security of that property, unless they follow the first mortgage bonds. The whole transaction is a matter of record. The creditor knows exactly what the value of the security is. On the other hand, a company with a surplus of $1,000,000 over interest charges may place its indorsement on a series of bonds issued by other companies whose stock it has acquired. These guarantees, if the borrowing companies do not prosper, may steadily shrink in value, as the margin between the amount which the guarantor may be obliged to pay under its indorsement, and its surplus income from the stocks of its subsidiaries, is reduced. The company with a surplus of $1,000,000 may assume the contingent liability of a guarantor up to $100,000 a year, and the bonds will be good aside from the earning power of the property which directly secures them. When, however, these guarantees aggregate $600,000 or $700,000 a year, the investor must look more closely into the condition of the borrowing companies, and must place correspondingly less reliance upon the security offered by the indorsement. There are some companies, such as the American Water Works Company, which have indorsed enormous amounts of bonds, and which are continually offering additional issues with the argument that they are also secured by indorsement. So far as the value of the guarantee extends, however, it is a question whether this unlimited indorsement is not a source of weakness rather than strength.

This objection to the security of a guarantee can be easily met, however, by including in the indorsement an obligation of the guarantor to limit his contingent liability. If, for example, his surplus earnings are $500,000 a year and he assumes a contingent liability to pay $250,000, it may be provided in the indorsement that no additional guarantees will be assumed by the indorser until the surplus earnings have reached $1,000,000. By preserving a safe margin between the payments which may be required by the contingent liability, and the surplus earnings out of which these payments must be made, the security of a guarantee may closely approach the security of a mortgage.

CHAPTER XXVI

THE COLLATERAL TRUST BOND

The method of financing new construction by the sale of bonds of subsidiary companies guaranteed by the parent company is advantageous only for strong corporations. Small issues of subsidiary company bonds with the additional security of a guarantee, when the guarantor is not abundantly able to meet all these contingent obligations without calling upon the issuer of the guaranteed securities, are not popular. One of the main reasons for issuing first and refunding or first and general lien bonds is to offer the investor a large issue and a direct obligation. It is increasingly difficult to sell the bonds issued by small companies.

When it is impossible or inexpedient for a company to issue first mortgage bonds, and unless it is of the first rank, so that its guarantee carries conviction, its best method of obtaining new funds is to issue its own debenture bonds secured by the deposit of stocks and bonds of subsidiary companies to which it makes advances for construction purposes. These bonds have already been described as collateral trust bonds. The value and the salability of these bonds depends not so much upon the earnings of the subsidiary company whose securities are pledged, as upon the solvency of the company which issues the obligation. It is not usual to issue collateral trust bonds secured only by the stocks and bonds of a single company. A number of issues of subsidiary companies are usually combined to furnish security for a large issue of the parent company's bonds.

One of the first cases where this method was employed

was by the Union Pacific in 1879. In 1873, in order to protect the second mortgage lien of the government to secure these advances in aid of construction, a law was passed prohibiting the Union Pacific from increasing its bonded debt. Any additional property which it might acquire must come under the lien of this second mortgage. As a result, the Union Pacific could build no branch lines nor extensions. It was necessary to build this additional mileage through subsidiary companies. The Union Pacific advanced the money for construction out of its current earnings, receiving the capital stock and first mortgage seven per cent bonds of the construction companies. To reimburse its treasury for these advances, the Union Pacific pledged these first mortgage bonds as collateral security for an issue of $7,000,000 of six per cent bonds.[1] In 1882, a second collateral trust issue was made by the Union Pacific for a similar purpose. Other railway companies which have made large use of the collateral trust bond in aid of construction are the Missouri Pacific, the Rock Island, and the Louisville & Nashville. A collateral trust bond secured by a lien upon the first mortgage bonds of subsidiary companies gives greater security than the contingent liability of a guarantee, since it is a direct obligation of the parent company. It is, however, inferior to the lien of a first mortgage, since a foreclosure of the collateral trust mortgage places the creditor in possession of other bonds, which necessitates additional foreclosure proceedings before he can get at the property which is the object of his search.

Collateral trust mortgages contain a number of safeguards designed to preserve the value of the collateral. When the security consists of bonds, it is stipulated that no more bonds of equal rank shall be issued by the subsidiary company, even though the subsidiary company's mortgage authorizes additional issues. To this end, the company owning the stock of the subsidiary company is required

[1] Thomas Warner Mitchell in the *Quarterly Journal of Economics*, vol. xx, 1905–06, p. 443.

to deposit this stock, or a controlling interest therein, with the trustee to make sure that the directors of the subsidiary company will not exercise their right to increase the issues of the bonds, and so weaken the value of the collateral trust bonds. When the bonds of a parent company are issued to obtain funds for making advances to subsidiary companies in aid of construction, it is important to stipulate that the parent company shall secure from the subsidiary companies evidences of their indebtedness in the form of bonds secured by mortgages, and that these bonds shall be at once pledged with the trustee of the collateral trust mortgage.

Greater care is taken in the framing of collateral trust indentures to protect the value of stock collateral than is necessary in case of bond collateral. The trust indenture securing the Northern Pacific-Great Northern-Chicago, Burlington & Quincy Collateral-Trust Bonds, contains a number of precautions of this character. The railway companies which acquired by the issue of these bonds about ninety-eight per cent of the stock of the Burlington, agree with the trustee that, in case there shall be issued any additional shares of the Burlington stock, except only treasury stock reserved for bond conversion, then the railway companies will assign to the trustee ninety-eight per cent of such additional capital stock. They bind themselves not to distribute any part of the surplus of the Burlington existing on July 1, 1901, since such a distribution would weaken the value of the stock. They agree also that they will cause all necessary repairs, renewals, and replacements to be made out of the earnings of the Burlington lines; that they will not permit the execution by the Burlington of any lease of any of the railways in its system unless such lease shall be made subject to termination by the Burlington, if the shares of the stock held by the trustee shall be sold in case of any default; and finally that they will not permit the sale of any part of the property of the Burlington, unless ninety-eight per cent of the proceeds of the sale is deposited with the trustee as security for the bonds.

Collateral trust bonds differ from call loans with collateral security in that they usually contain no provision for the substitution of collateral. We have seen that mortgages securing bonds by liens on real property allow directors, with the consent of the trustee, to sell any part of the property for which they have no further use, provided only that the proceeds of this sale be reinvested in place of the property withdrawn. The security of stock or bond collateral is, however, by no means so substantial as that furnished by the pledge of real property. Especially when the bonds run for a long term, the substitution of other collateral for that originally deposited is usually considered to give too much latitude to the borrowing company.

It is, however, possible to include the privilege of substituting collateral under adequate safeguards. An illustration of this method is furnished by the mortgage securing the four per cent refunding twenty-five-year gold bonds of the Oregon Short Line Railroad Company dated December 1, 1904. These bonds were secured by the capital stock of the Northern Securities Company, the Southern Pacific Company, and the Oregon Railroad and Navigation Company. Article 6 of the indenture allows withdrawal of the pledged securities and the substitution of collateral. Withdrawal may be made up to eighty per cent of the value of these securities ascertained by appraisement at the time of their delivery to the trustee. Section 2 authorizes the substitution of the stocks of securities of railroad, steamship, or terminal companies for collateral placed under the mortgage to a value equal to the value of the securities withdrawn. The method of appraisement is for two appraisers to be appointed representing the railroad company and the trustee, respectively, and for these appraisers to choose a third whose judgment as to the value of collateral is to be final.

The collateral trust bond is employed for a variety of purposes in addition to the financing of construction by subsidiary companies. A company whose only property consists of the stocks and bonds of other companies is usually limited to the collateral trust bond. The bonds issued by the large industrial corporations organized in the form of holding companies, whose chief assets consist of the stocks of a number of subsidiaries, furnish numerous illustrations of this method. In such indentures, either the stocks of subsidiary companies can be pledged under the mortgage, or the subsidiary companies themselves, in return for funds advanced to them by the parent company, can execute their own mortgage bonds, and turn these over to the parent company to be deposited under the collateral trust indenture. The precaution usually taken is to have all the securities, both stocks and bonds, of the subsidiary companies deposited under the indenture, and to provide in the mortgage that the parent company, in return for any advances which it may make to the subsidiary companies out of the proceeds of the collateral trust bonds, shall obtain from the subsidiary companies, and shall deliver to the trustee suitable evidences of indebtedness to furnish additional security under the collateral trust mortgage. Should default occur, the holder of the collateral trust bonds comes into the possession of bonds or notes of the subsidiary companies secured by direct liens on their property.

The collateral trust bond is also employed by corporations to acquire the stock of some other company which, when pledged as security for an issue of collateral trust bonds, furnishes the means for its own purchase without seriously taxing the credit of the purchasing company. Collateral trust bonds are, as already explained, plain obligations of the issuing company. They are promissory notes which, when issued by a solvent corporation, have a value apart from any special security which may be deposited. In order to give them greater currency and value, however, the stock of a company which has been purchased may be deposited as collateral security, in this manner providing the funds for its own purchase. Familiar examples of this use of the collateral trust bond are furnished by the Great Northern-Northern Pacific, Burlington Joint 4s already referred to; also by the issue of collateral trust three and a half per cent bonds by the New York Central, in 1897 to purchase the stock of the Lake Shore & Michigan Southern, and Michigan Central Railroad Companies.

In each of these cases, the stock security placed under the collateral trust bonds of the purchasing company has produced a revenue at least equal to the interest on the bonds, so that the income accounts of the parent companies have not been drawn upon, save temporarily, to pay interest on the collateral trust bonds. The credit of the parent company is, therefore, kept intact for the issue of other debentures for other purposes. With bonds amply secured by stock collateral, the investor does not consider the obligation as a burden upon the finances of the parent company. At the same time, however, the surplus earnings of the parent company stand back of the bonds to reassure any holder who may be uncertain of the value of the collateral security. For example, the Great Northern-Northern Pacific, Burlington Joint 4s have an interest charge of $8,000,000. The Burlington pays each year $8,000,000 in dividends, and earns far more than this amount, producing a considerable surplus over all interest charges. Besides this, however, the two purchasing companies had surplus earnings in their last fiscal year over their fixed charges amounting to $37,800,000, nearly five times the interest charges on the joint 4s.

When collateral trust bonds are issued by companies whose principal assets consist of the securities pledged under the lien of the collateral trust indenture, then the investor looks mainly to the value of the collateral, and the price of the bond fluctuates with the fortunes of the company whose stock furnishes its sole security. An illustration of a bond with no other security than stock is furnished by the collateral trust 4s issued by the Chicago, Rock Island, Pacific Railroad Company of Iowa, a company whose sole assets consist of the stock of the Chicago, Rock Island, Pacific Rail*way* Company of Iowa. During 1909, the price of the bonds showed an extreme fluctuation of nine and one half per cent. The bonds are highly speculative, since their interest must come solely from the dividends paid by the Chicago, Rock Island and Pacific Rail*way* Company. During the same year, however, the Burlington Joint 4s, whose interest absorbs a much greater proportion of the dividends on the Burlington stock than that proportion of the Rock Island Railway dividends which is required to pay interest on the collateral trust bonds which its stock secures, fluctuated only four per cent. The smaller fluctuations of the Burlington Joint 4s as compared with the Rock Island bonds show the high standing which collateral trust bonds issued by strong companies possess. At the same time, as already shown, unless the company issuing the collateral trust bonds secured by dividend-paying stock is obliged to make up the difference between the interest on the bonds and the dividends on the stock securing them, its credit is not seriously weakened by the issue of collateral trust bonds.

When such advances have to be made, however, as for a time was necessary in the case of the Atlantic Coast Line —Louisville & Nashville collateral 5s—the attention of the investor is directed to the nature of the collateral trust bonds, the direct obligation of the issuing company, altogether apart from the stock security underlying it. The existence of collateral trust bonds in such an event operates to subtract from the borrowing power of the issuing company, perhaps more than might be expected from the extent of this deficit between the dividends on the collateral stock and the interest on the bonds. The liability of the issuing company is then regarded in much the same light as the contingent liability of a guarantee when the borrowing company is not earning its interest and must call upon the indorser of its bonds to make up the deficit.

CHAPTER XXVII

BONDS SECURED BY THE ASSIGNMENT OF A LEASE

ANOTHER method of securing capital in the face of a closed first mortgage is by the use of the lease as security. The detailed discussion of the lease is postponed to a later chapter. At this point it is sufficient to define the lease as a contract by which the possession of property is transferred by the owner, known as the lessor, to some other person or corporation, known as the lessee, the title of the property remaining in the lessor but the lessee being allowed its possession and use under certain conditions set down in the lease.

The lease is largely used by railroad companies to borrow money for the purchase of equipment under a form of obligation, known as the car trust certificate, by which the property acquired serves as the security for the bonds, and which are also the direct obligations of the railroad company. This method of borrowing may be illustrated by the issue of the Lehigh Valley Car Trust Certificates, Series G. A syndicate, headed by E. T. Stotesbury, a leading Philadelphia banker, was organized to purchase and pay for a large number of passenger and freight cars. E. T. Stotesbury then executed an agreement whereby, in return for certain payments, and on the basis of certain covenants and stipulations, he leased to the railroad company from October 25, 1902, to August 1, 1910, the equipment which he had purchased, and which is carefully enumerated and described. The Lehigh Valley Railroad Company, for its part, in return for being allowed the use of the cars, agreed to pay $203,398.80 before the equipment was delivered to them and half yearly the following sums: First, a sum equal to $2\frac{1}{4}$ per cent on $800,000 to be reduced from time to time by $2\frac{1}{4}$ per cent on money paid by the railroad company in reduction of $800,000. Second, a sum equal to all expenses incurred by the lessor in enforcing the covenants and terms of the lease. Third, a sum equal to the taxes which the lessor might be liable to pay. Fourth, yearly the sum of $100,000, making in all eight annual payments of $100,000 each.

The deferred payments were evidenced by equipment notes the substance of which is as follows:

> The Lehigh Valley Railroad Company hereby acknowledges itself to be indebted to the bearer, or registered owner hereof, in the sum of $1,000 with interest at the rate of $4\frac{1}{2}$ per cent per annum. This certificate is one of a series of 800 for $1,000 each issued under the terms of a lease bearing date of the 25th day of October, 1902, between E. T. Stotesbury and the Lehigh Valley Railroad Company.[1]

In addition to these payments, the railroad company agrees with the lessor to keep the cars in good repair, to replace any which may be destroyed from any cause, to mark the name of the owner plainly upon the cars, and to furnish him each year a list of the equipment, not to sublet the equipment, and, in case of default under any of the provisions of the lease, to deliver to the lessor the equipment to which the lease relates. The lessor on his part agrees that after the payments have been completed, he will upon the payment by the railroad company of the additional sum of one dollar, transfer to the railroad company, as its absolute property, all the railroad cars held under the lease. The rental referred to in this agreement consists of three parts: First, a sum of cash which is usually considered to represent the expenses and profits of the syndicate acquiring the equipment; second, a sum which represents the purchase

[1] Only the essential portions of the Car Trust Certificate are given.

price of the equipment payable in installments; and third, interest on the unpaid installments of the purchase price.

E. T. Stotesbury, having now purchased the equipment, and having leased it to the Lehigh Valley, assigns the agreement as security for the certificates evidencing the deferred payments under the lease, to the Girard Trust Company substantially as follows:

> First, that the said E. T. Stotesbury hereby assigns unto the Girard Trust Company as trustee for the holders of the certificates hereinafter set forth, all the right, title and interest of said E. T. Stotesbury in and to a certain indenture of lease bearing even date herewith made by the said E. T. Stotesbury to the Lehigh Valley Railroad Company.
>
> Second, the said trustee covenants and agrees that it will certify and deliver to Drexel & Company (*for whom Stotesbury is acting*)[1] for distribution to the several subscribers to the said Lehigh Valley Car Trust Fund eight hundred certificates in the following form (*given above*),[1] which certificates shall be delivered in amounts and at times corresponding to the value and the time of delivery of the various lots of said railroad cars by the said E. T. Stotesbury to the Lehigh Valley Railroad Company. All of which certificates, when and as issued, shall be entitled to the security of all such railroad cars previously and subsequently delivered by said Edward T. Stotesbury to the Railroad Company under the terms of said indenture of lease of even date herewith.

These certificates were numbered consecutively from one to eight hundred and were payable in eight installments beginning August 1, 1903.

The agreement for assignment of lease, to which the Lehigh Valley Railroad Company is made a party, provides in detail for the protection of the holders of these certificates by the trustee. In case of any default in the payments under the lease, or the breach of any other covenant by the railroad

[1] Italics are the author's.

company, the trustee is authorized to retake possession of the cars, and to hold, or lease, or to otherwise dispose of all or any part of the equipment in such manner as it may deem beneficial, and also to recover from the company, for future accruing rent, any deficit which may remain after the sale or lease of the equipment, and the application of the proceeds to the claims of the certificate holders.

From the foregoing, the strong position of equipment trust obligations is evident. They are, in fact, debenture bonds of the railroad, with the additional security of a first mortgage upon railway equipment. They have the further advantage, explained in a former chapter in connection with the discussion of serial bonds—that their margin of security constantly increases, since the equipment is in existence at the time the last bond matures. Equipment trust obligations usually bear higher rates of interest than first mortgage bonds issued for long terms. They also yield higher returns to the investor than first mortgage bonds, while the security which they offer is practically perfect.

The Guarantee Trust Company of New York, in a circular dealing with the advantages of the equipment trust securities, summarizes these advantages as follows:

"The equipment of a railroad corporation is essential to its operation. It is the tool with which the railroad handles its business. If an individual mechanic becomes bankrupt, his tools are ordinarily exempt from seizure on the ground that possession of the tools is necessary for the mechanic to obtain his livelihood and ultimately satisfy his creditors. In the same way the courts, both State and Federal, have ruled that the necessary equipment of a railroad must be preserved for the Receiver of a bankrupt railroad in order to enable him to operate the railroad; and have generally placed the charges of principal and interest of equipment obligations upon an equality with charges for wages, materials and other operating expenses, and in priority to interest of even first mortgage bonds."

The record of equipment obligations issued by railroad companies which have subsequently gone into bankruptcy confirms this favorable judgment. Without exception the principal and interest on equipment bonds have been paid in full even by companies where all other bonds were reduced in interest or principal. This strong position of equipment bonds in bankruptcy is due to the fact that their security is not the property of the bankrupt corporation. The cars and locomotives which they represent are the property of another who has leased his equipment to the railroad company on certain definite conditions. Unless these conditions are met, the equipment can be hauled off the company's lines and sold. Property which is owned by the company can, as we shall see in a later chapter, be put out of reach of creditors, within the protection of the court. The court, however, can have no jurisdiction over property not belonging to the bankrupt corporation. The receiver, no matter if he defaults on the first mortgage bonds, must pay the interest on the equipment trust obligations.

The equipment trust bond represents the most familiar use of the lease as a means of obtaining new capital. Another method often employed is to organize a subsidiary company in the interest of a company desiring to obtain capital. This subsidiary company constructs or purchases the equipment or other property needed by the parent company, issuing for the purpose its own first mortgage bonds which may be guaranteed by the parent company. The property is then leased to the parent company for a rental sufficient to pay the interest on the bonds and to retire their principal after a term of years. In some cases, the rental is made sufficient to pay dividends on the stock of the subsidiary company. After the bonds of the subsidiary company have been retired, the property, upon the payment of a nominal sum, passes to the parent company. For the greater portion of bondholders, it is customary for the subsidiary company, in such a case, to assign the lease, out of which the money to pay the interest on the bond must come, to the trustee. If the rental is not paid, then the interest cannot be paid, the bonds are in default, and their holders can bring foreclosure proceedings. The trustee can sue the lessee company either upon its obligation of guarantee, in case it has indorsed the bonds of the subsidiary company, or under its contract of lease.

A third use of the lease as security is by the lessee company. The lease, being a contract for the use of certain property on the payment of certain stipulated sums, may be expected to show a surplus over the amount of the rentals. This surplus makes the leasehold interest, the value of the annual profits of the lessee, a valuable right which can be pledged by the lessee like any other thing of value as security for bonds. This form of security was employed by the Interborough Company which pledged its 999 year lease of the Manhattan Railway and its subway lease from New York City as the main security of $55,000,000 of mortgage bonds dated November 1, 1907. The Interborough, from the operation of these leased lines, in 1909 showed a large surplus over rentals, so that its leasehold interest represented a valuable property, furnishing ample security for a bond issue. It is unusual, however, to find leases showing such large earnings. While the leasehold interests are frequently conveyed as supplementary security to trustees, they are not often given a prominent position as a basis of bond issues.

CHAPTER XXVIII

CONSOLIDATION OF CORPORATIONS

THE consolidation of corporations offers a means of obtaining new capital without the necessity of providing funds for construction or purchase. It also enables companies to abolish or restrict competition and in this way to increase profits. In 1901, the Reading Company desired to obtain permanent possession of sufficient terminal facilities in New York. The Central Railroad of New Jersey possessed these facilities. The consolidation of the two companies gave the Reading the use of the valuable terminals of the Central Railroad of New Jersey in perpetuity. Numerous illustrations of the advantages of consolidation in restricting competition are furnished by the industrial trusts. These advantages have been fully discussed in a preceding chapter.

The methods of uniting corporations by consolidation are three: First, the merger; second, the purchase by one company of a controlling stock interest in another; third, the lease.

When a merger of corporations is accomplished, one or more of the companies concerned loses its identity in another. Suppose the case of two gas companies—A and B—competing for the business of the same town. A sufficient amount of the stock of B has been required in the interest of A, to control the sale of its assets and its dissolution. Two methods are available for merging B with A. A may offer its stock or bonds or cash in exchange for the stock of B, having acquired the amount of stock which by the laws of the state or the charter of B is necessary to assent to the disposition of B's assets. The directors of B now sell the property of that company to A. If all the stock of B has been acquired, the consideration need be only nominal. A now controls all the stock of B, and secures the dissolution of B, in the manner provided by law. The second method is for A to purchase the property of B, at its market value in securities or cash. B has then in its treasury the proceeds of the sale. B is then dissolved and the directors distribute its assets to its stockholders.

The method of merger is seldom adopted. There is usually some advantage to a company acquiring control of another company, in continuing the corporate existence of its subsidiary. Companies which have been in existence a sufficient length of time to establish a reputation have a certain good-will value in connection with their name which would terminate if their corporate existence were ended. Valuable privileges may also be lost if the method of merger is adopted. For example, the Boston Consolidated Gas Company, where the price of gas is fixed by law at eighty cents per thousand feet, owns stock of the Quincy Gas Light Company, the Chelsea Gas Light Company, and the East Boston Gas Light Company. In Chelsea and East Boston, where the population is not so dense as in Boston, the legal price of gas is $1 per thousand feet. In Boston the cost of distributing gas is less and the profit even at the lower price is greater. If the large lighting companies were merged with the consolidated company, the eighty cent rate would apply throughout the consolidated property. It is desirable, therefore, to maintain the corporate existence of these outside companies in order to secure the $1 rate in the suburbs. In consolidations of street railway companies possessing perpetual franchises, care is taken to preserve the corporate existence of the companies owning these valuable franchises.[1] There is no serious disadvantage in maintaining separate existences for corporations controlled by other companies. The salary ac-

[1] Lecture by F. E. Snow to Harvard School of Business Administration, Jan. 15, 1909.

counts of the subsidiary companies are nominal and the operation of their property can be merged if desired by leasing their property to the main system, or by operating them as divisions or departments of the parent company.

The second method of consolidation is that of stock ownership. One operating company can purchase the stock of another, giving in exchange cash or securities, or a company can be organized for the purpose of holding the stocks of other companies which by this device are brought under centralized control. How much stock is it necessary for a company to acquire to control another? The rule of law is that, in the absence of a provision allowing stockholders to accumulate their votes on one or two directors, thus insuring to the minority representation on the board, a bare majority of the stock can elect, if the owners wish, all the directors. While the rights of the majority are seldom pushed to this extreme, yet the holders of a majority of the stock always demand, with propriety, a substantial majority of the board of directors. There is no general reason, therefore, for acquiring ing all the stock of a corporation in order to control it.

Where the interest of the parent company may be opposed to the interest of the subsidiary company, there is no alternative, if it is desired to maintain the identity of the subsidiary, save for the parent company to acquire all of its stock, or to see that its control is held in the parent company's interest. Many of the consolidations of manufacturing concerns have resulted in the closing of badly located or otherwise unprofitable mills in order to concentrate the production in plants which are better equipped or more favorably situated. This policy makes for the interest of the parent company. It is, however, directly opposed to the interests of minority stockholders of the corporations owning the plants whose operation is discontinued. If their business were to be closed up in this manner, the minority stockholders would undoubtedly appeal to the courts which would give them effective protection against the depreciation in the value of their shares which would follow the suspension of dividends on their stocks. To avoid trouble of this character, it is usual to secure all the stock of the company to be consolidated, in case this can be purchased at reasonable figures.

If all the stock cannot be acquired, and in case the subsidiary company is to be exploïted for the benefit of the interests which control it, the method which has been employed in some cases is to guarantee a dividend on the minority stock of the subsidiary. This plan was followed by the Carnegie Steel Company in 1901 in guaranteeing four per cent on the minority stock of the Pittsburg, Bessemer & Lake Erie Railroad Company, whose principal freight, since its organization in 1897, had been ore destined for the Carnegie furnaces. The minority stockholders of the railroad company complained that their failure to receive dividends was due to the fact that the owners of the majority of their stock of the Carnegie Steel Company received such low rates on its ore that the railroad company was unable to make a profit. In order to quiet this criticism, the Carnegie Steel Company, through a subsidiary company, the Bessemer and Lake Erie, guaranteed a dividend on the stock, leaving itself free to fix rates as low as it thought best.

An exception to the rule that all the stock of a company, control of which is desired by another company, should be acquired, is furnished by large public corporations, such as railroad companies, where the object of the consolidation is merely to secure uniformity in rates or to arrange interchanges of traffic which will be mutually profitable. Here there is no temptation to the exploitation of one company by another, and the minority stockholders have no reason to feel aggrieved. Where the stock of a company is widely scattered, moreover, a controlling interest may be much less than a majority. The Pennsylvania Railroad Company for seven years exercised a potent influence in the directorates of the Baltimore & Ohio, the Chesapeake & Ohio, and the Norfolk & Western. At no time, however, did it own a majority of the stock of any of these companies. Any contest for control, however, during the period of the Pennsylvania's influence, would have been hopeless, owing to the control of the administrative machinery of these companies in the interest of their principal stockholder, and to the advantage which this control would have been given these officers in soliciting voting proxies.

Having settled upon the amount of stock required for control, our next question concerns the method by which this stock can be acquired. Stock may be purchased for cash, or with the stock or bonds of the purchasing company, or with stock trust certificates on which dividends are guaranteed by the company acquiring the stock. The consideration which will be offered and accepted in the acquisition of a stock control can be viewed from the standpoint of the purchasing company, and also from the standpoint of the individual stockholder. A purchasing company, if its surplus over its regular disbursements is substantial, can safely offer bonds or their cash equivalent to holders of stock which it desires to purchase. Other things being equal, an offer of bonds is desirable. If there is no identical interest represented in both companies to be considered, if the purchaser is in a strong financial position, and especially if there is a prospect that the stock purchased will become much more valuable in the hands of the purchaser, the method of purchase by bonds is likely to be adopted. The stockholders who receive bonds for their holdings surrender all right to future participation in the profits of their company over the amount guaranteed on their bonds. The purchasing company, by giving them a secured claim, succeeds to their right to the increase in profits over the amount paid in interest.

In some cases these purchases of stock with bonds have proven immensely profitable. In 1898 the New York Central purchased $45,000,000 out of $50,000,000 of the capital stock of the Lake Shore, Michigan & Southern, giving in exchange its 3½ per cent bonds at the rate of $200 in bonds for $100 in stock. The seven per cent dividends on the Lake Shore stock represented the equivalent of the interest paid on the bonds issued in payment. From 1899 to 1903, the Lake Shore paid seven per cent, from 1904 to 1906 inclusive, eight per cent, in 1907 twelve per cent, in 1908 fourteen per cent, and in 1909 twelve per cent. The purchase of the Lake Shore stock has proven most fortunate for the New York Central. Indeed, had it not been for the large profits made on this purchase, the Central would have had much difficulty in maintaining its five per cent dividends during 1909. The joint purchase of the Burlington by the Great Northern and the Northern Pacific has also been profitable, although the purchasing companies have not as yet taken any direct profit into their income accounts out of the large surplus earnings which the Burlington is showing over the dividends necessary to pay interest on the bonds issued to purchase this stock. There is the more reason to adopt the method of purchasing stock with the bonds of the purchaser, if the stock desired is a dividend payer, since then a substantial portion of the interest on the bonds can be provided out of the stock purchased.

When any doubt exists, however, concerning the ability of the purchasing company to meet the interest on a sufficient bond issue to buy the stock which it desires, prudence demands that stock be employed. Cumulative preferred stock gives almost the security of bonds, with the added advantage of a higher return. At the same time, the failure to pay dividends on such stock does not work the bankruptcy of the company. The United States Rubber Company in a circular to its stockholders recommending the purchase of stock of the Rubber Goods Manufacturing Company, stated the argument against bonds and in favor of preferred stock as follows:

"If no better means were provided, it might be advisable to make such purchase by the use of collateral trust notes, but it occurred to the management that rather than subject their stock to the prior fixed charges of such collateral trust notes, the stockholders might prefer to provide the means of purchase by an increased issue of stock, the preferred stock of the Rubber Goods Manufacturing Company to be acquired by an issue of new first preferred stock of the United States Company in amount equal to that of the Manufacturing Company, and with dividends limited to eight per cent annually."

Even where bonds can safely be employed, the importance placed upon preserving the credit of the purchasing company influences the use of its stock to acquire other stock. The New York, New Haven & Hartford, for example, at the time of its acquisition of the Boston & Maine, could undoubtedly have purchased this stock with bonds. The Boston & Maine stockholders had been in receipt of a seven per cent dividend for many years, and had no reasonable expectation of any higher return. It is not to be doubted that they would have accepted the debenture bonds of the New York, New Haven & Hartford secured by their own stock quite as readily as they received the stock of the purchasing company. By acquiring the Boston & Maine stock with its stock, however, the New Haven & Hartford maintained its credit unimpaired. Any mistake in its calculations as to the increased value which association with the Boston & Maine would confer upon that company's stock, would not damage the credit of the purchasing company, but would fall upon its stockholders.

From the standpoint of the stockholder, the acceptance of an offer for his stock may be influenced by various considerations. If he is not satisfied with the prospects of his own investment, there is little trouble in inducing him to accept a fair offer. For example, at the time of the formation of the United States Steel Corporation, the Carnegie Steel Company threatened with its competition every one of the large industrials whose stockholders were asked to exchange their holdings for United States Steel stock. The advantages of eliminating this competition, and of being associated in the same company with the strong Carnegie Steel Company, were sufficient to induce a practical unanimous acceptance of the offer of the United States Steel Corporation to the stockholders of the separate companies.

If, however, the stockholder is receiving good dividends and is not apprehensive of their discontinuance, strong inducements are usually required to persuade him to sell. Instances are not lacking where stockholders have given up dividend paying stock in return for stock which paid them nothing. A case in point is that of the Atlantic Transport Company, whose stockholders went into the International Mercantile Marine Company, exchanging their stock, on which they had been receiving regular dividends, for the stock of a large company on which they have received nothing. With a weak company or a new company offering to purchase, and especially when a corporation is organized with the sole purpose of acquiring the stocks of other companies, unless there are strong reasons urging consolidation, and unless bonds are not available, stock will not, as a rule, prove attractive. The stockholders demand either collateral trust bonds secured by the stock purchased, and with the provision in the indenture that in case of default the bonds can be employed to purchase the stock, or they demand cumulative preferred stock bearing a high rate of dividend. By the stockholders of the strong companies comprising the trusts, a bonus of common stock in addition was usually exacted.

As a compromise between the stock and the bond, a company purchasing stock may employ the stock trust certificate. In 1909, for example, the Minneapolis, St. Paul & Sault Ste. Marie Railroad Company acquired most of the preferred stock of the Wisconsin Central with its leased line stock certificates secured by a deposit of the stock purchased, on which four per cent is guaranteed for ninety-nine years. These stock certificates do not differ essentially from a collateral trust bond. In case of default, the holders of the certificates receive back the stock from the trustee and can sue for unpaid dividends. The obligation of the certificate is, however, a contingent obligation, and on that account is more acceptable to the stockholders of the purchasing company.

No matter what form of consideration is offered for the stock, the acceptance of the offer is not certain. Some stockholders will always be found to demand cash for their holdings, and some there are who will not sell at any price. This situation necessitates the usual employment of the underwriting syndicate in such transactions, which guarantees the provision of the cash required, and, in some cases, guarantees the delivery of the amount of stock necessary. The official circular announcing the joint offer of the Great Northern and the Northern Pacific to purchase the stock of the Chicago, Burlington & Quincy stated that "The purchasers will pay cash instead of bonds to an amount not exceeding in the aggregate $50,000,000 to those shareholders who shall prefer to receive payment partly in cash; and J. P. Morgan & Company, as managers of a syndicate, have undertaken to provide such cash, and to take therefor such bonds at par and accrued interest. You are accordingly offered the privilege of selling your stock at $200 per share, payable wholly in the four per cents described above, or in bonds to the amount of $160 and cash to the amount of $40."

Another precaution usually in such offers is to make the offer contingent upon its acceptance by a certain percentage of the stockholders to whom it is made. The offer just referred to was for not less than two thirds of the stock of the Burlington. When the syndicate guarantees the delivery of a certain amount of stock, a buying campaign is usually the preliminary feature of the transaction. Preceding the purchase of the Burlington stock, and also preceding the Rock Island consolidation, the stocks of these companies showed a large increase in value, owing, it was believed, to the operations of the syndicates interested in promoting the consolidation. The purchasing company can, of course, take no official part in this buying campaign, however essential though it may be to the execution of its designs. The company would not be justified in using its funds in buying stock for which it might have no use. The profits of syndicates under these circumstances, although severely criticised, have been defended on the ground that in no other way could the delivery of the amount of stock required be insured than by allowing the syndicate to make what profit they could in purchasing the stock below the figure at which, as they are informed, the company for which they are acting is prepared to purchase it.

CHAPTER XXIX

THE HOLDING COMPANY

THE holding company is a corporation organized for the purpose of acquiring the stocks and other securities of other corporations. These securities are acquired either by direct exchange of its own stocks and bonds, or by their sale for cash which is used to purchase the securities desired. The ownership of the stocks of various companies gives to the holding company the right to elect their boards of directors and to completely dominate their policy, thus accomplishing a combination between them which is as perfect as though the different corporations had merged their existence in that of the company which has acquired a controlling interest in their stocks.

Holding companies are formed both for legal and financial reasons. The primary purpose of forming a holding company is to effect a combination of allied enterprises which cannot be accomplished by the use of any one of the corporations which it is intended to include. The legalization of consolidation has, in most states, been deferred until recent years. If corporations are organized under the laws of different states, there is no method by which they can be directly consolidated. We have already referred to the formation of the trusts. These companies have been generally organized by means of holding companies formed under the laws of the State of New Jersey. The conditions out of which this device for consolidating competing enterprises developed will show in detail the principal legal reason for the use of the holding company.

Many attempts had been made before 1898 to lessen the recognized evils of competition. These attempts had usually taken the form of pools, many of which, especially in the iron and steel trades, were organized during the last industrial depression. A pool is a voluntary association of sellers who place the marketing of their product under some central control or general restriction. The primary object of such agreements is to secure profitable prices, either directly or by means of payments from a central treasury, to the members of the association. The methods by which these profitable prices have been secured are in general as follows: (1) The output of the mills included in the association is restricted, so that prices can be advanced by the limitation of supply; and (2) the buyer is held to the regular quotations, and is unable, by playing off one competitor against another, to obtain special concessions. The pool may go further than the regulation of prices and output; it may secure favorable terms on material purchased; it may deal as an association with railroads to obtain such concessions as are granted to large shippers, and it may assist its members in dealing with organized labor. As a general proposition, however, the purpose of a pool is to regulate production and control prices, leaving the details of management to the separate companies.

The pool is usually organized with a central governing or advisory body which conducts all routine business, and receives and distributes the funds of the organization. A matter of such importance as a change in prices would generally be decided at a meeting of all the members of the association, or by some executive committee composed of the larger manufacturers. Within these lines, the pool has assumed a variety of forms.

The Bessemer Steel Pool, which was organized in 1896, furnishes an illustration. This organization included the majority of the producers of crude steel and finished material in the Central West. Every mill was given a percentage allotment which it was allowed to sell—say, 500,000 tons, or one seventh of the total estimated output of the association.

At the end of each month the shipments from all the mills were reported to the officers of the pool. If any mill was found to have exceeded its percentage allotment, it was required to pay into the pool treasury $2 per ton of such excess, while an equivalent was paid out of the treasury to those who did not ship their allotment. For example, if the mill which was allotted 500,000 tons sold 700,000 tons, while the sales of another mill fell 200,000 tons short of its allotment, it would receive out of the pool treasury the amount which Mill No. 1 would pay in—viz., $400,000. The existence of this penalty operated to prevent price cutting among the members of the pool. In the Wire Nail Association, which held control of the nail market during 1895 and 1896, the central office fixed prices and assigned to each producer his share of the output, which it was believed could be marketed at the price agreed upon. It often happened in the management of a pool that the output of the association would be produced by a few of the best-equipped or best-situated plants, the owners of the idle plants being paid a certain rental to keep out of business.

The essential weakness of this form of organization is its inability to enforce its agreements. The necessity of voluntary assent on the part of every member of the association, the liberty of each to withdraw on short notice, and the difficulty of establishing relations of mutual confidence among competitors, all unite to emphasize this defect. The members of a pool have long since formed the habit of closely scrutinizing the moves of those in the same business, and even a small misunderstanding often creates a feeling of mutual distrust and apprehension which work the destruction of harmony and the final dissolution of the organization.

The successful management of a pool is peculiarly difficult during a period of business depression, when business at remunerative prices is hard to get. Strong producers at such a time are suspected of attempts to obtain more than their allotted share of orders by methods which are contrary to the spirit, if not the letter, of the pool agreement. For example, the Bessemer Steel Pool, above referred to, originally applied only to the tonnage of steel billets, ingots, bars, or slabs. The steel which was rolled into merchantable shapes did not count in the allotment. Some of the large producers took advantage of this fact to market as much as possible of their output in the form of finished material, by this method of indirection far exceeding the limits of their allotment, and they could not be penalized for so doing. Such offenses against the pool agreements made their permanent continuance impossible.

The following quotation from the *Iron Age* of December 10, 1896, shows the usual fate of these associations and the results which follow their dissolution: "The Billet Pool, or Bessemer Steel Association of the United States . . . is now in session. . . . The meeting promises to be a stormy one, as there is considerable ill feeling against certain concerns who are charged with having violated the pool agreement. The pool was practically dissolved as soon as the resignation of the Bellaire Steel Company was in the hands of the secretary. There has been an open market on Billets, Sheet and Tin-plate Bars since Saturday morning, and a scramble for business on the part of some mills. Probably 25,000 tons of Sheet Bars have been sold this week at very low prices, the deliveries running up to the close of 1897. There have also been considerable sales of Billets and Tin-plate Bars at low prices."

The prices which follow the dissolution of a pool, when confidence has been destroyed, and when manufacturers are making concessions to secure business, are often even lower than the low prices which had brought the producers together. Before the dissolution of a rail pool, in February, 1897, the price of steel rails at Chicago was $27.50 per ton. Owing to the dissatisfaction of the Lackawanna Iron and Steel Company with its allotment of seventeen per cent of the total output, and its consequent withdrawal from the association, and owing to the demand of the Illinois Steel Company for all territory west of Pittsburg, the pool was disrupted. Steel rails were immediately offered by the Carnegie Company for delivery at Chicago at $17 per ton, a reduction of $10.50 from the pool price. In 1895, for six months before the organization of this pool, the price of rails averaged $21 per ton. After the dissolution of the pool, the price did not again reach this figure until January, 1899. The breakdowns of pooling agreements in the steel trade during the period 1892–98 occurred with such periodical regularity that large buyers were accustomed to wait for the dissolution before making their purchases. After the break in the rail pool in February, 1897, the Eastern sales resulting from the reduction in price amounted to 200,000 tons. The Illinois Steel Company in the West booked orders amounting to $5,000,000. The railroads hastened to load up the rail mills with large orders, often for delivery eighteen months in the future.

Not only were the pool agreements unstable, but their regulation of prices was frequently very foolish. The determination of the policy of a pool is, in most cases, a question of majority rule, and the majority of producers in any trade are unlikely to be possessed of a broad grasp of business situations, or to be able to see further than the immediate future. When they found themselves in control of the supply, the various associations frequently raised prices to figures which seriously interfered with demand and which stimulated immediate and general competition. The policy of the nail pool above referred to offers a good illustration of this tendency to extortion. In the face of a general decline in prices, and a severe depression affecting every important industry, the price of a keg of wire nails was increased from 87 cents to $2.55, a rise of almost 200 per cent, and this high price was maintained for six months.

The *Iron Age* characterized this policy as follows:

"Looking at the matter even from the manufacturer's standpoint, it would seem the part of wisdom to have put the price of nails at a reasonable figure rather than attempt to maintain a price which in the very nature of things must be temporary, and may, perhaps, end in disaster. Only those in close touch with the trade are aware of the influence which the policy of the association has in encouraging the establishment of new plants, whose competition must be troublesome, while at the same time it invites the importation of foreign nails. . . . The trade are aware that the present price of nails is abnormally high as a result of agreement between the manufacturers—so high, in fact, that it is constantly under suspicion. The trade will doubtless continue to limit their purchases to their imperative requirements so long as nails are held at their present figures."

Pooling agreements among manufacturing competitors are inherently defective. They have no firm basis in mutual confidence. They usually result in such an unreasonable increase of prices as to check consumption and stimulate competition. In few cases have they been productive of more than a temporary advantage in profits to their members.

The "Trust" movement of the eighties promised a more satisfactory restriction of competition. In this form of organization, agreement among manufacturers as to prices and output was secured by depositing the stocks of the constituent companies with trustees in exchange for trust certificates. These entitled the holders to such dividends as might be declared on the stocks, and also empowered them to vote for the trustees in the same manner as the stockholders of a corporation elect their directors. The trust certificates, moreover, could be dealt in on the stock exchanges in the same way as the certificates issued by the voting trust of a corporation. The trustees, being in control of the stock of the several corporations included in the trust, directed the management of these companies, and secured a uniform policy upon prices and output. Permanence of control was secured by making the transfer of stock to the trustees, except by the formal dissolution of the trust, as provided for in the articles of association, irrevocable.

The trust, so far as it included former competitors, furnished a more satisfactory restriction of competition than the pool. It was open to fewer objections; its organization was permanent; its government was centralized, responsible, and representative. The control of the constituent corporations by the central organization—the trustees—was complete, for the trustees elected the board of directors of each of the constituent companies. Because it was permanent and centralized, the trust pursued a more enlightened policy as to prices than the pool. The Standard Oil Trust made a considerable reduction in the price of refined petroleum, and the Sugar Trust, although for some years in practical control of the market, did no more than to restore prices to a living basis. The Whisky Trust attempted to charge excessive prices, but the complete failure of its attempt, owing to the growth of competition, justified the wisdom of the more conservatively managed organizations. The Cotton Oil, Linseed Oil, and Lead Trust showed no disposition to practice extortion upon the consumers of these products. The trust, as a device for the control of competition, was satisfactory. Its legal position, however, was inherently defective.

Beginning with the Granger agitation against the railroads in 1870, there had grown up throughout the United States a pronounced sentiment against monopoly, understanding by monopoly any attempt on the part of a railroad or manufacturing corporation to increase rates or prices by reason of its control of a particular market. The laws of most of the states forbid monopoly. Many state constitutions contain similar provisions. In 1890, sixteen states, either in their constitutions or by statute, prohibited any combination in restraint of trade; and the common law, which was generally applicable throughout the states, also forbade any combination of this nature. The antitrust law of Missouri, for example, prohibited any "pool, trust, agreement, combination, confederation, or understanding with any other corporation, partnership, individual, or any other person or association of persons, to regulate or fix the price of any article of manufacture." In 1890, Congress passed the Sherman

Antitrust Act, which declared that "every contract, combination in the form of trust, or otherwise, or conspiracy in restraint of trade or commerce among the several states or with foreign nations, is hereby declared to be illegal." This legislation was backed up by a vigilant public opinion rancorously hostile to large corporations. It was not to be expected that the trusts would long survive in such an unfriendly atmosphere.

The pool was also specifically designated by most of these statutes as an unlawful combination, but the pool was a secret agreement whose details were not a matter of record and against which it was difficult to secure evidence. The Addystone Pipe and Tube Company is the most conspicuous case of the dissolution of a pool by legal process, and here the evidence against the organization was only secured through information given by a disaffected stenographer. That such pools existed was common knowledge, but to obtain conclusive evidence was difficult.

The trust, however, which was a permanent pool, and which was expected to realize the benefits of the pool while avoiding its mistakes, lay open to attack. The trust agreements were matters of record. Their organizations were made under the usual legal forms, and the details of these organizations could not be concealed. The trustees could not refuse to disclose their authority for issuing the trust certificates which were dealt in on the exchanges. Any stockholder could enforce his right to examine the constitution and working of the trust which held his property. Neither could the fact be concealed that these corporations, whose identity and active life had been preserved, were, under the trust agreement, no longer masters of their own actions. They had surrendered their delegated powers to the trustees. A perfect "combination in restraint of trade" had been effected, and in view of the manifold statutes prohibiting these self-evident combinations, the dissolution of such combinations waited only for an attack upon their right to exist.

The attack came in 1890, when the Attorney-General of New York brought suit against the North River Sugar Refining Company under the common law. The case was decided against the company, not only on the ground as stated in the opinion of the Circuit Court, that the North River Sugar Refining Company was a combination . . . "the tendency of which is to prevent competition in its broad and general sense and to control, and thus at will enhance, prices to the detriment of the public, . . . but because the corporation, entering the trust, had exceeded the powers of its charter. The defendant had disabled itself from exercising its functions and employing its franchise as it was intended it should by the act under which it was incorporated, and had, by the action which was taken, placed itself in complete subordination to another and different organization to be used for an unlawful purpose, detrimental and injurious to the public. This was a subversion of the object for which the company was created, and it authorized the Attorney-General to maintain and prosecute this action to vacate and annul its charter." The Standard Oil Trust was also declared illegal on similar grounds by the Supreme Court of Ohio in 1892.

The result of these suits showed that even without the new menace of the Federal antitrust law the legal position of the trust had become impossible. The states had prohibited all combinations in restraint of trade. The corporation is the creation of the state, and the state can revoke the powers which it has granted when these powers are exceeded or unlawfully exercised. Certain corporations had combined into trusts in order to limit competition—e. g., to restrain trade. These corporations had exceeded their powers, they had violated the laws of the states which had created them, and their charters were therefor forfeited. Unless some new device could be discovered by which the hardships of competition could be alleviated, the pool whose existence, though illegal, could be partially concealed, and which was ordinarily safe from legal attack, whenever regulation was required, must still be employed. Its defects were generally admitted, and it often aggravated the very evils which it was designed to cure; but if the trust was to be forbidden, the pool seemed to be the only form of combination possible.

In 1892 the Standard Oil Trust solved the problem presented by the illegality of the trust agreements by the application of the principle of community of interest to the managment of its various constituent companies. This trust was dissolved, and the stock was returned to the holders of the trust certificates, which were then canceled. A majority of the stock of each company, however, was retained by nine men who had been prominent in the affairs of the trust, and unanimity of action was in this way secured. Such an arrangement is always open to objection. It depends for its success upon the maintenance of harmony among the members of a group of individuals, and upon the tensile strength of the ties of self-interest supplemented by the bonds of friendly association and personal regard. The control of the various Standard Oil companies was held by the members of a single family and their close personal associates. These men had long been identified with a single interest, and the feuds of the competitive struggle had not divided them. The principle of community of interest proved to be, in this case, a working substitute for permanent organization.

Generally speaking, however, mutual self-interest backed by the friendship of members of a group of business men is a precarious foundation for stability of prices or rates. Self-interest may lead men one day together and the next day it may lead them apart, and when the paths of self-interest diverge, friendship is usually powerless to prevent a break. Community of interest, as applied to railroads on May 9, 1901, did not solve the difficulty. Yet the threatened catastrophe of renewed competition among the members of the trust must be prevented, not only to secure the advance toward stability of prices, which had already been made, but to furnish similar solutions for other vexing problems of competition.

Before 1889, when the corporation law of New Jersey was revised, the laws of no state authorized the chartering of a corporation for the general purpose of owning the stocks or property of other corporations. Consolidation of corporations was more generally permitted, but the purchase of stocks of other corporations by a holding company was not considered to fall within the field of corporate privilege. There were but few exceptions to the general rule that a corporation should be organized for a specific purpose or for closely allied purposes. Pennsylvania had gone so far as to prohibit incorporation for more than one purpose.

Now it was plain that the trusts could be preserved if a new corporation could be formed which was empowered to purchase, either for cash or with its own stock, the stocks of the several companies which were included in the trust, and which it was desirable to keep united under some form of permanent control. The only changes which would be made by such an arrangement in the organization of the combination would be these: (1) To substitute for the certificates of the old trust the shares of the new corporation; (2) to change the relation of trustee and trust into the relation of owner and property; and (3) to substitute for a board of trustees a board of directors. The result would be a single corporation whose assets were the securities of other corporations, each one in the full possession of its corporate faculties and exercising all of its lawful corporate activities; but the affairs of all would be placed under the permanent direction of the company owning a controlling interest in the stock of each, and competition among these companies would thus be prevented. The holding company, if this course seemed preferable, after acquiring the stocks of a corporation, could dissolve it, remaining in possession of the property which the canceled stock represented, and the securities holding company could also purchase the property of partnerships or individuals without resort to the expedient of organizing them into corporations in order to place their ownership in trust, as was formerly necessary.

It is true that this proposition of the holding company, first broached about 1890, did not differ in principle from the illegal trust which it was intended to supersede. The same combination in restraint of trade existed as before. If anything, the new combination, which was one of ownership and not of trusteeship, was more perfect than the form which had just been declared illegal. The suggested plan was a violation of both the spirit and the letter of the antitrust laws which had just been successfully invoked against the Sugar Trust. A company whose sole reason for existence was to control the ownership of previously competing corporations had manifestly effected a combination in restraint of trade. All this was admitted. Moreover, no state in which the sentiment against monopoly was strong enough to pass and to enforce the antitrust law could be expected so to amend the statutes of incorporation as to permit the organization of corporations to evade that law. However attractive the proposition might be, there seemed to be no way to bring about the authorization by one set of laws of a kind of corporation whose reason for existence and whose purposes of organization the laws of another commonwealth explicitly forbade.

The difficulty seemed to be insurmountable. For the sake of profits competition must be restricted. The law said that its restriction was illegal. No state legislature would have run the risk of legalizing the formation of corporations to perform *within that state* acts which would have necessitated the repeal of an antitrust law in order to make them lawful, and which would have been further in violation of the common law. But in these three italicized words lay the salvation of the trust. Although no state would empower a corporation to defeat the intention of its own statutes, a state was found to pass an act of incorporation which rendered void and of no effect the antitrust laws of every state attempting by statute to preserve competition. That state was New Jersey.

In 1889 the Legislature of New Jersey amended its corporation laws so as to include among the lawful objects of incorporation the right to purchase the stock of any company or companies owning mining, manufacturing, or producing materials, or other property necessary for their business, and to issue stock in payment therefor.

Under the provisions of this act, a body of men could form a corporation under the laws of New Jersey which, among other manifold privileges, might purchase and own the stocks, or other property of any corporation engaged in any kind of business in any state, providing the formation of this corporation did not violate any law of New Jersey, on complying with the following easy requirements: (1) To pay a small fee and a small annual tax; (2) to maintain a principal office in the State of New Jersey at the entrance to which the name of their company is conspicuously displayed, and where a legal representative of the company can be found upon whom process may be served; (3) to keep the stock transfer books of the company open to the inspection of any stockholder at its New Jersey office; (4) to make an annual report to the Secretary of State; (5) to hold their annual stockholders' meeting at the New Jersey office of the company; and (6) to have as one of their directors a resident of New Jersey.

For momentous consequences, this statute of New Jersey is hardly to be equaled in the annals of legislation. Sixteen sovereign states had passed searching and stringent laws in prohibition of any attempt to restrict competition; laws whose detailed minuteness of specification could hardly be improved upon; which had been proved effective against the only permanent form of competition regulation yet attempted, and which undoubtedly represented the conviction of a majority of the people of the United States—a conviction finding more general and authoritative expression in the Sherman Antitrust Law, and strengthened by the antimonopoly provisions of the common law; a well-nigh unanimous sentiment opposed to any form of trust or pool; and the little state of New Jersey, containing two per cent of the population and one and three tenths of the wealth of the United States, by the simple act of amending its corporation law, nullified the antitrust laws of every state which had passed them.

A trust could not exist in New York. The courts of New York would not allow the creation of a holding company to perpetuate the trust under another and slightly different form. Here are, say, ten corporations, all located in New York, which were formerly engaged in competition, later organized into a trust, and more recently dissolved by the New York courts. The owners of these corporations, having experienced the benefits of combination, wish to continue their organization under another form. They apply to the New York Legislature for permission to charter a new company which shall purchase all their stock, and whose officers can thus control their united policy. The Legislature refuses the application on the ground that the new corporation would be the old trust under a new name, and would therefore be existing in violation of the same law which had been recently employed against its predecessor. The case of the stockholders seems hopeless. They are citizens of New York. Their corporations are chartered by New York. New York absolutely forbids them to combine in restraint of trade. What are they to do?

In despair they turn their eyes southward. There, upon the other side of the North River stands the State of New Jersey, beckoning them with welcoming hands. For a franchise bonus or fee, New Jersey will come to their assistance. New Jersey will authorize them to form a corporation which is empowered to buy the stocks of their ten companies. New Jersey will allow them, as a New Jersey corporation, to perfect the combination in New York—for operation in New York—which the laws of New York absolutely forbid. New Jersey will thus deprive the State of New York of the right to control, in the interests of what her Legislature considers to be public policy, the corporations which New York has created and over which it assumes sovereign power. New Jersey will perform a similar office for any body of individuals who may wish to evade the antitrust laws of any state in the Union. As a New Jersey corporation, they may combine and coalesce for the operation of any number of competing plants, anywhere in the United States, with none to molest or make them afraid.

The State of New Jersey, by the amendment of its corporation laws in 1890, preserved the principle of combination, and made the modern trust possible. It is true that Delaware, West Virginia, Maine, and New York have followed the example of New Jersey. From present appearances, moreover, the general exodus of incorporators to those states which offer them the largest privileges, and charge the lowest incorporation fees, bids fair to compel most of the other commonwealths to relax their restrictions. New Jersey, however, was the first state to liberalize its corporation laws, and to New Jersey belongs the honor of first discovering that a foreign corporation may do many things in a state which a domestic corporation is by the laws of that state forbidden to do.

The difference between the old-time trust and the trust as we know it to-day, and the nature of the change in combination-organization which has taken place, may be illustrated by the table on page 361, which shows the metamorphosis of the Sugar Trust in 1891.

Industrially, the two organizations are identical. Their resources, their equipment, their organization, and their market are the same. Legally, however, between the "trust" and the "industrial combination" there is a great gulf fixed. It is impossible for the law to take cognizance of the fact that the American Sugar Refining Company is the old Sugar Trust under another form. In the eyes of the law, the Sugar Trust died when the shares which it held were turned back to their respective owners. The law is in no way concerned

THE SUGAR TRUST

STOCK OF CONSTITUTENT COMPANIES IN HANDS OF TRUSTEES—TRUST CERTIFICATES OUTSTANDING

THE AMERICAN SUGAR REFINING CO.

	Capital Stock	Capital Assets	Capital Stock
1. The Havemeyer & Elder Sugar Refining Co......	$500,000	$500,000	
2. The Dick & Meyer Co.....	200,000	200,000	
3. The DeCastro & Donner Sugar Refining Co......	350,000	350,000	
4. The Moller & Sierck Co....	210,000	210,000	
5. The Oxnard Brothers Co...	100,000	100,000	
6. The F. O. Matthiessen & Wirchers Sugar Refining Co..................	400,000	400,000	
7. The Brooklyn Sugar Refining Co..............	300,000	300,000	
8. The Havemeyer Sugar Refining Co..............	1,000,000	1,000,000	
9. The Forest City Sugar Refining Co............	300,000	300,000	
10. The Boston Sugar Refining Co..................	650,000	650,000	
11. The Standard Sugar Refining Co..............	1,000,000	1,000,000	
12. The Bay State Sugar Refining Co..............	225,000	225,000	
13. The St. Louis Sugar Refining Co..............	755,000	755,000	
14. The Louisiana Sugar Refining Co..............	450,000	450,000	
15. The Planters' Sugar Refining Co..............	250,000	250,000	
	$6,690,000	$6,690,000	
	Valuation	$50,000,000	$50,000,000

with the subsequent sale of these stocks to a New Jersey corporation.

There have not been lacking critics to scoff at the change in the legal form of the trust as being a thing of little consequence—a mere trick—a subterfuge to evade the law. A senator not many years since aroused much ridicule by stating that the trust no longer existed. There has been, however, no more far-reaching change in the organization of industry than that which converted an illegal combination in restraint of trade into a corporation organized to manufacture and sell securities, and to own the stocks and properties of other corporations engaged in the manufacture and sale of commodities.

By reconstructing the "trusts" to conform to the law, by capitalizing these permanent pools, the builders of the trusts made possible a widespread reorganization of competitive industry along more profitable lines, and opened the way to the creation of the huge mass of industrial securities which represent the capitalization of manufacturing industry in the United States, from participation in whose profits the public has before been excluded. Without this device of corporate organization, escape from competition would have been impossible. By its aid, however, the profitable regulation of competition was, at least prospectively, secured.

The legal position of these trusts is, however, by no means certain. The permanent success of Missouri in excluding from its boundaries two subsidiary corporations of the Standard Oil Company on the ground that, by allowing their stock to pass into a common control, they had incapacitated themselves from obeying the antitrust law of the state, shows that if the state authorities care to exert themselves they may enforce their anti-combination laws in such a manner as to deprive the holding company organized under the laws of another state which of course they have no power to reach, of control over properties which come under their own jurisdiction. The most serious danger to the trust lies in the recent attempts to enforce the Sherman Antitrust Law. This law was passed in 1890. Its important sections are as follows:

> Section 1. Every contract, combination in the form of trust or otherwise, or conspiracy, in restraint of trade or commerce among the several states, or with foreign nations, is hereby declared to be illegal.
>
> Every person who shall make any such contract or engage in any such combination or conspiracy, shall

> be deemed guilty of a misdemeanor, and on conviction thereof, shall be punished by fine not exceeding five thousand dollars, or by imprisonment not exceeding one year, or by both said punishments, in the discretion of the court.
>
> Section 2. Every person who shall monopolize, or attempt to monopolize or combine or conspire with any other person or persons, to monopolize any part of the trade or commerce among the several states, or with foreign nations, shall be deemed guilty of a misdemeanor, and, on conviction thereof, shall be punished by fine not exceeding five thousand dollars, or by imprisonment not exceeding one year, or by both said punishments, in the discretion of the court.

The first suit brought under the Sherman Antitrust Law to test the position of an industrial combination was in 1894 in the case of the United States vs. E. C. Knight Sugar Refining Company. That company had just purchased four independent refineries in Philadelphia, and action was brought to enjoin the purchase on the ground that a combination in violation of the Sherman law had been formed. The Supreme Court, however, to which the case was carried on appeal, held that the Sherman Act applied only to combinations in restraint of interstate trade; that the business of the American Sugar Refining Company was primarily manufacturing, and that it engaged in commerce only as an incident to manufacture. The court, therefore, stated that the United States had no jurisdiction over the combination since, if the contrary view should be upheld, the effect would be to give the Federal government control of all enterprises whose operations cross the line of a state, and this unusual control, which would reduce the power of an individual state to a nullity, it was never intended that Congress should possess.

This decision was rendered in 1895. Until 1902 it was regarded as furnishing complete protection to the industrial combinations. In 1902, however, suit was brought against the Northern Securities Company, a New Jersey corporation organized to acquire in exchange for its own stock the stock of the Northern Pacific and Great Northern under the Sherman Antitrust Law. The defense was that the Northern Securities Company was merely an investor, and that the United States had no jurisdiction over the lawful investments of a corporation organized under the laws of a state. The Supreme Court, by a bare majority, held that a combination in restraint of trade was accomplished by the joint ownership of the stock of these two companies by the Northern Securities Company, and ordered the Northern Securities Company to return the stock to their original owners. This decision struck at the holding company principle. Its application to railroads was not, however, regarded as weakening the legal position of manufacturing combinations. The recent suits against the Standard Oil Company, the American Tobacco Company, and other combinations, however, brought under the Sherman Act by the Department of Justice, strike directly at the holding company in the field of manufacturing enterprise. These cases are still before the Supreme Court, which has shown no disposition to hurry its decision.

The question at issue turns upon the definition of commerce. If the decision in the E. C. Knight case is upheld, although certain trading and shipping activities of the Standard Oil Company and the American Tobacco Company may be prohibited, it is unlikely that these holding companies will be dissolved. If, however, the court reverses its opinion expressed in the E. C. Knight case and interprets the Sherman Act as prohibiting combinations of manufacturing concerns which ship their products to all parts of the United States, then the legal position of every one of the combinations is unsound. In the Tobacco Trust case in the Circuit Court of the Southern District of New York, Judge Lacombe said: "The Sherman Act must be construed as prohibiting any contract or combination whose direct effect is to prevent the free play of competition and thus tend to deprive the country of the services of any number of independent dealers, however small. As thus construed the statute is revolutionary. But every aggregation of individuals or corporations formerly independent, immediately upon its formation terminates an existing competition, whether or not some other competition may subsequently arise. The act as above construed prohibits every contract or combination in restraint of competition. Size is not made the test. Two individuals who have been driving rival express wagons between villages in two contiguous states who enter into a combination to join forces and operate a single line restrain an existing competition and it would seem to make little difference whether they make such combination more effective by forming a partnership or not." The amendment of the law is apparently impossible.

Holding companies are not formed solely for legal reasons. Important considerations of financial expediency favor the use of this device when it is desired to bring under single control within a short time a number of properties in the same line of business. When it is desired to form a combination, for example, of a number of steel manufacturing concerns, one of the operating companies can be used as a holding company, or a new company can be formed. Even if no legal obstacles intervened, however, the holding company will be the device usually selected.

Mr. Robert F. Herrick, in a paper entitled "Holding Companies," originally presented before the Harvard Graduate School of Business Administration, has summarized the financial reasons for employing the holding company in such a case as follows:

"The natural purpose, then, of a holding company and the one for which it is used is the combination of allied and generally though not necessarily competing enterprises. Theoretically, such a combination or purchase could be effected by any one person or group of persons with sufficient capital. Further, it could be effected by the purchase outright, either by private individuals or a corporation, of the various properties or business. Practically, however, a great many combinations would never be brought about except for the holding company, and practically all of the great recent consolidations, such as the United States Steel Company, the Amalgamated Copper Company, and others, have been holding companies. It would have been practically impossible for the United States Steel Corporation to have been formed in any other way. It is necessary in the getting together of such a group of properties to act quickly and at a favorable time. It is necessary, so far as possible, to get along without new cash. The amount of cash necessary to buy the properties consolidated into the United States Steel Corporation would have been impracticable to raise. It is necessary, further, as much as possible to retain the interest of a large number of stockholders in the older companies in the new consolidated company. It is necessary to provide a practical working method of bringing them all together, and particularly necessary to provide for the contingency that it may be impossible or impracticable to actually sell the property of one of these corporations to the consolidated company, or that it may be impossible to get the consent of certain of those interested in the selling company to the consolidation.

"The stockholders act naturally like a flock of sheep. In the main they follow the lead of the directors, and if the details of carrying the plan through are so arranged that the stock in the new company has an apparent money value greater than the stock of the old company for which it is offered, the exchange once started takes place generally, and when a majority of the stock in the companies is exchanged practically the consolidation is effected. The difficulty in bringing enterprises together in any other way can be realized when you appreciate that in many states it is impossible for a corporation, even a private manufacturing corporation, to sell out its entire property, including franchises and good-will. It has been held in some jurisdictions that such a sale is foreign to the whole purpose for which the corporation was formed and that when the time for such a sale comes, it means the dissolution of the corporation and a final disposition of its assets among its stockholders. There is further in certain states the absolute prohibition for a corporation of greater than a limited amount of capital to do business in the state. This alone would prevent the amalgamation of a number of properties into one great corporation directly owning all the properties."

Another reason for choosing the holding company for the consolidation is that to employ an operating company as the purchaser of the stocks of other corporations, would require a large increase in the stock of this company, and this increase might, under the laws of the state or the charter of the corporation, require the consent of three fourths or even a larger proportion of the stock. Stockholders of the proposed holding company might object to this reorganization of the capital account for a purpose of which they might not approve, and the combination might be halted at its outset by embarrassing litigation resulting from the efforts of minority stockholders to protect what they considered to be their rights whatever the motives back of the litigation.

A holding company has various other uses in addition to that of accomplishing a combination. It is largely employed as a finance company. One of the best illustrations of holding companies organized for this purpose is furnished by the corporations manufacturing electrical apparatus and appliances. The products of the General Electric Company, for example, are purchased by corporations engaged in the operation of electric railroads, power and lighting companies. When these companies are started, their promoters usually welcome assistance in providing the funds for construction. They are willing not merely to make liberal arrangements in the way of stock bonuses, but also to give to the construction companies affiliated with the banking or financial concerns which give them assistance in putting through their project, exclusive contracts, not merely for construction, but also for all materials and appliances which may be needed for a long time to come in the maintenance and extension of the plant.

The companies manufacturing electrical appliances have, therefore, placed themselves in a position to render financial assistance to new companies in order to secure a market for their machinery. The General Electric Company owns the entire capital stocks of the Electric Securities Corporation and the Electric Bond & Share Company. Both of these companies are finance companies; they take part in the underwriting of securities of electric companies of various kinds, and also purchase the bonds of such companies, sometimes taking with the bonds a bonus of stock. They obtain the funds for these purchases, not merely because of the high credit which the backing of the General Electric Company gives them, but also by selling their own bonds secured by the stocks and bonds which they purchase. The Electrical Securities Company, for example, in 1904 offered $500,000 out of $1,000,000 collateral trust five per cent bonds secured by $1,250,000 par value of first mortgage bonds of nine electric railway, power and traction companies located in different parts of the United States. These companies earned a surplus over fixed charges, and the Electrical Securities Corporation was required to keep the principal acquired out of its interest-paying bonds under pledge equal at all times to at least 125 per cent of the principal of the collateral trust bonds outstanding. When a favorable opportunity occurs, bonds may be withdrawn and sold, a corresponding amount of the collateral trust bonds being paid off. In other cases, the substitution of collateral, according to the method already explained in the discussion of the collateral trust bonds, is permitted.

By pledging the bonds which it purchases as collateral for loans, a corporation of this character is able to free its capital for new employment without selling unseasoned bonds at the low prices which such securities bring. The bonds can be put away under the collateral trust mortgage until the companies issuing them have reached an assured position, when they can be sold at a substantial advance over the price paid. Bonds purchased by such corporations, moreover, often carry a bonus of stock, and the stock can either be held for dividends or sold as soon as it reaches a proper figure.

A limit is usually placed upon the amount of collateral trust bonds which such a corporation can issue. In the case of the Electrical Securities Company, for example, the "total indebtedness of the corporation, secured and unsecured, direct and contingent, shall never in the aggregate exceed four times the amount of its paid-up and unimpaired outstanding capital stock and surplus." Bonds of such a corporation, issued under these restrictions, furnish very good security. The fact that the collateral pledged represents the bonds of a number of different enterprises adds to the safety of these obligations.

The object of the Electrical Securities Corporation and the Bond and Share Company is to assist the owner of their stock, the General Electric Company, in pushing its business. It is not their object to retain permanently the bonds which they purchase. As fast as these show a substantial profit, they are sold and the proceeds reinvested in other securities. Other companies have been organized on this model for the purpose of permanent income to be derived from the securities yielding the high rate of return purchased with their own bonds at a lower rate. The Mortgage Bond Company of New York, for example, owns first mortgages in a large number of cities, and from time to time issues bonds secured by these mortgages with the proceeds of which other mortgages are purchased. The bonds of this company must at all times be secured by deposit with the trustee of first mortgages equal in face value to the value of the bonds outstanding on improved real estate in cities having a population not less than 40,000, subject to the right of the company temporarily to deposit cash, Government bonds, or New York City bonds at a valuation of five per cent below the market value thereof. All the mortgages used as collateral are limited to one half of the value of the mortgaged property as appraised for the company. With cities having a population of 300,000 or over, such mortgages may equal three fifths of the value of the property, and in New York City, two thirds of the value. These bonds are issued at low rates of interest, and their proceeds can be loaned at rates which show a substantial margin of profit for the stock. The mortgage bond indebtedness of the company is limited to fifteen times the capital stock outstanding at the time of issue. Other illustrations of holding companies organized for permanent control of properties are the American Water Works Company, the American Pipe Manufacturing Company, the American Gas Company, the American Light & Traction Company, and the United Gas Improvement Company.

The finance holding companies which have been described are similar to the organization of the investment trusts which are numerous in Great Britain. These corporations are organized to make available to the general investor the stocks and bonds of other companies, thereby relieving him of the task of finding safe investments for his money. Investment Trusts issue shares or debentures bonds to the investor, and with the funds obtained, they purchase large blocks of securities in various companies, many of them located outside of England. It is not regarded essential that these interests should be controlling interests. In some cases, new flotations can get their capital from such investment trusts. The purpose of these investment holding companies is indicated in the prospectus of the General Investors & Trustees, Limited, which says:

> This company has been formed to conduct the business of a trust and investment company. . . . The directors believe that the present is a favorable time for engaging in such an enterprise, securities being generally free from inflation, and the conditions of trade throughout the world being of a satisfactory character. It has been shown by experience that a well-managed investment company enjoys many advantages which are not usually within the reach of a private individual, who cannot generally exercise that

> vigilance essential to successful results. The former is in a position, while as a rule a private investor is not, to make the investigations necessary to ascertain the real position and intrinsic value and prospects of the undertakings in which it contemplates investing its capital. The information now required to be given by companies under recent legislation in conjunction with their annual reports and accounts, provides a useful index to their merit, and furnishes an invaluable aid to the operations of a trust and investment company. The business of participating in the underwriting of new issues of Home, Foreign, and Colonial Loans, and of bonds, debentures and debenture stocks, and shares and stocks of approved companies, will form a prominent feature of the company's operations.

The advantages of such a company are many. In the first place, it can act as an underwriter in taking over the stocks and bonds of new corporations in which it has confidence at very low prices, receiving occasional bonuses of stock, and selling its own shares or debenture bonds on an investment basis. This is essentially the same plan as that followed by railroad companies which build branch lines through subsidiary companies, and then sell securities of these companies in the form of their own collateral trust bonds to the public. The Investment Trust Company has also this advantage over the investment banker because the latter is compelled to turn over its capital quickly, and is forced, in order to market securities purchased, to give the purchaser lower prices than those which could be obtained for these securities if they were held until the company had fully demonstrated its earning power. The English investment trust, moreover, may retain its purchases, or may sell these securities when they appreciate in value as result of increased earnings. In either case, its shareholders obtain the full benefit of appreciating value which the American banker is forced to divide with his customers. The second point in favor of the investment holding company is that it spreads its investments over a wide field, by which it can, in the same manner as life insurance companies, reduce the risk of loss to a minimum. The investor in its debentures or shares can also be safeguarded by reserve funds built up out of the dividends and interest which it receives.

CHAPTER XXX

THE LEASE

THE lease has already been defined as a contract by which possession of certain property is transferred from the owner known as the lessor to some other person or corporation known as the lessee. Corporate leases contain the following provisions:

First, a description of the property, usually in the form of a complete inventory, which must be kept up to date, since the nature of corporate property is likely to be constantly changing. For example, the property of a street railway company, where the motive power is in turn changed from horse power to cable, then to the overhead trolley, and finally to the underground trolley, may be entirely different at the end of a ten-year period from what it was at the beginning. If this property is to be leased to another company, it is important that the inventory be revised at regular intervals.

Second, the length of the lease. It is usual to make corporate leases for long terms, ninety-nine years being common, and 999 years not unusual. When leases are made for shorter periods, options of renewal on certain terms are usually inserted.

Third, payments under the lease. With hardly an exception, corporate leases provide that taxes, insurance, interest, and expenses of maintaining the organization of the lessor shall be paid by the lessee. In addition, the payment for the lease to the lessor is usually made in the form of a dividend upon the capital stock of the lessor as then outstanding. It may also be provided that the lessee shall pay as rental for the property a certain proportionate part of the gross earnings or of the net earnings. This method places no limit to the participation of the owner in the profits of the property. These payments are frequently made on a sliding scale so as to permit the stockholders to share in the expected increase in profits.

Corporate leases provide, in even greater detail than private leases, for the maintenance of the property. This point needs to be far more carefully guarded in short term leases than when, for example, ninety-nine year leases are made. If the maintenance of leased property is not carefully looked after, as the date when the lease expires approaches, the lessee, unless he expects to renew the lease, will allow the condition of the property to deteriorate, making as much money as possible during the last year or two of his occupancy. In order to protect the lessor against such an abuse of his rights by the lessee, there may be reserved to the lessor the privilege of examining its physical condition. A typical provision for maintenance is the following, taken from the lease of the property of the Manhattan Railway Company to the Interborough Rapid Transit Company:

> The lessee covenants and agrees, at its own proper cost and expense, to maintain, operate and run the demised railroads and property during the said term in the same manner as the lessor is now or shall at any time hereafter be required or authorized by law to do; and shall and will keep all insurable property insured in reasonable amounts and rebuild all buildings and replace all property destroyed or deteriorated by fire or otherwise, to such an extent as to be unfit for use; and shall and will maintain, preserve and keep the railways and property hereby demised, including all property hereafter acquired, and every part thereof, in thorough repair, working order and safe and efficient condition, and supplied with rolling stock and equipment, so that the business of the said demised railways shall be preserved, encouraged and developed, the business thereof be done with safety and expedition, the public be accommodated in respect

thereto, with all practicable convenience and facilities, and the future growth of such business as the same may arise or be reasonably anticipated be fully provided for and secured.

The lessee further covenants and agrees, at the expiration or termination of this lease for any cause, to return and deliver the said railroad and railroads, real estate, and properties by this lease demised, including, among other things, all property, additions, improvements and equipments which shall be furnished, constructed or completed out of the proceeds of sale of the stock, bonds or property of the lessor, to the lessor in as good order, condition and repair as they were at the date this lease takes effect, or at the date when the same came into the possession of the lessee, and to surrender said franchises, rights and privileges, easements and properties unimpaired by any act of the lessee; excepting, however, all property of the lessor sold pursuant to the terms hereof, the proceeds of which shall have been applied as herein provided.

The lessee further covenants and agrees that it will, at all times during the continuance of this lease, at its own expense, keep the said rolling stock, and tools, equipment, machinery and implements necessary for the operation of the road, in good order, condition and repair, and will, as the same shall be worn out and rendered unserviceable, replace the same at its own expense, so that the said railroad and railroads shall always be kept, maintained and equipped in good and safe condition and effective working order.

The lessee further covenants and agrees that it will at all times during the continuance of this lease, at its own expense, comply with all lawful requirements with respect to the construction, maintenance and operation of said railroads, extensions or branches thereof.

In corporate leases, when the instrument covers, for example, a large and complex street railway system, it frequently happens that some portion of the property of the lessor is no longer of use to the lessee. It is for the interest of both parties that this property should be sold. Provision is usually made, therefore, for the sale of such property, with or without the consent of the lessor, but invariably with the stipulation that the proceeds of the sale are to be invested in improvements upon the lessor's property. In other respects the language and form of a corporate lease closely follows the corporate mortgage, the main objects being to preserve the physical condition of the property and to protect the lessor against any claims or charges arising from the nonfulfillment of any obligation connected with the property released. If the property is mortgaged, such a stipulation is, of course, necessary, and the consent of the trustee of the mortgage must be obtained.

A proposition made by a strong company to stockholders of another corporation to lease their property at a rental corresponding to the dividends which they are then receiving or of which there is an immediate prospect, is very attractive, and it is not so essential to make sure of their acceptance by purchasing enough stock to control the board of directors of the lessor company, as when a proposition is made to purchase the stock. A typical proposition of this character is indicated in the following offer:

> The Indianapolis Terminal and Traction Company offers to lease the property of the Indianapolis Street Railway Company, guaranteeing the payment of interest, taxes, etc., and also dividends on the street railway stock of one per cent on January 1; next, and thereafter semiannually 3 per cent for the first year, 4 per cent for the second year, 5 per cent for the third year, and from July, 1908, 6 per cent. The term of the lease is for thirty years, which is the unexpired life of the Indianapolis Company's franchise from the city.

The advantages of the lease, from the standpoint of the lessee, are equally evident. The lessee company obtains the control of property without the outlay of any money, and usually on terms which leave them a margin of profit after making the payments required by the lease. If property is to be built a large amount of financing is necessary. Bonds or stock must be sold, and extensive construction operations entered into. If, however, the property desired can be rented from its owners, the lessee company comes immediately into the possession of a fully completed property, manned by an operating organization and on a profitable basis. The same result, from the standpoint of control, may be reached by purchases of the stock of the company owning the desired property, which can be pledged under an issue of collateral trust bonds. This method has already been explained. Here, however, the question of financing arises, the bonds must be sold, or a sufficient sale must be insured by a syndicate to purchase the amount of stock desired. The question of stock, moreover, as we have seen, usually involves the entire issue of the company which owns the desired property, and the financing may be extensive. To acquire control by the method of lease, however, involves only dealing with the board of directors, and the submission by them of a proposition to the stockholders. If the offer is advantageous, and with the prestige of the directors behind it, it is likely to be unanimously accepted.

Leased property has objections from the point of view of the lessor. It is not available as security for loans to pay for improvements which may increase its value. While the property of a street railway system is in the possession of the lessee company, and while its operation is entirely controlled by the lessee, title to the property remains in the lessor. In the natural course of improvement, with a steady growth of population, large extensions and additions, and a considerable amount of reconstruction of the property, are reasonably certain. The progress of invention has completely revolutionized the methods and mechanism of street railway corporations. The motive power, types of cars, the methods of generating power and the types of track, have been greatly improved. The cost of all these improvements and extensions which are made upon the property of the lessor, in the absence of special provisions in the lease, must be borne by the lessee company. With a short term lease, the improvement of the lessor's property may be the ground for a successful demand for higher rental from the lessee, and improvements are likely to be deferred or abandoned on this account. With a long term lease, the only objection to improving the lessor's property is the difficulty of financing the cost of these improvements. In such cases, the only property right held by the lessee is the lessor's interest obtained by capitalizing the profits of the lease. This right may in some cases be very valuable. We have already seen that it was one of the assets pledged by the Interurban Rapid Transit Company as security for a recent issue of bonds. In few cases, however, are the profits so large as to make the lessor's interest of great value, and great difficulty may be experienced in financing improvements which are absolutely essential to the development of the system, and which may, in fact, be demanded by the public authorities.

A recent illustration of the difficulty experienced by the lessee company under these circumstances is furnished by the Philadelphia Rapid Transit Company which holds under lease the street railway property of the Union Traction Company which preceded it in control of the street railway system of Philadelphia. In September, 1908, the Rapid Transit Company sent a letter to the shareholders of the Union Traction Company which is as follows:

"On July 1, 1902, you turned over to this company your property on a rental basis. You had acquired this property seven years before, had expended your money in the development of it, and while in later years you had shown a surplus from operation, that surplus had not, up to that time, been sufficient to justify the payment of a dividend.

"This company, by the terms of the lease, undertook to pay you a dividend from the start, equal to the largest earnings which you had shown up to that time, and increasing until they should reach, as they now have, double that amount. In the past six years we have spent approximately $20,000,000 in building the new elevated and subway railway and $20,000,000 upon improvements and extensions of the system which you turned over to us. This company has been subject to severe criticism for having assumed to pay a dividend upon the par value of your stock, only thirty-five per cent of which has been paid in, but the answer is that we have (in effect) spent upon this system not only the 19½ millions remaining unpaid upon your capital stock but 10½ millions additional, with respect to which $30,000,000 no fixed charge has been assumed and no return has been paid.

"The increased cost of operation, the recent depression in business and unavoidable delays in the completion of the subway have necessarily upset, to a certain extent, the calculations upon which the rental obligations were based. These conditions, however, have merely postponed the fulfillment of our expectations, and the management has full confidence in its ability to place the property upon a substantial paying basis, provided it is able to do the financing always necessary for a growing property.

"Since we took over this property we have secured a contract with the city in which the Rapid Transit Company has given up valuable privileges for the purpose of securing to your company immunity from the threat of hostile legislation. This contract is of the very greatest benefit to the Union Traction Company and its underlying lines.

"As already stated, nearly half of the $40,000,000 capital raised by this company has been expended directly upon the surface system. Several millions of dollars went to the building of what are practically new lines, although they have been built under extensions of your old charters, principally the Twenty-second Street and Allegheny Avenue Passenger Railway Company in which you own every share of stock, and the West Philadelphia Passenger Railway Company (under which new lines have been built on 52d, 58th, and 60th streets) in which your company owns a controlling interest.

"The Rapid Transit Company has now made the final call upon its capital stock and this has been practically exhausted by the expenditures already detailed. It is now necessary to relay many miles of surface track and to add equipment of a more modern character calculated to serve the public better, and to collect a much greater percentage of the fares. These expenditures will be made directly upon your property, rendering the security of your lease that much better, both as to the value of the property and its earning power."

It appears from this letter that, unless the Rapid Transit Company could make use of the credit of the Union Traction Company, the financing of necessary improvements would be impossible. A proposition was, therefore, made to the stockholders of the Union Traction Company to permit the former to use a large number of valuable securities enumerated in the list and intrusted to the Rapid Transit Company as collateral security for an issue of $5,000,000 of collateral trust bonds. The proposition was accepted by the Union Traction Company, and the funds provided. Evidently, however, the lessee company cannot always count upon the acquiescence of stockholders of lessor companies in placing encumbrances upon their property for the benefit of that property. In recent leases, provisions have been inserted whereby the lessor company is obliged, under certain conditions, to finance improvements upon its own property.

One of the most carefully drawn leases ever executed is that which gave to the Boston Elevated Railway Company the control of the West End Street Railway. The lease bound the Boston Elevated to pay seven per cent per annum on the common and eight per cent on the preferred stock directly to the stockholders without any reduction, the lease stating that these dividends were to be "net" amounts. The lease further explicitly provided that the Elevated Company should pay all damages to persons or property; all sums due for taxes — federal, state or municipal — upon the lessor's property, franchise or capital stock; and all sums "by law required to be deducted from any amounts payable upon the lessor's stock." The lease, on the other hand, stipulated that all saving from refunding of the West End Company's bonus should accrue to the lessee, the Boston Elevated Company. The lessee also assumed definitely the interest on the bonds of the West End Company, and on the existing indebtedness of any street railway that the West End Company was under obligations to pay. It also assumed all liabilities under the contract with the city of Boston touching the subway.

The provisions in this lease regarding the right of the lessee to issue stock or bonds of the West End Company for improvements, particularly deserve attention. The West End Company was required to issue stock or bonds, from time to time, at the request of the lessee, in order to meet the cost of improvements and additions to the lessor's property. The West End Company must be informed of the purposes for which it is proposed to issue the securities, and if it dissent from the expediency of the expenditure, and withholds its consent to the issue, a board of arbitrators must pass upon the matter. If the arbitrators, by a majority opinion, do not approve the same, the lessee cannot insist upon the issue being made. One arbitrator is to be chosen by each of the parties to the lease, and the third by the two so chosen, or by the State Board of Railroad Commissioners, or by the Chief Justice of the Supreme Court of Massachusetts. The lessee company has the right to decide whether the issue of security by the lessor shall be stock or bonds, and it may fix the rate of interest which the bonds shall bear, but it is provided that "no bond shall be issued in excess of the outstanding capital stock" of the lessor. This reservation in the lease is of great importance to both the lessor and lessee. It enables the lessee to use almost at will the credit of the lessor for the purpose of improving property out of which it may be making a large profit.

It is true that the lessor is protected by the Arbitration Board, but still further safeguards are demanded. There is set down in detail in the lease the expenditures which the lessee can capitalize for the account of the West End Street Railway. These are especially limited to the following permanent additions and improvements:

1. The abolition of grade crossing.
2. Additional rolling stock and equipment.
3. Additional track mileage and its equipment.
4. Additional real estate.
5. Additional stations, power and car houses.
6. Additional buildings, bridges and other structures.
7. Renewals of or substitutes for stations, bridges, buildings and other structures, track and equipment, "so far as the cost of such renewals and substitutions exceeds the cost, when new, of the things received or the things replaced."

The provision just described is now often included in leases of properties where it is necesary to provide for capital expenditures. Another method sometimes employed, and which a proper organization of the capital account makes possible, is for the lessee, when it takes over the property of the lessor, and assumes the obligation to pay interest on its bonds, to take over also any unissued bonds authorized under existing mortgages, and to issue these at will subject to the restrictions of the mortgage. This method is preferable to that employed in the Boston lease which is apt to lead to endless discussions and bickering over the propriety of particular expenditures. If the restrictions in the mortgage are carefully drawn, the lessee can, without danger to the lessor's property, and in fact with great benefit to the lessor, freely employ the credit arranged for in the mortgage for the benefit of the lessor's property. In this manner provision can be made for the expansion of the business carried on with the leased property.

CHAPTER XXXI

READADJUSTMENT OF THE CAPITAL ACCOUNT

THE capital account of a corporation has been described as a statement of assets and liabilities. From time to time, it becomes necessary or advantageous for a company to readjust its capital account, changing the form of assets, exchanging assets for liabilities, distributing assets or evidences of liabilities to stockholders, or changing the form of liabilities. The methods employed in making these readjustments can be grouped under the general title of readjustment of the capital account.

Reorganization of the capital account is usually required in the event of bankruptcy, if the business is to be continued. This form of reorganization will be considered in a later chapter. We are here concerned with the reorganization of the capital accounts of solvent companies.

Reorganization may relate either to assets or liabilities. The first condition under which reorganization may be necessary is when it is desired to change the form of assets. The property of a corporation is constantly changing. A railroad company, for example, may wish to sell a part of its equipment which is no longer suited to its purposes, or certain real estate put out of use by the rearrangement of a terminal. Similar occasions are constantly arising when it is desirable for a corporation to dispose of certain of its property. When securities are owned, and when the control over the companies which have issued these securities is no longer important to the corporation which owns them, opportunity sometimes arises to sell these securities, and to reinvest the proceeds, either in improvements or in other securities showing higher rates of return. The testimony of Mr. E. H. Harriman before the Interstate Commerce Commission in its investigation of the alleged illegal combination between the Pacific companies in 1907, explained a transaction of this character as follows:

"We had, as the result of the Northern Pacific purchase, $82,000,000 of Northern Securities stock, at a cost of about $79,000,000. Then we were forced by the decision of the Supreme Court to take Great Northern, which we did not want, and a lesser amount of Northern Pacific than we had deposited with the Northern Securities Company. At the time the Great Northern and Northern Pacific was forced upon us, it had a market value of about $100,000,000. . . . Instead of disposing of it at that time, we held it until the market price increased in value to somewhere near $145,000,000 to $150,000,000. We sold some of it gradually as it went up, but at that value the returns from the Northern Pacific and Great Northern were less than three per cent on the stock that we held. Therefore we concluded that it was better to sell those stocks and invest the same money in other securities that would give us greater returns. So that, following out that line, we have sold enough of those stocks to realize $116,000,000."

Mr. Harriman further stated that the income from the securities purchased was approximately $5,500,000, instead of $3,250,000 on the Great Northern and Northern Pacific stock.

The working capital of a company, its cash, materials, and bills receivable, varies with the volume of its business. It is offset, in part, by current liabilities. With a falling off in business, a part of this working capital becomes unnecessary. It may then be employed to pay off the current debts of the company.

In some cases corporations may be unable to meet short term indebtedness at maturity, and may be obliged to sacrifice some of their property to take up their loans. The Colorado Fuel and Iron Company, in 1903, "found it necessary, in order to meet its obligations under contracts previously made, and for the extensive work of construction and betterments upon which the company entered a year or two ago, and also for its general corporate purposes, to raise money from persons interested either as stockholders or directors, or both, by means of loans and sales (the sales, however, being subject to a contract permitting repurchase by the Fuel Company within a specified time)." This property was afterwards repurchased by the corporation at an advance in price, the stockholders being allowed to participate in the profits of the repurchase.

The disposition of assets by the various methods above indicated presents no difficulty if the assets are not pledged as security for some loan. In case they are pledged, however, it becomes necessary to obtain the consent of the trustee, whose duty it is to make sure that the proceeds of the sale are used, either to reduce the amount of bonds secured by the mortgage under which the property sold was pledged, or reinvested for the protection of the bonds.

Taking up next the readjustment of liabilities, we come first upon the capital stock. The increase of capital stock as a means of distributing the surplus has already been referred to in Chapter XVIII. We are concerned with the conditions under which the amount of capital stock may be reduced. When the company has outstanding an amount of stock so great as to make it improbable that its earnings will ever reach a point where dividends can be safely paid, and especially when there has been such an accumulation of unpaid dividends on preferred stock as to make payment of dividends on common stock highly impracticable, the question arises, Shall the capital stock be reduced to a dividend paying basis? When the value of the stock, because of the remoteness of dividend payment, has fallen to a nominal figure, this question should be answered in the affirmative.

A company, for example, with $500,000 of surplus earnings applicable to dividends cannot, as a rule, safely pay out more than $300,000. If $250,000 of this $300,000 is required to pay preferred dividends, and if the amount of common stock is $10,000,000, the $50,000 remaining equals only one half of one per cent on the total common stock. There may also be accumulated dividends on the preferred stock, making the payment of dividends on the common stock even more improbable. Common stock, under these circumstances, will usually sell for a nominal figure, under $5 a share. Very little of it can be sold at any price. If, however, the $10,000,000 of common stock could be reduced to $1,000,000, and the accumulated dividends on the preferred stock readjusted, the company would have enough surplus earnings to pay five per cent on its common stock, which might be expected to sell at from $50 to $60 a share. The proposition made to the common stockholders to exchange, say, ten shares of the old stock for one share of the new stock should be aceptable, since they obtain an income at once, and also a free market for their securities. In case the increased earnings of the company eventually make it possible to pay a high dividend on this reduced capital stock, the stock retired may be returned to the stockholders in the form of stock dividends, maintaining a dividend rate at a reasonable figure, and placing them again in their original position so far as concerns the par value of their holdings. This method was employed by the General Electric Company, which in 1898 reduced its stock 40 per cent in 1902 returning the amount to its stockholders in a special dividend. Several corporations which were grossly overcapitalized at the outset have reduced their capital stocks to a dividend paying basis. The American Malting Company and the Distillers' Securities Company, among others, have made such reduction.

Reduction of capital stock to place it upon a dividend paying basis can only be accomplished, unless the company is to be dissolved and its property taken over by a new corporation, by unanimous consent of the stockholders. This unanimous consent is comparatively easy to obtain when the stock has only a nominal value, and where the directors are able to point out an immediate gain to the stockholder in taking the new securities. When, however, the stock, even though nondividend paying, has a speculative value and a free market, due to the prevalence of rumors concerning its prospects and earnings, or to reports that a contest for its control will be waged, or that it is to be consolidated with another corporation, it is then practically impossible to obtain the consent of the stockholders to reduce the value of their holdings sufficiently to enable the immediate payment of dividends.

Take, for example, the Erie. This company has outstanding \$112,378,900 of common stock. The present company is now over fifteen years old, and the common stock has received no dividends. During the last fiscal year, the surplus over fixed charges was barely sufficient to pay four per cent on the \$63,892,400 of preferred stock, which, however, received nothing. The preceding year showed a deficit of \$2,199,226. In order to place the Erie upon a dividend-paying basis, even making allowance for the expected improvement in its earnings due to the reconstruction of its property which has been in progress for some years, it would require a reduction of the common stock to about one fifth of its present amount, to enable the payment of a moderate dividend within the near future. And yet the market price of the Erie is to-day (Aug. 29, 1910) \$25¾ a share, and even in 1908, when its fortunes were at the lowest ebb, and when a receivership was anticipated, the lowest figure reached by the common stock was \$12 a share. To reduce the common stock of the Erie from \$112,000,000 to \$30,000,000, placing it upon a four per cent basis, might result in a market price of \$75 a share. A proposition to reduce this stock to a dividend paying basis would, therefore, be equivalent to asking the stockholders of the Erie to surrender about \$120 worth of market value with a fair prospect of higher prices in the future, in return for four per cent stock which might be sold for \$75 a share. If the Erie stock were held by investors, this proposition might be acceptable, but since such stocks are held either for control or for speculation, it would be impossible to secure unanimous consent to a proposition to reduce this amount.

Illustrations of this situation are furnished by the Missouri, Kansas & Texas which earned last year $420,000 on $63,300,000 of common stock, but which sells at $42.50 a share on the prospects of consolidation with some other road, and the Southern Railway which showed a surplus of $3,511,100 on $120,000,000 of common stock which sells, however, at $27 a share. A reduction of the capital stock of small corporations whose securities have no speculative value to a dividend basis is feasible and desirable since it stops the accumulation of interest on the cost of the original stock to its holders. With large public corporations, however, whose stock contains an element of speculative value, this method is not often available.

An easier method of favoring the common stock in a reorganization is to fund accumulative dividends on preferred stock. Suppose a case like the following: A company issues $5,000,000 of preferred stock and $5,000,000 of common stock. The preferred stock carries seven per cent of cumulative dividends, and thirty-five per cent of unpaid dividends stand against the common stock. The company earns $500,000 a year net over charges, sufficient to pay the current dividends on the preferred, and leave $150,000 to be applied to the accumulated dividends. At this rate it will require eleven years to pay the accumulated dividends, during which time the common stock will receive nothing. A proposition is made to the preferred and common stockholders that the company shall issue five per cent debenture bonds or five per cent second preferred stock in exchange for these back dividends which amount, as already stated, to about $1,750,000 on $5,000,000. The debentures should sell, on the company's showing of surplus earnings, at about 80. The fixed charges of the corporation would be increased by the issue $87,500 per year.

This proposition would appeal to the two classes of stockholders as follows: The preferred stockholder receives, instead of a contingent right to \$1,750,000 of dividends, that amount par value of debenture bonds with a market value of \$1,400,000. There is little doubt that the preferred stockholder would accept a proposition so favorable. The common stockholder is equally advantaged by such a plan. The earnings available for the common stock, after adding \$87,500 to the fixed charges of the company, are \$262,500, or five and two tenths per cent on the par value of the stock, out of which three per cent can be safely paid. Without any reduction of the par value of his security, the common stockholder at once receives an income. Such a case as this is, however, seldom encountered. Preferred dividends, when cumulative, are usually paid, even at the sacrifice of the permanent interest of the corporation. There are few cases of accumulation so great as to seriously depreciate the value of the common stock, and when this has occurred, as in the Republic Iron and Steel Company, and the Crucible Steel Company, earnings have usually recovered so as to permit the discharge of these back dividends without any scheme of reorganization. Wherever preferred dividends are allowed to accumulate to unmanageable proportions, however, the method above outlined will be found in most cases desirable.

Stock may also be reduced by exchanging into bonds with the consent of the statutory proportion of the stock. This method is applicable to seven and eight per cent preferred stocks issued by companies which are later able to place junior issues of bonds at fair prices. The most notable instance of such a conversion is that of the United States Steel Corporations bond conversion in 1902. On April 17, 1902, the president of the United States Steel Corporation issued a circular to the stockholders, which invited their coöperation in a plan to raise \$50,000,000 of new capital. Half of this amount was to repay loans incurred by the constituent companies for construction work which was, in part, rendered unnecessary by the merger, but which, owing to advance commitments, could not be suspended. In addition, $25,000,000 was required for improvements, which, it was stated, would effect an annual saving of at least $10,000,000. The plan proposed to the stockholders for raising this money was "to rearrange your corporation's capitalization (which, in round numbers, now consists of $300,000,000 of bonds, $500,000,000 of preferred stock, and $500,000,000 of common stock) by substituting for $200,000,000 of the preferred stock, $200,000,000 of sinking fund sixty-year five-per-cent mortgage gold bonds, and by selling $50,000,000 of additional bonds of such issue for cash. As the preferred carries seven per cent dividends, while the bonds would bear but five per cent interest, the $50,000,000 desired could, in this way, be added to the corporate resources, and the aggregate of the annual charges for interest and dividends, instead of being increased $3,500,000, would be decreased $1,-500,000 as compared with the present sum total of these two requirements."

The plan offered to each preferred stockholder the right to subscribe to the new bonds to the extent of one half his holdings of preferred stock, forty per cent of each subscription to be payable in preferred stock, and ten per cent in cash, or the subscription could be limited to forty per cent, in which event no cash payment was required. This transaction was assailed in the courts, and was delayed for a long period by injunctions. It was finally abandoned after $150,-000,000 of preferred stock had been converted. Conversion of stock into bonds such as this plan provided, can only be justified when the company making the conversion is so strong in surplus earnings that the issue of the new bonds will not jeopardize its solvency. Given this assurance, the advantage to the common stockholder is in the reduction of the payments which must precede his dividends, from the rate on the preferred stock to the rate of interest on the bonds issued in exchange.

We next take up the readjustment of the debt liabilities

of the company, dividing these into current liabilities, short term notes, and long term bonds. Current liabilities, when they exceed the normal amount in a particular industry, must be paid, either by the sale of some of the assets, or by the sale of bonds or notes. The methods of handling short term notes have already been discussed in Chapter XXIII.

When these are issued on the security of collateral, if a favorable opportunity arises to sell the collateral, provision is usually made for its retirement before maturity. When they mature, the method employed is either to sell the bond collateral and so obtain the means of payment, or to extend the notes, or to issue a new series of notes, or to take up the notes with an issue of stock. In most extension agreements, inducements are offered, usually in the form of higher rates of interest, or better security on the new issue. A syndicate may be organized to purchase the securities which are to be issued to take up those maturing, and then to offer to the holders of the maturing obligations the right to take the new securities on a favorable basis. The ordinary inducement is a cash premium.

The method of carrying through such a transaction is shown by the refunding of the $6,000,000 of four and one half per cent collateral trust notes issued by the Chicago, Rock Island & Pacific Railway Company in 1906. When these matured in April, 1908, the bond market was not in a condition to justify the offering of a long term security. The company, therefore, notified the note holders that it had arranged with Speyer & Company for the extension of these notes for one year, with interest at six per cent, subject to redemption at the option of the company on sixty days' notice. It was stated that "Holders who desire to extend their notes must present them, the April 1st coupon, at the office of Speyer & Company, on or before March 23d. A cash payment of $5 on each $1,000 note extended will be made to the holders availing themselves of this offer. Holders who do not desire to extend will receive par for their notes on April 1."

Speyer & Company had arranged with the Railway Company to purchase such an amount of the new notes as were not taken by the holders. The six per cent notes were offered at 99.5, yielding $6\frac{1}{2}$ per cent per annum, so it is fair to presume that Speyer & Company did not pay over 95 or 96. The more advantageous the extension offer is made, the easier will be the terms that can be arranged with the syndicate, since every note replaced with a new note lessens the financial liability of the bankers.

A special method of funding floating debt, which has been used for the relief of embarrassed companies, is the funding or deposit of interest coupons. This may be accomplished by several methods: arrangements may be made with a syndicate to purchase the amount of coupons which it may be impossible for the corporation to pay, taking the corporation's bonds as security, or the bondholders may be asked to take stock or bonds in lieu of their coupons, or they may be asked to deposit their coupons with some designated agent or trustee, foregoing their claim for interest during the period. The first plan of funding coupons is illustrated by the following announcement to certain bondholders of the Erie by President Underwood on June 11, 1908:

To the Holders of Prior Lien Bonds and General Lien Bonds Under the First Consolidated Mortgage:

"The extraordinary business depression, which has seriously affected all the railroads throughout the United States, has so reduced the net earnings of the Erie Railroad that there will be a deficit below the amount necessary to meet fixed charges for the current fiscal year ending June 30, 1908. While it is confidently expected that with any return to normal business conditions this deficit will promptly be made good, it is necessary for the company temporarily to obtain the amount from other sources.

"To this end, among other things, it has been arranged that the coupon for interest falling due at any time prior to July 1, 1909, may be purchased for cash and, with unimpaired lien, deposited and pledged under the collateral indenture of April 8, 1908, as additional security for the six per cent collateral gold notes issued and to be issued thereunder, thus making the notes more available to the company as a means of obtaining further cash if required, such notes to be accepted at par by the purchasers of the coupons for the amounts advanced for such purchase. While such temporary relief will probably suffice for the maintenance and operation of the property during the current calendar year, it will not be sufficient for the completion of the improvements begun two years ago, but which have not yet reached a condition where they are available for producing additional revenue for the company.

"It was anticipated that the funds for such improvements could be provided from the sale of your company's general mortgage bonds, but, principally owing to the injury done to your company's credit by the falling off in earnings during the existing business depression, such bonds are not now salable, except at prohibitive prices.

"As these improvements all serve to strengthen the security of the prior lien and the general mortgage bonds, it is expected that a plan will shortly be prepared for funding the coupons maturing on these bonds for a period sufficiently long to enable the company, out of its current funds, to complete the improvements now under way, and thus get the benefit of the large expenditures already made, but which, as above stated, remain as yet unproductive.

"You are therefore notified that your coupons, falling due July 1, 1908, will be purchased at par for cash by J. P. Morgan & Company, upon presentation and surrender thereof, on or before June 30, 1908, at their office, No. 23 Wall Street, New York."

The foregoing plan involved the sale to a syndicate of a sufficient amount of the collateral trust notes of the company to take up maturing coupons. The coupons so purchased, aggregating $3,160,480, were to be pledged under the indenture of the collateral trust notes, and the bankers accepted for their advances an equal face value out of $4,500,000 of the $15,000,000 note issue of 1908 which had been reserved. When these notes were paid, the liability of the company, on account of these coupons, lapsed.

This relief to the finances of the Erie was not considered sufficient, and a further proposition was made to the bondholders, that they should accept bonds of the company, instead of cash, for the coupons. This proposition, as finally approved by the Public Service Commission for the Second District of New York, was as follows: The company was to issue $30,000,000 par value of collateral trust thirty year five per cent bonds secured by general mortgage bonds which had been authorized but which, as the statement of President Underwood shows, could not be sold at reasonable prices. These bonds were to be exchanged for coupons on the general lien and convertible four per cent bonds up to the amount of $11,380,000, on the basis of par value of bonds for the face value of the coupons. The company, on its part, agreed to expend from income every six months, for improvements and additions to the property, an amount equal to the interest so funded which had accrued during the six months, this arrangement to continue for the five years during which the funding of coupons was to go forward. The advantages of this arrangement to the company and to the holders of these junior mortgage bonds were as follows:

The company was relieved of the necessity of paying interest, which at that time was not being earned, and was assured of $11,380,000 of new capital within five years on which it paid five per cent interest. The refunding scheme did not relieve it from the obligation of providing the money necessary to pay the interest on these junior lien bonds, but enabled it to apply this money to the improvement of the property. To the bondholder the advantages of the reorganization were even more apparent. They were set forth in a statement issued on behalf of the company as follows:

"We have put into the property in the last few years upward of $16,000,000 that has not been capitalized—$8,154,381 charged against income and $8,345,829 charged to capital account, and not yet represented by any bonds. In seeking to capitalize these expenditures, we are asking the assistance of our bondholders instead of outside investors, believing that we can get such assistance from the bondholders on much more favorable terms. As you will notice, the coupons are to be exchanged for the new bonds at par, whereas on the balance of the issue not consumed by the funding of the coupons or the refunding of the three year notes, the Public Service Commission fixes a net price to the company of 87½.

"We have, awaiting completion, on the Erie & Jersey Railroad and the Genesee River Railroad lines and others, important improvements in the shape of cut-off and low-grade lines into which we have put millions of money. We are not yet in a position to reap the benefit of these improvements because it will require several millions to complete them, and we do not feel that we can take the amount necessary to complete them from operating income. Therefore we are undertaking to defer the interest on the general lien and the convertible four per cent bonds and to put the equivalent amount into the completion of the improvements in question, so that at the end of the five years, the road will be in a position to take up all its obligations and operate at a profit.

"There is hardly any question as to our ability to do this. In every year from the reorganization until last year the Erie showed a surplus, including coal properties, of from $4,000,000 to $7,000,000 over its fixed charges. Last year, on account of the extraordinary conditions, there was a deficit, but the first six months of the current fiscal year show a surplus from operation, and when the revenues from its coal are taken in, there is a surplus of $2,000,000 for the six months. This is after all the interest has been paid, including that which it is now proposed to defer, so that I do not think there is any reasonable possibility of our being unable to put the required amount into the property out of income from year to year."

If the Erie did not obtain new capital, it must abandon improvements on which a large amount of money had already been expended and which were as yet unproductive. Unless this work could be carried through, the prospects of the company were gloomy. With the new capital, however, there was every reason to believe that the Erie could be placed on a basis of assured solvency, and that no such desperate remedies as that explained in the announcement of President Underwood would in fact be necessary. The bondholders were not asked to forego their interest. They were merely invited to invest their interest in the five per cent bonds of the company, which would be well secured and marketable at a price near par. The plan of the Erie for the funding of coupons was unusually favorable to the bondholders. They were to receive their interest in the form of salable bonds, but were assured that the amount of the interest would be invested in the property. It was not found necessary to put this plan into operation, owing to the improvement in the bond market, which enabled the Erie to obtain the necessary money by selling its bonds as originally contemplated.

In most cases, the bondholders do not receive so much consideration, the alternative being presented to them of either depositing their coupons and foregoing, for a time, their claim to interest, or taking the chances of bankruptcy. In return for the deposited coupons, the company may issue negotiable receipts. The usual method, however, is a simple postponing of interest without equivalent. The first method is illustrated by the plan for funding the coupons due from August 1, 1908, to February 1, 1912, on the first mortgage bonds of the Hudson River Electric Power Company. This contemplates the issue of $4,000,000 collateral coupon notes in exchange for the coupons dollar for dollar: "In case of default for thirty days in payment of interest, then so much of the principal of the notes as is represented by deposited coupons whose dates of maturity shall have been reached, shall, at the election of the trustee, upon the request of the holders of sixty per cent of the outstanding notes, become immediately due and payable. And in case of thirty days default in the payment of any portion of the principal of the notes, the trustee shall, upon demand, restore to the respective holders the coupons uncanceled." The deposit of coupons without a return from the company is illustrated by the action of the bondholders of the Deschutes (Oregon) Irrigation Company who unanimously agreed on February 10, 1908, to surrender to a committee of the bondholders the coupon due March 1, 1908, and also, if the committee so requested, the coupon due September 1, 1908. The company was expected eventually to pay these coupons with interest at six per cent, but in the failure to do so, or in the event of a receivership, the bonds themselves were to be deposited with the committee. Here is a postponement of interest for the benefit of a temporarily embarrassed corporation. Action such as the foregoing is prudent. The bondholders do not care to take over the property with the responsibilities of its management. The expenses of receivership and reorganization might subject them to heavy losses. When they can be readily reached, and the proposition clearly presented to them, it should not be difficult to persuade bondholders to defer their demands for interest, in order that the company may bridge over a temporary embarrassment.

Taking up now the readjustment of long term bonds, we have, first, the conversion of bonds into stock; this has been already fully discussed under the head of convertible bonds. In Chapter XXIV it was shown that the advantage to the company in using convertible bonds which were eventually exchanged for stock was, in effect, the sale of stock at a higher price than could have been obtained for the stock in the market and also, upon conversion, a reduction of its fixed charges and a resulting improvement of its credit. The advantage to the stockholder is an opportunity for a speculative profit, or to exchange his four or five per cent security, for a stock whose dividends may rise to such an amount as to show him a large yield on his investment.

The usual adjustment necessary in long term bonds is the conversion of one issue into another. We have already discussed at some length (in Chapter VII) the general inexpediency of providing for the payment in cash of bonds at maturity. Such provision can only be made by the accumulation of a fund in interest-bearing securities, or to pay off the debt, during its life, by installments, out of the income. Since a growing corporation is continually in need of money for improvements, and since the return on such expenditures is usually far greater than the return on any securities which could be purchased for the sinking fund, it is for the interest of the company, instead of accumulating a sinking fund in bonds, to spend the equivalent of the sinking fund on its property. Such a policy, however, makes no special provision for the repayment of bonds at maturity. Its object is to make the corporation so strong in assets and earnings that when its bonds mature, there will be no difficulty in placing a new issue which can either be exchanged directly for the maturing bonds, or can be sold for cash for an amount sufficient to pay off those bonds whose holders wish to change their investment.

An additional reason for refunding bonds, instead of accumulating a sinking fund to pay them, is found in the fact that new enterprises usually pay high rates of interest, owing to the limited demand for such unseasoned securities. If the corporation succeeds, its credit will improve to the point of placing bonds at much lower rates. When bonds mature, a considerable saving can therefore be made by taking them up with other bonds bearing low rates.

Refunding of bonds may take place either before the bonds mature, or at maturity. If bonds are issued subject to call at a fixed price, no difficulty is presented in retiring them. If, for example, a corporation issues $1,000,000 of six per cent bonds at 90, callable at 105 after three years, and if its credit improves to the point of selling a five per cent bond at 95, it is profitable for the company to call the six per cent bonds, replacing them with an issue of 5s. The economy of the transaction can be represented as follows:

Amount of five per cent bonds at ninety-five required to produce $1,050,000	$1,105,262
Interest at five per cent on these bonds	55,263
Interest on the six per cent bonds which are retired,	60,000
Annual saving	4,737

Conversion before maturity is sometimes made in order to provide for new financing with first mortgage bonds without the provision in the mortgage that these bonds can be issued for securities purchased. The opportunity may arise for acquiring control of desired properties, by exchanging bonds which carry stock control with them. The bonds outstanding under the first mortgage, however, present an obstacle to this transaction. In such a case, the bonds could be called and replaced with a new issue secured by a mortgage containing the desired provision. When such a conversion is contemplated, the cost can be greatly reduced if a large amount of the bonds, whose holders are not entitled to information concerning the intention of the buyers, can be purchased at the regular market price. The five per cent bonds, for example, which might be callable at 105 would not sell for more than 95. In anticipation of the conversion, arrangements could be made with the house which placed the bonds to accumulate as many as possible, in the interest of the corporation, at the market price. In this way, the premium need only be paid on those bonds which it is impossible to secure.

When bonds are not callable before maturity, and if they cannot be purchased at reasonable prices in the interest of the company, certain inducements must be offered to the holder. These may take the form either of better security on the new bonds, or a higher market value in the new bonds than those which are retired, or a bonus of cash or stock. An illustration of the method of accomplishing such a refunding is furnished by the readjustment of the bonded debt of the St. Louis & San Francisco in 1901. It was proposed to take up thirteen underlying issues secured, for the most part, by first mortgages on certain portions of the company's property, by issuing a refunding fifty-year mortgage bond, of which $62,500,000 were reserved for refunding purposes. By unifying the indebtedness of the sytem, the company not only reduced interest charges, but was also enabled to finance additions by selling bonds having an established market value. A syndicate was formed under the management of J. & W. Seligman, which agreed to purchase for refunding purposes $30,000,000 face value of the refunding mortgage bonds. The syndicate then made the following offer to the holders of the underlying bonds:

"*To Holders of the Following Underlying Bonds:*—

"As Syndicate Managers of a syndicate formed under an agreement dated April 4, 1901, we have arranged with the St. Louis & San Francisco Railroad Company to purchase, for refunding purposes, $30,000,000, face value of its proposed Refunding Mortgage Gold Bonds, to bear interest at the rate of four per cent per annum, and hereby offer to exchange such refunding bonds (to the extent to which they may be so issued and acquired by the syndicate), for underlying bonds of the railroad company's system, on the following basis:

For Each $1,000 Face Value of the Following Outstanding Bonds	In Refunding Bonds, Face Value	Cash	Market Price (*Added*) Range on June 8, 1901
1. 6% Second Mortgage A, B and C Bonds........	$1,166.66	113¾ and int.	112–114⅛
2. 6% Missouri & Western Division First Mortgage Bonds..........	1,282.05	125 " "	
3. 6% Trust Bonds of 1880..	1,282.05	125 " "	
4. 6% General Mortgage Bonds..............	1,369.23	133½ " "	134–135¼
5. 5% General Mortgage Bonds..............	1,194.87	116½ " "	118–118½
6. 5% Trust Bonds of 1887..	1,179.49	115 " "	102½–112
7. 6% St. Louis, Wichita & Western First Mortgage Redeemable Bonds..............	1,179.49	115 " "	
8. 6% Fort Smith & Van Buren Bridge First Mortgage bonds (redeemable)..........	1,128.20	110 " "	
9. 5% Southwestern Division Bonds (redeemable).	1,025.64	100 " "	
10. 4% Central Division Bonds (redeemable)...	1,051.28	102½ " "	
11. 4% Kansas City Division Bonds (redeemable)...	1,000.00	97½ " "	
12. 3% Kansas City Division Bonds (redeemable)...	876.93	85½ " "	
13. 4% Northwestern Division Bonds (redeemable)..........	1,051.28	102½ " "	
14. 4% Red River Division Bonds..............	974.35	95 " "	
15. 4% Consolidated Bonds..	1,025.64	100 " "	

"At the time of deposit, holders of underlying bonds will receive payment in cash of the unmatured interest accrued and accruing upon their deposited bonds to July 1, 1901, from which date the refunding bonds are to bear interest."

A comparison of these two tables with the third, giving the current market quotation of the more important of these underlying bonds, shows the advantage to the holders of accepting the syndicate's offer. The price offered was, in every case, higher than the current market quotation. Furthermore, the bondholders received in exchange for bonds included in various small issues, the bonds of a large issue which they could readily market, and which would be accepted by banks as collateral security to a high percentage of their par value. These bonds were offered on an exchange basis, at prices which were, on the whole, more favorable than could have been secured in the market. The offer in cash was slightly below the offer in bonds, and the only question which could arise in the minds of the holders concerning the acceptance of the bond offered, was whether the new four per cent bond would sell at par. At the time, there was every indication that the new bonds would sell at a high price. For the nine months ending March 31, 1901, the St. Louis & San Francisco had shown surplus earnings over fixed charges of $1,451,817, and it was estimated that, for the year, these surplus earnings would be $1,725,000. The direct saving in interest by the refunding, in case all the bonds were got in, was $70,000. In addition, it was expected that earnings would be largely increased as a result of capital expenditures then in progress. The sequel proved, however, that of the holders of the underlying bonds, those who accepted the cash offer chose the better part. The general four per cent bonds have sold below par ever since that date. The offer by the syndicate of these favorable terms was intended to reduce the amount of cash required. If all the bonds could be called in and exchanged, the syndicate could pay for the $30,000,000 of refunding bonds with the old bonds, advancing only a small amount of money, and retaining the surplus amount of bonds for sale.

When bonds are called at maturity, they may be taken up with stock or with new bonds or with notes, or the old bonds may be extended. The methods of accomplishing these various forms of refunding have already been considered in connection with the handling of maturing note issues and require no extended discussion here. The usual method is to employ the bonds of an issue previously authorized for the purpose of refunding. Careful provision is made in the mortgage for satisfying the claims of all maturing bonds, and for releasing the property from the underlying mortgages in order that it may come directly under the security of the general mortgage. When the bond market is unfavorable, notes may be employed to fund maturing bonds, or the bonds may be extended. In the latter case, extra inducements must be offered to the holders of maturing bonds to induce them to defer their claims.

CHAPTER XXXII

RECEIVERSHIPS

In our study of the corporate mortgage we have seen how large and sweeping are the powers of the trustee in reference to the disposition of the corporate property in the event of bankruptcy. The trustee has the authority to enter upon the property of the corporation and to operate it, collecting the receipts. Out of the receipts he is to pay its debts. He may also proceed against the company, and secure a sale of the property under the mortgage, applying the proceeds to the liquidation of its indebtedness. The theory of the mortgage, therefore, is that the property of a corporation which fails to pay its debts is to be seized by the trustee and sold, the proceeds being applied in satisfaction of its obligations. The powers of the trustee of a corporate mortgage have been taken over from the language of real estate mortgages. It is the custom, in case of default of interest or principal on debts secured by real estate mortgage, for the creditor to realize on the property of the bankrupt by having it forthwith sold under the authority of the court, compelling the owner to either bid enough at the sale to pay off the indebtedness or to forfeit possession of it. It is also customary in the settlement of the affairs of mercantile houses which become insolvent that the creditors should seize their stocks of merchandise and forthwith have them sold by the court for their benefit. While similar remedies are apparently preserved to the creditor of a corporation in the terms of the mortgage by which his bonds are secured, the theory of the corporation mortgage cannot, in many cases, be carried out.

Most business corporations are organized in the field of manufacturing, mining, or transportation. They conduct their business with properties, which, unlike real estate or merchandise, are highly specialized to some particular use, and can be used for no other purpose. Take, for example, the property of a railroad. It consists of terminals, on which stand certain buildings which can be used for nothing else than the purposes of the railroad, of certain real estate in the form of strips of land 100 feet wide and thousands of miles in length, between which runs the track, consisting of rails, spikes, fish plates and ties, and laid in ballast. Over this track runs the railroad equipment consisting of cars and locomotives. We have here a different kind of property from a store building or a farm. The property of the railroad can be used for no other purpose than the transportation of passengers and commodities. If sold, it must be sold to another railroad company.

Furthermore, a railroad property is a unit. To the successful operation of a railroad, all the items above enumerated are essential. A railroad must have main lines and it must have branch lines. In many cases it must control coal mining companies which furnish it traffic. It must own large amounts of real estate at its terminal points, and must have the necessary number of cars and locomotives, a stock of materials and a cash balance. All of this property is necessary to the operation of the road. No part of it can be separated from the others and sold without destroying a large part of its value. Furthermore, a railroad company may have valuable charter and franchise privileges, without which its operations could not be conducted. It has built up over a number of years a wide-spreading business organization by means of which it obtains traffic. The value of this property depends on the income which can be obtained from its use. If we look on the value of the company's property as the capitalization of the net earnings accruing from the operation of that property, we must admit that, to the earning of these profits, not merely a physical property but franchises and business organization are indispensable.

It follows, therefore, that if the creditors of the company should enforce the liens of their mortgages, and should take the property away from the company, especially in those cases where the different mortgages cover different portions of the property, in which event the enforcement of their liens will break the property to pieces, a large part of the value of this property will be immediately destroyed. In this value of the property, based upon its earning power, consists the security of creditors and the equity of stockholders. If, however, the creditors' claims are allowed to take their natural course of suit, judgment, attachment, and execution, the property of the company will be broken up, its working capital seized, the equipment hauled off its lines, its terminals taken from it, its organization destroyed, the franchises are perhaps lost and its earning power reduced to nothing. The effect is generally to make it impossible for the stockholders to recover any value from the wreckage, and to seriously jeopardize the security of even underlying mortgage bonds supposed to be fully protected by surplus earnings.

When a corporation approaches bankruptcy, it usually occurs that different portions of its property have been pledged as security for various issues of bonds. If the company is operating a railroad, for example, there are several first mortgages covering the different divisions of the main line of the railroad. Then over these is probably spread the lien of a general or blanket mortgage. Tributary to the main line of the railroad are a number of branch lines, and each one of these may carry mortgages to secure issues of bonds. These bonds have probably been delivered to the parent company in repayment of advances to the subsidiary company. The parent company may have pledged the bonds as security for an issue of collateral trust bonds. The equipment of the company may be covered by the lien of a car trust lease. The company perhaps operates coal-mining companies which have bonds outstanding against them. The terminal properties may also be pledged as security for separate mortgages. In addition to all these complexities of obligations, there may be unsecured debentures outstanding, issues of short-time notes and bank loans, money due employés and to concerns which have furnished supplies and materials to the railroad. Suppose, now, each one of these creditors should undertake to enforce his claim against the company, which he has the undoubted right to do. Is it not evident that the property would be completely disintegrated in the contest of creditors? Each set of creditors would make off with a piece of the *corpus,* and the value of the property, after it had been torn to pieces by the creditors, would have little relation to its value as a going concern. The organization of the business would be broken up, its markets destroyed, its good will extinguished.

It is manifestly the concern of all parties that the creditors should be prevented from exercising their rights under their various mortgages and liens, and that the property of the company should be placed beyond their reach so that the continuity of its operations may be undisturbed, and its earnings may continue to accrue until such settlement of its affairs can be made as will preserve the value of the property. The unsecured creditors, if they obtain judgment and levy execution, can usually find some property to attach, some cash or materials which have not been pledged as security for any loan, but if they laid their hands upon the working capital of the company, they may compel it to cease operations, thereby reducing their chances of recovering anything more than what they have seized to zero. As for the secured creditors, if they sit passive and allow the merchandise and bank creditors to prey upon the company, they may find their own security rapidly disappearing. But if they enforce their rights, then neither stockholders nor unsecured creditors are likely to receive anything.

A typical situation resulting in an application for a receivership is described in a letter of President Bush, of the Western Maryland Railroad Company to the directors of that company in March, 1908, in which he sets forth the reasons leading to the receivership:

"The gross revenues of the railway for the six months ended December 31, 1907, increased $540,725, or 20.332 per cent, and the net revenues increased $350,176, or 30.224 per cent over those of the corresponding period of the last fiscal year, with a resulting surplus over all fixed charges, including the abnormally high cost of temporary loans and renewals.

"The company is not confronted with any failure of its revenues to cover its full fixed charges, and its business has maintained a steady growth with unmistakable assurance of continued development. It has, however, maturing obligations, arising out of its temporary provisions for capital expenditures, and it must at an early date encounter the problem presented by the commodity clause of the Federal rate law.

"As you are aware, this company has outstanding loans maturing April 1, 1908, to the amount of $3,776,750, secured by pledge of $5,037,000 of its first mortgage bonds. The market price of these bonds—originally in considerable excess over the loans, has, notwithstanding substantial increase in gross and net revenues, shrunk to a level below the face of the loans.

"It has now become apparent that the company will be unable to meet these loans or to provide additional collateral to secure their extension. In this situation, the company itself will, of course, be unable to borrow the money necessary to meet mortgage interest falling due on the first of April next."

It may be possible, in rare instances, to secure the coöperation of all creditors in deferring the enforcement of their claims, and to give the company an opportunity to recover itself without the expense of a receivership. When there are only bondholders to consider, in case the holders of the number of bonds without which the trustee cannot be forced to act, can coöperate with the trustee in protecting the company, the necessary relief can be afforded without a receivership. Sometimes bondholders' committees will advance funds to meet pressing claims. As a general rule, however, creditors cannot be brought together, and the property must be protected against their assaults.

The property can be placed beyond the reach of the creditors by invoking the aid of a court of equity, the direct representative of the sovereign power of the state which created the corporation, one of whose recognized duties is to take charge of the estates of bankrupt individuals, firms, or corporations, and to preserve this property until the creditors can make a settlement with the bankrupt, or until a sale can be made of the property on more favorable terms than can be obtained by the creditors acting each for himself. The court takes charge of the estate of a bankrupt corporation through its agent, who is known as a receiver. The receiver is an officer of the court to whose charge is intrusted the estate of the bankrupt corporation. The judge, in placing the property of the company in the hands of a receiver, takes it away from the corporation, puts it out of reach of the creditors, and places it in a position to be secured, both from the mismanagement of officers and directors and the attacks of its creditors.

The reason for the appointment of a receiver has already been indicated, namely, to conserve the value of the company's property. He is often appointed at the instance of the directors who see long before any creditor the impending insolvency of the company, and who, at the first threat of disaster, fly to the shelter of a court of equity. The situation is something as follows: A federal judge is approached by directors of some corporation which is in difficulty, either in his court room or privately. Accompanying the directors is a creditor of the company. The attorney of the company informs the judge, to whom in most cases he is well and favorably known, that his client, the A. B. Corporation, is insolvent and he produces a creditor as evidence of the fact. The creditor states that the company owes him certain money, and the officials of the company are there present to confirm that the debt is due, and that the company is unable to pay it. In the interest of all parties concerned, therefore, the court is asked to appoint a receiver to take charge of the property until a settlement of its affairs can be obtained. The plea is forcibly made that unless the court intervenes, by appointing a receiver, the creditors of the company will seize upon its property and will render it unable to perform its functions. It may be represented that the embarrassment of the company is due to special and exceptional causes, and that, if the court takes its property under its protection, a few months will suffice to extricate the company from its difficulties. This procedure is known as making out a *prima facie* case for the appointment of a receiver.

If the judge suspects no fraud in the matter, he forthwith appoints a receiver, first temporarily, until the other parties in interest can have an opportunity to be heard, and afterwards, unless good reason appears for discharging the receiver, the receivership is made permanent. While most bankrupt companies do not present such a complex situation as we have supposed, there are usually at least three conflicting interests to be considered: secured creditors, unsecured creditors, and stockholders. The stockholders, it is true, have no claim against the company for money loaned, but they have an interest in the company which will be sacrificed if its property is torn from it. It may happen, for example, that the embarrassment has been caused by the maturing of a note issue which, owing to the condition of the bond market, cannot be funded at that time. Otherwise, the company may be abundantly able to meet its obligations. The stockholders have here an interest which deserves recognition and protection.

The receiver whom the judge appoints is usually an official of the bankrupt corporation, often its chief counsel. The reason for making such an appointment is that the judge, not being familiar with the operation of a railroad or manufacturing concern, wishes to install one conversant with the business and who can carry it on successfully. If he appointed a stranger to the property, it might suffer injury. When a receiver is shown unfit to hold this position, or if it can be made to appear to the court that with a particular receiver in control of the property, bankers will not come to its assistance, the receiver may be removed. When large public companies apply for the appointment of a receiver, the court is usually careful that the appointment is acceptable to all interests concerned. President Bush, of the Western Maryland Railroad Company, for example, was appointed receiver of the property of that company. On the other hand, in 1893, President McLeod, of the Philadelphia & Reading Railroad Company, who was at first appointed receiver, was later forced to resign, owing to the opposition of banking interests who held him responsible for the failure of the company.

Immediately following his appointment, the receiver assumes possession of the property of the company under the authority of an order of the appointing court, which usually authorizes the receiver:

(1) To take possession of the property of the corporation; to keep this property in good condition and repair, and to operate the property just as the corporation operated it;

(2) to receive the income from the property and to apply this income under the direction of the court to the payment of operating expenses and fixed charges;

(3) to collect all debts due the company, and to defend all suits to which it may be defendant.

In the performance of these functions, the receiver may employ such counsel or agents as he may deem necessary.

He must ascertain as accurately as possible the status of the corporation, and make a report to the court. He must also make further reports from time to time, and must obtain express authority for any extraordinary action, such as the discontinuance of interest on bonds or the sale of certain property.

In carrying out his duties, it is necessary for the receiver to provide money. When he takes charge, he usually finds a large amount of wages and audited vouchers due and unpaid. The property of the company has usually been allowed to deteriorate, no money being spent out while the directors were endeavoring to tide over their period of trial. He also finds various issues of bonds whose holders set up a claim to the earnings accruing from the operation of the business. There are also claimants under the lease of property which it is necessary for the company to retain. This situation requires that the receiver should provide a large amount of money at once to liquidate the more pressing claims against the company. He must then take up the question of dealing with the various creditors who may in the meantime have brought suit, usually in the court which has taken charge of the property, to establish their various claims. In carrying out these duties, the receiver must raise a considerable amount of money. He has three sources to rely upon. First, such part of the income of the company as is not required to pay operating expenses, interest, and rentals; second, the interest and rentals themselves; and third, the use of a form of obligation known as the receiver's certificate.

The receivership may have been caused by the inability of the company to fund or extend an issue of short-time notes. Aside from this, the company may be solvent, able to pay all interest claims. If the property is earning more than enough to pay the fixed charges of the company from which it has been taken by the court, and in case the receiver elects to pay those fixed charges, he can use the surplus income in his hands to defray any proper expenses of the company. In but few cases, however, is this surplus income sufficient for the receiver's needs. He must obtain additional funds. These he gets, in the first instance, by reducing the fixed charges of the company, by simply declining to pay certain amounts of interest and rentals. The creditors are powerless. The property which secures their obligations is in the receiver's hands, they can obtain their interest only by an order of the court. If, in the opinion of the receiver, whom the judge usually supports, the needs of the property require such action, he need pay no interest, and may apply all of the money which would otherwise go to the creditors, to pay the pressing obligations of the company. As a rule, however, when interest has been earned, it is paid by the receiver.

The owners of leased property need not submit, unless they desire, to the forfeiture of the rentals. The receiver has no title to their property; his possession of it depends upon his carrying out the covenants of the lease under which the corporation secured it. The lessor company, in case he fails to pay their rental, may, at any time, resume possession of the leased property, and may sue as general creditors for any unpaid balance on the rental or for any other damage which they may have sustained. When leases are profitable to the lessee, there is no danger that the receiver will run any risk of losing control of the property. With unprofitable leases, however, this method of refusing to pay rentals which have not been earned has been largely employed. Stockholders in the lessor company, in such a case, are deterred from acting in defense of their rights by the practical impossibility of making an advantageous arrangement for the disposition of their property elsewhere. In few instances, however, does the receiver carry his powers to this extreme. He is usually satisfied to pay interest and rentals where interest and rentals have been earned, and to refuse to pay only in those cases where the property has not produced a sufficient revenue to meet the specific charges upon it.

The disbursement of the revenues coming into the receiver's hands is made under the supervision of the court appointing him. An illustration of the method usually followed is furnished by the following quotation from an order issued by Judge Lacombe, making permanent the receivership of the New York City Railway:

"In the matter of improvements the receivers are fortunately relieved, at least in part, from the burden of devising improvements in the system by the existence of the Public Service Commission.

"The receipts from car service will be devoted first to maintenance, including all necessary repairs and replacements. Next in order are certain fixed charges in the nature of rentals and interest falling due on various mortgage bonds of such roads, which by the terms of the leases, the New York City Railway Company has covenanted to pay. It would seem to be to the public interest, because of facility of transfer, that the roads which were being run by the City Railway when receivers were appointed, should be operated as a unit. For the present, therefore, the receivers will continue to pay such rentals and mortgage interest.

"This will not include the rental in the Third Avenue Railroad which will fall due the last of this month. A clause in the lease of that road provides that default in the payment of any installment of that rental cannot be availed of for six months. Long before that time sufficient information can be gathered (and made public) by the receivers to give such enlightenment as to the whole situation as will enable the court to deal understandingly will all questions as to payment of all these items of rent and mortgage interest.

"Before default is made in any case (except the one above referred to and the rental due October 15 to the Metropolitan Street Railway) petition will be filed setting forth all the facts bearing on the question and asking instructions, and a day will be fixed on which not only the parties to the suit, but all in any way interested (including the Public Service Commission) will be heard as to the most equitable and wisest course to pursue.

"Until further order, the receivers will also, if the other

parties to such arrangements consent, carry out the arrangements by which the New York City Railway Company operates certain railroads not under lease, such as the Dry Dock East Broadway & Battery Railroad and the Union Railway."

To obtain the money required, the receiver usually resorts to the use of receiver's certificates. A receiver's certificate is, in effect, a short-term note secured by a first mortgage upon all the property in the receiver's hands. It is true that when the property was in the possession of the company the title to the property may have been vested in trust for the payment of bonds with a trustee. By the appointment of a receiver, however, the court takes into its own possession the title to the property, and, like any other owner, can pledge any of its possessions as security for a loan. These certificates may be either without date, or they may run for a definite period. An illustration of the first kind of receiver's certificate is the following, issued in 1880 by the receivers of the Philadelphia & Reading Railroad Company:

> Receivers' Office, Philadelphia & Reading Railroad Company.
>
> Philadelphia, May 24, 1880.
>
> This is to certify that there is due to —— or order from Edwin M. Lewis, Franklin B. Gowen and Stephen A. Caldwell, receivers of the Philadelphia & Reading Railroad Company (and not individually) one thousand dollars, on account of money borrowed by said receivers, under order of court, for payment of wages and interest upon certain mortgage indebtedness of said company.
>
> This certificate is transferable by indorsement, and redeemable after ten days' notice by advertisement in one or more daily papers of the City of Philadelphia, of the readiness of the receivers to make payment at the expiration of which notice interest thereon shall cease.
>
> Receivers,
>
> (Signed) W. McKenna,
>
> Circuit Judge.

The later form of certificate is illustrated by those issued in 1910 by the receivers of the Illinois Tunnel Company:

> This is to certify that for value received Charles G. Dawes and David R. Forgan, as receivers of the Illinois Tunnel Company, and not individually, are indebted to the bearer hereof in the sum of one thousand dollars ($1,000), payable at the National City Bank of New York, in the City of New York, or, at the option of the holder hereof, at the Continental National Bank, in the City of Chicago, two years from the date hereof, in gold coin of the United States of America of the present standard of weight and fineness, with interest thereon at the rate of six per cent (6%) per annum, payable semiannually, in like gold coin, on the first days of October and April, upon presentation and surrender, at one of the places therein specified, of the coupons for said interest as they severally mature.
>
> This certificate is part of an issue of certificates of like tenor and date not exceeding in the aggregate the principal sum of three million five hundred thousand dollars ($3,500,000) at any one time outstanding, authorized by an order of the Circuit Court of the United States for the Northern District of Illinois, Eastern Division, dated the 16th day of March, 1910, and on said day filed in the office of the clerk of said court, entitled in two certain actions pending in said court and consolidated under the title of The Corporation Trust Company against Illinois Tunnel Company and Central Trust Company of Illinois, as Trustee, against the Illinois Tunnel Company, and others. This certificate is issued pursuant to and is entitled to the benefits and security specified in the foregoing order, subject to all the terms and provisions whereof this certificate is issued and held. Among other things it is provided in said order that:
>
> "Said certificates of indebtedness to the amount of the principal and interest thereof shall constitute a lien upon all the property of every nature and description of the defendant Illinois Tunnel Company, and upon the telephone system which may be constructed

> by the said receivers, and upon all equipment and other property that may be acquired or provided by means of the said certificates or the proceeds thereof, and upon all net earnings and income which may hereafter result from the operation of the property in charge of the said receivers, which lien shall be prior to the lien of the judgment received in this court by the Corporation Trust Company against the Illinois Tunnel Company on December 1, 1909, for $1,129,-428.64 and prior to the lien of the First Mortgage or Deed of Trust, dated December 1, 1903, made by the Illinois Tunnel Company to the Equitable Trust Company, Chicago as Trustee (under which indenture the Central Trust Company of Illinois is now the duly constituted and acting successor Trustee), and prior to the rights of the holders of any and all bonds issued under the said First Mortgage or Deed of Trust."

These obligations are managed like short-term notes. They may be issued to consolidate other issues of the same kind; they may be called at any time; or they may be extended at maturity.

Money is provided by receivers' certificates for various purposes. These obligations are usually issued in small amounts, soon after the receiver takes charge, to pay pressing claims, e. g., for wages and supplies. Larger issues may provide for repairs which are necessary to the operation of the property. As a rule, a receiver will go no further than this in asking authority to issue receivers' certificates. Bondholders can have no objection to the provision of money for the purposes indicated. It is true that the lien of the certificates precedes that of the first mortgage, but if the receiver did not provide the money, the property could not be operated economically and its value would dwindle to the injury of its creditors. Receiver Frederick W. Whitridge, who took possession of the Third Avenue Railroad on January 12, 1908, on May 9th, reported to the Chairman of the Bondholders' Committee, showing the situation arising out of the previous neglect of the property with which the receiver must promptly deal, if he is to maintain and increase its earnings. This portion of his report is, in part, as follows:

"*Physical Condition.*—The general conditions of the Third Avenue Railroad were very bad; there were no offices, no supplies, or material on hand; the shops had been neglected; the track was and is in very bad shape; the cars in need of extensive repairs. The power house alone was in good condition.

"The supplies and material immediately necessary, most of which has been received, amounted to $50,000. Sprinkling apparatus in all of the barns and the cost of the various other fire apparatus essential to secure new insurance, the old policies, after the repeated fires in the New York City Railway barns, having been nearly canceled, amounted to $135,000; I hope presently that the property upon the system will meet the requirements of the most exigent underwriters.

"*Car Repairs.*—Of the 567 cars delivered to me by the New York City Railway Company receivers, there was not one on which some work was not immediately necessary. I ordered a sufficient number of new motors and controllers (50) to fully equip every car in the system. I estimate the total cost of putting all the cars in order, including the new motors and other electrical equipment, to be approximately $300,000.

"*Repair to Track.*—In many places on the main line of the Third Avenue track the contact rail is completely worn away, the slot rail very thin, and the car rail worn to the breaking point. Paving of the tracks, in accordance with the city ordinance, with Belgian blocks, will save $5,000 or $6,000 a year in maintenance. Under a temporary arrangement with the New York City Railway receivers, we are to repair the crossings on joint account. Altogether there will be needed for the track this year about $436,000 and thereafter, with a liberal allowance for maintenance, I think no further expenditure will be necessary for some years to come.

"*Buildings.*—The building at Sixty-fifth Street and Third Avenue needs extensive repairs to the roof, and in order to enable the shops to do their work certain other structural alterations are required, bringing up the total cost to about $151,000 for $14,821 of which amount I have let contracts.

"At 129th Street and Third Avenue there is, in front of the car barn, a building used as a hotel and several tumbledown stores or saloons. I propose to clean out the main building and construct therein proper offices for the Third Avenue and other lines; also accommodations for a club for the employees, which are much needed. The whole improvement will cost nearly $106,000."

To meet the cost of these and other improvements and payments, the receiver stated:

"I intend to ask the court for authority to issue $2,500,000 of receivers' certificates, payable within one year and bearing interest at the rate of six per cent. With those and the earnings from the property I think I can do all of the work and make all the payments which I have herein enumerated. It may be desirable to issue a certain number of certificates of the Union Railway, to an amount necessary to pay for the car barns, the Bronx & Pelham Parkway construction, and for the power station, not exceeding in all, however, $750,000, which could later be taken up by the Third Avenue certificates; or it may be desirable, while having authority, to issue certificates for the Union Railway, as above mentioned, as I already have authority to issue certificates for the Forty-second Street and the Dry Dock railways of which I have not availed myself, to issue Third Avenue certificates for the whole amount of $2,500,000 directly, as the bankers may prefer those to certificates of the other roads. If the certificates of those subordinate lines could be used permanently, the Third Avenue certificates should be diminished *pro tanto,* but in any case only certificates for $2,500,000 for one year will be outstanding."

Cases may arise, however, when receivers must go much further in the issue of these obligations than the payment of accrued wages and the making of necessary repairs. The property of the company, as with the Illinois Tunnel Company, may be only in part completed. Unless it is finished at once, it may not be possible to secure profitable business. For example, in anticipation of the construction of a power plant, contracts with consumers may have been signed whose binding force depends upon the delivery of power before a certain date. The company may have failed, leaving the plant half finished, and a receiver takes charge of the property. He finds a rival concern ready to run lines into this section and seize the market for power. The receiver, under these conditions, may have no choice but to mortgage the property to obtain funds for its completion in order to deliver power and secure the benefit of the contracts. He takes this action as much in the interest of the creditors as of the stockholders. Unless receivers' certificates were issued, the power plant when finished would find its market absorbed by its rivals.

Existing creditors of the company are violently opposed to the issue of receivers' certificates of large amount and often appeal to the court not to allow the receiver to place this new encumbrance ahead of the lien on their security. Their pleas are, however, usually disregarded. The court stands by its own appointee, the receiver, and is usually guided, as to the necessity of the issue of certificates, by the receiver's recommendations. The amount of money which the receiver will spend upon the property depends on his conception of his duties. If he looks upon his obligation as merely to preserve the business, as it were, in a state of suspended animation, doing as little as possible to repair or improve the property, merely protecting it from the onslaught of creditors until the different interests can be adjusted and the receiver discharged, he is not apt to issue more certificates than are necessary to pay the claims which press upon him in the form of unpaid wages, etc., when he takes charge of the property. If, however, he interprets the word conservation in its broad sense, he may conceive it to be his duty not only to preserve the property, but also to do all things necessary to increase its efficiency. In carrying out this obligation he may borrow large sums of money, and he may do a considerable amount of important work and even new construction. An illustration of this conception of the receiver's duties is furnished by the receivership of the Baltimore & Ohio Railroad Company.

The receivers appointed for the Baltimore & Ohio in 1896 were Mr. John K. Cowen and Mr. Oscar G. Murray. They were confronted with a difficult situation. The property of the company was in need of entire reconstruction. Ties, roadbed, rails, bridges, piers, cars, and locomotives were sadly in need of replacement or repair. The equipment of the company was particularly defective, a large number of freight cars and locomotives being out of service, and the equipment available for use being entirely insufficient to take care of the traffic offering. Moreover, the competitive situation of the Baltimore & Ohio was at this time peculiarly unfortunate. To the north lay the Pennsylvania, equipped to handle traffic at the lowest cost. On the south the Chesapeake & Ohio was a vigorous competitor, both for through traffic from the West and for the rapidly growing coal traffic out of West Virginia. Unless the Baltimore & Ohio was to abandon the field to its competitors, it must be placed in a position to carry traffic at the lowest possible cost. In other words, the Baltimore & Ohio must be entirely reconstructed.

Should the receivers reconstruct the road, obtaining funds by the issue of their certificates, or should they content themselves with keeping the system together and in passable running order, leaving the work of rebuilding to the officers of the company after it had been provided with funds in a reorganization? The receivers wisely chose the first alternative, notwithstanding powerful opposition and a vigorous controversy between their friends and men who asserted that they were exceeding their authority as receivers. New capital had to be issued eventually. To delay the work of improvement meant at least temporary abandonment of the competitive field, and the loss of advantages which might never be regained. Mr. Cowen and Mr. Murray faced the issue squarely. As receivers of the Baltimore & Ohio they issued within two years $10,742,000 of receivers' certificates, in addition to a large amount of car-trust obligations. A portion of these certificates were exchanged for other evidences of indebtedness which had to be taken care of, but for the most part they were issued for new equipment, rails, and ties.

Immediately after taking charge of the property, in May, 1896, the receivers obtained authority to purchase five thousand new freight cars and seventy-five locomotives. In February, 1897, a thousand additional box cars were purchased, and in May of the same year five thousand one hundred and fifty more cars were acquired. During this year two thousand one hundred and fifty cars were obtained from coal companies on mileage contracts, and three thousand cars were leased from the Pullman Company. Besides these heavy purchases of equipment, during the first year of the receivers' administration two hundred and twenty freight engines, some of which had not turned a wheel for months, were sent through the shops and put into service. Special attention was also paid to the way and structure. The track from Baltimore to Pittsburg and Wheeling was practically all relaid with new and heavier rails and new ties. Bridges on the system, many of which were unable to bear the weight of heavy trains, were generally replaced; and large sums were spent on the construction of yards and sidings. Taking advantage of depressed times, one of the features of the receivership was the placing of an order for forty thousand tons of eighty-five-pound rail, said to have been the largest order ever placed for rails up to that time. The price was seventeen dollars a ton. Not all the funds for these improvements were raised by the issue of receivers' and car-trust certificates. Earnings were heavily drawn upon, and in many instances bondholders were forced to wait until the property on which they had a lien was put into condition to earn the interest. In a word, the Baltimore & Ohio receivers rebuilt the road from end to end, and turned a new road over to the stockholders when the reorganization was completed.

This work, as intimated above, was not carried through without severe opposition. Suit after suit was brought by security holders to restrain the receivers from increasing the burdens of the property. It was urged that they were destroying the value of first mortgage bonds by their reckless issue of certificates, and they were advised that if new equipment was needed, it should be borrowed and not purchased. Their policy was denounced as a gross usurpation of power because, as it was charged, they ran counter to every precedent which should regulate the conduct of receivers. To this the answer was made that precedents were indeed violated, but that the situation with which the receivers had to deal was itself unprecedented. The receivers contended, and in this they were sustained by the court, that their policy was conceived in the interest of the bondholders, and they insisted that it be carried through to completion.

The policy of the receivers of the Baltimore & Ohio was abundantly justified during their term of office. During a period when the gross earnings of its competitors declined the earnings of the Baltimore & Ohio, as the direct result of its larger equipment and lower operating cost, materially increased. In 1896, gross earnings were $25,582,000 and in 1898, after the reconstruction of the property had been practically completed, they increased more than $2,000,000 in spite of a steady fall in rates. The contribution of reduced operating expenses to the result is seen in the increase of the operating ratio from 69.26 in 1895, a ratio which directly reflected the inefficiency of the property, to 78.23 per cent in

1898, which represented the expenditure of a large amount of earnings upon improvements. The effect of these improvements upon the operating efficiency of the road is seen in a decline in the operating ratio from 76.70 per cent in 1899 to 65.63 in 1900. The Baltimore & Ohio receivers took great risks. They applied a desperate remedy to a desperate situation. Their success on this account was all the more conspicuous and brilliant.

A receivership is an extraordinary remedy for an extraordinary situation. Like a surgical operation, although it may save the life of a distressed corporation, it usually leaves the patient in a weakened condition from which his recovery is slow. And for the same reason that intelligent physicians only resort to the knife after all milder measures of treatment have failed, so the owners and creditors of a corporation which has got into difficulties, consult their best interests, when they unite to tide over the crisis without resorting to the protection of the courts. As yet, however, such a degree of coöperation cannot be expected, and it is fortunate for the investor that the courts have generally shown wisdom and foresight in the administration of properties intrusted temporarily to their keeping.

CHAPTER XXXIII

THE REORGANIZATION OF BANKRUPT CORPORATIONS

THE reorganization of a bankrupt corporation is a settlement of the claims of the different parties in interest on such a basis that the property can be released by the court and again managed as a going concern.

As soon as possible after the receivers have been appointed, efforts are set in motion looking to the rehabilitation of the bankrupt corporation. The interests of all concerned point to a speedy settlement of its difficulties. As long as a corporation remains in the hands of the receiver, the values of its securities are low, owing to its uncertain future. Those persons whose capital is invested in these bonds and stocks are unable to find purchasers for their investments at fair prices, or to make loans upon these securities with financial institutions. Banks and trust companies which have taken these securities as collateral are, for the same reason, unable to dispose of the collateral except at a loss, even if they consider it expedient to further complicate an already difficult situation by such a drastic action. All interests are, therefore, equally concerned to reach a speedy reorganization of a bankrupt company. Unless an attempt is made to treat some interest unfairly, the operation is quickly concluded and a settlement is reached which preserves the integrity of the business, and equitably apportions among the different claimants the losses which have been sustained. The courts have also assumed the necessity of speedy reorganization, and have sometimes gone so far as to recommend to creditors and stockholders that they hasten to arrive at a settlement of their difficulties in order that the receivers may be discharged.

The objects of the reorganization are as follows:

1. To pay off or fund the floating debt.

2. To provide funds for betterments and working capital and to arrange for future capital.

3. To reduce fixed charges within a conservative estimate of net earnings.

Reorganization, in almost all cases, requires that a large amount of cash should be provided. This money is required to pay certain kinds of current debt, to complete an unfinished plant, or for the reconstruction and repair of property whose physical condition has been allowed to deteriorate. Taking up first the floating debt which must be provided for, we find this usually divided into receiver's certificates and secured loans. The receiver's certificates, as already explained, constitute prior liens on the property, and must be paid in cash when due. We have also seen in the discussion of the issue of short term obligations that these are now almost invariably secured by a large margin of collateral. These notes have been usually taken by banks, trust companies or large individual capitalists. The collateral back of them consists either of bonds authorized under existing mortgages, or of securities owned by the corporation representing the control of properties which are indispensable to it. The holders of such notes are in a position to demand payment in full. Unless paid, they can sell their collateral and seriously embarrass those who are endeavoring to reorganize the company.

The physical condition of a bankrupt property is usually bad. In some cases the original financial plan has not provided sufficient funds to complete the plant which must be finished before it is of any value, and the property of going concerns has often suffered severely before receivers were appointed. The receiver, as we have seen, may do much to improve the physical condition of the property, but he is not likely to provide all the money necessary.

The reorganization plan should provide that the net earnings of the company, on a minimum estimate, should insure a safe margin above fixed charges. If the receivership has been due to the maturity of debt at a time when financing was not possible, a reduction of fixed charges may not be necessary. In the great majority of cases, however, adversity has disclosed the fact that fixed charges are too heavy for the earnings of the company, and opportunity is taken in the reorganization to reduce them. Unless this is done, at the next season of trial, net earnings may again fall below charges, and another surgical operation on the capitalization of the company will become necessary. It is seldom provided that fixed charges in the reorganization plan should be so much reduced that an estimate of net earnings based on present conditions will insure immediate payment of dividends. Such a course would be unfair to creditors. If reviving business increases earnings after the reorganization, to the point of dividend payment, that is the good fortune of the stockholders; but the creditors cannot be asked to submit to a greater reduction in their claims for interest and rentals than is sufficient to enable the company out of its net earnings to pay interest and provide for working capital, renewals and betterments. The information upon which any plan of reorganization must be based is usually supplied by the receivers who make for the court an exhaustive analysis of the situation of the company, its past earning power, the causes of failure, a schedule of its assets and liabilities, and an estimate of its cash requirements.

We see the objects of reorganization. How are these objects to be realized? The first step in carrying through a reorganization plan is usually the formation of committees to represent the owners of different classes of bonds. In some cases also committees are formed to represent stockholders. The purpose of forming committees is to secure united action on behalf of each interest concerned in the reorganization, and also to keep the various bonds and notes of the company from being thrown on the market and sacrificed. The formation of committees may not, it is true, be necessary. The receivers or the directors may themselves formulate a plan of reorganization, or they may appoint a committee to formulate such a plan to which they may afterwards invite the consent of the security holders. If the plan proves satisfactory, it may at once be put into effect. It is seldom, however, that such a quick method of settlement can be adopted. Holders of different classes of securities are unlikely to consent to any plan which they have had no hand in formulating.

The method usually employed in the formation of these committees is for individual bondholders to constitute themselves or their representatives a committee to take charge of the particular class of securities, and to invite the creditors or stockholders to signify their consent to this arrangement by depositing their securities with some disinterested agent, a trust company or bank. If a majority of the securities are thus deposited, the self-constituted committee becomes representative, and is recognized as such by the courts. The powers of these committees are very broad. The committee is vested with the legal title to all securities deposited with them, and is authorized to act in all respects in behalf of the depositors as though they were directors of a corporation elected for the purpose. The committee has all the powers of owners of the securities, and full discretion as to the methods of carrying out the agreement. The committee is authorized to institute suits or to intervene in suits, to sell the deposited securities under certain conditions, to employ agents, attorneys and counsel, to purchase property at foreclosure sale, to borrow money on the security of the bonds or stocks deposited with them, and also, usually, to prepare a plan of reorganization which, after reasonable notice has been given to the depositors under the agreement with the committee, and failing objection on their part signified by the withdrawal of their securities, is held to be binding upon all. The depositors are held to be liable for the necessary expenses of the committee up to a certain percentage on the amount of securities deposited. It is usually provided that the committee may at any time terminate the agreement, and also to allow the bondholders to terminate it by a certain vote. The effect of the deposit of securities is to constitute the members of the committee trustees for the depositors, to form, as it were, a temporary corporation for the attainment of certain objects.

The committee, after conference with bankers, whose assistance is indispensable to the consummation of a plan of reorganization, after examining the condition of the property, its assets and liabilities, its record of earnings, and also after conferring with large shareholders and creditors, announce a plan of reorganization. This plan they may either announce on behalf of themselves or through bankers or individuals whom they may designate as reorganization managers. For example, J. P. Morgan & Company on June 1, 1909, made the following announcement to the holders of debenture stock, Preferred stock A, Preferred stock B, and Common stock of the Chicago, Great Western Railway Company:

"At the request of the London Committee for Debenture Stock of the New York Committee for Debenture Stock, and of the New York Committee for Preferred Stock A, Preferred Stock B, and Common Stock, the undersigned have consented to act as Reorganization Managers in carrying out a Plan for the Reorganization of the Chicago Great Western Railway Company."

So far as the securities affected by the plan have been lodged with a committee, the assent of the committee to the plan is held to be binding on the depositing bond or stockholders unless they signify their dissent within the time named in the agreement with the committee, by withdrawing their securities. Holders of securities which have not been deposited are given a certain time to consent to the plan. This time limit is often extended, but unless the deposits are made within the time stipulated by the committee, nonassenting bond or stockholders are held to be excluded from the benefits of the plan and must take their chances like anyone else in a foreclosure sale.

Coming now to the consideration of the reorganization plan, we find that the property may be either returned to its former owner, or it may be transferred under foreclosure sale to a new company. It sometimes happens that there are distinct advantages in reorganization without foreclosure sale, employing the same company which controlled the property before the default. Companies may have valuable privileges in the form of exemption from taxation, or authorization from the state to engage in enterprises such as the carrying on of coal mining and railroad operations under the same organization, which may have been forbidden to corporations since a particular charter was granted. In such cases, the reorganization plan usually contemplates the return of the property to the existing company. The Philadelphia & Reading Railroad Company, for example, went through two reorganizations because its charter privileges were too valuable to be surrendered.

The usual method is, however, to organize a new company in which is vested after foreclosure sale such portions of the property of the old company as it is thought wise to retain, and which either assumes the obligations of the old company in their original form, or secures such modifications and reductions in their amount as are necessary to the success of the new company. The advantage of this method is that, by the foreclosure sale, all the rights of nonassenting security holders are extinguished, and the new company is placed in complete control of the property which it desires. It is customary, even when a new company is employed, to use a name closely resembling that of the old company. A rail*road* company, for example, will be succeeded by a rail*way* company, and *vice versa.*

After the new company is organized, it authorizes the issue of certain securities. The Chicago & Great Western

Rail*way*[1] Company, the successor of the Chicago & Great Western Rail*road*[1] Company, authorized $28,000,000 of first mortgage, fifty year four per cent bonds, $50,000,000 of four per cent preferred stock, and $46,000,000 of common stock. The Western Maryland was reorganized by the formation of a new company which took over the property of the old company subject to its first mortgage and its underlying and divisional bonds, and which authorized $10,000,000 of noncumulative four per cent preferred stock, and $60,-000,000 of common stock. The securities of this new company are now offered for subscription. The subscriptions are paid either in cash, or with the securities of the old company, or, in rare instances, with the guarantee of another corporation. In the fulfillment of the conditions of subscription, the objects of reorganization are accomplished.

Advantage is usually taken of this opportunity to simplify the capitalization of the company. Especially has this been done in reorganizations of large railway companies. The formation of a new company which issues its bonds and stock in exchange for those of the old, makes possible the concentration and simplification of the capitalization. It unites branch line and terminal certificates, car trust certificates, equipment bonds and other obligations under single issues which are more easily managed, better secured and of higher values than those which they displace. The property of the Northern Pacific Railway Company, for example, before its last reorganization, was owned by fifty-four corporations which had issued $380,000,000 of stocks and bonds. The circular of the reorganization committee described the old plan of capitalization as follows:

"As it now stands, the system, in its form of incorporation and capitalization, is a development without method or adequate preparation for growth. Scarce any single security is complete in itself. The main line mortgage covers neither feeders nor terminals. The terminal mortgages may be be-

---

[1] Italics are the author's.

reft of their main line support. The branch line bonds are dependent upon the main line for interchange of business, and the main line owes a large part of its business to the branch lines."

The plan of reorganization of this company reduced the number of these obligations, and greatly simplified the capitalization of the company by subjecting the entire system to the lien of two bond issues, one following the other. Sinking fund provisions, which have proven embarrassing to the corporation, may also be eliminated. An adequate bond reserve may be provided under which, with proper restrictions, future issues of bonds for the capital needs of the company may be made. The company may also save in the exchange of securities by retiring high interest bonds issued on branch lines where the security is not perfect, with lower interest bonds secured by mortgage upon the entire property. All these methods of reorganizing the capital account have been fully explained in Chapter XXI. They are freely employed in the reorganization of bankrupt corporations, because the transfer of the property from one company to another furnishes an excellent opportunity for such readjustments.

A more important use is found for the securities of the new company in providing the cash required in the reorganization, and making the necessary reduction in fixed charges. In most reorganizations, as already observed, a large amount of cash must be provided. The cash requirements of the Baltimore & Ohio reorganization plan, for example, in 1896, amounted to $36,092,000. The reorganization managers of the Erie had to provide $19,344,000. More recently, the Chicago Great Western, a comparatively small company, provided $24,892,274 in its reorganization. This cash is obtained by subscription to the bonds and stock of the new company.

Efforts are first made to interest the stockholders who are invited to participate in the reorganization. To the committee in charge of the reorganization is presented this problem: "If we take over the property at a foreclosure sale, and exclude the former stockholders, it will be necessary for us to provide the cash required. The money can probably be raised, it is true, by the sale of first, or first and refunding mortgage bonds, but since one object of reorganization is to reduce rather than increase the debt of the company, it is desirable to keep down the new bonds issued to the lowest possible figure. The only practical alternative is to induce the stockholders of the bankrupt company to furnish the funds required."

The offer to subscribe to the securities of the new company is made to the stockholders in one of two forms. They may be told that their company has failed; it is unable to pay its debts, its creditors have liens upon all its properties. Unless the stockholders are prepared to furnish the money necessary to pay these debts, the property must be sold by the court and the stockholders will lose all chance to recover their loss. In the foreclosure sale, the various evidences of debt, no matter how much their interest may be in default, or how worthless they may be in the market, will count, as against any inferior lien, at 100 cents on the dollar. Therefore, if the stockholders desired to compete at the sale, they would be at a hopeless disadvantage, since it would be necessary for them to match, dollar for dollar, with cash, the various bonds which will be presented as a means of payment by the creditors. The creditors, therefore, control the situation. They propose to organize a new company to take over the property of the bankrupt corporation, since they realize the necessity of keeping the property together.

The creditors, however, do not desire to take undue advantage of their position. They will give to the stockholders the privilege of joining with them in this new company. They make to the stockholders the following offer: to sell them preferred stock in the new company for, say, $20 per share, and common stock for $10 a share. "We have every reason," they say, "to believe that with the indebtedness paid, funded or reduced within a conservative estimate of earnings, and with good management, the new company will be more successful than the old. We are confident that if you purchase stock in the new company on the basis proposed, you will have no reason to regret your action."

This was the proposition which, in substance, was made to the stockholders of the Westinghouse Electric & Manufacturing Company, on April 8, 1908. The stockholders committee of this company sent out a circular letter outlining a plan of reorganization in substance as follows: Certain bonds of the company were to remain undisturbed. The floating debt was in part to be converted into stock and in part funded into bonds and notes. The stockholders were to subscribe at par for $6,000,000 of new stock. The proposition to the stockholders was as follows:

"The chief difficulty with the company and the principal cause of the receivership are found in the fact that, as the result of the rapid expansion of its business, too large a proportion of its investment is represented by debt. If a substantial reduction can be made in the debt by the sale of additional stock, it is believed that the receivership can be promptly terminated with every prospect of the company entering upon a career of renewed prosperity. On this point the committee, of which Mr. Jarvie is chairman, in their circular of April 2, 1908, say:

"'The committee believe that if the conduct of the business can promptly be restored to the stockholders under the direction of a strong board of directors, the company will continue to make substantial earnings. On the other hand, there can be no doubt that a continuation of the receivership for a considerable time, and a forced liquidation of the assets, would be disastrous to the creditors as well as to the stockholders.'

"The Merchandise Creditors' Committee have shown their confidence in the company and its future by undertaking to secure the exchange of, at least, $4,000,000 of the company's floating debt for 'assenting stock,' at par. They, however, impose the condition that the remaining $6,000,000 of the $10,000,000 of subscriptions required to terminate the receivership and place the company in a safe position shall be furnished by the stockholders. It is for the purpose of securing from stockholders subscription to this $6,000,000 of stock that the undersigned committee has been formed.

"The holders of the preferred and common stock of the company are, therefore, asked to subscribe for 'assenting stock' of the company at par, at the rate of at least one share of new stock for every four shares (or fraction thereof) of existing stock. Such subscriptions are to be payable in the following installments:

25	per	cent	on	May 25, 1908,
20	"	"	"	August 1, 1908,
20	"	"	"	November, 1, 1908,
20	"	"	"	January 1, 1909,
15	"	"	"	April 1, 1909.

The deferred payments are to bear interest at the rate of six per cent per annum, with the privilege to subscribers to pay their subscriptions in full at any time.

"The Merchandise Creditors' plan cannot be carried into effect unless the stockholders protect themselves by subscribing pro rata for their shares of this new stock. If these subscriptions are not forthcoming, the inevitable result will be that the Readjustment Committee, which was organized for the protection of creditors, will be forced to reduce the debt of the company to judgment, bring about a forced sale of the property and its acquisition by a new corporation organized in the interest of creditors. Such a course would result in enormous loss which would fall chiefly upon the stockholders of the company. That loss can be avoided only by the coöperation of stockholders in promptly subscribing for a sufficient amount of new stock to insure an early termination of the receivership.

"The committee wish to lay special emphasis upon the fact that the success of this plan for saving the company for its stockholders requires the unanimous compliance of stockholders, however small their holdings, with this request for subscriptions. The ownership of the stock of the company is divided among about 4,000 stockholders, the average holding (excluding the holdings of the Security Investment Company and its president) being only about eighty-three shares (par value, $50). Most of the stock owned by the Security Investment Company has been pledged as collateral in comparatively small amounts with a large number of banks which are being asked to subscribe to the new stock in proportion to their respective holdings."

Subscriptions to the stock of the Westinghouse Electric & Manufacturing Company were largely influenced by this express threat that failure to procure the required amount would subject the stockholders to the danger of foreclosure sale.

The situation of the Westinghouse Electric & Manufacturing Company is, however, different from that of most bankrupt corporations. With this company, the trouble was chiefly due to inadequate working capital which resulted in an excessive amount of funded debt calling for the payment of both principal and interest at a time when financing could not be done. The reorganization of the Westinghouse Company required nothing more than the funding of this current debt on which the company was abundantly able to pay interest. The stockholders' interest in the property was plain. Even during the receivership, the stock never fell below $8.75, (par $50) which indicated a considerable margin of value after the debts were paid.

In most cases, however, bankruptcy has been due to the failure of the company to earn interest on its funded debt. If the company cannot earn enough to pay interest on its bonds, then its property is not worth the amount of its debts, and there is nothing left for the stockholders. Their interest in the property has, long before the reorganization, entirely disappeared. They have already been "wiped out." To stockholders in this situation a proposition that they should subscribe to stock in a new company at the rate of $10, $15, or $20 per share might be unattractive. The response of many stockholders to such a proposition would be an emphatic negative. They would inform the reorganization committee that they did not propose to throw good money after bad; that they did not care to make a new investment in the company with which they had fared so badly; that, although the claims of the reorganization committee as to the future of the company might be borne out by results, for their part, they would prefer to await the materialization of those results, rather than risk any more of their money in a venture which had proven so disastrous.

When money is to be raised from stockholders where there is no equity in the property which they would naturally desire to retain, the proposition has frequently been presented to them in a different form. Instead of being invited to subscribe to stock of a new company, the offer takes the form of a proposition that they should pay an "assessment" upon their stock, "go through the reorganization," and recover, in the increasing profits of the company, the losses which they have sustained. In the Chicago & Great Western reorganization plan, for example, the conditions of participation in the plan were set forth to the stockholders as follows:

"Participation under the plan by holders of the several classes of stock is dependent on the deposit of the stock certificates with the undersigned, within the period limited therefor. The plan embraces only the stocks so deposited. No certificate for any stock of any class will be received on deposit unless in negotiable form.

"Debenture Stock and Preferred Stock A are to be received without payment as stated in the Plan.

"Depositors of Preferred Stock B must pay $15 in respect of each share of such Preferred Stock B so deposited, and will be entitled to obtain from the Syndicate mentioned in the Plan, Preferred Stock voting trust certificates of the New Company when issued, equal at par to such payment, and also Common Stock voting trust certificates of the New Company, when issued, to an aggregate amount at par equal to sixty per cent of the par value of their present Preferred Stock B so deposited.

"Depositors of Common Stock must pay $15 in respect of each share of such Common Stock so deposited, and will be entitled to obtain from the Syndicate, hereinafter mentioned, Preferred Stock voting trust certificates of the New Company, when issued, equal at par to such payment, and also Common Stock voting trust certificates of the new Company, when issued, to an aggregate amount at par equal to forty per cent of the par value of their present Common Stock so deposited."

A careful examination of this statement will show the difference in form, although not, as we shall see, in substance, between the proposition of an assessment and the proposition of a new subscription. The payments of cash are to be made *in respect of* and *in connection with* the deposit of common and preferred stock under the plan. The stockholder is informed that, if he will make a contribution on account of his present stockholdings, he will be allowed to receive stock in the new company. He does not, on the face of things, pay for the stock in the new company—that is given him in exchange for his old stock. He pays an "assessment" on his old stock, and, on account of this "assessment," he becomes entitled to receive new stock.

The proposition to the stockholders of the old company that they should subscribe to stock of the new company is put something as follows when a subscription is styled an assessment: "Your company is bankrupt; its creditors are in position to take the property, and they will take the property unless a certain amount of cash is raised. The creditors do not, however, desire to exclude stockholders from participation in the reorganization, but they must look to the stockholders to furnish the necessary money by paying a small assessment on the par value of their present holdings. If you will pay this assessment, you will be allowed to exchange your certificates of stock in the old company for a certain number of shares in the new company, and you will receive stock in addition to the amount of the assessment."

This proposition, it is evident, is precisely similar to the one first mentioned. It is an offer of stock in a new company. But, while many stockholders in a bankrupt and discredited corporation will not accept a proposition when presented to them as a subscription, when designated as an "assessment" on the stock which they already own, they have very generally accepted the proposition of reorganization committees, have paid their assessments, and received stock in the new concern. The second form of the subscription proposition appeals to the stockholders while the first does not. The "assessment" proposition presents to the stockholder the idea of an unfinished transaction. He hopes that, with one more effort, the payment of $10 or $15 per share, he can recover from the company the money which he has lost. The "assessment" proposition offers him apparently the opportunity to recoup himself, to justify to himself his judgment of the value of the stock in which, up to the present time, he has been so grievously disappointed. By employing this method of calling a subscription to stock in a new company an "assessment" on stock in an old company, reorganization committees have been able to obtain large amounts of money from stockholders, whereas if they had asked the stockholders to subscribe to stock in a new company, they would probably have been much less successful.

The assessments of stockholders are usually underwritten, a syndicate being organized to pay the "assessments," and to take the stock of those holders who do not participate in the plan. The commission paid to this syndicate varies, of course, with the risk which they assume, but the existence of the syndicate brings pressure to bear upon the stockholder by assuring him that others stand ready to accept apparently the same terms which are offered to him. In 1895, for example, the final Atchison reorganization plan announced the following:

"A contract has been made with a syndicate to furnish an amount of money equal to the assessments of *nonassenting* or *defaulting stockholders,* and such syndicate, by such payment, shall take the place of the *nonassenting* or *defaulting stockholders,* and shall be entitled to receive the new common and preferred stock, which *nonassenting* or *defaulting stockholders* would have been entitled to receive if they had deposited their stock and paid their assessment in full." The syndicate may actually purchase the new stock and offer it to those stockholders who pay their assessments, thus making an exceptionally forcible appeal. By employing this method of approach, reorganization managers, especially in railway reorganizations, have been remarkably successful in paying off most of the floating debt without resorting to the sale of bonds.

The difference between a reorganization "assessment" and a subscription to new stock is only in form; in substance they are the same thing. When stock is full paid, it is not liable to any assessment. A stockholder may have only paid $20 a share for his full paid stock, but the corporation has no right to demand any more from him. Any further payments to the company are at his own pleasure. And yet, so imperfect is the knowledge possessed by the average stockholder of his rights and obligations, that he is apt to feel, when an assessment proposition is made to him, that there is an obligation to pay the assessment and take the new stock. A reorganization assessment is looked upon as compulsory. Stockholders are informed that if they refuse to pay they are "debarred from all participation in the reorganization," that they "lose all chance to recoup their loss from their share in subsequent profits."

An examination of a large number of reorganization

---

[1] Italics are the author's.

plans recently promulgated, however, shows that "assessments" are now being stated in their true light as subscriptions. For example, the reorganization plan of the Newhouse Mines & Smelters under date of June 1, 1909, states that:

"In order to furnish the necessary working capital for development, payment of debts, expenses of foreclosure, reorganization and underwriting, the Stockholders will be required to subscribe to the capital stock of the new company and to pay one dollar for every share so subscribed. Every Stockholder so subscribing will receive one share of common stock of the New Company for each share now held by him."

It is impossible to approve the indirect method of raising money from stockholders, which is only recently being abandoned. The stockholder owes nothing to the reorganization managers, or to the creditors. If they secure his participation in the new company, they should make him an offer of a more attractive investment than he can obtain elsewhere. Unless the payment of an assessment on stock of a bankrupt corporation gives the stockholder, who desires to continue his interest in the company, the new stock at a lower figure than that at which he can purchase it in the open market, he should allow the creditors to advance the money necessary, and buy the stock after the reorganization has been completed. While by adopting such a course he may be "debarred from all participation in the reorganization," he does not "lose all chance to recoup his losses from his share in the subsequent prosperity." Dr. Stuart Daggett, in his book "Railroad Reorganization,"[1] gives a list of eight reorganizations in which the common stock was assessed, together with the price of the stock one month after reorganization, and six months after reorganization. In every case the stock could have been purchased in the open market directly after the reorganization at a lower price than it was purchased from the reorganization managers. It is desirable that stockholders should coöperate in making the reorganization plan

[1] P. 353.

a success, but the proposition should be presented to them in its true light, and not under the guise of an obligation or a necessity.

The offer to stockholders if foreclosure is not involved in the reorganization plan is usually more liberal than when the threat of foreclosure can be issued to induce subscriptions. If the method of foreclosure is not to be employed, then the stockholders must be persuaded into the subscription by an attractive offer. The adjustment plan of the Seaboard Air Line Railway, which was carried through without foreclosure, provided the cash required by the sale of $18,000,000 of par value of cumulative five per cent income bonds, called adjustment bonds. These were offered for subscription at seventy per cent of their par value to the extent of thirty per cent of the par value of their existing holdings. A syndicate was organized which, for a commission of five per cent on the par value of $18,000,000 of bonds, offered to the stockholders, guaranteed to purchase at this price any bonds that might not be subscribed and paid for by the stockholders. In this case there was no pressure put upon the stockholders to furnish any capital to the company. An attractive offer was made to them, and their acceptance of the offer was guaranteed by responsible bankers. Whether they subscribed or not, so far as the provision of cash was concerned, the success of the plan was assured.

If, or to the extent that stockholders will not advance money, the creditors must provide the funds required by subscribing to the securities of the new company. The creditors of a bankrupt company are potentially in the position of owners. They can obtain the property at a foreclosure sale, and if they cannot persuade or coerce the stockholders into advancing the money necessary for its rehabilitation, they will be obliged to take over the property, and themselves provide the necessary funds. Eliminating the stockholders, we have now to consider the methods by which creditors finance the cash requirements of a reorganization. Several conditions may be presented. There may be only one class of creditors, the holders of mortgage bonds. The company issuing these bonds has defaulted, and receivers have been appointed. These receivers have made certain expenditures for the benefit of the property, and certain other expenditures are necessary. The stockholders will advance no more money. As the reorganization committee of the Arnold Print Works stated in their announcement of a plan of reorganization:

"Reorganization with fresh capital contributed by the present stockholders is impracticable, as nearly all the stock is owned by Messrs. Houghton & Gallup, and apart from their interest in this stock they are now without substantial means."

The creditors in such a situation must depend upon them selves. They organize a new company to take over the property, thereby extinguishing all rights of stockholders and any minor claims of current indebtedness which may be outstanding. They capitalize this new company according to the exigencies of the situation. They may subject its property to the lien of a first mortgage bond which they may either take themselves or sell to bankers, obtaining in this manner all necessary funds, or they may subscribe to the stock of a new company, placing no funded debt upon it. The property is at their disposal; they can use it to support the credit of the company as it may be necessary. If they advance the required funds themselves, they may arrange the capitalization of the new company in any way they see fit. If, however, they sell the securities to outsiders they must consult the wishes of the subscribers.

A case in point came recently under the writer's observation. A water-power company had underestimated the cost of a power and transmission plant. When the plant was little more than half completed, funds were exhausted. Receivers were appointed and the bondholders eventually bought in the plant at a foreclosure sale, eliminating the stock interest. It was now necessary to provide funds to complete the plant. The following plan, after prolonged negotiations, was presented to the bondholders. A new company should be organized to take over the plant. This company was to issue first mortgage five per cent bonds to an amount sufficient to complete the plant, and certain of the bonds were to be held in reserve for extensions. The old bondholders were to receive noncumulative preferred stock for their bonds, and the new bonds were to carry with them all the common stock of the company as a bonus. The owners of the plant were offered the privilege of subscribing to the new bonds, and receiving their pro rata share of the common stock. The subscriptions to the bonds were guaranteed by a finance company, which undertook, for a commission, to take the bonds of nonsubscribing owners, and receive their share of the bonus of common stock.

Another condition may arise; there may be secured creditors and unsecured creditors, commonly known as floating debt creditors. We have already seen that when floating debt is amply secured by collateral, the reorganization plan must provide for its payment. It frequently happens, however, that the floating debt is unsecured. The Westinghouse Electric & Manufacturing Company at the time of its failure owed $5,000,000 for merchandise, and $8,000,000 to banks, for all of which there was no special security. In such a case, the holders of the floating debt, if the amount is large, in order to save something from the wreck, must advance the money required to put the company on its feet. They cannot ask the bondholders to make sacrifices, because, if the bondholders advance the necessary money, they may insist on retaining the stock of the new company. As for their own claims, the floating debt creditors, in case they manage the reorganization and provide the necessary funds, and in case, also, they do not disturb the position of the bondholders and safeguard the bondholders' interests in the reorganization, may arrange the capitalization of the new company as they please. In the Westinghouse reorganization, for example, already referred to, where the stockholders advanced the necessary funds, the holders of the company's notes, for fifty per cent of their claims, received convertible five per cent debenture bonds of the company which were in its treasury, and for the other fifty per cent of their claims, fifteen-year five per cent notes of the company bearing five per cent interest. As for the banks, if they objected to waiting so long for repayment, they were offered the privilege of taking amounts equal to thirty per cent of their claims in serial bonds due in four, five, and six years, on condition that, for the balance of the fifty per cent, they should accept stock of the company at par. In this case the floating debt creditors were able to negotiate successfully with the stockholders, on account of the large equity in the property. If, however, the stockholders had not advanced the necessary funds, it would have been necessary for the holders of the floating debt to themselves subscribe to a sufficient amount of stock in the new company to provide the cash required, taking in addition stock for their own claims, and eliminating the stockholders.

Occasions may arise where the bondholders and the floating debt creditors, when no money can be obtained from stockholders, divide the burdens of the reorganization between them, and partition the stock of the company in return for their cash advances. Even if the bondholders are obliged to take charge of the reorganization, and arrange for the financing, they may not eliminate the floating debt creditors, on account of special reasons. It may be possible, for example, to arrange with some outside company to guarantee an issue of second mortgage bonds in return for the common stock. In such a case there would probably be no objection to the floating debt creditors receiving preferred stock in the reorganization plan without cash advances. As a rule, however, if the general creditors do not subscribe, and if suitable arrangements cannot be made with outside interests, then the bondholders must provide the money. They will usually take the stock of the new company, eliminating general creditors of the old company along with its stockholders.

A further complication enters when there are several

classes of bondholders, as well as different floating debt interests, and stockholders. Suppose stockholders will not advance money, that the general creditors are also unwilling to invest in the securities of the new company, that there are first mortgage bonds upon the property whose interest has been fully earned and paid by the receiver, but that, in addition to the first mortgage bonds, there are first and refunding bonds—that is, second mortgage bonds. There may be also debenture bonds and car trust certificates. In such a situation the underlying bonds and the car trust certificates cannot be disturbed. Their security is ample, and there is no way in which the reorganization committee can get at them. If any attempt is made to impose upon them the burden of providing the money required, they will assert their rights at foreclosure sale, taking away the security and eliminating all junior securities. The holders of car trust certificates are also in an exceptionally strong position; they cannot be asked to furnish any money. The holders of the junior bonds, with or without the participation of the stockholders, must here provide the necessary funds.

A case in point is that of the reorganization of the Western Maryland. In this reorganization plan, securities aggregating $50,951,950 remained undisturbed. Their owners were not called upon to provide any new money. The $8,274,160 of cash required for the payment of maturing obligations and for improvements and betterments was raised by the sale of $20,685,400 of the common stock of the company to a bankers' syndicate which offered this stock to the general lien and convertible holders and to the stockholders. The junior bondholders were offered the new stock at forty per cent, up to fifty per cent of their holdings, and the holders of the common stock were offered the new common stock at the same price, up to 100 per cent of their holdings. The undisturbed securities, in this case, included the first mortgage bonds, $42,518,000; divisional bonds, $6,200,000; leased line bonds, $1,659,300, and leased line guaranteed stock, $574,650. Interest on the first mortgage bonds had been fully earned, and there was no reason for asking them to make sacrifices. The divisional and leased line bonds and guaranteed stock were so secured that an assertion by their holders of their rights under the contracts with the Western Maryland Railroad Company might have resulted in the disruption of the system. It was necessary, therefore, to appeal to the junior securities, and, in this case, the reorganization managers were fortunate in securing the coöperation of the stockholders. If the stockholders had not been able to respond, however, then it might have been necessary for the holders of the first mortgage bonds to have taken a part of the new stock, securing the coöperation of the general lien bondholders, if only to a partial extent, by allowing them to share in the new securities.

I have suggested only a few of the complications which may arise. A reorganization committee may be confronted with a great variety of situations. Its task is to obtain the money on the best terms possible with due regard to the legal rights of all interests concerned. The only rule which seems established in the preparation of this portion of a reorganization plan is first to impose the burden upon the stockholders if they can be induced to assume it, next in order to approach holders of unsecured floating debts, next the junior bondholders, and finally the holders of underlying securities. The appeal in each case is strengthened by the implied or express threat of complete loss to follow the foreclosure sale which would be controlled by the holders of the prior claims.

Finally, if money is to be raised from bankers or outside investors, a proposition must be made which is attractive to them. For example, if there are first mortgage bonds which cannot be disturbed, and if it is proposed to obtain the necessary funds without "compulsory" subscription by any of the old interests, by the sale of first and refunding mortgage bonds to a bankers' syndicate, the syndicate may insist upon a certain amount of stock. They may also insist that this stock shall be given special preference. In such a case, the new company would issue preferred stock A to bankers, and the other interests would take B preferred and common stock.

We have already observed in the consideration of these several cases that the underwriting syndicate is a necessary feature in every reorganization plan. The commission paid to the syndicate will vary. In some cases it may be large. The Western Maryland Syndicate, we have seen, was to receive a commission of five per cent. In the reorganization plan of the United States Shipbuilding Company, the committee announced that it had entered into an agreement with the Morton Trust Company and Thomas F. Ryan for the purchase and sale of the entire issue of $3,000,000 collateral trust sinking fund six per cent bonds at a price of 87½, so as to guarantee the cash requirements of the plant. These bonds were offered by the syndicate to the holders of the existing bonds. The low price offered the chance of a large profit to the syndicate.

The needs of the present have now been provided for, current indebtedness has been paid, and provision has been made for sufficient capital to bring up the plant to a condition of efficiency. The committee on reorganization now addresses itself to the task of reducing fixed charges so that they will come well within conservative estimate of the net earnings. We have already discussed the method by which the limit of fixed charges in the new company is to be fixed. This limit is, as already pointed out, the minimum net earnings of the company. The amount is usually based on the experience of the receiver, although some allowance may be made for an anticipated improvement in earnings. For example, in the Atchison reorganization of 1894 it was estimated that the minimum earnings of the property from 1891 to 1894 were $5,204,880, and the fixed charges proposed for the new company were $4,528,547. The lowest net earnings which the Union Pacific had ever reported had been $4,315,-077. The interest on the bonds issued by the new company which took over the property in 1897, was placed at $4,000,-000; the net earnings for the Northern Pacific in 1895, the smallest earnings for eight years, were $6,052,660; the fixed charges of its successor were placed at $6,015,846. Dr. Daggett,[1] in his summary of the results of a number of railroad reorganizations, states that the fixed charges in seven large reorganizations from 1893 to 1898 were reduced from $65,984,219 to $45,576,984. It is now well recognized that unless this principle of reducing fixed charges below the lowest point to which net earnings have ever fallen is followed, there is danger that the work will, at some later period of depression, have to be done over again. This principle was not recognized in many of the reorganizations prior to 1893. Since that time, however, it has been generally accepted and may now be taken as an almost invariable rule.

The fixed charges of a corporation may be divided into rental charges and interest charges. The charges for rentals can be more easily reduced than the charges for interest. As long as a company is solvent it must live up to its rental contracts. The contract is, however, made with the old company, and constitutes no lien upon its property. That is segregated for the protection of other creditors. The lessor is an unsecured creditor, and can be dealt with as such. The company which takes over the property at a foreclosure sale is entirely free from all the lease obligations of its predecessor. Bankruptcy has wiped out the score. The new company need assume only such contracts as its reorganizers consider to be necessary to its success. The receiver has usually terminated or modified unprofitable lease contracts, and the reorganization committee has only to follow in his footsteps. If a leased line has proven unprofitable, the reorganization committee can either dispense with it, or, if it is retained, its rental can be reduced. The reorganization committee has a free hand. They cannot be held to old agreements. Old contracts have lapsed and must be renewed by the new company before they can become binding upon it.

The history of railroad reorganization contains notable examples of the termination of lease contracts. The reorgan-

[1] "Railroad Reorganization," Stuart Daggett, p. 357.

ization of the Wabash in 1886 resulted in a reduction of 1,541 miles of leased lines, and the Richmond & West Point Terminal reorganization lopped off 4,479 miles. A more common method than the reduction of mileage is, however, the reduction of rentals. In the railway field, the owners of leased lines have usually no choice but to accede to any reasonable proposition of the reorganization committee for a reduction in their rentals. Their property is usually of little value outside of a large railway system, and, as a rule, the system with which it is most valuable is that with which it is already connected. From 1892 to 1898, the net reduction in lease rentals for American railways was $24,527,000, a large part of this representing reductions in reorganizations. A portion also represented the acquisition of leased lines, and the consequent conversion of rentals into interest.

We come now to the reduction of interest. Just as holders of some of the bonds may have been obliged to make sacrifices by subscribing to new securities, so they may also be required to sacrifice some of their claims for interest in order that the solvency of the new company may be secured. This reduction of interest is accomplished in the exchange of the securities of the old company for the securities of the new company. The methods by which such an exchange is accomplished have been already suggested. The new company offers its securities for subscription, in part in cash, and in part in the securities of the old company. If the old company has not been able to pay interest on $10,000,000 of second mortgage bonds, and if it is desired to eliminate this interest charge from the income account of the new company, the new company may offer the holders of the second mortgage bonds, $10,000,000 of preferred stock to be paid for with their bonds.

Some of the creditors of the old company must make sacrifices. Some of its bonds must be disturbed. Which bonds shall be disturbed? How shall their claims be modified and what compensation shall they be given for their sacrifices? Let us reverse the inquiry and ask what are the bonds which are not disturbed in a reorganization? In every reorganization we find some of these bonds. Take the Erie, for example; it has five divisional mortgages ranging from first to fifth on portions of the line which lie within the State of New York. These mortgages have survived three reorganizations, not being disturbed by any of them. In the same way, the Norfolk & Western Railroad, the Reading, the Baltimore & Ohio, have carried through their reorganizations certain issues of bonds, without, in any way, disturbing them save, in some cases, to consolidate them by making attractive conversion offers into large issues. These bonds are safe from the reorganization committee for the reason that their interest, even in the worst years, has been fully earned. Even the receivers have recognized their claims and have paid their interest. Bonds secured by mortgages upon important branch roads, terminal property or equipment, do not suffer in a reorganization for the reason that there is no way to get at them. The property which secures them is indispensable to the company. Unless the rights of these holders are properly recognized they may inflict serious damage upon the system by seizing the property which secures their bonds.

It may, however, be necessary for the holders of first mortgage bonds, even though their interest has been fully earned, to subordinate their lien to the lien of a new first mortgage, without which the necessary money cannot be secured. Along with this sacrifice may also go a reduction in their interest claims. Speaking generally, however, the holders of first mortgage bonds whose interest has been earned, are not called upon to sacrifice their interest in reorganizations. In companies which present a complication of securities; first mortgages, divisional mortgages, general mortgages, debentures, etc., the sacrifices in interest are usually apportioned according to the extent to which the different bonds have participated in the net earnings of the company. The net earnings of the company are taken as the basis of the new fixed charges, and the reorganization committee apportions the net earnings among the various disturbed securities according to the amount which the property back of each security has contributed to the total. In so far as the interest on a bond has been earned, this absolute lien, as a rule, has been retained. In so far as its interest has not been earned, the bond is reduced to its true position as preferred stock, a form of security whose return is not guaranteed, but is conditioned on the future earnings of the company. The method employed in this reduction is illustrated by a statement made by the reorganization committee of the Atchison in the reorganization of 1895 with reference to the position of the general mortgage bonds in the reorganization:

"After making a careful estimate as to how much of the existing lines, if retained in the system, could, under the circumstances, be avoided, or if these lines be left out, what amount the Atchison system would be able to earn without the auxiliary lines, the committee has arrived at the conclusion that it would not be safe to place upon the property a fixed charge of more than four per cent upon seventy-five per cent of the principal of the present general mortgage bonds."

The situation of holders of general mortgage bonds whose interest has not been earned is here exactly stated. Since the company cannot earn their interest, they cannot, in reason, refuse to consent to a reduction of fixed income. Suppose they should refuse, what can they do? The only alternative is to foreclose the mortgage. To do this, they must raise enough cash to pay off all the prior liens, for their mortgage is spread over and is subordinate to the claims superior to their own. This is practically impossible, so their only course is to submit, after holding out, as long as possible, for better terms. It is true that there is always the final resort to the courts, who may, at any time before the recording of the new securities, hold up the whole proceeding by injunction. This will be done, if it can be shown to the satisfaction of the court that any interest is being unjustly treated. Such interference, however, cannot, unless in cases of the most flagrant injustice, be secured by a minority. If a large majority of the bonds are deposited, the courts will usually refuse to interfere, holding that the consent of the majority should be binding upon all. The contest over the Erie reorganization in 1895 offers an illustration. A plan had been proposed which seemed unfair to the second mortgage bondholders. Nevertheless eighty per cent of these bonds had been deposited, when a suit was brought in the New York Superior Court to enjoin the company from recording the mortgage. The court refused to grant the injunction on the ground that the consent of so large a majority of the parties in interest had made the plan already operative, and as minority should not interfere.

The nature of preferred stock has already been fully explained. Dividends on the preferred stock are payable out of net earnings after the expenses of operation, repair and betterments, interest on the funded debt, rentals and taxes, the necessary cost of operating the business and keeping it out of the hands of the receiver, have been paid. The fixed charge of a mortgage bond whose interest must be paid, or foreclosure results, but which the company cannot earn in justice to its physical condition and under the circumstances of its business, is converted into a claim whose payment is conditioned upon the net earnings of the company. In the exchange of bonds on which interest is not earned, for preferred stock in the reorganized company, the relation of the former creditors to the property is defined precisely. The element of risk which they assumed when they purchased the junior lien bonds is exactly expressed in the contract which sets forth the relation of the preferred stockholder to the company.

The position of the junior bondholder is improved by the conversion of his bonds into preferred stock. Before the conversion, he is occasionally exposed to the risk of receivership which would depress the value of his securities, and cut off his income. By converting his junior lien bond into preferred

30

stock, he enables the company to preserve its solvency and improve its credit, and he places it in a position where it cannot only earn interest but pay him his preferred dividends. With the two exceptions of the Southern and the Erie, and these are only partial exceptions, the preferred stocks issued in the reorganizations referred to in the following table have paid dividends for many years. If they retain these stocks, the former bondholders have fully recovered the losses caused by the defaults which led to these reorganizations.

The extent to which the conversion of junior bonds into preferred stock was employed during the great railway reorganizations following the panic of 1893 is shown in the following table:

Name of Road	Amounts of Preferred Stock Issued			
	For Old Bonds	For Stock	For Assessments	Miscellaneous
Atchison, Topeka and Santa Fe	$96,740,000	....	$13,717,000	$9,200,000
Erie........ First preferred...	27,146,000	$8,537,000	....	2,854,000
Erie........ Second preferred	7,271,000		....	192,000
Norfolk and Western..........	22,833,000	....	....	167,000
Northern Pacific.............	54,880,000	17,620,000	....	2,500,000
Oregon Railway and Navigation Company...............	9,290,000	....	1,440,000	270,000
Reading..... First preferred..	7,184,000	....	....	20,816,000
Reading..... Second preferred	40,286,000	....	....	1,714,000
St. Louis and San Francisco First preferred .	8,214,000	....	1,150,000	3,850,000
St. Louis and San Francisco Second preferred	8,214,000	....	....	7,786,000
Southern Railway............	32,887,000	8,799,000	7,814,000	4,800,000
Totals....................	$314,945,000	$34,956,000	$24,121,000	$54,149,000

The bondholders may also be required to accept a lower rate of interest, or to postpone their interest altogether for a series of years, or to take a low rate of interest with a gradually ascending rate, or to receive a portion of their principal in mortgage bonds and the balance in some junior security. In most cases, the reorganization committee, as an inducement to security holders to accept a reduction in their claim for fixed interest, offers them a bonus in some other security. If general mortgage bondholders, for example, are asked to receive one half of the principal in first mortgage bonds of the new company, and preferred stock for the balance, they may be given $500 in new first mortgage bonds and $750 or $1,000 in new preferred stock. The principal amount of their securities is, by this operation, increased. If the prospects of reviving business materialize, and the new management is efficient, the reorganization may prove to them to have been a blessing in disguise. An increase of capitalization is a feature which usually accompanies a reduction of fixed charges in the reorganization.

In concluding the discussion of the exchange of securities, two illustrations may be given, showing the distribution of the securities of the Northern Pacific and the Norfolk and Western in their respective reorganizations, both of which were accomplished in 1896.

An examination of these tables shows that so far as the specific security of the property back of each bond had contributed the amount of the interest on the bonds to the net earnings of the system, to that extent it was exchanged for

I. BASIS OF EXCHANGE OF THE SECURITIES OF THE NORFOLK & WESTERN RAILWAY IN THE REORGANIZATION OF 1896

Old Company	New Company			
Name of Security	Cash. Per Cent.	First Consolidated Mortgage Bonds. Per Cent.	Preferred Stock. Per Cent.	Common Stock. Per Cent.
Adjustment mortgage, seven per cent bonds.... ...	7	130	20	.....
One hundred year mortgage bonds..............	.....	62½	75	.....
Maryland and Washington Division bonds........	.....	70	67½	....
Chester Valley Division bonds..................	.....	50	70	
Equipment mortgage bonds, 1888............ ...	.....	100	48	.....
Five hundred and ninety debentures of 1892..	.....	.....	100	.....
Roanoke and Southern Railway bonds...... . ..	.....	55	65	.....
Lynchburg and Durham Railway bonds..........	.. .	35	65	.....
Norfolk and Western common } Assessment $12.50 per share	}	.....	.....	75
Norfolk and Western preferred				112½
Roanoke and Southern Stock				75
Lynchburg and Durham Stock				75

II. BASIS OF EXCHANGE OF THE SECURITIES OF THE NORTHERN PACIFIC IN THE REORGANIZATION OF 1896.

Old Company	New Company				
Name of Security	Cash. Per Cent.	New Prior Lien Mortgage Bonds. Per Cent.	New General Lien. Mortgage Bonds. Per Cent.	Preferred Stock Trust Certificates. Per Cent.	Common Stock Trust Certificates. Per Cent.
General first mortgage bonds	3	135	.....	.....	.....
General second mortgage bonds	4	118½	.....	50	.....
General third mortgage bonds	3	.....	118½	50	.....
Dividend certificates	3	.....	118	50	.....
Consolidated mortgage bonds	1½	.....	66½	62½	.....
Collateral trust notes	.....	100	.....	20	.....
Northwest equipment stock	100	.....	.....	.....	.....
Depositors of preferred stock on payment of $10 per share	.....	.....	.....	50	50
Depositors of common stock on payment of $15 per share	.....	.....	.....	.....	100

new mortgage bonds. In so far as its interest had not been earned, preferred stock was given, usually to an amount greater than the par value of the securities which it displaced. The principle of apportionment is especially well illustrated in the Norfolk & Western reorganization. The bonds of four branch roads were disturbed. Of these, the Maryland and Washington, and Roanoke, and Southern had earned more than the other two, and their greater earning ability was recognized in larger proportions of preferred stock. The 100-year mortgage bonds also, whose interest had not been fully earned, were cut down 25 per cent, but 55 per cent in first preferred stock was given in exchange, so that in the long run the bondholders were no losers, the preferred stock in 1898 having sold for 63⅞. In the same way, the holders of the consolidated mortgage bonds of the Northern Pacific received 62½ per cent in new prior lien bonds, and 62½ per cent in preferred stock. In 1895, before the reorganization, the consolidated bonds did not rise above 36, while in December, 1898, two years after the reorganization, the prior lien bonds sold for

93, and the preferred stock for 78. In exchange for a bond worth \$360, the Northern Pacific bondholders received another bond worth, two years later, \$642, besides \$780 in preferred stock.

One more feature of reorganization plans demands attention. The bondholders have controlled the reorganization and have made sacrifices in order that the plan might be successful. They insist, as a condition of their participation, that they should receive some guarantee of the quality of the management. The stock of the new company, if placed upon the market, will command a low figure. It may fall into the hands of speculators who may exploit the property for their own benefit. The bondholders fear that they may have another default to suffer, another floating debt to take care of. To guard against this danger, it is almost invariably provided that the stock of the reorganized company shall be placed for a series of years in the hands of trustees who will issue to the holders securities of beneficial interest in any dividends which may be paid on the stock, the voting power, however, remaining with the trustees.

The nature of a voting trust provision is indicated by the following extract from the reorganization plan of the Pope Manufacturing Company:

"All of the stock of the new company except directors' qualifying shares will be issued to voting trustees, who shall issue to the various persons entitled to receive said stock suitable certificates containing an agreement to deliver said stock on or after August 1, 1911, or sooner if the voting trustees shall so determine, and in the meantime to pay to such persons an amount equal to any sums received as dividends upon said shares of stock. During the continuance of the aforesaid voting trust (1) no mortgage shall be put upon the property (other than the mortgage herein referred to) except with the consent of the holders of two thirds in amount of each class of stock; (2) the amount of preferred stock shall not be increased except with the consent of the holders of three fourths in amount of the certificates representing preferred stock and the holders of two thirds in amount of certificates representing common stock; (3) the amount of common stock shall not be increased except with the consent of the holders of two thirds in amount of the certificates representing preferred stock and the holders of two thirds in amount of the certificates representing common stock."

By this provision, not only were the interests of creditors safeguarded by the placing of control for a period of three years in the hands of trustees, but the stockholders were assured against any abuse of their power by the voting trustees.

These voting trust certificates, when issued on behalf of large public corporations, are listed on the public exchanges, and are dealt in exactly as are shares of stock. The voting trustees are usually named by the banking firm which carries through the reorganization. They represent primarily the creditors' interest. Their administration has been generally successful and they have materially assisted in restoring to public confidence the corporations for whose management they have been made responsible.

INDEX

FINANCIAL MANAGEMENT 1880–1934

Volume 4

Edited and Introduced by
Morgen Witzel

THOEMMES

Financial Management, 1880–1934

Edited and Introduced by **Morgen Witzel**

Volume 1
Twenty Years of Inside Life in Wall Street, or Revelations of the Personal Experiences of a Speculator ... Illustrated (1880)
W. W. Fowler

Volume 2
Trusts, Pools and Corporations (1905)
William Z. Ripley

Volume 3
Corporation Finance (1910)
Edward S. Meade

Volume 4
Corporation Finance. An Exposition of the Principles and Methods governing the Promotion, Organization and Management of Modern Corporations (1909)
William H. Lough

Volume 5
Concentration and Control: A Solution of the Trust Problem in the United States (1914)
Charles R. van Hise

Credit and International Trade: How they Work in Practice (1934)
Barnard Ellinger

Volume 6
Problems in Business Finance (1921)
Edmund E. Lincoln

Volumes 7 and 8
Collected Articles and Chapters

Printed in England by Antony Rowe Ltd, Chippenham

CORPORATION FINANCE

An Exposition of the Principles and Methods governing the Promotion, Organization and Management of Modern Corporations

William H. Lough

THOEMMES PRESS

This edition published by Thoemmes Press, 2001

Thoemmes Press
11 Great George Street
Bristol BS1 5RR, England

http://www.thoemmes.com

Financial Management, 1880–1934
8 Volumes : ISBN 1 85506 633 5

British Library Cataloguing-in-Publication Data
A CIP record of this title is available from the British Library

Publisher's Note

The Publisher has gone to great lengths to ensure the quality of this reprint but points out that some imperfections in the original book may be apparent.

This book is printed on acid-free paper, sewn, and cased in a durable buckram cloth.

Corporation Finance

AN EXPOSITION OF THE PRINCIPLES AND METHODS GOVERNING THE PROMOTION, ORGANIZATION AND MANAGEMENT OF MODERN CORPORATIONS

BY

WILLIAM H. LOUGH

SECRETARY, ALEXANDER HAMILTON INSTITUTE;
PROFESSOR OF FINANCE IN NEW YORK UNIVERSITY
SCHOOL OF COMMERCE, ACCOUNTS AND FINANCE

Modern Business
Volume VI

ALEXANDER HAMILTON INSTITUTE
NEW YORK

TABLE OF CONTENTS

INTRODUCTION

CHAPTER I.

THE CORPORATE FORM.

CHAPTER II.

LEGAL STATUS OF THE CORPORATION.

CHAPTER III.

INTERIOR ORGANIZATION.

CHAPTER IV.

WHERE AND HOW TO INCORPORATE.

CHAPTER V.

CORPORATE STOCK.

CHAPTER VI.

TYPES OF BUSINESS CORPORATIONS.

CHAPTER VII.

THE SOURCES OF CORPORATE FUNDS.

CHAPTER VIII.

SHORT TIME LOANS.

CHAPTER IX.

THE CORPORATE MORTGAGE.

CHAPTER X.

TYPES OF CORPORATION BONDS.

CHAPTER XI.

TYPES OF CORPORATION BONDS (*continued*).

CHAPTER XII.

CORPORATE PROMOTION — THE NEW ENTERPRISE.

CHAPTER XIII.

THE PROMOTER AND THE CORPORATION.

CHAPTER XIV.

CORPORATE PROMOTION — FORMING CONSOLIDATIONS.

CHAPTER XV.

THE UNITED STATES STEEL CORPORATION.

CHAPTER XVI.

SELLING SECURITIES — THE PROSPECTUS AND THE BANKING HOUSE.

CHAPTER XVII.

SELLING SECURITIES — THE WALL STREET MARKET.

CHAPTER XVIII.

SELLING SECURITIES — THE UNDERWRITING SYNDICATE.

CHAPTER XIX.

MANAGEMENT OF THE UNDERWRITING SYNDICATE.

CHAPTER XX.

INVESTMENT OF CAPITAL FUNDS.

CHAPTER XXI.

DISPOSITION OF GROSS EARNINGS.

CHAPTER XXII.

BETTERMENT EXPENSES.

CHAPTER XXIII

CREATION AND USE OF A SURPLUS.

CHAPTER XXIV.

DISTRIBUTION OF THE SURPLUS.

CHAPTER XXV.

MANIPULATION BY CORPORATION OFFICERS.

CHAPTER XXVI.

MANIPULATION BY DIRECTORS.

CHAPTER XXVII.

MANIPULATION BY AND FOR STOCKHOLDERS.

CHAPTER XXVIII.

INSOLVENCY AND RECEIVERSHIPS.

CHAPTER XXIX.

PRINCIPLES OF REORGANIZATION.

CHAPTER XXX.

THREE TYPICAL REORGANIZATIONS.

INTRODUCTION

Twenty years ago a knowledge of corporation finance was not essential to the average business man. Only the larger concerns, roughly speaking, were organized in the corporate form. We have only to look around us to see that the situation to-day in this respect is entirely different. The corporate form, though not yet universal, is far ahead of partnerships and of individual proprietorships in popularity and in influence on business methods. As its advantages become better known we may expect to see it adopted even by small and backward concerns. This tendency is bringing to the front numerous problems of corporation law and management with which every man in business should be familiar.

From this point of view the present volume is written. It is intended primarily for the information and guidance of business men of all stations and degrees. Most of what is said here will be found applicable both to large and to small corporations. The facts and illustrations, however, are largely drawn from the experience of the big industrial and railroad combinations. The chief reason for directing attention to the big corporations is that their methods are well developed and are worthy of study and imitation by the managers of smaller corporations. Most of us have a great deal to learn from the men who control the financial affairs of such companies as the United States Steel Corporation, the Union Pacific Railroad Company, and the Pennsylvania Railroad Company, to mention three of our greatest and best managed corporations.

INTRODUCTION

While the first object of the volume is to serve business men, the author trusts that it will prove useful also to at least four other groups:

(a) To stock and bond brokers and their employés, many of whom, the writer has observed, have only a fragmentary knowledge gained from experience, not a comprehensive knowledge, of financial operations.

(b) To lawyers, all of whom should have a clear understanding of the financial as well as the legal phases of corporate organization and management.

(c) To bankers, who are constantly dealing with all kinds of business corporations.

(d) To accountants, to whom a comprehension of corporation methods and problems is almost as essential as a knowledge of strictly accounting principles.

This list might be indefinitely extended. It is not too much to say that everyone directly or indirectly connected with modern business ought to possess for his own protection and advancement a correct understanding of the principles of corporation finance.

The thirty chapters in the volume may be conveniently classified into seven groups:

Chapters I–VI present the elements of corporation law. They may be omitted by lawyers, but are essential to all other readers.

Chapters VII–XI describe all the methods and instruments that are used in this country in raising funds for corporations.

Chapters XII–XV explain how corporations are promoted, and give in illustration a brief account of the United States Steel Corporation.

Chapters XVI–XIX discuss the four methods of selling the securities of a corporation.

Chapters XX–XXIV deal with the problems of honest financial management of a corporation.

Chapters XXV-XXVII discuss the schemes and tricks of dishonest manipulators.

Chapters XXVIII–XXX are concerned with the causes of insolvency and the problems of reorganization.

The reader should bear in mind that all these questions are treated from the standpoint of corporation officials, not from the standpoint of stockholders or of prospective investors. Additional light may be obtained from the volume on INVESTMENT AND SPECULATION, in which the interests of buyers of securities are kept to the front, and from the volumes on ACCOUNTING and on COMMERCIAL LAW.

W. H. LOUGH.

New York University
School of Commerce, Accounts and Finance.

CHAPTER I

THE CORPORATE FORM

1. *"Non-stock" corporations.*—Everybody knows in a vague way that a corporation is an association of individuals formed to carry on an enterprise. Comparatively few people, however, understand just what the corporation is in the eyes of the law or the extent and the limitations of its activities. Obviously, the first step in the study of corporation finance should be an examination of the powers and possibilities of this peculiar and wonderfully effective form of organization.

Corporations fall into two distinct groups. There are, first, corporations without capital stock, or "non-stock" corporations; to this class belong almost all churches, hospitals, chartered clubs, universities and other strictly social and charitable organizations. The prime characteristic of such corporations is that the members share equally in all the privileges of membership without regard to the amount of money that each may have contributed. There is no arrangement for transacting a money-making business and distributing profits or losses. In fact, non-stock corporations exist either for the common benefit of all the members or for the purpose of serving the public at large. Many interesting questions as to the rights and powers of such corporations might be discussed; but the discussion would be out of place in this volume.

2. *"Stock" corporations.*—We are here concerned only with the second class, namely, "stock" corporations;

to this class belong all business corporations. Two apparent exceptions, mutual insurance societies and stock exchanges, both of which are ordinarily "non-stock" corporations, may be noted; both organizations in their fundamental character, however, are simply clubs which, like many other clubs, offer to their members certain valuable privileges. "Stock" corporations, on the other hand, are formed with the object of carrying on business ventures; they have a capital stock divided into transferable shares; they are intended to make profits which are to be distributed to their members, or stockholders, in proportion to the number of shares each one possesses; each stockholder secures his shares by purchase for valuable consideration from the corporation or by transfer from some previous stockholder; each stockholder is an owner of the corporation and its assets to the extent of the number of shares that he holds.

3. *Definitions.*—The most famous definition of a corporation, and a definition that in its main features is as sound to-day as it ever was, is that given in the Dartmouth College case in 1819 by Chief Justice Marshall of the United States Supreme Court, who referred to a corporation as "an artificial being, invisible, intangible, and existing only in contemplation of law." Blackstone, author of England's greatest legal text-book, gives a definition that is almost as well-known as Chief Justice Marshall's in the following words: "A corporation is an artificial person created for preserving in perpetual succession certain rights, which being conferred on natural persons only, would fail in the process of time." You will note that this definition emphasizes the most striking distinctive feature of the corporation, namely, its artificial personality. The corporation is an entity or being in itself, apart from the persons who organize

and own it. Let us review some of the results of this legal fiction that the creation of a corporation brings into the world a new person,—artificially created, to be sure, but yet endowed with many of the powers of an ordinary human being.

In the first place, as the corporation has an existence apart from the lives of any or all its owners, it is not broken up by the death or withdrawal of any owner. In the second place, the corporation has the right to buy and sell and contract debts in its own name and for itself; it may even owe money or lend money to some or all of its owners. In the third place, it may sue and be sued in the courts, without thereby involving any of its owners. In the fourth place, it may enter into all kinds of legal contracts, just as an individual might do.

4. *The fiction of "corporate entity."*—Here, then, is the first and most fundamental fact about the corporation for the student to grasp and keep always clearly in view, that it is a separate, distinct artificial person. It is true that within the last few years the courts of the United States have shown a strong tendency to go behind this artificial personality and to throw responsibility on the owners and managers of a corporation, especially in case of fraud. Clark, the author of a standard legal work, says:

> That a corporation is a legal entity, separate and distinct from the members who compose it, is a mere legal fiction, introduced for the convenience of the corporation in transacting business, and of those who do business with it; and, when urged to an intent and purpose not within its reason and policy, the fiction will be disregarded, and the fact that the corporation is really a collection of individuals will be recognized, even at law. Courts of equity, in every instance, look behind the corporate

entity and recognize the individual members and will do so whenever justice requires.

Yet the fact remains that the corporation's existence, property, contracts and debts all adhere to the corporation itself and not to the individuals who together own the corporation. It is true, also, that this artificial person, the corporation, has neither mind nor body and cannot therefore think or act. The law, however, easily gets over this difficulty by treating the managers and officers of the corporation as agents empowered to carry on its operations.

5. *Corporations in ancient nations.*—This fiction of artificial personality seems to be at first sight an unnecessary and even absurd idea, and the results that follow from the adoption of this fiction appear more like the spinning of legal cobwebs than the working out of common-sense principles. But a little further study reveals that the corporate form substantially as it exists to-day has been used by many ancient and modern nations. It seems, therefore, that there must be some good reason or reasons for its widespread use. The archæologists tell us that as far back as the prosperous days of Babylon the inhabitants of that ill-fated country in their commercial transactions used corporations somewhat as we use them now. The Romans also developed and made great use of the corporate form of organizing enterprises. Indeed, it is asserted by Blackstone, and was at one time universally believed, that our modern corporations are descendants in a direct line of the ancient Roman corporations. Although this theory is no longer fully accepted, it remains true that the Roman law with regard to corporations has had considerable influence in the development of our modern corporation law. Without going further into this historical survey,

which is a little outside the scope of this book, we may lay down this generalization, that in almost every great active commercial nation the corporate form of organization has sooner or later come into existence. It must, then, we may be sure, have some clear and important business advantages.

6. *Popularity in modern times.*—This conclusion is confirmed when we reflect that along with the marvelous business development of the last century there has been apparent a more than proportional increase in the number and importance of corporations. At first only large enterprises, such as railroads, steamship companies and great manufacturing establishments were so organized. Later the smaller factories and wholesale establishments followed the lead of the larger concerns. Finally within the last few years we have witnessed both in Europe and particularly in this country the extension of the movement to small manufacturing and retail establishments. The drift in this direction is so apparent that it need not be dwelt upon at any length. Every reader of this book may look around and see within his own circle numerous concerns in corporate form which were conducted a few years ago by individuals or partnerships. Unless this tendency receives some unexpected check it will not be many years before the corporate form will be adopted by almost every business, large and small, in the United States.

7. *Adaptability to raising large amounts of capital.*—Evidently there must be great advantages in the corporate form; otherwise the landslide toward it would long ago have been stopped. It will be worth while to review briefly some of these advantages.

Originally, as has been said, corporations were confined almost altogether to large enterprises and were used principally because of the facilities which they afforded for raising and handling large amounts of capital. In this respect they are obviously far superior both to individuals and to partnerships. Not even the richest individual—not John D. Rockefeller nor Andrew Carnegie nor Lord Rothschild—would be able out of his own resources to build and operate one of the great railroad systems of the United States. Even if one of these men were able individually to take care of an enterprise of this size, he would not care to do it. Men of great wealth do not consider it advisable to put all their money into one business. They scatter their investments, so that if one proves a failure profits on the others may more than counterbalance the loss.

Nor would a partnership, great and wealthy as some partnerships have been, be an efficient method of bringing together the vast amounts of capital that are required for every great enterprise. It would be an extraordinary coincidence if several men of immense wealth, who might conceivably construct and own in partnership a big railroad or a big industrial trust, were able to harmonize inevitable differences of opinion and to co-operate efficiently in a partnership arrangement. It is probably safe to say that in the whole commercial history of the world we could not find a single instance of, say, a billion or even half a billion—perhaps even a hundred million—dollars of capital raised and managed under a partnership agreement. It is well to remember in this connection that even the greatest individual fortunes are mere dots compared to the total wealth of a vast country like the United States. Furthermore, of these individual fortunes only a small part ordinarily is free at any one time to be used or invested as the owner wills.

The corporate form, on the other hand, has infinite possibilities so far as the raising and managing of capital is concerned. Any number of people, large or small, may contribute funds. The American Telephone and Telegraph Company, for example, has over 25,000 stockholders, the Pennsylvania Railroad Company over 60,000, and the United States Steel Corporation not far from 110,000. A large number of owners of a corporation does not tend to break up and render inefficient the management, for the control of whatever capital the owners contribute is kept in the hands of the officers of the corporation. Thus the corporation, without losing in efficiency, may reach out into the highways and by-ways of the land, draw its capital from a thousand or from a hundred thousand individuals and heap up vast aggregations of capital that could not possibly be obtained in any other manner. For this reason it is inevitable that the corporate form should be used in the financing of practically every large enterprise.

This advantage of corporations, that they are able to collect and to make use of the small contributions of many individuals, though most prominent in great undertakings, is by no means to be overlooked in the case of smaller enterprises. Frequently an inventor or a retail dealer or any small business man who needs a few hundred or a few thousand dollars, could not obtain it from his own immediate relatives and friends. The same man, perhaps, may easily raise the capital he requires by organizing a corporation and selling small interests to a considerable number of people. Many a business man has thus obtained necessary capital which he has made the foundation of a fortune.

8. *Permanence.*—The second important advantage

of the corporate form is permanence. When an individual owner of a business dies, his business dies with him. It may, to be sure, be carried on by his family or bought by strangers; on the other hand, it may be that no practicable method of disposing of it except at an enormous sacrifice will be found. This is largely a matter of chance, because no organization for carrying on the business is in existence. A partnership is almost equally subject to chance. When a partner dies, the firm is thereby automatically dissolved. The surviving partner or partners may, of course, form a new firm and take over the interest of the deceased partner. In so doing, however, disputes are liable to occur, especially in those lines of business where the earnings are irregular and the value of the assets is not clearly defined. If the surviving partners are unable to continue the business properly or are disposed to drive a hard bargain, the estate of the deceased partner may be deprived of a large part of its rightful interest in the business. Here, again, there is no permanent machinery for managing the business. The partnership, like the individual business, is subject to all the uncertainties and calamities that beset the lives of individual human beings.

The corporation, on the other hand, exists until it becomes bankrupt, is allowed to lapse or is voluntarily dissolved. The death of any man, even if he owns 99 per cent of the stock of the corporation, does not affect the corporation itself. It is an "artificial being," a creature of the law not subject to the infirmities of human existence. It is so organized that if one officer dies or withdraws, a successor may be quickly chosen. As the corporation exists apart from the persons who own it and as control is vested in its officers, the death or withdrawal of an owner does not at all disturb its machinery, and the death or withdrawal of an officer means simply that someone else must be found and appointed to the position.

9. *Centralization of control.*—This brings us to the third important advantage of the corporate form, namely, its centralization of power and responsibility. In this particular feature it cannot be, of course, superior to individual ownership, but it is far ahead of the partnership. As the law does not recognize in the partnership anything but a group or association of individuals, it follows that each partner is empowered to conduct the business, to buy and sell the partnership assets, to make binding contracts and incur debts. Ordinarily, to be sure, the partners mutually agree to a fixed division of duties and powers, but this division is not supposed to be known or to be binding on outsiders. Each partner, so far as his dealings with outsiders are concerned, is the whole partnership. Obviously, therefore, no partnership should ever be formed except between persons who have entire confidence in each other; and even then a partnership often proves an unsafe and inefficient method of conducting business. Except by mutual agreement binding only on themselves, to repeat, there is no clear-cut division of powers and responsibilities.

Under the corporate form, on the other hand, business can be transacted only by the duly appointed officers; no owner, unless he is also an officer—even though he hold almost all the stock—has any authority to transact business for the corporation. Each of the officers of the corporation, as is explained in the chapter on "Interior Organization," has his sphere of duties carefully defined, both within the corporation and outside. Persons not connected with the corporation are expected to have their dealings only with the duly authorized officers, and if they do not exercise reasonable care in this respect may find whatever agreements or contracts they make invalid. This will be more clearly understood by the reader after a study of the chapters on agency in the volume on COMMERCIAL LAW. Furthermore, the relations of the corporate officers to each other are clearly defined and the gradations of authority are so marked that each one may understand clearly just how far he is empowered to act on his own judgment and what questions he should refer to his official superiors. The great advantage of this care in organization and in delegation of power is so obvious that it need not be dwelt upon at any length. A well-managed corporation carries on its affairs with the precision and smoothness of a well-disciplined army.

10. *Transferability of ownership.*—A fourth advantage of the corporate form is the ease with which its ownership may be transferred. An individual owner who desires to sell his property must find a purchaser for all of it at one and the same time. A partner who desires to sell his interest in the firm must either make some satisfactory arrangement with the other partners, which may be a difficult matter, or must find a purchaser who offers satisfactory terms and is personally acceptable to the other partners, and that is likely to prove still more difficult. Altogether the problem of withdrawing funds that have been invested in an individually-owned property or in a partnership is almost always hard and frequently insoluble. Under the corporate form the problem is much simpler. The ownership of a corporation is represented by shares, any or all of which may be transferred from hand to hand without interfering in the least with the stability of the corporation. An owner

of several shares need not, therefore, find any one person to take all his property off his hands; he may sell a few shares to one man, one or two to another, and so on, and thus dispose of his property piecemeal. Furthermore, as the corporation is managed directly by the officers, not by the owners, no consideration ordinarily need be given to the question as to whether or not a prospective buyer is a good business man or is acceptable to the other persons interested in the corporation. Women, old men, administrators and trustees of estates, institutions of all kinds—all are possible purchasers of corporate securities. Thus the owner of corporate shares finds his market much broader and his facilities for selling much better than does the owner of a partnership interest. The securities of large corporations are constantly dealt in on the stock exchanges of large cities, and thus a continuous and easily accessible market is afforded to every owner.

11. *Limited liability.*—The fifth and last important advantage of the corporate form is the fact that the liability and possible loss of each owner is limited. Generally speaking, the owner of any corporation security is safe in reflecting that though the security may become worthless and he may lose all that he paid for it, he cannot possibly lose more than that amount. The reader may perhaps think that to the owner of the stock of a failed corporation this statement affords but cold comfort; but compare his situation with that of a partner in a bankrupt firm. The partner may not only lose all that he invested in the firm, but in addition is personally liable for all the unpaid debts of the firm. As has been explained above, it is possible that these debts may have been foolishly or even fraudulently contracted by some other partner; yet that fact would not relieve any other partner from his personal liability. No doubt most

readers of this paragraph will call to mind instances in their own experience of individual owners or of partners in disastrous enterprises who have lost everything they owned, including even their homes and most of their personal property, by the failure of such enterprises. If a corporation fails, on the other hand, and its debts prove greater than its assets, the creditors have no claim on the property of the stockholders outside the failed business.

An important exception to this principle of limited liability exists in the case of stockholders of national banks. They are individually liable in case of failure not only for their investment but for an additional sum equal to the par value of their holdings of bank stock. A similar rule applies in Minnesota to stockholders of most corporations and there are one or two other exceptions which are referred to in Chapter IV. Even in such cases, however, though the liability of stockholders is somewhat greater than with the ordinary corporation, it is still strictly limited.

No doubt this principle of limited liability has been one of the main advantages of corporations that has led to their formation in a great many cases, and especially has encouraged in recent years the widespread movement to change partnerships into corporations. No business man, especially one who has considerable personal property and perhaps is advanced in years, likes to reflect that at any moment, through the fraud or mismanagement of some subordinate or partner, or through some unavoidable natural calamity, he may be compelled to give up his home and personal property in order to satisfy the demands of business creditors. The corporate form of business relieves him of this haunting spectre.

The prominent advantages of the corporate form, which have brought about its great extension in recent years, may then be summed up as follows:

(1) FLEXIBILITY. The owners of a corporation may be few or numerous. This makes the corporate form especially well adapted to collecting large amounts of capital by means of small contributions from a great many people.

(2) PERMANENCE. The life of a corporation is not dependent on the life or on the caprice of any individual.

(3) CENTRALIZATION OF CONTROL. Under the corporate form the officers of the corporation within carefully defined limits exercise complete control.

(4) TRANSFERABILITY OF OWNERSHIP. Corporate shares may be readily sold either in a block or piecemeal and have a wide market.

(5) LIMITED LIABILITY. The corporation alone, with certain minor exceptions, is liable for its own debts and the shareholders cannot lose more than their original investment.

12. *Disadvantages of the corporate form.*—In view of these advantages it may be asked why all kinds of business without exception are not organized under the corporate form. The answer is that certain minor disadvantages, which in some instances are sufficient to offset the advantages named, are inseparable from corporations. These disadvantages may be briefly summed up as follows:

(1) INCREASED EXPENSE. All states impose certain incorporation fees, license and franchise taxes on corporations, which taxes are in addition to the ordinary state and local taxes on property. These taxes are, however, uniformly small. The United States Government also imposes a tax on corporate income. In addition,

legal assistance is almost always necessary in forming corporations, and there may be an additional charge on this account of from $25 up. These corporate expenses are, of course, too slight to be worth much consideration, except in the case of very small enterprises, where they may sometimes be of sufficient importance to prevent the adoption of the corporate form.

(2) LIMITED POWERS. As the corporation derives all its powers from the state in which it is incorporated, and as all its powers should be distinctly stated in its articles of incorporation (see Chapter II), it may be somewhat hampered at times by lack of authority to carry on operations that would be profitable. This, however, is a superficial objection that may be readily dismissed; for a good corporation lawyer will always find it possible to include in the statement of the powers of the corporation authority for every act that would be necessary in practice. If not, it is always easy to form a new corporation for whatever specific action is desired. This point also is further discussed in Chapter II.

(3) LIMITED CREDIT. A lender of money would, of course, prefer, other things being equal, to lend to an individual or a partnership, rather than to a corporation, because the liability of the owners of the property in the former case is unlimited, and in the latter case, as has been explained, is limited. Thus a partnership which is converted into a corporation will sometimes be embarrassed more or less by reluctance of its creditors to continue extending credit as freely as before the conversion. This objection, which is of importance usually only in the case of a small and closely held business, may be overcome, if desired, by the officers or certain stockholders personally endorsing the corporation's notes and bills payable. By so doing they, of course, lose the

advantage of limited liability, but they retain all the other advantages of the corporate form. There are some business activities, however, in which the personal element is so prominent as to make unlimited liability desirable. A firm of accountants, for instance, could not be changed to a corporation without forfeiting to some extent the confidence of the business public, for every public accountant is and ought to be personally liable to the fullest extent for the honesty and accuracy of his work. The same thing may be said of bankers and engineers, and to some extent of business advisers and systematizers; for such activities the corporate form, on account of its limited liability feature, is ill-adapted.

(4) Governmental control. Some concerns are strongly averse, for good reasons, to any publicity whatever as to their operations and financial results. They may perhaps be making so much money that they desire to keep it secret in order to avoid attracting competitors; or their real business may be quite different from their ostensible business, and they would not desire to attract attention to this fact by the inclusion of unusual powers in articles of incorporation. For fear of governmental supervision, therefore, they retain the partnership, even with all its disadvantages.

The reader will readily see that this list of disadvantages of the corporate form does not include anything of great importance to most legitimate kinds of business. Certainly the disadvantages are of little weight in most cases in comparison with the obvious and substantial gains that may be had by adopting the corporate form. We are justified in concluding, therefore, that the tendency toward the corporate form of conducting business, which has been referred to above, will not diminish, but rather will increase in the coming years. The corporation is the efficient twentieth century means of conducting business. In city and in country, from the captains of finance to the smallest units in the army of business, in transportation, in manufacturing, in trading, even in farming, the corporation has come to be recognized as the best form yet discovered for organizing the production of wealth.

To confess oneself ignorant of the nature, the functions, the abuses and the possibilities of this mighty instrument is indeed a confession of business inefficiency and narrowness. The pages that follow are to be devoted to a discussion of the formation and management of corporations which, it is hoped, will place this truly important and somewhat difficult subject in a clear light before our readers.

CHAPTER II

LEGAL STATUS OF THE CORPORATION

13. *Defining and controlling instruments.*—The corporation, we have said, is a "creature of the law," and this statement is to be taken literally. This artificial creature has no existence, no powers, no privileges, no duties, except those which are conferred upon it either by express statement or by implication. The artificial creature, in other words, does not have what we may call the natural rights of an individual to live unmolested and to pursue whatever objects he pleases, so long as the rights of others are not interfered with, but only artificial rights. In order to determine in any particular case, therefore, what a corporation may or may not do and what its standing is, we must look to the particular instruments which give it being and control its actions. These instruments in every state in the Union are three in number:

(1) The Constitution of the State.

(2) The General Corporation Act.

(3) The Charter of each particular corporation.

Supplementing the charter, practically all corporations have a set of by-laws for their own guidance. In order to understand the legal status of a corporation we must consider briefly each of these instruments.

14. *Common law of corporations.*—It must be borne in mind, in connection with what follows in this chapter, that corporations of one kind or another have been in existence for a very long time, and that the courts of England and of the United States have given a large

number of decisions dealing with the duties and powers of corporations. These decisions form the great body of common law with reference to corporations; and this common law, for which search must be made through the precedents of many years, governs where it is not superseded. Corporations as forms of business organization, however—and especially as forms of organization for relatively small enterprises—are comparatively modern. From the very beginning the English Parliament and the state legislatures of this country have found it expedient to enact statutes in order to define clearly the powers and duties of corporations. These statutes in every state are now so explicit and comprehensive as to govern the great mass of corporate activities. They form the body of statutory law with reference to corporations. The reader will find in the volume on COMMERCIAL LAW a full exposition of the relations between common and statutory law and of the manner in which statutes of the legislature are interpreted by the courts. For our purpose it is enough to say that the statute law supersedes the common law wherever the two disagree and that statute law with regard to corporations is so voluminous that we need rarely go back of it to the common law.

15. *The state constitution.*—The fundamental law in each state of the Union is the constitution of the state, and no provision which conflicts with any clause in the state constitution will be legal. This is a point, not merely of theoretical, but also at times of distinct practical importance. For instance, the Constitution of the State of Pennsylvania prescribes that all Pennsylvania corporations shall elect their officers by what is known as "cumulative voting"—a method that is described at some length in Chapter V. In one case, with which

the writer happens to be familiar, certain stockholders of a small Pennsylvania corporation planned to pass a rule against cumulative voting and by means of that rule to elect all members of the board of directors. Great was their chagrin and surprise when they discovered that no Pennsylvania corporation is competent to enforce such a rule as they proposed. It frequently happens that some of the ordinary statute provisions of a state are found, when tested in the courts, to be in conflict with some provision of the state constitution and therefore null and void. The reader, then, should not forget that behind every enactment of the legislature looms the constitution of the state, a fundamental factor that should not be left out of his reckoning.

16. *Method of creating the corporation.*—The direct legislative authority to create a corporation may be given in one of two ways, by special enactment of the legislature for the benefit of this particular corporation, or by a general act which governs the creation of all corporations. Formerly the first named method was universal. It proved itself, however, both inconvenient and unfair. Authority to incorporate was granted arbitrarily by the legislature for certain enterprises and denied to others equally deserving. It was necessary to have a "pull" in order to get the desired enactment. Favoritism and corruption, coupled with unwise conservatism, were the natural results of this method. It has therefore fallen into disuse and is definitely prohibited by the constitutions of many states of the Union. One rather conspicuous exception to the general rule that corporations are no longer formed and managed under the provision of special enactments is the Bay State Gas Company, a corporation organized by Mr. J. Edward Addicks, and later controlled, it is understood, by Mr. Thomas W.

Lawson. This company was given large powers and privileges by a special act of the Legislature of Delaware during the time when Mr. Addicks was reputed to be the political boss of the State.

The present-day method of creating the corporation is by complying with the provisions of a general corporation act—in some states called an "enabling act." Such an act usually prescribes the general purposes for which corporations may be lawfully formed, the chief powers which they may possess—such as power to hold property in the parent and in other states, power to hold its own stock, power to hold stock of other corporations (not conferred by all states), power to borrow money, power to do business in other states, and so on—the number of incorporators and stockholders, the manner and lawful purposes of issue of capital stock, the rights of the stockholders, the minimum numbers of directors and of officers, the character and amount of taxes, the nature of reports required, the exact form to be followed in incorporating, and so on. Under such a general act any citizens of the state—sometimes of other states—who meet the requirements of the law may form a corporation. Thus the favoritism and corruption incident to the old method of special enactment are eliminated. The universal establishment of these general corporation acts is one of the most important reforms in business methods of the second half of the nineteenth century. Though many of these acts—as is pointed out in Chapter IV—are far from perfect, we all have reason to be profoundly thankful that they exist at all.

17. *Essential features of the charter.*—We come now to the immediate instrument of incorporation, the

charter—sometimes called the certificate of incorporation or the articles of incorporation. Where the charter is obtained under a general corporation act, it is drawn by the incorporators or their attorney and presented to the proper state official, usually the secretary of state. If the charter as drawn is approved, the secretary of state signifies his acceptance thereof, and the corporation comes into being. There is no favoritism in this procedure, as there is in the granting of charters by special acts; the secretary of state has no authority to refuse any charter which is properly drawn and which complies with the provisions of the state law.

A charter need not be a very lengthy instrument, although large companies sometimes find it desirable to prevent future misunderstanding by inserting into the charter a great many details not absolutely essential. In practically all states every charter must contain, among other things, the following information:

(1) The name of the corporation.

(2) The purpose or purposes for which it is formed.

(3) The amount of capital stock, and if there is a division into classes of stock, the rights of each class.

(4) The number of shares of stock.

(5) The location of the principal business office.

(6) The period of existence of the corporation, which is usually unlimited or perpetual.

(7) The names and usually the post-office addresses of the incorporators.

If the reader desires a more detailed statement of the requirements in any particular state, he cannot do better than to go direct to the statutes of that state. It would lead us too far afield if we were to enter here on any comprehensive legal study of charter forms and provisions. A few remarks, however, as to the essential features of a charter and the presentation of the sample form following will not be out of place and will help to make clear some points of corporation practice that might otherwise be obscure.

18. *A sample charter.*—The following is a very brief and simple charter, which conforms to the laws of the State of New Jersey. The form in other states would be slightly different. The writer is indebted to Mr. Thomas Conyngton for permission to copy this form from his manual "The Modern Corporation."

CERTIFICATE OF INCORPORATION
OF THE
CARHART DRUG COMPANY.

We, the undersigned, for the purpose of forming a corporation under and by virtue of the provisions of an act of the Legislature of the State of New Jersey, entitled "An Act concerning corporations (Revision of 1896)," and the several supplements thereto and acts amendatory thereof, do hereby severally subscribe for and agree to take the number of shares of stock of the said corporation hereinafter placed opposite our respective names, do further certify and set forth as follows:

First—The name of said corporation shall be

"CARHART DRUG COMPANY."

Second—The location of its principal office in the State of New Jersey shall be at No. 15 Exchange Place, Jersey City.

The name of the agent who shall be therein and in charge thereof, upon whom process against this Corporation may be served, is the Corporation Trust Company of New Jersey.

Third—The objects for which this corporation is formed are:

(a) To manufacture, prepare, compound, mix, combine, buy, sell and generally deal in all manner of chemicals, chemical products, drugs and pharmaceutical compounds and preparations, and to patent, register or otherwise protect the same.

(b) To obtain, purchase or otherwise acquire formulæ, patents and secret processes for the manufacture and preparation of chemicals, drugs and the compounds and preparations thereof, and to operate under, sell, assign, grant licenses in respect of, or otherwise turn the same to account.

(c) To enter into, carry out or otherwise turn to account contracts of every kind; to have and maintain offices within and without the State; to acquire, hold, mortgage, lease and convey or otherwise use or dispose of real and personal property in any part of the world; and in general to carry on such operations and enterprises and to do all such things in connection therewith as may be permitted by the laws of New Jersey and be necessary or convenient in the conduct of the Company's business.

Fourth—The total authorized stock of the corporation shall be twenty-five thousand dollars ($25,000), divided into two hundred and fifty (250) shares of the par value of one hundred dollars ($100) each, and the amount of capital stock with which said corporation will begin business is five thousand dollars ($5,000).

Fifth—The names and post-office addresses of the incorporators and the number of shares subscribed for by each are as follows:

Names	Addresses	Shares
Willis J. Carhart...	15 Exchange Place, Jersey City, N. J.	40
Sheldon McCammis.	" " " " " " "	5
John B. Whelan ...	" " " " " " "	5

Sixth—The period of existence of said corporation shall be unlimited.

In Witness Whereof, we have hereunto set our hands and

seals this 21st day of July, A. D. nineteen hundred and eight.

Willis J. Carhart. (L. S.)
Sheldon McCammis. (L. S.)
John B. Whelan. (L. S.)

In the presence of
Harmon Watson.
Thomas O'Connell.
(Execution in due form.)

19. *The corporate name.*—The name of a corporation is part of its property and sometimes—especially after the corporation has been long enough established to have acquired good will—is highly valuable property. For that reason, a new corporation is not allowed to assume a name already taken by a previously existing corporation nor even a name so similar as to cause confusion. If the older corporation, however, in such a case were not incorporated or licensed in the same state as the new company, the state authorities would have no right to reject the new company's charter on account of the similarity in name. Under such circumstances the only remedy of the older company would be to bring suit in the courts. Some states lay down certain arbitrary rules, such as that the prefix "The" must be used, or that the word "incorporated" or "limited" must follow the corporate name. Alabama, Colorado, Kentucky, Connecticut, Delaware, Kansas, Missouri, North Carolina and Virginia require the word "company" to be a part of the corporate name. As a matter of business, it is usually very desirable for a new corporation to adopt some distinctive, self-explanatory, short name, and to avoid so far as possible hackneyed words and phrases.

20. *The corporate purposes.*—There is no more important section of the charter than that in which the

corporate purpose or purposes are stated. For most corporations, the activities of which are to be confined to some one line of business, a brief and simple statement is all that is necessary. The incorporators and their attorney should bear in mind in this connection, however, that it costs nothing at the beginning to insert a very full and comprehensive description of all the possible activities of the corporation and that the absence of the right word or phrase may at some future time cause serious inconvenience. The corporation is not obliged to carry out all of the purposes named in the charter; on the other hand, it has no authority to do anything which is not so named or clearly implied. The courts, to be sure, are generally liberal in their interpretation of the implied powers of corporations; but it is better to keep out of the courts and to take a little care at the beginning so as to avert any future disputes as to whether proposed activities are beyond the purposes and powers of the corporation or not.

To illustrate the care with which the purposes of a large company are stated in order to comprehend and give legal authority for any possible future activity, the charter of the United States Steel Corporation, which was drawn by one of the great corporation lawyers of the country, the late James B. Dill, of New Jersey, may be cited. The section of the charter, in which the purposes of this great corporation are stated, is too long to be quoted in full. Nine paragraphs are devoted to describing all the manufacturing, landowning, mining, trading, contracting, inventing and patenting, security-buying, selling and holding activities which could be thought of by all the eminent lawyers and business men who helped Judge Dill to draw the charter. Then follow the two paragraphs quoted below, in which, as the reader will observe, the incorporators aim to provide for any other possible activity not already distinctly set forth. Note particularly the italicized clauses. A statement somewhat similar to these two paragraphs might be included to advantage in the charters of many much smaller corporations, and perhaps would dispose of otherwise troublesome questions of authority.

The business or purpose of the Company is from time to time to do any one or more of the acts and things herein set forth; and it may conduct its business in other States and in the Territories and in foreign countries, and may have one office or more than one office, and keep the books of the company outside the State of New Jersey, except as otherwise may be provided by law; and may hold, purchase, mortgage and convey real and personal property either in or out of the State of New Jersey.

Without in any particular limiting any of the objects and powers of the corporation, it is hereby expressly declared and provided that the corporation shall have power to issue bonds and other obligations in payment for property purchased or acquired by it, or for any other object in or about its business; to mortgage, or pledge any stocks, bonds, or other obligations, or any property which may be acquired by it, to secure any bonds or other obligations by it issued or incurred; to guarantee any dividends or bonds or contracts or other obligations; to make and perform contracts of any kind and description; and in carrying on its business, or for the purpose of attaining or furthering any of its objects, *to do any and all other acts, and things, and to exercise any and all other powers which a copartnership or natural person could do and exercise, and which now or hereafter may be authorized by law.*

A further illustration of the importance of a clear and full statement in the charter of the purposes for which a corporation is organized is contained in a decision of the New Jersey Court of Errors and Appeals handed down March 5, 1909. The case involved the right of a railroad company to acquire and hold the stock of certain trolley companies near Atlantic City. The court denied this right and said, among other things:

The power to purchase, hold, etc., stock and bonds of other corporations conferred by Section 51 of the general corporation act is to be exercised subject to the limitations imposed by Section 2 of the same act; that is to say, the power exists as a primary power only when the purpose to exercise it as such is expressed in the certificate of incorporation; and otherwise it exists as an incidental power only so far as necessary or convenient to the attainment of the objects that are set forth in the charter or certificate of incorporation. It is only by reference to the certificate of incorporation that the Attorney General and other officials interested on behalf of the people can readily determine what powers have been granted and whether the company is usurping franchises not granted by the state. It is by reference to the articles of association that investors can conveniently ascertain the character of the contract into which they are entering and the property rights they are acquiring in purchasing stock of the company.

It must not be forgotten that stock ownership by one company in another is only a mode by which the former company engages in the business of the latter. But since the second company (if Section 51 were unqualified in its effect) might likewise hold stock in any other corporation or corporations, and these might do the same *ad infinitum*, stock ownership in any company under such a system would not evidence a participation in any definite kind of business, but in effect a participation in a "blind pool" subject to the uncontrolled will of the majority. There would be an end at once of all practical force to the doctrine that incorporation evidences a contract between the state and the corporation or between the corporators and stockholders themselves.

Evidently the eminent lawyers who drew up the charter, or certificate of incorporation, of the railroad company in this instance were either careless or lacking in foresight. Otherwise, they would have avoided this adverse decision very easily by including among the powers granted by the charter the right to acquire and hold stock.

21. *Other important features of the charter.*—The amount of capital and the number of shares of a new corporation which are desirable depend on principles of capitalization that are discussed in Chapter VII and which need not be considered at this stage.

Most, though not all, of the state laws require that the principal office of the corporation shall be within the state where the charter is secured. Partly for this reason, other things being equal, it is better to secure a charter from that state in which most of the business of a corporation is carried on; but this is by no means an invariable rule, as will be pointed out in Chapter IV. It is also usual, although not universal, to provide that one or more of the incorporators shall be citizens of the state which grants the charter. The minimum number of incorporators in most states is three.

The number of directors of a new corporation is an important point to consider when the charter is obtained. Sometimes the number is stated not in the charter, but in the by-laws and may readily be amended from time to time; but where the number is fixed by the charter it cannot be easily changed. A small board obviously is apt to be more efficient than a large board. This is another question which will come up for fuller discussion in a subsequent chapter.

22. *The by-laws.*—The by-laws are simply a collection of permanent rules for transacting business adopted by the stockholders or directors. It is not absolutely necessary, though almost always very desirable, that a

corporation should have by-laws. The by-laws usually contain provisions as to:

(1) Issue and transfer of stock.

(2) Meetings of stockholders and directors.

(3) Election of directors and officers.

(4) Powers and duties of directors and officers.

(5) General directions as to the management of the corporate property.

As in the case of the charter, we will run over briefly some of the important features of corporate by-laws.

First, the reader should study with care the following set of by-laws, which is used by a New York corporation, but could be adapted with slight changes to any small company. This set is taken from Mr. Conyngton's excellent manual, "The Modern Corporation."

BY-LAWS
OF THE
STANDARD BLEACHING COMPANY,
NEW YORK CITY

Article I.—Stock.

1. Certificates of Stock shall be issued in numerical order from the stock certificate book, be signed by the President and Treasurer and sealed by the Secretary with the corporate seal. A record of each certificate issued shall be kept on the stub thereof.

2. Transfers of Stock shall be made only upon the books of the Company and before a new certificate is issued the old certificate must be surrendered for cancellation. The stock books of the Company shall be closed for transfers twenty days before general elections and ten days before dividend days.

3. The Treasury Stock of the Company shall consist of such issued and outstanding stock of the Company as may be donated to the Company or otherwise acquired, and shall be held subject to disposal by the Board of Directors. Such stock

shall neither vote nor participate in dividends while held by the Company.

Article II.—Stockholders.

1. The Annual Meeting of the stockholders of this Company shall be held in the principal office of the Company in New York City at 12 M. on the second Monday in January of each year, if not a legal holiday, but if a legal holiday then on the day following.

2. Special Meetings of the stockholders may be called at the principal office of the Company at any time by resolution of the Board of Directors, or upon written request of stockholders holding one-third of the outstanding stock.

3. Notice of Meetings, written or printed, for every regular or special meeting of the stockholders, shall be prepared and mailed to the last known post-office address of each stockholder not less than ten days before any such meeting, and if for a special meeting, such notice shall state the object or objects thereof. No failure or irregularity of notice of any regular meeting shall invalidate such meeting or any proceeding thereat.

4. A Quorum at any meeting of the stockholders shall consist of a majority of the voting stock of the Company, represented in person or by proxy. A majority of such quorum shall decide any question that may come before the meeting.

5. The election of Directors shall be held at the annual meeting of stockholders and shall, after the first election, be conducted by two inspectors of election appointed by the President for that purpose. The election shall be by ballot, and each stockholder of record shall be entitled to cast one vote for each share of stock held by him.

6. The Order of Business at the annual meeting, and, as far as possible, at all other meetings of the stockholders, shall be:

1. Calling of Roll.
2. Proof of due notice of Meeting.
3. Reading and disposal of any unapproved Minutes.
4. Annual Reports of Officers and Committees.

5. Election of Directors.
6. Unfinished Business.
7. New Business.
8. Adjournment.

Article III.—Directors.

1. The Business and Property of the Company shall be managed by a Board of seven Directors, who shall be stockholders and who shall be elected annually by ballot by the stockholders for the term of one year, and shall serve until the election and acceptance of their duly qualified successors. Any vacancies may be filled by the Board for the unexpired term. Directors shall receive no compensation for their services.

2. The Regular Meetings of the Board of Directors shall be held in the principal office of the Company in New York City at 3 P. M. on the third Tuesday of each month, if not a legal holiday, but if a legal holiday, then on the day following.

3. Special Meetings of the Board of Directors to be held in the principal office of the Company in New York City may be called at any time by the President, or by any three members of the Board, or may be held at any time and place, without notice, by unanimous written consent of all the members, or with the presence of all members at such meetings.

4. Notices of both regular and special meetings shall be mailed by the Secretary to each member of the Board not less than five days before any such meeting, and notices of special meetings shall state the purposes thereof. No failure or irregularity of notice of any regular meeting shall invalidate such meeting or any proceeding thereat.

5. A Quorum at any meeting shall consist of a majority of the entire membership of the Board. A majority of such quorum shall decide any question that may come before the meeting.

6. Officers of the Company shall be elected by ballot by the Board of Directors at their first meeting after the election of directors each year. If any office becomes vacant during the year, the Board of Directors shall fill the same for the unex-

pired term. The Board of Directors shall fix the compensation of the officers and agents of the Company.

7. The order of business at any regular or special meeting of the Board of Directors shall be:

1. Reading and disposal of any unapproved Minutes.
2. Reports of Officers and Committees.
3. Unfinished Business.
4. New Business.
5. Adjournment.

Article IV.—Officers.

1. The Officers of the Company shall be a President, a Vice-President, a Secretary and a Treasurer, who shall be elected for one year and shall hold office until their successors are elected and qualify. The positions of Secretary and Treasurer may be united in one person.

2. The President shall preside at all meetings, shall have general supervision of the affairs of the Company, shall sign or countersign all certificates, contracts and other instruments of the Company as authorized by the Board of Directors; shall make reports to the directors and stockholders and perform all such other duties as are incident to his office or are properly required of him by the Board of Directors. In the absence or disability of the President, the Vice-President shall exercise all his functions.

3. The Secretary shall issue notices for all meetings, shall keep their minutes, shall have charge of the seal and the corporate books, shall sign with the President such instruments as require such signature, and shall make such reports and perform such other duties as are incident to his office, or are properly required of him by the Board of Directors.

4. The Treasurer shall have the custody of all moneys and securities of the Company and shall keep regular books of account and balance the same each month. He shall sign or countersign such instruments as require his signature, shall perform all duties incident to his office or that are properly required of him by the Board, and shall give bond for the faithful perform-

ance of his duties in such sum and with such sureties as may be required by the Board of Directors.

Article V.—Dividends and Finance.

1. Dividends shall be declared only from the surplus profits at such times as the Board of Directors shall direct, and no dividend shall be declared that will impair the capital of the Company.

2. The moneys of the Company shall be deposited in the name of the Company in such bank or trust company as the Board of Directors shall designate, and shall be drawn out only by check signed by the Treasurer and countersigned by the President.

Article VI.—Seal.

1. The Corporate Seal of the Company shall consist of two concentric circles, between which is the name of the Company, and in the centre shall be inscribed "Incorporated 1905, New York," and such seal, as impressed on the margin hereof, is hereby adopted as the Corporate Seal of the Company.

Article VII.—Amendments.

1. These By-Laws may be amended, repealed or altered, in whole or in part, by a majority vote of the entire outstanding stock of the Company, at any regular meeting of the stockholders, or at any special meeting where such action has been announced in the call and notice of such meeting.

2. The Board of Directors may adopt additional by-laws in harmony therewith, but shall not alter nor repeal any by-laws adopted by the stockholders of the Company.

23. *Essential features of the by-laws.*—The sections with regard to stock are usually of a formal character and state simply that the ownership of stock shall be evidenced by the issue of certificates to each stockholder, and that transfers of ownership shall be made only upon the books of the company. The reader should thoroughly understand this provision, which is practically universal. Frequently the engraved certificate of stock

in the possession of a stockholder, which usually reads "This is to certify that John Doe is the owner of .. shares of the capital stock of the John Doe Company, transferable only on the books of the company, etc.," (see page 70) is incorrectly called and mistaken for stock itself. As a matter of fact, stock is an intangible thing; it is merely a right to a share in the company's assets and earnings. A certificate is only a convenient method of proving that a certain person is the owner of stock. A certificate may be lost or stolen or given away or sold and yet the ownership of the stock will remain unchanged. Only by transfer on the books of the company will a change in ownership be consummated. The usual method of transferring stock is to sign a blank form on the back of each certificate (see page 70) which authorizes the secretary of the corporation or some other agent of the owner to make the transfer.

The by-laws almost always specify the time and place of an annual meeting of stockholders for the transaction of important business. Special meetings may be called from time to time on request of a certain number of stockholders or in whatever manner the by-laws may lay down. The important point is that to make a special meeting legal every stockholder must have proper notice in writing mailed to his last-known address. Meetings of the directors also are usually required at stated intervals and it is set forth in the by-laws that the directors are to elect the officers of the company and otherwise to manage its affairs.

The essential officers of a corporation are the president, the secretary and the treasurer. The duties of each officer should be and usually are clearly specified in the by-laws. Ordinarily the president, briefly stated, is the chief executive officer; the secretary keeps the records of the corporation; the treasurer handles the corporate funds. The reader should clearly understand, however, that this definition of duties is not necessarily or universally followed. The by-laws may make the president the custodian of funds and the treasurer the chief executive officer, or may distribute the duties in any other manner. The law recognizes, however, that an outsider has the right to assume that the man who is given the title of president, treasurer or secretary is given the powers and duties that customarily belong to that position.

The by-laws usually declare that dividends shall be paid only out of surplus, not out of the capital of the corporation, although this is simply a formal statement of a principle which could not legally be violated in any case so long as the corporation has creditors. A corporate seal is usually adopted and briefly described in the by-laws. The procedure and necessary percentage of favorable votes in order to amend the by-laws are usually stated.

The board of directors or the stockholders may sometimes adopt new rules of action which will be binding until rescinded, without the formality of amending the by-laws, simply by passing a formal resolution. No resolution, it need scarcely be said, will be legally binding if it is contrary to any by-law provision. Resolutions are frequently used, however, to supplement and further elucidate the by-laws and to lay down a general permanent policy.

We have now covered very briefly the main points that the reader should bear in mind as to the legal status of the corporation and as to the instruments that confer and define that status. All this is rather dry and more or less technical matter; yet it must not be slurred over by anyone who desires to acquire that knowledge of the corporate form and understanding of its uses and misuses that is essential to every person successfully concerned with modern business. We cannot afford to forget that the corporation is created and maintained under certain specific provisions of the law to which all its actions must conform.

CHAPTER III

INTERIOR ORGANIZATION

24. *Rights of stockholders.*—In this chapter we shall treat as briefly as the subject will permit the relations to each other of the various groups of individuals who are interested in a corporation. Those groups are:

I. Stockholders.
II. Creditors.
III. Directors.
IV. Officers.

Every corporation must be so organized that the duties, the liabilities and the rights of each of these groups are clearly known and may be enforced.

The nature of stock—the fact that it is an intangible share in the corporation's assets and earnings—has already been discussed. Each owner of stock becomes to the extent of his holdings an owner of the corporation. His rights fundamentally are the same as the rights of other owners of private property, but the full exercise of these rights is under the corporate form much abridged and modified. To illustrate, the private owner of a piece of property has the right to sell or destroy or give away or use for his personal enjoyment the property and its earnings. A stockholder, however, cannot sell or destroy or otherwise tamper with his proportion of the corporation's assets, because under the corporate form he has committed those assets to the care of other people.

The rights of stockholders as a body are:

(1) To elect directors.

(2) To amend the charter or by-laws.

(3) To sanction or veto the selling or mortgaging of the permanent assets of the corporation.

(4) To dissolve the company.

The first two rights have been touched upon in the preceding chapter and need not be further considered. The third right is not universal in all states and under all charters, but is generally conceded. In some states the courts assume that the stockholders, having chosen directors, freely turn over to them the sole and complete management of the business without any reservations whatsoever. Even in such states, however, the directors, in order to avoid any charge of fraud that might be brought against them, generally prefer on such important actions as the sale of permanent assets to have the officially expressed concurrence of the stockholders. A clause is sometimes placed either in the charter or in the by-laws requiring unanimous consent or the consent of a very large percentage of the stockholders in order to validate a sale or mortgage of permanent assets. The right of dissolution is very seldom exercised inasmuch as an unsuccessful corporation may be very easily abandoned and its charter allowed to lapse by non-payment of taxes.

25. *The proxy and its uses.*—The rights of each individual stockholder are four in number, as follows:

(1) To receive notice of and to participate in all stockholders' meetings.

(2) To share in the assets of the corporation in proportion to his stockholdings in case of dissolution.

(3) To share in dividends declared by the directors in proportion to his stockholdings.

(4) To inspect the accounts of the corporation.

The first right has already been mentioned. It should be further observed, however, that a stockholder's right to participate in meetings is not confined to personal attendance at the meetings. If he does not go himself he may confer the right to represent him upon some other person. The instrument which confers this right is known as a "proxy" and generally reads somewhat as follows:

KNOW ALL MEN BY THESE PRESENTS, that I, the undersigned, do hereby constitute and appoint John Doe my true and legal attorney to represent me at all meetings of the stockholders of the Blank Company and for me and in my name and stead to vote throughout upon the stock standing in my name on the books of said company at the times of said meetings, and I hereby grant my said attorney all the powers that I should possess if personally present.

This is a form well adapted to conferring a simple, unlimited right to represent the stockholder who gives it. The proxy may be much more formal and may contain any limitations that the giver chooses to impose; for instance, it may be good only for one meeting or up to a certain time or for a certain purpose, such as giving an affirmative vote on a proposition that is to come before the meeting.

The use of proxies in this country is widespread and is an important feature of corporation management. In England stockholders are more likely to appear in person at the annual meetings. By means of proxies American corporation officials are accustomed to hold meetings with no one but themselves actually attending, but with a constructive attendance through their proxies of more than a majority of the outstanding stock. The

Union Pacific Railroad, for instance, which is incorporated in Utah and must hold its annual meetings in that state, whereas its principal office is in New York City, every year sends its secretary and a few minor officials from New York to Salt Lake City, each official carrying a satchel full of proxies. The annual meeting is then held and the election of directors carried out with all the formality that would characterize a fully attended meeting. Any lone stockholder who appears in person will find that his presence adds nothing to the effectiveness of the proceedings and does not change their character in the least. Of course, in smaller companies the stockholders are more likely to be present in person, although even there representation by proxy is the established custom.

One point about a proxy that should be impressed on the mind of every stockholder is that it is never under any circumstances irrevocable. The courts will not recognize an irrevocable proxy as a valid agreement. No matter what the wording of the original proxy may be, no matter if it clearly and emphatically states that it is irrevocable, a stockholder may, as a matter of fact and of law, revoke it at his will.

The second right, as has already been intimated, is of small practical importance.

26. *The right to dividends.*—The third right—to share in dividends—is so often misunderstood by stockholders that its limitations need to be carefully noted. In the first place, notice that nothing is said as to earnings. A corporation may be getting enormous yearly profits and yet an individual stockholder may not draw any dividends whatever; nor can the stockholder get at these earnings until dividends are declared. In the second place, it will be pointed out in connection with the

powers of directors that directors alone have the right to declare dividends and cannot be compelled by any legal action whatever to grant dividends to the stockholders until they see fit. A case in point, which attracted some attention several years ago, was that of the Midvale Steel Company, a fairly large and now prosperous company, located in a suburb of Philadelphia. The management of the company for the ten years 1887 to 1897 devoted all of its earnings to improvement of the plant, in spite of protests and strenuous efforts on the part of minority stockholders to force the declaration of dividends. The courts will not interfere with the policy of the board of directors in this regard unless fraud or mismanagement can be proved.

27. *The right to information.*—The fourth right—to inspect the corporate books and accounts—was originally universally admitted and was of considerable importance. Each stockholder could go into the company's office whenever he chose and demand that he be given access to all the books and accounts. Early in the history of business corporations, however, it became evident that the manager of a rival business could buy a single share of stock and thereby obtain trade information that could be used to the detriment of the corporation. Thus the anomaly was presented of a stockholder of a corporation being able to work against the corporation's interests. The courts, recognizing the situation, have greatly modified and almost nullified this original right. No stockholder can now on legal grounds demand that he be furnished with information as to the customers of the corporation, the persons from whom supplies are bought and their prices, the corporation's contracts, and other points of similar nature. In most states he gets all the information that rightfully belongs to him if he

obtains simply a summary of the profit and loss account for the preceding year and of the balance sheet at the end of the corporation's fiscal year. Indeed, he cannot in all states secure even this meagre and apparently innocuous information.

The movement in favor of publicity of corporate accounts, however, is now so general and strong, and the force of public opinion behind it is so great, that almost all the important corporations voluntarily give to their stockholders and to the public fairly complete annual reports. Railroads particularly under the Interstate Commerce Act, as amended in 1906, are compelled to render to the Interstate Commerce Commission and through the Commission to the public and to their stockholders, a very complete and detailed summary of their operations each year. One striking exception among the large corporations to this general tendency toward increased publicity is the Standard Oil Company, whose management has never yet given out anything more than a bare statement of the amount of the capitalization and of the dividends declared. Publicity of accounts is not to be confused with the right of the individual stockholder to have access to the corporation's books, for even the greatest degree of publicity extends only to general financial results of the corporation's activities, not to the corporation's individual purchases, sales and contracts. The right to actual inspection of the books, with few unimportant exceptions, is entirely a theoretical, not a practically important, attribute of stockholders.

28. *Liabilities of stockholders.*—The next topic to consider is that of liabilities of stockholders, which may be grouped under the following four heads:

(1) Their liability to the corporation or to unsatisfied

creditors of the corporation for unpaid installments on part-paid stock.

(2) Their liability to unsatisfied creditors of the corporation in case dividends have been paid out of capital assets.

(3) In New York State, their liability to employees and servants for wages due by the corporation.

(4) In the state of Minnesota, their liability (except manufacturing corporations) to corporate creditors up to an amount equal to the face value of their stock-holdings. In national banks the same rule holds good.

(5) In California the unlimited liability of each stockholder for his proportion of unpaid obligations incurred while he remained a stockholder of record. This liability continues even though he sells his stock.

With further reference to the liability first stated in the preceding paragraph, it should be observed that corporations frequently do not need at the beginning of their existence all the capital assets that will later be necessary. They therefore ask their stockholders to pay only a certain percentage of their stock subscriptions at the beginning and either set certain dates for the remaining payments or leave the dates to be fixed later by the directors of the company. In the latter case it sometimes happens that the corporation becomes so prosperous that the unpaid installments are not called for and in the course of years stockholders may almost forget that they are still unpaid. Then if the corporation later gets into financial difficulties, the owners of stock at the time may suddenly find themselves confronted by a demand for the immediate payment of unpaid installments. It is a very unpleasant and not especially uncommon situation. Buyers of stock should therefore be very certain that their certificates are marked "full paid and non-assessable," or else make sure that they can meet whatever installments are unpaid, when called for, without great inconvenience to themselves.

The payment of dividends out of capital instead of out of earnings is a practice which we shall have occasion to refer to later in this volume. All that need be said about it here is that it might obviously be used as a means of diverting to stockholders assets pledged to creditors of the corporation and for that reason is not permissible.

29. *Rights of creditors.*—The creditors of a corporation are of two distinct kinds, secured and unsecured. The secured creditors are those who have had set aside for them under some form of agreement certain parts of the property of the corporation which are to be devoted, in case the corporation fails at the specified time to meet its debt, to paying the creditor in full. The exact procedure will be discussed at some length in connection with corporate notes and bonds. The unsecured creditors hold simply a claim against the general unattached assets of the corporation.

Whether the creditors be secured or unsecured, they have no part in the organization or management of the corporation so long as the debts to them are fully and promptly met. Only in case of insolvency or bankruptcy may they step in and exercise any rights which may have been conditionally granted to them. We will therefore defer a study of their place in the corporate organization until we come to the subjects of insolvency, bankruptcy and reorganization.

30. *"Dummy" directors.*—The statutes of nearly all the states require that the directors of a corporation

shall also be stockholders. In most states the ownership of a single share is sufficient to meet this requirement. As an example of the striking difference at times between what the law intends and what it accomplishes, this requirement deserves special mention. Obviously it is intended to prevent any one man from "packing" the board of directors; in practice it serves to facilitate the creation of and control over "dummy" directors.

A dummy director is one who serves the interest of some other person and who votes as he is told. Sometimes he is an actual stockholder or is given stock outright in order to qualify him for his position, and the man who controls him depends on influences outside the corporation to retain his control. When any doubt exists as to that point, however, the "dummy" director usually receives a certificate of stock duly transferred to him on the books of the company—which thus qualifies him to act as director—but is required to endorse the certificate back to the real owner. Thus the owner of the stock always has a string tied to the "dummy" director. If his orders are not followed to his satisfaction, all that he needs to do is to send in the certificate, have the stock transferred back to himself and thereby disqualify the "dummy." Thus a majority stockholder may elect a whole board of directors who are absolutely subservient to his orders and represent only his interests. He may not himself be a member of the board at all, and yet may dictate its every action.

31. *Powers and liabilities of directors.*—In theory, however, even if not in practice, a board of directors is supposed to represent all the stockholders equally. Partly for that reason the board, as has already been

indicated, is given complete control over the corporation's assets and officers. Very seldom, indeed, will the courts restrain the directors from taking any action short of selling or mortgaging the corporation's permanent assets, unless fraud or wrongdoing is conclusively shown. Their powers are usually more or less modified, however, by the corporation's by-laws, and, like other officers, they are not at liberty to transgress or omit any of the duties specifically set forth in the by-laws. As a general thing they have power among other things to fill vacancies in their own number until the next annual meeting of the stockholders for the election of directors, to appoint and remove officers of the corporation, and under limitations to modify or enact by-laws.

Any or all of these powers the board of directors may delegate, if they see fit, to a standing committee chosen from their number. Where the board of directors is so large as to be unwieldy and difficult to assemble at regular intervals, such delegation of powers is customary. The board of directors of the United States Steel Corporation, for example, which consists of twenty-four members, delegates a large part of its functions to a standing committee of eight members known as the finance committee. The finance committee holds frequent meetings and conferences with the chairman of the board of directors, and between meetings of the full board has complete authority to settle most questions. It also handles with full authority such financial questions as in most corporations would be referred to the board of directors. The committee with these functions in most corporations is called the executive committee.

The usual duties of corporation officers have already been treated in the preceding chapter. One officer not mentioned there, who is in several large corporations of much importance, is the chairman of the board of directors. In the United States Steel Corporation, the New York Central Railroad Company, the National City Bank of New York, and other companies of like magnitude, the chairman of the board of directors is a prominent paid officer to whom the president of the corporation reports. It would not be far from wrong to say that the chairman represents the board of directors and the standing committees of the board in the intervals between meetings. To him, in other words, are delegated *ad interim* the full powers of the board.

Personal liabilities of directors may arise in four ways:

(1) By reason of neglect or wrongdoing on their part that results in loss to the company.

(2) By issuing stock as full paid that is not actually full paid.

(3) By paying dividends out of capital.

(4) By doing other acts specifically forbidden by the statutes of the state in which the company is incorporated.

These acts, it should be observed, in the eyes of the law are wrong and fraudulent. So long as the directors keep within the law, no liability will attach to them in their capacity of directors.

32. *The efficiency of corporate organization.*—The reader may now see more clearly perhaps why "centralization of control" was named in the first chapter as one of the important advantages of corporations. He may carry away a more vivid idea of the whole arrangement if he compares the corporation to a double pyramid, as shown in this diagram:

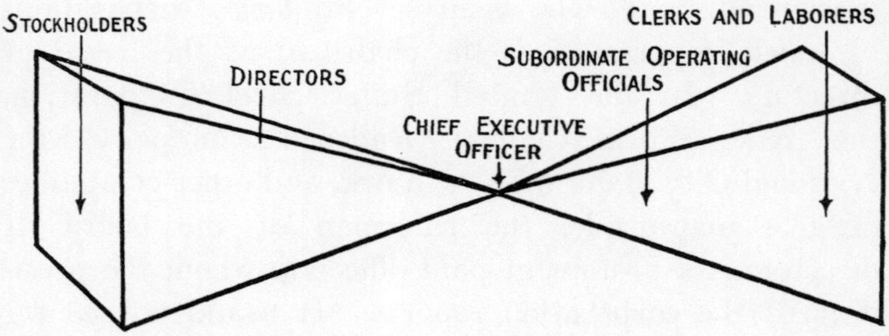

The base of one pyramid represents the body of stockholders or owners of the corporation who delegate their rights as owners to the directors, who in turn transfer all active authority to the president or other chief executive officer, who is at the apex of that pyramid. The other pyramid represents the subordinate officials and employees of the corporation. The chief executive officer is also the apex of this pyramid and transmits his orders through the various grades of subordinates to the clerks and laborers at the base of the pyramid. Thus responsibility and authority conferred by the stockholders and exercised over the employees are both centered in this chief executive officer. It is an organization almost ideally adapted, so far as efficiency and economy go, to the conditions of present-day industry.

CHAPTER IV

WHERE AND HOW TO INCORPORATE

33. *A corporation may be chartered in any state and do business in other states.*—The reader is probably well aware that a corporation need not necessarily take out a charter in the state in which it transacts its principal business. In fact, the great majority of the large industrial and railroad companies are incorporated in one state and carry on their operations in several states; in many cases none of their permanent assets worth mentioning are located in the state of incorporation.

This anomalous condition is made possible by the peculiar character of our American political system. Each state has the right to create corporations and by custom such corporations are recognized and allowed the usual rights and privileges in all other states. It should be noted at this point that such rights and privileges are granted as a matter of custom and of policy, or of "comity," to use the legal term, and not—as is sometimes stated even in legal text-books—under that clause of the Constitution of the United States which says that "the citizens of each state shall be entitled to all privileges and immunities of citizens in the several states." A corporation is not a citizen, but an artificial person created by law, which is an entirely different thing.

In an early case before the Supreme Court of the United States, The Bank of Augusta vs. Earle, the right of a corporation to make a contract outside the state of its incorporation was brought into question. The decision of the Court upheld this right as a legal presumption, but stated that the right might be withdrawn by any state legislature. The opinion written by Chief Justice Taney is so important and informing that some of the salient paragraphs are quoted below:

It is very true that a corporation can have no legal existence out of the boundaries of the sovereignty by which it is created. It exists only in contemplation of law, and by force of law; and where that law ceases to operate, and is no longer obligatory, the corporation can have no existence. It must dwell in the place of its creation and cannot migrate to another sovereignty. But although it must live and have its being in that state alone, yet it does not by any means follow that its existence there will not be recognized in other places; and its residence in one state creates no insuperable objection to its power of contracting in another. It is indeed a mere artificial being, invisible and intangible; yet it is a person, for certain purposes in contemplation of law, and has been recognized as such by the decisions of this court. . . . Now, natural persons, through the intervention of agents, are continually making contracts in countries in which they do not reside; and where they are not personally present when the contract is made; and nobody has ever doubted the validity of these agreements. And what greater objection can there be to the capacity of an artificial person, by its agents, to make a contract within the scope of its limited powers, in a sovereignty in which it does not reside; provided such contracts are permitted to be made by them by the laws of the place?

The corporation must no doubt show that the law of its creation gave it authority to make such contracts, through such agents. Yet, as in the case of a natural person, it is not necessary that it should actually exist in the sovereignty in which the contract is made. It is sufficient that its existence as an artificial person, in the state of its creation, is acknowledged and recognized by the law of the nation where the dealing takes place;

and that it is permitted by the laws of that place to exercise there the powers with which it is endowed.

It is nothing more than the admission of the existence of an artificial person created by the law of another state, and clothed with the power of making certain contracts. It is but the usual comity of recognizing the law of another state.

We think it is well settled, that by the law of comity among nations, a corporation created by one sovereignty is permitted to make contracts in another, and to sue in its courts; and that the same law of comity prevails among the several sovereignties of this Union. The public and well-known and long-continued usages of trade; the general acquiescence of the states; the particular legislation of some of them, as well as the legislation of Congress; all concur in proving the truth of this proposition.

34. *The regulation of "foreign" corporations.*—In the state in which its charter is granted a corporation is called "domestic"; in other states it is a "foreign" corporation. This word "foreign" must not be taken to refer to corporations of other countries than the United States; such corporations are known as "alien."

Every state in the Union regulates to a greater or less degree the business carried on within its borders by foreign corporations. In some states it is necessary to procure a license, which may be obtained by depositing with some official a certified copy of the corporation's charter and naming some agent on whom legal papers may be served. In other states it is merely required that the foreign corporation shall maintain an office and have an agent within the state. Some states restrict the power of foreign corporations to hold real estate. These regulations are not intended to apply to corporations which merely solicit orders or execute contracts incidental to their main business, but to those which are permanently established.

35. *Choosing the state of incorporation.*—Unless there is some reason to the contrary, it is generally much better for a corporation to get its charter in the state in which its principal business is located. This remark applies particularly to small companies operating wholly within one state. There are several reasons therefor. One is the fact that a foreign corporation must usually pay incorporation and annual franchise taxes in the state of incorporation and in addition a license fee or some other kind of a tax in the state in which it does business. Another reason is that the courts of each state are inclined to treat domestic corporations with greater consideration than foreign corporations. A third reason is that there is a popular prejudice, more or less well-founded, against those companies which go to other states for their charter. Creditors and prospective buyers of the corporation's securities are apt to ask embarrassing questions as to why the corporation cannot or does not comply with the legal requirements of its own state. A fourth reason is the inconvenience caused by the necessity of filing reports and generally of maintaining a separate office in the state of incorporation. If the managers of a small local concern, therefore, are considering where to incorporate, the answer will almost always be, "Get your charter in the state where you expect to do most of your business."

The answer to a similar question is not so easy, however, where the prospective corporation will be large, or where its business will be widely scattered through many states, or where its managers have in view some purpose or purposes not favored by the laws of the state in which its principal office is to be located. Neither is the answer so easy even for small local concerns in those ultra-conservative states in which the corporation laws are unduly burdensome or corporation taxes unduly expensive. Under all these circumstances, persons who are about to form a new corporation, or who are thinking of giving up their charter in one state, will naturally look about and compare the advantages obtainable under the laws of the various states. There are great variations among the states in regard to taxes, liberality of corporation laws and treatment of foreign corporations, and the problem of weighing all these factors and picking out the most economical and advantageous corporate home is often very difficult. The advice of a thoroughly competent corporation lawyer in all such cases is absolutely essential. Nevertheless, for his own protection, both in forming and in dealing with corporations, every business man should have a pretty accurate idea of the requirements and privileges in all the important states.

36. *Comparative charges in several states.*—The first and most obvious factor to consider in selecting the state of incorporation is the cost. This cost consists of organization fees, annual taxes and counsel fees. The following tables copied from a convenient manual by Thomas Conyngton, of the New York Bar, entitled "Corporate Organization," will give the reader an idea of how these expenses run in the five states which are most commonly used for incorporation by companies that expect to do business in other states:

COMPARATIVE TABLE OF ORGANIZATION EXPENSES.

(Including all Filing and Incidental Fees.)

Capital Stock of Company.	*New Jersey.*	*New York.*	*Delaware.*	*Maine.*	*South Dakota.*
$1,000	$35 00	$16.00	$25.00	$27.00	$13.00
5,000	35.00	17.50	25.00	27.00	13.00
10,000	35.00	20.00	25.00	27.00	13.00

Capital Stock of Company.	*New Jersey.*	*New York.*	*Delaware.*	*Maine.*	*South Dakota.*
25,000	35.00	27.50	25.00	67.00	13.00
50,000	35.00	40.00	25.00	67.00	18.00
100,000	35.00	65.00	25.00	67.00	18.00
500,000	110.00	265.00	65.00	67.00	23.00
1,000,000	210.00	515.00	115.00	117.00	28.00
5,000,000	1,010.00	2,515.00	365.00	517.00	43.00
10,000,000	2,010.00	5,015.00	615.00	1,017.00	43.00

COMPARATIVE TABLE OF ANNUAL FRANCHISE TAXES.

$1,000	$1.00	$1.50	$5.00	$5.00	None
5,000	5.00	7.50	5.00	5.00	"
10,000	10.00	15.00	5.00	5.00	"
25,000	25.00	37.50	5.00	5.00	"
50,000	50.00	75.00	10.00	5.00	"
100,000	100.00	150.00	10.00	10.00	"
500,000	500.00	750.00	25.00	50.00	"
1,000,000	1,000.00	1,500.00	50.00	75.00	"
5,000,000	4,000.00	7,500.00	150.00	275.00	"
10,000,000	4,250.00	15,000.00	275.00	525.00	"

South Dakota and Delaware are fair examples of what are sometimes called the "bargain counter" states, so far as incorporation expenses are concerned. Arizona also belongs in this class, and West Virginia and the District of Columbia might until recently have been included. As an example of the importance of this feature when large companies are formed, it has been estimated that if the United States Steel Corporation had taken out its charter in Pennsylvania, where most of its business is transacted, the organization expenses would have been about $3,500,000, whereas in New Jersey, where the charter was actually obtained, the corresponding expenses were only about $220,000. A great many companies which are organized to exploit mines or new inventions or other highly speculative enterprises may without impropriety issue very large amounts of stock, although the actual market value of their assets at the time of incorporation may be very small; in such cases it is customary and obviously economical to secure a "bargain counter" charter.

In those states where taxes and initial fees are small the necessary expense for legal assistance is apt to be at a minimum, for two reasons: first, because the state legislatures obviously are making a bid for the cheap incorporation business and will naturally make their forms and the necessary red tape of incorporation as simple as possible; second, because in such states incorporation agencies which carry on their business on a wholesale scale, are in existence, and high-priced legal talent is hardly necessary. In other states competent attorneys should always be secured, and their fees may be expected to range from $50 up. In this connection it may be well to remark also that the necessary corporate records, which are the secretary's minute book, the stock certificate book and the stockholders' register, may be obtained for from $10 to $500 per set. One of the cheaper sets is all that is necessary for most small companies. The reader now has sufficient data before him to form a rough estimate of the expense necessarily involved in the process of incorporation.

This factor of initial cost, however, in the case of companies which expect permanently to carry on an established business is, after all, a minor consideration. Among the other important points to bear in mind in selecting a corporate domicile, four stand out most prominently—the liberality of the laws, the permanence of the laws, the liabilities attaching to stockholders and the reputation of the state.

37. *Liberality of corporation laws in several states.*— The chief respect in which state laws differ, so far as liberality is concerned, is in granting or denying the right to buy and sell the securities of other corporations.

In 1889 New Jersey, first of all the states, enacted that corporations formed under its laws might hold the stock of other corporations. This privilege has proved of the greatest importance in the financial and industrial development of this country, as will be explained in the following chapter. The New Jersey act in this respect has been followed by Delaware, Maine, and New York. The great industrial trusts, for this reason primarily, have almost uniformly obtained New Jersey charters. An important case in the Court of Errors and Appeals of that state limiting and defining the right to hold shares in other companies has been mentioned in Chapter II.

Another feature in which the various states differ widely with regard to liberality is the issuance of stock for property. Most corporations as now organized turn over at least part of their stock in exchange for property, not cash. Some of the states make the estimate placed by the directors upon the value of the property so secured conclusive unless fraud is clearly shown. Other states hedge this general principle about with irritating and usually unnecessary restrictions. Liberality of the state laws as to other less important points will be considered by careful incorporators, but are too technical to be discussed here.

38. *Permanence of the laws.*—In those states in which the general corporation statutes have existed for some years practically unchanged, it is reasonable to expect that they are in fairly permanent form. Moreover, in such states the courts have given a large number of decisions on vital points. Both the statutory law and the interpretation of that law, therefore, may be considered well settled. This is a matter of prime importance to large corporations, which may expect, from the

very extent of their business, to be involved in more or less litigation. They want to know where they stand at all times and do not care to be confronted with sudden legislative enactments or with unexpected court decisions. In this respect New Jersey is particularly favored and this furnishes an additional reason why the large corporations tend so strongly to incorporate in that state.

The liabilities imposed upon stockholders have already been treated in the preceding chapter. The states of California, New York and Minnesota, as there noted, impose certain liabilities additional to the usual liability on capital stock. These liabilities are not apt to prove a serious matter. Yet corporations generally look with some alarm at any provisions of this nature.

39. *Reputations of various states.*—The reputation of the state of incorporation may have considerable effect on the sale of corporate securities. It is so well-known, for instance, that the laws of South Dakota and Arizona are lax that investors look with distrust on any corporation which operates under one of their charters. This statement, although to a much less degree, applies to Delaware and to Maine. New Jersey is so popular a state for incorporation that its provisions are well-known and its reputation is reasonably good. West Virginia and the District of Columbia do not rank nearly so well, on account of their record, although the District of Columbia law in 1905, on the recommendation of President Roosevelt, was altered and improved and the West Virginia law also has been changed. Connecticut, Massachusetts, Pennsylvania and Illinois have reasonably—Massachusetts perhaps unreasonably—strict requirements, and all as states of incorporation are in good repute. Among all the

states, New York, under its "Business Corporations Law," as amended in recent years, perhaps best combines the advantages of liberality and of high repute. Its laws, however, have not been so thoroughly tested and settled by the courts as the corresponding laws of New Jersey.

40. *Comparative summary of the advantages and disadvantages of the important states.*—For the benefit of readers who may desire to form a corporation or who may have occasion to consider the advisability of buying stock of a company incorporated in some other state than the one in which it does business we give below a brief summary of the advantages and disadvantages of several states:

ARIZONA.

Advantages:

1. Stock may be issued for money, property, or services. The fact that it can be issued for services may be an important advantage.

2. Directors' meetings may be held outside of the state.

3. The organization fee is very small. Moreover, there is no annual franchise tax.

Disadvantages:

1. Stockholders' meetings must be held within the state, unless at first meeting a by-law provision permitting subsequent meetings outside the state is adopted.

2. The corporation laws are unadjudicated.

CONNECTICUT.

Many promoters do not care to incorporate in Connecticut as they imagine that the advantages are not great. As a matter of fact, the high organization fee is the chief disadvantage.

Advantages:

1. Stock may be paid for in either cash or property. The judgment of the directors is final with regard to the value of

the property for which stock is issued, except in case of fraud.

2. Incorporators may be non-resident.

3. There is no annual franchise tax.

4. Corporations may hold stock in other corporations.

Disadvantages:

1. Stockholders' meetings must be held within the state. There is no provision requiring the meetings of the directors to be held within the state, but this may be inferred.

2. There is an inheritance tax on the stock.

3. The organization fees are comparatively high, from $25 to $2,510.

DELAWARE.

Advantages:

1. Stockholders' and directors' meetings may be held outside of the state, if the by-laws so provide.

2. Stock may be issued for cash, property or services.

3. Incorporators may be non-resident.

4. Corporations may hold stock in other corporations.

5. Provision may be made whereby bondholders will be permitted to vote. This provision makes a good market for bonds because bondholders will be assured that they will have a voice in the management of the corporation.

6. Organization fees are not very large, ranging from $20 to $765, including filing fees.

Disadvantages:

1. One of the directors must live in Delaware.

2. There is an inheritance tax on stock, applying both to residents and to non-residents.

3. There is an annual franchise tax.

DISTRICT OF COLUMBIA.

Advantages:

1. Very small cost of incorporation, probably not exceeding $10.

2. No franchise or inheritance tax.

Disadvantages:

1. A majority of the trustees, (the term trustee corresponds to the term director) must live in the District.

2. Stock cannot be issued for services, only for property or cash.

3. 10 per cent of capital stock must be paid in before beginning business. New York requires 50 per cent paid in before the end of the first year, but business can be carried on in the meantime. Here, no business can be done in the name of the corporation till 10 per cent is fully paid in.

4. An annual report of the corporation must be filed and published. This report must include amount of capital stock authorized, amount paid in and amount of existing debts.

5. The corporation cannot own stock in other corporations.

6. Corporation laws are unadjudicated.

MAINE.

Advantages:

1. Stock may be issued for property, cash or services. The judgment of the directors is conclusive as to value of the property—always provided there is no evidence of fraud.

2. Incorporators and directors may be non-resident.

3. Directors' meetings may be held outside of the state.

4. The corporation may acquire stock in other corporations.

5. Low organization fees, ranging from $10 to $517 for a $5,000,000 corporation.

Disadvantages:

1. Stockholders' meetings must be held within the state.

2. There is both an inheritance and an annual franchise tax; the latter, however, is very small.

MASSACHUSETTS.

Advantages:

1. Incorporators and directors may be non-resident.

2. Directors' meetings may be held outside of the state.

3. Stock may be issued for cash, property or services.

Disadvantages:

1. Stockholders' meetings must be held within the state.

2. The corporation cannot hold stock in other corporations.

3. A detailed annual report must be rendered to the state authorities.

4. There is an inheritance tax.

5. The organization fee varies from $10 for a $10,000 corporation to $1,200 for a $5,000,000 corporation; there is no filing fee.

NEVADA.

Advantages:

1. Incorporators and directors may be non-resident.

2. Stockholders' and directors' meetings may be held outside of the state.

3. Stock may be issued for cash, property or services. The judgment of the directors is conclusive as to value of property, providing there is no evidence of fraud.

4. Action of the majority of the stockholders or directors may be valid without regular meeting; that is, there may be an informal meeting held, without any notice whatsoever being given.

5. Bondholders may be given the right to vote.

6. Cumulative voting is allowed.

7. No annual franchise tax.

8. The organization fee is comparatively low, ranging from $15 to $700; there are no filing fees whatever.

Disadvantages:

1. In some cases an annual report must be prepared for the state authorities.

2. The state's reputation as a corporate home is not of the best.

NEW JERSEY.

Advantages:

1. Corporations may hold stock in other corporations. New Jersey was the first state to authorize the formation of holding companies.

2. Incorporators may be non-resident.

3. Stock may be issued for property or cash. Judgment of the directors is conclusive as to value of property. No provision is made for this judgment being set aside upon evidence of fraud.

4. Directors' meetings may be held outside of the state, if by-laws so provide.

5. Cumulative voting is permitted.

6. A voting trust may be created.

7. Laws are all well adjudicated.

Disadvantages:

1. Stockholders' meetings must be held within the state.

2. One of the directors must live in the state.

3. There is an annual franchise tax; also an inheritance tax, but this does not apply to non-residents. Fees are from $25 to $1,000; filing fee $10.

NEW YORK.

Advantages:

1. Stock may be issued for cash, property, or *labor*. Labor must be distinguished from "services" though there is no decision explaining the exact difference. The judgment of the directors is conclusive as to value of property, provided there is no evidence of fraud.

2. Directors' meetings may be held outside of the state.

3. Corporations may hold and control the stock of other corporations.

4. Cumulative voting is permitted.

5. A voting trust may be created, limited, however, to five years.

Disadvantages:

1. Stockholders' meetings must be held within the state.

2. One incorporator and one director must reside within the state.

3. One-half of the capital stock must be paid in within a year from incorporation.

4. Detailed books and accounts of the business are required.

41. *Agreements prior to incorporation.*—Sometimes a corporation is formed practically by and for an individual acting alone, who expects to take all the stock except what is necessary to qualify dummy directors and either hold it permanently or dispose of it whenever an opportunity arises later. Frequently, also, it happens that a corporation is organized to take over the business of a pre-existing partnership and the partners have come to an informal understanding as to how much stock shall be issued to each one. Under such circumstances, of course, no formal agreements previous to incorporation are necessary.

In many instances, however, corporations are formed by the harmonious action of a number of men who mutually agree as to the purposes, capitalization and other essential features of the new corporation and who each subscribe for a certain amount of stock. In such cases it is customary to draw up what is known as a "subscription contract" and to leave space at the bottom of this contract for each subscriber to write his name and fill in the number of shares that he agrees to take. The subscription contract should state among other things the par value of each share of stock, the total number of shares to be issued and the total number to be subscribed, in order to make the contract binding. Usually the subscription list is accompanied by a prospectus (described in Chapter XVI) which more fully states what the corporation is expected to accomplish. It should be noted that the subscription contract may be made immediately binding by having the amount of the subscription payable to certain specified trustees; or if not immediately binding, it will become binding as soon as the proposed corporation is properly organized and prepared to handle funds.

The remaining step in incorporation is very simple and has already been touched upon in Chapter II. It consists of drawing up a charter in proper legal form, filing it with the secretary of state or such other official as is designated by the laws of the state in which the charter is to be obtained, and receiving notice of his acceptance thereof.

42. *The wide range of choice in incorporation.*—If the reader has acquired by the reading of this chapter a clear conception of the freedom and liberality of corporation laws and of the ease with which almost any legitimate business may be put into the form of the corporation, the main purpose of the chapter will have been fulfilled. The advantages of the corporate form for almost all kinds of business were pointed out in the first chapter. One of the chief advantages named was flexibility, by which was meant the ease with which the corporate form could be adapted to small or to large enterprises. Now we are in a position to expand still further the meaning of that word "flexibility" in connection with corporations and to say that it means also the ease with which the corporate form may be adjusted to any sort of a business need. If the incorporators cannot find in one state the authority or the cheapness that they desire, they may pick out some other state in which those qualities are prominent in the general corporation law. If the incorporators desire permanence and legal stability above all things, they may go to still another state. The range of choice is wide. It takes only a little effort and ingenuity for a capable lawyer to fit out a business enterprise with the exact corporate powers and organization that will prove most advantageous.

CHAPTER V

CORPORATE STOCK

43. *Stock certificates not fully negotiable.*—As has already been said, corporate stock is not a tangible thing; it is simply a right to share under certain limitations in the management, the assets and the earnings of the issuing corporation. Stock is represented by certificates, which are in the possession of the owners. These certificates, however, it must not be forgotten, are merely evidence, not proof, of the ownership of stock. Actual ownership is proved by reference to the books of the company in which the names of the stockholders and the number of shares held by each one are entered. Certificates of stock are not, therefore, strictly speaking, negotiable instruments, but quasi-negotiable—a term which the reader will find defined in the volume on COMMERCIAL LAW.

The question as to whether stock certificates ought to be made negotiable or not has been much agitated, especially among lawyers. A committee of the Commission on Uniform State Laws, which is a body of lawyers appointed by the governors of forty-one states, issued a report in March, 1909, strongly advocating amendments to existing laws which would make transfer of ownership of corporate stock complete on delivery of endorsed certificates of stock without waiting for the formal transfer on the books of the corporation; in other words, the proposed amendments would make certificates of stock true negotiable instruments. The important sections of the text of the proposed amendments are as follows:

SECTION 1. Title to a certificate and to the shares represented thereby may be transferred.

(a) By the delivery of the certificate, if indorsed either in blank or to a specified person, signed by the person appearing by the certificate to be the owner of the shares represented thereby.

(b) By delivery of the certificate with a written assignment thereon, or a power of attorney to sell, assign, or transfer the certificate of the shares represented thereby signed by the person appearing by the certificate to be the owner of the shares represented thereby. Such assignment or power of attorney may be either in blank or to a specified person.

The provisions of this section shall be applicable although the charter or articles of incorporation or code of regulations or by-laws of the corporation issuing the certificate and the certificate itself provide that the shares represented thereby shall be transferable only on the books of the corporation or shall be registered by a registrar or transferred by a transfer agent.

SECTION 17. Nothing in this act shall be construed as forbidding a corporation to treat as owner in every way the person who may be registered on its books as the owner of shares.

In an editorial in *The Journal of Accountancy,* the writer said as to this proposed amendment:

Accountants, as well as lawyers and business men, have a direct interest in this proposition. If it is adopted by the states in which numerous corporate charters are granted, the effects will be felt in many different forms. Indeed, it is doubtful, judging from their explanatory notes, whether the commissioners realize what an extensive reform they are proposing. At first glance, to be sure, it does not appear that any considerable revision of present practice is intended; yet the act plainly points toward passing the rights and privileges of stockholders along with transfers of stock certificates.

The change would no doubt facilitate somewhat the purchase

and sale of stock by removing the technical requirement that transfers must be made on the books of the corporation. It would enable the stock exchange brokers to carry on their business more easily and more smoothly. It would make stock certificates more acceptable to banks as collateral for loans. These are the strongest arguments in favor of the act.

On the other side of the question, it should be remarked that making certificates of stock fully negotiable subjects them to increased danger of forgery, theft and loss. Many people, no doubt, would prefer the comparative safety of the present system, just as many investors, when a choice is offered, take registered rather than coupon bonds. This is a point of considerable importance. A far stronger argument against the proposed measure, however, is that it would destroy the value of a corporation's record of its stockholders and would thereby foster fraud. Accountants are only too familiar with cases in which corporations are organized simply for the purpose of transferring property from one hand to another in such a manner as to conceal profits or to swindle creditors. Under the present arrangement it is generally possible, if fraud is suspected, to get access to the stockholders' ledger and to learn who are the owners of the corporation. If a connection between the former owners of the transferred property and the stockholders of the corporation can be proven, a case of fraud may be made out. Under the proposed arrangement it would be impossible to discover the true owners of such a corporation. The stockholders' ledger, indeed, might be kept, but it would be of small value. The certificates of stock, and consequently the ownership of the corporation, might change hands a half dozen times without appearing on the corporation's books. Numerous similar cases will occur to any accountant.

We do not wish to go on record as absolutely opposed to this act. We have no doubt that it would be a convenience to corporation officials, bankers and business men generally if stock certificates were made fully negotiable. We would emphasize the fact, however, that this provision would also prove a great convenience where fraud or manipulation is intended. It would make secrecy as to corporate ownership even easier than it is now and would tend to lessen the responsibility that ought to attach to the stockholders of corporations. We think these evils important enough to outweigh the advantages that have been named. For that reason we suggest that the law with regard to transfers of stock ought to be left unchanged until further provision has been made for publicity of corporate accounts and for detection and punishment of the frauds which the corporate form already too much favors.[1]

44. *Par vs. market value of stock.*—Each share of stock in practically every case has a nominal money value. The most common nominal value of each share is $100; other nominal values commonly used are $50, $25, $10 and $1. This nominal money value of each share is sometimes called the "par value." To the uninitiated the par value of stock often seems quite an important matter. They are apt to regard it as being of much the same character as the face value, say, of a promissory note. A little reflection, however, will readily convince anyone that there is no close analogy between the par value of a share of stock and the face value of a note, and that the par value of a share throws very little light on the actual value of that share.

To make this proposition clear, let us suppose that three oil wells are discovered by three different individuals, the three wells being practically identical in location, quality of oil produced, amount of flow, permanence, cost of operation, access to markets, and other essential attributes. Each of the owners, we will say, interests some friends and outsiders and organizes a corporation to work his well. One owner is extremely conservative and therefore has his corporation issue only 1000 shares of a par value of $1 per share; the second

[1] *The Journal of Accountancy,* March, 1909.

owner, being somewhat more sanguine, thinks his well is worth more and, therefore, has his corporation issue 1000 shares, each of a par value of $10; the third owner is blessed with a vivid imagination which leads him to have his corporation issue 1000 shares, each of a par value of $100. Now what will be the actual value of a single share in each of these companies? Obviously each share entitles the owner to one one-thousandth of the assets and earnings of the well. As the wells, according to our supposition, are equally profitable, there will be no difference whatever between the three shares so far as their actual values are concerned.

Any number of further examples, drawn from experience, might be given to illustrate this truth. In fact, a simple inspection of the prices for stock bought and sold on the various stock exchanges of the country is sufficiently convincing. Most of the shares of stock there traded in have par values of $100; their market values will be found to range between next to nothing and $600 or $700—sometimes even more for bank stock.

The fact, then, that a certain share of stock has a nominal value is of small importance. Its practically valuable attribute is its right to a certain share in the corporation's assets and earnings. How much is that share to be? That question may be answered simply by knowing how many shares of stock are outstanding. If a corporation's assets are worth $1,000,000 and there are 1000 shares in the hands of stockholders, we know at once that the true value of each share is $1000 without reference to its par value.

This leads us to a question which was brought up several years ago by a prominent corporation lawyer and has been much discussed. Why not eliminate these useless par values and make each share in form as it is

Countersigned this ...... day of .... 19....
by .... Transfer Agent.

THE CORPORATION FINANCE COMPANY

Capital Stock $1,000,000

This Certifies that .... is the owner of .... Shares of the full paid Capital Stock of the Corporation Finance Company, transferable only on the books of the Company, in person or by Attorney, on surrender of this Certificate.

New York City, ... 19....

.... *Secretary.* .... *President.*

Shares $100 each.

[On stub.]

No.............

.... Shares

.... 19....

Issued to

....

....

Received above described Certificate,

.... 19....

....

[On back.]

For Value Received, ... hereby sell, assign and transfer unto .... Shares of the Capital Stock represented by the within Certificate, and do hereby irrevocably constitute and appoint .... Attorney to transfer the said Stock on the Books of the within named Company, with full power of substitution in the premises.

Dated .... 19....

....

In presence of ....

Registered this ...... day of .... 19....
City Trust Company of New York,
by .... Secretary.

in practice simply a right to a certain percentage of the assets and earnings of the issuing corporation? The form of a certificate of stock under the present system is given on page 70. The question before us is whether it would not be better to make the second line of the face of the certificate read instead of "Capital Stock $1,000,-000," "Number of shares 10,000," and to eliminate the last line, "Shares $100 each," altogether. Logically there could be no objection to the proposal; each share would be just as valuable—no more and no less—after the change as before. The chief advantage gained would be that misconceptions based on the idea that par value and actual value in some way correspond would no longer be possible.

Although this reform would be desirable, and is now legally permissible in New York and in some other states, it is not very seriously advocated and probably will never be adopted simply because the custom of assigning a nominal money value to each share has become well established and would be very difficult to eradicate. The same object will be attained in time, as people become more familiar with corporation practice, by the general recognition of the obvious fact that par value and actual value need not correspond; that the earning power of each share is the real test of value.

45. *Nature of preferred stock.*—In most corporations all the stock is of one class and each share has an equal right to its proportion of the assets and earnings. Such stock is called "common" because no share has any privileges which do not attach to all the other shares. In general, common stock may be defined as stock which does not possess any special or peculiar rights.

Other corporations, however, set aside certain amounts of stock in a separate class and grant to this class specific privileges. Such stock is called preferred. The usual preference consists in giving a fixed dividend to the stock preferred before any payment whatever is made to the common stock. This dividend may be "cumulative"; that is, if profits are not enough to pay it in full in one or more years, the unpaid portion remains as a claim against earnings that must be settled before any payment is made to the common stock. Or it may be "non-cumulative"; that is, if profits in any year, including usually the accumulated profits of preceding years, are insufficient to cover the preferred stock dividend, the unpaid portion is wholly lost to the preferred stockholders, no matter how large the earnings in succeeding years may be. Let it be kept clearly in mind, however, that preference as to dividends is merely the usual, not the universal, privilege given to preferred stock. When the single statement that stock is "preferred" is made, it is necessary to consult the charter and by-laws of the corporation in order to be sure as to the exact nature of the preference.

The stock may be preferred as to assets, as well as dividends, or as to both. Furthermore, cumulative preferred stock may get a fixed dividend, and no more, which is the customary arrangement; it may get a fixed dividend and then, after the common stock has secured a fixed dividend, all the rest of the earnings may be divided equally between the two stocks, which is the arrangement presumed by law unless an expressed stipulation to the contrary is contained in either the charter or by-laws; or it may get a fixed dividend and the common stock a fixed dividend and all the rest of the earnings may then go to the preferred stock, which is a very unusual arrangement.

Preferred stock had its origin in railroad reorganizations. In reorganization after bankruptcy it is necessary to cut down the claims of the various bond issues outstanding in order to put the reorganized corporation in a reasonably safe condition. The interest on the first mortgage bonds is usually scaled; some of the junior issues are perhaps turned into income bonds; and in the seventies some bright mind conceived the idea of changing the inferior bond issues into preferred stock. This process will be explained much more fully in our discussion of bankruptcy and reorganization.

46. *Uses of preferred stock.*—Although preferred stock was originally the offspring of receiverships, it proved to be such a useful instrument for some purposes that it has been retained and is now much used, especially by industrial companies. The railroad companies, for reasons that will be later discussed, are gradually giving it up.

Apart from its usefulness already alluded to in cases of reorganization, preferred stock serves four other purposes. First, it may be a convenient means of separating a company's stock into different voting classes. Sometimes the preferred stock has no vote at all; sometimes it elects a limited number of directors. In either case the owners of the majority of the common stock may elect a majority of the board of directors. Therefore, a much smaller interest will control the business than would be necessary if all the stock issued voted alike.

Second, preferred stock is often very useful in forming industrial consolidations. As we shall see in the study of these consolidations, they are usually capitalized for a great deal more than the combined capitalization of their subsidiary companies. Ordinarily the extra capitalization, which represents prospects, takes the form of common stock, and the present value of the plants and businesses absorbed is represented by bonds and preferred stock. The subsidiary company stockholders are much more inclined to exchange their common stock for preferred stock in the consolidation than they would be to exchange for common stock. If the subsidiary businesses have been successful and profitable it is reasonable to expect that dividends on the preferred stock can be paid, whereas nobody can foresee whether common dividends will be paid or not.

The third purpose of preferred stock is to facilitate the incorporation of a business which has been conducted as a partnership. In a partnership each partner has as much say with regard to affairs as any other partner, irrespective of the extent of his interest. It is true that in practice the senior partner usually controls, but in law they are all on the same footing. They may desire to preserve the same arrangement in the corporation, in which case they may create a non-voting common stock and assign that stock to each partner in proportion to his interest in the partnership and in addition may make a voting preferred stock, of which each partner receives an equal amount. In this case it is possible that the so-called preferred stock may have preference in nothing except voting power.

Fourth, preferred stock obviously may attract conservative investors who would not care to buy the more speculative common stock of a corporation. Preferred stock, in point of security, ranks between the lower grades of bonds, which are described in succeeding chapters, and common stock. The preferred stock of industrial corporations, on account of their fluctuating earnings, usually sells at much better prices than the common stock of the same corporations, even though the common stock may receive on the average as large or larger dividends.

Sometimes a certain amount of stock will be set aside at the organization of a corporation and given voting power, which right is denied to all the other stock. In such a case the corporation has in existence two classes of stock, "voting" and "non-voting." This is not at all a common arrangement and is rarely, if ever, adopted except when a partnership business is put into the corporate form. It amounts to the same thing as creating preferred stock with the preference confined to the privilege of voting.

47. *Cumulative voting.*—Originally the universal custom as to the voting power of corporate stock was to give one vote to each share. The custom is still general, at least so far as common stock is concerned, but is no longer universal. Certain important modifications of the custom, which have become more and more popular, should be noted.

The chief objection to the original custom is that it puts the control of the corporation absolutely in the hands of the owners of the majority of the stock. Under this custom they elect, not merely the majority, but all of the members of the board of directors. Hence the minority stockholders may find themselves unrepresented and absolutely powerless. This is unfortunately the condition of the minority in almost all American corporations.

In order to provide to some extent against this acknowledged evil and the abuses which are likely to to follow, it is very common in England to restrict the number of votes allowed to any one stockholder. Thus a man with ten shares or less may be allowed one vote for each share; for each additional share up to twenty he may get only one-half of a vote; for each additional share up to forty he may get only one-quarter of a vote, and so on. As each company prescribes in its by-laws its own rules as to voting, there are naturally a great many variations of this arrangement. The object evidently is to give the great body of small stockholders a voice in the management of the company and to make it impossible for any individual or small clique to gain absolute control without owning all or nearly all the capital stock. At first glance this arrangement seems admirable. It would be so easy, however, for a large stockholder to have his stock transferred in small lots to various employees and members of his family, and thus retain full voting power for that stock, that it is certain that the principal could never be made to work effectively under American conditions. The only reason that it is moderately successful in England is that stock is on the whole more widely scattered and held in smaller lots than in this country.

A far more effective method of attaining the same end is "cumulative voting." Under this method each share has as many votes in electing directors as the number of directors to be chosen. These votes may be scattered among the nominees or concentrated on one or two of them as the stockholder sees fit. The effect is to make it impossible for a majority to elect all the board; the minority at least secures representation.

To illustrate the working of this method, take a corporation in which there are 1000 voting shares and five members of the board of directors to be elected; each share, then, is entitled to five votes. We will suppose that there is an organized majority of 550 shares and an organized minority of 450 shares. Under the usual arrangement a majority vote would be cast for five nominees, all of whom would represent the majority stockholders. Under the cumulative voting system, however, each share having five votes, the majority would cast altogether 2,750 votes and the minority 2,250. The majority could safely give 916 2-3 votes to each of three nominees and thus elect a majority of the board, leaving the other two directors to be elected by the 2,250 votes of the minority. But if the majority should attempt to elect four directors they could give only 687½ votes to each of the four, whereas the minority, if well organized, could concentrate their votes on three directors and give each one 750 votes, thereby electing a majority of the board. To make the system and its possibilities perfectly clear, it would be well for each reader to construct mentally a number of similar hypothetical cases and to observe how readily a minority under this system may secure control of the board of directors, if the majority stockholders are too greedy.

Cumulative voting is an ingenious and generally a highly desirable method of conducting corporate elections. As was stated once before, the constitution of Pennsylvania contains a clause requiring that all corporations organized under the laws of that state shall conduct their elections by the cumulative voting method. Opinions may differ as to the propriety of including such a provision in a state constitution. There can hardly be a doubt, however, as to the wisdom of putting it into the charters of most corporations.

48. *Voting trusts.*—Another method of protecting the interests of minority stockholders and of the creditors of a corporation is the formation of a voting trust. This is an agreement under which a majority of the voting stock of a corporation is placed in the hands of trustees who are authorized to vote it under whatever limitations may be prescribed. The trustees usually issue in return

for the stock so deposited "voting trust certificates," which certify that the stock is held in trust by the trustees and which may be sold and transferred in the same manner as certificates of stock. As the trustees are usually men of high standing who are under instructions to vote the stock for certain officials or in behalf of certain measures, the minority stockholders may safely feel that so long as the agreement exists no radical change in the policy of the corporation can take place, and the rights of all stockholders alike will be respected.

A voting trust agreement which seriously restricts the freedom of the majority stockholders of a corporation is, of course, not likely to be acceptable to those stockholders. The agreement, therefore, as might be expected, is not often made except under strong pressure. It is most frequently used either when a corporation is first formed and can secure additional capital on no other terms; or when a corporation is in financial difficulties and its creditors are in a position to demand that the management be intrusted to certain men and that a well-defined policy be pursued.

CHAPTER VI

TYPES OF BUSINESS CORPORATIONS

49. *Further classification of corporations.*—So far, our only classification of corporations has been into the two groups, stock and non-stock. The non-stock corporation, as has been said, is adapted only for governmental, social, eleemosynary, educational or religious institutions, and not to business concerns, the prime reason being that the absence of stock leaves no machinery for obtaining capital, except borrowing, or for distributing profits. We have, therefore, dismissed the non-stock corporations as being altogether outside the scope of this volume.

Stock corporations may be further classified as quasi-public and private. Quasi-public corporations are those which perform a service for the whole community for the sake of profits to the owners of the corporation. The most conspicuous examples are steam and electric railroads, water companies, gas and electric light companies and telephone and telegraph companies. Quasi-public corporations are granted special franchises and powers, such, for instance, as the right of eminent domain, and, on the other hand, are peculiarly subject to legislative control. Private corporations are those which carry on any business, such as manufacturing, trading, and so on, without having any special franchise, entirely for the sake of profits to their owners. The great majority of corporations belong in this second classification.

We may further classify this last group on the basis

of number of owners into "close" and "open" corporations. Close corporations are those in which the shares of stock are held by a very small number of people who do not expect to transfer them. Such corporations are not much in the public eye, since their affairs are of interest to only a few individuals. Frequently a "family business," which has been organized as a kind of loose partnership for many years, is turned into a corporation and none but members of the family are stockholders in the corporation. Sometimes estates are put by executors into the corporate form for ease in transferring interests and in making the complicated adjustments attendant upon the settlement of a large estate. These are typical instances of the close corporation. By an open corporation is meant one, the shares of which are held by a considerable number of individuals and are traded in more or less. It is called open because anyone who has the money may readily buy some of its shares. Most business corporations belong in this class.

We shall have occasion frequently in this volume to refer to both "large" and "small" corporations. These words, of course, have no absolute meaning; yet in connection with corporations a fairly definite distinction between them may be drawn. Generally speaking, when large corporations are mentioned we shall have in mind the companies which operate several different plants or rail lines, particularly the big railroad consolidations and industrial trusts. A corporation which has only one plant, even though it be of considerable importance in its own community, for our purpose may be put into the class of small or local corporations.

Two types of business corporations that are both prominent and important in present-day industry are the parent company and the holding company. These two types are frequently, even usually, confused, although the distinction between them should be kept in view.

50. *The parent company.*—A parent company is one that for some reason does not desire to carry on operations in its own name over the whole country, and which therefore organizes and holds all or nearly all the stock of one or more subordinate companies. There may be several reasons for so doing. The parent company may wish to operate in other countries than the United States, in which case it will obviously be necessary to form a separate corporation in each country. Several English companies, for instance, have subordinate companies in this country and a great many American companies have British subordinate corporations. Another reason for this method of organization is to avoid excessive local taxation. As the capitalization of each of the subordinate corporations may be low, and as the parent company is not officially known to the authorities of the states in which the sub-companies are located, the taxes paid to these states are by this means much reduced. Another frequent reason is that it is desirable to have local men in charge of various plants of the corporation and to give these men a stock interest, not in the corporation as a whole, but in the branch under their control. This is best accomplished by the organization of a subordinate company at each branch. Obviously a parent company is also a holding company in the sense that it owns the stock of other corporations; but these subordinate companies have been created by its officers in its interest, and are in reality simply forms in which sections of its business are organized.

51. *Nature of a holding company.*—A holding company proper, on the other hand, using the term in a financial, not a legal, sense, comes into existence for the

purpose of buying control of pre-existing companies. Its ostensible object is the buying of securities of other corporations to be held for whatever revenues they will produce. The real object of its existence, however, is not accomplished unless it holds control of all its subsidiary companies and directs their operations. Sometimes this control consists in holding a bare majority of the voting stock of the subsidiary; but it is generally advisable to secure as much stock as possible, for the greater the extent of the control, the more readily may the holding company carry out its plans to achieve economies and fix prices. As we shall see in our later discussions of industrial combinations, the process of economizing frequently involves loss to one or more of the subsidiary companies; that is to say, production is often concentrated in the best plants and the poor plants are allowed to fall into decay. If there is a considerable minority interest in any of these poorly equipped subsidiary companies, there will inevitably be strong objections and legal obstacles to the plans of the holding company. It is also to the holding company's interest to own as much as it can get of the stock of those subsidiary companies the business and profits of which it intends to expand.

Thus a holding company almost always aims to become practically the sole stockholder in its subsidiary companies, so that it may operate their properties unhindered. Although in theory it merely holds securities, in practice it is the virtual owner of the railroads, the mines, the plants and the other property of its subsidiaries. We see an expression of this dual relation, the nominal and the virtual, in the reports of almost all holding companies. In these reports we almost always find two balance sheets and two income statements. The first balance sheet shows as assets of the holding company simply the securities in its treasury and the first income statement reports merely the dividends and interest received on those securities; the second balance sheet—usually called "consolidated" or "general"—shows as assets the physical property of the subsidiary companies and the second income statement shows their combined profits. A lack of knowledge of these simple facts has frequently caused confusion in the minds even of stockholders of holding companies, many of whom do not understand the status of their own company.

52. *The holding company as a means of organizing "trusts."*—The holding company is the method now used in organizing those vast industrial and railroad consolidations that are called trusts. Two former methods of forming such combinations were pools and trusts—this word being used in this instance not in its popular, but in its legal sense. The pool is a more or less formal agreement among manufacturers of any given commodity to limit production and to maintain prices; sometimes this agreement includes the organization of a central selling agency through which all the manufacturers dispose of their product. Trusts—in the legal sense—worked on a different principle; the holders of the voting securities of competing companies turned over at least a majority interest in each company to one man or a small group of men to hold in trust, and received in return what were known as trust certificates. In other words, a single voting trust for a number of competing companies was formed. The trustees had power to vote all the stock in their possession and thus exercise control over the policies of competing companies. Pools proved to be unworkable and trusts illegal, for reasons which it belongs to the science of economics rather than to corporation finance to discuss, and both have been given up in

favor of the modern form of combination, the holding company.

The holding company was first made possible in 1889 by an amendment to the corporation law of the State of New Jersey, which reads as follows:

Any corporation may purchase, hold, sell, assign, transfer, mortgage, pledge, or otherwise dispose of the shares of the capital stock of, or any bonds, securities, or evidences of indebtedness created by any other corporation or corporations of this or any other state, and while owner of said stock may exercise all the rights, powers, and privileges of ownership, including the right to vote thereon.

Professor Edward Sherwood Meade, of the University of Pennsylvania, includes in his valuable work on *Trust Finance* some remarks as to the meaning and results of this Act which are of such interest and importance that they are presented below in full:

For momentous consequences, this statute of New Jersey is hardly to be equaled in the annals of legislation. Sixteen sovereign states had passed searching and stringent laws in prohibition of any attempt to restrict competition; laws whose detailed minuteness of specification could hardly be improved upon; which had been proved effective against the only permanent form of competition regulation yet attempted, and which undoubtedly represented the conviction of a majority of the people of the United States—a conviction finding more general and authoritative expression in the Sherman Anti-trust Law, and strengthened by the anti-monopoly provisions of the common law; a well-nigh unanimous sentiment opposed to any form of trust or pool; and the little State of New Jersey, containing two per cent of the population and one and three-tenths per cent of the wealth of the United States, by the simple act of amending its corporation law, nullified the anti-trust laws of every state which had passed them.

A trust could not exist in New York. The courts of New York would not allow the creation of a holding company to perpetuate the trust under another and slightly different form. Here are, say ten corporations, all located in New York, which were formerly engaged in competition, later organized into a trust, and more recently dissolved by the New York courts. The owners of these corporations, having experienced the benefits of combination, wish to continue their organization under another form. They apply to the New York Legislature for permission to charter a new company which shall purchase all their stock, and whose officers can thus control their united policy. The Legislature refuses the application on the ground that the new corporation would be the old trust under a new name, and would therefore be existing in violation of the same law which had been recently employed against its predecessor. The case of the stockholders seems hopeless. They are citizens of New York. Their corporations are chartered by New York. New York absolutely forbids them to combine in restraint of trade. What are they to do?

In despair they turn their eyes southward. There, upon the other side of the North River stands the State of New Jersey, beckoning them with welcoming hands. For a franchise bonus or fee, New Jersey will come to their assistance. New Jersey will authorize them to form a corporation which is empowered to buy the stocks of their ten companies. New Jersey will allow them, as a New Jersey corporation, to perfect the combination in New York—for operation in New York—which the laws of New York absolutely forbid. New Jersey will thus deprive the State of New York of the right to control, in the interests of what her Legislature considers to be public policy, the corporations which New York has created and over which it assumes sovereign power. New Jersey will perform a similar office for any body of individuals who may wish to evade the anti-trust laws of any State in the Union. As a New Jersey corporation, they may combine and coalesce for the operation of any number of competing plants, anywhere in the United States, with none to molest or make them afraid.

This quotation is not intended to give the impression that holding companies are necessarily formed in every instance for unlawful or harmful purposes. On the contrary, the writer wishes to record here his conviction that some form of industrial and railroad combination under present conditions in this country is both inevitable and desirable. It is inevitable because by means of combination production as a rule can be carried on more cheaply than would otherwise be possible; it is desirable because through the working of economic forces the advantages gained by this cheapness of production will be distributed in the long run among all classes. To defend and illustrate this proposition would lead us too far away from our main subject. The statement is worth bearing in mind, however, especially by those persons who are prone to join in thoughtless outcry against the "trusts."

53. *Complexity of holding companies.*—Holding companies may be formed, not only to acquire stock of operating companies, but also to obtain control of other holding companies; then there is no reason, of course, why the stock of the second holding company should not be purchased sooner or later by a third still greater holding company. Thus there may be built up a most intricate and extensive organization, in which so many companies may be involved that it becomes a difficult matter to trace their relations to each other. Many examples, each of which would require considerable explanation, might be given. The reader will get a sufficiently clear idea, however, as to how complex organizations of this kind are built up if he will study the accompanying chart of the Interborough-Metropolitan Company, which was prepared for the Public Service Commission of the First District of the State of

New York. The Interborough-Metropolitan Company controls all the street car, elevated and subway railway lines in the principal boroughs of New York City. It was formed, as shown in the chart, by an exchange of its securities for the securities of two formerly competing companies, the Metropolitan Securities Company and the Interborough Rapid Transit Company. The relations of these two companies to each other, to their direct subsidiaries, and to the subsidiaries of their subsidiaries, are as clearly as possible presented in the chart.

54. *Organization of the Standard Oil Company.*—To illustrate further the extent, as well as the complexity, of the organization of a great holding company, there is presented below the most complete list ever published of the subsidiaries formerly controlled by the Standard Oil Company. The reader will find this list of value, not only for the present purpose, but for future reference. The Standard Oil Company of New Jersey was the "parent" of something over half of the subsidiaries shown in this list; it was a true holding company, in the sense in which that term has been defined in this chapter, so far as the other subsidiaries named were concerned.

I. COMPANIES WHOSE STOCK WAS OWNED DIRECTLY BY THE STANDARD OIL COMPANY

Name.	*Total Capital Stock.*	*Per Cent Owned by Standard.*
Anglo-American Oil Co., Ltd.	$5,000,000	100
Atlantic Refining Co.	5,000,000	100
Bedford Petroleum Co.	350,000	99.3
Borne-Scrymser Co.	200,000	99.9
Buckeye Pipe Line Co.	10,000,000	100
Carter Oil Co.	2,000,000	100
Chesebrough Mfg. Co.	500,000	55.5
Continental Oil Co.	300,000	100
Colonial Oil Co.	250,000	99.7
Crescent Pipe Line Co.	3,000,000	100

Name.	*Total Capital Stock.*	*Per Cent Owned by Standard.*
Clarksburg Light & Heat Co.	100,000	51
Deutsch-Amerikanische Petroleum Gesellschaft	2,250,000	100
Deutsch-Amerikanische Petroleum Gesellschaft (share warrants)	5,250,000	99.9
Empire Refining Co.	100,000	78.5
Empreza Industrial de Petrolio	500,000	70
Eureka Pipe Line Co.	5,000,000	100
Forest Oil Co.	?	?
Gilbert & Barker Mfg. Co.	40,000	100
Galena-Signal Oil Co. pfd.	2,000,000	74.4
Galena-Signal Oil Co. com.	8,000,000	70
Hazelwood Oil Co.	?	?
Hope Natural Gas Co.	500,000	100
Indiana Pipe Line Co.	1,000,000	100
Interstate Cooperage Co.	200,000	100
Lawrence Natural-Gas Co.	450,000	100
Mahoning Gas Fuel Co.	150,000	99.9
Marion Oil Co.	100,000	50
Mountain State Gas Co.	500,000	100
National Transit Co.	25,455,200	99.9
New York Transit Co.	5,000,000	100
Northern Pipe Line Co.	4,000,000	100
Northwestern Ohio Natural Gas Co.	2,775,250	59.4
Ohio Oil Co.	10,000,000	99.9
People's Natural Gas Co.	1,000,000	100
Pennsylvania Lubricating Co.	50,000	60
Pittsburg Natural Gas Co.	310,000	100
Romano-Americana	2,500,000	100
Reserve Gas Co.	2,225,000	50
Raffinerie Française	80,000	100
River Gas Co.	190,000	52.6
Solar Refining Co.	500,000	99.8
Southern Pipe Line Co.	10,000,000	100
South Penn Oil Co.	2,500,000	100
South West Pennslvania Pipe Lines	3,500,000	100
Standard Oil Co., California	17,000,000	99.9
Standard Oil Co., Indiana	1,000,000	99.9
Standard Oil Co., Iowa	1,000,000	100
Standard Oil Co., Kansas	1,000,000	99 9
Standard Oil Co., Kentucky	1,000,000	99 9
Standard Oil Co., Nebraska	600,000	99.9
Standard Oil Co., New York	15,000,000	100
Standard Oil Co., Ohio	3,500,000	99.9
Swan & Finch Co.	100,000	100

Name.	*Total Capital Stock.*	*Per Cent Owned by Standard.*
Underhay Oil Co.	25,000	98.8
Union Tank Line Co.	3,500,000	99.9
Vacuum Oil Co.	2,500,000	100
Waters-Pierce Oil Co.	400,000	68.6
West India Oil Refining Co.	300,000	50
West Virginia Oil Co.	200,000	50.6
West India Oil Co.	100,000	99.3
Washington Oil Co.	100,000	71.4

II. COMPANIES WHOSE STOCK WAS OWNED PRIMARILY BY SUBSIDIARY COMPANIES

Amerikanische Petroleum Anlagen	$187,500	100
Automaat Co.	10,000	100
Eschweiler Petroleum Import	7,500	25
Ghent Petroleum Co.	200,000	60
Hollandsche Petroleum Vereeniging	12,000	100
Mannheim Bremer Petroleum Actien Gesellschaft	750,000	100
Petrolifere Ghent	20,000	74.5
Petrolifere Nationale	10,000	100
Petroleum Raff. vorm August Korff	375,000	54.6
Societe Anonyme H. Reith Co.	412,500	61
Rheinische Petrol. Actien Gesellschaft	250	100
Actien Gesellschaft Atlantic	237,500	60
American Petroleum Co.	3,140,000	51.3
Street Tank Wagon Business-Duren	4,250	71
Gibraltar Petroleum Co.	25,000	100
Imperial Oil Co., Ltd.	4,000,000	83.1
Det Danske Petroleums Aktieselskab	756,000	51.3
Tidewater Oil Co.	20,000,000	31.1
Tank Storage and Carriage Co., Ltd. pfd.	300,000	100
Tank Storage and Carriage Co., Ltd., ordinary	42,195	100
Societa Italo-Americana pel Petrolio	1,000,000	60
Aktieselskabet Ostlandske Petrol. Cie	162,000	9.2
Krooks Petrol. and Olje Aktiebolag	270,000	10
Skanska Petroleums Aktiebolaget	135,000	60
Svenska Petroleums Aktiebolaget	27,000	75
Sydvenska Petroleums Aktiebolaget	98,550	24.7
Kestkustens Petroleums Aktiebolag	177,500	15.3
Koenigsberger Handels Compagnie	575,000	49.8
Petroleum Import Compagnie	30,000	100
Schweizerische Petroleum Handels Gesellschaft	60,000	60
Societe Anonyme Petrolea	30,000	66.5
Wachs. & Flossner Petrol. Gesellschaft	25,000	100

Name.	*Total Capital Stock.*	*Per Cent Owned by Standard.*
Westphalische Petroleum Gesellschaft	25,000	100
S. T. Baker Oil Co	50,000	100
Galena Oil Co.— Société Anonyme Française	40,000	100
Queen City Oil Co., Ltd	200,000	87.4
Connecting Gas Co	825,000	49.9
Cumberland Pipe Line Co	1,000,000	99.9
East Ohio Gas Co	6,000,000	100
Franklin Pipe Line Co	50,000	39
New Domain Oil and Gas Co	1,000,000	99.9
Prairie Oil and Gas Co	10,000,000	100
St. Paul Petroleum Tanks (Lim.)	250,000	55
Societa Meridionale pel Commercio del Petrolio	120,000	....
Societa per gli Olii Minerali	156,000	52.1
Société Tunsienne des Petroles	80,000	65
International Oil Co., Ltd	2,750,000	99.4
Vacuum Oil Co., Proprietary Limited	500,000	100
Vacuum Oil Co., Reszvenytarsasag	2,100,000	100
Vacuum Oil Co., Limited	275,000	99.9
Vacuum Oil Co.—Société Anonyme Française	400,000	100
Deutsch — Vacuum Oil Co	625,000	100
Vacuum Oil Co.— Societa Anonyme Italiana	100,000	100
Vacuum Oil Co.— Aktiebolag	27,000	96.6
Taylorstown Natural Gas Co	10,000	70
Total	$229,963,195	
Standard Oil Co. of New Jersey	98,338,300	
Grand total	$328,301,495	

CHAPTER VII

SOURCES OF CORPORATE FUNDS

55. *Summary of preceding chapters.*—The first six chapters of this book cover those fundamental features of corporation law which are essential to an understanding of the financial organization and management of corporations. We have taken up in turn among other topics: the advantages of corporations over other forms of conducting business; the legal powers of the corporation; the charter; the by-laws; the duties, rights and privileges of stockholders; of directors; of officers; the process of incorporation; the factors to consider in selecting the state of incorporation; the relative advantages and disadvantages of several states; the characteristics of common and preferred stock; the uses of cumulative voting and of voting trusts; the nature of a close corporation; of an ordinary operating company; of a parent company; of a holding company. All of this matter, although essential, is intended merely as an introduction to what follows. Our real subject is not the legal, but the financial, side of corporation practice, and this subject we are now ready to take up. It must not be forgotten at any stage of this study, however, that all financial measures must comply with and be in harmony with the legal principles that have been discussed.

56. *Four sources of corporate funds.*—In financing a corporation the managers may go for funds to six different sources, as follows:

(a) Active interests in the business
(b) Profits of the business
(c) Trade creditors
(d) Banks
(e) The investing public
(f) The speculative public.

There is no need of discussing in detail methods of raising funds from people who are actively engaged in the management of the corporation. Each one presumably will be fully informed as to the records and prospects of the company and will regulate his investments accordingly. In the case of close corporations the process of raising funds is simply to allow each person interested to invest as much as he can and will on terms that are settled by direct bargaining.

Profits that are not paid out from a surplus may be one of the most important sources of funds. The Carnegie Steel Company, as we shall see later, is a conspicuous example. This particular topic is fully discussed in later chapters and need only be mentioned here.

It may not be plain at first sight that the trade creditors of a concern are in reality furnishing part of the funds necessary to the business; but a moment's reflection makes it evident that a company which continually carries, say, $10,000 of accounts payable, thereby makes that amount available for its business. If the trade creditors should demand cash for every purchase, the concern would have to raise the $10,000 from some other source. In some lines of business, especially retail, a very small investment is sufficient to carry on comparatively large operations simply because long-time payments are permissible. Usually, however, the merchant or manufacturer who buys on credit also sells on credit, in which case the funds derived from trade creditors are promptly placed at the disposal of trade debtors.

Of course, it is possible also that a business may draw its funds from the advance payments of the people who buy its products; but this is so unusual a case that it is hardly worth mentioning.

Banks are institutions whose primary function is to furnish funds for commercial enterprises. Without going into the theory of banking, it may be pointed out that banks are dealers in credit. They buy the credit of other people in the form of notes and similar obligations and they sell their own credit principally in the form of deposits. Any reader to whom this statement is not altogether clear may turn to the volume on MONEY AND BANKING for further enlightenment. In order to make its credit good a bank must always be ready to redeem promptly every check that may be presented to it for payment. Therefore, a well-managed bank will never tie up its assets in permanent investments, but will keep them always "liquid." For that reason the corporation manager can look to banks only for short-time loans, usually not longer than ninety days. We will discuss the requirements of banks in detail in the next chapter. It is enough for the present to say that funds secured from banks will almost always be short-time loans in strictly limited amounts backed by unquestionable security.

57. *The investing public as a source of funds.*—The fifth source of funds is the investing public. This phrase covers, not only individuals, but institutions. The most important classes of investors are; (a) professional and salaried people who have no business of their own in which to place their savings; (b) women and minors who have inherited money; (c) estates held in trust;

(d) savings institutions; (e) insurance companies. Business men are not investors in securities of other corporations than those in which they are directly interested to any great extent, for the obvious reason that they are apt either to put their savings into their own concerns or to seek larger returns than are offered by strictly investment securities.

One of the great problems of raising funds for many kinds of business is to arouse interest and inspire confidence in this investing public. They may be appealed to by advertisements and circular letters—a plan which is seldom successful; or they may be reached—usually with much better results—through bond and brokerage houses whose business it is to retail investment securities to their clients. This is another topic that will come up for later discussion.

58. *Difference between investment and speculation.*—This is a good place to define the words "investment" and "speculation." The former word, as it is used in a somewhat technical sense by the leading financial papers, refers to a security or other property which is practically certain, so far as human minds can foresee, not to depreciate in value. No security in which the element of risk is prominent can properly be called an investment. If the probabilities are strong, but not conclusive, that the security or property will not depreciate in value, then the terms semi-investment or semi-speculative may be applied. To illustrate, a United States Government bond is certainly an investment, and so is a first mortgage bond on any of the standard railroads. Most of the industrial bonds, however, even where the earnings are large and the prospects apparently good, would be classed as semi-investments, because there is always danger that competition or some new invention will cut into

the business. In the same way high-grade preferred stocks of successful railroads and industrial companies would be called either semi-investment or semi-speculative issues. For our purposes in this book these finer distinctions are not necessary and would perhaps be confusing. We shall, therefore, use the word "investment" in a more popular sense to include both the true investment and the semi-investment or semi-speculative securities. We may define it, in its objective sense, as any security or other property the principal of which seems safe and returns on which (interest, dividends or rent) seem certain.

The great majority of corporate stocks would be classed as speculative; for no matter how promising they may be conservative brokers would not in most cases be willing to call them safe. Calling a security "speculative," the reader should understand, is not necessarily condemning it or objecting to its sale. As a matter of fact, few corporations comparatively have anything but speculative securities to offer. Moreover, it is only by more or less speculative purchases that returns on capital above 5, 6 or 7 per cent may be obtained. Nearly all investment securities have been at one time speculative in character. When the terms "highly speculative" or "purely speculative" are used, however, it is generally safe to assume that the writer intends to convey the idea that the security in question has a very remote chance of ever getting into the investment class.

59. *The speculative public as a source of funds.*—The speculative public may be roughly subdivided into three groups: (a) ill-informed people who do not know the difference between an investment and a speculation and who are continually placing their hard-earned money in the hands of unscrupulous promoters in the blind faith

that they are making an investment; (b) intelligent business and professional men who buy and hold for a rise speculative securities and property in the full knowledge that they are taking chances; (c) speculators who buy securities and property "on margin" in the hope of making a quick and large profit. Group (a) may be reached by means of circular letters and advertising; group (b), generally by personal solicitation or through the stock-market; group (c), usually through the stock-market. A detailed discussion of the methods of reaching and interesting possible buyers of corporate securities must be deferred. For the present our attention should be confined to the securities themselves.

Corporate funds fall into two classes: borrowed funds and owned funds. The borrowed funds are secured through accounts and bills payable, through bank loans or through bonds and mortgages. The owned funds are secured through issues of stock.

60. *Desirability of borrowing funds.*—Why should a corporation borrow funds at all? The reader will perhaps answer, as many people do, that it borrows from necessity; that as soon as possible it ought to pay off its debts, just as a man gets rid of the mortgage on his house as soon as he can. The fact is, however, that for a corporation to be out of debt is no credit to it, but rather a sign that it is either in a dangerous position or not intelligently managed. Only one method of raising funds is cheaper than borrowing, and that method is stealing. Therefore, a corporation should borrow as much as it can within the limits of safety.

To illustrate the desirability of borrowing part of the funds of a corporation: Suppose a manufacturing company needs $100,000 to carry on its business and produces an average net income of $6,000. If it raises the whole $100,000 by stock issues, it will only pay 6 per cent dividends—not enough to compensate for the risks and uncertainties of the business. Now suppose that the company is dissolved and the same business is carried on under a new company which sells $50,000 of 5 per cent. bonds, gets additional and larger credits to the extent of $10,000 and borrows $5,000 from banks at an average rate of 5 per cent. Then, only $35,000 stock need be issued, the income of which, after deducting interest charges of $2,750, will be $3,250, or 9.3 per cent, a satisfactory return.

Thomas L. Greene, author of "Corporation Finance," points out that a few years ago three-quarters of owned to one-quarter of borrowed funds was thought about right, whereas now the proportion in well-managed corporations is nearer one-quarter owned to three-quarters borrowed. The result has been to reduce the average rate of returns on capital and thereby to reduce cost of production and prices. In order to make profits at all under present conditions mercantile and manufacturing concerns must borrow heavily. Of course, there are limits to the safety and advantages of borrowing.

On the following pages are given five recent balance sheets (Herring-Hall-Marvin Safe Company, American Thread Company, Bethlehem Steel Company, A. Booth & Company, and United States Leather Company) selected practically at random, which will perhaps make these statements somewhat more vivid and concrete. Assuming that the balance sheet of the first-named concern is based on the actual value of the property (which is, to be sure, a pure assumption) we arrive at the real amount of funds utilized in the business by deducting from the total assets the item of "Patents, trade-marks, etc., $92,000," leaving approximately

HERRING-HALL-MARVIN SAFE CO.

Assets:	
Real estate and buildings	$202,652
Machinery, &c	298,864
Stocks on hand at cost	207,076
Work in process & materials	320,988
Bills & accts. rec. & cash	372,830
Insurance, &c., paid in adv	8,095
Stock of other companies	1,000
Patents, trade-marks, &c	92,000
Total	$1,512,506
Liabilities:	
Capital stock	$700,000
Debentures maturing to 1915	410,000
Bills payable	170,354
Accounts payable	92,561
Reserves for completion of contracts	64,208
Contingent liability reserves	16,000
Surplus of year's operation	59,383
Total	$1,512,506

AMERICAN THREAD CO.

Assets:	
Land, water, & steam power, mills, machinery, plant & effects	$12,694,896
Stocks-in-trade at net cost	4,960,971
Accounts receivable, net	1,016,445
Cash at bankers & in hand	341,483
Sundry investments	229,840
Advance payments	38,292
Total	$19,281,927
Liabilities:	
Com. stock ($3.50 paid up)	$4,200,000
5% Pfd. stock (fully paid)	4,890,475
4% 1st mtge. bonds	6,000,000
English Sew. Cot. Co. Ltd	351,164
Accounts payable	770,410
Bond int. accrued	60,000

Depreciation fund	2,076,987
Div. on com., payable July	588,000
Profit & loss	344,891
Total	$19,281,927

BETHLEHEM STEEL CO.

Assets:	
Property account	$37,857,260
1st mtge. bonds recd. in part payment for property	518,848
Inventories	6,795,542
Notes and accts. receivable	2,513,186
Cash on hand & in bank	4,230,418
Deferred charges	943,324
Total	$52,858,578
Liabilities:	
Capital stock	$29,770,000
Bonds of Bethlehem Steel Co	16,159,000
Notes & accts. payable, &c	5,735,154
Bond interest accrued	103,145
Reserved for depreciation	400,000
Reserved for relining furnaces, &c	97,885
Surplus	593,421
Total	$52,858,578

A. BOOTH & CO.

Assets:	
Cash	$510,777
Merchandise	937,976
Accounts receivable	1,556,689
Bills receivable	930,560
Unexpired insurance, R. R. mileage, etc	119,448
Treasury preferred stock	20,800
Treasury common stock	170,650
Plants, steamboats, real estate, etc	5,510,927
Total	$9,757,827

Liabilities:	
Common stock	$3,000,000
Preferred stock	2,500,000
Surplus	1,522,700
Undivided profits	202,138
Accounts payable	931,989
Bills payable	1,601,000
Total	$9,757,827

UNITED STATES LEATHER CO.

Assets:	
Cash	$2,505,159
Due by customers	10,761,665
Bills receivable	1,277,339
Doubtful debts. val	8,832
Other debtors	1,070,602
Hides & leather	15,269,784
Bark at tanneries	1,677,962
Sundries, pers. property, &c	654,627
Advance to other companies	1,920,921
Drawbacks	464,492
Railroad mortgage	100,000
Tannery plants, etc	6,847,706
Stock of other cos	56,760,181
Bonds of other cos	6,879,888
Real estate interests	490,235
Treasury stock	....
Good-will, &c	62,832,300
Unexpired insurance	106,293
Total	$169,627,987

Liabilities:	
Common stock	$62,882,300
Preferred stock	62,282,300
Bonds less in treas	5,080,000
Accrued interest, etc	67,960
Current accounts	609,585
Foreign exch. not due	2,072,904
Bills payable	13,080,000
Miscellaneous	639,729
Surplus	22,913,209
Total	$169,627,987

$1,420,000. The borrowings, including bonds, bills payable and accounts payable, are approximately $670,000, or something over 47 per cent of funds.

To arrive at the actual funds utilized in the property of the American Thread Company we should deduct from the $19,281,000 assets the depreciation fund of $2,076,000. Of the total funds, approximately $17,200,000, about $7,750,000 is borrowed (including bonds, debts to stock- and bond-holders and to English Sewing Cotton Co., and accounts payable). The percentage of borrowing is 45.

Deducting reserves for depreciation we find funds of the Bethlehem Steel Company to be approximately $52,500,000. Borrowings are about $22,000,000 or 42 per cent.

In the case of A. Booth & Company there are funds of about $9,750,000 and borrowings of $2,500,000, or 25.6 per cent. As the firm failed in September, 1908, this low percentage of borrowings tends to confirm what has already been said, to the effect that abnormally small borrowings indicate either a weak or a mismanaged company.

In estimating funds in the United States Leather Company, we should, of course, deduct "good-will." It is not improper also to deduct stocks and bonds of other companies, all of which were obtained in exchange for preferred and common stock. This leaves actual funds of approximately $42,700,000, against borrowings of $20,800,000, about 49 per cent.

It goes without saying that this analysis of the five balance sheets is superficial and that the results are merely suggestive. To ascertain the exact proportion of borrowed to owned funds in each case we should have first to learn the exact, not the nominal, value of the assets, which is an impracticable task. As it is reasonably certain that the cost in every case is less than the book value of the assets, the true percentages of borrowed to owned funds are in all probability greater than the figures given. Four out of these five corporations no doubt borrow more than half the funds they use. Other well-managed companies follow the same principle.

61. *Distribution of security issues.*—The next question to consider is: What issues of securities or credit instruments should a corporation put out and what proportion of its total funds should be obtained by each of these issues? In order to raise funds from each of the four sources outside the business itself named above the corporation manager will offer:

SOURCES	SECURITIES
(a) To trade creditors	Bills and notes payable
(b) To banks	Notes payable and endorsed notes receivable
(c) To the investing public	Mortgage bonds and perhaps preferred stock
(d) To the speculative public.	Stock.

The amount of each security offered will depend in part on the assets and in part on the earnings of the corporation.

Corporate assets in nearly every line of business fall naturally into six groups, as follows:

(a) Fixed investments essential to the business, such as real estate, buildings and machinery and, in the case of holding companies, securities of subsidiary corporations.

(b) Property that could be sold without breaking up the business, though the sale would probably be at a heavy sacrifice, such as, outlying real estate, securities of other companies control of which is not essential to the integrity of the corporation, raw materials, and goods in process.

(c) Finished products on hand.

(d) Accounts receivable.

(e) Cash.

(f) Intangible assets, such as good-will, trade marks, etc.

To the first five groups roughly correspond obligations for borrowed money, as follows:

(a) Mortgages and mortgage bonds obtainable as a rule on good terms up to 60 to 75 per cent of the appraised value of real estate; 50 per cent of buildings; 25 to 40 per cent of machinery; 50 to 90 per cent of securities.

(b) and (c) Income, profit-sharing and car-trust bonds, on a great variety of terms, preferred stock in some cases and to some extent short-term notes and bank loans.

(d) and (e) Accounts payable and bank loans.

Group (f) and the differences between the other assets and their corresponding liabilities are usually represented by stock issues and by surpluses. The reader will understand, no doubt, that this classification is merely approximate and is not always followed in practice; yet an analysis of balance sheets will reveal, on the whole, a close adherence by corporation managers to the principles just stated.

In all industries, more or less, and especially in railroads and stable manufacturing concerns, the creditors of the corporation, as we shall see later, pay more attention to the income account than to the balance sheet. The gross earnings of any corporation are necessarily devoted to the following purposes: (1) Operation; (2) maintenance; (3) fixed interest charges and rentals; (4) floating interest charges; (5) betterment and surplus; (6) dividends.

The stability and amount of the earnings will, of course, greatly affect—in fact, determine largely—the value of a corporation's assets, and in that way will affect the amount and kind of securities that it may wisely issue.

CHAPTER VIII

SHORT-TIME LOANS

62. *Trade credit as a source of funds.*—The preceding chapter named, without describing, the three forms in which corporations incur short-term or medium-term obligations, namely, trade credit, bank loans and notes sold to the public. We will now take up each of these forms in turn and see what we can discover as to the principles that should govern their use. Readers of this volume who are themselves engaged in an unincorporated business will perhaps read what is said as to the first two forms named with a more lively interest if they reflect that the principles laid down apply to partnerships or to individual proprietorships as well as to corporations.

The funds raised from the trade creditors of a corporation are secured simply by buying goods on credit. It is not customary in most lines of business to demand cash immediately on delivery of goods, except from concerns that are considered untrustworthy. Thirty days is usually allowed before trade creditors begin to press for payment and a company whose business is worth having can often considerably lengthen the average time of settlement, if that policy proves desirable. In some lines—especially when the sales are in large lots—sixty to ninety days, or even six months, is the usual allowance. For sixty days or over the debtor company generally gives a formal promissory note or else accepts a time draft which amounts to about the same thing.

As was indicated in Chapter VII, it is good business policy for a company to take as much trade credit as it can get on advantageous terms and with safety. These two qualifications are worth elaborating. A company does not obtain trade credit on advantageous terms: (a) when by so doing it acquires a reputation for "slow pay" which makes dealers unwilling to quote to the company their lowest prices; (b) when by so doing it loses the benefit of cash discounts larger than the prevailing discount on bank loans,—provided in this case that the company is not already borrowing as much as it should from banks. A company cannot accept trade credit with safety when by so doing its short-time liabilities are brought up nearly equal to its quick assets. Notice that the relation is not between total liabilities and total assets, but between quick liabilities and quick assets. A concern must have cash funds at hand to meet its accounts and bills payable when due and no other assets, no matter how valuable, will serve the purpose. A failure to realize just that simple fact has been responsible for many an unnecessary bankruptcy.

Taking the five balance sheets previously referred to (see pages 98–100), we find:

(1) That on the date of the balance sheet the quick liabilities of the Herring-Hall-Marvin Safe Company were about 70 per cent of quick assets and about 29 per cent of all the current assets, including stocks, work in process and materials.

(2) That the corresponding percentages for the American Thread Company were 58 per cent and 18 per cent. (Current liabilities, including debt to English Sewing Cotton Company, in proportion to current assets, including stocks, investments and advance payments.)

(3) That the corresponding percentages for the Bethlehem Steel Company were 85 per cent and 44 per cent.

(4) That the corresponding percentages for A. Booth and Company were 83 per cent and 64 per cent.

(5) That the corresponding percentages for the United States Leather Company were 100 per cent and 82 per cent.

We may infer from these five representative balance sheets that a conservative company will not, as a rule, allow its accounts, bills and notes payable to run much over 75 to 80 per cent of its quick assets. This percentage is, in fact, not far from normal. It would be foolish to try to lay down any absolute rule where so much depends on the custom of each line of business, on the seasons, on the nature of the company's assets, on the ease with which bank credit may be secured, and on the general commercial outlook. Enough has been said to indicate that trade credit, though a necessity to nearly every successful corporation, may become too extensive. Further discussion of this important phase of corporation finance must be deferred until we begin a study of the financial management of corporations.

63. *What reliance should be placed on bank loans?*—Bank loans are not usually to be had except on first-class security and for short periods. Perhaps the best method of considering the advantages and disadvantages of bank loans will be to run over hastily the detailed statements which many conservative banks now require applicants for loans to file with them. A blank form for such statements, adopted by the New York State Bankers' Association, and widely used, is presented on pages 108-109. Let us see how critically a banker will examine one of these statements when presented by a corporation with which he is not thoroughly

STATEMENT FORM FOR CORPORATIONS

FROM ....

ADDRESS ....

To KNICKERBOCKER NATIONAL BANK, NEW YORK.

For the purpose of procuring credit from time to time with you for our negotiable paper or otherwise, we furnish the following as a true and accurate statement of our financial condition on..........190 ..., which you are to consider as continuing to be full and accurate until we give you written notice of change.

ASSETS		LIABILITIES	
Cash on hand	....	Notes Payable given for merchandise	....
Cash in the following banks	....	Notes Payable negotiated to own banks	....
Name of bank		Notes Payable otherwise disposed of	....
" " "		Accounts Payable	....
" " "		Deposits of Money with Us as follows.	
....	....	By.. ..... $................	
Notes Receivable (not transferred)	....	By.. .. .. $................	
Accounts Receivable (not transferred)	....	By . ... . $................	
Notes and Accounts Receivable of officers (not transferred)	....	By sundry persons $.....	....
Merchandise finished (how valued ....)	....	....	....
" unfinished (how valued ....)	....	....	....
" raw material (how valued ....)	....		
Land owned by company used for this business	....	Bonds Outstanding....................	....
Buildings " " " " " " "	....	Mortgage Debt........................	....
Machinery " " " " " " "	....	Chattel Mortgages....................	....
....	....	Capital Stock.	....
....	....		
....	....	....	....
TOTAL		TOTAL	

CONTINGENT LIABILITY: Notes Receivable of customers Discounted or Sold and not included in assets enumerated above ....
Other contingent liability ....

We Have Not Pledged or Assigned any of the above Accounts Receivable; our Assigned Accounts Receivable amount to... ....
Other assets used as collateral.. ....

INSURANCE: on merchandise $.........buildings...........$.......machinery $........... Total Insurance ....

BUSINESS and RESULTS: Annual Sales for the year ended...........190. .or from. ....190...to ... ...190 ....

Gross Profits on Sales	For the same period ....
Expense of Conducting Business	" " " " ....
Net Profit	" " " " ....
Other Income, including investments	" " " " ....
Combined Profits	" " " " ....

DIVIDENDS PAID.................................. .from..........190...to.........190 ....

BAD DEBTS for the period from.. .. ..190...to... ....190 ....

OFFICERS: name ....
" ....
" ....
" ....

BANK ACCOUNTS: where kept other than above....................
MORTGAGES: on what assets a lien....................
Average TERMS on which we SELL....................
Average TERMS on which we BUY....................
DATE of ORGANIZATION of CORPORATION....................
TIME OF YEAR when NOTES and ACCOUNTS RECEIVABLE of CUSTOMERS, Uncollected, are generally maximum.......minimum.......
TIME OF YEAR when STOCKS of MERCHANDISE on hand are generally maximum..........minimum..........
TIME OF YEAR when LIABILITIES are maximum..........minimum..........
STATEMENT: is it based on actual inventory?..........if so, Date..........
VERIFICATION: have the books been audited by a Certified Public Accountant?..........if so, Name and Date of Audit..........
....

BUSINESS: what kind of business do you conduct?....................
BOOKS. what kind of books do you keep?....................
....

(Please sign corporation name)....................

Date Signed....................190 ..   By....................

Please Give Particulars of Each Parcel of Real Estate

Description	Street and number	City or town and state	Title in name of	Estimated value	Mortgages	Equity
....	....	....	....	....	....	....
....	....	....	....	....	....	....
....	....	....	....	....	....	....
....	....	....	....	....	....	....
....	....	....	....	....	....	....
....	....	....	....	....	....	....
....	....	....	....	....	....	....
....	....	....	....	....	....	....

familiar. What is said on this point is largely based on an article by Mr. William Post, Cashier of the Central National Bank of Philadelphia, in *The Journal of Accountancy,* Volume 1, page 181.

Take first the item, "notes receivable." In most lines of business notes are little given except by weak concerns, and a large amount of "notes receivable" outstanding, therefore, may indicate that a corporation has been in the habit of granting unsafe credits. Some of the principal lines in which note giving is still common are harvesting machines, plumbers' supplies and electric trolley supplies. Where notes are received to any considerable extent they are generally discounted at once by well-managed corporations. Corporations which show a large figure under this heading of "notes receivable," therefore, would be regarded by the banker with distrust.

"Notes and accounts receivable of officers," except in insignificant amounts, would naturally arouse suspicion. Ordinarily officers of corporations are expected to keep their personal obligations and the company funds entirely separate.

The valuation of merchandise should be made by means of an expert's inventory. In connection with these items a careful banker will take into consideration the possibility of extensive fluctuations in value, particularly in the case of staple articles such as pig iron, cotton, wool and metal.

The other assets specified are not of immediate interest to the banker, because they will not ordinarily be sold to meet short-time obligations. They may be considered, however, as a final protection to the banker in case the concern should go into bankruptcy.

Mr. Post suggests, "that in estimating the value of

plants, a sharp distinction should be made between buildings used for manufacturing and for merchandising purposes. A business structure, conveniently located for trade, is a good asset. It is not adapted specially to any one purpose. Even if the business which now occupies it should be withdrawn, it could be sold and applied to some other use. Its value can be easily appraised. The banker is justified, therefore, in placing a high net value upon such property when well located. With the manufacturing plant, however, the situation is entirely different. The whole building is often specialized to some particular use: if the business fails it is very difficult to apply the premises to other purposes." Machinery is even less salable, as a rule, than a manufacturing building. In general, a concern that is not making a success of its undertaking will very seldom find buyers, except at a very heavy sacrifice, for its fixed assets.

Turning to the liabilities, we have already laid down the rule that "notes payable" given for merchandise, except in the few lines of business specified above, are not required from first-class concerns. "The second and third items," says Mr. Post, "are distinguished in order to show how much paper a concern may have with its own banks and how much it may have negotiated through a note broker. It is quite important to the banker to know how much paper a borrower has sold, as the saying is, 'on the street.' If he finds that the borrower is choking his bank account and at the same time putting a large amount of paper out into the open market, the banker is likely to arrive at the conclusion that the borrower is not keeping available any particular resource or channel which he could utilize in case of a stringency in the money market. It is a fixed rule of financial management that a concern should not borrow largely at its bank and at the same time sell large amounts of its paper in the market. If the bank line is full, paper should not be upon the street; if made largely for the street, then the bank should be kept open."

"Accounts payable" is to be considered, of course, in contrast to "accounts receivable" and the proportions already mentioned in this chapter should be observed.

Ordinarily only close corporations would have any deposits made with them by individuals. Where there are such deposits they would be regarded as a possible source of danger, since the persons who make them are apt to be in close touch with the management and to be informed of any impending trouble in time to protect themselves—possibly at the expense of the other creditors.

Bond and mortgage debts should, of course, be proportioned to the fixed assets of the corporation. The mortgage should be very carefully examined in order to make sure that it does not cover more than the fixed assets. Sometimes a real estate mortgage will contain a clause making it a first lien also on the chattels or quick assets of the corporation. Chattel mortgages are unusual and do not often exist unless a corporation is already in serious straits.

A large amount of contingent liabilities would be regarded as a weakness. Especially is this true of the item "other contingent liability," which refers to endorsement of outside paper and to miscellaneous obligations.

Generally speaking, a corporation is not expected to assign its accounts receivable. There may be well-grounded exceptions to this rule but the exceptions require explanation.

The item "other assets used as collateral" would be filled out normally only by commission houses among which the custom is to put up bills of lading or warehouse receipts as collateral for loans. In the United States a manufacturing company is not expected to pledge any specific asset except its fixed capital. In Canada and in Europe manufacturers obtain funds from banks upon pledge of raw material and finished products.

The banker wants to be sure that a corporation is carrying sufficient insurance; otherwise a fire or some other accident may make the assets almost valueless.

The items under the head "business and results" are important, inasmuch as they tell the banker to what extent the company may meet its obligations out of income. An expert in any particular business can tell very often by an inspection of these items whether the company is well-managed or not, for he will know how large should be the percentages of gross profits and of net profits to sales. It is very difficult for an outsider to form any sound judgment on this point. "Dividends paid" will indicate how conservative the corporation is in providing against possible future losses. The item of "bad debts" obviously shows how carefully the corporation looks after its credits.

The succeeding items are intended to answer questions with regard to the balance sheet or profit and loss statement. The banker will, of course, observe very carefully what assets are covered by outstanding mortgages and bonds. He wants to know what bank accounts are kept other than those named in the balance sheet, because some concerns may keep additional secret bank accounts with the idea of inducing the bankers to favor them with loans. A knowledge of the average terms on which goods are bought and sold enables the banker to form an idea as to how pressing the corporation's accounts payable and as to how "quick" its accounts receivable are. By learning the time of year when accounts receivable, stocks of merchandise and liabilities are at their maxima and minima, the banker may better judge as to whether the balance sheet represents the normal condition of the corporation or not.

It goes without saying that to have the statement based on an actual inventory and to have it audited, before presentation, by a certified public accountant, will add greatly to its value in the eyes of any banker.

We have gone over this blank form at some length for two purposes: First, because it illustrates how a corporation's statement may be analyzed and how much information may be extracted from it; second, because it shows how strict and careful conservative bankers are in granting loans. The writer does not mean to say that every concern which borrows money from a bank presents such a detailed statement and has it so closely analyzed as what has been said may indicate. It is true, however, that the custom of demanding and of thoroughly inspecting such statements is growing. It is also true that a conservative corporation will not desire bank loans unless it can present a statement that would meet with the approval of any careful banker.

64. *Notes sold to the public as a source of funds.*—Promissory notes of a corporation may be given in order to raise funds from (a) concerns which supply merchandise, (b) banks or (c) the public. We have already seen how and to what extent they may be issued in the first two cases; we have now to consider the third case.

The form of the note is substantially the same in all three uses. It is a simple promise to pay and must contain the features that are essential to all valid negotiable notes, which are: (a) two parties to the contract, (b) transferability, (c) a definite sum of money, (d) definite day of payment, and (e) proper signature. It is worth noting here that as a general rule the power to bind a corporation in this manner does not belong to an officer unless it is expressly conferred on him. Nevertheless, the note of a corporation signed and in the hands of an innocent holder for value is usually binding, even if the signer acted beyond his powers. Technical objections to a note, based on its improper execution or on unauthorized uses of the money borrowed, are not usually upheld. It is worth noting also that the corporation signature should be used. Notes signed by officers in their own names, even if their corporate titles are given, or notes containing such words as "jointly and severally promise to pay" may be held as personal obligations.

The usual, although not a necessary, distinction between notes given in the ordinary course of trade or to banks and notes sold to the public is in the length of time of the debt. In the first-named cases they do not usually run over six months. Notes sold to the public are more likely to run from one tc ten years. Two or three years is about the average period, intermediate between sixty-days to six months notes, on the one hand, and ten to one-hundred-year bonds, on the other hand. They are issued in denominations varying from $100 to as high as $100,000.

The chief objection to these instruments is that they do not appeal to any large dependable body of purchasers. The commercial banks do not care for them because they are not "quick" enough. Comparatively few individual investors will buy them because they are to be cancelled within a comparatively short period, and the average individual investor does not choose to watch his investments closely and renew them frequently. His idea, on the contrary, is to get hold of a safe security that yields a steady return and to keep it indefinitely. The market for medium-term notes, therefore, is restricted, generally speaking, to persons of large means who are in fairly close touch with the financial world and who happen to have idle funds on hand. Such persons are most easily reached through the big financial houses and these houses almost invariably absorb note issues of any size and distribute them to their clients.

On account of the limitations of the market it is always difficult to tell in advance whether an issue of medium-term notes will be taken up by the public or not. It is still more difficult—in fact, impossible—to tell at the time of issue whether the notes can be readily renewed when the time of payment arrives. No conservative corporation manager will put out such notes unless he has first provided for their payment when due. This he may do in two ways: either by saving the necessary amount out of the corporation's income or by securing through bond issues the funds with which to pay off the notes. The first course involves cutting down the borrowings of the corporation which, as has been pointed out, is likely to be undesirable. Ordinarily the second course would be inadvisable, for if bonds are to be put out at all they might as well be issued in the first place.

This suggests the usual reason for the issue of notes

to the public, namely, as a temporary expedient when a bond issue is for the time being deferred. Sometimes a railroad is building a new branch or a manufacturing company is putting up a new building on which an issue of bonds is to be based. In the meantime medium-term notes may be issued to secure funds for construction. Again, a company in need of funds may find the general financial situation unfavorable to a bond issue and may put out notes with the intention of selling bonds before the notes come due. The practice, though often justifiable, is always more or less risky. In April, 1907, for instance, the Erie Railroad issued, for that reason, $5,500,000 of one year notes. In April, 1908, the conditions being still unfavorable, the railroad authorized an issue of $15,000,000 three year notes, of which $5,500,000 were exchanged at par for the first issue. In July, 1907, the Bethlehem Steel Company issued $1,187,000 of 6 per cent serial three, four, and five year notes, apparently for the same reason. In October, 1906, the American Locomotive Company issued $5,000,000 of one to five year notes for the purpose of paying floating indebtedness and of providing working capital. It is expected that these notes will be redeemed out of income. These examples will indicate roughly when and how medium-term notes are issued.

Although notes for the public are generally simply unsecured promises to pay, they may, especially for the longer terms, be based on certain definite property. A corporation's holdings of securities of other companies are frequently put up under mortgage as collateral security. It is difficult to draw a line between long-time collateral trust notes and short-time collateral trust bonds; in fact, notes and bonds merge into each other and the distinction between them is in some cases merely nominal.

In this chapter we have been dealing with the current obligations of corporations. The main point with regard to them to bear in mind is that they ought to be offset, if they are to be made good, by a more than equal amount of current assets, and no other kind of assets will serve the purpose. To issue notes and put the funds thus secured into fixed or semi-fixed assets without having on hand a large surplus of current assets is unsound and dangerous financing.

CHAPTER IX

THE CORPORATE MORTGAGE

65. *What determines the value of fixed assets?*—Now we take up the long-time obligations—especially mortgages and mortgage bonds—of corporations. Evidently they must be based on permanent, or fixed assets, and in amount will correspond roughly to the value of such assets.

Here we meet with the difficult and important question, What determines the value of fixed assets? Most people would be inclined to say that the cost of the assets must determine their value. A moment's reflection, however, shows this statement to be untrue. Suppose, for instance, that a man has put up a plant at an expense of $100,000 for refining copper, and afterwards discovers that there is no copper within hauling distance. The plant would not be worth the expense of demolishing it. On the other hand, suppose that he does put his plant in a rich copper country and secures such favorable contracts with the mine owners that he makes profits of $100,000 a year and may expect to continue such profits for an indefinite period. His plant, in that case, could be sold for perhaps a million dollars. Evidently cost of construction would have very little to do with the value of such assets.

The second opinion is that the value of fixed assets is determined by the expense of duplicating them. It is claimed, for instance, that to arrive at a fair valuation of the railroad property of the United States, all we need to do is to figure how much it would cost to reproduce this property under present conditions. The illustration already used, however, would apply in criticism of this second opinion as well.

The third opinion is that the value of fixed assets is determined by their earning power as in the above illustration. It takes no argument to show that this is actually the case in ordinary business practice. If you were going to buy anything in the nature of a fixed asset, from a university education to a steel mill, your first question as a business man would be, How much will this asset earn for me? Similarly, an investor in buying the securities of a corporation will inquire as to the value of the corporation's fixed assets, and will naturally estimate their value on the basis of earnings—not the present earnings altogether, but probable future earnings as well.

Bear in mind that this principle that earnings determine value is applicable only to fixed assets. The selling value of floating assets, such as raw material, tools, finished goods on hand, is another matter. That will be determined, normally, as the science of economics explains, by cost of production. The difference arises from the fact that fixed assets—land, buildings, machinery—are not intended for sale, but for use. They generally have little or no value except for the purpose for which they were intended; and their value for their purpose can be determined only by their earning power.

We have already intimated without going into details that the amount of investors' securities which may be issued by any corporation depends both on the value of its fixed assets and on the amount of its income available for interest charges. There is no contradiction between these two considerations. At bottom the important factor on which to base bond issues of a going concern is the amount and stability of income. We shall elaborate and emphasize this point a little later.

66. *Nature of a mortgage bond.*—The simplest method and the method most common among small corporations of borrowing long-time funds is by direct mortgage on the corporation's real property. An ordinary mortgage conveys "all right, title and interest" in a given piece of property to the mortgagee, with the proviso that the transfer is to become null and void in case principal and interest are paid as promised. Although the old common-law phrases, which would cause the whole property mortgaged to pass to the mortgagee in case of default, are generally retained in the mortgage indenture, yet the mortgage is universally regarded at law as in effect a lien. A simple corporate mortgage is in no important respect different from a mortgage by an individual or firm.

Where large sums of money are to be raised by a mortgage, however, the procedure is not quite so simple. In such a case it is customary to offer mortgage bonds in convenient denominations to the public. As the property mortgaged is for all practical purposes indivisible and as there are a large number of secured bondholders, it is impracticable to give a separate mortgage with each bond. It becomes necessary, therefore, to give the mortgage to some individual or concern, acting as trustee for the bondholders, in which case the mortgage indenture becomes a deed of trust. Each bond is a simple promise to pay, its phrasing being more formal, however, than that of a note. It is executed under corporate seal and contains a reference to the indenture between the corporation and the trustee. A study of the sample mortgage bond printed on page 123, will serve better than a long description to show the reader exactly what is contained in a bond.

The varieties of mortgage bonds will be considered later. For the present let us take up the terms of the deed of trust between the corporation and the trustee.

67. *Essential features of a deed of trust.*—Experience has demonstrated the necessity of making this deed very exact and comprehensive. The indenture of a large railroad mortgage may contain as many as 50,000 to 100,000 words. If printed and bound it would make a good-sized book. Of course, the ordinary industrial corporation would not find so lengthy and involved a description of the property and the terms of the mortgage necessary. To the lay reader even a comparatively simple indenture is apt to seem a mass of cumbersome and more or less nonsensical legal phraseology; but it must be borne in mind that every such deed is closely scanned by a large number of able and experienced lawyers, who will demand that no possible loophole for evasion or misinterpretation shall be left open. The rights and obligations of each of the three parties to the agreement, the corporation, the bondholder and the trustee, must be fully and explicitly set forth and the mortgaged property must be described so exactly that no conflict with other mortgages or obligations can possibly arise. The instruments have now come to follow certain models and are almost always arranged about as follows:

First, of course, come the date and the names of the parties to the indenture. Next follows the preamble, in which is a full statement of the legal status of the corporation, including the state in which it is incorporated, the amount of its capital stock and bonds, the

No........ UNITED STATES OF AMERICA. STATE OF OHIO $1,000

THE COLUMBUS CONSOLIDATED STREET RAILROAD COMPANY

First Mortgage Twenty Year Five per cent Gold Bond

For Value Received, The Columbus Consolidated Street Railroad Company, a corporation organized and existing under the Laws of the State of Ohio and operating street railroads in the City of Columbus, promises to pay to the Central Trust Company of New York, Trustee, or to the bearer or registered owner hereof, One Thousand Dollars, in gold coin of the United States of America, of the present standard, on the first day of July, 1909, and to pay interest thereon at the rate of five per cent per annum from the first day of July, 1889, on the first days of January and July in each year, on the presentation and surrender of the coupons hereto annexed as they severally become due, until said principal sum shall be paid, both principal and interest of this bond being payable at the agency of said Railroad Company in the City of New York. (This bond is subject to redemption on or after July 1st, 1894, at 110 per cent of the par value thereof, with accrued interest, out of a sinking fund of $22,500 a year, beginning with that date as provided in the mortgage herein described.) This bond is one of a series of Eight Hundred bonds, of like tenor, date and amount, numbered consecutively from One to Eight Hundred, both inclusive, and amounting in the aggregate to Eight Hundred Thousand Dollars, which are all equally secured by a mortgage of said Railroad Company in the nature of a conveyance in trust, dated July 1st, 1889, and duly recorded, conveying all the property and franchises of said Railroad Company to said Trust Company, in trust, for the benefit of the holders of said bonds, to all the provisions of which mortgage this bond is subject. In case of default for six months after due demand in payment of any interest on any of said bonds, the principal of all thereof may be declared due, as provided in said mortgage. The principal of this bond may be registered on the books of said Railroad Company at its said agency, and registration thereof noted hereon, after which no transfer thereof shall be valid, except on said books, until after registered transfer to bearer, when the principal of the bond will again become transferable by delivery. The coupons annexed to this bond will always be transferable by delivery. This bond shall not be valid unless authenticated by the Certificate of the trustee of said mortgage.

In Witness Whereof, said Railroad Company has caused its corporate seal to be hereto affixed, and this bond to be subscribed by its President and Secretary, and the name of its Treasurer to be engraved on the several coupons hereto annexed, at the City of Columbus, in the State of Ohio, this first day of July in the year Eighteen Hundred and Eighty-nine.

.... .Secretary. ....President.

[On the back.]

Trustee's Certificate.—The Central Trust Company of New York, Trustee, hereby certifies that this bond is one of the series of Eight Hundred mortgage bonds, described in the mortgage mentioned herein, bearing date the first day of July, 1889.

Central Trust Company of New York, Trustee.
By ... .*Vice-President.*

Notice!—No writing on this Bond, except by an officer of the Company.

Date of Registry.	In Whose Name Registered.	Transfer Agent.

[On the end, forty Coupons, numbered on the back, and dated each first day of January and July, from 1890 to 1909, the face of the first one reading:]

$25. Coupon No. 1.—On the first day of January, 1890, The Columbus Consolidated Street Railroad Company will pay the bearer, at its agency in the City of New York, Twenty-five Dollars, being the semi-annual interest then due on its First Mortgage Bond No...............

E. K. Stenorf, *Treasurer.*

amount and kind of property it owns. The preamble also presents the authority given by the stockholders and directors for the bond issue and the specific purpose of the issue. Then the full texts of the bond, the interest coupon, if it is a coupon bond, and the trustees' certificate of validity, which should appear on each bond (see form on page 123), are given.

The granting clause, which transfers the property to the trustee, and a detailed description of the mortgaged property follow. The duties of the trustee, including the statement that the property is granted only in trust, and a provision that the trustee shall certify to the validity of each bond are next set forth. This is followed by the covenant of the corporation to pay the interest and principal of the bonds at the time specified.

An important section of the mortgage is that which binds the corporation to keep the property insured, pay all taxes, assessments and charges, and in general to preserve the property and keep the lien valid. Another section retains for the company complete control of the mortgaged property and enjoyment of all the profits unless and until default is made of principal or interest.

Where a corporation has subsidiary companies it may be necessary to include a full statement as to the status and securities of each of these companies.

The sections following deal with default and foreclosures. Exactly what constitutes default must be definitely stated. Usually a short period of grace is allowed after interest payments fall due before the trustee can take action. The percentage of bondholders at whose request the trustee shall take active steps is stated, usually 20 or 25 per cent. The percentage of bondholders who must request foreclosure and sale in order to authorize the trustee to proceed to this extent is also given; usually a majority is required. The course of action of the trustee in case of foreclosure and sale is prescribed and the proceedings in case of receivership are set forth.

The responsibilities, liabilities and compensation of the trustee are presented and provision is made for the resignation of the trustee, or his removal upon request of a majority of the bondholders, and for the appointment of his successor.

It is customary, although seemingly hardly necessary, to absolve the officers and directors of the corporation from any personal liability.

In long mortgages there is frequently a separate section in which terms and phrases used in the indenture and open to possible misinterpretation are exactly defined.

At the end appear the signatures and seals of the corporation and of the trustee through their proper officers with formal attestation of the seals.

Frequently modifications of the original document are called for by changes in the legal status of the corporation or trustee or in the corporate property. Such modifications may take the form either of a supplementary indenture or of a supplementary agreement. The latter is less formal and usually relates to comparatively unimportant matters. Supplementary indentures are most common in case of reorganization. They must be authorized by stockholders and bondholders as well as by the two parties directly concerned.

68. *Classification of mortgage deeds of trust.*—Mortgages are conveniently classified as closed, open-end, and limited open-end. A closed mortgage covers a limited amount of bonds all issued at one and the same time and absolutely forbids any additional bonds secured by the

same mortgage. The open-end mortgage authorizes an indefinite amount of bonds, some of which are issued at once and some, under certain restrictions, in the future. This type has so far been restricted to railroad companies. The usual provision is that a given amount of additional bonds may be issued for each additional mile of track constructed.

The limited open-end mortgage, which is the common and for almost all purposes the best type, names a certain maximum amount of bonds to be based on the mortgage, part of which amount is issued at once. The rest may be sold under certain restrictions as to time; usually a given amount may be put out each year. Sometimes there are further restrictions, such as a requirement for the permission of the syndicate which bought the first installment; or the requirement that interest on outstanding bonds be paid for a given period before any new bonds are sold.

The merits of this limited open-end mortgage over either of the other two types are obvious. An absolutely closed mortgage may make it very difficult for a corporation to secure additional funds with which to carry on construction that is essential to its welfare. Possibly the corporation's earnings may thereby be restricted so as to invalidate the bondholders' as well as the stockholders' interests. The open-end mortgage, on the other hand, is too indefinite. The corporation may issue so many bonds under the mortgage and may raise its fixed charges to so high a point as to bring risk or even actual loss to the bondholders. We must not forget in dealing with mortgages and mortgage bonds that in principle the holders of these instruments are supposed to be free from even reasonable risk.

CHAPTER X

TYPES OF CORPORATION BONDS

69. *Classification of bonds.*—This and the following chapter are devoted to enumerating and describing the various types of bonds that are in common use. We would recommend that they be studied with particular care; for ignorance as to the exact nature and uses of each of the bond types named may very easily prove costly both to investors and to corporations. An error that is particularly frequent in small manufacturing corporations is to create a bond issue of a type that is not at all adapted to the financial status and prospects of the corporation. One attentive reading of these two chapters would have prevented many of these errors.

Bonds may be classified with respect to:

(a) The security for their payment,
(b) Their purposes,
(c) The manner of their payment,
(d) The conditions of their redemption.

As these classifications, which should be kept quite distinct, are frequently confused, the writer has made up the following list of the words commonly used in describing bonds, each word being placed under its proper heading:

A.—*Security of Bonds.*

1. First Mortgage,
2. Second Mortgage, Third Mortgage, etc.

3. Terminal, Divisional, Land-Grant, or other Special Mortgage,
4. General Mortgage,
5. Sinking-fund,
6. Collateral Trust,
7. Car or Equipment Trust,
8. Debenture,
9. Income,
10. Participating,
11. Profit-Sharing,
12. Joint,
13. Receivers' Certificates.

B.—*Purposes of Bonds.*

1. Unifying,
2. Refunding,
3. Construction,
4. Purchase-Money,
5. Improvement,
6. Extension,
7. Adjustment,
8. Consolidated.

C.—*Manner of Payment.*

1. Coupon,
2. Registered,
3. Registered as to principal, but dividends in coupon form.

D.—*Conditions of Redemption.*

1. Gold,
2. Redeemable,
3. Serial,
4. Convertible.

70. *Mortgage Bonds.*—A bond secured by a first mortgage on all the real property of a corporation—provided the corporation is stable and prosperous and the bond issue is not large—is regarded as a highly desirable investment. You could infer this from the quotations on the first mortgage bonds of the standard railroads and industrial companies, as shown in the three examples below. It should be noted that none of these three issues is secured by an absolute first mortgage. Such issues are usually small and their prices are hard to determine.

At present prices, Baltimore & Ohio first 4's yield about 4.05 per cent; Western Union first 4's, about 4.45 per cent; and Union Pacific first 4's, about 4.02 per cent.

A debt secured by a bona fide first mortgage cannot be interfered with by any inferior security and, unless the corporation goes into receivers' hands, no security of higher rank can be put out.

It is always possible, of course, to place a second mortgage on the same property covered by the first mortgage and to follow the second mortgage by a third, and a fourth, and so on. It is very seldom possible, however, to find buyers for anything junior to a second mortgage bond. Although bonds derive their value in large part from income, yet as they are nominally based on property, investors do not like junior bonds. Their dislike is not unreasonable, for in case of reorganization the heaviest loss would necessarily fall on the holders of junior securities. Many large corporations have made every effort to give each one of their bond issues, no matter how numerous these issues may be, the appearance of being based on a first mortgage. To this end many ingenious expedients and names have been invented.

For instance, there are many railroad divisional and terminal first mortgage bonds. Sometimes these bonds are based on property highly valuable in itself. Sometimes, however, they are first mortgages on branch lines or on terminal real estate that would be of very little use to any concern except the particular railroad that issues the bonds. In such a case the vaunted priority of the divisional or terminal bond is more or less of a fiction. A railroad could give up the branch line or the terminal real estate far more easily than the bondholders could afford to have the property separated from the railroad.

Another very common practice with both railroads and industrials is to have first mortgage bonds issued by subsidiary companies and then have a nominal first mortgage bond issued by the holding company. The holding company's bond is in reality based only on its holdings of subsidiary companies' securities and is inferior to all the subsidiary company bonds. Various names are given to these junior issues. Sometimes they are called "first and refunding" mortgage bonds, or "first general" mortgage bonds, or "first and unifying." The words "unifying," "consolidated," "refunding," and the like, used in this connection, are intended to signify that the underlying bonds will be retired as they fall due with the proceeds of the new issue. It would perhaps not be just to say that these names are intended to mislead; but at least it may be said that they put the most favorable possible construction on the terms under which the bonds are issued.

71. *Sinking fund bonds.*—In the case of mines and other enterprises which have a pretty definite lease of life it is necessary for the protection of bondholders to

establish a sinking fund for the redemption of mortgage bonds. In such cases the sinking fund is frequently obtained by setting aside a certain portion of the company's income. Lumber companies sometimes reserve a certain amount on each thousand feet of lumber cut and coal mining companies a certain amount on each ton of coal mined. It is more common, however, to set aside a fixed amount each year.

There are three methods of estimating the amount that should be set aside each year. One method is to divide the amount of the debt by the number of years that the debt runs and put into the fund each year the resulting amount. This is simple enough, but decidedly crude. As no account is taken of interest on the sums in the fund, the method ties up an unnecessarily large amount of money. The second method allows whatever is put into the fund to accumulate at compound interest and therefore calls for a much smaller annual payment than the preceding method. The third method is what is known as the installment or annuity method and consists in paying equal periodic installments to the bondholders, or their trustee, to settle principal and interest in a given number of years. It calls for somewhat larger payments than the second method, inasmuch as it takes care not only of the principal, but of the interest as well. A fuller discussion of sinking fund methods is unnecessary, as the subject has been covered in the volume on Accounting Practice.

The sinking fund method of guaranteeing that bond issues will be paid has been much used by industrial corporations, particularly when the permanence of their business is somewhat uncertain and investors consequently are inclined to look upon their securities with suspicion. In such a case it may be an advisable arrangement both for the corporation and for the bondholders. Where the corporation's assets, however, are of a permanent nature, the sinking fund is no longer regarded with favor. The objections to its use are clearly stated in the following selection from Professor E. S. Meade's "Trust Finance."

The sinking fund is of no benefit to the stockholder other than to ultimately decrease the liabilities of the company. During a long period, however, the corporation is under the necessity of paying interest, and at the same time of contributing to the sinking fund. The result of this double contribution is, for perhaps twenty-five years, to compel the stockholder to pay double for the money borrowed. The amount available for dividends is, therefore, reduced, and the stockholder suffers.

It may be argued that the stockholder will eventually receive full compensation for these smaller dividends in the reduction of fixed charges which the sinking fund will eventually bring about; but aside from the fact that it is a hardship for him to wait so long for this reward, there is the further objection that even after the reduction of liabilities by the cancellation of the bond principal, the owners of the company will have made, averaging the periods before and after the retirement of the bonds, smaller profits than if no sinking fund had been gathered. The reason for this permanent reduction of profits by the collection of a sinking fund is as follows: A sinking fund must be invested in securities. It cannot be put into betterments. In the form in which it is accumulated, a low rate of interest from the investment of these annual sums is all that can be expected. The compounding of these annual investments, it is supposed, equals the principal of the bonds at the time of maturity, and the corporation is thereafter freed from a portion of its fixed charges. This gain, however, is in reality a loss to the stockholders. If the money which has gone into the sinking fund had been spent upon improving the property, the stockholders would eventually have received a larger dividend.

It may be assumed that the corporation can earn a higher return on money invested in improving its own property than the return on securities purchased for the sinking fund. Under these circumstances, it is a good policy to devote all surplus funds to increasing the earning power of the company, allowing the debt to run without a special provision for repayment. In other words, by refunding bonds when they mature, and by refusing to make any deductions from profits to provide funds for debt payment, a corporation not only pays a larger dividend, but increases the value of its productive assets more rapidly than the value of its sinking fund would increase during an equal number of years. To put the matter in still another way, the accumulation of a sinking fund by a corporation decreases the proportion of debt to value of property less rapidly than when the annual amount of the sinking fund is invested in the equipment.[1]

For the larger corporations the sinking fund is usually in charge of a special trustee acting for the bondholders. With smaller corporations, however, it is customary to allow the sinking fund to remain in the custody of the corporation.

72. *Collateral trust bonds.*—With the growth of large holding companies a modified form of mortgage bond has come to be widely used. It is called a "collateral trust" bond because it is based on the securities of other companies owned by the bond-issuing corporation and deposited with a trustee as collateral security for the bondholders. The securities are covered by a deed of trust just as in the case of real property offered as security. The securities may consist either of stocks or of bonds of subsidiary companies or of a combination of both.

It would seem at first sight that a collateral trust bond would not be worth much, especially when the collateral

1 *Trust Finance,* pp. 241–243.

consists of stock. In such a case the collateral trust bond would be junior by several degrees to all underlying bonds of the subsidiary companies. In case any of the subsidiary companies go into bankruptcy and force the holding company to default, all that the trustee for the collateral trust bondholders can do is to take the stock posted as collateral. When he gets the stock he still is a long distance from having tangible property with which to satisfy the demands of the bondholders. Even when the collateral consists of bonds they are usually junior issues and the collateral trust bondholders in case of default are very uncertain as to getting possession of real property.

Nevertheless, collateral trust bonds are sold at high prices. The Northern Pacific-Great Northern collateral trust 4's, which are secured by the deposit of Chicago, Burlington & Quincy Railroad Company stock, have steadily sold close to par. Many other similar issues are well thought of in the financial district. One reason is that the income, out of which interest on the collateral trust bonds is paid, is derived from the interest and dividends on the collateral, and these latter returns are more regular than are railroad or industrial profits. A second reason is that securities, if they are worth anything at all, are almost always readily salable, whereas real property, even if its cost and value are high, is apt to prove unmarketable. Hence, the collateral trust bonds have great advantages in these respects which in the eyes of the financial public often outweigh their obvious disadvantages.

Strange as it may seem, it is not impossible for a holding company with subsidiaries, whose credit is poor, to take the stocks and bonds of these companies, post them as collateral and sell the collateral trust bonds very readily. It is not unnatural to feel a passing doubt as to the sanity of the financial world when one discovers that a promise to pay based on real property is less valuable than a promise to pay based on paper that is itself based on the same real property. Yet after all there is a sound reason for this apparent absurdity. Real property is hard to sell; paper representatives of property may be easily sold. Collateral trust bonds are therefore frequently excellent means of raising funds for subsidiary companies without much credit of their own.

They are also very useful at times in financing the process of buying control of subsidiary companies. The holding company borrows money from the banks and buys securities; then it issues collateral trust bonds based on these securities and with the funds thus obtained pays off the bank loans. Thus it finds itself with very little expenditure of its own funds in full control of the company whose stocks it has bought. Some companies have repeated this simple process time and time again. It is entirely legitimate, though somewhat risky.

To protect the bondholders, collateral trust mortgages generally provide against the issue of any securities by subsidiary companies ahead of those deposited as collateral. The mortgages also frequently have clauses to prevent unfavorable leases or other misuse of property represented by the deposited securities.

A further study of this type of bond belongs in the subject of investments rather than here. Enough has been said to indicate how a holding company may, by means of collateral trust bonds, borrow funds which it would probably be impossible for the subsidiary companies to reach.

73. *Equipment trust bonds.*—This form of bond is not used to any extent by other than railroad companies.

The equipment used as security for a bond issue of this kind does not belong to the railroad company at all. The manufacturers of the equipment usually turn it over to an intermediary company, which in turn leases it to the railroad, generally for a term of ten years or less, and hands over the lease to the trustee of the equipment trust bondholders. The railroad pays to the trustee the purchase price of the equipment in equal installments, together with interest on unpaid installments. When the payment is complete, the lease is cancelled and the title to the equipment passes to the railroad company.

In the meantime, in order to pay the manufacturers the intermediary company issues bonds to about 80 or 90 per cent of the cash value of the equipment. The bonds are in serial form so that as fast as purchase money is received from the railroad it may be devoted to their redemption, and the series is so arranged that when the last payment by the railroad is made the last bonds are redeemed.

The form of an equipment trust bond is given on page 137, and the following extract from the prospectus of one of the early intermediary companies in this field will further explain the working of this ingenious plan.

The business of the Railroad Equipment Company is to lease and conditionally sell on what is known as the Car Trust plan, to railroad and other corporations directly connected therewith, certain needed Rolling Stock.

A cash payment ranging from 10 per cent to as high even as 50 per cent is made at the outset, and the principal and interest of the balance due, represented by the promissory notes of the Corporation, maturing at fixed intervals over a term of years, is secured by a first lien or mortgage on the said Rolling Stock,

Series B132. $1,000 No. 0000.

THE RAILROAD EQUIPMENT COMPANY.*

Special Car Trust Loan of $375,000.

NEW YORK, APRIL 2ND, 1888.

For Value Received, THE RAILROAD EQUIPMENT COMPANY promises to pay to the bearer, or if this bond be registered, then to the registered holder hereof, ONE THOUSAND DOLLARS, on the First Day of April, 1896, with interest at the rate of Six per cent per annum, payable semi-annually, on the surrender of the coupons attached hereto, at the office of the Company in the City of New York, or E. W. Clark & Co. in the City of Philadelphia. This obligation is one of Series B132, bearing even date herewith, to the aggregate amount of $375,000 which are secured by a pledge or mortgage made by this Company to the Farmers' Loan and Trust Company, in trust, for the benefit of the holders of these obligations, of a lease of railroad equipment and rolling stock, under date of February 15th, 1888, made by this Company to the Atlantic and Pacific Railroad Company.

Said Lease is hereby specifically pledged as security for the payment of the series of obligations of which this is one, when and as they shall be or become due and payable, and in the order of their respective maturities, according to the terms set out in the pledge or mortgage made by this Company to the Farmers' Loan and Trust Company.

After registration, this bond is transferable only on the book kept by this Company or by its agent for this purpose. Such transfer to be noted by endorsement on this bond.

On presentation of this bond for registration, the coupons thereon shall be cut off and cancelled by this Company, and interest on this bond shall be thereafter payable only to the registered holder thereof.

.................................*Treasurer.* ....*President.*

[On the back.]

TRUSTEE'S CERTIFICATE.— This obligation is one of Series B132, bearing date April 2nd, 1888, which are secured by a pledge or mortgage made by The Railroad Equipment Company to the Farmers' Loan and Trust Company, in trust for the benefit of the holders of the said obligations, amounting to Three Hundred and Seventy-five Thousand Dollars, of a Lease of Railroad Equipment and Rolling Stock under date of February 15th, 1888, made by the Railroad Equipment Company to the Atlantic and Pacific Railroad Company.

THE FARMERS' LOAN AND TRUST COMPANY,

New York, April 2nd, 1888. by ....*President.*

DATE OF REGISTRY.	IN WHOSE NAME REGISTERED.	TRANSFER AGENT.

[On the end, fifteen Coupons, dated each first day of April and October, from April, 1889, to October, 1896, the face of the first one reading:]

Coupon No. 1. Series B132. $30.— The Railroad Equipment Company will pay to bearer, on April 1st, 1889, at the Banking House of Post, Martin & Co., in the City of New York, or of E. W. Clark & Co., in the City of Philadelphia, Thirty Dollars, being six months' interest on Bond No. 0000.

H. A. V. POST, *Treasurer.*

the whole of which remains as such security until the last note is paid.

These deferred payments extend over a period ranging from four to ten years, and during such periods and until the final payment is made and all the provisions of the Car Trust Contract have been fully complied with, the conditional purchaser uses the Rolling Stock as *lessee* only, and subject to the legal rights of the lessor, in whom the title to the property remains fixed and inalienable and unaffected by any liens or indebtedness of any kind of the lessee.

The lessee is also bound by the contract to keep the Rolling Stock in proper repair, to replace it if destroyed, and to hold it at all times subject to the inspection (it being readily identified, not only by the road numbers, but by the ownership plates invariably attached to each locomotive or car) of the lessor, by whom and for whose benefit it is fully insured.

In case of default of any of the payments, or of non-performance of the other provisions of the contract, the lessor has the legal right, not only fully recognized and confirmed by the United States Courts, but also protected by direct legislation in many of the States, to take immediate possession of the Rolling Stock wherever it may be, or however in use, to sell it at public or private sale, and to apply the proceeds to the payment of any indebtedness arising under the contract, whether matured or not, and in cases where a Receiver is appointed, the rule of the Courts is to order him to pay the Car Trust notes as they mature, rather than lose the use of the Rolling Stock and the benefit of the payment already made on it.

The securities arising under these Car Trusts are assigned to a Trust Company, and are held by it in trust, as security for certain Bonds of The Railroad Equipment Company issued against the same.

The holder of these Bonds has therefore as his security:

The direct obligation of the Railroad Equipment Company.

The direct obligations maturing at specified dates, generally monthly or quarterly, of the Corporation, the lessee of the Rolling Stock.

> The absolute ownership of such Rolling Stock which is kept in repair, insured, and replaced if destroyed, and the first cost of which, already reduced by the cash payment at the outset, is being steadily still further reduced by the periodical payment made by the lessee.

The security behind bonds of this character is excellent. In the first place, no railroad has ever yet defaulted on an equipment trust bond issue, because to do so would mean a loss of its equipment. All through the railroad receiverships of the 90's the receivers paid the interest and principal on these bonds regularly. In the second place, the railroad merely leases the equipment until the last payment is made and in case of default, therefore, no legal process is necessary in order to enable the trustee to take physical possession of the property. The leases usually provide that the equipment is to be kept in good repair.

In effect this form of security is a kind of chattel mortgage. From the railroad corporation standpoint it is open to the usual objection against chattel mortgages, namely, that it pledges a semi-fixed asset under a short term obligation which must be met at all hazards. It may well happen that the railroad, in order to meet this obligation, will have to part with funds necessary in order to meet other fixed charges. The best managed railroad corporations use these instruments with great caution. One reason for their existence is that many existing first and second mortgages on railroad property have what is called an "after-acquired property" clause, which makes the mortgage extend over all the property that the railroad owns at the time of making the mortgage and all that it acquires thereafter. Under this clause a straight mortgage on equipment would not be a first lien. The lease is the method by which this difficulty is overcome.

The market for equipment trust bonds is narrow, partly because the public does not thoroughly understand them and partly because the issues are relatively small. They are largely bought by banks, insurance companies and other financial institutions desiring to invest their reserve funds to the best advantage. The average yield on equipment trust bonds is considerably better than on ordinary mortgage bonds and their safety is almost perfect.

The principle of the equipment trust bonds is not applied to any considerable extent in industrial corporations and with very few exceptions it would be highly inadvisable for such corporations to buy equipment in this manner.

CHAPTER XI

TYPES OF CORPORATION BONDS (CONTINUED)

74. *Debenture bonds.*—There are two different uses of the word debenture which are somewhat confusing. In law any instrument which formally acknowledges a debt and promises payment, including any written bond secured or unsecured, is a debenture. In finance, however, the term has come to be restricted to a bond which is not secured by a lien upon any specific property. In other words, it is for all practical purposes, simply an unsecured promissory note running for a number of years. Being unsecured, the debenture bond, in case of insolvency, is legally on the same level as the general floating indebtedness of the insolvent corporation.

The debenture is much used in the financing of English corporations. Indeed, our American mortgage bond, in the case of railroads at least, is there almost unknown. It is used so largely because the English investors realize clearly that the earnings of the railroad after all are their actual security. As has already been pointed out, the holders of a railroad mortgage in case of foreclosure seldom take the physical property which legally belongs to them, because to separate any portion of a railroad's property from the rest is to diminish and perhaps destroy its value. Logically, therefore, the English custom is right and the American custom is wrong. In practice, however, it is probable that the American railroad managers have borrowed more funds on better terms than have the English railroad managers. An

English railroad corporation has only one kind of a bond—the simple debenture—to offer; an American railroad corporation may offer, as we have seen, an indefinite variety of mortgage bonds, each bond being secured by a lien on some part or section of the railroad property. The American junior bond, for that reason, looks better to the average investor than the English junior bond, and is more readily salable. Notice that this statement says "looks better," not "is better." If all American railroad mortgage bonds were to be exchanged for simple debentures arranged in the order of their priority, investors would be as well off as they are now.

Under the present system, however, the existing debenture bonds are for the most part far inferior in security and investment standing to mortgage bonds. Indeed, it would hardly be correct to call any of the present railroad debenture bonds, with a few notable exceptions, investments at all in the technical sense of that word, as previously defined.

If debenture bonds are so far inferior to mortgage bonds and therefore so much less attractive to investors, why issue them at all? There are several possible reasons. In the first place, a company may have reached its limit, so far as mortgage borrowings are concerned; it may have nothing of any great value left on which first and second mortgages have not already been placed. Third mortgages are so unpopular with investors that a simple debenture may be more easily sold.

Sometimes debenture bonds are created when a bankrupt railroad company is reorganized. The reorganizers may desire to lighten the load of mortgages that previously weighed down the company and perhaps caused its bankruptcy. In the general scaling down of the mortgage securities—a subject which we shall consider in detail when we take up reorganization—the junior mortgage issues are often replaced by debentures. This is the origin of most of our present railroad debentures.

A third possible reason may be that a conservative corporation is anxious to reserve some of its resources for future mortgage issues. Suppose a railroad, for instance, already has a first mortgage on all its property and desires to borrow a comparatively small additional sum. If it places a second mortgage on its property it will have used up much of its remaining borrowing capacity. If it issues simple debentures, however, it will still have a second mortgage to fall back upon. Usually debenture bonds issued under such circumstances are accompanied by an agreement between the corporation and the bondholders to the effect that if any new issue of mortgage bonds is subsequently put out the debenture bondholders shall be secured by the same mortgage as the new bondholders.

A fourth reason that has at times led to the issue of debenture bonds is that they are intended to be sold to European investors, among whom, as has already been stated, such bonds are highly regarded. In the reorganization of the Wabash Railroad Company in 1887, for instance, certain issues which are actually secured as to principal by a third mortgage were nevertheless given the name of "debenture bonds, Series A," because they were intended for English investors.

In this country the most successful railroad debenture bond issues are those of the New England railroads, for the obvious reason that the earnings of these roads are not only large, but particularly stable. The Boston and Maine R. R. Co. has outstanding four mortgage bond issues and seven debenture issues. All of the debenture bond issues commanded good prices and were considered sound investments. The earnings of this company have averaged six or seven times interest charges. Similarly the New York, New Haven and Hartford R. R. Co. has six issues of debenture bonds outstanding in addition to numerous issues of mortgage bonds of subsidiary companies. The net earnings of this company have been more than three and one-half times the interest charges. The practice of issuing debenture bonds seems to be gradually gaining favor among American railroads, and a number of lines have adopted the policy of replacing mortgage issues when they mature by simple debenture issues. The debenture bond is not much used by industrial corporations, however. These corporations do not usually have the confidence of investors and the stability of earning power which are necessary to make debenture bond issues successful.

75. *Income bonds.*—The income bond is a hybrid, partaking of the nature of both bonds and stock. As the name implies, the payment of interest charges can be demanded only when there is sufficient income for that purpose; if the interest charges are not earned they need not be paid. The principal, however, is usually secured by a mortgage. If there is no such mortgage, as happens in one or two cases, the word bond is a misnomer. For all practical purposes such an "income bond," so-called, is preferred stock without voting power.

Income bonds are usually the product of reorganization and are designed to take the place of junior mortgage bond issues which it is thought necessary to scale. Their advantage lies in the fact that they do not impose any fixed interest charges on the corporation. However, there is a great disadvantage in the fact that the principal is secured by mortgage and that therefore new mortgage bond issues in the future are hard to float. Another disadvantage is that there is apt to be dispute between the corporation and the bondholders as to whether the interest charges are actually earned or not. This objection can be obviated in part by inserting in the bond such a detailed statement of the method by which net income is to be determined as is given in the sample income bond shown on pages 146 and 147. The new system of railroad accounting under the Interstate Commerce Commission will probably aid in the settlement of this question in connection with railroad companies. For an example of the difficulties inherent in income bonds see the case of the Central of Georgia Railway Company cited in Chapter XXVII.

76. *Other types of bonds.*—The name of "participating bonds," is almost self-explanatory. A bond of this class usually gets a fixed rate of interest and in addition a share of whatever profits are earned by its underlying security. The best known issue of this kind was the Oregon Short Line participating 4's issued in 1903 and retired the next year, which were secured by all the stock of the Northern Securities Company, amounting to $82,-491,000 in the Oregon Short Line treasury. These bonds were to receive not only the regular 4 per cent. but whatever dividends over 4 per cent were declared on the collateral stock.

Profit-sharing bonds, which are infrequently issued, usually entitle the bondholder to get back his principal with the agreed interest and also to share in whatever increase in the value of the underlying assets may take place before the retirement of the bonds.

Joint bonds are direct obligations of two or more cor-

$500 UNITED STATES OF AMERICA. $500

ATCHISON, TOPEKA AND SANTA FE RAILROAD COMPANY.

No............ FIVE PER CENT INCOME GOLD BOND.

For Value Received, THE ATCHISON, TOPEKA AND SANTA FE RAILROAD COMPANY promises to pay to bearer, or in case of registration to the registered holder hereof, the sum of FIVE HUNDRED DOLLARS, on the first day of July, one thousand nine hundred and eighty-nine, together with interest thereon when earned at the rate of not exceeding five per centum per annum, payable only out of surplus net earnings, if any, on the first day of September, in the year 1890, and upon the same day in each year hereafter, on the presentation and surrender of the coupons annexed and to be annexed hereto, as they severally mature, both principal and interest being payable in gold coin of the United States of America, of the present standard of weight and fineness, or its equivalent, at the agencies of the said Atchison Company in the Cities of Boston or New York, or at the office of Baring Brothers & Company, London, England. The principal of this bond is payable only after the principal and interest of all the General Mortgage four per cent Bonds of the Atchison, Topeka and Santa Fe Railroad Company, dated July first, 1889, shall have been previously paid in full. Interest upon the principal sum of this Income Bond, if any is earned in any year ending June thirtieth, shall be paid upon the first day of September following, at a rate not to exceed five per centum per annum, from and out of the surplus net earnings only of the mortgaged property, provided that in the judgment of the Board of Directors of the Atchison Company such surplus net earnings shall be sufficient in amount to justify payment of interest on this Income Bond, and such payment shall be by said Board of Directors authorized to be so made. Such interest shall not be cumulative, and each successive holder of this Income Bond accepts the same subject to the agreement that the Board of Directors of the Atchison Company shall in their absolute discretion determine what are the surplus net earnings, if any, in any year ending June thirtieth, and applicable to such payment of interest, by deducting from the amount of the gross earnings during said year all operating expenses of every kind, and all fixed charges, including rentals of leased lines and other property, interest of all kinds, and taxes of all companies whose stocks are directly or indirectly pledged or mortgaged hereunder, and after providing for and deducting the amount of the interest upon and the sinking fund requirements of all bonds or obligations of the Atchison Company, including the above described General Mortgage Bonds, and of all bonds or obligations of other companies, the payment of the principal or interest of which has been guaranteed or assumed in whole or in part by the said Atchison Company, and after providing for and deducting the cost of the maintenance, renewals, repairs and improvements of the railroad, telegraph equipment, and appurtenances of the Atchison Company, and of the railroads which at the date hereof or during the life of said Income Bonds may form a part of the railroad system of the Atchison Company. The Atchison Company may at any time at its pleasure redeem this bond at its face or par value by giving notice of said proposed redemption six months prior to the first day of September in any year by publication once a week for three successive weeks in any newspaper of general circulation published in each of the cities of Boston, New York and London; and interest upon this bond, when so called for redemption, shall cease on and after the first day of September following such publication. All the provisions of the said General Mortgage are hereby expressly declared to be part of this bond and of every coupon hereto attached. No recourse shall be had for the payment of the principal or interest of this bond to any stock holder, officer or director of said Atchison Company, either directly or through the said Atchison Company, by virtue of any statute or by the enforcement of any assessment or otherwise. All payments upon this bond of both principal and interest are to be made without deduction for any tax or taxes which said railroad company may be required to pay or to retain therefrom by any present or future laws of the United States of America or any of the States and Territories thereof, said railroad company hereby covenanting and agreeing to pay any and all such tax or taxes. This bond is one of a series of Income Bonds, coupon and registered, of like tenor and date, the payment of which is secured by a General Mortgage or deed of trust, duly executed and delivered by the Atchison, Topeka and Santa Fe Railroad Company, the obligor, to the Union Trust Company of New York, Trustee, bearing date October fifteenth, 1889. This bond shall pass by delivery, or if registered, by transfer upon the transfer books of the Company. After registration of ownership, certified hereon by the transfer agent of the Company, the coupons shall remain negotiable; but no transfer of this bond, except on the books of the Company, shall be valid unless the last transfer is to bearer, which shall restore transferability by delivery, and it shall continue subject to successive registrations and transfers to bearer as aforesaid at the option of each holder; or the holder may, at any time, at his option, surrender this bond and the annexed coupons to the Company to be cancelled, and receive in exchange therefor a registered bond of the same issue, and thereafter it shall not be transferable to bearer, but the interest shall be paid to the registered holder. This bond shall be valid only when authenticated by the certificate hereon of the said Trustee, or its successor in said trust, that it is one of the Income Bonds issued under and described in the said indenture of trust or general mortgage.

In Witness whereof, The said Atchison Company has caused its corporate seal to be hereto affixed and these presents to be signed by its Comptroller or a Deputy Comptroller, and attested by an Assistant Treasurer, on this first day of July, 1889.

Atchison, Topeka and Santa Fe Railroad Company,

Attest........................*Assistant Treasurer.* By........................*Comptroller.*

No. .... $ ....

NEW YORK, WEST SHORE AND BUFFALO RAILWAY COMPANY.

Receivers' Certificate of Indebtedness.

This is to certify, that the bearer hereof is entitled to receive from Horace Russell and Theodore Houston, and their successors, as Receivers of the property of the New York, West Shore and Buffalo Railway Company, covered by the first mortgage to the United States Trust Company of New York, as Trustee, but not personally, the sum of .... dollars, upon the production hereof, and endorsement hereon of such payments on or before the first day of July, 1887, at the office of said Receivers in the City of New York, and interest thereon from the date hereof, at the rate of six per centum per annum, payable on the first days of each January and July, unless said sum and interest thereon, as aforesaid, be sooner paid by the Receivers out of the moneys coming into their hands from time to time, applicable thereto, or the moneys realized by them upon the sale of the mortgaged property in their hands. This Certificate is one of a series of certificates, amounting in the aggregate to a sum not to exceed five million dollars, and issued or to be issued under the authority and by virtue of the order of the Supreme Court of the State of New York, and under the authority and by virtue of the order of the Circuit Court of the United States for the District of New Jersey, in equity, and for the purposes and objects therein mentioned, said orders being made on the .... days of June, 1884, respectively in actions in said courts, wherein United States Trust Company of New York is plaintiff and complainant, and said railway company is defendant. Said certificates to the amount secured thereby are hereby declared to be a debt of the Receivers incurred for the benefit and protection of the mortgaged property in their hands, and until full payment thereof, to be a lien and charge thereon prior to the first mortgage and the interest thereon. This Certificate is not valid until countersigned by Franklin E. Worcester, Treasurer of the Receivers.

In witness whereof, we, as Receivers aforesaid, but not personally, have signed this Certificate this .... day of ...., one thousand eight hundred and eighty-

porations which join in issuing them. A well-known example is the Northern Pacific-Great Northern issue of joint collateral trust 4's. Somewhat the same effect is gained when a holding company guarantees a subsidiary company bond issue.

A corporate security which should be mentioned here, although it is not, strictly speaking, a bond, is a receivers' certificate. This represents money expended by the receivers of an insolvent corporation under authority of the court, as shown in the sample given on page 148. They constitute a claim on the property of the corporation superior to all other claims whatsoever. They go ahead of the first mortgage bonds. They do not, of course, usually exist in large quantities and a reorganized corporation will endeavor to refund and pay them off as quickly as possible. It is well to bear in mind, however, that in the case of an insolvent corporation this kind of a security may be used as a last resort when funds could hardly be secured in any other manner.

77. *Purposes, manner of payment, and conditions of redemption of bonds.*—The descriptive words applied to bonds indicating their purposes are almost all self-explanatory. "Unifying," "refunding," "adjustment" and "consolidated" imply that the previous bond issues are to be retired or rearranged in some way. "Construction," "improvement" and "extension" show that the funds secured from the bond issue are to be expended in some kind of development. "Purchase-money" bonds are sold before the property on which they are based is actually bought. Usually the funds secured by the sale of the bonds are turned over to a trustee to be held until certain specific property is purchased. Then the funds are paid out by the trustee and he receives in return a first mortgage on the property.

A registered bond is issued to an individual in the same manner as a certificate of stock and ownership can be transferred only on the books of the company. Interest is paid by checks which are sent out to the registered owner. Coupon bonds are usually payable to bearer and interest payments are represented by coupons attached to the bond, as indicated in the bond forms given on pages 123 and 137. When the interest date approaches, the coupon is detached from the bond and deposited in a bank just as a check on the corporation would be deposited. In fact, the coupons are practically simply post-dated checks. Sometimes coupon bonds are registered as to principal, in which case transfer of ownership is not made simply by delivery, but must pass through the books of the company. The interest coupons, however, are payable to bearer. Frequently an issue of bonds may be either coupon or registered at the option of the buyers.

There are obvious advantages in each form. The coupon form is very convenient, inasmuch as it may readily be sold or hypothecated. The registered form makes up in safety what it lacks in convenience. If it is lost or stolen it can be negotiated only by a forgery of the signature of the person in whose name it stands, in which case the transfer would not be valid. When a coupon bond is lost or stolen and is once sold to an innocent purchaser for value, the original owner must stand the loss.

A gold bond is one which specifies that payment of principal and interest shall be made in gold coin. If there is no such provision it is understood that legal tender will be acceptable. There have been times in the history of the United States, notably during the periods of greenback inflation and of free silver agitation, when this gold coin provision was regarded as highly important. At present not a great deal of attention is given to it.

Redeemable bonds are those which may be redeemed at the option of the corporation before date of maturity. Sometimes the selection of the particular bonds to be redeemed is made by lot and the terms of redemption are made attractive with a view to appealing to investors with a speculative twist of mind. The wisdom of issuing redeemable bonds is questionable. It introduces an element of chance which makes it very difficult to figure mathematically their exact value and which probably tends to depress their market price.

Serial bonds are redeemable in series extending over a term of years.

78. *Convertible bonds.*—This is a type of security that was revived a number of years ago, and has since become increasingly popular. It may be changed or converted under certain conditions into some other kind of security—usually into stock. The privilege of conversion may belong to any kind of a bond, mortgage, debenture, collateral trust or income. The usual arrangement is to permit a mortgage bond to be exchanged for preferred stock of the issuing corporation at a prescribed rate of exchange and within a certain definite period.

For instance, the Union Pacific Railroad issued in 1901, $100,000,000, of 4 per cent bonds which were convertible into common stock at par. As Union Pacific common sold in 1907 and 1908, at an average price much higher than par, practically all of this issue was converted long before the expiration of the time limit set.

The advantage of this scheme is that it gives bonds a speculative, in addition to their investment, value. The buyer figures that he gets as safe an investment security as he would have if there were no such privilege and in addition he may share, if he chooses, in any great upward movement of the stock. The privilege of convertibility enables the company to borrow at a lower rate of interest. A further advantage, from the corporation's standpoint, is that the company if successful may expect to be relieved by the process of conversion of the payment of interest on the bonds. Thus room will be made for additional future issues of bonds, if such issues are regarded as necessary.

From the investor's point of view the advantages of convertible bonds are summed up in a circular by Mr. Henry Hall issued in March, 1909. Notice that this circular recommends the bonds to the semi-investing rather than to the strictly investing public.

Convertible bonds belong to the sounder class of speculative investments, combining a reasonable degree of safety and certainty of interest return, with possibilities of substantial enhancement in value. Investors make from 25 to 50 per cent profit, sometimes more, on convertible bonds when properly bought.

Convertible bonds were first issued in this country forty and fifty years ago, when the financing of even the most promising of American railroads and at a high rate of interest was a difficult matter, and when it was occasionally necessary to offer special inducements to ensure the success of a new loan. Most of the financing of St. Paul, for instance, for twenty years or more after 1860, was accomplished through the issue of this class of bonds. It is said that as late as 1896, there were yet outstanding twelve separate convertible issues of the St. Paul. From 1880 to 1900, few or no issues of convertibles were made; but the requirements of the railroads then became so imperative and the multiplicity of competing issues became so great, that in 1900 and 1901 the convertible idea was once more resorted to.

In a general way, convertible bonds tend always to follow the price of the stock for which they are exchanged. This tendency is clearly exhibited by the quotations in this circular. Their fluctuations in price are therefore more lively than those of staid first mortgage and other strong issues. An ordinary bond of good standing seldom moves more than 5 to 10 points from year to year, while convertibles are apt to fluctuate from 10 to 30 points in a single twelve months. The ERIE 4s, Series A, fell from 109⅞ in one year to 46½ in the next and then rose to 80½.

Convertible bonds are always a direct obligation of the company. Some of these issues are secured by mortgage. Others are not, but this latter fact does not necessarily impair their value. It merely suggests a careful scrutiny of general conditions and the business of the company before buying them.

Of course there are corresponding disadvantages. The stockholder may well say that if the company is going to be successful it would be far better to let the bonds stand and thus save more of the income for the stockholders. On the other hand, if the company is not successful, the bonds will not be converted into stock. The stockholder sees loss for himself in either alternative. This would perhaps be an unanswerable argument, if it were not for the fact that the bonds are almost always offered at less than market prices to stockholders, so that the holders of convertible bonds and the holders of stock are likely to be the same persons; or at least the stockholder gets a valuable privilege in the form of a right to subscribe to the bond issues.

CHAPTER XII

CORPORATE PROMOTION—THE NEW ENTERPRISE

79. *The function of a promoter.*—A promoter is a man who organizes a new business and sets it going. The business need not necessarily take the form of a corporation. It may be handled as a partnership or a joint stock company. As new enterprises at the present time, if of any magnitude, are almost always conducted by corporations, however, it will be convenient and not far from the truth to speak as if the work of a promoter were confined to organizing and financing corporations.

The promoter is necessary because the great mass of the funds used in large corporate enterprises is passive; that is to say, the owners of investment funds are not primarily engaged in buying and handling business enterprises. They wait until a good proposition is presented to them. The function of the promoter, therefore, is to bring his proposition to the attention of the owners of funds in such a manner as to arouse their interest and confidence and induce them to buy the securities of his new corporation.

The word promotion has a tinge of discredit attached to it, partly because the promoter, from the very nature of his work, is apt to be over-sanguine and a little careless as to exact accuracy, and partly because the high-sounding word promotion is used by many swindlers who prey upon ignorant and foolish speculators.

One of these last mentioned gentry describes his operations in the following words:

> To-day THE PROMOTER—the 20th Century genii—takes an existent business enterprise, and, for every five dollars it *annually* earns, gives it *immediately* ninety-five dollars. He takes an Opportunity—an intangible, impalpable thing—and from it creates an *actuality*, a vigorous growing enterprise that showers wealth and happiness on thousands. He takes apparently irreconcilable interests, waves his promotion wand above them, and presto! they become associated by the bands of common interest; loyal to a single standard. Over business men he throws a mantle that protects their private means against bankruptcy, litigation or ruin. He carries a veritable Aladdin's Lamp—the Lamp of Knowledge, the Lamp of Power, through which he conjures opportunities into actualities, small businesses into large. His powers, legitimately employed, upbuild industry. Literally, in service to humanity, he stands with powers as beneficent as those exhibited by the Good Genii of our childhood tales.

The end of this quotation, when applied to men whose sole object is to draw into their own pockets as much as they can of the savings of their credulous victims, is sufficiently absurd. But when it is restricted to the true promoter, a man whose judgment and business instincts are sound and whose persuasive powers are used to secure funds for a legitimate business enterprise, the statements are not at all exaggerated. The promoter does, in fact, perform highly important tasks and often richly deserves the great rewards which fall to his share. Many of the great business men of America are promoters—though, as noted in the next chapter, such men do not usually spend all, or even most, of their energies in promotion. To this class belonged the men who between 1900 and 1907 formed great industrial "trusts," including H. H. Rogers, John W. Gates, D. G. Reid, W. H. Moore. Closely allied with them were financiers like J. P. Morgan, E. H. Harriman, George F. Baker and James Stillman.

80. *"Discovery" of a proposition.*—A promoter in handling an enterprise has three separate tasks before him. First, he must "discover" his proposition; second, he must "assemble" it; third, he must "finance" it.

The discovery of a proposition does not mean simply to find it, but includes a thorough investigation into all the surrounding conditions, and the solution in advance of all the difficult problems that are likely to arise in its development. Let us suppose, for instance, that a new invention which looks good on the surface is brought to the attention of a promoter. If he understands his business he will first of all examine critically every factor that points toward the invention's success or failure. He will find out whether it is patented and just what features the patent covers. If it is not patented, he will make sure, through a competent patent attorney, that the device is actually new and patentable. If he is prudent he will probably instruct the attorney to find out whether any similar invention is used in foreign countries or not. Next, he will consider whether other devices are in use which perhaps accomplish the same purpose as well or nearly as well as the invention. After making sure that the invention is what it purports to be, he will consider the possible markets for the article. The invention may be a new machine that could be used in only a few concerns, and perhaps these concerns would prefer to retain their present machines rather than expend any great amount of money for something new. In this connection the promoter will have to find out whether any incidental expenses are necessary in connection with the use of the invention. Generally speaking, the slighter the change from current methods, the more readily the invention may be marketed. The amount of advertising and selling expense called for must also be taken into account.

Next, the promoter takes up the cost of manufacturing. He finds out whether new and specially constructed machinery is necessary in manufacturing the invention, and whether any especial skill on the part of laborers is required. He considers the amount of experiment that will be necessary in order to perfect the invention and in addition figures a large amount of extra cost for unforeseen contingencies.

These are only a few of the factors that the promoter would investigate before taking any further action. Their number is sufficient to indicate, however, that any promoter who has a reputation to make or preserve, cannot afford to jump hastily at whatever proposition is presented to him. The process of discovery may take a long time, perhaps months or even years.

The case just cited is comparatively simple. Where a promoter is dealing with such an enterprise as a new railroad or a new mine or with a consolidation of manufacturing plants, he is confronted by a far more complicated situation. If the investigation is thorough and searching, the promoter will be able to give a well-grounded and satisfactory answer to every question that prospective buyers may raise.

81. *"Assembling" a proposition.*—By assembling a proposition is meant the process of getting temporary control into the hands of the promoter. If he is dealing with an invention, he assembles the proposition by getting an option on the invention or by making an agreement with the inventor on a royalty basis. In the case of a consolidation of plants or railroads into a new corporation, assembling is frequently much more compli-

cated and difficult. In such a case the promoter may have to get options or arrange the terms of purchase with every plant and perhaps with all the different classes of security-holders involved. Unless a promoter has these agreements or options in his own hands, it is as a rule foolish for him to go ahead with any further efforts. He might complete his arrangements for putting the new corporation on its feet and then find that in the meantime the original owners of the property had sold to other parties or had taken steps that would diminish the value of the property. Or he might find that after forming the corporation and bringing the owners of the funds and the owners of the property together, they would mutually agree to dispense with his services and would leave him, so far as his compensation is concerned, out in the cold.

82. *Financing a proposition—The initial development.*—Now we come to the most difficult part of the promoter's work, his financing of the new corporation. No hard and fast rules can be laid down to cover the promoter's procedure. There are some general principles, however, which apply to all enterprises and which should always be kept in mind.

First, it is advisable in practically every case to develop the proposition as far as possible with the promoter's own resources and those of his immediate friends before it is presented to outsiders. In making this statement it is assumed, of course, that the promoter really has faith in his proposition and is willing to take whatever risk is involved in developing it; otherwise the promoter will naturally spend as little as possible of his own money. In the case of an invention, for instance, which the promoter is trying to finance, it is far better to have the invention actually manufactured and a few of the articles on exhibition before any attempt is made to interest outside capital. If this is impossible, a working model at least should be on hand. The average capitalist is not likely to part with his money unless he sees before him something more tangible and impressive than a verbal description of what the inventor expects his as yet unborn machine to accomplish.

If a promoter is financing, let us say, a copper mine, he should do his utmost to have the ore bodies opened up and mining operations started, even if only on a small scale, before he starts to float his corporation. Where the promoter is consolidating several existing plants he already has some of his exhibits at hand in the form of the going plants and companies that are to be consolidated. Nevertheless, the combination itself is in reality a new enterprise and the promoter should spare no pains to secure some practical demonstration of its profit-making possibilities. Sometimes he may point to the success of previous combinations created under closely similar conditions. If he does not have examples, at least he can get exact figures as to the selling, administrative and operating expenses under the present arrangement which would be saved if the combination were effected.

In general the promoter must bear in mind that an enterprise which exists only on paper does not make anything like as powerful an appeal to the buyer of securities as an enterprise which has something tangible to show. It may be that the standing and prospects of the enterprise are in reality very little changed simply by producing some tangible results. Nevertheless, the confidence of people with funds is much increased and this, after all, is the promoter's main object.

83. *Foresight in providing funds.*—Second, the promoter should take care not to get his enterprise into such a condition that funds must be secured immediately on whatever terms are demanded. This is a situation that is quite apt to confront one who goes ahead with construction and development too rapidly. In his eagerness to make a favorable showing he may perhaps run short of funds, find the obligations of his corporation pressing and be compelled to make some very disadvantageous deals or see his corporation go into bankruptcy. Many a meritorious enterprise has suffered this fate.

To prevent such a catastrophe the promoter should see that his corporation is capitalized for a larger amount than he expects to need; thus there will always be unused securities which may be offered for sale without involving tedious and unnecessary formalities. It may be well to have this stock actually issued and transferred to the treasurer of the company in the manner which has been previously described.

Furthermore, the promoter should endeavor to raise in advance of any expensive construction or development all the funds that will be required for that purpose. The corporation which has a factory half-built, or mining machinery partially installed, or merchandise business half-stocked, is in an extremely precarious condition. Without additional funds it can go neither backward nor forward. It has no valuable assets or established trade on which to borrow funds, it has no trade credit, it has no record of sales and profits to present to prospective buyers or securities. It is therefore unable to secure any funds except from some individual or small group who may come to its rescue. The promoter may feel reasonably confident that their assistance will be purchased only with the sacrifice of his own control and probably of most of his profits.

84. *Advantages of a wide distribution of stock.*—Third, it is usually far better both for himself and for the corporation that the promoter sell his securities to a large number of small buyers rather than to a small number of large buyers. In the former case the stockholders are scattered and their holdings are too small to induce them to take any active interest in the business. Consequently the promoter, even if he fails to retain a majority of the voting stock, is left in absolute control. In the second case, the promoter is watched and perhaps hampered by the large stockholders; even if he holds a majority of the voting stock, he will probably not desire to arouse their objections and will therefore feel obliged to consult them or their representatives. Such an arrangement the promoter who has faith in his own abilities and ideas does not desire. He usually feels that he understands the proposition better than anyone else and that to him should be left the conduct of the business until it is well started toward success.

From the standpoint of the corporation, a large number of small stockholders is almost always desirable. The wider the distribution of the stock, the more friends the corporation has and the easier, probably, will be the selling of additional securities. Besides, the large capitalists who might be interested in the enterprise, should generally be kept in reserve for such emergencies as have been described. If the corporation does get into difficulties, in spite of all the care that its promoter may take, it can then turn as a last resort to these capitalists instead of drifting helplessly into insolvency.

85. *"Starting right" in the sale of stock.*—Fourth, if

the promoter is handling a legitimate small enterprise, he should look for his funds to the people of the locality where the enterprise is started. If the enterprise is too large for them, at least he should accomplish his preliminary financing—that is, the raising of sufficient funds to get the enterprise started, although not enough to carry it on to success—among the local people. Conservative bankers and business men always recognize the superior opportunities for getting exact information of local investors and have considerable confidence in their judgment. It is a great advantage to a promoter in presenting his enterprise to the public to be able to say that a large part of the funds have been subscribed by persons who are on the ground and in close touch with what is actually being accomplished. The same observations apply to people with technical training if the enterprise has many difficult technical features. The promoter of a corporation to manufacture a new electrical engine, for instance, ought to have the support of experts in that field—manifested not only in words, but by money—before he starts his campaign for subscriptions among outsiders.

86. *A concrete illustration.*—The practical application of the principles here laid down in the promotion and financing of interurban electric railroads has been well described in a lecture before the students of New York University School of Commerce, Accounts and Finance by Dr. Thomas Conway, Jr., of the University of Pennsylvania. Dr. Conway said:

The proposition having been discovered and thoroughly investigated, and the necessary options, for example the rights of way, etc., together with the necessary franchises, having been obtained, the promoter arranges to present the proposition to those who will furnish the money necessary. He accompanies his statement of anticipated earnings, with a map of the territory, showing population adjacent and tributary to his proposed lines, and he submits also engineers' estimates of cost of construction and cost of operation, based on the amount of traffic to be expected from the given population and its ratio of increase, and the grades and curves which will be encountered. He is now ready to arrange for the financing of his proposition. His first step is to organize a corporation, usually under the laws of a state in which his road expects to operate. This corporation will be organized with a minimum capital permitted by laws of the state in order to save initial taxes payable to the state. It will be organized with a minimum amount of cash payment and, if possible, requirements for actual contributions, will be satisfied by turning in options to the company. The charter of the company contains the authorization of the amount of capital which will be required to finance the enterprise. This capital consists of bonds, preferred and common stock. It is important that the amount of bonds per mile of road should be kept down to the lowest practicable figure as a large bonded debt immediately arouses a suspicion and suggests the advisability of a more skeptical and scrutinizing investigation of the promoter's representations. The amount usually fixed upon as conservative is $20,000 per mile. This may be exceeded in cases of especially expensive construction where interest on an excessive amount may be offset by lower cost of maintenance.

The preferred stock issue is usually for subscription in the immediate locality where interest in the new proposition must be aroused. It is advantageous to secure the largest possible amount in this manner, since it gets down the amount of bonds to be sold and makes their sale correspondingly easy. Two courses of action are now open to the promoter. He may either, after securing the proper introductions, address himself to a private banker in some financial center and offer to him the entire bond issue, or he may arrange for the financing of his enterprise in his own locality, approaching the city banker only after he has a record of earnings upon which to base his argument.

The investor to whom these securities must be sold, will not buy the bonds of an enterprise which has no recognized status, so long as it remains in formation and in chaotic condition. It is in his eyes a speculation and as such he is reluctant to put his money into its securities. If the bonds are, therefore, sold in the city, to the city banker, he must borrow the money to build the road, and must hold the bonds until at least a year's operation of the new property has been completed. The city banker will demand hard terms as a condition of advancing this money, if indeed one can be found with sufficient confidence in the new enterprise to risk his capital in its inauguration.

It is better, therefore, if possible, that the promoter should arrange for a preliminary financing of his scheme among local interests. This he does in the first place by securing subscriptions to preferred stock as already indicated. He also obtains a guarantee of purchase of the bonds of his corporation from local interests, bankers, institutions and capitalists, with whom he is acquainted, the condition of the guarantee being, that if the bonds are not sold within a definite time, say three years, above the price named in the contract of guarantee, the guarantors will take them at that price. The city banker would usually require that local interests guarantee at least a portion of the bonds, and it is therefore just as well for a promoter if he can accomplish this to secure guarantee of the entire issue. In order to make the stock of his company fully paid a device frequently resorted to is that of a construction company organized by the promoter and his friends and associates, who receive all the stock except what preferred stock may be prescribed for bonds of the new company in exchange for an agreement to construct and equip its lines in accordance with the plans and specifications of the engineers, which are made part of the agreement. At the time this contract is executed, all the common stock and sometimes such a portion of the preferred as may not have been provided for is turned over to the construction company, together with a small amount of the bonds. The remainder of the bonds are issued to a trust company, which acts as trustee for the holders, in installments corresponding to the completion of sections of the lines as certified to by the engineers representing the trust company. The promoter or his representative, acting for the construction company, which has now come into possession of all the securities of the new corporation, arranges with some trust company or bank to advance sufficient funds to build and complete the line. The security offered is the bond issue of the railroad company supplemented by the guarantees above mentioned and by a certain amount of the stock. The common stock of the railroad company, it should be mentioned, is divided up among the guarantors of the bonds. The trust company advances the funds, the banker finally sells the bonds, and what remains constitutes the promoter's profit. The amount of common stock, which must be given to each one of those interests, and that can be retained by the promoter, varies with circumstances. In return for making the loan, the trust company usually exacts a commission of say 2½ per cent to 5 per cent, besides the regular interest of 6 per cent or in some cases as high as 8 per cent, the loans running for two years. This money is advanced on serial notes of the construction company, corresponding to the completion of different sections of the road, and secured by the bonds which are issued to the construction company by their trustee as fast as the road is completed.

For example, we will suppose that the total amount of bonds is $1,000,000, and that these should be issued in ten installments to the construction company. The first installment of $100,000 is issued at the time the contract with the railroad company is executed. The construction company takes this note together with the guarantee of the purchase of these bonds, and $100,000 of bonds, and borrows from the trust company $100,000. With this $100,000 it pays for the completion of five miles of road. When it is certified to the trustee of the bonds that this mileage has been completed, another $100,000 of bonds is issued, another note negotiated and in this way by serial installments and notes, the trust company in time advances all the funds necessary to build the line. Prior to the completion of the lines some portion of the interest may be earned by the sections which may be put into operation. It is customary, however, to provide in the original capital issue sufficient funds for the payment of one or two years' interest.

If the calculations of the promoter have been correct, after the company has completed its first full year of operations, little difficulty will be experienced in arranging for an advantageous sale of the bonds to the city banker. Some stock may be demanded along with these bonds, but the amount will be small compared with what would have been asked if the banker had been obliged to advance the money for construction. In agreeing to take the bonds of an interurban electric railway the banker is running little risk, and is often able to dispose of all the bonds as soon as he has completed his payments for them. These bonds, until the notes which have been secured have been paid, remain in the custody of the trust company which advances the money to the construction company as fast as the bonds are delivered to the banker. He makes payment for them, and with these funds the notes of the construction company are satisfied and all the bonds have been taken up and paid for; the indebtedness of the construction company is discharged, and there remains in its hands a certain amount of cash and securities which are distributed to its stockholders. The construction company's work having been accomplished, it is then dissolved.

CHAPTER XIII

THE PROMOTER AND THE CORPORATION

87. *Professional promoters.*—It is time to say something about the promoter, his personality, his duties, his legal responsibilities, the services that he performs and the pay that he receives. Readers who are unfamiliar with the world of finance may have assumed from what has been said that a certain class or group of men make it their sole business to promote enterprises and that no one else ventures into this field. This would be an entirely erroneous impression. Anyone who is pushing a money-making scheme is a promoter for the time being, or at least he is performing some of the functions of a promoter. On the other hand, as not everyone by any means is well fitted by temperament, training or practice to make a success of the difficult work of promotion, comparatively few men are concerned with such work to any great extent.

We may classify the men who spend a considerable amount of their time and energy in promotion into four groups. Let it be clearly understood, however, that this classification does not pretend to be complete.

First come the professional promoters, the men who really do make it their main, and almost their sole, business to hunt for enterprises that promise profits and to finance those enterprises. This type is common in fiction, but rare in real life. So far as the writer recalls, he has met only one man who could be put in this class, a tall, lank, fervent individual with a persuasive air. At the time the writer knew him he was engaged in selling the stock of a Mexican rubber plantation company; he was also interested with others in the development of a tract of real estate near New York City; and he was investigating the possibilities of a copper mine in North Carolina. No doubt other plans were germinating in his mind. He was of the enthusiastic, visionary type, utterly incompetent to manage an enterprise, but skillful in appealing to the aspirations and emotions of others. On the whole, he was fairly successful; that is to say, he was making enough money on one enterprise to pay his losses on the others and to get a decent living in the bargain. He was unquestionably honest in his convictions; indeed, it was easy for him to be honest, for he possessed a mind that readily believed whatever he wished to believe. Probably he was used as a tool in many cases, although he never suspected it, by shrewder and less scrupulous men.

It might be said that Mr. John W. Gates, Judge W. H. Moore, Mr. Daniel G. Reid, and the others named in Chapter XII, are professional promoters. It would be more nearly correct, however, in the writer's opinion to classify these men as primarily brokers, or lawyers, or bankers, who have won a few great successes in the field of promotion. The man who does nothing but "promote" is not apt to achieve marked successes, one reason being that the really great opportunities are not usually stumbled upon by chance or disclosed to those who seek after them, but are revealed only to those who have an intimate acquaintance with the details of the business to be promoted. The only exception to this statement worth noting is when one who has already achieved success as a promoter is called in by men who thoroughly understand the business to be promoted and who place their knowledge at his disposal.

88. *Lawyers and bankers as promoters.*—The second class consists of lawyers and bankers in small communities. Such men have exceptional opportunities to inform themselves as to local conditions; they frequently take hold of some local enterprise, such as a steam or street railway, secure the assistance of experts for investigation and carry through the proposition to success. Still more frequently, however, so far as the writer has observed, such men underestimate the difficulties of the problem; they take it up with enthusiasm but are forced either to drop it or to call in men of wider experience.

The men to whom they generally turn constitute the third class of promoters, namely the larger bankers and brokers. The amount of promotion work performed by such men is limited and they usually confine their active participation—except for advice—to the financing of such enterprises as they take up. Mr. J. Pierpont Morgan stands out as the most prominent example of this class.

89. *Engineering firms as promoters.*—The fourth class—and this is a recent important development—consists of engineering firms engaged in construction work of various kinds. Certain large engineering concerns have established a wide reputation for success in operating street railroads, water works, electric lighting plants, and so on. These firms naturally have built up a large and well-equipped staff of experts in those fields. As the staff is expensive, it becomes a pressing problem to keep them profitably employed all the time. In the effort to solve this problem such firms have drifted into the custom of taking up new enterprises of merit

and performing the work of promotion themselves. Their prime object in so doing is to employ their own engineering talents and the abilities of their staff to the best advantage. Incidentally, of course, they have no objection to securing some of the other returns that naturally follow from successful promotion.

These engineering promoters have three great advantages which have told heavily in their favor:

(1) They are able to carry on a thorough investigation of any project that is presented to them without much extra expense; and as they are constantly engaged in such investigations, they have developed a body of experts who are able to give the best possible judgment as to the outlook for success in each instance. Consequently, they seldom go wrong.

(2) They are almost invariably big enough and have resources enough to finance the projects which they undertake themselves, if necessary. However, as they are primarily engineers, not financiers, they nearly always prefer to secure the greater part of the funds from other persons. This they accomplish by calling to their assistance some large banking and brokerage house, which will undertake to sell the securities of the corporations organized by the engineering firms. The alliance thus formed is of great advantage to the banking house, inasmuch as it may accept with confidence the results of the investigation carried on by the engineering firm's experts.

(3) The engineering firm, having a reputation to acquire and sustain, does not desert the new enterprise as soon as financed, as most promoters do, but sticks with it until it is a thoroughly established success. The engineering firm must have on its staff experts, not only in planning and building the street railroad or power

plant or whatever the new project may be, but also in operating the enterprise. It is in position, therefore, not merely to put the new corporation on its feet, but to give it a good running start toward success. Furthermore, if the corporation later gets into difficulties, the engineering firm may be relied upon to come to its assistance.

With these advantages there is no telling how far the tendency toward promotion by engineering firms will go. It would not surprise the writer to see almost all business of this kind except the largest projects turned over by common consent within the next few years to the well-established engineering firms. No doubt, as soon as this tendency becomes well known, cheap imitators of the reliable engineering concerns will come into the field. This difficulty, however, can be overcome, and in the end we shall perhaps find the business of promotion cleaner, more reputable and conducted with greater ability than under present conditions.

90. *Secret profits are illegal.*—No matter who the promoter of any particular enterprise may be, it is always necessary for him to raise funds from outsiders for his new corporation; and in the process of raising funds he must make representations as to the standing and prospects of the corporation. He also frequently enters into contracts on behalf of the corporation to be. His activities in both directions frequently raise knotty legal questions, which it is important for us to notice.

At law a promoter is in an anomalous situation, so far as his relation to his corporation is concerned. He is not, strictly speaking, an agent, because an agent must have a principal and the company promoted cannot be a principal because it is not yet in existence;

yet the courts have held that his activities in many respects are analogous to those of an agent. In addition, a promoter is in a sense a trustee of the interests of the corporation that he is organizing. He is under obligations to do his best for the corporation and to act always in good faith for its benefit. Furthermore, he must disclose all the pertinent facts in connection with the contracts and bargains that he makes for the corporation to its officers and stockholders when formed. Generally speaking, secret profits and fraud on the part of the promoter are not merely immoral, but are regarded by the courts as illegal as well. Where such transactions are discovered the corporation may bring suit and recover damages. The four cases given in abstract below illustrate different phases of this principle.

1. B agreed to sell land to X and Y, promoters of a corporation, for $12,000. He then associated himself with them and the three agreed to form a corporation which should buy the land for $40,000, out of which B was to receive the $12,000 he had originally demanded and in addition one-third of the profits of promotion. The company was formed, the purchase price of $40,000 paid and the stock of the company sold to outsiders. Subsequently the facts were discovered and the company filed a bill against the administrator of B's estate for the funds which B had received over and above $12,000, the ground of action being that B, as a promoter, was not entitled to make a profit by a sale of his land to the company at a fictitious value. The Supreme Court of Pennsylvania ordered a refund to the company of the amount received above $12,000.

2. B and C with the object of incorporating a mining company purchased oil lands for $10,000, and united

in organizing a company to buy the lands for $81,000. It was represented to prospective shareholders that B and C had purchased in the interest of the company and that the price paid by the company was the same as that paid by B and C to the original owners. The corporation sued B and C to recover the difference between the price paid in the first instance, and the figure at which the property was turned over to the corporation, and the suit was successful.

3. In a recent New York case it was shown that a promoter joined with the owner of a tract of land in procuring options of doubtful validity on adjoining tracts. The promoter then organized a corporation to purchase the land at an advanced price under an agreement with the owner that the profits thus secured were to be shared equally. The promoter bought the land for $66,223, though the deed to him recited $80,000 as the purchase price, and conveyed the land to the corporation for $80,000 and 400 shares of stock. He sold the stock to other stockholders and kept for himself the $13,777 profit. All of the money paid to the original owners of the land belonged to the corporation. It was held that the corporation was entitled to the $13,777 profits.

4. The promoters of a plantation company purchased land in Cuba for $40,000 and secured an option on additional land so drawn that it appeared they paid $20,000 for the option, making the total purchase price appear to be $60,000. In fact, nothing had been paid. They organized a corporation and represented to their associates that the plantation cost $60,000. They assigned their option to the corporation, taking $2,000 in stock as their share. Their associates retained the balance of the stock. It was held that the promoters were under a fidu-

ciary relation to the corporation and that the corporation was entitled as against them to the cancellation of the stock so issued to them.

It should be understood that there would be neither legal nor moral objection to a promoter's sale of property to his corporation at a higher price than he paid for it. The only obligation resting on him is that he should not conceal his profits. In practice it is very difficult to prevent concealment and the promoter may readily find methods of making sworn statements as to his profits that will be true, so far as they go, but will not be the whole truth. A scheme much used in buying property that is later to be sold to the promoter's corporation is to have it passed from the original owners first to another corporation owned by the promoter or to a friend of the promoter; then this corporation or friend will sell to the promoter at a price far in advance of what was paid to the original owner and the promoter will be able to assert that he turns it over to the corporation he organizes at cost to himself or at a very small profit. Sometimes the property may be made to pass through two or three intermediate hands in order to make detection more difficult.

91. *Misleading statements constitute fraud.*—Another feature of the promoter's work which should be considered relates to his statements with regard to the enterprise whether made verbally, in correspondence or in prospectuses. These statements are subject to the general principles of the law relating to fraud. The promoter is bound not merely to make his statements accurate, but not to omit any facts of vital importance.

Of course, the same difficulties that are found in all applications of the law relating to fraud are evident here. The promoter may state what he considers to be the facts and may omit features that he considers non-essential and it would be impossible to prove that his motives and intent were not of the best. We shall see in dealing with prospectuses how easy it is to give a misleading impression without actually making any misstatements.

92. *Contracts on behalf of the corporation and their acceptance.*—Difficulties sometimes arise in connection with the contracts which a promoter makes on behalf of his proposed corporation. As the promoter is not an agent, he has no right, strictly speaking, to act in behalf of the corporation. Courts of equity, however, have modified this strict rule to such an extent that the corporation accepts the contract by accepting its benefits. Acceptance need not be expressed in words; it may be reasonably inferred from the acts of the corporations.

93. *The promoter's pay.*—The most vital questions that arise between the promoter and his corporation are: How shall the promoter be paid for his services? How large shall his profits be? The promoter usually feels that he is entitled to all he can get. The corporation's stockholders, on the other hand, are apt to be dissatisfied even with a compensation that the promoter considers exceptionally small. The following extract from the Report of the Industrial Commission [1] states the essential facts.

There are various ways for the promoter to receive his pay. In certain instances, as, for example, the United States Rubber Company, the promoter received for his work 5 per cent of the total stock issued, but had to pay out of this the charges of lawyers, accountants, appraisers, and bankers.

A more usual form of remuneration is to give the promo-

[1] Second volume on "Trusts and Industrial Combinations," page VIII.

ter a certain amount of stock with which to buy the plants required and to pay expenses, permitting him to retain the surplus for his profits. In the case of the Rubber Goods Manufacturing Company the syndicate subscribers furnishing cash received for each $100 paid in $100 in preferred stock and $90 in common stock. The promoters had to purchase the plants and were given the entire issue of preferred and common stock. If they could buy the plants for the proceeds of 100 per cent of preferred stock and 90 per cent of common, they made the 10 per cent of common stock for their profit; if they had to pay more than that sum their profits were correspondingly lessened; if they could buy for less, naturally they made more than the 10 per cent of the common stock. They were under the express limitation that no preferred stock was to be issued in excess of tangible assets, and no common stock in excess of an amount determined by the earning capacity of the plants, as shown by previous experience, capitalized on a 7 per cent basis.

In the case of the American Smelting and Refining Company, syndicate subscribers for each $100 paid in cash received $100 in preferred stock and $70 in common stock. The promoters received the remaining $30 in common stock, out of which they had to pay the entire expenses of organization. They retained the remainder for their profits. Speaking generally, Mr. Chapman states that when a financiering syndicate receives for its subscriptions par in preferred stock and something less than par in common stock, the usual custom is for the promoters to receive the remainder of the common stock as pay for their services and for covering the costs of organization. In most cases their profits will depend upon the rigidity with which they can hold down their expense accounts, and, in many cases, where the purchase of plants is entirely in their hands, upon the skill which they can show in making purchases. Usually, of course, a careful appraisement has been made of plants beforehand, so that the basis of the stock issue is well known to all parties interested in the deal. A certain speculative chance is also often given to the promoters through the fact that it is within their discretion to buy for cash or stocks as they can best make agreements with the vendors. In that case they can sometimes make much better bargains for themselves by paying cash, or, on the other hand, by persuading the vendors to take securities, thus lessening the amount of cash that needs to be paid out. It is regularly the case that the promoter receives his pay in common stock.

Within the last two or three years there seems to have been a more conservative tendency shown by the bankers and others interested in financing the industrial combinations. The man who advances money to buy the various plants is, in many instances, taking a considerable risk and expects often to secure high pay therefor. The extent of his pay is dependent nevertheless largely upon his judgment as to the future course of development of the business of the combination in question. He practically buys securities of manufacturing establishments. If they earn high dividends his earnings will be great, provided he retains the securities; if he sells them his profits will be determined by the market rate of the securities, that being dependent again in the long run upon the earning capacity of the establishments. The more usual terms probably, under which within the last two or three years the financial agreements have been made, are that for each $100 cash paid in the subscribing member of the financial syndicate receives par in preferred stock with a bonus in common stock equal to the preferred less the amount reserved for the pay of the promoter. This reserve has sometimes been as high as 50 per cent of the common stock, sometimes 30 per cent, and sometimes only 10 per cent.

Instead of the plans mentioned above numerous others are of course found, especially where it is more desirable to issue bonds or where for some reason it seems desirable to make special terms, owing to the peculiar situation of some of the members entering into the combination. Promoters sometimes receive specified sums of money for their services; bankers practically always have to take for their services a percentage of the stock or the surplus left over.

94. *The promoter's risks and labors.*—Enough has been said to indicate that the promoter's labors and risks are heavy. If he does his work thoroughly he will probably spend a long time in careful investigation of the enterprise and in examination of all the possible causes of failure before he binds himself in any manner. If he is a man of sound judgment, as he must be in order to be successful, he will probably find serious if not fatal flaws in most of the enterprises that come to his attention. A professional promoter must expect, therefore, to spend a large amount of time and money in studies and investigations that bring him no return. Unless this part of his work is thoroughly done his efforts are foredoomed to failure.

In the process of assembling his proposition, the promoter must always take considerable personal risks. He buys options, enters into contracts, and perhaps spends money for further experiment, all of which will be absolutely lost unless his promotion proves successful.

In financing the enterprise, the promoter puts in jeopardy not only the time and money previously expended, but his business reputation as well. One notoriously unsuccessful promotion will probably end a promoter's activities, at least if he is engaged in an entirely legitimate line of business.

95. *Is the promoter overpaid?*—It is obvious also that the promoter must possess a rare and highly valuable combination of talents. He must be keen, shrewd, a good bargainer, farsighted, prudent, enthusiastic, persuasive, and, above all, he must inspire confidence. With this necessary combination of talents, labors and risks, it is not surprising that the promoter should subsequently claim and exact large profits. It is no doubt

true that a considerable number of men who have won success in this field have made millions and tens of millions of dollars in a very short time. To the on-looker it sometimes appears that these millions almost came dishonestly, that it is hardly possible that they are legitimate earnings. The average on-looker, however, has no conception of the amount or importance of the preliminary work which the promoter performs. Neither has he any conception of the large number of failures in this field. Probably the losses of promoters, who have spent their own time and both their own and their friends' money without benefit to themselves, would almost equal or perhaps exceed the total profits of successful promotions.

We must not forget to consider also the great importance to business and industry of their achievements. They are the men who have found and developed the inventions, the improvements and the better organization of industry which underlie our modern prosperity. Frequently the inventor complains that he has made less out of his invention than did the business promoter; the manufacturer complains that with all his years of effort he has made less out of his factory than did the promoter who takes it into a big consolidation; the mine owner complains that he has made less out of his land and ore than did the promoter who obtained the funds for its developments. All of these complaints are natural enough; yet they all alike fail to take into account the obvious fact that the promoter's efforts have not done them harm, but good. He has performed for each of them a great service; and even if he retains the larger part of the profits, they have no just ground for complaint.

CHAPTER XIV

CORPORATE PROMOTION—FORMING CONSOLIDATIONS

96. *The importance of small industrial combinations.* —Of late years the most conspicuous and perhaps the most important field for promoters has been the consolidation of manufacturing and railroad companies. The tendency toward consolidation has been even more widespread in the last few years than has appeared to the casual observer. Popular attention has been directed almost exclusively to what is called the trust movement, that is, the combinations of big companies with a view to controlling prices.

Of still greater importance, however, to the average business man has been the tendency to consolidate small local plants, not for the sake of achieving even a partial monopoly, but for the sake of the economies that result from manufacture on a larger scale than is possible by a small partnership or corporation. Among the most important economies that may be thus affected are: first, the elimination of wasteful competition in selling and advertising; second, the opportunity to use expensive and highly specialized machinery more constantly and thereby prevent the loss that results from allowing such machinery to lie idle; third, a position of greater advantage to business managers in their dealings with labor unions; fourth, bringing to bear the best brains and experience to be found in any of the plants consolidated on the problems of each plant.

No statistics have been or could be collected to show

exactly the extent of this movement. It is certain, however, that the great mass of the manufacturing capital of the United States is now employed by such consolidations and that the position of the small isolated manufacturer is daily becoming more precarious. Indeed, this result is inevitable, for the consolidation can usually effect the economies mentioned above without equally great disadvantages. The consolidation, therefore, although it may have no monopoly and no control over prices, either of raw materials or of finished products, easily undersells its small competitors. It is not worth while to rail against such a movement; business men will do better to recognize its inherent strength and get into line.

97. *Difficulties in the promoter's task.*—The formation of a consolidation through the medium of a holding company, which is the usual form, is by no means an easy task. It brings into play all the shrewdness, persuasiveness and business judgment that a promoter may possess. Usually managers and owners of the various plants to be taken into the proposed consolidation are so mutually jealous and antagonistic that it is next to impossible for any one of them to effect a friendly combination with all his competitors. Once in a while a successful manufacturer may buy outright the securities, or perhaps the physical assets, of competing plants; but this is an exception. Usually the promoter of a consolidation must come from the outside. He will probably be better off if he has had no connection with the business and therefore has no grudges and no prejudices to overcome. Sometimes the outside promoter is a banker friendly with all the interests to be combined; sometimes he is a well-known promoter who has made a name for fair dealing and success; sometimes he is a

security holder in one or more of the concerns to be consolidated, who has taken no active part in their management. He will of necessity have constantly at his command the expert knowledge of men directly concerned with the business.

For the sake of simplicity we will first consider the process of consolidating two or more small independent partnerships or corporations into a somewhat larger combination of some local importance; and after that we will consider the still more complicated problems that arise in the process of forming a big "trust"—using that word in the popular sense—a combination of previous consolidations.

98. *"Discovery" of a small consolidation.*—In organizing a small consolidation the promoter's first step, as has already been indicated, must be a thorough investigation of all the concerns which are to be included. Usually the promoter will not have the time or the facilities to undertake such an investigation personally or by means of his own assistants. But he should certainly be unwilling to accept the unsupported statements of the manufacturers; he will, therefore, use the services of competent engineers, of expert public accountants and perhaps of lawyers. The accountants' examination should produce the most important and significant results, and on these results the terms of the consolidation will probably be based.

The accountant's work in this connection should be even more extensive and searching than in the case of a regular audit. This is particularly true because the managers in the case of an audit presumably desire a correct report; in the case of this special investigation their interests lead them to favor over-valuation of assets, fictitious accounts receivable and a padded income statement. The accountant must get an accurate physical inventory of the property, if possible; he must verify the accounts and bills receivable as well as the accounts and bills payable; he should look into all indirect and contingent liabilities with great care; he must see that sales do not include goods sent out "on consignment" and "on approval" and that profits are not swelled by sales of what are in reality capital, not current, assets.

99. ***Basis of consolidation.***—The promoter's next step, if he is acting not simply on his own account, but as a sort of arbitrator for the various manufacturers, each one of whom is willing to go into the consolidation on reasonable terms, is to draw up a tentative "basis of consolidation." In an article in ***The Journal of Accountancy*** for November, 1908, Mr. F. H. McPherson, F. C. A., gives in illustration the following informal memorandum of agreement which was used as a basis in a certain consolidation of small companies with which he was concerned. The agreement is typical and is well worth careful reading. It is given in full below:

Basis of Consolidation:

A corporation to be formed under the laws of the State of Michigan, with a paid-up capital of ten million dollars, to be apportioned into 6 per cent preferred stock and common stock, as the parties interested may hereafter determine.

This corporation to purchase all the assets, property, goodwill, etc., of all the four companies and to pay therefor in preferred and common stock and by an assumption of the indebtedness of each company.

The amount of preferred and common stock, to be paid to each company, to be determined by the value of the net tangible assets and the valuation placed upon the earning power of each company.

In placing a value upon the tangible assets, same to be reached as follows:

(1) The land, buildings, machinery, tools, and patterns, to be determined by appraisers, to be chosen by a majority of a committee made up of one appointed by each of the companies; on failure of this committee to agree on appraisers the selection to be left to the committee who present these suggestions.

(2) Inventories of raw materials, work in progress and manufactured stock to be taken, and valuations placed thereon by the individual companies, and this to be done under the supervision of a disinterested party, to be named by the committee.

The inventories are to be made as of the same date, and to be taken at substantially the same time.

When completed the inventories are to be passed and agreed upon by a committee consisting of a representative of each of the companies and one to be named by the committee. The decision of these five to be binding.

(3) In reaching the value of the earning power of the several companies, consideration is to be given to the following details:

(a) That profits are incidental to the business and have not been anticipated.

(b) To the charging to operating expenses of items, exceptional or unusual, and which have had the effect of reducing profits below normal.

(c) The effect upon the earnings of the money paid out as interest upon borrowed capital, in case it be found that the borrowings (loans) made by the several companies are disproportionate to each other.

(d) That all charges to operating expenses are proper charges against the business and that they are made for and during the proper period.

(e) That proper and reasonable allowances have been made for repairs and renewals and that these have been charged against earnings.

(f) That charges against earnings for depreciation are adjusted upon an equitable basis.

(g) Such other matters as appear from an examination of the accounts and which would prejudicially affect the earnings of any of the companies, either advantageously or disadvantageously.

(h) The value of the earning power to be determined by a consideration of the business done by each of the several companies for the three years, 1903, 1904 and 1905.

(i) Accountants to be selected by the committee and questions which may arise as to treatment of various matters and about which there is difference of opinion, to be determined by the committee.

(j) All costs and expenses incurred in making appraisals, examination of accounts, or of performing the other duties in connection with the formation of the proposed new company to be charged to and borne by the new company; should the new company not be formed, then such costs, expenses, and disbursements to be borne by the four individual companies in proportion to the number of men employed by each.

It will be noted that the agreement just cited does not specify just when preferred and when common stock shall be paid by the holding company for the securities of the subsidiary companies. One very common arrangement is set forth in the following extracts from another actual agreement where several fair-sized manufacturing corporations and partnerships were to be consolidated. This agreement provided:

Each vendor executing this agreement also executes and delivers a schedule of the entire property, which it sells to said purchaser, setting forth briefly the various classes of property, with the sufficient description of the several items of real estate, plant and movables to identify the same, which schedule sets forth the value of the entire property so sold, the tangible and intangible property in separate items, the tangible property being valued as prescribed by subdivisions a and b in the Method of Appraisal hereinafter set forth, and the value of its intangible property ascertained and certified by one or more responsible public accountants, as prescribed by subdivision c of said Method of Appraisal, together with a statement of any additional facts, and of the valuations based thereon, which, in the vendor's judgment, may aid the Appraisal Committee in exercising the discretion conferred upon it by subdivision b of said Method of Appraisal. The valuations of the tangible and intangible properties so made by each vendor shall be considered as *prima facie* evidence of the true value of said vendor's property for the purposes of sale, but shall in no case be controlling upon the Appraisal or Executive Committee hereinafter appointed, such valuations or prices being subject in all cases to any investigation and modification which the said committee or committees may deem that justice requires; the total of such valuations as verified or modified according to the terms of this agreement, to be the purchase price which said vendor is to receive for its entire property so sold.

PURCHASE PRICE

The purchase price to be paid to such vendor for the property sold by it to the purchaser shall be the total value of its tangible and intangible property and shall be paid in stock of the purchaser at par, as follows:—

1. *Tangible property paid for in preferred, etc.*

Each vendor whose net earnings for the six months ending July 1st, 1898, amount to 4 per cent—that is, at the rate of 8 per cent per annum—on the value of its land and plant, ascertained as above, shall receive preferred stock for the full value of all its tangible property.

Any vendor whose net earnings for the said period of six months shall amount to less than at the rate of 8 per cent per annum on the value of its land and plant, shall receive preferred stock to the amount of twenty-five times its net earnings for said six months; and the balance of the value of said tangible property it shall receive in common stock.

Each vendor has upon its schedule set forth a statement of its net earnings for said period, which is subject to modification by said committee under the above rules applicable thereto.

2. *Intangible property paid for in common stock.*

The entire value of the intangible property, ascertained as per this agreement, shall be paid by the purchaser in its common stock at par.

Simultaneous with the sale and transfer of its properties each vendor shall receive from the purchaser in stock, or if permanent certificates are not ready, then scrip for the same, one-half of the purchase price to which it claims to be entitled by its schedule, less an amount of preferred stock equal to 125 per cent of its mortgage indebtedness, if any, and the remainder of said stock shall be withheld by the purchaser until the exact amount of the purchase price shall have been finally determined as herein provided, whereupon the vendor shall become entitled to the remainder of the purchase price, but the purchaser may out of such remaining stock retain an amount thereof sufficient to secure it against any defective title and against any indebtedness which is not otherwise sufficiently provided for.

APPRAISAL, ETC.

Each vendor expressly covenants and agrees that the property set forth by it in its schedule has been fairly and honestly valued in accordance with the following rules and methods, which shall be the rules and methods to govern the Appraisal and Executive Committees in their verification or modification of the same.

METHOD OF APPRAISAL.

(1) *Tangible Property.*

(a) Land:

Land shall be separately appraised at its actual value without reference to plants thereon, and consideration shall be given to special adaptability or want of adaptability to the business.

Plants shall be appraised apart from the bare land at their value to-day to a going concern for the purpose for which used, based upon present cost of construction at the same places respectively. No vendor shall set forth in its schedule any unimproved land or other property belonging to it which is neither a part of the plant of such vendor nor essential in the operation of the same, nor shall the same be purchased by the second party.

(b) Materials, Supplies and Manufactured Product.

These shall be appraised at what it would cost to replace the same at the place and date of the transfer of the same to the purchaser.

(2). *Intangible Property.*

(c) Intangible property shall be appraised by multiplying by ten the average yearly earnings during the past five and one-half years, which shall be ascertained as follows:—

In order to arrive at the earnings of the property sold by each vendor and to determine on a uniform basis fair for all, the earning power of the property so sold, each vendor shall add to its net profits such of the following items as have been theretofore deducted by said vendor in ascertaining its net profits during said period.

1. Interest on indebtedness.

2. Insurance of any description.

3. Arbitrary items of depreciation or wear and tear not paid out or actually incurred as a debt, and all items of new construction.

4. Also salaries and compensation paid to officers, directors, partners, trustees, superintendents of departments or works, general managers, auditors, cashiers and chief accountants, but all wages, salaries and compensation paid to laborers, servants, foremen, clerks and employees in subordinate positions shall remain charged against earnings.

5. The accountants must ascertain the amounts expended by each of said vendors for repairs, renewals and maintenance of plant which have been deducted from earnings during said period

of five and one-half years, and the said amounts so ascertained are set forth on the schedules of said vendors.

In order to place said vendors on a uniform basis as to the amounts expended, or which ought to have been expended, for repairs, renewals and maintenance of plant and charged against or deducted from the earnings during said five and one-half years or other period, each vendor shall add to said earnings any amount actually expended by it for repairs, renewals and maintenance of plant which it has heretofore charged against and deducted from said earnings, and there shall then be charged against and deducted from said earnings of each vendor ascertained as aforesaid, annually a sum equal to 3 per cent of the schedule value of the plant of said vendor completed prior to the last date of the five and one-half years or other period applicable to said vendor.

In the case of those vendors, if any, which shall not have kept a separate repair account the amounts expended by them for repairs, as required by this subdivision shall be ascertained as nearly as possible by the accountants and the committee of appraisal from the books of such vendors and from the condition of their plants and otherwise, and in default of information to the contrary it shall be assumed that they have expended in repairs a sum equal to 3 per cent of the value of their respective plants.

Having by the foregoing methods, ascertained the earnings, there shall thereupon be deducted from the average annual earnings of each vendor for said period, a sum equal to 5 per cent (5%) of the value of the land and plant sold and completed prior to the last date of the five and one-half years or other period applicable to such vendor, and the balance of said average annual earnings so ascertained shall be deemed for the purposes of this agreement the net profits of the respective vendors to be severally multiplied by ten as aforesaid.

Provided, however, that in case it shall be found that the aforesaid multiplier of ten will produce a grand aggregate of common stock greater in amount than the grand aggregate of preferred stock, the Executive Committee shall choose such lower multiplier as will limit the grand aggregate of preferred stock.

Provided, further, that in the event that the grand aggregate of the average annual net earnings of the vendors, ascertained as aforesaid, shall be found to exceed 12 per cent of the total value of the tangible property, then said Executive Committee in its discretion may choose such multiplier as will fix the volume of common stock as closely as may be at an amount upon which such past net earnings would show 6 per cent applicable to dividends upon such common stock after providing for the dividend on the preferred stock.

And thereupon such newly chosen multiplier (whatever the same may be) shall be the multiplier to be used in the case of each vendor.

The agreement that has just been cited in part deserves careful study. As the extracts given are self-explanatory, however, it will be left to the reader to work out for himself the exact methods employed by the promoters, and accepted by the owners of the plants in determining values. The substance of the plan, it will be seen, is that tangible property is to be represented by preferred stock in the consolidation and additional earning power by common stock. This puts the consolidation, so far as capitalization is concerned, on a conservative basis. The same plan, slightly modified, is widely used.

100. *The necessity for cash.*—Having investigated and assembled his proposed consolidation, the promoter must next arrange for its financing. It may be said at this point that the basis of consolidation in itself finances the new consolidation, inasmuch as it provides for the exchange of the consolidated company's securities for the subsidiary companies' securities. This financing is not sufficient, however, to provide for the needs of the

new corporation. Working capital, to a considerable amount, must certainly be obtained or the new corporation will plunge at once into bankruptcy. Furthermore, a consolidation almost always implies changes in methods of operation. New officers must be appointed, old ones dismissed. Some of the plants perhaps will be dismantled or put on part time; other plants will be remodeled and refitted with expensive modern machinery. Frequently the whole arrangement of the plants and processes of manufacture will be reformed in order to introduce the methods that belong to large scale production. All of these changes may be necessary in order to obtain the economies that belong to combinations. They may and probably will prove wise and in the end highly profitable. At the moment of forming the consolidation, however, they call for large amounts of new capital funds and bring to the front some of the most difficult problems of financing which a promoter has to face.

101. *One method of raising cash.*—Following the basic principles outlined in Chapter XII, the promoter of a small consolidation will endeavor to raise whatever cash is necessary first of all from local bankers and financiers. If he succeeds in obtaining the co-operation of these men, he is much more likely to find his proposition regarded favorably by larger banking interests. Two courses are now open to him: either he may issue bonds of the new company, which will not be first mortgage, but which he may name "first and refunding" or "first general" or "first consolidated"; or he may try to sell stock in addition to that which has been given to the owners of the consolidated plants. Either course has its disadvantages. The bond issue probably cannot be sold on advantageous terms because

the consolidation must necessarily be an experiment at the beginning and even its best securities will have a speculative character. Furthermore, in many cases the promoter will find the property of the subsidiary companies already mortgaged so that the bonds of the consolidated company, whatever title he may pick out for them, will be in reality junior liens. The sale of stock is undesirable because the stock issue in all probability is already large; it has to be large in order to make the terms offered to the owners of the subsidiary plants sufficiently attractive. If still more stock is issued to be sold to the public, it will be very difficult to pay dividends even on the preferred, not to speak of the common. This result, the promoter certainly does not desire. He has promised usually heavy cumulative dividends at once on the preferred stock and has held out hopes of early dividends on the common, and his reputation is staked on the fulfillment of these predictions. Moreover, he is himself usually a large holder of the common stock.

On balancing these considerations, the promoter usually finds himself strongly inclined to favor the sale of bonds if they can be sold at any reasonable price. His sanguine temperament—for that kind of temperament naturally belongs to a promoter—leads him to minimize the danger of increasing the new corporation's fixed charges and to exaggerate the probable profits. He therefore turns to local bankers for assistance in borrowing the necessary funds. Frequently, as the first step, he has the corporation put out a bond issue under a mortgage of the limited open-end type. The provision may be, and often is, that of the total issue one-half shall be offered for sale in the first year, one-fourth in the second, and one-fourth in the third year; of course, the length of time over which the sale is spread and the corporation's allotment each year may vary indefinitely, depending on the urgency of the company's need for cash. He then obtains a guarantee from local financiers, including perhaps some of the banks, to take the unsold bonds at the end of each period from the corporation at a low price which is specified. By this guarantee the corporation is protected from an absolute failure to secure cash. The guarantors must, of course, be paid, usually by a considerable commission on all the bonds that are sold. This kind of an arrangement, which we will consider at greater length later, is known as underwriting.

The promoter may now take his bond-issue—or part of it, if he has been able to get the sale of only a part guaranteed—to a friendly bank and secure a short-time loan, using the bonds as collateral security. He has thus provided for the immediate cash necessities of the new company at the beginning of its existence. As fast as he can sell the bonds, he pays off the bank loans and thus puts the corporation in a stronger financial position. If the issue is entirely successful, the corporation will soon have plenty of cash, obtained by this bond issue, and will be able to carry out the improvements in operation which are expected to make the consolidation a profitable venture.

The essential feature of this plan, it will be noted, is the distribution of the risk among several different parties. The bank is well protected in accepting the bonds as collateral by the guarantee of responsible parties to buy the bonds at the end of a certain period, if no purchaser willing to pay a higher price is previously found. The guarantors usually take little risk, for the price of the bonds to them is made low enough to be attractive. The corporation obtains at once whatever cash is necessary and its only risk is that it may have to sell its bonds to the guarantors at a low price.

Naturally the promoter in the period left to him before the guarantors' option becomes effective does his best to sell the bonds at a good price. The methods which he uses and the agencies through which he works are fully treated in later chapters.

102. *Problems in forming a large consolidation.*—There is no difference in principle between the promoter's functions in forming a small and his functions in forming a large consolidation. He is doing things on a bigger scale, however, and finds necessary several important variations in his methods.

In the first place, such a consolidation is almost always too large to be handled by any one man. In order to reach all the parties concerned and to inspire confidence, it is generally desirable for several promoters to work together, each performing a portion of the labor. When the United States Steel Corporation was formed, as described in the following chapter, almost all of the prominent, successful promoters of the country were concerned in one way or another. Apart from the necessity of dividing the work to be performed, it is very desirable to promote harmony and secure the best solutions of the difficult and complicated problems involved in such a consolidation by getting the ideas of a considerable number of able and experienced men.

In the second place, the promoter or group of promoters is dealing with such a large number of security owners of subsidiary companies that lengthy consultation with these owners and bargain-making is out of the question. Usually the heavy stockholders in the subsidiary companies are consulted and frequently they have some part in the scheme of promotion. The great mass of stockholders, however, are simply notified, when the proper time comes, of what is proposed and are invited to accept the offer which the promoters lay before them.

103. *Basis of consolidation.*—The amount and character of the security issues of the proposed consolidation, and the terms upon which these securities will be exchanged for the securities of the subsidiary companies, are fixed by the promoters in advance. This does not mean that the terms are unfair to the subsidiary companies' stockholders. On the contrary, they are usually extremely liberal. It must be remembered that it is very desirable for the holding company to have all the stock—certainly all the voting stock—of each subsidiary. The less subsidiary company stock there is left outstanding, the less is the chance of complaint and annoying legal processes on the part of the dissenting stockholders against the actions of the holding company. The promoters, therefore, try to offer such terms that all, or almost all, the stock of subsidiary companies will be exchanged for stock of the consolidation.

The usual arrangement is to divide the capital stock of the consolidation into preferred and common, the amount of the preferred being equivalent to the total market value of all the subsidiary company stock. Practically any amount of common stock may be issued; the promoter usually puts out as much as he thinks can possibly obtain dividends within a reasonable number of years. The stockholders of the subsidiary companies are then offered somewhat more than the market value of their stock payable in cash, or considerably more than its market value payable in preferred stock. If they take preferred stock, they will ordinarily receive in addition a substantial bonus of common stock. The first proposition is intended to catch the ultra-conservative; the second proposition is intended to be even more attractive. The stockholder is to receive in place of his present holding, having a fluctuating and uncertain dividend, a more than equal amount of stock preferred as to dividends, and in addition a considerable amount of the new common stock. Very few stockholders are likely to refuse so attractive an offer.

The application of these principles is well illustrated in the promotion of the biggest and one of the most successful consolidations that has yet been formed, the United States Steel Corporation. So important is this great company, not only in connection with our present study of corporation finance, but in its influence on industry in this country, that it has been thought best to devote a separate chapter to a review of its origin, its promotion, its financial history and its prospects.

104. *The Interborough-Metropolitan Consolidation.*—Another typical consolidation which was formed under very different conditions is the Interborough-Metropolitan Company, the holding company for the transportation companies of New York City. A chart showing the complicated internal organization of the company has been presented in Chapter VI. The terms of the consolidation are clearly set forth in the following extract from a lecture by Albert W. Atwood, Financial Editor of the *New York Press* and Lecturer on Investments in New York University.

1. Companies Taken Over.

Metropolitan Street Railway	$ 52,000,000	stock
Metropolitan Securities Co.	30,000,000	"
Interborough Rapid Transit Co.	35,000,000	"
	$117,000,000	

2. Capitalization of Inter-Met.

Bonds	$ 70,000,000
Preferred Stock	55,000,000
Common Stock	100,000,000
Total	$225,000,000
Deduct	117,000,000
Excess	$108,000,000

3. Basis of Exchange.

Interborough — one share received $200 bond and $99 common stock in the Inter-Met.

Metropolitan Street — one share received $100 preferred and $55 common in the Inter-Met.

Metropolitan Securities — one share, $75 paid up, received $93.50 common in the Inter-Met.

The Interborough-Metropolitan took over practically all the capital stock of the subsidiary companies. In 1902 the Metropolitan Street Railway, which had been the company which controlled and operated the surface lines, ran short of money and a scheme was devised to keep it going by leasing it to the New York City Railway (which had a comparatively small amount of stock) the stock of which was in turn all taken over by the Metropolitan Street Railway shareholders. By getting a large majority of the stocks of the Metropolitan Street Railway and the Metropolitan Securities Company the Inter-Metropolitan got control of the entire surface system and by securing the stock of the Interborough Rapid Transit it got control of the subway and elevated lines. The total of securities taken over was about $117,000,000 and the new company issued $225,000,000 of securities. The excess capitalization was $108,000,000, which in view of the fact that many believed the surface lines were already waterlogged, was a remarkable piece of finance. Three reasons are advanced for the excess capitalization:

1. The promoters say they honestly believed that within two or three years the common stock would be earning 2 per cent.

2. The merger was formed at the height of the business and

financial boom of 1906 and at that time the later financial and business reaction was not generally foreseen.

3. The holders of the securities of the old companies had to have an inducement to exchange their securities for the new ones. In other words, they had to be hypnotized into believing that they were getting something for nothing. Much was made of the growth of the passenger traffic in New York and the official prospectuses declared the common stock of the new combine would certainly be able to pay dividends in time owing to the growth of population.

These two illustrations will serve to indicate the general practice in exchanging a consolidated company's securities for those of the subsidiary companies. It may be observed that the steel consolidation was far more conservative than was the Interborough-Metropolitan consolidation. The second-named company was in a dangerous situation from the very beginning, for it was compelled to pay regular interest on its large bond issue or go into receivers' hands. The steel corporation gave only a small amount of bonds—relative to its total capitalization—and consequently was not in serious danger of insolvency. Even if it had failed to pay interest on its preferred stock it would not have been forced into a perilous position. The Interborough-Metropolitan financing was on its face so unsound as to arouse the suspicion that this particular consolidation was never intended to succeed.

CHAPTER XV

THE UNITED STATES STEEL CORPORATION

105. *Preparing the ground.*—1890 to 1900 is an important decade in the history of the steel business of the United States. Between 1890 and 1893 production was vastly increased, while the demand for iron and steel products practically stood still. As a result, prices were declining and a majority of the steel producers were in a precarious situation even before the severe crisis of 1893 began its work of destruction. The crisis hit the steel makers especially hard, and wiped out many of the small concerns. In the five years of depression that followed, individuals and partnerships as factors in steel production almost disappeared; their places were taken by comparatively large and strong corporations. These corporations not only managed to live, but even to thrive in a way, because they were able to buy new plants and enlarge old ones at bargain prices. By the year 1898 in all branches of the steel industry, including bar iron, rolled iron, steel rails, sheet steel, tin plate, wire, and other more highly finished products, a considerable number of fairly efficient and well-managed corporations, which had grown in strength during the depression, were prepared to handle the flood of new business that was expected to come with the revival of good times.

The flood came and with it such a rise in prices and a deluge of profits as would have seemed inconceivable two or three years before. Steel, in Andrew Carnegie's picturesque phrase, is either "a prince or a pauper."

The reason is that, as large amounts of fixed capital must be invested, the supply of steel products cannot easily be increased or decreased; whereas, as steel is not a prime necessity, the demand fluctuates violently. In other words, since supply and demand do not move up and down together, prices and profits jump from one extreme to the other with extraordinary rapidity.

106. *The steel consolidations preceding the formation of the United States Steel Corporation.*—In 1898, then, American steel makers had reached a higher level of prosperity than ever before and were moving rapidly upward; the business was carried on by a comparatively few fairly strong corporations in each line; at the same time, public interest in the advantages of industrial combinations and in their supposed opportunities for great profits was keen and the public appetite for the securities of such combinations, or "trusts," had been excited. Placing these three factors together, we see why the three years following, 1898–1901, were marked by a remarkable series of steel consolidations. We cannot take time here to tell the stories, interesting though they would be, of these consolidations. For our purpose it will be enough to name the important steel companies in existence in 1900.

1. The Federal Steel Company was formed in September, 1898, by combining the Illinois Steel Company, the Minnesota Iron Company, and the Elgin, Joliet and Eastern Railroad. Its authorized capital was $200,000,000, of which, however, only $99,700,000 was ever issued.

2. The American Steel & Wire Company was organized by John W. Gates in March, 1898. It was big enough to control virtually the entire production of wire goods. Its capital was $90,000,000.

3. The National Tube Company, formed in February, 1899, included over a dozen companies. It was the largest concern of its kind in the world and at the time the third largest concern in the iron and steel business, being surpassed only by Carnegie and Krupps, of Germany.

4. The National Steel Company, the American Steel Hoop Company, the American Sheet Steel Company and the American Tin Plate Company were organized in the period from December, 1898, to March, 1900, by Judge W. H. Moore, his brother, James H. Moore, Daniel G. Reid, William B. Leeds, and others who were later given the titles "Moore Party" and "Rock Island Crowd." Of these concerns the largest was the Tin Plate Company, which was a consolidation of forty companies, embracing about 95 per cent of the total output of tin plate in the United States.

5. The biggest and most powerful company of all, The Carnegie Company, was not a consolidation, but a growth. This great concern had been built up by the consistent policy, extending over many years, of putting most of its earnings into improvements instead of into dividends. The organizing genius of Carnegie, Frick, Phipps, and their co-workers, had made its body of workingmen the most efficient and its enormous plant the most economical in the world. Through its control of the H. C. Frick Coke Company, the Oliver Mining Company, the Pittsburg Steamship Company and the Pittsburg, Bessemer & Lake Erie Railroad, together with its fifty-year contract with the Rockefeller iron, mining and transportation companies, its supply of raw materials at low cost was assured for many years to come.

107. *A condition of unstable equilibrium.*—In one of

the most brilliant chapters in his well-known volume on "Trust Finance" Professor E. S. Meade has well described the conditions in the steel business in 1900. Industrially the situation might be said to be one of unstable equilibrium. It might have been expected that all of these consolidations would have been content to enjoy the prosperity, which was being showered upon steel makers, and would have desisted from intense competition with each other. Ordinarily competitive strife awakens in periods when business is stagnant and mills idle, while harmony is readily secured so long as orders are outrunning production. This would, in fact, have been the happy situation in the steel trade if it had not been for the appearance of a powerful new factor, the tendency toward integration. "Integration" is the economist's technical word for the control by one concern of the whole process of production from the raw material to the finished product. Ordinarily the manufacture of any finished article, say a tin can, is carried on through several stages, and at each stage passes from one group of producers to another group. In making the tin can iron ore must be mined; the miner sells his ore to a manufacturer who transforms it first into iron and next into steel; this manufacturer sells his product to a manufacturer of sheet steel, who in turn passes it on to the manufacturer of tin plate; finally the can manufacturer buys the tin plate and forms it into tin cans. At each stage of such a process there is a sale of the partly finished product and a profit is taken that enters into the final cost of production. Under the policy of integration, according to which all these stages are combined under the control of one great manufacturing concern, a twofold advantage is gained; first, the intermediate profits are all secured; second, a permanent, dependable supply of raw materials at lowest costs is assured. This second advantage is even more important than the one first named.

The Carnegie Company in 1900 up to a certain point was an integrated company; that is, it controlled great quantities of ore and coal, owned its own steamships and railroads for the transportation of these raw materials to its Pittsburg plants, and at the Pittsburg plants turned out steel rails and a large variety of half-finished products. It was partly for this reason that the company had become so strong and prosperous. Nevertheless, it was by no means wholly independent, for its chief customers were the other steel companies in the Pittsburg district which purchased its steel billets, ingots, bars, plates and slabs. The Federal Steel Company, also, was "integrated" up to a certain point, but like the Carnegie Steel Company was by no means independent of its large customers. A large part of its business consisted in furnishing wire rods to the American Steel and Wire Company and steel billets to the National Tube and the American Bridge Companies. The National Steel Company, a much smaller concern, furnished part-finished products to the other Moore companies, the American Tin Plate, American Sheet Steel, and American Steel Hoop.

The group of producers of finished steel products were by no means satisfied with their position. They desired to secure the advantages of integration for themselves; particularly they were anxious to free themselves from the domination of the concerns on which they were dependent for raw materials. Therefore, all of these companies in 1898, 1899 and 1900 were planning to purchase ore and coal lands, to get control of transportation companies and to construct furnaces and mills for the manufacture of part-finished steel products. The American Steel and Wire Company bought two thousand acres of Connellsville coal land and large ore properties. It already had partially under its control a fleet of twelve ore steamers. It now announced its intention to build large steel plants at Milwaukee and Pittsburg. The National Steel Company purchased iron mines and coal land and started to increase its furnace capacity. The National Tube Company began work on a large steel plant at Wheeling, West Virginia.

The completion of these projects meant heavy loss to the Carnegie Company and the Federal Steel Company. They were forced to fight back. The Federal Steel Company threatened to build wire mills unless the American Steel and Wire Company should abandon its proposed Milwaukee plant, and the threat for the time being proved effective. The Carnegie Company announced that it would construct a large tube mill at Conneaut, Ohio, and let it be understood that it would not hesitate to enter into active competition with all the producers of finished goods. There was no doubt in the minds of those who knew Andrew Carnegie but that these plans would actually be carried out. They recalled that "the wild Scotchman" had been successful in even more daring schemes.

The situation was full of dangers. The prosperity of the steel makers could not continue through the bitter competitive war that seemed to be in prospect. The officials of the Carnegie Company apparently were not seriously worried, for they felt confident of the ability of their organization to finance and make highly profitable in the end whatever new construction might become necessary. The officials of the other great companies, however, were not so complacent. All of the large consolidations were capitalized, as we shall see, up to the limit of their earning power, and their stock had been sold on the promise of large and regular dividends. Moreover, large amounts of the stock were still owned by the original promoters and underwriters. The managers, therefore, were far from eager to enter into a regime of severe competition. Under these conditions the suggestion that an immense holding company, the greatest trust in the world, be formed was favorably received. It furnished the only possible peaceful solution of the pending problems. The strongest financial houses, as well as the largest steel companies, were committed in advance to this plan, because it was the only means of protecting them from severe loss.

108. *Method of promotion.*—The promotion of the United States Steel Corporation was not, for the reasons that have been given, an especially difficult task. The chief obstacle was overcome when men of sufficient breadth, imagination and ability to form a clear conception of what was to be done had been found. So stupendous an undertaking could only be carried out by the giants of the financial, the industrial and the legal worlds. Fortunately for the project, the right men were at hand and were interested in its success; above all, the active support of Mr. J. P. Morgan, the most forceful personality in Wall Street, did more than anything else to make the plan practicable and ultimately successful.

The details of the promotion of the United States Steel Corporation have never been disclosed. Long investigation was not as necessary as in most promotions for the reason that the promoters were familiar at first hand with the concerns to be consolidated. The plan at first, it is known, was to combine only the great companies; the Carnegie Steel Company, Federal Steel Company, National Tube Company and the American Steel and Wire Company. The potential competition, however, of the four Moore companies looked so threatening that they also were brought into the combination. Certain other large companies, such as the Jones and Laughlin Steel Company, of Pittsburg, were approached, but no terms were agreed upon.

The United States Steel Corporation filed its certificate of incorporation in New Jersey on February 23, 1901, showing a capitalization of $3,000. Under its amended certificate of April 1, 1901, however, its capitalization was changed to $1,100,000,000, one-half common and one-half preferred. The charter, it may be noted, gives discretion to the board of directors to increase its capital stock.

109. *Prospectus of the corporation.*—In the light of the later history of the company and as an example of scientific prospectus-making, some extracts from the prospectus issued by the firm of J. P. Morgan and Company are given below. The reader should note how carefully each positive statement is qualified and how much more is implied as to prospective profits than is actually said. Yet the prospectus cannot be called misleading. If it is read as carefully as it was written, it will be found not only to contain technically accurate statements, but to give a correct impression as well. The difficulty comes in the fact that comparatively few persons are capable of giving it a careful reading. The prospectus also contains a sufficient account for our purpose of the basis of consolidation.

A syndicate, comprising leading financial interests throughout the United States and Europe, of which the undersigned are managers, has been formed by subscribers to the amount of $200,000,000 (including among such subscribers the undersigned and many large stockholders of the several companies), to carry out the arrangement hereinafter stated, and to provide the sum in cash and the financial support required for that purpose. Such syndicate, through the undersigned, has made a contract with the United States Steel Corporation under which the latter is to issue and deliver its preferred stock, and its common stock, and its 5 per cent gold bonds in consideration for stocks of the above-named companies and bonds and stock of the Carnegie Company and the sum of $25,000,000 in cash.

The syndicate has already arranged for the acquisition of substantially all the bonds and stock of the Carnegie Company, including Mr. Carnegie's holdings. The bonds of the United States Steel Corporation are to be used only to acquire bonds and 60 per cent of the stock of the Carnegie Company.

The syndicate offers for each $100 par value of stock of the class mentioned below, the amount set opposite thereto in preferred stock or common stock of the United States Steel Corporation at par:

Name of company and class of stock.	Amount of new stock to be delivered in par value.	
	Preferred Stock	Common Stock
Federal Steel Company:		
Preferred stock	$110.00	......
Common stock	4.00	$107.50
American Steel and Wire Company of New Jersey:		
Preferred stock	117.50	......
Common stock	......	102.50
National Tube Company:		
Preferred stock	125.00	......
Common stock	8.80	125.00

National Steel Company:		
Preferred stock	125.00	......
Common stock	......	125.00
American Tin Plate Company:		
Preferred stock	125.00	......
Common stock	20.00	125.00
American Steel Hoop Company:		
Preferred stock	100.00	......
Common stock	......	100.00
American Sheet Steel Company:		
Preferred stock	100.00	......
Common stock	......	100.00

With reference to the last four companies, the aggregate amount of stocks so to be offered was arranged with the principal stockholders of those companies, who have requested the distribution of such amount among the four companies, to be made in the percentages above stated.

Statements furnished to us by officers of the several companies above named and of the Carnegie Company show that the aggregate of the net earnings of all the companies for the calendar year 1900 was amply sufficient to pay dividends on both classes of the new stocks, besides making provisions for sinking funds and maintenance of properties. It is expected that by the consummation of the proposed arrangement the necessity of large deductions heretofore made on account of expenditures for improvements will be avoided, the amount of earnings applicable to dividends will be substantially increased, and greater stability of investment will be assured, without necessarily increasing the prices of manufactured products.

All shares of the United States Steel Corporation deliverable to or for account of the syndicate, which shall not be required for the acquisition of the stock of the Carnegie Company or for delivery to depositors under terms of this circular, are to be retained by and to belong to the syndicate.

It is proper to state that J. P. Morgan & Co. are to receive no compensation for their services as syndicate managers beyond a share in any sum which ultimately may be realized by the syndicate.

J. P. Morgan & Co.,
Syndicate Managers.

110. *Profits of the promoters.*—The sum which ultimately was realized by the syndicate was never made public, but it is easy to figure that it must have been in neighborhood of $240,000,000, face value, of common stock, against which should be off-set $25,000,000 cash furnished by the syndicate and the expenses of promotion. Assuming that the common stock was sold by the syndicate members at an average price of thirty, which is probably lower than the actual average, we have gross profits of $72,000,000. Deducting the $25,000,000 and assuming expenses to have been $1,000,000, we have left net promoters' and underwriters' profits of $46,000,000 —a huge sum and yet not too great, considering the risk and the financial power and ability required in the unprecedented undertaking.

The provision of cash by the syndicate was a somewhat unusual method of meeting this part of the financial problem involved in promoting a consolidation.

111. *Capitalization at the beginning.*—It is worth noting that the $160,000,000 Carnegie stock obtained in exchange $98,000,000 preferred stock, $90,000,000 common stock and $144,000,000 bonds of the Steel Corporation. In addition $160,000,000 Carnegie bonds obtained an equal amount of United States Steel collateral bonds. Thus the par value of the stocks and bonds given to Carnegie Company security holders was nearly one-half billion dollars, more than one-third the total capitalization of the corporation. The aggregate capitalization of the other seven original companies was $457,000,000 and the par value of Steel stock given in

exchange was $532,000,000, an increase of $75,000,000. The terms of exchange were so liberal that 98 per cent of the stock of the original eight companies was acquired.

Shortly afterwards two other companies were taken in, namely:

1. The American Bridge Company which had been formed in April, 1900. This company had absorbed twenty-six separate concerns and embraced over nine-tenths of the bridge-building interests of the United States.

2. The Lake Superior Consolidated Iron Mines Company, which owned and operated valuable mines in the Mesaba range of the Lake Superior iron region.

Practically all the securities of the Lake Superior Company were acquired and 85 per cent of the stock of the American Bridge Company.

The capitalization of the United States Steel Corporation at the end of the first year was as follows:

Capital Stock, Preferred	$ 510,281,100.00
" " Common	508,302,500.00
Capital Stock of Subsidiary Cos., outstanding	215,914.38
U. S. Steel Bonds	303,757,000.00
Other bonds	56,997,326.00
	$1,379,553,840.38

The figures following will give some idea of the enormous extent of the steel corporation's property at the beginning: 213 different plants and transportation companies; 41 mines; nearly 1,000 miles of railroad; a lake fleet of 112 vessels which constituted one-third total tonnage of Northern Lakes; controlled 78 blast furnaces, one-third of the number in United States; owned

57,000 acres of coking coal land; leased 50,000 acres Pocahontas Coal land, W. Va.; owned considerable areas of steam and gas coal in Illinois. The most important assets of all were the ore deposits in the Lake Superior region, which were estimated by Mr. Schwab at 750,000,000 tons.

112. *Additions.*—The principal additions to the steel corporation have been:

1—Shelby Tube Co.	1901
2—Union Steel Co.	1902
3—Holdings of Chemung Iron Co., Duluth	1903
4—Properties of Clairton Steel Co.	1904
5—Lease of Hill holdings in Lake Superior Region	1906
6—Tennessee Coal, Iron and Railroad Company	1907

The Shelby Steel Tube Company was a small and greatly over-capitalized concern which was, however, the largest maker of seamless tubing in the world.

The Union Steel Company was a consolidation of seven coke-mining, sheet steel, tin plate and steel companies in and near Sharon, Penna.

The Chemung Iron Company was a Detroit concern which owned a large and important block of Mesaba ore deposits.

The Clairton Steel Company was a Pittsburg concern which owned a large plant, 2,600 acres of coking coal land, 20,000 acres of mineral lands in the Marquette Range and considerable railroad and limestone properties.

On April 15, 1907, the notable lease of the Hill ore lands was ratified. The lease provides that a royalty of $1.65 per gross ton for ore of a fixed grade was to be paid in 1907 and the royalty increased 3 4-10 cents per ton each succeeding year. The minimum to be mined and shipped was 750,000 tons in 1907 and was to increase 750,000 tons per year until it reached 8,250,000 tons. The option was reserved, however, to the Steel Corporation to end the lease in 1915, and in 1912 the approaching termination of the lease was announced.

In November, 1907, the corporation acquired about $30,000,000, or practically all, of the outstanding common stock of the Tennessee Coal, Iron and Railroad Company. The stock was paid for at the rate of $11,904.76 par value of the 10-60 year sinking fund 5 per cent bonds of the steel corporation for $10,000 par of Tennessee common. Many readers no doubt will recall the circumstances surrounding this deal. It was made possible by the ability of the Steel Corporation to put up ready cash in the critical time of the October, 1907, crisis. The cash was used to buy in the Steel Corporation's own bonds with which to pay for Tennessee stock. The operation thus had a double effect of supplying cash to persons who needed it badly, and of supplying a security, which was acceptable as collateral, in place of the unavailable Tennessee stock. The Tennessee Company owned 16 blast furnaces, 450,000 acres of coal, ore and limestone and timber lands, large developed coal mines and a big steel rail mill at Ensley, Ala.

Besides these large purchases the steel corporation has also increased its holdings by building out of its earnings an entirely new plant. At Gary, Indiana, there has been erected a large modern steel rail mill at a cost of $75,000,000. The mill began operations in 1909. The Gary tract covers about 9,000 acres, of which 1,163 acres are devoted to the plant. The cost was nearly $80,000,000. This new plant was called for by the great increase in the western demand for steel.

113. *Financial changes.*—The chief event in the financial history of the Steel Corporation is its much discussed preferred stock conversion of 1902. In April of that year the management issued a circular to stockholders saying that $50,000,000 new capital was needed, one-half for redemption of temporary loans incurred by constituent companies and one-half for improvements. The plan proposed was to create a new issue of $250,000,000 5 per cent bonds, of which $200,000,000 was to be exchanged, dollar for dollar, for an equal amount of preferred stock and $50,000,000 was to be sold for cash. Each preferred stockholder was offered the right to subscribe to the extent of one-half his holdings, paying 40 per cent in stock and 10 per cent in cash, or to the extent of 40 per cent of his holdings, paying in stock alone. The argument urged for this plan was that the $50,000,000 would be raised and yet an annual saving in the company's charges of $1,500,000 would be effected. To this plan 99 8-10 per cent of the stock voted at the annual meeting assented.

The plan was objectionable, however, to certain stockholders for the obvious reason that a new issue was created superior to their own security without any corresponding enhancement in the value of the corporation's assets. The plan was further objectionable in that the issue was to be underwritten by a syndicate which included some of the corporation's directors. The syndicate agreed to take enough of the bonds to bring the total sale up to $100,000,000.[1] In return they were to have the privilege of subscribing to any or all of the bonds not taken by the stockholders and they were to get a 4 per cent commission on all the bonds sold to the stockholders or otherwise. It was objected that under this

1 See a copy of the agreement in Chapter XIX.

agreement the syndicate took a very slight risk inasmuch as it was practically certain that at least $100,000,000 worth of bonds would be sold, and got an excessive commission. The objections on this score were never satisfactorily answered.

The opponents of the conversion plan secured a temporary injunction and brought suit to restrain the directors from carrying out the plan. The decisions of the court, however, were in favor of the Steel Corporation management, on the ground that no fraud was shown and that the great majority of the stockholders had approved the issue. The danger of disaster to the corporation, on account of its great increase in bonded obligations, is somewhat lessened by the fact that the interest on these sinking fund 5's must lapse for two years before foreclosure proceedings can be commenced. This provision is a safeguard to the corporation, though, of course, it would not be of great value in a period of prolonged depression like that from 1893 to 1897.

The slump in the steel business in 1903 made it necessary for the corporation to economize. Several mills were dismantled and some of the sub-executive offices were abolished. It became desirable to change somewhat the financial organization of the corporation. In March, 1903, the original Carnegie Company of Pennsylvania, the National Steel Company and the American Steel Hoop Company were combined under the name of the Carnegie Steel Company of New Jersey and later in the year the American Sheet Steel Company and the American Tin Plate Company were combined as the American Sheet and Tin Plate Company. Early the next year the corporation's search for wider markets led to the formation of the United States Steel Products Export Company, which is the selling agency for all the foreign business of the corporation. The direct control of this company is in the Federal Steel Company.

114. *Basis of capitalization.*—Is the steel corporation over-capitalized? It is not worth while to rehash the wordy debate on this question, which has lasted for several years, but a few facts ought to be noted. The aggregate capitalization of the first ten companies to enter the corporation was approximately $710,000,000. In exchange for this amount of stock the corporation issued $868,000,000 stock and $144,000,000 bonds, an increase of $302,000,000. In addition the promoters of the steel corporation received for their services something over $240,000,000 in stock. Even though we should estimate that all the subsidiary companies' stock represented tangible assets, therefore, we should still have to conclude that $542,000,000 of United States Steel capitalization was water at the start.

But what are the facts as to the capitalization of the original companies? Daniel G. Reid, president of the American Tin Plate Company, testified before the Industrial Commission that of the $46,000,000 capitalization of that company, $18,000,000 (preferred stock) was supposed to represent the value of the property and $28,000,000 (common stock) represented hopes for the future and the pay of the promoter. It is well known that in the capitalization of the National Steel, American Steel Hoop and American Sheet Steel companies, all of which were promoted by the same interests as the American Tin Plate Company, the same principle was followed.

Similarly, Mr. John W. Gates testified that of the $80,000,000 capitalization of the American Steel and Wire Company, $20,000,000 to $30,000,000 was water. Of the $100,000,000 capitalization of the Federal Steel

Company, about $45,000,000 represented tangible assets and $10,000,000 cash assets, while the rest was water. These statements are enough to indicate that of the $710,000,000 capitalization of the original companies, a large share stood for nothing more tangible than good will and "prospects."

The suits to prevent the carrying out of the preferred stock conversion plan of 1903 brought out some interesting statements. One affidavit, by an engineer who was represented as an expert, said that the plants and properties of the corporation could be duplicated for about $200,000,000 and that the total assets, including good will and organization, were not worth $500,000,000, Another affidavit stated that the plants of the Carnegie Company, represented 44 per cent of the productive capacity of the steel corporation and that these plants had been valued on March 12, 1900, by the partners of the Carnegie Company in a legal proceeding at $75,000.000. On the other hand, Mr. Charles M. Schwab, then president of the steel corporation, submitted the following valuation:

1—Iron-ore Properties	$ 700,000,000
2—Plants, Mills, Fixtures, Equipments	300,000,000
3—Coal and coke fields, 87,589 acres	100,000,000
4—Transportation properties	80,000,000
5—Blast Furnaces	48,000,000
6—Natural Gas Fields	20,000,000
7—Lime Stone Properties	4,000,000
8—Cash and cash assets	214,278,000
	$1,466,278,000

There is not such a great difference between these two estimates as at first appears. More than one-half the assets, as given by Mr. Schwab, consist of ore and coal land in which he included unmined ore at a high value. Beyond question, such an estimate is uncertain and speculative. Technical progress may introduce new methods of treating ore which will greatly reduce the value of this large buried mass. Besides, Mr. Schwab had already counted the value of this ore once when he based his estimate of the value of the plants on their low cost of production and, as a factor in that low cost, counted in the cheapness with which they could secure raw materials.

In what has been said it has been assumed that the proper way to value a property is to arrive at the probable cost of replacing it. But there is another method of valuation which is more popular among business men, and, to the writer's mind, more scientific. This method is to capitalize earning power. The profits of the eight original sub-companies of the Steel Corporation in 1900 were $96,000,000. The record of the Steel Corporation in the first seven years of its history was as follows:

	Net Earnings
1902	$133,308,000
1903	109,171,000
1904	73,176,000
1905	119,787,000
1906	156,624,000
1907	160,965,000
1908	91,267,000
Average	$120,614,000

Now if we assume that 10 per cent is a fair rate on money invested in the steel business and capitalize profits on that basis, we get a result not a great deal below the present capitalization.

Our general conclusion on this point must be something like this: If the properties of the Steel Corporation were sold under the hammer, they probably would not fetch one-half or one-third the amount at which the corporation is capitalized. Even if we take into consideration good will, organization, financial connections, and so on, we could hardly say that the assets equal or nearly equal the capitalization. But, if we base our valuation on earnings, not assets, we can safely say that the over-capitalization is not very great.

The Steel Corporation is earning immense sums because it is well managed; because it has prestige; because in some lines it has almost a complete monoply. These things are not tangible assets, but they are sources of income; and income, according to ordinary business usage may properly be capitalized.

Even from the ultra-conservative standpoint, it may be said that the Steel Corporation is rapidly "squeezing out the water" for it has made it its policy to provide from its gross income for depreciation and for improvements. The figures following show that about $300,000,000 have thus been added to the tangible assets of the corporation since its formation.

Sinking Funds, subsidiary companies	$ 9,367,412
Sinking Funds, U. S. Steel Bonds	25,624,410
New Construction	176,137,166
Increase in surplus	82,223,107
	$293,352,095

115. *Operating policy.*—A careful study of the operating policy of the Steel Corporation belongs elsewhere. Our attention may be turned, however, to a few conspicuous facts.

The corporation's relations with its employés have so far been exceptionally harmonious. There has been no strike or serious trouble of any kind. At the end of 1902 the corporation started its famous profit-sharing plan under which a large amount of preferred stock has been sold to employees. The workers are divided into six classes, according to salary, and each class is allowed to buy a certain proportion of stock each year at a fixed price. The prices named have always been somewhat below the market prices. The corporation gives a bonus of $5 for each share which is held for five years. The result has been to give a considerable number of the 210,000 employees a lively interest in the success of the corporation, and to bind them more closely to the management. The scheme has proved practicable and has been probably of great benefit in maintaining industrial peace.

The corporation is, of course, simply a holding company and has only a general oversight over the sub-companies. Each subsidiary company manages its own internal affairs and buys and sells from and even competes with other sub-companies. Cross shipments, however, are avoided and raw materials are furnished by common agencies. The idea is to stimulate each company by internal competition and otherwise to the highest pitch of efficiency. The operating ratio or per cent of manufacturing costs to gross business has been very steady with a slight tendency downward since 1902. The ratio has not moved up very high in periods of depression, which is considered an indication of economical management.

116. *Steel securities.*—The securities of the United States Steel Corporation now outstanding are:

1—Underlying bonds	$ 160,877,877
2—Coll. Tr. Gold 5's, 1901	270,277,000
3— " " Skg. Fd. 5's, 1903	189,346,500
Total Bonds	$ 620,501,377
4—Preferred Stock	360,281,100
5—Common Stock	508,302,500
Total Securities	$1,489,084,977

The underlying bond issues are too numerous and too small in volume to be worth discussing here. Most of them are secured by direct first mortgages and are very closely held.

The collateral trust gold 5's of 1901, due April 1, 1951, are secured by the deposit of all the securities owned by the corporation. A sinking fund of $3,040,-000 per year is used to purchase bonds obtainable at 115 or less, and since April 1, 1911, has been applied to the redemption of the bonds drawn by lot. Almost all these bonds are held, it is understood, by Andrew Carnegie and are not on the market.

A more interesting issue to us is the collateral trust sinking fund 10-60 year gold 5's of 1903. The authorized issue was $250,000,000, of which $200,000,000 was reserved for exchange with preferred stock under the conversion plan. As a claim on the assets, these bonds rank next to the 5's of 1901. They are further protected by a sinking fund of $1,010,000 per annum to be used until 1913 for the purchase of bonds at 110 or less and after 1913 for the redemption of bonds, drawn by lot, at 110. This last named feature introduces a speculative element into the security which is supposed to enhance its value. If the estimates already quoted of the asset value of the property of the corporation are correct, these bonds have behind them chiefly the earning power of the corporation.

The preferred stock issue is 7 per cent cumulative. Dividends have not been missed since the formation of the corporation. The common stock drew 4 per cent in the first two years; ½ per cent in 1903; nothing from that date till 1906; 1½ per cent in 1906; 2 per cent until 1909, when 4 per cent was paid, and 5 per cent since 1909.

Steel has been a prince now for several years. Is it likely to become so much of a pauper that dividends or even interest will be threatened? There can be no doubt but that the corporation is still in danger; a bad slump or even insolvency is conceivable. On the other hand, there are at least two good reasons for believing that the danger is rapidly lessening and in a few years will be a thing of the past.

One of these reasons is that the physical condition of its properties is excellent, according to all reports, and is being constantly improved. We have already alluded to the large appropriations for depreciation and for betterments. It is estimated that following the completion of the Gary plant, the capacity of the corporation was increased about 75 per cent; yet the interest charges are practically the same as they were at the beginning. In addition, new ore deposits, it is said, of a value of $400,000,000 have been located on the lands of the Steel corporation. The second reason is that the demand for steel in this country is apparently insatiable. Steel rail production to-day is nearly three times that of 1881; yet this particular kind of product which was of great importance in 1881 is now only a fraction of the entire steel trade. The demand for structural shapes and for machinery, already enormous, is just beginning to grow.

To get an idea of what may be expected in the next ten or twenty years, let us observe the per capita increase in the production of pig iron in the last three decades as shown below:

1880	171	pounds
1890	329	"
1900	399	"
1905	619	"
1910	669	"

If the steel business, then, grows, as the biggest and most farsighted men in that line expect, and if the present policy of improving and enlarging the properties continues, as there is no reason to doubt, we may safely conclude that the earnings of the Steel Corporation will become very much larger than they are now. Of course, those earnings will not grow continuously. The steel business is speculative and erratic in its very nature and always will be, so long as periods of depression and of prosperity alternate. Yet the enterprise and efficiency of the United States Steel managers seem to be almost a guarantee that at the worst steel earnings will never sink so low that interest charges cannot be met; it is reasonable to expect that they will never sink so low that preferred dividends cannot be met; and it is even reasonable to hope that the common dividends will always be maintained at or above their present level.

CHAPTER XVI

SELLING SECURITIES—THE PROSPECTUS

117. *The four methods of selling securities.*—Whenever new securities—whether of an established company, of a new concern or of a reorganization—are issued, these are four possible methods of disposing of them. The first method is by an inside distribution of the securities to people already interested in the business. This method we have already considered. In the case of a close corporation the distribution of the securities is obviously a simple matter of bargain-making among the few people involved. In the case of a consolidation the distribution to insiders is carried on by exchanging the new securities for old securities as already explained.

The second method is to work through the Wall Street, or some similar, market, which is considered in the chapter following.

The third method is to sell them to the public through established bond or brokerage houses. This method will be discussed both in this chapter and under the head of underwriting.

The fourth method is by direct appeal to the public through newspaper and magazine advertising, through circular and individual letters and through salesmen. In a great many corporations the promoter finds the first three methods unavailable and is forced to resort to this fourth method. This is particularly true of speculative enterprises.

The principles that should be followed in the presentation and selling of corporate securities direct to the public are not different from the principles that should be followed in selling other articles. These principles are treated in the treatise on SELLING AND BUYING and need not be reviewed here. Something should be said, however, about the document in which the leading facts with regard to the securities are stated and the prospects of the company discussed, namely, the prospectus.

118. *General characteristics of a good prospectus.*—The promoter's prospectus should be, and with successful flotations usually is a work of art. A good prospectus will appeal to a large number of people, will arouse their interest, will hold their attention from beginning to end, and will engender confidence. A poor prospectus will nullify whatever success the promoter may have had in stimulating curiosity on the part of the prospective buyers of his securities.

It goes without saying that it should be well written and attractively printed. In this respect the same rules that apply to other selling literature should be followed.

Naturally the prospectus will emphasize the strong features and minimize the weak spots of the business. The promoter must take care, however, in so doing that he does not misstate or conceal any material fact. Otherwise he may be held liable for fraud, or at least anyone who subscribes to the corporation's securities on the strength of the prospectus may have good legal grounds for withdrawing from his contract. The skillful prospectus writer, who is presenting to the public securities which he knows to be highly speculative in character, must find some means of reconciling these apparently inconsistent requirements. He must present all the important facts and yet he must make his prospectus strong, attractive and convincing. Any well-trained writer should be able to do the trick if he studies his proposition carefully.

Obviously in any prospectus the strikingly attractive features of the enterprise will be made prominent and much will be said about them. Perhaps the statements with regard to them will be printed in bold face or other prominent type, so as to catch the eye of the reader at once. Statements as to the more doubtful and risky features of the enterprise will be tucked away in some obscure corner. Thus the law will be satisfied and at the same time it will take a very careful, intelligent reading to ascertain from the prospectus the real facts of the case.

Another means of avoiding legal objections is to make sweeping general statements without making the writer or any other definite person responsible for them. Such phrases as "competent judges have reported," or "after expert examination we believe," or "witnesses who have seen the property are thoroughly convinced," are very common introductions in prospectuses. The statements in themselves may be untrue; yet by using such phrases the writer may succeed in divesting himself of any personal responsibility.

Most prospectuses, as any reader of them will testify, are so vague, that what the writer implies assumes a much more prominent place in the average reader's mind than what he actually says. In a recent mining prospectus, for instance, we have the following typical sentence: "We have every reason to believe that the corporation will have assets at the end of the year that will astonish each and every holder of the stock, and it is our belief that claims, titles and rights cannot be bought outright for $1,000,000 or more." Notice that this sentence does not contain any single statement of fact to which the prospectus-writer could be bound down.

Another hoary trick that is worked over and over again in the prospectuses of new companies, is to call attention to the immense profits of other companies working in the same field. It is very seldom indeed that a copper-mining prospectus is issued that does not call attention in big type to the profits made by the holders of the original stock of Calumet and Hecla, the Copper Queen, Anaconda, and other classic examples. The reader is expected to infer that the new corporation will have a similar history.

119. *A typical speculative prospectus.*—The prospectus of a company designed to own and publish a magazine is given in part below. The reader will find in these few paragraphs illustrations of all the principles mentioned above. In this case, although the magazine is stated to have been in existence for twenty-eight years, not one word is said as to its record; instead, all the emphasis is given to "prospects," "purpose" and "possibilities."

It is a medium that can treat any subject with justice to itself and its readers; therefore, its pulling power for subscriptions, you will agree, covers possibly a greater field for circulation, than any magazine that you can recall. Its field of expansion is simply unlimited.

From an advertising standpoint, I might say, after years of experience, I do not know of a publication that has such prospects for money making as The Blank Company.

Being a practical publisher, it is my purpose to put The Blank Company in the place it should enjoy, and in order to do this, I have deemed it wise to share its future with a number of my friends, and am, therefore, organizing a company capitalized at $50,000 for the immediate expansion of The Blank Company. The stock is secured by the property, the name and the good will, which, if put up at auction, would be considered a bargain, if purchased at many times the amount of the company's capitalization.

If you have looked into the magazine field, you will know that although some of the larger magazines are capitalized for over a half-million dollars, they are all making phenomenal money for their early investors. The general magazine field I consider pretty well covered, but a magazine of the unique name that The Blank Company possesses, can be expanded and developed and larger profits made from it than any other publication enjoys.

To illustrate the earning power of magazines, permit me to say that one magazine was sold some time ago to a well-known newspaper publisher for nearly $700,000, in spite of the fact that at that time it had a circulation of only 250,000 and a shrinking in its advertising patronage.

Another well-known magazine, whose circulation had dropped down below 50,000 and had practically no advertising, declined an offer of $10,000 for its name and good will.

I will recall that if you had been able to buy a thousand dollars worth of *Munsey's* stock, on the ground floor basis (that you are now offered in The Blank Company) for your investment the thousand dollars in *Munsey's* now would be paying you $10,000 to $12,000 a year in dividends.

If you could have invested only $100 in *Munsey's*, your holdings would now be worth from ten to twelve thousand dollars and would be paying you $1,000 to $1,200 a year in dividends; a larger investment would have made you wealthy.

An English author, who ten years ago obtained $2,000 worth of *McClure's* Magazine stock in exchange for a manuscript, sold his holdings recently for $20,000, having received in dividends during that time the round sum of $14,000. For his $2,000 worth of manuscript he received in a decade $34,000 in cash, a profit of 1,700 per cent.

Everybody's, *The Ladies' Home Journal* and many other magazines, represent wonderful money-making investments.

The same opportunity is knocking at your door at this moment. The Blank Company, with its twenty-eight years of continuous existence, with an unlimited advertising field and with a subscription list that can be increased beyond that of any other publication in existence, offers you a rare opportunity in associating yourself with an enterprise which will make money for its stockholders very rapidly.

If you want to go in with me in developing and expanding The Blank Company, I will offer you some of its stock at its par value, $10 per share. This opportunity, however, will only remain open for a short while. Stock can be purchased on a basis of 3 per cent for cash with subscription, or 10 per cent down and 10 per cent per month.

120. *A typical investment prospectus.*—In the above remarks we have had in mind principally the prospectuses of highly speculative companies. We need not pass judgment here on the legitimacy of the methods that are used by such companies to obtain subscriptions for their stock. It is certainly improper to delude subscribers. On the other hand, it is unquestionably proper to present a new enterprise in a favorable light. Just where the dividing line between an honestly favorable and a dishonestly deceptive presentation comes is a question which every promoter must settle with his own conscience. The prospectuses of well-known, entirely legitimate investment securities often go to the other extreme. They present merely a dry, formal statement of the facts with sometimes a tabulation of the assets and earnings of the company or bald figures of some other kind.

For instance, several of the leading banks of the world—including Baring Brothers and Company of London, Comptoir National d'Escompte de Paris, Credit Lyonnais of Paris, Deutsche Bank of Berlin, J. P. Morgan and Company, the First National Bank and the National City Bank of New York—co-operated in issuing on March 1, 1909, a $50,000,000 5 per cent internal gold loan of the Argentine Government. Much might have been said as to the wealth, high standing and prospects of the Argentine Republic and as to the small amount of the loan in comparison with the great resources back of it. The bonds were sold at the price of 99 per cent of the face value, thus yielding to the purchaser something over 5 per cent, a high rate on the loans of a government of good standing. We can imagine, taking the examples that have been given above as a basis, how a promoter used to getting up prospectuses for speculative concerns would have reveled in the opportunities that this issue would have afforded him, how he would have enlarged on the Argentine Republic's reputation and prosperity, how many word pictures he would have drawn to illustrate his statements.

The prospectus issued by the great banks that have been named, however, compressed a description of the bonds, a statement of the terms on which they would be issued, and the argument on behalf of the bonds into the four brief, cold paragraphs that follow:

Provision is made for a sinking fund of 1 per cent. By the operation of this sinking fund the loan will be paid off in thirty-six years at the latest. The contract with the Argentine Government provides that said fund is to be applied half yearly to the purchase or tender of bonds at or under par or by drawings at par should the bonds be at over par. The first operation of the sinking fund will take place in the month of December, 1909. Drawn bonds will be payable on March 1st or September 1st following the date of the drawing. The Government undertakes not to increase the sinking fund or to redeem the whole of the loan before March 1st, 1914.

We reserve to ourselves the absolute right in our discretion to close the application list at any time without notice and to reject any or all applications and also to allot smaller amounts than applied for.

All applications should be made on forms which may be obtained at our offices, and must be accompanied by a deposit of $50 per bond.

If no allotment is made, the deposit will be returned in full, and if only a portion of the amount applied for be allotted, the balance of the deposit will be appropriated towards the amount due on March 10th, 1909. If any further balance remains, such balance will be returned. In case of failure to pay the balance of the subscription when due, all right in any previous payment will vest in us absolutely without accountability therefor.

Although such a presentation is unattractive, it is frequently effective. The coldness and dryness carry with them the sense of conservative safety. For that reason, a statement of this kind is sometimes put forward as a prospectus of what is in reality a highly speculative company; and this trick when skillfully executed has been known to succeed.

121. *The ideal prospectus.*—Even in the most formal prospectus, however, it is usually well to use untechnical expressions and to present facts in such a manner that they will be not merely significant, but interesting. Some such tendency is coming into evidence, even in the presentations of strictly investment securities. The number of people who are possible investors in such securities is constantly increasing and the amount of such securities is also increasing. In order to create a market for these immense issues among people who are not familiar with the technical jargon of the financial world, it is necessary to change somewhat the old-fashioned formal method of presentation. This change is undoubtedly for the better. As the intelligent in-

terest of the public in financial affairs grows, we may expect to see the typical prospectus of a speculative corporation and the presentation of a strictly investment security approaching each other more closely in tone and in form.

Although in this country the prospectus, as has been indicated, is so frequently used to present speculative and even swindling schemes in a false light that prospectus-writing has come to be regarded almost as a dishonorable method of securing money for an enterprise, and although this opinion is not without basis, yet it must be borne in mind, on the other hand, that there are such things as a legitimate direct appeal to the public for funds and an honest prospectus.

In England this method of raising funds is much more generally used for reputable enterprises than in this country. To take one instance, it is said that the English Eastman Kodak Company was floated without any assistance whatever from bankers or underwriters. About $5,000,000 of stock was sold to the public through direct newspaper advertising, circularizing and the issue of an attractive prospectus. That the method in this instance has been entirely successful is shown by the fact that the company's stock is now selling at the rate of about $675 a share. It is to be regretted that the number of similar instances in this country is so small.

122. *Selling through banking houses.*—The securities of almost all large legitimate corporations are sold through banks and brokerage houses. The advantage of this method to the investor is that he is protected more or less by the investigation and experienced judgment of his banker. The disadvantages are three: first, on account of his leaving the investigation to the banker he

does not acquire that first-hand knowledge of the enterprise in which he invests that it would be desirable for him to obtain; second, that he is thus left practically at the mercy of his banker; third, that the broker's commission, which is often not inconsiderable, intervenes between the buyer of the security and the selling corporation.

The advantage to the corporation of selling through a bank or brokerage house is that the corporation officials may feel certain that the issue will be successfully disposed of in this way, especially if it is "underwritten," as explained in Chapter XVIII. With a corporation of any size, the bond or brokerage house will probably be one of the large concerns that carry on their work in the Wall Street district of New York, the State Street district of Boston, the La Salle Street district of Chicago, or the corresponding financial center of some other large city.

123. *Requirements of reputable banking houses.*—The good Wall Street houses will not undertake to float issues of small size—certainly none less than $100,000 and preferably not that small—for two reasons; first, because there is not enough profit in selling small issues to pay for the expenses; second, because a small issue of stocks or bonds never becomes well-known to the public and is therefore not readily marketable. As to the kinds of enterprises that will be taken up, the better houses prefer in the order named, steam railroads, electric railroads and industrials. Most of them will not touch mines, oil companies, or any other highly speculative enterprise. The only practicable means for getting funds for such an enterprise from the public ordinarily is by direct solicitation.

There are not many high-class Wall Street houses

engaged in selling securities and there are a considerable number of imitation banking houses whose main object is to get their hands on the money of "suckers." The working plan of such swindlers is to receive persons who come to them with securities to sell, no matter how worthless the securities may be, with open arms, wax enthusiastic over the market for the securities, make numerous high-sounding promises as to the sales which they will be able to make, and in conclusion demand from the victim as his "guarantee of good faith" a sum of money for expenses. Of course this money is not honestly spent. The high-grade banking houses, on the contrary, will receive any new proposition that is presented to them, especially if it comes from a stranger, with skepticism; and, if they show any interest at all, it is to be expected that they will make a long and thorough investigation, before committing themselves in any manner. It is poor policy to approach one of these houses without having a business introduction of some kind. Generally speaking, it is well to present the proposition in writing in the first place, giving a clear and complete statement with all the supporting evidence that can be added. A Wall Street banker of the class that the writer has in mind is not likely to be carried off his feet by persuasive personal eloquence and is more likely to yield to cold figures than to impassioned appeals.

It takes a man who has spent a lifetime in the Street to tell absolutely what are the sound, reliable houses and what are the more or less shady concerns. There are Wall Street firms which, to the writer's knowledge, are regarded by Wall Street bankers as worse than banditti, which nevertheless have kept in existence and have apparently been prosperous for many years. Such firms may maintain expensive suites of offices, may have pious-looking personages at their head and may give an appearance of permanence and honesty. The only sure sign of their general unreliability, that the writer can give, is that they are out looking for business, that they make an effort to secure for themselves the flotation of securities of small corporations and that they are willing to pretend to sell such securities without having first made an adequate investigation. Even this symptom, however is not always present, for the heads of such concerns are shrewd and experienced enough to make a pretense at times of conducting an investigation before they accept the proposition that has been presented to them.

The first step in the investigation of an enterprise by a reputable house will be to get the complete record of all the men who have any connection with it. If there is a flaw in the reputation of any of them, the whole proposition will probably be dropped. Next, the prospects of the enterprise itself will be looked into. Every large house engaged in selling securities keeps on its own staff capable men who are qualified to form an expert judgment as to the merits of the common forms of business enterprises, such as street railroads, manufacturing plants, and so on. In addition, unless the house is absolutely satisfied, it will probably obtain reports based on searching examinations by three classes of professional experts, namely, engineers, lawyers and accountants. If all of these are favorable, from beginning to end, the proposition will perhaps be accepted.

The three essential factors in making a proposition acceptable are:

(1) Good reputation of the men connected with the enterprise.

(2) Absence of risky factors in the general nature of the business or in the general situation. For instance, a street railway company would not be taken up if the people of the locality in which it had been located were for some reason bitterly hostile to public service corporations. In the same way, as has been said, the good banking houses will not deal in the securities of undeveloped mines, no matter how promising.

(3) Practical certainty of profits sufficient to meet all fixed charges. This almost goes without saying; yet it is worth noting, because many people seem to imagine that if a new corporation promises to have considerable profits its securities are safe investments. It is necessary that these profits should not only be large in the aggregate, but should be steady enough and certain enough to guarantee that the corporation will never be compelled to pass any of its interest payments or other fixed charges.

124. *Their methods of selling securities.*—The good Wall Street houses are so exceedingly careful in their investigations because they sell most of the securities they handle, not to the public at large through advertising and through wide distribution of prospectuses, but to a comparatively small number of their clients. These clients include not only individuals, some of whom have regular sums to invest every year, but also such institutions as insurance companies, saving banks and trust companies. It is necessary in order to hold this clientele that the house should establish and maintain a reputation for the strictest integrity and conservatism. So long as this reputation is maintained there is seldom any difficulty in selling whatever securities the house may accept. The following extract from an article in

the "Bond Buyers' Dictionary" gives further details as to the methods of such houses.

It is through the retail bond dealers that the great investing public of the country is reached. The other day a retired merchant died in Pittsburg whose wealth was estimated by bankers to exceed \$50,000,000. Of the several million persons who read of his death in the newspapers the following morning only a few had ever heard his name before. There are thousands of similar capitalists in the United States, each possessing a fortune greater than was owned by any single individual in the country fifty years ago, whose names are entirely unknown to the average newspaper reader. There are several hundred thousand others who possess independent fortunes. It is with these individual investors that the retail bond merchant deals. All have a large list of wealthy customers, to which they are continually adding. The customers of some are mostly in New York or Pennsylvania, of others in New England, of others in Canada, of others in the West or the South. Some have wealthy foreign customers.

The number of regular customers may range from 5,000 to as high as 25,000. There is one retail bond house in Wall Street, which has been in business for seventy-five years, that has a list which could not be purchased for several million dollars. It includes 22,000 names, and these customers purchase, on an average, nearly \$5,000 of bonds a year apiece, or a total of more than \$100,000,000 a year. This house would not hesitate to purchase a block of \$5,000,000 or \$10,000,000 or even \$20,000,000, of municipal, county, or railroad bonds, knowing that it would be able to dispose of the entire block in the course of a few months in small lots to its regular customers.

Practically every large retail bond house in Wall Street now employs salesmen, who travel over the country selling bonds, very much as drummers sell tea or coffee. Some of the largest houses employ as many as forty salesmen; altogether, more than 300 are employed in Wall Street. Each has his own territory and possesses his own customers. Many make salaries of from

$10,000 to $15,000 a year, and some even more. All are, to some extent, experts on values. In addition to employing salesmen the retail bond houses advertise extensively.

The reputation of a bond house, and the following which it possesses among investors, is its principal stock in trade. The majority of the customers of a bond house purchase securities from it, not because of personal and expert knowledge of the security and safety of the bonds, but because of the reputation of the house. The average investor whether he invests $5,000 or $500,000 a year, after a superficial examination, purchases securities almost entirely on the recommendation of his bond dealer. The enormous profits the bond dealers make is the price they charge for lending this credit to corporations and municipalities. Practically every one of the leading Wall Street bond houses may boast that no investor has necessarily ever lost a single dollar through the purchase of bonds on their recommendation. With such a record, is it any wonder that, when such a bond house offers a block of bonds for sale, accompanied by a recommendation, that the entire issue is often oversubscribed within twenty-four hours of the opening of the books?

The profit of the banking house may take one of two forms, either a commission on the sales or the difference between the price at which it buys the securities and the price at which it sells them. Commission is more common and is regarded as more profitable. The amount of commission depends altogether on the size and reputation of the issue, and no definite statement on this point can well be made.

The question frequently comes before such a house, Do you absolutely guarantee the securities that you offer to be safe investments? Invariably the answer is: No, we give you freely the benefit of our experience and of our best judgment, but whatever risk is involved is yours, not ours; we guarantee nothing. Nevertheless, it is a well-known fact that almost all houses of the best character will protect their customers in case of loss or risk. In the first place, the house does not lose interest in the security as soon as the issue has been sold. It watches the future career of the issuing corporation with the closest attention and frequently exerts strong influence toward a conservative management of the corporation. If in spite of all its care and its efforts, the security depreciates in value, as will happen once in a long time, the house will probably offer to buy it back from its customers at the selling price. This is not laid down as an infallible rule, but as a custom. Of course, the house does not feel bound to follow that course unless it has very strongly recommended the security in the first place. Its motive in making the offer is simply to maintain its hard-won reputation for fair dealing.

CHAPTER XVII

SELLING SECURITIES—THE WALL STREET MARKET

125. *The principal stock exchanges of the United States.*—The stock exchange offers the best market for a great many corporate securities. Some readers are perhaps already familiar with the organization of that market and its manner of conducting business and will find much of the information given in this chapter already familiar. In spite of the importance of the Wall Street stock exchange, however, and in spite of the glib manner in which almost every one talks about it and against it, surprisingly few people have a correct understanding of its operations.

What is said about the New York Stock Exchange and Wall Street in this chapter applies in general, with slight modifications, to a considerable number of smaller stock exchanges in the larger cities of the United States. Chief among these exchanges are:

(1) The Boston Stock Exchange, on which local securities are bought and sold and which is the chief market for the stocks of copper-mining companies.

(2) The Philadelphia Stock Exchange, on which local securities and the securities of the Lehigh Valley, the Pennsylvania and the Reading Railroads are bought and sold.

(3) The Pittsburg Stock Exchange, the principal business of which is the handling of securities of the local steel companies, and of the United States Steel Corporation.

(4) There are stock exchanges also in Baltimore, St. Louis, Chicago and San Francisco, all of which are comparatively small and the operations of which are confined to local securities.

(5) In this group should be included the Consolidated Stock Exchange of New York, or the "Little Exchange," as it is frequently termed, whose members buy and sell the same stocks that are traded in on the New York Stock Exchange, or "Big Exchange." The transactions on the Consolidated are on a much smaller scale than on the "Big Exchange"; stocks are customarily bought and sold in ten share lots or multiples of ten, instead of in one hundred share lots or multiples of one hundred, as on the New York Stock Exchange.

The reader will see from this brief summary that large dealings in securities of corporations of national importance are confined almost wholly to the floor of the New York Stock Exchange. With some exceptions the stock of any corporation will be bought and sold on one exchange and one only; the chief exceptions, to most of which allusion has already been made, are: Amalgamated Copper Company stock, which is handled both in New York and in Boston; Pennsylvania Railroad Company, Lehigh Valley Railroad Company, and Reading Railroad Company, both in New York and in Philadelphia; United States Steel securities, in New York, Boston, Chicago and Pittsburg.

126. *Listing securities.*—In the first paragraph it was stated that the stock exchanges offer an excellent market for the sale of securities of certain corporations only. This limitation must be stated, because each of the exchanges confines its members, so far as trades on the floor are concerned, to a comparatively small number of

approved securities. On the New York Stock Exchange all new securities offered for approval are investigated before being "listed." The Exchange has strict rules governing the admission of securities to the "listed" class. There is a committee of five to whom are referred all applications for including securities among those listed. Accompanying the application, there must be filed a complete description of the property of the corporation, a full and true balance sheet, an income account, and information on certain other points. In the case of bonds a full statement of the terms under which the bonds are issued, a certified copy of the mortgage, and proof that the mortgage has been properly recorded, must be submitted. The exchange strongly recommends—a recommendation that has all the force of an order—that corporations whose securities are listed shall furnish to their stockholders complete annual reports at least fifteen days prior to annual meetings.

Many industrial corporations which are unwilling to comply with the requirements as to publicity, were formerly admitted to the "unlisted" class. This means that their securities were bought and sold on the floor of the exchange in the same manner as the listed securities, and so far as the general public was concerned there was no apparent difference between the two classes. There was, in fact, however, a very important difference, for the corporations whose securities were unlisted were not required to give complete reports as to their operations to the stock exchange committee or to their stockholders. Although the public did not appreciate the fact that such a distinction existed, men in the financial district were fully alive to its importance. Listed securities almost without exception were much more highly regarded by bankers and were more acceptable as collateral for bank loans.

For this reason, most corporations preferred to meet all the requirements and have their securities listed. About 85 per cent of the securities handled on the New York Exchange entered the listed department, and the unlisted group—partly on account of the force of the growing demand for publicity—rapidly declined in numbers and in importance. Among the last converts from the unlisted to the listed class were two industrial companies of great size and importance, the American Sugar Refining Company and the American Smelting and Refining Company. This entrance into the listed department was rightly interpreted as a final proof that the day of corporate secrecy, so far as stockholders are concerned, had gone by, and shortly thereafter the useless "unlisted" class was abandoned.

127. *The Curb Market.*—There are a considerable number of large corporations that are unwilling or unable to furnish even the very moderate amount of information that is necessary in order to have their securities entered on the Stock Exchange list. There are other securities that are very highly speculative in their nature, or that are issued by corporations which are not honestly and efficiently managed—"cats and dogs" such securities are called in Wall Street slang—which are bought and sold in considerable quantities in the Wall Street district. As such securities would not be admissible under the rules of any reputable exchange, an outside unorganized market has come into existence. This is known as the Curb Market, for the reason that the meetings of the brokers who participate in it are held in the open air in one of the streets in the Wall Street

district near the street curb. There are no written rules and no fixed organization for the Curb Market. Anyone may go among the throng of brokers standing on the street and buy or sell securities if he can find anyone else to trade with him. As a matter of fact, however, a stranger would not be able to transact any business, for no one would be sure that he would live up to whatever obligations he might contract. In practice, in order to do business on the "Curb," a broker must either have high standing and reputation on his own account or must be a representative of an established brokerage firm. Among the well-known and important corporations whose securities are bought and sold in the Curb Market we may mention the former subsidiaries of the Standard Oil and American Tobacco companies and a number of industrials, the stocks of which are also traded in on local exchanges outside New York, such as the Baldwin Locomotive Company, the J. I. Case Company, Cluett-Peabody Company, Goodrich Company and Studebaker Company. Most of the other active stocks on the Curb Market are of mining companies. The Curb Market is also the center of transactions in "rights" (which are described in Chapter XXIV) and in contracts for purchase and delivery of stock and bonds that are not yet issued. Such stocks and bonds are traded in "w. i.," to use the Wall Street abbreviation, which stands for "when issued."

128. *Stock Exchange methods.*—The scene on the floor of any of the regular stock exchanges and on the street where the curb brokers congregate always seems to an uninitiated observer strange and confusing. On the larger exchanges he sees a number of posts set up at regular intervals, each post bearing the initials of several of the corporations whose securities are listed on

that particular exchange. Around each post, if it is a busy day, are a large number of brokers, each armed with a pencil and a memorandum pad, and many of them engaged in making frantic signs to other brokers. The signs, which are unintelligible to the outsider, indicate offers to buy at a certain price or acceptances.

A broker who has the stock or bonds of any corporation to sell goes to the post to which that corporation is assigned, offers his stock and receives bids. Any reader who has never visited an exchange must not get the idea that this proceeding is as simple and unexciting as it seems when described in cold print. If the market is at all active, the seller may have to fight his way to the center of a struggling group, yell out his offer at the top of his voice, and accept one or more of the bids that may be yelled back at him in the twinkling of an eye. The noise that comes from the floor of a crowded stock exchange during an active business day resembles nothing so much as the roaring of wild beasts.

It has often been remarked, as an indication of the good faith and high standards of honor that must prevail as a rule among stock-exchange brokers, that in the midst of all this confusion and outcry a hasty sign from the purchaser and a nod from the seller of a block of securities may close a deal involving thousands of dollars. Each broker makes his own memorandum of the transaction and at the close of the day the houses which they represent compare notes and through the stock exchange clearing house settle their balances. It is very seldom that a serious error or even a misunderstanding occurs. Differences of opinion as to prices and quantities of securities are, of course, inevitable once in a while, but are usually adjusted in the friendliest manner.

The volume of business transacted in this manner on the leading stock exchanges is enormous. Million share days on the New York Stock Exchange, though somewhat above the average, are not at all uncommon. In other words, $100,000,000 worth of business is transacted. Of course it goes without saying that such quantities of shares are not bought outright, taken out of the market and placed in a vault. On the contrary, the great mass of the business of buying and selling is speculative. What is actually bought and sold is the right to receive or the right to deliver certain quantities of shares at the end of the day at the price fixed in the deals between brokers. In most cases no actual delivery is made. Through the stock exchange clearing house the transactions in the same stock offset each other and only the balances are delivered by those who sold to those who buy. Many floor traders seldom see any stock certificates because they make it a rule to sell during the day as much as they buy. They make both sales and purchases with the view to "scalping" small profits, 1/8 and 1/4 per cents.

129. *Importance of speculative dealings.*—Nothing need be said here as to the ethics of speculation, a subject which is adequately treated in another volume. It may be well to remark, however, that all these speculative transactions on the stock exchange, particularly the small transactions, perform at least one very useful service, namely, they tend to steady security prices. Obviously, if a stock starts to move up or down and a group of floor traders are at hand all trying to sell at each slight advance with a view to getting their small speculative profits, the price will probably not soar very rapidly. The same remark in substance will apply to all speculative dealings.

Enough has been said about the stock exchanges and stock and bond brokers to give some idea perhaps of their methods of operation. It is no part of the business of stockbrokers to buy and sell to any large extent on their own account, although many of them, to be sure, do not by any means abstain from so doing. Their main function, however, is to serve as agents for other persons who may desire to buy or sell securities. Some of these persons are true investors who are either parting with some of their stockholdings for cash or are buying securities outright with a view to holding them for the sake of dividends and of future increases in their value. Such persons, however, are in the minority; most of the buying and selling of stocks on the stock exchanges is speculative. Of this speculative business a small proportion is carried on by the outright purchase of stocks or bonds, which the purchaser hopes will rise in value within a short time so that he may sell at a substantial profit; or by the outright sale of securities which the seller hopes to be able to buy back within a short time at a substantial reduction. The great mass of speculative business, however, and for that matter of all the business transacted in Wall Street, consists of buying and selling "on margin."

130. *Buying on margin.*—By marginal transactions are meant those in which most of the necessary funds are borrowed and only a small percentage or "margin" is required of the person for whom the securities are bought or sold. The procedure in making a marginal speculative purchase is somewhat as follows: The speculator desires to own, we will say, one hundred shares of a stock which is selling at or near a par of $100; the least margin that will be accepted by reputable brokers in such a case will be $10 per share. The speculator, therefore, assuming that he does not already have an account with his broker, gives him a check for $1,000 and an order to buy the one hundred shares. A representative of the brokerage firm buys the one hundred shares on the floor of the exchange in the manner already described. At the end of the day he must be prepared to pay for the shares, which means an outlay of approximately $10,000 (100 shares at $100 each). In order to raise this amount the broker arranges with his bank to accept the shares, after they are bought, as collateral for a loan, which on standard stocks will be about 80 per cent of the market value, or on this block, $8,000. There still remains a difference of $1,000 which the broker must supply out of his own funds. If the stock shortly after this transaction advances, we will say ten points, the fortunate speculator will perhaps give an order to sell, and the broker will secure approximately $11,000 for the block. With this he repays the bank loan of $8,000, reimburses himself for his loan of $1,000 and after deducting interest on the $9,000 supplied by the bank and by himself and deducting his brokerage charges, he turns the rest over to the speculator. On the other hand, if the stock goes down seven or eight points the speculator is called upon to put up additional margin or, failing that, the broker sells the stock, repays the bank loan, reimburses himself, deducts interest and brokerage charges as before, and returns to the speculator anything that may happen to be left of his $1,000.

131. *Selling short.*—If the speculator chooses to sell on margin, or "sell short" in the Wall Street phrase, he deposits his $1,000 as before and orders the broker to sell. The broker's representative executes the sale on

the floor of the exchange and of course is called upon to make delivery at the end of the day. As neither the speculator nor the broker owns the stock that has been sold, it is necessary for the broker to borrow the stock from some owner. This he does in the "loan corner," as it is called, of the stock exchange, where stocks are loaned to "shorts" on payment of the market price. In form this loan is a sale of stock; it is provided, however, that on return of the stock the amount paid for the stock will be given back. This borrowed stock the broker uses to make delivery of the block that he has sold. If within a short time the stock goes down, the fortunate speculator orders his broker to buy a block at the lower price; the broker uses the block that he buys to repay the lender of the stock with which delivery was originally made. He turns over to the speculator his $1,000 margin plus the difference between the price at which the block of stock was sold and the price at which it was bought and minus brokerage charges. The brokerage house, when it borrowed stock with which to make delivery, paid to the lender the market value of the stock and is allowed interest on this sum; the speculator, therefore, in his "short" operations is relieved of interest charges. On the other hand, if the stock goes up several points in this case, the broker will call for more margin; failing that, he will buy a block of stock with which to repay the stock he has borrowed, will deduct from the speculator's margin the difference between the price at which the stock was sold and the price at which it was bought, together with brokerage charges, and will then return to the speculator anything that may be left of his $1,000.

132. *Stock exchange houses vs. bucket shops.*—The following quotation from a circular letter issued by a

large brokerage house gives an accurate statement of the terms upon which reputable brokers handle marginal transactions:

We execute commission orders for the outright purchase, in any amount, of listed stocks. Our charge is that fixed for all members of the New York Stock Exchange, 1/8 of 1 per cent of the par value, or 12½ cents a share, except that we make a minimum charge of $1 for any one transaction.

Our requirement for doing business upon margin is 10 per cent upon the par value of the active Stock Exchange issues quoted at 50 or below; 15 per cent for those quoted between 50 and 100; and 20 per cent for those quoted above 100. We reserve the right, when opening a margin account, to refuse to purchase those securities which either have not a ready market or are not available for collateral purposes. Those who desire to sell active stocks short, may do so upon a maintained margin of 15 per cent, in the case of stocks selling at par or below, and upon a margin of 20 per cent in the case of those selling above par, we, of course, to reserve the right to discriminate against any particular securities.

We do not buy or sell less than 100 shares of stock or $10,000 of bonds, upon margin, so that $1,000 is the least amount with which such an account can be opened. Our interest charges depend upon the cost of our own funds and are figured at the end of each month, so we cannot say in advance just what rate will be charged, but we will be glad to take this question up in detail at any time.

In opening margin accounts we require either a bank reference or an introduction from some of our friends.

We never open margin accounts for women or in the name of a woman, nor do we open margin accounts for bank officials or bank employees.

Just a word should be said here about bucket shops and swindling brokerage concerns of all kinds. The characteristic of all such concerns is that whatever money is turned over to them for buying and selling stocks never gets out of their own pockets. Whatever may be said as to the ethics of true stock exchange speculation, and as to its moral and economic effects, it is certainly true that Wall Street ought not to be blamed for the existence of the methods of the bucket shops. Wall Street brokers are, as a rule, entirely honorable in their dealings with customers. They make it their business to execute whatever orders are given to them by their customers under conditions which are fully and clearly set forth. If the customer misunderstands those conditions or misjudges the market, it is his own fault, not the broker's. A legitimate broker will make every effort to guide his customer aright and protect him from loss, for the broker's reputation and success depend directly on the success of his customers. The bucket shop, on the other hand, obviously prospers from the losses of its customers.

133. *The classes of Wall Street speculators.*—The Wall Street speculative contingent may roughly be divided into three classes: first, Wall Street men, bankers, brokers or corporation officials, who buy and sell securities on a large scale and who make it their business to keep in constant touch with all that goes on in the stock market; second, substantial men of property and business standing whose first interests are not in the Wall Street game, but who take a "flier" once in a while in some security or group of securities of which they have special knowledge; third, the hangers-on, the true lambs, a class made up largely of professional men, broken-down business men and women, who are suffering under the delusion that they can make money in Wall Street without having a special knowledge either of Wall Street methods or of the conditions in some particular line of industry. This third class is by no means so large as the moralists, the muck-rakers and the comic papers represent; yet it is true that its representatives are only too painfully in evidence. It is true also that the members of this class inevitably lose in the long run, and that too often they are infected with a poison that ruins them both financially and morally. It is more than doubtful, however, if Wall Street ought to be held responsible for the losses of such people. For the most part they are weak and foolish and it may safely be said that if they had not fallen victims to the Wall Street craze they would have found some other means of losing their money.

134. *A summary view of the stock market.*—What precedes is intended to present to the reader a bird's-eye view of the Wall Street market, or the stock exchange market, for securities. To recapitulate: only a comparatively few large corporations have their securities listed on any of the stock exchanges; those corporations whose securities are listed have a well-advertised, continuous and easily accessible market for their securities; this market is utilized both by investors and by speculators, but, so far as stocks are concerned, the speculative element is of chief importance; most of the speculation is carried on by means of marginal purchases and sales; the speculators may be classified under the three heads, Wall Street operators, business men and "lambs." With these leading facts before us, we are now ready to discuss briefly the process of selling a new security through the stock exchange markets.

135. *Stimulating speculative interest.*—If the new security is a small issue put out by one of the less important companies, the process of selling it through a stock exchange will not be much different from that

which has been described in previous chapters. The new security will be advertised, inquiries will be invited, an alluring prospectus will be issued, the new security will be listed and the corporation managers will then sit back and wait for orders to reach them.

Let us suppose, however, that a new stock of a large issue is to be put out by one of the well-known companies. In that case, the corporation managers, or the syndicate which is underwriting and handling the sale of that stock, will not only take all the means mentioned in the preceding paragraph to insure the success of the sale, but will go further. They will take measures to create a speculative interest in the stock and to "make a market" at a good price.

In addition to their advertisements and prospectuses, they will probably set to work other forces still better fitted to secure buying orders from marginal speculators. Now the average speculator is not much attracted by brass band announcements or even by newspaper stories, no matter how well written and convincing they may seem. But he rises to a tip like a hungry fish to the bait. He reasons that what is known to everybody will bring little profit to himself, but that information which comes to him confidentially by word of mouth gives him an exceptional opportunity. Therefore, Wall Street, from morning to night in an active market, hums with tips, rumors and gossip. The tips that are thus circulated are not all valueless by any means, although it must be admitted that a speculator who follows them too closely will probably be a heavy loser in the end. The first move, then, of the managers of a large new stock issue will probably be to see to it that rumors as to the extent and high quality of the issue, and above all, as to the "interests" that will support its market price, begin to circulate. Thus the appetite of speculators will be stimulated and large buying orders from them will probably await the first appearance of the stock on the market.

The next step will be to range the brokers in favor of the new issue, so that whatever advice they give to their customers will tend to favor its purchase. The most direct method of securing the brokers' favorable attention is by seeing to it that the new stock is acceptable as collateral for bank loans. Partly for this reason it is very important that among the persons interested from the beginning in the new issue should be representatives of large banking interests. If the broker feels sure that the stock will be acceptable as collateral, he knows that he will be able to carry large amounts of it for his customers on easy terms.

136. *Syndicate operations.*—The next step is to secure an agreement among the syndicate members and perhaps with large banking and brokerage interests outside the syndicate that the price of that particular security will be held at a given figure. Thus when the Interborough-Metropolitan Company, the great $240,000,000 merger of the transportation lines of New York City, was formed, the members of the syndicate were said to have agreed that the price of the common stock should not be allowed to fall below fifty. In order to maintain the price at this point they were compelled after the stock had been issued to purchase large blocks and take them off the market. In this particular case the syndicate, for reasons which need not be here discussed, went to pieces after about a year, and the price of the common stock suddenly broke very sharply. During the year, however, the agreement was lived up to. Where such an agreement is made and maintained,

the effect is to steady the price of the stock, or at least to hold it above the figure agreed upon, and thereby to attract both speculators and investors.

137. *Stock market manipulation.*—The fourth step in making a market for a new issue is to manipulate the price in such a manner as to gain the good will of speculators and brokers and arouse expectations of large profits. Manipulating a stock is a process that requires great skill, judgment and cool nerve. Several men in the Wall Street district have become famous for their abilities along this line; foremost among them is the well-known and successful operator, the late James R. Keene. To Mr. Keene was entrusted most of the large speculative stock flotations of recent years. He was almost uniformly successful.

One method by which a manipulator may fix a quotation for his security is by "wash sales," by which is meant selling with one hand and buying with the other. Brokers on the New York Stock Exchange, according to the rules of the exchange, are not allowed to be parties knowingly to such a process. They are not supposed to know, however, and as a matter of fact, cannot know, whether or not a selling order given to them is matched by a buying order simultaneously given to another broker. By means of such matched orders a manipulator may raise or depress the price of a stock almost at will with no further expense than brokerage commissions—provided, of course, that his plans are not interfered with by large buying or selling orders from other parties. It is customary for a stock market manipulator in this manner to fix or attempt to fix the price of a security at the beginning and then gradually raise its price and thus stimulate speculative interest in the security.

As the security advances in price and stockholders begin to send in their orders to buy, the manipulator, if his plans work out successfully, gradually feeds out small amounts of the stock that he has on hand. This process must be very gradual and carried on in such a manner that it cannot easily be observed; otherwise, the stock-market price will be depressed, stockholders will take warning and will begin to sell and the market will be spoiled. Furthermore, it is not well to allow the price to go up too rapidly or too steadily; otherwise the manipulation will be too apparent and furthermore no opportunity will be given to prospective buyers to purchase at slight recessions from previous prices. The price of a skillfully manipulated stock will move upward and downward by jerks, the tendency on the whole being upward. If the manipulation is secret and skillful, not even the most expert observer can be certain whether the price is subject to manipulation or not.

It will be impossible here to enter into a study of all the intricacies of manipulation and of the schemes which have been successfully worked in the past. The object of this chapter is attained if the reader sees that the securities, stocks especially, of large corporations may be sold through the stock market at much higher prices than would be possible if the same stocks were sold direct to investors. A further study of this interesting branch of our subject will be found in the volume on INVESTMENT AND SPECULATION.

CHAPTER XVIII

SELLING SECURITIES—THE UNDERWRITING SYNDICATE

138. *Origin of underwriting.*—One means of floating an issue of securities, we have seen, is to dispose of them through the agency of banking and brokerage houses. In such cases the financial houses may not merely undertake to sell the securities, but may make themselves responsible for the success of the sale. One method of so doing is by agreeing to take for themselves, if no other purchasers are found within a specified period, all of the unsold portion of the issue at a certain agreed price. Thus the issuing corporation is relieved of part of its risk and the buyers of the securities are made to feel that well-informed financiers have faith in their value. This process—modified more or less, as described later in this chapter—is known as underwriting.

The origin of underwriting is to be found in the famous London institution called Lloyd's. Lloyd's Coffee House was the place where the export and import merchants of London assembled in the 17th century to transact their business with shippers. As all such trade at that time was peculiarly subject to mishaps of all kinds, the practice grew up of dividing the risk on cargoes and shipments among a large number of merchants; each party to the agreement wrote his name under the contract and from this custom arose the name "underwriting." We are to discuss in this chapter the same principle as it is now applied to new issues of securities. The essential part of the arrangement is the insuring of someone against loss or failure. A secondary feature is the division of the risk among a considerable number of people, so that no one of the insurers is liable to suffer great loss.

139. *Advantages of underwriting to the corporation.*—There are several reasons why banking and brokerage houses may properly carry on this business of financial underwriting and why the business is usually profitable both to themselves and to the corporation which issues the underwritten securities. In the first place, the bankers are presumably experts in the valuation of securities. Their judgment as to the price which should be set on a new security or as to the terms of exchange, if the new security results from a conversion of an old security, is a valuable, authoritative judgment. In the second place, the bankers are also experts in selling securities and each house involved in the underwriting usually has an established clientele to whom it may readily dispose of almost any securities that it recommends. The corporation, on the other hand, has no facilities whatever for selling stocks and bonds; its activities are in the field of transportation, or industry, or trade, not in finance.

Two further reasons are even more potent in inducing corporation managers to have new security issues underwritten. First, even though the corporation can obtain expert financial advice and is reasonably sure to make a success ultimately of the sale of any securities it puts out, yet the time that will elapse before the sale is completed and the money received is always uncertain. Now the corporation ordinarily would not be trying to sell new securities if it did not need money at once or in the near future. It is disastrous to the success of many industrial or commercial operations to hold them in abeyance until the tedious process of selling a large block of bonds or stocks is completed; yet it is dangerous to go ahead so long as the sale is incomplete. This delay can be avoided by having the security underwritten, for the underwriters will pay the corporation within a definite period. The second reason that appeals strongly to corporation managers is that the credit of a corporation is seriously affected by any apparent inability to market its securities. One failure—or even a success that is too hard-won—would hamper the corporation greatly both in getting loans and in making future sales of stock.

140. *Advantage to the buyers of securities.*—There are telling advantages to the buyers of securities also in having them underwritten. As was pointed out in Chapter XVI, reputable banking houses never sell securities until after they have been satisfied by a searching investigation that the securities are all that they are represented to be. Though this does not mean a guarantee on the part of the banking house, it does mean that the buyer has the advantage of their expert, and presumably impartial, examination of every question, legal, financial, accounting, engineering or commercial, that pertains to the new security. This investigation is expensive; no ordinary investor could afford it on his own account. He is, therefore, willing to pay a little higher price for a security if this service has been performed.

Another advantage to the buyer is that he may be sure that the whole security issue has been sold by the corporation. A half-sold issue is a sign of weakness and a hindrance to the completion of the corporation's plans so serious as to reduce the value usually of the portion that has been sold. Suppose, for instance, that an industrial company desires to build a new plant at a cost of $10,000,000 and sells only $8,000,000 worth of the securities which are intended to finance the project. What can the company do? It can neither complete the plant nor return the $8,000,000. In all probability the money will be used unprofitably and the stocks or bonds sold by the company will be poorly secured. This danger is avoided when the whole block of securities is taken at one time by underwriters.

A third advantage to the buyer is that any reputable banking house will watch closely any security that it has underwritten, and will come to the assistance of the security-holders in case the corporation later gets into difficulties. As will be brought out in our study of reorganization, the committees formed to assist in devising plans to reorganize insolvent corporations almost always contain representatives of banking houses who are there to look after the interests of their clients.

For these reasons underwriting certainly adds to the value of securities. The underwriters naturally are not impelled by charitable motives; they expect a reasonable compensation for their risk and trouble, and frequently the compensation runs well up into millions of dollars. Barring collusion and graft, which have been only too apparent in isolated cases, it may be laid down as a general rule, however, that the underwriters give more than value received. There is no question in the writer's mind but that our corporation financing is cleaner and more efficient because underwriting is the general practice. It is hard to over-estimate the value of examination and supervision by fair-minded financial experts.

141. *When is underwriting advisable?*—It must not

be inferred that every new stock or bond issue ought to be underwritten. Small issues, say $500,000 or less, can usually be sold to a comparatively small number of investors by direct solicitation on the part of the corporation. Then again, well-established, successful corporations frequently sell new stock or bond issues to their stockholders at bargain prices. Ordinarily there is no risk in such a sale and consequently no necessity for underwriting.

An interesting concrete case, in which there is doubt as to whether new issues of bonds should be underwritten or not, was brought to public attention in March, 1909. At the annual meeting of the stockholders of the Pennsylvania Railroad Company Mr. Moorfield Storey, a Boston lawyer, submitted the following resolution:

Whereas, The Pennsylvania Railroad Company is to-day the first railroad corporation in the world, and its securities are entitled to rank with the best that can be offered, and, therefore, to command the highest price in the markets, both of this and foreign countries; and,

Whereas, There is now abundant capital in the hands of capitalists and combinations of capitalists the world over, who are seeking opportunities for buying such securities, and it is desirable that the directors of this company should take advantage of the opportunity which these conditions afford to obtain the highest price possible for such securities as the company now proposes to sell; and,

Whereas, The sale of railroad securities to the highest bidder after open competition will do much to remove the public belief that such securities are issued for excessive amounts, and thus tend to prevent legislation adverse to these corporations, which is now threatened.

Resolved, That the stockholders of the Pennsylvania Railroad Company desire to have the proposed issue of securities so offered as to be open to competitive bidding by responsible banking houses, and that the issue of securities should be advertised in advance, it being required that such bids shall be accompanied by certified check for such amount as may be necessary to insure good faith.

This reasoning sounds plausible at the first hearing, but is far from convincing. It fails to take unto account the risks involved in the proposed plan and the advantage to the railroad of having the right kind of banking connections in periods of financial stress. In the course of an able discussion of this proposal the *New York Evening Post* said:

Those who hold different views appeal to the Pennsylvania's own experience in 1903. Early in that year, when the stock was selling around 157, the shareholders were offered $75,000,000 new stock at 120. Before the time for closing the subscription list expired, the price of the old stock had fallen almost to 120, and the management was confronted with the difficulty that beset the Steel Corporation the same year, when bonds which had been offered to the shareholders at par were selling in the open market at 65. Needless to say, the Steel bonds were finally sold to a syndicate and not to the shareholders. When Pennsylvania dropped to around 120, in the spring of 1903, a banking syndicate was hastily formed to underwrite the new issue for which a commission of 2½ per cent was allowed. Before the whole operation was concluded the old stock had touched 110¾. Under favorable conditions a road in such high credit as the Pennsylvania, the St. Paul, the Great Northern, the Union Pacific, the Illinois Central, or the Northwestern could get a better price for an issue of bonds by shopping among the international banking houses than by confining negotiations to one banking firm. But all of the roads named have at one time or another been forced to borrow when the prices of investment securities were falling or when money market conditions were unfavorable.

A railroad which has established permanent banking connections has a guarantee that money can be raised in troublesome times, when necessary, as well as when investors are clamoring for securities. When acting in such capacity bankers are supposed to advise a railroad what kind of securities will find the readiest market, exactly when the securities should be issued, a very important point, and what price the public should be asked to pay for the issue. It is also the business of railway bankers to protect the market for a new issue until the securities reach the hands of investors.

142. *Why underwriting syndicates are formed.*—It would naturally be expected that each of the large financial houses engaged in the underwriting business would handle on its own responsibility whatever business comes its way, and that rivalry would prevent their co-operating to any considerable extent. The fact is, however, that these houses have long since learned that it is inadvisable for any one of them, no matter how powerful, to guarantee the success of a large security issue. It is true that the banker's judgment and experience should enable him to avoid heavy risks; yet a certain amount of risk is inevitable. A banker does not know what may happen in the financial world, does not know when the bankruptcy of some big concern or unexpected political events may create a sudden panic. If he is caught at such a time with his funds tied up in a large issue of new and unsalable securities, he may be forced into bankruptcy and is almost certain to suffer severe loss. It is not considered conservative banking, therefore, for any one house or even any two or three houses to underwrite a large issue. Many banking houses follow a definite policy in this respect and refuse absolutely to underwrite more than a certain sum, say $100,000 or $500,000 or $1,000,000, depending on the size of the house, even when the risk seems particularly small.

Another reason for co-operation among bankers is that each house desires to offer a variety of securities to its clientele. If it specializes too much or offers only a few securities, it cannot expect to attract and hold regular customers.

A third reason for co-operation is in order that a broad geographical distribution may be obtained and the sale of the security issue be made correspondingly easy. A Pittsburg steel company, we will say, is putting out a large new bond issue and gets a New York banking house to underwrite the issue. New York and Pittsburg investors may be loaded with similar bonds already; under such circumstances the New York banking house will certainly invite houses in Boston and Chicago and other centers, which are not yet saturated with such bonds, to participate in the underwriting.

For these reasons the banks and brokerage houses that handle this business on a large scale always band themselves together in the case of an issue of considerable size into an underwriting syndicate. By means of the syndicate the risk, the trouble and the profits are divided among several houses. The syndicate so formed may belong to any one of five types.

143. *Five types of syndicates.*—Originally the normal arrangement was to have the syndicate as a whole guarantee the price of the issue, and let the corporation attend to the selling. Under this plan, to give an example, a corporation putting out a $5,000,000 bond issue would offer the bonds to the public at a fixed price, say 95, and the syndicate would agree to accept any of the bonds not bought by the public at a lower price, say 90. This is underwriting in the original sense of the word; it is a species of insurance. Under such a plan the syndicate would have two sources of profit; first, a

commission on the portion sold to the public, or a fixed bonus; and, second, the difference between the wholesale price to them and the retail price at which they would ultimately dispose of the bonds. The ordinary commission would range between 2 and 5 per cent. This type is seldom used nowadays, principally for the reason already given that the corporation is not well equipped to attend to the sale of securities.

A second type, also rather unusual, is a syndicate formed to take an "underwriter's option." Under this plan the syndicate takes the block of bonds or stock at a fixed price, payable only as resold. As fast as the syndicate disposes of the bonds it turns over the proceeds to the corporation, after deducting whatever it receives above the fixed price. The corporation pays somewhat less for this service than for other kinds of underwriting, because the syndicate takes no risk; on the other hand, as the corporation cannot be certain when it will get its money, the type is not much favored by conservative corporation managers.

The third type of syndicate comes into existence when a large banking house has bought for itself a big security issue and wishes to distribute the risk. In such a case the original underwriter frequently calls upon other banking houses and upon individuals to take portions of the issue at prices low enough to be attractive. The agreement with the parties who are called in may be executed in anticipation of a contract that is about to be made between the original underwriter and the corporation. Full details as to an excellent example of this type of underwriting syndicate will be found in the agreement made in order to guarantee the conversion of the United States Steel Corporation preferred stock, which is given in full on pages 270–277.

144. *A fourth type—pooling the sale of the security.* —The fourth type of syndicate acts as a unit in making a contract for the purchase of an issue and pools the sale of the stock or bonds. The chief difference between the third and fourth types lies simply in the fact that the syndicate members deal directly with the corporation, not with a banking house. They thus secure for themselves all the profits of the underwriters. Such a syndicate is always managed by some one house or individual having complete authority. Its organization and management are further discussed below. On the whole, this is probably the best known and most common form of large syndicates.

To illustrate the workings of this type we will suppose that a syndicate has been formed, under the leadership of Speyer & Company, to underwrite a $25,000,000 bond issue at 90; to the public the price of the issue, we will say, is 95. One concern may agree to take $1,000,000, or one-twenty-fifth of whatever amount the public fails to buy; another concern may take $2,500,000, or one-tenth of whatever is left unsold, and so on. All the bonds are left, in this form of syndicate, with Speyer & Company, who offer the bonds to the public and sell all that they can. If the whole issue is taken by the public, each party to the syndicate receives his profits, after deducting expenses, without further trouble. If the public does not take the whole issue, each member must take his agreed proportion at the syndicate price, 90. In good times the risk in such a transaction is slight; if the public is indisposed to buy bonds, however, or if any serious mistake in their valuation has been made, the syndicate members may lose heavily.

145. *A fifth type—distributing the security.*—The pooling arrangement above described, although it se-

cures centralized and efficient management, is apt to prove unsatisfactory in that it does not bring into play the whole selling machinery of the various syndicate members. For this reason it has become more and more customary of late years to distribute the security issue among the members of the syndicate. This is the fifth type of an underwriting syndicate. Strictly speaking, of course, the distribution of securities is not an underwriting in any sense, but a sale. It is a sale at a special price, however, made under certain restrictions and designed to serve exactly the same purpose as true underwriting; the term therefore is freely applied to it in the Street. Chief among the restrictions on the sale is an agreement, either tacit or written, that the securities shall not be resold to the public at less than a certain fixed price. Frequently it is also agreed that some one or two of the syndicate members shall be given the first opportunity to advertise a sale of the securities, and that the other members are to keep out of the open market for a limited period. Such an agreement would not bar any of the syndicate members from selling the securities to their regular clients.

Among the members of a syndicate of this type there are frequently several individuals and institutions who are buying the securities, not for resale, but for investment; they are simply getting in on the ground floor, making their investment at the special syndicate price. Readers will perhaps recall that this practice was brought to public attention and much discussed during the great insurance investigation of 1904. Mr. George W. Perkins, later of the firm of J. P. Morgan and Company, and Mr. James H. Hyde, among others, alleged that their participation as individuals in syndicates, which was disclosed during the investigation, was for the purpose of buying bonds at especially low prices for the insurance companies which they represented. One objection to allowing investors to participate in syndicates of this type is that they may decide later to sell the securities allotted to them before the banking members of the syndicate are through selling, and may thereby break the price. With the view to avoiding such a result syndicate managers are exceedingly careful in choosing members who buy for investment, not for resale.

146. *The large underwriting houses.*—The *Wall Street Journal,* in a recent article dealing with the practice of the big corporations in disposing of bond issues to underwriting syndicates of the third, fourth and fifth types, says:

> One method is to sell the bonds in a block to one of the great underwriters. Pennsylvania, Baltimore and Ohio, Union Pacific, and many others, sell direct to Kuhn, Loeb & Company, get the money, and thereafter take only an indirect interest in the bonds. Rock Island sells to Speyer & Company, 'Frisco to Blair & Company and others, New York Central, Lake Shore, Southern Railway, Erie and others to J. P. Morgan & Company. The price at which these railroads sell their bonds to the underwriters is not generally known. It is taken to be a private matter, but it often leaks out.
>
> Another method, not uncommon, is to sell the bonds to the big retail bond houses who distribute them to a wide and wealthy public through advertising and through correspondence. Each of these houses has its clientele. Some are strong in New York, others in Canada, others in the South, etc. They are more or less specialists, and get to be known for a particular grade of bonds or stocks.
>
> These two methods, of course, overlap greatly. Harvey Fisk & Sons, for instance, known for years as a big retail bond house of wide clientele, frequently underwrite whole issues of

securities, as in the case of the Electrical Securities collaterals, recently brought out. Similarly, Fisk & Robinson took the whole issue of the new Buffalo & Susquehanna Railway 4½s. J. P. Morgan & Company, Kuhn, Loeb & Company and Speyer & Company generally participate to a greater or less extent in any extensive new bond issue, because their clientele demands it, even though these firms may not be the original underwriters.

Summing up what has been said with regard to the various types of underwriting syndicates, it is evident that the tendency is growing for the corporation to sell its new security issues at fixed prices to the large banking houses and then wash its hands of the business of selling the securities. Experience has demonstrated that this is the best method for the corporation. Banking houses also prefer this method to the original underwriting, which consisted simply in guaranteeing the price, for two reasons: first, because they can thus control the price and time of sale and bring to bear their skill in selling; second, because the underwriters, having full control of the securities, can post them as collateral and secure bank loans, thereby reducing their direct cash obligations.

In making this last statement the writer has in mind the distinction between "banking houses" and "banks" which may not be familiar to all readers. "Banking houses," so-called, seldom carry deposits to any great extent from other people, and do not make a business of loaning money. Their chief interests lie in buying and selling securities. "Banks," on the other hand, draw their profits mainly from receiving deposits and making loans.

CHAPTER XIX

THE MANAGEMENT OF THE UNDERWRITING SYNDICATE

147. *Informal agreements.*—As there are only a few large banking houses and institutions, even in the whole country, which ordinarily take part in large underwriting syndicates and as these houses are thoroughly familiar with each others' policies and resources, the agreements among them are frequently quite informal. In one large transaction recently, as was later brought out on the witness stand, J. P. Morgan and Company formed an underwriting syndicate simply by allotting a certain proportion of the security issue to each of several large firms and institutions. The members of the syndicate were not consulted at all or even advised in writing, but were merely called on the telephone and notified of their participation. The informality was possible in this case because the syndicate was expected to make good profits and J. P. Morgan and Company well knew that everyone concerned would gladly take as large an allotment as the syndicate managers would grant.

148. *A formal syndicate agreement.*—Ordinarily, however, a formal syndicate agreement is drawn up and signed. As these agreements are not generally made public, their exact terms seldom become known. The most elaborate and perhaps the most important agreement of this nature that has been given out, was produced on the witness stand in the famous suit to prevent the conversion of United States Steel preferred stock into bonds, referred to in Chapter XV. The agreement is

of such interest and importance that it is given in full below:

U. S. STEEL CORPORATION PREFERRED STOCK RETIREMENT SYNDICATE AGREEMENT.

An agreement made the 12th day of March, 1902, by and between J. P. Morgan & Co., co-partners, as Bankers, of the City of New York, parties of the first part, and the subscribers hereto (hereinafter called severally, parties of the second part).

Whereas, The United States Steel Corporation (hereinafter called the "Steel Company") proposes to make with J. P. Morgan & Co., a certain contract or contracts whereunder in behalf and on account of the Steel Company they are to offer to all of the preferred stockholders of the Steel Company, severally and ratably, the preferential opportunity of subscribing for and of taking at par the "Ten-Sixty Year" Five Per Cent Sinking Fund Gold Bonds of the Steel Company in even amounts approximately equal to 40 per cent of their several holdings of preferred stock, such subscriptions to be payable in such preferred stock at par, provided that every such subscription stockholder at the time of such original subscription payable in preferred stock shall have the right of his option then to make an additional subscription payable in cash for such bonds to an amount equal to 25 per cent of his stock subscription; such bonds to be authorized now for the principal sum of $250,000,000 and

Whereas, in and by such contracts J. P. Morgan & Co. are to guarantee to the Steel Company, that subscriptions for such bonds will be made for the aggregate sum of at least $100,000,000, payable in preferred stock to the extent of four-fifths of said sum, and in cash for the remaining one-fifth thereof; such contracts to provide for the payment or allowance to J. P. Morgan & Co., of a commission of 4 per cent upon the aggregate par amount of all such bonds, which shall be sold and delivered under their said offer, or to them, they having the prior right to take all of such bonds which shall be offered for subscription, and which shall not be taken by the preferred stockholders under such offer; and

Whereas, upon the terms of this agreement, and for the purposes above mentioned all of the parties hereto now desire to form a syndicate to provide and to furnish to J. P. Morgan & Co. for delivery to the Steel Company the preferred stock, and the cash required under their said guaranty, and to receive from J. P. Morgan & Co., four-fifths of the net commissions by them received under the said contract or contracts with the Steel Company, which contracts J. P. Morgan & Co. are authorized from time to time to make, modify and perform, as in the exercise of their unlimited discretion from time to time they may deem proper, do agree, as follows, viz.:

First. On signing this agreement each subscriber has delivered to J. P. Morgan & Co. certificates for preferred stock of the Steel Company in the amount indicated in his stock subscription hereto, which preferred stock, to such extent as may be required to meet the requirements of their said guaranty, is to be delivered to the Steel Company at par in exchange for the Ten-Sixty Year Five Per Cent Gold Bonds of the Steel Company for an equal amount at par, to be received therefor by any subscriber, and any such preferred stock not so delivered to the Steel Company is to be returned to the subscribers ratably according to their several subscriptions.

Second. Each subscriber further agrees to pay J. P. Morgan & Co. in cash the sum specified in his cash subscription hereto, for which cash J. P. Morgan & Co. shall receive from the Steel Company bonds as aforesaid at par equal to the amount of such cash payment by such subscribers.

Third. The several deliveries and undertakings of the several subscribers under this agreement shall be made and performed by the subscribers respectively when and as requested by J. P. Morgan & Co. or by the subscribers, of any of said Five Per Cent Sinking Fund Gold Bonds of the Steel Company.

Fourth. The several subscribers shall be called upon to

make payments of cash in respect of their several subscriptions only ratably according to the several amounts thereof; but each subscriber shall be so responsible to the full extent of the several undertakings regardless of performance or non-performance by any other subscriber. In the same proportion except as otherwise provided the several subscribers shall be responsible for loss resulting to the Syndicate under this agreement. Nothing herein contained shall constitute the parties hereto partners, or shall render any of the subscribers liable to contribute more than his several proportionate amount as herein provided.

FIFTH. In the case of the failure of any subscriber to perform any of his undertakings hereunder as and when called for by them, J. P. Morgan & Co. in behalf of themselves and the syndicate shall have, and at their sole and exclusive option they may exercise, the right to exclude such subscriber from all interest in the Syndicate, and in their discretion, without any proceedings, either at law or in equity, they may dispose of such subscriber's participation hereunder of any interest or right of such subscriber hereunder or under any of said proposed contracts, but nevertheless, each subscriber in default shall be responsible to J. P. Morgan & Co. for the benefit of themselves and the other subscribers hereto for all damages caused by any failure on his part. At any public sale under this article of any interest or right of any subscriber J. P. Morgan & Co. or any party thereto may become purchaser for their or for his own benefit, without accountability; but notwithstanding any sale, whether public or private, the defaulting subscriber shall be responsible to J. P. Morgan & Co. and to the Syndicate for all damages caused by such failure on his part.

SIXTH. J. P. Morgan & Co. shall have full power in their liscretion from time to time, to agree with the Steel Company upon the terms and provisions of any contracts such as are above referred to; and also, from time to time, to enter into any agreements with the Steel Company modifying the said contracts as they may deem expedient. They may deliver to the Steel Company a copy of this agreement, having annexed thereto a list of the subscribers; and thereupon to the extent of their several subscriptions, the subscribers, severally and respectively, but not jointly, and no one for any other, shall become responsible for the performance of such contracts with the Steel Company in discharge of the obligations thereunder of J. P. Morgan & Co. Any and all contracts with the Steel Company made by J. P. Morgan & Co. shall be open to inspection by any subscriber at the office of J. P. Morgan & Co.

SEVENTH. J. P. Morgan & Co. shall be the sole and final judges as to whether at any time it is to the interest of the Syndicate to proceed further under this agreement or under said proposed contracts; and wherever they may deem expedient, they may abandon the objects contemplated, in this agreement and said proposed contracts and all further proceedings thereunder. In such event all the cash or stock and bonds by them received and then held for account of the Syndicate, and the proceeds of such stock and bonds shall remain charged with the payment of all expenses and liability by them incurred hereunder and shall be applied:—

First to the payment of any and all expenses and obligations incurred by J. P. Morgan & Co. under any provisions of this agreement.

Secondly, in repayment to the subscribers (so far as the same may be sufficient for that purpose) of all amounts of preferred stock or of cash by them respectively delivered hereunder to J. P. Morgan & Co., such repayment to be made to the subscribers ratably.

EIGHTH. J. P. Morgan & Co. shall be sole managers of the Syndicate, and in behalf of the Syndicate they may make any and all arrangements, and may perform any and all acts, even though not herein provided for, in their opinion necessary or expedient to carry out the purposes of this agreement, or to promote or to protect what they deem to be the best interests of the Syndicate.

The enumeration of specific powers in this or in any other article of this agreement shall not be construed as in any way abridging the general powers of this article intended to be conferred upon or reserved to J. P. Morgan & Co.

NINTH. From time to time before October 1, 1903, J. P. Morgan & Co. in behalf of the Syndicate, may make sales of all or any part of the bonds received by them for account of the Syndicate. Any such sales may be made by J. P. Morgan & Co. either publicly or privately, by themselves, or in such manner as they may deem proper, and shall be upon such terms and for such price or prices as they may deem expedient. Each subscriber hereby assents to, and agrees to be bound by any such action.

No subscriber shall be entitled to receive any of said bonds before October 1, 1903. In the meantime, in their discretion, J. P. Morgan & Co. either themselves may retain all or any part of such bonds, or they may deliver to any subscriber his proportionate part thereof, upon his agreement to hold the same subject to sale by J. P. Morgan & Co. and to return the same upon call of J. P. Morgan & Co. at any time before October 1, 1903.

Should any subscriber desire to withdraw from sale the portion of bonds to which he may be entitled hereunder, J. P. Morgan & Co., in their discretion may deliver to any subscriber his portion of such bonds upon his agreement to hold the same for himself without sale until October 1, 1903, or until the complete sale by J. P. Morgan & Co. at an earlier date of all bonds held by or for the Syndicate.

TENTH. Until October 1, 1903, or until the final distribution hereunder, J. P. Morgan & Co. in such manner, at such prices, on such terms, and in such amounts as they may deem expedient, shall have power for account of the Syndicate, to make purchases of the 5 per cent gold bonds and of the preferred stock of the Steel Company, and they may resell any such bonds and stocks which they may have purchased and in their discretion they may make any further undertakings of any kind with any persons concerning any such bonds and stocks. They may apply towards any such purchases any sums realized from any sales of bonds and stocks of the Steel Company under any provisions of this agreement; and they may make advances, or may procure loans, and may secure the same to such amounts and in such manner as from time to time they may deem expedient for any of the purposes of this agreement.

Eleventh. J. P. Morgan & Co. shall issue to the subscribers suitable receipts in respect of payments made hereunder, and they may issue to the respective subscribers certificates of interest of such tenor and form as they may deem suitable. Such certificates of interest and rights and obligations hereunder of the respective subscribers may be made transferable in such manner and on such terms and conditions as J. P. Morgan & Co. may prescribe.

Twelfth. J. P. Morgan & Co. shall have authority from time to time and at any time to incur such expenses as they may deem proper in carrying out, or endeavoring to carry out, this agreement or said proposed contracts, or in doing any act or thing which they may deem to be in the interest of the Syndicate, and all such expenses shall constitute and be a prior charge in their favor upon any and all moneys, stocks and bonds by them received or held hereunder. Any and all moneys by them received hereunder shall hold by them as bankers in general account. They also shall have power and authority, in their sole and absolute direction, finally to fix and pay all compensations or depositaries, brokers, agents and counsel, or others, and in the expense account may be included brokers' commissions as usually paid.

Thirteenth. After the complete performance of the entire obligation of the Syndicate hereunder, but not before the first day of October, 1903, unless otherwise determined by J. P. Morgan & Co., in the exercise of their unrestricted discretion, payment may be made to the Syndicate by J. P. Morgan & Co. for the purpose of this agreement, out of any moneys for such purposes received or retained by J. P. Morgan & Co.

Fourteenth. J. P. Morgan & Co. shall not be liable under any of the provisions of this agreement nor for any matter therewith connected except for good faith in performing or in refraining from performing or carrying out, the obligations by them herein expressly assumed; the implication of any obligation not herein expressly assumed by them being hereby expressly denied and waived.

It is understood that, in the same manner as other subscribers, J. P. Morgan & Co. may become subscribers hereto, that as such subscribers they shall be liable for all subscriptions by them made, and that in all respects they shall be entitled to the same rights and benefits as any other subscriber. Any subscriber hereto may, on his own account, make any agreement with any other subscriber or with the Steel Company.

FIFTEENTH. This agreement shall bind, and is for the benefit of the parties hereto and their administrators and executors, severally and respectively, but no assignment hereunder shall be valid unless assented to in writing by J. P. Morgan & Co.

All rights and powers J. P. Morgan & Co. hereunder shall vest in said co-partnership firm, as from time to time constituted, without further act or assignment.

SIXTEENTH. Nothing herein contained shall be construed as creating any trust or obligation whatsoever in favor of any person or corporation other than the subscribers, nor any obligation in favor of the subscribers excepting only as herein is expressly provided.

SEVENTEENTH. Each subscriber shall set opposite his subscription hereunder an address, to which notices, calls or other communications may be sent, and any notice, call or other communication addressed to any subscriber at the address so given, and either at such address or mailed, shall be deemed actually given to such subscriber, and shall be sufficient for all the purposes hereof. If any subscriber shall fail so to furnish an address to J. P. Morgan & Co., he shall not be entitled to any notice of calls or offers, or any other notice hereunder, and he shall be deemed to assent to any action of J. P. Morgan & Co.

EIGHTEENTH. In consideration of the irrevocable rights in them vested hereunder, and the promises of the several subscribers, J. P. Morgan & Co. have become parties to, and in good faith will endeavor to consummate the purposes of this agreement; and, after receipt thereof from the Steel Company, they will, as herein provided, deliver to the Syndicate the said Five Per Cent Gold Bonds, or the proceeds thereof, and the said cash compensation.

In witness whereof, the parties of the first part have hereunto affixed their signatures, and the parties of the second part at various dates have affixed their subscriptions hereto, it being understood that for convenience this agreement may be subscribed in several parts and copies with the same force and effect as if all the subscriptions were on one part or copy thereof.

SUBSCRIPTION FOR FIVE PER CENT GOLD BONDS.

Name	Address	Preferred Stock	Cash

149. *Characteristics of syndicate agreements.*—The most prominent feature of this agreement, as the reader has no doubt observed, is the absolute and unrestricted authority retained by the managers of the syndicate. Such phrases as "J. P. Morgan & Company shall have full power in their discretion," "J. P. Morgan & Company shall be the sole and final judges," "J. P. Morgan & Company shall have authority from time to time and at any time," "J. P. Morgan & Company, in the exercise of their unrestricted discretion," and so on, abound. In this respect the agreement is typical of all underwriting syndicates. Indeed, it is easy to see that without such unrestricted authority the syndicate managers could not carry on their operations with the necessary promptness and secrecy. The real check to any abuse of this power is to be found in the necessity resting on each banking firm to preserve its reputation for integrity absolutely unstained.

For the same reason this agreement, like most other

such agreements, is marked by open dealing, so far as the essential things are concerned. At the very beginning of the agreement J. P. Morgan and Company state the commission which they are to receive. There is nothing on their part concealed from the other syndicate members; they state clearly what their profits and what the profits of each member are to be. The same rule holds true even in cases where the original underwriter is to make an extra profit over and above what goes to the other syndicate members. Secret profits are not permissible under the code of ethics that governs underwriting transactions.

Sometimes it happens that one of the underwriting firms finds its allotments too large for some reason, in which case it will probably form a sub-syndicate. The members of the sub-syndicate are usually individuals or smaller banking firms. They are not brought into contact at all with the original syndicate and have no part in its workings, but are responsible solely to the other members of the sub-syndicate.

150. *Functions of underwriting syndicates.*—Underwriting syndicates may handle the securities of

(a) Established corporations.
(b) Reorganized corporations.
(c) New corporations.

The first case is the one that has been kept in view so far in this discussion and need not be further considered. The second case presents some points of difference which will be referred to in the chapters dealing with reorganization. In both cases the syndicate is handling investment securities and its sole problem is to market those securities to the best advantage. The third case is closely allied with promotion; the syndicate methods in this case require some further consideration.

151. *Underwriting speculative securities.*—The securities of a new corporation, no matter how brilliant its prospects may be, are almost always speculative; the only exception is when a new corporation is formed to take over a business already established, and this exception we need not consider here. The first distinction, then, between a syndicate formed to underwrite the securities of a new corporation and other syndicates is that it is handling stocks and bonds of doubtful value which it cannot recommend unreservedly.

A second distinction is that the syndicate must be prepared to put up more cash or furnish more credit in proportion to the size of the security issues than would ordinarily be necessary. This follows from the fact that conservative banks are not willing to lend much money on speculative stocks and bonds.

A third distinction is that the syndicate must be prepared to carry the proposition through to the end; in no other way except at an enormous sacrifice can the money needs of the new corporation be met.

A fourth distinction lies in the fact that for their own protection the syndicate members must build up and maintain the credit of the new corporation.

Evidently there are several difficult and dangerous problems here to be solved. It is essential to their solution that the syndicate should absolutely control the new corporation. Without control measures may be taken that will impair the credit of the corporation and bring heavy losses upon the syndicate. Even with full control such enterprises are usually deemed too risky to be participated in by banking houses of the best class. At least if such houses do enter the syndicate they accept only small allotments, knowing full well the danger of becoming more deeply involved as the enterprise proceeds. No one can tell in advance what the cash requirements of a new corporation may be.

Each enterprise of this nature has its own variations of the difficulties and dangers that have been cited and requires a solution that will exactly fit its own peculiarities. Perhaps the best way of explaining the usual solution will be to present the facts of a particular instance with which the writer happens to be familiar.

152. *An example of speculative underwriting.*—In the spring of 1902 the promoter of a smelting and refining company in Mexico succeeded in convincing a number of Philadelphia financiers that his proposition was worth looking into. They made a thorough investigation, satisfied themselves that the proposed plant would certainly prove profitable, and undertook to finance its construction. Engineers' estimates called for an expenditure of something over $2,000,000 and a period of three years before the plant would begin to earn expenses. As a matter of fact, the expenditure was approximately $3,000,000 and the construction work was not completed until early in 1907.

A syndicate of Philadelphia and Baltimore capitalists and banking houses was formed to underwrite the enterprise. Next an entirely different syndicate of banking houses was organized, which agreed to take the notes when issued up to a certain amount of syndicate No. I, the notes to be secured by the stock of a corporation organized to construct the plant. The corporation was capitalized at $2,000,000, half preferred and half common stock. All its stock was sold to syndicate No. I, for $1,000,000. Syndicate No. I then posted the stock and gave notes to syndicate No. II, which loaned the $1,000,000. Thus syndicate No. I was not called upon for cash, except for expenses, and the construction company was supplied with $1,000,000 with which to begin operations.

Next, after expending the $1,000,000, the construction company issued $500,000 of its own notes, which being its only obligations were accepted by Philadelphia banks. The discount on this and the other sales, for the sake of simplicity, we will eliminate. Up to this point one-half the necessary funds had been secured and at the end of two years the work of construction had been more than half completed. Now a new corporation was formed which was to operate the plant. The reader will observe that the first corporation existed simply to carry on construction. The operating corporation at once took over the stock of the construction company, title to which up to this time had remained with syndicate No. I. Then the operating corporation put out a first-mortgage bond issue, based on all its property then owned and thereafter to be constructed, and sold during the next two years $1,500,000 of bonds. In this way the whole $3,000,000 necessary to built the plant was raised by borrowing and the members of syndicate No. I furnished nothing to the enterprise but their credit. The diagram on page 282 will perhaps assist the reader in arriving at a clear understanding of the whole series of transactions.

The plant at the date of writing has been running a little over two years. Earnings have been more than sufficient to meet all interest charges and other expenses, and it is expected that large profits will be earned in the future. Although the enterprise is not yet beyond the speculative stage, its chief difficulties have been overcome and its prospects appear bright. The first use to which surplus earnings will be devoted, according to the present plans, will be the paying off of the $1,000,000 of notes issued by syndicate No. I, and of the $500,000

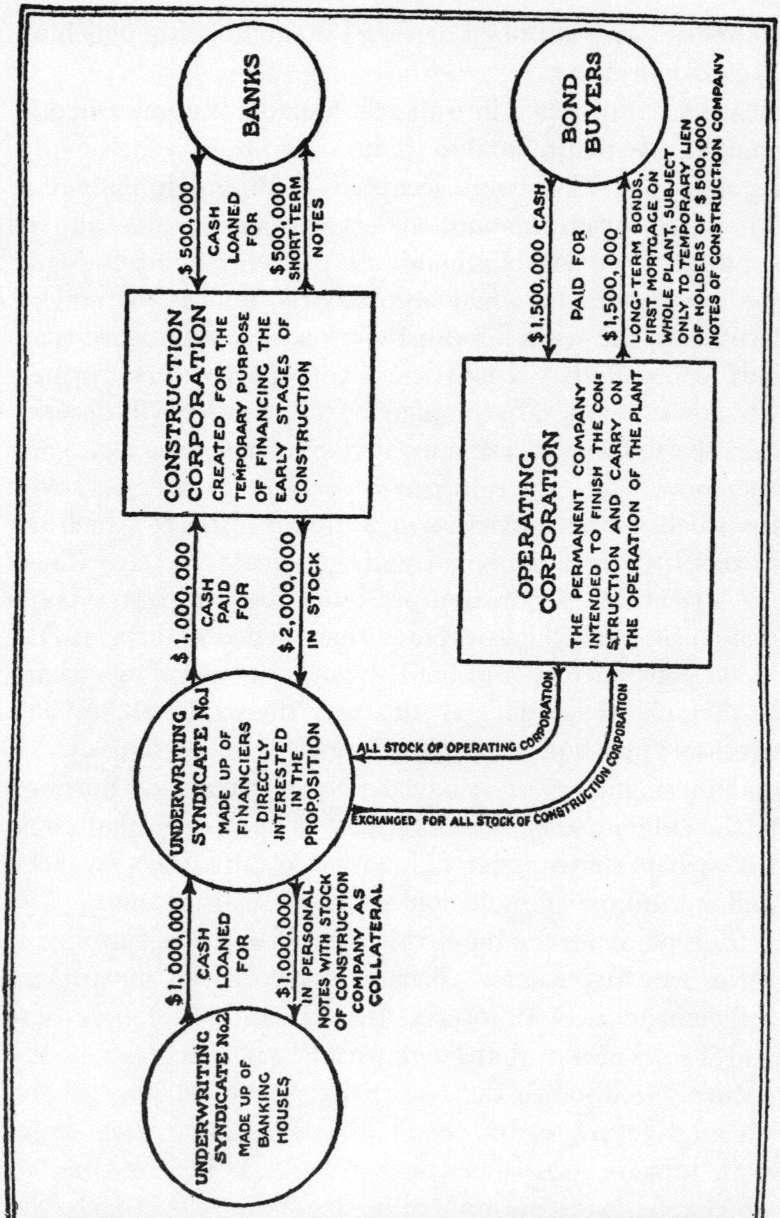
BANKS
$500,000
CASH
LOANED
FOR
$500,000
SHORT TERM
NOTES
CONSTRUCTION
CORPORATION
CREATED FOR THE
TEMPORARY PURPOSE
OF FINANCING THE
EARLY STAGES OF
CONSTRUCTION
$1,000,000
CASH
PAID
FOR
$2,000,000
IN STOCK
UNDERWRITING
SYNDICATE No.1
MADE UP OF
FINANCIERS
DIRECTLY
INTERESTED
IN THE
PROPOSITION
$1,000,000
CASH
LOANED
FOR
$1,000,000
IN PERSONAL
NOTES WITH STOCK
OF CONSTRUCTION
COMPANY AS
COLLATERAL
UNDERWRITING
SYNDICATE No.2
MADE UP OF
BANKING
HOUSES
BOND
BUYERS
$1,500,000 CASH
PAID FOR
$1,500,000
LONG-TERM BONDS,
FIRST MORTGAGE ON
WHOLE PLANT, SUBJECT
ONLY TO TEMPORARY LIEN
OF HOLDERS OF $500,000
NOTES OF CONSTRUCTION COMPANY
OPERATING
CORPORATION
THE PERMANENT COMPANY
INTENDED TO FINISH THE CON=
STRUCTION AND CARRY ON
THE OPERATION OF THE PLANT
ALL STOCK OF OPERATING CORPORATION
EXCHANGED FOR ALL STOCK OF CONSTRUCTION CORPORATION

notes of the construction company. As soon as these obligations are met the construction company may be dissolved and the operating company will begin to pay, it is expected, big dividends.

It may seem strange that a new plant could thus be constructed wholly with borrowed funds; yet there is nothing especially unusual about the operation. The secret of the success of the syndicate in this instance lay in the fact that they were themselves strong financially and could borrow the first $1,000,000 readily. This left a margin of safety to those who loaned funds directly to the two corporations. Furthermore, the syndicate members were shrewd and prudent enough not to use up all the available credit of their corporations at the beginning. On the contrary, the essential feature of their plan of operation was to leave the best lien till the last. Thus they were able to borrow $1,500,000 on first mortgage bonds at a time when most corporations under ordinary management would have been compelled to call on their stockholders for funds.

Much more complicated instances might have been cited. The principles followed in all those that have proved successful, however, have been the same, namely: utilize the credit of the backers of the corporation at the beginning and save the best security that the corporation can offer till the end. Working in this way, the underwriting syndicates of new corporations frequently borrow large sums on advantageous terms.

CHAPTER XX

INVESTMENT OF CAPITAL FUNDS

153. *The importance of wise investment.*—The next question that confronts the promoter or manager of a new corporation after he has succeeded by one means or another in raising the necessary funds is, How shall those funds be invested? This seems a very easy problem at first sight; and indeed the simple process of investing is easy enough. To invest capital funds wisely and to the best advantage for the future of the corporation, however, is a task that requires careful thought and foresight. A great many mistakes are made just at this point. The causes of failure of a great many failed corporations may be traced back unquestionably to errors in the original investment.

Of course, each corporation has its own peculiar conditions to meet and no general principles can be laid down that will take the place of keen observation and careful reflection over all factors in the particular situation that each manager faces. Nevertheless, there are some principles with regard to investment of capital funds so universal and some fatal errors so common that a short study of the problem is evidently worth while. Even if the result of this study is only a series of generalities, still experience shows that these generalities are worth making and worth keeping constantly in view.

154. *The installment method of getting cash as needed.*—In the first place, a new corporation as a rule does not require all of the capital funds that will be necessary for its development at the outset. On the other side, as was emphasized in connection with the subject of promotion, the corporation managers should have in sight from the very beginning all the capital funds that they are likely to need; for an effort to raise additional capital for an enterprise that is only half or two-thirds completed, and not on a paying basis, is painful and frequently unavailing. The manager or promoter of the corporation, then, looks for some method of reconciling these conflicting requirements.

The simplest and best method, from the corporation's standpoint, is to obtain subscriptions before the new concern is started for more than enough stocks and bonds to carry it through to success, but to have the cash for these securities payable in installments. This method is common and works very well with enterprises, the total capital cost of which can be accurately estimated in advance—such enterprises, for instance, as the erection of an office building or the construction of a railroad. In such cases the installments may be certain definite percentages due at days fixed in advance, say 10 per cent when the corporation is organized, 25 per cent at the expiration of three months, 25 per cent at the end of six months, 20 per cent at the end of nine months, and the remaining 20 per cent at the end of a year. In this way the sale of securities is facilitated, because buyers prefer usually to pay in installments, and the corporation gets its funds as needed.

The case is quite different, however, when the total amount of capital funds needed cannot be foretold. A corporation may be formed, for instance, to open up a mine or construct a tunnel or start a magazine. Nobody can foresee absolutely what obstacles the underground work of the mine or tunnel will encounter, or how quickly the magazine will "take" with the reading public. The promoter of such an enterprise, if he is honest with himself, will recognize that the corporation perhaps may need less and probably will need a great deal more capital funds than he anticipates. In order to meet this situation he will, if he can, induce people to subscribe capital funds to an amount greater than will probably be needed, issue part-paid stock when installments to a certain amount, say 50 per cent, have been paid and make the rest of the installments payable at the option of the corporation. Thus the corporation can get all the funds it needs and at the same time does not have to carry large sums for which it has no particular use. This is the ideal arrangement for such a corporation.

155. *Disadvantages of this method.*—Unfortunately this plan does not appeal to the average stockholder. He does not like the idea of being liable at all times for the unpaid installments, particularly as the calls for additional payments in many such enterprises are apt to come during periods of financial distress at the very time when it will be extremely disagreeable for him to meet them. Moreover, in large corporations such an arrangement gives to the managers of the corporation an opportunity for manipulation that they are not always virtuous enough to resist. Take the case, for example, of a well-known street railway company, which may be recognized by some of our readers, but whose name it would be improper to give in this connection: This company has a very large amount of part-paid stock outstanding, the remaining installments being due and payable at the option of the board of directors. It is strongly suspected that the board on several occasions have agreed among themselves in advance to issue a call

for an installment and have thus given themselves plenty of time to accumulate cash. Then the call has been issued and the installment made payable at a very early date, so as to make it difficult for most of the stockholders to meet the call. The result naturally has been in each instance that considerable amounts of the part-paid stock were thrown on the market and bought up at bargain prices by the directors and their friends. With the funds received from the installment the corporation has been in position to put its property in good condition and show excellent earnings for a year or two, thus allowing the directors to sell stock at high prices. After it was distributed the directors have issued another call and have repeated the milking process. Experiences like this have made buyers of securities very cautious in the purchase of part-paid stock. Generally speaking, it is a difficult thing to sell any stock that is not labeled "full paid and non-assessable."

156. *Other possible methods.*—It follows that the managers of a corporation, the needs of which for capital funds cannot be estimated in advance, are driven to take one of two courses: either they must sell at the beginning a far greater amount of securities than will probably prove necessary, and put their idle funds to some use outside the original purpose of the corporation, or else they must trust to luck that they will be able to sell more securities when additional capital funds are needed. Neither one of these alternatives is free from serious objections.

Here, then, is the first great problem in connection with the investment of capital funds, that of getting the funds when and if they prove to be needed. If that problem is not solved in just the right manner, either the corporation will have more funds on hand than it needs and its rate of profits on stock will thereby be diminished, or else it will not have enough funds and its development will thereby be checked.

157. *How much shall be invested in fixed capital?*—The next question to consider is, What proportion of the capital funds shall be put into "fixed" and what into "working" capital? The distinctions between fixed, semi-fixed, current and quick assets were discussed in Chapter VII. The fixed and semi-fixed assets together—those assets, in other words, which cannot be readily converted into cash—constitute the corporation's fixed capital. Working capital is somewhat different. It consists, not of the current assets, but of the difference between current assets and current obligations. In other words, it consists of that amount of current assets which is not furnished by trade and other short-time creditors and by temporary bank loans.

The amount of fixed capital required by any corporation depends, of course, on the nature of its operations. Industrial and mining corporations must have machinery; railroad companies must have track and rolling stock; trading companies must have office furniture before they can start business. The necessary total of fixed capital is not always so great as it appears to an outsider, for the reason that in most enterprises land, buildings and even machinery can be rented to better advantage than they can be bought. Accountants recognize this fact and are in the habit, in estimating the true cost of production in a manufacturing establishment, of charging an estimated rent for the land and buildings even though they be owned in fee by the corporation. It is well for corporation managers to consider this possibility, especially in starting a new enterprise, and where possible avoid the investment of large sums in fixed assets until after the success of the enterprise is assured.

One of the characteristics of fixed capital is that, although it may be essential and valuable to the corporation which owns it, it is likely to have very little value if put on the market for sale. Its value remains, in other words, only so long as the concern is "going." Therefore, the smaller the proportion of a corporation's capital invested in fixed assets, the better off it is in case of failure or bankruptcy.

158. *Forms of working capital.*—Working capital may take any or all of four forms:

(1) Cash, either on hand or in banks.

(2) Bills and accounts receivable.

(3) Raw materials and finished products in stock.

(4) Securities of other corporations held, not for control, but for temporary investment.

As an illustration take the following table, which shows the current assets and current liabilities of the United States Rubber Company for two recent fiscal years, as shown on the published balance sheets, and the working capital, or excess current assets over current liabilities:

CURRENT ASSETS.

Inventories	$18,404,726	$13,533,169
Cash	2,061,401	2,723,380
Bills receivable	3,681,126	994,250
Accounts receivable	8,687,631	8,494,234
Totals	$32,834,884	$25,745,033

CURRENT LIABILITIES.

Loans and notes payable	$ 6,821,077	$ 2,440,077
Accounts payable	737,384	362,634
Due General Rubber Co.	7,269,441	7,164,111
Reserve for discount	872,989	874,735
Totals	$15,700,891	$10,841,557
Working capital	$17,133,993	$14,903,476

159. *How much working capital shall be carried?*—The amount of actual cash needed by a corporation varies with the size of its pay-roll and other current demands for cash, with the amount and character of its accounts payable considered in connection with its accounts receivable, with the discounts that it may obtain on purchases by making cash payments, and with its facilities for securing temporary loans. The force of these considerations must be estimated by the corporation managers. Obviously there is a waste in carrying unnecessarily large bank balances; if any interest is received on such balances, it will not usually run higher than 3 per cent. On the other hand, every corporation naturally desires to stand well with banks and will carry large enough balances to make its deposits worth having. Otherwise, the corporation in times of difficulty may turn to banks in vain for temporary assistance.

The amount of accounts receivable cannot be determined by the financial management of a corporation, but depends on the volume of sales, on the custom of the trade as regards payment and on the efficiency of the credit department in granting credits and in making collections.

The amount of finished products and raw materials on hand is directly determined, of course, by the operating department of each company. Nevertheless, the executive heads of the company should and usually do exercise some discretion in this regard, particularly with a view to reducing the amount of working capital thus invested to a minimum. A great many manufacturing corporations, on account of improper purchasing and accounting methods, are wasteful in this regard. Careful perpetual inventories of goods in stock will often make it possible to buy and sell more closely without interfering in the least with the operating efficiency of the business. Although this is a topic which belongs rather to organization and accounting than to finance, its importance to a corporation's financial management should not be overlooked.

160. *The practice of large corporations.*—The following compilation made by the *Wall Street Journal* is of particular interest in that it shows the practice with regard to working capital of the largest and best-managed corporations.

A study of reports of the leading industrial companies shows that the United States Steel Corporation takes the lead in working capital, with the Standard Oil Co. second, the International Harvester Co. third and the General Electric Co. fourth.

Including sinking and reserve fund assets invested in securities, amounting to $32,442,400, the working capital of the U. S. Steel Corporation is $261,789,885.

The International Harvester Co., aside from the Standard Oil Co., probably has a larger working capital to gross business than any other corporation of consequence. Its working capital as of December 31, 1907, aggregated $77,087,811, while its gross business amounted to only $78,206,890.

The General Electric Co. also shows up well from the standpoint of working capital, reporting $61,235,724 on January 31 last, compared with its gross business of $70,977,168.

The following table gives the working capital of several of the prominent industrial companies, together with gross business and capitalization :

Company.	Gross Business.	Working Capital.	Capital Stock.
United States Steel Corp'n..	$757,014,767	*$261,789,885	$868,583,600
Inter. Harvester Company ...	78,206,890	77,087,811	120,000,000
General Electric Company ...	70,977,168	61,235,724	65,167,400
West. Elec. Mfg. Company ...	33,026,240	19,061,807	24,969,000
Lackawanna Steel Company ...	33,011,410	13,881,340	34,721,400
Republic I. & St'l Company ...	31,229,423	6,720,000	47,607,900
Bethlehem Steel Company ...	15,000,000	7,434,573	29,770,000
Am. Steel Foun. Company ...	19,463,521	4,834,843	17,184,000
Midvale Steel Company ...	....	1,804,929	750,000
Allis - Chalmers Company ...	....	12,522,074	35,790,000
Cambria Steel Company ...	....	14,597,865	45,000,000
Total		$730,970,851	$1,389,570,450

The above figures show that the twelve companies in question are well fortified with working capital. The aggregate working capital stands at $730,970,851, as compared with total stock capitalization of $1,389,570,450.

The figures given above indicate that the companies in question are in a strong position to weather any depression that may reasonably be expected.

* Includes sinking and reserve fund assets amounting to $32,442,401.

To invest working capital to any considerable amount in the securities of other corporations is not a very common or commendable practice. It is justifiable only in those companies that have great fluctuations in demands for cash and that cannot secure fair interest on bank balances. The buying and selling of securities is no part of the business of any corporations except the few which are distinctly organized for that purpose. Profits that are derived from this source are justly regarded as speculative and highly uncertain.

161. *Factors that affect working capital.*—Considering the situation as a whole the proportion of working to fixed capital in any business may be said to depend upon five factors, as follows:

(1) Volume of business.

(2) The regularity of supply of whatever raw materials are used and the savings which may be effected by buying raw materials in large quantities. If it is necessary for the corporation to pick up large batches of raw materials at irregular periods in order to get advantageous terms, of course the working capital must be correspondingly increased, for two reasons: first, because larger amounts of raw materials must be carried in stock than would otherwise be necessary; second, because larger bank balances must be maintained in order to meet these irregular demands.

(3) Regularity of the demand for the product of the corporation. The same considerations apply here as were named in connection with the preceding factor.

(4) Customs of payment in the business. Some manufacturing corporations normally buy on 90 days' time and sell on 30 days' time. This arrangement makes it possible to meet the accounts payable out of accounts

receivable and lessens the necessary amount of working capital.

(5) The length of time required to turn out the finished product. It takes three or four years normally to build a big steam vessel. During that period the ship-building corporation will necessarily pay out large sums for lumber and materials and a big working capital, therefore, will be necessary. The same remark applies to all concerns in which the period of manufacture is lengthy.

There is one great industry of the United States which can usually get along with a very small proportion of working capital, namely, railroad operation. The prime reason is that the railroads are manufacturing a commodity, that is, transportation, which is continually in demand and which is paid for ordinarily as soon as it is produced. There are no outlays to speak of for current raw materials; the only raw materials that railroads use are for fixed assets and may be regarded as part of the cost of securing fixed capital.

162. *The working capital of the Pennsylvania Railroad.*—Even among railroads there may be exceptional circumstances which make necessary large working capitals. The Pennsylvania Railroad, for example, in the early part of 1909 was completing its immense terminal improvements in and near New York City. In a sense it was engaged in the contracting business on a great scale, for it was building tracks, tunnels and stations. Therefore, it needed temporarily as much working capital as a manufacturing corporation should have.

Making a strict classification of current assets and liabilities, the Pennsylvania Railroad's cash position at the end of 1908 compared with its position twelve months before as follows:

CURRENT ASSETS.

	1908	1907	*Changes*
Cash	$56,025,898	$37,385,673	Inc. $18,640,225
Bills & accts. recv.	14,294,080	18,069,840	Dec. 3,775,860
Cash assets	$70,319,978	$55,455,613	Inc. $14,864,365

CURRENT LIABILITIES.

Payrolls & vouch.	$14,227,369	$20,226,164	Dec. $ 5,998,795
Int. accrued, etc.	3,231,248	2,875,982	Inc. 355,266
Miscellaneous	4,211,496	3,966,996	Inc. 244,500
Current liabilities	$21,670,113	$27,069,142	Dec. $ 5,399,029
Excess cur. assets	48,649,865	28,386,471	Inc. 20,163,394

This makes the company's net free capital, subject to the company's need of money to carry on its everyday business of transportation, more than $48,000,000 and $20,000,000 in excess of what it had been the year before. The other assets, not to be classed as quick items but more or less subject to liquidation in time, and deferred and contingent liabilities, compare as follows:

DEFERRED AND CONTINGENT ASSETS.

	1908	1907	*Changes*
Due on N. & W. & C. & O. stocks	$15,492,685	$15,492,685	....
Loans for cons., &c.....	12,403,834	18,412,493	Dec. $ 6,008,659
Due from controlled companies	3,159,784	462,218	Inc. 2,697,566
Materials on hand	10,449,483	15,929,925	Dec. 5,480,442
Sink. fund assets	8,148,208	7,772,627	Inc. 375,581
Total	$49,653,994	$58,069,948	Dec. $ 8,415,954

DEFERRED AND CONTINGENT LIABILITIES.

Car trusts chgd out	$ 2,043,803	$ 1,424,871	Inc. $ 618,929
Taxes chgd out	2,731,109	3,023,197	Dec. 292,088
Due Penna. Co.	....	2,290,897	Dec. 2,290,897
Extr. exp. fund.........	....	2,500,000	Dec. 2,500,000
Sinking fund liab.	10,339,057	9,815,956	Inc. 523,101
Total	$15,113,966	$19,054,921	Dec. $ 3,940,955
Excess def. & con. assets	$34,540,028	$39,015,027	Dec. $ 4,474,999

163. *General conclusions as to working capital.*—Many other industries, particularly those manufacturing staple articles of trade, require a comparatively small proportion of working capital. On the other hand, there are lines of business, such, for instance, as publishing, in which only a little fixed capital (office furniture, plates, etc., chiefly) is needed. This is true more or less of all trading corporations.

As was intimated at the beginning of this chapter, the principles herein laid down are of a very broad and general nature and can be successfully applied only by keen intelligence. Perhaps the chief practical conclusion is that the most careful thought must be given to securing a proper proportion of working capital. No matter how valuable the fixed assets of a corporation may be, if it does not have all the funds necessary to transact current business and to meet current obligations, it will inevitably prove a failure. Right here is where most of the mistakes and failures of the early stages of corporate management occur. Managers trust that the current sales will take care of current expenses; when the inevitable hitch occurs they have no other resources to use and the corporation suddenly plunges into the quicksands of financial trouble and discredit. This problem of providing sufficient working capital will crop out again when we come to consider the causes of corporate insolvency.

CHAPTER XXI

DISPOSITION OF GROSS EARNINGS

164. *Determination of income.*—The ordinary form of income statement of a corporation is somewhat as follows:

(a) Gross earnings from operation or manufacture.
(b) Deduct operating or manufacturing expenses.
(c) Net earnings from operation or manufacture.
(d) Add income from other sources.
(e) Total income.
(f) Deduct taxes.
(g) Balance applicable to fixed charges.
(h) Deduct interest.
(i) Deduct rentals.
(j) Deduct sinking fund and other charges.
(k) Balance applicable to dividends and surplus.
(l) Deduct dividends.
(m) Surplus from the year's operations.

It goes without saying that each corporation has its own methods of stating accounts and that there are many variations from this standard form. The essential items, however, are those stated above. It would be well for the reader to study with some care the income accounts of large corporations which are made public from time to time and which are printed in the financial columns of all metropolitan newspapers. If any of the items given above are not altogether clear, the reader should turn to the volume on THEORY AND PRACTICE OF ACCOUNTING and go over the explanation there given of the income statement.

The relations between accounting and finance are so close that a fair understanding of the basic principles of accounting is necessary in order to deal intelligently with the problems of financial management. In what is said below in reference to each of the items in the income account it will be assumed that the reader is familiar with accounting terms and with the elements of accounting practice.

165. *Honesty in stating gross earnings.*—Perhaps the only comment needful on the first item "gross earnings" is that it should be honestly stated. This remark is trite enough, and yet not uncalled for. A great many corporation managers are in the habit of including in their gross earnings sales that have been made to parties of doubtful credit which are represented merely by accounts receivable that are probably bad. In the case of holding companies it is not so uncommon as it should be to include in the gross earnings sales made from one company to another in the combination. Of course this is simply a juggling with figures. A still more flagrant instance of dishonesty was disclosed by Mr. Stephen Little, an accountant of wide reputation, who in 1894 was called upon to investigate the condition of the insolvent Atchison, Topeka and Santa Fe Railroad Company. Mr. Little found that the railroad had paid out millions of dollars in rebates to shippers which had not been deducted from its statement of gross earnings.

166. *What are operating expenses?*—Operating expenses are also often grossly misstated, although in this instance the fault is apt to be due, not so much to the

dishonesty of the corporation managers, as to their ignorance of correct accounting principles. The operating expenses ought always to include not only the actual expenditures for raw materials, labor and current repairs, but also a liberal allowance for anticipated repairs and renewals and for depreciation.

Repairs in the early years of a corporation's activities are seldom as great a burden as in later years. Accountants figure that most manufacturing machines will show a rising percentage of necessary repairs each year for the first five to ten years of their existence and after that a fairly steady ratio will be maintained. Now it is evident that unless some allowance is made during the first few years for the rise in this item during the following years, a misleading statement of operating expenses will be presented.

Corporations differ greatly in their handling of charges for renewals of machinery and equipment. Many of them figure that the new machines they buy are additions to their capital and therefore should not be charged against the income account at all. If the new machine, however, replaces to any extent an old machine, this reasoning is obviously incorrect. Only the difference between the value of the old and the value of the new machine could properly be charged to capital account. Conservative corporations in this country, railroads particularly, are in the habit of charging the whole cost of their new equipment, as a rule, as a part of operating expenses. The English railroad practice, on the other hand, is to charge the whole expense to capital and to raise new capital funds to meet it. We shall have occasion to consider this point further in connection with "betterment expenses."

167. *Necessity for depreciation reserves.*—The sub-

ject of depreciation is too large and important to receive full consideration in this place; a more extended treatment will be found in the volumes on accounting. As the desirability of allowing properly for depreciation ought to be indelibly impressed on the mind of every person interested in corporation management, however, some brief remarks on the subject, even at the risk of reiteration, are worth making here.

There are three general causes of depreciation, as follows:

(a) Failure to keep property in first-class working condition.

(b) The gradual breaking down of property in spite of all that may be done to keep it in good condition.

(c) Most important of all, obsolescence or the impairment of value because of new inventions and processes.

It is difficult for anyone not directly familiar with modern manufacturing enterprises to conceive of the rapidity with which changes in mechanical methods follow each other. Each important change is apt to make necessary a general revision of all the machinery and processes of manufacture. In the intense competition between industries, no concern that allows itself to fall behind in the race to install the latest and most economical devices will long be able to survive. American manufacturers have long been famous for the vigor and fearlessness with which they adopt new machinery and processes, even though the change may make almost worthless the expensive equipment that had previously been installed. The Carnegie Steel Company, it is said, time after time, has relentlessly sent to the scrap heap costly machines and even whole plants that were found to be inferior to new inventions.

This policy certainly pays in the long run, as the striking success of the Carnegie Steel Company shows. Where products are being turned out in great quantities, a very slight saving in the cost of producing each unit may prove to be the margin between bankruptcy and prosperity. Yet, though the policy is to be praised and followed, it must not be forgotten that it involves large losses for the time being whenever old machines are superseded by new. These losses ought to be foreseen and provided against when the first steps of an enterprise are taken. The only possible means of so doing is to charge as part of the operating expenses every year a liberal sum for depreciation—a sum that will take care, not merely of decay due to old age and lack of repair, but of obsolescence as well.

Anything like a scientific treatment of depreciation has unfortunately been conspicuously absent from the accounts of most American corporations. Manufacturers have been too willing to make rough guesses where fairly exact scientific deductions might have been drawn. Electric and steam railroads have uniformly declined to make any allowance whatever for depreciation on the ground that the value of their franchises is steadily rising and that this is sufficient to offset whatever depreciation of their property is going on. There is a certain amount of truth, to be sure, in this assertion; yet it reveals a woefully careless habit of thought. Such slap-dash methods fortunately are now being eradicated, so far as interstate steam and electric lines are concerned, through the control over their accounts now exercised by the Interstate Commerce Commission. Recent rulings of the Commission have very properly made it obligatory on railroads to form as accurate estimates as they can of the annual depreciation of their property and to set aside every year as part of operating expenses an adequate depreciation charge.

To avoid any possible misunderstanding by those who may not be familiar with accounts, it may be well to state at this point that depreciation reserves, so called, are not sums set apart and invested outside of the property, but are merely the total charges against gross earnings over a series of years on account of depreciation. The depreciation reserves are not separable from other capital funds invested in the business except as a matter of accounting.

168. *Income from other sources and deductions.*—We have now reached in our income statement the item "net earnings derived from operation." To these earnings should be added "income from other sources." In order to make the income account a clear and accurate statement of results of the year's operations, it is very important that this "income from other sources" should be stated separately and not confused with "net earnings from operation"; otherwise the corporation managers will be claiming credit for returns that are quite distinct from the company's own operation. Income from other sources includes dividends on the stocks of subsidiary and other companies, interest on the bonds of such companies, interest on bank deposits, rentals of property owned by the corporation and not used in its own operations, and other items of that nature. Such returns are frequently temporary or irregular, in which case, in order to make the situation clear, they ought to be specifically named in the income statement.

We now deduct taxes which, it will be noted in our model income statement, should not be included under fixed charges. There is some difference of opinion on this point. It is not a matter of sufficient importance, however, to be worth arguing over. The view here taken is that taxes are variable in amount, and are not, therefore, on the same basis as the regularly recurring fixed charges.

As to the nature of interest and rentals, little need here be said. Sinking funds have been sufficiently treated for our purpose in another place.

The deduction of fixed charges leaves as a balance the income applicable to dividends and surplus. Preferred dividends, as have previously been explained, are classified as cumulative and non-cumulative. Cumulative dividends, to the corporation managers, are often extremely disagreeable things. They are not so bad as interest charges, for they may be deferred as often as necessary. On the other hand, the fact that they are cumulative makes them pile up at an alarming rate, and in the course of a very few years, if they are not paid, they become a charge ahead of the common stock that makes common stock dividends seem an unattainable vision. For the best interests of common stockholders, therefore, it is usually very desirable to pay cumulative preferred dividends regularly. If a shrinkage in profits makes a temporary lapse necessary, the lost ground should be regained at the first opportunity.

169. *How much shall be paid out in dividends.*—The next question to consider in disposing of the earnings of a corporation is, How much shall be paid out in non-cumulative and in common dividends. Mr. Thomas F. Woodlock has well said that the payment of dividends is the only absolutely non-productive expenditure that an honest corporation makes. This may sound like a meaningless paradox, but it is literally true. So far as the corporation itself is concerned, whatever is paid out

in dividends is a total loss. On the other hand, it is also true that the only reason for the corporation's existence is that it may pay dividends to the stockholders. There is a conflict of interest here evidently and often a strong conflict of opinion between the managers of a corporation and the stockholders as to whether dividends should be paid or not. In the next chapter some striking examples will be cited.

Assuming that a corporation has a balance for the year applicable to dividends and surplus, and that all persons concerned are agreed that some dividends should be paid, the question takes the form, How large an amount shall be thus distributed to stockholders? The first and most natural answer to this question is that all the profits of each year belong to the stockholders and should be paid out in dividends; and this answer is deemed entirely satisfactory by many intelligent people. The English corporations almost invariably follow this practice, and some important American corporations as well. The New York Central Railroad Company, for instance, has for many years paid out in dividends each year almost all the net earnings of the year.

There are two distinct disadvantages in this practice: First, it does not permit the corporation to create a surplus of any considerable size; second, it makes the dividend rate irregular. The first disadvantage will be more fully discussed in Chapter XXIII. The second disadvantage is of great importance and calls for some explanation.

170. *Variability of profits.*—In all lines of business the profits necessarily vary from year to year. This is true because all the factors which enter into and determine profits are variable. These factors are:

(a) Volume of sales.
(b) Prices obtained.
(c) Prices of raw materials.
(d) Wages.

In no line of business is the volume of sales the same from year to year and in no line even where the general trend is upward, can the volume be expected to increase steadily and regularly. Some fair degree of regularity, to be sure, can be attained in the cases of large public service corporations, such as waterworks, street railways and steam railroads, that deal with great masses of people. Even here there are sometimes surprising fluctuations. In most lines of industry, prices are very unstable and show big variations from year to year. In general it may be said that those industries have the most regular prices and volume of sales which are concerned with the necessities of life; and the farther you get away from those necessities, the more violent are the fluctuations in those two items.

To make these statements more definite let us examine the records of some of the leading industrial, street railroad and steam railroad companies during the year of depression, 1908. The following gives the percentage of production of the leading industrial companies, compared with normal:

United States Steel Corporation	60
Republic Iron and Steel	90
Lukens Iron & Steel	60
Corn Products Refining	75
Standard Oil	95
General Electric	60
Westinghouse	60
Pennsylvania Steel	60
Maryland Steel	60

Jones & Laughlin	55
Amalgamated Copper	100
National Lead	95
American Smelting & Refining	80
Sloss-Sheffield Steel & Iron	80
International Paper	70
United States Rubber	75
Allis-Chalmers	65
American Can	75
American Car & Foundry	35
Pressed Steel Car	20
Railway Steel Spring	75
American Locomotive	40
Bethlehem Steel Corporation	50
International Harvester	100
United States Realty & Improvement	100

Orders for new railway equipment in 1908 were less than 40 per cent of those received during 1907 and hardly 20 per cent of orders booked in the big rush of business in 1905. The course of new business during the preceding four years may be gathered from the following comparison:

Year	*Loco. Orders*	*Fgt. Car Orders*
1908	1,182	62,700
1907	3,282	151,700
1906	5,642	310,315
1905	6,265	341,315

In striking contrast is the record of the following railroad and street railway companies. Notice particularly the small fluctuations in the street traffic in large cities. The decrease in street railway gross earnings was less than 1 per cent and in steam railroad gross earnings about 19 per cent.

ELECTRIC STREET RAILWAYS.

Company and Period	1908	1907	*Decrease.*
Boston, May–July	$ 3,596,000	$ 3,623,000	$ 27,000
Mass. Elec., Apr.–June	1,995,842	1,924,333	*71,509
Chicago Rwys., Mch.–May	2,625,533	2,574,324	*51,209
Twin City, Apr.–June	1,474,389	1,492,671	18,282
United St. Louis, Mch.–May...	2,645,364	2,735,406	90,042
Detroit United, Mch.–May.....	1,675,042	1,675,743	701
Total	$14,012,170	$14,025,477	$13,307

* Increase.

STEAM RAILROADS.

Company and Period	1908	1907	*Decrease.*
Lake Shore, April–June	$ 9,182,851	$11,160,400	$ 1,977,549
New Haven, April–June	10,913,741	12,670,010	1,756,269
Pennsylvania, Jan.–Mch.	31,375,489	37,203,589	5,828,100
Louis. & Nash., Feb.–Apr. ...	10,073,862	12,012,701	1,938,839
Missouri Pac., Feb.–Apr.	9,467,500	11,927,824	2,460,324
Boston & Maine, Apr.–June..	8,836,556	10,499,302	1,662,746
Total	$79,849,999	$95,473,826	$15,623,827

The explanation of the different manner in which the street railways and steam railroads have fared is largely to be found in the different character of their traffic. Street railway gross is 95 per cent derived from passenger receipts, while from 65 to 70 per cent of railroad gross is realized from freight; and in periods of universal curtailment freight earnings quickly feel the depression.

Even with an absolutely invariable volume of sales and level of prices any industry would still be subject to great variations in profits by reason of changes in raw material prices and in wages. This statement is obvious enough without any elaboration. It should be remarked that the amount of wages paid out is not dependent altogether on the nominal rate of wages, but also to a great extent on the efficiency of labor. When times are good and sales in all lines are heavy, it becomes necessary to employ workingmen of an inferior grade, who in bad times are always "out of a job." Taking on such men means a great reduction in the average efficiency of labor and in economy of production.

171. *Regularity of dividends desirable.*—We are safe in saying, then, that great fluctuations in profits are inevitable in most lines of business and cannot be altogether avoided, even by the large public service corporations which furnish the necessities of life. It follows that if all the earnings each year are paid out in dividends, the rate of dividends will fluctuate—in many cases fluctuate violently. The reader may perhaps ask at this point, Why not let them fluctuate? Let the stockholders in a corporation take their profits as they are earned, just as the owner of an individual business or partner in a firm would do.

The answer to this question is that stock, and especially the stock of large corporations, is widely held by people of all classes who are not in touch with business affairs and not prepared to take care of haphazard returns that drop into their laps from time to time, but who desire above all things a steady, regular and dependable income. Such people do not want lean years and fat years; they want a series of moderately good years. They belong, not to the speculative, but to the investment class. On account of the demand that such people create for regular dividend-paying securities, the market prices of such securities are far higher than they would otherwise be. For example, take two stocks, one of which pays over a series of five years, 4 per cent, 7 per cent, 6 per cent, 3 per cent and 5 per cent, averaging 5 per cent for the period, and compare it with another stock which has regularly paid 5 per cent each year; you will always find a marked difference in market price in favor of the second stock. The principal reason for this difference is that so many people prefer a regular dividend payer.

It is for the best interests of all a corporation's stockholders to pay regularly a steady rate of dividend, inasmuch as the market price is thereby enhanced. The corporation manager, then, is confronted with the problem of reconciling this demand with the irregularity of the corporate profits. The only safe method of accomplishing this result is to pay out in dividends no more than the minimum earnings of the corporation in its worst years. Thus the dividends may always be kept at a fixed rate and whatever is earned above the dividend requirements will go into the company's surplus.

172. *Prudence in paying dividends.*—This may seem an unnecessarily harsh rule, for it keeps the rate of dividends low and thereby unnecessarily, it may seem, cuts down the stockholders' income. In the long run, however, it works no injustice. As we shall see in succeeding chapters, whatever surplus is saved out of income, goes to increase the company's earning power and eventually its regular dividend rate.

Looking back over the ground covered in this chapter, we see that great care, prudence and foresight on the part of a corporation directorate in the distribution of gross earnings is necessary in order to give permanence and long-continued success to the corporation. The board of directors must see to it that the gross earning of each year are not overstated and that operating expenses are not understated. In connection with the latter item they must take care that sufficient reserve has been set aside to provide for accrued repairs and for depreciation. They must, of course, meet all the fixed charges of the corporation out of income under penalty of seeing the company forced into bankruptcy. They must pay cumulative preferred dividends so far as practicable, although in this regard some discretion is permitted to them. Finally they must resist unwise pressure from stockholders for larger dividends than the condition of the company in the long run will warrant. If they do not resist these demands, the company will be compelled probably sooner or later to reduce its dividend rate, thus removing its stocks from the class of desirable investments and lowering their market prices. The ideal corporation director will stand like Horatius at the bridge, defending the wealth and profits of the corporation from the onslaughts of hungry stockholders who do not possess either foresight or intimate knowledge of the business.

A corporation which has such a directorate is peculiarly fortunate and, whatever its line of business, may reasonably expect to attain a lasting success. A corporation which does not have such a board will perhaps prosper for a season and apparently enrich its officers and stockholders. In the end, however, it will prove to be but a mushroom growth. All the while its vitality is dwindling, its substance is being eaten out and sooner or later, to the surprise of unwary investors, it suddenly crumbles away.

CHAPTER XXII

BETTERMENT EXPENSES

173. *Two classes of betterments.*—All improvements and all expansions of property may be grouped under the general name "betterments." The question as to whether betterments should be made or not is primarily something for the operating officials of the company to decide. They should understand thoroughly the condition of the property, the cost of the proposed betterments and the prospects for additional business, and from the study of these factors should be able to draw pretty definite conclusions as to their advisability.

All betterments may be roughly divided into two groups:

(a) Those which are practically certain to bring about an immediate increase in revenue.

(b) Those which are expected to prove profitable in the long run, but which may or may not bring immediate returns.

As an example of the first class, we may suppose that a manufacturing company is about to put in a new and expensive engine; in such a case the proper officials should be able to calculate in advance almost exactly the annual saving that will be made possible by this particular improvement.

As an example of the second class, we may suppose that the same company is considering the advisability of building a Young Men's Christian Association reading room and gymnasium for the benefit of their employés.

Their motives, we may presume, are not in the least philanthropic; they expect the investment to yield big returns in the form of a better satisfied and more intelligent force of workingmen. The extent of the returns, however, cannot be calculated exactly and in any case will not be immediate.

The dividing line between the two classes is not always very clear and there may often be more difficulty than in the two examples just cited in assigning a proposed betterment to its proper class. The classification, however, consciously or unconsciously, is almost always made by intelligent corporate officials and directors.

174. *Sources of funds for betterments.*—Once a betterment expense has been agreed to, the next question is how to raise the necessary funds. This is a purely financial question, which deserves even fuller consideration than is possible within our space limits. At bottom the problem of raising capital funds for betterments is of the same general character as the problem of raising the initial capital funds when a corporation starts business. There are, however, as we shall see, some important variations in the problem.

The sources of capital funds, whether at the beginning or during the corporation's existence, are the same as have already been given, namely:

(a) The active managers of the corporation.
(b) Surplus earnings.
(c) Trade creditors.
(d) Banks.
(e) The investing public.
(f) The speculative public.

For our present purpose we may eliminate sources (a), (c) and (d). There is nothing to be said with regard to them that has not already been said in Chapter

VII. There remain: source (b), from which the funds may be obtained by one of two methods, either direct appropriations from surplus, or abnormally high operating expenditures; source (e), which may be reached either by the issue of medium-term notes or by the issue of bonds; and source (f) from which funds may be obtained by the sale of new stock.

175. *Appropriations from earnings.*—The safest and surest known method for providing for betterments and building up any concern is by making appropriations out of earnings. Expansion that is financed in this manner will be very slow, to be sure, unless the profits of the concern are inordinately large. This very slowness, however, is in some respects an advantage. It necessitates a gradual growth, a kind of evolution of the business, and thus automatically provides against waste and recklessness. It is practically certain that any concern which is built up altogether or in large part by means of appropriations from each year's surplus will be conducting its business along conservative lines. That it is not impossible by this method to construct in time an immense and profitable concern is proved by the history of two of our great industrials, the Carnegie Steel Company and the Baldwin Locomotive Works. The Carnegie Company had its inception in 1871 in an insignificant steel-making plant which was bought with the few thousand dollars that Andrew Carnegie and his associates were able with great difficulty at that time to command. It has since expanded until it is to-day worth, as a going concern, perhaps a half-billion dollars; and all that expansion has been the result of profits slowly turned back into the business. In this respect the history of the Baldwin Locomotive Works is closely similar.

176. *Objections to this method.*—Yet in spite of these great successes we must not overlook the two obvious disadvantages of this method of obtaining funds for betterments. The first and most vital objection is that the slowness of the process may occasion the loss of valuable opportunities. While an old, conservative company is thus gradually acquiring the funds necessary for the expansion of its business, it may well be that a somewhat more daring concern may borrow the funds necessary for expansion and thus capture the opportunity that was at first open to both of them. Conservatism undoubtedly is a business virtue; yet for the best results it needs to be mixed with a strong dash of speculative fervor. The second objection is that the ordinary stockholder in any concern desires to enjoy the profits of a business as they are earned and objects strongly to having those profits diverted to betterment expenses. It is true that an increase in the corporation's assets is an increase in his assets, for he is part owner of the corporation. It is true, also, that an increase in assets will be to some extent reflected in a rise in the market value of his stock, so that he may sell out if he chooses and put his money into a more liberal corporation. This last, however, is not a wholly satisfactory argument to the stockholder, for market values are based more largely on earnings and dividends than they are on underlying assets. This is a truth that will be found fully illustrated in the volume on INVESTMENT AND SPECULATION. Thus the body of stockholders is apt to oppose strenuously a reduction in their dividends in order to provide for betterments. It seems to them as if they were being compelled to make a sacrifice for the benefit of future stockholders.

177. *The attitude of stockholders.*—An example

that was conspicuous a few years ago was the determined struggle on the part of minority stockholders in the Wells-Fargo Express Company for larger dividends. This company was controlled by the Harriman party, and Mr. E. H. Harriman, following his usual policy, was, as it seemed, too much inclined to sacrifice dividends to financial strength. The minority stockholders stated that the Wells-Fargo Company had been piling up an enormous surplus, which was not needed or used in the business, but was invested in the securities of other companies. The majority stockholders—that is the Harriman party—rejoined that the security holdings of the Wells-Fargo Company were for the sake of control and for the prevention of ruinous competition; in other words, that earnings had been consistently devoted to betterments. The undeniable facts are that the company was highly prosperous, was paying relatively small dividends and was more or less harassed by a body of dissatisfied stockholders.

The objections by the stockholders in such cases may be induced by any or all of three motives:

(1) They may simply be anxious for present dividends, even though they be paid at the risk of reducing the corporation's future earnings and prosperity. Human nature is so constituted that to almost all of us \$1 this year looks better than \$2 five years from now.

(2) Some of the stockholders may have speculative tendencies which lead them to desire a good market price and a quick sale for their stock—perhaps with the idea that after a while the dividends will be cut and they will be able to repurchase stock at much lower prices. This motive will always be strong when many of the stockholders belong to the speculating, rather than to the investing class. Here is one of the best reasons

why a conservative corporation manager will desire to put his stocks on an investment basis from the very beginning, if possible.

(3) The stockholders in a corporation which has a large funded debt may reason that whatever sums are diverted from dividends to betterments go to increase the security and the value of the corporation's bonds rather than of its stock. We shall have occasion to deal with this motive and its results when we take up in Chapter XXVII the methods of manipulation for the benefit of the body of stockholders. It is enough to say here that this motive, although narrowly selfish, is still entirely legitimate and often has great weight.

Wherever these motives are at work—and some or all of them are likely to be strong in almost any body of stockholders—objections to heavy betterment expenditures out of earnings will be in evidence.

In the Wells-Fargo case the protesting stockholders, however disagreeable they might make themselves, did not have much influence with the management, because they were distinctly in the minority. It often happens, however, that the active managers of a corporation are more prudent or more farsighted than the majority of their stockholders and for the good of the corporation desire to pursue a policy of small dividends and large betterment expenses which would not be supported if it were clearly presented to the stockholders. In order to attain their object the corporation officers must keep the stockholders more or less in the dark; and this they do by the very simple process of charging expenditures for betterments under operating expenses.

178. *The case of the Lehigh Valley Railroad.*—The history of the Lehigh Valley Railroad so well illustrates the workings and the results of this species of well-inten-

tioned deceit that it is worth a rapid review. In the year 1897 new interests, which were represented in the active management by President Walters, came into control of this company. The five years following, 1898 to 1902 inclusive, were a period of remarkable development and prosperity for almost all the railroads and industrial corporations of the United States, and the Lehigh Valley was no exception. Gross earnings from operation increased 25 per cent; the revenue tonnage increased 150 per cent; at the same time the average freight rate per ton per mile showed a slight gain. On the other hand, the outlay per train mile for moving this tonnage decreased. Thus earnings were apparently going up while running expenses relatively were decreasing, and a largely increased net income would naturally have been expected to follow. The facts were, however, that the gross income (not gross earnings) decreased from $6,800,000 in 1898 to $4,800,000 in 1901 and $4,650,000 in 1902, when the anthracite coal strike was in progress.

An inquiring stockholder, who might have chanced to consider with care these strange and anomalous figures, would perhaps have turned to the balance sheet of the company in the expectation of finding therein revealed some noteworthy addition to assets purchased out of earnings. But our inquiring friend would have been disappointed. He would have found the comparative figures of the important assets of the road as follows:

ASSETS

	1898	*1902*
Cost of Road	$18,639,291.95	$18,639,291.95
Cost of Equipment	19,018,419.98	19,018,419.98
Securities owned	32,949,322.14	39,300,209.80

The only change here is an increase in the securities owned, which is not sufficient in amount to account for all that apparently should have been saved out of earnings. The book values of road and equipment, it will be noticed, have not been changed.

The true explanation could have been found only by analysis of the operating expenses of the railroad. In the first place, the proportion of total operating expenses to gross earnings from operations—or operating ratio, as it is called—had risen from 70 per cent in 1898 to 81 per cent in 1902. As a normal railroad operating ratio would be 60 to 65 per cent, it is evident that this extraordinarily high ratio of the Lehigh Valley in 1902 indicated one of two things: either bad management or inflated operating expenses. We may get some light as to which was responsible in the present case by a slight further analysis of operating expenses. In 1895 22 5-10 per cent of the total operating expense went to maintenance of way; in 1902 over 40 per cent. In 1895 the average train-load was 384 tons; in 1902, 467 tons. Evidently large sums had been devoted during the interim to betterments which greatly increased the economy and efficiency of the road's management. We are now informed that during the five years, 1898 to 1902, all new equipment, all side-tracking and other expansions of track, all contruction of bridges and buildings, all reballasting of track and similar items had been charged to operating expenses. Professor Edward Sherwood Meade, to whose searching analysis we are indebted for much of the information here presented, estimates that in these five years the Lehigh Valley under Mr. Walters' management, spent almost $13,000,000 on betterment expenses which ordinarily would have been provided for by new issues of stock or bonds; in other words, the $13,000,000 under a different management would have been distributed to stockholders.

In 1902 a new management came into power, and the report for the fiscal year 1903 shows some radical changes in accounting methods. Net income, for instance, which had been $4,650,000 the preceding year, suddenly jumped to $8,300,000. The new management, after appropriating $1,250,000 for betterments and after paying all fixed charges, was still able to show over $2,000,000 available for dividends; this, in the face of a deficit after allowing for fixed charges the preceding year of over $1,200,000. In 1904 the stock was given a dividend of 1 per cent. In 1905 it was put on a 4 per cent basis. Between 1901 and 1908 the gross earnings of the Lehigh Valley were increased about 33 per cent. Its net earnings were considerably more than doubled, and yet its fixed charges were increased scarcely at all. The figures below tell the whole story of this remarkable growth more plainly than it could be put in words.

	1908	*1901*	*Increase*
Miles operated	1,447	1,382	65
Gross earnings	$35,510,154	$26,683,533	$8,826,621
Gross, per mile	24,500	19,300	5,200
Net earnings	12,183,582	5,765,113	6,418,469
Net, per mile	8,420	4,170	4,250
Chgs, less other inc. .	4,813,008	4,364,800	448,208
Charges, per mile ..	3,320	3,150	170
Surplus	7,370,574	1,400,313	5,970,261
Surplus, per mile ..	5,100	1,013	4,087

Now, what is the meaning of these facts and figures? In the first place, it is plain that the road was in poor condition prior to Mr. Walters' administration and that he left it in such excellent condition that its net earnings afterward showed a phenomenal increase. There can be no question but that the millions which Mr. Walters poured into the property were wisely spent and have since been efficiently administered. To an investor or corporation manager this review should be an inspiring story of honest profits ably secured.

Nevertheless, it must be admitted that Mr. Walters' policy, so far as the stockholders were concerned, was one of evasion and deceit. True it is that whatever he did was intended for their own best interests; yet it is also true that they would not always have approved of his actions if they had known exactly what was going on. We do not need to enter into the ethics of the case. It is plain, however, that the stockholders, from any or all of the motives we have previously mentioned, might with justice have objected to Mr. Walters' course. As a matter of fact, they did finally become alive to the situation and helped in bringing a new management into power.

179. *Policy of the Union Bag and Paper Company.* —Another illustration of large operating expenses being used to beguile stockholders into putting a large portion of earnings into betterments is to be found in the recent history of one of the smaller trusts, the Union Bag and Paper Company. In a review of this company's condition, recently issued, we find the following remarks:

Benefit is now being derived from the liberality with which outlays for repair work, maintenance and improvements have been made. Since the formation of the company nine years ago, about $3,000,000 have been expended in construction, purchase of woodlands, etc., in addition to requirements for ordinary repairs and maintenance, which have been charged directly to operating expenses, and also in addition to the amounts expended in 1906 for the property of the Gres Falls Company and that of the Allen Bros. Company. All told over $6,000,000 have been expended, since the company's incorporation, for additional property and new construction, and the company has increased its capital obligations only to the extent of $2,439,000. While the company's physical and producing capacity has been undergoing improvement, its financial position has also been bettered, net working capital having been increased in the past four years by approximately $1,058,000 or about 100 per cent.

180. *Borrowing funds for betterments.*—The third means of raising funds for betterments is through issues of medium-term notes. It is not necessary to consider this method with great care, inasmuch as it has already been discussed in Chapter VIII. The examples given there were sufficient to show the dangers of this method. Obviously it cannot properly be utilized except to provide for betterments which are practically certain to yield large and immediate profits; otherwise the corporation will be incurring obligations that must be met out of income and that will perhaps become exceedingly dangerous.

A much better method, generally speaking, of securing the funds for permanent betterments is by means of long-term bonds. As has been previously explained, large well-established corporations do not usually expect to pay off these bonds when they fall due, but plan to refund them by new issues. In other words, what they actually do is to incur a permanent fixed charge. Now if a betterment is of such a character that it is practically certain to produce profits year after year larger than the fixed charges assumed in order to make the betterment, it is no doubt good policy to raise the necessary funds by the issue of long-time obligations.

181. *Policy of the Pennsylvania Railroad.*—The settled policy of the Pennsylvania Railroad is the best known and most consistent illustration of the working of this principle. This company, it is understood, separates all its betterment expenses into the two classes previously named: First, those which will in all human probability result in a permanent saving or profit more than equal to interest on the funds thus invested; second, those which will probably prove profitable, but which may or may not yield profits in the immediate future. To the first group the Pennsylvania management assigns such betterments as shortening and straightening a line, cutting down grades, providing new equipment where an increase in traffic is certain, and so on; to the second class they assign such betterments as a large part of the tunnel construction in and around New York City, providing new equipment for a hoped-for increase in traffic, operating passenger stations, and so on. The Pennsylvania Railroad's custom is to pay for all betterments of the first class by bond issues and for all betterments of the second class by appropriations from surplus. Thus the stockholders secure at the same time the maximum of returns and the maximum of safety. It is the ideal policy as regards betterments and will no doubt be more generally adopted in the future by railroad and industrial corporations.

To illustrate its workings in the concrete case of the tunnel into New York City and accompanying improvements, the following figures are presented. Up to the end of 1908 the total cost of the tunnel extension, as shown by the annual reports, was $77,528,664, of which only 60 per cent had been capitalized. The total cost is covered by the following charges on the books and appropriations of surplus profits:

Cost on Books, December 31, 1908	$46,528,664
Charged to surplus income of 1908	1,000,000
Charged to profit and loss account in 1907 . .	7,000,000
Charged to profit and loss account in 1906 . .	13,000,000
Charged to profit and loss account in 1905 . .	5,000,000
Charged to profit and loss account in 1903 . .	5,000,000
Total cost of tunnel extension at end of 1908 . .	$77,528,664

The cost on the books given above is the figure at which the Pennsylvania Railroad carried the work then accomplished as an asset. But in 1908 the Pennsylvania Railroad proper required the lines west of Pittsburg to assume a part of the burden and accordingly the Pennsylvania Company turned over $10,000,-000 in securities, deducting the value thereof from its profit and loss surplus. Assuming that the income derived from these securities will defray the interest charges on $10,000,000 of the capital invested in the tunnel, the Pennsylvania Railroad will have to look to the operation of that property to yield fixed charges upon capital borrowings for that purpose of only about $36,500,000.

182. *General conclusions as to the financing of betterments.*—The only remaining method to consider of securing funds for betterments is by means of stock issues. The comparative merits of increasing capitalization by means of stock, as compared with bond, issues are too obvious to need much discussion. A bond issue is a cheaper means of getting the necessary funds, for bonds can always be sold to better advantage than stock which yields the same return; on the other hand, bond issues

are objectionable insofar as they tend to increase the fixed charges and thereby imperil the safety of the company. New stock issues are safe enough, but of course tend to reduce the rate of distribution on the stock already outstanding. We may, perhaps, lay down this general rule, that betterments of the second class—following the classification we have given—ought to be financed either out of surplus or by means of new stock issues; betterments of the first class ought to be financed by bond issues, or in rare cases by issues of medium-term notes.

In what is said with regard to the financing of betterments, as in all other general questions of corporation policy, we must be content with broad conclusions. Corporation managers who differ from the general principles here laid down are not necessarily to be condemned offhand. They may have good reasons which do not appear on the surface. Every business man must base his actions, not so much on general principles, as on the important concrete factors that confront him. At the same time it is also true that a clear understanding of these principles and of the practice of large corporations will aid the corporation manager in handling more intelligently and more successfully whatever peculiar and difficult problems arise before him.

CHAPTER XXIII

CREATION AND USE OF A SURPLUS

183. *Definition.*—One of the most talked about topics in the field of Corporation Finance is the "surplus," its formation and its management. Yet in spite of all the discussion, there is still a great deal of confusion even in the minds of lawyers and men familiar with financial affairs as to what a surplus is and what it is good for. The main principles that govern the management of surplus are not different from those which should control the management of other capital funds, and are simple enough to seem obvious when they are once clearly stated. That they are not always clearly comprehended, however, is proved by the loose writing and thinking with regard to the subject that is so often manifest.

A brief satisfactory definition of surplus is that it is the difference between the assets and the obligations of a corporation, including under "obligations" all the outstanding stock of the corporation, as well as its reserves and debts. Suppose, for instance, that we have a corporation with assets of all kinds, having a total book valuation of $1,000,000, and having on the other side of the account debts represented by accounts payable, bank loans, notes and bonds of $500,000, depreciation and other reserves of $50,000 and outstanding capital stock amounting to $250,000; it is evident that the corporation must have secured $200,000 of its assets from some other source within the business; and that source we call surplus. The surplus account, as is explained in the volume on ACCOUNTING THEORY AND PRACTICE, appears on the liability side of the balance sheet, because it is an amount for which the corporation must render an account.

184. *Four sources of surplus.*—In our discussion of the corporation's surplus we will consider:

(a) How it is obtained.

(b) What is done with it.

(c) Its uses and management.

One possible, though very unusual, means by which a corporation obtains a surplus is by inheritance. Take, for instance, a corporation which is a consolidation of two companies, each having a surplus of its own. The consolidation may conceivably simply guarantee the bonds and other outstanding debts of the subsidiary companies, may issue dollar for dollar in stock for the stock of the subsidiary companies and may transfer the former surpluses bodily to its own accounts. As we have seen in our study of the formation of consolidations, however (Chapter XIV), the new corporation will usually issue securities far in excess of the market value of the assets of the old companies. The consolidation, therefore, will not only not start out with a surplus usually, but will be compelled greatly to overvalue its assets in order to make a balance sheet possible. We may dismiss this first possible source of surplus, then, with the statement that it is too uncommon to be worth much discussion.

The second source of surplus, which also is rather unusual, is the selling of the corporate stock or bonds above par. Evidently the corporation in such a case receives a sum of money greater in amount than the obligations which it incurs. Now this extra sum may be handled by an accountant in three or four different ways. One way is to include it in the corporation's surplus account. The propriety of this method may be disputed, but this is an accounting rather than a financial question.

A surplus may originate, in the third place, in whole or in part from the sale of a corporation's fixed or semi-fixed assets. Thus if a manufacturing company owns a plant which has become obsolete and worthless for manufacturing purposes, and the value of which has been fully covered by a depreciation reserve—in other words, written off the books—and afterwards sells this plant, the sum resulting would go into the surplus account. Of course, the reader will understand that if the value of the plant in such a case had not been written off the books, but was still included in the corporation's balance sheet, the only effect of its sale would be a transfer of the amount received from the property account to cash or notes receivable or whatever was taken in payment for the plant.

A similar source of surplus is a revaluation of the fixed assets of a corporation when the revaluation shows an increase in their value. This increase would naturally be represented on the liability side of the balance sheet by a corresponding gain in the surplus. Generally speaking—and it must be remembered that there are some exceptions to this rule—an upward revaluation of assets is not in accordance with correct accounting or financial principles. Therefore, this fourth source of surplus is not commonly found.

185. *The fifth source—saving.*—This brings us to the fifth and most common source of surplus, namely, saving from income. The uses to which income should be put have been discussed at some length in Chapter

XXI; and the final uses, after the fixed charges and reserves had been provided for, were found to be dividends and surplus. It will do no harm to reiterate the important principle there laid down that the dividends of practically every corporation should be maintained at a fixed rate and should move only to increase. Fluctuating dividends destroy the confidence of the investing public and greatly reduce the credit of the corporation below what it might possess. The proper policy, with few exceptions, is to ascertain the minimum net earnings of a company in the years of greatest depreciation and rigidly hold the dividends at or below that minimum. The rest of the net earnings will be transferred to the company's surplus account.

That this method of forming a surplus may build it up with great rapidity is shown by the record of that great industrial concern, the Standard Oil Company. The annual net profits, the sums appropriated to surplus and to dividends, and the totals of each item for seven years are as follows:

Year	*Profits*	*Dividends*	*Surplus after divs.*
1908	$ 80,000,000*	$ 39,335,320	$ 40,664,680*
1907	85,000,000*	39,335,320	45,664,690*
1906	83,122,251	39,335,320	43,786,931
1905	57,459,356	39,335,320	18,124,036
1904	61,670,110	35,188,266	26,481,844
1903	81,336,994	42,877,478	38,459,516
1902	64,613,363	43,851,956	26,761,307
Total	$513,202,074	$279,258,980	$233,943,094

*Approximated; not reported after 1906.

It is evident that in the case of any company which follows the principle just laid down, the proportion of dividends paid will vary with the fluctuations in earnings. The greater those fluctuations the more rapid will be the increase in surplus. The converse proposition is that a stable rate of earnings makes unnecessary the creation of a big surplus.

186. *Policy of the "trusts,"*—Professor Edward S. Meade's well-known volume on "Trust Finance" gives the result of a careful study of the dividend and surplus policy at the beginning and during the existence of all our important industrial combinations or "trusts." The prime object of the managers of almost all these combinations at the beginning, Professor Meade points out, was to pay dividends and thereby encourage the sale of stock. They were therefore averse, as a rule, to appropriating any considerable amounts to the surplus account. They even, in some cases, incurred a deficit in order to pay dividends. Professor Meade computes that twenty-six important consolidations, which he has studied with especial care, earned in the four years 1898–1901, $150,201,390. He says:

> This amount, although large in the aggregate, represents but little more than 3 per cent per annum. It would appear, as already stated, that every consideration of prudence would incline the directors of these companies to reserve practically all their profits in order to strengthen the financial position of their companies. So far from following the path of prudence, however, 61.9 per cent—almost two-thirds of these profits—were paid out in dividends, leaving 38.1 per cent for the surplus reserve. The inadequacy of this reserve may be better understood when it is compared with the outstanding capital whose permanent value it was intended to secure. A reserve of only 4.2 per cent is the net result of the operations of three years.

The industrial trusts are excellent examples of corporations which for reasons of their own were reluctant to keep dividends down to a conservative basis and to create large surpluses. The results of their imprudence are familiar to most of us—perhaps entirely too familiar to some. The common and preferred stock of most of these companies received dividends for a few years, but at the first hint of trade and financial depression, earnings fell off, dividends were stopped and the market prices of the stocks dropped with a thud. We have here presented an impressive lesson that ought to be mastered by every corporation director and stockholder—the lesson that in times of plenty provision should be made, through creation of an adequate surplus account out of income, for the seasons of famine that are sure to come.

187. *How should surplus be invested.*—We have next to consider what form the surplus of a corporation should take, or, in other words, how it should be invested. Its possible forms or uses are as numerous as the uses to which the original capital funds of a corporation may be put, and may be classified under the following heads:

(a) Cash.

(b) Securities.

(c) Decrease of current liabilities.

(d) Sinking fund.

(e) Increase in stock of raw materials or finished products on hand.

(f) Betterments.

(g) Extensions and additions to fixed assets.

It goes without saying that the surplus should be used to strengthen the weak spots, whatever they may be, in the corporation's capital equipment. We can be somewhat more specific, however.

188. *The surplus as a "rainy day fund."*—There are two distinct and opposed opinions as to the true function

of a surplus: one, that it should be merged with the rest of the corporation's capital funds; the other, that it should be set aside as an insurance against future losses. Let us first consider the justification and the results of this second opinion. Its advocates base their case on the assertion that the original investment of capital funds should be sufficient to carry on properly all the business of the company; if these funds are not sufficient, then they should be increased by borrowing or by bringing in new stockholders, not by saving out of profits. The arguments in favor of providing funds for betterment by borrowing, rather than by saving, have already been given and have been found to have considerable weight. The advocates of this opinion are convinced of the advisability of maintaining dividends at a stable rate and conceive it to be the true function of a surplus account to equalize the dividends over a series of years. In other words, the surplus account should be, in their view, as it has well been called, simply a "rainy day fund," to be drawn upon for dividends whenever the necessity arises.

It follows, if this opinion is correct, that the surplus ought to take the form of cash or something that may readily be turned into cash, for example, securities. Otherwise, it will not be readily available for dividends in periods of financial stress when it is most likely to be needed. It is true, to be sure, that a surplus may be invested in permanent assets and yet be treated as a "rainy day fund," for these assets may be made the basis of temporary loans to the corporation. The objection here is that it is uncertain whether such loans can be obtained when they are most needed and, moreover, it is unsafe to base temporary loans on a corporation's fixed assets. On the whole, then, we may say, that if the surplus account is to be regarded simply as a kind of reservoir in which future dividends for lean years are to be stored, that reservoir should be filled with cash or easily marketable securities.

The chief exponents of this policy are the great English and German shipping companies, particularly the Cunard Company and the Hamburg-American Line. The former company is said to have nearly one-third of its total assets invested in securities which have no direct connection with its shipping business. If the company runs into a period of intense competition during which it cannot earn dividends, or should it sustain severe losses, enough securities would be sold to maintain the regular dividend rate. There are obvious advantages in this course; on the other hand, there are disadvantages equally obvious and for most corporations of controlling importance.

The first disadvantage is that to build up a cash surplus is almost a waste of that much capital. It is a waste because capital in that form earns next to nothing. If it is kept as a permanent cash balance it may, to be sure, draw interest at 2 or 3 per cent, or in exceptional cases, even 3½ per cent; but this is a totally inadequate return on an industrial investment. If the surplus is in the form of marketable securities the case is almost as bad; for the only securities that are marketable in times of stringency are high-grade bonds which do not yield above taxes more than 3½ per cent or 4 per cent at the outside. As the second disadvantage, it must be borne in mind in this connection that funds so invested, though safe enough from the corporation's standpoint, do not give the corporation stockholder safety sufficient to compensate for the small yield. What is meant by this statement is that the surplus, however invested, is part of the corporation's capital and would be swallowed up by the corporation's creditors in case of bankruptcy. Thus the surplus goes to protect the creditor rather than the stockholder. The stockholder would be much better off, so far as safety is concerned, if his portion of the surplus were turned over to him individually and he would himself buy good securities with the proceeds.

189. *Putting the surplus back into the property.*—Having these disadvantages in view, corporation managers in this country have almost universally put the surplus of their corporations back into the property. Sometimes it is used to increase the cash balance where more cash is really needed in the business, or to buy securities of companies which it is desirable to control. In both these cases, however, the object is not to separate the surplus from the business, as it is when the rainy day fund is formed, but to make it productive in the business. Sometimes it goes into betterments, as explained in the previous chapter, or into extensions or into some other of the seven forms mentioned above. Just which form shall be chosen by the corporation management depends on considerations which have already been discussed in the chapter on "Investment of Capital Funds." As a normal return on capital invested in commercial enterprises in this country would run from 6 per cent on up, it is evident that as a rule the investment of surplus in the business in which it was produced is the best and most profitable policy.

Perhaps the stockholder may object at this point that the surplus is taken from the profits which ought to be turned over to him. The objection is superficial and fails to take into account the various methods by which a surplus may be, and in the end, must be, distributed to the corporation stockholders. Some of these methods are not well understood; indeed it is doubtful whether half the stockholders in business corporations realize how or when their surplus is distributed to them. This is the interesting topic which will be the subject of our next chapter.

CHAPTER XXIV

DISTRIBUTION OF THE SURPLUS

190. *Effect of a surplus on assets and dividends.*—Ordinarily, as stated in the preceding chapter, a surplus is formed out of savings from income and is invested in the capital assets of the corporation. Thus it becomes merged at once with the capital funds. The average stockholder feels that it is lost to him. He sees, to be sure, that the assets of the corporation are increased by the formation of a surplus, and he will admit probably, if you press him, that theoretically this increase in assets is a good thing for the corporation and for every stockholder and tends to increase the value of his stock. The admission, however, is apt to be grudgingly made and probably does not disturb the stockholder's conviction that whatever sums are devoted to surplus are taken out of the pockets of the owners of the corporation. He sees how these sums are taken away from him, but does not see clearly in what form they come back to him. The object of this chapter is to explain the methods by which the surplus may be and generally is returned.

It has already been mentioned—and, for that matter, is self-evident—that surplus wisely invested in capital assets increases the earning power of the corporation and therefore its ability to pay large dividends. Moreover, the surplus when properly invested so as to extend the sales of the corporation or its ownings of raw materials, or its control over competitive plants, tends strongly to make earnings more stable and therefore to make practicable a distribution in dividends of a larger proportion of earnings. This is a point not often alluded to and worth a word of explanation. It is evident that generally speaking the larger the business a concern does, the more stable and dependable will be its earnings—for slight local fluctuations up and down will almost always balance each other. If a big jobbing corporation loses trade for local reasons in one section of the country, it may reasonably hope that gains in other sections will at least counterbalance the loss. It is also true that control, even partial control, over the prices of raw materials or of unfinished products tends to make earnings more stable. It may well happen for these reasons that a relatively small surplus will have a more than proportionate influence on a corporation dividend rate—not so much, to reiterate, because it increases earnings, as because it makes them more uniform.

Frequently—and this is especially true of a close corporation—no individual stockholder would be able to save and invest to such good advantage as the corporation can do for him. Take once more the famous example of the Carnegie Steel Company. Does anyone suppose that any single stockholder in that company would have become as wealthy if the earnings had regularly been paid out to the stockholders in dividends instead of being put back year after year into the property? The stockholders did not receive very large dividends for many years, and some perhaps were inclined to complain that they were not getting the returns on their investment that were justly due them. In this case the stockholders were never given any considerable proportion of earnings, nor was the vast surplus of the company distributed, except to a limited extent, until the sale of the Carnegie Steel Company in 1901 to the

United States Steel Corporation. Then the extraordinary strength and riches of the company were suddenly revealed. Almost a half-billion dollars in cash or salable securities were showered upon the fortunate stockholders of the company. Pittsburg, like a night-blooming cereus, suddenly blossomed with millionaires.

191. *Distribution through stock watering.*—This chapter is not to deal, however, with the distribution of surplus through its effect on dividends or through the final sale of the company's assets, but rather with the more direct and usual methods. First among these methods to be mentioned is the declaration of an extra stock dividend. In the year 1880 the Chicago, Rock Island and Pacific Railroad Company was a highly successful corporation with large earning power, due in part to the fact that for many years a considerable proportion of the earnings had been put back into the property. The directors of the corporation thought it wise to increase their dividend payments, and yet on account of the popular prejudice against large railroad earnings did not wish to increase the dividend rate. They therefore adopted the plan of consolidating with themselves a small subsidiary railroad, the stock of which they already owned; they paid for that stock and for the stock of the Chicago, Rock Island and Pacific Railroad Company by an immense issue of stock of an entirely new corporation, the Chicago, Rock Island and Pacific Railway Company. This stock of the new corporation was distributed to the old stockholders in the proportion of two new shares to one old share. Then on all the stock outstanding they declared and maintained a dividend rate nearly equal to what had previously been paid. In effect this process was a capitalization of a surplus of the corporation and a distribution

of the surplus to stockholders. A more recent instance of somewhat the same kind is the well-known Chicago and Alton deal, which is discussed in Chapter XXVII.

The essential feature of such a transaction is the capitalization of surplus and distribution of this extra capitalization to stockholders. The reader may inquire as to the advantage of this course. Surely, he will say, two shares of a total capital stock of $2,000,000 are worth no more than one share of a total capital stock of $1,000,000. The two shares in the first instance represent no larger proportion of assets and earnings than the one share in the second instance. This reasoning is plausible and true so far as it goes; yet the fact remains that the stockholders gain something by a stock dividend. In the first place, the dividend rate is kept down by this means, and in the case of public service corporations public hostility is to some extent avoided. In other words, the stock is watered, and the dividend rate maintained. The American Telephone and Telegraph Company is one of the many examples of companies which have thus greatly increased their capitalization from time to time, apparently with this object in view. A discussion of the ethics of such a transaction would be interesting, but is outside the scope of this volume.

In the second place, it is well known to corporation managers and to all who have studied the stock market with any care that two shares of stock, each paying 4 per cent per annum, will have a combined market price higher than one share of stock paying 8 per cent per annum. This seems a curious anomaly, but is readily explained. There are more people able and willing to buy low-priced than there are to buy high-priced securities. Therefore, the market for the two shares in this illustration is wider than the market for the one share; that is to say, the demand for the two shares is somewhat greater and therefore their combined price will be higher.

This same principle leads the promoters of mining and oil and other highly speculative companies to fix the par value of their shares at a low figure, \$10 or \$1 or 10 cents, or even as low as 1 cent. Applying the principle to stock dividends we see that there may be a real gain to a stockholder in an increase in the number of shares he holds, even though there is no change in the amount of dividends he receives.

192. *Distribution through subscription privileges.*—We are ready now to discuss the most common and important method of distributing a surplus, namely, the granting of subscription privileges for new issues of stock. In most states, as the reader is already aware, stock cannot be regarded as fully paid if it is sold for less than its par value. No state, however, makes it obligatory under any circumstances to sell stock at more than its par value; yet the stocks of successful corporations which are able to maintain stable dividend rates of more than 6 or 7 per cent per annum, almost always have market values higher than par. Here is an opportunity for the corporation directors, if they see fit, to give the stockholders a valuable privilege—the privilege, namely, of buying new stock issues at less than the market prices.

The relative advantages of providing funds for improvements and extensions of property by bond issues, by stock issues and by appropriations from earnings, have been discussed in Chapter XXII. It was there laid down as a general principle that provision of permanent capital funds by means of stock issues is not advisable unless all the new stock is taken by the old stockholders. This condition will be fulfilled, however, when the old stockholders are given the valuable privilege of buying the new stock at less than its market value, and under such circumstances the raising of additional capital funds by stock issues is a very common and on the whole commendable method. We have now to consider exactly how surplus may be distributed by means of these "privileged subscriptions" and how each stockholder may best secure his share of the advantages that should accure to him.

193. *An opportunity thus given for cheap investment.*—The privilege of buying a certain amount of stock below the market price enables the stockholder, if he chooses, to make a new investment on exceptionally favorable terms. For instance, in 1902 the Illinois Central Railroad Company put out a new stock issue and gave to its stockholders of record the privilege of buying the new stock at par in any amount up to 20 per cent of their stockholdings. Thus if a man had 100 shares of old stock, he was given an oportunity to buy 20 shares of the new stock at par. The average price of Illinois Central stock during the six months following the date of the new issue was 156½, thus showing a large paper profit to those who bought the new stock. As this stock was then paying an 8 per cent dividend, those who bought and held it for investment were getting much more than the usual market return on their investment.

A great many stockholders, however, do not care to increase their capital investment, but prefer to take their profits at once. In such a case they have a choice among four different methods of securing the profits, as follows:

(a) A stockholder may buy outright the proportion

of new stock allotted to him as a speculation, and a little later at some favorable opportunity may sell it.

(b) He may sell "short" after the issue of new stock is announced and deliver when he gets his quota of new stock.

(c) Instead of selling "short" he may sell outright an amount of his old holdings just equal to the amount of new stock that he has a right to buy.

(d) He may sell his privilege or "right" to subscribe to the new stock.

It will be well to compare briefly the advantages of these four methods.

194. *Cashing the privilege.—The subsequent sale.*—The first-named method is the simplest, but not generally the best. The chief difficulty is that the stockholder must pay cash for his quota of the new stock; and that means that he must either borrow the money or must lose the interest on some of his own funds. Frequently the subscriptions to the new stock are payable in installments. There may be a period of several months or a year between the date of the first installment and the final issue of the stock. For many stockholders it may prove decidedly inconvenient either to use their own funds or to borrow money. Another disadvantage lies in the well-known fact that the market price of any stock after a privileged subscription has been allotted to it almost always tends downward. One reason obviously is that the new issue increases by so much the total amount of stock outstanding; the second reason is that after a "right" has once been granted, investors figure that there will be no additional rights for a number of years; a third reason is that the chief men interested in a corporation that is about to put out a new issue and the underwriters of a new issue will usu-

ally "bull" the previously outstanding stock in advance, in order to create a good demand for the new issue. Now a stockholder who follows the first of the four methods and does not sell his stock until after he has paid for and received it, will probably sell on a falling market and will not reap as much profit as one who follows either of the other three methods. On the other hand, it must be said for this first method, that it is absolutely safe—a statement which cannot be applied to the method next to be considered."

195. *Cashing the privilege.—"Short selling."*—The mechanism of "short selling" has already been treated in Chapter XVII. In the case immediately before us a stockholder who had the right to subscribe to twenty shares of a new issue might deposit a margin of 10 or 15 per cent with his broker and instruct him to sell short. The broker borrows the twenty shares in order to make delivery and keeps on borrowing until the stockholder is able to get his twenty new shares from the corporation and turn them over to the broker to repay the borrowed stock. Under this arrangement the stockholder will be more likely than under the first method to get the top market price, because he will sell immediately after a "right" is announced—sometimes, if he has inside information, even before such announcement is made. This method further makes it unnecessary for the stockholder to borrow any money. He simply turns over his rights to his broker who uses, in order to pay for the new stock, the money that he has received from the "short" sale.

All this sounds very easy and simple and, as a matter of fact, it usually works out all right. The difficulty comes in the fact that any man who sells short runs the risk of being caught in a bull movement of that stock or even in a "corner."[1] The reader may perhaps suggest that in such a case he may easily make delivery from his old stock and thus obviate any serious loss. The answer here, however, is that probably he has sold short the amount of his old stock as well as of his quota of new stock, or has in some other way tied up the old stock; otherwise, he would probably follow the third, rather than the second, method. Successful corners are not very common in Wall Street or any other market. When they do come, however, they bring disaster and ruin in their train.

196. *Cashing the privilege.—Sale of old stock.*—The third method is not open to either of the objections that have been specified. The stockholder is much more likely to get the best market price than under the first method; he is not involved in the dangers that attach to the second. He picks his own time to sell and from the proceeds of the sale has funds enough to buy the same amount of new stock with large profits in addition. The sale of part or all of the stockholder's shares will not impair in any way his right to subscribe to the new stock, inasmuch as this right is always granted to stockholders of record on a given day; it makes no difference whether the stockholder of record increases or decreases his holdings after that day. The only fault to be found with this method is that it is not practicable for all stockholders. A great many of them, in all probability, will have their holdings posted as collateral for loans, or for some other reason will not care to part with stock even temporarily.

197. *Cashing the privilege.—Sale of rights.*—The fourth method, the sale of "rights," is the next best plan

1 The meaning of the term "corner" is explained in the volume on INVESTMENT AND SPECULATION.

ordinarily and is much used by those who do not care either to increase their holdings or to decrease them even temporarily. It is customary when any of the large corporations give their stockholders a "subscription privilege" to a new stock issue, to send out to each holder of record a formal statement of the number of new shares to which he has a right to subscribe. Such documents may be endorsed and transferred in the same way as stock certificates and are bought and sold on many of the stock exchanges and on the New York Curb Market. These documents are themselves known as "rights," just as certificates of stock are loosely called "stock."

As was stated in Chapter XVII, there are confusing differences of terminology between the New York and some of the other stock exchanges, particularly Philadelphia. In New York a "right" is the privilege to subscribe to a certain amount, usually a fractional part of a share of new stock. A stockholder, therefore, has as many "rights" as he has shares. In Philadelphia, on the other hand, a "right" means the privilege of buying one of the new shares of stock. To illustrate, suppose that the Lehigh Valley Railroad Company, whose securities are listed on both exchanges, should issue new stock to old stockholders at less than the market price and should give the subscription privilege at the rate of one new share to every five old shares. In that case the holder of five shares would have one "right" to dispose of on the Philadelphia or five "rights" on the New York Exchange. Of course the Philadelphia "right" would be worth five times as much as the New York "right." The difference is merely in terminology.

It may be thought that the third and fourth methods

would yield practically the same returns, but this is an error. The third method is almost always more profitable, the reason being that there is a much broader demand for stock than there is for "rights" to subscribe to stock. As was explained in Chapter XVII, there is a large body of purchasers not directly concerned with the stock market, who are constantly taking the standard stocks out of that market and holding them for permanent investment. This demand does not exist in the case of "rights," because few people, outside of those whose business it is to know such things, understand how the value of a "right" is figured or even what it is. It would often be greatly to the advantage of these permanent investors if they did buy "rights" instead of stock. As the matter now stands, however, almost the only buyers are stock brokers and their immediate followers who buy as a quick speculation in the hope of making a quick profit. As they are willing to buy only in case they think they are getting a bargain, it follows that the price of rights is usually less than it should be theoretically.

198. *Theoretical value of a right.*—Let us see how the value of a right should in theory be ascertained. The reader may perhaps have jumped at the conclusion that the value would be the difference between the market price of the old stock and the price at which the new stock is sold to stockholders. This is incorrect, however, because it fails to take into consideration the change in the value of each share brought about by an increase in the amount of stock outstanding. The new stock, it must be remembered, is issued at less than the market price, and does, not, therefore, bring to the company's treasury its proportionate amount of assets. For this reason it is inevitable that the market price of

each share after the new stock has been issued should be less than it was before.

To illustrate these abstract and rather vague statements, take the case previously cited, that of the Illinois Central Railroad, which in August, 1902, increased its stock 20 per cent and gave to each five shares of old stock the privilege of subscribing to one new share at par. The market price of the old stock at the time the rights were granted was about 170, giving a premium, or excess above par, of $70 per share. Now there is to be added for each share of the old stock, $20 in assets, because each old share has the right to subscribe to one-fifth of a new share at par. At the same time there is to be added $20 to the capital stock for each $100 previously outstanding. The market value of each share, therefore, after the new stock has been issued, will be $\frac{170 + 20}{100 + 20} = 158\ 2/6$, which in theory would be the market price of each share after the new stock issue. As a matter of fact, the average price of Illinois Central shares during the six months following August, 1902, was 152 3-5. The value of the "right" belonging to each share of old stock would, of course, be in this case one-fifth of the difference between par and the market price of each share of new stock, or 1-5 of 58 1-3, approximately 11 2-3.

The following formula, commonly used on the New York Stock Exchange, gives directly the theoretical value of a right. Let P represent the premium on the old shares and R represent the percentage of increase. Then the value of a right will be found by the formula $\frac{P \times R}{1 + R}$. Applying this formula to the Illinois Central example, we would have $\frac{70 \times .2}{1 + .2} = \frac{14}{1.2} = 11.66$. As has been stated these theoretical prices for "rights" are seldom obtained because speculative purchasers of rights are not willing to go that high. Moreover, there are some assumptions underlying these mathematical formulæ which may or may not be true. It is assumed, for instance, that the stock market price of the old stock is a normal price uninfluenced by speculative factors. It is assumed, also, that the company's use of the funds which come to it from the sale of new stock will be neither more nor less remunerative than the use of the capital funds previously in its possession. It is assumed, moreover, that the market price after the new stock has been issued will be uninfluenced by speculative factors. There is a risk in all these assumptions, as the professional stock market trader well knows, and he is therefore unwilling to pay the full theoretical price for the rights.

Summing up, then, we may conclude that of the four methods of securing profits from privileged subscriptions, which have been described, the third method is, on the whole, likely to yield the largest returns. The second method comes next in that respect, but has the disadvantage of being dangerous. The fourth method comes next, and the first method is, on the whole, least desirable. It will not do to accept these conclusions as being true at all times and under all circumstances. They are merely generalizations based on experience.

199. *Privilege subscriptions as a method of stock watering.*—So far as distribution of surplus is concerned, giving "rights" to privileged subscriptions to new issues of stock produces the same effect, though not to an equal degree, as a stock dividend. The assets of the company in proportion to the number of shares are diminished, and the stockholder gets the benefit. If the old rate of dividends is maintained on all the stock

outstanding after the new issue, each stockholder may be truthfully said to have come into possession of some of the company's surplus. The privileged subscription is a device for increasing capitalization without proportionately increasing assets. In that sense it is "stock watering."

The meaning of the terms "stock watering" and "overcapitalization" have been sufficiently discussed and need not be given further attention. It is enough to reiterate that whatever may be said for or against the practice in connection with public service corporations, it is in private corporations, when properly used, a simple and legitimate means of making a corporation's capitalization correspond to its earning powers; and is in addition, as outlined in this chapter, a legitimate means of transferring to the stockholder a part of the surplus which his company has created for him.

CHAPTER XXV

MANIPULATION BY CORPORATION OFFICERS

200. *Ought we to study manipulation?*—So far we have been dealing with and endeavoring to formulate the principles of honest and efficient corporate management; the rest of this book will deal with dishonesty, inefficiency and failure. Sometimes any study of rascality is condemned offhand on the ground that it may suggest swindling practices to persons who otherwise would not have thought of them. Perhaps there is something to be said in favor of this view; if any readers of this volume feel themselves morally weak it may be well for them to omit the next three chapters. On the other side of the argument, we may say that a thorough knowledge of fraudulent methods does not by any means encourage fraud, for it reveals that almost all such methods, however cunning they may appear, are unsound and dangerous. Furthermore—and this is the important point—honest men ought certainly to acquire as clear an insight as they can into the methods of swindlers in order that they may be on their guard and may protect themselves and those who are dependent upon them.

201. *The corporate form favors manipulation.*—The corporation, as practically every business man now appreciates, is for most concerns the most convenient, useful and efficient form of organization that has yet been devised. It is likewise true that the corporation so far has proved itself a most efficient form in the hands of

rascals for transferring other peoples' rightful property into their own pockets. In an address on "Abuse of Corporate Privileges" printed in the *American Law Review* Mr. Seymour D. Thompson has described from the lawyer's point of view the present conditions. He says:

> Our corporate life is honeycombed with corruption. A corporation is formed; its business is put into the hands of certain managers holding some of its stock and expert in the management of its business. Debts are created and the managers become the creditors. The result is that rings are organized within rings, wheels within wheels, combinations within combinations. The managers, in the character of creditors, seize upon and foreclose the property of the corporation, and by well-known processes squeeze the other stockholders out and become themselves proprietors with larger holdings than they had before. This sweating process, dignified by the name of foreclosing and reorganizing, has come to be a regular industry in our courts of justice. Courts of justice have neither the time nor the means to take upon themselves the management of all the corporations in the country; and therefore the outraged and complaining stockholders are told that they cannot come into court until they have exhausted all the remedies within the corporation.

202. *Is manipulation a necessary evil?*—Now this deplorable condition, which is one of the chief evils of the American business world, is not, fortunately, a necessary evil. We may well doubt, indeed, whether the lawyers with their quibbles and conservatism will do much to remedy conditions. But we may expect much from the growing interest of the public in corporate affairs. The evil exists chiefly because the corporate form of organization is still a thing in which most people have had little experience and the workings of which they do not

clearly understand. The true remedy, then, for the evils of corporate manipulation, is publicity and education. These three chapters following, which constitute the first attempt, so far as the author knows, to classify and describe the methods commonly used for defrauding some of the owners of a corporation for the benefit of others, will fulfill their chief purpose if they have some slight influence in checking this evil.

Perhaps the words "fraud" and "swindling" in the preceding paragraphs should not have been used; they do not convey exactly the conception which is in the author's mind in writing these chapters. We are not to be concerned here with ordinary clear cases of fraud; a study of such cases belongs to law rather than to finance. Moreover, a clear-cut instance of fraud is not usually a very dangerous thing, because the victim may seek and obtain redress in the courts. The chief danger comes not from crude and obviously illegal larceny, but from acts that cannot be proven fraudulent and that belong in the shadowy borderland, bounded by shrewd dealing on the one side and on the other by plain swindling. Some of the practices to be described are allowable, although most of them are discredited under the rules of the business game as those rules are generally interpreted.

203. *Scope of the chapters on manipulation.*—It should be made plain also at the beginning that in these chapters not much will be said about "malefactors of great wealth" or about large "predatory corporations," although some of these corporations furnish shining examples which cannot be overlooked. We shall deal rather with everyday small business corporations and with those kinds of manipulation that may be found in every section of the country. The "sharks" of Wall

Street do not by any means have a monopoly, as some of the cases to be cited will show, on dubious finance.

As a basis of classification we will take up methods of manipulation under the four heads:

(a) Manipulation by officials.

(b) Manipulation by directors.

(c) Manipulation for stockholders as a body.

(d) Manipulation for controlling stockholders.

Of course, this classification is not exact. We shall find constant overlapping, for the obvious reason that any man or group who desire to manipulate will probably try to make their control as complete as possible, and will work through stockholders' meetings, directors' meetings, and officers' administration. Nevertheless, this classification will be found convenient and for the present purpose sufficiently accurate.

204. *Exorbitant salaries.*—The most obvious and common method by which a corporation official may milk a corporation of its profits is by paying himself an exorbitant salary. This is a practice so frequent and so easy that it would be superfluous to cite examples. A corporation official cannot, to be sure, absolutely fix his own salary, for that power is reserved to the directors. If the official, however, is a powerful stockholder, or if two or three officials can get hold of a majority of the stock, or if an official can bring outside pressure to bear upon the board of directors, he may cause a salary to be allotted to him far in excess of what he is actually worth to the company. It is not at all unusual for minority stockholders in small corporations to be deprived of profits because the president, or other official, who owns the controlling stock raises his own salary as fast as profits go up. It would be very difficult—practically impossible—in such a case to prove fraud. No

court would undertake to say that a salary was fraudulent, or that directors were acting beyond their powers in agreeing to it, unless the salary were beyond all reason.

205. *Fraudulent contracts.*—Another favorite method of manipulation by officers is the use, or rather abuse, of their power to purchase and to make contracts on behalf of the corporation. The evil of purchasing officers being in league with the firms from which they buy supplies and getting a rake-off on the corporation's purchases, has been so much exploited as to make unnecessary any further illustration. There is no question but that something of the kind does go on in many of the larger corporations. Yet the purchasing agent is generally a subordinate official whose policy is closely scrutinized by his superiors and who is subject to instant dismissal if any strong tendency on his part toward "grafting" is discovered. His delinquencies are not so interesting to us in this study as those of his superiors. Let us examine briefly a few instances in which high corporate officials have misused their power to bind the corporation.

In the Illinois courts some years ago suit was brought by H. P. Killjoy, a stockholder, against the Mandarin Brewing Association. He alleged, and seems to have proved to the satisfaction of the court, that in 1896 three brothers purchased a majority of the stock and obtained control of this brewing corporation. They elected themselves to the directorate and to most of the corporation offices. One of the brothers owned a piece of real estate which the corporation purchased at an amount alleged to have been far in excess of its true value. The brothers, as directors, paid themselves large salaries as officers and no dividends were forthcoming to the stockholders. The stockholders were kept in ignorance of the purchase of the real estate and of the size of the salaries. Although the court was so far convinced of the truth of these allegations that a receiver was appointed for the company, no criminal or civil action was taken against the three brothers.

The facts cited in a recent case in the Massachusetts courts are of interest in this connection. Samuelson, defendant in the case, was treasurer of the Easton Ferry Company. He sold bonds of the company and neglected to account for them. He charged the company for bank discounts larger than the bank charged, claiming that this extra discount was for his own personal indorsement, which appeared on the notes. He purchased coal in his own name at a low price and, as treasurer, bought the same coal for the company from himself at a high price. In this case the court ruled that Samuelson should be charged with the market value of the bonds that he had sold and should refund the difference between the market price of the coal and the price at which he had purchased it from himself for the company. Here again there was no hint of criminal liability or punishment.

Take another case, this time from the New York courts. Two officers of a paper company obtained an option to purchase a manufacturing plant for $75,000. The same plant was sold to the corporation, of which one of the defendants was president, for $100,000. The deed was taken directly from the owner of the plant to the corporation reciting a consideration of $1. The majority of the stockholders had no knowledge of the option price of $75,000 until later. On learning the facts they elected new officers who, on behalf of the company, brought suit against the defendants for the difference between the true purchase price and the price charged to the corporation. The suit was unsuccessful.

As this is not a legal treatise, a discussion of the exact legal reasons for the decisions of the court in each of the three cases cited is not necessary here. The important feature common to the three cases and common to practically all similar cases is that in the present state of the law an official may make contracts and purchases directly advantageous to himself and disadvantageous to the corporation without fear of punishment—provided, of course, that he and his lawyers make no legal blunders. Assuming that he avoids this pitfall, the worst that can happen to him through the operation of the law is a restitution of his ill-gotten gains, which is, of course, no punishment at all. His true punishment comes simply in the fact that sooner or later his dishonesty will be discovered and his reputation among honorable business men will be indelibly smirched.

206. *New companies for profitable business.*—A third method by which corporation officials often transfer an undue portion of corporate profits to themselves is by the formation of new companies for profitable business. Every corporation, whether it be railroad, industrial, trading or financial, will find some features of its operations more profitable than others. The ordinary stockholder may not know anything about the actual operation of the business or about the opportunities for large profits; obviously the officers who do understand the situation are under a strong temptation to use their knowledge for their own, instead of for the corporation's, benefit.

The writer, for instance, knows of a company of considerable size, which is in the business of buying and selling domestic rugs and carpets. The concern began to deal in a small way in oriental rugs and Smith and Jones, the president and office manager, respectively, discovered at once that in their town this business was extraordinarily profitable. Instead of taking hold of the business and developing it for the established corporation of which they were officers, Jones resigned his position, organized a new company, in which Smith was secretly a large stockholder, and quickly secured all the oriental rug trade of their city for the new corporation. The stockholders of the first corporation retain Smith as their president to this day and regard him highly for his business ability. At the same time, Smith is growing rich from the profits of the new corporation. The stockholders, even if they knew all the facts, would not be justified in saying that they had been defrauded. All that they have lost, in fact, is an opportunity. The ethics of the proposition is too big a question to be here discussed. Whether the action of the officials in this case be regarded as right or wrong, it is certainly true that its effect was to transfer possible profits from the corporation to the officers.

Take another instance, which has been related to the writer by a public accountant. The Automatic Door Fastening Company is a corporation with a large capitalization. It controls a patent device that can be cheaply manufactured and readily sold at a good price. The officers easily sold the stock to a number of small investors who were impressed with the high value of the patent and the large profits which would certainly be forthcoming as soon as it was put on the market. The corporation secured the necessary amount of capital funds, and manufactured the device; at this point the stockholders learned that a subsidiary corporation, owned by the officers, had been formed in each section of the country where sales were expected to be large and that every subsidiary corporation had a hard and fast contract with the parent company by which the subsidiary company got the device at a price that barely covered the cost of manufacture and was given exclusive selling rights in its own section. Practically all the profits evidently were thereby transferred from the corporation to the subsidiary companies.

There is nothing new in such an arrangement. Thirty-five years ago when the numerous short-distance railroads of the United States were first being consolidated into systems, railroad officials discovered that the most profitable traffic was that which moved over long distances. It was not long after this discovery before twenty-five or thirty "despatch lines" and "fast freight lines" were in existence, each of which handled the through long-distance traffic over two or more railroads under contracts by which much the greater portion of the large profits went to the despatch line companies. It is almost needless to add that the chief stockholders of these new companies were railroad officials.

The same principle was applied by Commodore Vanderbilt when the New York Central System was formed by holding in his own hands the stock of companies which owned the important terminals of the railroad. These terminals were then leased to the New York Central on terms that were not generally exorbitant, but that nevertheless yielded a large return to the Commodore. Although the Vanderbilt family for many years have not held a majority or anything like a majority of the New York Central stock, yet they have been able to dominate the management of that road and to secure for themselves large profits through their ownership of these terminal companies.

207. *Misuse of inside information.*—The fourth method of milking a corporation for the benefit of its officers is by making use of "inside" information. This is, on the whole, the safest and least disreputable method. Indeed the line between the proper and improper use of the information that necessarily comes into the officers' possession is so indistinct that no one has yet been able to trace it. We are all agreed, no doubt, that it is quite improper for the president of a corporation to make a business of speculating in the stock of his company, especially if he "sells short" and thereby puts himself under temptation to mismanage the company. On the other hand, probably few people would raise any objection to an officer's investing in some shares of his company's stock, if he has good reason to believe that the stock is selling below its true value; nor does there seem to be any valid objection to his selling this same stock, if later he discovers that speculative forces have raised it far above its true value. Now just where shall the line between what is proper and improper in this regard be drawn? No one can say. It is as shadowy as the line between speculative and investment buying.

Whatever doubt there may be as to whether the use of inside information by a corporation officer to guide his buying and selling of stock is improper or not, there can certainly be no question but that the use of such information by an officer in order to enrich himself directly at the expense of the corporation is wholly unjustifiable. The three cases cited below are fair examples of what is sometimes done:

(a) An officer of an oil refining company in Pennsylvania, who had no authority to sell stock for the corporation, received a buying order addressed to himself as an official of the corporation for 5,000 shares at 20 cents a share. He filled the order by transferring 5,000 shares from himself to the purchaser and then took for himself 5,000 shares of treasury stock at the special price of 2 cents a share. In this case, the facts being fully proved, the court ordered a refund of the difference between the two prices to the corporation.

(b) The XYZ Manufacturing Company, with capital stock of $500,000, one-half paid in, went into receivers' hands. The company had notes for $20,000 outstanding, bearing 10 per cent interest and secured by a mortgage on its property. The president, knowing the condition of the company, just before the failure, secured the notes in exchange for $30,000 face value of his stock in the company. Ten thousand dollars was paid on the notes when they fell due, but the other stockholders objected to paying the remainder. The president transferred his claim for the remaining $10,000 to an outsider and the court enforced payment of the claim.

(c) Robinson, the treasurer of a railroad company, which was in poor condition, bought up outstanding notes of the company at a large discount with his own money and as treasurer saw to it that the notes were paid when due at their full face value. The court held that the treasurer had done nothing illegal. He was at liberty to buy the notes for himself, as he was under no obligation to buy them for the road. He could meet them when due with the road's money, as that money was there to pay any or all of the road's debts and not any special debt.

The striking feature of these three cases, as in several of the other cases cited, is that although the officials were obviously unfaithful to their trust and were not acting in good faith as agents for the corporation, nevertheless they were able to escape legal punishment.

208 *Is manipulation by officers common?*—The four methods that have been given and illustrated, by which corporations are frequently deprived of part of their just profits by their own officers are:

(a) Exorbitant salaries.

(b) Collusion or fraud in marketing, purchases and contracts.

(c) Formation of new companies for especially profitable business.

(d) Misuse of confidential information which comes to officers by virtue of their position.

It would certainly be a gross exaggeration to say that all or a majority of the corporation officers of the United States are guilty of any of these practices. On the contrary, it is probably true that their dealings with or for the corporation which they serve are in most cases absolutely honorable. Yet it must be regretfully admitted that these four methods of milking a corporation are only too well-known and too skillfully practiced. As an accountant of wide experience says, in speaking of corporate manipulation by officers, "That this is constantly being done is obvious from the fact that so many men, drawing salaries with large corporations of $10,000 to $15,000 a year, become millionaires in a very short period. It is a mere matter of arithmetic to demonstrate that this is not done out of the money that they save."

CHAPTER XXVI

MANIPULATION BY DIRECTORS

209. *Usual methods.*—As has already been stated, it is difficult to draw the line between manipulation by officers and manipulation by directors, for in most cases more or less collusion between the two is essential to the success of any of their fraudulent schemes. It is possible, however, to draw a distinction between those forms of manipulation which are primarily intended for the benefit of officers and those forms which are primarily for the benefit of directors; with the latter class of manipulative methods we have now to deal.

The method that was given the first place in our consideration of manipulation by officers, namely, exorbitant salaries, is not worth attention here. Directors, to be sure, are frequently allowed fees for attending meetings, and sometimes these fees seem to be somewhat excessive. They are frequently prescribed, however, in the by-laws, in which case, of course, the stockholders as a body would have no ground for complaint against the directors as a body. In any case, the fees are not large enough to make it worth while for the directors to attempt to defraud the stockholders and enrich themselves by this particular method. Without much question the courts would set aside directors' fees for attending meetings much higher than \$10 to \$25 for each meeting and would look with suspicion on an especially large number of meetings.

Eliminating this possible method of manipulation, then, as of small consequence, we may set down four important and not uncommon means of transferring an undue proportion of a company's assets and profits to the pockets of its directors. These four methods are:

(a) Fraudulent purchases and contracts.

(b) Formation of new companies for especially profitable business.

(c) Deceiving the body of stockholders by means of juggled accounts.

(d) Forcing the corporation unnecessarily into bankruptcy or into receivers' hands.

The reader will observe that the first two methods have been discussed in the preceding chapter. There are, however, some variations that should be mentioned between the application of these methods by officers and by directors.

210. *Fraudulent contracts.*—The number of cases of fraudulent purchases and contracts by directors that have been brought before the courts are so numerous that it is difficult to make a selection. The following instances are typical:

(a) In an Alabama case the facts brought out were as follows: The promoters of a large electric manufacturing company obtained as a profit in its formation approximately $2,000,000 of stock and were thereby able to exercise considerable influence on the board of directors. The directors, in spite of the demands of several stockholders, neglected to seek to recover from the promoters any portion of their excessive profit. Suit was brought by a stockholder to compel the directors to act and they replied that they deemed the proposed attempt to recover inexpedient. It is intimated in the court's decision that they were improperly influenced by the promoters and the court ordered them to make the attempt.

(b) Three directors of a corporation formed to build a summer resort hotel caused the corporation to purchase the land on which the hotel was to be located from themselves at a 200 per cent profit to themselves. The land was purchased subject to a heavy mortgage. When only $25,000 had been subscribed toward the $90,000 required to erect the hotel, the directors made a contract to start construction of the building. Their object in so doing was to enhance the value of other land in that vicinity which they owned. The corporation became insolvent and the directors, on foreclosing their mortgage on the land, virtually became the owners of the land and of as much of the hotel building as had been erected. The court in this case held that the directors were liable to the stockholders for the depreciation in the market value of the stock.

(c) Two of three directors of a South Dakota corporation, for the purpose of securing control of the corporation for themselves, caused the issue and immediate sale to one of their friends of a large amount of new stock sufficient to give the two directors and their friend together a majority. The court held that as the friend knew all the facts, the sale of the stock conferred no rights upon the purchaser. It may be inferred from this decision that if the purchaser had been an innocent party, the transaction would have been valid.

(d) In a somewhat similar instance in New York a full board of directors authorized the issue of sixty-seven shares of stock to increase its capital. The president of the company reported at a subsequent meeting that he had received no subscriptions, and four of the seven directors thereupon took the stock without knowledge of the holder of the majority of stock previously issued, who was also a director. In this case the court allowed the purchasers to hold and vote the stock, but enjoined them from using it to the injury of the previous majority holder.

(e) A railroad company was organized in Minnesota to build a local road in that state. Capital stock of $2,000,000 and bonds to the extent of $1,500,000 were authorized. A director and owner of a majority of the outstanding shares drew up a contract with the XYZ Construction Company under which the company was to build the road and receive 331 shares of its capital stock together with first mortgage bonds to the amount of $20,000 per mile. The XYZ Construction Company then made a contract on its own account with the firm of A & B, under which the firm was to pay $5,446 for each $20,000 block of bonds and in addition was to furnish the material necessary to build the road. The director above referred to was interested with A & B and was to receive for himself an agreed share of the railroad bonds. The actual cost of construction was to be about $14,000 a mile. The contract came before the board of directors and two directors, whom we will call Smith and Jones, voted for the contract with the understanding that they also were to become interested with A & B and to receive a portion of the profits. Afterwards they offered to contribute one-fourth of the cash required for actual construction of the road in order to become partners with A & B. Their offer was refused. They then brought suit, exposed the whole transaction and asked to have the contracts declared void for fraud. The court held that there was no fraud on the face of the transaction but that fraud could plainly be inferred, inasmuch as the corporation was made to pay more than was necessary for contruction. They held, however, that the two directors, Smith and Jones, having knowledge of the transaction, did not come into court with "clean hands" and could not cry fraud because they lost what they had attempted to gain. The contract, therefore, was not set aside.

211. *Attitude of the courts.*—These illustrations, taken almost at random, indicate what opportunities for fraudulent manipulation are open to corporate directors and how slight is the danger of legal punishment. As may be observed over and over again, the courts assume that a corporation is honestly managed in accordance with the wishes of the stockholders unless the contrary is absolutely proved. Stockholders who object to the contracts and purchases made by their directors are apt to be told that their true remedy is to elect a new board.

Obviously this principle of the law, however far from applicable it may be in particular cases, works out, on the whole, for the good of the greatest number. Most corporations are honestly managed. Directors are rightly believed generally to have a far more extensive knowledge of the affairs of the corporation and of the contracts and purchases that should be made than the body of stockholders have. The courts, therefore, ordinarily do not desire to set aside contracts made by the directors or even by investigation to cast doubt upon those contracts. The attitude of the courts, it must be admitted, is correct. On the other hand, as the instances given above plainly indicate, it is also true that this attitude gives directors almost unlimited opportunities for fraudulent manipulation. The only practicable remedy in the long run is for the stockholders to be exceedingly careful to elect men of proved probity to their directorate.

212. *New companies for profitable business.*—The second method of manipulation by directors that has been named is the formation of new companies for profitable business. A few typical illustrations will best explain the working of this method.

(a) The directors of a New York building and loan association, the charter of which required the funds to be invested in first mortgages, nevertheless bought some second mortgages. The association became insolvent and receivers were appointed. Some of the directors then organized a realty company which took from the receivers the land and buildings owned by the association at 50 cents on the dollar and made part payment with additional second mortgages. The directors thus secured for themselves at small cost most of the valuable assets of the association. The court discharged the receiver and appointed another receiver to conserve the remaining assets.

(b) The Strong Lumber Company and the Hoffman Manufacturing Company elected three men, constituting a majority of both boards, directors of both companies. The Hoffman Manufacturing Company, which had the better credit, accepted time drafts drawn upon them by the Strong Lumber Company, although no consideration had been given. To secure themselves from personal liability the three men as directors of the Strong Company placed a mortgage on the property of that company and issued bonds which were turned over to the Hoffman Company. When the facts were presented, the court entered a decree setting aside the mortgage.

(c) The directors of a railroad company in Nevada were members of a syndicate which intended to build a connecting road. The road was built and paid for by the syndicate and was mortgaged heavily. The syndicate received all the bonds and stock and then transferred 51 per cent of the stock to the railroad company, of which they were directors, in consideration of this company's guaranteeing the bonds. The guarantee of the bonds allowed the syndicate to sell them at a good price. The court held that allegations of fraud were not sustained and that the whole transaction was legitimate.

In the last two cases the profit to the directors evidently came in the form of increased credit for companies in which they were interested. It seems clear in both cases that there was no corresponding advantage to the corporation; otherwise the corporation in each case would have made the arrangement on its own account. The reader will observe, no doubt, that directors have opportunities of the same kind as those which fall to officers, when it is discovered that some particular feature of a company's business is especially profitable. Either the directors or the officers, or both together, may organize a new company of their own to handle that business and thus may divert profits to themselves.

213. *Juggling accounts.*—The third means open to directors, who wish to manipulate corporate affairs for their own interests, is to tamper with the corporation's books and thus give the stockholders a wrong impression as to the company's condition. The methods that may be used to accomplish this object are so numerous and so complicated that it would be impracticable to enumerate all of them here. Indeed, this section of our subject belongs to accounting rather than to finance.

A few typical instances, however, which have been supplied by some of the most experienced and best known public accountants in the United States to the writer, may be enumerated. The reader will find further light on this important subject in the volume on AUDITING.

(a) The directors of a holding company, which owned the entire stock of four separate manufacturing companies, desired to present a favorable report of the year's operations to their stockholders. In order to do so they took into account dividends paid by three of the companies and ignored altogether a very heavy loss incurred by the fourth company. Their excuse for so doing—which excuse, however, carries very little weight—was that the holding company as a stockholder in the other companies was entitled to the benefit of all the dividends declared, but could not be called upon to make up any loss that might be sustained; this excuse obviously overlooks the fact that the loss incurred by the fourth company constituted a diminution of the assets of the holding company. A firm of certified public accountants was called upon to sign the misleading report prepared by the directors. The accountants were given access to the books of the holding company but were refused the books of the subsidiary companies. The firm lost the audit, which went to more pliable accountants (not holding the degree of certified public accountant), and the original report was presented to the stockholders. Presumably the directors seized the opportunity to sell their stock in the holding company at a high price. At any rate, the holding company went into bankruptcy not long afterwards.

(b) A railroad company, when the time for the annual report and audit approached, deliberately withheld the intertraffic claims of other companies, amounting to a considerable sum, by simply pigeon-holing the documents and not recording them as a part of their current obligations. This action was taken, it is stated, by order of the executive committee of the board of directors, who were about to ask authority for a new stock issue and who desired to bring out the issue shortly after the annual report appeared. The certified public accountants, who had charge of the annual audit, in this case discovered the deception through a general analytical study of the year's operations whereby it was seen that while such intertraffic claims ought to exist, they were not in evidence.

(c) An industrial company was enabled to maintain a market value for its stock through the payment of unearned dividends out of capital. The deficit was not shown on the books and was not known to the stockholders until after an audit by public accountants. Its existence, however, should have been known to the directors and in all probability was known during the period in which unearned dividends were declared. In this case judgment was obtained in the courts against the directors and restitution of the unearned dividends was obtained.

(d) In a case brought in the federal courts stockholders asked for the cancellation of stock alleged to have been fraudulently and secretly issued by the board of directors. It was stated that a person, to whom the certificate was issued without consideration to the company, executed to one of the directors a power of attorney authorizing him to vote the stock and delivered the certificate signed in blank. Thus, although no transfer appeared on the books of the corporation, the stock was actually owned and voted by one of the directors. As the stock of this corporation was widely scattered and as the reports to stockholders were fragmentary and misleading, the whole transaction would have passed unnoticed if it had not been accidentally revealed to one of the stockholders. The court in this case merely cancelled the certificate in question and neither civil nor criminal liability was found to attach to the directors.

214. *An accountant's observations.*—A certified public accountant, whose experience in handling such cases has been exceptionally large, has been kind enough to sum up for the writer the results of his observations in the following note:

The methods employed for the purpose of giving a wrong impression to the stockholders or the public as to the company's condition as shown by the published balance sheet are almost innumerable, but I will cite a few.

Where the accounts are subject to audit and it is desired to make a good appearance at the date of the balance sheet, the practice of borrowing a large sum of money from brokers or bankers for a few days is often resorted to. By this means at the date of the balance sheet the company has apparently a large amount of available funds, though in point of fact the loan is repaid a few days later. In the same way, where such a corporation as a loan and investment company finds itself holding securities of a speculative character, such as mining stock, it is quite customary to make a sale of these securities to brokers a few days before the date of the balance sheet, with the understanding that the company is to repurchase them at the same price less commission for the accommodation a few days later. In this way the company avoids showing on its published balance sheet any investments that are not of a gilt-edged character, and in both the instances quoted above it is very hard for the auditor to find any grounds for refusal to give an unqualified certificate to the balance sheet; the condition is as stated by the accounts at the particular date at which they are drawn up.

Again, where it is desired to conceal from stockholders the fact that the company is making large profits or, on the other hand, incurring heavy losses, the valuation placed upon investments in stocks and bonds of other corporations or the valuation placed upon merchandise on hand is often juggled, the officers of the company constituting themselves the arbiters as to what is really the actual value of such assets.

Another window-dressing plan often employed is to treat the balances due on current account from the branch houses of the corporation as though they were accounts receivable due from ordinary customers. Goods on consignment are often similarly treated as though they were accounts receivable and included in the balance sheet at sale price under this caption instead of at cost price.

215. *Remedies for this kind of manipulation.*—What little has been said here with regard to juggling accounts by directors is sufficient to drive home at least one truth, namely, that the only safety for stockholders lies in insisting upon frequent and thorough examinations by certified public accountants of the highest standing. The chief asset of a public accountant is his unquestioned reputation for penetration and integrity. The loss of that reputation means the loss of his professional standing and of his clientele. He has, therefore, the strongest motive to lay bare the true condition of any corporation which he is called upon to examine and to state the exact facts to the stockholders. The stockholders may safely place confidence in him—unless, to be sure, he happens to be one of those black sheep, a few of whom find temporary employment in all professions.

In England it is customary for the stockholders themselves to elect a public accountant to serve as the annual auditor of their company. It will be a fortunate day for American stockholders when this practice becomes prevalent also in this country. We may lay it down as a general principle that officers and directors who are worthy of their trust will not object to having their operations scrutinized at least once a year by an impartial and absolutely independent expert.

Another tendency which works indirectly toward the same result is the growing demand on the part of the people of the United States for publicity in corporation affairs. The demand for publicity is especially effective in the case of railroads and other public service corporations, most of which are now required to render complete annual reports either to the Interstate Commerce Commission or to some corresponding state authority. The primary purpose of this requirement is to obtain information that will aid legislatures and commissions in deciding upon reasonable rates and prices. It is doubtful, in the opinion of the writer, whether this result will be achieved. There can be no question, however, but that the interests of stockholders of such companies have been greatly advanced by a general adoption of this requirement. It is now possible for an investor to obtain such a complete and authoritative knowledge of the interior affairs of the principal American railroads as to make possible an intelligent judgment of the honesty and efficiency of the management.

Seeing the advantages that are thus gained, the stockholders of other large corporations are insisting more and more forcibly on a similar publicity and investors are refusing to buy the securities of companies which do not present satisfactory annual reports. That this attitude has for some years been making itself felt appears from the numerous conversions, referred to in Chapter XVII, of securities quoted on the New York Stock Exchange from the unlisted to the listed group.

216. *Inflicting loss on the corporation.*—The fourth important method of manipulation by directors is through forcing heavy losses and frequently even bankruptcy on their companies. Here again a few examples selected from a mass of cases which the writer has examined will best illustrate the principal variations of this method.

(a) The G. and R. Railroad Company, a Kentucky corporation, constructed a road from Graceton to Rawlings for which it was heavily indebted. Robinson, a director, with the assistance of other directors, used the profits of the road to make improvements and thus made impossible the payment of interest on the outstanding bonds. The company was thus forced into bankruptcy and at the bankrupt sale all the property and rights were sold to Robinson. Robinson and others then formed a new corporation to hold the road. Five years later the stockholders of the bankrupt corporation brought suit against the heirs of Robinson to have the court adjudge the road as held in trust for the G. and R. Railroad Company. The court found that Robinson had violated his duties of trust by willfully mismanaging the road and misappropriating the earnings and, therefore, returned the property to the original stockholders, compensation being allowed to Robinson's heirs for the amount actually paid by Robinson for the road. Evidently Robinson's actions in this instance, although finally declared unlawful, would have passed unchallenged but for the enterprise and persistency of one or two of the stockholders.

(b) In a recent case in the federal courts, certain

trustees of a building and loan association sold a valuable piece of real estate to a trust company, in which some of the trustees were also interested, in exchange for securities of doubtful value. A mortgage on the real estate was taken from the trust company as a guarantee that the securities would realize the price agreed upon for the property, but by agreement the mortgage was not recorded. Later the trust company desired to sell the property and the trustees passed a resolution authorizing the cancellation of the mortgage, and it was cancelled without the knowledge or consent of the stockholders. Shortly afterwards the trust company became insolvent, the securities held by the building and loan association were found to be worthless and next to nothing was obtained for the property that had been sold. This may be taken as a typical instance of loss willfully inflicted on a corporation by its own directors.

(c) A corporation was indebted to its directors and they caused mortgage bonds to be issued to them for the indebtedness. The bonds were immediately assigned to a rival corporation. Before anything further had been done the stockholders learned of this transaction and brought a suit for damages. The court held that the directors would be personally liable for whatever consequences of their acts might affect injuriously the interests of non-consenting stockholders.

(d) A stockholder of a Montana mining corporation in an action alleged that officers and directors in pursuance of a plan to depreciate the company's stock, in order to render practically worthless stock held by the plaintiff and others similarly situated, refused to sell treasury stock of the corporation in order to procure funds with which to prosecute assessment work on the company's mining claims essential to compliance with the state and federal laws. Further the directors systematically depreciated the value of the treasury stock by words and actions, refused to accept money offered therefor, removed the books of the company from the state, declined to give the plaintiff any information regarding the company's affairs and in general so conducted its business as to destroy the value of its shares. Their object in so doing was to make it necessary for the company to give up its mining claim in order that they might re-locate the property in their own names. In this case the court decided that fraud had been sufficiently shown and placed a receiver in charge of the property. The decision, however, would not have been reached except for certain imprudent remarks on the part of some of the directors.

217. *The danger in losing control of a corporation.*—The most interesting instance that has come to the writer's notice is given by a certified public accountant in one of the Western States, who vouches for its being a typical and actual case of manipulation by directors. He writes as follows:

A owned a majority of the capital stock outstanding in a manufacturing concern. Besides himself he had two dummies for the two other members of the board of directors. B desired to buy an interest in the concern and bought less than half of A's stock (leaving A still in control), with the understanding that B was to become a member of the board of directors, and that A and B should select another person whom they might interest at some future date when selling more stock. Therefore, they mutually decided to place a dummy temporarily on the board. B is a crook, as develops afterwards. C (the agreed-upon dummy) proves to be a bigger crook than B, thus giving B a majority in the board of directors. After this arrangement has been carried through, B and C trump up some imaginary charges against the methods of management of A, and thus the majority of the board depose A as president and manager of the concern. A opposes the action and the case is brought into the court. B and C being the majority of the board of directors, the court upholds their action and gives an injunction against A not to interfere with B and C.

B and C then buy some worthless vacant property for a few dollars, which they appraise at an excessive value and sell to the company, taking stock in payment at the increased values. This stock is then divided between B and C, thus leaving A in the minority as a stockholder. The factory then burns down and a low settlement is made with the insurance companies, because suspicion was directed toward B for having set fire to the property. Their assets having thus been reduced, and wishing to make an excellent impression upon the court, and further wishing to hide their fraudulent action in placing the excessive value on the vacant, valueless property, they decrease the capital stock to about 10 per cent of the original capital stock. Each stockholder obtains his proportionate share of the new stock. In this manner B and C beat A from a half interest to a sixth interest.

They then incorporate a new company called The Investment Company, of which B and C are the only stockholders and in which B and C put up $5,000, which they loan out on improved realty to the manufacturing company, obtaining therefor a note secured by a mortgage.

They then proceed to incorporate another company, which succeeds the old manufacturing company. They value the assets of the old company at about one-third of what they stand on the books. The new company purchases the assets at the reduced value, giving the stockholders of the old company stock in the new concern in proportion of one to three, thus reducing the holdings of A from a half to an eighth interest in the same assets of which he was originally the owner. The new company then contracts with D, who is another crook, to build it a factory. The contract made with him is at a figure which is about $5,000 higher than the ordinary contractor would have built it for.

In addition to this B and C give him a large block of stock as a part consideration for the building of the plant. This $5,000 in excess of the real cost of the factory is paid to D every other day in cash and the books indicate that such cash was for his pay-roll. But circumstantial evidence points to the fact that these payments are bogus transactions on the books and that in fact the money goes into the bank account of the Investment Company.

Then the Investment Company begins to play treasurer for the new company, because it has no funds. Thus it loans the $5,000 back to the manufacturing company. The new manufacturing company needing more funds, the Investment Company sells the $5,000 note above mentioned to the manufacturing company, permitting the manufacturing company to credit the Investment Company for this $5,000 on its books. The manufacturing company then puts up the $5,000 note as collateral for a loan of $3,000 at the Bank. The result is that the Investment Company secures a credit in its favor for $5,000 for an actual value of but $3,000. After this transaction the Investment Company shows signs of anxiety for the money it has advanced, $5,000 in cash and $5,000 in notes. It therefore secures its claims by a mortgage from the manufacturing company on its new plant for $10,000.

The plant is completed, the stock bonus issued to the contractor, and this stock transferred to the Investment Company. Circumstantial evidence shows that no consideration was paid by the Investment Company to the contractor for this stock. As the case stands at present, the Investment Company is trying to foreclose its mortgage and if successful, will entirely defeat the interest of A, who in less than eight months was beaten out of a more than half interest in a successfully-run factory.

I was employed in this case by order of the court upon the complaint of A that B and C were wasting the assets of the company. I cannot see how under the laws of the state A has any redress whatever, except to show fraud in the first issue of additional stock and in the subsequent decreasing of the capital stock. But from the point of view of law it will be exceedingly difficult to bring in this evidence. However, there is a ray of hope in the horizon; namely, that the state statutes forbid the directors to put a mortgage on a mining or manufacturing plant without calling a special stockholders' meeting and obtaining the consent of two-thirds of the stock. These directors had two-thirds of the stock and could have easily complied with the requirement, but their attorney evidently overlooked this point and we believe that we can have this mortgage set aside and a receiver appointed. In this case the receiver could start suit against B and C and then bring out these fraudulent transactions.

The cases that have been cited seem scarcely to call for comment. They all—and especially the last case—however, give point to one precept, which controlling stockholders would do well to keep before them, namely, DO NOT PART WITH CONTROL. A swindling or hostile board of directors can do more in one session to wreck a corporation and bring loss to its honest stockholders than a capable board can accomplish in years toward repairing the damage.

CHAPTER XXVII

MANIPULATION BY AND FOR STOCKHOLDERS

218. *Cheating creditors.*—The subject matter of this chapter is concerned with manipulation directed toward one of two objects; either toward depriving creditors of some of their just rights for the benefit of the body of stockholders; or toward increasing the profits of controlling stockholders at the expense of minority interests. In the first case the stockholders may be either acting as a body, or manipulation carried on primarily for the benefit of the majority stockholders may be of such a character that the minority can successfully obtain a share in its advantages. Generally speaking, manipulation by and for stockholders as a body is confined to small close corporations. We shall find, however, one or two notable exceptions to this rule.

We are all of us familiar, some of us perhaps to our loss, with the old trick of an individual or partnership buying a stock of goods on credit, disposing of it quickly and secretly, concealing the returns and shortly afterward going into bankruptcy. The trick may be worked by corporations as well as by partnerships or by individuals. Indeed, the corporation affords an additional advantage to the swindlers in that its bankruptcy need not affect them in the least. Credit-men understand the game in all its variations thoroughly and are especially cautious in granting credit to small close corporations, no matter how imposing may be their title and their capitalization. This scheme, of course, is simply a plain case of fraud and has no especial interest for us in this study.

A slightly different method of reaching much the same result is to have a corporation pile up a large debt on the strength of its assets and then to allow the assets to depreciate. Stockholders of a corporation whose outstanding bonded debt is high are always under temptation to encourage this policy. By so doing they may secure large dividends for themselves over a series of years and at the end leave assets of small value to satisfy the bondholders. As we have already found in our study of corporate mortgages (Chapter IX) properly drawn instruments of this character provide that the property mortgaged shall be maintained in at least as good condition as at the time that the mortgage is drawn, on penalty of having the corporation put into the hands of receivers. If the trustee under the mortgage performs his duties properly he will see to it that this provision is enforced. If the stockholders and directors acting for the stockholders really desire to evade the provision, it may require the closest attention and rigorous action on the part of the trustee to forestall them.

219. *The Chicago and Alton deal.*—The well-known instance of the Chicago and Alton Railroad deal illustrates another variation of the same principle. The facts with regard to the Chicago and Alton manipulation which were fully brought out in an investigation by the Interstate Commerce Commission in 1907, may be briefly summarized as follows: A close syndicate in 1898 bought about 80 per cent of the outstanding common stock of the Chicago and Alton Railroad Company. The company had been managed with great conservatism for several years and had saved from its earnings

and put back into the property a surplus of $12,500,000. Now a surplus is legally, of course, the property of the stockholders of a corporation. It is so unusual, however for stockholders to distribute this surplus directly to themselves that bondholders naturally look upon it as in part a protection to themselves and buy bonds with that understanding. Ordinarily, as has been explained, the surplus is invested in the form of permanent assets of the corporation, and the value of these assets is a strong factor in influencing the bond buyer. The syndicate of common stockholders in this case, determined to secure for themselves, and incidentally the other stockholders, the accumulated surplus of the company. They therefore issued new bonds to the extent of $32,000,000, which were sold at 65 and the proceeds, about $21,000,000, turned into the company's treasury. They then declared an extra cash dividend of 30 per cent and thus transferred a large share of the cash obtained by the bond issue into their own pockets. The action was much discussed at the time, was condemned by some and defended by others, but did not arouse much public interest until the investigation by the Interstate Commerce Commission in 1907 brought it into prominence. Then, probably to the surprise of the members of the syndicate, the verdict was practically unanimous against them. They were tried before the bar of public opinion and were found guilty of misuse of corporate funds which had been entrusted to their care. There can be no question but that this unanimity on the part of the public is highly significant. It means that between 1898 and 1907 a notable gain in the public's knowledge of corporation finance and in the public's conception of what is and what is not justifiable had taken place. The gentlemen who composed the syndicate ought not to be too severely criticised, for they merely acted in accordance with the custom of the period. We may well hope and believe that manipulation of this kind and of the other kinds that have been enumerated will become less and less frequent as our conceptions of the trusteeship implied in almost all corporate activities become clearer.

220. *Manipulation through subsidiary companies.*—Another method that is very commonly used when stockholders plan to get the better of the creditors of their corporation, is the device of interposing one or more corporations between the creditors and the assets on which they think they have a claim. A case in point which was recently settled out of court, and in which the names of the parties concerned, therefore, cannot here be given, is that of an amusement company operating a large park in one of the cities of the United States. The operation of the park was extremely costly and, as the price of admission was only ten cents, the returns were not sufficient to pay expenses. There were, however, a large number of shows and amusement enterprises in the park which were highly profitable. The stockholders of the corporation as individuals were interested in these sideshows and secured large profits. The corporation which owned the park, on the strength of its apparent prosperity, was able to borrow large amounts of money. When the time for settlement came the creditors learned the true state of affairs and were informed that their claims were practically worthless. Fortunately in this case they were able to bring such pressure to bear on the stockholders that their claims were settled. It is quite evident, however, that as a method of getting loans and avoiding re-payment the scheme is workable.

Here is another instance which shows that eminent and entirely respectable railroad directors are not above working the same trick for the benefit of their road. The N. E. Railway owned a majority of the stock of a small rail and boat line which had income bonds outstanding. The large company, being in control, was able to apportion traffic and earnings as it pleased and gave less than its share to the small line. Three of the boats owned by the small company were being paid for on the installment plan and one of these payments was allowed to lapse, thereby forfeiting the interest of the small company in the boats. The large railroad company then bought the boats from the vendors, being allowed the amount which had already been paid by the small company. Then a consolidation of the large and the small companies was determined upon and, as the earnings of the small company had been practically stopped, its shareholders received only one share in the new consolidated company for every ten shares in their possession. The income bondholders received no interest after the large company came into control and when the consolidation took place were compelled to consent to a great reduction of their claims. The case was threshed out in the courts and it was decided that all the steps taken were legal, except the voluntary passing of the payment on the boats.

221. *Central of Georgia income account.*—Another case in point, that several years ago attracted a great deal of attention in the financial world, was set forth in the suit of the income bondholders of the Central of Georgia Railroad Company for the payment of interest in full on the bonds. The reader will recall that in describing the nature of income bonds it was stated that they are falling into disuse on account of the in-

evitable disputes that arise as to what are and what are not profits. The bonds in question were issued in 1895 at the time of the reorganization of the old Central Railroad and Banking Company of Georgia.

This case well illustrates the subject now under discussion, inasmuch as it discloses one method of manipulation in favor of stockholders at the expense of creditors. The principal fact alleged by counsel for the income bondholders, and practically admitted by the railway company, was that a subsidiary corporation, the Ocean Steamship Company, almost all of the stock of which is owned by the Central of Georgia Railway Company, had been making large profits and that these profits had been appropriated by the railway company. Evidence disclosed that the Ocean Steamship Company kept no separate bank account but deposited all its funds to the credit of the Central of Georgia Railway Company. There were, however, separate books of account for the two companies and it was claimed at the suit, on behalf of the railway company, that the earnings of the steamship company were simply loaned to the parent corporation. These earnings, the reader should understand, were not used in order to declare dividends on the stock of the Ocean Steamship Company held in the treasury of the railway company, but were turned over bodily under the fiction of a "loan"; therefore the earnings of the steamship company did not appear at all in the income account of the railway company, and the railway company thereby avoided showing sufficient profits to pay interest to the income bondholders. The counsel for the railway company urged, according to the brief of petitioners' counsel, "that the net earnings of the steamship company should not be included in the income account of the railway company and that unless a dividend is declared by the steamship company no part of the net earnings of the steamship company belong to the railway company or are pledged to the bondholders, and that the question of declaration of a dividend is a matter of discretion lodged with the board of directors of the steamship company, with which a court of equity should not interfere. In other words, the railway company interposes the doctrine of 'corporate entity' and desires to have what it regards as the 'sacredness' of the doctrine taken cognizance of by a court of equity."

The decision of the court in this case, which was rendered after long and hard-fought litigation, was in favor of the complaining bondholders. It would certainly seem clear to a layman that the subsidiary corporation was here used as a device to prevent the income bondholders from securing profits justly due.

These cases are sufficient to show what risks creditors may unwittingly take on themselves and how careful they should be in fixing the terms of their mortgage. Especially is this true in dealing with corporations which carry on several activities and which may through separate companies readily divert their earnings from the rightful creditors to the stockholders.

222. *Squeezing the minority stockholders.*—We are ready now to take up the second group of manipulative methods to be discussed in this chapter, namely those methods which are designed to enrich controlling stockholders at the expense of minority interests. Let us consider first the following instance, taken from a Missouri court decision, of willful mismanagement:

The Olympic Theatre Company was organized in May, 1903, with a capitalization of $50,000. E. S. James, Sr., obtained 240 shares, par value $100, and

J. S. McIntosh, 150 shares; the other 110 shares were never issued. Three days after the organization the company obtained a hundred-year lease of a lot in St. Louis. Under the terms of the lease the company was to pay the owner a rent of $2,500 for the first two years and thereafter at the rate of 6 per cent of the appraised value of the lot. The company had the right to purchase at the appraised value at the end of five years. The lease was to become void by non-performance of any of its conditions and, in the event of its being voided, the owners of the lot were to get full title to whatever buildings the theatre company might erect on the lot. The company erected a building and conducted a theatre.

In 1905 McIntosh sold his stock to Robert Henry, and Henry became a director and treasurer of the company. E. S. James gave ten shares of stock to his son, E. S. James, Jr., and made him the third director. In 1907 James, Sr., transferred ten shares to another son, Alfred James, and ten shares to a clerk, L. R. Osgood. In the same year the new board of directors elected were James, Sr., James, Jr., and Osgood, thus forcing Henry out. In 1908, as the company was not strong enough financially to buy the lot, the stockholders gave the directors the right to dispose of the company's option to any stockholder. The directors immediately sold the option for $50 to James, Sr., who thereupon resigned as president and director and had his son Alfred elected in his place. James, Sr., then used his option to buy the lot for $50,000 and made an agreement with the company fixing its appraised value at $65,000 and its annual rental at $3,500. Alfred James then resigned his offices and his father was re-elected president and director. The board failed to pay the rent when due and James, Sr., as owner of the lot under the terms of the lease to the company, declared the lease void and was placed in possession of the lot and the building erected thereon. Henry, the minority stockholder, brought suit and it was finally decided that sufficient evidence of fraud had been produced to warrant the court in reinstating the lessee in possession of the theatre under the terms of the lease.

It may be inferred from the decision that two factors which decided the court in favor of the plaintiff were, first, that the James family were evidently acting as a unit, and, second, that the books of the corporation had been destroyed. These were tactical errors which might readily have been avoided; if they had not been present, it is safe to say that the whole series of transactions would have been found legal.

A more simple and common case is stated in a recent decision of one of the federal circuit courts. The officers and owners of a majority of the stock of a wire company voted as stockholders to lease the property of the company at a low rental to another corporation, all of whose stock was held by these same majority stockholders. No fraud was shown and the petition of the minority stockholders to set aside the lease was not granted.

In another federal court case it was shown that the majority stockholder of a gas company absolutely dominated the board of directors and induced the board to purchase worthless bonds of another corporation in which he was interested, by which he was able to make a large individual profit. Here again the minority stockholders, in spite of their unremitting efforts, were unable to prove fraud.

223. *A complicated real estate proposition.*—Here is an instance furnished by a prominent accountant

and which is stated to be typical of the operations of a certain group of companies. The Suburban Development Company is a close corporation which speculates in acreage and sells city lots on a commission basis. The company sells a piece of property belonging to an outsider, Smith, to the Redbank Realty Company. This last named company is in reality a subsidiary corporation, all of whose stock is owned by the Suburban Development Company. The Suburban Development Company collects a commission from Smith for selling his property.

The company now organizes a third corporation, the Long View Land Company, which buys the property at a handsome advance and assumes the mortgage which was on the property when Smith owned it. The Long View Land Company, in addition to assuming the mortgage, issues all its stock to the Suburban Development Company for the balance of its purchase price. The Long View Land Company now makes a contract with the Suburban Development Company whereby the last-named corporation sells the lots on a commission of 20 per cent. The Long View Land Company is also charged an exorbitant amount for office rent and pays large salaries to its officers, who are the stockholders in the Suburban Development Company.

The Suburban Development Company now pushes the sales of the lots owned by the Long View Land Company. When no outsiders can be induced to buy, other subsidiary corporations are formed which buy lots at high prices from the Long View Land Company. Thus this company is given a fictitious appearance of great prosperity and a surplus is created on the books. With such a showing it is easy to find purchasers of the stock of the Long View Land Company, which is in the treasury of the Suburban Development Company. After all but the controlling shares are sold, the subsidiary companies which have bought lots from the Long View Land Company go into bankruptcy, the lots are returned and the paper profits of the Long View Land Company suddenly vanish into thin air.

The object of this complicated series of transactions, as the reader will see, is simply to sell the minority stock of the Long View Land Company. The majority shares must be retained in the hands of the manipulators in order to avoid investigation and litigation. The company advertised and kept before the public in all these transactions is, of course, the Long View Land Company. All the time, however, the stockholders of the controlling corporation are calmly pocketing all the real profits.

The above illustrations are typical. It would seem impossible to enumerate all the possible variations in method. The feature common to them all, however, is the transfer of property from one corporation to another corporation owned by the majority stockholders of corporation number one. This is what the minority stockholder must always fear and, so far as possible, provide against. There is no other way of preventing such manipulation except by associating only with honest majority stockholders in companies where the fullest publicity obtains.

224. *Robbing a partnership to pay a corporation.*—One more instance should be added to the list already given, for it shows very clearly what may be accomplished in the way of defrauding helpless and ignorant minority owners.

James Ehrenbahn, a partner in the firm of L. A.

Ehrenbahn and Company, manufacturers of agricultural implements, died in the year 1896. He had an undivided one-fourth interest in the firm and in addition had loaned the firm $3,000. He also had a one-third interest in a credit against the firm of $12,000, the other two-thirds belonging to his brother, L. A. Ehrenbahn. The firm held property whose book value was approximately $260,000. Immediately after the death of James Ehrenbahn the surviving partners caused to be written off to profit and loss accounts and bills receivable alleged to be uncollectible amounting to $110,000, leaving a net book value of the property of the firm of approximately $150,000. L. A. Ehrenbahn was acting not only for himself but also for the estate of his brother, of which he had been appointed administrator. The surviving partners made no attempt to close the affairs of the firm, but continued in business and made large profits, of which they rendered no accounting. In continuing the business they used up money and property belonging to the estate of James Ehrenbahn.

About October 1, 1898, the surviving partners agreed to form a corporation, lease to it the plant and real estate of the co-partnership and sell to it on credit, the terms being indefinite, the personal property, accounts and bills receivable in the hands of the surviving partners. The corporation took over the inventory of finished products at an appraised value to be paid for out of money received from the sale of implements on hand. The organization of the corporation was in 1898 and its operations began the same year, but no stock was issued until 1903.

A peculiarity of the business thus transferred was that large amounts of agricultural implements were sold "on consignment" to agents who had the privilege of either returning the goods or of paying for them. The corporation now began to deal with these agents, sent them new stocks of goods and allowed them without protest to return the goods which had been sent them on consignment by the partnership; thus the accounts and bills receivable of the partnership were rendered worthless and their place was taken by accounts receivable of the corporation. Furthermore, the corporation used no diligence in collecting the accounts receivable of the partnership that were left outstanding.

In March, 1903, L. A. Ehrenbahn for himself, and assuming to act as administrator of his brother's estate, delivered a new lease to the corporation of the land and buildings belonging to the partnership at the excessively low rate of $1,000 a year. In the same year the partnership made a final sale to the corporation of the personal property for $20,000, although this same property had been valued in 1898 at $50,000. Between 1898 and 1903 the corporation paid nothing for the property or for its use. Beginning in 1904 the corporation paid annual 10 per cent dividends on a capitalization of $100,000. The record does not show what dividends were paid between 1898 and 1904. When the case came into court on complaint of the heirs of James Ehrenbahn decision in substance was that the corporation should be compelled to pay a price to be fixed after investigation by a master for the personal property and real estate. It was adjudged, however, in the case of accounts and bills receivable, that no legal liability lay against the corporation.

There can be no question, judging from the facts as presented to the court, that large sums had been deliberately withheld from the partnership and transferred to the corporation by the manipulation of the accounts and bills receivable. Yet this manipulation could be carried on so easily by the corporation that it was impossible to prove fraud or bad faith.

225. *Remedies for manipulation.*—The examples that have been cited in these three chapters on corporate manipulation seem to the writer not only interesting but highly instructive. It is an unpleasant duty to record instance after instance of cunning rascality, especially when the record to be truthful must set forth at least temporary successes on the part of the rascals. As was said at the beginning, the swindling operations are for the most part in a field which the law does not reach and their perpetrators are seldom given the legal punishment to which they are justly entitled. Fortunately the punishment of social opprobrium and loss of business standing is generally visited upon them.

The purpose of these chapters will have been secured if they serve to warn owners of corporate securities of the facilities which the corporate form affords for graft and dishonesty. The writer desires to reiterate that instances of the kind that have been narrated are rare compared to the vast amount of entirely honorable and legitimate business transacted under the corporate form of business organization. Nevertheless they are frequent enough to demand attention and, so far as possible, prevention.

One preventive is for security-holders to insist on complete and absolute publicity as to the affairs of their organizations.

Another preventive is for them to attend stockholders' meetings and take an active interest in all that goes on in the corporation.

A third preventive is to see to it that under the cumulative system of voting every stockholder gets a chance to be represented.

A fourth preventive is to insert explicit provisions in the corporate by-laws as to salaries of officers, amount of indebtedness to be incurred, amount of surplus to be set aside each year, and so on.

The best preventive of all, however—without which all the other measures will prove of small avail—is for the security-holder to investigate with the greatest care the reputations of all the officers and directors of the corporation.

CHAPTER XXVIII

INSOLVENCY AND RECEIVERSHIPS

226. *Two types of insolvency.*—The causes of insolvency have perhaps been sufficiently indicated in connection with the subject of management of capital funds and of earnings. At any rate, they may be inferred to be the reverse of the principles of sound corporate finance, which were there laid down. It will do no harm, however, to recapitulate briefly the principal causes. A great many business men, even the managers of large corporations, are evidently not fully alive to the dangers which threaten any corporation.

It is well to distinguish between two types of insolvency. The distinction for our purpose is important, although in law and in ordinary business language it has not been clearly kept in view. We may call one type "true" and the other "legal" insolvency. True insolvency exists where the value of an individual's, firm's or corporation's assets is less than its total debts. This, by the way, is substantially the definition given in the National Bankruptcy Act, but it is declared by eminent legal authorities to be a definition without precedent in the law. Such insolvency may or may not lead to failure. Certainly if failure is not to follow there must be an improvement in the condition of the business. It frequently happens, however, where debts are not immediately payable, that a concern insolvent in this sense will manage to pull out of its difficulties and meet its obligations when they finally mature.

Legal insolvency exists when a concern's cash assets are insufficient to meet its liabilities as they fall due. It may well be, and frequently is, true in such a case that the total assets would far overbalance the total obligations. As obligations are almost uniformly payable in cash and cash only, however, it really makes no difference how great the value of the firm's unsalable assets may be. Legal insolvency almost of necessity leads immediately to suspension or, in the case of small concerns, to bankruptcy. The only escape would be a compromise of some kind accepted by creditors.

227. *Causes of true insolvency.*—True insolvency may exist from the very beginning of corporate existence, although not usually without bad faith on the part of the incorporators. It is possible, however, that the value of a corporation's assets at the beginning may be honestly over-estimated, that the corporation may borrow an undue amount of money secured by such assets, and that the money thus obtained may be foolishly expended. In such a case, unless a marked rise in the value of the assets takes place, the corporation may be said never to have been truly solvent. It is only a question of time until the inevitable failure arrives.

A second cause of true insolvency may be a great and perhaps unavoidable decline in the value of a corporation's assets. If, for instance, a cyclone demolishes the property of a corporation that does not carry insurance against such a calamity, insolvency will necessarily be the result. The fall in the value of the assets may be due simply to ordinary causes, which are not offset by a depreciation reserve. Any one of a hundred other events, which will occur to every reader, may reduce the value of assets below obligations. It may be stated, however, that a conservatively managed corporation is not likely to suffer in this way. The principles of insurance and of depreciation are now so widely applied that a high degree of protection is afforded.

The third cause of true insolvency, especially with trading companies, is bad management in buying and selling goods. The lack of a proper system of cost accounting may lead corporation managers to a long-continued course of selling below cost. The fact that such a course has been followed may not become entirely apparent for a number of years; then it is found that the corporation has been gradually consuming its capital funds in order to pay running expenses.

The complexity of modern business is such that frequently an accurate and searching analysis carried on at considerable expense is necessary in order to determine whether a business is being carried on at a profit or not. Many a concern has seen its sales growing, its gross profits swelling and apparently its surplus increasing, while at the same time, owing to lack of care to maintain its fixed assets in good condition and to keep up its established trade, it has in reality been moving rapidly into insolvency. An anecdote is told of a large wholesale dealer in men's clothing who was selling quantities of goods at prices which expert accountants found to be considerably below cost, including in cost all the selling and administrative expenses. The accountant approached the manager of the company and asked him how he could afford to carry on his business. "Ah," was the naive reply, "you see our transactions are on so much larger a scale than those of any of our competitors." It seems needless to add that this particular concern did not long keep out of the bankruptcy court.

The fourth cause of true insolvency is actual fraud

or theft, a cause which need not be here discussed.

228. *One cause of legal insolvency—"lack of capital."* —As to the causes of legal insolvency, we have a valuable mass of information collected by the two great mercantile agencies, Bradstreet's and Dun's. The Bradstreet Company summarize their judgments as to the prime causes of all the business failures that occurred in the United States during the four years preceding the crisis of 1907, in the following table:

Causes of Failure.	*Percentages.*			
	1907	1906	1905	1904
Incompetence	22.6	22.3	24.4	23.1
Inexperience	4.9	4.9	4.8	5.1
Lack of capital	37.1	35.9	33.4	32.2
Unwise credits	2.3	2.6	3.5	3.4
Failures of others	1.4	2.0	2.2	2.5
Extravagance	.9	1.0	1.1	.8
Neglect	2.5	2.2	2.9	3.1
Competition	1.2	1.0	1.5	1.3
Specific conditions	16.3	17.3	16.3	19.1
Speculation	.7	.8	.7	.8
Fraud	10.1	10.0	9.2	8.6

The reader will notice that "lack of capital" heads the list and that personal incompetence comes second. Unfortunately no distinction is made between lack of permanent capital and lack of working capital. It seems safe to say, however, that lack of permanent capital does not usually in itself lead to insolvency; most businesses may be automatically adjusted to any reasonable amount of capital. The difficulty comes rather in the form in which the capital funds are invested, particularly in sacrificing quick in order to build up fixed assets.

To make this statement concrete let us examine the *Wall Street Journal's* analysis of two typical instances of financial difficulty. In February, 1909, the American Ice Company was reported to be facing insolvency and reorganization and the *Journal* commented as follows:

The annual report just submitted shows that the floating debt, about $650,000 a year ago, has now reached the threatening proportions of something like $1,250,000. Herein lies the whole trouble with the American Ice Company. The concern transacted a gross business during the year ended October 31, of $8,120,000, and it is clear that to maintain this volume of business ample liquid capital is essential. The report evidences the need of working funds in other ways; it shows that $72,728 was expended for interest on its floating debt.

Where the company will raise money is a problem. It is known that institutions friendly to the company which have helped it out of difficulties in the past, have withdrawn further support. The company has little credit of its own to borrow on. The treasury contains several hundred thousand dollars worth, par value, of securities of subsidiary concerns, but these are hardly sufficient for collateral for a loan as large as American Ice requires.

Evidently the company was in danger of legal, not true, insolvency. After the above paragraphs were written the ice company denied its allegations and asserted that it was not in serious need of financial assistance. Nevertheless the quotation indicates clearly enough where a trained financial writer looks for symptoms and causes of weakness.

229. *The case of the Detroit, Toledo and Ironton Railway Company.*—The paragraphs that follow constitute an attempt to explain the failure of the Detroit, Toledo and Ironton Railway Company.

The company in question, a reorganization of the old Detroit Southern, began business in the early part of 1905. When the management of the property again passed into the hands of the court this year, its new career had lasted about two and a half years, during no part of which had it succeeded in earning the fixed charges which the capitalization of the reorganization plan had fastened upon it. In the first full fiscal year of its operation as an extended system, the deficit after payment of interest charges and taxes amounted to $270,000; in the second fiscal year which ended June 30th last, the deficit reached the sum of $371,000. After that, presumably, the company ran still further behind.

As to the question of working capital, the Detroit, Toledo & Ironton's balance sheet of June 30, 1905, practically the beginning of its career, shows current assets of $1,218,524 and current liabilities of $390,194, making an apparent working balance of $828,330. Among these current assets was an item, "due from reorganization committee, $1,050,000." A year later this item had disappeared into equipment account, and the inference is that it never was a part of true working capital. In that case, the new company began without any working capital, but with an actual funded debt of about $200,000.

If President Zimmerman's theory that the receivership is primarily attributable to the clause of the Hepburn law which forbade the company to proceed with its Kentucky coal mining project is true, the Detroit, Toledo & Ironton as it exists was not a success to begin with. That is, it did not have and could not obtain a current revenue sufficient to carry its own obligations, aside from the cost of the Ohio River Bridge and Kentucky extension, and could only become a self-sustaining property by tapping an entirely new and rather distant source of traffic. Such a development naturally could not take place except through the investment of much additional capital and the completion of works bound to take a year or two in construction. Meanwhile the company was exposed in a perilous financial condition to the usual danger of adverse general conditions, which did not fail to arrive.

The two causes assigned in this case are: First, lack of earning power in the assets sufficient to meet fixed charges, which is a condition of true insolvency;

and, second, lack of current assets, or of working capital.

230. *Additional causes of legal insolvency.*—We have found in our study of financial management that it is not usually advisable for a concern to allow its accounts payable to exceed 70 to 80 per cent of its accounts receivable; that its bank loans should be represented for the most part by cash in the bank; and that its finished products on hand should not be offset by any corresponding liability. If these relations are not maintained, the company is apt to sink first into an unprofitable and next into a highly dangerous situation. The concern begins to lose profits, if its working capital is insufficient to permit taking full advantage of all considerable discounts for the prompt payment of bills. This point has already been discussed in connection with financial management. It is obvious that as working capital decreases the corporation manager is driven to depend more and more upon his current sales and accounts receivable for funds with which to pay his bills. If for any reason his sales fall off sharply or his debtors fail to pay promptly, he will be unable to meet his own obligations promptly. Unless he can secure extensions or arrange for loans from some other source failure is inevitable.

Let us give attention again—for this is an important point—to the fact that a concern may fail in this manner although its assets may be thoroughly sound and far in excess of obligations, its business large and growing, and its profits great. Carelessness or lack of appreciation of the necessity of keeping up working capital may thus be the sole cause of legal insolvency. As to the statement that the trouble with many concerns is "lack of capital," our analysis has indicated that the proper wording of this phrase in most cases would be "lack of working capital."

A slightly different cause of legal insolvency arises when a corporation, in order to pay dividends, unduly increases its quick obligations. It may well be in such a case that the dividends have been earned and are properly due to the stockholders. If the profits that are to be used for dividends, however, have been put back into the property or into any sort of a permanent investment, the payment of the dividends will involve borrowing money. Among conservative financiers this is universally regarded as a dangerous practice. Dividends ought to be provided for in advance by so large an accumulation of cash that their payment will not unduly reduce, even temporarily, the corporation's working capital.

A third frequent cause of legal insolvency is inability to renew medium term notes or refund long-time obligations when due. This situation may not be the fault, so much as the misfortune, of the corporation. The obligation may fall due during the height of a crisis when borrowing of money on any terms is next to impossible. It may have been entirely proper to issue the obligations in the first place; the assets may be far more than sufficient in value to cover them; and yet the actual cash to meet them may not be forthcoming. We shall have occasion in the following pages to discuss a recent case of failure and reorganization which falls within this class.

231. *Two methods of handling insolvency—Bankruptcy and dissolution.*—There is so much confusion—not only in the public mind, but even among lawyers—as to the exact nature of the remedy that should be applied when a corporation gets into financial difficulties, that it seems proper to preface our study of corporate

reorganization by a brief survey of the legal aspects of insolvency, receivership and bankruptcy. Much of what is said in this chapter will apply to individual proprietorships and to partnerships, as well as to corporations. Additional information on the topics here briefly treated will be found in the volume on COMMERCIAL LAW.

The reader is probably already aware that the constitution of the United States confers upon Congress the sole authority to establish a uniform law as to bankruptcy procedure for the whole country, and that the latest expression of this authority is found in the National Bankruptcy Act of 1898. Bankruptcy may be either voluntary or involuntary. It may be asked for by an insolvent individual or partnership in order to obtain a discharge from his or its debts; or it may be asked for by creditors whose claims are unsatisfied in order to obtain an equitable division of the property of the bankrupt. The Bankruptcy Act provides that a corporation cannot become a voluntary bankrupt, but that corporations engaged principally in manufacturing, trading, printing, publishing, mining or mercantile pursuits, owing debts to the amount of $1,000 or over, may be adjudged involuntary bankrupts. The converse of this statement is that all other corporations, including those engaged in banking and transportation, are incapable of becoming bankrupts. As a matter of fact, it is seldom to the interest either of stockholders or of creditors to force a corporation into bankruptcy. Indeed, the chief reason that may lead to such drastic action is the desire of unsecured creditors to prevent secret deals and transfers of the corporation's assets and to expose any past irregularities in the conduct of the corporation. Bankruptcy is especially valuable at times as a means of making invalid liens or judgments that have been secured by favored creditors within four months of the period of bankruptcy.

A second method of handling the affairs of an insolvent corporation is by a dissolution of the corporation and a distribution of its assets to creditors and shareholders. This method is even more infrequent than bankruptcy and is plainly out of place except for corporations, the organization and good will of which are not worth saving.

232. *A third method—Appointment of a receiver.*—A third method is the use of what is known in law as a "bill in chancery." The objects sought to be obtained by this method are, first, to come to an equitable settlement between the corporation and its creditors, and, second, to preserve the corporation's organization and continue its business. The "bill in chancery" is, in lay language, simply a petition presented to a court of equity asking the court for protection and supervision of the corporation's property and business until a settlement of the conflicting claims may be secured. If the petition is granted, the court at once appoints an officer responsible solely to the court known as a "receiver," whose business it is to conduct the corporation's affairs until he is discharged. The petition may be presented by any one of four parties: (a) the corporation itself; (b) the stockholders; (c) secured creditors; or (d) unsecured creditors.

A petition of this character presented by a corporation in its own name is unusual and instances of its being granted by the court are still rarer. It is also somewhat unusual to find petitions by stockholders presented and granted. A complaining stockholder is usually told by the court that his proper course, if he is dissatisfied with the management of the corporation, is to elect new directors. Moreover, a complaint by a stockholder that his corporation is insolvent and should be placed in a receiver's hands is seldom necessary, for in such a case creditors will be more than likely to take the initiative. Where the corporation itself is willing that a receiver should be appointed the petition is usually presented by friendly unsecured creditors. This is, in fact, the usual method of securing what is known as a "friendly receivership." It is doubtful, however, in many states, whether an unsecured creditor can successfully apply for a receivership in the face of opposition on the part of a corporation. Secured creditors have a far stronger case and a petition on their part based on the proved insolvency or mismanagement of the corporation is not generally denied.

Unlike petitions in bankruptcy, bills in chancery may be presented either in the federal courts or in any of the state courts which have jurisdiction. Here is a frequent cause of much confusion and frequently of conflict between courts. The legal questions involved are entirely too complicated and technical to be discussed in this chapter. All that need be said is that where large inter-state corporations are involved the tendency is growing to apply to the federal courts for relief. One reason is that the judges of these courts are especially familiar with cases of this kind; another reason of still greater importance is that federal judges in different parts of the country work together more harmoniously than do the judges of different states.

233. *Duties of a receiver.*—If the corporation is carrying on simply a trading business and goes into bankruptcy, the activities of the receiver in bankruptcy will be comparatively simple. He will dispose of the assets as rapidly as he can and will use the funds thus obtained, so far as they will go, to settle with creditors. There may be a considerable waste in this process, for the established trade and business connections of the failed company will go for nothing. Yet, on the whole, it is the quickest and most certain method of satisfying the obligations of the company, and it is usually followed. Unless the corporation's borrowings have been far in excess of the value of its tangible assets, the obligations will be met and the loss will all be borne by the stockholders. In an ordinary bankruptcy the stockholders' interests are very little considered.

Where the failed corporation is a large manufacturing or railroad company with a great amount of fixed capital and a receiver is appointed by a court of equity, his duties are entirely different. He has as his object in this, as in the former case, the payment of corporate obligations. It is very seldom, however, that this object, when the corporation has large fixed assets, can be attained by the sale of these assets. Ordinarily there is no one to buy them except at a tremendous sacrifice. It would evidently be quite impossible to find cash buyers for the millions of dollars of property of any of the great industrial combinations or of any of the great railroads. Therefore, the receiver is permitted in such a case to go on with the business. No profitable activities of the concern are allowed to cease. It goes on manufacturing or transporting, or whatever its business may be, under the receiver's administration, just as it did under the administration of its own officers. As the holders of claims against the failed corporation cannot hope for immediate payment in cash, a settlement with them must be made in some other manner—usually through a reorganization, a subject to which considerable attention is given in the following chapters.

234. *Receiver's powers.*—The receiver is a very powerful official. So long as no actual fraud or obvious mismanagement on his part is proven, he is at liberty to make such disposition of the assets and earnings under his charge as he sees fit. He may use his power altogether for the benefit of the creditors, or he may use it in part also for the benefit of the stockholders. If he has the latter object in view, he will naturally do what he can to delay a settlement until a favorable period arrives and will thus preserve as much of the property as possible for the stockholders.

In view of his power it is always very important to the stockholders—and frequently more equitable to every one concerned—to have a receiver of their own choosing appointed. In recent years it has become customary for corporations which are getting into difficulties to secure from the court the appointment of what are generally known as "friendly" receivers. Frequently the friendly receivers are officers of the corporation. In order to get this result there must be collusion between one or more of the creditors and the corporate officials. The creditor or creditors and the officials go secretly—often at dead of night—to some judge who has jurisdiction; the creditor complains that his debt is unpaid and the officials confess insolvency; then the creditor asks for the appointment of some man previously agreed upon to act as receiver, and the judge then and there duly appoints him. Of course, the judge must be fully aware of this scheme and must approve it. On account of the conflicting jurisdictions of our state and federal courts, however, it is usually a very easy matter to find one among the several judges with the proper authority who will do what is wanted.

It will not do to say off-hand that in every case the appointment of friendly receivers is absolutely wrong, or that the judge who makes the appointment is corrupt. As has been intimated, insolvency sometimes results from causes beyond the control of corporate officials and hasty action on the part of receivers would cause heavy unnecessary loss. We cannot absolutely condemn, therefore, either the officials who request the action or the judge who complies with the request. Nevertheless, the transaction, being secret and more or less irregular, seldom reflects credit on any one concerned.

Since the receiver, however he may be appointed, is a court officer, his expenses are court expenses and until paid constitute a lien on the corporate assets that goes ahead of all other claims. This fact has already been referred to in the discussion of receivers' certificates. Receivers' certificates may be issued in order to secure funds for practically any purpose that the receiver deems proper. The funds may be used to purchase new supplies or equipment or to improve and extend the property. If the development of a corporation has been greatly hampered by lack of funds a receivership may thus prove a very desirable thing, for the receiver has an opportunity to put the company into prime condition. Receiverships have been known in this way to prove the salvation of an insolvent concern.

The receiver usually charges and gets a very large fee for his services. There has been much complaint and agitation at times on this account, especially in connection with bank receiverships. The size of receiver's fees during the panic year, 1907, in New York City became almost a public scandal. This, however, brings up questions which do not properly fall within the scope of corporation finance.

CHAPTER XXIX

PRINCIPLES OF REORGANIZATION

235. *Reasons for reorganization.*—There are two general classes of reorganization: first, those that are necessary as the result of insolvency; second, those that prove desirable in order to readjust the securities and the means of control of a company. The principles of reorganization also are somewhat differently applied in railroads and in manufacturing concerns. In order to bring out these distinctions we shall take up in the following chapter three typical reorganizations: First, of an insolvent railroad; second, of a solvent railroad; and, third, of an insolvent industrial. In this chapter our attention will be confined to the general principles which apply in all kinds of reorganizations.

The reasons for reorganization in lieu of a simple sale of property have already been alluded to. In order to make them plain, however, we should give them some further consideration. The complexity of the financial organization of a large corporation is one factor to take into account. In the case of a railroad the parent company will probably own the securities of a number of subsidiary companies. Each one of these subsidiary companies will have one or more mortgages on its line. The stock and perhaps some of the bonds of the subsidiary companies will be owned by the parent company and will perhaps be posted as security for a collateral trust bond issue. The parent company will perhaps own a main line and several branch lines, and will have outstanding mortgage bonds based on each of the branch lines, mortgage bonds based on the terminals and real estate holdings, and very likely, in addition, a general mortgage bond issue to cover whatever property is left. Then there will probably be preferred and common stock and short-time claims, including accounts payable, accrued wages and bank loans. Such a group of corporate relationships and obligations may be taken as typical. It is, in fact, not half so complex as the financial organization of many large railroad and industrial companies.

In contrast to this complicated financial scheme we find the railroad property to be practically, for operating purposes, an indivisible unit. The word "indivisible," as here used, does not mean, of course, that the property is actually physically merged into one. It would be possible for the branch line bondholders to mark out and segregate their property and take it for themselves; for the terminal bondholders to do the same; for the main line bondholders to do the same; and so on. It is indivisible, however, in the sense that a division of the property would destroy most, if not all, of its value. This statement applies only to a well-constructed, unified railroad system. If any part of the system is superfluous, it may be lopped off and taken by its own bondholders. This, for instance, was the case with the St. Louis and San Francisco Railroad, which was owned by the Atchison, Topeka and Santa Fe, up to the bankruptcy of the latter road in 1893, and was then taken over by the St. Louis and San Francisco bondholders. The same thing was true of the Oregon Short Line, which was temporarily cut off from the Union Pacific System in the bankruptcy of 1893.

Assuming that a failed corporation possesses property which is commercially indivisible, the question that arises in case of bankruptcy is, What arrangement can be made to prevent the property from being split up into segments by the conflicting claims of the various security-holders? How can it be held together, put back on its feet and restored to its rightful position as a valuable profit-making business? Every bondholder, as well as every stockholder, is keenly interested in finding the right answer. The value of any bond, as has already been shown, depends in large part on the earning power and prosperity of the issuing corporation.

236. *The formation of committees.*—In the process of getting an answer the first step is to ascertain as nearly as possible the exact status of each of the corporation's obligations. Usually this task is left to the receivers or to such persons as are selected to act as a reorganization committee. Each class of bondholders chooses representatives whose duty it is to represent the interests of that particular class. These representatives are usually called a committee and are selected in various ways. Sometimes a meeting of the bondholders of one class is called and the members of the committee are elected. Sometimes banking houses which have underwritten one or more of the bond issues come forward and offer to serve on reorganization committees. Generally these members of the committee are self-chosen, and are of such character and standing that they readily secure the support of their fellow bondholders. Shortly after the breakdown of a big corporation it is quite customary for one of the heavy bondholders of each class to send a circular letter to the other bondholders of that class stating that they should be represented in the pending negotiations and asking that they place their interests in his hands. Usually he states in the

circular that his only interest in the matter is to secure the rights of the persons to whom he appeals and that he will act in good faith with that sole object in view. The bondholders signify their consent by depositing their bonds with some stipulated trust company. If a majority of the bonds of a given class are deposited, the self-appointed representative or committee is authorized to act on their behalf. We should bear in mind, however, that the committee's authority is only that of a representative. It cannot bind the bondholders to any terms whatever. Whether the bondholders accept the plan which their committee approves or not will depend largely on their estimate of the character and intelligence of the members of the committee.

Within a few days after an important insolvency is announced, there will usually come into existence a number of different duly authorized committees, one representing the general mortgage bondholders, one the bondholders of each of the subsidiary companies, one the debenture bondholders, if there is such an issue, and so on. Ordinarily it is not necessary for the bona fide first mortgage bondholders to organize. They are so well protected that they can afford to sit quiet while the other claimants fight it out. Usually also the stockholders do not organize. They have practically no voice in the reorganization, anyway, if the receivership is unfriendly; if it is friendly their interests are already protected. Sometimes, however, the stockholders as a body, or the preferred and common stockholders, each acting as a class, will appoint committees of their own when burdensome assessments seem imminent.

Once the committees are appointed the "jockeying for position" and the arguments pro and con as to the strength of each of the competing claims on the corporation's assets begin. If many different claims are involved, it will probably be necessary for the committee of each class of security-holders to appoint a single representative and have these representatives form a general reorganization committee. It is the duty of this committee to discuss terms of reorganization and finally to agree upon a plan which may be submitted to the security-holders.

237. *Why not foreclose.*—The reader may well inquire at this point why the bondholders as a whole or some class of bondholders do not foreclose and sell under their mortgage and thus get enough cash to meet their own claims, or failing that, bid in the property for themselves. It may correctly be suggested in this connection that for the purpose of buying the property when it is sold, each bond would be accepted at its par value.

This question has already been answered in part by the statement in the last chapter to the effect that it would be next to impossible to sell a large corporation to an outsider for cash, because the amount involved is too large. Besides, an outsider who wished to get control of the property could accomplish his purpose much more economically by buying the securities of the failed corporation at the low prices at which they naturally sell during the period of reorganization.

In answering the second part of the question we must consider that the bondholders whose securities are close to the property would not have anything to gain by a sale. Their principal and interest, presumably, are well protected and they could not by any process of juggling get more than principal and interest. With the junior mortgage bondholders the situation is somewhat different. They might at times, if the reorganization scheme appears unfavorable to them, have something to gain by compelling foreclosure, and bidding in the property. In this case, however, they might be forced to settle all the claims that rank ahead of their own in cash, which would ordinarily be too large an undertaking. However, the possibility of such action on their part is always recognized by the reorganization committee and their claims are in consequence treated with greater respect than they would otherwise command. The result is that foreclosure proceedings are usually only a form. After reorganization plans have been completed foreclosure is simply a method of transferring the property of the old corporation to a new corporation.

238. *Problems confronting the reorganization committee.*—The reorganization committee, then, once formed has a reasonably free hand. At the same time it must act with due circumspection in order not to arouse the hostility of any powerful body of security-holders. It must treat everybody with apparent justice; it must reconcile conflicting claims and interests. The success of whatever plan of reorganization it adopts will depend upon the extent to which the plan is accepted by security-holders. As noted above, the first and perhaps most important duty of the committee, therefore, is to form some working estimate of the relative values of the different classes of securities.

First, they must consider whether there has been an impairment of assets and earnings sufficient to affect the first mortgage bonds. Usually this question may be answered in the negative. If an affirmative answer has to be given, any attempt at reorganization might as well be given up, for nothing can be done except to allow the first-mortgage bondholders to take whatever property is left. Assuming that the first mortgage bondholders are still in an entirely safe position, the reorganization committee next considers the situation of the bondholders secured by mortgages on outlying or small sections of property. Mortgages of this nature on railroads are usually divisional, terminal, branch line or real estate; with industrial corporations there may be mortgages on unessential plants or property. For instance, a consolidation may originally have taken in twenty plants, and may have found ten of the plants so uneconomical that it has transferred almost all their business to the other ten; or a merchandising corporation may have gone into general trucking; or a paper mill may own a great expanse of forest land, not all of which is essential to its business. In such cases the outlying mortgage bondholders may be allowed to take their property, and their claims may then be eliminated from further consideration. It may well be, on the other hand, that the separate pieces of property so mortgaged are highly essential, in which case the bondholders would be able to insist on a settlement of their claims in full. Thus a railroad could not well get along without its terminals or without equipment, and the reorganization committee would have to allow full value to all bonds based upon such property. A manufacturing corporation may derive its chief profits indirectly from its control of the sources of raw materials, in which case the reorganization committee would arrange to pay bonds based on such property in full, even if the property taken in itself were not of great value. Disputes are bound to arise in connection with many of these claims on specific pieces of property.

A railroad branch line, for instance, may earn very little revenue for itself, according to the railroad's method of figuring, and may have absolutely no value except as an adjunct to the failed railroad. Yet it may turn over to that railroad a large and highly profitable traffic. The bondholders will naturally point to this traffic as justification for a demand that their claims be paid in full. The other interests involved will point to the isolated position of the branch line apart from the railroad as sufficient ground for attaching very little value to the branch line bonds. Usually a compromise is necessary. Both parties have much to lose and nothing to gain by a permanent separation of main and branch lines. Each side will probably "bluff" so far as it dares, and each will finally concede something.

The reorganization committee next takes up the claims of the general mortgage bondholders and endeavors to ascertain how much assets and earnings are left for them after satisfying prior claims. This may or may not be a particularly difficult task; that all depends on the nature and complexity of underlying mortgages. The value of the general mortgage bonds will depend to a great extent on the wording of the mortgage. It may cover only such property as was in existence when the mortgage was drawn or may contain an "after-acquired property" clause. Next in order of consideration are the debenture bonds. As these bonds are chiefly claims on earnings, not on assets, the reorganization committee in estimating their value will try to find out how much of the corporation's income is left for them after paying prior interest charges.

Finally, the reorganization committee will consider what must be done for the preferred and common stockholders. Sometimes in heavily over-capitalized concerns the common stock will be wiped out absolutely. It is more usual, however, to try to preserve something for the stockholders, with the proviso, usually, that the stockholders pay certain cash assessments.

239. *Necessity for cash.*—Another factor in reorganization not previously mentioned is the current or floating debt of the corporation. This debt may take the form either of loans and medium-term notes having specific security or of unsecured obligations, such as accounts payable. Whether secured or unsecured, this floating debt must be paid in cash; otherwise the creditors of this class will certainly attach the assets of the corporation and effectually prevent the success of reorganization. The only path of escape from the floating debt would be through foreclosure and sale of the property, and this path does not lead to reorganization. The reorganization committee, therefore, must by some means raise cash sufficient to meet all this floating debt in order that the reorganized company may begin business. Furthermore, there must be enough cash left over to provide the reorganized company with a fair working capital; otherwise it will begin at once to get into new difficulties, as is well illustrated by the career of the Detroit, Toledo and Ironton Railroad reviewed in the last chapter. The committee also, if it desires to have the reorganized company prosper, must see to it that its fixed charges are not larger than its minimum net earnings. We have thus, four main objects of every reorganization: (a), to pay the floating debt; (b), to provide working capital; (c), to bring the property up to at least normal efficiency; (d), to reduce fixed charges below minimum earnings.

The first three of these objects require cash in large amounts; especially is this true since a company which is approaching insolvency almost always lets its accounts payable accumulate, its working capital decline, and its property become impaired. Of course, this may not be the situation at all if the corporation has simply met with some temporary reverse, which brought it into a condition of legal insolvency. In such a case the problems of reorganization are comparatively simple. As a general thing, however, the reorganization committee will find it necessary to raise cash from every available source. As sufficient cash makes the attainment of the first three objects named above easy, we may say that the reorganization committee will consider two things of prime importance: first, to raise cash; second, to reduce fixed charges.

240. *Raising cash by assessments.*—There are three possible methods of securing cash: first, by the sale of some of the corporate property; second, by the issue of new securities; third, by assessments on the security-holders. The first method is almost never practicable. If the corporation possesses outlying property non-essential to its business, it is more than likely that this property has been heavily mortgaged and must be turned over to the mortgagees. The second method, as a general thing, is equally impracticable. Obviously a corporation is not likely to fail unless it has already exhausted its borrowing power, and the sale of the stock of an insolvent corporation is out of the question. These considerations again do not necessarily apply when the corporation is not a true insolvent but has merely suffered a temporary setback. Even in true insolvency cash is sometimes raised through considerable issues of receivers' certificates, which in reorganization are funded along with the first mortgage bonds into a new first mortgage issue. At times this may be entirely proper and expedient. The efficiency of the

corporation's assets may have become impaired and a little cash raised by receivers' certificates may put them into such a condition as to enhance its earning power vastly more than the amount of the extra fixed charges thus imposed.

The third method—assessment on the security-holders—is almost universal. Naturally the first and heaviest assessments fall on the common and preferred stockholders. The possibility of raising cash by this method is limited by the stockholders' estimate of the value of the stock of the reorganized company. They are given the choice either of paying the assessment or of forfeiting their equity in the corporation's assets. If the assessment is made too high evidently the stockholder will choose to forfeit whatever rights remain to him, rather than to pay what is asked. The reorganization committee will therefore endeavor to keep the assessment down to what it considers a reasonably low figure.

Under these conditions the average stockholder almost always finds it worth while to pay his assessment and retain an interest in the company. If he cannot raise the necessary cash he will sell his stock in the open market for whatever it will fetch to someone who has both the courage and the means to meet the assessment. It is almost always true that the stock of a failed company sells at an abnormally low figure. It is frequently true that a short time after reorganization, the stock of the reorganized company sells at a price considerably above the price of the old stock during the receivership plus the assessment. In other words, experience has demonstrated that the stockholder will do better if he sticks with the company than if he forfeits or sells his shares. By paying the assessment he reduces his losses.

Sometimes, although rarely, it becomes necessary to assess the junior bondholders also. It seems strange that a creditor of the corporation should ever be forced to pay an assessment in order to remain a creditor, yet the logic of the situation compels the bondholders, when they are thus assessed, to accept it with as good grace as they can muster. The bondholders will not and cannot equitably be compelled to pay unless the burden is too heavy for the stockholders to carry alone. If the amount of cash needed is so large that most of the stockholders would rather lose their equity in the property than furnish their proportion of the cash, the bondholders find themselves in an unpleasant dilemma. Either they must take some of the burden off the stockholders' shoulders, or they must take the whole burden themselves and eliminate the stockholders altogether. Almost always they prefer the former alternative. When the Atchison, Topeka and Santa Fe Railroad, for instance, was reorganized in 1894, the cash requirements were so large that each stockholder would have been compelled to pay in the neighborhood of $14 per share, and it was more than doubtful if the stock of the reorganized company was worth this amount. The reorganization committee, therefore, imposed $4 of the assessment on the junior bondholders.

Usually the cash needed by the company is not required at once, and the terms of payment of the assessments may therefore be made fairly easy, thus reserving some of the cash resources of the corporation. Another means of providing funds for future use is to base the bond issues of the reorganized company on a limited open-end mortgage, so that the company need not be hampered for many years to come by a dearth of funds.

241. *Reducing fixed charges.*—Having provided the reorganized company with sufficient cash, the reorganization committee now takes up its final and most difficult problem, reduction of fixed charges. The fixed charges that may be affected are of three kinds: guarantees, rentals and interest. A company may be dissolved in reorganization, in which case it is, of course, released from its previous contracts and the reorganized company may or may not renew them. If guarantees of interest and dividends on subsidiary company securities have proved burdensome and unprofitable, the reorganization committee has an opportunity to dispense with them. It does not follow that the committee will always take this action. The guarantee may be necessary in order to hold control of the subsidiary companies. Frequently, however, the holders of the guaranteed stock and bonds will submit to a reduction of the guarantee rather than take back their property.

Much the same thing may be said of rentals. The owners of a leased property would ordinarily have great difficulty in leasing it to any other corporation and could not very well operate it themselves. Especially is this true when the leased property has been constructed in the interest of the failed corporation. The owners, therefore, have practically no choice in the matter. They must submit to any reasonable reduction that the reorganization committee demands.

Far more important usually in its effect on fixed charges is the substitution for the interest-bearing securities of the old corporation of dividend-paying securities of the new corporation. Sometimes, also, old securities which bear interest at a high rate are converted into new securities bearing interest at a low rate. The result of this readjustment, if the reorganization is to prove successful, must be to bring the total fixed charges below the net earnings of the corporation even in the worst years. Ordinarily the reorganization committee will first make a conservative estimate of the lowest earnings likely to occur in the future and will cut down interest charges accordingly. Of course this reduction is not proportionate on all the bond issues, but is adjusted in accordance with the relative strength of the various claims against the corporation, as already indicated.

One of the great advantages of reorganization is the possibility which it affords of unifying and simplifying the complicated and sometimes conflicting obligations that have been imposed at various times. The reorganization committee will usually arrange for a few comprehensive, well-defined mortgages in place of the numerous mortgages previously existing and will increase the amount authorized under each mortgage. This principle, however, cannot be extended too far. The committee cannot, for instance, without getting into legal difficulties, absorb any of the old bond issues, interest on which has unquestionably been earned for several years previous. The old first mortgage issue and the first mortgage bonds on highly important specific pieces of property will therefore generally be left untouched. On top of them, however, the committee may impose a new general mortgage bond issue of large size sufficient to refund all the existing issues that are to be absorbed, to refund the old first mortgage bonds when they finally fall due and to provide for necessary improvements and extensions. This general mortgage issue will be designed evidently to become in time a first lien on all the corporation property. For these new general mortgage bonds the old junior bonds will be exchanged on such terms as may be finally agreed to.

242. *Capitalization of the reorganized corporation.*—Assuming that the reorganization committee has succeeded in determining the relative values of the various issues of mortgage bonds, it may now proceed to a corresponding allotment of the new general mortgage bonds. Suppose, for instance, that there had been outstanding $1,000,000 second mortgage bonds, $500,000 branch line bonds and $1,500,000 debenture bonds, and that the new general mortgage issue available for exchange is fixed on the basis of the lowest earnings at $2,000,000; suppose also that the reorganization committee estimates the first-named issue on the basis of lowest earnings to be worth 80 per cent of its par value, the second-named issue, 60 per cent, and the third-named issue, 60 per cent: It would then offer to the bondholders of the first class $800 in new general mortgage bonds for each $1,000 of the old bonds, and to the bondholders of the second and third classes, $600 in the new bonds for $1,000 of the old bonds. As the values of the old issues and the amount of the new issue are figured on the same basis, lowest net earnings, they must, of course, exactly correspond. Not every case is so simple by any means, as our illustration. The same principle, however, would always be applied.

It is felt to be equitable, as well as necessary in order to satisfy the bondholders, that they should be compensated for the reduction of their interest-bearing principal. This is accomplished by giving them at least enough dividend-paying principal to bring the par value of their holdings in the reorganized company up to an equality at least—sometimes considerably more than an equality—with the par value of their old securities. Formerly it was customary to give them the difference between the par value of their old bonds and the par value of their allotment of new interest-bearing bonds in the form of income bonds. Income bonds have already been described and characterized. They are a fallacy and a delusion and at the present time are practically unused. Their place in reorganization has now been taken by preferred stock. The debenture bondholder in our illustration who got $600 in new bonds for $1,000 in old bonds would under the present practice probably get also at least $400 in preferred stock. He thus has a chance to share in the future prosperity of the company. He may well hope and even expect that in the end he will more than recover his losses. The same principle is applied to all the other bondholders, so far as practicable, and even to the preferred and common stockholders. It follows that one usual and almost necessary result of a reorganization is a great increase in capitalization. The reorganization committee endeavors to remedy the failures and disappointments of the past and present by drawing heavy drafts on the future. It is only fair to say that in this country these drafts have usually sooner or later been honored.

The final problem which the reorganization committee must settle is whether to revive the old company and the old charter or to take out a new charter and organize a new company. The first course involves a maintenance of all the previously existing contracts and obligations of the company not provided for in the reorganization scheme. Its advantage, of course, lies in the retention of the charter which may perhaps confer valuable privileges. The question is at bottom legal rather than financial. In truth, it is a matter usually of no very great consequence.

To insure stability of financial management, until after the reorganized company is well started, it is not uncommon to place the new stock in the hands of a voting trust for a period of years. The nature and operations of such a trust have already been described.

243. *Summary of the chapter.*—Briefly the principles and the results of reorganization may be summed up as follows:

(a) The reorganization must remove the immediate causes of bankruptcy by providing cash and at the same time reducing fixed charges.

(b) The reduction of securities bearing fixed charges may well be and usually is accomplished by a great increase of dividend-paying securities.

(c) In determining who shall stand the losses caused by the company's insolvency, the reorganization committee will first rank the securities in the order of their safety and will then impose the losses in inverse order.

(d) In so doing the directors must of necessity consider primarily the ability of the security-holders to make trouble for or to wreck the reorganized company if their demands are not satisfied.

(e) In raising necessary cash they will naturally impose the first and heaviest assessments on stockholders, but they must bear in mind that if they go beyond certain limits the stockholders will forfeit their shares rather than pay the assessments.

The working out of these principles will be further discussed in connection with the illustrations cited in the following chapter.

CHAPTER XXX

THREE TYPICAL REORGANIZATIONS

244. *Growth of the Santa Fe System.*—The principles of reorganization laid down in the preceding chapter will be much better understood if we consider their application in a few typical instances. For this purpose we will take, first, the forced reorganization of the insolvent Atchison, Topeka and Santa Fe Railroad Company in 1894; second, the voluntary reorganization of the prosperous Chicago, Rock Island and Pacific Railway Company in 1902; third, the forced reorganization of the Westinghouse Electric Manufacturing Company in 1908.

It is necessary to go back several years in order to get a typical case of a large railroad receivership and reorganization, for American railroads in the last fifteen years have enjoyed extraordinary, and up to 1907 almost uninterrupted, prosperity. It is true that a considerable number of railroad systems, including the Seaboard Air Line, the Chicago Great Western, the Detroit, Toledo and Ironton, the Chicago, Cincinnati and Louisville, the International and Great Northern, the Western Maryland and the Macon and Birmingham went into the hands of receivers as the result of the financial panic of October, 1907. None of these roads, however, is of first-rate importance and their problems did not prove as intricate and difficult as the problems of the numerous railroad reorganizations following the great crisis of 1893. We shall find it therefore more instructive—even if not of so great current interest—to study one of the 1893 reorganizations rather than one of later date.[1]

Like most of our great railroad systems, the Atchison, Topeka and Santa Fe has grown by leaps, so to speak. It was chartered in Kansas in the year 1863, and contruction on the first section of the road was begun in 1869. The main line from Kansas City to Colorado, thence in a southerly direction to Albuquerque, New Mexico, and thence southwest to a connection with the Southern Pacific Railroad at Deming, Arizona, was not completed until 1881. In 1882 the Atchison exchanged its stock for the stock of the Sonora Railroad, and thus secured an entrance to Guaymas, Mexico. The company by using a section of the track of the Southern Pacific had a through route from Kansas City to the Pacific Coast. To appreciate the importance of reaching the Pacific Ocean it must be borne in mind that traffic from any of the Pacific Coast ports may move readily and cheaply by water to any other of these ports. The Santa Fe was therefore in a position to take through business by its part-water-and-part-rail route from any port on the Pacific Coast to the East.

This route, though important, could not, however, bring to the Santa Fe a large proportion of the traffic to and from the Pacific Coast in the face of the existing competition of the all-rail routes, particularly of the Santa Fe's chief competitor, the Southern Pacific. President Strong of the Santa Fe therefore entered into

[1] Acknowledgment should be made here, in connection with the following reviews of the Santa Fe and Rock Island reorganizations, of the information obtained from Mr. Stuart Daggett's "Railroad Re-Organization." Most of what follows as to these two companies is based on Mr. Daggett's researches. He is one of the first to bring to bear on financial problems the thorough, scientific methods of university scholarship.

an alliance with the St. Louis and San Francisco Railroad, which owned the charter of a company known as the Atlantic and Pacific Railroad Company. By the terms of this alliance the two roads jointly financed the operations of the Atlantic and Pacific and by means of purchase and of new construction endeavored to secure a through rail route to San Francisco. In 1885—one of the great railroad building years of the United States—the Atchison, by construction, purchase and lease combined, managed to reach Los Angeles. The main line of the road still had its eastern terminal, however, at Kansas City and the system did not reach the Gulf of Mexico, or in fact any of the rapidly developing agricultural country south of Kansas. To remedy this defect a road, known as the Gulf, Colorado and Santa Fe, had been constructed, partly in the interest of the Santa Fe, from Galveston to a point about two hundred miles north, and another line known as the Southern Kansas Railroad was built south from Arkansas City to connect with the track of the Gulf, Colorado and Santa Fe. In 1886 the stock of the last-named road was bought by the Atchison and the bonds, to the extent of about $17,000 per mile, were assumed. In 1887 the Atchison purchased the Chicago and St. Louis Railroad between Chicago and Streator, Illinois, and other subsidiary companies constructed new track up to Streator. By 1888 it had thus obtained its Chicago entrance.

In the meantime between '86 and '89 it had built a large number of branch lines in all directions largely for the purpose of forestalling competition. "The method of financing these competitive extensions varied," says Mr. Daggett. "Sometimes the parent company guaranteed the principal and interest of the branch line bonds; sometimes it took these into its treasury and issued collateral bonds against them; sometimes, perhaps more frequently still, it leased new roads for a rental equivalent to the annual interest on their bonds. If the branches could have earned their fixed charges, the burden of the Atchison would have been nominal, but as in large part they could not, it was real and serious."

The results of the rapid expansion of the Santa Fe from 1884 to 1888 are well summarized by Mr. Daggett in the following table:

	1884		*1888*
Mileage	2,799		7,010
Bonds	$48,258,500		$163,694,000
Stock (Atchison)	60,673,150		75,000,000
Gross earnings	16,699,662		28,265,339
Operating expenses	9,410,424		21,958,195
Net earnings from operation	7,289,237		6,307,145
Net profits excluding dividends	5,147,883	def.	2,933,197
Net profits, including payments for dividends and interest on floating debt		def.	5,557,323

It should be noted that while the bond indebtedness (including the assumed bonds of subsidiary companies) had considerably more than tripled, gross earnings had increased only about 70 per cent and net earnings from operation had declined. Evidently, unless this tendency should be speedily reversed, the company was doomed to insolvency. In addition the floating debt had increased from approximately $3,300,000 in 1884 to over $8,000,000 in 1888, and the road had consequently been forced to authorize, in October, 1888, $10,000,000 of three-year notes.

245. *First reorganization of the Santa Fe and its results.*—The situation was so obviously dangerous that a committee of the directors was appointed in 1889 to bring about a friendly reorganization and thereby to avert bankruptcy.

About one-third of the $163,000,000 of bonds were direct obligations secured by mortgages on the Atchison's own property, while the other two-thirds consisted of obligations of thirty-two subsidiary companies. From what has been said in the preceding chapter, it will be seen that the entanglements and conflicts of these various issues were almost beyond unraveling. The directors first aimed at simplification and with that object in view suggested that two large issues be put forth, one of 4 per cent general mortgage bonds, to the amount of $150,000,000, and one of 5 per cent income bonds to a total of $80,000,000. Some $14,000,000 were to be sold in order to raise necessary cash and the remainder of the two bond issues was to be exchanged for the numerous existing issues. Income bonds were much used in reorganization at that period and were not received with the distrust which they now excite. The proposal to the original bondholders that they should exchange their mortgage bonds in part for income bonds was not, of course, altogether palatable; yet it must be remembered that the bonds which were to be thus exchanged had always been regarded as more or less speculative in character and had for that reason been sold, for the most part, well below par, and, furthermore, that the branch line bondholders would have lost rather than gained by a forced bankruptcy and foreclosure sale. Moreover, the basis of the exchange was such as to compensate them in part for their loss of fixed interest payments by a larger principal. In other words, as usually happens in reorganizations, the company proposed to cut down its current fixed charges and held out in place thereof hopes of high optional payments in the future. The reorganization plan was accepted and put into effect.

After this reorganization, the Atchison policy of rapid expansion was apparently renewed with fresh vigor. In 1890, by an exchange of securities, the St. Louis and San Francisco Railroad was brought into the Atchison system. This acquisition of 1,300 miles at one stroke did not prove nearly as profitable as was anticipated. In the same year the Colorado Midland, 346 miles long, was purchased.

When the $10,000,000 note issue of 1888 fell due in 1891, the directors found themselves unable to meet the payment out of earnings and therefore arranged for a two-year extension. In 1892 the need of additional funds for improvements and extensions, which, as the reader may have noted, had not been at all provided for in the reorganization of 1889, made necessary a new issue of second mortgage bonds. As the terms of issue of the $80,000,000 income bonds forbade any prior lien (except the first mortgage) being placed upon the property, it was necessary before placing a second mortgage to arrange for the protection of the income bondholders. This was accomplished by making the second mortgage cover an issue of $100,000,000 4 per cent bonds, $80,000,000 of which were to be exchanged dollar-for-dollar for the income bonds, and $20,000,000 to be sold for cash. Thus in 1893, by a coincidence, which may be called unfortunate, but which with wise management would never have occurred, the Atchison had to face largely increased fixed charges and the payment of the $10,000,000 note issue, both coming at the same time with the panic and the traffic losses of that disastrous year. In January, 1894, the inevitable insolvency arrived.

246. *Second reorganization and its results.*—Several bondholders' committees, according to the custom in reorganization, were quickly formed. Among others the English holders of second-mortgage bonds sent over a strong committee which put forward what was known as the English plan of reorganization.

This plan involved foreclosure either by the first or second mortgage bondholders. In either case the first mortgage issue would be left undisturbed and overdue interest would be paid either in cash or in new securities. A new income mortgage bond issue was to be exchanged for the second mortgage bonds and was also to provide compensation for an assessment of $12 per share on the stockholders. By paying this assessment the stockholders would retain their stock interest in the road, as well as receive income bonds. The income bonds were to have voting power. The substance of the plan, it is evident, was to reverse the former conversion of income bonds into second mortgage bonds. In the reconversion the English bondholders were to secure an increase in principal and the important privilege of voting. The plan was not acceptable to the stockholders, however, who felt that part of the load thus imposed upon them ought rightfully to be borne by the second mortgage bondholders.

Before the argument had been carried far a new factor was introduced into the situation, namely, the publication of the report of Mr. Stephen Little, an expert accountant who had thoroughly investigated the Atchison books. Mr. Little found that by means of peculiar fictitious accounts—most important of which was an account that carried rebates by the company as an asset—the recorded earnings of the railroad had been deliberately inflated. The annual net earnings, according to the company's reports, had been as follows:

1891	$ 7,631,598
1892	10,953,896
1893	12,126,866

According to Mr. Little they should have been:

1891	$ 5,204,880
1892	7,853,173
1893	8,085,608
1894	5,956,615

This startling announcement completely changed the plans which had been formulated. It was evident that a far more radical reduction of fixed charges would be essential.

A new committee proposed the second and final reorganization plan in March, 1895. The purposes of this plan were stated to be:

(a) To reduce fixed charges to a safe limit;
(b) To provide for future capital requirements;
(c) To liquidate the floating debt;
(d) To reinstate existing securities upon equitable terms in the order of their priority;
(e) To consolidate and unify the system.

The committee proposed foreclosure under the first mortgage and the formation of a new railway company which was to issue

(a) Common stock....................$102,000,000
(b) 5 per cent non-cumulative preferred stock $111,486,000

(c) General 4 per cent bonds............$96,990,582
(d) Adjustment[1] 4 per cent bonds.......$51,728,310

Old common stockholders were to receive share for share new common stock provided they paid an assessment of $10 per share and for this $10 were to receive $10 in new preferred stock. An underwriting syndicate guaranteed to take the place of defaulting stockholders. The old general mortgage bondholders were given 75 per cent of their holdings in new general mortgage bonds and 40 per cent in adjustment bonds. The second-mortgage bondholders were to be assessed $4 for every $100 of their holdings and were to receive 113 per cent in new preferred stock. It was provided that additional bonds under the general mortgage might be issued at the rate of $3,000,000 per year up to a limit of $30,000,000 and that thereafter additional adjustment bonds might be issued at the rate of $2,000,000 per year up to a limit of $20,000,000.

The St. Louis and San Francisco Railroad and some other smaller subsidiary lines were not included in the reorganization plan, but were turned over to their own bondholders.

It will be seen that this plan accomplished the five purposes named by the committee. It brought about a very radical reduction of fixed charges affecting even the first mortgage bondholders. It gave room for additional issues of bonds under certain restrictions to provide for future improvements and extensions. It brought in about $14,000,000 cash to meet current obligations. It retained the relative claims of the various security-holders to the road's assets and earnings. Finally, by lopping off nonessential lines, it helped to consolidate and unify the system.

[1] The so called adjustment bonds were in reality income bonds.

The principal opposition to the plan came from some of the minority stockholders who believed that the former management had proved untrue to their interests and that this management had not been entirely eliminated. This opposition, however, was unable to muster enough votes to defeat the reorganization plan.

The high credit and prosperity of the Atchison in the last few years indicates that the reorganization was carried through on sound lines. There has never been a question raised since the reorganization but that the company could easily meet all its obligations. The road has been greatly improved and strengthened physically and earnings have grown far more rapidly than expenses. The changes in the decade following 1897 are shown in the following tabulation:

	1897	*1907*
Mileage	6,479	9,273
Gross earnings	$30,621,230	$93,683,407
Net earnings	7,754,041	32,153,692
Annual surplus	1,452,446	21,168,724

Naturally the market price of the Atchison securities has steadily risen. Nobody suffered in the end from the reorganization. On the contrary, all the security-holders who retained their interests have seen them steadily appreciate in value. The Atchison reorganization of 1895 may well be taken as a fair type of a highly successful readjustment of charges.

247. *Growth of the Rock Island System.*—We will consider now an entirely different kind of reorganization —one in which not necessity but desire for quick speculative profits was the controlling factor. In order to understand the situation it will be well to review hastily the history of the Rock Island Railroad. The line was completed between Chicago and Rock Island in 1854,

and from Rock Island to Council Bluffs in 1869. The company was prosperous almost from the beginning. Its road ran through a well-settled and fertile territory where traffic was large and certain and construction was cheap. Capitalization was very moderate, especially as compared with many other western railroads whose construction was paid for not in cash but in extravagant allotments of stocks and bonds to the contractors. In 1880 the road was earning so much and paying such large dividends that it seemed desirable to water the stock. This was accomplished by an exchange of the stock of the Chicago, Rock Island and Pacific Railroad Company for the stock of a new Chicago, Rock Island and Pacific Railway Company in the ratio of about two to one. The new Railway Company also took in some other properties previously controlled by the Railroad Company, and was, therefore, in form, though not in fact, a consolidation.

The new railway company did not continue to be as prosperous as it was in the beginning. The middle '80s were hard years for western railroads, for all of them were forced into competitive railroad building, which for the time being was largely unprofitable. The Rock Island dividends and the market prices of the road's securities suffered severely. Nevertheless, the road's management was conservative and able and the company not only survived, but even paid dividends through the trying depression of 1893–1897. After 1897 the road shared in the renewed prosperity of the United States and began in its conservative way to plan for further expansion and development.

In 1901, however, the conservatism of the company suddenly disappeared as if the earth had swallowed it. Directors and officers who had served for years and decades were removed, and new men—younger men of an entirely different type—were put into their place. With the older men there vanished also the former ideals and purposes of the company and a very different path toward success and prosperity was entered.

The reason for these changes is to be found in the fact that during 1900 and 1901 a small coterie of speculative promoters known as "the Moore crowd," of whom we have heard in connection with the formation of the United States Steel Corporation, had quietly bought a majority of the common stock in the Wall Street market. The process of buying had been carried on so patiently and warily that it was hardly suspected and the price of the stock was very little increased. The financial world first got an inkling of the situation when in April, 1901, Mr. William H. Moore and Mr. D. G. Reid were elected to the directorate.

The principal men in the new party, which now rapidly assumed full control of Rock Island affairs, were Mr. W. H. Moore, his brother Mr. J. H. Moore, Mr. D. G. Reid and Mr. William B. Leeds. No one of these men had had any experience in railroad managerial positions and none of them had ever been prominently identified before with railroad operations. All of them, however, were bold and successful speculative promoters and all of them were well versed in the ways and wiles of the speculative security market. Their successes had been gained in the promotion of the companies which were taken into the United States Steel Corporation. Their interest in railroad affairs, therefore, it was easy to see, was entirely financial. They did not take, and as a matter of fact never have taken, any active part in the operating management of their road. All their energies have been given to maintaining its financial status and at the same time directing for their own benefit its financial operations.

In the two annual meetings of June, 1901, and June, 1902, the stockholders increased their capital stock from $50,000,000, at which it had been placed in 1880, to $75,000,000. Also the stock of some smaller roads, including the important Choctaw, Oklahoma and Gulf, was bought by the Rock Island, payment being made partly in cash and partly in Rock Island securities.

248. *Rock Island reorganization.*—The "Moore crowd" now brought forward the scheme of reorganization which they had devised primarily, it appears, with a view to selling a large part of their stock without losing control. The plan involved two holding companies and a double exchange of securities. It is perhaps the most complex and ingenious scheme on a large scale for attaining the purpose just named that has yet been successfully put through.

The operating company under this scheme remained the same as it had been since 1880, the Chicago, Rock Island and Pacific Railway Company. The first holding company (whose prime object, apparently, was to meet any legal objection that might afterwards arise to the consolidation of competing railway companies) was the Chicago, Rock Island and Pacific Railroad Company, incorporated in Iowa. The second holding company was the Rock Island Company, incorporated in New Jersey. The outstanding bonds and other securities of the old "railway" company were left undisturbed. The new "railroad" company issued stock to the amount of $75,000,000. The Rock Island Company issued $96,000,000 common and $54,000,000 preferred stock. The last-named company then delivered $127,-

500,000 of its preferred and common stock to the Chicago, Rock Island and Pacific Railroad Company of Iowa in exchange for all the $125,000,000 common stock of the Iowa company. After this transaction the last-named company had in its treasury most of the common and preferred stock of the Rock Island Company; it also had the right to issue $75,000,000 bonds. It now offered for each share of the railway company's stock, one share of its own 4 per cent bonds, one share of Rock Island Company common stock and $70 of Rock Island Company preferred stock. These bonds were to be collateral trust secured by the deposit of all the "railway" company shares obtained by the "railroad" company. Thus the "railway" stockholders would, in case of default, get back exactly the stock which they had exchanged.

The "railway" stockholders readily accepted this proposition, which was equivalent to giving a large stock dividend, and figured that even if they retained in their own hands all the securities which they received in exchange they could not lose and might benefit by the exchange. If they did not care to retain all the securities they received, they could easily dispose of their Rock Island common and preferred shares and thus get a large immediate cash payment.

We shall understand better why the "Moore crowd" desired this reorganization if we examine the charter provisions of the Rock Island Company. One of the important clauses reads as follows:

> There shall be five classes of directors. The first class shall contain a majority of the whole number of the directors as fixed at any time by the by-laws. The holders of the preferred stock shall have the right to the exclusion of the holders of the common stock to chose directors of the first class.

Thus a majority of the Rock Island Company preferred stock could elect a majority of the board of directors of that company and this board, through the company's holdings of "railroad" stock could completely control all the affairs of the Chicago, Rock Island and Pacific Railway Company, the operating company. Now the outstanding preferred stock of the Rock Island Company is only a little over $45,000,000; therefore the ownership of approximately $22,500,000 par value of this preferred stock would be sufficient to give complete control over the whole Chicago, Rock Island and Pacific Railway Company, having a total capitalization of about $225,000,000. Indeed, if this $22,500,000 preferred stock were carried on a margin of $20 a share, $5,400,000 cash would suffice to secure control.

The advantage of this reorganization to the "Moore crowd" may readily be seen if we compare the price they paid for control in the "railway" company with what is necessary for control in the Rock Island Company. Assuming that they bought all their stock outright and paid in the neighborhood of 140, which was not far from the average market price while they were buying control of the "railway" company, their investment would have been $52,500,140. In exchange for this under the reorganization scheme they obtained stock and bonds which at the market prices of the early part of 1903 were worth:

Rock Island Company common	$18,375,049
Rock Island Company preferred	21,918,808
Chicago, Rock Island & Pacific Railroad Co. 4% bonds	32,765,712
Total	$73,059,569

As the preferred stock was all that was necessary for control they were left free to sell their bonds and common stock, and it will be observed that this sale would have brought to them just about as much cash as they had originally paid for control of the Chicago Rock Island and Pacific Railway Company. In other words, control of the Rock Island Company, carrying with it control of both subsidiary companies, cost them in cash next to nothing.

In addition, the Rock Island Company later obtained control of another great railroad system, the St. Louis and San Francisco. The Rock Island directors accomplished this by offering to exchange for each share of common stock of the St. Louis and San Francisco $60 par value in the common stock of the Rock Island Company and $60 par value in a new issue of 5 per cent gold bonds, the bonds being secured by deposit of the "Frisco" common stock as collateral. It will be observed that this great addition to the Rock Island system did not disturb in any way the controlling force of a majority of the relatively small issue of Rock Island Company preferred stock. Thus by reorganization and purchase the "Moore crowd" with a very small expenditure of cash, have under their control a system with an aggregate mileage of 14,270 miles.

249. *Westinghouse reorganization.*—This reorganization of 1908, although not essentially different in principle from the Santa Fe reorganization, introduces some new features that are worthy of attention. Owing to space limits it is necessary to confine our attention to these peculiar features.

This is a typical instance of a company which was strong in equipment and ability and which was doing a large and profitable business and yet suddenly found itself technically insolvent. Its difficulties resulted from a lack of sufficient working capital. The company's assets were too largely fixed, and quick assets were relatively too small, considering the amount and character of the company's business. In prosperous times the company was able to prosper with the rest of the country. In the period of strain, however, it was very quickly stripped of cash and, being unable to obtain capital, necessarily went to the wall.

It naturally followed that the most active and influential body of creditors in planning the reorganization were merchandise creditors; next to them came the bank creditors; the bond and note holders were little consulted and their claims were not disturbed.

The problem before the reorganizers of this company differed from that which confronts most reorganizers in that the company needed simply to be tided over a bad period. No one apparently felt any question as to the renewed prosperity of the company as soon as normal business conditions should be restored. The permanent fixed charges were met even during the period of reorganization. All that was necessary, therefore, was to take care of the floating debt.

The main elements in the floating debt were notes payable to banks, $7,919,000, and merchandise debts, $4,762,000. After much discussion and consideration of two or three plans, the merchandise creditors, through their committee, finally agreed to accept new common stock of the company at par in full settlement of their claims on certain conditions specified below:

(a) Such of the bank debt as would not accept new common stock to be provided for partly by convertible bonds of an issue already authorized previous to the bankruptcy and partly by 5 per cent notes running for an average period of 5 years.

(b) The existing issues of convertible bonds, debenture certificates and collateral notes not to be disturbed.

(c) The preferred and common stockholders each to pay a 25 per cent assessment in cash.

It will be observed that none of the sacrifices under this plan were to be made by the bond and note holders. Indeed, it would have been impossible to impose sacrifices upon these classes or to refuse or modify their claims, for in that case they would certainly have been prompt to bring foreclosure proceedings, buy the property at a forced sale and thus reduce the unsecured claims and wipe out the stockholders. The bond and note holders, in other words, were in an impregnable position because the company, even in the worst times, was more than earning the permanent fixed charges.

The bank creditors came next in order of preference, and their only loss, therefore, was an extension of time of payment of their obligations. The unsecured creditors, knowing the weakness of their position, were willing to accept stock in payment. Under the circumstances it was both expedient and just that the stockholders should be called on for a particularly heavy assessment. It was expedient because the prospects of the company were excellent and the stock, even through the reorganization, sold at fairly good prices. The stockholders, therefore, could well afford to pay this assessment rather than forfeit the stock. It was just that they should pay because the difficulties of the company could have been prevented if less had been paid out in dividends and more cash had been reserved for an emergency. Such protests as were made by the stockholders for these reasons proved unavailing and the plan as outlined above has been carried into effect.

The company operating under this plan has re-established itself as a firm and prosperous corporation. There was no reason to fear the result. The plan provided for all the floating debt incurred before the reorganization, it enlarged only very slightly the fixed charges of the company, and it introduced new and conservative elements into the management of the company. The cash working capital on hand after reorganization was sufficient for the needs of the next two years, even if business had been very poor indeed. In addition it was at once clearly stated on good authority that dividends on the new common stock of the company would not be paid for at least two years, thus giving time for the accumulation of a substantial surplus. These drastic measures proved effective in strengthening the company's financial position and enabling it to go forward steadily, almost as if no setback had occurred.

QUIZ QUESTIONS

(*The numbers refer to the numbered sections in the text.*)

CHAPTER I

1. What are "non-stock" corporations?

2. What are "stock" corporations? For what purpose are they usually organized?

3. What is the most striking distinctive feature of the corporation compared to other forms of business association?

4. In what sense is "corporate entity" a fiction?

5. In what nations have corporations been prominent features of business life?

6. Show briefly how the use of corporations has spread in recent years.

7. State how and why the corporate form is well adapted to raising large amounts of capital.

8. In what sense is a corporation more permanent than a partnership or than individual proprietorship? How is this attribute an advantage?

9. Show how and why the corporate form better lends itself to an efficient, centralized control of a business than the partnership form.

10. Can an interest in a corporation be more readily transferred from one person to another than an interest in a partnership? Why?

11. What is the principle of limited liability of corporate stockholders? Is the principle universally applicable? Name the principal advantages of the corporate form of organization.

12. Name the principal disadvantages of the corporate form. Mention two kinds of enterprises in which these disadvantages outweigh the advantages.

CHAPTER II

13. What are the legal instruments that define and control a corporation's activities?

14. How far is the common law applicable to corporations?

15. Is it important to consider the provisions of the constitution of the state in which a corporation is formed? Why?

16. Discuss the relative advantages of two methods of securing authority to incorporate.

17. What is a charter? What is a certificate of incorporation? What are articles of incorporation? What information should a charter ordinarily contain?

18. Draw up a charter for a company (imaginary or otherwise) following the model given in the text.

19. Can a new corporation assume a name which has already been adopted by a corporation chartered in some other state? Do any of the states prescribe any part of the names of corporations organized under their laws?

20. Why is it important to state the purposes for which a company is formed fully and carefully in the charter? Why did the New Jersey Court of Errors

and Appeals hand down a decision adverse to the railroad company in the instance cited in the text?

21. What is the minimum number of incorporators in most states? of directors?

22. What topics are usually considered in the by-laws of a corporation? Draw up a brief set of by-laws for a company (imaginary or otherwise) following the model given in the text.

23. What are the usual by-law provisions as to stock, meetings, officers, dividend payments and by-law amendments? How may new rules of action be adopted without the formality of amending the by-laws?

CHAPTER III

24. What are the four fundamental rights of the body of stockholders of a corporation? May a board of directors ordinarily sell the assets of their corporation without the consent of the stockholders?

25. Name the four fundamental rights of each individual stockholder. What is a proxy? Write a proxy conferring the right to vote in favor of a proposed amendment at a special meeting called for the purpose of considering the amendment. When is a proxy irrevocable?

26. Can stockholders force a board of directors to declare a dividend, provided the company is admitted to have earned large profits? What is meant by the "right to dividends"?

27. Does a stockholder have a legal right to inspect the books of his company? How does the movement in favor of publicity of accounts work in favor of stockholders?

28. What are the two chief universal liabilities of stockholders?

29. What are the two classes of creditors? Has either class a right to interfere in the internal management of the debtor corporation?

30. What are "dummy" directors? How are they sometimes kept under control?

31. What in general are the powers of a board of directors? May those powers be delegated? Under what circumstances do directors become liable for loss suffered by their corporation?

32. Why is it stated in the text that the corporate form is "almost ideally adapted, so far as efficiency and economy go, to the conditions of present-day industry"?

CHAPTER IV

33. By virtue of what legal principle do corporations chartered in one state of the Union extend their operations to other states? Give the gist of the decision of the Supreme Court in the case of The Bank of Augusta vs. Earle.

34. May a state regulate in any manner corporations doing business within its borders, but chartered in another state? If so, how?

35. Give three reasons in favor of securing a charter from the state in which a corporation has its principal office. Why are not these reasons decisive in all cases?

36. From the tables given in the text estimate the organization fees and the annual franchise taxes of a corporation with $50,000 capital stock in New Jersey, New York, Delaware, Maine and South Dakota. What

other expenses will probably be incurred in starting a new company?

37. Name four states which have liberal incorporation laws?

38. Why is it desirable to secure a charter in a state which has an established and well-adjudicated corporation law?

39. Name three states which bear poor reputations as states of incorporation. Name three states which bear good reputations.

40. If you were about to incorporate a manufacturing company, located in Massachusetts, designed both to operate a plant and to buy up the stock of several competing companies, the capitalization to be $2,000, 000, in what state would you take out a charter? What other states would you be inclined to consider favorably? Base your answer on the data given in the text and state your reasons fully. An excellent method of getting familiar with the main features of the various state laws is to make up a number of similar hypothetical cases and consider each one carefully.

41. What is a "subscription contract" and when is it used?

42. What is meant by the statement that a capable lawyer can generally fit out any corporation with the exact powers and privileges that will prove most advantageous.

CHAPTER V

43. In your opinion should stock certificates be made fully negotiable? Give your reasons in full.

44. What is the "par value" of a share of stock? The

"market value"? Is there any good reason foı the custom of giving shares a nominal value in money?

45. Define fully "preferred stock," showing wherein the preference may consist.

46. Name and discuss four uses of preferred stock. What is "voting stock"?

47. What is the object of "cumulative voting"? How is that object attained?

48. What is a "voting trust"? What is the usual plan of organization? What is the usual object in establishing a voting trust?

CHAPTER VI

49. Define "quasi-public corporations," "private corporations," "close corporations."

50. What is a "parent company"? What is the difference between a "parent company" and a "holding company"?

51. Why does a holding company usually aim to secure more than a bare majority of the stock of its subsidiary companies? What is the distinction between the ordinary balance-sheet of a holding company and its "consolidated" or "general" balance sheet?

52. Under what plan were the early "trusts" organized? Why do most "trusts," so-called, now take the form of holding companies?

53. Taking the chart of organization of the Interborough-Metropolitan Company, show what relation of ownership and control exists between the New York City Railway Company and the Interborough-Metropolitan Company.

54. How many companies are directly controlled by

the Standard Oil Company of New Jersey? How many indirectly?

CHAPTER VII

55. Enumerate from memory the principal topics covered in the first six chapters of this book.

56. What are the six sources of corporate funds? In what sense may profits be called a possible source of funds? In what sense do trade creditors supply corporate funds? Can a corporation manager or promoter ordinarily sell the stock or bonds of his company to a bank? If not, why not?

57. What are the important classes of investors?

58. How would you distinguish between an "investment" and a "speculative" security?

59. What are the important classes of buyers of speculative securities?

60. Why is it desirable that a corporation should borrow a considerable proportion of its funds? What proportion of the funds used by the five companies named in the text are borrowed?

61. What kinds of securities ordinarily will a corporation offer in order to secure funds from (a) trade creditors, (b) banks, (c) the investing public, and (d) the speculative public? Name and describe the six important groups of corporate assets. What securities may be issued corresponding to each group? In determining what securities a corporation shall issue are the earnings of the corporation, as well as its assets, taken into consideration? If so, how?

CHAPTER VIII

62. How are corporate funds secured from trade creditors? What two qualifications limit the general statement that a corporation should buy as much as it can on credit? What is a conservative percentage of accounts, bills and notes payable to quick assets?

63. What are the main points that will be considered by a careful banker in determining how much credit he is willing to extend to a corporation?

64. What are the essential features of a valid negotiable promissory note? What is the chief objection to using short or medium term notes sold to the public as a means of securing corporate funds? Under what circumstances is it good financial policy for a corporation to issue such notes? In general should the short-time obligations of a corporation ever be based on the corporation's permanent assets?

CHAPTER IX

65. What three opinions are prevalent as to the chief factor that determines the value of fixed assets?

66. What are the characteristic features of a mortgage? What is a mortgage bond? What is a mortgage deed of trust?

67. What are the essential and usual provisions of a corporate deed of trust?

68. Define "closed," "open-end" and "limited open-end" mortgage deeds of trust? Which of the three types is generally the best? Why?

CHAPTER X

69. Give from memory the principal descriptive words applied to corporate bonds indicating (a) their security, (b) their purposes, (c) their manner of payment and (d) their conditions of redemption.

70. What is a junior mortgage bond? How is the fact that it is a junior bond sometimes disguised?

71. What are sinking fund bonds? What are the principal objections to their use?

72. What are collateral trust bonds? Why may they sometimes be sold more readily than the securities on which they are directly based? How may they be used to finance the process of buying control of subsidiary corporations?

73. What is an equipment trust bond? Why are they so highly regarded by investors?

CHAPTER XI

74. Compare English with American practice with reference to the use of debenture bonds. What reasons lead to the issue of debenture bonds from time to time by some corporations in this country?

75. What are income bonds? What is the chief objection to their use?

76. Define "participating," "profit sharing" and "joint" bonds and "receiver's certificates."

77. What are registered bonds? Coupon bonds? What are the advantages and disadvantages of each form? What are redeemable bonds?

78. What are convertible bonds? What are their advantages and disadvantages to the corporation?

CHAPTER XII

79. What is a promoter? Does he have a legitimate and useful function or not? Give your reasons.

80. What is meant by the promoter's "discovery" of a proposition? Illustrate in detail with reference to some hypothetical case, such as a new gold mine in Alaska or a proposed creamery in a small country town.

81. What is meant by "assembling" a proposition? Illustrate in detail with reference to the same hypothetical case used in the previous question.

82. What are the first steps in financing a proposition? What is the advantage of carrying the development of the proposition as far as practicable before asking outsiders to supply funds?

83. Why should a promoter usually endeavor to raise more money in advance of complete development of a proposition than he expects will be needed?

84. Why is it usually better for a promoter to sell to a large number of small buyers than to a small number of large buyers?

85. To whom should a promoter go first, generally speaking, for funds? Why?

86. Show how the principles of promotion laid down are applied in the illustration given in the text.

CHAPTER XIII

87. Why are professional promoters usually unsuccessful in the long run?

88. Why do lawyers and bankers in small communities do a considerable amount of promotion work? To

what extent do the large metropolitan bankers and promoters enter the field of promotion?

89. What are the advantages of engineering firms as promoters?

90. Is a promoter in any sense an agent of his corporation? A promoter buys a manufacturing plant for $10,000 and sells it to a corporation which he promotes for $20,000, representing this latter sum to be the price he paid for the plant: is he legally entitled to his $10,000 profits? If not, what course may he pursue in order to evade the law?

91. Why is it difficult to enforce the principle that misleading statements by a promoter are fraudulent?

92. A promoter makes a contract on behalf of his corporation which is not yet formed: how may the corporation become bound by this contract without formally ratifying it?

93. How did the promoters of the Rubber Goods Manufacturing Company receive their pay? Of the American Smelting and Refining Company? In general what two plans of determining a promoter's profits are most commonly used?

94. What are the chief risks and tasks that a promoter must generally assume?

95. Do you think that promoters in general are or are not overpaid? Give your reasons.

CHAPTER XIV

96. Why is there a strong tendency toward consolidation among small as well as among large industrial establishments?

97. What are the principal difficulties that are apt

to confront a promoter who undertakes to consolidate several existing concerns?

98. Describe briefly the process of "discovering" a consolidation.

99. What is the usual method of "assembling" a consolidation? What is a "basis of consolidation"? What are the characteristic features of the two agreements cited in the text?

100. Why is it important for the promoter of a consolidation to consider with especial care the means of providing his new corporation at the outset with sufficient cash?

101. Why does the promoter of a consolidation generally try to raise cash by means of a bond issue? How may he manage to dispose of bonds issued by a new corporation with small or uncertain assets?

102. How does the problem of forming a large consolidation differ from the problem of forming a small consolidation?

103. What is the usual basis of consolidation or exchange and how is it determined?

104. What was the basis of exchange in the formation of the Interborough-Metropolitan Company? In what respects was it faulty?

CHAPTER XV

105. What were the conditions under which the steel business of the United States was conducted in the decade, 1890–1900?

106. What were the chief steel companies in the field in 1901 and why had most of them been formed in the three years, 1898–1901?

107. What is meant by "integration" of an industry? How did this factor operate to bring about the formation of a great steel combination?

108. Why was not the promotion of the United States Steel Corporation an especially difficult task? Why were the four Moore companies included in the combination? What was the original capitalization of the United States Steel Corporation?

109. Was the prospectus issued by the promoting syndicate misleading? How much cash did the syndicate furnish?

110. What were the approximate profits of the promoting syndicate?

111. What percentage of the stock of the underlying companies was secured by the Steel Corporation? Give from memory a list of some of the important assets of the corporation.

112. What have been the principal additions to the Steel Corporation? Give briefly the terms of the Hill ore lease and of the Tennessee Coal, Iron and Railroad Company deal. What is the approximate cost of the steel rail mill at Gary, Indiana?

113. Describe briefly the preferred stock conversion plan of 1902. What objections were raised to the plan? What important changes in the interior financial organization of the corporation have been made?

114. Give briefly the argument tending to show that the Steel Corporation is greatly over-capitalized. Give briefly the argument on the other side of the question.

115. What in general is the policy of the Steel Corporation toward its employés? Do the subsidiary companies of the corporation compete with each other?

116. What are the principal outstanding securities of the Steel Corporation? What reasons may be given

for expecting that these securities over a period of years will rise in value?

CHAPTER XVI

117. Name the four methods of selling corporate securities.

118. What are the characteristics of a good prospectus? Why are statements in speculative prospectuses usually vague?

119. Show that the characteristic features of speculative prospectuses are present in the example cited in the text.

120. What are the characteristics of strictly investment prospectuses? Is it safe to assume that these characteristics are never apparent except when the security offered is of the highest grade?

121. What would be the characteristics of an ideal prospectus?

122. What are the advantages and disadvantages to a corporation of selling its securities through large bond and banking houses?

123. What are the characteristics of large, high-class banking houses in contrast to disreputable concerns and what are the essential factors that make a proposition acceptable to them?

124. What are the usual banking house methods of selling securities? Do such houses guarantee the safety of the securities they sell?

CHAPTER XVII

125. Name the principal stock exchanges of the United States.

126. What percentage of the securities handled on the New York Stock Exchange are "listed"? What are the requirements for listing?

127. What is the "curb" market and what classes of securities are bought and sold in this market?

128. Describe briefly the method of handling transactions on the floor of a stock exchange.

129. What is the relative importance of speculative as compared with investment business, and what function is performed by the speculative business?

130. Describe the process of buying securities "on margin."

131. Describe the process of selling securities "short."

132. What are the characteristics of stock exchange houses in contrast to "bucket shops"?

133. Into what three classes may Wall Street speculators be divided?

134. Give from memory a brief review of the characteristics of the Wall Street security market.

135. What measures may be taken to stimulate speculative interest in a security that is about to be issued?

136. With what object is a syndicate frequently formed to assist in the flotation of a security?

137. By the use of what methods may the price of a stock market security be manipulated and kept under control?

CHAPTER XVIII

138. What is underwriting? How did the practice and the word originate?

139. What are the chief advantages to the corporation in having its new issues underwritten?

140. What are the advantages to the buyers of securities?

141. When is underwriting inadvisable? What is your opinion as to the merits of the Pennsylvania Railroad controversy referred to in the text? Give your reasons.

142. Why do the underwriting houses in almost every case band themselves together into syndicates?

143. Describe three types of syndicates.

144. Describe the type of syndicate in which the sale of the security is pooled.

145. Describe the type of syndicate in which the underwritten issue is distributed among the members of the syndicate.

146. Name some of the principal underwriting houses. What is the distinction between a bank and a banking house?

CHAPTER XIX

147. Why are underwriting syndicate agreements frequently quite informal?

148. Make an abstract showing the principal points covered in the agreement of the syndicate formed to underwrite the preferred stock conversion of the United States Steel Corporation.

149. Mention two general characteristics of underwriting agreements.

150. With what three classes of corporations do underwriting syndicates deal?

151. What are the peculiar problems and difficulties involved in underwriting the security issues of new or speculative corporations?

152. Review from memory the example of speculative underwriting given in the text and make sure that you understand thoroughly all the operations involved. What conditions made possible the construction of a new plant in this case wholly with borrowed funds? What principles followed in this case are applicable in all cases where it is desired that an undeveloped corporation should borrow as much as possible?

CHAPTER XX

153. What mistake is frequently made in the investment of the original capital funds of a corporation?

154. What are the advantages of the installment method of getting funds for a corporation only as the funds are needed?

155. What are the disadvantages of this method?

156. What are the other possible methods of getting cash as needed, when the total amount necessary cannot be accurately foreseen?

157. What considerations determine how large an amount must be invested by a corporation in fixed capital? What is working capital?

158. What are the four forms which working capital may take?

159. What factors determine how large an amount of working capital should be carried by a corporation?

160. Of the companies named in the text which one

has the largest percentage of working capital to gross business? Can you suggest any reason?

161. What are the five factors that immediately affect working capital and determine its amount? Why do railroads require only a small proportion of working capital?

162. About how much working capital did the Pennsylvania Railroad Company carry in 1908? Why was this amount greater than that carried by most railroad companies?

163. Why is it of the utmost importance that a corporation should be supplied with the proper amount of working capital?

CHAPTER XXI

164. Draw up from memory a model corporate income statement, arranging the items in their proper order.

165. By what common methods may a company's statement of gross earnings be padded?

166. What expenditures and what reserves should always be included under the head of operating expenses?

167. What are the causes of depreciation? What is a depreciation reserve? What method of allowing for depreciation has been in common use among steam and electric railroad companies? Is a depreciation reserve usually set aside as a separate sum to be invested outside the corporate business?

168. Why should "income from other sources" be stated separately? Why should cumulative preferred dividends be paid regularly, if practicable?

169. Should a corporation ordinarily pay out all its profits in the form of dividends to its stockholders? If not, why not?

170. What four factors determine the amount of profits? What industries are apt to have the most regular profits? Why are the profits of railroad equipment companies so variable?

171. Why is it desirable that a corporation should establish and maintain from year to year a regular dividend rate? How may regularity of dividends be secured in spite of irregularity of profits?

172. Why is great prudence and foresight on the part of the directors in declaring dividends essential to the best interests of a corporation?

CHAPTER XXII

173. What are the two important classes of betterments?

174. What are the three important sources of funds for betterments?

175. What are the advantages of providing for betterments by appropriations from earnings?

176. What are the two objections to this method?

177. What three motives may lead stockholders to oppose a policy of providing for betterments by appropriations from earnings? How do corporation officers sometimes manage to follow this policy without the consent of even a majority of stockholders?

178. Review briefly from memory the case of the Lehigh Valley Railroad Company and show how President Walters for some years pursued the policy referred to above.

179. Show how the Union Bag and Paper Company is now profiting by reason of having previously pursued this policy.

180. When and how may funds for betterments safely be borrowed?

181. What policy as to provision for betterment expenditures is followed by the Pennsylvania Railroad?

182. What are the comparative merits of bond and of stock issues as means of raising funds for betterments?

CHAPTER XXIII

183. Define "surplus."

184. Give and discuss briefly four sources of surplus.

185. What is the fifth source of surplus? Can a surplus be built up to any considerable amount by this method?

186. What was the policy of most of the industrial trusts as to surplus in the first few years of their existence? What were the results of their policy?

187. How may a surplus be invested? What general principle should be followed?

188. What is meant by using the surplus as a "rainy day fund"? What companies follow this practice? What is the argument in its favor? What are its disadvantages?

189. What is the usual practice in this country with reference to the use of a surplus?

CHAPTER XXIV

190. What should be the effect on dividends of putting a surplus back into the property of a corporation? Is the effect ever to increase dividends in a proportion greater than the proportion of surplus so invested to the original corporate capital? If so, when?

191. How may stock-watering be a method of distributing a surplus to stockholders? Give an illustration. Why is it that a stock paying a regular dividend of 4 per cent often sells for more than half as much as a stock paying an equally regular and certain dividend of 8 per cent?

192. What are subscription privileges? How may they be used as a method of distributing surplus?

193. How does a subscription privilege give an opportunity for cheap investment? What four methods may be used by stockholders in order to secure quick cash profits?

194. What is the method known as the "subsequent sale"? What are the objections to its use?

195. What is the "short selling" method? What is the objection to its use?

196. What is the method known as "sale of old stock"? Why cannot it always be used.

197. What is the method known as "sale of rights"? What is meant by a "right" in New York? What does the same word mean in Philadelphia? What is the objection to the use of this method?

198. What factors determine the theoretical value of a right? What is the formula commonly used on the New York Stock Exchange? Why is the market value of a right usually less than its theoretical value?

199. Is the granting of privileged subscriptions a method of stock watering? Are they objectionable on that account?

CHAPTER XXV

200. What good reason can you give for taking up the study of corporate manipulation?

201. Is it true that the corporate form favors manipulation? Why?

202. Is any force at work in the financial and industrial world which has a strong tendency to check manipulation?

203. What four classes or bodies of persons may endeavor to manipulate a corporation for their own benefit?

204. How may high salaries be used as a method of manipulation?

205. How may the power to bind a corporation by purchases and contracts become a means of manipulation? Is it usually possible to find a legal remedy or punishment?

206. How may the power to form new companies to handle especially profitable business be used as a method of manipulation? How was this principle applied by Commodore Vanderbilt?

207. How may a corporate officer manipulate a corporation by reason of having "inside" information?

208. Is there reason to think that the use of these four methods of manipulation is not uncommon?

CHAPTER XXVI

209. Why do not directors who wish to manipulate a corporation in their own interest enrich themselves by voting exorbitant fees to themselves? What four methods do such directors commonly use?

210. How may directors misuse their power to make contracts on behalf of their corporation? Illustrate by reference to the case of the Minnesota railroad company cited in the text.

211. Why do not the courts interfere in such cases?

212. How may directors manipulate by forming new companies or transferring credit or assets of their company to some other company? Give an illustration.

213. State a few methods of juggling the accounts of corporations which are not infrequent. How may directors profit by juggling the accounts of their corporation?

214. What is meant by "window-dressing"? How may it be used by directors as a method of manipulation?

215. What remedies for this kind of manipulation may be suggested?

216. How may directors secure gain for themselves by inflicting loss or even bankruptcy on their corporation? Give two illustrations.

217. Review the essential features of the case cited in the text. How might the manipulation of the corporation in this case have been prevented?

CHAPTER XXVII

218. How may stockholders fraudulently secure profit for themselves at the expense of the creditors of the corporation?

219. What are the essential facts in the well-known case of Chicago and Alton Railroad Company?

220. How may subsidiary companies be used as a

means of manipulating a corporation and defrauding creditors? Illustrate.

221. Review the main facts in the Central of Georgia Railway case cited in the text.

222. Show how the minority stockholders in a corporation may be "squeezed" by wilful mismanagement on the part of the majority stockholders and illustrate by reference to the case of the Olympic Theatre Company cited in the text.

223. Review from memory the series of transactions in the real estate proposition cited in the text and show exactly how the minority stockholders in the Long View Land Company were defrauded.

224. Review from memory the series of operations carried on by L. A. Ehrenbahn cited in the text and show how they all worked in favor of the manipulation of his deceased brother's estate in his own interest.

225. Mention four measures preventive of manipulation that should be taken by honest stockholders.

CHAPTER XXVIII

226. Distinguish between "true" and "legal" insolvency.

227. Mention four possible causes of true insolvency.

228. What are the chief causes, according to Bradstreet's table, of legal insolvency? What is the real meaning of the phrase "lack of capital" when used in this connection?

229. What were the two causes, according to the *Wall Street Journal,* of the failure of the Detroit, Toledo and Ironton Railway Company in 1909?

230. Mention three immediate causes of legal insolvency in addition to "lack of capital."

231. What is bankruptcy? Can a corporation become a voluntary bankrupt? Can all corporations become involuntary bankrupts? Is dissolution of the corporation a common method of handling insolvency? If not, why not?

232. What is a "bill in chancery"? By whom may it be presented? How may a friendly receiver for a corporation be obtained? What courts have jurisdiction in cases of corporate insolvency and receiverships?

233. What, briefly stated, are the duties of the receiver of a failed corporation?

234. From what source does he obtain his authority? How are his powers limited? May he incur debts binding on the insolvent corporation? Does he receive a fee?

CHAPTER XXIX

235. Why is it usually necessary and desirable to reorganize large insolvent corporations rather than to sell their property and distribute the assets among the creditors?

236. Why is the formation of committees usually the first step in reorganization? How are these committees appointed? How much authority do they possess? How may a general reorganization committee be formed.

237. Why are bondholders usually ready to agree to a reorganization rather than foreclose and force a sale and distribution of assets?

238. What are the main problems and difficulties that confront a general reorganization committee? How

are the relative standing and value of the various issues of mortgage bonds and other claims on the corporation determined? What concession is usually made to the stockholders of the corporation?

239. Name the four main objects of every reorganization. Why is it necessary usually to raise considerable amounts of cash?

240. What are the three possible methods of raising cash? Why do almost all reorganizations of insolvent corporations involve assessments on security holders? How large may the assessments on stockholders be made? Under what circumstances may bondholders be induced to pay assessments?

241. What three classes of fixed charges are usually reduced in reorganization? What threat may be used to force an acceptance of a reasonable reduction? What principle is usually followed in determining the maximum total amount of fixed charges to be imposed upon the reorganized company?

242. How are bondholders usually compensated for the reduction in their yearly interest? What is the effect on the total capitalization of the company? What factors determine whether or not the reorganized company shall operate under the charter of the old company? Why is a voting trust frequently formed at the time of organization?

243. Summarize briefly from memory the principles of reorganization laid down in this chapter.

CHAPTER XXX

244. Sketch from memory the growth of the Santa Fe System. What were the effects on the company's

financial strength of the rapid expansion in the years 1884–1888?

245. What were the main results of the reorganization of 1889? What were some of the events that led up to the failure of the company in 1893?

246. What was the substance of the so-called English plan of reorganization? Why was it not adopted? What were the main features of the plan that was finally adopted? What have been the results of this reorganization?

247. Sketch from memory the growth of the Rock Island System.

248. Outline the plan of reorganization brought forward in 1902. What was the prime object of this reorganization? Was that object attained? Show how control of the Rock Island System may have been secured by the Moore crowd without any permanent outlay?

249. Why did the Westinghouse Company fail? What was the main problem that confronted the reorganization committees? What were the main features of the plan adopted?

INDEX

FINANCIAL MANAGEMENT
1880–1934

Volume 5

Edited and Introduced by
Morgen Witzel

THOEMMES

Financial Management, 1880–1934

Edited and Introduced by **Morgen Witzel**

Volume 1
Twenty Years of Inside Life in Wall Street, or Revelations of the Personal Experiences of a Speculator ... Illustrated (1880)
W. W. Fowler

Volume 2
Trusts, Pools and Corporations (1905)
William Z. Ripley

Volume 3
Corporation Finance (1910)
Edward S. Meade

Volume 4
Corporation Finance. An Exposition of the Principles and Methods governing the Promotion, Organization and Management of Modern Corporations (1909)
William H. Lough

Volume 5
Concentration and Control: A Solution of the Trust Problem in the United States (1914)
Charles R. van Hise

Credit and International Trade: How they Work in Practice (1934)
Barnard Ellinger

Volume 6
Problems in Business Finance (1921)
Edmund E. Lincoln

Volumes 7 and 8
Collected Articles and Chapters

Printed in England by Antony Rowe Ltd, Chippenham

CONCENTRATION AND CONTROL

A Solution of the Trust Problem in the United States

Charles R. van Hise

CREDIT AND INTERNATIONAL TRADE

How they Work in Practice

Barnard Ellinger

THOEMMES PRESS

This edition published by Thoemmes Press, 2001

Thoemmes Press
11 Great George Street
Bristol BS1 5RR, England

http://www.thoemmes.com

Financial Management, 1880–1934
8 Volumes : ISBN 1 85506 633 5

British Library Cataloguing-in-Publication Data
A CIP record of this title is available from the British Library

Publisher's Note

The Publisher has gone to great lengths to ensure the quality of this reprint but points out that some imperfections in the original book may be apparent.

This book is printed on acid-free paper, sewn, and cased in a durable buckram cloth.

CONCENTRATION AND CONTROL

A SOLUTION OF THE TRUST PROBLEM IN THE UNITED STATES

BY

CHARLES R. VAN HISE

AUTHOR OF "CONSERVATION OF NATURAL RESOURCES IN THE UNITED STATES," ETC.

REVISED

New York
THE MACMILLAN COMPANY
1914

PREFACE

It is the aim of this book to present an outline picture of the situation regarding concentration of industry in the United States, and to suggest a way to gain its economic advantages and at the same time to guard the interests of the public. The book is written because this is the most pressing problem now before the people and before Congress and state legislatures. No other problem is likely to have so large discussion in the political campaign now waging. If this book has the good fate to assist in the rule of enlightenment, reason, fair play, mutual consideration, and toleration, and thus advance the solution of the problem, the author will have been repaid many fold for his labor in its preparation.

The scope of the treatment does not include the public utilities. They are only considered in so far as their development and control throw light upon the other industries.

The reader who is familiar with trust literature will recognize the influence of Ely's "Monopolies and Trusts," Jenks's "The Trust Problem," von Halle's "Trusts or Industrial Combinations of the United States," Ripley's "Trusts, Pools, and Corporations," Montague's "Trusts of To-day," Nolan's "Combinations, Trusts, and Monopolies," Collier's "Trusts," Wyman's "Control of the Market," and Macrosty's "Trust Movement in British Industry."

Aside from these standard works, the most important sources of information in presenting a picture of the situation as it is at the present time are the special reports on manufactures in 1905 by the Census Office, reports of the Commissioner of Corporations upon Standard Oil, tobacco, steel, beef, lumber, and water powers, and the hearings and reports before the committees of the Sixty-second Congress. Especially important in this connection have been the hearings before the United States Senate Interstate Commerce Committee, the report of Mr. Hardick for the special Committee of the House of Representatives to investigate the Sugar Refining Industry, and the reports of the House Committee of Investigation for the United States Steel Corporation.

Further, I had the opportunity to see the manuscript of a book now published by Dr. Charles McCarthy, upon "The Wisconsin Idea," from which I have taken material concerning the situation in that state. Professor T. K. Urdahl has prepared for insertion a summary account of the steel combinations of Germany. Professor Richard T. Ely and Professor Urdahl have kindly read the manuscript and made many suggestions of value to me. Professor E. A. Gilmore has done the same for the chapter upon the law regarding coöperation. To these men I am especially indebted. Also I have had many valuable suggestions from other members of the staff of the University of Wisconsin in the departments of political science, political economy, history, and sociology. Finally, a number of the students in that university, under the direction of Mr. W. I. King, have given me important assistance in looking up decisions and summarizing material along special lines; these are S. A. Barrett, W. K. Braasch, Harlow Brown, F. A. Buechel, N. B. Bunin, W. H. Butt, J. S. Josiassen, J. C. Pritzlaff, John Schmidt, R. A. Weir, E. E. Witte.

In preparing the book, it has been the purpose to put in a small volume the information which is essential to reach a sound conclusion regarding the handling of the great problem of concentrations of industry, both in the way of legislation and administration. Following a statement of facts, the conclusions of the author are given in these matters; and it is hoped that these may appeal to the judgment of the reader. However, even if the conclusions are not followed in all respects, it is still hoped that the summary of facts bearing on the problem of concentration may be helpful.

The material published in the magazines and newspapers, even much of the testimony before the committees of Congress, shows a lamentable lack of comprehension of the facts involved in concentration of industry; and in many cases conclusions are presented without taking into account more than a very small part of the facts. It is hoped that a brief and clear presentation of the more important factors of the problem may help in leading to logical thinking, and thus assist in reaching a consensus of opinion which may finally result in sound remedial legislation.

CHARLES R. VAN HISE.

The University of Wisconsin,
April, 1912.

TABLE OF CONTENTS

CHAPTER I

THE GENERAL FACTS REGARDING CONCENTRATION

CHAPTER II

SOME IMPORTANT ILLUSTRATIONS OF CONCENTRATION

CHAPTER III

THE LAWS REGARDING COÖPERATION

CHAPTER IV

THE SITUATION IN OTHER COUNTRIES

CHAPTER V

REMEDIES

CONCENTRATION AND CONTROL

INTRODUCTION

The history of industry in the United States may be divided into two great periods, that antecedent to the Civil War of 1861–1865, and that following this conflict. In the years preceding the Civil War the Middle West became settled. A few railroads had crept as far west as the Mississippi River. The large cities east of that great north-south water thoroughfare were thus connected. The railroads were wide apart; their efficiency as compared with present times was small. West of the Mississippi River the population was sparse. That part of the country was still in its frontier stage, with the exception of portions of California and Oregon.

The Civil War divides two industrial periods.

Under the conditions above given many small manufactories had grown up to meet the needs of the communities in which they existed. Indeed manufacture in a small way had begun in the eastern cities before the end of the eighteenth century.

During the first half of the nineteenth century there was steady and slow expansion of manufacture, not mainly by increasing the size of plants which already existed, but by the multiplication of plants wherever a clientele was found in the township, county, or district. Thus in the Middle West during these times almost every community had its gristmill run by the power of the adjacent creek or small river. Similarly there were many small plants for the smelting of iron. For the most part these were located adjacent to small banks of iron ore, and especially in districts where coal and limestone were near at hand to serve for fuel and flux. The great drift to the cities had not yet begun, and a large proportion of the population was rural, 87.5 per cent in 1850, and 83.9 per cent in 1860.

THE SELF-SUFFICIENT COMMUNITY

The farmstead a workshop.

The farmer in the sparsely settled districts of the Middle West was largely self-sufficient. For heat he cut his own wood. He raised his own wheat and corn, took the same to the adjacent mill and returned, after paying proper toll, with flour and corn meal for his family and bran for his stock. He raised and killed his own meat; in the winter he had fresh meat; in the summer, salt pork and corned beef. As a matter of course each farmer raised his own vegetables; he had cows which furnished him with milk, butter, and perhaps cheese; he had his poultry yard, which might include chickens, geese, and ducks. The farmer of the North produced his own wool and many had a crop of flax. In the South cotton was the stable for textiles. In the earlier part of the nineteenth century the wool was cleaned and carded at the house, but at a little later stage of development was taken to a factory in the adjacent small town to be cleaned and made into rolls ready for spinning. The equipment of the farmer's house included the spinning wheel and often the loom. With spinning wheel the wool and flax were made into yarn or thread to be later transformed into stockings, mittens, or cloth. The home loom produced either somewhat coarse cloth or carpets. Cotton very early found its way to the factories, which before the Civil War were largely located along the streams of New England. The village or town contained a shoemaker, whose raw material frequently came from leather supplied by the farmer. In a town of a few thousand inhabitants, there was likely to be a small agricultural implement factory.

Not every farmstead would have all of the equipment indicated, but all would be found in the neighborhood; and by barter among the farmers, or trade between the farmers and the villagers, the chief necessities not produced at home were supplied.

The articles not produced in a community were mainly those which are relatively light as compared with their value, sugar, tea, coffee, starch, tobacco, and cloth-cotton or woolen.

These were the staples which the farmer purchased from the sales of a part of his wheat or other crop.

From the above, it is apparent that each community of fair size was essentially self-sufficient; and this was true without reference to the different parts of the United States, although there were differences as to the approach to completeness of the self-sufficient character of the community, the approach to this situation being nearer in the North than in the South. A city, and in many cases a county, if cut off from the rest of the world would have gotten along without any special hardship. Some luxuries and conveniences would have been missed, but no far-reaching change would have been made in the habits of the community.

The situation above described has now ceased to exist for the United States, with the exception of those communities which, isolated by natural barriers, have been left behind in the industrial movement. Some such communities have remained nearly as they were a hundred years ago, not affected by the great stream of progress which has moved past them. In the coves of the Great Smoky Mountains to-day may be found essentially the situation described, and that not more than twenty or thirty miles from a city of considerable size, for instance, Cades and Tuckaleeche coves, a short distance east of Knoxville. In one of those coves, only a few years ago, I saw upon the porch of a little cabin the complete change from wool to stockings going on at the same time, one of the three daughters carding the wool, the second spinning it into hard yarn, and the third knitting it into stockings. What is true for the coves in this country still obtains for great regions in less-developed countries. For instance, in Brazil, in the province of Minas Geraes, the people are substantially self-sufficient. The articles which they raise are not the same as those produced in the United States. Their products are beans, bananas, other fruits, tobacco, coffee, etc. In the district are still running many small bloomeries for the manufacture of iron, the most primitive type known to man. From the blooms are wrought iron for rods, nails, horseshoes, etc. The walls

Self-sufficient communities still exist.

of the houses are constructed of a lacework of poles between which mud is filled in, and the roof is of tile burned from clay close at hand.

THE CIVIL WAR AND CONCENTRATION

In the United States, before the Civil War, industry was dispersed, the shops and factories being small; indeed, every farm to a considerable extent was a shop and factory. In any community the shops and factories mainly supplied the needs of the people.

The Civil War demanded large scale operations.

The Civil War, the most gigantic strife which to that time had existed among men, required that things be done on a great scale. More than a million and a half of men were in the field at one time from the North and the South together. The North built up the greatest navy that the world had then seen. The great armies required similar equipment for more than a million men, — a million blankets, a million muskets, etc. The artillery required great quantities of iron, and the newly devised monitors more. Metal was used upon a scale never before approached in this country. Above all, the million men must be fed. Thus as a result of the demands of civil strife the large manufactory grew up especially adapted to producing the materials and munitions of war. These supplies must be transported to serve a vast and shifting army.

But even more important than the great factory was the training of many thousands of men, both South and North, to do things in a large way through the use of a multitude of men, in order that a given big result might be reached at a definite time and place.

One of the most far-reaching effects of the Civil War was the acceleration of concentration under the tremendous necessity to do things on a great scale.

THE DEVELOPMENT OF TRANSPORTATION AND COMMUNICATION

Beginning with the Civil War the period of concentration in industry was on; but a condition precedent to its full growth was the development of transportation and communication.

Following the Civil War came the time of great railway building. The increase in the number of miles of railway in the United States by decades from 1850 to 1910 and the percentages of increase per decade are shown by the following table: —

Table 1. Railway Extension by Decades since 1850[1]

Year	Miles	Per Cent
1850–1860	9,012 to 36,626	306.0
1860–1870	36,626 to 52,922	44.4
1870–1880	52,922 to 93,262	76.3
1880–1890	93,262 to 166,703	78.7
1890–1900	166,703 to 194,262	16.4
1900–1909	194,262 to 238,356	22.6

Concurrently with the expansion of the railways was the extension of the telegraph lines, and finally, with the centennial exhibition in 1876, came the telephone. When the Union Pacific Railroad was completed in 1869, it was thought to be a mighty achievement; and it was accomplished only through liberal, indeed extravagant, federal grants and guaranties. At the present time there are six continental roads stretching from the Mississippi to the Pacific coast. Also the increase in the railway mileage east of the Mississippi has gone on with accelerating speed.

Railways everywhere.

Thus the country is now linked together by agencies of transportation and communication. A large proportion of the population lives within a half dozen miles from a railway; it is only in the sparsely settled sections of the country that a railway is ten or twenty miles distant. Railway speeds and weights have been increased. A few trains move passengers and the more valuable freight a thousand miles in twenty-four hours. A single train with one locomotive may carry five thousand tons of iron ore. The telegraph and the telephone make communication instantaneous.

[1] Poor's "Manual of Railroads," 1910.

Decreasing freights.

The freight and passenger rates have steadily fallen. In 1864, the charge on a bushel of wheat, in carload lots, from Chicago to New York, was from 48 to 96 cents; in 1902, 7.8 to 9.6 cents, one sixth to one tenth as much. The heavier, cheaper products, such as coal and iron ore are transported in great quantities at a cost of about one fifth of a cent per ton mile, and the rates for such commodities at various places are less than one half a cent a ton mile. It may cost the farmer who lives twenty miles from a railroad more to get his wheat to the station than it does from the railroad point to the central market.

It is not meant to imply that the railways are the only means of transportation, although from the present point of view they are dominant

Navigable streams.

Before railways existed, navigable streams furnished means of communication and transportation for commodities heavy and light for those communities which were fortunate enough to be thus reached. Thus there grew up in the early part of the nineteenth century a great traffic upon the Mississippi, Ohio, and upon many other rivers of smaller size. The Great Lakes furnished cheap transportation from Buffalo to Chicago and the head of Lake Superior. Inevitably, settlement and development proceeded much more rapidly along the naturally navigable waters than elsewhere. But even where the conditions were most favorable, navigable waters furnished transportation facilities to only a small part of the country, and for that part at a very low speed.

The vanishing water traffic.

The next stage in transportation development was the system of canals. The Erie Canal connected the Hudson and the Great Lakes. Many other less important canals were built. But even at best the construction of canals was expensive; the transportation of materials upon them slow; and only a small part of the country was ever reached by them. With the era of railroad development, canals began to wane. Many of them were acquired by railroad companies and put out of commission. Upon the Mississippi itself, through the acquisition of terminals, purchasing boat lines, cutting rates, refusing to prorate, etc. the railroad companies have reduced river transportation above St. Louis almost to a negligible quantity.

The country as a whole, even at the present time, has very few good highways. Only a few sections of the country have well-made roads. Before the Civil War, and locally since, until our own time, toll roads have connected some of the great cities. Upon the toll and free public roads wheel vehicles move; but before the automobile appeared speeds were limited to ten miles per hour, and quantities to a few tons per load. Consequently, by 1875 railroads had a leading place in transportation in this country, and they are now dominant.

Transportation and concentration.

It is not meant to imply that the development of transportation went on without concentration of industry taking place at the same time. Naturally there was action and reaction between them. Without concentration of industry and, consequently, large amounts of goods to ship, the railroads would not have developed so rapidly; and on the other hand, without the development of transportation and communication, concentration of industry would have been impossible.

The development of transportation and communication furnished the fundamental basis for concentration of industry, because through them it became possible at a moderate cost to transport goods long distances in a short time and easy to communicate with the customer who desired goods. As soon as the freight rates became sufficiently low so that the advantages of concentration were greater than the cost of freight and doing business at a distance, the small concerns began to suffer in competition with the large manufactory.

The treatment of the subject of concentration and control will be divided into five chapters: I, The General Facts regarding Concentration; II, Some Important Illustrations of Concentration; III, The Laws Regarding Coöperation; IV, The Situation in Other Countries; and V, Remedies.

CHAPTER I

THE GENERAL FACTS REGARDING CONCENTRATION

THE general facts regarding concentration of industry will be considered under the sections: 1, The economic advantages of concentration; 2, The causes of concentration; 3, The purposes of concentration; 4, The kinds of business most likely to become concentrated; 5, The extent of concentration; 6, The forms of organization; 7, The kinds of competition; 8, The break-down of competition; 9, The wastes of competition.

SECTION 1

THE ECONOMIC ADVANTAGES OF CONCENTRATION

What are the economic advantages of manufacturing in a large plant and doing business on a large scale, and how important are they? Different industries differ among themselves very greatly in these respects, and any general statement will need modification when applied to a particular case. What is said will be more applicable to those groups of industries which are better adapted for concentration.

(1) *The Handling of Material.* — The handling of material on a large scale in itself gives great economy. In any manufactory the material must be there assembled. For instance, if it be an iron manufactory, and we have a primitive bloomery depending upon an adjacent bank of ore, it will not pay to go to any great expense in providing for transportation of the ore to the bloomery; and the ore will be hauled in a cart. When the bloomery changes to the blast furnace, the quantity of ore needed will be so great that the ore is brought with trams or some kind of mechanical haulage. The same is

true of the coal. Thus the economies due to mere magnitude of operation in this industry become very great. Also in the manufacturing process itself the large furnace has an advantage in economy of fuel and efficiency over the small furnace.

(2) *The Use of Machinery and Departments.* — In the large manufactory it is possible to use machinery to an extent not possible in the small establishment. The introduction of labor-saving machines is well known to be one of the greatest causes of economic efficiency. The illustration of the cotton gin is classic. Where there are many processes in the manufacture of an article, if the concern be a large one, it is possible to have a separate machine or a number of them for each process.

Similarly for different departments. In making agricultural implements, if the plant be a large one, the iron and wood departments will be separate. These again will be specialized for different lines of work. The parts of iron and wood will be assembled in another department; and finally the painting and varnishing will be done in still another.

(3) *Subdivision of Labor.* — In most manufactories an article must go through many processes before it is completed. In the old primitive shop, the shoemaker at the bench did all of the different stages of work in making the entire shoe. In the large manufactory the part that any one man does has been steadily lessened until now in the making of a single shoe many persons participate. In the making of a wagon or a binder in a large manufactory scores of people take part. In the wagon shop which served the country community one man, or one man with his helper, made the wagon in all its parts except that the iron in bars or rods was furnished to him. Specialization of labor is only possible in the large manufactory, and it is generally agreed that such specialization gives increased efficiency.

(4) *Integration.* — A further step in the development of concentration of industry is its integration; that is, a corporation handles not one stage of manufacture only, but a number or even all of the stages from the raw material to the

finished product. This again gives increased economy and efficiency, because all the different units of the integrated industry are in harmony, one with reference to the other. Thus the United States Steel Corporation mines its raw materials, assembles them, smelts the ore into pig iron, changes the iron to steel, and the steel into structural forms, — plate, wire, or nail. Other illustrations of integrated industries are oil, sugar, etc., described pp. 104–150.

While there is great economic advantage in integration for almost every industry, that of iron and steel furnishes one of the best illustrations. When the blast furnace was independent of the converter, the molten pig iron was allowed to cool, and was melted for the Bessemer converter. The steel from the converter was again allowed to cool in the ingot and was reheated before rolling into the rail. At the present time the molten pig iron goes to the converter, is transformed into steel, and then after solidification but before cooling goes to the rolls where it is wrought into rails. Similar methods are introduced for other products. The saving of energy by integration is great, as is also the saving in labor. Independent blast furnaces, Bessemer converters, and rolling mills cannot possibly give the economic efficiency of integrated establishments combining the three.

(5) *Parallel Consolidation and Specialization.* — The concentration of management goes not only to the point of the manufacture on a large scale, integration, and saving of by-products, but extends to the point of ownership of manufactories of the same general kinds at various points. Under these conditions it is possible to make the same product at the different plants, or to specialize the different manufactories under the same organization so that one shall handle one line of work, and another another. Further, the work of any one branch may become standardized and require comparatively little shifting or changing of machines. Thus the shapes, forms, and sizes of the manufactured iron which comes from a given plant may remain the same month after month, or even year after year; and this very greatly promotes efficiency. If the industry be tobacco, one manufac-

tory may produce cigarettes, and another cigars. A proof of the superior efficiency of completely equipped concerns is fully admitted in the case of tobacco, as is shown by the objections filed by Messrs. Brandeis and Levy against the plan of disintegration of the American Tobacco Company (see pp. 183–187). As counsels for the independent companies they say that no independent tobacco company is now completely equipped to do tobacco business covering all the main branches of the tobacco trade, and that any plan to restore competition will be ineffective which does not compel each of the elements of the disintegrated tobacco company to confine itself to one line of business. They state: "It follows that any corporation taking over a part of the plug tobacco business or smoking tobacco business of the trust shall not take over any of the cigarette or cigar business; that a corporation taking over a part of its cigarette business shall not take over any of its smoking tobacco business, plug tobacco business, or cigar business; and that a corporation taking over any part of the cigar business shall not take over any of its smoking tobacco business, plug tobacco business, or cigarette business."[1] There can scarcely be stronger evidence of the economic efficiency of parallel consolidation and specialization under a single corporation than the above remonstrance of Messrs. Brandeis and Levy upon behalf of the independent tobacco companies.

The consolidation in management of plants making the same class of products at different points is especially economical for those articles in which transportation is an important factor. Cross freights are avoided to a large extent when the manufactories of one district supply the markets of that district. For articles which are heavy as compared with their cost, for instance salt and steel rails, this factor may be one of controlling importance.

(6) *Saving By-products.* — A further advantage of magnitude is the use of by-products. The small manufactory

[1] Hearings before the Committee on Interstate Commerce United States Senate, Part VII, p. 319.

cannot spend much money in such utilization, although the coarser of them may be saved. In the production of meat, the by-products,—hides, fat, bone, etc. are a very important part of the income. These materials are much more largely utilized in the large abattoir than in the small slaughter-house.

For the great oil refiners, if kerosene be regarded as the chief, as it was the original product, then lubricating oil and gasoline are by-products. Also in addition to these scores of other by-products are saved. In fact for all chemical and metallurgical industries by-products are the source of a large part of the profits. But to save these materials economically requires large scale manufacture.

(7) *Consolidation of Allied Industries.* — The final stage in consolidation is the union of allied and connected industries. This frequently goes beyond integration, in that the lines of manufacture are absorbed which use as raw material the by-products of the central organization. Thus the United States Steel Corporation has begun the manufacture of cement, using slag, a by-product of the blast furnace, for that purpose; but the manufacture of cement is itself a great industry which requires a large and expensive plant, and slag is therefore a by-product which it is not possible to save except in plants of great magnitude.

The big beef firms have entered lines of business related to their own. Those having refrigerator cars have begun the transportation of fruit. They are largely interested in the stockyards. In order to use the by-products the packing house companies have formed fertilizer companies, soap companies, glue companies, curled hair companies, and felt companies; all of which industries are large users of materials furnished by the packing industry.

(8) *Keeping Establishments Up to Date.* — The large company uses only the most modern manufactories which have complete and highly efficient machinery and practices, including the latest labor-saving devices and the best technical improvements. The weak company will frequently continue to use an inadequate plant because it has not and cannot get sufficient capital to put its plant into an up-to-date

condition. The American Sugar Refining Company after organization built one large new plant fully equipped with the most modern machinery, simply as a safeguard in case of increased demand or stoppage of other factories. Shortly after it abandoned altogether a number of refineries acquired at the time of consolidation, because of their inefficient equipment or disadvantageous location, or both.

(9) *Investigating Departments.* — Not only is the large organization able to use the most modern methods, but it is able to have an investigating department in order that discoveries may be made for still further improvements. The economies which have come from such a department are strongly emphasized by many men connected with great organizations. The Cotton Oil Company has an experiment station. The Standard Oil Company carries on chemical investigations of the most elaborate and extensive kind in order to utilize fully the by-products of the oil; as a result of which they have on the market some three hundred by-products, many of which come from the part of the oil which otherwise would have been thrown away.[1] The United States Steel Corporation, the General Electric Company, and indeed practically all great organizations have investigating departments in which large sums of money are spent.

Mr. Louis Brandeis,[2] who is strongly opposed to the existence of large concentrations, recognizes the economic advantage of investigative departments to be so great as to threaten the practicability of retaining relatively small industrial units under the competitive system; this is shown by the fact that he urges that all investigations which are necessary for the advancement of applied science should be carried on by the government. Apparently, he does not realize the enormous expense that this proposal, if taken seriously, would entail. Says Mr. Brandeis, "Whenever industry requires for its advance investigations of the character which are so expensive that only a huge concern can assume

[1] Ernst von Halle, "Trusts or Industrial Combinations in the United States," pp. 66–67.

[2] Hearings before the United States Senate Committee on Interstate Commerce, Part XVI, p. 1169.

the burden, then it is the government's function to secure the information for all the people."

In favor of this position he cites the investigations by the government for the farmer. This illustration seems scarcely applicable, since the most distinctive feature of the farmer's business is the vast number of those following it and the average smallness of a single holding of land. Because of this the individual farmer is wholly incapable of carrying on the necessary investigations. Hence the government, national and state, has undertaken the function. The proposal of Mr. Brandeis, if carried to its logical conclusion, would blot out, or at least profoundly modify, our patent system, under which discoverers are protected to the extent of monopolistic use for a limited period. No stronger testimony than the proposal of Mr. Brandeis could be given as to the economic advantage of concentration of industry gained through investigating departments.

(10) *Business Advantages of Concentration.* — Thus far the industrial advantages of concentration only have been given. Upon the business side there are also great economies. Some of the more important of these are as follows: —

(*a*) Big organizations are able to buy in large quantities and thus gain the advantages of the lowest rates of purchase.

(*b*) Big organizations are able to sell in large quantities and most advantageously. A large part of the cost of business under new conditions is the marketing of products. In the marketing there are great costs in commercial travelers, in advertisements, etc. (see p. 89). With the large concentration the advertising cost per unit of sale is much lower than with the small industry. Work is organized so that a traveling salesman or agent does the work in a given community for a large concern instead of several for the different plants of that concern. When the American Steel Hoop and Wire Company was formed, about two hundred salesmen were discharged. Similarly with the formation of the whisky combination three hundred salesmen were spared. With the organization of the International Harvester Company the expense of marketing was reduced by $500,000 a year.

Marketing products.

(*c*) When there is a single great federated establishment, orders can be received at a central office and from that office distributed to the different plants as best required by efficiency in manufacture, taking into account the expense of transportation.

(*d*) Also the mere size of an establishment, so that it may be able to take a large order at almost any time and fill it promptly, gives a great advantage over smaller concerns.

Foreign trade and concentration.

(*e*) For entering foreign trade the business economies of concentration are undoubtedly very great. Sending agents to foreign countries to build up a trade for an industry is an expensive undertaking. Especially is this the case when the markets are already in the possession of foreign competitors. In this respect the great corporations of the country, such as the United States Steel Corporation and Standard Oil Company, have proved themselves to be economically superior to smaller organizations, more than 90 per cent of the export business in their respective lines being done by United States Steel and Standard Oil. Moreover, the foreign trade in iron and oil has been almost wholly built up since the organization of the steel combination and the Standard Oil Company.

(*f*) The losses through poor debts are less with large organizations than with small ones. Frequently where there are many organizations having keen competition with a large number of travelling salesmen, sales are made without careful reference to the ability of the purchaser to pay. To illustrate, it is stated that after the American Steel and Wire Company was formed, the loss from bad debts for the constituent companies was reduced from one half of one per cent to one twentyfifth of one per cent.[1]

Regulation of output.

(*g*) One of the greatest advantages of concentration with coöperation of the independent units is the regulation of production. As we shall see in other connections, with the competitive system, underproduction alternates with overbuilding and overproduction. Where instead of fierce competition there is coöperation (and this is only possible where there are large units), the great losses are avoided which re-

[1] "Trusts of To-day," G. H. Montague, p. 43.

sult from investments of capital in manufactories which run only a portion of the time and before they shut down produce more goods than can be sold at a profit.

Efficiency of capital.

(*h*) Another advantage of concentration is that a less amount of capital is necessary in order to handle a combined business than would be necessary if a great organization were subdivided. If a concern be fairly independent of the banks and the necessity to pay excessive rates of interest, it must keep a considerable amount of ready cash on hand to handle its business. A very large concern, in which the variation in the demands for the different products compensate for one another to some extent at least, is able to handle its business with a relatively small cash reserve. This is one of the advantages which the United States Steel Corporation has had since its organization. By keeping from $50,000,000 to $75,000,000 in cash, a very large amount as a whole, but rather small as compared with its total business, the corporation has always had sufficient money on hand to meet its needs without borrowing, and therefore has been independent of the banks at times of financial depression.

(11) *Opportunity for High Order of Ability.* — It may be that a final advantage of concentration will be the opportunity for the display of ability of the highest order. A farmer who can successfully run a dairy with twenty cows may fail with a hundred. A man who can handle a single manufactory may be unable to see the broader comparative aspects of a dozen. The manager of each factory will be required as before; but also there will be needed the man who, while giving large liberty to the individual manager, will see the work of the whole in its broader relations. Concentration of industry will demand the highest and best trained intellect along all lines.

Says Macrosty[1]: "Rule of thumb is dead in the workshop, the day is with the engineer and the chemist with their methods of precision; in the countinghouse and board room there is no longer a place for the huckster or gambler, the future is with the commercial statesman whether in a large individual business or a combination."

[1] "The Trust Movement in British Industry," H. W. Macrosty, p. 337.

(12) *Other Advantages of Concentration.* — Other advantages of concentration are frequently claimed. Among these are: steady employment of labor, better wages, better protection against industrial accidents, the maintenance of superior quality, etc. These points are not here introduced as advantages of concentration, since in reference to them there is a marked difference of opinion. In some cases it appears that concentration of industry has led to the steadier employment of labor, improvement in wages, and lessening of industrial accidents. In other cases the great industrial corporations have been careless or openly regardless of the conditions of the laboring population, and instead of improvement there has been no improvement or even retrogression. Theoretically the advantages mentioned should be possible with concentration, and under proper control they should become available; but they cannot be claimed as general advantages of the great corporations as they now exist. (See pp. 104–154.)

Wages and social conditions.

Total Advantages of Concentration. — It is not easy to give the economic advantages in terms of percentages for any industry which result from the large factory, the subdivision of labor, the full use of mechanical appliances, the specialization of departments, integration, utilization of by-products, entrance into allied industries, distribution of plants of the same kind, using only the most efficient plants, maintenance of investigating departments, economies of business management, and reduction of amount of capital; but it is safe to say that the gain is very great for the large concentration as compared with the small plant.

While percentages cannot be given, the economic advantages of concentration have been conclusively proved for many consolidations. Thus under the competitive system some businesses became greatly overbuilt, as, for instance, whisky distilling. At the time consolidation took place when the whisky trust was organized, it was found advantageous to concentrate the business in a few plants. It closed 68 of its 80 distilleries, doing the entire business of the country with the remaining 12, furnishing

Evidence of economies.

the same output, and in a short time even an increased output. Von Halle[1] mentions as evidences of efficiency that the cotton oil trust shortly after its formation closed more than a dozen of the small old-fashioned plants. The sugar trust after formation was able to supply the whole market with one fourth of its refineries. According to the census of 1900, many of its plants were idle. Under one of the pool arrangements in steel the Carnegie Company paid to a Maryland company which did not operate at all $300,000, this sum being paid to close the mill; but the form was gone through of having the orders come to this mill while the rails were supplied by the Carnegie Company. It was more economical to close the mill and pay $300,000 than to produce the rails in the smaller mill.[2]

Without further development of the economic gain of concentration, it is evident that the advantages are so great as to enable the large organizations to pay the freights to markets that are not local and to pay the expenses of marketing products at a distance. Thus transportation once developed, concentration became inevitable. As already indicated the two have acted and reacted; for once a market secured at a distance, freight and passenger service improved so as further to encourage the development of concentration, which in turn further assisted transportation, and so on continuously.

Small manufactories disappearing.

The small manufactory in the little town, except for specialities and patent-protected articles, has either disappeared for the most part under the stress of competition, or else by combination has become a unit of a larger organization. The larger proportion of the small manufactories of standard and widely used articles have been discontinued; but an occasional concern has been saved by becoming a part of a combination. Those whose years number fifty have seen the gristmill on the small stream become intermittent in its running, then cease altogether, although here and there one favorably located still continues its small business. The many widely dispersed

[1] Von Halle, Trusts, pp. 65–66.

[2] *Ibid*, pp. 62–63.

small furnaces for smelting iron ore have gone, and their place is taken by the relatively few great blast furnaces. No longer is the spinning wheel or the loom found in the house. The work has gone to the great factory located where labor is available and adjacent to some stream which furnishes adequate power, or where coal is sufficiently cheap so as to furnish energy at a reasonable rate. The shoemaker of the village has become the cobbler, the shoes are manufactured at great industrial centers, such as Boston and vicinity.

Growth of cities and concentration.

The concentration of industry during the past fifty years has been one of the chief factors which has led to the phenomenal growth of the cities, the inevitable centers for manufacture because of their transportational facilities and the abundance of labor. Thus Chicago, at the head of Lake Michigan, having cheap water transportation to all lake ports, and the center of the greatest railroad system in the world, has become a colossus among the manufacturing cities of the nation. The same is true of New York, the gate of the continent, and the great group of cities which cluster about that harbor. Boston and Philadelphia are centers less in importance only to the two mentioned.

Magnitude and efficiency.

While it seems clear that the above statement regarding the economic advantages of concentration cannot be gainsaid, there may be a limit beyond which additional economic advantages may not occur from further increase in magnitude or from federation of great establishments. Also in some industries in this country the concentration and federation may have gone beyond the stage of magnitude which does give economic advantage. This point of view has been strongly presented by Mr. Louis D. Brandeis.[1] Mr. Brandeis mentions a number of trusts which have been financial failures. He states that since the United States Steel Corporation was organized our foreign trade in iron has increased but slightly in ten years, from 1,114,000 tons to 1,533,000 tons; whereas the German foreign tonnage has increased during that time from 838,000 to 4,868,000; and that of the

[1] Hearings before the Interstate Commerce Committee, United States Senate, Part XVI, pp. 1146–1166.

United Kingdom from 2,213,000 to 4,419,000. On the other hand, he gives illustrations of manufactories in which the business is fairly competitive, as that of book paper, in which there has been a steady increase in efficiency and decline in price. Unfortunately the illustrations given do not prove the general case. Had the Standard Oil or American Tobacco companies been considered, instead of United States Steel, an immense expansion of foreign trade could have been shown.

Further, the question of prices is not the one under discussion at the present time; the question concerns the cost of production. It will be held in another place that the prices charged by the great organizations have been too high and that they should be lowered. Furthermore, if we consider only the cost of production we have dealt with but one half of the problem. As has been seen, the economic advantages which come from concentration are largely those on the business side of the enterprise, buying, selling, finance, etc. Therefore, the problem for consideration is not the cost of production at the factory, but the cost at which a given article can be placed upon the market.

Magnitude and cost of production.

Taking the entire problem into account, it is believed future quantitative investigations will show that concentration must go far in order to give the maximum of efficiency, although it is not held that it should go to the extent that the element of monopoly enters. If the public be able to secure a price based upon investment instead of capitalization, or what the traffic will bear, it is believed the price in most cases will be sufficiently low to justify the existing concentrations.

While it seems to the author that the weight of argument is strongly in favor of the increased efficiency of very large concentrations of industry upon the average, the opinions of Mr. Brandeis have been brought forward to show that this view is not universally accepted. The position which one holds at the present time for most industries must depend upon qualitative statements, since there have been few investigations of the cost accounting in the same industry for different magnitudes, and under similar conditions.

SECTION 2

CAUSES OF CONCENTRATION

Thus far only the inevitable and legitimate causes which have led to concentration have been considered. There are in addition very important promoting causes of concentration about the legitimacy of which there will be difference of opinion.

(1) *The Limited Liability Corporation.* — The first of these is the rise of the modern limited liability corporation. Before the Civil War an occasional manufactory had a capital of a million or even two million dollars. These concerns were usually partnerships rather than joint stock companies. The general corporation act of New York was passed in 1848. Similar acts were later passed in other states. These laws were taken little advantage of until after the Civil War. The limited liability company gives immensely greater opportunities in the way of magnitude than the partnership. The owner of stock in such a company is not responsible for the debts of the company beyond his investment in the stock. A partnership at best is limited to a few; the owners of a corporation may be thousands or even many thousands; thus even relatively small individual holdings may make possible a large capitalization. A corporation which would have been regarded as large before the Civil War may have the majority of the stock in holdings of $10,000 or less. In fact it is not too much to say that without the device of the modern limited liability corporation, it would not have been possible to unite the enormous capital necessary for the great industrial combination under the control of a small group of men, the officers and directors of a corporation.

(2) *The Protective Tariff.* — The second of the promoting factors is the tariff. It has been the policy of the United States to develop its industries and place a tariff upon foreign goods sufficient to protect the American manufacturer. The theory upon which such tariff has been based has varied from time to time. First, it was to protect the infant industry. The Republican party, still defending a protective

tariff, has now come to the principle that the tariff should be sufficient to compensate for the difference of labor cost at home and abroad. The Democratic party stands by the position that the tariff should be for revenue only. It will scarcely be held by any one familiar with the situation that either party, when responsible for change, has framed the tariff in accordance with the theory held. Whatever views one has regarding the tariff, it will be conceded by all competent persons that the tariff on many articles has been more than sufficient to pay the differences of cost of labor at home and abroad; that it has been greater than necessary to give the maximum revenue; and thus has afforded a margin beyond either of these principles to protect the home manufacturer. This has made possible a development of concentration in industry which might not otherwise have occurred. Not only so, but the high tariff, often prohibitive, has enabled the manufacturer to sell commodities at home as high as the tariff permitted and the markets would bear, and to dispose of his surplus in the foreign markets at a lower rate. This practice has been so common that no detailed evidence regarding it is needed, but one or two illustrations may be mentioned. The Steel Corporation sells its products abroad to meet the world's markets at a lower rate than the same articles are sold for at home where the freight is lower. Steel rails from the great steel companies of the United States cost the railway companies of Canada less than do the same kind of rails the companies of the United States.[1] As shown on another page, a similar situation obtained for Standard Oil, that article having been sold in the markets of various parts of the world at a much lower rate than in America, when transportation charges are taken into consideration. (See p. 108). The same situation has obtained to a large extent with respect to agricultural implements.

(3) *Railway Rebates and Drawbacks.* — Another important cause for the development of concentration in the past

[1] Hearings, House Committee of Investigation, Steel Corporation, No. 57, p. 5135.

has been secret arrangements between the railroad companies and manufacturing corporations under which rebates were given.

The published rates applied to the small or weak manufactory. Many large concerns in various lines of industry received rebates greater or less in quantity, and frequently so great as to make it possible for the large manufactory to sell at a profit; whereas the weaker competitor, obliged to pay the published tariff, could sell only at a loss. This practice was common before the interstate commerce law was passed in 1887, and has only ceased within a few years. It has had powerful influence in the concentration of industry, since the rebates were usually larger the stronger the corporation; and hence a strong impetus toward concentration.

Perhaps the best illustration of the importance of this factor in producing concentration was the Standard Oil Company, but the influence on other companies has scarcely been less important. In one respect Standard Oil perhaps surpassed all others in profiting by unfair freight rates, in that it not only received rebates upon its own shipments, but drawbacks upon the shipments of its competitors. In other words, the rebates which should have gone to the competitor went to the Standard Oil. Under these conditions the destruction of the weak corporations was inevitable.

(4) *Local Underselling.* — Another factor very influential in promoting concentration is that of local underselling, the purpose being to drive out the weaker competitor. The great corporation having the advantage of a large business and wide markets may sell even at a loss in a given community, until the competitor is obliged to discontinue, the loss to the large company being recouped by large profits elsewhere. This practice has been engaged in by many corporations; but probably the chief one was Standard Oil, which organization almost to the time of its dissolution followed this method of killing competition with great success. Not infrequently the Standard Oil Company used for the purpose a company which was supposed by the public

to be independent, but which secretly belonged to the Standard Oil.

(5) *Patents.* — Another factor favoring concentration is the control of patents. The patent itself gives monopoly. If to produce a given article a certain patent is necessary, all other competitors are driven out unless an equivalent result can be reached in some other way. A complicated manufacturing business is likely to have many details which are covered by patents, so that many great corporations have the partial protection of monopoly through scores of patents. Such organizations are illustrated by the Westinghouse and General Electric companies.

In some specialized lines of machinery, the patents may be so important as to become absolutely necessary for the industry, and in that case control may be secured by refusing to deal with a party unless all the machinery or all the material is purchased from the concern controlling the patents. This has been the practice of the United Shoe Machinery Company. Not only so, but this corporation has gone to the point of so fully controlling the machinery necessary for the cheap manufacture of shoes that it refuses to sell; it merely installs the machines in the factory at a rental. The Shoe Machinery Company has absorbed or driven out all its competitors.

(6) *Manufacturers' Rebates.* — Another practice of the large corporations, very successfully pursued, to secure the market, is to give a rebate upon the list price of the article at the end of a given period, provided the buyer has purchaesd exclusively from the corporation. This practice was very extensively followed by the American Tobacco Company. Thus, if at the end of the year a buyer had purchased only from that company, he could get a rebate of 5 to 7 per cent upon his purchases, the rate depending upon the magnitude of his business.

(7) *General Statements.* — It is now universally agreed that many of these practices are unfair and should be prohibited. That of rebates by the railroads for interstate transportation was forbidden by the interstate commerce law, and many

states have passed similar laws to apply within the states. While these laws were undoubtedly violated by the railroads upon an extensive scale after their passage, at the present time it is agreed upon all sides that rebates by railroads are morally indefensible; and it is believed that rebating has nearly ceased in consequence of investigations of commissions, federal and national, with attendant prosecutions.

The protection of the tariff still holds; but at the present time the tariff is being investigated by a commission and will probably be readjusted soon. It is generally agreed that such readjustment is necessary. The advantages gained from patents are legal under existing law, and they can only be overcome by a thorough revision of the patent laws.

The legality of giving rebates by manufacturers upon purchases made, provided they are exclusive, has been upheld by the courts in some cases; but such rebates are now regarded as contrary to law. In many of the states there is no law which prevents underselling to drive out a competitor, but in some states statutes and decisions place a ban on this practice (see pp. 170–202). Many people have now come to the point of view that corporations should be required to make their charges in different parts of the country correspond to factory charge plus transportation. It is fully understood that there would be great difficulty in carrying out this idea, since it is one of the fundamental conceptions of the competitive system that a man who owns a thing may sell or refuse to sell; and if he decides to sell, he is without restraint as to the price he may ask; also it has been a universally accepted principle of trade that it is legitimate to sell a large quantity of goods at a lower rate than smaller quantities.

Section 3

THE PURPOSES OF CONCENTRATION

The purposes which have led to federation and concentration, in addition to the economic advantages already considered, are the elimination of competition, the regulation of output and division of business and territory, the maintenance of prices, and the profits of readjustment.

(1) *Elimination of Competition.* — The elimination of competition is the most potent force which led to coöperation and combination. When in a village there are two competitors and they are able to coöperate, competition is partly eliminated; when they unite it is wholly eliminated. This principle extends in its operation from the country cross roads to the great industries. In another place it is shown that keen competition leads to lessening of profits and oftentimes to wiping out profits altogether, or even to loss. It is obvious that the situation may be met by the union of the competing concerns; thus competition itself frequently leads to combination. The elaborate investigation of the Industrial Commission of 1900 led to the conclusion that "among the causes which have led to the formation of industrial combinations, . . . competition, so common, so vigorous, that nearly all competing establishments were destroyed, is to be given first place." [1]

A study of the history of any one of the great combinations which exist in the United States will show that a main purpose in the establishment of the combination was the elimination of competition. Therefore only a single illustration will be mentioned. An elaborate investigation of the United States Steel Corporation shows that the first and most important of the purposes, not only in the formation of the groups constituting the steel corporation, but later in the union of the groups, was the elimination of competition.[2]

(2) *Regulation of Output and Division of Business and Territory.* — Under the competitive system, to be more fully discussed later, at times of large demand and prosperity, manufactories are likely to become overbuilt. Then follows overproduction in the attempt to reduce cost by a large output, and with this falling prices. When this situation is reached

[1] Industrial Commission, Preliminary Report on the Trusts.

[2] Hearings, House of Representatives, Investigation United States Steel Corporation, 53, Part I, p. 3638.

and a time of depression comes, the production of the factories running full time would far outrun the demands. Manufactories in an industry which would, at fair price, give a profit if built for the normal demands of the country, when overbuilt, often become unprofitable or run at a loss, at least for many concerns, because of inability to dispose of their goods, or because of interest on capital and depreciation when idle or not running full time, or partly both.

The extent to which overbuilding may go is illustrated by the whisky industry, which before the trust was formed had distilleries with a capacity three or four times as great as the demands of the country. When after a time of prosperity a time of depression came on, as in the panic of 1873, there was a strong desire on the part of the manufacturers to reduce the output of the different distilleries; but unless they were united, it was very difficult indeed to control them so as to make the output of each fairly proportional. This the manufacturers could not do through coöperation without breaking the law regarding restraint of trade. Thus greatly overbuilt, they were almost driven to combination to regulate output. A situation similar to that which led to the whisky combination led to combination in various industries.

Overbuilding and combination.

(3) *Maintenance of Prices.* — The competitive system inevitably leads to great irregularity in price. One of the chief purposes of all coöperation in industry is the maintenance of prices. When the demand exceeds the supply, prices will be high and there will be little tendency to cooperate; but when the supply exceeds the demand, there will be falling prices, and this leads to coöperation for their maintenance. The coöperations may take the form of agreements or pools, or may extend to consolidation. The extent of the control of prices will depend in large measure upon the proportion of the business which is included in the combination.

(4) *Profits of Promoters.* — The fourth important purpose of union and concentration are the profits to promoters and capitalists in putting through the reorganizations. At each

consolidation or reorganization, the capital obligations of the company are increased without the investment of additional money. The inflation takes the form of bonds or stocks, or partly both, of which the stock-holders get a large share, but great blocks often go to the promoters and underwriters.

As we have seen on another page, the American Tobacco Company was first formed; then there was another company formed, to which the American Tobacco Company was subordinate; and then another reorganization made the American Tobacco Company the dominant one. Similarly, the development of the United States Steel Corporation went through several stages, the two chief ones being the consolidation of the elements of the great subsidiary companies into units, and later the union of these units.

Usually at each consolidation the bonds and the preferred stock of the new company represent the actual value of the constituent companies; and this frequently upon a very liberal estimate, sometimes much above the market value of the outstanding bonds and stocks. The common stock issued at such time is usually the capitalization of the good will, the patents, and the economies which are believed will be effected. Since there is no way to calculate accurately in advance the amount of resulting economies, the issue of common stock depends largely upon the constructive imagination of the promoters. It is the aim to capitalize the consolidation sufficiently so that the bond and stocks floated will fully utilize the earning power of the combination. The common stock is speculative, and the profits of the reorganization frequently depend upon the success of the stock promoters, financiers, and manipulators in getting the public to take the common stock, which usually is at the time *aqua pura;* or if not that, it has no more substantial backing than the capitalized somewhat hazy good will, including the trade marks and patents, and economies to be effected. As we have seen, the majority of the great concentrations of industry have gone through two or three stages of such reorganization, the promoters and financiers each time profiting greatly, and sometimes enormously.

Common stock pure water.

An illustration is furnished by the American Tobacco Company, which between 1890 and 1904 at its various reorganizations capitalized the good will of the company in stock to the extent of more than $110,000,000,[1] which, however, between 1904 and 1908 was reduced by $18,000,000. Another illustration of great overcapitalization was that of the United States Shipbuilding Company. According to James Smith, Jr.,[2] who was appointed receiver for this company when it was unable to meet its obligations, the real value of the properties which were taken over was about $12,440,000; whereas it was capitalized at $67,997,000, or more than five times as much. The directors of the company, according to him, appeared to have made a gift of $55,000,000 worth of stocks and bonds to various members interested in the manipulations.

Tobacco.

Shipbuilding company.

Probably the largest amount of water that went on to the market at one time was placed by the United States Steel Corporation; more than $500,000,000 of common stock when issued represented no substance whatever; but this is not the present situation (see pp. 115–117). The speculative character of this stock is indicated by its wide market variations. This stock was placed on the market at about 45; went below 30 in 1902; in 1903 it ranged from 39 to 10; since that time, in 1909, it reached 94⅞, and March 30, 1912 had a market value of 68. Many other instances could be given of the very wide ranges of the common stock of the great corporations, varying from those like the writing paper trust, the upper leather trust, and the union paper bag trust, the common stock of which has ranged from 50 cents a share up to $4 or $5 a share, to those in which the common stock has in large measure been made substance.

Steel.

The trusts that failed.

As illustrations of common stock which have gone far above par may be mentioned American Tobacco and Standard Oil. American Tobacco has been above 525 and Standard Oil has reached 900.

Even the preferred stock of the better industrials had very

[1] Report of Commissioner of Corporations, "Tobacco Industry," Part 2, p. 13. [2] "Trusts, Pools, and Corporations," Ripley, pp. 197–198.

wide ranges in their market values in their earlier years; but there has been a tendency toward solidity and uniformity in the prices of the better class of American preferred industrials, a considerable number of which are now above par. This is shown by the following table: —

TABLE 2. RANGE OF PREFERRED STOCK FOR SOME IMPORTANT INDUSTRIALS FOR 1900 AND 1910

	1900[1]		1910[2]	
	Highest	Lowest	Highest	Lowest
American Car and Foundry . . .	72	$57\frac{3}{8}$	120	109
American Cotton Oil	100	$73\frac{1}{2}$	107	100
American Smelting and Refining .	99	85	$112\frac{3}{4}$	$98\frac{1}{4}$
American Sugar Refining . . .	$118\frac{1}{4}$	106	124	110
American Tobacco	143	128	$99\frac{3}{4}$	$90\frac{1}{2}$
General Electric	200	120	$160\frac{7}{8}$	134
Laclede Gas	$102\frac{1}{4}$	95	$116\frac{1}{2}$	$93\frac{3}{4}$
National Lead	$107\frac{1}{4}$	83	110	$101\frac{3}{4}$
Pressed Steel Car	89	$70\frac{1}{8}$	$107\frac{1}{2}$	90
Pullman	204	176	200	$153\frac{3}{4}$
Republic Iron and Steel	$70\frac{3}{4}$	49	$104\frac{1}{4}$	$82\frac{3}{4}$
Union Bag and Paper	$77\frac{3}{4}$	$56\frac{1}{4}$	73	$52\frac{1}{8}$
United States Rubber	$105\frac{1}{2}$	$74\frac{1}{2}$	$116\frac{1}{2}$	99
United States Steel (1901) . . .	$101\frac{7}{8}$	69	$125\frac{3}{8}$	$110\frac{1}{2}$

Many consolidations organized in the United States have put a variable amount of watered stock upon the market from a small sum to the $500,000,000 of the United States Steel Corporation.

The most serious of the evils of overcapitalization are as follows: —

(*a*) That portion of the stock which is pure water or is largely diluted, through stock manipulating campaigns, is sold to the public, oftentimes for several times its real value.

(*b*) When watered stock is placed upon the market, the

[1] Bradstreet's, January 5, 1901, p. 8.
[2] *Ibid.*, December 31, 1910, p. 251.

officers of a company try to make earnings sufficient to pay dividends upon it; and in order to do this, if practicable, excessive prices are charged.

(*c*) Sometimes the officers of a company, which has a large amount of watered stock, put earnings back into the business with the purpose of making the water substance; to do this further adds to excessive prices.

(*d*) Oftentimes the necessity of paying dividends upon watered stock makes it difficult to accumulate a sufficient reserve to protect the business; and when a time of depression comes, the concern is likely to fall into the hands of a receiver.

Stock manipulation.

Closely connected with overcapitalization are the profits which come to the financiers in connection with the manipulation of the stock on the market, especially the common stock. In this country there is no law which prohibits officers and directors from dealing in the stocks of their own companies. Having inside information, they are able to take advantage of the situation, buying when there is likelihood of a rise, selling when there is likelihood of a fall. Indeed, it is certain that the officers of some companies, by giving favorable and unfavorable information, by timing the news to their purposes, and in other ways, have both bulled and beared their stock, having as their aim their own personal advantage rather than the benefit of the stockholders. Such practices are unlawful in European countries and should be prohibited in America. It is but just to say that for the majority of the greater corporations there is no evidence that this grosser form of manipulation has been practiced on a large scale. In general the officers and trustees of a company have tried to increase the value of its stock, since in most cases they are holders of the securities of the company.

Section 4

THE KINDS OF BUSINESS MOST LIKELY TO BECOME CONCENTRATED

Certain classes of business are especially adapted to concentration. These classes are as follows: —

(1) Industries in which the element of natural monopoly enters are likely to become concentrated. Here are included the public utilities. For a long time it was supposed that the railroads were on the same basis as any other business, and that the desirable thing to do was to have as many companies as possible. Parallel lines were regarded as advantageous because they would compete for trade and in price. The disastrous costliness of this theory was clearly brought out by the paralleling of the Vanderbilt lines between New York and Chicago by the West Shore and the Nickel Plate. As the railroad business developed it became evident that if great sums of money were put into unnecessary railroads the public must bear the expense; that if there were two railroads between two given points when one could do the business, the rates must be higher rather than lower in the long run in order to pay interest upon the investment. This view was accepted only after ruinous competition had occurred upon a great scale with enormous economic loss.

The West Shore road.

The principles of this part of the subject are so well known that they need not be elaborated. It is now accepted doctrine that railroads, electric lines, both city and urban, telegraph and telephone, and other means of transportation and communication, should only be developed sufficiently to do the required business. The business is best done when the number of railroad lines from one city to another are just sufficient to handle the traffic, when a single company controls all of the city railways, when the telegraph business is done by two companies instead of by a score, when the telephone business of the country is substantially controlled by a single organization. Indeed, these facts are so well recognized abroad that in Europe the means of communication are always government monopolies, and the means of transportation largely or exclusively so except in Great Britain.

Public utilities and monopoly.

(2) Businesses depending upon a natural resource limited in quantity and localized in its occurrence are likely to become concentrated. This is well illustrated by anthracite coal,

all of which for the United States is contained in one small area in Pennsylvania of about five hundred square miles. The entire anthracite business is now substantially controlled by a half dozen corporations.

Limited natural resources.

(3) Businesses in articles which can be standardized, and which in quality are sometimes controlled by inspection, are likely to become concentrated. Here are included sugar, oil, salt, whisky, and to a less extent those industries in which there are standard forms and dimensions, as, for instance, steel, matches, etc. Salt is inspected and must reach a definite quality; oil must meet the test of the public inspector for safety; sugar is easily tested by the polariscope. It is notable that the early group of trusts included salt, whisky, oil, and sugar.

Standardized articles.

During recent years by large scale manufacture there have developed various lines in which articles of commerce in themselves very complex may be regarded as standardized. A manufacturer by producing a very large number of machines of exactly the same kind is able to standardize the machinery and standardize methods of operation and thus reduce cost to a minimum; whereas this would not have been possible without such standardization. Common illustrations of this type of standardization are certain kinds of automobiles, cash registers, and typewriters.[1]

(4) Articles which are demanded over a wide territory are likely to become concentrated in production. In this connection the development of transportation is of paramount importance. If an article be used throughout the country, a company producing it may be very large and have many plants even if the object itself be small; thus the Diamond Match Company produces the greater part of the matches of the United States.

Widely used commodities.

The strength of a very large corporation producing an article of wide use may lie not in a single plant at one locality but in many plants of the same kind in different localities. Thus a single lumber company may have hundreds of yards in

[1] Hearing before the committee on Interstate Commerce, United States Senate, Part XXI, p. 1784.

as many cities; a hardware company may have shops distributed throughout a large part of the country; and recently, we have seen the development of shops under one company in various cities for groceries, dry goods, and other commodities.

Protection by patents.

(5) Businesses protected by patents are especially likely to become concentrated A patent gives a monopoly by law, and thus the same principle applies to the making of patent-protected products that applies to a natural monopoly. Here also are to be included trade-marks, which, protected by law, have the same effect as patents, although their influence upon concentration is by no means so far-reaching.

Large capital.

(6) Businesses which in themselves are of a kind to require a large amount of capital are likely to become concentrated. To build a sugar refinery costs several millions of dollars. To build a steel plant adapted to one line of product, as, for instance, steel rails, may involve the expenditure of many millions of dollars. As will be seen in another place, there is likely to be greater fierceness of competition among relatively few and large companies than among many small ones. At the time of the formation of the sugar trust, in consequence of the killing-competition, consolidation became inevitable. At that time, in 1887, there were forty sugar refineries in the United States, and the combination only occurred after some eighteen had gone into bankruptcy.[1]

Section 5

THE EXTENT OF CONCENTRATION

The manufacturing census of 1905 enables us to trace the stages of concentration, so far as the establishments are concerned, for a number of decades. By establishment is meant a plant which is owned by a single individual, firm, or corporation, located in a single city, town, or county, and engaged in a single industry.

Concentration in Management Greater than Concentration in Plants.—There are certainly hundreds of corporations in the

[1] "The Trust Problem," Jenks, p. 19.

United States to which the term "trust" has been popularly applied, because each represents a consolidation in management of establishments once independent. No list of organizations of this kind is available, but it has been estimated that there are five hundred or more such in the United States.

The number of trusts.

Often a considerable number of establishments of different kinds and of the same kind located in different parts of the country are owned or controlled by a single corporation. The greater corporations control several scores of establishments, and some of them, illustrated by the United States Steel, more than two hundred.

If a list of organizations were available controlling more than one establishment, and the number of establishments constituting each organization were known, it would be practicable to give a more accurate estimate of the extent to which concentration has gone than is now possible.

Statistics Confined to Factory System.—The census reports are confined to those establishments which are included within the factory system. They do not include such plants as the small custom grist and saw mills, the small shop such as the blacksmith shop, or manufacture in the household.

Considering all industries together, the census report of 1905 for the country as a whole includes 216,262 establishments. As showing the extent to which the large establishments control industry, the 24,181 establishments which have products exceeding $100,000 per annum, being only 11.2 per cent of the total number, have control of 81.5 per cent of the capital, employ 71.6 per cent of the wage earners, and produce 79.3 per cent of the value of the products. In some lines of industry every establishment has a product exceeding $100,000 in value. Here are included rubber, glucose, locomotives, smelting and refining of zinc.

Dominance of large establishments.

Localization of Industries.—In connection with concentration there has grown up, as a corollary, a localization of many industries, the larger part of an industry for the country perhaps being located in a state, and sometimes even in a county. In other cases the localization is in a great section of the country in which the conditions are similar. The localization in connection with concentration is dependent upon a number of causes. Sometimes the resources upon which the industry is based are found only in one section of the country. Another frequent cause for localization is that when once an industry has become established in a certain district, there may be found trained workmen for it. In consequence, when the existing corporation is enlarged, a plant is built in the same vicinity; or when a new company enters the business, it builds its plant in the locality in which there are available workmen. Other factors favoring localization are nearness to markets, water power, and favorable climate.

If an industry be an important one, it may have a number of centers, and in these few centers a large part of the business be located. In no case is any industry completely localized; there will be chief centers in which we find the larger number of great plants, and in the other parts of the country the industry may exist in a more dispersed form.

As illustrating the localization principle may be mentioned the following industries:—The chief center for the manufacture of agricultural implements is the upper Mississippi Valley, with New York and Pennsylvania. The iron and steel industry is very largely localized in the states of Pennsylvania, Ohio, Illinois, and Alabama. The meat-packing industry is mainly in the four states of Illinois, Kansas, Nebraska, and Missouri; however, Massachusetts, Iowa, California, Minnesota, and New Jersey are important states. As an illustration of extreme localization, 77.2 per cent of the ammunition of the country is manufactured in Connecticut. This is connected by the Census Bureau with the fact that in the manufacture of side arms, rifles, shotguns, and revolvers, Connecticut has a prominent place. The manufacture of rubber boots and shoes is done in New England to the extent of 90 per cent.

Concentration in Representative Industries.—For a number of selected industries the facts as to the increase of concentration are tabulated for one or more decades. The numbers other than percentages are taken directly from the census reports; the latter have been calculated. For each product these tables give the number of plants, the value of the products, the capital per establishment, and the value of product per establishment, for a number of decades, in some cases as far back as 1850, in other cases only for one or two decades. Since the reports are from the census of 1905, the last numbers are for a half decade.

Brief comments will be made regarding each of the foregoing tables.

It will be seen for *iron and steel* (Table 3), not only that the number of establishments has not increased since 1870, but that it has decreased each decade; and that the total number of establishments in 1905, 606, is 25 per cent less than in

TABLE 3. IRON AND STEEL — COMPARATIVE SUMMARY WITH PERCENTAGES OF INCREASE 1870–1905, BY PERIODS

YEAR	NO. OF ESTABLISHMENTS	CAPITAL	VALUE OF PRODUCTS	TONS OF PRODUCTS	CAPITAL PER EACH ESTABLISHMENT	VALUE OF PRODUCTS PER ESTABLISHMENT	TONS OF PRODUCT PER ESTABLISHMENT
1870 . . .	808	121,772,074	207,208,696	3,263,585	150,708	256,446	4,039
1880 . . .	792	209,904,965	296,557,685	6,486,733	265,032	374,442	8,190
% of Increase	**−2.0**	**72.4**	**43.1**	**98.8**	**75.8**	**46.0**	**102.8**
1890 . . .	719	414,044,844	478,687,519	16,264,478	575,862	665,768	22,621
% of Increase	**−9.2**	**97.3**	**61.4**	**150.7**	**117.3**	**77.8**	**176.2**
1900 . . .	669	590,530,484	804,034,918	29,507,860	882,706	1,201,846	44,107
% of Increase	**−7.0**	**42.6**	**68.0**	**81.4**	**53.3**	**80.5**	**94.9**
1905 . . .	606	948,689,840	905,854,152	34,844,933	1,565,495	1,494,809	57,499
% of Increase	**−9.4**	**60.7**	**12.7**	**18.1**	**77.3**	**24.4**	**30.3**
% of Increase 1870–1905 .	**−25.0**	**679.0**	**337.1**	**967.7**	**938.8**	**482.8**	**1,323.6**

1870. This is the situation, notwithstanding the fact that each decade the capital of the business has increased from 42 per cent to 97 per cent, and even for the five years between 1900 and 1905, 60 per cent. Similarly the value of the products has increased each decade from 46 per cent to 80 per cent, but the proportional increase was not so great for the five years from 1900 to 1905. In the same way, if we go by tons of product, the increases for the three decades were 103 per cent, 176 per cent, and 95 per cent, an average per decade for the thirty years of more than 100 per cent; that is to say, the output of each decade between 1890 and 1900 was more than for all previous decades. In 1905 the average capital per plant was more than $1,500,000, and the value of the products annually $1,500,000. The capital per establishment in 1905 was more than ten times as great as in 1870, the value of the product more than five times as much, and the output itself fourteen times as great. Thus the output has increased faster than the price.

While the number of iron and steel establishments in 1905 was 606, seven great companies, now reduced to six, owning the great establishments, controlled more than 90 per cent of the output of the country.

By inspection of the other tables statements might be made parallel to that which has been made regarding iron and steel, but this hardly seems necessary since a most cursory examination of them renders the facts apparent. Therefore only such general points will be added as are brought forth by the tables.

Coke (Table 4) is an industry which has very rapidly expanded and is one in which the number of plants has steadily increased. This is due partly to the great expansion of the

TABLE 4. COKE — COMPARATIVE SUMMARY WITH PERCENTAGES OF INCREASE FROM 1880–1905 BY PERIODS

YEAR	NO. OF ESTABLISHMENTS	CAPITAL	VALUE OF PRODUCTS	CAPITAL PER ESTABLISHMENT	VALUE OF PRODUCTS PER ESTABLISHMENT
1880	126	4,769,858	5,359,489	37,856	42,536
1890	218	17,462,729	16,498,345	80,104	75,680
% of Increase .	**73.0**	**266.1**	**207.8**	**111.6**	**77.9**
1900	241	36,502,679	35,585,445	151,463	147,657
% of Increase .	**10.6**	**109.0**	**115.7**	**89.1**	**95.1**
1905	278	90,712,877	51,728,647	326,305	186,074
% of Increase .	**15.4**	**148.5**	**45.4**	**115.4**	**26.0**
% of Increase, 1880–1905 .	**120.7**	**1,801.9**	**865.2**	**761.9**	**337.5**

iron and steel industry, in which coke is mainly used. Also, the manufacture of coke distributes itself naturally, either adjacent to the coal fields from which it is made, or to the iron furnaces which use the product.

Shipbuilding (Table 5) shows from 1850 to 1905 a slight increase in number of plants, capital multiplied nearly twenty-

TABLE 5. SHIPBUILDING — COMPARATIVE SUMMARY WITH PERCENTAGES OF INCREASE FROM 1850–1905 BY PERIODS.

YEAR	NO. OF ESTABLISHMENTS	CAPITAL	VALUE OF PRODUCTS	CAPITAL PER ESTABLISHMENT	VALUE OF PRODUCTS PER ESTABLISHMENT
1850	953	5,373,139	16,937,525	5,638	17,773
1860	675	5,952,665	13,424,037	8,819	19,887
% of Increase .	**−29.2**	**10.8**	**−20.7**	**56.4**	**11.9**
1870	964	11,463,076	21,483,967	11,891	22,286
% of Increase .	**42.8**	**92.6**	**60.0**	**34.8**	**12.1**
1880	2,188	20,979,874	36,800,327	9,588	16,819
% of Increase .	**127.0**	**83.0**	**71.3**	**−19.4**	**−24.5**
1890	1,006	27,262,892	38,065,410	27,100	37,838
% of Increase .	**−54.0**	**29.9**	**3.4**	**182.6**	**125.0**
1900	1,107	77,341,001	74,532,277	69,865	67,328
% of Increase .	**10.0**	**183.7**	**95.8**	**157.8**	**77.9**
1905	1,097	121,623,700	82,769,239	110,869	75,451
% of Increase .	**−0.9**	**57.3**	**11.1**	**58.7**	**12.1**
% of Increase, 1850–1905 .	**15.1**	**2,163.5**	**388.7**	**1,866.4**	**324.6**

fold, and the value of product fourfold. Probably this striking discrepancy is related to stock manipulation described, pp. 28–31.

Electrical machinery, apparatus, and supplies (Table 6) show a history only from 1880, because these industries have mainly arisen within the past three decades. As would be expected under these circumstances, the increase of plants has been very great, as has also the capitalization per establishment and the value of the output. While there are in this industry a large number of establishments, 784, two great companies, the General Electric and Westinghouse, produce a large per cent of the value of the output of the country. This illustrates how much farther concentration of management has gone than increase in the magnitude of establishments.

TABLE 6. ELECTRICAL MACHINERY, APPARATUS, AND SUPPLIES — COMPARATIVE SUMMARY WITH PERCENTAGES OF INCREASE FROM 1880–1905 BY PERIODS.

YEAR	NO. OF ESTABLISHMENTS	CAPITAL	VALUE OF PRODUCTS	CAPITAL PER ESTABLISHMENT	VALUE OF PRODUCTS PER ESTABLISHMENT
1880	76	1,508,758	2,655,036	19,865	34,934
1890	189	18,997,337	19,114,714	100,515	101,136
% of Increase .	**148.7**	**1,158.3**	**619.9**	**405.9**	**189.5**
1900	581	83,659,924	92,434,435	143,993	159,095
% of Increase .	**207.4**	**340.4**	**383.6**	**43.3**	**57.3**
1905	784	174,066,026	140,809,369	222,023	179,604
% of Increase .	**34.9**	**108.1**	**52.3**	**54.2**	**12.9**
% of Increase, 1880–1905 .	**931.7**	**11,429.4**	**5,203.5**	**1,017.7**	**414.1**

For *petroleum* (Table 7), in 1905 there were 98 refineries, but as is shown in another place one company, the Standard

TABLE 7. PETROLEUM REFINING — COMPARATIVE SUMMARY WITH PERCENTAGES OF INCREASE FROM 1880–1905 BY PERIODS

YEAR	NO. OF ESTABLISHMENTS	CAPITAL	VALUE OF PRODUCTS	CAPITAL PER ESTABLISHMENT	VALUE OF PRODUCTS PER ESTABLISHMENT
1880	86	27,325,746	43,705,218	317,741	508,200
1890	94	77,416,296	85,001,198	823,577	904,268
% of Increase .	**9.3**	**183.3**	**94.5**	**159.2**	**77.9**
1900	67	95,327,892	123,929,384	1 422,804	1,849,692
% of Increase .	**−28.7**	**23.1**	**45.8**	**72.7**	**104.5**
1905	98	136,280,541	175,005,320	1 390 618	1,785,769
% of Increase .	**46.3**	**43.0**	**41.2**	**−2.3**	**−3.5**
% of Increase, 1880–1905 .	**13.9**	**398.7**	**300.5**	**337.6**	**251.3**

Oil, controlled a sufficient number of these so as to produce more than 95 per cent of the oil of the country.

Clay product establishments, (Table 8), from 1850 to 1905 became twice as numerous with a seventeenfold capitalization, and a sixfold value of product per establishment. The increase in number of clay product establishments is explained by the very wide distribution of clay and the weight of the articles manufactured. The manufactory is

TABLE 8. CLAY PRODUCTS — COMPARATIVE SUMMARY WITH PERCENTAGES OF INCREASE FROM 1850–1905 BY PERIODS

YEAR	NO. OF ESTABLISHMENTS	CAPITAL	VALUE OF PRODUCTS	CAPITAL PER ESTABLISHMENT	VALUE OF PRODUCTS PER ESTABLISHMENT
1850	2,121	5,217,231	8,189,359	2,459	3,861
1860	2,240	9,707,952	13,987,828	4,333	6,244
% of Increase .	**5.6**	**86.1**	**70.8**	**76.2**	**61.7**
1870	3,959	26,776,011	36,368,151	6,763	9,186
% of Increase .	**76.7**	**175.8**	**160.0**	**56.1**	**47.1**
1880	6,383	35,039,939	41,810,920	5,489	6,550
% of Increase .	**61.2**	**30.9**	**15.0**	**−18.8**	**−28.7**
1890	6,535	108,705,670	89,827,785	16,634	13,745
% of Increase .	**2.4**	**210.2**	**114.8**	**203.0**	**109.9**
1900	6,423	148,038,323	95,533,862	23,048	14,873
% of Increase .	**−1.7**	**36.2**	**6.4**	**38.5**	**8.2**
1905	5,507	230,882,977	135,352,854	41,925	24,578
% of Increase .	**−14.3**	**56.0**	**41.7**	**81.9**	**65.2**
% of Increase, 1850–1905 .	**159.6**	**4,325.3**	**1,552.7**	**1,604.9**	**536.5**

located near the clay bank so as not to entail heavy freights in reaching the market.

Glass (Table 9), like clay products, is one of the industries in which there has been an increase in the number of plants and at the same time a great increase in the value of the capital and the output.

Salt (Table 10) is one in which the normal process of concentration is well illustrated. We find a decrease in the number of plants in 1905 to less than one half those in 1850, and multiplication of capital per establishment twenty-twofold, and value of product tenfold. As is seen in another place, salt is derived from a natural resource limited in amount, confined to definite areas, and the product is standardized; therefore it is of a kind in which the

TABLE 9. GLASS — COMPARATIVE SUMMARY WITH PERCENTAGES OF INCREASE FROM 1850–1905 BY PERIODS

YEAR	NO. OF ESTABLISHMENTS	CAPITAL	VALUE OF PRODUCTS	CAPITAL PER ESTABLISHMENT	VALUE OF PRODUCTS PER ESTABLISHMENT
1850	94	3,402,350	4,641,676	36,195	49,379
1860	112	6,133,666	8,775,155	54,764	78,349
% of Increase .	**19.1**	**80.3**	**89.1**	**51.3**	**58.7**
1870	201	14,111,642	19,235,862	70,207	95,700
% of Increase .	**79.5**	**130.1**	**119.2**	**28.2**	**22.1**
1880	169	18,804,599	21,154,571	111,269	125,174
% of Increase .	**−15.9**	**33.3**	**10.0**	**58.5**	**30.8**
1890	294	40,966,850	41,051,004	139,343	139,629
% of Increase .	**74.0**	**117.9**	**94.1**	**25.2**	**11.5**
1900	355	61,423,903	56,539,712	173,025	159,210
% of Increase .	**20.7**	**49.9**	**37.7**	**24.2**	**14.1**
1905	399	89,389,151	79,607,998	224,032	199,518
% of Increase .	**12.4**	**45.5**	**40.8**	**29.5**	**25.3**
% of Increase, 1850–1905 .	**324.4**	**252.7**	**1,615.0**	**519.0**	**304.1**

manufacture is especially favorable to concentration. Salt manufacture was the first industry in which the tendency toward consolidation in management appeared. At one time the entire output of the country was controlled by a single combination. (See pp. 101–103.)

Manufactured ice (Table 11) is one of the industries in which the movement has been contrary to the usual rule. The first decade, that from 1870 to 1880, was an experimental one. The permanent tendency of the manufacture is shown by the figures from 1880 to the present time. Using these, it will be seen that the number of plants has increased very greatly. This increase is due to the nature of the product. Ice is an article which is heavy in proportion to its cost; not only so, it is one which must in the warm weather be transported in cold storage, which still further increases the transportation-cost. Hence where ice does not naturally form reasonably close at hand, it is cheaper to manufacture it than to transport natural ice to the locality. Similarly, it is cheaper to manufacture the ice at each important center

TABLE 10. SALT—COMPARATIVE SUMMARY WITH PERCENTAGES OF INCREASE FROM 1850–1905 BY PERIODS

YEAR	NO. OF ESTABLISHMENTS	CAPITAL	VALUE OF PRODUCTS	CAPITAL PER ESTABLISHMENT	VALUE OF PRODUCTS PER ESTABLISHMENT
1850	340	2,640,860	2,177,945	7,767	6,405
1860	399	3,692,215	2,289,504	9,253	5,738
% of Increase .	**17.4**	**39.8**	**5.1**	**19.2**	**−10.4**
1870	282	6,561,615	4,818,229	23,268	17,085
% of Increase .	**−29.3**	**77.7**	**110.4**	**151.4**	**197.8**
1880	268	8,225,740	4,829,566	30,693	18,020
% of Increase .	**−5.0**	**25.4**	**0.2**	**31.9**	**5.5**
1890	200	13,437,749	5,484,618	67,188	27,423
% of Increase .	**−25.4**	**63.4**	**13.6**	**118.9**	**52.2**
1900	159	27,123,364	7,966,897	170,587	50,106
% of Increase .	**−20.5**	**101.8**	**45.3**	**153.8**	**82.7**
1905	146	25,586,282	9,437,662	175,248	64,641
% of Increase .	**−8.2**	**−5.7**	**18.5**	**2.7**	**29.0**
% of Increase, 1850–1905 .	**−57.1**	**868.8**	**333.4**	**2,156.3**	**909.2**

than to transport it from one to another. Hence we find 1320 plants in 1905 as compared with 35 in 1880. The capital per establishment has increased about 50 per cent from 1880 to 1905; but the value of the product per establishment has not radically changed since the earlier date.

For *lumber and timber* (Table 12), the number of establishments from 1850 increased and then later decreased until the total number was not much greater in 1905 than in 1850.

TABLE 11.—MANUFACTURED ICE—COMPARATIVE SUMMARY WITH PERCENTAGES OF INCREASE FROM 1870–1905 BY PERIODS

YEAR	NO. OF ESTABLISHMENTS	CAPITAL	VALUE OF PRODUCTS	CAPITAL PER ESTABLISHMENT	VALUE OF PRODUCTS PER ESTABLISHMENT
1870	4	434,000	258,250	108,500	64,562
1880	35	1,251,200	544,763	34,720	15,565
% of Increase .	**775.0**	**188.3**	**110.9**	**68.0**	**– 75.9**
1890	222	9,846,468	4,900,983	44,354	22,077
% of Increase .	**534.3**	**687.0**	**799.7**	**27.8**	**41.8**
1900	787	38,204,054	13,874,513	48,544	17,629
% of Increase .	**254.5**	**288.0**	**183.1**	**9.4**	**– 20.2**
1905	1,320	66,592,001	23,790,045	50,448	18,022
% of Increase .	**67.7**	**74.3**	**71.5**	**3.9**	**2.2**
% of Increase, 1870–1905 .	**32,900.0**	**15,243.8**	**9,112.0**	**– 53.5**	**– 72.1**

TABLE 12.—LUMBER AND TIMBER PRODUCTS—COMPARATIVE SUMMARY WITH PERCENTAGES OF INCREASE FROM 1850–1905 BY PERIODS

YEAR	NO. OF ESTABLISHMENTS	CAPITAL	VALUE OF PRODUCTS	CAPITAL PER ESTABLISHMENT	VALUE OF PRODUCTS PER ESTABLISHMENT
1850	18,769	41,444,364	60,413,187	2,208	3,218
1860	20,659	74,530,090	96,715,856	3,607	4,681
% of Increase .	**10.1**	**79.8**	**60.1**	**63.3**	**45.4**
1870	25,832	143,493,232	210,159,327	5,554	8,174
% of Increase .	**25.0**	**92.5**	**117.3**	**53.9**	**74.6**
1880	25,708	181,186,122	233,268,729	7,047	9,073
% of Increase .	**– 0.5**	**26.3**	**11.1**	**26.9**	**11.0**
1890	22,617	397,861,928	437,957,382	17,591	19,364
% of Increase .	**– 12.0**	**119.6**	**87.8**	**149.6**	**113.4**
1900	23,053	400,857,337	555,197,271	17,388	24,083
% of Increase .	**1.9**	**0.8**	**26.8**	**– 1.2**	**24.3**
1905	19,127	517,224,128	580,022,690	27,041	30,324
% of Increase .	**– 17.0**	**29.0**	**4.5**	**55.5**	**25.9**
% of Increase, 1850–1905 .	**1.9**	**1,147.9**	**860.1**	**1,124.6**	**842.3**

However, the capital per establishment for 1905 is more than twelve times, and the value of the product per establishment more than nine times, those of 1850. The explanation of the maintenance of a large number of establishments for lumber and timber is of course the weight of the material as compared with its value. In the manufacture a large part of the wood of the logs is removed, and therefore the product is usually handled near its source.

Paper and wood pulp (Table 13) is an industry in which there has been an increase in the number of establishments,

TABLE 13.—PAPER AND WOOD PULP—COMPARATIVE SUMMARY WITH PERCENTAGES OF INCREASE FROM 1850–1905 BY PERIODS

YEAR	NO. OF ESTABLISHMENTS	CAPITAL	VALUE OF PRODUCTS	CAPITAL PER ESTABLISHMENT	VALUE OF PRODUCTS PER ESTABLISHMENT
1850	443	7,260,864	10,187,177	16,390	22,995
1860	555	14,052,683	21,216,802	25,320	38,228
% of Increase .	**25.3**	**93.5**	**108.3**	**54.5**	**66.2**
1870	677	34,556,014	48,849,285	51,808	73,237
% of Increase .	**22.0**	**145.9**	**130.2**	**104.6**	**91.6**
1880	742	48,139,652	57,366,860	64,878	77,313
% of Increase .	**9.6**	**39.3**	**17.4**	**25.2**	**5.6**
1890	649	89,829,548	78,937,184	138,412	121,628
% of Increase .	**– 12.5**	**86.6**	**37.6**	**113.3**	**57.3**
1900	763	167,507,713	127,326,162	219,538	166,875
% of Increase .	**17.6**	**86.5**	**61.3**	**58.6**	**37.2**
1905	761	277,444,471	188,715,189	364,578	247,983
% of Increase .	**– 0.3**	**65.6**	**48.2**	**66.1**	**48.6**
% of Increase, 1850–1905 .	**71.8**	**3,721.1**	**1,752.4**	**2,124.4**	**978.5**

but a much greater increase in the capital and the value of the output per establishment. The reasons for this situation are the same as those for lumber, the raw material for paper and wood pulp being the forests.

Printing and publishing (Table 14) is one of the industries in which there has been increase in number of plants, no great increase in capital, and no great increase in the value of the product per establishment. It gives the best illustration of any of the tables of the lack of tendency toward concentration. The explanation undoubtedly is that the great majority of printing and publication establishments publish newspapers. Every community of any size has a newspaper, and the large city has a considerable number, each one of which has its own plant. Local news can only be handled locally. The news of the day is demanded

TABLE 14. PRINTING AND PUBLISHING — COMPARATIVE SUMMARY WITH PERCENTAGES OF INCREASE FROM 1880–1905 BY PERIODS.

YEAR	NO. OF ESTABLISHMENTS	CAPITAL	VALUE OF PRODUCTS	CAPITAL PER ESTABLISHMENT	VALUE OF PRODUCTS PER ESTABLISHMENT
1880	——	——	179,988,415	——	——
1890	16,566	195,387,445	275,452,515	11,794	16,627
% of Increase .	——	——	**53.0**	——	——
1900	22,311	292,516,642	347,054,430	13,110	15,555
% of Increase .	**34.7**	**49.7**	**26.0**	**11.1**	**– 6.4**
1905	26,422	385,008,604	496,061,357	14,571	18,774
% of Increase .	**18.4**	**31.6**	**42.9**	**11.1**	**20.7**
% of Increase, 1880–1905 . .	——	——	**175.6**	——	——
% of Increase, 1890–1905 .	**59.5**	**97.1**	**80.1**	**23.5**	**12.9**

in the evening or the morning. Concentration of the printing industry is therefore impossible.

In *agricultural implements* (Table 15), concentration has gone very far, the number of plants being not half as great in 1905 as in 1850; but the value of the output of each establishment is more than thirty times as great as in 1850. Agricultural implements illustrate the class of product which is very widely used, can be standardized, and hence is favorable to concentration in manufacture. These factors are more important than the freight, although agricultural implements are heavy.

TABLE 15. AGRICULTURAL IMPLEMENTS — COMPARATIVE SUMMARY WITH PERCENTAGES OF INCREASE FROM 1850–1905 BY PERIODS.

YEAR	NO. OF ESTABLISHMENTS	CAPITAL	VALUE OF PRODUCTS	CAPITAL PER ESTABLISHMENT	VALUE OF PRODUCTS PER ESTABLISHMENT
1850	1,333	3,564,202	6,842,611	2,674	5,133
1860	2,116	13,866,389	20,831,904	6,553	9,845
% of Increase .	**58.7**	**289.0**	**204.4**	**145.1**	**91.8**
1870	2,076	34,834,600	52,066,875	16,779	25,080
% of Increase .	**−1.9**	**151.2**	**149.9**	**156.0**	**154.7**
1880	1,943	62,109,668	68,640,486	31,966	35,327
% of Increase .	**−6.4**	**78.3**	**31.8**	**90.5**	**40.9**
1890	910	145,313,997	81,271,651	159,685	89,309
% of Increase .	**−53.2**	**134.0**	**18.4**	**399.4**	**152.8**
1900	715	157,707,951	101,207,428	220,571	141,549
% of Increase .	**−21.4**	**8.5**	**24.5**	**38.2**	**58.5**
1905	648	196,740,700	112,007,344	303,612	172,851
% of Increase .	**−9.4**	**24.8**	**10.7**	**37.6**	**22.1**
% of Increase, 1850–1905 .	**−51.4**	**5,419.9**	**1,536.9**	**11,254.2**	**3,267.6**

TABLE 16. BUTTER, CHEESE, AND CONDENSED MILK — COMPARATIVE SUMMARY WITH PERCENTAGES OF INCREASE FROM 1880–1905 BY PERIODS.

YEAR	NO. OF ESTABLISHMENTS	CAPITAL	VALUE OF PRODUCTS	CAPITAL PER ESTABLISHMENT	VALUE OF PRODUCTS PER ESTABLISHMENT
1880	3,932	9,604,803	25,742,510	2,442	6,546
1890	4,552	16,016,573	60,635,705	3,518	13,320
% of Increase .	**15.8**	**66.8**	**135.5**	**44.1**	**103.4**
1900	9,242	36,303,164	130,783,349	3,928	14,151
% of Increase .	**103.0**	**126.7**	**115.7**	**11.7**	**6.2**
1905	8,926	47,255,556	168,182,789	5,295	18,842
% of Increase .	**−3.4**	**30.2**	**28.6**	**34.8**	**33.2**
% of Increase, 1880–1905 .	**127.0**	**392.0**	**553.3**	**116.8**	**187.8**

Butter, cheese, and condensed milk (Table 16) represent an industry with an increase in number of establishments, and no rapid increase in the capital per establishment and the value of the output. The explanation is that the raw material, milk, is being produced over a steadily widening territory, and if transported, must be transported rapidly. This is expensive; hence it is advantageous to have numerous establishments of fair size distributed throughout the producing area.

TABLE 17. BEET SUGAR (1890 DATA NOT GIVEN) — COMPARATIVE SUMMARY WITH PERCENTAGES OF INCREASE FROM 1880–1905 BY PERIODS

YEAR	NO. OF ESTABLISHMENTS	CAPITAL	VALUE OF PRODUCTS	CAPITAL PER ESTABLISHMENT	VALUE OF PRODUCTS PER ESTABLISHMENT
1880	4	365,000	282,572	91,250	70,643
1900	30	20,141,719	7,323,857	671,390	244,128
% of Increase .	**650.0**	**5,418.3**	**2,491.8**	**635.7**	**245.5**
1905	51	55,923,459	24,393,794	1,096,538	478,309
% of Increase .	**70.0**	**177.6**	**233.1**	**63.3**	**95.9**
% of Increase, 1880–1905 .	**1,175.0**	**15,221.5**	**8,532.7**	**1,101.7**	**577.1**

Beet sugar (Table 17) is another industry which has a short history. In this case, there is a very great increase in the number of establishments, capital per establishment, and value of product per establishment. The former shows dispersion of the industry with the expansion of the beet-growing territory, and the latter increase in the magnitude of the establishments. Beets are heavy as compared with their cost; they cannot be transported far, and wherever a district undertakes the growing of beets, a manufactory must be located near the source of supply.

Starch (Table 18), one of the standardized articles, has had something of a decrease in the number of establishments from 1850 to 1905, but a multiplication of more than eleven-fold in capital, and of sevenfold in the value of the output per establishment.

Tobacco (Table 19) is an industry in which there has been a great increase in the number of establishments. The number in 1905 was thirteen and one half times as great as in 1860. While there has been a steady and moderate

TABLE 18. STARCH — COMPARATIVE SUMMARY WITH PERCENTAGES OF INCREASE FROM 1850–1905 BY PERIODS

YEAR	NO. OF ESTABLISHMENTS	CAPITAL	VALUE OF PRODUCTS	CAPITAL PER ESTABLISHMENT	VALUE OF PRODUCTS PER ESTABLISHMENTS
1850	146	692,675	1,261,468	4,744	8,640
1860	167	2,051,710	2,823,258	12,286	16,906
% of Increase .	**14.4**	**196.2**	**123.8**	**159.0**	**95.7**
1870	195	2,741,675	5,994,422	14,059	30,741
% of Increase .	**16.8**	**33.6**	**112.3**	**14.4**	**81.8**
1880	139	5,328,256	7,477,742	38,332	53,797
% of Increase .	**−28.7**	**94.3**	**24.7**	**172.7**	**75.0**
1890	80	4,929,155	8,934,517	61,614	111,681
% of Increase .	**−42.4**	**−7.5**	**19.5**	**60.7**	**107.5**
1900	124	11,671,567	9,232,984	94,125	74,459
% of Increase .	**55.0**	**136.8**	**3.3**	**52.8**	**−33.4**
1905	131	7,007,695	8,082,904	53,494	61,701
% of Increase .	**5.6**	**−40.0**	**−12.5**	**−43.2**	**−17.1**
% of Increase, 1850–1905 .	**−10.3**	**911.8**	**540.8**	**1,027.6**	**614.1**

increase in the capital per establishment and an increase in the value of the product per establishment, these have not been large. Thus tobacco is a case in which, so far as number of establishments is concerned, the industry is much dispersed.

But these statistics might lead to quite erroneous conclusions; for, as we have seen in another connection, this is one of the industries in which a few of the great manufactories are doing a large part of the business, and one in which a single concern reached a position of monopoly. The American Tobacco Company, before its dissolution, controlled more than 50 per cent of the business of the country, and controlled from 59 to over 90 per cent of all of the lines of tobacco business with the exception of cigars. This illustration shows how far the statistical tables of the census fail to give an idea of the extent of concentration of management which has taken place.

In the *slaughter and meat packing industry* (Table 20), the number of establishments has greatly increased from 1850 to 1905, being five times as numerous; and during the same time the capital per establishment has become thirteenfold, and the value of the product per establishment fifteenfold.

TABLE 19. TOBACCO — COMPARATIVE SUMMARY WITH PERCENTAGES OF INCREASE FROM 1860–1905 BY PERIODS

YEAR	NO. OF ESTABLISHMENTS	CAPITAL	VALUE OF PRODUCTS	CAPITAL PER ESTABLISHMENT	VALUE OF PRODUCTS PER ESTABLISHMENT
1860	2,104	12,529,960	30,889,313	5,955	14,681
1870	5,204	24,924,330	71,762,044	4,789	13,789
% of Increase .	**147.3**	**98.9**	**132.3**	**−19.6**	**−6.1**
1880	7,622	38,905,950	116,772,631	5,104	15,320
% of Increase .	**46.5**	**56.1**	**62.7**	**6.6**	**11.1**
1890	11,351	90,359,143	195,536,862	7,960	17,226
% of Increase .	**48.9**	**132.3**	**67.5**	**55.9**	**12.5**
1900	14,959	111,517,318	263,713,173	7,454	17,629
% of Increase .	**31.8**	**23.4**	**34.9**	**−6.4**	**2.3**
1905	16,828	323,983,501	331,117,681	19,252	19,676
% of Increase .	**12.5**	**190.5**	**25.6**	**158.2**	**11.6**
% of Increase, 1860–1905 .	**699.8**	**2,485.6**	**971.9**	**223.2**	**34.0**

The explanation of the numerous plants is the fact that concentration has not gone to the point so that the small community does not have its own slaughterhouse. However, as is shown in another place, more than 50 per cent of the business of the country is done at the great abattoirs of the large cities. So far as management is concerned these are under the control of six great concerns; and these six are charged with coöperating in business. The average capital per establishment is large, more than a quarter of a million; the ratio between capital and output per establishment is 1 to 4, a much higher ratio than obtains for most industries.

The *leather* business (Table 21) is one of great concentration. The number of plants in 1905 is less than one sixth as many as in 1850, the capital per establishment more than sixtyseven times as great, and the value of the product thirtyseven times as great. Tanning is a complex, chemical

TABLE 20. SLAUGHTERING AND MEAT PACKING — COMPARATIVE SUMMARY WITH PERCENTAGES OF INCREASE FROM 1850–1905 BY PERIODS

YEAR	NO. OF ESTABLISHMENTS	CAPITAL	VALUE OF PRODUCTS	CAPITAL PER ESTABLISHMENT	VALUE OF PRODUCTS PER ESTABLISHMENT
1850	185	3,482,500	11,981,642	18,824	64,765
1860	259	10,158,362	29,441,776	39,221	113,675
% of Increase .	**40.0**	**191.7**	**145.7**	**108.3**	**75.5**
1870	768	24,224,692	75,826,500	31,542	97,430
% of Increase .	**196.5**	**138.5**	**157.5**	**−19.6**	**−14.3**
1880	872	49,419,213	303,562,413	56,673	348,122
% of Increase .	**13.5**	**104.0**	**300.3**	**79.7**	**257.3**
1890	1,118	116,887,504	561,611,668	104,550	502,336
% of Increase .	**28.2**	**136.5**	**85.0**	**84.4**	**44.3**
1900	882	188,800,181	783,779,191	214,059	888,627
% of Increase .	**−21.1**	**61.5**	**39.6**	**104.7**	**76.9**
1905	929	237,714,690	913,914,624	255,882	983,762
% of Increase .	**5.3**	**25.9**	**16.6**	**19.5**	**10.7**
% of Increase, 1850–1905 .	**402.1**	**6,725.9**	**7,527.6**	**1,259.3**	**1,419.**

process, requiring a large plant. The raw hides in large number come from the great packing houses and from importations. That portion derived from the dispersed slaughterhouses can readily reach the great tanneries, since hides are not heavy as compared with their value. Another factor localizing the tanneries is the necessity for tanbark. This largely locates the industry in the parts of the country where this material is not at a great distance.

TABLE 21. LEATHER, TANNED, CURRIED, FINISHED — COMPARATIVE SUMMARY WITH PERCENTAGES OF INCREASE FROM 1850–1905 BY PERIODS

YEAR	NO. OF ESTABLISHMENTS	CAPITAL	VALUE OF PRODUCTS	CAPITAL PER ESTABLISHMENT	VALUE OF PRODUCTS PER ESTABLISHMENT
1850	6,686	22,774,795	43,457,898	3,406	6,499
1860	5,188	39,025,620	75,698,747	7,522	14,591
% of Increase .	**−22.4**	**71.4**	**74.2**	**120.8**	**124.5**
1870	7,569	61,124,812	157,237,597	8,075	20,773
% of Increase .	**45.9**	**56.6**	**107.7**	**7.3**	**42.4**
1880	5,628	73,383,911	200,264,944	13,039	35,583
% of Increase .	**−25.6**	**20.1**	**27.4**	**61.5**	**71.3**
1890	1,787	98,088,698	172,136,092	54,890	96,326
% of Increase .	**−68.2**	**33.7**	**−14.0**	**320.9**	**170.7**
1900	1,306	173,977,421	204,038,127	133,213	15,623
% of Increase .	**−26.9**	**77.4**	**18.5**	**142.7**	**62.2**
1905	1,049	242,584,254	252,620,986	231,252	240,820
% of Increase .	**−19.7**	**39.4**	**23.8**	**73.6**	**54.1**
% of Increase, 1850–1905 .	**−84.4**	**965.1**	**481.3**	**6,689.5**	**3,605.5**

The manufacture of *boots and shoes* (Table 22), a severely competitive industry, and a business which has been freely entered by competitors, shows a decrease in the number of

TABLE 22. BOOTS AND SHOES — COMPARATIVE SUMMARY WITH PERCENTAGES OF INCREASE FROM 1880–1905 BY PERIODS

YEAR	NO. OF ESTABLISHMENTS	CAPITAL	VALUE OF PRODUCTS	CAPITAL PER ESTABLISHMENT	VALUE OF PRODUCTS PER ESTABLISHMENT
1880	1,959	42,994,028	166,050,354	21,947	84,763
1890	2,082	95,282,311	220,649,358	45,764	105,979
% of Increase .	**6.3**	**121.6**	**32.9**	**108.5**	**25.0**
1900	1,599	99,819,233	258,969,580	62,426	161,957
% of Increase .	**−23.2**	**4.8**	**17.4**	**36.4**	**52.8**
1905	1,316	122,526,093	320,107,458	93,105	243,243
% of Increase .	**−17.7**	**22.7**	**23.6**	**49.1**	**50.2**
% of Increase, 1880–1905 .	**−32.8**	**184.9**	**92.8**	**324.2**	**188.1**

establishments as compared with 1880 of seventeen, and as compared with 1890 of thirty-two. In this industry, as elsewhere, the capital per establishment and the value of the output per establishment have considerably increased, although not so largely as in some others. In 1905 the average capital per establishment was $93,105 and the value of the output per establishment $243,243, a ratio of one to two and a half. This ratio, like that of the meat industry, is much higher than the average.

Leather gloves and mittens (Table 23) illustrate an industry in which the number of manufactories has steadily increased

TABLE 23. LEATHER GLOVES AND MITTENS — COMPARATIVE SUMMARY WITH PERCENTAGES OF INCREASE FROM 1850–1905 BY PERIODS

YEAR	NO. OF ESTABLISHMENTS	CAPITAL	VALUE OF PRODUCTS	CAPITAL PER ESTABLISHMENT	VALUE OF PRODUCTS PER ESTABLISHMENT
1850	110	181,200	708,184	1,647	6,438
1860	126	594,825	1,176,795	4,720	9,339
% of Increase .	**14.5**	**228.3**	**66.2**	**186.6**	**45.1**
1870	221	2,340,550	3,998,521	10,590	18,092
% of Increase .	**75.4**	**293.5**	**239.8**	**124.3**	**93.7**
1880	300	3,379,648	7,379,605	11,265	24,598
% of Increase .	**35.7**	**44.4**	**84.6**	**6.4**	**35.9**
1890	324	5,977,820	10,103,821	18,450	31,184
% of Increase .	**8.0**	**76.9**	**36.9**	**63.8**	**26.8**
1900	381	9,004,427	16,721,234	23,633	43,887
% of Increase .	**17.6**	**50.6**	**65.6**	**28.1**	**40.7**
1905	339	10,705,599	17,740,385	31,579	52,331
% of Increase .	**−11.0**	**18.9**	**6.1**	**33.6**	**19.2**
% of Increase, 1850–1905 .	**208.2**	**5,808.2**	**2,405.0**	**1,817.4**	**712.8**

until it was threefold as great in 1905 as in 1850; but the capital per establishment and value of the products per establishment increased at a much greater rate. In the respect of increase in number of establishments there is contrast between this industry and the manufacture of boots and shoes.

TABLE 24. COTTON GOODS — COMPARATIVE SUMMARY WITH PERCENTAGES OF INCREASE FROM 1850–1905 BY PERIODS

YEAR	NO. OF ESTABLISHMENTS	CAPITAL	VALUE OF PRODUCTS	CAPITAL PER ESTABLISHMENT	VALUE OF PRODUCTS PER ESTABLISHMENT
1850	1,094	74,500,931	61,869,184	68,099	56,533
1850	1,091	98,585,269	115,681,774	90,362	106,033
% of Increase .	**−0.3**	**32.3**	**87.0**	**32.7**	**87.5**
1870	956	140,706,291	177,489,739	147,182	185,658
% of Increase .	**−12.4**	**42.7**	**53.4**	**62.8**	**75.1**
1880	756	208,280,346	192,090,110	275,503	254,087
% of Increase .	**−20.9**	**48.0**	**8.2**	**87.2**	**36.8**
1890	905	354,020,843	267,981,724	391,183	296,112
% of Increase .	**19.7**	**70.0**	**39.5**	**42.0**	**16.6**
1900	973	460,842,772	332,806,156	473,631	342,041
% of Increase .	**7.5**	**30.2**	**24.2**	**21.1**	**15.5**
1905	1,077	605,100,164	442,451,218	561,838	410,818
% of Increase .	**10.7**	**31.3**	**32.9**	**18.6**	**20.1**
% of Increase, 1850–1905 .	**−1.7**	**712.1**	**615.1**	**724.9**	**626.2**

TABLE 25. WOOL MANUFACTORIES — COMPARATIVE SUMMARY WITH PERCENTAGES OF INCREASE FROM 1860–1905 BY PERIODS

YEAR	NO. OF ESTABLISHMENTS	CAPITAL	VALUE OF PRODUCTS	CAPITAL PER ESTABLISHMENT	VALUE OF PRODUCTS PER ESTABLISHMENT
1860	1,476	38,814,422	73,454,000	26,297	49,765
1870	3,208	121,451,059	199,257,262	37,858	62,112
% of Increase .	**117.3**	**212.9**	**171.3**	**43.9**	**24.8**
1880	2,330	143,512,278	238,085,686	61,593	102,183
% of Increase .	**−27.4**	**18.2**	**19.5**	**62.7**	**64.5**
1890	1,693	245,886,743	270,527,511	145,237	159,792
% of Increase .	**−27.3**	**71.3**	**13.6**	**135.8**	**56.4**
1900	1,414	310,179,749	296,990,484	219,363	210,035
% of Increase .	**−16.5**	**26.1**	**9.8**	**51.1**	**31.5**
1905	1,213	370,861,691	380,934,003	305,739	314,043
% of Increase .	**−14.2**	**19.6**	**28.3**	**39.4**	**49.5**
% of Increase, 1860–1905 .	**−17.8**	**855.4**	**418.6**	**1,062.6**	**531.0**

The cotton and wool manufactories (Tables 24 and 25) afford cases in which the number of establishments has decreased (for cotton slightly, and for wool considerably), and in which the concentration has been in the increase of the capital and the output per establishment.

Hosiery and knit goods (Table 26) illustrate a product in which the number of establishments has increased very

TABLE 26. HOSIERY AND KNIT GOODS — COMPARATIVE SUMMARY WITH PERCENTAGES OF INCREASE FROM 1860–1905 BY PERIODS

YEAR	NO. OF ESTABLISHMENTS	CAPITAL	VALUE OF PRODUCTS	CAPITAL PER ESTABLISHMENT	VALUE OF PRODUCTS PER ESTABLISHMENT
1860	197	4,035,510	7,280,606	20,485	36,957
1870	248	10,931,260	18,411,564	44,078	74,240
% of Increase .	**25.9**	**170.9**	**152.9**	**115.1**	**100.9**
1880	359	15,579,591	29,167,227	43,397	81,246
% of Increase .	**44.8**	**42.5**	**58.4**	**−1.6**	**9.4**
1890	796	50,607,738	67,241,013	63,578	84,473
% of Increase .	**121.7**	**224.8**	**130.5**	**46.5**	**4.0**
1900	921	81,860,604	95,482,566	88,882	103,672
% of Increase .	**15.7**	**61.8**	**42.0**	**39.8**	**22.7**
1905	1,079	106,663,531	136,558,139	98,854	126,559
% of Increase .	**17.2**	**30.3**	**43.0**	**11.2**	**22.1**
% of Increase, 1860–1905 .	**447.7**	**2,543.1**	**1,775.6**	**382.6**	**242.4**

greatly, since in 1905 there were more than five times as many as in 1860. The capital per establishment is nearly five-fold, and the value of product per establishment nearly three and one half fold. Thus we have here concentration so far as size of establishments is concerned, but not concentration of establishments. The reason for the contrast in tendency so far as number of establishments is concerned between hosiery and knit goods and cotton and woolen is not clearly apparent. All are industries in which invention and improvement of machinery during the past fifty years has been most marked; but it may be suggested that the size of the machines is not nearly so great in hosiery and knit goods as in cotton and woolen manufacture.

In silk manufacture (Table 27), the number of establishments from 1860 to 1905 has multiplied more than fourfold, the capital per establishment more than eightfold, and the output per establishment more than fourfold. This

TABLE 27. SILK MANUFACTORIES—COMPARATIVE SUMMARY WITH PERCENTAGES OF INCREASE FROM 1860–1905 BY PERIODS

YEAR	NO. OF ESTABLISHMENTS	CAPITAL	VALUE OF PRODUCTS	CAPITAL PER ESTABLISHMENT	VALUE OF PRODUCTS PER ESTABLISHMENT
1860	139	2,926,980	6,607,771	21,057	47,538
1870	86	6,231,130	12,210,662	72,455	141,984
% of Increase .	**−38.1**	**112.9**	**84.8**	**244.1**	**198.6**
1880	382	19,125,300	41,033,045	50,066	107,416
% of Increase .	**344.2**	**206.9**	**236.0**	**−30.9**	**−24.3**
1890	472	51,007,537	87,298,454	108,066	184,954
% of Increase .	**23.6**	**166.7**	**112.8**	**115.8**	**72.2**
1900	483	81,082,201	107,256,258	167,872	222,062
% of Increase .	**2.3**	**59.0**	**22.9**	**55.3**	**20.1**
1905	624	109,556,621	133,288,072	175,571	213,603
% of Increase .	**29.2**	**35.1**	**24.3**	**4.6**	**−3.8**
% of Increase, 1860–1905 .	**348.9**	**3,643.0**	**1,917.1**	**733.8**	**349.3**

industry affords a contrast to the manufacture of hosiery and knit goods and wool manufactories in the great increase in the number of establishments.

Combined textiles (Table 28) show very well the normal tendency for increase of concentration per establishment. The number of establishments from 1850 to 1905 increased fivefold, the capital per establishment nearly eightfold, and the value of the output per establishment over sixfold.

For *needles, pins, hooks, and eyes* (Table 29), the number of establishments, while greater than in 1860, is less than in 1870. In 1905 as compared with 1860 the capital per establishment is sixfold and the value of the products more

TABLE 28. COMBINED TEXTILES (COTTON GOODS, COTTON SMALL WARES, HOSIERY AND KNIT GOODS, WOOL MANUFACTURES, SILK AND SILK GOODS, FLAX, HEMP AND JUTE PRODUCTS, DYEING AND FINISHING TEXTILES) — COMPARATIVE SUMMARY WITH PERCENTAGES OF INCREASE FROM 1850–1905 BY PERIODS

YEAR	NO. OF ESTABLISHMENTS	CAPITAL	VALUE OF PRODUCTS	CAPITAL PER ESTABLISHMENT	VALUE OF PRODUCTS PER ESTABLISHMENT
1850	3,025	112,513,947	128,769,971	37,195	42,568
1860	3027	150,080,852	214,740,614	49,581	70,942
% of Increase .	**.1**	**33.3**	**66.8**	**33.3**	**66.7**
1870	4,790	297,694,243	520,386,764	62,149	108,640
% of Increase .	**58.2**	**98.3**	**142.3**	**25.3**	**53.2**
1880	4,018	412,721,496	532,673,488	102,718	132,572
% of Increase .	**−16.1**	**38.7**	**2.3**	**65.3**	**22.0**
1890	4,276	767,705,310	759,262,283	179,538	177,564
% of Increase .	**6.4**	**86.0**	**42.5**	**74.8**	**33.9**
1900	4,312	1,042,997,577	931,494,566	241,883	216,024
% of Increase .	**0.8**	**35.8**	**22.7**	**34.7**	**21.7**
1905	4,563	1,343,324,605	1,215,036,792	294,395	266,280
% of Increase .	**5.8**	**28.8**	**30.4**	**21.7**	**23.3**
% of Increase, 1850–1905 .	**50.8**	**1094.0**	**843.6**	**691.5**	**525.5**

TABLE 29. NEEDLES, PINS, HOOKS, AND EYES — COMPARATIVE SUMMARY WITH PERCENTAGES OF INCREASE FROM 1860–1905 BY PERIODS

YEAR	NO. OF ESTABLISHMENTS	CAPITAL	VALUE OF PRODUCTS	CAPITAL PER ESTABLISHMENT	VALUE OF PRODUCTS PER ESTABLISHMENT
1860	25	453,200	725,086	18,128	29,003
1870	48	801,050	1,225,436	16,689	25,529
% of Increase .	**92.0**	**76.8**	**69.0**	**−8.0**	**−12.0**
1880	45	1,564,738	1,748,101	34,772	38,847
% of Increase .	**−6.3**	**95.3**	**42.7**	**108.3**	**52.2**
1890	55	2,269,707	2,109,469	41,267	38,354
% of Increase .	**22.2**	**45.1**	**20.7**	**18.7**	**−1.3**
1900	52	4,617,552	3,237,982	88,799	62,269
% of Increase .	**−5.5**	**103.4**	**53.5**	**115.1**	**62.3**
1905	46	5,331,939	4,750,589	115,911	103,273
% of Increase .	**−11.5**	**15.5**	**46.7**	**30.5**	**65.8**
% of Increase, 1860–1905 .	**84.0**	**1,076.5**	**555.1**	**539.4**	**256.1**

than threefold. The materials are light as compared with the value; they may be standardized; and thus they illustrate the natural tendency toward concentration. The table is introduced mainly for the purpose of showing that the tendency to concentration may be just as marked with small and relatively unimportant articles as with large and important ones.

Pens and pencils (Table 30) are industries in which the number of establishments has steadily increased, being

TABLE 30. PENS AND PENCILS — COMPARATIVE SUMMARY WITH PERCENTAGES OF INCREASE FROM 1860–1905 BY PERIODS

YEAR	NO. OF ESTABLISHMENTS	CAPITAL	VALUE OF PRODUCTS	CAPITAL PER ESTABLISHMENT	VALUE OF PRODUCTS PER ESTABLISHMENT
1860	15	39,150	134,000	2,610	8,933
1870	32	704,400	827,380	22,012	25,855
% of Increase .	**113.3**	**1,699.2**	**517.4**	**743.2**	**189.4**
1880	23	894,247	976,488	38,880	42,456
% of Increase .	**−28.1**	**27.0**	**18.0**	**76.6**	**64.2**
1890	41	4,116,247	3,025,664	100,396	73,796
% of Increase .	**78.3**	**360.3**	**209.9**	**158.1**	**73.8**
1900	55	3,671,741	4,222,148	66,758	76,766
% of Increase .	**34.1**	**−10.8**	**39.5**	**−33.5**	**4.0**
1905	62	7,101,366	7,673,777	114,538	123,770
% of Increase .	**12.7**	**93.4**	**81.8**	**71.5**	**61.2**
% of Increase, 1860–1905 .	**313.3**	**18,038.8**	**5,626.7**	**4,288.4**	**1,285.5**

sixtytwo in 1905 as compared with fifteen in 1860. The capital per establishment and the value of product per establishment have greatly increased, being respectively fortythree and thirteen times greater than in 1860. While like needles, pins, hooks, and eyes, so far as magnitude of establishments is concerned, the two are unlike in that for pens and pencils the number of establishments has increased.

General statements. — The foregoing tables show that

while concentration has not taken place for every industry, in the great majority of the more important ones, it has been steady and in some cases amazing, being marked by great decrease in the number of plants and relative increase in the magnitude of the plants and the value of the output. Concentration general.

For certain industries, while the business done by the several plants has increased, the actual number of the plants has increased. However, in most cases the increase in number of plants is much smaller than the increase in the value of the product, showing that even in the cases where there is increase in the number of plants, concentration has been taking place.

The different industries differ greatly among themselves in the ratio between the capital per establishment and the value of the product per establishment. From this point of view for 1905 I shall classify them into three divisions: those in which the value of the product per establishment is less than the capital per establishment by 20 per cent or more; those in which the value of the product per establishment does not differ more than 20 per cent from the value of the capital per establishment; and those in which the value of the product per establishment is greater than the capital per establishment by 20 per cent or more. Variable ratio between capital and product.

The industries in which the value of the product per establishment is less than the value per establishment by 20 per cent or more are the following: coke; ship building; clay products; salt; manufactured ice; paper and wood pulp, agricultural implements; beet sugar; cotton goods; and of these, in the cases of salt, ice, and beet sugar, the value of the output is less than half the capitalization.

Those industries in which the value of the product per establishment does not vary more than 20 per cent from the capital per establishment are the following: iron and steel; electrical machinery, apparatus, and supplies; glass; lumber and timber products; printing and publishing; tobacco; leather; wool manufactories; combined textiles; needles, pins, hooks, and eyes; and pens and pencils.

Those industries in which the value of the product per establishment is 20 per cent or more than the capitalized value per establishment are the following: petroleum; butter, cheese, and condensed milk; starch; slaughtering and meat packing; boots and shoes; leather gloves and mittens; hosiery and knit goods; silk manufacture; and of these, in the case of butter, cheese, and condensed milk, and meat, the value of the output per establishment is more than three times as great as the capitalization, and for boots and shoes more than twice as great.

If there were available detailed histories of each of these industries so that we might know to what extent the capitals of the different classes are inflated and to what extent they represent substance, the very great differences in ratios might be partly explained. Possibly for the slaughtering industry and boots and shoes, we have industries in which there is not over capitalization; whereas in some of the cases where the value of the output per establishment is not more than half as great as the capitalization there may be inflated capitalization.[1]

Section 6

FORMS OF ORGANIZATIONS

The development of the laws concerning combinations in this and other countries will be considered in another place (see Chapter III); but it is to be said that the principle of statute law, prohibiting restraint of trade, has had a powerful influence in the forms which concentrations of industry have taken. Combinations during their history have passed from those of the loosest kind to those in which there is complete unity of management. The different kinds of associations and combinations may be roughly classified as follows:

(1) *Informal or Formal Associations for the General Protection or Advancement of a Business.*—These are illustrated by the various business associations. Almost every industry has such an association, and some of them many. Thus

[1] The situation regarding concentration of industry in 1900 is fully given in the Reports of the United States Industrial Commission for 1901, Vol. I, p. 1325; Vol. XIII, p. 1013; Vol. XIX, pp. 595–724.

there are associations of brewers, butchers, bankers, hardware men, lumbermen, cattlemen, fruit growers, wine makers, butter makers, and of practically every producing industry. Similarly there are associations of salesmen, wholesalers, and retailers in each of the various industries, whether they be hardware, drugs, dry goods, or groceries. These sales associations may be national, state, or local, or they may be national with state and local branches. The importance of the local associations depends upon the size of the town. The merchants' or manufacturers' association in a great city may have large importance, and the retail grocers' association in a small town may be of little consequence. Not only are there associations of tradesmen and salesmen, but there are associations of people engaged in the same service, teachers, dentists, doctors, laborers, etc. The laborers' association may be for the entire country or for a definite industry, as, for instance, the American Federation of Labor, and the Brotherhood of Locomotive Engineers.

Multitude of associations.

The purpose of all of these associations is to advance the interests of the group concerned. This is done in the loosest form of association in the public convention at which views are compared, experiences exchanged, papers presented, the purposes of which are to benefit one another merely by the exchange of information, without any implication whatever that any one will feel impelled to abide by any view presented.

Thus the members of the retailers associations meet and exchange information to the common advantage. One of the items concerning which information is exchanged is as to the manufacturers that sell to the so-called mail order house, the severest competitors of the retailers. The purpose of such information is clearly that the members may buy of wholesalers and jobbers that do not deal with the mail order houses; but now the retailers feel that even such exchange of information with no implication that it will be used as indicated comes under the ban of the Sherman act.[1]

Exchange of information.

Another aim in this exchange of information is to secure

[1] Hearing of Senate Interstate Commerce Committee, XIII, p. 937.

common prices for standard articles. There need not be, indeed usually is not, a formal agreement in a community or association upon this matter. One way to secure a common price is by means of a printed list or catalog.[1] Even without any formal agreement among the dealers, they all understand that the price list is to be followed. Sometimes these lists are prepared by the retailers, in others by the wholesalers or jobbers. In the latter case the catalog gives the retail prices and the retailer has a discount from the printed price. An excellent illustration of this plan of regulating prices is furnished by wire rope. The manufacturers have a common catalog which they distribute to the retailers and the retailers all sell at the list price. The Southern Wholesalers' Association printed lists of prices for the information of its members until enjoined by the court. It might be supposed that a loose arrangement of this kind would not work; but as a matter of practice it is successful. A. F. Huston[2] well states the force which holds men to the understanding in the following words: "Let me say that it is a general broad principle that if a certain price is felt to be a fair and right price, each one for himself feels that he ought to maintain that price and not vary from it to the detriment of his fellows without he should let them know, but without any agreement, express or implied, to that effect." However, in some cases the understood prices are departed from. In such a case, if one decides to cut a price, the others may remonstrate; but if he persist, except it be as a leading line for a short time, the others may meet the cut, and a new minimum be fixed. Similarly as a result of informal discussion of the conditions of the market, prices are put up or down in unison.

Common prices.

The regular and uniform rise and fall of the price of anthracite during any year illustrate the situation. In early summer the price is the lowest; it is increased by regular increments as the autumn comes on. The price is the same in a given community from each dealer for purchases at a given

[1] Investigation U. S. Steel Corporation, 10, pp. 604–615.
[2] Investigation U. S. Steel Corporation, 11, p. 693.

time under similar circumstances. The result is almost as certain and as uniform as if it came about by formal agreement put into legal form.

The stage of the association for exchange of information easily passes into the second phase in which regulations are adopted by the association to control the actions of its constituents; as, for instance, methods to be pursued in advertising, quotations, and even scale of prices. Actions of this kind are well illustrated by the brewers' association, which decides as to the price to be charged for beer in the retail trade, issues regulations about rebates to retailers, and even goes into such minor details as the treating of drivers, and the extent to which favors are to be given by advertising, etc.

Regulations of associations.

When the members of an association are numerous, the extent to which they coöperate in these respects is a matter of public knowledge; but in case an industry is concentrated in several or at most a few corporations, a secret gentlemen's agreement may be reached which acts powerfully in restraint of trade. Thus it is charged that at the weekly meetings of the Chicago packers, which in the past regularly occurred, a definite understanding was reached as to field of operation, output, prices, and margins, which were to obtain for the following week.

Secret agreements.

Similarly it is charged that at the so-called Gary dinners an informal understanding was reached concerning these points for iron and steel. What happened, according to Mr. E. H. Gary, was that the steel makers met together and exchanged information with reference to one another's affairs, their outputs, prices, etc., in order that each might have full knowledge of the transactions of other producers to guide his own judgment. In the case of the Chicago packers there can be little doubt that the understanding was much more definite than in the case of the steel conferees; but so far as the public was concerned, the results were substantially the same; output was regulated, prices were maintained.

Informal understandings binding.

It is charged also that the group of men who control the anthracite industry meet regularly to fix output and prices at the various commercial centers, and that this practice has

Anthracite coal prices fixed.

been in vogue for many years. That this charge is true can scarcely be doubted, although it might not be easy to prove. Also, there is no doubt that the railroads in the early stage of their coöperation entered into agreements and understandings as to the portion of business to be handled, the prices to be charged, and rebates to be allowed.

Similarly it is charged that produce exchanges agree upon and control prices; thus it is stated that the association of butter makers centering in Elgin fix prices on dairy products, and especially butter, for a large part of the country.

The character and influence of these associations have become widely known through the prosecutions by the United States Attorney-General under the Sherman antitrust act. One of these, the Southern Wholesalers' Association, without going to trial, admitted many of the practices above described and accepted a comprehensive decree enjoining the members from coöperating. A number of other associations, illustrated by the lumber associations, are under attack. These cases bring clearly to light the real significance of a form of organization which pervades the commerce of the country.

While associations formal and informal are the least definite of the various combinations, they are probably the most important because their scope is coextensive with the country and with its business.

(2) *Formal Agreements.* — In certain lines of business, corporations have made definite agreements about the management of the business of the uniting parties. The arrangements, usually called pools, (1) divided the production in a definite manner between the different companies; (2) divided the markets; (3) regulated the sales for the home market, perhaps leaving freedom in the matter of export; or (4) placed the entire profits in a common fund or pool to be divided according to an agreed plan. With the foregoing features, there sometimes went agreements as to prices; but this was not essential, since when controlling outputs, dividing markets, regulating sales, and apportioning profits, it is to the interest of all to keep prices at a high level.

Pools.

As the railways developed in this country, competition became so severe as frequently to lead to operation at a serious loss. Relief from this situation was found by pools under which the business between two points was definitely divided, and an agreement was made as to rates. Thus it might be agreed that each of the trunk lines between Chicago and New York should handle a definite percentage of the business.

Railway pools.

The pool so largely used by the railroads was also extensively applied to the industries. Under the manufacturers, pools, which began as early as 1860, each manufacturer was usually allotted a certain percentage of the business. A manufacturer who received more than the allotted percentage paid into the pool a sufficient amount to balance the excess; while the manufacturer who received less than his percentage received from the pool a sum sufficient to make up the deficiency. The business was done through a supervisor who acted in the capacity of a clearing house. For violation of the agreements of the pool, penalties were imposed upon its members usually in the way of fines or a percentage charge on business done outside the pool.

Industrial pools.

Pools are very well illustrated by the numerous agreements which were made by the iron companies among themselves before the organization of the United States Steel Corporation.[1]

In the case of the Michigan Salt Association, the organization developed to a state intermediate between the pool and the trust. This association, formed in 1876, soon controlled 85 per cent of the business of the state. The stockholders were the salt manufacturers of the state; and each manufacturer was allowed shares in the association in proportion to his production. The capitalization of the association was nominal. The association fixed the output of salt for each manufacturer and managed the entire selling business, including the determination of prices. The manufacturer gave up the entire management of his business to the Salt Association, excepting the running of his manufactory.[2] (See pp. 101–103.)

The Michigan Salt Association.

[1] Investigation U. S. Steel Corporation, 24, pp. 1813–1817.
[2] "Pools and Trusts," *Quarterly Review*, Vol. 199, p. 185.

Fruit growers' exchanges.

Very analogous in form of organization and conduct of business to the Michigan Salt Association, long since dead, are numerous fruit growers' exchanges. Some of these exchanges are district in their character, precisely as was the Michigan Salt Association. In others the district exchanges first formed have gotten together into a national exchange. In some instances such an exchange handles as much as 80 per cent of the entire crop. The stockholders of the exchange for a definite fruit or group of fruits are those engaged in growing the product. The exchange is usually a selling agency, charging commission for its services. While a fruit grower may sell a part of his crops other than through the agency, he pays the same commission that he would if the entire crop were disposed of by the exchange.

When the crop of fruit begins to come upon the market, the exchange sets a price for a certain period, which may be raised at the beginning of a second period and again at a later period. For fruits that keep well the usual plan is to start the price sufficiently low so that the fruit will begin to be marketed promptly, and to advance the price rapidly enough so that there will be a supply to the normal termination of the season. For some fruits the prices for early products may be high; later the prices are reduced; and still later, when the height of the season is over, they are again advanced. If prices be placed too high, some of the fruit will go to the dump at the end of the season; if they be placed too low, there will not be a sufficient amount to supply the market during the latter part of the season. To carry out wisely the above plans, careful estimates are made of any crop for the year. Inspectors are employed by the exchange to supervise the harvesting, storing, sorting, packing, and shipping of the fruit so as to get definite and uniform grades, and to have the fruit shipped under the most favorable circumstances. The growers retain their own brands.

Advantages of exchange.

The fruit exchanges do not regulate output; they do control prices; they aim to get the product as directly as possible to the jobbers and grocers without falling into the hands of speculators. The marketing costs are lessened by the exchange. Prices start at a reasonable level and have graded changes so that the producers are sure of a fair return. The public cannot be disregarded in fixing prices, since one kind of fruit competes with another, and since to a certain extent fruit is an abundant but desirable luxury which will not be disposed of if the prices are excessive. Products are inspected and standardized. It would seem that the credits due the fruit exchanges are considerable; that the public is better off than under the old hit or miss methods of disposal of the crop which have sometimes been characterized as mob methods; and that exchanges should be encouraged and retained.

These fruit growers' exchanges are illustrated by the Fruit Growers' Association of California.[1] For this exchange the contract between the grower and the local association requires that the grower shall sell only to the association, and that if he fails to pack and deliver his fruit within five days after demand is made upon him the association may enter the orchard, take possession of the premises, pick, pack, and market the fruit, all at the expense of the owner. The district exchanges of this association are under contract to sell only to the general exchange and as called for by that exchange. It is perfectly clear that the purpose of the citrous fruit growers of California is the control of the market.

Other lines of coöperation[2] among the farmers are the elevator systems for marketing grain and the warehouse exchanges for marketing cotton. It is said by Mr. E. H. Coller that there are in the neighborhood of twenty-five hundred or three thousand buying or selling organizations in the United States which are in the interests of better prices.[3]

Mr. T. J. Brooks, representing the Farmers' Educational Coöperation Union, suggests that since these farmers' cooperative associations are so advantageous they should be exempted from the prohibition of the Sherman antitrust law.[4]

[1] Hearings, Interstate Commerce Committee, XXVI, pp. 2336–2353.
[2] Edward G. Dunn, Farm and Fireside, March 16, March 30, April 13, 1912.
[3] Hearings, Interstate Commerce Committee, p. 1344. [4] *Ibid.*, p. 2337.

This is an appropriate suggestion, for it can be asserted without fear of contradiction that fruit exchanges organized as indicated are as clearly in violation of the Sherman anti-trust law as the selling agencies of manufacturers which have been declared to be illegal by the courts.

If the farmers' selling agencies are admitted to be beneficial to the farmers and to the public, it may be said that fully as strong a case may be made for other selling agencies, among which is coal. Yet when a number of coal operators whose market was Chicago conceived the idea of establishing a selling agency which did not combine more than four per cent of the consumption of that market, they were warned by the federal authorities that such action would be combination in restraint of trade.[1]

Reign of the pools.

The pools in the seventies and early eighties occupied an important place in the development of combination; their chief reign was from 1879 to 1887, about ten years. With the passage from the partnership to the corporation, the principles of the law applicable to individuals and to partnerships were carried over to corporations. But the pool was in effect a partnership of corporations, or at least, if not a partnership, such coöperation of corporations, as to amount substantially to the same thing. Partnerships of corporations were illegal, and consequently the pool contracts were non-enforcible.[2]

Weakness of pools.

The non-enforcible agreement gave the pools a fundamental weakness. Any member that became dissatisfied could withdraw at any time. Also, since the courts refused to enforce the arrangements made under pools, compliance with the regulations depended exclusively upon the honor of those entering them; and, in consequence, there were frequent secret violations of the pool agreements. A railroad or a manufactory would exceed its percentage, or in order to get business would reduce rates. Further the men and corporations entering into the pools were in danger of penalties from the courts. As we have already seen, the selling agency,

[1] Hearings, Interstate Commerce Committee, XXVI, pp. 2320–2321.
[2] "Trusts of To-day," G. H. Montague, pp. 144–145.

having many of the weaknesses of the pools, still retains an important place in business.

(3) *Trusts.* — Since the pool was a failure, in order to attain the objects striven for by it, the trust was devised. Under the trust, each unit of the combination transferred its stock to trustees. Thus the entire stock of the constituent companies was held by a group of trustees who had complete authority over the business of all the companies entering into the trust. An establishment or company retained its own officers and conducted its business, but under the direction of the trustees, as to line of product, amount of output, and price. The trust was able to prevent overbuilding and overproduction, to prevent competition in price between its units, to apportion business, to consolidate buying and selling, and thus gave all the advantages of unity of organization, as described, pp. 8–20, due to concentration of industry. Well-known types of this organization were the Standard Oil trust, the sugar trust, the cotton-seed oil trust, the whisky trust. The great period of the trust was from 1888 to 1897.

If the pool was a partnership of corporations, it was even more clear that the board of trustees controlling the business of a number of corporations through their trust certificates was such a partnership. In consequence of this, in the late eighties trusts were declared to be illegal, and this led in the early nineties to the next stage of combination.

(4) *Holding Corporations.* — Under the trust each of the constituent companies was an independent legal entity. The stock was simply placed in the hands of the trustee for management. In the holding corporation, the stock is transferred to the holding concern so that this corporation actually owns the stock of the constituent companies. So far as management and operation are concerned, the situation is precisely the same as under the trust and the advantages the same, only the constituent companies are subsidiary companies instead of nominally independent. The subsidiary company maintains its officers, carries on its business, and competes so far as efficiency is concerned with

the other companies of the combination; but as to nature and quantity of output and price, the policy is completely controlled by the corporation of which it is a constituent member. The era of the holding corporation began in the nineties, and has extended through that decade and the first decade of the twentieth century. Great examples are the Standard Oil Company and the United States Steel Corporation.

While some of the holding corporations have remained merely managing companies, others of them, and some of the more important, have also become manufacturing companies.

Holding corporations also manufacturing ones.

In these instances some plants are under the direct management of the directors of the corporation, while other parts of the business are run by subsidiary companies. This stage of development is intermediate between the strictly holding corporation and the merger, next to be spoken of.

Under the common law the stock of one corporation could not be held by another; therefore the holding corporation was declared to be invalid.[1] This situation was met by

State laws come to the rescue.

the enactment of corporation laws under which it was valid for a corporation to hold stock of other corporations. The first of the states thus to reverse the common law principle was New Jersey. She has been followed by several others, notable among which are Delaware, West Virginia, and Maine. The liberal, not to say lax, corporation laws of these states have led to the holding corporations being organized under their laws, and mainly under the laws of New Jersey and Delaware. According to Frederick W. Kelsey, the state of New Jersey profits to the extent of over $3,000,000 per annum because of its pioneer position in passing liberal corporation laws.

Holding corporations attacked.

However, the corporations which are in whole or in part holding companies, organized under the laws of these states, are now being attacked in the United States Court. In 1911 orders were given for the dissolution of the Standard Oil and the American Tobacco companies, the first of

[1] People *v.* Chicago Gas Trust Co., 130 Ill. 268; also other cases.
[2] Hearings, Interstate Commerce Committee, XVII, p. 1358.

which was strictly a holding company and the second of which was both a manufacturing and holding company. (See pp. 181–187.) Many other holding corporations are now attacked by the Attorney-General of the United States and must fight for their existence.

The holding corporation began in 1897, but the great consolidations did not begin until in 1899, since which time the holding corporation has been the dominant form of consolidation.

(5) *Complete Merger.* — This is the final stage in concentration of management. The stock of the constituent companies of the combination is actually bought in and canceled, the only stock being that of the master company. If, for instance, the different companies of the United States Steel Corporation — the Federal Steel, the Carnegie Steel, and others — cease to exist by their stock being canceled and stock of the Steel Corporation be the only existing issue, we should have the final stage of corporation management for this gigantic company.

Coming of the complete merger.

Since the recent decisions of the United States Supreme Court (see pp. 180–181), which seem to indicate that holding companies will be in a stronger position if they are actually manufacturing companies, it is easy to predict that the great consolidations, now forming, so far as practicable will become unified corporations. The merger began to become important about 1904, and since that time its growth has steadily continued, although, as already pointed out, the holding company is still the dominant form of concentration.

Just as the pool, the trust, and the holding corporation have been successively attacked in the courts, there can be little doubt that the great merger will also there be attacked. Indeed, for intrastate commerce such attack has already been begun. For instance, the Diamond Match Company which bought outright the properties of competing concerns engaged in the manufacture of matches, was declared to be an illegal monopoly in the state of Michigan.[1] Similar attack is likely to follow for interstate commerce under the Sherman act.

The merger on defense.

[1] Richardson *v.* Buhl, 77 Mich. 632.

The laws have accelerated consolidation.

General Statements. — It is to be noted that the development from pool to trust, from trust to holding company, from holding company to complete consolidation, has been accelerated by the laws which exist in restraint of trade. The dissolution of pools by the courts led to the trust; the dissolution of the trust led to the holding corporation; the dissolution of the holding corporation at the present time is now leading to the consolidated company.

The actions which have led to the above development have been partly under common law and partly under statute law. The common law, forbidding unreasonable restraint of trade, may be invoked to prevent any form of pool, trust, holding company, or merger, which goes to the point of producing monopoly. Actions under statute law, to be successful, must of course comply with its terms, somewhat variable in the different states. (See pp. 192–200.)

Other accelerating causes.

By the above statements it is not meant that the law against restraint of trade is the only cause which has led to the development described. As we have seen, pp. 26–27, fierce and unrestricted competition has led directly to combination, or else elimination of the weaker by destruction, until the remainders are reduced to a manageable number, usually all strong and at least of the same order of magnitude, if not exactly the same size, when they combine. Also there are other important factors leading to combination which have been discussed, pp. 8–20.

Section 7

THE KINDS OF COMPETITION

There are different kinds of competition. For present purposes the more important are, competition in quality, competition in price, and competition in service.

(1) *Competition in Quality.* — The better the quality, the easier it is to do business. For certain articles the quality is easily determined and so becomes a very important factor in competition; for other things it is not easy to settle.

With such articles as tea, tobacco, coffee, the quality is not an absolute thing, but depends upon the taste of the customer. We frequently hear the story of the retail dealer who takes a chest of a poor or medium quality of tea, divides the same among three caddies upon which he puts prices of thirty-five cents, sixty-five cents, and one dollar per pound. A person who can afford to pay but thirty-five cents quickly takes that kind; the person who is able to afford somewhat more takes from the intermediate caddie; the third, to whom the matter of a dollar is of little consequence, at once takes the tea having the highest price.

The same tea with three prices.

There is no doubt that this sort of performance has occurred and is occurring at the present time upon an extensive scale in thousands of retail shops.

If for such articles as tea, tobacco, and coffee there is no definite standard, this is even more markedly so with the so-called "articles de Paris," or if we use the American term, "Yankee notions." There is no standard by which the price of a lady's hat can be fixed. The price that is charged usually depends more upon the make-up than upon the cost of its materials. Indeed in this class of goods the artistic quality enters, or if not the artistic quality at least the conventional quality, which itself has a market value, and this makes impossible any standardization. The price of a hat is very largely fixed with reference to what the traffic will bear. Thus a lady's hat in a town in which the customer is able to pay $50 might have a price one fifth of that amount in a town in which the customer was able to pay only $10. Another illustration: The success of the manufacturer of silver articles who wishes to sell his goods in India will depend very largely upon producing forms which please the Indian taste. Thus for many articles, whether or not a sale is made depends not only upon the cost of the material in the article, but upon whether it pleases the customer. Competition in these lines of business is not close because there is no basis upon which to compare prices.

Yankee notions.

The value of a lady's hat.

From the class of articles in which success in business depends not upon standardization or upon cost, but upon adaptability to the customer, we have every stage to those in which the material of the article becomes the chief factor.

Standardization and price.

(2) *Competition in Price.* — When we come to deal with articles the quality of which may be definitely determined competition immediately enters in price, and becomes more and more important as we approach standard products. Granulated sugar is a standard article, which is the same whether purchased of one dealer or another; the same is true of oil, which has a certain fireproof test; and to a large extent is true of cement and coal, at least they may be made to meet standard tests. The same is true of the more important forms of steel rails, structural forms, etc., and for many other products. For articles in which quality is standardized, competition enters mainly in the matter of price. These standard articles, as we have seen, are also those which usually have very wide use, and are those which are especially subject to combination.

Blind faith in competition.

Competition in price is the one in which the public as a whole is most deeply interested. Indeed, this is so dominant in the minds of many, that the securing of a fair price is regarded as the sole purpose of the competitive system. In purchasing, the price that one can afford to pay is the paramount consideration for all but a minute fraction of the people. This applies alike to the man or woman buying the necessities of life for the family and to the lady in the middle walks of life purchasing clothes or jewels. The number of people who can afford to ignore the question of price is less than one per cent of the population. It is the general belief that competition is the best means of securing a fair price that has held many with unswerving faith to the competitive system.[1]

[1] The best formulation of this faith which I have seen is that of General Roger A. Pryor, as follows: —

"1. Competition between buyers of the raw material enhances the price to the producer.

"2. Competition between sellers of the manufactured article reduces its price to the consumer.

"3. Reduction of price multiplies the number of consumers.

"4. Increase of consumption stimulates production to supply the increased demand.

(3) *Competition in Service.* — In addition to competition in quality and in price there is competition in service. This is best illustrated by those cases in which competition does not exist for the first two. Thus in standard articles in a town, such as ice, there is no competition in quality; there is no competition in price; the only competition is in service. Similarly for railways, now that competition in prices has ceased, competition is reduced to the nature of the service, — the number of trains run, the convenience of the schedules, the excellence of the cars, etc.

The personal element in competition

It is in the matter of competition in service that the personal element largely enters. Where quality is standardized and the price is the same, the decision as to where one shall deal depends upon the agreeable qualities of the firm. Are the employees polite and considerate? Is the service promptly rendered? These factors are so important that agents having a pleasant personality and a persuasive way of putting things are highly paid by corporations, their sole business being to show that the service rendered will be of the highest quality and the attention of the best. So important is this factor of service that many, indeed a majority, of the people are influenced by it in the selection of the firm with which they will deal; and with the well-to-do it is frequently the dominating consideration. Even where competition in quality and in price are eliminated there may be the keenest competition in service.

"5. Increase of production implies an increase in the employment of labor.

"6. Competition between the employers of labor enhances the wages of labor.

"7. Enhancement of the wages of labor involves the material and moral amelioration of the condition of the laboring class.

"8. Competition to sell stimulates to improvements in the quality of the article offered.

"9. Competition to sell urging reduction in the cost of the article, ingenuity is quickened to the invention of expense-saving and labor-saving machinery, and so a stimulus is applied to the progress of the useful arts and sciences.

"In short, competition ministers to the welfare of all classes of the community, and augments the resources and power of the state. But the evil of excessive competition is counteracted and arrested by the principle of self-interest and the operation of the law of supply and demand."

Section 8

THE BREAK-DOWN OF COMPETITION

The Faith in Competition. — Competition for the control of prices and quality of goods has been a faith which has been believed in by the great majority of people of America; it has been the fundamental principle of the common and statute law upon which our court decisions controlling trade have been built up. Every proposal to legalize coöperation in trade has been stoutly resisted as interfering with the inflexible law of competition, the bulwark of our industrial liberty.

The producer may do as he pleases with reference to quality; he may ask the price he can get; but he cannot combine with another producer in the regulation of price or do anything which may be interpreted to interfere with complete independence in trade. The theory is that the quality will be kept up and the price kept down by competition, and that the purchaser needs no further protection.

The Failure of Competition adequately to regulate Quality. — This faith in the power of competition has gone so far in the past that any manufacturer might call an article by any name he pleased, provided the name did not have a trade mark, regardless of whether or not it had any relation to the product so labeled. An article could be called pure fruit jelly and have no fruit in it; it could be called corn whisky and not a grain of corn be used in its manufacture; it could be named strained honey and a bee never have had anything to do with its making; it could be called maple sirup and never a drop of maple sap have entered it; it could be called butter and have no relation with milk or cream; it could be called boneless chicken and consist of immature veal. A hundred other illustrations could be given. As already indicated, if the producer could to his own advantage use names that had no relation to the product, he did so. The purchaser was not obliged to buy. If he wished an article

The failure of competition to prevent fraud.

which had a relation to the name, he was to ascertain this for himself.

These practices have obtained both for intrastate and interstate commerce until within a few years; but now a large number of states (see p. 245) have pure food laws. Most of these laws are comprehensive in their character and they apply to all foods, drugs, and drinks. To illustrate, it is no longer possible to sell oleomargarine as butter; indeed, it is not possible in some of the states to color oleomargarine in such a manner as to make it appear like butter to the user. Finally, after many years of struggle against tremendous opposition, a comprehensive pure food law was passed in 1906 by Congress, under which the same principles which had been applied in some of the states for intrastate commerce were applied to interstate commerce.

Pure food laws.

In addition to the pure food laws, some states have enacted laws prohibiting the importation of weed-infested seed, regulating the importation of nursery stock, especially to prevent the spread of insect pests, and requiring that fertilizers shall meet definite standards.

Thus for food and drugs it may now be said to have become an accepted principle that competition in the control of quality has broken down, and similarly that competition has not furnished sufficient protection in certain other classes of commodities. For protection to the customer in these matters of fundamental importance we now understand that we must depend upon regulation. This regulation has for its basis law; but the success of the laws has been dependent upon the creation of special machinery other than the courts for their enforcement, viz., administrative commissions, etc. (See pp. 245–247.)

Competition has failed to secure quality.

While there is a wide range of articles in which competition as a regulator has been abandoned, there are many articles in which competition is left as the guard. Thus a dealer may sell cloth as pure silk which is largely composed of cotton; he may sell cotton as linen; he may sell shoddy as woolen. While these things may be contrary to law, the public, as a

The feeble guard of competition

matter of fact, is wholly unprotected; for the law is not enforced. Quality, so far as it is satisfactorily controlled, is securable only through law as administered by commissions or other special officers under a broad exercise of the police power.

The Failure of Competition adequately to regulate Price. — During the same time that competition has ceased to control quality there has been a break-down of competition in the control of prices. This is now admitted for the so-called public utilities. It was the theory in the early days of railroad building that we must get as many lines as possible and have them compete in charges. The frightful wastes of that method, bankruptcy, receiverships, financial depression, alternately excessively high and low rates, show that for this line of business competition in price is a hopeless failure; and it is now a tacitly accepted doctrine that so far as railroads are concerned, prices for the same manner of service, whether freight or passenger, between two points is to be the same over the different lines. This is done through mutual understanding of the supposed competing lines. That a half-dozen railroads between New York and Chicago could have the same complicated freight schedules for all classes of articles without coöperation is incredible. Everybody knows the rates are agreed upon by the various traffic associations. Yet such coöperation and agreements are just as illegal as they have ever been in the past. The parties to them under the law are subject to criminal and civil prosecution; yet nobody prosecutes; nobody complains. Why is this so? Because the public through its commissions is able to secure fair rates. So far as interstate commerce is concerned, the price is fixed by the railroad and controlled by the Interstate Commerce Commission. Within many of the states, the prices are fixed by the corporations, but may be modified by the commissions.

Railroads do not compete in price.

In cities the street car lines, gas companies, and electric companies, each have monopoly in a given city, or the two or more agree upon identical rates. Competition has ceased to control prices. Where prices are controlled it is through a public utilities commission.

Public utilities do not compete in price.

Just as there has been a complete collapse in competition in prices for railroad transportation and city utilities, so there has been complete collapse in charges for communication. The post office is a public monopoly; the rates are fixed. The telegraph business of the country has become consolidated into two great corporations the prices of which are identical. The telephone business is now mainly under the control of a single corporation. The foregoing facts show that the only present effect of the theory that competition gives adequate control of prices, so far as the railroads and other public utilities are concerned, is to bring the law into contempt.

Closely allied to the natural monopolies are the great companies which for each industry are controlled by a single organization or by a number of organizations working together under open or secret agreements or understandings and not competing in price. Here are included anthracite, steel, oil, beef, whisky, sugar, and other great industries. When prices are maintained at the same level for steel rails for a decade during times of panic and great expansion alike, it is certain that competition has ceased to control adequately prices for iron products. The same applies to anthracite, oil, and many other commodities.

Trusts do not compete in price.

For some articles, the producers, instead of uniting their concerns and informally agreeing on prices, have united in a selling agency and in this way succeed in holding up the prices and maintaining a like price for each producer. Thus the Michigan Salt Association, as first organized (see pp. 101, 103), was a selling agency. One of the largest of the selling agencies is the United Metals Selling Company. It markets upward of 500,000,000 pounds of copper annually. It is the sales agent for the Amalgamated Copper Company and affiliated corporations. The commission charged the Amalgamated was 1½ per cent before 1906, but now is 1 per cent. The company has been highly successful, having paid dividends upon its capital stock of $5,000,000 of from 20 to 30 per cent since 1904, with one extra 50 per cent dividend in 1909.

Selling agencies.

At one time there was a producers' association for oil, the association selling only through its regularly appointed agencies, and only to the refiners' association and its members.[1] In a like manner the manufacturers of wall paper organized a selling company to handle their entire output, selling only to such persons as entered into a prescribed agreement; but this organization got into court, was declared to be illegal, and was therefore dissolved.[2]

Selling agencies in the industries have existed in a number of lines, but there is a tendency at the present time for them to disappear so far as manufacturers are concerned, since it is recognized that they are violations of the laws, national and state.

Selling agencies among farmers.

While the selling agency is disappearing among the manufacturers, coöperative selling agencies are arising among the farmers. These are illustrated by the fruit growers' exchanges of the West in Washington, Oregon, and California, by the nut growers' associations of the South; indeed at the present time all over the country there is a strong movement for coöperation of the farmers not only to buy through coöperative associations, but to form selling associations for marketing their products (see pp. 66–68).

Bad and good selling agencies.

The selling agencies of the manufacturers which have held up prices have been denounced. The proposals to create selling agencies for the farmers' products have been generally commended. It is difficult to see wherein the principle differs in one case from that in the other. If it is not legal for the copper producers or wall paper manufacturers to have joint selling agencies, it is difficult to see how the fruit producers can legally have such an agency.

To a large extent competition has ceased adequately to control the prices for many articles not in great combinations, and this is true both in the wholesale and retail businesses. The various associations of business men have, as one of their chief purposes, the maintenance of prices. Many articles which are protected by patents or trade marks are

[1] Tarbell's "History of Standard Oil Company," Vol. I, p. 341.
[2] Continental Wall Paper Company *v.* Louis Voigt & Sons, 212 U. S. 227.

How price agreements are maintained.

sold to the dealers only on condition that the prices fixed by the manufacturer shall be maintained. The manufacturer of a definite automobile apportions the country into districts and requires of the dealers in each of the districts that the prices fixed by the manufacturer shall be charged. The same thing is true of hundreds of articles, from sewing machines to talking machines, and so on down to an atomizer. In this class of trade there is competition to a certain extent between the different manufacturers; there is no competition between the tradesmen selling the same articles. Frequently the prices for a definite line of goods are held up by agreement or understanding among the different manufacturers producing the same line of goods, they agreeing among themselves regarding the prices which shall be charged by the retailer; and in many cases the different manufacturers are in a definite combination.

Penalties for violation of price agreements.

While the courts would not enforce any penalties for a violation of these agreements, the manufacturer or jobber usually has sufficient power through refusal to sell the article to prevent the agreement from being broken. Thus the saloon keeper who would sell a glass of beer for less than five cents, or who would use a glass holding more than the agreed maximum amount, could no longer purchase beer from the brewers. Through this method of control competition in price has broken down completely among retail dealers for many articles.

Local dealers agree on prices.

But this does not indicate anything like the extent to which competition in price has disappeared. The retailers in a given city or community have an association either formal or informal, and there is among the members a definite understanding that prices shall be maintained. It makes no difference from what dealer one buys anthracite, or sugar, or bacon, or flour, or any other standard article, in the majority of the small towns and cities of the country; the price asked by each is the same, with possible slight variations in some cases. It may be that for a time a retailer will cut the price on some standard article in order to increase his trade, in which case there is likely to be a cut by some other retailer on another standard line in order to equalize this advantage. But soon they get together and the prices are again the same.

For some concerns which have a large part of the business of a town, either through a single retail shop or a number of them, an additional shop may be there established by this firm under another name, apparently in complete independence, in order that there may be an appearance of competition. From time to time if there be danger of outside parties entering the field, the stool pigeon establishment may reduce prices under the direction of the controlling organization.

The extent to which there is combination among the retailers has led Professor Laughlin, of the University of Chicago, before the Senate Interstate Commerce Committee, to testify that competition among retailers has completely broken down. Says he: "We do not have competition; it does not exist. To-day there is really no competition between the retail men who sell meat or groceries to different classes of people."[1]

While the statement is substantially true for most communities, it does not fully express the facts for all of them. There still exists competition in prices between the small shops and the great mail order houses. Indeed, this competition is so severe that it is feared by the ordinary retailers, who oppose vigorously a parcels post because they believe that this would make the mail order houses even more formidable competitors. Also there is competition between the small retailers and the great department stores; and since the latter have begun to introduce branch houses in this country as has been done extensively in England, the competition is likely to become more serious. Further, there is competition between the regular retailers and the coöperative stores; but in this country the latter are relatively few in number, although numerous in England.

Competition between different classes of dealers.

A statement nearer the truth about the retail trade would be that competition in price for standard articles has ceased to exist between shops of the same class in the same

[1] Hearings, Senate Interstate Commerce Committee, Part XIV, p. 1005.

community. The regular retailer's prices for a town are the same; the prices for the department stores are the same; the prices of the mail order houses are the same.

Declining influence of competition in the retail trade.

In short the retail trade is the one in which concentration has not gained dominance; and we are in a transition stage between the old and new order of things. One who has watched the rise of the great department store in this country and England and who now sees their expanding branches, one who has seen the rise of the great mail order house within the last score of years, need have little prophetic sense to realize that concentration is to rule in the retail trade, the same as it has in manufacture. The retail trade as pointed out by Macrosty, is the "last stronghold of competition."[1]

But even in that business competition has largely broken down, and presently there, as elsewhere, coöperation will become general. The small retailer can only hold his place to the extent that he best performs a service to the community.

Agreements in the dark.

General Statements. — As to the extent of combinations and agreements in the industries, Mr. Samuel Untermeyer, who certainly ought to know the facts, said before the Senate Interstate Commerce Committee: "I have known of hundreds of them being dissolved where they were under written agreements. There are safes in New York stuffed with the written evidences of these conspiracies with big men's signatures to them. Those are gone, but in their places you have associations for the betterment of trade, etc.; there are any number of dinner and luncheon clubs and reunions and general understandings, winks, and telephone messages, that are far more difficult to get at."[2]

If any one doubts the above statement regarding the extent to which there is coöperation in prices in all parts of the United States and in all lines of business, it is suggested that such doubter talk with the business men of the country, from the retailer to the great manufacturer. This the author has done with many, and in no instance has he found

[1] "The Trust Movement in British Industry," H. W. Macrosty, p. 244.
[2] Hearings, Senate Interstate Commerce Committee, Part V, p. 214.

Testimony of business men.

a man who does not say that in his business coöperation exists everywhere and that competition does not control in prices; that they are matters of agreement, formal and informal; that prices are fixed at what seems to the organization as a fair amount, or to such a level as can be maintained without encouraging additional competition.

Limit to excessive prices.

In making the statement that prices of many articles, from the great natural monopolies to matches, are controlled by some form of combination or agreement, is is not meant to imply that any price can be charged for an article. There is a limit beyond which, if the price be raised, competitors will enter a business. This so-called potential competition makes the combinations careful not to place the prices at so high a level as to lead to additional competition. Although this is the situation, if the combination be a powerful one, it may go far; for the man thinking of entering the field knows that if he attempts this, the price of the product may be depressed by the great organization, and he fears to enter the enterprise. In the earlier stages of combination in this country the danger mark was frequently overshot; and competitors appeared, sometimes to the detriment of the organizations, but more often with disaster to themselves. By practice the great combinations have become skillful in exacting as much as possible without danger to themselves.

Prices what the market will bear.

Beyond the amount which is a fair profit there is a limit to the excess which can be taken year after year without bringing in competitors; but the total excess may be vast in amount. Sufficient evidence of this is furnished by the great corporations which are especially considered. (See pp. 104–154.) The United States Steel Corporation, in addition to paying interest on its bonds and ample dividends on all of the real valuation of the stock, has been able to put back into the business in a decade more than five hundred million dollars. This was accomplished in ten years by this corporation coöperating with the other corporations in the iron business, through holding the prices as high as the domestic trade would bear, but always sufficiently low so that a protective tariff prevented competing iron from coming into this country from abroad. At the prices fixed, as large sales were made as possible in the United States and the excess was sold abroad at a lower rate. Precisely the same situation has obtained for the Standard Oil Company. The enormous profits of the past decade, far beyond reasonable amounts (see pp. 108–109), have been accomplished by an excess margin of somewhat more than two cents a gallon. This seems small; it may be so, — perhaps not more than twenty-five cents each for every man, woman, and child, in the United States, — but even on this basis the excess would be more than twenty million dollars per annum.

The same principles apply all along the line down to the local grocers. The advantages of prompt and convenient delivery enable the retail dealers of a town or city to coöperate in maintaining their prices above a normal profit by a definite margin. The limit to this margin is that it cannot be made so large as to make it advantageous for the consumer to purchase in a large city or in a neighboring town; although it may approach so close to this that some of the more careful and astute do make outside purchases.

The margin of profits which may be gained beyond a fair price is known as monopoly price. The law of monopoly price has been carefully analyzed by Ely. He says: "The greater the intensity of customary use, the higher the general average of economic well-being, and the more readily wealth is generally expended, the higher the monoply charge which will yield the largest net returns." [1] If the price be raised too high, sales will diminish and therefore returns be lowered. It is the aim to hold the prices sufficiently high to give the largest possible return with the least expansion of business. In this connection it should be understood that the principle of monopoly price applies where monopoly does not fully exist; that it applies in greater or less degree as long as there is any coöperation of a group engaged in a given trade.

The law of monopoly price.

As illustrating the principle that if a local combination goes beyond the monopoly price, outside competitors will come in, is the case of ice at Madison, Wisconsin. Madison

[1] "Monopolies and Trusts," R. T. Ely, p. 103.

is situated between two lakes upon which ice forms each winter; ice houses are located along the lakes; and thus the ice dealers should be able to furnish this product at a low rate. For a moderate sized house until two or three years ago the price of ice furnished for family use was at the rate of $1.50 for five hundred pounds, or $18 per annum. The price was raised to a flat rate of $2 a month in 1909, which price was so high that the Knickerbocker Ice Company entered the field in 1910. This company fixed the price at $1 for five hundred pounds, and the local companies met the cut. But later, when the business of the new company was established, they and the local companies got together and raised the rate to $1.50 per five hundred pounds.

Entrance of outside competition.

Just as with public utilities, manufacture, and trade, competition has broken down as an adequate regulator of price, so in great measure competition has broken down in the price of labor and service. Thus the physicians of a given town usually charge exactly the same rate for the same kind of a service. Not to do so is regarded by the physicians as contrary to good medical ethics. The same practice obtains in other professions. And yet so far as the principle is concerned, an understanding by which a common price is charged for a like service is just as unlawful in proportion to the importance of the matter as any other combination in which there are price agreements.

Professional men agree in prices.

Not only do professional men agree about prices, but also those who perform services of an entirely different character. The most fundamental purpose of the trades-union and all combinations of labor is to do combined bargaining, the chief point being the price. A union scale of prices is fixed by which all members of the union must abide. Not only do the regulations of the labor unions prescribe the price which is to be charged by the laborer, but the methods under which he is to work. In many instances in which the price is fixed regarding the day's wage, the laborer must not do more than a prescribed amount of work. The idea of individual bargaining by the laborers in the industries, and their competition among themselves as proper regulators of prices, has broken down

Labor combinations and prices.

absolutely; and necessarily so, because the laborer as an individual was simply helpless against the great concentrations of capital. The only way that the laborers can be put on anything like an equal footing with capital in industry is to unite and so give themselves the strength of concentration, and thus do joint bargaining. From time to time the representatives of labor unions for coal, for railways, for the building industries, meet with the employers of labor, and agree with them upon a scale of prices which are to be charged for a given period of time. In this way competition in the price of labor between individuals is destroyed; not only so, but the fluctuation in price is wholly eliminated for a definite period.

The foregoing description of the situation cannot but convince any man who will look the facts in the face that the blind faith that prices are adequately controlled by competition in the United States is no longer justified, if indeed it ever was justified. Unrestrained competition does not as a matter of fact exist for many articles, except to a very limited degree at the present time. Everywhere there is restraint of trade by agreement or combination, either lawful or unlawful. So inevitable is this situation that we have seen how the law forbidding restraint of trade has accelerated concentration of industry from the loose agreement to the pool, from the pool to the trust, from the trust to the holding company, and from the holding company to the giant completely consolidated industry.

Blind faith in competition not justified.

In making the foregoing statements, it is not meant to imply that competition has not been a most useful economic force in the past, nor that it will not continue to be a useful force. Competition has been powerful in stimulating men to effort; it, under some conditions for some industries, has been potent in improving quality; it has limited margins within monopoly prices, and has often been helpful in a wider sphere; it has been dominant in improving service. From the smallest firm to the greatest corporation there has been an increase rather than a decrease in the power of competition in improvement of service. Even if competition were

Usefulness of competition.

wholly destroyed as to quality and as to price, competition in service would still remain of the keenest.

Competition must be supplemented by regulation.

While therefore agreeing that competition has been a great and highly useful economic force, it has been the purpose of the foregoing pages to show its severe limitations; to show that it is not adequate alone to control quality or price, and that where relied upon for these purposes, it has been a lamentable failure. For these, competition must be supplemented by regulation in order to give satisfactory results. In another place it is proposed that we shall retain the advantages of competition and also secure the advantages of regulation. (See pp. 249–252.)

Section 9

THE WASTES OF COMPETITION

On previous pages the economic advantages of concentration have been given. The obverse of these are the wastes of competition. The economic gains through concentration are possible savings, which, if not taken advantage of, are at least losses in the sense that better things could be done even if they are not technically wastes. Therefore, in one sense all of the advantages of concentration should be here listed as gains not securable through competition. The various points discussed (pp. 8–20) will not here be repeated, but a brief statement will be made of some of the evils of competition which can manifestly be called wastes.

(1) *Expenses of Salesmen.* — One of the largest of the wastes is the unnecessary expenditures for salesmen under the competitive system. Where there is competition, the sales agents everywhere overlap one another in their work. In a small town or village there may be a half-dozen men selling the same kind of article within a week; whereas, if coöperation existed, many different brands could be exhibited by a single salesman and the expense greatly reduced.

A number of illustrations of such losses have already been given. (See p. 14.) Many more might be included; but one of the best is the enormous loading in the life insurance business, which has resulted from the competitive system due to the expense of salesmen selling life insurance, usually men receiving high pay and high commissions. Indeed, for many companies a large percentage of the conduct of the business and a considerable percentage of the income has gone to compensate salesmen of insurance.

(2) *The Expense of Advertising.*—The money spent for advertising is enormous. This varies from the frantic efforts to push patent medicines, through many specialties, such as automobiles, to staple articles, such as soap, clothing, and foodstuffs. It is a well-known fact that the great daily newspapers would be losing enterprises, as conducted, if it were not for the advertising; indeed their major profits come from this class of business. The same is true of the weekly and monthly magazines, many of which give more space to advertising than to reading matter. If one looks through the magazines and makes an estimate of the amount of money which is spent in the advertising of such an article as soap for a single month, he will find that this reaches tens of thousands of dollars. The enormous cost of advertising will scarcely be appreciated without knowing the cost per page and the number of pages carried per month for the different magazines. The cost of advertising per page for each issue of some of the standard magazines is as follows:

Ladies' Home Journal, $6000; *Saturday Evening Post*, $4000; and such magazines as the *Century, American, Harper's, McClure's, Munsey's, Cosmopolitan, Everybody's*, from $250 to $600, depending upon the circulation.[1] Exceptional positions, such as the back covers and the pages next the covers have special rates greater than the above. The average number of pages of advertising for the *Ladies' Home Journal* is about 35, and the *Saturday Evening Post* is about 25. This makes the advertising cost for a single issue for these publications $210,000 and $100,000 respectively.

(3) *Competition and Conservation.* — The heaviest of the wastes of competition with reference to the future of the race

[1] Mahin Advertising Company Data Book, 1912.

are those due to the unnecessary destruction of natural resources in order to put an article on the market at a competitive price.

Of the wastes of natural resources through competition probably those of fuels and gas are the worst. Holmes says, regarding coal: —

"Those who are less familiar with the mining industry than you are with the metallurgy may not be aware of the fact that for every ton of coal brought to the surface in the bituminous or soft coal mines of this country, not less than one half a ton is left under the ground, and it will not be possible to bring it to the surface in the future at any reasonable cost, if at all. But more shocking still is the fact that in our anthracite coal fields, which are so limited in extent as to be confined to a territory comprising less than four hundred square miles, even with all modern improvements, not more than 50 per cent of the anthracite coal of the areas mined is being brought to the surface. The remainder of it, now aggregating 80,000,000 tons a year, is being left underground in such condition as to make its future recovery difficult, if not impossible.

One third of bituminous coal lost.

"In the early days of anthracite mining there was brought to the surface an average of between 30 and 40 per cent of the coal, so that from 60 to 70 per cent remained under the ground, which was sufficient to give strength to the roof; and to-day mining engineers are bringing to the surface a part of the coal which was left in the mines 30 or 40 years ago. But as the percentage of coal mined has increased, from time to time, the possibility of recovering what is left behind diminishes. It has been estimated that since the beginning of coal mining in the United States, more than 2,000,000,000 tons of anthracite coal and 3,000,000,000 tons of bituminous coal have been left underground in such condition as to make its future recovery doubtful or impossible.

Half of the anthracite left in ground.

"I know of no other American industry which to-day is in so deplorable an economic condition as is the bituminous

[1] *Journal of Industrial and Engineering Chemistry*, "Carbon Wastes," J. A. Holmes, pp. 160–162.

coal industry. The operators, unable under existing laws to combine and fix prices of coal or any trade agreements, are adopting what appears to be the only alternative — ruinous competition, which encourages or enforces wasteful and dangerous mining. It seems essential that federal or joint state legislation be enacted authorizing such reorganization of this great industry as will permit reasonable returns on the money invested and at the same time properly safeguard the public interests. You realize that it is often less expensive per ton for the operator to bring the first half of his coal to the surface than it is for him to bring out the remaining half, because this second half will support the roof while the first half is being removed; but while he removes the second half he must often temporarily support the roof with timbers; this entails additional expense, to meet which there is generally neither an accumulated surplus from which to draw, nor a temporary profit from which to meet this extra expense; hence the coal is abandoned. It is only fair to the coal operator that he is not in the mining business for his health, but to make a living by earning a reasonable return on his investment. Therefore, what we may consider a waste may be a necessary waste under existing economic conditions; a waste, however, that is preventable and should be prevented by improvements in our economic conditions, and necessary legislative requirements."

Competition produces waste.

The above admirable statement by Holmes regarding the inevitable waste of coal under the competitive system may be made more concrete by illustrations.

Mr. Walter S. Bogle, speaking for the coal operators of the state of Indiana, says that the proposed formation of a selling agency by a number of small operators was declared by the federal officers to be in restraint of trade, and notice was given that if such selling agency were established, those contemplating its formation would be subject to criminal and civil prosecution.[1] This is the situation even if the operators contemplating a selling agency are together able to put no more coal upon the market than a single large

[1] Hearings, Interstate Commerce Committee, XXVI, pp. 2320–2327.

concern. The Indiana coals are of a kind that deteriorate rapidly when taken out of the mine. Several varieties and sizes of coal are produced; to obtain one size other sizes must be made. If an order comes to a mine for a certain size, corresponding orders may not come for the other sizes; but such orders may come to an adjacent mine. If a group of mines may coöperate so that the orders will equalize themselves among the different varieties and sizes of coal, it is evident the waste will be greatly reduced.

Mr. G. W. Traer,[1] speaking for the Illinois Coal Operators' Association, says in that state there are about three hundred independent coal producing companies; that the demand for the Illinois coal is about 50,000,000 tons a year, but that the capacity of the mines is about 75,000,000 tons. It is necessary to have a greater mining capacity than the average demand, since the demand in the winter months greatly exceeds that of the summer months.

The Illinois coal, like the Indiana coal, deteriorates if unused for several months. Thus if the mines be developed sufficiently to meet the demands for the year, they must lie idle for a portion of the time. As a matter of fact the average running period of the mines per annum is about one hundred seventy days. If the mine operators do not agree among themselves regarding limitation of output during the summer months, it is inevitable that there will be overproduction, deterioration, and great waste; yet it is certain that under existing laws agreements to limit output are illegal.

Mr. J. F. Callbreath [2] states that there are 5000 operators of bituminous coal in the United States which have the ability without opening new mines to produce 200,000,000 tons of coal per annum more than the present markets demand. Under existing laws no group of these operators may coöperate. He states that three fourths of the members of the American Mining Congress are consumers of coal, not producers, and they urge that there be coöperation among the coal mines in order to secure regularity of out-

[1] Hearings, Interstate Commerce Committee, XXVI, pp. 2353–2359.
[2] *Ibid.*, XXVI, pp. 2372–2380.

put and uniform prices. According to him an investigation of the bituminous coal mining industry for 1910 shows the following situation: The average cost of production for 1910 was "$1.07 per ton, 95 cents for mine labor and supplies and 12 cents for general expenses. It shows that there was invested in the industry $585,000,000. The average price obtained at the mine during 1910 was $1.11 — 4 cents per ton to cover selling costs, depreciation of machinery, exhaustion of resources, and interest upon capital invested.

"The sworn testimony of the Pittsburg Coal Co., before the Interstate Commerce Committee in November, 1911, shows that in the previous 17 months the company mined 3,522,500 tons of coal at a cost of $1.1148, and the average selling price for that period was $1.0930. It showed further that the product of 20 of its mines, out of a total of 52, produced 5,350,594 tons at a cost of $1.0788, and when the money actually spent in selling this coal is added to the given cost and the interest on bonds of the company it appears that the cost of this coal was actually in excess of $1.15 per ton run of mine." [1]

Under such conditions it is certain that the mining will not be carried on economically; that only the coal will be taken out which can be mined cheaply, and the remainder left in the mine to be crushed by the gradually sinking roof. "To avert these conditions there are but two possible remedies. One, that the coal shall be sold at a greater average price; the other, a greater economy in operation by which the same price will yield a profit. Neither of these remedies is possible under the system of cutthroat competition which now exists. It is only by general coöperation that any relief can be obtained except by a process which would eliminate the greater number of those now in the business." [2]

Nor will it be possible under these conditions to introduce in the mines those devices which are necessary for the preservation of life; and plainly it will be impossible to

[1] Hearings, Interstate Commerce Committee, XXVI, pp. 2372–2373.
[2] *Ibid.*, p. 2376.

give the miners wages adequate to introduce good social conditions. In view of the above situation the operator asks that conditions be created covering the following points: —

"First. Proper protection to the lives and health of the miners.

"Second. Prevention of waste and proper conservation of fuel resources.

"Third. A fair profit to the operator.

"Fourth. A fair and uniform price to the consumer." [1]

No one can gainsay the desirability of creating the above conditions, but it is absolutely certain that they can never be established except through coöperation, and coöperation of a kind which is illegal under existing laws.

Waste of natural gas

Regarding gas, Professor Holmes says: "Our waste of natural gas is a crime, and thoroughly discreditable to the nation. It is far worse than the waste of coal. The statistics for 1910, according to the Geological Survey, showed that some 480,000,000,000 cubic feet of gas were turned into the atmosphere and forever lost. In the above as in other cases, the individual operator finds it easier to save a part, than all, of these resources, yes, cheaper for him to waste a large part of these resources than to save all. In the case of natural gas he says: 'I want to get oil, and if I can get the oil cheaper by letting the gas escape, that is the operation I will pursue.' And the state and the nation stand by and watch the operation.

Waste in making coke.

"There are many other examples of extensive and serious carbon waste in this country. Thus, in the coking industry the beehive coke ovens have turned into the atmosphere more than 100,000,000,000 cubic feet of valuable gas, which, if properly treated, will yield not only gas but other important carbon by-products."

Statements have been made at some length regarding fuel and gas because of their paramount importance; but for some of the metals a similar situation exists and must continue to exist under the severely competitive system.

[1] Hearings, Interstate Commerce Committee, XXVI, p. 2379.

This is illustrated by lead and zinc. Putting together all the losses in mining, concentration, and smelting, they probably amount on an average to at least 40 per cent of the metal of the ore, and in some instances the losses run as high as 60 or 70 per cent. These losses are in large measure due to the extreme competitive system under which excessive royalties are charged to the operators.[1] Waste of lead and zinc.

Untermeyer[2] calls attention to this situation for copper. Methods of competition involve overproduction for this country and exportation of the excess, when the copper ore in sight is probably not sufficient to last more than fifty years. If the copper producers were allowed to coöperate in the regulation of production, rational action could be secured both as to quantity of copper which is to be mined and as to methods of mining. Waste of copper.

Small production and competition in all mining enterprises lead to great and irreparable wastes, the effects of which must be borne by succeeding generations.

Another of the numerous wastes is that in metallurgy. For instance, sulphur is being burned upon a great scale, and the products are being passed into the atmosphere to the injury or destruction of surrounding vegetation. With reference to agriculture this loss of sulphur is likely to become irreparable, since sulphur is one of the limiting and crucial elements among plant foods.[3] Waste of sulphur.

A situation obtains for timber similar to that which applies to the metals and coal. With unrestricted competition the timber is cut and only the choicest parts of the logs are marketed, the remainder being left in the woods. If coöperation were possible, it would be practicable to have conservative timber cutting, the additional expense of saving the wasted material slightly adding to the price. Mr. D. E. Skinner[4] illustrates the situation regarding timber in Waste in timber.

[1] "Conservation of Natural Resources in the United States," C. R. Van Hise, pp. 80–85.

[2] Hearings, Senate Interstate Commerce Committee, Part V, p. 184.

[3] "Sulphur Requirements of farm crops in relation to the Soil and Air Supply," Research Bulletin 14, Agricultural Experiment Station, University of Wisconsin.

[4] Hearings, Interstate Commerce Committee, XXII, pp. 1909–1911.

the western part of the United States. Since under the Sherman act coöperation is not possible the weaker operators are bound to make sales, and they will at such prices as they can get. For the lower parts of the trees the average sale price is $15 per thousand feet board measure, and for the upper part $7 per thousand feet. In California it costs in round numbers $5 a thousand feet for logging and $5 for milling. Under these circumstances it naturally follows that the tops of the trees and the small down timber which will not produce lumber selling at about $10 a thousand, are left to rot in the forest; and this leaves on the ground from twenty to thirty per cent of the material which should have been taken off. The only possible remedy for the above situation is to allow coöperation so that a price may be secured which will permit the utilization of the upper parts of the trees. For our wild orgy of competition in the lumber industry succeeding generations will pay heavily.

Conditions in older countries.

In making the above statements, it is realized that in a new country, with abundant resources and a relatively sparse population, we cannot expect the same severe economies that are practiced in the older, more densely settled countries. It would be impossible to introduce the extreme economies and labor costs of the intensive agriculture of China into the United States under present conditions. The smaller twigs and limbs of timber cut in lumbering cannot be saved in this country as yet. Where labor is cheap, savings are possible which cannot be practiced in the United States. While this is the situation, upon the other hand, reckless extravagance in the use of natural resources is not warranted. Under present conditions, we can and should introduce all practicable economies in the use of our natural resources along every line.

Responsibility to posterity.

Everywhere the necessity to meet severe competition, combined with the desire to produce large profits, results in extravagant and wasteful use of resources limited in quantity. It is our duty to our descendants to conserve our fundamental resources, to use them economically, to prevent their unnecessary waste or destruction; and if by so doing a ton of anthracite or iron costs us a few cents more, we should bear this additional expense. Under unrestricted competition there is no hope for economical use of our resources, no hope for conservation.

The Consumer pays for the Wastes of Competition. — Ultimately all the losses and wastes of competition come back to the consumer and are added to the price which he must pay. If, as a result of overbuilding, concerns fail and factories are dismantled, the cost finally must be borne by the community. The enormous expense of traveling salesmen and advertising is paid by the consumers of the articles sold. The men who carry life insurance support the numerous high-priced agents. Succeeding generations will suffer for our reckless exploitations of natural resources.

Says Nettleton: "The waste of wealth due to unrestrained competition would, if saved, go far to enrich the community every year. And this waste finally falls for the most part on the general body of consumers, — the much enduring public." [1]

Wastes of Competition drive to Combination. — Because of the situation described, not only has restraint of trade existed in a thousand matters in contravention to the Sherman act and the various state antitrust acts; but it will continue to exist either lawfully or unlawfully, because of the frightful wastes of the competitive system. If where fierce and unrestricted competition exists, this goes on until the weaker competitors are driven from the business and the others are on the verge of bankruptcy, in order to prevent the destruction of the group, a combination or coöperation of the remaining companies will be formed either secretly or openly. In consequence of this principle, because of the law against restraint of trade in this country, innumerable secret combinations have been formed.

Combination permitted abroad.

In Germany and England, where combination is free as well as competition, the organizations of fair size have coöperated through one of the looser forms of organization, and have thus avoided the losses of fierce competition; but in America the loose agreements not being enforcible in the courts, in order

[1] "Trusts or Competition," A. B. Nettleton.

to save themselves from destruction, the competing units have been obliged to combine formally in a manner which it was supposed the courts would protect. We have seen that many of the whisky distilleries of the country had gone into bankruptcy before the remainder combined. Similarly it was the still fiercer competition between the Federal Steel and the Carnegie Steel and other steel companies that led to the formation of the United States Steel Corporation.

Railroads violate laws against restraint of trade.

When the stage of competition resulting in enormous losses was reached between the great railroads, agreements and pools were first formed; and finally a way was found to exempt the railroads and other public utilities from the laws forbidding combination in restraint of trade by control through commissions. To this plan the public gives general assent and no prosecutions follow, although the agreements regarding prices are as clearly in violation of the law as were those of the packers or those of the Standard Oil Trust.

Combinations on the ocean.

A like situation exists between the Atlantic liners. With modern conditions we have seen the ships grow larger and larger. We have now the *Lusitania* and the *Mauretania* of the Cunard line and the *Olympic* of the White Star line. Occasionally there has been severe competition in price between these lines and the other great lines, such as the North German Lloyd, Hamburg-American, etc.; but at the present time for definite seasons of the year there are substantially like prices for similar accommodations, the prices being raised and lowered for the same accommodations at different seasons of the year, being perhaps twice as high in the summer as in the winter.

The illustrations given show that the inevitable consequence of unrestricted competition is bigness and finally monopoly. Even Brandeis,[1] who strongly advocates competition, says: "Unrestrained competition will lead necessarily to monopoly." Along the same line, Untermeyer[2] says: "The logical outcome of unrestrained competition is legalized monopoly." Laughlin puts the case that with

[1] Hearings, Senate Interstate Commerce Committee, Part XVI, p. 1162.
[2] *Ibid.*, Part V, p. 183.

"free competition you must inevitably expect to have bigness and also monopoly." [1]

Ruin or Combination. — In the past, the disastrous competition which has led to ruin has been largely confined to the small concerns. When there is severe competition of many small manufacturers or sellers, a number of them with relatively small capital fail. The fact that from 10 to 20 per cent of them go to the wall may not so seriously affect business as to be generally noticed; but its total effect is great, and, so far as the man whose business is destroyed is concerned, it is an individual disaster. As the many drop out, the competitors become fewer and the competition becomes ever keener. Finally a situation arises where this can no longer be endured.

Numerous illustrative cases could be given in which fierce and unrestrained competition has driven business men to the verge of destruction or to complete ruin. I select one or two recently brought before the United States Interstate Commerce Committee.

Vinson [2] testified that in West Virginia the small coal producers cannot compete with the large concern because they cannot coöperate through a selling agency. He says that if the small concerns are not allowed to coöperate so as to have the advantage of the large concentration, the only alternative is bankruptcy.[3] Untermeyer reports that a dozen of the paper manufacturers had failed because they were unable to compete with the big fellows; and that they had made a temporary trade agreement in order to save themselves from destruction; but that in consequence they were indicted and fined for violation of the antitrust law. Says Untermeyer: [4] "Requiring the enforcement of unrestricted competition calls upon people either to make criminals of themselves or to ruin themselves in obeying the law." Says Walker: [5] "Competition is the life of trade;

[1] Hearings, Senate Interstate Commerce Committee, Part XIV, p. 996.
[2] *Ibid.*, Part III, p. 30. [3] *Ibid.*, Part V, p. 194.
[4] *Ibid.*, Part V, p. 183.
[5] "Unregulated Competition Self-destructive," Aldace F. Walker, *Forum*, December, 1881.

competition is the death of trade: one phrase is as true as the other." And again: "Unrestrained competition as an economic principle is too destructive to be permitted to exist."

The fierceness of modern competition is the inevitable result of the development of transportation and communication. Until these were in a highly advanced condition it was not possible for an organization to reach a great territory with its products. With highly efficient transportation and communication the strong organizations, even if far apart, meet one another in the wide markets; and the destructive struggle is inevitable unless they coöperate.

Coöperation in industry imperative.

A situation similar to that which existed with the railroads before coöperation in charges was actually agreed upon is now reached for the great manufacturing industries. They have found a way by consolidation to prevent the evil effects of unrestricted competition. It is now proposed through the courts to break up these combinations and restore competition. If this be done, it is safe to say that even greater disasters will befall the country for the great industries than those which the country suffered when the same situation existed with the railroads.

Alternative, lawlessness or failure.

With the alternative before the business men of coöperation or failure, we may be sure that they will coöperate. Since the law is violated by practically every group of men engaged in trade from one end of the country to the other, they do not feel that in combining they are doing a moral wrong. The selection of the individual or corporation for prosecution depends upon the arbitrary choice of the Attorney-General, perhaps somewhat influenced by the odium which attaches to some of the violators of the law. They all take their chance, hoping that the blow will fall elsewhere. With general violation and sporadic enforcement of an impracticable law, we cannot hope that our people will gain respect for it.

CHAPTER II

SOME IMPORTANT ILLUSTRATIONS OF CONCENTRATION

Now that a general statement has been made of the economic advantages of concentration, its extent, the wastes of competition, its consequent break-down, etc., it seems advisable as the next step to make the situation more concrete by giving an outline statement concerning some of the greatest combinations, including the benefits and evils which have appeared in connection with them.

With two exceptions, the illustrative industries selected for description are those upon which reports have been made by the United States Commissioner of Corporations. The earliest of these reports, viz., that upon beef, was made when James R. Garfield was Commissioner. The other reports were issued during the time that Herbert Knox Smith has held that office. The corporations reported upon by the Commissioner are those of the first magnitude, and the facts concerning them are presented with a fullness not available for the corporations not investigated by this bureau.[1]

SECTION 1

THE MICHIGAN SALT COMPANY[2]

Beginning with 1860, there was a rapid development of salt production in Michigan. About 1865 came overproduction and unrestricted competition; the weaker companies were driven to the wall. It was recognized that the solution of the difficulty was combination. By 1866 the manufac-

[1] The great combinations as they existed twelve years ago are described in the Report of the Industrial Commission, Vols. I and XIII.

[2] Summarized from an article by J. W. Jenks, contained in "Trusts, Pools, and Corporations," Ripley, pp. 1–21.

turers united their interests for selling the product. In 1868 there was formed an association called the Saginaw and Bay Salt Company, which handled four fifths of the salt shipped from the Saginaw Valley. This association continued until 1871, when it was broken up as a result of dissensions; but declining prices and lack of prosperity led to the formation of the Michigan Salt Association in 1876. The agreement forming this association was for five years, but it was renewed in 1881 under the name of the Salt Association of Michigan, and again in 1886 under the name of the Michigan Salt Association.

Changing name.

The associations were essentially pools; they had a very small capital, $200,000, which was distributed among manufacturers of salt in proportion to their capacity. After providing for the expense of the business, there was an annual dividend of only 7 per cent upon the stock. After paying this dividend and the expenses, the remainder of the income was distributed to the manufacturers in proportion to their output. Under the articles of agreement a contract was made every year with each manufacturer to make salt wholly upon the association's account, of the best quality, to be delivered to the association according to the conditions of the contract. If a manufacturer violated his agreement, he paid ten cents upon every barrel of the salt so sold. There was no restriction imposed upon the output of the various concerns. This lack of limitation was due to the fact that the salt manufactories obtained their heat from the by-products in lumber manufacture.

Conditions of the pool.

The economic advantages accruing to the manufacturers through the association were reductions in the amount of selling costs due to the maintenance of a single selling agency at each of the commercial centers, and reasonable prices, as well as the avoidance of cross freights. After the association was formed in 1866 the prices were somewhat increased; they reached a maximum in 1868, when the price of salt was $3.25 a barrel at Chicago. From this time on prices continued steadily to fall until in 1881, when the Chicago prices were $1.05 per barrel. In 1871 the salt com-

Economic advantages.

bination was extended to include not only the Michigan salt producers, but those of Ohio and New York. Prices were fixed by the combination at various points. The outputs of the fields were apportioned in 1871, and reapportioned in 1881. The pool broke up in 1882, after which there was a further decline in the price of salt. At Chicago in this year it became as low as 80 cents.

Jenks places to the credit of this association the following points: —

As a result of the action of the association a system of state inspection was established under which every block of salt placed upon the market was rigidly examined. In consequence, each manufacturer was obliged to produce an article which came up to the standard set by the association and by the state. The prices were reasonable and steadily declined during the life of the association. In consequence of the combination, less capital was required to conduct the business; better rates of transportation were secured; there was no loss by cross freights; the cost of marketing was reduced; there was a reduction in the losses through bad debts.

Credits to pool.

It would seem that the history of the Michigan Salt Association was a creditable one, in that dealing with an essential article, the output was increased, the quality of the product improved, the cost of manufacture reduced, so that there was placed upon the market a superior article at a price much less than when the association was organized.

The association very well illustrates the instability of the pool, since not having the sanction of law and the support of the court (see p. 68) any member or group might withdraw at any time, or violate any of the articles of agreement and refuse to pay the penalty; consequently the history of the association, as of other pools, was one of ups and downs and finally inevitable dissolution.

Pools unstable.

Section 2

THE STANDARD OIL COMPANY[1]

The report of the Bureau of Corporations upon the Standard Oil Company was published in 1907, and includes an account of the business to and including the year 1906. The facts here stated are to be considered as of that date.

The Standard Oil Company, with its various affiliated concerns, handled 84.2 per cent of the crude oil which goes to the refineries in the United States. One refinery, that at Bayonne, New Jersey, consumed more crude oil than all of the independent plants of the country.

The Rise of the Company. — The rule of the Standard Oil Company began with the union of several large refining companies into a partnership known as Rockefeller, Andrews, & Flagler, in 1867. Three years later this partnership was succeeded by the Standard Oil Company of Ohio, with a capitalization of $1,000,000; and with its organization began the campaign for the control of the refining business of the country. When the company was formed, it did not control more than 10 per cent. Within ten years the Standard Oil and associated companies controlled about 90 per cent. Monopoly was accomplished in a decade.

Monopoly swiftly accomplished.

Not only did this company control the refining business, but it controlled every important pipe line in the oil fields. The only serious competitor was the Tide Water Pipe Line Company, which, however, in a few years passed to the Standard. Thus the Standard for many years had no rival in pipe line transmission of oil to the Atlantic coast; and at no time was there more than one independent pipe line to the seaboard and this much smaller than those of the Standard Oil.

In 1882 the Standard Oil interests formed the Standard Oil Trust, under which the entire stock holdings of fourteen companies and a majority interest in twentysix additional concerns were held by trustees. The capitalization of the trust

[1] Report of the Commissioner of Corporations on the Petroleum Industry: Part I, "Position of the Standard Oil Company in the Petroleum Industry"; Part II, "Prices and Profits." Washington Government Printing Office, 1907.

at that time was $70,000,000, and the appraised value of its property in excess of $55,000,000. Of the $70,000,000 trust certificates nine of the trustees owned more than $46,000,000. The appraised value of the trust by 1892 had accumulated to $126,600,000. As a result of a decision against the Standard Oil Company of Ohio in 1882 (see p. 174) and contempt proceedings, the Standard Oil Company of New Jersey was organized, but not until 1897.

Capitalization of the trust.

Thus, the Standard Oil Company of New Jersey, a holding concern, was a direct successor to the trust, the only difference being that the holding company owned all of the stock of the subsidiary companies, instead of being a trustee for this stock; each alike controlled the business of the subsidiary companies, and received and distributed all dividends. The officers of the constituent companies in one case had their orders from the trustees, in the other from the officers of the corporation composed of substantially the same men.

Trust and holding company the same in essence.

The authorized capital of the Standard Oil Company of New Jersey was $100,000,000, of which $98,338,300 was issued. The Standard Oil Company included in America eleven companies mainly engaged in refining, five lubricating oil companies, three crude oil companies, fourteen pipe line companies, a tank line company, six marketing companies, and sixteen natural gas companies. Its business abroad was done through sixteen companies. In addition to these companies seven pipe lines and refining companies were closely affiliated with or controlled by the Standard Oil Company.

Scope of operations.

The Monopolistic Position of the Company. — While the statistics of production show that the Standard Oil Company was dominant in all departments of the business, it did not hold this position through a direct monopoly of the ownership of the wells; since in 1905, of approximately 135,000,000 barrels of crude oil, not over one sixth came from the wells owned by the Standard, and in no one district did its own wells produce more than 50 per cent of the output. But while the Standard did not control the wells, it controlled the pipe lines, which are the only means by which oil may be cheaply transported. Thus the Standard was almost the

Standard purchased oil.

sole purchaser for the oil owned by others. The control of the pipe lines controlled the situation because the refinery at the distant town was not able to pay the railway rates upon crude oil, which are very high as compared with the pipe line transportation.

Monopoly of pipe lines.

The Appalachian, Lima-Indiana, Illinois, and Mid-Continent are the four great fields which produce the most valuable oil for illuminating purposes; and in these four fields there was only one pipe line other than the Standard's, that of the Pure Oil Company, a line less than 550 miles in length. The percentage of business of these four fields handled by the Standard varied from 84 to 96 per cent.

Monopoly in refining.

In the refining industry the plants of the Standard were favorably located and of high efficiency. In 1904 it produced 86.5 per cent of the refined illuminating oil, leaving 13.5 per cent to the independent refineries. Of the export business, Standard Oil handled, in 1904, 13,240,113 barrels, or 87 per cent, of the total for the country.

Efficiency in marketing.

In the marketing business Standard Oil was in an especially strong position because of the wide and wise distribution of its plants, because of its pipe lines, tank cars, and many local storage plants. This system of distribution was so complete that, for the most part, it eliminated the jobber, and dealt directly with the retailer or with the individual consumer. For the United States the known Standard concerns marketed 88.7 per cent of the illuminating oil.

The causes which led to the dominating position of the Standard Oil Company were efficiency of organization, magnitude, integration, utilization of by-products, and unified marketing; in short, all of the advantages which are described (pp. 8–20) as economic causes for concentration. But in securing the position which Standard Oil occupied there is no doubt that very important, if not determining, factors in reaching it were the following special causes: —

Railroad discriminations in favor of Standard Oil were continuous from the formation of the Standard Oil Company of Ohio until the railroads under the Interstate Commerce

Commission were compelled to discontinue these practices. The rebates secured by Standard Oil from western Pennsylvania to the seacoast were frequently a considerable part of the cost of transportation. At one time when the open rate from Pennsylvania to the coast was $1.44½, 80 cents was the rate for the Standard Oil. Another form of advantage was to give lower rates on oil in tank cars than on oil in barrels. At other times the published rates were reduced for short periods after previous notice to the Standard, so that large shipments could be made by that company, after which the rates were again advanced.

Railroad discriminations.

Another advantage which the Standard Oil had was through its pipe lines. These gave it almost complete monopoly of the cheapest form of transportation. Even after the pipe lines were declared to be common carriers, the Standard Oil Company still refused to transport the oil of its competitors; or if it transported the same, it was with excessive rates, under such conditions as to make competition extremely difficult. Where there was a competing line the Standard would attack it by purchasing the crude oil of the wells in the vicinity of the independent line at excessive prices, sometimes from 15 to 20 cents a barrel more than the current price. In this way, even at a loss, the Standard prevented the competing lines from getting business, recouping the loss by profits from other parts of its system. If the pipe lines had in fact acted as common carriers, and transported oil at reasonable rates at points as asked, a very important element in the growth of the monopolistic power of the Standard would have been lacking.

Unfair use of pipe lines.

The Standard Oil Company maintained a monopoly from the establishment of the Standard Oil Trust in 1882 until the time it was dissolved by the order of the Supreme Court in 1911. Because of this the organization was able to charge excessive prices which gave enormous profits. According to the Commissioner of Corporations, the following points appear regarding prices: —

Monopoly prices.

1. There was a marked increase in the margin between the price of crude oil and its leading finished products, after the

formation of the Standard Oil Trust, and even during the past ten years.

2. Standard Oil has sold illuminating and free petroleum products cheaper abroad than at home, the difference being very great in 1902.

3. Standard Oil discriminated greatly in fixing prices in different sections and different towns, charging exorbitant rates when there was no competition, very low rates, and even prices so low as to give a loss, in places where there was competition.

4. The profits of the Standard Oil Company especially in its domestic business were excessive.

5. The real source of the Standard's power was not in superior service but in long-continued use of unfair methods of competition.

6. The Standard by using its influence as a larger shipper secured excessive prices for lubricating oil from the railroads of the country.[1]

Margins and Profits.—The margin between crude oil and illuminating oil increased markedly from 1897–98 to 1903–04. In 1898 it was 5.3 cents; in 1903, 7.1, an increase of 1.8. Similar increases of margins applied to gasoline and lubricating oil. Even if the profits due to increase in margins be placed at only 1.5 cents per gallon, on 1,400,000,000 gallons produced in 1904, the increased profit would mean $21,000,000. Similar calculations give $25,000,000 for 1903. Corresponding with this calculation, the profits of the company in 1896–97 were in the neighborhood of $34,000,000; whereas, in 1903 they were $81,000,000, an increase of $47,000,000. In 1893–94, when the margins were the lowest, the profits of Standard Oil on the capitalization of the company were between 11 and 12 per cent; in 1896 they had reached 23 per cent; and since that time to dissolution there were enormous profits, due to the increase of margins. Prices in the United States for two years, taking into account both grade and freight, have been from one to nearly three cents higher than those which obtain in London and Hamburg.

Excessive margins.

[1] "Petroleum Industry," Part 2, 1907, pp. 1–2.

Price Discriminations.—Sectional price discrimination was shown by the very great variation in price among the different cities, being relatively low where competition was keen, and very high where monopoly was complete or nearly so. In 1904 at Los Angeles the price was 6.7 as compared with 12.3 at San Francisco. Prices have been as high as 16.61 at Butte at the same time they were as low as 7 in other cities. Illustrating the situation very well, in New York City and vicinity, the very seat of the Standard's greatest refineries, the price was 10.5, while at Worcester it was 7.5, and at Cincinnati and Cleveland 7 or less.

Excessive Profits.—The total dividends paid by the Standard Oil Company from 1882 to 1906 were over $550,000,000, on an average over $22,000,000 a year. This, however, does not represent the total net earnings, since there were large accumulations not declared as dividends. From 1882 to 1896 the profits on the capital stock and trust certificates averaged about 19 per cent. In 1903 they had reached 83 per cent and the average from 1903 to 1905 was about 68 per cent, annually. The total profits from 1897 to 1906 are believed to be somewhere from $790,000,000 to $850,000,000; and this upon properties the value of which originally aggregated not more than $75,000,000. These figures show that after monopoly was obtained and improvements made in transportation and manufacturing, it was possible because of this situation to secure these enormous profits.

It is notable that excessive profits came about, not by taking any very large amount from a single gallon of oil, not more than two or three cents, and yet these two or three cents multiplied by the enormous number of gallons used by the people of the United States led to the vast profits above given. The Standard Oil industry very well illustrates the principle that if a commodity is widely needed, even if one family uses a relatively small amount, and the average annual tribute levied upon that family is small, if there be a moderate excess beyond that of a fair price, the total illegitimate profits of the organization may be fabulous; not only so, but the accumulation of these enormous profits in the hands of a few men may enable them to invest in other lines of business which have monopolistic elements, and they thus gain a commanding influence in the industry of the country. It is well known that the excessive profits which have gone to the owners of the Standard Oil Company have enabled them to enter many other great lines of business, so that they, with their railroads, industrial organizations, trust companies, and banks, are one of the two great dominating centers which in large measure control the money of the United States. The disintegration of the Standard Oil Company by the order of the courts is discussed on pp. 181–183.

Summary of Evils. — In summary the Standard Oil Company illustrates very clearly a number of evils which have risen in connection with great combinations.

This company has engaged in the following practices: —

1. From the railroads it has secured rebates and drawbacks; has had better service than competing corporations; has had rates manipulated for its own purposes; has had lower rates on oil in tanks than in barrels; has secured information as to business of competing companies.

2. It has owned pipe lines; by its position of ownership it has had great advantages through refusing in good faith to execute the duties of common carriers to competing organizations.

3. Because of its monopoly it has been able to increase its margins beyond reasonable amounts, and thus has secured excessive profits.

4. It has disposed of its products cheaper abroad than at home.

5. It has had greatly varying prices in different sections of the country, the prices being made very low whenever competition appeared, the purpose being to destroy competitors, and it has succeeded in many instances.

6. It has pursued methods of espionage upon competing concerns in order more advantageously to compete with and destroy them.

7. It has used secret companies to kill competitors.

Section 3

THE UNITED STATES STEEL CORPORATION[1]

Early Consolidations. — Before the organization of the United States Steel Corporation, consolidation of the iron and steel industry had made much progress. Prior to 1898 the steel business was distributed among a large number of relatively small companies, although even at that time a number of steel companies had obtained considerable prominence, among which were the Illinois Steel Company and the Carnegie Steel Company. The organizations producing the more finely finished materials were almost altogether separate from those which made pig iron, steel billets, and the relatively heavy and simple finished products, such as rails, structural material, and plates. In 1898 there began a series of mergers which resulted in the development of a number of very large companies, each one having as elements a number of organizations before independent. The earliest of these was the Federal Steel Company incorporated in 1898 with a capital of $100,000,000. This included the former Illinois Steel Company, the Minnesota Iron Company, the Lorain Steel Company, and the boats and railways owned by these companies. By this merger the steel business was for the first time integrated from the ore to the coarser of the finished products.

The National Steel Company was formed in 1879 with a capital of $59,000,000. The plants acquired were mainly in Ohio.

In 1900 the Carnegie interests were organized into the Carnegie Company of New Jersey, with a capitalization of $320,000,000. This new organization united the Carnegie Steel Company, the H. C. Frick Coke Company, and the Oliver Iron Mining Company. The company also had

[1] Report of the Commissioner of Corporations on the Steel Industry: Part I, Organization, Investments, Profits, and Position of the United States Steel Corporation; Part II, Cost of Production. Washington Government Printing Office, 1911. Hearings before Committee on Investigation of United States Steel Corporation, Parts 1 to 63 inclusive, p. 5594.

control of a railway from Lake Erie to Pittsburg and owned boats on the lakes. Thus there was even greater integration than in the case of the Federal Steel Company, in that a great coke company was included.

The three great companies mentioned were engaged chiefly in the manufacture of crude material or the coarse finished products such as pig iron, steel billets, rails, beams, plates, and bars.

During the same period the companies producing the more refined products were also largely consolidated into the American Tin Plate Company in 1898, the American Steel and Wire Company in 1898, the National Tube Company in 1899, the American Steel Hoop Company in 1899, and in 1900 the American Sheet Steel Company, the American Bridge Company, and the Shelby Steel Tube Company. Each of these organizations, with the exception of the Shelby Company, which was smaller, had a capitalization varying from $33,000,000 to $90,000,000.

In addition to the above consolidations, all of which later entered into the United States Steel Corporation, there were enlargements and consolidations of other important companies, operating in the northeastern quarter of the United States, among which are notably the Republic Iron and Steel Company, the Pennsylvania Steel Company, the Cambria Steel Company, the Lackawanna Steel Company, and the Jones and Laughlin Steel Company. These companies, at the times of the reorganizations or later, increased their capitalizations to amounts varying from $27,250,000 to $47,500,000.

In the South the important Tennessee Coal, Iron, and Railroad Company had continued to expand during the same period, as had also the Colorado Fuel and Iron Company in the West.

Causes of Consolidation. — The Commissioner of Corporations gives as the causes which led to the consolidations described the desire to restrict competition among the constituent companies and the desire for integration. Both of these purposes were for the time accomplished. For instance, the constituent companies of the Federal Steel did not compete among themselves. The matter of integration will be considered later.

During the period before consolidation the competition had been severe and prices alternately high and low, depending upon the trade conditions and the extent of coöperation. For a time excessive prices would be maintained; but at times of depression sooner or later agreements or pools would break and prices would go down. Thus upon the breaking up of an agreement, prices for steel rails fell from $28 per ton in 1896 to $17 or $18 in 1897 and 1898. After the combination had been reëstablished, prices for rails went to $35 per ton in 1899 and 1900, but in the earlier part of 1901 fell to $26. Steel billets went from $16.25 per ton to $39.50 and back to $16.50 between December, 1898, and October, 1900. During the same time wire nails went from $20 to $50 per ton and then back to $30. These figures show how unequal and unsatisfactory were the conditions as to prices. When the independent mills or the combined companies could get together, and demands were large, prices would become abnormally high; as the demands decreased and the full capacity of the mills was not required, the combination would break and the prices become abnormally low.

Unstable prices under competitive system.

Organizations of the Corporation. — Before the consolidations of the companies producing highly finished products, the constituent companies bought their steel billets from the primary companies. After the consolidation they began to acquire ore and coal lands, to build blast furnaces, and to manufacture their own steel ingots; and thus they were planning to cease buying crude steel from the primary companies. This led the Carnegie Company to plan to build several plants for making the finished products. Similar plans were made by the Federal Steel Company. This contemplated extension of the two groups to become completely independent was the final factor which led suddenly in 1901 to the formation of the United States Steel Corporation. If the great companies of both groups could be united into a single corporation, the iron industry would be completely integrated. The different lines of work could be divided among the subsidiary companies, and there would be great economy. Obviously also the combination would be in a more advantageous position to maintain prices than a number of independent companies. It was plain that the combination could not succeed unless the Carnegie Company could be acquired. Successful negotiations were entered into with Mr. Andrew Carnegie to this end, and thus, in April, 1901, the United States Steel Corporation was formed, consisting of the Carnegie Company of New Jersey, the Federal Steel Company, the American Steel and Wire Company, the National Tube Company, the National Steel Company, the American Tin Plate Company, the American Steel Hoop Company, and the American Sheet Steel Company. Shortly afterward there were acquired the American Bridge Company, the Lake Superior Consolidated Iron Mines, the Bessemer Steamship Company, and the Shelby Steel Tube Company. Each one of the manufacturing organizations included a number of manufacturing plants distributed at various points as well as other properties necessary to integrate the business, such as ore companies, coke companies, dock companies, railroad companies, gas companies, water companies, etc.

Companies consolidated.

The Steel Corporation as organized was essentially a holding company, having the stock of all of the subsidiary companies. These subsidiary companies held their subordinate properties in two classes, in fee and the stock of the subordinate companies. Thus the Carnegie Company of New Jersey was the holding company of the stock of twenty companies, ranging from the various works of the Carnegie Steel Company of Pennsylvania to the great Frick Coke Company.

A holding company.

The United States Steel Corporation, when formed, had steel works with an annual capacity of 9,400,000 tons of crude steel, 1000 miles of railway, 112 lake ore vessels, iron ore deposits estimated to contain from 500,000,000 to 700,000,000 tons of ore, and more than 50,000 acres of high grade coal lands and numerous related properties. The total number of plants under the control of the corporation exceeded 200. Since its organization it has acquired three steel companies in the same region in which were located the other properties of the corporation, namely, Union Steel, Sharon Steel, and Clairton Steel, these being acquired between 1902 and 1904. Finally, there was added in 1907 the great southern property, the Tennessee Coal, Iron, and Railroad Company.

Capacity and resources.

Overcapitalization. — The capitalization of the company in 1901, after acquiring the Shelby Company, was as follows: —

Preferred stock	$510,205,743
Common stock	508,227,394
Steel Corporation bonds	303,450,000
Underlying bonds	59,091,657
Purchase-money obligations and real-estate mortgages	21,872,023
Total	$1,402,846,817

As a result of careful investigation, the Commissioner of Corporations concluded that a fair valuation of the entire physical property of the United States Steel Corporation at the time of its organization was $676,000,000. If the valuation were made upon a basis of the market value of the properties acquired, it would be approximately $793,000,000, and this figure should include the good will of the going business. Using the higher figure, the capitalization of the United States Steel Corporation exceeded its face value by $609,000,000. This shows conclusively that the common stock at the time it was issued was all water and that other securities were inflated. Indeed, the managers of the corporation justified their capitalization only by placing the ore deposits at practically one half of the complete valuation, $700,000,000, a dollar a ton; which, as any one who was or is familiar with the situation knows, was an excessive valuation in 1901, especially as a large part of the ores are not owned in fee, and royalty must be paid to the fee holders. This valuation by the company was later admitted to be

Overcapitalization.

excessive, since in 1907 the value placed upon the ore by the company was about fifty cents a ton, which if correct would indicate that the value in 1901 was still lower. The Bureau's estimate of the value of the ore at the time of the organization is about $100,000,000. The comparisons between the estimated value of the properties by the corporation and by the Bureau is shown by the following table: —

TABLE 31. VALUE OF TANGIBLE ASSETS ACQUIRED BY STEEL CORPORATION IN 1901, AS COMPUTED BY BUREAU, COMPARED WITH ESTIMATE OF CORPORATION SUBMITTED IN THE HODGE SUIT IN JUNE, 1902

CLASS OF PROPERTY	BUREAU'S ESTIMATE OF TANGIBLE VALUES IN 1901	CORPORATION'S ESTIMATE OF TANGIBLE VALUES IN 1902	DIFFERENCE [1]
Ore property . .	$100,000,000	$700,000,000	$600,000,000
Manufacturing plants, including blast furnaces .	250,000,000	348,000,000	98,000,000
Railroad, steamship, and dock property . . .	91,500,000	120,340,000 [2]	28,840,000
Coal and coke property . . .	80,000,000	100,000,000	20,000,000
Natural gas property	20,000,000	20,000,000	——
Limestone properties	4,000,000	4,000,000	——
Cash and cash assets	136,000,000	164,660,000 [3]	28,160,000
Total . . .	$682,000,000	$1,457,000,000	$775,000,000

[1] A part of the differences between the two estimates is accounted for through additions made to property during the interval from April 1,1901,to July 1, 1902, such additions, of course, being included in the corporation's figures.

[2] This figure includes $40,340,000 of indebtedness which was not included in the estimate of the corporation, this addition being made in order to render the estimates comparable.

[3] In arriving at this figure purchase money obligations and real estate mortgages of $16,369,000, which were deducted by the corporation, were restored by the Bureau to make the amounts comparable.

As an incident to the organization of the company, of the stock issued by the corporation in 1901, $150,000,000, including $40,000,000 preferred, was for promoting and underwriting services. The cash received from this stock was probably in the neighborhood of $100,000,000.

Since the corporation was organized in 1901, its earnings have been sufficiently large so that aside from paying interests on bonds, full dividends of 7 per cent on the preferred stock, and from 2 to 4 per cent on the common stock, sufficient money has been saved so that the net additions to the investments, December 31, 1910, amounted to $504,928,653; thus, if the market value of the consolidating companies is taken as a basis, the excessive capitalization had at that time been reduced to about $105,000,000. Using a more conservative valuation of the property made by the Commissioner of Corporations, the amount of water at the end of December, 1910, would be $215,000,000.

Water made into substance.

If the iron ore be now appraised on the basis of assessed valuation, and this seems reasonable, the ores controlled by the corporation are worth not less than $380,000,000 (see pp. 129–132). But a considerable portion of these ores are subject to a royalty to the feeholders. If one fourth be deducted to compensate for this, the value of the ore to the corporation would be $285,000,000. Using this figure, rather than $100,000,000, for the present value of the ores, the appraisal of the properties of the corporation exceeds its capitalization by $70,000,000. Apparently the mighty flood of water put upon the market when the United States Steel Corporation was organized has largely or wholly been transformed into substance.

Earnings. — The net earnings of the Steel Corporation by years from 1901 to 1910 are shown by Table 32.

TABLE 32. ACTUAL EARNINGS OF STEEL CORPORATION ON ITS TOTAL INVESTMENT, AS COMPUTED BY BUREAU, 1901–1910

YEAR	NET EARNINGS AS SHOWN BY ANNUAL REPORTS	ADJUSTMENTS BY CORPORATION IN SUNDRY ACCOUNTS	INTEREST ON BONDS, MORTGAGES, AND PURCHASE-MONEY OBLIGATIONS OF SUBSIDIARY COMPANIES	LOCKED-UP PROFITS IN INVENTORIES	EXCESSIVE DEPRECIATION ALLOWANCES	TOTAL ADJUSTED EARNINGS
	$	$	$	$	$	$
1901[1]	75,006,230.89	——	4,500,000.00[2]	[3]	−1,765,000.00	77,741,230.89
1902	108,534,374.25	−1,207,886.84	6,113,584.34	[3]	8,062,272.00	121,502,343.75
1903	83,675,786.51	−5,427,540.33	6,553,861.06	[3]	9,354,851.00	94,156,958.24
1904	57,791,196.80[4]	+ 13,108.34[4]	6,573,146.54	−1,254,336.48	−631,165.00	62,491,950.20
1905	96,432,595.93	− 99,253.78	6,710,214.73	6,307,189.83	3,480,088.00	112,830,834.71
1906	125,966,938.13	− 90,501.19	6,561,478.70	2,739,403.74	8,216,388.00	143,393,707.38
1907	133,244,929.28	− 681,515.52	6,492,195.42	9,744,692.51	6,616,572.00	155,416,873.69
1908	74,882,529.11	+ 394,034.59	7,401,205.18	426,983.85	1,688,543.00	84,793,295.73
1909	107,773,099.96	+ 548,445.08	7,887,178.18	2,617,395.54	1,981,460.00	120,807,578.76
1910	116,738,157.80	− 818,182.64	7,263,453.66	2,751,307.08	1,281,348.00	127,216,083.90
Total	980,045,838.66	−7,369,292.29	66,056,317.81	23,332,636.07	38,285,357.00	1,100,350,857.25

[1] Nine months.
[2] Approximated; this amount never computed by the Corporation.
[3] In these years these inventory profits were not deducted by the Corporation and hence need not be restored.
[4] After deducting employees' bonus fund, which in this year was taken out after stating net earnings, but which in other years is deducted before determining the net earnings.

According to the Commissioner of Corporations the net earnings on the actual investment of the Steel Corporation from 1901 to 1910, ten years, was 12 per cent. It thus appears, according to the Bureau, that the earnings of the corporation for ten years have been $1,100,000,000, or $110,000,000 a year.

According to Mr. F. J. MacRae, for the nine years from January 1, 1902, to December 1, 1910, the adjusted net earnings amounted to $1,029,685,389, or approximately $13 per ton. He concludes that the percentage of net earnings for sales to outside consumers for this period amounted approximately to 29 per cent; and that 29 per cent of the selling price is equivalent to 40 per cent of the cost.[1]

Proportion of Business. — The proportion of the iron and steel business of the country done by the organization is shown by the following table: —

Table 33. Proportion of Output of Principal Iron and Steel Products for United States Steel Corporation and for Independent Companies, Respectively, in 1901 and 1910

Products	Steel Corporation's Percentages		Independent Companies' Percentages	
	1901	1910	1901	1910
Pig iron, spiegel, and ferro	43.2	43.4	56.8	56.6
Steel ingots and castings	65.7	54.3	34.3	45.7
Rails	59.8	58.9	40.2	41.1
Structural shapes	62.2	47.0 [4]	37.8	53.0 [4]
Plates and sheets of all kinds [2]	64.6	49.7 [4]	35.4	50.3 [4]
Black plate produced in tin mills	79.8	52.9	20.2	47.1
Coated tin-mill products	73.1	61.1	26.9	38.9
Black and coated sheets produced in sheet mills	67.3	38.9	32.7	61.1
Wire rods	77.7	67.3	22.3	32.7
Wire nails	68.1	55.5	31.9	44.5
Wrought pipe and tubes [3]	57.2	38.2	42.8	61.8
Seamless tubes [3]	82.8	55.3	17.2	44.7

[1] Investigation U.S. Steel Corporation, 53, Part I, pp. 3613–3614.

[2] Includes sheets for tinning, galvanizing, and other coatings.

[3] These percentages are based on capacity and not production. The capacity of independent companies is, moreover, partly estimated.

[4] For 1909; figures for 1910 not available.

Reduce percentage of output.

The total production of the iron and steel of the country by the Steel Corporation fell from 60.6 per cent in 1901 to 51.6 per cent in 1909, and of steel ingots and castings the total fell from 65.7 in 1901 to 54.3 in 1910. While there has been a decrease in the percentage of the domestic production, the total business of the corporation has vastly increased. The crude ingots produced increased from 9,743,918 tons in 1902 to 14,179,369 in 1910, or 45.5 per cent. The foreign business has been greatly extended, and of this line the Steel Corporation controls about 95 per cent. In 1911 there were exported by the corporation 1,719,272 tons of steel and other finished products. Such products are sold considerably cheaper abroad than at home, the differences per gross ton for 1910 being as follows: Steel rails, $3.84; plates, $3.93; standard shapes, $4.50.[1]

The foreign business is done through the United States Steel Products Export Company.[2] This company now controls ninety per cent of the total steel export trade of the United States. Until 1904 the company was allowed a three per cent commission on its business; but in 1904 it was reduced to two per cent. Any surplus over the actual requirements of the export company are to be rebated to the different companies, the products of which are sold. As a matter of fact the commission is fixed so that it meets the operating expenses of the company. The advantage to the Steel Corporation of the selling company is that the foreign business is handled as a unit and this is a matter of fundamental importance in the export trade. See pp. 222–224.

Cost of Production. — In Part II of the Report of the Commissioner of Corporations, the cost of production of steel is considered. Since this is the most elaborate available investigation of cost of production of a great fundamental article, and especially since it contains comparisons of the cost of the large and small companies engaged in the business, the summary of results is reproduced.

"Certain salient points are brought out by this investiga-

[1] Investigation U.S. Steel Corporation, No. 57, p. 5135.
[2] *Ibid.*, 53, Part I, pp. 3691–1695.

tion of costs. These points will be discussed in detail, but for convenience are here stated in summary form, as follows: —

"1. That cost statements for iron and steel products vary greatly on account of differences in scope of operations and in legal organization and accounting methods of different companies. Therefore, the statement and use of such cost data require the most careful discrimination.

"2. That the 'book costs' of highly integrated concerns (that is, those companies which link up under one control successive stages of production of materials and finished commodities) are not net costs, because they include large items of intermediate profit. These profits occur as the materials pass from one stage of production to another, because these materials are transferred from one department or subsidiary to another at market prices or at arbitrary 'transfer' prices, instead of at cost.

"3. That the average costs differed greatly, according as such intermediate profits were included or excluded, is shown by Table 34.

TABLE 34. COSTS OF VARIOUS PRODUCTS, INCLUDING INTERMEDIATE PROFITS

PRODUCTS	COST INCLUDING ALL INTERMEDIATE PROFITS	COST EXCLUDING INTERMEDIATE TRANSFER PROFITS ON MATERIALS [1]
Lake ore	$2.64	[2]
Bessemer pig iron	13.89	$12.10
Large Bessemer billets	20.11	17.90
Bessemer standard rails	21.27	18.80

"The above are average costs for companies having a very large proportion of the total production in the United States for the five years 1902 to 1906.

"4. That if all these companies are divided into two groups, large highly integrated companies, and small companies

[1] This cost does not exclude, however, transportation profits, which are considerable in amount for the Steel Corporation, as explained later.

[2] No difference except for a trifling amount of intercompany royalty.

which generally were not well integrated, the average costs of the two groups differed decidedly. These differences were more marked when intermediate profits were excluded. The facts are shown by Table 35.

TABLE 35. COMPARATIVE COSTS OF SEVERAL PRODUCTS IN LARGE AND SMALL COMPANIES

PRODUCTS	COSTS INCLUDING ALL INTERMEDIATE PROFITS		COSTS EXCLUDING INTERMEDIATE TRANSFER PROFIT ON MATERIALS[1]	
	Large companies	Small companies	Large companies	Small companies
Lake ore	$2.67	$2.49	[2]	[2]
Bessemer pig iron	13.86	14.27	$11.93	$14.21
Large Bessemer billets	19.89	22.54	17.56	21.69
Bessemer standard rails	21.27	——	18.80	——

"These differences between the two groups are, of course, largely due to the fact that the more steps in production controlled by one concern the more intermediate profits go to that concern, instead of being paid to outsiders. Accordingly, when intermediate profits are excluded, the net cost for an integrated concern is less than for one not so highly integrated. It should be observed that the above figures show costs exclusive of transfer profits on materials, and not exclusive of transportation profits. Such transportation profits are earned by certain large companies, and above all by the Steel Corporation

"5. That while highly integrated concerns have a lower net cost than non-integrated concerns, and therefore a higher margin (not rate) of profit between costs and prices; yet, on the other hand, being so integrated, they have a larger investment to be covered by this margin of profit over net cost.

"6. That the costs for this period (1902 to 1906, inclusive) are substantially representative of present conditions. This

[1] This cost does not exclude, however, transportation profits, which are considerable in amount for the Steel Corporation, as explained later.

[2] No difference except for a trifling amount of intercompany royalty.

is shown by a comparison of costs for a number of important selected plants for several products from 1902 to 1906, inclusive, and for 1910.

"7. That the United States Steel Corporation has a special advantage in cost of production on account of its complete integration, particularly in producing all the ore and coke it uses, and in having railroads for ore transportation, which branches of its business yield great profits. The costs of the Steel Corporation are especially reduced if these intermediate profits are excluded, as is shown by Table 36.

TABLE 36. COMPARISON BETWEEN BOOK AND INTEGRATED COSTS OF SEVERAL PRODUCTS FOR THE UNITED STATES STEEL CORPORATION

PRODUCTS	BOOK COST	INTEGRATED COST EXCLUDING INTER-COMPANY PROFITS ON MATERIALS AND TRANSPORTATION
Lake ore	$2.88	$2.40
Bessemer pig iron	14.39	10.21
Bessemer standard rails . .	21.53	16.67

In considering these integration costs of the Steel Corporation, the much more extensive and diversified investment of that company should also be taken account of.

"8. That the indicated investment per ton of product for Bessemer steel rails for the period 1902 to 1906, taking conditions of business then prevailing, ranged from $80 to $55 per ton of rails. On the basis of a price of $28 per ton for rails the profit for all companies whose costs (excluding transfer profits only) would be from 11 to 17 per cent on the investment.

"9. That the prices of lake ore have been kept for many years at an unreasonably high level compared with the cost of production and the cost of the investment in the producing ore properties. Consequently, integrated concerns, transferring such ore to the pig-iron producing departments of the business at those high prices, necessarily show an unduly high book cost for pig iron and for various steel products made from pig iron.

"10. That this policy in regard to ore prices has two important results. For companies selling ore it tends to make renumerative the investment in vast ore reserves which are not at present utilized, and to unduly enhance the value of such properties. It also tends to make the cost of iron ore excessively high to companies which must purchase it in the open market, and thus prevents them from becoming effective competitors in pig iron or in steel products made therefrom."

In the above statements and what is to follow the large companies are interpreted to include the following: —

1. The United States Steel Corporation, total capitalization, $1,402,846,817.

2. The Lackawanna Steel Company, common stock $60,000,000, preferred stock $10,000,000, bonds $75,412,000, total capitalization $145,412,000.

3. Jones and Laughlin Steel Company, stock $30,000,000, bonds $24,487,000, total capitalization $54,487,000.

TABLE 37. AVERAGE BOOK COST PER GROSS TON OF LAKE ORE AT LOWER LAKE PORTS, EXCLUDING INTERCOMPANY ROYALTY AND DISTINGUISHING LARGE AND SMALL COMPANIES, 1902–1906

ITEMS OF COST	ALL COMPANIES (106,268,728 tons)	LARGE COMPANIES (84,920,942 tons)	SMALL COMPANIES (21,347,786 tons)
Labor	$0.45	$0.44	$0.50
Other operating	.37	.38	.34
Royalty	.23	.23	.21
Mine cost	$1.05	$1.05	$1.05
Rail freight	.67	.69	.58
Lake freight	.74	.74	.74
Lower Lake cost	$2.46	$2.48	$2.37
General expense, depreciation, and taxes	.16	.16	.12
Total cost at lower Lake ports	$2.62	$2.64	$2.49

TABLE 38. TOTAL COSTS PER GROSS TON FOR SPECIFIED PRODUCTS, ARRIVED AT BY ADDING TO THE AVERAGE MILL COSTS, AS SHOWN BY THE COST SHEETS, AN ASSUMED NORMAL CHARGE IN PLACE OF ADDITIONAL COSTS (GENERAL EXPENSES AND DEPRECIATION) 1902–1906

	All Companies		Small Companies		Large Companies		Difference between Small and Large Companies	
	Book Cost	Excluding Transfer Profits	Book Cost	Excluding Transfer Profits	Book Cost	Excluding Transfer Profits	Book Cost	Excluding Transfer Profits
Bessemer pig iron, furnace cost	$13.13	$11.34	$14.18	$14.12	$13.04	$11.11	$1.14	$3.01
Total cost (with assumed addition of $0.50 per ton)	13.63	11.84	14.68	14.62	13.54	11.61	1.14	3.01
Basic pig iron, furnace cost	12.29	11.30	13.81	13.59	12.17	11.11	1.64	2.48
Total cost (with assumed addition of $0.50 per ton)	12.79	11.80	14.31	14.09	12.67	11.61	1.64	2.48
Bessemer billet ingots, works cost	16.64	14.55	19.96	19.10	16.45	14.28	3.51	4.82
Total cost (with assumed addition of $0.60 per ton)	17.24	15.15	20.56	19.70	17.05	14.88	3.51	4.82
Bessemer rail ingots,[1] works cost	16.54	14.70	—	—	—	—	—	—
Total cost (with assumed addition of $0.60 per ton)	17.14	15.30	—	—	—	—	—	—
Large Bessemer billets, mill cost	19.01	16.80	22.51	21.66	18.69	16.36	3.82	5.30
Total cost (with assumed addition of $1.10 per ton)	20.11	17.90	23.61	22.76	19.79	17.46	3.82	5.30
Heavy Bessemer rails,[1] mill cost	19.98	17.51	—	—	—	—	—	—
Total cost (with assumed addition of $1.30 per ton)	21.28	18.81	—	—	—	—	—	—

[1] No small companies.

4. The Republic Iron and Steel Company, common stock \$27,171,000, preferred stock \$25,000,000, bonds \$18,439,500, total capitalization \$70,630,000.

5. Cambria Steel Company, stock \$45,000,000, iron company stock \$8,468,000, bonds \$6,000,000, total capitalization \$59,468,000.

For the years 1902 to 1906, the book costs, the transfer profits, and relative costs of the large and small companies are given for a number of products in the preceding tables. The data used includes only the Buffalo plant of the Lackawanna and only the Johnstown plant of the Cambria.

The costs of steel for the years 1902–1906 above considered do not differ greatly from those less thoroughly investigated for later years; this is shown by Table 39.

TABLE 39. COMPARISON OF AVERAGE BOOK COST PER GROSS TON OF LAKE ORE AT LOWER LAKE PORTS FOR 1902–1906, INCLUSIVE, WITH 1907–1910, INCLUSIVE, FOR THE STEEL CORPORATION AND TWO OTHER LARGE COMPANIES.

ITEMS OF COST	1902–1906 (88,082,551 tons)	1907–1910[1] (88,833,156 tons)	ITEMS OF COST	1902–1906 (88,082,551 tons)	1907–1910[1] (88,833,156 tons)
Labor	\$0.43	\$0.35	Rail freight	\$0.70	\$0.74
Other mining	.21	.20	Lake freight	.74	.72
Stripping and development	.03	.11	Cost at lower Lake ports	\$2.49	\$2.54
Depreciation	.13	.13	General charges	.09	.16
Royalty	.25	.29			
Cost at mine	\$1.05	\$1.08	Total book cost	\$2.58	\$2.70

The comparisons of different years for Bessemer pig iron and for Bessemer rails are shown by the following tables: —

[1] For 1910 includes the costs of the Steel Corporation only.

TABLE 40. COMPARISON OF BOOK COST PER GROSS TON OF BESSEMER PIG IRON AT THREE FURNACE PLANTS OF THE STEEL CORPORATION FOR 1902–1906 WITH 1910

ITEMS OF COST	1902–1906 (13,051,404 tons)	1910 (2,668,230 tons)
Net metallic mixture	$7.39	$8.77
Coke	4.05	3.94
Limestone	.40	.40
Labor	.67	.48
Other operating	.73	.43[1]
Furnace cost [2]	$13.24	$14.02

TABLE 41. COMPARISON OF BOOK COST PER GROSS TON OF HEAVY BESSEMER RAILS AT TWO PLANTS OF THE STEEL CORPORATION FOR 1902–1906 WITH 1910

ITEMS OF COST	1902–1906 (5,944,409 tons)	1910 (923,651 tons)
Ingots	$16.94	$17.86
Labor	1.01	1.14
Fuel	.10	.17
Other operating	.94	1.06
Works cost [2]	$18.99	$20.23

For 1910 the book, intercompany profits, and integration costs for some of the principal products of the Steel Corporation are shown by the following tables: —

[1] The items covered in this figure show a lower aggregate sum in 1910 than for the previous period chiefly on account of credits for gas used in other departments of the works.

[2] This does not include any allowance for "additional costs" shown on profit and loss accounts.

TABLE 42. STEEL CORPORATION'S FURNACE COST PER GROSS TON OF BESSEMER PIG IRON, AS SHOWN BY PRODUCING SUBCOMPANIES' COST SHEETS, APPROXIMATE INTERCOMPANY PROFITS INCLUDED THEREIN, AND INTEGRATION FURNACE COST, AS SHOWN BY THE RECORDS OF THE CORPORATION, FOR 1910 (6,269,534 tons)

ITEMS	COMPANY OR BOOK COST	INTERCOMPANY PROFIT (APPROXIMATELY)	INTEGRATION COST (EXCLUSIVE OF ANY RETURN TO INVESTMENT OR ANY ANTERIOR STAGE OF PRODUCTION OR TRANSPORTATION)
Net metallic mixture	$8.63	$3.68	$4.95
Coke	3.79	.49	3.30
Limestone . . .	.42	.01	.41
Labor	.55	——	.55
Other operating .	.50 [1]	[2]	.50
Furnace cost [3] .	$13.89	$4.18	$9.71

TABLE 43. STEEL CORPORATION'S MILL COST PER GROSS TON OF HEAVY STANDARD BESSEMER RAILS, AS SHOWN BY PRODUCING COMPANIES' COST SHEETS, APPROXIMATE INTERCOMPANY PROFITS INCLUDED THEREIN, AND INTEGRATION MILL COST, AS SHOWN BY THE RECORDS OF THE CORPORATION, FOR 1910 (923,651 tons)

ITEMS OF COST	COMPANY OR BOOK COST	INTERCOMPANY PROFIT (APPROXIMATE)	INTEGRATION COST (EXCLUSIVE OF ANY RETURN TO INVESTMENT ON ANY ANTERIOR STAGE OF PRODUCTION OR TRANSPORTATION)
Ingots	$17.86	$4.83	$13.03
Labor	1.14	——	1.14
Other operating .	1.23	.03 [4]	1.20
Mill cost [3] . .	$20.23	$4.86	$15.37

[1] The amount of this item was $0.69 before deducting credit for furnace gas used in other department, namely, $0.19.

[2] Intercompany profits $0.002 and losses $0.002.

[3] This does not include any allowance for "additional costs" shown on the profit and loss account.

[4] In fuel, steam, materials, and provision for rolls.

TABLE 44. STEEL CORPORATION'S MILL COST PER GROSS TON OF HEAVY OPEN HEARTH RAILS AT NORTHERN AND SOUTHERN PLANTS, AS SHOWN BY PRODUCING COMPANIES' BOOKS, APPROXIMATE INTERCOMPANY PROFITS INCLUDED THEREIN, AND INTEGRATION MILL COST, AS SHOWN BY THE RECORDS OF THE CORPORATION, FOR 1910

ITEMS OF COST	NORTHERN (530,955 TONS)		INTEGRATION COST (EXCLUSIVE OF ANY RETURN TO INVESTMENT OR ANY ANTERIOR STAGE OF PRODUCTION OR TRANSPORTATION	SOUTHERN (323,061 TONS)
	Company or Book Cost	Intercompany Profit (approximate)		Company or Book Cost (which does not include any intermediate profit)
Ingots . . .	$18.37	$3.54	$14.83	$14.86
Labor . . .	1.19	——	1.19	1.72
Other operating	1.35	.02	1.33	2.66
Mill cost[1] .	$20.91	$3.56	$17.35	$19.24

The value of iron ore. — The iron ore holdings of the United States Steel Corporation are very important for the future. Excluding the Hill ore leases, which are to be dropped in 1915, the United States Steel Corporation controls 60 per cent of the available Lake Superior ores or about 800,000,000 tons. The total holdings of the corporation are placed at 1,200,000,000 to 1,500,000,000 tons. The author is aware that these figures are lower than those of others, but they are based upon careful estimate from the most reliable original sources of information. The Steel Corporation in Minnesota owns railroads from the ore fields to the mines, and also owns ore roads from the Lake Erie to the Pittsburg district. Further, it owns the boats it uses on the lakes. It is thus in a commanding position in resources.

Amount of ore owned or controlled.

The ore is the fundamental resource upon which rests the entire steel industry. Therefore the question of ore costs is one of paramount importance. For the year 1902 to 1906 these are shown by the following table: —

[1] This does not include any allowance for additional costs shown on the profit and loss accounts.

TABLE 45. AVERAGE COSTS, PRICES, AND PROFITS ON LAKE ORE, PER GROSS TON, BY YEARS, 1902–1906

Year	Tonnage	Cost per Ton	Price per Ton	Profit per Ton
1902	20,111,011	$2.77	$3.34	$0.57
1903	17,627,423	2.70	3.57	.87
1904	16,555,393	2.70	3.06	.36
1905	26,093,788	2.58	3.18	.60
1906	29,036,426	2.64	3.47	.83
1902–1906 . .	109,424,041	$2.67	$3.33	$0.66

As we have seen, the Commissioner of Corporations computed the value of the ores when the organization was formed at $100,000,000; at the close of 1910, he placed the total investment in ores at about $134,000,000. This makes a capital account of $7.50 to $7.55 per ton of production. On this basis a profit of 66 cents per ton would be equivalent to about 9 per cent. The Commissioner regards this valuation as excessive. He thinks that on the basis of carrying an ore reserve of from thirty to thirty-five years, the amount invested per ton of ore probably would be less than $5 and that a profit of 66 cents per ton on the ore is too large by at least 25 cents.

Profits on ore.

In this matter, the question may well be raised whether the Commissioner of Corporations has not overlooked one very important factor. In order to justify the vast investments of the United States Steel Corporation in the improvement of the mines, development of transportation, and the construction of the great mills, the industry must have a considerable future. If the Steel Corporation owns only enough ores to carry on its business for thirty years, it must not only provide for current depreciation, but the entire capital account must be written off before the end of that period. When the ores are exhausted, the entire capital outlay is valueless.

Ore the basic resource.

For the larger part of the investment of the Steel Corporation the situation is similar to that in a mine. It is not only necessary to provide for the outlay and improvements at the mine, but it is necessary by the dividends to write off the entire capital account by the time the ore deposit is exhausted.

It may, however, be said that only the high grade ores are now considered in the estimated resources and that the corporation owns great reserves of low grade ores, which will enable the company to carry on its business when the high grade ores are exhausted. This is undoubtedly true; but if lower grade ores are used, those from 35 to 45 per cent metallic iron, the cost of manufacture will be greatly increased; and if this be so, it would be reasonable to allow much more than the profit of an ordinary manufacturing business for the rich ore from the mines. Until this factor is taken into account it cannot be said what profit should be allowed to the ores.

High valuation of ore justified.

Fundamental natural resources, limited in quantity, have an exceptional value because of their early exhaustibility; and methods of computation based upon the hypothesis that illimitable quantities may be acquired, as convenient, cannot but lead to fallacious results. The extremely limited quantity of known high grade iron ores, as compared with the certain needs of this century, justify a corporation having the great manufacturing and transportation properties of the United States Steel Corporation in acquiring ore reserves as far ahead as they can be obtained at reasonable figures, and after obtaining them in placing a high value upon them.

The above reasoning is fully confirmed by the rapid increase in the assessed valuation of the Lake Superior Iron lands. In 1906 the assessed value of the iron-bearing lands of Minnesota was $64,486,409; in 1910 it was $224,669,845, or nearly four times as much. This assessment was made upon the basis of forty per cent of real value; therefore the value of the iron ores of Minnesota for 1910 was not less than $561,674,612.[1] Of this ore, excluding the ores of the Hill leases, the United States Steel Corporation owns or controls sixty per cent. According to these figures the value of the ores controlled by the corporation in Minnesota

[1] Iron Ore Manual, Lake Superior District, 1911. Rukard Hurd, p. 24.

would be $337,004,767. In 1911 the ores of the corporation in Michigan, on the theory of full valuation but as a matter of fact below the value, were assessed at $42,645,000.[1] Therefore the ores in Michigan and Minnesota controlled by the corporation on the basis of assessment have a value of not less than $379,649,767, or nearly three times the estimate of $134,000,000 given by the Commissioner of Corporations.

As further evidence of the soundness of the above position may be cited the rising price of timber. It is pointed out (pp. 159–160) that good timber, well located, during the past twenty years, has increased in value from six to fifty fold; and that the larger part of this increase has occured during the second half of this period. Much of the increase is unquestionably due to the limited quantity of this resource; although it is true that a part of it is due to the consolidation of holdings. The existing timber will be likely to meet the needs of the nation as long as the discovered high grade iron ore; and there is this difference: the timber is renewable, indeed, is being renewed one third as fast as it is cut, whereas the iron ore cannot be increased by a ton through any effort of man. It would seem that the fortunate owners of high grade iron ore are justified in increasing its valuation at least as rapidly as the owners of timber.

Practices of the Corporation.— Regarding methods of consolidation, the United States Steel Corporation illustrates only a single phase of the process. Before this organization was formed, the trust had been declared to be unlawful, and consequently the steel company became a holding company for all of the stock of its subordinate companies; and in turn each of these subordinate companies is to a greater or less extent a holding company of subsidiary companies. As we have already seen, the Carnegie Company of New Jersey was strictly a holding company. The dividends of the subsidiary companies, the stock of which is owned, goes to the Steel Corporation, and the Steel Corporation in turn declares dividends, it being the only stock which the public holds.

[1] Investigation U. S. Steel Corporation, 28, p. 2020.

In the matter of combination with other companies there is no charge that the Steel Corporation, as such, has entered into a formal agreement to regulate prices and outputs. However, there have been meetings of the men engaged in the iron and steel business of the United States, representing nearly 90 per cent of the total, in which the entire situation has been gone over; and there has been an informal understanding as to spheres of influence and prices, under which, while there has been competition for business, there has been no severe fluctuation in price. In fact, steel rails have been held at $28 per ton since the time the corporation was formed.[1]

Mutual understandings of companies.

In the complaint made by the Attorney-General, petitioning for the dissolution of the Steel Corporation, it is alleged that at these meetings, the different corporations "reached a common understanding which was followed under solemn admonition that they were bound by an obligation more estimable than life. These meetings brought about the maintenance of prices. It was understood by them that they were traveling together, and that they were going to stand together. They understood and acted upon the understanding that a statement as to what one would do as to prices or output was a promise and a pledge upon honor to the others. At the meeting of January 11, 1911, and other meetings, there was a general expression of opinion that prices should be maintained, and in pursuance of this understanding and agreement they were maintained. When an understanding was reached, individual declarations were made of intention to follow the movement. It was recognized that they followed the policy laid out by them by the head of the corporation. This meeting of January 11, 1911, was attended by about 80 representatives of iron and steel concerns, being a large majority in number and output of such concerns in the United States. They understood that the purpose was to consider the prices of iron and steel, that the consensus of opinion was that the prices should not be lowered, but that they should be maintained, and that by virtue of what occurred, they were in honor bound to each other to maintain

[1] Investigation U. S. Steel Corporation, 57, pp. 5138–5139.

them. In fact, they, in pursuance of this action, did maintain them." In the answer to the complaint, it is denied that at any "time was there any attempt to reach any agreement or understanding with respect either to output or to prices, nor was anything said or done which was calculated or intended to suppress competition or restrain trade, and there never was nor is there now any such agreement or understanding."

To what extent the charges made will be proved to be true is yet to be seen; but there can be no doubt that since the formation of the United States Steel Corporation, prices have been steady as never before in the steel trade in this country when conditions of severe and sometimes destructive competition alternated with pools or gentlemen's agreements. The regulation of prices appears to be the chief objection which has been made against the corporation. That the corporation has a steadying influence upon prices is undoubtedly true. Also it seems that the profits of the corporation, as given pp. 117–119, have been excessive. Further, the corporation has required unreasonably long hours of labor from a part of its force, and has opposed labor unions.

The Efficiency of the Corporation.—The economic advantages which have resulted from the Steel Corporation include all of those which have been assigned in the general discussion as a justification for concentration. However, there are certain points in which the concentration has led to especially important savings. These will be briefly mentioned.

Complete integration.

The complete integration of the industry has given very high efficiency. The company, owning its ore, coal, and limestone, and owning its transportation lines, including railroads to and from the lakes and the steamboats on the lakes, has been able to get to its various furnaces the material in quality and quantity as desired. Owning a very wide variety of ores, the ores of different qualities have been brought to a given furnace in such proportions as to give the proper mixtures for the particular grade of iron needed at that point. If for Bessemer use, the material is low in phosphorus; if for conversion into steel by the open hearth process, it is somewhat higher in this element; if for foundry iron, the phosphorus is much higher.

Since the many millions of tons of ore needed by the corporation must go to the lakes and down the lakes to the docks or to the furnaces during approximately seven months of the year, the advantage of control of the transportation for the ores has been very great. Indeed, it is extremely doubtful if, without such control, it would have been possible for the corporation to have retained the highest efficiency.

Since the corporation has a set of mills to produce articles of various kinds at the great industrial centers of Pittsburg and Chicago, and to a less extent at many other points from Superior to Cleveland, cross freights have been reduced to a minimum. To illustrate, the products needed south and west of Chicago are furnished by the mills about that city. As the corporation has a large number of plants, it has been able to specialize its mills, in many cases a single mill giving almost its entire energy to a certain product, or if not to a single product, to a set of similar products. This has enabled the corporation to go far in standardizing its goods, which is a very great source of economy. Bridge materials are turned out in definite lengths, widths, thicknesses, and forms; so also iron rods, bars, etc. These practices obviate frequent changes in the rolls.

Specialization of mills.

The manufacture of iron and steel is one which is constantly requiring scientific investigations. The magnitude of the corporation has enabled it to keep a strong investigating department for improvements, mechanical and chemical; and this department has carried on extensive experiments which could not have been undertaken by a small company. Through the investigating department many advances have been made. Thus it has been ascertained that with the Pennsylvania coal a very considerable percentage of Illinois coal can be mixed and a satisfactory coke be secured for the manufacture of iron. This has markedly decreased the expenses for coke at the furnaces in the Chicago district.

Investigating department.

It is sometimes held that the great corporation does not secure as efficient management of its individual plants as smaller organizations; but this cannot be said to be true of the Steel Corporation. This is a holding corporation; the officers of the subsidiary companies are retained, the same as before the consolidation. These officers have had the stimulus to efficiency, not only of general published results, but of actual comparison of the results of one management with another by parallel columns under the strictest system of cost accounting. Indeed, the competition for efficiency between the different subsidiary companies of the Steel Corporation has been nothing short of terrific. However, before the consolidation, the competition was of the keenest between the different mills of the same class in the Federal Steel and Carnegie corporations. There is a general belief that the alertness of management and the efficiency under the Steel Corporation have not deteriorated as compared with the situation before its formation.

Comparison of management.

Relative Efficiency of Large and Small Steel Companies.—All of the above conclusions rest upon qualitative rather than upon quantitative studies. While the report of the Commissioner of Corporations does not give the data to enable us to make a statistical statement regarding the economic advantages of the Steel Corporation as compared with other companies, it does furnish material to make a comparison in this respect between the Steel Corporation together with four other large concerns (Lackawanna Steel Company, Jones and Laughlin Steel Company, Republic Iron and Steel Company, and Cambria Steel Company), and the small concerns.

Tables 37 and 38 (pp. 124–125) show that while the cost of ore at the lower lake ports for the small companies is somewhat less than for the large companies, \$2.49 as compared with \$2.64, that for the manufactured products the cost is always greater for the small companies than for the large companies; and this is so whatever the basis of comparison. Thus taking book costs: Bessemer pig iron costs the large companies \$13.04 per ton as compared with \$14.18 for the small companies, a difference of \$1.14; basic pig iron costs the large companies \$12.17 as compared with \$13.81 for the small companies, a difference of \$1.64; large Bessemer billets cost

Costs greater for small companies.

the large companies $18.69 as compared with $22.51 for the small companies, a difference of $3.82.

If transfer profits be included, even greater differences appear. Thus the costs of Bessemer pig iron on this basis are for the large companies $11.11 per ton as compared with $14.12 for the small companies, a difference of $3.01; for basic pig iron $11.11 for the large companies as compared with $13.59 for the small companies, a difference of $2.48; and for large Bessemer billets, $16.36 for the large companies as compared with $21.66 for the small companies, a difference of $5.30.

In the above statement the advantages which the large companies have in the matter of transportation are included. For the Steel Corporation it is estimated that the average profits on transportation amounted to 60 cents per ton upon the ore; this would be roughly equivalent to $1 a ton on the products above mentioned. The profits of the Steel Corporation on transportation were undoubtedly much greater than those of the other companies, and therefore for the average of the four companies $1 for the profits of transportation are too high; 75 cents may perhaps be accepted as a rough approximation. If this amount be subtracted from the excess profits of the large companies, they still have a wide margin over the small companies.

Economic merits of large and small companies.

The above data do not give a basis upon which to compare the economic merits of the large and small companies, since in the integrated industry the production of a ton of steel involves a larger capital per ton of output than for the small companies. The capital of the small companies includes only the cost of mills to transform billets into steel products, whereas for the larger companies much capital is invested in the part of the industry anterior to the billets.

Unfortunately the report of the commissioner does not give the capital accounts of the large and small companies, nor determine the amount which should go to interest on this account per ton of product, and thus enable us to ascertain the net advantage of the larger company per ton over the small company, nor even to determine whether such net advantage exists.

However, the facts available show, if ruthless competition were to occur regardless of interest on capital, that the large companies would be able to destroy the small ones; because by eliminating transfer costs the great companies have their materials at the final mills at a lower rate than the small companies. At a figure for final products which would eliminate all profits for small companies, the large companies would still have a profit on pig iron and billets of from $2.48 to $5.30, as shown by the last column of Table 38. Thus the large companies, if they were willing to reduce profits below the above amounts and pay a very small interest on capital, could compel competitors to close up or run at a loss.

Great companies may destroy small ones.

The figures of the commissioner seem to show beyond question that if competition be carried on without reference to the percentage of profit on the capital invested, the large steel companies could crush the smaller ones.

Relative Efficiency of the Large Steel Companies. — The very interesting question as to the relative strength of the United States Steel Corporation, as compared with the other four companies reckoned as large, is not taken up by the Commissioner. Would a similar comparison of the Steel Corporation with these companies, excluding transfers, show a greater profit per ton than the other four large companies? The high integration of the Steel Corporation would seem to render this possible. If this be so, just as the large companies could crush the small companies, so the Steel Corporation could crush the other large companies, if the competitive system were pushed to the limit with the aim of destroying all competitors.

This comparison raises the question whether the consolidation of the great constituent companies of the United States Steel Corporation because of that fact increased their joint efficiency; that is to say, could the companies of the size of Federal Steel, Carnegie Steel, and the American Steel and Wire Company have continued their business with an efficiency equal to that of the Steel Corporation? This is the crux of the question concerning the relation of economy and extent of consolidation for iron and steel. It is agreed by all, that in this industry an organization to be highly efficient must be large; that it is necessarily one of great concentration. Is a capitalization of from $50,000,000 to $100,000,000 for a steel corporation sufficient to give the maximum economy? Some men believe that the undoubted economies due to complete integration, avoidance of cross freights, specialization of work in the different mills, etc., enjoyed by the United States Steel Corporation are more than compensated by deterioration which it is charged has been introduced because of the gigantic size of the corporation. It is, in short, asserted that magnitude has gone beyond the stage giving increased efficiency.

Relative efficiency of great companies.

On the other hand, it is held by Mr. Gary,[1] Chairman of the Steel Corporation, that none of the great independent companies could hold their ground against it if competition was driven to its final limit.

This view is confirmed from other sources. The *Wall Street Journal* states that in 1911 the net profits of the Steel Corporation were close to $11 a ton; whereas the hightest profits of the independent companies were approximately $7 per ton; and the average of the independents not much more than $4 per ton. These figures are confirmed by the elaborate investigations of Mr. Farquhar I. MacRae for the Congressional Committee. It therefore appears that if unrestrained competition were introduced into the iron and steel industry it would be possible for the United States Steel Corporation to crush its competitors.[2]

To throw further light upon this subject, it is to be hoped that the Commissioner of Corporations will compare the cost of production of the large steel companies among themselves as he has the larger companies with the

[1] Investigations U. S. Steel Corporation, 53, Part I, pp. 3690–3691.

[2] See also testimony Chauncy M. Dutton, Hearings Senate Interstate Commerce Committee, XIX, pp. 1672–1699.

smaller ones. Also it is to be hoped that these investigations will take into account interest on capital in order that we may have exact data to base a conclusion concerning the relative economic efficiency of the large independent organizations, and of these as compared with the small companies.

Summary of Evils. — In conclusion, the chief evils which have appeared in connection with the United States Steel Corporation are: —

1. Unparalleled overcapitalization.
2. Large sums paid to organizers and manipulators at the time of the conversion of the preferred stock into bonds.
3. Excessive prices; these have resulted in enormous earnings.
4. Selling products cheaper abroad than at home.

Section 4

THE AMERICAN TOBACCO COMPANY[1]

The tobacco industry is one of those in which a single combination controlled a large percentage of the business of the United States until the organization was dissolved by order of the Supreme Court into fourteen companies.

History of Company. — The dominant corporation in the tobacco industry during recent years has been the American Tobacco Company. This company had three great subsidiary companies, the American Snuff Company, the American Cigar Company, and the British-American Tobacco Company. All four of these companies controlled a large number of subsidiary companies, the total number of companies under the combination doing business in the United States, Porta Rico, and Cuba being eighty-six.

This group of companies in 1909 controlled 92.7 per cent of the cigarette business of the country, 62 per cent of the plug tobacco, 59.2 per cent of the smoking tobacco, and in 1901,

[1] Report of the Commissioner of Corporations on the Tobacco Industry: Part I, Position of the Tobacco Combination in the Industry; Part II, Capitalization, Investments, and Earnings. Washington, Government Printing Office, 1909, 1911.

the first year it entered the snuff business, 80.2 per cent of the snuff. Later the American Tobacco Company entered the cigar business and by 1903 it had acquired about one sixth of the cigar output of the United States. The capitalization of the companies of the combination in stocks and bonds, when reported upon in 1909 by the Commissioner of Corporations, was, without counting duplication of stock by interholdings, $316,346,281.

Monopolistic position.

The business of the American Tobacco Company included the manufacture and handling of chewing and smoking tobacco, of cigarettes for domestic consumption, and little cigars, together with enterprises allied with the tobacco industry. The American Snuff Company confined its operations to the manufacture of snuff. The American Cigar Company, with its subsidiaries, handled the cigar business of the combination. The British-American Tobacco Company handled all the foreign business of the company. The dominating organization was the American Tobacco Company, which held a majority of the capital stock of the American Cigar and the British-American Companies, and over 40 per cent of the stock of the American Snuff Company.

Scope of business.

The total number of companies absorbed in building up the combination was in the neighborhood of two hundred and fifty. The organization went through three stages. It began with the formation of the American Tobacco Company in 1890. This company, beginning with the manufacture of cigars and cigarettes, soon expanded its operations into the plug tobacco business. By carrying on a vigorous war, the American Tobacco Company acquired a number of its competitors, and in 1898 united with the strongest of the others into the Continental Tobacco Company. Following this, in 1900, came the snuff combination under the name of the American Snuff Company. This presents the first stage of combination.

Two hundred and fifty companies absorbed.

In 1901 the Consolidated Tobacco Company was formed, which took over the Continental and American Tobacco Companies, being itself strictly a holding corporation. As a result of a campaign of the new combination to push its business in Great Britain, the British-American Tobacco Company was formed in 1902 for the foreign tobacco business outside of Great Britain and the United States.

After the decision of the Supreme Court dissolving the Northern Securities Company (see p. 180), the companies above mentioned were merged in 1904 into one corporation, the reorganized American Tobacco Company.

Stages of development.

In the process of growth of the American Tobacco Company, we have illustrated all of the stages of most of the great concentrations of industry, with the exception of pools and trusts, which stages of development had been gone through before the organization of the first American Tobacco Company. These included the consolidation of numerous companies into a large company, then control of groups of companies through holding companies, and finally a single consolidated combination, the American Tobacco Company.

Overcapitalization. — At each step in the development of the American Tobacco Company, there was opportunity for increasing its securities, both stocks and bonds; and this was done at each transformation upon a great scale; accrued earnings and good will were capitalized and common stock was issued as a bonus. Each company when taken into a new organization was treated most liberally in the estimate of values, in some cases the amount of bonds issued being double stock previously held. In 1908 the good will of the American Tobacco Company represented a capitalization of $105,000,000; whereas its cash value according to the Bureau of Corporations was only about $39,000,000, or 37 per cent. Altogether, the transformations resulted in the enormous capitalization mentioned.

Expansion of stock.

As illustrating the amount of the expansion, it may be said that the capital of one of the constituent businesses of the company in 1885 was $250,000. When the American Tobacco Company was organized this went in on the basis of $7,500,000 in stock. By 1908 the readjustment of this amount had reached $22,000,000; and cash dividends and interest had amounted to $16,900,000. Thus an original investment of $250,000 had by 1908 realized in stock, bonds, dividends, and interest $39,000,000, or one hundred fifty-six times the value of the business in 1885.

Illegitimate Competition. — After the combination formed, the methods of ruthless competition were used. Having control of several lines of business, when a new line was entered, there were put upon the market certain brands which were sold either at no profit or at a loss. These were called "fighting brands." In the case of plug tobacco, one of these was appropriately called "Battle Ax"; another was known as the "Horse Shoe." In order more effectively to carry on destructive competition some twenty or more companies were secretly purchased, and, while a part of the American Tobacco Company, were supposed to be independent firms. These companies were used in the campaign of underselling; and in this way public disapproval of the illegitimate campaign was avoided by the American Tobacco Company. Exclusive contracts were made with sellers, and bonuses given for compliance with the same. The business of competitors was placed under secret espionage. The methods of competition were so fierce as often to destroy the weaker competitors. Others found too strong to be killed by the illegitimate methods of competition were purchased from time to time, usually at very high prices. Continuity in the plans for expansion and monopoly was secured through a group comprising only about half a dozen men who always controlled the business of the American Tobacco Company, the center of the organizations and reorganizations.

International Combination. — After the American Tobacco Company had acquired a dominant position in the United States, the British market was vigorously entered. In order to meet the competition of the strong American company, many British companies united into the Imperial Tobacco Company; and thus the forces of the war were equalized. This led to a mutual agreement upon the part of the combinations, each to respect the territory of the other, leaving the British field free to the British Company and the American field to the American Company. At the same time the two combinations united to form an additional company, the British-American Tobacco Company, which was to push vigorously the tobacco business in all other parts of the world, except the United States and Great Britain. Thus the formation of the great combination in America led to a similar combination in Great Britain, and also made a step toward world combination.

Expansion into Allied Businesses. — As is usual when a great combination is formed, the companies concerned went into allied businesses. Since licorice is one of the important materials used in the manufacture of tobacco, this was one of the businesses which was entered; and the American Tobacco Company obtained more than 95 per cent, nearly a complete monopoly, of the licorice business of the United States.

In addition to acquiring allied manufacturing businesses, the American Tobacco Company had a stock interest, often controlling, in the concerns of the country which were engaged in the distribution of tobacco.

Concentration of Manufacture. — The organization concentrated the manufacturing of tobacco in a limited number of large plants, the small plants which were acquired from time to time being closed. Also the manufacture of tobacco was specialized, a given great factory devoting itself to one line of product. Thus, while there were two hundred and fifty or more plants acquired, the main part of the business of the company was carried on in the great plants. The cigarette and little cigar business was conducted in nine plants; all of the business in plug and twist tobacco was carried on in six plants, and about seven eighths of this amount in two plants. About 30 per cent of the business was distributed among ten subsidiary companies, of which the relation of eight with the American Tobacco Company was kept a secret. Half of the business of the fine-cut tobacco was done in nine plants and the remainder in subsidiary plants. The entire snuff business of the company was conducted in ten plants, four directly owned and six subsidiary. Thus through size and specialization the combination had a marked advantage over its competitors; and still further advantage was gained by the control of more efficient machinery for marketing.

Excessive Profits. — The profits of the combination were very large. After the formation of the reorganized American Tobacco Company in 1904, the average earnings upon actual investments to 1908 were 19 per cent, or $31,200,000 yearly; and this upon the basis of a capitalization of $316,000,000, which we have already seen was reached by several manipulations, each with great expansion of the stock and bonds.

The combination was greatly assisted in securing these enormous profits through changes in the internal revenues. In 1898, as a result of the Spanish War, taxes were greatly increased upon tobacco and prices were raised accordingly. In 1901–1902 this tax was reduced to its former level; but by this time the combination had become sufficiently powerful to hold up prices, so that practically all of the advantage of the reduction of the tax on the manufactured tobacco from twelve cents to six cents per pound went, not to the consumer, but to the combination, in this way adding many millions to its income.

War tax benefits combination.

The enormous profits of the combination were thus due largely to the following causes: the reduction of the Spanish war tax, the capitalization of the good will of the business at each consolidation or reorganization, putting in surplus to increase the capital stock, exchanging at inflated values at times of reorganization, and issuing common stock as a bonus.

These enormous earnings were derived from an article mainly sold in small packages. Much the greater proportion of the retail sales of tobacco is in amounts of fifty cents or less; but tobacco is very widely used. The American Tobacco Company, by adding a little additional tribute to the purchases of millions of people, has made fabulous profits.

According to the Commissioner of Corporations the rates of profit obtained by independent concerns average much lower than those of the combination.[1] The average rate of earnings of forty-eight independent companies for 1906 was 15.9 upon the total tangible assets; whereas, for the same year the earnings of the American Tobacco Company were 40.9 of its tangible assets or more than three times as much.[2]

Monopoly and Competition. — Notwithstanding the great advantage which the American Tobacco Company had through large plants, specialization of business, and control of machinery, the competitors of the combination steadily gained in their business; and this in spite of the fact that they were put to great expense for advertising to meet the "fighting brands" of the American and illegitimate competition through secret companies. This was possible because of the enormous profits which the combination was taking. These facts go to show that even a combination of gigantic size, controlling 80 per cent of the business of the country along various lines, may exist, and competitors gain upon it, if the prices charged are very excessive and the profits correspondingly great. They indicate that there is a limit beyond which extortionate charges may not be levied. If the amount of tribute be made too great, even fear of a mighty combination will not prevent capital from entering a business in order to share in the great profits. Upon the other hand, the facts clearly show that excessive prices may be retained sufficient to give the combination enormous profits. This is true for the American Tobacco Company, even upon the basis of the fictitious capitalization; and if we consider the great gains made by the chief manipulators of the company at the various transformations, the profits for these men are nothing short of amazing.

The limits of tribute.

It is the opinion of the Commissioner of Corporations that almost from the outset it was the aim of the American Tobacco Company to acquire monopoly. This plan was first applied to one line of business, the cigarette and little cigar; from this it was extended to plug tobacco and

Aim to gain monopoly.

[1] "The Tobacco Industry," Part II, p. 314.
[2] *Ibid.*, pp. 326, 328.

later to snuff and fine-cut tobacco. The purpose was largely accomplished in these lines, since the combination succeeded in getting four fifths of the business of the country; but the combination never accomplished its purpose in the cigar business, the maximum proportion gained in this line being about one sixth. The dissolution of the American Tobacco Company by order of the courts is discussed pp. 183–187.

Summary of Evils. — The chief evils illustrated by the American Tobacco Company are: —

1. Overcapitalization, and especially excessive capitalization of good will, exchanges at each reorganization at inflated values, and giving common stock as bonus.

2. Stock manipulation. The reorganizations were made in such a manner as greatly to benefit those who were on the inside.

3. Excessive prices due in large measure to monopolistic position. The high prices lead to enormous and unwarranted earnings.

4. The use of secret companies to kill competitors.

5. The compelling of purchasers to deal exclusively with the American Tobacco Company.

6. Espionage of competitors' business with other unfair practices in connection with the same.

SECTION 5

THE AMERICAN SUGAR REFINING COMPANY[1]

Commanding Position of Company. — The initial organization of the sugar combination was the Sugar Refineries Company. From 1887 to 1891 this company purchased refineries in various parts of the country until finally twenty refineries were controlled. In 1891 this organization incorporated under the laws of the state of New Jersey as the American Sugar Refining Company, with a capital of $50,000,000. Most of the plants purchased were abandoned,

[1] House of Representatives, 62nd Congress, 2nd Session. Report by Mr. Hardwick from the special committee to investigate the American Sugar Refining Company, and others.

all the refining being done in seven establishments. The American was engaged in the refining of cane sugar. When organized it controlled 75 per cent of that class of business. Shortly after the organization of the New Jersey corporation the Spreckles Company of the West united with the American, so that as early as 1892 the combination controlled 90 per cent of the sugar refining business of the country. From this time until 1898 the company had practical monopoly of the refining business in the United States. In 1898 Arbuckle Brothers entered the refining business, and for a time there was fierce competition; but the two companies got together in 1903 and the war ended.

Beginning with 1901 the American Company began to acquire an interest in the beet sugar companies and soon secured a large interest in that line of business.

In 1900 the American Sugar Company refined 67 per cent of the sugar. This proportion declined, until, in 1910, it refined only 42 per cent. But the company also owned stock or controlled a number of so-called independent companies. As a result, it is calculated that of the cane sugar refining business and beet sugar manufacture of the United States in that year the American Sugar Refining Company controlled 62 per cent.

Increase in Margins. — During the years in which the American Company has had approach to monopoly the margins for refining have been increased. During the four years prior to the formation of the Sugar Refinery Company, competition was severe and the average margin was 79.6 cents per hundred pounds. As soon as the refiners became well organized the margin was raised to $1.25. At the time of the competition between the Havemeyer, the Spreckles, and the Arbuckle interests, it fell to between 70 and 75 cents, and in 1899 was as low as 50 cents. After the Arbuckle war closed, in 1901, it rose to $1; but since 1905 has gradually declined, and while variable from time to time, in 1911 it was 89.2 cents.

Price of Raw Material. — There is complaint on the part of the sugar planters of Louisiana that the price for cane raw sugar has been unduly depressed, being made 15 cents per hundred pounds lower at New Orleans than at New York; but doubtless at least a part of this difference is justified on the ground of the transportational advantages of New York. The sugar planters of the Hawaiian Islands, Porto Rico, and the Philippines are united and have been able to protect themselves. Similarly the prices paid to the farmers for beets have been satisfactory, there being no evidence of a combination between manufacturers to depress prices.

Overcapitalization. — The Sugar Refining Company when organized with a stock of $50,000,000 was greatly overcapitalized. As other companies were united they were taken in at excessive values, and this led to a capitalization of $90,000,000 by 1901. At least 50 per cent of the common stock is regarded as water, of which the insiders and promoters got a large portion.

Excessive Profits. — The preferred stock has paid 7 per cent and the common 9.4 per cent, an average of 8.2 for the whole stock issue, or at least 15 or 16 per cent on a fair valuation of the properties and business. The promoters of the organization and the manipulators have, with the exception of a single firm, sold these watered stocks to the public at a price of from $120 to $130 per share, so that at the present time a large part of the stock originally owned by fifty men is now in the possession of nineteen thousand people scattered all over the country, but largely located in New England and the North Atlantic states; of these nineteen thousand, ten thousand are women.

Evils Illustrated. — The American Sugar Refining Company has engaged in exceptionally objectionable practices.

(1) Through collusion of the officers of the sugar company and the officers of the government, duties were paid upon the basis of short weights. There were recovered from the company on account of these weighing frauds $1,835,486. The secretary-treasurer of the American Sugar Refining Company and the general manager of the Brooklyn Refinery were convicted for participation in them.

(2) In the investigation of the weighing frauds illegalities

were also discovered under which the company had received drawbacks for exported syrup in excess of the amount justly due. The company settled the case with the government by the payment of $700,000.

(3) The company has been convicted of taking rebates from a number of railways; and in consequence of those practices has been fined sums aggragating $98,000.[1]

(4) In addition to the above, the Congressional Committee finds strikingly developed several evils which they regard as characteristic of combinations. These are as follows: —

"*a.* Original overcapitalization of great industrial corporations resulting in increased cost of production, if a profit is to be made (as is always insisted upon) on the inflated capitalization, and higher prices of the product to the consuming public.

"*b.* The temptations of the persons who organize and control these large corporations to earn dividends on watered stock as soon as possible, so that such stock may be unloaded in the open markets upon the investing public. These dividends can rarely if ever be made without increasing prices to the consumer.

"*c.* Exploitation not only of the consuming public and of the investing public, as already set out, but also of the corporations themselves, by their officers, directors, and trustees, who do not hesitate to overburden the consumer, to deceive the investor, and to take advantage of the corporations that have trusted them, whenever it will line the pockets of such individual trustees."

Section 6

THE MEAT PACKING INDUSTRY[2]

The Big Six. — Another industry in which a large part of the business has been concentrated with a few companies is

[1] Report of the Attorney-General, 1910, pp. 12–142, 1911, p. 21.

[2] Report of the Commissioner of Corporations on the Beef Industry. Washington Government Printing Office, 1905.

meat packing. The report of the Commissioner of Corporations is based upon facts available to the end of 1904, and the statements below should be considered of that date. The large packing companies are: Armour, Swift, Morris, National, Schwartzchild & Sulzberger, and Cudahy, frequently called the "Big Six." These control 50 per cent of the beef packing industry of the United States. Also these companies handle hogs, sheep, calves; and they do an extensive business in the purchase, storage, and sale of dairy and poultry products. The by-products of these companies are very important; some of these are hides, fat, and fertilizer. Each of the companies owns refrigerator lines for the transportation of products, and each does a general refrigerating business.

Percentage of business.

While the total business of the "Big Six" is only about 50 per cent of the whole, in the large cities of the East they do a much larger proportion; for instance, in New York 75 per cent, in Boston 85 per cent, in Philadelphia and Pittsburg 60 per cent. On the other hand, in cities west of Pittsburg, such as Cleveland, Cincinnati, and Indianapolis, not one half of the business belongs to these companies. Even in the small towns in New England these companies control about three fourths of the business; but in the Western states, in cities having populations of fifty thousand or less, they usually control less than half of the business.

The total capitalization of these companies in 1905 was $93,000,000, which included $5,000,000 in bonds. The gross business of the six companies was about $700,000,000 per annum. With one exception these companies have largely grown up as a single corporation and have increased in size as business has grown, although to a certain extent the growth has been by accretion through the purchase of other companies. However, the National Packing Company is an exception to this, in that it was organized in 1903 through the consolidation of a number of existing companies. In 1906 there was comparatively little interownership among the large companies.

The big companies have either owned or are largely interested in a number of subsidiary packing companies and other companies, the business of which is allied to the packing business. Thus the Armour Company of Illinois owns or controls packing companies in New Jersey and Louisiana, car lines, fertilizer works, soap works, and glue works. Also owned or controlled by the company are the Armour Grain Company, the Armour Elevator Company, the Continental Fruit Express, and large interests in stockyards at Omaha, Fort Worth, Sioux City, St. Louis, and Kansas City. A similar but not identical line of business is owned or controlled by each of the other large companies. This is especially true of the Swift and the National Packing companies. Each of the large companies owns large packing houses in various cities; for instance, the Swift Illinois corporation has packing houses at Chicago, Omaha, Kansas City, East St. Louis, St. Joseph, St. Paul, and Fort Worth.

Enter allied business.

Capitalization and Profits.—It was the opinion of the Commissioner of Corporations, at the time his report was rendered in 1906, that these companies are not largely overcapitalized. At any rate, they are in a very marked contrast with the American Tobacco Company, a business of much less importance; but in which the capitalization is between three and four times that of the six beef companies combined.

At the time the Commissioner made his report he did not regard the profits of the companies as excessive as compared with the business. Thus the profits of Swift in 1904 were placed at $3,850,000, and this profit includes that on private cars, or 1.9 per cent on the entire transactions of the company. In no case, from 1902 to 1904, did the profits of the company exceed 2 per cent on the sales. However, if the profits be looked at from the point of view of capitalization, for Swift, $3,850,000 would represent a profit of 11 per cent on the capitalization of $35,000,000. The net profits of the Cudahy Company are reported to be $927,969 in 1904, 1.8 per cent of the volume of the business. If the car lines be considered separately, the profits on this part of the business are greater, from 14 to 17 per cent on the capital invested on the basis of $1000 per car.

If the price of cattle and the price at which dressed beef is sold are compared, it is found that there is a rough parallelism between the two. However, when the price of cattle rose, there was a tendency for the price of beef to rise to a somewhat greater extent, giving a larger margin of profit. This was especially marked in 1902.

The above statements refer to the wholesale prices of beef; the retail price is quite another matter. It is probable that the retailer has been able to secure a larger profit upon his sales than was possible before the combinations existed. This is not due altogether to the great combination, but to the tendency for retail men at a given point to coöperate, this tendency being synchronous with the general movement in recent years toward combination of the men engaged in the same business in the United States.

Principles Illustrated. — Concentration in the packing industry has given various economic advantages, among which are the following: The returns from the by-products are a considerable portion of the entire business, the value being roughly 25 per cent of the total. The small slaughter-house is at a great disadvantage in respect to these by-products; a large abattoir may save everything. A second advantage of concentration is the location of abattoirs by the same company in different cities. Through this arrangement cross freights are saved. The beef cattle for the packing house at a given city are acquired from the territory contiguous to that city. The demands for beef in that territory are supplied by that plant. Furthermore, for the eastern part of the United States there is an advantage in that the beef cattle are killed near the source and only the dressed product shipped to the market, thus reducing greatly the amount of freight to be handled, since the weight of the dressed beef is only from 54 to 57 per cent of the weight of the live cattle.

Economic gains.

There can be little doubt that, since the organization of these six great beef companies and their combination with affiliated companies in controlling the stockyards, it has become more difficult for an additional great company to enter the business. The large interstate business of the country is in very great measure controlled by the "Big Six"; the local business is still largely with the small company.

In 1905 an indictment was brought against a considerable number of the officers of the "Big Six," charging that they were in combination and in restraint of trade and that they had "an agreement, understanding, and arrangement among themselves whereby they fixed, regulated, and controlled prices."[1] The trial of those charged under the indictment did not take place until in 1912. On March 26, the long contest was closed by the jury finding that the officers of these companies were not guilty under the criminal section of the Sherman act against conspiracy in restraint of trade.

SECTION 7

THE LUMBER INDUSTRY[2]

In the United States concentration of the ownership of standing timber has progressed far.

The General Situation. — "Certain basic facts in the lumber industry are as follows: —

"First. The entire remaining supply of standing timber in continental United States (excluding Alaska) is now about two hundred and eighty billion board feet, of which about twenty-two hundred billion is privately owned. (The unit 'board foot' is a foot square and an inch thick.)

Timber supply.

"Second. There has come about, and there is still proceeding, a very remarkable concentration in the ownership of this remaining standing timber in the hands of a comparatively few interests. This concentration results chiefly from the speculative holding of timber lands for future profit, primarily made possible by our long-standing public land policy.

Concentration of ownership.

"Third. From the time when the vast majority of our

[1] United States of America *v.* Louis F. Swift *et al.*, Decision, p. 2.

[2] Summary of Report of the Commissioner of Corporations on the Lumber Industry, Part I, "Standing Timber."

present timber supply left the hands of the one great original owner, the United States, till the present there has been an enormous increase in the value of standing timber. This increase has varied greatly, according to local conditions, but practically everywhere it has been manyfold — sixfold, tenfold, twentyfold, thirtyfold, and in some cases fifty-fold. The present commercial value of the privately owned standing timber in the country, not including the value of the land, is estimated (though in the nature of the case such an estimate must be very rough) as at least $6,000,000,000.

Increase in value.

"These conditions must be considered in the light of the further facts that our standing timber is a natural resource created almost exclusively by nature; that where it has not been destroyed it is substantially in the same condition as when it left the hands of the government; that human effort, or the private owners that hold and have left it, have added practically nothing to it; that while a certain amount of reforestation is possible, standing timber is a resource in the main quite similar to our ore and coal measures; that our present annual consumption of timber is about three times the annual growth, and the demand is steadily increasing; that speculative holding of timber land for future rise in no way improves the character of the timber and does not give such public service as is given by those who acquire lands for actual present use and improvement. While the profits of speculative timber holding have been enormous, as will be hereafter shown, the risks of such holding and the services rendered by the holders are peculiarly small in comparison with those profits.

The unearned increment.

"These great facts have brought about certain results of tremendous significance from the standpoint of the public welfare. The timber supply is a diminishing natural resource. Its increasing concentration into a comparatively few strong hands has conferred upon those strong holders a vast power over the timber industry and over prices therein; and has itself greatly accelerated the enormous rise in timber values."

Rise in prices and concentration.

The lumber industry is one in which the units of manufacture are not of extremely large size, because the material is so heavy as compared with its value that it cannot be transported a great distance advantageously. The logs, by stream in favored localities and by railroad in others, must be transported to the mill. Where the logs float downstream the expense is not great. For the lumber so located that it must be transported by rail the cost increases more rapidly with distance, so that there is a limit beyond which it is not advantageous from the point of view of economic efficiency to transport logs, and this fixes the size of the mill to that adapted to the work of sawing the logs for the tributary area. "The largest sawmill in the country cuts less than one half of one per cent of the total annual output of lumber." Since the control of the market is not readily secured by concentration of sawmills, it has been secured by the concentration of the ownership of standing timber.

Limit in size of mill.

Concentrated Ownership of Timber. — Of the merchantable saw timber of the United States 20 per cent is still owned by the government, leaving 80 per cent in private hands. Of the vast amount of timber in private holdings the concentration of ownership is shown by the following table: —

Four fifths in private ownership.

TABLE 46. CONCENTRATION OF TIMBER OWNERSHIP BY GROUPS, SHOWN CUMULATIVELY, IN ENTIRE INVESTIGATION AREA

	NUMBER OF HOLDERS	AMOUNT OF TIMBER OWNED IN BILLIONS OF FEET	PER CENT OF TOTAL
Total	—	1747.0	100.0
Group 1	3	237.5	13.6
Groups 1–2 . . .	8	339.5	19.4
Groups 1–3 . . .	22	459.0	26.2
Groups 1–4 . . .	48	574.3	32.8
Groups 1–5 . . .	90	690.5	39.5
Groups 1–6 . . .	195	839.7	48.0
Groups 1–7 . . .	385	972.1	55.6
Groups 1–8 . . .	658	1068.5	61.1
Groups 1–9 . . .	1147	1153.3	66.0
Groups 1–10 . .	1802	1208.8	69.2
Group 11 . . .	—	538.2	30.8

"From this table it will be seen that three holdings include no less than 237.5 billion feet, or nearly 11 per cent of the privately owned timber in the entire country, and over 13.5 per cent of the privately owned timber in the investigation area. These three holders are the Southern Pacific Company, the Weyerhaeuser Timber Company, and the Northern Pacific Railway Company. Five other holders ranking next in importance own in the investigation area an aggregate of 102 billion feet, or 4.6 per cent of the total privately owned timber of the country and 5.8 per cent of that in the investigation area. Thus the eight large holders together own approximately 340 billion feet of timber, or 15.4 per cent of the total privately owned timber of the country and 19.4 per cent of that in the investigation area.

The big three.

"Twenty-two holders own 26.2 per cent of all the timber in the investigation area; 195 holders own 48 per cent. Stated in another way, more than one eighth of the total timber in the investigation area (this representing 80 per cent of the total privately owned timber of the United States) is owned by only 3 holders; more than one fourth is owned by only 22 holders. Almost one half is owned by 195 holders.

"The most marked concentration is in the hands of the comparatively few large holders of the upper groups; the lower groups control a much less important percentage. Thus, while the 385 holders in groups 1 to 7, inclusive, control 55.6 per cent of the timber in the investigation area, the 273 holders in group 8 control only 5.5 per cent, the 489 holders in group 9 only 4.9 per cent, and the 655 holders in group 10 only 3.2 per cent.

"Furthermore, these 10 groups, 1802 holdings, embrace nearly 70 per cent of the total timber in the investigation area, while group 11, the remaining holdings, aggregating unnumbered thousands, have in all only 538.2 billion feet, or 30.8 per cent of the total."

An organization is regarded as holding a property when it has more than one half of the stock of a corporation. Even the above statements do not indicate the real extent of concentration of ownership, since many great timber holders have stock in several companies. Further, where in great holdings of timber small holdings are blocked in, they are practically controlled by the large holders, since the owners of the smaller blocks can only sell to the surrounding holders or get the timber out through coöperation with such holders.

Of the three great companies, the Southern Pacific is first, the Weyerhaeuser is second, and the Northern Pacific is third, the holdings of the three together constituting 23.5 per cent of all the privately owned timber in the five states of the Pacific Northwest. In order to appreciate the magnitudes of the Southern Pacific holdings it may be said that the timber of this company "stretches practically all the way from Portland, Ore., to Sacramento, Calif., a distance of 682 miles. The running time of the fastest train between these two points is thirty-one hours; yet during all that time the traveler is passing through lands a large proportion of which for thirty miles on each side of him belongs to the corporation over whose track he is riding, and in almost the entire strip, 60 miles wide and 682 miles long, this corporation is the dominating owner of both timber and land."

Enormous holdings in Pacific states.

The holdings of these three great companies are based upon government grants. That of the Southern Pacific was acquired almost exclusively by government gift, and the Weyerhaeuser holdings were largely purchased from the government-granted lands of the Northern Pacific. The original vast grants were made more valuable by the law which permitted the exchange of lands in the forest reserves and parks for other lands. Much of the land released in the Pacific forest reserve and Mount Ranier National Park had comparatively little timber, and in exchange the great companies selected heavily timbered land.

The timber given away.

While the concentration in timber holding is great for the country as a whole, it is still greater in single regions. At the present time the largest quantity of the most valuable timber is in the Pacific Northwest. Concentration in this region is shown by the following table: —

TABLE 47. CONCENTRATION OF TIMBER OWNERSHIP BY GROUPS, SHOWN CUMULATIVELY IN PACIFIC NORTHWEST

	NUMBER OF HOLDERS	AMOUNT OF TIMBER OWNED IN BILLIONS OF FEET	PER CENT OF TOTAL
Total	——	1013.0	100.0
Group 1	3	237.5	23.5
Groups 1–2 . . .	8	338.9	33.5
Groups 1–3 . . .	20	436.3	43.1
Groups 1–4 . . .	38	507.3	50.1
Groups 1–5 . . .	64	571.9	56.5
Groups 1–6 . . .	131	663.8	65.6
Groups 1–7 . . .	217	723.0	71.4
Groups 1–8 . . .	313	757.3	74.8
Groups 1–9 . . .	489	789.1	77.9
Groups 1–10 . .	711	807.4	79.7
Group 11 . . .	——	205.6	20.3

"The pronounced concentration of timber ownership in the Pacific Northwest is at once apparent from this table. The 3 largest companies own over 23 per cent of the total, or almost one fourth, while 5 more own 10 per cent, these 8 holders having a little more than a third of the total for this region. The next 12 holders own over 9 per cent, giving the 20 principal holders 43 per cent of the total. The next 18 own 7 per cent; thus no less than 50 per cent of the total privately owned timber in this vast region is in the hands of 38 holders. The next 6 groups, comprising 673 holders, together own less than 30 per cent of the total."

Concentration of ownership in the southern pine belt and in the lake region, while great, is not so far advanced as in the Pacific Northwest. In all regions the concentration is greater for the high class timber, such as fir, pine, and cypress, than it is for the less valuable hard wood.

Rising Prices.—Since timber is a natural resource, which is diminishing in quantity, it is inevitable that in anticipation of a lack of supply, the prices for timber are continually rising; for timber is being cut at the present time about three times as fast as it is renewed. However, the enhancement of price has been greatly accelerated because of the concentration in ownership. Many illustrations could be given as showing the increase in the value of timber. For instance, upon the average for Minnesota, the state has received from its pine lands a steadily increasing amount. In 1880, the average price per thousand feet was $1.47; in 1890, $2.25; in 1900, $5.17; and in 1909, $7.53, or more than five times the price in 1880. Other illustrations of the rise in price during the past twenty years are as follows: from $5 to $30 an acre, $7 to $40, $20 to $150, $1 to $13, $4 to $140, $1 to $50.

Multiplication of prices.

The government gave its lands as bonuses to railroads, canals, and wagon roads, or received $1.25 or $2.50 per acre for the same. In short, our reckless liberality in giving away our natural resources and our defective land laws were the chief underlying causes which have led to the extraordinary concentration in ownership of one of the great natural resources of the country, the timber.

Our heritage squandered.

Section 8

THE WATER POWERS[1]

The water powers of the country have in recent years become of rapidly increasing importance. This has followed as a consequence of the improvements in the electrical transmission of power. It is now possible to transmit power economically from a given center to a distance of two hundred miles and over an area of one hundred thousand square miles.

The Amount and Distribution. — The minimum potential water power of the United States is estimated at 32,083,000 h.p., and the maximum at 61,678,000 h.p. Assuming an

[1] Report of Commissioner of Corporations on Water Power Development in the United States. Washington Government Printing Office, 1912, p. 220. "Conservation of Natural Resources in the United States," C. R. Van Hise, pp. 118–161, The Macmillan Company, New York, 1910.

efficiency of 75 per cent for this potential horse power, the water powers would give a minimum effective energy of 26,736,000 h.p., and a maximum of 51,398,000 h.p. By minimum horse power is meant the average available for the two weeks of lowest water during a period of seven years; by the maximum is meant that which is available during a period of not less than six months each year.

From 1905 to 1907 the amount of mechanical energy used in the United States was approximately 23,000,000 h.p., of which 3,432,000 h.p., or 15 per cent, was produced by water, the remainder being developed by steam and internal combustion engines. In June, 1911, the developed water power installations, greater than 1000 each, amounted to 4,016,127 h.p., and that in units less than 1000 h.p., to 2,000,000 h.p., making a total in round numbers of 6,000,000 h.p.

Of the water power installations nearly 50 per cent of those developed for sale and for public service corporations was located in five states, as shown by Table 48.

TABLE 48. SHOWING COMMERCIAL WATER POWER IN FIVE STATES

	PER CENT
California	14
New York	13
Washington	10
Pennsylvania	6
South Carolina	5
Total	48

The water power which is used for manufacturing is even more concentrated than the "commercial" water power, as is shown by Table 49.

TABLE 49. WATER POWER IN A NUMBER OF STATES EMPLOYED IN MANUFACTURE

	PER CENT
New York	30
New England States	36
Minnesota and Wisconsin	17
South Carolina	5
Total	88

M

Concentration of Ownership. — There are strong economic forces which tend to concentrate the ownership of water powers.

The demand for energy is very unequally distributed, both as to time and place. There are variations in the amount of power needed in winter and in summer; there are even greater variations in the demands during a given day. If, for any district, the different water powers are coupled up, a greater amount of energy can be utilized than if each be managed separately. Consequently the most efficient use of water power is gained by "gathering into a single unit all the power available for a given market or group of markets using the same system of transmission lines." Another reason for concentration is that the limit of two hundred miles for economic transmission of power makes it impossible for the water powers of one district to compete with those of another. Therefore, if all the water powers of a single district or a large portion of them can be acquired by a single concern, there will be monopoly in that district. Concentration has also been promoted by the close connection between the manufacturers of hydro-electric machinery and the water power companies, and by a union of these with financial concerns especially interested in these lines of business.

Reasons for concentration.

In consequence of the foregoing factors, in each of the principal regions in which water powers are developed on a large scale, the control of the greater part of the same is by one or two companies.

"In California the bulk of the power produced in the northern half of the state is controlled by a single interest, and that in the southern half by only two companies. In Montana two companies control 96 per cent of all the developed power of the state; and in Washington a single interest controls the power situation in the Puget Sound region, while another interest, more or less closely affiliated with it, controls the developed power elsewhere in the state. All the developed power in the vicinity of Denver, Colo., and nearly 70 per cent of the total developed power in that state, is controlled by one interest. In South Carolina one corporation owns 75 per cent of the developed commercial power, while in North Carolina 45 per cent of such power, developed and under construction, is controlled by a single interest. One group of interests practically controls 58 per cent of all the commercial power, developed and under construction, in Georgia. In the Lower Peninsula of Michigan a single group owns 73 per cent of all such power. The great development at Niagara Falls on the American side is controlled by only two companies."

Strong position of great companies.

Not only is there concentration in control of districts, but the same companies have large interest in water powers in different districts.

"The General Electric interests control the water power situation in large portions of Washington, Oregon, Colorado, Montana, and elsewhere. The Stone and Webster interests exercise control (based largely, however, on management rather than ownership) in localities in Washington, Iowa, and Georgia. The Pacific Gas and Electric Co., practically dominates the power situation in a large number of localities in the northern half of California. The Southern Power Co., controls the power situation in South Carolina and has a strong foothold in North Carolina. The S. Morgan Smith interests dominate the power situation in the vicinity of Atlanta, Ga. The Telluride Power Co. controls absolutely a large territory in Utah and Idaho. The Commonwealth Power, Railway, and Light Co., which is a part of the Clark-Foote-Hodenpyl-Walbridge interests, dominates the power situation in the Lower Peninsula of Michigan. The Gould interests control the best of the available water power sites in the vicinity of Richmond, Va."

Also there is a very close relation between the water power companies and the public service corporations, since the largest use of the power is for street railways, electric lighting of cities, etc.

"In the country as a whole, water power companies, or companies affiliated with them, own or control and operate street railways in no less than 111 cities and towns in the

United States, electric lighting plants in 669 cities and towns, and gas plants in 113 cities and towns. These companies, moreover, supply power to municipal lighting plants in a considerable number of cities and towns. Many of these are among the most important municipalities in the states involved. Furthermore, in many cities and towns in the United States all the public utilities—street railways, electric lighting and gas plants—are controlled by water power interests."

Community of interests.

Finally there is very close interrelation of the large water power interests through common financial houses, common directorates, and common ownership of public utilities.

The use of the 6,000,000 h.p., now developed, saves at least 33,000,000 tons of coal. If the amount of water power used could be made fourfold, this would save annually more than 130,000,000 tons of coal. So great a saving of a fundamental resource would mean much to the future of the nation. It is clear, therefore, that the greatest "waste of water power is its non-use." But we must recognize that its rapid development can only be accomplished by unification of storage, coupling up, and coöperation with public utilities corporations. Thus water powers probably furnish the best illustration of the tendency toward concentration of a natural resource limited in quantity.

Saving of coal.

Public Control.—The prices charged for water power at present are substantially those that the traffic will bear. If the prices are made too high, public utilities and manufactories using water power will not be rapidly developed. It is obvious that the price for water power cannot be made higher than for equivalent energy produced by coal; therefore in the part of the East where coal is cheap, water-developed energy is relatively low. In localities where coal is expensive, as in the Pacific Northwest, the traffic will bear more; and the price of water-created energy is placed very high by the controlling companies, in some instances as high as $40 per horse power per annum to the large consumers.

Price of water-created energy.

The amount of water in the United States even when fully

developed will be far short of the energy which in the future will be required for the industries and public utilities. This is evident by the fact that there is already in use almost as much energy as the entire minimum horse power available for the United States. For the great, densely settled regions, it will not be possible to gain through the use of water more than a relatively small fraction of the energy needed. Hence there is a sound reason for not placing the price of energy derived from water on the market at a lower rate than that derived from the consumption of coal, otherwise those who are obliged to obtain their power from coal would be at a disadvantage.

Since, however, energy derived from water power is upon the whole very cheaply produced, requiring only a capital investment of from $40 to $300 per horse power for installations of moderate size, and the expense of the operation is very low, it is clear that the profits from the development of water power upon the average are large. The public should gain the advantage of this natural source of power which will be available in perpetuity. In all cases in which the public still retains the right to the energy of falling water, some plan should be devised which will give to the public a large part of the difference between the cost of producing energy by water and of producing an equivalent amount of energy by coal. Where the government or the states retain the water power sites this will be easily accomplished through a lease or rental system.

Public should gain profits.

Fortunately the United States government still owns the land adjacent to many of the streams in the western part of the United States, and has all the water rights for a large number of water power sites. Some of the states, illustrated by Illinois and New York, also own some of the water power there located. A number of municipalities own water powers, among which Los Angeles has first place, controlling more than 100,000 h.p.; and Chicago, Augusta, Ga., Seattle, and Tacoma, are very important, each controlling from 12,000 to 76,000 h.p. In several of the Western states, illustrated by Colorado, California, North Dakota, Washington, Wyoming, Idaho, and Oregon, the use of water for all purposes has been declared to be a public use; and in some of them the water in its entirety has been declared to belong to the public.

Future importance of water powers.

Whatever public rights to the use of water for the development of energy exist, they should be jealously guarded; for in the distant future, when the coal is gone, the power of falling water is the only source of cheap energy of which we have knowledge at present. When that time comes, the owners of the water powers will control the industries of the nation. The energy from falling water so far as publicly owned or controlled should be sold for a limited term of years at a rate sufficiently low to lead to prompt development, and thus displace as much coal as possible. A large part of the margin between the selling price and the cost of development should go to the public.

In those states in which the energy of falling water has been given through legislative enactment or judicial decision to the riparian owners, the problem of water power control is more difficult. In such instances one way to secure control by the public would be to condemn privately owned water powers, and after such condemnation have them operated as public utilities.

CHAPTER III

THE LAWS REGARDING COÖPERATION[1]

SECTION 1

ENGLAND

IN England, in the time of Edward VI, a very strict statute was passed by Parliament against "forestalling, enhancing, regrating, and engrossing." Without going into details the things prohibited by these laws were roughly as follows: Forestalling was the offense of going out on the road and buying merchandise which was coming to the market, with the intention of selling at a higher price upon its arrival. This applied especially to wheat, or as it is called in England, corn. Enhancing defines itself; it applied to buying a product, one of the necessities of life, with the intention of selling again at an increased price. Regrating was the offense of going into the market and buying products in a greater quantity than needed for consumption with the intention of selling in the same market at a higher price. Engrossing was buying corn growing, or any other corn, butter, cheese, fish, or other dead victual, with intent to sell the same again. Under these old laws transactions were prohibited which raised the price of an essential article. Many of the regulations went so far as to fix prices.

Early rigid statutes.

While at this time these offenses were made statutory, they apparently had been offenses against the common law at a much earlier date. Indeed, so far as we can ascertain, the common law in the Middle Ages was very strict against combinations in restraint of trade, as well as against regrating,

[1] For full information concerning this part of the subject, see Eddy on Combinations, Callaghan & Co., 1901; Noyes on Intercorporate Relations, Little, Brown & Co., 1902; Wyman on Control of the Market, Moffat, Yard & Co., 1911, and Jenks Report of the Industrial Commission, Vol. II.

forestalling, and engrossing. Since the statutes were found to have a tendency to prevent free trade and to enhance the price of essential commodities, they were repealed during the reign of George III. Notwithstanding this fact some of the judges held that the common law against these offenses still existed and penalties were imposed for them. In order to clarify the situation, in 1844, Parliament definitely abolished the offenses of badgering, engrossing, forestalling, and regrating, for Great Britain as a whole, and repealed a large number of acts which had been passed prohibiting restraint of trade. The repealed acts included those which required foods to be sold at reasonable prices, which allowed justices of the peace to fix the rate of wages of laborers, various statutes fixing the prices of different articles, and finally acts which prevented men from engaging in allied lines of business, such as not permitting "an hostler to make horse bread," and prohibiting a butcher from being a grazer. Thus, at one stroke Parliament repealed the statute laws against restraint of trade. This repealing act guarded against fraudulent or unfair practices by adding the following clause: —

Rigid statutes repealed.

"Provided always and be it enacted, that nothing in this act contained shall be construed to apply to the offense of knowingly and fraudulently spreading or conspiring to spread any false rumor, with intent to enhance or decry the price of any goods or merchandise, or to the offense of preventing or endeavoring to prevent by force or threats any goods or wares, or merchandise being brought to any fair or market, but that every such offense may be punished as if this act had not been made."

Combination in trade may be defined as the coöperation of two or more persons, partnerships, or corporations to achieve a given result. According to Eddy[1] the purposes of combination are to reduce the cost of producing and marketing products, to control prices, and to discourage and if possible to suppress, competition. Since 1844, the law in England has permitted combination in all commodities including the essentials of life even if the purpose of the same were to

[1] Eddy on Combinations, Vol. I, Sections 167, 176, 184.

enhance the price. Any combination is permitted which does not involve immoral, unlawful, and oppressive acts, is not contrary to public policy, and does not go to the extent of monopoly. Magnitude alone does not make a combination illegal; but monopoly is prohibited in order to retain competition. It is realized in England that "competition has it disadvantages as well as its advantages, and may be the death as well as the life of trade." [1]

Law permits corporation.

In England also in early times the common law restrictions were very severe upon *contracts* in restraint of trade. By contract in restraint of trade is meant any contract "whereby any party binds himself to not follow some particular occupation, trade, calling, or profession, or engage in some particular business or enterprise for a period within a particular territory." [2] Gradually the rigidity of the early rule forbidding contracts in restraint of trade was modified, so that in England at the present time whether contracts in restraint of trade are lawful is dependent upon their reasonableness. They may be sustained even if they be indefinite, both as to time and place; but such contracts, to be lawful, must be essential for the protection of the legitimate interest of the contractees, and must be reasonable.[2]

Early limitations on contracts removed.

The above statement shows that at the present time the laws have so developed in England that there is freedom to combine in trade to any extent, provided that the combination is not immoral, unlawful, or oppressive, is not contrary to public policy, and is not a monopoly. Thus there is freedom to combine in trade as well as freedom to compete. This great policy is in accordance with the principle of *laissez faire* which for many years has had such a vast influence in England. It is a very radical departure from the early decisions under the common law and the policies of the old statutes. As we shall see, freedom for combination as well as freedom for competition has had a very far-reaching influence upon the development of trade in the United Kingdom.

Freedom to combine and freedom to compete.

[1] Eddy on Combinations, Vol. I, Section 308.
[2] *Ibid.*, Section 688. [3] *Ibid.*, Section 713.

Section 2

THE UNITED STATES

The laws of England regarding trade, both common and statute, were brought over to this country; and here they have gone through the same stages of development as in Great Britain.

The statute laws, originally severe, were gradually ameliorated and finally wiped out. The common law regarding contracts and combination in restraint of trade went through the same stages of development as in England, until finally they permitted combination and contracts which were reasonable. The purposes of contracts may be to restrain trade, to suppress competition, or to control the market. It has been held that contracts in restraint of trade which go to the extent of the entire United States for an unlimited time are unreasonable. Contracts in partial restraint of trade, such as not to use a trade in a particular place for a definite term, if founded on a good consideration and for a proper and useful purpose, were valid; and they were so even if an entire state was comprised by the contract.

Partial contracts in restraint allowed.

The limits of the combinations which were permitted are given in general terms by Noyes [1] as follows: —

Principles limiting combinations.

"(1) Any combination of corporations or individuals the object of which is, or the necessary or natural consequence of the operation of which will be, the control of the market for a useful commodity, is against public policy and unlawful.

"(2) Any combination of quasi-public corporations, the object of which is, or the necessary or natural consequence of the operation of which will be, the increase of charges beyond reasonable rates, or the curtailment of facilities afforded the public, is against public policy and unlawful."

Under the above principles the following have been held to be lawful, viz., combinations which had for their object maintenance of a fair price, union of rival manufacturers,

[1] Noyes on Intercorporate Relations, Section 352.

agreements in selling price or division of profits, and exclusive trade agreements. Even if such combinations tended to raise the price of a commodity, they were lawful. Also, agreements to remove a rival from the field are legal unless they result in monopoly.[1]

Extent of combination allowed.

From actual cases which have been considered by the courts,[2] Eddy gives the following statement regarding the nature of combinations which were permitted before the statutes of recent years were passed: —

"Combination to control competition is legal where oppressive monopoly is not intended." — "Combination by consolidation of competing companies, by the formation of a new corporation to take over the assets of the competing companies, the object being to diminish competition, is legal." — "Combination among individuals by the formation of a partnership to handle produce or merchandise and control competition in a given market is legal where no fraud or deception is practiced." — "Combinations among competitors, the object of which is to realise a fair price for the goods manufactured and sold, do not contravene any rule of public policy, even though they operate in some respects as in restraint of trade." — "Combination of all competitors to control trade and prices by formation of new corporation to take entire product and act as exclusive selling agent is legal." — "Combination by voluntary association among competitors for the purpose of suppressing ruinous competition and establishing better prices through the appointment of an exclusive selling agent and a supervisory committee, held legal." — "Combination to prevent competition by subsidizing competitor is legal." — "Combination to suppress competition by means of contracts with independent manufacturers for their entire products is not illegal so long as there is not a conspiracy to monopolize the market." — "Combination of workmen for protection and to increase wages is legal; so also is the combination of common carriers to guard against undue competition and the reducing of

Illustrations of combinations.

[1] Eddy on Combinations, Vol. I, pp. 124–127.
[2] *Ibid.*, Chapter 7, pp. 131–198.

freights below a fair compensation." — "Combinations between individuals or firms for the regulation of prices, and of competition in business, are not monopolies, and are not unlawful as in restraint of trade, so long as they are reasonable and do not include all of a commodity or trade, or create such restrictions as to materially affect freedom of commerce." — "An agreement between a number of persons to act concertedly in fixing prices at which they will sell a particular commodity in a particular city is not illegal as being in restraint of trade unless it appears that they have a monopoly of that commodity." — "I know of no rule of law ever having existed which prohibited a certain number (not all) of the producers of a staple commodity agreeing not to sell below a certain price."[1]

The general principle regarding contracts in restraint of trade was admirably stated by Justice Guthrie as follows:[2] "That all contracts in partial restraint of trade are not void as against public policy is too well settled to be gainsaid; while, on the other hand, it is as fully established, as a general rule, that contracts in general restaint of trade are against public policy and, therefore, absolutely void."

Freedom for fair competition.

While combinations and contracts in restraint of trade are permitted in England to a large degree and were permitted in America to a similar extent under the common law, in both countries it is a fundamental principle that there must be freedom for fair competition. Contracts must not be tainted with fraud, against public policy, or contrary to the statutes. All claims on the part of any person or partnership to have the exclusive right or monopoly in any business have universally been denied the protection of the law, whether such exclusive privilege was claimed as a general right or because of a contract. Moreover, freedom of competition under the common law has not been allowed to go to the point of establishing business to injure a person through a malicious purpose, nor so far as to allow the breaking of one contract to make another on more advantageous terms. If

[1] Eddy on Combinations, Vol. I, Sections 270, 271, 272, 276, 277, 278, 280, 281, 282, 313, 315, and 316.

[2] 35 Ohio State, 666.

fraud be used in competition, it is illegal; as, for instance, the misleading use of a firm name. A company manufacturing watches in Waltham was not allowed to call the same Waltham watches, since this was a well-known manufacture of a previously established company. Libelous statements may not be used to secure business. Intimidation or coercion to secure trade or to compel exclusive employment of a certain class, such as the members of a business, has not the protection of the common law.

Since by reference to Eddy the very numerous cases in which combinations in restraint of trade have been permitted in this country under common law may be easily found, they are not here repeated. There will be mentioned a few cases showing how far contracts in restraint of trade have been permitted.

In New Jersey a contract not to manufacture anywhere in the United States except in Nevada and Arizona for fifty years was held to be valid so far as the state of New Jersey was concerned.[1] In New York a contract not to engage in the manufacture of matches for ninety-nine years except in the state of Nevada and the territory of Montana was held to be partial and not general restraint of trade, and therefore valid.[2] In another case in that state it was held that a contract under which a steamboat company paid another company not to run a competing line of steamboats was valid on the ground that it may be a benefit to keep competition from becoming too strong.[3]

While it is clear under the common law in this country that there was great liberality regarding combination and contracts in restraint of trade, when such contracts and combinations affected partnerships of corporations, they were uniformly declared to be illegal.[4]

Here falls the famous case of the People *v.* the North River Sugar Refining Company under which the shares of the capital stock of the constituent companies were transferred to a board of trustees. This was the case in which

[1] 56 N. J. Eq. 680. [2] 106 N. Y. 473. [3] 110 N. Y. 519.
[4] 121 Ill. 530; 58 S. W. Rep. 853; 86 Tenn. 598.

the trust was first brought before the court. Speaking of the trust, Justice Barrett of the circuit court says that the acts of this trust are unlawful for two reasons: "1. They constitute the corporation a partner and a corporation is not allowed by law to enter into partnership. 2. Any combination, the tendency of which is to prevent competition in its broad and general sense and to control, and thus at will enhance prices to the detriment of the public, is a legal monopoly, and is against public interest." Justice Finch, of the court of appeals, declared "that defendant corporation has violated its charter and failed in the performance of its corporate duties, and that in respects so material and important as to justify a judgment of dissolution." [1]

Under this principle the Standard Oil Trust of Ohio was declared to be illegal.[2] In this case the action of the corporation was held to be *ultra vires*, against public policy, and therefore ground for the forfeiture of the charters of the offending companies. Apparently in this decision was also the element of monopoly since Justice Minshall declared that under the trust form of combination "by the invariable laws of human nature, competition will be excluded and prices controlled in the interest of those connected with the combination or trust."

Numerous cases could be cited which have declared combinations which go to the extent of monopoly to be contrary to public policy as intending to control the market, but the principle is so well known that details will not be given.[3]

Section 3

THE SHERMAN ANTITRUST LAW [4]

The law as above described in Section 2 for this country was a natural development under which the law conforms to the conditions of trade. Large liberty was permitted.

[1] 121 N. Y. 582. [2] 49 Ohio State 131, 1892.

[3] 139 N. Y. 105; 145 N. Y. 267; 47 Ohio 320; 111 Pa. 473; 77 Mich. 632.

[4] For the full text of the law see Appendix I. Many discussions of the Sherman antitrust act and its influence on law and trade have been published. Some of the more enlightening are the following: "The Federal

Suddenly, in 1890, a new policy was introduced by statute law, the principle of which was to go back to severe restrictions regarding trade, not so severe as in the Middle Ages in England, but far in that direction. This policy was inaugurated by the Sherman antitrust law. Combinations of the kind above mentioned and which before had been regarded as legitimate were by congressional act for interstate commerce declared to be unlawful. The Sherman act clearly stated that restraint of trade in any degree is illegal. How marked is the contrast between this law and the previously existing common law is shown by the following summary of its important provisions.

Sudden reversal of policy.

Provisions of Sherman act.

Sections 1 and 3 of the Sherman act make "every contract, combination in the form of trust or otherwise, or conspiracy in restraint of trade or commerce" illegal. This provision applies as among the several states and territories, the District of Columbia, and foreign countries; as between persons, corporations, and associations engaged in interstate commerce; and as between one of any of these groups with any member of another group, except contracts between two foreign countries.

Section 2 provides that "every person who shall monopolize, or attempt to monopolize, or combine or conspire with any other person or persons, to monopolize any part of the trade or commerce among the several states, or with foreign countries, shall be deemed guilty of a misdemeanor." Thus the law forbids both restraint of trade and monopoly or attempt at monopoly. Violation of any of the above provisions of the act is made a misdemeanor and is punishable by a fine not exceeding $5000, or imprisonment not exceeding one year, or by both.

Section 7 provides that any person who is "injured in

Antitrust Act," Robert L. Raymond, *Harvard Law Review*, Vol. XXIII, pp. 353–379; "The Standard Oil and Tobacco Cases," Robert L. Raymond, *Harvard Law Review*, Vol. XXV, pp. 31–58; "Antitrust Legislation and Litigation," annual address before the American Bar Association, Boston, 1911, by William B. Hornblower; "Recent Interpretation of the Sherman Act," George W. Wickersham, *Michigan Law Review*, Vol. X, pp. 1–25, Hearings, Senate Interstate Commerce Committee, Albert H. Walker, Part XIX, pp. 1537–1571, and Victor Morawetz, *Ibid.*, pp. 1629–1642.

his business or property by any other person or corporation by reason of anything forbidden or declared to be unlawful by this act . . . shall recover threefold the damages by him sustained and the cost of suit including reasonable attorney's fee."

Other sections of the Sherman law provide for instituting proceedings by the Attorney-General of the United States and the conduct of cases by the court.

Amendments to the Sherman law have extended the inhibition of combinations to importers, and have given cases which arise under the law precedence over others. While the act is called the Sherman antitrust law because introduced by Senator Sherman, it was more largely written by Senator Edmunds than any other one man, although some clauses were based upon drafts by Senator Sherman and other clauses were written by Senators Hoar and Ingalls.[1]

Early decisions.

The Sherman antitrust act has now been on the statute books for twenty-two years, and many cases have been decided under it. Some of the early decisions were of a kind which gave little promise of the effectiveness of the law.

Thus in 1890 some seventy distilleries united, capable of producing 77,000,000 gallons of whisky. Their output was three fourths of that of the United States. The combination approached if it did not reach monopoly. The distilleries were located in different states. The products were shipped into states other than those in which the distilleries were located. It was held by the court that these acts did not constitute an unlawful agreement under the antitrust act.[2] Again it was held to be a legal act for two or more traders to agree among themselves that they will not deal with those who purchase goods of any designated traders in the same business.[3] An agreement to make exclusive purchases from a dealer with the provision that this would entitle the purchaser to a rebate if the agreement was carried out, was held not to violate the law.[4]

When dealers in lumber in different towns and cities of

[1] Hearings, Senate Interstate Commerce Committee, XXVI, pp. 2422–2431. [2] 51 Fed. 205. [3] 55 Fed. 851. [4] 51 Fed. 213.

the states of Wisconsin, Minnesota, Iowa, Illinois, and Missouri agreed to raise the price of lumber fifty cents per thousand feet in advance of the regular market price of pine lumber, it was held that the agreement did not necessarily raise the price generally and that the combination to come under the statute must be such that the members of the combination through the combination controlled the price of the entire output.[1] In other words, if the combination was not such as to introduce the element of monopoly, it was not illegal.

Early decision disconcerting.

Even more important than this case was that of the American Sugar Refining Company. This corporation, organized under the laws of New Jersey, secured control of four Philadelphia refineries, thus gaining practical monopoly of the business. It was held by the court that monopoly in the *manufacture* of an article necessary to life is not interstate commerce, and that combinations which restrain interstate commerce indirectly are not under the ban of the law.[2] This decision was all the more disconcerting because the manufacturers who combined were located in different states. While the decision did not say so, it was supposed that manufacturers in different states could combine and the company afterwards dispose of the products without reference to state lines. Apparently this was not the intention of the decision, or if so it was reversed by later decision.

The Kansas City Live Stock Exchange was a voluntary association doing business in Kansas and Missouri. The business was essentially that of a selling agency for cattle. The association had very strict rules regarding the methods of dealing of its members and also rules forbidding members of the exchange from buying of non-members. In this case it was held that the effect of the agreement in restraining interstate commerce was only indirect and therefore not under the ban of the act.[3]

The Traders' Live Stock Exchange, which at the Kansas City yards bought live stock coming from more than one

[1] U. S. *v.* Nelson, 52 Fed. 646.
[2] U. S. *v.* E. C. Knight Co., 156 U. S. 1.
[3] 171 U. S. 78.

state, differed from the above exchange in that cattle were bought and sold. The members of the Traders' Exchange coöperated under strict rules as to the method of conducting their business, among which was the provision that the exchange would not recognize any trader who was not a member. The undoubted effect of the arrangement was coöperation in prices and in other ways in buying and selling. In this case, it was held that if there was restraint of trade, it was not direct, but only an indirect result of the operation of the association; and that the business, all being done in Kansas City, was intrastate rather than interstate commerce, although the cattle came from more than one state.[1]

Reasonable and unreasonable immaterial.

While the above decisions seemed to promise little for the effectiveness of the Sherman act, even in early years there were other decisions which looked toward its effectiveness. Thus, combinations fixing price and contracts for exclusive dealing were declared to be in restraint of trade,[2] also all the earlier decisions held that whether the restraint of trade was reasonable or unreasonable was immaterial.[3]

The more important of these decisions were the Trans-Missouri[4] and the Joint Traffic[5] cases. In the Trans-Missouri case, Justice Peckham said it is "urged that the statute in declaring illegal every combination in the form of trust or otherwise, or conspiracy in restraint of trade or commerce, does not mean what the language used therein plainly imports, but that it only means to declare illegal any such contract which is in unreasonable restraint of trade while leaving all others unaffected by the provisions of the act." With this view the court disagreed, and held that all combinations in restraint of trade without exception or limitation are prohibited by the act. This was a bare majority decision. In the same case it was held that the Sherman act applies to railways and other public utilities as well as to industries. In the Joint Traffic case the same justice shaded this sweeping decision somewhat, by saying, "The act of Congress must

[1] 171 U. S. 604.
[2] 432 Fed. 898.
[3] 85 Fed. 252; 115 Fed. 610; 166 Fed. 290; 167 Fed. 721.
[4] 166 U. S. 327.
[5] 171 U. S. 566.

have a *reasonable construction*," and he indicated in his opinion that certain combinations were not necessarily inhibited by the act.

The decisions under the Sherman act have uniformly held that exchanges and selling agencies and combinations, where the commerce was clearly interstate, which fix prices, divide territories or business, or limit output, are illegal.[1] This statement is slightly modified by a decision [2] concerning a boat company which sold to another company with the agreement not to do business between Cincinnati and Portsmouth for five years after the sale. This agreement was held to be valid.

Combination permitted by common law illegal.

In the case of an agreement between a number of manufacturers to market their entire output through a selling agency at specified prices, it was held that a selling agency organized to control all the business of the manufacturers was in restraint of trade and contrary to law. Combinations of companies for the purpose of preventing others from entering a business are in restraint of trade.[3]

Selling agencies illegal.

All combinations which have been shown to have the element of monopoly, or agreements which attempt to produce monopoly, have been declared to be illegal. This principle has been applied not only to industry, but to transportation, both boats and railways. While the decisions have been uniformly against monopoly, it has been decided that mere size does not constitute monopoly.[4] Unfair practices, the aim of which was to drive from business and thus secure monopoly, are illegal.[5]

Mere size does not constitute monopoly.

The antitrust act forbids combinations of labor in restraint of commerce as much as it does combinations of capital. For laborers to interfere with interstate commerce is illegal under the act. It is illegal for an organization to attempt to compel an establishment to employ none but union men. Boycotts have been declared to be illegal. It is immaterial whether the persons who combine in a boycott

Act applies to laborers.

[1] 175 U. S. 211; 196 U. S. 375; 203 U. S. 390; 212 U. S. 227.
[2] 200 U. S. 179.
[3] 209 U. S. 423.
[4] 172 Fed. 455.
[5] 193 U. S. 38; 196 U. S. 375.

are themselves engaged in interstate commerce.[1] As illustrating these principles may be cited the award of $222,000 against the striking hatters of Danbury, Connecticut, same being against about two hundred working men.[2]

Of the more important decisions which have laid down broad principles affecting the future interpretation of the Sherman act the following may be mentioned: —

Legality of holding company.

The Northern Securities Company[3] was a holding company, possessing all or the majority of the stock of several railroads. This company was declared to be in retraint of trade. The decision was rendered comparatively early, and the question of reasonable or unreasonable restraint of trade was held to be immaterial. This decision, like the Trans-Missouri and Joint Traffic decisions, was by a five to four vote.

While Justice Brewer was with the majority, he dissented from the opinion given by Justice Peckham already cited that every contract or combination in restraint of trade was within the statute. This decision is of far-reaching importance, in that it appears to raise a doubt as to the legality of the great holding companies.

Recently there have been broad decisions declaring the Standard Oil, the American Tobacco, and the Dupont Powder Companies to be illegal combinations.

Word "reasonable" introduced into statute by decision.

As has already been pointed out, the earlier decisions of the Supreme Court, under the first section of the Sherman act, insisted that the reasonableness or unreasonableness of the restraint was immaterial; and in this position the court followed the literal statement of the law as it looked to Peckham and as it still looks to a layman. The interpretations of the act in the cases of Standard Oil and American Tobacco shows a change in the position of the court. In the future it will declare only business to be interdicted by the act which is in undue restraint of trade. The second and third sec-

[1] 54 Fed. 994; 208 U. S. 274.

[2] Hearings, Interstate Commerce Committee, XX, pp. 1729–1730. For full presentation of the two sides of the Sherman act as applied to laborers see Hearings, Senate Interstate Commerce Committee, XX, pp. 1727–1778; XXIII, XXIV, pp. 1979–3102.

[3] 120 Fed. 72.

tions of the Sherman act are apparently interpreted together. It seems to be the argument that the first section, prohibiting all combinations and contracts in restraint of trade, is meant to cover the same ground as the second section, which prohibits monopoly or attempt to monopolize; and thus the interpretation seems to be that restraint of trade which monopolizes or attempts to monopolize is interdicted by the law. This is the restraint of trade which is undue, and being undue is unreasonable; that is, undue and unreasonable are made synonymous terms.[1]

Return to common law principle.

The court gives the opinion that it was the intention of Congress that "the standard of reason, which had been applied at the common law and in this country in dealing with subjects of the character embraced by the statute, was intended to be the measure used for the purpose of determining whether in a given case a particular act had or had not brought about the wrong against which the statute provided." The court says, "The fact must not be overlooked that injury to the public by the prevention of an *undue restraint* on, or the monopolization of trade or commerce *is the foundation upon which the prohibitions of the statute rest*, and, moreover, that one of the fundamental purposes of the statute is to protect, not to destroy, rights of property."

Apparently the decision of the court goes as far as practicable towards reintroducing the common law regarding combinations and contracts in restraint of trade. Combinations and contracts may take place provided they are reasonable; but the sweeping decrees regarding the disintegration of the Standard Oil and American Tobacco and other companies make it appear that it was not the intent of the court to go as far toward freedom as was permitted by the common law. Thus we are left in doubt as to how far the court will in the future permit combinations and contracts in restraint of trade.

The effects of the Standard Oil and American Tobacco decisions upon those organizations were as follows: —

The Standard Oil Company. — The Circuit Court of the

[1] The Supreme Court of the United States, No. 398, October term, 1910; *Ibid.*, Nos. 118 and 119.

United States for the Eastern district of Missouri on November 20, 1909, declared the Standard Oil Company to be an illegal combination; that the officers of the Standard Oil Company and thirty-seven constituent companies have combined and conspired to monopolize and have monopolized a substantial part of the commerce in oil among the states and in the territories and with foreign nations. The officers of the Standard Company were prohibited from voting the stock of the subsidiary companies, and the officers of the subsidiary companies were enjoined and prohibited from paying any dividends to the Standard Oil Company, although they were not prohibited from distributing rateably to the shareholders of the company the shares of the subsidiary companies. The subsidiary companies were enjoined from acquiring stock interests in potentially competitive companies, or from placing the control of any of the corporations under a trustee and making any agreement, implied or expressed, as to the management of other corporations, or to regulate prices, sales, rates of transportation, or outputs.

Standard Oil Company a monopoly.

On May 15, 1911, this decree of the Circuit Court was affirmed by the United States Supreme Court,[1] except in the minor modifications of time for executing the decree and for continuance of business during the time necessary to carry out the decree. The time for the dissolution of the corporation was extended to six months from the 21st of June, 1911, and pending the dissolution the Standard Oil Company continued business in the United States.

Disintegration of Standard Oil Company.

As a result of these decisions and orders the Standard Oil Company has now been broken into thirtyeight companies. These companies are not to have common officers or directors. The stock of the Standard was not widely distributed and the new companies have common owners. The officers of seven of the more important new companies remain in the same quarters which the Standard Oil Company before occupied, 26 Broadway.

[1] The Standard Oil Company of New Jersey *et al.* *v.* The United States, Appeal from the Circuit Court of the United States for the Eastern District of Missouri, May 15, 1911. U. S. Reports, Vol. CCXXI, p. 1.

Ex-President Taft announced that the plan of the administration in prosecuting trusts was to secure "a degree of disintegration by which competition between its parts shall be restored and preserved."[1] Will this result be reached in the case of the Standard Oil Company? Will the officers of the seven large companies in different rooms at 26 Broadway really compete in prices? That this will occur has been widely doubted by the public from the outset; and on February 29, 1912, it was announced that the Waters-Pierce Company of Texas had alleged that the disintegrated companies are combining, and this company had instituted an investigation in order to show the facts.

Is coöperation destroyed?

Antecedent to the dissolution, during the years 1909 and 1910, the stocks of the Standard Oil Company ranged from about 600 to 700. When the case was in court a low level of 585 was reached. At the time the decision was rendered the price was about 670. For a few months the prices ranged somewhat lower; but, beginning with 1912, Standard Oil stock began to rise and by August the price had gone above 1000. Since that time the prices have never been lower; in 1914 they ranged from 1260 to 1400. In other words, the Standard Oil stocks are worth on the market about double what they were worth before the company was attacked. It is clear that experience has shown that the decision of the court has not resulted; nor is it likely to result, in a reduction of the great profits which the Standard Oil Company and the other companies, originally forming this organization, have enjoyed.

Effect of dissolution on price of stocks.

The American Tobacco Company. — On May 29, 1911, the Supreme Court of the United States declared the American Tobacco Company to come within the prohibition of the first and second sections of the Sherman antitrust act.[2] The combination of itself as well as the elements composing it, both corporate and individual, were collectively and separately declared to be in restraint of trade and were found to be

Comprehensive terms of decision.

[1] Speech at Detroit, September 18, 1911.

[2] American Tobacco Company *v.* The United States, Appeal from the Circuit Court of the United States for the Southern District of New York, May 29, 1911. U. S. Reports, Vol. CCXXI, p. 106.

attempting to monopolize and monopolizing the tobacco business. In order to carry out the effect of this decision the lower court was ordered to ascertain some plan of dissolving the combination, or recreating out of the elements a new condition which should be in harmony with the law. To accomplish this a period of six months was allowed. If at the end of that time some plan had not been devised in harmony with the law for disintegrating the company, it was to be restrained from engaging in interstate business. In the meantime, the company was restrained from enlarging its powers or extending its business.

In accordance with this decree and order the Circuit Court of the United States for the Southern District of New York, on November 6, 1911, approved a plan for disintegrating the American Tobacco Company, which, as we have seen, represented a consolidation of some two hundred and fifty corporations, into fourteen companies.

The fourteen companies are enjoined from coöperating in business in any way; they must not occupy the same offices; they cannot hold the stock of one another, or even stock in companies in which other companies hold stock. Each company must do business in its own house, and the products of each must bear the firm name. For five years they are enjoined from having common offices or directors or the same sales agents.

The stock of the American Tobacco Company was, in a manner like that of Standard Oil, distributed proportionally to his holdings to each stockholder of the fourteen companies. There were twenty-nine men who held a dominating position in the old corporation, and they in like manner hold a dominating position in the three new companies into which the chief assets of the old company have been divided.

As a matter of fact we now have fourteen tobacco combinations which have the sanction of the courts instead of one that did not.

Dissolution and price of stocks.

It is notable that after the order was given by the Supreme Court to dissolve the corporation, the stock of the American Tobacco Company fell to 390 per share; but that after the decision of the Circuit Court as to the kind of disintegration which was to take place, the common stock rose to as high a price as ever before in the history of the company, with the exception of a single day, $529 per share.[1] This was the result of more than four years' litigation which cost the independent companies and the American company vast sums of money, and the government as large or larger sums; all of which will ultimately be paid by the public.

There remains to be mentioned the most notable feature of the tobacco decision. The Supreme Court said: "While in many substantial respects our conclusion is in accord with that reached by the court below, and while also the relief which we think should be awarded in some respects is coincident with that which the court granted, in order to prevent any complication and to clearly define the situation we think instead of affirming and modifying, our decree, in view of the broad nature of our conclusions, should be one of reversal and remanding with directions to the court below to enter a decree in conformity with this opinion and to take such further steps as may be necessary to fully carry out the directions which we have given."

The court undertaking administrative work.

The radical feature of the decision is contained in this last clause, "to take such further steps as may be necessary to fully carry out the directions which we have given." As we have already seen, the lower court in complying with this request approved a plan for the disintegration of the tobacco trust which had been proposed by the tobacco combination and had been approved by the Attorney-General. Thus this court took on the function of giving an order to the lower court to do administrative work, of a kind which has usually been done by a commission (see pp. 233–244), and for which a commission is much better adapted. When the order was executed as directed, the members of the disintegrated trust had the advantage of having the sanction of law. The administrative work of the court in disintegrating the American Tobacco Company, already severely criticized and generally believed to be futile, is

[1] Hearings, Senate Interstate Commerce Committee, Part XVIII, p. 1368.

one of the best evidences of the lack of adaptation of the courts to the handling of the complex administrative problems of great concentrations in industry.

The Du Pont Powder Company. — In the case of the E. I. Du Pont de Nemours Powder Company,[1] known as the powder trust, the company was dissolved and the broad principle was laid down by the Supreme Court, "that a combination cannot escape the condemnation of the antitrust act merely by the form it assumes or by the dress it wears. It matters not whether the combination be 'in the form of a trust or otherwise,' whether it be in the form of a trade association or a corporation, if it arbitrarily uses its power to force weaker competitors out of business or to coerce them into a sale to or union with the combination, it puts a restraint upon interstate commerce and monopolizes or attempts to monopolize a part of that commerce in a sense that violates the antitrust act."

Form of combination immaterial.

The Shoe Machinery Case. — In the Shoe Machinery case a further important step has been made in the interpretation of the Sherman act. The combination attacked was one formed by the union of several companies, each of which manufactured machines for different purposes. In regard to this case the Court says:[2]

Integration of industry lawful.

"But taking it as true, we can see no greater objection to one corporation manufacturing 70 per cent. of three non-competing groups of patented machines collectively used for making a single product than to three corporations making the same proportion of one group each. The disintegration aimed at by the statute does not extend to reducing all manufacture to isolated units of the lowest degree. It is as lawful for one corporation to make every part of a steam engine and to put the machine together as it would be for one to make the boilers and another to make the wheels."

This decision seems to make it clear that combination which results in integrating an industry, the different parts

[1] Annual Report of the Attorney-General of the United States, 1911, p. 8.
[2] The United States *v.* Sidney W. Winslow *et al.*, Supreme Court of the United States, No. 620, October Term, 1912.

of which may be operated as independent enterprises, is not violation of the law. Thus, for instance, union of ore companies, manufacturing companies, and coal companies might take place, if for no one element of the integrated industry there is monopoly.

The Union Pacific and Southern Pacific Merger. — It is evident that the Sherman act is to be pushed, also, against the public utilities as well as against manufactories and corporations. Already a final decree has been rendered which compelled the Union Pacific Railroad Company and the Oregon Short Line Railroad Company to dispose of shares of the Southern Pacific Company held by them.[1] These shares were disposed of to the Pennsylvania Railroad Company in exchange for shares of the Baltimore and Ohio Railroad Company. The result of the exchange was to give the Union Pacific Company and the Pennsylvania Company a large number of shares in lines which are not immediate competitors in the same territory in place of shares in a system belonging in the same territory.

The Sherman act and the public utilities.

Dissolution by Mutual Agreement. — In addition to dissolution of corporations by the court, after full trial and conviction, there is another class of cases in which, as a result of complaint, the company without trial has agreed with the government as to the violation of the Sherman act; and decrees have been issued in accordance therewith with the consent of the company against which complaint was made.

The most important illustration of a public utility corporation which under pressure from the Attorney-General has agreed to discontinue its alliance with another corporation is that of the American Telephone and Telegraph Company (Bell Telephone System) and the Western Union Telegraph Company. The Bell Company agreed to dispose of its entire holdings of stock in the Western Union Telegraph Company in such a manner that the control of the latter

The Bell Telephone Company.

[1] The United States of America *v.* The United Pacific Railroad Company, the Oregon Short Line Railroad Company *et al.*, District Court of the United States. District Court of the United States for the District of Utah. Final Decree.

will be entirely independent of the Bell system. The consent to do this by the officers of the Bell system led to a commendatory letter from President Wilson in which he stated: "It is very gratifying that the company should thus volunteer to adjust its business to the conditions of competition."

A notable case of dissolution by mutual agreement was that of the General Electric Company. This company was charged with having a monopoly in the manufacture of incandescent electric lamps. This monopoly was secured through secret companies, and by having the exclusive rights in this country to use tantalum and tungsten filaments. This right through exclusive agreement was used to require that any firm buying lamps of these kinds should also buy all their carbon filament lamps from the General Electric Company. Through unfair methods, such as fixing prices, exclusive agreements, rebates, etc., monopoly was secured, the company having obtained 97 per cent. of the incandescent lamp business of the country. In consequence, excessive charges for lamps were made, being seventeen cents apiece in this country, while the same lamps are sold abroad at ten cents.

Unfair methods of competition.

A most comprehensive decree was issued restraining the General Electric Company from the various unlawful acts set forth in the petition, and particularly the following were ordered: That all subsidiary companies of the General Electric Company should be known as such and should conduct their business in the name of that company; exclusive contracts of all kinds were forbidden, such as requiring another company to sell goods exclusively to the General Electric Company, combining with other companies to fix prices, requiring that those who purchase tantalum and tungsten lamps should also purchase from the General Electric Company their carbon lamps. The company was enjoined from making a discount depending upon quantity of lamps purchased when the result is to combine or aggregate the discount on an unpatented and a patented lamp; it was further enjoined from making prices or terms of sale for the purpose

Sweeping decree.

of driving out of business any rival manufacturer; "provided that no defendant is enjoined or restrained from making any prices for incandescent electric lamps to meet, or to compete with, prices previously made by any other defendant, or by any rival manufacturer; and provided further that nothing in this decree shall be taken in any respect to enjoin or restrain fair, free, and open competition."[1]

Another interesting case is that of a business association. In October, 1911, a most sweeping decree was given by agreement of both the United States and Southern Wholesale Grocers' Association. The members of this association were perpetually enjoined from restraining trade by having a list of dealers to whom special privileges were granted, including selling only to members of such association. They were enjoined from making any agreement regarding prices, or even preparing a list of prices for the information of one another, from giving rebates or bonuses from any dealer because he is a member of the association, from boycotting any manufacturer who is not a member of the association or does not maintain limited selling prices. In short, the decree in most comprehensive terms enjoins the association from restraining trade in any way by fixing prices, making exclusive agreements, or granting exclusive privileges to members of the association. Under the decree it is difficult to see how there can be any combination of the members in restraint of trade either reasonable or unreasonable.[2]

Grocers' agreements illegal.

Another case of dissolution by mutual agreement is that of the New Departure Manufacturing Company,[3] engaged in the manufacture of bicycle and motorcycle coaster brakes. The independent members of this combination were forbidden from fixing sale and resale prices, from holding any meetings

Sweeping terms of decree.

[1] United States of America *v.* General Electric Company *et al.*, In Equity, Circuit Court of the United States for the Northern District of Ohio, Eastern Division. Petition and Final Decree.

[2] The United States of America *v.* The Southern Wholesale Grocers' Association *et al.*, Circuit Court of the United States for the Northern District of Alabama. Decree of Injunction.

[3] The United States *v.* The New Departure Manufacturing Company *et al.*, District Court of the United States for the Western District of New York.

the purpose of which is to arrange concerted action, from having any joint arbitrator, referee, or commissioner, from giving preference to any manufacturers or dealers, and from fixing by any mutual agreement or understanding discounts, trade rebates, or terms of credit.

Other decrees by mutual agreement have had similar sweeping provisions. It is apparent that more rigid terms have been imposed by the Attorney-General, where there has been dissolution by mutual agreement, than has been applied in those cases which have gone before the United States Supreme Court. In short, it appears that a serious abuse has grown up, in connection with dissolution by mutual agreement. Corporations under the threat of attack from the Attorney-General consent to conditions more drastic than those it is probable the court would have imposed. This they do under the threat of prosecution. Rather than go to the great expense and prolonged delay of litigation, agreements are entered into not to engage in various things, many of which are probably lawful.

Abuses in dissolution by mutual agreement.

Other Corporations under Attack. — In addition to the cases which have been terminated by trial or by agreement, there are a very large number of organizations now under attack. The cases are in different stages of procedure, from those in which the petition for dissolution has just been filed by the Attorney-General, to those which have been argued before the United States Supreme Court and are awaiting decision, and to those in which decisions have been rendered regarding the principles which apply but details of the application of the principles have not been worked out by the Attorney-General and the parties concerned. The largest number of these cases concern corporations engaged in manufacture alone, or in manufacture and commerce. Another set of cases concern commerce alone. Others apply to boards of trade and similar associations. Some of these boards are dealers only in agricultural products. Illustrations of the last are the Elgin Board of Trade dealing in butter and butter fat, and the Board of Trade of Chicago dealing in grain. Other cases have special features in that

All classes of business attacked.

the companies attacked deal in natural resources, such as timber and coal. Still another class of cases relate to combinations of labor. Others concern the public utilities, including railroads, telephones, and steamship-companies engaged in the coasting and in foreign trade. It is therefore plain that the law is being invoked in almost every line of trade and industry.

Perhaps the most important industrial cases are those of the United States Steel Corporation and the International Harvester Company; and the most important public utilities case that of the New York, New Haven, and Hartford Railway.

General Statements. — In recent years whenever cases have been in the court under the Sherman act, pools, combinations, or agreements, producing restraint of trade, have been declared to be illegal. From the tenor of the decisions the conclusion might be reached that the law had been fairly effective in producing the results which were sought when the act was passed, at least for later years; but an examination of the situation shows the contrary to be true.

Railways coöperate.

All of the railways connecting any two points in the United States charge exactly the same prices for the same service, be it freight or passenger. As already pointed out, it is a matter of common information that competition in price between the railroads does not exist; and this fact is tacitly accepted by the public and by the Attorney-General of the United States, although every person having common sense knows that the situation is only possible by agreements through informal understandings, traffic associations, etc.

Law drives combination from one entrenchment to another.

For twenty years the major effect of the decisions has been to change the forms of combination, from the informal agreement or pool to the trust, from the trust to the holding company, and finally there is the beginning of the transformation from the holding corporation to the complete merger. At the same time this evolution has been going on for the great industries, hundreds of informal associations of exactly the same kind as those which have been declared to be illegal have arisen, such as the various retailers' and wholesalers' associations, the fruit growers' associations, the butter makers' associations, etc. Indeed, a comparison of the situation in the United States with other countries, such as England and Germany, in which combination is open, shows that at the present moment combinations exist to a greater extent in the United States than in either of those countries, in which trade agreements are enforced by the courts.

In other countries where coöperation of corporations is permitted, if not such as to be contrary to public policy, there has been no such rapid concentration of industry as in this country. A man who builds up a business is reluctant to surrender his autonomy. He has a pride in the house. If the situation becomes such that it is necessary or advantageous to coöperate with his neighbors, this he will do; but he will not surrender his independence. In consequence of this principle, the great combinations called cartels in Germany are much looser aggregations than the holding corporations of this country. They consist of a large number of coöperating organizations each largely independent, rather than a great organization such as the United States Steel Corporation.

Relative independence in Germany.

Could there be more positive evidence than this of the failure of the law to destroy combination and coöperation? The impotency of the Sherman act to accomplish the results for which it was made has been admitted by all, alike by those who would have it amended so as to give greater freedom in combination and by those who would have it amended so as to give a very strict construction, with the vain hope that it might thereby destroy coöperation.

Defects of Sherman act.

The public not benefited by dissolution.

Much satisfaction has been expressed by many at the dissolution of the Standard Oil Company, the American Tobacco Company, the American Telephone and Telegraph Company, the Union Pacific-Southern Pacific merger, and other organizations. But what advantage has the public derived from the disintegration of these corporations?

The chief interest of the public in whether an article is manufactured by one company or by ten companies is the price paid for the product. Is the retail price of kerosene, tobacco, beef, or paper lower because there have been dissolutions of great organizations engaged in the manufacture of these articles?

Prices increased by disintegration.

While the evidence is not altogether conclusive, so far as it goes, it indicates that the effect of the dissolution of industrial corporations has been to increase rather than to diminish prices. One of the strongest indications of this is the greatly enhanced price of the stocks of the Standard Oil and American Tobacco companies since their dissolution. (See pp. 183–185.)

No advantage to the public by dissolution of utilities.

In those cases where public utilities organizations have been separated, it has not been made clear what if any advantage the public has gained or will gain in the future from their disintegration.

Wherein will the public be benefited by the dissolution of the Union Pacific and the Southern Pacific Railways? Are rates lower for passengers or freight than they were before the separation? And are they likely to become so? The only effect one can foresee so far as the public is concerned in the separation of these railroad companies is that there will be fewer through trains, greater expense in accounting, and less close coöperation between the separated systems in handling the freight and passenger business of the public.

The Bell Telephone Company.

Wherein will the public be benefited by the voluntary separation, under the pressure of the Attorney-General, of the Bell Telephone Company and the Western Union Telegraph Company? The business of the two is closely analogous, —the carrying of messages partly by one and partly by the other is of advantage to millions of people. From the point of view of economy in doing the work of the two, the closer the coöperation, the better. At numerous places in the United States, one small room would furnish adequate quarters for the service of both the telephone and telegraph; indeed this is the situation in a number of European countries. In very small exchanges a single person on duty at one time could handle the necessary work of telephone attendant and an operator for the telegraph. But more important than these is the use of the same set of wires and poles for telephone and telegraph, — by far the most expensive part of the installations for both lines of business. At the same time wires are being used to telephone, they are also available to telegraph. For the trunk telephone lines, two wires may be used simultaneously for a telephone circuit and for four telegraph circuits. Thus a very large part of the telegraph business of the country could be done over the telephone wires. The advantages of the joint use of poles are obvious. Why then should the public be compelled to pay rates which will give fair returns on large sums of unnecessary capital required for the independent installation of telegraph systems, when by proper coöperation it would be possible within a few years to handle the larger part of the telegraph business of the country over the telephone system of wires.

The economies of joint operation of telephone and telegraph are so evident that if both were administered by the government in this country, as is the situation in various other countries, no one would for a moment think that they should be independent. In that case, it would be agreed by all that there should be as close interlocking as possible in the use of the necessary facilities and of the force.

Government monopoly recommended.

Indeed, the Postmaster General of the United States, in February, 1914, transmitted to Congress the report of a departmental committee, consisting of the First Assistant Postmaster General, the Chief Clerk of the department, and the Superintendent of the Division of Salaries and Allowances upon the proposal to make the telephone and the telegraph business a public monopoly. That committee recommended that the government acquire the telephone and telegraph business of the country in order that they might be operated as a unit in connection with the mails. This committee thus recognizes the numerous economies obtainable by the joint operation of the telephone and telegraph.

Gains to public through coöperation.

Why then should the Bell Telephone Company and the Western Union Telegraph Company cease to coöperate and thus become less efficient? Wherein will the public be benefited by the separation of the two companies? Have the rates been lowered by the telephone and telegraph companies, in consequence of the separation? Are they likely to be lowered in the future because of this separation? It is to be remembered in this connection that it was after the alliance of the two companies that the lower rates involved in the night and day letters were introduced under the joint management. Also the telephone and telegraph companies are public utilities and under the control of the interstate and state commerce commissions; therefore, if the increased economy which in the future would result from their coöperation, permits excessive earnings at existing rates, the commissions on behalf of the public should reduce the rates to reasonable amounts. Further, if the rates charged at the present time by the telephone and telegraph companies are unreasonable, this matter should be investigated by the Interstate Commerce Commission and the companies ordered to put in force reasonable rates precisely as has been done with the express companies. This, clearly not separation, is the direction of progress for the operation of the telephone and telegraph, if the committee of the Post Office Department is sound in its recommendations that all telephone and telegraph companies of the country be acquired by the government.

Remedy other than dissolution.

In the above statements concerning the dissolution of public utilities, it is not meant to imply that all consolidated companies have been well managed. This assertion could be no more made than that the separate parts of the consolidated companies before their union were always well managed. But upon the whole there can scarcely be a doubt that the great railroad systems, illustrated by the Pennsylvania, New York Central, the Baltimore and Ohio, the Northwestern, the Burlington, etc., every one of which has been built up by the consolidation of many independent and competing companies, have been far more efficiently managed and to the greater satisfaction of the country than were the several small independent elements which composed each of them.

Bigness not always successful.

When glee is expressed at the disintegration of a great corporation, which is not a monopoly, we should have a satisfactory answer to the question, "Where does the public come in?" before we join in the mirth. If the public

Where does the public come in?

has gained nothing in price reduction for standard articles or for service by the destruction of the great corporations, would it not have been wiser to take steps to see that their profits were made reasonable, to see that the great advantages which come from their magnitude, efficiency, and coöperation should be shared in large measure by the public?

Since the Sherman act was passed a child born has attained his majority. While there has been gain in the elimination of unfair practices, there has been no gain in preventing combinations in restraint of trade, the fundamental purpose of the law. It would seem that the time had now come for a rational consideration of the principles which should apply to the situation in order to secure reasonable results both for combinations and for the public without interfering with great economic tendencies. Any attempt further to amend the law so as to make it more rigid as against coöperation cannot but be futile. The problem of combination in restraint of trade is one too large, too complex, and too irresistible to be handled by the courts. This situation has been clearly seen by Knox, by Wickersham, and by others who have attempted to secure the results aimed at by the Sherman law; they have found themselves baffled. The constructive side of the case is presented on pp. 238–266.

Time arrived for rational solution.

Section 4

STATE LEGISLATION AGAINST TRUSTS

Many of the states have constitutional provisions or statutes which embody the same principles as the Sherman act. Among the states which have constitutional provisions against combination in restraint of trade or monopoly are: Alabama, 1901; Arkansas, 1836; Idaho, 1889; Kentucky, 1891; Maryland, 1867; Mississippi, 1890; Montana, 1889; North Carolina, 1875; North Dakota, 1889; South Carolina, 1895; South Dakota, 1896; Tennessee, 1870; Texas, 1875; Utah, 1895; Virginia, 1902; Washington, 1889; Wyoming, 1889.

The Statute Laws. — The names of some of the states

and the date of the statutes against restraint of trade and monopoly are as follows: Alabama, 1907; Arkansas, 1897, 1899, 1905, and 1907; California, 1907; Florida, 1897; Georgia, 1896; Illinois, 1891, and 1893; Indiana, 1897, 1899, 1908; Iowa, 1897; Kansas, 1889, 1897, and 1899; Kentucky, 1903; Louisiana, 1890, 1892, and 1894; Maine, 1899 and 1903; Massachusetts, 1908; Michigan, 1889 and 1903; Minnesota, 1891, 1899, 1905, and 1907; Mississippi, 1890, 1906, and 1908; Missouri, 1891, 1899, and 1907; Nebraska, 1897; New Mexico, 1891, 1897, and 1907; New York, 1892, 1897, and 1899; North Carolina, 1899 and 1905; North Dakota, 1890, 1897, and 1907; Ohio, 1898, 1905, and 1906; Oklahoma, 1890 and 1908; South Carolina, 1897, 1899, and 1902; South Dakota, 1890, 1897, and 1899; Tennessee, 1889 1891, 1897, and 1903; Texas, 1895, 1899, 1903, and 1907; Utah, 1898 and 1907; Wisconsin, 1893 and 1897.

It is notable that only two of the states had antitrust acts prior to 1890, the year the Sherman act was passed. The State antitrust acts were the natural response to the public demands within the states for prohibition of restraint of trade in intrastate business, similar to that which had been enacted regarding interstate business. As would be expected, under the circumstances, while the phraseology varies, the prohibitions of the state laws are substantially like those of the Sherman act, except that they, of course, contain no reference to trade between the states and territories or with foreign countries. In a number of instances, trusts, pools, and holding companies which have the purposes of regulating output, dividing the market, or controlling prices are specifically prohibited. In a few states there are special features which should be noted, as giving additional insight into the situation.

The contagion of legislation.

In *Georgia* is a provision that the general assembly of that state shall have no power to authorize any corporation to buy shares of stock in any other corporation in that state or elsewhere, or to make any contract or agreement whatever, with any such corporation, which may have the effect to defeat or lessen competition in their respective businesses, or to encourage monopoly; and all such contracts and agreements are declared to be illegal and void. This is the only instance in which the law specifically forbids the interholdings of stocks, a remedy which is advocated by many for interstate commerce.

In the *Illinois* and *Louisiana* laws there is a clause which states "that the provisions of the act shall not apply to agricultural products or live stock while in the hands of the producer or raiser"; and in the Louisiana law is the additional clause that the law shall not be construed to affect any combination or confederation of laborers for the purpose of increase of their wages or redress of grievances. The legislatures of Louisiana and Illinois in passing an antitrust law apparently fully appreciated the fact, practically unnoticed in the public discussions, that the selling agencies of the farmers for marketing their produce may be as clearly a combination in restraint of trade as are similar selling agencies of manufacturers. The exempting clause for agricultural products was declared to be void by the United States Circuit Court of Illinois as being class and special legislation.

In *Massachusetts* it is a criminal offense to impose "the condition in a sale of goods that the purchaser shall not sell or deal in the goods of any person other than the seller." [1] This law has been held to be constitutional.

In *Michigan* is a provision of the law declaring illegal contracts "not to engage in any avocation, employment, pursuit, trade, profession, or business, whether reasonable or unreasonable, partial or general, limited or unlimited." This state law specifically goes beyond the common law principle of reasonable restraint. This law accords with the decisions of the Supreme Court of the United States which had been made up to that time. It was not until 1911 that the courts introduced, by interpretation into the Sherman act, the word "reasonable."

In *Oklahoma* the antitrust law prohibits several unfair practices. Thus it is prohibited to discriminate by sale at a lower rate in one section than in another, "or at the same rate or price at a point away from that of production or manu-

[1] 191 Mass. 545.

facture as at the place of production, etc., if the effect or intent is to hinder competition or restrain trade." Also, the Oklahoma law is very specific regarding trusts, holding corporations, limiting output, and marketing. It is declared unlawful to issue or own trust certificates, or to enter into any combination, etc., for the purpose of placing the management or control of such combination, or the conduct or operation of the same, or the output or produce thereof, or the marketing of the same in the hands of any trust or trustees, holding corporations, etc., with the intent to limit or fix prices, lessen the production or sale of any article, or the use and consumption of the same, or to prevent or restrict, the manufacture or output of any such article. Further, in this state the following very significant provision is inserted in the law: "Whenever any business, by reason of its nature, extent, or the existence of a virtual monopoly therein, is such that the public must use the same in such a manner as to make it of public consequence, or to affect the community at large as to supply, demand, or price thereof, or said business is conducted in violation of section 1 (6679), said business is a public business and subject to be controlled by the state, by the corporation commission, or by an action in any district court of the state, as to all of its practices, prices, rates, and charges." This paragraph clearly looks toward the point of view that the great concentrations of industry become public utilities; indeed, whenever the element of monopoly or restraint of trade to the extent of affecting the community enters as a whole it makes them so. When this situation is reached for any business, it comes under the same principles of control as the common carriers.

Industries having a public interest.

In *South Dakota* the law especially protects the farmers, as follows: Any combination to prevent competition by raising the price beyond the reasonable cost of production or that tends to advance the price to the user of farm machinery, implements, tools, supplies, lumber, wood, and coal, imported into this state from any other state, territory, or county, beyond the reasonable cost of production and sale of same or which tends to and does induce a sale of wheat, corn, oats, barley, flax, cattle, sheep, hogs, or other farm or agricultural products for less than they are worth at time of sale, or for what they would sell at in open market, if such contract did not exist, is declared to be unlawful.

In *Utah* it is seen that when professional men agree on prices the principle is the same as in other combinations, and the law says, "Any combination having for its object the controlling of the prices of any professional services, any products of the soil, any article of manufacture or commerce, or the cost of exchange or transportation is prohibited and declared unlawful."

The *Nebraska* antitrust law of 1897 was most sweeping in its character. It very definitely makes all combinations in restraint of trade to whatever extent a trust and declares the same to be illegal. Also it prohibits in comprehensive terms all classes of coöperation. It, however, excludes from its provisions all assemblages and associations of workingmen and provides that "there is thereby reserved for them all the rights and privileges now accorded them by law." [1] This act was declared to be unconstitutional by the federal courts as depriving persons of their liberty in violation of the federal Constitution and also as exempting labor organizations from its provisions, thus denying equal protection of the laws to persons not members of such organizations.

In *Texas*, refusing to buy or sell to another any article of merchandise is declared to be conspiracy in restraint of trade. Also, agreements to boycott or threaten to refuse to buy are made illegal. The state statute prohibits all combinations in restriction of competition or trade, but exempted agricultural products and live stock while in the hands of the producers or raisers.[2] This law was declared by the federal courts to be a violation of the amendment to the Constitution of the United States, which declares that no state shall deny any person within its jurisdiction equal protection under the laws.

The Illinois, Nebraska, and Texas decisions seem clearly to

[1] 110 Fed. 816, 1901.

[2] 79 Fed. 627, 1897.

show that the antitrust laws in those states which contain exemptions in favor of any class will be held to be unconstitutional by the Supreme Court of the United States.

Decisions under the Statutes. — In this brief book there is not space to discuss in detail the decisions which have been rendered under the statute laws. In general, the statutes regarding combinations and contracts in restraint of trade have gone much farther than the common law in imposing restrictions upon commerce. The author knows of no instance in which state statutes have moved in the direction of the English Parliamentary act in enlarging the scope of combination. The effort of the statute law has been to reach restraints of trade which would have escaped the ban of the common law. Pools, trusts, combinations, and monopolies have been declared not to be legal. For the most part restraint of trade taking the form of contracts regarding division or restriction of territory, or regulation of output or prices, have been declared unlawful. Such decisions have been rendered in many states,[1] although, under the common law, many of the forbidden agreements would have been allowed. It is not necessary to give the details of decisions covering these points, and only those having some special feature will be summarized.

Restrictive trend of state laws.

Agreements regarding the fixing of price for insurance have been held to be illegal. In Iowa this has been applied to a group of local insurance agents who agreed upon the price for each class of risk.[2] In Minnesota a combination by which twenty-eight independent companies agreed to place the control of their business with one company to the extent of fixing the rate was held to be in restraint of trade and a violation of the code.[3] In Missouri, an agreement of insurance companies regarding rates was declared illegal.[4]

A local agreement to raise the price of beer in Kentucky

[1] 147 Cal. 115, 1905; 107 Pac. 712, 1910; 65 Ill. App. 502, 1896; 182 Ill. 551, 1889; 171 Ill. 391, 1898; 65 Kas. 240, 1902; 112 Ky. 925, 1902; 119 Mich. 255, 1899; 134 Mich. 103, 1903; 140 Mich. 538, 1905; 187 Mo. 244, 1905; 116 N. W. 302, 1908; 177 N. Y. 473, 1904; 139 N. Y. 251, 1893; 72 Ohio State, 210, 1905; 61 Ohio State, 520, 1900; 106 Pac. 969, 1910; 128 S. W. 599, 1910.

[2] 102 Ia. 602, 1897.

[3] 75 Minn. 28, 1897.

[4] 152 Mo. 1, 1899.

$1 a barrel was declared to be illegal, although it had for its purpose the raising of the price of an intoxicant, the increased use of which the law does not favor.[1]

It is not necessary that a combination shall secure a practical monopoly of the product in order to be in restraint of trade under some of the state statutes.[2] Transactions creating a local monopoly for a limited period (ten years) have been declared to be illegal.[3] In Oklahoma this principle has been carried so far as to hold that a combination by three companies manufacturing ten per cent of a product is in restraint of trade.[4]

Contracts for exclusive dealing have been declared to be unlawful in a number of states. In Kansas exclusive contracts of agents to handle International Harvester machinery were declared to be in restraint of trade.[5] In Michigan agreements to sell all the salt manufactured to a single concern and to stop the manufacture of salt upon the payment of a certain rental was held to be illegal.[6] In Texas an agreement to buy oil and beer from a single firm, to sell at a fixed price, and not to sell to competing dealers, was declared to be in violation of the laws in restraint of trade.[7]

In general, agreements made by associations by which their members would have the advantages of exclusive dealing or which discriminate against non-members regarding prices and other matters, have been held to be unlawful.[8]

Thus produce exchanges which discriminate in prices between members and non-members have been declared to be in restraint of trade.[9] In Michigan it has been held that a contract to sell lambs where the buyer agrees not to purchase any other lambs to a fixed time is held to be void, since under the statutes all contracts designed in any manner to prevent or restrain price competition is unlawful.[10]

In Oklahoma an agreement not to enter business within one

[1] 112 Ky. 925, 1902. [2] 214 Ill. 421, 1905. [3] 128 S. W. 599, 1910.
[4] 59 S. W. 709, 1900. [5] 81 Kas. 610, Feb., 1906.
[6] 134 Mich. 103, 1903.
[7] 19 Texas Civ. App. 1, 1898; 90 Texas 277, 1896. See also 119 Mich. 255, 1899, and 97 Miss. App. 280, 1902.
[8] 211 Mo. 181, 1908; 75 Neb. 637, 1906; 103 Tenn. 99, 1899.
[9] 82 Minn. 173, 1901. [10] 119 Mich. 255, 1899.

hundred miles of Oklahoma City was declared to be in conflict with the statute which provides for disposal of good will on an exclusive basis only to the extent of a specified county.[1]

In Minnesota it has been held to be a violation of the statute to sell kerosene, as has been done by the Standard Oil Company, at different prices at various localities, with the intent to destroy business of competitors and create monopoly.[2]

Selling agencies are under the ban of the law in some states. In New York City there was created an agency for the buying and selling of milk at wholesale and retail. The majority of the stockholders in this agency were milk dealers in the city of New York. The board of directors fixed the price at which milk should be purchased by the stockholders. This price so fixed, controlled the markets and the combination was declared to be unlawful.[3] Similarly the producers of bluestone combined in an association to regulate the price and apportion their output under which separate companies made the sales for each participant. This arrangement was declared to be unlawful.[4]

Restraint allowed to limited extent.

The above sufficiently illustrates the dominant trend of the decisions against restraint of trade. Some of the states have allowed contracts in restraint of trade to a very limited extent. In California, when a merchant purchased a certain quantity of olive oil, agreeing not to sell the same below a certain price per gallon, this agreement was held not to be in violation of the code restraining monopolies.[5] In New York in one case it has been held that an agreement under which wholesale dealers, manufacturing certain proprietary articles, sell their goods at a uniform jobbing price only to such dealers as would conform to the manufacturers' price list is legal.[6] Along the same line it has been held lawful for manufacturers to give jobbers rebates who would agree not to sell for less than the list price prescribed by the manufacturers.[7]

In New York an agreement between a builders' association and a bricklayers' union, under which the association gave

[1] Wilson's "Review and Annals," St. Okl., 1903, sections 819–820.
[2] 126 N. W. 527, 1910. [3] 145 N. Y. 267, 1895. [4] 164 N. Y. 401, 1900.
[5] 156 Cal. 611, 1909. [6] 175 N. Y. 1, 1903.
[7] 40 N. Y. App. Div. 513, 1899.

preference to the members of the union, and no member of the bricklayers' union could work for any one not complying with the regulations, was declared not to constitute a monopoly within the New York statute.[1] An agreement of the Duluth board of trade providing that all members of the board shall charge uniform rates of commission for selling grain to non-members was declared not to be a violation of the Minnesota antitrust act.[2]

Contracts for limited exclusive agencies, and to refrain from business for a limited time and place, have been held to be legal. In Mississippi a contract for an exclusive agency for a definite territory to sell a certain article manufactured by a single company was held not to be in restraint of trade.[3] In Arkansas an agreement to refrain from soliciting insurance in Jefferson County for five years was held to be lawful.[4] It has been held to be reasonable for shopkeepers to agree as to the hour of closing their shops.[5]

General Statements. — The foregoing discussion of the situation within the states shows that the statute laws have been very strictly construed regarding restraint of trade. The great majority of the decisions under the laws have been against combinations and contracts in restraint of trade, and against regulation of output, division of territory, and agreements in prices. However, the last set of cases cited show that contracts restraining trade to a very limited degree have been allowed.

The statute laws are as strongly against combination or restraint of intrastate trade as is the Sherman antitrust act for interstate commerce. Upon the whole the situation within the states with regard to restraint of trade under the laws and decisions is practically the same as with interstate commerce under the Sherman act.

The legislation against the trusts among the states along the same lines as that of Congress shows the influence of contagion, and the willingness of legislatures to act upon a generally accepted faith such as that which prevails

[1] 169 Fed. 256, 1909. [2] 101 Minn. 506, 1909. [3] 77 Miss. 476, 1899.
[4] 121 S. W. 293, 1909. [5] 54 S. W. 969, 1900.

concerning the power of competition adequately to regulate commerce.

As already pointed out, combinations in prices, formal or informal, exist everywhere, from the two or three grocers at the country crossroads to the great business concerns. Just as the effect of the Sherman law has been steadily to increase the concentration of industry, so the legislation in the states regarding restraint of trade has been an influence in the same direction.

The foregoing makes it clear that where a sound and powerful economic tendency appears which appeals to the common sense of the community as necessary for the general welfare, a law, however drastic, cannot stand in its way. Burke said in his address upon Conciliation with America, "I do not know the method of drawing up an indictment against an whole people." If at the present time the laws against combination in this country are to be strictly enforced, it will be necessary to draw an indictment against the larger part of the business men of the country.

The great combinations which have been selected for indictment have been those against which popular clamor has been directed. The selection of them has been largely due to this cause combined with their magnitude. Is it not a most unfortunate situation when tens of thousands are guilty, that here and there one is picked out for prosecution?

One of the most serious evils in connection with the situation arises from this fact. The business men, knowing that coöperation is not possible under the law, are driven to secret understandings and gentlemen's agreements. In the dark, serious abuses appear in connection with coöperation which would not arise if the coöperation were legal and therefore there was no reason to hide the facts from the public. In this respect the business men of England and Germany are in an advantageous position as compared with those of the United States. In those countries they may coöperate; in the United States they may not.

It would indeed have been fortunate had we allowed the common law to stand, and instead of enacting statutes to prohibit coöperation, had undertaken its control through some administrative instrumentality. While it is believed that the present campaign, by the Attorney-General, to destroy coöperation and return to competition will not be successful, yet if it should be successful, trade, manufacture, and commerce will again be in the position that they were when England and America were under the old restrictions of common and statute law. If it should turn out that business is forced to this situation, we shall again be obliged to go through the same stage of development that both countries have once undergone, — amelioration of the law until reasonable coöperation is again permissible. In that case we shall, by our unwise attempt through statute law to stem the tide of great economic forces, make America go through two cycles of evolution to reach, permanently, reasonable trade conditions, whereas one cycle has been sufficient for all other civilized countries.

CHAPTER IV

THE SITUATION IN OTHER COUNTRIES [1]

To describe adequately the situation regarding concentration in industry for other countries would involve for each a book as large or larger than this; therefore there can be inserted but the briefest summary of the principles which have controlled combinations and restraint of trade in several of the more important countries.

SECTION 1

ENGLAND

The situation in England is fully described by Macrosty,[2] and from his book this statement is mainly taken.

As already pointed out, the law of England originally prevented combination in restraint of trade. This principle was abandoned many years ago, and the doctrine was accepted that freedom in trade gave freedom to combine as well as freedom to compete, provided the combination did not result in monopoly. Under these circumstances there have grown up extensive combination and coöperation in almost every line of industry in Great Britain; but, not being driven from one position to another by prohibition of combination, the movement toward giant holding companies or mergers has not been so far-reaching as in this country. To a considerable extent the combinations are through coöperations and federations rather than mergers, although in a number of cases consolidation has gone far; and there are

Federations rather than mergers.

[1] The situation regarding industrial combinations in Europe to the year 1900 is fully described by J. W. Jenks, Report of the Industrial Commission, Vol. XVIII, pp. 343.

[2] "The Trust Movement in British Industry."

a few industries in which a single combination controls more than half of the business.

In the iron and steel industry amalgamation is far advanced, so that at the present time the larger part of the business is controlled by a few large combinations. The greater consolidated companies are united into an association under which there are agreements or understandings regarding prices, markets, and allotments. Says Macrosty:[1] "Summing up the situation in the iron and steel industries, the conclusion forced on us seems to be that the tendency is towards the evolution of a comparatively few large units in each branch, and then that these units should combine into a loose organization for the regulation of their trade." The combinations in iron and steel include both horizontal combination, that is, union of plants of the same kind, and vertical combination, or union of the industry from its raw material to the finished product.

Large units in the iron trade.

In coal mining and cement making, consolidation and coöperation have taken place, but the process has not gone so far as in iron and steel.

In the textile industries concentration has extended very far. This combination, unlike that of steel, is mainly of the horizontal kind. The first great success in amalgamation in this business was the J. & P. Coats consolidation. This business has expanded so as to become an international company. The success of this combination led to similar ones for various textiles, although large combinations as yet have not extended to all lines of the business, nor for all have they been successful.

Textile combinations.

In the chemical industries, combinations have extended very far. Concentration has been rapid in the grain-milling industry. In tobacco there is one great consolidation, the Imperial Tobacco Company, which occupies a position in Great Britain analogous to that of the former American Tobacco Company in this country. Even in the retail business, which Macrosty points out is the last stronghold of competition, combination and coöperation exist upon an extensive scale.

Tobacco combination.

[1] "The Trust Movement in British Industry," p. 82.

While in the various consolidations of Great Britain over-capitalization and promoters manipulations have been frequent, these have not gone so far, nor been so widespread, as in this country, where consolidation has been stimulated by adverse laws, and where combination has had the protection of a tariff. Macrosty says:[1] "The weakness of every form of combination in the United Kingdom is due to the free admission of foreign competition." He states that if that condition can be removed, the combinations will be enormously strengthened. The combination which confines its operations strictly to Great Britain is at a disadvantage as compared with combinations in countries which have a protective tariff, for the reason that the excess products of the foreign countries can enter Great Britain without payment of duties; whereas the reverse is not the case. This situation has resulted in international combinations for a number of the more successful of those which center in or do business in Great Britain. Such international combinations are illustrated by the Imperial Tobacco Company with a capitalization of £17,500,000, the United Alkali Company with a capital of £8,200,000, the W. Cory & Sons Coal Company with a capital of £2,800,000, the J. & P. Coats Thread Company (this combination includes England, America, and Belgium), the Nobel Dynamite Trust Company with a capital of £3,000,000, and the international steel rail combination.

Combination and tariff.

British combinations not confined to United Kingdom.

Macrosty summarized the situation as follows: —

"The position of the British combinations in regard to the interests of the community may be summed up as not at present dangerous but containing, like every new development, great and unknown possibilities alike for good and for evil. Over prices their powers are not great but are growing. So far they have shown no increased power over their employees, and with a strong trade union they need not have." . . .

Cannot go back to early conditions.

"Nothing could be more fatal than in a panic to try to turn back a great industrial movement. So far as can be seen the great amalgamations are the best instruments of

[1] "The Trust Movement in British Industry," p. 342.

production yet devised, and to break them up into their original components would be foolish if it were not in most cases impossible. Crude methods of suppression are always wrong, nor does it seem sensible to search among legal principles relevant to a different stage of industry for weapons to hamper and obstruct." . . .

Futility of repressive legislation.

"Repressive legislation could only affect the outer form of combination. Amalgamation cannot be prohibited without forbidding the union of even two firms, while to make monopoly illegal would be fruitless where no formal monopoly exists, and there is no way of determining the greater effectiveness for evil of a merger including eighty per cent of the trade over one containing only fifty. No law can suppress the Gentlemen's Agreement, where there are no rules, no constitution, no contract, but common action is effected verbally and informally, and yet some of the most oppressive combinations have been of that form. Neither combination nor agitation should be driven underground, and it is significant that to-day complaints are generally raised in the United Kingdom, *not against the legally recognized amalgamations but against associations which have no existence in the eyes of the law and work in secret.* To strike at the methods adopted by combinations is not easy without at the same time repressing measures blamelessly adopted by the individual trader. Boycotting, dumping, selling at a loss to crush competition, maintaining prices at the highest level which the market permits — these are no monopoly of combinations, but are weapons in everyday use by manufacturers, merchants, and shopkeepers. It would be indeed an extraordinary thing to strike at competition in the name of competition."[1]

Section 2

GERMANY

In Germany, combination has gone farther than in England. In 1897 Liefmann gave a list of 345 combinations in

[1] "The Trust Movement in British Industry," pp. 343–345.

that country. Usually the combinations, called cartels, are contracts among independent establishments which limit output, divide markets, and control prices. Oftentimes these are accomplished through central agencies. It is clear that these cartels for each of the lines of business, concerning which they exist, act powerfully in restraint of trade. Many of them comprise substantially the feature of the typical trusts of the past in America which have been dissolved by the courts. But in Germany, violations of these contracts are held to be immoral. In other words, the principle is broadly accepted and enforced by the courts, that freedom in commerce involves freedom to combine as well as freedom to compete.

Extent of combination in Germany.

As illustrations of these cartels, the Steel and Potash combines will be briefly described.

The German Steel Combine. — Combinations in Germany have extended farthest in the iron industry. One of the largest and most successful of these combinations is that of the steel producers. This combination is especially important because of its analogy to the United States Steel Corporation, the fundamental difference being that the German steel combination is within the pale of the law, while the United States Steel Corporation is attacked by the United States Attorney-General as being interdicted by the law. The statement given below is by Professor T. K. Urdahl: —

Steel Combine lawful in Germany.

"The German Steel Combine is the largest private industrial undertaking in the world outside of the United States. The aggregate capital of the combined firms amounts to over 1,250,000,000 marks, and the average annual value of its products exceeds this sum. The contracts and articles of incorporation upon which this giant combination is based were signed on the 29th of February, 1904. Its duration was originally limited to three years, but in 1907 it was renewed, and to-day it stands as one of the strongest organizations in the industrial world, controlling, as it does, 95 per cent of the steel output of Germany.

Magnitude of steel combine.

"The scheme was not devised at a given moment by the

brain of a genius, but, like the modern political state, was preceded by a long series of experiments.

Origins. "Each of the organizations representing the stages in the evolution of the steel combine was more complex and more perfectly adjusted to its environment than were its predecessors.

"Instead of swallowing up and assimilating the many competing elements, as have the American trusts, the German Steel Combine represents a confederation in which the individual members retain much of their independence and autonomy. In one sense, it is a syndicate of syndicates, since it grew out of and took over the functions of six large cartels, each controlling one large line of steel products.

"There were:

(*a*) Half-manufactured Products Combine, Düsseldorf.

(*b*) Steel Beam Combine of Lower Rheinish-Westphalian District, Düsseldorf.

(*c*) German Steel Rail Association, Düsseldorf.

(*d*) German Steel Tie Association, Düsseldorf.

(*e*) South German Steel Beam Association, St. Johann a. d. Saar.

(*f*) German Steel Beam Association, Wiesbaden.

"TABLE 50. SHOWING RELATIONS OF GERMAN STEEL CARTELS

ORE	PIG IRON	IRON AND STEEL		FINISHED STEEL PRODUCTS
		Asso. for sale of half-manufactured products, Düsseldorf	STEEL COMBINE	Armor plate
				Sheet iron
				Tin
		Steel Beam Asso., Lower Rhine, Düsseldorf		Sheet steel
	Pig Iron Syndicate			

Ore	Pig Iron	Iron and Steel		Finished Steel Products
	Düsseldorf	German Steel rail Asso., Düsseldorf		Wire nails
				Wire rope
	Pig Iron (Thomas iron) Sales Bureau, Düsseldorf			Woven wire
Asso. for sale of Siegerland iron ore		South German Steel Beam Asso., St. Johann		Steel tubes
		German Beam Association, Weisbaden	Steel Combine	Tin cans
	Asso. for sale of Siegerland pig iron, Siegerland			Enameled ware
		German Ry. Tie Association, Düsseldorf		Gas pipe
	Upper Silician Pig Iron Syndicate, Zabrze	Upper Silician Steel Combine		
				Steel Beam Dealers' Association
				Hardware Manufacturers' Association
				Steel Spring Manufacturers' Association

"Each of these was organized to handle and sell its special products in its own field, and had developed a successful organization to carry out special purposes.

"In organizing the steel *combine* it was necessary to devise a scheme to do the work of the above named cartels and in addition to perform similar duties for a large variety of firms and associations, altogether thirty-six, out of which the combine was formed. Among these there were some relatively simple manufacturing plants known as 'pure roller mills,' steel mills without smelters of their own, engaged in transforming pig iron and steel ingots into roller mill products. There were other firms that not only combined smelters with roller mills, but owned and operated coal and ore mines and conducted wire nail and steel rail mills as well.

"In order to carry on the marketing of this great variety of material the steel combine established three main divisions or bureaus for handling *A* products: 1. half-manufactured products (ingots, pig iron, steel blocks, etc.); 2. heavy railroad material; light railroad material (ties and rails). 3. structural iron; (I and U beams, etc.). Each division has separate bureaus for taking care of domestic trade and of exports.

A products.

"In handling all *A* products the steel combine has complete control of the purchase and sale, and becomes the owner of the product during the brief space of time intervening between the purchase from the smelter and sale to the manufacturer. This system is an improvement upon the scheme that prevailed in the earlier syndicates whereby the syndicate acted merely as an agent for the individual members. Furthermore, the combine exercises the power to determine what the maximum output shall be, and apportions among the different firms their quota of the total output of all the mills.

"In handling *B* products, which include all other roller mill goods, the syndicate pursues an entirely different policy. Here all orders are received, either directly from the consumer or through the members, and are distributed by the central bureau among different works according to certain

B products.

rules. These are: First, each member shall receive orders until its output, when compared with its allotment, is relatively as large as that of the other members of the combine. Second, cheapness of freight charges and avoidance of cross freight shall be considered. Third, so far as possible orders shall be so distributed as to stimulate territorial division of labor. Whenever an order is sent to a steel firm it must at once be forwarded to the central bureau, which then places the order with the firm entitled to it under the above rules. The wishes of the person placing the order are not considered unless his desires conform with what is deemed desirable from the standpoint of the combine.

Terms of sale.

"All producers of *B* products are divided into groups. Every group has allotted to it a certain quota of output, which quota is always established by a resolution of the entire steel combine. The combine may increase or decrease the quota of any group at pleasure, but, thus far, no radical reduction has been attempted. Instead, a gradual increase, amounting in ten years to nearly 33 per cent has been authorized. All goods bought from the syndicate must be paid for on the fifteenth of the following month, and the syndicate itself settles with the individual members on the twentieth of the following month.

Price at works.

"The price paid to the producers is fixed by the syndicate, and is generally called the table price (Tabellen-preise), which is supposed to cover roughly the cost of producing. Prices to the consumer are generally quoted free on board for railroad material at the works, — for structural iron at Diedenhofen; and for half-manufactured products at certain centers for groups of producers, five of which are specified in the syndicate agreement. Freight to the center is paid by the works, and freight from the center is paid by the consumer. Should the consumer be located nearer to the works than to the center, he is still compelled to pay freight from the center. This saving in freight is given to the works enjoying the advantage. All general sales prices are fixed quarterly and apply usually for the next two quarters. These prices are known as standard prices, and only in an exceptional case is any one allowed a rebate or a lower price. For extra quality or exceptional forms of steel goods the combine establishes exceptional prices. The difference between the table price and the selling price is noted for each group of products. Careful accounts are also kept of losses and administrative expenses connected with each group of production. After these losses and expenses have been deducted from the surplus, the remainder is distributed pro rata among the members of the group in quarterly payments.

"Since 1902 there has been in existence, in Düsseldorf, a bureau maintained and originally organized by the four syndicates producing half-manufactured goods, but at present jointly maintained by the coal syndicate, the raw iron syndicate, and the steel combine. When the syndicate exports to foreign countries, it pays the producers the regular table prices, and the loss involved, if any, is charged against profit and is thus shared by all members of the group producing the exported products. In order to promote exports a system of export premiums has been established. These premiums amounted in 1907 to the following sums:

Rules of export.

"Marks 1.50 per ton for coal used up in the production of steel exported.

"Marks 2.50 per ton for iron ore used in the production of steel exported.

"Marks 15 per ton for partly manufactured steel (inclusive of the coal and iron ore premium).

"Marks 20 per ton for steel rails of all kinds (inclusive of the premiums on coal and raw iron).

"In addition to these premiums others are added by special cartels, such as the wire nail syndicate, the wire syndicate, etc. Premiums are ordinarily paid to works in proportion to the amount of raw material, coal, etc., used in the production of its exports; but a firm which owns its coal and iron mines is not always entitled to the maximum amount authorized by the bureau. Only firms that use coal and iron included in the output authorized by the syndicate are allowed this privilege. The premiums granted are also established by the syndicate and may change from time to time as the conditions warrant.

Effect of export policy.

"The manufacturing industries claim, and apparently with good grounds, that the export policy of the steel combine will in the long run prove disastrous to the exports of the German machine industries. Whenever the home market is unable to absorb the amount of steel that the producers place at the syndicate's disposal, it is generally forced to reduce its price to foreign buyers in order to get rid of the output. In this way, the foreign manufacturer of machines, by obtaining his raw material from the German combine, is placed in an unduly advantageous position in competing with the German producer. In 1904, for example, pig iron was sold abroad at from 69 to 71 marks, whereas the domestic buyer was forced to pay from 82½ to 92½ marks. The steel combine admits this charge, but claims that its importance has been greatly exaggerated by critics of the syndicate.

Fines and penalties.

"The combine is bound by contract to receive and pay for all the product of each individual member, provided the same does not exceed the quota allotted to the firm in question. The steel thus purchased is sold by the combine to industrial and other concerns at a uniform price known as standard price. Only in very exceptional cases is any steel disposed of to a domestic concern at any other price. The standard price is established by the directors of the combine at the beginning of each quarter. The quota assigned to each relates exclusively to products offered for sale. Any member of the combine may use as much steel and iron as it pleases in its own factories.

"If any member violates the contract of the syndicate by selling directly *A* products to consumers, he is compelled to pay a fine of one hundred marks per ton for each ton of goods sold. Every other violation of the contract is punished by a fine of 1000 marks for each offense. A restricting penalty of twenty marks per ton is imposed upon the firms for each ton they produce in excess of the amount of *B* products allotted to their plants. If any firm produces *A* products in excess of its quota, it is required to pay a fine of five marks per ton. In the same way, firms producing less than their quota are entitled to five marks per ton premium from the syndicate. No member of the combine is allowed to sell or rent his plant to an outsider without the consent of the syndicate. He is also forbidden to establish new plants or to own shares in any company outside the combine. All differences of opinion between members of the combine are to be settled by a Board of Arbitration, and under no circumstances are to be carried into the courts. The syndicate exercises no control whatever over the method of securing iron ore or other raw material by the individual members. It also refrains from interfering with labor struggles, strikes, or other disputes.

"The combine has secured sufficient orders to enable all its members to increase their output about 33⅓ per cent and at the same time has secured gradually increasing prices. Increased output in large scale production necessarily results in cheapening the cost per unit of production to the limit of maximum efficiency.

Increase in prices.

"As a result of the combine, the profitableness of steel works and the value of steel stocks has increased materially since the syndicate came into existence. Apparently, therefore, the syndicate has been decidedly beneficial to the plant owner. Still it must not be forgotten that the period in which it has been in existence has been one of favorable industrial conditions. The gross profits of fourteen of the largest works increased, in the year 1904–1905, 31.8 per cent, whereas the capital invested in the works in question was increased only 8.6 per cent. Averages, however, do not indicate fully the influence of the steel trust upon each individual member. Generally the larger and more powerful members have benefited more than the weaker ones through its activity, and in some cases the condition of the weaker members has deteriorated rather than improved. While some companies have undoubtedly been able to remain in existence as a result of the syndicate's activity, that would under the competitive system have been forced to the wall, others that might have developed under the competitive system have

Increase in profits.

apparently been held back by the cartel's policy of combination.

"If the combine had not been created, the smaller works would probably have been swallowed up, one after another, until the steel industry of Germany developed into a trust-like consolidation resembling the United States Steel Corporation. This tendency has been restrained rather than eliminated, since numerous consolidations have been made within the combine during the period in which the steel syndicate has existed.

"The most important advantage which the steel syndicate has secured for its members is a diminution in the costs of handling and sale of steel. The average per ton cost has amounted to only 25 pfennig, whereas it is claimed that the cost for the same service in the American steel combination is $2 per ton. The comparison is not correct, however, since the $2 per ton in the latter includes a large number of overhead charges, which in the German works are borne by the individual firms.

Lowered costs.

"Costs of production have also been cheapened by the steel combine as a result of the increased division of labor made possible by its creation. Under the cartel contract it has been possible for one mill to exchange orders for certain kinds of goods for which its equipment was inadequate with another mill whose facilities for making this class of goods were more up-to-date. In this way it has been possible for some mills to produce on a large scale relatively few kinds of steel products, such as steel rails, beams, etc.

"Another advantage obtained by the members from the existence of the cartel is in dealing with strikes and labor difficulties. Whenever a strike threatens, the concern can transfer its quota to some other mill where there are no labor difficulties. Furthermore, the syndicate contract contains a provision releasing the mill from obligation to deliver goods whenever a strike is on. Such an arrangement would have been impossible under the competitive system, and losses growing out of strikes would undoubtedly have been much greater if the syndicate had not existed.

Advantages in strikes.

"In general it is feared that the organization of the steel industry in the form of the steel combine will result in a gradual deterioration in the quality of steel products and that the chief object of the combine will become quantity rather than quality. On the other hand, it is also clear that the steel works will be able to specialize much more successfully under the cartel régime than has been possible under the competitive system. The steel producers are now able to devote themselves solely to the problem of production, since the cartel takes over the entire distribution of the products. In addition to this tendency, the owners of smelters are not forced to devote so much time to the problem of the purchase of raw materials, since this side of the business has also been systematized so that purchases are made on a large scale by joint agreements between iron ore owners and steel producers.

Quality of steel.

"It is also asserted that the steel combine has secured much greater stability in the iron and steel market than was possible before it came into existence. This stability has made it practicable for manufacturers to avoid losses which formerly were almost inevitable. It has been possible for the cartel to shift the burden more and more upon the less organized manufacturers who use steel products as raw material. Consequently the last and unorganized stages of steel product manufacture, *e.g.* machine making, etc., have been forced to bear the greater proportion of the burdens caused by a gradual increase in prices. These manufacturers will undoubtedly be able to shift a part of the burden upon the final consumer. As yet, this process has not been entirely completed in a great many lines.

Stability.

"In times of business prosperity the steel combine fulfills its contracts only partially and this also constitutes ground for complaint on the part of purchasers of steel goods.

"Many complaints are also directed against the strict conditions of sale imposed by the combine. It is maintained that the wishes of customers are not given due consideration, that they are compelled to take the quality of steel which the combine sees fit to give them, regardless

Harsh sale conditions.

of the special needs of their business. Furthermore, it is asserted that the combine delivers steel to certain firms, from different plants, which makes it difficult for the manufacturer to secure as uniform a grade of goods as he had been able to obtain when he bought all his steel from the same firm. The steel syndicate claims that most of these complaints are based upon prejudice and imaginary differences in quality.

"A comparison of the total output of steel in Germany with the total steel output of the United States during the last ten years demonstrates the fact that for some reason or other the steel production has been much more stable in Germany than in America. The crises of 1903 and of 1907 resulted in a violent slump in the production of America. These crises had relatively little effect upon the work of the steel mills. Whether the absence of fluctuation in Germany can be traced back to the steel cartels, or whether it is due to the fact that German industrial conditions are more stable than they are in America, is a question which cannot be easily answered. It is probable, however, that the German cartels have solved the problem of adjusting the supply to probable demands about as successfully, if not more successfully, than the American steel combine."

Effect on steel output.

For the great German steel combine, thus described by Professor Urdahl, controlling ninety-five per cent of the industry of the country, it is clear that coöperation is allowed to proceed to the extent of monopoly, and that without any administrative control by the government or attempt to prevent the combination from fixing prices which the markets will stand. It is notable that the combination sells steel abroad lower than at home; in some cases as much as twenty per cent cheaper, in this respect following the same policy as the United States Steel Corporation. This is possible because Germany, like the United States, has a protective tariff; and therefore the foreign producer cannot enter the domestic trade of these countries. This is reserved for the home corporations. If it were not for the fact of Germany's tariff, it is plain that it would not be

Surplus sold abroad at low prices.

possible to keep the level of prices for iron and steel higher at home than they are in the world's markets. The same is of course true for the United States.

The Potash Industry.[1] — One of the most interesting of the combinations in Germany is that of the potash industry. In the Stassfurt district are the greatest potash mines of the world. A comprehensive law concerning potash was passed in 1910 creating a board of apportionment. This board fixes the amount which is to be sold during any year; it determines the proportion that each producer — and they are some fifty in number — shall be allowed to mine. Any producer may exceed his allotment by ten per cent; but if he does, the excess is deducted from his next year's allowance. If a company exceeds this maximum it must pay a greatly increased tax upon the excess. The companies are forbidden to lower grades. The maximum price is fixed for each grade of the product; and not only this, but freight rates are adjusted, so that the prices are equalized at different commercial centers, just as the anthracite combination fixes the price of that article at Boston and Buffalo. The law also provides that the price of potash in Germany shall not be greater than it is abroad. The taxes on the potash companies are reserved for the administration of the governmental machinery necessary to control the industry. Each company must give a full report of all its transactions. The books are open to the board of apportionment. There is an appeal from the board of apportionment to a commission, just as in the proposed plan allowing coöperation in America there is appeal from the commission to the courts. (See pp. 242–243.)

Allotments and prices fixed.

Before the above law was passed there was a syndicate which controlled the potash industry. When this syndicate agreement terminated, two companies broke away and made contracts for large sales of potash in America. This situation led to the above law, which embodies many of the regulations previously contained in the syndicate

[1] The full text of the potash law is given Hearings, Senate Interstate Commerce Committee, Part IX, pp. 489–497.

agreements. The law was therefore a direct outgrowth of previous experience under the pressure of an emergency. One reason which was strongly urged for its passage was that it would result in the conservation of the potash resources in Germany. Before combination, the potash industry had all the difficulties of many competing concerns with regard to a natural resource limited in extent. Prices were too high or too low. The plan of controlling the potash industry in Germany promises to work to the satisfaction of the producer, and to the satisfaction of the government, which is a part owner in the potash mines.

Combinations result of development.

It is notable that for the potash industry, in which complete monopoly is allowed, restrictions are introduced which are not regularly applied to the cartel in Germany. The board of apportionment has authority to control prices; not only so, but to prohibit the selling of material abroad cheaper than in Germany. In both of these respects the policy of the government is an advance over that which applies to the steel combination. That combination, while not a complete monopoly, controls 95 per cent of the output of the country; and there is no government regulation of prices either at home or abroad. In consequence of this, as we have seen, prices are kept up at home and reduced abroad sufficiently to sell the surplus product.

Complete monopoly allowed.

While in Germany coöperation is permitted to an almost unlimited extent, the laws are there very severe against unfair competition. The types of unfair competition are closely defined, and a party who is injured through their violation may recover damages.

Section 3

AUSTRIA

In Austria the laws make illegal all agreements to raise prices and other contracts to the detriment of the public. There are exceptions to the extent that agreements which maintain prices in times of crises, reduce prices, and secure more favorable conditions of production, such as lowering of freight rates, large scale purchases, etc., are lawful. While, upon the whole, the law of Austria is against cartels, the industrial situation is similar to, but not identical with, that of Germany. Combinations extensively exist. Some of the more successful ones are those in iron, sugar, and petroleum. Ordinarily these combinations control outputs and prices. This may be accomplished through selling bureaus and by division of markets.

Law against cartels.

The courts, acting under the laws stated, have been less favorable to the combinations in their decisions than the courts of Germany. While, in some cases, contracts for the division of the market, fixing of prices, etc., have been declared illegal, these decisions have not been any more successful in checking the tendency toward combination than have similar decisions in this country; indeed, they have somewhat accelerated mergers in Austria as they have greatly in this country. According to Jenks[1] the tendency to combination has been retarded to some extent by the regulation requiring publicity in business, and because of the fact that taxes are heavier on corporations than on private firms.

Combination continues.

Looking toward the future in Austria, a government commission has recommended the recognition of combinations by law and their supervision and regulation by government authority.

Section 4

FRANCE

In France the laws provide heavy penalties against price agreements for food products. The courts have held that combinations which do not have the purpose of raising prices, but to prevent prices from falling and to regulate their fall, are lawful. Also combinations which do not strive to raise prices but only to secure a market so as to put them in a position to compete with their rivals have been held to be lawful.

Law against combinations.

[1] "Ency. Brit.," 37, 338.

One of the effects of the laws against combinations and agreements in France has been to drive them to secrecy, the same as in this country. It is therefore difficult to ascertain the extent to which combinations exist, but it is certain that they are widespread.

Coöperation goes on.

Selling bureaus have been established which receive orders and fix prices for the establishments concerned. This form of organization has not been successfully attacked in the courts. These agreements and selling agencies affect many industries, including sugar, petroleum, and porcelain.[1]

Section 5

GENERAL STATEMENTS

Belgium has many cartels which are very similar to those of Germany, and often the cartels in the two countries are closely related. Some other countries having cartels for various products are: Bulgaria, Egypt, Italy, Portugal, Roumania, Spain, Scandinavia, Switzerland, and Russia.

The faith of Britain and Germany in coöperation.

From the foregoing summary regarding the situation in foreign countries it appears that the premises with which Great Britain and Germany start concerning combination in restraint of trade is just the reverse of our own. Our faith is in competition; their faith is in coöperation. Clearly the theory of the United States or that of Great Britain and Germany is wrong. In this country there exists a popular distrust and fear of combination and the desire to strike it wherever it appears; in Germany and Great Britain combination is accepted as a necessary step in commercial progress. The expanding trade of Great Britain and Germany gives strong evidence of the merit of their point of view. Those who have watched the development of Germany since the Franco-Prussian war have been amazed at the rise of that country to a position in commerce at home and abroad second to no country in the world. In many lines of manufacture, for instance, steel,

[1] "Ency. Brit.," 37, 338–389.

the foreign trade of Germany and Great Britain vastly exceeds our own; not only so, but it is more rapidly expanding. It, of course, cannot be held that the astonishing advance of Germany in commerce and the increase in foreign trade of Germany and Great Britain are due exclusively to freedom to coöperate in business as well as freedom to compete; but it may be safely asserted that this was one of the essential conditions to their great success.

Section 6

INTERNATIONAL COMBINATIONS

Combinations not only exist in the European countries and in the United States, but for many industries international coöperation has begun between the great companies in different countries. Macrosty[1] says that "rails, tubes, nails, screws, sewing thread, bleaching powder, borax, nitrates, and tobacco are to a greater or less degree brought under international control, while, at least till lately, dynamite was so controlled, and repeated efforts have been made similarly to syndicate the whole steel trade." The forces which have produced such international combinations are the same as those which have resulted in those confined to one country, the maintenance of prices, division of territories, and limitation of production.

Wide extent of international combination.

Perhaps the most important of these combinations is the International Rail Syndicate, which was formed in 1883 between Great Britain, Germany, and Belgium. Under this agreement England was awarded 66 per cent of the business, afterwards reduced to 63½ per cent; Germany, 27, afterwards 29 per cent; and Belgium 7, afterwards 7½ per cent. Later this pool was broken up with a fall of prices, but in 1904 it got together again on a different basis, that of division of territory. In 1905 the United States was taken into the arrangement. Also, there have been international combinations for a number of other iron and steel products.

The steel rail syndicate.

[1] "The Trust Movement in British Industry," pp. 63–64, 342.

One of the most important of the international combinations is that of the marine interests. In 1902 the International Mercantile Marine Company was organized under the laws of New Jersey, with a capital of $120,000,000, one half common and one half preferred stock. The combination included the following lines: Leyland (49 vessels, 295,000 tons); White Star (29 vessels, 181,000 tons); Atlantic transports (23 vessels, 183,000 tons); American and Red Star (24 vessels, 181,000 tons); Dominion (14 vessels, 110,000 tons).

The marine syndicate.

Without being a member of the International Mercantile Marine Company, the Hamburg American and North German Lloyd Companies, with 190 vessels and 1,093,000 tons, have entered into a working agreement with it by which a committee composed of four representatives, two of which are named by the International Mercantile Marine Company and two by the German company, are authorized to fix rates, distribute steerage passengers, etc.

TABLE 51. SHOWING CONSTITUTION OF SHIPPING COMBINE

a. International Mercantile Marine Company	Combination	Cartel, known as Shipping Combine
North German Lloyd Hamburg-American Company	Cartel	
b. Belgian Red Star Line.		
c. Holland-American Line.		
d. Compagnie Trans-Atlantique.		
e. Cunard Line.		

Another shipping combine is said to control the freight business between New York and the Far East. Both of these marine companies are under attack for violation of the Sherman antitrust law.[1]

[1] United States *v.* Hamburg-Amerikanische Packetfahrt-Actien-Gesellschaft, and others, U. S. Circuit Court, Southern District N. Y. 2d Dist.; United States *v.* American-Asiatic Steamship Company, and others, District Court of the United States for Southern District of N. Y.

At Jena there is a central bureau. Each member of the cartel sends a statement to the bureau, giving the freight and passenger business of the company. If a member of the combination has carried more than his share, he pays the surplus into the treasury or pool, which in turn reimburses the companies whose businesses have been curtailed.

Oil is one of the businesses in which the international combination and coöperation have gone far, in some places there being union, in others division of territory.

As we have already seen the American Tobacco Company made an agreement with the Imperial Tobacco Company under which each was to respect the home territory of the other, and a combination company was created, the British-American Tobacco Company, through which the two handled their foreign business.

The nitrate combination regulates prices and output. Some businesses have become international by one of the great companies buying other companies in the same business, or establishing branches in foreign countries. The latter applies to a number of the greater companies of the United States, illustrated by the Westinghouse Company.

Combination world-wide.

It is not the intention to give a detailed description of international combinations, since this would unduly expand this book. That international combination has gone so far shows the world-wide extent of the tendency for coöperation in business.

The United States cannot successfully compete in the world's markets without large industrial units. When combination and coöperation are permitted not only in foreign countries but as between foreign countries, if the manufacturers of the United States are excluded from uniting and from taking part in international coöperations, they will not be important factors in the world's markets. No nation can walk by itself in the world's trade. If the Sherman act is rigidly enforced in its present form, and the administration apparently regards this duty as resting upon it, American manufacturers must look mainly to their home markets.

CHAPTER V

REMEDIES

Section 1

SPECIFICATIONS TO BE MET

Before presenting a constructive plan to meet the existing situation in trade, it will be well to give specifications regarding the things that are to be accomplished and the things that are to be avoided, the same being based upon the statement of facts contained in the previous chapters. In making these specifications, the aim will be to present a consensus of opinion, not personal views.

1. While the existence of a non-competitive field, that of the public utilities, is admitted, and in many cases for such monopoly must exist, outside of public utilities there is still a large field for competition. Competitive conditions should be retained in the industries. Certainly there should remain competition for business; there should remain competition for quality; there should remain competition in prices so far as this is consistent with other specifications. A condition should not be allowed to arise such as to render competition in prices, quality, or service impossible. In order to retain freedom of competition it will be necessary to prevent monopoly. In those industries in which freedom of competition does not now exist, the facts regarding individual industries (given pp. 104–150) show that this condition has arisen and has been maintained very largely through unfair practices or by monopoly.

Competition to be retained.

2. Unfair practices must be prohibited and unfair advantages must not be permitted. Only so will it be possible to

Unfair practices.

retain competition.[1] Some of the more important regulations should be as follows: —

(*a*) All corporations should be placed upon the same basis with reference to common carriers. Discrimination, rebates, drawbacks, and exceptional services should not be allowed.

(*b*) Business should not be allowed to be carried on by secret companies or combinations. The complete organization of any corporation should be open. No company should appear to be independent which is not so.

(*c*) The grosser forms of unfair competition, such as espionage of business competitors, bribing of men in the employ of competitors, etc., should be prohibited.

(*d*) No agreement should be allowed requiring exclusive dealing; nor should any rebate or advantage be gained from exclusive dealing.

(*e*) Local selling at or below cost to kill competition should be prohibited.

Coöperation to be permitted.

3. Reasonable coöperation between corporations should be permitted. It is believed that in business under modern conditions, coöperation not competition should be the controlling word. Sufficient coöperation should be allowed to prevent fierce and unrestrained competition which goes to the extent of reducing prices below a reasonable amount. Only by coöperation can the enormous wastes of competition be avoided. In this connection the form of the solution which may be adopted to secure coöperation may depend very largely upon the definition of reasonable and unreasonable. If all restraints of trade are reasonable which do not produce monopoly, then we may accept the common law principle that unreasonable restraint of trade is not to be allowed, and under this principle secure coöperation. But if unreasonable restraint is to be narrowly construed, so as to interdict all combinations which divide territories, regulate outputs and make price agreements, then unreasonable restraint of trade must be redefined by statute in order to secure the benefits of coöperation. Much of the confusion in

[1] Details as to the kinds of unfair practices which have arisen in business may be found by reference to Chapter II.

the thinking and discussion concerning concentration is at this point, some persons having in their minds that all restraints of trade are reasonable which do not go to the extent of monopoly, and others holding that almost any form of coöperation in business is unreasonable restraint of trade.

Just as coöperation of capital should be allowed, so coöperation of laborers should be permitted. The laborers find themselves prevented from coöperation by the Sherman law precisely as have the industrial combinations.[1] It is clear that unless laborers may unite in trade unions, in joint bargaining, and in all legitimate matters which concern them, they will be helpless. Not only should coöperation between capitalists and coöperation of laborers be allowed, but coöperation of the two groups should be permitted. In short, it is advocated that the principle of coöperation should control in commerce, including both laborer and capitalist.

4. Corporations should be allowed to be of sufficient magnitude to give the highest economic efficiency in order that (*a*) they may be able to supply the needs of our own people at the lowest practicable rate, and (*b*) to secure an increased proportion of foreign trade. As to magnitude which may be allowed without the presumption that in consequence of this there is unreasonable restraint of trade, it may be suggested as a working basis that no one corporation, including all its subsidiary companies, should be permitted to control more than 50 per cent of any line of business of the country. There is no sanctity in the number 50, and this may be reduced to 40 per cent or increased to 60 per cent if either be more acceptable to the public. This rule is not only to apply to a corporation as a whole but to each of the different lines of business which may be covered by it. If this principle be accepted, it is natural to say that any corporation which has more than 50 per cent of the business of the country is a monopoly, and that monopoly is unreasonable restraint of trade.

Sufficient magnitude for efficiency

[1] Hearings, Part XX, pp. 1727–1778.

5. It must be possible to secure the freedom of competition defined under 1 and the prohibition of the unfair practices under 2 practically without cost to the complainant. It is the theory that all are equal before the law, but everybody knows this theory is unsound. Under modern conditions, in which there are giant corporations with substantially unlimited funds, the man who has a small business is not equal to such organizations before the law because of his inability to bear the expense of the contest. If concentrations of industry be allowed to exist, some machinery must be devised under which the weak man may be sure of fair practices and an open field.

Justice without cost to complainant.

6. For all businesses in which there is any restraint of trade, reasonable or unreasonable, through coöperation, there should be full publicity. As soon as coöperation is permitted, the business as a matter of fact is invested with a public interest; and even if not declared to be a public utility, if any privileges are given for coöperation, or for magnitude, which involves restraint of trade to the extent of controlling the market, all the operations of the company, including the profits, should be matters of public knowledge.

Full publicity.

7. Corporations should be required so to conduct their businesses as to conserve the natural resources. This will involve the restraint of competition so as to prohibit waste. With reference to the future, this specification is one of paramount importance. The difficulties regarding production and distribution of wealth we are sure to solve. In the meantime there may be loss and waste and unjust distribution. There is not of necessity permanent loss. If, however, natural resources of great value are allowed to be wasted or destroyed, this is a perpetual loss to the race. Thus, as has already been pointed out (pp. 89–94), if a large percentage of coal be wasted under severely competitive conditions of mining, if there be waste in the mining of our metals so that a considerable part of the deposits are left in the ground in such a condition that they cannot in the future be recovered,—this is an irreparable loss which permanently impoverishes our people.

Conserve resources.

8. Coöperating corporations should give just rewards to labor. The wages paid should be fair; and fair wages for a man means wages such that he can support a family under decent conditions so that his children may have open before them the avenues of opportunity.

Just rewards to labor.

9. The business of the great corporations should be conducted under good social conditions. It has been charged that some of the great corporations require too long hours of labor, and that the work is carried on under very unfavorable conditions. On the contrary, with regard to other great corporations, it is claimed that in these respects the larger organizations are in a better position than the smaller ones. Both of these statements appear to be true. So far as large businesses are allowed to exist, because of their magnitude, these social factors become of special importance; and the great concentrations which have exceptional strength or magnitude should not be allowed to take advantage of labor in hours, service, sanitation, or other social factors.

Good social conditions.

10. Fair prices should be obtainable by individuals or groups selling to the great corporations. Corporations should no more be allowed unduly to depress prices for materials necessary for their manufactories than they should be allowed unduly to depress prices of labor.

Fair prices.

11. Corporations should not be allowed to charge excessive prices to the consumer. So far as the public in general is concerned, the greatest complaint with respect to the concentrations of industry has been the excessive prices; that is, the stockholders of the great corporations rather than the public have gained the major part of the advantages of their exceptional efficiency. If great organizations are allowed to exist and to coöperate, it is clear that they cannot remain without restraint in fixing prices. Some way must be found to prevent excessive charges and thus guard the interests of the public. In order that fair prices may be secured, it is necessary that certain other things be prohibited; among which are the following: —

The public to share in the profits.

(*a*) If great concentrations of industry be permitted to exist, there must be some method of guarding the capitalization of the mergers and consolidations in order to protect the public against the ill-advised purchase of watered stock, and against the payment of dividends upon watered stock. It is fully appreciated that this matter of overcapitalization is one of extraordinary difficulty concerning which it is not easy to formulate definite rules. This will be appreciated if the report of the Railroad Securities Commission of 1911, on public utilities, be examined. In some cases it is fair to a certain extent to capitalize good will, trade marks, and patents. Also in passing from the competitive system to the coöperative system, it may be necessary to take into an organization some plants which cannot be utilized but which must be paid for. In such cases there is loss in either method, by operating under the competitive system or by capitalizing under the coöperative method. This is well illustrated by the whisky combination. When this consolidation was formed, it was found economical not to utilize a considerable number of plants taken into the combination. So far as such plants could not be used for some other purpose than that of distilling they became a complete loss. Thus, while some capitalization of unproductive property and good will is allowable, this should be on a conservative basis. Capitalization of hoped for earning power may not be legitimate.

Overcapitalization.

(*b*) Excessive costs of organization and manipulation by promoters should not be allowed. It is clear that while fair charges for promotion, including underwriting, are permissible and should be included in the capitalization, one of the great evils of the recent era of consolidations has been excessive charges in these particulars.

Promoters' charges.

(*c*) Speculative management should be guarded against and payment of unearned dividends prevented. While these evils are not peculiar to the great corporations, as an organization increases in size it becomes of increasing public interest, and therefore should be considered in an exceptional way in proportion to the magnitude of the enterprise.

Speculative management.

12. Finally the scope of the powers of the United States and the several states should be clearly defined in the control of commerce. Mr. Bryan said at the White House in 1908:

"There is no twilight zone between the nation and the state, in which exploiting interests can take refuge from both."[1] If this phrase were changed from "there is" to "there should be" it would precisely express the situation. Nothing is plainer than that there is a twilight zone between the nation and the states where the great corporations have taken refuge from both. This has clearly appeared in the prosecutions carried on by the Attorney-General of the United States in attempting to enforce the Sherman act.

The twilight zone.

Minimum Specifications. — It cannot be expected that at once a scheme will be enacted into legislation to meet all of the above specifications. It may be doubtful, indeed, if it be advisable to present a complete plan to meet them, since any such plan would be sure to be profoundly modified in all but its essential features before the time was reached for the enactment of the more remote parts of it. It will be the work of many years to secure a system of legislation, state and national, which will meet the specifications made in regard to which there seems to be a consensus of opinion. It must be remembered that the temper of our people is such that in handling any complex situation by legislation, advance is made step by step, each one being very short. This is very well illustrated by the legislation for handling public utilities to be subsequently spoken of.

Conservative temper of our people.

It is therefore essential, if possible, that we select the fundamental points among the specifications upon which a consensus of opinion can be reached, and propose a program which deals definitely only with those points, leaving the other specifications to be handled by later amendments.

Of the specifications given it appears to me that two are fundamental and paramount to the others.

The first is that the weak and the strong shall alike have full opportunity to secure justice from the great corporations. That this is the situation at the present time no one would claim. There have been a few recoveries of damages by important companies or combinations against greater com-

[1] Conference of the Governors of the United States, Washington, 1908, p. 201.

binations which have been in restraint of trade; but so far as the general public is concerned, the individual who has been overcharged, the small company that has been weakened or destroyed by unfair practices, has had substantially no redress. The law may have been such that if the individual or the small company had unlimited money, and the courts proceeded with ten times the expedition that they now do, an approximation to justice might be reached; but these are not the facts; they never will be the facts. No sane man can deny that the existing laws or any other possible ones, however severe they might be made against the great concentrations of industry, would be of no avail to the workman who is overcharged for an article of daily consumption, or to the small producer. If we are to retain the essentials of a democracy, and are not to become a plutocracy, some plan must be devised under which the weak as well as the strong has redress for wrongs, has his rights respected. If the most ardent advocate of court method of procedure against corporations in restraint of trade through amendments of existing laws to be enforced by the courts believes that there is any possibility of redressing the wrongs of the individual and securing the rights of the weak, he must indeed be blind to the experience of the past fifty years of development and be content with faith without works.

The weak and strong to be equal.

Second if the arguments in the earlier chapters of this book are approximately sound, we must now accept for this country the principle of coöperation in business. Even the most ardent defender of the competitive system says that competition must be regulated; and he says that the alternative is between regulated competition and regulated monopoly.[1] The writer holds that there is no such alternative. We should not accept competition as the controlling principle on one side, nor monopoly as the controlling principle on the other side. We should accept the broad principle that reasonable coöperation should be allowed in business as it is allowed everywhere else in our social structure.

Reasonable coöperation.

[1] Brandeis says: "The real issue is regulate competition or regulate monopoly." Hearings, Part XVI, p. 1162.

We have seen that the laws against great concentration of industry have been without avail to give justice to the individual. Similarly, they have been without avail in preventing coöperation. The Sherman law and some of the state antitrust laws are now over a score years old. At the time the Sherman law was enacted it was supposed that the courts would be competent to regulate the trusts so as to produce reasonable rather than unreasonable coöperation. That this would not be the case Professor Richard T. Ely [1] clearly foresaw a dozen years ago. He says: "If there is any serious student of our economic life who believes that anything substantial has been gained by all the laws passed against trusts, by all the newspaper editorials which have thus far been penned, by all the sermons which have been preached against them, this authority has yet to be heard from. Forms and names have been changed in many instances, but the dreaded work of vast aggregation of capital has gone on practically as heretofore. The writer does not hesitate to affirm it as his opinion that efforts along lines which have been followed in the past will be equally fruitless in the future."

Failure of courts.

As has been clearly developed in the earlier parts of this book, the views which Professor Ely held at that time have been fully justified. The laws against trusts and the actions of the courts in their enforcement not only have not prevented the existence of concentrations and the enlargement of the trusts, but have greatly accelerated their development.

Section 2

COMMISSION CONTROL OF PUBLIC UTILITIES

In marked contrast with the situation for industry during the past score of years, there has been sound development in control of one great line of concentration, that to which the term public utility applies. For many years it was an accepted faith that the wrongs to individuals perpetrated

[1] "Monopolies and Trusts," p. 243 (1899).

by the great public utilities corporations were to be redressed through the courts of law and that competition was to regulate prices. Under this faith, millions of wrongs went unredressed; and competition led to unnecessary duplication, great loss to the public, destruction to the weak, and finally, complete dominance of the great public utilities and especially the railroads.

Wrongs unredressed.

The well-recognized maxim upon which the traffic managers worked under the old régime was to impose all the traffic would bear, to make the kind of service rest exclusively upon the returns. In short, the theory originally enunciated, it is alleged, by William H. Vanderbilt, "The public be damned," if not always announced openly, was the real feeling which was dominant in many of these corporations. They were regarded as private properties to be run for those who owned the stocks and bonds and not for the advantage of the public. All the laws made against the public utilities corporations and their enforcement through the courts by action for damages or by state's attorneys to protect the public rights accomplished practically nothing. But the fact that these organizations were public utilities in law and therefore did have an exceptional relation to the public led step by step to another method of control, — that by commission.

"The public be damned."

Early Commission. — As early as 1869, the state of *Massachusetts* created a railroad commission, upon which was imposed the duty of supervising all the railroads of the state, "whether operated by steam, horse, or other motive power." It rested upon the commission to ascertain whether the railroad company complied with the laws of the state and to consider the complaints of citizens. However, the commission had only the right of suggestion. It might inform the railroad company that the rates charged were too high; it had no authority to enforce a lower rate.

California, in 1876, established a railroad commission called Commissioners of Transportation, the powers of which went far beyond those of the Massachusetts commission. They included the establishment of stations, the prohibition of discrimination, and the power of examination of books.

New York established a state railroad commission in 1882. This commission had power to investigate accidents resulting in injury or loss of life, had the power of examining the books, had imposed upon it the duty of calling to the attention of the company any violation of the law, unfair practices, excessive rates, inadequate facilities, etc., with recommendations. If these recommendations were not complied with by the railroads, the commission could present the facts to the attorney-general, who was to secure redress through the law.

These cases illustrate the beginnings of commission control of public utilities in this country. In this brief statement, it is not possible to give a history of the application of commissions to public utilities, for adequate consideration of the commission laws would involve a book much larger than the present one. In general, however, it may be said that these early commissions had the power to investigate and make suggestions and recommendations to the railroads. If these recommendations were not complied with, they might be presented to the Attorney-General for prosecution in the courts. While the early commissions accomplished something, there was no fundamental change in the situation. The railroad company need do no more than it desired to do in any of the matters recommended, except as compelled by action of a court of law; and, as we have already seen, this method of procedure has been a failure for the control of concentration of industry from the outset.

Power limited to recommendation.

From these beginnings, the commission idea of control of railroads extended to many other states; and there was a gradual expansion of their power until finally in some states rate-making authority was given.

The first state to pass a comprehensive law including this power was *Iowa*. In 1897 a law was passed in that state which gave to a commission of three members general supervision over all the common carriers of the state. The inhibitions of the act and the powers of the commission were substantially the same as those contained in the interstate commerce act of 1887 (see pp. 238–239), and the latter law

Iowa fixed rates.

undoubtedly served as the model for Iowa. If the railroad companies failed to obey the order of the commission, the commission could petition the district court to enforce the order.

The Iowa law went farther than the interstate commerce law in that it gave the commission the power to prescribe maximum rates. After hearing the evidence in a case "the board shall prescribe a reasonable maximum rate. Such finding of the board shall in a judicial proceeding against the railroad company be considered as *prima facie* evidence of the unreasonableness of a rate higher than that prescribed by the board."

The Wisconsin Commission. — It was in Wisconsin, when U. S. Senator R. M. La Follette was governor, that the full solution was first reached. In that state, in 1905, W. H. Hatton was chairman of the committee on transportation in the state senate. He laid down the principle "that it was as much the duty of the state to furnish transportation facilities as it ever had been to make roads or build bridges, and that if the function was delegated to any one, it was the duty of the state to regulate it so that the agent should be required to furnish adequate service, reasonable rates, and practice no discrimination."[1] Senator Hatton further said regarding the proposed bill to accomplish the above: "I want this procedure so simple that a man can write his complaint on the back of a postal card, and if it is a just one, the state will take it up for him."[2]

We have here enunciated the two principles now generally recognized as applying to public utilities, regulation so as to get reasonable rates and no discrimination, and machinery so simple as to give justice to all.

The act passed by the Wisconsin legislation gave the commission the power of regulation regarding rates, service, and discrimination, for railroads and correlated organizations, such as refrigerator lines, sleeping car, and dispatch companies. In the regulation of service the power of various state commissions had been gradually extended, and the Wisconsin bill merely carried this phase of the matter to its

[1] "The Wisconsin Idea," Charles McCarthy, p. 39. [2] *Ibid.*, 41.

logical conclusion. The first fundamental new point of the law was that while the onus of fixing the rates rested upon the railroads, the commission could investigate by its own initiative or by complaint any rate or charge; and if the same was found to be unreasonable, the commission could order a new rate, which new rate must be substituted for the old one. Thus, the commission was given a possible task. It was not assigned the task of at once fixing all rates, but the task of readjusting unreasonable rates.

Power to adjust rates.

The second fundamental principle of the law was that the alterations of service and rates were accomplished by the commission without cost to the complainant; and thus justice was as certainly obtainable by the man who had imposed upon him an excessive charge for shipping a single article as by a great corporation. There was no escape from the decision of the commission by the railroad except by an appeal to the court; and the appeal was against the commission, not against the individual who made the complaint. As a matter of course both complainant and defendant had full opportunity to present their cases in public hearing before the commission in advance of action.

The power of the commission secures justice.

The third important principle introduced into the law was that, in case of appeal, the burden of proof that the order of the commission was unreasonable was upon the appealing railroad. Still further, if evidence was introduced into court which did not come before the commission, the court was obliged to stay its proceedings and remand the case to the commission for a rehearing, thus preventing the holding back of evidence by the corporations to discredit the commission.

New evidence.

All the provisions of the bill were such as to make the powers given the commission lie within those which may be delegated by a legislature. The legislature is to make the law; is to lay down the rules which control; the commission does nothing but administer the law; the commission cannot legislate, but it can make regulations under the rules of law formulated by the legislature. In this Wisconsin bill we have fully fledged the administrative commission. Its

Regulation under rules of law.

regulations are sometimes called administrative law as opposed to legislative law.

Following from the powers and duties of the commission, there have come many corollaries. In order to determine just rates, it has been necessary to make a physical valuation of the public utilities. In the valuation of the properties, both physical and good will, it has been necessary to use trained experts, both in engineering and in economics.

The powers of the railroad commission of Wisconsin were by three laws in 1907 extended to apply to all public utilities within the state. In the same year a comprehensive public utilities law along somewhat different lines was passed in New York, that state being divided into two districts, one including New York City and the other the remainder of the state.

This principle of control of public utilities through commissions, first put into full force in Wisconsin and New York, has been accepted by a number of other states.

The Interstate Commerce Commission. — Just as the states have undertaken the control of public utilities for intrastate business, the United States, by the interstate commerce act of 1887, has instituted a system of control for interstate commerce. This act creates a commission of five members, later increased to seven, appointed by the President, who hold office for six years. The original act applies to railways and to boats engaged in the transportation of passengers or property when the same is interstate. Violations of the act are made a misdemeanor punishable by a heavy fine for each offense. Unreasonable charges, unjust discrimination, and unjust or undue preference to some particular person are all illegal. Railroads must afford all reasonable and proper facilities for the interchange of traffic, and discrimination in the rates through such connection is prohibited. The law provides for the posting of schedules and requires advances of the same to be preceded by ten days' notice. No variation from published rates are to be permitted. All schedules are to be filled with the commission.

Charges to be reasonable.

The commission has power to inquire into the management of the business of common carriers and to obtain full information concerning them. Any person sustaining damage may make complaint to the commission or bring a suit in his own behalf in the District Court or Circuit Court of the United States; but he cannot do both. If complaint is made to the commission, this organization will investigate; and if the complaint is well founded the commission will recommend that reparation be made.

The chief defect of the law of 1887 was that the commission was a purely advisory body. Further, the commission was not given sufficient appropriations to make investigations upon which to determine whether charges were reasonable. Notwithstanding these limitations, the rebate evil was reduced, and a great number of cases were satisfactorily adjusted without going into court.

In 1906 and 1910 the interstate commerce law was amended. It now applies to all common carriers engaged in interstate commerce and also to companies engaged in communication, such as telephone, telegraph, and cable. In 1906 was given the power to fix maximum rates, and in 1910 to suspend increase of rates pending investigation. The charges both in transportation and communication are to be just and reasonable; unjust and unreasonable charges are declared to be illegal. A charge for a short haul shall not exceed the charge for a longer distance over the same road, provided that the Interstate Commerce Commission may grant relief in special cases.

All public utilities included.

Whenever the charges are found unjust or unreasonable the commission is authorized and empowered to determine and prescribe what will be a just and reasonable rate. Increases in rates must first be passed upon by the commission, and the burden of proof is upon the carrier to show the reasonableness of the advanced rate. If the carrier fails to comply with an order of the commission, the complainant may sue the carrier in the Circuit Court, where the finding of the commission shall be *prima facie* evidence against the carrier. Also the Interstate Commerce Commission may appeal to the Commerce Court for the enforcement of its order.

Power to regulate rates.

The amendments adopted gave the commission the necessary authority to make the interstate commerce law effective; and many decisions have been rendered declaring rates to be unreasonable, and reasonable rates have been fixed. In many cases railways have been found guilty of discrimination, orders have been given for such discriminations to cease, and proper damages have been awarded. In numerous cases where the joint rates exceeded a combination of the different local rates, the joint rates have been reduced so as not to exceed the combined local rates. Special rates have been declared to be unlawful; and unfair regulations, the effect of which is to favor some shipper (in one case the Standard Oil Company), have been abated.

Effectiveness of law.

At the same time the last amendment was passed giving the Interstate Commerce Commission power to regulate rates, a Commerce Court was created. This court has exclusive jurisdiction of all cases arising under the interstate commerce act "otherwise than by adjudication and collection of a forfeiture or penalty or by infliction of criminal punishment, or any order of the Interstate Commerce Commission than the payment of money." The pendency of a suit in the Commerce Court does not in itself stay or suspend the operation of an order of the Interstate Commerce Commission; but the Commerce Court may at its discretion suspend such order pending final hearing or determination of the suit. There may be appeal from the Commerce Court to the Supreme Court of the United States, and such cases are to have priority except over criminal cases. Complainants interested in a case before the Commerce Court have the right to appear and may be made parties thereto.

Commerce Court.

Of the cases of appeal from the Interstate Commerce Commission to the Commerce Court, there have been many affirmations and also many in which the orders of the Interstate Commerce Commission have been temporarily suspended or reversed.

In some instances, charges which the commission declared to be unreasonable have been declared to be reasonable by the court. In other instances where charges have been declared to be unreasonable by the commission, the court has declared that the order was based upon insufficient evidence. In one case a through railway rate had been lowered until it met a combined rail and water rate. This resulted in the railway getting the major part of the business, so that the water competition was eliminated. The higher rate was then resumed. In this case the commission condemned the advance in the rates as unjust and unreasonable; but the Commerce Court held that there was not sufficient evidence to sustain this finding. This decision is of great consequence, since the method that the railway pursued is that which has been frequently followed to drive out water competition, — viz., lowering rates until water competition is destroyed, then raising the rates and taking increased profits.

Decision likely to eliminate water competition.

In another case the Commerce Court held that the commission exceeded its authority when it laid down a hard and fast rule to apply to a large part of the United States in regard to the long and short haul clause. Finally, the Commerce Court has held that its jurisdiction extends to those cases in which orders are for the payment of money only. In one class of cases the court has gone farther than the commission. It was held by the commission that the complainant could not recover the excess charges exacted by unreasonable rates previous to his complaint to the commission; whereas the court held that the complainant could recover from the time the unreasonable rate was inaugurated.

Right of review.

Some of the chief differences between the commission and the court are as follows: The commission holds that the court has no right to review the orders of the commission concerning charges, except such orders as are confiscatory; whereas the court holds that it may review the action of the commission as to the reasonableness or unreasonableness of charges.

Commission hampered.

The Commerce Court held that the commission has no right to require information concerning intrastate business, since the same is not interstate commerce. Probably this is the decision of the court that has most hampered the commission in that it made it impossible for the commission to obtain information concerning intrastate business. Without this knowledge the commission found it very difficult to determine the reasonableness or unreasonableness of interstate rates, since the reasonableness of a charge for a given class of business is dependent as one factor upon the entire business done by the road. Fortunately this decision of the Commerce Court has been reversed by the United States Supreme Court. Also decisions of the Supreme Court rendered in July, 1914 have fully sustained the authority of the Commission to regulate interstate commerce.

General Statements. — From the early public utilities commission of the sixties almost every proposal to create a commission or to extend its powers has been denounced as wildly radical, as socialistic. It has been said that if the laws proposed were passed, we might as well at once go to the socialistic doctrine and have business carried on by the government. The officers of the public service corporations clearly foresaw that the commissions meant sooner or later the destruction of the principles of imposing rates that the traffic would bear and the attitude, "the public be damned." Also with this appreciation by them there was undoubtedly an honest fear on the part of many that their properties would be unjustly raided; but the old situation was intolerable. The public service corporations and the people were at war; and under conditions of war there was rancor and distrust on both sides, an obstinate determination on the part of the railroad companies to resist every encroachment in the matter of control and determination on the part of many of the people to find a weapon by which they might smash the corporations.

Resistance to regulation.

In a half dozen years this state of mind both on the part of the owners of the public utilities and upon the part of the people has largely disappeared. Where before we had war, we now have peace.

Those who have studied the orders of the commissions to the public utility corporations know that commission rule, upon the whole, results in reasonable requirements regarding service and rates. If an unreasonable rate be imposed, there is appeal to the courts; and if the corporation can show that the rate imposed is confiscatory under the 14th amendment of the United States Constitution, the order of the commission will be reversed by the courts. To bring a suit in court imposes no especial hardship upon the railroads, since these great corporations have the money to carry their cases to the highest courts of the land. In consequence of the adequate, indeed unique, protection which property possesses in this country under the 14th amendment, as compared with any other country, some orders of the commissions have been reversed and property has been completely protected.

Protection of property rights.

The commissions, as a matter of pride, desire to avoid having their orders found unreasonable, desire not to have them found to be of a kind which confiscate property; and thus the commissions upon the whole have been conservative in their actions in the lowering of rates.

If there be any advantage upon either side through commission rule, it is with the corporations. Notwithstanding this, the people know that the weakest one of them is no longer subject to unjust discrimination which would ruin his business; he is certain that his stronger competitors are not directly receiving rebates and drawbacks; he is certain that his rates are not exorbitant; he accepts the situation even if he thinks the rates are somewhat high.

In making the above statement it is not meant to say that everything is all that could be desired. This state of affairs never will be reached in a progressive, industrial democracy. So long as the conditions are dynamic rather than static, no one will ever be completely satisfied. Many of the more important railroad men, in private, make complaint of some of the orders of the commissions, both state and interstate, because of what they regard as their too theoretical character due to lack of knowledge of practical difficulties involved in executing the orders. There are complaints as to divisions of cost between freight and passenger traffic; there are complaints of orders regarding stations, frequency of service, etc. Upon the other hand some of the people complain that, because of the protection of property under the 14th amendment,

Complete satisfaction unattainable.

the commissions have been too conservative and that the rates have not been sufficiently reduced; that adequate service has not been secured. That each side should unduly stress its own point of view and not see with perfect fairness the point of view of the other side is natural, indeed inevitable. But neither side would go back to the old condition of affairs. The wiser railroad men would far prefer to be under commissions than to be under blackmail through holdup bills at every session of many state legislatures. The pressure of these holdup bills was so great that many a railroad man in high position and of unquestioned business standing has felt it necessary in the past to bribe legislatures. No longer does this extremely distasteful, disgraceful, and unlawful performance generally exist. On the other hand, while the people may not be completely satisfied, they realize that they are far better off than when rebates and drawbacks existed, when there was discrimination between men and discrimination between different localities.

Perfect contentment we shall never have; but the results achieved in the control of public utilities by the administrative commissions are so great that we may be sure that from this time on the steps will be forward rather than backward in commission control of public utilities. The fundamental principle of regulation of the public utilities by commissions is substantially sound. It remains only to extend the principle worked out to the remaining states of the country and develop details necessary for the perfection of the method of control.

Movement forward.

So satisfactory upon the whole is the situation that, as already pointed out, the people accept with equanimity the principle of coöperation among the public utilities. Everywhere the latter coöperate in fixing rates so as to prevent destructive competition. No officer of any state or of the United States thinks of bringing suit against the public utility corporations for violation of the antitrust acts, although they are as flagrant violators of these laws as any in the United States. In short, the administrative commission has secured for the public utilities reasonable justice to all and by common consent has permitted coöperation.

Coöperation accepted.

Section 3

PURE FOOD AND DRUGS LAWS

At the same time that one class of commissions has arisen to control charges and service of public utilities, another class of administrative body has arisen to control the quality of commodities. As we have seen (pp. 74–78), the dogma of competition is that it is to control quality and price. For the industries, we have further seen that in controlling quality competition has been an unqualified failure; indeed, so disastrous was the failure and so menacing to public welfare, especially with reference to health, that the great majority of states have passed pure food laws, under which it is necessary for the label to tell the truth concerning an article. These laws prevent the introduction into food of preservatives inimical to health and prevent the adulteration of foods, drinks, and drugs.

Failure of competition to secure quality.

The states and possessions having pure food laws include the following: Alabama, 1907; Alaska, 1906; Arizona, 1906; Arkansas, 1907; California, 1907; Colorado, 1907; Connecticut, 1907; Delaware, 1907; Florida, 1907; Georgia, 1906; Hawaii, 1903; Idaho, 1905; Illinois, 1907; Indiana, 1907; Iowa, 1906; Kansas, 1907; Kentucky, 1908; Louisiana, 1906; Maine, 1907; Maryland, 1910; Massachusetts, 1882; Michigan, 1881; Minnesota, 1905; Mississippi, 1910; Missouri, 1907; Montana, 1907; Nebraska, 1907; Nevada, 1909; New Hampshire, 1907; New Jersey, 1907; Ohio, 1904; Oklahoma, 1909; Oregon, 1907; Rhode Island, 1908; Philippines, 1906; New Mexico, 1906; New York, 1909; North Carolina, 1907; North Dakota, 1907; Pennsylvania, 1907; Porto Rico, 1906; South Carolina, 1907; South Dakota, 1907; Tennessee, 1907; Texas, 1907; Utah, 1903; Vermont, 1907; Virginia, 1908; Washington, 1901; West Virginia, 1907; Wisconsin, 1903; Wyoming, 1907.

It is noticeable that with two exceptions these laws were formulated from 1903 to 1910. The salient point in connection with the present discussion is that for each state having

The administrative commission.

pure food laws, special administrative officers are assigned the duty of their enforcement. These officers may constitute a commission or a board. The duty may rest upon a single designated individual, in a number of instances called commissioner.

United States pure food law.

The same principles which were first applied within the states in the control of quality through commission was recognized by the United States when the pure food law was passed for interstate commerce in 1906.

This law makes it a misdemeanor to manufacture adulterated foods or drugs or to misbrand same or to sell adulterated or misbranded foods or drugs; it provides for examination of products upon the market by the Bureau of Chemistry; it provides that the secretaries of agriculture, of the treasury, and of commerce and labor shall issue rules and regulations for the enforcement of the act; the violation of these rules is to be punished by fine or imprsonment or both. Misbranded or adulterated foods or drugs are to be condemned.

A meat inspection amendment was added to the pure food laws providing for the inspection of all slaughtered carcasses. This amendment applies both to commerce between the states and between the states and foreign countries. Before passing any carcass it is to be found in a healthy and sound condition. This work is to be done by the Department of Agriculture.

Regulation under rule of law.

In general, the pure food laws, both state and national, lay down the general principles to be obeyed; the commissions or other administrative officers formulate definite detailed regulations under the general rules of law. These pure food officials have created laboratories for analyses of foods and drugs; they send their investigators to the various parts of the country to ascertain whether the laws are being complied with. They issue necessary orders in connection with their duties. In short, they are administrative bodies having imposed upon them the duty of seeing that the laws for the protection of the public regarding quality are complied with. Finally, the pure food officials may prosecute in the courts for failure to comply with the regulations issued.

Under the theory that competition would regulate, the public would have remained without protection. Had it not been for the creation of the administrative officials to enforce the quality laws, the only redress of the injured individual would have been to take his case to the courts. In the majority of cases the damage was small and an injured individual could not afford to do this. Just as with the public utilities, redress should be obtainable without expense to the individual. The situation was saved by the recognition of legislatures and Congress at the time they made the pure food laws, that they must create administrative officers to enforce them.

Redress without expense to the individual.

Just as there was resistance by the railroads and other public utility corporations to commission form of control and the principle was established only as a result of many years of severe contest, so there was prolonged and determined, indeed fierce, opposition by many of the manufacturers to the pure food laws. There was great commercial gain by exploiting the public through deceit, and this advantage they were determined not to lose. Resistance was so powerful that it was only when there was an aroused public sentiment in favor of the passage of the laws that the states and finally Congress enacted the same.

Resistance to pure food laws.

A case of most determined resistance was that of meat. False brands were used; the conditions in some of the abattoirs were unsanitary; diseased meat was sold. The packers opposed bitterly the necessary inspection to secure wholesome meat. The public was of no consequence as compared with increased gain. Meat inspection was so strongly resisted that the law as finally enacted by Congress was only gotten through by the government taking upon itself the cost of the inspection.

The public sacrificed for gain.

Even to the present time there is determined resistance by some manufacturers to the execution of the laws, and pressure is brought to bear upon the Department of Agriculture to suspend or modify its rulings. Other wiser and more public-spirited manufacturers are cheerfully conforming, indeed assisting, in the enforcement of the pure food laws. In general the revolution has taken place and a new situation exists. This being so, it seems almost unthinkable that the nation was allowed to be exploited for so long a time by the unscrupulous manufacturers who wished to gain through deceit at the expense of the public.

Section 4

THE CREATION OF TRADE COMMISSIONS

Following the inductive method, and taking steps in advance with the greatest care only as justified by the experience of the past, is not the conclusion inevitable from the evidence presented in the previous section that the machinery which has been applied so successfully to the control of public service corporations and to the control of quality so far as essential articles are concerned, should be applied to the great industrial corporations? The failure of the competitive system for the adequate control of the price and service for public utilities and quality for manufactures cannot be gainsaid.

Control by trade commissions.

The thesis is presented that commissions should be created to control industrial corporations affected with a public interest just as they now control the public service corporations, as they control quality in industry.

That some method of administrative control for the combinations must be created is shown by the case of the American Tobacco Company, in which the inferior court in coöperation with the Attorney-General undertook extraordinary administrative work of a new kind and to which the court is not adapted. (See pp. 183–187.) Regarding the dissolution of the American Tobacco Company, the Attorney-General said the problems involved were economic rather than legal. He adds: "But neither the courts nor the department of justice is properly equipped to work out such problems save in exceptional cases." He points out that in the particular instance in which a complex economic duty was imposed upon the court, it so happened that the Bureau of Corporations had made an elaborate investigation and had the facts in its possession necessary to base a plan for carrying out the decree. The bureau was called upon by the Attor-

Courts not adapted to control.

ney-General for the *extra-official* duty of advising him regarding the manner of disintegration.

The Attorney-General suggested that the duty of the bureau might be enlarged so as to include investigations and reports upon plans for disintegration of monopolistic combinations, which either voluntarily or by pursuance of decree are adjudged to be in violation of the antitrust act. He further suggested that the bureau might be availed of as the nucleus for "an administrative board under whose supervision consolidations or mergers for lawful purposes might be formed." This proposal is a first step in the direction of that which is herein made that administrative commissions should be created upon which should rest the duty of supervision of combinations which exist in restraint of trade. To combine the duties of the commissions with the courts, as suggested by the Attorney-General, would be most unfortunate; since of necessity the courts must remain the body to which appeals may be made from the commissions. The duties of administrative commissions and the courts should be kept wholly distinct.

Administrative commission.

SECTION 5

PROPOSED MINIMUM AMENDMENTS TO ANTITRUST LAWS

To accomplish control of combinations through administrative commissions, it will be necessary to make the following amendments to the antitrust laws: —

(1) *Business of a Public Interest.* — The law should declare that those industrial organizations, which of themselves are so large as to be affected with a public interest, or which by coöperation control the market, are subject to regulation under the same principles as the public utilities. No one can doubt that the greater corporations are just as much affected by public interest as are the railroads. The United States Steel Corporation, Standard Oil Companies, and the American Sugar Refining Company, each of which produce commodities required by the larger portion of the population, have relations to the public as a whole. This principle has already been recognized by some common law decisions; and, in consequence, one class of business which earlier was regarded as purely

Great corporations public utilities in fact.

private has become a public utility. Elevating grain, as a result of a long contest, was declared to be affected with a public interest, and therefore to be under the same obligations as other public utilities.[1] In the case of Munn *v.* Illinois, Chief Justice White, speaking for the court, said: "Property becomes clothed with a public interest when used in a manner to make it of public consequence, and affect the community at large." Judge Vinje, of Wisconsin, in discussing this matter, summarizes the conclusions of the United States Supreme Court in the following words: "We find that private property or business becomes affected with a public interest when used or carried on in a manner to make it of public consequence, and affect the community at large, and when thus affected such property or business becomes subject to legislative control in all respects necessary to protect the public against dangers, injustice, and oppression."[2]

Great business affects community at large.

Therefore we have but to apply the principle of law already recognized by the United States Supreme Court to businesses which exist in restraint of trade. Indeed, in the case of Oklahoma, this principle has already been embodied into statute law in most comprehensive terms. In that state, whenever any business by reason of its extent or by virtue of monopoly is such as to make it of public consequence or to affect the community at large in reference to supply and demand or price, such business is declared to be a public business and to be under control of the state through the Corporation Commission or by an action in any district court of the state (see p. 195). Thus existing common law and statute law for one state are in accord with the principle here advocated. It remains only to embody the principles enunciated into statute law for the several states and for the nation.

Big business of public interest.

(2) *Coöperation Reasonable.* — The law should define reasonable restraint of trade in such a manner as to permit coöperation. Regarding the extent to which coöperation should be permitted, there will doubtless be difference of opinion;

[1] Munn *v.* Illinois, 94 U. S. 113; Budd *v.* N. Y., 143 U. S. 517.
[2] "The Legal Aspects of Industrial Consolidations," Reports of Wisconsin State Bar Association, Vol. VI, pp. 159–181.

but, as already indicated, the most logical place at which to stop is the point fixed by the common law principle, and declare restraint of trade unreasonable that gets to monopoly. To make the law exact it should declare any corporation which, with its subsidiary companies, controls a definite percentage of the business a monopoly (see p. 227). This is in accordance with the proposal recently made by Mr. W. J. Bryan, who mentions 50 per cent in this connection. The difference between the view of Mr. Bryan and the position taken here is that he apparently regards this regulation alone as sufficient to insure competition, and he believes in the adequacy of the control of business by competition. If the meaning of the court in the decisions regarding Standard Oil and Tobacco are that undue restraint of trade means restraint of trade which extends to monopoly (see pp. 181–187), then the only additional point embodied in the above proposal beyond existing law is that monopoly be definitely defined.

Reasonable coöperation does not permit monopoly.

However, amendments to the law must extend beyond the proportion of business if coöperation be permitted in prices, outputs, etc.; for, as shown by the decisions of the federal and state courts, coöperation, except to a very limited degree as to time and space, is under the ban of the law as it now exists.

In this connection it should be mentioned that it has been proposed as a solution of the problem of combination that the amount of business which one company may control shall be reduced to a relatively small fraction. Some have said that no one corporation should be allowed to produce more than ten per cent of a product. Others would limit the capitalization of a business; and this is another way to accomplish the same purpose.[1] Even if the limitation were severe regarding portion or capitalization, it would still be possible for the corporations to coöperate, secretly or openly, and thus act substantially as a unit. Indeed, at the present time we know that there are many more than ten companies engaged in the same business coöperating in various ways in its control. Therefore the limitation of amount of business alone or of capitalization is wholly futile. If coöperation be permitted,

Futility of limiting corporations to small fraction of business.

[1] Hearings, Senate Interstate Commerce Committee, Part XX, p. 1593.

and that it should be seems to me to have been established, the coöperating units must be under the supervision of some authority in order that the public may secure fair treatment.

(3) *Competition to Remain Free.* — The law should declare any restraint of trade unreasonable which does not permit free competition. While reasonable coöperation should be possible, no coöperation should be permitted which in any way prohibits another person or corporation from freely entering a business. Similarly coöperation of labor should be under the same supervisory authority as coöperating capital.[1]

(4) *Unfair Practices should be Prohibited.* — In the enumeration of unfair practices to be prohibited, there doubtless would be difference of opinion. One enumeration is given, pp. 225–226.

General Statements. — But how are these proposed rules of law, state and national, to be enforced? Clearly, if the argument to this point be sustained, — by the creation of trade commissions, both national and state, an interstate trade commission to control interstate industrial commerce and state commissions to control intrastate commerce. Court procedure would be as futile to secure the enforcement of the above rules of law as it has been with the existing laws; but commissions granted the broad powers to enforce these rules of law, being administrative bodies, able to take action without complaint, and acting on complaint without expense to the complainant, may be reasonably expected successfully to enforce the proposed laws.

It is not necessary again to give in detail the powers which these trade commissions should have, since in general they should be the same for the industries as those already existing for public utilities. (See pp. 233–244.)

These powers should be ample to enforce all the above provisions. Penalties should be provided for violation of the principles enunciated. The findings of a commission should be accepted as *prima facie* evidence of their correctness and

[1] Hearings, Senate Interstate Commerce Committee, Part XIX, S. P. Bush, pp. 1642–1644.

should go into effect at once. In case of appeal to the courts no new facts should be introduced, provided same could have been presented to the commission. If material facts are brought forth, which for any reason could not have been presented to the commission the case should be remanded to the commission for a rehearing. In this way it will be possible to prevent withholding evidence when a case is before the commission in order to get the same into the court.

There is no question that the creation of trade commissions to administer the general principles enacted by Congress and state legislatures would be legal and constitutional. It is to be noted that the principles of law suggested are stated in broad and simple terms, the idea being to leave the formulation of detailed regulations to the commissions. Thus the law should forbid unfair practices, but the specific unfair practices should not be enumerated; this would leave it to the commission to stipulate those practices which are unfair. By this procedure the list of unfair practices and their definitions could be modified from time to time as the exigencies demand; whereas if the unfair practices were enumerated in detail in the statutes, there would be sure to arise situations which are not adequately covered.

Similarly, regarding coöperation, the law should merely prescribe that reasonable coöperation is allowable, and the commission should work out details as to what is permissible under the rule.

Again, under the rule of law laid down by the courts prohibiting monopoly, the matter of deciding whether a given corporation falls under that rule should rest with the commission. Not only so, but if a corporation be found to be a monopoly and therefore to be unreasonably in restraint of trade, the commission should give the orders as to the modifications of the business which are necessary so that the corporation shall cease to be a monopoly. Such orders might go to the extent of disintegration of the existing organization, if the monopoly be such that the public interests cannot be adequately protected without such action.

The above provisions present an irreducible minimum to which the antitrust laws, state and national, must be amended in order to secure freedom of competition, freedom of coöperation, destruction of monopoly, and justice to all. If such a program be adopted, the first conservative fundamental step will have been taken to stop the present perfectly futile attempts to regulate concentration of wealth by destructive litigation, adequately to protect any corporation entering a business, and at the same time, to give protection to the individual and to the public.

It should be noted that the plan to this point permits coöperation to no greater extent than is allowed in England and Germany. Indeed, coöperation in Germany, as is shown by the steel combination, is allowed to go to the extent of monopoly, and in this has the protection of the courts; although if the prices were made so excessive as to excite general complaint, it would be possible for the courts to order a modification of the combination as being contrary to public policy. No disastrous consequences have come in those countries because of the ability of their business men and manufacturers to coöperate. Indeed, there is general agreement in these nations that the gains from coöperation are far greater than the disadvantages of the unrestrained competitive system.

The proposal made does not permit coöperation to go to the extent of monopoly, as is allowed in Germany. Furthermore the coöperation which is allowed to exist in restraint of trade is under the supervision and regulation of an administrative commission, and therefore the proposal made is a much more conservative one regarding recognition of concentration of industry than exists in England and Germany.

Section 6

FURTHER EXTENSION OF POWER OF COMMISSIONS

While the above is a minimum program, adequate grounds can be adduced for further extending the authority of the commissions. If this be done, it will be necessary to enact additional principles into law, which have been mentioned in the specifications, given pp. 225–231, as desirable. The additional points will be enumerated in the order in which they are likely to be acceptable to the public, not in the order of their importance.

(1) *Publicity Required.* — All corporations which exist in restraint of trade should be subject to full publicity. For any one of them the public should know the amount of outstanding stocks and bonds of each class; it should know the physical valuation of the property; it should have full information concerning the conduct of the business, including the amount of the profits which goes for improvements, depreciation, sinking fund, and dividends. In short, for each corporation allowed to coöperate with others, the public should have full knowledge of all of the facts necessary to pass a judgment upon the nature, extent, and effects of its business.

If this principle be agreed to, the requisite amendment to the antitrust laws should include another clause stating in broad terms that the commission has full power of investigations, including access to the books of the company, with authority to make public any facts concerning the business which are regarded by the commission as having a public interest.

(2) *Regulation of Prices.* — While the above provisions will make a great advance over the present situation, it is by no means certain that they are sufficient to protect the public in the matter of fair prices. Turning again to the commissions regulating public utilities: they were first given various powers regarding service, publicity, etc.; but the public was never adequately protected until they had authority to regulate prices, not the responsibility of fixing prices, but the authority to order modification of prices upon complaint or by their own initiative. I am aware that at this point there will be great difference of opinion; therefore I have carefully refrained from including it as an essential part of the proposed remedial plan. But it is inevitable that sooner or later the logic of events will demand

that the rule of law be made that all coöperating corporations which control the market shall charge reasonable prices. Under this simple rule of law the commission will be directed to see that such reasonable prices be maintained. If this principle can be agreed to, the situation is adequately covered; for if an unreasonable price be charged, the commission will have authority to fix maximum and minimum prices as is required to make the price reasonable.

Reasonable prices must be maintained.

In justification of this principle it may be said all that it is necessary to do is to apply the practice of the past concerning monopoly prices to the present situation and to place the enforcement of this rule of law with the commission rather than the court. In early historical times, indeed until the nineteenth century, transportation was so poorly developed, that it was possible to have monopoly in a relatively small area. Even in a township or county, the difficulties in transportation were sometimes such that it was not easy to carry needed articles from one place to another, and an individual, or two or three individuals, might have monopoly for some product essential to the community. Under these circumstances, it was wholly natural that the control of monopoly should have been a function of the state — it was so under Roman law and under the common law of England. Control went so far as to regulate prices. This was very common in Rome. In England, prices were fixed by law at different times for many commodities; among these were books, beer barrels, coal, wheat, rye, bread, and labor. In Massachusetts the revised laws of 1649 limited the prices of wages, freight, ferryage, mill tolls, wharfage. In both Massachusetts and New York the scale of wages was fixed for farm laborers, mechanics, and teamsters. Many other illustrations of fixing prices could be given.

Fixing of price in early times.

These laws show with perfect clearness that the public has a right to a fair price; that in this matter as in others "the welfare of the people is a supreme law." Whenever it becomes advisable for the welfare of the people that the state authority be invoked to regulate prices, this may be done. The question of so doing is merely one of expediency.

The right of state regulation of prices is beyond question.[1] It has merely been suspended for a time because inexpedient to exercise it.

With the modern development of transportation, it became more difficult to maintain monopoly; the competitive factor became more important; and it was less necessary for prices to be controlled by regulation. By the beginning of the nineteenth century, with minor exceptions, this country had gone over to the theory of the regulation of prices by competition. As we have seen, during the nineteenth century we had a period in which the system of letting everybody alone, of freedom of competition, was our faith. If we could only get free competition, we believed, we should have the remedy for our ills, so far as prices were concerned.

Regulation of prices by competition.

But as we have seen with the great development of transportation and concurrent concentration of industry during the latter half of the nineteenth century and especially during the last twenty-five years, conditions have recurred for large sections of the country similar to those which obtained in the smaller community during the early history of the nation. The factors which have led to such concentration have been discussed, pp. 8–31. Concentration has gone far for all industries; and at the present time for many important commodities has gone to the extent of monopoly, either through a single corporation or by the coöperation of a number of corporations. Staples in which the monopolistic factor clearly enters are steel, sugar, oil, anthracite, beef, tobacco, matches, shoe machinery, electrical appliances, and many others. For some of these commodities a single corporation controls from fifty per cent to as much as ninety per cent of the product.

As has been fully shown (pp. 77–78), not only where monopoly exists, but where there is coöperation far short of

[1] "Government Regulation of Prices," Eugene A. Gilmore, *Green Bag*, 1905. Address before the Illinois State Bar Association, Charles Carroll Bonney, *American Law Review*, Vol. 25.

Excessive prices where there is monopoly.

monopoly so far as any one organization is concerned, prices may be maintained by mutual understanding, without regard to whether such prices are reasonable or unreasonable; simply with reference to the dividends which may be secured by the corporations. It is believed by many, if corporations are made subject to publicity, that they will not dare to charge unreasonable prices; but the public should place no confidence in this conclusion, and therefore should place the power with the commissions to make orders regarding prices in such cases as in fact they are found to be unreasonable.

Excessive profits.

It is safe to say that under court enforcement of laws against trusts and combinations, the prices charged by single companies or companies working in coöperation have been such as to give unreasonably large profits. This has been shown to be true for some of the corporations, facts concerning which are given (pp. 104–150). In order to reinstate the matter in the mind it may be recalled that the Commissioner of Corporations says that in the United States Steel Corporation, upon the actual investment, from April 1, 1901, to December 31, 1910, the profits have been twelve per cent per annum. Since the bonds bear five per cent, this gives a much higher rate of profit than twelve per cent upon that part of the stock which represented substance and not water. The Commissioner says that the earnings have been so great that the company has been able to put back into extensions and improvements, into the sinking fund, and into the treasury together, from the net earnings, the collossal sum of $435,000,000. This is in addition to the dividends which have been declared on the stock, including both substance and water, and the interest on the bonds.[1] Again, the profits of the American Tobacco Company, according to the Commissioner of Corporations, have increased with amazing rapidity, and in 1908 were $40,000,000 upon an investment of $240,000,000, or nearly seventeen per cent. In addition to the net profits declared, enormous

[1] Summary of Report of Commissioner of Corporations on the Steel Industry, Part I, p. 49.

returns have been derived from the inflation of securities.[1] Further, it has been seen, when the element of monopoly entered in the American Sugar Refining Company and the Standard Oil Company, the margins for manufacture were increased so as to give enormous profits. The Commissioner of Corporations says that the dividends of Standard Oil, from 1882 to 1906, averaged above twenty-four per cent, and the profits due to the increased margins were more than $200,000,000. The total profits for three years were about $790,000,000 upon an investment of not more than $75,000,000. Thus in fifteen years the profits have been more than ten times the capital originally invested.[2]

In view of these and similar facts regarding other corporations, it seems unsafe to believe, if coöperation be permitted, that the corporations will have so great a change of heart as to treat the public fairly. If coöperation be permitted, with this must go control, else the public will be without protection. It is perfectly clear under modern conditions that the determination of prices by legislation is an impossible task. However, as already indicated, under the clear legislative right to control prices, Congress and state legislatures may enact the rule that prices shall be reasonable, and authorize administrative commissions to regulate prices under this rule. The reserve power to require modification of unreasonable prices should be placed with the commissions.

With coöperation must go control.

In this connection it is notable, for the potash industry in Germany, where complete monopoly is allowed, that this industry is placed under control of a commission with authority to regulate prices. Therefore, at the present time in Germany the plan of regulating prices by commission is in operation for one industry.

It may be said that the burden of controlling prices will be so great that it cannot be performed by commissions. Precisely the same statements were made regarding rail-

[1] Report of the Commissioner of Corporations on the Tobacco Industry, Part II, pp. 310–313

[2] Report of the Commissioner of Corporations on the Petroleum Industry, Part II, p. iv.

roads when it was proposed to control prices of public utilities by commission. It may be asserted, without fear of successful contradiction, that there is no problem of adjustment of prices more difficult than that of freight rates. Different rates apply to different classes of commodities; rates are variable under different conditions of shipment, such as quantity, distance, etc. Furthermore in fixing the price on freight it must be made reasonable; and this can only be determined by finding the valuation of the enormously complex and variable class of railroad properties, taking into account the extremely complicated business operations. Notwithstanding these difficulties, which by the railroad men were declared to be absolutely insuperable and impossible to perform except by the experienced railroad man, the commissions have been, if not wholly successful, at least reasonably so. Therefore, the arguments regarding the impracticability of regulating prices by commission falls to the ground. It is not to be presumed that every price would be regulated all of the time; quite the contrary; only exceptionally would prices be regulated by the commissions. Whenever a complaint is made that the market is controlled and a price is unjust, then a commission would investigate and make an appropriate order; or if a commission reached the conclusion that a case needed investigation, it could do this on its own initiative.

Control of prices a practical problem.

It should be emphasized that it is not proposed that the commission shall have the power to regulate all prices, but only this power where there is monopoly or the market is controlled through coöperation. Also a commission need go no farther in a given case than to fix a maximum price or a minimum price, or both, as may be required by the situation, leaving competition to regulate further within the prescribed limits. As at present, competition would remain the sole regulative of prices in the vast number of instances where the market is not controlled. These qualifications enormously simplify the task of the commissions.

Maximum and minimum prices.

The very fact that the commissions have authority to regulate prices, when they become unreasonably high or unreasonably low, would act as an important restraining force upon those controlling the market and tend to keep prices reasonable, and thus reduce the number of cases in which it would be necessary for the commissions to act. This power of the commissions, we know, has been a restraining influence with the railroads; it will be a restraining influence in preventing unreasonable prices if extended to the industries.

Thus, so far as we can foresee, the task of the commissions, which to some men seems dreadful, will in all probability turn out, as a matter of fact, just as with the railroad commissions, practicable. The misconceptions which arise in connection with controlling prices may be illustrated by statements made by Mr. William B. Hornblower.[1] He says it means "the right to control the prices of the necessaries of life to the ultimate consumer. What the average American and his wife and children shall eat and drink and wherewithal they shall be clothed depend upon the prices to be paid for such necessaries of life." Apparently Mr. Hornblower is appalled by the dread of the catastrophe; but who fixes the prices of these necessities now? The gigantic corporations certainly in large measure. It seems plain that the public would be safer if some organization, having responsibility to it, had a part in the process. The situation will, as a matter of fact, be substantially as it is at present, in the initial fixing of prices. The most that is proposed is that, whenever the market is controlled for any commodity, a commission fix maximum and minimum prices from time to time when prices are found not in accordance with the rule of reason.

Control of price by corporation or commission.

We may return to a state of subdivision of industry in which the economics of concentration are not available, and depend upon competition to control prices. If it were possible to secure "tolerant" competition, to use a phrase which has been proposed, under these conditions it is probable that the prices would be higher than they are with concentration, even with coöperation and without control.

[1] "Antitrust Legislation and Litigation," pp. 35 and 36.

That we can return to such a condition contrary to the world-wide tendency is extremely improbable, almost unthinkable. The other alternative is to have large units; if we have large units, coöperation becomes inevitable; and with concentration and coöperation the prices unregulated will become unduly high. The only protection for the public is regulation in some way; and such regulation is best accomplished through a commission which has authority to place maximum and minimum prices at reasonable levels. This situation has been very clearly seen by Attorney-General Wickersham. He says: "If we permit the existence of organizations or combinations of producers under such conditions that they can fix prices, there is no means of securing justice to the consumer except through the government's asserting its right to step in and dictate prices, or at least to require that they shall not be raised above reasonable limits." [1]

Regulation the only way.

It has been repeatedly asserted that the proposal to give commissions authority to order prices to be changed, when found unreasonable, is socialism. Precisely the same statements were made when it was proposed to give the railroad commissions similar powers a few years ago. Socialism to the extreme conservative means anything with which he does not agree; but the meaning of socialism is the taking over and management of property by the state.

Regulation not socialism.

The plan presented does not involve taking over property or its management. Indeed, it does not involve anything whatever except securing to the public a reasonable price in the same manner that reasonable prices have been secured from the public utilities, the only way in which it has been found practicable to do this. It is probably the only satisfactory way in which fair prices can be secured from the great industrial corporations. Under the plan proposed the industrial concentrations remain private property in charge of those who own them just as at present. Being granted the privilege of coöperation in restraint of trade, they are forbidden to take advantage of the public by charging unrea-

[1] *Century Magazine*, Vol. LXXXIII, No. 4, p. 619.

sonable prices; and if forbidden so to charge, there must be some organism which will enforce the prohibition. The prohibition probably could be enforced by lawsuit under common law; and therefore the proposal made simply gives to an efficient administrative body authority to do what the courts probably have power to do under the common law, but which they could not efficiently perform. Those who hold up the bogy of socialism because of the modest proposal to allow commissions to regulate prices, if they reflect, must conclude that they have only a bogy.

(3) *Conservation Enforced.* — It should be made unlawful for any person, firm, or corporation unreasonably to waste or maliciously to injure, destroy, or impair any natural resource. This rule has been made a statute in Wisconsin.[1] Upon the commissions should be imposed the duty of requiring the enforcement of this rule for all corporations which exist in restraint of trade. Under this simple regulation the major portion of the great wastes of the natural resources under the competitive system (described pp. 89–97), so disastrous to the future of the race, could be prevented. The unnecessary and unreasonable wastes never will be prevented under the competitive system; indeed, they are compelled under that system. Regulation of the kind proposed is likely to be of little avail if enforced only by the courts. But, if any case of unnecessary waste of a natural resource by any corporation can be brought to the knowledge of a commission by an individual, and the commission is thereby compelled to investigate the same and give appropriate, reasonable orders, we may expect that progress will be made in the protection of our natural resources.

Unnecessary wastes prevented.

Preventing unnecessary waste of a natural resource may somewhat raise the price of certain articles because of the increased cost of so conducting the business as to give this result. Indeed, it is certain in coal mining and in various other industries, that if as large economies as practicable be secured, there will be slight increases in prices. In such cases, if it be necessary for the future welfare of the race,

[1] Ch. 143, Laws of 1911.

this generation should be willing to bear the small additional expense.

(4) *Good Social Conditions Securable.* — The rule of law may be laid down that corporations which exist in restraint of trade shall conduct their business in accordance with good social conditions. Under this rule the administrative commissions would have power to formulate reasonable regulations in these respects and to enforce them. From the point of view of many, the possibility of introducing reasonable social conditions for the labor force of great corporations will be one of the greatest arguments in favor of commission supervision. To others this will seem to be going very far; but it is certain under the competitive system that the social conditions for labor are very unsatisfactory. The mining industry is extremely hazardous. Many of the great manufacturers press their labor to the limit, and this under dangerous conditions.[1] To introduce safe and sanitary conditions will involve greater expense in production. Under commission regulations the necessary additional expense may be compelled, and the additional price warranted may be allowed by the commissions. Like other regulations which have been suggested, that regarding social conditions stands upon its own merits; is not a necessary part of the plan to remedy the most pressing evils of the competitive and court system of control of industry.

(5) *Fair Wages Realizable.* — If desirable, the rule of law may be laid down that corporations doing business in restraint of trade shall pay fair wages. If this rule be adopted, again it would rest upon the commissions in cases of complaint to determine what are fair wages under the conditions which exist in a given instance. Like other suggestions under consideration, this is not an essential part of the plan of control, but it is believed to be one of the advantages which may in the future accrue from it.

When the author wrote the preceding it seemed somewhat radical even to him; but since that time in England,

[1] Hearings, Senate Interstate Commerce Committee, Part XXVI, p. 2322; Investigation U. S. Steel Corporation, pp. 2835–3152; 3255–3454.

a country commonly spoken of in America as conservative, Parliament has enacted a law establishing the principle of a minimum wage for coal miners, under which local boards each fix such wages for its district. This is a definite recognition by statute that wages must be paid which are adequate to furnish at least a livelihood, even if upon a somewhat low scale. Probably there will be a wide difference between the minimum wage of England and a fair wage in this country, but the principle involved in each is the same.

(6) *Control of Capitalization.* — If advisable, the law may lay down rules controlling the issue of stocks and bonds in order to prevent overcapitalization and stock manipulation. This subject, however, is one of such complexity that the author does not venture to formulate a rule of law to cover it. An appreciation of the difficulty of so doing may be gained by referring to the report of the Railroad Securities Commission upon stocks and bonds of railroads.[1] The same principles which apply to the railroads apply to a large extent, if not altogether, to the great industrial corporations.

(7) *Delimitation of Powers of State and Nation.* — A clear rule of law should be formulated regarding the limits of interstate commerce. The early decisions under the Sherman act inclined toward narrowly construing the power of Congress. The later decisions of the court have gone much farther, and it now looks as if the United States Supreme Court would sustain the position that Congress has the right to control all businesses in which any part is interstate in character. This seems the only logical place at which to stop. If this position be accepted, the necessary federal commissions would have under their regulation corporations having any interstate business. The state commissions would have the authority to deal with those businesses which are strictly within the states. This would include a vast field, for instance, practically all of the retail business of the country; not only so, but the vast numbers of small manufactories in various lines, and in

[1] Report Railroad Securities Commission, Washington, D.C., 1911.

many cases the coöperation of laborers and professional men.[1]

General Statements. — We have now covered the specifications given on pp. 225–231 relating to what is desirable to accomplish by amending the antitrust legislation. A bill must first be passed covering the essential points mentioned, (1) to (4), pp. 249–252. If this can be accomplished, the existing futile and exasperating situation will cease to exist. Justice will be equally obtainable by all. The frightful wastes of the competitive system will, in a measure at least, cease. The business men may coöperate, and thus be able to carry on their business without becoming criminals under the law. Monopoly will not be permitted. Competition will remain open.

With these essentials accomplished the advantages of the additional proposed rules of law, (1) to (6), pp. 255–265, may be introduced as fast as practicable. Regarding some of them, possibly a consensus of opinion of the lawmakers may soon be reached; but if this does not prove to be true, they may be added from time to time, as justified by experience and demanded by public opinion.

Section 7

OTHER PLANS FOR AMENDMENT TO SHERMAN ANTI-TRUST LAW

The plan above proposed for handling the existing situation in this country concerning concentration of industry is not necessarily contradictory to, but may be regarded as supplementary of, a number of other plans which have been proposed.

Federal registration or license, federal incorporation, and federal tax have all been suggested. Senator Newlands[2] would permit all corporations that comply with definite regulations, including publicity, engaged in interstate commerce,

[1] See Senator Newlands, Hearings, Senate Interstate Commerce Committee, Part XIX, p. 1598.

[2] Hearings, Senate Interstate Commerce Committee, Part I, pp. 1–4.

doing a gross business of more than $1,000,000 per annum, to have federal registration, which registration would grant certain privileges. Low [1] would require a federal license for all corporations having $2,000,000 of assets or paid up capital. Mr. Elbert H. Gary and Mr. George W. Perkins [2] also favor a license system for corporations doing an interstate or international business. Untermeyer [3] would require every corporation engaged in interstate commerce, having gross assets of $1,000,000 or more, to secure federal incorporation. Low [4] and Wickersham [5] would permit, but would not require, federal incorporation.

The industrial commission proposed a franchise tax upon corporations in proportion to the actual value of stocks and bonded debts less the local assessment on the real estate, and in addition a graded tax upon the incomes of the corporations.[6] An allied proposal is that of an increasing tax upon the capital of corporations. Thus W. S. Dwinnell,[7] of Minneapolis, suggests "a graded annual tax upon the capital of every corporation engaged in interstate commerce, whose capital exceeds a certain amount." Senator Newlands makes a similar suggestion.[8]

Another class of proposals is in the direction of limitation of corporate powers. Some men would altogether prohibit holding corporations from engaging in interstate commerce. Among these is Mr. Seth Low.[9] He thinks the evils of holding companies are such that this class of corporation should no longer exist. According to his idea, each company should be independent. This would require the disintegration of a great many companies or their complete merger. Others have argued that one corporation should not hold any stock in any other corporation in any way whatsoever. A number of men have taken this position before the Interstate Commerce Committee. Some men would not go

[1] Hearings, Senate Interstate Commerce Committee, Part XVI, p. 520.
[2] *Ibid.*, XXVI, pp. 2407–2412 ; XV, p. 1091.
[3] *Ibid.*, Part XVI, pp. 487, 488.
[4] *Ibid.*, Part V, p. 19.
[5] *The Century Magazine*, Vol. LXXXIII, pp. 619–620.
[6] U. S. Industrial Commission, Vol. XIX, pp. 1067–1068.
[7] Hearings, Senate Interstate Commerce Committee, Part III, p. 90.
[8] *Ibid.*, Part VIII, p. 482.
[9] *Ibid.*, Part IX, p. 488.

so far as to prohibit holding companies, but would require that the voting power of stocks owned by holding companies should be eliminated. Here is included Mr. Frederick W. Kelsey.[1] Still others would place a limitation upon community of directors so as to make sure that companies, apparently independent, are really so. Among these are Mr. Louis Brandeis.[2]

None of these proposals will be argued. Each must stand upon its own merits and justify itself if it is to be adopted by Congress and the state legislatures. None of these proposals interfere with the plan which has been suggested. If it seems advisable to do any of these things either by independent act or as additional amendments to the antitrust laws, this may be done without interfering in any way with any of the proposals made by the author on previous pages.

However, it is notable, that a number of those who have suggested the above measures desire to place their execution as well as the execution of the Sherman antitrust act with an administrative commission. Among these are Newlands,[3] Untermeyer,[4] Low,[5] and Perkins.[6] Further, in some cases the proposals have gone so far as to include the regulation of prices; for instance, Untermeyer would lay down the rule that the maximum price which may be chargeable "does not allow an undue profit."

Section 8

PATENT MONOPOLY [7]

There is another important problem in connection with combinations in restraint of trade which has not been considered. This is patent monopoly. Many of the businesses in restraint of trade are so in large measure because they

[1] Hearings, Senate Interstate Commerce Committee, Part XVII, p. 1364.
[2] *Ibid.*, Part XVI, p. 1179.
[3] *Ibid.*, Part I, pp. 1, 2.
[4] *Ibid.*, Part IX, pp. 487, 488.
[5] *Ibid.*, Part IX, p. 520.
[6] *Ibid.*, Part XV, p. 1102.
[7] For full information regarding the patent situation, see Hearings before the Committee on Judiciary, House of Representatives, 1912, Patent Legislation, Series No. 1.

own patents. The very idea of a patent is monopoly. Under the new conditions of consolidation the patent monopoly has taken an entirely new aspect. The great manufacturing corporations, such as the General Electric Company, the United States Shoe Machinery Company, and the National Cash Register Company, have acquired a large part of the patents which affect their businesses. Some of these they have used; others they have simply acquired to prevent use by others. A combination of patents under one ownership, as compared with a single patent, has produced a situation regarding patents somewhat analagous to that which arose when partnerships of corporations were formed from corporations, by means of the device of trusts. The vast importance of this question of patent monopoly has become even more clear through a recent decision of the Supreme Court of the United States.[1] Previous decisions have made it clear that the patentee may restrict the time, place, or manner in which a patented machine may be used. The recent decision of the court, however, goes farther than this in that it is held that restrictions may be made regarding other things necessary for the use of the patented article, even if such things are not patented. Chief Justice White and Justices Hughes and Lamar strongly dissent from this opinion. They hold this principle to be dangerous and give as illustrations of these dangers the following. The quotations are from the Chief Justice:—

The danger of combining patents.

"Take a patentee selling a patented engine. We will now have the right by contract to bring under the patent laws all contracts for coal or electrical energy used to afford power to work the machine or even the lubricants employed in its operation. Take a patented carpenter's plane. The power now exists in the patentee by contract to validly confine a carpenter purchasing one of the planes to the use of lumber sawed from trees grown on the land of a particular person or sawed by a particular mill. Take a patented cooking utensil. The power is now recognized in the patentee to bind by con-

[1] Henry et al. *v.* A. B. Dick Company, U. S. Supreme Court, 20, October Term, 1911.

tract one who buys the utensil to use in connection with it no other food supply but that sold or made by the patentee. Take the invention of a patented window frame. It is now the law that the seller of a frame may stipulate that no other material shall be used in a house in which the window frames are placed except such as may be bought from the patentee and seller of the frame. Take an illustration which goes home to every one — a patented sewing-machine. It is now established that by putting on the machine, in addition to the notice of patent required by law, a notice called a license restriction, the right is acquired, as against the whole world, to control the purchase by users of the machine of thread, needles, and oil lubricants or other materials convenient or necessary for operation of the machine.

"My mind cannot shake off the dread of the vast extension of such practices which must come from the decision of the court now rendered. Who, I submit, can put a limit upon the extent of monopoly and wrongful restriction which will arise, especially if by such a power a contract which otherwise would be void as against public policy may be successfully maintained?"

It is clear that the situation is such that the patent laws under the new conditions will require amendments to protect the public. However, this matter lies outside of the scope of this book. It is mentioned because so closely related to that under consideration; indeed, for many concentrations of industry, patents have been the basis upon which monopoly has been secured.

Section 9

POSSIBLE OBJECTIONS TO PLAN OF REGULATION PROPOSED

In order that the remedial plan proposed may be fairly before the readers of this book, the writer will now consider some objections which may possibly be raised regarding it.

(1) It may be said that the commission form of regulation is new and untried; that the great corporations desirous

of controlling the commissions will be too powerful for them; and that the public will not be protected. In the minds of many, this will be a serious objection to the proposals made; and the danger is one which must be especially guarded against. One of these guards should be that all of the business of a commission should be open. The complaint made, the conduct of a case, the facts brought out, the reasoning relating to the facts, and the conclusion reached should all be made public. In short, in order that the people shall be protected, there should be the same publicity in the actions of a commission as is now demanded regarding the actions of a corporation. In time, methods of public bookkeeping will be developed and rules formulated to guide the commissions in their work and thus enable them to perform their duties, notwithstanding the great pressure which may be brought to bear upon them.

Public must hold commission accountable.

If it be desirable, a further precaution may be inserted similar to that which exists concerning commissions in Europe. Upon the request of a certain number of senators or representatives of Congress or of state legislators a commission may be summoned before the creating legislative body and be required to give answers to written interrogatories and be interrogated regarding any matter which is before the commission. Further, if the above are not sufficient to guard the public interest, provision may be made that any member of a commission may be removed for cause by the President or governor, or by Congress or legislature upon the passage of a joint resolution. By these various methods the public may be amply protected against any failure of a commission to perform its duty.

While there is the possible danger on one side that the powerful interests will control, on the other side there will be the fear by the corporations that the commissions will go too far and raid property. But on this side there is adequate protection under the Constitution, since from the commission there is appeal to the courts; and the courts under the 14th amendment are obliged to prevent the confiscation of property. If on both sides there be fear of the power of trade commissions, it may be regarded as probable that a judicial balance will be maintained.

While the early experience in this country with commissions for control of railroads was not especially encouraging, the experience we have had with the railroad commissions later appointed, especially illustrated by that of Wisconsin, and by the Interstate Commerce Commission, since it has been given adequate authority, is very hopeful.

Doubtless difficulties will appear in connection with the administrative work of the commissions; but these do not seem likely to be nearly so serious as those which confront us if the Sherman act is invoked to destroy great concentrations in industry to the extent that will be necessary in order to return to adequate control of prices through competition.

(2) It may be said that the greater corporations will destroy the smaller corporations in the same business. The experience of other countries where coöperation is permitted gives no just ground for this conclusion. We have seen in this country under the competitive system and under severe laws against combination, that many small corporations have been destroyed. Upon the other hand, in England and in Germany, where the various corporations have been allowed to coöperate, while there has also been a strong tendency to consolidation, the concentration has not gone nearly so far as in America. Also the smaller competitors in most cases have been made a useful part of the coöperative or consolidated system rather than destroyed.

(3) If the amendments include the regulation of prices, it may be said that it will be especially difficult to control prices in those industries where the corporations do not manage the business from the source to the final product. As we have seen, the United States Steel Corporation handles its materials from the ore, limestone, and coal to the finished product. In such a case the problem of controlling prices is easier than the control of the prices of freight. But in cases illustrated by tobacco, beef, sugar, and oil, the combination is a buyer as well as a seller. In such an instance if

the corporation too greatly depresses the price of its supply, the product will not be furnished. In the long run, if the farmers do not get a fair price, they will not produce beef cattle nor tobacco; they will raise something else.

Cannot unduly depress prices.

This is illustrated by the beet sugar industry. For any district the purchase of beets by the sugar factory corporation is a practical monopoly, because transportation is so expensive for the heavy product, beets, that they cannot go to distant factories. This being the situation, the farmer will not plant beets unless he knows in advance the price he will receive. The sugar corporations are obliged to offer a price for beets which will induce the farmers to raise a sufficient supply for the adjacent factory. If the price offered is not sufficient, the factory will lack material for its run.

As we have seen, pp. 148–149, there is little complaint that the American Sugar Refining Company has unduly depressed the price of raw sugar. It has been charged that the packers at different times have unduly depressed the price of beef cattle; but if this practice existed, it has largely ceased, for it is now realized by the combination that it must maintain a reasonable price for beef, cattle, hogs, sheep, etc., in order to secure a sufficient amount of raw material through the years. The farmers will only permanently raise material for this industry when it is not as profitable to them as other products.

Precisely the same principle applies to tobacco. While undoubtedly there have been causes for complaint against the American Tobacco Company, if this organization had been allowed to continue permanently, it is certain that it would have been obliged to be fair and reasonable in prices paid for the raw material; otherwise, the combination would not be able to secure a sufficient amount to meet the demands.

For many years the great monopolistic company, Standard Oil, bought by far the larger portion of the crude oil for its refineries from hundred of sellers. In the early days of Standard Oil there was complaint regarding depression of prices; but for many years the prices paid by the Standard have been sufficient to induce drillers to search for and obtain sufficient oil to supply the market. Indeed, there has been upon the whole an oversupply, which, from the point of view of conservation, is a detriment to the nation. So long as the prices paid for a natural resource produced from the interior of the earth are sufficient to supply the market not only in this country, but for a large part of the world, this is evidence that the price of the raw material has not been unduly depressed.

The principle which applies to the above commodities applies to all commodities in which the corporations are buyers as well as sellers. While there may have been occasion for complaint from time to time, probably the producers of raw products for the great corporations have had as equitable prices as are ordinarily secured for those commodities concerning which unrestrained competition completely controls.

In further answer to the statement that there will be cause for complaint regarding prices paid for materials by the great corporations, it may be said that if prices at which the products of the combinations are sold, are subject to control of commissions and profits cannot be excessive, there will be no strong motive to depress unduly the purchase prices of the materials which must be bought. Indeed, it is a probable advantage of the plan proposed that fair and reasonably uniform prices will be secured for the products needed by the combinations.

(4) It may be said under the plan in which prices are held at a reasonable level that the income on the bonds and stocks of a corporation, so far as they are substance, not water, will be guaranteed; and, therefore, an organization will rest on its laurels, and progress will be stayed. The answer to this objection is that the proposal made eliminates only competition in prices; it does not interfere with competition in service (see p. 75). If a ton of freight be shipped from New York to Chicago, it makes no difference what road is used; the rate is the same. But has competition ceased between the railways running between New York and Chicago? On the contrary, it is of the keenest. The agents of these roads are everywhere soliciting business, explaining advan-

tages, promising to put through freight promptly. Similarly, for passenger service; the speeds have been increased; new steel cars have been introduced; more trains are run. In many ways the service is becoming safer, more reliable, convenient, and satisfactory. Why is this true when prices are the same? Because the road which makes most progress and is most efficient will do more business, and be able to pay a larger profit than its competitors. Those who know the facts appreciate how keen is the competition between the New York Central and Pennsylvania systems; each has done its best to increase and extend its facilities in order to get the largest possible proportion of business.

At this point we see a fatal defect of another proposal which has been made regarding combinations, viz., that prices be controlled through limiting profits or dividends.[1] This proposal would stifle competition in business, and hence progress; because, if an organization be sufficiently efficient so that it gives just the returns allowed, five or six per cent on its bonds, and seven per cent on the stock, why do anything more? Hence the proposal to control the trusts by limiting incomes and dividends is economically fallacious. The corporation which is efficiently managed should pay a higher dividend than the poorly managed concern. Indeed, in Boston the gas company is allowed to pay higher dividends in proportion as it lowers the price of gas. The commissions may find it advantageous to use this principle and thus give strong inducements for high efficiency.

Controlling profits or dividends unsound economically.

Therefore, it is insisted that the plan advocated does not do away with competition in service. It does not interfere with technical improvements, as held by Clark;[2] it does not interfere with the installation of cost accounting, nor any of the advantages of the competitive system, except competition in prices; and, as already seen, competition in prices is far from an unqualified gain.

(5) It may be objected to the proposal to allow concentra-

[1] Professor J. Laurence Laughlin, Hearings, United States Senate Interstate Commerce Committee, Part XIV, p. 1000.

[2] *Ibid.*, Part XIV, p. 972.

tion and industrial coöperation that this will result in putting the major portion of the money for the great lines of business in a few centers; in short that it will promote the so-called money trust. Indeed, this objection has been made regarding large concentrations of industry by Mr. Brandeis.[1]

Banking reform.

The reform of our banking system is a question to be handled by separate legislation. We already have a report by the Aldrich Monetary Commission upon improvements of the banking system of this country, which admittedly is far behind that of other great industrial nations. Many other plans have been proposed. Our banking system is now being investigated by Congress and is the subject of special study by the National Citizens' League for the Promotion of a Sound Banking System. As to what should be done to improve the situation in banking, the author will venture no opinion; but he insists that this problem is one which of necessity must be solved by special laws and independently of the general plans for conducting industry.

Numerous commissions may be necessary.

(6) It may be said that the plan for regulating all concentrations and coöperations in industry which go to the point of controlling the market will create a great series of commissions, national and state. This is undoubtedly the fact. It may well be in the future that in addition to an interstate trade commission, which has the position in industry of a supreme commission, there may be subordinate to it another class of commissions to which must first go certain questions exactly as law cases commonly first go to district and circuit courts. In the states, it is probable that a single commission with its scientific staff of experts will be sufficient to handle the business that will come before it; but if necessary, there may be created in the states two classes of commissions precisely as there is more than one class of courts. Certainly whatever cost is necessary in order to relieve the present chaotic condition of affairs and to secure justice and development, that cost is justified.

(7) It may be said that the plan proposed provides no method of punishment for those who have violated the

[1] Hearings, Senate Interstate Commerce Committee, Part XVI, p. 1189.

national and state laws against restraint of trade. The answer is that there is nothing in the proposals made which relieves any individual or corporation from the sins of the past. Some men believe that those who have violated the trust laws, and especially those who have engaged in the grosser unfair practices, should not escape punishment. Upon this point the author has merely to say that he is far more interested in the future than in the past. The proposals which have been made are for the future. They leave the question of punishment of individuals for violation of existing laws to be settled by the good sense of the community. It may be that there will be advantage in punishing some of those who have indulged in the more outrageous forms of unfair practices. When in the future we have rational laws with administrative commissions to enforce them, we shall have a situation for industrial corporations like that we now have for the railroads. There will be comparatively few who will violate the laws, and it will be possible to punish those who do violate them.

Shall the guilty escape?

Section 10

CONCLUSION

In conclusion there is presented as the solution of the difficulties of the present industrial situation, concentration, coöperation, and control. Through concentration we may have the economic advantages coming from magnitude of operations. Through coöperation we may limit the wastes of the competitive system. Through control by commission we may secure freedom for fair competition, elimination of unfair practices, conservation of our natural resources, fair wages, good social conditions, and reasonable prices.

Concentration and coöperation in industry in order to secure efficiency are a world-wide movement. The United States cannot resist it. If we isolate ourselves and insist upon the subdivision of industry below the highest economic efficiency and do not allow coöperation, we shall be defeated in the world's markets. We cannot adopt an economic system less efficient than our great competitors, Germany, England, France, and Austria. Either we must modify our present obsolete laws regarding concentration and coöperation so as to conform with the world movement, or else fall behind in the race for the world's markets. Concentration and coöperation are conditions imperatively essential for industrial advance; but if we allow concentration and coöperation, there must be control in order to protect the people, and adequate control is only possible through the administrative commission. Hence, concentration, coöperation, and control are the key words for a scientific solution of the mighty industrial problem which now confronts this nation.

APPENDIX

THE SHERMAN ANTITRUST LAW

[Act of July 2, 1890 (26 Stat., 209)]

AN ACT to protect trade and commerce against unlawful restraints and monopolies.

Be it enacted by the Senate and House of Representatives of the United States of America in Congress assembled,

SEC. 1. Every contract, combination in the form of trust or otherwise, or conspiracy, in restraint of trade or commerce among the several States, or with foreign nations, is hereby declared to be illegal. Every person who shall make any such contract or engage in any such combination or conspiracy, shall be deemed guilty of a misdemeanor, and, on conviction thereof, shall be punished by fine not exceeding five thousand dollars, or by imprisonment not exceeding one year, or by both said punishments, in the discretion of the court.

SEC. 2. Every person who shall monopolize, or attempt to monopolize, or combine or conspire with any other person or persons, to monopolize any part of the trade or commerce among the several States, or with foreign nations, shall be deemed guilty of a misdemeanor, and, on conviction thereof, shall be punished by fine not exceeding five thousand dollars, or by imprisonment not exceeding one year, or by both said punishments, in the discretion of the court.

SEC. 3. Every contract, combination in form of trust or otherwise, or conspiracy, in restraint of trade or commerce in any Territory of the United States or of the District of Columbia, or in restraint of trade or commerce between any such Territory and another, or between any such Territory or

Territories and any State or States or the District of Columbia, or with foreign nations, or between the District of Columbia and any State or States or foreign nations, is hereby declared illegal. Every person who shall make any such contract or engage in any such combination or conspiracy, shall be deemed guilty of a misdemeanor, and, on conviction thereof, shall be punished by fine not exceeding five thousand dollars, or by imprisonment not exceeding one year, or by both said punishments, in the discretion of the court.

Sec. 4. The several circuit courts of the United States are hereby invested with jurisdiction to prevent and restrain violations of this act; and it shall be the duty of the several district attorneys of the United States, in their respective districts, under the direction of the Attorney-General, to institute proceedings in equity to prevent and restrain such violations. Such proceedings may be by way of petition setting forth the case and praying that such violation shall be enjoined or otherwise prohibited. When the parties complained of shall have been duly notified of such petition the court shall proceed, as soon as may be, to the hearing and determination of the case; and pending such petition and before final decree, the court may at any time make such temporary restraining order or prohibition as shall be deemed just in the premises.

Sec. 5. Whenever it shall appear to the court before which any proceeding under section four of this act may be pending, that the ends of justice require that other parties should be brought before the court, the court may cause them to be summoned, whether they reside in the district in which the court is held or not; and subpœnas to that end may be served in any district by the marshal thereof.

Sec. 6. Any property owned under any contract or by any combination, or pursuant to any conspiracy (and being the subject thereof) mentioned in section one of this act, and being in the course of transportation from one State to another, or to a foreign country, shall be forfeited to the United States, and may be seized and condemned by like proceedings as those provided by law for the forfeiture, seizure, and condemnation of property imported into the United States contrary to law.

Sec. 7. Any person who shall be injured in his business or property by any other person or corporation by reason of anything forbidden or declared to be unlawful by this act, may sue therefor in any circuit court of the United States in the district in which the defendant resides or is found, without respect to the amount in controversy, and shall recover threefold the damages by him sustained, and the costs of suit, including a reasonable attorney's fee.

Sec. 8. That the word "person," or "persons," wherever used in this act shall be deemed to include corporations and associations existing under or authorized by the laws of either the United States, or the laws of any of the Territories, the laws of any State, or the laws of any foreign country.

APPENDIX II

THE CONGRESSIONAL SITUATION

AN INTERSTATE TRADE COMMISSION

Growth of public sentiment.

SINCE this book was written public sentiment has developed very rapidly in regard to the trust question. The control of corporations through trade commissions therein advocated was at the time of its first imprint favored by few; but the idea has rapidly gained ground. It was placed in the platform of the Progressive Republican party at their convention held in Chicago in June, 1912. During the following campaign the proposal was vigorously opposed by both the Democratic and Republican parties. However, the constructive features of the plan steadily gained in the favor of the country. When President Wilson, on January 20, 1914, sent a message to Congress on the control of the trusts, he had accepted the idea and strongly advocated it. He said:—

Views of President Wilson.

"And the business men of the country desire something more than that the menace of legal process in these matters be made explicit and intelligible. They desire the advice, the definite guidance and information which can be supplied by an administrative body, an interstate trade commission.

"The opinion of the country would instantly approve of such a commission. It would not wish to see it empowered to make terms with monopoly or in any sort to assume control of business, as if the Government made itself responsible. It demands such a commission only as an indispensable instrument of information and publicity, as a clearing house for the facts by which both the public mind and the managers of great business undertakings should be guided, and as an instrumentality for doing justice to business where the processes of the courts or the natural forces of correction outside the courts are inadequate to adjust the remedy to the wrong in a way that will meet all the equities and circumstances of the case.

"Producing industries, for example, which have passed the point up to which combination may be consistent with the public interest and the freedom of trade, cannot always be dissected into their component units as readily as railroad companies or similar organizations can be. Their dissolution by ordinary legal process may oftentimes involve financial consequences likely to overwhelm the security market and bring upon it breakdown and confusion. There ought to be an administrative commission capable of directing and shaping such corrective processes, not only in aid of the courts but also by independent suggestion, if necessary."

More than eighty bills relating to the trusts have been introduced into the 63rd Congress. Many of these provide for an interstate trade commission. Among these were administrative measures introduced into both the House and the Senate. An interstate trade commission bill, the so-called Covington bill (H. R. 15613), passed the House.

The Interstate Commerce Committee of the Senate, to which this bill was sent, reported a substitute. This substitute is supposed to represent the final or semi-final ideas of the administration. The first part of the substitute provides for the creation of a federal trade commission composed of five members. This commission is to take over the duties of the Bureau of Corporations.

The administration bill.

The more important powers of the proposed commission are contained in Sections 3 to 6, inclusive. These sections read as follows: —

"SEC. 3. The commission shall have power among others:

"(*a*) To investigate from time to time, and as often as the commission may deem advisable, the organization, business, financial condition, conduct, practices, and management, of any corporation engaged in commerce, and its relation to other corporations and to individuals, associations, and partnerships.

Broad power of investigation.

"(*b*) To require any corporation subject to the provisions of this Act which the commission may designate to furnish

Corporations required to furnish information.

to the commission from time to time information, statements, and records concerning its organization, business, financial condition, conduct, practices, management, and relation to other corporations, or to individuals, associations, or partnerships, and to require the production for examination of all books, documents, correspondence, contracts, memoranda, or other papers relating to or in any way affecting the commerce in which such corporation under inquiry is engaged or concerning its relations to any individual, association, or partnership, and to make copies of the same.

Uniform annual reports.

"(*c*) To prescribe as near as may be a uniform system of annual reports from such corporations or classes of corporations subject to the provisions of this Act, as the commission may designate, and to fix the time for the filing of such reports, and to require such reports, or any special report, to be made under oath, or otherwise in the discretion of the commission.

Commission to make reports.

"(*d*) To make public, in the discretion of the commission, any information obtained by it in the exercise of the powers, authority, and duties conferred upon it by this Act, except so far as may be necessary to protect trade processes, names of customers, and such other matters as the commission may deem not to be of public importance, and to make annual and special reports to the Congress and to submit therewith recommendations for additional legislation.

"(*e*) In any suit in equity brought by or under the direction of the Attorney-General as provided in the antitrust Acts if the court finds for the complainant it may, upon its own motion or the motion of any party to such suit, refer the matter of the form of the decree to be entered to the commission as a master in chancery; whereupon the commission shall proceed in that capacity upon such notice to the parties and upon such hearing as the court may prescribe, and shall as speedily as practicable make report with its findings to the court, which report and findings having been made and filed shall be subject to the judicial procedure established for the consideration and disposition of a master's report and findings in equity cases.

Commission may act as master in chancery.

"(*f*) Wherever a restraining order or an interlocutory or final decree has heretofore been entered or shall hereafter be entered against any defendant or defendants in any suit brought by the United States to prevent and restrain any violation of the antitrust Acts, the commission shall have power, and it shall be its duty, upon the application of the Attorney-General, to make investigation of the manner in which the order or decree has been or is being carried out, and as to whether the same has been or is being violated and what, if any, further order, decree or relief is advisable. It shall transmit to the Attorney-General a report embodying its findings as a result of any such investigation with such recommendations for further action as it may deem advisable and the report shall be made public in the discretion of the commission.

Commission may investigate carrying out of decree.

"(*g*) If the commission believes from its inquiries and investigations, instituted upon its own initiative or at the suggestion of the President, the Attorney-General, or either House of Congress that any corporation, individual, association, or partnership has violated any law of the United States regulating commerce, it shall report its findings and the evidence in relation thereto to the Attorney-General with its recommendations."

Report findings to Attorney-General.

"For the purpose of prosecuting any investigation or proceeding authorized by this section the commission, or its duly authorized agent or agents, shall at all reasonable times have access to, for the purpose of examination, and the right to copy any documents or writings of any corporation being investigated or proceeded against.

Books open to commission.

"(*h*) The commission is hereby directed to investigate, as expeditiously as may be, trade conditions in foreign countries where associations, combinations, or practices of buyers, dealers, or traders may injuriously affect the export trade of the United States, and also to investigate whether American exporters have combined with each other or with foreign producers or dealers to control prices abroad, and to report to Congress thereon from time to time.

Foreign trade conditions.

"Sec. 4. The powers and jurisdiction herein conferred

Power over all corporations except utilities.

upon the commission shall extend over all trade associations, corporate combinations, and corporations as hereinbefore defined engaged in or affecting commerce, except banks and common carriers.

Unfair competition prohibited.

"SEC. 5. That unfair competition in commerce is hereby declared unlawful.

"The commission is hereby empowered and directed to prevent corporations from using unfair methods of competition in commerce.

Commission may issue orders regarding unfair competition.

"Whenever the commission shall have reason to believe that any corporation has been or is using any unfair method of competition in commerce, it shall issue and serve upon such corporation a written order, at least thirty days in advance of the time set therein for hearing, directing it to appear before the commission and show cause why an order shall not be issued by the commission restraining and prohibiting it from using such method of competition, and if upon such hearing the commission shall find that the method of competition in question is prohibited by this Act it shall thereupon issue an order restraining and prohibiting the use of the same. The commission may at any time modify or set aside, in whole or in part, any order issued by it under this Act.

Commission may take case to court.

"Whenever the commission, after the issuance of such order, shall find that such corporation has not complied therewith, the commission may petition the district court of the United States, within any district where the method in question was used or where such corporation is located or carries on business, praying the court to issue an injunction to enforce such order of the commission; and the court is hereby authorized to issue such injunction.

Penalties.

"SEC. 6. That if any corporation subject to this Act shall fail to file any annual or special report, as provided in subdivision (*b*) of section three hereof, within the time fixed by the commission for filing the same, and such failure shall continue for thirty days after notice of such default, the corporation shall forfeit to the United States the sum of $100 for each and every day of the continuance of such failure, which forfeiture shall be payable into the Treasury of the United States, and shall be recoverable in a civil suit in the name of the United States brought in the district where the corporation has its principal office or in any district in which it shall do business. It shall be the duty of the various district attorneys, under the direction of the Attorney-General of the United States, to prosecute for the recovery of forfeitures. The costs and expenses of such prosecution shall be paid out of the appropriation for the expenses of the courts of the United States."

Paragraphs (*a*), (*b*), (*c*), and (*d*) relate to the ascertaining of facts regarding corporations. These powers are those which have already been exercised by the Bureau of Corporations. But beginning with (*e*), there is new substantive law.

Significance of bill.

One of the great difficulties in the enforcement of the anti-trust act through the Attorney-General has been the dissolution of corporations found to have violated the law. The Interstate Trade Commission, under (*e*), may be appointed a master of chancery to make a report to the court regarding the form of the dissolution or the nature of the orders which should be given regarding the offending corporations. Moreover, under (*f*) the Commission may, at the request of the Attorney-General, investigate the manner in which the final decree is carried out.

But even more important than these provisions is that contained in section 5, making unfair competition unlawful and empowering the Commission to give orders to corporations to discontinue practices which are found by the Commission to involve unfair competition.

Another excellent feature of the bill is that contained under (*h*), which requires investigation of trade conditions in foreign countries in relation to the antitrust laws.

Section 4 extends the jurisdiction of the Commission over all organizations engaged in or affecting interstate commerce, except banks and common carriers; and in this respect the bill follows a sound principle.

The above summary of the principal provisions of this bill is made in order that its essential effects may be clearly appreciated apart from the details relating to their enforcement. Undoubtedly this bill, if enacted into law, will be an admirable instrument in assisting the Attorney-General in prosecuting corporations suspected of violating the Sherman act and in the dissolution of corporations found guilty by the courts of contracts or combinations in restraint of trade. Moreover, the provision of the bill, which gives the Commission authority of itself to give orders in regard to unfair competition, is a great constructive advance, in that it empowers the Commission to deal directly with the corporations rather than having that body auxiliary to the court.

Incompleteness of measure.

However, the bill seems to fall short of meeting the full situation, in that it does not authorize corporations of themselves to ask the advice of the Commission, as suggested by the President, in regard to whether existing or proposed practices are in accordance with the law. The Interstate Trade Commission should have the power to pass upon the legality of both existing and proposed practices and coöperation as advocated in the earlier part of this book and as also favored by the President in his statement to Congress. The author has suggested that there be added to the interstate trade commission law the following clause: —

Proposed additional power of Commission.

"Any person, association, or corporation, subject to the jurisdiction of the Commission, may present to the Commission for its approval any existing or proposed practice or plan of coöperation. If such existing or proposed practice or cooperation is found by the Commission to be in accordance with law, the Commission shall issue an order authorizing said practice or coöperation, either for a specified time or until further order is given. If the existing or proposed practice or plan of coöperation is found by the Commission not to be in accordance with law, the Commission shall issue an order forbidding said practice or coöperation either for a specified time or until further order is given. Orders of the Commission shall be prima facie evidence of their lawfulness to such time as changed by the Commission or reversed by the courts through action of the Attorney-General."

In favor of granting the proposed Interstate Trade Commission the powers proposed by this clause are, among others, the following reasons: —

While the Sherman act has been a law for more than twenty years, the business man does not know and cannot find out where the courts will place the boundary line between legitimate coöperation and unreasonable restraint of trade. It is only fair that business men should have some machinery by which they can ascertain whether or not any existing or proposed coöperation is in accordance with law without going through the enormous expense and great delay of litigation extending from the District Court to the Supreme Court, which ordinarily involves an expenditure of many thousands of dollars and from three to five years of time. **The uncertainty of the law.**

In dealing with complex business questions involving economic principles, the administrative commissions in this country, with their simple, direct methods of procedure, have shown themselves to be immeasurably superior to the complex methods of the courts.

Various objections have been urged against granting the proposed power to the Commission, but they are identical with those which were urged against the State and Interstate Commerce Commissions for the control of the public utilities. They are founded upon hypothetical fears which have been shown, in the case of the public utilities, to be without foundation.

The Clayton Bill

Several other important administrative measures relating to the trusts are embodied in a complex bill, the so-called Clayton bill (H. R. 15657). This bill has passed the House, and has been reported from committee to the Senate with amendments. This bill amends and supplements the Sherman act in various particulars. Among its provisions are those regarding price discrimination, the control of resale prices, exemption of laborers' and farmers' organizations from the Sherman act, the holding by any corporation of the stock of other corporations, interlocking directors, injunctive relief, etc.

A make-shift bill.

In large part this bill is indefensible in that it deals with classes and special cases rather than in accordance with a principle. The features are not here discussed in dctail, since it is uncertain whether or not the Senate will accept the bill in its present form. Of the various unwise features of the bill, only the most objectionable is here quoted, that relating to farmers and laborers. This section reads as follows: —

Exemption of laborers and farmers.

"That nothing contained in the antitrust laws shall be construed to forbid the existence and operation of labor, agricultural, or horticultural organizations, instituted for the purposes of mutual help, and not having capital stock or conducted for profit, or to forbid or restrain individual members of such organizations from lawfully carrying out the legitimate objects thereof; nor shall such organizations, or the members thereof, be held or construed to be illegal combinations or conspiracies in restraint of trade, under the antitrust laws."

Objections to exemptions.

There can be no possible defense for having one law for merchants and manufacturers and another law for farmers and laborers. The interpretation which the court will place upon the above clause is of course unknown and unknowable. Already there exists the widest divergence of view in regard to the intention of the clause. However, it is clear that certain farmers' and laborers' organizations are to have special consideration.

This section, and indeed several of the other special sections, are but lame and imperfect attempts to amend the Sherman act by consideration of particular cases rather than by a broad general principle; and, in this respect, they are in marked contrast to the remarkably comprehensive language of the Sherman law itself.

The Sherman act, as shown by Appendix I, lays down the broad principle that every contract and combination in restraint of trade is illegal; also that monopoly is illegal. As has been shown in this volume, the courts have found it necessary to modify the literal meaning of these words by inserting the qualifying word "reasonable," thus prohibiting, as interpreted by the court, only unreasonable combinations and contracts.

What is now needed is a principle which shall define what is reasonable and what is unreasonable restraint of trade rather than a complex bill dealing with special classes or particular practices. Such a principle is easily formulated. A simple addition to Section 1 of the Sherman act as follows will meet all cases: "The restraint of trade or commerce meant by the Sherman act is that restraint of trade which is detrimental to the public welfare; and the presumption is that any restraint of trade is thus detrimental."

Proposed amendment to Sherman act.

In the Australian antitrust law this principle is the fundamental qualification which affects all of the prohibitions. The law of that country states that it will be a defense against any of the things prohibited "that the matter or thing alleged to have been done in restraint of or with intent to restrain trade or commerce was not to the detriment of the public." [1]

The Australian Law.

If the amendment to the Sherman act, above proposed, were adopted, it would be possible for all corporations, organizations, and associations of whatever kind to enter into any coöperation which was not detrimental to the public welfare; and it would rest upon a corporation to prove that the practiced or proposed coöperation is not detrimental.

Inimical coöperation to be prohibited.

Does any one seriously hold that practices or coöperation not detrimental to the public welfare, should be prohibited? If not, the law should be specific upon this point, and thus make clear to laborers, to farmers, to manufacturers, the principle under which they may rightfully coöperate.

If the proposed amendment were adopted, the public would be perfectly protected, because the presumption is against any restraint of trade. Any organization wishing to engage in restraint of trade, to any degree, must show that such restraint is not detrimental to the public welfare, before the Court, or Commission, preferably the latter, because of the simple and effective procedure of a commission as compared with a court.

Legitimate coöperation should be permitted.

[1] Laws of Trusts and Monopolies, Domestic and Foreign, Revised Edition, Washington, Government Printing Office, 1914, pp. 364, 366.

If the Interstate Trade Commission were given the power to advise above advocated, and the proposed amendment to the Sherman act were adopted, there would be no necessity of special legislation, such as the proposed exemption of laborers and farmers. The labor organizations would be free to coöperate in all legitimate ways; and this is all that they should ask. The farmers could go forward with their coöperative movement along all desirable lines. Finally, the merchants and manufacturers would be restrained, where restraint is needed, but could coöperate where such coöperation is fair to the public. In short, there would be one law for all, in accordance with principle rather than class legislation, as proposed by the Clayton bill. Class legislation would be sure to lead to bitterness, occasioned by injustice; and thus tend toward industrial warfare; whereas, one law for all, because just, would tend to promote industrial peace.

Statesmanship demanded.

If the present Congress rise to the statesmanlike view of handling the great composite trade situation by principle rather than by piecemeal carpentry, we shall have a final solution of the most extraordinarily complex problem of concentration of industry, the most difficult economic problem, which has yet confronted this nation.

MADISON, WIS.,
August 1, 1914.

INDEX

CREDIT AND INTERNATIONAL TRADE

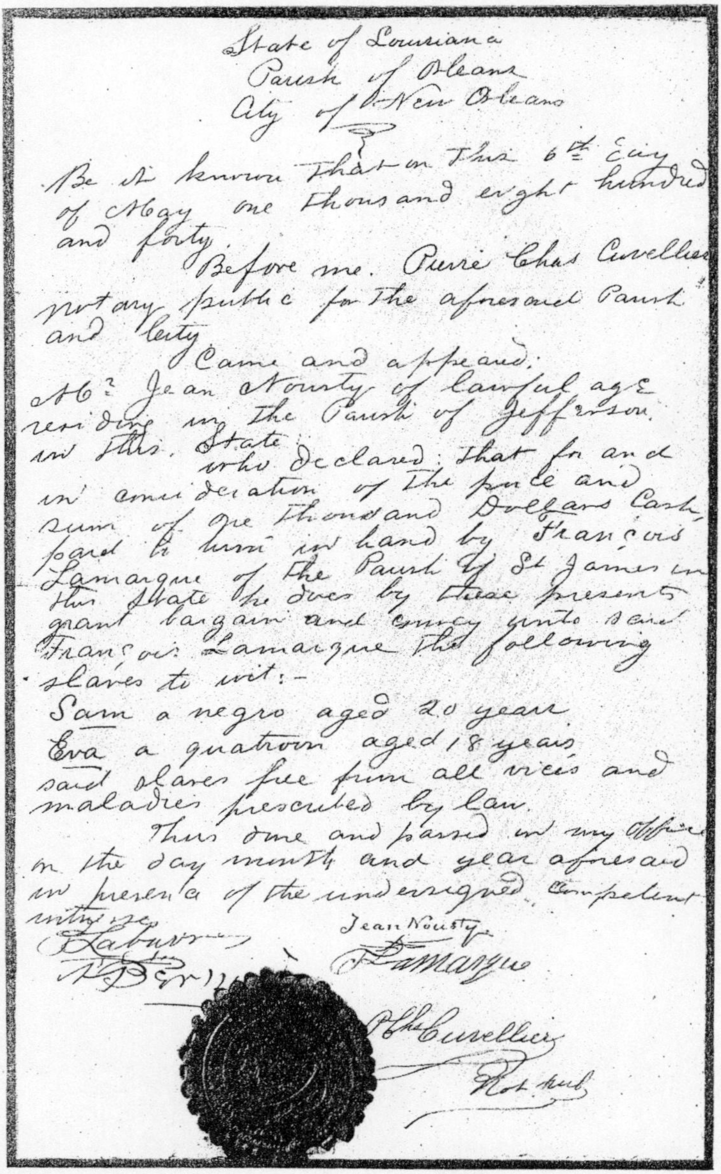

State of Louisiana
Parish of Orleans
City of New Orleans

Be it known that on this 6th day of May one thousand eight hundred and forty.

Before me. Pierre Chas Cuvellier notary public for the aforesaid Parish and City

Came and appeared.

Mr Jean Nousty of lawful age residing in the Parish of Jefferson in this State

who declared: that for and in consideration of the price and sum of One Thousand Dollars Cash, paid to him in hand by François Lamarque of the Parish of St James in this State he does by these presents grant bargain and convey unto said François Lamarque the following slaves to wit:-

Sam a negro aged 20 years

Eva a quatroon aged 18 years

said slaves free from all vices and maladies prescribed by law.

Thus done and passed in my Office on the day month and year aforesaid in presence of the undersigned competent witnesses.

Jean Nousty

Labarre

Lamarque

Chs Cuvellier
Not. pub

A SLAVE CONTRACT

Reproduced from the original by kind permission of Messrs. Reynolds & Gibson, Liverpool

CREDIT AND INTERNATIONAL TRADE

HOW THEY WORK IN PRACTICE

BY

BARNARD ELLINGER, C.B.E.

WITH AN INTRODUCTION

BY

SIR CHARLES ADDIS, K.C.M.G.

MACMILLAN AND CO., LIMITED
ST. MARTIN'S STREET, LONDON
1934

PREFACE

THIS book is concerned with the world's international trade in commodities and describes how these commodities are carried round the earth on an endless belt of credit.

About one-half of our imports are received from countries to which same countries we send a corresponding value of exports. We pay for the remainder of our imports in two ways; partly by sending exports to countries from which we have not received a corresponding value of imports, and partly by our invisible exports, that is, services which we render to the rest of the world or which have been rendered in the past. Balances which remain owing between nations are, in the last resort under gold standard conditions, regulated by the transference of gold; explanations of these operations are only referred to incidentally but can be found fully described in any text-book on money.

In order to give life to the transactions, names have been given to all the people who produce and handle the various commodities described. All the names (with the exception of the New Orleans Federal Compress & Warehouse Company and those of the United States Government institutions for giving credit to the farmers) are fictitious, but the transactions themselves are typical of actual business transactions which are taking place every day.

This book is a practical not a theoretical book,

describing business transactions as actually handled by business men. For the sake of students, examples of actual credit instruments which are used in daily practice are shown in Part II of Chapters I, II, IV, V. Explanations which are given of these credit instruments are from the business standpoint, and not from the legal or banking point of view. Lawyers and bankers have their text-books which deal with credit instruments, but the intention here is to fill the void in the education of the student of economics who is taught what business men do and why they do it, but is often at a loss to know *how* they do it. Any reader who is not interested in the actual credit instruments should omit Part II of these chapters, which can be done without any loss of sequence in the remainder of the book.

It is one of the aims of the book to bring home to the reader the fact that international trade is carried on between individuals and not between nations. Other aims are to show the complexities of production and distribution, the use of credit in helping in the producing and moving of commodities, and the dislocations which can be caused in the world's economy by changes in the habits of people or in the wants which they desire to satisfy. The transactions which have been selected are illustrative of trade in the multiplicity of commodities which are produced and distributed throughout the world, and the credit instruments shown in the book are a selection of the very many different types of credit instruments which are used in achieving this end.

I must express my gratitude to Sir Charles Addis, K.C.M.G., for writing the Introduction to this book. It will be noted that there is no bibliography; I have, however, during the making of the book, received comment, criticism, and information from so many friends in the academic, industrial, commercial, and financial world, that their names may be considered to form a human bibliography, and to all of them I must tender my sincere thanks. Among the large number I must particularly mention in the academic world Professor Henry Clay; also Professor G. W. Daniels, Messrs. T. S. Ashton, H. Campion, E. W. Mead, all of the University of Manchester; and Principal Henry L. Marsden, and Mr. G. A. Taylor of the Municipal High School of Commerce, Manchester, and also Miss Dorothy Smith; in the cotton world Colonel John J. Shute, M.P., and Sir John Reynolds, Bart., of Messrs. Reynolds & Gibson, Liverpool; Messrs. G. H. McFadden & Bro., Jenks Gwynne & Co., H. Hentz & Co., all of New York; and Mr. S. Skinner of Manchester; in the produce world Mr. G. Darling of the Co-operative Wholesale Society, Ltd., Mr. Robert Graham, a director of the Manchester Chamber of Commerce, Mr. P. F. H. Howlett of the English & Scottish Joint Co-operative Wholesale Society, Ltd., Mr. H. T. Karsten, Mr. E. Kraunsoe, Danish Consul in Manchester, and Mr. R. Schlee; in the banking world Mr. T. Y. Lee, Co-manager of the Bank of China, London, and Mr. W. Ewart Shepherd; in the shipping world Dr. L. Isserlis of the Chamber of Shipping of the United

Kingdom, and Messrs. R. S. Dalgliesh, Ltd., W. L. Runciman, and W. A. Souter & Co., Ltd.; and last but by no means least, my thanks are due to my indefatigable and long-suffering secretary, Miss Astra Kamberian, whose candid criticism was always helpful and constructive. The responsibility, however, for everything in the book rests solely with myself.

B. E.

August 1934.

CONTENTS

CHAPTER IX

CHAPTER X

CHAPTER XI

CHAPTER XII

APPENDICES

LIST OF ILLUSTRATIONS

INTRODUCTION

This is a book full of instruction. It is also highly entertaining. The student whose mind is bemused by the subtleties of abstract economics will find his ideas refreshed and clarified as he follows this plain and simple narrative of the fortunes of a bundle of cotton, from the field where it was grown by a negro "cropper" in Mississippi, to its appointed goal as a shirt on the back of Mr. Wu in an inland town in China. The author is the possessor of an agreeable and lively style and he brings out very clearly the way in which credit enters into every stage of the long journey.

We may dismiss the "cropper" as a direct user of credit since his field is tilled on the half-and-half system, that is to say, he supplies the labour and receives in exchange one-half of the cotton he is able to produce. But he presents the sole exception in a continuous chain of credit operations. For the land on which he works is mortgaged to the bank who provided the purchase money, and the owner has to obtain credit to buy the seed which he supplies to the "cropper". Then the local merchant, who buys the cotton from the owner, pays for it by a bill on the merchant in New Orleans, who in turn draws on the firm in Liverpool to whom he exports it. Credit is required to transport the cotton across the Atlantic, and to spin, weave, and bleach it when it reaches the other side, before it is ready to be exported to China in the form of cloth.

Up to this point the combined operations would appear to have been effected by nothing more than a series of book entries, in which credit is given to one after the other of the various factors of production, without any commodity having actually changed hands except, of course, the cotton itself. Here the author intervenes to show, not without a touch of humour, how the cotton not only changes hands repeatedly but is transmuted in the course of its long itinerary by the magic wand of credit into a whole series of commodities, so that Mr. Fu, the middleman at the Treaty port in China, is enabled to pay for the cotton cloth which is sold to Mr. Wu by shipping tea and sharks' fins and birds' nests to Manchuria and pigs' bristles to England. To pay for the tea and sharks' fins and birds' nests, Manchuria ships soya beans to Denmark. England settles her American account by shipping the pigs' bristles received from China to the United States, and Denmark pays for the soya beans received from Manchuria by shipping butter to England.

The circle is now complete. What appeared at first sight to be a mere series of book entries is now seen to be resolved, through the medium of credit, into a series of actual exchanges, in which the claims of each country concerned are satisfied by receiving the commodities of other countries in exchange for its own. So far as England is concerned, the net result is that she receives Danish butter in exchange for her labour in manufacturing the cotton goods.

The book is not intended, as the author reminds us, to be an exposition of the theory of Credit and International Trade. His more modest purpose is a description of how credit actually enters into commercial transactions of which he happens to possess first-hand knowledge. Nevertheless, despite his modest self-abnegation, we may be permitted to doubt whether his masterly handling of the complicated details of credit and international trade, and the presentation of his subject in so simple and attractive a manner, could have been achieved without a good deal more than a passing acquaintance with its theoretical implications.

The experienced man of business may read *Credit and International Trade* with profit and pleasure, but it is to the young banker or merchant who takes an intelligent interest in his business and wants to understand something of the reality veiled by the various documents he has to handle in the course of the daily business routine that I would especially commend this book as the best introduction I have seen to the economics of foreign trade and particularly of foreign banking.

C. S. ADDIS

August 15, 1934.

CHAPTER I

PRODUCTION AND MARKETING OF RAW COTTON

PART I

THE story begins with Hezekiah Godbehere, a negro tenant-farmer, or cropper as Americans call him, who lived in Mississippi and grew cotton; or rather it starts with his father Zachariah, who was born in 1844 and is still hale and hearty at the age of ninety. Zachariah was also interested in cotton in his youth. He was set to pick it at the age of nine, and worked for Mr. John B. Robinson senior, until he was twenty-one. In fact, he belonged to John B. Robinson, for he was a slave and only freed in 1865 when slavery was abolished in America on the termination of the Civil War.

We do not know how much was paid for Zachariah, but a selling contract dated 1840 (see frontispiece) affords an indication of the prices ruling (500 dollars per slave), about the time of Zachariah's birth.

We may go still further back; Zachariah's grandfather was born aboard a slaver about the year 1738. The vessel was sailing from the Gold Coast to Virginia and was not very successful as a commercial venture, for 65 out of the 123 negro slaves which she carried died on the voyage.

These slavers were owned by Liverpool merchants, some having an eighth share, others a sixteenth or a thirty-second, but "BIG BUSINESS" was beginning to make itself felt, for, forty years later, ten shipping firms controlled half the trade and carried two-thirds of the slaves. It was a triangular trade, for the vessel loaded cotton from Virginia for Lancashire, where it was manufactured into cloth, sent to the Gold Coast and there exchanged for slaves, and the slaves were then carried to Virginia. The first record which we have of a slaver belonging to Liverpool merchants dates from the year 1700 and the vessel enjoyed the singularly appropriate name of *The Blessing*.

Daniel Defoe, writing in 1728, said: "The Trade carried on here," (that is, the West Coast of Africa), "whether by the *English* or other European Nations, consists in but three capital Articles viz. *Slaves*, *Teeth*, and *Gold*; a very gainful and advantageous Commerce, especially as it was once carried on, when these were all purchas'd at low Rates from the Savages; and even those low Rates paid in Trifles and Toys, such as Knives and Sissars, Kettles and Clouts, Glass Beads, and Cowries, Things of the smallest Value, and as we may say next to nothing; but even this Part of the Trade is abated in its Goodness, since by the Strife and Envy among the Traders, we have had the Folly to instruct the Savages in the Value of their own Goods, and inform them of the Cheapness of our own; endeavouring to supplant one another, by underselling and overbidding, by which we have taught the Negroes to supplant both, by holding up the Price of their own Productions and running down the Rates of what we carry them for Sale.

"Thus that gainful Commerce once superior to all the Trades in the World, which carried out the meanest of all Exportations and brought home the richest, is sinking daily into a Kind of Rubbish as to Trade; and we are sometimes said to buy even the Gold too dear."

We are not concerned, however, with Hezekiah's great-grandfather, but rather with Hezekiah himself and how he grew and sold his cotton in the year 1934.

Hezekiah rented a farm of ten acres from John B. Robinson junior, on the half-and-half system. Robinson owned about 100 acres which he let in small lots to other negro croppers on the same system. The tenants supplied the labour and half the fertilizers, but Robinson supplied everything else: land, cabin, tools, work-stock, feed for work-stock, seed, and one-half of the fertilizers, and granted the tenant the privilege of getting wood for fuel. When the crop was grown the tenant received half and John B. Robinson half, but the tenant often sold his half to or through Robinson.

It was necessary before planting the new cotton to obtain seed, and John B. Robinson, who was short of money, borrowed from a Production Credit Association set up by the Department of Agriculture's Credit Corporation, pledging as security the cotton crop when grown, and the Department of Agriculture watched that only good seed was supplied to Robinson (Part II: Credit instruments Nos. 4 and 5). Formerly Robinson would have borrowed money from his local bank with which to buy the seed, but after the American crisis, which began in 1929 and led to difficulties of many banks, the Government formed this Credit Corporation in order to help the farmers.

John B. Robinson did not only require to borrow money for his seed, but owing to the bad times, was also obliged to borrow in order to buy his farm implements, stock, and even to pay his taxes. He had borrowed on mortgage 4000 dollars on his farm on which he had to pay 6% interest, and for other money which he owed he had to pay as much as 8% interest. Times were so bad that he could not raise the interest, and the people who had lent him the money had threatened to seize his farm and sell it so as to recover the debts due to them. This state of affairs was fairly common among farmers in the United States between 1929 and 1933, in which latter year Congress passed the Emergency Farm Mortgage Act. As a result he was then able to borrow (from institutions set up by the Government) enough money to pay off his mortgage and settle his other debts (Credit instruments 1, 2, and 3). He contracted to repay this loan in annual instalments over thirty years but was only obliged to start repayment after five years, during which period he had to pay interest only, and even then at the rate of 4½% per annum instead of the 6 to 8% which he had been paying. Robinson had to undertake to leave 5% of the borrowed money with what was known as the National Farm Loan Association for investment in that Association's capital, as part provision of a fund to protect the

Association against loss, and enable the money which was to be lent to the farmers to be raised from the public at cheap rates by the issue of bonds.

The National Farm Loan Association was founded by the Government for the purpose of making loans on easy terms to the farmers. The Government guarantees the interest on the bonds, and care is taken that loans are only made on sound value in order to ensure that the principal is safe. The 5% investment of each individual borrower serves as a mutual guarantee fund for all the borrowers.

In due course Hezekiah's crop was harvested. His ten acres yielded about 1800 lb. of cotton, but the cotton when picked was full of seed, and Hezekiah sent it to the local gin, the Mississippi Ginning Company, in order that it might be ginned, that is, the seed separated from the cotton. Hezekiah had to drive his wagon with his cotton several miles to the nearest gin. The ginner not only removed the seed from the cotton lint, but took out a certain amount of dirt and then packed the cotton, when ginned, into a bale. Some ginners purchase the cotton before it is ginned, but otherwise they keep sufficient of the seed to repay themselves for their work, returning the remainder to the farmer. Usually about one-third of the unginned cotton is lint and two-thirds seed, but sometimes the proportion is as high as half and half. Cotton seed is a valuable commodity, and from the seed four products are obtained: oil (the most valuable) which is used for salad oil, vegetable shortening (fat used for cookery), soap and sardine packing; linters (the fibre which is left on the seed after ginning) is used for felt, writing-paper, explosives, varnishes, absorbent cotton, photograph films, and nowadays in the manufacture of rayon; the hulls or husks are used for cattle food and fertilizers; and the material left after extracting the oil from the seed has also a large market for the same purposes. A ton of seed will yield approximately 330 lb. of oil, 825 lb. of cake or meal, 595 lb. of hulls, and 150 lb. of linters. When Hezekiah received back his lint and seed from the ginner, he handed it all, including his own share, to Robinson so that he might sell it.

John B. Robinson drove every day into the country town with two or three bales of cotton which had been grown by Hezekiah and other negro croppers. In the country town he might have sold the cotton to a "scalper", a man who buys a few bales every day on his own account and usually sells them in the evening of the same day. There are also other buyers of cotton; for instance, a man who is known as "the supply merchant", possibly he is the store-keeper in the town and has given credit to Robinson for fertilizers and implements. Having made his profit in this way he would sometimes pay a price rather higher than the market price for the cotton in order to set off the value against the money owing to him. If the supply merchant bought the cotton, he would probably immediately re-sell it to a "merchant's take-up man" who buys for some large merchant, or possibly to an "exporter's agent" who usually buys from other buyers for some large exporting firm. But John B. Robinson sold to a "f.o.b. man" (who also more frequently buys from other buyers than from the farmers direct). The term f.o.b. means "free on board" and it is one of the functions of the f.o.b. man to care for putting the cotton free on board the train and arranging for it to be forwarded to his buyer. This f.o.b. man, Marcus B. Levine in this instance, had been in the habit of buying Hezekiah's cotton every season, because he knew that he had a buyer for the special quality which Hezekiah grew, and he had probably arranged the price with his buyer before he purchased the cotton from John B. Robinson (Credit instrument No. 9).

Levine, before buying the cotton from Robinson, cut a hole in a bale, took a sample of the cotton, examined it, and then made his bargain regarding the price. He then carted the cotton to the town's cotton-yard or warehouse, where it was weighed by the public weigher. If Marcus B. Levine had sufficient cash, he might use it to buy his first few bales of cotton, or, failing this, he would arrange a loan with a local bank, giving them some bonds or shares as security. He would pay John B. Robinson out of these funds (Credit instrument No. 6), and when John B. Robinson sold his cotton, he would repay the loan which he obtained for the seed from the Production Credit Association and also his annual instalment in repayment of the mortgage. The bales which Levine bought were loosely packed and if loaded in that condition would have cost an unnecessarily large amount in railway freight, so Levine sent them to a pressing company which pressed them into bales of smaller compass and warehoused them for Levine until he was ready to forward them by rail to his customer. Levine then took the warehouse receipt (Credit instrument No. 7) to the bank and obtained a further loan against the cotton which he had stored in the warehouse. This enabled him to make a new purchase of cotton, and with every new purchase he obtained a warehouse receipt which he pledged with the bank, and obtained a still further loan which enabled him to continue his purchases. But the bank would probably see that it only advanced about 75 to 80% of the market value of the cotton, thus keeping themselves covered against any possible fall in the value of the security which might occur owing to a decline in price, and Levine would have to find the remaining 20 to 25% out of his own money.

When Levine had collected sufficient cotton to send a load to his buyer, Silas J. Hocking in New Orleans, he went to his bank and obtained from them an order to the warehouse to release the cotton on his promise (Credit instrument No. 8) to hand over to the bank the railway bill of lading (that is, the railway's receipt for the cotton) when he had loaded it, which the bank would then hold as security in place of the warehouse receipt. He then made out his invoice charging Silas J. Hocking with the cotton, and at the same time he wrote out a draft (similar to Credit instrument No. 6), but instead of being drawn on a bank, it was drawn on his buyer Silas J. Hocking, who was obliged to pay it to anybody to whom Levine endorsed it. He then took the draft and the railway bill of lading to his local bank. The bank deducted from the value of the draft the loan which it had made to Levine, its charges for interest and any other charges, and credited Levine's account with any balance which remained over. The local bank sent the bill of lading and the draft to a bank in New Orleans, which collected the money from Silas J. Hocking and in exchange handed to him the railway bill of lading, the bank in New Orleans remitting the money to the local bank from which it had received the bill of lading.

Part II

CREDIT INSTRUMENTS

Credit instrument No. 1: In this instrument there are three points which should be noted. First, by it John B. Robinson offers his farm as security for the money which he asks should be advanced to him and which he undertakes to repay by instalments; so that the debt would be liquidated in thirty years. Secondly, he agrees to purchase stock to the extent of 5% of the money advanced, in a National Farm Loan Association if the money is obtained from the Association or (if the money is obtained from the bank), in the bank. Thirdly, if the money is obtained from the bank, he agrees to unite with other borrowers at some future time in forming a National Loan Association, from which, when formed, he may obtain a reduction of $\frac{1}{2}$ or 1% per annum in the rate of interest charged for his loan. In addition, this document, which is signed by John B. Robinson, contains detailed information concerning his property, debts, and the purpose for which the loan is required.

CREDIT INSTRUMENT NO. 1.—APPLICATION FOR LOAN

Form 1321—Consolidated—Rev. 7-20-33.

(THIS APPLICATION MUST BE FILLED OUT WITH PEN AND INK OR TYPEWRITER)

Kind of Loan(s) Closed............, Rate............, Appraisal Fee, $............

Application	Land Located in Territory of	Amount Applied for	Amount Loaned	Loan
FLB No........	............N. F. L. A.	FLB $........	FLB $........	FLB No........
LBC No........	Classification	LBC $........	LBC $........	LBC No........

(Do not write above this line) (Space above the line for Farm Credit Administration use only)

APPLICATION OF

JOHN BENJAMIN ROBINSON (Applicant's full name—Print or type) P.O. VICKSBURG (Town) (R. F. D.) MISSISSIPPI (State)

EVA JEAN ROBINSON (Husband's or wife's name—Print or type) P.O. VICKSBURG (Town) (R. F. D.) MISSISSIPPI (State)

TO THE FEDERAL LAND BANK OF NEW ORLEANS

(Hereinafter termed "bank")

and

TO THE LAND BANK COMMISSIONER

(Hereinafter termed "Commissioner")

Paragraph 1. Amount of Loan: I, the undersigned, hereby apply for a loan of Six thousand dollars (Multiples of $100) ($ 6000) Dollars, to be repaid in 30 (annual—semi-annual) installments.

Paragraph 2. Loan from Bank: I apply to the bank for a loan of so much of the amount desired as can be granted by it on the security offered, such loan to be made through a national farm loan association serving the territory wherein the security is located, if the endorsement of such association is acceptable to the bank, and if such endorsement is not acceptable I desire a direct loan from the bank. I agree to purchase stock to the extent of $5.00 for each $100.00 lent by the bank, such stock to be in the association if the loan is made through it, and in the bank if a direct loan is made. I agree that the cost of the stock may be deducted from the loan. If a direct loan is made I do (do—do not) desire to covenant in my mortgage to unite with other borrowers later in forming a national farm loan association in order to obtain a reduction of ½ of 1% in the rate of interest on my loan in accordance with Section 7 of the Federal Farm Loan Act, as amended. I agree to comply with all the terms and conditions of, and rules and regulations issued under, the Federal Farm Loan Act, as amended.

Paragraph 3. Loan From Commissioner: If the bank cannot lend any or all of the amount desired, I apply to the Commissioner for the balance or so much thereof as he can lend on the security offered. I agree to comply with all the terms and conditions of, and rules and regulations issued under, part 3 of the Emergency Farm Mortgage Act of 1933.

Paragraph 4. As hereinafter used the term "Loan" shall be deemed to refer to any loan or loans made to me by the bank and/or the commissioner pursuant to this application.

A. DESCRIPTION OF LAND OFFERED AS SECURITY:

5. I offer as security for the loan a first (first—second) mortgage on the real estate described as follows: (Give legal description which must be in sufficient detail to identify the property and its bounds.)

Credit instrument No. 2: This report is not merely a report on the condition and value of the farm, but also on the applicant's character and farming experience; also on the probability or otherwise of the applicant being able to earn sufficient from the farm to keep his family and gradually pay off the loan. At the foot of the form is a certificate from the National Loan Association stating that John B. Robinson is either a charter member (or as we should call him, a founder member) or has been elected a member of the National Farm Loan Association, and that the board of directors by a majority vote approves the application for the loan and recommends that the Federal Land Bank of Mississippi should grant it.

CREDIT INSTRUMENT NO. 2

Form 1321-A—Rev 7-20-33.

—FOR LOAN THROUGH N. F. L. A ONLY—
(CONFIDENTIAL)

REPORT OF THE LOAN COMMITTEE TO THE FEDERAL LAND BANK OF MISSISSIPPI

NOTE: Section 10 of the Farm Loan Act, as amended, provides that the loan committee may designate someone to make an investigation of the security and the applicant in its behalf, or the committee itself may make the investigation. The result of the investigation must be approved and the report signed by every member of the loan committee.

1. The land on which this report is based is the indentical property described in the application hereto attached and signed by JOHN BENJAMIN ROBINSON

2. The farm offered as security is in a (good—~~fair—poor~~) location. It shows (~~good~~—fair—~~poor~~) management. It is in (~~good~~—fair—~~poor~~) condition.

3. The soil is (describe kind) black loamy of good quality, 95 acres can be profitably cultivated,

4.

Kind		Value Uninsurable Buildings	Value Permanent Insurable Buildings
Dwelling	(Bldg. No. 1)	$	$
	(Bldg. No. 2)		
Huts ~~barn~~	(Bldg. No. 3)		200
	(Bldg. No. 4)		150
	(Bldg. No. 5)		150
	(Bldg. No. 6)	120	
	(Bldg. No. 7)	90	

VALUATION OF LAND
(The acreage classified must agree with total acreage offered as security for this loan)

No. of Acres	Classification	Value per Acre	Total Value
95	Cultivated	$ 170	$ 16150
5	Uncultivated		
	Orchard		
	Grove		
	Pasture		
	Timber		
	Waste Land		
	Total Value of Land		$ 16150
	Value of Insurable Bldgs. to Farm		500
	Total Value of Farm		$ 16650

5. The present sale price of the property is $ 16650

6. The applicant's character and habits are (good—~~bad~~). He is (slow—~~prompt~~) in meeting obligations.

7. The applicant (is—~~is not~~) by virtue of actual farming experience, training and temperament, qualified and capable of making a success in the operation of this farm.

8. This farm (will—~~will not~~), under the management of the applicant, produce a sufficient revenue to sustain the family of the applicant and enable him to meet amortization payments as they become due.

9. The applicant is in (good—~~poor~~) health. He is (White—~~Mexican-Spanish~~-American—~~Negro~~)

10. Give any further information you have bearing on this loan

11. The applicant (will—~~will not~~) accept the loan as herein recommended.

Based upon the investigation of the property, its earning power under normal conditions, the solvency, character, and qualifications of the applicant, I recommend that a loan be granted for an amount not to exceed $ 6000

The foregoing is a report of an investigation made the 12th day of May, 1934.

Ezra Jones Wilks.
Investigator for Loan Committee.

We, the Loan Committee of the WARREN National Farm Loan Association, have carefully considered this application and the report of our Investigator, or have personally investigated the security, and recommend that a loan be granted for an amount not to exceed six thousand dollars $ 6000

No member of this committee nor any person who made the investigation is interested, directly or indirectly, in the loan sought by the within-named applicant.

Dated at VICKSBURG

4th day of June, 1934

Angus P. MacMahon
Secretary-Treasurer.

(This report MUST be signed in ink by all members of the Loan Committee.)

Nathaniel R. Sykes
Robert G Horner
Philip A. Soady

ACTION OF THE BOARD OF DIRECTORS

The undersigned Secretary-Treasurer of the within and above-named National Farm Loan Association, hereby certifies that the within-named applicant is a charter member of or has been admitted to membership in said Association by a two-thirds or more vote of the Board of Directors. I further certify that the Board of Directors of said Association by a favorable vote of a majority of the entire directorate, at the casting of which vote no interested director participated in any manner, has approved and recommended to the Federal Land Bank of Mississippi that said applicant, on the land described in this application, be granted a loan not exceeding six thousand dollars $ 6000

Witness my official signature this 14th day of June 1934

Angus P. MacMahon
Secretary-Treasurer.

Note to Secretary-Treasurer: In connection with consolidated application form 1321 (Rev. 7-20-33), the above report must be filled in completely and sent to the Bank with each application, except in cases where loans cannot be made through your association and in cases where you know that a loan can be made only by the commissioner.

THE R. L. BRYAN CO., COLUMBIA, S. C. 190709

Credit instrument No. 3: This is a direct loan from the Federal Land Bank of New Orleans, the National Farm Loan Association referred to in document No. 1 not having been established at the time the loan was made. The loan is repayable plus a certain percentage per annum, in an agreed number of years according to the amortization tables approved by the Land Bank Commissioner. These are tables which show how long it will take to repay a given debt by annual payments which are applied partly in payment of interest and partly as an instalment towards the repayment of the capital, or what we should call a Sinking Fund. In Robinson's case the interest was $4\frac{1}{2}\%$ per annum; the capital commenced to be repayable only after five years, and the table would show how much a year would have to be paid over the whole thirty years in order to wipe out both interest and capital. The document also contains many legal clauses, too numerous to reproduce here.

FLB FORM NO. 596
7-20-33

DIRECT LOAN

Deed of Trust

State of Mississippi,
County of WARREN

OFFICE COPY
FORM SUBJECT TO CHANGE
WITHOUT NOTICE.

FEDERAL LAND BANK
OF NEW ORLEANS

Know all Men by These Presents:

That WHEREAS,

JOHN BENJAMIN ROBINSON

hereinafter called Grantors, whether one or more, is/are indebted to **THE FEDERAL LAND BANK OF NEW ORLEANS**—hereinafter called the Bank—in the sum of six thousand DOLLARS, for money lent by it, which indebtedness and the interest accruing thereon, at the rate of 4½ per centum per annum from the date hereof, is repayable in 30 installments, according to amortization tables approved by the Land Bank Commissioner, the terms of which are hereby agreed to, in varying amounts and at times as follows, to-wit:

On the 24 day of April, 1939, the first installment, comprising interest from date hereof on the principal amount of such indebtedness, plus the principal portion of the said first installment of the amortization table which is printed on the back of the note hereinafter described and herein secured; and the remaining installments successively, including principal and interest, one on the same day of each year thereafter until all have matured; on an amortization plan, in the order and in the several respective amounts as the same are set forth in, and fully in accordance with, the amortization table printed on the back of the note hereinafter described in and identified with this deed of trust, the terms of which are hereby accepted and made a part of this deed of trust, to the same extent as if the said note, including the said amortization table, were recited verbatim herein. Said indebtedness repayable in said annual installments is evidenced by a note of even date herewith for the said principal sum, which, with the interest therein provided, is repayable in the amounts and at the times aforesaid, at the office of the Bank, in the City of New Orleans, Louisiana:

AND WHEREAS, the undersigned desire to secure the payment of said indebtedness as the several installments thereof respectively fall due and the performance of all obligations, agreements, and conditions herein assumed:

NOW THEREFORE, in consideration of the premises as well as the sum of Five Dollars to them paid by John Benjamin Robinson as Trustee, hereinafter called the Trustee, the receipt whereof is hereby acknowledged, the Grantors do hereby convey and warrant unto said Trustee the following described real estate, situated in the County of WARREN State of Mississippi, to-wit:

one farm of 100 acres.

Comprising five huts.

In the postal district of Vicksburg. Box No: 270

CREDIT INSTRUMENT NO. 3 (*continued*)

Witness the signature of the Grantors on this the 16th day of March, 1934

John B. Robinson

State of Mississippi,
County of WARREN

Before me, the undersigned authority in and for the County and State aforesaid, this day personally appeared the within named

John Benjamin Robinson

who acknowledged that he signed and delivered the foregoing instrument on the day and year therein mentioned.

Given under my hand and official seal this 24 day of April, 1934.

Joshua R. Watts.

(SEAL)

Credit instrument No. 4 is an indenture, that is an agreement by which John B. Robinson who is the Grantor, acknowledges a loan from the Production Credit Association and undertakes to repay the same with interest. He gives promissory notes as security which bear interest from the date of the note (Credit instrument No. 5). He also gives as collateral security (i.e. additional security, literally security which runs alongside the original security) his growing crops, and other chattels. This security is given by selling the whole of his crops grown or to be grown, to a trustee for one dollar. The trustee holds them on trust until the debt to the Production Credit Association is paid, after which they revert to John B. Robinson. It will be remembered, however, that half the crops belong to John B. Robinson's tenants, and of course, Robinson cannot give a lien (that is, pledge) on his tenants' share of the crops. In order to get over this difficulty there is attached to the indenture a "waiver" which is signed by Robinson's tenants in which these tenants agree to waive any rights which they have in the crops in favour of the Production Credit Association to the extent of the Association's claim. Formerly it was not possible, under the ordinary law of the United Kingdom, to give a lien on growing crops, unless this was coupled with a lien on the land. But in the Agricultural Mortgage Act of the United Kingdom, an exception was made in this respect. However, the American indenture would not ordinarily be legal in this country, as it would still involve the necessity for giving a bill of sale.

CREDIT INSTRUMENT NO. 4.—CROPS AND CHATTELS MORTGAGE

P. C. A.-M. 403

CROPS AND CHATTELS

State of Mississippi,
County of WARREN

THIS INDENTURE, this day made and entered into between JOHN BENJAMIN ROBINSON of VICKSBURG, Mississippi, hereinafter designated as the GRANTOR; JOSHUA R. WATTS of VICKSBURG, Mississippi, TRUSTEE; and the JACKSON Production Credit Association of WARREN, Mississippi, hereinafter designated as the ASSOCIATION.

WITNESSETH: That whereas the GRANTOR is justly indebted to the ASSOCIATION in the full sum of four hundred DOLLARS ($ 400) for money loaned and to be loaned as evidenced by the GRANTOR'S 4 promissory notes of even date herewith, in favor of the ASSOCIATION, bearing interest from date until paid at the rate of 4½ % per annum, and being due and payable as follows:

No. 1 for $ 100 due September 10th 1934	No. 5 for $, due
No. 2 for $ 100 , due October 10th 1934	No. 6 for $, due
No. 3 for $ 100 , due November 10th 1934	No. 7 for $, due
No. 4 for $ 100 , due December 10th 1934	No. 8 for $, due

All of said notes provide that in the event they are placed in the hands of an attorney for collection, or if suit is brought on the same, or any portion thereof, or if collected by any court proceedings, the GRANTOR agrees to pay a reasonable attorney's fee.

WHEREAS, the said GRANTOR is willing to secure the prompt and full payment of the indebtedness hereinbefore specifically described, and also such future and additional advances as may, within one year from the date hereof, be made to the GRANTOR by the ASSOCIATION, such additional future advances not to exceed the sum of $ 100 , together with any other indebtedness that may become due and owing under the terms of this instrument:

NOW, THEREFORE, in consideration of the premises, and the further consideration of One Dollar ($1.00) cash in hand paid by the aforesaid TRUSTEE the receipt of which is hereby acknowledged, the GRANTOR does hereby sell, convey and warrant unto said TRUSTEE, any and all crops of cotton, cotton seed, corn, hay, truck and any and all agricultural products, of any and all kinds whatsoever, grown and to be grown by said GRANTOR and by any and all tenants, share-croppers, laborers and/or any employees of said GRANTOR during the crop year 1934, on any and all lands cultivated and controlled by said GRANTOR and particularly on the land situated in the County of WARREN Mississippi, described as follows, to-wit:

1 farm of 100 acres

in the postal district of VICKSBURG.

Box. No.270

John B. Robinson

15th February 1934

CREDIT INSTRUMENT NO. 4 (*continued*)

State of Mississippi
COUNTY OF WARREN

Personally appeared before me the undersigned authority, in and for the jurisdiction aforesaid, the within named JOHN BENJAMIN ROBINSON who acknowledged that he signed and delivered the foregoing deed of trust on the day and year therein mentioned.

Given under my hand and official seal this the 15th day of February, 1934.

AFFIX OFFICIAL
SEAL HERE

James S. Neale
Notary Public.

WAIVER AND AGREEMENT

Date 1st February 1934

In consideration of the loan to be made by the JACKSON Production Credit Association of WARREN, Mississippi, to the GRANTOR named in the foregoing deed of trust, which is to be a lien superior to any lien, claim or interest of the undersigned upon the crops and chattels mentioned therein, the undersigned, as owner and/or mortgagee of the land therein described and/or prior mortgagee, sharecropper, tenant or lienor of the crops and chattels so mortgaged and/or the present owner and holder of a rent note, mortgage note, agreement, or land-sales contract entitling the holder to a legal interest in said crop or chattels and/or the present legal equitable owner of any interest of any kind or character in and to the land described therein or in said crops and chattels, does hereby waive, subordinate and release in favor of said Jackson Production Credit Association of WARREN, Mississippi, or its assigns, all or any right, lien, claim or interest which the undersigned or any of them may now have or may hereafter have under whatever claim or right, in or to the said crops and chattels or the proceeds from the sale thereof, to the extent of the claim of the said Association thereto, and do hereby covenant and agree that the enforcements of their said rights, liens, claims or interests in the said crops and chattels shall be deferred until such claim is fully paid, satisfied and discharged. And for the consideration aforesaid, the undersigned do further covenant and agree: (1) That he is the present owner and holder of all notes or other documents evidencing the indebtedness due him; (2) Not to transfer, pledge, hypothecate, sell or assign any rent note, mortgage note, agreement, land-sales contract, mortgage, or other lien or claim held by them against the said crops or chattels without first obtaining the written consent of the said Association until its aforesaid mortgage or lien is fully satisfied or paid; and (3) That in the event loans or advances are made by said Association for the purpose of harvesting and marketing the said crops, it is agreed that the money so advanced may be repaid from the proceeds derived from the sale thereof prior to the satisfaction of any lien, claim or interest of the undersigned.

Hezekiah Godbehere
Augustus Moses Livingstone
Pompey Green
Adam Samuel Mason
Lazarus Ferguson.
Seth Johnson

Credit instrument No. 5 is a promissory note undertaking to pay by various instalments the amount borrowed plus interest from the date of the note. It contains a clause agreeing that the Association's right, to call upon any guarantor of this promissory note to pay it in the event of Robinson failing to do so, shall not be affected by the Association's failure to give notice that Robinson has not paid on the due date. Further, the Association's rights against the guarantor shall not be annulled if the Association agrees to give Robinson an extension of the time for payment.

CREDIT INSTRUMENT NO. 5

INSTALLMENT NOTE

$ 200 .... 15th February 19 34

For value received, I, ~~we or either of us~~ promise to pay to the order of the JACKSON PRODUCTION CREDIT ASSOCIATION of WARREN MISSISSIPPI the sum of Four hundred Dollars ($ 400) with interest at the rate of 4½ % per annum from date, until paid, payable at its office in the City of VICKSBURG MISSISSIPPI in installments as follows, to-wit:

$ 100 on September 10th 19 34	$ .... on .... 19 .....
$ 100 on October 10th 19 34	$ .... on .... 19 .....
$ 100 on November 10th 19 34	$ .... on .... 19 .....
$ 100 on December 10th 19 34	$ .... on .... 19 .....
$ .... on 19	$ .... on .... 19 .....
$ .... on 19	$ .... on .... 19 .....

Interest on each installment to be paid at maturity thereof.

Upon the failure to pay any of the said installments, or interest thereon when the same becomes due, then the entire indebtedness, at the option of the holder may be declared to be due and payable.

The makers, sureties, endorsers and guarantors of this note hereby severally waive presentment for payment, notice of non-payment, protest and notice of protest, and diligence in the enforcing of payment hereof and all right of exemption under the Constitution and laws of the State of Alabama as to personal property, and consent that time of payment may be extended without notice thereof to any of the sureties of this note. It is further expressly agreed that if this note, after the maturity of any of the installments or payments, above referred to, is placed in the hands of an attorney, for collection, whether suit is brought on the same or not, then and in that event to pay the owner or holder of this note ten per cent additional of the principal and interest due thereon as attorney's fees for collection. This note is secured by chattel mortgage dated 15th February 1934 ; executed by the makers hereof to the payee herein on property more particularly described in said mortgage.

No. 1679 .... John B. Robinson

Due September - December 1934

Address P.O. Box 270 VICKSBURG

Credit instrument No. 6 calls for no comment. It serves the same purpose as an ordinary English cheque.

CREDIT INSTRUMENT NO. 6.—CHEQUE

MARCUS B. LEVINE
COTTON MERCHANTS

$ 168.30 Vicksburg, Mississippi October 3rd 1934.

At sight

Pay to the order of John B. Robinson

One hundred and sixty eight *Dollars*

thirty cents

VALUE RECEIVED AND CHARGE TO ACCOUNT OF
for cotton 3 bales Marcus B. Levine

To Mississippi Cotton Banking Corporation
MISSISSIPPI

(signed) Marcus B Levine

No. 3192

Specimen

Credit instrument No. 7 requires little explanation. The words "without novation" mean without the right to substitute some other debtor or trustee for the debtor or trustee mentioned in the document.

CREDIT INSTRUMENT NO. 7

THE COMPRESSION Co. INC.
SHIPPING AGENTS
HOUSTON :: GALVESTON :: CORPUS CHRISTI
DALLAS :: LAKE CHARLES
VICKSBURG

TRUST RECEIPT

Vicksburg, Miss.
(Office)

October 3rd 1934.
(Date)

Received in Trust from Marcus B. Levine

three bales cotton

for account of Mississippi Cotton Banking Corporation

The documents above described are held by us IN TRUST and WILL NOT BE DELIVERED without surrender of this Receipt. This delivery being temporarily made to us for convenience only, without novation, or without giving to us any title to the documents or the property they represent except as trustee and agent for the above mentioned parties

THE COMPRESSION Co. INC.

BY J. Harrison

Specimen

Credit instrument No. 8 is an application to withdraw the cotton from the warehouse for the purpose of putting it on the railway. In this document Levine agrees to hold the cotton in trust for the bank, and to hand over to the bank the railway bill of lading directly he receives it. By this "application" the bank is asked to give Levine permission to substitute the railway bill of lading (or "way-bill" as it is also called) for the warehouseman's receipt for the cotton. In order that the bank may not lose its hold on the security, it is assured by this document that Levine only handles the cotton in transit from the warehouse to the railway only as a trustee for the bank.

FORM 1 9-12-50M

Form adopted by the New Orleans Clearing House Association

APPLICATION AND TRUST RECEIPT

Vicksburg, Miss., 30th October 1934

Mississippi Cotton Banking Corporation

I hereby make application to withdraw, on the terms and conditions of the subjoined TRUST RECEIPT, the certain documents hereinafter described, which said documents and the property represented thereby are pledged with you to secure advances made to me on one obligations dated October 3rd 1934.

for one or both of the following purposes, viz.:

First, for delivery, of the property represented by said documents, to Y. & M.V. Railway (Name of steamship or railroad) for shipment to New Orleans (Destination)

Second, for substituting and changing said documents for warehouse receipts or other documents representing and describing the identical property, to be obtained from The Y. & M.V. Railway (Name of warehouse, etc.)

Said document~~s~~ to be withdrawn ~~are~~ is viz.:

MARKS, NUMBERS AND DESCRIPTION OF COLLATERAL PLEDGED

Trust Receipt dated October 3rd 1934

for 3 bales cotton

Signature Marcus B. Levine

TRUST RECEIPT

Vicksburg, Miss. October 30th 1934

Received in trust from The Mississippi Cotton Banking Corporation the bills of lading, press or warehouse receipts, or other documents or securities described in the foregoing application, held by said Bank as collateral pledged to secure advances made to the undersigned, and in consideration thereof, the undersigned hereby expressly agrees to pay over to said Bank or its assigns, on demand, the proceeds of the sale of the property described in and/or represented by said documents, or should the amount of said proceeds exceed the entire indebtedness to said Bank, in principal and interest, the undersigned expressly agrees to pay over to said Bank or its assigns, on demand, a proportion thereof, equal to the full amount of said entire indebtedness, in principal and interest.

It is stipulated that the payments herein contemplated shall be specifically applied against the identical advances secured by the aforesaid property.

In the event that the undersigned withdraws said documents for the purpose of substituting and/or changing them for warehouse receipts or other documents, representing and describing the identical property pledged, it is expressly agreed that said new documents shall be delivered to said Bank or its assigns within one (1) day from the receipt thereof by the undersigned.

In either or both of the above cases it is expressly agreed that this delivery is being temporarily made to the undersigned for convenience only, without novation of the original debt, or giving the undersigned any title to said property and the undersigned is given possession thereof solely as trustee for said Bank, and as such to receive the avails thereof or the documents therefor for account of the said Bank.

It is further stipulated, that the undersigned shall not, under any circumstances whatsoever, repledge the property withdrawn under the terms of this TRUST RECEIPT, or, use or sell said property, so withdrawn, for any other purpose than that of paying the indebtedness for the security of which the said property was pledged to said Bank.

(Any violation of the terms and conditions of this TRUST RECEIPT is made a felony by Act No. 9, of 1914, printed in full on the back hereof.)

Signature Marcus B. Levine

Form No. 9 is not a credit instrument. It is a contract of sale for the cotton sold by Levine to Silas J. Hocking, that is for 20 bales of cotton at 11·85 cents per lb. The cost, freight, and insurance is included in the price, and an allowance of 6% of the value of the cotton is made for tare, that is, the approximate weight of the material used in packing the cotton, or in other words, the "tare" is the difference between the nett and the gross weight.

FORM NO. 9.—CONTRACT OF SALE

SALE NOTE No. 412

FROM

MARCUS B. LEVINE

Vicksburg, Miss. October 30th 1934

To Mr. Silas J. Hocking

New Orleans

We have this day Sold to you: 20 bales cotton

as sample in your possession marked: B.A.Z.

@ 11.85 cents per lb.

Specimen

TERMS: Cost Freight, Insurance and 6 per cent. for Tare, October Shipment

To New Orleans

Reimbursement by draft

All other terms in accordance with our general agreement. Marcus B. Levine

CHAPTER II

THE EXPORT OF RAW COTTON FROM NEW ORLEANS TO LIVERPOOL

Part I

We have now carried the story up to the point where the cotton was received in New Orleans.

Silas J. Hocking placed the cotton in the New Orleans Public Cotton Warehouse, the largest port cotton warehouse in the world. It covers 33 acres, it warehouses 461,800 bales, 250 cars can be unloaded at one time, and there is a wharf accommodation for four large ocean-going steamers. When the cotton had been warehoused, with many other bales which Silas J. Hocking had bought in various cotton centres, he graded the cotton according to quality, and marked the bales with distinctive marks. For instance, his mark for Hezekiah's quality was B.A.Z., which he also used for cotton bought from other farmers equal to Hezekiah's quality.

It might happen that some time elapsed before Silas J. Hocking sold his cotton. If, in the meantime, he wanted money to pay drafts for new cotton which was coming in, he might take his warehouse receipt (Credit instrument No. 10) to his bank in New Orleans and obtain a loan against the security of the cotton. Or, he might issue to his bank in addition, his own promissory note, *i.e.* his promise to pay on demand or on a certain date a given sum of money (Credit instrument No. 11), or, if he were sufficiently wealthy and well known, sell it through a broker; that is a man who sells it in the open market to anyone who will buy it, earning a commission for his services (Credit instrument No. 12).

One day Silas J. Hocking might receive a cable from Birdhead & Co. in Liverpool offering him a price —we will suppose of 12·10 cents per lb.—for 1000 bales of B.A.Z. mark, shipment 200 bales a month October/February. If he was willing to accept the price, he would cable Birdhead & Co., who, by arrangement, would open a credit with a bank in Manchester, Liverpool, or London, authorizing Silas J. Hocking to draw a ninety-days Bill of Exchange (Credit instrument No. 13) on the bank for the amount of the shipment of cotton, on condition that the ocean-going bill of lading (Credit instrument No. 14) and a marine insurance policy (Credit instrument No. 15) were handed over to the bank as security. Generally speaking there would be no credit instrument for opening the credit. Birdhead & Co. would simply go to their bankers and ask them if they were willing to accept drafts drawn on the bank by the sellers of cotton in New York for shipments to Birdhead & Co. An amount would be fixed and the bank would agree to accept drafts say up to £50,000. This is the manner in which these cotton credits are usually arranged. It sometimes happens, however, that an American seller might sell cotton to a firm in Liverpool of whose financial standing the seller was uncertain. In this case, he might ask the buyer to open an irrevocable confirmed credit (Credit instrument No. 16).

Silas J. Hocking having accepted Birdhead & Co.'s offer, the bales were pressed once more into still smaller compass before the cotton was shipped, in order to save ocean freight. Silas J. Hocking on receipt of his credit, drew, from time to time as he shipped the cotton, Bills of Exchange on the bank, (say the North-Western Bank, Ltd., in Liverpool), for the value of each shipment. The value of a particular shipment of cotton was say £250, so Silas J. Hocking's bill was an instruction to the North-Western Bank, Ltd. to pay to himself or his order, the sum of £250 ninety days after sight (that is ninety days after the North-Western Bank, Ltd. had seen the bill, or, as it is usually expressed, had "sighted" the bill). Silas J. Hocking then endorsed the bill to his New Orleans bank, which had the effect of instructing the North-Western Bank, Ltd. to pay the amount to the bank in New Orleans or to anyone to whom the New Orleans Bank might order it to be paid. In order to take the goods (which were pledged to the bank) out of the warehouse, Silas J. Hocking made application to the bank in the same way as Credit instrument No. 8 and gave the bank as security a Trust Receipt undertaking to hand over the bills of lading when received. This Trust Receipt would be in a similar form to Credit instrument No. 8, but would refer to ocean bills of lading, whereas the former referred to railway bills of lading. Along with the Bill of

Exchange, Silas J. Hocking handed to his New Orleans bank the ocean bill of lading when he received it, the marine insurance policy, and his invoice for the cotton, all of which were forwarded to the bank's agents in Liverpool. The New Orleans bank deducted from the value of the sterling Bill of Exchange the equivalent in dollars of the amount of any loan plus interest which it had made to Silas J. Hocking, and credited his account for the surplus, if any.

The New Orleans bank then sent the Bill of Exchange and all the other documents to a New York bank, who forwarded it to agents in Liverpool; or possibly the New Orleans bank sent the Bill of Exchange and other documents direct to its agent in Liverpool. Whichever way it was done, the agents in Liverpool on receipt of the Bill of Exchange and documents, presented them to the North-Western Bank, Ltd., and left the bill of lading and insurance policy, etc., with the bank against the return of the Bill of Exchange with the word "accepted" written across it and the signature of the North-Western Bank, Ltd., indicating that the bank was willing to pay it after ninety days (Credit instrument No. 17). If the New York or New Orleans bank desired to receive the money immediately, the accepted Bill of Exchange would be discounted with a discount broker or with a bank in England and the money remitted to New York or to New Orleans by a demand draft on an American bank, or else used to make payments here in England on behalf of the New

York or New Orleans bank. The discount broker or bank would thus have given ninety days credit to the New York or New Orleans bank, and it would be said that the shipment of cotton had been financed in England. On the other hand, if the New York or New Orleans bank did not require the money, it might hold the bill until maturity, that is, until payment became due after ninety days had elapsed. In such a case the cotton would have been financed in America, for it would have been by money provided by the New York or New Orleans bank that Silas J. Hocking received credit for the ninety days which had to elapse before his cotton was paid for by Birdhead & Co. in Liverpool.

Before accepting the bill, however, the North-Western Bank, Ltd., received a request from Birdhead & Co. asking them to accept it (Credit instrument No. 18). After acceptance of the Bill of Exchange, the bank handed over the bill of lading to a warehouse-keeper or to a shipping agent in Liverpool in order to enable them to obtain the cotton from the ship in exchange for this bill of lading, and the shipping agent or warehouse-keeper undertook to hold the cotton in trust for the bank (Credit instrument No. 19), and to hand to the bank the warehouse receipt for the cotton when it was stored.

Later on, when Birdhead & Co. sold the cotton, in order to deliver it to their buyer (the Diamond Spinning Co. Ltd.), they requested the bank (Credit instrument No. 20) to instruct the warehouse-keeper to deliver the cotton to Birdhead & Co.; this firm undertaking to hand over the proceeds of the cotton directly they received them from their buyer. The bank then released the cotton (Credit instrument No. 21) and used the proceeds, when received from Birdhead & Co., to pay the Bill of Exchange drawn by Silas J. Hocking.

When the bank received payment from Birdhead & Co., for the cotton which had been delivered to the Diamond Spinning Co., Ltd., the bank credited Birdhead & Co., in their account with the bank, which was called the "Provision for Acceptances" account, and the money in this account was used by the bank to pay the Bill of Exchange drawn on the bank by Silas J. Hocking. If, by the time the Bill of Exchange was due, all the cotton was not sold and paid for, the bank would make a loan to Birdhead & Co. for the value of the unsold cotton, and Birdhead & Co. would use this loan to fulfil their obligations to pay the bank sufficient cash to meet the Bill of Exchange.

The banks concerned held the cotton as security (either by means of warehouse receipts or by the bill of lading), for all credit which was given to Silas J. Hocking from the time that he bought the cotton from Levine until he was finally paid by Birdhead & Co. ninety days after the Bill of Exchange arrived in Liverpool. From the time, however, when Levine delivered the cotton until final payment, a period of five or six months might elapse. For the last ninety days of this period the American bank would be fully covered because they held the acceptance of the North-Western Bank, Ltd. But, for the first part of the period, if cotton fell to a price which, when sold, would be insufficient to reimburse the bank for its advances to Silas J. Hocking, and if this latter firm were unable to make good the deficiency, then the New Orleans bank would lose. In the same way, if the cotton fell to a price which made the total value less than the value of the Bill of Exchange "accepted" by the North-Western Bank, Ltd., and if Birdhead & Co. could not pay the difference, the North-Western Bank, Ltd., would lose.

Neither Silas J. Hocking nor Birdhead & Co. were speculators. They bought their cotton in order to sell it at their normal profit, and this was all they desired to make. They expected a profit to remunerate them for the services they rendered to the ultimate consumer, which consisted in bringing the cotton to the place where it was wanted and at the time it was wanted, in order that it might be spun into yarn. They did not look to make a profit through the possible rise in the price of cotton, but, on the other hand, they wished to safeguard themselves against a possible loss through a fall in the price of cotton between the time when they bought it and the time when they sold it.

In order to ensure that the value of the security of the banks was always maintained at the value which it had when the credit was given, and in order to ensure that Silas J. Hocking and Birdhead & Co. did not make losses through a fall in the price of cotton, the cotton when purchased was immediately "hedged" by Silas J. Hocking, and later by Birdhead & Co.

The system of hedging is as follows. When Silas J. Hocking bought his cotton from Levine, he would immediately sell it for delivery at some future time ahead; he would not sell the actual cotton, because this he expected Birdhead & Co. to want at some future date, but he would sell "futures", *i.e.* he would enter into a contract to deliver so many bales of cotton at some future period. When the time came, he would be entitled to deliver cotton of a quality equal to certain standards such as MIDDLING, LOW MIDDLING, etc., according to universal standards which are recognized by the chief cotton exchanges of the world. For instance, if he had bought in November, 1000 bales of B.A.Z. mark, he might sell 1000 bales of "futures" for delivery in March. The price he paid for B.A.Z. would, of course, bear some relation to the price of MIDDLING quality on the same day, more or less according to whether B.A.Z. was better or worse than that quality. Now when Birdhead & Co. bought the B.A.Z. cotton some months later, Silas J. Hocking would lose if, in the meantime, the price of cotton had fallen. On the other hand, he would be able to buy cotton at a corresponding reduction to deliver against his contract for "futures" which had to be settled in March, so that what he lost with Birdhead & Co. he would gain on his "futures" contract. But whenever Silas J. Hocking sold to Birdhead & Co., the price at which he sold would be higher than the price at which he could replace the cotton on that day, the difference representing the remuneration which he received for his services. If the price of cotton rose between his purchase and sale of B.A.Z., then he would get a higher price from Birdhead & Co. and make an extra profit, which extra profit, however, would be swept away because he would have to pay a higher price in order to complete his deal in March "futures". By this method of "hedging", then, Silas J. Hocking could not suffer any loss through a fall in the price of cotton, and would always be able to make good the deficiency (if any), to the bank which advanced him money.[1]

We have now traced the cotton from the time when Hezekiah planted the seed in his ground, until the cotton was finally landed in Liverpool. We have seen that even before the cotton was planted, John B. Robinson held his farm on credit; that the fertilizers for the land were bought on credit; that the cotton seed was bought on credit; and that the cotton was moved from Hezekiah's farm into the warehouse in Liverpool on a continuous belt of credit. This credit enabled everyone in America who grew or handled the cotton to be paid for his efforts, but nothing, that is, no specific thing or things, had as yet (in the transactions which we have described) been received by America in exchange for the cotton which she had sent to England.

In describing the sale of Hezekiah's B.A.Z. cotton,

[1] The hedge described is not absolutely watertight, because an alteration in demand for a special quality of cotton may cause a variation in the price of that quality, irrespective of a variation in the price of the standard qualities.

we have used this transaction as illustrative of hundreds of others which are taking place daily between the United Kingdom and United States in all kinds of commodities. The commercial and financial relationship of two countries is, however, not confined to the export and import of commodities, but embraces other transactions also which are called "invisible" imports and exports. By this term is meant the exchange of services, such as the ocean freight earned for carrying goods; insurance premiums; and commissions and interest on borrowed money. The term also includes the buying and selling of bonds and shares belonging to the nationals of one country to the nationals of another; money remitted home from people living in a foreign country and money spent in a foreign country by visitors from abroad; film rights and various other items.

When we say that America received nothing in exchange for Hezekiah's cotton, we do not mean, of course, for this one special transaction. Nor do we mean that America did not receive goods and services in exchange for goods and services sent and rendered to us, but as she sends us three or four times the value of commodities which she receives from us, there must remain a balance in her favour. This balance can only be regulated either by invisible exports, the shipment of gold, or through methods of indirect payment which it is one of the objects of this book to describe.

Part II

CREDIT INSTRUMENTS

Credit instrument No. 10: This is an acknowledgement from the New Orleans Federal Compress and Warehouse Company, that they have received one bale of cotton as described on the receipt, but that they have not insured it against fire, so this would have to be done by Silas J. Hocking. The warehouse company has a lien on this cotton for the charges for storage on this bale. The space on the left-hand of the receipt is to enable the cotton to be graded by the examiners of the Board of Agriculture if desired. A separate receipt is given for each bale.

CREDIT INSTRUMENT NO. 10.—COTTON WAREHOUSE RECEIPT

TAG AND RECEIPT

Nº 216004

OLD TAG NUMBER

U. S. DEPARTMENT OF AGRICULTURE – BOARD OF COTTON EXAMINERS

Nov. 7. 34

	GRADE M	RED. FROM	%	STAPLE
TENDERABLE	1 Bale			$1\frac{1}{8}$
UNTENDERABLE				

PURSUANT TO THE U. S. COTTON FUTURES ACT WE CERTIFY THE CLASSIFICATION OF THE COTTON DESCRIBED HEREIN IS THAT STATED ABOVE

BY Charles. B. Pell
CHAIRMAN – BOARD OF COTTON EXAMINERS

REVIEWED AND DETERMINED TO BE AS SET FORTH BELOW

19	GRADE	RED. FROM	%	STAPLE
TENDERABLE				
UNTENDERABLE				

BY
CHAIRMAN – BOARD OF COTTON EXAMINERS

GOV'T LOT NO. ______ OLD LOT NO. ______

SPACE AT LEFT FOR USE BOARD OF COTTON EXAMINERS

FEDERAL COMPRESS WAREHOUSE, New Orleans, La.
FEDERAL COMPRESS & WAREHOUSE COMPANY, Proprietor. License 2-958
Located on Tchoupitoulas St., between St. Mary and St. Andrew Sts.
Incorporated under the laws of Delaware

TAG AND RECEIPT

Nº 216004

WAREHOUSE CLASSIFICATION: GRADE ______ STAPLE ______ WEIGHT ______ CONDITION ______
ACCORDING TO THE OFFICIAL COTTON STANDARDS OF THE UNITED STATES

BANDS	COMP'N	DATE WEIGHED	WEIGHT	DATE REWEIGHED	REWEIGHED	PATCHES NO. LBS	MISC.
3		7. Nov. 34	512	---	---	2 2 lbs.	

LICENSED AND BONDED UNDER THE UNITED STATES WAREHOUSE ACT

Copy—Not Negotiable

Received for storage from Silas J. Hocking

THE ONE BALE OF COTTON DESCRIBED HEREIN AND STORED IN THE ABOVE NAMED WAREHOUSE, FOR WHICH THIS RECEIPT IS ISSUED SUBJECT TO THE UNITED STATES WAREHOUSE ACT, THE REGULATIONS THEREUNDER FOR COTTON WAREHOUSES AND THE TERMS OF THIS CONTRACT. SAID COTTON IS NOT INSURED BY THE UNDERSIGNED WAREHOUSEMAN AGAINST LOSS OR DAMAGE BY FIRE OR LIGHTNING UNLESS EXPRESSLY STATED OTHERWISE ON THE FACE OF THIS RECEIPT. SAID COTTON IS ACCEPTED FOR STORAGE FOR ONE YEAR ONLY FROM THE DATE OF THIS RECEIPT, BUT UPON SURRENDER BY THE HOLDER, THIS RECEIPT MAY BE EXTENDED OR A NEW RECEIPT ISSUED AS PROVIDED IN SAID REGULATIONS. THE UNDERSIGNED WAREHOUSEMAN IS NOT THE OWNER, EITHER SOLELY, JOINTLY, OR IN COMMON WITH OTHERS, OF THE COTTON COVERED BY THIS RECEIPT UNLESS EXPRESSLY STATED OTHERWISE HEREIN. THE UNDERSIGNED WAREHOUSEMAN CLAIMS A LIEN ON SAID COTTON FOR CHARGES AND LIABILITIES AS FOLLOWS: STORAGE AT THE RATE OF 1 CENT PER BALE PER DAY ON STANDARD AND HIGH DENSITY COMPRESSED COTTON AND 1 CENT PER BALE PER DAY ON UNCOMPRESSED COTTON FROM THE DATE OF STORAGE, PLUS OTHER ACCRUED CHARGES THEREON ACCORDING TO TARIFFS OF THE COMPANY PUBLISHED AND IN EFFECT DURING THE LIFE OF THIS RECEIPT. UPON THE RETURN OF THIS RECEIPT AND THE PAYMENT OF ALL CHARGES AND LIABILITIES DUE THE UNDERSIGNED WAREHOUSEMAN, AS STATED HEREIN, SAID COTTON WILL BE DELIVERED TO BEARER FOR HYPOTHECATION IN ACCORDANCE WITH THE LAWS OF THE STATE OF LOUISIANA

STORAGE BEGINS 7 Nov. PRO ISSUED AT NEW ORLEANS, LA.

FEDERAL COMPRESS & WAREHOUSE COMPANY
LICENSED WAREHOUSEMAN

WEIGHT DETERMINED BY A WEIGHER LICENSED UNDER THE U. S. WAREHOUSE ACT.

STORAGE .004 PER DAY

BY Thomas Westcott.

THE ISSUANCE OF A FRAUDULENT RECEIPT, OR ILLEGAL CONVERSION OR REMOVAL OF THE COTTON REPRESENTED BY THIS RECEIPT, IS PUNISHABLE BY A $10,000.00 FINE, OR IMPRISONMENT FOR TEN YEARS OR BOTH

Credit instrument No. 11 is a promise to pay after 30 days the sum stated plus 5% interest per annum and agreeing that the cotton warehoused, as shown by Credit instrument No. 10, shall be held by the bank as collateral security for the payment of this promissory note, and that Silas J. Hocking will give further collateral security to the bank if demanded. It further agrees that any other property or money which the bank may hold belonging to Silas J. Hocking is pledged to the bank for the payment of this note, and gives the bank the right to sell any security which it may hold, if the note is not paid on the due date. If Silas J. Hocking becomes insolvent, and under other similar circumstances as stated, this note becomes due immediately.

FORM DIS. 11

$ 1000 New Orleans, La., 7th November 1934

thirty days after date, I, whether maker, endorser, guarantor, surety, or other party hereto, promise to pay to the order of New Orleans & Overseas Bank at METROPOLITAN BANK OF NEW ORLEANS one thousand Dollars, for value received, with interest, at the rate of 5 per cent per annum from 7th November 1934 until paid

All parties hereto hereby severally waive presentment for payment, demand, notice of non-payment, protest, and all pleas of division and discussion, and agree that the payment hereof may be extended from time to time, one or more times, without notice, hereby binding themselves, in solido, unconditionally and as original promisors, for the payment hereof, in principal, interest, costs, and attorney's fees.

All parties hereto bind themselves to pay the fees of any attorney-at-law who may be employed to recover the amount hereof, or any part hereof, in principal or interest, or to protect the interests of the holder hereof, or to enforce the pledge herein contained, or to compromise, or to take other action with regard hereto, which fees are hereby fixed at ten per cent. (10%) on the amount then owing hereon and sought to be collected, protected, or preserved, which fee is secured by the pledge herein contained.

The property described on the reverse hereof, and any property that may be substituted therefor or added thereto, and all other property that may now or at any time hereafter be given or left in the possession of the Whitney National Bank of New Orleans, for any purpose by any party hereto, or any property belonging to any party hereto, that may come or be in the possession of said Bank, or that may be in transit to or from said Bank, for any purpose, are hereby pledged and delivered to said Bank to secure the payment of this note, and of any note given in extension or renewal thereof, as well as for the payment of any other obligation or liability, direct or contingent, of any of the parties hereto to said Bank, whether due or to become due and whether now existing or hereafter arising, with interest, attorney's fees, expenses, and costs, up to the amount of $500,000.00. All parties hereto severally consent and agree that the property hereby pledged may be exchanged or surrendered from time to time without notice to or assent from any party hereto, and without in any manner releasing or altering their obligations hereunder.

Should any of the pledged property decline in value, each of the parties hereto agrees upon demand to deliver and pledge, on the terms here stated, to said Bank satisfactory additional property as security and to make payments to said Bank's satisfaction on account of this note. On the non-performance of this agreement, or upon the non-payment at any maturity of any of the obligations or liabilities of any party hereto, or upon the death, suspension, failure, or insolvency, or upon any application for the adjudication in bankruptcy, or upon the commencing of dissolution proceedings, or proceedings for the appointment of a liquidator or liquidators, of any party hereto, or upon the application by or against any party hereto for a respite, assignment, or receivership, then and in any such case this note and all other obligations and liabilities, direct or contingent, of the parties hereto, and each of them, to said Bank, shall forthwith mature and become due and payable, without demand, notice, or putting in default, anything herein contained to the contrary notwithstanding; and full irrevocable power and authority are hereby granted and given to said Bank, thereupon, or upon this note not being paid at maturity, to sell, assign, transfer, and effectively deliver the whole of the property of every kind pledged hereby, or any part thereof, or substitutes therefor, or additions thereto, at public or private sale, without recourse to judicial proceedings and without either demand, appraisement, advertisement, or notice of any kind, all of which are hereby expressly waived. At any such sale, said Bank may itself purchase the whole or any part of the property sold, free from any right of redemption on the part of any party hereto, which right is hereby waived and released. In case of any sale or other disposition of any of the property aforesaid, after deducting all costs, attorney's fees, and expenses of every kind, said Bank may apply the residue of the proceeds of sale or sales, pro tanto, to the payment of any or all of the obligations or liabilities of the parties hereto or any of them, whether then due or not due, up to the amount of $500,000.00, making proper rebate for interest on obligations or liabilities not then due and returning the overplus, if any, to the maker hereof.

All parties hereto hereby authorize and empower said Bank, at any time, to appropriate and apply to the payment and extinguishment hereof and/or of any of the obligations or liabilities, direct or contingent, of any of the parties hereto, whether now existing or hereafter arising, and whether then due or not due, up to the amount of $500,000.00, said Bank being authorized to impute the payments as it sees fit, any and all moneys, stocks, bonds, or other property of any kind whatever now or hereafter in the hands of said Bank on deposit or otherwise to the credit of or belonging to any party hereto, including any moneys or other property in transit to or from said Bank for any purpose. All parties hereto do hereby further irrevocably authorize and empower said Bank, at any time to collect, and appropriate, and apply to the payment and extinguishment hereof, the interest, dividends, or other income accruing and payable on any of the property pledged to secure the payment hereof, and, to facilitate such collection, all parties hereto agree that any of the said property may be transferred, at said Bank's option, to the name of said Bank, or its nominee, on the books of the company issuing same.

Any holder hereof may transfer this note and may deliver said collateral security or any part thereof to the transferee or transferees, who shall thereupon become vested with all the powers and rights herein given in respect thereto; and any holder making such transfer shall thereafter be forever relieved and fully discharged from any liability or responsibility in the matter. No delay on the part of any holder hereof in exercising any rights hereunder shall operate as a waiver of such rights.

All parties hereto further severally agree that this note evidences and sets forth their entire agreement with the holder hereof, that they hereby consent to all the terms and conditions hereof, and that no modification hereof shall be binding unless hereon endorsed in writing and signed by the parties.

$ 1000 Silas J. Loveking

Due 7th December 1934

Credit instrument No. 12 is the promissory note which Silas J. Hocking might sell in the open market through a broker. No comment beyond that already made for Credit instrument No. 5 is necessary.

CREDIT INSTRUMENT NO. 12.—UNSECURED PROMISSORY NOTE

FORM D.S 12

$ 1000 New Orleans, La., November 7th 19 34

thirty days after date, I, whether maker, endorser, guarantor, surety, or other party hereto, promise to pay to the order of The New Orleans & Overseas Bank at METROPOLITAN BANK OF NEW ORLEANS

one thousand Dollars, for value received, with interest at the rate of 5 per cent per annum from 7th November 1934 until paid

Upon the non-payment at any maturity of any of the obligations or liabilities of any party hereto, or upon the death, suspension, failure, or insolvency, or upon any application for the adjudication in bankruptcy, or upon the commencing of dissolution proceedings, or proceedings for the appointment of a liquidator or liquidators, of any party hereto, or upon the application by or against any party hereto for a respite, assignment, or receivership, then and in any such case this note and all other obligations and liabilities, direct or contingent, of the parties hereto, and each of them, to the Whitney National Bank of New Orleans, shall forthwith mature and become due and payable, without demand, notice, or putting in default, anything herein contained to the contrary notwithstanding.

All parties hereto hereby authorize and empower said Bank, at any time, to appropriate and apply to the payment and extinguishment hereof and/or of any of the obligations or liabilities, direct or contingent, of any of the parties hereto, whether now existing or hereafter arising, and whether then due or not due, said Bank being authorized to impute the payments as it sees fit, any and all moneys, stocks, bonds, or other property of any kind whatever now or hereafter in the hands of said Bank on deposit or otherwise to the credit of or belonging to any party hereto, including any moneys or other property in transit to or from said Bank for any purpose.

All parties hereto bind themselves to pay the fees of any attorney-at-law who may be employed to recover the amount hereof, or any part hereof, in principal or interest, or to protect the interests of the holder hereof, or to compromise, or to take other action with regard hereto, which fees are hereby fixed at ten per cent. (10%) on the amount then owing hereon and sought to be collected, protected, or preserved.

All parties hereto hereby severally waive presentment for payment, demand, notice of non-payment, protest, and all pleas of division and discussion, and agree that the payment hereof may be extended from time to time, one or more times, without notice, hereby binding themselves, in solido, unconditionally and as original promisors, for the payment hereof, in principal, interest, costs, and attorney's fees.

All parties hereto further severally agree that this note evidences and sets forth their entire agreement with the holder hereof, that they hereby consent to all the terms and conditions hereof, and that no modification hereof shall be binding unless hereon endorsed in writing and signed by the parties.

$ 1000 Silas J. Hocking

Due 7th December 1934

Credit instrument No. 13 is the Bill of Exchange drawn by Silas J. Hocking on the North-Western Bank, Ltd., in Liverpool. The Bill of Exchange is drawn in duplicate and the second copy sent by a different mail from that of the first, so that if the first were lost, the second would be presented for acceptance and eventually for payment. Silas J. Hocking endorses the bill to the New Orleans & Overseas Bank, which bank credits him for the amount.

CREDIT INSTRUMENT NO. 13.—BILL OF EXCHANGE

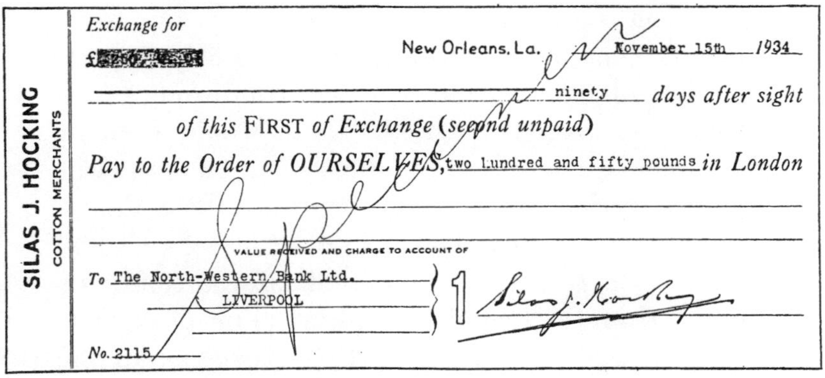
SILAS J. HOCKING
COTTON MERCHANTS

Exchange for
£[redacted]
New Orleans, La. November 15th 1934
ninety *days after sight*
of this FIRST *of Exchange (second unpaid)*
Pay to the Order of OURSELVES, two hundred and fifty pounds *in London*
VALUE RECEIVED AND CHARGE TO ACCOUNT OF
To The North-Western Bank Ltd.
LIVERPOOL
1
No. 2115

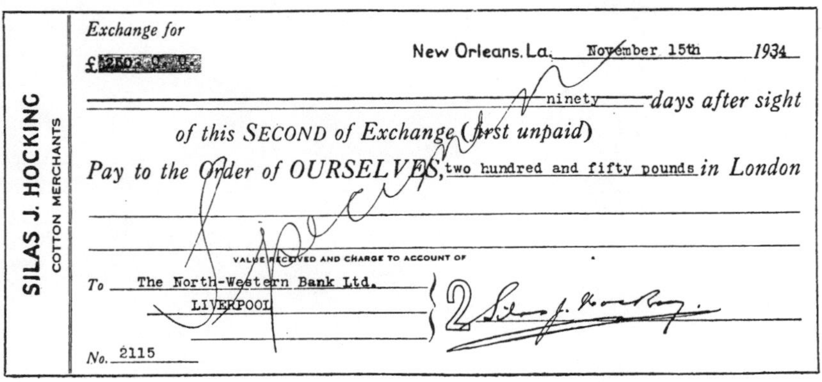
SILAS J. HOCKING
COTTON MERCHANTS

Exchange for
£[redacted]
New Orleans, La. November 15th 1934
ninety *days after sight*
of this SECOND *of Exchange (first unpaid)*
Pay to the Order of OURSELVES, two hundred and fifty pounds *in London*
VALUE RECEIVED AND CHARGE TO ACCOUNT OF
To The North-Western Bank Ltd.
LIVERPOOL
2
No. 2115

Credit instrument No. 14 is the bill of lading used for the ocean transport of the cotton. It is a transferable acknowledgement by the shipowners of the receipt of the cotton in apparent good order and condition, and stating to which port it has to be carried. On a bill of lading there are always a large number of clauses detailing the conditions under which the cargo is carried. These would take up too much space to reproduce here, but students who require further information regarding these clauses should refer to text-books like Scrutton's *Charter Parties and Bills of Lading*, or if information is required from the technical banking point of view, to Grant's *Law of Banking*, Hart's *Banking*, or similar standard text-books.

CREDIT INSTRUMENT NO. 14.—OCEAN BILL OF LADING

NEW ORLEANS U-K LINE

owned and operated
by
William Jemson S.S. Co., Inc.

General Offices
New Orleans Houston
Galveston

U.S. Gulf Ports
to
UNITED KINGDOM

SHIPPER'S MARKS AND NUMBERS

B.A.Z. 20 Bales

OCEAN FREIGHT AND WHARFAGE PREPAID

Freight on 9833 lbs.
@ 33 cents per 100 lbs.

Issued under Agreement with the Liverpool Bill of Lading Conference Committee with respect to shipments of Cotton.

S.S. Contract No. Port

Bill of Lading No. 424 1934

Received in apparent good order and condition from Silas J. Hocking to be transported by the American steamship NEW ENSIGN from the port of New Orleans, La., and bound for EUROPEAN PORTS or failing shipment by said vessel by a subsequent vessel, carrying vessel having liberties as to routes and ports of call as hereinafter provided: the following goods:

Twenty Bales (20) High Density Compressed Bales Cotton

WEIGHING 9833 LBS.

being marked and numbered as per margin (quality, quantity, gauge, weight, measurement, contents, and value unknown), and to be delivered in like good order and condition at the port of Liverpool, England or as near thereunto as the vessel may safely get, and always lie afloat, unto ORDER OF

SHIPPER

or to his or their assigns, on payment of freight and charges thereon in cash without deduction, credit, or discount, immediately on discharge of the goods at the rate as per margin, unless prepaid (all collect freights under this bill of lading, including any short paid freight, shall be converted at the current sight rate of exchange on New York on the date the vessel enters customs at the port of discharge), and upon the following terms and conditions:

[*Here follow usual Clauses.*]

CREDIT INSTRUMENT NO. 14 (*continued*)

IN ACCEPTING THIS BILL OF LADING the shipper, owner, and consignee of the goods and the holder of the bill of lading agree to be bound by all its stipulations, exceptions, and conditions, whether written, printed or stamped on the front or back hereof, as fully as if they were all signed by said shipper, owner, consignee, or holder, any local custom or privileges to the contrary notwithstanding.

IN WITNESS WHEREOF, the Master or Agent of said vessel has affirmed to Two bills of lading, all this tenor and date, one of which being accomplished, the other to stand void.

Dated at New Orleans, La., November 14th 1934.

For the Master:

WILLIAM JEMSON S.S. Co., INC.

By A. J. Dempster.

Credit instrument No. 15 is a marine insurance policy. It declares that the insurer has represented that he is interested in the cargo, because in order to insure he must have an interest which might be injured in the event of a loss, and an outsider who has no such interest, cannot insure the cargo. Subject to many clauses and provisions which are not shown here, the insurance company, in consideration of the arranged premium, undertakes to reimburse the insurer for any insured loss which he may sustain. Students who wish to pursue the matter further should read the clauses of an ordinary marine insurance policy, or, if they are interested from the banking point of view, the books mentioned at the foot of the preceding credit instrument, while for the legal aspect they should refer to Gow's *Marine Insurance* or other standard text-books.

CREDIT INSTRUMENT NO. 15.—MARINE INSURANCE POLICY

The London & National Marine & General Insurance Co., Ltd.

Head Office: 14, FENCHURCH AVENUE, LONDON, E.C.3.

Stamp 6d

New Orleans Agency

No. 34 / 5846

PAYABLE IN Liverpool

At the current exchange of the day for a Bank Demand Draft on London

In case of loss or claim apply to Company's Office——

the Agents of the Company in Liverpool

Whereas Silas J. Hocking has represented to THE LONDON & NATIONAL MARINE & GENERAL INSURANCE COMPANY LIMITED that he is interested in or duly authorised as Owner Agent or otherwise to make the Insurance hereinafter mentioned and described with the said Company and promised or otherwise obliged himself to pay forthwith to the said Company the Sum of Fourteen shillings and threepence as a premium or consideration at and after the rate of ——one quarter—— per Cent. for such Insurance

Now this Policy of Insurance witnesseth that in consideration of the premises and of the said Sum the said Company doth promise and agree with the said Assured his Executors Administrators and Assigns that the said Company shall be subject and liable to pay and make good all such Losses and Damages hereinafter expressed as may happen to the subject matter of this Policy and may attach to this Policy in respect of the Sum of Two hundred and seventyfive Pounds hereby insured which Insurance is hereby declared to be upon

Twenty bales cotton B.A.Z. 1/20

to the Ship or Vessel called the New Ensign and/or steamer or steamers whereof is at present Master or whoever shall go for Master of the said Ship or Vessel lost or not lost at and from

New Orleans to Liverpool

Subject to the conditions of the printed clauses

(HERE FOLLOW PRINTED CLAUSES)

Including the Risk of Craft. Each Craft or Lighter to be deemed a separate Insurance.

In Witness whereof, We the Agent(s) for THE LONDON & NATIONAL MARINE & GENERAL INSURANCE COMPANY LIMITED, have subscribed our name(s) to two Policies of the same tenor and date one of which being accomplished the other to be void this Fifteenth day of November in the Year One Thousand Nine Hundred and thirty-four

For and on behalf of THE LONDON & NATIONAL MARINE & GENERAL INSURANCE COMPANY LIMITED

Exd. 94

Nicholas Huron & Co
Agent(s)

Credit instrument No. 16 is a request to the bank to open an irrevocable confirmed credit, which once being granted by the bank cannot be withdrawn, so that Silas J. Hocking with a credit of this description would be sure that he could get his money for his cotton even if Birdhead & Co. became insolvent before it was delivered. Banks often charge a somewhat higher rate of commission for these irrevocable credits than they do for an ordinary unconfirmed credit, which latter they are at liberty to withdraw before use. Birdhead & Co. undertake in clause 1 to provide the North-Western Bank, Ltd., with money to pay out-of-pocket expenses and sufficient money to pay the Bill of Exchange; such money to be in the hands of the bank three days before the bill falls due. The effect of clause 2 is to give the documents, the cotton, and any money received from the sale of the cotton, to the bank as security. Clause 5 is an agreement on the part of Birdhead & Co. that if they fail to pay the bank sufficient money as mentioned in clause 1, the bank shall hold any goods or money as security against money owing to them by Birdhead & Co. on *any* account and not merely for anything owing against this special transaction. Clause 6 frees the bank from any responsibility regarding the quantity, quality, and value of the cotton against which they have accepted the Bill of Exchange.

CONFIRMED (IRREVOCABLE) CREDIT. No. 120

November 2nd 1934

To **THE NORTH-WESTERN BANK, LIMITED**

*Delete mail or cable.

We request you to open on our account by ~~mail~~ cable at our risk and cost a confirmed credit with The New Orleans & Overseas Bank at New Orleans in favour of Silas J. Hocking of New Orleans for an aggregate amount of £ 12500 (say Twelve thousand five hundred pounds) available by their drafts on your Liverpool office at ninety days sight for the amount of their invoices purporting to cover shipment of

from October 1934 to February 1935

the drafts to be accompanied by the following documents :—

(a) Invoices

(b) Full sets of bills of lading to Order endorsed in blank.

(c) Delete if all insurance effected here.

(c) Policies or Certificates of insurance endorsed in blank covering all risks, including War Risks, for approximately 10 per cent. above C.I.F. value payable in England.

(d) Insert any additional documents required.

(d)

† Delete if shippers are to insure.

~~Insurance payable in England covering all risks ... to be effected and maintained by us.~~

This credit is not to be available in New Orleans after the 28th day of February 1935

IN consideration of your opening the above credit :—

1. We will put you in funds in cash to meet your disbursements and we will provide you with funds to meet your acceptances three days before their maturity.
2. We hereby charge the above mentioned documents and the goods and all proceeds thereof in your favour as a continuing security for the payment to you on demand of all moneys payable by us hereunder with interest, banking charges and expenses.
3. In case we should fail to do so we authorise you to pay and debit to our account cost, insurance, freight and any other charges and expenses in respect of the goods or otherwise.
4. We will assign to and lodge with you the policies in respect of the above mentioned insurance and any money paid thereunder shall forthwith be paid over to you and until so paid shall be held by us in trust for you.
5. If we fail to put you in funds as aforesaid you may debit all sums paid under or in connection with this credit and all bills as they mature to our current or any other account and this security shall be a continuing security for all moneys then or from time to time owing by us to you on any account and for all liabilities incurred by you on bills, guarantees or otherwise for us alone or jointly with others on any account whatsoever, and on default in payment on demand of any money hereby secured you may take possession of and sell the goods or any part thereof when and in such manner as you think fit and may collect any insurance moneys due or to become due and repay yourselves all money hereby secured with all costs and expenses of and incidental to storage and realisation, including your commission and all your other charges and expenses whatsoever, and on demand we will pay to you any deficiency.
6. You incur no liability hereunder beyond the due acceptance and payment of drafts drawn in accordance with the terms hereof and in particular you and your Correspondents shall not be responsible for the quantity, quality, value or description of any goods nor for the terms or sufficiency of any insurance and your rights hereunder shall not be prejudiced or affected by any invalidity, insufficiency, irregularity or misdescription in any document.
7. This Agreement shall continue in force notwithstanding any change in the constitution of any firm or company referred to herein.
8. We agree to pay you a commission of 1 per cent. on the amount of this credit.
9. This Agreement and all matters arising thereout shall in all respects be construed according to English law.

6D. STAMP.

Birdhead & Co

Credit instrument No. 17 is the same as credit instrument No. 13, but it has now been "accepted" by the North-Western Bank, Ltd., in Liverpool by writing across it the word "accepted". For convenience, as most bills are discounted in London, when the bill is accepted, it is made payable in London.

CREDIT INSTRUMENT NO. 17.—ACCEPTANCE

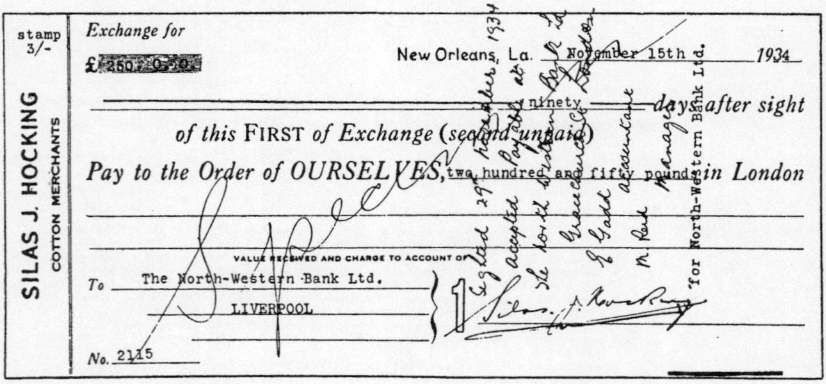
stamp 3/-

SILAS J. HOCKING
COTTON MERCHANTS

Exchange for

£ 250 : 0 : 0

New Orleans, La. November 15th 1934

ninety *days after sight*

of this FIRST *of Exchange (second unpaid)*

Pay to the Order of OURSELVES, two hundred and fifty pounds *in London*

VALUE RECEIVED AND CHARGE TO ACCOUNT OF

To The North-Western Bank Ltd.
LIVERPOOL

No. 2115

for North-Western Bank Ltd.

Credit instrument No. 18: In this document Birdhead & Co. ask the North-Western Bank, Ltd., to accept the Bill of Exchange. They guarantee the validity of all the documents and authorize the bank to hold the cotton as security, but as a continuing security, that is, a security for all present and future debts. They give the bank an estimate of the day's value of the cotton, and undertake to pay the bank sufficient cash to make up any deficiency in the event of a fall in the price of cotton. They also undertake to provide the bank with cash to meet the bill either at or before maturity.

CREDIT INSTRUMENT NO. 18.—CUSTOMER'S REQUEST FOR ACCEPTANCE

To the North-Western Bank Ltd. . November 21st 19 34

We understand that pursuant to our instructions the Vendors named below have delivered to you the bills of lading relating to the cotton specified below together with the undermentioned drafts for your acceptance and that the said cotton is now in your possession, you holding either the bills of lading or the warehouseman's receipt therefor.

Please accept the said drafts and debit the amount thereof to our acceptance account. In consideration thereof we hereby guarantee the validity of the said documents and drafts and authorise you to retain possession of the said cotton as security not only for our liability to you on the said accepted drafts but also as a continuing security for every debt or liability however arising which we have incurred or may incur with or be or become under to you whether solely or jointly with others and whether as principal debtors or sureties and whether such debt or liability be absolute contingent mature or immature.

The net value of the cotton at to-day's price we estimate to be about £250. 0. 0. after deducting freight and all charges. In the event of any fall in the value, we engage from time to time forewith to deposit with you cash and/or security to your approval equivalent to the amount of such fall.

We further engage to provide you with cash funds to meet the drafts at or before maturity.

Yours faithfully,

Birdhead & Co.

DRAFTS				PROPERTY			
NO.	DRAWN BY	TENOR	AMOUNT	MARKS	BALES	GROWTH	SHIP
2115	Silas J. Hocking	90 days sight	£250	B.A.Z 1/20	20	American	S.S. New Ensign

Credit instrument No. 19: This is the document by which the warehouse-keeper or shipping agent undertakes to hold the cotton in trust for the bank, and to hand a warehouse receipt to the bank when the cotton is stored. The only point to be noted in regard to this document is the fact that it bears the marks and numbers of the bales, thus identifying the property of the bank, so that if the warehouse-keeper were to become bankrupt or to be in liquidation, the liquidator could not claim the cotton, as the marks would enable the bank to prove which actual cotton was the bank's property.

CREDIT INSTRUMENT NO. 19.—WAREHOUSE TRUST RECEIPT

To The North-Western Bank Ltd. November 27th 1934

In consideration of your handing to us the documents for the cotton as specified hereunder, we undertake as your Agents, until further instructed by you, to hold the said documents and the cotton thereby represented in trust for the Bank, and not to part with the said documents or cotton for any purpose whatsoever.

We also undertake to retain entire control thereof and to store in your name with the Liverpool Cotton Warehouse Co. Ltd. all the cotton represented by the documents and to direct to you the relative warehouse receipt in due course.

We further undertake to keep the cotton fully covered by insurance in trust for the Bank and to pay any insurance monies we may receive to you specifically.

Yours faithfully,
Liverpool Cotton Warehouse Co. Ltd
Peter Walsh.

NO.	MARKS	BALES	SHIP
207	B.A.Z. 1/20	20	S.S. New Ensign

Received the above mentioned documents

Liverpool Cotton Warehouse Co. Ltd
Peter Walsh.

Credit instrument No. 20: When Birdhead & Co. require the cotton in order to deliver it to their buyer, the Diamond Spinning Co., Ltd., they sign credit instrument No. 20 in which they request the bank to give them (Birdhead & Co.) a delivery order authorizing the warehouse company to hand the cotton over to them. They undertake, in return, to hand over to the bank the payment for the cotton when they receive it from the Diamond Spinning Co., Ltd. (It is assumed in this instance that the cotton has been in store in Liverpool for a period of about seven months.)

CREDIT INSTRUMENT NO. 20.—REQUEST FOR DELIVERY ORDER

To The North-Western Bank Ltd. July..11th 1935

We desire to obtain possession of the undermentioned cotton now in the hands of the

Liverpool Cotton Warehouse Company Limited.

on your behalf and shall be obliged if you will sign and hand to the bearer the enclosed delivery order. In consideration of your so doing and without prejudice to your right to require repayment of the balance of our account at any time we hereby expressly undertake to deliver the goods to the said purchasers and to receive and hold the net proceeds of the sale thereof and of any insurances thereon in trust for you and to pay all such proceeds direct to you specifically and immediately on receipt thereof or each portion thereof as the case maybe, and to hold the said delivery order and/or the goods and/or proceeds of sale and/or insurance thereof only in accordance herewith and as trustees for you.

ACCEPTANCE NO.	MARKS	BALES	GROWTH	SHIP
2115	B.A.Z. 1/20	20	American	S.S. New Ensign

Yours faithfully,

Birdhead & Co

Credit instrument No. 21: This is merely an order to the warehouse company signed by the bank, authorizing the cotton to be delivered to Birdhead & Co. on payment of the storage and other relevant charges.

CREDIT INSTRUMENT NO. 21.—DELIVERY ORDER

12th July, 1935

To The Liverpool Cotton Warehouse Company Limited.

You are authorised to transfer to Messrs. Birdhead & Co.

or order the undermentioned cotton which you now hold for account of this Bank upon payment by them of all relevant charges.

Yours faithfully,

North-Western Bank Ltd.

sub-manager: Lester Hampton

NO.	MARKS	BALES	GROWTH	SHIP
207	B.A.Z. 1/20	20	American	S.S. New Ensign

CHAPTER III

CHINESE PURCHASE OF LANCASHIRE COTTON GOODS

Mrs. Wu lived in Fuen-choo, a town in the province of Shan-si in China. Fuen-choo is about a thousand miles from Shanghai, an old Chinese walled city the gates of which were shut every night. The streets were very narrow, and in summer they were shaded from the sun and protected from the rain by matting which could be rolled to close or open as desired. The shops and houses were lighted by electric light, but were not very well lighted.

It was summer and Mr. Wu sat outside in the street stripped to the waist, fanning his stomach with a paper fan. He was very fat and looked rather like the Chinese god of which we see porcelain figures in the shops here. Mr. Wu sold pork in his shop. All the shops in Mr. Wu's street sold pork, and all the shops in the next street sold fans; at right angles ran a street in which nothing but dried fish was sold, and opposite, a street full of grocery stores, for in China the shops are not all higgledy-piggledy as with us, but all in one street sell the same kind of goods.

One day Mrs. Wu set out for the street of cotton cloth merchants, because she wanted to buy twenty-one feet (a Chinese foot is about 12·3 inches) of the same cotton cloth which she had bought annually for the past five years, in order to make new shirts for her husband. The trade mark under which this cloth was sold was called the "Nine Dragon Chop", and every piece bore a beautiful paper label on which nine Chinese dragons were printed in gold on a black ground. Mrs. Wu and her friends knew that the material which bore this ticket made shirts which washed well and lasted a long time.

As Mrs. Wu entered the shop, she met the proprietor, Mr. Feng, who said to her: "Ah, Mrs. Wu, I have long been without the benefit of your felicitous face and your instructions", to which she replied, "I am much obliged and hope for your happiness". "I failed", said Mr. Feng, "in not being here to welcome you". "How can I presume to accept such a compliment", said Mrs. Wu, and to his enquiry "Are all in your honourable house well?" she replied, "I am much indebted for your enquiries". These phrases are the literal translations of the customary greetings between Chinese people, but neither Mr. Feng nor Mrs. Wu realized their original meaning; any more than we do when we say "I am very pleased to meet you" or even "How-do-you-do", to which enquiry we never expect to receive any answer. But when Mrs. Wu began to talk to his salesman, business was business, and all these flowery compliments were dropped and the following conversation took place :

Mrs. Wu: "What is the price of this Nine Dragon Chop?"

Salesman: "Thirty coppers a foot."

Mrs. Wu: "But that is a great deal more than I paid last time. Why has the price gone up?"

Salesman: "Well, you see, Mrs. Wu, this Chop is very popular and we have had to renew our stock since you bought last time. All foreign goods cost more now owing to the Tariff increase—and, besides, exchange has moved against us. The rate on Shanghai is 112 now, whereas a year ago, you'll remember, it was under par. You know, too, Mrs. Wu, that copper cents have fallen badly. Why, a year ago the rate was 130 to the dollar and to-day it is 153. All prices are up. It is difficult for all of us to buy and sell in these times, but worst for us dealers in foreign goods."

Mrs. Wu: "Well, perhaps some of this national cloth might do. What is the price of that 'Three Tigers?'"

Salesman: "Ah, that is less expensive, it is true. But I know that you, Mrs. Wu, always take the best and there is nothing like Nine Dragon for good finish and hard wear."

Mrs. Wu: "But I can't pay at this rate. I'll give you twenty-five coppers."

Salesman: "How many feet do you want?"

Mrs. Wu: "Twenty-one feet."

Salesman: "I'll tell you what, Mrs. Wu, you take a little more than twenty-one feet and that will finish off the piece. Then I'll take the responsibility of reducing the price by three coppers."

Mrs. Wu grumbled a bit, but her husband's shop had done fairly well lately, and she was very particular about keeping him and her children neatly clothed, so she paid the price and took the extra length.

It may seem very peculiar to us that Mrs. Wu knew all about the rate of exchange, but she did, as do all Chinese people, because their own money varies from day to day and from province to province. For instance, nominally there are 100 coppers to a silver dollar, but the number of coppers given in exchange for a dollar has greatly increased and alters continually. It is as if on some days we received 13d. for a shilling, on other days 13½d., and on others 11½d., and so on; and not only that, but as if the exchange value of copper and silver coins coined in Lancashire altered continually in comparison with those coined in Middlesex, Northumberland, etc.

After Mrs. Wu had made her purchase and left the shop, the Chinese salesman went to Mr. Feng, the owner, and told him that they had sold so much of the "Nine Dragon Chop" during the last few days that they had very little stock left. Mr. Feng said that as the season was drawing to an end he would not buy any more but that he would write to his business friend, Mr. Chang, in Shanghai from whom be bought the cloth, and tell him that in about nine months he would require for his next spring trade two cases of forty pieces each of the "Nine Dragon Chop" instead of the one case which he had bought last year. So he wrote the following letter to his friend Mr. Chang in Shanghai.

The envelope bore the inscription: "For the honoured Mr. Chang to open", and inside the letter commenced: "This letter respectfully begins". But these phrases mean no more to the Chinese than "Dear Sirs", and "Yours very truly" mean to us. It is an extraordinary thing how grotesque the motes in the eyes of foreigners appear to us, while we quite fail to realize the curious contours of the beams in our own.

The letter continued as follows: "The last consignment of 'Nine Dragon Chop' has gone well, but if the price continues to go up like this, I don't think business in it will continue for long. Please send me two cases as soon as possible, and try to get it from the foreign firm at the old price. Please examine the market thoroughly." (Literally: Let there be a falling of the water till the stones on the bottom appear.) "A further rise will mean that the market will disappear. All my customers, although they prefer such goods as 'Nine Dragon' and have used it for many years, are beginning to ask for national goods, which as yet, we must admit, are not quite up to standard. Still, one can't squeeze money out of empty purses, and price decides. I tell you this because we've been friends for so many years" (literally: You and I have been as closely connected in our business as the upper and lower teeth of the jaw) "and I know the whole of your business is in the import trade. I should not like to have to go elsewhere for my supplies."

On receipt of this letter Mr. Chang went to call on the English importing house, G. Townsend, Ltd., from whom he had bought twenty cases of these goods in the preceding year, because he sold this quality not only to Mr. Feng but to other shopkeepers in different towns in China. The Chinese dealers do not converse in Chinese with English importers but in what is known as "pidgin English". Mr. Chang said to Mr. Townsend, "My think more better you puttee book forty case Nine Dragon shirting suppose you can catchee six and a half pence per yard shipment five moon. My think come next year this Chop can walkee velly well."

G. Townsend, Ltd., had other customers besides Mr. Chang for this cloth and, in consequence of this conversation, which took place in May, cabled an offer to their suppliers in Manchester, Rathbone Baxter & Co., Ltd., saying that they were willing to buy forty cases "Nine Dragon Chop" at sixpence farthing a yard December shipment. This offer was at a farthing a yard less than the price Mr. Chang was willing to pay so that G. Townsend, Ltd., could make a profit.

When Rathbone Baxter & Co., Ltd., received from G. Townsend, Ltd., the offer for forty cases of shirting cloth at sixpence farthing per yard c.i.f. Shanghai, shipment December, they had to make certain calculations, in order to find out whether the business could be accepted and still leave them a profit. (C.i.f. stands for Cost, Insurance, and Freight, so that the price of sixpence farthing had to include in addition to the cost of the cloth plus the profit, the cost of insuring the goods on the ocean voyage, and the charge for freight for carrying the goods from Manchester to Shanghai.) Rathbone Baxter &

Co., Ltd., started their calculations with the figure of sixpence farthing. From this they had to deduct a certain percentage, possibly 5%, to cover their overhead charges. The freight to Shanghai varies, of course, at different times, but when this particular order came through it was 55 shillings per ton—this is not per ton of weight, it is 55 shillings per ton of 40 cubic feet. The number of yards, therefore, which are contained in 40 cubic feet will vary according to the thickness of the cloth. Rathbone Baxter & Co., Ltd., calculated how many yards of this "Nine Dragon Chop" were contained in 40 cubic feet and thus found out how much was to be deducted for the cost of ocean freight. In addition they deducted $\frac{1}{4}$% of the value of the goods for the cost of marine insurance. Then the goods had to be forwarded from Manchester to Birkenhead, whence the China steamer sailed. This might cost about 10s. a ton weight, so they had to find out the weight of the cloth, ascertain how many yards went to a ton weight, and made deductions accordingly. There were other small items which had to be taken into consideration; for instance, the charges of the Liverpool agent for putting the goods on to the steamer and the cost of obtaining the bills of lading, which latter are subject to a small Government stamp. The firm also calculated for the cost of providing the shipment patterns, and for the cost of cabling and other incidental expenses. Then the goods had to be packed in a tin-lined wooden case, the cost of which had to be deducted from the price. The Manchester exporter bought these goods in the unbleached state, or, as they say in Lancashire, "in the grey". But the goods needed bleaching before shipment, so the charge for bleaching had also to be deducted from the price of sixpence farthing. They also deducted for the loss of interest on the cost of the grey cloth while the goods were being bleached, because they paid cash for the grey cloth and only received their money back when the goods were shipped.

Having made all these calculations, Rathbone Baxter & Co., Ltd., knew how much they could then afford to offer to the manufacturer, the Blackburn Weaving Co., Ltd., who wove the unbleached cloth. In order to make a profit on the goods, they would offer the Blackburn Weaving Co., Ltd., something less than the nett price which G. Townsend, Ltd., in Shanghai was willing to pay, that is, the figure which represented the resultant price after taking into consideration all the deductions enumerated.

The Blackburn Weaving Co., Ltd., before deciding whether they could accept Rathbone Baxter & Co., Ltd.'s offer, had also to make certain calculations in order to see whether they could accept the price. The Blackburn Weaving Co., Ltd., had made this cloth before for Rathbone Baxter & Co., Ltd., and had bought the yarn from which it was woven from the Diamond Spinning Co., Ltd., of Oldham. In order to produce exactly the same quality of cloth again they would have to buy the same quality of yarn as that which they used to weave the cloth on former occasions. They, therefore, wished to buy their yarn again from the Diamond Spinning Co.,

Ltd., of Oldham and informed this firm of the price which, according to the calculation they had made, they could afford to pay and yet leave a margin of profit on the transaction. The spinners (the Diamond Spinning Co., Ltd.), however, could not accept, as the price was too low. The Blackburn Weaving Co., Ltd., therefore told Rathbone Baxter & Co., Ltd., that they would require $\frac{1}{8}$d. per yard more than the price which was proposed to them. This latter firm cabled this information to G. Townsend, Ltd., in Shanghai, who asked Mr. Chang if he was willing to pay the increased price. Mr. Chang said "Can do", and G. Townsend, Ltd., cabled to Manchester accepting the price. Rathbone Baxter & Co., Ltd., then bought the goods from the Blackburn Weaving Co., Ltd., who in their turn bought the cotton yarn from the Diamond Spinning Co., Ltd.

How did the Diamond Spinning Co., Ltd., obtain exactly the correct quality of cotton which they required to spin the yarn, in order to give the same quality of cloth which the Blackburn Weaving Co., Ltd., had sold on previous occasions to Rathbone Baxter & Co., Ltd., who exported it to G. Townsend, Ltd., in Shanghai, who sold it to Mr. Chang, who sent it to Mr. Feng in Shan-si, who sold it to little Mrs. Wu, who insisted on having the same "Nine Dragon Chop" which she had always bought?

The Diamond Spinning Co., Ltd., had many customers for this special quality of yarn spun from a special brand of cotton which they had always bought as the B.A.Z. mark, from Birdhead & Co. in

Liverpool. As we know, that Liverpool firm in their turn, purchased this cotton from Silas J. Hocking in New Orleans, who obtained his supplies, in part, from the cotton grown by Hezekiah Godbehere.

The Diamond Spinning Co., Ltd., knew that they always used a certain amount of this B.A.Z. cotton annually, and in order to make sure that they would be able to obtain it when required, bought it in November from Birdhead & Co. in anticipation of their requirements and for delivery one-third of the quantity in May, one-third of the quantity in June, and the remaining third in July. They bought 300 bales, but they did not fix the price of the cotton at the time at which they bought it. The B.A.Z. mark was superior to the standard quality of "MIDDLING" as fixed by the Liverpool Cotton Association. In November it was worth 75 "points on", that is seventy-five hundredths of a penny more than the standard "MIDDLING", and although the Diamond Spinning Co., Ltd., did not wish to fix the price in November which they would have to pay for the cotton in May/June/July, they did wish to fix this basis of 75 "points on" which would be in addition to the price of standard "MIDDLING". Birdhead & Co. only paid 50 "points on" when they bought the cotton from Silas J. Hocking, so that when they sold it to the Diamond Spinning Co., Ltd., at 75 "points on" they made twenty-five hundredths, which is equal to $\frac{1}{4}$d. per lb. profit. If the B.A.Z. mark had been an inferior quality to "MIDDLING", it would have been sold at a certain number of "points off" MIDDLING.

When the Diamond Spinning Co., Ltd., received their order for yarn from the Blackburn Weaving Co., Ltd., in May, they calculated the price which they were offered for the yarn on the basis of 75 "points on" the price of standard "MIDDLING" cotton ruling on the day when they were offered the order from the Blackburn Weaving Co., Ltd. They then told Birdhead & Co. in Liverpool that they wanted 100 bales delivered out of their contract in May at this price. This is termed "calling" the cotton, and after calling the 100 bales the Diamond Spinning Co., Ltd., had still 200 bales "to call" out of their contract.

Why did Birdhead & Co., who were not speculators, sell cotton in November to the Diamond Spinning Co., Ltd., at a price which would not be fixed till May/June/July, and on which they would lose if the price of cotton fell from the time they had purchased it until the Diamond Spinning Co. "called" it? Birdhead & Co. safeguarded themselves in exactly the same way as Silas J. Hocking had done, that is to say they "put out a hedge". When they bought their cotton they sold "futures" for delivery May/June/July, and when the Diamond Spinning Co., Ltd., wanted the B.A.Z. cotton, they delivered the actual cotton to them at the market price and bought enough cotton in the market to enable them to fill their contract for the sale of the "futures" which they had made in November.

To summarize this short history. Mrs. Wu bought the Nine Dragon Chop cotton cloth from Mr. Feng in Shan-si. Mr. Feng, in order to replenish his supplies, ordered further quantities from Mr. Chang in Shanghai for delivery nine months ahead. Mr. Chang ordered the cloth from G. Townsend, Ltd., in Shanghai, who bought it from Rathbone Baxter & Co., Ltd., in Manchester. This latter firm gave an order to the Blackburn Weaving Co., Ltd., to make the cloth who, in their turn, bought the yarn from the Diamond Spinning Co., Ltd. This firm (although they had not fixed the price) had some time previously entered into a contract to buy the special cotton they required from Birdhead & Co., in Liverpool, who obtained it from stock held by Silas J. Hocking, in New Orleans. This cotton was known as the B.A.Z. mark and part of it had been bought by Silas J. Hocking from Marcus B. Levine, who had acquired it from John B. Robinson, who obtained it from Hezekiah Godbehere's crop. So that it was really Mrs. Wu (and of course thousands of other women) who caused Hezekiah Godbehere's cotton to be sent from Mississippi to Lancashire, where it was made into cloth and sent out to China.

CHAPTER IV

COTTON SPINNING, WEAVING, AND MERCHANTING

PART I

WE must now examine the means by which the different people involved in these transactions in Lancashire were paid, and what part credit played in providing the necessary money. We must commence with the spinner, but, in order to understand the position, it is necessary to say something about the origin of spinning firms in Lancashire. These may, perhaps, be classified under four headings. First there are the very old firms; the history of a few going back as far as 150 years. These firms had very small beginnings. They may have been started by an operative spinner who hired a room and a few spindles; profits were made, the profits were put back into the business and probably, sometime during the last fifty years, the business was turned into a private limited company, usually all the shares of which are still held by members of the original family and their friends. A private limited company may not have more than fifty shareholders, and it is under no obligation to publish its balance-sheet. In some cases, however, some of these old concerns were formed into public companies, the shares being held, not only by the family, but also by members of the public.

The second type of spinning companies, formed about the end of the nineteenth century, consisted at that time of new businesses, the shares of which were generally subscribed by the families of the people who were to *manage* the business, and by their friends. There were, as a rule, no debentures issued (*i.e.* no money was obtained by loan against security of the machinery and buildings), but operatives and other employees, and outsiders who wanted a short-term investment, were allowed to deposit with the company sums of money bearing 4 or 5% interest per annum, which deposits were payable on demand or short notice (Credit instrument No. 22). These deposits in the spinning firms (in which respect they differed from loans by employees in other trades) were not invested in good securities outside the business and held as a separate fund, but the money was used in the business, and not separated in any way from the other moneys of the concerns.

The third type of mill was similar to the second type, except that it was formed in the boom of 1907 and the architects, builders, machine makers, and other suppliers often took a proportion—perhaps 20 or 25%—of the sums owing to them in the shape of shares in the company. In some cases even spinners and other operatives took shares in order to be employed in the mill.

The fourth type has brought great disaster to Lancashire. In 1920 there was an enormous boom during which profits were very large, and this opened up a great field for the enterprise of company promoters. They suggested to the owners of the mills that their buildings and machinery should be revalued, and that new companies should be formed with a capital based on the then earning power, which was five or six times greater than that previously earned on the original capital. For example, they would offer the owner of a mill to purchase the business which had a capital of £100,000 for perhaps £300,000 in cash and £300,000 in shares of the new company which they intended to form, and at the same time they would secure a rich harvest for themselves. They would raise the £300,000 cash by selling shares in the new company to the public. The gambling fever became very widespread, and operatives, small shopkeepers, clerks, and others, all wanted to buy shares in the companies which had taken over the old concerns. In the great majority of cases these people had little or no money with which to do this, so the company promoters arranged that part of the new shares should only be partly paid up, that is, that a man could acquire a £1 share for 2s. 6d. or 5s. cash, the remainder being a liability, which he might be called upon to meet should necessity arise; but in those halcyon days it was not expected that the necessity would ever arise, as it was thought that the mills had more than enough money with which to carry on their businesses.

These reconstituted firms (which are called in Lancashire "turnover" firms) issued no debentures, but still continued to take deposit loans from their operatives and others. In certain cases the "turnover" mills were formed into large amalgamations of several companies, and these amalgamations did issue debentures to the public against their land, buildings, and machinery.

The company promoters had to find the cash which they had to pay to the people who had sold the old companies to the new owners. The promoters could not obtain this cash until they had sold the new shares to the public, or in some cases, obtained deposit loan money, or made profits. They, therefore, borrowed money from the banks on behalf of the new companies. As long as the boom was in full swing, these loans were paid back directly the public subscribed for the new shares, but when the boom came to an end, the public suddenly would not subscribe for any new shares and there was no money with which to repay the banks. The banks then insisted that they should receive as security what is known as "a floating charge" on all the assets of the new companies (Credit instrument No. 23), that is, not only on the land, buildings, and machinery, but also on any stocks of yarn or cotton belonging to the companies and any debts due to the companies including the liability for uncalled capital on the partly paid-up shares, for which the operatives, clerks, shopkeepers, and others who had bought these shares were responsible.

These debts, owing by the new companies to the banks, were increased because of the losses which were sustained when the slump came, and these losses, which persisted for a long time, eventually forced other mills which had not originally been indebted to the banks, to borrow from them also against "a floating charge" on their assets. The effect of these "floating charges" is—in the event of a liquidation—to put the banks in the position that they are paid off before any other creditors of the company, including the loan-holders.

These transactions illustrate two direct forms and one indirect form of credit which the mills obtained. The money deposited by the loan-holders was lent to the company and was a direct form of credit, as was the money obtained from the banks on the security of the "fixed" and "floating" assets of the company. These assets, however, were increased by the liability of the holders of the partly paid shares for the amount of the uncalled capital, and this liability to the companies enabled them to obtain larger loans from the banks than they could otherwise have done, and this may be considered a form of indirect credit.

The methods which have been described were the main sources of credit obtained by the spinning mills, but formerly the Liverpool cotton brokers often gave credit to the spinners by drawing bills on them payable after two months. Owing to the bad position of the Lancashire spinners, this credit has ceased and all cotton has now to be paid for on the tenth day after delivery, and, in the case of weak firms, very often on delivery. This facility having been withdrawn, the hiatus has been made good either by calling up and using the balance of partly paid capital, or by increased loans from the banks. The banks occasionally advance money on cotton for spinning companies, such cotton being warehoused in the bank's name. This is frequently done where cotton is bought from India or from Egypt, the shipment being financed against a bank acceptance credit, as in the case of Birdhead & Co.

The only other form of credit which spinners enjoy is that accorded by the suppliers of mill stores, coal, oil, and other necessaries. These things are usually paid for on the average about six weeks after delivery, and very often after the stores have been consumed, and the yarn into whose cost they have entered, has been paid for.

After the yarn has been spun in the spinning mills, it is sold to those firms whose business it is to weave it into cloth. For this purpose credit again plays some part.

The weaving sheds in Lancashire are mostly either private family firms or private limited companies, the shares of which (with few exceptions) are held by the founders of the firms and their friends. Until recently the credit which these firms obtained from their suppliers of yarn and mill stores did not, as a rule, exceed three weeks. Generally speaking, their working capital was sufficient for their purposes; but it sometimes happened that they held unusually heavy stocks of yarn, and in order to pay for these they required money. It might be they were short of money because they had to give extended credit to their merchant customers or hold up deliveries of goods for them owing to bad conditions ruling in their markets. Under these circumstances, the manufacturers[1] sometimes found it necessary to have recourse to their banks. The bank would examine their balance-sheets, and if the concerns which required temporary accommodation were good and had been making profits, the bank would grant an overdraft on the strength of the surplus of assets over liabilities. This is usually a verbal agreement and there is no credit instrument used. In more recent years many weaving concerns have made no profit and have even made losses. Balance-sheets do not look as healthy as they formerly did, and the banks, before granting overdrafts, would now require some security. This security might take one of two forms. It might be a specific charge on the "fixed assets", *i.e.* the land, mill, and machinery, which of course always remain the same, and a floating charge (Credit instrument No. 23) on the "liquid assets", *i.e.* on the stock and book debts, which, of course, do change from day to day. Or, on the other hand, it might take the form of collateral security, perhaps in the shape of a deposit with the bank of some bonds or other securities belonging to the directors and their friends, or possibly a guarantee to the bank by the directors or their friends of the overdraft which the bank granted to the company.

The merchant who buys the goods from the manufacturer also requires credit. He pays the manufacturer seven to ten days after receipt of the goods, and unless they are to be shipped abroad in the

[1] In the Lancashire cotton trade the term "manufacturer" only applies to the owners of the weaving sheds.

"grey" state, they require dyeing, bleaching, or printing, which may take a couple of months. During this time the merchant is out of his money, while his own capital may, to a large extent, be locked up in credit which he has given to those customers upon whom he does not draw bills. The conditions under which he can obtain loans or overdrafts from his bank are similar to those which we have outlined in the case of the manufacturers, except that the merchant has, as a rule, no fixed assets which he can give to the bank as security. Whether his bank will or will not require security will depend on the financial strength of the firm, its reputation, and its profit-earning capacity.

During the present century there has grown up another system by which merchants obtain credit from their banks or possibly from London finance houses. By this method they pledge the actual goods which are in process at the bleachers, dyers, or printers (Credit instruments Nos. 24, 25, and 26). This system is not looked upon with much favour by the banks. While they are in process at the bleachers, dyers, or printers these firms have a lien or charge on the goods belonging to the merchant. This lien is not only for the value of the work done on these specific goods, but extends to any money which may be owing by the merchant to the processing firms. The banks, therefore—if the security has to be realized because the merchant cannot pay his debts—never know how much will be left for them after the dyer, printer, or bleacher has been paid. It is, perhaps, mainly for this reason that they look with little favour on this method of giving credit.

The merchant pays the dyer, printer, or bleacher for work done on his goods, towards the end of the month following that in which the goods have been returned to him in the finished state.

Thus up to this point, *i.e.* until the goods are ready for shipment, the credit which the merchant receives is first, seven to ten days on the unfinished cotton cloth; secondly, an average of about five to six weeks from the bleacher, dyer, or printer on the cost of the work which he has done on the cloth; and thirdly, sometimes an overdraft from his bank to carry him over the time while the goods are in process. The credit which he receives on exporting the goods will be dealt with in the next chapter.

Part II

CREDIT INSTRUMENTS

Credit instrument No. 22 is the receipt given by the Diamond Spinning Co., Ltd., to one of its loan depositors, Ebenezer Murgatroyd, and calls for no comment.

CREDIT INSTRUMENT NO. 22.—SPINNER'S LOAN ACKNOWLEDGEMENT

No. 499

DUPLICATE.

Loan Acknowledgment.

Date January 17 1920 Folio 101

Name Ebenezer Murgatroyd

Address 131 Burton St

Oldham.

twelve Pounds

ten Shillings, and

Six Pence, £ 12 : 10s. 6 d.

Present Claim......£ 56 : 17s. 6 d.

Examined by Peter Tait

No. 499

THE DIAMOND SPINNING Co. Ltd

OLDHAM January 17 1920

Folio 101

Directors' Receipt.

To Mr Ebenezer Murgatroyd
Oldham

We have pleasure in notifying you that your Loan Account with this Company was duly credited with twelve *Pounds* ten *Shillings, and* Six *Pence, on the* 12th January 1920

The total sum at your credit is now £ 56 · 17 · 6

If this amount differs from your Loan Book we shall be glad to be advised immediately.

John Horsfield
James Richards } *Directors.*

Tom Platt *Secretary.*

Credit instrument No. 23 is the "floating charge" which the Diamond Spinning Co., Ltd., give to the bank as security for a loan. It is a long document containing many clauses setting out the conditions under which the loan is granted. The effect of the document is to give to the bank as security for any money owing at the time, or which might become owing:

(1) The mill, machinery contained therein, and the freehold land on which it was built.

(2) All the other assets of the Company, present and future, including uncalled capital and the goodwill of the concern.

Further, the Company undertakes:

(*a*) To pay to the bank on demand any money which may be owing. This enables the bank to demand payment at any time, and if not paid, to sell the security.

(*b*) That the bank's security shall rank before any other security and that the Company will not dispose of any of its assets.

(*c*) That any money received for uncalled capital shall be paid to the bank and no uncalled capital will be called up without the consent of the bank.

(*d*) To supply all information regarding its affairs to the bank when required.

(*e*) To keep its property insured.

Banking students wishing to make a closer acquaintance with this type of document should consult Grant's *Law of Banking* or Hart's *Banking*, and those seeking legal knowledge on these instruments should consult Coote's *Treatise on the Law of Mortgages* or other standard text-books.

CREDIT INSTRUMENT NO. 23.—FLOATING CHARGE

THIS INDENTURE made the seventeenth day of January One thousand nine hundred and thirty-three Between THE DIAMOND SPINNING COMPANY LIMITED, whose registered office is situate at Diamond Mill, Oldham, in the County of Lancashire (hereinafter called "the Company" which expression shall where the context requires or admits include the assigns of the Company) of the one part and THE LANCASHIRE & CHESHIRE BANK LIMITED, whose registered office is situate at 12 Mosley Street in the City of Manchester (hereinafter called "the Bank" which expression shall where the context requires or admits include the assigns of the Bank) of the other part.

WHEREAS the Company has at the request of the Bank agreed to give to the Bank such security as is hereinafter contained as well for the moneys (if any) now owing as for any moneys which may hereafter during the continuance of this security become owing by the Company to the Bank either alone or jointly or otherwise as hereinafter mentioned NOW THIS INDENTURE WITNESSETH that in pursuance of the said Agreement and in consideration of the premises the Company as beneficial owner hereby charges in favour of the Bank with the payment to the Bank of all and every sums and sum of money for which these presents are hereinafter declared to be a security FIRST the premises described in the Schedule hereto (hereinafter called the specifically mortgaged premises) and SECONDLY the undertaking and goodwill of the Company and all its other property assets and rights whatsoever and whatsoever both present and future including its uncalled capital for the time being (all of which premises secondly hereby charged are hereinafter referred to collectively as the general assets).

[*Here follow the usual Clauses and Signature.*]

Credit instrument No. 24 is an instruction from the Manchester exporting merchants, Rathbone Baxter & Co., Ltd., to the Quicksilver Bleaching, Dyeing & Finishing Co., Ltd., instructing the latter to hold the goods mentioned in the schedule to the order of the London & Manchester Bank, Ltd. The point which calls for comment are the words "subject only to your lien for charges for work done to the goods". This means that the Quicksilver Bleaching Co. has a prior claim on the goods to the claim of the bank, but only for the amount of the cost of the work which the Quicksilver Bleaching Co. has done on the goods. The general lien referred to on page 74 will thus not operate in this case.

CREDIT INSTRUMENT NO. 24.—INSTRUCTION TO HOLD IN TRUST

Enclosure 2nd October 1935

To

THE QUICKSILVER BLEACHING, DYEING & FINISHING CO. LTD.
DROYLSDEN

DEAR SIRS,

We have handed you goods as per Schedule hereunder. Please hold the same to the order of LONDON & MANCHESTER BANK LTD. MANCHESTER, subject only to your lien for charges for work done to the goods.

Will you kindly sign and forward to the Bank the enclosed acknowledgement.

(Signed) RATHBONE BAXTER & CO. LTD.
Director, AMOS BAXTER.

SCHEDULE

Description of Goods
500 pieces 32 inches 120 yards Shirting—Lot 340 (part delivery against order No. 312)

Credit instrument No. 25 pledges the goods to the bank as security not only for the specific loan relating to these goods, but for any other money which Rathbone Baxter & Co., Ltd., may owe at the time or at some future time to the bank. It is a continuing security; that is to say, even if this specific loan is paid off, as long as the bank holds the security, it is available as security against any other money owing, or against any fresh loan which may be made.

2nd October 1935

To The London & Manchester Bank Ltd.

Dear Sirs,

We have delivered to The Quicksilver Bleaching, Dyeing, & Finishing Co. Ltd. Droylsden, goods as per Schedule hereunder to be held to your order.

In consideration of advance made and/or to be made to us from time to time we hereby charge the said goods in your favour as a continuing security for the payment to you on demand of all sums and liabilities now due or hereafter to become due from us to you upon any account whatsoever including guarantees and either alone or jointly with another or others with interest, banking charges and expenses.

This is without prejudice to any other lien which the Bank may have or might have had apart from this security.

We will keep the said goods fully insured against all risks and will, if required, deposit with you the policies of insurance and insurance cover notes and premium receipts, and in the meantime will hold in trust for you such policies and all moneys received under them.

Dated this second day of October nineteen hundred and thirty-five.

(Signed) RATHBONE BAXTER & CO. LTD.
Director, Amos Baxter.

6d.

Schedule

123—S&S.1/25.

Description of Goods.		Value.		
500 Pieces 32 inches 120 yards Shirting—Lot 340		£750	0	0

Credit instrument No. 26 is a confirmation from the Quicksilver Bleaching Co. to the bank that they hold the goods for the bank, subject only to their lien for charges for work done on these specific goods. The instrument also informs the bank that the goods are insured by the Quicksilver Bleaching Co., and that any money which may eventually be received under the policies, belongs to the bank, subject to the above-mentioned lien.

CREDIT INSTRUMENT NO. 26.—CONFIRMATION OF LIEN

3rd October 1935

To The London & Manchester Bank Ltd.

Dear Sirs,

We have received from Messrs. Rathbone Baxter & Co. Ltd. goods as per Schedule hereunder which we hold to your order subject only to our lien for charges for work done to the goods.

As regards all such goods for the time being insured in our name we undertake in case of damage or destruction by fire that the money payable under the Policies shall belong to you subject only to our lien as aforesaid.

(Signed) THE QUICKSILVER BLEACHING, DYEING & FINISHING CO. LTD.

Director, W. Twemlow.
Secretary, Henry Karolson.

Schedule

Description of the Goods.

500 Pieces 32 inches 120 yards Shirting—Lot 340

CHAPTER V

EXPORT OF COTTON GOODS FROM MANCHESTER, AND MARKETING IN CHINA

PART I

WE may now return to our story and describe how the shirting cloth which was manufactured by the Blackburn Weaving Co., Ltd., and sold to Rathbone Baxter & Co., Ltd., was dealt with by the latter firm.

When G. Townsend, Ltd., sent the order in May for the cotton cloth to Rathbone Baxter & Co., Ltd., the former immediately opened a credit in favour of Rathbone Baxter & Co., Ltd. This credit was opened with the China Exchange Bank, Ltd., in Shanghai, and by it the bank instructed their branch in London to make cash advances to Rathbone Baxter & Co., Ltd., for the value of the goods which they had to ship to G. Townsend, Ltd., in Shanghai, in December. Although the bank could cancel this credit before the goods were shipped (as it was not an irrevocable credit), this would not be done in normal circumstances, and so by the opening of the credit, Rathbone Baxter & Co., Ltd., were assured that they would be able to get their money in London in December when they shipped the goods. (Credit instrument No. 27).

When the goods were ready, they were packed

and forwarded to Birkenhead to be put on a steamer sailing for China. Rathbone Baxter & Co., Ltd., procured from the shipowner a Bill of Lading, that is a receipt for the goods, and insured the goods against loss or damage on the voyage to the Far East. They made out their invoices, charging the goods to G. Townsend, Ltd., in Shanghai. Having done this, they sent the Bill of Lading, Insurance Policy, and invoices to the China Exchange Bank, Ltd., in London, accompanied by a Bill of Exchange, drawn by them on G. Townsend, Ltd., and instructing that firm to pay the amount stated in the Bill of Exchange (which sum was for the value of the goods shipped). The Bill of Exchange which G. Townsend, Ltd., had undertaken to "accept" (Credit instrument No. 28), was drawn at four months sight, so that G. Townsend, Ltd., would pay it four months after they had seen it, that is, four months after it had been presented to them for acceptance. If the bill, for any reason, could not conveniently be paid at the end of four months, it would usually be renewed for a further period of three months by arrangement between the bank, Rathbone Baxter & Co., Ltd., and G. Townsend, Ltd.

To make the transaction perfectly clear, we may explain that "opening a credit in favour of Rathbone Baxter & Co., Ltd." simply means that the China Exchange Bank, Ltd., inform them that when the goods are shipped and the bank has received the Bill of Lading, Insurance Policy, Invoice and Bill of Exchange on G. Townsend, Ltd., it will lend to the suppliers of the goods (Rathbone

Baxter & Co., Ltd.) the amount of the bill. The Bill of Exchange contained a clause which instructed G. Townsend, Ltd., to pay—in addition to the amount stated on the bill—a sum equivalent to 5% interest per annum from the date the bill was drawn, until the approximate time when the money, which had been paid in Shanghai to meet the bill, would arrive in London (Credit instruments Nos. 28, 29, 30, and 31). By this means Rathbone Baxter & Co., Ltd., recovered the interest for the four months' interval which elapsed from the time the bill was presented for acceptance until payment was made, and also for the time of transit of the bill out to China and the money back to England. The interest varies according to the rate charged to Rathbone Baxter & Co., Ltd., by the China Exchange Bank, Ltd. Rathbone Baxter & Co., Ltd., endorsed the Bill of Exchange, the effect of which was that G. Townsend, Ltd., were instructed to pay the money when due to the China Exchange Bank, Ltd., or to their order, *i.e.* to whomsoever the bank might, in turn, instruct it to be paid. G. Townsend, Ltd., being in Shanghai, only possessed Chinese dollars and not pounds sterling. In order, therefore, to avoid all questions regarding the rate of exchange at which the bill should be paid, a clause was inserted which ensured that G. Townsend, Ltd., paid sufficient dollars to provide the necessary amount of pounds sterling, calculating the exchange at a rate at which the bank was willing to sell pounds sterling for Chinese dollars on the date when the bill fell due.

The rate of interest which the China Exchange Bank, Ltd., charged would usually be 1% higher (but with a minimum of 5%) than the rate of discount charged by the Bank of England (bank rate) for discounting bills, the bank's remuneration being included in the rate of interest which it charged on the loan.

Under certain circumstances there is a cheaper method by which Rathbone Baxter & Co., Ltd., might obtain their money against the bill which they drew on G. Townsend, Ltd. If the rate for discounting bills in the London discount market were very low, the China Exchange Bank, Ltd., instead of lending *cash* to Rathbone Baxter & Co., Ltd., might allow them to draw a bill on the China Exchange Bank, Ltd., in London (Credit instruments Nos. 32 and 33). Rathbone Baxter & Co., Ltd., could discount this bill with their own Manchester bank or with a London discount broker at a rate which (after paying the commission of the China Exchange Bank, Ltd., and the other charges for their services) would work out cheaper than if they had borrowed the cash from the China Exchange Bank, Ltd., at 5% or 1% over the Bank of England rate, whichever was more (Credit instrument No. 34). For example, if Rathbone Baxter & Co., Ltd., could discount a bill on the China Exchange Bank, Ltd., for 2% per annum, and if the bank's charge for "accepting" the bill were 1½% per annum, then the credit would cost Rathbone Baxter & Co., Ltd., 3½% per annum, plus bill stamp and collecting commission, instead of the 5% which they would have to pay if they obtained a cash loan from the bank. Where a cash advance is taken from the bank, interest is only charged from the date of the advance until the bank is paid, so that if part of the goods, against which the bill is drawn, is delivered before the maturity of the bill, a rebate of interest would be allowed on this part for the unexpired period of the bill. In this respect the system of taking a cash advance has an advantage over the method of drawing a bill on the bank in London, for in the latter case the charge for discounting the bill is payable for the full period for which the bill runs.

By one of the two means, credit was given by Rathbone Baxter & Co., Ltd., in Manchester to G. Townsend, Ltd., in Shanghai for a period of at least four months in addition to the time that the mail took for the voyage and for the time necessary to bring the money back to England. Rathbone Baxter & Co., Ltd., were enabled to grant this credit through the help of the China Exchange Bank, Ltd., and possibly through the additional help of their own Manchester bank, or a London discount broker, if they used the second method of obtaining credit from the China Exchange Bank, Ltd.

When the goods arrived in Shanghai, the Bill of Exchange drawn on G. Townsend, Ltd., was presented to them by the China Exchange Bank, Ltd., and the firm wrote across it the word "Accepted", which meant that they were willing to pay the bill when due. They then advised Rathbone Baxter & Co., Ltd., in Manchester that they had accepted the bill (Form No. 31). Having once "accepted" the bill, they could not refuse to pay it, even if the goods turned out to be not in accordance with their order. In such a case they would, of course, have a legal claim against Rathbone Baxter & Co., Ltd., in Manchester, but in any event they would have to pay the amount of the bill to the China Exchange Bank, Ltd. It is obvious that the banks would not grant credit freely if their reimbursement could be affected by disputes between buyer and seller.

The Bill of Exchange having been "accepted" and the goods discharged from the ship, they were placed in a bonded warehouse in Shanghai, that is, a warehouse under the control of the Chinese Customs authorities. It was not necessary to pay import duties on them until they were taken out of this warehouse. They were placed in the warehouse either in the name of the bank or in the name of G. Townsend, Ltd. In the latter event G. Townsend, Ltd., would sign a receipt saying that they held the goods in trust for the bank. During the time that they remained in the warehouse, G. Townsend, Ltd., was obliged to keep them insured against fire (Credit instruments Nos. 35 and 36).

Mr. Chang, the Chinese who bought the goods from G. Townsend, Ltd., was advised by the latter firm when the goods had arrived. According to the general custom he could only obtain possession of the goods by paying cash for them, but he was at liberty to leave them lying in the warehouse for two months before he need take delivery—a period which in bad times is often extended. The interest for the two months was included in the price of the goods, but Mr. Chang was liable to pay interest for any longer period for which he left them in the warehouse. Although Mr. Chang received the goods only when he paid for them, the arrangement by which they could lie in the warehouse until he was ready to pay, was in itself a kind of credit, and pending delivery of the goods to Mr. Chang, G. Townsend, Ltd., could obtain a loan from the bank against the security of the goods, provided they had paid Rathbone Baxter & Co., Ltd.'s Bill of Exchange.

Rathbone Baxter & Co., Ltd., did business in other parts of the world, and in some countries they, or their European customers, allowed the native dealers to receive delivery of the goods on arrival against their promise to pay; so that these dealers, because they had the goods in their possession and could sell them, enjoyed a greater degree of credit than that which was accorded to the Chinese merchants in Shanghai who received the goods only when they paid for them.

Mr. Chang, when he obtained delivery of the goods, had to send them to the shopkeeper Mr. Feng in Shan-si. It took a long time for the goods to reach Shan-si, and even then Mr. Feng could not pay for them until he had sold them, because his stock in his shop was always much greater in value than the amount of his capital, so that he was obliged to obtain credit from Mr. Chang. Mr. Chang in his turn, also had to obtain credit in order to be able to give credit to Mr. Feng and his other customers, for he did a large business, and the value of his stock plus the amount of money owing to him at any one time was always greater than the amount of his capital.

We must now consider how Mr. Chang obtained his credit. Twice a year every Chinese settles his debts; once at the Midsummer Festival, and once at the Chinese New Year. After the New Year settlement, the Chinese merchant goes to his native banker and arranges with him for an overdraft sufficient, with his own capital, to enable him to carry on his business and give credit to his customers. If his banker was the old-style native bank, Mr. Chang would obtain his overdraft purely on his personal standing, and possibly without giving the bank any security; his overdraft might be as much as five or ten times his own capital but a very high rate of interest would be charged, that is anything from 12% per annum upwards. Not every firm could obtain an overdraft without security, but only approved firms, the standing of whose partners was well known to the bank. In recent years, modern Chinese banks have come into existence which work on the same principles as the foreign banks. They charge a much lower rate of interest than the old-style native bank, probably from 6% per annum upwards, but they give no overdrafts to anyone without security (Credit instrument No. 37).

Mr. Chang, having arranged his overdraft, obtained from his native bank a "native bank order" for the amount which he had to pay to G. Townsend, Ltd., in order to obtain delivery of the goods which he wanted to send to Mr. Feng in Shan-si. This native bank order is a promissory note of the Chinese bank promising to pay the sum stated on it after ten days. These native bank orders are accepted by the European banks in China as the equivalent of cash. Mr. Chang paid this native bank order to G. Townsend, Ltd., who took it to the China Exchange Bank, Ltd., with which they had pledged the goods, and obtained a release note from the bank authorizing the warehouse to deliver the goods (Credit instrument No. 38). This release note was then handed to Mr. Chang, who obtained the goods from the warehouse and put them on a steamer in Shanghai which transported them to the nearest port from which they could be sent to Mr. Feng in Shan-si.

Mr. Chang could now wait for his money to come from Mr. Feng and then pay it into his native bank, or (since the growth of modern banks in China), he could draw a bill on Mr. Feng and take it with the Bill of Lading and Insurance Policy to the modern Chinese bank and obtain an advance against the security of the Bill of Exchange and the Bill of Lading in exactly the same way that Silas J. Hocking sent his cotton to Birdhead & Co. in Liverpool, and as Rathbone Baxter & Co., Ltd., financed the shipment of their goods to G. Townsend, Ltd., in Shanghai. Mr. Feng who, in his turn, gave credit to his customers, would obtain credit from his native bank, probably without giving it any security. These native banks are private partnerships of unlimited liability, in addition to which their liabilities are guaranteed by the Native Bankers' Guild.

Our transaction in Chinese shirting is now complete. We have seen that, from the negro cropper to Mrs. Wu (who received fifty dollars' credit from Mr. Feng), the whole business was carried on by credit. Nothing tangible had been exchanged; it had all been done by bits of paper. Although the negro cropper, and all the manufacturers and merchants in the chain of transactions, were paid, America received no commodity or service in exchange for her cotton, nor did the United Kingdom receive any goods in payment of the labour, etc., which she expended in manufacturing the raw cotton into shirts.

We must remind ourselves here of what we said at the conclusion of Chapter I. When we say that America and the United Kingdom received no commodities in exchange for the cotton and cotton goods, we do not mean that these countries received no goods and services in exchange for all the goods which they exported and all the services which they rendered. America, however, sends more to the United Kingdom than she receives from the United Kingdom, and the United Kingdom sends more to China than she receives from China, and in our story, no goods or services have been exchanged up to this point in payment for these surplus exports, visible and invisible. In order to see how America and the United Kingdom ultimately were paid, we must carry the transactions four stages further.

Part II

CREDIT INSTRUMENTS

Credit instrument No. 27 is the credit which G. Townsend, Ltd., in Shanghai opened with the China Exchange Bank, Ltd., in favour of Rathbone Baxter & Co., Ltd. Through this document the opening of the credit is advised to Rathbone Baxter & Co., Ltd., by the China Exchange Bank, Ltd.'s office in London. It stipulates that the freight on the goods shall be paid to Shanghai and that all the documents shall be hypothecated, that is pledged, to the bank. Part of these documents consists of Bills of Exchange drawn by Rathbone Baxter & Co., Ltd., on G. Townsend, Ltd., in Shanghai. The credit stipulates that Rathbone Baxter & Co., Ltd., are to remain responsible as drawers of the bills in the event of them not being paid by G. Townsend, Ltd.

CREDIT INSTRUMENT NO. 27.—LETTER OF CREDIT

(Outward Bills Department)

THE CHINA EXCHANGE BANK LTD.,
19 Lombard St., LONDON, E.C.

1st February 1935.

Messrs. Rathbone Baxter & Co. Ltd.,
Rathbone House,
Whitworth Street,
MANCHESTER.

DEAR SIR/S,

We beg to inform you that we are instructed by the Manager of our Branch at Shanghai to negotiate, as offered, your documentary Bills drawn at 4 months' sight on G. Townsend, Ltd. to the extent of not exceeding £1400 (Fourteen hundred pounds) for full Invoice cost of 40 Cases Cotton goods shipped to that Port.

The Bills must be accompanied by full sets of Bills of Lading, made out to the order of the Shippers, for account of the Consignee, and be duly endorsed by the said Shippers, also marked by the Shipping Company "Freight paid", together with Invoices and Policies of Insurance for Marine and War Risks, all duly hypothecated to the Bank against payment of the Bills.

Please note that this is not to be considered as being a Bank Credit and does not relieve you from the liability usually attaching to the Drawer of a Bill of Exchange, also that although it is considered to be open until 15/1/36 it may be cancelled by us upon giving you notice.

Bills drawn under the above-mentioned instructions must be plainly marked "Shanghai D/C 82/1386" and must be accompanied by a letter quoting this reference number.

Postage Charge at the rate of 2/– per Bill upon each Documentary Bill under £100 will be deducted by us when making payment.

Marine and war risk insurance to be effected in England.

Yours faithfully,

(Signed) THE CHINA EXCHANGE BANK LTD.
E. PHILLIPS, Manager

Credit instrument No. 28 is the bill drawn by Rathbone Baxter & Co., Ltd., on G. Townsend, Ltd., in Shanghai. The bill is for £1327 : 4 : 10, but states that interest is to be added to this sum at 5% per annum from the date of the bill until the approximate time of payment of the money in London. As G. Townsend, Ltd., in Shanghai will only have Chinese dollars, the bill stipulates that the money shall be paid at the rate of exchange at which the China Exchange Bank, Ltd., is willing to sell demand drafts on London on the day the bill is payable. The bill further stipulates that the documents (that is the Bill of Lading and the Insurance Policy) may only be handed over by the bank to G. Townsend, Ltd., on payment of the bill.

CREDIT INSTRUMENT NO. 28.—BILL OF EXCHANGE

BILL OR NOTE
FOURTEEN SHILLINGS
21. 12 35

Shanghai D/C No. 82/1386

£ Sterling 1327 - 4 - 10 Manchester. 21st December 1935

Four months after sight pay this first of Exchange second unpaid to the order of Ourselves Thirteen hundred and twenty seven pounds four shillings and ten pence sterling with interest added thereto at five per cent per Annum from date hereof to approximate due date of remittance Payable at the current drawing rate for The China Exchange Bank Ld's Demand Bank Drafts at Shanghai on London Documents to be given up to the drawee on payment of the bill Value received against

G 123 T LTD 1/40

per SS "Antenor"

To messrs. G. Townsend Ld
Shanghai

For and on behalf of
Rathbone Baxter & Co. Ld

E. Gadson Director.
J. Smith Director.

No 526

Credit instrument No. 29: This is the letter from Rathbone Baxter & Co., Ltd., handing the documents including the Bill of Exchange to the China Exchange Bank, Ltd., in London, and instructing the bank to pay the amount of the advance, *i.e.* the amount of the Bill of Exchange, to the London & Manchester Bank, Ltd., in London, to Rathbone Baxter & Co., Ltd.'s credit with the bank's Head Office in Manchester.

CREDIT INSTRUMENT NO. 29.—REQUEST FOR ADVANCE

Rathbone House,
Whitworth Street,
MANCHESTER,
21*st December* 1935

The China Exchange Bank Ltd.,
LONDON, E.C. 2.

DEAR SIRS,

Shanghai D/C. No. 82/1386.

Against the credit granted in your favour of the 31st October 1935 we beg to hand you herein first and second of exchange to order ourselves at four months' sight

1 draft for £1327 : 4 : 10.

Attached to this draft is a complete set of B/Lading in duplicate, Marine and War Risk Policy in duplicate and relative invoice and copies covering goods sold and shipped to drawees as per particulars below.

Documents are only to be given up against payment of the bill.

Thereagainst please pay tomorrow the 1st prox. the amount of the abovementioned bill to the London & Manchester Bank Ltd., Cornhill, E.C., to our credit with their Head Office here.

We are, dear Sirs,

Yours faithfully,

For and on behalf of

(Signed) RATHBONE BAXTER & Co. LTD.
E. GADSON, Director

G T
123
LTD. 1/40

per ss. "Antenor"

Credit instrument No. 30 is the means by which Rathbone Baxter & Co., Ltd., pledge the Bill of Exchange and the shipping documents to the China Exchange Bank, Ltd., as security for their advances. This hypothecation does not refer to this transaction only, but to all transactions of this nature which the bank may have with the firm.

CREDIT INSTRUMENT NO. 30.—GENERAL LETTER OF HYPOTHECATION

General Letter of Hypothecation

To the China Exchange Bank Limited.

1. As you may from time to time purchase from or negotiate for me/us Bills of Exchange drawn or endorsed by me/us with collateral securities, it has been agreed between us that the stipulations contained in this Memorandum shall be deemed to be continuing and ambulatory, and are to apply to all cases in which such Bills of Exchange may at any time either directly, or through other persons, be negotiated with or sold to you by me/us and this Memorandum shall have the same force until I/we shall give you notice of my/our intention to terminate it, as if a separate Memorandum were signed by me/us on each purchase or negotiation.

2. I/we authorize you, or any of your Managers, or Agents or the Holders for the time being, of any such Bill or Bills as aforesaid (but not so as to make it imperative) to insure any goods forming the collateral security for any such Bill or Bills of Exchange from sea risk including loss by capture, and also from loss by fire on shore, and to add the premiums and expenses of such insurances to the amount chargeable to me/us in respect of such Bill or Bills and to take recourse against such goods in priority to any other claims thereon, or against me/us, without prejudice to any claim against any endorser or endorsers of the said Bills, for reimbursing yourselves, or other the person or persons paying the same, the amount of such premiums and expenses, and also to sell any portion of such goods which may be necessary for payment of freight, insurance, and expenses, and generally to take such measures and make such charges for commission, and to be accountable in such manner, but not further or otherwise than as in ordinary cases between a merchant and his correspondent. And I/we consent to the goods being warehoused at any public or private wharf or warehouse selected by the Drawees or Acceptors of the Bills, unless you offer an objection to such wharf or warehouse.

CREDIT INSTRUMENT NO. 30 (*continued*)

3. I/we hereby also authorize you, or any of your Managers, or Agents, or the Holders for the time being of any Bill or Bills of Exchange as aforesaid, to take conditional acceptances to all or any of such Bills, to the effect that, on payment thereof at maturity, the Documents handed to you as collateral security for the due payment of any such Bill or Bills shall be delivered to the Drawees or Acceptors thereof, and such authorization shall be taken to extend to cases of acceptances for honour. Subject nevertheless to the power next hereinafter given, in case the Drawee shall suspend payment, become bankrupt, or go into liquidation during the currency of any such Bill or Bills.

4. I/we further authorize you, but not so as to make it imperative, at any time or times before the maturity of any Bill or Bills of Exchange as aforesaid, to grant a partial delivery or partial deliveries of such goods, in such manner as you or the Acceptors of such Bill or Bills of Exchange, or their representatives may think desirable to any person or persons on payment of a proportionate amount of the invoice cost of such goods, or of the Bill or Bills of Exchange drawn against same.

5. I/we further authorize you, or any of your Managers, or Agents, or the Holders for the time being of any Bill or Bills of Exchange as aforesaid, on default, being made in acceptance on presentation, or in payment at maturity, of any such Bill or Bills, or in case of the Drawees or Acceptors suspending payment, becoming bankrupt, or taking any steps whatever towards entering into liquidation during the currency of any such Bill or Bills, and whether accepted conditionally or absolutely, to sell all, or any part of the goods forming the collateral security for the payment thereof at such times and in such manner as you, or such Holders may deem fit, and, after deducting usual commission and charges, to apply the net proceeds in payment of such Bill or Bills with re-exchange and charges; the balance, if any, to be placed at your or their option against any other of my/our Bills, secured or otherwise, which may be in your or their hands, or any other debt or liability of mine/ours to you or them, and subject

CREDIT INSTRUMENT NO. 30 (*continued*)

thereto, to be accounted for to the proper parties. In case of loss of ship or goods insured at any time I/we authorize you, or the holders thereof, to realize the policy or policies, and charge the same commission on the proceeds as upon a sale of goods, and to apply the net proceeds, after such deductions as aforesaid, in manner hereinbefore lastly provided.

6. In case the net proceeds of such goods shall be insufficient to pay the amount of any such Bill or Bills, with re-exchange and charges, I/we authorize you, or any of your Managers, or Agents, or the Holders for the time being of such Bill or Bills as the case may be, to draw on me/us for the deficiency, without prejudice nevertheless to any claim against any endorser or endorsers of the said Bills for recovery of the same or any deficiency on the same; and I/we engage to honour such Drafts on presentation, it being understood that the Account Current rendered by you or by such Holders, shall be sufficient proof of sale and loss.

7. I/we further authorize you, or any of your Managers, or Agents, or the Holders for the time being of any such Bill or Bills as aforesaid, whether the aforesaid Power of Sale shall or shall not have arisen at any time before the maturity of any such Bill or Bills, to accept payment from the Drawees or Acceptors thereof, if required so to do, and on payment to deliver the Bills of Lading and Shipping Documents to such Drawees or Acceptors; and, in that event, you or the Holders of any such Bill or Bills are to allow a discount thereon *not exceeding five per cent* per annum for the time they may have to run as follows :—

At one-half per cent per annum above the advertised rate of interest for short deposits allowed by the leading London Joint Stock Banks, if payable in Great Britain.

At the current minimum rate of discount of the National Banks of France, Italy and Belgium, if payable in those countries.

At the current minimum market rate of discount, if payable in Germany.

CREDIT INSTRUMENT NO. 30 (*continued*)

At the current rate of rebate for Documentary Bills, if payable in Switzerland or the United States.

At the current rate of rebate allowed by the Exchange Banks if payable at any place east of Suez.

8. Lastly, it is mutually agreed that the delivery of such collateral securities to you shall not prejudice your rights on any of such Bills in case of dishonour, nor shall any recourse taken thereon affect your title to such securities to the extent of my/our liability to you as above, and that notwithstanding any alteration by death, retirement introduction of new partners or otherwise in the persons from time to time constituting our firm or other the style or firm under which the business at present carried on by us may be from time to time continued, this Letter and the powers and authorities hereby given are to hold good as the Agreement on the part of the firm as aforesaid with you and that each negotiation of a Bill or Bills hereunder is to be treated as a renewal by or on behalf of the firm as then existing of the terms of this Agreement. It is also agreed that you are not to be responsible for the default of any Broker or Auctioneer employed by you for any purpose.

Dated at Manchester this twentieth day of April One Thousand Nine Hundred and Thirty-Five

Witness to the Signature of Amos Baxter

(Signed) MARY HODEN, *Witness*

SECRETARY, *Occupation*

RATHBONE HOUSE, MANCHESTER, *Address of Firm*

(Signed) RATHBONE BAXTER & CO. LTD.

AMOS BAXTER, Director.

Form No. 31: This is not a credit instrument but is merely the advice which will reach Rathbone Baxter & Co., Ltd., in due course from G. Townsend, Ltd., advising the former firm that they have accepted the bill of £1327 : 4 : 10, and informing them on which date the bill will fall due. As it is a four months' sight bill, that is, payable four months after acceptance, Rathbone Baxter & Co., Ltd., cannot know the due date of the bill until they know on what date G. Townsend, Ltd., have accepted it.

FORM NO. 31.—ADVICE OF ACCEPTANCE

PLEASE RETURN TO 25th. January 1936

MESSRS. RATHBONE BAXTER & Co. Ltd.
MANCHESTER

Dear Sirs,
We beg to advise having during the week accepted the following drafts against shipment made by you

We are, dear sirs,

Yours faithfully,
For and on behalf of:-
G. TOWNSEND LTD.

Documents against payment.

[signature] Director.

Date of Acceptance		Steamer	Marks and Numbers		Usance	Amount £	s.	d.	Due Date of Draft	
1936 Jan.	25	Antenor	G T 123 LTD.	1/40	4 m/s	1327.	4.	10	May	28

Credit instrument No. 32: This is the bill drawn by Rathbone Baxter & Co., Ltd., on the China Exchange Bank, Ltd., in London, because this method of finance was, at that time, cheaper than taking a cash advance from the China Exchange Bank, Ltd.

CREDIT INSTRUMENT NO. 32.—BANK'S ACCEPTANCE

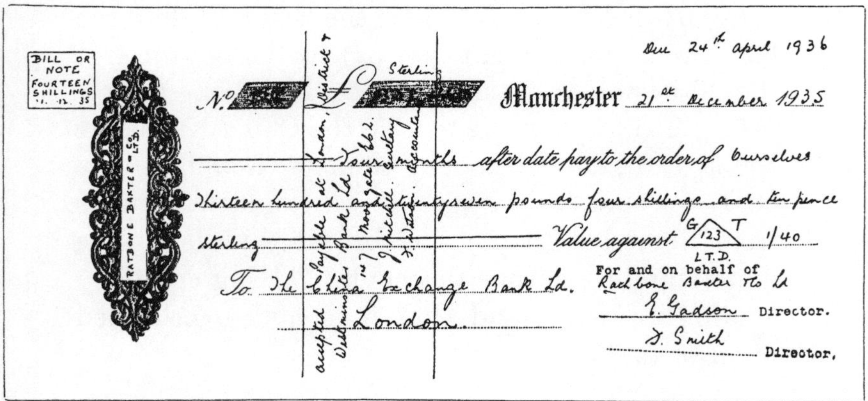

BILL OR NOTE FOURTEEN SHILLINGS 21. 12. 35

RATBONE BAXTER & CO. LTD.

Due 24th April 1936

No. [redacted] £ [redacted] Sterling

Manchester 21st December 1935

Four months after date pay to the order of Ourselves

Thirteen hundred and twentyseven pounds four shillings and ten pence

sterling Value against G T 123 LTD. 1/40

To The China Exchange Bank Ld.
London.

Accepted payable at London, District & Westminster Bank Ld 1 Moorgate EC2.

For and on behalf of Rathbone Baxter & Co Ld

E. Gadson Director.

D. Smith Director.

Credit instrument No. 33 is the letter sending the bill (Credit instrument No. 32) for acceptance. It should be noted that in this letter Rathbone Baxter & Co., Ltd., undertake to give the China Exchange Bank, Ltd., enough money to meet the bill in case G. Townsend, Ltd., have not sent sufficient funds from Shanghai to pay the bill at due date. The understanding is that the bank is giving credit by lending its name, and that it is not to be called upon to find any cash.

CREDIT INSTRUMENT NO. 33.—PRESENTATION FOR ACCEPTANCE

Rathbone House,
Whitworth Street,
MANCHESTER,
21*st December* 1935.

The China Exchange Bank Ltd.,
LONDON, E.C.2.

DEAR SIRS,

We have pleasure to hand you herein first and second of exchange to order ourselves at four months' sight

1 draft for £1327 : 4 : 10.

Attached to this draft is a complete set of B/Lading in duplicate, Marine and War Risk Policy in duplicate and relative invoice and copies covering goods sold and shipped to drawees as per particulars below.

Documents are only to be given up against payment of the bill.

Thereagainst we have today drawn upon your goodselves at four months' date 1 draft for a like amount and this draft we enclose for your kind acceptance and return.

We undertake to put you in funds to meet your acceptance at maturity should proceeds not have been received from Shanghai and at all times to keep you out of cash advance.

In settlement of your accepting commission we enclose our cheque for £6 : 12 : 9 of which kindly acknowledge receipt.

We are, dear Sirs,

Yours faithfully,

G T
123 1/40
LTD.
per ss. "Antenor".

For and on behalf of
RATHBONE BAXTER & CO. LTD.
E. GADSON, Director. (Signed).

Credit instrument No. 34: The cash for the above credit instrument was found by the London & Manchester Bank, Ltd., and Credit instrument No. 34 shows that the bank has discounted the bill at the rate of $1\frac{1}{4}\%$ per annum. (This is an abnormally low rate of discount, but discount rates during 1932–34 were lower than they had been for forty years.)

CREDIT INSTRUMENT NO. 34.—DISCOUNT NOTE

LONDON & MANCHESTER BANK Ltd

BILL DEPARTMENT. Manchester, 24th December 1933

Bills discounted for Messrs. Rathbone Baxter & Co Ltd.

Amount			Due		Days	Rate	Discount			Drawee
1327	4	10	April	24	122	1¼	5	10	11	China Exchange Bank Ltd.
£ 1327	4	10				£	5	10	11	Debited to a/c

Specimen

E. Mason.
pro Manager.

Credit instrument No. 35: is an application from G. Townsend, Ltd., to the China Exchange Bank, Ltd., asking for the Bill of Lading in order that they may obtain the goods from the ship, and store them in a neutral godown (warehouse) to the order of the bank.

CREDIT INSTRUMENT NO. 35

APPLICATION FOR BILL OF LADING

SHANGHAI, 15th February 1936.

The Manager,

CHINA EXCHANGE BANK, Ltd

SHANGHAI.

Dear Sir,

Kindly hand to us Bill of Lading relating to our acceptance as stated below. We hereby agree to land and store the goods in a neutral godown to your order and to send you Landing Account in due course.

We shall effect insurance and send you the Policy.

Yours faithfully,

G. TOWNSEND LTD.

Gregory Townsend

DIRECTOR.

SPECIMEN

ACCEPTANCE			BILL OF LADING		
Bank No.	Amount	Due Date	Steamer	Wharf	Marks & Nos. of Packages
D/C No: 82/1386	£1327.4.10	May 28.36	S.S. "Antenor"	Pootung	G T 123 LTD 1/40.

Credit instrument No. 36 is similar to No. 35 except that in this case the goods are stored in the name of G. Townsend, Ltd., who undertake to hold them for the bank as trustees. As the bank has been instructed by Rathbone Baxter & Co., Ltd., only to hand the goods over against payment, the responsibility for handing them to G. Townsend, Ltd., without payment, rests with the bank.

CREDIT INSTRUMENT NO. 36

TRUST RECEIPT

(Hypothecated Shipping Documents)

Shanghai, 17 February, 1936.

To the Manager,

CHINA EXCHANGE BANK LTD

SHANGHAI

Dear Sir,

In consideration of your handing to $\frac{\text{XX}}{\text{us}}$ Shipping Documents for goods, as per particulars at foot, hypothecated to the Bank as collateral security for the due payment of the undermentioned draft drawn upon $\frac{\text{XX}}{\text{us}}$ by Messrs. Rathbone Baxter & Co. Ltd. and accepted by $\frac{\text{XX}}{\text{us, we}}$ hereby engage to land, store and hold the said goods as Trustee for and on behalf of the Bank, and in the event of the goods or any portion thereof being sold and delivered before full payment of the said draft the proceeds of such sales shall be received by $\frac{\text{XX}}{\text{us}}$ as Trustee for the Bank, and paid to the Bank when and as received, $\frac{\text{I}}{\text{we}}$ at the same time specially advising the Bank of the account on which such payment is made.

$\frac{\text{X}}{\text{we}}$ undertake not to sell any part of the goods on credit unless with your previous consent in writing.

$\frac{\text{X}}{\text{we}}$ also undertake to keep the goods fully insured against fire as against marine risks, and to hand over to the Bank all amounts received from the Insurers, the Policies of Insurance being in the meantime, held by $\frac{\text{XX}}{\text{us}}$ as Trustee for and on behalf of the Bank.

SPECIMEN

Yours faithfully, G. TOWNSEND LTD.

Gregory Townsend.

DIRECTOR.

PARTICULARS OF DRAFTS AND GOODS.

A.B. No.	Amount of Bill			Due		Description of Goods	Vessel
12	£1327	4	10	May 28	1936	Cotton Shirtings	S.S. "Antenor" G 123 T LTD. 1/40

I

Credit instrument No. 37 shows the form that Mr. Chang signed when he obtained his overdraft from the modern Chinese bank against security which is mentioned on the back of the instrument. It empowers the bank to sell the security in case Mr. Chang should not pay back the loan on demand, and Mr. Chang obliges himself to keep the value of the security up to the original amount, and to find fresh security to make up the amount if it should decline in value.

III

SECURITY FOR OVERDRAFTS.

To the

CHINA EXCHANGE BANK, Ltd

$\frac{I}{we}$ Chang hereby acknowledge to have deposited with the **CHINA EXCHANCE BANK Ltd** established at the port of Shanghai the property, goods, merchandise, documents and security for property or money mentioned on the other side, as security for the payment of all $\frac{my}{our}$ joint or several indebtedness to the said Bank at any time and on whatsoever account and more especially for the payment of $\frac{my}{our}$ overdraft with the said Bank to an amount not exceeding $20,000 (twenty thousand dollars) and of interest thereon at the rate of 6 (six) per centum per annum and of the costs and charges of keeping the said property as a security or otherwise incurred in connection therewith and undertake to do all things which may at any time be required by the Bank for more effectually granting to and maintaining in the said Bank an effective pledge of the said property, and in case $\frac{I}{we}$ should make default in paying the said overdraft or any other indebtedness to the said Bank on demand or at due date as the case may be, or in any other obligation by $\frac{me}{us}$ hereby undertaken $\frac{I}{we}$ hereby authorise and empower the said Bank to sell or otherwise dispose of the said property in such manner as it may think most advisable without any reference to $\frac{me}{us}$ or consent on $\frac{my}{our}$ part, and $\frac{I}{we}$ further authorise the said Bank to reimburse itself for and pay out of the proceeds of the said property in the first place the costs, charges, and expenses of keeping and selling the property, or otherwise incurred in connection therewith, but so that the said Bank shall not be responsible, for any loss through or by any broker or auctioneer employed in the sale of the said property or in any other manner whatever in respect of the said property, and in the next place the amount of the said overdraft and the interest and charges thereon, and should any balance remain over the said Bank shall be entitled to place the amount of such balance against all or any sums or sum of money which may at the time of such sale be due or owing from or by $\frac{me}{us}$ to the said Bank upon or in respect of any debt, advance, promissory note, bill of exchange, or other engagement, although it shall happen that such sums or sum of money shall not be due at the time of such sale and $\frac{I}{we}$ further engage to pay on demand to the said Bank the balance (if any) of such overdraft or other debts remaining unsatisfied with interest and $\frac{I}{we}$ further engage to execute deliver *and do and do* hereby appoint the said Bank and its Manager or other recognised officer at Shanghai $\frac{my}{our}$ attorneys and attorney jointly and severally to execute deliver and do all such deeds document and acts as may be found necessary or expedient effectually to vest in the said Bank the said property and documents and to enable it to sell or transfer the same, and $\frac{I}{we}$ further engage to keep up the value of the said security as mentioned on the other side to the full amount of dollars 20,000 (twenty thousand dollars) according to the market rate of the day either by payment of money or (at the option of the Manager or other recognised officer for the time being of the said Bank at Shanghai) by deposit of other property equivalent in value to the market deterioration of the undermentioned property and in the event of $\frac{my}{our}$ failing so to do $\frac{I}{we}$ hereby authorise the said Bank to sell at any time all or such portion of the said property as may be necessary for the full payment of $\frac{my}{our}$ overdraft and other indebtedness (if any) with interest and charges as aforesaid, and to retain or pay out of the proceeds the amount of such overdraft indebtedness, interest and charges, and all further security added is to be subject to the foregoing stipulations, and $\frac{I}{we}$ further agree and engage not to revoke or make void this or any other power of attorney or other authority which $\frac{I}{we}$ have given or may give to the said Bank to enable it to sell and transfer the said property and documents, and $\frac{I}{we}$ agree that the said Bank shall not be answerable or responsible for any damage or depreciation which any of $\frac{my}{our}$ property may suffer while in its possession under this agreement.

Dated this twenty third day of May 1936

Chang

Credit instrument No. 38 is the delivery order which Mr. Chang obtains from the China Exchange Bank, Ltd., when he has paid for the goods, and it authorizes the godown man (warehouse-keeper) to deliver the goods to Mr. Chang.

CREDIT INSTRUMENT NO. 38

CHINA EXCHANGE BANK. Ltd.

DELIVERY ORDER.

No. 12 Shanghai, May 23rd 1936.

GODOWN MAN OF: G. Townsend Ltd's Woosung Warehouse

Deliver to Chang or order

the under-mentioned goods charges thereon to be paid by the holder :—

Marks & Numbers	Number of Packages	Description of Good.
G T 123 Ltd 1/40	40	Cotton Shirtings

CHINA EXCHANGE BANK Ltd.

CHAPTER VI

THE EXPORT OF TEA FROM CHINA TO MANCHURIA. HOW TEA IS GROWN

BEFORE the Japanese invasion of Manchuria in 1931, the town of Mukden was the seat of government, where Chang Tso Lin, the Overlord of three Manchurian provinces, had his residence. Mukden in those days was the home of many wealthy Chinese who, like wealthy people the world over, were fond of luxurious food. Among other dishes they liked birds'-nest soup, sharks' fins, and bamboo shoots. Birds'-nest soup is a greater luxury in China than turtle soup is in this country. The soup is made of the nests of a kind of swift. The bird uses neither sticks nor twigs, but as the Chinese say, makes it "all out of its own head"; that is, by means of a gelatinous saliva. Birds'-nest soup is an acquired taste, and to a novice it seems something like badly made junket. The Chinese consider it strengthening and stimulating, and usually cook it with pigeons' eggs, a little ham, and sometimes with the addition of sugar candy. The young shoots of the bamboo are very tender and have a pleasant taste, rather like truffles. Sharks' fins are sun-dried, steamed, and eaten with crab and a little ham. They are neither shark nor fin, but the delicate portions of the swordfish, and they are imported into China mainly from Nova Scotia. Birds'-nest soup is served at all important dinners given by the rich, but no wedding party is complete without sharks' fins. A wedding dinner of the rich will comprise perhaps forty-six courses, and that of the more humble folk about eighteen, but the bill of fare of both would contain sharks' fins.

These dishes have not been described because they are fantastic; if they appear so to us, it is merely because we are not familiar with them and do not ourselves eat them. There is nothing more peculiar in eating a bird's nest made from the saliva of a bird than in eating honey, the excretion of a bee's honey sac, and the Chinese might find it as strange to eat caviare or herrings' roes as we should to consume sharks' fins. The reason for mentioning these articles is because Mr. Hsu Chiang sold them to his rich customers in Mukden and sent an order for them to his friend Mr. Fu in Shanghai. But Mr. Hsu Chiang had also customers who were less wealthy, and as Chinese of all classes drink tea, he did a large business in that commodity, which he ordered from Mr. Fu at the same time.

Mr. Fu in his turn bought the tea from Mr. Li, who lived in Hankow. Tea is grown in various parts of China, but best of all on the hill-tops and mountain slopes; sometimes as high as 4000 feet; mostly in inaccessible districts and hundreds of miles from the Treaty Ports. The seed is sown in a nursery bed, and the seedlings, when ready, are transplanted. The tea is ready to be picked in five or six years from the time of planting, and when the tree has come to maturity it yields four crops a year. The first crop, which yields the tenderest leaves, is harvested before the Tomb festival, that is, in the first week in April; the second picking takes place in the third or fourth week in that month, before the Grain Rain festival, and the tea from these two pickings is called Spring tea. After the beginning of the Summer festival, in the first week of May, the third picking takes place, and the fourth about one month later. These two crops are called Summer tea; the leaves being full-grown are somewhat astringent with a bitter taste, and this tea is mainly consumed by the poorer classes. Tea should be picked in the early morning or at dusk, otherwise the sun spoils the leaves. The highest plant does not exceed seven feet, and the picking is usually done by women and children who earn about the equivalent of fourpence per day. They earn more for the Spring than for the Summer tea, the work being harder, as, from the former only two or three leaves can be picked from each bud. Green and black tea are the same, varying only in the method of preparation, the green colour being obtained by twisting the leaves in a particular manner. In order to produce dark green tea, the leaves are rubbed by hand and dried by fire, and black tea is the result of rubbing them still further, treading them underfoot, steaming, and then drying them in the sun. Semi-fired green tea keeps better than black, and individual factories need not have such a high weekly output as the tea will not deteriorate while awaiting preparation. When the tea is sent away from the tea-growing district, it has probably been incompletely prepared by the farmer, and the wholesale merchant in the town to which it is sent will see to the final preparation. Some authorities estimate that only about 20% of the tea produced in China is exported.

Mr. Hsu Chiang ordered Spring tea for his rich customers and Summer tea for his less wealthy clients, but he also ordered from Mr. Fu considerable quantities of brick tea. The production of brick tea is said to date back a thousand years. It is used by nomadic tribes in Inner Mongolia, where it is often bartered for spices, furs, wool, and medicinal herbs. It is carried into Mongolia by caravans on pack animals, and it is made into bricks to lessen the bulk and prevent damage by rain, as the journeys may last a couple of months.

China is a land of small peasant proprietors and the growing of tea is in the hands of a large number of small farmers. Except in very mountainous districts, where the soil and conditions are unsuitable for other crops, it is grown as a side line, just as in England a farmer might have a small orchard on his farm. The bushes receive very little care or cultivation. Some of the farmers who grow tea, rent their land, the rent equalling about 10% of the yield of the tea harvest, but many others are themselves the owners of their farms. The farmers sometimes obtain credit by mortgaging their land, and often the growing crop, to money-lenders at high rates of interest, but the modern Chinese banks in an endeavour to help the farmers, are now trying to set up co-operative loan societies. There also exists a type of mutual loan association organized by the farmers themselves or other borrowers, and these are formed by anyone who wants to borrow money and can find twenty others to join him. All the members pay monthly contributions into a common fund, the whole of which they borrow in turn. The member who offers the highest rate of interest has the right to borrow for that month, but no member can obtain a loan twice until everyone has had his turn. The man who starts the loan association is entitled to the first loan and is absolved from paying any interest in view of the fact that he manages the association and keeps all the accounts. Mr. Dyer Ball has compared this system (although it is more complicated) with that of the "Clubs" which are formed in so many of the Lancashire factories.

When Mr. Li in Hankow wished to buy the tea from the farmers, he engaged the services of a *chahong*, who usually specializes in the tea of one or two districts. He acts as an intermediary between the farmer and the wholesale merchant, and when the farmers are short of cash they often obtain credit from these *chahongs*. The *chahong*, in visiting the farms to purchase the tea, takes with him strings of cash, each string being approximately a thousand copper coins, or nowadays more probably he takes silver dollars. In some districts farmers are becoming more accustomed to the notes issued by the Bank of China and will accept these instead of silver dollars. Sometimes the *chahong* obtains his funds from the nearest local centre by means of drafts drawn on these centres, a system of remitting funds which has been in use among the Chinese for centuries. Very often tea is sold by a grower to a wholesaler at the beginning of the season without the price being fixed or any money changing hands. This happens when the parties cannot agree upon the market price, so the grower sells the tea at "Market Price" and the manufacture begins. The actual price may not be settled until several weeks later.

Mr. Li in Hankow was a member of a private partnership with a capital of 60,000 dollars. When he wanted credit, he obtained it from Mr. Fu, the Shanghai tea merchant, but on condition that he sold all his tea through Mr. Fu's Shanghai firm. If he did not wish to do this, he might go to a native bank and obtain an overdraft without security, for which he would have to pay about 12% per annum, or he might borrow from one of the new modern banks at about 6% per annum, but only against approved security as Mr. Chang did for his cotton goods.

When Mr. Li had prepared the tea, he sent it to Mr. Fu in Shanghai, who paid cash for it, less 2% discount, or, he might have asked Mr. Li to draw a Bill of Exchange on him payable after forty days.

When Mr. Fu shipped the tea to Mr. Hsu Chiang in Mukden, he took the Bill of Lading, Insurance Policy, and invoice to a modern Chinese bank as well as the Bill of Exchange drawn on Mr. Hsu Chiang, and obtained an advance from the bank in a similar manner to that obtained by Rathbone Baxter &

Co., Ltd., in Manchester when they shipped cotton cloth to G. Townsend, Ltd., in Shanghai.

The farmer and Mr. Li and Mr. Fu had now all received payment for their tea, but China had received nothing from Manchuria in exchange for the birds' nests, sharks' fins, bamboo shoots, black, green, and brick tea which had been sent to that country. China had really received in exchange for these commodities the cotton cloth which she obtained from Lancashire, and for which she gave the United Kingdom nothing in exchange.

Neither the United Kingdom nor America had as yet received anything in exchange for the commodities which they exported, and in order to see how they were ultimately paid, we must carry the transactions three stages further.

CHAPTER VII

THE PRODUCTION OF SOYA BEANS IN MANCHURIA, AND EXPORT TO DENMARK

CHINA is divided from Manchuria by the Great Wall, which is 2000 miles long and was commenced in 255 B.C. and lengthened and completed in 214 B.C. The object of the Wall was to keep out the hordes of Manchurian and Mongolian raiders but, in spite of this protection, the Manchus conquered China and ruled it from A.D. 1644 till 1912, when the Emperor was dethroned and China became a republic. In 1931 the Japanese invaded Manchuria and rechristened the country Manchoukuo. In 1934 the former ex-Emperor of China, sometimes known as Mr. Henry Pu, was crowned Emperor of Manchoukuo.

The country is rich in minerals and has a fertile soil, and one of the chief products, the soya bean, has become an important article of international trade. Soya beans account for more than one-third of the agricultural produce of Manchuria and over 70% of the crop is exported. More than one-half of the population depends directly or indirectly on the cultivation of this bean and the railway system of the country relies mainly on the freight earned by the transport of this commodity, while an export duty thereon has, in the past, furnished a considerable part of the national revenue. Of the world's production of soya beans 80% is centred in China and Manchuria, but Manchuria is by far the largest exporting country of this bean, and in 1928–29, out of a total world production estimated at 353 million bushels, Manchuria produced 222 millions.

The soya bean is the shape and size of a pea and is grown in various colours—in Manchuria mainly yellow. The bean contains a large amount of oil which the Chinese have used for edible purposes for many centuries, but the export trade to Japan and Europe has arisen during the last thirty years. For hundreds of years the Chinese have also used the oil for lighting purposes, but in other countries it is employed in manufacturing soap, sauce, margarine, paint, and during the Great War it was also used for making glycerine. After the oil has been expressed, the residual bean-cake is used for cattle food and as a fertilizer. The soya bean has become a serious competitor to the cotton seed which we described in the first chapter, some of which was grown on Hezekiah Godbehere's farm, as the two commodities are used for many similar purposes. Cotton seed, however, is still the more important article, furnishing 30% of the world's consumption of vegetable oils, whereas the soya bean supplies only half this quantity.

The United States both grows and imports soya beans, but Manchuria also exports to Japan, England, Germany, Holland, and Denmark, and it is with the export to the latter country that this chapter will deal.

Contracts for the purchase of soya beans are usually made in July and August, long before the crop is harvested. The delivery of the beans by the farmer and merchants takes place in October to December when the mud on the roads is frozen, enabling the carts to make their way. Few of the farmers own their own land and they cannot, therefore, mortgage it, but like farmers all over the world, many of them are in the hands of the money-lenders. At one time it was customary to make advances to the farmer while his crop was growing, for the full amount of the beans which he had promised to deliver during October to December; this the Japanese call "buying the beans green on the field", but so many defaults took place on these contracts that advances are now rare, except perhaps to the extent of 6 to 8% of the value of the beans. One reason why these advances ceased was owing to extensive floods which occured in Manchuria washing away nearly the whole of the crop before it had been warehoused, and thus entailing severe losses on the buyers who had made advances.

Since the new kingdom of Manchoukuo has been formed, efforts have been made to introduce one standard currency because the number of kinds of money which had been employed previously in the purchase and sale of beans enormously complicated these transactions. The "tiao" for which Manchurian peasants formerly sold their crop has practically become obsolete, but there still existed up to the time of the Japanese occupation, the local dollar, the gold yen, the silver yen, the Russian chervonetz, and the pound sterling, all of which currencies were employed in the business, the rates of exchange constantly varying between them.

The farmers sell their beans to Chinese wholesale dealers who collect them from the farms and store them at the principal railway centres, or along the rivers in Manchuria. The wholesale dealer pays cash to the farmers and is refunded by the large exporting firms who, in turn, buy the beans from him and who pay for them as soon as they are received in the railway and river warehouses, which is usually a long time before the beans are shipped or before they are even forwarded to the port of shipment. Sometimes the exporter pays the wholesale dealer on his promise to hand over the warehouse receipt as soon as the beans are warehoused (the Credit instruments used would be similar to Nos. 8 and 10).

In former days, when advances were made to the farmers against the growing crop, the money was also found by the exporting firms, who obtained it either from their own head-office in Europe, or by drawing "anticipatory bills" on London and discounting them with the local bank. The arrangement made in these cases was that the exporting house drew a bill on a London bank or finance house, giving as collateral security the Bill of Lading for the shipment of the beans. The "anticipatory" bill was one drawn in anticipation of the time when the beans would be shipped and the Bill of Lading received by the exporter. In this case the exporter would undertake to the bank that he would hand the Bill of Lading over when the beans were loaded on the vessel. The exporting house nowadays obtains the money to pay the wholesale merchants either from its head-office in Europe or from local banks in Manchuria, from whom it obtains credit against railway waybills or barge Bills of Lading, which later, when the beans are shipped, are exchanged for ocean Bills of Lading. These local banks in Manchuria are repaid out of the proceeds of the bill which the exporter draws on London when he ships the cargo, and which bill he sells in Manchuria. These bills, which are at three or four months' sight, are drawn against credits which have been opened by a London bank. (See Credit instruments 8 and 10, and 13–18 inclusive.)

Beans sold to Denmark are usually sold direct to the oil mills. Under the credit which the Danish oil mill opens with a London bank, the oil mill receives the beans on arrival, and is only obliged to reimburse the bank in time for it to pay its acceptance, that is, three or four months after the arrival in Denmark of the beans. The oil mill thus secures credit during the process of manufacture and will, in most cases, have received payment from the buyer of the oil and bean cakes before it has to pay the bank. The oil is sold to margarine factories, principally in Denmark, and the firms owning the factories in many cases really belong to the oil mills. The bean cake for cattle fodder is sold to provincial merchants on one or two months' credit, and the merchants in their turn sell it to the farmers on similar credit terms.

China exports more goods to Manchuria than it

receives from that country, and for the purposes of our argument we may assume that among the other commodities which formed the excess of exports, was the tea, etc., sent by Mr. Fu to Mr. Hsu Chiang, and that for this China received no commodities from Manchuria in payment; on the other hand, she had given no commodities in exchange for the cotton cloth which she received from the United Kingdom. Manchuria received nothing from Denmark in payment for the soya beans, for Denmark exports little or nothing to that country. Manchuria really received, in exchange for the soya beans, the tea and other commodities which it obtained from China. In order to see what Denmark gave in exchange for the soya beans and how the United Kingdom and America were ultimately paid for the cotton and cotton goods, we must carry the description of the transactions two stages further.

CHAPTER VIII

SHIPMENT OF BUTTER FROM DENMARK TO ENGLAND, AND OF PIGS' BRISTLES FROM CHINA TO AMERICA

We have seen that bills were drawn upon London in payment of soya beans which were shipped to Denmark. In order to find the money, that is, the pounds sterling, to pay for the soya beans, Denmark had to send something to the United Kingdom which she could sell and thus procure the sterling with which to reimburse the banks upon whom the bills for the soya beans had been drawn. We are assuming that the "something" which Denmark sent was butter, and that it is this butter which the United Kingdom received as the real payment for the services which she had performed in manufacturing Hezekiah's cotton into cotton shirting for Mrs. Wu's husband.

Cotton comes from America, tea from China, and soya beans from Manchuria because, owing to climatic reasons, these countries are peculiarly suitable for the production of these commodities. What are the conditions which render Denmark particularly suitable for the production of butter? A short survey of the Danish agricultural economy will help us to answer this question.

Of the total area of Denmark, 76% is used for agriculture. There are over 200,000 farms, 65% of which vary in size from $1\frac{1}{2}$ to 36 acres, and while the number of farms occupying 36 to 150 acres is under 30% of the 200,000, these farms cover more than half the total acreage occupied by farmers. Only 10% of this acreage consists of farms between 150 and 300 acres and under 9% are farms over 300 acres. Denmark is thus a country of small farms and this fact has had a widespread influence on Danish agricultural economy. There exist in Denmark laws prohibiting the conversion of small farms into large farms, and 90% of the farms are owned by the farmers themselves.

Denmark formerly was a grain-growing country, but when competition, about fifty years ago, became very acute and most countries imposed tariffs on the importation of grain, Denmark adopted a policy of free trade, and concentrated her energies on the raising of cattle instead of on the production of corn. To-day the most important branches of her agriculture are dairy-farming, the raising of pigs, and to a smaller extent, the production of eggs. The food value produced in Denmark in 1929 was over 50% greater than that of 1920. In order to provide winter feed for her cattle, she has largely increased her production of root crops. She imports grain and fodder, and uses also her own production of barley and oats (mixed together) for cattle food. Over 80% of the total yield of small and medium-sized farms is due to animal husbandry; and of the total production of grain, cattle consume four times the quantity of that consumed as human food or used for industrial purposes.

In 1929 Denmark produced over 5 million tons of milk; 115,000 tons were made into cheese, 15,000 tons into condensed milk for export, and about 400,000 tons were consumed by her own people; about 4¼ million tons were used for making butter, almost entirely for export, as the Danes themselves mostly eat margarine. Butter forms one-third of the total value of the whole of Danish exports, and of 159 million kilogrammes exported in 1929 Great Britain took 108 millions and Germany 43 millions. It takes 26·3 lb. of milk to make 1 lb. of butter. Most of the butter is carried in Danish ships, as is also a considerable quantity of the soya beans which come from Manchuria.

Denmark has always been a great cattle country. At present to every hundred of human beings in the country there are 86 head of cattle, of which 45 are dairy kine, and during the present century the number of cows has increased over 60% and in 1930 was 1,692,000; the yield of milk increased about one-third, the butter-fat content being 40%.

Agricultural labourers are engaged on half-yearly contracts and are paid only twice a year, but usually, if requested by the wage-earner, monthly advances are made to him. In 1927 the annual wage of men was £36 a year plus board and lodging, £31 for women over eighteen, and £24 for girls under eighteen, the working hours varying from eight hours from December to February, to ten hours from April to November.

Some writers emphasize the fact that the Danish agricultural population is much better educated than similar classes in this country, but the success of agriculture in Denmark must be mainly attributed to the co-operative system. The Danish farms, both large and small, are now organized on a co-operative basis for the purchase of the requirements of the farms. Co-operative dairies exist for making the butter and other co-operative units for marketing it, and this system gives to the small and medium-sized farmer the same advantage as those normally enjoyed by the big farms. Modern dairies require such expensive plant that it does not pay even the largest farmers to make their own butter. The co-operative societies were formed on the initiative of the farmers without State assistance and without State propaganda. They are organized on a democratic basis; anybody can join, profits are divided in proportion to each member's turnover, but every member has an equal voice in the management irrespective of the size of his farm. The only help which the co-operative societies receive from the Government is a grant towards research work and the provision of remuneration for expert advisers. Of the farmers, 90% owning 86% of the cows are members of co-operative dairies, of which there are 1382 with a membership of 180,000 and a turnover of about £40,000,000.

Of the quantity of butter exported, 90% is made in co-operative dairies. There are 11 co-operative butter exporting societies of which the co-operative dairies are members. They handle about 40% of the export of butter. Of the remainder, about 30% is dealt with by private exporters and another 30%

is purchased by the British Co-operative Wholesale Society and the Maypole Dairy Co.

There are four large co-operative societies for the importation of feeding-stuffs and they deal with about one-third of the total quantity imported; their annual turnover being about £8,000,000. In 1916 there was formed a Danish Co-operative Manure Purchasing Society which, in 1928, had 1376 local branches, about 57,000 members, and a turnover of nearly £1,500,000, which was about 40% of the total importation of fertilizers. Seeds are also purchased and sold co-operatively.

The co-operative societies which we have so far described are all producers' societies, but there exist also consumers' co-operative societies whose chief business is the supplying of the household requirements of the farmers.

Co-operative societies in Denmark perform a useful function for their members by the collection of statistics which are circulated and help the farmers to keep their farms up to date. Workers in the co-operative dairies are highly trained; they have constant meetings for discussion and it is said that no one has ever kept an invention concealed from his colleagues, and "everything that experiment and science could do to help them on the way forward, has been taken into use".

Members bind themselves, usually for ten years, to deliver all the milk produced to the society. Farmers are paid for the milk by the co-operative dairies once a week according to the quality as ascertained after testing, and profits are divided half-yearly or yearly, each farmer receiving in proportion to the amount of milk delivered. The farmers originally subscribed enough money to cover the societies' first outlays and all the members are jointly and severally responsible for the liabilities of their own co-operative dairy. Directly the butter is churned it is handed over to the co-operative marketing organization which pays the dairies every week for it, thus enabling the dairies to pay the farmers weekly. The co-operative marketing organizations when sending the butter to the United Kingdom draw ten-day drafts on the importers which they hand to their bankers, and thus obtain the funds enabling them to pay the dairies. When the butter arrives in England it is sold weekly to the shops on about one month's credit.

If the farmer buys his bean-cake from a merchant and not through a co-operative society, he probably receives one to two months' credit, while the co-operative societies which supply him with seeds, implements, and other necessaries, sometimes give him credit and sometimes sell to him for cash.

The Danish farmer possibly does not require as much credit as farmers in other countries owing to the system of only paying wages half-yearly, but the mortgage system by which he obtains the credit which he needs, is more developed than in many other agricultural countries. Farmers in Denmark often have three mortgages on their farm. With one exception, the institutions which grant first mortgages are also co-operative. They are associations of farmers who require loans and who are jointly and severally responsible for all money borrowed. This system enables the mortgage society to issue bonds bearing a low rate of interest, which in 1929 was not more than $4\frac{1}{2}$%. When the farmer mortgages his farm, he receives these bonds in payment and can sell them on the open market, and before the Great War they were commonly saleable in France and England. On the first mortgage the farmer can obtain an advance of 50 to 60% of the value of his farm. The rate of interest charged in 1934 was $3\frac{1}{2}$ to $4\frac{1}{2}$%; the second mortgage, which is for 20 to 30% of the value of the property, would be subject to $4\frac{1}{2}$ to 5% interest. This class of mortgage is granted by "Hypothec" Societies, but sometimes also by private people. Third mortgages are practically always in the hands of private people and the money could be borrowed in 1934 at 5 to 6% per annum, the percentage advanced on the value of the property being a matter of individual arrangement. The mortgages only cover immovable property and in all cases a $\frac{1}{2}$% per annum is added to the interest payment as part payment of the capital amount.

In this chapter, we have carried the butter from Denmark to England, and we have assumed that it is this commodity which we received in exchange for the work done in manufacturing the cotton goods which we sent to China.

In order to complete our circle, we must still show what America received in exchange for the raw cotton which she sent to the United Kingdom, and we will further assume in our story that

America received pigs' bristles in exchange for her raw cotton, which bristles came from China to the United Kingdom and were transhipped thence to the United States.

Pigs' bristles are exported mainly from China and Russia. Chinese farmers are not celebrated for modern ideas on sanitation, and regard their pigs as scavengers; this may lead (unless care is taken) to transmission of disease, particularly anthrax, through the medium of the bristles. Sanitary provision is, however, taken against this danger: exporters treat the bristles before they are shipped, and, if the shipment is certified by the Port Health officers, it can be taken that the bristles are free from contagion. The best quality comes from Hankow, but in some parts of China special pigs are raised for their long hair, and Dr. W. H. Bolton, an authority on Chinese bristles, states that about 70% are under three inches in length and 30% over three inches, while practically the reverse is true of Russian bristles. The Chinese are a pork-eating nation and consequently will not allow their pigs to grow to full age for the purpose of obtaining longer bristles. Although the Russian bristle, then, has an advantage in length, it has the disadvantage that the bristles have mixed with them a percentage of wool, or soft hair which is objectionable and which is not to be found in Chinese bristles. Bristles similar to those which come from Russia are also exported from Manchuria, but are inferior in quality.

China produces annually about 100,000 piculs

($133\frac{1}{3}$ lb. equal a picul) of which two-thirds are exported. It is estimated that 90% are black in colour and come mainly from North China, but white bristles are produced in the south and south-western provinces.

Bristles are collected in winter when the hair is crisp, and the average Chinese hog produces half a pound of spinal, and a quarter of a pound of side bristles. Tientsin is the largest collecting centre and the total value exported is about one million taels annually.

Some of the large firms have their own purchasing agents in the interior towns, but buyers and peddlers also go about the country making purchases in small lots, often by payment in kind. When collected, the bristles are sorted according to length, colour, and quality, and are then tied in bundles, disinfected, and packed according to sizes in boxes of one picul nett. In this form they are exported to the United States, where they are mainly used for making paint-brushes.

Our circle is now complete.[1] We may imagine that some of the imported Chinese bristles, after being made into paint-brushes, found their way to the store in Hezekiah's home town and that Hezekiah, wanting to paint his barn, bought one of these paint-brushes which came into the country in payment of the B.A.Z. cotton which he had raised. If we stretch our imagination still a little further we can envisage a coincidence by which the bristles in Hezekiah's paint-brush are from a hog slaughtered

[1] See Appendix No. 2.

by little Mrs. Wu's husband, who, it will be remembered, was a pork butcher, and that the profit which he made by selling the bristles and the meat which this hog yielded, enabled Mrs. Wu to buy the poplin shirting which was manufactured from Hezekiah Godbehere's B.A.Z. cotton. In that case Mr. Wu's bristles would have paid America for the cotton in Mr. Wu's shirt!

CHAPTER IX

THE COMPLETE CHAIN—THE PART PLAYED BY BANK LOANS IN MARKETING COMMODITIES

We have now seen how Hezekiah Godbehere and John B. Robinson were paid for their cotton out of the money borrowed by Levine from the local bank. We have also seen how John B. Robinson reimbursed the banks for seed and paid the instalment on his mortgage, and how Levine reimbursed the bank when he received payment of the bill which he had drawn on Silas J. Hocking, to whom he had sold the cotton. Silas J. Hocking, who sold the cotton to Birdhead & Co. in Liverpool, was reimbursed by the New Orleans & Overseas Bank, to whom he gave the bill against the cotton which he had drawn on the North-Western Bank, Ltd., in Liverpool.

Birdhead & Co. obtained the money to pay the North-Western Bank, Ltd., by selling the cotton to a spinner (The Diamond Spinning Co., Ltd.). This spinner might have borrowed money from his bank in order to pay Birdhead & Co., in which case he could have paid his bank back when he had sold his yarn to the manufacturer of the cloth. In his turn the manufacturer (the Blackburn Weaving Co., Ltd.) might have obtained the funds which he needed to pay the spinner by borrowing from his bank, in which case he could have paid his bank back when he received payment from the merchant (Rathbone Baxter & Co., Ltd.) to whom he sold the cloth. Rathbone Baxter & Co., Ltd., might have borrowed money from their bank in order to pay the Blackburn Weaving Co., Ltd., in which case the former could have paid the bank back out of the proceeds of the bill drawn by them on G. Townsend, Ltd., in Shanghai, on which they received an advance from the China Exchange Bank, Ltd., to whom they gave the bill.

G. Townsend, Ltd., in Shanghai could have paid the China Exchange Bank, Ltd., in Shanghai out of the money received from Mr. Chang, who probably borrowed it from a native bank and paid it back out of the money received from Mr. Feng, who sold the cotton cloth to Mrs. Wu, who paid for it out of the profit which Mr. Wu made by selling pork.

Mr. Fu, the tea merchant, perhaps borrowed money from his native bank in order to pay Mr. Li in Hankow and enable the latter to pay the *chahongs* who paid the farmers. Mr. Fu would pay back his native bank out of the money which he received from the modern Chinese bank in Shanghai for the bill which he had drawn on Mr. Hsu Chiang in Mukden. The bank in Shanghai would send the bill to its branch in Mukden, and when the bill fell due Mr. Hsu Chiang could pay the amount to the bank in Mukden out of the money which he received from the sale of the tea.

In the same way, the soya-bean farmer might have been paid by the merchant out of the money which he borrowed from the exporting firm. The exporting firm could have borrowed money (on the railway receipts) from a Manchurian bank, which it perhaps paid back out of the proceeds of the bill which it drew on London against shipment of soya beans to Denmark, which bill it gave to a bank in Manchuria.

Again in a similar way all the people involved in the butter transaction in Denmark were paid in their turn, the farmer by the co-operative dairies, co-operative dairies by the co-operative marketing organization, and the latter either by exporting merchants or by bills drawn on foreign importers, for which the co-operative marketing organizations would receive cash from the Danish banks.

It thus becomes clear how, throughout these transactions, the people who supplied the commodities, and the internal local banks which supplied the money, were all paid. We still have, however, to describe the means by which the various overseas banks were reimbursed; for instance, the New Orleans & Overseas Bank, which paid Silas J. Hocking; the China Exchange Bank, Ltd., which found the money for Rathbone Baxter & Co., Ltd.; and so on throughout the chain of international dealings in the various commodities.

In order that we may understand the position, we must bear in mind that the United Kingdom bought cotton from America and butter from Denmark. She sold cotton goods to China, the value of which included the value of the cotton which she bought from America.

We will assume that the value of the cotton goods which Rathbone Baxter & Co., Ltd., sold to G. Townsend, Ltd., in Shanghai (and similar transactions between other firms) was £100,000, and that the cost of the cotton bought by Birdhead & Co. from Silas J. Hocking and manufactured into these goods was £50,000; the other £50,000 representing the value of the work which had been done in Lancashire and the cost of transporting the cotton goods to Shanghai.

Our next assumption is that in exchange for this £100,000 of cotton goods, Mr. Fu in Shanghai sold tea, birds' nests, sharks' fins, and bamboo shoots to Mr. Hsu Chiang in Mukden (and others) to the value of £50,000, and sent £50,000 worth of bristles to the United Kingdom and that the bristles were re-exported from the United Kingdom to America. Manchuria sent £50,000 worth of beans to Denmark, for which she drew bills against credits opened in London, on London banks. Finally Denmark sent £50,000 worth of butter to the United Kingdom and drew bills for that amount on London.

The position then was, that banks in the United Kingdom had to *pay* the following Bills of Exchange:

(*a*)	For raw cotton, bills amounting to Drawn from America.	£50,000
(*b*)	For soya beans, bills amounting to Drawn from Manchuria (shipped to Denmark).	50,000
(*c*)	For butter, bills amounting to . Drawn from Denmark.	50,000
(*d*)	For bristles, bills amounting to . Drawn from China.	50,000
		£200,000

The banks in the United Kingdom had to *receive*:

(*e*)	From China for the value of cotton goods . . .	£100,000
(*f*)	From America for the value of bristles	50,000
(*g*)	From Denmark for the value of soya beans . . .	50,000
		£200,000

The United Kingdom had to receive £100,000 from China for the bills drawn against shipment of cotton goods, but China drew bills on London for £50,000 for bristles which ultimately went to America, so that Great Britain only had to receive the balance of £50,000. Shanghai might pay this £50,000 balance by sending London the bills for £50,000 which had been drawn on Manchuria for the tea, or more probably give the bills to a

European bank in China with its head-office or branch in London. This would be the same thing as telling Manchuria to pay to London the money which it owed to China, and this would cancel out (*a*) the £50,000 which Manchuria had drawn on London against the soya beans; (*b*) the debt owing by Manchuria to China; and (*c*) the transactions for cotton goods and bristles between the United Kingdom and China.

The United Kingdom owed Denmark £50,000 on the bills which had been drawn against the shipments of butter, but Denmark owed the United Kingdom £50,000 for the bills which had been drawn on London for the soya beans received by Denmark from Manchuria, so these two transactions cancelled out and the account was settled between Denmark and London.

England owed America £50,000 for the bills drawn for cotton shipped to Liverpool, and America owed England £50,000 for bristles imported into England and re-exported to the United States, so that these two transactions cancelled each other.

All the international banks concerned were thus paid. If the bill on America for bristles were held by the China Exchange Bank, Ltd., in London, all that would be necessary would be for the North-Western Bank, Ltd., in Liverpool, which had to pay the bill for the cotton, to pay the amount to the office of the China Exchange Bank, Ltd., in London (which had to receive £50,000 for the bills drawn on the New York bank against the shipment of bristles). To regulate the position in America, the New Orleans & Overseas Bank, which had to receive £50,000 for the bills drawn for cotton, could be paid this sum by the bank in New York on which the bills for the bristles had been drawn. All the banks would thus have been paid and no money would have passed internationally. The result of all these transactions as far as the United Kingdom was concerned would have been that she received butter in exchange for the work she had done in manufacturing the cotton goods.

Of course in practice things do not always work out as exactly as this. There may still remain a balance owing when all transactions for the exchange of goods, and services for freight, insurance, bank commissions, interest on investments, and money spent by travellers, money remitted home by emigrants, film rights, and sale of such stocks and shares as are internationally marketable, have been set off against each other. If the debit balance has arisen through the importation of such things as railway materials or materials for harbours and docks, repayment will probably not be due except very gradually over a long series of years. The bills drawn against the materials for the railways and docks will of course have to be paid, but as far as the international banks are affected, these will be cancelled out by loans raised in the exporting country or other countries in order to find the means of building the railways and docks in the importing country.

It must not be supposed that an account of international transactions is drawn up at particular times and the balance then settled; transactions are going on continually, and balances still owing (after all the items which we have enumerated have had their effect), are reflected in the rate of exchange ruling between the different countries. If at any time England owes more money to America than America owes to England on balance (that is after all possible cancelling out has been done), then there will be a demand for dollars on the part of the people who have to pay money in dollars, which, however, will not be offset by any corresponding demand for sterling from America. The increased demand for dollars will send up their value, we shall have to pay more pounds sterling for the dollars, or, in other words, the rate of exchange will be against us.

Any balance which is unsettled may remain owing until it is rectified by a change in the visible and/or invisible imports and exports. The maladjustment in the trade between any two countries will, by affecting the rates of exchange, act as a warning to bankers and others. Credit in the country which owes the balance, and whose exchange will fall, will become restricted, prices will fall and imports will be discouraged and exports encouraged not only of goods but also of those Stock Exchange securities which are dealt in internationally, and in this way the balance may be rectified. If it is not, it may be settled by the transfer of balances held abroad by the different banks. Central Banks and banks engaged in international trade hold balances in banks in foreign countries in the currency of those foreign countries. If for instance we have a balance owing to France which is not settled by any of the aforesaid means, then it may be adjusted by our banks transferring to French banks, out of their balances held in Paris, as many francs as may be necessary to readjust matters. In the last resort, and if all these other means are exhausted, the balance will be settled (under Gold Standard conditions) by the transference of gold from the debtor country to the creditor country, but even in this case it need not be a physical transfer. If the balance is against England and in favour of France, gold need not actually be shipped from England to France, but it will suffice if gold belonging to the Bank of England is transferred or, as we say, "earmarked" for the Bank of France. Gold in this case would still remain in the vaults of the Bank of England, but the ownership would have passed from the Bank of England to the Bank of France, and the Bank of England would then merely hold it as a warehouse-keeper or agent for the Bank of France.

CHAPTER X

BORROWERS AND LENDERS

HAVING seen how all the banks were paid back for the credit which they gave, we may now enquire whence they obtained the money which they lent.

The amount of credit given by banks far exceeds the amount of capital owned by them. They are really only channels through which credit can be obtained, and the funds for providing this credit emanate from the savings of the people, including the undistributed profits of business concerns if invested outside the businesses. These savings are deposited with the banks and lent by them to the borrowers, or the savings are lent by the savers for a term of years in the form of mortgages, debentures, or bonds. Just as Employment Exchanges function as intermediaries between those seeking employment and those having employment to give, so the banks function as intermediaries between those seeking to borrow and those who are willing to lend.

Not all trade is carried on by means of credit, although a very large part is transacted by this method. If a customer buys a motor-car and pays cash for it, no credit is involved, but if the motor-car manufacturer sells him a motor-car on the understanding that he will pay for it after a lapse of time, then the motor-car is obtained on what is called "trader's credit", and if the motor-car manufacturer's capital is sufficient to allow him to give his customers such credit, then no bank credit is involved in the transaction. But the motor-car when bought, although not yet paid for, belongs to the customer, and the motor-car manufacturer has no security for the debt owing to him. Most cars, however, are sold on the deferred-payment system. This is a different form of trader's credit, for the manufacturer owns the motor-car until it is paid for, or, in other words, he is really lending it, and it is only finally sold when all the instalments have been paid. In transactions of this nature in the motor and other trades, bank credit is also involved. The motor-car manufacturer insures with a company against the risk that his customer will not pay all the instalments, and gives this insurance policy to some bank or financial institution which advances him money, thus enabling him to deliver the car against deferred payments by his customers.

We may now turn to an examination of what it is that the lender actually lends and for what purposes it is borrowed.

What is it that the borrower desires to borrow? We have seen that all credit is obtained from the banks in exchange for credit instruments, warehouse receipts, Bills of Exchange, and similar documents, but while it is said that man cannot live by bread alone, it is equally true that he cannot live on bits of paper. Of what, then, does credit really consist? Let us look at the chain once more in order to see what it is that the people have borrowed. What is actually borrowed is *purchasing power* which enables the borrowers to acquire the commodities which they need in order to produce, or to satisfy their wants. In a community in which money did not exist it would be the commodities themselves which would be borrowed, but in a modern community it is purchasing power which is borrowed, the borrower himself, by means of money, acquiring the commodities which he needs. John B. Robinson acquired his farm. Hezekiah Godbehere rented part of the farm from Robinson and acquired the cotton seed on credit. Levine, the f.o.b. man, bought cotton from Robinson with money advanced from his bank; virtually the bank lent the purchasing power to Levine, Levine acquired the cotton, and later some other bank again lent purchasing power to Silas J. Hocking in New Orleans in order that he might acquire the cotton from Levine, and still another bank lent purchasing power to Birdhead & Co. in Liverpool in order that they (Birdhead & Co.) might acquire the cotton from Silas J. Hocking. Throughout the transactions it was the actual bales of cotton which the purchasers desired to acquire on credit. The spinner who bought the cotton mortgaged his mill by a floating charge, that is, he really acquired his machinery, building, or possibly cotton and other commodities, by means of the purchasing power which he borrowed from the bank. The manufacturer who wove the cloth wanted yarn and obtained credit which was for the purpose of acquiring yarn, while the merchant borrowed purchasing power to enable him to acquire the cloth and hold it during the period when it was being bleached, printed, and shipped to China; and the firms in China also acquired it by means of credit until little Mrs. Wu, who bought it on credit, finally paid for it out of her savings. The tea was acquired by somebody in China on credit until it was actually paid for by Mukden; the soya beans and the fertilizers for growing them were acquired on credit, while the Danes, in order to produce the butter, obtained fertilizers on credit from the co-operative societies, and purchasing power from the Mortgage Associations (which they used to acquire their farms), and finally the English shopkeeper acquired the Danish butter and remained indebted for it until he had sold it over the counter.

When purchasing power is borrowed, it is always in order to acquire commodities; that is, commodities in the widest sense including farms, factories, ships, railways, and the commodities which are necessary to maintain the labour used in producing goods. It is obvious then, that the limit of credit which is available at any time for new production is measured by the amount of purchasing power which people are able and willing to lend, and which other people are able and willing to borrow in order to acquire the commodities which they want. But the quantity which the borrower can acquire of these commodities at any given time is limited by the quantity of actual stock which the holders are able and willing to sell. On the one hand, the willingness of banks or other people to lend purchasing power will not increase production unless there are borrowers able and willing to borrow it in order to acquire the commodities. On the other hand, an alteration in the amount of purchasing power which people are able and willing to lend and other people able and willing to borrow will (unless a corresponding alteration takes place in the amount of commodities which people are able and willing to sell and other people are able and willing to buy), only alter the price of the available stock of commodities, but cannot increase or decrease the actual stock available at any moment. An alteration in the available amount of purchasing power, however, may encourage or discourage future production, or it may increase or decrease the willingness of holders of stock to sell, and the willingness of buyers to buy.

It must be remembered that this is not a theoretical book on Capital and Credit, but a description of how credit actually enters into and is used in commercial transactions. Let us take an example. We will suppose the stock of American cotton existing in the world and available for sale on June 1st is 6 million bales. We will further suppose that this cotton has been bought by the present holders at a price of £10 a bale by means of purchasing power borrowed from the banks; that is, the holders have borrowed £60,000,000. We will assume that the demand for cotton on the part of cotton merchants and speculators increases. This will send the price up perhaps to £11 a bale, and as cotton is parted with by the original holders and passes into the hands of the new buyers, they will require to borrow purchasing power at the rate of £11 a bale. The total amount of purchasing power required to be borrowed in order to hold the 6 million bales will be increased, while the stock of the actual cotton will remain the same until the next year when new cotton can be grown or until the present stock passes into actual consumption.

The rise in the price of cotton, made possible by the increase in purchasing power which has been lent, may induce farmers to grow more cotton in the next year, just as a fall in price might induce them to grow less. But the increased credit obtained to market the existing stock of cotton at £11 instead of £10 a bale does not increase the quantity of that stock, nor will it directly help any more cotton to be raised in the next crop. It will induce a cotton farmer to try to raise more cotton, but he will only succeed in doing this if he can find a lender able and willing to lend him the purchasing power which he will require in order to buy the necessary increased supply of seed and fertilizers. In the same way, if the farmer grows more cotton, having obtained the necessary increase in purchasing power, no more cotton yarn will be produced, if the spinners (possibly because their credit is bad and they have no more security to offer to the banks) are unable to borrow the increased purchasing power necessary to absorb the greater quantity of cotton.

During the cotton famine of 1864 there was plenty of cotton in America which the Americans were willing to sell and the Lancashire spinners anxious to buy, but (owing to the blockade of the southern ports), although they were willing, they were not able to sell it because it could not be transported to Lancashire. There was, however, plenty of purchasing power which people were willing and able to lend, and others willing and able to borrow in order to acquire the cotton. The consequence of this was that the price of cotton soared to four or five times the pre-famine price, while the Lancashire mills were standing idle for lack of the raw material. We had an example of the reverse position in 1933 when again there was plenty of purchasing power available to be lent or to be borrowed in order to acquire the cotton, and large stocks of raw cotton which the holders were very anxious to sell. But Lancashire mills again stood idle, and the price of cotton fell to abnormal depths because the spinners, owing to the existing trade depression, were unwilling to borrow the purchasing power (even if they could), as they did not wish to acquire the cotton, fearing that they would be unable to sell the yarn at a profitable price.

We may now ask who lends the purchasing power used to acquire all these commodities? As a rule, obviously not the people who produce them. Hezekiah cannot afford to sell his cotton and wait for payment until the Lancashire spinner has bought it. The spinner cannot afford to sell his yarn on long credit; he already owes money to his bank for his mill and machinery. The farmers in China and in Manchuria cannot afford to sell the tea and the soya beans and wait for payment; they are probably already in the hands of money-lenders.

The amount of money which the banks lend far exceeds their own capital. Somebody, or rather many people, save up money, and it is by means of these savings that Hezekiah's cotton is acquired by Levine. These people who save, do not themselves buy the cotton from Hezekiah and then lend it to Levine, but they deposit their savings in the banks and allow the banks to lend them to the Levines who wish to buy the cotton from the Hezekiahs. Although the banks lend their customers' money, they guarantee the savers the safety of their deposits and it is the banks which take the risk of lending the money to the borrowers.

If Hezekiah himself sells the cotton on credit, he can only do so if he has saved up enough other things (or enough money to purchase other things) to subsist until he receives payment for the cotton. He can only sell the cotton on credit if he has accumulated capital. When the banks lend money it is also capital, but the capital of someone else, which they are lending.

There may be at any given time, and there generally is at all times in some commodities, a stock of things which people are not willing to sell at that particular time because they think that by withholding the stocks from the buyers they will, at some future date, obtain a higher price for them. On the other hand, there are times when buyers are not prepared to buy the stocks, because they think that by withholding their purchase they will acquire them later on at a cheaper price. There are also times when the banks and other lenders of purchasing power are not prepared to lend freely, either because they lack confidence in the ability of the borrowers to pay them back, or because they think that later on they will get a higher rate of interest for their money. Similarly, there are times when borrowers are not prepared to borrow, either because they lack the necessary confidence to undertake new enterprises or expand their present undertakings, or because they think that by delaying their borrowing, they will obtain the money later on at a lower rate of interest.

We have seen that the money which people are able and willing to lend affects the price of the stock of things which the borrowers are able and willing to acquire. If the money which is being lent at any given time is greater than the amount of money lent at some previous time and no alteration in the meantime has taken place in the stock of commodities available for selling, then the effect of the increased money credit is only to increase the price of these commodities but does not increase the existing stock. The reverse is equally true if the amount of money which people are willing to lend in relationship to the commodities has decreased instead of increased, and it is also true if an alteration has taken place in the amount of commodities available for sale, without a corresponding alteration in the money available for loans. But an alteration in the price of commodities may induce the holders to expedite or retard their sale, and consequently their passing into the hands of people able and willing to use them, and in this way may affect future lending and production. On the other hand, an alteration in the price of commodities may have an effect in stimulating or retarding enterprise and thus increase or diminish the willingness of borrowers to borrow.

Realization of the fact that all credit is founded on somebody's savings should help us to understand why it is that in the chain of international transactions which we have described, America and the United Kingdom are the last of the countries involved to receive payment in commodities for the goods which they have exported. The reason is that the people of these two countries save a large amount annually, and it is they who either own a large part of the surplus stocks of the world, or own the means of purchasing them, and who are able and willing to lend these stocks to people in other countries. The stocks themselves may, of course, not be in the United Kingdom or America, but in other countries. The English people, for example, have invested a considerable amount of their savings in China in railways, docks, and similar undertakings, and on these savings receive interest. If they are willing to lend this interest to foreigners they may possibly deposit it with the China & Exchange Bank, Ltd., in Shanghai, which bank could, in its turn, lend it to Mr. Li, who could lend it to Mr. Fu in Hankow, who could lend it to the *chahong* who bought the tea from the Chinese farmer. Thus someone in the United Kingdom would have given the credit necessary to buy the tea in China. It may happen, and it does, of course, happen very often, that the Englishman who is entitled to receive interest on his investment in a Chinese railway for instance, needs the money to spend in England and does not want to reinvest it in China, but as long as there are other Englishmen who have savings which they are willing to invest in China, the investment will still take place; the first Englishman will sell, directly or indirectly, the interest which he is entitled to receive in China to the other Englishman who is willing to lend it in China, the latter paying the amount to the former in England.

The United Kingdom is the country in which the technique of lending money abroad is most fully developed, and for this reason London is the greatest money market in the world. She has the longest experience and the best organization for foreign lending. It is only comparatively recently that America has become an important international lender, and during the nineteenth century she was indeed an international borrower. France and, to a lesser degree, Holland are also important lenders to foreigners, but this type of business is nowhere as fully developed as it is in England.

CHAPTER XI

THE BREAKING OF A LINK, AND ITS CONSEQUENCES

OUR chain is now complete. We have seen how the cotton brought from America has been exchanged for bristles imported from China into England, and exported thence to the United States. Lancashire exported cotton goods to China; part of the value of these goods represented the value of the raw cotton used in their manufacture, and we may consider that this part was exchanged for the bristles, and for the remainder (that is for the work done on the cotton), the United Kingdom received Danish butter. China gave in exchange for the cotton goods, partly bristles, exported to the United Kingdom and thence to the United States, and partly tea, birds' nests, sharks' fins, and bamboo shoots, which were exported to Manchuria. In exchange for these Manchuria sent soya beans to Denmark, and in payment for the soya beans Denmark sent butter to the United Kingdom.

We have mentioned a few of the people, firms, and banks involved in these transactions, but there were, of course, many people and business concerns indirectly involved; for instance, those concerned in making the agricultural implements used by the various farmers whose dealings in produce we have described. There were also the railways and ships, which carried the produce, and all the people who helped in maintaining the railways, running the ships, and mining the coal which was used for these purposes.

It is apparent that in all these transactions many different interests were involved, and that many complex considerations might arise. The breaking of a link in our chain might cause dislocations having consequences, some of which it would be very difficult to foresee. The effect of these consequences might be so widespread that it is worth while describing some of the possible reactions which might result, in order that the reader may understand how dislocations in commerce and industry sometimes arise. We must remember, however, that all the time new chains of transactions are coming into existence which may minimise the consequences of the breaking of some links in the old.

We can classify the principal causes of the breaking of the chain under the following headings:

(1) Failure, or alteration in consumptive demand.

(2) Failure of production, or alteration in the nature of production.

(3) Failure to release or acquire stocks of commodities.

(4) Failure to lend or to borrow the money to finance the moving of stocks of commodities.

(5) Government interference with the normal flow of trade through the imposition of tariffs, exchange restrictions, quotas, subsidies, and other hindrances to trade.

All these have one common feature; they all

cause dislocation in the exchange of commodities which results in dislocation in industry and commerce, and dislocation means unemployment for somebody. We will consider these causes in the order which we have mentioned them. First, failure or alteration in consumptive demand.

It will be remembered that little Mrs. Wu married a pork butcher who lives in Shan-si. We will assume that one year the province is inundated by terrible floods (which frequently occur in China). Crops are destroyed, people generally impoverished, demand reduced, and Mr. Wu's trade suffers equally with that of his neighbours. Consequently Mrs. Wu cannot afford to buy the "Nine Dragon Chop" of shirting for her husband's shirts, so that she decides to buy a lower quality, that is one which is cheaper in price. We may also assume, and the assumption is quite probable, that the motives which induce Mrs. Wu to economize induce, at the same time, thousands of other women who are accustomed to buy the "Nine Dragon Chop" or similar qualities, to satisfy themselves with cheaper cloths. If Mrs. Wu substitutes another English quality for the "Nine Dragon Chop", she may either choose a cloth which contains a smaller quantity of cotton, or she may choose one which is made from a cheaper quality of cotton. In the former case, the demand for Hezekiah's quality of cotton, the B.A.Z. mark, will decline and, in order to get rid of his crop, Hezekiah may be forced to lower his price somewhat. But if Mrs. Wu's new purchase is made from a different quality of cotton, then the demand for the B.A.Z. mark for the purposes of the "Nine Dragon Chop" will be entirely lacking, and Hezekiah may have to lower his price considerably in order to sell all his cotton. This will reduce Hezekiah's income and Robinson's income; their general purchasing power will decline, and they will have greater difficulty than before in meeting the interest payments on the money which they have borrowed. The decline in Hezekiah's purchasing power will tend to cause a certain amount of unemployment among those people who have been manufacturing commodities, such as farming implements, clothing, and other necessities, to meet his requirements. If instead of the B.A.Z. mark other American cotton is used, the increased demand for such cotton will tend to increase the purchasing power of the growers thereof and stimulate their demand for the commodities which they require. But they may be different commodities, or those farms may be situated in a different State in America, and the improvement of the demand in that State will not prevent the dislocation and consequent unemployment in Hezekiah's State.

It is possible also that the new quality of shirting is not manufactured from American cotton at all, but perhaps from cotton grown in some other country, in which case prosperity in that country might be increased at the cost of unemployment in the United States. Let us suppose, however, that Mrs. Wu decides to buy a cloth which is manufactured in Japan and made half from American and half from Indian cotton. A different set of reactions would arise. Imports of American and Indian cotton into Japan would increase, giving more employment to the ships that carried the cotton from India. On the other hand, as America would only be supplying half the amount of cotton to Japan for Mrs. Wu's shirts that she had supplied to England, the demand for ships carrying cotton from America would decline. Levine, the f.o.b. man, would have less business to handle; the American ginners, less cotton to gin; the railways, less cotton to carry; and the warehouses, less to warehouse; the loans demanded from the banks would decline; and Silas J. Hocking would lose part of his business. Hezekiah, not having been informed, however, by Mrs. Wu that she had ceased to buy shirts made from his cotton, would possibly think that the decline in the demand for his quality of cotton was purely temporary and, therefore, plant his usual quantity of seed for next season's crop instead of some other crop, and thus prolong the period of his loss of purchasing power. The cumulative effect of all this would be unemployment in America.

The Liverpool warehouses would have less cotton to warehouse; Birdhead & Co. would lose part of their business; the railways would carry less cotton to the Diamond Spinning Co., Ltd., in Oldham, who would have less cotton to spin and to send to the Blackburn Weaving Co., Ltd., in Blackburn, who in their turn would have less cloth to weave and to send by motor lorry to the bleachers in Droylsden, who would have less cloth to bleach. The

Manchester packers would have less goods to pack, causing a decline in the demand for paper, timber for cases, terne plates, and nails. Rathbone Baxter & Co., Ltd., would lose part of their business; the shipowners who carry goods from Birkenhead to Shanghai would lose part of their freight. All along the line unemployment would be caused in the United Kingdom because Mrs. Wu in Shanghai and her thousands of countrywomen had decided to buy Japanese cloth as it was cheaper than the English "Nine Dragon Chop".

The reactions would go further than this. Manchuria would still require tea from China, and Denmark soya beans from Manchuria, but Japan would now import something in exchange for her shirting cloth, and India something in exchange for her cotton. America, on the other hand, would only have to receive half the former amount of bristles because she had sent half of the amount of cotton to Japan which she formerly sent to the United Kingdom. Her diminished export of cotton would lessen the purchasing power of her people and she might find her demand for bristles reduced; if not, she would have to export some other article to replace the cotton or reduce other imports. The United Kingdom would have to receive nothing from China in exchange for the cotton goods which she had ceased to export, but she would still want Danish butter (perhaps in a somewhat reduced quantity owing to unemployment); she would have to find some new export to pay for the Danish butter, or reduce some other import, or lend less money to foreign countries as she would have a smaller surplus.

In Japan and India the reverse would happen to that which would happen in the United Kingdom and America. There would tend to be more employment in the former countries; and greater employment would lead to a greater demand. For instance, Japan's increased prosperity might lead to a greater demand for wool from Australia with which to clothe her people, and in turn, Australia might buy perhaps more agricultural implements from the United Kingdom and improve the demand for labour in that industry, but the dislocation would still exist because the increased demand for labour in the agricultural implement industry would not absorb labour trained to spin yarn and weave cloth, which labour would consequently tend to remain unemployed. India having experienced a greater demand for her raw cotton, might increase her demand for machinery, Ford tractors, or for machinery from America, causing more employment in those trades but not helping Hezekiah, Robinson, Levine, the cotton ginneries, warehouses, and all others employed directly or indirectly in the export of cotton from America.

If Mrs. Wu decided to buy cotton cloth made in China from Chinese cotton, the same dislocation and loss of business would occur in the United Kingdom and America as if she had bought the cotton cloth in Japan. China, owing to the extension of her cotton industry, would want more machinery. We should send her machinery instead of cotton cloth, and this would mean more employment for our mechanical engineers, but would not help the spinners and weavers who had been thrown out of work, except possibly to the slight extent that the increase in the machinery trade might stimulate employment in the home demand for cotton goods. China, on the other hand, might buy the machinery from Germany. The circle would then be widened and the dislocation extended, but in the end if Germany's exports increased, her imports would also increase.

The action of Mrs. Wu might set up changes in prices other than in the price of cotton cloth; for instance, the demand for Chinese cotton would be increased and for American cotton diminished, consequently the price of Chinese cotton would tend to rise and that of American cotton would tend to fall which, in its turn, might cause some goods formerly made of Chinese cotton now to be made from American cotton. If this took place to a sufficient extent, the equilibrium between the prices would, in time, be restored. Or again, if unemployment in the cotton trade in this country reduced the demand for Danish butter, it might increase the demand for margarine, causing a larger demand for the soya bean oil in order to make margarine, but a decreased demand for the by-product, namely, the bean-cake which is used to feed the cattle which give the milk which makes the butter.

Mrs. Wu's change (and all the other Mrs. Wus'

changes) in the purchase of the quality of shirting which she buys might also cause considerable financial disturbance because, if the dislocation in the United Kingdom and America led to unemployment and reduced the purchasing power of the people, that might (and probably would) affect the total value of goods imported into the United Kingdom and America, possibly from countries outside our chain. On the other hand, exports of cotton from America to us (that is our imports) and our cotton cloth exported to China would be reduced. If our imports were reduced, the amount of Bills of Exchange drawn on London would also be reduced, and the rate of exchange between the exporting countries and England would consequently be altered. America would have a less amount of bills to draw on us, which would affect the rate of exchange between America and England, and Manchester would have fewer bills to draw on Shanghai, which would affect the rate of exchange between England and China. In time, other forces operating would readjust the position, but in the meantime a certain amount of dislocation in the foreign exchanges might have been caused.

Mrs. Wu's action would also have an effect on the London Discount Market. As fewer bills would be drawn on London, there would be a smaller amount offering in the market for discount; discount brokers would, therefore, be more eager to acquire the bills and consequently would charge a lower rate of interest for discounting. (The rate of interest charged for discounting a bill is the price which discount brokers charge for lending their money). It is not the purpose of this book to discuss all the repercussions of an alteration in the discount rate, but any reader interested in pursuing this further, should refer to a text-book on money.

So much for Mrs. Wu. Although we have described some of the reactions caused by the decline in her purchasing power, these are only the first ripples caused in the pond by the stone which she has thrown; the effects which result from her action continue in ever-widening circles.

We have now to consider the reactions set up by failure of production or alteration in the nature of production. What about our friend Hezekiah Godbehere?

Hezekiah might decide to plant maize instead of cotton. This might be due to the fact that the price of his cotton had fallen considerably and he hoped to make more money by growing maize; or his reason might be that the last crop of cotton suffered seriously from the ravages of the boll-weevil of which trouble he feared a recurrence. But—whatever his reason—by his failure to re-plant cotton he would cause various kinds of dislocation similar to those which we have described, although perhaps different people might suffer in different ways and in different countries. If other planters who produced the same quality of cotton as Hezekiah also curtailed their production, then the price of this particular quality of cotton would become dear relatively to the price of other qualities. Mrs.

Wu might consequently have to pay more for her "Nine Dragon Chop", and might decide to do so even if that necessitated the postponing of the purchase of the new silk jacket which she had promised herself for the coming New Year's festivals.

The demand for Chinese silk would then be reduced. The price of cocoons would fall to the detriment of the farmers who depend to some extent on sericulture, and unemployment would be caused in the silk filatures in Shanghai, until Mrs. Wu and all the other women who had had to abjure their new silk garments owing to rise in price of cotton cloth, had saved sufficient money to resume their purchases of silk goods. But a more serious reaction on the silk market might take place. Mrs. Wu, instead of foregoing her new coat, might buy one made of artificial silk. She might be so pleased with this that she would continue to buy artificial silk goods instead of real silk goods, and the demand for real silk would permanently decline while that for artificial silk would be increased.

Another reaction to Hezekiah's reduction of production would affect an entirely different trade. If less cotton were produced there would be a smaller supply of cotton seed. Cotton seed, relatively to other seeds used for oil pressing, would tend to become dear. In some cases soya beans might be used in place of the cotton seed; the demand for soya beans would increase, bringing prosperity to Manchuria and a greater demand (among other things) for sharks' fins for wedding feasts, thus stimulating the export from Newfoundland, whence these delicacies emanate. On the other hand, the unforeseen demand for soya beans would tend to increase the price; the raw material for margarine would become dearer and the English shopkeeper would have to pay a higher price to the Danish producers. Higher prices might also be asked for bean-cake which is used as a fertilizer, and some farmers who had hesitated between the use of bean-cake and chemical manures might be induced to turn to the latter, and if they found them more satisfactory, adhere to that form of fertilizer and cause a permanently increased demand for the products of the chemical works in England, Germany, and other countries in which they are manufactured.

We have assumed that Hezekiah and many other cotton-growers turned over for the time being from cotton to maize. Perhaps the growers of maize in the Argentine might not know that this had occurred and would continue to plant their accustomed acreage of that cereal. This might lead to excessive world stocks of maize, the price of which, if lowered, would drag down with it the prices of competing feeding stuffs, reduce the purchasing power of the farmers, and consequently the demand for the manufactured goods of the industrial countries of the world. All these dislocations would, if sufficiently widespread, cause bad trade, losses, unemployment, business failures, and in the end create a feeling of want of confidence, with the consequent disinclination on the part of the producers, on the one hand, to undertake new enterprises, and on the other hand, on the part of people who lend money, to encourage the undertaking of new enterprises.

This brings us to our third point, which is the failure to release or acquire stocks of commodities. Hezekiah and John B. Robinson, if they realised that the low prices which they received for the B.A.Z. cotton was due to an over-supply of their quality of cotton in the world, would be discouraged from planting and consequently would need less cotton seed than before. Robinson would still require, however, some fertilizers and some farm implements, but the man who had these in stock, knowing that Robinson had had continued severe losses over a series of years, might be disinclined to sell them to him on credit. Silas J. Hocking in New Orleans, and Birdhead & Co. in Liverpool, would be equally nervous, and would reduce to a minimum the amount of stock held by them and necessary to satisfy their customers' requirements; Silas J. Hocking, possibly because he was nervous of Birdhead's position, perhaps might not wish to ship him too much cotton, for which, after all, he would have to give credit by means of the ninety days bill which he would draw. Birdhead & Co., in their turn, might be uneasy about the position in Lancashire and consequently not wish to buy the cotton from Silas J. Hocking, even on credit, not desiring to be overloaded with stock which they might have difficulty in selling. If the lack of confidence continued for sufficiently long, then fewer warehouses would be required to store the diminished quantity of cotton, fewer ships to carry it, less machinery to manufacture it; consequently new enterprise in the provision of these would be discouraged. As a result, the stocks of commodities available for use in such new enterprises would remain in the hands of their owners who would be afraid to release them, while producers would be unwilling to acquire them fearing that they could not be turned to a profitable use.

The same motive would underlie our fourth cause of dislocation, which is the failure to lend or to borrow the money necessary to finance the moving of stocks of commodities. Bankers, owing to the general lack of confidence, might become chary of lending the money necessary to enable the possession of stocks of commodities to pass from the owners into the hands of those whose ordinary business it is to buy them. The banks might be willing to afford the necessary financial facilities only to people whose soundness was beyond question. But those people would probably be of a very careful and conservative nature and not only would not want to borrow fresh money (because they would be frightened of undertaking new ventures), but might indeed actually pay back to the banks money which they had previously borrowed, and thus pile up uninvested savings in the hands of the banks. If the banks were frightened of lending money, they would ask a high rate of interest in order to deter borrowers from borrowing. As, however, the unused money continued to lie idle in the banks, their policy would gradually change, and they would become willing to take a very low rate of interest to encourage sound borrowers to seize the opportunity of cheap money in order to start new enterprises. But this provision of cheap money might last a considerable time before the confidence of sound borrowers was restored.

The last of the causes of dislocation in our chain, namely: government interference with the normal flow of trade through the imposition of tariffs, exchange restrictions, quotas, and subsidies, is the most serious of them all. For, while all the other dislocations might right themselves within a comparatively short time, when restrictions on trade are once imposed by one country they tend to spread to many other countries, and it may take years before they are removed. Mrs. Wu might, as we have seen, have caused a reduction in the exports from some countries and a dislocation in the rate of exchange of their currency. Such countries would have an increasingly unfavourable balance of trade and in an endeavour to reduce it, might restrict imports by the imposition of tariffs and quotas, which restrictions their statesmen would advocate as a means of absorbing the labour which had become unemployed as a result of a reduction in the exports. Reduction of imports in one country means reduction of exports from some other country. This loss of exports may, in some countries, make it more difficult to obtain the foreign currency requisite to pay interest on loans which had been raised in other countries. This would lead the government of the borrowing country to impose exchange restrictions on operations which might otherwise result in a still further depreciation of their rate of exchange. The imposition of tariffs, quotas, and exchange restrictions, in the various countries of the world might also lead to political repercussions, the discussion of which lie outside the scope of this book.

If Mrs. Wu knew what she had done, she would have been unable to sleep at night.

CHAPTER XII

CONCLUSION

We have described in the previous chapter some of the consequences of a reduction in the production of Hezekiah's cotton or an alteration in the consumption of cotton goods by Mrs. Wu. We have used cotton as an illustration, because the production of cotton, and the manufacturing and distribution of cotton goods, covers a large field of industrial and commercial activity. Cotton illustrates the production and marketing of a raw material and it affords an example,—the greatest example—of America's export trade, while at the same time it shows how an important commodity is handled when entering the United Kingdom. It goes through many processes in the course of manufacture in Lancashire, and, owing to the horizontal structure of the industry, these processes are carried out by several different manufacturing units. It exemplifies the export of manufactured goods from one country, and the import of these goods into another, as well as demonstrating how this is carried out, and how the goods are marketed in the importing country from the time of entry until they are finally bought over the shop's counter by the consumer.

Perhaps another reason for choosing cotton is that the author is more conversant with this trade than with any other; although he has handled commercially all the other commodities described in this book, with the exception of birds' nests, sharks' fins, and bamboo shoots, which he has only handled comestibly.

Cotton forms a useful illustration in another way, because the length of time elapsing from the planting of the seed until the consumption of the finished article is so great. The object of credit is to cover the period between production and consumption and the longer this period is, the longer is the time for which credit is required. The more complex and numerous the processes of production, manufacturing, and distribution are, the more complex are the kinds of credit required and the greater the variation in the types of credit instruments used. This fact is clearly demonstrated in this book because at least 90% of the credit instruments which have been reproduced appertain to the cotton industry, although most of them are equally applicable in aiding the movement of the other commodities described. Not only in America but in all civilized countries means are provided by which a farmer who is short of money owing to bad times, can obtain credit by mortgaging his farm and avoiding the necessity of selling it directly the bad times come upon him. In the same way in most agricultural countries, means are provided, if necessary, for supplying the farmer with seed and his other requirements in aid of production on credit until he is able to pay after having harvested his crop.

Methods of "hedging" in the cotton industry

have been described at length because in dealings in other kinds of produce "hedging" has also been created in order that risks may be minimized and the giving of credit facilitated. At one time banks regarded "hedging" as a type of speculation, but have now come to see that by this means their interests are safeguarded, and in many cases now will only grant credit if the produce is "hedged". In order to obtain credit when required, all owners of factories (not only cotton factories), issue debentures or pledge their fixed and often their floating assets. The custom of granting overdrafts to merchants exists in many other trades besides the cotton trade. The system by which Silas J. Hocking in New Orleans, obtained credit for the cotton which he shipped to Birdhead & Co. in Liverpool, by drawing Bills of Exchange on the latter firm and obtaining from banks advances against them in cash, is common to all international transactions in commodities.

Of course, the credit instruments which have been reproduced here are only samples. Each bank, each trade, each district, each State, and each country use credit instruments which, although similar in principle, vary in detail. We have mentioned in this book only a very few of the commodities which enter into international trade. His Majesty's Customs has scheduled over four thousand items of different commodities imported into this country, and the variety alone in types of raw cotton, in types of cotton yarn and cotton cloth, and the uses to which they are put, would run into many hundreds.

Quite apart from the commerce in imports and exports, there is a trade carried on which forms part of our invisible imports and exports. Our ships not only carry goods to and from this country, but also goods which neither reach nor leave our shores, but which are borne between different ports all over the world. The profit which is earned by British insurance companies in insuring them, and the profit earned by our banks and financial houses in financing them (for they are mostly carried on credit by means of bills on London), all form part of our invisible exports, and the fact that these boats are largely consuming English coal increases our exports of this commodity.

In order to exemplify the varied and widespread voyages of these boats, the actual itineraries of three tramp steamers, which may be taken as typical, are given in Appendix 1.

Only the credit necessary to move the raw cotton, the manufactured cotton shirting, the tea, soya beans, butter, and bristles has been described, but the production and distribution of these commodities involved the use of a great volume of other credit. Credit was required for mining the iron used in making the ploughs for all the Hezekiahs; credit was required by the chemical trades manufacturing the fertilizers, and the insecticide for killing the boll-weevil. Credit was required for obtaining the timber to build the railway trucks and for building the railways themselves, and credit to build the ships which carried the goods, and the warehouses which warehoused them, and for the coal mines which produced the coal for the ships' bunkers. Credit was required for the sizing material for sizing the yarn, for the bleaching powder for bleaching the goods, for mining in the Straits Settlements and transporting the tin for the packing-cases in which the goods were packed, for felling the trees in Scandinavia, and for preparing the pulp from which the paper was made in which the goods were wrapped. Credit was required for mining and transporting the lead used in China for the lining of the tea-chests, and credit was also required for producing jute in Bengal in order to make and transport to Manchuria the gunnies in which the beans were packed, and so on *ad infinitum,* because all these things required other things to help in their production, and all those other things required the aid of credit in order that they could be produced and marketed.

Finally, it must be remembered that trade is not carried on between nations, but between individuals. Hezekiah Godbehere and little Mrs. Wu have been created merely as an illustration of millions of other Hezekiahs and Mrs. Wus in the world,—counting their children they number about two thousand millions—all of whom are busy exchanging commodities between themselves. It is this urge to exchange commodities, in order to satisfy human wants, that increases the wealth of the world, and it is only by using the world's savings in the form of credit that these commodities can be produced and exchanged.

APPENDIX No. 1

VOYAGE ITINERARIES

From Barry in May 1933 for Port Said with . *coals.*
Thence Aden to Chittagong with . . *salt.*
,, Burmah to Hamburg with . . *rice.*
,, Danzig to Albany, U.S.A., with . *rye.*
,, Cuba to Marseilles with . . *sugar.*
,, North Pacific to Sydney, N.S.W., with *lumber.*
Will load *grain* in South Australia for home.
Due about June 1934.

Tyne/Trinidad, Port Royal, West Indies . *coal*
then
Galveston, Houston or New Orleans/Japan and China *via* Panama . . . . . *cotton*
then
Philippine Islands, Manila, Ilo. Ilo/Galveston, New Orleans, Baltimore, Philadelphia, New York or Boston *via* Panama . . . *sugar*
then
Newport News for *bunkers*
Cuba, San Domingo, Jamaica, Trinidad or Barbados/Montreal . . . . *sugar*
Montreal/United Kingdom . . . *grain*

The following is a typical example of a tramp steamer, the voyage occupying a total of 435 days: The vessel loaded a cargo of *coal* Dunston (Newcastle-on-Tyne) to Servola (Italy); she then proceeded in *ballast* to Casablanca (Morocco), and loaded a cargo of *phosphate* for Japan, proceeding *via* the Panama Canal. After discharging *phosphate* in Japan she proceeded to Ocean Island (one of the Gilbert Islands in the Pacific-British) in *ballast* and there loaded a cargo of *phosphate* which she discharged at Bunbury (W. Australia) and Freemantle (W. Australia). She then proceeded to New Caledonia in *ballast* and loaded at Paagoumene (New Caledonia in the Pacific-French) a part cargo of *nickel ore*, completing her loading at the Solomon and Fiji Islands (Pacific-British) with *copra*, which she discharged at Marseilles, Valencia (Spain) and, Passages (Spain), afterwards proceeding to New York to discharge the balance of her *nickel ore*. From New York she proceeded to St. John, N.B., in *ballast* and there loaded a cargo of *bulk grain*, discharging this at Oneglia (Italy), Genoa, Naples, and Milazzo (Sicily), proceeding thence to the Tyne in *ballast* for dry docking and overhaul.

APPENDIX No. 2

CHAIN OF TRANSACTIONS

Raw Cotton

Hezekiah Godbehere in Vicksburg, Miss., sent cotton to ginner: The Mississippi Ginning Company (for ginning).
From ginner to Hezekiah.
From Hezekiah to Marcus B. Levine in Vicksburg through John B. Robinson.
From Levine to Silas J. Hocking in New Orleans.
From Silas J. Hocking to Birdhead & Co. in Liverpool.
From Birdhead & Co. to the Diamond Spinning Co., Ltd., in Oldham (to be spun into yarn).

Cotton Yarn

From Diamond Spinning Co., Ltd., to the Blackburn Weaving Co., Ltd., Blackburn (to be woven into cloth).

Cotton Cloth "in the grey state"

From the Blackburn Weaving Co., Ltd., to Rathbone Baxter & Co., Ltd., in Manchester (for examination).
From Rathbone Baxter & Co., Ltd., to the Quicksilver Bleaching, Dyeing, & Finishing Co., Ltd., in Droylsden (for bleaching).

Cotton Cloth "in the bleached state"

From the Quicksilver Bleaching, Dyeing, & Finishing Co., Ltd., to Rathbone Baxter & Co., Ltd., in Manchester (for packing).

From Rathbone Baxter & Co., Ltd., to Birkenhead for shipment to G. Townsend, Ltd., in Shanghai.

From G. Townsend, Ltd., to Mr. Chang in Shanghai.

From Mr. Chang to Mr. Feng in Fuen-Choo (province of Shan-si).

From Mr. Feng to Mrs. Wu also in Fuen-Choo (to be made into shirts for Mr. Wu).

Tea

From Chinese farmer to the *chahong* (buyer's intermediary).

From *chahong* to Mr. Li in Hankow (for final preparation).

From Mr. Li to Mr. Fu in Shanghai.

From Mr. Fu to Mr. Hsu Chiang in Mukden, Manchuria (for sale to consumers).

Birds'-Nests and Bamboo Shoots

From Mr. Fu in Shanghai to Mr. Hsu Chiang in Mukden.

Sharks' Fins

From Newfoundland to Mr. Fu in Shanghai.

From Mr. Fu to Mr. Hsu Chiang in Mukden.

Soya Beans

From Manchurian farmer to wholesale merchant.

From wholesale merchant to railway warehouse or barge.

From railway warehouse or barge to exporter in Dairen.

From Dairen to oil mills in Copenhagen (for extraction of oil).

From oil mills in Copenhagen (as soya oil) to margarine factories.

From oil mills in Copenhagen (as soya bean-cake) to farmers as fodder for milch cows and other cattle.

Butter

Milk from cows to co-operative dairy (to be made into butter).
From co-operative dairies to co-operative marketing organization.
From co-operative marketing organization to Manchester butter importers.
From Manchester butter importers to shops in Lancashire (who sell the butter to cotton spinning, and weaving operatives).

Pigs' Bristles

From the backs of Mr. Wu's pigs in Fuen-Choo to Shanghai.
From Shanghai to London.
From London to New York.
From New York to Vicksburg (in the form of paint-brushes).
From Vicksburg to Hezekiah Godbehere (who used the brushes to paint his barn where he stored his cotton).

INDEX

Printed in Great Britain by R. & R. Clark, Limited, *Edinburgh.*

FINANCIAL MANAGEMENT
1880–1934

Volume 6

Edited and Introduced by
Morgen Witzel

THOEMMES

Financial Management, 1880–1934

Edited and Introduced by **Morgen Witzel**

Volume 1
Twenty Years of Inside Life in Wall Street, or Revelations of the Personal Experiences of a Speculator ... Illustrated (1880)
W. W. Fowler

Volume 2
Trusts, Pools and Corporations (1905)
William Z. Ripley

Volume 3
Corporation Finance (1910)
Edward S. Meade

Volume 4
Corporation Finance. An Exposition of the Principles and Methods governing the Promotion, Organization and Management of Modern Corporations (1909)
William H. Lough

Volume 5
Concentration and Control: A Solution of the Trust Problem in the United States (1914)
Charles R. van Hise

Credit and International Trade: How they Work in Practice (1934)
Barnard Ellinger

Volume 6
Problems in Business Finance (1921)
Edmund E. Lincoln

Volumes 7 and 8
Collected Articles and Chapters

Printed in England by Antony Rowe Ltd, Chippenham

PROBLEMS IN BUSINESS FINANCE

Edmund E. Lincoln

THOEMMES PRESS

This edition published by Thoemmes Press, 2001

Thoemmes Press
11 Great George Street
Bristol BS1 5RR, England

http://www.thoemmes.com

Financial Management, 1880–1934
8 Volumes : ISBN 1 85506 633 5

British Library Cataloguing-in-Publication Data
A CIP record of this title is available from the British Library

Publisher's Note

The Publisher has gone to great lengths to ensure the quality of this reprint but points out that some imperfections in the original book may be apparent.

This book is printed on acid-free paper, sewn, and cased in a durable buckram cloth.

PROBLEMS IN BUSINESS FINANCE

BY

EDMOND EARLE LINCOLN, M. A. (*Oxon.*) Ph. D.,

ASSISTANT PROFESSOR OF FINANCE,
HARVARD UNIVERSITY GRADUATE SCHOOL OF
BUSINESS ADMINISTRATION;

AUTHOR OF
"THE RESULTS OF MUNICIPAL ELECTRIC LIGHTING IN
MASSACHUSETTS," "CENTRAL ELECTRIC LIGHT AND POWER
STATIONS, 1917," etc.

A. W. SHAW COMPANY

NEW YORK CHICAGO LONDON

To

the Students of the Harvard University Graduate School of Business Administration Whose Critical Interest and Appreciation Have Led to the Writing of This Book for Them,

and to

the Many Business Men and Bankers of Boston, New York, and Elsewhere, without Whose Generous Cooperation This Book Could Not Have Been Written.

PREFACE

IN preparing this book of PROBLEMS IN BUSINESS FINANCE the purposes are many. First, the author wishes to provide in readily usable form problems in finance to be used by his own large classes in Harvard University, which are conducted solely by the "case" method of instruction. Secondly, the aim is to present primarily those problems, too frequently ignored, of the small and medium-sized business concerns of various sorts. Further, the financial problems which are common to all kinds of business units, large or small, are also developed. The normal, day-to-day, intimate problems have been stressed, rather than those of a spectacular and public sort. Finally, the constant purpose has been to show the interrelation of financial operations in business, the effects of general business policies on the financial program, and the desired coordination of a concern's activities through central financial control—all in relation to the Business Cycle.

The problems are real ones, drawn directly by the author from the financial experiences of a large number of business men and bankers. More than 125 totally different kinds of business and industry are represented, and hundreds of separate concerns. Many of these instances have come under the writer's personal observation. Only a small proportion have been publicly known, and, in using such cases, the writer has usually managed to secure additional first-hand information of an illuminating sort.

On account of the confidential nature of most of the material presented, it has usually been necessary to disguise or delete names or places, and occasionally to change incidents and the character of the business. Actual names have been used sparingly, and then only when the facts have been published by the general financial press. On rare occasions, also, the author has combined two problems in order to make a better case for discussion. In no instance, however, has the force of the original situation been lost.

For pedagogical reasons, an effort has been made to include in most of the problems used a sufficient amount of first-hand data to enable the reader to reason out the logical conclusion. Very frequently, also, actual solutions have been given with a view to eliciting critical comment. In pursuance of this policy, therefore, much material bearing on the internal financial conduct of business concerns has been collected, which is probably not elsewhere available in printed form. The Appendix contains some significant statistical data, a large part of which is now published for the first time and much of which is not readily accessible. These facts should make the book of more use and interest to the general reader as well as to the student.

Since the problem method of teaching business subjects is still in its infancy, it is no simple task to secure financial data which will effectively serve the purpose of the instructor. Time is required for the "ripening" process. The present book of problems has been put together with a good deal of haste, primarily for the benefit of the author's own students. He is, accordingly, conscious of many shortcomings in the work, some of which may be remedied in future editions if the public calls for them. Hence, suggestions and criticisms of every sort, from any source, will be doubly welcome.

The author's indebtedness to others is greater than he can ever repay. His thanks are primarily due to the large number of business men and bankers in many places who have so generously supplied him with first-hand material and whose interest in the problem method of teaching Business Finance has been unflagging. He hopes that they may at some time be in a small measure compensated for their pains by the better trained young men who go out from the schools to enter their service.

Mention should also be made of the constant interest taken in this work by Dean Wallace B. Donham, to whom is largely due the introduction of the "case" method of instruction in the Harvard Business School. Finally, the faithful services of his secretary, Miss Margaret A. Randall, should not go unnoted by the author.

E. E. L.

Cambridge, August 8, 1921.

TABLE OF CONTENTS

PART I—INTRODUCTORY

CHAPTER I

INTRODUCTION AND GENERAL SURVEY OF THE FIELD

CHAPTER II

FINANCIAL AND GENERAL CONSIDERATIONS INVOLVED IN BEGINNING A BUSINESS

PART II—SOURCES OF CAPITAL

CHAPTER III

THE PROBLEMS OF RAISING FIXED CAPITAL

E. FINANCING MORE OR LESS DOUBTFUL UNDERTAKINGS

B. EMPLOYEE OWNERSHIP

C. COOPERATIVE OWNERSHIP

CHAPTER V

THE PROBLEMS OF RAISING WORKING CAPITAL

B. OPEN MARKET BORROWINGS

C. THE USE OF THE TRADE ACCEPTANCE

D. MISCELLANEOUS METHODS OF RAISING WORKING CAPITAL

PART III

PROBLEMS OF INTERNAL FINANCING

CHAPTER VI

FINANCIAL ASPECTS OF PURCHASING GOODS

CHAPTER VII

FINANCIAL ASPECTS OF PRODUCING GOODS

A. COSTS AND FINANCE

A. REDUCING COSTS THROUGH INCREASED SIZE—COMBINATIONS HORIZONTAL AND VERTICAL, AND DEVELOPMENT OF SUBSIDIARIES

CHAPTER VIII

FINANCIAL ASPECTS OF SELLING GOODS

A. GENERAL PROBLEMS OF THE CREDIT DEPARTMENT

B. RELATIONS BETWEEN CREDIT DEPARTMENT AND SALES DEPARTMENT

C. COOPERATION WITH THE CUSTOMER

D. SALES POLICIES

E. PRICE POLICIES

CHAPTER IX

THE ADMINISTRATION OF EARNINGS

PART IV—FINANCIAL DIFFICULTIES AND THEIR SIGNIFICANCE

CHAPTER X

FINANCIAL INVOLVEMENTS, ADJUSTMENTS, RECEIVERSHIPS, BANKRUPTCIES, REORGANIZATIONS, ETC.

PART V—GENERAL PROBLEMS

CHAPTER XI

GENERAL SURVEY PROBLEMS

STATISTICAL APPENDIX

OUTLINE AND BIBLIOGRAPHY

Outline and Bibliography for a General Course in Business Finance Dealing Primarily with Small- and Medium-Sized Industrial Concerns and Developed by the "Case" Method of Instruction

A. BRIEF OUTLINE

Note: This outline should be carefully looked over by the student before the problems are taken up.

I. General Survey

1. Importance of the small- and medium-sized industrial concern.
2. "Industrial" Finance *vs.* "Corporation" Finance.
3. The financial problems of Industrial concerns as compared with those of Public Utilities and Railroads.
4. General differences existing between the financial policies of different types of industrial concerns.
5. Relation of Business Finance to the Business Cycle.
6. What are the sound Principles of Business Finance?

II. Financial Considerations Involved in Beginning a Business

1. Is the launching of a new enterprise financially justified?
    - a. The idea.
    - b. The time.
    - c. The place.
    - d. The management.
    - e. The demand.
    - f. The source of supply.
    - g. The competitive situation.
    - h. The investment market, etc.

2. From the financial point of view, what Form of Organization shall be chosen?
   Incorporated or unincorporated?
3. Where shall the business be incorporated?
   a. Financial considerations depending upon State Legislation.
   b. Other considerations.
4. Methods of Promoting the new concern.

THE SOURCES OF CAPITAL

III THE PROBLEMS OF RAISING FIXED CAPITAL

a. For the new business
b. For the old business.

1. The following, among other methods, should be considered with reference to the Type of Business and the Business Cycle.
   a. Individual investment.
   b. Investment of partners.
   c. Earnings put back into the business.
   d. Taking new members into the concern.
   e. Borrowing from friends.
   f. Mortgages.
   g. Advertising for funds.
   h. Stock issues,
      Common,
      Preferred,
      No par value, etc.
   i. Customer ownership.
   j. Investment by employees.
   k. Note issues.
   l. Bonds.
      Mortgage,
      Debenture,
      Collateral, etc.
   m. Dealer credit.
   n. Bank loans.
2. In connection with financing for Fixed Capital purposes, such questions as the following should be touched upon:
   a. How much capital is needed?
   b. How much capital should be furnished by the parties in control?

c. Bases of Capitalization.
    i. Earnings, past, present and prospective.
    ii. Physical value.
    iii. Valuation of intangibles.
        Cost of development.
        Patent rights.
        Good will, etc.
    iv. Over-capitalization *vs.* under-capitalization.
    v. "Stock watering."
d. The Prospectus and its analysis.
e. The local investment market.
f. Investment "fads."
g. Selling the securities.
h. In what proportion shall the various types of securities be issued?
i. Financing with a view to the Business Cycle.
j. The relation of the different kinds of permanent financing to each other.
k. Holding in reserve a new method of financing.
l. The desirable distribution of ownership in the business.

3. When and why does a concern need New Capital?
    a. Financing past losses.
    b. Financing changes in ownership
    c. Raising new capital to make possible changes in methods of operation.
    d. Raising new capital in order to change the character of the business.
    e. The turning point from a small to a large business.
    f. Shall other concerns be taken over?
    g. Financing an expansion—
        Relation to the Business Cycle.

IV. THE PROBLEMS OF RAISING WORKING CAPITAL

a. For the new business.
b. For the established business.

1. The following should be considered:
    a. The Amount of Working Capital needed in the different kinds of business.
    b. Money furnished by individual owners or partners.

- c. Money secured through sale of stock.
- d. Earnings put back into the business.
- e. Using the dealer's credit.
- f. Borrowing from the banks.
- g. Borrowing from the commercial paper house.
- h. The use of trade acceptances.
- i. The use of bankers' acceptances.
- j. The pledging of receivables.
- k. The sale of stock.
- l. The sale of notes or bonds.
- m. Borrowing through "Finance Corporations."
- n. Newly developed methods of financing sales and purchases through specially organized banking concerns.
- o. Miscellaneous.

2. Special attention should be given to the following topics:
   - a. Borrowing from Banks.
     - i. What the borrower should know about his bank.
     - ii. What the bank should know about the industry.
     - iii. The intangible items.

       Character.
       Capacity.
       Good-will, etc.
     - iv. Sources of credit information.
     - v. The Statement and its analysis.
     - vi. The Line of Credit,

       How arrived at.
       Variation according to type of industry.
       The Terms of Sale.
       The Age of the borrowing concern.
       Past performance.
       Future prospects.
       The Turnover and its relation to Profits.
       Relation to the Business Cycle, etc.
     - vii. What should the bank do for its borrower?
     - viii. Cooperation between the bank and its customers.

ix. From how many banks should a concern borrow?
x. Conditions in the past and outlook for the future.

b. The Commercial Paper House.

i. Practice and procedure.
ii. Relation to the type and size of business.
iii. Relation to bank borrowings.
iv. Advantages and disadvantages.
v. The present situation.

c. The use of Trade Acceptances.

i. The development of the practice.
ii. Relation to the size and type of business.
iii. Relation to other forms of temporary financing.
iv. Advantages and disadvantages.
v. Abuses and possibilities.

THE PROBLEMS OF INTERNAL FINANCING

V. Financial Aspects of Purchasing Materials

1. Methods and considerations.
2. Contracts and commitments.
3. Open market prices *vs.* contract prices or fixed prices.
   a. Purchasing in the buyer's market.
   b. Purchasing in the seller's market.
   c. Purchasing from a monopoly.
4. Hedging to protect purchases.
5. Under what considerations should excess purchases be made?
   a. Should a producing concern speculate in its raw material?
   b. The evils of "over-buying."
   c. Is there danger of "under-buying"?
6. The seasonal and cyclical considerations.
7. Special methods of financing purchases.
8. Relation to the general financial program.

VI. Financial Aspects of Producing Goods

1. The function of Cost Accounting.
2. The engineer's function.

3. Elimination of Waste and its significance.
4. The possible financial significance of Standardization.
5. The interrelation of Material Costs, Labor Costs, and Capital Costs.
6. The problem of reducing costs through increasing the "scale of production."
7. Relation of the production program to the general financial program and the Business Cycle.

VII. Financial Aspects of Selling Goods

1. Mercantile Credit.
    a. Standards and policies.
    b. Sources of information.
    c. Credit Interchange, etc.
2. Relation between the Credit Department and the Sales Department.
3. Financial Cooperation between Dealer and customer.
4. The Turnover of inventory and Business Profits.
    Methods of "speeding-up" sales, etc.
5. Relation between the Sales Department and the Production Department.
    a. When, if at all, should goods be sold under cost?
    b. "Over-selling."
6. Relation between Price Policy and the general financial policy.
    a. Price maintenance.
    b. Price guarantees.
    c. Price reductions, etc.
7. Terms of Sale.
    a. Usual arrangements.
    b. Selling on Instalment.
    c. Selling on Consignment.
    d. Seasonal Datings, etc.
8. Discounts.
    a. Cash.
    b. Quantity.
    c. Trade.
9. Contracts and Cancellations—
10. Collections.
    Methods, policies, etc.
11. Credit Insurance, safeguards, etc.
12. The Advertising program in relation to the general financial program.

VIII. Financial Coordination and Control

1. Relations which should exist between the various departments.
2. Budget-making.
   Its possibilities.
   Its significance.
3. The location of Financial Control.

IX. The Administration of Earnings

1. Maintenance and Depreciation policy.
   a. Effect on present and future earnings.
   b. Relation to present and future financing.
2. Reserves.
   Nature and investment.
3. Dividends.
   a. When shall they be declared?
   b. How much shall the dividend be?
   c. Various alternative uses for earnings.
   d. Relation to financial "set-up," etc.
4. The Surplus.
   a. How shall it be invested?
   b. How large shall it become?
   c. The advantages or disadvantages of a large surplus, depending on the type of business, etc.

MISCELLANEOUS PROBLEMS IN FINANCING

X. Financial Standards for the Various Types of Industries

1. Can they be determined, and of what use may they be—
   a. To the banks?
   b. To the business concerns?
2. Their relation to the Credit Structure and to the Business Cycle.

XI. Financial Gains and Losses of Size

1. A consideration of the relation of the Scale of Production to Business Profits.
2. The supposed Economies of Combination, either horizontal or vertical, etc.

XII. FINANCIAL COOPERATION
1. Between large and small industries.
2. Through Trade Associations, etc.
3. Between business concerns and their employees.
4. Between business concerns and their customers.
5. Between business concerns and their banks.
6. Cooperation in purchasing.
7. Cooperation in production.
8. Cooperation in marketing.
9. Profit Sharing and Business Profits.

FINANCIAL DIFFICULTIES AND THEIR SIGNIFICANCE

XIII. WHEN CONCERNS GO WRONG
1. Financial Failures and their causes.
2. Adjustments and Compositions.
3. Receiverships.
4. Bankruptcies.
5. Reorganizations.

THE LAW AND BUSINESS FINANCE

XIV. RELATION OF LEGISLATION TO BUSINESS FINANCE
1. Federal and State Regulation.
2. "Blue Sky Laws" and their possible effects on the financing of sound concerns.
3. Government Price Fixing.
4. Effect of Tax Legislation on—
   a. Methods of financing.
   b. Form of organization.
   c. Maintenance policy.
   d. Dividend policy, etc.

B. BIBLIOGRAPHY

Bibliographical Note

THE following brief Bibliography, roughly classified according to the main topics developed by this book of Problems, may be helpful to the general reader as well as to students and teachers of Business Finance. Both general and specific references are from time to time made to some of the books here listed in connection with the problems which follow. While it is by no means essential to the study of the problems that many of these books be looked into, yet it is thought that even the smaller college libraries can, without undue expense, provide themselves with the more important books here listed. No attempt is made to give a bibliography of the "Trust" problem or of "Corporation" Finance in the wider sense. Nor is the subject of Public Utility or Railroad Finance touched upon.[(1)]

There are many points brought out in the problems which are not touched upon in any text-book on the subject of business finance. In fact, in many cases the problem itself has served as the vehicle for imparting the information needed by the student in finding the proper solution. However, those books which have proved most helpful in connection with the use of the problems are marked with an asterisk (*).

For the sake of the beginning student who may be unfamiliar with the better current publications on financial subjects, a list of the more important periodicals, newspapers, manuals, and the like, is given. Those marked with an asterisk (*) will probably be most useful.

A preliminary knowledge of accounting is essential to the profitable study of the problems which follow. Those students who have not already had a course in accounting can probably acquire a working knowledge within a short time under the instructor's guidance. They will, however, find it necessary to do considerable outside studying on this subject. Some of the most helpful books on accounting for the beginner are such as the following: Cole, W. M.,

[(1)]For general books on these fields the student is referred to *The Financing of Public Service Corporations*, by M. B. Ignatius, The Ronald Press Co., 1918, and to W. Z. Ripley's, *Railroads: Finance and Organization,* Longman's, Green & Co., 1915.

Accounts, Their Construction and Interpretation; Dickinson, A. L., *Accounting Practice and Procedure;* Hatfield, H. R., *Modern Accounting;* Kester, R. B., *Accounting, Theory and Practice* (published in three volumes; Vol. I is particularly valuable for the beginner); Montgomery, R. H., *Auditing Theory and Practice.*

The student or general reader who has not already acquired a working knowledge of Business Finance, is strongly advised to glance through one of the standard text-books on the subject. For a general survey which will be most helpful in connection with these problems, the writer has found Lough's *Business Finance* to be easily the most satisfactory.

I. General Books on Business and Corporation Finance, Etc.

The following books cover the various aspects of Business and Corporation F nance in a general way. Certain parts of these books will be useful in connection with the more detailed topics. For this purpose, however, references will be made in connection with the problems them elves when it seems desirable.

Bennett, R. J., *Corporation Accounting.* New York, The Ronald Press Company, 1920.

Bentley, H. C., *Corporate Finance and Accounting.* New York, The Ronald Press Company, 1911.

*Conyngton, H. R. *Financing an Enterprise.* New York, The Ronald Press Company, 1921.

Cooper, F., (Pseudonym), *Financing an Enterprise.* New York, The Ronald Press Company, 1906.

*Dewing, A. S., *Corporate Promotions and Reorganizations.* Cambridge, Harvard University Press, 1914.

*Dewing, A. S., *The Financial Policy of Corporations.* New York, The Ronald Press Company, 1920.

*Dewing, A. S., *Problems to Accompany The Financial Policy of Corporations.* The Ronald Press Company, 1921.

Friday, David, *Profits, Wages, and Prices.* New York, Harcourt, Brace, and Howe, 1920.

Gerstenberg, C. W., *Materials of Corporation Finance.* New York, Prentice-Hall Company, 1915.

*Gerstenberg, C. W., *Problems in Private Finance.* New York, Prentice-Hall Company, 1916.

*Gertenberg, C. W., *Principles of Business.* New York, Prentice-Hall Company, 1918.

*Gerstenberg, C. W., *Syllabus of Corporation Finance.* New York, Prentice-Hall Company, 1920.

Greene, T. L., *Corporation Finance.* New York, G. P. Putnam's Sons, 1908.

Jenks, J. and Clark, W. E., *The Trust Problem.* New York, Doubleday, Page & Company, 1917.

*Jones, E. D., *The Administration of Industrial Enterprises.* New York, Longmans, Green & Company, 1919.

Keir, M., *Manufacturing Industries in the United States.* New York, The Ronald Press Company, 1920.

*Lough, W. H., *Business Finance.* New York, The Ronald Press Company, 1917.

*Lough, W. H., *Corporation Finance.* Chicago, De-Bower, Elliott Company, 1909.

*Lyon, Hastings, *Corporation Finance.* Boston, Houghton Mifflin Company, 1916.

*Mead, E. S., *Corporation Finance.* New York, D. Appleton and Company, 1920.

Mitchell, W. C., *Business Cycles.* Berkeley, California, University of California Press, 1913.

*Moulton, H. G., *Financial Organization of Society.* Chicago, The University of Chicago Press, 1921.

Moulton, H. G., *Principles of Money and Banking,* Part II. Chicago, The University of Chicago Press, 1916.

*Pratt, E. S., *Work of Wall Street.* New York, D. Appleton and Company, 1912.

Prendergast, W. A., *Credit and Its Uses.* New York, D. Appleton and Company, 1920.

*Regan, J. M., *Financing a Business.* Chicago, LaSalle Extension University, 1920.

Shaw, A. W., *An Approach to Business Problems.* Cambridge, Harvard University Press, 1916.

*Shaw, A. W., Company, *How to Finance a Business.* Chicago, 1912.

*Walker, W. H., *Corporation Finance.* New York, Alexander Hamilton Institute, 1917.

II. General Problems of Organization—Legal Aspects, Etc.

*Conyngton, Thomas, *Corporate Organization and Management.* New York, The Ronald Press Company, 1917.

*Conyngton, Thomas, *Business Law.* New York, The Ronald Press Company, 1918.

Gerstenberg, C. W., *Law of Bankruptcy (with problems).* New York, Prentice-Hall Company, 1917.

*Gerstenberg, C. W., *Organization and Control.* New York, Alexander Hamilton Institute, 1917.

Haney, L. H., *Business Organization and Combination.* New York, The Macmillan Company, 1920.

Machen, A. W., *Modern Law of Corporations.* Boston, Little, Brown and Company, 1908.

Moore, W. H., *The Law of Commercial Paper.* New York, D. Appleton and Company, 1918.

*Robinson, M. H., *Organizing a Business.* Chicago, La Salle Extension University, 1920.

*Schaub, L. F., and Isaacs, N., *The Law in Businsse Problems.* New York, The Macmillan Company, 1921.

Stetson, Byrne, Cravath, *et al.*, *Some Legal Phases of Corporation Financing, Reorganization, and Regulation.* New York, The Macmillan Company, 1917.

Williston, Samuel, *Commercial and Banking Law.* New York, American Institute of Banking, 1918.

Wrightington, S. R., *Law of Unincorporated Associations.* Boston, Little, Brown and Company, 1916.

III. The Problems of Raising Fixed Capital

Atwood, A. W., *The Exchanges and Speculation.* New York, Alexander Hamilton Institute, 1918.

Bonds as Investment Securities. Annals of the American Academy of Political and Social Science, 1907.

CHAMBERLAIN, LAWRENCE, *The Work of the Bond House.* New York, Moody's Magazine, Book Department, 1912.

*CHAMBERLAIN, LAWRENCE, *Principles of Bond Investment,* Part I. New York, Henry Holt and Company, 1911.

*COLLVER, CLINTON, *How to Analyze Industrial Securities.* New York, Moody's Investors Service, 1921.

EMERY, H. C., *Speculation on the Stock and Produce Exchanges in the United States.* New York, The Macmillan Company, 1904.

*JONES, E. D., *Investment.* New York, Alexander Hamilton Institute, 1917.

*JORDAN, D. F., *Investments.* New York, Prentice-Hall Company, 1920.

*LAGERQUIST, *Investment Analysis.* New York, The Macmillan Compang, 1921.

RAYMOND, W. L., *American and Foreign Investment Bonds.* Boston, Houghton Mifflin Company, 1916.

SIMPSON, K., *The Capitalization of Goodwill.* Baltimore, Johns Hopkins Press, 1921.

Stocks and the Stock Market. Annals of the American Academy of Political and Social Science, 1910.

STOCKWELL, H. G., *Net Worth and the Balance Sheet.* New York, The Ronald Press Company, 1912.

Most of the general books listed under Topic I give a good deal of attention to this subject.

IV. THE PROBLEMS OF SECURING WORKING CAPITAL

American Acceptance Council. Various pamphlets on the problem of acceptances are useful.

*BABSON, R. W., and MAY, R., *Commercial Paper.* Wellesley Hills, Mass., Commercial Institute, 1920.

*GREENDLINGER, L. G., *Financial and Business Statements.* New York, Alexander Hamilton Institute, 1917.

KEMMERER, E. W., *The A. B. C. of the Federal Reserve System* (4th ed.). Princeton, The University Press, 1920.

*KNIFFIN, W. H., *The Business Man and His Bank.* New York, McGraw-Hill Company, 1920.

*KNIFFIN, W. H., *Commercial Paper, Acceptances, and Analysis of Credit Statements.* New York, Bankers' Publishing Company, 1918.

KNIFFIN, W. H., *The Practical Work of a Bank.* New York, Bankers' Publishing Company, 1915.

LANGSTON, L. H., *Practical Bank Operations.* New York, The Ronald Press Company, 1921.

*MATHEWSON, PARK, *Acceptances: Trade and Bankers.* New York, D. Appleton and Company, 1921.

MATHEWSON, PARK, *Budgets and the Banker.* Benton Harbor, Mich., Successful Banking, 1920.

*PHILLIPS, C. A., *Bank Credit.* New York, The Macmillan Company, 1920.

*SHAW, A. W., Company, *Credits and Collections.* Chicago, 1918.

WALL, ALEXANDER, *Bankers' Credit Manual.* Indianapolis, The Bobbs-Merrill Company, 1919.

*WALL, ALEXANDER, *Credit Barometrics.* Detroit, National Bank of Commerce, 1919. (Also in Federal Reserve Bulletin, March, 1919.)

V. FINANCIAL ASPECTS OF PURCHASING GOODS

*BRACE, H. H., *The Value of Organized Speculation,* Chaps. II-IV. Boston, Houghton Mifflin Company, 1913.

FIELD, C. C., *Retail Buying.* New York, Harper and Brothers, 1917.

RINDSFOOS, C. S., *Purchasing.* New York, McGraw-Hill Company, 1915.

*TWYFORD, H. B., *Purchasing and Storing.* New York, Industrial Extension Institute, 1917.

There are chapters on this subject in such books as Gerstenberg's *Principles of Business*, Jones' *Administration of Industrial Enterprises*, and Kimball's *Principles of Industrial Organization.* No satisfactory bibliography, however, is available.

VI. Financial Aspects of Purchasing Goods

*Basset, W. R., *Accounting as an Aid to Business Profits.* Chicago, A. W. Shaw Company, 1918.

Berndt, I. A., *Costs: Their Compilation and Use in Management.* Chicago, H. P. Gould, 1920.

Church, A. H., *Manufacturing Costs and Accounts.* New York, The McGraw-Hill Book Company, 1917.

Ficker, N. T., *Industrial Cost Finding.* New York, Industrial Extension Institute, Inc., 1917.

Goldman, O. B., *Financial Engineering.* New York, John Wiley and Sons, 1920.

*Jordan, J. P., and Harris, G. L., *Cost Accounting Principles and Practice.* New York, The Ronald Press Company, 1920.

Mitchell, W. C., *History of Prices During the War.* Washington, Government Printing Office, 1919. (War Industries Board.)

Nicholson, J. L., and Rohrbach, J. F. D., *Cost Accounting.* New York, The Ronald Press Company, 1919.

*Sammons, Wheeler, *Keeping up with Rising Costs.* Chicago, A. W. Shaw Company, 1915.

*Scovell, C. H., *Cost Accounting and Burden Application.* New York, D. Appleton & Company, 1916.

Shaw, A. W. Company, *Operation and Costs.* Chicago, 1915.

Spooner, H. J., *Wealth from Waste.* London, George Routledge & Sons, Ltd., 1918.

U. S. Federal Trade Commission, *Fundamentals of a Cost System for Manufacturers.* Washington, Government Printing Office, 1916.

Webner, F. E., *Factory Costs.* New York, The Ronald Press Company, 1911.

See also various titles under Topic IX, Financial Standards and the Financial Economies of Size.

VII. Financial Aspects of Selling Goods

Aspley, J. C., *What a Salesman Should Know About Credit.* Chicago, The Dartnell Corporation, 1921.

BEEBE, D. E., *Retail Credits and Collections.* New York, Harper & Brothers, 1919.

BLANTON, B. H., *Credit, Its Principles and Practice.* New York, The Ronald Press Company, 1915.

*CHERINGTON, P. T., *Advertising as a Business Force.* New York, Doubleday, Page and Company, 1913.

*DUNCAN, C. S., *Marketing, Its Problems and Methods.* New York, D. Appleton and Company, 1921.

*ETTINGER, R. P., and GOLIEB, D. E., *Credits and Collections.* New York, Prentice-Hall, Inc., 1917.

*FREDERICK, J. G., *Modern Sales Management.* New York, D. Appleton and Company, 1920.

HAGERTY, J. E., *Mercantile Credit.* New York, Henry Holt and Company, 1913.

LAWRENCE, H. C., *Cash Discount Piracy.* St. Louis, Consolidated Publishing Company, 1919. (Also *Making Him Pay*, and *Making Him Buy*, by the same author.)

Mercantile Credits. New York, The Ronald Press Company, 1914.

MEYER, C. A., *Mercantile Credits and Collections.* New York, The Macmillan Company, 1919.

MITCHELL, W. C., *History of Prices During the War.* Washington, Government Printing Office, 1919. (War Industries Board.)

MURCHISON, C. T., *Resale Price Maintenance.* New York, Longman, Green & Company (for Columbia University), 1919.

National Association of Credit men, *Credit Man's Diary,* published annually. New York.

NAYLOR, E. H., *Trade Associations.* New York, The Ronald Press Company, 1921.

ROGERS, E. S., *Goodwill, Trade Marks, and Unfair Trading.* Chicago. A. W. Shaw Company, 1914.

SHAW, A. W., Company, *Credits, Collections, and Finance.* Chicago, 1914.

Terms of Sale. A Series of articles in the Federal Reserve Bulletin from December, 1919, to October, 1920.

U. S. Federal Trade Commission, *Digest of Replies Relative to the Practice of Giving Guarantees Against Price Decline.* Washington, Government Printing Office, 1920.

VIII. Administration of Income and Financial Control

*Dewing, A. S., *Financial Policy of Corporations.* Vol. III, *The Administration of Income.* New York, The Ronald Press Company, 1920.

*Lough, W. H., *Business Finance,* Part IV, pages 355–524. New York, The Ronald Press Company, 1917.

Lough, W. H., *Corporation Finance,* 297–393.

McKinsey, J. O., A series of articles on *Budgetary Control,* in *Administration,* beginning in January, 1921. New York, The Ronald Press Company. (To be published later in book form.)

*Mead, E. S., *Corporation Finance,* Chaps. XIV-XVIII.

Shaw, A. W., *An Approach to Business Problems,* Ch. XVIII. Cambridge, Harvard University Press, 1916.

Some of the other books listed touch upon these subjects, but comparatively little has hitherto been written. The magazines, *Administration* and *System,* frequently publish helpful articles bearing on the subject.

IX. Financial Standards and the Financial Economies of Size

Very little scientific writing had been done on this subject. Most of the material is of a fugitive sort. The following, however, will be helpful to those who wish to make a beginning:

**Corporate Earnings and Government Revenues,* 65th Congress, 2nd Session, Senate Document No. 259. Washington, Government Printing Office, 1918. (Contains much useful "raw" material.)

Costs, Merchandising Practices, and Sales in the Retail Distribution of Clothing. In 6 volumes, covering the years 1914, 1918 and 1919. New York, Prentice-Hall Company, 1921 (Prepared by the Bureau of Business Research of the Northwestern University School of Commerce in cooperation with the National Association of Retail Clothiers.)

Dewing, A. S., *Corporate Promotions and Reorganizations*.

*Dewing. A. S., *The Financial Policy of Corporations.* Vol. IV., Chap. II, "The Law of Balanced Return," and Chap. III, "Industrial Combinations."

*Harvard Bureau of Business Research. Very interesting and helpful bulletins have been published dealing with the expense side of the question on the following distributing businesses: *Retail Drug, Retail Grocery, Retail Hardware, Retail Jewelry, Retail Shoe, Wholesale Grocery.* Other bulletins are to be published shortly, some of which will probably deal with manufacturing concerns.

*Lincoln, E. E., *Central Electric Light and Power Stations, 1917*, Chap. X. Washington, Government Printing Office, 1920.

*Lough, W. H., *Business Finance*, Ch. XXII. New York, The Ronald Press Company, 1917.

Massachusetts, *Abstract of the Certificates of Corporations* (published annually), Public Document No. 10. Boston, Wright & Potter.

Massachusetts, *Statistics of Manufactures* (published annually), Public Document No. 36. Boston, Wright & Potter.

Robert Morris Associates, *Barometrics.* Lansdowne, Pa., 1920.

Robert Morris Associates, *Financial Statements.* Lansdowne, Pa., 1920.

*Sallee, A. D., *Standard Retail Statements.* Pittsburgh Association of Credit Men, 1921.

Shaw, A. W., Company, *How to Run a Retail Lumber Business ata Profit.* Chicago, 1918.

Shaw, A. W., Company, *How to Run a Store at a Profit.* Chicago, 1913.

Shaw, A. W., Company, *How to Run aWholesale Business at a Profit.* Chicago, 1918.

*Shaw, A. W., Company. The Bureau of Business Standards of the A. W. Shaw Company, publishes from time to time suggestive reports on the subject of standards, costs, etc.

Statistics of Income, compiled from the returns for 1918 by the Commissioner of Internal Revenue. Washington, Government Printing Office, 1921.

United States Census Bureau, *Thirteenth Census of the United States*, 1910, Vol. VIII, *Manufactures*.

(This volume is perhaps the most serviceable published by the Federal Census of Manufactures, since it contains more detailed information on the various classes of production expense than can be found in any preceding Census. The *Abstract of the Census of Manufactures* for 1914 is also helpful in places.)

United States Commissioner of Corporations, Reports on the *Petroleum Industry*, the *Tobacco Industry*, the *Steel Industry* (Part I),. and the *Lumber Industry*.

United States Federal Trade Commission, Reports on the following industries are helpful: *Anthracite and Bituminous Coal, Coal (Pennsylvania Bituminous), Beet Sugar Industry, Book Paper, Copper, Commercial Wheat Flour Milling, Flour Milling and Jobbing, Farm Operating Equipment Leather and Shoe Industry*, the *Meat Packing Industry* (particularly Part V, 1920), *News Print Paper Industry, Sugar Supply and Prices*.

United States Fuel Administration, *Report of the Engineers' Committee, 1918-1919*. Washington, Government Printing Office, 1919.

United States Tariff Board, Reports on the *Pulp and Paper Industry*, and *Wool* and *Cotton Manufactures*. Washington, Government Printing Office, 1911, 1912.

United States Tariff Commission, *Costs of Production in the Dye Industry, 1918-1919*. Washington, Government Printing Office, 1920. (Also, *Costs of Production in the Sugar Industry*.)

United States, War Industries Board. (A mass of useful financial and cost data was collected by the War Industries Board to serve as a basis for price fixing and Government regulation during the war. Some of this data is now available in various Government departments, though a large part of it is filed away in Washington and is apparently inaccessible.)

VAN HISE, C. R., *Concentration and Control* (Revised edition). New York, The Macmillan Company, 1914.

*WALL, ALEXANDER, *Credit Barometrics* (published in the Federal Reserve Bulletin for March, 1919 and also privately circulated as a monograph.)

*WOOLEY, G. L., *The Financing of Cotton*, Bulletin of the Robert Morris Associates, July 1920.

Some of the references under Topic VI., Financial Aspects of Producing Goods, are closely related and will be helpful. A number of interesting studies on the subject of "Financial Standards" and the financial results of "Size" have been made, under the author's direction, by second-year students in the Harvard University Graduate School of Business Administration for their graduating theses.

X. FINANCIAL INVOLVEMENTS, ADJUSTMENTS, RECEIVERSHIPS, BANKRUPTCIES, REORGANIZATIONS, ETC.

DEWING, A. S., *Corporate Promotions and Reorganizations*. Cambridge, Harvard University Press, 1914.

*DEWING, A. S., *Financial Policy of Corporations*, Vol. V., "Failure and Reorganization."

GERSTENBERG, C. W., *The Law of Bankruptcy*. New York, Prentice-Hall Company, 1917. (The problems presented in Part IV, together with the answers to these problems published in a separate pamphlet, are particularly helpful.)

*LOUGH, W. H., *Business Finance*, Part V. New York, The Ronald Press Company, 1917. (Also, *Corporation Finance*, 394-443.)

LYON, HASTINGS, *Corporation Finance*, Part II, 220-307. Boston, Houghton Mifflin Company, 1916.

*MEAD, E. S., *Corporation Finance*, Chaps. XXX-XXXII. New York, D. Appleton and Company, 1920.

There are also helpful chapters dealing with these problems in other general books listed under Topics I and II. In the various books on the subject of Credit, listed under Topic VII, Financial Aspects of Selling Goods, will be found helpful chapters. Particular reference may be made to the following:

BLANTON, B. H., *Credit, Its Principles and Practice*, pp. 170-228.

*Ettinger and Golieb, *Credits and Collections*, pp. 307-357.

*Hagerty, J. E., *Mercantile Credit*, pp; 247-377.

*Meyer, C. A., *Mercantile Credits and Collections*, pp. 141-163, and pp. 179-254.

Mercantile Credits, pp. 196-245. The Ronald Press Company.

XI. The Relation of Legislation to Industrial Finance

*American Economic Association, *Report of the Committee on War Finance.* March, 1919 (Supplement.)

Baruch, B. M., *American Industries in the War*, (Report of the War Industries Board.) Washington, Government Printing Office, 1921.

*Burton, T. E., *Corporations and the State.* New York, D. Appleton and Company, 1911.

Clabaugh, William, *Income and Profits Taxes* (A series of lectures delivered before the Y. M. C. A.) New York, The Association Press, 1920. (The questions and problems contained in the Appendix, pp. 261-334, are in places useful.)

*Davies, J. E., *Trust Laws and Unfair Competition.* Washington, Government Printing Office, 1915.

Elliot, J. M., *Annotated Blue-Sky Laws of the U. S.*, Cincinnati, The Anderson Company, 1921.

Haig, R. M., *The Taxation of Excess Profits in Great Britain.* American Economic Review, Supplement, December, 1920.

Holmes, G. E., *Federal Income and Profits Tax.* Indianapolis, Bobbs-Merrill Company, 1920 (with Supplement for 1921.)

*Jones, Eliot, *The Trust Problem in the United States.* New York, The Macmillan Company, 1921.

Litman, S., *Prices and Price Control in Great Britain and the United States During the War.* New York, Oxford University Press, 1920. (Published for the Carnegie Endowment for International Peace.)

Montgomery, R. H., *Income Tax Procedure,* 1921. New York, The Ronald Press Company.

Montgomery, R. H., *Excess Profits Tax Procedure, 1921.* New York, The Ronald Press Company.

Orth, S. P. (editor), *The Relation of Government to Property and Industry.* Boston, Ginn and Company, 1915.

Ripley, W. Z., *Trusts, Pools and Corporations* (Revised edition.) Boston, Ginn and Company, 1916.

Stevens, W. S. (editor), *Industrial Combinations and Trusts.* New York, The Macmillan Company, 1914.

Stevens, W. H. S., *Unfair Competition.* Chicago, The University of Chicago Press, 1917.

U. S. Federal Trade Commission, *Decisions,* Vols. I and II. Washington, Government Printing Office, 1920.

Various reports of the United States Commissioner of Corporations and of the Federal Trade Commission, some of which have been already referred to, are helpful in this connection. The student may also refer to some of the titles listed under Topic II.

XII. Suggestions Regarding Current Material of Various Sorts

A. Financial Periodicals

Acceptance Bulletin (Published monthly by the American Acceptance Council, New York.)

The Annalist (Weekly, New York, Times Publishing Company.)

Banker's Magazine.

Banker and Tradesman.

Bulletin of the Investment Bankers' Association (Published by the Association, Chicago.)

**Commercial and Financial Chronicle* (Weekly, with many supplements.)

The Credit Monthly (Formerly the *Bulletin* of the National Association of Credit Men.)

Dun's Review (The Annual numbers are particularly helpful.)

**Federal Reserve Bulletin* (Published monthly by the Federal Reserve Board, Washington.)

Journal of the American Institute of Banking.

Journal of Accountancy.

Monthly Review of Credit and Business Conditions (Published by the Federal Reserve Bank, New York.)

Economic Conditions, Government Finance, and United States Securities (Published monthly by the National City Bank of New York.)

B. PERIODICALS WITH USEFUL ARTICLES

**Administration* (Published monthly, beginning January, 1921, by the Ronald Press Company.)

Business Organization and Management (London, Sir Isaac Pitman & Sons.)

FACTORY (Monthly, A. W. Shaw Company.)

Forbes Magazine (Bi-weekly.)

Industrial Management (Monthly.)

Journal of Political Economy (Published monthly by the Economics Department of Chicago University.)

Magazine of Wall Street.

Monthly Labor Review. United States Bureau of Labor Statistics, Washington.

Printers Ink (Weekly.)

*SYSTEM (Published monthly by the A. W. Shaw Company.)

C. FINANCIAL AND BUSINESS DAILIES

Boston News Bureau.

Daily News Record (New York.)

Journal of Commerce (New York.)

New York Commercial.

Wall Street Journal.

The financial and industrial pages of such newspapers as the *Boston Transcript*, the *New York Times*, the *New York Evening Post*, and the *Chicago Tribune* are particularly helpful.

D. MANUALS, STATISTICAL SERVICES, AND MISCELLANEOUS

Massachusetts, *Abstract of the Certificates of Corporations;* Public Document No. 10 (Annual.)

Massachusetts, *Statistics of Manufactures;* Public Document No. 36 (Annual.)

MOODY'S and POOR'S *Manual of Industrial Securities.*

MOODY'S and POOR'S *Analyses of Industrial Securities.*

Review of Economic Statistics (Published monthly by the Harvard University Committee on Economic Research.)

Standard Corporation Service (The Daily and Cumulative reports are invaluable, and the Manual of Unlisted Securities is also helpful.)

Standard Daily Trade Service.

United States, *Abstract of the Census of Manufactures, 1914,* as well as volumes dealing with *Manufactures* at the Decennial Census periods, contains some useful material.

United States, *Statistical Abstract* (Published annually by the Bureau of Foreign and Domestic Commerce).

The various Trade Directories such as Bennett's *Hand Book of Textile Securities,* Davidson's *Textile "Blue Book,"* Lockwood's *Directory of the Paper, Stationary and Allied Trades,* the *National Iron and Steel Blue Book,* the *Official Textile Directory,* and Thomas' *Directory of Manufacturers,* or Hendrick's *Commercial Register of the United States,* may help the student in some of his investigations.

Many of the Trade Associations collect financial data from their members to which it is sometimes possible for the student to gain access. Material collected by the various Cedit Reporting Agencies is also helpful.

PART I

INTRODUCTORY

NOTE TO TEACHERS, STUDENTS, AND THE GENERAL READER

IN the problems which follow, an attempt has been made to include all the detail which may be essential to an intelligent class-room discussion. It is assumed, however, that in addition to reading the Introductory Chapter, the student will have secured, either through his own outside reading or from a few informal lectures by the instructor, an understanding of the commoner terms used and a general knowledge of the principles of Business Finance. For those students who have never had a general course in finance, the writer has found it helpful, as a preliminary, to require the rapid reading of such a text-book as Lough's "Business Finance."

A working knowledge of accounting is also practically essential to the most intelligent handling of the problems. This book, can, accordingly, be used with most profit by those who have had an elementary course in accounting, though here again the individual teacher can himself fill any gap in the student's preparation, if he has the time and inclination to do so. Mention has already been made in the Bibliographical Note on page xxxv of some of the more useful texts on the subject of accounting.

The teacher himself should find it helpful to make extensive use of the bibliography given. It should be stated, however, that on many of the problems presented there is no published material which will prove particularly helpful. In such cases, enough information is given in the problem itself to enable a satisfactory answer to be arrived at by common sense.

In addition to the preliminary preparation which has been mentioned as being highly desirable on the part of the student, he would also do well to consult some of the readings listed at the beginning of each chapter. These will frequently give the key to problems which follow. Occasionally, also, a special reference is appended to the individual questions, for the student's guidance and information, rather than because such reference is absolutely necessary to a correct solution of the problem. The student will occasionally find it helpful to glance at the statistical material in the Appendix, much of which is wholly new. Some teachers, also, may find it desirable from time to time to preface their class-room discussions of the various topics by a brief preliminary survey.

So far as the problems themselves are concerned, the author has endeavored to arrange them in such an order that the subject can be logically developed. It should, however, be very helpful to the reader to consult the general outline above given, in order to get a preliminary view of the general relations of the topics to be presented. In many instances, also, it must be admitted that the arrangement of the problems can be reduced to no logical scheme, inasmuch as there are many natural overlappings of the subject. Some instructors, therefore, may not care to follow the author's order in all cases.

The aim of the problems has been to present actual financial situations in different lines of business as they arise. Hence, many different types have been used. Sometimes the problem conveys its own solution, and the student's judgment is tested by critically analyzing this solution or by attempting to discover a desirable or possible alternative. At other times, two or more alternative courses are open, and the student is asked to choose that solution which seems best. Frequently, also, the problem is so stated as to test the student's ability to think comparatively and to reason analogically. Again, in certain problems the student may be led into a seeming *cul de sac* and asked to find the way out.

In many cases, solutions have not yet been reached by the business men who have given the problems. This fact should add considerable zest to the discussion.

For problems of this type, also, there is frequently no one *correct* solution. The answer may be largely a matter of personal judgment. In all such cases, however, the student should be vigorously pressed to defend his position.

It should further be noted that in many of the problems the proper solution hinges on some small point which at first glance may be wholly overlooked by the student, or at any rate may seem relatively unimportant. A very slight change in a business situation frequently leads to momentous consequences—a fact which cannot be too strongly impressed upon the reader.

In order to facilitate the student's preparation, as well as the class-room discussions, numbered questions stressing the more important points have been appended to each problem. These questions are merely meant to be suggestive, not exhaustive. Teachers can follow them or not as they see fit. In the author's own experience, also, it had proved very useful to make frequent summaries of the various points discussed in the separate problems, as well as to give more general summaries at the conclusion of the discussion of the different divisions of the subject.

In the discussion of the problems, teachers may find it desirable to have the main points at issue summed up by a student prior to the general discussion, as is customarily required in those law schools where the case method is used. This exercise will aid in developing power of analysis and terseness in expression, and will insure full preparation on the part of the student. As a matter of course the student's text should always be brought to the class-room, so that he can constantly follow the development of the various problems and jot down important memoranda.

Some teachers will probably find it advantageous to require a certain amount of written work from the student, either in the nature of class-room tests or occasional reports. The author would suggest that brief class-room tests on outside reading, assigned as a preparation for the problem discussion, will in many cases prove extremely valuable, especially for those students who have had no previous preparation in finance. The Exercises preceding some of the chapters will also be helpful as outside reports, which will give the student a better understanding of many of the problems. Occasionally, it may be worth while to require written solutions of the problems themselves.

The material in this book is ample for a full year's course, though by making the proper selection it can readily be adapted to a half-year's course. The author himself uses it for a half-course in Industrial Finance with students in the Harvard Graduate School of Business Administration. Depending upon the nature of other required courses, some teachers may wish to omit certain problems, topics, or even chapters. Such omissions can be judiciously made without in any way breaking up the continuity of the whole. To the author's knowledge, no other book or collection of books attempts to cover the vital phases of Business Finance from the same angle or in so comprehensive a manner as the present volume. Hence, even if a textbook is being regularly used, this book should prove useful as required collateral reading.

Finally, it should be stated that, while there is really no mystery connected with the subject of finance, as is sometimes supposed, yet many apparently simple problems are far more significant than may at first appear. Practically every one of the topics developed and problems presented has been carefully discussed with well-known business men and bankers of New York, Boston, or elsewhere. The keen interest which such men, after many years of outstanding financial success, have taken in every aspect of the work, leads to the conclusion that the more intensive is the business equipment and experience of the reader, the more good he will probably get out of a perusal of the following problems. Accordingly, the author is emboldened to hope that many men actively engaged in the financial conduct of industry will find within the covers of this book material which will be of interest to them.

CHAPTER I

INTRODUCTION—GENERAL SURVEY OF THE FIELD

WHEN Henry Ford was reported to be in financial difficulties early in 1921, and when it was thought that he needed new financing to the extent of $75,000,000 or more, many of the "wise ones" said, "What a fool! This is an example of the evils resulting from one-man control in industry. Ford has ignored banking and finance and now the bankers will have a few things to say to him when he comes with hat in hand seeking their assistance." In fact, one banker is reported to have gone so far as to pay Mr. Ford a special visit in order to suggest to him who the treasurer of his refinanced organization should be. Within a few weeks, however, Ford himself announced that he was not seeking any financial assistance, and, further, that if he should wish to arrange for credit he would do so at a time when he did not need the help.

Three or four months after this announcement by Mr. Ford, the same "wise ones" were almost fulsome in their praise of Ford's financial skill because he had managed to "turn the corner" without any outside assistance. His example was referred to as one of the most inspiring instances on record of what one man's ability and determination can accomplish in troubled times like these.

Probably neither of these extreme assertions regarding Mr. Ford are wholly correct. Yet it may be that in the long run some of the policies recently adopted by Mr. Ford, which have been the subject of much criticism, may lead to his financial undoing. Nevertheless, the fact that he so successfully weathered the storm while others were sinking, suggests that his past financial policies and the financial structure of his organization were preeminently sound and worthy of study.

At the very time when the largest automobile company of its kind in the world was coming safely through this troubled period, the world's largest maker of rubber tires, Mr. Seiberling, was being ousted entirely by the Goodyear Company's creditors from the control of the mammoth organization which he had built up in twenty years, with practically no original capital. These two organizations were integral parts of the same great industry. They began in much the same manner and both were preeminent in their respective fields. Why did Mr. Ford apparently succeed, and why did Mr. Seiberling fail? The causes for the difference in the financial position in which these two great companies find themselves at the middle of 1921, can be readily ascertained and merit careful study.

During the first six months of the present year, one of the great commercial agencies reports 9,035 business failures with aggregate liabilities of $310,671,000. In amount of liabilities, during the first half of 1921 the failures have been about 60 per cent greater than in any similar period in our history. Many a hitherto "successful" business man is now being forced to reflect on the underlying causes of the present situation. During the long upward swing of prices for more than twenty years, it was comparatively easy to make money, since some of the increasing expenses of production always tended to lag behind the selling price of the finished product. During the period of rapidly rising war-time prices many a concern found it easier than ever to be "successful." In fact, mere upstarts in business were disposed to regard themselves as financial leviathans, because of the unprecedented temporary profits which they were fortunate enough to make.

As the tide of business prosperity is waning, however, it becomes apparent to the thoughtful man that many of the present financial difficulties are due, not to the catastrophes wrought by the Great War as is habitually asserted, but to the failure of business concerns themselves to "read the handwriting on the wall," and to follow the simple rules which are inseparable from lasting financial success. While the post-war boom was on, it was easy to forget that there is a Business Cycle, that very definite results inevitably follow certain causes, and that all the activities of a business are intimately related and ultimately have a profound effect on its financial condition.

No matter how apparently prosperous a business may have been, there are times when financial difficulties cannot possibly be avoided unless the "rules of the game" have been consistently followed from the very beginning. Hence it is at this time decidedly worth while to examine the financial problems which have been and now are faced by typical business concerns. Thus it may be possible to discover causes, account for results, and draw certain valid conclusions, which without a first-hand study would seem to be little more than academic theorizing.

Nor is it desirable for present purposes to center much attention on the larger business units. Their financial position and problems are frequently not typical and are usually fairly well-known. Rather, it would seem that the greater benefit can be derived from a study of the problems of the medium-sized and smaller industrial concerns. Those businesses which may properly be designated as being in this classification, in 1914 constituted 98.6 per cent of the total number of manufacturing concerns in the United States, and produced more than 52 per cent in *value* of product.* In addition there are literally hundreds of thousands of trading, financial, and personal service concerns of various types, most of which are unincorporated. Accordingly it now seems desirable to devote attention largely to the daily problems of this numerous

*All manufacturing concerns the annual value of whose product was less than $1,000,000 are included in this classification. It is interesting to note that 87.7 per cent of the total number of manufacturing establishments reported to the United States Census Bureau in 1914 showed an annual value of product less than $100,000.

group of smaller businesses, and to those problems which are common to all types of business whether large or small.

Since most books on the general subject of finance have in the main discussed the problems of so-called "corporation" finance and "trust" finance, giving a good deal of attention to railroads and public utilities, it may be helpful at this point to call the reader's attention briefly to some of the outstanding characteristics which tend to make many phases of railroad and public utility finance different from industrial finance.

(1) In the first place, it may be noted that public service corporations of all sorts must secure franchises from public bodies to enable them to use the highways, and the like. The railways in particular can exercise the right of eminent domain. (2) This of course suggests the fact that local public utilities, at any rate, are as a rule more cheaply and conveniently carried on as monopolies. (3) Further, interesting problems arise because of the fact that the service furnished by utility companies and railroads must be consumed in connection with the plant which renders it. Therefore, the question of the distribution of product and its financing is a far different one from that which arises in the case of industrial concerns. (4) Probably, also, on account of the nature of the service rendered by public utilities and particularly by railroads, the economic principal of "joint cost" is more in evidence than in the case of the average factory operation. Hence it should be easier to determine the actual costs of a manufactured product than to discover the true cost of a given service rendered by a transportation company. (5) It is also significant that the average industrial concern can within limits change the nature of its product, produce side-lines, or engage in subsidiary or by-product operations, all of which activities are practically impossible for any public utility. (6) The average industrial concern can expand its plant with considerable ease without consulting any parties

but the owners. No such possibility exists in the case of the various transportation corporations. (7) After a certain point has been reached it is practically impossible for a public service corporation to grow larger, inasmuch as it is already serving the full needs of the community. For industrial concerns, however, there is practically unlimited opportunity for growth in some new direction.

(8) It is further significant that in the public utilities and railroads the investment is high relative to the annual gross income. In fact, the "gross" is ordinarily not more than 20 to 25 per cent of the investment and frequently much lower. In manufacturing concerns, however, the proportion of gross income to investment is often 100 per cent or more, and in the case of those trading businesses which turn their inventory rapidly, it is frequently many hundred per cent. (9) Public utilities can, as a rule, count on a relatively steady income, since the demand for their service is reasonably constant. This condition holds true for the railroads to a much less degree, but for many manufacturing concerns the income is very sporadic and uncertain, and the demand for the product cannot readily be predicted. (10) Should serious financial difficulties arise, there is always the possibility of selling the plant of a public service corporation, for its services are needed no matter what happens. The plant of an industrial concern, on the other hand, may be practically worthless under a forced sale no matter how carefully constructed that plant may be.

On account of the conditions indicated, it has been possible to bring the finances of railroads and public utilities to a reasonable degree of standardization. Because of the direct public interests involved, general public regulation of public service corporations has developed, and this regulation has tended to bring about an even higher degree of standardization. The finances of industrial concerns, on the contrary, have hitherto only in a very indefinite sort of way been regulated by public bodies. The latter have accordingly been much freer in their methods of financing.

Though from a financial point of view there are very interesting and definite contrasts between industrial concerns and public service corporations, yet it must also be borne in mind that striking differences exist between business concerns themselves. In fact, an almost endless classification might be made on the basis of the type of organization, the nature of the product, and the size or age of the establishment. Further, great differences of much financial significance exist between those concerns which produce staples and those which deal only in specialties or novelties. Again, those concerns engaged in seasonal businesses of various sorts are in an entirely different position from the ones which turn out a product for which there is a steady demand. The seasoned type can also be readily distinguished from the more spectacular kind of undertaking. The concerns which are engaged in manufacture may be set off, with regard to their financial problems, from the trading companies or the organizations which merely render service, such as the banking business, amusement companies, and so on.

Finally, it must be observed that even in the same line of industry there has not hitherto been much standardization, due to important differences in location, plant construction, management, and the like. In an industrial concern, therefore, of whatever type it may be, the personal factor tends to play a far more important part than in the case of public service corporations. Hence one might normally expect to find a wide variation in the financial problems of industrial concerns, and it is easy to fall into the error of thinking that the principles of finance which apply in one case will have little or no relation to another case. It is of course true that, on account of the changes in the general business conditions, what is apparently good financing at one time may be very bad financing at another. It is further true that the financial "set-up" of certain types of industry must from the nature of their operations differ greatly. Yet, in spite of these apparently important differences, it is probable that the fundamental principles of sound business financing can be reduced to a comparatively small number of simple rules.

In the following survey, the point of view will be a conservative one. The suggestions made are meant merely to serve as a guide to the student and general reader. There are no absolutely fixed rules of finance; but for the beginner it is well to set up certain ideals as a standard.

Most of the attempts to promote new enterprises "fizzle out." Yet, in spite of this fact it appears to be comparatively easy to raise enough money to launch any kind of a new concern—as evidenced by the Federal Trade Commission's report that probably half a billion dollars was recently sunk in worthless securities in the space of one year by the people of the United States. Even for those whose intentions are the best, it seems to be easier to raise capital to be thrown away than to decide whether there is any financial justification for launching the new concern. Unless there is some very special financial advantage connected with a new concern as compared with others in the same line of business, such as the ownership of a "100 per cent patent," which will confer a monoply for a period of time, the occupation of a very superior location, the certain securing of lower operating expenses through improved methods or lower construction costs, or something of the sort, it is very doubtful whether there is in the long run any economic reason for launching a new enterprise, unless, of course, there should be a very rapidly growing and probably continuous demand for the commodity produced.

The mere fact that there is a "market" for the goods to be produced does not in itself decide that a given concern should be launched. There may be others, more effective, coming into the field. Even granting that all other conditions are favorable, the stage of the Business Cycle may be wrong for the starting of a new enterprise, on account of the high absolute costs, and the possibility of a depression in the near future.

For launching a concern in order to develop an absolutely new idea, after the *other* logical requirements are met, the chief question is that of demand for the commodity to be produced or the service to be rendered. Many a financial miscarriage has resulted from the failure to realize that no matter how admirable the idea or how secure the patent rights, and the like, the public may have no use for the new commodity. Most failures which result ultimately from such an unpropitious beginning are an economic waste. Yet, if the start is honestly made, is it not possible that the lessons taught by some unfortunate experience of this sort serve a useful purpose? And may it not also be true that the possibility of such easy launching of new concerns tends to foster a spirit of wholesome competition from which the public ultimately gains?

Assuming honest intentions throughout, it may be stated with regard to the problem of securing capital to launch a new, small concern—and all successful concerns have small beginnings—that the original financing should be done largely in a private manner. Ownership and responsibility for the outcome should go hand in hand. Ordinarily, outsiders should not be expected to risk their money, unless the proposition is understood by them to be a largely speculative one, until the business has demonstrated its capacity to earn a return on the initial investment. In most cases the beginning should be modest, with the minimum investment in fixed assets. Ample provision, however, should be made for working capital—a caution usually overlooked. All obligations such as mortgages should whenever possible be avoided. If the unlimited risks of individual ownership or partnership are to be escaped, there may be, aside from tax considerations, a good reason for incorporating. In the long run, the safest rule is for an industrial corporation to finance itself solely by means of common stock issues. Preferred stock, however, is frequently used as a temporary bait to call forth the investment of those who are willing, for a stipulated low return, to hold the financial bag, while the common stock holders, often with only a negligible original investment of their own, but with sole control, reap all the rewards which come from the use of the money of outsiders.

As a rule, the strong business concern, like the strong body, grows slowly, financing itself out of earnings until the time comes when the reinvested earnings cannot be made to yield as high a return to the owners by being put back into the business as the owners could themselves realize by investing these earnings in some other manner. Certainly this is true of a closely held concern. It is a most unwise policy for any company to expand rapidly with a view to securing business which may prove only temporary. The earnings may be high for a time, but after that the deluge! The overhead expenses have a way of holding their own while profits shrink. If a concern manages to grow out of earnings, and no permanent borrowing is necessary, the pressure of hard times will be less severe. However financed, expansions and developments should usually be made only at the beginning of a period of prosperity or during a lull, when capital costs are low.

If it has become necessary to resort to public financing in order to expand and develop, the easiest terms are usually secured by that concern whose past financial history is sound. If a public offering of securities is made and the stock listed on some exchange, the future financing of the company will probably be done partially with an eye to the stock ticker. In view of the speculative raids on listed securities and the rumors which constantly float around, it seems sometimes that the concern is safest whose stock is unknown on 'change. For the smaller concerns, however, the problem is not usually a serious one, since their market for funds is only local.

Another important feature of the new financing should be noted. The concern seeking new funds must watch the investment "fads." Not many years ago all but railway and public utility securities were considered speculative. But the public became sadly disillusioned in this matter and turned to industrials. Within the last few years industrial preferred stock and bonds have come largely into the "investment market." The sentiment has swung to the opposite point of the compass. But this is not the whole story. Four or five years ago it was easy to sell industrial preferred stock on a 7 per cent basis, without noticeably stringent protective provisions. Gradually the rate basis grew to 8 per cent or more, with much more drastic protective features. Next, the public called for debenture notes instead of preferred stock. These at first were notes maturing within three to five years. At the next stage ten year debentures were called for, and at present it is difficult to secure capital even for working purposes without issuing first mortgage bonds!

Nor does the story end here. The protective provisions relating particularly to sinking fund and redemption requirements, to the maintenence of a stated ratio of current assets to current liabilities, or to keeping the net current assets at a certain fixed and high percentage of the securities outstanding, have frequently made it necessary for a really strong concern to refinance under great difficulties in order to abide by the terms of its indenture. A weak concern may often be made even weaker by these provisions, which are meant to protect the securities held, but which are too inflexible for the financial needs of the particular business. All of these things should be considered by the business which publicly seeks new capital.

Furthermore, obligations incurred in order to finance an abnormal or sudden growth should be self-liquidating. The officers of the concern should see their way out before they get in too deep. This rule applies particularly to times of rapidly rising prices, when securities have frequently been issued for working capital purposes. Finally, the concern should always leave open some satisfactory alternative method of financing, just as strategy demands that even a victorious army assure itself of a line of retreat.

Yet the average business concern inclines to follow the tide, buy its capital on the dear market, and then sell its goods a little later on the cheap market. Many a corporation which rushed boldly into public financing in order to expand and "gobble up" war-time profits, is now slinking around with hat in hand, begging the bankers or the small investor directly to take their first mortgage bonds at an almost unthinkably high rate. It is really pathetic to count the number of formerly conservatively financed concerns, which flashed into a momentary glory during the war, and which will probably be working for their creditors for the next generation, if indeed they manage to avoid bankruptcy in the near future. In all these matters it would appear to be a generally safe rule in financing, as on the stock exchange, to do about the opposite of what the average business man feels like doing.

In connection with this all-important question, one more point should be mentioned. When an industrial concern passes through the adolescent period and emerges into a good-sized corporation, two mistakes are commonly made. In the first place, the cautions of the earlier years tend to be forgotten and the energies of the management frequently become divided. The day of small things is too often despised—as if the fundamental rules for success are any different for the large concern than for the small one! It is a well recognized American business trait to make up in bigness and advertising for what is lacking in financial soundness.

Secondly, many concerns grow large in size while their officers fail to grow up with them. They continue to think and act in small terms when their business demands unusual scope and vision, which can result only from profound study of the situation, combined with great natural capacity. To attain success, the growth of a business must be coordinated in all its parts. No doubt many a man whose business has grown too big for him looks back with regrets to the earlier years, and rightly so, for his grasp is loosening. It requires almost more than eternal vigilance to guide a large corporation through the business shoals for many years, and usually only one hand can hold the rudder.

That small concern is fortunate indeed which starts with an adequate supply of Working Capital, so that it will not need to look for further assistance until it has demonstrated its capacity as a money-getter. Even though the company's own funds are inadequate, arrangements should, if possible, be made to take the cash discounts on purchases rather than to pay what amounts to high interest rates to the dealer. Hence resort should be made to the bank, and requests for loans should be accompanied with a full statement of condition and information regarding the purpose of the loan. Many a struggling concern has grown powerful as a result of the disinterested guidance of a friendly banker.

The small business man does not as a rule sufficiently realize the banker's function. He either goes in fear and trembling, dreading lest he be swindled, exterminated, or devoured by the unscrupulous banker, and endeavoring to conceal all information regarding his business which might "incriminate" him, or, on the other hand, he rather arrogantly demands that the bank make wholly unwarranted and even unnecessary commercial loans, frequently on no better security than his fixed assets! This lack of understanding of the bank's true function is partially accounted for by the attitude of the banks themselves. They have frequently failed to acquaint themselves with the nature of their client's business, and have sometimes not cared to be bothered with the smaller accounts.

In general, however, the great competition in banking in the United States has led to a particular cultivation of the small borrower. In fact, credit has probably been far too easy in this country. We have reaped the results in rapid growth, accompanied by numerous failures. Again, competition in banking has made it possible for many a stronger concern to ignore its bank and refuse to give the information regarding its financial condition, which is essential to intelligent credit granting.

Though there is much loose talking about banker control of industry, this criticism cannot properly be directed against the average commercial bank. If a customer is frank with his bank, and lives up to the requirements, he can usually get any service within reason. Investment bankers sometimes insist that they be represented on the directorate of companies which they have helped finance—frequently to the discomfort of the original owners, who now have to work to pay off their debts. A concern which does not fancy financial control of this sort will do well to keep its house in order and to walk humbly in the days of its prosperity.

There yet remains a vast field, as yet little cultivated, for the development of financial cooperation between banks and industries. The banks have not made sufficient use in an analytical way of the invaluable material in their possession. Nor have they until recently secured detailed statements of condition with sufficient frequency from their clients. There has been too much guessing on the part of the lender and borrower. It should be the banker's function to obtain more information and carefully to analyze and interpret the data in his possession. Thus by making a dynamic study of the credit situation in the different types of industry, and by reducing the results to approximate financial standards, it might be possible to give such constructive financial advice to business men as would enable them to avoid many of the pitfalls into which they now tumble through a failure to conduct their operations with a view to the current trends in business conditions.

All economic laws are but approximations. No rigid rules can be laid down. To base credit granting solely on statistical standards is as unsafe as to make only character and capacity the criterions. Yet the statistics, when properly interpreted, no doubt usually reflect the character and capacity of a concern's officers in a rather intimate way. The fact that we still have so many business calamities, so many peaks and valleys in our Business Cycle, shows that there is some "maladjustment" somewhere which probably can be remedied when the causes are sufficiently understood. It would seem that the banks, through a more careful study, and through greater cooperation with each other and with industrial concerns, might give constructive advice and force compliance with this advice on the part of the borrowers, in time to prevent many a catastrophe. Thus the curves of the Business Cycle might gradually be somewhat flattened out, much to the financial gain of the business concerns themselves, the banks, and the community at large.

Finally, it cannot be stressed too strongly that the average concern tries to do too much business on credit. Many a business has failed and many a bank has lost money, because temporary borrowings have been used for investment purposes. This situation might be avoided if the bankers would insist that their customers pay off all loans at least once each year. This rule is not ordinarily observed, except by the very small concerns which are not large enough or "shrewd" enough to use the open market or some other bank as an alternative source of funds. Some borrowers make it a practice to flit in and out, from bank to bank, or from bank to open market and back again, and then to call it "cleaning up" the loans! This practice simply means a lack of permanent working capital on the part of the borrowing concern, with the many attendant dangers.

The Commercial Paper Market is not for the small borrower. Many medium-sized concerns, however, resort to borrowing through note brokers in order to secure temporarily lower rates of interest and to avoid keeping the usual deposits required by their banks. The open market is useful in the case of large concerns whose banks cannot, according to law, lend them enough money, and which do not care to maintain adequate deposit requirements in a large number of separate banks. But for the smaller company the open market appears to have few advantages. These little fellows tend to use the note broker as a competitor of the bank instead of as a useful adjunct. Usually they neglect to live up to the bank's deposit requirements, and then when the market suddenly closes on them they are in a dangerous position. All lines should be kept open as long as possible.

Further, a concern selling its paper on the open market is subject to much investigation and gossip which very frequently works injury. Finally, the small interior banks, which in recent years have absorbed great quantities of commercial paper, act pretty much like sheep. They buy some paper which is really far from "prime" because they "know" the name of the borrower or the issuing concern. They turn against or refuse other paper of a much higher grade because the name is not so well known or because of prejudice arising from unfounded rumors. For example, if the paper of a concern in one line of industry goes bad, there is a tendency to avoid all paper put out by any concerns engaged in this particular industry. Beyond a doubt that company rests easiest which does not need to reckon with situations such as these.

Many enthusiastic claims have been made for the Trade Acceptance as a method of financing for working capital. Some have gone so far as to say that the working capital of a concern would be doubled if the trade acceptance were used on all accounts, since these acceptances could be discounted. The obvious reply to this line of argument is that if a firm's collection of customer's accounts is prompt, a bank will lend to the limit on the current ratio. Trade acceptances in such cases are not needed to improve the quality of a concern's receivables. If, on the other hand, accounts receivable are customarily slow, the acceptances may be used to make payments more certain. Trade acceptances arising in this manner, however, might not be looked upon with much favor for rediscount purposes. At any rate, no reputable banker cares to lend twice on the same assets, nor does he care to have his customers' trade acceptances, which become two-name paper, discounted on the open market or with finance corporations, after a bank loan has already been made. The real function of the trade acceptance would seem to be remedial—to improve the quality of a concern's receivables and so improve its credit position and increase the turnover of its working capital.

The various emergency methods of financing for working capital purposes require little mention in this place. As a rule, no concern should pledge its receivables or borrow on other security except as a last resort. Additional working capital above what the banks can safely lend should be secured from earnings reinvested, rather than through public financing. When it becomes necessary through hard luck or bad management to sell senior securities in order to protect the current position, one can only say, "God help the unfortunate borrower!"

Just as no family can thrive permanently without proper food, and no salaried man can save unless his wife is a careful buyer, so no business concern can hope for success unless it knows how to buy *right*, in quality, in quantity, in price, and in time. No concern is stronger than its purchasing policy. Unwise buying, buying too much and at the wrong time, has wrecked the largest companies. Few concerns during the past year have failed to suffer bitterly because of the heavy shrinkage in high cost and unnecessarily large inventories. As the housewife lays in an enormous stock of 25-cent sugar, though when it costs only 7 cents per pound she buys only from hand to mouth, so when prices are high and goods apparently scarce, the business man seems unable to resist the temptation to "load up." In the case of the retailer, the overbuying is usually the fault of the salesmen, who talk high prices in order to make present sales. The losses due to a wrong purchasing policy, even though there be no inventory shrinkage, are serious because of the slower turnover of working capital, if for no other reason.

The dangers of underbuying are relatively too small to be noted. In a small manufacturing business, in which the various operations are coordinated in one man, there sometimes seems to be less danger of excess buying than in the larger corporations where the labor of supervision is divided. Nor is it a safe policy for an industrial concern to speculate on the raw material which it uses; it is much like stock market gambling—a few gain but most lose.

Finally, the fact cannot be too strongly stressed that the firm which *buys for cash* has the world at its feet. As Petrarch puts it, "There is no place so strong but that an ass laden with gold will find his way in." Better still, to paraphrase the words of Adam Smith, "There will never be any scarcity of wine for him who hath the wherewithal to pay for it." The buyer who has ready money can always get the best prices because he is beholden to none.

In the production end of most manufacturing concerns great financial losses arise. The true costs are frequently not known with sufficient accuracy or frequency. By many smaller competing concerns goods are even sold at an actual loss. They make money until they fail! Nor are the most profitable methods of production utilized. According to the much discussed "Hoover Report" more wastes in production are charged to the management than to labor, which has ordinarily been blamed for inefficiency. Whatever the theories may be, it is true without question that the wastes arising from wholly unnecessary labor turnover are enormous. The economic wastes arising from style changes, lack of standardization, and similar causes, are vast, and in the long run mean lower profits for all industries. At a given time, however, it is difficult to know how great this effect may be. Nor should it be overlooked that there are intangible gains coming from the mental satisfactions derived from constant variety in goods produced.

So much has been written about the economies of large scale production and the advantages of horizontal and vertical combination, that the topic seems hardly worth mentioning in this connection. It may be noted, however, that very frequently the alleged decrease in cost of production resulting from an increase in the size of the organization is illusory. While from the engineer's point of view the so-called manufacturing costs may be lessened, because of plant specialization, or the use of more economical units of equipment, and the like, yet as a business grows larger through the absorption of other concerns, there are many added expenses not incurred by the smaller productive units. These unforseen increases between factory cost and price to customer seem frequently to devour a considerable part of the original economy. A one man concern grown large is frequently an exception to this rule, as are also the smaller concerns which are centrally managed though not actually combined.

This entire subject, and the allied question of integration and development of subsidiary companies, furnishes a fruitful field for further study. This book is not concerned with the financing of combinations as such, which frequently amounts to a mere juggling of balance sheets and is not a part of the normal financial conduct of an industry.

In recent years attention has been directed to the volume of sales in dollars, rather than to the number of units sold. Hence comparisons now being made with the preceding years prove rather depressing, though in many cases there is really not much cause for gloom. People cannot eat much more food or use more of the staples just because prices are falling—nor will they.

It is an American commercial trait to overrate the selling end of the business. Salesmen are paid an exceptionally high salary because they "get the business." It is very true that most businesses could not long exist without their salesmen and their advertising. Yet the fact remains that a great part of the energy expended in selling goods is in the main an apparent economic waste. Were it not for the nature of our industrial competition and the fact that "everybody's doing it," it should not be necessary to incur so much expense in trying to convince the customer that Chesterfield cigarettes are better for him than Fatimas! Since the public is willing to pay the bills, there must be some intangible gain, and no doubt competition in selling keeps up the standard of efficiency so as to lower costs. This again is a matter for further investigation, particularly in so far as the ultimate financial results of advertising are concerned.

It is much more significant that many business concerns are constantly out of breath in their endeavors to keep up with their salesmen, who "over-sell" certain lines of goods when the selling is easy, and then call on the management for more plant capacity in order to supply a demand which proves to be only temporary. Many a concern, having expanded under such pressure during recent years, has now been effectively *sold* into the receiver's hands or the bankruptcy court.

Mention should also be made of another reprehensible sales policy—that of making special concessions to customers, particularly in the way of granting unduly long terms. It is not the function of a selling concern to act as a banker; the practice is dangerous for the seller and doubly dangerous for the customer. The latter fools himself into thinking that he is a business success when he is really hovering on the brink of failure. Many an incompetent upstart bursts into business because of the fact that dealers are willing to carry his accounts for a long time. The results are in the long run usually disastrous all round, and the ultimate consumer again pays the bills. Collections should at all times be prompt. It is no kindness to let a customer form the habit of being slow and losing his discounts.

Finally, it should be the aim of every concern to keep its stock rapidly moving, even though the margin of profit is lower. Money tied up in inventory yields no income. If values shrink and losses must be taken, they should be taken early. The business can thus, after cleaning out the old stock, put itself in a strong position to buy at the best market, and to start competition with lower costs. The importance of the same policy should be impressed on customers. It is criminal to urge them to overbuy, while such a policy inevitably reacts on the finances of the selling house.

As to the Administration of Earnings, little need be added. If the management is honest, there will be no doubt about the policy followed. In fact, with reasonable intelligence, there is less likelihood of going wrong at this point than at most others. Adequate maintenance should be provided for, ample depreciation allowed, and liberal surpluses built up against less prosperous years. Improvements should be made out of earnings and not out of capital. After this point, the rest is comparatively simple. If the business is privately owned, the question of dividend policy is frequently not raised. If the stock is more widely held, however, dividends should not under any circumstances be paid until a margin of net income equal to at least one year's reasonable dividend payments has been accumulated. If the future looks ominous, dividends should rarely be paid, even though earned by a considerable margin.

With these considerations in mind, the dividend policy will be determined largely by the exigencies of the particular case. If the holders of common stock have actually paid cash for their shares, they are entitled to a fair return for the risks taken. Yet, it is always a conservative policy to put back into the business one dollar for every dollar paid out in dividends, until such time as it appears that the accumulated profits of the stockholders would yield a higher income if invested by them outside the business. In the light of these general suggestions, particular cases regarding expansion out of earnings can be decided. When the earnings permit, this should ordinarily be the rule; for the expansion should not be planned unless the owners feel that the proposition will pay well, and that their income from the added construction will be high.

According to the statistics of the Treasury Department, in 1918 there were 115,518 business corporations in the United States with no annual net income. Inactive concerns having been deducted, the number was 71,907, or more than 26 per cent of all active business corporations in the country. Of those corporations reporting net income, 118,370, or 58.6 per cent, had a net income below $5,000, while only 1,026, or one-half of one per cent, reported a net income in excess of $1,000,000 annually.

This preponderance of very small incomes is striking. When the two groups are combined, it appears that 190,277, or more than 69 per cent of all *active* business corporations in the United States, either reported no net income, or an annual net income under $5,000. The figures are still surprising, even when due allowance is made for the well-known methods of tax evasion. It is obvious that the average industrial concern was not making fabulous profits, although 1918 was an unusually prosperous year. Of course, a majority of these concerns were small, but some were no doubt very large.

During this same year the number of failures reported by Bradstreet's was 10,146, of which only 222 had liabilities in excess of $100,000. The financial difficulties of the present are leading to much larger failures than ever before. Yet it appears that the smaller concerns are the ones which usually suffer most. Many of the larger industrial units borrow so heavily from their banks that the latter find it more worth while to carry them over the crisis than to let them go into bankruptcy, when the plant would sell for almost nothing.

At the present time it is customary for failing concerns to attribute their difficulties to the post-war conditions, to labor squabbles, to legal restrictions, or what not. These, to be sure, are important factors in the situation. But such causes could not have operated so effectively had the internal financial weakness not already been present. In other words, with the timely application of reasonable foresight and intelligence, probably the majority of recent failures could have been averted.

It is unnecessary here to enumerate the specific causes of failure. They can be readily deduced from the preceding discussion. It should be stated, however, that in many cases it is probably well for the failures to come. There are a large number of wholly inefficient little concerns which should never have been launched. Then there are the "war babies," in the begetting of which a momentary pleasure was realized, but which were doomed from birth. The pity of it all is that so many otherwise good concerns are failing largely because of fundamental ignorance of business conditions and economic principles.

It has from time to time in the past two years afforded rather gruesome diversion to read statements by certain alleged leaders of business, explaining the reasons for their great success and formulating general rules of sound finance; then to learn a few months later that the corporations which they had developed were in a receiver's hands and that they themselves were ejected from the management. *Sic transit gloria mundi.*

The rules of the game are after all very simple—so simple that comparatively few recognize them. Probably little new light on the fundamentals of business finance has been discovered for many generations. It is to be hoped that the extraordinary degree of cooperation which has arisen out of the present emergencies—cooperation between banks and business concerns, and between various business concerns themselves—will in a measure continue during more settled days, and that the lessons in the fundamentals of finance now being learned in bitterness of spirit will, because of this cooperation, not soon be forgotten.

CHAPTER II

FINANCIAL CONSIDERATIONS INVOLVED IN BEGINNING A BUSINESS

References:

*Conyngton, *Financing an Enterprise*, particularly pages 3-161.
Conyngton, *Corporate Organization and Management*, 39-48.
*Duncan, *Marketing, Its Problems and Methods*, 21-60; 277-314.
*Jones, *The Administration of Industrial Enterprises*, 21-56.
Keir, *Manufacturing Industries in America*, 61-85.
Lough, *Business Finance*, 11-63.
*Lough, *Corporation Finance*, 49-64.
Mead, *Corporation Finance*, Chapters II and III.
Regan, *Financing a Business*, 1-47.
*Robinson, *Organizing a Business*, 29-67, 186-20.
Shaw, *An Approach to Business Problems*, 25-52, 115-130.

Throughout the book it is assumed that the student will have a general knowledge of the subject such as can be derived from the rapid reading of a text like Lough's *Business Finance*. The most helpful references are marked with an asterisk (*). Where it will facilitate the work of the student, an appropriate reference is also given by author's name following particular problems. The general Outline and Bibliography at the beginning of the book should also be consulted.

COUNTLESS attempts are made to launch enterprises which cannot under any circumstances be successful. Provided the idea in itself seems good, many people look no further. Hundreds of millions of dollars are wasted every year on utterly futile propositions. The following problems, closely related to the problems in Chapter III, attempt to direct attention to some of the vital financial considerations involved in connection with the launching of a new enterprise.

Problem 1

General Problem in the Launching of Various Types of Businesses*

Consider yourself an impartial *financial adviser*, chiefly interested in the smaller business concerns. Your expert advice is asked upon the following propositions:

A. Smith, who can depend upon sufficient financial backing and who is supposed to have good business sense, wishes to start a small rubber factory in an Ohio town in 1919. He is 45 years of age, energetic, of excellent character, and has a thorough knowledge of the rubber tire business.

Questions

1. What advice would you give him? Indicate in detail the reasons for your decision and the considerations involved.

*The following suggestions are pertinent:

"There are certain fundamental factors which enter into the selection of every plant site. It is the weighing of these factors and establishing the relative importance of each that assists most in drawing scientific conclusions and deciding upon the proper location for the plant. The main factors may be classified as follows: Market, foreign, domestic, national or local. B—Raw materials, principal and secondary. C—Transportation, rail, water, motor trucks. D—Labor, male, female, skilled, unskilled. E—Power, coal, fuel, oil, electric. Secondary facts: A—Climatic requirements, if any. B—Public utilities required. C—Dependency upon municipal environment. D—Dependency on municipal laws or ordinances. E—Advertising value of plant. F—Financial aids, capital, bonus, free site. G—Disposal of plant wastes. In outlining the above factors it will be seen that the primary ones are those which usually enter most prominently into the production and distribution costs of the product, which, as stated previously, are kept at a minimum by a properly selected site. These are the items, then, that should receive careful and thorough study and should be weighed in relation to each other for any particular industry. It is understood, of course, that in various industries the importance of these factors will differ and in some industries some of the secondary factors will assume major importance. But the more consideration that is given toward establishing the relative value of these factors, the more likely it is that the proper site will be chosen."

(Adapted from H. H. McCanna, in *Industrial Management*, June 1, 1921, p 396.)

2. Would you have given the same advice in 1913?

3. Would your advice have been the same if the prospective location of the factory had been in Cambridge, Massachusetts? San Francisco, California?

(See Jones, *et al.*)

B. Brown has worked for 20 years in a shoe factory and knows the manufacturing end thoroughly, having held all positions from that of errand boy to that of foreman. He has saved $10,000. As the concern for which he is working is a family affair, he decides that there is no real future for himself if he remains. Since the shoe business is the only one that he knows, he wishes to start a little shoe factory of his own in Brockton, Massachusetts, in 1910.

Questions

1. How would you determine the probabilities of success in the new venture?

2. What kind of advice would you give him?

3. If Brown had wished to begin the business early in 1920, in Minneapolis, would you have given the same advice?

(Reference: Keir, *Manufacturing Industries in America*, p. 235, ff.)

C. Jones, who has an ordinary education and has worked in subordinate positions in retail grocery stores as well as in candy making concerns, inherited $5,000 early in 1919. As he wished to be more independent, some of his friends advised him to start up a candy-making business and others advised him to open a retail candy store.

Question

What would be your analysis of the proposition, and how should you have advised him?

D. Dr. F, a professor of chemistry in............ University, discovers a new process for making a rare shade of dye, which hitherto has never been produced in this country. Being hard pressed for funds, late in 1920 he offers to sell his process to a friend, B. This friend was formerly engaged in the manufacture of chemicals, but has been inactive since the end of the war. For a consideration of $10,000 he offers his secret process, together with his services in getting the plant started. It was estimated that an additional $40,000 would be necessary to install the plant. The total cost, $50,000, was just equal to B's entire capital. Hence, he was desirous of knowing definitely whether the business would be profitable.

Question

Indicate the various considerations involved, and the steps in reaching your decision.

E. To summarize the concrete result of the foregoing discussions, under what conditions is the launching of a new enterprise financially justified?

(Reference: Conyngton, *Financing an Enterprise*, p. 35-77.)

F. In each of the foregoing cases what form of organization would you consider the most desirable and why—individual ownership, partnership, or corporation?

(Reference: Robinson, *Organizing a Business*.)

G. 1. Is it financially desirable for a business concern to be incorporated in the state where it operates? Why or why not?

2. Will your decision differ depending upon the size or nature of the business?

(References: Lough, *Corporation Finance*, 49-64; Conyngton, *Corporate Organization and Management*, 39-48.)

Problem 2

Shall a Chain of Toy Shops Be Financed?

Recently the following advance information was privately circulated regarding the organization and financing of the United Toy Shops:

Two Big Objects

Two big objects will be attained through the establishment of a chain of United Toy Shops across the country. The American factories will have their business stabilized and be practically assured of a continuity of operation twelve months in the year, rather than depending upon a short seasonal rush. This fact, coupled with the ability of a chain store organization to buy in large quantities for a great many stores, will enable the American boy and girl to secure toys at a more stable price than is possible under the present methods of high-pressure seasonal demand.

A New Industry

Prior to the War, we depended on Germany and other countries for our toys. There was little incentive here for the investment of capital in the toy business. However, since the War and with the advent of high-grade mechanical toys, to take the place of foreign gimcracks, new factories by the hundreds started up, and the American toy makers began a career of production and development that has been equaled only in the automobile field. In fact, a new industry has been created in this country, jumping overnight from a production of a few million dollars to one approaching one hundred millions in 1920. The great toy fair held in New York this year opened our eyes to perhaps America's fastest growing industry, and just as we have led the world in automobile production, so we are already leading the world in toy production.

An All-Year Business

Toys are a product that do not seem to feel business depression, as it has been noticed that in periods of "hard times" toys are apt to sell even better than ever. Furthermore, just as the automobile business has been changed from a summer trade to an all-year-round one, so toys are coming into their own for all times of the year. Easter season, for example, is becoming as great a toy season as Christmas, and by the methods to be employed by United Toy Shops in publicity and advertising, the business will be a constant one throughout the year—with naturally increased demand around the various holidays.

Advance Financing

During the organization period of United Toy Shops and prior to the selection of officers, directors, etc., an opportunity is afforded to participate in the advance financing on a very satisfactory basis. This is a real chance to get into a big chain store enterprise at the very start. We believe this is the first time the public generally has been invited to participate in a retail chain store organization at the outset.

The Company as it progresses will need hundreds of active men and women for executive and other positions and those who participate in the advance financing have naturally an excellent opportunity along these lines.

Capitalization

United Toy Shops will be one holding company operating its various shops just as Woolworth's, Ligget's, etc., are operated from one main office with district offices and managers.

Capitalization of the Company is to be as follows:

8% Gold Coupon Ten Year Debenture Bonds	$1,000,000
Class A Common Stock No Par Value	50,000 shares
Class B Common Stock No Par Value	5,000 shares

Stock to be Full Paid and Non-Assessable.

Class B stock is to be owned by the founders, but will not receive any dividends until the Company has earned at least $5,000,000 in any year—that is, Class A stock will be entitled to dividends up to $100 a share annually before any dividends are paid on Class B shares. Then the balance will be divided between the two classes.

As the Class A stock will be sold in a large measure, according to present plans, with the Debenture Bonds, it is seen that the stock will no doubt be owned chiefly by the public and not controlled by any special interests.

The plans are for the Company to make application to list both the Debenture Bonds and Class A shares on the New York Stock Exchange when the Company is fully financed.

Earnings

Careful consideration has been given to the prospective earnings of United Toy Shops. Based on the fact that the profit in toys is large and that the Company will no doubt do a good mail-order business from each store through its catalogs, distributed in the towns surrounding the city where there is a shop, in addition to the sales in the shop, it is felt that a profit of approximately $70 a day per shop is very conservative. This would amount to about $20,000 annually. One hundred shops on this basis would show a profit of $2,000,000 a year, which would be equivalent to nearly $40 per share on the entire 50,000 shares of Class A stock.

Three hundred shops on this basis would thus readily show earnings of $100 per share on the Class A stock. What the possibilities are in years to come when the Company is able to operate, say, 1,000 shops, it is difficult to estimate.

That the above figures are reasonable can be seen from the fact that Woolworth's net income last year was around $10,000,000, selling five- and ten-cent articles, whereas the average purchase at a United Toy Shop would no doubt be several times that of a Woolworth store, and a great deal larger volume of business per store is expected with larger profits per dollar sale and smaller selling or clerk hire expense.

Subscription Prices

Subscriptions may be placed for United Toy Shop securities on the following basis:

$100 Face Value Debenture Bonds and 10 Shares Class A stock @ $100.

$200 Face Value Debenture Bonds and 20 shares Class A stock @ $200.

$300 Face Value Debenture Bonds and 30 shares Class A stock @ $300.

$400 Face Value Debenture Bonds and 40 shares Class A stock @ $400.

$500 Face Value Debenture Bonds and 50 shares Class A stock @ $500.

Larger units in proportion. Above special offer is for immediate acceptance for a limited amount only and will positively be withdrawn as soon as organization of Company is completed, after which the Class A stock will be sold at a price consistent with its possible earning power and the showing of the Company.

What United Toys Offers as an Investment Possibility

Taking figures under "Earnings" as a basis, United Toys seems to offer an excellent investment possibility.

Figuring on a subscription of say $300, you receive $300 in Debenture Bonds to yield 8% yearly and 30 shares of Class A stock given as a bonus.

With 100 shops showing earnings of around $40 a share, this will be equivalent to $1,200 on your 30 Class A shares. With 300 shops in operation and estimating dividends at $100 a share, this would net you $3,000 annually. In this case the value of your shares, figuring on a basis of 10% for valuation, would be around $30,000.

While we cannot make any promises or guarantees of any kind with reference to earnings or dividends of United Toys, yet we feel that the Class A shares offer unusual speculative possibilities, and even the large possible returns cited above are small compared to what other concerns have paid to those who invested at the beginning. The man who invested $500 in United Cigars at the beginning is said to have earnings from the stock of $4,000 a year and the stock to be worth around $40,000.

We feel that the toy business will be one of our leading industrials within a few years, and on this basis United Toy Shops should justify all our expectations of earning power.

Subscription Understanding

Subscriptions are now being received for the securities of United Toy Shops with the understanding that the name

United Toy Shops, Inc.

has been approved by the Secretary of State of New York, and of other states, and that the corporation papers will be put through as soon as all legal details have been taken care of, final draft of charter approved, etc.

All subscriptions are being received by the United Toy Shops Organization, to whom checks must be made out. The United Toy Shops Organization guarantees to deliver the bonds and stock as specified in subscription form if same is accepted.

Questions

1. Do you approve of launching such an enterprise at this time?
2. Do you approve of the financing by means of debenture bonds?
3. What is your opinion as to the earning power and future prospects of this concern, granting that it can be financed?
4. What advice would you give to a friend asking you whether he should invest in this proposition?

Problem 3

Shall a Company for Exploiting a New Mechanical Device be Launched?

A small investment house sends out the following account of the method by which a machine known as the Kuick Koin Kalkulator is to make money for those who invest in the company formed to exploit the patent rights:

KUICK KOIN KALKULATOR

This machine is designed to take care of the postage stamp business in public places, such as hotels, office buildings, drug stores, railway stations or any place where the sale of postage stamps has become a nuisance. This machine actually does take care of the postage stamp business because it will accept any coin from a nickel to a 25¢ piece and sell to the customer any quantity of either 2¢ or 1¢ stamps or both, which may be desired, and deduct the amount purchased from the coin inserted and give back the change due, less 1¢. The change is always short 1¢ because each and every time this machine operates it charges 1¢ for service so that every time the machine is operated it earns 1¢ for itself.

From a mechanical standpoint this machine is a very remarkable machine because it is called upon constantly to do varying work. All coins are inserted in the same inlet slot, and the same push-button is used whether you buy one stamp or 24¢ worth of stamps, and the same change-button is used whether you are getting change for a nickle or change for a 25¢ piece. The machine is the same class of mechanism as cash registers, adding machines, and typewriters, but unlike these machines our machine is fool-proof. Operators have to be taught how to operate cash registers, adding machines and typewriters or they will ruin the machines, while our machine cannot be gotten out of commission by the operator. This feature of the machine is essential because the machine is left by itself to take care of its customers as well as itself. The machine always deals correctly with the operator, and if for any reason the machine becomes exhausted of its supply of postage stamps or change so that it cannot accommodate the customer, it immediately locks itself up so that it cannot be operated until its merchandise is replenished.

The machine is equipped with a very clever coin-detecting mechanism and throws out spurious coins and slugs as well as foreign money. For instance, a Canadian 25¢ piece will immediately be returned to the customer as will a telephone slug or any such slug made.

The machine as a machine is a complete and individual business in itself. It takes care of itself in every way. It also takes care of the customers and it records each and every deal that is made and balances its cash after every transaction, so that any time we call upon the machine we know exactly how much the machine has earned, and so on, so that the machine actually does run a business of its own, as well as do its own bookkeeping and cashier work.

To sum up the whole machine from a machine or mechanism standpoint, it is considered by all engineers who have investigated it as well as worked upon it, to be the most remarkable piece of mechanism ever completed and perfected, and all engineers know as soon as they look at this machine, that it was developed only after many years of work and after the expenditure of many hundreds of thousands of dollars.

This because the machine is entirely new from an invention standpoint and there is nothing to date of record in the Patent Office from which assistance could be gotten in the development of this machine, because it is the first machine ever attempted which would sell a varying quantity of merchandise out of one coin. The machine goes farther because it sells varying quantities of varying commodities, out of either one coin or varying coins.

Plan of Operation

These machines are not for sale but are being placed in public places, such as above mentioned. The reason the machine is built to sell postage stamps is because the postage stamp business is one of the largest lines of business in America in actual volume of dollars and cents and it is the only business which is actually built up and in existence which no one wants who has it. Whenever a concern is found which has a nice large postage stamp business, we find they are very anxious to unload this business on someone else, because it is a constant nuisance to them as well as a constant expense, so that we are relieved of the common cost in selling devices of this character, and the selling cost of such machines has been proven to be very high. All we have to do is to manufacture our machines and haul them around and install them in places where they have the stamp business already established for us. Immediately after the machine is installed it begins to earn money, real cash money, and it continues to do this earning practically indefinitely.

Looking our whole proposition over from every angle and basing our possible earnings on machines which are actually in operation and which have been in operation for a period ranging from one and one-half years to six months, it does not seem as though there is any limit to the possibilities for big profits in this business, because on an output of five thousand machines per year we could hardly take care of the new drug stores, new hotels, new office buildings, etc., which are being opened up each year in the United States. In addition to this, the stamp business is doubling and has doubled every five years in the large cities, ever since the Government took over the operation of the postage stamp business. Some of the cities have doubled their stamp business every two years for a period of years. The postage stamp business of the entire United States has doubled on an average of every eight years, but, of course, the cities increase faster than the rural districts, hence the reason for the cities doubling every five years. This ratio of increase is certainly to continue because mailings constantly increase with the increase of education.

There are just three questions to be decided in a person's mind as to whether or not this proposition will be a success. The questions follow:

First: Does the machine do the work?
Second: Is there a field for the machine?
Third: Will the public pay the penny toll for the service?

Answering the above:

First: Four machines placed for six months in the Grand Central Station earned $6 to $8 per day. One machine at the Morrison Hotel in Chicago earned over $1,500 per year for three years.

Second: There is certainly a field for the machine because 90% of the postage stamps sold in large cities to the people who actually put the stamps on the mailings are retailed outside of the post-office.

Third: People are now paying the toll which this machine exacts and are doing it gracefully. By standing around one of these machines which is being operated by the public one will learn that every person who works this machine thinks it is worth the money and they all marvel at how the machine can accomplish what it does. Even though we had not already proven that the public would pay the toll, it has been proven many times in recent years that the public are willing to pay for service provided that by paying for the service, they can save time or save annoying someone else, and it is a proven fact that any device which saves time and sells service is a success and always a big money maker.

Our proposition is strictly a public service proposition and is not unlike the telephone, which is nothing more or less than a time saver. If you want to mail a letter you have to have a postage stamp and you have the privilege of paying us for serving you or walking to the post-office and securing a postage stamp at its face value. You have the same proposition in the telephone because you can always walk or ride to where the party is to whom you want to talk, but in most cases it is good business to pay a nickel and use the telephone. The difference between our proposition and the telephone is that one telephone is no good to anyone and will make no money, a complete exchange system being necessary before the telephone system can be operated, while in our proposition each machine is a money maker itself and has no connection with any other machine and no wire connections and no franchises or central girls are necessary to the machine in order that it earn money.

There never has been another proposition in the world, of which we have been informed, which had as many attractive features connected with it as this proposition, which has a greater field in which to expand, and it would be silly for any man to even assume what the ultimate earnings of this proposition will be.

Questions

1. Discuss critically the claims made for this machine as a money maker.

2. Granting that the machine itself is all that is claimed, do you think that a business launched to deal in the machines would be a financial success?

3. Assuming that you favor the launching of this new enterprise,

   (*a*) How do you think the proposition should be financed?

   (*b*) What form of organization should be followed?

   (*c*) Should the concern manufacture its own machines?

(Reference: Conyngton, *Financing an Enterprise*, 81-94, 147-163.(

Problem 4

Harnessing the Tides!

On January 1st, 1921, the following material, with illustrations, occupied a full page of a widely read and very conservative eastern daily:

New Year's Greetings to the people of New England from the Universal Tide Power Company!

(*Author's note:*—Under this were photographs of the pleasant conditions enjoyed by the "subscribers to the Universal Tide Power Company" whether at home, on the railways, or in the factories.)

Do you want to eliminate your coal bill? If so, you are cordially invited to call at the home of the Universal Tide Power Company.

The Knowlton Hydraulic Air Motor, which generates light, heat and power from the tides. Patents issued in the United States, Canada, Argentina, Chili, England and France. Demonstration plant now under construction.

The Universal Tide Power Company is organized under the laws of Massachusetts and capitalized at $10,000,000.

Patent rights to first town accepting.

New England community building initial tide power plant will get preference.

One of the greatest boons that this northern climate has ever known will come when the method invented by John A. Knowlton to generate power from the tides is put into practice. A demonstration plant to show the practicality of this system is now being built at East Saugus by the Universal Tide Power Company.

"As inventor of the Knowlton hydraulic air motor and treasurer of the Universal Tide Power Company," declared Mr. Knowlton, "it has been my great desire to put heat in the homes at a minimum cost."

This is the season of the year which above all others brings with it the desire to give, to help, and in that spirit the company is renewing its offer of the past and will give the rights free to the first city of Massachusetts or the first New England state which will build a plant. The city or state the first to build, would be able to furnish not only the needed heat to its people, but light and power as well, and all for a nominal cost to them. Further, this could not fail to lower taxes, which together with the low cost of heating, should be followed by lower rents. The Universal Tide Power Company has sent a letter making this offer to the mayor of every city in Massachusetts and to the Governor of each of the New England states.

With the completion of the demonstration plant, within the next few months, this offer will be withdrawn. The company is not making this offer for selfish gain, but from our honest desire to serve the public well, and as practical expression of gratitude to the masses of the people of New England whose generous support has made its success possible. While the people will necessarily benefit eventually from the installation of tide power plants the added saving to them in money from the prompt acceptance of this offer would be great and relief from dependence upon coal would be immediate.

I am making this public announcement for the Universal Tide Power Company because it can serve the people only through the officials who represent them, and desire the people of this state and of New England to know that this opportunity is theirs, and that only through inaction on the part of their executives can it be lost to them.

I believe the company will receive the cooperation from these officials which the people have a right to expect, and I have cordially invited them to send the best hydraulic engineers which the Government—state or nation—can furnish, to inspect the Universal Tide Power plant at East Saugus, see the plans and specifications and the working model at the home office, and to make their expert opinions known.

Six months later the company was sending out literature as follows:

The Press unanimously declare that power can be derived from the tides.

Understanding your opportunity pays.

BILLIONS IN INVENTIONS

An estimate made ten years ago shows that American manufactures, which have for their foundation inventions—fully protected by Government patents—amounted to the enormous sum of $21,000,000,000.

The men and women who get these billions are the men and women who invested in inventions and the industries inventions build. This is Your Opportunity!

ACT NOW! Price of Shares Now $3.00 DON'T DELAY

Bonus on All Cash Sales

CASH

From One Share up for Cash

$ 75.00 buys 27 Shares
$ 150.00 buys 55 Shares
$ 300.00 buys 110 Shares
$ 600.00 buys 220 Shares
$1050.00 buys 385 Shares

TERM PAYMENTS

$75.00 buys 25 Shares $15 down and 4 monthly payments of $15.

$150.00 buys 50 Shares $30 down and 4 monthly payments of $30.

$300.00 buys 100 Shares $60 down and 4 monthly payments of $60.

$600.00 buys 200 Shares $120 down and 4 monthly payments of $120.

$1050.00 buys 350 Shares $210 down and 4 monthly payments of $210.

FINANCES

The financial standing of the Universal Tide Power Company is very satisfactory. We have no debts, our liabilities consisting of outstanding shares and current bills only. Our assets consist of deposits in the bank. Bills collectible amounting to a considerable sum—our holdings at Saugus, to which may be added the value of work done there, and several hundreds of dollars worth of other properties; such as models, films and projectors, office furniture, tools and automobiles used in our business.

IMPORTANT: The plant now being built by this company at East Saugus, Massachusetts, is for demonstration purposes only. Dividends and profits will come later from the sale of patent rights.

This invention is patented in six countries and is designed to utilize the tremendous possibilities of the waste waters of the world.

After installation there will be but slight cost for maintenance of plant, the ENERGY for which (WATER) will cost nothing, against the ever-increasing cost of coal.

THE TIDES WILL PERSIST IN WORKING PERPETUALLY,
THUS MAY THE USE OF COAL BE ELIMINATED

Price of Shares soon to Advance

Questions

1. Granting that the men back of this proposition are honest, and granting that electricity can be generated in the way which they state, do you think that there is any financial justification for the launching of this concern? Why?

2. Specifically, what important considerations, if any, appear to you to have been overlooked in connection with this proposition?

3. Assuming for the moment that so far as can be determined the company will *ultimately* prove

successful, do you believe that it should be financed in the way indicated?

(Reference: Conyngton, and Jones, *Investments*, 310-328.)

Problem 5

Launching a Fire Insurance Company in 1921

Early in 1921 a group of men in Wisconsin were endeavoring to launch a new fire insurance company. In their attempt to secure money for financing this proposition, they stressed particularly three things:

In the first place they attempted to show by means of statistics that fire insurance companies both in number and in volume of business done had by no means increased in proportion to the actual increase in building valuation during the last few years.

Secondly, they showed that in proportion to the building valuation in the State, people in Wisconsin were carrying far less fire insurance than in most of the larger states, and relative to the possibilities for fire insurance business, the State was not well supplied with fire insurance companies. Hence there should be a very good field for a new fire insurance company.

Finally, they suggested that the fire insurance business, as demonstrated by the experience of the old-line companies in the Eastern States, is a highly profitable undertaking with relatively steady earnings.

Questions

1. Should you expect that the launching of a new fire insurance company at the time and place indicated was justified?

2. What is your opinion of the reasons given by the promoters for the formation of this company?

3. Do you think it desirable that a fire insurance company be operated as a corporation or as a mutual benefit association?

(Reference: Zartman and Price, *Property Insurance*, 121-147, 309-322.)

4. If the attempt had been made to launch a new life insurance company at the same time and place, analogous arguments having been presented by the promoters, what would your answer have been?

(Reference: Zartman and Price, *Personal Insurance*, 75-94, 297-309.)

PROBLEM 6

AN ATTEMPT AT FINANCING A COMMERCIAL PAPER HOUSE

In May, 1921, the following prospectus of a new stock issue appeared privately in Boston:

Tax Free in Massachusetts

NEW ISSUE Free of Normal Federal Income Tax FIRST OFFERING

$350,000

.....................Company

Established 1916 (A Massachusetts Corporation) Incorporated 1921

8% CUMULATIVE PREFERRED STOCK
Par Value $100

Redeemable at $110 and accrued dividend

Dividends payable quarterly on the first day of January, April, July and October.

1,750 Shares Common Stock
No Par Value

The following is summarized from a letter of Mr.........., President:

The Company is an established commercial paper house. It maintains offices at ...., Devonshire Street, Boston, and will establish and maintain offices in the principal financial centers.

The capital is always liquid and has been turned over better than 110 times in the year of 1920, yielding a gross profit of 30% on its capital.

Among the company's clients are some of the leading manufacturing and mercantile companies in the country. The house is favorably known to, and does business with, the leading banks.

The business in which this company is engaged is permanent and is becoming of greater importance every year.

The growth of the business since 1916 has been steady and conservative with all safety. Profits have also increased steadily each year.

We offer this stock in units of:

2 Shares of 8% Cumulative Preferred (par value $100 per share).

1 Share of Common Stock (no par value).

Accompanying the prospectus was a letter from the president of the new company, from which the following excerpts are made:

BUSINESS

COMMERCIAL PAPER BROKERS—The primary business of a commercial paper house is dealing in three to six months' notes of manufacturing and mercantile concerns, whose credit is of sufficiently high standing, disposing of the same to banks who purchase for short-time investment as secondary reserve. These notes being rediscountable with the Federal Reserve Bank when having not more than ninety days to run.

SALES AND EARNINGS

For the past five years we give the number of times our capital was turned over and our gross profit each year.

	Capital Turned Over	Gross Profit
1916	50 times	18%
1917	87 "	23%
1918	95 "	24%
1919	100 "	28%
1920	110 "	30%

Customers

The customers on our books at this time include cotton manufacturers, rubber companies, woolen mills, candy companies, shoe and leather concerns, jobbers and various mercantile businesses.

Commercial Paper Scope

National in Scope—About four billion dollars of commercial paper is sold by brokers annually. Practically all large manufacturing, mercantile, and textile concerns now seek the open market for temporary capital through the sale of their short-time notes to commercial paper brokers.

Offices are established in principal financial centers, and business is solicited from corporations and firms of highest standing, and their paper distributed to banks in the section of the country where funds are most plentiful at the moment, as it may often happen that the demand for funds for business is heavy in the East, while the banks in the Middle West have surplus funds to loan, or vice versa.

There are only about fifteen large commercial paper houses in the country, most of which are operated as partnerships. They occupy a unique position in the banking world, cooperating as they do with the banks and soundest commercial establishments, and they enjoy the highest reputations.

Capital

With a capital of $1,350,000 paid in, this company should take a position as one of the leading commercial paper houses of the country. This amount paid in would allow us to do a business of at least $125,000,000 a year.

Profits

Assuming we turn our capital but one hundred times a year and make a gross profit of but 25%, we would show the following profit on our capital:

Capital			$1,250,000
Estimated gross profit		$312,500	
8% Preferred Stock	$100,000		
Expenses, Taxes, etc.	75,000		
	$175,000	175,000	
Net		$137,500	
Sinking-Fund (Director's Discretion not to exceed 25%)		34,250	
Balance		$103,250	

Leaving a balance of $103,250 applicable to the common stock, or $8.26 per share.

Safety

Under the present methods of credit investigations and audits by certified public accountants, the risk from loss is very small. The writer cannot recall in over twenty years' experience a single failure of a commercial paper house.

Liquidation

This Company deals, as stated above, only in obligations of the strongest corporations and firms, which are approved by the most conservative banks, and it can readily be seen that its assets, consisting as they do of notes and acceptances having *not more than six months to run, completely liquidate themselves in that period of time.*

Questions

1. Analyze this prospectus critically.
2. Do you approve of this method of securing capital for a commercial paper house?
3. Does this seem to you to be a desirable time for launching a new commercial paper house, or expanding an old one?
4. Who should you expect to buy this stock?
5. Assuming yourself to be the president of an industrial concern, would you wish to sell your commercial paper through this house?
6. As a buyer of commercial paper, should you be disposed to purchase the notes sold by this house?
7. Would you expect that the services of university graduates, with business school training, could be secured to assist in the stock-selling campaign?
8. What is your prediction as to the future of this concern?

(References: Phillips, *Bank Credit*, 260-262; Moulton, *Financial Organization*, 428-430.)

Problem 7

Launching a Small Investment Company in 1921

The . . . . . . Investment Company was organized in 1921 with a small amount of capital privately subscribed. Its chief purpose was to act as a distributor of the shares of the . . . . . . Company described in Problem 6. The officers further said that they expect to make a good deal of money buying and selling securities of such well-known concerns as the Cities Service Company, as well as of some concerns not so well known and of rather uncertain financial standing.

Questions

1. What is your opinion as to the desirability of launching this business from the financial point of view?
2. What should you expect its future to be?
3. Do you think an investment banking house should be incorporated or unincorporated?
4. From the point of view of incorporation, is a commercial bank in any different position from an investment banking house?

(References: Conyngton, 639-651; Moulton, 215-217.)

PART II

SOURCES OF CAPITAL

CHAPTER III

THE PROBLEMS OF RAISING FIXED CAPITAL

References:

Collver, *How to Analyze Industrial Securities.*

*Conyngton, *Financing an Enterprise*, 165–651.

Dewing, *Financial Policy of Corporations*, Vol. I. (*passim*) and *Vol. II, 48–60, 104–168.

*Jones, *Investments*, 218–344, and *passim.*

*Lough, *Business Finance*, 64–104, 130–353.

Lough, *Corporation Finance*, Chapters VI, VII, IX–XIV, XVI–XIX.

*Lyon, *Corporation Finance*, Part I, p. 1–143, 166–219, also Part II.

Mead *Corporation Finance*, Chapters IV–XIII, XIX–XXVI.

Regan, *Financing a Business*, 48–122.

*Walker, *Corporation Finance*, 290–310.

MUCH depends upon the methods whereby a business concern is originally financed. Financial difficulties frequently arise from the adoption of a plan not suited to the nature of the industry, the size of the organization, or the period in the Business Cycle. Many concerns expand too soon. The usual tendency is to overbuild. Often a business man who is highly successful as an organizer, a producer, or a seller, has very nebulous ideas regarding the best methods of financing. The results of this lack of balance are often highly disastrous.

In the problems which follow, some of the more important aspects of the subject of Fixed Capital financing are touched upon. Many of these problems are closely related to those given in Chapters II and V.

Exercise I

How Much Capital is Needed?

Estimate the minimum amount of capital needed to begin any one of the following different kinds of businesses, indicating clearly the considerations involved and the reasons for your conclusions:

1. An Agricultural Implement Factory
2. An Automobile Factory
3. A Candy Factory
4. A Chemical Plant
5. A Cotton Mill
6. A Cutlery Factory
7. A Hosiery Mill
8. A Paper Mill
9. A Pottery
10. A Printing Establishment
11. A Rubber Tire Factory
12. A Shoe Factory
13. A Steam Laundry
14. A Steel Plant
15. A Watch and Clock Factory
16. A Woolen Mill

(Suggested references: Massachusetts, *Statistics of Manufactures*; U. S. Census, 1910, Vol. VIII, *Manufactures*, Chapter X; Regan, *Financing a Business*, 48–67; Walker, *Corporation Finance*, 206–212.)

A. GENERAL METHODS OF RAISING FIXED CAPITAL

Problem 8

General Problem in Raising Fixed Capital for a Small Business

Two printers in an Iowa town who had decided to take over a plant, got together one evening to figure out how to raise the necessary money. Every conceivable method of financing their plant was discussed, item by item; material resources, loans, investments.

Fredericks had a house and lot worth three thousand dollars mortgaged for one thousand dollars. Barnes had several influential friends he thought might consent to a loan, some stock in a doubtful proposition, and his life insurance. Together they had eight hundred dollars in cash.

The first suggestion, the issue of stock, involved the probable interference of stockholders, and furthermore they saw that it would be as easy to secure outright lenders as investors. They could get no initial help from supply houses because the plant was already equipped and the owner demanded cash. The moneyed partner offered nearly the same objections as the stock issue. Finally they decided that to borrow on all their available resources would almost finance the enterprise. They did this:

Fredericks raised:	
On house and lot by second mortgage	$ 800
On household effects	200
Cash	400
	$1400
Barnes raised:	
From friends on personal note	$ 500
On his life insurance	300
On his $1000 unlisted stock	200
Cash	400
	$1400

Twenty-eight hundred dollars was the total amount they were thus able to raise. They needed thirty-two hundred dollars to buy out the plant, and an additional five hundred dollars for their expenses. They worked together now, and fortunately they had begun to plan far enough ahead so that there was still time to proceed with caution. The partner was the only recourse. First they canvassed among their friends. Those who had money, however, had already been drawn upon for loans. As a last resort they advertised for another investor. From among those who replied they found one man who consented to put seven hundred dollars into the business and remain a silent partner. He had been watching the records of the printers and was satisfied that he was making a good investment.

This amount raised their capital to thirty-five hundred dollars. They still needed two hundred dollars.

This was for a part of the running expense. To cover this amount they solicited work in advance. The owner of the building where the plant was situated gave an order for work which he accepted in payment of the rent. The other minor expenses were met in the same way.

(Quoted from Shaw, *How to Finance a Business*, 13–15.)

Questions

1. Examine critically the arguments of these two men.
2. What seem to you to be the strong or weak points of this plan of financing?
3. Do you see any other alternatives than those selected?

Problem 9

Dealer Help in Financing Fixed Capital

It is common for manufacturers of machinery used by printers to sell on receipt of an initial payment, frequently not higher than one-third of the price, and to take the balance on the customer's notes payable over a considerable period of time. This time is frequently extended over two or three years.

Questions

1. Do you approve of this policy?
2. In what specific ways might this policy affect:

    (*a*) The finances of the newly organized printing establishments,

    (*b*) The finances of the old established printing concerns?

Problem 10

Two Simple Methods of Financing a New Pottery

A. Some twenty-five or thirty years ago, several business men in a small town in the Middle West, decided that it would be profitable to build a pottery. Although none of them knew much about the business from actual experience, they had friends in an adjoining city who had found the pottery industry very profitable. Accordingly, they formed a partnership agreement, each putting into the business a few thousand dollars. No money was borrowed. After a few years of up's and down's, the management discovered that their knowledge of the market was not sufficient to enable them to get orders enough to make the business profitable. Accordingly, they secured for manager a man who was known as a first-class salesman of chinaware, in the hope that he would bring to the business what they found lacking in themselves.

B. To the same town, a few years later, came a man whose entire life had been spent in the pottery business. He had worked himself up from the lowest paid jobs to the position of superintendent in a pottery in a nearby city. He had no capital of his own, but felt that he could make a big success if he could have an opportunity to organize and manage his own factory. Accordingly, he proposed the following plan to the people of the town, assuring them that, as a result of the business activity and increased property values which would come through the establishing of a new industry, they would be the decided gainers. The proposals adopted were as follows:

(*a*) The factory site was donated by one of the well-to-do farmers on the outskirts of the town, who hoped to be able, after the business was started, to sell a good amount of his land for town lots.

(*b*) Through a public common stock subscription of $15,000, raised to a large extent by the business men who expected to be the ultimate gainers, enough money was secured to erect the building.

(*c*) In order to raise enough money to equip the plant, shares of preferred stock were sold to people of the community, many of whom had already subscribed to the common stock. Thus about $20,000 was obtained.

(*d*) The additional amount needed until the business could get on its feet, about $5,000, was secured by placing a mortgage on the property which was to be carried by the local bank.

The business was incorporated with the promoter as president and general manager, and he received $15,100 in common stock as his "bonus."

Questions

1 Which of the plans appears to you to have been the more satisfactory? Why?

2. Examine the strength and weakness of each.

3. What would be your prediction of their success?

Problem 11

Financing a Small Rubber Tire Factory

In 1909 a new rubber tire plant was launched in a middle western state by a man whose life had been spent in the hotel business in the city of Pittsburgh. He had $50,000 of his own to put into the business, and it was found that $500,000 more would be needed in order to put the factory in running shape.

Accordingly, a corporation was formed, all the common stock, with no par value, being issued to the promoter and his family; while the additional capital was raised by the sale of preferred stock, largely to people in the locality. The dividends on the preferred stock were cumulative at 7 per cent, and it was to be redeemed by the company at 110, at its option, within next five the years after a two-year period had expired.

The funds for retiring the preferred stock were secured largely through the sale of additional common stock, after the concern began to do a fair business and the prospects seemed good. In selling the new common stock the company's chief selling arguments were as follows:

(*a*) The factory had brought many new residents to the town, and so had made more business for all and had greatly increased property values.

(*b*) Those who had invested in the common stock of the Firestone and Goodyear companies had within a few years received in dividends many times their original investment.

Questions

1. Do you consider this a satisfactory plan of financing for the enterprise in question? State your reason clearly.
2. Would you have advised a friend to subscribe to the new common stock of the company in 1915? In 1919?

Problem 12

Public Financing of a Hotel

In January, 1921, the following news item appeared in a city paper:

> That Providence may realize on scheduled time its long-cherished project of having one of the noteworthy hotels of the country, the contractors who are building the $5,000,000 structure are pushing the work every hour every day except Sundays and holidays.

Interest in the development of this great hotel is general throughout Rhode Island, for the imposing 19-story structure has been financed largely by popular subscription. The scheme took concrete form under an impulse furnished by the Providence Chamber of Commerce. Aside from its importance as a much needed improvement to the now inadequate accommodations for the entertainment of traveling men and other visitors to this business city, the building will go far to develop the civic centre to which Providence people point with pride.

The first efforts of the chamber of commerce were made almost 10 years ago. The hope then was to have a 12-story building. High costs of labor and other commodities because of the war discouraged the project, and the matter lay quiescent for awhile. It was then revived, and with its revival the ambition grew to one for a 14-story building, then for 16 stories and finally the present plan for 19 stories was settled on.

When the armistice was signed the chamber returned to its hotel enterprise with renewed energy. By hard teamwork, stock to the amount of $2,500,000 was sold by popular subscriptions. Large blocks of this stock were taken by corporations and financiers, mostly of Rhode Island; many shares were sold to relatively small investors.

Hundreds of clerks and others in Providence hold stock in the project. The spirit behind taking this stock was deemed to be not that of gain so much as registering faith in the future of Providence. The slogan of the chamber, "Do it for Providence," made an excellent motto for this campaign.

The Providence-Biltmore Hotel is to be of steel frame construction, with limestone, brick and granite as its principal materials. The architectural style will be simple and colonial, in keeping with the traditions of Providence. The building will be fireproof in every particular, its architects assert.

It will contain 560 rooms, arranged to accommodate 800 guests. The 18th and 19th floors will be devoted mainly to a ballroom, supper rooms and other facilities for social functions. The 19th story will be so arranged that it can be used as a roof garden in summer.

Those who have been working for the project say they have at last succeeded in putting their city on the hotel map and believe that the Biltmore will give Providence a chance to become one of the important convention cities in the country.

Question

Do you approve of this plan for financing the construction of a hotel?

B. VALUATION OF INTANGIBLES

Problem 13

Valuation of Patents and Other Intangibles in an Old Concern

The.......... Company, engaged in the making of gear shapers, was solely the creation of one man's brain. It had been operating for about twenty years. During this time the aim had been to perfect gear cutters which would be as accurate as human ingenuity could make them. The man at the head of the concern thought little of profits and put all the earnings back into the business. Further, a large amount of money was spent in experimenting with a view to developing the most effective machinery for making the output. In many cases, long years of development lay back of an apparently simple piece of machinery. Most of the machines were patented. There was no other concern in the United States which was able to turn out such perfect gear cutters and appliances. The product was used extensively by practically all automobile manufacturing concerns and automobile accessory companies. The market was more than nation-wide, and since no other concern could make as desirable a product, the.......... Company may be said to have enjoyed a monopoly.

A year or two ago, the man at the head of the concern realized that he was growing old, and that it would probably be desirable to reorganize the business and distribute the ownership more widely. Consequently he wished to know just what the value of his business was, with a view to capitalizing the enterprise at a reasonable figure.

Various accountants and engineers worked over the proposition in detail, and it was finally agreed that the capitalization should be on the basis of 40 per cent for tangible assets and 60 per cent for intangibles. The latter included development expenses, 10 per cent; and patent rights, 50 per cent.

Questions

1. In a business of this sort, suggest how the engineers might arrive at a fair value for the patent rights.
2. Do you believe that it was a wise policy for the ....Company to patent most of its machines?
3. Do you believe that it would have been desirable for the..........Company to capitalize its intangibles in the manner indicated?
4. From the point of view of selling the common stock of this company to effect a change in ownership, do you see any advantages or disadvantages in capitalizing the intangibles at a high rate?
5. Assuming that the..........Company had been producing goods which were distributed under a trade-mark, should you have considered the case in favor of the capitalization of intangibles to be stronger or weaker than under the present situation?

(Reference: Conyngton, *Financing an Enterprise*, 188–227).

Problem 14

Valuation of Patents in a New Concern

An officer of a concern organized early in 1921 gives the following account of the purpose of the concern and the financial plan under which it has been organized:

A refrigeration engineer, Brown, has made improvements in ice manufacturing processes which will lower the cost of manufacture about 40 per cent. These improvements are being patented and the patents properly protected. This engineer wished to build a small ice manufacturing plant, partly for the profit to be realized from the plant itself, and partly for the purpose of demonstrating the value of his improvements. The plant which Brown decided to build will produce 25 tons of ice a day at a profit of more than $3 per ton in excess of that earned by the ordinary plant. This profit in itself will mean a very considerable income from the business, but it is planned further to make arrangements with other ice manufacturers which will allow them to use the improved methods through the payment of a royalty of 50¢ per ton. Thus it is expected that the profits will constantly grow greater, as more ice manufacturers become interested in the new processes which will make money for all.

Brown had little capital of his own, but wished to maintain control of the business. In order to effect this end, a company was incorporated with an authorized issue of $125,000 in common stock and $125,000 in preferred stock. The engineer, Brown, received in exchange for his patent rights $62,510 of the common stock. The plant cost about $27,000, and $3,000 additional was needed to get the business under way. Hence the total amount, $30,000, was raised by selling preferred stock, cumulative at 7 per cent. With each share of preferred stock was given a share of common. The balance of the stock is for the present unissued.

The tentative balance sheet of the new company as of June 1, 1921, is as follows:

Assets

Plant and equipment	$ 27,000
Cash	3,000
Patent rights, etc	92,510
	$122,510

Liabilities

Common stock (outstanding)	$ 92,510
Preferred stock (outstanding)	30,000
	$122,510

Questions

1. Is the launching of a new business under the conditions outlined financially justifiable?

2. Is the company justified in putting so high a value on its patent rights, and other intangibles?

3. From the financial point of view, do you think it was advisable for this company to patent its new processes?

4. Do you consider the original plan of financing sound?

5. Would it have been good policy to raise the needed capital by selling stock to ice manufacturers?

6. What do you expect to be the financial future of this company?

Problem 15

General Problem on Capitalization of Goodwill

In recent years goodwill has been very highly valued by a number of large concerns as a basis for issuing common stock. Some outstanding examples are the following: B. F. Goodrich Company, $57,798,000; American Tobacco Company, $54,099,430; Woolworth Company, $50,000,000; Liggett & Meyers Tobacco Company (including trade-marks, brands, and the like), $40,709,711; Cluett Peabody Company, $18,-000,000 (out of total assets of $27,759,912).

Most of the tobacco and cigarette companies have valued their goodwill at a high figure. This is particularly true, also, of a number of the chain stores and rubber companies.

Questions

1. When, if at all, is it desirable to capitalize "goodwill"?

2. Does the size of the concern or the nature of the industry have any bearing on the question?

3. On what basis can the value of goodwill be properly arrived at?

(References: Conyngton, *Financing an Enterprise*, 340—357; Greendlinger, *Financial and Business Statements*, 120–138; Lough, *Business Finance*, 191–197; Simpson, *Capitalization of Goodwill, passim.*)

C. FINANCING CHANGES IN OWNERSHIP

Problem 16

Financing a Change of Ownership in a Closely Held Concern

The following problem is given by a Cleveland business man:

A manufacturing corporation, long established, and with a profitable business on staple commodities in every-day use, finds itself obliged to make some new financial arrangements. The total assets of the company are about $2,000,000.

When the company was organized some thirty-five years ago, the stock was held by ten or twelve different stockholders. From time to time, as opportunity offered, the president and treasurer of the company, who are its principal executive officers, have bought up such stock as was offered, until at the present time, they own practically all of the stock of the company in equal shares. The treasurer is the younger man of the two, and has been extremely active in the management of the company's affairs. He suffered from a severe attack of nervous prostration in December, 1919, and from that time until the present (Feb. 1, 1921) has taken no active part in the business.

The president was thoroughly experienced in all departments of the business and carried along the duties of the treasurer during his enforced absence, with the expectation that he would sooner or later recover and return to his usual line of work. He appeared to gain considerably in health during the summer of 1920, and there seemed every reason to expect that in a few months he would be back at his post. But on February 1, 1921, he informed his associate he had decided that he did not care to undertake active business again, and would prefer to sell out his interest.

The president was very loth to continue to carry on the business alone, as he had himself expected to retire, and had assumed that the treasurer, being several years his junior, would naturally take charge until the younger men in the employ of the company were fitted for the more important positions. Under the circumstances the president decided to offer the business for sale, so that both he and the treasurer might withdraw. It was advertised in the financial papers, and quite a number of responses were received, but it was at a time when financial conditions were unfavorable for new investments, and the offers received were not interesting. The records showed that the business had been steadily profitable, and the goodwill was important, but no capitalists seemed to be interested to take over the business on a basis which would recognize to the full extent the actual assets of the business.

The president of the company hesitated seriously at the thought of taking the whole thing on to his own shoulders, as the amount involved in the purchase would be large, and the work and responsibility very arduous, at least until such a time as the younger men in the employ of the company could be fitted and trained for the more important duties. But as there seemed no other way to preserve the goodwill and secure the full value of the work done for many years in building up the organization and establishing the quality of and creating a demand for the goods manufactured, he finally decided to undertake it.

Practically all of the property of the president was invested in the stock of the company. He had available outside but two or three hundred thousand dollars which could be used in the transaction.

The problem is, "How should this change of ownership be financed?" Conditions were such in the money market at the time that a sale of preferred stock was out of the question, except at a serious sacrifice. The possibility of issuing serial notes convertible after a time into preferred stock was also suggested. The best of good feeling existed between the officers, but the retiring treasurer felt that he should have a substantial part of his investment in cash.

Question

1. In what manner could the change be effected with the least disturbance and expense?

Problem 17

Financing a Complete Change of Ownership Which Will Make Possible a Continuance of the Policies of the Former Owners

The..........Company has been operated by a conservative management for many years. A real goodwill has been created and the equity of the few stockholders is very great, though not much money was originally invested in the concern. The company is really a very important ente prise in its locality, employing more workers than any other concern. The townspeople consider it one of the local institutions to which they can point with pride.

The men who have been responsible for the success of this concern are growing old and they have no sons or relatives who can succeed them in the management. Further, they hold the majority interest in the stock. If they should die the concern would be left wholly without proper guidance.

The problem now confronting these men is that of a reorganization or refinancing which will prevent the concern from being grabbed and exploited by outsiders after their death, and which will insure against any radical changes being made in the conduct of the business.

The present managers have asked for advice as to e financial policy which will be most likely to insure he continuance of the business along the lines which have made it a profitable and highly thought of local institution.

Question

What steps would you advise them to take in order to attain this end?

Problem 18

Refinancing to Effect a Change in Organization

The following data, submitted by a well-known business manager, show the financial condition of a manufacturing company in 1919:

Statement

Assets		Liabilities	
Cash..........	$34,323.95	Notes payable.	$315,000.00
Liberty Bonds.	115,000.00	Accounts payable........	91,451.76
Notes and Accounts receivable........	269,801.65	Reserve for income tax....	3,765.00
Inventories....	547,960.90	Capital stock..	510,000.00
Fixed assets...	187,015.93	Surplus.......	241,598.97
Prepaid expenses	7,713.30		
Total	$1,161,815.73	Total	$1,161,815.73

Record of Sales and Profits

	Sales	Profits
1916	$ 866,210.66	$ 77,225.28
1917	1,028,940.51	44,490.92
1918	1,035,251.41	65,190.02
1919 to July 16th	859,948.74	122,203.76

The business has been very conservatively managed. The full amount of depreciation has been written off each year and both the inventories and the fixed assets have been valued low.

This manufacturing business was originally started by one man. Later he took in two partners, and the partnership gave him notes to the amount of $300,000. These notes were carried with accounts and notes payable, and this constituted a quick liability which made the financial statement less satisfactory from the standpoint of an investment banker. Subsequently, in order to take in two additional partners who had no money, the business was incorporated, and $500,000 in 6 per cent cumulative preferred stock was issued. Of this stock, $300,000 was exchanged for the notes held by the original owner. The remaining $200,000 of preferred stock was owned by the other two members of the partnership; $10,000 of common stock was issued and held by the three owners and the two new partners. It was provided that the preferred stock should be non-voting so long as the dividends were paid regularly.

At the time of the incorporation a voting trust composed of two of the stockholders was formed to hold $200,000 of preferred stock and all the common stock. The receipts from the dividends on this stock were to be used by the voting trust to purchase the $300,000 preferred stock held by the founder of the business. In approximately two years $100,000 of the preferred stock had been retired. This leaves $200,000 preferred stock still to be retired. The voting trust holds the $100,000 that has been retired, and the dividends on this, as well as on the stock first placed in the hands of the voting trust, are used for liquidating the remainder of the preferred stock. If the present plan is carried out, it will take about two years to retire this sum.

The business is now an absolutely closed corporation, but one of the preferred stockholders wishes to have some plan adopted for refinancing the business in order that he may regain full rights on his preferred stock and dispose of it in the open market. The problem is: What plan shall be adopted for refinancing? The current rate of interest for such securities as this preferred stock is generally 7 per cent at the present time (1919).

Question

What possible solutions of this problem can you suggest?

D. FINANCING THE EXPANSION

Problem 19

Financing the Growth Solely Out of Earnings

About three generations ago, an ambitious young man who was trying to make his fortune in the jewelry business in Boston went on a business trip to New York City. While in the latter place he found that an attempt was being made to manufacture jewelry cases of different sorts out of fancy cardboard. Realizing that there might be possibilities for additional profit in this side-line, he bought a quantity of cardboard out of his cash in pocket and carried it with him back to the home of his father, who was a shoemaker in New Hampshire. Arrangements were made whereby the father, who had not made any particular success of his trade, would make up a number of jewelry cases in his own little shop, which the son planned to sell in Boston.

The distance between the place of manufacture and the possible market was relatively great, because poor means of transportation existed. Some market, however, was found for the goods turned out, so that the gross sales for the first year amounted to two or three thousand dollars.

In two or three years, as the sales began to increase, the father found it impossible to do all the work by hand, and accordingly designed a simple machine to do the cutting. All the proceeds of the business to date were used up in making this machine. However, within a short time the sales increased pretty rapidly and some net profits were made.

As the years went on, various members of the family still at home assisted in turning out the goods, and, as the scale of operations grew, the original "shop" was extended to the attic of the house and finally to the barn. As these quarters were outgrown, some of the work was parceled out to various families in the community, until finally a considerable number of people in the adjoining villages were engaged in helping make these jewelry cases. This, of course, necessitated the hiring of wagons and teams in order to collect the goods made by the people in the different localities.

However, the central factory was not built until about twelve years after the first orders had been placed. This factory was paid for in full out of the accumulated earnings of the past, which had resulted largely from the activities of the entire family. At this time the gross earnings were about $100,000 per year.

Questions

1. Comment on this method of starting a business.
2. Was it desirable to have the production carried on so far from the nearest market?
3. Should the factory have been built sooner?
4. Should money have been borrowed for this purpose?
5. Should you expect a business started in this way to prove successful or to have a long existence?

Problem 20

Ford's Method of Financing Expansion and Securing New Capital

The following paragraph appeared in the *Boston News Bureau* on January 22, 1921:

> "Mr. Ford never believed in finance, or banks, or stocks, or bonds. He wanted only one shareholder, and that himself, in the Ford Motor Company. When his factory closed, he turned to Finance, and Finance has turned to ask some questions of Mr. Ford. Indeed, rumor is abroad that Finance will dictate. He may call it Jew Finance or what he likes; others may call it common sense finance."

In this connection the following general suggestions regarding Ford's early methods of financing should be borne in mind:

About twenty years ago, when Ford was experimenting with the possibilities of cheap automobiles, he is said to have mortgaged his house, used up his wife's savings bank account, and borrowed some money from friends. When he finally succeeded in developing a car which customers were willing to buy, he found himself with barely sufficient funds to buy the needed material for making one car.

Finally a company was formed in 1903 with $28,000 capital paid in, Ford himself owning about one-fourth of the stock. The usual method of financing, however, was the hand-to-mouth method, until enough profits had been earned to make it possible to build proper factories. Within a few years after the business had been incorporated, the majority of the stock was held by Mr. Ford himself, and the remainder by a very small group of friends. In 1919 Ford bought out all the other stockholders at a price of nearly $100,000,000.

He has always been opposed to the policy of borrowing, except in recent years for temporary financing. Due to his unusual expansion policy, however, with a view to "digging automobiles out of the ground" and "eliminating the middleman," it had now apparently become necessary for the company to raise from $75,000,000 to $100,000,000 new capital. The fact that during the past year or two practically all the old officials had severed their connections with the company, seemed to point to something wrong internally. However, Ford himself denied that he needed any more funds and no loan was effected.

Incidentally, it is interesting to note that even though the total assets of the company are several hundred million dollars, the total amount of stock outstanding until 1920 has never exceeded $2,000,000, and there is no bonded indebtedness. The price of Ford cars was reduced in the autumn of 1920, while other makers were attempting to keep prices up. Though during 1920 more cars were sold than ever before, all of Ford's factories closed at the end of December and remained closed for several weeks. Within two or three months after the resumption of operations, however, the company was turning out more cars than ever before.

In the *Boston News Bureau* for July 14, 1921, the following eulogy regarding Ford's financing appeared:

How Ford Turned the Corner

A Brilliant Financing Scheme Which Turned 125,000 Surplus Cars Into Cash—Still the Sensation of the Motor Industry

Little more than six months ago Henry Ford had all but completed arrangements for borrowing $75,000,000 in the face of what appeared to be desperate necessity. His plants were closed, there was little demand for his cars. Ford owed the Government $55,000,000 in taxes. Notes for nearly $30,000,000, originally issued to buy out his minority partners, were due within a few weeks. Cash and treasury bonds together aggregated only $23,000,000. Unsold cars were piled high in the factory and choking salesrooms over the country. The public was not buying automobiles of any kind.

Yet Ford did not borrow from the banks, but paid them up, and today his sales are the greatest in history. How was the corner turned?

It was first turned by transferring the load. Marvelously recuperated markets completed the process. Ford pushed his 125,000 surplus automobiles up the hill off his own inventory account and into the hands of his 17,000 dealers. He shipped automobiles over the world to willing and unwilling consignees and drew against them. The tide of cash returned—$69,000,000 before April 1.

He also gave notes or acceptances to some extent for supplies and parts furnished when he started up.

* * * * * * *

The Ford recovery was probably the most inspiring event possible to the motor industry, and the manner in which it was accomplished was most salutary to the Ford organization. Had Ford been able to obtain the desired $75,000,000 without restrictions as to who should be his treasurer, company extravagances might have continued. Angered at banker "dictation" on one hand, and advised by banker friends on the other, he decided to go it alone. To make the hill he had to economize.

As a result, Ford combed his entire organization, and there is probably no more efficient industrial unit in the country today. Where he formerly employed 60,000 men to produce an average of 4,000 cars daily, he now obtains an output of 4,500 daily with 45,000 men. The $6 minimum wage had been retained, but foremen have been put to work, tasks doubled up, and adjustments averaging 20 per cent to 25 per cent reduction made in wages.

A day or two later most papers wrote eugolistic editorials about Mr. Ford, stating that there is "only one Henry Ford," and so on. They referred with great approval to the fact that he had offered to purchase the Government's nitrate plant and water-power developments at Muscle Shoals, Alabama, calling for an initial payment of $5,000,000, and the assumption of a 100-year lease necessitating an additional payment of $1,500,000 annually. Some of the very bankers who ridiculed Ford's financial methods a few months earlier, even suggested that he might be able to solve the great problem of the railroads in the United States, since he appeared to be effecting remarkable economies on the little road which he had bought.

Questions

1. Do you approve of Ford's early methods of financing?

2. What do you consider to be the strength or weakness of individual ownership of so large a business?

3. In days of business depression which concern is in the stronger position if it seems advisable to stop producing goods for a time, the concern whose stock is widely held and quoted on the stock exchange, and which perhaps has bonds outstanding, or the concern which is closely owned and has no bonded indebtedness?

4. Do you approve of the recent policy of "expansion" which appears to interest Henry Ford?

5. How do you account for the diametrically opposite points of view expressed in the papers at the two separate times?

6. What, in your mind, is the real explanation of Ford's financial success?

7. Granting that Ford continues to follow his more recently developed policies of "expansion" along lines not essential to effectiveness in *factory* production, what do you think his financial future will be?

Problem 21

Raising Fixed Capital Through a Novel Preferred Stock Issue

On July 6, 1921 the following notice appeared in the Boston *Transcript*:

Free from Massachusetts Income Tax and Normal Federal Income Tax

$1,250,000
NEW ENGLAND POWER COMPANY
6% Cumulative Preferred Stock

Preferred as to earnings and assets. Not subject to call.

Dividends payable quarterly, January 1, April 1, July 1, and October 1st.

Each share now offered carries a transferable profit-right certificate calling for payment of $2.50 additional to holder each year from July 1, 1921, to July 1, 1931, to be paid quarterly out of surplus or net earnings otherwise available for common dividend.

OUTSTANDING CAPITALIZATION
(With that proposed to be issued)

First Mortgage 5% Bonds	$9,054,000*
Preferred 6% Stock (shares $100 par value)	5,349,200
Common Stock	3,800,000

*Including $186,000 held alive in the Sinking Fund.

BUSINESS—The New England Power Company, through the New England Company Power System, supplies electric power at wholesale in about two hundred cities and towns including Boston, Providence, Worcester, Nashua, Fitchburg and Fall River.

PROPERTY—The New England Power Company has five hydro-electric generating stations with capacity of about 48,000 H. P. and with further available development of an additional 75,000 H. P. (This financing includes the building of plant No. 9, which will generate an additional 5,500 H. P.) The company also owns 250 miles of transmission and distribution lines, together with a reservoir at Somerset, Vermont, with a storage capacity of over 20,000,000,000 gallons.

SECURITY—The present properties of the Company, together with additional property resulting from the present financing, will have a valuation over $5,500,000 in excess of the amount of bonds and preferred stock to be outstanding upon completion of this financing.

EARNINGS—Earnings for the 12 months ended March 31, 1921, were over 2.93 times the preferred dividend requirements.

PRICE $100 and accrued dividend per share (with profit rights).

YIELDING 8½% for ten years, and 6% thereafter.

Questions

1. Why do you suppose this company issued preferred stock under the conditions indicated?
2. Would you consider this to be a satisfactory method of financing for an industrial concern?
3. Do you think it would have been possible for the average industrial concern to issue preferred stock in this way in 1921? Give your reasons.

Problem 22

Prospectus Covering the Flotation of a Small Bond Issue

January 1921 New Issue.

We Offer for Private Subscription

$160,000

FIBREBOARD COMPANY

(A Massachusetts Corporation)

First Mortgage 8% Sinking Fund Coupon Gold Notes

Dated January 3, 1921 Due January 1, 1936

Interest payable January and July 1st at the Old Colony Trust Company, Boston, Mass.

Coupon Notes in the denomination of $1,000, $500 and $100. Registerable as to principal

Subject to redemption at 100 and accrued interest up to and including July 1, 1926, and thereafter up to and including July 1, 1935, at 102 and accrued interest, upon sixty days' notice from the Company, except that the notes may be called by lot for sinking fund purposes on any interest date at 100 and accrued interest.

Old Colony Trust Company, Boston, Trustee

Sinking Fund

The company agrees that until the entire issue is retired, it will pay on January 20, 1922, and each month thereafter, a sufficient amount into the sinking fund so that the entire issue will have been retired on or before January 1, 1936.

Summary

This issue of notes is secured by an absolute first mortgage on the entire property of the company, now owned or hereafter acquired, the present appraised value of which is over 3½ times the amount of the outstanding notes.

The average net earnings for the past seven years and nine months have been at the rate of almost two and one-half times the interest requirements of this issue. The business of the company, as it is to be conducted, should in the opinion of the management provide net earnings of about $5 per share on the common stock.

The plants of the company are so located that it is able to supply its customers with either large or small orders at a minimum transportation cost and with quick deliveries.

The sinking fund requirements are sufficient to maintain a steady demand for these notes in any market. (Provisions here omitted.—*Author*).

All legal matters connected with this issue will be approved by Messrs . . . representing us, and by Messrs . . ., representing the Fibreboard Company. Copies of their opinions will be furnished upon application.

Price and Yield (Details omitted.—*Author*).

Under the terms described above the noteholders cannot receive less than 8.60% income on their investment, if held to maturity, and they may receive a net return as high as 11.70%.

The following information was given in a letter written by the president of the company:

General Information

The Fibreboard Company is the successor of the Hideite Leather Company of Brockton and in addition to that plant has recently acquired a second fully equipped plant and established fibreboard business at Amesbury, Mass., so that it now owns two manufacturing plants, each constituting complete units, centrally located in the City of Brockton, Mass., and in the town of Amesbury, Mass. Each of these factories is of brick and heavy mill construction, thoroughly protected by sprinkler systems, thus assuring the lowest possible insurance rates. The property of the company is insured for a total sum of not less than $350,000.

The factory at Brockton is located on the Middleboro division of the main line of the New York, New Haven & Hartford Railroad. As the company owns a side track extending the full length of its plant it can deliver raw material into its stock sheds and coal into its coal pocket at the boiler room doors. This plant is near to the class of labor which we employ and is on a street car line running to the center of the city.

The factory at Amesbury is well located in the center of the town on the Powow River and has two railroad side tracks connected with the Boston & Maine Railroad, thus enabling easy delivery of raw material to the warehouse and of coal at the boiler room door. This plant is also near to the class of labor which we employ.

The machinery and equipment of both plants are of modern and up-to-date type, excellent condition in all respects, and have recently been appraised at $333,011. The total appraised value of real estate, buildings, and equipment of both factories is $488,011.

Kinds of Fibre Products Manufactured

"Hideite Leather"—The Company manufactures a patented leather fibreboard. known as "Hideite Leather," which has been used in the manufacture of the better grade of shoes in New England for a period of ten years. "Hideite Leather" is used principally for heel lifts to take the place of the regular tanned leather lifts, and represents to the shoe manufacturer a saving of over 50% in the cost of a corresponding amount of leather in the production of the heel. This percentage of saving is figured by taking into consideration the *normal* cost of genuine leather used for such purposes.

The patents protecting the manufacture of "Hideite Leather" have been sustained in the Patent Courts of the United States and we and those authorized by us to do so, are, and legally, can be, the only producers of a waterproof leather substitute for these purposes in the United States, Canada. and European countries.

The following are a few of the shoe manufacturing firms which are large consumers of "Hideite Leather."

Churchill & Alden Company, Brockton, Mass.
W. L. Douglas Shoe Company, Brockton, Mass.
P. B. Keith Company, Brockton, Mass.
Whitman & Keith, Brockton, Mass.
M. A. Packard Company, Brockton, Mass.
F. M. Hoyt Shoe Company, Manchester, N. H.
Rice & Hutchins, Rockland and Marlboro, Mass.

Hamilton & Brown Shoe Company, St. Louis, Mo.
Commonwealth Shoe & Leather Company, Whitman, Mass.

This list fairly represents the class of manufacturers who have used this product for years.

"Bullseye" Wadding Board—This wadding board is manufactured by us under patented processes and will be used extensively in the production of shot shell cartridges by such firms as are mentioned below. This wadding board has been thoroughly tested by these firms and found to be as good as hair felt for over 90% of their purposes in the manufacture of cartridges. For the past fifty years, no other material costing less had ever been found that could be used with as good results as hair felt.

The normal price of the hair felt is 30c to 35c per pound, while the present price of our "Bullseye" wadding is 15c per pound, which represents a tremendous saving in the production of cartridges.

Since the tests were completed by the following concerns, substantial orders have been received from all but one of them, which concern was under contract to buy hair for all its requirements until January 1, 1921:

Dominion Cartridge Company of Canada, Montreal, Canada.
Remington Arms and Union Metallic Cartridge Company, Bridgeport, Conn.
United States Cartridge Company, Maurer, New Jersey, and Lowell, Mass.
Western Cartridge Company, East Alton, Illinois.
Winchester Repeating Arms Company, New Haven, Conn.

A modified form of this "Bullseye" wadding can also be used at a considerable saving for insulation purposes, as shown by exhaustive tests made by Prof. Gordon B. Wilkes, of the Massachusetts Institute of Technology, as well as for other construction purposes. This possible use represents a large outlet for this product.

Counter Board—The "Hercules" and "Atlas" brands of counter board are manufactured by this company for use extensively in the manufacture of boots and shoes as counters instead of leather. These two products are recognized in the market as being of highest quality and there is an increasing demand for them among shoe manufacturers. A counter made from "Hercules" or "Atlas" brands costs the shoe manufacturer about two cents a pair, as compared with the cost of a leather counter of from eight to twelve cents per pair, and is entirely satisfactory for the shoe worn by the great consuming public.

The following are a few of the firms which are extensive users of the "Hercules" and "Atlas" brands of counter board:

The Appleton Counter Company, Haverhill, Mass.
Wm. E. Bixby & Son, Haverhill, Mass.
Colonial Counter Company, Lynn, Mass.
D. J. Mulligan & Sons, Salem, Mass.
The Three Line Counter Company, Newburyport, Mass.
Wilkinson Counter Company, Salem, Mass.

Record of Earnings

The business of the Hideite Leather Company was established in 1907 and the present factory at Brockton was constructed in 1908 and 1909.

The record of earnings of that company covering a period of seven years and nine months, during which the company handled no war orders and which reflects no profits from sales of wadding board or counter board, shows average annual net earnings available for interest, dividends, and depreciation of $30,912.03, or nearly two and one-half times the interest requirements on this issue of $160,000, 8% notes.

Financial Statement

Assets		Liabilities	
Real Estate and Buildings	$155,000	Common Shares 22,000 (no par value)	
Machinery and Equipment	333,011	Preferred Stock (par value $100)	$335,000
Inventory, Cash, etc.	101,200	8% First Mortgage Notes (this issue)	160,000
Patents, Processes and Good Will.........	250,000	Serial Notes	55,000
		Surplus	289,211
Total	$839,211		$839,211

Estimate for 1921

In response to your request for an estimate of earnings for the calendar year of 1921, I wish to state that the average output of the Hideite Leather factory for the past nine years has amounted annually to 2,030 tons of product, and that during the past six months we have been producing wadding board at the rate of 500 tons per year.

The tonnage of the Amesbury factory on "Hercules" and "Atlas" counter board during the calendar year of 1920 has been at the rate of 1,500 tons per year.

Taking, as a basis of figuring, sales of 750 tons of "Hideite Leather," 500 tons of wadding, and 1,750 tons of counter board, which I believe can be accomplished during the year 1921, and using for cost figures present prices of labor and materials, I find that after taking care of all note interest, sinking fund requirements, depreciation, dividends on preferred stock, but before Federal Taxes, the company should show a balance of approximately $85,000 for the Common Stock.

Return of Normal Business Conditions

With the return of normal business conditions the output of the two factories should increase to at least 4,000 tons per year, in which case this balance for the Common Stock should increase from $85,000 to between $140,000 and $160,000.

In making this estimate no account has been taken of royalties, due from foreign "Hideite Leather" factories, or of export sales to foreign agents.

Signed——————
President.

Questions

1. Analyze this prospectus critically and in detail, summing up all the strong and weak points of the proposition.
2. What is your conclusion regarding the financial present and future of the company?
3. What do you consider the essentials of a good prospectus?

Problem 23

Banker Control

One of the partners in a large and influential investment banking house in New York City stated that his organization would not under any circumstances put through any important piece of financing without securing a place on the board of directors of the refinanced concern. This he stated to be the only proper course for them to follow if they expected to have those policies of sound management, for which they prided themselves, carried out under all circumstances. By insisting upon this sort of management in connection with their financing they felt that they would be in a position to see that the various companies refinanced by them lived up to their obligations. Thus they feel that they are building up an excellent reputation with the buyers of their securities.

One of the members of a large Boston private banking firm at about the same time stated that it was absolutely contradictory to their policy to let themselves be represented on the directorate of any concern whose securities they sell. Even though the companies may insist on this arrangement, feeling the need of sound financial advice, this banking house has uniformly refused to accede to such requests. They consider themselves "investment bankers" and not business managers. They are, however, always ready to advise those concerns whom they finance as to the proper financial policies for them to follow.

Questions

1. With which point of view do you agree? State the reasons for your position.
2. Would you draw any distinction between an investment bank and a commercial bank in this matter?

Problem 24

Getting New Capital for an Old, Closely Owned Concern

The M. Company, engaged in the manufacture of enamel-ware, began business in 1903. It has always been largely a one-man concern, though incorporated. Aside from a small issue of serial bonds in 1907, the business has been financed out of earnings and out of the small original capital. The prosperity of this business was affected very little by the war.

In 1919 it was felt by the management that in order to develop the business properly it would be necessary to double the plant capacity. The original plant had been secured very cheaply and was hopelessly antiquated. There was not sufficient warehouse room, nor was it possible to handle orders with sufficient speed. Further, there had heretofore been no very active attempt to increase the volume of sales. On the contrary, the business had grown naturally and surely, largely because of the excellent quality of goods turned out. The company has never used its own trademark, and has sold only to a comparatively few large customers. It was felt, however, that with the changed business conditions following the war it would probably be necessary to carry on the business in much larger volume and with more aggressiveness, in order to make good profits.

Accordingly, in 1919 the new building campaign was launched in spite of the excessively high prices, and the expenses were financed partially through an increase of common stock very narrowly distributed and partially through the sale of some additional bonds, which had been authorized in connection with the earlier issue. The bills payable to banks increased rapidly during the year 1920, and these loans were used primarily for building purposes.

The new plant was finished late in 1920. Though the cost of this additional construction was high, the average cost of all the fixed assets was very moderate because of low original outlays. The management feels that very high returns will be realized on the added investment as soon as general conditions improve.

It should further be explained that this business is practically free from the seasonal element and sells its goods largely to jobbers, the usual terms being 2 per cent 10 days, 60 days net. Ordinarily the customers discount their bills promptly. The volume of sales for the fiscal year ending November 30, 1920, was $1,269,557, and the entire loss from bad debts during the year was less than 1/200 of 1 per cent.

The cost of these sales during the year, less discounts on purchases, was $1,087,053. After the various allowances for reserves, fixed charges, etc., the net profit amounted to $106,649, or more than 10% on the total assets of the business. It should be stated, however, that during the latter half of 1920 the profit on sales was very much smaller than normal, due to general high expenses.

Along in 1921, the management began to grow very much concerned about its relatively high floating debt, not because there was any present fear that the banks might cut down their lines of credit, but because business was falling off, and inventory was large, receivables were growing slower, and so on. All in all, it appeared in the spring of the year that by the end of 1921 the current ratio might be dangerously low and that it might then be difficult to do any new financing if there should be need for it.

The following comparative and much abbreviated financial statements will indicate what has happened to the finances of the company between the end of 1919 and the end of 1920, and it must be admitted that any undesirable changes shown have been exaggerated during the past six months:

COMPARATIVE STATEMENT OF THE M. COMPANY
November 30

Assets	1919	1920
Real estate, buildings, etc.	$165,000	$324,000
Equipment, machinery, etc.	112,000	185,000
Goodwill	32,000	32,000
Inventory		
Raw materials	132,000	190,500
Work in process	22,000	41,000
Finished work	29,000	49,000
Cash	44,000	24,500
Liberty Bonds	10,000	....
Accounts receivable	80,000	130,000
Bills and acceptances receivable	500	6,000
Personal advance	5,000	6,000
Miscellaneous	18,000	22,000
	$649,500	$1,010,000

Liabilities

Capital Stock	$290,000	$435,000
Bonds	30,000	98,000
Surplus	101,000	17,000
Profit for year	86,000	107,000
Vouchers payable	14,000	67,000
Bills payable		90,000
Bills and acceptances discounted		4,000
Dividends payable		6,500
Reserved for depreciation	56,000	67,000
Reserved for taxes	16,000	50,000
Miscellaneous Reserves	39,500	47,500
Accruals	17,000	21,000
	$649,500	$1,010,000

The following alternatives are now being considered by the management:

(*a*) Should the business continue to finance itself on the present basis, going ahead modestly and taking a chance on reducing its current indebtedness in the hope that business will begin to improve by the end of the year? If this program were followed, there would be no further expansion of plant, though it is thought to be wise to invest from $25,000 to $50,000 more in this item, and no future financing would be contemplated.

(*b*) Shall an attempt be made to secure additional capital with a view to taking up some of the floating indebtedness, furnishing more working capital, etc.? If so, how shall this capital be secured and how much should be secured?

(*c*) Shall the concern struggle along as best it can until new capital can be secured on more favorable terms and then do its financing?

Questions

1. In the light of all the facts at your disposal, do you believe that the expansion was justified at this time?

2. Accepting the situation as it now is, what financial policy should you advise the management to follow?

3. If you agree that there should be new financing, what method would you advise taking?

Problem 25

Securing More Capital for a New Concern

The following problem was received from the president of a newly organized company in February, 1921:

The writer has organized four successful selling agencies, the latest one of which was the New York territory for the..............Machine Company. This firm manufactures and distributes the.......... Package Sealer, used in stores for dispensing a properly moistened piece of gummed paper tape for the sealing of parcels, and the like.

The machine is rather complicated for the ordinary clerk, as it contains a lever, cutting-off knife, gears, pawl movement, etc., that give more or less trouble which the ordinary clerk cannot adjust, thus necessitating the return of the machine to the factory for repairs. The selling price of this machine is $28, which is prohibitive to the small concern.

The writer invented a new tape machine, which will retail for about $10, do all the work that the above mentioned machine can do, do it more quickly, with practically no chance of the machine's getting out of adjustment, because of its simplicity. Fifty-two points were applied for in the patent application, of which fourteen were allowed, thus making what is termed a 100% patent.

The writer then oıganized a corporation, incorporated under the laws of the State of New Jersey, with a capitalization of 1,500 shares, par value $50, all common and non-assessable. He accepted $3,000 in stock for his patent rights. For selling the stock of the company and to maintain the majority holdings of stock in the company he is given one share of stock for each share sold. The present standing of the company is as follows:

Stock of tape (used in the machines) on hand	$1,530.86	
Office fixtures	325.00	
Cash in bank	779.39	
Cash on deposit with manufacturing concern	100.00	
Accounts receivable	200.00	
Notes payable		$800.00
Capital stock		11,800.00
Patent rights, operating expense, incorporating expense, patterns, etc.	9,665.00	
	$12,600.00	$12,600.00

Approximately $1,300 will pay for three dies needed to make die-cast tanks, rollers and platen. This will also include the first 1,000 of each of these castings. After the cost of the dies has been taken care of, it will cost approximately 55¢ for the three castings for each machine. The first 1,000 machines complete, ready for sale, will cost approximately $3.50, and after the first 1,000, in 1,000 lots the machines will cost approximately $2.75 each. The condition of the company at present is such that we need more money to carry on. After the first thousand machines are sold and the second thousand are being sold, we shall need money to continue the business unless purchasers are prompt in paying their invoices.

I have arranged with a foundry and machine shop combined to manufacture machines and deliver to me completed machines ready for sale at the cost of about $3.00. If I were equipped to manufacture, or rather to assemble machines from material from foundry, I could reduce the cost of the machine to approximately $2.25. The cost of an assembling plant would be approximately $2,000 for outlay, and a weekly expense of about $200 extra. I estimate that inside of one year 1,000 machines a week would be the output.

A bank has signified its interest and may loan us some money on "accounts receivable." I am practically certain of about $1,000 more coming in from the sale of stock within a week or two. The less stock we have out, the more profit there will be for the stockholders. The company has been embarrassed for lack of cash because about $700 of the owner's money has been tied up for several months in a bank which failed.

I have been a successful master mechanic, a successful sales manager, and have invented several successful articles that did not bring me any great remuneration because I was under contract. I have tried to step aside here and build up a business for myself, for I am now 48 years old. I am convinced that I have an article of real merit, as it has been demonstrated to the three largest possible users of such devices, who have given it their unqualified indorsement. The limit of my own and my wife's personal resources have been invested in the company, and I have resigned from the New York managership of the other company at a salary of $10,000 a year to play this game. I have been offered and have refused $20,000 for 60 per cent of the capital stock.

In this connection I should explain that I already have a good market for gummed tape, which I handle as a jobber. As my machine is sold it will logically follow that the purchasers will also buy gummed tape from me. On this tape there is a very good profit, and I have already made an agreement with one of the largest gummed tape producers in the country to supply me with all the tape that I wish. I also have had registered a trade name for a special quick-drying tape which is being prepared for me and which should be in great demand.

Should I try to operate on the smaller capital, of course getting some more stock out, say $5,000, or should I get busy and sell enough stock to get, say, $20,000 or $25,000 more with which to operate? Selling stock at present would take time, delay production, and the results would be uncertain, while expenses would continue. Expenses, by the way, have been reduced to a minimum and the actual cash output each month is under $300.

In other words, should I concentrate on production or on capitalizing?

My idea on marketing the machine was to make a trip through the country, appointing general agents on a commission basis in some places and appointing wholesale paper jobbers as distributors in others. The machine should cost (manufacturing and packing) about $3, and to my thinking should sell to the general agent for $5.50, to the sub-agent for $6.50, and should retail for $10, 5 per cent off in lots of 10, 10 per cent off in lots of 25, 15 per cent off in lots of 50, and 25 per cent off in lots of 100.

What would be your suggestion for marketing?

Questions

1. In view of the information given, do you think that the launching of this new enterprise is financially justified?
2. Granting that the machine is all that is claimed for it, what steps should you advise the president to take in order to insure financial success?
3. What are your answers to his specific questions?
4. Do you think that the present president is the right man to head the concern?

Problem 26

General Problem in the Financing of a Company Making Patent Caps and Jar Covers

The following interesting problem is submitted by the manager of the E. Z. Lid Company:

The E. Z. Lid Company manufactures a patent cap or cover for bottles, jars, cans, and the like. These covers are a marked improvement on any now used for similar purposes, and the more important ones are covered by patents which expire in 1930. The products have been on the market for two years. The company buys containers to sell along with the covers.

Officials of the company feel that a great potential market exists for their product, but in order to secure the proper volume of business it will be necessary to inaugurate an extensive campaign of national advertising and increase their manufacturing facilities. All of these things would require a considerable amount of new capital. It is understood that their chief competitor spends a quarter of a million dollars each year on advertising alone.

Sales have held up well during the period of depression. During 1920 orders were received amounting to $135,000. However, because of difficulties in obtaining containers—especially glass containers—from the factories supplying them, the gross sales were reduced to only $100,000. This unfortunate difficulty in securing containers was the result of unusual business conditions, and should not be a normal situation.

Owing to the cost of obtaining business and the expenses attendant upon promoting a new commodity, this volume of sales ($100,000) was not sufficient to produce any profit. In fact, because of the relatively high sales and advertising expenses, the deficit last year amounted to $12,017. It is estimated that about four times this volume of sales could be handled with only a slight increase in present operating and overhead expenses, under which circumstances net profits on sales would be about 25 per cent.

The line carried by this company is being added to from time to time. The last addition, an improved fruit jar cover, has promise of a big market when its superior features have been made generally known. In spite of all the difficulties encountered, the officers of the E. Z. Lid Company have great faith in the future of the business, and are working for smaller salaries than could be obtained elsewhere.

The company's balance sheet for December 31, 1920, was as follows:

BALANCE SHEET OF THE E. Z. LID COMPANY AS OF December 31st, 1920

Assets			
Current Assets			
Cash in bank..........	$9,895.64		
Petty cash on hand....	368.13		
Accounts receivable....	29,706.59		
Notes receivable.......	40,000.00		
Upressit Cap Co. of Canada, Ltd........	104.00		
Total Current Assets.		$80,074.36	
Working and Trading Assets			
Raw materials—glassware—advertising matter—moulds, etc..		32,366.25	
Fixed Assets			
Patents (U. S.)........	$4,148,068.69		
Drawings.............	2,454.32		
Machinery............	23,223.06		
Dies.................	9,341.76		
Tools................	575.61		
Factory fixtures.......	2,195.49		
Office furniture and fixt.	2,649.87		
Trade-mark...........	75.00		
		$4,188,583.80	
Deferred Charges to Expenses			
(Packing and shipping material—office supplies—insurance, taxes and commissions paid in advance, etc.)		5,678.28	
Total Assets........		$4,306,702.69	
Net Loss—1920.....		12,017.89	
Total Assets.......			$4,318,720.58
Liabilities			
Accounts payable........		$12,555.13	
Capital stock			
Common.............	$4,000,000.00		
Preferred (outstanding).	275,000.00	4,275,000.00	
(Authorized $1,000,000.00)			
Treasury stock subscribed and paid*............		31,165.45	
Total Liabilities....			$4,318,720.58

*Treasury stock subscribed and unpaid, $70,389.55.

PAR VALUE

Preferred stock, $100. Common stock, $10.

The company, having in the last few months received payment on the "Treasury stock subscribed and unpaid for," now has close to $75,000 in cash, this reserve being necessary to tide them over the present business depression. The management of the E. Z. Lid Company now raises some of the following questions:

Questions

1. What suggestions can you make regarding the desirability of launching this company early in 1919?
2. What light, if any, does the above balance sheet throw in the problem? What criticisms have you to offer?
3. Would it be more desirable for this company to endeavor to raise additional capital and to continue to operate independently, or to be taken over as a subsidiary by some large going concern, as for example the American Can Company.
4. Granting that you approve of the continued independent operation of the company, what plans can you suggest for securing adequate funds for the necessary advertising campaign and the extension of manufacturing facilities?
5. Do you think it wise for the company to buy containers to be sold along with its covers? Why do you suppose the company does this?
6. Again, assuming that the company is to be independently operated, should you advise them to continue buying the glass jars and containers from other concerns, manufacturing only the caps and covers, or should the company avoid a recurrence of the situation which confronted them last year, by beginning to manufacture containers as well?
7. As an impartial adviser, what further suggestions, if any, can you make as to the past, present, and future financing of the company?
8. How, if at all, would your answers to the above questions differ if you were an officer of the E. Z. Lid Company?

PROBLEM 27

AN EXPANSION WHICH NECESSITATES A CHANGE IN ORGANIZATION

Mr. H., an official of a large New England paper company, the D. Company, is heavily interested in a small paper mill operated by two or three partners. Unless the mill is considerably enlarged there is little hope of receiving more than a moderate return on the investment in the future, though war-time earnings were very large, and the present financial position is excellent. H. asked his auditor for a report on the proposed new financing, and received the following analysis in reply:

Memorandum to Mr. H.,

"I have made a careful analysis of the financial requirements for building the M. Paper Company to a two-machine paper mill. We have very definite figures covering the requirements in the way of cash, notes receivable, inventories, plant, etc., from the D. Company's reports. It is comparatively easy, therefore, to set up a balance sheet which should represent the financial requirements of a business of the size you mentioned. Having arrived at these figures in this manner, we are able to check them very definitely by the engineering data furnished by Mr. Y. (chief engineer), and by other means, and I believe that the balance sheet presented herewith would closely approximate the financial condition of the company after reorganization. As you will note, the plant would be carried at a value of $2,500,000. This is upon the basis of the present valuation of $1,000,000 as placed upon the plant by the present owners, and the addition of two machines with all the subsidiary machinery required, at an estimated cost of $1,500,000.

The financing required to attain this condition would be exceedingly difficult, due to the fact that it would be almost entirely a construction proposition. In other words, the present business as carried on by the M.

Paper Company would not justify the raising of $2,000,000, either in the form of bonds or stock issues. It is perfectly evident that no banks would be inclined to loan the money upon any security which the M. Paper Company as an organization has to offer. It seems to me that probably the only way in which you could secure the required money would be to secure the support of interests who are familiar with the business and with the opportunity which exists for its development.

If this is not possible, a bond issue, consisting of construction bonds to be paid in instalments as the work progresses, would probably float it. You would find, however, that the cost in the form of premiums and interest would probably be prohibitive. Preferred stock might be disposed of if you could secure subscriptions from interested parties for a large percentage of the issue, thus offering to the public only a small part for subscription. The D. Company might be persuaded to take a block of such stock, and the distributors a portion.

Either of the three methods outlined would result in securing $2,000,000 of outside capital, $1,500,000 of which would be used to build plant, and the other $500,000 to furnish working capital to carry on the business.

I have prepared operating statements showing the results of operations after the installation of the necessary machinery, based upon an output of 18,000 tons of paper per year, and 9,000 tons of soda pulp, at present selling prices of paper and at 7 cents per pound for soda pulp.

Analysis of the cost of manufacture indicates that at present prices for raw material and labor, and with reasonable efficiency, paper could be manufactured at a cost which would net about 20 per cent on sales. As will be seen from the operating statements, corporate requirements, allowing common stock dividends of 10 per cent, preferred stock dividends of 8 per cent, and with provision for the retirement of the preferred stock in 10 years, would be $560,000. In addition to this, Federal Taxes would have to be met. The figures shown are based upon different percentages of profit, and you will note that net profits would have to be maintained at 20 per cent or better in order to meet corporate requirements, and to leave any surplus for improvement of the corporation's financial condition. It is, of course, a fact that the preferred dividend requirements would be constantly reduced until they finally disappear at the end of ten years, so that a profit of even 15 per cent on sales would in two or three years show up very favorably, and at the end of ten years would leave the corporation in excellent financial condition. In the lower part of the table you will find the corporate requirements based upon a 6 per cent common stock dividend, 7 per cent preferred stock dividend, and a sinking fund of 5 per cent. Upon this basis it is evident that earnings might drop as low as 10 per cent, based on the selling prices mentioned, and still leave the corporation in fair shape. In this case it is also true that the condition would be better year by year as the preferred stock was retired, until at the end of twenty years the preferred would be entirely eliminated, the entire equity in the business resting in the common stock, and the financial condition of the corporation being very good.

It must be borne in mind in talking of a reorganization upon any such basis as this, that the net return to the present owners of the business is not apt to be as large as at present, due to the fact that considerable sums of money would be withdrawn from the business in the form of preferred dividends, which amounts are now distributed to the owners of the business. It is also a fact that due to the very low valuation at which the plant now stands, and due to the very peculiar arrangement with the D. Company,* the capital invested in the business is very small for the business done. Due to the present high cost of construction, the amount of capital required to produce the added

*The D. Company manages the M. Company, and affords numerous facilities at low cost.

sales in the form of paper is entirely out of proportion. The new Corporation would find itself with a very heavy capitalization for the amount of business which it would then do. This, of course, adds to the fixed charges, and means that the net earnings which could be withdrawn would be correspondingly reduced.

Another factor which must be borne in mind is that as at present organized there are no fixed requirements in the form of preferred dividends, sinking funds and taxes. Thus if poor years are encountered no particular harm is done. As a matter of fact, as at present organized, a loss for any one year for the M. Paper Company could be deducted from your other income on your personal tax returns and the Government would thus pay a part of the loss. This would not be true of a corporation. A loss in any year means that preferred dividends would accumulate, sinking funds could not be met, and these would constitute a preferred liability, and the common stock equity would be impaired. No part of the loss could be deducted in submitting tax returns.

This preliminary memorandum cannot, of course, be expected to cover all the phases of the proposition, but may be of some value and interest to you.

BALANCE SHEET OF M. COMPANY
(After proposed new financing)

Cash, Accounts and Notes Receivable	$ 500,000	Cash, Accounts and Notes Payable		$ 500,000
Inventory	500,000	Capital Stock Com.	$1,000,000	
Plant	2,500,000	Pref.	2,000,000	3,000,000
	$3,500,000			$3,500,000

ESTIMATED OPERATING STATEMENT

Gross Sales—Paper	18,000 tons @ $200	$3,600,000
Pulp	9,000 tons @ 140	1,260,000
		$4,860,000

Gross Sales	$4,860,000	$4,860,000	$4,860,000	$4,860,000
Per cent of Profit	25	20	15	10
Net Profit	$1,215,000	$972,000	$729,000	$486,000

A. Requirements:				
Dividends—Common @ 10%......	$100,000	$100,000	$100,000	$100,000
Dividends—Pref. @ 8%	160,000	160,000	160,000	160,000
Sinking Fund @ 10%...	200,000	200,000	200,000	200,000
Taxes.......	407,400	295,920	183,500	92,980
Total.....	$867,400	$755,920	$643,500	$552,980
Available for Corp. Use.	$347,600	$216,000	$85,500	$66,980
B. Requirements:				
Dividends—Common @ 6%....	$ 60,000	$ 60,000	$ 60,000	$ 60,000
Dividends—Pref. @ 7%	140,000	140,000	140,000	140,000
Sinking Fund @ 5%....	100,000	100,000	100,000	100,000
Taxes.......	407,400	295,920	183,500	92,980
Total.....	$707,400	$595,920	$483,500	$392,980
Available for Corp. Use...	$507,600	$376,080	$245,500	$93,020

Questions

1. Has the auditor in his report considered all phases of the problem?
2. In view of the information given in the memorandum, what action do you advise Mr. H. to take?
3. Do you see any better methods of financing than those suggested by the auditor?
4. What would have been your advice if the date were 1910 instead of 1921?

Problem 28

Financing an Expansion which Necessitates a Change in the Nature of the Business

The.......... Company of Philadelphia, engaged largely in the manufacture of cardboard packing cases, began as a small undertaking owned by three men just before the war. The owners were poor business men and grew very much discouraged with the undertaking, though their earnings had been reasonably good. Early in 1917 a fourth man, Mr. B., then 37 years of age, who had little money but who had a good general knowledge of this kind of business, was taken into the organization. After several months it became evident to B. that the business could not prosper with so many different hands in the management, nor did he have any confidence in the capacity of the men who had originally started the business. Consequently, he decided if possible to secure the sole control of the concern. The financial statement of the business in the spring of 1917 was as follows:

Assets		Liabilities	
Equipment	$5,775.64	Capital Stock[2]	$11,125.00
Merchandise Inventory		Notes payable	2,500.00
		Accounts payable	6,794.50
Cash	11,050.34	Surplus (mostly earned the year before)	
Receivables[1]	1,240.05		
	11,218.55		8,865.08
	$29,284.58		$29,284.58

1. Of this amount, $4,000 was bad.
2. Of this amount $9,200 had been paid in cash.

Mr. B. already owned some stock in the company, and, although his outside personal resources at the time amounted to less than $1,000, he was able with this sum to make an advance payment to one of the other owners, who agreed to sell out his stock. The balance was to be paid in notes over a period of time. In this way B. secured the controlling interest in the business. Having once secured control, it was not a difficult matter for him to induce the remaining owners to sell out to him. Though B. found it necessary to strain his credit to the limit and to "kite" a few checks with friends in order to effect this change in ownership, the deal was finally put through and B. became the sole owner, with a number of personal notes yet to pay. By allowing himself a high salary, as sole owner, he soon secured sufficient funds to pay off these notes.

Through personal connections, B. managed to secure the trade of several large manufacturers who agreed for the immediate future to buy the greater proportion of their boxes from him. Much attention was paid by the new company to "personal service" and to making the kind of goods which would appeal particularly to the consumer.

During the next three years the business grew rapidly. The number of employees grew from less than 40 to about 200, the gross sales increased from $68,000 in 1917 to $281,331 in 1920, the net worth increased from about $20,000 at the end of 1917 to more than $40,000 at the end of 1920, while the production and selling costs were actually kept lower than in most competing concerns. The owner did his own selling through personal contacts. In the meantime very liberal allowance had been made for depreciation and the owner had been paying himself a salary of $12,000 a year, all with a view to avoiding high income taxes.

In the early part of 1921 the.......... Company began to feel the effects of the general business depression. Since it depended almost solely for its income on the patronage of a few manufacturers whose business was now practically at a standstill, it was now in a particularly precarious position. In the first place, most of the customers were in financial difficulties for one reason or another, and found it almost impossible to pay their bills. Further, those customers who were not actually in serious financial straits, found their sales so much curtailed that they could give only small orders for packing cases. As a result, the.......... Company found it difficult to meet its own bills, as it had always financed itself on a very close margin of working capital. It became necessary to put off the less urgent creditors by means of notes and promises, and to pay only those who threatened suit in case of non-payment. The following statements show the more recent financial history of the company:

Assets

	Dec. 31 1919	Dec. 31 1920	Mar. 31 1921
Cash	$ 2,340	$ 588	$ 1,617
Accounts receivable	9,475	16,596	29,609
Merchandise	25,365	54,888	44,464
Liberty Bonds	2,000	....	....
Machinery, fixtures, etc	17,130	36,264	37,546
Total	$56,210	$108,336	$113,236

Liabilities

Notes payable	$18,951	$ 7,344	$ 16,144
Accounts payable	24,021	61,652	48,632
Reserve for taxes	......	4,963	3,868
Capital Stock Common	11,125	1,925	1,925
" " Preferred	......	15,600	15,600
Surplus	2,113	16,852	27,067
Total	$56,210	$108,336	$113,236

In the second quarter of 1921 business began to fall off very rapidly, until the owner felt that the company would no longer prosper unless the business could be more widely diversified. It did not appear that there would be any speedy recovery in the demand for packing cases on the part of his present clients, particularly in view of the fact that sales to his type of customer are always low during the summer months.

Accordingly, B. endeavored to discover some kind of product to which his organization might profitably be turned either as a temporary side-line or, more desirably, as a permanent part of the business. He now has two or three definite projects in mind. The possibility which seems to him most feasible is that of making cigar boxes out of specially prepared heavy cardboard, which he could "process" in his own factory, but no attempt has yet been made to patent this process. Upon investigation he has found that cigar manufacturers can use the type of box which he plans to make as a substitute for the usual wooden boxes, at a very great saving. He further finds that several important manufacturers of cigars are ready to contract with him for their entire supply of boxes for the year, if he can soon be in a position to furnish them.

In order to develop this new line of work, which it appears would be highly profitable, it will be necessary to raise additional capital of about $200,000. The problem at present confronting B., who is now thoroughly convinced that it will be to his financial advantage to undertake the new business, is, "How in the middle of 1921 can he raise the necessary capital for expanding and changing his present organization?" Unfortunately he has no close friends on whom he can call for financial assistance, and his health is very uncertain.

Questions

1. What is your estimate of B.'s financial ability and of the financial soundness of his business at present?
2. Do you think that B.'s present business should be refinanced in any way?
3. Do you think it wise for B. at this time, to expand his business in the direction indicated?
4. Granting that you favor this expansion, what appears to you to be the best method of securing the needed funds?

Problem 29

Shall a Small Concern Expand Quickly During a Period of Rising Prices?

The..........Company was a small concern engaged in manufacturing a staple commodity. Its growth had been slow and sure. During the war there was a sudden increase in the demand for its product and there seemed to be excellent opportunities for slightly changing the nature of the enterprise in such a way as to lead to enormous profits.

The management of the company, seeing their various competitors putting themselves in a position to get more business, decided that the only policy for them to follow was to expand and seize their profits while prices were still climbing. They were not content to expand gradually out of their large war-time earnings, but wanted to sell bonds or notes if possible. They hoped in this way to be able to trade on their equity and make higher profits, since the small number of present owners would not be possible if they financed by means of stock issues.

The concern was, however, really too small for a bond issue or a note issue, as general purchasers could not be interested in the proposition. Nor was it large enough to interest outsiders in a new stock issue, for not more than $200,000 additional investment was actually needed. So far as a preferred stock issue was concerned, the company did not have a record of earnings extending far enough back to assure financing by this method. It would have been necessary to float such an issue on the security of prospective profits after the new organization was effected, instead of on the security of past "performance" when the company was small. It should also be stated that the company was using its credit to the limit with its banks and tradespeople, so that no temporary help could be expected from these sources.

Confronted by this situation, desirous of expanding quickly, but uncertain of the best method of doing so, the company approached a private banking house for advice. At the same time they stated that from their point of view a sale of preferred stock would seem to be the most satisfactory, all things considered.

Questions

1. Should such a concern have attempted to expand?
2. Granting that the expansion was desirable, what method of financing should the bankers have suggested to them?
3. If the concern had wished to increase its profits by a slight change in the nature of the business carried on, so as to take up a more profitable line, would your answers to the foregoing questions be the same?
4. Are there considerations other than financial which might have justified the expansion during the war?

Problem 30

Expanding a Garment Manufacturing Concern to Take Over a Textile Mill in 1919

The.......... Overall Company had for a number of years been noted for its conservative and shrewd management. They had put the minimum amount of money into plant and equipment, consistent with a high degree of efficiency in production. They always took advantage of their discounts in buying material. They always collected their receivables promptly, and upon the whole had an excellent standing among bankers in different sections of the country.

The company's investment in fixed assets was only \$200,000 at the end of 1918. In 1920, however, it appeared from their statement that their fixed capital had increased to more than \$1,000,000, though there was practically no increase in their gross sales. Accordingly, one of the bankers made inquiry regarding the matter and was informed by the president of the company that they had found it necessary to buy one of the textile mills which had been supplying them with cloth for making the overalls.

The company's explanation of this move was to the effect that the concern from which they had been buying always drove hard bargains with them and practically forced them to contract for a large amount of material well in advance of the company's needs. Finally, the textile concern had insisted that the overall makers agree to take all of their annual output during the year 1920. Otherwise, business relations between the two would be severed. Therefore, owing to the uncertainties of the business, the management of the overall company decided that it would be best to buy out the textile concern, and so be free to conduct their business along their own lines. The president further explained that it was at the time (late in 1919) extremely difficult to secure satisfactory material at reasonable prices from any other mill.

Questions

1. Analyze critically the wisdom of the expansion policy followed by the overall company, and the reasons given.
2. How would you have advised the management?

Problem 31

Financing the Expansion of a Conservative Paper Company in the Post-War Period

The.........Paper Company was an old-fashioned concern which had been under the same family management for many years. It operated on a small scale, although it was a somewhat integrated industry, owning some timberlands for the supply of its pulp mill. The plant was rather old-fashioned, but good. They had apparently always been making a good return on their investment. Their credit was the highest possible for a concern of their size and type.

When the boom in the paper business came during the war period, with rapidly mounting prices, a good deal of pressure was brought to bear to induce them to enlarge their plant, so that they might accept more orders and get a larger proportion of the business. For two or three years they withstood this pressure, meanwhile operating their plant to its utmost capacity and making extraordinarily high returns on their investment. Yet their actual and potential customers, on account of the goodwill which attached to the high grade of paper put out by them, continued to urge orders upon them. Finally, therefore, they felt that circumstances beyond their control were forcing them to expand, and decided to build their plant greater in order to take more of the business which was being thrust upon them.

As a result of their decision, a program was outlined, which called for the acquisition of more timberlands, more water power, and a considerably increased plant. These plans began to be carried into effect late in 1919.

There was no funded indebtedness of any kind against the old plant, though some preferred stock was outstanding. The company had also built up a very large surplus out of past earnings, much of which was kept in a liquid condition. Consequently, though the expansion ultimately called for a more than doubled investment in fixed assets, they were able in the beginning to finance themselves by means of their large cash resources and by extensive borrowing from their banks, who at first raised no objection, because of the initial high current ratio which their statements showed, and because of their excellent standing in the past.

In 1920, as the general depression came in this industry, the current assets of the company, while still relatively good, became more or less frozen. Further, the banks were no longer in a position to be able to loan as extensively as heretofore for what appeared to be largely a capital expenditure. As a matter of fact, the company's construction program was launched at a time when prices of needed materials and labor were at the peak, but when the demand for the company's goods was soon to decline. However, all the people engaged in similar lines of industry thought that the high prices for paper would continue for at least two years, and they could see no clouds on the horizon.

The next step was to float a mortgage loan secured by their plants and timberlands at the 1920 valuations. They had little difficulty in convincing the engineers and investment bankers who handled the proposition that it was a very desirable piece of financing, and the larger part of the issue was immediately sold without much trouble.

It now became evident that the money raised by this mortgage would not be sufficient to pay off all their bank obligations and provide the necessary additional funds for construction and working capital. Costs were greater than had been expected. Accordingly, before the entire issue of bonds had been sold, they were forced to attempt to raise additional capital. This they tried to do by means of an issue of short-time, high-interest-bearing notes which had an attractive sinking-fund provision.

While they were in the midst of these transactions, the bottom rather suddenly fell out of the paper market. Prices were considerably cut by the larger concerns, and the independents were forced to follow suit. This company, therefore, found itself with a still unfinished expansion program on its hands, borrowing from its banks beyond any safe limit, and with some of its senior securities still unsold. An appeal was then made to the stockholders to furnish the needed working capital by subscribing to junior securities, and a little money was raised in this way.

Questions

1. In view of the fact that all of this company's financial advisors decided that it would be in a stronger position in every way after the expansion was carried through, do you think this paper company was justified in expanding at the time it did?

2. Granting that you approve of the extension, do you approve of the method used to secure the needed funds? If not, what alternatives would you suggest?

3. When the paper market broke, what different policy, if any, should have been followed by this company?

4. If you were called upon to outline the future financial policy, what would be your advice?

5. In the light of the data supplied, what do you expect to be the financial future of this company?

Problem 32

Shall a Concern Own Real Estate or Pay Rent?

The..........Candy Company is a concern which until the war period grew slowly and always had the reputation of being very conservatively managed. Its product is of the highest grade and has been sold on the strength of quality rather than by means of high-pressure advertising. No real estate was owned, but a rather antiquated building had for some years been rented. By operating in this fashion, the overhead had been kept very low, so that this company was one of the most advantageously situated in the trade. It was a source of considerable annoyance, however, to find that in the rush season work could not be comfortably carried on in these quarters, and as the volume of business grew, it was frequently necessary to turn away some orders because of the congestion. Further, the owners of the building would lease the property only by the year and were constantly raising the rent.

In volume of sales, the business of this company grew about as follows: 1913, $450,000; 1914, $525,000; 1915, $600,000; 1916, $720,000; 1917, $850,000; 1918, $995,000; 1919, $1,250,000.

Because of the greatly increased sales figure toward the end of 1919, the management began to think that the company was at last going to come into its own, particularly since this result had been achieved with practically no general advertising. It was further perfectly evident that the old rented quarters would be wholly inadequate if the business should expand any more. At its utmost capacity the old plant could not turn out under present price conditions more than $1,300,000 worth of product. With the more normal prices which might ultimately be expected, the output would have been limited to about $900,000. Also, it was felt that much valuable goodwill was being lost because of the unavoidable delays in filling orders, as well as because of the orders which actually had to be turned down. If the demand should continue at the present rate, it seemed to the management that their sales for the year 1920 would be in excess of $1,500,000, and many expected that the $2,000,000 mark would be reached.

In view of these considerations, it was decided to build a plant which would insure sufficient capacity under all conditions. As this company's credit was excellent, there was little difficulty in raising $250,000 additional capital by an issue of preferred stock. Of the amount received it was planned that $150,000 should go into the plant and the balance was to be used for additional working capital. It was also estimated that at least $400,000 profits could be made during the year 1920, which would put the company in a very strong position with the banks and enable it also to retire some of the preferred stock. As the work progressed during the year, it was found that more working capital was needed than had been anticipated, so that the concern had to borrow about $500,000 from the banks, at the peak, instead of $250,000 or

$300,000 as had been customary. Further, it was found that when all allowances were made the building would necessitate an increase in fixed assets of at least twice as much as had been originally planned for.

Hence, after the sale of the preferred stock, instead of having an increased amount of working capital the company was forced to draw on its former cash balance to the extent of $50,000 for building purposes, as well as to use some of its bank borrowings for the same purpose. The net earnings expected during the year did not materialize. There was an inventory shrinkage of about $45,000, and during the last two months of the year an actual loss in operation of $30,000 was incurred. The volume of sales for the year had dropped considerably below the volume for the preceding year, and the surplus resulting from many years of conservative management was largely wiped out.

The first of the year 1921 saw the company in its new quarters. By this time it was realized that in order to break even, with its new plant, the company would need gross sales of at least $1,500,000. Yet not only had prices now fallen greatly, but the demand which had the year before been thought permanent seemed to grow constantly less. During the first five months of 1921 there was an actual loss in operation of $150,000. It appears that this loss will continue until the autumn, after which time, with reasonable luck, an even break may be expected until January. It is very probable that the volume of sales for the year will not exceed $750,000. In the meantime, the company owns a very superior plant, has no fear of rent increases, and has a good deal of extra space which might profitably be leased.

Questions

1. What are the chief lessons to be derived from this episode?

2. What steps should you advise the company to take in order to improve its financial position?

Problem 33

How Fast is it Safe for a Business to Grow?

The Standard Parts Company is a manufacturer of various automobile and vehicle accessories. Its products are also used by many other industries, including manufacturers of metal furniture, machine tools, metal beds, electrical appliances, go-carts, chandeliers, and the like. According to the published balance sheets, the assets of this company increased more than 50 per cent in the last six months of the year 1917. This increase is indicated as follows:

General Balance Sheet of Standard Parts Co.

	Dec. 31, 1917	May 31, 1917
Assets—		
Property account	$9,430,723	$9,960,618
Sundry securities owned, etc.	142,548	47,356
Patents and licenses	1,317,813	....
Goodwill, contracts, etc.	3,110,972	....
Marketable securities	134,284	....
Other permanent investments, stocks of other companies, etc.	2,179,855	2,110,467
Inventories	6,300,518	3,741,769
Accounts receivable	2,212,017	1,125,309
Cash	1,043,059	194,405
Notes receivable	106,134	74,653
Deferred assets	172,726	68,339
	$26,150,649	$17,322,916
Liabilities—		
Common stock	$13,112,599	$8,661,800
Preferred stock	6,798,700	5,551,800
Notes payable	2,245,783	272,610
Patent liability	178,200	....
Accrued payrolls, taxes and dividends	286,870	180,323
Accounts payable	943,864	736,814
Depreciation and reserves	447,568	1,207,214
Capital surplus	10,000	....
Appropriated surplus	750,000	....
Profit and loss	1,377,065	712,355
	$26,150,649	$17,322,916

In January, 1918, the president of the Standard Parts Company wrote as follows on the subject of "Making a Small Business Big": (SYSTEM, January 1918, p. 21 ff.)

"I entered business eleven years ago with a cash capital of $100, and $55 of this was spent for lawyers' and incorporation fees; we began making automobile springs in an abandoned smithy. Today we have a $35,000,000 corporation owning and operating thirteen plants. Why and how did we grow so quickly? Is there anything supernatural in the transit from single dollars to millions?

The difference between big business and little business is largely one of vision. The bars to success are commonly self-made."

He sums up under the following heads the principles which seem to him most significant in connection with the growth from a small to a large business:

"I. Business secrets are of the past; the corporation taking a vote on an action that could not be spread broadcast is ill-managed, for good management connotes fair, open dealing.

II. The fellow who has a little business calls himself a small business man, wants to know only about other small business men, and dismisses the lessons from larger affairs with the remark, 'That's all right for him—he's a big fellow, but it won't do for me,' is the man destined for petty concerns.

III. Some men think that I am too willing to try out something new, and I have been severely criticized at times for making expenditures for the future, but I will, as a fundamental principle, spend any amount within reason in the prospect of shortening the work and thus saving in the end.

IV. Striving for cheapness at the expense of quality is an earmark of little business. Nothing need to be 'put across' on other than its merit in the concern which has a through ticket for the larger affairs.

V. Money is a business tool—and nothing more. Translate money into terms of what it will buy and you have the real rule for figuring its worth.

VI. I thought for some years that everything had to pass over my desk. I worked in the office until eight or nine o'clock in the evening and reached home dog tired. It was only gradually that I learned that the business was not bound up in me and that others could take over certain responsibilities."

The subsequent history of this concern may be briefly summarized as follows. In the latter part of 1919, there were rumors that the Standard Parts Company was not being well managed, that its cost accounting system was inadequate, that it had been trying to carry on too large a business for its capital, and so on. Its credit with its banks was very seriously impaired.

In a signed statement under date of December 31, 1919, the president of the company having stated that in some of their operations they were losing money, and having attributed the loss partly to the post-war competition, and partly to the shortage of working capital over a period of years, said:

"The president assumes full responsibility for the management of the business, and any failure must be charged to him."

On February 16, 1920, the management accordingly changed hands. It was found that the operating loss for the year 1919 had been $1,611,349, which had been increased to $2,444,238 as a result of the payment of unearned dividends.

In spite of the change of management, a receiver was appointed for this company on September 4, 1920.

After numerous attempts at reorganization, the following notice appeared on April 14, 1921:

"On April 12, 1921, the creditors of the Standard Parts Company approved a reorganization plan providing for a new company to have $1,000,000 preferred stock, par $100, and 125,000 shares no par common stock, and $6,500,000 mortgage notes maturing January 1, 1924. The old stockholders will have the right to purchase new notes and common stock within ninety days of this offer."

On June 17, 1921, the following statement was made:

"On June 15, 1921, the stockholders of the Standard Parts Company voted down the plan of reorganization proposed by the creditors. Both preferred and common stockholders agreed to hold out for an extension of the receivership until the depression ends."

Questions

1. Was the launching of this enterprise financially justified?
2. Do you agree with the "principles" of growth laid down by the president of the Standard Parts Company?
3. From the facts given regarding this company's career up to 1918, should you have expected it to continue to be a financial success?
4. What are your own theories regarding the financial policy of this corporation?
5. How fast is it safe for a business to grow?

(Reference: SYSTEM, August, 1921, p. 145 ff.)

PROBLEM 34

FINANCING THE EXPANSION AND THE CONTRACTION

The following statement was made in July 1920:

"The scramble of corporations doing a large volume of business on borrowed money, to get in out of the wet, as the banks gradually curtailed credit accommodations in the last six months, is reflected in the tremendous volume of the new financing which has been done in that period. These corporations have tried two methods of making themselves secure against a calling in of their bank loans at maturity. They have invited more partners into the concern, or have borrowed money from investors for long-term periods.

During the first six months of 1920, corporate financing broke all records, as to number of new securities and amounts. The aggregate reached $2,117,066,470, against $1,124,475,325 in the same period of 1919. In the full year of 1919, new financing aggregated $2,944,-988,000, the record figure up to that time. Financing may drop off considerably during the balance of the year and yet set up a new record for twelve months.

A feature of this year is the comparatively small amount used for refunding, 6.4 per cent against 21.8 per cent in the first six months of 1919.

The largest part of new money this year was for expansion of industrial corporations, principally oil and motor industries. Considerable financing was also necessary to obtain additional working capital by reason of high prices of raw material and other commodities."

The new financing for 1920 is said to have reached an aggregate of $3,322,264,000, of which nearly $2,400,-000,000 was by industrial concerns.

During the first four months of 1921, the total amount of corporate financing reported is $1,040,547,-000. Of this amount, about 35 per cent is said to have been for refunding purposes, much of which was a forced refunding brought about by the protective provisions of earlier security issues which required a definite minimum ratio of net quick assets or the like. The balance of the financing, while stated to be for "new capital," was almost solely emergency financing with a view to securing additional working capital needed to maintain the current position or to pay off mercantile and bank creditors during the period of inventory shrinkage, order cancelations, and general business depression.

Question

What significant relations exist between the financing of 1919-1920 and the financing of 1921?

E. FINANCING MORE OR LESS DOUBTFUL UNDERTAKINGS

Problem 35

Floating a New Automobile Company in 1920

In 1920 the Pan Motor Company, a Minnesota corporation, sold stock to some 54,000 persons, from whom the promoters received the aggregate sum of $4,723,811. Of this amount nearly $1,200,000 was paid to salesmen in commissions. Over $650,000 was retained by the boss promoter for his services as fiscal agent, and over $500,000 went for advertising and other expenses, so that nearly one-half the receipts were absorbed in getting the money.

Questions

1. What do you expect the future of this company to be?

2. Would your answer be different if the company had been launched in 1910?

3. Taking the long-run point of view, how do you think an automobile company should be financed? Give your reasons clearly.

4. Do you think it desirable for the common stock of an automobile concern to be widely distributed?

PROBLEM 36

FINANCING A FRUIT COMPANY IN AN UNUSUAL MANNER

The..........Fruit Company was formed in 1916 with none but doctors for common stockholders. The scheme provided as follows:

The doctors, who purchased common stock, were to prescribe for their patients only the kind of fruit handled by the..........Fruit Company, which it was intended would be of superior quality, raised in the company's orchards, and kept in their own storage plant. It was assumed that because of the stockholders' personal interest the sales of the company would be excellent.

Common stock of no par value to the extent of 10,000 shares was taken by several hundred physicians, the amount paid being in most cases very little. The promoters, one broker and two physicians, issued to themselves the major part of the stock as a reward for their services. In order to raise the additional capital needed to start operations on a small scale, an attempt was made to sell 7 per cent sinking fund, ten-year gold notes to the extent of $200,000.

Questions

1. Should this company have been launched?
2. Is the common stock plan a good one?
3. Would it have been better to sell common stock to the patients.
4. Why did the promoters not sell preferred stock?
5. Would you be willing to invest in the company's debentures?
6. What do you expect the outcome of this proposition to be?
7. Does the date of the formation of the company in any way affect your answers?

Problem 37

Financing an Automobile Finance Corporation

The following words of praise regarding the G. Company appeared, in 1920, in a New England paper:

The question arises why a concern which has been in existence not over three years has risen to such a pinnacle of success as the G. Company.

Why is it that this company, starting with a small office on State Street three years ago, has grown to the proportions which it now takes, in 115 branch offices throughout the principal cities of the East, employing upwards of two thousand men and women.

* * * * * * * *

If you will investigate, you will find the answer to the question, why the company has been so successful.

The G. idea is founded on the principle that the investor is entitled to more than the rental value of his money. He is entitled to the full earning power of his savings.

* * * * * * * *

These savings represent the difference between the amount produced and the amount consumed. These savings are represented in our railroads, in our general business of supplying the necessities and comforts of life.

On the other hand, if you look at the increase of the annual wealth, extended over a period of fifty years, you will find a disproportionate distribution of the annual investment due to the production that was made possible by the savings of the people. If you analyze the causes of the situation, it is found that the methods of financing that have been indulged in during this period of financing that have been indulged in during this period of progress have worked against the small investor.

Mr. G. saw in the commercial banking field, and especially in the field of funding or loaning on automobile paper, an opportunity that would provide a business that would be profitable and at the same time as safe as human ingenuity can make an investment.

* * * * * * * *

It is, therefore, this appeal to sound, common sense, based upon work in a field that has proven profitable, that forms the basis of the success.

Author's explanations: When the G company and its subsidiaries and imitators were endeavoring to sell stock to small savers in order to begin the business, they stressed particularly the fact that the banks had heretofore been making all the money; that they had taken in the savings of the people at the low rate of 4 per cent and had used and reinvested the money in such ways as to make 20 per cent—30 per cent—50 per cent—yes, and 100 per cent or more on their capital. To lend further support to this argument, it was stated that the Federal Reserve Bank of New York City had during the last year made more than 100 per cent on its capital.—This happened to be true.

In this connection, the following explanations regarding so-called "Automobile Finance Corporations," and the like, should be borne in mind:

The reasons for the development of the automobile bank are inherent in the nature of the distribution end of the automobile business. The automobile, despite the current assertions that it is a necessity, has always been looked upon by the commercial bankers as in a different class from staple products—as involving relatively large risks. Automobile dealers, as distinguished from the manufacturers, commonly have relatively small resources; they buy cars largely on credit and in turn sell them largely on credit. It has been estimated, indeed, that 65 per cent of the passenger cars and 90 per cent of the trucks are sold on time. Since the automobile is ordinarily in the nature of a luxury, it quickly becomes a drug on the market in a period of business depression, and since second-hand cars are subject to a very heavy depreciation, commercial banks have not been willing to extend credit to automobile dealers in proportion to their requirements in periods of rapid expansion. Hence the necessity of and the opportunity for the automobile banker.

The work of the automobile bank is similar to that of commercial paper houses and discount companies. It is something more than a broker in that it advances the funds to borrowers, and it is something less than a bank in that as a rule it promptly shifts to the regular banks the burden of carrying the loan. While similar to the institutions already described, it has nevertheless evolved certain distinct financial methods.

There are two types of automobile financing operations to be described. First, certain large credit companies extend what may be called wholesome credit to automobile dealers; second, there are many smaller financing corporations which specialize in the making of retail loans secured by the instalment notes of the ultimate purchasers of cars.

1. THE WHOLESALE PLAN—The financing conducted under the first plan is designed to enable the dealer to secure the funds with which to pay the manufacturer for the cars without waiting for their sale to, or at least without waiting for final payments from, customers. In a sense they are therefore financing the manufacturers themselves. The loans are made to the automobile dealer, who gives his promissory note to the automobile bank, together with chattel mortgages on the cars in his possession. It should be stated, however, that it is only in certain states that we find the chattel mortgage. In some states a trust receipt is used, and in still others a conditional sale agreement is employed, the particular type being determined by the varying laws of different states.

While each particular loan is in fact secured by a chattel mortgage on a particular car, the main reliance is nevertheless placed upon the dealer's general responsibility. Loans made to dealers in this way commonly run for two or three months. While the loans are made to the dealer, it should be added, however, that where cars are held in storage, it is customary for the manufacturer to guarantee the payment of the loan. Thus, the automobile bank often has two-name paper. Such companies derive their profits from a gross "service charge."

2. THE RETAIL PLAN—A concrete illustration of the practice followed by a particular discount company will indicate the difference between this method of financing and that which we have just described. Let us assume that a dealer has sold a car valued at $6,000 and has received $1,000 down and for the remainder instalment notes of $500 each, payable monthly. A chattel mortgage is also given by the purchaser. The dealer borrows $4,000 from the automobile banker, putting up the $5,000 in instalment notes as collateral security. The dealer usually guarantees the payment of such notes. The bank loan is typically, as in this case, 80 per cent of the value of the notes offered as collateral security. Since the purchaser's notes are paid in monthly instalments, the dealer is required to pay his loan to the automobile bank in monthly instalments.

It is the common practise with these smaller companies to discount the dealer's notes, usually at 5 per cent. And since the notes usually bear interest at 7 or 8 per cent, the company always secures 5 per cent on the face of the note, plus 7 per cent interest on that portion of the loan which it finances out of its own resources. Moreover, since the company can usually borrow from the commercial banks on its own note, secured by the instalment notes received from dealers as collateral, at a rate lower than that which the notes themselves bear, it will be seen that some additional profit is thus procured. It will be apparent, however, that it is the 5 per cent discount that constitutes the main source of income.

The extent of the gross profits that may be obtained, therefore, depends largely upon the volume of loans that can be made. Since the dealer is required to pay his loan to the automobile bank in monthly instalments, this bank is in fact in a position at the end of each month to make a new loan of several thousand dollars, on the basis of the instalment receipts, borrowing as before 80 per cent of the amount from a commercial bank, on the collateral security of the new dealer's note and chattel mortgage. These monthly payments, it will be observed, will prove cumulative as additional loans are extended, each of which calls for monthly payments. In fact, by virtue of its ability to borrow from the commercial banks, a company is in a position rapidly to pyramid the volume of its business. It is commonly believed that loans may safely be made to eight or ten times of the company's capital.

The funds employed by *automobile banks* are procured in a variety of ways. First, they may borrow from the commercial bank or through commercial paper houses, on their single-name promissory notes, without other security. Second, they may borrow from commercial banks on their promissory notes, secured by the instalment notes of the purchasers of cars. The officers of the credit company also frequently endorse the notes. Third, they may raise the funds by selling the company's unsecured debenture bonds in the investment market. This method is apparently not very commonly employed. Finally, they may secure the money by selling in the investment market collateral trust notes or bonds.

(Moulton, *Journal of Political Economy*, Dec., 1920, pp. 833-837.

Questions

1. Analyze, critically, the methods of securing capital used by the G. Company.

2. Do you think such financing was justifiable in 1919?

3. From the general social point of view, are such companies necessary? Desirable?

4. How, if at all, should you expect the future financial experience of concerns like this to differ from their past history? Why?

Problem 38

Public Financing of a New "Private" Banking House

Early in 1921 the following notice appeared in a widely read eastern newspaper:

—17%—

The yield in Cash and Participations at par for 1920 was the above.

The C. N. Company Debentures.
Price $115 per Share.

Apply to your own bank or broker, or write to us direct.

The .... Company, Inc.
Boston, Mass.

In reply to an inquiry regarding this advertisement, the "investment" company which was responsible for the notice replied as follows:

When you have carefully read and digested the contents of the enclosed folder, and perhaps discussed it with your banker, we think it will be apparent to you why the C. N. Company debentures are recognized as being an extremely safe investment with a decidedly attractive earning power.

We would call your attention to the fact that this security embodies all the strength of a well-selected, diversified group investment.

The following information derived from the prospectus material enclosed will be instructive:

THE BUSINESS OF THE C. N. CORPORATION

The C. N. Corporation aims to keep in touch with manufacturers in many lines of business in many parts of the country. It invites them to submit their needs for money to be used in their enterprises. The facts in each case are reviewed by the Executive Committee, composed of three officers of the Company. If these facts are not inviting, the matter is dropped. If the facts warrant further investigation the Executive Committee asks for an auditor's report by an outside auditing company and obtains from the real estate board in the manufacturer's locality or from some well-known appraisal company, an official appraisal of the company's physical property. The proposition then goes before the Board of Directors, which passes final judgment on the subject before an investment in an enterprise is made or an underwriting undertaken.

As the investment is made or the sale of a manufacturing company's stock is undertaken and developed, the C. N. Corporation binds itself more and more closely into that business through representation upon the company's Board of Directors, its Executive Committee and Finance Committee, and through the acknowledged right of audit and inspection of such company's books and property at any time without notice, together with an agreement for the Fiscal Agency for the financed company for a period of years, usually not less than five. In consequence of these stipulations the C. N. is always in a position to know all the details in reference to the business of the companies it finances. Therefore, the interest in the corporation does not cease when an underwriting has been completed, but this control and supervision follows through the administration of the funds provided—to the very end—and it will keep a constant watch on the way in which such company's business is developed.

Such a policy, steadfastly followed, goes as far as humanly possible towards safeguarding the constantly increasing investments of the public in C. N. Debentures, and from the growth the Corporation has had it bids fair to become in due time a national institution of considerable importance.

THE SOURCES OF PROFIT

The C. N. Corporation has several sources of profit, chief among which are the following:

FIRST—Through the financing of sound, industrial enterprises—buying or underwriting of the preferred stocks at a certain figure, usually accompanied by a substantial bonus of the common stock, which is held in the treasury of the C. N. C. N., as it appears advisable, either holds in its treasury for revenue or in due time sells the Preferred Stocks at a higher figure. The net profit is usually at least 5 per cent on each transaction on the preferred stock alone, and the annual profit from this source depends only on the number of operations that can be successfully handled. For instance, ten underwritings per annum of, say, $250,000 each, at a profit of no more than 5 per cent, represent a turnover of two and a half million, yielding $125,000 IN CASH PROFIT ALONE, enough to pay the guaranteed dividend on the total authorized Debentures more than two and a half times.

SECOND—The profit in common stock acquired as a bonus—which is seldom less than 10 per cent, and frequently more. Therefore, the C. N., in addition to the above cash profit, would also have in its treasury at least $250,000 of the Common Stock of the companies it had financed. *The acquisition of this bonus of stock permits, from time to time, the declaration of very attractive stock dividends.*

THIRD—The sales organization of the C. N., through which it sells its Debentures and the various preferred stocks, comprises the wholesale investment security house of Blank & Company, Inc., its Fiscal Agents, in which it owns all but three incorporators' shares. Blank & Company, Inc., in turn, own or control an increasing number of retail investment security houses in various other cities. These houses function in a capacity similar to branch offices, but in this way C. N. shares in their profits, and its overhead is decidedly reduced since they are officered by men of strong local reputation, and transact business under their own names and their own responsibility.

FOURTH—C. N. plans, through its affiliated houses, to conduct a regular commercial paper business, making temporary loans to companies in which it is interested, taking their paper therefor and placing it with banks in the usual manner. This in itself is a staple and profitable business and has its place in the C. N. service to business concerns.

FIFTH—The Corporation acts as Registrar and Transfer Agent. The average fee for acting in this capacity is $600 per annum for the registration, transfer or issue of 500 certificates, any amount in excess thereof being paid for at the rate of 15c per certificate. This phase of the business entails practically no additional expense and is, therefore, almost entirely clear profit.

SIXTH—The salaries of the executives are limited, and the lives of the President and Vice-President, the two most active heads of the business, are insured to the corporation to the extent of $50,000 each. The Treasurer of the Corporation functions under a bond of $100,000 and great care was taken in drawing its Charter and By-Laws by one of the most prominent law firms of the country, Messrs........ &.........., to protect the interests of the Debenture holders in every possible way through its profits from all sources, as well as its investments and assets of every nature.

THE PARTNERSHIP POSSIBILITIES OF DEBENTURE HOLDERS

It is seldom, as a holder of Preferred Stock in any corporation, you have the chance to participate like a partner in the profits above the fixed dividend rate on your stock. More rarely still do you have a chance for such participation in an investment banking institution such as the C. N. Corporation.

YOU NOW HAVE A MANY-FOLD OPPORTUNITY IN C. N. DEBENTURES

FIRST—The opportunity of securing through the ONE investment the automatic diversification of your money into many lines of business, each under the watchful eye of the C. N. Corporation, an investment banking institution.

SECOND—Participation like a partner in the profits and opportunities of the business over and above the fixed dividend on your Debenture—for instance:

Suppose you put $100, $500, $1,000, $5,000, or the most that any one man can invest in C. N., namely, $10,000—into these Debentures, what do you get?

First, *you get the security of diversification*—your money goes, say, partly into a stove business, partly into a bread business, partly into a foundry, partly into a chain store system, partly into a typewriter factory, partly into an adding machine factory, partly into a shoe factory, and so on, all of which are under the careful watch of the C. N. to produce as much revenue as possible.

Second, *all of the assets of the C. N. Corporation of every kind whatsoever are back of your Debentures* before anything is applied at all to the Common Stock of the C. N.

Third, *every year C. N. must pay 7% cash return on your money* before the Common Stock can receive a penny.

Fourth, after $7.00 has been paid on each of your Debentures and $10.00 a share has been paid on the Common Stock, *you receive dollar for dollar, share for share with the*

Common Stock in additional cash dividends declared by the Corporation.

Fifth, from time to time *you receive special participations* in the way of distributions of stocks from the treasury of the C. N., accumulated through its financing operations. Such special participations have equaled 10% in par value over and above the cash dividends. It is not expected that they will be less, but rather, in line with treating Debenture holders as much like partners as possible, such participations are apt to be more generous as time goes on.

Sixth, *when the preferred stocks of companies financed are put on the market, you are entitled to a discount from the price* in advance of public offering.

Seventh, in order that you as a Debenture holder may always be informed of the status of your Company *a business statement is furnished you by the Treasurer every 60 days.* This statement shows you how and where the business stands. Most concerns issue statements annually, some semi-annually, but so far as we know, this is the only institution that issues a statement every 60 days. Through these statements, you are kept constantly informed of the progress of the business in which you are a Debenture holder and partner.

Furthermore, as a Debenture holder, *you are entitled to the same voting privileges as held by the Common Stock* of the Corporation, which is one vote at all meetings of the stockholders for each Debenture held. This assures you a voice in the administration of C. N. affairs—a voice that in the majority of companies is denied the holders of anything other than the Common Stock.

The Human Element

The average corporation is apt to be a cold proposition. With the C. N. every effort is made towards the other extreme. The policy of your officers and directors to humanize the C. N. to the greatest possible extent has met the approval of Debenture holders everywhere. Your officers alternate in visiting all localities where there is a sufficient number of Debenture holders to gather in a meeting to hear personally and informally about the progress and plans of the C. N. business. These meetings also offer the opportunity of acquaintance and fellowship with each other, and as Debenture holders in every community are substantial men, this is an opportunity highly appreciated.

In localities where there are fifty or more Debenture holders this meeting takes the form of a quarterly or semi-annual dinner, at which not only the officers, but some or all of the Board of Directors endeavor to be present.

This program of humanizing the Corporation has been adopted advisedly in the belief that the soundest foundation of any institution or organization lies in the complete understanding and confidence of all concerned, and it is being systematically made a most practical source of strength to the Corporation. Therefore, in buying C. N. Debentures you not only make an investment as safe and profitable as humanly possible, you not only have as much of the opportunities of a partner in an investment banking business as possible, but you become one of a large and constantly growing circle of Debenture holders which is almost in the nature of a club.

From the prospectus it appears that the officers of the C. N. Corporation are identical with the officers of the Blank Investment Company.

Questions

1. Do you believe that the financial plan of the C. N. Corporation is a sound one? Why?
2. Do you think it wise to finance such a corporation in 1920-21?
3. If you were a business man should you appeal to this company for assistance in financing?
4. Would you advise your friends to invest in the Debentures of this corporation?
5. Is it desirable that an investment banking business be incorporated? Why?

Problem 39

Financing a Mortgage Company

Early in 1921 the following literature was sent out by a newly organized mortgage company of Akron, Ohio, whose active manager is a university graduate of about ten years standing:

PUTTING YOUR DOLLAR TO WORK!

VALUABLE INFORMATION FOR THE SMALL INVESTOR

The .... Company is formed by the banding together of the resources of thousands of men and women of moderate means for the purpose of investing their money in the safest security known—namely, Mortgages on improved, income-producing property.

Individually their money would have rental value only.

Collectively it has the earning power of capital in large amounts employed in a purely financial institution.

Mortgages are the one class of security that has withstood the onslaught of changing conditions in America for a hundred and fifty years.

Their fundamental safety is acknowledged by savings banks, insurance companies, trusteeships and guardianships, all of which are required by law to invest in properly selected mortgages.

The .... Company combines the safety of a mortgage investment with the earning power of large capital frequently turned in the great and well-lubricated machinery of the modern financial world.

Stockholders in such financial institutions have received with absolute safety and certainty returns of hundreds and even thousands of per cent on their original investments over a period of years.

As a part owner in this company, which has already demonstrated its earning power in the prompt payment of its quarterly dividends, you are offered a share in the large earnings it has every right to expect as its assets and earning power increase from year to year.

What the ...... Company Is

The .... Company is an Ohio corporation. It is a mortgage company restricted by the terms of its charter to deal in one class of security only—mortgages on improved income-producing real estate. It can also own property in its own name.

It can buy mortgages, make first-mortgage construction loans, and by placing these mortgages in trust it can issue bonds against them, thus getting the use of the original amount invested a second time and making additional profits from the reinvestment of its funds.

How Profits are Made by Purchasing Mortgages

We buy first-class real estate mortgages on improved, income-producing property only. Our appraisals are most conservative. Bear in mind the fact that the lower the appraisal, the less money we have to pay for a mortgage, and you will understand why our appraisals may at all times be said to be "ultra conservative."

The profit on the average mortgage purchase may be computed in the following manner:

Face value of mortgage	$1,500.00
Purchase price (20% discount)	1,200.00
Profit	$300.00

This $300 is 25% profit on the $1,200 invested, made the moment the transaction is completed, with no waiting, no further expense and no guesswork.

All mortgages pay 7% on their face value in this locality, so we receive 7% interest on the $300 profit, as well as the 7% on the $1,200 we invested, or a total of 8¾% on the actual amount of money invested.

The first year's profit on the above transaction would therefore be 8¾% plus 25%, or 33¾%.

How Profits are Made in First-Mortgage Construction Loans

Suppose a building operator desires to erect an apartment house or other income-producing building which will cost a total of $100,000 and wishes to secure a first-mortgage construction loan.

He must have $40,000 in cash himself before he can secure a loan from us.

After thorough investigation of the man and his proposition we will loan him up to $60,000—or 60% of the value of the property.

The method of making the loan is as follows: His $40,000 is deposited with us first. When the first floor of the building is completed we pay the contractor part of his money upon advice of our own supervising engineers; when the second is completed another part; and so on until the building is finally completed.

Note particularly that we pay out the $40,000 that has been deposited with us first; and, secondly, we pay out the $60,000 loan over a period of six months to one year.

Suppose the loan is for three years. We charge a commission of 2% a year, amounting to a total of 6% on $60,000, or $3,600.

In addition to this we have had the use of $40,000 for a period of from four to six months.

The borrower pays us 7% interest on the first-mortgage construction loan from the date the papers are signed, which is always three to six months in advance of his receipt of the actual cash.

When the building is completed we have a first mortgage worth $60,000 on income-producing property worth $100,000 in addition to the value of the building lot. This first mortgage is a marketable security, which we can sell by offering it to a bank, insurance company or a trust company.

Or we can dispose of it by putting it in trust and issuing first-mortgage bonds against it in denominations of $500 and $1,000. These bonds are sold to individuals and banks.

In this way we get our money back before the maturity of the mortgage and put it to work again.

Money is made on the quick turnover of capital. Suppose we make this kind of a turnover every two months. This means that we make a commission of 6% on each loan six times per year—or 36% in commissions in one year on first-mortgage construction loans, with accrued interest in addition.

Our Three Sources of Getting Money to Invest

Cash comes in to this Company from three sources—

1. Sale of stock.
2. Payments of interest and principal on mortgages held by us.
3. Borrowing capacity, including short-term bank loans and bond issues.

Cash received from the sale of stock is the first money received by this company, and is immediately used for the purpose of buying mortgages at a discount, and of making first-mortgage construction loans.

Many of our mortgages are monthly payment mortgages on which both the interest and part of the principal are paid back to us each month, thus constantly reducing the amount of money invested in the mortgage, and making our equity and margin of safety constantly larger and larger.

The..........Company has a borrowing capacity from banks which are permitted to make short-term loans. This money is also immediately used to purchase mortgages, proper provisions being made to pay back the loans as soon as they fall due, from income on mortgages.

Bond Issues

The largest source of cash, however, that this company has, comes from its ability to issue bonds against mortgages held in trust by a trust company. This process is very simple, and operates as follows:

We take part of the mortgages we have and place them in the vaults of a bank or trust company, under a trust agreement which provides that the bank or trust company must see that sufficient mortgages are maintained in trust to back up the bonds issued against them.

The trust agreement also provides that sufficient funds must be placed in a sinking fund at the bank to pay the bond coupons and principal when they fall due.

This sinking fund is maintained by the payments on the mortgages themselves, so that the whole plan works automatically, and the payments on the mortgages automatically liquidate the bonds when they come due.

In addition to this security, the..........Company is liable, as a company, for the bond issue; and if default should ever occur in the payments on any one mortgage, this company must make good the default by placing another mortgage in trust, and by making up the amount due out of its other resources.

The extreme care, however, that this company takes in purchasing only first-class mortgages makes it possible for us to say that we have never had a mortgage go bad on us—nor have we ever had to foreclose a mortgage in order to enforce payment.

Many mortgage companies throughout the United States have bond issues outstanding many times the amount of their original capital stock. The more bonds this company can sell, the more money it makes—and the greater will be the cash returns to the stockholders.

Free From Taxes

Shares in the........Company are tax-free in Ohio and free from normal federal income tax under the present laws. This means that such taxes as are levied by the State upon this business, comparatively small in amount, are paid by the company.

The 7% dividends on the preferred and the dividends on the common are given to you in full amount, with nothing deductible for the State.

Dividends Payable Quarterly

Dividends both on the preferred and common shares are payable in January, April, July, and October of each year. These dividend checks are mailed promptly on the last day of each month preceding the dividend-paying month, and should be in the hands of stockholders on the first of the month. The common is now on a 20% dividend basis.

Preferred Shares Redeemable

At the option of the Board of Directors the preferred may be redeemed in part or in whole at any time after January 1, 1921, at $110 per share and accrued dividends.

The company makes no promise as to when this redemption will occur, but it is for the interest of the stockholders to have this preferred redeemed, and every effort will be put forth by the officers to start redemption as soon as this policy will benefit the stockholders.

Terms of Purchase

Shares in the..........Company may be purchased for cash, or on varying terms to suit the convenience of the purchaser. When shares are purchased for cash, the preferred begins to earn 7% dividends from date of purchase, plus regular dividends on common.

6% Interest on Deposits Compounded Quarterly

When shares are purchased on the Easy Payment Plan, all money deposited with the Company draws 6% interest, compounded quarterly, until such time as stock is paid in full.

The..........Company Thrift Plan

$10 Per Month Buys—

6 shares of preferred at $100, and
3 shares of common at $20; total $660

$15 Per Month Buys

8 shares of preferred at $100, and
4 shares of common at $20; total $880

$20 Per Month Buys

10 shares of preferred at $100, and
5 shares of common at $20; total $1,100

$25 Per Month Buys—

12 shares of preferred at $100, and
6 shares of common at $20; total $1,320

$30 Per Month Buys—
16 shares of preferred at $100, and
8 shares of common at $20; total $1,760

$35 Per Month Buys—
18 shares of preferred at $100, and
9 shares of common at $20; total $1,980

$40 Per Month Buys—
20 shares of preferred at $100, and
10 shares of common at $20; total $2,200

How Thrift Plan Pays 18$\frac{3}{5}$% Per Year

When Interest is Compounded Quarterly on six-share purchase at $10.00 per month.

No. Years	Paid on Principal	Interest Compounded Quarterly
1 year	$120.00	$ 3.96
2 years	240.00	15.52
3 years	360.00	35.14
4 years	480.00	63.34
5 years	600.00	100.64
5½ years	660.00	122.87

Average yearly payment on principal	$120.00
Total amount of compound interest 5½ years	122.87
Average yearly interest	22.34
Average yearly rate of interest	18$\frac{3}{5}$%

What You Get

While you are paying for your securities in full, they are deposited with us and are increasing in value constantly.

When shares are bought on the small-payment plan, the common alone—by the time they are paid for in full—should have a ready market value of upwards of $200 *per share.* This prediction is borne out by the history of other mortgage companies.

(Here follows a detailed statement of the earnings of several New York mortgage companies—*Author's Note*).

Finally the following suggestions are made:

"The man who shut his eyes and purchased a few shares in new financial institutions has made more money and suffered less loss than in any other investment field known to man. He has enjoyed the maximum of profits."

Hon. Leslie M. Shaw,
Sec. of the Treas. U. S. for 5 years

A MESSAGE TO WOMEN

How many women of your acquaintance have that enviable possession—an independent income?

Among the 1,500 partners who own the..........Company at least 300 of them are women. The president of this company has often made the statement that women are good investors of money. They usually refuse to take chances, and insist on fundamental safety rather than promises of large and quick returns.

A small investment in the shares of this company will grow over a period of years into a considerable amount if constantly reinvested. The fear of poverty need never haunt the woman who has her money invested in the kind of mortgages this company handles.

A small monthly saving is easy for you to put aside now. Put it in the securities of the........Company, and you will always have the knowledge that no matter what happens, you will have a regular income not dependent on your own efforts to produce.

The manager of this real estate company, earlier referred to, was recently making a rather energetic attempt to enlist the services of advanced college students in connection with the company's security-selling campaign. Some university employment offices are said to have recommended the position as being particularly attractive at this time.

Questions

1. Would you be willing to sell the stock or the 6 per cent first mortgage bonds of this company?

2. What should you expect the financial experience of this company to be during the years 1921 and 1922?

3. Analyze the proposition

(*a*) From the point of view of its financial soundness.

(*b*) From the point of view of the economic service rendered.

Problem 40

Financing a Fisheries Company During the War Period

At the end of 1917, a fisheries company was organized in New England. As Liberty Loans had been taking up the slack in the investment market, an attempt was made to interest small subscribers in the stock of the company. In selling the stock, the management stressed that fact that, due to the war conditions, the price of pork and beef had risen to such an extent that people were being advised to eat fish instead of their customary flesh food. They further pointed to the conservation campaign being carried on by the Federal Food Administration, and to the fact that people were being advised, for patriotic reasons, to eat fish instead of the food which was needed by our own troops and our allies abroad.

Further use was made, in selling the stock of the concern, of a letter which had been written by the United States Commissioner of Fisheries, in which he wrote as follows to the management:

"I have had occasion to examine the plans and note the prospects of this company and have become satisfied that it is in a position to do a very large and remunerative business. No more favorable time could have been chosen for launching a new fishery company, for the country is fish hungry, and the demand for fish food far exceeds the supply and will continue to do so. It is my opinion that the stock of this company is a safe investment, and I do not see how it can fail to yield handsome returns."

The following prospectus was used in selling the first stock issues to small investors:

$3,000,000
7% Cumulative Preferred Shares.

Full Paid, Non-Assessable — Tax Exempt in Maine

E. Fisheries Company

Incorporated Under the Laws of Maine.

Registrar	Transfer Agent
Equitable Trust Company	Empire Trust Company
New York City	New York City

Capitalization

Bonds	None
7% Cumulative Preferred	$5,000,000 Par $100
Common Shares	$5,000,000 Par $10

The E. Fisheries Company is a profitably producing company, operating out of Boston, Portland, Gloucester and New York. The proceeds of this issue, already largely subscribed, are for the enlargement of this company's fishing equipment, by the addition of further highly productive steam trawling vessels. The Company has 4 large food-producing vessels in regular operation and is adding several additional trawlers. The Company's latest steam trawler, the S. S. "Pelican," nearing completion in the shipyards at Portland, Maine, is of the same large size and efficient type as the S. S. "Seabird" lately added to the Company's producing fleet. The plans of the Company are in accord with those laid down by the United States Government.

Through alliance with the largest fisheries interests in this country, the company is highly favored with an efficient, practical management and strong advisory talent long identified with the fishing industry.

Salient Points of Merit

First—The Preferred Shares are preferred as to assets and dividends. Dividends are payable quarterly on the first day of January, April, July and October. The preferred shares are redeemable, in whole or in part, at the option of the directors at $115 per share and accrued dividends.

Second—The ships operating and under construction for the company are tangible assets with ready market value.

Third—The company's ships and equipment are all insured to the full amount of their cost.

Fourth—No bonded indebtedness can be placed on any of the company's property while this issue is outstanding, except by the written consent of two-thirds of the outstanding preferred stock.

Fifth—Actual records of the steam trawlers now operating on the East Coast substantially indicate that all the ships of this company, when in full operation, should earn more than eleven times the preferred dividend.

Sixth—The E. Fisheries Company has no indebtedness. It owns its entire operating equipment free and clear. All ship-construction contracts are paid in full to date.

Seventh—The Company pays regular dividends of 7%.

EARNINGS

Estimated Net Operating Earnings for Twelve Months:

15 Trawlers, when in full operation, per annum,	$2,700,000
Dividend requirements on 7% Preferred, approximately	210,000
Balance available for Surplus	$2,490,000

This estimate is based upon the actual earnings of steam trawlers now in operation.

LEGALITY

All legal matters pertaining to the incorporation of this company and to this issue have been approved by Wilber, Norman & Kahn, New York City.

We recommend the purchase of these shares as a SOUND INVESTMENT. Price on application.

I. M. TAYLOR & CO.
Incorporated
7 Wall Street, New York

BUSINESS

American Fisheries is our last great undeveloped natural resource. Ranking next to the beef industry, it is but beginning to feel the hand of modern enterprise. The primitive methods that have for centuries governed this vast and important food industry are giving way to the world's imperative food needs.

The steam trawler works fast between an *unlimited* supply and an *unlimited* demand. What the harvester is to agriculture, the steam trawler is to the fisheries industry. With its giant nets it drags the near-by bottom of the sea where the "ground" fish are permanently feeding. It saves an enormous amount of time as it is not subservient to the elements. It can harvest in a few days 250,000 to 350,000 pounds of fish and, with its high speed, returns quickly to market where a heavy demand awaits it.

The Great Fishing Banks, off the North Atlantic Coast, are the richest in the world. The "ground" or "bottom" fish, permanently obtained there, are standard for food purposes and command high prices. Our Great Banks alone could supply the food-fish demands of the entire world.

This business is a safe and dependable one. The steam trawler harvests this food product rapidly and regularly, in large quantities and in all seasons and under all weather conditions. The shiploads are quickly landed and cash is promptly received on delivery.

The great superiority of the big steam trawler over the common type of fishing schooner is thoroughly demonstrated over a long period. One steam trawler has a greater capacity for production than a fleet of fishing schooners.

At the outbreak of the war some 7,500 of these steam trawlers were regularly operating in Europe. On this side of the Atlantic there are less than 20 operating at the present moment. Many more are urgently needed. The present and immediate plan of the E. Fisheries Company is to add an additional fleet of these profitable steam trawlers. It is for the enlargement of the company's successfully operating fleet that the company is making the present offering of its preferred stock.

Fish by-products constitute an important industry of unlimited opportunity. All fish by-products are produced by very simple and well-established processes. They find a ready market and yield enormous profits. A big demand, far in excess of the supply, always exists for fish-oil, fish-glue, fish fertilizer, fish-leather and for chicken and cattle food elaborated from fish.

Directors

F. O. Bezner, Capitalist, New York City.

I. M. Taylor, of I. M. Taylor & Co., Bankers, New York City.

L. F. Nagle, President of Nagle Steel Company, Pottstown, Pa.

W. F. Birch, President, Dover Boiler Works Co., Dover, N. J.

C. E. Knoeppel, of C. E. Knoeppel & Co., Counsellors on management, New York City.

Irving Cox, of Cox & Stevens, Naval Architects, New York City.

W. G. Timothy, Vice-President, James, McCreery & Co., New York City.

Richard Cole, of P. K. Wilson & Son, New York City.

Walter P. Wells, President, Williams & Wells, New York City.

Mark W. Norman, Vice-President, Home Bank & Trust Co., Darien, Conn.

W. E. Aughinbaugh, Chair of Foreign Trade, New York University; Foreign and Export Editor, N. Y. Commercial, New York City.

I. M. TAYLOR & CO.

Questions

1. As a business proposition, do you think it was desirable to float a new fisheries company in 1918?
2. Do you agree with the claims made and the methods used by the E. Fisheries Company?
3. What is your opinion of the directorate of this Company?
4. What is your opinion of the letter written by the United States Commissioner of Fisheries?
5. Should you expect that the stock of this company could be sold in 1918?
6. What should you expect the financial future of this company to be?
7. Do you believe that any fisheries company should be publicly financed? Why?

Problem 41

Financing a New Theatre in 1921

Late in 1920 the following financial advertisement appeared in the *Harvard Crimson.*

THE STATE THEATRE

Massachusetts Avenue, Boston

Management—The management is substantially the same as "Loew's, Incorporated," capital $35,000,000, of New York; Marcus Loew, President; M. Douglas Flattery, of Boston, Managing Director. The State Theatre is expected to open January 1st; and is to have 25 per cent greater capacity than the Orpheum Theatre of Boston, also under the same management and which earned net last year $346,213.

Earnings—If the State Theatre profits equal the Orpheum record of last year there will be 34.6 per cent earned for the

$1,000,000 State Theatre Company common stock. Revenue from leases on the property other than the theatre will be sufficient to pay preferred stock dividends.

This amounts to capitalizing for only $1,000,000 a 4,000-capacity Loew Theatre in an excellent location. The Orpheum Theatre having less capacity is capitalized at $2,712,500 and yet is paying 14 per cent on its common stock besides 7 per cent on its preferred stock.

STOCK FIRST LIEN—There will be no mortgage. We estimate the total value of the State Theatre property will be $3,152,000, being capitalized at only $1,250,000 preferred and $1,000,000 common stock.

We suggest a certificate as an ideal Christmas Gift; one which will benefit the recipient and remember the giver quarterly for years to come.

Subscribe for the Common Stock now at par, $10 a share, or send for circular.

On February 21, 1921, there appeared a notice from a local investment house stating that to subscribe to common stock of the State Theatre Company was "Like buying $140 worth of real estate for $100 and having 20 per cent on your investment." It was further stated that "The last of the common stock of the State Theatre Company is now offered at par, $10 a share."

On June 6, 1921, there appeared in one of the leading Boston newspapers a financial notice to the effect that the State Theatre Company was offering an issue of $1,200,000 first mortgage, 7 per cent, convertible gold bonds due June 1, 1946, Federal income tax to the extent of 3 per cent to be refunded. The following information is quoted from this notice:

THE CONVERTIBLE CLAUSE AND ITS VALUE

On June 1st, 1926, and December 1st, 1926, and each 6 months thereafter, 1½% of the outstanding bonds will be redeemed in the usual way at 103% (see deed of trust for particulars). But up to June 1st, 1926, no bonds will be redeemed, and at any time during this period the owner of a bond can exchange it for an equal amount of common stock at par. The common stock has been sold at a premium, and if earnings equal or exceed estimates, the premium on the common stock may increase to 50% or more—which would reflect on the bonds and make them worth an equal percentage of premium above par.

STATEMENT AS OF SEPTEMBER 1ST, 1921
(Estimated after giving effect to present financing.)

Assets		Liabilities	
Land, buildings, machinery, equipment, etc.	$2,400,000	Mortgage Bonds, (this issue).....	$1,200,000
Cash from deposit on leases (est.).	50,000	Deposits on lease (est.)..........	50,000
		Capital Stock—	
		Preferred......	177,500
		*Common......	1,000,000
		Surplus......	22,500
Total.......	$2,450,000	Total.........	$2,450,000

*$1,200,000 additional common stock authorized for the purpose of redeeming bonds.

The proceeds of this bond issue it is estimated will be sufficient to pay off all indebtedness and finish and equip the buildings so that the company will start business owning the property subject only to this issue and with no debts of any kind outstanding, leaving all net profits available for dividends.

Revenue from leases and rents (without theatre profits) to amount to $125,000, is about 1½ times interest requirements on this bond issue.

PRICE 100% AND INTEREST
Denominations $1,000 and $500

Questions

1. What is your estimate of the claims made by the State Theatre Company at the end of 1920?

2. As a general proposition, which theatre should you expect to be most successful financially—a large one or a small one?

3. How do you account for the first-mortgage bond issue of this theatre?

4. Would you at any time have been willing to buy the securities of the State Theatre?

5. What should you expect to be the financial future of such an amusement house launched in 1921?

Problem 42

Problem in Securing Capital to Develop an Old Gold Mine

Mr. B., who had had some experience in other promotion work and in selling stocks of a speculative character, was approached by a group of men who had formed a company to promote a gold-dredging proposition in one of the western states. From their statements and his inquiries through a competent engineer, he found out the following facts:

The property in question had been originally owned and worked in the 50's for a number of years by a "placer" mining company, and several million dollars' worth of gold had been taken from the location. After the accessible benches had been worked out the property had been abandoned.

In the 90's, a process of extracting free gold from low-grade gravel was successfully evolved in California. Later one of the most successful of the men engaged in this sort of mining, who had properties in Alaska and California, sent his engineer to prospect this particular property. The engineer found that there was a large volume of low-grade gravel with a sufficient supply of ore to make extraction by dredging possible. His employer purchased the property from the rancher who owned it, and had just installed a small dredge, which had been previously worn out in the Alaskan fields, when he died, leaving the property to his several children. His sons took over the management of their father's Alaska and California properties, but not wishing to bother with this property, offered it for sale.

The engineer who had prospected the location for their father believed it was a profitable property, but was unable himself to purchase it. He interested two other men, whom he had known in Alaska, in this proposition. These two men had about $40,000 between them. Finally, the engineer and his two friends incorporated a company and issued to themselves 400,000 shares, out of a total of 1,000,000 shares of common stock, as their promotion bonus.

This company next executed an agreement with the heirs of the property to purchase it for $250,000, paying the $40,000 cash which they had. The balance was to be paid in instalments and the dredge was to be allowed to stay on the property and be operated, the proceeds from its work to go, one-half to the new company and one-half to the heirs, until the property was paid for. The new company had a year in which to pay for the property and the dredge.

The members of the new company attempted to sell the stock, but failed because of their lack of experience in this line. They did succeed, however, in selling 20,000 shares at $1 per share. In addition, they managed to borrow about $40,000 from a local bank, depositing as collateral most of the remaining stock. Most of the money realized from this bank loan was used in their attempts to promote the company, in selling stock, and so on, and in keeping up current payments on the property to the owners as the instalments fell due. At the end of a year there was no money in sight, current payments had been postponed, and they were faced with the alternative of raising $200,000 or letting the property revert to the original owners.

Mr. B. had been approached by these men when the company was first beginning to get into financial troubles. He had looked the proposition over and refused to touch it unless he had control of the company. At this point he was called in for the second time. He believed the property was a good property and would produce profits, with adequate investment. His estimate was that in addition to the $200,000 needed to pay for the property, there should also be raised $150,000 for a power line and a new dredge, the old one being now absolutely worthless.

Mr. B. engaged a competent engineer to examine the property and found from him that the small dredge had been able to produce $445 worth of gold per day at an expense of $100 per day. The recovery during the time that this old dredge had been operating was 81¢ per cubic yard. The content was about $1 per cubic yard.

The property consisted of a valley five miles in length and about one thousand feet wide, the gold-bearing sand and gravel in the bottom averaging eight to twenty feet in depth. About seventy prospect holes were sunk throughout the length and breadth of the valley. The gravel from these holes showed from 70¢ to $1.21 per cubic yard. These prospects were all made by the engineer engaged by Mr. B. and the result seemed to be perfectly satisfactory.

Mr. B.'s problem was to raise $350,000 capital which would enable him to meet the final payments to be made to the original owners, and to install an up-to-date dredge as well as a power line. This was in 1919. Mr. B. could raise about $50,000 on his own account. The balance of $300,000 must be secured from outside sources.

Questions

1. Should you expect it to be worth while to attempt to raise further capital for this proposition? Does the date affect your decision?

2. Granting that the proposition is worth while, suggest, with details, the best method of raising the needed capital at this time, bearing in mind the various interests involved?

(References: Jones, *Investments*, 290–309; Dewing, *Financial Policy*, Vol. II, pp. 152-168.)

Problem 43

The Financial Methods of a Small Oil Company

Late in 1919 a considerable quantity of stock was sold in the Tex-La-Homa Company, largely to people of moderate means, including tradesmen and professional people, who on account of the high cost of living felt that the return which they received from their Liberty Bonds was inadequate. The company was pictured to be in a most flourishing condition.

One or two dividends are said to have been paid. Shortly after the next dividend was due, it was reported to the stockholders that one of the officers of the company had been dishonest and had "robbed" the concern of many hundred thousand dollars. Further reports indicated that the company was in a "receiver's" hands by the end of 1920. Advices came in from time to time, however, to the effect that the property was being successfully developed and that the concern would soon be in a prosperous condition once more.

Not long after this time, some of the stockholders received the following letter:

S. Securities Company
Investments
Commerce Building
Kansas City, Missouri.

To the Stockholders of the
Tex-La-Homa Oil Corporation:

You have been receiving, for some time past, circulars from different concerns requesting you to send money to assist them in protecting your interests. It is quite unnecessary for us to mention the companies' names who have constituted themselves in some instances self-appointed "Protective Committees," and in other instances trying to form committees to reorganize, but we do want to call attention of the stockholders to the fact that J. R. S. & Company* has for the past eight months been representing the stockholders who are, to a large extent, clients of this house, without requesting any contribution whatsoever.

* Initials used throughout for obvious reasons.

The expenses that we have incurred in looking after your interests are exceedingly heavy (we are heavy stockholders in Tex-La-Homa Oil Corporation), but we have not asked you to send us one dollar to assist in defraying these expenses.

We bought tens of thousands of dollars' worth of stock, both Preferred and Common, and are today one of the largest stockholders in the Tex-La-Homa Oil Corporation. Naturally, we are interested in seeing some means or plans worked out that will protect everybody, and without going into details would state that at the present a reorganization of both Corporations is under consideration by bankers holding the Corporation's notes. Also by the directors and endorsers for the Corporation who are working in connection with your duly appointed Stockholders' Committee of Boston, headed by Mr. H. C. G., Chairman.

It is our belief that, without question, a reorganization of Globe and Tex-La-Homa will be effected within a very few weeks, and an announcement will be made to each and every stockholder by the Trustees in Bankruptcy just as soon as the plan has been definitely worked out and determined upon.

Pending receipt of authentic information either from the trustees in Bankruptcy or Mr. G.'s committee in Boston, we would suggest and recommend that the Tex-La-Homa stockholders pay no attention whatever to information coming from any other source and especially those who are asking for contributions.

J. R. S. & Company is doing everything in their power to effect a reorganization which will mean, in the long run we hope, the working out of all interests concerned without any loss whatsoever.

Less than six months ago, the writer and his associates organized the S. Securities Company.

At that time we believe we offered you an opportunity to join with us when the stock could be obtained at the first price of $10 per share. In less than six months we have declared five monthly 2 per cent cash dividends, making a total cash return of 10 per cent. We have paid 10 per cent stock dividends, making total dividends for less than six months, 20 per cent, and we have increased the value of the stock where today we believe it is worth twice what we originally sold it for—all of this, mind you, in less than six months' time.

Today, the S. Securities Company is a closed corporation. There isn't any stock for sale. Our stockholders are more than pleased with the success which we have gained for them. Our cash dividends of 2 per cent per month have been earned for many months in advance. We have piled up a substantial reserve—we have many different oil properties—we have substantial production, and we are a successful, live, going concern today. More than that, we anticipate some very generous disbursements to our stockholders in the near future.

This is not the sort of results you obtained through your investment in Tex-La-Homa. The fact that Tex-La-Homa was not a tremendous success is not the fault of the writer nor this organization.

Management is the secret of success in any enterprise, whether it be oils, industries, or banking. I have succeeded in my own business right here in the Commerce Building during the past eleven years. I have sold millions and millions of dollars' worth of high-class bonds and dividend-paying stocks, and the only company whose securities have been offered by the house of S., that as yet have not proven successful, are the securities of the Tex-La-Homa and Globe.

I reiterate that the failure of these companies to make good cannot be charged to this office. I take a pardonable pride in the fact that out of the one hundred and seventy-five different issues of municipal bonds and high-grade securities, every investor through this house has found his principal and interest paid when due, and found his investment a profitable one, with possibly one exception.

I don't want a single dissatisfied customer in the house of S. I don't want to sell any living man a security that will not prove a profitable investment. I feel very keenly the Tex-La-Homa situation. By reason of this fact, and actuated by a desire to prove of real assistance to you, the following proposition is being outlined for your consideration, and your acceptance or rejection promptly is earnestly solicited.

If there ever was an opportunity in the world to engage profitably in the production of crude oil, today is that day. A dollar today in the oil industry will do the work of ten. Now the opportunity is right here for a body of men, clubbing together and putting their money in one pot, to build up a real, independent oil company that can be made most profitable for all concerned. We have for months been working along these very lines. We have secured options and we have negotiations pending for some most excellent properties.

We are, at the present time, organizing a new corporation which will be managed along the lines that we have found successful in the S. Securities Company—a company whose office will be right in the Commerce Building with its records and its books and its cards on the table—a company that will furnish to every stockholder, complete information and actual facts regarding its affairs at all times—a company that will treat every stockholder as a partner in the institution, consulting his wishes and listening to his suggestions—not a company officered by a few men attempting to "hog" it all.

This company, yet unnamed, is to be organized along fair and square lines, with a guarantee of a square deal to everyone. How much money, or how little money, it will make remains to be seen. Whatever the facts are, every stockholder will know. Whatever the profits may be, he will receive his pro rata share.

This company will have two classes of stock—an 8% preferred profit-sharing stock, and a common stock of nominal or no par value. The writer is to receive a large block of this common stock for services rendered, and for certain options and properties that will be turned over to the company. This will be the individual stock, issued to and belonging to J. R. S. I am not at this time writing you or suggesting that you subscribe, or purchase any of the stock of this company.

I am going to give you an interest in this corporation. I am going to give it to you out of my own personal stock. For every share of Tex-La-Homa preferred, par value $100, that you may own, you may have 100 shares of my stock (common) in this new company, and for every share of Tex-La-Homa (common) that you own, you may have 50 shares of my stock (common). I only ask that you forward 5c per share of the new stock, or at the rate of $5 per share on your Tex-La-Homa, which money will partly reimburse me for my expense in organizing this company and in securing the options and properties that I will turn over to the company.

None of the preferred stock of the new company is to be sold for less than par, and it is this preferred stock that will provide the money with which to finance the company. Common stock is in reality bonus stock, or promotion stock, or anything that you may like to call it. I am banking on its being worth a very great deal of money, and not only recoup me for the money I may lose in Tex-La-Homa, but also giving you an opportunity to secure, without cost to you, a stock that should make you more money during the next year than we ever invested and lost in Tex-La-Homa (and I don't think we will, for there is yet a great chance for Tex-La-Homa to be put back on its feet).

Now, I don't want you to feel that you are exchanging Tex-La-Homa stock for the stock of this new company. That isn't the idea. I want you to keep your Tex-La-Homa stock. I am keeping mine. I am giving you this opportunity to share part of the holdings that are coming to me in this new company, for the reason that I believe this new stock will make you some money, and will, in turn, enable you to say within a year from today that you never lost a dollar through the house of S.

Don't get the idea that I am posing as a philanthropist, because I am not. I am doing this for purely good, selfish business reasons. If I had the money today I would buy every share of Tex-La-Homa stock that you have and pay cash for it—the full amount of cash you paid for it—and I believe that I would be doing good business by doing so.

I have been in business right here for the past eleven years and I expect to be here a great many years more. I certainly believe that your friendship and your patronage is worth more to me than the amount of money you invested in the Tex-La-Homa.

Now, if I can lead this new company to success, and I believe that I can with the assistance of my able associates, and if I can take this stock I am giving to you from my own personal holdings and make it of real value to you, then regardless of the outcome of Tex-La-Homa you will be unable to say that you ever lost a dime through the house of S.

I am telling you frankly what I can do, how I will do it, and why I will do it. I am not even going to suggest that you take advantage of this offer that I am making. I wish you would read this letter over carefully, weigh the matter in your own mind, and decide for yourself whether or not you wish to accept the portion of my stock that you will be entitled to under this arrangement, at a nominal cost to you, which will merely represent a small proportion of the organization and incidental expense.

Thanking you for the past favors and awaiting your early reply, I am

Yours very truly,
J. R. S.
President.

Some time after this letter had been sent out, an "investment" house in New York sent a letter to stockholders of the Tex-La-Homa Company stating that it was reported to them on good authority that J. R. S. was making valiant efforts to improve the financial condition of the company. They stated that there was every reason to believe that within a short time losses would be made good and dividends would be resumed.

This New York house also suggested that it had for sale a limited amount of the preferred stock of the Tex-La-Homa Company which had a par value of $100, but which they would be willing to sell to common stockholders at the rate of $2.25 per share, if they would purchase immediately. It was further stated that the stock would no doubt be "brought to par" in the near future.

It was represented by this "investment" house that they were fellow sufferers in the Tex-La-Homa difficulties and that they were now merely passing the "good word" along, so that a few stockholders who had lost on the common might recoup themselves by buying a very limited amount of preferred. For the convenience of the recipient of the letter, also, a telegraph blank was enclosed, properly filled out and requiring only the signature of the prospective customer.

A number of the Tex-La-Homa stockholders immediately sent in their order for their "allotment" of the preferred stock.

In June, 1921, an attempt was made to find out something more definite regarding the J. R. S. Securities Company as well as the Tex-La-Homa Company. In reply to an inquiry sent to a well-known and thoroughly dependable source of information in Kansas City, the following letter was received:

Kansas City, June 18, 1921.

Dear Sir:

I regret that we cannot tell you much about the inside workings of the Tex-La-Homa Oil Company. Mr. J. R. S., of the S. Securities Company, Commerce Building, Kansas City, Missouri, assures us that his company lost heavily in this company, which went into the hands of the receivers, and that they are trying with might and main to recover what is possible from the company for the benefit of stockholders.

The S. Company, we understand, are putting through some wells in Louisiana and it is apparently with the idea of interesting Tex-La-Homa stockholders in the Louisiana proposition that they are offering subscriptions. This plan is one which is used by a number of companies in the oil-promotion business who offer an opportunity to stockholders in a new company when they have been losers in a former enterprise.

Of course, the oil business as carried on by promotion companies is more or less of a gamble and there is no telling until the drill hits the oil sand whether your money is lost or not. Even if oil is struck, sometimes bad management on the company's part, or the greed of some insider, may filch from the company the legitimate earnings of the stockholders.

The attached bulletin issued by this Bureau last fall will give you a little idea of the methods of promoters in the oil business. One of the big promoters cited in this bulletin —Mr. N. F. W., who was connected with the J. R. S. Company, has been driven from this city, and S. claims that W. defrauded him before he got through with W., and had he known W.'s true character he would not have allowed him to associate with his concern.

I regret that we cannot give you any more information about Tex-La Homa.

There is such a maze of contradictions about Tex-La-Homa's affairs that we doubt whether anyone can with certainty, at this stage, tell exactly what the standing of the company is.

Questions

1. What is your opinion of the original financing and the present position of the Tex-La-Homa Company?
2. What is your estimate of the financial standing of the S. Company?
3. Would you be willing to "take a chance" on any of the stock above described?

Problem 44

Advertising for Capital

Out of about 100 advertisements for "Capital Wanted," appearing in a prominent New York paper on April 17, 1921, the following are selected for purposes of discussion:

1.—Progressive fancy knit-goods house, in order to branch out, desires a wide-awake salesman who can invest $25,000; open for closest investigation; exceptional opportunity.

2.—Established concern, manufacturing and selling well-known line cosmetics, needs additional capital to branch out; will consider offers with or without active services.

3.—Business Man with $5,000 and services wanted to join inventor manufacturing and selling meritorious $5 appliance; unlimited field, big demand.

4.—Sales Manager—Cigar manufacturing concern needing additional capital, has an opening for a party who will invest $5,000 to $10,000; will pay salary and 10% on investment; only capable man with references need apply.

5.—Opportunity—Good income on small investment; publisher periodical wishes to obtain $5,000; will issue preferred stock cover same; also guarantee by second mortgage on home worth $20,000 above first good bonus.

6.—Well-Established business manufacturing special product national in scope. Beginning rapidly to attain popularity, desires additional capital with or without services, to handle the increased business; substantial profits already shown; fullest investigation asked.

7.—Partner or capital wanted to build corporation to finance surprising novelty; new system to make decorative painting like silk on furniture; best investment; enormous profits; no agents; sample furniture on exhibition.

8.—Wanted—Party with $100,000 to finance patented snap fasteners used on clothing, gloves, etc.; revolutionary in principle, with many advantages and big saving in cost of production over present type.

9.—Advertiser desires a party who can invest or furnish $50,000 to develop and build homes within the limits of the City of New York, 5 to 12 minutes' walk to two railroad stations; 30 minutes to Pennsylvania Station.

10.—MOVING PICTURE THEATRE on busiest street in Boston, Mass.; have thirty-year lease; figuring lowest admission and highest expenses, weekly net profits are over $1,000; need one or more with $100,000 for renovating; I am in N. Y. now.

11.—UNUSUAL OPPORTUNITY—Investor join group to finance corporation combining some of largest firms in certain supply lines; merger assures excellent earnings; personnel highest; endorsed by leading men; principals only.

12.—MANUFACTURING BUSINESS, well established, needs capital for expansion; articles thoroughly covered by patents; growing too rapid under present working conditions; strict investigation invited.

13.—CORPORATION owning valuable U. S. and foreign patent rights on automatic machinery for important industry, desires investment of $5,000 to $50,000; take active part in business if desired; unlimited possibilities.

14.—AN EXPERIENCED BUILDER desires a party who can invest or furnish $25,000 to build one-family houses, 30 minutes from Pennsylvania Station; building loans arranged for.

15.—WANTED, a partner in a wholesale bakery, with $15,000 to $20,000; present drawings $75 per week; $10,000 yearly profit; business man only preferred.

16.—WANTED IN A LEGITIMATE REAL ESTATE BUSINESS IN NASSAU COUNTY, L. I., partner with $10,000 to $12,000; practical builder preferred; advertiser is thoroughly experienced and will invest equal amount; money to be used solely for house construction and secured by mortgage; will bear searching investigation.

17.—GENTLEMAN with capital, $20,000 to $30,000, as partner in jobbing business; must be active and give full time; $10,000 required for immediate investment; balance as needed; business is well established and well known; full information only by personal interview; this proposition will stand the fullest investigation.

18.—FOOD PRODUCTS—Manufacturer highest grade food products wishes gentleman to invest up to $15,000 in business for half interest and working capital, preferably one who is qualified to take charge of finances and sales; concern has been ten years in the business, its goods are well known, but working capital and experienced sales manager are needed; principals only.

19.—Owner of tire factory within 200 miles of New York, capable of producing about 22,000 tires this season, wishes to meet party with $15,000 who will receive one-third interest; this money is needed for operations; about one-half of production is sold at good profit; factory can clear about $40,000 this year. Do not answer unless you have money required.

20.—Executive Partner Wanted for well-established high-class specialty shop carrying millinery, gowns, and wraps, vicinity 57th street and 5th avenue; executive ability; reference and conscientious efforts of paramount importance; will bear complete investigation as to character, experience and business integrity; investment of $30,000 to $40,000 required.

21.—Corporation (Western New York), an old-established business, protected by basic patents, requires services of experienced business executive, able to finance new selling corporation holding exclusive contracts, to put their product on the market for household use; unlimited market to develop both here and abroad; only requires introduction to become household staple; goods ready for distribution; capital required, $250,000.

22.—Well-Established sales agency, controlling entire factory outputs of two substantial products (one a food product) wants an active man, capable of taking entire charge of sale and distribution of the food line; must have $5,000 to $10,000 to finance sales; right man can secure half interest in business.

23.—Steel Merchant and importer, Christian, representing American and foreign mills in Eastern States, many years' clientele, desires partner with $15,000 to $25,000 additional capital to arrange New York stock in American, British and German steel specialties; firm agencies; established since 1915; fullest confidence guaranteed and asked; principals only.

24.—Established leather goods house. A1 selling force, making soft fabric bags and novelties, looking for good sample maker and all-around man, who can make investment $3,000 to $5,000; wonderful opportunity for right man; will stand strict investigation; state experience.

25.—German Import House—Established import house; best German pre-war connections, representing leading manufacturers' staple lines in this country; large credits and consigned merchandise; wants partner with $15,000; unusual opportunity.

26.—AN OPPORTUNITY to make a good profit on an investment of $10,000 to $15,000 for the period of four months; money secured by merchandise; orders on hand; demand for merchandise created by using previously proven and successful method; quick action necessary.

27.—WANTED—Third partner in newly established advertising business with unlimited possibilities; $5,000 to $10,000 cash; preferably man who wishes to make an investment rather than take an active interest in business; no risk.

28.—PARTNER WANTED—Well-known promoter requires additional working capital for enlargement of his business; an attractive proposition will be made to one who is capable of making a substantial investment; best banking and other references exchanged.

29.—WANTED—PARTY WITH CONSIDERABLE CAPITAL and unquestioned high standing to help launch unique publishing enterprise susceptible great extension and large financial returns.

30.—IS THERE SUCH A MAN?—Capable office manager having the following qualifications: able to earn $5,000 per year; possessing vision sufficiently broad to enable him to pass on nation-wide credits; able to collect accounts and keep customers' goodwill; ready to invest $15,000 in clean-cut manufacturing business with more than ordinary profit possibilities; able to become congenial associate with two young men who have already invested over $75,000 in cash in business; no brokers; personal interview arranged.

31.—ASSOCIATE WANTED—Having obtained United States agency for the finest French automobile and truck upon exceptional terms, I require the cooperation of a gentleman or organization; $25,000 to $50,000 required; trucks in New York now; exceptional opportunity for a man with vision who can act quickly.

32.—WANTED—Wanted to borrow $50,000 on 20,000,000 feet of original growth large yellow pine, located in the vicinity of Aiken, S. C., 35,000-foot-capacity saw mill, 3 steam dry kilns, electric lighting plant, 7 miles standard-gage logging railroad, 2 steam skidders; low freight rate to all points from Norfolk to Boston, which advantage is sufficient to pay for this loan; will make attractive proposition to party loaning the money.

33.—A BOSTON CORPORATION furnishing insurance, appraisal, engineering and management service to many high-grade New England manufacturers desires to expand into the New York field, and requires services of a really big business man, not over 35 years old, who can invest in company approximately $50,000, which will secure a large share of control; business was started six years ago and has doubled its income every year; this is an opportunity which comes but once for the right man.

34.—PROSPEROUS BUSINESS, established 8 years, supplying a necessary service to the wealthy families of Manhattan; all cash, no credits, no losses, no debts; my net profits 1920 25%; increasing expansion compels my purchase of larger building; I require $25,000 additional money to secure an ideal building which I have selected; I invite an associate to join me; his or her services optional; investment secured; full particulars, highest banking and social references furnished acceptable associate.

35.—WANTED, partner (lady or gentleman), with services and $5,000 to $10,000 for enlarging long-established and prospering art embroidery and crochet beading trade school; capital necessary for materials sold pupils during course; lady now operating school has long years of practical experience and many excellent ideas that with required capital will prove most profitable; business will stand strictest investigation; good income from beginning; business references given and required.

36.—A MILLION DOLLAR chain store corporation, operating in Pennsylvania and New Jersey, seeks for its Brooklyn branch which it is about to establish, a plant manager, credit manager and sales manager; only highest calibre men able and willing to invest $5,000 will be considered; we have also openings for several high-grade salesmen, fully experienced, and who could invest $2,000. Write, giving fullest details.

37.—MAN with $25,000 to help buy out retiring interest in staple manufacturing concern to fill position as secretary; business controlled by young men; the potential possibilities are very great; it is necessary to have a man associated with the company who has funds to invest, and who may be capable of handling the financial development of the work as the volume of business increases; we are a very big company in the making; we wish no replies from brokers or professional introducers; we want a few minutes' audience with a man who can qualify; we can prove up our end to his entire satisfaction.

Questions

1. After a careful study of the above financial "ads," indicate those propositions which seem to you

deserving of financial assistance and which you consider are "safe" propositions. Indicate clearly the reasons for your conclusions.

2. Under what circumstances, if any, is a small business concern justified in endeavoring to secure new capital in this way?

3. Would you reach the same conclusions for all types of businesses and for all stages in the Business Cycle?

F. RAISING WORKING CAPITAL BY THE METHODS COMMONLY USED TO SECURE FIXED CAPITAL

While the following problems might logically be presented in the Chapter on Raising Working Capital, yet inasmuch as these methods of financing are those ordinarily used for fixed capital financing, it is thought best to include them in this chapter. The computations which are called for in the third of these problems will be very valuable as a preparation for analysis of the problems in Chapter V.

Problem 45

Selling Stock by the Company

The C. Rubber Shoe Company found its business at a low ebb early in 1921, and being hard pressed for working capital attempted to sell additional preferred stock to the public direct. The company achieved this end by sending out on a selling campaign many of its employees for whom there was no work in the factory. Through the following up of replies to advertisements, and frequently by means of house-to-house canvassing, the company sold a considerable quantity of stock, though this would have been impossible except for the fact that the concern was well known in the locality. This stock, paying 7 per cent dividends, was sold to the small investor at par. The previous issue of preferred stock was not listed on any exchange, but from time to time sales were being made on the open market for less than 80 (par 100.)

Questions

1. From the point of view of this concern what seem to you to be the advantages or disadvantages of following the policy outlined?

2. Do you approve of a company's selling its stock directly?

3. Will your answer differ according to the size or age of the concern, the kind of industry, or the stage in the Business Cycle?

(Reference: Lough, *Business Finance*, 291–318).

4. Would it be easier for a company to market "no par value" stock than stock having a definite par value? Why?

5. Specifically, what are the arguments for or against issuing stock with no par value?

(References: *Administration*, January, 1921, 87–94; Bonbright, *Railroad Capitalization*, 100–131; Conyngton, *Financing an Enterprise*, 385–400.)

Problem 46

Raising Working Capital for a Small Rubber Tire Company Through a Preferred Stock Issue at the End of 1919

The following notice of a new preferred stock issue appeared in some of the middle western papers on November 6, 1919:

$2,500,000.

The ——— Tire & Rubber Company

Factories: E. P., Ohio   General Offices: Cleveland, Ohio.

$2,500,000 7% Cumulative Sinking Fund, Preferred.
5,000 shares No Par Common.

Both Classes exempt from the Personal Property Tax in the State of Ohio and from the Normal Federal Income Tax.

Par value of Preferred Stock $100, preferred as to assets and dividends. Dividends payable quarterly, January, April, July and October 1st. Redeemable at 110 and accrued dividends. Dividends on the preferred stock will accrue from October 1st.

Capitalization
(Upon Completion of Present financing)

	Authorized	Outstanding
7% Cumulative Sinking Fund Preferred Stock	$5,000,000	$2,500,000
Common Stock (No Par Value)	100,000 shs	100,000 shs

No Bonds or Mortgages

We call attention to the following facts given in a letter to us from the president of The ——— Tire & Rubber Company:

History—The ——— Tire & Rubber Company plant is located at E. P., Ohio, with general offices in Cleveland, Ohio. The Company has been in successful operation for ten years, and manufactures cord and fabric automobile tires, truck tires and inner tubes of the highest quality. The growth of the Company is evidenced by the increase in net sales from $746,000 in 1912 to over $7,000,00 (3 months estimated) in 1919.

Purpose of Issue—The entire proceeds of this issue, after retiring the old preferred stock, will be used as working capital, and will be applied against the Company's current indebtedness.

Assets—After giving effect to the present financing, the Company's statement shows net quick assets of $138 per share and net tangible assets of $193 per share for each share of preferred stock. Quick assets amount to four times current liabilities. The net tangible asset value of the common stock is $23.25 per share. A recent appraisal made by the American Appraisal Company shows the present value of the Company's plant to be approximately $458,000 in excess of the valuation carried in the balance sheet.

Earnings—The average net earnings, certified by Ernst & Ernst, for 5 years and 9 months ending August 31, 1919, after Federal taxes, and allowing for interest, have been $503,360, or nearly three times the annual dividend requirements on this preferred stock issue. The estimated earnings for 1919, based upon the report of Ernst & Ernst for 9 months, are $573,980,000. After payment of the dividend on the preferred stock, this amounts to $4 a share for the common stock.

Redemption—During each year ending June 30, 1921, 1922 and 1923, 2½% of the largest amount of preferred stock at any one time outstanding and annually thereafter, an amount equal to 10% of net earnings shall be redeemed at 110 and accrued dividend, by lot or by purchase in the open market. It is provided, however, that such amounts after 1923 shall not be less than 5% of the largest amount of preferred stock at any one time outstanding.

Protective Features—The preferred stock of the company will have the following characteristics:

No mortgage shall be placed on any of its property.

Net quick assets of 100% and net tangible assets of 180% of the largest amount of preferred stock at any time outstanding shall be maintained.

Restrictions regarding issuance of the remainder of the authorized preferred stock.

Management—The present management of the company is in the hands of the same men who were responsible for its past success.

The accounts have been audited by Messrs. Ernst & Ernst, certified public accountants.

Price, 10 shares Preferred Stock 2 shares Common Stock	$1,000 and accrued dividends on the Preferred Stock from October 1st.

In this connection, it should be explained that the ....Tire & Rubber Company paid dividends of about 12% on the market value of its common stock during 1917 and 1918. After the first quarter of 1919 no further dividends were paid. During this time, however, the officers of the concern were receiving the usual war-time salaries, a number of them being paid amounts ranging from $20,000 to $40,000. The amount of "old" preferred stock outstanding was at this time negligible.

Questions

1. What is your opinion of a tire concern which finds it necessary to secure working capital by a preferred stock issue at this time?
2. Analyze critically the above prospectus. What, if anything, is lacking?
3. How do you expect the finances of this concern to stand at the beginning of 1921?

Problem 47

General Problem in Alternative Methods of Raising New Working Capital for an Old Concern, Through Public Security Issues

The R. Company, well known in New England, is a relatively small subsidiary of a very large and strong national concern. It is engaged in processing some of the important by-products of the parent industry. In January, 1921, the company furnished the following financial statement:

STATEMENT OF THE R. COMPANY
January, 1921

Assets	
Real estate, buildings, machinery, etc	$ 650,000
Inventory	800,000
Accounts receivable	500,000
Notes receivable	50,000
Cash	150,000
Liberty Bonds (at market)	10,000
Russian and German Government bonds	10,000
Stocks and bonds of industrial companies	50,000
Prepaid insurance and rent	5,000
Total	$2,225,000

Liabilities	
Common stock (par $100)	$ 500,000
Notes payable (bank loans)	800,000
Accounts payable	200,000
Accrued wages	5,000
Accrued local taxes	10,000
Reserve for bad debts	20,000
Reserve for decline in inventory value	100,000
Reserve for reduced value of Russian bonds	8,000
Reserve for reduced value industrial stocks	20,000
Reserve for Federal income tax	50,000
Reserve for depreciation of plant	150,000
Surplus (undivided profits)	362,000
Total	$2,225,000

It further appears that the net profits of the R. Company available for interest on floating debt, dividends and the like, over a period of three years have averaged $168,000 per annum. The business of the company is relatively free from seasonal fluctuations, and is not ordinarily much affected by changes in the Business Cycle.

Exercises

A. Set up the Assets and Liabilities of the company as shown on the above balance sheet so as to show in the usual manner the following:—

1. The total assets.
2. The quick (or "current") assets.
3. The total net assets ("net worth").

4. The quick (or "current") liabilities.
5. The net quick (or "current") assets (sometimes called "working capital").
6. The total indebtedness of the company.
7. The book value of the common stock.
8. Ratio of current assets to current liabilities ("current" or "quick" ratio).

B. In the light of your revised balance sheet, answer the following questions:

Questions

1. Does the R. Company need any new financing?
2. Is the R. Company in a position to seek further outside financial assistance?
3. Assuming that the R. Company does need some refinancing, what methods appear to be open to it?

C. As a matter of fact, the R. Company in the spring of 1921 did go to a well-known investment banking house in the city of Boston with a view to effecting some new financing in order to improve its current position. The three following alternatives were considered by the investment house:

(*a*) The possibility of funding all the notes payable (bank loans) into an unsecured "debenture" note issue running from ten to fifteen years at about 8 per cent.

(*b*) The possibility of funding only one-half of the notes payable, or $400,000, by creating a first mortgage on the assets of the R. Company. (Why not on the "fixed" assets only?)

(*c*) The possibility of taking up one-half of the notes payable by the creation of a first mortgage as indicated above (*b*), and retiring the remainder out of the proceeds of the sale of preferred stock either to existing stockholders or to new investors.

Based on the information already given, what are your answers to the following questions:

Questions

1. Which of the proposed methods of financing would leave the R. Company in the strongest position so far as its senior security holders are concerned?
2. Which method of financing do you suppose would be most feasible?
3. Can you suggest any alternative methods which seem to you more satisfactory than any of the above?
4. In the light of the facts given, and your knowledge of general conditions, do you expect that the investment house applied to for assistance decided to put through any new financing for this concern?
5. Assuming that the investment house refuses to assist the company, what steps should you advise them to take?

(References: Collver, Greendlinger, Jones, or the "Introduction" to Moody's *Analyses of Industrial Securities*.)

CHAPTER IV

THE PROBLEMS OF RAISING FIXED CAPITAL (*Continued*): CUSTOMER OWNERSHIP AND EMPLOYEE OWNERSHIP

WITHIN recent years much interest has been shown in the question of selling stock to customers and employees of business concerns. Many public utility companies and some industrials have marketed securities widely to the users of their service or product. The movement in favor of giving the employee a vested interest in the company for which he works is even more marked.

The motives back of this movement are varied. However, the more obvious gains which companies may derive from these newer policies are probably threefold. First, to sell stock to customers or employees is sometimes a comparatively easy and cheap method of raising additional funds. Secondly, in times when public agitation is frequently directed against business concerns, it may be highly advantageous to have as wide a distribution of ownership as possible and to have as stockholders those who, as customers or employees, might otherwise be in a position to work injury. Finally, the extension of employee ownership is thought by many to be one of the best methods for reducing the prevailing labor unrest.

Some of the plans of employee ownership now being devised are utterly unsound from a financial point of view. To the extent that they may help the company to raise much needed funds, they may jeopardize the real interests of the employees. On the other hand, to the extent that the employee's financial position may be carefully protected, he may feel that he is being treated in a too paternalistic fashion. Beyond a doubt there are many difficulties and dangers arising from the plans now being tried out. Some of the more important considerations are indicated by the problems which follow. Very little scientific writing has been done on the question.

A. CUSTOMER OWNERSHIP

Problem 48

Financing a Large Electric Light Company by Selling Stock to Customers

The Commonwealth Edison Company of Chicago, having 12,000 shares of common stock to sell, recently (1920) organized teams of salesmen (voluntarily) among their employees outside of working time. They sold the entire amount in three days, and by the end of the week had sold 20,000 shares. The company now has 14,000 stockholders, mostly customers.

No preferred stock has been issued, but the bonds outstanding are about equal to the common stock. The company probably does the largest electric lighting business of any in the world.

Questions

1. Does this indicate a strong financial position?
2. As a rule, would the common stock of a public utility company be a sound investment for the small saver? Why?
3. Does the size or type of public utility have anything to do with the question? Why?
4. As an investment for the customer, how would the common stock of this company compare with that of a large industrial concern? Of a small industrial concern?

Problem 49

Financing a Small Light and Power Company by Selling Preferred Stock to Customers

A small public utility company in the West financed itself largely by selling preferred stock to its customers. As time went on the company was absorbed by a holding company in New York City. During the "bad times" of 1917-18 the holding company decided to defer dividend payments.

Questions

1. Inasmuch as the stock had been sold to customers and nearby residents as an investment which was perfectly safe for "widows and orphans," do you consider that this was a proper method of financing, and should the dividends have been deferred, even though the treasury of the company was exhausted?
2. Should you deem it advisable for an industrial concern to finance itself in the same way?
3. How does this case compare with the preceding one?

Problem 50

Financing the Expansion of a Small Telephone Company Solely by the Sale of Common Stock to the Users of the Service

A small telephone system was installed by a poor but progressive citizen in one of the towns of North Dakota. All the service in the beginning was performed by the owner and his family. As calls came for extension of service, the owner refused to meet the demand unless the customers would buy shares of common stock in the business. In course of time the service was gradually extended to an adjoining municipality. The customers had purchased enough common stock to enable the extension to be made without incurring any debt.

Questions

1. Do you consider this a satisfactory method of financing?
2. Would it have been a sound policy for a small industrial concern to follow?
3. How does this case compare with the preceding one?

Problem 51

Financing the Expansion of a Small Power Company by Means of Preferred Stock Issues Sold to Customers

The..........Power Company was originally a small, conservatively managed, electrical generating company, having some water power development as well as a small steam plant. Some years ago a consolidation was effected with other properties in the State and the ownership which had before been largely local began to be widely scattered.

A rather extensive construction programme was attempted shortly after the consolidation. More water power was secured, additional steam plant capacity was provided, and a heavy investment in transmission lines was incurred in order to take care of the new business. Owing to the market conditions at the time, the additional capital needed for this programme was secured largely by the issue of bonds, which, because of the excellent reputation of the concern in the past, carried a very low rate of interest. At the time of the consolidation, some additional stock had been issued, but this was almost solely accounted for by capitalization of prospective earnings.

Due to the unexpectedly high costs during the following years, and the refusal of the Public Utility Commission to allow a corresponding increase in rates, the company for some time has been unable to pay dividends on its common stock, part of which, as previously indicated, was water. Yet in order to hold their business, and to develop the new business which seemed essential for the future, it was necessary to continue a moderate programme of new construction.

The capital needed for this purpose could no longer be raised by bonds, because the earnings were not sufficiently high to allow the usual margin of safety. In fact, it was about all the company could safely do to meet the interest on its heavy bonded indebtedness and to provide adequate reserves of different sorts. The company, therefore, managed to meet its capital outlays by selling preferred stock in small amounts to people in the territory served by them.

Recently it was decided that the earnings could be greatly increased by further expansions which called for a considerable capital expenditure. In order to finance these extensions, an appreciable amount of additional preferred stock was again sold to local purchasers to whom the issue was described as being particularly attractive.

Questions

1. Do you think that the policy of financing by means of preferred stock followed by this company was desirable—

    (*a*) From the point of view of the common stockholders?

(*b*) From the point of view of the bond holders?

(*c*) From the point of view of the customers and others who purchased the preferred stock?

Problem 52

The Method by Which the United Drug Company Originally Secured the Interest of Retail Druggists

The following eulogy appeared in the *Boston News Bureau* in February, 1921:

> "New England should be proud of any man who by sheer energy, business ability, and enthusiasm, builds within the Commonwealth, over the short period of seventeen years, one of the country's largest corporations. Not only that, but Louis K. Liggett manages and heads the biggest drug business in the world. He is to drugs what Duke was to tobacco, what Hill was to railroads, what Rockerfeller was to oil.
>
> "Coming to Boston when a young man with only a dream, supported by the qualifications which have made America's captains of industry, he launched into a field which had not been conquered."

The United Drug Company was first organized at the end of 1902. Forty friends of Mr. Liggett subscribed $4,000 each, so that the original capital was $160,000. It was further arranged that the company would manufacture and sell drugs only to those stores which were preferred stockholders of the company. There was to be only one such drug store in each town. Business was started in 1903 with one hundred fifty retail druggists as local stockholders.

Questions

1. Specifically, what were the real gains from this arrangement?
2. From the financial point of view, do you see any drawbacks?

Problem 53

Extending the Customer Ownership in the United Drug Company

In referring to plans being made for increasing the sale of stock among the retail druggists who purchase from the United Drug Company as well as to their clerks and customers, President Liggett wrote as follows to present stockholders on March 18, 1921:

I think the most valuable idea that I got from the Boots Company in England when we bought it was the fact that they had 40,000 Preferred Stockholders, and that those 40,000 were customers of the Boots Stores, who bought the stock of the Boots Company over the counters of the Boots Retail Stores. I was astounded when this information came to light. They had 40,000 influential citizens throughout England who were actively boosting the Boots business as compared with our having 8,000 Druggist Stockholders who are boosting our business, and approximately 4,000 investment stockholders who probably, too, are boosting our business.

At the annual meeting of our Directors, held last week, I discussed the situation with them; I discussed the comparison; I told them of my plans for the consolidation, sometime later this year, of Liggett's International and United Drug Company; I pointed out to them what the possibilities of this consolidation were going to bring about from the standpoint of earnings, etc.; then I told them that a year ago the stockholders had voted the Board of Directors the right to dispose of any unissued Common stock that was in the Drug Company's Treasury, and I said to them, under the circumstances—what do you think ought to be done with this stock? Should it be offered to all Common stockholders *pro rata*, or should it be offered to the Rexall Retail Stockholder Agents of the Company, or should it be sold to bankers? Their decision was without hesitancy and unanimous that in view of the points that had been made there could be no question but that the Rexall Stockholders should have (and as they expressed it) the immediate opportunity of taking this stock, not only for themselves, but for their clerks, and for their customers' interests. As one Director said,—"I want the opportunity of selling this to a dozen friends of mine because of the influence in the community; it would help my retail business, and help the United Drug Company." Another one promptly said,—"I want to interest the Doctors in my town in this stock because it will materially break down the antagonistic feeling on the part of the Doctors toward the United Drug Company."

As a result, I was authorized to immediately put through the necessary formalities so that the Rexall Agents could have the first opportunity to purchase this stock.

You know we live by experience. I remember in 1914, right after the war broke out, that I offered the last block of stock in the old Company to our stockholders, and it was immediately oversubscribed. A year and a half later every man who bought a share of that stock received three and one-quarter shares in exchange for the one share he bought, in addition to his regular dividends. In other words, if he had sold his shares for par he would have taken a profit of $225. That is analogous to the present condition. The United Drug Company has in its Treasury $4,723,300 of Common stock over and above what it must hold for conversion purposes. In my opinion there never will be any more of this Common stock issued. Unless something unforeseen occurs we will be able to bring about consolidation during this year of all of our interests under one name with this one corporation stocks issued and listed. We will have concentrated our businesses—manufacturing, wholesaling and retailing of all kinds in this country, Canada and England, into one big organization representing a volume of business in excess of $120,000,000 with substantial profits from it, and with every indication and prospect of materially increasing these profits over what we have shown in the past.

We are so developed in our manufacturing business, that we can take care of the next five years' growth without new buildings or more machinery, with a possible exception of some additions to warehouses in England.

As I see the future, the more we develop the plan of having the Retail Druggist Stockholder, his clerks, and his customers, interested as investors in our Company, so do I see a pulling power that will make for volume such as no other plan could accomplish. This has been working constantly in my mind since the day that I discovered what Boots had done toward interesting his customers in his business, but not until recently did it occur to me that we had a way of working it out here. When our consolidation takes place I am going to give you a fixed plan for accomplishing this in your own community. Can you see the effect of having, as Boots has, between 700 and 800 stockholders surrounding each one of his stores? What I am suggesting in this letter is the initial step to make a foundation among a few prominent people in your town, who will materially profit by the consolidation, and their interest will interest many more. If we are to make a profit in bringing about this consolidation that profits should as far as possible go into the hands of those who have in the past, and are now, supporting our business by their efforts. That is TRUE COOPERATION!

The United Drug Company has for years continuously paid its dividends. As an industrial it has a record that is clean and wholesome. It at present pays 8% per annum. Its development in volume has probably been second to none. Its stock within the last two years has sold in the market as high as $150 per share in substantial amounts, even when it was paying less dividends than it is paying now. Its Common stock sold in the market today at $95. I have been buying it constantly at from $145 a share down, and I know that every officer in the Company and the employees have been doing the same thing. If you stockholders collectively went into the market in the next month to buy even a million dollars' worth of our stock, let alone $4,700,000, you would probably force the market up to $125 or more per share.

The company itself cannot sell its stock for less than 100. If we were to employ the bankers to sell it for us we should have to pay them a five per cent commission on the par value to do it. What I am proposing to do is that you and other retail agents should act as our agents in the sale of this stock, in place of the bankers, and we will pay you a cash commission for your services of $5 per share on each share of stock for which you obtain a subscription. In this way, at the same expense, our stock will be placed with our retail druggists, their clerks and friends, rather than with investors.

The terms of remittance will be 25% on the first of April of whatever amount you subscribe to; 15% on the first of May, and 15% on the first of each month thereafter until the stock is paid for.

I want to close this letter by saying that I was never more confident of the future of this business than I am right now. No industrial organization in this country will be able to compare with our growth in the next five years when our full cooperative plans are developed.

Believing as I do that this opportunity will never come again, I strongly recommend that you take advantage of it, and am glad that you, your clerks and friends are having this chance.

Under date of April 6, 1921 Mr. Liggett again wrote as follows, after the stock selling campaign was started:

I am not thinking so much about the money brought in directly to the Company—that is not it—I am thinking about the increased business of The Rexall Stores when these new stockholders commence to wield their influence in their communities. I wish it were possible for me to describe what I believe their participation in this last offer of the United Drug Company Common stock will mean to them before another year has passed, and also what it will mean to The Rexall Stores in those towns from which subscriptions come. I know also, that the new stockholders who come in now will get the full benefit from the plans we are perfecting and will therefore be better boosters for your business and the Rexall products that you control. If every Rexall Agent sent in as long a list of subscriptions as some have sent in, it would be impossible to fill one-tenth of them from the limited number of shares in this allotment. What I specially want to impress upon you is, that the stockholders you now get among your friends should be the representative people in your communities—people who can do you and your business the most good. These will be essential to the foundation of the ideal condition I have in mind. I do not want a single town in the United States where there is a Rexall Store to be without that foundation which is required for a tremendous publicity campaign for you personally and your stores.

I have pressed for eighteen years a policy which I believe to be right—COOPERATION—and nothing ever had better support than this policy has had from the present 10,000 Rexall Agents. We have gone far with it, but not far enough. True and thorough cooperation in business means the manufacture, distribution and consumption of trade-marked articles with a unified interest, and this we propose to pursue until it becomes a reality, with you controlling the situation in your own town. I have always believed in this policy. When I observed what the Boots Company had accomplished by actual practice in England, as stated in my previous letter, I made up my mind that the moment had come to bind these businesses together for the stockholders who stand as the exponents of this broad policy, and who will reap the benefits arising from it.

* * * * * * * *

I am told that my recent letter to you on this policy got into Wall Street last Thursday. Evidently some of the professional traders did not relish the idea that the United Drug Company stock is tightly held by those interested in the business, nor did it seem to like the plan to place more of it in the hands of the Rexall Agents, their friends and customers, and thereby lessen the opportunity of these professional bear traders to manipulate the market for their own benefit. They consequently attempted a so-called "bear raid" and started to sell the stock "short." They offered it in large blocks and hammered the price down to $85 per share. Many of them contracted to sell what they did not have to deliver, expecting to buy the stock cheaper than they sold it, but when they started to buy for delivery they ran the price back very quickly to $90 and then to $95 the next day. I am told that some of them are still short and must cover some time at some price.

They find it dangerous to sell United Drug Common "short"—the floating supply is small—people buy our stock to keep it because they know what we have done in the past, and they have confidence in the future. I have never believed anything with a stronger conviction in my life than that United Drug will repeat its past performances both in growth and earnings and will far excel anything we have yet accomplished.

It doesn't matter whether you buy the stock in the market or from the Company—do whichever you want; but this I do know—that the offer I made saved money, because if I had taken all the subscriptions that we have received here and bought the stock in the market to fill them, the stock would have cost nearer $125 and I probably would not have been able to fill the subscriptions at that price.

In conclusion, let me say that the United Drug Company's business with its stockholders was nearly as large in March as it was in January and February combined—I was never more confident of our business for this year. I cannot account for our showing in any other way than that The Rexall Stores are seeing the wisdom of enlarging their purchases from their own Company on their own controlled goods. Now you are reaping the benefits of the exclusive agency on merchandise which is not subject to the smashing prices by Tom, Dick and Harry. We don't make a product that is not of good value for the money the customer pays, and your profits are protected.

Liggett's Retail Stores are ahead in March over the same month of last year. Indeed, I can now see many indications of a big year ahead of us with conditions improving every day!

On June 6, 1921, a notice appeared in the financial papers to the effect that the United Drug Company was putting out an issue of $15,000,000 twenty-year, convertible bonds at 8 per cent interest. The purpose of the new issue was stated to be the payment of short time notes coming due on June 15th and the reduction of outstanding bank loans.

The indenture under which the bonds was issued provided as follows:

(1) So long as any bonds of this issue are outstanding, none of the United Drug Company or of its subsidiaries (other than the real estate now mortgaged as above stated) shall be mortgaged or pledged unless the present issue of bonds are equally secured with the other obligations covered by such mortgage or pledge; provided that the company and its subsidiaries shall have the right to purchase additional property, subject to existing mortgages, or may mortgage or pledge any property heretofore acquired, other than its quick assets.

(2) The Company agrees that the ratio of quick assets to quick liabilities, as described in the indenture (and including the present issue of bonds and the 5½ year notes) of the Company and its subsidiaries, shall be maintained at at least 125 per cent. In case such ratio is not maintained, no dividend shall be paid on the Common stock of the Company until it is restored.

Since this date there has been talk of additional financing.

Questions

1. Analyze critically the claims made by the United Drug Company.

2. Do you think it was wise at the time indicated for the company to attempt to sell more stock to customers and employees?

3. Do you think the same arguments for customer or distributor ownership in the United Drug Company which applied at its beginning, apply to the present situation?

4. What is your opinion of the stock selling methods used?

5. How do you expect that the future financial experience of the company will affect those customers who have recently increased their holdings?

Problem 54

Giving Preferred Stock as a Bonus to the Customer

"Two men in New York City, possessing an extensive knowledge of selling and a new process for producing after-dinner confections, determined to finance a new $50,000 company on their customers' capital. Very little equipment was needed, as the product consisted of an assortment of attractive five cent packages, made in one shape and from one substance, but possessing different flavors and labels. The selling expense, however, would normally be very high, and particularly the cost of introducing the brand.

"With a few hundred dollars, these men first contracted for a small quantity of their product from a reputable manufacturer, who supplied the product, labels, cartons and all, at a stated contract price. Then a small, but attractive prospectus was issued in pamphlet form, describing in glowing terms the advantages of the product and the splendid business which the new company would doubtless develop. The authorized capitalization was $500,000, although the promoters only expected to raise $50,000 in cash.

"With the samples and prospectus in hand, the two men individually canvassed a portion of the retail trade in New York City. Their proposition to the retailer was that he should place with them a contract for the confection equal to his full annual requirements, at the usual prices prevailing for similar confections, which were clearly no better than the new product. As a consideration for doing so and for ordering by mail as required, thus avoiding the expense to the seller of frequent sales calls, the retailer was to get a full-paid certificate of eight per cent preferred stock, to the par value of one dollar, with each ten-dollar carton of goods ordered, in addition to the usual quantity discount on larger orders. The preferred stock was to be delivered on payment of the invoice. All orders were taken for future delivery, with the exception of the first ten-dollar carton, which was delivered then and there upon an order calling for payment within ten days.

"It will be noted that under this plan the retailer was paying no more than usual for his goods, but was receiving in addition a ten per cent bonus in preferred stock. This made him a stockholder in the new company and presumably a regular customer. On the other hand, the new company was giving away nothing, since the preferred stock delivered to retailers represented merely the amount which would otherwise have been paid to retail salesmen, or advertisers, to market the product. The usual profit would accrue to the company from the manufacture and sale of the goods. The plan was based upon a clever device to reduce the expense of selling repeat orders, the saving being refunded to the purchaser in capital stock to insure his continued support. The issue of stock under these circumstances was equivalent to selling it for cash and then using the capital to advertise and sell the product of the company.

"All stock was originally issued to the two promoters in exchange for the full right to the process, names, designs, etc., under which the product would be produced. The $150,000 preferred stock would finance sales up to $1,500,000, on which the normal gross profits to the company were expected to be $300,000. Out of this profit were to be paid dividends on the preferred, the cost of selling introductory orders, and administration expenses. It was calculated that $100,000 would remain, half for dividends on common, and half as cash capital donated by the common stockholders to finance the business. By the time the preferred stock would become exhausted the business would be established on a profitable basis, they calculated, leaving the company free to increase the capitalization or change the form of their selling contracts, which expired annually."

(Quoted from Walker, *Corporation Finance*, 297–299.)

Question

What is your opinion regarding the soundness of this scheme and its possibilities?

PROBLEM 55

A NOVEL METHOD OF SELLING STOCK TO THE CUSTOMER

On May 20, 1921, the following note appeared in the *Boston Herald* regarding the stock selling campaign of a small company recently formed to operate a chain of gasoline filling stations:

> "Giving away common stock as a bonus is nothing new. It has been done by many industrial concerns. A local brokerage house which

is selling stock in a gasoline filling station proposition goes this one better by making the following offer for $50: Four shares of 8% preferred, par $10, three shares of common, par $5, and 5 gallons of 'Socony Gasoline.'

"Of course, throwing in plenty of gas is no innovation in the stock selling game. This article is a part of the stock-in-trade of many security salesmen."

Two or three days later there appeared on the financial page of the same paper a good sized "ad" in which the above note was reproduced in a rather striking form and backed up by the following suggestions:

"Boston & Maine Railroad for generations gave to its stockholders free rides.

"It is common practise for companies to seek to interest the stockholders in their properties.

"The above company wants its stockholders to patronize the stations it owns at the following locations: (*Four different stations are here mentioned.*) It is a satisfaction when buying Socony Gas at the lowest prices quoted to be at the same time earning dividends on your own stock."

Question

Do you think that this company should have difficulty in financing itself?

Problem 56

Getting new Capital for an Automobile Concern by Selling Stock to Customers in 1920

"An automobile manufacturing company has hit upon a unique method of increasing its working capital, while at the same time providing for an increase in the sales of its automobiles. It has been decided to sell 2,000 of what are termed 'Ownerships of Motors,' these being apportioned among the various states on what appears to be a population basis.

"To become one of the so-called owners one has to subscribe for twenty-five shares of 8 per cent participating preferred stock, which participates in earnings after dividends on the preferred and after 6 per cent has been paid on the common. This stock may be purchased at $5 a share, and ownership entitles the holder to subscribe to seventy-five additional shares of preferred stock at the par of $5 a share at such times as the Board of Directors may declare the books of the corporation open for further subscription.

"The bearing of the ownerships to the sale of cars is bound up in a clause in the circular which states that the holder of a membership is entitled to purchase one car manufactured by the corporation at a discount of 20 per cent from the list price at any time within two years from the date of subscription, provided that at such time he shall have signified his intention to take up complete ownership by subscribing to seventy-five additional shares. The subscription to the first twenty-five shares is payable, should it be so desired, in four instalments, making $125 in all, but there is a discount of 2 per cent to be had for cash so that the subscription in this case would cost $122.50.

"In letters to prospective 'Owners of Motors' some glowing details are set forth of the earnings which automobile companies are enjoying, but there is no specific mention of what these companies' earnings amount to with relation to outstanding stock. The situation is, however, summed up in these words: 'In acquiring an ownership in the corporation now you are putting yourself in line to share in profits of this money making industry by an investment which is safe, moderate in amount and very easy to make.' From 'safe' to the end of the sentence the words are underlined to give added force to the statement. With the additional capital to be supplied by the 2,000 new owners for the immediate expansion of its business, it is asserted there is an opportunity for profit that is unmatched today."

(*New York Times*, Oct. 23, 1920.)

Questions

1. What do you think of this method of getting new capital, and the arguments used?

2. From the point of view of an industrial company, is it wise for customers in general to buy stock as a speculation? Why?

Problem 57

A Drive for Customer Ownership in a Chain of Lunch Rooms

On January 25 and 26, 1921, half-page advertisements appeared in the *Boston Herald*, inserted by the president of the Waldorf Lunch System. In summary, the material appearing in these advertisements was as follows:

Waldorf

How Less Than 2 cents Profit Per Meal
Built an $11,000,000 a Year Business.

A Real Opportunity for the Small Investor.
Why I Want Waldorf Customers to Share
in Our Proceeds

There is a great human story, a business romance, in how one poor man with his hard earned savings and borrowings from friends started with only $1,800 and lived to see the idea grow into the largest chain of lunch rooms in the country, with restaurants in twenty-eight different cities and assets of over $5,000,000—Waldorf System, Inc.

The Waldorf System had its inception in the founding of the first Waldorf Lunch at Springfield, Massachusetts in 1904, with an initial investment of only $1,800.

No such remarkable success would have been possible had there been behind the project only the thought of profit. The foundation idea of the Waldorf System, Inc., was to establish lunch rooms of real public service in providing the people at large with food of unquestionable quality, correctly and uniformly prepared in absolutely clean, sanitary kitchens, at such a price as to place it within the reach of every man, and woman, at a profit of a few cents a meal.

In the desire to increase valuable good-will and to establish closer relations with those it serves, Waldorf System, Inc., cordially invites every one of its patrons to become part owners in this great business by becoming owners of a small amount of its common stock, and thus share in the profits which their patronage helps to create. Waldorf System, Inc., has no common stock to sell and therefore, obviously, would not profit or receive one cent from such a purchase. The stock may be purchased—like any other stock—in the open market.

This company would benefit indirectly in turning its customers into partners, so to speak, with all the natural increase in interest which ownership inspires in a customer of a business. This company, therefore, desires to have its common stock owned by thousands of its customers in small amounts rather than owned by several hundreds in larger amounts, as at present. This sound business policy has been advocated for years by the larger public utility companies which, like the Waldorf System, deal directly with thousands of people. Further encouragement is given by such companies to have its stock owned in small amounts by a large number of its customers. A representative example is the American Telephone & Telegraph Company, whose stock is owned by 138,000 different stockholders.* America's greatest corporation, the United States Steel Corporation, is another conspicuous example, as the profits of that great enterprise are shared by nearly 100,000 people.

We have chosen this particular time to make this announcement, as this period offers the most striking evidence of the desirability of an investment in the common stock of the Waldorf System. Compare the steady growth and prosperity of the Waldorf System, Inc., right through the period of businessd epression, which in a large number of cases has entirely cut off the dividends of some of America's best known and heretofore most successful corporations. The fundamental reason for Waldorf prosperity is apparent—people must eat, however they may restrict other purchases.

The best and safest investment will have both stability and steadiness of earning power. The present business

*Stated to be about 200,000 by the end of August, 1921.

period has strikingly shown that an investment may be both safe and be in a stable business, yet not possess a steady earning power. It profits the investor little to have his money in a stable business if it does not earn money for him steadily. Compare the record of the thousands of investments (whose earnings are entirely cut off) to the record of earnings of the Waldorf System, Inc., during the same period of business depression.

There are hundreds of people eating daily at the Waldorf Lunches who every three months are paid back by the Waldorf the money they spent in the meantime for their lunches. They have found one of the most profitable methods of reducing the cost of living.

They are the men and women who have put their savings in the common stock of the Waldorf System, Inc., and own enough shares so that the dividends they have received pay for their lunches the year round.

I am taking this method of talking to our thousands of patrons, as a great many of them are not investors, or are not in touch with investment houses and are therefore not likely to know what an unusually safe and profitable investment the common stock of the Waldorf System, Inc., is.

The net earnings for 1919 were at the rate of $385,467 a year. Although the increased costs of provisions reduced the company's proceeds per meal during 1920, the new restaurants acquired (30) and the large increase in the volume of business, with careful, efficient management, enabled the company to show net earnings at the rate of $626,703 for 1920. (There are now 89 restaurants in the chain.)

In 1919 dividends on the common stock were at the rate of 10% per year, cash dividends. In the year just closed, 1920, there were a cash dividend of 10% and two stock dividends of 5% each. Based on the present outlook, I can see no reason why future earnings should not equal or exceed past earnings.

Neither this company nor its officers have any common stock to sell. It may be purchased like any other stock in the open market, through any stock exchange member. The market price is shown daily on the Boston Stock Exchange.

If you have no broker connection, or if you are not familiar with investment matters, I shall be glad to advise you of the name of some responsible investment house through which you can buy Waldorf common stock. I shall welcome you as a part owner of this business, no matter how few shares you can buy. And you'll have the satisfaction of having your money invested in a business that has proved safe.

Questions

1. What seems to you to be the real purpose of this advertising?
2. Analyze the apparent strength or weakness of the Waldorf Company at present?
3. Do you agree with the arguments presented by the president of the company?
4. Is "customer ownership" of a restaurant of any real advantage?

B. EMPLOYEE OWNERSHIP*

Problem 58

Some Typical Methods of Promoting Employee Ownership

The following instances of selling stock to employees, many of which have been publicly noticed, show the recent tendencies toward employee ownership. These cases have been selected at random for purposes of discussion.

A. The United States Steel Corporation

The United States Steel Corporation announced yesterday that the annual stock offering to employees would be made this year at $81 a share, the lowest price at which the shares have been put out since 1914, when the offering price was at $57 a share. The highest price was in 1917,

*There are really no worth-while references on this topic. Some help may be gained on one aspect of this subject by consulting "*Profit Sharing; Its Principles and Practice*" by Burritt, Dennison, Gay, *et al.*, pp. 199–234. See also suggestions on page 197, *infra*.

when the subscription was available at $107 a share, and last year the offering was made at $106. The number of shares taken in 1920 was the largest on record, totaling 167,407, and the subscriptions of 1919 totaled 156,680 shares, when the 100,000 mark was crossed for the first time in the history of the corporation. It is expected that the present subscription will take at least 175,000 shares and possibly cross the 200,000 point, since the price is low as compared with recent years.

An employee of the corporation who subscribed for every offering of common stock and who took his subscription this year would find that the average price of his shares was slightly in excess of $79. It was the custom of the Steel Corporation in its earlier years to offer employees the right to subscribe to preferred stock, but no allotment of preferred was made available after 1914. The lowest price at which the common stock has ever been offered was in 1909, when the figure was $50 a share.

So far as the offering this year is concerned, it conforms in every way with the offerings of the past, except as to price. The employees have the privilege of subscribing to stock in proportion to their salary, those receiving $795 or less being entitled to take one share, and those with a salary between $19,000 and $32,000 being entitled to fifteen shares. Payment for the stock may be made monthly over a period of three years. There is a $5 a year bonus for a period of five years that goes with each share of stock held continuously by a subscriber for that time. This cuts down the actual outlay of cash by the subscriber by $25." (January 1921.)

B. The General Electric Company

A special meeting of the stockholders of the General Electric Company has been called for the purpose of voting upon a proposition to authorize the sale of shares in the company to employees. C. A. Coffin, chairman of the board of the company, in sending out the call for the special meeting, says that it has long been the view of the directors that ownership of stock by employees is greatly to be desired, both as a means of investing their savings and of creating a direct and personal interest in the company's welfare. The amount of stock it is proposed to sell the employees is not to exceed 50,000 shares.

In the letter accompanying the call for the special meeting Mr. Coffin says, in part:

Acquisition of such stock by employees in a large way is not practicable except through some plan permitting the purchase upon instalment payments. Until recently it has not been possible for your company to adopt such a plan for the reason that stock was not available for this purpose. But under the New York Stock Corporation law as amended in 1919, a corporation now may, with the consent of its stockholders, sell stock to its employees.

It is under the provisions of this statute that you are now asked to vote authority to the Directors to sell not more than 50,000 shares of the authorized and unissued capital stock to the company to its employees.

It is proposed that the subscription price shall be substantially the market price at the time the offer is made, payment for the shares to be made by periodical deductions from the payroll. In order that all complexity and detail shall as far as possible be avoided, there will be no allowance or adjustment for interest either on payments made or on unpaid balances; but upon completion of the subscription payments the company will give a credit to the employee which shall represent approximately the net return had he been an actual holder of the stock and had received the dividends thereon from the date of his subscription.

It is proposed that an employee whose subscription is canceled because of illness, unemployment or other reason may receive back the money deducted from his pay with interest at the rate of 6 per cent per annum.

Certificates of stock will not be delivered until completion of subscription payments. (January, 1921.)

C. The Eastman Kodak Company

The adoption of plans under which employees are given a chance to purchase stock is now being contemplated by a number of large- and medium sized concerns in all parts of the country. These will be interested in one of the most successful employee stock subscription plans which has come to notice, that of the Eastman Kodak Company, Rochester, N. Y. In July, 1919, it is stated, this company extended to the wage earning and salaried employes in the service of the company, or in any of its allied companies, at the time the application for shares was made, the privilege of buying a prescribed number of shares of stock at par. Of the amount set aside for distribution, Mr. Eastman donated 10,000 shares of common stock, par value $1,000,000, and the company set aside the same number of shares of like value. At the time this stock was set aside the company's stock was quoted at 600. Both Mr. Eastman and the company reserve the right to reject the application of any employee to participate in their respective donations. The money realized from sale of the stock donated by Mr. Eastman, as well as the interest on unpaid balances, is turned over to the company to be used in welfare work for the employees and administered under rules and regulations mutually agreed upon by Mr. Eastman and the board of directors. Employees, who on January 1, 1918, had served continuously for two years or more, but not five years, are permitted to purchase an amount of stock equal to 2 per cent of the total salary or wages earned in five years of continuous service. Applications to participate are entirely voluntary. By applying for shares the employe assumes no debt. He may pay the whole par value of his shares at once, or may make payments thereon from time to time, as may be convenient, or he may pay for the shares by means of the dividends received thereon by the managers from the company.

D. The Montana Power Company

The Montana Power Company is offering its common stock for subscription to employees at $53 a share on terms of 20% of the purchase price down, and 20% thereafter annually. The previous offering of stock to employees about eight months ago was at $60 a share. (1920-1921).

E. The Midvale Steel & Ordnance Company

Midvale Steel & Ordnance Company is offering officers and employees opportunity to subscribe for not to exceed an aggregate of 6000 shares at $35 per share. About a year ago it offered employees and officers privilege to subscribe to 8000 shares at $50 per share. The quota was oversubscribed by 6046 shares. (Early in 1921).

F. A Rubber Company

The.............. Rubber Compnay organized a Thrift Club among its employees for the purpose of enabling them to purchase preferred stock of the company if they so wished to do. In accordance with the plan adopted, the amount agreed upon beforehand was deducted from the weekly wage of the employee and put on deposit in the "Thrift Bank" until a sufficient amount was saved to enable the employee to purchase one share of preferred stock.

G. The Standard Oil Company

The subscription price to Standard Oil of New Jersey common stock by employees during 1921, has been fixed at 155 by the Trustees for employee stock purchase plans. This is the first price fixed under the recent plan for stock ownership by employees with assistance of the company. The last sale of stock on the Exchange was 160½.

Initial payments commence with the first pay-day in February and will continue for a period of five years unless sooner terminated. The plan provides that employees can subscribe for stock up to 20% of their salary, and for every dollar so subscribed the company will pay an additional 50¢.

(January 28, 1921.)

Questions

1. Analyze critically these different plans of employee ownership.

2. Summarize the chief features of each plan for comparative purposes.

3. Indicate, with your reasons, which plan or plans seem to you best (*a*) immediately, (*b*) in the long run,

   i. From the point of view of the industry itself.
   ii. From the point of view of the employee.
   iii. From the point of view of the public.

4. Do you think that any of the companies above listed go too far or not far enough in the matter?

5. What effect do you think that employee ownership will have on the profits of the concerns in question?

6. What seem to you to be the real reasons for the company's encouragement of employee ownership in the above cases? Distinguish the individual instances.

7. Do you attach any particular significance to the fact that many of these schemes were being more actively promoted in 1920–1921 than ever before?

8. Is employee ownership more to be desired in a public utility or in an industrial concern? Why?

9. Should an employee take any speculative risks in this matter?

10. As an employee, indicate whether you would subscribe to the stock of the above concerns, giving your reasons in each case.

Problem 59

Employee Ownership in Two Old and Highly Successful Manufacturing Concerns

A. The Dennison Company

The Dennison Manufacturing Company of Framingham, Massachusetts, is engaged in the manufacture and distribution of tags, labels, paper boxes and many other paper products and novelties. The company, dating back to 1844, has always stressed "quality" and fair dealing. In order to make the business successful, it must require from its managers and workers long training in detail, concentration of effort, and peculiar natural aptitude. One of the reasons for its success has been its ability always to get a new idea or product on the market ahead of its competitors.

The Dennison Company operated as a partnership until 1878, since which time it has been organized as a corporation. In 1911, however, an important change in organization was made leading to re-incorporation. Regarding this change, the company writes as follows:

> The chief motives which led us to re-incorporate the Dennison Manufacturing Company in 1911 in the form of an Industrial Partnership were: first—to provide a better means of distribution of whatever profits there might be in excess of a fair return on capital; second—to make cetain that the voting power would always remain in the hands of those intimately acquainted with the Company's affairs. From the early days of the Company, stock has been offered to employees at a figure below its actual value, but this plan proved insufficient, unsatisfactory and unfair in many ways.
>
> * * * * * * * *
>
> Actually, the Dennison Manufacturing Company, is as the name of its voting stock suggests—not a normal financial corporation, but a true industrial partnership.
>
> In so far as its corporate fund is the property of investors, it is in the form of preferred stock, which gives to its owners a fixed return, representing interest and compensation for risk. But this preferred stock gives no share either in the net profits or in the control of the corporation. The investors are in the position of lenders and not in any sense a part of the body corporate.

Each year, the profits remaining after dividends on all outstanding stock of any kind have been paid are re-invested in the business and against this investment shares of stock are issued called Industrial Partnership Stock.

Two-thirds of this stock is voting stock and issued to the Managerial Industrial Partners in proportion to their relative salaries. These are the managerial employees of the company—employees who have been with the Company at least 5 years, and whose positions require the exercise of managing ability and control over methods of manufacturing and marketing, such as an executive, principal foreman, chief clerk, or principal salesman; or whose work shows the use of a high degree of imagination, tact or business judgment.

Since this is the only voting stock, the entire control of the Company is in the hands of the managerial employees, and since this stock is non-transferable and must be exchanged for second preferred stock when an Industrial Partner leaves the Company, the control will always remain exclusively in their hands.*

The remaining one-third of the Industrial Partnership stock is voting, and is distributed among the Employee Industrial Partners in relation to the length of their service. These consist of all employees other than the managerial industrial partners, who have been over three years with the company. All employees who have been with the Company long enough to have become thoroughly identified with it, thus share in the profits of the Company.

* * * * * * * *

Cash Dividends on Industrial Partnership Stock cannot exceed 20%, and cannot amount to more than one-half of the profits remaining after Preferred Dividends are paid. This will make it certain that new men will always receive stock if profits have been earned and that some of the earnings will be put back into the business.

But if I. P. Stock is to be issued in any year, there must be paid a cash dividend of at least 5% upon the I. P. Stock already outstanding, so that there will not be successive issues of stock upon which no cash is realized.

The exact amount of the profits need not be issued in I. P. Stock each year, but if desirable, part may be held as temporary surplus in a Surplus Account, which must not exceed 10% of the amount of all kinds of stock outstanding and must be materially reduced at least once in eight years.

* * * * * * * *

Since its establishment the results of the Industrial Partnership plan have been as follows:

*Except, of course, when the control is transferred to the preferred stockholders in the case of foreclosure for failure to pay dividends.

	Shares Distributed	Number of Principal Employees
March, 1913......	15,122	167
March, 1914......	18,604	211
March, 1915......	12,779	218
March, 1916......	12,884	228
March, 1917......	43,752	260
March, 1918......	19,015	288
March, 1919......	30,740	320
March, 1920......	57,363	364

Average cash dividend rate on outstanding I. P. stock 10 per cent.

B. *The Studebaker Corporation*

The Studebaker Corporation dates from 1852, and was incorporated in its present form in 1911. Beginning as a maker of vehicles, the concern has developed into one of the most successful automobile companies of the United States.

The following plan of employee ownership is followed by the Studebaker Corporation:

In addition to the plans under which regular employees receive anniversary checks, annual vacations, pensions and life insurance, the directors offer this opportunity whereby employees may become copartners in the business, and share to a still greater extent, as stockholders, in the profits resulting from its operations. The directors believe that a large increase in the number of employee stockholders will develop the relation of co-partnership in its broadest sense.

The plan is as follows:

1. Continuous service is necessary to entitle employees to purchase stock of the corporation under the liberal terms of this plan, although absence of thirty days or less due to sickness, vacations, suspension of operations, or leave of absence will not be regarded as interruptions of continuous service. Absences without leave, aggregating six full working days or more in employee's anniversary year, will operate as a rupture of continuous service. Employees who have been absent in the war service will not, thereby, affect their continuous service record.

2. Employees who have been in the service of the corporation for three months or more, may have common or preferred stock purchased annually for them by the corporation for their account, in an amount not exceeding Three Hundred ($300) Dollars market value of the stock at the time of the purchase, and in the aggregate not exceeding

five (5) shares of stock, but in neither case to exceed twenty per cent (20%) of their annual rate of earnings.

3. Applications for purchase of stock must be accompanied by an initial payment of 10 per cent of the estimated purchase price, and the remaining 40 per cent thereof, which is payable by employees, must be paid in four years in installments of one-fifteenth of the amount every three months after the date of purchase.

4. The corporation will fully absorb the remaining 50 per cent of the cost of the stock (provided employees keep up their payments and remain in its service continuously for four years), by crediting employee's accounts every three months with one-sixteenth of its half of the cost of the stock purchased.

* * * * * * * *

6. From the above table (*here omitted*) it will be seen that should an employee withdraw from this plan on September 1, 1922, after two years' participation, he would have paid $31.36, and his credit from the corporation would be $25.04, making a total of $56.40 against the original cost of the stock, viz.: $100.00 leaving an unpaid balance of $43.60. He could pay this balance and receive his stock or, if he so desired, he could order his stock sold at the then prevailing market price, and receive cash for the balance to his credit. If, for example, the stock was sold for $110.00 per share, he would receive $66.40, which would be the $31.36 which he had paid, plus $35.04 consisting of $25.04 in credits from the corporation, and $10 in profit from the sales of the stock.

7. All stock purchased under this plan will be charged to employee's accounts at cost, and interest will be charged quarterly at the rate of 6 per cent per year on the unpaid balance of the purchase price, after deducting payments by employees, and credits by the corporation. All cash dividends (and stock dividends paid on the common stock) will be credited to the accounts of employees and the excess of dividend credits over interest charges will act as a reduction in the amount of the final payment to be made by employees in the last year.

8. Stock certificates purchased for the account of employees will be held by the corporation in its name until the expiration of the fourth year, when, if payments are completed, they will be delivered to employees.

9. Fractional shares will not be purchased for employees or delivered to them upon settlement of their accounts.

10. Employees will not be allowed to assign or transfer their rights to stock undelivered under this plan, which rights are personal and contingent upon continuous service.

11. As participation in this plan is voluntary and in no way compulsory, employees may, at any time, withdraw from participation, in which event the credits by the corporation will cease as of the quarterly date preceding withdrawal, and will be forfeited altogether if the withdrawal is made inside of six months from the date stock was purchased. Employees who withdraw within six months, shall receive the actual amount paid in by them, without deductions or additions. Employees who withdraw after six months may either—(1) pay the balance due on the purchase price of their stock and receive stock certificate, or (2) authorize the sale of stock held for them at the prevailing market price, and receive in cash the balance due them, if any, consisting of the difference between the orginal cost of the stock, plus interest charges, and the payments by employees, credits by the corporation, dividends, and sales proceeds of their stock. Employees withdrawing from the plan shall not be permitted to renew participation within one year thereafter.

12. Employees who resign or are dismissed, or who fail to maintain their instalment payments when due, will automatically be withdrawn from the plan on the same basis as above provided for voluntary withdrawal.

13. In the event of death of a participating employee, his heirs or legal representatives may pay the balance due on his stock, either in full or in instalments, and receive stock certificates, or may authorize its sale on the terms herein provided for voluntary withdrawals.

In a letter regarding this plan of employee ownership, President Erskine of the Studebaker Corporation writes as follows under date of July 8, 1921:

The rewards paid the men are for value received, and in no sense may be considered charity or welfare distribution. We do not like these words, and the men resent them. We claim that experienced employees are more valuable than inexperienced ones, and that we can afford to pay for this value. The payments under these plans are fixed charges of operating the business, and come before dividends to stockholders. This year the aggregate payments will exceed $2,000,000. We have had the plan in effect since September 1, 1919, and are very much pleased with the results accomplished. Our labor turnover, at all plants, for the first five months of this year was 5.6% against 108.9% last year, and while, of course, the lack of employment may account for a large part of the decrease in turnover, we believe that the maintenance of the continuous service records by employees has actuated them to stick to their jobs.

Questions

1. Contrast carefully the Studebaker and Dennison plans of employee ownership.
2. Could the same plan of employee ownership be advantageously used by the two companies? State clearly the reasons for your position.
3. To what extent, if at all, do you believe that the present success of these companies is due to employee ownership?
4. What are the essential differences between employee ownership and profit sharing?

Problem 60

Employee Ownership of Preferred Stock in a Paper and Pulp Mill

A large New England Paper Company, until recently unincorporated and very much of a family affair, has for years encouraged its employees to save. Formerly the company even acted in the capacity of a savings bank for the employees until they accumulated several hundred thousand dollars.

Due to very high war-time earnings, however, the concern incorporated about three years ago in order to keep down its taxes. At the time of incorporation, the employees were given an opportunity to invest in a prior preference stock, cumulative at 7 per cent. No other type of stock will be sold to employees.

This prior preference stock is followed by an ordinary preferred stock and by a large common stock issue.

The major part of the prior preference stock was taken by the employees, while almost all of the preferred stock and the common stock is in the hands of a very few men in whose families ownership of the mill has become a tradition. In amount outstanding, the par value of the preferred and common stock is about three times as great as the prior preference stock.

Some of the protective provisions of the prior preference stock are as follows:

While any prior preference stock, Series A, remains outstanding, the corporation shall not do any of the following things without the written consent or the authorizing vote at a stockholders' meeting called for the purpose by the holders of not less than eighty (80) per centum of the prior preference stock, Series A, then outstanding:

A. Change the purpose for which the corporation is formed or the nature of its business;

B. Dispose by sale, lease, exchange, consolidation, merger, or otherwise of all or the principal part of its property and business;

C. Create any mortgage, pledge, or other lien of or upon any of its property or transfer any of its property as security; provided, this shall not apply to purchase, money mortgages of real estate to be acquired for corporate purposes for not exceeding seventy (70) per centum of the cost or market value of the property, whichever is less, or to mortgages given for the purpose of refunding mortgages given by the corporation and outstanding on February 1, 1919, to secure notes of a par value not exceeding the par value of the notes secured by the said mortgages existing on February 1, 1919, issued and outstanding at the time the refunding takes place;

D. Issue or guarantee any bonds, notes, or other evidences of indebtedness maturing later than one year from the issue thereof, or incur any obligations for money borrowed maturing later than one year from the incurring thereof, except as permitted in subdivision (*C*) of this paragraph;

E. Issue prior preference stock, Series A, which together with the prior preference stock, Series A and Series B, then outstanding shall be in excess of the par value of four million (4,000,000) dollars, and then only in case—

(*a*) After such issue the net quick assets are not less than one hundred (100) per centum of the total par amount of prior preference stock, Series A and Series B, then outstanding, plus the amount then to be issued, and

(*b*) The average annual net earnings of the corporation before the payment of any dividends on the prior preference stock, Series A and Series B, or other stock, for a period of twenty-four (24) calendar months preceding the date of such issue, shall have been at least equal to three (3) times the annual dividends on the prior preference stock, Series A and Series B, outstanding and then to be issued;

F. Authorize or issue any other class of stock on a parity with or having priority over the prior preference stock, Series A, in respect of dividends, of the sinking fund applicable thereto, or of payments in liquidation or dissolution.

Questions

1. Is there any need for protecting the employee stockholders to the extent that this company has done?
2. Do you think it would be advisable for the company to let the employees buy common stock also if they wish?
3. Just what does the company gain by this scheme?
4. What do you think should be the attitude toward employees of a company which sells stock to them?

Problem 61

Selling Common Stock to Employees During a period of Depression in Order to Secure Working Capital

The G. Company had a very good reputation in the trade and was perfectly satisfactory to its bankers. When the business depression came in 1920, more working capital was needed in the business. But the manager who held the majority of the stock, wished to retain his control. In order to do this he arranged to sell additional common stock to his employees, who were to make a payment of 20 per cent with their subscription, the balance to be paid over a period of several months. This scheme resulted in the securing of some immediate cash for the more pressing needs.

However, as money was needed more rapidly than the subscriptions were due, the owner pledged the notes which he had received from his employees, covering their total subscriptions, as collateral for a six-months' loan at the bank.

When the depression grew serious later in the year the employees were unable to meet their payments on this stock and hence the value of the bank's collateral was impaired.

Questions

1. Analyze the strength or weakness of this attempt at employee ownership.
2. What would be your advice to the company at the present time?
3. What do you expect to be the nature of the future relations of this company with its employees?

Problem 62

Employee Ownership Resulting in Speculation

The........Company makes a product for which there is a wide market and usually a steady demand. Its business is of such a sort that it was not particularly affected by war conditions. This company's dividend record had for many years been an excellent one. It had no preferred stock and no bonds outstanding.

In order to reduce the labor turnover, increase goodwill, and encourage thrift among the employees, the company offered to sell them new stock at par, at a time when annual dividends of 14 per cent were being paid, and the stock was quoted on the market at about 180. Several methods of paying for the stock were open to the employees. Those who had saved a sufficient amount of money could pay outright; those who had security, such as their homes or liberty bonds, and the like, could borrow from the banks in order to make payment; and others were given the opportunity to pay in instalments over a considerable period of time.

A large number of employees, accordingly, bought new stock about the end of the year 1919. Encouraged by the hope of an apparently sure and high return, many of the purchasers of stock went further and tried to buy on a margin on the open market. Speculation in shares of this company became common at this time. Naturally the market price of the stock began to fall off after the new issue had been sold on this basis. Further, with the 1920 decline in business, a reduction of dividends became absolutely necessary. Consequently both the employees who had been speculating and those who had been buying in a perfectly legitimate manner were panic-stricken, and appealed to the company for help.

In order to prevent a real catastrophe, the company tried to lend from its own funds to those employees who were holding stock on a margin so as to prevent their being sold out. This was at a time when the company was sorely pressed for funds. When the stock fell below par, there was naturally great dissatisfaction on the part of all employees who had purchased stock in an entirely legitimate manner, since there seemed to be no likelihood of any early upward swing in the market price.

Eventually this company went into a receiver's hands and the value of the common stock dropped to a merely nominal figure. Under the reorganization plan, so many senior securities were issued that it is certain the common stockholders will probably never be able to realize par on their stock and it will probably be years before they receive any dividends.

Questions

1. From this instance, what conclusions can be drawn as to the advantages and disadvantages of selling stock to employees?

2. Specifically, what are the chief advantages and chief disadvantages of employee ownership?

C. COOPERATIVE OWNERSHIP

Some who advocate employee ownership wish to carry that ownership so far that the employees will actually control the industries in which they work. In a number of cases this result has been achieved in a small way. Usually, however, such ownership has been effected only when the workers themselves have established their own enterprises, as in the case of the Brotherhood of Locomotive Engineers and their $1,000,000 bank in Cleveland, or the Brotherhood of Maintenance of Way Employees and Railway Laborers, who are reported to have invested about $3,000,000 in cooperative factories. Cooperative associations for marketing purposes have been much more common and no doubt more successful than cooperative productive enterprises.

Though there has recently been much discussion of this question, the movement is of comparatively little interest to the student of finance except in so far as it may be an outgrowth of customer or employee ownership, or may occasionally raise some problem of competition. The two problems here given indicate in a general way two types of cooperative ownership.*

PROBLEM 63

FINANCING A NEW PACKING COMPANY BY SELLING STOCK TO STOCK RAISERS

In 1920, a company known as the "Associated Packing Company of Des Moines, Iowa," sold $3,800,000 of stock, having gone no farther with the construction than to secure a set of blue prints. Promoting and advertising expense consumed nearly one-half the amount subscribed.

The stock was sold mostly to farmers upon the representation that the undertaking was a cooperative enterprise, and the ground was well prepared by the exaggerated reports that had recently been circulated about the profits of the big meat packers.

The investors could have bought the stocks of the long established Chicago companies in the open market at less than their book value, at the very time they were making their subscriptions to this new concern's stock. The farmers bought in blocks, frequently of $5,000 and $10,000, and gave their notes, which were discounted in neighboring banks, where they will have to be held until they are paid off by the produce of the farms.

It was particularly stressed by the sellers of the stock that they were trying to "beat the trust," that they would "eliminate the middle man," that they wanted the farmers, "to be in on the ground floor" and make profits which were now being diverted into the pockets of the five big packers. They did not want business men from Des Moines as stockholders—they wanted farmers. And 98 per cent of the stockholders *were* farmers.

*Those who are interested in this problem will find scattering suggestions in Harris, E. P., *Cooperation the Hope of the Consumer*, New York, The Macmillan Company, 1918; Finn, J. J., *Cooperative Ownership*, Chicago, Langdon & Company, 1916; and in Wolff, H. W., *Cooperative Banking*, London, P. S. King & Son, 1907.

Questions

1. Do you see any objection to making stock-raising farmers the chief stockholders of a packing company?
2. What do you think of this proposition?
3. What might be the result if the producers of raw material generally controlled the manufacturing or distributing concerns which use or handle their goods?

Problem 64

Financing the Construction of Buildings by Selling Stock to Members of the Building Trades Unions

The following circular was sent to members of the Building Trades Unions in Boston in the late summer of 1920:

Homes to be Built

By the Building Trades Unions' Construction and Housing Council.

Preamble

The title of the organization shall be "Building Trades Unions' Construction and Housing Council."

The body shall consist of five delegates from each of the building trades unions of Greater Boston.

To defray expenses of organizing, an entrance fee of ten (10) dollars shall be charged each union.

The purpose of the council shall be to carry on building construction in its entirety.

The immediate work of the Council shall be to stimulate building of homes.

First—By taking charge of construction for those prepared to build.

Second—By the cooperation of the trades in the elimination of all unnecessary overhead charges.

Third—By furnishing sufficient workers to construct each home quickly and economically, consistent with good workmanship.

To finance the movement the Council proposes the creation of a Building Fund.

First—By selling shares to organized labor at ten (10) dollars per share.

Second—By organizing a Cooperative Bank.

Possibilities of the Council

This Council, formed by the rank and file of union men engaged in the building trades of Greater Boston, is truly representative, being made up of five delegates from each local union, and is unique in that its three committees, Finance, Construction, and General Council, each include one of the delegates, thus giving every local represented an equal share in the deliberations and activities of the parent body.

The Finance Committee to have charge of the raising and disbursement of all financial transactions of the Council.

The Construction Committee is to furnish plans, specifications and estimates of building activities; to act as a board of appraisers on land, property and material; appoint a supervisor for general construction; to employ such technical or expert service as conditions may warrant.

All action of the two committees to be subject to review by the General Council.

The Council shall be incorporated under the state laws of Massachusetts, and shall be known as The Building Trades Unions' Construction and Housing Council, with a capital stock of five hundred thousand (500,000) dollars, divided into fifty thousand (50,000) shares of a par value of $10.00 per share. Shares to be sold to organized labor at the rate of $10.00 per share, payment for which may be made in full or on instalments of $1.00 per week per share for ten weeks.

Each shareholder having one vote in electing officers or determining the policies of the Council.

All money resulting from the sale of shares will be used for construction work and expenses incidental thereto. From the earnings of the Council, after a certain percentage has been set aside for a reserve fund, the Council may declare semi-annual dividends.

The Council proposes to organize a Cooperative Bank for the purpose of assisting home builders.

Buildings do not grow, they are constructed by the building trades mechanics, each performing his part. The building becomes a standing fact. Since the building trades workers are the construction force, the organization of the workers is the only thing necessary in order that they may carry on construction in its entirety, thus eliminating the so-called overhead cost and so construct economically.

One could not conceive of an organization better equipped, both for devising policies and performing the work of actual construction, than this Council made up of men whose daily tasks, from superintendent to laborer, eminently qualify them for the duties at hand.

With no desire to criticize others engaged in the study of the housing problem, such a Council as this should command the support of every true union man. It is not too much to say the entire plan is a practical one.

The financing of such a plan as this should not be a very difficult problem. The money now paid for rent could be used to purchase a home. Let every worker who pays rent put $1.00 or more a month into the COOPERATIVE BANK which this Council will create, and each member of organized labor purchase one or more shares of stock. The building of homes could start at once, and in a short time there would be homes complete. Rent coming in could be used for increased building; the rents need not be any higher than pre-war rates. Inside of ten to twelve years you would own what you would still be paying rent for and someone else would own.

The entire plan is cooperation through which the workers shall participate in the management of industry. Every union member should cooperate and purchase stock; every rent payer should cooperate and purchase shares in the COOPERATIVE BANK.

Every shareholder has a vote.

Questions

1. Analyze the strength or weakness of this plan.
2. What do you expect the outcome to be?

CHAPTER V

THE PROBLEMS OF RAISING WORKING CAPITAL

References:

Babson and May, *Commercial Paper*, 9–130.
Greendlinger, *Financial and Business Statements*, (*passim*).
Kniffin, *The Business Man and His Bank.*
*Kniffin, *Commercial Paper, Acceptances, and Analysis of Credit Statements*, (see particularly pages 90–159 for statement analysis.)
*Kniffin, *Practical Work of a Bank*, 371–502.
*Mathewson, *Acceptances*, Chaps. II, V, VI, XI–XIII, XVII, XX–XXVI.
Moulton, *Financial Organization of Society*, 427–456.
*Phillips, *Bank Credit*, 160–234, 260–294.
*Shaw, A. W. (Co.), *Credits and Collections*, 77–124.
Wall, *Banker's Credit Manual*, (*passim*).
*Wall, *Credit Barometrics.*

MOST books which have been written on Business Finance go little farther than the subject of raising fixed capital with the attendant problems. The securing of permanent capital, however, is a problem which confronts a business man only at comparatively rare intervals, while the question of raising funds for temporary financing is forever present. The problems of fixed capital financing are more or less publicly known, whereas the vital issues relating to current financing are of a much more intimate sort.

No academic line can be drawn between "fixed capital" and "working capital." Some of a concern's so-called "current assets" are as permanently invested in the business as if they had been sunk in plant and equipment. Very frequently both fixed and working capital are raised by the same financial operations.

This chapter, however, is primarily concerned with the securing of those funds for current needs, in purchasing, carrying, or selling, the obligations for which can and should be liquidated within a year or within a much shorter period of time. The problems which follow cover the more important phases of bank borrowing, borrowing through commercial paper houses, and the use of trade acceptances, as well as some of the less common methods of temporary financing. As many concerns have recently been forced to raise capital for current needs through public borrowing, some attention is also given to this situation. (See also Chapter III, Section F.)

Exercise II

Problem in Working Capital, Financial Standards, Etc.

1. Select three or more companies engaged in a similar line of industry, preferably manufacturing, but wholesaling or retailing accepted, and tabulate complete financial statements, together with profit and loss statements if they can be secured, over a five-year period for each concern.

2. Compute the following ratios:

   a. Current Assets to Current Liabilities.
   b. Current Assets to Fixed Assets.
   c. Current Assets minus Inventory to Current Liabilities.
   d. Net Current Assets ("Working Capital") to Fixed Assets.
   e. Receivables to Inventory.
   f. Cash to Current Assets.
   g. Cash to Total Assets.
   h. Inventory to Payables.
   i. Receivables to Payables.
   j. Inventory to Sales.
   k. Receivables to Sales.
   l. Net Worth to Capital Stock.
   m. Net Worth to Sales.

3. Tabulate and present your results in graphical form.

4. Draw conclusions, where possible, from the above studies:

a. As to the meaning and significance of the ratios.
b. As to the normal proportions of working capital which may be expected, depending upon the type of business.
c. As to the effect which changes in general business conditions have had on the industry
d. As to the credit position of the industry.

Suggested References: Moody's *Manuals; Abstract of the Certificates of Corporations* (Massachusetts); *Standard Corporation Service* (Cumulative); Wall, *Credit Barometrics*; Lough, *Business Finance,* Chaps. XVII, XXII.

A. BORROWING FROM THE BANK

Problem 65

What is Meant by Bank "Loyalty"?

Not long ago the .... Bank was lending heavily to the........Steel Company whose financial condition was very bad and had constantly been growing worse. The management of the bank, however, had confidence in the character and capacity of the officers of the steel company and decided that they could probably save them from disaster if they continued to extend generous credit. Yet, at no time was it apparent that the .... Steel Company was on the road to financial success. Finally, it failed and in its failure broke the lending bank.

On the morning after the bank's doors were closed, the president said:

"Loyalty of our firm to its customers has caused its financial embarrasment."

A financial writer in one of the daily newspapers, commenting on this occurrence, said:

"The policy of 'loyalty' to customers in times of stress is one of the poorest recommendations for any bank for it is an indication of departure from business principles which must inevitably lead on to disaster."

Questions

1. As a business man, can you reconcile these two statements?
2. How can a bank best show its loyalty to its clients in times of stress?

Problem 66

The Character of a Bank's Officials

A small manufacturing company was successfully financed by the son of a prominent local citizen who was one of the influential directors of the leading bank. Owing to the father's influence the stock was speedily sold and very ample bank accommodations were secured. The son, however, was wholly devoid of business ability and proceeded to drive the concern upon the financial rocks. The father, aware of the situation, urged the bank to make further loans. Finally, he himself advanced the company several thousand dollars more, taking a first mortgage on the property as security.

The new funds sufficed to carry the company over a four months' period so that the preference created by the bonds could not be set aside under the Bankruptcy Act.

At the end of four months, the company was thrown into bankruptcy by the father who bought it in at twenty-five cents on the dollar and satisfied his claims as the only secured creditor. The other creditors, including the bank of which the man was a director, received practically nothing.

Eventually the business was re-organized and became highly successful under the direction of the father who, until his death, remained in management and also maintained his position as director of the bank.

(Adapted from Walker, *Corporation Finance*, p. 293, ff.)

Question

Analyze this case from the point of view of a new industrial concern wishing to borrow from this bank.

Problem 67

What Should the Business Man Know About His Bank?

In the winter of 1920-1921 a new bank was orgaized in the city of Cleveland, having a capital of $2,000,000. The officers have been successful and conservative bankers in various cities of the state. On the Board of Directors there are bankers and business men whose reputation is of the highest in business circles in New York, Chicago, and Cleveland.

There has been a good deal of discussion regarding this bank by business men. Exactly opposite conclusions have been drawn regarding the probable success of the bank. Many have felt that it would not be a safe place to do banking, and have particularly stressed the fact, that, as they allege, the bank was founded at a very inauspicious time.

Questions

1. Do you agree with the business men who felt that it would not be good policy to patronize this new bank? Why, or why not?

2. Specifically, what consideration should be borne in mind by the business man in selecting his bank? Enumerate.

Problem 68

Securing Credit Information from a Bank

A. The .... Company of New Haven, Connecticut, wrote to the .... Bank of Boston for credit information concerning a business house which had no dealings whatever with the bank. The information called for was detailed, covering the latest financial condition, as well as the character and connections of the officials, the standing of the company in the trade, and the like.

The company about which the information was asked had never had an account with the bank.

Questions

1. Do you think the company was reasonable in making this request?
2. How should you expect the bank to handle the inquiry?
3. If the request had come direct from a New Haven bank which had no connections whatever with the Boston bank, instead of from the company, how should the matter have been handled?

B. This same bank recently received an inquiry from a business house in another state regarding the credit standing of a small concern about which the bank had never heard. Upon looking further into the matter, it was discovered that the concern was not listed in the Greater Boston Directory. There was no possibility that the company requesting the information would be a customer of the ...... bank.

Question

1. Under the circumstances, what kind of a reply should you expect the bank to send to this letter of inquiry?

PROBLEM 69

THE "INDUSTRIAL SERVICE" OF THE BANK

Some of the largest commercial banks have developed extensive "industrial service" departments, the functions of which vary widely. In some cases this department confines its activity largely to supplying significant trade information to the bank's borrowers upon request. In other cases an active attempt is made to meet the customer more than half way in this matter. In fact, some bankers as well as some business men feel convinced that the solution of many of our industrial difficulties can be largely attained through more active banker cooperation of this sort, since the bank is in a position to supply the borrower with important information, backed up by constructive advice which could be secured from no other source.

At the same time there are other bankers who are vigorously opposed to the entire scheme of industrial service as above outlined. To paraphrase the words of one whose successful record is well known, "The bank's business is to lend money to its customers, having assured itself that their condition warrants a loan. It is not the proper function of a bank to tell its customers how to run their business, nor in any way dabble into the affairs of its clients."

Questions

1. With which point of view do you agree?

2. To which type of bank would you resort for a loan if you were starting up in business?

3. Specifically, what, if anything, does a bank gain through this policy of "industrial service"?

4. What does the borrower gain?

5. Does such a policy entail any losses,
   (*a*) to the bank,
   (*b*) to the borrower?

6. What do you expect the future tendency along this line to be? Why?

Problem 70

Lending to a Concern Without a Statement of Condition

A. One of the officers of a very large bank in New England says that until recently they have not, in most cases, secured financial statements from woolen manufacturing concerns and that in almost no instances were the annual sales given.

He explains this condition by saying that the companies are more or less family affairs and that they simply refuse to divulge information which might in some way get into the hands of their competitors. He further suggests that anyway the woolen manufacturing business is a well seasoned one, and that most of the concerns make high returns on their investment. Therefore, it has not been necessary to insist on the sales figures, even when financial statements were secured. The general statement of the treasurer or other officer of the mills to the effect that they were making money was considered adequate.

B. The .... Company of Boston engaged in a very large retailing business has never furnished a financial statement to any of its banks, who consider its credit to be A-1 in every respect. When some of these bankers were asked why they did not require a statement they gave two reasons:

First, that the concern had always refused to give a financial statement and threatened to do its banking elsewhere if they insisted.

Second, as the management was so well known to them and so conservative, they thought that no risk was being run.

Accordingly, certain Boston bankers continue to lend many hundreds of thousands of dollars annually to this company, with little accurate knowledge of its affairs.

Questions

1. Do you approve of this way of doing business?
2. Would it be any gain for the company to be required to give frequent statements of its financial condition and earnings? Would it help the banks?
3. To which of these concerns do you think it would be safest to lend without a financial statement?
4. What effect, if any, does competition in banking have on the above situation?
5. If you attribute this situation to competition among banks for the borrowers' patronage, should you advise doing away with competition in banking? Why or why not?

Problem 71

The Relative Importance of Character, Capacity, and the Financial Statement

"We do not believe in this intensive and comparative statement analysis in connection with credit granting. After all, it is character and capacity which really count. There are men to whom we would not lend a cent, even though they showed the best statement in the world. There are others who might open a good line of credit with us, though they produced no statement whatever. Too much time is wasted over mere figures. J. P. Morgan says that he has frequently lent as much as a million dollars without security to men who to his knowledge did not have a cent in the world."

Questions

1. Analyze and criticize from the business man's point of view the foregoing statement made by a "banker."

2. Is the position here outlined in any respect a correct one?

3. Would you differentiate in your answer between a country bank and a city bank? Between a commercial bank and an investment bank? Why?

4. In making a straight commercial loan should "character" and "capacity" ever be considered more important than the financial condition?

5. Just what is the relation, if any, between the financial statement of a concern and the "character" and "capacity" of the officers of the concern?

Problem 72

The Desirability of Giving Full Information to the Bank

Questions

1. What seem to you to be the chief advantages and disadvantages, if any, from the point of view of a business concern in giving complete financial statements and profit and loss accounts to bankers?

2. Do you consider that additional information should also be given?

3. What features should be most carefully considered by the bank in granting loans to business customers?

4. Should the bank be informed of all "contingent" liabilities, such as endorsements, commitments to purchase goods, and the like? Why?

5. What are the lender's chief sources of information regarding the financial condition of the smaller business concerns? Estimate the comparative value of these different sources.

6. Should a borrower let his bank know the purpose for which he desires a loan?

7. How often should statements be given? Does the size of the business, its age, nature, or the time in the Business Cycle affect the problem?

Problem 73

To What Extent, if at All, Should a Bank Lend on "Fixed" Assets?

"A manufacturing concern, established only a short time and doing a good business, sought its first loan. Its chief officer made application in person at the bank president's office. With some pride, he exhibited photographs showing the plant, exterior and interior.

" 'We have the finest little factory in the city,' he said 'and it's paid for. We own the equipment, free of debt. Except for raw material, we do not owe a dollar. We sell our product on long credits. We want to grow, but we haven't the money to carry more accounts. We want the bank to help us extend our credit lines.'

"The banker fumbled the photographs for a moment and complimented their artistic finish. Then he tossed them aside abruptly. Tempering his words with a kindly smile, he said:

" 'Photographs do not represent the best security. We do not lend on real estate or factory equipment. A factory may be the best in the world, yet be idle tomorrow. In the applications that come to us, it is very common for business men to emphasize their fixed assets and minimize those that are liquid.' "

(Shaw, *Credits and Collections*, *108*.)

Questions

1. Do you agree with the banker?

2. Are there circumstances under which you would consider "impressive" quarters an important element in negotiating a bank loan?

3. What steps would you advise this man to take in order to secure working capital?

4. Why should a commercial bank, as a rule, not lend on the security of "fixed" assets?

5. Would it be satisfacto y for the bank to take a mortgage on plant and equipment, and the like? Wehn or Why?

Problem 74

The "Two to One" Ratio

It has for many years been customary among the banks to insist that a borrowing business must show at least a "2 to 1" current ratio in order to secure loans. Frequently little else has been considered.

Questions

1. What considerations are back of this "rule of thumb"?
2. Do you agree that a "2 to 1" ratio is necessarily desirable?
3. Under what circumstances, if any, should it be higher or lower?
4. Does such a ratio, after all, really mean anything?
5. What items in the current assets should be most carefully watched? In the current liabilities? Why?

Problem 75

The Analysis of the Current Ratio

Questions

A. 1. Should you deem a "2 to 1" current ratio satisfactory if the cash and accounts receivable are less than the notes and accounts payable?

2. Which appears to you to be the more liquid asset, merchandise or receivables?

3. Will your answer differ according to the nature or age of the industry, or the stage in the Business Cycle?

B. 1. Would a business concern be justified in expecting a bank loan equal to its "accounts receivable"? Greater than its "accounts receivable"?

2. Will your answer differ depending upon the nature of the business, the age of the business, or the stage in the Business Cycle?

(References: Wall, *Credit Barometrics; The Annalist*, May 2, 1921, 496–97.)

Problem 76

Exercise in Statement Analysis

A—General Statement

Assets		Liabilities	
Fixed Assets	$100,000	Stock	$125,000
Cash	30,000	Notes payable	60,000
Accounts receivable	50,000	Accounts payable	55,000
Merchandise	150,000	Surplus	90,000
	$330,000		$330,000

Sales, $200,000.

Question

Examine this statement with the view to determining the type of concern and its soundness from the credit standpoint.

B—Statement of a Wholesale Grocery House
Oct. 1, 1920

Assets		Liabilities	
Real Estate and Equipment	$1,800,000	Preferred Stock	$1,800,000
Goodwill	1,500,000	Common Stock	1,200,000
Cash	300,000	First Mortgage bonds	1,500,000
Accounts receivable	1,825,000	Notes payable	1,200,000
Merchandise	1,775,000	Accounts payable	300,000
		Surplus	1,200,000
	$7,200,000		$7,200,000

Sales, $19,200,000.

Analyze this statement critically, bearing in mind the following among other questions:

Questions

1. Does the concern discount its bills?
2. Is the merchandise inventory properly valued and salable?
3. What elements of weakness, if any, are to be found in the statement?
4. What would be your opinion of the "capacity" of the management?
5. Do you expect that this concern should be able to borrow more money from its banks or commercial paper houses? If so, how much?

C.

Questions

1. Analyze the following statements with a view to determining the elements of strength and weakness indicated thereby, and the amount which the bank can safely loan. Bear in mind also the light which they may throw on the quality of management.
2. Using the same statements, but assuming the dates of the first two to be two or three years later, and the dates of the last two to be two or three years earlier, make the same analyses.

(*a*) STATEMENT OF A PACKING COMPANY
Nov. 1, 1914

Assets		Liabilities	
Plant, etc.	$400,000	Stock	$600,000
Cash	125,000	Bills payable	450,000
Accounts receivable	225,000	Accounts payable	50,000
Merchandise	425,000	Surplus	75,000
	$1,175,000		$1,175,000

Sales, $7,500,000.

(*b*) STATEMENT OF A PIANO MANUFACTURING COMPANY

July 1, 1917

Assets		Liabilities	
Cash	$15,000	Bills payable	$150,000
Accounts receivable	50,000	Accounts payable	50,000
Bills receivable	500,000	Capital Stock	300,000
Merchandise	300,000	Surplus and Undivided Profits	465,000
Plant, Real Estate	100,000		
	$965,000		$965,000

(*c*) STATEMENT OF A MAKER OF LADIES' STYLE SHOES

July 1, 1920

Plant, etc.	$100,000	Partners' capital	$150,000
Cash	20,000	Accounts payable	75,000
Accounts receivable	50,000	Notes payable (to bank)	35,000
Notes receivable	30,000		
Merchandise	100,000	Surplus	30,000
	$300,000		$300,000

(*d*) STATEMENT OF THE .... WORSTED MILLS

July 31, 1920

Assets

Cash on hand and in banks		$1,527.45	
Accounts receivable		243,262.86	
Inventory		668,508.96	$913,299.27
Real Estate			363,794.63
Machinery, Tools and Fixtures			305,853.40
			$1,582,947.30

Liabilities

Notes payable		$192,000.00	
Accounts payable		85,797.28	$277,797.28
Bonds on Real Estate and Machinery due 1921			500,000.00
Capital Stock			500,000.00
Surplus July 31, 1919		$338,939.25	
Less: 6% Int. on Bonds	$30,000		
2% Div. paid	10,000	40,000.00	
		$298,939.25	
Net profit for Year		6,210.77	
Present Surplus Account		$305,150.02	305,150.02
			$1,582,947.30

Volume—$1,451,960.91.

(Signed) ...... WORSTED MILLS

By ...., President

D

Comparative Statement of a Rubber Tire Company
(0,000—omitted)

Statements made as of October 31st of each year

Assets

	1920	1919	1918	1917	1916	1915	1914
Cash	$167	$1,040	$635	$378	$345		
Notes & a/cs rec.	1,255	2,364	1,387	1,638	1,001	$785	$647
Merchandise	4,117	3,557	3,051	2,850	1,694	776	457
Fixed Assets	5,512	3,526	2,579	2,494	1,269	785	681
Investments in & advances to subsidiaries	4,257	558	554	522	248	...	...
Miscellaneous	.....	917	708	289	315	226	304
Deficit	1,565	.....	...	...	...	...	...
	$16,873	$11,962	$9,314	$8,171	$4,872	$2,572	$2,089

Liabilities

	1920	1919	1918	1917	1916	1915	1914
Notes payable	$2,388	$950					
Accts. payable	1,710	1,049	$808	$2,103	$917	$194	$67
Reserve for Taxes	.....	137	.....	.....	.....	...	...
Capital (prefer.)	6,613	3,667	3,878	2,439	1,750	665	700
Capital (com.)	5,990	2,076	2,047	2,028	1,750	838	799
Surplus	......	3,333	2,071	1,276	225	703	405
Reserve	172	750	510	325	230	172	118
	$16,873	$11,962	$9,314	$8,171	$4,872	$2,572	$2,089

Contingent Liabilities, $860. *Not reported.*

	1920	1919	1918	1917	1916	1915	1914
Sales	$18,900	$16,900	$13,100	$11,100	$6,400	$3,600	$3,100

Dividends Preferred 7%, Common 12% during the entire period.

Questions

Analyze the above statements comparatively with a view to determining,

(*a*) Whether the managerial policy has been a wise one;

(*b*) What elements of weakness or strength are indicated;

(*c*) When, if at all, was the turning point passed which portended financial difficulty?

Problem 77

Looking Beyond the Balance Sheet

"Banking and investment losses are occasioned by ignorance even by corporations themselves of vital conditions, plant location, nature of the product, manufacturing methods, industrial and trade relations, and general and financial policies among features requiring expert analysis. Some companies n the last year or two have caused their bankers losses running into the mi lions because the officers of these companies and of the banks did not have a knowledge of world supplies of such raw material as sugar or copper. There are many other factors that a balance sheet does not reveal. Take the matter of the location of the plant. Such days of competition as the present ones will seek out the uneconomical'y located plant and close it up, and the bankers who floated the securities of such a corporation and the stockholders who first bought them, will be left with the bag to hold if they have not seen the handwriting on the wall and unloaded on to others. As another instance, consider the labor situation. Take certain of the New York clothing manufacturers, who won battle after battle with their labor, to wind up only a jump or two ahead of the sheriff. The problem is much too broad for any method of basing credit on the fixed assets or moral character of a company. The difference between corporate success and failure is often the difference between 99 and 101 per cent, and this narrow zone can be affected in many ways."

(Adapted from *The Annalist*, April 25, 1921.)

Questions

Do you agree *fully* with the above statement? If not, why not?

Problem 78

The Twenty Per Cent Deposit Requirement

It is customary for most banks in the eastern section of the country to require that their commercial borrowers shall keep on deposit with them an amount of cash equal to 20 per cent of the maximum line of credit extended during the year. No interest is ordinarily paid on such deposits. This requirement, while frequently departed from, is theoretically in effect irrespective of the average amount of borrowing during the year. In normal times there are numerous instances in which a concern will keep this amount on deposit without borrowing anything from the bank.

Questions

1. How do you account for the origin of this custom?
2. Do you approve of the practice?
3. Does it seem to be a necessary requirement? If so, why? If not, what improvements or changes can you suggest?
4. What does the bank gain from this requirement?
5. Does the borrower gain anything?
6. Should the bank pay interest on this compulsory deposit?
7. What should be the bank's attitude toward a customer who, when not actually borrowing, lets his deposits fall below the stipulated per cent?
8. Will your answer to the above question be affected by the nature or size of the borrowing concern, or the stage in the Business Cycle?

Problem 79

Need for Maintaining the Required Bank Balances

The A. B. Shoe Manufacturing Company is a closed corporation, the stock being almost solely held by a few relatives who are men of experience in the shoe business, though this particular concern is relatively new. According to the financial statement of the company submitted to its banker as of December 31, 1919, the business was making a good deal of money and its current position was apparently satisfactory. A net worth of $300,000 was shown, and on the strength of its statement it was an easy matter for the A. B. Company to extend its lines of credit with its old bank to the amount of $75,000 and to open up new lines of credit of an equal amount with two other banks. While actually borrowing from these banks the customary deposit of 20 per cent of the line was kept.

During the first half of 1920 the concern continued to make money but still carried a relatively heavy inventory. The old bank at this time cautioned the company to go easy and to be sure to keep an ample deposit with the two new banks with which lines of credit had been established. However, as the lines from the other two banks had been of a temporary sort, it let the balances drop low as soon as it was able to "clean up". During the second half of the year 1920 the concern began to lose money rapidly, because of returned goods, cancelation of orders, shrinkage of inventory, and so on, so that by the end of the year not only had the appreciable profits of the first half-year been wiped out, but also the capital was impaired to the extent of $100,000.

Early in 1921 the concern applied to its old bank for an additional loan as well as for advice. The bank, however, was very reluctant under the circumstances, in view of the impaired equities and frozen condition, to extend any further loan, and asked the A. B. Company if it could not use its lines at the other two banks. Particular inquiry was made regarding the proportion of deposits kept at these other banks, whereupon it appeared that instead of keeping the customary 20 per cent of the line which would have been about $15,000 in each bank, a deposit of not more than $1,000 to $2,000 was being kept in each, the other cash resources having been absorbed by the unsatisfactory transactions of the past six months. The A. B. Company, however, seemed to feel confident that the line of credit would be extended to the full amount of $75,000 if desired.

Fearing that this was an impossible situation, an officer of the first bank went to the other two banks along with a representative of the A. B. Company. These banks stated that they would not under any circumstances make a loan unless the full 20 per cent balance was kept with them. The company, however, was at the end of its resources and knew of no way of providing such a balance. Finally it was arranged that the old bank would extend its line, now being used to the limit, to the amount of about $30,000, which it furnished in cash to the A. B. Company.

The company thereupon deposited this sum in equal amounts with the two other banks, who then agreed to extend credit as needed and not to press for immediate payment. The official of the old bank who was responsible for this temporary solution of the difficulty, says that their own line was extended and increased, and they had used their influence with the other banks in their customer's behalf, solely because of their confidence in the character of the customer. The customer's finances by the middle of 1921 had grown worse rather than better, though practically all merchandise customers were paid off and the inventories were being liquidated.

Questions

1. What particular weaknesses in financial management are shown in this problem?

2. Should the old bank have come to the assistance of the A. B. Company in the way indicated?

3. Should the other two banks have been willing, under the circumstances, to lend further to the A. B. Company?

4. Can you suggest any better way whereby the A. B. Company could have financed itself over this period?

5. What do you expect to be the outcome of the present situation?

6. What specific light does this problem throw on the general financial situation in 1921?

Problem 80

Should a Borrowing Concern Pay Off All of Its Bank Loans at Least Once Each Year?

The statement is frequently made that theoretically the borrowing concern should at least once during the year "clean up" its bank and commercial paper loans, that is, it should pay off all its temporary borrowings. In practice, however, most bankers admit that this rarely happens.

Questions

1. What seems to be the reason for such a "rule"? Is it really desirable that a borrowing concern follow it?

2. Can you think of concerns, which, from the nature of their business, should "clean up" oftener than once per year? Less frequently?

3. Would you make any distinction between a "seasoned" business and a new business in this matter? Why?

Problem 81

How Extensively Should a Business Borrow?

It is the practice among some business concerns to arrange for a line of credit with several banks, though they confine their borrowing largely to one or two institutions. Some follow the practice of opening lines of credit in cities remote from the place where their business is done. Some of the concerns which follow this policy say that it not only gives greater credit protection but also has a useful advertising value.

A well-known business man recently said that he considered it to be a wise policy for a business not only to arrange for a larger line of credit than it expects to need, but also even to borrow money temporarily which is not needed in the business, for the purpose of letting the bank know "Who's Who."

Question

1. From the point of view of the business itself, what seem to you to be the chief advantages or disadvantages of borrowing in the manner indicated?

Problem 82

How Much Business Can a Concern Afford to Do on Credit?

A well-known banker recently wrote as follows:

"How much can I afford to sell? How much business can I afford to do?

"The usual answer pertly given, would be 'All that I can. How else can I go forward?' It seems ridiculous to think that a man may have more business than is good for him. Yet it has been my experience that a large portion of the business difficulty which results in financial difficulty, comes through failing to ask whether or not orders should be taken beyond a certain amount. This amount will vary according to circumstances and according to the business. It can be regulated by principles, but not by fixed rules.

* * * * * * * *

"There is only one chance in a thousand of staying in business, say, five years if credit is forced to serve as capital."

(W. F. H. Koelsch, in SYSTEM, August 1921, p. 145 ff.)

Questions

1. How can a concern determine how much business it is safe to do on a given amount of capital?
2. When, if at all, is it wise to use temporary borrowings for investment in fixed assets?
3. What factors determine the relative amount of working capital needed in a business?

(Reference: Lough, *Business Finance*, 380-414.)

PROBLEM 83

BANK LOANS AND GOVERNMENT REGULATION

"Shortly after the income tax law became effective, a manufacturer of metal goods filed a statement of his financial condition, and when it was turned over to the credit department for analysis, a sharp decrease in net worth was uncovered. As the various items on the comparative statement were balanced one against the other over a period of years, the latest statement showed evidences of manipulation.

"The outside investigator was sent to the customer's plant with instructions to make a survey of the business for the past year. As was usually his line of action, the investigator did not attempt a detailed audit, but endeavored rather to look over the stock, prove up the condition of the trade, and gather other pertinent information of a general character.

"While he was at the plant, the manufacturer hastened to the bank and sought out the credit manager.

"'Why did you send an investigator to my plant?' he asked, half angrily, half like a boy whose pride has been wounded. And, without giving the other man a chance to answer, he launched forth a violent protest against the bank's action. 'I've been a good customer of this bank and I'll not be watched like a criminal,' he said, emphasizing his words by pounding on the top of the mahogany desk.

"In the midst of this tirade the investigator walked in and reported there was nothing to indicate a reduction in the concern's net worth and that there must be some mistake in the last statement. Calmed by this unexpected interruption, the manufacturer changed his attitude and confessed that he had purposely made an artful error in the statement.

"'That was a copy of the statement I submitted to the government,' he explained, 'and I left it the same for you so if it were checked up at any time it would show no discrepancies.'"

(Shaw, *Credits and Collections*, 68-69.)

Questions

1. What in your opinion, have been the chief effects of the national tax laws on the relations existing between business concerns and their banks?

2. How has the Federal Reserve Act affected the situation?

B. OPEN MARKET BORROWING

Problem 84

A Small Company Borrowing on the Open Market

The .... Overall Company referred to in an earlier problem* had in recent years been selling a little paper on the open market. There had been consistent growth for several years, but the financial statement had shown little change so far as the various relations were concerned, until 1919. Further, so large a surplus had been built up out of earnings, as a result of conservative management, that the reputation of the company was apparently very high with those bankers and merchants who had dealings with the concern.

By 1920, however, as a result of the expansion policy earlier described, the balance sheet showed some marked changes, though the current ratio remained practically as before. The following financial statements indicate the general condition:

Assets	1919	1920
Plant account, etc.	$200,000	$1,000,000
Inventory	100,000	400,000
Accounts receivable	70,000	100,000
Cash	30,000	50,000
	$400,000	$1,550,000
Liabilities		
Capital Stock	$100,000	$1,000,000
Bonds	....	225,000
Accounts payable	25,000	100,000
Notes payable	75,000	175,000
Surplus	200,000	50,000
	$400,000	$1,550,000

The larger number of notes payable were those which had been sold to various banks by note brokers, who, owing to the excellent record of the company in the past, found no difficulty in placing the small issues. During the fall of 1920, one of the holders of this company's notes failed to receive payment when the

*Problem 30

note was due. Accordingly an inquiry was sent by this bank to its correspondent bank in New York City with the request that the financial standing of the company be carefully checked up.

The New York Bank accordingly made use of its various channels of information, securing letters from banks which held the company's paper or had loaned it money directly, from merchants who had had dealings with the concern, and from commercial agencies. All reports received were uniformly favorable. The excellent management of past years, in which there had been no changes, was particularly stressed.

Questions

1. What would be your analysis of the situation here indicated?

2. Should this concern be selling paper on the open market? Why?

3. Should you agree with the reports submitted by the various sources? If not, how do you account for their favorable reports?

4. Would the company's financial position be better at the present time if it had borrowed solely from the banks? Why?

(Consult Phillips, *Bank Credit*, 260-294.)

Problem 85

Is the "Quality" of Commercial Paper Related to the Nature of the Industry Engaged in by the Borrowing Concern?

"The nearer the inventory is to the absolute raw material of standard size and fineness, the more liquid it is and hence the more advantageous as an asset."

Questions

1. Do you agree with this statement?
2. If so, indicate briefly those concerns whose commercial paper should have the readiest market.

Problem 86

The Commercial Paper Market and the Business Cycle

It is reported (1920-21) that many of the largest banks both in Boston and New York have purchased no commercial paper for three or four years. On the other hand, many of the smaller "country" banks are investing rather heavily in commercial paper. In fact, had it not been for these "country" banks, it is estimated that many of our large business concerns would have failed during the past year.

Questions

1. How do you account for the situation here indicated?
2. Should you expect to find a different state of affairs in normal times? Why?
3. Is the above situation a safe one? Why or why not?

Problem 87

General Questions on the Use of Commercial Paper

Questions

1. Should a concern borrowing on the open market give more information to the broker regarding its financial affairs than it would ordinarily give to its bank?

2. Should you expect it to be possible for a financially weak concern to sell its paper to note brokers?

3. Can you suggest any limitations on open market borrowings dependent on the size or type of business attempting to sell its commercial paper?

4. Is it a wise policy for a business to borrow only through commercial paper houses?

5. Do you consider it sound policy for a bank to buy the commercial paper of a concern to which it is already extending a line of credit? How, if at all, might this practice affect the business situation?

6. (*a*) From a point of view of a business concern, what are the advantages and disadvantages of open market borrowing?

(*b*) Sum up the situation, also, from the point of view of the bankers.

(Reference: Phillips, 260-294.)

Problem 88

What a Supposedly Strong Concern Can Do by Borrowing Through Note Brokers

A striking illustration of what can happen to a concern using the open market, is furnished by the borrowing operations of the H. B. Claflin Company of New York, which failed in 1914.

"This concern, which was one of the largest wholesale dry goods houses in the world, had affiliated with it a manufacturing concern and twenty or more retail stores. The retail stores bought of the wholesale house on open account, until the accounts reached certain amounts when notes would be given in payment of the accounts. These notes the H. B. Claflin Company would endorse and steadily offer for discount over a wide area, generally through note brokers. As to the amount of endorsed paper outstanding at any time, brokers, fearful of losing the lucrative business, were reluctant to inquire and bankers only guessed. The key to the explanation of the willingness of bankers to buy paper offered under such uncertain conditions was the personal esteem in which Mr. H. B. Claflin, the head of the concern, was held. One of the foremost citizens of the metropolis, he had cultivated a personal acquaintance with prominent bankers over extensive territory.

"It was known that everybody held Claflin paper and it developed at the time of the failure that the Claflin receivables or endorsements were diffused among 2000 to 3000 banks. If everybody wants the paper, the bankers seem to have reasoned, it must be good. The very knowledge that everyone else is carrying the paper of a given house that a banker thinks well of, is a source of satisfaction to him. If failure should occur others would share his disappointment.

"In June, 1914, with tight money prevailing, the concern was unable to market more paper through its brokers and asked for temporary additional assistance from its bankers. The bankers interested cooperated in making an examination of the affairs of the company, uncovering direct indebtedness of $9,000,000 and contingent liabilities of almost $32,000,000, representing the endorsed notes of the retail stores, the condition of which was a depressing revelation to the bankers concerned. Quick assets amounted to approximately $12,000,000. In spite of having long paid five or six per cent dividends the concern had been insolvent for several years. The note brokerage system had prolonged the life of the company at the expense of the banks."

(Quoted from Phillips, *Bank Credit*, 285-286.)

Question

What conclusions can be drawn from this incident regarding open market borrowing and its relation to direct bank borrowing?

Problem 89

How a Small Concern Borrowing Solely on the Open Market Deceived Its Creditors

Not many years ago, a concern in the Middle West failed to the extent of nearly $1,000,000. Of this amount less than $100,000 had been borrowed directly from the bankers. However, about $800,000 in commercial paper had been sold through note brokers to small banks throughout the country. On this paper they suffered a complete loss. None of the paper had been placed in the city where the business house was located, and, further, the concern had practically no accounts payable for merchandise outstanding. In fact, so far as the trade was concerned, its credit seemed to be A-1.

Questions

1. How do you account for this episode?
2. Could this situation have arisen if the concern had done most of its borrowing from local banks?
3. Does this failure reflect most discredit on the borrower, the note brokers who sold their paper, or on the banks which bought it? Give your reasons.

Problem 90

What Steps Shall be Taken When the Commercial Paper Market is No Longer Open?

The B. Company is engaged largely in the manufacture of woolen dress goods. It has always had the reputation of being very conservatively managed and its credit with the banks has been excellent. Even though small it has been able to sell its paper on the open market without question. However, the banks are now much concerned about the company's present credit position. The following financial statements show the financial condition of the company at the end of 1919 and at the end of 1920.

Comparative Statement of the .... Manufacturing Company

Filed with the Massachusetts Commissioner of Corporations November 30, 1919 and 1920.

Assets	1919	1920
Real Estate	$293,335	$481,015
Machinery	204,738	254,799
Merchandise	1,213,597	1,618,661
Furniture and Fixtures	....	8,744
Mortgage	....	6,500
Cash and accounts receivable	591,976	486,584
Securities	166,198	248
Deferred assets	14,221	32,669
	$2,484,068	$2,889,224
Liabilities		
Capital Stock	$500,000	$500,000
Mortgages	....	10,000
Floating debt	863,000	1,545,000
Accounts payable	401,146	231,990
Surplus	939,601	551,018
Reserve	141,019	51,215
	$2,484,068	$2,889,224

Questions

1. What essential changes have occurred between the two dates, and how do you account for these changes? Could they have been avoided?

2. Should you expect this concern to be able to sell any paper on the open market in 1921?

3. Should you expect that any bank would rediscount loans made by this company with other banks?

4. Assuming that the major part of the floating debt is in the form of commercial paper, what do you expect the company's financial position to be at the middle of 1921?

5. What financial advice would you give this concern at the present time?

Problem 91

Attempting to Renew Relations With a Former Note Broker in 1921

The F. Hardware Manufacturing Company had formerly been a customer of the N. Commercial Paper House. For four or five years, however, they had not raised any money by the sale of notes, though this banking house had from time to time made non-committal offers of service. However, the F. Company had managed to finance itself almost solely through its banks and did not appear to be interested in trying the commercial paper market. The moral risk of the concern was excellent.

In June, 1921, they approached the commercial paper house for a loan, presenting the following statement of condition as of December 31, 1920:

Assets		Liabilities	
Real Estate......	$586,030	Capital..........	$569,100
Machinery.......	282,743	Accounts payable.	378,992
Cash............	142,516	Notes payable....	505,000
Accounts receivable	480,262	Surplus and reserves.......	1,845,995
Investments.....	251,217	Accrued items....	10,815
Notes...........	6,873		
Merchandise.....	1,279,250		
Furniture, fixtures	256,439		
Autos, trucks, teams.........	9,641		
Patent rights.....	5,461		
Prepaid expenses.	9,470		
	$3,309,902		$3,309,902

The trade checkings on this concern were found to be excellent, and their commercial bankers considered them A-1 in every respect.

Questions

1. Should the F. Hardware Manufacturing Company have expected the N. Commercial Paper House to buy its commercial paper at this time with the condition indicated on the statement?

2. As the credit man of the N. Commercial Paper House, what would be your decision?

PROBLEM 92

SEEKING A NEW NOTE BROKER IN 1921

The Q. Company is a consolidation of several smaller concerns and is at present engaged in making miscellaneous clothing accessories, particularly suspenders, garters, and the like. At the time of the consolidation in 1915 their chief financial adviser was a firm of private bankers, the A. Banking Co., who dealt in some investments as well as in commercial paper. In fact, these bankers were well represented on their board of directors.

The credit of the new company was from every point of view considered excellent. At this time also a commercial paper house, the B. Banking Co., which had frequently sold the paper of one of the important consolidating companies, offered its services to the new organization. This offer was from time to time repeated during the next two or three years, but on account of the influence of the group of bankers back of the consolidation the offer was not accepted.

During the early part of 1921, however, the ...... Company began to put out feelers with a view to interesting the B. Banking Company in an offer of commercial paper. They stated that while the A. Banking Company had heretofore taken care of their commercial paper loans, they were not averse to finding out what terms the B. Banking Company would make them. They further let it be known that though they had been in the past and still were borrowing heavily from their bankers, they would be glad to have their paper sold more extensively on the open market.

Accordingly, the B. Banking Company looked into the situation. They found it difficult, however, to secure a financial statement, in view of the fact that the company had been considered very prosperous and had been dealing solely with bankers who were financially interested in the business. Finally, the following statement was obtained from the records filed with the Commissioner of Corporations:

STATEMENT OF THE Q. COMPANY
Dec. 31, 1920

Assets		Liabilities	
Real Estate	$1,462,165	Capital Stock	$3,731,650
Machinery	1,290,178	Mortgage	*none*
Furniture, fixtures & merchandise	1,978,152	Accounts payable.	78,325
Notes	126,298	Notes payable	1,011,000
Accounts receivable	387,288	Subscriptions to capital stock	9,337
Cash	204,267	Reserves	773,843
Securities and Investments	267,124	Surplus	1,233,745
Patent Rights	283,986		
Trade marks	675,282		
Treasury stock	106,550		
Development expenses	56,610		
	$6,837,900		$6,837,900

Questions

1. From your analysis of the balance sheet do you think that this concern was being properly managed?

2. What should you expect to be the credit rating of this concern (*a*) in "the trade," (*b*) by the banks with which it has been dealing?

3. On what basis should you expect the second commercial paper house to form its decision?

4. Do you expect that this company was able to sell its paper through the second commercial paper house?

Problem 93

Should a Concern Finance Itself Largely Through Note Brokers?

The W. Company was engaged largely in the manufacture and export of shoes to South America. Though the company had lines of credit with two banks it had grown so rapidly during the war years that these lines, $50,000 at each bank, were wholly out of proportion to the amount of business done. Further, the company had been depending almost solely on the open paper market until the first of 1920, at which time it had outstanding about $500,000 in notes, with an average maturity of about three months.

When the depression came in the South American trade, and many orders began to be cancelled, the company found itself pressed to meet the notes coming due. In view of the shrinkage in inventory value, and the frozen and uncertain condition of their receivables, concerns engaged in a similar line of industry were unable to sell paper on the open market. Though the W. Company's position was still relatively good, the market, due partially to the general prejudice, simply would not absorb its paper. The company, therefore, resorted to its banks for an extension of credit. However, the bank lines arranged, based on the condition of two or three years earlier, before the business had become so widely expanded, were not more than sufficient to take care of one-fifth of the open market borrowings.

As the moral risk of the management of the concern was wholly satisfactory, the two banks felt that the financial tie-up was due as much to the general business conditions as anything else, though they had reason to criticize the policy of their customers, who had failed to keep their lines sufficiently large. Notwithstanding, they agreed in each case to double their line of credit to the concern, making it $100,000, provided the W. Company could secure in addition lines of credit to an equal amount from three other banks. This would enable the concern to pay off its open market borrowings. The additional lines of credit were finally arranged in time for the W. Company to pay its notes at maturity and continue in a solvent condition.

Questions

1. Was the W. Company justified in expecting its banks to extend further credit at this time?

2. What light does the problem throw on the relations existing between open market borrowing and bank borrowing?

Problem 94

Conflict of Interests Between Open Market Borrowing and Bank Borrowing

The .... Company, manufacturer of a well-known product for which there is a world-wide market, has nearly always depended for its current financing on the commercial paper market. As the concern has been prosperous there has always been a ready sale for its paper and only stereotyped questions have been asked by the commercial paper houses. The concern is unincorporated, and the partners were supposed to have extensive resources outside this particular business. Under the circumstances, their commercial paper was considered "gilt-edged."

It should further be explained that this company, while never borrowing much from its banks, always arranged for large lines of credit and always maintained at least a 20 per cent cash deposit against these lines. Consequently its reputation with its bankers was excellent, and this excellent reputation increased the eagerness with which its paper was bought throughout the country.

In the first part of 1921 rumors came that the partners of the concern had invested their outside resources in all manner of questionable undertakings which had now either failed or were in serious financial difficulties. A few days before this time a well-known commercial paper house had bought outright, and sold under the usual options, $200,000 worth of this firm's paper. The concern had a deposit of $40,000 in a well-known New England Trust Company which entitled it to a line of $200,000. Only $50,000, however, was being borrowed.

When the company endeavored to use its line of credit at the bank more extensively, questions were immediately raised, whereupon the precarious condition of the concern became evident. Fearing bankruptcy proceedings which might result in very extensive loss, the bank immediately exercised the legal right to demand 60 days' notice before the withdrawal of the customer's funds. This action of the bank at once gave them an 80 per cent protection.

The action of the bank and the rumors regarding the solvency of the partners of the concern immediately became known, through the usual sources of information, to the banks which were buying the latest issue of commercial paper on option. They therefore returned the paper to the note brokers who had just bought it. The note brokers, therefore, whose function is merely that of a go-between, became unsecured creditors to the extent of $200,000.

Question

1. What light does this problem throw on the desirability of selling paper on the open market by an unincorporated concern,

   (*a*) From the point of view of the concern itself.

   (*b*) From the point of view of the purchasers of its paper?

Problem 95

The Nature of the Business, the Business Cycle, and the Note Broker

The M. Company are dealers in masons' supplies. On June 15, 1921 they applied to a commercial paper house for as large a loan as the latter would be willing to grant. They presented the following balance sheet, as of December 31, 1920:—

Assets		Liabilities	
Real Estate......	$14,427	Capital..........	$400,000
Cash............	20,485	Accounts payable.	237,621
Accounts receivable...........	498,348	Notes payable....	380,000
Investments.....	10,892	Surplus..........	167,352
Notes...........	38,219		
Merchandise.....	516,391		
Furniture, fixtures and tools	26,816		
Autos, etc.......	29,459		
Patent rights.....	700		
Goodwill........	20,000		
Patterns.........	1,000		
Miscellaneous....	8,231		
	$1,184,973		$1,184,973

Questions

1. What is your analysis of the balance sheet furnished?

2. Should the company in June, 1921 expect to sell its commercial paper on the strength of this balance sheet?

3. Irrespective of general business conditions, do you think that a concern such as this should be selling its paper on the open market?

4. As the investigator for the commercial paper house what further information, if any, should you call for?

5. What decision do you expect would be handed down in this case?

C. THE USE OF THE TRADE ACCEPTANCE

Problem 96

Claims Made for the Trade Acceptance by One of Its Chief Advocates

"Thousands of business men owe the present liquid condition of their concerns to the use of this form of paper (*i. e. the trade acceptance*), whereas abuse has been due to practices of the individual not the instrument. Within the past three years the best minds in the business and banking world have given the system a most thorough study, applying the acid test of experience and finally pronouncing it worthy of their approval. The principal mission of the trade acceptance is to liquefy credit, improve the turnover and minimize credit losses. To maintain its place as a high grade credit instrument it will therefore be used with the best class of current accounts. Where goods have previously been sold on open account basis and the credit department record of the customer shows that his account is usually settled with due regard for the credit terms, the acceptance is used to the best advantage.

"It is a matter of record that more than one-third of commercial failures are due to insufficient working capital. If trade acceptances were substituted for open accounts, thus enabling the merchant to discount them at his bank, thereby providing additional capital, the strain would unquestionably be relieved and the merchant would be in a position to do twice the amount of business possible under the open book method."

Questions

1. Does a concern derive any particular advantage from using the trade acceptance with "the best class of current accounts?"

2. Do you agree that a concern using the trade acceptance could do at least twice as much business as could be done under the open account method?

3. Would the discounting of trade acceptances, as suggested, really supply more working capital in a business which lacks it?

4. If a concern's credit is already good at the bank and it is borrowing in the usual commercial way, would a good bank be likely to discount its trade acceptances?

5. Would it be wise for a concern which is already borrowing to the limit from its banks to discount its trade acceptances in other quarters?

6. If a concern's credit is such that the banks are not interested in its ordinary commercial account, would its credit position be improved by changing its open accounts to trade acceptances?

7. Granting that the above statement is true, how would the universal use of the trade acceptance in the manner indicated affect,

(*a*) The price of commodities,
(*b*) The general credit structure,
(*c*) The number of commercial failures?

Problems 97

What Do Figures Prove?

Early in 1921, Mr. E. W. Shepard, General Credit Manager of the Western Electric Company, wrote substantially as follows, regarding their experience with the trade acceptance:

"Early in 1918 we started the use of trade acceptances. During 1919 and 1920 their use has developed. In

1919 both the number and volume increased over 200 per cent. In 1920 the number and volume have increased over 200 per cent. Our losses on trade acceptances for the first two years were much smaller than our losses on open account. An analysis gives us the following comparison:

	Per cent loss to sales on open account	Per cent loss to sales on trade acceptances
1918.......	0.39	0.03
1919.......	0.27	0.07

"Some opponents tell us that trade acceptances lengthen terms, but when used properly they shorten terms or quicken the turnover, and most users have found that they do. Our turnover during 1919 was increased 15 per cent, and this year our average turnover for ten months has been nearly 12 per cent better than during the same time in 1919, notwithstanding conditions of the last four or five months. A considerable part of this improvement is due to the use of trade acceptances. The real credit problems at present are: 1. Increasing failures. 2. Slow collections. The first means increased expense, and the second means increased expense in carrying the accounts and decreased turnover. In finding the solution of these problems don't overlook the value of the trade acceptance. I believe the credit man has a real opportunity to show that he is a constructive force in the industry. Let us, therefore, take advantage of this instrument which, when used properly, will help us in accomplishing better results than in the past."

Questions

1. Do the figures above given "convince" you of the value of trade acceptance?
2. Should you expect this company to have more or less favorable experience with the use of the trade acceptance than would a smaller concern? Why?
3. Which type of concern should you expect to reap most advantage from the use of trade acceptances, a manufacturing or a "trading" concern? Why?

Problem 98

Trade Acceptances and the Rapid Increase of Prices

The following statement was made in 1919 by the president of a medium-sized concern dealing in iron ore, coal and coke:

"It was during the beginning of the great expansion of business that we adopted the trade acceptance. Prices of iron jumped overnight from approximately $16 per ton to almost $50. It required three times as much capital to do business satisfactorily during the war as it required to do business before the war. Had it not been for ample and generous banking facilities—and our case was probably typical of thousands of other business houses—we would have found our own cash resources quite inadequate to meet the situation. As it was, we found that we had in open book accounts four or five times as much money due us as we had ever had due us at any time previously; and in order to swing our trade and keep our own credit good, discounting our own bills and meeting all payments on their due dates, we were owing banks, not a sum of money out of proportion to the money due us, but an amount which was much larger than our capital, and which four or five years ago, would have seemed impossibly large.

"This was our situation when we adopted the trade acceptance. The results were absolutely miraculous. In less than four months' time we had reduced our open book accounts to a comparatively small figure; we had paid every dollar of indebtedness due the banks, and more than that we were carrying a large cash balance, and, in addition, had trade acceptances in our safe which we called a cash reserve, because it could be instantly converted into cash. These trade acceptances ran into large figures.

"Now, there is our record. That is what the trade acceptance did for us."

Questions

1. Is this concern really in a strong position?
2. If so, is their position a result of the use of the trade acceptance?
3. What should you expect their experience to be at present?
4. What difficulties might confront a similar concern beginning the use of the trade acceptance at present?
5. Would a *manufacturer* of steel products find it easier or more difficult to use trade acceptances than a distributor of raw material needed by the manufacturer? Which would probably gain most from their use?

Problem 99

Introducing the Use of the Trade Acceptance With Concessions

The .... Shoe Company never had enough working capital to put it in a comfortable financial position. Further, under the prevailing open account method of selling to customers, their collections tended to be very slow. Several years ago their condition was so dubious that their old bank refused to lend them any more money in the usual way.

Finally, the bank agreed to lend them for a short time on their best accounts receivable up to about 80 per cent of the face value. It was arranged, however, that the bank should collect the accounts and that the company in the meantime should work out a plan for more speedy collections.

At last the .... Shoe Company decided to give trade acceptances a thorough trial. Their chief problem, however, was to persuade their customers to accept bills drawn on them in this way, as many thought it was too great a reflection on their credit standing. Accordingly, as an inducement, the company agreed to disregard the usual terms of sale, 2 per cent in 10 days, 30 days net, so that the time for payment indicated on the acceptances was extended 15 days. This induced most of their customers to give acceptances, taking advantage of the delay in payment and still receiving the cash discount. In about a year's time nearly three quarters of the company's sales were financed by the use of trade acceptances. These were readily discounted by the bank and the threatened failure of the company, due to insufficient working capital, is said to have been permanently averted.

Questions

1. Should these concessions have been made?
2. Should the bank discount acceptances obtained in this way?
3. Should the company continue its present policy?

Problem 100

Using the Trade Acceptance as an Aid to Selling

The .... Company, wholesale cloth merchants, in 1920 were very eager to sell their goods as usual to a large customer in New York City. The customer, already having suffered a good deal of loss on inventory, having his assets in a comparatively frozen condition, notwithstanding price reductions, protested that he feared that he could not pay for the goods at the usual time and hence preferred not to buy.

The .... Company, however, made him what seemed to be a very fair price, suggesting that he could give a three-months "acceptance" for the goods, and that if he should be unable to honor it at the expiration of this period, they would gladly renew the acceptance until he could be in a position to pay. Thus the company hoped, by increasing their accounts receivable, to make a more favorable showing with their own bank when they wished to borrow. They further supposed that they had it in their power to discount the acceptance at once, provided they needed cash. So the deal was closed.

In a short time the company found that its banks were not in a position to make further loans for current financing. Consequently an attempt was made to discount this acceptance to the extent of about $100,000. Upon making inquiry, their bank discovered that the acceptor would probably be unable to pay his obligations when due. Thus a tacit agreement for continued renewal was brought to light. This, of course, made the acceptance ineligible for rediscount, the company's banks would have nothing to do with the matter, and it became necessary to resort to a finance corporation, which bought the acceptance at a very heavy discount. This corporation immediately forced payment at the maturity of the acceptance, and so brought about the bankruptcy of the company's customer.

Questions

1. Analyze the conditions herein presented.

2. What light does this problem throw on the use of the trade acceptance,

(*a*) From the seller's point of view;

(*b*) From the buyer's point of view?

3. As a rule should a concern discount the trade acceptances which it receives from its customers or hold them till maturity? Why?

Problem 101

Can the Open Account Prove More Satisfactory Than the Trade Acceptance?

An electrical supply concern finds the use of the trade acceptance a poor policy with poor customers who have no bank accounts. They merely buy all they can and put off the time of payment as long as possible by signing trade acceptances. For example, if the credit extended is for 60 days, they will have bought at least two months' supply before the first payment comes due, and very probably they will use their credit with the first concern in order to establish credit with other concerns, the result being that they manage to secure a considerable amount of goods which they proceed to sell off as rapidly as possible, so that when the acceptances come due there is practically nothing to attach, and payment cannot readily be forced. Further, the fact that they have no bank accounts makes it an extremely troublesome process to collect from them, even if their intentions may be good.

The .... Electrical Supply Company, therefore, contends that with an open account it can manage to get a little money from time to time without running the risk of waiting a long time for the initial payment, which almost invariably means a large or a total loss. Hence this company expresses itself as being vigorously opposed to the use of the trade acceptance.

Questions

1. Is the difficulty which this concern encounters due to the use of the trade acceptance?

2. What advice would you give to the management in the matter?

Problem 102

Under What Circumstances Shall the Trade Acceptance be Adopted?

A wholesale grocery house operating under the usual conditions in an Ohio city showed the following financial condition on December 31, 1919:

Statement of ...... Company
Dec. 31, 1919

Assets		Liabilities	
Cash on hand...	$3,374.42	Accounts Payable	$16,587.62
Accounts receivable..........	124,026.22	Notes payable...	95,000.00
Notes receivable.	10,893.91	Other liabilities..	
Merchandise inventory......	312,086.87		
Equipment inventory......	4,455.75		
Others Assets—			
Real Estate...	124,191.67		
Bonds........	2,484.00	Balance........	569,425.22
	$581,512.84		$581,512.84

Net Sales..........................	$1,354,788.03
Gross Profit..........................	$160,507.84
Credit and collection expense........	$2,260.50
Losses from bad debts..............	$2,938.30
Total Expense......................	$124,012.31

This firm does business with about 1200 retail customers. It employs eleven salesmen who call on the customers weekly. These salesmen also make collections. A number of the customers, however, pay by check, and take cash discounts amounting in the aggregate to about 1 per cent of the annual net sales.

An advocate of the trade acceptance endeavored to persuade the management of this concern that they should use trade acceptances with all of their customers who were not taking the cash discounts offered. It was stated among other things that such a practice would reduce collection expenses as well as losses from bad debts. An officer of the concern has now asked for advice on the matter.

Questions

1. Do you think that this concern should adopt the trade acceptance? Why, or why not?

2. Indicate, specifically, under what conditions you think it desirable to use the trade acceptance?

PROBLEM 103

THE BANKER'S POINT OF VIEW ON THE TRADE ACCEPTANCE

"A concern taking the acceptances of its customers will be using its credit in the same way that it would if it took its note to a bank and got a loan. The same questions will arise regarding the concern's credit standing. Whether it discounts its notes or its customers' acceptances—the basic security, which briefly is the ability to sell and collect on sales, remains the same.

"The experience of bankers so far shows that the proof of the responsibility and capability of the acceptor of a trade acceptance is obtained for the most part from the maker, who at the same time becomes the indorser when he presents the paper for rediscount. The credit manager, then wants to be sure that the information regarding the acceptor is correct, even though the financial standing of the indorser is first class. The temptation, investigation indicates, is for the maker to put the acceptor's best financial foot forward when he comes to the bank with trade acceptance paper.

"For this reason, suggests one banker, the data thus obtained should be minutely scrutinized. The indorser may not always be the best source of information because unconsciously at least he may, as the representative of the selling house, be too anxious to increase sales and make as many turnovers as possible. 'Second-hand' information of this sort might, if distorted in any way, defeat the whole purpose of trade acceptances as especially desirable two-name paper for the bank. Such data might indeed make the offering of security poorer from the standpoint of dependability than a commercial short-time note."

Question

Do you agree with the point of view here expressed?

Problem 104

Conflicting Opinions of Bankers On Trade Acceptances

A. A partner in one of the largest commercial paper houses in the country recently made the following statement regarding trade acceptances:

"Judging by the experience of the past two or three years, I think the trade acceptance is one of the worst calamities that could have possibly happened in the financial world. It has lead to inconceivable abuses and has weakened the position of many a concern which would otherwise have been strong. While there may be in certain instances, something to be said in its favor, so far as our house is concerned we will avoid its use to the uttermost and will have no dealings with a company which gives trade acceptances."

Question

Why should a commercial paper house "feel" this way about it?

B. A well-known banker recently said, "The use of the trade acceptance is growing rapidly. It has been the salvation of many a concern which during the past two years without its use would certainly have gone on the financial rocks."

On the same day that this statement was made, another leading banker said, "The use of the trade acceptance is dying out. In two or three years more no one will give them. Personally, I wish the whole d——— business were dead and buried."

Questions

1. Analyze these conflicting statements with care.
2. Account for the differences of opinion expressed.
3. What are your own conclusions on the matter?

Problem 105

Trade Acceptances and the Turnover of Inventory

From the point of view of the general credit situation, should you consider it more desirable to use trade acceptances in the various stages of an industry in which the turnover of inventory is slow, or in one in which the turnover is comparatively rapid? Why?

Problem 106

General Questions on the Trade Acceptance

Questions

1. Can you formulate any rules as to the type and size of business concerns which can most profitably use the trade acceptance in place of open accounts?

2. Does the use of the acceptance depend at all upon the type of customers, their number, or the average size of their orders?

3. Specifically, what relation, if any, does the use of the trade acceptance bear to the Business Cycle?

4. Summarize the advantages and disadvantages of the trade acceptance:

a. From the point of view of the drawer;
b. From the point of view of the acceptor;
c. From the point of view of the commercial banker;
d. From the point of view of the note broker;
e. From the point of view of the general credit situation.

D. MISCELLANEOUS METHODS OF RAISING WORKING CAPITAL

Problem 107

Conservatism in Securing Working Capital

A concern manufacturing a large line of articles marketed all over the country through jobbers, retailers, and direct to customers, has throughout its history been able to attain its desired growth by reinvesting its profits above a normal return on the investment. Borrowing has usually been restricted to a small per cent of its invested capital and to the period in each year when its inventory was at the highest. During the balance of the year the concern was able to build up its cash, which at the lowest inventory period usually about equaled its borrowing. Money was borrowed from banks on promissory notes.

During the war period, rising prices and increased business led to a large increase in inventory and bills receivable. The company found itself in need of more funds and the question arose as to whether it should increase its capital stock, borrow on notes, or increase its borrowings from its banks. The possiblity of using trade acceptances was scarcely to be considered, since this company sold its goods at 30 days net, and the terms were usually strictly observed.

It was decided not to increase the capitalization for the following reasons: (1) It was not thought that the need of more funds was a permanent need such as would not be overcome by falling prices and gradual accumulation of reinvested profits. (2) Any increase in capitalization would necessarily be at a high rate of interest, which would permanently increase the company's fixed charges, or at a high rate of dividend.

Selling its notes through commercial paper houses was rejected, first, on account of the old-fashioned but conservative objection to having the company's paper sold generally throughout the country. This would be poor financial advertising, in some people's minds. This plan was further opposed because of the difficulty and high cost of issuing notes at the time when funds were needed. Finally, it was felt that concerns who usually borrow on the open market are frequently unable to get sufficient funds, and can, in case of real need, only with difficulty obtain additional help from their banks, whose funds are being conserved for their old customers.

The question of changing some of the slower open accounts to the trade acceptance basis was casually mentioned, but it was felt that the company's credit at the banks might be injured if they should attempt to discount their two-name paper.

Questions

1. Do you think that this company considered all the desirable alternatives for the financing indicated? If not, what further methods can you suggest as reasonable possibilities?

2. (*a*) Do you agree with the conclusions reached regarding certain specific methods of financing as given above?

(*b*) Do you agree with the specific reasons given for arriving at these conclusions?

3. What method or methods of raising the additional working capital would you have advised this concern to follow?

4. What method do you believe the company actually adopted, and what should you expect to be the results?

Problem 108

Getting Credit from the Supply House

John Black, a dry-goods salesman, decided to put ten thousand dollars into a dry-goods business. After he had selected his location, the first problem was the purchase of fixtures. Next he was obliged to place a limit upon the credit he would extend to customers. This was a vital problem, and one that would affect the credit standing of his store. Deducting the amount tied up indefinitely in fixtures and in customers' credits, he had left a working capital of six thousand dollars. On this capital he should be able to secure four thousand dollars' credit from his supply house. This would enable him to carry ten thousand dollars' stock. As he could turn it three times a year, he was in a position to do an annual business of thirty thousand dollars.

His expenses were not to be more than twenty per cent of the total sales—six thousand dollars per annum, or one thousand dollars every sixty days. His bills fell due in sixty days. On the basis outlined his business was conducted thus:

Original cash capital	$10,000
Fixtures	2,000
	$8,000
Customer's accounts	2,000
	$6,000
Credit from jobbers	$4,000

Stock carried	$10,000
Sales for year	30,000
Sales every sixty days	5,000
Deduct expenses and personal withdrawals for sixty days	1,000
Cash, including profits, to apply to accts. payable	4,000

(which last entry proves up with the item, "Credit from jobbers.")

John Black was able to establish a successful business. He planned not only to put his business on a sound basis, but he considered also his credit standing. He limited his outlay for fixtures; he limited the amount of his accounts receivable; he planned his business and took collection precautions; so that he could meet his notes when due; he accepted an amount of credit well proportioned to his working capital.

(A. W. Shaw Company, *How to Finance a Business*, 30-31.)

Questions

1. Do you see any weakness in this plan?
2. Would it have been better for Black to borrow from the local bank?
3. Was it wise for him to carry so large an amount of stock?
4. Should you advise him to continue to finance himself in this way?

Problem 109

Business Borrowing on Personal Collateral

The Unit Company, a concern making important machine accessories, is solely a one-man concern and unincorporated. During the war years it was extraordinarily successful and secured heavy loans from one bank. As its business dropped off heavily in 1920, not only was it impossible to pay off this loan, but in order to avoid failure additional bank loans were needed.

The bank was finally on the point of forcing the concern into liquidation with a view to salvaging a part of the loan, as it seemed improbable that the concern would be able to work its way out. The manager and sole owner, however, was a large holder of good securities, which he agreed to pledge with an officer of the bank, not as collateral for his loan, but as a guarantee to the bank which would protect them against any loss. He did not wish the word to go out that he had been reduced to the extent of borrowing on collateral. The amount of securities thus voluntarily handed over by him, according to the banker's statement, was several times the extent of the bank's loan. The bank on its part, also, has attemped to conceal the details of this transaction.

Question

1. From the point of view of the borrowing concern, what appear to be the elements of strength or weakness in the policy followed by the owner of this business?

Problem 110*

Pledging Receivables

Mr. B, a dealer in automobile supplies and accessories, had enough capital of his own to start his business. As his trade expanded, however, he found that he did not have sufficient working capital to finance the expansion and to buy under the most favorable

*The following account of the practices regarding the pledging of receivables by different types of concerns should prove valuable:

(1) Assigning of accounts by concerns that are financially involved.

Suppose a certain business, which has $10,000 of accounts receivable, is in financial straits and must have immediately, say, $5,000 in cash. Unable to borrow on its own note, having neither customers' notes nor trade acceptances available for discount at a commercial bank, it still has in its accounts receivable a resource which can be converted into cash through the intermediation of a discount house. By purchasing these accounts at a substantial discount and collecting them in full at maturity, the discount company can at once provide the necessary financial assistance to the enterprise in question and earn a profit for itself. The discount company receives the funds which it advances, partly from its shareholders, but more largely from the commercial bank from which it borrows on its promissory note, secured by the purchased accounts as collateral. The amount of the discount varies somewhat, but in the nature of the case the rates are very high, usually ruinously so.

(2) The sale of accounts by "well-rated" concerns as a means of increasing working capital.

In periods of very active business, particularly, many concerns find that after having utilized the full line of credit extended them by the commercial banks, they could make a profitable use of more funds. Indeed, even before the maximum line of credit at the bank has been utilized, a concern often resorts to the sale of receivables in order to keep some of its bank credit available for an emergency. The money borrowed may be devoted to expanding the volume of business through the purchase of additional raw materials or merchandise, or it may be used to pay off trade bills, thereby saving the discount that is offered for early cash payments. While rates charged for such funds are high, the cost is usually less than the amount of the cash discount on trade bills, which can thus be saved.

The character of the business concerns which make use of such credit sources may be seen from the fact that one discount house in 1918 made 77½% of its $55,000,000 of loans to customers whose commercial ratings were of the first or second classes. Nearly 75% of the customers, moreover, were concerns rated above $35,000, some of them at more than $1,000,000, the average size being between $50,000 and $75,000. It should be clearly understood, however, that while the concerns which borrow in this way may typically be well rated, and of fair size, a resort to the sale of accounts receivable as a means of raising funds indicates a credit condition, temporarily, such that commercial banks are unwilling to lend them more. Concretely, the concern's ratio of quick assets to current liabilities is, as a rule, considerably less than what is customarily insisted upon by the commercial bankers.

conditions. At first he made arrangements to borrow from a local bank on his promissory notes, endorsed by his wife, who owned a small amount of real estate. These notes ran for three months, and in accordance with the agreement made with the bank it was necessary for him to pay off the greater portion of the loan by the end of that time. It was his practice, however, to renew these notes at the end of the three months, so that he was a continuous borrower from the bank.

The business prospered, but with its growth there was a constant need for more working capital, since the original investment had been entirely too small. The bank thereupon made arrangements to lend more heavily on condition that the best accounts receivable should be pledged and turned over to them for collection. These served as collateral for B's borrowings, until ultimately about three-fourths of his accounts receivable were really in the hands of the bank. Directions had been issued to his customers that they should pay month by month at the bank, but to the credit of the account of the business. Though the rate charged by the bank on this loan, being a monthly rate, was much higher than the usual discount rate, the borrower found it possible to "clean up" his loans frequently, until finally he reached a position in which it was no longer necessary for him to borrow except when his business was at the peak.

Recently, B, whose business is now on a firm footing, wishing to erect a new building in order to expand his business further, tried to negotiate a loan with the bank whereby a portion of the necessary funds might

The high-grade credit companies engaged in such financing operations sometimes discount the accounts receivable, but more commonly they make a "service charge" instead. For instance, one large commercial credit company advances about 80% of the face value of each account at the time of purchase, and the balance as it is collected. It derives its profits by a gross charge of 1/25 of 1% on the net face of accounts for each day or a little over 1% per month, plus $5 per $1,000 on the first $100,000 worth of purchases from any concern in any one year. In order that the customers of a concern may not be disturbed, an arrangement is made whereby the borrower may do his own collecting; thus the customers need not know that their accounts have been sold. This is known as the "non-notification" plan. (Moulton, in *Journal of Political Economy,* Dec. 1920.)

be raised by a mortgage. However, his old bank, with which he had done business for many years, refused to make the loan.

Questions

1. Analyze the strength or weakness of this method of financing, taking into consideration the point of view of the bank as well as that of the business.

2. Was the bank justified in refusing the loan for plant expansion?

3. How would "pledging the receivables" of a stationary or declining concern differ from the present problem?

4. Would your answer be the same if the receivables were to be sold to a "discount" company instead of to a commercial bank? Why, or why not?

Problem 111

Securing Working Capital Through the Issue of Notes Secured by Inventory

In February, 1921, the Copper Export Association, composed of a number of the largest copper companies in the United States, issued $40,000,000 of 8 per cent secured gold notes maturing in one, two, three and four years from February 15, 1921. The security back of these notes was 400,000,000 pounds of refined copper held for export, and the sums required for the payment of principal and interest were guaranteed by seventeen copper producing companies, members of the Copper Export Association.

As both the foreign and the domestic demand for copper was very much below normal at the time, and as it was uncertain when the export companies would be able to liquidate their inventory, the purpose of this issue was to relieve the banks of their heavy export loans and put the companies in such a position that they would be free from immediate worries regarding their current financial position.

A good deal of satisfaction was expressed in financial circles at the "discovery" of this new method of financing, based on the security of a commodity. During the next few months there was talk of raising funds in the same way to finance cotton merchants who found themselves with a large amount of depreciated inventory on their hands, which they had expected to export. There has also been talk of creating a farmers' export association with a view to financing the export of those farm products, particularly grain, which have for some time been held in excessive quantities in this country.

Questions

1. Do you consider this method of financing for working capital sound?

2. Would you make any distinction in your answer between this method of financing as applied to exports of copper, and the financing of cotton or farm products in a similar manner?

3. Should you approve of this method of financing if, as farmers have wished, the purpose would be to enable the holder of such commodities in this country to avoid selling inventory produced at a high cost, at the prevailing low prices?

4. Would your answer be the same if the commodity to be financed were a manufactured article?

5. What important effects, if any, should you expect this export financing to have on the finances of the export companies?

6. What seem to you to be the essential differences between borrowing on notes secured by inventory and "pledging receivables"? Which do you consider the safer method of borrowing?

Problem 112

A Distress Method of Raising Working Capital

The X. Paper Box Company prided itself on its ability to please its customers. Being a small concern it would make up special orders of all sorts on demand, and would frequently use a special quality of cardboard selected by its clients. One of the large clients had formed the habit of buying his own cardboard and selling it at cost to the X. Paper Box Company, which thereupon would make up the material according to specifications. Early in 1921, when business was very bad, this client, whose business had very markedly fallen off so that he required few boxes, sent to the box company $20,000 worth of cardboard which he had purchased several months before, when it appeared that business in this particular line would continue active. The client, already in serious financial difficulties, though at present very little indebted to the box company, asked the latter to pay cash for this shipment of cardboard from which the future orders of boxes would be made. This was, of course, a method of getting some ready money from the box manufacturer, who already had on his hands more inventory than he knew what to do with.

Question

Under the circumstances, what policy should the box manufacturer follow in dealing with this customer?

Problem 113

How Can a Successful Woolen Firm Improve Its Credit Position in 1921?

The Old Company is a firm of wool merchants practically owned by one elderly partner, all of whose resources are in the business. Its financial position on January 1, 1921, was as follows:

Statement of the Old Co.
January 1, 1921

Assets		Liabilities	
Cash	$365,000	Notes payable (to banks)	$900,000
Accounts rec.	89,000	Notes payable (to officers)	124,000
Merchandise (actual value)	343,000	Accounts payable	2,000
Merchandise consigned	193,000*	Surplus	1,285,000
Liberty bonds	316,000		
Other securities	834,000		
Rest Estate	164,000		
Miscellaneous	17,000		
	$2,311,000		$2,311,000

(*This item really covers notes receivable from wool growers whom the merchants are financing and whose clip is consigned to them.)

This firm of merchants has now (June, 1921) used up the greater part of its cash in financing this year's crop of wool and it has been unable to reduce its bank loans. The banks recently have been much disturbed by the condition of the business, as indicated by the statement above given, as well as because of the general depression in the industry, and are debating whether they shall refuse to renew the loans now outstanding.

Questions

1. As indicated by the above statement, is this a "bankable" proposition?

2. In order to put themselves into a more satisfactory financial position (*a*) immediately (*b*) ultimately, what steps should you advise this concern to take?

Problem 114

Recently Developed Methods of Securing Working Capital

Since the conclusion of the World War, numerous methods have been suggested or actually put into operation in this country for financing the sale of goods to European manufacturers who would apparently be induced to buy in much greater quantity or who would apparently reap a considerable gain if they could postpone payments until business comes back to normal. One important consideration, from the point of view of the European purchasers, has of course been the unfavorable exchange rates with this country, so far as they are concerned. This exchange condition is due partially to the depreciated currencies of foreign countries and partially to the huge public and private loans which have been made to them by this country, as well as to the fact that they have in recent years found it necessary to import our goods more heavily than ever before. Such a condition naturally makes it necessary, provided they finance their purchases on a cash or short-time credit basis, to pay the added cost resulting from their depreciated exchange, in addition to the relatively high prices which are charged by the American producer. So far as the American exporter is concerned, he argues that an important part of his market will be unavoidably lost unless hitherto unusual steps are taken to enable the foreigner to purchase his goods.

As a result of this situation, various foreign finance corporations have been organized in this country by mercantile and banking interests, with a view to making possible the extension of much longer credits than have heretofore been customary among our exporters. The United States Government, also, passed the Edge Act at the end of 1919, providing for the creation of special banking houses for foreign trade purposes, the capital of which may be subscribed to by national banks, and which are under the supervision of the Federal Reserve Board.

Much pressure has also been brought to bear on the Federal Government to make loans direct to the producers in this country, so that they can finance themselves while selling to foreign users of their goods under a long-time credit arrangement which would make it impossible for ordinary commercial banks to extend their assistance.

Recently, in connection with the League of Nations, a plan has been suggested by a Dutch banker, named after him the ter Meulen plan, whereby it might be possible for those needing imported goods, provided they can satisfy an international committee that their credit is sound, to receive from their respective governments national bonds, presumably secured by collateral satisfactory to the issuing government. These bonds would be due at a future time, not at all related to the time needed for effecting the transaction or for transferring the imported goods. The exporter would then receive these bonds as payment, and could either hold them until maturity, or no doubt sell them on the open market.

Questions

1. Viewed as a general proposition, do you consider such methods of financing the sale of our goods abroad financially sound?
2. How should you expect the financial position of our industries to be affected in the long run if these methods were generally used?
3. How should you expect the finances of foreign industries using our goods to be affected?
4. How should you expect the general price level to be affected by these methods?
5. Should you approve of any method of financing which would enable producers to hold their merchandise inventory in the hope of keeping up prices when the general trend of prices is downward?
6. Would your answer be different if the capital for this sort of financing were to be furnished by the Government?

Problem 115

Shall a Concern Whose Financial Standing Has Been Excellent Sell New Securities at a High Rate in Order to Improve Its Current Position?

The .... Company, engaged in the making of steel products, has been excellently managed. Its growth has been continuous but not spectacular. The company has for many years made high profits, until by the end of 1920 it had a surplus equal to about 60 per cent of all the capital stock outstanding. During the year 1920, after the payment of dividends on preferred and common stock, there was added to surplus an amount equal to about 11 per cent on the common stock. In fact, 18 per cent had been earned on the common stock, and in addition a considerable amount of bonds had been retired out of earnings. Liberal allowance had also been made for depreciation and for tax reserves. The net worth of this company on December 31, 1920, was equal to 160 per cent of the par value of the stock.

During the early months of 1921 the company suffered a decline in business because of the general depression. Within the first six months of the year it probably did not operate at more than one-third its full capacity. But it turns out a very wide variety of products and its market was one of the last to decline and will be one of the first to improve. The president of the company now thinks (July, 1921) that they will be operating at about two-thirds' capacity by autumn.

On account of the small volume of business done, the company naturally operated at a deficit during the first half of 1921, for in accordance with earlier experience it would have been necessary for the plant to operate to about 75 per cent capacity in order to break even. Every effort, however, has been made to reduce overhead expenses and effect economies until it is now believed that the company can avoid a deficit if the plant is operated to 60 per cent capacity.

Due to the generally unliquid business conditions this company unavoidably has a high merchandise inventory, which, to be sure, has been written down to market. Its bank borrowings are also higher than they have ever been before, though not in excess. The current ratio was at the beginning of the year about 2.4 to 1. This ratio has naturally been reduced since that time, but is still a very good one considering business conditions.

The management of this concern, not being used to reporting deficits to stockholders and desiring to maintain the financial independence of the company, is wondering whether it would be a good plan to do some financing in the near future, so that it would not be necessary to secure from the banks constant renewals of notes payable.

The bank lines are still more than sufficient to take care of all present borrowings, but the president feels that since the financial showing for 1921 will be decidedly subnormal, it will probably be extremely difficult to do any new financing in the following year, if that should become necessary.

With investment conditions such as they are at the present time, it would probably be impossible for the company, in spite of its excellent record, to secure any new funds except through an issue of bonds. This would introduce a new difficulty into the situation, since there is already outstanding an issue of 5 per cent first mortgage bonds on the fixed assets of the company. The management, therefore, feels that it would be difficult at the present time to float a new bond issue junior to this issue. At any rate, if this were done, the charges would be almost prohibitively high.

Hence the question arises as to whether it would be good policy to attempt to sell new bonds to provide for the needed working capital, and to retire the present bond issue. At this point another complication is raised inasmuch as the entire present bond issue is held as an investment by another company. This company refuses to sell these bonds back to the subject company except at par, though if they were on the market they would be selling at a much lower figure.

Questions

1. In the light of the facts given, do you think it is wise for this company to attempt any new financing of any sort at the present time?
2. If there is to be new financing, should you advise retiring the present bond issue?
3. Assuming that the management decides to raise additional working capital, what method would *you* suggest?

Problem 116

The Cumulation of Credit Operations in the Automobile Industry

The .... Automobile Company was in the habit of drawing sight drafts on the wholesalers to whom their cars were sold. The company paid the makers of accessories and parts, from whom they bought, by trade acceptances drawn for the usual term. The wholesalers had been financing themselves by discounting, sometimes with banks but usually with finance corporations, their short-time promissory notes secured by chattel mortgages or trust receipts on the cars in their possession. They were in the habit of meeting these notes at maturity largely out of the funds secured from the retail dealers,who financed the sale of cars to customers in the manner already described in a previous problem. (Problem 37.)

A great slump in sales came in 1920, but this company, thinking that the market was off only temporarily, continued to manufacture cars.

Questions

1. Analyze the advantages or disadvantages of these several methods of financing, from the point of view of the automobile industry.
2. What financial difficulties would the company encounter when the sales practically stopped?
3. How could it have been extricated from these difficulties?
4. Do you approve of their policy in continuing to manufacture the cars?
5. What new financial difficulties, if any, were raised by this policy, and how could they be met?

Problem 117

Paying Off Unsecured Creditors With New Security Issues

One great corporation owning many millions of dollars has worked out a "plan" for the liquidation of its debts. This "plan" calls for the issuance of a lot of new securities to be used in paying off creditors whose claims are either partly secured or not secured at all. And in the "plan" it is pointed out that these securities may be used by the creditors as collateral against which they may borrow at the banks. Just how this is to help the banking situation is not clear.

Questions

1. Is this a satisfactory "plan"?
2. How will it help the corporation?
3. How will it affect other corporations?

Problem 118

The Inter-relation of Credit Operations in the Different Stages of an Industry

Jones, a cotton broker, had been selling raw cotton in large quantities to a fabric mill. It was his custom to draw drafts at 90 days on the mill. This ordinarily gave ample opportunity for the raw material to be made up and sold before the draft became due. Drafts, when accepted by the mill, were discounted with a large national bank.

The fabric mill to which Jones sold had been in a very strong financial position while prices were on the upward trend. It had accordingly arranged for a liberal line of credit at several different banks, one of which was the same bank which customarily discounted the broker's paper.

In the early part of 1920 the fabric mill was under contract to deliver a large part of its output on very favorable terms to the M. Rubber Tire Company. These goods were sold on open account and ordinarily payment was made at the first of each month. During the year 1920, however, the tire company became a little slow in its payments.

The M. Rubber Tire Company was selling a good deal of paper in the open market. This paper was rated as prime paper by all the banks and was held in considerable quantity by the national bank already referred to.

The M. Rubber Tire Company sold a part of its output direct to a well-known automobile manufacturer whose business fell off rapidly in the latter part of 1920. The M. Tire Company, hoping to continue its output, even in the face of this depressing situation, at the end of the year began selling tires to dealers at a price concession, dating for spring delivery, and receiving from the dealers trade acceptances drawn for 90 days. As the payments from the automobile manufacturer became slow, some of these acceptances were discounted with several different banks by the M. Tire Company.

The automobile company to which this tire company was selling went into a receiver's hands early in 1921. This catastrophe, together with the delayed payments from other sources, and the losses due to price reduction, inventory shrinkage, and the like, forced the M. Tire Company also into a receivership.

Just at this time the bank examiners, in looking over the loans of the national bank before mentioned, found that they held the commercial paper of the M. Tire Company, were making direct loans to the fabric mill, and had discounted the drafts of Jones, the cotton broker.

As the tire company had now become practically insolvent, it was evident that neither the fabric mill, nor in turn the cotton broker, could hope to receive payments which would enable them to liquidate their obligations to the bank. In practical effect, therefore, all of these different types of bank loans were being made to the now financially embarrassed tire company. The aggregate loan thus arrived at was much in excess of the legal maximum of 10 per cent of the bank's capital and surplus which could be lent to one borrower. This situation was pointed out to the bank, which was asked to remedy the condition as soon as possible.

The fabric mill is still perfectly solvent. Its current assets, however, are temporarily rather frozen. The bank finds it easiest to bring pressure to bear on the mill and to curtail its line of credit. The situation having developed thus far, the president of the fabric mill asks what his next step should be.

Questions

1. What weaknesses in our credit structure, if any, are indicated by this problem?

2. Is the position in which the fabric mill finds itself the result of the present disorganized financial situation or of an unwise policy on the part of the management?

3. What suggestions can you offer to the president of this fabric mill?

4. From the point of view of what is probably best for the industry, what advice would you give to the bank?

Problem 119

Current Financing and the Business Cycle

"The Government has not paid the railroads, and the railroads, in their turn, are not paying what they owe. This one interruption multiplies the hardship on the whole community, and it is multiplied again when the companies and individuals to whom the railroads owe moneys are rendered incapable of making prompt payment to their creditors because of the slowness of pay by the railroads. And so it goes down the line, with the amount "frozen" steadily and rapidly mounting each time it is passed to a new class. If the Government pays the roads, the roads can pass the proceeds along to their creditors, and their creditors can pass the money along to the next group, and so on. The original debt of \$350,000,000 to \$400,000,000 blocks probably several billions of payments, and the freezing process becomes a real factor in the credit situation.

In the second place, there is the West and the South. Neither the West nor the South liquidated last fall. It did some liquidation, but it was little more than going around the edges. The great agricultural sections were caught in the price decline, and at first would not sell and later could not sell. It is one thing to say, now that the collapse of commodity prices has become real, that liquidation should have taken place. But it is distinctly another to offer workable ways for liquidation now that collapsed prices are an actuality.

Commodities have fallen too rapidly to allow of a real liquidation now. Cotton, for instance, which was the greatest export crop we had last year in point of dollar value, has declined some 69 per cent in value since the last week in July, 1920. The July price may have been too high, and was, as a matter of fact, an artificial value, but even so, a 69 per cent depreciation is a thing to be reckoned with, even when it is from absurd levels. And if the stocks of cotton now being carried were to be thrown on the market, the depreciation probably would run closer to 90 per cent, or more than to the present 69 per cent.

In the same way wool has suffered. There are huge stocks of wool on hand now, and probably they could all be liquidated at a price. But that price would ruin the wool industry. Sheep have to be kept not only for current needs, but for those of next year and the year after, and the year after that. Herds cannot be dissipated, and if present market prices are too low to allow of realization on current herds and current stocks of wool, the stocks and the herds have to be carried until they can be sold.

These things are being carried. They are being carried by banks which, for the time being, cannot realize on their loans. They could in a pinch take over the collateral on which they have made advances, and doubtless some of them have done so already. But that does not alter the situation. The banks cannot sell the collateral and reimburse themselves, so they would be no better off in a broad general way than they were before.

And then there are the "limping corporations," as they have been called. This, perhaps, is a much more serious situation than generally is realized. The public, for obvious reasons, has not been informed as to the number or the condition of many large corporations which are having difficulty in meeting their bank loans.

Last fall, when the time arrived for final payment of Federal income and profits taxes, a good many corporations—and more than a few individuals, too, for that matter—had to be helped out by the banks in order to meet their tax debts. How many of the loans made then have been paid off subsequently cannot be told, but bankers, speaking of their individual experiences, say that the total is not large."

(Statement made early in 1921.)

Questions

1. Do you agree with the *opinions* above expressed.
2. Discuss critically and constructively the steps which might have been taken to avoid the financial difficulties here described.

PART III

PROBLEMS OF INTERNAL FINANCING

CHAPTER VI

FINANCIAL ASPECTS OF PURCHASING GOODS

References:

Brace, *Value of Organized Speculation*, 50–179.
*Gerstenberg, *Principles of Business*, 373–399.
Rindsfoos, *Purchasing*, 1–69.
*Twyford, *Purchasing and Storing*, 14–133, 157–172.

MANY a concern which has been originally well financed, falls into serious financial difficulties as the result of overbuying or buying at the wrong time. Some of the astounding failures of the post-war period have been largely or solely due to an improper purchasing policy. While prices are tending continually upward, it may be possible to attain an apparent financial success even though unwise methods are followed. The acid test of the policy, however, comes in the period of falling prices.

Since most businesses, from the least even unto the greatest, are in danger of going wrong at this point, largely through failure to correlate the purchasing policy with the general financial program and the Business Cycle, it has seemed worth while to include some suggestive problems on a few of the financial aspects of purchasing goods. Some of the problems in Chapter X may also prove helpful in this connection.

Problem 120

General Problem in Purchasing and Credit

J. C. Penney writes as follows regarding his early purchasing and credit policy:

"After three years the partners began to consider opening a store in Kemmerer. By that time I had saved $500. The store was planned to start with a capital of $6,000 and they offered me a third interest if I could raise the money; I borrowed $1,500 and took their offer.

* * * * * * * *

Within five years I had paid off my loan and bought out my partners. We, however, continued our joint buying trips to the East until my buying was large enough to gain the quantity advantage. I never bought from a salesman and never asked for credit. In those days I did not even borrow from the bank. Everything was on a cash basis and I bought and sold only staple lines of dry-goods and notions. They sold quickly because the price was low, the quality high, and the guarantee of satisfaction was absolute. I found that I had to make more than two trips a year to market, and also I found, that buying frequently permitted me always to dispose of my stock on the buying price. My sales expense never exceeded 10 per cent and was usually lower. I could make a good profit at prices the other stores could not touch and so I never had to hold a mark-down or bargain sale.

* * * * * * * *

The panic of 1907 had not touched me; it had only enabled me to buy at very low prices for cash and hence gave me a still greater advantage over competitors who wanted to buy on credit—when credit was hard to get.

* * * * * * * *

The original merchandising plan of the shack at Kemmerer is still the plan under which we operate. We never rent a store in what is supposed to be a good location and at a high rental. We try to locate in a fairly central position in a town, but rarely on the main street. We want low rents. We take to a side street and if the side streets are expensive, then we go to the edge of the business section or wherever the rents are cheap. We find that people will come to our stores to buy without regard to location; if we paid high rents, we could not sell at a profit and keep within the line of our small mark-up, So we pay no attention at all to the number of people who habitually use a street on which we plan to open a store. If 1,000 people a day pass one point and the rental is high, we should not hesitate to go to a street where only 50 people pass in a day—if the accommodations are good and the rental low.

* * * * * * * *

Our policy is to buy frequently and for cash. We hold that it is no part of the merchandising function to speculate in goods value. We might make large future contracts on a rising market and profit by the increased value of the goods. But on the other hand, future contracts would be losing ventures in a falling market. We should have to alter our principle of merchandising to sell the cheaply bought goods at the market instead of at cost, while the goods bought in a falling market could not be sold at cost over a long period. So instead we buy frequently, get the goods out instantly to the stores by express and sell at cost plus our mark-up. Our stores turn their stocks on an average of five times a year, so by the time any large change in price has reached the retail market we are buying and sending out at the new price.

Neither the branches nor the stores carry inventories above what might be termed current needs. With our fingers always in the primary markets and with cash in our pockets, we are content with hand-to-mouth buying and permit the other man to do the guessing on price.

We do not gamble against the market; we buy what we need and not what the other man wants to sell to us. In the end we obtain our goods at a lower price than the average buyer who attempts to get the better of the market and we are never stuck with great lots of high-priced goods. Therefore, we have no special sales of any kind throughout the operation of adjusting our inventories. A man with cash can always buy what he needs.

We buy only staples; we do not carry fancy or unusual goods of any kind. Our appeal is to the middle class that wants honest merchandise.

We do not want the whole trade anywhere; we want only that trade to which we can promise to give the largest value for the dollar. That we have always done, but we could not continue to do it if we experimented with styles or laid wagers against the course of prices.

If we wagered against prices, customers would lose while prices were going up, and we should lose when they were going down. We are distributors of merchandise, not speculators, and during our 19 years of business life we have never had to take a serious loss on merchandise."

(SYSTEM, February, 1921.)

Questions

1. Analyze critically the financial methods and policies followed by the above concern.
2. Do you expect that such a concern would ever get into financial difficulties? Why?
3. Do you approve of the methods of purchasing followed by this company?
4. Would such methods be satisfactory for all concerns?

Problem 121

Buying from Hand to Mouth

The owner of a large grocery store writes as follows:

"We always buy less than we expect to sell. That way we protect ourselves against unexpected developments. We get our profit; and when we have sold the lot we go into the market and buy whatever we need to finish the season. We make a moderate profit, certainly no loss, on that business."

Questions

1. What are the real gains, if any, resulting from this policy?
2. Should you have considered this to be a satisfactory policy in 1917?
3. Would it be safe for every type of business to follow this policy?

(Reference: System, April 1921, p. 544, ff.)

PROBLEM 122

RELATION BETWEEN THE PURCHASING POLICY, THE TURNOVER, AND PROFITS*

The vital question is not how many goods can be bought with a given amount, but how much net profit can be made; and the net profit depends, not on the first cost of the merchandise, but entirely on the turnover.

On such staple lines as hosiery and underwear, a retailer could well afford to pay 10 per cent more for an article, if by doing so he could increase his rate of turnover.

This seems almost like a foolish statement, but actual facts will prove it sound.

Suppose a merchant uses 60 dozen of a hose in two months, which could be bought direct from the mill at 95 cents, or at $1.05 from the wholesale house. If he buys from the mill, he has to get at least 60 dozen, but in buying them from a jobber he could get along with only 10 dozen, which would give him 5 dozen for his forward stock and the same amount in reserve.

Buying direct, the stock (60 dozen) amounts to $57, and the total purchases for the year (360 dozen) to $342.

If these goods are sold at two pair for a quarter, the year's gross business on the item would amount to $540. A 20 per cent cost of doing business on this would be $108, leaving $432. Deducting the cost, $342, gives a net profit on the $57 investment, of $90.

*Elwood Sampson, Chairman, Public Relations Committee, National Association of Purchasing Agents, Detroit, writes in an interesting manner regarding "Profits from Purchases" in the *Michigan Manufacturer and Financial Record*, for May 14, 1921. Some of his remarks may be summed up as follows:

"The most evident possibility of purchasing profit is in foretelling the trend of prices. Although this is so recognized by almost every business man, still the development in this direction, with a few exceptions, is still in an infantile state. The general method at present of judging the market trend is to talk the situation over with this one and that one who ought to be in a position to be fully informed concerning his particular commodity; read the various trade papers; note what various competitors are doing, and then act accordingly. In this method judgment is based mostly upon surface indications. The danger of this is that surface signs apparently all point one way. Also, they have a most unhappy faculty of completely reversing themselves overnight. Today everything looks rosy. Tomorrow is just the opposite. On the other hand, here and there in Detroit and throughout the country have been buyers who have operated upon a carefully worked-out scientific plan of forecasting the market. For such, final judgment is based upon a consideration of the underlying fundamental factors and not merely on surface indications. These men were not buying heavy a year ago, for fundamental signs all pointed to a heavy decline during the latter part of 1920."

To illustrate how this is done, the author takes a tried and proved plan (not an academic one) and reduces it down to a classified outline of the factors considered.

In buying from a jobber the stock (10 dozen) would cost \$10.50, and the yearly purchases (360 dozen), \$378. The selling price and the cost of doing business are the same, no matter how the goods were bought, so deducting \$378 from \$432 shows a net profit of \$54.

This apparently shows a loss of net profit on this particular transaction, of \$36.

(SYSTEM, July 1921, p. 40, ff.)

Questions

1. Is the above reasoning applicable to all cases? Is any loss involved?

2. What would be the annual gains resulting from buying in the smaller quantities?

PROBLEM 123

THE RESULTS OF "OVERBUYING" IN A RETAIL STORE*

Mr. X. was a retail men's clothing merchant in a small middle western town. For a man in his position his education was fair and he had more than the average knowledge of accounting, which had been secured through local business schools and correspondence schools. He was a fairly active member of one of the local churches, to all appearances had no bad habits, was married and the father of two children. In fact, he was a perfectly respectable and desirable citizen of his community, though he was practically without capital of his own and without any connections which would enable him to borrow local private capital or to secure funds from the local bank.

In 1911, Mr. X. decided to launch into the merchandising business, and, as might be expected, he fell into the rather common error in this line of business—he overbought. This overbuying, he explained, was due to the fact that salesmen offered him such a liberal

* See also problems in Chapter X for further results of "overbuying."

extension of credit that the time of payment seemed far away. Of course, when he accepted the terms offered he was not able to take the usual cash discounts because of his lack of capital. Nor did he at the time fully realize how much could be saved by using the cash discount. In course of time, it became evident to him that it would be impossible to dispose of all the goods which he had bought, in the town where his store was located. Accordingly, feeling that he had already made a misstep which could not be rectified without taking a great chance, he decided to open up a store in an adjoining town in order to dispose of his surplus. This move was apparently successful, inasmuch as he managed to clean up his stock and pay off his maturing obligations.

Somewhat elated by his seeming success, he again launched optimistically into a buying campaign, urged on by the same salesmen who had before induced him to overpurchase. As he did not yet have enough capital in his business to enable him to borrow from the local bank, he did not have the opportunity to secure bankers' advice, which might have prevented this mistake. Consequently, he again overbought, and, trusting to his past luck, opened a third store in another town in order to dispose of the surplus goods which he found could not be marketed by the first two stores.

By this time our dealer had developed for himself a fairly careful system of accounting which enabled him to tell with reasonable accuracy where his finances stood at the end of each month. He knew what it cost him to do business and how long it would take him, provided business was reasonably good, to pay off his mercantile creditors. Unfortunately, however, the European war broke and business fell off markedly, so that Mr. X. was threatened with bankruptcy. The line of goods which he already had was turning slowly, so that there was good reason to expect that it would eventually be sold. On the other hand, it was quite apparent that he could not keep his trade unless he could secure several thousand dollars' worth of additional new goods to attract the holiday trade. Yet in view of the fact that most of his accounts were already past due, there seemed to be no possibility of getting further credit.

Confronted with this situation, with absolute failure apparently inevitable, Mr. X. thought that boldness coupled with downright honesty might save the day, for it was clear that no other resource remained. Accordingly, having prepared a careful statement of his financial condition and having drawn up a set of figures to show his costs of doing business, he wired his chief mercantile creditors that he would be in their office in Cleveland at 10 o'clock the next morning. In accordance with this message he arrived on the stroke of 10, asked for the manager, put before him the statement of his financial condition and his cost sheet, and said:

"Mr......., we are up against it. Failure stares us in the face. We owe money to a large number of selling houses (at this point showing the list of his creditors), and your firm is our largest creditor. We have foolishly overbought, though we would have been able to work our way out had it not been for the depressed conditions. Now we throw ourselves on your mercy absolutely. If we fail, you will lose a good deal of money. If you help us to pull through, you will have our everlasting gratitude and all the future business that we can give you. We know where we stand financially, and know what the trouble is, and know what it costs us to do business, and know that our costs are relatively very low, and feel certain that we can pay off our obligations at the end of several months. However, in order to hold and develop the trade and to retrieve our past mistakes, it will be necessary for us to buy more goods. In fact, we now need from you a bill of $5,000 worth of holiday goods. What will you do for us?"

Questions

1. Should Mr. X. have opened up new stores to dispose of his surplus goods, when he did not even have enough capital to run one store?

2. In view of the fact that he persistently overbought, do you believe that he was a man whom dealers were justified in trusting?

3. What kind of financial advice, if any, do you think the various salesmen should have given him?

4. Can you suggest any method whereby he might have put himself in a position to take advantage of the cash discounts instead of financing himself through dealer credit?

5. Did Mr. X. follow a correct policy in approaching his largest creditor in the manner outlined and what do you expect would be this creditor's response?

6. Indicate, with reasons therefor, what you expect would be the financial future of Mr. X'.s business.

Problem 124

The Goodyear Company's Purchasing Policy

In System for August, 1920, there appeared an article by President Seiberling, of the Goodyear Tire & Rubber Company, on the financial policy of purchasing goods, in which statements such as the following were made.

In referring to the early days of the Goodyear Company, some twenty years ago, he said:

"Because we had so little money we learned how to buy.

The company usually had to pay cash because it was so little known and so poor that credit could not properly be extended to it.

The fact that in the beginning we had to buy our raw materials for cash allowed us to pick and choose.

"Because when we were small we planned our buying ahead—that is one of the reasons that today we are large.

"If you know how to buy and to make, the world will make a path to your door."

He further defends the policy of controlling a part of the source of supply of goods needed on the ground; first, that it gives the manufacturer a line on the fair price which should be paid, and second, that it makes the concern more independent. He also suggests that such a policy may help to stimulate "backward markets." In line with this reasoning, he describes in glowing terms the gains which have come to the Goodyear Company from purchasing and developing a coal mine, cotton plantations in Arizona, fabric mills in New England, and rubber plantations in Sumatra.

When the Goodyear Tire and Rubber Company failed in the autumn of 1920, the chief criticisms made by the bankers who worked out the plan for the future financing of the company, which resulted in Seiberling's having all connections severed, were two—first, that the Goodyear Company had recklessly expanded its fixed investment by attempting to control or develop the source of supply of raw materials, the fixed investment having more than doubled in one year's time. Secondly, they were appalled by the very high merchandise inventory and the commitments for purchases which had been made at high prices. The company had been trying to "buy up" the rubber market. It was necessary to write off many millions of dollars because of this situation, and a surplus of more than $30,000,000 in 1919 was changed to a deficit of more than $15,000,000 by the end of 1920.

Questions

1. Do you agree with the statements made by Mr. Seiberling regarding the proper purchasing policy?

2. If the general principles which he outlined are sound, how do you account for the condition in which

the Goodyear Company was found shortly after Seiberling's article was written?

3. What light, if any, does this problem throw on the financial considerations involved in purchasing raw materials?

Problem 125

The Possible Results of Accepting One's Commitments When Others are Canceling

The N. Cotton Cloth Mill carries on solely weaving operations of a specialized sort. It is a very old mill with an excellent credit reputation, having financed itself out of earnings until its resources were very high. During the year 1919-1920, owing to the conditions then prevailing, it was common for mills of this sort to have contracts with makers of yarn so as to be assured of the needed supply. This mill was no exception to the rule.

When the general market slump came in 1920, the N. Cotton Cloth Mill, proud of its past record, continued to accept all the yarn which it had agreed to take, at the high prices prevailing at the time the contracts were made. Thus the inventories piled up, the cash position became weak, and the notes payable increased.

In the months of depression which followed, most of the competitors of this mill either could not or would not accept the shipments of yarn which they had agreed to take. Some of them, by the way, were purchasing from the same yarn mills which furnished goods to the N. Company. They either canceled their orders altogether, or managed to secure an adjustment of prices. Thus they hoped to save their present credit position by throwing the burden back on the spinner. They were further putting themselves in a position to buy yarn at a much lower figure, as the price of cotton rapidly dropped. Hence, they expected to be in a position, when operations were resumed, to cut under the price for cloth at which their larger and erstwhile stronger competitor could afford to produce.

Questions

1. From the long-run financial point of view, do you think the N. Company acted wisely in continuing to accept the contracts made when prices were much higher?

2. Do you think that the smaller competitors would be justified in cutting their prices below their larger rivals?

3. If the competitors should cut the price below that which can be made by the large concern, what would you expect the ultimate effect to be,

(*a*) On the finances of the group of smaller companies,

(*b*) On the N. Company?

4. Assuming that the N. Company's current ratio is far below the danger line, also that no securities can be sold for additional financing except to rival mill owners, how, if at all, can this company save itself from financial ruin?

Problem 126

Hedging Operations

There appears to be little uniformity in the methods followed by cotton mills in financing their sales. Some goods are made up largely to order at a firm price, while in other cases the goods are manufactured before actual receipt of orders. Though there is a wide margin between the cost of the raw cotton used and the selling price of the finished goods, in the case of a cloth mill, yet at times changes in the market price of raw cotton may become very significant.

With an organized cotton exchange it is possible for mills to protect themselves against loss on finished goods by buying and selling cotton futures. The extent to which this practice is carried on by the mills themselves is difficult to ascertain, but it does not appear to be so common in this country as in England, where there is a greater specialization in the various processes of cotton manufacture. However, opinions differ widely as to whether "speculation" of this sort is a proper function of the manufacturer.

In the case of flour milling, there is a comparatively narrow margin between the cost of wheat and the market price of flour. It is commonly reported that the mills very frequently protect themselves against price changes by buying and selling futures on the wheat exchange.

Questions

1. Under what circumstances, if at all, is it desirable for a cotton mill to buy and sell futures?

2. Should you expect "hedging" operations to be carried on more commonly by those mills which produce solely yarn, or by those mills which do not make their yarn, but only weave the cloth?

3. Are there any reasons why you would expect the practice of "hedging" to be more common in the case of flour mills than in the case of cotton mills?

4. So far as the raw material is concerned, what conditions seem to be requisite in order to make it possible for futures to be bought and sold?

(References: *Textile Recorder*, June 21, 1921, p. 67; Brace, 151-159.)

Problem 127

Speculating for a Rise in Price

A. In 1917, the dean of a well-known school of commerce wrote as follows:

"In 1898, a manufacturer whose raw material was steel had his attention called to some facts which set him thinking—that the price of steel was lower than it had been for many years; that prices in general had been falling for over twenty-five years; that business had been prostrate since the panic of 1893; that the increasing output of gold must soon have an effect upon the level of prices; that there were many reasons to expect a revival of business in the near future. That was in June of 1898. The manufacturer was so impressed that he immediately ordered a quantity of steel sufficient to last him for three years if the demand for his product did not increase. In September business in general began to pick up and by the end of the year this manufacturer was in the market again buying steel. The lively demand for his product had used up all that he had bought in June.

In June his partners said he was crazy; in December they doubtless thought he had made a lucky stroke. He was neither crazy nor lucky. He made money simply because he had good judgment and relied upon it."

(Johnson, J. F., *Business and the Man*, 195-196.)

B. A well-known private banker and successful business man, whose interests have been largely in the iron and steel industry, referred in March, 1921, with great approval to the policy reported to be followed by one of the important makers of steel products in the United States, in accordance with which the company purchases large quantities of steel when prices are very low and sells the material to other companies when prices have risen.

This particular company has never issued any bonds or notes and has been financed almost solely by common stock issues. Further, it has built up a surplus out of earnings which is about equal to its outstanding common stock. The outstanding preferred stock amounts to little more than 20 per cent of the common stock. The company has had an excellent dividend record since its organization in 1899. It is reported to have made a good deal of money by this practice of buying steel at low prices far in excess of its own immediate future needs, and selling out later at much higher prices.

C. The treasurer of a very large and prosperous company which manufactures paper products, and which has had an enviable financial history over a long period of years, stated in July, 1921, that it was wholly contrary to the policy of his company to buy any material in excess of their needs for the near future. He says that no matter how low prices of material may be, it is not the business of his company to speculate in the goods which they use. The company is thoroughly opposed to any "excess purchasing," no matter how good the price looks, and this policy has beyond a doubt saved the business many a financial setback. This concern is the largest of its kind in the country, and sells its finished goods to many thousands of relatively small customers.

Questions

1. Considered as a general principle, do you think that the policy outlined in case "A" is a financially sound one?
2. What is your opinion of the wisdom of the practice followed in case "B"?
3. Do you approve of the policy outlined by the treasurer in case "C"?
4. How, if at all, would you draw the line between forehanded purchasing and speculation in materials used?
5. Will your answer to the foregoing questions be influenced in any way by the nature, size, or methods of financing of the business under consideration? By the period in the Business Cycle?

Problem 128

Shall a Concern Whose Resources are Low Purchase Heavily in Order to Get a "Bargain"?

The . . . . Company is a manufacturer of surgical dressings. Between November, 1918, and January, 1920, it lost a good deal of money as a result of the dumping of surgical supplies on the market by the War Department and the Red Cross.

As a result of heavy liquidation of old stocks, the particular number of grey cloth needed for making the surgical dressings was selling at 90¢ per pound as compared with $1.15 per pound for numbers finer and coarser. Practically all the goods suitable for this purpose was made by mills in the city of Fall River.

In the aggregate, these mills had on hand about 5,000,000 yards of the material, and their sales had been slight since the conclusion of the armistice.

In January, 1920, the . . . . Company was in so precarious a financial condition that it could scarcely purchase on any large scale. The management, having carefully looked over the situation, estimated that the liquidation of old stocks was about complete and that they would be able to use the 5,000,000 yards now held by the mills within about six months. Consequently, the treasurer of the . . . . Company quietly secured options to purchase this entire supply of suitable grey cloth at 90¢ per pound. The option called for delivery of such a portion of the entire supply at a succession of dates, that not more that $250,000 would be needed to finance the purchases at any one time. With $50,000 cash as a deposit, the remaining $200,000 could be borrowed from the banks on warehouse receipts as the cotton cloth was being used.

At 5:45 p. m. of the day upon which the options were to expire at 6 p. m., the treasurer of the . . . . . . Company went to a financier, B., with the following proposition:

If B. would purchase the cotton as needed through a syndicate, or some such arrangement, the . . . . Company would guarantee B. against any loss, would pay 6 per cent for the money advanced plus 2 per cent commission on the quantity purchased, and would divide equally any profits made, based on the difference between the market price of the product at the time taken and the purchase price of 90¢ per pound secured by the option.

Questions

1. Was the .... Company following a sound financial policy in attempting to purchase cloth under the conditions outlined?

2. How should you expect the market price of this cloth to be affected if the plan proposed by the .... Company was carried through?

3. Had you been in B's place, what action would you have taken?

Problem 129

Financial Difficulty Arising from Buying, Due to "Guessing" the Market Wrong

The Z. Company is a partnership engaged in the leather export business. For some years it had made a specialty of dealing in a low grade of kid leather which was used in some European countries, particularly England, for making cheap shoes. The concern had for several years made high earnings on its original capital of $150,000. It dealt only with one bank and had regularly followed the practice of taking its trade discounts, so that it normally carried a very low proportion of accounts payable.

During the year 1919, as it was thought that there would be a post-war boom in European countries, the

Z. Company stocked up heavily with inventory, borrowing from its bank about $200,000, an amount considerably in excess of its own capital, in order to carry this inventory. About October, 1919, the export market for this grade of leather was very suddenly cut off, due to foreign conditions, so that both the inventories and receivables became frozen. The European market now being shut off, there seemed to be no possibility that a domestic demand for this type of leather could be created. Hence the inventories shrank so rapidly that all equities were wiped out and there seemed to be no possibility that the bank could secure payment of its notes except in the distant future.

In January, 1921, the bank was still carrying this concern, having continuously renewed the original loan of $200,000. This loan was a straight commercial loan, and practically the only security which the bank had for repayment was the inventory, now so greatly depreciated that the value was wholly problematical and amounted to only a fraction of the bank's loan. The company had almost no fixed assets, as it leased its real estate. The moral risk of the partners had always been considered good. The only possibility of the bank's recovering on this loan apparently depends on the active renewal of European trade.

Questions

1. What particular elements of financial weakness are apparent in the case of this concern?

2. Could the Z. Company have followed another course since the slump in trade, which would have left it at present in a stronger position?

3. What steps, if any, do you believe should now be taken,

(*a*) By the Z. Company?

(*b*) By its bank who is the sole creditor?

Problem 130

A Problem on Financing Imports

During the war an American importing house with relatively small capital wished to import some very large orders for its well-known and responsible customers. The orders were so large that it would have been impossible for the company to finance the transaction in the usual direct way by letting bills of exchange be drawn on itself. Further, the price of the commodity to be imported (indigo) was many times higher than normal, so that the goods themselves could scarcely be considered as safe collateral for any banker, even though the parties supplying the goods were thoroughly dependable.

As the customers were very eager to obtain the goods, and were not in a position to import on their own account, the importer secured the assistance of an international banking house, which issued a letter of credit in favor of the importing house, so that it was merely necessary for the importer to pay the usual commission to the bankers for their services, without himself putting up any capital. The goods were, of course, held in trust by the banking house while being sold. The difference between the import price and the selling price, minus the banker's small commission, was passed on to the importer as the goods were delivered to the customers.

The quality of the goods was guaranteed to the customer by the importer, but in order to save any delays and to avoid any risks being taken by the banker, the customers were induced by the importing house to sign an agreement to the following effect—this agreement to be held by the banking house:

"As we are desirous of facilitating this transaction . . . . . . we agree to accept delivery on arrival and pay for against domestic bills of lading . . . . without any question as to quantity, quality, or substance."

Questions

1. What seem to be the conditions essential to financing a purchase of goods in this way?

2. Should you consider it desirable for a medium-sized business concern to attempt to finance directly the purchase of materials from abroad? Why or why not?

3. Under what circumstances, if at all, is it financially desirable for a large manufacturing concern to import directly the goods which it uses?

CHAPTER VII

FINANCIAL ASPECTS OF PRODUCING GOODS

IN many kinds of manufacturing it is no easy matter to determine the exact Cost of the goods produced. Until recently, too much has been taken for granted. There has also been an all too common assumption, fostered by the theoretical economist, that the costs of production can be more or less indefinitely lowered as the size of the productive unit increases. Hence many exaggerated claims have been made for the large-scale producer and the horizontal or vertical combination of business concerns.

It is only by relating the production program of a business to the general financial program, over a considerable period of time, that a concern can hope to be successful. The exigencies of the war period have directed attention to the possibilities of conservation through standardization, elimination of waste, and improved efficiency methods. While prices were rapidly raising, however, business profits were high. Many unnecessary items of expense were incurred, and many a needless expansion of fixed assets was made. Very frequently the selling end of the business was able to bring unwarranted pressure on the production department. With prices falling, the very concerns which were most prosperous on the upward swing, tend to be hardest hit by the depression. Profits are now shrinking into deficits, while the overhead expenses stubbornly refuse to come down. As it should be the aim of every well-conducted business to reduce its costs to the minimum, a few problems bearing on some of the financial aspects of producing goods are here given.

A. COSTS AND FINANCE*

Exercise III

Problem on the Relations Between the Business Cycle, Costs of Production, Net Profits, etc.

Select three industries from the Census of Manufactures, 1909, for each of which the total value of product is $100,000,000 or more. Tabulate the following data, making your own computations whenever necessary:

1. Number of establishments.
2. Capital invested.
3. Value of products.
4. Total expenses.
5. Net income.
6. Ratio of value of product to capital.
7. Ratio of net income to capital.
8. Ratio of net income to value of product.
9. Ratio of total expenses to value of product.
10. Cost of services.
11. Cost of materials, etc.
12. Miscellaneous costs.
13. Ratio of cost of services to total expenses.
14. Ratio of cost of materials, etc., to total expenses.
15. Ratio of miscellaneous costs to total expenses.

In the light of the above data—

(*a*) Explain the varying degrees of prosperity enjoyed by *each industry* at the end of 1914, 1917 and 1920.

(*b*) Compare the probable financial condition of the *several industries* at these same dates.

Source: *The Thirteenth Census of the United States, 1910,* Vol. VIII, pages 518-537.

Reference: Mitchell, *Business Cycles*, Chapters X and XI, pages 452-511.

Additional suggestions: Mitchell, *History of Prices During the War; Review of Economic Statistics; Monthly Labor Review;* the various financial and trade publications.

*There are no specific references which will be particularly helpful in connection with the problems in this section. The student, however, is referred to some of the titles under Topics VI and IX of the General Bibliography. Sammons', *Keeping Up With Rising Costs* may be read with profit.

Problem 131

How Shall the Overhead Be Reduced?

A certain business in 1914 sold 100,000 units for \$1,000,000, and the overhead amounted to 10 per cent of the total sales, or \$100,000, equal to one dollar for each unit of sales (approximate figures are used.)

The increase in sales during the war boom brought the total units, in 1919, to 200,000, amounting to \$4,000,000, and the overhead still remained at 10 per cent on the gross sales in dollars, or \$400,000, equal to two dollars on each unit sold. This shows a large increase in overhead, both as to dollars and to amount on each unit, but the increase in prices kept pace and not only allowed this increase to be met, but showed a more than satisfactory margin of profit.

The present year will show a drop in gross sales to approximately 150,000 units, amounting to \$2,250,000; and the overhead, which will be little diminished in total dollars, will run at about \$350,000, or over 15 per cent on the gross dollars of sales, and at the rate of $2\frac{1}{3}$ dollars on each unit of sale. This shows a substantial increase in overhead in the per cent, gross dollars, and the unit cost, which results in a material inroad into the net earnings for surplus and profits.

The following table illustrates the situation:

	Sales Dollar		
	1914	1919	1920
1. Production.....	60%	50%	60%
2. Marketing.....	10%	8%	15%
3. Administration.	10%	10%	15%
4. Profit.........	20%	32%	10%

Questions

1. How, if at all, could this situation have been prevented?

2. What steps should now be taken to improve the situation?

(Reference: *The Reduction of Merchandising Expense*, published by the Chamber of Commerce of the United States, April, 1921.)

PROBLEM 132

REDUCING COSTS THROUGH SPECIALIZATION IN PRODUCTION

The.................... Woolen Company was a relatively small and narrowly owned concern. The father, who had organized the business and who had managed it with a reasonable degree of success, was about ready to retire. His son, who had gained in the schools some knowledge of cost accounting, decided that he could make a *real* success of the business by finding out the type of goods which could be produced at lowest cost and then turning out only such goods. Accordingly, by a series of computations he discovered that their mill would incur the lowest expenses of operation if it specialized in coarse homespuns. Not only was their plant of such a sort that they could make this material more cheaply than any other, but it was common knowledge that this kind of cloth was usually in good demand.

Hence, contrary to the advice of his father as well as to that of the company's selling agent, the son turned the factory into making this one product, which theoretically should be a great profit maker.

Questions

1. Do you think this company was well advised in attempting to make only one fabric, whereas it had previously turned out several fabrics of somewhat different sorts?

2. Why do you suppose the father and the selling agent advised against this policy? Do you agree with their advice?

3. What do you expect was the immediate outcome of this change in policy? Should you expect the ultimate outcome to be different?

Problem 133

Reducing Costs Through Quantity Output

The .... Textile Mill was one of the largest concerns of its sort in the country. It specialized in the making of staple cotton goods, depending upon mass production for its profits. However, on account of the large original investment in plant and equipment, the company was from the beginning hampered by the lack of adequate working capital. Accordingly, for several years it had been forced to follow the "hand to mouth" policy, taking whatever orders it could secure and running them off as speedily as possible. Along with this they frequently experimented in making up a certain quantity of staple goods, which they were then forced to sell at the immediate market price because of their lack of funds. As the business was conducted, the plant was never operated at more than two-thirds' capacity. The result was that on account of the very large fixed assets, the unit costs of operation were unduly high and the company was never able to make a reasonable return on the investment, in spite of the hopes with which it had been originally organized.

Finally, the old management decided to give up the task which they had not yet been able satisfactorily to cope with. The new management decided that since the physical equipment was so satisfactory for mass production, it would be worth while to find out what their costs would be provided they produced to full capacity, as no attempt apparently had hitherto been made to approach the problem in this way.

With the new unit cost as the basis, it was reasoned that there would be good ground for expecting that this company could undersell practically all its competitors. On the theory that nothing could now be gained without taking a chance, the old conservative policy was thrown overboard and the mill was operated at full capacity. Thereupon it was found that the unit costs were very much lower than any heretofore realized by the .... Company. They were, in fact, so low that there was no difficulty in underselling the market for those staple goods.

Questions

1. Do you think that the new management followed the correct policy?

2. How should you expect this policy to affect (*a*) immediately, and (*b*) ultimately

(*x*) The finances of this mill?

(*y*) The finances of other mills engaged in making similar products?

Problem 134

"Making Money at a Loss"—Selling Below Cost

"What the United States—the world, in fact—wants today is not alone increased production. We had that during the war, and have now to get over it, because that increase was brought about by cost increase. Our necessity now is an increase in production carrying with it a decrease in cost. Many look to labor to give us this; but such an increase is the task not so much of labor as of management. There is more production being lost right now through lack of efficient management than there is through lack of efficient labor.

Here's an instance: Recently I visited a foundry where the product varied from castings weighing less than a pound to those weighing several tons. Their production was worked out on the "average" basis, with ruinous results, as you will quickly see. A molder at $9 a day working on small castings, does well if he produces 250 pounds of castings a day.

Another molder at the same wage, but working on larger castings, may easily produce 1,750 pounds of castings a day. The two men will therefore produce 2,000 pounds of castings for an average labor cost of 90 cents per 100 pounds. From a bookkeeping standpoint that figure tells a true story; but see how misleading it is when applied to cost as a basis for sale prices. The labor cost for the small castings is not 90 cents per 100 pounds but $3.60 per 100 pounds, while the labor cost in the large castings is only just over a half of 90 cents per 100 pounds. Naturally when the foundry quoted on a basis of 90 cents per 100 pounds for the small castings, it was overwhelmed with orders for those castings and lost $2.70 on every 100 pounds weight made. At the same time it lost all business in the heavier castings, because its quotations were too high."

Questions

1. Should costs for such a concern be computed on the "pound" basis?
2. What solution can be suggested for the apparent financial difficulties of the above concern?
3. Under what circumstances, if any, is it financially justifiable for a producer to sell below cost of production?

Problem 135

Should the Selling Price Be Uniform Irrespective of Costs?

It is reported to be the practice for some makers of knit underwear to charge the same price for all sizes irrespective of cost, the only distinction made being that between children's and adults' sizes.

Questions

1. From the financial point of view, what should you expect to be the results of this policy?

2. Would the same reasoning apply in the case of a concern which makes men's ready-to-wear clothing and follows a similar policy? In the case of a custom tailor?

Problem 136

Is a Concern Well Advised in Making Some Goods For Which the Market Is Small?

The .... Company, engaged in the manufacture of various kinds of machinery accessories, produces 17,500 different items, many of which have a very limited sale. The president of the company, feeling that the turn-over of inventory was not sufficiently rapid, had an investigation made, whereupon he discovered that 600 items out of the total accounted for about 67 per cent of the annual business. It was further discovered that many of these items had been manufactured merely to suit the whims of particular customers whose business it was thought might better be kept or be increased by this practice. In other instances, the articles had been manufactured because certain salesmen had found them easier to sell than some standard lines. Also there were some cases in which the production of the article had been due to the salesmen's trying to get business by agreeing to minor changes from the standard products, or by urging that some special article be made to sell along with the standard line.

Questions

1. Do you approve of the policy which led to the making of so many different articles?
2. Would it now be good financial policy to reduce the number made?
3. From the point of view of the producer, as well as the consumer, what financial gains or losses might result from the policy which you advise?

Problem 137

Ignorant Competition, Cost, and Failure

The President of the .... Company engaged in the making of chemicals, recently said:

"We have no fear of intelligent competition. In fact, we like it, for it helps us to bring our own business to a higher degree of efficiency. During the last two or three years, however, the competition which we have had to face has been of an unusual sort, rarely encountered in more normal times. It has been *ignorant* competition. Many concerns have been started by those who have little understanding of the technicalities of the business, whose sole aim has been speedy profits and then a quick 'get-away.' The selling prices of many of these "competitors" have not been based upon true costs. They have supplied goods at almost any price which would enable them to get a market. In many instances, these concerns and similarly conducted ones in other lines of industry, have sold their goods without any regard to the present or the future and have gone on with this reckless competition until they have failed. In the meantime, they have worked untold injury to the soundly managed companies frequently causing them also to fail. Ignorant competition is the worst possible enemy of a business."

Questions

1. To what extent do you agree with the point of view expressed by this manufacturer?

2. Do you believe that there is much "ignorant" competition of the sort indicated.

3. Has a really efficient concern anything to "fear" on this account?

4. Generally speaking, what are the chief financial advantages of competition,

   (*a*) From the point of view of the consumer of the goods;

   (*b*) From the point of view of the producer?

Problem 138

What Effect Would a Reduction in the Number of Styles Have on the Cost of Production?

In referring to the wastes in industry, it was asserted by a member of the American Engineering Council's Committee on Elimination of Waste in Industry (the "Hoover" Committee) that probably the greatest single waste in the industry of today arises from the change in styles, particularly the changing styles for women.

In reply to this charge an officer of the Associated Dress Industries of America "came back" strongly as follows:

Style is the outstanding element which makes the textile industry the second largest in this country. Clothing would be worn if it possessed no style, because of necessity, but it is style which creates volume in new orders every season, and repeat orders always. It is style in clothing that gives employment to hundreds of thousands of well-paid workers; it is style in clothing that runs the output into billions of dollars annually; it is style that fills factory lofts with millions in rentals and calls for huge building projects. The elimination of style from clothing would be an economic and industrial catastrophe.

Questions

1. From the financial point of view, state clearly your reasons for agreeing with the "Hoover Committee" on this point, or with the officer of the Associated Dress Industries.

2. In your answer would you make any distinction between the immediate and ultimate financial effects of a possible reduction in the number of styles?

Problem 139

The Possible Financial Gains of Greater Standardization in Production

Questions

1. From the point of view of the producer and of the consumer, what appear to be the financial gains of greater standardization in production?

2. Do you think that there are considerations other than financial which are sufficient to justify the present lack of standardization?

B. REDUCING THE COSTS THROUGH INCREASED SIZE—COMBINATIONS HORIZONTAL AND VERTICAL, AND DEVELOPMENT OF SUBSIDIARIES

References:

Dewing, *Corporate Promotion and Reorganizations*, 546-576.
Dewing, *Financial Policy of Corporations*, Vol. IV., 3-68.
Jenks and Clark, *The Trust Problem*, 31-50, 198-216.
Lincoln, *Central Electric Light and Power Stations* (*1917*), 126-142.
Van Hise, *Concentration and Control*, 8-166 (particularly 8-20.)

Exercise IV

The Financial Economies of Size

Group a number of reasonably comparable concerns engaged in the same line of industry according to their size. From a careful analysis of their significant financial figures, try to discover the most "profitable" size of industrial unit.

Suggested reference: Lincoln, *Central Electric Light and Power Stations*, 126-142.

Suggested source of material: *Corporate Earnings and Government Revenues* for the year 1917.

The various corporation manuals as well as some of the other references mentioned in the bibliography should also be of service.

Exercise V

The Financial Results of Combinations of Various Sorts

Select several companies in a given line of industry which are the result of combinations of smaller units. Compare the financial record of each company over a period of years after the combination with the financial performance of the constituent companies over a similar period. Make this study for integrated concerns as well as for those which are horizontally combined.

Suggested reference: Dewing, *Financial Policy of Corporations*, Vol. IV., 33-68.

Suggested sources: The corporation manuals, etc.

Problem 140

Financial Advantages of Size

It has been stated that some small makers of electrical appliances can produce their goods at a lower price per unit than is possible in the case of large concerns like the General Electric Company. Similarly it has been asserted that in certain lines small specialty paper makers can produce their goods more cheaply than a large concern like the Dennison Manufacturing Company can produce them. Other examples might be given, and while in some cases this may be mere assertion, in other cases it has been definitely proved to be true.

Questions

1. Granting the truth of the foregoing statements, would it be correct to say that it is financially desirable for industry to be carried on under conditions of small scale production whenever it is found that the unit costs of production under such circumstances are less than when the goods are produced by large plants? Why or why not?

2. Specifically, what are the financial gains or losses arising—

(*a*) From large scale production;

(*b*) From the combination of industries engaged in similar lines of production?

Problem 141

Financial Considerations Involved in Combinations

Questions

1. Sum up all the important considerations which should be borne in mind by a small concern which wishes to increase its profits by taking over one or more other small concerns engaged in the same type of business.

2. In what respects, if any, would different considerations enter in if the plan were to take over one or more concerns engaged in different stages of the same industry—for example, with a view to controlling one of the sources of supply or one of the channels of distribution for the particular industry?

Problem 142

Financial Advantages of the Chain Store

Questions

1. What particular financial gains, if any, should you expect a small chain of retail stores to have over the single store?

2. Which chain of stores should you expect to be more successful, one developed by buying out established stores or one which has built up new stores?

Problem 143

Financial Problem of a Department Store

Specifically, what are the financial advantages or disadvantages of the small department store,

(*a*) As compared with the store which sells only one type of goods, and

(*b*) As compared with the chain stores?

Problem 144

Certain Financial Considerations Involved In the Integration of a Business

The A. Press Company confines its operations largely to art printing, the bulk of its business being the preparation of high-grade advertising material. Experience has shown that its business is most active in periods of general business depression, though in times of prosperity the volume of business is sufficiently good. However, it has been the policy of this concern to build up its plant and equipment on the basis of the normal amount of business to be expected in the duller periods, and to work on double shifts when orders are heavy. Further, the company does not attempt to do any general printing business or even much of its binding. This sort of work is really incidental to the business of art printing, and whenever the pressure becomes too great for its limited capacity such work is given to job printers of different sorts. Nor does the company employ regularly artists and photographers whose services are from time to time needed. Rather it is their plan to hire such persons as occasion demands.

The B. Press Company is a much larger organization engaged in the general job book printing business. It has a large plant, equipped to carry on every phase of printing and publishing. In addition to a very extensive printing plant it has developed an unusually large bindery. On account of the scope of its business, the B. Company has also taken over a small textile mill to supply the cloth used in binding. The balance of the mill's output is sold on the general market.

Questions

1. Which policy outlined above should you expect to lead to the greatest financial success?
2. Do you think it would be wise for both of these companies to follow the same policy? Why?
3. Which company should you expect to have the fewer financial difficulties in 1921?

Problem 145

Possible Financial Gains of Vertical Combination or "Integration"

Many engineers have cited the Ford plant in Detroit as an outstanding example of efficiency in production, due to large scale operations. The Ford Company has until recently been engaged solely in the making of cars and parts. About the first of 1921 Ford is said to have stated that it was his ambition to "dig his automobiles out of the ground." In other words, he planned to develop an integrated business, which would control metal and coal mines and forests, for the supply of raw material, and even some railway facilities for transporting raw materials and finished product. Thus he hopes still further to reduce his costs of production and the price of his car to the consumer.

Question

1. In what ways, or to what extent, can the unit cost of the product be lowered through vertical combination, that is, the linking up under one management of concerns engaged in successive stages of a given industry?

Problem 146

The Development of Subsidiary and Affiliated Companies

1. What appear to you to be the advantages or disadvantages, from the financial point of view, in developing separately financed subsidiary companies for carrying on the accessory and by-product production for the parent industry?

2. Do you see any gains to be secured from having the selling or purchasing branch of a business organized separately from the production end of the business?

3. Is it a wise financial policy for a company to own affiliated businesses, one or more of which may be operated at a loss, merely for the purpose of keeping competitors out of the field?

CHAPTER VIII

FINANCIAL ASPECTS OF SELLING GOODS

References:

Beebe, *Retail Credits and Collections.*
*Cherington, *Advertising as a Business Force,* 3-28, 47-67, 380-460.
Credit Man's Diary (*passim.*)
*Duncan, *Marketing, Its Problems and Methods,* 225-247, 448-468.
*Ettinger and Golieb, *Credits and Collections* (*passim.*)
Mercantile Credits (Ronald Press Company.)

IT has not been customary in general books on Finance to give much attention to the financial aspects of selling goods. Just as the purchasing and production activities of a business have usually been thought of as largely separate from the general financial programme, so the credit man and the sales department have been customarily passed by. The former has frequently been considered a necessary evil, particularly by the sales department, while the latter, with little understanding of finance, has attempted to make itself the most important part of the business.

Great are the economic and financial wastes resulting from the wholly unwarranted attempts to stimulate demand for goods. Many a business has been wrecked by its sales department, particularly within the last few years when the unhealthy pressure of easily secured orders has led to greatly increased plant capacity. "Over-selling" may be an even more serious financial crime than "over-buying." Only by a proper financial coordination of all the branches of a business can real and lasting success be attained. Hence in the following problems brief attention is given to some of the more obvious financial aspects of selling goods.

A. GENERAL PROBLEMS OF THE CREDIT DEPARTMENT

Problem 147

Standards For Credit Granting

The credit manager of a large manufacturing concern illustrates some of his problems as follows:

The business in mind produces a great variety of manufactured goods, some of which are sold to every line of trade, from "shoe cobbler" to a "million dollar concern" of any kind. The usual terms of sale are "net, 30 days."

The principles of Credit approval are built around three different things, viz.: "Character," "Capacity," and "Capital."

The application of these principles varies, naturally, in comformity with the nature of the business to which they are applied.

It would take "volumes" to explain in detail all the possibilities of the above combination of words, but a few concise, *actual cases in point*, will serve to give one a clear idea upon which to work.

The illustrations which follow show the result of judgment, and in them will also be seen "discrimination."

Character

Company A.—This concern is rated over one hundred thousand dollars, "high," but is on a "cash-in-advance" basis. Why? Because their policy is to take cash discount regardless of whether it is allowable. In other words, they lack "character" in their dealings and are not a desirable credit risk.

Company B.—Here, the opposite is true. This company is rated at less than ten thousand dollars, but we credit as high as two thousand dollars at one time—a strong "moral" risk.

Capacity

Company C.—A very large corporation with many millions of capital,—passed through a financial crisis recently, which was caused by a lack of proper management or capacity. The "Personnel" of the concern has been completely changed and it is again in good credit standing. Full confidence is placed in the new organization.

Company D.—Has capital rating of only $5,000 to $35,000. They have a great "capacity" for "quick turnover." Purchase nearly two thousand dollars' worth every month and pay *each bill* at maturity. No fear of failure here.

Capital

Company E.—It is rated $50,000 to $75,000, but third-grade credit. This concern is sold for "cash" only. Although unquestionable in regard to "character," there is always a lack of "capital" to carry the amount of business done, and this tends also to show a lack of "capacity." These are sure signs of ultimate failure and credit men should be forewarned.

Company F.—This is rated $35,000 to $50,000 (first-grade credit). Just the opposite to the preceding account. Plenty of capital to successfully carry on the business. They are sold as high as a thousand dollars at a time and payments are made promptly on maturity dates.

Questions

1. Should you consider it desirable for the credit man of this concern to follow more definite rules in his credit granting than are here indicated? For example, would it be a wise plan for him to limit the amount of credit to a certain fixed proportion of the capital, net worth, or current assets of the customer?

2. Would your answer differ,

   (*a*) If the concern granting the credit were relatively small?

   (*b*) If the business were not so widely diversified?

3. Indicate clearly the essential differences and similarities between "mercantile" credit and "commercial" or bank credit.

Problem 148

The Credit Policy and the Business Cycle*

The following statement of the policy followed in a particular case was submitted by the credit manager of a large and prosperous manufacturing concern, which sells to many thousands of small customers, the average yearly orders being less than $300 per customer:

This customer has purchased goods from us since 1914. During that year and 1915, which were better known as "slump years," we extended credit for this company's entire requirements in our line, which often were as high as $200 at a time. It was a very active account with ten or twelve charges a month. The terms of sale, however, were never observed, as payments were made from 90 to 120 days, instead of at the 30-day period as they should have been. This question was often discussed with the customer, but we were unable to educate him so that he might show

*The following cautions are particularly suggestive in this connection:

We have congratulated ourselves, and rightfully so, in preventing heavy failures through cooperative action. Banking and merchandise creditors have exerted a tremendous force in this direction. It is true that numerous failures have occurred lately, greater in number than in former years, but the total in dollars and cents does not by any means represent what would have been the failure toll had not cooperation prevailed. All honor to the men who have stood the task at and done their work well.

Throughout the country there is still a large sum of frozen credits representing receivables that cannot be thawed out at once. Improvements will depend upon the warming rays of a new summer sun.

Let us not deceive ourselves in the present situation. Thanks to cooperation much has been done, but, in truth, only the beginnings have been made and complete success in the operation will not come until the thawing out process is accomplished. The granting of new credits, when we have such a large sum in a frozen condition, demands unusual care and discretion. The credit manager must be saved from self-deception. He must have constantly in mind the deferred receivables, and base his present calculations for new credits on the sum that he is carrying and what is perfectly safe for him in his new credits to undertake.

The situation suggests largely a marking of time, no great chances taken in one direction or the other until the thawing time arrives. The usual skill of the credit manager must be exercised in an unusual manner these days, and, granted the proper attitude and discreet action, liquidity in credits will eventually come, and that which is now frozen will have passed once again into circulation. The frozen credit is something that the credit manager must watch over so that there will be no chipping away of the block to the hurt of the creditor's interests, and the volume of liquid will finally represent the frozen equivalent. *General Letter No. 11*, May 1, 1921, National Association of Credit Men.

improvement in this direction. We needed business, however, during those years, so we continued to struggle with the account.

As we got well along into the year of 1916, which was the beginning of better times, we made our requests upon him more urgent for prompt payments, with the same results as formerly. So we finally told him that he would be required to pay cash in advance for anything that he might wish in our line. This was, of course, a severe blow to him, and we, of course, ran the chances of entirely losing his business. As a matter of fact, this is just what we were hoping would happen, since this year as well as the four which followed were "Seller's Market" years. Our plant was so overloaded with work that we could not begin to take care of our first-class credit customers, and to solicit new businss was out of the question. One of the ways therefore that we had in which to work out of the difficulty was to apply the knife to undesirable and doubtful credit risks.

Today the times are entirely different. Business is scarce and hard to get. We are obliged to assume risks that are doubtful. This very account that we turned down a few years ago was reopened on our regular terms only this month, with the understanding that we will supply goods to the amount of the former credit level on our regular terms of thirty days net. This Company has not made any great advancement during the years of prosperity, but it has managed to hold its own and show some slight improvement.

Question

Show clearly your reasons for approving or disapproving of the policy above outlined.

Problem 149

The Small Concern and the Mercantile Agency

The .... Company has been quietly and soundly built up by one man who is still the dynamo of the business and the sole owner. From a beginning of a few hundred dollars the concern has grown until its net worth is more than $200,000. All bills are promptly paid and very little is borrowed from the banks.

This concern has been repeatedly approached by representatives of a standard mercantile agency for information which would enable them to give it a satisfactory rating. The proprietor, however, has always taken the position that inasmuch as the business is solely owned by him and always takes its discounts and never troubles anyone for credit, there is nothing to be gained from having its financial position made public property. Consequently he has refused to give the usual information regarding his financial affairs to this agency. The agency accordingly has given him a "third-grade" credit rating in view of the fact that the owner would give out no information regarding his business.

Questions

1. Is it desirable that a closely owned concern be "rated" by the mercantile agencies,

    (*a*) From the point of view of the concern itself?

    (*b*) From the point of view of the creditors of the concern?

2. Was it justifiable under the circumstances for the mercantile agency to give this business a "third-grade" rating?

3. What appear to be the advantages or disadvantages of the standard mercantile reports,

    (*a*) From the point of view of the "rated" concern?

    (*b*) From the point of view of the creditors of the concern?

4. Should you expect the same advantages or disadvantages to exist in the case of the various *trade* credit agencies?

Problem 150

The Abuse of Credit Interchange

"No bureau for credit interchange can rightly be conducted with more than one purpose in view. When a bureau takes the information gathered through interchange and sells it, or a service based upon it, then we have an abuse of confidence. The interchange loses its original constructive and protective sides and, becoming commercialized, takes its information to destroy credit. A bureau, getting through the interchange department unfavorable information, may use that information to force a debtor into a still weaker condition. The bureau may, unless a claim it has be paid, threaten to expose the weakness. The result may be putting the man out of business—when intelligent care might have saved him.

An agency wrote a debtor as follows:—

'We are checking credits for nearly 4,000 manufacturers and jobbers. You failed to pay an account of .... for $... This will necessitate an adverse report to our credit department and the placing of claim with local attorney. Wire if remitting; save costs.' "

(System, April, 1921, p. 521.)

Questions

1. Do you agree with the point of view above expressed?

2. What seem to you to be the reasons for the exchange of credit information? The objections to it?

3. Do you approve of the above letter? Why?

Problem 151

Is Credit Interchange Dependable?

The following statement appeared recently in a house organ:

A certain enterprising merchant has a chain of a dozen stores. He bought rather liberally last year and was disappointed in his sales. As a result he is having considerable difficulty in paying his bills; but he had been a good customer and his creditors, while they realize that he is in difficulties, do not want to see him go to the wall. They are not inclined to ship more goods to him, but are distinctly willing that someone else ship him goods that he may continue in business, get on his feet again, and buy from them later on. So when he gives their names as reference they all report him paid up, and this information would normally find its way into a report.

The *Letter* of the National Association of Credit Men sent out in June, 1921, comments as follows upon the above statement:

The man who wrote this story has just awakened from a quarter century sleep. In the early nineties a story citing these circumstances might have received credence, Now, however, nobody will accept it. The impression at once is that the purpose was to sell some kind of service. We question absolutely its accuracy as reflecting present-day conditions in credit interchange, for nowadays no credit manager, and certainly no group of them, would be so foolish as to falsify their information. They know that the lie would be discovered quickly and, when discovered, would not only bring discredit upon them but eliminate them from that reciprocal credit service which has been established among credit men who have confidence in each other.

It is most unfortunate that anyone should try "to put over" a story of this kind. Accuracy and faithfulness in the interchange of ledger experiences can be almost absolutely depended upon in the relations between credit guarantors. No credit department could survive the circulation of a lie. No house could survive that founds its work on mere expediency, or which defends itself from losses by resort to the falsification of information.

The reading of this story will fill credit grantors to a man with feelings of indignation. They could not be satisfied until they have branded it as absolutely false and misrepresentative of present conditions.

Questions

1. In the light of your knowledge of business conditions do you believe that the statement of the house organ is true, or do you agree with the view expressed by the National Association of Credit Men?

2. Can you think of any reason why the house organ should have distorted the facts?

3. Have you any reason for believing that the National Association of Credit Men has misrepresented the situation?

Problem 152

Extending Credit on the Financial Statement*

A credit man who not long ago asked a corporation of Carson City, a brand new customer, for a financial statement, received the following reply:

Gentlemen:—In regard to your request for a statement, would say that we have just made a financial statement to the commercial agencies and beg to refer you to them for same.

Very truly yours,

............Corporation.

*The importance of the "intangible" factors in mercantile credit granting is illustrated by the following interesting episode:

"This party, whom we will call Jones, was proprietor of a general store, had been a customer for fifteen years, knew every head man in the concern, was an important man in his community, held local offices, was a prominent church worker, had been for several years the superintendent of the biggest Sunday-school in his town. He owed the house in question in amounts running from $500 to $3,000, and was generally and all along had been a very satisfactory payer, but here was the credit man returning from his trip recommending that Jones be cut off from any further accommodations.

"Naturally, this aroused prompt and vigorous protest, for the credit man was unable to set forth any such specific reasons for cutting out Jones' account as in the other cases cited. He had not learned that Jones drank or gambled or had fallen into any pernicious habits, could not find that he had been keeping irregular hours, that he had been

The credit man was not at all suspicious in the matter and naturally wished at this time to gain as much dependable business as possible. Accordingly, he wrote the commercial agencies for the rating and statement of the .. .. .. Corporation. Their statement showed a net worth of $61,000, as follows:

Assets	
Merchandise	$35,000
Cash	3,000
Accounts Receivable	6,000
Real Estate	10,000
Machines	5,000
Fixtures	3,000
	$62,000
Liabilities	
Owing for Merchandise	1,000
	$61,000

On the strength of this statement the credit man passed an order for $600, and goods were shipped to the .. .. .. Corporation.

inattentive to business, that he had an extravagant wife or a spendthrift son, yet the credit man stoutly maintained that something was wrong with Jones, that he was no longer a safe credit risk. He had spent three of four days in the little town on the pretense that he was taking a few days of enforced vacation because of ill health, had seen him in his store, had been introduced at his house, had observed him in his relation to his family, and had satisfied himself that there was something wrong, something amiss. He found that the very clerks in the Jones store had an air as if something were impending, and he wanted his house to cut Jones off.

"The principal adviser of the house, who acted as court of last resort in cases of dispute, objected to the acceptance of the credit man's advice in the case of Jones, declaring that he had known Jones personally for fourteen years, that Jones had paid them thousands of dollars and would patronize them for years to come. He said that within the past three months Jones had spent a Sunday with him as his guest, had accompanied him to church, and addressed a Bible class acceptably, and that he must be a man of the highest type of character and his credit must not be curtailed, but his wants supplied to the limit. This was the final decision of the house, and it was not weakened when the credit man acknowledged that Jones had $18,000 to $20,000 of good assets and could show a net worth of from $11,000 to $12,000 and none of his accounts with the house was past due.

"It was five months later that the morning papers contained a racy elopement story of a country merchant named Jones who had quietly converted his property into cash, deserted his wife and skipped to Canada with the family servant girl with whom he had been enamored for some time past, this information of course being followed with the usual comments on the alleged tendencies of church leaders."—*Credit Monthly*, March, 1921, 256-7.

Questions

1. Should the credit man have been satisfied with the above statement? Why?
2. Should he have shipped any goods on the strength of the above statement? Why or why not?
3. What do you expect was the outcome of this transaction?

PROBLEM 153

THE STATEMENT AND THE BUSINESS CYCLE

"It is to be remembered that after the period of unwise and inflated buying, the man who faces the facts is the best risk, and also it is to be remembered that he is likely to show the worst statement, for he will have marked his whole inventory down to the market.

This is no time for collection agency methods and threats; the big thing is not to get the money at all costs but to get business back to normal with the fewest possible number of capable people being hurt in the process. There is a difference between a collection agency and a credit department."

Question

Do you think that a "bad statement" may "indicate a good risk," either from the point of view of granting mercantile credit or bank credit?

Problem 154

Easy Credit Granting and Low Debt Losses

The credit manager of a large merchandising house wrote as follows some three years ago:

When I tell you that practically none of our business is for cash, but that most of it is on thirty days' time, you may think that either the strain on me is terrific or that I have unusual facilities for getting credit information.

On the contrary, I am quite easygoing, as a rule. I pass practically all orders from new customers even though I can get no information on them from the credit agencies. I'll tell you how I came to take this attitude on extending credit.

When, years ago, I started in as credit man for this concern—we sell coffee to retailers—I would not pass a new order unless it looked iron-clad. I laid great stress on credit ratings and net worth, and felt that it was up to me to throw every safeguard that I could around an order.

After a few months' experience I made two startling and discouraging discoveries. One was that an order from a new account had only about a 50–50 chance of passing me—that made me unpopular with everyone in my concern.

But the other discovery hurt me even more, for it was so unlooked for; it was that, of the orders I passed, the ones that went bad were as often as not those which had stood up best under my scrutiny.

Often I found that a history of years of prompt pay, good ratings by the agencies, first-class references, and a satisfactory net worth, did not keep a customer from failing to pay. I mulled over these facts and came to a conclusion.

It was the simple one that if all signs failed sometimes, as they seemed to, I might as well pass any order that did not look bad on the surface. But before jumping in over my head I decided to test my theory out on several hundred orders.

These I took as they came, provided no order was for goods worth more than $50, and passed it blind if there were no unfavorable reports on it. I did not care about ratings or property, nor did I look for unusually good past performances.

Exactly 98 per cent of these new accounts were paid for in reasonably good time; 2 per cent were written off. And that is a ratio that I find holds true with us.

(System, November, 1919, page 665, ff.)

Questions

1. Do you believe that the policy now followed by this credit man is a sound one?

2. Do you believe that a similar policy would be safe for all types of concerns? At all times?

3. How, if at all, should you expect this easy credit granting policy to be supplemented in order to insure no greater losses from bad debts?

4. What is your opinion of this credit man?

5. Should you expect him to handle his credits in a similar manner in 1921?

Problem 155

Guaranteeing the Account by Officers of the Buying Concern

"It is true that men of standing hesitate to accept personal liability in corporate matters, but if the matter is presented to them in the proper light very frequently such guarantees can be arranged. One very successful argument is, "How can you expect us to take the risk, if you who are in control of the corporation's affairs are unwilling to take the risk?" And it is a fact that if a responsible individual has control of the destiny of a corporation and is unwilling to loan that corporation strength, after assuring the seller that the bills will be promptly paid, as long as he is connected with it, it is no fit subject for a credit man to take a chance on."

Question

Is the argument above presented a sound one?

Problem 156

Does Easy Mercantile Credit Cause Retail Failures?

Commercial agencies give the following causes for the majority of failures:

Incompetence, inexperience, lack of capital, unwise granting of credits, speculation outside of regular business, bad habits, personal extravagance, fraudulent disposition of property.

Very little attention, however, appears to be given to the *fundamental* causes of failure. A careful study of retailing methods in this country, in England and in France, together with a study of the successes and failures of individual concerns, leads to the conclusion that the fundamental causes of failure in the retail business in this country are due to dishonesty, lack of preparation, and expanded credit, *with which may be coupled too much capital.* A national trait in this country is for people to do things about which they know the least. The farmer who makes money on the farm goes to the city or village and buys or starts a store and in this way loses his money. The man who makes money in the city goes to the country and buys a farm, only to find it a permanent source of loss. In the end, too much capital causes more failures than lack of capital. As a matter of fact, the writer has never been able to find a single case where lack of capital has caused a failure of a retailer. What has been called lack of capital was merely an expanded credit.

If the history of those retail businesses who have been in existence for forty years or more be studied, it will be found that nearly every one of them was established by men who lacked capital. They were so limited in regard to credit and capital they had to watch every penny to make it go just as far as was possible.

Questions

1. Analyze critically this point of view.

2. Do you agree that "what has been called lack of capital is merely expanded credit"?

3. Do you agree as to the fundamental causes of retail failures?

4. What constructive suggestions can you make as to methods of granting retail credit?

5. In principle, is the extending of "dealer" credit sound or unsound?

B. RELATIONS BETWEEN CREDIT DEPARTMENT AND SALES DEPARTMENT

PROBLEM 157

SHALL THE CREDIT MAN ANTAGONIZE HIS SALESMAN AND TURN DOWN A "SURE PAY" CUSTOMER?

Mr. X is a storekeeper in a small country town. He is one of the wealthiest men of the community, having large outside interests and lending a good deal of money to the surrounding farmers. Exclusive of his stock of goods, store building, and the like, he is probably worth at least $100,000. He has practically no liabilities of any kind, is a leader in the community, and an exceptionally high moral risk.

In 1920 and 1921 the farmers in this community suffered greatly from the drop in prices and were disposed to purchase nothing but absolute necessities. When Mr. X was beginning to be worried about his small amount of sales, a clever salesman managed to convince him that the reason for his low sales was that his stock of goods was largely out of date and not kept in first-class condition. The salesman explained that by laying in a large new stock an appeal could be made to the buyers, who now might be unable to pay cash, but whose credit in the long run undoubtedly would be good. Finally, therefore, Mr. X agreed to buy $25,000 worth of new stock which will presumably be sold on long credits, and the salesman in turn offered to grant exceptionally long terms.

Mr. X has now been convinced that he needs this additional amount of goods and that customers will want them. There is no question about his solvency, and little doubt that the selling company will receive payment in due time.

Questions

1. Did Mr. X act wisely in agreeing to these new purchases at such a time?

2. Was the salesman well advised in urging Mr. X to buy so extensively?

3. If you were the credit manager of the wholesale house wishing to sell to Mr. X, how would you pass on this order?

4. What do you think would be the nature of the future relations existing between Mr. X and the selling house if the order is passed?

(Reference: SYSTEM, July, 1921, p. 37, ff.)

PROBLEM 158

COOPERATION BETWEEN THE SALES AND CREDIT DEPARTMENTS*

The credit manager of a large manufacturing concern writes as follows regarding his handling of the credit problem:

I now have my salesmen working in such harmony that for a couple of years back I have not found it necessary to keep a "turn-down" record. The only accounts which it is necessary to turn down come from new salesmen who

*The following points may well be borne in mind:—"Can a man sell a firm's credit policy while selling its goods?" "No," says one executive; another says, "Why not? Our men do." Every one of our salesmen is a self-constituted credit man. A half-way observant salesman can get the information right in the course of his sales talk. "Suppose, for instance, that the salesman is calling for the first time on a retailer. Say the retailer is a hardware dealer. The salesman, walking in and glancing around the store, can see many things that are pertinent to

haven't quite caught the idea. The salesmen making the greatest amounts of money are the men who also have the fewest losses among their accounts. This is proof enough that assisting the credit department does not militate against commissions. The whole thing is in getting everybody around to the same viewpoint.

* * * * * * * *

I send the men on the road complete reports concerning their customers and the state of their accounts. If there is a dispute or trouble threatened, I refer it to the salesmen in the territory to get on the job rather than write directly to the customer—the salesman has, and I have not, an intimate personal knowledge of the situation.

I never turn down an order without finding out what the salesman has to say about the debtor. If the salesman's report differs from the reports of the agencies, or from the report of a local attorney, I go over the matter with him and try to find out who is right. After looking at all the facts, it is very rare that the salesman and I fail to agree on whatever action we happen to take.

I do not ask my salesmen to be "inquisitive." I would rather that they did not ask for any kind of a statement from the customer unless they are absolutely certain that the statement will be willingly forthcoming and is made out of a desire to keep the credit line in good condition.

* * * * * * * *

In the case of a new account, the salesman is expected to turn in a report which includes a financial statement and two or three references, with his personal opinion.

(SYSTEM, July, 1917, p. 40, ff.)

credit. On the shelves, for instance, he'll see somebody's paints. There's a lead to be reported to the credit man in the home office. In the show cases he'll see somebody's cutlery and some other concern's tools, and on the floor he'll see some firm's wringers and another manufacturer's lawn mowers. There are more leads. A general size-up of the store will tell the salesman pretty accurately just what sort of merchandiser the retailer is. "But specifically," I asked, "just what is a salesman to look for?" "These," said Mr. Meriam, "are some sound suggestions: First—Who is the manager of the business, and is he a capable man? Second—What is the policy of the concern in meeting local obligations? Third—Is it an old established concern, or a new enterprise? Fourth—What is its local reputation? Fifth—Does the concern carry a large or small stock of goods, and is the stock in good condition; or would it be subject to depreciation if placed on the market at a forced sale? Sixth—To what class of trade does the concern cater? Seventh—Is the concern up-to-date in its methods? Eighth—What condition, such as crop shortages, strikes and the like, would have an effect upon the business of the concern? Ninth—From what other manufacturers and wholesalers does the concern buy goods, and on what terms? Tenth—Taking all matters into consideration, what is your opinion of the concern as a credit risk?—Adapted from *Business*, May, 1921, page 20.

Questions

1. Do you approve of the extent to which "cooperation" is carried in this concern?

2. From the point of view of the concern itself would it be possible, or at any rate desirable, to carry cooperation between the sales and credit departments to this extent in all lines of industry?

PROBLEM 159

"PUTTING IT UP TO THE SALESMAN"

A salesman of the . . . Company, on his monthly rounds, discovers that the business operated by one of his former customers has recently changed hands, without the knowledge of the concern which he represents. The new management has agreed to continue business on the old terms granted to their predecessors and they wish to buy a large order on credit.

The salesman is in doubt as to what policy he should follow. Accordingly, he telegraphs to his firm for instructions and receives word that the credit man is away for the day. His assistant replies, however, that if everything looks all right he sees no harm in taking a chance on the order. By the time this reply is received, the salesman has been advised by two banks and several business men that they would not extend credit to the new management, even to the extent of ten dollars.

Question

What course would you advise the salesman to follow under these circumstances?

Problem 160

The Value of References Secured by the Salesman

Brown, a salesman for the . . . Company, was a very kind-hearted individual who disliked to do anything which would offend his customers, many of whom had come to be close personal friends. His firm had been having some difficulties in collections and had decided that they must exercise more care in granting credits. Accordingly, he had received instructions to the effect that more than the usual caution should be exercised in the opening of new accounts, and it would be necessary to secure several responsible references before credit would be extended to a new customer.

Brown, with his usual civility, approached a prospective customer apologetically, as follows:

"By the way, Mr. Ben, our credit man has been getting a little grouchy and insists that we send in several references regarding the financial standing of new customers before goods will be shipped on credit. Of course, you understand that I am not concerned about this little thing and don't want to bother you, but to keep the office in good humor I shall have to send in a few names. Suppose you let me have the names of a few of your friends who will put in a good word for you, if our credit man wishes."

Questions

1. Did this salesman follow the proper policy?
2. Did the credit office follow the right policy?
3. How might dependable credit information be secured without offending the new customer?

Problem 161

Relation Between The Credit Risk and the Method of Paying Salesmen

How should you expect the credit experience of the concern whose salesmen sell on straight commission to compare with that of the concern whose salesmen receive a stated salary? Why?

(Reference: *Printer's Ink*, April 7, 1921, page 6.)

Problem 162

Should the Credit Department Tolerate "Irregular" Terms of Sale Given By the Salesman?

Jones, of the . . . Company, was a very energetic salesman and proud of the record which he had made in the past. As business conditions became rather unsettled toward the end of 1919, his firm informed him that in the future no special concessions of any sort would be made to customers. Heretofore Jones had been in the habit of giving a slight extra discount or a few days extra time to desirable customers, and because of the large business which he secured his company had tolerated the practice.

Shortly after the new ruling had been passed, Jones was asked by one of his biggest customers for the usual "extra" time, and was given to understand that the order would be placed elsewhere unless this concession were made. Jones wished to make the sale, but not caring to assume the responsibility of losing this particular customer, wired his house to find out if they would be willing to make the concession in this case.

Questions

1. Was the earlier policy of Jones' company a wise one? The later policy?

2. Did Jones follow the correct policy?
3. What effect do you think his policy would have—
   (*a*) On his company?
   (*b*) On his customer?
4. How should you expect the selling house to reply to his telegram?

Problem 163

How Far Should the Salesman Be Trusted?

"The signs of retrogression are too well known to an experienced salesman to require much comment. The office observes them in the merchant's falling behind, in failing to take discounts, in irregular payments, in paying on account, or in checks returned from the bank marked 'no funds.' But these indications, while evidence of poor management and a signal to 'slow down,' are not in themselves conclusive. A customer may have invested heavily in bonds, or in real estate, and for the time being put himself in a tight place financially. Or he may be doing too much business for his capital. In such cases, it is not always advisable to shut off a man's credit, at least not until after you have looked into the matter with some race.

In 1907, during the money stringency, it was reported by the credit agencies that a big New York department store was in a tight place. Immediately those manufacturers who had been selling the store began to apply the brakes. The more cautious refused point blank to give another cent's worth of credit. But there was one corset manufacturer who refused to be stampeded by the report and asked the salesman on the territory to look into the matter before taking summary action.

It so happened that this particular salesman was of the type that believed in representing his house first, and selling goods secondly. Times without number he had shown his whole-hearted interest in the general welfare of the business by sending in tips, which in several cases had enabled the firm to avoid a loss. So the credit department felt safe in putting the whole matter up to the salesman and leaving it for him to decide whether or not the account should be closed out.

The salesman got on the job at once, and after doing some clever 'gum shoe' work learned that the store in question had plenty of money, but that it was tied up in the construction of some new buildings. With this information in his pocket the salesman went to the manager of the store and said:

'I know that other corset manufacturers have shut down on you. I have also found out that you've got money, but it is tied up. We'll sell you all the merchandise you want and give you an extension of time, but you will have to pay interest.' "

(Quoted from Aspley, *What a Salesmen Should Know About Credit*, pp 47-49.)

Questions

1. Discuss critically. Did the salesman follow a correct policy?

2. Would you approve of the same policy under similar conditions, in 1921?

C. COOPERATION WITH THE CUSTOMER

Problem 164

Dealer Cooperation

An example of what a credit department can do in the way of constructive dealer help is furnished by the "Business Service Department" of the M. & S. Co. of Brooklyn, N. Y., which sells varnish to the hardware trade and general stores.

This company has "a business department" under the control of the credit manager. The object of the department is to help dealers in the conduct of their business, by advice and counsel; to avoid their going backward; to help them escape the courts; to avoid losing their money; in short by suggestion and personal assistance to help make successful merchants.

The aim of the department is to help educate the dealers wherever a weakness is evident, to analyze the weakness and serve the proper nourishment. The dealer who can be educated to give "service" as an important object in his business makes a far better credit risk.

The credit manager can best teach those principles that go to make up the right sort of merchant.

The salesmen locate the customers who need the service of the department. The salesmen are provided with printed forms which contain on them ninety-five different points by which a business could be affected. The salesman through talks with the customer learns the weaknesses of his business methods and checks these on the form provided and mails it to the house. The case may be taken up either by mail or by personal visit of the credit manager where possible or by the salesman.—Most of the work done and advice given by the department is in the matter of accounting, credits, buying and selling, insurance, taxation and legal matters.

(*Bulletin*, National Association of Credit Men, January, 1915, pp. 9-10.)

Questions

1. Do you see any real gain from the point of view of the M. & S. Co. in carrying cooperation to this extent?

2. Would the answer which you give apply to other types of concerns?

3. Just how much do you expect the customers to gain through this policy?

4. To what extent do you consider that the relation between the selling house and the purchaser is analogous to the relation existing between the bank and its commercial borrowers?

PROBLEM 165

FINANCIAL COOPERATION BETWEEN DEALER AND CUSTOMER

The W. Rubber Company does an annual business of more than $30,000,000 of which about 75 per cent is in rubber footwear and allied lines, while the remainder consists of rubber tires. In the footwear part of their business for the year 1920 there were sales of about $7,000,000 to 15,000 retail customers. The balance of nearly $17,000,000 worth of goods was sold to about 100 jobbers. About 90 per cent of the tire sales, or nearly $8,000,000, was made to 4,000 retail customers. The tire business of this concern is relatively very recent, having been developed largely within the last three or four years.

For nearly twenty years this company has been a strong believer in dealer cooperation. In order to help their customers toward better financing, as well as to protect themselves, they have gradually developed a corps of traveling auditors, who periodically examine the finances of those concerns which buy from them. These auditors, or "traveling credit men," in the case of jobbers are sent directly from the home office. For the retail customers, however, auditors are sent from the thirty or more branch offices which manage the tail trade.

The dealer cooperation is carried to such an extent through this method that the majority of the customers now feel slighted unless they receive their periodic audits, although there was earlier a good deal of opposition. Further, the company makes every attempt to train its customers in the best methods of financing. Even though they may be in serious financial difficulties, if they appear to be honest and attempting to do the right thing by their creditors, every assistance is extended.

According to the records of this concern, it appears that the sales of footwear during the past twenty years have been $200,000,000, with a bad debt loss of only $10,000. The average loss from bad debts in business of similar types is at least one-half of 1 per cent, frequently much higher. In the year 1919, however, the tire sales of $6,500,000 showed a bad debt loss of $31,000.

Questions

1. Does the above case indicate that cooperation of this sort "pays" in dollars and cents?
2. How do you account for the much larger bad debt losses in the tire business?
3. Analyze critically the *pros* and *cons* of the situation.

Problem 166

Educating the Customer to Buy Light And Take Losses Early

"With prices falling, the people who sell at all are bound to sell at a loss or without profit. If they have not accumulated a surplus during the rising market, they will naturally be short of money and will dread the selling at a loss. They will want to hold their goods until the market turns—they will be in the position of the speculator who is always hoping that if he only holds on long enough he will get out of the hole in which he finds himself.

We know from experience that although one may now and again in the stock market succeed in winning out by delay, the expert trader takes his loss early. It is easier to hold a share of corporate stock through a period than it is to hold a stock of goods; the average stock of goods held until the market price goes up is apt to be worthless. So it is for the benefit of all hands that losses be taken quickly; the best means to this end is firm collecting. The profits in a declining market are to be made by the quick turning of stocks—a turning of them before the price has had a chance to go down. This quick turning cannot be made without quick collections all around so that the rapidity of turnover may extend through every operation in the process of manufacture and distribution.

The danger of advocating quick collections is that the quickness may be overdone and the collector become panic-stricken and thus force a quite unnecessary loss. Panic is most infectious and utterly destructive of orderly trade. On the other hand, personal contact and an explanation of the necessity for turning swollen inventories into money may be used further to strengthen the position of the customer. It can be shown that the collections are being made in the interest of the buyer as much as of the seller and that it is all a part of the necessary readjustment to the lines of normal business.

This also involves a responsibility on the part of the seller; it is not fair business to load up a customer with a large stock of goods on long credit on the assertion that by thus buying he will save paying higher prices that are later and most mysteriously going to come about. That is not only encouraging speculation, but is in a class with selling fake mining stocks on the pretense that they will fetch fortunes if only they are held long enough. It should be the duty of the seller to expect his customer to make money on the selling of what he buys and not on speculating in it."

(SYSTEM, January, 1921.)

Question

Specifically, what are the financial disadvantages of "over-selling" a customer?

D. SALES POLICIES

PROBLEM 167

SEASONAL DATINGS

Many concerns which manufacture goods for which there is a seasonal demand, make a business of dating their sales ahead, that is, they will endeavor to get orders in December, for example, for goods which will not have a market until spring. Having received the orders, they proceed to make up the goods and deliver as soon as possible. The accounts rendered, however, call for payment at some future time when the sale of the goods will be active. For example, a season dating for goods thus ordered in December might be April 1st or May 1st. This means that the usual cash discount would be given for payment within 10 days from the future date, or that the ordinary cash terms will prevail from this date.

Question

1. What seem to you to be the advantages or disadvantages arising from this practice—

(*a*) In the case of the producer?

(*b*) In the case of the purchaser?

(Reference: Ettinger and Golieb, 72-74.)

Problem 168

Pushing Sales by a Bold Method

"When business began to limp last summer (1920), the . . . Petticoat Company found itself much in the same situation as most other concerns in the ready-to-wear garment trade. It was anything but a pleasant situation.

The house was stocked to the ceiling with piece-silk goods, most of which had been bought at prices far above the current market. Orders had practically stopped coming in. Only depression talk was heard as to the future. How the situation was going to develop was fairly obvious. Watching it develop would not help. Plants were slowing down. Prices were going down.

Then the . . . . Petticoat Company took a position which called for considerable pluck. Instead of slowing down, as its neighbors were mostly doing, this concern put its factory on double time."

(*Printer's Ink,* March 3, 1921, page 25, ff.)

The company used its own trade-mark and made up no goods for the job or lot trade. The main appeal was direct to the retailer. The company did not wait for orders, but went out to get them. They bought more silk at low prices even before their old supply was used up. They determined to cut the wholesale price whenever necessary to get the business.

Questions

1. Do you think the . . . Company was well advised in following this increased production policy at a time when its inventories were so large and sales seemed to be stopping?

2. What steps should you expect the . . . Company to take in order to make a financial success of this policy?

3. What do you suppose was the outcome of their unusual policy?

4. Are there gains other than financial to be derived from such a policy?

5. Should you expect that a similar policy, if generally followed, would lead to financial success?

Problem 169

"One Cent" Sales

The Rexall Stores frequently put on a "one cent" sale, that is, two articles are sold for the price of one plus one cent.

Questions

1. In the long run what do you expect to be the financial gains, if any, from following such a policy?

2. When should you consider it most advisable for a retail establishment to have such a sale? Why?

3. Can you lay down any principle as to the type of retailer who might profitably use this method?

Problem 170

The Turnover and Business Profits*

"The aim of all business concerns is to obtain the largest possible net return on the capital employed. There are really only three factors which effect net return: 1. Gross profit. 2. Expenses. 3. Turnover.

*The following example is illuminating on this subject:—"Offers to the merchant of special prices on large orders have been productive of short-sightedness in buying, and accounts, in many instances, for large stocks of goods that fail to move from the shelves. Only one who has seen the tremendous overstocking of goods among the merchants in the smaller towns can understand what a dead weight rests on the back of the majority of retailers, and yet they almost invariably believe that they are saving money by buying in large orders. Only rarely

It is usually recognized that gross profit added to the cost of merchandise should be large enough to cover all overhead expense incident to the business and should include a fair net profit. It is also recognized that the expenses must be kept below *gross* profit in order to show a *net* profit. It is admitted, however, that there are many retailers who fail to appreciate the effect of turnover on the net return; and because of this fact net profits are often dissipated by slow-moving assets.

Assuming sales of $120,000 per year, also an average investment of six months' sales in merchandise and accounts receivable, and a net profit of $6,000, the net return on the investment in comparison with an investment of four and two months' sales in these two assets works out as follows:

	Investment 6 mos. sales	Investment 4 mos. sales	Investment 2 mos. sales
Merchandise	$30,000	$20,000	$20,000
Accounts receivable	30,000	20,000	0
	$60,000	$40,000	$20,000
Turnovers	2	3	6
Net profits on sales	5%	5%	5%
Net return	10%	15%	30%

It will be noticed that by lowering the investment, or working capital, the turnover increases and the net

has one of these merchants been heard to admit that he was overstocked, and even then, nothing more than a guess could be made as to what lines were in excess. This lack of knowledge of the existence of overstocking, makes education especially useful, and, where it has been given, flatteringly productive.

"That the merchant in most cases loses money by this method of purchasing can be shown by an illustration. Suppose a merchant every month buys an article that costs him 75 cents a dozen and sells a dozen every month at the price of $1. At the end of the year this merchant has turned this 75 cents twelve times, making 25 cents every time, or, in other words, has made $3 on an investment of 75 cents.

"Then a specialty salesman comes along and says, 'You are paying too much money for those goods. I can sell you that same article at $6 a gross.'

"It looks like a saving so the merchant takes a gross. During the year following this purchase he sells a dozen a month or the entire gross, at a profit of $6. In other words, he has made $6 on a $6 investment, or 100 per cent, while under the former method of buying he made $3 on a 75 cent investment or 400 per cent."—*Administration*, April, 1921, page 450.

return increases in the same ratio. Likewise raising the investment lowers the turnover and decreases the net return."

(*Credit Monthly*, April, 1921, p. 46.)

Questions

1. What is the relation of "turnover" to expense?
2. Is the "turnover" of merchandise a more significant factor in net return than "turnover" of receivables? Why?
3. How, if at all, can the "turnover" of receivables be increased without changing the terms of sale?
4. Does the above example clearly indicate the effect which an increased "turnover" has on business profits?
5. What is to be said for or against the elimination of the investment in receivables—
   (*a*) In the case of retail businesses?
   (*b*) In the case of wholesale businesses?
   (*c*) In the case of manufacturing concerns?
6. If the investment in receivables were greatly reduced or eliminated, how might it affect the "turnover" of inventory?

Problem 171

Can the Dealer Prevent "Bargain Sales"?

"What happens to your merchandise when the market goes down? Your retailers put on bargain sales and take sacrifices which they want you to pay for the next time they buy your merchandise. Why not find some way to give the retailer twelve turnovers a year instead of two? Every clearance sale in which your merchandise is represented is a disgrace to your business management, to say nothing about being a direct liability for which, some time, you must answer."

Question

1. Do you agree with the point of view here expressed?

Problem 172

The Financial Significance of the Sales Policy—Selling to One Large Customer

The Blank Brothers were skilful mechanics who developed their little repair shop into a small factory for the making of metal lamps. As their work was conducted on a very small scale, it was not possible for them to reduce their costs enough to enable them to sell these lamps at a particularly attractive price. However, because of the excellent quality of their work, they managed to build up a very satisfactory little business, financing themselves solely out of earnings. Yet the brothers realized that they could never hope for much volume of business until they could reduce their prices. Since they were not skilled in "finance," they did not feel that they could run the risk of reducing prices until they were assured of a larger patronage.

When the business had been developed to this extent, the owners found that a large mail order house was handling in large quantities a lamp similar to the one which they made, and decided that it would be worth their while to try to supply this house. Accordingly, they calculated their costs at what they thought to be the lowest possible figure for producing the probable number of lamps, added a reasonable margin for profit, and made known their terms to the mail order house.

The purchasing agent of this house, a very shrewd man, called in a metal expert to advise him whether such a lamp as they offered him should cost as much as they had estimated. He stated that with the most approved method of producing the lamps the cost to the manufacturer should be considerably lower.

The purchasing agent, accordingly, offered to buy a large number of these lamps from the brothers at a price based on this lower cost of production. The quantity called for was so great that it would entail the building of a new plant and the employing of many workers. Though the brothers felt that their profits might be almost wiped out if they accepted the figure offered by the mail order house, yet the bigness of the proposition appealed to them and they decided that it would be to their advantage to make the venture. In accordance with this decision they contracted to give all of their greatly increased output to the mail order house for a fixed period of time, at the end of which a new contract might be made or relations might be severed.

Having launched on this new program, the brothers found that their costs could be reduced much lower than they had originally anticipated, so that they actually made a good deal of money on the contract. When the period of the contract expired, the mail order house refused to make a renewal except on terms which the manufacturers felt would be suicidal. The brothers, therefore, found themselves with a large investment in plant and a considerable force of workers employed, apparently confronted by two alternatives—either they might continue to produce in volume at what they deemed to be a sure loss, or they might close down most of their plant and operate on a smaller scale, which would probably not even yield them enough return to pay a reasonable interest on their investment.

Questions

1. Under what circumstances, if any, would you expect it to be to the advantage of a producer to sell his output to only one purchaser?

2. Do you think that this concern followed the right policy in refusing to renew its contract with the mail order house?

3. If you were advising these brothers as to the "next step," what would you tell them?

4. If the expansion of plant had been secured largely by means of a mortgage, would you give the same advice as if the plant had been paid for out of earnings?

E. PRICE POLICIES

Problem 173

Relation Between a Fixed Sales Price and The Financial Program

There are many manufacturing concerns which produce a well-known, standard article which was sold by the retailer before the war at a fixed price, allowing a fair profit both to producer and retailer. In the case of these commodities the brand and the price became inseparably connected in the minds of the buying public. Examples of this sort are furnished by the Ingersoll dollar watch, Uneeda Biscuits at 5 cents a package, Ivory Soap at 5 cents a cake, Campbell's Soups at 10 cents a can, and other cases too numerous to mention.

This selling price, while not necessarily maintained by all distributors, was understood and expected by the buying public. Furthermore, the prices had been arrived at during a period of slowly rising prices when the increase in the cost of production was probably largely, if not wholly, offset by the increase in efficiency of production.

When the cost of material mounted with unprecedented rapidity during the war period, such concerns were confronted by an extremely difficult financial problem. If they should attempt to raise their standard prices in order to cover their increased costs they must immediately reckon with the public opposition, which would result from the advertising policy that had been followed and from the association in the minds of buyers of a stated price with the brand in question. It was sometimes a problem to know whether an increase in prices would cut down sales and give a competitor an opportunity to establish himself. Further, if quantity or quality should be altered, with a maintenance of the old price scale, there would almost certainly be a loss of goodwill which it had taken years to build up. Yet, unless some definite steps had been taken, many of these concerns would have become financially embarrassed.

Questions

1. What suggestions can you offer as to the best method of solving the problem above presented?
2. Will your answer apply to all types of products?
3. How, if at all, does the position differ of those concerns which sell a product at a standard price and which have many competitors in the field selling a similar product at the same price—for example, makers of men's collars retailing at two for a quarter, and makers of cotton thread selling ordinarily at 5 cents per spool?
4. As a general proposition, do you consider it financially desirable to stress the selling price in advertising brands of the sort above indicated?

Problem 174

Price Guarantees

The E. Wholesale Hardware Company had a large inventory on its hands. Its customers were afraid to buy because of business uncertainties, yet unless the inventory was turned over the company could not pay its maturing bills.

To meet the situation the E. Company decided to offer its goods at such a price as would insure a very low profit, and to give its customers a guarantee against loss resulting from a drop in the price of goods within a specified time, the period of guarantee being that normally required for the turnover of this particular type of inventory in the best managed stores among the E. Company's customers.

Questions

1. What should you expect the financial effects of this policy to be, (*a*) immediately, (*b*) ultimately
   (*x*) On the selling house?
   (*y*) On the customers?
2. If this policy had been generally followed, what effect would it have had on recent business conditions?
3. If such a policy were followed by only one representative concern in a particular industry, what should you expect the financial outcome to be?

(Reference: System, July, 1921, p. 41 ff.)

Problem 175

Increasing the Turnover and Decreasing Cancelations by Reducing Prices Even on Goods Already Sold

A Philadelphia manufacturer of shirts writes as follows regarding the development of their business and their relations with their customers during the period of depression:

Eleven years ago when our company decided upon a campaign of national advertising, we made it a fundamental policy to maintain continuous, uninterrupted production based on average yearly conditions in this country rather than to fluctuate production to meet temporary current demands. The result has been a steady, continuous growth.

Twice during the past five years we have been put to the crucial test of standing staunchly by that policy, come what may, or of abandon ng it completely and shaping a new.

The first test came during the war, when business all over the nation was expanding and the general temptation was to reach out and grab for all that might be had. The second came at the outset of the recent depression when the temptation was reversed and the impelling inclination—the easy way—was to shut down the plant, halt production and wait for the turning of the tide.

By refusing to yield to the common impulse on the first occasion, though it cost us a very considerable loss of more than 20 per cent in orders at the time, we were largely enabled to successfully pass through the second. During the entire period of dull business, as a result, our cancelations have not amounted to more than 10 per cent; our factory has been running at full time; there have been no reductions in hours or working forces other than those of a normal nature, and the volume of our business stood at within 10 per cent of our record normal of the past few years.

* * * * * *

During the boom days of the war and the immediate post-war period we stopped going after new business, which was available on all sides and allotted our product to our established accounts.

We did not expand, build new plants, and disregard our standard of quality to secure increased production. We centered our efforts almost exclusively on improving the facilities we already had and so were able to appreciably increase production with the same working force, and keep our labor turnover at less than 5 per cent.

Then, when the tide began to go out and the business skies grew black, we had reason to congratulate ourselves on having laid down a principle and having had the courage to stick to it. Our organization was sound; our finances were in excellent shape; we were prepared to cope with emergencies, to stand the racket when it came.

While our prospects, when the slump struck us, were no brighter than those of others, behind us we had a goodwill and public demand born of 10 years of consumer advertising. In the spring of 1920 our salesmen went out and booked the greatest volume of fall business in our history. As a matter of fact it exceeded the allotments we had given them by more than 10 per cent. Then, in the fall, depression started to sweep the country; cancelations started to come in; factories about us and in the same line were closing down or going on short time; no new business was in sight.

At the first indication of this we moved to forestall cancelations of orders as far as possible. Realizing that the retailer's price on our product would be governed largely by what he had paid us, it seemed desirable, if our goods were to sell to the public, that price reductions be made not only on goods awaiting shipment from the factory, but also on goods shipped earlier and on the retailer's shelves. Consequently on September 1 we notified our retailers by mail to this effect.

* * * * * *

This action, together with the fact that we had undersold the demands of our fall market, had the desired effect. Cancelations immediately slowed up and in total were only sufficiently large to balance evenly against the 10 per cent excess in orders the salesmen had turned in over their allotment. Our volume of business for the fall season was the largest in our 40 years' existence, and our working force and our plant were practically at normal in every respect excepting wages.

(SYSTEM, May 1921, p. 653, ff.)

Questions

1. Do you think this liberal price reduction policy would have had the desired effect in all lines of business?

2. Do you see any essential connection between the expansion policy followed by this company and the outcome of their price policy as reported?

3. Do you see any connection between the success of this policy and the character of the company's customers or the nature of the terms made with them?

Problem 176

Effect of Price Reductions

Questions

1. Should a manufacturing concern which makes goods having a largely seasonal sale, cut the price on its product immediately after the majority of its customers have been supplied?

2. What would be the financial effect of such a policy, (*a*) immediately, (*b*) in the long run, on

(*x*) The selling concern?

(*y*) Its customers?

Problem 177

Relation Between Price Policy and General Financial Policy During a Period of Depression

The D. F. Company, a firm manufacturing ladies' suits, followed the usual policy of those in the trade during the year 1919 and the first part of 1920. They looked for continued increase in prices, and urged their customers to buy at once in order to benefit by the present "bargains" and to assure themselves of good quality. The retailers and the few jobbing houses to whom they sold were still in a buying mood in the first part of 1920, and ordered their goods far ahead. As a consequence, the company stocked up heavily with inventory at the highest prices so as to be in a position to deliver goods for the following winter trade.

While a large quantity of their material was still unmade or "in process," there began to be rumors of a break in the prices of woolen goods. The "buyers' strike" began to be serious, and orders were being canceled, or even refused after shipments had been made. Hence the D. F. Company, though it had made a great deal of money during the war and had been successfully financed in earlier years, found itself in a decidedly embarrassing position.

It had borrowed to the limit from its banks in order to buy materials which it expected to sell in finished form at a large profit, and now its inventories were rapidly shrinking in value. On account of cancelations "receivables" were changing back into "merchandise." Further, those customers who had ordinarily taken their cash discounts began to be slow. Hence "accounts receivable" on the company's books became practically frozen as the distributors of their goods were feeling the effects of the "buyers' strike." By September, 1920, their financial position was approximately as follows:

STATEMENT OF THE D. F. COMPANY
September, 1920

Assets

Machinery, equipment, etc.	$100,000
Cash	5,000
Accounts receivable	200,000
Notes receivable	25,000
Inventory:	
Unmade and in process	300,000
Finished goods	300,000
	$930,000

Liabilities

Partners' capital (original investment)	$100,000
Notes payable (mostly bank loans)	400,000
Accounts payable	125,000
Sundry payables and accruals	25,000
Surplus	280,000
	$930,000

At this stage the company was seriously in need of more money to pay its current bills as well as to satisfy some of its mercantile creditors. Their bank, however, was so heavily involved that it could not be induced to lend further credit. Hence the owners of the company felt that the alternatives confronting them were, (1) a receivership forced by the creditors, (2) later involuntary bankruptcy, or (3) raising of additional working capital from some new source.

The company finally decided to do everything in its power to avoid a receivership. Since all the personal resources of the members of the firm were already invested in the business, they could not secure any additional capital on their individual credit. As their sales had not yet wholly ceased, they decided that their best course was to sacrifice their inventory at any price which they could obtain, before conditions became worse. They accordingly made a considerable cut in their prices, with the unexpected result that sales instead of increasing, decreased, and more orders were canceled. Everyone seemed to be waiting for prices to go still lower.

Questions

1. What other alternatives, if any, could you have suggested to the management?

2. Do you see any method whereby the company can now avoid ultimate bankruptcy?

3. Would the financial condition of this concern have been better if it had been incorporated? Why do you suppose it grew to this size without being incorporated?

4. What specific lessons does the above problem teach regarding,

(*a*) The proper price policy at various times?

(*b*) The sound principles of finance?

Problem 178

The Relation Between Cost of Production And Market Price

A small factory making a well-known product was started in one of the Southern cities some years ago. The owners were skilful workmen who themselves performed the more important operations in connection with the manufacture of their product. They had no very definite idea of costs, but thought that they could readily undersell a larger concern making the same lines of goods in the same place. Accordingly, they began on a small scale by sending out one salesman who offered to deliver the article at a price from 20 per cent to 30 per cent under the market price then prevailing.

The larger company making the same line of goods heard of the lower prices offered by the salesman of this concern, and in order to hold its customers, reduced its price, though the reduction would almost wipe out all profits.

Soon this cut was reported to another concern in an adjoining city, and the second concern likewise cut its prices to meet the competition. Thus the movement continued, the prices for this particular product being generally cut, and no one seeming to know where the cut started.

In about a year the little factory which originally made the low price failed. In the bankruptcy proceedings following, it was found that slightly more than $20,000 worth of goods had been sold by this concern, while the "competing" and larger concerns had sold more than $1,000,000 worth of goods at the reduced price.

Questions

1. What particular significance can be attached to this incident?

2. What seem to you to be the best means of preventing the development of a situation like this?

F. DISCOUNTS

Problem 179

Quantity Discounts

One of the advantages which large retailers have had in the past over small retailers has come from the quantity discounts which have been extended by some sellers. Recently, with the increased cost of doing business, there has been a tendency toward the formation of associations of small retailers for cooperation in buying. For example, the retail druggists in Toronto have worked out a scheme in accordance with which each druggist is assigned the task of buying enough of certain goods to supply all the druggists participating in the plan. He then turns over the goods to the others at the cost price. Each druggist, in reality, becomes a jobber along certain limited lines.

Commenting on this tendency, a business man recently wrote as follows:

> Nevertheless the cooperative buying agitation is something that has to be met in a constructive way. It can't be soft pedaled out of existence. The main thing, it seems to us, is to eliminate the dealers' fear of the big chains through showing them that the independent retailer who will adhere to certain primary laws of good storekeeping, merchandising and advertising can always have a prominent place regardless of what the chain may do. Time was when the retailer thought the retail mail-order house was going to push him out of business. He loudly called to the jobber and manufacturer for prices that would enable him to compete with the catalogue houses. He has learned now that mail-order business can be kept in its place. The chain store is a harder nut to crack. But it is up to the manufacturer to show the retailer that buying in quantity prices will by no means solve the question so far as the retailer is concerned.
>
> And what is still more important, is that manufacturers should determine, once and for all, the justice or injustice, as the case may be, of the quantity discount system. As long as the quantity purchased determines the discount that is to be given, the chains are always going to have a certain buying advantage over the independents. This will inevitably cause retailers to band themselves together for the

purpose of getting discounts that are equally as large as those given the chains."

(*Printer's Ink*, Feb. 24, 1921, p. 52.)

Questions

1. Is the practice of granting quantity discounts financially desirable from the point of view of the selling house?

2. Should the seller who grants quantity discounts, approve of cooperative purchasing?

3. How may "quantity" buying affect financially—

(*a*) The seller?

(*b*) The buyer?

(*c*) The ultimate consumer?

Problem 180

Relation of Trade Discounts to Quantity Discounts

"The Dennison Manufacturing Company is a well-established business with its headquarters and plant located in New England. Branch sales offices are maintained in about thirty of the large cities of this country, Canada, South America, England and Denmark. In addition retail stores are maintained in four of the larger cities of the United States. These retail stores are established primarily for promotional purposes and do not compete to any substantial degree with the retailers carrying the company's products.

The company manufactures a varied list of paper products, such as shipping tags, marking tags, gummed labels, crepe paper products, jewellers' cases, boxes, and findings. Although the company sells a large quantity of special goods direct to consumers, this problem is concerned with their regular stock goods. In these regular stock goods there are approximately

8,000 items. Most of these items are used by the ultimate consumer in small quantities, and the unit value is small. Consequently they are distributed largely through retailers.

These stock lines are catalogued and priced by the unit and in many cases also by the carton, containing six, ten, twelve, or more units. The retail price given in the company's catalogue is quite generally observed by the retail trade, except in the Far West, where high freight rates make it necessary to charge a higher retail price. The intention of the company is that the consumer who buys from the retail merchant shall pay the price which is stated in the catalogue. When the goods are boxed in cartons containing more than one unit, the price stated for the carton is called the list price, and the consumer purchasing a whole carton would be given this list price by the dealer. When goods are sold in less than carton lots, the unit price is slightly higher than the price per unit in carton lots. From the retail price or from the carton or list price, when that exists, the discounts to the trade are figured.

The wholesale stationer who can handle practically everything that the company makes, receives a discount of 40 per cent from the list price, provided he sells not less than $200 worth of merchandise in a calendar year. Under certain conditions he may also receive in addition certain quantity discounts. The minimum of $200 is a nominal amount and is established merely as a guarantee of good faith on the part of the wholesaler.

A large portion of the company's sales of stock goods are made direct to retailers through the company's travelling salesmen. A substantial number of these retailers also carry on a wholesale business, wholesaling to smaller retailers.

A retailer who sells $500 worth or more of the company's products a year receives a discount of 40 per cent the same as the wholesaler. To those retailers selling less than $500 a year, a discount of 30 per cent from the list price is given. Under certain circumstances, the retailer, just as the wholesaler, may receive quantity discounts, regardless of the annual purchases. Two-thirds of the sales of stock goods are made to retailers who receive the 40 per cent discount. Out of 10,000 dealers who carry the Dennison goods, something over 2,000 are in the 40 per cent class, and their purchases average about $1,500 a year.

The company's salesmen call on dealers in towns of 25,000 population and up. Small purchases by dealers in these towns, however, are usually made from wholesalers because of the saving in freight. All the goods are shipped from the company's factory and the buyer pays the freight.

Numerous objections have been raised to this discount plan. In the first place, it has been suggested that there is an element of unfairness in having the amount of the dealer's profit depend on the quantity of goods which he sells for the company. Nevertheless, the requirement of $200 a year for the wholesaler and $500 for the retailer is well within the reach of those of the trade who take sufficient interest to give the line adequate display and promotive attention.

Again, while it is the company's intention immediately to advance the discount when a wholesaler or retailer reaches the minimum requirement, it is often difficult with 10,000 accounts to put the increased discount into effect as soon as the merchant is entitled to it. If the company fails to make this change at once, its oversight is resented by the merchant.

There are also frequent occasions when a merchant reaches $500 in sales one year only to fall below that amount the next year, thereby reducing his discount in the third year. After a dealer is once placed in the $500 class, he remains there until for one calendar year he has fallen below that limit. Reductions in the discount, however, are fairly frequent owing to the fluctuations in a merchant's business and also because a merchant may go over the minimum in one year, due to an unusually large order for Dennison goods that he may have received from one of his customers, as, for example, from some government agency or from a railroad company.

One object of the high discount is to reward the merchant who takes an interest in this line, and it is naturally desirable from one standpoint to hold forth the inducement of the high discount as an incentive to the merchant who has not yet attained it. It has been found, however, that this stimulus is rather dangerous as it may encourage a merchant just under the line to pad his orders near the end of the year in order to go over the $500 mark. Having padded his orders in one year he inevitably runs the risk of requiring less goods the next year and thus may fall below the minimum amount.

Friction is also encountered with the merchant who may have failed to reach the minimum by only a few dollars and who claims that an injustiec is being done to him when he was so near the mark. This difficulty has been particularly pronounced during the period of unusually heavy demand and the shortage of many items. Under these conditions the company has frequently been unable to ship to a merchant all the goods he ordered. Consequently the merchant has claimed that if the company had made shipments to him in accordance with his orders, he would have been well over the $500 line.

The company is embarrassed also when it comes to opening an account with a new customer. He may be in prospect a promising 40 per cent account; perhaps he already has a large established business; or he may just be starting a business of his own on an unusually large scale because of experience that he has had in some large store.

Such a merchant believes that he is entitled to the 40 per cent discount because of the future possibilities of his business. In many of these cases the company would prefer to give the men as great an inducement as possible to put in a full line of goods if it could be done without breaking down the established custom.

In the last few years there has been a rapid advance in prices and $500 worth of merchandise represents much less in bulk than it did in 1914. Consequently, by virtue of these high prices, many dealers are coming into the 40 per cent class. If prices and the volume of sales go back to a more normal level, some of these merchants will again drop into the lower class.

The company is also troubled from time to time with the pooling of orders whereby two or more small dealers entitled only to 30 per cent discount combine in ordering their goods in order to get over the $500 mark. The company cannot stop this abuse provided the combination of dealers has the goods shipped and billed to one address. The company does decline to grant the discount if such dealers ask to have the goods shipped or billed to more than one place.

One of the suggestions that has been made for the solution of this problem is to give the entire trade, both wholesalers and retailers, the discount of 40 per cent. This would be objected to by the wholesaler as cutting off his trade with the smaller retailers. The wholesaler now sells to the smaller stores in urban districts and especially to the stores in the rural districts and small towns.

Another suggestion has been to eliminate the minimum sales requirement, to give to retailers 40 per cent off and an extra 10 per cent discount to wholesalers. One of the drawbacks to this plan is, that numerous retailers are also wholesalers. They would immediately claim the extra discount, and it would not be long before other large retailers would be demanding the same discount as their competitors. The company also fears that the introduction of the extra 10 per cent discount to wholesalers who are also retailers would result in price cutting."

(Quoted from Copeland, *Marketing Problems*, 336-340.)

Questions

1. What are the chief purposes of the "trade discount"?

2. What is the relation of the "trade" discount to the "quantity" discount?

3. What is your opinion of the Dennison Company's policy?

4. What steps would you advise them to take?

Problem 181

The Cash Discount—Theory *vs.* Practice

"I cannot conceive of any argument that would defend the practice of taking (or stealing) extra time on a cash discount or a net maturity. Since the discount offered is much more than the use of the money is worth, the basic principle is offering a reward for keeping a contract, and appealing to the instinct of cupidity, instead of to the higher ideals of justice and right.

* * * * * *

"The offer of a fair rate of interest for anticipated payment is the only cash discount that is correct in principle and a large discount is only defensible on the ground of expediency.

"Then the question is raised, 'Will not a cash discount enable us to approach nearer to the goal of prompt receipt of the net amount?' Emphatically it will not. A discount for cash in ten days is impossible of strict enforcement, for in but few cases can a shipment be received and the account put through the various necessary channels and the remittance made to reach the shipper in ten days. When almost daily shipments are made, what firms will discount each separately? They 'bunch' the invoices, 'average' the dates and the average is usually later than the list invoice. With so few exceptions as to make it distinctly the rule, the best and largest firms construe ten days' cash discount to be payment by the tenth of each month for the previous month's shipments.

"What I would advocate as a basis for general agreement is, 'Net cash 30 days,' for a month is a unit of time in business."

Questions

1. What appear to you to be the real advantages, if any, of the cash discount?
2. Do you approve of the opinion above expressed?

(For specific information on "terms of sale" consult Ettinger and Golieb, 66-76, also articles in *Federal Reserve Bulletin.*)

Problem 182

The Cash Discount "Piracy"

"We would protest that there is no more justification for a merchant to take advantage of 2 per cent discount, after discount terms have been past, than there would be for the seller to exact an additional 2 per cent on selling price when payment is made."

Questions

Do you agree? Why or why not?

Problem 183

Letters on the Cash Discount

Criticize the following letters regarding the "Cash Discount Piracy":

A. We regret, however, that you are offended by our insistence in this matter of discount, but hope that upon further consideration it may appear to you in a different light.

The effort of any house to maintain its terms deserves commendation, not censure; in equity to all who purchase under them, it would not be fair to grant one account special terms not enjoyed by all. In other words, were the circumstances reversed you would not want to have 1% or 2% discount more to pay than another one of our customers under conditions which are identical.

We have always endeavored to make no exceptions, play no favorites. Is it not well to be assured that you are getting the same value and service that every merchant on our books enjoys?

Could you afford to be satisfied with less? Join hands with us for a square deal for all, all the time.

Won't you forget our little misunderstanding?

B. We are returning your check amounting to $......,

We dislike, each time your remittance is received, to find it necessary to complain about your method of discounting, which you can see is utterly contrary to our terms. We have explained this to you several times and are surprised that you do not cheerfully meet our requests, as it surely is apparent to you that you are not justified in the discount deductions you make.

Won't you kindly favor us with your better attention to this matter and let us have your check for the correct amount?

C. We regret that we cannot allow the discount you deduct, however, and are accordingly returning your remittance, preferring to receive it a week hence for the full amount of your account.

When you purchased this bill of us you had the privilege of two terms of payment, i. e. you could pay within ten days and deduct 2% cash discount as a reward for prompt payment, or you could remit the face of the account at the end of the net thirty-day terms.

Your remittance, just received, does not contemplate a choice of these two terms, but included both—you remit in twenty-two days and take advantage of the ten-day discount terms.

We should like to please you in this matter but feel that we cannot consistently do so when we take into consideration our own requirements and the necessity of being scrupulously careful to treat all our friends and customers alike, which we would not be doing were we to create a preference in the present instance.

(All quoted from Lawrence, *Cash Discount Piracy.*)

G. COLLECTIONS

Problem 184

Charging Interest on Past Due Accounts

A. "When we come to analyze our books we find our customers divided into six classes, and that terms which are rigidly enforced on us for payments, mean little or nothing to a very large percentage of our trade. This is owing to our country being largely agricultural, affording but one general pay day, so to speak, making large lines of credit and long time a necessity of liberal trade in this section. This condition, however, but adds strength to our argument. Of the above-named classes we give the discounter first place, and this class is growing, owing to our fine local conditions. Next we name the man who pays when due on regular terms, much prized, but in our business so small in number as to be scarcely recognizable in comparison with the whole. Thirdly, the customer who settles by note, representing a most respectable number and volume, and among our most valued trade. The next, and possibly the class representing our greatest volume in dollars, are those who pay on accounts as they can and make one or two note settlements a year. Among these are many of that peculiar temperament who will pay interest on a note, but object to the charge on open account, and we strike our first snag. The fifth class, numerically larger than all the others combined, is composed of those who make payments from time to time, require carrying generally, want all there is coming to them and then some, give you only a portion of their trade, object to note settlement, and won't pay interest if they can avoid it. And lastly, but not soon forgotten, those who won't pay at all.

"Returning to the main issue between our customer and ourselves, what is the argument? Briefly this: The charge of interest is made to reimburse us in part for an outlay solely in his behalf, which in all justice can only be covered by a direct charge on his account, at a rate usually less than he could obtain it from his own banker, and without one penny's worth of security. Justice is so manifest in this brief argument, that further discussion should not be necessary, but we have often been met with the reply from customers, that they cannot or do not charge interest, hence we should not charge them."

B. "It has been my experience that to charge interest every month often has the effect of stirring the customer to an effort to collect his accounts, that he may pay his bills when due and thus save interest, and it often happens that he will pay us and make the one who does not charge interest wait for his money. One might charge a slow pay customer more for his goods than he does the one who is prompt, but that would be a discrimination not justifiable and in the end would prove unsatisfactory. It sometimes happens that the slow customer, by industry, economy and close attention to business, succeeds in accumulating capital sufficient to pay promptly or to discount, and when that time comes the jobber who has held him up and robbed him will lose the business.

"A jobber cannot in justice to himself or his customer fail to charge interest from maturity of bills. If one will figure interest at 6 per cent on an account from maturity he will be astonished to learn how short a time it takes to eat up the entire net profit. It is an unfair proposition to furnish one man $500 or $1,000 or more as capital in his business to compete with equally good customers who pay promptly, unless the current rate of interest is charged and even then there is an element of unfairness in it.

"I maintain that not to charge interest is discriminatory as between customers and unfair to those who pay promptly. It places a premium upon slowness. The customer on one side of the street who pays his bills promptly undoubtedly is at times compelled to go to his banker and borrow money to enable him to be prompt. The customer on the other side of the street who compels the jobber to carry his account instead of going to bank and borrowing the money, is buying his goods cheaper than the prompt-pay customer just to the extent of the interest he would have to pay, if the jobber does not charge it, and the prompt-pay customer is at a disadvantage."

Questions

1. Examine critically the above reasoning.
2. Should interest be charged on past due accounts? How should you answer this question—
   (*a*) In the case of a new customer?
   (*b*) In the case of an old customer?
   (*c*) In the case of a new selling concern?
   (*d*) In the case of an old selling concern?
3. Would your answers to this question be the same for 1917 as for the present period?

Problem 185

Collections and the Business Cycle

A. "During a time of falling prices, the best reasons in the world may be put forth by debtors for not paying their bills and these reasons are so nearly like those which in normal times are good reasons that one has to give not a little thought to the distinguishing of the good from the bad.

"For instance, under ordinary circumstances it is not good business to push a man for money if he has not been able to sell what you have sold to him. We have to consider credits and collections in their larger sense and recognize that the creditor is interested in preserving a customer and a business unit as well as in getting his money. Hence pressing a solvent and merely unfortunate man is not good business.

"Today it is not good business to delay the payment of your own bills or to allow debtors to delay in paying you on the plea that the goods bought are still unsold on the shelves."

B. "The debtor who fails to respond to admonition for an overdue account and appears to be slipping, should not be held up too hastily. The facts on which the account was opened should be reviewed. The debtor should be treated as one who but needs a little help to mend his ideas and methods and produce the desired results."

Question

Can you reconcile the points of view here presented?

Problem 186

The Cost of Small Collections

Questions

1. Assuming that the average cost of writing collection letters is 30¢ to 50¢ do you think that a business house should be persistent in its attempts to collect very small overdue accounts?

2. Do you see any method of eliminating the expense in connection with these small accounts?

Problem 187

Trade Acceptance *vs.* Collection Letters

"One way to cut unnecessary expense—a way most business men might not think of—is to avoid writing collection letters. It takes some preliminary measures to get the plan under way; but once it starts, it brings in the money promptly and cuts the cost of getting it. Why not recognize that on the part of many customers who do not take the 10-day discount, there is not the slightest expectation of being able to pay in 30 days, and on the part of others who can, no intention of doing so? That, of course, is after allowing for those who make a practice of observing net terms. And, having gone that far, why not endeavor to place these customers on terms which they can and will observe and reserve regular open-account terms for those who are able and disposed to fulfil them? There is one best way to shortcut collection expense. That the trade acceptance can be used to make collection letters unnecessary admits of no argument. Getting a customer on trade acceptance saves all the collection letters you would otherwise send. There is not, after all, anything really formidable about the trade acceptance. It is more than anything else, perhaps, a post-dated check, at least where it is not discounted. In fact, some of our acceptance customers charge acceptances against their bank accounts when they are accepted and then promptly forget about them."

Question

In the light of your knowledge of trade acceptance use and practice, to what extent do you consider the above claims justified?

PROBLEM 188

COLLECTING THE BILLS OR ACCEPTING THE RETURNED GOODS

A successful and very highly esteemed millinery merchant, Mr. A., states that in the first ten years of his experience it annoyed him greatly when the ladies attempted to return hats which they had purchased from him and had worn one or more times. It was his earlier custom to endeavor to collect from his customers and make them keep the goods.

In the second ten years of his experience, A. decided that it was not worth his while to argue with his clients about the matter, and usually accepted the returned goods, himself bearing with rather bad grace the losses which resulted from this policy. During the last decade, however, he has followed a much more liberal policy. When hats are returned, he receives them with apparent satisfaction, stating that he is glad the customer brought the goods back if in any way they failed to give satisfaction. In fact, he has carried his liberality so far that even when he has made up hats to special order, which he knows have been worn by the purchaser for a special occasion, but which are returned on some pretense or other, he replies somewhat as follows:

"Madam, I am delighted to have this hat back. I really think a great deal of it and am sorry that I let you have it at the low price made. Really, you know, I made you a special price which was too low for profit, because I value your trade so highly. It will be money in my pocket to have the hat back, for several women have been looking for just such a hat and are willing to pay almost any price for it. I can assure you that you have really done me a favor by bringing the hat back."

Mr. A. states that his policy of the last decade has resulted in great financial success.

Questions

1. How do you account for the financial "success" which A. says has resulted from his more recent policy?

2. To what extent, if at all, should you expect the general policy outlined by Mr. A. to prove successful in other lines of retailing?

3. Should you expect such a policy to bring financial success—

(*a*) In the mail-order business?

(*b*) In the wholesaling or jobbing business?

(*c*) In the case of manufacturers who have a large number of customers?

Problem 189

Novel Collection Methods

A. "Occasionally a credit man or collector is found with a check on his hands that is returned unpaid—sometimes post-dated and sometimes bearing the current date, given in the ordinary course of business—with the reason for nonpayment endorsed by the bank 'insufficient funds,' and in many bankruptcy proceedings creditors are found holding checks dishonored for that very reason. A practice that seems to be little followed is that of determining how much short the check is, and then depositing to the credit of the debtor enough money to make the check good.

"For instance, if you are given a check for $100, by diplomatically handling the matter with the bank you can find out how much the debtor's account is short. If you cannot discuss the matter with an out-of-town bank, possibly you can send the check to a traveling salesman and have him call at the bank and get him to ascertain how much the account is short. In the case recited, if you learn, for instance, that there is but $90 on deposit, while you have a $100 check, you can deposit $10 to the customer's credit, or have the traveling man do it, and the check will be cleared."

B. "If all efforts to obtain security have failed and the account is in a precarious condition, efforts should be made to offset the obligation by purchasing from the debtor something that can be resold. Such an offset, in the absence of fraud, is good even if a bankruptcy petition should be filed shortly afterward. For instance, if your customer runs a lumber mill, purchase the lumber even if you know you have no use for it, and sell it at a slight discount if you anticipate a loss on his account. In fact, no matter what the debtor produces, or resells, if there is any reasonable market for it you can usually find that market and make a ready sale of the product by allowing some slight discount under the market. This is much better than to find your debtor is so involved that the account will drift along, with the prospect that you will ultimately face a much larger loss than the slight discount you know you will lose if you accept the wares of your customer to apply as a credit on your claim against him. This procedure will often enable you to realize even after some other creditor has obtained security."

Question

Do you approve of the collection methods outlined above?

Problem 190

Sample Collection Letters*

Criticize the following "Collection" Letters:

A. A novel way to collect small past-due accounts is being used by an eastern manufacturer, who, after failing to get any response to his letters requesting a check, sends the customer a receipted statement worded:

This statement is marked "paid in full" and receipted because we have exhausted every means to get you to make payment.

The bill is small, and if your conscience should ever tell you to send us your remittance, which is rightfully due us, we shall, of course, be glad to get the money.

B. "It seems that the only way we can get any remittance from you on account is to wire you inquiring what you intend doing. This is rather expensive and we have not made very great headway as it is. The present balance remaining due, $.........., is really ... months past due and is more than one-half of those bills which matured on ...... Now, this isn't satisfactory.

"Our draft of ...., as we wrote you before, came back with the endorsement: 'Will send check in a few days,' and here it is two weeks without a word from you in reply to our letter of the .... We will not wait until you get ready to pay us. Unless we have some assurance that something will be done, we are going to hand an itemized account

*The following suggestions may be helpful:—"The wheel that squeaks the loudest gets the grease. Therefore, it behooves every collection manager to be consistent in dunning and insistent in demands for payment. His follow-up must be regular and not spasmodic and one must take advantage of every available means to 'bring home the bacon.' There are a great many other points that can be brought out, but principally, (a) We never let the follow-up get behind. Try to be one or two days ahead of schedule rather than one day behind. (b) Never bluff. (c) Never let a customer forget his promises. (d) Don't use 'rubber stamp' collection methods. Individualize. (e) Handle each account on its merits and don't threaten to sue some customer when a nice, diplomatic letter would have made the collection. A harsh letter not only antagonizes the customer, but, no doubt, loses him for the firm. The real collection manager not only gets the money, but retains the good will of the customers and keeps the accounts out of the attorney's hands. Under the present method we not only keep our accounts up to the standards, but have reduced the number of employees in the collection department to half the number previously employed under the old methods, making an annual saving on the payroll of over $3,000 a year."—(Adapted from an article by A. M. Tamwrath, Collection Manager, American Slicing Machine Co., Chicago, in *100%*, May, 1921, p. 98.)

to our collectors, one week from today. If you desire us to bear with you in this case, you must send us a remittance upon which to base our leniency. We believe in being perfectly frank in the matter, and, this being the case, we must tell you we are thoroughly disappointed with the present condition of your indebtedness with us."

C. "We return herewith your note, etc. We could not possibly accept a sixty-day note, at the present time for your entire account—not that we are unwilling to do so, but we cannot, for this simple reason that we will need this money before.................. We had been depending upon receiving your remittance, and must, under the circumstances, request you to make other arrangements, either through your bank or some available source, and let us have settlement in the next week or two."

D. "It certainly seems strange to us that you permit our drafts to come back, do not write, and send us nothing to apply on your past-due account. We have regarded you as perfectly good, and have not felt apprehensive about your finally paying us, but must confess our inability to understand your treatment of us. We will be frank and say that we want something to apply on your account, and will ask you to let us hear from you before the ... day of May."

E. "The Collection Department refers your account to us, this morning, and we cannot help but think that if the payments you made us gave us half the pleasure it did to receive your orders, what a pleasant time we would have doing business together. Usually, when one buys goods in ..., even under the most unfavorable conditions, he certainly should have disposed of enough of them to send us at least a liberal remittance thereon in ... ; but you are owing us entirely for purchase from ... on—in fact, ... of the balance now shown is owing on invoices for ...

We are just telling you how the matter looks to us here. The Collection Department seems unable to get your balance adjusted, and, of course, we always desire, if possible, to have these little matters settled amicably, so that we can maintain pleasant relations. The slightest consideration of the matter must show that we have been very lenient thus far; caused you no trouble, simply writing you from time to time endeavoring to have you make settlement. This is our policy as regards every account which we regard as highly as we do yours; but there does come a time when we must insist upon payment. We shall expect to hear from you promptly, and in the meantime have taken the liberty of over-ruling the suggestion of the Collection Department, but desire to have a remittance from you."

(Last four quoted from Lawrence, *Making Him Pay*)

H. FINANCIAL ASPECTS OF ADVERTISING

Problem 191

Relation of Advertising to Sales

"The real way to decrease your advertising expenses is to increase it. It will start your business growing and pretty soon you will find the advertising expenditures can't keep up with the growth. The truth is that a decent advertising appropriation is an investment, not an expense."

In support of this statement the following data are given regarding a distributor of men's clothing:

	First Half 1918	Second Half 1918	Second Half 1919
Percentage of advertising appropriation to sales of previous period	2.40%	6.35%	9.46%
Percentage of sales of current period to sales of previous period	63.78%	126.40%	197.80%
Percentage of advertising expenditure of current period to sales of current period	3.77%	5.00%	4.78%
Gross profit	41.40%	38.60%	37.70%
Net profit	4.81%	8.24%	11.02%

"As you increase your advertising, you increase your business so fast that your expenditure turns out to be a much smaller percentage than the percentage of your appropriation."

Question

Do you agree with the statements made and the conclusions drawn?

PROBLEM 192

WAS ADVERTISING RESPONSIBLE FOR THE FINANCIAL SUCCESS OF THIS CONCERN?

Recently there appeared an article in an advertising periodical which attributed the growth of the Habirshaw Electric Cable Company almost entirely to its method of advertising. Briefly stated, the company endeavors by means of its advertising to push the use of those appliances not made by it, but in conjunction with which its product is used. The following claims are made:

"Very rarely does the average man purchase even a few yards of electric wire. He certainly never buys electric cable. Habirshaw makes nothing but electric wire and cable. Yet for five years this company has been addressing the bulk of its advertising to Mr. General Person. A purely technical product has been advertised to the general public. When the company started advertising on these lines, it began with an appropriation of $12,000, of which about $10,000 was spent on the man in the street. This year the company will spend something like $200,000 on advertising, and at least $150,000 of it in efforts to reach people who do not buy electric wire. If that seems to deepen the mystery, listen! Five years ago the company was doing an annual business of only $800,000, and it stood twenty-eighth on the list of electric wire and cable manufacturers. Today it claims to be the largest house of its kind in the world, and is reported to be doing a business of $16,000,000 a year. In five years the business has been increased 2,000 per cent, and the advertising appropriation 1,500 per cent. At the same time the selling cost, including the advertising, has been reduced 50 per cent. It is a remarkable record—and none of it, it is said, was due to the war. The Habirshaw Company ascribes this great and rapid growth almost entirely to its manner of advertising, plus the merchandising idea on which the advertising and practically all of its selling efforts were based."

(*Printer's Ink*, March 24, 1921, p. 49, ff.)

Question

Based on the information above given, do you believe that advertising has played the important part claimed in the financial success of this company?

Problem 193

The Financial Gains From Advertising

Advertising is a curious thing. It has had to be taken on faith for the most part. You can't usually measure its effect. Men who advertise and find their business prospering keep on advertising. Men whose business has been slow sometimes try advertising and find their business suddenly growing. Then they keep on advertising. That's the reason you can't measure its results. Many merchants pay for advertising and get only publicity.

Question

How can a concern determine the amount of money which should be spent for advertising?

Problem 194

Advertising and Business Profits

Many concerns, in 1919, due to unusual business activity, made an extremely high return on their investment. Business seemed to be growing better. In fact, many lines of goods seemed almost to sell themselves at any price asked by the producer.

Question

Under these circumstances, would it have been sound financial policy for such concerns to incur heavy expenses for advertising?

(Reference: *Printer's Ink*, June 30, 1921.)

Problem 195

Advertising To Aid "Seasonal" Business

It is a well-known fact that a good many lines of business are more or less "seasonal." Commenting on this condition, a recent writer has said:

"One of the great things that this powerful force of advertising can do for American business is to help straighten out sales curves. If you were sure of an even market, month by month throughout the year, how much would it save you? How much do you lose during your low months—not how much do you lose in actual dollars and cents, but how much do you lose in momentum?

(*Printer's Ink*, Feb. 24, 1921, p. 89, ff.)

Questions

1. What, specifically, are the chief financial losses of seasonal selling?
2. To what extent do you believe that advertising can remedy the evils?
3. In the case of manufactured products, are there *necessarily* goods which have only seasonal sales?

Problem 196

Dealer Advertising and the Distributer

"You hear a lot of talk about the "cancelation evil" these days. A lot of manufacturers declare that many retailers have been guilty of a moral misdemeanor because they have canceled their orders, and that they have thrown a great burden upon industry. I am not advocating the practice, but what about the manufacturer who sells you goods largely on the strength of his work with consumers to help you dispose of them, and then turns around and cancels his advertising?"

Questions

1. Are the manufacturers who at present cut their appropriations for advertising, playing the game fairly with their retail distributers?
2. Would it be justifiable for a retailer, under the circumstances, to cancel his contracts with the producer?
3. Is continued or increased advertising, under present conditions, financially justifiable?

Problem 197

Does Advertising Aid the Credit Seeker?

"Investors tumbled over themselves to buy the recent $20,000,000 bond issue of the Vacuum Oil Company. At the same time the great city of New York had to take its hat in hand and go from bank to bank, begging for enough money to pay its current bills. The security in each case was unquestioned, but, nevertheless, the partiality of the investor for the private borrower was decided. Something similar has happened on many other occasions recently. Why?

The answer is that ten credit risks are offered for every one accepted. The lender selects his risks with extreme care. Any margin of value in favor of one, usually decides the choice. In many cases advertising is this margin. How it helps the borrower is explained by the following list of recent short-term notes of big national advertisers, the rate of interest and asking price of which is due somewhat to the prestige gained through consistent advertising."

Security	Rate	Due	Asked
American Tobacco.......	7	Nov., 1921	100⅜
Cudahy Packing Co......	7	July 15, 1926	99
H. J. Heinz Co..........	7	Dec. 1, 1930	98
Liggett & Myers.........	6	Dec., 1921	99½
Proctor & Gamble........	7	March, 1922	100⅜
R. J. Reynolds Tobacco...	6	Aug., 1922	97¾
Swift & Co..............	7	Aug. 15, 1921	99½
Westinghouse Elec. Co....	7	April 19, 1925	99¾

(Reference: *Printer's Ink,* April 14, 1921, page 1.)

Questions

1. Do you think that the comparison above made is a fair one?

2. In what types of concerns, if any, do you think that national advertising of the product will aid in securing credit at a more favorable rate?

3. Fundamentally, what are the chief causes which make a borrowing concern a "prime" risk?

Problem 198

How Much Can a Candy Company Afford To Spend in Advertising?

The following problem was submitted by the treasurer of a good-sized candy manufacturing concern in April, 1921. The proper answer to the questions which he raises will be of very vital interest to him, since the sales have been falling off rapidly and the company which he represents has recently completed a new plant.

I. Character of Business.

a. High-grade confectionery, chocolates, fancy packages, retailing at $1.00 to $1.50 per lb.

b. Good-grade bulk.

c. 5c, 10c and 15c specialties.

"*a*" Is on trade-mark goods and represents desired kind of distribution. "*b*" Is to take up suplus production. "*c*" Is for added profit, representing character of goods that can be sold without extra sales cost through existing dealers.

II. Distribution. Distribution now through 4,000 to 5,000 retailers, largely drug stores, throughout states east of the Mississippi. Sales through force of twenty salesmen. Three or four jobbers together with their salesmen are used in certain territories.

III. Volume. Volume $1,250,000 to $1,750,000. Distribution is not as intensive as it should be or volume would be larger for the number of dealers and the territories covered.

The relation between possible volume and total investment is from three to five times as great as the total net worth of the high-grade confectioner. The ratio between fixed investment, including machinery and fixtures (but not including real estate, as it is often leased)and possible volume, may be 1 to 7, 8, 9, or 10, that is, the volume may be eight or more times the fixed investment.

IV. Margin of Profit. The net margin after all expenses on business of this character is generally from 7 per cent to 10 per cent of the volume. Roughly, the gross margin above actual manufacturing expenses at the stock room is from 30 per cent to 38 per cent. Manufacturing costs in good candy plants is necessarily from 62 per cent to 70 per of the manufacturers' sale price. Out of the 30 per cent or 38 per cent must come administration, selling, and publicity, bad debts, interest. For a package for which the manufacturer gees $1.00, the retailer will get from $1.35 to $1.50. Retailer aims to get at least 30 per cent on the retail price.

V. Publicity. Business is about fifteen years old and previous publicity has been almost entirely in the form of store signs (both temporary and more or less permanent), sample boxes, and window displays, a little incidental theatre program and college magazine advertising, and some advertising in local newspapers. Total store help and sign advertising about 2 per cent to 2½ per cent of volume. 1½ per cent or 2 per cent is always necessary, regardless of what other publicity is undertaken.

Questions

1. On how small an expenditure can one hope to get appreciable increase in volume, and through what means of publicity?

Author's Note:—Candy manufacturers in general do not appear to have spent a large relative amount on advertising. The low-grade producers are evidently the heaviest advertisers, while among the high-grade producers almost nothing, or at any rate less than 1 per cent of their sales, is said to be spent for this purpose. In this connection, it should be noted that the ten best retail advertising men in the country recently gave the following figures as the proper amount of gross business to be set aside for advertising:

	Per Cent		Per Cent
Department Stores	3½	Electrical Stores	6
Women's Specialty Shops	5½	Jewelry Stores	5½
Shoe Stores	4	Men's Clothing and Furnishing	5
Millinery Stores	4	Miscellaneous	4
Music Stores	5½		
Furniture Stores	5½		

2. In what respects, if at all, are the financial aspects of advertising in the candy manufacturing business different from what would be found in the examples given?

CHAPTER IX

THE ADMINISTRATION OF EARNINGS

References:

*Dewing, *Financial Policy of Corporations*, Vol. III.
*Lough, *Business Finance*, Part IV.
Mead, *Corporation Finance*, XIV-XVIII

IN the problems which have preceded an attempt has been made to illustrate the sound principle of finance which should be followed, step by step, from the inception of the business to the time when its earnings come in. If the financial edifice has been soundly built to this stage, there is little danger that the management will go wrong in its disposition of earnings. However, with a view to illustrating a few of the typical situations which may arise, the following problems are given.

Problem 199

Should a New Building Have Been Financed Out of Surplus Earnings?

"A large department store was organized in a city of the Middle West. The store was well located and the capital should have been sufficient. At the start there was little competition and the business prospered.

The prosperity, however, was brief. The owner of the store concentrated his attention on selling and buying. He neglected credit. He paid all small bills upon their presentation at the cashier's window; larger bills upon receipt of invoice. He took no measures to keep idle funds active; he did not try to establish a business reputation among bankers and moneyed men;

he adopted no plan to equalize his supply of capital with demand.

At length the business required a new building. The younger members of the firm advised establishing their credit and borrowing the money they needed. A new competitor had begun to build and was making improvements. One of the merchant's sons, exasperated by this move, spoke to his father. "See here," he said, "we're behind time. Take the railways, the skyscrapers, and all the great industrial works for that matter. Could they have been built up by following our method? Do they keep their capital idle while waiting for it to grow? Why not borrow the money for this new building? We may be obliged to ask for credit some day to carry on our business. It is better to establish it now while we can."

The senior member of the firm, however, was obdurate. He would do nothing until he had accumulated a surplus sufficient to cover the expenses of the improvement, though he admitted that lack of space was a handicap.

The first two years, the firm managed to build up a considerable surplus. This money was kept in a savings bank, drawing 3 per cent interest. The third year, however, the competition had so grown that no surplus was earned. The fourth year began with a general business depression. The balance in the bank sank. Still the old policy continued."

(Quoted from Shaw, *How to Finance a Business*, 7-8.)

Questions

1. Did the father follow correct policies—
   (*a*) In his current financing?
   (*b*) In the disposition of the surplus earnings?
2. Do you agree fully with the son's arguments?
3. What steps, if any, should you now advise taking in order to improve the financial condition of this business?

Problem 200

General Problem on Dividend Policy

The American Telephone and Telegraph Company has for many years been referred to as an outstanding example of a conservatively financed concern. Its present form of organization dates back to 1900, during the last fifteen years of which time dividends of 8 per cent on the common stock have regularly been paid. In addition to liberal maintenance and depreciation charges the company has built up a large surplus mainly out of earnings, but including some premiums realized on the sale of new securities. Only common stock has been issued. It has always been the policy of the management to avoid placing any mortgage on the property, and to date the outstanding bonds are of the debenture or collateral type.

The price range of the stock has been as follows:

1901–1905, High—186; Low—117¼ (dividend rate at this time 7½%.)

1906–1917, High—153⅛; Low—88 (during the panic of 1907.)

1918–1920, High—109¼; Low—90⅝.

1921 (till Aug. 1st), High—108½; Low—95¾.

(Since February 1, 1921, the stock has not sold below 99½. On July 30 it sold at 105⅜.)

In February, 1921, there was a rumor to the effect that the company was planning some new financing. This report was denied by the management. Near the end of March, however, the directors authorized the president to announce their decision to establish 9 per cent as the regular annual rate of dividend to be paid upon the company's shares, beginning July 15, 1921.

In deciding upon this change of policy it was stated that the management was influenced by the "conclusion that a higher rate of return is necessary to attract the portion of capital which must come from shareholders in order that an extension of telephone service to keep pace with the growth of the country and the demands of the public may go on."

It was further stated that there had been no time during the last ten years when the company's earnings had not been sufficient to pay a higher rate of dividend than 8 per cent. The president further states:

The change in dividend rates is nothing more than an adjustment to a new set of conditions. It has always been the policy of the company to pay such a dividend as would maintain the market value of the stock at a premium sufficient to attract subscriptions to new stock issues.

The issue of a fair proportion of new capital rather than an increased debt to take care of the growth is a necessary part of any sound financial program. Before the war the 8 per cent dividend maintained the stock at a satisfactory premium.

Since the war, with efficiency and earnings equivalent to pre-war standard, its stock is bought and sold at only about par. Par value indicates satisfactory absorption of the present issue, but not demand for more at the same rate of return. Stock must be quoted at a premium to indicate a readiness to absorb further issues.

Not only present financial conditions governing the status of this and other investment securities have been considered, but also the probable conditions in the future.

In commenting on this action of the American Telephone and Telegraph Company, the financial editor of one of the daily papers wrote as follows on March 30, 1921:

Some criticized, some condemned directors of American Telephone for increasing the dividend. The increase naturally attracted more attention than would a change in the dividend in any other corporation in the country, partly because the company serves so many people, partly because more people own stock of the American Telephone Company than of any other corporation in the world. The number of stockholders is in the vicinity of 140,000.* Some said yesterday that the dividend increase was the most stupid thing directors ever did. Others said that it was the most clever thing they ever did.

Those who argued that it was stupid said it was a poor time to advertise corporate prosperity when there is so much labor unrest and especially when the company's largest subsidiary, the New York Telephone Company, is pleading poverty as an excuse for increased telephone rates

**Author's Note.*—The reported number of stockholders had increased to about 160,000 by the first part of July, 1921.

in its territory. The increase in its rates recently allowed has not yet been made permanent by the up-state public service commission of New York.

The dividend increase was characterized as the wisest thing directors have ever done by those who were looking at it from the standpoint of a financial operation, pure and simple. The last few years the company has been unable to raise money for extension purposes by selling stock, for it must sell its stock at par or better. Bonds and notes have been the media of financing. Bankers have not looked with good favor on this policy, for in order to maintain the credit of any corporation it is necessary to maintain a certain ratio between fixed and contingent liabilities. Financing through bond or note issues entails an increase in fixed liabilities, while an increase in stock means an increase in contingent liabilities. So, in order to maintain the highest credit for the company, it was necessary to come to a point where new money would be raised by the sale of stock rather than by the sale of additional fixed interest-bearing securities. That could not be done with the stock on an 8 per cent dividend basis. It can be done with the stock on a 9 per cent basis.

Earnings fully justify the new rate.

On May 11, 1921, it was announced that the directors had voted to offer $90,000,000 new stock to stockholders at par, stockholders of record on May 20th being entitled to subscribe until July 20th for new stock in the ratio of one new share for each five shares held. Latest information indicates that this new issue has been rapidly absorbed through the direct selling method.

Questions

1. What appear to you to be the real reasons for this increase in dividend?

2. Taking the long-run point of view, do you consider this increase in dividends a sound policy?

3. Would the same reasons exist for increasing the dividend on the stock of a large industrial concern? Of a small industrial concern?

4. Would a concern whose stock is not listed on any exchange be faced with a similar problem?

5. Would a concern whose stock is narrowly owned be confronted by such a problem?

6. Should you expect the continuance of this rate of dividend (9%) to be more certain in the case of a public utility than in the case of an industrial concern? Why?

7. What relation, if any, does the wide distribution of ownership and the customer ownership of shares have to the financial program above outlined?

Problem 201

Relation of Dividend Declaration to Emergency Financing

The S. Rubber Tire Company is a well-managed concern with generally excellent credit. It has had a very satisfactory dividend record. It had been borrowing largely in the open market, keeping its bank lines in reserve. By the end of 1920, however, even though its credit was still good, there was practically no market for commercial paper, because of the generally depressed business conditions. This concern was forced to resort to its banks early in 1921 in order to borrow enough money to pay off its maturing paper.

The S. Rubber Tire Company sold its tires largely to manufacturers of automobiles. With the general slump, therefore, orders practically stopped and a large portion of its receivables became frozen. Further, they had made commitments for the purchase of fabric to which they were definitely held. Hence they were in the position of being forced to buy a good deal of this material at a high price when the market was off. On the whole, the company was in an *unfavorable* rather than in a *dangerous* position, since its earnings for the year 1920 had been very good, and the company through conservative management had built up a large surplus. Its current ratio, from the quantitative point of view, was highly satisfactory, nor were its current liabilities higher than in normal times. Though sales for the first six months of 1921 were low, the business of this company began to pick up about the middle of the year; yet, because of their commitments, and the like, the profit on these sales was very low. A good deal was also owed to the trade.

Thus the concern was in the middle of 1921 confronted with the problem of financing its purchases of materials for the next year's business. In order to pay for these materials which would be coming in during the winter months, an amount of credit far in excess of that which the banks would be willing to lend was needed.

Finally, the management decided to raise the needed funds to pay off their creditors and extend their bank lines by selling ten-year serial debentures, carrying a high rate of interest. Just at this time, however, the dividend on the common stock (very little preferred stock had been issued) was coming due. This stock was very widely held. The dividend had been earned by a considerable margin, and, as stated before, the company had a very creditable surplus. The directors of the company, therefore, were confronted with a double problem (*a*) that of financing their next year's purchases, (*b*) that of passing or declaring their dividend.

Questions

1. Do you think the company chose the best method of raising working capital needed to finance its purchases? If not, what alternatives can you suggest?

2. In view of the situation presented, what action should the directors have taken on the matter of the dividend payment?

3. Will your answer be the same whether or not the stock is listed on some exchange?

Problem 202

Shall Dividends be Declared or Shall Earnings be Used for Plant Extensions?

The A. B. C. Shoe Company has had a highly creditable financial history dating back for almost one hundred years. It has always been their policy to make liberal provision for depreciation and maintenance. The common stock is rather closely held, being largely in the hands of six men, almost all of whom are also officers of the concern. The preferred stock, cumulative at 7 per cent, is widely held. This stock was issued with the provision that if dividends in excess of 10 per cent should be declared on the common, the preferred should share equally with the common. The agreement under which the preferred stock was issued also provides that the ratio of current assets to current liabilities shall never be allowed to fall below 175 per cent, and if it should fall below this point the voting power shall vest solely in the preferred stockholders, who otherwise have no voice in the control. The company is under no obligations to retire the preferred stock out of earnings at any time, nor can it convert the preferred into common stock or other types of securities. No bonds or debentures are outstanding and no mortgages can be placed on the plant without the consent of 75 per cent of the preferred stockholders.

During the year 1920 this company, as was the case with practically all shoe concerns, lost a good deal of money, so that by the end of the year, though the current position was still reasonably satisfactory from the banker's point of view, the common stockholders began to fear that the preferred stockholders might get the control. However, the company took its inventory losses at once, cleaned out its old stock, and early in 1921 put itself in a relatively strong position.

As the old inventory had been worked off, the A. B. C. Company was able to buy raw material at the lowest market. Accordingly, its costs of production were lower than those of any of its active competitors making the same grade of shoes. Because of this favorable position, the company was able to make lower prices to the trade than could be made by other important producers. Consequently, orders began to come in rapidly, so that by July, 1921, there were enough advance orders on hand to keep the entire factory going at full capacity until early in 1922. These orders are at a figure which will insure high profits to the company and are secured by very definite contracts which give the company the right to cancel whenever it may see fit, while the customers are firmly held. The contracts were made binding in this manner largely because of the company's unfortunate experiences with cancelations in 1920. At the same time, most factories turning out a similar product are doing very little business.

The A. B. C. Company, in spite of its large orders on hand, has not been able to operate its factory at more than 70 per cent of normal capacity, because of labor difficulties which it appears may continue for many months. These difficulties center largely around the question of a reduction in wages.

In order not to let its orders get so far behind, the A. B. C. Company has, from time to time, been having part of its work done by another company, the N. Company, whose business is slack. However, the goods produced by the N. Company go out under the trade-mark of the A. B. C. Company. This situation makes it necessary for the latter to watch more carefully the quality of the work done by the N. Company, as there is danger of inferior workmanship which might injure the goodwill of the A. B. C. Company. But the arrangement has been, upon the whole, a mutually satisfactory one because the N. Company, filling its own valleys in production by means of these orders, can afford to do the work even more cheaply than it could have been done by the A. B. C. Company. It should further be explained that the A. B. C. Company also owns a little subsidiary company which is engaged in making shoes of the A. B. C. brand. This plant is managed by a man who can always be depended upon for promptness and large output at a low cost, but who is not keeping up his work to the quality standard demanded by the A. B. C. Company.

On July 1, 1921, the audited statement of the A. B. C. Company showed a current ratio of fully 3 to 1. The cash on hand was relatively high, the inventory was being purposely kept very low, while the receivables, because of the contract provisions already referred to, were all of prime quality. The current liabilities were practically all in "accounts payable," averaging not more than ten days, as the company was taking all the cash discounts. Comparatively little was owed to the bank. The surplus reported was relatively smaller than it had been for some years, because of the losses which had been suffered in 1920. However, it had been considerably increased during the first six months of 1921, until it now amounted to somewhat more than 10 per cent of the total assets. For about a year no dividends had been declared on the common stock, though the surplus might have permitted a conservative dividend.

In July, 1921, therefore, with the first half year's record an excellent one, and with the prospect of a still better record for the succeeding six months or more, the question of declaring a common stock dividend was naturally raised. As already explained, the common stock is in the hands of a very few men, who are both officers and directors of the A. B. C. Company. In fact, three officers control the stock.

At a meeting held on July 15, 1921, the question of declaring a dividend of 20 per cent on the common stock, to cover the year's operations, was seriously discussed. It was felt that as practically no dividends had been paid in 1920 and as the 1921 business appeared to justify the policy, the stockholders were now entitled to their rewards. The declaration of a dividend of this amount would, of course, have necessitated a rather heavy payment to the preferred stockholders, so that the aggregate dividend payment would have required a large amount of cash. The company's cash position, however, was sufficiently strong to enable it to do this and still have left a very comfortable margin and a current ratio still in excess of 2 to 1. At this meeting, however, a very interesting division of opinion arose and several alternative policies were discussed.

Mr. A., one of the heaviest stockholders, who manages the production end of the business, is much in need of some ready money and is very desirous of having the high dividend declared. He prefers for the plant to continue to operate as at present, feeling that he will be able to put the large orders through within a reasonable time.

Mr. B., who is in charge of the sales end of the business, is absolutely opposed to A. in this matter. He has grown very much annoyed because of the pressure brought to bear on him by customers, whose orders are being frequently delayed, due to the lack of "capacity" production in the plant. He fears that if this condition continues the company will lose very valuable goodwill. His chief desire is to keep the company as strong as possible. Though there are at present no clouds on the horizon, he is not so optimistic as the others regarding the outlook for 1922. He is opposed to the declaration of any dividend at the present time and feels that the company should wait at least six months longer before taking up this matter.

B. urges, moreover, that the proper course for the company to follow is to relieve the present congestion in the plant and keep the goodwill of the customers, by investing the larger part of their cash in a new and cheaply constructed plant, which could be built in about six weeks' time at a town some distance away in an adjoining state, where an adequate labor supply can be readily secured.

This suggestion is considered an excellent one for several reasons. In the first place, the A. B. C. Company has always employed a number of carpenters and general repair men, who could generally supervise the construction of the new plant, thus greatly reducing the cost of building. Further, it would be possible for the company to send some of its idle machinery to the new plant. Also, as the job could be put through in a hurry, it is practically certain that the company could thereby keep itself in a strong position with the trade because of its ability to fill their orders more promptly.

Mr. C., who controls the purchasing end of the business, has troubles enough of his own, and takes no very active part in the discussion of policy. He feels, however, that it might be better merely to declare a small dividend at the present time, which would not make necessary the payment of additional dividends to the preferred stockholders. He then advises waiting until the end of the year before taking any other definite steps.

Mr. D., a junior officer of the company, has still another plan to present. He suggests that since their subsidiary company is so successful in quantity output and speedy production, though the quality tends to suffer somewhat, it would be well to divide the operations of the A. B. C. Company, which turns out two grades of shoes, so as to give all the low-grade work to the subsidiary. The subsidiary plant, however, is already working to full capacity, and the congestion could not be relieved by this change in policy unless an addition were made to the plant. Hence, D. advises that the cash now on hand be spent for extending the plant of the subsidiary company.

Mr. E., who is only slightly interested as a stockholder but whose opinion is usually given some weight, advises a still different policy. He thinks that it would be better to conserve the cash, probably paying no dividends at present, or at any rate a very low dividend. He suggests that the filling of orders might be speeded up by letting out more of the work of the A. B. C. Company to some of the other shoe companies whose plants are largely idle.

Such is the line-up of opinion in the directorate of the A. B. C. Company at the end of July, 1921. No action has yet been taken. Mr. A., the heaviest stockholder, is still vigorously contending for the high dividend. He has, however, now agreed with B. and D. that some kind of an expansion should be made in order to enable the A. B. C. Company to fill its orders more rapidly. This he thinks should be provided for by borrowing money or by selling more preferred stock.

Questions

1. Give your reasons specifically for agreeing or disagreeing with any one of the conflicting points of view expressed by the directors.

2. If the decision of the matter should be left in your hands as an impartial arbiter, what policy should you advise the A. B. C. Company to follow,

(*a*) With respect to declaring any dividend at all?

(*b*) With respect to the amount of the dividend declared?

(*c*) With respect to relieving the present congestion in the A. B. C. Company's plant?

3. Would your answer be any different if the preferred stock provisions did not have to be considered?

4. As a preferred stockholder, how would you feel about the matter?

5. Though this company's bank has not yet been consulted, what advice do you think it would give on the questions raised? Why?

Problem 203

How Large a Surplus Should a Concern Have?

An officer of a large investment house was on one occasion asked, "How large a surplus should the average industrial concern build up out of earnings?"

As he was uncertain what answer should be given, he accordingly made a study of the actual surpluses shown by fifty-seven leading industrial concerns in the United States at the end of 1918. These concerns were all engaged in different kinds of enterprise and their combined balance sheet showed total assets of $4,641,287,412. It was further found that the combined balance sheets disclosed a surplus equivalent to 18.11 per cent of the total assets (or liabilities.) As a result of these computations, the answer was made to the inquirer that obviously from 15 per cent to 20 per cent would be a very satisfactory proportion which the surplus should bear to the total assets.

A later study of the companies whose balance sheets were included in the analysis made by the investment house, reveals the fact that by June, 1921, seven of these corporations had passed both common and preferred dividends, nine others had passed their common dividends, two had reduced their common dividends, while three had never paid dividends on their common stock, and one had been absorbed by another company in order to avoid bankruptcy. This entire group of concerns was composed of those which are ordinarily regarded as among the financially strongest in the country.

A member of another investment house, not so large but even more conservative, expressed his opinion to the effect that, in the long run, for safe financing an industrial concern should put a dollar back into the business for every dollar paid out in dividends on common stock. This opinion is based, he says, on his study of the most conservatively financed concerns, with the longest record of success.

Questions

1. Based on the evidence given, should you consider it safe to assume that 18.11% of the assets is a satisfactory surplus for an industrial concern to build up?
2. Would the fact that a third of the companies cited were in more or less serious financial difficulties in the first part of 1921 influence your opinion on this matter?
3. Would you agree with the general rule laid down by the second investment house?
4. Should you consider it more or less desirable for a small industrial concern to build up a comparatively large surplus than for the same policy to be followed by a large concern?
5. Do you see any reasons for following a different policy in regard to the creation of a surplus for a public utility company than for an industrial concern?
6. How, in your opinion, should a surplus be invested?
7. Do you see any particular disadvantages which might result from the building up of a large surplus in a business?

Problem 204

Shall Competitors Be Bought Up With Surplus Funds?

The Z. Cotton Manufacturing Company found itself heavily stocked with raw cotton at the time when sales began to slump. The management, feeling less optimistic than its competitors, began to protect itself against the probable drop in prices by selling its cotton for future delivery, when there seemed to be no market for the finished goods. Accordingly, within a few months, while the competing mills were without orders and had all their resources tied up in inventory bought at top prices, the Z. Company had cleared out practically all of its inventory, had a large amount of cash on hand, and was ready to buy raw cotton at the bottom of the market.

The president of the Z. Company says that several questions having to do with the financial policy of the company are now being considered by his organization:

A. Shall the Z. Company cut its prices on cotton cloth to a point where many of its competitors will be forced into bankruptcy?

B. Should the Z. Company use some of the surplus funds which it now has to buy out its failing competitors?

C. Assuming that the Z. Company is agreeable to purchasing some of the competing mills, provided it can get them cheap, the question is raised, "When is a cotton mill cheap?"

At the present time it would cost two or three times as much to reconstruct a mill as before the war.

(*a*) Would a mill, therefore, be worth buying if it could be taken over at the pre-war cost of reproduction, less depreciation?

(*b*) Even if this low figure could be secured, would it be a wise financial policy to buy out competitors?

Questions

1. What advice would you give the president of the Z. Company on the various questions raised by him?

2. If you do not advise buying up competitors, just what would you advise the Z. Company to do with its surplus?

3. Do you think it advisable for a concern to follow a "fluctuating" dividend policy, or is it wiser to keep the common stock dividends fairly even from year to year? Does the nature of the business or the extent and character of its ownership affect your decision?

PART IV

FINANCIAL DIFFICULTIES AND THEIR SIGNIFICANCE

CHAPTER X

FINANCIAL INVOLVEMENTS, ADJUSTMENTS, RECEIVERSHIPS, BANKRUPTCIES, REORGANIZATIONS, ETC.

References:

*Dewing, *Corporate Promotions and Reorganizations*, 518–576.
Dewing, *Financial Policy of Corporations*, Vol. v., 13-65, 162–187.
*Ettinger and Golieb, *Credits and Collections*, 307–357.
*Lough, *Business Finance*, Part v.
*Lyon, *Corporation Finance*, Part ii., 220–307.
Mead, *Corporation Finance*, xxx–xxxii.
Mercantile Credits (The Ronald Press Company), 196–245.

IT has been the aim of this book to deal with the common financial problems of the small and medium-sized concerns. Yet, just as some of the greatest advances in physiological and medical science have been made possible by the examination of the abnormal and by the dissection of the dead body, so it is frequently easiest to illustrate the sound principles of Finance by calling attention to the difficulties which result when these principles are departed from. Furthermore, so few concerns are really successful, and so many of the smaller ones fail, that financial difficulties of some sort can almost be said to be a very common thing, particularly at present. It is hoped, therefore, that the following problems will help to drive home the lessons which the preceding problems have been meant to teach.

Exercise No. VI

What Has Been the Actual Financial Position of Business Concerns at the Time of Failure, Classified According to the Nature of the Business, and What Dividends Have the Creditors Received?

The following letter has been received from the partner of a large investment house:

I am very interested in securing from some source statistics covering a period of, say, ten years, in connection with the liquidation forced by business difficulties of various lines of jobbers and manufacturers. I thought possibly this might come under your research work.

In order to make myself clear, I might state that the information I am seeking is along the following lines: Suppose a wholesale grocery concern, which showed Capital and Surplus of $300,000, Quick Assets of $450,000, Fixed Assets of $50,000 and total current debt of $200,000 (these figures indicating a ratio of 2.25 of Quick Assets to Current Liabilities), should be forced to liquidate through conditions caused by crop failures, bank failures or other causes beyond their control, what has been the average results of the liquidations in respect to the payment of the indebtedness?

I took this matter up with credit insurance companies and also with both of the large mercantile agencies, but none of them had this particular information. I thought on account of the classification risks that the credit insurance companies would have it, but the only information which I could get from them was that in their experience (which, of course, was limited when compared to the mercantile agencies), they had found, for instance, in the jobbing lines that hardware liquidated to a greater extent than groceries.

(By consulting the records of the local Bankruptcy Court it should be possible for the student to make a significant study of this problem. A few preliminary suggestions of value can be secured from the Annual Number of *Dun's Review*, and particularly from the *Annual Report* of the Attorney General of the United States.)

Problem 205

The General Credit Situation in 1921

About the middle of December, 1920, the "economist" of one of the large New York banks wrote as follows:

"The position of most large businesses is exceedingly strong. They have 'ploughed under' a very high percentage of the abnormal profits of the past five years. Additions to corporate surpluses made out of profits have been incredible. On the face of the record more than $16,000,000,000 was added to corporate surpluses in the United States from 1914 to the end of 1919, and this has been on the basis of exceedingly conservative bookkeeping. Unincorporated businesses have added very much more, but the figures cannot be given. The most conservative bookkeeping policies have been followed; plant and other fixed assets have been generally estimated at pre-war values, while betterments, and even additions to plant, have often been charged to 'cost' rather than entered into capital account."

At practically the same time the president of a large credit organization wrote as follows:

"We have all heard too much about failures and rumors of failures.

* * * * * * * * * * *

"These general rumors of business troubles that have been circulated so freely in the market this season are an absolute insult to the intelligence of the average business man in a normal state of mind. I happen to have direct access to information on all concerns in every branch of industry, selling their notes to banks through note brokers. It might be of interest to you to know that 4,395 concerns offered their paper in the open market this year. Out of this number, the notes of only thirty-one concerns have been withdrawn from the market, after being offered, for credit reasons.

"At least fourteen of these have had no trouble at all. Their direct banking connections were found sufficient to take care of their requirements and their paper was withdrawn, as the ratio of quick assets to liabilities was not quite up to the open market standard.

"In all probability, twelve or thirteen of the remaining names will continue without interruption, while two or three will not pay in full, due to causes that would have been fatal ultimately under any circumstances."

In connection with these statements the following facts should be borne in mind. During the last three months of the year 1920 one of the leading mercantile agencies reports 3,498 business failures with liabilities aggregating $128,544,334. In amount of liabilities this was far in excess of any previous year in our history, not excepting the last quarter of 1893, when the record of failures was 4,824, with total liabilities of $95,430,529. These 1920 failures averaged almost twice as high in individual liabilities as in any previous year in our financial history. During the first six months of 1921 the same agency reports 9,035 failures, with aggregate liabilities of $310,671,000. In amount of liabilities the failures for the first half of 1921 have been about two-thirds greater than during a similar period in any preceding year. In actual number, for this period, the failures of 1921 have been exceeded only twice in our history.

In addition to the unprecedented seriousness of failures reported during these nine months, there have been innumerable extensions, reorganizations and adjustments of various sorts, which have saved both large and small businesses from going bankrupt. Some of these cases are commonly known in the financial world, such as that of the Goodyear Company, which in itself might have involved an excess of liabilities over assets amounting to at least $50,000,000, had it been allowed to fail. Innumerable other cases are being quietly handled by the banks through their private committees, or by mercantile creditors through adjustments of various sorts. In fact, the writer is in a position to know that the actual failures during the period mentioned would probably have been at least two or three times as great as those reported, had it not been for the unprecedented development of "financial cooperation" among business concerns and the banks during the past year.

Statistics available by the end of June, 1921, show that about seventy of our large and well-known and supposedly strong business companies, practically all engaged in manufacturing, with an outstanding capital stock of about $1,000,000,000, passed their dividends on common or preferred stock, or both, during the year 1921, subjecting the stockholders to a loss in income of about $25,000,000. A large number of other concerns passed their dividends during the last quarter of 1920. In addition to this extensive passing of dividends by concerns still solvent, a very large number of companies have either reduced their dividends or paid them in stock in the hope that future earnings may justify this policy.

Finally, it should be noted that during the first four months of 1921 business corporations in the United States issued more than $1,000,000,000 in new securities, about two-thirds of which was said to be for the purpose of raising "new capital," and the remainder for "refunding" purposes. However, a general analysis of the situation shows that by far the greater part of these issues meant "distress" financing. In the first place, many a concern was forced to refund outstanding issues of bonds and debentures because it was unable to maintain the ratio of current assets to current liabilities or of total assets to total liabilities, called for by the bond indentures. Hence there was no alternative but to do new financing or become bankrupt. In the second place, most of the "new capital" issues were either in the form of debenture bonds, with very stringent sinking fund or other protective provisions, or in the form of mortgage bonds. In fact, some of the largest and supposedly best managed corporations were forced to issue first-mortgage bonds in order to secure "new capital" to protect their current position, frequently because of the protective provisions of an earlier preferred stock issue. Most of the so-called "new" financing was merely a change in the nature of the obligation, from banking or open market loans, or from notes and accounts due to mercantile creditors, to mortgage loans. These loans, because of the high rates of interest at which they were floated and because of the extremely rigid protective features introduced, will in many instances hamper perfectly solvent concerns for many years.

Questions

1. In the light of the facts which have been given, how do you explain the quoted statements made by men who, from the nature of their positions, are supposed to be in intimate touch with the actual financial situation?

2. Does the fact that the notes of only a negligible proportion of all concerns selling their paper on the open market in 1920 were withdrawn for credit reasons after being offered, throw any light on the actual credit situation?

3. Does the fact that large amounts were added to corporate surpluses in the United States during the war period argue for the solvency of these concerns? Why or why not?

Problem 206

Will Failures Increase as Industry Revives?

In the spring of 1921 the following statement appeared in the financial columns of the *New York Evening Post*:

> "While trade is dull and producers and dealers seem content to drift along and merely take care not to rock the boat, many leaky business craft can manage to keep afloat, but when the tide turns and it becomes necessary to quit bailing and take to the oars such concerns will be submerged. Many firms that are able to hold together in a

slack season will later succumb to the blows of their more vigorous competitors. This will raise the rate of business mortality for a short time, but this should not be regarded as a bad sign. It means the elimination of the unfit, and the resulting failures are the cost of progress."

Question

Do you believe that the above reasoning is correct? Why?

Problem 207

How Far Should Creditor Cooperation be Carried in Critical Periods?

"Cooperation among creditors has unquestionably gone a long way towards ameliorating failures; and the wisdom of a liberal policy on the part of creditors at present is generally accepted. The suggestion is ventured, however, that an attitude of leniency is detrimental to the mutual interests of both debtor and creditor.

* * * * * * * * *

"Some of those who are now asking the indulgence of their creditors were enormously prosperous during the upswing in prices. Instead of building up a sinking fund or other surplus, they made additions or alterations to plant, or overexpanded their business. The result has been that the outgoing tide finds them well up on the beach. They do not accept their situation as the natural sequence of their own improvidence and of an era of abnormally high prices.

* * * * * * * * * *

"A manufacturer should not be expected to perform a banking function and cannot do so profitably, even at the banker's rate of interest. Too much is taken for granted by some embarrassed debtors."

(Reference: *Credit Monthly*, June, 1921, p. 32 ff.)

Question

1. Should you consider it a wise policy for creditors to invariably press those concerns whose present financial difficulties are the result of war-time over-expansion or failure to build up adequate reserves, and the like causes.

PROBLEM 208

IMPROVING THE CREDIT POSITION OF A SMALL, CLOSELY OWNED CONCERN BY JUGGLING THE SECURITIES

An old Massachusetts shoe manufacturing concern whose stock is closely held by a few individuals, owing to abnormal conditions prevailing during 1920, found its surplus (accumulated during several years of successful operation) completely wiped out, and a large deficit showing on the asset side of the annual statement. This company had always enjoyed a good reputation and was considered to be very conservatively managed. Its paper was readily sold on the open market, supported by well-balanced figures reflecting good earnings. The unfavorable financial statement would hereafter prevent the company from placing its paper on the open market, although it was perfectly solvent, having ample assets to meet its liabilities.

To meet the situation, the few stockholders agreed to cancel $100,000 of the common stock which they held. This enabled the company to wipe out its deficit and to draw up a new statement making a more attractive showing.

The following figures show approximately the condition of the company before and after stockholders had donated $100,000 of the common stock, which was canceled, and after an additional issue of $25,000 preferred stock exchanged for a note held by one of the officers of the company for money loaned by him to the corporation.

Assets

	Before	After
Cash	$57,000	$57,000
Receivables	86,000	86,000
Inventory	395,000	395,000
	$538,000	$538,000
Plant	159,000	159,000
Prepaid	20,000	20,000
Patents	13,000	13,000
Profit and loss deficit	99,000	......
	$829,000	$730,000

Liabilities

	Before	After
Bills payable	$200,000	$200,000
Accounts payable	28,000	28,000
	228,000	228,000
Due to endorser	50,000	25,000
	$278,000	$253,000
Capital Stock:		
Preferred	125,000	150,000
Common	426,000	326,000
Surplus		1,000
	$829,000	$730,000

Questions

1. What was the real significance of this action on the part of the stockholders?

2. Should you now expect it to be possible for this concern to secure additional credit?

3. Granting that most of the bills payable are commercial paper loans, and since these loans cannot be renewed at maturity, should you expect this company's bank to be willing to lend an amount sufficient to pay the maturing commercial paper?

4. Does this problem suggest any particular advantages which may accrue in times of financial stress to the closely owned business?

Problem 209

Improving the Current Position by a Readjustment of Ownership

The A. Company, engaged in the paper and pulp business, was rapidly expanding and always suffered from the lack of working capital. Toward the end of 1915, when it was necessary to make out the annual financial statement, the company found that its current assets were not enough in excess of its current liabilities to enable it to borrow from the banks. The ratio was about 1.25 to 1.

It should further be explained that the A. Company owned extensive timber-lands, owned the entire capital stock of a subsidiary, the B. Company, having a par value of $500,000, and one-half of the capital stock of a small semi-defunct company, C. The other half of the C. Company stock was owned by one of the stockholders of the A. Company, who also owned a considerable amount of timber-land.

The A. Company had outstanding first-mortgage bonds on its plant and timber-lands. The indenture of these bonds provided for the release of any portion of the property originally covered by the mortgage and the substitution therefor of cash or of other property at 75 per cent of its cost or value, whichever was lower. After puzzling over the situation for some time, the president of the A. Company decided to improve his current position in the following manner:

The stockholder who owned one-half of the stock of the C. Company was persuaded to sell a large amount of his timber-lands to the C. Company, and the A. Company agreed also to sell an equal amount of its timber-lands to the C. Company. The aggregate value of the lands thus to be sold, at a fair valuation amounted to several hundred thousand dollars. Payment for the lands was made by issuing first-mortgage bonds of the C. Company to the A. Company for its portion of the timber-lands, while the stockholder agreed to take second-mortgage bonds, plus a 10 per cent bonus in second-mortgage bonds, for his portion of the timber-lands sold to the C. Company. The first-mortgage bonds were readily marketed by the A. Company, which thus secured $500,000 in cash and was able to show a very creditable current position at the end of the year. In order to comply with the provisions of its mortgage indenture, the A. Company dissolved the B. Company, whose stock it owned, and substituted the physical property of the erstwhile B. Company for the timber-lands sold.

Questions

1. Is this method of raising working capital to be approved from the point of view of the lending banks?

2. From the point of view of the A. Company, examine the strength or weakness of the steps taken.

Problem 210

The Part which Protective Provisions Surrounding a Security Issue May Play in a Company's Solvency

The . . . . Company has sufficient inventories on hand to take care of its normal manufacturing program for six months. However, sales have almost wholly stopped and it is probable that business will not pick up again for at least three months. If the company should shut down completely, its overhead expenses would still be $250,000 per month and there is very little cash in the treasury. The direct labor expenses when the plant is running at normal capacity would be $75,000 per month.

The net quick assets of this company early in 1921 were $1,600,000. The current liabilities amounted to $500,000.

The company has outstanding $1,000,000 in debenture bonds. The bond indenture provides that the company shall maintain net quick assets equal to at least 150 per cent of the outstanding debentures, and that failure to maintain this ratio shall constitute a default, in which case the bonds shall become due and payable.

Questions

1. Should this company close down the plant or continue to operate at normal capacity?

2. Do you see any method of avoiding a receivership without new financing?

3. Assuming that the company has outstanding $1,000,000 in preferred stock instead of debenture bonds, but with the same security provisions, would its present financial difficulties be any less serious? Why?

Problem 211

Avoiding a Serious Financial Dilemma Through a Debenture Issue

The L. Company is engaged in making several types of machine tools, together with accessories. About 50 per cent of the business in volume is normally carried by the accessories, while the remainder is divided between two types of machines for which there is an alternate demand. While the volume is about equally divided between accessories and the machines, about 80 per cent of the profits are ordinarily made on the accessories, which normally must be bought by those who are using the machines. Before 1914 the business of this company was relatively unprofitable. In this year, however, the management was changed, and for the next four or five years the concern was an excellent money-maker.

In 1919, acting on the advice of experts in the field, the management decided to expand its plant with a view to providing sufficient room for manufacturing in larger quantities, as unit costs could thus be considerably decreased and as it would then be possible to make more speedy deliveries. Orders were at the time booked far in advance, and it was a real source of annoyance to customers that they had to wait so long to have their orders filled. The plant was accordingly increased in size until the balance sheet item for real estate was doubled.

When the depression in this line of business became marked about the middle of 1920, the new plant was erected but was not yet equipped with machinery and fixtures. Fortunately, also, no commitments had been made for the purchase of equipment. The business depression found this company in July, 1920, with an inventory larger than normal in quantity, and naturally from two to three times larger than normal in value. In August there was a sudden change in demand for the machines being made, which left the concern with a very badly balanced inventory. The financial situation confronted by the concern may be summed up as follows:

The business was capitalized at $400,000 preferred stock (cumulative at 6 per cent), and $350,000 common stock. Both the preferred stock and common stock was held largely by the same parties, about thirty stockholders constituting from 15 to 20 per cent of the entire number of stockholders and owning a majority of the stock. There was no mortgage on the plant, the expansion having been financed through personal loans of several well-to-do stockholders and some bank loans. The volume of sales of the company reached a peak of more than $600,000 in 1919 and shrank very rapidly during the year 1920, until during the last quarter there was an actual loss in operation, after interest on current loans was paid, but without allowing for depreciation, and other charges, of $30,000. Preferred dividends were passed at this time.

In December, 1920, in order to get the jump on its competitors, who it was thought would probably reduce their price from 12 per cent to 15 per cent, a price reduction of 33⅓ per cent was made on the machines manufactured. No reduction, however, was made on the appliances, which were almost invariably sold along with the machines or to those who were already using the same. This reduction, of course, tended to hasten the turnover of the company's inventory, even though at a loss.

It should further be stated that the company had had very few cancelations of orders during this period, because of the fact that it sold principally to 18 or 20 dealers who were secured by contract against a drop in the market, provision having been made for reimbursing the customer in case of price reductions. Accompanying this guarantee against loss from price reduction were stipulations as follows: (*a*) a dealer would have the exclusive right to sell in his own territory, (*b*) he should not handle competing goods, and (*c*) he should carry a complete line of accessories.

The current ratio of this company, which in January, 1920, had been more than 2 to 1, had been reduced to a little more than 1 to 1 by the early part of 1921. The current liabilities at this time were composed as follows: 52 per cent due to home banks, 20 per cent due on note to large stockholders, and the balance of 28 per cent was covered by open accounts in the trade, accrual items, and the like. The gross business of the company had dropped from $600,000 in 1919 to an estimated $60,000 in the first half of 1921. Further, there was an operating loss of $33,000 during the first quarter of 1921, and a probable loss of $3,000 during the second quarter.

The problem which confronted the management in the spring of 1921, therefore, was apparently either bankruptcy proceedings or some kind of financing which would improve the current position and enable them to pay off their trade creditors and part of their bank loans which had been several times extended. The following plan was worked out:

The company offered to its preferred and common stockholders \$300,000 in 10-year, 8 per cent debentures to be subscribed to in cash at 93½ or to be taken at par, 75 per cent in cash and 25 per cent in preferred stock. (The preferred stock was not listed on any exchange and was normally very inactive, though there had been a few recent sales at about 45).

The results of this offer to the stockholders were as follows: About \$95,000 of debentures were sold to about 30 of the heavier stockholders, two of whom did not own any preferred stock. Only three of these stockholders paid for their bonds in preferred stock in accordance with the arrangement made. The others paid cash at the rate of \$93.50 per \$100 in debentures.

This financing resulted in an improvement of the current position by about \$80,000, brought about by the exchange of the stockholders' notes for debentures to the extent of \$50,000, and an increase in cash by about \$30,000. In all, about \$10,000 in preferred stock was retired.

Questions

1. Was this company justified in 1919 in expanding its plant for the reasons given?

2. Was it a wise policy for this company to have guaranteed its dealers against loss, even though by so doing cancelations were generally avoided?

3. Do you consider that the company adopted the best method of getting out of its present financial difficulties?

4. Can you explain why only three of the stockholders who subscribed to the debenture issue exchanged their preferred stock for bonds in the proportion allowed?

Problem 212

Possible Consequences of Heavy Commitments

When prices were tending rapidly downward, when purchases were falling off, and supposedly good contracts were being canceled, the A. B. Company, a cotton-manufacturing concern of high repute, found itself in the following financial condition so far as its current position was concerned:

Quick Assets

Cash	$ 500,000
Accounts receivable	950,000
Bills receivable (from customers)	100,000
Merchandise inventory:	
Raw material	1,500,000
Semi-finished goods	900,000
Finished goods	2,550,000
	$6,500,000

Quick Liabilities

Accounts payable	$ 275,000
Notes payable	2,825,000
Reserve for taxes	140,000
	$ 3,240,000

This statement indicates a current position of more than 2 to 1, which in a good cotton mill is usually considered highly satisfactory. The company had been making money during the first half of the year 1920, and as indicated by the reserve for taxes has been highly prosperous. The surplus and undivided profits amount to $250,000. As a result of the caution of the management, a reserve of $300,000 has been set up against possible depreciation in merchandise inventory. The capital, all paid in, amounts to $3,000,000.

Upon investigation, it was found that this company had earlier made commitments to purchase cotton at the high price then prevailing. This would call for the payment of about $5,000,000. The business of this concern practically closed down in the autumn of 1920, while the price of cotton inside of three months dropped about 50 per cent. Even though there were no other increase in liabilities, the company would be subject to a shrinkage of about 50 per cent on the merchandise inventory which it had on hand in August, 1920, and of fully 50 per cent on the new cotton which it was under contract to purchase. In other words, if the mill should continue to take in raw cotton according to its agreement, it would by the end of the year increase its quick liabilities by about $5,000,000, while its quick assets, on account of the shrinkage on the merchandise on hand, would have increased very little, if at all.

Questions

1. If you were the president of this company, would you have canceled your contracts when you found the price of cotton dropping so rapidly? If not, what would you have done?

2. As the banker of this concern, what advice would you give?

Problem 213

Threatened Failure Due to "Overbuying"

The . . . Leather Company had been conservatively managed over a period of years. It had the highest credit rating among the banks and the trade. Its stock was largely held by a few wealthy men, though there was a sprinkling of small stockholders. Acting on advices which had been given by people in the trade and on various reports by the United States Department of Commerce, the company invested very heavily in inventories in 1919, placing orders for a large quantity of hides from the Argentine. The deliveries came in gradually after several months.

In the meantime, on account of the credit conditions prevailing and the high prices, the sale of shoes was practically stopped. The manufacturers who had been placing orders with the leather company curtailed or canceled their purchases, so that in less than a year the . . . Company was left high and dry with practically no working capital but its inventory, which earlier in the year had been valued at about $8,000,000. Late in 1920, however, due to the drop in the price of leather, the inventory was cut in half and the company was forced to take a loss of about $4,000,000. This loss wiped out the accumulated surplus of years, thus reducing the current ratio to little more than 1 to 1. Notes to the banks for large amounts were coming due, and it seemed that the concern would be thrown into bankruptcy.

It was apparent that now when hides had reached practically the lowest price in history, the company might be able to recoup some of its earlier losses by buying at the current market and holding for higher prices. Not only would this have proved a safe speculation, but it probably would have been possible in a year or two to effect a great saving on the cost of production by purchasing surplus hides now. Under the circumstances, however, this policy seemed wholly impossible, as no further credit could be secured.

Question

1. What, under the circumstances, can this concern do in order to regain a solvent position?

Problem 214

How Far Should the Stockholders Go in Their Attempts to Save a Company from Failure?

The National Conduit and Cable Company was organized in 1917 out of previously existing companies which had apparently been successful. Its capitalization consisted of 250,000 shares of no par value common stock, marketed at $35 per share, and $5,000,000 first-mortgage, sinking-fund, ten-year, 6 per cent bonds. The bond indenture provided that an annual payment of $125,000 should be made to the sinking fund for retirement of bonds, either by purchase in the open market or by calling by lot at a price which after April 1, 1919, should not exceed $105 and interest. The indenture also provided that the company "shall at all times maintain net quick assets at a figure in excess of the aggregate bonded indebtedness."

Almost from the beginning this company failed to make money, though its various balance sheets showed assets ranging from fifteen to twenty million dollars. Its net sales for the year 1920 were $13,733,903, as compared with sales of $10,557,836 in 1919. On April 7, 1921, the following notice was sent to the bondholders by a Protective Committee representing the principal bondholders:

> The statement of the financial condition of the Company as of December 31, 1920, which has been filed with the Trustee pursuant to the terms of the mortgage, shows that the Company is not complying with its covenant to maintain net quick assets, as defined in the mortgage, at an amount in excess of the outstanding bonds, which at that date amounted to $4,438,500 face value. The deficiency was in excess of $900,000 according to the statement and has since increased.
>
> We are advised that the Trustee has served written notice of this default on the Company and that the period of grace will expire on or about April 19th, after which date remedies under the mortgage may be invoked against the Company.
>
> The unfavorable results of the Company's past operations indicates that the existing deficiency in net quick assets, which already endangers the bondholders, is more likely still further to increase than to diminish. In these circum-

stances, and in view of the fact that the liquidation of the Company may be advisable, it is important that the holders of the First Mortgage, 6 Per Cent, Ten-Year, Sinking Fund Gold Bonds unite for the protection of their interests. The undersigned, representing a large amount of the bonds, have agreed to act as a Committee for that purpose.

Sherman & Sterling, Counsel.	CHARLES E. MITCHELL, President, The National City Co.
Sherman Allen, Secretary, No. 55 Wall Street New York City.	JAMES H. PERKINS, Montgomery & Co. WILLIAM O. GAY, W. O. Gay & Co. *Committee.*

THE NATIONAL CITY BANK OF NEW YORK, Depositary,
No. 55 Wall Street, New York City.

About the same time a committee of the stockholders was endeavoring, if possible, to save the company from bankruptcy. They employed an engineering firm to look into the company's finances and prospects. This firm estimated that if $1,500,000 new money were put into the concern, it could, after a period of six months, show net earnings of $500,000 a year, which would be sufficient to pay their interest and leave about $1 per share for the stock.

It was admitted by this committee that the National Conduit and Cable Company had lost $1,063,438 in 1919 and $1,222,752 in 1920. In fact, the balance sheet as of December 31, 1920, showed a profit and loss deficit, accumulated since 1917, of $3,178,869.

In the face of this situation the Stockholders' Protective Committee recommended that the stockholders put up the extra money indicated, amounting to about $6 per share, on condition that the bondholders accept less drastic provisions regarding the security of their bonds than now existed. Various other methods were also suggested for solving the difficulty through reorganization of some sort which would improve the current position. One suggestion was an 8 per cent cumulative preferred stock issue. Another step talked of was the issue of a new mortgage carrying a higher rate of interest, the proceeds of which might be used to retire the bonds already outstanding. At this time, however, it was found that these bonds had been selling recently on the open market at 60 and that the common stock, which is listed on the New York Exchange, was quoted at from $1\frac{1}{2}$ to 2.

Questions

1. What light, if any, does this problem throw on the possible financial results of combinations?
2. As a bondholder, what course would you follow?
3. Granting that the bondholders do not force liquidation, should you advise the stockholders to put up the additional amount of money supposedly needed to save the situation?
4. Of the other steps suggested, which would seem to you to be most feasible?
5. What do you expect the financial future of this company to be?

Problem 215

Banker Control and the Credit Problem in Times of Financial Stress

The Oak Company is engaged in the tanning and handling of a kind of leather which ordinarily has a very good market. The affairs of the concern have been very closely kept, inasmuch as the chief officers are important bankers who are largely using their own bank for financing the business. Recently, however (April 1, 1921), on account of rumors which have been afloat, some of the banks holding the commercial paper of this company, as well as some which had rediscounted their commercial loans, began to make inquiries into the actual financial condition of the company. Heretofore the excellent reputation of the bankers interested in the concern had been sufficient to enable the company to sell its paper on the open market and to enjoy the rediscount market without any question.

After much difficulty, the following statement of condition as of February 1, 1921, was secured:

STATEMENT OF OAK COMPANY
February 1, 1921

Assets	
Cash	$43,500
Accounts receivable	385,000
Merchandise	3,512,000
Land and buildings	613,500
Investments	93,500
Prepaid items	40,000
	$4,687,500
Liabilities	
Notes payable for borrowed money (including the open market)	$2,364,000
Accounts payable (including trade acceptances)	155,500
Reserved for taxes, wages	47,500
Dividends	18,000
Capital:	
Preferred stock	1,250,000
Common stock	288,500
Surplus	564,000
	$4,687,500

The outside bankers holding the paper of this company were considerably alarmed at the situation presented. The officers of the bank which was lending most heavily on straight commercial loans were then appealed to for information as to how the affairs actually were standing. However, the replies were rather elusive, and about all that could be learned was that the company had in three months' time reduced its indebtedness to this bank by $400,000, though it was admitted that practically no business was being done. It was further stated that there was normally, and would be ultimately, a very good demand for their product and that the company would be one of the very first to profit when business conditions were changed for the better. The opinion was given that unquestionably the company was, considering business conditions, in a very satisfactory condition and would soon be in a really strong position.

On the same day that this information was received from the prominent banker who was financially interested in the concern, word was also received from a former minor officer of the company, whose record with them seems to have been unquestioned and whose reputation with his present employers is of the best, to the effect that he knew personally that the larger part of the inventory of this company was unsalable, some of it having been ruined in handling, and some having seriously depreciated as a result of long storage.

The problem now confronting the outside banks is whether they should consent to renew their loans and rediscounts, as the company is obviously not in a position to "clean up"; and the problem confronting the banker officers of the concern is, what steps they shall take if the outside banks demand their money.

Questions

1. From an analysis of the statement presented what conclusions do you draw regarding the character and capacity of the management of this concern?

2. From the problem as presented, what conclusions, if any, do you draw regarding the advantages or disadvantages of a good-sized industrial company's having for its officers important officials of banks,

(*a*) From the point of view of the industry itself?

(*b*) From the point of view of the banking community?

3. What do you expect the financial future of this concern to be?

Problem 216

Difficulties Arising Through Attempting to Finance an Expansion by Means of Current Loans and Dealer Credit

A Chicago confectionery manufacturing concern, with prospects of excellent business ahead, made extensive additions to its plant which greatly increased its current indebtedness. Owing to the general slump in this particular line of business, they were caught with a large amount of merchandise which they could not move, and were pressed by their creditors who had furnished the material, labor and equipment for the plant extension. In this position the company was unable to get further bank credit, unless the present large creditors would be willing to wait for their money and would give some assurance that they would not push their claims until a definite future date.

The company then issued a sufficient amount of three-year, 7 per cent notes, secured by a first mortgage on its land, buildings and equipment, which were accepted by some of the large creditors in settlement of their claims. Others were sold to furnish cash to enable the company to continue through the depression prevailing in this particular industry.

The following figures show the condition of the company before and after placing a $245,000 mortgage on its plant and fixtures, against which were issued three-year notes, of which a large part were given to creditors to settle their claims on account of new construction and equipment furnished.

Assets

	Before	After
Cash	$12,000	$8,000
Receivables	67,000	125,000
Inventory	153,000	169,000
	$232,000	$302,000
Plant	$592,000	$617,000
Prepaid	49,000	24,000
Capitalization expense		67,000
	$873,000	$1,010,000

Liabilities

Bills payable	$25,000	$15,000
Accounts payable	224,000	115,000
Accrued	34,000	22,000
	$283,000	$152,000
Mortgage notes		245,000
	$283,000	$397,000
Capital Stock:		
Preferred	$443,000	$443,000
Common	44,000	44,000
Surplus	103,000	126,000
	$873,000	$1,010,000

Questions

1. Indicate the fundamental mistakes made by this company before they got into financial difficulties.

2. What is your opinion of the method taken by this concern to secure temporary relief, and what do you expect the outcome to be?

3. As a mercantile creditor, would you have been willing to have your claims settled in the way indicated?

4. Should a commercial bank ever knowingly make loans for fixed capital purposes?

Problem 217

Shall a Strong Concern Which is the Victim of Hard Luck be Allowed to Fail?

The Peerless Confectionery Company of Philadelphia had outstanding $340,000 in preferred stock and $100,000 in common stock. A considerable amount of the stock was still owned by the members of the private banking house which had originally financed the concern. No new financing had been done since the outbreak of the war. The business of this company was very well managed and had proved to be extremely profitable during the war. In 1919, net earnings before the payment of taxes amounted to more than $800,000. After the payment of $250,000 in excess profits taxes, net earnings available for dividends amounted to more than $550,000. The earnings of this year were typical of the war-time earnings. Some of the common stock was sold early in 1920 at $1,200 per share.

As a result of the inconvenience and delay which had been caused largely by the conservative purchasing policy of this company during the preceding year, as well as because of the great difficulties encountered in securing needed commodities, the company in 1920 began to buy more raw materials, so that it would not have to turn away or delay its orders. Finding that they could buy more cheaply by taking a whole cargo, they placed a large order for cocoa beans. They also purchased sugar and peanuts in considerable quantities. In addition they committed themselves for these large purchases at war-time prices.

The company's affairs became seriously involved because of the strike of shipping employees early in the year, which resulted in holding up for many weeks some of the shipments which they were to receive. Consequently, an attempt was made to secure additional cocoa beans from Europe and a large cargo was contracted for in Spain. Immediately afterwards, however, there was a serious strike and a "revolution" in Spain which delayed shipment for several weeks, so that the company was forced to pick up some large shipments elsewhere in order to carry on its business.

The outcome was that late in 1920 the company became stocked up with an unusually large amount of inventory, at a time when prices were rapidly dropping and business was speedily declining. The result of the year's operations indicated a loss due to cancelations, inventory shrinkage, and the like, of $1,400,000. Cocoa beans which were bought at 19½ cents per pound in 1920 could in the early part of 1921 be purchased for a little more than 5 cents; peanuts which had been bought in large quantities at 14 to 15 cents per pound could now be bought at about 3 cents, and sugar laid in at $22\frac{1}{2}$ cents per pound could be purchased for 5 or 6 cents per pound.

This concern's current liabilities early in 1921 amounted to more than $2,000,000, the major part of which was owed to the banks either on straight commercial loans or on banker's acceptances covering the import of goods, and the company was at this time practically insolvent.

Questions

1. Do you see any means whereby this concern can avoid bankruptcy? If so, what steps should be taken?

Problem 218

Attempting to Save a Concern Engaged in the Cuban Trade by a Further Extension of Bank Loans

The Y. Company is a partnership in Baltimore engaged in the shoe jobbing business. It is, however, practically a "one-man concern," having in 1919 a net worth of about $300,000. This concern did business principally with foreign countries and was particularly interested in the Cuban export trade. Early in 1920 business was booming in Cuba and everyone was spending liberally. In fact, most of the shoes were being shipped to Cuba at this time, and the banks apparently considered the credit of a concern thus engaged in the export trade particularly good. The company accordingly had lines of credit with three banks in the city to the extent of about $100,000 each, most of which were being used to the limit. After the "sugar crisis" came in the autumn of 1920, the concern found itself at the end of the year in the following condition:

Assets

Inventory	$190,000
Receivables	400,000
Cash	10,000
Miscellaneous	10,000
	$610,000

Liabilities

Notes payable to banks	$300,000
Accounts payable	125,000
Trade acceptances and miscellaneous payables	25,000
Partners' capital	160,000
	$610,000

Of the receivables, approximately $300,000 was due from customers in Cuba. These receivables were for the time being practically worthless. It was perfectly apparent that only a small proportion of them would be paid. Further, in the course of a few months, fully one-third of the receivables turned back into merchandise as the company managed to get back some of the goods already sold to customers who now were bankrupt.

During the first five months of 1921 about $50,000 was collected from Cuba. This was used to cut down the bank loans. Also, the company opened up several retail stores in order to dispose of the returned merchandise at a great sacrifice. It does not appear, however, that more than $25,000 can be realized on the $100,000 worth of merchandise thus being disposed of. So far as the inventory in this country is concerned, the home market, which had never been considered seriously, is a very uncertain element.

A number of the smaller mercantile creditors are now pressing the company and threaten to throw it into bankruptcy. The banks, however, have agreed to loan further to the Y. Company. A plan is now being worked out, in accordance with which the company is offering to pay its mercantile creditors a "composition" of fifty cents on the dollar, which is probably decidedly more than the dividend which would be received as a result of bankruptcy proceedings, since all unsecured creditors would then share alike. The bankers think that they will ultimately be able to work out of their difficulties, though it will be a very long pull.

Questions

1. As a financial expert analyze the financial weaknesses of this concern in its period of prosperity.
2. Do you think it is following the proper method of solving its present problems?
3. As a mercantile creditor, would you be willing to accept the "composition" offered?
4. As the manager of this concern, how should you expect to raise the money to pay off the mercantile creditors?
5. What is your opinion of the policy being followed by the banks?

Problem 219

The Reorganization of a Cotton Manufacturing Concern by a Bankers' Committee

A banker presents the following problem:

The . . . . Company is a cotton manufacturing concern whose principal business during the past year or two has been the manufacture of tire fabric. The following statement shows the condition of this company as of April 1, 1921, at about which time they passed into the hands of a bankers' committee:

STATEMENT OF THE . . . COMPANY
April 1, 1921

Assets		
Cash on hand and on deposit	$653,521	
Accounts receivable	660,508	
Merchandise	3,189,136	
Current Assets		$4,503,165
Real estate and buildings		1,967,615
Investments		639,115
Prepaid expenses		83,800
Treasury stock		52,531
Goodwill		400,000
		$7,646,226
Liabilities		
Notes payable for borrowed money	$2,710,000	
Accounts payable	248,715	
Accrued liabilities	49,255	
Taxes	150,000	
Current Liabilities		$3,157,970
Capital:		
First preferred		$1,420,500
Second preferred		974,900
Common		703,000
Surplus		1,389,856
		$7,646,226

In addition to the figures given above the company had manufacturing contracts of about $12,000,000, and had outstanding commitments for cotton of about $5,000,000, against which they had advanced $1,000,000, the present market for this cotton being about one-third less than at the time of contract. Under ordinary conditions their cotton contracts would have taken care of their business for about four months.

The company were borrowing from the banks about $2,160,000, against which they had lines of credit with their banks of about $2,200,000. Besides this, they were owing for paper sold through the brokers about $550,000.

The company's receivables were all good and the merchandise item in their statement included the

$1,000,000 paid against cotton. On the remainder of the merchandise they would undoubtedly have to take about a 33⅓ per cent shrinkage. The item of "investment" was practically all made up of the stocks of subsidiary companies.

The plan of agreement put through by the Committee was substantially along these lines:

To stop paying the paper placed by the brokers, these notes to rank the same as the obligations of the company's bankers. The banks are to extend the full amount of loans until May, 1922, with interest at 8 per cent. Merchandise creditors are to extend until November 1, 1921, with interest at 8 per cent. Cotton and yarn people agreed to postpone delivery until May 1, 1922. Whatever cotton is withdrawn is to be paid for by a preferred obligation of the company running three months, for the market value of the cotton at the present time. The difference between this price and the contract price is to be covered by a note payable May 1, 1922, and ranking equally with the other extended notes of the company. No new cotton shall be bought until all existing cotton contracts have been taken up, unless a quality different from that contracted for is needed.

Questions

1. Why should this concern have been taken over by the banker's committee?
2. What is your opinion of the equitableness of the plan of agreement put through by the Committee?

Problem 220

How Shall a Company be Saved from Bankruptcy, Part of Whose Business is Good and Part of Which is Being Carried on at a Loss?

The S. Leather Company, a closely owned corporation, has owned and operated a tannery at the city of W. for more than fifteen years. Its practice was to tan leather on contract, and also to buy hides in its own name for tanning and subsequent sale. In order to finance its operations, the company was in the habit of issuing drafts to be accepted by bankers and banking corporations, drawn at ninety days' sight. Sometimes hides in the warehouse waiting tanning operations would be pledged to secure the acceptances, and at other times the acceptances would be made against a shipment of the tanned hides. In addition to this use of "bankers' acceptances" it was customary, also, for the company to borrow from several banks without security.

Late in 1919, the market for leather began to decline rapidly, and the S. Leather Company was facing the possible loss of its large inventory, together with the cancelation of orders for tanned hides. However, the immediately maturing loans were renewed and the banks carried the company for eleven months longer. During this time the leather market became exceedingly dull, so that the secured creditors found themselves with box leather on their hands which had declined in value to an unprecedentedly low figure and for which there was practically no market at any price.

The balance sheet of this company for December, 1920, shows that the capital was badly impaired; current liabilities at the time exceeding the estimated current assets by $26,000. At the end of the year, the company had on hand a large stock of black box leather, but in addition found itself with a considerable number of orders to do tanning on contract. It owed the banks $465,000, of which $125,000 was considered "secured," as there was back of the debt a pledge of box leather which ordinarily would have furnished more than a sufficient margin of safety for the loan. The mercantile creditors were comparatively few in number and their claims were not large.

At this time the eight interested bankers came together to plan for a reorganization of the S. Co., since it had no money with which to carry on operations. Moreover, on account of the decline in the value of the property and the probability of continued decrease in prices, the current assets were estimated to be insufficient to liquidate the bank obligations. Even the banks which had demanded pledges of leather now really found themselves in the position of unsecured creditors. Consequently, payment of a large part of the company's obligations would have to depend upon the problematical future earnings, if it were allowed to continue in business.

Upon investigation it was found that the stock of leather which the company had on hand, and part of which it had pledged, when given a reasonable market value was worth not more than 75 per cent of the advances made against it. On the other hand, the company had plenty of contracts to do tanning but not money for carrying on the operation, whereas most tanneries found it difficult at the time to secure orders enough to keep their plants in operation.

It should be explained that this "contract" tanning was carried on by the following method. The hides were shipped on consignment to the S. Leather Company, which put them through the tanning process and then sold them, receiving 5 per cent commission on the net sales price, in addition to being paid for the cost incurred in tanning. From the proceeds of the sale the company reimbursed itself for tanning, took its selling commission, and turned over the balance to the owners of the hides. There had been no losses on the contract work and the company had always promptly paid off its debts to the owners of the hides.

The question which the bankers now had to face was whether the business should be allowed to continue, in the hope that future earnings would provide for their reimbursement, or whether it should be wound up and a *pro rata* distribution of assets be made before prices of leather should drop further. If the company were to be allowed to continue in business, an additional loan of $50,000 or more would have to be made immediately in order to allow tanning operations to be carried on.

Questions

1. Indicate clearly how you think this problem should be solved:
   (*a*) From the point of view of the mercantile creditors,
   (*b*) From the point of view of the company itself,
   (*c*) From the point of view of the banks?
2. Would your answer be the same,
   (*a*) If the stock were widely held,
   (*b*) If the mercantile creditors were numerous?
3. If the bank loans were relatively small and the "accounts payable" large, what would be your solution?

Problem 221

Bankruptcy of a Small Concern and Reorganization by Its Bank

The M. Company was a one-man concern engaged in making elevators and dumb-waiters as well as in repair work on elevators. The business had developed largely out of original repair shop work until it had become a very prosperous small company in 1918. The owner was an excellent mechanic and a man of unquestioned integrity.

Owing to war demands practically all the foundries which supplied castings and various accessories needed in the construction of elevators were busy to capacity and had orders far ahead. The M. Company, therefore, found it almost impossible to secure needed materials, and in order to get them at all it was necessary to pay extremely high prices.

Consequently, the owner, having more land than he needed for his assembling plant, decided that he would himself construct a small foundry to supply his needs and to enable him to expand his business more rapidly, without any of the uncertainties and losses which seemed inevitable while he was forced to "beg" for his materials. Accordingly, late in 1919, the M. Company, without consulting the only bank from which it had ever borrowed, and which, on account of the war-time prosperity, had been scarcely resorted to by the company for loans during the last two or three years, began to construct a foundry which it was expected would cost from $40,000 to $50,000. As bills came due covering the cost of construction, all the available cash of the M. Company was used up, and they also began to put off some of their creditors in order to pay the new bills incurred for construction of plant.

Early in 1920, when the job was about half done, the company found that unless they could raise more money they were in danger of being forced into a receivership by their various creditors. At this time, therefore, they appealed to their bank for advice, but their current position was so weak that not more than a few thousand dollars additional could be raised on a straight commercial loan. Finally, the bank, thinking that the M. Company would probably work its way out if business continued to be reasonably good, agreed to take a first mortgage on the entire plant to the extent of about $35,000, and thus tide them over immediate difficulties. Within a few months, however, business conditions had become so strained that the M. Company was again wholly tied up.

The bank was their chief creditor. There were in addition about 200 small mercantile creditors. The approximate financial condition of the company at this time was as follows:

Assets

Plant, etc.	$80,000
Receivables	10,000
Material in process	18,000
	$108,000

Liabilities

Capital stock	$10,000
Mortgage	35,000
Notes payable	40,000
Accounts payable	23,000
	$108,000

In view of the fact that the assets still apparently exceeded the liabilities the concern was not yet technically bankrupt. Consequently, in order to save the business if possible, an equity receivership was arranged by the chief creditors so that the assets might be "conserved and increased" for the benefit of all.

The manager and owner of the business then endeavored to effect some kind of settlement with his creditors, which would enable him to continue solvent. After trying different plans, he finally asked them to take 8 per cent cumulative preferred stock for the amount of their claims against the company. This stock was to be redeemed out of the first earnings of the company, and provision was to be made whereby a portion of the issue would be retired every six months. It was necessary, however, that all the creditors agree to this "composition," as otherwise it could not be made legally binding.

Eventually, 95 per cent of the creditors, both in number and amount, agreed to the proposition, but one creditor to whom the company owed about $2,000, and two or three very small ones, refused to give their assent. Hence this plan could not be carried through. By this time, however, the liabilities had slightly increased. On a revaluation there was enough shrinkage in the assets, particularly in the "materials in process," so that the liabilities somewhat exceeded the assets, and the concern was now actually insolvent beyond a doubt.

Hence the case was taken over from the equity court to the bankruptcy court, whereupon the lending bank, as the only secured creditor, discovered that an offer exactly like that made during the receivership would be legally binding if accepted by the *majority* of the creditors. Inasmuch as it appeared that on any forced sale a dividend of not more than 20 per cent could be realized, the same creditors who had earlier agreed to the composition offer of preferred stock to the full extent of their claims again accepted the offer. This was confirmed by the court and thus all debts of the company, except the mortgage due to the bank, were paid. The technical change effected really resulted in the creation of a new company with much greater capital and no current liabilities.

The corporation was turned back from the bankruptcy court to be managed under the direction of a committee of three trustees, composed of the principal creditors, who were to exercise supervision over its affairs until the new issue of preferred stock should be retired.

In order to reduce the overhead and to gain money for a more speedy retirement of the stock, the trustees advised that the foundry be sold. They were fortunate in finding a buyer who was willing to pay $27,000 for the property, a sum considerably lower than the actual cost, but which would have been very satisfactory under normal conditions. This purchaser agreed to pay from $4,000 to $5,000 annually on the property taken over, and gave the trustees a second mortgage on the foundry as security. The bank still held the first mortgage which covered the entire assets of the original company. The trustees were also given by the agreement general supervision over the new management of the foundry, in order to see that the assets were not wasted by the owner with a view to "milking" the business before the mortgage should be paid.

In order to effect further economies, part of the machine shop, which was now really too large for the original concern, was rented, the overhead expenses were substantially cut, and the owner is now carrying on almost solely the elevator repair work, and the like, which requires very little capital to be tied up in materials. Accordingly, at present practically no current obligations are being incurred and the receivables are turning over rapidly.

In this connection an alternative solution of this part of the problem, proposed by the bank member of the trustees, should be mentioned. He suggested that the machine shop and foundry be separated, and that the latter should be organized into a new corporation. In accordance with this plan the old concern would have owned 49 per cent of the stock of the new corporation, while the trustees would have kept the balance of power by holding temporarily 2 per cent of the stock. Thus the new concern could have been operated separately for the benefit of the original company.

Questions

1. In view of the steps which had earlier been taken by the M. Company, should they have expected the bank to lend them money on a mortgage?

2. Do you consider that it was good banking policy to advance money in this way at this time?

3. As a mercantile creditor would you have been disposed to accept preferred stock to cover the full extent of your claims?

4. What is your opinion of the method actually followed in adjusting the company's affairs?

5. Is there any reason to expect that the alternative scheme proposed by the banker trustee would have been better than the plan actually followed?

6. Would you be willing to sell material on credit to this concern as reorganized?

7. What do you expect to be the ultimate results of this reorganization?

8. On general principles do you consider that the business was worth saving?

Problem 222

Readjustment of Debt and Capitalization of the Goodyear Tire and Rubber Company*

Till the middle of 1920 the Goodyear Tire and Rubber Company was considered the leading factor in the automobile tire trade, and was generally supposed to be in a strong financial position. However, it borrowed very little directly from the banks, depending for current financing largely on the commercial paper market. The company's salesmen had sold nearly $25,000,000 worth of new 7 per cent preferred stock at par during the summer, much of the stock being taken by small investors. This expedient afforded only temporary relief. With an oversupply of high-cost inventory, and a rapid decline in sales, the sharp business depression found the company in a condition in which it was unable to meet the demands of the situation. The result is the Readjustment Plan summarized herein. This plan affords an interesting example of the recon-

(*See problem 124.)

struction of a company's financial structure without the preliminary step of a receivership.

History

The Goodyear Tire and Rubber Company was incorporated in 1898, and has grown to be the largest manufacturer of rubber tires in the world, besides doing a large bus ness in mechanical rubber goods, such as hose, belting, packing, and similar articles.

The company's operations in the past have been extremely successful, and its growth since its incorporation has been enormous. One year ago it was regarded as one of the eminently prosperous corporations of this country. The present difficulties are generally ascribed to the tremendous and rapid expansion program undertaken in a period of inflation which culminated in the investment of $54,000,000 in new plants and subsidiary enterprises at the very peak of inflated business and prices. The resultant strain on its cash resources, coupled with huge inventory losses, plunged the company into virtual insolvency.

Property

The main factory of the company is at Akron, Ohio, and the plant comprises 14 modern and well-equipped buildings, with a total floor space of 113 acres.

In addition, the company maintains stations in most of the large cities of the country, and through stock ownership controls a large number of subsidiary companies engaged in similar lines of business.

Earnings

Below is given the income account of the company for the years 1916–1920, inclusive.

Yrs. ended Oct. 31st	Sales	Net Income
1916	$59,122,281	$7,456,877
1917	103,558,669	15,067,765
1918	122,675,726	16,176,808
1919	158,258,892	23,759,989
1920	188,866,024	10,384,908*

Capitalization—Prior to Readjustment

7% Preferred Stock	$ 65,082,600
Common Stock	61,000,000
Total	$126,082,600

*As of October 31, 1920, inventories were written down to market values by a deduction from this figure of $9,970,000.

After completion of readjustment

First Mortgage 8% Bonds	$ 30,000,000
10-Year 8% Debenture Bonds	27,500,000
Total Funded Debt	$ 57,500,000
Prior Preference 8% Stock	$ 30,342,000
7% Preferred Stock	65,082,600
Management Stock	10,000
Common Stock	1,000,000*
Total Stock	$ 96,434,600
Total Capitalization	$153,934,600

*Consisting of 1,000,000 shares without par value figured at $1.00 a share in this capitalization.

Description and Distribution of New Securities

$30,000,000 20-Year First Mortgage 8% Sinking Fund Bonds. This issue is secured by a first mortgage on all the fixed assets of the company, and by pledge of subsidiary stocks. The entire issue will be redeemed by sinking fund at 120 through semi-annual drawings beginning November 1, 1921. The proceeds from the sale of these bonds are to be used in part to retire bank loans, and in part to provide working capital.

$27,500,000 10-Year 8% Debenture Bonds. This is the total authorized issue of these debentures with the exception of $2,500,000 to be held in the treasury. Under the Trust Agreement the holders of these debentures will be entitled to 10 shares common stock on or after May 1, 1922, without additional payment.

A cumulative sinking fund is provided in the amount of $1,500,000 a year, or 25% (whichever is the greater) of any balance after payment of interest and sinking fund on the First Mortgage Bonds, interest on Debentures, and dividends on Prior Preferred Stock. This sinking fund will retire bonds up to 110. These bonds, or proceeds from their sale, will be used in settlement of that part of the company's bank debt not taken care of by the proceeds of the First Mortgage Bonds.

$30,342,000 Prior Preference 8% Stock. This amount is to be presently issued out of a total authorized issue of $40,000,000, the balance to be used as collateral or reserve for creditors not yet assenting to the Plan. This stock is entitled to 8% dividends cumulative from January 1, 1921, before any dividends on the Preferred or Common Stock, or before the redemption of any Preferred Stock. The stock will be utilized in settlement of the company's merchandise debt.

Before dividends may be paid on the Preferred or Common Stock a sinking fund is to be provided of not less than 8% of the principal amount of all First Mortgage Bonds and Debentures retired during the preceding year.

$65,082,600 7% PREFERRED STOCK. This stock is to be issued in exchange share for share for the present Preferred Stock now outstanding in the hands of the public. The balance of the authorized issue, $450,000, will remain in the treasury. This stock is entitled to 7% dividends, subject to the rights of the Prior Preference and Management stock.

$10,000 MANAGEMENT STOCK. This stock will remain in the hands of a banking committee composed of Messrs. Clarence Dillon, of Dillon, Read & Co., John Sherwin, Chairman of the Board of the Union Trust Company, Cleveland, and Owen D. Young, Vice-President of the General Electric Company, or their successors. The right to elect the majority of the Board of Directors is vested in this stock, and the stock is entitled to maximum dividends of $30,000 a year.

1,000,000 SHARES COMMON STOCK. This stock is largely to be offered in exchange, share for share, for the old stock now outstanding.

Questions

1. What appear to you to be the *real* causes of the Goodyear Company's financial difficulties?

2. Criticize this Readjustment Plan from the following points of view:

(*a*) The point of view of the former common stockholders,

(*b*) The point of view of the preferred stockholders who bought in 1920,

(*c*) The point of view of mercantile creditors,

(*d*) The point of view of the bankers.

3. Do you consider any of the provisions of the "Readjustment" too drastic? If so, which ones, and how do you account for them?

4. Would it have been a wiser policy for the company to have borrowed more heavily from the banks in normal times? Why?

5. Did the bankers act wisely in putting the president, Mr. Seiberling, entirely out of the organization?

6. What do you expect the financial future of the Goodyear Company to be? State your reasons clearly.

7. What are the essential differences between the recent financial history of the Goodyear Company and the Ford Company?

(See Problem 20)

Problem 223

A History of the Financial Difficulties and the Private Reorganization Plans of a Small Automobile Company

The O. Automobile Company was organized before the War to build a low-grade car selling for about $800. Owing to the type of car and to the name, which was of foreign origin and hence not satisfactory for advertising purposes, the public never became particularly interested in the proposition. Even when the make of car was changed so that the company was putting out a medium to high-grade car, beginning in 1918, the indifference of possible buyers continued, so that the O. Company did not expand as rapidly as the better automobile companies. Its growth, however, though slow, was apparently sure, and at the end of 1918 a large "surplus" was recorded on the financial statement. This surplus appears to have been partially earned and partially only a book surplus resulting from a mark-up of some of the tangible assets. It seems to have resulted largely from the fact that no dividends were ever paid on the common or preferred stock of the company.

The end of 1918 found the O. Company with an abnormally high proportion of "accounts receivable," largely resulting from their failure to receive prompt payment on various war orders which they had filled. During the following year there was some improvement in the current financial position, though the financial statement showed an abnormally high amount of finished cars on hand as well as a great deal of inventory of other sorts. While "accounts receivable" continued to decline, the relative proportion of inventory increased during the year 1920, and the cash on hand became constantly less.

Finally, about the middle of 1920, the O. Company found themselves in an intolerable financial position, as they could no longer finance their sales in the usual way—that is, by sight drafts on the dealers to whom they sold. This situation resulted from the generally strained credit conditions which caused the Federal Reserve banks to regard automobile loans at that time as in the highly speculative class of risks. The actual trouble commenced because the Federal Reserve bank of one of the middle western states refused to rediscount the automobile "dealer paper" which had already been discounted by member banks.

It should be explained at this point that for some time it had been the practice of the O. Company, when hard pressed for funds, to discount the sight drafts drawn on western automobile dealers at its local bank, which would then send them on for collection. However, when it became known that the western banks were refusing to discount the "dealer paper" of this automobile concern, the local bank refused to continue its discounting of the sight drafts on the ground that, unless the dealers could raise funds by discounting their paper, it would be impossible for them in turn to honor the sight drafts of the manufacturer. To heighten the difficulty, also, a good deal of friction resulted between the producing company and its western distributors, because of the piling up of demurrage charges on shipments of cars which had been made and which were not turned over to them because of their inability to meet the sight drafts. This friction was made even more unpleasant because it had been the policy of the O. Company to require a deposit of from 10 to 15 per cent of the value of the cars at the time when the orders were placed, and in most cases the demurrage charges rapidly ate up the initial deposit.

In the face of all these difficulties the O. Company continued for some time to build cars. This policy is accounted for by two reasons. First, they had unwisely laid in a large inventory which was now rapidly falling in value and which could be no source of income to them until the cars were built. Secondly, the management of the O. Company felt that the situation would be bound to improve by the end of 1920 or early in 1921, and planned to be ready to supply the trade at a reasonable figure as soon as the period of depression should turn for the better.

It now became necessary for the O. Company to give trade acceptances for any new material which they bought, thus losing the benefit of the cash discount. In many instances they also took up accounts slightly past due by giving trade acceptances to their creditors. When these acceptances came due they usually found themselves unable to make payment and were accordingly forced to give their notes. Before the end of the year, also, they had quadrupled the small mortgage which had been originally placed on their real estate, and had in this manner raised a secured loan from their bank.

In spite of all these attempts to tide the O. Company over current financial difficulties, their condition became worse and worse with the general business depression. They constantly put off all creditors, the payment of whose accounts could be postponed, and under the circumstances their banks would not come to their assistance. The officers of the O. Company frequently found it necessary to use their personal funds in order to meet the weekly payroll.

Consequently, by the end of the year production had temporarily stopped. Before conditions had reached their worst, the O. Company endeavored to raise cash for meeting its notes payable by making a financial arrangement with the R. Motor Company, in accordance with which, for a consideration of $250,000, the O. Company would agree to stop building its own motors and use only those made by the R. Motor Company. While this concession might have been attractive in prosperous times, the R. Motor Company now naturally stalled, and negotiations were broken off.

Thus the O. Company came to the beginning of 1921 with its mercantile credit very seriously endangered, with its bank lines practically cut off, with cash almost wiped out, and production practically at a standstill. It had even been impossible to get any investment house sufficiently interested to help in floating a bond issue, the proceeds of which would have been used to furnish working capital.

At this point, the management of the O. Company decided to take the only chance which remained between them and absolute failure by reorganizing the old company, or organizing a new company, changing its name, and changing the type of car made. In order to effect this reorganization, they incorporated their own investment company, for the purpose of selling their securities in small amounts to a widely diversified list of purchasers.

The following data give in detail comparative financial statements of the O. Company over a period of three years, together with the plan of reorganization, and the relation of the securities of the two newly organized companies to the old company, as drawn up by the officers of the company. Some of the material is now being used in connection with the private sale of stock.

Financial Statements of the O. Company[1]

Assets

	Dec. 31, 1918	Dec. 31, 1919	Dec. 31, 1920[2]
Cash	$102,644.46	$43,878.53	$6,105.37
Notes receivable of customers	21,531.48	7,649.61	7,649.61
Accounts rec. of customers	475,725.13	105,955.61	83,753.28
Merchandise			
–Finished	132,980.22	310,816.31	260,096.34
–Unfinished	11,299.76	101,618.59	127,295.19
–Raw	55,591.18	125,044.27	169,778.10
–Supplies	69,737.55	11,363.79	34,506.92
Liberty Loan Bonds	18,900.00	56,150.00	41,150.00
Quick Assets	$888,409.78	$762,476.71	$730,434.81
Land—Buildings	353,887.17	349,623.37	621,000.00
Machinery—Furn.—Equip.	505,294.91	492,718.92	531,743.33
Investments (Capital Stock O. Sales Corp.)		40,000.00	40,000.00
Deferred charges—Prepaid items	4,727.22	2,267.58	12,244.65
Total	$1,752,319.08	$1,647,086.58	$1,935,422.79

Liabilities

	Dec. 31, 1918	Dec. 31, 1919	Dec. 31, 1920[2]
Notes payable for borrowed money	$12,920.00	$24,950.00	$55,550.00
Notes payable for mdse.			220,000.00
Accounts payable	281,451.03	47,430.75	27,374.38
Sundries—Accruals	10,444.16	25,729.85	6,898.63
Current Liabilities	$304,815.19	$98,110.60	$309,823.01
Mortgages on Real Estate	42,000.00	42,000.00	186,000.00
Reserve for depreciation	209,733.20	250,811.21	322,464.43
Reserves	12,666.83	12,675.27	12,675.27
Capital: Preferred	124,500.00	124,500.00	124,500.00
Common	200,000.00	200,000.00	200,000.00
Surplus	858,603.86	918,989.50	779,960.08
Total	$1,752,319.08	$1,647,086.58	$1,935,422.79
Sales	$831,191.67	$1,011,101.08	$1,285,308.46
Net Profits	3,946.92	10,622.37	

[1] Taken from the Company's books—not certified.

[2] Estimated

Reorganization of the O. Company

The following reorganization schemes are proposed:

Condition on October 1, 1920.

Estimated value of Current Assets based on actual inventory at current market	$737,329.44	
Current liabilities	302,874.38	
Net liquid assets		$434,455.06
Permanent investment at values by Amer. Appraisal Co., preliminary survey, December 17, 1920	$941,250.00	
Less mortgages	186,000.00	
Net equity in fixed assets		755,250.00
Total net worth		$1,189,705.06

It is indicated by The American Appraisal Representatives that the detailed appraisal of the O. Plant will show values several hundred thousand dollars more than above.

Present Capitalization—

Common Stock	$250,000	
Unissued	50,000	
Outstanding		$200,000
Preferred	$250,000	
Unissued	125,500	
Outstanding		124,500
Total		$324,500

Increase capital of O. Company by an increase of the preferred stock to $675,000. Declare stock dividend of 250% on the common stock payable in preferred with the following result, and a stock dividend of 27% on the preferred stock to cover the accumulated dividends to date.

Common	$250,000	
Unissued	50,000	
Outstanding		$200,000
Preferred	$675,000	
Unissued	16,885	
Outstanding		658,115
Total		$858,115

Exchange O. stock for stock in X. Company which is to be organized for the purpose of financing and operating the O. Company, $240 par value of X. common to be given for each $100 par value of M. common and $100 of X. preferred for each $100 of O. preferred. After stock dividend the following result is achieved. The original subscribers to the stock of the O. Company received $100 of O. 6% preferred and

$100 of O. common stock for $100, and as a result of the stock dividend and in the transfer to the X. Co. will receive:

$100.00 O. 6% pfd. orig. sub.—	$100.00 X 8% pfd.	$8.00 an'l div.
250.00 O. 6% pfd. st'k div.—	250.00 X 8% pfd.	20.00 an'l div.
27.00 O. 6% pfd. pfd. div.—	27.00 X 8% pfd.	2.16 an'l div.
100.00 O. Com. orig. bonus—	240.00 X Com.	
$477.00 To'l O. st'k aft. div.	$617.00 Total val. X.	$30.16 an'l div.

Which means that the present O. stockholders will receive $617 worth of X. stock for each $100 they originally invested, and preferred dividends of $30.16, or 30% on the original investment without taking into account any dividend on the common stock.

Financial Plan of the X. Company

X. Company—To be organized for the purpose of financing and operating the O. Company.

Capital 1,000,000 shares common, par $ 1.00		
250,000 shares preferred, par 10.00		8% cumulative.
Common stock to be distributed	480,000	to O. stockholders *pro rata*.
	520,000	to new stockholders, employees, underwriters and Investors' Service organization.
	$1,000,000	
Preferred stock to be distributed	658,115	to O. stockholders *pro rata* for their holdings in the O. Co.
	225,000	to Investors' Service, Inc. for 125,000 cash.
	1,616,885	to new stockholders for cash
Total.	$2,500,000	

X. Company to sell immediately upon organization to Investors' Service, Inc., $225,000 preferred for $125,000 cash to secure sufficient cash to finance sale of new stock and to furnish necessary cash to O. Co. to get into operation to take care of the spring demand for automobiles. All money advanced to the O. Company by the X. Company will be in the forms of loans secured by bond issue to be placed on the O. plant, equipment, etc.

The preferred stock of the X. Company to be sold to the public, it is estimated will be sold at a maximum cost of 22%, with the result that the $1,616,115 par value preferred will be sold at a minimum of 78%, or $1,287,390 cash, with following result in the financial condition of the X. Co. after giving effect to this financing:

Assets		Liabilities	
Cash		Preferred	$2,500,000.00
From Investors' Serv.	$ 125,000.00	Common	1,000,000.00
From pfd. stock sales	1,261,170.30	Surplus	531,590.06
O. common	200,000.00	Total	$4,031,590.06
O. preferred	658,115.00		
O. surplus	331,590.06		
*Contracts and other reorganization items	1,455,714.70		
Total assets	$4,031,590.06		

*This item is to offset the common stock, the preferred stock bonus to the Investors' Service, Inc., and the cost of selling the preferred stock to the public.

This statement does not take into account the greater value of the O. plant and equipment which is indicated by the American Appraisal Company to be approximately $250,000 more than shown by the O. statement. It does show a surplus which assures dividends on the entire issue of 8% preferred stock for almost three years to come.

Stock-Selling Campaign

The X. preferred stock will be sold to the public:

First.—Through a mail-order campaign patterned after the campaign used by two other motor companies, one of which sold $900,000 worth of stock during the last seven months, and the other started a campaign October first and has averaged $50,000 worth of stock monthly since that time. Neither of these companies has the plant, the assets, or the past record of earnings of the O. Co., which is the foundation of the X. Co. The cost of selling the stock of one of these companies has averaged approximately 12%.

Second.—By organizing a sales force consisting of high-grade, experienced stock salesmen, who have been district managers and representatives of investment banking houses, specializing in selling safe and attractive preferred stocks to the small investor, by intensive selling methods. We have a nucleus of this organization already arranged for. One of the organizations with which we are familiar has sold on an average of $300,000 worth of such stock per month for the past year in one state at a cost not to exceed 18%.

Third.—By turning over to brokerage houses lots of $50,000 to $100,000 to offer to their regular clients—at a cost not to exceed 20%.

We estimate selling a minimum average of $60,000 monthly, the first twelve months, and $100,000 monthly the second twelve months.

Purpose of Organization of the X. Company

The X. Co. has been organized for the following purposes:

First.—To supply the necessary funds to properly finance the operations of the O. Co.

Second.—To properly advertise and merchandise its products.

Third.—To have a Board of Directors composed of successful men of mature judgment to insure the best policy of operations.

Fourth.—To supply management of past proven success to thoroughly develop every facility of the O. Co. by putting its operation on the most modern and efficient basis, to insure dividends for the stockholders, and a progressive institution.

Fifth.—To develop the present product, the Master Six, and a new four-cylinder car, the X. Four, to complete the line, which will make possible better dealer representation, and give greater volume of production of a less fluctuating character.

The X. Four, which Mr. O. is now designing, will stand out in comparison with the four-cylinder cars now on the market because of its advantage in:

Lower first cost
Greater gasoline mileage
Greater tire mileage
Finer appearance
Easier riding qualities

and meet the trend of the industry and demand for economy and luxury at low initial cost.

Estimate of Profits of X. Company

The past experience of the O. Co. indicates that, with the adequate capital and other facilities made possible by the reorganization, there will be a minimum production for the first year of 3,000 cars, which, on a minimum net profit of 8%, would show:

2,000 Master Six Cars @ $1,400 net =	$2,800,000	
1,000 W. Four Cars @ $1,000 net =	1,000,000	
	$3,800,000	
	8%	profit
NET PROFIT..............	$ 304,000	
Less dividend requirements on $1,500,000 preferred.	120,000	
Available for dividend on common stock..........	$ 184,000	or *18%*

As the O. Plant has produced as high as 40 cars per day, a much greater production is possible in future years, and with the complete line of both a six-cylinder and a four-cylinder car a much greater demand can be expected. If this first year's estimated production is only tripled in succeeding years and but 12% profit is realized, the earning will be:

4,000 six-cylinder cars @ $1,400 net =	$ 5,600,000
5,000 four-cylinder cars @ $1,000 net =	5,000,000
	$10,600,000
	12% profit
	$ 1,272,000
Less dividend requirements on entire $2,500,000 preferred	200,000
Available for dividends on common stock	$ 1,072,000 or *107%*

And the new financing should put the company in a position to pay out big dividends to the stockholders, instead of keeping the profits in the business to make expansion possible.

Management

President and Consulting Engineer., C. H., who has concentrated his energy on the development of the automobile industry since its beginning, having previously devoted his activities to manufacturing and engineering enterprises.

Vice-President and General Manager, M. C., formerly Vice-President and General Manager, Blank Bronze Corporation, who, though still a comparatively young man, has a record of successful accomplishment as a manufacturer and sales and financial executive. A director of the P. Association of Credit Men, the Blank Bronze Corporation, the P. Stamping Co., and other successful enterprises.

Treasurer and Counsel, W. J. B., Attorney at Law, director of the C. National Bank.

Secretary, E. H., law student at Cornell University previous to his twelve years' association with the O. Co., as sales manager, manager of branches, and more recently as president.

The Board of Directors to be composed of such men as:

G. W. B., Chairman; Vice-President, A. Trust Co.; President R. Motor Co., and B. Products Corp.

C. H., President and Consulting Engineer; Founder and active head of the O. Co.

W. J. B., Treasurer and Counsel; Director, The C. National Bank.

M. C., Vice-President and General Manager; Director, Blank Bronze Corporation, P. Stamping Co., Civic Building and Loan Association.

C. J., Secretary, E. Watch Co.

EXHIBIT A

On May 6, 1921, a new firm of accountants drew up the following comparative statement, indicating that the O. Company is to be absorbed by the X. Company.

L. E. B. & Co.
Certified Public Accountants,
Philadelphia, Pa.

Exhibit *re* the O. Company and the X. Company, *Refinancing Plan.*

1st. Financial condition of the O. Company as of December 31, 1920, per its books. Plant account being adjusted to accord with the American Appraisal Company's valuations or with *bona fide* bid prices; inventories priced conservatively, and with adequate reserves for losses in current assets.

2nd. Giving effect to an issue of $2,500,000 Preferred and $1,000,000 Common Stock of the X. Company, to acquire the assets of the O. Company as of December 31, 1920, and provide additional working capital, increase plant facilities, and reduce liabilities.

Assets

	No. 1 O. Company Dec. 31, 1920	No. 2 X. Company with Financing Plan in effect
Cash, Accounts Receivable, Inventories.	$645,627.29	$1,731,296.83
Investments: Bonds, Real Estate, Mortgages (Net Equity)	137,756.57	137,756.57
Plant and Equipment, Less Depreciation (O. Co., per American Appraisal Co.)	1,306,474.11	1,406,474.11
Prepaid, Interest, Insurance, etc	9,357.73	9,357.73
	$2,099,215.70	$3,284,885.24
Intangibles:		
Contracts, Goodwill, etc		900,000.00
Refinancing Costs Estimated		355,572.46
	$2,099,215.70	$4,540,458.70

Liabilities

	No. 1	No. 2
Notes and Accounts Payable	$364,797.78	$164,797.78
Accrued Accounts, Taxes, Interest, etc.	3,436.81	3,436.81
Mortgage on Plant	150,000.00	150,000.00
Reserve for possible Inventory Depreciation	59,417.65	59,417.65
	$577,652.24	$377,652.24
Capital Stock:		
Preferred	$158,757.00	$2,500,000.00
Common	200,000.00	1,000,000.00
Surplus	1,162,806.46	662,806.46
	$2,099,215.70	$4,540,458.70

On March 1st, 1921, the O. Company authorized $600,000 of bonds, pending the consummation of the above financing plans, when the bond issue will be retired.

The above balance sheet of the O. Company, as of December 31, 1920, is in accord with said Company's books, and the balance sheet for the X. Company, showing the effect of the refinancing plan as outlined, in our opinion is correctly stated.

(Signed) L. E. B. & Co.

EXHIBIT B

Plan of the Investors' Service Co., Inc.

Organized to finance the sales of X. Company preferred stock:

Capital

1,250 shares no par value stock.
1,250 shares 8% cumulative preferred stock, par value $100.

To be offered to stockholders, officers and employees of O. Company and others interested in the development of the O. Company.

Offering:

1 share preferred, par	$100
1 share no par value common	
For	$100
Assessment for expenses	1
	$101
Total issue preferred, 1,250 shares.	
Total income	$126,250
Initial corporate set-up Cash	$126,250
Total Assets	126,250
Preferred stock	$125,000
No par value (1,250 shares) common.	
Surplus	1,250
Total liabilities	$126,250

Investors' Service to enter into a contract to buy first $125,000 of preferred stock in X. Company and to be given bonus of $100,000 preferred stock and $62,500 common in consideration of making the initial investment to finance the sale of the preferred stock issue of the X. Company.

Financial set-up of Investors' Service after purchase of X. preferred.

Assets

Cash	$1,250
Securities	125,000
and $100,000 X preferred (distributed direct to stockholders *pro rata.*)	
X common	12,500
and $50,000 X common (distributed direct to stockholders *pro rata.*)	
Total	$138,750

Liabilities

Preferred stock	$125,000
No par value (1,250 shares) common	
Surplus	13,750
Total	$138,750

RESULT: A subscriber to $1,000 worth of Investors' Service, Inc., preferred, would get immediately his subscription is paid:

	$1,000	Investors' Service 8% preferred
	800	X. Co. 8% preferred
	400	X. Co. N. P. V. common.
	$2,200	Value of securities.
Payment	$1,010	Cash—$1,000 for stock and $10 for expenses.
Gain	*$1,190*	*greater value of securities than investment*

Investors' Service to receive commission of 1½% on the $1,600,500 preferred stock in X. Company to be sold to public, and 25% of the saving or difference between 22% and the actual cost of selling the X. preferred. It is estimated that this plan will make possible marketing the X. stock at a cost not to exceed 16%, which will mean a saving of 6%, or 1½% for the Investors' Service, which will make the income of the Investors' Service, Inc., as follows, over the two years' period required to sell the stock:

Income

Stock sales, Investors' Service	$125,000.00
Assessment for expenses	1,250.00
Commission on X. stock sales	24,757.50
Bonus on saving in cost of stock sales	24,757.50
2 years' dividend on X. preferred stock	20,000.00
	$195,765.00

Disbursements

Purchase of X. preferred	$125,000.00
Expense of organization	1,250.00
Dividend 2 years on Investors' Service preferred	20,000.00
Balance on profit	49,515.00
	$195,765.00

This will show a statement at close of 2 years of Investors' Service, Inc.

Cash	$49,515.00
Securities—X. preferred	125,000.00
Securities—X. common	12,500.00
	$187,015.00
Preferred outstanding	125,000.00
No par value (1,250 shares)	
Surplus	62,015.00
	$187,015.00

1,250 shares N. P. V. worth $62,015. Surplus = $49.61, value each share common.

For original investment of $1,010:

10 shares Investors' Serv. pfd.	@	$100 par	=$1,000.00
80 shares X. preferred	@	10 par	800.00
400 shares X. common	@	1 par	400.00
10 shares Investors' Serv. no par value			496.10
2 years dividend 8% X. Co.			128.00
2 years dividend 8% Inv. Serv., Inc.			160.00
Total securities and income			$2,984.10
Less investment			1,010.00
197% net profit within 2 years			*$1,974.10*

This plan will be adopted for the purpose of financing the X. Co. at a lesser cost and on a more satisfactory basis, with the same results as if the stock were underwritten by the usual investment banking house. Still a nice profit is possible for the stockholders of the Investors' Service, Inc., who in effect form an underwriting syndicate.

Every stockholder subscribes on exactly the same basis and shares in the profits proportionately.

There will be no expense to the operation of the Investors' Service, Inc., other than the $1,250 collected originally for this purpose. *Hence all the income will be profit.*

Questions

1. What is your opinion of the financial management of the O. Company before the attempted reorganization?

2. Analyze critically and from all points of view, the plans for refinancing the O. Company and organizing the X. Company and the Investors' Service Corporation.

3. What do you expect the future of this concern to be? State your reasons clearly.

PART V

GENERAL PROBLEMS

CHAPTER XI

GENERAL SURVEY PROBLEMS

THE excuse for this final chapter is the following problems themselves. They touch in an unusually significant manner upon most of the principles of financing a small business which have already been discussed.

The first problem (224) is a refreshing example of the sort of success that can be achieved by a man of no original business training, who is guided solely by an unusual native common sense—where one might least expect to find it.

The second problem (225), which might have been included in the preceding chapter, paints the life history of a typical "war baby." It might well have been labeled "From Birth to Death in Four Years."

The third problem (226) very nearly runs the gamut of all the financial experiences which a small, recently launched concern might meet. The manager of this little concern should be able to draw some helpful lessons from the other two problems.

PROBLEM 224

THE FINANCIAL GROWTH OF A SMALL MUSICAL CONCERN

Some twenty years ago, Mr. Y. was employed as a musician playing in theatre orchestras in one of the leading cities in the United States. Having left school at the age of twelve, he had spent more than twenty years of his life on trivial jobs of various kinds, though his chief interest was music. On one occasion he wished to purchase an improved type of the wind instrument which he usually played, and which it was necessary to import from Europe. The only dealer who at the time handled instruments of this sort in this city was unwilling to take the trouble of importing the instrument desired.

Being disappointed, Mr. Y. ordered an instrument from the European firm which dealt in the article. As this was the first order which they had received from that locality, they offered to make Y. their agent on a small scale. He thereupon decided that it might be worth while to conduct this little business as a side line, since he would have an opportunity to sell some instruments to his friends.

Accordingly, with practically no capital, he began to take orders from his friends, securing advance payment so that he could import the instruments from abroad. For convenience he soon opened up a little store composed of one room nine by eleven feet in size, and began to do a small jobbing business in other instruments as his friends desired. During this time, also, various requests came to him for repair work in connection with the type of instruments which he dealt in. Some of the simpler repairs he was able to make himself, though he was not by any means a mechanic, and some he managed to have done by a repair man of unusual skill.

At the end of a year, Y. had saved about $1,000. As the business grew, he persuaded the repair man, Z., to work for him regularly so as to repair satisfactorily all the instruments that Y's friends brought, and paid him a fair amount for his goodwill. Thus, Y. really secured a monopoly on the wind instrument repairing business, and it grew steadily during the next two years, within which time the dealer who had originally refused to purchase the needed instrument for Y., fell into financial difficulties and was forced to sell out to Y., who took over the importing part of his business. This Y. did by paying the dealer $2,000 in cash and the balance of $18,000 in notes due over a period of five years.

In two or three years more, Y. started a small music publishing business in connection with his importing and repair work. This part of the business was combined with another small publishing company and eventually the entire interest was bought out by Y.

During this time Y. and his repair man had begun to manufacture some small articles which were needed in connection with wind instruments, to supply the needs for repair purposes. In the course of time it was natural that they should occasionally attempt to make for their friends instruments which at the time, for some reason or other, it was difficult to import. This sort of work was, of course, at first regarded merely as an experiment, but it gradually grew to be a serious part of the business. When Y. found that the profits in manufacturing were much higher than the profits on the goods which he imported, he began more actively to push the production of instruments. It was fortunate, therefore, that the repair man, Z., had two sons who were skilful mechanics and who learned the art of making certain of the instruments. In a few years other skilful workers were added to the force of employees, until manufacturing became the chief part of the business.

It was not long before Y. discovered that his old repair man, trained in Europe, and following antiquated methods, failed to realize the possibilities of scientific mass production. He attempted to perform all of the making operations himself. Y., though having no precedent to follow, decided that the work was of such a nature that the operations could be greatly simplified. His aim was to divide the task to such an extent that individual operations would be simple and could be carried out by workers having only a reasonable degree of skill, in many cases by young persons. It accordingly became necessary for Y. to pension his repair man, whose skill had started the manufacturing, and to leave the guidance of the work largely to Z's sons, who had by this time thoroughly mastered the production end of the business. In course of time, also, machinery was developed for performing the simpler operations.

The introduction of machinery gave Y's business a definite advantage over that of other producers both in this country and in Europe, inasmuch as his labor costs were greatly reduced. Further, it was possible to keep his plant operating rather evenly throughout the year by hiring during the summer young persons who could readily be taught to perform the simpler operations connected with the making of instrument parts, later to be assembled as the orders came in. After Y. began to know his market, he followed the policy of making up parts for twice the number of instruments called for by the orders on hand. He found that the unit cost of making them in this manner was very greatly reduced.

In 1915, Y. found it necessary to change his quarters in order to get all of his manufacturing business under the same roof. He accordingly waited for an opportunity to buy a satisfactory building which was on the market under a forced sale. This building was in a locality slightly removed from the business and manufacturing center of the city, but as there was an opportunity to secure the building for about 60 per cent of its assessed value, Y. thought it best to buy and so keep down his overhead. In order to purchase this building, he assumed a first mortgage of $10,000, and borrowed the balance of $12,000 from the one bank with which he had made connections. Y. explains that the bank loaned solely on the strength of his character and success in business.

During the war the import market was cut off, and Y. had a number of opportunities to take over large orders from the Government. He refused, however, to accept any orders that would make it necessary for him to launch upon a policy of expansion, which would necessitate an increase of capital and plant and a resultant growth in fixed investment. He contended that there is no real and worth-while growth but slow growth.

In July, 1921, Y's current position was as follows:

Current Assets		Current Liabilities	
Cash	$13,000	Accounts payable (during the month.)	$3,000
Receivables	50,000		
Inventory	75,000		$3,000
	$138,000		

The inventory consisted of about $30,000 in metal plates, for printing music and instruction books to be used with the type of instruments made, $15,000 in finished goods, and $15,000 in goods partially finished, the balance being in raw materials. The inventory is relatively higher than is normally carried.

The receivables consisted of about $12,000 due from the Government on a large order which the company is now filling. The rest is due partially on open account, partially on goods consigned to small and preferred dealers, and the balance on goods sold to jobbers and agents through a conditional sales agreement.*

The liabilities shown are negligible. Y. explains that he has built up his business solely out of profits and always takes his cash discounts. He has never borrowed, for working capital purposes, more than $8,000 from his bank at one time, and his total bank borrowings since he began his business have been little more than $150,000. This concern, being unincorporated, has never been required to file a statement of condition with the State authorities, nor has the owner ever given his bank a statement. Mr. Y. is so conservative that he has not even given the information which would enable him to get a rating from Dun's or Bradstreet's.

Y. is uncertain as to the exact value of his fixed assets. The building and real estate which were bought at a

*It should be explained that the terms of sale of this concern are rather flexible. Due to the lack of competition on high-grade instruments it is possible to make very high profits on many articles sold, hence it frequently happens that a chance is taken on a customer whose credit may not be wholly certain. While the usual terms given are 2%–10 days and 30 days net, large quantities of goods are sold to jobbers and agents on conditional sales contracts, and many are sold to small or preferred dealers on consignment. The company is willing to take back goods which its purchasers are unable to sell (See *Credit Man's Diary*, 1921, pages 109-121.)

bargain are now probably worth many times what he paid for them. Further, the very considerable amount of machinery which he uses has been gradually installed in his factory over a period of years, and no patents have been taken out on any of the machines. No records have been kept which would make it possible to estimate the actual cost of these machines. Finally, as the business is unincorporated, no attempt has been made to put a value on developmental expenses, goodwill, secret processes, and the like, which in this case are extremely valuable.

The gross earnings of this business in recent years have been as follows: 1919, $200,000; 1920, $185,000; 1921, $250,000 (estimated).

At this time (July, 1921), Y. employs about eighty people, divided between the instrument factory and the publishing house. Y. explains that the depreciation in connection with the publishing end of the business is extremely high, and that no particular attempt has been made to make money out of it directly. The aim, however, is to publish and keep up to date music and text books, for the type of instruments manufactured. In doing this, every effort is made to secure the services of the highest authorities in the field. Even though this end of the business has not more than paid for itself, Y. says that he considers it a very desirable thing for him to engage in.

Such is the general history and present financial condition of the . . . . Company. When the owner was asked what had been his most difficult financial problems, he replied that he could not recollect ever having had any. He said that he had begun with only a few dollars, had paid all his bills as he went, and had been extremely slow to expand.

He further states that his son, who has recently graduated from a business school, tells him that he is decidedly a "back number" in business, that he knows nothing about accounting or financing—a charge admitted by the father—and that in course of time his business will probably fail, if it continues to be conducted as at present. Y. is still in his prime (age 53), but hopes to retire within the next ten years. He wishes very much to have his son conduct the business after him. Yet he feels that the son has no sympathetic understanding of the problems of this business and no appreciation of the principles which have led to what Y. considers a reasonable success.

At this juncture two general questions are raised by Mr. Y. (*a*) What weaknesses, if any, are to be found in the financial conduct of his business? (*b*) What steps should be taken to insure continued prosperity of the business when the present owner ceases to be its active administrator?

Questions

1. Was the starting of the business under the conditions outlined, financially justified?

2. Was it a wise policy for this concern to finance itself solely out of earnings?

3. Was it financially justifiable to go into the music publishing business?

4. Was Y. justified in refusing to expand rapidly during the war period?

5. Should the machinery used be patented?

6. Do you approve of the sales policy indicated?

7. Do you approve of Y's policy in refusing to give figures to the mercantile agencies, and in avoiding a statement to his bank?

8. Was the bank justified in lending this man $12,000 to put into fixed assets?

9. Is it financially desirable for this concern to be unincorporated?

10. What elements of weakness, if any, can you find in the finances of this business?

11. What seem to you to be the chief elements of strength in the financing of this enterprise?

12. What steps, if any, should you advise the owner to take in the future?

Problem 225

Promotion, Expansion, Receivership and Sale of Assets Within Five Years

The N. B. & F. Company making for the most part boiler-room equipment, began business in a small way in May, 1915, and was incorporated November 20, 1915, with a capital of $20,000 preferred stock and $30,000 common. The authorized capital was increased on April 4, 1917, to $100,000 preferred and $100,000 common. All the common stock was held by the three main officers of the company.

The president and general manager of the company, Mr. N., was thirty-eight years of age, of good character, and reputed to be an able inventor. At one time he had been associated with a firm of machinists and was in charge of their shop. This firm, however, was not successful. Upon its failure N. leased the plant and continued to manufacture blowers and furnaces individually until he organized the N. B. & F. Company. He was not reputed to have much capital of his own.

The vice-president, B., was a widower, sixty-nine years old, of excellent character. He had earlier organized a wholesale provision and commission house and had been president of the . . . Fruit and Produce Exchange. He was supposed to be worth about $100,000.

The treasurer, M., was forty-nine years old and had been for thirty years receiving teller of the Five Cent Savings Bank. He was also interested in a number of other propositions, but was not supposed to have much personal means.

The following figures, taken from various reports, show the financial condition of the N. B. & F. Company at different times:

Condition shown in reports to Commissioner of Corporations:

	Total Assets	Total Liabilities	Net Worth
March 6, 1916	$100,230	$ 48,600	$51,130
January 1, 1917	298,286	150,398	47,880

Statement of the N. B. & F. Company
March 31, 1917

Assets

Cash	$ 2,454.57		
Accounts receivable	46,370.65		
Stock on hand	91,367.43		
Labor accrued	11,274.90		
Machinery	161,473.03		
Equipment	56,493.33		
Furniture and Fixtures	4,105.01		
Autos	5,591.61		
		$379,140.63	
Patents		2,000.00	
Treasury stock		16,500.00	
Total			$397,640.63

Liabilities

Accounts payable	$108,660.60	
Notes payable	62,659.90	
F. B.	3,500.00	
Advances on Products	676.25	$175,496.75
Excess of Assets over Liabilities		$222,143.78

Represented by:

Common Stock	$20,000.00
Prefer ed Stock	30,000.00
Depreciation reserve	18,566.54
Surplus	153,477.24
	$222,143.78

At the end of 1917 the company is reported to have employed about 300 hands. For a period of two years the company's growth was extremely rapid, due largely to war contracts. On May 23, 1918, they stated that they had been obliged to give a chattel mortgage to the M. R. Company as security for liabilities incurred on a contract which they had attempted to fill for the Russian Government. After the entrance of the United States into the war, they canceled a number of their foreign contracts and entered into others with the United States Government.

A statement prepared by a well-known C. P. A. as of December 31, 1918, reveals the following condition:

STATEMENT OF THE N. B. & F. Company
December 31, 1918

Assets

Cash	$40,040.92
Accounts receivable	270,570.82
Investments	3,606.37
Stock on hand	185,707.19
Machinery	363,139.54
Equipment	95,804.98
Autos	16,716.11
Furniture and fixtures	7,998.00
Patents	2,500.00
Treasury stock	94,500.00
	$1,088,593.93

Liabilities

Accounts payable	$191,518.99
Mortgage notes payable	165,236.92
Machinery notes payable	70,491.61
Merchandise notes payable	57,998.55
Capital stock	200,000.00
Reserve for depreciation	65,250.74
Surplus	338,097.12
	$1,088,593.93

Total sales for 1918 were	$2,225,092.05
Total gain	$347,350.94

This report showed apparently large profits, but it should be borne in mind that the business was practically all war business. There was a large investment in machinery covered by chattel mortgages to the M. R. Company, and a large amount held under leases from various dealers and manufacturers.

In the latter part of 1919, the N. B. & F. Company began to have serious financial difficulties. They could not secure cash to pay their creditors. It was apparent that some other work beside war work would be necessary to keep the plant busy. The company accordingly began to manufacture a special make of tractor which was the pet project of the president of the concern. The company having had no previous experience in this line of work found it necessary to invest heavily in new equipment in order to turn out the tractors. A statement filed August 25, 1919, purports to show the following condition:

Statement of the N. B. & F. Company
August 25, 1919

Assets	
Machinery	$418,407.89
Manufacturing stock and materials	185,707.19
Cash and debts receivable	831,443.39
Patents	2,500.00
Investments	82,565.12
	$1,520,623.59

Liabilities	
Capital stock	$105,500.00
Accounts payable	181,518.99
Funded debt	159,255.14
Floating debt	663,322.19
Surplus	331,027.27
Contingent liabilities	80,000.00
	$1,520,623.59

At this time, four mercantile creditors reported that they found the company from one to four months slow and that they did not consider their account satisfactory.

On September 23, 1919, proceedings were filed in a bill of equity in the United States District Court for the appointment of a receiver. At this time there was apparently an excess of assets over liabilities amounting to several hundred thousand dollars. Accordingly, on September 26, 1919, the judge appointed Mr. C. as the receiver, under bond of $50,000. Mr. C. was a member of an old-established firm of machinery dealers. He was about forty years of age and a son of the founder of his firm. Though he had an excellent reputation, he had never had any factory experience.

On the day of his appointment as receiver, C. was authorized by the court to sell $200,000 in receiver's certificates at an interest rate not exceeding 7 per cent. On January 10, 1920, he was authorized to sell $50,000 additional. These certificates were all purchased by the . . . National Bank. The receiver retained N., the former president and manager, with him in the business.

During the next year the receiver's chief aim seems to have been to keep the plant in operation. He accordingly proceeded to finish up the war contracts on hand. He is said to have employed a practical factory manager formerly with the . . . Arms Company and to have secured outside advice and approval on all important contracts. He also continued to manufacture the N. Tractor, the making of which was already under way. These tractors proved defective, however, and this part of the business turned out to be a heavy loss to the company. The receiver further made contracts with different concerns for machinery parts for certain appliances, which also porved to be unsatisfactory. Not the least of his operations was said to be the production of certain accessories, to be sold to his own company, the making of which required the installation of a good deal of new equipment.

Some time after the appointment of the receiver, a reputable firm of accountants was employed to report on the financial condition of the N. B. & F. Company. However, the accounts were so confused that it took three months for the accountants to make their report. Their preliminary report showed that the assets had been greatly overvalued. The definitive report filed July 31, 1920, showed the following condition:

STATEMENT OF THE N. B. & F. COMPANY
July 31, 1920

Assets

Inventory	$328,000	
Accounts receivable	105,000	
Cash	2,500	
Investment in affiliated companies	54,000	
Machinery, equipment, etc.	472,000	
Tools, patterns, patents, etc.	204,000	
Total	$1,165,500	

Liabilities.

Receiver's Liabilities		$552,000
Receiver's Certificates payable to S. B. Co.	$250,000	
Receiver's Certificates payable for merchandise	233,000	
Other payables and accruals	69,000	
Secured Loans		508,000
Mortgages notes payable	113,000	
Machinery lease notes	56,000	
Manufacturers' Finance Corporation	76,000	
Blank Trust Company	68,000	
Blank Bank	195,000	
Unsecured Obligations		509,000
Accounts payable	304,000	
Notes payable	107,000	
Taxes, accruals, etc.	98,000	
Total Liabilities	$1,569,000	
Excess Liabilities	430,500	

The receiver gave out no statement of his operations before July 31, 1920. Shortly after this date the following information was given:

RECEIPTS AND DISBURSEMENTS OF THE N. B. & F. COMPANY UNDER THE RECEIVERSHIP FROM SEPTEMBER 26, 1919, TO JULY 31, 1920.

Receipts		$832,000
From current sale of product	$490,000	
From loans	266,000	
From collections	27,000	
From miscellaneous	49,000	
Disbursements		$835,000
For wages and salaries	559,000	
For materials, supplies, etc.	213,000	
For miscellaneous	63,000	

By this time the new creditors, who naturally considered themselves secured under the receivership, were growing extremely restless, as it was not possible for them to obtain payment of their bills, and checks of the N. B. & F. Company were being dishonored.

On August 27, 1920, F. & A., attorneys for the P. G. Company, filed a petition to have the receiver removed, claiming mismanagement and failure to render proper accounts. It is understood, however, that such a bitter attack was made that the court did not feel justified in removing the receiver, but did appoint as co-receiver a lawyer of high standing.

On October 28, 1920, without bankruptcy proceedings, the failure being so obvious, the Court authorized the receivers to sell the property at public auction, in order to satisfy the outstanding claims. This auction took place on November 17, 18, 19, and 20, 1920, and the amount realized from the sale was $259,606.73. The details of the sale and apportionment of the proceeds were gradually worked out and submitted to the Court on June 1, 1921, within two weeks after which time a hearing of the creditors was to be held. An advance survey of the report to be presented to the creditors at that time is given as follows by one of the largest creditors:

Creditors' Claims on the N. B. & F. Company Arranged as Nearly as May Be in Order of Priority

1. Leased Machinery. As previously stated, a large amount of machinery was held on leases which were partly paid for. Whatever was received from the sale in excess of these leases went to the receivers. If the property sold for less than the amount of the leases, the owner would lose the difference. The total amount realized from the sale of the leased machinery was $83,425.62. Of this amount it required $53,934.24 to clear the leases. From the difference a proportionate share of the expenses of the sale must be deducted.

2. Chattel Mortgage. As already indicated, a large amount of the machinery was secured by chattel mortgages from the M. R. Company. The machinery so covered was valued at approximately $160,000. From the sale of this

mortgaged machinery $91,000 was realized, from which must also be paid a proportionate share of the cost of the sale.

3. Rent Expenses (Under Special Judgment.) On February 11, 1921, the Court issued a special decree giving preference for the charge for rent amounting to approximately $21,000.

4. Expenses of the Sale. The expenses of the sale will be approximately $26,000, of which $14,000 will cover actual outlays for assistance of various sorts. The auctioneer will also probably claim about $12,000 for his own services, extending over a considerable period both before and after the sale. This claim must be approved by the Court.

5. Accrued Pay-Roll. At the time of the sale there was an accrued pay-roll amounting to about $16,000.

6. Manufacturer's Finance Corporation. This corporation has a secured claim of $26,000, but the total amount of their claim is $76,000. They will fight for the full amount on the basis of their agreement with the N. B. & F. Company which covered all subsequent loans. This claim must be settled by the Court, and so far as the total amount is concerned the results are doubtful.

7. Receiver's Claims (Following the Order of Sale.) The amount of these claims is not known. However, it will probably be from $15,000 to $25,000 depending on the judgment of the Court.

8. Receiver's Claim (Preceding the Order of Sale.) The amount of this claim is not yet known. It may be contested that the receiver is not entitled to any compensation on account of negligence, and the creditors (headed presumably by attorneys F. &. A.) may also endeavor to secure the forfeiture of the receiver's bond of $50,000. The Court is apparently friendly to the receiver and it is doubted whether anything will come of this action, since attorney A., though a responsible man, is rather hot headed and inclined to raise ill feeling.

9. Receiver's Certificates. After the receiver's expenses are paid, or disallowed, will logically come the claim of the . . . National Bank for $250,000 loaned on Receiver's Certificates. In case there should be no property left to meet this claim, however, there is a very real question as to whether the claims of the receiver's creditors may not be placed on an equality with those of the bank. The argument is made that there is no justification for preference.

10. RECEIVER'S CREDITORS. After the Receiver's Certificates (or on a par with them), will come the claim of the Receiver's Creditors. It is understood that these claims will total from $160,000 to $180,000. Of these the largest is probably that of the A. L. Iron Works amounting to more than $30,000, followed by that of the Blank Foundry Company (amount not known), and by the C. & F. Company, of which the receiver, Mr. C., is an officer, amounting to possibly $10,000 or $12,000.

11. UNSECURED CLAIMS. Following all these claims would come the unsecured claims of creditors of the company for debts incurred before the receiver was appointed. These claims do not change appreciably from the condition shown in the statement on July 31, 1920.

Questions

1. Summarize under appropriate heads the definite conclusions which can be drawn from the foregoing problem regarding the sound principles of Industrial Finance.

2. What special conclusions, if any, do you draw regarding the financing of this concern under its receivership?

3. What light, if any, does the problem throw on the question of granting mercantile credit to a concern which is in a receiver's hands?

4. As the president of the A. L. Iron Works Company would you have sold goods on credit to the N. B. & F. Company?

5. What steps, if any, should you advise taking at this time by the A. L. Iron Works Company, the chief mercantile creditor under the receivership?

6. As the situation has been presented, granted that no legal action is taken by the receiver's creditors, under the most favorable conditions what dividend can the A. L. Iron Works hope to receive on its claims?

7. Assuming that you had been the president and manager of this concern, what steps, if any, would you have taken to avoid the conditions which led to the receivership in 1919?

8. Assuming that you had been appointed receiver of the N. B. & F. Company, what definite steps would you have taken to save the company?

Problem 226

The Financial Problems of a Small, Newly Organized Refrigerator Company

Mr. X. is the highly efficient district sales manager for the East North Central States of one of the largest refrigerator companies in the United States. He has a thorough knowledge of the production and the selling end of the refrigerator business. The company which he represents makes only standard sizes and styles of refrigerators in large numbers, and has continually refused to accept any orders calling for special construction, on the ground that it is more profitable for them to depend for their profits on mass production.

Mr. X., however, discovered that it was necessary, because of his company's policy, for him to turn away on the average several thousand dollars' worth of business per month. Accordingly, he decided that it would be a worth-while experiment to do a little manufacturing himself, in order to fill some of the special orders which he was forced to turn away from his own company. He reasoned that so long as he did not take away customers from the concern which employed him, it would be a perfectly ethical thing for him to do, though he did not at present wish the fact to be known by his employers. Nor did he have at this time more than a few hundred dollars' capital to put into the new venture.

In accordance with the policy which Mr. X. had decided upon, he took a few orders in the spring of 1920, and hired a firm of carpenters, skilled in the art of making refrigerators, to do the work. As he required a large deposit when each order was accepted, he managed to finance the operations for a few months in this way.

Orders began to come in rapidly by July, 1920, and it soon became evident that if this "side line" of Mr. X's was to be continued, he must have a more definite organization for carrying on the work. Yet it was also apparent that his position would be in danger if his identity should be disclosed in this connection before his side line had become sufficiently important to demand all of his attention.

Consequently a plan was worked out for incorporating the company in order to conduct the business more effectively. A president and a treasurer were found, who were willing to put a little money into the business and to act more or less as "silent partners." Mr. X. himself also put in a few hundred dollars. No real estate was purchased, but the services of the firm of carpenters were secured to carry on the manufacture of refrigerators by allowing them $2,000 in cash for their work already in process and the goodwill of their business. They accordingly became employees of the new concern. In all, including the amount paid for this goodwill, not more than $3,500 in cash was originally put into the business. Capital stock was issued as follows:

500 shares of preferred, with a par value of $50.
500 shares of no par value common.

The common stock carried all the voting power, and the majority control was given to Mr. X. as the active promoter of the organization. A very little of the preferred stock was sold to outsiders. Another small portion was taken and paid for by the officers above mentioned, while the remaining portion was donated and deposited as "treasury stock," and was carried on the asset side of the balance sheet.

As the months went on, business was turned to this new concern by Mr. A, though he was always careful not to reveal his own connection with the new company. Finally, he conceived an additional project, which, as he thought, might eventually make his company a great success. Realizing from his former experience that the butcher, for example, is desirous of placing with the same concern an order for some of the other general equipment needed in addition to refrigerators, such as scales, meat cutters, meat blocks, and the like, he decided to act as a jobber for these appliances, and so add a profitable side line to his refrigerator business.

There is a very wide margin between the purchase price and the selling price of such goods, and no added salary expenses were incurred by this policy.

In the meantime, Mr. X., who has little knowledge of accounting and finance, was endeavoring to keep the books of his concern and to exercise general supervision after his day's work was done for the company which employed him. By February, 1921, however, his affairs were in such a condition that he decided to engage the services of a new accountant, who would also act as "assistant treasurer," to help in straightening out his finances. The first balance sheet drawn up showed the following condition:

STATEMENT OF . . . REFRIGERATOR COMPANY
February 1, 1921

Assets	
Machinery, equipment, etc.	$2,000
Inventory:	
Raw material	1,000
In process	1,500
Receivables:	
Accounts	2,000
Notes	2,500
Cash	500
Goodwill	7,000
Treasury stock	14,000
	$30,500

Liabilities	
Capital Stock:	
Preferred (par val. $50)	$25,000
Common, 500 shares (no par value)	500
Accounts payable	5,000
	$30,500

At this point it should be explained that it was now the usual practice of the . . . Company to require 25 per cent cash with all orders, 25 per cent more C. O. D., and the balance over a six months' period, covered by notes due each month for one-sixth of the amount unpaid at the time of delivery (50 per cent of the selling price). These terms are common in the "trade." But the terms granted to the company when purchasing materials were as a rule not more than sixty days net, and they were never able to take their cash discounts because of their lack of working capital. In fact, they were rarely able to pay their bills at the expiration of the net period. They usually tried to put off their smaller creditors on the ground that their financial position would soon be more satisfactory, and that they would then pay cash for their orders. Consequently, this concern, while giving long term, did not itself secure any of the advantages in purchasing which come from prompt payments and an abundant supply of working capital, nor was it possible at this time to borrow any money from the local banks, because of the extremely unsatisfactory current position. It should further be explained that long terms were also given to the customers who bought the accessories carried as a side line, though in this case again the credit terms to the . . . Company were much shorter.

One salesman was now put on the road on a commission basis, ranging from 5 per cent to 10 per cent, depending upon the articles sold. Orders began to come in rapidly within the next two or three months, until by spring the company was almost literally swamped with work which there was no possibility of completing for several months. The management, however, was disposed to encourage these orders, because a certain amount of cash was received with each order—and more cash was absolutely necessary for the business if it was to continue.

Practically every expedient had been tried in order to secure and conserve working capital. For example, neither the president nor the treasurer received any salary, and the "assistant treasurer and accountant," while nominally receiving a small salary, had drawn out practically nothing. Part of the salesman's commissions were not for the present being paid. Further, though an excellent trade-mark had been devised, it had not been registered because of the expense which would thereby be incurred. Some difficulty had always been experienced in meeting the absolutely necessary payroll, and frequently checks were "kited" by the officers between different local banks, with a view to securing temporary funds before demands were made by creditors. Frequently, also, Mr. X. drew on his personal account in order to pay the weekly bills.

By the end of March, an officer of the concern, through an influential friend who was well known to one of the banks in an adjoining town, managed to arrange for the discount of some of the customers' notes held by the . . . Company. This arrangement brought only temporary relief.

In April, 1921, the financial statement submitted to the State Tax Commissioner was as follows:

Statement of . . . . Refrigerator Co.
April 1, 1921.

Assets	
Machinery, equipment, etc.	$2,500
Inventory:	
Raw material	2,000
In process	3,000
Notes receivable	3,000
Cash	1,000
Goodwill	7,000
Treasury stock	13,500
	$32,000
Liabilities	
Capital Stock:	
Preferred (par val. $50)	$25,000
Common, 500 shares (no par value)	500
Accounts payable	4,325
Deposits due to customers on account of unfilled orders	2,000
Surplus	175
	$32,000

The accountant also discovered that the volume of business since the organization of the company in July, 1920, had been about $50,000, and that the sales were rapidly increasing. In fact, during the next month of April, $10,000 worth of goods were sold. The terms of sale were at this time made somewhat more flexible, much business being done for cash and some on open account. By May 15th, the Company was discounting $2,500 of its notes receivable, and the financial condition, as given by the treasurer, was as follows:

STATEMENT OF . . . . REFRIGERATOR COMPANY
May 15, 1921

Assets

Machinery, equipment, etc.	$3,000
Inventory:	
Raw material	2,300
In process	2,800
Finished goods*	2,600
Notes receivable:	
Under 6 months	2,500
Over 6 months	1,200
Accounts receivable	4,800
Cash	600
Treasury stock	14,100
Goodwill	1,000
	$34,900

* Mostly samples of side lines for display purposes.

Liabilities.

Capital Stock:	
Preferred (par val. $50)	$25,000
Common, 500 shares (no par value)	500
Accounts payable	5,000
Due to customers	1,000
Liability for notes discounted	2,500
Surplus	900
	$34,900

On the strength of the above statement a loan of $1,000 was now secured from the local bank. All of the short-time notes receivable were also being discounted by several small banks.

Mr X. is becoming more and more enthusiastic about his little company as the orders are rolling in, and he is now spending most of his nights on his pet project, though still retaining his position as sales manager for the . . . Refrigerator Company, in which he gives entire satisfaction. He is making all possible sacrifices and feels that he has a proposition which will ultimately bring him a fortune. His wife is also much interested in her husband's new company, but is naturally extravagant, and it has not been possible for Mr. X. to put into the company any considerable amount of the earnings received from his present position. After October, Mr. X. plans to devote all of his time to the new business. (He is still under forty.)

Questions

1. Do you approve of launching a new enterprise under the conditions above outlined?

2. Could you suggest any better method of financing the business in the beginning?

3. Do you think it was financially desirable for the company to take on the "side lines" mentioned?

4. Analyze the elements of weakness which you believe are shown by the balance sheets submitted. What important changes, if any, took place between the various dates? Explain any unusual item.

5. Do you approve (*a*) of the selling and (*b*) of the purchasing policy of the concern?

6. (*a*) As an actual, (*b*) as a prospective mercantile creditor, what would be your attitude toward this concern?

7. Are the banks well advised in discounting the customers' notes of this concern? Should an unsecured loan have been made?

8. What steps, if any, would you advise taking in order to secure more adequate working capital?

9. What do you expect to be the future of this company under present management?

10. Assuming that you should have an opportunity to buy out the concern, and were willing to do so,

(*a*) How much would you be disposed to pay and

(*b*) How, if at all, would you reorganize its finances?

STATISTICAL APPENDIX

STATISTICAL APPENDIX

THE following Tables of Statistics are in the main arranged so as to parallel the various chapters in the text. In some of them have been incorporated significant data here worked out for the first time. Others contain material which has been published, but not widely circulated. It is hoped that the material here listed may prove of considerable value to the student and general reader in connection with the preceding problems.

I. Number and Size of Industrial Concerns in the United States

The following summary tables, based on the Census of Manufactures for 1914, show the general development of business concerns over a fifteen-year period:

A. Manufacturing Industries in the United States*

Item	1914	1909	1904	1899
Number of establishments	275,791	268,491	216,180	207,514
Persons engaged	8,263,153	7,678,578	6,213,612	(1)
Proprietors and firm members	262,599	273,265	225,673	(1)
Salaried employees	964,217	790,267	519,556	364,120
Wage earners (average No.)	7,036,337	6,615,046	5,468,383	4,712,763
Primary horsepower	22,547,574	18,675,376	13,487,707	10,097,893
Capital	$22,790,979,937	$18,428,269,706	$12,675,580,874	$8,975,256,496
Salaries and wages	$5,366,249,384	$4,365,612,851	$3,184,884,275	$2,389,132,440
Salaries	1,287,916,951	938,574,967	574,439,322	380,771,321
Wages	4,078,332,433	3,427,037,884	2,610,444,953	2,008,361,119
Paid for contract work	$198,876,826	$178,645,635	$145,322,516	(1)
Rent and taxes (including internal revenue)	$582,039,665	$457,883,110	(2) $131,964,825	(1)
Cost of materials	$14,368,088,831	$12,142,790,878	$8,500,207,810	$6,575,851,491
Value of products	$24,246,434,724	$20,672,051,870	$14,793,902,563	$11,406,926,701
Value added by manufacture (value of products less cost of materials)	$9,878,345,893	$8,529,260,992	$6,293,694,753	$4,831,075,210

(1) Figures not available. (2) Exclusive of internal revenue.

*Preliminary figures for 1919 put the Number of Establishments at 288,376, with a total Value of Product amounting to $62,588,905,000.

B. Manufacturing Concerns in the United States Classified According to Size

Value of Product	Establishments		Wage Earners		Value of Products		Value Added by Manufacture	
	Number	Per cent distribution	Average Number	Per cent distribution	Amount	Per cent distribution	Amount	Per cent distribution
All Classes:								
1919	288,376	100.0	....	100.0	$62,588,905,000	100.0	....	100.0
1914	275,791	100.0	7,036,337	100.0	24,246,434,724	100.0	$9,878,345,893	100.0
1909	268,491	100.0	6,615,046	100.0	20,672,051,870	100.0	8,529,260,992	100.0
1904	216,180	100.0	5,468,383	100.0	14,793,902,563	100.0	6,293,694,753	100.0
Less than $5,000:								
1914	97,061	35.2	129,623	1.8	$233,381,081	1.0	$151,739,764	1.5
1909	93,349	34.8	142,430	2.2	222,463,847	1.1	144,246,008	1.7
1904	71,147	32.9	106,353	1.9	176,128,212	1.2	114,781,124	1.8
$5,000 to $20,000:								
1914	87,931	31.9	429,037	6.1	905,693,168	3.7	507,430,875	5.1
1909	86,988	32.4	470,006	7.1	904,645,664	4.4	509,907,934	6.0
1904	72,791	33.7	419,466	7.7	751,047,759	5.1	424,129,643	6.7
$20,000 to $100,000:								
1914	56,814	20.6	999,600	14.2	2,550,229,411	10.5	1,238,879,430	12.5
1909	57,270	21.3	1,090,449	16.5	2,544,426,711	12.3	1,258,317,991	14.8
1904	48,096	22.2	1,027,047	18.8	2,129,257,883	14.4	1,090,271,887	17.3
$100,000 to $1,000,000:								
1914	30,166	10.9	3,002,071	42.7	8,763,070,135	36.1	3,888,094,982	39.4
1909	27,824	10.4	2,896,532	43.8	7,946,935,255	38.4	3,572,746,038	41.9
1904	22,246	10.3	2,515,064	46.0	6,109,012,538	41.3	2,782,641,883	44.2
$1,000,000 and over:								
1914	3,819	1.4	2,476,006	35.2	11,794,060,929	48.6	4,092,200,842	41.4
1909	3,060	1.1	2,015,629	30.5	9,053,580,393	43.8	3,044,043,021	35.7
1904	1,900	0.9	1,400,453	25.6	5,628,456,171	38.0	1,881,870,216	29.9
Average per establishment:								
1914	....	.....	25.5	.....	$87,916	.....	$35,818	.....
1909	....	.....	24.6	.....	76,993	.....	31,767	.....
1904	....	.....	25.3	.....	68,433	.....	29,113	.....

II. Analysis of the Balance Sheets of Leading Industrial Concerns for the Year 1918

An analysis of the combined balance sheets of more than fifty of the leading industrial concerns of the United States for the year 1918, made by a well-known investment house, shows the following interesting relationships:

Combined Balance Sheet of 57 Leading Industrials for the Year 1918

Assets		Per Cent of Total
Cash	$ 251,601,600	5.42
Receivables	547,318,307	11.79
Inventories	988,340,287	21.30
Securities and other investments	429,952,082	9.26
Deferred or prepaid accounts	55,101,574	1.19
Plant account, Tangibles	1,938,819,088	41.77
Plant account, Intangibles	430,154,474	9.27
	$4,641,287,412	100.
Liabilities		
Common stock	$1,279,074,519	27.56
Preferred stock	971,365,327	20.93
Bonds	500,114,093	10.78
Notes payable	206,941,018	4.46
Accounts payable	409,870,973	8.83
Accrued taxes, dividends and interest	47,844,797	1.03
Reserves	347,171,940	7.48
Special obligations	38,150,932	.82
Surplus	840,753,813	18.11
	$4,641,287,412	100.

1. Statement of Net Quick and Total Net Assets

Current Assets		Per Cent of Current Assets
Cash	$ 251,601,600	11.35
Receivables	547,318,307	24.68
Inventories	988,340,287	44.58
Securities and Other Investments	429,952,082	19.39
Total Current Assets	$2,217,212,276	100.

Current Liabilities		Per cent of Current Liabilities
Notes payable	$206,941,018	19.71
Accounts payable	409,870,973	39.03
Accrued Accounts	47,844,797	4.56
Reserves	385,322,872	36.70
Total Current Liabilities	**$1,049,979,660**	**100.**

		Per Cent of Total Net Assets
Net Quick Assets	$1,167,232,616	36.9
Deferred and Prepaid	55,101,574	1.8
Plant Account, Tangibles	1,938,819,088	61.3
Total Net Assets	$3,161,153,278	100.
Represented by:		
Bonds	$ 500,114,093	
Preferred Stocks	971,365,327	
Common Stocks	1,279,074,519	
Surplus (Less Intangibles)	410,599,339	
	$3,161,153,278	

Ratio of Net Quick Assets to Preferred Stock and Bonds		.79
Ratio of Total Net Assets to Preferred Stock and Bonds		2.15
Total net earnings (after depreciation and taxes)		$324,378,143
Per cent on capital	10.97%	
Relation of preferred stock to common stock	75.9 %	
Relation of bonds to common stock	39.1 %	

2. Relation of Working Capital to Gross Sales

An analysis of the balance sheets and income accounts of 37 large industrial concerns shows the following interesting relations:

Working Capital (Net Quick Assets)	$1,625,243,713
Gross Sales	$7,150,943,372
Turnover of Working Capital	4.4 times

III. Statement of the Capital and Financial Results of Operation of More than 250 Important Industrial Companies for Each Fiscal Year (in Millions of Dollars)

A study of more than 250 of the leading industrial companies, for the period 1911-1918 inclusive, classified in the following manner—

A. Farm and household supplies
B. Industrial material and equipment

shows the following significant relationships*:

A. Farm and Household Supplies

Item	1911	1912	1913	1914	1915	1916	1917	1918
1. Total Assets	$2,252	$2,759	$3,218	$3,416	$3,668	$4,398	$5,251	$5,278
2. Total Liabilities (Excl. funded debt)	288	374	484	528	544	699	1,152	1,389
3. Net Worth	1,964	2,385	2,734	2,888	3,124	3,699	4,099	3,889
4. Funded Debt	313	280	323	339	350	392	383	407
5. Capital Stock	1,317	1,646	1,892	1,964	2,067	2,382	2,499	2,349
6. Net Income	144	189	227	203	284	488	522	371
7. Interest paid on funded debt	15	14	17	17	18	20	20	18
8. Amount Earned for Capital Stock	128	175	211	186	265	468	502	353
9. Dividends paid on Capital Stock	73	101	192	135	150	200	193	169
10. Rate of Return Earned (per cent):								
On Net Worth	7.38	7.93	8.30	7.03	9.08	13.20	12.98	9.53
On Capital Stock	9.74	10.61	11.13	9.46	12.84	19.65	20.10	15.03

B. Industrial Material and Equipment

Item	1911	1912	1913	1914	1915	1916	1917	1918
1. Total Assets	$4,604	$5,013	$5,227	$5,306	$5,890	$6,809	$8,155	$8,382
2. Total Liabilities (Excl. funded debt)	378	441	527	531	854	941	1,651	1,937
3. Net Worth	4,226	4,572	4,700	4,775	5,037	5,868	6,504	6,445
4. Funded Debt	974	1,069	1,071	1,062	1,010	1,025	1,132	1,112
5. Capital Stock	2,784	2,981	3,062	3,160	3,295	3,469	3,589	3,402
6. Net Income	265	309	342	229	444	999	886	627
7. Interest paid on Funded Debt	43	46	47	46	46	47	51	52
8. Amount earned for Capital Stock	222	263	295	183	398	952	835	574
9. Dividends paid on Capital Stock	189	167	183	157	224	360	424	323
10. Rate of Return Earned (per cent):								
On Net Worth	6.27	6.76	7.30	4.78	8.81	17.02	13.62	9.72
On Capital Stock	8.00	8.82	9.63	5.80	12.08	27.45	23.25	16.89

*Based on a study made by a well-known certified public accountant.

IV. Percentage of the Various Types of Securities Outstanding in Typical Industrial Companies

An analysis of the capitalization of groups of typical industrial companies shows the following relationships and changes in the nature of the securities outstanding between 1900 and 1920*:

A. Coal and Iron Companies

Type of Security	1900	1905	1910	1915	1920
Common Stock	71.5	55.1	45.5	50.	50.2
Preferred Stock	4.	2.5	13.3	14.2	18.
Mortgage Bonds	5.	13.	7.7	12.3	8.7
Debenture Bonds	.....	1.1	.4	3.	4.
Miscellaneous and Subsidiaries' bonds	19.3	28.2	32.8	17.3	18.6
Notes	.....	.....	.....	3.2	.....
Shares of no par value (000 omitted)	.....	.....	1,500	1,500	1,500

B. Iron and Steel Companies

Type of Security	1900	1905	1910	1915	1920
Common Stock	56.	37.	37.2	36.1	38.
Preferred Stock	44.	27.	25.	24.6	25.
Mortgage Bonds	.....	.25	2.6	4.5	3.2
Debenture Bonds	.....	.....	.8	.15	2.1
Miscellaneous and Subsidiaries' bonds	.....	35.3	34.25	33.7	31.6
Notes	.....	.....	.5	.75	.03
Shares of no par value	.....	.....	.....	.....	2,344,000

C. Mining Companies

Type of Security	1900	1905	1910	1915	1920
Common Stock	86.	79.	78.5	78.5	71.7
Preferred Stock	9.9	19.3	21.	15.7	12.1
Mortgage Bonds	4.	1.	.15	1.7	4.1
Debenture Bonds	.....	.6	.....	2.	6.
Miscellaneous and Subsidiaries' bonds	.....	.2	.....	.....	5.9
Notes	.....	.....	.12	2.6	.27
Shares of no par value	.....	.....	.....	.....	5,052,000

D. Oil Companies

Type of Security	1900	1905	1910	1915	1920
Common Stock	.....	.....	.....	65.	54.5
Preferred Stock	.....	.....	.....	12.8	30.
Mortgage Bonds	.....	.....	.....	10.3	1.7
Debenture Bonds	.....	.....	.....	9.	2.7
Miscellaneous and Subsidiaries' Bonds	.....	.....	.....	2.5	1.
Notes	.....	.....	.....	.....	11.
Shares of no par value	.....	.....	.....	.....	9,156,000

*Based on a study made by a second-year student in the Harvard Graduate School of Business Administration.

E. Railroad Equipment Companies

Type of Security	1900	1905	1910	1915	1920
Common Stock	53.5	51.	48.	50.7	54.5
Preferred Stock	46.5	46.	42.8	38.8	39.
Mortgage Bonds	......	1.7	1.8	4.9	4.3
Debentures	......	......	......	......	....
Miscellaneous and Subsidiaries' Bonds	......	1.3	3.7	4.4	2.4
Notes	......	......	3.7	1.5	....
Shares of no par value	......	......	......	......	220,000

F. Sugar Companies

Type of Security	1900	1905	1910	1915	1920
Common Stock	58.	55.	55.	50.	46.
Preferred Stock	41.	45.	44.5	43.	52.5
Mortgage Bonds	......	......	......	......	.3
Debenture Bonds	1.	......	......	.3	....
Miscellaneous and Subsidiaries' Bonds	......	......	.4	6.5	....
Notes	......	......	......	......	.8
Shares of no par value	......	......	......	......	605,000

G. Tobacco Companies

Type of Security	1900	1905	1910	1915	1920
Common Stock	47.8	18.4	24.7	45.3	42.
Preferred Stock	52.2	32.8	35.8	36.	31.6
Mortgage Bonds	......	......	......	......	....
Debentures	......	48.7	39.4	18.5	13.1
Miscellaneous and Subsidiaries' Bonds	......	......	......	......	3.3
Notes	......	......	......	......	10.3
Shares of no par value	......	......	......	......	90,000

H. Automotive and Automobile Accessory Companies

Type of Security	1900	1905	1910	1915	1920
Common Stock	......	......	......	52.	44.3
Preferred Stock	......	......	......	44.3	52.
Mortgage Bonds	......	......	......	......	....
Debentures	......	......	......	......	....
Miscellaneous and Subsidiaries' Bonds	......	......	......	......	....
Notes	......	......	......	3.8	3.8
Shares of no par value	......	......	......	......	22,472,000

V. Standards for Credit Granting in Various Industries

One of the most interesting studies on the subject of "Financial Standards" was made by Mr. Alexander Wall, Secretary and Treasurer of the Robert Morris Associates (formerly of the Detroit National Bank of Commerce), at the request of the Federal Reserve Board. From this study, which appeared in the Federal Reserve Bulletin for March, 1919, the following tables are given. In interpreting these tables, the reader should remember that they cover only one year. The average results of an analysis covering a period of years might show different relationships.

1—Wholesale Dry-Goods—Type 1.

Statements	Section	Current Assets	Current Liabilities	Debt	Receivables	Merchandise	Fixed Assets	Net Worth	Sales
6	1	$11,215	$4,646	$5,067	$5,039	$5,674	$2,037	$8,191	$29,749
7	2	11,690	5,436	6.048	5,500	5.400	2,026	7,659	25,266
12	3	12,680	5,093	5,125	4,831	7,209	2,623	10,184	23,783
6	4	4,287	1,497	1,497	1,920	2,340	472	3,494	7,817
4	5	9,203	4,216	4,466	4,104	4,055	1,551	6,290	13,598
12	6	42,364	21,648	21,648	19,137	20,442	9.654	26,546	82,025
27	7	31,834	13,118	13,128	12,106	16,392	7,020	25.752	61,409
4	8	1,849	698	698	743	1,058	837	1,987	4,027
5	9	7,854	3,178	3,178	2,956	4,006	546	5,525	12,659
83	....	$132,976	$59,530	$60,855	$56,236	$66,576	$26,766	$95,628	$260,333

2—Wholesale Hardware—Type 2.

Statements	Section	Current Assets	Current Liabilities	Debt	Receivables	Merchandise	Fixed Assets	Net Worth	Sales
2	1	$ 788	$ 352	$ 352	$ 319	$ 325	$ 193	$ 833	$1,974
10	2	6,428	2,410	2.791	1.706	4,155	1,372	4,949	13,760
14	3	8,898	2,253	2,603	3,318	5,234	3,446	9,578	18,192
25	4	19.791	7,281	7,327	8,077	10,655	2,693	15,530	36,303
8	5	21,262	8,074	8,108	8.487	11,805	5,810	18,765	41,161
13	6	8,989	2,359	2.434	2,309	5,904	1,182	7,536	18,290
16	7	10,865	4,278	4,359	3,734	6,306	1,466	7,642	19,856
4	8	4,851	1,899	1,899	1,732	2,977	1,741	4,651	9,949
7	9	10,417	3,595	3,655	3,006	6.808	1,887	8,512	18,175
99	....	$92,289	$32,501	$33,528	$32,688	$54,209	$19,790	$77,996	$177,660

3—Wholesale Grocer—Type 3.

Statements	Section	Current Assets	Current Liabilities	Debt	Receivables	Merchandise	Fixed Assets	Net Worth	Sales
5	1	$3,207	$1,578	$1,643	$1,470	$1,470	$ 451	$2,027	$10,037
24	2	17,858	7,794	10,707	6,835	9,213	9,326	16,568	59,128
29	3	24,420	10,038	10,095	7,423	15,601	6,477	20,642	80,095
47	4	20,139	7,574	7,646	9,242	9,526	3,623	16,387	64,039
15	5	20.638	8,683	10,319	8,812	10,455	4,067	13,957	60,143
27	6	24,384	10.228	10,348	8,499	14,443	5,079	18,968	75,238
16	7	34,425	15,383	15,658	14,013	18,134	4,373	22,898	96,495
5	8	1,811	562	562	761	977	195	1,429	4,790
7	9	5,591	2,229	2,262	2,292	3,067	872	4,200	17,727
205	....	$152,473	$64,069	$69,240	$59,247	$82,886	$34,463	$117,076	$467,692

4—Tanners—Type 5.

Statements	Section	Current Assets	Current Liabilities	Debt	Receivables	Merchandise	Fixed Assets	Net Worth	Sales
6	1	$22,709	$10,847	$10,847	$8,332	$12,790	$1,870	$12,554	$45,226
7	2	9,051	3,452	3,721	3,028	4,717	2,632	7,889	14,474
8	3	17,443	5,561	6,989	4,517	11,894	7,195	16,857	33,697
1	4	203	99	99	61	128	15	119	479
2	5	20,241	8,635	8,635	4,978	14,255	9,302	20,880	31,983
1	6	435	167	167	147	273	73	341	871
1	7	1,536	226	226	883	454	339	1,645	5,632
2	9	4,263	1,761	1,787	1,368	2,521	1,099	3,576	5,848
28	....	$75,881	$30,738	$32,481	$23,314	$47,032	$22,525	$63,861	$138,210

5—Drugs—Type 6.

Statements	Section	Current Assets	Current Liabilities	Debt	Receivables	Merchandise	Fixed Assets	Net Worth	Sales
2	1	$18,427	$6,749	$6,749	$3,913	$13,011	$35,461	$42,532	$44,711
3	2	5,755	2,154	2,154	1,640	3,430	3,892	7,050	12,234
3	3	1,906	939	939	806	970	554	1,478	4,211
4	4	2,405	794	996	944	1,368	556	1,962	4,743
4	6	2,401	412	412	844	1,471	535	2,503	5,265
1	7	806	213	238	291	482	168	739	2,156
1	8	512	73	73	149	347	33	467	1,122
3	9	2,812	1,006	1,006	852	1,823	336	2,106	5,597
21	....	$35,024	$12,340	$12,567	$9,439	$22,902	$41,535	$58,837	$80,039

6—Farm Implements—Type 7.

Statements	Section	Current Assets	Current Liabilities	Debt	Receivables	Merchandise	Fixed Assets	Net Worth	Sales
2	2	$2,798	$1,360	$1,360	$1,070	$1,453	$1,886	$3,323	$6,618
5	3	7,806	2,983	4,483	1,141	5,093	9,758	12,818	13,475
1	4	764	280	280	361	390	152	636	941
3	5	31,971	5,858	11,871	12,376	15,776	14,910	31,413	22,176
6	6	4,491	1,597	1,669	1,876	2,334	2,103	4,693	6,239
1	7	208	53	53	75	103	86	242	502
2	9	8,888	3,869	3,869	2,236	5,681	3,185	8,203	13,123
20	....	$56,926	$16,000	$23,585	$19,135	$30,830	$32,080	$61,328	$63,074

7—Lumber—Type 9.

Statements	Section	Current Assets	Current Liabilities	Debt	Receivables	Merchandise	Fixed Assets	Net Worth	Sales
4	1	$3,522	$1,312	$1,359	$1,654	$1,612	$2,220	$4,391	$8,056
3	2	2,533	1,059	1,059	1,175	802	948	2,410	6,300
6	3	12,309	4,432	4,607	3,199	7,656	14,970	20,690	23,148
2	4	1,437	664	664	675	597	562	1,339	2,566
11	5	13,273	5,516	6,220	6,595	5,953	4,154	11,163	22,210
15	6	8,984	3,551	3,552	3,556	4,551	3,702	9,315	13,495
4	7	2,030	412	412	938	968	2,612	4,232	2,188
7	8	5,315	2,116	2,116	2,550	2,467	2,295	5,416	11,430
2	9	1,789	697	697	696	922	3,550	4,675	4,264
54	....	$51,192	$19,759	$20,686	$21,038	$25,528	$35,013	$63,631	$93,657

8—Packers—Type 12.

Statements	Section	Current Assets	Current Liabilities	Debt	Receivables	Merchandise	Fixed Assets	Net Worth	Sales
1	1	$ 641	$ 430	$ 430	$ 290	$ 282	$ 688	$ 797	$2,629
1	2	1,120	175	175	278	751	2,189	2,685	2,652
10	3	397,286	169,890	251,470	146,215	176,792	157,932	297,443	1,490,928
3	5	6,087	2,950	2,950	1,754	3,505	4,059	7,155	33,864
1	6	220	118	118	20	195	155	257	916
1	8	1,776	1,046	1,046	591	1,108	1,272	2,003	4,987
2	9	10,330	3,663	3,663	2,584	5,268	9,114	12,212	22,805
19	....	$417,460	$177,272	$259,851	$151,732	$187,901	$175,409	$322,552	$1,558,781

9—Boots and Shoes—Type 13.

Statements	Section	Current Assets	Current Liabilities	Debt	Receivables	Merchandise	Fixed Assets	Net Worth	Sales
20	1	$51,265	$23,669	$24,083	$23,200	$23,871	$13,678	$41,616	$109,817
14	2	43,765	20,216	20,241	12,860	24,570	1,503	24,473	53,080
9	3	6,258	2,025	2,137	2,742	3,243	816	4,922	13,438
1	4	815	216	216	470	324	71	669	914
7	5	9,082	3,930	3,930	3,847	4,417	1,695	6,722	16,126
10	6	52,600	22,904	23,084	19,374	29,979	26,212	33,822	121,073
2	7	2,179	673	673	798	1,237	222	1,729	3,290
1	8	211	118	118	98	80	156	249	401
2	9	1,638	698	698	519	987	146	1,086	3,397
66	....	$167,813	$74,449	$75,180	$63,908	$88,707	$44,499	$115,288	$321,536

10—Dry-Goods—Type 1.

Sections	1	2	3	4	5	6	7	8	9	National
No. of statements	6	7	12	6	4	12	27	4	5	83
	Per cent.	*Per cent.*	*Per cent.*	*Per cent.*	*Per cent.*	*Per cent.*	*Per cent.*	*Per cent.*	*Per cent.*	*Per cent*
Current ratio	241.39	215.04	248.96	288.37	218.28	195.69	242.67	264.89	247.13	223.38
Receivables—merchandise	90.41	101.85	67.01	82.05	101.21	93.61	73.85	70.22	73.48	84.61
Worth—fixed assets	402.11	378.03	388.29	740.25	405.54	274.97	366.83	237.39	1,011.90	357.27
Sales—receivables	590.37	459.38	492.29	407.13	331.33	428.16	507.26	541.49	428.24	462.10
Sales—merchandise	524.30	467.88	329.90	334.05	335.33	401.25	374.62	380.62	316.00	391.03
Sales—worth	363.19	329.88	233.53	223.72	216.18	308.99	238.46	202.66	229.12	272.23
Debt—worth	61.86	78.96	50.32	42.84	71.00	36.36	50.97	35.12	57.52	63.66

11—Hardware—Type 2.

Sections	1	2	3	4	5	6	7	8	9	National
No. of statements	2	10	14	25	8	13	16	4	7	99
	Per cent.	*Per cent.*	*Per cent.*	*Per cent.*	*Per cent.*	*Per cent.*	*Per cent.*	*Per cent.*	*Per cent.*	*Per cent.*
Current ratio	223.22	266.72	394.94	271.82	263.33	381.05	253.97	255.45	289.76	283.95
Receivables—merchandise	98.15	41.06	63.39	75.80	71.89	38.84	59.21	58.17	44.15	60.29
Worth—fixed assets	431.60	260.70	277.94	576.68	322.97	637.56	521.28	267.14	457.00	394.11
Sales—receivables	618.80	806.58	548.28	449.46	484.98	792.11	531.76	574.42	604.62	543.50
Sales—merchandise	607.38	331.16	347.57	340.71	348.67	207.70	314.87	334.19	266.96	327.73
Sales—worth	236.97	278.03	189.93	233.76	219.34	242.70	259.83	213.91	213.52	227.78
Debt—worth	42.25	56.39	27.17	47.15	43.20	32.29	48.86	40.82	42.93	42.98

12—Grocers—Type 3.

Sections	1	2	3	4	5	6	7	8	9	National
No. of statements	5	24	29	47	15	27	46	5	7	205
	Per cent.	*Per cent.*	*Per cent.*	*Per cent.*	*Per cent.*	*Per cent.*	*Per cent.*	*Per cent.*	*Per cent.*	*Per cent.*
Current ratio	203.26	229.12	243.27	265.89	237.68	238.42	223.78	322.22	250.82	237.98
Receivables—merchandise	100.00	74.18	47.58	97.56	84.26	58.84	77.27	77.89	74.73	71.60
Worth—fixed assets	499.41	177.66	318.69	452.58	343.17	373.45	523.62	732.82	481.65	339.71
Sales—receivables	682.78	865.07	1,079.03	692.91	682.51	885.25	688.61	629.43	773.42	788.06
Sales—merchandise	682.78	641.77	413.39	672.25	575.25	520.93	532.12	490.29	577.89	564.25
Sales—worth	495.16	356.87	388.01	390.79	430.91	396.65	421.41	335.19	422.07	399.47
Debt—worth	81.05	64.61	48.90	46.65	73.93	54.55	68.38	39.32	53.85	59.14

13—Tanners—Type 5.

Sections	1	2	3	4	5	6	7	8	9	National
No. of statements	6	7	8	1	2	1	1	....	2	28
	Per cent.	*Per cent.*	*Per cent.*	*Per cent.*	*Per cent.*	*Per cent.*	*Per cent.*	*Per cent.*	*Per cent.*	*Per cent.*
Current ratio	209.35	262.19	313.66	205.05	234.40	260.47	379.64	....	241.28	246.86
Receivables—merchandise	65.14	64.19	37.97	47.65	34.92	53.84	25.59	....	54.26	49.57
Worth—fixed assets	671.33	299.73	234.28	793.33	224.46	467.12	487.90	....	325.37	283.51
Sales—receivables	542.79	359.33	746.00	785.24	642.98	592.51	637.82	....	427.48	592.81
Sales—merchandise	353.60	306.84	283.31	374.21	224.36	319.04	1,240.52	....	231.97	293.86
Sales—worth	360.25	183.47	199.89	402.53	153.17	255.42	342.37	....	166.53	216.42
Debt—worth	86.40	47.29	41.46	43.35	41.35	48.97	13.37	....	49.97	50.86

14—Drugs—Type 6.

Sections	1	2	3	4	5	6	7	8	9	National
No. of statements	2	3	3	4	0	4	1	1	3	21
	Per cent.	*Per cent.*	*Per cent.*	*Per cent.*	*Per cent.*	*Per cent.*	*Per cent.*	*Per cent.*	*Per cent.*	*Per cent.*
Current ratio	273.03	267.17	202.98	302.89	....	582.75	378.40	701.36	279.52	283.83
Receivables—merchandise	30.07	47.81	83.09	69.00	....	57.37	60.37	42.94	46.73	41.21
Worth—fixed assets	111.94	181.14	266.78	352.87	....	467.85	439.88	1,415.15	626.78	141.85
Sales—receivables	1,142.62	745.97	522.45	502.43	....	623.81	740.89	753.02	656.92	847.96
Sales—merchandise	343.64	356.66	434.12	346.71	....	357.91	347.30	323.33	307.02	349.48
Sales—worth	105.12	173.53	284.91	241.74	....	210.34	291.74	240.25	265.76	136.05
Debt—worth	15.86	30.55	63.53	50.76	....	16.46	32.20	15.63	47.76	21.35

15—Farm Implements—Type 7.

Sections	1	2	3	4	5	6	7	8	9	National
No. of statements	....	2	5	1	3	6	1	....	2	20
	Per cent.	*Per cent.*	*Per cent.*	*Per cent.*	*Per cent.*	*Per cent.*	*Per cent.*	*Per cent.*	*Per cent.*	*Per cent.*
Current ratio	....	205.73	261.68	272.85	545.78	281.21	483.61	....	329.72	355.78
Receivables—merchandise	....	73.64	22.40	92.56	78.45	80.37	72.81	....	39.35	63.50
Worth—fixed assets	....	176.19	131.35	418.42	210.88	223.15	281.39	....	257.56	191.17
Sales—receivables	....	618.50	1,180.98	260.66	179.18	232.56	569.32	....	586.86	329.62
Sales—merchandise	....	455.47	264.57	241.28	140.56	267.30	487.37	....	230.99	209.33
Sales—worth	....	199.15	105.12	147.95	70.59	132.94	207.43	....	150.97	102.84
Debt—worth	....	40.92	34.97	44.02	37.79	35.56	21.90	....	47.16	38.45

16—Lumber—Type 9.

Sections	1	2	3	4	5	6	7	8	9	National
No. of statements	4	3	6	2	11	15	4	7	2	54
	Per cent.	*Per cent.*	*Per cent.*	*Per cent.*	*Per cent.*	*Per cent.*	*Per cent.*	*Per cent.*	*Per cent.*	*Per cent.*
Current ratio	268.44	239.18	277.72	216.41	240.62	252.99	492.71	251.18	256.67	259.08
Receivables—merchandise	102.60	146.50	41.78	113.06	110.78	78.13	96.90	103.36	75.58	82.37
Worth—fixed assets	97.79	254.21	138.20	238.25	268.92	251.62	162.02	186.43	131.68	181.73
Sales—receivables	487.06	536.17	723.60	380.14	336.77	379.49	233.26	448.23	612.64	445.18
Sales—merchandise	499.75	785.53	302.35	429.81	373.08	296.52	226.03	463.31	462.47	366.87
Sales—worth	184.46	261.41	111.87	191.63	198.96	144.87	51.70	211.04	91.20	147.18
Debt—worth	30.94	43.94	22.25	49.58	55.71	38.13	43.92	39.06	17.90	32.50

17—Packers—Type 12.

Sections	1	2	3	4	5	6	7	8	9	National
No. of statements	1	1	10	....	3	1	....	1	2	19
	Per cent.	*Per cent.*	*Per cent.*	*Per cent.*	*Per cent.*	*Per cent.*	*Per cent.*	*Per cent.*	*Per cent.*	*Per cent.*
Special current ratio	....	....	157.98	....	....	....	....	....	....	160.65
Current ratio	149.06	640.00	233.84	....	206.33	186.44	....	169.79	282.00	235.49
Receivables—merchandise	102.83	37.02	82.70	....	50.04	10.25	....	53.33	49.05	80.75
Worth—fixed assets	110.02	122.65	188.33	....	176.27	165.80	....	157.46	133.99	183.88
Sales—receivables	906.55	953.95	1,019.68	....	1,093.67	4,580.00	....	843.82	882.54	1,027.30
Sales—merchandise	932.36	353.12	843.32	....	766.16	469.74	....	450.00	432.89	829.57
Sales—worth	329.86	98.77	501.24	....	473.06	356.42	....	248.97	186.74	483.27
Debt—worth	53.95	6.50	84.54	....	41.22	45.91	....	58.22	29.98	80.56

18—Boots and Shoes—Type 13.

Sections	1	2	3	4	5	6	7	8	9	National
No. of statements	20	14	9	1	7	10	2	1	2	63
	Per cent.	*Per cent.*	*Per cent.*	*Per cent.*	*Per cent.*	*Per cent.*	*Per cent.*	*Per cent.*	*Per cent.*	*Per cent.*
Current ratio	216.59	216.48	309.03	377.31	231.09	229.65	323.77	178.81	234.67	225.40
Receivables—merchandise	97.18	52.34	84.55	145.06	87.09	64.62	64.51	122.50	52.58	72.04
Worth—fixed assets	204.25	1,628.27	513.18	942.25	396.57	129.05	778.82	159.61	743.85	259.07
Sales—receivables	473.34	412.75	490.08	194.46	419.18	624.92	412.28	409.18	654.52	503.12
Sales—merchandise	460.04	216.03	414.36	282.09	365.08	403.85	265.96	501.25	344.17	362.46
Sales—worth	263.88	216.89	273.01	136.62	239.89	357.97	190.28	161.04	312.79	278.89
Debt—worth	57.86	82.70	43.41	32.28	58.46	68.25	38.92	29.82	64.27	65.21

19—National Type Ratios.

Types	1	2	3	5	6	7	9	12	13	....
No. of statements	83	99	205	28	21	20	54	19	66	....
	Per cent.	*Per cent.*	*Per cent.*	*Per cent.*	*Per cent.*	*Per cent.*	*Per cent.*	*Per cent.*	*Per cent.*	
Current ratio	223.38	283.95	237.98	246.86	269.35	355.78	259.08	235.49	225.40	
Special current ratio	....	....	....	....	....	....	....	160.65	....	....
Receivables—merchandise	84.61	60.29	71.60	49.57	41.21	63.50	82.37	80.75	72.04	....
Worth—fixed assets	357.27	394.11	339.71	283.51	141.65	191.17	181.73	183.88	259.07	....
Sales—receivables	462.10	543.50	788.06	592.81	847.96	329.62	445.18	1,027.30	503.12	....
Sales—merchandise	391.03	327.73	564.25	293.86	349.48	209.33	366.87	829.57	362.46	....
Sales—worth	272.23	227.78	399.47	216.42	136.05	102.84	147.18	483.27	278.89	....
Debt—worth	63.66	42.98	59.14	50.86	21.35	38.45	32.50	80.56	65.21	....

20—National Mixed Type Ratios

Sections	1	2	3	4	5	6	7	8	9	National
Number of statements	91	138	165	107	72	144	127	36	41	981
	Per cent	*Per cent*	*Per cent*	*Per cent*	*Per cent*	*Per cent*	*Per cent*	*Per cent*	*Per cent*	*Per cent*
Current ratio	233.43	234.65	236.02	261.20	270.85	237.02	252.40	305.55	256.81	241.24
Receivables—merchandise	69.76	59.95	61.17	82.43	70.05	66.09	71.89	69.51	56.11	64.64
Worth—fixed assets	191.48	184.06	165.15	289.95	199.47	186.80	345.43	178.84	239.77	184.47
Sales—receivables	586.16	659.48	890.14	558.87	515.08	766.26	627.90	568.12	776.04	734.61
Sales—merchandise	408.91	395.39	544.55	460.68	360.82	506.48	451.58	394.94	435.46	473.44
Sales—worth	209.21	200.71	281.55	248.97	188.94	297.60	293.25	142.52	246.22	249.34
Debt—worth	43.28	43.35	52.46	43.38	46.13	46.14	48.98	22.16	38.58	47.19

VI. Financial Standards in the Rubber Tire Industry

An analytical study of the finances of the smaller rubber tire companies in the United States, covering the last decade, shows the following interesting relations*:

*The figures were compiled under the author's direction by a second-year student in the Harvard University Graduate School of Business Administration.

BALANCE SHEET RATIOS OF SMALL RUBBER TIRE PLANTS

Averages of Ratios for the Group of Smaller Tire Companies (*100 per cent=1.*)	1910	1911	1912	1913	1914	1915	1916	1917	1918	1919	10-Year Average	Last 6-Year Average	Last 3-Year Average
Fixed Assets to Total Assets	.40	.35	.35	.35	.35	.35	.32	.26	.27	.25	.33	.30	.26
Current Assets to Total Assets	.60	.65	.65	.65	.65	.65	.68	.74	.73	.75	.67	.70	.74
Current Assets to Plant	1.6	1.8	2.2	2.2	2.3	2.0	2.2	2.9	3.3	3.4	2.4	2.7	3.2
Cash to Total Assets Investment	.04	.03	.04	.07	.06	.06	.03	.03	.09	.06	.05	5.5	.06
Net Worth to Total Assets	.73	.67	.70	.75	.85	.90	.70	.60	.70	.70	.73	.74	.67
Net Worth to Fixed Assets	1.8	2.0	2.4	2.4	2.5	2.5	2.2	2.5	3.0	3.0	2.4	2.6	2.8
Net Current Assets to Total Assets	.37	.33	.35	.35	.45	.55	.40	.39	.45	.48	.41	.45	.43
Net Current Assets to Plant Investment	.9	1.0	1.5	1.2	1.7	1.6	1.3	1.4	2.0	2.1	1.5	1.6	1.8
Cash to Plant Investment	.11	.12	.18	.19	.16	.16	.13	.13	.33	.22	.17	.19	.22
Cash to Current Assets	.13	.06	.07	.12	.09	.10	.05	.05	.13	.08	.09	.08	.08
Receivables to Current Assets	.19	.35	.33	.29	.35	.41	.39	.33	.31	.32	.33	.35	.34
Inventory to Current Assets	.68	.59	.59	.58	.55	.48	.54	.59	.55	.58	.57	.55	.57
Receivables to Inventory	.29	.60	.55	.40	.61	.78	.56	.53	.59	.68	.55	.61	.54
Receivables to Sales	.05	.14	.20	.21	.16	.19	.18	.19	.14	.15	.16	.17	.16
Sales to Inventory	4.0	4.8	4.3	4.1	4.1	3.5	3.2	2.7	3.6	3.4	3.8	3.4	3.2
Sales to Fixed Assets	8.0	5.6	6.8	5.5	6.1	4.4	5.1	3.6	6.9	5.5	5.7	5.3	5.3
Sales to Net Worth	3.8	2.4	2.3	1.9	2.1	1.5	2.1	1.6	2.4	2.2	2.2	2.0	2.1
Sales to Net Current Assets	7.5	4.8	3.1	2.7	2.9	2.2	2.9	3.0	3.9	3.0	3.6	3.0	3.3
Profits to Net Worth	.25	.12	.18	.15	.18	.14	.12	.13	.11	.14	.14	.14	.13
Profits to Total Assets	.25	.10	.16	.13	.16	.16	.10	.10	.10	.11	.13	.12	.10
Profits to Fixed Assets	.50	.30	.35	.27	.32	.40	.40	.30	.32	.38	.35	.35	.33
Profits to Sales	.11	.03	.10	.11	.14	.14	.10	.07	.05	.08	.09	.09	.07
Current Assets to Current Liabilities	5.5	2.1	3.5	3.7	4.5	10.0	3.0	3.0	3.9	3.4	4.3	4.6	3.4
Receivables to Debt	1.1	.75	1.0	1.2	1.7	1.9	1.3	.95	1.0	1.1	1.2	1.3	1.0
Cash to Debt	.52	.14	.33	.73	.52	.77	.21	.13	.39	.35	.41	.40	.29

VII. Financial Standards in the Automobile Industry

A comparative study of the financial condition of all automobile companies in the United States for every year since 1910 shows the following interesting balance sheet relations:*

Ratio of	High	Low	Modal Average
1. Current Assets to Current Liabilities	4.	2.4	3.3
2. Cash to Current Assets	.24	.04	....
3. Cash to Current Liabilities	.85	.1	.25
4. Receivables to Merchandise Inventory	.55	.15	.27
5. Receivables to Current Liabilities	1.0	.20	.50
6. Merchandise to Current Liabilities	2.75	1.00	2.00
7. Current Assets to Plant Investment	3.0	1.5	2.0
8. Net Current Assets to Plant Investment	2.5	1.0	1.5
9. Net Worth of Plant Investment	3.5	2.0	2.8
10. Total Debt to Net Worth	1.0	.4	....
11. Net Income to Capital Stock	.32	.1	....
12. Net Income to Sales	.18	.04	....
13. Receivables to Sales	.27	.5	....
14. Sales to Merchandise	6.	2.5	....

*This study was made under the author's direction by a second-year student in the Harvard University Graduate School of Business Administration.

VIII. Financial Standards in the Cotton Industry

The following interesting ratios of concerns engaged in the cotton business were worked out by Mr. G. Livingston Woolley, Manager of the Credit Department of the Hibernia Bank and Trust Company of New Orleans, and published in the July, 1920, *Bulletin* of the Robert Morris Associates.

A. Average Statement of Cotton Broker
Based on 43 Names

Assets

Cash	.1246
Bills and accounts receivable	.2220
Acceptances receivable	.0013
Cotton on hand	.4896
Liberty Bonds and War Savings Stamps	.0243
Advances	.0089
Real estate, fixtures, etc.	.0306
Stocks and bonds	.0739
Sundries	.0066
Due from brokers—hedges	.0182
Total	1.0000

Liabilities

Bills and accounts payable	.6008
Acceptances payable	.0057
Money on deposit	.0328
Due brokers on hedges	.0149
Accruals	.0311
Capital accounts	.2313
Undivided profits	.0755
Capital reserves	.0079
Total	1.0000

B. Average Statement of Cotton Mill,
Based on 80 Names

Assets

Cash	.0526
Accounts and bills receivable	.0595
Merchandise	.2524
Due from selling agents	.0366
Liberty Bonds and War Savings Stamps	.0679
Building, plant and equipment	.4950
Stocks and bonds	.0129
Other accounts receivable, including due from officers, etc.	.0052
Fuel and supplies	.0114
Sundry, including good-will, etc.	.0065
Total	1.0000

Liabilities

Accounts and bills payable	.1438
Trade acceptances	.0008
Due selling agents	.0012
Money on deposit	.0012
Due affiliated companies	.0004
Accruals	.0431
Bonded indebtedness	.0020
Capital	.2810
Surplus	.3644
Reserves, including depreciation	.1621
Total	1.0000

IX. Classification of Expenses in Manufacturing Industries Having Products Valued at More than $100,000,000 in 1909

Computations made from the United States Census of Manufactures for 1909 show the following interesting relations:

AMOUNTS IN MILLIONS OF DOLLARS

Number	Industry	Number of Concerns	Capital	Value Of Product	Net Income	Total Expenses	Salaries and Wages	Cost of Materials	Miscellaneous
	All Industries	268,491	$18,428	$20,672	$2,217	$18,455	$4,366	$12,143	$1,94
1	Agricultural Implements	640	256	146	28	118	39	60	
2	Automobiles, etc.	743	174	249	38	211	58	132	
3	Bakeries	23,926	213	397	57	340	73	238	
4	Boots and Shoes	1,918	222	513	35	478	117	333	
5	Canning and Preserving	3,767	119	157	16	141	27	102	
6	Carriages and Wagons	5,492	175	160	21	139	46	82	
7	Car Building	110	140	124	6	118	32	79	
8	Cheese, Butter, etc.	8,479	71	275	16	259	15	236	
9	Chemicals	349	155	118	24	94	20	64	
10	Clocks, watches, etc	120	58	35	5	30	15	11	
11	Clothing, men's	6,354	275	568	55	513	133	298	
12	Clothing, women's	4,558	129	385	44	341	99	209	
13	Coke	315	152	96	12	84	18	64	
14	Confectionery	1,944	68	135	15	120	25	81	
15	Copper, tin, etc.	4,228	218	200	23	177	50	113	
16	Cotton Goods	1,324	822	628	74	554	147	371	
17	Cutlery, etc.	959	67	53	7	46	22	18	
18	Electric Mach.	1,009	268	221	19	202	70	109	
19	Explosives	86	50	40	9	31	5	23	
20	Fertilizers	550	122	104	14	90	12	70	
21	Flour Mills	11,691	349	884	56	828	34	768	
22	Foundries	13,253	1,514	1,228	151	1,077	415	540	1
23	Furniture	3,155	227	240	27	213	81	109	
24	Gas (artificial)	1,296	916	167	53	114	33	52	
25	Hosiery	1,374	164	200	24	176	52	110	
26	Iron and Steel	446	1,005	986	96	890	189	658	
27	Leather (tanning) etc.	919	333	328	22	306	39	248	
28	Leather Goods	2,375	70	105	12	93	25	60	
29	Liquor, distilled	613	72	205	10	195	5	36	
30	Liquor, malt	1,414	671	375	75	300	64	97	
31	Lumber	40,671	1,177	1,156	160	996	366	508	
32	Musical Instruments	507	103	90	9	81	28	44	
33	Paint and Varnish	791	104	125	14	111	19	79	
34	Paper	777	409	268	31	237	50	165	
35	Petroleum Ref. etc.	147	182	237	15	222	14	199	
36	Pottery, terra cotta	822	141	76	10	66	36	22	
37	Printing	31,445	588	738	119	619	268	202	
38	Railway Shops	1,145	238	406	.....	405	199	199	
39	Rubber Goods	227	99	128	14	114	20	82	
40	Shipbuilding	1,353	126	73	5	68	29	31	
41	Silk	852	152	197	20	177	46	108	
42	Slaughtering	1,641	383	1,371	54	1,318	72	1,203	
43	Smelting—lead	28	132	167	7	160	7	152	
44	Sugar ref.	19	115	249	8	241	7	226	
45	Tobacco	15,822	246	417	51	366	86	177	
46	Woolen & Worsted	985	431	436	48	388	83	283	

PERCENTAGE RELATIONS

Ratio of Value of Product to Capital	Ratio of Net Income to Capital	Ratio of Net Income to Value of Product	Ratio of Expenses to Value of Product	Ratio of Cost of Services to Total Expenses	Ratio of Cost of Materials to Total Expenses	Ratio of Miscell'n's Expenses to Total Expenses	Number. . .
112	12	10.8	89.2	23.7	65.8	10.5	. . .
57	11	19.2	80.8	32.9	51.1	16.0	1
143	21.8	15.2	84.8	27.6	62.5	9.9	2
186	26.7	14.4	85.6	21.5	69.9	8.6	3
231	15.8	6.8	93.2	24.5	69.6	5.9	4
132	13.4	10.2	89.8	19.0	72.0	9.0	5
91	12.	13.2	86.8	32.7	58.9	8.4	6
88	4.3	4.8	95.2	27.3	66.7	6.0	7
387	22.5	6.0	94.0	5.7	91.0	3.3	8
76	15.5	20.3	79.7	21.5	68.2	10.3	9
60	8.6	14.3	85.7	50.6	37.2	12.1	10
206	20.	9.7	90.3	25.9	57.9	16.2	11
300	34.1	11.4	88.6	29.0	61.1	9.9	12
63	8.0	12.5	87.5	20.7	75.5	3.9	13
200	22.1	11.1	88.9	20.7	67.9	11.4	14
91	10.5	11.5	88.5	28.2	63.7	8.1	15
76	9.0	11.8	88.2	26.6	66.9	6.5	16
79	10.4	13.2	86.8	47.8	40.1	12.1	17
82	7.0	8.6	91.4	34.5	53.8	11.7	18
80	18.	22.5	77.5	17.3	72.5	10.2	19
85	11.5	13.5	86.5	13.2	77.2	9.7	20
252	16.0	6.3	93.7	4.1	92.8	3.1	21
82	10.	12.3	87.7	38.5	50.1	11.4	22
106	11.9	11.2	88.8	38.1	51.0	10.9	23
18.2	5.8	31.7	68.3	29.4	46.2	24.5	24
122	14.6	12.0	88.0	29.8	62.7	7.4	25
98	9.6	9.7	90.3	21.3	73.9	4.8	26
99	6.6	6.7	93.3	12.7	81.2	6.1	27
150	17.1	11.4	88.6	26.5	64.6	8.9	28
285	13.9	4.9	95.1	2.6	18.4	79.0	29
57	11.2	20.	80.	21.3	32.2	46.5	30
96	13.4	13.8	86.2	36.8	51.0	12.2	31
87	8.7	10.0	90.0	35.1	54.2	10.7	32
120	13.5	11.2	88.8	16.8	71.1	12.2	33
65	7.6	11.5	88.5	21.2	69.7	9.1	34
130	8.3	6.3	93.7	6.2	89.6	4.2	35
54	7.1	13.2	86.8	54.2	33.4	12.5	36
125	20.2	16.1	83.9	43.3	32.6	24.1	37
. . . . . .	. . . . . .	. . . . . .	. . . . . .	49.0	49.2	1.8	38
129	14.1	10.9	89.1	17.1	72.0	10.9	39
58	4.0	6.8	93.2	43.4	46.2	10.4	40
130	13.2	10.2	89.8	26.	60.8	13.2	41
358	14.1	3.9	96.1	5.4	91.3	3.3	42
126	5.3	4.2	95.8	4.3	94.8	0.9	43
216	7.0	3.2	96.8	3.0	93.8	3.2	44
170	20.7	12.2	87.8	23.5	48.4	28.0	45
101	11.1	11.0	89.0	21.3	72.9	5.8	46

X. Classified Expenses in Retail Stores

Figures recently issued by the National Association of Newspaper Executives show the common experience in percentage of net sales in the principal branches of retail trade. These figures are compiled from data furnished by the Harvard University Bureau of Business Research and some of the retail research organizations. They were recently published in the *Retail Public Ledger* (March 16, 1921).

	Department	Grocery	Drug	Hardware	Furniture	Men's Clothing	Shoe	Jewelry
Rent	3.24	3.07	4.02	3.41	5.04	3.04	3.21	4.98
Salaries	9.65	8.46	10.95	10.11	9.73	9.49	10.51	10.96
Advertising*	4.67	1.83	2.76	1.12	3.72	3.16	2.65	2.85
Heat and Light	.54	.39	.69	.43	.92	.62	1.10	.61
Delivery	1.02	2.53	.51	.91	.94	.65	.46	.09
Supplies	.38	.37	.35	.60	.41	.43	.30	.89
Insurance and Taxes	1.08	.58	1.21	.99	1.57	1.07	1.03	1.32
General expenses	4.15	.45	4.49	2.01	1.10	2.31	4.36	3.95
Depreciation and Shrinkage	1.11	.76	.47	.52	2.14	2.16	.50	.95
Bad debts	.21	.47	.19	.31	1.94	.34	.10	.21
Total percentage of expenses to sales	26.05	18.91	25.65	20.41	27.51	23.27	24.22	26.81

*Specialty store advertising can run as high as 5.5 per cent.

Extremely valuable computations of a more detailed sort are being made annually by the Harvard University Bureau of Business Research for the following lines of business: *Retail Grocery, Wholesale Grocery, Retail Shoe, Wholesale Shoe, Retail Hardware, Retail Jewelry, Retail Drug.*

XI. The Annual Turnover of Stock in Retail Stores

There are presented herewith figures regarding the turnover of inventory, collected from various sources.

This following table (A) is based on the result of questionnaires sent to about 5,000 different concerns, the results of which were published in the *Bulletin* of the National Association of Credit Men (April, 1917, page 240):

A. General Retail Stores

Business	Stock Turnover	Percentage Cost of Doing Business (on Net Sales)
Groceries	10	16
Department Stores	7	26¼
Drugs	4	24¾
Dry-Goods	4	23
Hardware	3½	19½
Furniture	3	24
Boots and Shoes	2	23¼
Clothing	2	20¼
Jewelry	1½	25¾

The annual average turnover of the following lines of stock in several hundred department stores has been estimated by the Bureau of Business Standards of the A. W. Shaw Company as follows:

B. Turnover of Stock in Department Stores

Type of Goods	Stock Turnover	Type of Goods	Stock Turnover
Notions	9	Hosiery	4
Corsets	8	Gloves	3.5
Women's ready-to-wear clothing	6	Dress goods	3.2
		Silks	3.1
Wall paper	4.2	Domestics	3
Men's furnishings	4.2	Carpets	1.5
Underwear	4.1		

The annual stock turnover in the Rexall chain of drug stores was some years ago reported to be as follows:

C. Turnover in Rexall Stores

Type of Goods	Stock Turnover	Type of Goods	Stock Turnover
Soda water	52	General merchandise	8
Candy	20	*Total Store*	10
Cigars	15		

XII. Relative Advertising Expenses in Typical Concerns

A study covering 1,489 cases, the results of which have recently appeared in System (May, 1921, p. 673, ff.), shows the following interesting relations of advertising expenses and total selling expenses to net sales, in manufacturing concerns:

Percentage Expense on Net Sales

Business	Advertising	Total Selling
Trunk manufacturing	5 %	12.25%
Hardware manufacturing	4.29%	8. %
Dry-goods jobbing	1.6 %	7.33%
Hosiery manufacturing	1.88%	10. %
Food products manufacturing	4.55%	14.3 %

XIII. The Relation of Net Income to Invested Capital

A study of the relationships which exist between the invested capital, capital stock, and the net income of various types of manufacturing concerns, based on the general figures given in the Treasury Report on Corporate Earnings and Government Revenues for the year 1917, shows the following significant facts:

A. Investment and Income Statistics of Garment Manufacturing Concerns, Grouped According to Invested Capital. (Thousands omitted.)

Group	1917						1916				
	1	2	3	4	5	6	7	8	9	10	11
	Number in each Group	Capital Stock	Invested Capital	Net Income	Per cent 4 to 2	Per cent 4 to 3	Capital Stock	Est. Invested Capital	Net Income	Per cent 9 to 7	Per cent 9 to 8
Under $10,000.....	17	5.4	7.	4.2	77.	60.	5.2	6.7	2.8	57.	44.
10,000–20,000.....	29	11.6	14.	2.4	21.	17.	6.1	7.4	1.9	31.	26.
20,000–50,000.....	108	24.	32.	9.	35.	26.	22.	29.	8.	36.	27.
50,000–100,000....	57	50.	72.	17.	34.	24.	45.	65.	15.	35.	24.
100,000–200,000...	37	103.	145.	40.	39.	27.	100.	141.	33.	33.	24.
200,000–500,000...	25	191.	321.	80.	42.	25.	201.	336.	67.	33.	20.
500,000–1,000,000..	9	388.	663.	183.	47.	28.	416.	711.	145.	35.	20.
1,000,000–2,000,000	7	618.	1176.	480.	78.	41.	544.	1033.	227.	42.	22.
2,000,000–5,000,000	2	1075.	2349.	561.	52.	24.	825.	1798.	312.	38.	17.

B. Investment and Income Statistics of Steel Manufacturing Concerns, Grouped According to Invested Capital (thousands omitted)

1. Castings

Group	1917						1916				
	1	2	3	4	5		6	7	8	9	
	Number in Each Group	Capital Stock	Invested Capital	Net Income	Per Cent		Capital Stock	Estimated Invested Capital	Net Income	Per Cent	
					4–2	4–3				8–6	8–7
Under $10,000	6	12.2	9.2	7.8	64.	85.	6.	4.5	.33	5.5	7.3
10,000– 20,000	12	11.8	16.	6.3	54.	39.	11.2	15.2	4.6	41.	30.
20,000– 50,000	27	25.	36.	13.	51.	36.	23.	33.	10.	46.	32.
50,000– 100,000	41	51.	74.	29.	58.	40.	43.	62.	15.	35.	24.
100,000– 200,000	41	98.	148.	54.	55.	36.	85.	127.	35.	40.	27.
200,000– 500,000	35	167.	324.	155.	92.	48.	153.	298.	97.	63.	32.
500,000–1,000,000	15	402.	665.	280.	70.	42.	272.	449.	305.	112.	68.
1,000,000–2,000,000	9	833.	1478.	534.	64.	36.	837.	1482.	298.	36.	20.
2 000,000–5,000,000	5	1343.	3278.	2217.	165.	68.	743.	1814.	2375.	320.	131.
10,000,000–20,000,000	1	8000.	12299.	3672.	46.	30.	7949.	12241.	1463.	18.	12.
20,000,000–50,000,000	1	2625.	20199.	5898.	225.	29.	14731.	113281.	668.	4.5	59.

B. INVESTMENT AND INCOME STATISTICS OF STEEL MANUFACTURING CONCERNS, GROUPED ACCORDING TO INVESTED CAPITAL (thousands omitted)

2. FORGING AND FOUNDRY

Group	1917						1916				
	1	2	3	4	5		6	7	8	9	
	Number in Each Group	Capital Stock	Invested Capital	Net Income	Per Cent		Capital Stock	Estimated Invested Capital	Net Income	Per Cent	
					4–2	4–3				8–6	8–7
Under $10,000	6	6.2	8.2	4.7	76.	57.	6.	8.	1.4	19.	15.
10,000– 20,000	13	18.	17.1	11.	61.	64.	11.8	11.2	5.2	40.	42.
20,000– 50,000	59	22.	34	11.	51.	32.	21.	33.	7.	34.	22.
50,000–100,000	43	38.	70.	18.	49.	26.	34.	62.	15.	43.	23.
100,000–200,000	40	84.	142.	42.	49.	29.	81.	14.	26.	32.	19.
200,000–500,000	36	160.	341.	103.	65.	30.	136.	290.	66.	48.	23.
500,000–1,000,000	4	372.	561.	257.	69.	46.	214.	320.	131.	61.	41.

B. Investment and Income Statistics of Steel Manufacturing Concerns, Grouped According to Invested Capital (thousands omitted)

3. Machine Tools

Group	1917						1916				
	1	2	3	4	5		6	7	8	9	
	Number in Each Group	Capital Stock	Invested Capital	Net Income	Per Cent		Capital Stock	Estimated Invested Capital	Net Income	Per Cent	
					4–2	4–3				8–6	8–7
Under $10,000	4	8.	9.2	5.	63.	54.	8.2	9.2	5.5	67.	58.
10,000–20,000	7	11.4	18.4	8.4	74.	46.	11.4	18.4	7.6	66.	41.
20,000–50,000	20	23.	36.	15.	64.	40.	19.	30.	13.	67.	42.
50,000–100,000	19	43.	74.	24.	56.	32.	25.	43.	27.	105.	62.
100,000–200,000	20	66.	132.	41.	62.	31.	596.	119.	45.	75.	38.
200,000–500,000	14	125.	289.	109.	87.	38.	119.	274.	94.	79.	34:
500,000–1,000,000	10	285.	686.	215.	75.	31.	255.	614.	217.	85.	35.
1,000,000–2,000,000	5	702.	1482.	704.	100.	47.	546.	1152.	691.	127.	60.
2,000,000–5,000,000	5	1723.	2893.	1058.	61.	37.	1744.	2912.	1043.	60.	36.
10,000,000–20,000,000	1	25000.	17301.	5092.	20.	29.	25000.	17250.	5780.	23.	34.

XIV. Corporation Income Distributed by Industrial Groups

The Report on Statistics of Income for the calendar year 1918, recently published under the direction of the Commissioner of Internal Revenue, furnishes the following significant data:

Distribution of Corporation Income by Industrial Groups and Into Those Reporting Net Income and Those Reporting no Net Income, Calendar Year 1918

Industrial groups	Total number of corporations reporting	Corporations reporting net income				
		Number	Per cent of total number of corporations reporting in each group	Gross income	Total deductions	Net income
Agriculture and related industries	7,887	4,406	55.86	$420,465,998	$ 367,801,978	$52,664,020
Mining and quarrying	10,661	5,524	51.82	3,597,203,674	3,029,426,465	567,777,209
Manufacturing:						
Food products, liquors, and tobacco	12,657	9,778	77.25	8,891,356,833	8,361,459,707	529,897,126
Textile and textile products	8,363	7,018	83.92	6,612,560,029	5,847,322,392	765,237,637
Leather and leather products	1,724	1,434	83.18	1,679,523,585	1,563,146,831	116,376,754
Rubber and rubber goods	565	412	72.92	1,036,684,977	935,089,865	101,595,112
Lumber and wood products	6,520	4,985	76.46	1,802,007,281	1,628,138,448	173,868,833
Paper and pulp products	1,529	1,277	83.52	967,078,872	870,892,369	96,186,503
Printing and publishing	7,198	5,192	72.13	858,142,262	792,200,046	65,942,216
Chemicals and allied substances	5,215	3,576	68.57	3,868,858,346	3,474,445,341	394,413,005
Stone, clay, and glass products	2,822	1,856	65.77	627,788,574	544,741,706	83,046,868
Metal & metal products	13,706	10,539	76.89	12,924,990,763	10,871,663,262	2,053,327,501
All other manufacturing industries	6,975	5,138	73.66	2,666,098,499	2,354,494,040	311,604,459
Total Manufacturing	67,274	51,205	76.11	41,935,090,021	37,243,594,007	4,691,496,014
Construction	7,731	5,297	68.52	1,664,583,913	1,529,721,290	134,862,623
Transportation and other public utilities	18,246	12,564	68.86	[1] 3,226,579,289	[1] 2,448,301,447	778,277,842
Trade	70,149	58,466	83.35	20,163,971,759	19,109,498,395	1,054,473,364
Public service-professional, amusements, hotels, etc.	14,899	9,745	65.41	865,515,406	800,113,370	65,402,036
Finance, banking, insurance etc.	68,132	49,589	72.78	4,575,929,180	3,891,268,733	684,660,447
Combinations—predominant industry not ascertainable	8,944	5,220	58.36	3,256,848,358	2,924,969,139	331,879,219
Inactive concerns	43,656	45	.10	471,550	453,075	18,475
Total	317,579	202,061	63.63	79,706,659,148	71,345,147,899	8,361,511,249

[1] Gross income and total deductions incomplete

Distribution of Corporation Income by Industrial Groups and Into Those Reporting Net Income and Those Reporting no Net Income, Calendar Year 1918—*Continued*

Industrial groups	Corporations reporting net income			
	Income tax	War profits and excess profits tax	Total tax	Per cent of total tax
Agriculture and related industries	$4,540,664	$8,201,050	$12,741,714	0.40
Mining and quarrying	49,177,732	142,186,645	191,364,377	6.06
Manufacturing:				
Food products, liquors and tobacco	41,443,420	165,310,172	206,753,592	6.55
Textile and textile products	48,936,351	344,513,264	393,449,615	12.46
Leather and leather products	9,750,340	31,779,565	41,529,905	1.31
Rubber and rubber goods	8,526,354	29,814,808	38,341,162	1.21
Lumber and wood products	14,815,718	40,857,770	55,673,488	1.76
Paper and pulp products	7,810,532	28,524,482	36,335,014	1.15
Printing and publishing	5,548,846	11,848,801	17,397,647	.55
Chemicals and allied substances	30,215,221	130,391,973	160,607,194	5.08
Stone, clay and glass products	6,471,882	25,584,478	32,056,360	1.01
Metal and metal products	140,489,116	862,542,151	1,003,031,267	31.76
All other manufacturing industries	23,915,597	102,953,969	126,869,566	4.02
Total Manufacturing	$337,923,377	$1,774,121,433	$2,112,044,810	66.86
Construction	7,421,237	64,538,221	71,959,458	2.28
Transportation and other public utilities	82,540,725	66,813,028	149,353,753	4.73
Trade	79,304,014	290,597,346	369,901,360	11.71
Public service—professional, amusements, hotels, etc.	5,116,179	9,825,743	14,941,922	.47
Finance, banking, insurance, etc.	59,093,798	60,993,402	120,087,200	3.81
Combinations—predominant industry not ascertainable	28,080,757	88,289,071	116,369,828	3.68
Inactive concerns	....	....	....	....
Total	$653,198,483	$2,505,565,939	$3,158,764,422	100.00

DISTRIBUTION OF CORPORATION INCOME BY INDUSTRIAL GROUPS AND INTO THOSE REPORTING NET INCOME AND THOSE REPORTING NO NET INCOME, CALENDAR YEAR 1918—*Continued*

Industrial groups	Corporations reporting no net income				
	Number	Per cent of total number of corporations reporting in each group	Gross income	Total deductions	Deficit
Agriculture and related industries	3,481	44.14	$103,714,716	$126,031,758	$22,317,042
Mining and quarrying	5,137	48.18	397,839,320	469,312,449	71,473,129
Manufacturing:					
Food products, liquors, and tobacco	2,879	22.75	534,303,851	565,721,271	31,417,420
Textile and textile products	1,345	16.08	146,889,000	154,572,788	7,683,788
Leather and leather products	290	16.82	46,583,571	49,327,175	2,743,604
Rubber and rubber goods	153	27.08	12,677,340	14,491,719	1,814,379
Lumber and wood products	1,535	23.54	197,010,348	213,713,504	16,703,156
Paper and pulp products	252	16.48	43,116,320	46,587,807	3,471,487
Printing and publishing	2,006	27.87	114,873,962	124,719,826	9,845,864
Chemicals and allied substances	1,639	31.43	208,779,844	223,650,483	14,870,639
Stone, clay and glass products	966	34.23	62,201,989	69,939,369	7,737,380
Metal and metal products	3,167	23.11	433,001,430	477,257,444	44,256,014
All other manufacturing industries	1,837	26.34	432,623,882	449,456,429	16,832,547
Total Manufacturing	16,069	23.89	$2,232,061,537	$2,389,437,815	$157,376,278
Construction	2,434	31.48	281,716,215	298,330,231	16,614,016
Transportation and other public utilities	5,682	31.14	[1] 495,416,523	[1] 594,195,053	98,778,530
Trade	11,683	16.65	1,497,772,270	1,550,664,341	52,892,071
Public service — professional, amusement, hotels, etc.	5,154	34.59	232,412,501	252,774,793	20,362,292
Finance, banking, insurance, etc.	18,543	27.22	1,313,832,572	1,519,807,399	205,974,827
Combinations—predominant industry not ascertainable	3,724	41.64	200,965,243	242,156,466	41,191,223
Inactive concerns	43,611	99.90	1,891,267	4,684,220	2,792,953
TOTAL	115,518	36.37	$6,757,622,164	$7,447,394,525	$689,772,361

[1] Gross income and total deductions incomplete

XV. Income and Deductions

Distribution of Corporation Income by Industrial Groups and by Nature of Deduction, Calendar Year 1918

Industrial groups	Total number of returns	Total gross income	Cost of goods	Compensation of officers	Interest paid	Domestic tax
Agriculture and related industries..	7,887	$524,180,714	$267,209,346	$16,144,097	$21,588,942	$11,605,066
Mining and quarrying............	10,661	3,995,042,994	1,806,562,618	53,143,770	67,010,715	50,610,967
Manufacturing:						
Food products, liquors and tobacco.....	12,657	9,425,660,684	7,350,838,662	133,675,818	106,856,996	105,712,538
Textile and textile products.	8,363	6,759,449,029	5,077,052,283	142,205,906	69,942,988	30,929,710
Leather and leather products	1,724	1,726,107,156	1,397,470,708	34,413,531	20,555,060	6,373,911
Rubber and rubber goods.	565	1,049,362,317	745,382,666	8,813,332	17,366,622	5,059,957
Lumber and wood products	6,520	1,999,017,629	1,377,307,423	52,352,467	35,663,129	20,986,571
Paper and pulp products.....	1,529	1,010,195,192	726,550,541	21,683,953	12,186,155	9,277,321
Printing and publishing...	7,198	973,016,224	437,356,863	43,438,431	8,875,311	4,869,458
Chemicals and allied substances......	5,215	4,077,638,190	2,909,227,462	67,652,445	44,721,679	23,135,176
Stone, clay and glass products	2,822	689,990,563	419,109,992	31,306,980	14,808,449	4,798,166
Metal and metal products.....	13,706	13,357,992,193	8,849,955,775	272,272,653	174,539,551	84,152,534
All other manufacturing industries.....	6,975	3,098,722,381	2.173,134,296	84,813,629	33,699,055	16,902,796
Total Manufacturing..	67,274	44,167,151,558	31,463,386,671	892,629,145	539,214,995	312,198.138
Construction......	7,731	1,946,300,128	1,215,621,964	53,383,912	14,316,342	5,410,319
Transportation and other public utilities............	18,246	[1] 3,721,995,812	[1] 371,657,480	[1] 138,960,885	[1] 478,794,461	[1] 94,969,112
Trade............	70,149	21,661,744,029	17,137,499,331	618,424,858	599,615,687	115,303,662
Public service—professional amusements,hotels,etc.	14,899	1,097,927,907	328,811,931	56,809,318	18,979,185	17,297,918
Finance, banking, insurance, etc....	68,132	5,889,761,752	1,624,564,798	347,275,631	817,548,352	187,411,435
Combinations–predominant industry not ascertainable............	8,944	3,457,813,601	2,239,404,068	48,575,540	75,233,818	32,848,878
Inactive concerns..	43,656	2,362,817	1,159,945	196,103	538,371	226,993
Total.......	317,579	86,464,281,312	56,455,878,152	2,225,543,259	2,632,840,868	827,882,488

[1] Gross income and total deductions incomplete

Distribution of Corporation Income by Industrial Groups and by Nature of Deduction, Calendar Year 1918—*Continued*

Industrial groups	Exhaustion, amortization, and depletion	Miscellaneous expense	Total deductions	Net income before deducting tax	Income tax, war profits, and excess profits tax	Net income after deducting tax
Agriculture and related industries...	$17,583,142	$159,703,143	$493,833,736	$30,346,978	$12,741,714	$17,605,264
Mining and quarrying...	442,089,772	1,079,321,072	3,498,738,914	496,304,080	191,364,377	304,939,703
Manufacturing:						
Food products, liquors and tobacco	177,917,440	1,052,179,524	8,927,180,978	498,479,706	206,753,592	291,726,114
Textile and textile products..	119,768,730	561,995,563	6,001,895,180	757,553,849	393,449,615	364,104,234
Leather and leather products..	11,180,989	142,479,807	1,612,474,006	113,633,150	41,529,905	72,103,245
Rubber and rubber goods....	25,893,669	147,065,338	949,581,584	99,780,733	38,341,162	61,439,571
Lumber and wood products.....	75,465,694	280,076,668	1,841,851,952	157,165,677	55,673,488	101,492,189
Paper and pulp products......	35,464,962	112,317,244	917,480,176	92,715,016	36,335,014	56,380,002
Printing and publishing	21,671,620	400,708,189	916,919,872	56,096,352	17,397,647	38,698,705
Chemicals and allied substances	162,604,867	490,754,195	3,698,095,824	379,542,366	160,607,194	218,935,172
Stone, clay, and glass products..	29,487,788	115,169,700	614,681,075	75,309,488	32,056,360	43,253,128
Metal and metal products..	526,605,594	1,441,394,599	11,348,920,706	2,009,071,487	1,003,031,267	1,006,040,220
All other manufacturing industries...	85,654,397	409,746,296	2,803,950,469	294,771,912	126,869,566	167,902,346
Total Manufacturing	1,271,715,750	5,153,887,123	39,633,031,822	4,534,119,736	2,112,044,810	2,422,074,926
Construction	41,365,546	497,953,438	1,828,051,521	118,248,607	71,959,458	46,289,149
Transportation and other public utilities....	[1] 176,598,869	[1] 1,781,515,693	[1] 3,042,496,500	679,499,312	149,353,753	530,145,559
Trade.......	202,557,766	1,986,761,432	20,660,162,736	1,001,581,293	369,901,360	631,679,933
Public service—professional amusements, hotels, etc..	37,588,270	593,401,541	1,052,888,163	45,039,744	14,941,922	30,097,822
Finance, banking, insurance, etc...	107,461,984	2,326,813,932	5,411,076,132	478,685,620	120,087,200	358,598,420
Combinations—predominant industry not ascertainable.	118,367,048	652,696,253	3,167,125,605	290,687,996	116,369,828	174,318,168
Inactive concerns......	137,501	2,878,382	5,137,295	[2] 2,774,478	....	[2] 2,774,478
Total..	2,415,465,648	14,234,932,009	78,792,542,424	7,671,738,888	3,158,764,422	4,512,974,466

[1] Gross income and total deductions incomplete [2] Deficit

XVI. Corporation Income and Deductions by Industrial Groups, Showing Amounts Expressed in Percentages, Calendar Year 1918

Industrial groups	Total gross income	Cost of goods	Compensation of officers	Interest paid	Domestic tax	Exhaustion, amortization, and depletion	Miscellaneous expenses	Total deductions	Net income before deducting tax	Income tax, war profits, and excess profits tax	Net income after deducting tax
	P. ct.	P.ct.	P.ct.	P.ct.	P.ct.	P.ct.	P. ct.	P. ct.	P. ct.	P.ct.	P.ct.
Agriculture and related industries	100.00	50.98	3.08	4.12	2.21	3.35	30.47	94.21	5.79	2.43	3.36
Mining and quarrying	100.00	45.22	1.33	1.68	1.26	11.07	27.02	87.58	12.42	4.79	7.63
Manufacturing:											
Food products, liquors, and tobacco	100.00	77.99	1.42	1.13	1.12	1.89	11.16	94.71	5.29	2.19	3.10
Textile and textile products	100.00	75.11	2.10	1.03	.46	1.78	8.32	88.80	11.20	5.82	5.38
Leather and leather products	100.00	80.95	1.99	1.19	.37	.65	8.26	93.14	6.59	2.41	4.18
Rubber and rubber goods	100.00	71.03	.84	1.66	.48	2.47	14.02	90.50	9.50	3.65	5.85
Lumber and wood products	100.00	68.89	2.62	1.78	1.05	3.78	14.02	92.14	7.86	2.78	5.08
Paper, pulp, and products	100.00	71.92	2.15	1.21	.92	3.51	11.11	90.82	9.18	3.60	5.58
Printing and publishing	100.00	44.96	4.47	.91	.50	2.23	41.19	94.26	5.74	1.78	3.96
Chemicals and allied substances	100.00	71.33	1.66	1.10	.57	3.99	12.03	90.68	9.32	3.94	5.38
Stone, clay, and glass products	100.00	60.74	4.53	2.14	.70	4.28	16.69	89.08	10.92	4.65	6.27
Metal and metal products	100.00	66.24	2.04	1.30	.63	3.95	10.80	84.96	15.04	7.50	7.54
All other manufacturing industries	100.00	70.13	2.73	1.09	.55	2.77	13.22	90.49	9.51	4.09	5.42
Total manufacturing	100.00	71.23	2.02	1.22	.71	2.88	11.67	89.73	10.27	4.78	5.49
Construction	100.00	62.46	2.74	.74	.28	2.13	25.58	93.93	6.07	3.70	2.37
Transportation and other public utilities	(1)	(1)	(1)	(1)	(1)	(1)	(1)	(1)	(1)	(1)	(1)
Trade	100.00	79.11	2.85	2.77	.53	.93	9.17	95.36	4.64	1.71	2.93
Public service—professional, amusements, hotels, etc.	100.00	29.95	5.17	1.74	1.57	3.42	54.05	95.90	4.10	1.36	2.74
Finance, banking, insurance, etc.	100.00	27.59	5.90	13.88	3.18	1.82	39.51	91.88	8.12	2.04	6.08
Combinations—predominant industry not ascertainable	100.00	64.76	1.40	2.18	.95	3.42	18.88	91.59	8.41	3.37	5.04
Inactive concerns	100.00	49.09	8.30	22.78	9.60	5.82	121.81	217.40	[2]117.40	....	[2]117.40
TOTAL	100.00	65.28	2.57	3.04	.96	2.79	16.48	91.12	8.88	3.65	5.23

[1] Not given, due to incomplete data. [2] Deficit.

XVII. Corporation Returns Distributed by Income Classes, Calendar Year 1918

Income classes	Number	Net income	Income tax	War profits and excess profits tax	Total tax	Average amount of tax	Per cent of total tax to net income
Reporting net income:							
0 to $2,000	68,973	$ 55,281,461	....	....	....	....	....
$2,000 to $5,000	49,397	162,073,156	$ 7,275,952	$ 2,504,236	$ 9,780,188	$ 198	6.03
$5,000 to $10,000	29,780	213,305,243	16,441,379	12,069,321	28,510,700	957	13.37
$10,000 to $50,000	37,053	800,570,917	70,090,289	133,925,666	204,015,955	5,506	25.48
$50,000 to $100,000	7,224	507,215,825	41,567,639	138,743,794	180,311,433	24,960	35.55
$100,000 to $250,000	5,383	838,508,564	66,636,178	262,601,787	329,237,965	61,163	39.26
$250,000 to $500,000	2,054	713,779,767	54,454,610	247,027,672	301,482,282	146,778	42.24
$500,000 to $1,000,000	1,171	815,090,903	61,947,717	286,745,920	348,693,637	297,774	42.78
$1,000,000 to $5,000,000	846	1,701,416,343	131,803,287	574,088,712	705,891,999	834,388	41.48
$5,000,000 and over	180	2,554,269,070	202,981,432	847,858,831	1,050,840,263	5,838,001	41.14
Total	202,061	8,361,511,249	653,198,483	2,055,565,939	3,158,764,422	[2] 23,734	[2] 38.03
Reporting no net income	115,518	[1] 689,772,361	....	....	....	....	....
Grand total	317,579	7,671,738,888	653,198,483	2,505,565,939	3,158,764,422	....	....

[1] Deficit [2] Average for returns reporting net income of $2,000 and over

XVIII. The Record of Business Failures in the United States

It may be of considerable use to the reader to have before him general statistics of business failures over a period of years. The following tables, therefore, based on Dun's and Bradstreet's annual reports are here given:

A. Failures, Assets, Liabilities and Number in Business in the United States Yearly Since 1881. (Bradstreet's)

Year	No. failures	Per cent increase or decrease	Actual assets, millions	Total liabilities millions	Per cent assets to liabilities	Number in business	P. ct. failing
1920	8,463	+53.4	$274.1	$426.3	64.3	1,958,042	.43
1919	5,515	−40.8	55.3	115.5	47.9	1,843,066	.29
1918	9,331	−28.3	69.3	137.9	50.9	1,824,104	.51
1917	13,029	−21.0	84.8	166.6	50.9	1,828,464	.71
1916	16,496	−13.3	86.1	175.2	49.1	1,790,776	.92
1915	19,035	+13.4	160.8	284.1	56.5	1,770,914	1.07
1914	16,769	+15.2	197.2	357.1	55.2	1,749,101	.95
1913	14,551	+5.3	159.0	292.3	54.3	1,718,345	.84
1912	13,812	+9.2	98.5	198.9	49.5	1,673,452	.82
1911	12,646	+9.2	102.0	188.1	54.2	1,637,650	.77
1910	11,573	−2.3	94.2	188.7	49.8	1,592,509	.72
1909	11,845	−15.6	69.3	140.7	49.2	1,543,444	.76
1908	14,044	+36.8	168.4	295.9	56.9	1,487,813	.94
1907	10,265	+9.3	287.9	383.7	75.0	1,447,680	.70
1906	9,385	−5.9	63.1	127.2	50.0	1,401,085	.66
1905	9,967	−4.3	65.0	121.8	53.3	1,352,947	.73
1904	10,417	+6.5	75.7	143.6	52.7	1,307,746	.79
1903	9,775	−1.9	84.1	154.3	54.5	1,272,909	.76
1902	9,973	−6.3	50.4	105.5	47.7	1,238,973	.80
1901	10,648	+7.4	61.1	130.1	46.9	1,201,862	.88
1900	9,912	+2.8	60.1	127.2	47.2	1,161,639	.85
1899	9,642	−16.9	60.1	119.8	50.1	1,125,873	.85
1898	11,615	−11.2	73.1	141.6	51.6	1,093,373	1.06
1897	13,083	−13.3	86.5	158.7	54.5	1,086,056	1.20
1896	15,094	+16.4	147.8	246.9	59.9	1,079,070	1.40
1895	12,958	+1.8	87.6	158.7	55.2	1,053,633	1.23
1894	12,724	−17.9	83.2	151.5	54.9	1,047,974	1.21
1893	15,508	+51.0	231.5	382.1	60.6	1,059,014	1.46
1892	10,270	−17.1	54.7	108.6	50.3	1,035,564	.99
1891	12,394	+16.1	102.9	193.1	53.3	1,018,021	1.21
1890	10,673	−9.0	92.7	175.0	52.9	989,420	1.07
1889	11,719	+10.7	70.5	140.7	50.0	978,000	1.20
1888	10,587	+9.7	61.9	120.2	52.0	955,000	1.10
1887	9,740	−7.8	64.6	130.6	50.0	933,000	1.04
1886	10,568	−4.9	55.8	113.6	49.0	920,000	1.15
1885	11,116	−4.3	55.2	119.1	46.0	890,000	1.25
1884	11,620	+13.0	134.6	248.7	54.0	875,000	1.32
1883	10,299	+34.0	90.8	175.9	52.0	855,000	1.20
1882	7,635	+28.0	47.4	93.2	51.0	820,000	.93
1881	5,929	......	35.9	76.0	47.0	780,000	.76

B. FAILURES IN THE UNITED STATES AND CANADA

CLASSIFIED ACCORDING TO CREDIT RATINGS, TO LIABILITIES AND TO CAPITAL EMPLOYED. (BRADSTREET'S)

	1920		1919		1918		1917	
	No.	*P. ct.*	*No.*	*P. ct.*	*No.*	*P. ct.*	*No.*	*P. ct.*
Credit Ratings of those who failed.								
Total number of failures U. S. and Canada	9,442	100.	6,141	100.	10,146	100.	14,139	100.
Number failing which had Very Moderate or no Credit rating	8,807	93.3	5,995	97.6	9,825	96.8	13,698	96.9
Number failing rated in Good Credit	557	5.9	117	1.9	282	2.8	398	2.8
Number failing rated in Very Good Credit or higher	78	.8	29	.5	39	.4	43	.3
Liabilities of those who failed.								
Total number failures U. S. and Canada	9,442	100.	6,141	100.	10,146	100.	14,139	100.
Total with less that $5,000 Liabilities	4,191	44.4	3,346	54.5	6,001	59.1	11,262	79.7
Total with $5,000 liabilities and over	5,251	55.6	2,795	45.5	4,145	40.9	2,877	20.3
Total with $5,000 to $20,000 liabilities	3,206	34.	1,967	32.	2,957	29.1	2,134	15.1
Total with $20,000 to $50,000 liabilities	1,119	11.9	519	8.5	752	7.4	487	3.4
Total with $50,000 to $100,000 liabilities	447	4.7	164	2.7	229	2.3	142	1.
Total with $100,000 to $500,000 liabilities	363	3.8	127	2.1	182	1.8	101	.7
Total with $500,000 liabilities and over	116	1.2	18	.3	25	.3	13	.09
Total with $1,000,000 liabilities and over	61	.6	16	.2	15	.1	6	.04
Capital employed by those who failed.								
Total number failures U. S. and Canada	9,442	100.	6,141	100.	10,146	100.	14,139	100.
Total with $5,000 capital or less	8,474	89.8	5,740	93.5	9,078	89.5	13,304	94.1
Total with over $5,000 and less than $20,000	613	6.5	264	4.3	745	7.4	617	4.3
Total with $20,000 and less than $50,000	217	2.3	87	1.4	227	2.2	153	1.1
Total with $50,000 and less than $100,000	69	.7	23	.4	50	.5	39	.3
Total with $100,000 and less than $500,000	59	.6	26	.4	44	.4	25	.2
Total with $500,000 and over	9	.09	1	.02	2	.02	1	.007
Total with $1,000,000 and over	1	.01	.....	......	1	.01	.....	......

C. FAILURES BY BRANCHES OF BUSINESS—FIVE YEARS (DUN'S)

MANUFACTURERS	Number					Liabilities					Average
	1920	1919	1918	1917	1916	1920	1919	1918	1917	1916	1920
Iron, Foundries and Nails	35	23	38	44	41	$4,083,973	$1,520,780	$1,209,574	$1,347,467	$1,519,093	$116,684
Machinery and Tools	248	177	193	218	209	27,066,318	12,868,454	11,103,534	7,205,325	3,803,781	109,138
Woolens, Carpets and Knit Goods	18	6	8	22	20	1,836,218	94,001	78,869	451,871	502,428	102,012
Cottons, Lace and Hosiery	30	21	26	33	28	1,446,678	1,456,138	2,347,417	1,953,989	1,125,375	48,222
Lumber, Carpenters and Coopers	207	240	337	517	455	13,345,872	4,442,536	9,044,451	17,181,812	13,164,602	64,472
Clothing and Millinery	435	174	336	535	565	10,551,074	1,721,845	4,066,727	6,130,915	4,938,885	24,255
Hats, Gloves and Furs	93	26	34	53	65	3,091,431	305,150	415,707	1,026,457	1,280,170	33,241
Chemicals and Drugs	45	38	35	54	22	3,222,836	1,128,960	1,094,514	1,489,757	643,481	71,618
Paints and Oils	11	8	15	11	16	310,416	169,073	188,133	140,646	514,949	28,219
Printing and Engraving	50	59	146	145	204	2,509,071	824,870	2,400,808	1,668,508	1,879,247	50,181
Milling and Bakers	282	172	175	305	495	3,606,130	2,477,628	1,398,853	1,936,730	3,352,367	12,787
Leather, Shoes and Harness	91	73	86	81	103	3,485,696	895,417	1,922,804	1,495,047	2,256,663	38,304
Liquors and Tobacco	61	49	79	101	133	1,371,535	934,089	4,593,935	1,495,028	3,476,121	22,484
Glass, Earthenware and Brick	26	45	77	96	93	1,344,809	1,809,836	3,699,509	4,876,375	6,289,805	51,723
All Other	1,003	774	1,181	1,476	1,742	50,720,414	20,965,439	29,816,859	31,143,580	28,252,613	50,568
Total Manufacturing	2,635	1,865	2,766	3,691	4,196	$127,992,471	$51,614,216	$73,381,694	$79,543,507	$72,999,580	$48,573
TRADERS											
General Stores	618	425	593	975	1,391	$10,143,829	$4,412,395	$4,509,165	$7,662,600	$11,542,200	$16,413
Groceries, Meat and Fish	1,713	1,359	1,969	3,129	3,599	13,058,862	8,256,917	9,296,954	14,206,187	12,929,101	7,623
Hotels and Restaurants	369	324	437	530	650	4,175,359	3,158,861	8,728,222	4,441,529	6,268,720	11,315
Liquors and Tobacco	160	214	479	732	936	1,858,623	1,522,640	3,253,560	4,587,393	5,253,554	11,616
Clothing and Furnishing	566	325	645	836	1,089	7,672,954	2,760,100	5,798,818	5,974,142	8,928,253	13,556
Dry-Goods and Carpets	377	206	296	478	712	8,096,949	3,073,446	5,108,528	6,220,403	11,525,923	21,477
Shoes, Rubbers and Trunks	162	120	174	229	376	1,954,013	1,090,104	1,362,692	1,430,960	2,357,730	12,061
Furniture and Crockery	74	78	148	249	287	743,455	805,037	1,417,118	2,773,802	2,647,602	10,046
Hardware, Stoves and Tools	83	81	152	208	349	1,434,922	1,211,738	1,390,426	2,069,519	4,090,516	17,288
Chemicals and Drugs	112	130	280	362	490	914,705	789,261	2,225,692	2,182,039	2,351,209	8,167
Paints and Oils	16	21	39	63	54	324,963	758,623	294,081	904,007	425,318	20,310
Jewelry and Clocks	103	73	178	222	293	1,669,599	699,733	1,644,854	1,787,026	2,790,361	16,209
Books and Papers	21	21	42	51	99	229,287	176,337	400,842	462,029	549,430	10,918
Hats, Furs and Gloves	135	21	32	37	51	7,365,158	288,887	370,121	516,799	452,990	54,556
All Other	1,023	615	1,030	1,329	1,547	28,915,669	8,866,364	12,109,898	14,898,234	19,260,921	28,265
Total Trading	5,532	4,013	6,494	9,430	11,993	$88,558,347	$37,670,443	$57,910,971	*$70,110,669	$91,373,828	$16,008
Agents, Brokers, etc	714	573	722	734	874	78,570,987	24,006,578	31,727,314	32,781,195	31,838,848	110,043
Total Commercial	8,881	6,451	9,982	13,855	16,993	$295,121,805	$113,291,237	$163,019,979	$182,441,371	$196,212,256	$33,230

[NOTE.—Iron, Woolens and Cottons include all the branches of those manufactures; Machinery includes vehicles, shipbuilding, hardware, fixtures and implements; Lumber includes saw, planing, sash and door mills and furniture; Clothing includes tailors, men's and women's clothing, also furnishings; Chemicals include chemical fertilizers; Printing includes books and maps; Leather and Shoes include saddlery and trunks; Liquors include wines, brewers and

D. Causes of Failures in the United States (Bradstreet's)

Failures due to	Number		Assets		Liabilities	
	1920	1919	1920	1919	1920	1919
Incompetence	2,753	2,109	$32,455,312	$11,730,114	$56,522,786	$26,068,530
Inexperience	556	307	7,725,694	1,740,312	14,268,745	5,510,902
Lack of capital	2,735	1,669	60,396,251	15,837,726	113,612,638	29,378,542
Unwise credits	131	72	12,625,729	2,869,310	15,578,242	4,534,615
Failures of others	105	97	2,389,931	2,046,947	3,476,379	3,844,066
Extravagance	105	59	642,160	612,889	1,268,384	1,374,864
Neglect	110	93	1,057,127	340,426	2,021,429	934,622
Competition	112	59	728,628	476,852	1,266,060	945,009
Specific conditions	1,221	623	144,002,263	12,095,267	194,121,666	23,671,566
Speculation	43	37	4,761,745	1,112,845	8,119,845	2,640,534
Fraud	592	390	7,363,014	6,498,608	16,115,341	16,646,409
Total	8,463	5,515	$274,147,854	$55,361,296	$426,371,515	$115,549,659

FINANCIAL MANAGEMENT
1880–1934

Volume 7

Edited and Introduced by
Morgen Witzel

THOEMMES

Financial Management, 1880–1934

Edited and Introduced by **Morgen Witzel**

Volume 1
Twenty Years of Inside Life in Wall Street, or Revelations of the Personal Experiences of a Speculator ... Illustrated (1880)
W. W. Fowler

Volume 2
Trusts, Pools and Corporations (1905)
William Z. Ripley

Volume 3
Corporation Finance (1910)
Edward S. Meade

Volume 4
Corporation Finance. An Exposition of the Principles and Methods governing the Promotion, Organization and Management of Modern Corporations (1909)
William H. Lough

Volume 5
Concentration and Control: A Solution of the Trust Problem in the United States (1914)
Charles R. van Hise

Credit and International Trade: How they Work in Practice (1934)
Barnard Ellinger

Volume 6
Problems in Business Finance (1921)
Edmund E. Lincoln

Volumes 7 and 8
Collected Articles and Chapters

Printed in England by Antony Rowe Ltd, Chippenham

COLLECTED ARTICLES AND CHAPTERS

I

THOEMMES PRESS

This edition published by Thoemmes Press, 2001

Thoemmes Press
11 Great George Street
Bristol BS1 5RR, England

http://www.thoemmes.com

Financial Management, 1880–1934
8 Volumes : ISBN 1 85506 633 5

British Library Cataloguing-in-Publication Data
A CIP record of this title is available from the British Library

Publisher's Note

The Publisher has gone to great lengths to ensure the quality of this reprint but points out that some imperfections in the original book may be apparent.

This book is printed on acid-free paper, sewn, and cased in a durable buckram cloth.

CONTENTS

FORMS OF CORPORATE ENTERPRISE[1]

Thomas L. Greene

When a firm, established long enough to give its returns some stability, desires to sell its business, it soon finds that the easiest way to accomplish this result is by incorporation. When the company is decided upon or formed, the bonds or shares become available for public sale or subscription in any desired amounts. In this way a large business with its plant can be sold by piecemeal, as it were, at a total valuation which could not be obtained in any other way. The larger the business the more difficult is it to find partnership purchasers.

The usual course in such matters is to consult some banking or promoting house which can be induced to finance the project (*i. e.*, to furnish any money required during the transfer), and which has facilities for disposing of the new bonds or shares to its customers and the public. It is a tendency of the times to give the sale of public securities into the hands of those whose profession is that of judging of the values of the securities to he offered. The majority of the investors have their own concerns to look after, and in any case are not good judges of bonds or shares or of the prospects of success of special enterprises. Such persons in the end take the advice of trusted banking houses. Since the reputation of such houses is very important to them, they take pains not to recommend purchases which may involve their customers in losses. Conversely their recommendation is much sought after for new enterprises, and to pay their charges is the cheapest way in the long run to "float" a public corporation. These remarks, of course, do not apply to cases where all of the new capital is retained by the old partners.

Where such houses are consulted by the would-be incorporators there is usually a difference as to the value to be put upon the enterprise; the owners are perhaps over-sanguine; the banking

1 [Chapter 2 of *Corporation Finance*, New York: G.P. Putnam's Sons, 1897]

house, if conservative, goes through the submitted facts and figures in cold blood. It knows, too, approximately, what the public will be willing to pay. The capitalization is then fixed at a sum which it is supposed will allow of a small distribution of profits even in poor years.

There is first the division of the capital into bonds (or preferred stock) and common shares. In order that money may be borrowed at the lowest rate of interest, and thus every possible profit be reserved for the common stock, it is necessary that bonds should be issued only to the minimum value of the property. When preferred stock has a preference not only as to dividends but also as to assets in cases of failure, it takes the place of bonds and should be regarded in the light of a debt. What this minimum value is, is not an easy question to determine. Sometimes it is taken to include the values of the buildings, machinery (or other contents), and the raw material on hand or in process of manufacture. Whether this is safe depends in part upon the nature of the business. Sometimes real-estate experts are asked to appraise the plant as a basis for bonds; but here care should be taken as to the instructions given to such appraisers. If they are required to give an opinion on the value of the ground, buildings, etc., for the use of that particular business, they may honestly put their appraisal at figures far above anything which could be obtained at forced sale in case of insolvency, and security in such an event is the very thing sought for by the bondholder. In the same way and under similar instructions an extravagant valuation may be put upon the machinery, which may not be new, and indeed may already be in process of supersedure as to kind in other and competing establishments. The raw or half-worked up material should be also computed at prices which allow for possible fluctuations because of changes in fashions or by reason of any circumstances which may affect the particular business under consideration. Yet bonds aggregating a larger sum than the valuation of the plant at forced sale may be legitimate and safe because of the stable nature of the manufacturing or trading to be taken over by the new company. But in such cases it should be distinctly understood that a part of such bonded debt rests for security upon success rather than upon real-estate values, *i. e.,* upon the "good-will."

The amount of common stock to be issued does not occasion so much trouble. Allowing for the ups and downs of business, the common capital should fairly represent the fluctuating possibilities of the new concern. To estimate this future properly, the number of common shares should be conservatively small; but the difficulty here, as everywhere else in corporation financiering, is the dislike of the public to the payment by a corporation of dividends higher than the normal rate of interest. It is better financiering to pay good returns in good years, thus allowing for a decline in periods of depression, than to capitalize the company up to the highest point with the possible result of making the whole common issue of little or no value in poor years – and worthless shares are always a menace to honest business.

In asking for subscriptions to bonds or shares in a new corporation formed to take over a manufacturing or trading business, it is usual to employ reputable public accountants who are required to make a report stating what the profits have been for a number of. years. These accountants' certificates have had great weight with purchasers, but recent events have limited their importance. Too much meaning was found in such certificates by small capitalists; they were construed practically to guarantee the whole corporation and its future. As a matter of fact, those certificates were valuable as giving an expert statement of the books of the old partnership as they stood; but they were not intended to explain or to sit in judgment upon the commercial facts which lay behind those books. Being employed by the old partnership or by the promoting house, such accountants may have examined only such accounts as they were requested to, made statements in the form desired, or omitted items, which they were not paid to investigate. A firm of accountants might certify that the average annual profits for three years were a given sum, and stop their report at that point. If the partners had a year previously formed the resolution to incorporate, they might easily swell their revenues greatly during the last year. The discrepancy would be detected if the earnings were; given for each year separately, but not if an average alone were stated. Again, the form of such a certificate might be that the accounts and bills receivable exceeded those payable by a given sum which might be added to the assets to be covered by the proposed share capital; and such a statement, while true, might be misleading. The accounts receivable might be such as were always outstanding, for which working capital should be provided in the plan of capitalization. If so, and every business needs more or less of such working sums of money, simply to offset them by bills payable – meaning money borrowed from the banks – is, under the circumstances, manifestly improper. Borrowed money is a debt, and the plan of incorporation under discussion assumes that the bonds or preferred stock covers the whole of that debt. This particular error in incorporating is sometimes ventured upon in order to give to the old partners all the money subscribed by the public for the bonds and common stock, but it conceals the real status of the finances and leaves unguarded a possible danger. Moreover, bills payable must be met in full while the running accounts of customers may not be worth their face, leaving a deficiency not covered by such a plan of incorporation. The rise and fall of the Thurber-Whyland Company in New York City furnishes an example.

It may be that the certificate unintentionally misleads in another way. The books may be exact in giving the earnings and expenses for the previous year, and yet the resulting profits may not be a proper basis for corporate capitalization; for the reason that selling prices may have been exceptionally high or the cost of raw material or of some important item of expense exceptionally low, so that the year's profits may be too good for an estimate of the future. The case of the Allsopp Brewery in England is an illustration. For these reasons, the course for those proposing to incorporate themselves, or to promote such incorporation, or to purchase the bonds and shares in the new company, is to supplement the information furnished by the accountant with other expert knowledge regarding the circumstances and conditions under which the particular business has been and is likely to be carried on.

A matter which should be considered is that of management. Practiced experience, as well as the best economic theory, lays emphasis upon the importance of an able manager. Nothing can take his place; and his rewards in the shape of salary or returns upon his shares, must be commensurate with his importance. In building up a business the personal element is a great factor. In railways there has been developed in the process of time a body of specialists who are trained in their work of superintending and managing railroad operations, and from whom men may always be had by any company to take control. This same thing will in time be true of all corporation work which concerns the production or distribution of staple goods or necessaries, and, indeed, this is true already of certain lines of work; but it is a point to be considered by all interested in new corporations whether expert management can be had, particularly if those who brought the old firm up to its place of importance are soon to drop out of control through age or lack of interest. When our important corporations have passed their experimental stage, proper management will be largely a question of proper payment.

Aside from the advantages which the corporate form offers for the gathering of capital in small sums for some great enterprise, for the massing of men and machinery at some proper spot, and for the conduct of a large business at a small expense per unit of output, there are benefits to other and smaller concerns by the transfer into corporations. It often happens that partnerships are turned into companies without intention to become public concerns. Perhaps a number of persons acquire an interest in a business established and built up by a father and uncle, a business which it is intended to keep in the family. But the multiplication of owners occasions much difficulty, while another death or two may put the whole enterprise in peril, perhaps require a selling out to other parties in order to determine the value which would then require to be divided. These perils lying in the path of firms having many partners, some minors, some women, are well understood. Some of them may be guarded against by such devices as insuring the lives of the managing partners; but many of such instances are best solved by organizing a corporation to carry on the business; in this way the proportion of each partner or heir can be set aside in shares, which can be transferred or sold in any proportion or at any price without affecting the business itself. Nor will death destroy the living of the remaining owners; for corporations do not die with the death of shareholders. One of the arguments against trading corporations is that the new company may lose the advantage of the zeal and ability of the manager who has brought the business up to its present state of profitableness, but who having now no such interest in the result will drop out altogether, or will not give it the old and close attention. In scattered instances this may be a good objection, for we should not omit the personal equation from our calculations. To supply a class of managing specialists in trading or manufacturing is a work of time; but if a particular line of trading or manufacturing is large enough to demand expert management and to give remunerative employment to those who will study the business, such a class will surely arise to meet that demand. The only danger is that until a good manager is born and made, the business may suffer to a certain extent. It is proper to take the contingency into account in estimating on the probable future values of the bonds and shares of a corporation if offered for public subscription or sale. In some cases the contingency may be provided for by arranging to have the old managers retain a large interest for a certain number of years, or in any way which will make future success an advantage to the old partners.

But to partners who form a company for family reasons, these possible objections do not apply. The status of such companies is directly affected by the fact that no bonds or shares are to be sold to the public therefore the public are concerned with the success or failure of such a family company only so far as that company may wish to borrow money from the banks or ask for credit on goods purchased. In such cases equity requires a complete exhibit of their affairs to those who have a right to that information. For the public at large, and for the information of the state which granted the charter of incorporation, a statement of the assets and liabilities in brief form is properly demanded. The profits of a family company is not a matter with which the state need concern itself. The limits of liability under a corporate form are well understood, and if liability is limited, so also is the credit; no undue advantage is taken of anybody by incorporation. Bank officers when asked for loans will either accept the signature of the company through its proper representative, or will demand the personal endorsement of some individuals; the matter of credit in family corporations regulates itself.

A defect in our general laws touching corporations is often the neglect to distinguish between those companies which are public in their nature and those which are private. A company whose bonds or shares are held by the public and which depends upon public support for its financiering, ought to be compelled (if it does not agree of its own motion) to give out its business accounts in such detail that the holders of its bonds or preferred or common stocks can form a clear idea of the profitableness, of the financial standing, and of the managerial success of their company. But private or family companies are under no obligations to the public as to their affairs except as already noted, and should not be required to make returns in detail. The distinction between public and private corporations would at times be difficult to draw; no rule could be made which would not sometimes err. Perhaps a limit to the number of stockholders would furnish a practical test under which such a distinction could be made.

It is sometimes thought that the legal restrictions imposed upon corporations and the state oversight to which they are subjected, are such drawbacks to the corporate form as to balance the advantages already referred to. Such restriction and such oversight will probably never be withdrawn; indeed, the tendency of the times – as evidenced as much in economic discussion as in actual legislation – is toward further restraint. The matter of stock or bond watering often has business effects which a prolonged strike or some other commercial event can alone make clear; the whole discussion as to "monopoly," though somewhat crude as yet, may, as regards future legislation, turn in the end upon the question whether the profits arising from combination or from huge corporations have been equitably divided between the three parties in interest: the company itself, the consuming public, and the employees. To answer such a question, the widest information will be necessary. Corporations, therefore, should not look forward to any general reduction in the amount of state regulation.

But while this seems to be true generally, it by no means follows that corporations will find that form of doing business less favorable than before. If we keep in mind the fact that a corporation – a public company – implies a well-established business on a scale so great as to require large capital and a large and well equipped plant, it will be seen that the best success cannot come from the partnership form. If we accept a large output or traffic and a correspondingly low cost per unit of production as the criterion of a well-managed company, we necessarily imply a large business enjoying good credit and with years of experience behind it, things which are not so hopefully to be expected from a firm. Such a company must, in the nature of the case, have an element in its business which, from want of a better word, may be called monopolistic; if that advantage is used for the public good there should be no complaint; it is an advantage in the hands of a skilful manager for which the company may well pay by giving publicity to its affairs. Nor should it be forgotten that in such cases publicity does not have the drawbacks urged by small trading companies – that it invites competition. If our supposed company is well managed and is doing business at a low ratio of profit, publication of its affairs rather repels competition by showing the hopelessness of success to a new company.

Precisely because a large volume of transporting or manufacturing is essential to the stability and long-continued success of an ideal corporation, so such corporations tend gradually to absorb the production of such articles as can be carried or manufactured in large quantities, and, of course, consumed by the public in like amounts. Generally such articles are the necessaries of life, or if not strictly speaking necessaries, then those with which the consuming public are especially concerned. From this point of view also we must expect in the future additional legislation. The best defence of corporations against unduly severe laws is full publicity. The history of a company, its early losses and struggles, the prices of the commodity when the business was begun compared with prices now, the cost of production per pound or gallon or barrel, showing the reduction, and in view of such facts the moderate profits of to-day – statements such as these will prove to be the best defence against drastic legislation before the bar of public opinion. But a company relying upon such a defence must be sure that its course as regards prices and policy is one which cannot be fairly attacked. For these reasons, while the restrictions imposed by the state are sometimes onerous and often foolish, yet the advantages of the corporate form for the prosecution of a large and stable business must outweigh the disadvantages. Probably the question of taxation is a serious one for most corporations. Their form and their business seem to invite taxation. It may be that for a time corporations will be obliged to carry more than their proportionate share of the common burden in this respect. In the end this question will run into the more general one of the rightful profits to be made; but meanwhile taxes are things for which incorporations must be prepared.

Corporations formed to carry on a business semi-public in its nature, like that of supplying water and gas to the citizens of cities and towns, do not need extended discussion. So far as the arrangement of their finances is concerned, it should not depart greatly from the principles already laid down for the formation of manufacturing companies. Into the matter of governmental ownership it is not purposed to enter here but regarded from the financial point of view the amount of bonded indebtedness should not exceed the safe value of the property conservatively estimated. Gas and water companies do not indeed often offend in these particulars, since in successful cases the shares have so increased in value as to leave no doubt of the conservatism of the original financial plan. The investor should look into the probability of losses by reason of a change in policy on the part of the community, or because of the beginning of the enterprise on a scale of expenditure not warranted by the probabilities. Yet water and gas are modern necessaries of life, and the supplying of these necessaries, when done by private companies under a conservative plan, is a proper and safe business for the investment of money.

Another form of industrial enterprise destined to assume an important position in investment finance, is that of supplying street transportation to the inhabitants of cities and towns. The rapid growth in the use of electrical power has carried the matter of surface railways in and between cities and villages to a position of great importance. As forming the basis for the investment of capital there can be nothing better than the street traffic of our cities. Experience has demonstrated that such traffic is even more constant and stable than that of steam railroads, and is capable of yet greater development, as surface car lines are extended to meet the demands of a spreading population and as travel increases in proportion as the facilities of easy and rapid transit are increased.

But while the safety of street travel as a basis for the investment of capital cannot be disputed, there may remain questions about the values of the bonds and shares of individual street railway companies for whose settlement further time is required. Some six or eight years ago the motive power of street lines was the horse; but electricity, it was soon found, upset all the old calculations of receipts and expenses. The capitalization of the company was increased by the cost of the new power but so was the volume of travel, so that great profits were shown to have been earned.

The demand for electric equipment led to its manufacture in such quantities and under such uniformity of detail that the prices of new motors and the like fell to one half the old figures. Study and experience found ways of keeping rolling stock and motors in repair at a cost formerly believed impossible; and meanwhile the traffic receipts continued to increase steadily and regularly as the public came to realize the improvements in street conveyance and to take increasing advantage of them.

In the cases of companies freshly established and operating in large cities, it may be assumed, for the purposes of a rough calculation, that the roadbed will require a complete renewal in ten or twelve years, the overhead construction (if the trolley is used) within fifteen years, the electric station and buildings in from twenty-five to fifty years, the car bodies in twelve or fifteen years, and the motor trucks in ten or twelve years, with the steam machinery in fifteen years. These averages of life should, of course, be extended in cases where circumstances would make such a test too severe, as, for instance, in interurban lines using the turnpikes. When, however, fair averages can be obtained and the cost of such renewals estimated, it will be possible for those interested in a new road to make a hypothetical calculation of the average annual earnings for the future, leaving the expected increase in traffic as an offset to any possible error in the calculation.

We are now accumulating a mass of experiences and figures about street railway companies which will place the bonds and shares of those companies on as sure a basis as those of steam railroads and as fully entitled to the good opinion of the investing public. Meanwhile, an approximate result can be obtained by any one who will take the time and trouble to make a thorough analysis of the condition and circumstances in any particular case.

A matter to be considered also is the life of the charters of the street companies and the rights to the use of the highway. Generally speaking, the American public are not disposed to be unfair, and a practical seizure of street railway property by a forfeiture of the charter or by a refusal to renew the same without compensation is not to be expected. On the other hand, it is often a matter of importance how far the company is protected against competition perhaps on adjoining streets. It is well also to examine the provisions of the charter to see whether they contain requirements which may prove onerous in the future.

Throughout this book the form of corporation discussed is that of the company whose capitalization rests directly upon the property, and whose shares are owned by individuals. There is, however, a company of another sort formed under the laws of certain States, particularly New Jersey, which permit corporations to hold the shares of other corporations. In such instances the company does not itself hold property or manage a business, but issues its bonds or shares upon the bonds or shares of other and operating companies held in its treasury; it is, in short, a corporation of corporations.

In certain lines of business such financing companies are the logical result of the movement toward consolidation, of which the simple company was the first outcome. In some cases no other method of concentration seems possible. Perhaps the production of some article requires that the various processes shall be conducted in as many different States whose laws demand that the business within that State shall be conducted by a company incorporated by that State. If all these subsidiary companies are to work in harmony there must be some method of uniform management, brought about most easily by a common ownership of the different shares. Economically speaking, such financing companies are to be judged by their results, precisely as in the case of simple corporations.

Companies are sometimes formed to hold the shares of other companies, principally to prevent competition and to stop the reduction in prices that perhaps previously to such common ownership was bringing disaster upon all concerned. Financial insolvency is a thing to be dreaded for its own sake; and when it would apparently lead to no better conditions than before, it confers no benefit upon the community. Such companies are, as before, judged by their ultimate results, society at large being adverse to such combinations only as they may prevent genuine progress through the formation of still larger single companies able to reduce costs to themselves and prices to the consumer. Such combinations are sometimes made through Trust agreements, which purport to give to the old proprietors in lieu of their old title, a trustee's certificate stating that they are entitled to such a proportion in the equity of all the combined businesses as their original property bore to the whole, these various values being previously fixed by negotiations between those concerned. The public at large are hostile to such Trusts, believing them to be secret agreements in restraint of trade and against the interests of the community. Moreover, they appear to be unnecessary, since all the essential advantages of a Trust can be secured under the form of a lawful corporation either simple or compound.

Where the properties sought to be combined have been owned by firms or individuals, it has often been found expedient to transfer the title of such properties, perhaps lying in different

States, directly to the combining company in return for the issue of bonds and shares of the new company in agreed proportions. In such cases the possible advantages are that it may give to the new company the knowledge and skill possessed in different degrees and about different parts of the process by the old proprietors, for common use; that it may prevent frauds in weight and quality which the previous extreme competition may have brought about and that it may allow a concentration of buying and selling at the least expense and with better results. If a reasonable share of these advantages is given to the public in one form or another, the new company has a strong argument for its existence.

As to the finances of such huge corporations, or of companies holding the shares of other companies, they do not differ in principle from the rules already quoted regarding simple corporations. The bonds issued (including the underlying liens, if any) should not exceed in amount the minimum worth of the property, and the shares should fairly represent the fluctuating values remaining. The bonds and shares of such great combining corporations, generally speaking, are not quoted on the exchanges at as high a range as those of railways. This may be due partly to the fact that the business of the company may be, from the nature of the case, highly speculative in character, and therefore uncertain as to results in any particular year; or its affairs may be in the hands of men perhaps experienced in that particular line of business, but who have not yet acquired a reputation with the investing public; or perhaps there may be on its board of directors or among its officers no one in whom capitalists have confidence as experienced in financial management, for the department of the finances in corporation affairs requires special care and ability just as does the manufacturing or trading. Time will be required to bring about a settled public opinion as to the degree of value which can safely be put upon the businesses of huge industrial combinations or corporations.

COMBINATION AND MONOPOLY[1]

Jeremiah W. Jenks

There is much difference of opinion as to whether or not the large combinations of capital of the present day are to be considered monopolies; and since the decisions of the courts regarding combinations are based largely on their views regarding monopoly, the question has a decidedly practical aspect. When a monopoly is found to exist, there seems to be also a difference of opinion as to the force by which the monopoly is retained. Of course circumstances are likely to differ in the different cases. Some of the larger combinations have succeeded in obtaining control of practically all of the valuable patents in certain lines of manufacturing, thus giving them a legal monopoly which would be protected by the courts. Practically all of the barb wire made in the country at the present time, as well as the wire fencing, is in the hands of the American Steel and Wire Company, because that company owns all of the valuable patents, with one or two exceptions, in those lines of manufacturing.

No one questions the fact that the so-called "industries of increasing returns" or "natural monopolies," such as the railways, the telegraphs, the telephones, the street railways, gas and electric-lighting plants, etc., do, as a matter of fact, in most cases possess a real monopoly. It is, of course, true that this monopoly is probably in no instance entirely without some competing force in operation against it. A gas company may supply all of the gas used in a city, but some of the more thrifty individuals will use wax candles or kerosene lamps instead – a kind of competition which may often materially affect the dividends of the gas companies. There may be but one street railway company in a city, but if its prices are high, or if they are even at the ordinary rate, there is always more or less competition

[1] [Chapter 4 of *The Trust Problem*, New York: McLure, Philips & Co., 1900.]

from carriages, omnibuses, and bicycles. In all of these instances, however, the fact that there is more or less business carried on by others does not prevent the existence of what is properly called a monopoly.

Most of the instances which have been cited of the savings of the wastes of competition which come from the combination of different establishments, have dealt with organizations that are neither "legal monopolies" nor "natural monopolies," as those expressions are ordinarily understood, but are simply combinations with a very large capital; although in some cases, like the Standard Oil Company, which controls pipelines, there may be united with them some natural monopoly, or they may receive some special favors, such as those just mentioned of freight discrimination or of favorable tariffs, which may aid them in maintaining their position. The advantages of freight discriminations and tariffs are to be found also in the case of nearly all large manufacturers or shippers, even though they have not been able to secure what may be considered a monopolistic control of the market.

It is even sometimes asserted that the possession of very large capital is in itself never sufficient to secure a monopoly in any industry, while the popular opinion clearly is that practically all of the so-called Trusts, whether recipients of these special favors or not, possess monopolistic power, and are properly called monopolies. Any differences of opinion that arise over such a question arc usually differences coming from misunderstandings regarding terms. Late decisions of the courts and the common usage of later days justify the use of such expressions – which, strictly speaking, are often self-contradictory – as "partial monopoly," "temporary monopoly," "virtual monopoly," etc. It should be kept in mind that these expressions themselves call attention to the difference between those conceptions and that of, let us say, a legal monopoly. In the case of the legal monopoly, the monopolist has absolute control of the market, and may forbid under penalty of law any competition whatever. The monopoly price, then, will be fixed on the basis of the greatest net returns to the manufacturer. In determining this price, the cost of production for our purpose here being assumed to be constant, the manufacturer takes into account mainly two factors, the number of sales that can be made, and the price, or, to put the matter in another way, the effect of price upon the demand. Will the net returns be greater with more numerous sales at lower prices, or with fewer sales at higher prices? The question of competition does not enter into the problem. Only the demand need be considered.

On the other hand, it seems to be generally conceded (at any rate the courts and popular usage concede it) that it is proper nowadays to use the word " monopoly" even when the element of competition is not entirely eliminated. A manufacturer who controls, let us say, 90 per cent. of the output of any product is enabled to put prices considerably higher, for the time being, than could any one of ten active competitors, each one of whom controlled not much more than 10 per cent. of the output, or than fifty competitors, no one of whom controlled more than 3 or per cent, of the output. The manufacturer with 90 per cent. of the output must, for the time being, supply a very large majority of would-be purchasers. If he puts his price above former competitive rates, even to a considerable degree, it will still be true that a majority of the customers must buy from him, since the other sources of supply are not sufficient to meet their needs. To be sure, exorbitant prices cannot be held for any great length of time without calling competitors into the field; but, in many instances, a rival powerful enough to make really effective competition could not build and equip a new plant, costing possibly some millions of dollars, short of two or three years. While one may grant that under those circumstances the monopoly would be only temporary, it clearly seems proper, as it certainly is common, to say that the manufacturer possesses, at least temporarily, a monopoly. He certainly is exercising and can exercise for a considerable length of time a really monopolistic power. It is also, however, true that in fixing prices so as to secure under the circumstances the greatest net returns, he has to take into consideration this third factor – that of potential competition – which does not enter into the problem when the monopoly is legal in its nature.

He may find it best to secure the greatest returns possible for only a short time, knowing that, if he follows that course, competitors will comparatively soon force him to lower his prices. Perhaps the best example of a temporary monopoly following this plan is to he found in the case of the Wire Nail Pool, which existed in the years 1895-96. The Pool was enabled to increase the prices rapidly from \$1.45 per hundred to \$1.80, to $2.15, to $2.65, to $2.85 – where it held them six months – to $3, for two months, and finally to $3.15, where it held them six months more before the break came. By the end of that time, after some eighteen months of monopoly, competitors had succeeded in providing facilities for manufacture, so that the Pool was broken, and prices fell back to a competitive rate, although not quite so low as they had been before the organization of the Pool. Indeed, in this case, the boldness of the Pool managers in pushing prices so very high doubtless extended the time of their monopoly. Competitors enough to break the Pool would have arisen sooner, had not each one anticipated its speedy collapse on account of its high prices promising enormous profits. Each believed that some one else must very soon enter the field.

On the other hand, it may be that the so-called capitalistic monopoly may consider it wiser to attempt to secure its returns permanently. In that case, while it may perhaps keep prices somewhat above former competitive rates, it must keep them low enough so that the temptation for competitors to enter the field will not he great, and it must be able to put them without absolute loss lower than it would be possible for an ordinary rival to manufacture and sell.

It would probably be granted by all that an organization controlling for the time being 90 per cent. of the output of any product, by putting its prices down, can compel its few rivals to follow; while, on the other hand, it may put prices up above former competitive rates, and can still for a considerable length of time control sales, inasmuch as the other sources of supply cannot fill the demand. If its competitors, controlling only 10 per cent. of the output, put prices up, they will make practically no sales, inasmuch as the combination can supply on short notice the entire market; while, on the other hand, if they put prices down be low the market rate, the combination will not be compelled to follow in all places, inasmuch as the competitors cannot supply the entire market. It need meet their prices only in their own localities. In fact, it is not infrequently the case that the small competitor, owing to the fear of customers that he may not be able to supply their orders, will be compelled to sell very generally at something below the market rate as fixed by the combination. Late testimony, given before the Industrial Commission, as has been previously stated, seems to show that some of the competitors of the American Sugar Refining Company have during the past year, for a considerable part of the time, been compelled to sell at one-sixteenth of a cent per pound below the market rate.

Will now experience justify the contention that mere possession of great capital will give substantially no monopolistic power permanent in its nature, unless some element of legal or natural monopoly or some special favor, such as comes from the tariff or from discriminating rates on railroads, be also secured? Of course this question cannot be settled absolutely on a basis of fact until after more years of experience; but certain advantages come from the possession of large capital which clearly under our present system of laws tend toward monopoly; and, so far as we have a basis of experience in fact, that experience seems to justify the belief that monopoly within certain limits *(i.e.,* monopoly as the word is at present used, meaning unified control enough to hold competitors well in check, as evidenced by the power to put prices higher than former competitive rates while still excluding nearly all competitors), as has been intimated, may be secured simply by the possession of large capital. This power to get higher rates depends generally upon the ability to put goods on the market without loss at lower rates, if need be, than can its rivals.

A large combination, controlling from 75 per cent. upward of the output, with its manufacturing plants favorably located in different sections of the country, would certainly have a decided advantage in freight rates, especially if its products were bulky, over any competitor who would set up in business, unless that competitor were to enter the contest with substantially equal capital. If such a rival entered the field, there would be in operation manufacturing plants which, on the whole, could readily supply one-half more product than the country needed. It may readily be granted that if capital were on hand to be invested in such large amounts, the new organization could force the old combination to sell at former competitive rates or lower. Those, however, who take the position that potential competition will prevent prices from going at all above former competitive rates, overlook the fact that new capital is not at all likely to be invested under such circumstances, unless the profits of the combination are put very high indeed. The reason for it is perfectly evident. It is absolutely certain that, if competition of that kind is tried, prices will be forced down not merely to the normal competitive rates among small manufacturers, but far below that, and those investing their capital for purposes of competition are certain to make, instead of the high profits of the existing combination, very low profits or none at all.

The same situation exists, regarding the advantages of a large organization with branches in different parts of the country in the possibility of its lowering prices to cost or lower in special localities, for the sake of forcing out its smaller rivals, while keeping prices elsewhere above competitive rates among small manufacturers. This power of destructive competition alone, which may depend solely upon its large capital shrewdly invested, is sufficient to enable it to crush out any small rival. On the other hand, if a rival powerful enough to meet its cuts in substantially all markets were to enter the contest, it would be with the absolute certainty that, instead of securing high prices and the consequent high profits of the existing combination, the result must inevitably be a competition so fierce that prices would be forced below usual competitive rates, and profits would entirely disappear. If it be suggested that such competition might be started with the idea of selling out to the combination, the fact still remains that this enlarged combination, organized with the certainty that it would possess plants sufficient to supply considerably more than the normal demand of the country at remunerative rates for a period of years, would, in all probability, make low profits on the total capital invested. If it attempted to make high ones, its prices would need to be put so high that still other competitors would enter the lists, and in course of time a reorganization must take place which must result in great loss of capital. This ultimate result will make the first strong would-be competitors wary.

This same line of argument applies to practically all of the advantages that are to be secured by a large industrial plant. The only difference between the large business and the capitalistic monopoly is, after all, one of size and power which come from capital. A large manufacturing establishment which does not supply more than 10 per cent. of the output of the country may, perhaps, as regards the division of labor in the manufacturing plant itself, be able to manufacture as cheaply as a great combination which controls 90 per cent. of the output. On the other hand, in many lines of industry, it does not have the same facilities for marketing its product, owing to increased cost of transportation and a relative increase in the cost of advertising. Its power of competition is also smaller, since it cannot so readily make cuts in special localities against small competitors while keeping up its prices elsewhere, and since, also, supplying so small a part of the market, it cannot get its prices even temporarily above normal competitive rates. Neither can it secure the numerous other advantages of a great combination which have already been cited.

This element of fear on the part of the small would-be competitor, who knows that he can be crushed out, is the influence which keeps him from investing his capital until the combination is securing considerably more for its product than competitive rates among small manufacturers. The certainty which keeps the large would-be competitor out, even when prices are considerably above such competitive rates, is that after he has entered the business the existing combination must force the competitive fighting so hard that profits will entirely disappear during the contest; and the knowledge that if a combination with the competitor is made, it must be with so large a capital and so much surplus productive capacity that even for a goodly time in the future the profits must be comparatively low, or more probably non-existent; while the endeavor to make profits would push prices up again which might tempt in new rivals.

The only competition that is likely to prove effective, if any does, is that from another great combination in a collateral line of work. For example, a great steel combination might effectively add to its plants some tin-plate mills. This movement has already begun, both in the way of competition and of combinations which attempt to include all steps of manufacture from the mine to the highly finished product. Such combinations will probably extend still further; but this fact does not change the principles laid down. It simply points to larger consolidations.

It will thus be seen that we may make properly a distinction between merely large capital and capital large enough to give an organization a virtual monopoly. It also seems certain that the sources of savings of a great combination, added to this fear of the attacks by great capital, are sufficient, in spite of potential competition, to enable a large combination to secure permanently under existing laws profits considerably above those which could be secured under a competitive system of smaller men, although not so high as might readily be secured by a legal monopoly or by a natural monopoly. This fact seems to justify the use of the expression "capitalistic monopoly," although of course one may readily concede that the power of monopoly in this case is not so complete as in the others.

One may grant still further that experience so far does seem to show that these larger combinations have ordinarily pushed their prices so far above usual competitive rates that other capital has entered the field and pushed prices from time to time back to, or often below, former competitive rates. On the whole, however, the fact that, during the twelve years of its existence, the American Sugar Refining Company (with capital stock not a little watered, if one judges on the basis of cost of reproduction and running cash capital) for more than nine of these years has been able to keep its margin between raw and refined sugar considerably above the former competitive margin, and has paid dividends of 7 per cent. on its preferred stock and 12 on its common stock, while laying up a surplus, seems to show that its large capital has secured more than former competitive prices, and that it has had certain monopolistic power. The nature of competition between large competitors as compared with that among small rivals is considered at length in the chapter on Prices.

The assertion made that the Sugar Combination has also received special favors from the railroads may or may not be true. It certainly has not been proved, while the other reasons, and the undeniable facts regarding the increase in the margin between raw and refined sugar, as shown in the chapter on Prices, furnish sufficient cause for the high dividends. A somewhat similar assertion may be made regarding the Standard Oil Company. It was doubtless true that in earlier years it received great favors from the railroads. It is possible that it has received special favors from the railroads at times since, but it has not been proved that such favors in the form of discriminations (except those coming directly from its large capital, which enables it so to locate refineries and supply markets that it has an advantage) have been received to any material extent, if at all, of late years, while it has been proved that its profits have been much greater during these later years than before.

The other advantages claimed for the capitalistic monopoly, in crushing competitors by local cuts in prices, in transportation, and in other ways that are perfectly legal and normal in their nature, however unjust they may be, certainly seem in themselves enough to explain part at any rate of its high profits. Similar experiences are found in the cases of other combinations of lesser note; and yet it ought to be repeated that so far most combinations have overreached and have paid the penalty of trying to secure exorbitant profits. More experience is needed to teach most of them the art of permanent monopoly – an art that, when it is learned, will need to be kept under careful control by society.

Even as regards the special discriminating favors that are mentioned by those who believe that there is no such thing as capitalistic monopoly, it might readily enough be claimed that those special favors in themselves are secured only by virtue of the power of large capital, but that would be a technical claim which need not be made.

Possibly the chief influence in the long run in promoting combinations of capital, as well as their most far-reaching effect, is the element of personal ambition which is fostered by monopoly. There can be no doubt that, in the case of the larger industrial combinations, the belief on the part of the managers that a virtual monopoly can be secured, is a powerful element toward bringing about their formation. The pride of power, and the pleasure which comes from the exercise of great power, are in themselves exceedingly attractive to strong men. As one with political aspirations will sacrifice much and take many risks for the sake of securing political preferment in order that he may in this way rule his fellows, so a successful organizer of business derives keen satisfaction from feeling that he is practically directing alone the destinies of a great people, *so* far as his *one* line of business is concerned. Mr. Havemeyer says that his ambition is to refine the sugar of the American people. Mr. Gates says that it was the ambition of the organizers of the American Steel and Wire Company to control the wire output of the world. One cannot say that these ambitions are not as worthy as those of politicians, and as natural. No one can question that these elements of personal satisfaction and pride are most powerful factors in all lines of social intercourse, and this pride could not be gratified in business short of the belief on the part of these men that they can secure a practical monopoly. This ambition will not be gratified by the control of merely a very large business. Napoleon was not content to be the head of a great state. His ambition would brook no rival. May not the ambition of a sugar king or a petroleum magnate well be of like imperial nature, though in a more restricted field?

Connected with this belief in the power of monopoly within the home market is that of the ability of the great combination to enter new, and especially foreign, markets. Much more capital is required to introduce into a foreign market a special product than would be required for the extension of the sale of that product within one's home country. The power of great capital thus enables the combination to extend its trade as could otherwise not be done, although this power by no means necessarily implies monopoly. The American Tobacco Company has developed a great market in Japan, India, and throughout the Far East. In some instances even, it is said, it has been forced practically to create the taste for tobacco and to break down religious scruples in order to introduce its product. One may question the value to those peoples of this "educated taste"; one cannot question the skill and power needed to accomplish the result. The Standard Oil Company has pushed its products into practically all the markets of the world. In neither case could these industries have so expanded without the possession of very large capital; and this ability to manage the foreign market in conjunction with the home market, is beyond doubt an advantage of the large organization which the small competitor does not possess. The possession of a secure foreign market gives the large manufacturer still further power in handling the home market, so as to give him a virtual monopoly.

Granting, then, all that can be said with reference to the special advantages that come from legal monopolies and from natural monopolies, it still seems reasonable to believe that without them what must, under the present usage of terms, be called monopoly, does, through the power of capital, exist, temporarily at least; and apparently it may exist permanently, exerting, if it wishes, some if not all of the power exercised by other monopolies, and needing like them the restraining hand of the state through courts and legislatures to prevent abuse. The term "capitalistic monopoly" has been given to this kind of business organization, and until a better expression is found, it seems well to make use of that.

PROMOTER AND FINANCIER[1]

Jeremiah W. Jenks

If several different firms or corporations are to combine into one, or if a large corporation is to be organized, it is ordinarily true that some individual must undertake the task of carrying on the negotiations among the different establishments or individuals concerned, of providing a plan of organization, and of persuading the different individual owners that it is to their ad vantage to enter into the combination on the terms suggested. This persuasive optimist who can succeed in convincing each that it is for his interest to join the organization is the promoter.

In the organization of many of our later industrial combinations, the large pay of the promoter has come directly or indirectly through the issuance of watered stock. To see fully the common practices in connection with such work, we may profitably sketch hastily in review the more usual processes and forms of organization of corporations.

A certificate of stock is essentially a receipt for a certain amount of capital paid into a company to enable it to carry on business. This capital is divided into shares, usually of $100 each, and the certificates of stock stand for a certain number of shares. It is ordinarily supposed that the certificates of stock represent capital paid in cash or an equivalent of cash, so that ten shares of stock would represent $1,000 in cash or in an equivalent of cash. If stock is issued only for cash, there is little likelihood of injustice being done, or of either the investors in the stocks or those who are doing business with the company being deceived with reference to the terms on which the business is organized.

In most cases, however, when a company is organized, considerable amounts of property need to be purchased, either land, or buildings, or tools, or property in some other form, adapted for carrying on the business. In many cases persons who wish to

[1] [Chapter 5 of *The Trust Problem*, New York: McLure, Philips & Co., 1900.]

invest their money in the organization are themselves the owners of this desired property. In consequence, it is a matter of convenience that shares be issued directly or indirectly for this property instead of for cash. Sometimes, to avoid the appearance of issuing stock for property, the managers of the company agree upon a price in stock at par value at which a special piece of property will be purchased. The managers then go through the form of handing their checks to the property owners for the sum agreed upon, and receiving in turn the checks for an equal amount of the owners of the property for stock issued then and there. In a late case certified checks of a leading Trust Company were used to pay for the properties – a loan for the amount for one day having been made for that purpose – and the checks of the mill-owners paid the loan the next day. If the property is tangible, such as land or buildings, and the estimate placed upon its value is conservative and fair, there seems to be no reason why the shares should not be issued directly for this property, if there were no danger of injury to any person. Likewise, if the property is intangible, as a patent or a copyright, or possibly the good-will of a business, its value may be as great as that of land or buildings.

Naturally the inventor and the promoter are hopeful of large profits, and will therefore set a high price upon the patent. If, as is often the case, the invention proves a successful one, the patent may prove to be worth more capital than was estimated at the beginning, and shares of stock therefore issued in payment for it will be worth more than their par value in cash. On the other hand, if the undertaking proves a failure, there will be no tangible property left against which the shares were issued, and the shares themselves may become valueless. In case like this, where the organization is founded chiefly on hope, there are great opportunities, and the temptations are also very great to issue stock to large amounts, even though the hopes are not well founded.

It may be that in other cases the services of some individual peculiarly skilled in the business may be taken in lieu of cash. Under the partnership form of doing business, it is not in frequently the case that one partner contributes capital in the form of cash or tangible property equivalent to cash, while another partner contributes his skill and time in the form of services, the two partners dividing the profits equally. Likewise in the formation of a corporation: one individual, whose knowledge or skill or services are thought to be peculiarly valuable to the business, may have allotted to him in the organization of the company a certain number of shares of stock for the services which he is to perform for the organization in the future; or, if he is a promoter whose work has been of special service in putting the organization into a situation to earn large profits, stock may be issued to him in payment for services already performed. Some of our States forbid the issuance of stock for services; others permit it. It is readily seen how a skilful promoter, who may have succeeded in bringing together a large company whose profits, on account, it may be, of some monopolistic feature, bid fair to be large, may readily assume that his services have been of great value to the company, and receive a large amount of stock in consequence. Here again, however, the stock is issued largely on hope, and its value may partake of the fleeting nature of its foundation.

If a business is so profitable that it can earn considerably more than the rate of interest common in the locality upon well-secured loans, it may be wise for its managers to borrow money to enlarge the business. If a firm or corporation can earn 10 per cent. upon capital invested, it is surely profitable for it to increase business so long as these earnings continue. Even though a half of the capital required to furnish these earnings may have been borrowed at 6 per cent., there has been a net gain of 4 per cent. When the expansion of a business, or even perhaps its present success, depends, therefore, upon the handling of comparatively large sums of money, it is the usual custom to borrow a considerable portion of this capital. Indeed it is not unusual for public service corporations, such as railroads, gas companies, and other like institutions, which possess some natural monopoly, or which have the grant of some franchise that practically gives a monopoly of a certain line of business, to borrow enough capital to pay the entire cost of building the plant, whether railroad or factory. If the establishment can pay anything more than the regular interest on the debt thus created, all of the surplus may go as profits to the stockholders, the persons in whom the legal title of the road rests. It is not at all uncommon for our street railways or our railroads to be in debt – that is, to be bonded – to an amount fully equal to the entire cost of the road and its equipment. It is customary also in such cases for stock to be issued to an amount at least equal to the cost of building, so that the railroad thus built, which can pay the interest on its bonds and pay dividends on its stock, gives to the first holders of the stock a pure profit to the extent of whatever the money value of the stock may come to, as well as a regular annual profit of whatever dividends may be paid. This issuance of stock beyond the cost value of the road is, of course, what is generally known as stock watering.

The new industrial combinations, which are believed by many of their organizers and promoters to be able so to control the conditions of the business that they may possess a virtual monopoly, are also in many cases in a position to borrow in some form or other a large part of the capital needed for the creation and carrying on of the business, and to leave their stock partly or wholly as a bonus in the hands of those who have organized the company, to draw dividends upon, provided the company can earn more than the interest upon its bonds and a small amortization fund.

Under the laws of our States, of course, a firm or corporation which fails to pay the interest on its debts is adjudged insolvent, and is placed in the hands of a representative of its creditors, to be managed in their interest. If a business is more or less speculative in its nature and is heavily indebted, there is always danger that in some period of depression it may fail to pay interest on its bonds, and may thus have the management taken out of the hands of its directors. In consequence of this danger, it has been customary of late years for those organizing the somewhat speculative industrial combinations to issue certain classes of preferred stock in lieu of bonds. For example, a company, the cost value of whose plants was not less than $500,000, might issue preferred stock to the extent of $500,000, representing substantially cash to that amount. If the business were fairly well managed, it might be expected that there would be no trouble whatever in paying some interest – say 6 or 7 per cent. – upon this amount of capital. Persons buying the preferred stock might therefore be assured that their investment would be substantially as safe as if the corporation had borrowed that much money and issued bonds in its stead. In case the company should fail in any one year to earn the full amount of the 6 or 7 per cent. interest mentioned as due the holders of preferred stock before any profits are paid to holders of the common stock, the company would not be adjudged bankrupt, as in the case of the issuance of bonds, but the management of the property would still remain in the hands of the stockholders through their directors as before.

The preferred stock is sometimes given the still further advantage of being cumulative – that is, if in any year or series of years the company fails to pay the dividends mentioned in the conditions upon which the stock is issued, say the 6 or 7 per cent., the amount falling short remains as a charge upon the future profits of the organization, and no dividends can be paid to the holders of the common stock until after this charge has been met. In this way preferred stock becomes substantially as secure in all particulars as bonds. Practically the only difference is that in the case of the failure of the preferred stock to secure its dividends, the management of the company remains in the hands of the Board of Directors; whereas in the case of failure to pay interest on bonds, the management of the company is placed in the hands of a receiver.

As has been intimated, a large proportion of the new industrial combinations issue preferred stock instead of bonds, the preferred stock often representing what is supposed to be the fair cash value of the plants themselves. For each share of preferred stock there is also frequently issued to the holder thereof one or more shares of common stock as a bonus, which may fairly be considered "water," and which takes the place of the common stock so often issued by public service corporations when the cost of building has been substantially raised through the selling of bonds. If the company should be successful in making large profits, dividends will be paid on the common stock in proportion to its degree of success. If the company is less successful, while holders of the common stock will receive no dividends, they will still have a voice in the management or possibly indeed the entire management of the business of the corporation, and the fluctuating chances for future business and future profits will give the common stock a more or less range of value as time goes on.

It is largely through his skill in arranging all these details of organization and of issuance of stock that the promoter gets his profit. In most cases, as it has been his special labor to bring together the corporation or the combination of corporations whose profits are largely a matter for the future to determine, his pay is justly enough given him in part or altogether in the more speculative securities of the company organized – that is, in common stock. For example, testimony given before the United States Industrial Commission seemed to show that in the organization of the Standard Distilling and Distributing Company, for each $100,000 cash value that was secured, in the form of either cash or tangible property, there was issued to the promoter $150,000 in common stock. In addition to this, $100,000 in preferred stock and $100,000 in common stock were issued to the seller of the property who entered into the combination, and $100,000 preferred and $150,000 of common stock were issued to the underwriters, the nature of whose services will be spoken of hereafter. It will be noted that each $100,000 cash valued property was presumed, if dividends were to be paid, to earn interest on $600,000. Would the attempt to do this put prices up, especially if the organization had some monopolistic power?

An account of the organization of the American Tin Plate Company will show one way in which a promoter may receive his pay. Most of the manufacturers of tin plate in the United States, feeling severely the lessening of profits that came from competition and depression in business, thought it wise to organize a combination which should practically control the market. To that end they asked Judge William H. Moore, of Chicago, to aid them. He visited the different tin plate manufacturers and secured an option of purchase for cash at a fixed sum upon the plants of each one of the firms or corporations which contemplated entering the combination. After these options had been secured, Judge Moore organized a company with an authorized capitalization of $50,000,000, of which about $46,000,000 were later issued. For this capital stock there were to be furnished to the company some $4,000,000 in cash as running capital and the plants of all of the companies which entered into the agreement. It was understood that the cash options on the plants amounted to something less than $18,000,000, although as the contract was made with each establishment separately, and as each one of the options was a purely private matter between the promoter and the person selling, it was not publicly known exactly what sum was agreed upon for the value of each separate plant.

It was understood that in most cases the choice was given to each company to receive for its plants either cash or preferred stock, of which the par value should be an equal amount with that of the cash option, together with a like amount of common stock as a bonus. In this way it was supposed that about $18,000,000 of preferred stock and the same amount of common stock were issued, as against the properties and cash, whereas $10,000,000 more of common stock went to the promoter to pay him for his services and for all of the expenses of getting the organization together. It was, of course, necessary that organization fees, lawyers' fees, etc., be paid. It was also probably true that in order to raise the necessary cash certain commissions had to be paid to bankers and others who advanced it. It might have been also true that, instead of the preferred and common stock being taken on the terms suggested before, better terms in certain instances had to be given, and it is even possible that in other instances less favorable terms may have been accepted. Inasmuch, however, as at the time that the company was organized one share of preferred and one share of common stock together sold for considerably more than $100, it seems fair to assume that the promoter had the opportunity of making very large profits indeed out of the $10,000,000 in common stock assigned him for covering the cost of formation and for his pay for services rendered. It will be noted that aside from this $10,000,000, he had the opportunity of making much more if he could make close enough bargains with those who entered into the organization so as to buy their plants at less than the $18,000,000 which seems to have been generally agreed upon as the value of the plants with the cash capital; whereas, on the other hand, if he could not secure them for that sum, his profits would be correspondingly diminished.

With the promoter ordinarily works the "financier" or the underwriter. If the company is to be a success, it is necessary that the stock be sold in order that the needed capital in the form of either plants or cash, or both, be secured to carry on the business. Private bankers are ordinarily chosen to negotiate the sale of stocks and bonds, and very frequently they are persuaded also for a consideration more or less large to underwrite the stock. By this "underwriting" is ordinarily meant an agreement to secure the sale, at a named price, of a certain amount of the stock of the company. If persons not connected with the company or the banker concerned purchase all of the stock under the agreement at a price as high as that named in the contract, the banker has no further responsibility. If, on the other hand, all has not been sold at the time agreed upon, the banker takes the remainder at the rate mentioned and furnishes the cash to pay for it. In that case, his profits or losses will depend upon the price at which he may be able thereafter to sell the stock; or in case he holds it, upon the dividends that may be paid by the company in its regular course of business. It is commonly believed that the sums asked by the underwriter are as high or higher than those of the promoter. A banker agreeing to furnish millions of dollars to a company in order to enable it to enter upon a line of business in the way in which its promoters prefer, often takes, of course, considerable risk, and will wish corresponding pay. The pay of the underwriters in the organization of the Standard Distilling and Distributing Company has already been noted. High officers in some of the industrial combinations have stated that the cost of organization, including the pay of the promoter and financier, amounts often to from 20 to 40 per cent. of the total amount of stock issued, dividends having therefore, if possible, to be paid upon this amount of stock at least in addition to that which represents the cost value of the plants or the amounts paid for them.

Not infrequently the work of the financier and that of the promoter are combined, the profits depending upon the terms at which the stocks are bought and sold. The case of the Distilling Company of America is one in point. Its authorized capital is $55,000,000 of 7 per cent, cumulative preferred stock, and $70,000,000 of common stock. Of this total sum, $31,250,000 of preferred stock and $46,250,000 of common stock were put into the hands of the organizers or promoters of the combination for the purpose of bringing about the organization. The company was incorporated to purchase and hold the stocks of four existing companies, each in itself a combination, and to secure control of certain rye distilleries. The organizers or promoters were to use the stocks placed in their hands to exchange in certain named proportions for the entire stock of each of the existing combinations, to furnish also $1,500,000 in cash for working capital, and to buy two rye distilleries owned by the Hannis Distilling Company and a rye distillery in St. Paul. A large proportion of the stocks of these different companies were as a matter of fact secured, considerably more than 90 per cent, in each case. It was testified that the rye distilleries cost some $2,000,000. If the entire stocks of all of the four companies had been exchanged at the rates agreed upon, there would have remained in the hands of the organizers $10,710,000 of preferred and $13,360,000 of common stock, for which they were to secure the $3,500,000 needed for purchasing the rye distilleries and furnishing the $1,500,000 to be used for working capital. At the rate at which the stocks of the new company sold very soon after its organization, these stocks would have given a net profit to the promoters and financiers, had they been able to sell them promptly, of from $3,000,000 to $4,000,000 for their services; but one must remember, of course, that the effect on the market of an attempt to sell these promptly would probably have been very de pressing. The speculative nature of such a business is readily seen, when one notes that the stocks declined rapidly in value, so that if the organizers had them left in their hands six months later, they would have barely sufficed to furnish the $3,500,000 necessary to enable them to fulfil their contract.

There can be little doubt that many of the promoters and financiers have in the past agreed to aid in the organization of industrial combinations with the hope of securing large profits by the sale of stocks without themselves taking any material interest in the business. This method of furthering combinations has, beyond question, proved one of the greatest evils connected with them, inasmuch as it has given a decidedly speculative turn to industrial stocks, such as was found in the market for railroad stocks and bonds fifteen or twenty years ago.

Those companies that have been organized with a fair degree of conservatism have often assumed or have compelled the constituent companies to pay off all their debts before the parent company began business. The effect of this policy in large sections of the country has been to relieve many small banks of the burden of carrying, with considerable risk at times, the business of these companies. At the same time it has deprived many of these small banks of their best customer. On the other hand, many of the large city banks, from underwriting or accepting as collateral the stocks of the new parent companies, find themselves carrying a heavy burden which it is very difficult to shift. The instability of these securities, with the large numbers of them thrown upon the market, has tended during the last year to make bankers much more conservative in accepting the stocks as collateral for loans, or in attempting to place the stocks upon the market; so that the worst period of this speculative organization has, in all probability, passed.

Perhaps the worst feature from the social point of view, connected with this method of promotion of industrial companies, has been the practice (a practice commonly stated and believed to be exceedingly common, although rarely proved) of securing the influence of bank officials – presidents, cashiers, or directors – through the payment to themselves individually of large amounts of stocks or even of cash, to persuade their banks to accept these securities as collateral on loans, or to underwrite the stocks and thus furnish cash for the companies. It seems most unfortunately to be true that in many cases officials of banks and trust companies have failed to realize to the full the nature of their trusteeship as it concerns their stockholders and depositors. Nor can we over look the indirect influence of such acts by these prominent financiers. The mere fact that a prominent bank or a successful capitalist is willing to invest in the stock of a company is enough to lead hundreds of small investors to follow, often to their injury. And beyond the financial evil, in the long run, is to be feared most of all the lowering of moral tone in business circles if such practices were to continue. The essence of successful business as well as of social and political success of the highest type is faithfulness to a trust, a keen sense of honor. This evil of speculation, coming from the work of the promoter and financier, which has led to the substantial bribery of bank officials and to excessive stock watering on the part of the industrial combinations, is to be counted among the great evils which have attended their organization. They should be so conservatively capitalized and managed that their stocks will prove as safe an investment as farm mortgages, and a far more convenient. one for the man of small means.

THE BASIS OF CAPITALIZATION[1]

Jeremiah W. Jenks

So much has been said of late years with reference to the evils of over-capitalization and of fraudulent practices in connection with stock watering, that it may be worth while to consider briefly the actual and the proper basis of capitalization of industries. It is ordinarily assumed in discussion by those who are opposed to what is generally called "stock watering," that stock ought to be issued for cash or for what is called the "actual cash value" of the property taken. It is generally assumed that the actual cash value will represent fairly well the cost of reproduction of the properties in present condition together with needed running capital in the form of cash on hand. Such an issuance of stock in an ordinary manufacturing business, under conditions of fair competition, will give dividends in the long run probably not materially different from, but perhaps somewhat higher than the usual rate of interest in the community.

It seems to have been the purpose of the corporation law of Massachusetts, and of some other States and countries, to secure capitalization on this basis. The new law for Puerto Rico, lately passed by Congress, takes this position, and shows how conservative it has tried to make its action on this subject. In Massachusetts, not merely must the directors or organizers of a corporation, part of whose stock is issued against property, make oath that the property has been received at its actual cash value, and that the stock is issued at this rate at par, but the Commissioner of Corporations of the State must also certify that he is satisfied that this is the case. Let us note just what this means. This is the capitalization of the plant and running capital, not necessarily that of the business as a going concern.

On the other hand, most business men are of the opinion that the value of any property depends upon its earning capacity, its

[1] [Chapter 6 of *The Trust Problem*, New York: McLure, Philips & Co., 1900.]

value as "a going concern," and that it is wise and just to issue stock of a corporation upon that basis. In the case of corporations, such as those mentioned in the paragraph above, the probability is that the reproduction value of the establishment would correspond closely with the capitalization of its earning capacity at current interest rates. On the other hand, it must be remembered that much higher rates of profit can often be made, either (a) in times of more than usual business prosperity, or (b) under exceptionally skilful management, or (c) with the possession of considerable monopolistic power, from whatever source derived, whether the possession of patents, or of exceptional good-will, or of a very large capital. Mr. Bryan's dictum that only in the case of monopoly can you secure dividends upon stock that does not represent money invested is not always strictly accurate but it is so generally true that it ought carefully to be noted. The times of prosperity when this can be done without monopoly may be fleeting. The exceptional skill or the monopolistic power are likely to endure for a longer season. Under those circumstances, with any of these advantages, the corporation might readily pay dividends of the usual rate of interest on a capitalization twice or three times more than the reproduction cash value of the plants.

Attention is frequently called to the case of a newspaper with a tangible property of, say, $100,000. Such a newspaper, ably edited, with a strong constituency of subscribers and a large advertising patronage, might readily pay good dividends on $1,000,000 or more. Why should the capitalization not be placed at $1,000,000, regardless of what the plant might cost? The earning capacity may be due largely to the skill of the editor, or to the fact of connection with some political party, or to the peculiar business skill of its advertising manager, or to the good will gained through many years of skilful catering to the public taste. Why, it is asked, should not the capitalization be made upon its earning capacity rather than with reference to the cost of the plant.

Most business men, as has been intimated, prefer capitalization on the basis of earning capacity. In the first place, if the dividends declared seem to be at about the normal rate of interest, it conceals the actual state of the business from all persons not so situated that they either know the details of the business of this special establishment, or know that kind of business so well that they may readily judge the profits from external signs. This concealment of large profits lessens the temptation to rivals to enter the business, and lessens also the danger of popular disapproval, which is often expressed against those who make large profits upon capital invested, even though such profits may have been made more by the special individual skill of the manager than by the advantage that comes from the possession of capital. A prominent stockholder in a large gas company lately expressed the fear that it might be necessary soon to lower the price of his gas. The profits were becoming too large to please the public, and it seemed difficult to find an excuse for issuing more stock, though such excuses in the past had been found and for a time had served to conceal the rapidly increasing profits.

Again, a large capitalization is more advantageous, provided the stockholders wish to sell. If in any line of securities, for example, the stock of corporations that regularly pay dividends at 6 per cent, stand at par, those of similar nature and class of which the dividends are regularly 3 per cent, will usually stand at more than 50. People seem to like to deal in large figures, and there is also a greater element of speculation present perhaps in the latter case, though either motive is probably largely an unconscious one. But, because they will sell for more usually, a large capitalization is often de sired, even by conservative business men.

Still more is this the case if the business is speculative in its nature. Doubtless the stocks of many industries which have been largely over-capitalized are more pleasing to speculators on that account. They may not pay dividends; it cannot be expected that they will pay dividends in the near future; but on account of the instability of the business, their fluctuations up and down are more readily affected by rumors or by other slight influences on the stock market – and speculation flourishes on fluctuations.

It is claimed by many that the public is little affected by stock watering, and has little interest in the basis of capitalization. If the capitalization is high, the value of the stock will be correspondingly low, and vice versa. Business men will invest their money, it is thought, on the basis of actual values, as shown by earning capacity, regardless of the par value of the stocks, and neither prices nor investors are materially affected, whatever the basis of capitalization. After a business has been long established and its methods of management are well known, this contention is largely true. On the other hand, when new corporations are organized, and only those who are closely connected with the management know on what terms properties are purchased for which stock is issued, there is great opportunity for deception. Even a public statement of actual earnings of different corporations for a series of years past may be so arranged that the results will be decidedly misleading. Average profits over a period of five years might well be 10 per cent., when if a period of seven years were taken the average would be not more than five. Even the profits of the last two years might be nil. The ordinary investor, who has not had the opportunity of studying the details of organization, is unable to judge.

Even capitalization at the reproduction value of the plants may be as misleading in many ways as capitalization on supposed earning capacity, because unskilful management or a changing state of the market may either double the value of the plant or halve it within a year or two, if we are to take as the basis of value what it might actually bring in the market, which depends again, as has been intimated, on its earning capacity.

There can be no doubt, too, that a high capitalization brings pressure to bear upon officers of corporations to raise prices of their products. Payment of dividends is likely to seem their first duty, and they push prices as high as the market will bear.

The only just method of preventing the evils which are likely to come through the capitalization of any establishment, is to place clearly and fully before all investors, at the time of the organization, the plan of organization itself, the amounts actually allowed for all and each of the properties taken into the establishment, with as complete information as possible regarding these properties, so that a fair judgment can be made regarding both their cost and their earning capacity. In like manner the condition of the business from year to year must be impartially set before the public, so that its earning capacity can be fairly known. Whatever capitalization is then made at the beginning, the value of its stock will in the main be based upon its fair probable earning capacity, while the changing conditions of business from year to year being made fully known would determine with even justice among thc different parties concerned the changing values.

The chief evils of our over-capitalization in recent years have appeared in those organizations that have issued stock far beyond any reasonable likelihood of dividends on the common stock, short of monopoly, and whose promoters have been primarily, not business men, but gamblers.

A proposition has been made to avoid all evils connected with capitalization by providing that shares of stock, representing dollars as their par value, should not be issued, but that a plan reported by a committee of the New York State Bar Association should be adopted, which it was thought would afford a remedy for all these evils. The proposition is as follows:

"To permit the formation of a distinct class of business stock corporations, whose capital stock may be issued as representing proportional parts of the whole capital without any nominal or money value.

"The effect of such amendment would be to provide for the measurement of the interest or shares of the members of such a corporation by a statement of proportion, as in case of the part owners of a ship, and not by an arbitrary assignment of money value, which is delusive in the case of every corporation whose capital stock has a market value either more or less than its nominal par value.

"Such an amendment, though somewhat radical, is not altogether novel. It embodies a principle adopted in corporation laws in Germany.

"It would relieve any possibility of injury to the public from misleading representations as to the money value of corporate stock, and would also relieve from embarrassment conscientious corporate officers often compelled to deal with legal fiction as to which they have no personal knowledge, as though it were a reality within their own observation."

The suggestion is valuable and would apparently prove effective; but there is no general interest in a change, and it is probably, for the present at least, not practicable.

The effect of over-capitalization upon prices will be discussed briefly in a later chapter.

METHODS OF ORGANIZATION AND MANAGEMENT[1]

Jeremiah W. Jenks

Before the compact combinations of the present day were known, various forms of specific agreements among independent corporations and individual competitors were common, such agreements often being called pools, although the earnings of the different companies were not put into one common stock from which profits were to be distributed.

For some years before the organization of the Whiskey Trust, competition had been very fierce among the different distillers, and agreements were usually made from year to year which fixed the amount that each distiller should produce during the year. At other times, under agreement, an assessment was levied which each distiller should pay upon each bushel of corn mashed, in order to export the goods at a loss, and thus, by relieving the home market of its surplus, make sufficient provision for selling the domestic production at a remunerative price. These so-called pools were not stable. Ordinarily, within a year, some one of the parties to the agreement would be discovered distilling more than his proportion of the normal output, and the result would be a break in the pool.

Agreements for fixing the price of the product or for dividing territory are perhaps still more common. A noteworthy late case is that of the Addyston Pipe Company, in which the different parties agreed not to enter into competition with one another. The contract was to be carried out in the following way: a committee consisting of a representative from each corporation entering into the agreement set the price for each job of work, and the corporation that offered the largest bonus for the job, secured it, the others putting in higher bids to make an apparent compe-

[1] [Chapter 7 of *The Trust Problem*, New York: McLure, Philips & Co., 1900.]

tition. It will be seen that, although in this agreement there was no uniform fixing of price or of profits, competition was done away with, and the agreement may fairly be considered as one tending to create a monopoly, or, at any rate, to bring about all the evil effects of a monopoly and to oppress the consumers.

An agreement of a quite different nature has been formed among coal dealers in one of our cities. A committee of several of the leading dealers determine the price at which coal shall be sold by all wholesalers and retailers. They also keep a supervision of the trade, seeing that full weight is given, that the quality of coal is exactly as represented, and that the consumers are protected against dishonest dealers as well as the dealers against excessive competition. If any dealer cuts the price to any of his consumers, he is heavily fined by the central committee. If he refuses to pay the fine, an agreement with the mines stops his securing a sufficient supply of coal to meet the needs of his customers. The initial cause of this agreement was said to be excessive competition. Some of the dealers finding the prices so low that they could not make a profit, came to the conclusion that some must be giving light weight. An investigation and a re-weighing of several loads proved this. The combination was then formed, which maybe said to exist primarily to protect the dealers and incidentally the consumers against this unfair kind of competition, which resulted in their detriment. Prices are fixed at a rate which is said to give only moderate profits to retailers and wholesalers, and fair prices to the consumers; while the consumers, as has been said, are secure against light-weight loads and poor quality of coal. It should be noted that those who fix the "fair" prices are interested parties; but experience may have shown them what is really wise and fair for all. All those dealers who are willing to conduct their business fairly and honorably at the rates fixed are allowed to make a reasonable profit. Longer experience may perhaps show different results. At present reports are favorable.

Owing to the fact that ordinary pools and agreements of the kind mentioned above cannot usually be well enforced, the Standard Oil Company in 1882 organized the Standard Oil Trust, a form followed afterward by the so called Whiskey Trust (the Distillers' and Cattle Feeders' Trust), and also by the Sugar Trust. The form of organization is substantially this: the stockholders of each of the separate companies assign their stock to a certain number of trustees – seven or nine – giving thus an irrevocable power of attorney to these trustees to vote the stock as they see fit. The trustees issue trust certificates to the stockholders in lieu of their assigned stock, and it is upon these certificates that profits are divided. All of the earnings from all of the different members of the combination are put into a common treasury, and whether one of the manufacturing establishments is running or closed makes no difference in the profits received by the stock holders of that special company. The trustees, by having in their hands the voting power of all of the separate corporations, of course elect whatever officers of the corporations they see fit, and direct thus, as seems to them wise, the affairs of each separate corporation.

The decision of the New York Court of Appeals against the Sugar Trust, declaring that the act of a corporation in thus putting its stock into the hands of trustees and abdicating its own independent power of self-direction, was *ultra vires,* together with hostile legislation in other States and an apparent hostility of public opinion, led the old Trusts to give up this form of organization and to reorganize. The Sugar Trust and the Whiskey Trust organized as individual corporations, the certificate holders becoming stockholders in a new corporation which owned all of the plants that had been owned by the individual corporations before the formation of the Trust. In both cases there was substantially no change in the management, the trustees of the former Trust becoming directors of the new corporation and the officers of the new corporation remaining substantially the same as the officers of the Trust. It was a change in name, a change in technical legal form, but no change as regards the practical management of the organization.

The Standard Oil Trust followed a different plan. It so happened that the nine trustees of the Trust owned a large majority of the Trust certificates. The Trust then dissolved into separate corporations, the holders of Trust certificates being given shares pro rata in each one of the twenty corporations into which the Trust was divided. Inasmuch, however, as the former trustees then owned a majority of the stock in each one of these twenty different corporations, they were enabled, without any formal organization among themselves, to direct the affairs of all these corporations in perfect harmony just as efficiently as they had done while acting as trustees and holders of a majority of the

Trust certificates. Here, again, there was a change in form; but in this case, instead of the Trust becoming a single corporation, it became twenty corporations, the majority of the stock in each being held in the same few hands, and all of the corporations being managed in perfect harmony.

A comparatively late change in this company of a different kind has been made. One of the separate corporations, the New Jersey corporation, has increased its stock, and so arranged that it can take control of the business of all of the different companies. The stocks of the separate companies are therefore now being exchanged gradually for the stock of the New Jersey corporation, and in the course of time it is expected that this one corporation will own all of the stocks of the twenty different corporations, so that the management will thereafter be not merely practically one, but also technically and legally one under the directors of one corporation, they voting all the stock of each of the corporations. It is practically a return to the Trust form in all but name.

A voting Trust, somewhat different from the kinds of Trusts described before, is also frequently found. In this form the Trust applies ordinarily only to one corporation. The holders of a majority of the stock of this corporation put into the hands of some few trustees or possibly of a trust company the voting power of the stock, with specific instructions in certain instances as to the way in which this stock is to be voted and the affairs of the corporation carried on. In other cases the power is left to the trustees to carry on the business of the corporation as seems to them wise in accordance with a certain general line of policy laid down beforehand. The individual shareholders may then pledge or sell or dispose of their stock in whatever way seems to them best, but the voting power remains in the hands of the trustees. The purpose of such a voting Trust is, of course, to secure continuity of the policy which, for whatever reason, the stockholders prefer. In some cases it may be that the majority of the stockholders of the original corporation think it desirable to devote all the earnings for a specific period to the improvement of the property instead of to the payment of dividends. It might be impossible to continue such a policy with a shifting body of stockholders, many of whom might wish to receive annual dividends. If, however, the stock can be transferred, but the voting power remain in a few hands, the policy can be carried out consistently for a fixed period of years.

In the case of the Pure Oil Company and other competitors of the Standard Oil Company, it was thought desirable to place the majority of the stock in the hands of a few trustees, because many stockholders felt that otherwise the Standard Oil Company might in time buy from individual stockholders a controlling number of shares, and thus succeed in absorbing more or less completely one of its chief rivals. It is claimed by the managers of the Pure Oil Company that, owing to experience with some other companies, they had reason to believe that this was the purpose of the Standard Oil Company, and, in consequence, the Pure Oil Company had its stock placed in the hands of a voting Trust.

It will be noticed that in all of these cases the difference between this form of voting Trust and the original Trust as seen in the case of the Sugar Trust, is that in the later cases provision is made simply for the management in a specific way of the affairs of some one corporation, whereas in the other case the intention of the Trust was to unite many different corporations under a single management and possibly in certain cases to secure a virtual if not a complete monopoly of the output.

After the dissolution of the old Trusts, the form of organization into one great corporation that should own the separate plants, became most common. Under that form, as, for example, in the case of the organization of the American Tin Plate Company or of the National Steel Company, each one of the separate corporations sold its plant outright to a new corporation, and the original corporation then dissolved. When the combination was completed, there remained in existence only the one great corporation owning the plants that had belonged before to the separate corporations or to individual partnerships or owners. In no essential particular did the legal aspect of the single new corporation differ from that of the separate corporations which had preceded it.

The form of organization that seems to have become most common within the last year or two is one that is closely allied to the old Trust form in its essential character. In this case, when a combination is about to be perfected, a new corporation is formed whose purpose it is to buy up all, or at least a controlling share, of the stock of all of the separate corporations that are to come together. The different corporations then maintain their separate legal existence, but their stock is held by the one company. The officers of the great corporation having thus in their hands the control of the stock of all of the separate corporations, and voting that stock as they see fit, elect, of course, from year to year the directors of all of the corporations, and thus by this absolute control of the officers, direct the affairs of the different corporations. In some cases the "parent corporation" (so called, though born from the others), besides owning the stock of the individual corporations, owns also independently some properties of its own; but in other cases the parent corporation owns only the stock of the separate ones which have entered into the combination. The profits of the individual corporations are made, of course, as before; their dividends are declared; and these dividends are the only source of profit of the parent corporation.

While this form of combination probably doubles the total capitalization in par of stocks, it should be noted that there is no increase in capital, and that there need be no stock watering – although there often is. Neither need there be any more speculative securities created. This fact is often overlooked by those who are appalled by the huge capitalization of industries during the past few years. While new companies have formed, old ones have died that they might live, or the constituent companies pay all their dividends to the parent company to enable it to pay its bills. In this way the earnings of the separate corporations are pooled as effectively as they were in the old Trust. The management is kept as effectively in the hands of the officers. The only difference seems to be a legal one. The parent corporation now owns the stock of the different corporations. In the other case a Board of Trustees held this stock in trust without themselves having any separate legal corporate organization. These new corporations are, it is true, amenable to the courts in a somewhat more direct way than were the former trustees; otherwise there seems to be no essential difference between these two forms of combination. In this later form of combination the constituent companies have their separate boards of directors, their separate officers, and carry on their business independently, managing it, however, under the general direction of the officers of the parent company. It follows of necessity that the work of all the different corporations is carried on harmoniously. Someone of them may have its plants closed for a time in order to suit the supply of product to the demand; on the other hand it may even be that prices will be fixed by the officers of the several companies but in case of need they can always be readily controlled.

It should be noted that among these various forms of combinations there are two kinds, as was indicated earlier in Chapter II, essentially different in nature. The first is made up of companies that have been active competitors before the combination was made, as in the case of the original Sugar Trust and Whiskey Trust. In these cases the combination was sought for the special purpose of lessening competition, together with the elimination of the competitive wastes. The combination simply took different competitors out of the market and enabled the price of the product to be fixed by the central organization.

In the second kind of combination, the constituent members have often not been competitors in the same line of work before the combination was made, though they each seek a share of the value of the final product. Instead of being competitors in the same line of business, they have been producers of different products at different stages in the same industry. For example, the Federal Steel Company is a combination of several companies that were not competitors. The Minnesota Iron Company owns iron ore property, also the Duluth and Iron Range Railroad Company, which connects its mines with Lake Superior at two points. It owns ore docks and also twenty-two steel lake vessels that can carry a large proportion of its products each year. The Federal Steel Company bought all its stock.

It also bought all of the stock of the Lorain Steel Company, which manufactures chiefly steel rails for street railways, although some steel billets; it bought all the stock of the Johnson Company, which is engaged chiefly in manufacturing frog switches and crossings for street railroads, as well as electric motors. Another company, all the stock of which it purchased, is the Illinois Steel Company with several plants, which produce pig iron, steel rails, steel billets, steel plates, etc. This company is also the owner of the stock of the Chicago, Lake Shore and Eastern Railway, which connect its plants in the neighborhood of Chicago, and also gives these plants an outlet to the general market over all of the railroads in the country. It also owns large tracts of coal property on which it manufactures coke used in its plants. From this statement it will be seen that the Federal Steel Company by its formation lessened only to a very slight extent, if at all, the competition in the same lines which had existed before. Its purpose was different. Through the combination the mines are furnished with a sure customer, provided they need one, for a large part at least of their output; while, on the other hand, the Illinois Steel Company, in its manufacture of steel rails, billets, etc., is assured of a steady supply of its ore for the carrying on of its manufacture. In this way contracts can be taken for a long period of time in advance with perfect certainty of their being carried out on time without any excessive losses that might otherwise come from possible changes in the price of ore. Before the organization, of course, each of these separate companies tried to get the largest share possible of the value of the finished product. Now, while the contest may be the same, the motive has been weakened. The profit which the mine foregoes, may be made by the rolling mill or the fleet of transports. It is, of course, true that the business of each one of these separate companies is managed independently; it is still further true that at times the mining company can sell its ore to better advantage to outside manufacturers than to the other constituent members of the Federal Steel Company, they in turn buying their ore to better advantage from some other mine. But, while the work can be ordinarily and is ordinarily carried on independently, and while at times each of the separate constituent companies deals largely with outsiders, this perfect union in management enables them to be secure at all times as regards the supply of raw material on the one hand, and a proper sale of the raw product on the other, advantages that can by no means be lost sight of.

Some other companies without any formal organization are managed in largely the same way. For example, the American Tin Plate Company, the National Steel Company, and the American Steel Hoop Company, while entirely independent in their organization, have nevertheless to a considerable extent the same men as large stockholders and as directors. While each one can thus work independently, and while legally each one does so work, there is to a considerable extent the same knowledge on the part of each of the business of the other and the same harmonious working that is found among the constituent companies of the Federal Steel Company, of the Distilling Company of America, and of others that have united through the holding of the stock of the constituent companies by one parent company.

Whatever the form of organization, however, the one essential requirement is efficiency and an opportunity for saving any of the waste that might come if the different corporations or companies were working independently. It is desirable, of course, from the one point of view that this efficiency be used to serve the public in the way of better goods and lower prices. On the other hand, from the standpoint of the combination itself, the efficiency points simply to the cheaper cost of production and the more efficient control of the process of manufacture, whereas the service to the public in the way of cheaper prices is of course a secondary consideration, and is sometimes even contrary to the wish of the corporation.

The form of organization will naturally determine to a considerable extent the method of management of one of these combinations. Ordinarily there is no difference in appearance between the management of a large corporation called a Trust and any ordinary corporation. Any student of corporation law, upon reading the charter and by-laws, can readily tell from the power that is put into the hands of the directors whether they are in a position to manage the corporation in their own interests as against those of the stockholders, or whether the stockholders are given power of control.

If one may judge from the fluctuations of the shares of several of these larger corporations on the Stock Exchange, it would seem that the power at any rate is given to the directors so to manipulate the stock that they as individuals, by buying and selling at suitable times, may make large individual profits at the expense of the majority of the stockholders – a most dangerous power.

In the first place, the stockholders in many cases are prevented by the by-laws from having access to the books of the corporations, except under the most extreme circumstances. The directors make no reports to the stockholders that give them any clear insight into the methods of management of the business, and the public who may be intending to invest in the stock have no means of judging what the financial condition of the corporation is. When the charter and by-laws thus enable a board of directors to conceal absolutely from the stockholders the condition of the business, one may at least be justified in the opinion that if the affairs of the corporation are not managed for speculative purposes by the directors, it is because they are men above temptation of that kind.

In some instances, also, the Boards of Directors are so classified and the terms of their office so arranged that those who are first put into control as directors by the organizers of the company may keep that control for a period of years without any possibility of being ousted by the shareholders, unless their methods of management are so palpably fraudulent that the courts will order their removal. Under those circumstances the directors and officers are in a position of strong temptation to manage business in their own interests with comparatively little danger of being found out for a considerable length of time. Here, again, an investor who sees in the articles of incorporation and by-laws provisions which deprive him and his fellow shareholders of all effective power over the directors for a period of years, buys the stock knowing his own risk.

It is not intended, of course, to overlook the fact that too great power given to the shareholders, or too close a knowledge of the interior management of a corporation by the shareholders, may easily result in injury to the interests of the great majority of them. It is not desirable for a corporation to have its competitors know the details of its management. If any shareholder were at liberty to examine the books of the corporation at any time, or if the directors were compelled to give to the share holders the privilege of examining closely the details of their management, it would be a comparatively easy matter for the manager of a rival company to buy a few shares of stock in order that the lawful and proper secrets of the corporation might become his. It would also be possible for an individual shareholder practically to levy a blackmail upon the corporation, which it will promptly, however unwillingly, pay, in order to prevent proper secrets of management from becoming public property. While one may readily grant that these dangers to the real welfare of a corporation exist if too great power is given to the shareholder, one must not overlook the fact that the other extreme is no less dangerous.

It would be very desirable if more careful study were made of the forms of organization, as shown in the charter and by-laws of corporations. Intending investors would in many cases by such study be prevented from putting their money into corporations organized evidently for purposes of speculation, or for the special advantage of the directors and officers against the interests of the shareholders.

So, too, if more attention were paid to this feature of corporation organization and management, there would soon be some decided improvements in our corporation laws.

Of course these statements regarding Trusts apply to all large corporations, but the opportunities for speculation against the interests of the shareholders and of the public are so much greater in the case of the very large corporations, which have some monopolistic power, that the offence becomes almost of a different kind.

A SUGGESTION FOR NATIONAL LEGISLATION ON CORPORATION FINANCE[1]

Edward S. Meade

The first essential to such a reform in our corporation law is national control of all corporations. As long as the States are permitted to bid against each other for corporation fees by the offer of large priveleges to incorporators, no measure of restriction can be expected. The stringent regulations of one State can be set aside by the more liberal laws of another. It is not altogether clear that Congress possesses under the Constitutional right to regulate interstate commerce, the implied power to charter all corporations winch conduct an interstate business. A constitutional amendment is generally considered to be an essential preliminary to national control of corporations, and this, it must be admitted, would be difficult, although not impossible, to secure. Without, however, entering into a discussion of ways and means, it is important to observe that the States, in surrendering their powers of incorporation to the National Government, supposing this can be brought about, would not give up any rights which they now possess. On account of the large powers which the law gives to a foreign corporation, the States have not been able to enforce their provisions of regulation against those of their citizens who wished to do business within their borders under the privileges of a charter granted by some other State.

It is not required, as some corporation officials seem to fear, that the full measure of publicity which is necessary to acquaint the investor with the facts about a property, should surrender the secrets of the business to competitors. A Philadelphia accountant, in conversation with the writer, recently illustrated the possibility of harmonizing publicity with necessary secrecy. This gentleman

[1] [Chapter 20 of Trust Finance, New York: D. Appleton & Co., 1903]

was engaged to make a report on a newspaper property which was about to be sold by order of the court. The report was especially full and detailed, but not sufficiently explicit to suit certain persons, who requested information as to the returns from advertising and the amount paid for salaries. The Master in Chancery refused to allow this information to be given on the ground that competitors would discover the secrets of the business. The accountant pointed out to the writer, however, that by presenting merely the totals, without mentioning individual items, this danger could be avoided, and at the same time the investor could be fully informed. The competitors of this paper could not have profited from information as to the aggregate salaries paid or the total amount of advertising receipts. What they were concerned to discover, was the amount paid to certain individuals on the staff, and the terms of particular advertising contracts. This information would be of no service to the investor.

It is impossible, in most manufacturing enterprises, to conceal from competitors the cost of operation. This can be told from the known facts of the industry. The special arrangements with individual buyers and sellers, however, can be kept back from the public, while at the same time, abundant information as to the financial condition of the company can be given. It would be difficult to discover from the admirable reports of certain leading railway corporations, the existence of the system of rebate agreements which has been recently brought out in court. As for the other elements of the scheme of public regulation and control which have been suggested, their utility is conceded and they need no longer detain us.

If we had no supervision of banks, and it was proposed to adopt such a system of supervision, examination, and control of the affairs of banks as is now provided for by the National Banking Law, and worked out through the Comptroller's office, it is probable that the average bank officer would say that such a course would be absolutely ruinous, and that no bank could possibly submit its affairs to such scrutiny by public officials. But, as a matter of fact, we find that the publicity enforced by the National Banking Act, and the provisions as to paid-up capital, reserve, surplus and loans which the law enjoins, and the Comptroller enforces, are most salutary and do not interfere with the proper conduct of a bank's business. If the affairs of industrial corporations were subject to a similar scrutiny, if we had perhaps a Federal Comptroller of Corporations, with the same power over corporations that the Comptroller of the Currency has over National Banks, the result would be most beneficial.

Up to this point, our scheme of corporation reform has placed a certain class of corporations under Federal control, and has provided for full publicity in their accounts. But is this sufficient? Will publicity prevent the evils which such a law should remedy? On the basis of the discussion which has preceded, publicity alone would be insufficient. New companies of the character of the trusts look to the future for their results. They do not. base their promises of dividends upon the earnings of their constituent concerns. Their prospectuses expressly state, in many cases, that these former earnings were only sufficient for dividends on the preferred stocks. It is in the profits of consolidation that they find the basis of their proposition. A firm of New York promoters, who make a specialty of mining propositions, the most risky to the general speculator, and where the desirable certainties are usually picked up by insiders without public subscription, make a great point of publicity in all their transactions, even going so far as to send monthly statements of the operations of each one of the properties, giving the fullest information concerning receipts, disbursements and prospects, to each one of their stockholders. It is evident, however, that the speculator who buys their stocks can not see any further into the earth because of these elaborate tabulations and reports. No amount of publicity can make the future clear to the present.

Moreover, the class of individuals who buy these speculative securities would not be greatly influenced by an accountant's report, no matter how detailed and explicit it might he. On this point, a quotation from the Commercial and Financial Chronicle of March 10, 1900, is pertinent: "Occasionally, as was the case last spring, the public will fairly go crazy, and literally insist on putting its money into enterprises of which it knows nothing, and of which it makes no effort to learn anything. No restrictive legislation can help in such a case as this. The phenomenon...is psychological rather than financial, and the mischief may easily be done in stocks of companies which make no concealment of their earnings. The heaviest of all the losses in last year's carnival of speculation...were not in the industrial stocks, but in one or two street railways which published periodically income accounts and balance-sheets. We do not doubt the wisdom of requiring reasonably full and frequent statements of their condition by the trusts; but all the legislation on earth could not provide the brains to enable investors to understand and properly reason from such statements. We should like to know what proportion of the shareholders in an industrial company making annual statements are really wiser than they were before, after examining the complicated entries of allowance for depreciation of plant, for bad accounts, and for actual value of real estate and machinery."

The advocates of the "publicity cure" for the evils resulting from speculative promotion could not be better answered than the Chronicle has answered them. Those who bought the stocks of the trusts would not have been deterred by an examination of any number of balance sheets. They were investing in futurity. No amount of publicity could have deterred them.[2] Reform in our corporation law must go much further than the enforcement of publicity, if low-priced stocks are to be banished from the exchanges. It is true that publicity is a necessary element of a scheme of corporation reform. Without full information, the provisions of the law can not be enforced. But it should be borne in mind that publicity is only a means to the end of regulation.

In suggesting what seems to be an essential feature of a scheme of regulation which will destroy or at any rate diminish speculative promotion, it is believed that time reader has already arrived at the correct answer to the question propounded. The discussion of the preceding chapters has shown that, in order to market the stock of a speculative proposition, the syndicate managers must promise immediate and large dividends, and that, as far as possible, these promises must be kept if the stock is to be sold within the time of the underwriter's agreement. It has also been shown that this immediate disbursement of profits is

[2] It should also be noted that the margin speculator delights in uncertainty. The more mysterious the operations of a company are, the greater speculative favorite it is likely to be. It would be an actual unkindness to the margin speculators to enforce complete publicity on speculative corporations. The "investor," whose interest the states man is so anxious to protect, is usually a 5- or 10-per-cent margin speculator, who regards interference with his gambling utensils as pool-room betters would regard an interdict on horse-racing.

opposed to the permanent welfare of the company which demands that the capitalization should be fortified by a large reserve out of earnings. The amount of the capitalization is of no consequence if only the reserve be accumulated.

The situation, then, is as follows: The profits of the promoters and underwriters of a new company can only be realized by the promise of large dividends followed by a free disbursement of profits to stockholders. If this is done, the shares can, as a rule, and unless the company is reorganized, never attain an investment position. The solution of the problem of eliminating speculative promotion lies, therefore, in the enforcement of a conservative disposition of profits. If these are paid out to shareholders, the stock will continue for an indefinite period on a speculative basis. If they are turned into surplus, the shares are straightwav put on the road to an investment position. The regulation which would attain the desired end of increasing the number of investment securities is, therefore, a requirement that until a certain percentage of reserve has been accumulated, no more than a certain proportion of profits, say one-third or one-fourth, shall be paid to stockholders. Only when the rate of dividend is fully protected by an adequate reserve of ascertained earning power, should the corporation be given a free hand in the disposition of its earnings.

It will be observed that no restriction of capitalization is suggested. It is a matter of no consequence into how many shares the ownership of a company may be divided, providing the reserve bears the necessary proportion to capital. Given an adequate reserve, and the value of any number of shares may be made secure. The necessity of collecting this reserve before dividends could be paid, would probably operate to make original capitalizations sufficiently conservative. What the proportion of reserve should be, is immaterial if only it be large enough. Fifty per cent is probably none too small for manufacturing companies, and 25 per cent for railway corporations.

It will be further observed that nothing has been suggested as to the regulation of the depreciation account or the floating debt. These can be safely left to the judgment of the representatives of the investor, who would, as a result of the reserve requirement, in a few years, come into control of the company. Furthermore, during the period of underwriter's control, the good opinion of the investor would be sedulously cultivated. With the necessity of appealing to the speculative demand removed, there is no reason to question the ability of the financial management of American corporations.

The question of cumulative preferred stock could also be safely left to the judgment of the directors. If these were elected by investors, such stock would be issued, if at all, probably with prevision for early retirement. All such matters would take care of themselves, if only the investor is placed in control. Let the law see to it that the dividends of new companies are made secure, and the investor can be trusted to safeguard his interests by providing for competent management.

The result of such a regulation would be to seriously interfere with the activity of the speculative promoter. The speculator would not be attracted by a proposition to wait perhaps for years for a large return on his money. He would have little to do with stocks which were condemned by too much security. Under such a system of corporation regulation, when a promoter has assembled a proposition, he must, as a rule, organize it on a basis winch would appeal to the investor, since otherwise he could not get it underwritten by the banker. The underwriter, moreover, since he might be obliged to carry for years the securities whose sale he guaranteed, would see to it that the proposition was one which commended itself to his judgment.

The promoter, under such a reserve requirement, must get down to the bed-rock of reality. He could no longer profitably indulge his fancy in painting gorgeous word pictures of what is "reasonably certain," or "likely to be realized," or "assured in the opinion of experts." The gains of promoters and underwriters would, under such a system of regulation, be moderate, in keeping with the moderate risks assumed. It is not unreasonable, moreover, to believe that the ultimate result of a system of corporation regulation, such as has been outlined, with an adequate reserve requirement as its central feature, would be an advance in the yield on good securities as a consequence of an increased supply of investments, and a larger measure of stability and security in general business conditions.

THE DEVELOPMENT OF INDUSTRIAL COMBINATION[1]

Gilbert Holland Montague

Competition is proverbially the life of trade; but, from the standpoint of the seller, it has always been the death of profits. In spite of the efforts of legislatures and of markets, from mediaeval times to the present, to keep alive competition in every community and in every business, the seller still tries to restrain it. Even among the trades men of a small community the tendency is eternally at work. The local grocer and the dry-goods dealer each notes the prices of his competitor's goods and makes his similar. From time to time he marks down the prices of a few articles, trusting that the increased patronage induced by the blazoning of these "leaders" may increase the sales throughout his store. Aside from these occasional cuts, which seldom affect a considerable fraction of the business, tacit and informal agreement everywhere restrains competition in retail markets.

The Tendency to Combination in Large Businesses

In the wholesale trade, however, competition is always more troublesome. Compared with retail consumers, the wholesale buyers are more eager for small savings, better acquainted with the conditions determining prices, and shrewder at driving hard bargains. The wholesale sellers, because their stocks are necessarily less various than those of retail shopkeepers, can less easily recoup on the rest of their business what they lose by unremunerative "leaders"; and because their trade is more wary than the untutored public, must exert proportionately greater efforts in marketing their products. In good times and in bad they must command the attention of the trade by expensive advertising in the public prints, in street cars and on billboards, and by

[1] [Chapter 1 of *Trusts of Today*, New York: McLure, Philips & Co., 1904]

persistent canvassing by highly paid commercial travellers. In order to hold his customers during a season of reduced demand, the manufacturer must make burdensome concessions: he must pay freight instead of shipping F. 0. B.; he must grant net cash ninety days instead of net cash thirty days; he must allow cancellation or modification of orders, and a discount for storing the goods in the buyer's wareroom, and must uncomplainingly allow excessive claims for lack of merchantableness. Lest his business go over to his rival, when trade picks up and prices advance, the manufacturer must contract with his buyer twelve or eighteen months ahead, at the low prices current at the moment the market begins to turn. As a result, during the first year or two of advancing prices the producer realises far less 'than the "current price for immediate delivery" – with its illusion of extraordinary profits – seems to promise. In November, 1899, for instance, while steel billets were quoted at $34, the mills were chiefly occupied in filling contracts at $16. Finally, when the time arrives for making new contracts, the buyer and the seller cannot get together on the current price, and in order to dominate his territory the seller is once more obliged to grant a reduction. And no sooner does he attain his dominance than his competitor five hundred miles away reaches in with advertising and with agents and with more attractive terms.

The Pools in the Whiskey and the Oil Industries

Among producers and wholesale sellers, accordingly, something more tangible than tacit, informal agreement is needed to restrain competition. So long as industry was localised by imperfect transportation and by the relative smallness of capital invested, formal combinations were as unnecessary among manufacturers as they are generally among shopkeepers. With the rapid development of business after the Civil War, however, together with the extraordinary stim ulus given to certain lines of industry – by internal-revenue legislation, for example, in the case of the manufacture of spirits, and by the discovery and the utilisation of petroleum in the arts – came all the distressing effects of acute competition among manufacturers. The spirits business had attracted such a large sum of capital that the producing capacity grew far beyond the country's normal demand. To dispose of surplus stock, prices were cut until the business became notoriously speculative and discredited; booms and depressions, due sometimes to changes of the law, but chiefly to the accumulation of stocks of whiskeys, made and ruined, with every shift of trade, hundreds of distillers. With a view to placing the business on a sound basis, combinations of seventy or eighty distilleries, organised to reduce the output, were formed as early as 1882. The Western Exporters' Association, for example, determined the producing capacity of each distillery and distributed to each its pro rata share of the consuming capacity of the country. Sometimes only twenty-eight per cent. of the producing capacity was thus utilised, and seldom was more than forty per cent. required. Distilleries producing an excess were obliged to export from the country at their own cost, and any fortuitous excess was exported at the expense of the association and the loss met by assessment. By a similar development the petroleum industry had even earlier attained the same form of combination. Further discoveries of petroleum in 1865, like the internal-revenue legislation in the spirits business, over-stimulated production; and throughout the next decade there were abortive attempts to regulate the output of oil. Early in the seventies the more important refiners, under the leadership of Mr. John D. Rockefeller, reached an informal agreement regarding prices and had come to be known as the Standard "alliance." After eliminating competition among its own members, the group availed itself of the peculiar railway conditions of the time to assert its dominance over the trade. Railroads had not as yet consolidated, and competition for traffic at common points was excessive and unprofitable. To save themselves from insolvency the railroads agreed with one another and with large shippers to divide the traffic, and to pool on agreed percentages the freight earnings. The Standard "alliance," being the most conspicuous group of shippers in the trade, was in this way generally made the "evener"; and in return for this service obtained from the railroads such concessions as raised it, in 1879, to dominance in transportation facilities and to the control of ninety-five per cent. of the refining business of the country.

The Weakness of Pools

The purpose of the pool, as shown in the experience of the distilling and refining industries, is to regulate prices and to meddle as little as possible with details of management in the constituent companies. The output of each concern is so restricted that prices may be advanced by limitation of the supply. The prices are determined at a meeting of all the members of the association or by the executive committee of the pool; and the buyer, being held to the regular quotations, is unable to play off one competitor against another or to obtain special concessions.

In the Addyston Pipe Pool of 1897 the manufacturers of cast-iron pipe in thirty-six States agreed not to compete with one another; whenever a consumer called for bids a committee of the pool, made up of representatives of each mill, set the price for the job and assigned the contract to the mill that gave the largest bonus for it; to keep up an appearance of competition the other members of the pool put in higher bids. The Bessemer Steel Pool, organised in 1896 and including most of the manufacturers of crude steel in the Middle West, assigned every month to each mill a fraction of the total output of the association. At the end of each month, when the shipments were reported to the central advisory body, any mill which had exceeded its allotment was required to pay into the common treasury $2 per ton for such excess, which was distributed proportionately among those who had not shipped their allotment. In the Wire Nail Association of 1895 the central body fixed prices and allotted the output; and in times of slack demand the output was produced by a few of the best adapted plants, and the others received a certain rental for keeping out of business. By its very nature, however, this form of organisation is weak. The policy of the pool is determined by majority rule; and, as each producer is concerned only with the immediate future, the management of the association seldom takes a broad view of the situation. In the midst of a general decline in prices the Wire Nail Association raised prices 200 per cent. Similar short-sighted extortion in the whiskey pools time and again broke down the market. The necessity of voluntary assent on the part of each member and the liberty of each to withdraw without notice have made it impossible to enforce pooling agreements. No relief is to be had in the courts. By one of the firmest principles of the common law a pooling agreement which actually controls the market is unenforceable because it restrains and tends to monopolise trade. In addition to the common law, the Sherman Anti-Trust Act of 1890 – as the Addyston Pipe Pool learned to its sorrow – expressly forbids, with forfeiture of property and threefold damages, every restraint of trade, reasonable or unreasonable, between the States. The difficulty of establishing relations of mutual confidence among former competitors emphasises all these defects. A small misunderstanding creates mutual distrust. Strong producers are always suspected of obtaining business beyond their allotments by methods contrary to the spirit, if not the letter, of the pooling agreement. Having pooled and allotted the production of crude material, these producers increase to the utmost their output of finished goods and thus evade the calculations of the pool. From all these causes the dissolution of pooling agreements is periodical and anticipated by the trade. As the prices following the breakdown of the pool are often lower than the prices current before the pool, large buyers have been accustomed to wait till the dissolution before placing their orders. In February, 1897, owing to the dissatisfaction of the Lackawanna Iron and Steel Company with its allotment of seventeen per cent. of the output and the demand of the Illinois Steel Company for the territory west of Pittsburg, the Steel Rail Pool dissolved; and steel rails, which before the pool had sold at $21 per ton and during the pool at $27.50, were offered by the Carnegie Company at $17 per ton.

Combination Through "Trust Agreements"

The managers of the Standard "alliance" early discovered that pools regarding prices and output did not give sufficient power, either to control the market or to secure the most efficient methods of production. Consequently this association devised and put into effect, in 1882, the original "trust agreement" of the Standard Oil Trust – the first attempt to give binding legal obligation to the unenforceable agreements of the pool – which has since lent its technical name to the entire class of the industrial combinations. A board of nine trustees received in trust from each of the parties to the "trust agreement" either an assignment of stock with voting power or, in some other form, the absolute control of the separate properties. The trustees issued in return for these assignments "trust certificates" representing the valuation of the plants. Except for three or four shares left with the officers of each corporation to qualify them as directors, the trustees could vote all the stock of all the committees. They elected from their own number the directors of each constituent company and thus managed all the properties in complete harmony. As stockholders of the companies composing the trust, the trustees collected all the dividends, and distributed the gross sum among the holders of the "trust certificates" in the form of dividends on the certificates, regardless of whether the original property for which one had received "trust certificates" was making profits or was idle. Success in harmonising divergent interests in the refining business led to similar arrangements in other industries. In 1887 eighty distilleries which had previously maintained a precarious association in pools united for more perfect union into the Distillers' and Cattle Feeders' Trust; and soon after the Sugar Refineries Company was organised.

As a device for controlling the market and for securing the most efficient production, the trust was thus far the most practical form of combination. Through the board of trustees the control over the constituent companies was no longer persuasive but legally enforceable; and measures too drastic to be assented to by informal agreement could easily be accomplished by the trustees in the exercise of their legal rights. Immediately after the formation of the Distillers' and Cattle Feeders' Trust, out of eighty distilleries which joined all were closed except the twelve largest and best equipped, which ran at full capacity. The Standard Oil Trust dismantled such of its refineries as were poorly located, improved the equipment of the rest, and built new works at strategic positions commanding the markets of the entire country. Since these combinations were unincorporated there was no means by which outsiders could learn the nature of their business. They were permanent in organization, centralised in government, responsible and representative; and, being permanent and responsible, they pursued a broader policy than did the pool. Excepting the Distillers' and Cattle Feeders' Trust, no trust exacted the extortionate prices demanded by the pools: the Standard Oil Trust effected a steady reduction in prices; the Sugar Refineries Company raised prices above the competitive rates which before the trust was formed had ruined eighteen out of forty refiners, but maintained them at a point no higher than English and Continental prices. In ease of organization and efficiency of administration the trust form of combination has always supplied the most satisfactory restriction of competition. Economically and commercially it is a unit – and therein lies its strength; legally, however, the trust is not an entity but an association of persons. A rancorous legislature, merely by enacting that any combination of individuals to restrain trade shall be forbidden, could make the "trust agreement" not only unenforceable – as were the pooling agreements – but also illegal and penal. In 1890 sixteen States had thus forbidden combinations within their borders; the Federal Government by the Sherman Anti-Trust Act had forbidden combination in interstate trade, and the common law, as generally applied throughout all the States, was also understood to forbid such combination. During that same year the Sugar Refineries Company was declared illegal by the New York courts, and two year later, when the Standard Oil Trust was similarly declared illegal by the Supreme Court of Ohio, it became realised that the trust form of combination must be abandoned.

Combination Through "Community of Interest"

The dissolution of the "trust agreement," unlike the breakdown of the pools, was not followed by cut-throat competition. The members of the combinations had too long enjoyed the sweets of restricted competition ever to relapse again into their former condition. In one form or another of association the constituent companies continued their harmony of management. Since both pools and "trust agreements" were forbidden, the lawyers were thrown back on other devices. The Standard Oil Trust was dissolved in 1892, and in surrendering their "trust certificates" the owners were given a proportionate amount of stock in each of the constituent companies. By chance the nine trustees under the original agreement owned in their own right a majority of the "trust certificates," and under the new arrangement, by voting together, could control each particular company of the trust. Furthermore, the years of association with one another in the earlier Standard "alliance" had brought about in these men a remarkable singleness of interest and purpose. The experience of most pools proves that mutual self-interest and friendship of a group of business men is an unstable foundation for common action. Among the nine men controlling the Standard interests, however, the ties of family, of personal regard, and of long and close association proved sufficient. For seven years that intangible bond which has become known in the operation of railroad systems as "community of interest," held together the strongest combination of industry in the United States.

Community of interest, however – as appeared in 1901 in the struggle for the Northern Pacific Railroad – is generally precarious. The same self-interest that one day brings men together is likely on another day without warning to leave them far apart. Only by an unconditional surrender of control to some central body can an enduring union be reached; and as the law forbade such a union, so long as its members retained their legal entity, the most natural substitute seemed to be a new corporation which should buy the properties of the smaller companies and sink their legal existence in its own. In 1890 the Distillers' and Cattle Feeders' Trust, which had feared hostile treatment in the courts, reorganised under the corporation laws of Illinois as the Distilling and Cattle Feeding Company. Of the $35,000,000 of capital stock all but $1,000,000 was turned over to the owners of "trust certificates" in payment for the properties of the trust. Shortly afterward, on account of an Illinois statute forbidding payment for properties in stock instead of in money, the new corporation was declared illegal. A new company, the American Spirits Manufacturing Company, was accordingly formed, into which the stockholders of the unlucky Distilling Company transferred their stock, and from which they received, dollar for dollar, new shares. In order to control the distributing business, this company in 1896 organised the Spirits Distributing Company, and soon after sought to combine a number of outside distilleries in the Standard Distilling and Distributing Company and the Kentucky Distilleries and Warehouse Company. By these devices was continued the consolidation of the distilling industry.

Combination Through "Holding-Corporations"

There remained one form of combination more attractive than either community of interest or outright purchase of the properties. In many particulars it resembled the old "trust agreement"; but there were sufficient points of difference to convince most lawyers that it was quite legal. The "trust agreement" had failed be cause it was a "conspiracy" of several persons. If, instead of a combination of persons, a single person could control the several companies, this difficulty could be avoided. The more careful promoters after creating this legal entity – the Distilling and Cattle Feeding Company, for instance – caused it to buy outright the works of the constituent concerns. The more venturesome organisers, however, regarded such complete absorption as unnecessary. A private individual, by owning a majority of the stock in two companies, might elect directors who would effect a unity of management. Why not, then, create a legal person – a giant "holding-corporation" – who should purchase a voting majority of the stock of the several concerns; whose directors, having been elected as usual by the shareholders of the giant corporation, should vote in the meetings of the component companies, precisely like the trustees under the "trust agreement"; who might thus bring about permanent harmony of control? This device had patent advantages over an outright purchase of the properties. The charter of many business corporations – as is wellnigh universal among railroad charters – forbade the sale of the entire business properties; the effect of which was, of course, to make complete absorption impossible. Furthermore, in the sale of plant and goodwill, the higgling of owners and stockholders over the price is for the promoter both expensive and exasperating. To go into the market and buy the voting majority of the stock is quicker and generally less expensive. If desired, the buying may be concealed under the usual daily trading in the stock, and the unsuspecting owners will not be prompted to hold off for an exorbitant price. Finally, the capital of the "holding-corporation" need not be so large, or so difficult to raise, as that of the corporation which purchases properties. Assuming the voting control of the constituent companies to vest in a bare majority of their stock and their shares to be at par, a "holding-corporation" of $501,000 paid-in capital could as effectively control companies whose aggregate capitalisation was $1,000,000 as could a corporation of $1,000,000 by outright purchase of the properties. In an actual case like the preceding the exorbitant prices – either in money or in stock – which the owners would demand for their properties and the unfavorable rates at which the new stock must be placed on the market in order to provide means of payment, would require for an absorbing corporation a capitalisation greatly in excess of $1,000,000. All these disadvantages in absorbing corporations and advantages in "holding-corporations" induced most combinations to assume the latter form.

Before 1889 the laws of no State authorized the creation of a "holding-corporation"; the purchase of stocks of other companies was not considered a desirable power, and, excepting private individuals, no legal person could exist for the general purpose of owning property in other corporations. In 1889 New

Jersey supplied the want by including among the lawful objects of corporations the purchase of stock in any companies owning, mining, manufacturing, or producing materials or other property necessary for their business, and the issue of stock in payment therefor. According to the comity among the several States guaranteed by the Constitution, this new legal entity could extend its operations throughout the whole United States. For a small franchise fee New Jersey offered to provide all corners with this convenient legal person. Connecticut, Delaware, and, with slight reservations, New York and West Virginia followed the example. The Sugar Trust was among the first to avail itself of the New Jersey law. On the dissolution of the Sugar Refineries Company, in 1891, the "trust certificates" were exchanged, share for share, for the stock of the American Sugar Refining Company. Every whit as effective as the "trust agreement"; and after a narrow decision of the United States Supreme Court – in a case to test the applicability of the Sherman Anti-Trust Act to the American Sugar Refining Company[2] – generally regarded as immune from every law against combinations on both State and Federal statute-books, this form of combination promised shelter against ruinous competition within and hostile legislation without.

The Rush to Combination 1897-1902

The depression following 1893 retarded consolidation. But when the revival came, in 1897, an unprecedented rush to combination began. With the large harvests of 1898 and steadily rising prices the prices of securities rose. To the clamorous desire of producers for combination was added an artificial stimulus even more potent. Capital which had long held aloof from the investment market returned to find the supply of securities inadequate to the demand. The old standard stocks, which for so long had been the playthings of speculation, were now in the strong hands of investors beyond the reach of the professional stock-operator. If the increasing desire for speculation were to be satisfied there must be provided new counters for the game. The promoter who in ordinary times found his reward among the manufacturers whom his combination saved from competition, now made, in addition, a most extraordinary profit in supplying securities for the market. In almost any association of separate

2 United States *vs.* E.C. Knight Co., 156 U.S. 1 (January, 1895).

businesses insuring partial or complete control of the industry the control of the output and the economies of production promise an increased profit; and when the big corporation is formed this increased earning capacity may as fairly be capitalised as the inventory-value of the plants. The promoter, however, tempted by the gullible demand for mere quantity in the stock-offerings, used the undoubted economies of combination as the basis for an enormously inflated issue of stock. Very few of these corporations had a capital of less than $1,000,000; the great majority had a capitalisation exceeding $5,000,000. Before 1897 only sixty-three of these combinations had been formed; in the next three years 183 were organised – seventy-nine in the year 1899 alone – with a total capitalisation of over four billions of dollars. This enormous sum – one-twentieth of the total wealth of the United States, nearly twice the amount of money in circulation in the country, and more than four times the capitalisation of all the manufacturing consolidations organised between 1860 and 1893 – was owing entirely to the fever of speculation which culminated in the short panic of May, 1901.

The anxiety of manufacturers to avoid competition, the frenzy of speculation in the security market, and the facilities afforded by new corporation laws in a "holding" or absorbing corporation conspired to bring about consolidation in almost every industry. Wherever a semblance of monopoly could be obtained a promoter was ready to organise, and the public was eager to buy his securities. In rapid succession the various branches of the steel business were combined in purely "holding-corporations." In 1899 the Distilling Company of America was incorporated in order to purchase a controlling interest in the stocks of the four existing combinations in the whiskey business. For this purpose capital stock to the amount of $125,000,000 was authorised, $80,000,000 of which was placed in the hands of the promoters to acquire the entire stock of each company, with the condition that if any part of such stock could not be acquired a proportionate number of the shares entrusted to the promoters should be returned to the treasury of the new company. In fact, the promoters purchased about ninety-five per cent. of the stocks of the several combinations. The mode of payment, which was fixed by a committee of the promoters and the large stockholders of the existing combinations, followed the general plan of a merger. For every preferred share of the American Spirits

Manufacturing Company fifty per cent. in preferred stock of the Distilling Company of America was allowed, and for the common stock twenty-five per cent. in common stock of the new company; for Kentucky Company common stock, seventy per cent., and for preferred stock, eighty-five per cent. in preferred and fifteen per cent. in common; for the Standard Company preferred, eighty-five per cent. in preferred and fifty per cent. in common, and for common sixty per cent. in common; for the Spirits Distributing Company first preferred, eighty per cent. in preferred and twenty per cent. in common, and for the second preferred, twenty per cent. preferred and twenty per cent. common. Like all "holding-corporations," the Distilling Company of America was authorised to acquire properties as well as stock. Accordingly, the promoters sold on the market enough of the stock in their hands to net $3,500,000 cash, $2,000,000 of which they used in the purchase of three independent distilling properties, and the remainder they turned into the company for working capital. So attractive appeared this new form of combination that in 1899 the Standard Oil combination, which had cautiously clung to the informality of community of interest since the "trust agreement" of its own contriving had gone awry, ventured to avail itself of the New Jersey law. The old Standard Oil Company of New Jersey was granted enlarged powers and an increase of stock from $1,000,000 to $110,000,000. Its purpose was eventually to take all the stock of the different Standard interests into the larger company, so that, when the transfer was finally complete, the Standard Oil Company of New Jersey might own outright the stock or the properties commonly known and mentioned together as the Standard Oil Company. Since 1900, about $97,000,000 of the capital stock of the New Jersey company has been used to purchase at par the stocks or properties of the other Standard companies, the capitalisation of which was approximately $97,000,000, but whose goodwill and earning power as represented by the market value of the stock aggregated $650,000,000. The same principles of merger and of outright purchase appeared in the United States Steel Corporation, organised in 1901 with a capitalisation of $1,404,000,000 for the purpose of acquiring the stocks of ten of the largest corporations in the world. By 1901 a sufficient number of combinations had been incorporated to familiarise the public with their organisation.

In the opinion of the legal profession at large, and among public prosecutors generally, the difficulties of the anti-trust laws had been surmounted. A certain amount of doubt – which has lately been strengthened by the decision against the Northern Securities Company – still attached to the principle of combination by mere ownership of stock through a "holding-corporation," but in most cases – railroads everywhere were the great exception – their charters allowed the constituent companies to consolidate and the "holding-corporation" to buy either the stock or the properties. A consider able body of judicial decision, particularly clear in New Jersey, where alone the question was likely to arise, held in effect that combination through ownership of the properties was unassailable. The ease of changing, when ever convenience demanded, from a holding to a purchasing corporation afforded, accordingly, a security which no attack on the principle of merger seemed likely to threaten. To the heated imagination of the public, meanwhile, the profits of combination seemed enormous. During the depression after 1893, it was remembered, the combinations in steel, in oil, in rubber, in sugar, and in tobacco were scarcely inconvenienced; during this period the dividend of the Standard Oil Company had grown from twelve per cent. to forty-eight per cent. Controlling the output of staples for which the demand could never entirely abate, and relieved from the hardship of competition, these companies enjoyed a conspicuous prosperity. The economies of combination, as both manufacturer and public were aware, lay chiefly in the control of the market. The promoter found the manufacturer weary of competition and eager either to combine or to sell; he found the public clamorous to capitalise visionary profits of combinations and to buy the shares as fast as he could provide them. With such incentives it is not surprising that in the four years ending in 1901 he succeeded in consolidating one-seventh of the manufacturing interests of the country.

The Decline in Industrial Securities 1898-1903

The year 1901 marks the second period of flood tide in the trust movement. The first had occurred fifteen years before, when the example of the Standard Oil "trust agreement" had been followed in the sugar and the whiskey businesses. Hostile legislation, expressed in anti-trust statutes on State and Federal statute-books, obstructed the course of combination in the late eighties and early nineties. The disillusionment of the public in regard to the securities of the new combinations has for the present stopped the wild rush to consolidation. The very years that have seen an increase in the value of established railroad stocks of more than one hundred per cent. have witnessed in the industrial stocks listed since 1898 on the New York Stock Exchange a steady depreciation of sixty-five per cent. The decline in the stocks of twenty-one leading industrials alone has inflicted during this period a loss on the community of a billion of dollars. In every case these losses represent the discrepancy between the promise and the performance of the anticipated profits of combination over competition. The evils which in the early nineties led to the restriction of the trust movement affected the consumer, the competitor, and the State – in short, the entire community outside the trust. But the ills which at present are emaciating the great industrials are internal; the evils of unscrupulous promotion, over-capitalisation, and bad management fall upon the individual stockholders, and only indirectly affect outsiders and the State.

The steps that have led to the present situation are clear. Loose association among producers in specially stimulated industries after the Civil War led throughout the later seventies to pools for the regulation of prices. The device of the "trust agreement," which gave legal force to combinations illegal as pools, was eagerly adopted throughout the eighties and early nineties by the consolidating industries. When the "trust agreements" had been declared illegal, and the statutes against combination were growing more harassing, a few commercial States relaxed their corporation laws and created enormous business companies – henceforward known as trusts – which absorbed the members of the combination by the purchase of their properties or their stock. An unparalleled period of speculation in the four years following 1897 stimulated trust promotion, until in 1901 one-seventh of the manufacturing industry had been consolidated.

The Evils of Industrial Combination

The evils of industrial combination, as they have shown themselves in the development of the trust and as they exist to-day, arrange themselves in two classes. First, those inherent in combination, however it be conducted, because of the mere fact that it is a practical monopoly. Most familiar of these is the temptation to raise prices, to get secret discriminations from railroads, to fix destructive prices in order to crush smaller rivals, to corrupt legislation, and to depress individual initiative. Since the reign of Elizabeth, every English-speaking jurisdiction has enforced laws directed against these evils. The fact that monopoly threatens everyone outside itself – consumer, competitor, and employee – has for three hundred years raised against it the hand of the State. It is only natural that the first protest in the late eighties against trusts should be the restatement, with stricter prohibition, of the common-law abhorrence of monopoly. In the present situation, an easy device for evading the statutes has left the first class of evils as alarming as ever, and has added another sort, at present and in the immediate future likely to be more ruinous than the first. This second class of evils results from the particular form and method of organisation prevalent in existing combinations. Unscrupulous promotion, over-capitalisation, and bad management, which have notoriously resulted in financial discredit, affect primarily the investor; and, in so far as present forms of organisation make it difficult to enforce the law upon an elusive citizen, they also affect the State.

The Trust Problem

Briefly stated, the trust problem resolves itself into this: If the trust deserves to live, the savings of combination must be found real and legitimate; the first class of evils, flowing from the mere fact of monopoly, must be proved either self-corrective or able to be corrected by statute; the second class of eyils, resulting from the particular form assumed in the organisation of existing combinations, must be shown to be self-corrective or capable of correction by statute. The extended bearings of the problem have only gradually been realised. Till 1902, interest was centred upon the prevention of the first class of evils. The statute-books bristled with laws against combination and monopoly, but not a single remedy was attempted for the second class; indeed, certain "charter-granting" States had hastened to remove such protection against these evils as their early corporation laws afforded. Since the publication in 1902 of the report of the Industrial Commission, and since the decline in industrial securities, interest has centred about the second class of evils. As the difficulties of the problem become more clearly defined, suggestion grows more sober and cautious.

The commercial forces and the governmental principles, which together form the sinew and the nerve of the nation, are seen to be involved in the answer. By realising the transcending importance of the situation, the first step toward its solution has been taken.

AN INQUIRY INTO THE INTER-RELATION OF THE INDUSTRIAL AND THE FINANCIAL WORLD[1]

Hugo Bilgram

Not long before his death the late Senator Mark Hanna expressed his belief that the then prevailing prosperity had come to stay. Unfortunately, events have since shown that his words were the reflection of a desire rather than a prophetic inspiration. In the light of our experience the periodical recurrence of business depressions seems to be a persistent characteristic of the modern industrial era. The present time may be opportune to propound the question whether these recurring depressions are really an inevitable concomitant of industrial progress. If their cause can be discovered, it may be possible to suggest a remedy.

This inquiry must take into account all the symptoms accompanying the alternating periods of prosperity and depression, for no attempted explanation can be accepted as correct unless it can account for them.

One of the most prominent features of dull times is the apparent deficiency of effective demand for both labor and its products. A demand is "effective" if coupled with the intention and ability to give an equivalent in exchange for the thing demanded.

Considering that money is merely a medium for exchanging commodity for commodity, or commodity for service, or service for service, the offer of any commodity or service implies an effective demand for some other commodity or service. Each application for employment, each offer, in the market, of service or merchandiser is accordingly the measure of an effective demand for some other commodity or service in exchange. In

[1] [*Annals of the American Academy of Political and Social Science* 25 (1905), January: 87–100]

other words, each actual supply constitutes an effective demand, and it manifestly follows that an exact equality constantly exists between total actual supply and total effective demand. While it is possible that in any one branch of production or in any one profession there may be an excess of supply over demand, this very condition is proof of the existence of an excess of the demand over the supply of the products of some other trade or the services of some other profession.

Apparently, this theory is contradicted by the facts developed during periods of stagnation. In every trade the supply exceeds the demand, in every branch of production goods accumulate for the lack of demand, the volume of traffic shrinks far below the capacity of the railroads; in short, everywhere, and especially in the labor market, the actual supply exceeds the effective demand. Yet, according to the above law this excess of supply must somewhere be balanced by an equal excess of demand or deficiency of supply. Is our theory defective? Or is the equalization effected in some way not apparent on the surface and in quarters where the lack of supply has hitherto not been clearly recognized?

A close study of our system of production and exchange may furnish a clue. The modern industrial era is distinguished by a most minute specialization of production, entailing a correspondingly complicated system of exchanges. The practical impossibility of effecting these exchanges by any system of barter is obviated by the use of a medium of exchange, which has therefore become an indispensable instrument of commerce. The historic evolution of this medium of exchange from cattle and other things of value to silver and gold, then to these metals in coined form and ultimately to credit instruments is too well known to need disquisition here.

In the present system practically all merchandise and nearly all services are primarily offered for a money consideration. Barter and payments in kind have almost completely disappeared. But the introduction of a medium of exchange cannot affect the law according to which the sum total of supply must equal the sum total of effective demand. We have still good reason for concluding that there is an insufficient supply somewhere.

Inasmuch as all merchandise and services offered in the market represent primarily an effective demand for the medium of exchange, an excessive supply of the offerings of the market constitutes an excessive demand for money and its substitutes. The observed facts, then, point to "money" as that of which the supply is deficient and short of the demand, the deficiency being equal to the over-supply of merchandise and services.

This over-supply, ordinarily regarded as "over-production," is accordingly capable of only one logical interpretation. Currency being an institution whose legitimate object is to facilitate the exchange of merchandise and services, for which purpose it is further supplemented by the modern check system, the above reasoning points to the conclusion that even when so supplemented our currency is inadequate to perform all of the work for which it was devised and instituted. Stagnation in business, then, finds a ready explanation in the deficiency of our mechanism of exchange.

This contention is by no means a new one. It has already been discussed by John Stuart Mill,[2] but while admitting an under-supply of money, he failed to pursue this line of investigation to its logical conclusion. Also other writers have referred to it, many of whom consider it untenable, for reasons, however, which are open to dispute.

The substitution of credit instruments for actual currency in many of our business transactions is often claimed to cover every possible shortage of currency. But in the present banking system the volume of that credit which can be used in lieu of cash, namely, bank accounts, never can exceed more than a limited number of times that portion of our currency which is held in banks as reserve, and is therefore strictly limited by the limited volume of currency. While the check system, in performing the function of money, greatly adds to our exchange facilities, yet its limitation prevents it from supplying the entire demand, which is constantly increasing; for the volume of exchanges tends to increase with every progress in the specialization of industries, and this increasing demand has simply outrun the increased supply.

However, the most plausible objection to the conclusion that we are suffering from a dearth of money is based on the fact that business depressions are not permanent, but alternate with periods of prosperity, while the volume of currency in existence

[2] Princ. Pol. Econ., Mill, Book III, Chapter 14.

during both periods of the cycle is practically the same. Indeed, during times of depression banks are, as a rule, amply supplied with funds which they offer at a low rate of interest. This very fact is generally considered to indicate the existence of a surfeit of money. But this conclusion can be shown to be erroneous, since it is possible to account for business fluctuations even on the assumption that the volume of currency were a strictly constant quantity.

It should be remembered that at times a large portion of the existing currency is virtually withdrawn from circulation, not only by hoarding, but also by holding funds for the purpose of lending. Only that portion of the total volume of currency and bank accounts is in actual circulation which is in control of those who intend employing it in commercial pursuits, such as buying things or paying wages. That portion which is held for lending is temporarily withdrawn from circulation. Not until the lender finds an acceptable borrower will it be restored to its natural function, unless, indeed, the owner changes his intention of lending it and employs it in the market directly.

A distinction should therefore be made between funds in circulation and funds held for lending. The latter are in a passive state as regards demand for goods or services and cannot be classified as money in circulation. The total volume of currency and bank accounts should accordingly be divided into two parts, the volume of passive and that of active funds, the one embracing that portion which is held for lending, the other that which is held for buying things and for paying wages. It is true that this distinction is rather indefinite, depending upon the subjective factor: "Intention of the Owner," which in many cases may not even have been formulated, but as in the present investigation only actual transactions need be taken into account, the subjective factor, "Intention," can virtually be transferred to the province of the objective by a proper classification of those transactions. Let us assume that the intention is determined by the nature of the transaction which immediately precedes, leaving departures from this rule to be considered separately.

For this purpose certain qualifications and premises must be agreed upon. In the argument here adduced the term "Debt" will be strictly confined to those relations between creditors and debtors resulting from the lending of funds, excluding those which are contracted in the regular course of business and which merely constitute a delay of payment for merchandise and services. Investments in stocks of a stock company, for instance, cannot be regarded as money loans, while investments in bonds distinctly belong to this category. Moreover, the principal of a loan should be strictly distinguished from the interest, a discounted note being, of course, a loan of the discounted sum only, and the discount itself simply interest. For the purpose of our discussion, as regards "Intention," it will be reasonable to assume that not only the principal of collected "Debts" but also the incomes from such investments will again be applied to similar investments and they will accordingly be assigned to the volume of passive funds, while incomes from industrial investments are similarly to be assumed as intended for industrial investment and will therefore be assigned to the volume of active funds. To be sure, departures from this rule will frequently occur, as already indicated, and these will be considered in their proper place.

After these preliminary remarks, the import of which will become more apparent further on, we may again return to our subject.

In the regular course of business a continuous circulation of funds takes place between the two divisions noted. There are three channels through which money may flow from the volume of passive to that of active funds and three in which the flow is in the opposite direction. This circulation can be illustrated by the diagram, Fig. 1, in which the sum total of all funds is represented in an enclosure divided into two compartments containing the respective divisions of these funds by a partition with openings through which the various currents are passing to and fro.

One current from the passive to the active division results from "Loans," that is to say, from the process of lending. From this cur rent must obviously be excluded all loans to those who but lend again, such intermediation having no effect on the actual volume of loans. A second current results from a direct restoration to activity of funds that had been in the passive state, for instance, when a portion or all of the interest received on loans or of the principal of paid debts, instead of being again used for loans, as assumed in our premises, is used for living expenditures or is invested in industrial or commercial pursuits. This is one of the departures to which we have above adverted. There is still a third current in the same direction, though comparatively insignificant, consisting of commissions paid to agents and trust companies for attending to loans and collecting debts and interest, as well as of taxes, where the business of lending is burdened with taxation. These cover payments for services rendered and other items constituting "Cost," which term is here confined, of course, to the expense of conducting the business of lending.

To facilitate our investigation, these currents may be denominated by the letters: L (Loans), E (Expenditures), and C (Cost).

The first current flowing from the active to the passive division consists of funds applied to the payment of "Debts," related to which is the second current consisting of the payment of interest. In this latter current is of course included the interest paid on bonds, but not dividends paid on stocks, inasmuch as we are here considering only loan transactions. We have next to consider another departure from our assumed premises, a departure which forms a third current from the active to the passive state. We had assumed that funds employed industrially or commercially are in the active state. But as such funds are frequently diverted into loans, which we have assumed as flowing from the passive division, it follows that such funds must previously have been transferred to that division, a transfer which is to be recognized as the third current. Thus, for example, workingmen take part of their earnings to savings banks where the funds are loaned out, merchants or manufacturers lend out some of their profits by investment in bonds, or stockholders apply some of their dividends to loan on mortgage. Such lending of funds previously in circulation is accordingly a dual process, namely, a transfer from the active to the passive division through "Savings," and another passage in the opposite direction through "Loans." This double passage must be recognized for reasons that will appear later.

Reverting to the subject of the second current we should consider that the market rate of interest paid on loans is determined by three economic factors and should accordingly be divided into three parts, namely:

First, "Cost," comprising the current expenses of lending, such as commissions paid to agents attending to the business of lending as well as other items of cost. This part is equal to the previously discussed current C.

Second, the insurance against "Risk" which inevitably attends the business of lending.

Third, the net profit on money loans or "Interest Proper."

Let us denominate these currents by the letters P (Payments of Debts), C+R+I (the three parts of gross interest: Cost, Risk and Interest Proper) and S (Savings devoted to Lending).

If we now further denote by V the volume of active funds and by dV the change or differential of this volume within a given period, and if we disregard, for the time being, any possible changes of the total volume of funds, such as may result from coinage, the issue or withdrawal of currency, the expansion or contraction of bank deposits, etc., it follows that the change of volume, dV, within a given period is determined by the volumes flowing through the several channels within the same period, hence:

1. $dV=L+E+C-P-(C+R+I)-S=L+E-P-R-I-S.$

This formula will be used later for further deductions.

In studying the cycle of prosperity and depression there is another item demanding consideration. It is well known that periods of business depression are invariably preceded by more or less pronounced financial crises manifesting themselves by an increased number of business failures. This would indicate that the indebted ness of the industrial to the financial world exceeds the ability of borrowers to pay their debts. To be sure, in this connection we must not leave out of sight that we are here concerned only with money loans and the indebtedness thereby accruing.

The volume of this indebtedness is increased by that current of funds from the passive to the active division which is dominated by the letter L in the preceding deduction and is reduced by the reverse current P. There is, however, another factor reducing the volume of debts, namely, the depreciation of their value due to the insolvency of debtors. A vast amount of lenders' assets is annually ruled off to loss on this account. But in the aggregate this loss is balanced by that portion of the gross interest known in economics as insurance against risk, which has been discussed above and designated by the letter R. It follows then that these three currents are the factors which bring about an increase or a decrease of the volume of indebtedness, according as the opposing currents predominate in the one or in the other direction. If now the letter D is used to designate the volume of indebtedness and dD the change or differential of this volume during a given period, it is evident that

2. dD=L–P–R.

The reason for carefully defining the term "Debt" as well as for considering the lending of money previously in active circulation to constitute a dual process will now be understood, for only on these premises will the currents embraced in this formula be identical with those of equal denomination in equation 1, and both equations may accordingly be combined and solved for I, the resulting equation being:

3. 1=E–S+dD–dV.

This equation will reveal some very instructive information if subjected to careful analysis. As it refers to given periods, it is true for short as well as for long oties. The terms E and S will increase approximately in proportion to the time embraced in the period, while the differential terms dD and dV will merely fluctuate. At times they will be positive, at times negative; in short, they are not cumulative with the increase of time. If long periods are considered, the last two terms will for this reason be insignificant in relation to the others and become negligible. The equation will then assume the form:

4. 1=E–S.

Fig. 1.

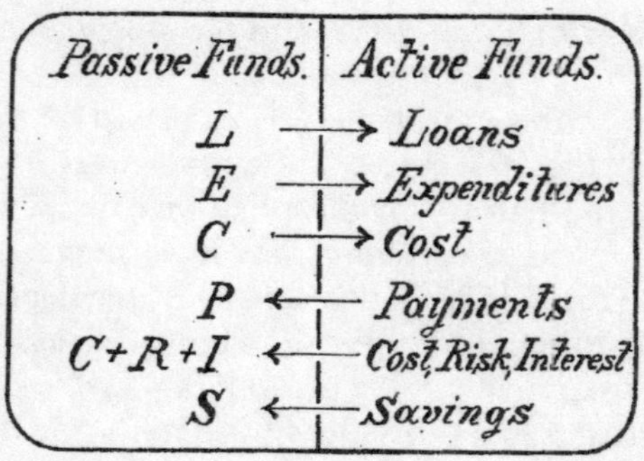

It will be remembered that I is the volume of the net incomes from money loans, E is the volume of funds transferred as "Expenditures" from the passive state into the field of activity by being laid out in living expenses or being put out into business ventures, while S is the volume of funds taken out of the field of activity and put as "Savings" into condition to be loaned. The current S being a current of processes which are the reverse of those making up the current E, the quantity E–S may properly be termed "Lenders' Net Expenditures." With this in view, formula 4 conveys the information that the aggregate of the lenders' net incomes depends upon and is equal to their "Net Expenditures" when long periods of time are considered. The aggregate incomes from loans, then, are increased by more liberal "Expenditures" of those incomes and are diminished by the "Savings" of industrial earnings and their investment in loans.

This may appear to be a startling proposition. But its truth is unassailable and may be better understood when it is considered that the concept "Lender" is here used not so much in a personal as in an economic or functional sense. The function of lending is that of facilitating the distribution of the available funds into those commercial or industrial channels in which they can perform the most efficient service. It were therefore an error to apply the above conclusion to the individual instead of to the function. To the "Lender," in this exclusive sense, all investments in industrial enterprises are as much "Expenditures" as are outlays for personal necessaries or luxuries. The proposition simply indicates that the field of lending is strictly limited and that accordingly the volume of loans cannot be indefinitely expanded. This is indeed confirmed by the fact that numerous representative financiers have of late gone beyond their normal province of "Lending" and have acquired large industrial interests. Their field in the financial world being limited, they find room for expanding their influence in the acquisition and in the creation of giant enterprises, especially those to which of late the term "Trusts" has been applied.

That same conclusion, namely, that the aggregate net incomes from loans are increased by the "Expenditures" of those incomes and are diminished by the factor denominated "Savings," applies of course to the community as a whole. To the individual lender it is inapplicable, inasmuch as an individual lender cannot increase his personal income by spending his resources more freely while other lenders are restricting their outlays and reinvesting the major portion of their incomes in loans.

So far we have dealt only with long periods of time, on basis of which alone our formula 4 is wholly valid. Within shorter periods the quantities dD and dV of formula 3 cannot be neglected and can be shown to have a definite significance in the cycle of industrial conditions.

In this respect four periods can be distinguished, according as the predominating features are, in rotation, at first a positive dD, followed by a negative dV, then by a negative dD and finally by a positive dV, which means, respectively, an increasing volume of indebtedness, a decreasing volume of active funds, a decreasing volume of indebtedness and an increasing volume of active funds. Of course, these periods are by no means sharply defined. They gradually pass one into the other, not without considerable overlapping. Only when specific causes intervene, such, for instance, as wars or other far-reaching influences, may a comparatively rapid passage from one to the other be observed.

It is perhaps worth noting that in the first two periods the quantity I exceeds the quantity E–S, while in the last two this relation is. reversed. This agrees with the law expressed by formula 4, according to which any excess of I over E–S during one period must be balanced by an equal deficiency during another period.

The diagram Fig. 2 graphically represents the fluctuations, in the course of the cycle, of the two factors, D, the volume of indebted ness and V, the funds in active circulation. This diagram will be found to fully illustrate the following analysis of the progress of the cycle.

Fig. 2.

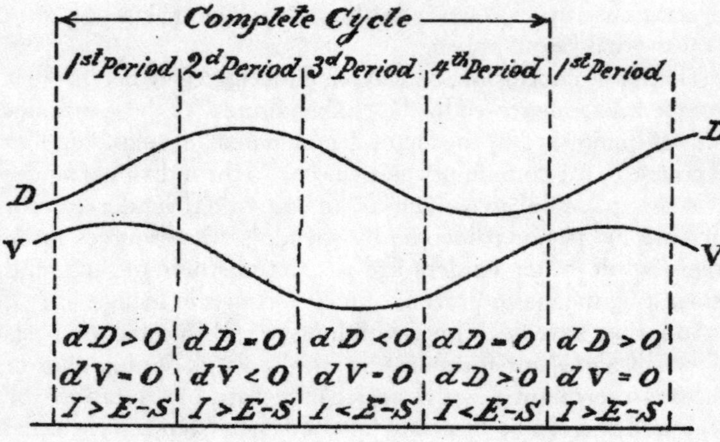

The first period is that in which dD is positive, *i. e.,* in which the volume of indebtedness is increasing, while dV is practically nil, *i. e.,* the circulating volume is practically stationary. This is the prosperous period in which commerce flourishes, business increases and new enterprises are established. Expanding business absorbs all available passive financial resources. Those who have funds for lending have no difficulty in making loans on satisfactory terms. Interest rises to the highest rate. Because of the ease with which acceptable borrowers can be found, the bulk of funds is kept in active circulation, for every accretion to the passive volume is promptly returned to circulation. There are comparatively few business failures, hence only a small fraction of the gross interest need be devoted to cover losses from bad debts, the greater portion of interest being net profit.

Trust companies and other financial institutions must reinvest the incomes from loans in their care, they having practically no choice in the matter. Individual lenders also, spending only a part of their incomes, naturally desire to invest the remainder. It is thus apparent that the "Net Expenditures" of lenders are less than their net incomes, in other words, the quantity E–S is less than the quantity I, hence the flow of funds from the active to the passive division preponderates, at least as regards the channels E, S and I. The primary effect is an accumulation of funds in the passive state, but they are readily restored to circulation by an excess of the current L over P. This, however, is attended by a constant increase of the volume of indebtedness and with it by an increasing obligation to pay interest, which still further hastens the flow of funds from the active to the passive division through the channel I. So long as these funds are again released by borrowing, the total indebtedness increases with accelerating rapidity and, in the nature of things, must ultimately exceed the ability of borrowers to furnish adequate security. The borrowing which has heretofore restored to circulation the funds accruing to lenders is then reduced and we enter upon the second stage of the cycle in which dV appears as a negative quantity, in other words, in which the active volume V is decreasing, because of the accumulations in the passive state. "Cash" in business becomes scarce, the payment of accounts becomes tardy, long credits are asked in business transactions. The steady diminution of the quantity of money in active circulation invites hoarding, which makes matters worse. But the flow of funds due to the excess of

I over E–S continues to reduce the volume of active funds. Finally the increasing scarcity of money in circulation renders it impossible for many of the debtors to meet their obligations and the number of business failures increases, often amounting to a crisis. Business, that is to say, the exchange of products and services, becomes stagnant for the same reason. This marks the advent of the third period in which the term dD of formula 3 becomes negative, indicating a diminution of the volume of indebtedness. Those business men who can do so pay off at least part of their debts, since a smaller working capital suffices for the reduced volume of business, but the sum total of debts is also reduced by reason of the numerous business failures, and since a greater portion of the gross interest must now be devoted to cover losses, the remainder, constituting interest proper, is materially reduced, even though the rate of gross interest is not changed at once. This is the typical period of business depression. The law according to which the net income of lenders cannot, in the long run, exceed their net expenditures asserts itself. By the force of circumstances over which the lenders have no control, their net incomes fall below their net expenditures in the measure in which they formerly exceeded the latter. Money is now freely offered for loans at a low rate of interest, provided complete security is given, but the scarcity of funds in circulation, combined with the inability of business men already indebted to the limit of their borrowing power to furnish the security demanded for further loans, causes such a stagnation in business that even those not already overburdened with debts cannot afford to borrow.

Finally the third period is succeeded by the fourth in which dV is positive and which ends in gradual recovery. The net income of lenders is still low, principally for two reasons. In the first place, most of the remaining debts have been renewed at a lower rate of interest and, in the second place, the volume of indebtedness is at an ebb, while the chances for investing the money held by lenders are comparatively few. The low volume of indebtedness during this period is clearly shown in diagram Fig. 2. By an excess of the "Lenders' Expenditures" (as previously defined) over their incomes, the passive funds are finally restored to circulation. Thus the fourth period merges into the first of the next cycle and the play is repeated.

In reviewing the cycle as here outlined, it will be noted that each period presents conditions which inevitably bring about the results that characterize the succeeding period. The power of money to command interest exceeding "Cost" plus insurance against "Risk," or C+R, creates a tendency of funds to concentrate in the hands of the lenders. In prosperous times these funds are readily restored to circulation by lending, which, however, correspondingly increases the volume of "Debts." When the increasing indebtedness begins to exhaust the ability of borrowers to furnish security, the accretions to the volume of passive funds are no longer released and the consequent reduction of circulating funds deprives borrowers of the means of meeting their financial obligations. This leads, largely through business failures, to a reduction of collectable debts and incidentally to a reduction of the rate of actual or net interest. The lenders' income is reduced and eventually the accumulated passive funds find their way into circulation through their owners preferring to expend them in industrial or commercial ventures rather than hold them idle indefinitely. in the resulting fluctuation of the volume of active funds the periodicity of business depressions finds a logical explanation. Cause and effect follow each other in their natural sequence, completing a continuous, ever recurrent cycle of the four periods described. It is hardly possible to present a better proof for the correctness of this explanation than the complete agreement of the hypothesis with the facts.

In practice the play of economic forces, as above traced out, is perhaps slightly modified by the constant fluctuation of the total volume of currency and bank deposits, by changes and improvements of industrial and commercial methods, by the practice of hoarding and by other factors, but these influences are sporadic and do not affect the ultimate conclusion, namely, that the capacity of our present system of currency and banking is inadequate to mediate the enormous volume of exchanges required and entailed by the modern system of production.

A remedy can be looked for only in improved methods of mediating exchanges. As one of the possible remedies the writer would suggest that business men establish a commercial clearing house through which their mutual accounts can be cleared practically without the use of current funds. Such a system, if surrounded by proper safeguards, would virtually permit the payment of accounts payable with accounts receivable. In the measure in which business men would thus make themselves independent of the money market, exchanges would be facilitated and stagnation prevented. Indeed, a universal application of such a system may be the means of ultimately eliminating business depressions and of establishing perpetual prosperity.

FINANCING OF CORPORATIONS[1]

Albert H. Putney

Section 54 – Capital of Corporations.
The capital stock of a corporation is the par value of the stock which it is authorized to issue by its charter.

"There is a distinction between the capital of a corporation and its capital stock, though they are often used as interchangeable terms. The capital stock is clearly not the same as property possessed by the corporation; for the capital stock remains fixed, although the actual property of the corporation varies in value and is constantly increasing or diminishing in amount. What the amount of the capital shall be is within the discretion of the man agers, but the amount of capital stock is limited and determined by the charter and the laws governing it. It follows, therefore, that a limit imposed upon the capital stock of a corporation does not restrict the amount of property which it may own."[2]

Section 55 – Corporate Securities.
Corporate securities fall into two general classes, stocks and bonds.

There are many classes both of stocks and bonds, but all the classes in each division have many resemblances, while a most fundamental distinction is to be observed between the two divisions of securities.

Stock is an evidence of ownership. A stockholder is the owner of a certain definite but undivided part of the assets of the corporation, although he does not have the right to have any special part of the assets of a corporation set aside for his share, at least. while the corporation is still a going concern.

In general, the rights of bondholders can only be enforced in connection with the rights of other bondholders.

[1] [Chapter 2 of *Corporations: Organization, Financing, Management*, Minneapolis: Cree Publishing, 1909]

[2] Beach on Private Corporations, Vol. II, p. 761

Section 56 – Stock – How Acquired.

Stock maybe acquired in any one of three ways:

First. By original subscription.

Second. By transfer, either by purchase or otherwise.

Third. Through the issue of a stock dividend.

Section 57 – Subscriptions for Stock.

Subscriptions for stock may be made either before or after the incorporation of the corporation. If made after incorporation the contract is binding, even when executory. There has been much difference of opinion as to the effect of a contract of subscription to stock made before the charter of the corporation was issued. The better rule seems to be that if the subscription was in pursuance of a step expressly authorized by law to be taken in the creation of a corporation, such a contract is binding but otherwise not. Contracts to subscribe for stock are generally, but not always, held to come under the provisions of the Statute of Frauds. In some States it is necessary that all stock of the corporation be subscribed for before the corporation begins doing business, but in other States this requirement does not exist.

In some States all stock subscribed for must be paid for in full in advance. In most States a portion may be paid and the payment of the balance deferred.[3] Stock may be paid for either in money or in property or labor.[4]

[3] For the liability of the stockholders under such circumstances, see section 92.

[4] "A corporation may receive in payment of its shares of stock any property which it may lawfully purchase, and in general, may receive any consideration which is suitable and applicable to the purposes for which the corporation was organized. A railroad corporation may receive payment in contract work, in right of way, or in any kind of material or labor applicable to its construction. A manufacturing corporation may receive payment in the good-will of a business or the stock in trade. Land may be taken in payment when the corporation would be allowed to purchase the same. Promissory notes may also be taken, under the corporate power to give credit and extend the time of pay ment of debts. But a bank may have no power to accept the subscriber's notes in payment of a subscription to its stock, and the directors are personally liable for so doing, unless the notes were good or the directors had reasonable cause to believe they were good. Fully paid-up stock may be issued by an irrigation company, in payment for pipe lines, wells and ditches. It is legal for a corporation to issue stock as fully paid to a person in consideration of his leaving an employment in which he is engaged and of assuming the presidency of the corporation. Services rendered by a director after he had subscribed for stock are a good con sideration in payment therefor, in accordance with an agreement to that effect. A person to whom a corporation issues full-paid stock in settle ment of a claim is not bound by any prior contracts of the corporation in regard to that stock where he took the stock, without notice of the contracts." Cook on Corporations, Vol. I, pp. 82–5.

In some States the value of such property must be passed upon by some State official and in many cases where there is fraud in the valuation of property the party paying for stock with such property may be held liable to the creditors of the corporation.

"The good will and trade name are a species of property that may be valued and sold, and the purchaser protected in their enjoyment the same as any other property; the same is true with trademarks.

The assignment of trademarks may be made to the same extent as other property, but with one important exception – the trademark must (with few exceptions) accompany and pass to the party who purchases the good will of the business; any general assignment of the good will, will carry with it the trademarks in use, without any special reference to such trademarks in the assignment, and this is equally true of the trade name in use.

While it is, of course, impossible to fix the value of the good will of a business with mathematical precision and accuracy, still such value may be arrived at with sufficient certainty for all practical purposes. The common rule adopted for valuing the good will is, to first ascertain the net earning capacity of the business for a given period, usually for a sufficient number of years to reach the general average of such earning capacity, then to divide the amount thus obtained by the number of years over which the estimate extends, and this will constitute the general average profits upon which the value of the good will depends. Then as to the value, it must necessarily vary according to the circumstances of the particular case.

A common practice in determining and fixing the value of the good will (where common stock is to be issued therefor) has heretofore been to place the amount at a sum upon which the annual net earnings would pay a dividend equal, at least, to the legal rate of interest prevailing in the State where the transaction occurs. As an example, suppose the average annual net earnings to be fifty thousand dollars ($50,000); this would be five per cent (5%) on one million dollars ($1,000,000), and that sum would constitute the value of the good will. But this is purely arbitrary and without foundation in reason, as the good will differs so widely in character from actual money or money's worth that to make it a basis of value upon its earning power is to go farther and place its intrinsic worth equal to money as well. Besides, the good will of a business has no value aside from its immediate connection with the business itself, and upon the winding up of the enterprise, by law or upon liquidation, the property vanishes.

As before intimated, no inflexible rule will apply in fixing the value of the good will of a business; its age, standing and earning capacity are elements of its value only.

The trademarks are integral parts of the business as a unit, and their individual value is not important, except as elements in the valuation of the good will and their relative value and importance to the future of the enterprise.

Here, as with patents, it is difficult to value 'future prospects and possibilities,' and this must depend upon the particular circumstances of the case under consideration; for if the business has been organized and established with skill and experience behind it, its future prospects and possibifities may be of far greater value than its present good will, and in this, at least, intangible property differs from that of tangible, viz., in that of their valuation."[5]

Section 58 – Acquisition of Stock by Transfer.
Stock may be acquired from a former owner by practically any method by which any form of personal property may be acquired; for example, by gift, will, assignment, judgment, forfeiture, insolvency, or intestacy.

Section 59 – Stock Dividends.
Whenever a corporation has acquired a surplus in its treasury, which might lawfully be used for the payment of dividends, it is legal for them to add such surplus to their capital and to issue additional stock to their stockholders as a stock dividend.

Section 60 – Classes of Stock.
Stock is classified and described in various ways. Among the various kinds which must be considered are the following:

Common stock,
Preferred stock,
Guaranteed stock,
Deferred stock,
Convertible stock,
Special stock,
Issued stock,
Non-issued stock,
Over-issued stock,
Treasury stock,
Founders' stock,
Full paid stock,
Partly paid stock,
Bonus stock,
Watered stock.

[5] Frank on Science of Organization and Business Development.

Section 61 – Common Stock.

The common stock of the corporation is the ordinary stock without any special rights or protection. The control of the corporation is generally in the holders of the common stock, although sometimes both common and preferred stock is given the voting power. The common stock of a corporation is always the last of the securities upon which dividends or interest are paid.

Section 62 – Preferred Stock.

The name preferred stock is given to that stock which is "preferred" in payment of dividends. In other words, stock which receives dividends in advance of common stock.

Preferred stock may be classified in several ways. The first classification would be into voting and non-voting preferred stock. Some preferred stock carries with it the right to vote at stockholders' meeting, and other preferred stock is without any share in the management of the company.

Another division of preferred stock is that into cumulative and non-cumulative stock. In non-cumulative preferred stock each year's business is considered by itself and if the company fails to earn enough to pay the dividend to which the preferred stock is entitled one year, such deficiency cannot be made up out of the earnings of the following year. In the case of cumulative preferred stock, any back deficiency due on preferred stock, must be paid before the common stock may receive anything.

For example, let us suppose that a company is incorporated for $100,000 common stock and $100,000 five per cent preferred stock, and that one year the company makes a net profit of $2,000, which could be applied on dividends, and next year a profit of $10,000. In the first year the preferred stock will, of course, receive the whole of the $2,000, whether the stock is cumulative or not, and in either case there will be a deficiency of $3,000. If it is cumulative stock, this $3,000 will be paid out of the $10,000 earnings the second year, which means that the preferred stock this year will receive $8,000 and the common stock only $2,000 as dividends, while if the preferred stock is non-cumulative, both common and preferred stock will receive $5,000 each.

The third classification of preferred stock is into preferred stock which can never receive a larger dividend than that which is paid before the common stock receives anything, and preferred stock which will receive an equal dividend with the common stock if enough is earned to pay both a dividend higher than that to the extent of which the preferred stock is preferred.

For example, to take our former illustration of a company with $100,000 common stock and $100,000 five per cent preferred stock; if the company earns $5,000, this will of course go to the preferred stock. If it earns $100,000, both common and preferred stock will receive $5,000, that is, a dividend of five per cent. If it earns $15,000 in a year, in the case of the first class of preferred stock under this classification, the common stock would receive $10,000, that is, a dividend of ten per cent, while the preferred stock will still be restricted to the five per cent dividend, but in the case of the second class of preferred stock both the common and preferred stock will receive a dividend of seven and one-half per cent.

A fourth classification of preferred stock is that into preferred stock which may be retired by a vote of the common stock and preferred stock which cannot be so retired.

Section 63 – Guaranty Stock.
Cumulative preferred stock is sometimes called guaranty stock, but the proper use of the latter term is to describe the stock of a corporation which is leased to another corporation. The lessee corporation guarantees the dividends of the stock of the lessor corporation.

Section 64 – Deferred Stock.
Deferred stock is any stock which is paid dividend after certain other classes of stock. The term is not a usual one. In any corporation where there is any preferred stock the common stock is deferred stock.

Section 65 – Convertible Stock.
Convertible stock is stock which may be converted into the bonds of the corporation at the option of the holder of such stock, This is a recent species of stock and it is generally held that it can only be issued in pursuance of express statutory authority. Such stock is permitted in New Jersey and in some other States which pattern after the New Jersey corporation system.

Section 66 – Special Stock.

"In Massachusetts incorporated companies are permitted by statute to issue a peculiar kind of stock, known as 'special stock.' It is something essentially different from preferred stock. Its chief characteristics are that it is limited in amount to two-fifths of the actual capital; it is limited in amount to two-fifths of the actual capital; it is subject to redemption by the corporation at par after a fixed time, to be expressed in the certificate; the corporation is bound to pay a fixed half-yearly sum, or dividend, upon it as a debt; the holders of it are in no event liable for the debts of the corporation beyond their stock, and the issue of this special stock makes all the general stockholders liable for all debts and contracts of the corporation until the special stock is fully redeemed. Special stock can be issued only by a vote of three-fourths of the general stockholders of the company at a meeting duly called for that purpose. The guarantee of dividends of special stock in Massachusetts is an absolute one, and not in any degree conditional upon the earning of sufficient profits by the corporation."[6]

Section 67 – Issued, Non-Issued, Over-Issued Stock.

Issued stock or outstanding stock is such stock as has been purchased or otherwise disposed of and is the private property of some individual.

Non-issued stock is that part of the authorized capital stock of a corporation which has not been disposed of and still remains the property of the corporation. In some States such stock is not permitted.

Over-issued stock is stock which has been issued beyond the amount authorized by the charter of the corporation. It is held that over-issued stock is void.

The leading case on the subject is the case of New York & New Haven B. R. Company vs. Robert Schuyler, William Cross, and 324 others. In this case, "the capital authorized by the charter was limited to $3,000,000, represented by thirty thousand shares of stock, all of the shares except seventy-eight having been issued and the capital paid in, less about $700 on the seventy-eight shares, several years since. Transfer books of the stock were kept at the city of New York and two other places, where

[6] Cook on Corporations, Sec. 276.

transfers of the stock were made and certificates issued as occasion required. From the organization of the company, in 1846, to the 3rd of July, 1854, Robert Schuyler was the president and transfer agent of the company, having his station and place of business at the office of the company in New York. As early as October, 1843, he commenced a series of fraudulent acts, extending over the whole period of time intermediate that date and the 3rd of July, 1854, during which time, unknown to the plaintiff, he issued and disposed of a large number of certificates of stock of the company, which on their face purported to be genuine, were executed and signed in the same manner as genuine certificates, and undistinguishable from them, but which in fact were fraudulent over-issues for his own private purposes. Some of these he issued to a firm of which he was a member; the others were issued to divers other persons.

In other instances, after making transfers of stock for other parties on the books of the company, he failed to cancel the old certificates which were surrendered for that purpose, but fraudulently reissued them as genuine certificates of stock owned by himself.

In furtherance of his designs he allowed clerks of his firm and himself a false credit on the stock ledger of the railroad company, by which it was made ostensibly to appear that such firm and himself had stock to their credit on the books of the company to the amount of $1,000,000, when in truth it owned none. These false certificates purporting to be genuine, and those originally genuine certificates which instead of being cancelled were reissued, were used by Robert Schuyler in his own, and in the business of the firm, under representations that they were genuine, chiefly for the purpose of borrowing money; were sold openly in the market as genuine stock in some instances, and have passed in this way into the hands of the defendants, the present holders.

In some instances this overissued stock has be come commingled with genuine, by having, in the regular course of business, been transferred and incorporated into a certificate with the genuine.

The whole false issue amounted to near $2,000,000.

Nine thousand three hundred and eighty-three shares now stand on the books of the railroad company, in the names of twenty-nine persons and firms to whom it had been transferred by the firm to which Schuyler belonged. The balance of such over-issues has gone into the hands of two hundred and sixty-six persons and firms at different times, in different amounts, from different persons, and many of these holders are also the holders of genuine stock.

Intermediate the 29th of June and the 3d of July, 1854, Schuyler, the president and transfer agent of the company, being sick, Mr. Worthen, the vice-president, who was also one of the directors, undertook, but, as the plaintiff says, without authority, to act as transfer agent in the place of Schuyler, and unaware of Schuyler's frauds, transferred four thousand four hundred and forty-six shares of that false stock for twenty-one different persons and firms, supposing the certificates he received and transferred to be genuine.

Some of the holders of this over-issue, as the complaint alleges, took, knowing the certificates were fictitious; some with reason to believe so; some on usurious contracts; many under circumstances which should have put them on inquiry; and many others under circumstances and upon considerations unknown to the plaintiffs.

They all claimed rights against the company; some that they are stockholders; others that they are either stockholders or have a right of action against the company for their losses. Some claim damages to the full nominal par value of the certificates they hold; others for the money that they have actually advanced; while all assert a claim upon the company in some form. It is not averred that some of these fraudulently issued certificates have not gone into the hands of entirely innocent parties, for value.

Several of the defendants sued the company. Some suits were pending in the Supreme Court, some in the Superior Court, and some others in the Common Pleas of New York City. Other suits were threatened. The complaint joined in this suit Robert Schuyler and all the alleged owners or holders of this over-issued stock and prayed that the certificates be decreed illegal and void, and surrendered up and cancelled; that until these questions were settled, those who sued be stayed in their proceedings; that those who have not, be enjoined from suing; that the suits which were pending be consolidated with this, and closed with the usual general prayer for such further and other relief as is meet and proper."

The defendants demurred to the bill and the Court of Appeals of New York overruled the demurrer, saying in part:

"This extraordinary fraud could not fail to place the corporation in a situation of extreme difficulty and embarrassment.

What was to be done with the spurious stock certificates? Were the holders to be recognized? Were they to share in the dividends, and were they entitled to vote at elections? Was the stock of the company practically increased to $5,000,000 when the charter confined it to $3,000,000? If this could not be done, then was the company bound to pay, in damages to each holder of these false instruments, the value which the genuine stock has borne in the market? These were grave questions, about which gentlemen of great eminence in their profession, and the courts also, differed. In the courts of original jurisdiction it was determined, after the institution of this suit, that the corporation was, in some form, bound to make good the false certificates. On appeal to this court we held them void to all intents and purposes, and that the corporation and its genuine stockholders were entirely unaffected by them.

Such was the situation of this company on the discovery of these acts of Mr. Schuyler. As a pure creation of law, the corporation was not a sentient being; but the law, nevertheless, clothed it with authority which enabled it to act, by its board of directors, as a natural person, within the sphere of its powers and duties. It had therefore the rights of which a natural person would have in analogous situations, and in order to evolve the principle of this controversy, we may suppose that a natural person is clothed with the legal title to, and is in possession of, an extensive line of railroad, receiving the gross earnings for the purpose of dividing the net profits among a large class of individuals, whose right, in certain fixed proportions, is evidenced by a certificate or declaration of trust, which each one held, signed by the legal owner or his authorized agent. If, then, a new class of individuals should come forward claiming the same rights, and presenting, as the evidence thereof, instruments of the same kind in all respects, bearing on their face all the appearance of genuineness and authority, but in fact unauthorized and spurious, what would be the rights and the duty of the legal owner in that exigency? Upon the settled principles of equity, it would be his right and his duty to call the false claimants into court in order to remove the cloud upon the equitable interests of those whom he represented. It would be his right, as owner of the legal estate, to bring to a determination every claim upon that estate, in law or equity, resting upon facts and documents giving to it, prima facie, all the appearances of genuineness and validity. It would be his duty to call for such a determination as the representative of numerous equitable interests carved out of his estate and placed under his protection. These are principles so familiar and elementary that citations from the books are not required to support them.

With the aid of these analogies, we can come to a conclusion as to the rights of this corporation in the exigency which had arisen at the commencement of this suit. It stood, as we have seen, in a quasi trust relation to its shareholders, holding, as it did, in the legal estate, and they having, as individuals, an equitable right in the net earnings or income of the same estate. They also had the right to vote at the elections of the company, to the exclusion of all other persons. If the corporation yielded these rights to the holders, of its original and genuine stock, and rejected the claims of those who held the false certificates, it became at once exposed, not merely to one, as we have seen, but to a multiplicity of suits, questions of no inconsiderable difficulty. In these circumstances, its right of resort to a court of equity, in order to have the spurious certificates cancelled and annulled, does not admit of a doubt, provided those instruments were such, in character and appearance, as to bring them within the principles on which courts of equity administer protective and preventive justice. There is no head of equity jurisdiction more firmly established than that which embraces the cancellation of instruments which are capable of a vexatious use after the means of defense at law may become impaired or lost, or when they are calculated to throw a cloud upon the title or interest of the party seeking relief. But the jurisdiction does not universally attach on the mere ground that the deed or other contract is invalid. If the invalidity plainly appears on the face of the writing, so that no lapse of time or change or circumstances can weaken the means of defense, it is held that no occasion arises for a suit in equity to decree its cancellation. And the doctrine now is, that such instruments do not, in a just sense, even cast a cloud upon the title or interest, or diminish the security of the party against whom the attempt may be made to use them. If, on the other hand, the invalidity does not appear on their face, the jurisdiction is not confined to instruments of any particular kind or class. Whatever their character, if they are capable of being used as a means of vexation and annoyance, if they throw a cloud upon title or disturb the tranquil enjoyment of property, then it is against conscience and equity that they should be kept outstanding, and they ought to be cancelled. These principles of general jurisprudence are believed to be decisive in favor of the right of this corporation to demand the cancellation of the false stock and to maintain a suit in equity for that purpose. On their face, as we have seen, the certificates of this stock are undistinguishable from those which are genuine and true. They confer, therefore, upon each holder, a prima facie right as a stockholder. The evidence of such right must in every case be repelled by showing that the certificate does not represent the actual stock of the company, and it is impossible to say that the means of repelling these claims will always be as per fect as they were when the frauds in which they originated were first discovered.

It is true, we held in the case already mentioned, that the company could successfully defend an action brought against it for refusing to recognize one of these certificates; but the defense rested, as it must, if actions were to be brought upon every other certificate, upon the extrinsic facts to be proved. Conceding, even, that every one of these claims may be defended, at whatever distance of time and under whatever circumstances they may be pressed upon the corporation, this by no means meets the equity of the case. If, as we have held, no just claim against the corporation arises out of these certificates, it is plainly unconscientious and inequitable that they should be kept on foot. Their very existence, outstanding, is unjust, because it must of necessity exercise a most depressing influence upon the real stock of the corporation. We all know how sensitive are values in property of this description; and what conceivable facts could cast a deeper shadow, over every genuine shareholder's interest than a spurious issue of $2,000,000 of stock, evidenced by certificates apparently valid, and under which every holder boldly and confidently asserted his claim? The fact is not alleged in the complaint, but we can scarcely err in supposing that, on the dis covery of these frauds, every share of valid stock must at once have lost nearly one-half of its market value. That depression must continue in a greater or less degree, while the certificates are allowed to stand. A decision against one of them, in an action founded upon it, is not a determination against any other one, and cannot, while the others are outstanding, restore to the genuine stock the value which justly belongs to it. To say that the shareholders must remain in such a condition of insecurity and doubt, and must hold their shares under such a depression, would be to sanction a species of injustice which ought to be prevented. These shares of stock are a description of property as much entitled to invoke the protective remedies peculiar to courts of equity as any other.

For this reason there is a great difficulty in sustaining the present suit as one brought by a trustee to be advised and directed in regard to the proper line of duty toward the cestui que trust, and those who claim to stand in that relation. But the same reason unerringly indicates the corporation as the organ through which the shareholders are to be heard when legal wrongs are to be redressed or equitable remedies are to be invoked. If, therefore, I have been successful in showing that the fraudulent certificates of stock are instruments of such annoyance and vexation, in depressing values and disturbing the fair enjoyment of rights, that they ought not to be allowed to stand, then this suit by the corporation rests firmly upon that branch of equity jurisdiction which includes the cancellation of such instruments.

The views which have been taken assume the validity of all the certificates fraudulently issued by Schuyler. Upon the facts stated in the complaint, which the demurrer adnüts to be true, and upon the principles laid down in the case of the Mechanics' Bank against this company, it is impossible to say that any one of them is a valid representative of stock, or a claim of any kind against the corporation. It appears, indeed, that most of the certificates have passed into the hands of third parties, in good faith, paid for or advanced value upon the shares. On that ground it was further assumed that their rights were superior to those of the corporation and the holders of its actual and genuine stock. This is a view of the question which holds a prominent place among the reasons given for dismissing the complaint. But since the court below pronounced its judgment, the other case mentioned came before us on appeal, and the contrary doctrine was very precisely determined, and upon the fullest consideration. Adhering as we do to that decision, and looking at the case as the complaint states it, all the certificates in question must share the same fate; and the present case will not be embarrassed by the necessity of rendering different judgments in respect to different parties. In saying this much, however, it is not designed to prejudge the rights of any person in special circumstances, to be defensively alleged and proved, differing in their character from any yet called to our attention."[7]

[7] Keener, Cases on Equity, Vol. I, pp. 121–6.

Section 68 – Founders' Stock.

"Founders' shares are a new class of stock in America, and are not in general use. They are more common in England. To this class of stock belong the surplus profits of a corporation, or a portion of the surplus profits, which remain after paying fixed dividends on the preferred and common stock, and, perhaps, after setting aside also a given amount of the profits for the reserve fund, whenever a distribution of the surplus profits is determined upon. Suppose a corporation is organized with $500,000 capital stock, $300,000 of which is preferred and $200,000 common. Suppose $50,000 of this common stock is set aside as founders' shares, and after six per cent is paid out of the net earnings as a dividend on the preferred stock, the surplus profits are to be divided equally between the. common stock and the founders' shares. This would make the founders' shares worth four times as much as the common stock on the basis of earnings. Founders' shares may be issued under the New Jersey laws, but under the laws of most of the other States they are not possible. There is no particular advantage that can be derived from their issue that cannot be had from the judicious issue of common or preferred stock. Founders' shares are commonly used as compensation for promoters or others who, by lending names or influence, have for warded the interests of a corporation."[8]

Section 69 – Treasury Stock.

Treasury stock is stock which is once issued and which has then come back into the possession of the corporation.

If this stock has once been fully paid for it retains the characteristics of full paid stock even if it is later sold by the corporation below par. A method often resorted to for the purpose of relieving purchasers of stock below par from further liability is to issue a large amount of stock to some person for a small amount of property and then to have such party return a portion of such stock to the treasury. This method has many dangers and cannot be recommended.

Section 70 – Full Paid Stock and Partly Paid Stock.

Full paid stock is that the par value of which has been paid either in cash, property or labor. Partly paid stock is stock upon which

[8] Wood on "Modern Business Corporations," p. 117.

a balance remains unpaid. The liability of holders of partly paid stock will be discussed in Chapter IV.

Section 71 – Bonus and Watered Stock.
Bonus stock is stock given without additional compensation to purchasers of bonds or preferred stock. Bonus stock is one form of watered stock, but the latter term is a much broader one.

"Watered stock or fictitiously paid-up stock is stock which is issued as fully paid-up stock when in fact the whole amount of the par value thereof has not been paid in. All stock which has been issued as paid-up stock, but the full par value of which has not been paid into the corporation in money or money's worth, is watered to the extent that the par value exceeds the value actually paid in. Watered stock is, accordingly, stock which purports to represent, but does not represent in good faith, money paid into the treasury of the company, or money's worth actually contributed to the capital of the concern.

The issue of shares of stock as 'paid up,' when in fact they are not paid up, gives rise to some of the most complicated questions connected with the law of corporations. A share of stock is supposed, in theory, to represent its par value in money or money's worth paid in or to be paid in to the corporation. Accordingly when it is issued as paid up, it is bought and sold in the open market on the supposition that it is full-paid stock. Upon this basis, transactions in paid-up stock, involving millions of dollars, are of daily occurrence in the commercial centers of the country. The fact is, however, that where stock is issued in payment for property, the actual value of the property is rarely equal to the par value of the stock issued for it. Especially is this the case with the great industrial corporations. Hence it becomes important to know what liability is attached to such stock; who is liable; to whom the liability arises, and when the liability may be enforced.

There are four different ways in which watered stock is issued: First, by the issue of certificates of stock for an amount of money less than the par value of the stock, although the certificates assert on their face that the full value has been paid in; second, for property or construction work taken at an overvaluation; third, by a stock dividend, the equivalent par value of which has not been added to the capital stock; and fourth, by consolidation under a statute. Each of these four methods may be the means of issuing stock which has been paid up in good faith. Each also, is available for the issue of 'watered' stock. The second method particularly – that of taking property at an overvaluation – is well calculated to conceal the fictitious character of the issue, and to accomplish the purposes of the participants.

Where a corporation has acquired shares of its own paid-up capital stock, either by purchase or by forfeiture for non-payment of calls, it may legally re-issue and sell the same at less than the par value thereof.

There have been various opinions, generally dicta, as to the character of stock issued as paid-up, when in fact it has not been paid for. The customary expression is that such an issue is a fraud upon the law and upon the public and upon the stockholders; or that it is against public policy; or is a fraud on subsequent purchasers of the stock so issued. The law now is, however, that an issue of stock as full paid-up stock, under an agreement that the full par value shall not be paid, is not necessarily a fraudulent transaction, but that as between the parties thereto it is a legal and valid agreement, and violates no principle of public policy."[9]

The liability of the holders of watered stock will be fully treated in Chapter IV on the liability of stockholders.

Section 72 – Bonds.

A bond is merely a promissory note of the corporation secured by the property or income of the corporation.

Bonds have been classified as follows:

1. Mortgage bonds.
2. Equipment bonds.
3. Land credit bonds.
4. Collateral trust bonds.
5. Prior lien bonds.
6. Debentures.
7. Income bonds.

Bonds to be binding must be issued under proper authority and signed by the proper officials. The face of the bond will specify the time when such bonds will become due and the rate of interest.

[9] Cook on Corporations, Secs. 28–30.

Section 73 – Mortgage Bonds.
"In order to create the mortgage lien, no peculiar form of instrument is necessary. Thus a trust deed is in legal effect a mortgage. And car trust agreements for the purchase of rolling stock by installments regarded as rental only upon forfeiture according to the condition of the contract, are held to constitute mortgages. So also where bonds are expressly made a lien upon the property of the company issuing them, either by statute or stipulation to the bonds is unnecessary. And, if a statute be clear, and explicit, in creating a lien of this character it is not necessary that the bonds should make any mention of the statute. Bonds of this character cover all property, presently owned or afterward acquired, and must be foreclosed to become available, in the manner provided by the statute, in all respects as a general mortgage lien. But notes given for money borrowed to pay interest on railroad bonds, each of which stipulates that a certain amount of the gross earnings of the road from date 'is pledged in liquidation of this note,' are not thereby given priority over the bonded debt, as the stipulation is ineffectual."[10]

Section 74 – Other Bonds.
"Equipment bonds are issued to acquire rolling stock, and are secured by a mortgage thereon. Akin to them are Car Trust Certificates (not quoted in the market), by the aid of which rolling stock can be bought on the 'easy payment' system. These certificates are due at frequent intervals – usually semi annually – and are secured by a lien upon the roffing stock in payment of which they are given.

Land grant bonds pledge lands granted by the Government as a guarantee for regular payment of dividends. The land being gradually sold, and the proceeds applied to the retirement of land grant bonds, the majority of these securities have been redeemed. Owing to the low prices realized for land, and considering the rapid rise in the value of real estate, it would probably have been more advantageous to railways to have retained their lands for some time to come, but need of funds and the advisability of reducing fixed charges usually induced them to accelerate these sales.

[10] Beach on Private Corporations, Sec. 741.

Collateral trust bonds are issued against no other security than funds of other railways. Many of the greater companies own vast amounts of stocks or bonds of subsidiary concerns, which gives them control; the Pennsylvania Railroad Company, for instance, possesses upward of $150,000,000 (nominal) of similar securities. When new funds are required they are often obtained upon the security of bonds of subsidiary concerns, which are given in trust to trustees. The value of trust bonds, like that of all mortgages, depends upon the value of the security upon which the advance is made, but usually the securities given in trust yield more than is required for the service of the collateral bonds, in which case the surplus, as a rule, goes toward a sinking fund, out of which trust bonds are redeemed.

Debentures are not frequently met with. They are bonds without any special collateral security, ranking after specified mortgage bonds, and their value depends entirely upon the financial status of the company by which they are issued.

Prior lien bonds likewise are not frequently met with. They are usually issued to pay debts enjoying precedence over mortgage bonds, and in consequence they rank before all other mortgages.

Income bonds more resemble preferred shares than bonds, no dividend being paid unless earned. At the same time they are akin to debentures, inasmuch as they are not issued upon any special security. They differ from preferred stock because no voting rights attach to them, and from debentures inasmuch as interest upon them in the majority of cases is non-cumulative."[11]

Section 75 – Promotion of Enterprises.

The first step in the business of a corporation is raising the capital upon which to do business. Occasionally the parties organizing the corporation themselves put up the capital. And in some cases, a going business formerly owned either by an individual or by a partnership is turned into a corporation.

Corporations are generally organized by persons known as promoters. The function of a promoter has been thus described:

"The word 'promoter' has not yet a legal definition, but it is a business term familiar in corporate finance. The promoter in business practice is one who seeks fields for investment in new

[11] The A, B, C of Wall Street, pp. 245.

enterprises or in the extension of diversification of established industries, and for a consideration forms and organizes a corporation to develop a particular field he has chosen. The promoter commonly attends to everything connected with a floating of an enterprise. In the first place, he finds an enterprise with prospects of good returns on the money he has invested; he employs technical experts in the line of industry to prepare the figures of costs and prospective returns, so he and those to be interested with him may know as exactly as may be what they have and what they may expect; he prepares the prospectus based on the expert's figures; he secures legislation where that is necessary; he secures options and leases where they must be secured; in short, he 'assembles' the proposition; then he employs a corporation lawyer to prepare the articles of incorporation and secures the necessary subscribers to the articles, sees that the articles are recorded and filed; that a certificate of incorporation is issued, and pays the incorporation costs; he sells the stock of the company directly to the public or to bankers or other underwriters whom he has usually provided for before organizing the corporation, and ordinarily, he takes his own profits out in stock. His relation to the corporation is fiduciary; the promoter has to create value to entitle him to profit. He provides a new or original means of making money and makes the means productive through the development of a 'going' concern for the utilization of that means."

A promoter is not an agent for the corporation because the principal is not yet in existence. Such corporation can therefore only become liable for the contracts made by the promoter by ratifying them. Promoters are themselves liable on all previous contracts, either as partners or as individuals, according to the terms of their agreement. Promoters are liable on an action of deceit for any fraudulent representations.

Section 76 – Trading in Stocks and Bonds.

In small corporations stocks and bonds will be treated in much the same way as other forms of personal property. The security of the larger corporations are listed in Wall Street and the operation is thus described in the recently issued "A B C of Wall Street":

"Transactions in stocks are usually made for quick delivery. A broker buys or sells, and receives or delivers the stock or bonds dealt in on the day following the transaction. While odd lots of stocks are dealt in, say 1, 10 or 57 shares, yet 10 and multiples of 10 are the common trading amounts. Commission brokerage houses will not buy and carry on a margin less than 10 shares. Most firms will not accept orders for less than 100. The lots most in vogue in Stock Exchange trading is the 100 share lot, but blocks of as high as 20,000 shares have been sold in one transaction. The par or nominal value of a share of stock is usually $100, and the par value of 10 shares is $1,000, and of 100 shares $10,000. When bought or sold outright the share certificates are delivered to the buyer or by the seller, after an exchange of checks representing the actual or market value. When you speculate in shares on a margin, the margin is usually 10 per cent of the par value. Thus a 10 per cent margin on 10 shares is $100, on 100 shares $1,000. Some brokers require 20 per cent margin and some will accept 5. If you buy, in expectation of an advance, 100 shares of stock at par, or $100 a share, you deposit $1,000 or 10 per cent margin. Should you sell the stock at 110, your broker will give you a check for $2,000, representing your margin and your profit of ten points, or $10 a share, less his commission, the war revenue stamps and the interest paid to carry the stock. The commission is one-eighth of 1 per cent each way, which means $1.25 to buy or sell 10 shares, or $12.50 for each $100. A complete transaction representing the purchase and sale of 100 shares represents a broker's commission of $25. Brokers are not allowed to charge non-members of the Stock Exchange less than the regular fee, but they trade for fellow members at the rate of $2 for each 100 shares. The war revenue tax calls for a $2 stamp on each 100 shares. If you buy and pay the full cash value of your stock you have no interest to pay, but if you pay on a 10 per cent margin the broker is required to borrow the $10,000 which he paid for your stock, unless he carries it himself, and as money always commands interest, you have that interest to pay, and it is usually 6 per cent, but sometimes more and again less. The interest begins on the day the stock is received and expires on the day it is delivered.

Speculators who buy on a margin are credited with the dividends declared on the stocks they buy during the time they hold them, and at times they offset the interest charge. Should you sell 100 shares of stock at 100 with the expectation of buying it back at 90, you would have no interest to pay. In that event your broker would borrow the stock and deliver it to the broker he sold it to. The broker he borrowed it from would pay your broker interest for carrying it, as it represents just as much money. When you bought back the stock you sold at 100 it would be received by your broker and returned to the one from whom he borrowed it, thus closing the transaction. In this case (short trading) the rule of trading says that the interest belongs to your broker, and there are exceptions in the matter of interest, for at times when a certain stock is scarce borrowers have to pay a premium to get the stock, and it would then repre sent the equivalent of interest. (See Fiat in Dictionary.) In the quotations of stock fractional parts of 1 per cent play a prominent part. The smallest fraction employed in trading is 1/8 per cent, or $12.50 on each 100 shares.

Stock Exchange fractional profits or losses are shown in the following table:

Stocks. Fractional profit or loss.	Shares.	Amount. Profit or loss.
⅛ per cent	100	$ 12.50
¼ per cent	100	25.00
⅜ per cent	100	37.50
½ per cent	100	50.00
⅝ per cent	100	62.50
¾ per cent	100	75.00
⅞ per cent	100	87.50
1 per cent	100	100.00
5 per cent	100	500.00
25 per cent	100	2,500.00

You will bear in mind that your broker has the right of calling for more margin when your margin becomes impaired.

Thus if you are trading on a $1,000 margin, and your trade shows a loss of $700, your broker can request you to deposit more money, Or place a limit within your margin on your loss.

It is also well to always remember that when you buy and sell 100 shares of stock it costs you 1/4 per cent more than the price of the stock, this fraction being the commission, to which is added the revenue stamps and interest. It was stated above that the par value of stocks is usually $100, but there are exceptions (about half a dozen stocks on the list which have a par value of $50). They are designated as 'half' stocks, but in trading the custom is to buy 200 shares of a 'half' stock, which would be equivalent to the usual 100 shares of 'full,' or $100 a share stocks. All stocks are quoted at a percentage of par, or 100. To illustrate, the Stock Exchange and the newspapers quote stocks as follows:

Jan. 31. Sales.		Highest.	Lowest.	Closing.	Net. Change.
148,615	Am. Sugar	121⅜	117¼	118⅛	−1¾
27,915	Atch., Top. & S. F. pf..	62½	61	62⅛	+1⅜

In this illustration, two active stocks are used, one an industrial and the other a railroad stock. It will be seen that on January 31, 1900, 148,615 shares of American Sugar Refining stock were bought and sold. The highest price was $121.37 a share, the lowest price $117.25, and the closing price $118.25, while the net change for the day represented by the minus sign was a loss of $1.75 (the equivalent of $175 per 100 shares), as compared with the closing price of the previous day, January 30. On January 31, 37,915 shares of Atchison, Topeka & Santa Fe preferred railroad shares were bought and sold. The highest price was $62.50 a share, the lowest $61, and the closing $62.12, while the net change for the day represented by the plus sign was a gain of $1.37 a share (the equivalent of $137.50 per 100 shares).

Bonds are traded in very much the same way as stocks. Bonds are usually of the denomination of $1,000, although there are some $500 bonds. In speculation on a margin a $1,000 bond is the equivalent of 10 shares, and 10 bonds the equivalent of 100 shares of stock. Single bonds, however, are sold more often than fractional lots of stocks. The dealings in bonds outside the Stock Exchange are very large, and they call for men who are skilled in this single department of securities.

Stock Exchange fractional profits or losses are shown in the following table:

Bonds. Fractional profit or loss.	Amount of bond.	Amount. Profit or loss.
⅛ per cent	$1,000	$ 1.25
¼ per cent	1,000	2.50
⅜ per cent	1,000	3.75
½ per cent	1,000	5.00
⅝ per cent	1,000	6.25
⅞ per cent	1,000	7.50
¾ per cent	1,000	8.75
1 per cent	1,000	10.00
5 per cent	1,000	50.00
25 per cent	1,000	250.00[1]

HANDLING OF CORPORATE FINANCES[1]

W. J. Jackman

This is a matter directly within the duties of the board of directors, and embraces a wide field of action. It covers the obtaining and distribution of funds in the broadest possible sense. It is for the directors to decide, subject in most instances to the approval of the stockholders, what securities shall be issued and how they shall be classified and disposed of; what loans, if any, shall be contracted; how surplus funds may be distributed or invested; what dividends shall be paid; in short, everything affecting the financial welfare and management of the corporation.

Economy in Raising Funds.
One of the most important features of financial management is that of the issuance of corporate securities. This is one of those occasions when the utmost nicety of human judgment is required to protect the corporation against loss, or at least effect a decided economy in expenses.

At first thought, for instance, it would very naturally be held that it would be cheaper to get money by the issuance of 5 per cent bonds than by selling stock. But this would often be fallacious. True, the interest on the bonds would be 2 per cent less than that on the stock, but it must be remembered that the 5 per cent interest on the bonds must be paid regularly regardless of the condition of the corporation treasury, while the interest on the stock may be deferred or skipped entirely, being in reality a dividend payable only out of earnings.

Close Judgment is Essential.
This is one of the frequent cases in which an error in judgment may be frightfully expensive. In the case of a prosperous concern earning

[1] [Chapter 10 of *Corporations: Organization, Finance and Management*, Minneapolis: International Law and Business Institute.]

large profits and abundantly able to meet its obligations promptly, the issue of bonds would be decidedly the most economical. On the other hand, should there be uncertainty as to the future – unknown, of course, to the investing public – it would be to the best interest of the corporation to issue the stock, as no positive liability to meet interest payments at certain dates would be incurred.

But in this connection there is another vitally important condition to be taken into consideration. What price can be obtained for the respective securities? No matter which kind may be issued, the interest accrues on the par, not the market value. Consequently, the question of selling price becomes a vital one.

Market Price a Factor.
Bonds, owing to the manner in which they are secured, generally command a higher market or selling price than stock, particularly if the corporation issuing them is not paying large dividends. It is frequently the case that bonds will readily sell at par when the stock of the same concern sells at 50 or less.

In a condition of this kind it would manifestly be to the advantage of a corporation to sell bonds rather than stock, despite the fact that the interest on the former is a fixed charge. Let us see how it works out. A corporation issues $100,000 in 5 per cent bonds which are sold at par and it thus obtains $100,000 in cash. The interest charge is $5,000 yearly. If stock is sold at 50 the corporation obtains only $50,000 for the $100,000 par value of the stock, while the interest charge, provided dividends are paid, will be $7,000 or 7 per cent on the full par value of $100,000, 14 per cent on the amount obtained.

Problem a Serious One.
It thus becomes a serious problem as to which means of raising the desired funds will be to the best interest of the corporation. Everything depends upon the condition of the market and the condition of the corporation. It is a problem which must be solved by the directors according to their best judgment.

Let us imagine an opposite market condition, one that is not by any means unusual. In the case of a sound, prosperous corporation the bonds, owing to their earning power being limited to 5 per cent, sell at par, while the stock, earning large dividends, sells at 150. In this event the corporation would obtain only $100,000 from an issue of bonds, at an annual cost of $5,000, while the sale of $100,000 in stock (provided it was not taken on stockholders' "rights") would net $150,000. Here again we encounter the problem of dividend charges.

Allowing that the stock is limited to a straight 7 per cent, the sale of this security in preference to bonds would be of great advantage to the company, as it would get the use of $150,000 for $7,000 a year, or less than 5 per cent, with no obligation to keep up the payment should anything occur to greatly lessen its earning power.

When Debt May Be Incurred.

It may be argued that a prosperous corporation has no excuse or necessity to incur indebtedness. This is an error. In fact it is only prosperous concerns that can afford to incur obligations of this kind. The larger and more profitable the operations the greater will be the urgency for additional capital. There are eminent authorities who maintain that for a growing, prosperous corporation to be out of debt is an evidence of poor financial management.

Many conditions arise which may make indebtedness advisable and even profitable. Take the case of a corporation which, in order to fill a large contract to advantage, requires a considerable addition to its equipment. Wise business policy will dictate the purchase of the necessary equipment, as through it an additional profit is secured, much larger than the cost of carrying the debt incurred by the purchase of the additional equipment.

Lack of Capital a Handicap.

Lack of capital may also narrow the opportunities of a corporation by limiting its capacity to carry the accounts of perfectly responsible customers. Here again it is an act of wisdom to incur an obligation by borrowing funds so that the business of the corporation may proceed to its full capacity.

Profit in Borrowed Money.

Some years ago it was considered wise, conservative business policy to limit borrowed funds to one-quarter of the amount of actual owned capital. That day has passed. The rule now in force is exactly the opposite – the borrowed capital is generally three times as great as the owned capital. The additional profits made possible by the borrowed capital more than overbalances the interest charges.

If money can be borrowed at not more than 7 per cent, and it usually can, and the additional product made possible by the use of this borrowed money can be disposed of at a net profit, less the interest, of 12 per cent, there can be no question of the wisdom of the transaction. It means an additional 5 per cent for the stockholders earned without the investment of any more of their own funds. It is equivalent to borrowing money at 7 per cent, loaning it out at 12, and pocketing the difference.

How to Borrow Money.

Loans obtained through banks are uncertain, limited as to tenure, and also limited in amount. As a general rule banks will advance funds only on a sworn statement of bills receivable and payable, backed with satisfactory collateral, and then only to a moderate percentage of what appears to be reasonably safe assets. It is not within the province of banks to do otherwise. Their loans must be made with a view to quick conversion into cash in time of emergency. Consequently all accommodation of this nature is for a comparatively short time, thirty, sixty, or at the most, ninety days. Besides this they are, in many instances, "call" loans, payable on demand regardless of the time for which they are made.

While it is expedient and proper for corporations to raise small amounts of funds in this manner from time to time, the only satisfactory method where the use of large amounts is required for long periods is by the sale of bonds or stocks. The former are redeemable only at the end of the stated period for which they are issued, be it five, ten, twenty or thirty years, and no demand can be made on the maker so long as the interest payments are maintained.

Distributing Profits in Stock.

It is frequently the case that the profits of a well-managed corporation are so large that distribution in the form of dividends becomes a serious problem. This is mainly true of the better class of industrial corporations. In some instances it might be unwise to distribute these profits in cash, lest the amount thus distributed provoke hostile criticism. In such cases recourse is had to what are known as stock dividends.

When the shares of a corporation are selling at a big price, stock dividends are preferred by the shareholders of record, and with good reason – they get more money out of them than they would if the actual cash were handed out.

Advantage of Stock Dividends.
Stock put out in the form of dividends is always issued at par regardless of the market price. When a shareholder is entitled to a dividend of $100 in cash he gets a certificate for one $100 share of stock, and the money which would otherwise have been given to him is covered into the corporation treasury in payment for such stock.

If the stock of such a corporation is selling on the market at a premium the shareholder may at once dispose of such shares as he may receive in the way of dividend, and thus secure an extra profit.

The Singer Mfg. Co., with a capitalization of $30,000,000, has declared a stock dividend of $30,000,000, thus giving every stockholder an amount equivalent to his original holding. This, in the parlance of stock dealers, is known as "cutting a lemon."

Deciding Amount of Dividends.
Another important feature of financial management is the fixing of the rate of dividend to be paid – provided that the corporation is earning enough to warrant such payment. A corporation that is making a profit of 20 per cent on its capital stock is not justified in declaring a dividend of 20 per cent – far from it. The rate which may be safely fixed upon may not be more than one-half, or even one-quarter, of 20 per cent; perhaps nothing.

In deciding upon this rate the ordinary rules of business prudence should govern. Having ascertained the net income over and above all expenses and charges of every kind, provision must be made for a depreciation account and, in the case of wise, conservative management, of a surplus account, which may come in handy when times are less prosperous and the business of the corporation less profitable. It is impossible to give any fixed rule that will apply in all cases as to the proper percentage of dividends to net earnings, but it is reasonably safe to say that not over one-quarter of these net earnings may be safely paid out.

How to Determine Income.
First take the gross earnings as derived from the output, and from this deduct the cost of operation. To the difference add such income as there may be from other sources, like rentals, returns from investments, etc. This will give the total income. From this net income should be deducted all fixed charges, such as taxes, interest on outstanding bonds, amount required for sinking fund (bond redemption), rentals on leased property or patents, etc. The balance, if any, is the amount available for division between the depreciation, surplus and dividend accounts. Following is an illustration of this method:

GENERAL HYPOPHOSPHITE COMPANY.

Gross earnings	$3,000,000
Operating expenses	2,000,000
Net earnings	$1,000,000
Income from other sources	300,000
Total income	$1,300,000
Taxes	100,000
Interest on $500,000 bonds	25,000
Rentals on leased lands	20,000
Sinking fund	25,000
Actual net income	$1,030,000

Allowing that the capital stock of the General Hypophoshite Company is $3,000,000, this would show net earnings of 33 1/3 per cent on the total stock. But a wise administration would not pay out this 33 1/3 per cent in dividends, or anything like it.

Protection of the Stockholders.
Careful, conscientious directors will look far into the future with a view to protecting the interests of the stockholders. They know that the plant and equipment, the buildings and machinery will in time wear out. Renewal must be provided for. This will be done by covering a certain proportion of the net income or profits into the depreciation account, so that the necessary renewals in the plant may be made without calling upon the stockholders for more funds.

"Rainy days," bad times, are liable to come to every business enterprise. Wise men guard against them by creating a surplus fund. Into this another big share of the 33 1/3 per cent profits will go. The larger this surplus, the stronger will be the corporation in time of adversity, and the better able it will be to weather such business squalls as may overtake it.

Under a competent business administration the 33 1/3 per cent in net profits would probably be divided (approximately) among the three accounts as follows: Depreciation account, 8 per cent; dividend account, 10 per cent; surplus account, 15 1/3 per cent.

Benefit of Depreciation Fund.
Many stockholders, not understanding the conditions, will object to such division. They will claim, and justly so, that all the net earnings belong to them. This is true, but their objections lose force in view of the fact that these net earnings are not actually taken away from them. If no depreciation fund were maintained the stockholders would in time, owing to the decay of the plant, be compelled to either abandon business or find money with which to provide new equipment. The maintenance of a depreciation fund enables them to continue indefinitely the operation of a profitable business and thus insures a continuation of dividends which would otherwise cease. Besides this, proper maintenance of the plant keeps the bondholders assured of the sufficiency of the security, and prevents them from throwing their bonds on the market and thus depreciating the value of the corporation securities to the detriment of the stockholders.

Stockholders Own Surplus Fund.
It is virtually the same with the surplus fund. The credit of a corporation with a big surplus is rarely attacked, except for stock-jobbing purposes, and this does not affect the solvency of the corporation itself. Not only is the maintenance of a surplus account a strong financial bulwark in perilous times, but it is a savings fund for the stockholders. Should, for any reason, the dissolution of such a concern be decided upon the stockholders would each get a proportionate share of the surplus as well as a pro-rata division of the proceeds of the general property of the corporation. Consequently there is little force to the clamor some times raised against the covering of a large share of the net earnings into the depreciation and surplus accounts. It comes largely from ignorant people unacquainted with the merits of the proposition, or is started by speculators who have selfish objects to attain.

Danger of Dishonest Action.

All this presupposes the fact that the directors are honest and trying to conduct the financial affairs of the corporation for the best interests of all concerned. Without violating the law, without in any way laying themselves liable to criminal or civil action, it is within the power of the directors to so act in their official capacity as to make large fortunes for themselves, while wrecking the corporation and the other stockholders.

A majority of the board, having sold the market short may, for instance, so manipulate the financial affairs of a corporation, and seemingly with honest intent, as to make the payment of dividends impossible. The concern will be just as solvent, probably more so, than ever, but the passing of dividends will depress the price of the stock, and the members of the clique will reap big profits. Having covered their short sales, they will buy on the decline and, at the next opportunity, restore the dividends, when, presto, up goes the stock again and another profit is raked in.

How the Trick is Worked.

But how, may be asked, is it possible to juggle with dividends in this manner? It is the easiest thing in the world, provided the jugglers are without conscience and calloused as to their responsibilities to their brother shareholders and the general public. Big earnings may be covered up by the payment of extra large salaries, by purchases of material and equipment really not needed at the time, by the passing of abnormally large amounts of money to the depreciation and surplus accounts.

To perform juggling of this kind in an open, careless manner would be to invite detection. The jugglers are too smart for that; they are sleight-of-hand artists. They have before them a statement showing large earnings. They make a few "passes" over it, and it becomes a case of "now you see it, and now you don't." Glib of tongue, gifted with the "patter," or talk which must accompany all tricks in magic, they make explanations which, while seemingly plausible, do not really explain, and the mystified stockholders do not awaken to a realization of the actual conditions until the job has been done.

This sort of transaction, while not unknown, is fortunately rare, save in cases where the corporation has been organized mainly for speculative purposes.

Corporate Form Encourages Rascality.
There is no question but what the corporate form offers some opportunity for rascally manipulation. It could not well be otherwise when the financial management is entrusted to a few directors, and yet it is practically impossible to adopt any other method. It would be difficult, in fact impracticable, to get together a majority of the stockholders every time action is to be taken. The only safeguard against manipulation or dishonesty is in the moral character and disposition of the men selected as directors. The corporate form in itself is all right; it possesses many advantages for legitimate business and endeavor impossible to secure in any other way. Its sole weakness lies in the fact that it offers opportunity for dishonesty, not for downright stealing, but tricky manipulation, the results of which are virtually the same as those of actual, plain larceny.

The Only Real Protection.
But, while the general plan of corporate management is in this respect in need of revision and improvement, such dishonest manipulation as occurs under it is due more to the knavery of individuals than to defects in the system. That the general system might be strengthened with a view to making it more difficult to carry out plans for tricky manipulation is certain, but the protection of the stockholders lies more in the personal uprightness of the directors and officials than in such barriers as might be erected in the by-laws.

In a number of corporations, notably the larger ones like the United States Steel Corporation, manipulation and other forms of dishonesty are made difficult, if not impossible by the close supervision of a finance committee, a body consisting of the president and the chairman of the board of directors, who are members *ex officio,* and such other members, elected from among the directors, as may be provided for in the by-laws.

Powers of Finance Committee.
This committee is supposed to be in continuous session, especially in the interims between the sessions of the directors, and to have general absolute control over all financial matters. When the board of directors is in session the committee reports to that body, but at all other times it acts on its own initiative. No moneys can be paid out, no debts incurred, no investments made, in short, no

financial action of any kind taken, without the express consent and approval of the finance committee.

This arrangement is by far the best yet suggested as a check upon extravagance and dishonesty. Of course it still leaves open the possibility for crookedness, but to take advantage of this there must be collusion between the board, the committee, and the general officials, and this would entail the taking of too many people into the secret.

FAILURES, DISSOLUTIONS, REORGANIZATIONS[1]

W. J. Jackman

While the causes producing insolvency in corporate enterprises are in the main the same as those prevailing in individual failures, the effects are radically different. It is possible for a corporation to be insolvent and yet continue in business at a profit; in fact it is rarely that insolvency leads to the actual winding up of a corporation and its retirement from business, especially if it be a concern of any particular magnitude. In the case of individuals, insolvency almost invariably means a retirement from business, compromise with creditors, or the taking in of new capital.

What Is Insolvency.

Literally translated in a commercial sense, insolvency means inability to pay debts in cash at maturity. This, in turn, means failure and bankruptcy. Because a corporation is unable to meet its obligations promptly, how ever, does not necessarily imply that the enterprise is unprofitable. Many corporations doing an immensely profitable business are insolvent because of the very magnitude of that business – their working capital is not large enough to meet the demands upon it; they have outgrown the financial resources at their command. A corporation in this condition may have ample assets so far as tangible property is concerned, but these assets are not readily convertible into cash, hence there is an inability to meet obligations and a condition of insolvency exists.

This, judged solely from the viewpoint of commercial law, means failure, and in the case of an individual would be met by the creditors with a demand for a receiver, or the filing of proceedings in bankruptcy, unless a showing could be made which would warrant a compromise or extension of credit.

[1] [Chapter 11 of *Corporations: Organization, Finance and Management*, Minneapolis: International Law and Business Institute.]

General Course with Corporations.
It is seldom that creditors thus interfere with the operation of a corporation no matter how marked the signs of insolvency may be, and the larger the corporation the less likelihood there will be of any interference. Creditors, as a rule, prefer to leave the concern unhampered, realizing that in this course lies the greatest possibility of eventually getting their claims paid. Proceedings under the bankruptcy act are markedly infrequent. One reason for this is that the line of corporate enterprises coming within the scope of the bankruptcy act is limited to those engaged in manufacturing, trading, printing, publishing, mining or merchandising. Action in the case of these must be by involuntary petition by three or more creditors. No corporation can file a voluntary petition.

Exemptions From Bankruptcy.
Corporations engaged in a common carrier or other service of a public utility nature, such as railroading, etc., can not be forced into bankruptcy, no matter how badly their finances may be involved. In cases where the protection of creditors demands legal action, the proceedings are invariably in the nature of an application for a receiver, and the official thus named by the court operates the business of the insolvent corporation and is supposed to see that its affairs are honestly and impartially administered with a view to the protection of all concerned.

Powers and Duties of Receivers.
When a receiver is named for a comparatively small corporation the successful operation of which in the future is a matter of doubt a winding up of the company's affairs and an abandonment of business is in order, provided the property can be disposed of without serious loss. In all large enterprises, however, where a continuation of business tends to improve the security of the creditors, and prevents a sacrifice of the assets, it becomes the duty of the receiver to keep the corporation going; to handle its affairs exactly the same as if he were the president of the company, responsible only to the board of directors and stockholders.

Effect on Public Utility Corporations.
This is particularly true of enterprises of a public utility character where the corporation owes a duty to the public as well as to its creditors. In fact an effort to dissolve or discontinue a corporation

of this kind would meet with serious opposition from the courts unless ample provision were made to protect the public against an abandonment of the service. The theory of this is that, if a corporation is chartered to perform a service of public necessity for profit it can not voluntarily abandon that service because it turns out to be unprofitable, or the corporation becomes financially embarrassed. The receiver may, with the permission of the courts, borrow such money by the sale of "receiver's certificates," or in other ways, as may be necessary to conduct the business; or in like manner he may contract with some responsible party to continue the public service should the dissolution of the corporation be deemed advisable.

Dissolution Rarely Resorted To.

In nearly all the States provision is made for the exact method of procedure in case dissolution is resorted to. This provision, however, is seldom taken advantage of except in the case of what may be termed insignificant concerns. No matter how badly the finances of an important, or reasonably important, corporation may be involved, the franchise it holds is almost invariably of too great a value to be lost, or deliberately surrendered by voluntary dissolution. This applies to all large merchandising and manufacturing concerns as well as those of a public utility nature. The United States Steel Corporation, for instance, is solely and exclusively a manufacturing company. There was a time when its stock was greatly depressed in price, and there were rumors of impending dissolution. Shrewd investors did not accept these rumors because they knew that, regardless of the question of the corporation being operated at a profit, its franchise was worth too much money to admit of dissolution being even seriously considered.

Dissolution means an absolute retirement from busi ness, a complete surrender of all franchise and other rights, a physical and financial breaking up of the corporation. Consequently it is rarely resorted to; never, in fact, if there is anything left worth saving.

Modern Plan of Reorganization.

In the place of dissolution we have the modern plan of reorganization. Human nature is selfish and it sometimes happens that corporations are deliberately wrecked by those in control with the object of advancing their own interests. It is also not infrequently the case that big corporations are shattered on financial reefs unintentionally. In either event relief is to be had by reorganization. Incidentally it may be remarked that in this reorganization process, while absolutely necessary to save a corporation's life, fortunes have been made by those conducting it.

Illustration of the method and active principles of reorganization may best be had in the suppositious case of a railroad which has become so hopelessly involved in debt that further operation in its existing form is impracticable. Does this mean dissolution of the corporation, or abandonment of the property? Not at all. Of course it would be possible to sell the physical property at some price, but the amount of this price would depend upon how badly somebody wanted it.

How Reorganization is Effected.

The first move in reorganization is the appointment of a receiver. So long as this officer of the courts is in charge creditors and others who may be hostile to the plan can not interfere. Next various committees representing the bondholders and other vitally interested parties are formed. These committees, sometimes as a whole, but generally through specially named members, get together and select a reorganization committee which is representative of all the interests concerned.

It is the duty of this latter committee to formulate an equitable plan of readjustment, one that will make each of the interests bear a fair share of the financial load, and assure to each an equally fair share of the property to be reorganized. In arriving at this conclusion there are four main points to be considered:

First, total amount of indebtedness; second, fair valuation of property; third, equitable proportion of each interest; fourth, amount of working capital required.

Further Course of Committee.

Having decided upon a general plan which appears equitable, the report of the reorganization committee is submitted to the committees representing the bond holders and other interests for approval or rejection. If approved, the work of reorganization goes on; if the report is rejected, a new reorganization committee is appointed, or the old one does the work over again. The end sought for is a plan which will be acceptable to the various interests and, until this is secured, there can be no actual progress toward reorganization.

The committee must evolve a plan that will satisfy the creditors, relieve the corporation from its pressing indebtedness, furnish adequate working capital, and at the same time protect so far as possible the holders of the corporation stock. Frequently this latter is an impossibility so far as owners of common stock are concerned, and they are wiped out entirely, left without interest of any kind to represent their original investment.

Settling the Financial Problem.

Sometimes the reorganization plan provides for the formation of a new corporation, which assumes the liabilities and assets of the old concern. The securities of the new company are then exchanged for those of the old at an agreed-upon price, and settlement made with the nonsecurity-holding creditors, either in securities, or part cash and part securities. In such event the new corporation requires all the rights, privileges and property of the old. It is virtually a continuance of the insolvent company. Frequently the change in name is so slight as to be barely recognizable, as in the case of a certain transportation company which became insolvent as the ______ *Railway* Co., but worked out its financial salvation as the ________ *Railroad* Company.

It is possible in some instances for the debtor corporation to preserve its corporate identity and effect a satisfactory settlement by retiring its old bonds and securities, issuing in their place new ones at a lower ratio. This requires the consent of the holders of the securities, but the plan is by no means an unusual one.

How Exchange System Works.

The first bonds of an insolvent corporation are selling, say, at 60, but the company is responsible for their redemption at maturity at the par value of 100 regard less of the market. Under the reorganization plan the holder of old bonds would be offered $800 in new bonds for each $1,000 (par value) of old. Similar tenders, at a lower scale, would be made to the holders of the junior, or secondary issues, perhaps as low as $500 on the $1,000 for those of more doubtful security. Should these tenders be accepted, and they generally are, the corporation would thus start in scaling down its bond obligations materially. An original bond indebtedness of $5,000,000 could in this manner be cut down to

$3,500,000 or less, and the corporation relieved of indebtedness to just this amount.

Unsecured creditors who are pressing in their claims are treated in the same way so far as the price of the bonds offered them is concerned, but are sometimes given in addition a bonus in stock, and a partial payment in cash. Once the details of reorganization are decided upon it is a comparatively easy matter to effect a settlement with the bondholders and creditors.

The Raising of Cash.

In all reorganization plans the raising of a considerable sum of money in cash is a necessity, and the question of how to do this to the best advantage is a serious one. As a rule this cash is raised by assessments on the stock, but care must be taken to make these as sessments moderate or the shareholders will decline to meet them and allow their holdings to be forfeited. Should the amount which can be actually raised from the stockholders be insufficient an assessment must be made on the junior bondholders, but this is seldom done.

Necessity for levying tribute from the bondholders may be averted by making the assessments on the stock payable in installments, and where large sums are to be raised this is the usual practice.

Occasionally conditions are such that the raising of any considerable amount of cash means the wiping out, the entire elimination, of the common stock. The assessments may be so heavy, even after the junior bonds have been called upon for a fair share, that it amounts to a confiscation of the stock. And yet it is a matter of record that shares in a reorganized corporation in variably advance sharply in value. The history of the Union Pacific affords a notable example of this.

Effect of Scaling-Down Process.

This scaling-down process, while reducing the amount of the corporation indebtedness so far as present necessities go, and making liquidation comparatively easy, does not actually reduce the volume of liabilities. On the contrary, every reorganization loads the corporation with additional debt. Thus a corporation owing $10,000,000 may succeed, through the scaling-down process, in securing a reduction of its present liabilities to $7,500,000 and settle at that figure. But this does not mean that an actual saving of $2,500,000 has been effected.

In order to raise the $7,500,000 required for liquidation and provide a working capital it has become necessary to increase the corporation indebtedness to $15,000,000 by the issue of new bonds and stock. It is in effect a gamble on the profits of the future – a speculation that, under the new order of things, these profits will be enough larger to make the assuming of the addi tional $7,500,000 of liabilities a paying transaction.

Analysis of the Transaction.
Take the case of a corporation which owes $10,000,000, payment of which is demanded and impossible to meet. One of two actions are optional: the corporation – provided it is not of the public utility kind – may quit business and allow its property to be seized and sold for the benefit of its creditors. This plan satisfies nobody. The members of the corporation lose everything they have invested, and the bondholders and other creditors obtain only a part of their claims.

Study of the situation warrants the belief that, if the pressing claims can be taken care of and a working capital provided that will permit of operation on a more extended scale, large profits can be made, and, instead of dissolution and collapse, reorganization is decided upon.

This is equivalent to saying: "We cannot pay $10,000,000 now; the concern is insolvent, but if we can raise funds to operate on we can easily pay $15,000,000 twenty years from now and disburse a large amount of interest in the meantime."

Much Depends Upon Receiver.
Having perfected a plan of reorganization that is acceptable to the creditors, the next move is to report conditions to the court and secure the discharge of the receiver. Necessity for his serving as a buffer between the corporation and its creditors no longer exists. With rare exception this official is of the kind known as "friendly"; he serves in the interests of the corporation, or those who control it, rather than of the creditors, although he is supposed to be the representative of the latter. On his honesty or dishonesty depends entirely the matter of actual corporate wreckage or rehabilitation.

The powers of a receiver are practically limitless. In the case of a "friendly" receiver his acts, no matter how cleverly disguised, are always in the interest of those in control. If these men desire to actually wreck the concern they encourage extravagant administration on the part of the receiver. As the debts incurred by the latter constitute a prior lien on the corporation assets, it is easy for a receiver and his friends to make money at the expense of the corporation.

A Trick in Receiverships.

It is not even necessary, to secure the appointment of a receiver, that a corporation should be insolvent, provided the application is made by the right people. It simply requires collusion between the corporation officials and the parties making the application. In considering this proposition we must keep in mind the fact that failure to pay a matured debt on demand constitutes insolvency.

Two or more people conspire with the officials to wreck a corporation. They secure possession of claims against it, and demand payment. In pursuance of the plot payment is refused, care being taken to so manipulate the finances in advance that the treasury for the time being is exhausted, although the corporation is perfectly sound financially.

Application is made at once – sometimes at night – for a receiver. On the *ex parte* showing that an admission of insolvency has been made by failure to pay the claim in question, the judge names a receiver. This receiver is almost invariably the one suggested by the complaining creditors, and in this way the conspirators get complete control of the corporation.

Other Evils Besides Dishonesty.

The evils in this system, aside from the opportunity afforded for dishonest administration, are to be found in the fact that honest creditors and stockholders are left without protection. If the officials of a corporation see fit to contest an application it is practically impossible, or at least very difficult and prohibitively expensive, for a creditor, acting in good faith, to secure the appointment of a receiver even when an act of insolvency has been committed.

Neither can stockholders who find the assets of a corporation being mismanaged or misdirected obtain the appointment of a receiver, unless the directors consent. Action of this kind is very uncommon, but it has been taken in a few instances with the result that the applicants were told by the judges that their only relief was in the election of new directors.

This discrimination is made possible by the fact that when the officials admit insolvency there is no contest, and this admission is seldom made except in cases of collusion and to further an improper purpose.

MARKETING OF CORPORATE SECURITIES[1]

W. J. Jackman

It is only in connection with corporations of large capital – $1,000,000 or over – that the question of the marketing of securities need be considered. In the case of smaller concerns the matter is one which takes care of itself. In these latter instances the securities are generally taken by those interested in the organization of the company, or by people who have personal knowledge of the purposes and prospects of the enterprise, and are reasonably convinced as to the chances for success.

With large corporations, however, the matter of making a market for securities, not only those contemplated at the time of organization, but such subsequent issues as may be necessary, is one of serious import. It is essential that this market should he a positively reliable one so that there may be no delay or uncertainty when the time comes to raise funds.

Floating of New Securities.

All corporations, of course, desire to have their securities command good prices, but there are occasions when certainty of sale at some price is of more importance than the price itself. This brings us face to face with a most curious condition.

It is a general rule (statutory) in nearly all the States – in fact, it is practically universal – that a corporation cannot dispose of its stock until it has received its full par value. There is, generally speaking, no limitation as to the price at which bonds may be disposed of, but the stock put out *must* represent an equal amount of cash or property actually turned over to the treasury of the corporation. This would seem to bar the sale of stock by the corporation at less than par, but, thanks to the ingenuity of the modern financier, it has no such effect. Were this law strictly

[1] [Chapter 13 of *Corporations: Organization, Finance and Management*, Minneapolis: International Law and Business Institute.]

adhered to it would make impossible the successful flotation of monster corporations.

How the Law is Evaded.

It is rarely the case that the general public will pay par, or anything like par, for the stock of a large corporation, the success of which is an unknown quantity. Despite this the stock, or a large part of it, must be floated on the public market. The original incorporators, even in monster concerns, take only an insignificant fraction of the total in the way of actual, bona fide subscriptions. The public must take the rest. It is sold to them at a price far less than par, but the law is not violated; it is simply evaded.

In the case of a new railway company, the "insiders," the original incorporators, organize a construction company with which the railway corporation contracts for the construction of its road. The railway corporation has no funds with which to pay for the work, so it makes payment in advance in stock, turning over to the construction company all the authorized common stock, ostensibly at its full par value, but in sufficient quantity to admit of the contractors disposing of it at a big reduction from its face value, and still obtaining money enough to pay for the work. It's simply a matter of a difference of opinion as to the value of the work, and of this the directors are the sole judges.

Getting Securities Into Circulation.

In various ways this stock, the disposition of which would otherwise be impossible, begins to make its way into the hands of the public. One favorite method is for the contractors to distribute it as a bond bonus. As fast as a section of road is constructed bonds are issued, usually to the amount of $20,000 a mile. These bonds, or a good part of them, also find their way into the hands of the contracting company, which uses them as collateral on which to secure funds for the work.

The bankers or trust companies which advance the money for building purposes accept the bonds and stock as security with the understanding that they are to dispose of them to their customers at the best obtainable price. If this is less than the amount advanced the borrowers make good the difference.

Thus far the market is a limited one, and of a purely personal nature, being confined to such deals as can be made between the corporation and the people with which it has dealings, and between the latter and the bankers who advance funds. Being an uncertain proposition all around, with profits a matter of the future, such values as can be established are naturally low.

Stock Exchange the Real Market.

It is not until corporation securities are listed on a stock exchange that a certain market can be depended upon. To secure this listing the officials of the corporation must make formal application to the secretary of the stock exchange on which listing is desired. The matter then comes before the governing board for action. This body in turn calls upon the corporation for complete details of its financial condition. If these details are satisfactory the stock is listed. If they are not considered favorable the application is rejected.

Once listed a security becomes to a certain extent the ward of the exchange. This latter body does not in any way guarantee the solidity of the stock, beyond a state ment of the facts obtained in the investigation. It does, however, exercise to a considerable extent active control over corporations the securities of which are thus listed. One feature of this control is the requiring of a complete annual report at least fifteen days in advance of each annual meeting. A copy of this report in detail must be mailed to every stockholder.

Public Favors Listed Securities.

The fact that a security is listed shows that the exchange officials are satisfied with the financial condition of the corporation issuing the security, and that it is a reasonably safe trading proposition. This tends to establish a market in which the values, while purely speculative, may be taken advantage of at any time by those desiring to buy or sell. It is a certain market so far as getting action is concerned, and at the same time a very uncertain one as regards the obtainable prices. Its quotations, however, are accepted the world over as a basis of transactions even between private parties.

It is, by way of example, practically impossible, save in rare instances, to borrow money in a legitimate way on an unlisted security. On the other hand, loans may always be negotiated on listed securities, the amount of the loan being regulated by the market value of the security which it is desired to hypothecate as collateral.

One Great Central Exchange.

The one great stock exchange of the United States is the New York Stock Exchange, known in technical parlance as Wall Street. The professionals seldom or never refer to "the exchange." It is invariably "Wall Street does this," or "Wall Street does that."

There are other exchanges at Boston, Philadelphia, Pittsburg, Baltimore, Chicago, St. Louis, Denver and San Francisco, but most of them are of minor importance, dealing either in a limited number of specialities or local securities exclusively. Of these Boston is by far the most important, the specialties being local gas stock and the shares of copper mining companies. The volume of business in these lines is respectably large.

New York, however, is the one great central security market. In addition to the listed department, the New York Stock Exchange maintains an unlisted department; there is also the Consolidated Stock Exchange, and last of all a "Curb" market on which securities not otherwise handled are dealt in.

Dealing In Unlisted Securities.

Because a stock is not listed it does not necessarily follow that it is a weak or dangerous security. It may be that, for good reasons, probably to keep the information from competitors, that the officials decline to give the complete details demanded by the exchange as a pre-requisite to listing.

For the convenience of corporations of this kind – which are principally "industrials" – the New York Stock Exchange maintains an "unlisted" department, in which a large volume of business is transacted daily. There is a demand for some details of corporate conditions in the unlisted department, but the range of investigation is greatly limited as compared with that prevailing in the listed department. As a consequence the "unlisted" securities are not looked upon by investors and loaners of money with as much favor as those which are listed.

What the "Curb" Means.

"On the Curb" is the term used to designate transac tions on the open street in securities which are not dealt in on the exchanges. The term is a literal one; it means just what it says. Every day, immediately after the adjournment of the regular exchanges, a great throng of men open a market "on the curb" and buy and sell every imaginable sort of security.

This market is an unorganized one; there are no officers, no members. All the dealing is between individuals without an overseeing or controlling power; everything is done on honor. On the regular exchanges any attempt at dishonest practice to evade a trade, to escape from an unprofitable transaction, would be met by punishment, either in the form of a fine or by expulsion.

On the "Curb," while the opportunity for dishonesty is unrestrained, actual occurrences of this nature are very rare. This is because the trading is done exclusively between men who know one another, either in a personal or a business way. While in theory the market is open to everybody, an unknown person would find it impossible to obtain recognition as a trader.

Gilt-Edged Stocks Dealt In.

While the so-called "securities" of many shady corporations are dealt in on the Curb, numerous gilt-edged stocks are also handled there. American Tobacco, selling at 432, and Standard Oil, for which there is a demand at 623, are prominent in Curb transactions. Western Pacific and Burlington railway 5 per cent bonds are also favorites.

In short, it is possible to sell anything, not listed on the regular exchanges, "on the Curb." There is a market, at some price, for everything from gold dollars down to shares in Prof. Bird's Flying Machine Co. This is what makes the stock market the most popular means of marketing corporation securities. While the market thus made, as previously explained, is largely, almost entirely, a speculative one, this very speculation furnishes a basis on which actual sales and deliveries of stocks may be made.

Sales By Underwriting Process.

Another method of disposing of corporation securities is by the underwriting process, which is a sort of insurance of sales. This method has one strong and one weak feature. The strong feature is that it assures a fixed, positive price to the corporation and also assures a market at this price for the amount of securities offered. The weak feature is that the returns of cash from the sale may be long delayed, as the process is a slow one. When a concern is in immediate need of funds this latter feature becomes an almost insurmount able obj ection. Per contra, it may well be argued that all well-managed corporations will provide well in advance for their financial needs, and thus avoid being pinched.

Preferable to Forced Sales.
As a general proposition, provided equitable arrangements can be made, the underwriting method is preferable to forced sales on a stock exchange. But here again we are confronted with several features which require close study. The first of these is that there is a limit to the amount of securities which can be assimilated, or disposed of, by underwriting, unless the project is enormously large, so large and prospectively profitable as to command the attention of men who underwrite only mammoth enterprises, men like J. P. Morgan, or Kuhn, Loeb & Co. The capacity of the stock exchange for assimilation is unlimited. Effort to take full advantage of this capacity, however, would undoubtedly cause a decided shrinkage in value, while the price set by underwriting is unchangeable.

Details of Underwriting Method.
In the underwriting process arrangements are made with some responsible individual or firm to take the entire issue at an agreed-upon price. A corporation has decided to issue $500,000 in bonds. The underwriter agrees to take them all at 90 cents on the dollar. This does not always mean that the bonds have been actually sold for immediate delivery at that price, and that the money will be forthcoming on delivery of the securities. The general plan is for the underwriters to place the bonds among their customers at 95, or to advertise them for sale to the public at the same figure. On the portion thus sold the underwriters receive, either the difference between the underwriting and the market price (5 points) or an agreed-upon commission. Such bonds as may remain undisposed of are taken by the underwriters at 90. Settlement is made in cash for the bonds sold as fast as the bonds are disposed of. Those remaining in the hands of the underwriters are paid for at the close of the sale, a fixed date for this closing being always named.

This, in many ways, is to the advantage of the corporation in cases where the stockholders will not, or cannot, take up the issue at par. The underwriters pay all expenses of publicity in connection with the offering of the bonds, and carry all the risk of the issue not selling at 90 or more. In other words, the commission, or division of profits paid to the underwriters, is in the form of a premium for the insurance of this price.

Deals With Big Underwriters.
Some underwriters, having taken a risk of this nature, divide it with other firms in the same line, each firm carrying a fair proportion of the risk, and sharing pro rata in the profits. There are some big corporations, notably the United States Steel Corporation, and the leading railways, like the New York Central, the Pennsylvania, in fact all of them, which have regular, permanent underwriters who handle their securities year after year. The New York Central deals through the firm of J. P. Morgan & Co., the Pennsylvania with Kuhn, Loeb & Co., the Rock Island with Speyer & Co., etc.

In such cases the matter of guaranteed price is a business secret between the parties interested. There is no bidding for the underwriting privilege. Firms like those mentioned take an entire issue, no matter how large it may be. Deals of $100,000,000 in this way are not uncommon.

Risks In New Enterprises.
Securities of all new corporations which have not attained the "going" stage – are not already engaged in a profitable business – are by force of circumstances purely speculative. Nobody can foretell with any degree of accuracy what these securities may be worth a month or a year after they are issued. Nobody of business sense and reputation will attempt to do so. Hence, if an underwriting agreement can be made, which is uncertain, the underwriters assuming this risk will naturally demand a much larger margin of profit than they would in the case of a well-established proposition.

The actual, tangible assets upon which the bonds, etc., are based – the real property and equipment of the new corporation – may be vastly more valuable than those of an older concern, and yet the security represented by these assets be of less real value than in the latter case.

How Credit is Established.
Take two corporations, each owning $500,000 worth of property, and each seeking to float an issue of $250,000 in bonds. One is an old-established concern, its plant is rather dilapidated and has depreciated much below its original value, but the company is "going," and doing a profitable business. The other is a new concern, its plant is modern and up-to-date, would

bring much more at forced sale than that of the first-named concern, but it is not "going" yet; its earnings are small and uncertain; its profits purely prospective.

Which corporation will find the readiest, surest market for its securities on advantageous terms? Every experienced underwriter will agree that those of the old concern will be the safest, most inviting as an investment, despite the fact that the tangible security is not apparently as great.

Income vs. Non-Income Property.

A parallel illustration may be found in the case of two large business buildings, each representing the same actual value in money. One of these buildings is profitably rented; the other is empty and returning no interest on the investment. Which would be considered the more valuable as security for a loan?

One thing may be depended upon. No reputable underwriter will attempt to float the securities of a corporation until he has made a searching inquiry into the affairs of the concern, particularly a rigid investigation as to the nature and value of its assets on which the securities are based. To a certain extent the underwriter stands in the position of a guarantor of the securities he handles. True, he does not actually guarantee the payment of interest or principal, but he has a business reputation at stake which makes it imperative that he use every possible precaution to protect his creditors. To this end the underwriter not only investigates the nature of the security and the business affairs of the company, but he retains expert lawyers to pass upon the validity of the securities, to make sure that they are legally issued.

CERTAIN CHANGES IN NEW YORK'S POSITION AS A FINANCIAL CENTER[1]

E. M. Patterson

During the last year much attention has been given to the dominant position of New York City in our banking system. The extent of the control exercised by New York has been and is so great that several important changes that are taking place have escaped general notice.

That the position of New York City as a banking center has undergone a change in the last few years is shown by the facts: (1) that a smaller amount of cash is being withdrawn from there each fall for crop-moving purposes; (2) that a relatively smaller amount of cash is held by the New York banks than in former years; (3) that New York holds relatively less of the reserve funds of the entire country than in the past; (4) that the total banking resources of New York have been growing less rapidly than those of other parts of the country; and (5) that strong banking centers are rapidly being developed in other sections. The rest of the United States is apparently becoming more and more independent of New York for cash and for the financing of relatively small enterprises. With the financing of large ventures and with the general question of extension of credit this paper does not deal.

That the fall movement of cash out of New York is less than in former years is a fact which few people seem to have noticed. Probably very few indeed are aware that the net movement during the fall months is now in the other direction. Several years ago this movement was carefully analyzed, for the years 1899-1908 inclusive, by Professor E. W. Kemmerer in his report to the National Monetary Commission.[2] He averaged the

[1] [*Journal of Political Economy* 21 (1913): 523–39.]

[2] *Seasonal Variations in the Relative Demand for Money*, etc., pp. 124–29.

movement for this period and found a definite flow of money out from New York each fall – a movement averaging $3,434,000 in the thirty-eighth week of the year (the latter part of September) when it was at its maximum. The maximum movement into New York he found to be $6,895,000 and to occur in the latter part of January.

Since these statistics were prepared, an important change has occurred. Professor Kemmerer relied upon two sources of information: (1) special reports for 1905-8 from the New York clearing house banks to the Monetary Commission, and (2) the weekly figures from these same banks for the net interior movement of cash into and out of the banks during the ten years 1899-1908. In this paper, of course, only the latter source of information is available, and all statistics of cash movements have been compiled from the weekly statements in the *Commercial and Financial Chronicle*. All statements of interior movements as reported in this publication include telegraphic transfers by the New York Subtreasury.

TABLE I

NET MOVEMENT OF CASH BETWEEN NEW YORK CLEARING-HOUSE BANKS AND THE INTERIOR (000 OMITTED)

(The sign + indicates movement to New York)

YEAR	MONTHS					TOTAL FOR FIVE MONTHS
	August	September	October	November	December	
1899........	$+ 3,984	$−18,884	$− 9,211	$− 3,311	$+ 3,806	$− 23,616
1900........	+ 8,478	−15,657	−22,495	+ 3,148	− 69	− 26,595
1901........	− 755	−12,940	−13,597	+12,592	+ 1,409	− 13,291
1902........	+ 3,173	− 9,077	− 6,973	+ 71	+ 2,413	− 10,393
1903........	+15,733	− 5,491	−18,948	−13,584	+ 6,615	− 15,675
1904........	+ 3,228	−12,994	− 7,676	+ 4,975	+14,925	+ 2,458
1905........	+ 326	−19,906	− 4,585	− 4,993	+ 2,762	− 26,396
1906........	− 4,470	−19,966	−24,605	+ 138	+ 5,131	− 43,772
1907........	+ 115	− 6,582	−29,525	−84,953	−23,193	−144,138
1908........	+23,149	− 2,675	+ 56	+ 1,114	+13,656	+ 35,300
1909........	+ 9,430	− 4,687	− 3,200	+ 2,850	+23,663	+ 28,056
1910........	+19,317	− 3,120	− 2,836	+ 8,674	+ 9,042	+ 31,077
1911........	+27,676	+ 8,353	+ 5,958	+16,891	+45,012	+103,890
1912........	+22,343	+ 6,357	+ 6,734	+ 8,707	+23,570	+ 67,711

An examination of this interior movement as presented in Table I shows that a very pronounced change has taken place since 1907. Before that date the movement during the fall months, August – December inclusive, was out of the city. The figures given begin with 1899 (Professor Kemmerer's starting-point) and are continued through 1912 – a total of fourteen years.[3] Prior to 1908 New York was the loser in every year except 1904, when her gain was slight; but even in that year there was a heavy net loss in September and October. The heaviest total loss appeared in 1907 because of the large withdrawals during the panic. With 1908 came a change. Since that time New York has gained rather than lost during the fall months. In 1908 only September shows a loss, and in 1909 and 1910 only September and October; while for 1911 and 1912 every month shows a gain for New York. In 1911 the total gain for the period was $103,890,000, and in 1912 it was $67,711,000. In 1911 there were net losses in only three weeks – those of September 9, October 7, and October 14. In 1912 there were likewise only three weeks of net loss – $1,855,000 for September 14, $423,000 for October 26, and $837,000 for November 30.

It may be urged that the dullness of business since the panic of 1907 is the explanation. But whatever may be said of other years, 1912 was a year of bumper crops, expanding business, and general prosperity; and in September of that year the gain for New York was the largest for any September during the years under review with the exception of 1911. In October, 1912, the gain was the heaviest for any October of the period. Evidently some other change has occurred. It is not true that the out-of-town banks are no longer sending their money to New York. Table II gives, in column II, the net interior movement for the entire year and shows clearly that, in absolute amount, New York is gaining more than ever. Prior to 1908, every year except 1906 and 1907 shows a gain; but beginning with 1908 and continuing through 1912 this gain has been much larger than

[3] The *Chronicle* is published each week on Saturday, and it is impossible to follow closely the limits of each calendar month. Instead, the dates on which the paper appeared have been used as the basis. Thus if an issue of the *Chronicle* was dated January 1, the movement recorded for the week has been credited to January instead of to December. This is arbitrary but in no way affects the general conclusions presented. It has been adopted because of the difficulty of assigning the proper amount to each month when a week is divided between two months. Net monthly results have been secured by first combining the net weekly movements as given and then combining these monthly figures to secure the totals for each year.

before, reaching a maximum of $325,158,000 in 1912. Prior to 1907, New York's greatest gain was $134,940,000 in 1904, but since that date the gain has never been less than $213,591,000. It is clear that the out-of-town banks are sending their money to New York in larger absolute quantities than ever before.

The reason for this movement of cash into New York is generally understood to be the offer of interest by the New York banks for out-of-town deposits. The legal requirements as to reserves must be met by outside banks, but cash held in their vaults is earning nothing. Since a part of the reserve may be transferred to approved agents in reserve cities where it will receive 2 per cent, the natural thing is for the out-of-town banks thus to deposit it. The change in the direction of the fall movement seems to be explained by the increasing tendency on the part of these out-of-town banks to lend their money directly on the New York market. It is currently reported that high money rates in 1905 and 1906 led the banks to begin the practice. Their New York reserve agents hesitated to perform the service but were forced into it by the trust companies who offered to do it free of charge if the national banks would not.

The statistics prepared for the Congressional committee investigating the alleged "Money Trust" show an increase in the practice as follows:[4]

LOANS BY SUNDRY NEW YORK FINANCIAL INSTITUTIONS FOR THEIR CORRESPONDENTS

	January	July	November
1908	$106,621,000	$ 89,248,000	$ 85,011,000
1909	103,524,000	121,648,000	168,557,000
1910	208,260,000	160,185,000	125,201,000
1911	143,876,000	128,804,000	148,820,000
1912	140,901,000	141,028,000	240,480,000

4 *Money Trust Investigation,* p. 1193. The loans as given are those "outstanding on or about January 1, July 1, and November 1 in each of the years 1908 to 1912, inclusive."

The tables prepared for the committee show a slight increase in the amount loaned on stock-exchange collateral by the New York banks for themselves, but a very much larger increase in the amount loaned by them for their correspondents. They also show that although these correspondents are lending more at all times of the year than formerly, the amount so loaned in the fall has grown much more rapidly than the amount at other seasons. On November 1, 1912, the total was nearly three times that on November 1, 1908.

The opportunity to lend these large sums at the high rates current each fall for demand loans goes far to explain the reason why there is now a movement of cash into, rather than out of, New York during the fall months. The out-of-town banks no longer content themselves with the 2 per cent allowed them by their reserve agents. If they have any surplus funds over and above their required reserves, a direct loan will yield perhaps 4, 6, or 8 per cent, or even more. The inducement to use funds in this manner is very strong. Money so used does not, of course, count as a part of reserves as it would if left on deposit with the reserve agent, but any excess above the amount needed for reserve purposes may be thus loaned. The lending bank may and in some cases does pass upon the collateral given as security, but often, especially if the lending bank is small, all is left to the discretion of the New York agent, and the out-of-town bank is merely sent later, for approval, a list of the securities held. Thus any surplus above reserve requirements may be employed to advantage and anything that may be spared from local needs may also be sent on for a similar use. When the out-of-town bank finds it necessary to build up its reserves these loans may be called, the New York bank still acting as agent in the transaction. The money thus secured may be left on deposit in New York and counted as a part of reserves or, if necessary, the cash may be withdrawn from the city.

There is another change that aids in explaining the lessened autumnal demand on New York. Checks are being used to an increasing extent in rural communities. Just how much of a change has occurred it is impossible to determine, but numerous inquiries addressed to western bankers have found them agreed that there is a constantly decreasing demand for cash for local needs. Farmers and merchants ask for less actual money and prefer accounts against which checks may be drawn. Even if this practice should greatly increase, the demand for cash would not be entirely eliminated but merely lessened. It would still be necessary to withdraw cash from New York and other centers to build up local reserves, but the amount needed would not be nearly so great as before.

That the continual flow of money, into New York does not result in a large accumulation of cash in that city is explained by the losses to the Subtreasury and through gold exports. An examination of Table II (in which the net interior movement is given in columns I and II, the Subtreasury and import and export movement in columns III and IV, with a combination of both in columns V and VI) shows that the net result is no great gain in cash for the New York banks for the entire year, and only a relatively slight loss during the fall months.

TABLE II

NET CASH MOVEMENTS INTO (+) AND OUT OF (−) NEW YORK CITY CLEARING-HOUSE BANKS (000 OMITTED)

Year	Interior Movement		Subtreasury and Gold Imports and Exports		Total Net Movement	
	I Aug.–Dec.	II Entire Year	III Aug.–Dec.	IV Entire Year	V Aug.–Dec.	VI Entire Year
1899	$− 23,616	$+ 37,116	$− 18,715	$− 58,859	$− 42,331	$− 21,743
1900	− 26,595	+ 52,563	− 117	− 21,732	− 26,712	+ 30,831
1901	− 13,291	+ 77,569	− 18,050	− 66,422	− 31,341	+ 11,147
1902	− 10,393	+ 50,067	− 23,144	− 54,675	− 33,537	− 4,608
1903	− 15,675	+ 87,954	+ 251	− 55,242	− 15,424	+ 32,712
1904	+ 2,458	+134,940	− 45,258	− 56,608	− 42,800	+ 78,332
1905	− 26,396	+ 71,862	− 30,395	−105,019	− 56,791	− 33,157
1906	− 43,772	− 36,143	+ 11,337	+ 75,621	− 32,435	+ 39,478
1907	−144,138	− 92,255	+134,211	+135,765	− 9,927	+ 43,510
1908	+ 35,300	+264,100	− 35,757	− 48,653	− 457	+215,447
1909	+ 28,056	+223,553	− 71,735	−147,297	− 43,679	+ 76,256
1910	+ 31,077	+213,591	− 50,368	−122,666	− 19,291	+ 90,925
1911	+103,890	+302,377	−103,858	−193,364	+ 32	+109,013
1912	+ 67,711	+325,158	−103,616	−277,566	− 35,905	+ 47,492

The interesting change has come since 1907. Since that date each autumn shows a Subtreasury and export loss greater than in any year up to 1907, except that the loss of $45,258,000 in 1904 exceeded that of $35,757,000 in 1908. For the entire year a similar change has been taking place. A combination of these two movements in columns V and VI shows no change of any significance. New York has been the gainer in eleven of the fourteen years, although a loser in the fall months during every year but one. The total net movement shows no important change except in 1908.

All the facts thus far presented lead to no conclusion relative to a change in New York's position except that there has not been for several years past a net loss to New York for crop-moving purposes. Instead, New York gains from the interior during this period, but has lost through the Subtreasury and gold exports an amount sufficient to offset these gains.

Professor A. P. Andrew, in a letter appearing in the *New York Evening Post* of January 8, 1913, contends that New York lends large sums to the interior each autumn and that if these "loans to correspondents" were included "it would doubtless be evident that any apparent increase in the net balance of out-of-town money in New York about November 1 of the present year was more than offset by an increase in loans made by the New York banks to their correspondents." However, he introduces no facts in support of this contention and it is difficult to see why the New York banks would send money out of the city in large quantities when interest rates are such as to bring such large sums into the city.

TABLE III

AMOUNT AND NATURE OF RESERVE HELD BY NATIONAL BANKS ON OR ABOUT OCTOBER 1 OF EACH YEAR (00,000 OMITTED)

Year	Reserve Cities (except Central Reserve Cities)		Localities Other than Reserve Cities		Entire United States	
	Lawful Money	Due from Reserve Agents	Lawful Money	Due from Reserve Agents	Lawful Money	Due from Reserve Agents
1902........	$128,2	$129,8	$144,9	$150,7	$523,8	$280,5
1903........	139,2	122,1	162,6	155,8	572,9	277,9
1904........	152,0	141,4	164,0	163,8	681,9	305,2
1905........	166,1	156,6	178,7	181,9	688,9	338,4
1906........	172,0	164,0	193,7	204,7	651,6	368,6
1907........	196,6	165,7	216,8	226,7	729,0	392,4
1908........	227,0	188,9	235,0	220,1	899,1	409,0
1909........	232,9	207,9	240,4	241,5	886,6	449,5
1910........	229,4	204,6	251,0	258,3	884,8	462,9
1911........	246,6	224,4	256,6	273,8	929,8	498,2
1912........	251,7	236,8	271,6	299,9	931,0	536,7

That New York holds relatively less cash than formerly is another change of importance. This is shown by Table III, which has been compiled from the reports of the Comptroller of the Currency, beginning with 1902, rather than with 1899 as do the previous tables, because a change at that date in the method of presenting the facts makes accurate comparisons with earlier years impossible. The table gives the reserve in millions of dollars held by the national banks of the reserve cities, of localities other than reserve cities, and of the entire United States, respectively. The figures have been taken in every case from the report nearest to October 1. The reserve is given in its two parts: (1) lawful money held (including redemption fund at Washington), and (2) the amount with reserve agents. Table IV shows the amount in cash as compared with the amount with reserve agents in percentage form.

TABLE IV

PERCENTAGE OF LAWFUL MONEY AND OF DEPOSITS WITH RESERVE AGENTS IN THE RESERVES OF NATIONAL BANKS ON OR ABOUT OCTOBER 1 OF EACH YEAR

Year	Reserve Cities (except Central Reserve Cities)		Localities Other than Reserve Cities		Entire United States	
	Lawful Money (Percentage)	With Reserve Agent (Percentage)	Lawful Money (Percentage)	With Reserve Agent (Percentage)	Lawful Money (Percentage)	With Reserve Agent (Percentage)
1902........	49.6	50.3	49.0	50.9	65.1	34.8
1903........	53.2	46.7	51.0	48.9	67.3	32.6
1904........	51.8	48.1	50.0	49.9	69.0	30.9
1905........	51.4	48.5	49.5	50.4	67.0	32.9
1906........	51.1	48.8	48.6	51.3	63.8	36.1
1907........	54.2	45.7	48.8	51.1	65.0	34.9
1908........	54.5	45.4	51.6	48.3	68.7	31.2
1909........	52.8	47.1	49.8	50.1	66.3	33.6
1910........	52.8	47.1	49.2	50.7	65.6	34.3
1911........	52.3	47.6	48.3	51.6	65.1	34.8
1912........	51.5	48.4	47.5	52.4	63.4	36.5

There has been no change of importance during the period in the practice of the banks as to the percentage of reserve held with reserve agents. The amount of cash held as compared with the amount of deposits with reserve agents is about the same in the later years as in the earlier. Such changes as have occurred since 1908 have been in the direction of a larger rather than a smaller percentage with reserve agents.. Thus for the country as a whole this proportion has increased from 31 per cent to 36per cent, for the country banks from 48 per cent to 52 per cent, and for the reserve city banks from 45 per cent to 48 per cent. In each case this is a return to conditions prior to 1907. Apparently the banks for a time hesitated to intrust a large proportion of their reserves to banks in other cities, but this hesitation has gradually disappeared until now conditions similar to those which preceded the panic have returned. The national banks are still taking advantage of their legal right to leave a part of their reserves with approved reserve agents. They are not hoarding their cash in their own vaults.

TABLE V

LAWFUL MONEY RESERVE (INCLUDING REDEMPTION FUND) HELD BY NATIONAL BANKS ON OR ABOUT OCTOBER 1 OF EACH YEAR (00,000 OMITTED)

Year	New York		Chicago		St. Louis		Other Reserve Cities		Localities Other than Reserve Cities		Entire United States	
	Amount	Percentage of 1902 Reserve	Amount	Percentage of 1902 Reserve	Amount	Percentage of 1902 Reserve	Amount	Percentage of 1902 Reserve	Amount	Percentage of 1902 Reserve	Amount	Percentage of 1902 Reserve
1902..	$186,1	100	$45,9	100	$18,7	100	$128,2	100	$144,9	100	$523,8	100
1903..	205,3	110	47,3	103	18,5	98	139,2	108	162,6	112	572,9	109
1904..	289,9	155	54,1	117	21,7	116	152,0	118	164,0	113	681,9	130
1905..	256,0	137	60,9	132	27,1	144	166,1	129	178,7	123	688,9	131
1906..	201,5	108	60,0	130	24,2	129	172,0	134	193,7	133	651,6	124
1907..	221,3	118	66,6	145	27,6	147	196,6	153	216,8	149	729,0	139
1908..	340,1	182	70,3	153	26,6	142	227,0	177	235,0	162	899,1	171
1909..	304,6	163	77,4	168	31,3	167	232,9	181	240,4	165	886,6	169
1910..	294,0	157	82,9	180	27,3	146	229,4	178	251,0	173	884,8	168
1911..	305,8	164	89,7	195	30,8	164	246,6	192	256,6	177	929,8	177
1912..	288,5	155	89,7	195	29,4	157	251,7	196	271,6	187	931,0	177

But the New York national banks hold relatively less of this amount than formerly. Table V presents the same figures in a different manner. In this table the amounts of cash reserve held by the banks in 1902 are viewed as 100 and the amounts at later dates calculated as percentages of them. The results show that while the lawful money reserve held by the national banks of the entire country increased from 1902 to 1912 by 77 per cent, the amount held by the New York banks increased only 55 per cent.

St. Louis increased 57 per cent, while Chicago increased 95 per cent or nearly doubled. The other reserve cities as a group gained 96 per cent, while the country banks increased 87 per cent. New York gained a little less than St. Louis, much less than Chicago, and also much less than the other banks of the country.

TABLE VI

AMOUNTS DUE FROM NATIONAL BANKS (00,000 OMITTED)

Year	I Due from Reserve Agents (all National Banks)	II Due from National Banks Not Reserve Agents (all National Banks except New York)	III Total Due (Columns I and II Combined)	IV Due to National Banks (New York City only)	V Percentage Ratio of Column IV to Column I	VI Percentage Ratio of Column IV to Column III	VII Difference between Column IV and Column III	VIII Percentage Ratio of Column VII to Column III
1899...	$414,1	$184,2	$598,3	$252,7	61	42	$345,6	58
1900...	450,7	187,4	638,1	260,0	57	40	378,1	60
1901...	456,6	208,8	665,4	252,3	55	37	413,1	63
1902...	465,6	218,9	684,5	248,3	53	36	436,2	64
1903...	454,9	221,0	675,9	230,5	50	34	445,4	66
1904...	562,6	256,4	819,0	311,4	55	38	507,6	62
1905...	605,4	277,4	882,8	303,1	50	34	579,7	66
1906...	616,1	288,5	904,6	297,5	48	32	607,1	68
1907...	614,4	289,0	903,4	259,2	42	28	644,2	72
1908...	711,9	326,0	1,037,9	359,0	50	34	678,9	66
1909...	719,3	335,9	1,055,2	331,3	46	31	723,9	69
1910...	688,7	329,0	1,017,7	315,0	45	30	702,7	70
1911...	744,6	350,1	1,094,7	332,0	44	30	762,7	70
1912...	812,1	407,2	1,219,3	345,0	42	28	874,3	72

The same general situation may be made clear in another way. It has been shown above that the banks of the country are redepositing their reserves as much as ever. The New York banks, however, are receiving a much smaller part of these deposits than in earlier years The facts given in Table VI are the ones that show the change. These also are taken from the reports of the Comptroller of the Currency, the report selected for each year being the one nearest October 1, as in the three preceding tables. The first column gives the amount "Due from Reserve Agents" for the entire United States. As there is no such item for central reserve cities, New York City is in no way included. Column IV, "Due to National Banks," gives for New York City the item that indicates (not exactly but in a general way). the amount held by the New York banks as reserve agents for the banks in the interior. The growth in the amount left with reserve agents (column I) has been rapid, and, with the exception of 1903, 1907, and 1910, it has been steady. The amount held in New York (column IV) has also grown but with much less rapidity. A high point was reached in 1904, followed by a decline to $259,200,000 in 1907. In 1908 came a large increase soon followed by a drop to $315,000,000 in 1910. In 1912 the amount was only $345,000,000, much less than in 1908. The changes are best shown in column V, which states the facts in percentage form. In 1899 New York owed the national banks of the country an amount equal to 61 per cent of the total amount due the national banks from reserve agents. This declined to 50 per cent in 1903, increased to per cent in 1904, fell to 42 per cent in 1907, rose to 50 per cent in 1908, and has steadily declined ever since, until it was 42 per cent in 1912. A comparison with Table V shows a marked correspondence in the fluctuations in the amount o lawful money held by the New York banks and the amount due from them to other banks. New York banks held no more lawful money reserve in 1912 than in 1904 and owed only a little more to national banks. New York's cash holdings declined in 1906 and 1907 and increased in 1908. The same changes are shown in Table VI in the amount due to national banks. Since 1908 both items have declined. It is also to be observed that the decline in the percentages given in column V of Table VI has been almost constant.

Lest this should not seem to be an entirely fair statement of the case another item has been inserted in Table VI. Column II gives for all the national banks of the country (excluding New York) the item "Due from National Banks – Not Reserve Agents." This includes many exchange items which are purely temporary, but also includes many more permanent accounts. Column III combines columns I and II, while column VI compares this total with New York's item "Due to National Banks" in column IV. The same fluctuations and the same general decline are to be noticed. The 42 per cent of 1899 becomes 28 per cent in 1912, a drop of 14 per cent. Put in another way, the rest of the country has gained 14 per cent. Column VII gives the difference between columns IV and III, or, approximately, the amount held by the rest of the country.[5]

[5] Throughout the discussion of Tables V and VI, sight must not be lost of the duplications due to the practice of banks in Chicago and St. Louis sending their surplus funds to New York.

Nor have the total resources of the national banks of New York increased so rapidly as those in other parts of the country. This fact has been presented with great clearness and force by Professor A. P. Andrew,[6] and need only be summarized briefly here. Table VII presents the percentage changes in number, capital, and resources of the United States national banks from June, 1900, to June, 1912, as given by him. It is evident that the banking strength of the South and West has been growing more rapidly than that of the East.

TABLE VII

PERCENTAGE CHANGES IN NUMBER, CAPITAL, AND TOTAL RESOURCES OF ALL REPORTING BANKS FROM JUNE, 1900, TO JUNE, 1912, BY GROUPS OF STATES

Groups of States	Percentage Change		
	Number of Banks	Capital	Total Resources
New England	−2.2	−8.8	61.6
Eastern States	62.7	71.0	103.6
Southern States	275.3	191.3	259.9
Middle Western States	124.6	108.4	175.1
Western States	203.5	174.4	227.2
Pacific States	252.8	192.7	240.8

There remains for discussion the question of the present distribution of banking reserves. It seems clear that the country is less dependent on New York for cash than in former years; that a relatively smaller amount of cash and of "Due from Reserve Agents" is held by the New York banks than in former years; and that the total banking resources of New York have grown less rapidly than those of other parts of the country.

Have other centers been developing? If so, the fact would be evidenced in each case by growth in total banking resources, in cash held, in "Due to Other Banks" and in the cash movements into and out of such centers. The last of these points would show the extent to which the autumnal strain has been shifted

[6] See *New York Evening Post,* December 7 and 14, 1912, and January 8, 1913. These articles are reprinted in Senate Document 1003, 62d Congress, 3d session.

TABLE VIII

GROWTH IN STRENGTH OF THE NATIONAL BANKS OF CERTAIN CITIES FROM 1899 TO 1912 (000 OMITTED)

Cities	Total Resources			Specie and Legal Tenders			Due to National Banks		
	1899	1912	Percentage Increase	1899	1912	Percentage Increase	1899	1912	Percentage Increase
New York City	$985,682	$1,762,727	78	$171,834	$286,157	66	$252,785	$345,018	36
San Francisco	34,138	240,847	605	6,585	16,628	152	1,609	22,215	1238
Washington, D.C.	24,750	50,484	103	2,911	3,161	8	363	2,822	682
Chicago	241,467	571,760	136	37,127	88,972	139	67,797	164,436	142
Indianapolis	23,686	62,872	165	2,703	4,607	70	4,094	8,845	116
Des Moines	8,217	23,717	188	545	1,896	247	1,630	4,931	202
New Orleans	24,598	46,652	89	2,089	2,742	31	1,542	4,043	162
Baltimore	71,340	114,007	59	4,557	5,759	26	10,286	17,378	60
Boston	302,910	357,580	18	24,629	29,354	19	51,808	37,744	26*
Detroit	29,165	65,094	123	2,458	6,803	176	2,951	5,514	86
Minneapolis	23,288	95,324	309	1,928	7,611	294	3,477	15,323	340
St. Paul	24,547	52,961	115	2,712	4,364	60	2,723	8,756	221
Kansas City	44,959	121,551	170	3,281	7,824	138	11,711	30,974	164
St. Joseph	5,761	19,623	240	503	1,436	185	1,021	3,612	253
St. Louis	90,575	213,752	135	10,814	28,623	164	20,334	58,364	187
Omaha	28,481	61,548	116	2,349	5,193	121	6,375	12,255	92
Albany	19,940	62,192	211	1,565	4,644	196	6,771	23,576	248
Portland, Ore.	10,354	39,941	285	1,086	4,436	308	1,300	4,669	259
Philadelphia	234,593	440,526	87	19,204	35,933	87	49,562	80,285	161
Pittsburgh	111,876	295,086	163	9,875	23,089	133	15,391	47,241	206
Houston	6,322	48,939	674	1,475	3,250	120	514	8,204	1496
Milwaukee	37,039	73,315	97	3,689	5,662	53	4,975	6,143	23
	1906								
Galveston†	3,392	7,940	134	293	923	215	831	1,256	50
Salt Lake City†	14,429	22,113	53	1,344	2,133	58	1,440	2,361	63
Seattle†	28,973	50,049	72	2,685	4,456	65	1,885	3,443	82

* Decrease.
† The reports of the Comptroller of the Currency do not give data for these three in 1899 as they became reserve cities at a later date.

from New York to these other centers, but unfortunately no reliable statistics are available. Such as have been gathered are admittedly incomplete, and are for such a short period as to make satisfactory comparisons impossible.

Information on the other points is, however, more easily secured. Table VIII shows the growth in total resources, specie and legal tenders,[7] and "Due to National Banks" for the leading reserve centers of the country from 1899 to 1912. In this table the cities, except New York, are arranged in the alphabetical order of the states in which they are situated. New York City has gained in the three specified items 78 per cent, 66 per cent, and 36 per cent respectively. Compared with these gains, those of Chicago were 136 per cent, 139 per cent, and 142 per cent, and those of St. Louis were 135 per cent, 164 per cent, and 187 per cent.

A fair comparison must take into account both the rate of growth and the present actual amounts. Such a comparison reveals the gradual development of a number of financial centers in the interior. Whether in each of these cases the growth will continue is by no means certain, but the growth of the past is not open to question.

In Table IX are grouped by sections sixteen cities whose geographical location, recent growth, and present strength are indicative of their influence. In New England, Boston is the only city which can be looked to as leader. Although her amount of "Due to Other Banks" has declined by 26 per cent during the period, it is still large, and the amount of cash held and of total resources have increased. Aside from the need for a center at some point in New England it is probable that the Boston practice of collecting out-of-town items through the clearing-house has been, and will be, a very important factor.

In the Eastern States New York City is, of course, leader, with Philadelphia second. The size of Philadelphia and its prominence as a manufacturing center account in part for its financial importance, but some of its growth, as well as that of Albany, may be attributed to the New York practice of charging exchange on out-of-town items. The New York clearing-house banks divide the

[7] The item "Specie and Legal Tenders" is not the same as "Lawful Money Reserve" used in Table V and so slight differences appear. Also in Table V the first year given is 1902, while in Table VIII it is 1899.

TABLE XIX

GROWTH IN STRENGTH OF THE NATIONAL BANKS IN LEADING CITIES OF CERTAIN SECTIONS OF THE UNITED STATES (000 OMITTED)

Cities	Total Resources			Specie and Legal Tenders			Due to National Banks		
	1899	1912	Percentage Increase	1899	1912	Percentage Increase	1899	1912	Percentage Increase
New England—									
Boston	$302,910	$ 357,580	18	$ 24,629	$ 29,354	19	$51,808	$ 37,744	26*
Eastern States—									
New York City	985,682	1,762,727	78	171,834	286,157	66	252,785	345,018	36
Albany	19,940	63,192	211	1,565	4,644	196	6,771	23,576	248
Philadelphia	234,593	440,526	87	19,204	35,933	87	49,562	80,285	161
Pittsburgh	111,876	295,086	163	9,875	23,089	133	15,391	47,241	206
Baltimore	71,340	114,007	59	4,557	5,759	26	10,286	17,378	60
Southern States									
New Orleans	24,598	46,652	89	2,089	2,742	31	1,542	4,043	162
Houston	6,322	48,939	674	1,475	3,250	120	514	8,204	1496
Galveston†	3,392	7,940	134	293	923	215	831	1,256	50
Middle States—									
Chicago	241,467	571,760	136	37,127	88,972	139	67,797	164,436	142
Minneapolis	23,288	95,324	309	1,928	7,611	294	3,477	15,323	340
St. Louis	90,575	213,752	135	10,814	28,623	164	20,334	58,364	187
Kansas City	44,959	121,551	170	3,281	7,824	138	11,711	30,974	164
Pacific States—									
Seattle†	28,973	50,049	72	2,685	4,456	65	1,885	3,443	82
San Francisco	34,138	240,847	605	6,585	16,628	152	1,659	22,215	1238
Salt Lake City†	14,429	22,113	53	1,344	2,133	58	1,440	2,361	63

* Decrease.

† Comparisons are for 1906 and 1912.

country into three sections. Localities in the first section are discretionary points on items from which exchange may or may not be charged. All items from a second section farther distant must, according to the rules, be charged at least one-tenth of 1 per cent, while items from more distant points must be charged at least one-fourth of 1 per cent. The effect of this is that many banks in near-by cities, e.g., Trenton, send to Philadelphia for collection large sums that might otherwise go to New York, because the Philadelphia banks have no such agreement and take all items at par. The only loss incurred by collecting through Philadelphia is due to the fact that in the latter city the banks have agreed to defer interest payment for three, five, or seven days, on amounts deposited, the length of time being determined by a grouping similar to that of New York in charging exchange. This deferring of interest in Philadelphia has been in effect only since September 1, 1911. Recently New York has attempted to offset some of the losses sustained through her exchange charge by extending the number of discretionary points to include other cities, provided the banks in those cities will meet certain requirements as to prompt remittance. It is too early to forecast the effect of this change. Albany has undoubtedly been a gainer, for the reasons which have favored Philadelphia, but her nearness to New York will probably make it difficult, if not impossible, for her to maintain her position. The growth of Pittsburgh has been remarkably rapid and that of Baltimore also deserves attention.

None of the cities in the South are as yet large enough for comparison with those of the East and Middle West, but New Orleans has been gaining rapidly and Houston and Galveston are growing. Houston now surpasses New Orleans in all three items given and shows a remarkable percentage increase. It seems probable that the use of the Panama Canal may send enough traffic through these southern ports to aid their growth very materially.

In the Middle States there are several cities, e.g., Cincinnati and Indianapolis, which are larger than some of those mentioned in the South and West, but they are surpassed by the ones selected for the table. Chicago, Minneapolis, St. Louis, and Kansas City have geographical advantages and such prestige that their future seems beyond question.

In the inter-mountain region, Salt Lake City is still relatively small but will probably maintain her position of leadership as the country develops. San Francisco has an undoubted advantage in position and has been growing with remarkable rapidity. Seattle at the north will develop with the further growth of the Northwest and with the increasing business of the railroads with termini at Puget Sound.

There is nothing in the facts presented in this paper to indicate that New York is in the least danger of losing her position as the financial leader of the United States. There is ample evidence, however, that her growth is less rapid than that of other sections of the country and that other cities are now relatively of more importance than in the past. More capital is being invested in banking, more cash is being held, and more deposits of other banks are being collected. These deposits are largely being sent on to centers like New York and Chicago, but increasing amounts are being held in the West. Though there may still be an autumnal demand for New York cash, this demand is now meeting with little response.

DIFFERENCE BETWEEN SPECULATION AND INVESTMENT[1]

Thomas Conway

1. *Close similarity of speculation and investment.* – No subjects have a more wide-spread interest or excite more keenly the imagination and interest of the ordinary person than speculation and investment. Every man is in a sense a speculator. Every prudent person sooner or later becomes an investor. We speculate when we change from one position to another, or when we choose our careers; we take chances when we enter into almost any of the ordinary common contracts. Every one fortunate enough to possess an income in excess of his material necessities, if he is at the same time prudent, endeavors to invest safely a portion of his earnings.

The dividing line between speculation and investment many authors have attempted to locate. The distinction is at best a narrow one, and the authorities do not agree upon the nature of the division which should be made. There are a large number of points in which the two subjects bear a close similarity. As a consequence it is really impossible to discuss speculation without reference to the investment view-point, and in the same way every investment when intelligently purchased must be considered from a speculative standpoint.

One of the most common distinctions made between speculation and investment is that the investor buys securities or some productive piece of property in order to secure an income, while the speculator buys not to secure a steady return upon his money but to take advan tage of an increase in the price of his purchase. The illustrations used for this distinction are largely stereo typed. The man who buys a government bond is frequently taken as an illustration of an investor. He realizes that the value of government bonds is almost fixed, and that its price will fluctuate very slightly

[1] [Chapter 1 of *Investment and Speculation*, New York: Alexander Hamilton Institute, 1914.]

if at all, during its life. He purchases the security because he has surplus funds which he desires to put at work, thereby adding to his income. The return, or interest, which is paid upon the security, and the assurance that at the end of the period his money will be returned, are the inducements which prompt him to make the purchase. On the other hand, the man who buys the stock of a bankrupt railroad company quoted at an almost nominal figure, believes that the security will rapidly enhance in value, and that although he may receive no return upon the stock he will make a large profit because of the advance in its price.

This distinction is weak and unsatisfactory because it establishes an unreal test. For example, many railroads at the present time have a reasonably satisfactory financial history, and their earning power seems to be sufficient to meet their probable needs, yet their bonds sell at a price considerably below par. The purchaser of these securities may be prompted by a double motive – first, securing a return upon the investment, and second, profiting by the advance in the price of the security to or above par through the growth in the prosperity and financial stability of the company. To classify this individual according to the test which we have considered. would be impossible. Viewed from one position he is a speculator, while looked at from another he is an investor.

2. *Distinction between speculation and investment.* – The second test, which is very generally accepted, is succinctly described by S. S. Pratt in "The Work of Wall Street." He says:

> Speculation is an investment of money in which large risk is taken in expectation of great gain. But it is not easy to draw the line where investment ends and speculation begins, in Wall Street such a line is drawn, but it is an arbitrary division. When a security is bought and paid for in full, put away in a place of safe keeping and held for the income it yields – that is called an investment. The great bulk of the dealings in bonds are for investment. When a security is bought on margin and held for sale as soon as the price advances – that is speculation. The bulk of the dealings in stocks is speculative.

There is an element of speculation in most investments. Investors who pay outright for their securities are generally ready to sell them again at a profit. They buy them for the incomes, but if the advance in price is large enough, the profit in selling may be more attractive than the profit in keeping. On the other hand, the speculator buys on a margin to sell again on a rising price, but he buys and sells on an income basis the same as the investor. All wholesale business in modern trade is done on credit which is only another form of the Wall Street system of margins. The merchant who restricts his purchases to the amount his cash capital can pay for in full, must do a comparatively small business. The wholesaler's capital, in a certain sense, corresponds to the speculator's margin. The former buys on time and borrows of the bank the money to pay for the goods as the time for payment approaches. With a capital of $100,000 he may buy, perhaps, $500,000 worth of goods.

It is only by a system of credits that the great operations of modern business can be conducted. The speculator buys stocks, like the merchant, on credit. With a capital of $10,000 the investor can buy 100 shares of stock, selling at par value of $100 per share, and pay for them in full. But with $10,000 deposited as a margin the speculator can buy 1,000 shares. Of course the risk is much greater. If the price declines the speculator may lose his entire margin or capital; but the merchant also runs a risk in buying goods in excess of the amount of his capital. Except that there is a greater mobility in the stock market than in other markets so that changes in prices are more rapid and extreme, the risk in both cases is equal.

3. *All men are speculators.* – The operations of the merchant and the speculator are therefore, in the last analysis, essentially the same. If all business, whether in stocks or in trade, were conducted strictly on the cash, or investment basis, the transactions would be very limited. Credit means expansion and activity. In times of panic, when credit is withdrawn, speculation ceases and all business becomes of the investment order. Then stagnation sets in, wages fall, and widespread suffering is caused. Someone has said that speculation is "a disease of the mind"; but Henry Clews, in his testimony before a legislative committee which investigated cor ners in 1881 gave a serious and better definition. He said:

> Speculation is a method for adjusting differences of opinion as to future values, whether of products or of stocks. It regulates produdion by instantly advancing prices when there is a scarcity, thereby stimulating production, and by depressing prices when there is an overproduction.

The speculator may be defined as a man who, making a study of business conditions and of the earning power of the companies in whose stocks he purposes to trade, buys because he believes that prices ought to advance, or sells because he believes they will fall; and does so on a margin ample to protect him against any ordinary vicissitudes of the market. He exercises the same foresight and conservatism as does the merchant who places a large order for goods.

The gambler in stocks is one who "goes it blind," who buys and sells without study of conditions or of the property in which he invests, who trusts to chance. He often risks more than he can afford to lose, perhaps wasting the savings of many months in one transaction. He might as well risk his money on a horse race or a roulette table. Wall Street is full of gamblers of this kind. "People will deal in chance," said Jay Gould to a United States Senate committee. "Your minister, doctor and barber have all the same interest in speculation."

The distinction which Mr. Pratt makes between investment and speculation is regarded by many as not entirely satisfactory. It consists of a comparison of extremes. It is necessary that this radical difference be understood before a more careful distinction can be made. Investment consists in the exchange of money for property which is believed to be of such stable value that the principal sum may be recovered either by the sale of the security or through its redemption at some definite date by the issuing company. In addition the purchaser must be assured that he will receive a satisfactory and constant return for the use of his money. Furthermore, the wise investor demands that his money shall not only be secure and that a satisfactory income be assured, but also that there shall be a sufficiently wide market for his investment to enable him to dispose of it quickly and rapidly in case he desires to convert his holdings into cash.

Speculation, as Mr. Pratt says, is the taking of long chances in expectation of great gain. A shrewd man speculates with his eyes open to the risks which he is taking. He calculates them as accurately as possible and then decides whether the chances of profit are sufficient to compensate him for his chances of loss.

The criticism most commonly made is that one man may regard a proposition as an investment which another declares to be a speculation. The world is full of illustrations of this. Day laborers, men of meager salaries, in fact almost every class whose earning are limited and who must husband every resource, will plunge into glittering wild-cat schemes which are declared by their promoters to be safe investments, but which in reality are desperate speculative snares. A few of these may turn out partial or even satisfactory successes. The great majority of them never have a chance of becoming solid and substantial propositions. The deluded buyer may for a time regard the disposition of his savings as an investment. He later finds, to his sorrow, that in reality it was a foolhardy speculation.

This criticism loses much of its force if the definition is applied, not from the stand-point of an inexperienced person, but from the point of view of the collective judgment of acute and experienced investors and observers of conditions. The consensus of opinion of those who have made a study of the particular security, and a business of judging of properties of this class, gives to each offering its proper category. It is not much the judgment of the individual as the collective judgment of the community which must be considered. Thus a security may at the time it is first floated be regarded as a rank speculation, but wise management and the development of latent and too generally discounted resources may so improve its earning power and com pletely demonstrate the value of its property as to cause a reversal of opinion and the placing of its securities in the class of high grade investments.

4. *Practical importance of understanding difference.* – The distinction between speculation and investment is, however, an academic question to which we need give but little attention. The important point for us to remember is that the speculator and investor look at the securities or properties in which they are trading from different stand-points. The speculator is an opportunist. He places his faith to a large degree upon a quick turn based many times upon conditions which have little or nothing to do with the considerations entering into the decision of the investor. The experienced speculator, it must be understood, generally makes a careful study of the business conditions and the earning power of the companies in whose stocks he proposes to trade. He discounts both of these factors to the fullest degree in forming his judgment. He, however, feels but a temporary and transient interest in the property he buys, for he hopes to sell it again in a short time. The investor regards himself in a certain sense as becoming a partner in the business enterprise. As such

he makes a careful and intimate study of its probable future, its assets and its earning power. The speculator regards himself as one who has no intention of making a permanent connection, but rather secures an option upon certain property in the belief that it may turn out to be valuable. This is particularly true where the speculator trades upon margin or buys a privilege. The strongest proof of the correctness of this diagnosis is found in the fact that there is but little speculation in bonds. If there is no possibility of a large advance in their price they are sought only by investors. It is the stocks of corporations which furnish a medium for most of our speculative transactions, for it is here that the largest possibilities of fluctuation are to be found. The speculator regards the shares of stock which he buys largely as pawns in the game which he is playing.

THE MARKET FOR SECURITIES[1]

Thomas Conway

5. *Where securities are dealt in.* – The study of Investment and Speculation concerns itself with the securities issued by governments, states, municipalities and private corporations. Naturally the first question which arises has to do with the markets which exist for these securities. If we do not know where bonds and stocks are bought and sold and who sells and buys them we cannot progress far with the study of their characteristics or values. Anyone may buy and sell securities, but where the transactions reach a large scale markets spring up, and where the markets are taken in charge by regular organizations and controlled by rules such markets become stock exchanges. It does not follow, however, that all important transactions are made upon the stock exchanges, although the importance of these organizations is constantly becoming greater. The largest American stock exchange is in New York City and here for the past decade there have been average annual sales of shares of 196,500,000, at prices involving an average annual turnover of nearly $15,500,000,000; bond transactions in the same period averaged about $800,000,000 a year.

6. *Stock Exchange the largest single market.* – From these figures it will be seen that a much larger proportion of the stock than of the bond business is concentrated on the exchanges. This shows how large a part speculation plays in Stock Exchange operations, speculation being largely confined to stocks and but little existent in bond dealings. It is generally estimated that not more than one-third the total bond sales in New York City take place on the Stock Exchange. In the case of Government bonds more than nine-tenths of the sales are made directly by two or three dealers and prices reported from the "board," as the

1 [Chapter 2 of *Investment and Speculation*, New York: Alexander Hamilton Institute, 1914.]

Exchange is often termed, are little more than nominal. Fully nine-tenths of the transactions in municipal bonds take place in other quarters than on the Stock Exchange. This business, also, is largely in the hands of dealers and New York City bonds are the only ones which find a ready market on the exchange.

The New York Stock Exchange is, however, by far the largest single market in the country, both for bonds and stocks. There is seldom a year in which at least half a billion of new bonds are not listed on this exchange and during years when the output of new securities is on really a large scale listings run in excess of that. There is also a smaller exchange in New York, the Consolidated, and large dealings in both stocks and bonds are also carried on in Broad Street under the name of the Curb. This market is but little organized, although the totals of its transactions are large. There are important stock exchanges in other cities, particularly in Boston, Chicago and Philadelphia, and finally there is a great amount of buying and selling of securities, especially of bonds, among the banking firms, Stock Exchange firms with bond departments, and banks and trust companies with bond departments. Although, as already stated, the greater portion of all dealings in bonds and especially in United States governments and municipals, is carried on privately, or "over the counter," the tendency toward employing the Stock Exchange as the major market is steadily increasing. Many issues, formerly traded in only among dealers, now find a market on the board and the value of a Stock Exchange membership is more appreciated by the bond houses than formerly. Indeed every small bond house is ambitious to own a Stock Exchange seat. It is often ad vantageous for purposes of record to have important transactions carried through on the board and the information which the Exchange requires from all corporations seeking to have securities listed is of assist ance in arousing the interest of investors in these securities.

7. *Markets created by savings.* – If for a moment we drop the subject of speculation and consider only the more important matter of investment we will find a significant relation between investment and geography. Primarily, dealing in securities is greatest where the investment demand is greatest and the extent to which funds seek investment is determined to no small extent by locality. The reason for this is the fact that generally in the older communities a much larger proportion of all wealth has

been saved and is available for investment. In new communities every resource is employed in developing the land and putting up dwellings, but in New England, New York and a few other eastern states there are hundreds of thousands of persons, many of them women, who have more money than is immediately needed for carrying on the pressing daily business of the locality in which they live and this money finds its way chiefly into the securities of public and private corporations.

As the West grows richer there is an increasing surplus for investment, but it is still true that the central investment markets are in the East and especially in New England, New York City and Philadelphia. Here the bulk of the trading in securities is carried on. The same situation rules in Canada.

8. *Functions of the savings banks.* – The best proof of the foregoing statements may be found in the relation of the mutual savings banks of New England and New York to the investment situation. In these states there are savings banks, entirely mutual in character and managed solely in the interest of the depositors, there being no stock or dividends, which receive very small sums from millions of depositors and which in turn invest the money largely in high grade bonds. These banks have about $2,000,000,000 invested in bonds and their purchases prove a most far-reaching factor in the investment markets. The larger life insurance companies are nearly all located in New England, New York and Eastern Pennsylvania and these companies are as large buyers of bonds as the savings banks. The fire insurance companies also are purchasers to be reckoned with in both the stock and bond markets and the majority of such concerns are in New England and New York. Finally there are many trust estates, universities, colleges and philanthropic institutions in the great eastern centres of population which are constantly seeking investments.

9. *Chicago a growing investment centre.* – In New York there are 391 firms dealing in securities. In Boston we find 129 and in Philadelphia 122. Chicago is a poor fourth with 101 and then come Baltimore, Cincinnati, Pittsburgh and St. Louis with 44, 42, 39 and 35 respectively. These figures plainly show how the East still holds the supremacy in investment affairs but similar figures ten years from now will probably reveal a wholly different situation. The Chicago Stock Exchange is being enlarged and many corporations which formerly maintained transfer offices

only in New York and permitted their securities to be traded in on the New York Exchange alone are opening offices in Chicago and adding their stocks and bonds to the Chicago Exchange. According to competent authority the bonds houses of Chicago distributed $250,000,000 of bonds in 1909, but a decade later they will be expected to distribute twice that amount annually.

10. Stock exchanges as speculative markets. – Bonds and stocks which are bought for permanent investment may be, and in the case of certain classes of securities usually are, traded in outside the regular stock exchanges but when we come to the study of speculative operations in securities we find that such operations are almost always confined to the stock exchanges. Even here no transaction takes place and the customer of what by courtesy alone is termed a "broker" places a bet on the change in prices as indicated by actual transactions made by other persons, the bucket shop where he gambles often pretends to have made a sale or purchase on some more or less mythical stock exchange. Whatever the evils of speculation may be it should be thoroughly understood at the start that the purchase nd sale of securities on any of the larger exchanges are real, actual transactions. By means of collusion and various private arrangements the capital invested in peculative transactions may be small but the delivery of the securities has to be made and paid for just the same as if a savings bank were buying for permanent investment.

11. Element of speculation present in all business. – Nor should it be supposed that only on the Stock Exchange does speculation occur. It is found in every walk of life. The ordinary merchant who buys a large stock of goods in anticipation of a rise in price due to advance in the tariff schedule is a speculator. The man who buys a store property upon an important retail street in a large city, feeling certain that with the growth in the community its value will be increased, is a speculator. The shrewd observer who believes that because of a small crop the price of a product will rapidly advance in the months preceding its harvest, and who buys large quantities in anticipation of such a rise, is a speculator.

The bulk of speculation, however, is carried on in connection with either the stock exchange or the produce exchange for the reason that they afford a quick and instantaneous market in which purchases can be resold. The merchant who buys his stock of goods in anticipation of a rise in price through a tariff change, for example, can only realize his profit after he has slowly disposed of his stock in the ordinary course of trade. This may take many months. The speculator in the stock or grain market can take his profit in five minutes with a single transaction upon the exchange.

ORGANIZATION AND OPERATION OF THE STOCK EXCHANGE[1]

Thomas Conway

12. *The New York Stock Exchange.* – The keystone of the structure of speculation is the stock exchange. The New York Stock Exchange as being by far the most important merits a detailed study. To begin with it is an unincorporated organization.

Its object as stated in its constitution, "shall be to furnish exchange rooms and other facilities for the convenient transaction of their business by its members; and to promote and inculcate just and equitable principles of trade and business." These three objects are faithfully carried out by the exchange.

The home of the exchange, situated in the heart of the financial quarter of New York usually known as "the Wall Street district," is unexcelled in point of magnificence and convenience.

The managers of the New York Stock Exchange have been successful in their efforts to maintain prescribed standards of integrity among its members. Membership in the exchange is a very valuable privilege, which in boom times is eagerly sought after. The membership having reached the limit, entrance can be secured now only through the purchase of the seat of a deceased or insolvent member or of some one about to retire from business. The word "seat" is a misnomer. In early days the brokers had seats in a room arranged like the ordinary legislative chamber, but at the present time the business of the exchange is handled upon a great floor, the brokers standing or moving around to transact their business. The sale of a "seat" merely gives the member the right of entrance to the floor, which is open only to members or their representatives and to the employés of the exchange. The qualifications for membership in the exchange are simple. The applicant must be a citizen of the United States

[1] [Chapter 3 of *Investment and Speculation*, New York: Alexander Hamilton Institute, 1914.]

and at least 21 years of age. All applications for membership and all applications for reinstatement of suspended members are referred to the Committee on Admissions.

13. *Government of the exchange.* – The government of the stock exchange is vested in a Governing Committee composed of the president, treasurer and forty members. The members of the Governing Committees and the secretary constitute the officers of the exchange. One-fourth of the membership is elected each year. The Governing Committee is all powerful in the exchange Its powers correspond in a general way to those of the board of directors of a corporation. Among its duties, for instance, are the following: (1) It determines the manner and form by which its proceedings shall be conducted; (2) it has the power to appoint all committees and regulate their jurisdiction; (3) it has supervisory jurisdiction over all matters referred to sub-committees; (4) it has the power to try all members for alleged offenses and punish them if found guilty; (5) it has control of the finances of the exchange and fixes the amount of fees; (6) it is vested with all powers necessary for the guidance of the exchange and of its members.

The officers of the exchange are president, secretary and chairman. The president directs the enforcement of rules and regulations and may preside over the exchange whenever he may care to do so. He is also the presiding officer of the Governing Committee. The chairman of the exchange is appointed by the Governing Committee. It is his duty to preside over the exchange during business hours, to maintain order, enforce the rules and impose fines and penalties. He is not permitted to buy or sell personally upon the floor of the exchange.

14. *Exchange committees.* – In addition to the Governing Committee there is a large number of so-called standing committees, to each of which is assigned special duties. The number of these committees vary, being larger in the New York Exchange than in other exchanges. The most important of these standing committees in the case of the New York Stock Exchange are:

1. Committee of Arrangements, composed of seven members, which makes and enforces all rules necessary to the conducting of business on the exchange. It considers all complaints of violation of rules, controls and regulates the quotation service and all telegraph or telephone connections with the exchange. In

addition this committee has charge of the employés of the exchange and of the physical condition of the property.

2. Committee on Admissions, composed of fifteen members, passes upon all applications for the transfer of seats and of suspended members for reinstatement to the usual privileges. A vote of two-thirds of the committee is necessary to elect to membership or to reinstate a suspended member.

3. Arbitration Committee, which investigates and decides all claims and differences between members of the exchange arising out of contracts subject to the rules of the exchange. If the committee is unable to decide, or if the parties both desire, the controversy between the members may be brought into the courts in the regular manner. The decision of the committee, when rendered, is final in all cases, unless an appeal is taken by a member of the committee. All controversies involving $2,500 or over may be appealed by either party to the Governing Committee, which may finally adjudicate the case or advise the parties to secure their remedy at law or direct a re-hearing by the Arbitration Committee.

The fourth committee is the Committee on Clearing House. This committee is composed of five members and has charge of the clearing of the business of the exchange and the preparation of the financial reports arising out of the performance of this work.

In addition to this there are a number of other committees whose names indicate their duties. The most important are the Committee on Commissions, regulating and enforcing the commissions to be charged by members; Committee on Constitution, Finance Committee, Committee on Insolvency and Law Committee.

The Committee on Securities makes the rules regulating the delivery of securities from one member to an other and the settlement of contracts between members.

The Committee on Stock List considers all applications for placing securities upon the list of the exchange.

This organization of the exchange at first glance seems complicated, yet in reality it is very simple when compared with the magnitude of the business involved and the complexity of questions which constantly arise. A considerable number of these committees are very inactive, meeting infrequently and having little work to consider. The exchange is a self-governing body whose operations have been eminently successful. The rigidity of the discipline maintained and the swift punishment meted out to all offenders make infractions of the rules comparatively infrequent.

15. *Method of doing business.* – The main part of the exchange consists of two floors. The lower is used by employés and members for cloak rooms and other necessary purposes. The main floor of the exchange is surmounted by a high dome, through which light and air are obtained. Around the walls is a seemingly endless series of telephone booths, each of which is leased to some member of the exchange and is used by him many times each day in communicating with his office for the purpose of receiving orders and reporting the success of his negotiations. The major portion of the main floor is given up to the exchange "floor." This is a great open space, scattered over which are a large number of posts. Each of these posts bears a sign upon which are printed the names of the stocks which are traded in at this point. Sometimes a single stock will be given a post, while sometimes a number of stocks will be grouped together at one post. There is, therefore, some particular spot in the room for the purchase and sale of each security. For example, there is the sugar post where the stock of the American Sugar Refining Company is traded in. There is another post at which stock may be borrowed for delivery on short contracts, and still another for the sale of call money. When a member secures an order to buy stock he goes to the proper post and cries out how much he wants and the price which he will pay, starting, of course, at or below the last quotations. All the other brokers who have that stock for sale gather around the post, each crying out the price at which he will sell the quantity desired. At first the buyer and seller are at extremes – one may offer 65 and the other may demand 671/8. Each rapidly approaches the other – one offering an eighth more than his previous offer, the other dropping, if he sees fit, in the same degree. This continues until the broker offers the stock at the price which is agreeable to the buyer. The latter shouts "Taken," and both make a simple memorandum upon a little pad which they carry in their hands. All that is set down is "bought" or "sold," the number of shares, initials representing the names of the stock, the price, and name of the other party. Thus amid a ceaseless roar which is utterly unintelligible to the uninitiated – seeming like the cries around the Tower of Babel to the inter-

ested visitor in the gallery – is transacted in a simple and informal manner millions of dollars of business during each working, day. The exchange, which to the outsider at all times, seems turbulent, becomes an arena of fighting, frenzied men whenever there is great activity in the market and sharp variations in prices. When a broker has bought or sold in the exchange he reports the transaction as soon as convenient by telephone to his office. Within an hour from the closing of the exchange each office sends out a slip or ticket memorandum covering each transaction to the other firm involved. This comparison is intended to check up mistakes which may have occurred. As a matter of fact, it is remarkable how few differences exist. In spite of the fact that large transactions are constantly being made, that the contracts are oral and are made amid turmoil and confusion, the agreements are honorably fulfilled by the members and compara tively few controversies ever arise.

16. *Penalties for insolvency of members.* – An inexorable condition of membership in the Exchange is that no member shall be allowed to trade upon the Exchange after he has become insolvent. The business of a stockbroker is hazardous. During good years large profits are made, but these may be wiped out by a single mistake of judgment or lack of caution in an hour of panic. The trading of members with each other is upon the faith of the ability of each to carry out his part of the contract. The failure of one house frequently drags down with it firms which would otherwise be solvent. Under such conditions rigid rules are in force in all our exchanges governing the insolvency of members. Let us again take the New York Stock Exchange as our example. The rules provide that a member who fails to comply with his contracts, or becomes insolvent, or who is associated as a partner in a firm registered upon the exchange which fails to carry out its agreements, shall immediately inform the president in writing of the insolvency of himself, or of his firm. The president immediately suspends him from membership and this suspension continues until he is able to settle with his creditors and has been formally reinstated by the Committee on Admissions.

17. *Reinstatement of members.* – The unfortunate member is given one year in which to arrange a settlement with his creditors and apply for reinstatement. If he does not succeed in doing so within this period of time, his membership is disposed of by the

Committee on Admissions, the proceeds being turned over to the representative of his creditors. The committee, however, is given the option of extending the period of time if it deems such a course advisable. In order to secure reinstatement a member must submit conclusive evidence of having settled with his creditors. The Committee on Admissions then posts his name for a period of at least three days. At the end of this time a ballot is taken, and if the applicant succeeds in securing a favorable vote of two-thirds of the entire committee he is entitled to reinstatement to full privileges. The applicant is given the right of choosing the meeting of the committee at which his application is to be passed upon. His failure, however, to secure the affirmative two-thirds vote of the committee does not destroy his hope of reinstatement, for he can present his petition at any one of the five subsequent meetings of the committee which he may select. It is necessary, however, that the second presentation of his name occur within one year from the date of his suspension. If the committee is still unwilling to accept the delinquent, he has one other alternative. He may appeal within ten days of the last rejection to the Governing Committee, which may, by an affirmative vote of not less than twenty-five of its members, reinstate the applicant. If, however, his appeal to the Governing Committee shall fail, the Committee on Admissions is then charged with the duty of disposing of his membership and turning over the proceeds of the sale to him.

The Committee on Admissions usually reinstates members when no evidence has been presented of reckless or unbusinesslike dealing. Whenever this has occurred, however, the committee usually refuses to approve of the application for reinstatement, and if the matter reaches the Governing Committee, it submits the facts substantiating these allegations to this body. The Governing Committee is empowered to declare ineligible for reinstatement any member who in its opinion is guilty of irregular practices by a resolution passed by a two-thirds vote of the total number on the committee. In the same way the Governing Committee can by a two-thirds vote expel any member whom it finds to be guilty of fraud or fraudulent acts.

18. *Exchanges try to prevent competition.* – The stock exchanges jealously guard the monopoly which they possess by providing penalties for every member who transacts business through any outside organization which permits dealings in

securities traded upon in the regular exchange. As a consequence the irregular or outlaw exchanges lead a precarious existence and usually die a natural death, except where they take up a field of activity not covered by the regular exchanges. The penalty for members of the regular exchange who are connected directly, by partnership or in any other manner, with an irregular exchange is suspension for a period not exceeding one year, or expulsion, as the Governing Comittee may determine. In addition, a member making a transaction with a non-member in the quarters of the exchange is subject to suspension for a period of one year.

19. *Gratuity fund.* – An interesting feature of our American exchanges is the so-called gratuity fund which exists for the benefit of the families of deceased members. In the case of the New York Exchange every person who becomes a member must pay to the trustee of the gratuity fund the sum of $10 before he is admitted to the privileges of membership. Whenever a member of the exchange dies an assessment of $10 is levied upon every member. The income from these two sources is used to fulfill the pledge of the exchange to pay to the executors of the deceased member's estate within one year after his death the sum of $10,000, or so much thereof as may have been collected and unexpended.

20. *Fictitious transactions prohibited.* – The rules of the exchange furthermore provide that no fictitious transactions be permitted on the floor under a penalty of suspension for a maximum period of one year. These fictitious transactions are commonly called "wash" sales. This device is intended to give fictitious values to securities. Two brokers might conspire, let us say, to ad vance the price of stock. One would offer it on the floor in the regular way. His confederate would bid the price up beyond what others would be willing to pay and would then buy it in. The continual succession of these high sales would attract interest to the security and give to it unnaturally high quotations.

The practice, though prohibited, exists in a modified form, which seems to be beyond the scope of the rules. An operator who desires to advance or depress the price of the stock now does so by "matched" orders, as they are called. In these transactions he uses different brokers, some of whom he instructs to buy and others to sell, naming the price limit in each case according to his desires. In most cases the broker is ignorant of: the object in view and executes the transactions in good faith. Nevertheless a large operator with ample resources can by this method secure the same ends as he formerly attained with the "wash" sales. The only disadvantage is that in this process he may be forced to absorb a large amount of stock which is offered by outsiders and which is naturally purchased in good faith by the innocent broker in preference to that offered by his unknown ally. This stock must, of course be paid for in the regular way. The purchase of this stock at high prices materially reduces the profits of the operator in his stock market campaign.

21. *Recommendations of the Hughes Committee.* – The committee appointed by Governor Hughes of New York to investigate speculation made this recommendation in regard to the manipulation of prices and fictitious transactions:

> There have been instances of gross and unjustifiable manipulation of securities, as in the case of American Ice stock. While we have been unable to discover any complete remedy short of abolishing the Stock Exchange itself, we are convinced that the Exchange can prevent the worst forms of this evil by exercising its influence and authority over the members to prevent them. When continued manipulation exists it is patent to experienced observers.
>
> So far as manipulation is based upon fictitious or so-called "wash sales," it is open to the severest condemnation, and should be prevented by all possible means. These fictitious sales are forbidden by the rules of all the regular exchanges, and are not enforceable at law. They are less frequent than many persons suppose. A transaction must take place upon the floor of the Exchange to be reported, and if not reported does not serve the purpose of those who engage in it. If it takes place on the floor of the Exchange, but is purely a pretence, the brokers involved run the risk of detection and expulsion, which is to them a sentence of financial death. There is, however, another class of transactions called "matched orders," which differ materially from those already mentioned, in that they are actual and enforceable contracts. We refer to that class of transactions, engineered by some manipulator, who sends a number of orders simultaneously to different brokers, some to buy and some to sell. These brokers, without knowing that other brokers have countervailing orders from the same principal, execute their orders upon the floor of the Exchange, and the

> transactions become binding contracts; they cause an appearance of activity in a certain security which is unreal. Since they are legal and binding, we find a difficulty in suggesting a legislative remedy. But where the activities of two or more brokers in certain securities become so extreme as to indicate manipulation rather than genuine transactions, the officers of the Exchange would be remiss unless they exercised their influence and authority upon such members in a way to cause them to desist from such suspicious and undesirable activity. As already stated, instances of continuous manipulation of particular securities are patent to every experienced observer, and could without difficulty be discouraged, if not prevented, by prompt action on the part of the Exchange authorities.

The state of New York recently passed a law levying a tax of 2/100 of 1 per cent upon all shares transferred upon the exchange or elsewhere. This tax, while producing considerable revenue for the use of the state, was intended also to diminish the amount of the fictitious business which was being carried on.

22. *Members' fees.* – The fees which members are allowed to charge for their services are fixed by the rules of the exchange, which are rigidly enforced. Three rates of compensation are named. The first applies to all business transacted for parties who are not members of the exchange and for firms on which the member of the exchange is only a special partner. Upon this class of business it is provided that the commission shall not be less than one-eighth of 1 per cent on stocks selling at $1 or over, except mining stocks. On all stocks selling at less than $1 per share the commission is $1 per hundred shares, and on mining stocks selling at less than $10 and over $1, the commission is $6.25 per hundred. The purchase of 100 shares, therefore, entitles the broker to $12.50. If the seller of the stock is also a non-member, he has been forced to pay the same price. The total compensation, therefore, which is received by exchange members for each transaction for outsiders amounts to $25. The practical effect of this is that there must be an advance of at least one-fourth of 1 per cent in the par value of the stock to enable the sale to net an amount sufficient to pay the commissions for the seller. For he has paid the amount of $12.50 when he bought the stock and will have to pay the same amount when he sells it. Any

advance over the sum of $25 on each 100 shares represents the profit of the member. From this it is usual to deduct the interest on the money invested during the time the stock is held and advanced to the customer by the broker.

The second rate is for members of the exchange who purchase securities for other members of the exchange, but who do not give the name of the member for whom they act. The commission for this business is fixed at one-thirty-second of 1 per cent, or about $3.12 for each 100 shares. When, however, the member gives up the name of a principal who is also a fellow broker of the exchange, the rate is one-fiftieth of 1 per cent or a charge of $2 for the purchase or sale of 100 shares.

23. *Two-dollar brokers.* – At first glance it would seem strange that any member should take the trouble to execute the orders of other members. There are, however, a number of brokers who do not care for a business involving a large number of accounts, negotiations with customers and the maintenance of an expensive establishment, but who would rather execute the floor business for other brokers who have a large clientele. These "two-dollar brokers," of whom there are about two hundred and fifty, must do a large volume of business in order to make any considerable profit. They rely upon the efficiency and speed in which they can execute orders for the continuance of their trade and become very proficient in carrying out commissions. Their services are especially sought after during rush times.

24. *Room traders.* – There is another large class which does not come into direct contact with the public, and in fact, cares little or nothing about its business, except in so far as it affects the stock quotations. These are called "room traders." These brokers are sometimes called professionals. They do not buy or sell for others, but trade on their own account, making their profit out of their speculations rather than out of their services for others. "Room traders" do not try to make large profits on any transactions. They only expect a very small profit on each share and rely upon the volume of their transactions to give them their income. Being on the floor of the exchange at all times and not having to rely upon the mechanical devices to convey information concerning the movement of prices, which in rush times are several minutes behind the actual happenings upon the floor of the exchange, they are able to take advantage of every slight fluctuation, selling upon the slightest upward movement and

buying again when prices begin to sag. They usually specialize on a few stocks which they study closely so as to guard against being caught in any general movement of prices. Most of them endeavor to balance up each day's business at the end, carrying over very little stock to the next day. That is to say, they endeavor to have their purchases and sales nearly equal so that in the final settlement very little cash is required.

25. *Specialists.* – The third class of members who do not come into direct contact with the public are the "specialists." This class is made up of those brokers who make a specialty of a few selected securities. In some cases brokers confine their entire operations to one security, although usually three or four are carried. To this they give continuous and expert attention. In most cases the business of these brokers comes from the execution of orders given to them by other brokers.

LONDON AND NEW YORK AS FINANCIAL CENTRES[1]

E. L. Stewart Patterson

Since the beginning of the present European war there has been a great deal of discussion in the financial papers and elsewhere as to the effect of the war on London's position as the financial center of the world and the probability of New York succeeding in assuming and keeping the position. It is, of course, natural that the serious interruption in shipping, commerce and exchange throughout the world would minimize for the time being London's supremacy, especially when the stupendous task of financing not only Great Britain's munition requirements but those of her Allies devolves upon her.

There is no question that at the end of the war, New York's position as an exchange and financial center will be vastly enhanced but not necessarily at the expense of London. Sovereigns and dollars are the only two important mediums of exchange that have been at all reliable since the war commenced and this will no doubt put both of these exchanges immeasurably ahead of the exchange of any other country at the end of the war.

The Reasons for London's Supremacy

London has been for centuries the commercial clearing house of the world. This is due not only to its central situation, its immense foreign trade and its large mercantile navy, but also because, through its highly perfected banking system, it provides facilities of such magnitude and of such entire efficiency for the final settlement of exchange operations, that drawers or negotiators of bills in every quarter of the globe gave preference to sterling over any other form of exchange. It has been estimated that nearly 90 per cent of all letters of credit issued throughout the

[1] [*Annals of the American Academy of Political and Social Science* 68 (1916), November: 264–77.]

world were, prior to the war, drawn in English money. Lloyd George, in commenting on the unique and commanding position of Great Britain in international trade and the consequent serious responsibility placed upon her at the outbreak of the war, said in November, 1914:

> We had not merely our own business to run; we were an essential part of the machinery that ran the whole international trade of the world. We provided the capital to raise the produce; we carried half the produce, not merely of our own country, but of the whole world. More, we provided also the capital that moved that produce from one part of the world to another, not merely for ourselves, but for other countries.
>
> I ask anyone to pick up just one little bit of paper, one bill of exchange, to find out what we are doing. Take the cotton trade of the world. The cotton is moved first of all from the plantations, say, to the Mississippi, then it is moved down to New Orleans; then it is moved from there either to Germany or Great Britain or elsewhere. Every movement there is represented by a paper signed either here in London or Manchester or Liverpool; one signature practically is responsible for the whole of those transactions. Not merely that, but when the United States of America bought silk or tea in China the payment was made through London. By means of these documents accepted in London, New York paid for the tea that was bought from China. We were transacting far more than the whole of our own business; we were transacting half the business of the world as well by means of these paper transactions. What is also important to establish is this: that the paper which was issued from London has become part of the currency of commerce throughout the world.

In considering the possibility of New York being a successful rival for supremacy as the exchange and financial center of the world, we can do no better than review some of the principal reasons why London has hitherto held that position and, it will be realized that New York must duplicate these conditions in great part if not in entirety before London can be dethroned. These reasons and conditions can be tabulated briefly under three headings, physical, psychological and economic, those coming under the first heading are of course unalterable, under the second heading can be remedied in time through education and training and under the third heading are matters of legislation and custom.

I. Physical Conditions Favourable to London

London is situated on the threshold of Europe in the heart of the world's commercial activities, directly opposite the estuary of the Scheldt and nearly opposite that of the Rhine and is within a short distance of every important exchange center in the world with the exception of New York. This alone may be considered as an in superable obstacle to New York's ambition.

London has the advantage of ice and fog free water lanes to every large port in the world with the exception of New York; the climate is equable and liquids and perishable goods run little or no danger of freezing in winter.

The restricted insular area of Great Britain, a little larger than the state of Minnesota, is also an important factor, as it not only affords an immense seaboard compared with its size, but concentrates the population. A frequent and rapid transit service makes Great Britain practically one large city with London as the business center. Every bank in the country has a branch or correspondent in London, carries its reserves there and clears direct with every part of the country through its London agent. The economy of resources effected by this natural concentration of funds is seldom realized and is worthy of study. The insular position of London renders it comparatively free from the danger of invasion and seizure by a hostile power and this immunity has been a factor in making London a world depository.

The geographical situation of Great Britain, coupled with her willingness to invest money in international utilities, has placed her in a unique position as regards mail and cable facilities. Through her immense mercantile navy London has direct communication by fast steamers with every important port in the world and consequently acts as a foreign mail clearing house for all other countries. If French, German or Dutch steamers afford a faster service to any point they can be utilized with little or no loss of time.

As Great Britain owns and operates two-thirds of the submarine cable mileage of the world, it is natural that London should be a great cable center with practically direct communication the world over. This service is now supplemented by a far flung system of wireless stations. Furthermore, under normal conditions, every main railroad on the continent of Europe gives its best service and equipment to its London mail train. The Trans-Siberian Railway already gives access by rail to the Pacific and it is only a question of time to the establishment of through connections with India, China and South Africa.

In dealing in foreign exchange and stocks London is the center of the world as regards time. She knows the conditions in eastern markets before they close and is open long enough to operate in New York before her own markets close. Her position is therefore pivotal as regards time and distance. Time is the essence of an exchange transaction, a day's delay may turn a profit into a loss and, granting that New York has the means and enterprise to create an efficient steamship and cable service in due course, how can she eliminate the more serious handicap of distance by water from all other financial centers?

II. Psychological Conditions

Perhaps a better heading than this would have been national characteristics. Great Britain is a land of slowly acquired fortunes and the banker and merchant there are content with small profits and slow returns. They have long realized the fact that trade follows the loan and have therefore been willing to invest money in foreign countries with no prospect of recovering immediate returns or large profits, and the financing of these loans abroad has been an important factor in making the London money market so supreme. It is doubtful if the American is adapted temperamentally for operations of this kind or for the small profits of the exchange operations connected therewith. The United States has still a vast area in proportion to its population, its natural resources are not yet fully developed and it is a country of large and rapidly acquired fortunes. It will, therefore, be many years before the investors and entrepreneurs are forced to direct their attention to foreign fields. Great Britain, before the war, invested over a billion dollars annually in foreign enterprises and at the beginning of the war had between twenty and thirty billions so invested. The United States at the same time was a debtor nation for over six billion dollars, and allowing that some two billions of this amount has been paid off or absorbed in the past two years of the war she will still have to invest nearly twenty-five billion before she is on an equal footing with Great Britain in this connection.

The average family of Great Britain is large compared with that of the United States and there is little room and few opportunities at home for the younger sons. This class man the army, the navy and the mercantile marine and go abroad as clerks, etc., to foreign and colonial banks and commercial houses, the more venturesome, as soon as they acquire experience, carry British trade and prestige to new and undeveloped countries, – British subjects are found everywhere, no matter how remote the place.

The young American, on the other hand, has so many oppor tunities at home that there is little inducement to venture abroad except for pleasure. He is probably the only son of the family and takes up his father's business or is assisted in setting up in business for himself. If he does go abroad, he is not content with a subordinate position, but wants to be his own master and strike out for himself. Preferably he goes back home to do this. We might instance the experience of the International Banking Corporation, a state bank, chartered in Connecticut with foreign branches chiefly in the Orient. This bank, though an American institution, is manned principally by Englishmen. It will be interesting to watch the personnel of the staff of foreign branches of the national banks established under the Federal Reserve Act.

Sectional Jealousies in the United States

To be a world center of finance it is essential that a city must in the first place. be the unquestioned financial center of its own country. London is indisputably recognized as the financial center not only of Great Britain but of the British Empire. No local jealousy is evinced by Birmingham, Liverpool, Glasgow or other large cities as to London's supremacy in this regard. New York is the principal financial center of the United States, but it is not the only financial center. Chicago, St. Louis, San Francisco and other important centers are strong competitors with New York for domestic business and to a certain extent for foreign business. Aside from sectional jealousy, the vast area of the United States makes this competition inevitable. Will these cities abandon selfish motives and aid New York in her ambition? Will not the expansion of the country's foreign trade accentuate rather than diminish this competition? Chicago and Minneapolis will share in the development of the great Canadian West, San Francisco will become more and more important with the extention of business with the Orient and New Orleans will benefit by the opening of the Panama Canal and the expansion of trade with South America. The United States is not a country but a collection of countries or commonwealths of which New York State is only one. The tendency is to minimize New York's financial supremacy rather than to assist it. A study of the discussions on this feature preceding the passing of the present Federal Reserve Act will bear out this statement.

It is not a question of the ability and enterprise of the American, but one of his overcoming the handicaps of temperament, environment and tradition and we might add prejudice and suspicion as the world has not yet forgotten the frequent and serious crises in American financial history.

Mr. Hartley Withers in his excellent book, *The Meaning of Money*, puts the case succinctly as follows:

> It is a cherished ambition among Americans to see New York some day established as the monetary center of the universe, and with their vast natural resources and population there is no doubt that the United States can achieve any material tasks that they choose, if they can learn the necessary lessons and develop the necessary character. At present the characteristics of the typical American businessman seem to fit him to do most things better than banking. His haste to grow rich, his eager enthusiasm and buoyant optimism followed by plunges into apprehension and depression, his quickness and versatility, his keen sensibilities, his craving for speculative excitement, and his genius in exaggeration – all these qualities make him an excellent producer, a first-rate distributor, a miraculous advertiser, an unapproachable gambler, and a somewhat questionable banker. There are hundreds of good bankers in the United States, who take a scientific interest in the problems of their business such as is comparatively rare among their English brethren. But they are developed in spite of their environment, and of the atmosphere of eager enterprise which makes it difficult to observe the humdrum laws and limitations of banking.

London's supremacy is the cumulative result of numerous forces, political as well as economic, spread over a long series of years during which time the world has learned to think in terms of British money and the bills of exchange on London have been raised almost to the dignity of an international currency, while the safety of the Bank of England and the value attached to the word "sterling" have become proverbial. Sovereigns and to a great extent Bank of England notes pass current the world over without recourse to money changers. The dollar and the dollar bill must be made equally well-known and acceptable.

The Influence of Custom and Tradition

It must not be overlooked that, when an international business is so long established and well centralized as the money market of London, the world will continue to use it as a matter of convenience rrespective of the possibly superior facilities of New York. The financial roads to London are well defined by much travel, and business tradition will favor the old stand; it is human nature the world over to follow the cow track across a pasture no matter how oblique its direction.

One of the main foundations upon which London's position rests is the world's estimation of its credit. This credit is tried and sound, backed by great resources, and has been reared upon the trust and confidence in the honorable tradition of British business ethics and it is unlikely that the world will have cause to revise its opinion after the war is over. In a recent article in the *London Bankers' Magazine* a writer (Mr. Benjamin White) says in part:

> As to what will be the credit of the British Empire among the nations of the world after the war, there is no reason to imagine that it will be diminished. The burden of financing our great allied nations has fallen upon her shoulders. The bonds of trade between the Allies will be forged closer, and it will be done in Great Britain's workshops. If the British nation were effete and decadent, there might be some reason to fear that hands which tried in vain to snatch the trident from its grasp might rob it of its financial crown. But the fact that four to five million of the Birtish race have flown to arms voluntarily in order to defend their heritage gives to such an insinuation the lie direct. The British race is still virile and the world will not be discouraged from leaving its balances in London when it reflects that London's sons have shed their blood willingly in Flanders to maintain the honor and credit of British plighted word. British banking will not attract less confidence abroad

when it is found that the shock of the greatest war the world has ever seen has not disturbed its equilibrium. A liner in foreign ports flying the British flag will be none the less welcome because the British navy will have crushed a revival of piracy upon the main, and by so doing will have secured the freedom of the seas to all peaceful traders.

III. Economic Factors

The principal economic factors which tend to enhance London's position as a financial center may be considered under the following heads:

Free Gold Market
Liquid Discount Market
Stability of Money Rates
Immense Mercantile Navy
Great Foreign Export and Import Trade
Tariff
Excellent Banking System at Home and Abroad
The Numerous Branches of Foreign and Colonial Banks Established in London
Freedom from Panics and Financial Disturbance
Free Navigation Laws
Marine Insurance, etc., and reliable Ship Registration

London a Free Gold Market

Of the four great exchange centers of the world, London, New York, Paris and Berlin, London is the only one that can always be depended upon to meet every legitimate trade demand for gold, which means that there is no delay or premium entailed in realizing gold on a bill expressed in English money. It is payable in pounds sterling which represent a definite and immutable weight of fine gold. Great Britain adopted the gold standard unequivocally in 1816, over one hundred years ago, and has not departed from it since, even to the extent of charging a fractional premium on gold or by restricting its export by legal or sentimental embargoes. Even war conditions did not deprive the Englishman of the privilege of converting Bank of England notes into gold and, if he were willing to take the risk of shipping it, he could pay a debt in Europe or America without let or hindrance. Hon. Walter Runciman, President of the British

Board of Trade in speaking recently of Britain's trade and financial power said:

> It never has been necessary for us to prohibit the export of gold. We are prepared to meet our liabilities on a free gold basis. Since August 1914 Great Britain has exported £13,850,624 gold bullion and coin in the *ordinary course of business,* in addition to large sums exported by the Bank of England for Government account, and no individual is prevented from meeting his liabilities abroad in this way if he prefers to settle by bullion transactions.

Even in normal times other nations have not assumed this position. The Bank of France always reserves the right to pay in either gold or silver so that in times of stress it could charge a premium on gold. The Imperial Bank of Germany though theoretically obliged to pay gold makes it very uncomfortable for any bank or customer who has the temerity to demand gold for export purposes. Both France and Germany, since the war, have abandoned any attempt to maintain a gold basis.

New York, though generally willing to part with gold for export purposes, was – at least up to the establishment of the Federal Reserve system – handicapped by the lack of machinery for the efficient and economical mobilization, and control of the gold reserves of the country.

England is not only committed to an undeviating policy to maintain a free gold market but enjoys peculiar advantages in this connection. Great Britain is not oniy the largest creditor nation of the world but also controls and supplies, within the British Empire, nearly two-thirds of the raw gold output of the world and has the control automatically, independent of any exchange movements, of over $350,000,000 newly mined gold each year. Owing to this natural gold income Great Britain has been able to maintain her position as a free gold market during the whole period of the war and its bank notes and treasury notes have been and still are redeemable in gold at the Bank of England on presentation.

It is true that since the war London's activities as an international gold market have been curtailed owing to the disturbances in trade routes and difficulty and risks of ocean transportation, but, so important is the certainty of the English monetary standard and financial policy to the merchants and brokers of the world, that it is unlikely that the war will cause more than a temporary recourse to other methods of settling international obligations.

Also a Liquid Discount Market

The natural complement of a free gold market is a liquid money market capable of absorbing bills of exchange to an almost unlimited amount. This unique feature of the London market makes a first-class bill of exchange on London as acceptable as gold. The strength and broadness of the London market, apart from the natural resources of the country, lie in the ebb and flow of foreign capital through the machinery of the branches of foreign and colonial banks established there.

Although London does not particularly encourage the es tablishment of foreign banks, it, on the other hand, does nothing to restrict the movement and allows freedom in banking privileges to all corners of good standing. This broadminded policy though it perhaps affects to a certain extent the individual interests of some of the British banks is recognized as of great importance to London and the country in general, and therefore indirectly to the banks themselves. These branches of foreign banks, with their network of correspondents throughout the world, in addition to their direct influence on the exchange situation, give invaluable assistance to the Bank of England in preserving the equilibrium of the money market.

The policy of New York in connection with foreign banks is just the reverse of that of London and is apparently based on a local and narrow point of view. New York bankers have always discouraged the establishment of foreign banks in their midst and have evoked state legislation and other means to this end. A few foreign banks are represented by agents, not by branches, they cannot take deposits or discount commercial paper and their activities are practically restricted to making call loans and dealing in foreign exchange.

The London discount rates are controlled by a central institution, the Bank of England, and changes in the rate are not only infrequent but seldom rise above 6 per cent. By this control of the money market through the bank rate as it is called, the Bank of England has been able to attract gold to London by raising the rate whenever the exigencies of commerce and the exchange situation require it.

Reference has already been made to the ability and willingness of Great Britain to invest its large surplus income in foreign and colonial securities and thus provide foreign countries with the means of paying for British merchandise and machinery. The movement of such investments forms a large part of the so-called invisible exports and imports and is necessarily an important factor in creating exchange and adjusting international balances.

The Mercantile Navy and Tariff

The absence of a tariff in Great Britain except on a few specific articles is of great importance, as not only do foreign goods find a ready market, but it permits British merchants and others to import goods into Great Britain free of duty and export them at their convenience. London and the other important seaports of Great Britain correspond to the freight yards at railway centers, cargoes consisting of goods of every description pour into these ports from all parts of the world and are there sorted into mixed cargoes to be despatched to various countries. In other words London also acts as a clearing house for cargoes.

The United States is so irrevocably committed to a high tariff that it is unlikely that any appreciable modification will be possible for some time to come, though this obstacle in New York's path might be removed in great measure by the establishment of free ports.

Large amounts of British capital have been invested in the establishment of British banks in her colonies and in foreign countries with head offices in London, and these render invaluable assistance in the operation and preservation of British foreign trade and commerce.

Great Britain possesses a mercantile navy second to none in the world. This not only means an immense toll on the world's commerce in the way of freight, etc., but also enables Great Britain to govern to a great extent the destination of cargoes. Incidentally, with her large ship owning, Great Britain is naturally interested in marine insurance, and owing to the excellent standing of her insurance companies does an immense business in foreign marine insurance. Lloyds, an association of English underwriters of marine insurance, collects and distributes by cable reliable maritime intelligence through its agencies established in every part of the globe; it also issues Lloyds Register, giving the rating, etc., of every British and foreign ship.

British navigation and shipping laws are liberal. A foreign ship is in the same position as a British ship with regard to British trade, and foreign ships engaged in the coasting trade are not subjected to higher port rates than British ships (141 Custom Law Consolidation Act 1876). British law affords equitable protection to both British and foreign seamen, but avoids emasculating the service by undue paternalism.

The navigation laws of the United States have always been a serious handicap to her shipping business and the recently passed La Follette's Seamen's Law will still further embarrass the unfortunate American ship owner.

England's Enormous Foreign Trade

Under normal conditions Great Britain has an immense export and import trade with every part of the world. This great commerce is not only of material benefit to the country generally but the constant flow of inward and outward remittances forms an invaluable nucleus for London's foreign exchange operations, and bills of exchange can be bought and sold in London drawn on any place in the world, no matter how remote. For the year ending December 31, 1913, the imports of Great Britain were £768,734,739 against exports of £634,820,326 representing shipments from and to every country of the world. At the end of 1915, excluding certain goods belonging to the British and allied governments, the figures for which are not available, the exports were £483,444,459 against imports of £853,756,279 a shrinkage of about 23 per cent. It is evident that Great Britain is still able to maintain the bulk of her export trade notwithstanding war conditions and the shortage of bottoms.

Great Britain has a fully developed banking system, eminently adapted to the requirements of her international trade and finance, which has been ably and successfully conducted through a long series of years by highly trained bankers, in whose judgment and conservatism the British public have every confidence. Consequently the country is practically immune from panics and other financial disturbances. The banking laws are simple and impose no unwise restrictions as to legal reserves, etc., leaving such questions to the individual judgment of the banks themselves. Experience has shown that good banking is obtained not so much by good laws as by good bankers.

We have now reviewed briefly the principal reasons to which London owes her financial supremacy and though the events of the past two years have brought New York into a position of financial eminence and power, it remains to be seen how much of this power has been thrust upon her temporarily and how much she has acquired permanently at the expense of London.

New York's Present Dominance Temporary

Since the war commenced the United States has gradually changed from a debtor to a creditor nation, principally owing to the fact that vast exports of munitions, etc., have been made to belligerent countries, thus creating an abnormal trade balance in her favor. With this shifting of international balances, large amounts of gold have been received from debtor nations, a considerable volume of American securities held abroad have been absorbed by the New York market and large loans made to the belligerent nations, as well as to Canada and other countries of the American continents.

Owing to the position of the United States as a wealthy neutrai nation, far removed from the scene of conflict, a wide demand has also developed for dollar exchange and dollar credits, not only in the United States but in foreign countries. In other words, the abnormal conditions induced by the war called upon New York to take the position of international bankers heretofore played almost exclusively by London. This role was assumed by New York, not so much of her own volition as by force of circumstances. Will these war time opportunities, when peace is declared, be sufficient to retain for New York the position which London with all her advantages took centuries to acquire? Before New York can do this to any great extent the United States must learn to think internationally and not provincially. It must increase its foreign trade tremendously and revise its navigation and alien labour laws and its tariff, all with a due regard to the comity of nations; sound per manent banking and currency systems, removed from legislative tinkering must also be established, and finally foreign banks should be encouraged to establish branches in New York and other centers without unnecessary restrictions as to the business they may under take.

One of the leading banks in New York, the Mechanics & Metals National Bank, has expressed itself as follows in a recent monthly letter:

Today, to be sure, there is more trade passing in and out of the harbor of New York than in and out of any other port of the world. Before the war, the trade here was less than that of either London, Hamburg or Liverpool. But more than 60 per cent of New York's present trade is with four countries of Europe, and a great deal of it is due to the purchase of war material for the Allies. This is a state of affairs that cannot be enduring, or even if enduring, that is not designed to shift away from London its historic supremacy among the world's money markets.

In order permanently to fix a new place for ourselves, we must become really a world trade center. Time will show whether we are sufficiently developed for that. To ship to world markets and cultivate them permanently for our manufacturers and merchants, we must become lenders of wealth on a big scale. One of the most familiar axioms of international trade is that commerce will flow where capital flows; one reason for European supremacy in oversea trade has been the tremendous outside investments made by England and France, and more recently by Germany. Our people are not yet educated to loan money abroad in large quantities; in spite of our apparently large loans in the past eighteen months we cannot yet be called in a true sense an international loan market. For example, at the present time, London, with a high interest rate, is unable to attract our gold, while we with comparatively low rates are receiving from London more than we want.

Abnormal conditions have for the present destroyed the power of interest rates to direct the flow of gold, but were we an international loan market on a scale demanded, we would energetically seek a way to overcome those conditions. Eventually the normal laws of economics will again assert themselves and then will come a fairer test of our position. If then we can meet the situation in a big way, and conduct our affairs in a manner in keeping with a world outlook, it ought to be possible for Wall Street at least to share with Lombard Street the financial premiership of the world, and the responsibilities that go with it.

In conclusion, I am of the opinion that the financial center of the world will always remain in Europe, if only for geographical and national reasons, but there is need and room for another strong financial center in addition to London and it would always be desirable that such an alternative center should not be located in Europe, as the present European crisis has amply demonstrated.

New York is already the financial center of the new world; she should strengthen and broaden her claim to this position and, as a coadjutor, relieve and assist London in her great responsibility as the world center. In the reconstruction that must follow the close of the war Great Britain and the United States will undoubtedly play a great part and London and New York will find it more and more necessary to cooperate in the performance of their several functions. London is ready now. When the time comes will New York be equally prepared and able to do her share?

New York will doubtless benefit permanently from the advantages and experience gained during the war. Great Britain will profit also from the intimate intercourse with France, Italy and Russia, likely to result from the war which will undoubtedly tend to reestablish, if not strengthen London in her former position. Great Britain has financed her Allies generously through the war and will not only have these large amounts refunded to her in due course but will receive collateral advantages which should more than offset the business lost to New York.

The conditions, however, that will obtain after the war are too much a matter of conjecture at the present stage of the conflict to warrant an opinion of any value. No one knows how or when the war will end and the whole world, including the United States, may yet be involved.

THE CORPORATION, A PRELIMINARY SKETCH[1]

William H. Walker

1. *Scope of corporation finance.* – Corporation finance, as distinguished from other branches of finance, relates to the methods and policies involved in securing capital and managing the finances of incorporated business enterprises. A simple example will serve to illustrate the scope of the subject.

When an individual desires to extend his business more rapidly than his earnings or means will permit, he can do so by borrowing or by taking in a moneyed partner, who will thereafter share with him the risk, management and profits of the business.

If these partners later desire to extend their activities beyond their own resources, they may do so by borrowing, or by admitting other new partners who will bring in additional capital, and who, like the original partners, will share the risk, management and income of the enterprise. But there are, generally speaking, rather definite limits to the expansion of partnerships thru the admission of new members. Each partner participates in the management and assumes full secondary liability for the debts of the concern beyond his own share, thereby guaranteeing creditors against the incompetence or dishonesty of his associates. Furthermore, the life of a partnership is limited by the life of each individual partner and by the terms of the partnership agreement. New partners cannot be admitted or old one dropped without unanimous consent. Under such conditions men will not freely invest capital. Obviously, if the business under discussion expands further, some form of organization other than the partnership will be required to interest new capital.

[1] [Chapter 1 of *Corporation Finance*, New York: Alexander Hamilton Institute, 1917.]

The next expansion will call for incorporating the enterprise under a charter from the state. Here for the first time corporation finance enters this business. The new association is a corporation and the right to participate in the control, risk, income and assets of the business is called capital stock. The members are stockholders, with rights in the company proportioned to their respective holdings. To obtain capital for the company by the sale of stock, or by borrowing, involves corporation finance. The management of the business is now delegated by the stockholders to a hoard of directors, and, with the proper legal sanction, the capital of the enterprise may be indefinitely expanded by the sale of new shares whenever funds are needed and investors can be found to buy them.

In changing the form of the business from individual ownership to partnership, and from partnership to corporation, no change has been made in the methods of buying, producing, selling, shipping, billing or collecting for goods or services sold. The form of association does not affect the manner of conducting these fundamental financial operations involved in production and distribution, and corporation finance does not deal with them, except incidentally.

But it should he noted that the methods of raising additional capital are entirely changed in converting the enterprise from a partnership to a corporation. Partners are associated personally on a basis of mutual confidence; stockholders may be entire strangers, not acquainted with the business, and it takes great skill to interest them to the extent of investing capital in it.

To finance an enterprise means to provide the capital necessary to begin and maintain its operations. Corporation finance, therefore, relates only to the assembling of capital thru the sale of corporate securities – stocks, bonds and notes – and to matters of financial policy affecting the distribution of control, risk and income among the holders of such securities.

2. *Nature of a corporation.* – One hundred years ago, Chief Justice Marshall of the United States Supreme Court, defined a corporation as "an artificial being, invisible, intangible, and existing only in contemplation of law." This definition conveys the essential fact that a corporation is not a natural person, but a separate legal entity, to which the law assigns a perpetual or continuous existence, independent of the lives of the persons composing it. The stockholders, in their collective capacity,

compose the corporation, but it is governed by duly appointed directors and officers. The company, as an artificial person, cannot exist or act, except thru human agency, and, like natural persons, must be held responsible for wrongful acts and omissions. The law therefore holds its officers, directors and stockholders responsible for the misdeeds of the corporation and visits upon them appropriate punishment for corporate offenses.

The charter is the birth certificate of the corporation; and the corporation ceases to exist when ever the charter is annulled or abandoned. Since the corporation is not a natural person, it has no natural rights and privileges but only such as are specifically extended to it by law and charter or may be reasonably implied from them. The charter is a grant from a sovereign legislature, obtained by special enactment or by appropriate procedure under general laws.

Altho the corporation is an old institution, its extensive use is modern, over nine-tenths of the corporate activities of the United States having been initiated since the Civil War and fully half of them in the past fifteen or eighteen years. Obviously, it must possess great administrative and financial advantages to receive such general adoption.

Within the memory of our older citizens, means of communication and transportation were crude and expensive, and nearly all enterprise was local in character. The investment of capital, production and distribution of goods, and the extension of credit were local and personal affairs, man to man, friend to friend. Competition, accordingly, was local and not over severe, and margins of profit were higher than now.

With the vast development of railroads, telegraph lines, telephone and steamship lines following the Civil War, conditions were changed. Following the lead of the great railways and a few great industrial concerns, larger business units were formed to conduct interstate trade and to outsell the smaller local concerns. This was the result of cheap communication and transportation, together with the possibility of financing and managing large aggregations of capital thru the corporate form. Economies of large scale production and distribution, with the resulting interstate competition, soon reduced profits to a point that drove many of the smaller concerns out of business or forced them in time to combine or enlarge under the corporate form.

The passing of the small localized business marked the death of the partnership as the principal form of association and ushered in the age of the corporation. Business now demands the large capital that may be secured only by a wide distribution of ownership, together with expert centralized management, and these the corporation affords. The development of corporations has been so rapid in recent times that the science of corporate finance and management is always several years in advance of the law and the courts.

3. *Formation of corporations.* – To form a corporation, stock subscriptions are first taken on lists provided for that purpose, after which a few of the subscribers, acting as incorporators, draw up a request that the state grant a charter to the proposed corporation. This is known as an "application for charter," or a "certificate of incorporation," and must show the name of the proposed corporation, the location of its principal office, the nature of its business, and other essential facts regarding it, followed by the signatures and addresses of the incorporators. Usually, a list of stockholders and the number of shares subscribed by each is included. When this certificate has been filed for examination in accordance with law, and the application granted by the proper state authority, it becomes the charter of the corporation. Each state, thru general corporation laws, prescribes in detail the method of forming the corporation, extent of its powers, and the rights of stockholders, directors and creditors. Upon receiving the charter, the stockholders meet for the purpose of adopting by laws, electing directors, and otherwise perfecting the internal organization of the company, which is then ready to do business. Unpaid subscriptions are called by directors as rapidly as funds are needed, or as provided in the subscription lists.

The real difficulty arises in securing adequate capital and this is the work of the promoter, or financier. If corporations could do business without capital, all of us would be great corporation executives – for a time. Any good lawyer can take care of these formal details of incorporation and organization, but to depend upon him further for business and financial advice is no more sensible than taking a broken leg to the dentist.

4. *The lawyer in corporation finance.*– Candor compels the statement, based upon the grievous experience and careful observations of business men, that lawyers give notably unsound

financial advice. Corporation law is a far different thing from corporation finance. There are, of course, some well informed financial lawyers, found mainly in the very large cities, but ninety-nine lawyers in a hundred have given no study to finance, and matters of financial expediency are outside their realm.

If this appears hard on the profession, it is nevertheless true and is a self-inflicted fault. The writer can cite many cases of business failure due to the financial advice of lawyers, and yet the victims would never have thought for a moment of reversing the process and seeking legal advice from a financial expert. The fault lies as much with the business man who seeks such advice in the wrong place as with the lawyer who thinks he has learned finance by studying law. Of course, our reader, if he be a lawyer, will understand that he is the one out of a hundred, above referred to, who gives sound financial advice.

5. *Powers of the corporation.* – The corporation receives limited powers from the constitution and laws of the state and from its charter, including the power to engage in a certain line of business, to contract, sue and be sued, borrow, and own certain kinds of property. Unlike an individual, who has general power to do anything not prohibited by law and custom, the corporation is restricted to powers specifically granted or reasonably implied.

A corporation does not extend, except by courtesy, beyond the jurisdiction of the state which chartered it. A New York corporation, for instance, cannot own property or conduct a branch in Pennsylvania, unless the latter state chooses to extend these privileges. Outside the state of its creation, it is called a foreign corporation. Foreign corporations, by the comity existing between states, are recognized in every state of the Union; in fact, are welcomed because of the business which they bring into the state and the taxes which they pay there.

If corporations exceed their powers, they may be punished by forfeiture of charter, fines, forfeiture of right to sue and recover, or other appropriate penalty. The corporations must abide by the laws of both the state which chartered it and the one in which it does business as a foreign corporation.

6. *Capital stock.* – The stockholders of a corporation are its owners, subject, of course, to the claims of creditors for advances to the company. A share of stock is one of many equal parts of, or divisions of interest in, the corporation, and the interests of

various stockholders are in proportion to the number of shares owned. Stock certificates are issued as evidence of the ownership of the stock itself. The earnings of the corporation available for distribution are paid to the stockholders in the form of dividends upon the stock. These may be at the rate of so many dollars a share or a percentage of par value; thus, if the par value of a share is one hundred dollars, the dividend may be either five per cent on par or five dollars a share.

Par value is the price which the original subscriber is supposed to have paid, in cash or property, for the share. It has no necessary relation, as we shall see later, to the actual value of the share or the actual amount paid for it. It is usual for all shares of the same issue to possess the same par value. The par value of the stock of the corporation is limited by the state at the time of charter and is called the authorized capitalization. The authorized capitalization may be increased from time to time with permission from the state, so that new securities may be sold to obtain additional capital.

Capital stock may be of different classes, so that some holders are preferred over others in the extent of risk assumed, control granted, or priority of dividends. Stock with any such preference is called preferred stock, and all other issues are called common stock. It is customary to limit the return upon preferred stock to a certain rate, usually six or seven per cent, in exchange for the preference which it enjoys in the distribution of assets, earnings and voting powers.

7. *Management* of *the corporation*. – Altho the stockholders are the owners of the corporation, they are not its managers, this being one of the essential differences between a partnership and a corporation. Management of the corporation is vested in a board of directors, and in certain officers chosen by the board or the stockholders. The officers and directors are limited in the exercise of their duties by the provisions of by-laws which the stockholders have enacted. The individual stockholder, acting alone, has no power whatever in the management. Acting together, however, stockholders may, in meetings duly assembled and formally conducted, direct or control the management in important matters of policy, such as the material enlargement of the business, issue of new securities, mortgaging of assets, sale of capital assets, merger, dissolution, receivership, etc. Outside such formal meetings, in which each stockholder may vote directly or

by proxy proportion to his interest, the stockholders have no power in management. Even in meeting assembled, their power is limited to the election of directors and to voting upon certain important policies which vitally affect their interests.

8. *Right of stockholders to dividends.* – Dividends represent the division of corporate earnings among stockholders. They are the only means, aside from fraud or manipulation, by which the earnings of the company may reach its owners. We shall see later that the dividend policy of a corporation is an important element in its financial management.

Stockholders have no rights to dividends until they have been declared by the directors, and directors have no right to declare dividends unless they have been actually earned. To pay dividends otherwise than out of net earnings impairs the capital of the company and is unlawful unless the stockholders vote to reduce the capital or dissolve the company. Stockholders have a right to know, and directors are under obligation to insist that the paid-in capital of the company be kept intact so as not to impair the stockholders' investment.

Even tho dividends have been earned, the stockholders cannot compel the directors to declare or pay them unless they can prove to a court that there has been fraud, oppression or gross mismanagement in the affairs of the company, by reason of which dividends are being improperly withheld. The courts are loath to interfere in the management of corporations and will not extend relief to stockholders unless it is clear that every other remedy has been exhausted. This rule often seems harsh, but it is for the best interests of all concerned.

9. *Right of stockholders to information.* – Theoretically stockholders have the right to examine the affairs of their company and for this purpose to employ counsel to assist in the examination of the general hooks. This right is supposed to exist where a stockholder has good reason to suspect fraud, oppression, or flagrant mismanagement, and is supposed to be respected by the corporation when the exercise of the right will not interfere materially with the running of the business nor open the affairs of the company to the scrutiny of competitors.

As a matter of fact, however, the right of inspection does not exist in practice. It is clearly impossible for large corporations to open their books to the inspection of stockholders. To do so would involve unnecessary inconvenience and place their affairs as an open book before competitors, who could easily gain access by the purchase of a few shares of stock. Companies uniformly refuse requests of this kind, and the courts protect them by demanding very clear circumstantial evidence of fraud, oppression or mismanagement before ordering such a disclosure of corporate affairs.

As a matter of policy, most companies submit periodic reports to the stockholders, containing more or less satisfactory information. It is proper to add that the management seldom accuses itself of any thing but hard work and good results in such reports.

10. *Negotiability of shares.* – A partnership is founded upon mutual consent and confidence. Interests in a partnership are therefore not transferable, except by unanimous consent. Stockholders of corporations, however, do not have or require a choice of associates, since they are liable for corporate debts only to the extent of their investment and have individually no voice in management. Stock may therefore be sold and transferred, or pledged to secure debt, at the will of the stockholder. Such transfers are facilitated by the fact that the stockholder's liability is limited to his investment.

Since the ownership of stock is evidenced by registration in the name of the owner upon the books of the company, and by the issue of certificates, a transfer must usually be recorded upon the books before the new owner has any right to vote or to receive dividends. The registered owner possesses these rights, and any adjustment of dividends upon the sale of stock is ordinarily made by adding accrued dividends, at the established rate, to the selling price of the stock.

In practice, shares are delivered by merely handing over the certificate, with the power of attorney upon the back signed in blank by the former owner, authorizing the holder to register the shares upon the books of the company in the name of the new owner. This new owner's name need not be designated until the certificate is actually surrendered and a new certificate taken out. The burden rests upon the purchaser to record his shares properly upon the books of the company. By means of this signed blank, power of attorney certificates may be bought and sold without formal written assignment, and passed freely on delivery, thus facilitating transactions and minimizing expense. Stock certificates are not technically negotiable instruments in the sense that commercial paper is negotiable, since mere delivery of the certificate, with power of attorney properly signed, does not complete the delivery of the stock. The transfer must be recorded on the company books before it is complete, in order that the company may know who is entitled to vote and receive dividends on its stock. Nevertheless, stock is readily negotiable, that is, it may be easily transferred from one owner to another. Negotiability must not he confused with marketability, as stock is often not salable at any price.

The case of issuing and transferring corporate shares in small amounts makes them a favorite form of investment and enables corporations to draw funds from many thousands of small and scattered investors. Large organized markets for trading in shares have naturally grown up to supply the demands of investors, the chief of these being the London and New York Stock Exchanges, Paris Bourse, and other exchanges of similar type. Thousands of banking and brokerage houses are engaged in the business of buying and selling stocks and bonds, a business which depends entirely for existence upon the great utility, convenience and popularity of corporate stock as a form of investment

11. *Powers of directors and officers.* – It must not be supposed that officers and directors are unrestricted in their powers of management. Legally speaking, they are the agents of the stockholders in the management, but not subject to detailed interference on the part of stockholders. Directors are usually elected annually by the stockholders, who may thus exert control by removing incompetent or distasteful directors from office.

The directors in turn usually choose the officers, who hold office during the pleasure of the directors. Both directors and officers are subject to the provisions of the by-laws, and, in certain leading matters, to the direction of stockholders, upon formal resolution in meeting assembled. The by-laws govern the internal organization and distribution of authority. They are usually subject to change by the stockholders upon some majority vote, such as two-thirds of all shares outstanding, or some other proportion.

The directors have individually no powers of management, but possess full access to the affairs of the company. To be binding, all acts of directors require formal resolution in meeting duly assembled, unless the board has delegated authority in certain matters to individual directors. In this manner, by resolution properly recorded, the directors may, but seldom do, regulate the actions of officers to the minutest detail. Directors meet periodically, and also hold special meetings to transact important business and determine matters of policy, leaving the officers in charge of all details.

The officers, as paid servants of the company, are not responsible for losses arising from ordinary business mistakes, so long as they exhibit integrity, good faith and reasonable care in the affairs of the company. The directors, who are usually not paid for their services, are bound only to exert ordinary diligence and prudence in directing the company.

Both officers and directors, however, may become individually responsible to stockholders or creditors for fraud, gross negligence, or exceeding their authority. Officers are usually directors, and their knowledge of the affairs of the corporation frequently enables them to dominate the board. From the financial viewpoint, this fact is important, and the reader is asked to note carefully that the control of corporations is customarily pyramided into the hands of the directors and officers, the board of directors controlling the policy of the company, and the administrative officers dominating the board.

12. *Advantages of the corporation.* – By this time, it must be clear what the business and financial advantages of the corporation are. The principal ones may be summarized as:

(a) Perpetual existence, without regard to the lives of stockholders. If a stockholder dies, his interest merely passes to his descendants, and the corporation continues without interruption.
(b) Limited liability of stockholders, making it unnecessary for them to choose their associates or to participate directly in the management.
(c) Transferability of interest, creating a broad market for corporate shares.
(d) Divisibility of interest, making it possible for stockholders to have large or small interests in the corporation, divided according to their means or desires, including wide distribution of shares among absentee owners, and making possible large aggregations of capital under centralized management.
(e) Delegated and centralized management by directors and officers representing stockholders in the aggregate, relieving individual owners from the cares of administration and the risks of partnership association.

Other advantages of the corporate form might be mentioned, but the above will suffice here.

13. *Disadvantages of the Corporation.* – Certain disadvantages of the corporate form, most of them of small importance, may also be mentioned:

(a) Lower credit, due to the limited liability of stockholders. California affords an interesting exception, for in that state, stockholders are liable to creditors beyond their investment in the capital stock.
(b) Limited powers. Corporations possess only the powers granted to them by law, while individuals and partnerships possess all except those prohibited by law.
(c) Unusual expenses, such as charter fees, various special forms of taxes upon domestic and foreign corporation, taxation of corporate stocks and bonds, etc. The partnership and trusteeship escape some of these forms of taxation.
(d) Government regulation. The Federal and state governments closely regulate the activities of corporations, and require frequent reports of their condition and business. This regulation is best typified by the control of the Interstate Commerce Commission over railroads, and of the Federal Reserve Commission over industrial companies.

14. Is *there a substitute for the corporation?* – The increasing taxation and regulation of corporations by the Federal and state governments, imposing in some instances burdens that are almost prohibitive, have stimulated renewed interest in an old and recognized form, the business trust, under which certain parties, known as trustees, are vested with the legal title and management of property for the benefit of others, described by the law as beneficiaries or cestuis que trustent. Certain flexibility of interest is obtained by issuing negotiable certificates of beneficial interest, divided into equal units, somewhat similar in effect to certificates of capital stock. These certificates refer to the trust agreement under which the trustees are acting and set out the principal rights of holders and the extent of their interest in the enterprise.

This form of association has reached its greatest development in Massachusetts, and is variously designated as the Massachusetts Trust, Expressed Trust Business Trust, etc. Its weakness lies in the fact that certificate holders cannot control the trustees to the extent that stockholders control their directors. The trustees, once elected, are not agents of the certificate holders, but act independently as legal owners of the property. The courts recognize the business trust as an attempt to dodge the liabilities of the corporate form, and whenever the trust agreement subjects the trustee to any considerable control by beneficiaries, the courts are likely to construe it as a partnership agreement, with the certificate holders as partners and the so called "trustees" as their agents. These decisions have tended to limit the use of the trust as an instrument of business and make it doubtful whether the business trust will ever supersede the corporation on any large scale. Of course, it lies within the power of the state to declare such business trusts illegal, or to subject them to the same taxation and control as corporations. It would be very difficult, however, to prohibit or restrict them by law without hampering the use of the trust form for other necessary and desirable purposes.

15. *Corporate combinations.* – One company may own the stock of another, and if a large proportion is owned the latter is termed a subsidiary company. If the subsidiary company grew naturally out of the extension of the business, the original corporation is termed the parent company. If a company is formed principally for the purpose of acquiring the of two or more other companies, it is known as a holding company, because its purpose is merely to effect a combination by holding and voting the stock of these companies.

Corporate combinations may he effected by a holding company, or by one company acquiring the stock of another, or by trustees acquiring voting control in the stocks of several companies. Of course, a physical merger of assets may be effected, and the former competing units done away with altogether by one company purchasing outright the assets of competitors, who thereupon dissolve and cease to exist as separate companies; or by dissolving the competing companies and placing their assets in charge of trustees, whose certificates of beneficial interest are issued to former security holders in exchange for their stocks and bonds. Pools, such as were prevalent among railroads in the seventies, or the leasing of competing properties, may also secure like results of combination.

It should be noted, however, that a corporation can not become a partner in any enterprise, as that would partly subject its assets to the control of other partners outside the company, who have not been elected by stockholders. This would be a departure from the principle of agency, under which the directors, and directors only, manage corporate property and affairs in the interests of stockholders.

THE CAPITAL OF THE CORPORATION[1]

William H. Walker

1. *Care in the use of terms.* – In considering corporation finance it is necessary at the outset, to learn its language and to distinguish carefully certain terms relating to capital and capitalization, particularly the following:

Capital
Capital Funds
Capital Investment
Capital Assets
Capitalization
Capital Stock
Authorized Capital
Outstanding Capital

The first four of these expressions refer to capital, the last four to capitalization.

The capital of a corporation consists of its assets. Land, buildings, machinery, stock, cash, patents, and all other forms of property owned by the company constitute its capital. Throwing aside fine economic distinctions, we may state that, for practical purposes, the value of assets is determined either by their earning power or by the price which they will bring in the market. The market price in turn is itself determined mainly by earning power, since investors purchase securities for the dividends which they will bring, after making due allowance for depreciation, risk, etc. Productive efficiency, or earning ability, is therefore the prime test of the value of assets. In fact, the actual capital is seldom accurately known, altho it may be closely approximated by modern accounting methods.

[1] [Chapter 2 of *Corporation Finance*, New York: Alexander Hamilton Institute, 1917.]

2. *Capital investment.* – Taken literally, the words capital investment apparently refer to the actual original cost of the assets of the company, the total amount invested in the business from every source. Since the assets fluctuate constantly in value, they are likely to be worth at any given time more or less than their original cost, and accordingly the capital investment and the capital have no fixed relation, except at the time the investment is originally made. If a new company gets its money's worth, its capital in the beginning should equal the capital investment.

A less accurate, but more commonly used, definition refers to capital investment as the total amount received from the sale of the corporate securities. This definition eliminates the investment of new capital out of the profits of the business itself, on the theory that profits do not belong to the stockholder until they have been declared in the form of dividends and that the investment consists only of contribution which security holders have made from outside sources. It is, of course, apparent that an increase of capital out of earnings changes neither the capitalization nor the investment. On the other hand, the payment of unearned dividends reduces both assets and investment without affecting the extent of capitalization.

In this text, we shall use the more popular definition, and refer to capital investment as the actual amount received by the company from the sale of its securities. Funds thus secured are known as *capital funds,* because they are invested permanently in the business and have been secured by increasing the outstanding capitalization.

3. *Capital and current assets.* – The capital of a concern consists partly of assets which are fixed or essential to the business, known as *capital assets,* and partly in assets of a current nature, employed from day to day in conducting the business, but no particular part of which is essential to its continuance. These latter are known as current assets. Some companies, such as steel mills, have a greater percentage of capital assets, whereas others, such as wholesale groceries, have a greater percentage of current as sets. Both together equal the capital of the concern.

Land, buildings, machinery and other similar items not regularly bought and sold by the company are capital assets. Raw and finished stock, cash, accounts receivable, etc., are current assets. Current assets are not a part of the plant.

4. *Capitalization.* – The word "capitalization" is one of the most misused expressions incorporation finance, in addition to capital stock, corporations issue other securities known as notes and bonds. Capital secured from the sale of stock is called owned capital, whereas capital secured from the sale of stocks and bonds is called loaned or borrowed capital. The ownership, control, management and risk of the enterprise is divided in various proportions among these securities. The term "capitalization" refers to the amount and character of the securities and should be distinguished carefully from the key word "capital," which relates to the *assets* of the company and not to its *securities*.

Capitalization is of two kinds – quantitative and qualitative:

Quantitative. The capitalization is the total par value of the outstanding stock, bonds and long term notes of the company. Trade credit, bank loans, and other current indebtedness are not included.

Qualitative. Capitalization is the plan of distribution of the control, risk and income of the business among the various security holders. This definition relates to the kind of securities, and not to the amount; whereas the first definition relates to the amount of securities, and not to the kind. To avoid confusion, we shall refer to this qualitative definition as the plan of capitalization.

5. *Authorized and outstanding capital.* – Legal theory does not always harmonize with financial fact. Out of this discrepancy grow many terms in common usage that are not justified by accurate definition. The term "authorized capital" is one of these. By this term is really meant "authorized capitalization." The state, in chartering a company, limits the number of shares or the par value of the shares which the company may issue, and this limit is known as "authorized capital." The state fixes no limit on the value of the company's assets, but merely on the par value of the stock, and it is therefore capitalization and not capital that is authorized.

The outstanding capitalization of the company consists of the total par value of all its outstanding securities, regardless of their real value, or the amount authorized to be issued. The "authorized capital" does not include bonds. Every company has the inherent right to borrow for the purpose of conducting its business without authority in the charter, and bonds are issued under this general borrowing power.

Thus, we say that the United States Steel company has an authorized capitalization of $550,000,000 common and $530,000,000 preferred stock. But its actual outstanding capitalization includes also $304,000,000 in bonds.

6. *Kinds of corporate capital.* – The corporate capital, somewhat in the order of its bonding value, may be classified as follows:

(1) Land.
(2) Buildings.
(3) Equipment.
(4) Securities owned and necessary to the business.
(5) Securities and other unattached or outlying properties not necessary to the business.
(6) Raw material and supplies.
(7) Work process.
(8) Finished product.
(9) Bills and accounts receivable.
(10) Cash.
(11) Good will, including secret processes, patents, copyrights, and trade-names.

While all forms of corporate assets are supposed to be productive, as otherwise the corporation would not have acquired them, nevertheless they represent different degrees of productiveness and risk. Many forms of assets cannot be converted readily into cash, except at great sacrifice. Second hand machinery, for instance, is often difficult to sell, altho it may be of great value to a running business. Capital tied up in unproductive assets or in forms not easily convertible into cash is naturally not good security for loans. Such assets, therefore, must be provided by the sale of capital stock, which absorbs the risk of corporate ventures, while bondholders provide funds to purchase the more staple and productive assets. This fact lies at the basis of every scheme of capitalization and renders necessary the close analysis of each enterprise before attempting to finance it.

7. *Compensating the owner of capital.* – We have already defined capitalization as the method of distributing control, risk and income among security holders. Those who contribute capital to a corporation must be paid for its use. Corporations are formed to conduct business for profit, and these profits

appear in the form of dividends upon stock or interest upon bonds and notes. But the element of risk is ever present in corporate enterprise, and for assuming it the security owner demands more than mere interest for the use of his capital. This additional charge may be designated as "premium for the assumption of risk."

On the other hand, there are special advantages to be had from participating in the management or control of certain corporations, aside from the dividends or interest received. Directors of banks and insurance companies, or of large industrial and railway corporations, for instance, feel that the prestige of their position is worth something apart from the direct earnings upon their investments. How, then, shall the owners of this capital be compensated for its use?

There are four elements which enter into this question, and the answer involves the entire plan of capitalization. These elements are:

(1) Control
(2) Management
(3) Risk
(4) Income

These elements must be so arranged in the scheme of capitalization as to compensate the investor for:

(1) Use of his capital
(2) Risk of losing it

Let us examine what value each of these factors possesses for the various classes of investors.

8. *How control is acquired.* – By control we mean the power to direct the policy of the company. Control is exercised thru the voting power of security owners, and to some extent, in the case of bonds, thru the power to foreclose in the event of default. Obviously, the chief advantage of control lies in the ability to prevent loss thru the mismanagement or manipulation of others. Actual control requires a majority voting power, tho, as we shall see, this does not necessarily require the ownership of a majority of the outstanding stock. Voting power may be extended to certain classes of securities and withheld from others, or it may

be contingent upon a certain event. Preferred stock, for instance, may be given a vote if dividends are not paid, but not permitted a vote when dividends are paid regularly. It often happens that even a minority of the voting stock may control, as when the shares are divided among a great many smallholders, many of whom do not exercise the voting privilege. This leaves the few larger interests in control; altho having merely enough votes to carry a poorly attended election. Control may also be secured thru the voting trust, in which stockholders transfer their voting priveleges to trustees, or by gathering proxies from other stockholders.

9. *Relation of controlling and minority interests.* – A voice in the control is an important consideration to security-holders who desire to lessen, or in some extent to govern, the risks of their investment. Sometimes, however, control is bought purely for the purpose of manipulating corporate affairs, or gaining prestige or some other outside advantage. Such a control is always a dangerous one for the corporation and for the minority interests, for it affords a strong temptation and a splendid opportunity of profiting personally at the expense of the company. This has been frequently demonstrated in the railroad field, where certain large stockholders of railroad companies, having become directors thru their voting power, have used their positions to secure preferential contracts from the roads for concerns in which they are interested, for the underwriting of securities, or for the purchase of equipment. Excessive profits have been made at the expense of the railroad which they were supposed to represent. The practice became so general that a clause was inserted in the Clayton Act to stop it by subjecting such contracts to open competition, under the supervision of the Interstate Commerce Commission.

Sometimes the controlling interests, while seeking no individual advantage, endeavor to secure preferences for their own classes of securities at the expense of other securities. In this ease it is plain that it is important for the other security-holders to have a voice in the management, which will enable them to upset any such preferences and to insure a square deal to themselves. Ordinarily, extending a voice in the control to a certain class of security is intended merely to lessen the risk of that security, or to offset the natural risk which surrounds it. Common stockholders usually control the corporation, because they have given preferences in liens or income to bond holders and preferred stockholders. The further application of the principle of control will be left until later chapters. It is sufficient here to point out that control is a factor of great importance in the financial plan.

10. *Element of risk.* – Every business and every security possesses an element of risk. Indeed, one cannot own wealth without assuming the risk of losing it in one way or another. United States government bonds are considered so safe that they are sold upon approximately a three per cent basis, and yet only sixty years ago six per cent bonds of the United States government could be purchased at 40 per cent par.

In the field of business thousands of failures occur annually, ranging from that of the large corporation with many millions of dollars invested, to that of small companies, partnerships and individual enterprises. The statement has often been made, and is probably true, that nine out of every ten corporations within ten years from the date of formation are either dissolved, failed, reorganized, or swallowed up by other companies. Very few companies survive a period of twenty-five years without financial difficulty. Railroad securities are the most substantial issues in the United States, and yet over half the railroad mileage of the country has been under receivership and reorganization within the past fifteen years. No wonder the owner of common stock lies awake nights.

A substantial percentage of all new corporations practically fail before they get under way, owing to faulty or fraudulent promotion. In many cases, the promoter very generously pockets the entire capital in exchange for a patent which he has purchased for little or nothing. One promoter was heard to remark that the investor always got his money's worth, but that he usually got it in experience. This is undoubtedly true, and it is also true that experience is the most costly school in the world. It is a very important financial fact, too, that very few people are smart enough to learn from the experience of others. If this were not true, there would be neither so many worthless promotions nor such a large number of "lambs" constantly led to the slaughter. Fatherly advice has never played a large part in corporation finance. The average man dies just about the time his experience has become valuable. The new generation then begins all over again, without analyzing the experience of their predecessors or profiting much from it.

11. *Payment for risk-taking.* – Such are the risks of business, and for assuming this risk, the investor must be paid. Therefore, loaned capital demands not only an interest rate for its use, but also an added rate to compensate for the risk assumed. The rate paid for the use of the capital may be called the true interest rate. It averages perhaps between 3.5 and 4 per cent in this country. The balance of the interest paid upon bonds, and of dividends paid upon preferred stock above the true interest rate, represents the compensation to the owners of those securities for assuming the risk of investing in them. The only reason why some securities sell below the true interest rate is that they are limited in amount and are prescribed by law for certain purposes, such as the investment of trust funds, the circulating privilege upon two per cent government bonds, etc. The fact that bondholders and other holders of preferred security receive anything for the risk of their investment shows how hazardous the common stock must be, for it stands legally between them and disaster.

12. *Management and income.* – Management must be differentiated from control. Certain stockholders owning a majority interest may control a corporation, and yet not manage it. The management is usually vested in a certain few chosen officials who are satisfactory to the controlling interests, but who themselves may not possess the actual control of the business. The manager has a double inducement for investing in the company. First, it secures him an income as manager, and secondly, it enables him to watch his investment and guard it intelligently.

Since, however, only a very limited number may be managers, the influence of this factor upon the plan of securing capital is very slight in the aggregate. Usually control, risk and income are mentioned as the factors which determine the financial plan, and management is omitted entirely.

Income is the chief purpose of investment and is received in the form of dividends or interest. These will be treated at length in succeeding chapters.

13. *Capital for new enterprises.* – In discussing how capital is obtained for corporate enterprises one must consider not only the various forms in which capital can be raised and the various persons from whom the capital can be secured, but also the stage of development of the enterprise. The latter will to a considerable extent determine the means by which money can be obtained, as well as the persons to whom an appeal can profitably be made.

When an enterprise is wholly new and is not formed to take over some existing concern, capital is obtained usually in the form of cash and by the issue of common stock. The enterprise being new and its earning capacity untested, it involves a large element of risk, which all who participate must be willing to share. In such cases the capital stock is usually subscribed in small amounts by a relatively large number of persons.
The conditions under which preferred stock can be issued do not obtain in such case. On the one hand, investors have no guarantee that the dividends on the preferred stock will be paid. On the other hand, the subscribers to time common stock cannot afford to promise a definite return to the holders of other stock when the whole issue of time enterprise is so problematical.

14. *Incorporating existing enterprises.* – As a matter of fact, few corporations outside of the banking business and a few other limited fields start as absolutely new ventures. More commonly the corporation is formed to take over an existing concern. When this is done the past record of the enterprise which is absorbed in the new corporation gives a basis upon which a distinction can be made between common and preferred stock.

In this case cash subscriptions are apt to be only a part of the total contribution to the capital stock, the remainder consisting of the assets of the concern which is being taken over by the new corporation. Under the conditions which have been described, the two forms of stock are frequently employed. There is not as a rule an opportunity to secure capital by the issue of bonds. In the case of holding companies, the new bonds or stocks are given in exchange for the securities of the constituent companies.

15. *Extending the capital of an existing corporation.* – It is when a corporation is already in existence and desires to extend its operations that the most interesting problems of corporation finance arise. The ways of raising capital are varied, the sources from which capital can be drawn are numerous. As a going concern, the corporation can avail itself of the same means and sources of capital supply as are open to similar concerns organized on the basis of individual proprietorship or partnership, and can adopt other methods and draw upon other sources by virtue of its corporate form. But as all of these means and sources play an important part in the financing of corporations, it is well to make the statement comprehensive. In order that the reader may gain a clear idea of how capital is raised by

an existing corporation and of who furnishes it, the diagram on page 36 is presented.

In the left-hand column are noted the various means of securing capital; in the right-hand column are given the principal persons or classes of persons who furnish it. The connecting lines show the persons from whom capital can be obtained by each method here noted.

Of the five methods here named, the first four. it will be plainly recognized, are not peculiar to the corporation, and might be equally applicable to a partnership. The fifth group, the issue of securities, is a very broad one. Were it not that the chart would be too confused it would be well to consider the sale of bonds and long-term notes, the sale of preferred stock, and the sale of common stock as three separate and distinct methods.

If attention is directed to the right-hand column, it will be noted again that the sources of capital supply numbered from 1

METHODS OF RAISING CAPITAL AND SOURCES OF SUPPLY

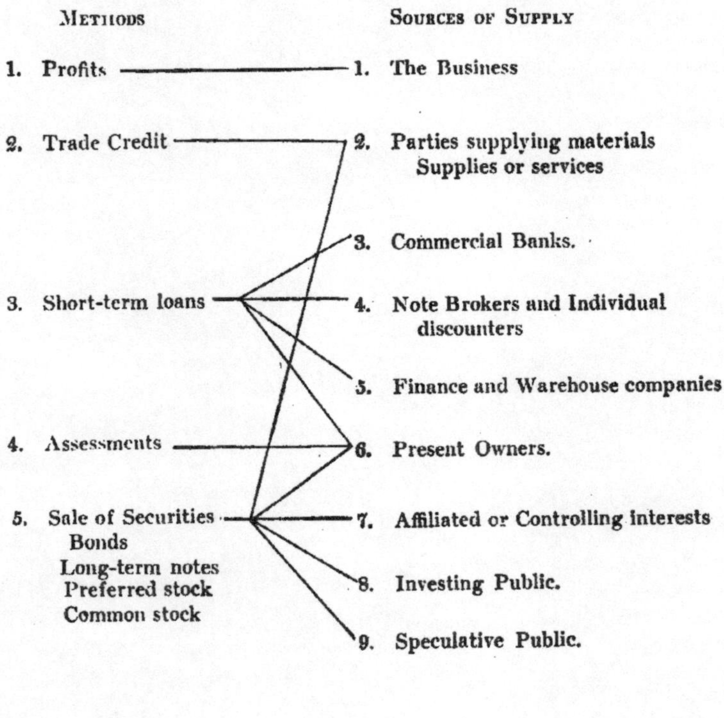

to 6 are, in the main, open to a business organized as a partnership as well as to a corporation. The single qualification of this general statement is found in the fact that concerns with which the corporation has dealings may, thru the purchase of securities, contribute to the capital of the company.

16. *Fixed and working capital.* – It will be noted, further, that in the main the corporation can acquire working or fluid capital by the same means and from the same sources as the partnership. It differs from the partnership in its acquisition of fixed or permanent capital. While the partnership can draw for such purposes only on the resources of the partners, the corporation can enlist the capital of any one who will purchase the securities it issues.

The foregoing summary of how capital is obtained by the corporation is intended merely as a sketch. The detailed consideration of the different methods of raising corporate capital and the circumstances under which each applies will form the subject matter of succeeding chapters.

CAPITAL STOCK[1]

William H. Walker

1. *Stock and non-stock corporations.* – Capital stock has already been defined as the vested interest which the owners of a corporation have in the company. A share is merely one of the equal parts of the capital stock. The share-owners are the owners of the corporation; in fact, in their collective capacity the shareholders are the corporation, since it can have no existence without them. Most corporations are stock corporations.

Another form of corporation, also composed of individuals associated under a charter from the state, is known as a non-stock corporation, because the interests of the associates are not represented by transferable shares. The interested parties in this case are called members, instead of stockholders. Non-stock corporations are formed for public or mutual benefit, and not for private gain. Contributions are in the form of donations, from which profits are not expected or received. Churches, universities, Young Men's Christian Associations, charitable and cemetery associations, institutions for promulgating art and civic improvement, mutual benefits, etc., are familiar types of non-stock corporations. Altho an interesting volume could probably he written upon the methods of raising funds for these worthy purposes, such associations cannot be classed as business companies and their methods of raising funds do not be long to the subject of corporation finance.

2. *Subscriptions to capital stock.* – It is usually desirable, and frequently necessary, that some provision for securing the capital of the corporation be made before the charter is taken out. And yet the corporation itself, until the charter is received, has no existence and no power to contract for capital. This situation is met by employing subscription lists, which may be used either before or after the charter is received.

[1] [Chapter 3 of *Corporation Finance*, New York: Alexander Hamilton Institute, 1917.]

A subscription to capital stock may be, in effect, a mere promise to take stock after the corporation is chartered, or it may be a contract between the corporation and the subscriber, or between the subscriber and trustees who are acting for the proposed corporation, as the case may be. The laws of some states vest authority in certain state officials to act as trustees in receiving stock subscriptions for the benefit of corporations which are about to be formed. Such subscriptions immediately become as binding as any other contract, because the trustees have legal capacity to contract.

In the case of subscriptions to the stock of corporations not yet formed, when trustees are not acting, the subscriptions take the form of a mere or continuing offer, which cannot be enforced at law until the corporation has received its charter. When the charter is obtained the offer becomes a binding contract between the subscriber and the corporation. Under most state laws the offer is automatically canceled upon the death of the subscriber, or if he becomes insane, and may be canceled by him at any time prior to the incorporation of the company. In view of this regulation, which applies quite generally, it would seem advisable, from the financial standpoint, to secure the charter of the company as soon as possible after the subscription books are opened.

3. *Form of the subscription.* – Lists or books – prepared for the purpose – known as subscription lists, may be used for subscriptions, or the subscriptions may be entered on separate cards for convenient filing.

Altho subscriptions may be taken by telephone or telegraph and are as binding orally as other forms of contract, it is always advisable to have oral subscriptions confirmed by letter, or signature on the prescribed form, in order that indisputable evidence of the subscription may be on file. The subscription should always be signed and show in printing, or preferably in the handwriting of the subscriber, the date and the actual number of shares subscribed for. Oftentimes, the par value of each share and of the entire subscription is inserted, as a check upon the amount subscribed.

The list should also clearly describe the stock issue to which it refers, and briefly the purpose of the corporation. No statement should be with held the omission of which might afterward justify a suspicion of fraud or sharp dealing. If, for instance, the list states that the company is being formed to manufacture automobiles, whereas, in fact, it is chartered to make both automobiles and bicycles, the omission of this fact from the list might enable subscribers to resist effectively the collection of the amount subscribed. Subscriptions cannot be successfully resisted, as a rule, unless they have been obtained by fraud or material misrepresentation on the part of the company or its authorized representative. If the misrepresentation is not of consequence, or is made by one who is not acting authoritatively in receiving subscriptions for the company, or is a mere statement of opinion or a prediction, no court will relieve the subscriber of his contract to take the shares.

4. *Advantages of using several lists.* – When lists are employed, oftentimes a number of them are circulated in order that the proposition may be placed before many prospective subscribers without delay. Even in smaller companies, several lists are some times used, one for large subscribers, another for subscribers of moderate amounts, and still others for smaller subscribers. It would be a mistake to present to a possible subscriber for a large amount a list upon which had been entered a large number of small subscriptions. It would in turn discourage the small subscriber in many cases if a list were presented to him containing a number of very large subscriptions and 110 smaller ones.

It is customary to head each list with the subscription of some well known and highly respected citizen, whose signature will lend confidence to the enterprise and serve to induce others to subscribe. Such men often receive free stock in return for the use of their names on the list. The writer remembers one instance in which a man of broad success in corporation work was given twenty-five hundred dollars' worth of stock merely because he allowed his name to stand at the head of a new subscription list.

5. *Paying for capital stock.* – Sometimes payments upon stock subscriptions must be made before the corporation is actually chartered. The State of Pennsylvania, for instance, before a charter is granted, requires a certificate to the effect that ten per cent of the authorized capitalization has been paid. In this case, funds are deposited in the bank to the credit of some one who acts as trustee for them until the corporation has been chartered and officers duly elected. If payments are made from this fund before the corporation is chartered and authority is granted by the directors, the trustee is liable for the amount personally, unless the corporation subsequently ratifies the expenditures.

Sometimes, the actual requirement of the law is avoided by borrowing funds from the bank, and leaving them there on deposit long enough to file a certificate that ten per cent has been paid in; after that the loan is repaid by checking the funds back to the bank. This, of course, leaves the incorporators responsible, but avoids tying up the cash until required by the corporation. The bank protects itself by making the loan on a demand note to the incorporators, with the verbal agreement that the funds will not be checked out. If a check against the fund should be presented, contrary to the agreement, the bank will at once call the loan and return the check unpaid.

After the corporation has once been chartered, the payments upon stock subscriptions of course go directly into the treasury of the company, and may be paid out only by officers, and for corporate purposes, in the usual manner. Once the corporation is formed, subscribers are liable to the amount of the paid value of the shares they have subscribed for, or, if no par value has been assigned to the shares, as is often the case in New York State, they are liable for the amount they have agreed to pay for the stock, at a stated price per share.

Subscriptions may be paid up at once or by installments, according to the terms of the contract or the calls of the directors, but in any case certificates marked "full paid" cannot be legally issued until the par value, or stated price per share, has been paid to the corporation. The joker in this legal provision appears in the fact that stock need not be paid for in cash, but in most states may be settled for in other property, or in services, at the option of the directors, who assign their own value to such services or property. Obviously, the placing of an exorbitant value upon them has the practical effect of the issuance of shares at less than par, altho marked "fully paid and non-assessable."

6. *Assessable stocks.* – When capital stock has been paid for at par in cash, or in services or property acceptable to the directors, it is known as "fully paid and non-assessable stock," and this information is printed upon the stock certificate.

It sometimes happens, however, that the corporation does not need its new capital all at one time. This is often the case with mining companies, whose capital requirements depend largely upon the unseen and uncertain deposits of nature, and therefore can not be accurately forecasted. The capital required and the time when it will be needed cannot be definitely predicted, and yet the company may desire to have its capital all subscribed in advance to insure against the uncertainties of future financing. If the highest estimates are accepted, the task of financing is correspondingly greater, and, in this case, if the shares are issued fully paid, the company may find that requirements have been overestimated and that it has more capital on hand than it can productively employ.

7. *Embarrassment of excess capital.* – The excess capital probably cannot be invested safely and profitably outside the business, even if power to do so exists. Either the funds must lie idle, thus depressing dividends and encouraging extravagant management, or be returned to the stockholders thru a reduction of capitalization, or be employed in a forced expansion of doubtful expediency. Such a situation is likely to discredit the management, tho it is by no means as serious as a shortage of capital. The second United States Bank failed in 1836 from the attempt to find use for its excessive capital, and a number of modern concerns owe the beginning of their downfall to the same cause. A more chronic difficulty, however, is the shortage of capital. Who ever knew a business man under fifty who was not short of cash?

8. *Difficulties of capital shortage.* – If the lower estimates are adopted and full paid stock issued accordingly, the company may later find itself embarrassed on account of lack of funds with which to complete the undertaking. The failure to provide adequate capital will then reflect unfavorably upon the enterprise and cause distrust of the management. The stockholders cannot legally be called upon to pay more on their full-paid shares and may not be willing either to authorize or to purchase additional stock. Their distrust will naturally spread to outside investors and the banks.

Under such conditions, if additional funds are procured at all, it will probably be on most unfavorable terms, such as will permanently injure the credit of the company and discredit the management. The fear of loss easily stampedes the investment and loan market, even if based upon nothing more serious than the failure of the management to estimate correctly and provide adequate capital in advance.

9. *Remedy found in part-paid stock. – To* provide against such exigencies, part-paid or assessable stock is sometimes issued. A typical certificate of full paid and non-assessable common stock

appears upon the following page. The term "assessable stock" means merely that the stock is issued before its full par or stated value has been paid to the company, part being paid at the time of issue and the balance being payable on stated future dates or upon the call of directors. Certain restrictions may be placed upon these calls, as, for instance, the requirement that the directors shall not call more than ten per cent in any one month, but in any event the stockholder is not liable for more than the par or stated value, and the stock becomes full paid and non-assessable when the par or stated value has been paid. The certificates representing assessable stock are supposed to indicate that fact, and may or may not show the amount paid upon the stock or the amount still subject to call. The full par value of the stock may never be called if not required.

The uncertainty of the demands that. may be made upon stockholders in the future renders assessable stock unpopular with investors. A stockholder may lose his stock entirely thru inability to meet an assessment, or he may hesitate to pay an assessment, fearing that the condition of the company is unsound. If this fear is justified, to pay the assessment may be only to send good money after bad. And yet there is the hope that additional funds may enable the company to survive. What shall he do, pay or refuse to pay? Only a few weeks before this chapter was written, the writer was under the painful necessity of advising a young man who had purchased ten thousand shares of stock at twenty-five cents a share to forfeit his stock rather than meet another assessment of ten cents a share which the directors had just levied. In this case investigation proved that the mining company needed an undertaker instead of additional capital. It should be noted that the predicament of the stockholder would have been about as serious had the company been good, but be unable to find a market for the shares or to raise the funds required to meet the assessment. Those who do not pay such assessments are usually shut out by judicial sale in favor of a syndicate representing those who do pay.

10. *Paying for stock in instalments.* – Assessable stock should not be confused with subscriptions paid by instalment. The investment of capital funds is a gradual process usually, and the corporation does not require all of its subscribed capital at one time. It may take, for instance, two years to construct and place in operation a steel mill, during which time the construction will

COMMON STOCK CERTIFICATE, FULL-PAID

Certificate No. 25
For 20 shares.
Issued to
W. H. Walker,
323 Fourth Ave.,
Pittsburgh, Pa.
Dated December 10, 1912.
From whom Transferred,
Original Issue.
Dated Dec. 10, 1912.

No. Original Certificate	No. Original Shares	No. of Shares Transferred

Received Certificate No. 25
for Twenty Shares this
12th day of Dec., 1912.
W. H. Walker.

No. 25 20 Shares

Incorporated under the Laws of The State of New Jersey

THE DUQUESNE IMPROVEMENT COMPANY

Capital Stock..................$150,000
Common Stock............$100,000
Preferred Stock............$50,000

Full-paid and Non-assessable

THIS IS TO CERTIFY that W. H. Walker is the owner of Twenty Shares of the Capital Stock of The Duquesne Improvement Company transferable only on the books of the Company by the said owner thereof in person or by duly authorized attorney, upon surrender of this Certificate properly endorsed.

{CORPORATE SEAL}

Witness the seal of the Company and the signatures of its duly authorized officers this tenth day of December, 1912.

R. S. JONES, Treasurer.

J. B. SMITH, President.

Shares, $100 each

be paid for as rapidly as completed. Working capital may not be required until the plant begins operation. Nevertheless, stock subscriptions are taken in the beginning for the full capital, with the intention of issuing full-paid and non assessable stock. Obviously, gradual payments upon these subscriptions will not inconvenience the company, while investors may be more easily interested if the stock can be paid for out of their incomes on the instalment plan. This is particularly true of small investors, who are afraid of assessable stock but will buy non-assessable shares on the instalment plan. One instance is recalled in which subscriptions were payable 20 per cent down and 20 per cent every four months.

When payments are arranged on this plan, interest is often allowed on them from the date made until the full subscription is paid and the stock issued, when the regular dividends begin to apply. The better practice, however, is to issue full-paid stock to the extent of each payment as made, the regular dividend rate applying thereon from the date issued, so that the amount of stock issued by the company at all times agrees with the amount received upon subscriptions. When the company desires for some good reason to withhold issuing certificates until subscriptions have been paid in full, interest should be paid at the same rate as the prevailing rate of dividend, if possible; otherwise, at the current rate of interest for short-term notes. The usual reason for withholding the issue of certificates is to support the market for the stock, which might otherwise be broken by a flood of selling offerings interfering with the further collection of subscriptions and the trade credit of the company.

It is becoming more and more the practice of corporations to enlist the interest of their employees in the welfare of the concern by giving them an opportunity to become stockholders. When this is done, subscriptions are usually taken which are payable in small monthly instalments. Interest is allowed on the partial payments, and when the amount subscribed has been fully paid, stock certificates are issued.

11. *Stock notes.* – It appears to be illegal in many jurisdictions for a corporation to accept the note of a subscriber as full or part payment for stock, particularly unless the issue of certificates is withheld until the note has been paid. A note is not payment, but a promise to pay. It can hardly be construed to fulfil the statutory requirement that stock shall not be issued until it is paid for.

If no stock is issued against it, such a note should be entered and considered as a mere accommodation to the company on time part of the subscriber, and not a settlement for stock. The note may in this manner be taken, indorsed and discounted without fear of exceeding corporate powers or violating the law. When it is paid, the accommodation is automatically discharged and stock may be issued.

When such notes are taken in exchange for stock, contrary to the intent of the law, banks with a knowledge of the circumstances should not discount them, for they may prove to be uncollectible. The courts of most states, however, enforce the payment of such notes, and, when stock may be legally issued for property other than cash, the subscriber may apply in payment of subscriptions the notes and bonds of others which he owns, if the directors will accept them. The issuance of stock notes is always of doubtful financial expediency because of the legal difficulties surrounding their use.

12. *Treasury stock.* – It is well at this point to in dictate the difference between certain terms that are often confused. The following terms should be clearly distinguished from one another: (1) Authorized Stock, (2) Issued Stock, (3) Unissued Stock, (4) Treasury Stock, (5) Bonus Stock.

The authorized stock, as already stated, consists of the number of shares, or the total par value of shares, which the company's charter permits it to issue. The issued stock consists of that portion of the authorized capital represented by outstanding certificates. The technical point should be noted that stock which has not been issued may have been paid for. The term, "issued stock," refers to the certificates actually is used, and not to stock subscribed and paid for. But the term, "outstanding stock," more properly applies to the actual amount of stock that has been paid for, whether certificates have been issued or not, since the certificate is not essential to the ownership of the stock. "Unissued stock" is merely that part of time authorized issue not represented by outstanding certificates. Issued stock plus the unissued stock equals the authorized stock. It is customary for paid or outstanding stock to be issued immediately.

Unissued stock is frequently confused with treasury stock. Treasury stock consists of shares which have been paid for and issued by the corporation and have come back into the possession of the company by purchase or gift. In most states companies are permitted to buy their own shares and to receive their own shares in gift. Unissued stock can be sold only by the corporation for its par value in cash, property or services. But treasury stock may be sold at any price, or given away, if desired, since it has already been once legally paid for and issued. Treasury stock, as we shall see, is frequently acquired by the corporation at a nominal price from promoters who have purchased it originally from the company in exchange for greatly overvalued property or services. Having been legally issued in this manner as full-paid stock, and returned to the treasury of the company, such shares are at the disposal of the officers to be given away with bonds or preferred stock, as an inducement to investors.

When stock is given out in this manner, to assist in securing additional capital, it is called bonus stock. Treasury stock need not necessarily be used for the purpose of paying bonuses, but may be sold for cash to secure working capital.

Unissued stock, on the other hand, cannot be legally given away as a bonus. But note how easily the rule is thwarted. The corporation has power to borrow on whatever terms it is able to procure, and therefore, to sell its bonds at any price. All that is necessary, therefore, to legalize the stock bonus is to offer the stock and bonds together at a lump sum, inferring a discount on the bonds equal to the par value of the accompanying stock. In other words, the amount of stock given with the bonds is treated legally not as a bonus, but as a reduction in the selling price of the bonds. For example, if a company desires to market debenture bonds, and is only able to do so by giving a 25 per cent bonus in common stock, it will legally accomplish this by selling to the investor $250 in common stock at par and $1,000 in its debenture bonds at seventy-five, receiving in exchange one thousand dollars in cash. This is really giving unissued stock as a bonus, without receiving payment at par, but the books should show that the discount is upon the bonds and not upon the stock, in order that the law may be satisfied.

13. *Transfer of stock.* – After stock has been subscribed, paid for and certificates of stock issued, the holder may desire to sell it. Enough has been said to indicate the general procedure of transferring stock. The subject is of great legal interest, because of the mass of litigation between conflicting claimants. A few of the principles of law which have emerged from this litigation about the negotiability of shares, bearing directly upon the financial plan of the company, require mention.

It is apparent that the more readily negotiable the shares can be made, the more marketable the stock will become. At the same time, it is necessary to safeguard the issue of certificates and to identify clearly the legal owners of stock for the purpose of voting and receiving dividends. Stock certificates may be lost or stolen, certificates may have been issued for stock fully paid, or several certificates may have been erroneously issued for the same stock. Stock certificates may be forged or counterfeited; in fact, numerous circumstances may arise which make it necessary to have some other and better evidence of stock ownership than the certificate.

In order that stock certificates may be a valuable means of identifying the owner of shares, the law places upon the corporation the burden of issuing and properly recording them. The innocent purchaser of a stock certificate, unless it has been forged, may therefore feel quite certain that the assignment of it places him in position to demand a new certificate in his own name and to have it recorded on the books of the company.

To make this transfer, the original owner of the stock may appear personally and surrender this certificate, authorizing a new certificate to be issued to the new owner, or he may sign a power of attorney, authorizing another whose name is mentioned to appear for him and transfer the stock in like manner. By reason of this signed blank, power of attorney, printed upon the back of the stock certificate, enables any future holder to insert his own name and have the stock transferred to himself on the books, the certificate becomes highly negotiable, passes by delivery, and may be sold, or pledged as collateral upon a loan, without further assignment.

STOCK NOT PAID IN CASH[1]

William H. Walker

1. *Cash payment not the universal rule.* – A careless reading of the incorporation statutes might easily give the impression that the capital stock of a corporation must always be paid in cash. But this is not the case, and a more careful search of the statutes will discover provisions which make it possible to issue stock against property of various kinds, or sometimes serv ices, with the sole qualification that these shall be estimated at their true value. Thus arises a wide variety in the payment of stock subscriptions, some forms of which must be considered.

2. *Paying for assessable stock out of profits.* – A successful concern has issued assessable stock, and has not called for full payment, the withholding of dividends has the practical effect of paying up the stock, since it relieves to that extent the necessity of calling the balance of the payments, and increases the capital of the company as much as tho regular dividends had been declared and an assessment for a similar amount had been made against the stock. From the accounting and legal standpoint, however, this stock is still only partly paid. The earnings with held by the company appear on its books as surplus, and have not reduced the amount still callable on the stock before it becomes fully paid. The surplus may render financial difficulties less likely, and, of course, the credit and stability of the company is enhanced by retaining both the surplus and the additional stock liability of subscribers.

But stockholders desire to avoid the uncertainties of assessable stock, preferring the more marketable and less risky full-paid shares. It is therefore customary, under these circumstances, for the company to declare a special dividend equal to the callable and unpaid portion of the subscriptions, at the same time making an assessment of an equal amount to pay up the shares. Stockholders

[1] [Chapter 4 of *Corporation Finance*, New York: Alexander Hamilton Institute, 1917.]

may then take out full-paid certificates and the amount of the dividend is charged to surplus and credited to capital stock account on the books of the company. The effect of this transaction is to pay for stock out of earnings.

3. *Converting profits into stock.* – In a company which has issued only full-paid and non-assessable shares, upon which regular dividends have been paid, the surplus may be similarly distributed in payment for stock by declaring a special stock dividend, which will likewise transfer the credit from the surplus account to the capital account of the corporation. Each stockholder will then receive a new certificate for additional full-paid shares to the extent of his dividend. Thus, if a stock dividend of 25 per cent is declared, the holder of one hundred shares of the par value of one hundred dollars each, will receive a new full-paid certificate for 25 shares. We shall see later, in the discussion of dividend and capital accounts, the effect of such a transaction upon the balance sheet of the company.

The value of each share of stock outstanding will be decreased about 20 per cent in the above illustration, because there are now 125 shares outstanding against property formerly represented by only 100 shares. But the stockholder may find himself a trifle better off after the stock dividend than before, as the 125 shares will probably have a slightly higher aggregate market value than the 100 shares did before, and the established rate of dividend which he formerly received upon only 100 shares, will now probably be continued on the 125 shares, thus substantially increasing the income and marketability of the stock.

4. *Building up a surplus.* – Paying for stock out of earnings must not be confused with the increase of stock values thru the creation of a surplus. The common stock of the United States Steel Company, for instance, was not paid for directly by its holders out of the earnings of the company, but it has achieved a real value from the accumulation of surplus earnings re-invested in the business. When the stock was issued it represented largely the expectations of future earn ings. By good management and a conservative dividend policy the United States Steel Company has increased its assets until the common stock now rests largely upon tangible values in the business.

5. *Paying for stock with property.* – When stock is paid for with property rather than with cash, the directors may place their own valuation upon the property. If they are bargaining

with an outsider, they will of course give as little stock for the property as the owner is willing to accept. If they or their friends control the property, however, and it is desired to water the stock of the company, that is, to issue it without receiving full money's worth at par, they may do so by assigning an exorbitant value to the property which is exchanged for the stock. The stock will then be issued as full paid, in conformity with law, and may be sold or given away at their pleasure, either by the promoters personally or as treasury stock of the company. This overvaluation of property in exchange for stock effectively nullifies the legal theory that stock cannot be issued unless paid for at par.

Two well-known cases will serve to illustrate the point. When the United States Steel Company was formed in 1901, it entered into a contract with a syndicate, headed by Mr. Morgan, in which it agreed to turn over its securities in exchange for the securities of the ten large steel companies that were to compose the combine and $23,000,000 in cash. Under this agreement, the Steel Company delivered practically its whole authorized capital stock to the par value of $530,000,000 common, $550,000,000 preferred, and also $304,000,000 in bonds, in exchange for $25,000,000 in cash and the securities of ten steel companies. The par value of the United States Steel securities was perhaps double the actual value of the securities taken in exchange. The common stock represented a capitalization of the anticipated economies of combination; in the expectation, since realized, that increased earnings would enable dividends to be paid on a larger capitalization than had been possible under ten separate and competing companies. Here, then, is an instance in which property, consisting of the securities of other companies, was over-valued in order that full-paid and non-assessable stock of the new company might be issued.

The United States Leather Company, formed in 1893, represents a typical voluntary combination. Without much assistance from outside promoters and by agreement between the companies interested, committees were appointed to appraise the holdings of the various concerns. The consolidated company then paid $100 in common and $100 in preferred, par value, for the assets acquired, based upon the appraisals of these committees. In other words, the company paid for the tannery and bark properties with its preferred stock, giving an equal amount of common stock as a bonus. The capitalization thus overvalued its assets two to one.

6. *Effect of issuing stock for overvalued property.* – If the company has not received money's worth at par for its stock, the creditors, in the event of the company's becoming insolvent, may usually recover from stockholders, by proving the fact that the stock was issued for overvalued property or services, making allowance in favor of stockholders, of course, for reasonable differences of opinion as to the value of the property or services received. Only the state, or creditors of the insolvent company, may question the transaction, and the lapse of considerable time does not remove their remedy. In many instances courts have assessed, for the benefit of creditors, shares marked "full-paid and non-assessable." Such cases, however, usually arise in companies of small or moderate size in connection with the attempt of promoters to defraud subscribers or creditors and secure exces sive profits.

7. *Liabilities of directors and rights of subscribers in overvaluation.* – In many states, directors who knowingly issue stock for overvalued property or services may be held accountable to the creditors of the company, if it afterwards becomes insolvent and, in a few states, they may be imprisoned. The modern tendency is to hold directors and officers of corporations personally responsible for all the wrongful acts and omissions of the company. Fining a corporation only results in reducing its profits, thus imposing the punishment upon innocent stockholders. But the imprisonment or fining of officers and directors places the responsibility and punishment for intentional violation of the law where it belongs.

When a subscriber who has paid money's worth for his stock at par, finds that other subscribers have been permitted to pay less, he is entitled to have his subscription canceled and his money returned on the grounds of fraud. But if the subscriber takes his stock and new stock is afterwards sold for overvalued services or property, he has no relief except to prevent by legal means or otherwise the issuance of the new shares. Subsequent issues of stock are frequently put out at a discount, with the consent of stockholders, in order to get much needed additional capital. The innocent holder, who subsequently purchases such stock without knowledge of the circumstances attending its payment, cannot usually be held liable to creditors, since he is entitled to the assumption that the stock which he is purchasing has been legally issued in the first place.

Of course, a contract to buy or sell shares at less than par cannot be enforced, since it is ultra vires on the part of the corporation. If executed on one side, however, the courts will usually compel performance by the other, or a reinstatement of the parties to their original position. Thus, if a subscriber has paid for stock at less than par, under the terms of the contract, and a subsequent officer refuses to issue the certificate, the court will ordinarily compel the company to issue the certificate upon payment of the balance due, or return the money of the subscriber and cancel his subscription.

Since promoters rely mainly upon watered stocks for their compensation, it is evident that a strict enforcement of the rule that stock must be paid for at par, in actual value, would prevent the promotion of many new enterprises.

8. *Intangible property as a basis for watering stock.* – Patents, trade marks, and good-will are personal property. Intangible assets of this nature possess such uncertain values, that directors are safe in issuing almost any amount of stock in exchange for them. Who would undertake to prove, for instance, that the patent processes and good-will of the ten steel companies, whose control was acquired by the United States Steel Company, were worth less than the half billion dollars par value in common stock issued for them? The law permitted the Steel Company to acquire the stock of other companies, and the directors of the Steel Company were under the necessity of fixing a price upon the value of the shares to be acquired. A large part of this value arose from the possession of intangible assets of problematical value.

9. *Capitalization of patent rights.* – No one can tell the value of a patent. A new invention may at any time be superseded, or it may be annulled in court for infringement. The protection which it affords is limited by law to seventeen years, and its value as a patent expires with this protection. The entire value of a patent, if carried as an asset, and oftentimes of the capital investment required to exploit it, disappears when the protection afforded by law ceases.

It is plain that the value of any patent actually depends upon the profit which results to the company from its use or possession. The cost of acquiring, protecting and exploiting the patent are elements influencing its value, and the shorter its period of life the smaller will be the product and the greater will be the unit cost of production. Therefore any time lost in taking advantage of a patent, or time and money lost in establishing its validity, or fighting infringements, materially affects its value as an asset. These factors cannot be foreseen, and no one, therefore, knows the value of a patent.

One of the world's greatest inventors, who has since died, a few years ago patented a device and organized, to exploit it, a company capitalized at $1,500,000, practically all the stock of which was issued to him for the patent. The company then succeeded in borrowing $100,000 working capital from a bank. The only real capital of the concern consisted in the borrowed money, and upon this beginning a small and fairly prosperous business has been erected. And yet in the same city of Pittsburgh, three men of mechanical genius, but limited means, have perfected and patented a similar device, superior in every way to that of the great inventor, but having, as yet, no financial backing. What is the relative value of these two patents?

In the one case a bank, with almost criminal carelessness, loaned $100,000 of its depositors' good money upon the strength of a patent which had not yet demonstrated its success and which is now superseded by a better device. The loan was secured really upon the name of the inventor and the bold front of a prominent attorney. On the other hand, the invention of the three mechanics, altho now several years old and rapidly approaching expiration, has represented nothing but expense and trouble to them, the difficulty being that they, themselves, are unable to produce and market the device and yet are unwilling to sell at a sacrifice price to those who have the adequate capital. No patent, as a rule, can be marketed for a large sum until it has been thoroly demonstrated, and these three gentlemen are not able to invest the capital required to properly demonstrate their invention. As each year elapses, their expense grows greater, and the value of their patent becomes less. The capitalization of patented processes, unseen natural resources and good-will at excessive values is the most ordinary form of "painless dentistry" used to extract safely the savings of the unwary.

Secret processes are even a poorer basis of capitalization than patents. Not only is a process subject to all the risk of a patent, except the time limit of its existence, but it is likely to be divulged and thus lose any special advantage the company had thru its use.

Being secret, investors have no way of judging in advance the value of the process, except by the output, and it may be discovered too late that a process has been capitalized which has never existed, or which is nothing more than a matter of common knowledge in the industry.

10. *Valuation of good-will.* – The good-will which attaches to a trade name is of more definite value than either patents or trade processes, but even here the same inability to measure the value of the good-will is apparent. How is any one to tell whether the success of an established concern has been due to the superior management of certain men connected with it, or whether the good-will attaches to the concern itself? Many cases could be cited in which the withdrawal of a single individual from an established business has resulted in practically wrecking its good-will within two or three years.

One instance is recalled in which an established and successful lithograph company, making annual profits between $40,000 and $60,000, or at the rate of from 20 to 30 per cent upon its capitalization, was practically wrecked in five years by an incompetent new management. And yet the good-will of this business had been capitalized in combination at more than $300,000. Under the old management, never less than 10 per cent had been paid on this inflated capitalization. Under the new, the trade-name was soon dropped and dividends almost ceased. Two questions are of interest here. Was the good-will over valued at $300,000? If not, what salary was the old manager worth, and what salary the new?

The capitalization of intangible assets, such as have been mentioned above, formed the basis of the stock watering operations of the industrial trusts and of the enormous profits which the promoters of those trusts were able to secure. The safest way apparently to overcapitalize a company is to assign an extravagant value to intangible assets which are exchanged for securities. The only test of the value of such assets is found in their probable earning power, and this is so uncertain that rarely can a capitalization based upon it be successfully attacked in the courts.

The matter of a good-will and its place in the balance sheet is still the subject of periodical discussion in Canada. A large industrial company of the Dominion for years carried good-will in its balance sheet at $1,000,000. It then reduced the item to the nominal sum of $1. The company's explanation was as follows:

> "A recent appraisal of the company's properties, made by competent valuators, established their real value at over $2,000,000 in excess of the figures at which they were being carried on the books of the Company; and the directors therefore felt justified in adding $830,304.03 of this excess to property accounts. This, with $169,694.97 transferred from the profit and loss account, enables the company to write down the item of $1,000,000 for good-will, trade marks and patent rights to the nominal figure of $1."

In valuing good-will or other intangible assets of companies, it is noticeable that there is a greater difference in such valuations than is found in the valuation of physical assets. Naturally, allowance must be made for differences of opinion in estimating values.

FINANCIAL MANAGEMENT
1880–1934

Volume 8

Edited and Introduced by
Morgen Witzel

THOEMMES

Financial Management, 1880–1934

Edited and Introduced by **Morgen Witzel**

Volume 1
Twenty Years of Inside Life in Wall Street, or Revelations of the Personal Experiences of a Speculator ... Illustrated (1880)
W. W. Fowler

Volume 2
Trusts, Pools and Corporations (1905)
William Z. Ripley

Volume 3
Corporation Finance (1910)
Edward S. Meade

Volume 4
Corporation Finance. An Exposition of the Principles and Methods governing the Promotion, Organization and Management of Modern Corporations (1909)
William H. Lough

Volume 5
Concentration and Control: A Solution of the Trust Problem in the United States (1914)
Charles R. van Hise

Credit and International Trade: How they Work in Practice (1934)
Barnard Ellinger

Volume 6
Problems in Business Finance (1921)
Edmund E. Lincoln

Volumes 7 and 8
Collected Articles and Chapters

Printed in England by Antony Rowe Ltd, Chippenham

COLLECTED ARTICLES AND CHAPTERS

II

THOEMMES PRESS

This edition published by Thoemmes Press, 2001

Thoemmes Press
11 Great George Street
Bristol BS1 5RR, England

http://www.thoemmes.com

Financial Management, 1880–1934
8 Volumes : ISBN 1 85506 633 5

British Library Cataloguing-in-Publication Data
A CIP record of this title is available from the British Library

Publisher's Note

The Publisher has gone to great lengths to ensure the quality of this reprint but points out that some imperfections in the original book may be apparent.

This book is printed on acid-free paper, sewn, and cased in a durable buckram cloth.

CONTENTS

THE TOMORROW OF FINANCE[1]

S N. Patten

A man to whom I was quoting figures exclaimed: "I cannot think in terms of billions." This inability illustrates a defect in the popular thought. Men educated in a particular industry can think in its terms but they become lost when a national budget is presented. In most cases the situation is even worse for they think only in terms of a family budget. The majority of families have not even risen to this concept but merely spend when they can and seek credit for their deficit. It is no wonder that they become confused when the nation's budget is presented and even with the best intentions make serious mistakes when they undertake to handle government problems. Whether we will or no, the national budget is in terms of billions and solutions of national problems can be found only when a budgetary view of national affairs is adopted. Huge as the railroad problem is by itself, it cannot be settled apart from the other problems of national finance. Nor can we settle the food problem, the fuel problem or the shipping problem without a like reference to the related problems, each represented by its billions in national finance.

This popular confusion of thought is represented by the action of Congress which appropriates 20 billions for war purposes and authorizes only 4 billions of taxes. Revenue measures all have this same defect – a lack of realization of the magnitude of the problems to be faced. It is easy to suggest means of raising 2 billions or even 4 billions of taxes. The proposer thinks he has done his duty by suggesting some small increase of taxation, forgetting that the deficit he leaves unprovided for will disorganize not only public credit but also private enterprise unless it is met in some adequate way. If private enterprise is not to be

[1] [*Annals of the American Academy of Political and Social Science* 76 (1918), March: 257–271]

disorganized capital must be forthcoming regularly. The capital needs of the railroads have been forced upon our attention and must call for consideration under any system of government regulation, control or ownership. The problem of capital is but part of the larger problem of a national budget. Capital can come from two sources – profits or savings. Latterly it has come from profits. In the tomorrow of finance it must come from savings. This is the issue that the railroads – indeed, all industry – must meet.

This brief introduction brings me to the heart of the problem and indicates the way the problems of national finance should be met. Our railroads, our food and our industry are parts of a national budget which we must visualize before any one issue can be adequately faced. The year 1914 was the last year of normal peace conditions. By contrasting the budget of this year with that of 1918 the exigencies of our present situation can be clearly seen.

National Budget

1914	Billions	1918	Billions
Total production	40	Total production	70
Waste	10	Waste	18
Earned income	10	Earned income	16
Surplus	20	Increase of government expenditure	15
Annual increase of capital	2	Increase of currency	3
Annual increase of values	5	Excess of exports over imports from 1914 to 1918	8
Stock	12	Decrease of stock	8
Ground rent	4	Decrease of industrial capital	2
Total bank deposits	18½	Decrease of security values	10
		Government bonds held by banks and other credit institutions	4
		Total bank deposits	26½

The year 1914 was a year of sound prosperity and of it the facts are well known. The basis of my budget is the income of that year which is usually placed at 30 billions. The addition I have made, which is the only unique feature of the table, is an endeavor to estimate the waste of the year. We overestimate the evils of economic stress if we do not show the economy which reduced income imposes. A war budget of 10 billions does not mean a like diminution in national welfare. The reduction of waste eases the situation and prevents acute suffering.

By waste I mean any loss of material which does not result in full production. If the material for three suits of clothes passes into the consumer's hands only as two suits, there is waste. If a hotel buys twice the quantity of food which the consumers get, there is waste. So also is it waste if willing workers can find no employment or if they are prevented from working by unnecessary sickness. Add all these maladjustments together and the sum of annual waste becomes a striking magnitude. It is a modest statement to affirm that the production which does not reach the ultimate consumer plus the failure to produce which known methods could have prevented, amount to one-fourth the real production. Waste is not important in estimating the income of past years. It is significant only as it alters the pressure which a period of national stress imposes. Far more important is the estimate of the annual amount of earned income as contrasted with the surplus enjoyed. Here estimates are widely different, not because the facts are in question, but because of differences in opinion as to where various items should be placed. The ordinary business man reckons the surplus as the amount left when the year's expenses are paid. He thus regards it the same as the annual increase of security values which amount to five or six billions a year. A single taxer assumes it to be the same as the total amount of ground rent which is perhaps 4 billions a year. Capitalists regard their interest as an earned income and professional men likewise count their earning as a payment for their costs.

These estimates I have discarded as expressions of personal feeling which creates a bias in each group in favor of its own form of income. All the confusion about the distribution of wealth is involved in this discussion and all the uncertainty of its results. If the various claims were added they would not tally with the known national income but would greatly exceed it. The general result is the denial of the power of the government to make large expendi tures. Each class wants its share exempted and what is left may suffice to meet the ordinary expenses of government but it is not enough to meet the expenditure of a great war. Can we meet the expenses agreed to by Congress for the year 1918? "No" must be the answer if these class estimates are accepted.

Who has discovered how to raise more than four billions on the basis he accepts? It was impossible to raise the tax rates higher than they were placed, so great was the pressure from many groups each with its own special interests to guard.

The solution is not to accept any of these pleas but to base exemptions on vital needs measured objectively. The real surplus is the difference between the amount produced and that needed to maintain the personal welfare of the population. We now have accurate measures of the demands for food, shelter and clothing. The figures show that they are from $600 to $800 a year, varying with the size of the city in which people live. But this $800 for large cities represents food prices as paid in retail stores. There are profits to someone on these sales and on the house rents repre senting land values. Labor costs would thus be these prices minus the profits of storekeepers and landlords. A fair estimate of labor costs would be about $500 a year per family or $100 a year per person. A sum of 10 billion dollars a year is thus needed to support the population of 1914 at the prices then prevailing. What is not included in these costs is surplus. With it the people buy the comforts and luxuries they enjoy but which they could forego with out physical detriment if a period of national stress demanded the sums thus expended for national purposes. We may therefore assume that in 1914, of the 30 billions of income, 10 billions was needed for the physical welfare of the people and that 20 billions was a surplus which might be diverted to national purposes without a lowering of the standard of life. No such sacrifice of comforts and luxuries has been demanded nor is it likely to be. It, however, represents what Germany is doing and why the German people have held out so long and so well. Such suffering as Germany has had to endure is not the result of the reduction of income which has been demanded but of wrong estimates made at the beginning of the war. The new view of food values was not accepted by the Germans at the beginning of the war. As a result they killed off their livestock too rapidly and could not replace it when they found their shortage was in fats and not in proteins. Such a mistake may be fatal to a blockaded nation like Germany but it does not affect America with its generous supply of all needed commodities. We could feed, clothe and house our people for $100 per person. The rest is surplus on which the nation has a first claim.

Such are the problems of sustenance. The increase of prosperity on which the increase of surplus depends is largely a question of the increase of capital. A conservative estimate of this increase is 2 billion dollars a year. This means that production exceeds consumption by this amount. The sum, however, grows with every improvement in the processes of production or in the utilization of the labor force. These improvements add about 200 million to the surplus each year and show our rate of annual progress. But far different from these estimates are those of the increase of values. The increase of values is the increase of security values determined by the market price of stocks and bonds. Of these prices, our knowledge is fairly complete and indicates an increase of values from 4 to 6 billions a year. The increase of security values is thus more than double the increase of capital as measured in stock and physi cal improvements. This is due to the low rate of interest which gives high security values. We have a nominal rate of interest (4 per cent) in which values are estimated when the real rate is nearer 8 per cent. So long as the two rates are so far apart, the rapid rise of security values is inevitable. The values thus made are not real but estimates based on the rate of interest. We are said to be worth 200 billions but a rise of the interest rate from 4 to 5 per cent would take a quarter from these estimates.

The budget of 1918 represents the conditions of January 1 and is therefore subject to change as the facts of the year become more fully known. The essential difference is due to the rise of prices. Of this, various estimates have been made varying from 60 to 100 per cent. The cost of living has risen 88.5 per cent according to the figures of the Federal Department of Labor. Agricultural produce of practically the same amounts valued at 10 billions in 1914 were valued at 21 billions at the close of 1917. It would seem therefore that an increase of 75 per cent was a conservative estimate and on this basis the money value of the national income would rise from 40 billions in 1914 to 70 billions in 1918. The figures I use for waste do not mean an increase in the amount wasted but in the value of what is wasted. Rises in wages are difficult to estimate as they are different in the various occupations. Unskilled labor has perhaps gained a net advantage through the rapid rise in its rate of payment but skilled labor and the lower range of salaries have gained but little. Between groups as varied as they are it is hard to strike an average. There can, however, be little doubt but that the workers and the salaried groups have as a whole suffered by the change. A rise of 60 per cent is probably an overestimate of the advantage they have received.

On this basis the money value of the national surplus would be about 40 billion dollars of which the government takes 15 billion in taxes and bond issues. This would leave 5 billions still in the hands of producers as extra profits, an estimate which is probably below the actual figures.

Great inroads have also been made in the stock of goods, so great in fact as to change the surplus of 1914 in many cases into a deficit. This shortage we are beginning to feel and will feel more severely as the year progresses. The 12 billions of stock held in 1914 has been reduced to below 4 billions. My estimates are based on these facts. The excess of exports over imports for the three years from 1914 to 1917 inclusive was 8 billion dollars. In return for this we have received about 5 billions of American securities held abroad and 3 billions in cash. As there has been little or no reduction in the amount consumed, the condition of today differs from that of 1914 namely in the reduction of stock. Goods have gone out while securities and gold have flowed in.

In addition to this change there has been an actual loss of industrial capital. The railroads have not kept up their rolling stock, the evil effects of which we now keenly feel. Manufacturers have saved by using their machines and tools for a longer time and thus reduced current expenses at the expense of the future. Many factories have been transformed into military establishments which process reduces the industrial capital. Such a factory must be rated, not as it yields for war purposes, but as it will yield when it is again put to industrial uses. The income of war plants is not national income but a part of the expenses of war.

The loss in security values has also been equally severe. The amount of securities listed on markets are estimated at 40 billions and the average decline in value has been 25 per cent, thus making a loss of 10 billions in values to be added to the loss of 10 billions in goods. The amount of bank deposits were 18 1/2 billions in 1914 and 26 1/2 billions in 1917. This seems a gain but if the rise in values has been 75 per cent the deposits of 1917 would purchase 6 billions less goods than would the deposits of 1914 at the prices which now prevail. These all represent pre-war losses. Our war expenses come under another head. Of the bonds sold at least 4 billions were still in the hands of the banks or related institutions at the beginning of the year. The public have promised to take much of this, thus relieving the pressure on the banks, but it must be done by a contraction of expenditure on their part in the year 1918. It is a deficit weighing on national resources until these promises are fulfilled.

The equilibrium in terms of the budget of 1914 left a surplus of 2 billions for future investment. Given the same disposition to spend in 1918, an increased government expenditure of 15 billions would leave a deficit of 13 billion dollars. A new equilibrium thus demands a decrease of nearly a third in personal expenditure. There is little in the history of the last three years to show that measures thus far devised will produce the desired result. The year 1917 shows no net decrease in personal expenditure. Many have doubtless promised to save in the year 1918 but promises are valueless unless measures are devised to make them effective. Were the situation merely a result of the war, we might regard it abnormal and wait for peace to restore what the war has disturbed. There is, however, much evidence that the situation is the normal outcome of far-reaching changes which were manifest before the war but which have become active forces only under the pressure which the war has created. Had 10 billions of extra funds been demanded at any time in the last ten years, the same crisis in national finance would have occurred. The reason is that there has been a sharp increase in the urgency of consumption due to the cheapening of comforts and luxuries which thus produces an increased desire to spend. At the same time the increased security of salaried incomes has reduced the willingness to save. An annual expenditure in the form of life insurance will give a stability to family life which a real saving fails to secure. We have ceased to be a nation of savers and have become a nation of life insurers. This means security and increased happiness but it does not involve that rapid increase of capital which former methods encouraged. The low birth rate adds to the intensity of present expenditure and is probably its result rather than its cause. But it tends to an equilibrium between expenses and income which shuts out saving. There is still some saving among families whose incomes are under $1,200 a year. The uncertainties of work, of health and of life keep active many of the older economy motives and make an annual surplus a necessity. But if the class whose incomes range from $1,200 to

$4,000 were put in a group by themselves, they would probably owe society more than society owes them. They have ceased to own houses for apartment life suits them better. They own automobiles, but they are in debt for them. They may go to high priced theaters less but they patronize motion pictures more. They are well housed, well clothed and enjoy summer vacations, but all these add to the urgency of present expenditure and leave less room for the saving by which capital is increased. If we add to this the rapid increase in display advertising and the growth of department stores we com plete the picture of the growing power of expenditure over the saving instinct.

These facts are not war facts but a statement of tendencies clearly evident before the war came on. I have frequently called attention to them as a social change to which industry must adjust itself. The war has made a crisis in that it increases national expenditure without reducing the pressure of individual wants. The growing deficit of pre-war times becomes a startling fact when it is coupled with the present war expenses. I say pre-war deficit because the pressure of deficit would have been felt then if it had not been covered by the savings of the small class whose incomes exceed $5,000 a year. Their profits have been high, leaving an excess for saving in the face of increased expenditure. The rich in this sense had probably a gross income of 10 billions before the war, of which they saved perhaps one-quarter. This would account for all the saving made at that time. If people with smaller incomes had no deficit they were fortunate. Certainly the class as a whole contributed a negligible sum to the national saving. Many complaints are made that all the increase of wealth goes to the rich, but with the lack of motive to save it is hardly possible that it would be otherwise. Only the prosperous have an income which exceeds their urgent wants. Families with medium income live as they go and the workers save only to meet the exigencies arising from sick ness and non-employment.

I picture this pre-war situation so as to show the crisis the nation then faced. The period from 1900 to 1910 were flush years in which large profits were made. The industrial surplus was placed on the investment market and the rate of interest forced thereby to below 4 per cent. At the same time the sources of amusement and pleasure were vastly increased making a pressure for consumption by which the income of the average family was used up. The people thus ceased to save; but the loss of these savings was not felt because of the vast surplus made in the newly enlarged industries. Capital thus ceased to be savings and became industrial profit. The low rate of interest forced up security values to such a degree that one dollar of real capital became two dollars of values in security.

By 1910, the sources of the great surplus in the large industries were in a measure reduced and the supply of fresh capital fell off. A check on the increase of capital was thus created which could be met in only two ways. Either a higher rate of interest must be offered and popular saving evoked, or higher rates must be charged so that the industrial surplus would be sufficient to permit the proper increase of capital. If a higher rate of interest were offered security values would fall. A 5 per cent rate instead of 4 per cent would decrease security values by a quarter. Naturally this solution did not appeal to the nation's financiers. They chose the other plan of forcing up rates so that the increase of capital would come from the surplus thus acquired. This policy is apparent in the case of railroads whose values would be most affected by a rise in interest rate. Everyone is familiar with the struggle about rates between the Interstate Commerce Commission and the railroads. The rates were held down. The railroads refused to offer higher rates of interest, stopped making improvements and practically ceased to increase their rolling stock and other equipment. A crisis in railroad finance was thus approaching even if the war had not intervened. Low profits and a low rate of interest do not match. One or the other must yield. But the issue was put off by the war which has for the time brought high profits and has reversed the tendency for lower rates. The element desiring that capital be created out of profits is again supreme and will probably remain so while the war lasts. But the issue, although delayed, cannot be avoided. A system of finance that depends on profits to create new capital must move in one direction while a democracy must go in another. The increase of capital as well as the expense of the war must come from high profits or from popular economy. Of the former plan all are familiar since it is the method of finance on which recent prosperity has depended. With democratic finance we are less familiar and to use it would reverse many well-established financial maxims.

Every reduction of the interest rate adds to the value of what the prosperous have and creates a sharper gulf between them and the less fortunate classes. The less the rate the more difficult is the advance from lower to higher social ranks. It may seem that a reduced rate is of popular advantage as when the mortgage rate of interest is lowered. But the advantage is to present holders only. They gain by an increase of values while to others the difficulty of acquiring farms grows. A low rate of interest means high farm values and a growth of tenant workers. It is hard to find a locality where the rate of interest has fallen below 6 per cent without break ing up the community life of farmers and substituting in their place a much lower class of tenant farmers. The problem is not solved, however, by dealing with a specific class no matter how important they are. The real problem is what motives can be placed around a people so they will do their own saving. A 4 per cent rate will not do this. There never has been in the past much popular saving below a 6 per cent rate but even this rate may fail under the new pressure for increased consumption. While the rate which will evoke sufficient popular saving cannot be stated, the general issue may be seen by contrasting the conditions of a farming community with a 4 and an 8 per cent rate of interest. An 80 acre farm with an 8 per cent rate would be worth $4,000. ($50 an acre) while with a 4 per cent rate it would be worth $8,000 ($100 an acre). If a working man can make a net saving of $100 a year and he must pay one fourth of the purchase money to buy a farm, he can become a land owner in 8 years if the rate of interest is 8 per cent while it will take him 18 years to save enough to buy the farm if the rate is 4 per cent, thus making the selling price $8,000 of which he must pay one-fourth down. It is easy to see that in the first case, workers will become landholders and the standards of the community will be maintained, while in the second case the long wait will lead to discouragement and to the migration of the better workers to some other occupation. There is no way in which a unified community standard can be upheld where such high values and low rates of interest persist. A social split is sure to occur dividing the community into a leisure class and a large mass of dependent workers. The same tendencies show themselves in industrial occupations although it is not so easy to contrast the motives which operate to discourage one class and to give advantage to the other. But democracy demands the same in both cases and the solution is not different. Suppressed motives must be evoked and the obstructions to social unification set aside.

To make the bearing of these statements plain it is necessary to define more clearly the meaning of an economic democracy. An economic aristocracy is a society where the capitalists are a self-perpetuating class distinct from the workers both in occupation and in motive. Capital once saved is perpetuated and gives to its holder advantages denied to other classes. Low rates of interest with extraordinary inducements for individual enterprise are the basis of this condition. The high personal rewards give the basis of large fortunes and the low rates of interest stop the growth of competing capital. In contrast to these conditions a democratic economy is one in which privileges do not endure. All personal advantage is slowly reduced so that in time any family or class loses its industrial superiority and sinks back to the common level from which it must take a fresh start if its advantages are to be renewed. From shirt sleeve to shirt sleeve in three generations is an old adage which has a social significance if it means that the superior energy of one generation does not lift a family into a self-perpetuating leisure class. The adage implies that the descendents will be extravagant and thus lose their superiority. Socially, however, the advantage should not be lost in this way but by conditions which prevent the self-perpetuation of capital. This self-perpetuation is now favored because it is believed to be the only means by which an adequate supply of capital can be obtained. But the need of this perpetuation depends on the rate at which new capital is secured. Low rates of interest check the increase of new capital while high rates encourage it. The problem of democratic finance is to get a rate of interest which will produce a growth of new capital large enough to supply an increasing industry and to replace the decrease which is actually taking place in old capital. If, for example, old capital decreased at the rate of 2 per cent a year while an increase of 3 per cent a year was demanded to supply the increasing need of industry, the annual increase of new capital must be at least 5 per cent a year. If this condition were brought about, we would have democratic finance and the permanance of class distinctions would cease. Everyone would be permitted to gain whatever advantages his superior advantages permitted but what he left to his heirs would not be a self-perpetuating fund; it would be merely an annuity which would finally disappear.

The difficulty is not in preventing this self-perpetuation, but to secure the requisite capital to take its place. We now think of capital as a permanent fund and do not realize how an industrial system could work without it. The advantage of capital now seems to lie in elevating one's family into the leisure class. A democratic view would not be this but the creation of a period of economic leisure for one's old age. We realize the advantage of limiting the hours of labor in each day, but we do not in a similar way see the advantage of limiting the years of labor. We stop work at 5 p.m. but we do not stop industrial activity at sixty. This lack of a social concept is largely due to the shortness of life in the past and to its uncertainty. Just as men were glad to get work they were glad to work until they dropped dead. The decrease of disease and the growth of sounder views of life permit us to think of a thirty-year working period as we now think of an eight-hour day. Should this view become prevalent a new attitude about saving would result. Men would save freely during their working period and spend freely in their old age. Their capital would become an annuity and not a permanent fund. Each generation would supply the capital for its successor who in turn would save for those which follow. A continuous destruction and replacement of capital would result with no permanent class enjoying its advantage. The old would lend to the young and the young would save for their old age leisure.

The longer life and the better living are now realities and will engage more attention no matter what financial system we use. The choice is between low rates of interest with a permanent leisure class and high rates with democratic saving by the whole population. The heredity of the upper and lower classes are not different. It is conditions which evoke saving habits and they may be made general by calling them into activity with the proper inducements. When a region is new and capital scarce, there is no difficulty to arouse the proper amount of saving. It is when the inducement fails because of low interest rates that the division into classes appears. If taxation had prevented this self-perpetuation of capital the general inclination to save would have continued and fresh capital would have appeared each year to replace that lost by taxation.

A democratic society must think more of its health, more of the length of life and more of leisure both in old age and from day to day. It must be a working organization active and efficient but it cannot afford to be 100 per cent efficient in work and only 20 per cent efficient in its amusement, recreation and leisure.

Production and consumption must complement each other and each bring its joys. Democracy is a many-sided life and not an alley leading to a single goal.

These statements I assume will be accepted in a vague way by most people who read them. We have become so used to the presentation of Utopias that we read of them with pleasure and for get them with equal readiness. It is only as they are transformed into facts that they become realities for the realization of which practical plans may be devised. I shall try to do this by presenting figures which show how the ends desired may be reached. We must begin this with a study of the prosperous for it is with changes in their attitudes that we are mainly concerned. We are as a class quite willing to lecture the workers but we do not take home the lessons taught. Many budgets have been presented of workers and we know fairly well of the merits and defects of their expenditure. We lack a like picture of the upper middle class whose expenditures are more than any other factor the cause of the present situation and the obstacle to its improvement. I shall present not the usual budget of the workers which visualizes the minimum of necessities needed by working families, but a budget of those whose expenditures represent the lower limit of good living. These "good livers" represent the tendencies of the prosperous and the pressure to spend forced on them by the social life they enjoy. In the cost of an automobile I have included depreciation charges. A $1,200 automobile run by the owner will cost him $300 a year on this basis. The rule for wise insurance is that the income to be derived from it should equal half the family income.

The Minimum of Good Living

Annual Budget

Rent	$800	Summer expenses	300
Automobile	300	Amusement	200
Service	300	Generosity	200
Clothing	300	Taxes	100
Food	600	Extras	200
Household expenses	100		
Insurance	600	Total	$4,000

The defect in this budget is not from the personal but from the social viewpoint. The comforts of life are provided for but there is no pressure to encourage thrift. Such a standard is therefore incomplete and undemocratic. It is incomplete in that the thrift instinct must be aroused to make a normal man. A thriftless man is as liable to degeneration as is a man who does not work. Such families, however pleasant and wholesome, sink in intelligence and vital power. They are also undemocratic because if they do not save there must be a capitalistic class to perform this function, and back of them, a predatory class to amass the fortunes which the capitalist class inherit. Oniy when energy and thrift are combined and simultaneously evoked, will a democratic family appear which is thus independent and self-determining. To bring this about a thrift item must be added to their budget and thrift motives evoked by a sufficing rate of interest.

The working epoch of each man should be followed by a period of leisure in old age. During the working period he saves, in old age he spends. What sum of annual saving will give a thirty-year period of work and saving coupled with a period of twenty years' leisure in old age? If the sum of this saving sufficed to keep up the capital of the country there would then be a replacing capital instead of the permanent fund now sought. There could then be fresh capital saved each generation to replace the spending of their predecessors of the past generation. Capital in one sense would be permanent for enough would always be at hand, but it would be temporary in the sense that the capital of each generation would go as they go. To bring this about would demand an annual saving of $400 a year if the rate of interest remained at 4 per cent while an annual saving of $200 a year would suffice if the rate of interest was 8 per cent. It is plain that $400 a year of saving would exceed present possibilities while a saving of $200 a year is practicable. If the actual return on capital is now 8 per cent there is no external obstacle to an unified democratic society. It is the thrift-pressure which we need and this cannot be evoked while the rate of interest remains at 4 per cent.

Such a picture the reader may regard as picturesque if he will. It is not this which I have primarily in mind but to show the dilemma in which the nation is at the present time. We have had in the past a society more or less predatory in its nature. The gains of the few were at the expense of the many and out of these gains came the capital of the nation. The "good liver" is an adjunct and completed product of this epoch. But against this régime the people have of late revolted and pressure has been put in ways which have reduced profits. However, capital came from these high profits and with their reduction comes a failure to supply the capital needed for industrial enterprise. This restrictive economy is thus bound to fail. The check to the increase of capital must be obviated either by a return to the epoch of high individual profit or by pushing on to a more democratic society in which the people do their own sav ing. Such a choice the American people face and to which they will turn I cannot say. But I can say that a policy of restriction will not work. I can also say that a more fully democratic society is a practical expedient if the mental attitude of the people is altered to meet the new situation. The struggle of coming years is thus not a struggle with nature but a struggle of conflicting motives. Our democratic ideals may become real forces, or a keen desire for good living may keep active the forces on which our social class distinctions depend.

WHAT MONEY SHOULD COST[1]

Walter H. Cottingham

Fundamental facts in business financing

"Money is merely a commodity and it is not so much what you can afford to pay for its use as what you have to pay. What you expect to make out of the money gives an easy guide as to what you can afford to pay."

That sounds like quick and comprehensive dismissing of the whole subject of finance in so far as the worth of money is concerned. I have heard the formula given many times with facile assurance. It is a favorite speech of the money shark. Following it, has, I think, brought about more bankruptcies than any other single cause. For it expresses a dangerous half-truth. It is responsible for people starting in business with a heavy load of interest charges that presently become a crushing weight. It is responsible for borrowing money at ruinous rates to carry through a contract which at the time of taking seems able to support the burden – and the interest eats up all the profit.

It is responsible for men giving chattel and other mortgages with monthly interest charges that, visualized on a yearly basis, would quickly show them that they were paying for money alone more than they could legitimately expect to earn out of the whole business.

When Borrowing Complicates Troubles

There are emergencies when large sums can be paid for the temporary use of money. But for one such real emergency there are a thousand supposed emergencies in which the money borrowed will not meet but only postpones the crisis. And then the final failure will be all the more disastrous.

[1] [*System* 37 (1920), May: 944–45.]

The unfortunate part of attempting anything in the way of a general denial that money can ever be considered solely as a commodity is that sometimes it can be so considered.

In any business where the manufacturing and the selling phases are comparatively unimportant, as compared with the raw material, then that raw material, as for instance in cotton manufacturing, is carried on borrowed money. That is the cheapest way to conduct such a business. The money has to be borrowed at the market and paid for at the market rate, unless the borrower happens to have luck.

The money is loaned on the character of the owner but it is expected that he will use it only to buy and fabricate raw materials that will readily be sold and turned into cash. Throughout such trades, borrowing is universal, and the cost of the money is as recognized a factor as, say, the cost of the raw cotton. Money is then almost a commodity.

Always, in short-time borrowing. you can afford to pay for it only that sum which, added into the price of the goods or services that the money will purchase, will not make either the price of the finished goods too high to sell or so cut into the margin of profit that it will be inadequate. Every penny of this money has to go around the circle of business and return to its starting point. If you pay a high discount and your competitor uses his own money, then you are at a very considerable disadvantage. It is the small and not the large business that is likely to pay too much for its money, because the small business – having only local facilities – may be forced to resort to the personal money lender or to one of those agents who seem able to open the money boxes of certain banks upon the payment of a sufficient commission. And again the small man frequently does not seem to appreciate the necessity of getting money into his business before it is needed and leaves his financing until the funds are urgently required. Then he has no time to look around or see what best he might do.

This matter of money is today in the fore with practically every business man. The high prices of materials and the high prices of labor have made it necessary to use more money in the conduct of business than at any previous time. Because profits are also high or at least the aggregate total of the profits is large, the initial disposition is to hope that somehow the profits will be great enough to take care of the increasing demands for working capital and plant extension. In nearly every instance this hope fails of realization.

However large the gross profits, the average man is today extremely lucky if he can preserve even a normal percentage of profit.

This percentage of profit will not commonly result in a sufficient surplus for reinvestment in the business to meet the growing capital needs.

It is dangerous to dodge the exposition of capital requirements and to imagine that the shortage of money is but temporary and can be tided over by borrowing. This course will inevitably lead to a confusion between legitimate short-time borrowing for the purchase of materials, supplies, and the like, and illegitimate borrowing for capital requirements. Money for fixed or working capital is not a commodity but a tool.

But when one sets out to get additional money, one is immediately confronted with the fact that it is not to be had unless a round price be paid for it. The wages of money are high just as are all other wages; with gilt-edged bonds selling between 80 and 90 and yielding up to 7% or 8%, the ordinary merchant or manufacturer cannot expect to go into the market and get money for less than those concerns which have enormous resources and long records of profits back of them.

Curiously enough, here again it is that the business man of comparatively small resources and without familiarity with finance frequently stands in his own way by imagining that a discount is an evidence of financial insecurity and hence bitterly resents offering any type of security at less than par.

The man without experience in finance will have no hesitation in indignantly insisting that any stock he issues must be bought at par regardless of the fact that many of the soundest stocks in the country sell considerably below par. Almost every day one comes across the man who declares that he is not going to be held up, that anything he stands behind is worth 100 cents on the dollar, and that it would be a confession of near-insolvency if he disposed of promises to pay issued by him at less than their face value.

What is the Relation Between Par Value and Worth?

There is even a fairly widespread delusion that the value stamped upon the face of a stock or a bond is, or should be, the worth of that particular piece of paper. As a matter of fact the par value, as everyone of experience knows, has nothing to do with the actual market value. When we issue a security of fixed return as a 6% bond or a 7% cumulative preferred stock, what we really offer for sale is the right to receive $6 or $7 a year as the case may be, with the additional right to receive in certain eventualities, instead of the yearly income the flat sum engraved upon the bond or certificate.

In some states the laws and everywhere the banking custom decree that the physical property behind the bond or preferred stock issues should be reasonably worth considerably more than the face or par value of the issues, on the theory that tangible property is the thing – is the security. And so it was years ago when concerns were small. But the really big asset of today is the good will – an asset which those of us who are very conservative wrongly hesitate to put upon our statements of condition. The character and skill of management alone make the inert property of value, and it is the power to earn money and pay the charges that is of moment, and not the dividend in bankruptcy. No one would think of investing in a bond only to realize its face value on foreclosure, nor of buying a stock on the chance that when the company wound up get more than he paid. There is a real difference between investment and junk dealing. The only excuse for a corporate offering of bonds or stocks is the ability to pay an income on the paper offered. These are not the strictly legal delineations of bonds and stock but they are convenient definitions or points of view for the man who is financing. It is easier to grasp what the sale of securities means when we think of selling a certain annual payment rather than a share in the corporation, for then we realize that we are competing on a price basis with others who offer investors incomes.

Thus the procedure is taken out of the discount class and put into that of investment. Considered on this basis we can arrive at an idea of how much we can afford to pay for money. A rule might be phrased somewhat in this fashion: The amount that can be paid is the comparison between the annual charge put upon the business by the new money and the additional income which the new money will provide by furnishing additional facilities.

Working out this rule not only sends us at once to the examination of our present statement of condition and statement of operations – more particularly the statement of operations – but also compels us to look ahead to see what business we may reasonably expect to do in the future. Then we find that instead of working forward from a plant of a certain capacity to a market we must work back from the market to the plant.

This would seem self-evident were it not that the country is dotted with idle plants that are losing money because they were built before the sales capacity was known. They were financed on output instead of as they should have been – on sales.

It is the sales that determine the plant capacity and the amount of money required, and it is my view that no financing can be intelligent unless first a definite sales plan is formulated and carried through. I look at a plant or a store in its relation to its ability to fill the demands of the selling force and not as a means of providing something to sell. It is the sales that determine the size of the plant. That is the plan we have carried out with our own company.

The price of labor and of material and the cost of selling all have increased to such a degree that we found it impossible to preserve the same percentage of profit that we had when it cost less to do business. All of our raw materials, even though we produce them ourselves, cost more than ever before because of the increased charges for labor and transportation. It costs more to manufacture these materials, it costs more to transport them, and everyone knows how enormously the expenses of salesmen have risen.

At the beginning of 1918 I determined in spite of the fact that business prospects were then none too good to set a sales mark of $1,000,000 gain each month for 1918 and to make our plans for the year on that basis. Increased sales of that size would cause such a rapid rate of turn over that we could make a larger gross profit with less than our usual percentage of profit per dollar. It is my belief that when business seems to be dull is the time to make a mighty drive for high sales.

Back in 1907, when the panic had gripped the country, I bet a suit of clothing with one of our directors at the Chicago convention that the company would sell more in 1908 than it had in 1907, in spite of the fact that at that moment the business of the country was flat on its back. So confident was the director that he wanted to add an overcoat. I lost the bet but I lost it by only 1-10 of 1%.

To start a drive with the conditions as they were in January, 1918, seemed to be flying in the face of Providence. Perhaps it was.

In such times I believe in flying in the face of Providence rather than into the cyclone cellar. For the first few months our men did not hit the quota; but by June they were going a quarter of a million over the quota. Now, similarly, I have planned gradually increasing sales for some five years ahead – and when I say planned, I mean that unless everything that we now think we know turns out to be wrong we are going to get those sales. I believe in drives. I believe in setting marks and forcing forward to those marks with every possible known effort, and also I believe that the concern that does not press itself forward by planned effort must go back. I do not believe in lounging about and saying, "I guess this will be a good year" or "I guess this will be a bad year."

There is always someone who wants to buy and enough of those someones can always be found. In 1907 when the railroads and the big corporations could not buy paint we made a drive for the smaller consumers, even for individuals, with the argument that then, in the general dullness, was a good time to do their painting. On that line we pulled ourselves out of a possible hole.

The first step in finance is to plan sales. Steadily increasing sales on a prearranged plan will require a steadily increasing productive capacity for a plant and will require a steadily increasing amount of money. These calculations will show how much of a charge can be carried for the new money – that is, whether the sales can be increased to such a figure and consequently the plant output increased to such a figure as properly to distribute the money charge so that the finished goods can be sold at a reasonable profit.

The amount that can be paid thus depends on circumstances and each man will have to work out a rule for himself, but the figure is not difficult to arrive at if today's costs are known and tomorrow's costs are planned.

And of course anyone who has not taken the trouble thoroughly to acquaint him self with the costs of his business is not justified in asking an outsider to place money with him.

There are several ways of borrowing money. Bank credit, as I have already said, has nothing to do with the permanent financial requirements; it is in a sense a commodity credit. The two leading ways of getting new money into a business are through the issuance of bonds secured by mortgage and the issuance of preferred or common stock.

Take bonds: when money rates were lower, this was a favorite mode of financing. The money was cheap, the amount to be paid was fixed, and no new stock holders were created to interfere with the management of the concern.

But the interest upon bonds must be paid whether or not it is earned. It is a continuing charge like the rent of a property and must be distributed into the cost of the goods.

This tends to give a higher production cost than that of a competitor who does not have to include mortgage interests in his factory overhead. This interest is properly charged into the cost of production because unless it be regularly paid, production cannot continue; the holders of the bonds will step in through their trustee and foreclose on the mortgage.

But money rates have made industrial bond issues very expensive. Unless bonds at 6% can be sold above 90 – and today they cannot be sold at any such price; the average industrial concern will be lucky to dispose of 6% bonds between 85 and 90 – it is in my personal opinion a dangerous way of getting new money unless the amount borrowed is very small.

I would personally say, roughly, that an industrial concern is not justified in borrowing on bonds unless it cannot with the utmost conservatism figure out a year in which the bond interest could not be met. A transportation company or a public service corporation can make such a calculation but very few industrial concerns can, in good conscience, do so – and especially if the amount raised is at all large.

A public utility has some income, whatever the times, for of course the people must live – but an industry can be shut down and its income cease. In addition to the interest burden is the ordinary sinking-fund requirement which stands on a footing equal with that of the interest payments.

If a concern has a reputation it may sell its common stock, but that involves the danger of losing the voting control – that is, of losing the management which makes the stock worthwhile. Or again, a non-voting class of common stock may be issued by those corporations with a long record of large profits, but in my opinion the safest for the company and the most profitable for the investor is the preferred stock with a cumulative dividend and a sinking-fund to retire it.

A corporation offering preferred stock and without funded indebtedness gives to the investor practically as high a security as a mortgage bond, and also it gives something that is really an additional security – the assurance that a disastrous year will not result in the break-up of the company through the foreclosure of a mortgage.

For no matter how prosperous has been a company, if it hits the rocks in a bad year and goes through a reorganization it will rarely again get on its feet.

The big point in preferred stock is that the money is not borrowed. The buyer of that stock comes in as a partner and he receives his dividend only if it is earned – no reasonably sane company will declare a dividend that threatens to cripple it financially. Therefore, the stock can be disposed of at a price attractive to the investor and at the same time the company will have the full opportunity to use the new money to make more money. The corporation does not borrow money – it admits limited partners.

A Precaution for Small Concerns

The small business does not raise additional funds easily. No money is raised "easily" – it has to be bargained for. But I think a part of the smaller man's difficulty may be traced to two reasons. The first is a lack of planning ahead and of a consequent scheduling of money requirements for at least several years in advance. This carelessness naturally results in a panicky getting of money only when it is urgently needed. The second difficulty is in analogy; because he has not planned, the owner has no clear comprehension of just what he can afford to pay for money, and is likely to insist upon too low a price until suddenly he finds himself "up against it." Then he pays too high a price – if he gets the money at all.

Planning both sales and money ahead gives a freedom that cannot otherwise be had. We, like most new companies, began with only a small capital; then when we needed more money we issued a preferred stock, and later we issued another series. Always the money had to be raised in what amounted to a makeshift way, for the money plans followed the sales plans instead of going hand in hand with them.

When we made a sales plan, the question at once arose, "Can we get the money to carry this through?" That fear of money hampered and constrained. The better plan is to take care of all reasonable future requirements at once.

If you need only a certain amount today but know that you will need double that amount next year, do not issue stock only for today's amount; instead, authorize an issue that will meet the requirements for a long time ahead, and then offer for sale only that amount which is necessary for today. There is a slight additional expense in the authorization of the larger amount, but that expense will prove to be less than the added premium that one usually has to pay in order to get back previously issued stock that must be retired before a new issue is put out.

What you can afford to pay for money is thus not an abstract calculation but is the result of a coordination of the sales and productive sides of the business.

EARNING POWER AS A BASIS OF CORPORATE CAPITALIZATION[1]

James C. Bonbright

This article is written with a definite purpose. Its object is to show that a certain widely accepted principle of corporation finance – the principle that capitalization should be based on earning capacity rather than on actual cost – is not only unsound in theory but is also vicious in its practical application. None of the points to be adduced in support of this view are original with the author. At one time or another they have all been noted implicitly or explicitly by earlier writers. Yet they have never been presented with sufficient emphasis to carry conviction, if one may judge from the fact that the "earning power basis" not only persists among recent text book writers, but is accepted by them uncritically, without even an attempt to meet the arguments that can be urged against it.

Before considering the earning power basis, let us first note its alternatives. Two other possible bases are usually mentioned by writers: actual cost of assets, and replacement cost. To illustrate the three different possibilities, let us assume the case of a corporation whose property, save for a negligible amount of current assets, consists entirely of buildings and grounds that were purchased in 1910 at a cost of one million dollars. At the present time, in view of higher prices and appreciation in land values, the cost of replacing that property would be two million dollars. But the company is very prosperous and gives assurance of earning an average net income of $200,000 per year. Capitalizing this income at a nominal rate of interest, say 5 per cent, one arrives at four million dollars as the present value of the enterprise as a going concern. In a case like this, it makes a deal of difference which of the above three bases is to be accepted as the test of the

1 [*Quarterly Journal of Economics* 35 (1921), May: 482–90.]

proper amount of security issues. On the basis of actual cost, the limit is one million dollars; on the basis of replacement cost, it is two million dollars; while on the basis of earning power, a capitalization of four millions is permissible.

Of course the relationship assumed in the above figures is only hypothetical. Often capitalized earning power would be less than actual cost or replacement cost. A capitalization based on an estimate of earnings is not necessarily a high capitalization; that is, it is not necessarily high in theory, altho it is almost invariably high in practise, owing to the extremely liberal estimates of earning power made by financiers.

With this introduction, let us consider the reasons that are presented in defense of the earning power basis of capitalization. All supporters of this basis use the same general line of defense, but no one has stated the case more clearly and uncompromisingly than has Lough in his volume on *Business Finance*.[2] We shall, therefore, find it convenient to analyze Lough's argument, as fairly representing the position of those who accept the earning power standard.

Lough begins his discussion by stating that "The question: 'What is the right basis of capitalization?' is almost identical with the question: 'What is the best measure of wealth?'" In other words, a company is properly capitalized when the par value of its outstanding securities corresponds roughly to the actual value of the assets that these securities represent. If we accept this position, our problem is then simple: it is to find the best measure of the value of the assets. Is this best measure original cost? Certainly not; for if a corporation can earn little or nothing for its security holders, what matters it that its physical property may have cost many millions of dollars? Aside from bare scrap value, assets are worth only what they will earn, and not what they may have cost. But if we rule out original cost, how about cost of replacement? Even this basis, according to Lough, would not be satisfactory: for it does not correctly measure value. While it may fairly indicate the value of the tangible assets, it does not take account of intangible values. "To every piece of property there attaches a certain intangible value. A man running a successful retail shop would not be willing to part with it,

[2] William H. Lough, Business Finance (New York, 1917), chap. viii.

ordinarily, in exchange for another shop which was just as well fitted up and carried the same stock but which had been unsuccessful. It is possible – at least theoretically – to reproduce physical assets, but it is impossible to reproduce goodwill, organization, prestige, and the like. Hence, the attempt to measure wealth by figuring the cost of reproducing properties breaks down as soon as we begin to measure the value of intangible assets."

Following the above line of reasoning, Lough is led to conclude that the correct measure of value is earning power. "If we take into account not merely current earnings but also potential earnings, then we have here a measure of wealth which must be a true and satisfactory measure. After all, in buying property for business reasons, what do we buy? Not merely so much real estate or so many articles. We are buying income."

Lough concludes: "If the answer that earning power is the best measure of wealth is granted, and if the proposition that 'capitalization' of an enterprise is an approximate estimate of its wealth is accepted, then it would seem to follow that the correct basis of 'capitalization' is earning power. This answer, however simple and sound it may appear to us, is not a principle of the law governing corporations, which, on the contrary, assumes that investment is the only correct basis of capitalization."

The argument as stated by Lough is delightfully clear and simple, and its logic seems impregnable if we accept its two premises – (a) that capitalization should correspond to the actual value of the assets, and (b) that this value is measured by the earning capacity of the enterprise. But can we accept the premises? Let us consider first the second – that value is measured by earning power.

This, in the approximate sense in which it is meant, is doubtless correct. The fact that other factors than present or expected earnings are of influence in determining value merely qualifies without destroying the truth of the statement. But one should take careful note that if earning power is to be accepted as a measure of value, this earning power must be estimated and capitalized at whatever figure is determined by the market. For value, in the economic sense, is simply market value. It is the valuation which the investing public places upon a particular property. In making such a valuation, the public will have its own ideas of future earning power and will capitalize those expected earnings at a rate of interest depending, among other things, on the element of risk involved. In short, if one is really serious in asserting that capitalization should represent value, one must accept the conclusion that the total par value of outstanding securities should not exceed their market value. Of course, merely to state this condition is to indicate that the advocates of the earning capacity basis do not really want to base capitalization on *value*. In practise, they would estimate future earnings at a very liberal figure, and then they would capitalize this figure, not at the market rate of interest – which would be high, owing to the great risk in a new enterprise – but rather at some conventional rate such as 5 or 6 per cent. The resulting capitalization, of course, does not represent value at all. At best it represents what the promoters hope that the value may sometime be. More likely, it is a pure fiction.

But let us overlook this discrepancy between the *theory* that capitalization should represent value, and the *practise* of issuing securities in excess of the real value. What about the theory itself – the principle that capitalization should represent the value of the assets? This assumption is stated by Lough and others without any attempt at justification. Apparently it seems to them self-evident, not even requiring to be proved to the uninitiated reader. But as a matter of fact, is it really so obvious and necessary an assumption? Is it not based rather on a disregard for some of the most fundamental principles of accounting? The fallacy in the assumption – at least what seems to the present writer to be a fallacy – lies in the failure to bear in mind that capitalization is not an asset at all, and is not even a measure of total assets. It is rather the sum of the fixed liabilities (the outstanding funded debts) and a *certain part* of the proprietorship – capital stock. These two accounts are found on the right side of the balance sheet, and they seldom alone equal the value of the assets as noted on the left-hand side. The difference between assets and capitalization is registered in the various surplus and deficit accounts. To assume that capitalization is a measure of the value of the property is to overlook the fact that capital stock does not alone represent the total proprietorship and hence does not indicate the total net assets. What it does represent is "capital" as distinct from surplus, the capital being the amount that must be retained in the business and the surplus being the amount that may be drawn upon for dividends. Capital stock may thus be compared to a low-water point on a boiler; it no more represents the value of the assets than does the low-water point measure the actual amount of water in the boiler. It simply fixes a limit below which assets must not be distributed in dividends, a point fixed by law at the amount of capital actually contributed by the shareholders.

If those who insist that capitalization is a measure of value were really prepared to accept the logic of their position, they would be forced to hold that any material change in the value of the property should be accompanied by a corresponding change in nominal capitalization. Of course, such a position is untenable. Value, whether measured directly by stock and bond quotations or indirectly by earnings, is constantly changing with the ups and downs of the business. This year it is low; next year it may be high; the following year it may again be low. To change the par values of outstanding securities so as to make them correspond to the shifting property value would be quite out of the question from a practical standpoint, even if it were desirable in theory – which it is not. Defenders of the earning power basis recognize this difficulty and therefore do not attempt to carry their theory to its logical conclusion. Instead, they propose simply that, at the outset, an estimate of value based on earning power should be made, and that this estimate should determine once for all – or at least for a long time – the capitalization.

But this concession is fatal. For it destroys the entire force of the argument that the *value* of the property, as something distinct from the *cost,* should be taken as the basis of capitalization. It is only after a lapse of time that a discrepancy ordinarily arises between the value of assets and their costs. At the outset, sound accounting would not sanction a valuation at a higher figure than the actual costs. Only after the business has developed a goodwill or a surplus from reinvested earnings can there be adequate ground for holding that the value of the property exceeds the price that has been paid for it. Hence, the notion that value as distinct from original cost should be the basis of capitalization collapses when it is admitted that capitalization cannot be shifted to correspond to a fluctuating value. Critics of original cost as the basis of capitalization have objected to it on the ground that it soon becomes out of date – that it represents a mere historical fact instead of a present condition. In this respect, however, the earning power basis has no better claim to favor than does its rival, original cost. Indeed, the claim of the former is not so good, for whereas original cost is a historical fact of real significance, an out-of-date estimate of earning power is of little or no consequence.

It would be interesting, and perhaps illuminating, to discover how this fallacious notion that capitalization should represent the value of the assets has been accepted so uncritically by writers on corporation finance. One may conjecture that a partial explanation lies in a confusion between partnership accounts and corporation accounts. In a partnership, no distinction is made between the capital contributed directly by the partners and the surplus from reinvested earnings. Both amounts are covered in one general account on the liabilities side of the balance sheet – "proprietorship." This proprietorship, since it represents original capital plus surplus or minus deficit, is therefore an actual measure of the net assets; that is, it represents the difference between the value of the assets and the amount of the debt. But with corporate accounts it is different. Here there is no single proprietorship account. A distinction is made between capital contributed by shareholders and surplus from reinvested earnings. It is only by adding surplus to capital, or by deducting deficit from capital, that one arrives at the net value of the corporate assets. If corporate earnings increase, if the value of the assets rises, this fact may be shown, not by a credit to capital stock, but rather by a credit to surplus. If assets decline in value, the fall is registered, in the absence of a reorganization, not by a reduction in capitalization but by a reduction of surplus.

To many practical men of affairs the foregoing objections to the earning power basis would seem hopelessly theoretical. Admitting all that has been said about the failure of this basis to square with strict accounting theory, they would hold that as a practical business matter, earning power is the only sensible measure of proper capitalization. For is it not earnings, present and prospective, that determine the value to investors of their securities? To this question the reply is that earnings certainly do largely determine the value of the shares, but that it does not follow that such a value should be registered in the nominal capitalization, in the par value of the securities. For what proper object is there in making par values represent market values, or earning power? These two items can be seen simply by noting the market quotations on the stock and the reported annual earnings of the company. It would be useless to attempt to register this market value, or to capitalize these earnings, in the form of a stated par value of the shares. And in any event the attempt is sure to be a vain one, for par values are relatively fixed, while market values and earning capacity are constantly fluctuating.

But if the earning power basis of capitalization is both unsound in theory and impracticable in application, why is it so generally supported by American financiers? The answer is fairly clear: it is that the earning power basis of capitalization gives promoters the opportunity to set the nominal capital at whatever figure they think will give the securities their highest market value. One of the strange but well recognized phenomena of the financial market is that an enterprise capitalized at a liberal figure is very apt to seem more valuable to the investing public than would that very same enterprise if capitalized at a lower amount. The "magic of par value" often has a decided influence. American promoters are past masters in the art of taking advantage of this preference for a large nominal amount of stocks and bonds. And in this game their best ally is the highly sanctioned theory that capitalization should properly be determined by earning power. For by estimating future earnings at an extravagant figure and then by capitalizing these earnings at a very low rate, the promoters are able to justify an issue of securities far in excess of the actual cost of the property.

Of course it may be argued by supporters of the earning power basis that this inflation of capitalization beyond the reasonable value of the property condemns merely the abuse, but not the proper use, of the principle. As a practical matter, however, this defense carries little weight. It is idle to expect that promoters and bankers who are personally interested in putting a high valuation on their properties will make a conservative and impartial estimate of the earning power of their enterprise. Even when they are honest – and honesty is a relative term – they are almost sure to be overoptimistic; that is their nature. The fact is that earning power (i. e., prospective earning power) is largely a matter of conjecture. There can be no adequate objective tests. And to expect a conservative capitalization to be set up in the absence of objective tests is simply utopian.

As to those financiers who make no effort to find a theoretical defense of their methods of determining capitalization, but who more or less frankly issue whatever amounts of stock will give their holdings the best market, nothing need be said in this place. All that is here insisted upon is that such practise should not be allowed to seek shelter – as it has done in the past – under a "theory" of capitalization that is said to have the support of sound economics."[3] Is it unfair to suggest that those writers on corporation finance who have afforded such a shelter should hold themselves in some slight measure responsible for the notorious prevalence of inflation in American corporate finance?[4]

So much space has been devoted to a criticism of the earning power basis of capitalization that there is no opportunity here to discuss at length the other possible bases. The writer's position will be infered from the very objections that he has urged against the earning power principle. Briefly it is this: since capitalization is a measure of liabilities rather than of assets, it should equal the principal of the funded debt plus the amount of capital actually subscribed for by shareholders. This is the orthodox theory. Its merit is the simple one of truthfulness, for it requires that the par value of a share shall mean just what it purports at law to mean – namely, the actual contribution made by the shareholder.

Doubtless it is often impossible for a corporation to market

[3] The most recent and most carefully written treatise on corporation finance – that by Dewing – recognizes frankly the fictitious nature of nominal capitalization as it is usually determined. "The common stock," it states, "may be issued to any amount that suits the convenience of the promoters; probably the amount should be large so that a considerable number of shares can be distributed to bankers, investors, lawyers, and the like, and the promoters still retain a controlling majority." Financial Policy of Corporations (1920), vol. ii, p. 60. While many will not be able to accept the principle that capitalization should be a mere fiction, they will admit that it is far better frankly to recognize its fictitious character than to maintain the pretense of a reality that does not exist.

[4] The reader may recall the defense by George Kennan of one of the most ill-advised and harmful cases of stock watering, the Chicago & Alton capitalization of 1899–1900. Mr. Kennan bases his case in large measure on an attempt to prove that the proper test of capitalization is not actual cost but earning power. In support of this position he cites the opinion of eminent authorities in the field of finance. Kennan, The Chicago & Alton Case: A Misunderstood Transaction (1916), pp. 28–34.

its shares at part. Until recently, corporations under such circumstances were probably justified in issuing "full paid" shares at a discount. But this excuse is no longer generally valid. For it is now possible, under the laws of many states, to issues shares of stock without par value and thus to avoid the necessity of marketing shares at a discount. The very fact that such a practicable alternative now exists should make governmental authorities and courts far more rigid than they have been in enforcing the liability of stockholders to make full payment for their subscriptions as represented by the par value of their shares.

SOME RECENT FINANCIAL DEVICES[1]

Charles O. Hardy

The participating bond is one of the rarest devices in American corporation finance.[2] The Disco Milling Company, an Illinois corporation, is now financing the development of a new flour-milling device through an issue of participating bonds which present certain novel features. The capital required for the purchase of a building and the installation of equipment is to be secured through the sale of $500,000 of twenty-year 6 per cent first-mortgage bonds which carry the privilege of participation in the profits of the corporation on the following basis: 10 per cent of the net earnings of the company is to be set aside for retirement of the principal of the bonds. Whenever the fund so accumulated amounts to $25,000, it is to be applied to the retirement of the principal of the bonds, the face of *each* bond being reduced pro rata. To facilitate this operation, $50 principal coupons are issued to make up each $1,000 bond. Of the remaining profits, 25 per cent goes to the bondholders and 75 per cent to the stockholders. As no *stock* is offered to the public, this 75 per cent represents the equity of the inventor, the promoters, and others concerned with the earlier development of the invention, and with its financing. Retirement of part or all of the principal of the bonds through the operation of the sinking fund or through maturity does not affect the participation, each bondholder continuing to draw his proportion of the net earnings until 1981. In order to avoid the danger of this participation being treated by thc courts or the administrators of the Blue Sky laws as really a distribution of bonus stock, a trustee is interposed between the company

[1] [*Journal of Political Economy* 29 (1921), Marc: 249–51.]

[2] Three cases of its use are cited by Dewing *(Financial Policy of Corporations,* I, 87), all of them obsolete bonds, and no others seem to have been noted by the authors of current financial literature. The writer's attention has been called also to a participating bond issued by McNally-Peck & Company, an Indiana onion producer, four or five years ago, which is still extant.

and the bondholders. Title to the property is held for the bondholders by the trustee, a reputable trust company, and the property is leased to the operating company. The interest, sinking fund, and share of profits are all due to the trustee as rent. This, it will be noted, makes the claim of the bondholders to their share of undistributed profits a creditor's lien.

Another new financing device is the ten-year convertible first mortgage 9 per cent bond issued by the Rio Blanco Syndicate, Incorporated, of Colorado, to finance the development of a project for extracting oil from shale. The novel feature of this bond is the provision that the 9 per cent interest is due and payable only on the date of maturity of the bond. The conversion privilege consists of a right to convert each $100 bond into $400 par value stock of the corporation "at such time prior to its maturity as said conversion may be offered by the Syndicate." The Syndicate agrees to make such offer at some date prior to the maturity of the bond. Apparently, however, there is no limitation on the amount of stock which may be issued, so that the actual proportion of the profits accruing to the holders of $400 of stock is left to the discretion of the management.

Another device for raising capital which has been in use for some years, but seems to have escaped the attention of financial writers is the certificate of beneficial interest in oil leases held by a trustee. The plan of operation is as follows: An individual promoter or a small group buys either the leases on properties more or less remote from oil production, or a share of the one-eighth royalty interest which under the standard type of oil leases is reserved to the landowner. These leases are then assigned to a trustee, in small deals usually one of the promoters, and certificates of beneficial interest, representing small fractions of the equity, are sold to speculative investors. The total interest covered by the deed of trust varies from a single quarter-section to a consolidated royalty interest in thousands of acres, with a corresponding variation in the number of shares. The financial principle is that title to property of unknown value can usually be sold in small fractions for a much greater amount than it can be sold for in block. Not infrequently 1 per cent interests in a lease are sold for about one-fiftieth the cost of the lease to the promoters, but there is no standard rate of profit in this type of transaction. As one promoter puts it, "If there is oil there, the lease is worth more than we can possibly get for it; if there is none there, it isn't worth anything. So any price we can get is a fair price." No financial obligations are assumed by the certificate-holders or the trustee, except office expenses and rentals due under the lease. If the syndicate holds an interest in a lease, annual rentals will be due to the landowner; if the holding is an interest in the landowner's royalty, the rentals will be a source of income to the syndicate. If the holding is a lease the trustee is empowered to sell out to an operating company or to negotiate a contract for drilling out the property on a royalty basis. Normally, such a contract cannot, of course, be secured at the outset, but if the prospects are improved by wells being brought in near by, it becomes possible to secure a contract to have a well drilled on a basis which leaves the syndicate an equity of one-eighth or one-fourth. In case the operators are successful, either in selling out the holding or in securing a drilling contract which results in a discovery of oil, the duties of the trustee are simple, consisting merely of the collection of the proceeds and their distribution to the stockholders. In case the lease gets a black eye through the drilling of dry holes near by, or in case drilling operations are unsuccessful, the duties of the trustee are still further simplified. Where the syndicate holds a royalty interest in the farmer's reserved eighth in property on which the leases are held by operating companies, the trustee has no duties until a well is brought in by the lessee; then he collects and distributes the royalty. Certificates of beneficial interest in these "trusts" are transferable, and are freely bought and sold.

The possible bearing of recent Blue Sky legislation on the development of financial devices is noticeable. There is as yet no uniform body of rules or decisions interpreting the Blue Sky laws, but in various states it has been held that certificates of participation in a trust are not securities within the meaning of the law and that first mortgage bonds on real estate are not speculative securities. The advantage of utilizing these financial devices for speculative projects are obviously increased by this circumstance.

RECENT TENDENCIES IN CORPORATION FINANCE[1]

Albert S. Keister

American industrial corporations passed through two financial crises in the past six years. Perhaps one ought to say they have passed through one crisis and are now passing through the second. From 1916 to 1920 the upward swing of one of the most pronounced business cycles this country has ever known brought serious problems to our corporations – problems of financing an expanding volume of business at an increasing price level, complicated by war taxes. From the middle of 1920 on, equally serious difficulties have been confronted in the down swing of the cycle – problems of writing down and working off high cost inventories, meeting fixed charges in addition to operating deficits, paying off bank loans, dodging receiverships.

It is to be noted that the railroad and public utility corporations have experienced a cycle the reverse of the above. With fixed rates, rising tardily and against strenuous public resistance, 1916 to 1920 were lean years. Since 1920 the financial pressure has eased and many of them are "in clover." For these a period of extensions and betterments is at hand.

How have our industrial and public utility corporations weathered these two storms? What types of securities have they used when appealing to the public for capital? Have they in these sobering moments occasion to regret some of the covenants so freely entered into during the intoxicating years of prosperity? Have the investment bankers seized the opportunity to strengthen their control over our industrial machine? These and many other interesting questions are raised by the financial events of the past six years.

[1] [*Journal of Political Economy* 30 (1922), April: 257–73.]

In order to throw some light on these problems an examination was made of the changes in capitalization, occurring between 1916 and 1921, of 211 industrial corporations and 72 public utilities. About half of the concerns studied are well known, with their securities listed on the leading exchanges. The other half are small but none-the-less representative corporations.

The 211 industrials made a total of 405 issues of securities during the five years, of which 269 were stock and 136 were bonds and short-term notes. This means that in two-thirds of the cases the appeal was made to the "ownership element" while in one-third of the cases creditors were interested. Since these proportions were reversed in the case of the public utilities (two-thirds bonds, one-third stock) these facts afford some evidence that the industrials are observing the old principle that companies with fluctuating earnings should "go easy" on bonds. However, as pointed out below, one of the most significant tendencies is to make of preferred stock a security which will straddle these two interests and catch the very large group of buyers who do not care to be "speculative" stockholders nor "conservative" bondholders.

Of these 269 issues of stock, 136 were of common and 133 were of preferred. Easily the most striking feature of the common stock issues was the pronounced trend toward no-par stock. Almost half (62 of the 136 issues) were "common of no-par value."[2]

Considering that New York authorized this type of security as recently as 1912, that practically all other states permitting its use have done so since that year, and that to date less than half the states have legalized stock without par value, its growth in popularity has been phenomenal. What is to be said for and against it?

Advantages of No-Par Stock

Advocates of this type of security are willing to have it tested from three points of view – that of the corporate finance manager,

2 Among some of the more prominent companies using no-par common are American Chicle, Cuba Cane Sugar, Columbia Graphophone, Chandler Motor, Famous Players-Lasky, Goodyear Tire and Rubber, General Motors, Goodrich Rubber, General American Tank Car, International Cement, Montgomery Ward, Maxwell-Chalmers, Pierce Arrow Motor, Stewart Warner Speedometer, Stutz Motor, Wilson and Co., and Western Electric.

the creditor, and the stockholder. Since the kind of securities employed has practically no relation to either the labor or the price policies of the company, it is evident that the three classes mentioned include all the groups vitally concerned.

First, as to the corporate financier. No-par stock is flexible and elastic. The original issue can be put out at any price per share that the directors deem expedient. Successive issues can be sold above or below this original price. No question is raised regarding the stock being full paid, so long as the price is made in good faith and that price is actually received in cash, property, or services. The subterfuges used to get around the legal prohibition against issuing stock for less than its par value are abolished. No longer need promoters turn in to the new corporation property and services at twice their actual value in order to receive a large amount (in par value) of stock, then donate back half of it to become treasury stock, after which it can be "legally" sold at a discount or given away as bonus stock. This has been repeatedly practiced when it was impossible to market stock at par. If no-par encourages straightforward dealing in the formation or expansion of corporations it shall assuredly score one on that issue.

Second, as to the creditor. It has been claimed that par value reveals at a glance the amount that the stockholders have invested, hence tells creditors how much equity there is back of their loan. To this there are two replies: The par value never represents, either at the start or subsequently, the real equity of the stockholders, and furthermore credit is never extended nowadays, if indeed it ever was, on the basis of what the stockholders originally invested. The shrewd creditor looks not at the proprietorship items, but at the assets, at the important ratios, at the earning power, at the personnel of management, and at the business outlook. Hence it is evident creditors are no worse off with no-par than with par value and indeed may gain if no-par tends to promote more honest accounting.

Third, as to the stockholder. So long as a considerable class of security buyers persist in believing that there is some mysterious law that will eventually pull the market value up to the par value, society must welcome anything that will help shatter such a belief. No-par stock puts the prospective investor on his guard. "What is it worth?" leads him to not inquire as to par value and buy if the price is below par, but to inquire as to the actual worth. And he may ask: "What is a share of stock anyway?" And the answer should come: "Simply a fractional part of the ownership, your proportion of the equity remaining after prior claims to income and capital are satisfied." This should lead him to inquire as to the prior claims, the income, and the capital assets. If he gets that far the victory for sober investing will be won. The advocates of no-par stock do not regard it as a cure-all. "Suckers" will still be born every minute and Blue Sky laws will still be needed; but if it does nothing more than dispel the notion that the par value and the actual value are or ever will be the same, it will have justified its existence.

Disadvantages of No-Par

First, because it is an innovation, people do not understand it, business customs are set against it. Obviously this in itself will not stay the onward march of this youthful security.

Second, much of our state taxation is based on par value. One might argue over the proposition whether par value *ought* to be the basis of any tax but remembering that taxes have a hard time finding any basis we may pass that by. Suffice it to say, New York, Illinois, and many other states legalizing no-par stock have not let the no-par corporations escape their burdens.

Third, the law measures the liability of the stockholders of some corporations, such as banks, by the par value. For these corporations one might either take the position that they should continue to use par value since very few or no abuses surround their stock issues, or that no-par could be used coupled with the proviso that in case of failure the holder is liable for an amount equal to what was originally paid in for the stock.

Fourth, the law generally holds stockholders of any corporation liable for the difference between the par value and the amount of value turned in for the stock. If the stock has found its way into the hands of innocent purchasers the law holds the original buyer. Hence it is claimed par value gives creditors a measure of the liability of stockholders where inflated assets are traded for stock and the concern later goes bankrupt. This protection is more apparent than real. In the first place it is difficult to establish the "fair" value of property and services turned in to a corporation; the courts are reluctant to overrule the judgment of the board of directors in such matters. Realizing this, creditors seldom try such litigation. In the second place, whatever protection there is in such a law can be carried over into no-par stock. Why not say that original owners of no-par shares are liable for the difference between the price set on the shares and the value of the property and services they gave in exchange?

Fifth, the balance sheets of corporations using no-par stock are unstandardized. Some companies, such as General Motors, carry the stock at its original issue price and then have a surplus account. Others, such as Famous-Players, carry the stock at present market value with a surplus account. A third group carry their stock at a nominal figure, e.g., Pierce-Arrow at $5 per share, and show a surplus. A fourth method, used for example by General American Tank Car, is to divide the equity of the common stockholders by the number of shares and thus get a book value per share and show no surplus. Although this objection does not strike at the merits of no-par stock, nevertheless it would be well to standardize these reports. Of the four methods in common use that of reporting the stock at market value is the least defensible, since the figure given on the balance sheet is obsolete by the time the report is published and if one is really interested he can ascertain the market price without looking up the corporation report. Two of the other methods are valuable to certain parties; to know the original investment and how much of the profits made have been reinvested in the business (surplus) is important information to some people, as is the present book value of the stock. There is no reason why both should not be reported on the balance sheet.

On the whole the champions of no-par stock seem to have the better of the argument and we may confidently expect its wide extension. In fact the no-par arrangement is even creeping into preferred stock. The Lucey Manufacturing Company issued in 1920 a Class A no-par stock which is cumulative in dividends at $5 per year per share until 1923 and thereafter is cumulative at $8 per share per year, and a Class B no-par common. The Disco Milling Company has issued a preferred whose dividends are cumulative at $6 per share per year; the Shotwell Manufacturing Company issued in 1920 a Class A stock carrying 80 cents per year per share dividend ranking ahead of the Class B no-par stock; Montgomery Ward and Company in 1919 issued a Class A stock of no-par value, with cumulative dividends of $7 per share per year, followed by no-par common.

The foregoing cases point also to another recent tendency, namely, to break away from the old simple classification of stocks into preferred and common, and create other varieties of stocks. In England "founders" shares, coming after the common or "ordinary" shares, have been in vogue for a long time. Here we find the Armour Leather Company, formed in 1919, issuing preferred, common, and founders shares. General Motors is using cumulative preferred, cumulative debenture stock, and no-par common. Goodyear's recapitalization in 1921 brought out prior preferred, preferred, management stock (loaded with voting power to give the reorganization committee control) and no-par common. American Chain Company has a 7 per cent preferred, a Class A 7 per cent cumulative but receiving up to 10 per cent if earned, a Class B 7 per cent cumulative receiving up to; 10 per cent if earned, and no-par common. Armour and Company recently changed their capitalization to a 7 per cent preferred followed by Class A receiving 8 per cent, then Class B receiving a like percentage, then A and B share equally. Channell Chemical Company changed their capitalization in 1920 to provide for a Class A stock, no-par $6 per share per year cumulative dividend, and Class B no-par, with $6 per share per year cumulative dividend, after which both participate equally.

While most of these stocks differ more in name than in fact from the old-fashioned preferred and common, yet they are certain to bewilder investors and may be the beginning of a practice which will finally give us as great an assortment of stocks as we now have of bonds. Should that unhappy day arrive the financial page of the newspaper will contain references to and quotations on as many varieties as the famous Pittsburgh pickle firm boasts.

Preferred Stock

One of the most interesting recent tendencies is for corporations to develop a flexible capital instrument in the form of preferred stock. As stated above 133 issues of this type were brought out by the 211 industrials as compared with 136 issues of common. Considering that some of these companies were started during this period and hence had to issue common, the fact that the number of preferred issues practically equaled that of common proves that the preferred stock was adapted to the occasion. In fact there were two major forces at work to popularize this instrument. The first was that corporate financiers had to raise capital in large and increasing amounts throughout this period and desired if possible to do this without sharing control or creating fixed charges; the second force was the excess profits tax of the federal government.

To consider the second proposition first. This tax, passed in 1918, levied progressive rates on profits made in excess of 8 per cent on invested capital. At once the troublesome query arose: "What is invested capital?" Among the rulings forthcoming from the Treasury Department on this moot question was one which held that capital derived from the sale of stock was " invested" capital while that obtained from the sale of bonds or notes was not invested. Instantly the corporations seized upon the straight, old, 6 per cent cumulative preferred and dressed it up in all sorts of strange costumes. Patriotic urgings to pay taxes willingly fell on deaf ears as clever financiers stripped the covenants off of bonds to clothe their new creations. Aside from the fact that these preferred stocks rank after the loans, it would take more than an "expert" to find any essential differences between some of these war-evolved preferred stocks and bonds.

The other force at work causing the recent widespread use of preferred stock was more economic in nature. As the war prosperity, beginning in 1915, accumulated and intensified more capital was imperatively demanded. Plants had to be enlarged, payrolls went up, materials steadily advanced; the longer the war continued the more pressure there was to transfer this burden from the commercial banks to the investment market, corporate managers – representing, theoretically at least, the common stockholders – did not want to undertake the burden of fixed charges in post-war years. They were afraid a collapse of demand would sink their "net" below the zero point. Hence they were strongly inclined to use stock rather than bonds. Fortunately for them the war boom, which created the need for more capital, created the profits which made their outstanding stocks sell at attractive figures. The market was in a receptive mood for stocks. But why not use common stock? Common stock was in fact extensively employed; in many cases, however, the common stockholders did not want to share their advantageous position with others. They desired more capital but did not want it represented by bonds, neither did they want more common shares. The non-voting, cumulative, sinking fund preferred met the need.

How extensively stocks predominated over bonds during the boom period is shown in the following table:

KINDS OF SECURITIES USED, BY YEARS

	1916	1917	1918	1919	1920	1921 (Till May)
Common stock........	27	21	8	30	41	3
Preferred stock.......	18	22	8	31	21	5
Bonds...............	14	13	2	14	15	13
Notes...............	4	4	7	10	27	5

It will be remembered that little public financing was permitted by the government in 1918. The table shows how extensively stocks were used until the bubble burst in May, 1920. After the period of liquidation began, profits shrank and stocks were useless as a capital-raising device. Then it was the short-term note became popular and by 1921 bonds were overwhelmingly predominant.

Voting power. – In devising the special features of these recent preferred stock creations it should be recalled that corporate managers did not want to share control with the capital furnishers. To deny a share in control means depriving the security of voting rights. Such is the pronounced tendency in these recent preferred stocks. Examination of 157 preferred stocks disclosed only 20 per cent with full voting power; 25 per cent gave no voting power under any circumstances while the remaining 55 per cent conferred conditional voting power on the holder.[3]

The special conditions which confer voting power on the preferred stockholder are various. The one most frequently found is that when preferred dividends are in arrears for a certain period (usually four quarters) then the preferred shall have voting power. In some cases more teeth are put into the voting power by providing that if dividends are passed for a certain period then

[3] Recently the Supreme Court of Illinois ruled that under the constitution of the state no corporation chartered in Illinois can deprive any stockholder of voting power.

the preferred shall have exclusive voting power, thus turning control of the management over to the preferred. An increasing number of companies are saying to their preferred stockholders: "If we do not maintain quick assets at a 2 to 1 ratio to current liabilities," or more commonly, "If we do not maintain net quick assets (working capital) equal to 150 per cent of outstanding preferred stock then we will allow you to vote for directors."

Thus it is evident that the modern tendency is to ask preferred stockholders to keep hands off so long as their principal is safeguarded and their dividends are regularly forthcoming; but whenever things break badly and either principal or income is threatened then to invite the preferred either to participate in management or take it over altogether.

Callable features. – Of the 157 preferred stocks examined 90 per cent are callable. The call price varies from par to 125 but almost half the entire number made the call price 110, so that may be taken as typical. But giving the corporation the right to buy back its stock and actually buying it back are very different things. To what extent are these companies actually retiring their preferred stocks? A surprisingly large proportion impose sinking fund requirements on themselves and use the fund to retire the preferred stock. No less than 82 per cent of the companies having callable provisions obligate themselves for sinking funds.

There are two fundamental principles on which these sinking funds are based, with a great many varieties of detail from each of the main bases:

A. A specific, flat amount to be set aside each year and applied to the retirement of the preferred. This flat amount is sometimes stated in dollars, as $110,000 per year; more frequently as a percentage of the maximum amount issued, as 3 per cent of the maximum issue to be retired annually. Among the 157 cases over half of the companies with sinking funds used this flat amount method. It is the less desirable of the two from the standpoint of good, corporate, financial management. It ties the corporation to a special equal burden each year, regardless of business conditions. Whether the firm is making money or not, it has covenanted to set aside and use so much income to retire preferred stock. In years of business depression it is certain that many firms will not be able to live up to this requirement.

B. A percentage of the net earnings each year. This basis, being elastic, is much better for the company and in the long run for the preferred stockholder as well. In lean years it is better to forego retirement of part of their stock than to add to the troubles of a financially embarrassed management. When a corporation is finding it well-nigh impossible to meet operating expenses and fixed charges, it goes without saying that it cannot be forced to buy in some of its own preferred stock.

If careful financial management dictated the sinking fund provisions it is difficult to see how the first of these two methods should ever find a place.

Covenants and penalties. – Another tendency strongly evident in recent issues of preferred stock is for the corporation to make various covenants which, ostensibly at least, protect the stockholders' principal, and to place in the hands of a trustee an indenture containing these covenants and the penalties attaching for their violation. These covenants are of three general kinds:

A. Regarding sinking funds. These have been considered above. In general no penalties attach to their violation. Occasionally a company gives preferred stock voting power or says no dividend shall be paid on common if such a covenant is broken.

B. Regarding maintenance of assets. To safeguard the investment it is common to find covenants to maintain *net quick* assets at from 100 to 150 per cent of the outstanding preferred and *net tangible* assets at from 200 to 300 per cent of outstanding preferred. Here again the majority of concerns are long on promises and short on penalties. However, one finds more penalties than in A above. When punishment is provided it takes the form of stopping dividends on common or giving voting rights to preferred. Whether these covenants will be violated or not would seem to depend on the honesty of the accounting policy of the corporation. It would be comparatively easy to have the books show such ratios at the time statements are published, even though the company did not actually have the necessary assets.

C. Regarding issues of additional securities. These are of two sorts: mortgage bonds and additional preferred stock. As to mortgage bonds 111 out of the 157 covenant not to place any future mortgage (except purchase money mortgages) on any of the fixed assets of the company without the consent of a large percentage (usually 75 per cent) of the preferred stock. Since these covenants closed the door to mortgage bonds we have witnessed a great many issues of short-term notes and debenture bonds. As to additional preferred stock being issued, such is usually allowed if two-thirds or three-fourths of that already outstanding votes favorably and if the net quick assets and net earnings are ample to safely permit taking on additional shareholders. These covenants are practically self-enforcing. If the three-fourths vote is not obtained the mortgage bonds cannot be issued. (But the funds can be obtained by issuing debenture bonds or short-term notes which of course rank ahead of the claims of the preferred stockholders.) If the net quick assets are not up to covenant, which is usually that such assets must be kept at 200 per cent of the total preferred including the proposed new issue, then the new issue cannot be brought out. Likewise the covenant regarding net earnings is self-enforcing. If the net earnings are not equal to at least three times the dividend requirements on the total preferred issued and to be issued, then the proposed issue is tabled.

Reflecting on these various provisions in recent preferred stocks one cannot help feeling that such a security more nearly resembles a bond than it does a stock. The dividends are cumulative – so is bond interest. The holder under ordinary circumstances gets no vote for directors – neither do bondholders. The holder, however, gets a voice in management or assumes it altogether if his dividends are in arrears – so does the bondholder through foreclosure. The preferred stock is callable with a sinking fund to redeem it – so with bonds. Protective covenants safeguard the principal of the preferred stockholder – so it is with recent bonds and short-term notes. Indeed about the only similarity between common stock and these new-fashioned preferreds is that the law regards them both as evidences of ownership, not creditorship. Legally, preferred and common stock resemble each other; in practically every other way they are different. It would appear that in this instrument corporation finance had struck an unusually flexible and facile device to tempt that large strata of capital suppliers who want neither a pure speculation nor the conservative 5 or 6 per cent mortgage bond. Surely also, corporate management must realize that there is no small advantage to itself in being relieved of the fear of receivership in case default on dividends occurs. Receiverships are notoriously expensive. The general public will gain if they are reduced to a minimum. Undoubtedly the recently devised preferred stock will contribute to that end.

Let no one be deceived, however, into thinking that any type of security is a substitute for cautious discrimination on the part of the investor, nor for sound business policy on the part of corporate management. These must be relied on always to be the truly effective means toward a sounder financial basis for our corporations.

Short-Term Notes and Bonds

During the recent boom period, as we have seen, stocks were the favorite instrument of capital raising. As soon as the index number of commodity prices turned downward, the corporations had to turn to borrowing. The reasons are apparent. When prices stopped rising and then began to fall orders were canceled, profits turned into losses, high-cost inventories piled up and simultaneously stocks tumbled. Indeed the "key" stocks broke as early as November, 1919, discounting the decline which occurred six months later. With stocks on the toboggan it was useless to think of trying to market new issues of any kind of stocks. Not even the most elaborate covenants in preferred could make them palatable. Yet the industrials were in imperative need of funds. The banks had been furnishing them large amounts of working capital. Now the banks began pressing the corporations to fund, their indebtedness into securities and pay off or reduce materially their bank loans. Throughout the latter half of 1920 short-term notes, mostly of five or ten years maturity, appeared in great numbers. The circulars describing these notes stated with monotonous frequency: "Purpose, To pay off current indebtedness and provide additional working capital."

Many of these notes were made convertible, the advertisements playing up the high prices of the company's stock during the preceding five years as a reason why the conversion privilege should be highly regarded. Doubtless many investors accepted this dubious argument. Another interesting feature of these recent short-term notes is the surprisingly large proportion (43 per cent) that mature serially. To the corporation there are two noteworthy disadvantages in this type of security. First, it involves a different market price for each maturity of the series, thus rendering it less marketable; and second, in years of depression it imposes the same definite obligation to redeem part of the notes as is imposed in years of prosperity. Already this second disadvantage is of more than academic importance to some companies.

Finally by the end of 1920 the market became surfeited with notes, even 8 per cent interest not being sufficiently attractive to market them in the face of the apathy of investors. Then it was that the industrials were driven to bonds. It was an unfortunate time to have to use this instrument. Market rates of interest were high, hovering around 8 per cent for industrial bonds. This would mean that by the time underwriting commissions were paid money would cost the corporation from 9 to 12 per cent or even more. There was every prospect that by late in 1921 interest rates would be lower and would continue to fall after that. It would have been a propitious time to use the short-term note as a borrowing instrument. But the short-term note had worn out its welcome. Under these circumstances the corporations had to make the best of things, issue their bonds at expensive rates and extract what comfort they could from the fact that they made these bonds callable. If the interest rates for this type of security fall to 5 1/2 or 6 per cent, which is another way of saying that if the market price of these bonds rises considerably above par, it will be profitable for the issuing companies to pay another underwriting commission and have the old, high-rate bonds called in and paid off with the proceeds of the sale of new, lower-rate securities. Indeed it is possible that within the next five years stocks may recover a considerable part of their recent losses in which case capital funds might be secured cheaply from the sale of preferred or common stock and these 7 and 8 per cent bonds retired with the proceeds. If such a situation should come about it would mean that the corporations that used the convertible bond might find themselves rid of their debt without going through the investment banking channels at all.

A final observation on these industrial notes and bonds. The government educated a vast number of people to the bond-buying habit during the Liberty Bond campaigns. It is estimated that there were only a half-million bondholders in this country prior to the war, whereas in 1919 they were said to number twenty millions. The vast majority of these could not hope to buy corporate bonds of a denomination even as high as $500. So the tendency has been to try to catch these small bond-buyers by offering the "baby" bond of $100 denomination and combining with it the instalment plan of purchase. Whether this will pay the investment houses remains to be seen. It costs practically as much to sell and handle a $100 bond as it does a $1,000 bond even if bought outright, while with the instalment payment plan it probably costs considerably more. However, if enough of these small purchases grow into $500 and $1,000 accounts, the bond houses will be repaid. Probably also, the tendency to reduce the par value of stock to $25 and $10 goes back to marketing considerations.

Public Utilities

As stated above 72 public utilities were studied to see wherein their financing differed from that of industrials. These concerns made 142 issues of securities of which 47 were stocks and 95 were bonds and notes. Why should we find here two-thirds of the issues bonds and notes whereas the industrials used stocks in two-thirds of all their cases?

It is safer for public utilities to borrow than for industrials because, first, the demand for their product is stabler than for that of most industrials; second, they are protected against competition; third, their rates in the larger communities are fixed by public authority and insure a reasonable return on the "fair" value of the property employed; fourth, they have a heavy investment in fixed assets to offer as mortgage security for bonds. It is not surprising therefore that they should so successfully appeal to the bond-buying classes. Another significant difference between the public utility and industrial issues is that 30 per cent of the public utility bond issues were for refunding purposes, while practically none of the industrials were so. It is clear that the public utilities are coming to regard their debts as perpetual. When one bond issue matures another takes its place. In this respect these concerns are following the example of the railroads.

Another difference is the fact that public utilities seldom give as the purpose of the security issue, the raising of working capital.

Less than 7 per cent of the issues mentioned working capital as a purpose. Are the public utilities ashamed to admit they go to the investor for working capital or are they not in need of the working capital that industrials must have? The truth seems to be that they need relatively small amounts of working capital and that the public furnishes what they do need in other ways than through interest-bearing securities. They need less because the typical electric light, or gas, or telephone, or street railway company has few accounts and notes receivable and those of short-time duration, mostly 10 to 30 days; furthermore they collect in advance for many of their services, such as street-car rides, thus being furnished with their working funds by the consumer; they carry relatively small inventories for they sell services rather than commodities. Hence the maintenance of adequate working capital is no problem for them.

It is common observation that the holding company movement is proceeding rapidly among the public utilities. Evidences of this are apparent in their financing. For example, where the purpose of the issue could be determined it was found that 54 per cent of the bond issues were for expansion. "Expansion" does not necessarily prove the growth of holding companies but it probably points to that in a large proportion of the cases. Further evidence of the holding company movement is seen in the large number of issues secured by collateral; 30 of the 95 bond issues were so secured. In most cases this collateral means stocks and bonds of subsidiaries, put up by the parent as security for its own bonds.

There are certain economic advantages in this holding company movement. In the first place the parent company needing large blocks of capital at one time can raise the funds more cheaply than the small separate concerns could. Second, these securities are better for the investor both because they are more marketable and because his funds find their way into the productive property of subsidiaries in different communities thus spreading his risk. Third, the holding company benefits by virtue of the fact that it draws its income from the income of its scattered subsidiaries; such subsidiaries are likely to produce a fairly uniform and steady income for the parent since lessened demand in one community is likely to be offset by improving conditions in another. Fourth, economies in management especially in purchasing and reduction of overhead can be effected by the holding company. Fifth, the holding company can plead its cause before public utility commissions more effectively than small separate companies. Sixth, large holding companies alone can make a reality of the potential marvels of hydroelectric development.

So far as stocks are concerned the public utilities seem to be sticking close to the old-fashioned preferred and common. There is scarcely any tendency to adopt no-par stock, neither are they creating variations from preferred and common. Middle West Utilities is one of the exceptions, having provided in 1921 for no-par common and a prior-lien stock ranking ahead of preferred. Cities Service Company has had for several years "Bankers' shares," each share representing one-tenth equity in a share of their high-priced common.

Creditors' Control

When a corporation found itself insolvent under the old system of things the officers moved for a receiver and at frightful cost the affairs were reorganized, after which the bankers, representing the creditors, insured themselves control for the ensuing critical years by tying up the common stock in a voting trust. The management was under the control of the financiers, who were acting for the protection of their clients, the security buyers.

The recent tendency is to avoid these expensive receiverships and organize a "rescue party" composed of the interested banking houses. This rescue party moves in when "technical" insolvency is reached, proceeds to do a thorough job of financial reorganization, looking carefully after the interests of the various classes of creditors and, if rumor has it right, taking pretty generous commissions for their own services. They then proceed to sew up control of the affairs of the company in their own hands during the life of the new bonds. Instead of using the old voting trust arrangement, the tendency now is either to issue to themselves a special kind of voting stock or have an ironclad agreement with the stockholders that the management selected by the financiers shall be kept in power. It is not usually difficult to get the stockholders' consent to relinquish their voting power. The bankers simply tell them that the alternative is receiver ship. To this powerful argument is added the practical help that only a few of the larger stockholders take an active interest anyway, and since these few are usually involved in the management their co-operation is assured.

The friendly reorganization of the Goodyear Tire and Rubber Company in 1921 resulted in the creation of $10,000 management stock, heavily loaded with voting power and held by the reorganizing bankers, who immediately ousted President Sieberling and put in a new management. The circulars announcing the $10,000,000 First Mortgage twenty-year bonds of the Fisk Rubber Company stated:

> During the life of these bonds control of the management of the Company through the right to elect two-thirds of the Board of Directors, will be vested in Messrs. James Dean, of Dillon, Read and Company, Otis H. Cutler, Chairman of the Board of American Brake Shoe and Foundry Company, and H. T. Dunn, President of the Fisk Rubber Company, or their successors, through the issue of Management Stock.

The Cuba Cane Sugar and Moline Plow companies came through their friendly reorganizations with the financial powers in control.

What does it mean? Are we in for an era in which the policies of industries are to be finally passed or vetoed by the financiers? Can the "protection of investors" justify such vigorous measures as "firing" the old management and naming the new? Has it come to this, that however medieval a corporation's *labor* policy may be nothing will happen, unless perchance the laborers force a change, but if the corporation's financial policy gets the company into difficulty the bankers must immediately take charge? Perhaps so. Perhaps the results to the public will justify these measures. The defense of the investment bankers is. that their clients must be protected. Capital must be safeguarded. They probably would not deny that labor and the public need safeguarding also, but the simple fact is that capital is organized and on the job while the other interests are not. Such a procedure, we are assured, is better for all concerned than receivership.

But the question may be raised: If the financiers are to supervise management after the corporation's finances have come to the point of insolvency, why should they not supervise them before they reach such a condition and thereby prevent the trouble? If this logical development works out then what becomes of stockholders' control? Would management by financial houses in the interests of creditors be any worse for the public than management by a small group of common stockholders, who alone take any active interest in the exercise of their voting power? Might it not be better? Or might it not be best of all to have all the parties interested – creditors, stockholders, laborers, and the public – share the management responsibilities? It is a long way to that goal, perhaps, but the growing tendency for creditors to get protection by representation in management may be a step in that direction.

Summary

Two-thirds of the public utility financing is done by borrowing while two-thirds of the financing of industrials is done by sale of stocks.

During the boom period preferred stock was the favorite instrument; immediately after the break of prices in 1920 short-term notes predominated, while the depression of 1921 has been prolific of bond issues.

There is a pronounced trend toward no-par stock among industrials; little evidence of it as yet among the public utilities.

The industrials are tending to create varieties of stocks, other than preferred and common.

Recent preferred stocks are being made callable, are carrying attractive covenants regarding maintenance of large working capital, net tangible assets, and sinking funds for retirement of such stock; many of which covenants are certain to be violated and no penalty suffered.

Public utility companies are coming to regard their debts as perpetual, whereas industrials nearly always provide sinking funds or use the serial type of bond.

The holding company movement is gathering speed among the public utilities and offers promising advantages to the public, pro vided of course that regulation is effective.

The $100 denomination of bonds and short-term notes is becoming common.

The friendly "rescue party" is supplanting receivership as a method of reorganizing insolvent concerns and is increasing the tendency for bankers to either participate in or actually control the management of our industries.

CORPORATE FAILURE[1]

Arthur S. Dewing

The Importance of Reorganization. – The failure of a corporation is distinctly different from that of a partnership. In the latter case the business would ordinarily have no bonded debt, and the bank and merchandise creditors would either force the business to liquidate, or else compel the partners to offer some plan involving the partial or complete payment of the debts. The case of the small corporation is similar. In the case of a large corporation, on the other hand, there are many different persons interested in the business. It is a complex organization. No one is personally liable for the debts in case, on liquidation, the business does not sell for the amount of its liabilities. Furthermore, the large business has usually valuable intangible assets, such as good-will, which retain a value only if the business is continued. So that even when it appears that the business may be disintegrated and the parts sold for an amount sufficient to meet the creditors' claims, the stockholders themselves will probably deem it expedient to invest sufficient new money to pay these claims immediately and thus save the business and its organization from complete disruption. In this way a new or reorganized business, free from immediate embarrassment, starts with the same stock holders as the old.

If the corporation furnishes a public service it cannot be closed up, even if the various parties concerned are willing. The courts take the attitude that a railroad, or an electric light or gas plant, supplies a public necessity and that the rights of the public come before the wishes of the stockholders or even the debts of the creditors. Except in extreme cases when there is abundant evidence to show that there exists no public need, the courts will insist that the embarrassed corporation shall operate its trains or

[1] [Chapter 24 of *Corporation Finance*, New York: The Ronald Press, 1923.]

its lighting plant through the agency of a receiver, and that its stockholders and creditors shall ultimately adjust their difficulties and reorganize the corporation so that it may continue its business as a solvent and progressive enterprise. The court may even issue securities in the name of its receiver which take precedence over the claims of every creditor of the corporation; it may decide which creditors' claims shall be paid and which shall not; and it may otherwise conduct the business in an arbitrary manner, provided such usurpation of power is necessary to safeguard the interests of the public. From all these causes the probability is very slight that an unprofitable or bankrupt business, meeting an obvious need of the public, will be disintegrated and the parts sold; it will be voluntarily or forcibly reorganized.

Distinction Between Fundamental and Superficial Causes. – In discussing the causes of corporate failure it is convenient to distinguish between three phases of the general subject – the fundamental causes of failure, the superficial causes or conditions, and the outward signs. These three are usually confused, even by economists. We may go even further and say that ordinarily neither the men who are responsible for the business failure nor the financial experts who constitute themselves an investigating committee, ever note the difference between the fundamental and abiding causes of financial distress and the mere external symptoms that stand out clearly in the foreground. Business men are usually unreflective. In a very true sense that makes them aggressive and quick of response, because action is not imperiled by irresolution. It does not, however, make them successful in diagnosing their own troubles or those of their associates. They cannot see the causes of business failure in their true perspective. After the most exhaustive and illuminating analysis of economic causes of business failure, there must stand out always the fact that a business fails because the managers do not possess the necessary intuitive skill, foresight, initiative, perseverance, and intellectual power to compel its success. Any discussion of economic advantages or disadvantages must be subordinate to the conscious recognition of personal characteristics. Yet recognizing fully these psychological conditions leading to failure, one may still speak of fundamental economic causes, in the sense of economic conditions which will, under the leadership of any but a business genius, lead to failure. In this category may be included four – excessive competition, unprofitable expansion, a change in the public demand for the commodity, and the distribution of capital as ostensive profit.

Fundamental Economic Causes – 1. Competition. – Competition is a necessary and wholesome element in all business enterprise. Within broad limits, the keener the competition the greater will be the business efficiency and the higher the range of executive ability required for success. It becomes a true cause of failure only when it becomes so keen that the most efficient competitors are required to sell at less than cost. In the case of a business requiring small capital, a business which can be created or liquidated in a short time, the most efficient will never be compelled to sell for less than cost. Instead, the less able managers of the less efficient plants will wisely stop producing or even retire from business. But if large amounts of capital are invested, or if the service is required by the public, or if the business carries itself forward by the sheer momentum of its past, it can neither stop producing nor go into liquidation. A railroad is a case in point. It cannot cease to exist. If the rates it collects for its services are insufficient to pay for its operation, it must still run its trains. A local public service company is ordinarily protected by the utility commission of the state in the exercise of monopoly powers, provided it renders good and reasonably cheap service to its customers. Competition is a relatively unimportant factor for such businesses, unless one considers the competitive influence of two utilities – gas and electricity, omnibuses and street-cars. In manufacturing businesses the plea of severity of competition can be advanced but seldom as a fundamental cause of failure. A manufacturing business can curtail production even at the expense of its organization rather than dispose of its product at less than cost. It is true competition is alleged to be the true cause of many failures, but the allegation is merely an excuse to obscure the deeper defect in business management. Too keen competition is invariably the excuse of the weak.

2. *Unprofitable Expansion.* – Unprofitable expansion is a much more serious and a much more common cause of failure than drastic competition. It is the besetting sin of a fairly successful corporation with a relatively large margin of gross profit based on a small output. It is also the usual cause of disaster among

corporations favored with an unusual capacity for borrowing money. While overmastering competition occurs only when there is a large capital investment, the temptation to overexpand is present in every business. It is commonest in a country like the United States where the margin of profit shows marked fluctuations and where the temperamental bias of optimism is magnified by an inclination to regard hopes for the future as things predestined. As a keen judge of business conditions remarked to some students, "When you have a business that is growing very rapidly, you are apt to be a little blinded by the rapidity of it, and look at your gross sales rather than your net profits."

The number of instances in which the cause of failure is overexpansion are legion, but for the present purpose it suffices to note three, drawn from the manufacturing, the public service, and the railroad industries.

Overexpansion of a Manufacturing Industry. One of the striking instances of failure due to overexpansion of an other wise successful manufacturing business is afforded by the history of the Westinghouse Electric and Manufacturing Company. Starting in 1886 with sales amounting to less than $150,000, the business grew by leaps and bounds. During the year 1894, a period showing relatively little business activity, the Westinghouse Company, on a capital including bonds and current debts of less than $10,000,000, showed a net profit of over 16 per cent. Expansion continued. The company organized foreign departments and finally foreign factories. It financed interurban electric railway lines for the purpose of exploiting its inventions; it advanced large sums to unproductive subsidiary companies. By 1906 its total funded and current liabilities and stock had risen to $45,000,000 but the net profit was only a little over $3,000,000, or only 5 per cent. No theoretical economist ever discovered a clearer illustration of the law of diminishing returns. As a small business in a year of depression, the Westinghouse Company earned 16 cents on every dollar of invested capital; as a large business in a year of marked prosperity, it earned 5 cents on each dollar. It failed the year following.

Overexpansion of a Public Service Holding Company. The second type of illustration comes from the field of the holding company, or more particularly the public service holding company. As explained in another connection, this type of enterprise became very popular in the years following the panic of

1907, when capital was seeking new channels of investment. The first two or three of these companies were successful from the beginning, notably the original United Gas Improvement Company, and later the American Light and Traction and the American Gas and Electric companies. In finance, as in all other fields of endeavor, there are always hosts of imitators whenever a new development seems to point the way to an easy success. Public service holding companies sprang up all over the country. As their profits consisted entirely in the increment of earnings remaining to generous issues of common stock of the local operating companies, it seemed to the operators of these companies that the greater the number of utilities controlled the greater must be the profit. The success of the American Light and Traction Company was due to the careful selection of properties to be acquired, conservative management, and shrewd finance. Its imitators, however, lacked these three elements of success – they lacked particularly care in selecting new properties. Economy was sacrificed to mere size. This foolhardy mania for expansion reached its climax toward the end of 1911 just before the decline of the stock market values which ended in the close of the Stock Exchange, July 30, 1914. Subjected to a shrinking market for credit, these recently organized holding companies were in dire straits. Most of them resorted to the issue of short-time notes, either to meet the demands of their subsidiaries, or to fulfil already existing contracts. Some of them used borrowed money to maintain the interest on their bonds. Several went into the hands of receivers. Others passed their preferred stock dividends or gave scrip for them. They all advanced excuses – a tight money market, increased taxes and labor costs of the operating companies, and latterly a difficulty in selling securities because of the Great War. But the fundamental reason was not given. The companies had spread their resources and their credits so thin that the cover had begun to break.

Overexpansion of Railroads. In the field of railroad enterprise the influence of unwise expansion was much more potent than that of keen competition even during the decade before the panic of 1893, although excessive competition has been advanced as the primary cause of the numerous receiverships of that time. When the Northern Pacific passed into the hands of receivers the road was facing an annual loss of over $1,500,000, caused very largely by its unprofitable branch extensions. The Atchison in its foolish expansion from 1884 to 1888 illustrates the principle clearly. In the former year with 2,800 miles of line the road made net earnings of $2,600 a mile; in the latter year with 7,000 miles of line it earned only $700 a mile. In the former year the road had over $5,000,000 available for its stockholders; in the latter year there was a net deficit of $3,000,000. Looking at the matter another way, the Atchison system earned 6 1/2 per cent on its total outstanding bonds and stock in 1884, and 2 1/2 per cent in 1888.

Among eastern roads the failure of the Reading in 1880 was due directly to the purchase, at a cost of $73,000,000, of coal lands valued at the time at $30,000,000, and the receivership of 1884 to the lease of the Central Railroad of New Jersey which guaranteed a dividend of 6 per cent on its stock when the interest on its bonds was not earned. The Reading's failure of 1893 can be traced to the burdens of the Central New Jersey and Lehigh Valley leases, together with wild speculations in the stocks of New England railroads. So that each of the three failures of the Reading can be attributed, unhesitatingly and without a suspicion of doubt, to unprofitable expansions.

The most conspicuous railway failure of the last few years due to unprofitable expansion is that of the New Haven system. Brushing aside for the moment all the secondary causes that led to one of the most unfortunate and unnecessary failures of railroads, the primary fact stands out that the New Haven Railroad itself was ruined by the insane craze of its bankers and directors so to extend its sphere of control as to embrace a monopolistic system of transportation covering all of New England. Sustained by the hope of ultimately securing monopoly profits and thereby justifying the outlay, stimulated by the surreptitious profits obtained by its directors and by the ease with which it received credit from New England investors, the road plunged headlong into a series of expenditures which embraced traction companies, steamship lines, connecting railroads, even gas, light, and water companies, until the legitimate profits from the railroad were more than offset by the losses on the outside enterprises. Thus in 1899, on a total capitalization of $80,000,000, including bonds and stocks, the company earned, above operating expenses and taxes, almost exactly $10,000,000, or approximately 12 per cent on the capitalization. This was before any outside operations were undertaken. In 1914, after the completion of the policy of expansion, the total outstanding capitalization had increased to $417,000,000, while the railroad mileage stood at exactly the same figure. The net income available for interest and dividends on capital had increased to $21,500,000, but that was only 5 per cent on the outstanding stock and debt – less than half what it was before the period of outside speculations. In brief, during the fifteen years between 1899 and 1914 the railroad mileage of the New Haven system was not increased. Yet during the period invested capital became five times as great and the earnings only twice as great.

All these failures due to unwarranted extensions illustrate the economic law of diminishing returns. This is more than a mere academic doctrine of scholastic economists. It is a vital force operating in actual business. If a certain investment, say of $1,000,000 in a manufacturing plant or a railroad, yields a net profit of 10 per cent, it does not follow that an investment twice as great will yield twice as great a profit. On the contrary, wastes incident to the bigger business will creep in, so that the profit, although perhaps greater in actual amount, will be smaller proportionately. And if the investment be continued without limit the decline in actual earnings with the later investments will even obliterate the profit on the earlier investments. In brief, after a certain point, as capital is added to any industry, the rate of return on each dollar invested grows smaller. It is true that up to a certain point, the point of saturation, as it were, the profit tends to increase. But this point is early reached. The optimism of business men, the avarice of bankers, and the enthusiasm of engineers easily carry the business beyond it.

3. *Cessation of Public Demand.* – A third deep-lying economic cause of failure is the change in the conditions of public demand. Such a case, however, is relatively rare. The failure of the old American Bicycle Company is a case in point. This combination acquired in 1898 some 48 bicycle plants producing upwards of 65 per cent of the bicycles made in the United States. According to reliable auditors the annual profits of these plants had together averaged nearly $5,000,000 for the preceding four years. Appraisal by reliable independent experts showed actual property to the value of over $22,000,000, of which upwards of $12,000,000 consisted of net quick assets. All this augured well for the combination. The total number of bicycles sold fell from

860,000 in 1899 to 100,000 in 1902. Suddenly, with no warning, the public ceased to use its toy. As a result the millions of dollars of property set aside for the manufacture of bicycles became useless and the company failed. Even after $2,500,000 in new money was added to adapt the factories for the manufacture of automobiles, it was no more successful. The reorganized company failed twice thereafter.

4. Excess Payment of Capital Charges. – The fourth of the group of fundamental economic causes of failure is entirely financial. It is the payment of excessive interests or dividends due to a mistaken belief in the profitableness of the enterprise. Such payments may often be excused on the ground of unconservative but technically correct principles of accountancy – principles which, for example, may be theoretically defensible but are unquestionably unjustifiable in practice. The corporation which employs them becomes insolvent whatever the textbooks of accountancy may say. At other times the payment of interest or dividends in excess of profits cannot be justified by any theory and can be called nothing short of fraud. Thus the American Malting Company, in a notable case that came before the courts, paid out nearly $900,000 in dividends, while its gross profit, without allowing for depreciation or special reserves, amounted to $500,000. In 1872 the old Erie Railway was rescued by Daniel E. Sickles from the notorious Drew-Fisk clique. In the three following years the road earned a profit of $1,008,775, but its directors represented the profit to be $5,352,573, on the basis of which dividends were paid on the preferred and common stocks. Meanwhile, $6,000,000 of bonds were sold. From 1888 to 1895, or in seven years before its failure, the Baltimore and Ohio paid out $6,269,008 in dividends, whereas an independent auditor found that less than $1,000,000 had been actually earned. In 1887 the directors of the Atchison road increased the dividend rate from 6 to 7 per cent at a time when the net earnings of the road were actually falling short, by over $2,000,000, of the interest and rental requirements. And this situation is present in the contemporary railroad troubles. Although the failure of the St. Louis and San Francisco Railroad in 1913 was due primarily to unprofitable extensions, it was aggravated in no small measure by the payment of excessive charges on the securities of the Chicago and Eastern Illinois. The weak ness of the Toledo, St.

Louis and Western Railroad, which passed into the hands of receivers in October, 1914, was due to the excessive capital charges resulting from the burdensome charges of the Chicago and Alton Railroad.

It is important to observe also that although the occasion for the payment of unearned dividends and interest may be traced back to overexpansion, and for that reason overexpansion is to be regarded as the fundamental cause of distress, still the payment of unearned capital charges has in many cases directly precipitated failure.

This is particularly true of railroad systems constructed out of numerous component parts, and of industrial combinations promoted in the expectation of receiving monopoly profits. Thus, of 24 cases of industrial failure examined in another connection, it was found that "18 out of the 24 paid either unearned interest on bonds or unearned dividends on stock in the year just prior to the failure or reorganization," and that "every corporation paid out interest or dividends in the face of falling earnings and none need have suffered serious financial difficulties had the amounts paid in interest and dividends been conserved."

While it is entirely possible and safe to draw on a large surplus in order to maintain interest or dividend payments for a single year or even two years of reduced business, the policy is at best questionable. No doubt the New Haven Railroad's plight was aggravated by the fact that in the four years from 1910 to 1915 the dividend payments every year exceeded the profits available. No sufficient excuse for the mistake can be found in the desire to protect the small investor or in the hope of maintaining the company's credit among savings banks. This entire matter has been discussed in its proper place before, but it is important to note again that the continued payment of interest or dividends in excess of earnings can have only one outcome, however successful the policy may appear to be for a short period.

REORGANIZATION METHODS[1]

Arthur S. Dewing

Contraction of Financial Plan. – When a corporation fails or becomes embarrassed its financial plan is usually remolded. This is reorganization. It is a redrawing of the financial plan, but with a view to contraction, not to expansion. Whether the new plan provides for contraction or expansion, new money is required, but an expanding and profitable business may ordinarily solicit new capital on the basis of its past success, whereas a bankrupt business secures capital only through coercion. Unwillingly its security-holders add more money merely to save that already invested. So easy is it to obtain money for the expansion of a successful business by one of several ways that the question is merely one of financial expediency; so difficult is it, on the other hand, to obtain the money necessary to reorganize an unsuccessful corporation that the success of the reorganization depends primarily on selecting that plan which shall achieve this one end with the least friction.

Factors Involved. – Owing to the delicacy of the situation and the judgment required, corporate reorganization is the most intricate phase of the whole field of finance and the one in which generalizations and precedents are least significant. It is a subject which has as its elements a mass of conflicting legal precedents, the makeshifts of mere temporary expedients, and, permeating the whole, the psychological bias and prejudices of thousands of dissatisfied human beings whose interests are in fundamental conflict. The primary purpose of every reorganization is justice to all concerned. But the justice is tempered – one might almost say obscured – by motives of expediency. Compulsion is exerted at one or more points. This requires the arm of the law. Moreover, even when the statutory law presents no difficulties,

[1] [Chapter 25 of *Corporation Finance*, New York: The Ronald Press, 1923.]

there are always conflicting precedents and legal opinions. In addition to the legal aids and impediments there are important financial questions of mere judgment – the ease with which an underwriting may be obtained, to what extent the stockholders may be counted on to add money, what may be the opportunity for selling bonds during the first year of the new company's life. In answering these questions in any one particular case precedents are of little value. Each reorganization is different from all that have occurred before in one or more important respects.

Importance of Study of Reorganization. – Yet in spite of its intricacy, a study of the reorganization of corporations is one of the most important in the field of finance. In the past, hundreds of millions of dollars of actual property investment have been involved in reorganizations. Great railroad systems like those of the Atchison and the Reading, great traction systems like those of the New York City and the Chicago surface lines, great manufacturing industries like that of the Westinghouse Company, involving thousands of laborers and the production of necessities of modern civilization, have all been subjected to the uncertainties of reorganization. These enterprises have involved much more than the mere fortunes of the wealthy; they have been concerned with the savings of a great multitude of people, including the very poor. Frequently the savings of a man's lifetime have been jeopardized by a single man's interpretation of justice in a reorganization plan. Probably the ablest men in law, finance, and productive industry have given some of their best efforts to the solution of the intricate problems involved. The regrettable feature is that in spite of all precedents each new reorganization is quite as perplexing as those that have gone before. Only the most vague and inexact theories and generalizations can be made.

Reorganization of a Large Corporation. – A large business is not ordinarily closed, its property sold, and the proceeds divided up among the creditors. It is reorganized. Sometimes this is done publicly, with all the dislocation and notoriety that usually attends business misfortune; sometimes it is done quietly through conferences and concerted action by all the persons concerned. The former is a reorganization through a court receivership and the latter a reorganization through a friendly committee. The former method was and still is pursued in case of the failure or expected failure of a large corporation with many security-holders and creditors of diverse interests. Under these circumstances close co-operation is impossible and the whole readjustment must occur under the supervision of the court.

The procedure followed at the present time in effecting the reorganization of a large business corporation has developed through a series of precedents, each one of which was established originally more through accident than forethought. Ordinarily a fundamentally important mode of procedure, in financial as well as other social affairs, results from a slow and tempered growth of precedents, all of which are firmly rooted in the common or the statutory law, and all of which are constantly balanced off against contemporary social opinion. The history of the organization of the business corporation, the history of the public franchise, the history of the practice of corporate taxation, are all illustrations of the orderly and well-regulated development of a body of well-considered precedents, consistent at all times with the law and with public opinion. Not so the present practices governing the reorganization of financially embarrassed corporations. They have arisen through immediate necessities; they have come into existence at times when any action, legal or illegal, impetuous or reflective, was better than no action.

Motives Governing Procedure. – Three separate and often antagonistic sets of motives govern the procedure to be followed in the reorganization of any kind of large corporation. The most important and usually the least apparent is concerned with the human or psychological elements. Most writers on finance, taking their promptings from published circulars and reports, forget the interplay of human motives, ambitions, antagonisms, and friendships that underlie every financial episode of importance. A corporation is reorganized by men, not puppets; its officers, its creditors, its security-holders, the attorneys, and the judges, are not mere thinking machines, but ordinary men subject to human emotions and weaknesses. First then, the procedure must be such as to allay, not aggravate, the friction incident to the conflict of personalities. The second set of motives governing reorganization procedure is economic. Leases must be continued or abrogated, contracts rewritten, rights enforced or surrendered, in accordance with the single question – Is it profitable? No corporation can be permanently successful and serve the public well which does not pay its operating expenses, including fair wages to its employees, with adequate upkeep of its plant, and in addition a fair rate of return on the invested capital. And the reorganization procedure must recognize this simple economic imperative. The third set of controlling motives is legal and judicial. Experienced students of legal practice have worked out certain more or less clearly defined lines of orderly procedure. Some of these lines of procedure have been prescribed by the courts, others are merely tolerated by the courts because they facilitate the regular course of the reorganization, and others, arising from the ingenuity of lawyers, are followed until some court decision condemns them. Lawyers are apt to exaggerate their own importance and the significance of their legal machinery in determining the form and details of reorganization procedure, forgetful that a reorganization is primarily an adjustment of human motives and economic conditions, circumscribed rather than determined by the law. The present orderly, and on the whole socially expedient, procedure in connection with the reorganization of all corporations large and small, has been built up from the interplay of these three underlying motives.

Events Immediately Preceding Failure. – The explicit failure of an industrial company may come suddenly, as the immediate consequence of a labor strike, a panic, or a bank failure, or even the death of an important director. A railroad failure, or the failure of a local utility, invariably due to deep-seated, slow-acting causes, may often be postponed or quickened at the discretion of those in immediate control. At all events, when the financial and operating conditions of the corporation reach such a pass that a crisis seems inevitable to the management, it takes one or both of the two steps – the organization of protective committees, and the petition for the appointment of a receiver. Sometimes committees close to the management are formed before failure has reached a critical stage, one of the avowed purposes being to prevent or forestall receivership proceedings; and sometimes receivership proceedings are brought suddenly, and almost at the last moment, before the management has an opportunity to organize a "stockholders' committee." Thus no general rule can be laid down covering the order of these two events, but the public acknowledgment of financial failure is indicated if one or the other or both of them occur.

Formation of Committees. – The organization of protective committees is more important than the receivership proceedings, the latter being a legal formality now dispensed with when the corporation is small, the parties concerned few, and the fundamental difficulty easily ascertained and remedied. The committees arise from two different sources. There is, first, the stockholders' committee, usually dominated by the old directors of the corporation. This committee acts on the defensive; throughout the whole course of the reorganization proceedings the stockholders' committee is engaged in explaining and justifying the past management and haggling with the other committees in regard to the extent of the sacrifices which the old stockholders must undergo in order to regain the control of the corporation. The other types of committees are representative of different classes of creditors. In the reorganization of a small industrial corporation there is, in addition to the stockholders' committee, only one committee of creditors. In intricate industrial reorganizations there may be separate committees representing the merchandise creditors, the bank creditors, and the public holders of the notes and debentures. In intricate railway reorganizations there may be committees of junior bondholders, of senior bondholders, of branch and divisional line bondholders, and of the bondholders of subsidiary lines or terminal properties controlled through leases or operating contracts. The committees of the holders of the floating debt are usually formed and dominated by the large bank creditors. The committees of bondholders are formed and dominated by the investment banking houses which were responsible for the original sale of the bonds to the public; if the bonds were distributed long ago, prominent trust companies or life insurance companies may assume the guiding hand.

The committee or committees representing the floating debt, the junior bonds, the notes and debentures, will stand antagonistic to the committee of stockholders. The committees of senior bondholders will assume throughout an attitude of watchful waiting. In the majority of cases, especially if the property is a railroad and the lines covered by these liens are strategically important for the unity of the railway system, these committees will be called upon to take little part in the reorganization. If, as is the case in comprehensive railroad reorganizations, they are required to fund their bonds under new first and general mortgages, they will be able to prescribe the conditions which the junior bondholders and stockholders must accept. It facilitates matters very much if the important committees agree among themselves upon the formation of a general reorganization committee upon which representatives of the different committees serve.

Classifications According to Legal Procedure. – The character and the significance of the legal aspects of a reorganization depend very largely on whether or not a receiver is appointed to administer the business during the period between the financial crisis and the final consummation of the reorganization. This in its turn depends on whether or not there is likely to be acrimonious and prolonged dispute among the various security-holders, and whether or not a recalcitrant group of security-holders is likely to try to impede or even frustrate an amicable settlement of conflicting interests. If the failure is very serious, thus entailing large losses to all concerned, or if it involves a large railway embodying many conflicting interests, or if there are burdensome leases and contracts which must be abrogated at all hazards, then receivership proceedings are necessary.

A drastic but fair reorganization can be carried through in an autocratic manner if a receivership is resorted to, because in the end, by a judicial sale of the bankrupt corporation's property, the court can force a recalcitrant minority to accept what it considers a just reorganization plan or extinguish the interests of the minority. But if the reorganization is that of a small industrial corporation, the opposing parties of which are two or more closely knit factions who are able to compose their differences, or if the crisis is merely temporary so that little permanent sacrifice is required of any body, then the various security-holders can probably arrange a plan of reorganization among themselves without resort to the machinery of the courts. A reorganization consummated without compulsory pressure exerted by the courts through judicial sale, even though a receiver be appointed at some stage in the proceedings, is called "voluntary," one consummated through the coercive authority of the courts, represented by a judicial sale of the property of the old corporation and the reorganization of a new corporation, is called "involuntary." The vast majority of railroad organizations are involuntary and follow a court receivership, although from time to time voluntary reorganizations have been attempted for large railway systems, and sometimes they have been successfully consummated. There have been many voluntary reorganizations of large and small industrial and local public utility corporations.

The paramount advantage of a voluntary reorganization is that it preserves valuable rights. The whole reorganization can be carried out with little outward formality and without harming the general credit of the corporation or any good will values belonging to its trade-marks or franchises. The objections to such a reorganization lie entirely in the difficulty of its execution and in the large amount of securities which must be issued in order to please everybody concerned. In several large and important reorganizations of this kind it has been found expedient to carry on parts of the reorganization under the protection of the court. The number of these voluntary reorganizations, aside from minor capital readjustments, has been relatively small. And in all respects, except in certain details of legal procedure, voluntary reorganizations are similar to those consummated through foreclosure sale.

Appointment of a Receiver. – In the vast majority of cases, the first step in the legal procedure of the reorganization is the appointment of a receiver by a court of equity. Brushing aside exceptional conditions, the usual practice in the consent receiverships may be very briefly stated. The necessity or desirability of a receivership having been agreed upon by the directors (usually in a secret meeting), some friendly general creditor with a claim in excess of $3,000, not residing in the same state as that in which the corporation has its main office, is asked to allow his name to be used in the receivership proceedings. Accordingly the attorneys for the corporation prepare the necessary bill of complaint to which the creditor complacently signs his name. The attorneys at the same time prepare the corporation's answer, which admits the allegations of the creditor's bill and prays for the appointment of a receiver. The court grants the prayer and appoints one or more receivers. Subsequently, the trustee of the general junior mortgage brings a foreclosure bill in the court of primary jurisdiction and the same receivers are appointed as under the creditor's bill. At least one receiver is one of the old officials of the corporation, familiar with routine administration, whose name is suggested to the court at the time. The other receiver is a lawyer or publicist in whom the court has explicit confidence.

As soon as the receiver of a corporation has been appointed he assumes the management of the business. Ordinarily, especially with large corporations, such as railroads and traction companies, the receiver makes very few changes in the personnel of his organization, although he may alter entirely the general policy of the corporation in many important contracts. For permission to enter into or cancel important contracts, a receiver will usually seek the consent of the court; he must also obtain permission of the court in order to issue receiver's certificates and to expend large sums for the improvement of the property. But in all details of actual management the receiver is free to follow his own judgment.

Investigations Succeeding Receivership. – During this period, while the receiver is in actual control of the property of the corporation, the various committees are at work seeking to find a substantial, basis upon which to establish their plan of reorganization. This requires a knowledge of at least three sets of facts.

First, they must ascertain by competent auditors whether or not the published reports of the corporation in the years preceding the failure were approximately true. The audit must not only verify the technical correctness of the books, but it must also determine whether or not the depreciation accounts were adequate, and if they were not – as was probably the case – the extent of the deficiency. The auditors must also ascertain whether or not all the equipment – machinery, merchandise, or rolling stock – claimed to be in fit "usable" condition, is actually in use or in fit condition; they must check all the rentals, insurance policies, and intercompany contracts to be sure that the old managers have protected the company's contractual rights.

The second set of facts is supplied by attorneys, acting for the reorganization committee. They have to do with countless legal matters resulting from the general tangle: what contracts may be safely abrogated and what contracts must be fulfilled even at temporary losses, the amounts required to settle with parties holding contingent claims in order to forestall troublesome delays, the probable outcome of pending suits, and the approximate expenses of the receivership and reorganization.

A third set of facts the reorganization committees must supply themselves, and since there are among their number distinguished bankers, they require no independent expert advice. These facts cover the general probability for the successful negotiation and sale of the securities of the reorganized road. The committees must assess accurately the probable effect of their reorganization plan on the market values of old and new securities; they must determine the limit of sacrifice stockholders will make without surrendering their interests, the relative marketability of long- and short-term bonds, the expenses and fees of underwriters, and similar financial matters.

Formation of the Reorganization Plans. – From the results of these investigations the general committee works out a single reorganization plan which is based on the most accurate and comprehensive knowledge available. No definite plan is now advanced in haste. But this orderly procedure has developed, however, only within the last twenty years. Formerly plans were propounded by one committee after another, beginning almost as soon as the rumors of the impending disaster were heard. In contrast to the reorganizations before 1900, it may therefore be said that the contemporary practice is to lengthen the period of preliminary investigation and adjustment, during which time no reorganization plan is published, and, so far as possible, to shorten the period of public discussion over the plan through a preliminary agreement on the part of all the influential interests to support the final plan as soon as it is published. Practically all the recent reorganizations of large corporations have run along smoothly in an orderly manner, to outward appearances. The Chicago, Rock Island and Pacific, the St. Louis and San Francisco, the Pere Marquette – all of them reorganizations of railroads involving a multitude of conflicting interests – were consummated without apparent external friction, once a definite and final plan had been agreed to secretly by the various committees which represented the important securities.

The most difficult and important step in the reorganization procedure is to secure a complete outward harmony of all important interests, so that all may work for the success of a common plan. All, except perhaps the senior bondholders, must make some sacrifices. But the determining power lies usually with the committee representing those securities – usually the junior mortgage bonds or debentures – of which some sacrifice is required, but which is nevertheless in a relatively secure position as compared with the holders of the floating debt and the stocks. In other words, the determination of the plan is likely to be left to the factions which must make sacrifices, Of these, the party making the least sacrifice will probably have the deciding voice.

Out of the conflict of opinions and interests, a plan of reorganization is finally evolved which has the acknowledged support of all the committees representing the conflicting interests. This plan is published before the receiver surrenders the property, or even before the foreclosure sale. It is published with the recommendation of all the committees that it be accepted by the various groups of security-holders. The latter are asked to become parties to the "reorganization agreement," which is the formal legal document that invariably accompanies "the plan." By so doing, they assent to the terms of the reorganization and on paying their assessment, if any is called for, receive their allotted securities in the new corporation. Those who do not care to accept the terms of the reorganization are allowed to withdraw the securities originally deposited, usually on the payment of a small fee to cover expenses of the committee. If, as is probably the case, a very large proportion of the security-holders consent to the conditions, the reorganization committee declares the plan operative, and the reorganization is finished except for the legal formalities.

Execution of the Plan. – To carry out the obvious will of the great majority of assenting claimants and security-holders, the reorganization must be forced through and the dissenting minority and obstructionists settled with in a just and open manner fully approved by the court. This is accomplished by the judicial sale of the old corporation's property through a decree of foreclosure, by which the court preserves the outward form of a foreclosure sale. Owing to the fact that the foreclosure of the property of a great corporation requires far more capital than a single man or group of men can command, the court recognizes that there will be no competition at the foreclosure sale of the property. In order to prevent the various parties who have agreed among themselves upon a workable plan of reorganization from conspiring together to purchase the property for little and thus defeat the just claims of other creditors who have not pooled their interests, the court ordinarily fixes a minimum or "upset" price. It is the amount which the receivers must realize from the property in order that the court shall confirm the sale. It amounts, practically, to the determination by the court of the price at which the reorganization committee may acquire the property of the old corporation at a public sale, and also of the conditions under which the committee must settle with the creditors who have not consented to its plan. There is, theoretically at least, a chance that other persons may care to pay more for the property than the reorganization committee, and the general creditors not embraced in the committee's plan should be given – theoretically at least – an opportunity to bid in the property in satisfaction of their own liens.

The reorganization committee, having acquired the property, immediately turns it over to the new corporation. This the committee has caused to be formed even before the final settlement. The same name is retained in the case of reorganization of a public service corporation, except that "railroad" may be changed to "railway" or "company" to "corporation." But in the case of industrials the name of the new corporation is almost invariably made different from the old one.

Adjustment of Opposing Interests. – The most difficult problem remaining to the reorganization committee after the sale is that of the final adjustment of conflicting interests. The questions connected with this problem have been affecting all the tentative plans and later stages of the work of the various reorganization committees. They represent the loose ends and possible sources of embarrassment and litigation that invariably cast their shadows about every reorganization of importance. In case all the bonds are of one class, are all deposited with the reorganization committee, and no other creditors exist, the transition from control by the receivers to that of the new corporation occurs without a possibility of friction. But such simplicity is seldom if ever present in any reorganization of considerable size. There are always claims to be adjusted. If the upset price exceeds the face value of one or more issues of underlying bonds, these bonds are not affected; in the vocabulary of finance they are "undisturbed." If the upset price does not equal the face value of a bond issue, some adjustment is necessary with those of the bond holders who have not consented to enter the reorganization and they are invariably paid off in money raised by the reorganization committee as part of their plan. The amount each non-assenting bondholder receives is the proportional part the face value of his bond bears to the sum received by the court from the sale of the actual property securing them. Unless the bonds are secured by very valuable physical property the amount given the non-assenting bondholders is small.

PROMOTION – THE WORK OF THE PROMOTER[1]

Charles Gerstenberg

Scope of book. – When a business man speaks of Finance, he may have one of two ideas in mind; he may be thinking of the way money is coined and how funds are created by banks to be exchanged in foreign and domestic banking, or he may be thinking of how individuals and corporations obtain and use funds and distribute the profits derived therefrom. The former idea carries one naturally into the field of Banking; the latter into the field of Business Financing. In this book we shall study the latter idea: how businesses acquire funds, how they use them, and how the profits of the business are distributed. We shall have to consider also what will happen to a company when it has insufficient funds or when its operations result in losses.

The relation of financing to other branches of business. – Finance is intimately related to the other branches of business, namely, Marketing, and Accounting. When production is inefficient, funds will be wasted, if, indeed, they can be attracted at all to be used by the inefficient concern. The principles of marketing will have to be drawn upon by the financier, first in studying whether to engage funds in a given enterprise, and second, in discovering how to market stocks and bonds. Accounting is intimately connected with finance, for the financial manager must rely upon the accuracy and scientific arrangement of the records of a company to guide him in managing the in-flow and out-flow of funds. In this book, therefore, it will be necessary at times to refer to principles of Production, Marketing, and Accounting; but only so much of these subjects will be drawn upon as is absolutely necessary to explain the principles that are usually included in a study of finance.

[1] [Chapter 1 of *Financial Organization and the Management of Business*, New York: Prentice-Hall, 1924.]

Promotion. – Promotion is the first step in finance. Promotion may be defined as the discovery of business opportunities and the subsequent organization of funds, property, and managerial ability into a business concern for the purpose of making profits therefrom. A man with funds is a master of many people's destinies. By contributing to this enterprise or to that, he dictates which of the public's desires for goods or services shall be realized. This responsibility is a great one and is committed by most sensible people to investment banks whose business it is to investigate enterprises calling for funds to see whether they will serve a public demand urgent enough to earn a return sufficient to pay all operating expenses, interest on the capital invested, and to yield, in addition, a profit that will encourage the managers to carry on the business with the utmost efficiency. Investment bankers, however, do not initiate enterprises. They simply check them up and decide whether or not funds shall be invested in them. The original idea of the business, if it is a new one, arises in the mind of a promoter. It is the work of the promoter to search for new public demands and to find means of satisfying them. Frequently, the promoter will carry his work beyond the stage of promotion and undertake to conduct the promoted business. Such men really are entrepreneurs who promote their own enterprises. The out-and-out promoter, however, – a man like Charles R. Flint,[2] who promoted the American Chicle Co., and a number of other companies – ordinarily does not interest himself in managing the business after it has been promoted. For the present, we shall confine our attention to promotion pure and simple and to the work of the promoter as such.

The promoter and competition. – A promoter may undertake to launch an enterprise because he feels that some other concern is making monopoly profits or conjunctural profits, a part of which he can share. Every time a new business is started in a field in which there are already competitors we have an illustration of this form of promotion. The promoter ought to be well assured that there are some available monopoly or conjunctural profits. If, however, his purpose is to promote a concern to earn what the economists call "pure profits," he must be reasonably sure that the standard of efficiency of those already in the field is so low

[2] See his "Memories of an Active Life."

that a new concern will be able to produce at a lower cost, for it must be remembered that every new concern that enters a given field of production increases the available supply of products and thus tends to bring down the price of that product.[3]

On the other hand, the promoter may seek to eliminate competition through the consolidation of several competing units. During the period of the formation of the industrial trusts, say from 1880 to 1905, promoters found their largest profits in this form of promotion work.

Economic function of the promoter. – The successful promoter makes large profits, so large indeed that it is sometimes thought that he is over-paid for the services he renders. The fact is that he not only takes huge risks but that he performs unusually valuable services to the public. In an action brought against Thomas F. Ryan by Harry Haskins, a promoter, the latter stated in his complaint that he had spent $50,000 in investigating the feasibility of consolidating a number of in dependent lead plants and in obtaining options on those plants.

An engineer's report on a projected interurban railway or electric light and power plant and distributing system may easily cost as much as $10,000 or more and the result of the report may be to show that the project is not feasible. There is a well-known engineering firm in this country whose specialty it is to investigate patents for new inventions to see whether the patents are secure against infringements and whether they are commercially exploitable. A fee of from ten to fifteen thousand dollars, we are told, to ascertain the business value of an automobile accessory is not unusual. In another case a promoter spent $30,000 for investigations, plans, and like material preliminary to the organization of an engine works. All such expenses are paid by the promoter, and if his investigations prove the inadvisability of such an undertaking – as they did in the case of the engine works, above mentioned – the entire cost is borne by him as a loss.

The promoter performs a public service whenever he produces a successful concern. As we have seen, he either creates a new demand that helps us to do our business more

3 The reader who is unacquainted with economic theory will do well to read the chapter on profits in Ely and Wicker, "Elementary Economics."

readily, or to live more comfortably, or he supplies older utilities in a cheaper way, or he saves the ruining wastes of competition with its long trail of duplications, unnecessary advertising, and similar extravagances.

The promoter has been much maligned. He is not a prestidigitator. Rufus Wallingford no more represents the real type of promoter than Sherlock Holmes represents the true type of detective. The true promoter may have his moments of elegant ease, but he knows what real work is. We are told that one of the best-known promoters in the country had a load of mules aboard ship on the way to Europe in 1914 a few days after the declaration of war. You can imagine how this man worked night as well as day in getting the contract and in filling it. As we shall see, the promoter's work of discovering, assembling, and financing is a matter of close attention to details.

Steps in promotion. – The promoter accomplishes his purposes in three distinct steps: first, he makes the discovery of the idea, then he assembles the elements of the business, and finally procures the funds to put these elements into operation.

Discovery. – A promoter makes a discovery when he deter mines that an opportunity exists for exploitation. The opportunity is at this stage a mere idea which may involve the creation of a new demand or the satisfaction of an old demand that is not yet well or completely satisfied. For example, when the United States entered the World War, a demand for "service" flags was created by the invention of the "service" flag, and it is safe to say that this idea meant thousands of dollars not only to the inventor, but to a great many other people who were in the business of making flags or who went into that business. On the other hand, there has been in existence for some time a demand for a simple method of wrapping up bundles and the man who first conceived the idea of using gummed paper tape was at the moment of discovery a promoter. Frequently, an idea is refined by future promoters as was the case in the use of gummed tape when a young man conceived the idea of an interlocking device that would permit the use of gummed tape without completely sealing the package. This young man was a promoter and his idea will probably save thousands upon thousands of dollars to shippers who must have an unsealed package for use in parcel post to save high rates of postage.[4]

Steps in discovery. – Discovery is essentially a matter of investigation as was intimated in the previous paragraph. The idea itself may come as a flash to an inventor, or it may be an inspiration on the part of some people engaged in a similar business to expand into a somewhat new field,[5] or it may painfully develop in the minds of competitors who see in it an escape from the ruin that a continuation of competition will entail. The threat of Carnegie to go into the semi-finished steel products industry to forestall the plans of Morgan who was taking steps preparatory to going into the iron ore industry is a familiar example. But the feasibility of the idea must be investigated by a person whose training and experience fit him to weigh impartially all of the elements of advantage and risk that lurk in a projected enterprise. In the very nature of things, a person who has conceived the idea usually is an optimist and an enthusiast; his viewpoint is warped by prejudice. It would be much better for him to turn over his idea to an impartial investigator, a trained promoter who can weigh the elements that will have to be taken into consideration in making a fair forecast as to whether the enterprise will be profit-making or not. It will be seen, therefore, that the mere conception of an idea is not all there is to discovery. This step in promotion includes not only conception but investigation and this latter process may again be divided into three steps of which the first is a rough estimate, the second, a detailed investigation, and the third, checking up or verification.[6]

A rough estimate. – Let us suppose an idea is brought to you and that you are asked to promote it into a business enterprise. You will first inquire who originated the proposition, and in obtaining the answer to this question you may save much unnecessary

[4] Since writing the above the author has learned that the Post Office has changed its rules and that the promoter's business has faded away. Such are the risks of the promoter.

[5] The E. I. du Pont de Nemours activities, for example.

[6] It is interesting to note how practical matters can be "squared" with theoretical principles. Compare, for example, these three steps in discovery with the steps in scientific reasoning. C. W. Gerstenberg, "Principles of Business," page 63.

labor later, for the unlikelihood of a feasible idea coming from an incompetent person is so great that the first rule of the promoter is that a proposition must be properly sponsored. An example of good sponsoring could be found in the case of a bright young man who has had experience in the line of business and sees improved methods in that line which do not appeal to his old-fogy employers.

The promoter will then seek to determine the basic idea in this business. Is it a manufacturing or a marketing idea? Does it satisfy an old want in a new way, or does it depend upon the stimulation of a new demand? The promoter, it will be seen, should be a man of wide experience who can sense the possible value of new ideas and reject without laborious investigation those which are palpably defective. The aim of this first step should be to determine whether it will pay to spend the time and money necessary to make a detailed investigation.

Who makes detailed investigation. – At this stage of his inquiry the promoter will have no more than a "hunch" that he is on the track of a profitable idea; but it will not pay him to spend his time or to risk other people's money in testing out in actual operation the value of a "hunch." He must make, or cause to be made, a detailed investigation. The cost of this investigation is comparable to an insurance premium. It costs money, to be sure, but it is a protection against a much larger loss.

If the enterprise is one that involves difficult production problems, investigation will be carried on chiefly by an engineer. If it depends for its success upon the possible existence of a demand and the discovery of a proper method of reaching that demand, the services of a marketing analyst should be secured. If, on the other hand, the promotion is in the nature of a consolidation, the investigation will be carried on chiefly by accountants and appraisers whose business it is to determine the values of the constituents of consolidation. Additional specialists may be required, such as chemists, patent-lawyers, and others.

Scope of detailed investigation. – For the present we shall not consider the promotion of consolidations. The analysis of a projected new enterprise from the standpoint of the promoter may be divided into three parts: first, the computation of the capital cost, second, the estimate of probable gross revenue, and third the calculation of the operating costs. These three steps may be stated in another way as follows: will the projected enterprise take in enough to pay the costs of operation, pay interest on the capital invested, and leave sufficient profit to compensate the owners for their risks and their services?

The capital costs. – Money will be needed for the capital as sets – so-called – of any enterprise. Not only are the land and buildings, the machinery and fixtures, and the raw materials to be acquired, but also a certain amount of working capital to get the operations started and to keep them running smoothly. The amount of capital funds required will depend on the nature of the business. A public utility such as a gas company or a telephone company will require much more in proportion to the size of its business than a simple trading company. Then there is to be taken into consideration the proposed scope of the projected business. It may be desired to start out on a large scale or it may be thought wise to begin in a small way and to expand the organization gradually out of profits. Finally there is the problem of whether all branches of the business are to be carried on or only a few. For example, it is possible to start in the cotton goods business, and to operate only the function of buying the product and reselling at a profit. The production will be done by an independently owned mill, and the accounting, financing, and collecting will be done by a fiscal agent.

Determining scope of enterprise. – At the outset, then, after the nature of the business is determined, and before the capital to be raised can be estimated, the projectors will have to determine whether they want to start on a small scale and gradually expand, or whether they want to start full-fledged. Where a large-scale business is contemplated the underlying motive is usually the timeliness of the project. To get the market when it is just right is a great advantage. But certainly there are many disadvantages in trying to build up an organization with money only and without regard to the element of time. Mistakes are sure to be made and these will be costly in proportion to the size of the business. The personnel of the concern will be difficult to handle, especially as compared with an organization where the different grades of responsibility are gradually consigned to men whose ability to shoulder responsibility has been tested. In short, the full-fledged, full-panoplied proposition is likely to be a forced hot-house plant.

Next, the projectors must determine whether or not the product is to be marketed only, or is to be manufactured as well as marketed. Some very prosperous concerns have been built up on products produced outside the business itself. Such concerns, for example, are the mail order houses. The options that are open to a projector are more numerous than are generally suspected. (1) The concern may do its own manufacturing with its own machinery, either (a) buying the plant or (b) leasing it. This method of conducting the business gives the concern the manufacturing as well as the selling profit, insures uniformity in quality and quantity of output, and holds out the possibility of meeting competition through reduction of manufacturing costs. On the other hand, profits may be cut down through such contingencies as strikes and fluctuations in costs of material; the manufacturing effort may be great compared with the selling effort, while the profits from the former may be relatively small and the time and effort required to get the manufacturing started may preclude large profits that could be obtained by getting to the market immediately. (2) The concern may contract to have its product manufactured for it, (a) owning none of the machinery, or (b) owning the patterns and special tools. The arguments for and against this plan are about the reverse of what they were for plan 1. (3) The concern may contract for the manufacture of its product but may itself buy most of the raw material, thus saving the buying commission, which in the case of paper in publishing concerns is usually about ten per cent. Moreover, this plan insures a steadiness of output in times when materials are scarce. (4) The concern may assemble its product, and may (a) make none of the parts, or (b) make some of the parts. Many automobile concerns use outside parts almost exclusively and probably none of the manufacturers in this country makes the entire automobile. The problem here hinges on large-scale production. One concern, for example, may not require enough axles to enable it to produce them in large quantities and thus get the benefits of large-scale production.

The reader can easily determine for himself, with but little consideration, which of the methods of operating a concern will require the greater amount of initial capital.

Factors that enter problem of home and outside production. – Very briefly we shall outline some of the general questions that must be considered by the projector in determining which method of manufacturing shall be chosen. These questions will be listed and only briefly considered.

1. Difficulty of raising capital. – Where the project is inherently so small or of such a nature that the usual channels for raising money cannot be used or cannot be used profitably, and where the promoters have not the necessary financial connections, the method that requires the smallest initial outlay will usually be chosen.

2. Load factor. – In order to manufacture its own goods a concern may have to buy a considerable amount of machinery only part of which can be used steadily. These part-time machines will be charged with interest twenty-four hours a day and three hundred and sixty-five days in the year. They may produce income only fifty per cent or even only ten per cent of that time. In such cases it may be better, till the business has grown, to contract for the manufacture of the product with some other concern which through other similar contracts en joys the benefits of large scale production.[7]

3. Hazard of the experiment. – If there is any danger that the marketing at a reasonable price will be difficult, the experiment should be tried with a minimum of invested capital.

[7] This problem of the load factor is only beginning to be understood. In commenting on the success of the six-hour day of the famous Leverhulme plant in England, H. K. Webster explained the situation thus:

"You are a manufacturer. The labor cost of the thing you, make is one dollar, and the overhead, on the basis of the eight-hour day, is one dollar. That is to say, the interest on the capital invested, rent of premises, depreciation, taxes, salaries of executive officers – all expense, in a word, that does not increase as the volume of the product increases, works out, when you divide it up by the number of articles you make on an eight-hour, one-shift basis, to as much per article as the wage of a man while he is making one. In this case, one more dollar. So the total cost of the article, outside raw material, is two dollars.

"Now you adopt the six-hour day with two shifts. You pay the worker his four dollars for three articles instead of for four. Another worker then comes on and you pay him the same. At the end of the day you have six articles instead of four, but you have paid eight dollars for them. Now add in the overhead. That remains constant at four dollars, since it does not increase with the increased production. Four dollars, then, added to the eight. And a gross cost of twelve dollars for six articles, where, on the other basis, you had a gross cost of eight dollars for four articles. So it comes to the same thing? By no means. You've been selling those articles at a profit, haven't you? Say of fifty cents. You have an output now – without increasing your investment in plant – of six as against four. A profit, therefore, of three dollars as against two.

4. Secrecy of quality. – Where the enterprise depends for its "selling point" on superior quality the business will likely have to manufacture its own goods. In practice this point is probably less important than it seems. Certainly in the standardized – so-called – brands of canned food and toilet articles many concerns boast of quality though they have little to do with the direct production.

5. Intricacies of the business. – Where one department is likely to interfere with another, the most profitable part, usually the marketing, will probably be retained and the other department omitted. Thus comparatively few publishers print their own publications.

"And we're not at the end of our tether yet, either. If two shifts, why not – if the demand warranted – three? A shift going on at 8:30 p. m. and coming off at 2:45 a. m. Inconvenient hours, rather, but it would be only one week in three that you would have it to do. How does that work out? Labor cost for the three shifts, $12. Overhead, $4. Total, $16. And you have nine articles at the former gross cost of eight. And nine articles to make a profit upon as against four under the old system." From "Lord Leverhulme and the Six-Hour Day," *Metropolitan Magazine*, July, 1919.

PROMOTION – METHODS OF INVESTIGATION[1]

Charles Gerstenberg

Methods of making investigation. – Having now considered the broad problems that arise in determining the amount of funds that will be required, we may turn to a consideration of the three methods of investigating specific enterprises; that is, the methods that are used in estimating probable capital requirements, probable gross earnings, and probable operating costs. These three methods may be stated to be the statistical method, the canvassing method, and the comparison method.

In the statistical method, units are devised and all calculations are made on the basis of these units.

The canvassing method does not use abstract units; actual estimates of the cost of building the proposed plant are made, and a survey is also made of the particular field that is to be served by the products of the projected company.

The comparison method involves the study of the balance sheets and income statements of companies of about the same size as the projected company and doing a similar work.

What funds are required. – Before showing the exact methods of estimating the amount of funds required for a new concern it seems advisable to classify the purposes for which funds for the new business will be needed, in the following way:

1. Promotion expenses.
(a.) Preliminary investigation of the project.
(b.) Assembling parties who may be willing to participate.
(c.) Preliminary engineering, legal, accounting, and marketing advice.

[1] [Chapter 2 of *Financial Organization and the Management of Business*, New York: Prentice-Hall, 1924.]

(d.) Estimates of costs, income, and expenses.
(e.) Procuring options.
2. Organization expenses.
(a.) Incorporation of the company.
(b.) Expenses of keeping corporate organization going until company begins operations.
(c.) Taxes and interest due before company begins operations.
(d.) Miscellaneous legal and accounting expenses.
3. Cost of fixed assets.
4. Cost of establishing the business, which includes all expenses including canvassing and advertising for business from the time the company begins operations till its income is sufficient to meet the expenses.
5. Regular working capital.
6. Financing, including banker's commissions and promoter's profits.[2]

In estimating the total amount of funds necessary for these six purposes the investigator will not necessarily follow throughout one of the three methods mentioned in the previous sections. He will, perhaps, use the statistical method for estimating the promotion expenses, and the cost of establishing the business, the canvassing method for estimating the cost of fixed assets, and for the remaining items he may use the comparison method.

Importance of detailed classification. – This classification may seem to be extraordinarily detailed and applicable only to large enterprises. The fact is that it is important in the smallest as well as in the largest projects. Some of the items, to be sure, may be very small, but this statement is likely to be true only *absolutely* and not *relatively.* At any rate, the promoter entering upon any project will do well to use a table like that contained in the foregoing paragraph no matter what undertaking he has in hand, for then he will be less likely to fall into the grave error of making his estimates too low. This, after all, is the great danger against which the promoter must guard. The promoter is an optimist; he would like to see his concern launched with a small initial outlay, for in that way his enterprise will better engage the interest of capitalists. But there is a fundamental rule of

[2] See *Elements of the Cost and Value of a Gas Plant,* C. W. Gerstenberg, "Materials of Corporation Finance," page 455.

finance that the last dollar is always the most valuable dollar. If $100,000 has been invested in a concern and $10,000 more is needed, the people who furnish the final $10,000 are likely to demand as large an interest for their money as those who furnish the first $100,000. Without the last $10,000, the first $100,000 will become worthless. The promoter then must see to it that his estimates are ample and that no money is tied up till the full amount is in sight.

Statistical method of calculating capital requirements. – We are now ready to explain the methods of calculating the capital requirements of a new concern. In the statistical method the various elements of outgo are broken up as far as possible into uniform units. After the cost of each unit is estimated and the number of units of each kind that will be needed is ascertained, it is simply a matter of mathematics to arrive at the total cost.

1. Promotion expenses. – The statistical unit that can best be used in calculating the promotion expenses is probably a unit of time. All the promotion expenses can be reduced to a matter of paying the promoter and his engineering, accounting, and marketing experts for the time required to make their investigations. Some money probably will have to be given in a lump sum to bind the options, such as an option on a patent, but frequently even the consideration for the options will be the promoter's promise to undertake and prosecute the promotion of the company. An estimate on the statistical basis of the promotion expenses of a concern to exploit a patented automobile accessory to be sold but not manufactured would appear as follows:

Promoter's expenses, including preliminary investigation, engaging experts, assembling, etc., 100 days at $50 a day..................	$5,000.00
Engineer's report on validity of patent and feasibility and economy of patented device, 10 days at $100 a day......................	1,000.00
Commercial analysis of proposition by marketing analyst, 20 days at $25 a day..	500.00
Total..	$6,500.00

2. *Organization expenses.* – In the same way the organization expenses may be estimated as follows:[3]

Incorporation of company:		
Filing fees	$40.00	
Organization tax, $1,000,000 capital stock at 50c per $1,000	500.00	
Lawyer's fees, 5 days at $100 a day	500.00	
Legal expenses, stenographer	20.00	
		$1,060.00
Office expenses for 8 weeks at $40 a week for clerical help, and $75 a week for manager		920.00
Rent of office for two months at $75 a month		150.00
Miscellaneous expenses, stationery, telephone, etc.		80.00
Total		$2,210.00

3. *Cost of fixed assets.* – We will assume here that the company is merely to sell its product and is to have it manufactured by a contractor. This will simplify our procedure while we are making a general survey. Later we shall take up in detail the problem of estimating the cost of fixed assets. Our estimate of cost of fixed assets, therefore, need include only office furniture, the actual cost of preparing the patent papers, and legal expenses incidental to getting the patent.[4]

Patent	$225.00
6 desks at $60	360.00
2 typists' desks at $50	100.00
3 filing cabinets at $60	180.00
2 typewriter machines at $100	200.00
2 tables at $55	110.00
12 chairs at $7.50	90.00
2 rugs at $50	100.00
Total[5]	$1,365.00

[3] These expenses run from the time an office is engaged until the company is organized, the funds are raised, and the company begins operations.

[4] It is assumed that the company is to pay the expenses of getting the patent, and that in addition stock will be given the inventor for his invention. Additional stock will be issued to the promoter for his services. Hence the capitalization of the company is $1,000,000.

[5] Other equipment may be required later, such as an addressograph, check protector, multigraph, etc., but at the outset these devices can probably be dispensed with.

4. *Cost of establishing the business.* – In large enterprises, such as public utilities, the cost of establishing the business gives rise to the capital asset known as "going concern value." in a well-known rate case, the New York Court of Appeals defined "going concern value" as follows: "I define 'going value' for the rate purposes as involved in this case to be the amount equal to the deficiency of net earnings below a fair return on the actual investment due solely to the time and expenditure reasonably necessary and proper to the development of the business and property to its present stage, and not comprised in the valuation of the physical property." The value of "going concern" may be represented as follows:

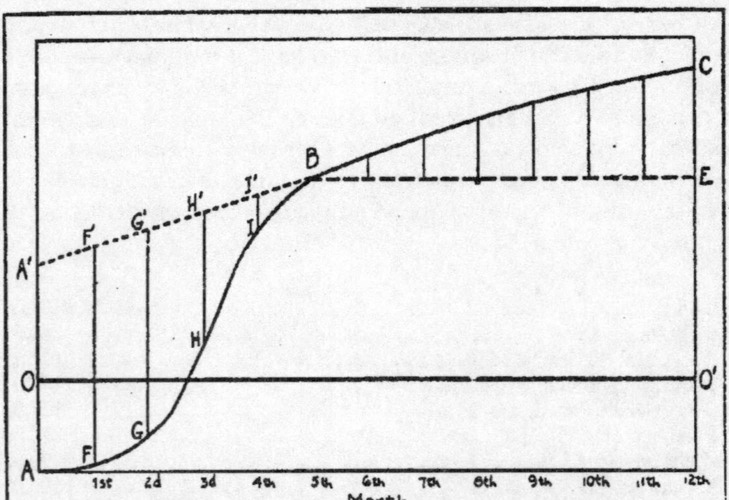

CHART ILLUSTRATING MEASUREMENT OF GOING CONCERN VALUE AND OF GOODWILL

A, B, C is the line of net earnings. The vertical lines mark off months during which the business is in operation. When the net earnings reach *B,* at the end of the fifth month, they have reached the normal and increase with the normal in crease in general business in the industry. If we carry this trend line backward to A^1, we will find what would have been the normal earnings if the company had had its business fully established. The sum of the amounts represented by the distances FF^1, GG^1, HH^1, and II^1 is the value of the company's "going concern." It is the deficiency of earnings that every company must be ready for if it is to overcome the inertia of getting established.[6]

This is all very well, the reader will say, to value the in tangible asset known as "going concern value" after it has been established, but our problem is to estimate at the outset what it is going to cost to develop the business. The objection is well taken; the explanation given above was intended as a definition of "going concern value," rather than as a method of determining how much it costs to acquire it. We shall return to our simple enterprise, the development of the business of marketing a new automobile accessory, and attempt to determine the cost of going concern value in this case. The marketing expert's analysis of the feasibility of the enterprise will probably include a plan for marketing, with estimated costs, and a statement of the time it will, take to bring cash income up to cash outgo. We may assume that for the sixth month after operations begin, and thereafter, sales can be made at the rate of $5,000 a month. The total development costs, or costs of establishing the business, may be summarized thus:

Rent for six months		**$450.00**
Stenographic and clerical help, per week—		
Two stenographers	**$55.00**	
Bookkeeper	**35.00**	
Manager	**100.00**	
Salesmen's drawings	**250.00**	
	$440.00	

[6] We may use the same diagram to illustrate what is meant by the term "goodwill." If the distance between the line 00^1 (the base line of nothing) and the line *BE* represents the net earnings necessary to pay a fair return on the stock of the company (or more correctly the owner's investment), then the distance between *BC* and *BE* capitalized will equal the company's goodwill. While "goodwill" is usually entered on the balance sheet at a definite amount, theoretically its value varies with the fortune of the concern.

Twenty-five weeks at $440 per week....................		11,000.00
Advertising, magazine (about 800,000 circulation spread over six months at $2.50 per M)...........................		2,000.00
Circulars and mailing same, 200,000 at 6 cents..........		12,000.00
Miscellaneous expenses, including stationery, telephone, general office supplies, at $50 per month...............		300.00
Total....................................		$25,750.00
Less expected revenue, as follows:		
Sales second month, 100 at $2.50 [7]............	$250.00	
Sales third month, 300 at $2.50	750.00	
Sales fourth month, 700 at $2.50	1,750.00	
Sales fifth month, 1200 at $2.50	3,000.00	
Sales sixth month, 2000 at $2.50	5,000.00	
		10,750.00
Net amount of funds required to start business and run it till income will take care of outgo....................		$15,000.06

5. *Regular working capital.* – We shall discuss in a separate chapter the problem of the funds required for regular working capital. Here our problem is to discover how much funds the company ought to have at the outset beyond the amount required to establish the business. Some margin of liquid capital will be required for contingencies and to give the company a good credit standing.[8]

In the case we have in hand we can assume that goods are sold on thirty days credit, and that the manufacturer gives the same credit. A fair estimate for regular working capital for this concern would be about a month and a half's operating expenses. These we found above to be $25,750 for six months; the amount required therefore would be about $6,500.

6. *Cost of financing.* – We must pause now to see how much money will have to be raised. Our summary will be as follows:

[7] The $2.50 represents the total income per unit of product less the cost of manufacture.

[8] In view of the more complete discussion of working capital (see Chapters XXIII–XXV) the discussion here is very brief.

1. Promotion expenses	$6,500.00
2. Organization expenses	2,210.00
3. Cost of fixed assets	1,365.00
4. Cost of establishing business (net)	15,000.00
5. Regular working capital	6,500.00
Total	$31,575.00
Add for contingencies, 10 per cent	3,158.00
Total amount of cash to be raised	$34,733.00

The sum of money to be raised is comparatively small. No investment banker with an established business and clientele probably could afford to handle it as a proposition to be dealt with as are larger propositions. It may be suggested that the promoter ought to be able to raise the money. Strictly this is not his function. His function is to discover, assemble, and arrange for the financing, the latter step of which in large concerns is accomplished through the aid of an investment banker. In a proposition as small as this the promoter may well undertake to raise the money himself. In so doing his expenses, including commissions that he may have to pay intermediaries, may amount to from 10 to 15 per cent of the amount raised. It would be necessary for this concern, there fore, to have from $37,500 to $40,000.

If the sum needed had been in excess of $100,000 the promoter might have found some security house to handle the sale of stocks necessary to yield this amount. Such houses are rare. They will hardly be found in New York where the investment houses have discovered, according to the best information we have been able to obtain, that an issue of less than $1,000,000 is unprofitable. Or the promoter might hire an experienced salesman to "peddle" the securities. Cost of selling securities of an issue of less than $1,000,000 will be about 25 per cent of the amount raised.[9] The regularly established security houses may be interested in large concerns requiring more than $1,000,000. Their charges and disbursements will run, for a new concern, from 1 or 2 per cent of the amount to be raise a to 25 per cent, depending on the size of

[9] See the complete discussion in the chapters on selling securities (Chapters XX–XXI).

the issue, on the nature of the enterprise, and on the people who are behind it.

Another example of estimates of cash required. – In the preceding example we carried through the calculation for a relatively small concern and we used the statistical method. Let us see now how the second method of investigation, the canvassing method, can be applied to a larger concern, whose demand for fixed assets is large because it is to do its own manufacturing. We may in fact take an interurban railway. The following figures are in part a summary of an actual engineer's report.[10]

General scope of the proposition. – The first problem of the promoter is to decide just what he wants to do. Shall his road run from X to *Y* or continue to *Z,* or shall there be a branch line from *M* on the road *XY* down to *A*? The problem here is very much the same in its parts as in its entirety: will the extra capital outlay be justified by the business possibilities of the extension?

We cannot go into all the detail; that is an engineer's job. All we can do is to explain what the promoter can expect the engineer to do. The promoter himself, or through his associates, will have made, we will suppose, the rough estimates which have justified him in procuring his franchise and the necessary options on the right of way.[11] The engineer will then survey the ground and determine about what the construction problems will be. To this end he will divide the entire length of the line into parts each of which presents rather distinct problems. In the report which we are considering, and which may serve as a guide, the entire road was projected to connect up three cities, of which Lima and Marion, both in Ohio, are about 55 miles apart, the third city, Kenton, being about midway between them. The entire route was divided into six sections, numbered for convenience from 0 to 5, of which the

[10] The original report is printed in full in C. W. Gerstenberg, "Materials of Corporation Finance," pages 456, et seq. Although that report is now somewhat old, the method is unchanged. The figures as they are given for 1906 may be used, since costs are now variable and any reasonable figures may be used to illustrate the method.

[11] In the case of any utility the preliminary survey would include a consideration of competition and of supporting population. The American Investment Bankers Association has pointed out that a public utility security does not present a sound investment unless the utility will be supported by a population of 500,000.

shortest section was the first, 2.17 miles, and the longest was the fifth, 14.77 miles. The construction of the roadway was divided into sixteen elements as follows:

(a) Clearing and grubbing: All cutting of trees and underbrush, and removing of stumps along right of way.
(b) Excavation and embankments: All earth work to sub-grade.
(c) Bridges: All plate girders, steel trusses, and wooden trestles.
(d) Concrete: All masonry in wall or arch for culverts and abutments for steel spans.
(e) Ballast: All cost of material, loading, transportation and placing.
(f) Rails: All "T" and girder rails and special work in main track, sidings and switches.
(g) Spikes: All used in main track, sidings and switches.
(h) Splices and bolts: All used in main track, sidings and switches.
(i) Ties: All used in main track, sidings and switches.
(j) Track laying and bonding: All labor connected with this part of construction.
(k) Fencing: All cost of one line on private right of way paralleling roads; two lines where passing through property.
(1) Highway crossing: All cost of cast iron pipe in place.
(m) Culvert pipe: All cost of cast iron pipe in place.
(n) Bonds and cross-bonds: All cost of 0000 copper bonds in place under splice bar and cross-bonds every 500 feet.
(o) Platforms and shelter houses: All costs for stations along line.
(p) Repaving: All cost for taking up and relaying pavement in Kenton and Marion.

How capital investment is estimated. – In a preliminary statement some of the essential features of the nature of the construction are explained, as for example, that "rail, along private right of way, to be 70-pound standard tee rail, joined with four-bolt splice bars. Through village streets it is in tended to use 9-inch 95-lb. girder rail."

The report then proceeds to examine each of the six sections and to estimate the cost separately of each of the sixteen elements. A summary brings together the costs of the six sections. The power plant and stations are described and their costs estimated. The total cost of the sections, of line construction (that is, poles, overhead wires, insulators, and so forth), of buildings, power plant, substations, and rolling stock (passenger cars, combination passenger and freight cars, freight cars, locomotives, work cars, and flat cars) is estimated at $1,198,626. To this is added "for supervision of construction, engineering, contingencies, and first year's carrying charges," 7 per cent of the total or $83,904, making a total estimated capital investment of $1,282,530.

Canvassing the territory to estimate probable gross receipts. – The second step in investigation, we saw, is the estimate of gross income. We will now describe this step and incidentally illustrate what we have termed the canvassing method of making an analysis – that is, making a survey of the particular field to be covered.[12]

In the report on the interurban railway, after the engineer has made his estimate of capital costs, he proceeds to canvass the territory in order to estimate the probable gross receipts. This is not a simple matter. An actual count is made of the business and social activities of the various towns and cities and from these the engineer judges whether the people are progressive, and whether their activities are such as will likely lead them to use the projected road. So important is it that this be done carefully and accurately that we shall appropriate the space to show how, in the case under consideration, one of the cities is described:

"Marion, the county seat of Marion County, is a thriving railroad and manufacturing city located forty-four miles north of Columbus.

"The Columbus, Delaware and Marion Railway is in operation south to Columbus, and a line is now under construction north to Bucyrus. This line gives excellent passenger and freight service, having hourly schedule from six a. m. to nine p. m. to Columbus, and ten and eleven p. m. to Stratford. Cars arrive from Stratford at six, seven, and eight a. in., and from nine a. m. to eleven p. m. from Columbus. The running time from Marion to Columbus is two hours and twenty-five minutes, and from Marion to Delaware one hour, making connections at Prospect for Richwood and at Delaware for Magnetic Springs. The fare from Marion to Columbus is seventy-five cents, round trip one dollar forty-five cents; from Marion to Delaware forty cents, round trip seventy-five cents.

[12] The canvassing method as applied to the analysis of capital costs consists in obtaining from contractors, builders, equipment houses and others, actual estimates of the cost of building and equipping a plant designed for the particular enterprise to be promoted. A theoretical example of the statistical method of calculating the consumption, that is, computing gross income, will be found in Harry Tipper, "The New Business," pages 154 et seq.

"Four railroads pass through Marion – The Big Four, Erie, The Columbus, Hocking Valley and Toledo, and the Columbus and Sandusky branch of the Pennsylvania.

"The Erie Railroad freight tonnage at Marion for last year was eight hundred fifty thousand tons; the passenger earnings at Marion Station were eighty-five thousand dollars. This covers outgoing business in both directions.

"The principal manufactures are steam shovels, contractors' tools and harvesting machinery. The limestone quarries have an enormous output of crushed rock, building stone, and lime.

"The growth of Marion in recent years has been phenomenal – the population in 1890 was 8,327, in 1900 11,862, and at present it is estimated at 17,000.

"The value of property, according to tax duplicates is six million seven hundred thousand dollars; actual real estate values eighteen million two hundred fifty thousand dollars.

"The industries of the city are carried on by about fifty manufacturing companies giving employment to more than five thousand persons with an annual payroll in excess of three million dollars.

"The numerous enterprises of the city are listed as follows:

Municipal:
18 Miles of Paved Streets
Water Works
Sewer System
Garbage Disposal Plant
4 Parks
3 Fire Departments
1 Patrol Station

Steam Railroads:
The Big Four
The Erie
Columbus, Hocking Valley & Toledo
Columbus and Sandusky

Electric Railroads:
Columbus, Delaware and Marion Railway
Marion Railway, Light and Power Plant

Manufacturing:
Marion Steam Shovel Company
Huber Manufacturing Company
2 Brick Manufacturing Companies
2 Planing Mills
2 Ice Companies
3 Stone Quarries
1 Brewery
1 Silk Manufacturing Company
3 Cigar Manufacturing Companies
1 Monumental Works
3 Wagon Manufacturing Companies
8 Blacksmiths

Financial:
5 Banks
3 Building and Loan Associations

Commercial:
1 Bottling Works
5 Piano Stores
9 Hardware Stores
10 Hotels
10 Liveries
6 Jewelers
44 Saloon and Liquor Stores
53 Groceries
11 Dry Goods Stores
11 Druggists
3 Express Companies
2 Telegraph Companies
2 Telephone Companies
5 Dairies
8 Clothiers
9 Wood and Coal Yards
2 Furniture Stores
5 Feed Stores
19 Meat Markets
4 Restaurants
2 Wholesale Grocers
20 Barber Shops

2 Daily Newspapers
2 Semi-weekly Newspapers
4 Weekly Newspapers
22 Shoe Dealers
8 Confectioners
8 Millinery Stores
5 Cigar Stores
2 Florists
2 Laundries
3 Undertakers

Educational:
10 Public Schools
1 Public Library

Amusements:
Opera House
Fair Grounds
1 Skating Rink

Charitable and Religious:
2 Hospitals
Young Men's Christian Association
23 Churches
40 Secret Societies[13]

A summary is then made of the population. The report says: "In estimating passenger income, the total population has been taken four miles from located line for direct traffic. For tributary passenger income, an estimate has been made of the population along steam and electric roads out of Lima, Kenton and Marion to the principal city or village at a distance not exceeding fifteen miles from the Lima-Eastern Railway." In estimating the population in the eight-mile strip (four miles on either side of the located line) the population for each township involved is listed, the percentage of the township that lies within the eight-mile strip is approximated, and the same percentage of the population of that township is tabulated as being within the directly tributary strip of territory. Thus the population of one township, Liberty, was 1,410, the

[13] C. W. Gerstenberg, "Materials of Corporation Finance," pages 481–3.

percentage of the township lying within the directly tributary territory was said to be 40 per cent, and the directly tributary population, therefore, was listed at 564. Where villages or cities are involved the figures for the latest two decennial censuses were given and from these the estimated population was derived, on the principle that the *rate* of growth in population during the ten years between the two censuses has continued since the latest census. The population that will be directly served by the projected road is estimated in this way to be 76,740. The tributary (that is outlying) population is figured out in the same way to be 41,735.[14]

The report then examines the nature of special activities, such as mail, package freight and express, dairy products, and general freight to see if they offer possibilities for income.

The summary of estimated total revenues is as follows:

REVENUE AND OPERATING EXPENSE

ANNUAL REVENUE

1. Passenger Traffic:		
(a) Directly on line, 76,740 at $2.25	$172,665.00	
(b) Tributary to line, 41,735 at $0.22½ (1-10 of above rate)	9,390.00	
(c) Transfer of passengers from distant points on roads, from and between steam and electric railroads, in Lima, Kenton and Marion	2,500.00	
		$184,555.00
2. United States Mail		7,500.00
3. Package Freight and Express		9,300.00
4. Dairy Products:		
(a) Milk	$5,760.00	
(b) Butter, eggs, etc.	1,000.00	
		6,760.00
5. Freight:		
(a) Coal	$1,500.00	
(b) Farm products	6,000.00	
(c) Miscellaneous	200.00	
		7,700.00
Total estimated revenue		$215,815.00

[14] This method is considered by L. E. Fischer in his "Economics of Inter urban Railways" to lead to erroneous results. Fischer contends that the population of the principal, or, as he calls it, the primary terminus, should be omitted, and that it is unnecessary to pay any attention to the strictly rural population between towns, since if the towns are large and close together the rural population is likely to be correspondingly dense, while if the towns are small and scattered the rural population is likely to be sparse. Of course, in estimating what the *per capita*

Importance of correct estimates of probable income. – The importance of estimating correctly the probable income of a projected enterprise of this kind cannot be exaggerated. Two points need consideration: one is, how many people are there, and the other is, how many of these people on the aver age will be interested in using the service, and to what degree? The first point merely requires accuracy in collecting and manipulating simple statistical data. The other point, unfortunately, is not accurately determinable. Thus if the engineer had estimated that each person "directly on line" would use, on an average, $3 worth of service per year instead of $2.25 the total revenues would have been increased by $57,555–a sum equal to about 25 per cent of the total estimated revenues and equal to considerably more than all the revenue estimated to be forthcoming from all sources except from "passenger traffic directly on line." What shall determine whether $2.25 or $3 shall be used as a multiplier? Here we must fall back on the third method of investigation – the comparative method, which we shall illustrate farther on. In brief, the problem may be stated somewhat like this: what is the correct multiplier in a given case where a road has been in operation; that is, what average use have people in other places made of similar interurban railway service? A proper allowance is then made for the difference in economic and social activities in the respective fields, and the multiplier for the projected road is in that way estimated. The important thing to be observed is that the estimates must not be guesswork. Every available bit of information should be brought forward and care and skill should be used in applying the results of the operations of other similar enterprises to the situation under consideration, making proper and reasonable allowances for differences in conditions.

Estimates of operating costs. – A simple statement of the financial transactions of a business for a given period may be represented as follows:

income will be, Fischer would use a much larger multiplier to show the *per capita* contribution than does the engineer making the report under consideration. While Fischer's method is much simpler and perhaps equally as accurate (his contention that the population of the primary terminus should be omitted seems incontestable where one of the termini is conspicuously superior in size), the estimate of total income made by the engineer is about the same as that determined by Fischer's method.

(a) Operating revenues	$1,000,000.00
(b) Operating expenses	600,000.00
(c) Net revenue	$ 400,000.00
(d) Interest on bonds, taxes and insurance	300,000.00
(e) Profits	$ 100,000.00

Item (e) and most of item (d) go to the people who put up the money to run the business. Before they can get any return, however, wages must be paid, materials purchased, and other expenses of operation must be met. The big problem we have under discussion is whether items (d) and (e) will be large enough to compensate the people who put up the money and take the risks of the business. Obviously this question cannot be answered until items (a) and (b) have been determined. We have seen how a canvass is made to deter mine (a).

How, now, are the operating expenses to be estimated? The entire subject is handled in the report under examination in the following brief summary:

OPERATING EXPENSE

Per Car-Mile:		
Maintenance	$0.025	
Power Plant Operation	0.030	
Operation of Cars	0.055	
Miscellaneous	0.020	
Per Car-Mile	$0.130	
Car-Miles:		
Passenger Service	743,200	
Express, Freight, Work Trains, etc.	137,600	
Total Car-Miles	880,800	
880,800 Car-Miles at $0.13		$114,505.00
Gross Income (see page 24)		215,815.00
Gross Income, less Operating Expenses		$101,310.00

This method appears to be very simple. One only has to determine how many times during the day a car will cover the 55-mile trip from one end of the line to the other, multiply that number by 55 miles and the resulting number by 313 (365 days less 52 Sundays) and add to the result the car-miles estimated for the 52 Sundays. It will be noticed that the passenger cars and freight cars are treated separately in estimating the car-miles, but not in estimating the cost of each car-mile.

The cost of operating is divided into four parts: (1) the cost of upkeep or maintenance; (2) the cost of operating the power plant; (3) the cost of operating the cars (chiefly what is known as platform wages, that is, wages of motormen and conductors); and (4) miscellaneous costs including briefly the general administration expenses.

Criticism of method used for estimating operating expenses. – While this report was made for conditions as they existed a number of years ago, it is unlikely that the estimate of operating costs was adequate even then. But aside from any quantitative mistakes, the mistakes of method are glaring enough to be condemned. And while the problem involved is some what technical for a treatise built on as broad lines as is this book, the error must be pointed out, to emphasize the fundamental principle that in making estimates care must be exercised to use facts and figures with due regard to their proper relations. The maintenance costs are set down as 2 1/2 cents a car-mile. The error here lies in the fact that some of the maintenance costs cannot be measured by the car-mile, for there is no necessary and inevitable relation between them and the car-miles. The costs referred to are the expenses of keeping the track, roadway, buildings, and other structures in repair. These costs will run whether the company produces one or one million car-miles. The repairs will be necessary only partly because cars run over the tracks. The greater part of the repairs will be due to the actions of nature, such as rain, winds, freezing, and thawing. The cost of repairs due to these latter causes will have some relation not to the car-miles operated by the company, but to the number of miles of track that are exposed to the elements. It is customary, therefore, to divide maintenance costs of railways into two parts – maintenance of equipment, which may properly be measured by the number of car-miles, and maintenance of road and structures, which is usually measured by the miles of road.

The same question may also be asked here as was asked in respect to the multipliers in estimating the revenues. How do we know whether to take as the unit cost for "operation of cars" 5 1/2 cents or 25 1/2 cents? And the same answer must be given here as was given in the case of revenues. We must arrive at these unit costs from an examination of enterprises in operation. For some businesses, as, for example, the railroad business, these unit figures are readily ascertainable from published reports. But if we are to find out how much it will cost to operate a steamship per ton capacity, or how much to run a mill per spindle capacity, we shall have to go to people who have such information and who are willing to divulge it. This may not be so difficult as it seems, for while Jones may not be willing to tell you the exact costs in his own factory, he may give the limits of costs – high and low – as he believes them to be in his line of business and this information can be checked against similar opinions from Jones's competitors.[15]

Summary of economics of a projected enterprise. – We have, now, all the elements necessary to determine whether it will pay to build an interurban electric railway from Lima to Marion. For the moment we may accept the figures of the engineer as correct. We are interested here in the qualitative side of the subject, in the methodology, in the *how to investigate.* Later we shall take up the third step in investigation – verification – and we shall then have occasion to come back to the engineer's figures to test them.

The whole situation may be summed up as the engineer sums it up:

Total estimated cost of construction	**$1,282,530.00**
Capitalization—Bonds placed at 90[16]	**1,425,000.00**
Gross earnings less operating expenses	**$ 101,310.00**
Fixed charges—Interest at 5 per cent	**71,250.00**
Net income	**$ 30,060.00**

[15] For some interesting analyses of costs, see W. L. Webb, "Economics of Railway Construction." Engineers, accountants, and market experts may be found who have such information, gathered from years of experience in ministering to many enterprises. See also F. W. Doolittle, "Studies in the Cost of Interurban Transportation Service."

[16] It is doubtful if at any time in the last twenty years bonds for an inter-urban to be built could have been sold at 90 if they paid only 5 per cent. Probably 6 per cent bonds at 90 would represent about what could have been done for a sound project during the first decade of the twentieth century.

Plan of financing the proposition. – While this is not the place to consider methods of financing, it is interesting to note, in passing, the engineer's ideas on this subject in this particular case. According to the engineer's figures, it would appear that all the money necessary to be raised could be obtained by selling $1,425,000 of per cent bonds and that after paying the interest on these bonds, amounting to $71,250, there would be left, each year, $30,060. This sum would pay dividends of five per cent on $601,200 of stock or dividends of six per cent on about $500,000. While there is nothing said in the report on the subject of cost of financing (item 6, page 17), the plan of the promoter undoubtedly would be to issue to himself for his services and expenses, from $500,000 to $600,000 of common stock. This, of course, he would sell, and from the proceeds he would replenish his own treasury from which would be drawn the expenses of the next promotion. The banker who placed the bonds would undoubtedly be expected to reimburse himself from the difference between the price paid by the investor and the $90 to be turned over to the company.

It may be well to state here that the road from Lima to Marion was never built. But that is another story which will engage our attention later.

PROMOTION – INVESTIGATION *(concluded)*, Checking Up, Assembling, Legal Phases[1]

Charles Gerstenberg

How to use the comparison method of investigating. – In the comparison method of determining what amount of funds will be necessary and whether those funds can be profitably employed in a projected enterprise, the important consideration is to find a number of concerns of similar size and conditions from the statistics of which we can estimate what will be required and what will be the results. Certain errors may creep into the investigation of which the financier must be wary. First, an analysis of a single concern may be misleading. We are reminded of the promotion of such magazines as *Hamptons* and *The Columbian* about fifteen years ago. The promoters pointed to the wonderful success of *Munsey's*, but overlooked the hundreds of failures that did not have a Frank Munsey to guide them. Secondly, in making comparisons we must select enterprises that are somewhat similar to what our own is likely to be. For example, a single track interurban railway connecting small towns and designed to carry light traffic may cost but $30,000 a mile to build, whereas the heavier rails and larger stations of a more pretentious transportation system may entail a minimum initial expenditure of at least $100,000 a mile.[2] It would not be fair, therefore, to state that the projected road can be built for $30,000 a mile because a road has been built for that amount.

[1] [Chapter 3 of *Financial Organization and the Management of Business*, New York: Prentice-Hall, 1924.]

[2] The reader will appreciate this point if he will study, for example, the operating and financial statistics given for Class A, Class B, and Class C utilities by the Wisconsin Railway Commission in its annual report. See also an excellent article by F. W. Doolittle on "Anatomy of the Interurban Report" in the *Electric Railway Journal*, vol. 49, page 242.

Another error is sometimes committed in using the comparison method. Instead of finding the average costs and the average operating results of a number of concerns, the investigator may erroneously use different individual concerns for comparison purposes at various stages of the calculations. Thus the argument may run: road *A* cost so much to build, therefore, road *X* will cost the same to build; road *B* cost so much to operate, therefore, road *X* will cost the same to operate. The fact may be that road *A* was poorly constructed, with no regard to the saving in operating costs that might have been realized by the elimination of grades or by the use of crushed stone ballast instead of sand or cinder ballast. Road *B*, on the other hand, may have cost a great deal to build, the original cost including provision for elimination of grades and sharp curves, the use of heavy rails, preserved ties, and first class ballast, all of which make for low operating costs.

Special cases of investigation. – Since many investigations are similar in that they center about some central idea such as a patent or a peculiar piece of property, such as a mine or a timber tract, we may pause for a moment to consider very briefly the principles involved in one or two of these classes of enterprises.

Investigation of inventions. – The investigation of inventions may be intrusted to capable and experienced engineers and patent attorneys, but a few simple principles every promoter should understand. The risks are enormous, and, in the experience of the author, who has observed a number of such instances, the inventor is likely to shilly-shally with his device, to neglect perfecting it for commercial exploitation, as soon as he finds a promoter ready to take up his patent and when, therefore, the doubt about the next day's livelihood has been removed.

Whether the invention is patented or not these questions should be asked:

1. Is the device worth while? The records of the patent office are swarming with applications for silly devices, as a bed that will eject the lazy sleeper, a device for keeping the feet warm by conveying to them the warm breath exhaled from the lungs, and so forth.[3]

[3] The reader is referred to "Gulliver's Travels" for other examples not more ridiculous than those occurring in actual life.

2. Is the idea practicable? In the chemical business, for example, a laboratory reaction may be obtainable, though the production of the same result on a commercially large scale may not be attainable.

3. Will the device accomplish the purpose for which it is designed? We are reminded of the patent obtained on the idea of preventing fraud in the sale of cigars. The fraud consisted in putting high class bands on plebeian tobacco, and the remedy was to weave into the high grade cigar a silk thread. The claim was made by the deluded inventor that while the defrauders might substitute bands they would not dare infringe the patent of weaving a silk thread.

4. Is the device merchantable? Safety razors, toilet preparations, and the like are hard to sell, however meritorious.

If the patent has been obtained, these questions may be asked about it:

1. Is the patent good, in the sense that its claims have not been anticipated?

2. Are the claims broad enough? A German doctor obtained a patent on the solution of a certain East Indian gum in turpentine. Along came a chemist who patented the solution of the gum in any hydrocarbon other than turpentine.

3. How old is the patent? The life of a patent is only seventeen years.

Secret processes are difficult to investigate since the results obtained may be very expensively brought about. It can hardly be expected that the inventor will divulge his process, and reliance must therefore be placed upon his integrity as to his statement of costs.[4]

Investigation of timber tract. – Another example of the hazards that must be run in connection with a seemingly simple proposition is the timber tract. It would seem that practically no risks are run by the man who puts up money to place a mill on a timber tract and pays for cutting and transporting the lumber. However, there is first the question of title. Vast tracts of virgin forests in Tennessee, Kentucky, and Virginia have not been worked because it is almost impossible to get a clear title. Then

[4] For further information on this interesting subject, see Mois H. Avram, "Patenting and Promoting Inventions."

there is the problem of fire risk. A fine stand of timber today may be a charred desert tomorrow. There is also the problem of getting the timber out. The mountain sides may be steep and the streams practically useless. Moreover, the difficulty of getting a reliable "cruise" or estimate may result in gross overestimates of value.[5]

Need for checking up the investigation. – The investigation is, as we pointed out, made by an independent expert, perhaps an engineer or a marketing analyst. In any event, the investigators are supposed to be competent and impartial. Frequently an incompetent investigator is chosen because the promoter can afford to pay for his services while the services of a reputable investigator would be beyond his means. Some times the investigator is partial because he has an interest in the subject of the investigation. For example, promoters have frequently chosen State geologists to make a report on a proposed cement plant. The State geologist is interested in attracting industry to the State; that in effect explains "the reason for being" of his office. While the prestige of his office is likely to be accepted as a point in his favor, it should, in fact, be a cause for suspicion. Then, too, there is the question of fees. The promoter is anxious to have a favorable report; the investigator knows that. And because the fee is to be paid by the promoter and because the promoter, if successful in launching this enterprise with other people's money, is likely to have other projects on which he will need a report, the investigator is likely to resolve doubts favorably to the project. Moreover, the investigator will probably meet the promoter frequently and will become infected with the latter's contagious enthusiasm.

[5] The following books will be found helpful in investigating propositions: *General texts on methods:* Carl S. Duncan, "Commercial Research"; J. George Frederick, "Business Research and Statistics"; "Source Book of Research Data," by the New York University Bureau of Business Research; Percival 'White, "Scientific Analysis and Organization of Markets." *On specific lines of industry see:* F. W. Doolittle, "Studies in the Cost of Interurban Transportation Service"; L. E. Fischer, "Economics of Interurban Railways"; J. C. Pickering, "Engineering Analysis of a Mining Share"; Joseph E. Pogue, "The Economics of Petroleum"; A. T. Shurick, "Coal Mining Costs"; Northwestern University, "Retail Clothing Survey"; Harvard University Bureau of Business Research, Studies in Retail Jewelry, Department Stores, Retail Shoe Stores, Wholesale Grocery Stores, Retail Grocery Stores, and Retail Drugs. See also "Analysis of a Business Case" in L. C. Marshall, "Business Administration" (slate quarry in Vermont).

Checking up is all the more important because there is an insidious guarantee of accuracy in an array of figures. Let a promoter outline in detail the probable cost of operations and the probable income, and the would-be investor, ignorant of such matters and ignorant even that he is not investing, but is speculating, immediately accepts the statements as gospel truth. The number of facts included may be complete, the conclusions from those facts may be inevitable, and still there may be the simple fault of inaccurate facts.

The report evidently must be checked up by somebody who represents the capitalists' interests rather than the promoter's interests. This somebody is likely to be the statistician of the financial institution to whom application is made by the promoter for the funds indicated by the report to be required for launching the project. Whoever it is that represents the sought-for capital, he must be a man of clear judgment, with habits of carefulness and diligence, and he must have some experience or training in examining reports.

Experience teaches men to look for the glaring errors. Suppose we return for a moment to the interurban report. The cost of the 55 miles of line was estimated at $1,282,530, or about $23,300 a mile. The experienced statistician would have known that this was possible in the days for which the report was made. Again the revenues were placed at $215,815. This the statistician would probably accept as a fact to be verified later if all the other facts more readily tested proved the enterprise feasible. He indeed would be justified in doing this in this case, for the third element, operating costs, is so far from what was possible that the report should be rejected even though the revenues are accepted as true. The car-mile cost of operation was placed at 13 cents. The statistician could turn to railway reports, or could call upon operating officials of interurban railways and would readily learn from these sources that 25 cents was a minimum. Using this minimum we would get these results:

Total estimated revenues (page 24)	$215,815.00
Operating costs, 880,800 car-miles (page 26) at 25 cents	220,200.00
Operating deficit	$ 4,385.00

No wonder the road was never built.[6]

Methods of checking up investigation. – There are practically three methods of checking up an investigation. One is to examine the report itself to see if it contains errors in mathematics, omissions, or false reasoning. The second method consists simply in comparing results of one method of investigation with the results obtained by another method. A third method involves really a trial of the enterprise on a small scale.

1. *Examining the report.* – Some of the errors contained in a report were pointed out when the method of investigating the projected line from Lima to Marion was explained. The report referred to, for example, assumed that the rail and structures would wear out in proportion only to the number of cars that were operated and the distance they ran. The report left out entirely a consideration of the repairs necessitated by fire, flood, frost, wind, and rain. Moreover, there are certain omissions in that report in estimating the capital requirements. The sixteen elements that enter into the construction of the roadway (page 19) do not include roadside tools and waiting rooms. A very frequent omission is illustrated by the investigation of a hypothetical concern to sell a new automobile accessory (page 17). An allowance for contingencies was made in that case, but it is frequently omitted. It is usual in large enterprises such as an interurban rail way to allow as much as from ten to twelve per cent of the estimated capital requirements for contingencies.

2. *Checking up by comparison.* – A simple method of detecting mistakes is to check up a report carefully with known results. If, for example, we take the illustration of the so-called statistical method of investigating where we found that about $40,000 was needed, and compare that sum with the investment in similar trading concerns we can get some assurance of the accuracy or worthlessness of the details. Or perhaps a projected cement

6 It must be remembered that all figures given here refer back to the year 1905. Operating expenses do not vary much from place to place; hence the person checking up the report would likely know that 25 cents was more appropriate. He could not check up the revenues so readily because revenues do depend on the character of the particular community to be served.

company may be shown to be a very profitable prospect since its cost of operations is reckoned to be 60 cents a barrel, whereas examination of even highly successful companies may show a minimum cost of 65 cents a barrel. If the plant is a modest one, say, of 800,000 barrels capacity, the difference in the estimated costs of operation will be reflected in an excess of profit amounting to $40,000.

In checking up by the comparison method the chief object is to find a unit for the basis of comparison. In estimating capital costs, the unit is usually the unit of capacity, such as the kilowatt capacity of an electric light plant, the mile of track of a railway, the net tons of a ship, the barrel capacity of a cement plant or an oil refinery, and the spindle capacity of a cotton mill.

In estimating probable revenues comparison is frequently made on the per capita or customer basis. For example, in comparing gas plants the first figure to get is the number of possible consumers per 100 population, then the estimated consumption of gas per consumer and this with the price of gas per thousand cubic feet will give the probable gross earnings. In checking up these figures we simply inquire: what revenue per capita does this amount to for every person in the territory served? We know in a general way what the limits of expected revenue are, and that if the investigator's estimates of per capita revenue do not fall within those limits, something is probably wrong. In checking up costs of operation the unit of comparison is usually the cost per unit of product of actual production. Thus, as we have seen, we may compare the operating costs of two cement plants on the basis of the cost per barrel of output.

3. Checking up by trial. – Where marketing costs are an important factor in the success of an enterprise, estimates are likely to be quite at variance with the results. In other words, the margin of error is likely to be large. The best way to reduce a possible loss to the minimum is to check up estimates by making trials. For example, it is planned to form a company to market a new trade-marked brand of coffee. Instead of carrying out a campaign throughout the entire country a test may be made in one community and the same factor of error in calculating may be assumed for the entire country as appears in the selected community from an actual attempt to market the new brand in that community.

Second step in promotion. – After a discovery has been made and it is decided to go ahead, the elements of the business must be brought together. The important elements from the standpoint of financial plans are: (1) the fundamental idea; (2) property necessary; and (3) managerial ability. Funds, of course, are necessary, but the problem of raising them is considered under the third step in promotion, that of financing.

Assembling the idea. – The basic idea may be the discovery of some demand that is not being filled, or it may be a better way of filling a demand, or a method of reducing costs by consolidation of existing plants. How can this "idea" be contributed, and the value of it protected? An idea is not patentable; only the device for carrying *out* an idea can be patented. Neither can an idea be copyrighted. If now an "idea" without any device or property attached to it is to be brought to a promoter, only two methods of protecting it against piracy are open. One is to present it only to promoters who are known definitely not to be pirates. The other is to protect it by contract. The difficulty of drawing a binding agreement is almost insuperable. How can the discoverer of such an idea, for example, as the building of a gas plant at such and such a place, prevent anybody else from building at that place? The fact is that the person who discovers the idea usually tries to protect himself, and does so to a certain extent by doing a part of the assembling himself. For example, he may obtain the special franchise to build the gas plant and in that way practically prevent others from coming in. But even in such a case the special franchise may be rendered practically useless by non-user.

The case of Harry Haskins against Thomas F. Ryan is well known and interesting.[7] Haskins conceived the idea of consolidating a number of independent lead companies and procured options on their plants. These he took, so he alleges, to Thomas F. Ryan, who professed an interest in taking up the options. Instead of taking up the options, Ryan, so the story goes, on one pretext or another, delayed the consummation of the plan till the options expired, and then went about the consolidation himself. In a word, Haskins was "frozen out."

[7] For a statement of facts see the complaint in C. W. Gerstenberg, "Materials of Corporation Finance," pages 489–495.

Methods of taking property. – Control of the essential property connected with an idea, whether the property be a patent or secret process, a special franchise or the plants of the constituents of a consolidation, may be acquired in one of several ways. First, the promoter may take title in his own name. Second, title may be taken in the name of a small corporation to be expanded later or from which title may be taken by the final corporation. This apparently was the method used in the promotion of the United States Steel Corporation.[8] Another method is the trustee or escrow method, whereby the title to the property is placed in the hands of a trustee to be turned over by him to a corporation upon the performance of certain conditions, such as the payment of certain sums of money for the use of the company that is being promoted.[9] A fourth method is to procure an option, which, if not taken up, will entail only the loss of the money necessary to bind the option. To be sure, the loss may be considerable, since the persons originally owning the property may be unwilling to give binding options unless a large sum is paid. It is said that Henry Frick lost a clean million when he failed to get the necessary funds to take up his option on Carnegie's plants a year or so before the formation of the United States Steel Corporation. Finally the property may be controlled by a contract to buy. If the contract is not put through the promoter will have to stand ready to pay damages for breach of contract.

Valuation of properties. – When properties are to be acquired the question always arises: what shall be paid for them? This problem is somewhat different from the problem of capitalization. For example, it may be planned to promote a company that will be. a consolidation of companies *A, B,* and *C.* The problem here is, how much are the properties of the several companies worth separately. The problem of capitalization is to determine how much they will be worth when brought together. Incidentally it may be remarked that the difference between the aggregate of the separate values and the collective value measures somewhat accurately the value of the promoter's services.

[8] See A. Cotter, "Authentic History of the United States Steel Corporation."

[9] See, for example, C. W. Gerstenberg, "Materials of Corporation Finance," page 500.

Several methods of valuation may be mentioned. The first may be called scientific appraisal. In this method a definite, and more or less scientific, plan is agreed upon and the actual figures to be paid are arrived at by applying the plan to the property. Thus a patent on an automobile accessory may be valued somewhat as follows: Assume that one in every 100 automobile owners will buy a device once in two years, and will pay a profit of one dollar. The annual profits may then be capitalized at 20 per cent and the result will be the price of the patent.[10] Real estate, it may be agreed, shall be valued by taking late sales in the neighborhood and applying rules of appraisal understood by expert real estate operators and appraisers.

A second method of valuation is simply to name the appraisers and to agree to abide by their verdict.

A third method may be called negotiation. The negotiators agree upon a price, being guided perhaps, though not necessarily, by some scientific rules of valuation.

Frequently valuations are made by negotiating for part of the property and agreeing upon terms of any appraisal for the rest. Thus where a plant is to be bought, it may be stipulated that a certain sum shall be paid for the intangible property, such as trade names, patents, and so forth, but that the tangible property shall be valued through an appraisal.[11]

Valuation of goodwill. – When the goodwill of a business is to be sold, it is usually valued in the following way. The average earnings of the business over a period of time are capitalized and from that sum is subtracted the appraised value of the tangible property of the concern. The remainder will be the value of the goodwill.[12] Thus company A is about to sell all its assets to X. Its earnings for the previous five years have been, in thousands, \$100, \$200, \$150, \$250, \$300. Its average annual earnings are \$200,000. This may be capitalized at about 7 per cent (the rate depending on the nature and risk of the business) or at

[10] For more detailed methods of valuation see C. W. Gerstenberg, "Materials of Corporation Finance," pages 499–541.

[11] See, for example, the Deering Harvester Agreement, reprinted in C. W. Gerstenberg, "Materials of Corporation Finance," page 499.

[12] The diagram on page 15 with the footnote on goodwill indicates another method of arriving at the same result.

$3,000,000. If now, a physical appraisal of the tangible property shows it to be worth $1,000,000, the value of the concern's goodwill will be $2,000,000, that is, the difference between the total value of $3,000,000 and the appraised value of the physical assets.[13]

Assembling managerial ability. – The importance of managerial ability is generally too well understood to be dwelt upon here. The promoter ought not to be successful in his quest for funds for a new company unless he can show that he has available the kind of managerial ability necessary to success. Securing managerial ability, however, is very generally a matter of paying the right price. A greater difficulty may be experienced by the promoter in getting rid of incompetent managers. The following situation recently came to the author's attention. A concern wanted to make a definite step in expansion, amounting in effect to the promotion of a large company to take over its business and add to it large sums of new capital. The new capitalists were quite willing to pay a large salary to the inventor of the basic process to induce him to use his efforts to introduce improvements, but they were somewhat non-plussed as to what arrangement to make with the other half-owner, who had been the general manager. It was felt that his limitations might quickly develop when he undertook the management of a much larger concern. It was finally agreed to pay him a large salary for a stipulated number of years, a part of the agreement, however, being that the capitalists might remove him from authority at any time, though in such event his salary was to continue.

Presenting the proposition. – When an idea has been discovered, that is, when it has been conceived, investigated, and checked up, and when the necessary assembling has been made, the promoter has what is popularly called a "proposition." His next step is the financing of the proposition. However this is done, the previous work will have to be organized for presentation to the prospective capitalists. A careful promoter will keep a file of all papers and correspondence connected with the discovery and assembling. These will be available to the capitalists in checking up the

[13] See Kemper Simpson, "The Capitalization of Goodwill," and P. D. Leake, "Commercial Goodwill, its History, Value, and Treatment in Accounts."

accuracy of statements made by the promoter in his formal presentation. This latter document should be a well-organized, clear, concise statement of the proposition, supported by copies of engineer's and accountants' reports, lawyers' opinions, copies of legal documents, copies of government reports, pamphlets, and material relied upon to show the value of the plan. The document of formal presentation will be much more voluminous than a prospectus designed to sell securities of the company to the general public. It will be neatly gotten up and will convey in its physical appearance some degree of the care exercised in making the discovery and accomplishing the assembling.

Financing. – The third step in promotion is financing. By financing is meant the actual acquiring of funds with which to procure the necessary property, tangible and intangible, and with which to perfect the organization, start operations, and keep them going until the business is on a self-supporting basis. We cannot properly study this subject till we have considered the instruments with which such funds can be raised, and the legal organization which the financing entails.[14] For the present, then, we shall omit the consideration of financing and turn our attention to organization, ownership, and credit instruments and to an analysis of possible financial plans. In short, our next problem is, what can the promoters offer the owners of the funds in exchange for them – shares in a partnership, participations in a syndicate, stocks, bonds, what? But first let us consider a few indispensable questions of the law of promotions.

Some legal considerations in promotion. – While this is not a book on law, there are some legal questions connected with promotion that every promoter will care to know. They affect to such an extent the work that the promoter is doing or can do that expertness in promotion cannot be achieved without knowing something about them.

[14] However, it should be said here that the cost of financing the promotion up to the point where the final proposition is presented to the capitalists should be borne by the promoter himself. If the project fails to mature into a promoted concern, the promoter will be out of pocket; if the financing is successful, he will reimburse himself from the contributions of the participants to whom interests in the business are sold.

Who is a promoter? – Anybody who undertakes to organize or to assist in the organization of a corporation. or other association is a promoter. A promoter can hardly be said to be an agent because the principal for whom he is working is not in existence.

It will be noticed that any person who assists in the promotion of a company is a promoter. This statement is literally true, for if a person knowingly engages in work connected with the promotion of a company he is to act fairly and not to conspire with the acknowledged promoter to make unreasonable profits out of the new enterprise.

When does a promoter begin to promote? – This is an important question, as will be seen from the following illustration. A man owns a piece of property and has held it for a long time. He promotes a corporation to take over the property. At what price must he yield it to the company? The property may have appreciated year by year and he is entitled to no profit through his holding that may accrue during the time of promotion. On the other hand, he is not bound to turn it over to the company at the very small price he may have paid for it when he first bought it. The answer is that he must give it to the company at what it was worth at the time he became the promoter, and this time is fixed at the moment he conceived the idea of promotion. Since it is hard to read men's minds a more practical rule is that the promoter begins to promote when he first does something in connection with that operation.

When does a promoter cease to promote? – A promoter need not continue his promotion unless he has bound himself in some way to some individuals to continue his work. For example, you may give him one thousand dollars to be paid for in stock of the corporation later, on condition that he will raise a certain number of thousand dollars from other people. Under these circumstances he would be compelled to promote the company until he raised the stipulated sum.

In the example given in the preceding section it was said that the promoter could not make any profit from the moment he became a promoter. This was not altogether true for he may have completed the promotion of his company and permitted the stockholders to elect directors; thereupon he would cease to be a promoter and could deal with the corporation at arm's length.

In other words, he could have said to the permanent directors, "If you care to buy this property I'll sell it at such a price," and the bargain, in the absence of any misrepresentations, would be binding on the company.

Adoption of promoter's contracts. – We have seen in connection with the assembling of a proposition that various contracts are made for acquisition of property and for engaging the services of employees of one grade or another. Some times these contracts are made with trustees for the corporation. At other times they are made in the name of the corporation. In any event, they are not binding on the corporation until the corporation knows all about them and adopts them. The corporation cannot be said to adopt any contract the terms of which it does not know fully. It is improper, therefore, for a promoter to turn property over to a corporation stating that he is to make a profit on it or that the corporation's directors can find out how much the profit will be by consulting certain deeds.

Remedies for fraudulent acts of promoter. – Where the promoter did not make a full, frank, and fair statement of the profits he was making out of a transaction with the corporation during the period of promotion, the directors, when they learn of the secret profits, may either rescind the contract, return the property and receive back the stock or cash paid for the property, or they may sue the promoter for the secret profits, or they may sue for any other damages. For example, a promoter cannot permit people with whom he deals to make unreasonable profits out of the corporation. If the promoter did permit such unreasonable profits to be made, the corporation would not be bound to recover those profits from the third person, but could sue the promoter for the damages which would be measured by the unreasonable amount of profit paid to the third person.

Subscription contracts. – A promoter should know the law on the subject of subscriptions in the State in which his corporation is to be organized. If the corporation is not organized and the subscription agreement therefore cannot be made with the corporation, it should be made with a trustee for the corporation. It is usual to put in the contract a clause stating that the consideration for the subscription is the subscriptions of other subscribers.

SUBSCRIPTION AGREEMENT

THIS AGREEMENT dated the 15th day of October, 1912, between the undersigned Subscribers severally, as the first parties, and HENRY L. DOHERTY & COMPANY, a partnership doing business at No. 60 Wall Street, New York City, New York, hereinafter described as the Bankers, as the second party, WITNESSETH:

WHEREAS, a plan has been devised for the acquirement of certain electric and gas companies, traction companies and other corporations engaged in the furnishing of service to various municipalities in the United States of America and the Dominion of Canada, which plan is as follows:

PLAN

A corporation is to be formed under the laws of the State of Delaware, or some other suitable state, to be known as Utilities Improvement Company or some other suitable name, which said corporation is to have an authorized capital as follows:

1st. Fifteen million dollars ($15,000,000) par value of common stock, to be divided into one hundred and fifty thousand (150,000) shares of the par value of One hundred dollars ($100) each.

2nd. Twenty-five million dollars ($25,000,000) par value of six per cent. cumulative preferred stock, to be divided into two hundred and fifty thousand (250,000) shares of the par value of One hundred dollars ($100) each, which said preferred stock shall be redeemable at any time upon the payment of one hundred and twenty per cent. of par, plus accrued dividend and to be non-voting so long as dividends are paid thereon.

Of the above authorized issues, Ten million dollars ($10,000,000) par value of the preferred stock and Ten million dollars ($10,000,000) par value of the common stock are to be issued forthwith for the properties above specified (subject to present indebtedness). It is further understood and agreed that neither the new corporation, its stock or bond holders, nor any one else, shall have any right to question any contract or transaction through which said bonds or said stock shall be issued or acquired, although there may result to said Bankers, or anyone else, a profit therefrom; and

WHEREAS, all other and further details of said plan are to be determined by the Bankers; and

WHEREAS, the Bankers expect to acquire and secure some or all of the stock and bonds so to be issued, and to be in position to sell and dispose of any portion of the same;

NOW, THEREFORE, in consideration of the premises, each subscriber hereby severally, but not jointly, agrees with the Bankers upon the terms and conditions hereinafter specified, to purchase from the Bankers preferred stock of the said new Company of the par value set after his signature hereto (together with common stock of the par value of forty per cent. of the par value of such preferred stock) or such smaller amount as the Bankers may allot, it being understood that, prior to allotment, the Bankers may reduce or reject entirely any subscription.

The price is to be

One thousand dollars ($1,000) for { One thousand dollars ($1,000) par value of Six Per Cent. Cumulative Preferred Stock Four hundred dollars ($400) par value of common stock.

Payment therefor is to be made to the Bankers or such depositary as the Bankers may designate, in instalments, the first instalment to be twenty per cent. (20%) of the par value of the preferred stock for which subscription is made, and to be payable upon the signing hereof, and the balance to be payable from time to time after allotment in instalments of not more than twenty per cent. (20%) of the amount allotted, upon not less than ten (10) days notice and not less than thirty (30) days between dates of payment.

Preferred stock to the nearest integral amount, or interim receipts therefor, shall be delivered as payments are made, and upon completion of such payment, any balance of preferred stock, with adjustments for interest, and the common stock certificates, will be delivered. After allotment, the subscriber may pay the whole or any part of the subscription before it shall become payable as aforesaid.

Should any subscriber fail to pay any instalment of the purchase price when due, the Bankers, or their assigns, may, if they so elect, re-sell, at public or private sale, without notice and upon such terms as they may determine, the stock hereby agreed to be purchased by such subscriber, and shall thereupon be accountable to the subscriber only for the excess, if any, of the net amount received upon such sale over the amount still payable by him hereunder, the subscriber to remain liable to the Bankers for any deficit.

Any call, notice, or other communication under or in connection with this agreement shall be sufficiently given or made to any subscriber if delivered at, or mailed, telegraphed or cabled, to the address written after his signature hereto.

No partnership or joint relation of any kind results from this agreement and the same is made in and is to be construed according to the laws of the State of New York.

Subscriptions will be received until October 26th, 1912, and allotments will be made immediately thereafter.

Dated, New York City, New York, October 15, 1912.

NAME	PAR VALUE OF PREFERRED STOCK	ADDRESS

Special technical rules may prevail in certain jurisdictions. For example, in New York State a subscription to be binding must be accompanied by ten per cent of the consideration. Even an option to take stock would probably not be binding unless accompanied

FORM OF SUBSCRIPTION AGREEMENT

Each of the undersigned in consideration of the subscriptions of the other subscribers hereby subscribes for the number of shares of stock of the ....of the class set opposite his signature, and hereby agrees to pay the par value thereof in cash, to the treasurer of the corporation as follows: ten per cent on the signing of this subscription, and the remaining ninety per cent at such time or times as the board of directors may require by resolution and notice, in writing, to the subscribers, but such requirement shall be uniform and pro rated among all the subscribers according to the amounts of their several subscriptions.

Signature	Number of Shares	Class of Stock	Amount of Subscription	Date
....	....	....	....	....
....	....	....	....	....
....	....	....	....	....

by ten per cent of the option price. A form of subscription to a corporation about to be organized, and a simple form of subscription for a corporation already in existence, follow.[15]

Compensation of promoters. – It has been shown that a promoter cannot make any profits out of a corporation except those that arise out of the contracts made with the promoter after the corporation is organized and has its own directors – dummy directors appointed by the promoter will not do – or where the profits made are known to the permanent directors when they adopt the transactions previously made by the promoter. It is true, however, that a promoter like any other person who acts in a trust position is entitled to reasonable compensation for his services. It is altogether reasonable, therefore, for a company to give stock to the promoter in payment for his services as long as the amount of such stock is reasonable.[16]

[15] For other forms see S. Gordon, "Annotated Forms of Agreement," forms 88–99.

[16] For a study of promoters' profits see W. Z. Ripley, "Trusts, Pools and Corporations," Chapter XIII, The Asphalt Combination. W. M. Fletcher's "Cyclopedia of the Law of Private Corporations" is a standard recent work on corporation law; it is in nine volumes with periodic supplementary volumes.

FORMS OF ORGANIZATION
– Individual Proprietorship, Partnerships, Joint Adventure, and Joint Stock Company[1]

Charles Gerstenberg

Importance of correct selection of legal form of organization. – No step in business building and management is more important than that of selecting the legal form of organization, for upon the form of organization depend not only the division of the profits of the business, but the risk which all those interested run, the amount of money that can be raised, the placing of control, and many other incidental questions. Before we can go into these interesting and important questions we had better briefly describe the forms of organization that are used in English-speaking countries.

Legal forms of organization. – The common forms of organization, are: (1) the individual proprietorship; (2) the general partnership; (3) the limited partnership; (4) the joint adventure; (5) the joint stock company; (6) the limited partnership association; (7) the Massachusetts or business trust; and (8) the corporation.

Prevalence of different forms of organization. – The desirability of the different forms of organization for large concerns and small concerns is indicated by the prevalence of the several forms in American business. It will be noted from the following table that both the individual form and the miscellaneous forms of organization have decreased relatively while corporations have increased. The parts of the table showing number of wage-earners, the value of the product, and the value added by

[1] [Chapter 4 of *Financial Organization and the Management of Business*, New York: Prentice–Hall, 1924.]

manufacture, indicate that corporations have grown in number most notably in those industries in which the units are large.[2]

TABLE No. 1

STATISTICS OF FORMS OF ORGANIZATION

Character of Ownership	1919		1914		1909		1904	
NUMBER OF ESTABLISHMENTS AND PER CENT OF DISTRIBUTION								
	Number	*%*	*Number*	*%*	*Number*	*%*	*Number*	*%*
Individuals...	138,112	47.6	142,436	51.6	140,605	52.4	113,946	52.7
Corporations..	91,517	31.5	78,152	28.3	69,501	25.9	51,097	23.6
All others....	60,476	20.8	55,203	20.0	58,385	21.7	51,137	23.7
AVERAGE WAGE EARNERS PER ESTABLISHMENT								
	Per cent		*Per cent*		*Per cent*		*Per cent*	
Individuals...	4.0		5.0		6.0		7.0	
Corporations..	86.0		72.0		72.0		76.0	
All others....	10.0		12.0		18.0		21.0	
VALUE OF PRODUCT AVERAGE PER ESTABLISHMENT AND PER CENT DISTRIBUTION								
	Dollars	*%*	*Dollars*	*%*	*Dollars*	*%*	*Dollars*	*%*
Individuals...	25,605	5.7	13,518	7.9	14,523	9.9	14,944	11.5
Corporations..	598,188	87.7	258,255	83.2	235,121	79.0	213,399	73.7
All others....	68,413	6.6	38,726	8.8	39,203	11.1	42,768	14.8
VALUE ADDED BY MANUFACTURE—PER CENT DISTRIBUTION								
	Per cent		*Per cent*		*Per cent*		*Per cent*	
Individuals...	6.2		9.1		11.4		13.1	
Corporations..	87.1		81.9		77.2		71.9	
All others....	6.7		8.9		11.5		15.0	

The individual proprietorship. – The individual proprietor ship needs little explanation. When a man goes into business all by himself, he owns all and risks all. If he cares to, he can incorporate his business, and still own it, giving to others nominal interests and making them co-directors, but requiring that they shall consent to a practical surrender of all authority to him through the simple device of electing him president and writing into the by-laws of the corporation a provision that the president shall be the general

[2] The Abstract of the Census of Manufactures for 1919, published in 1923, contains all the information available on the classification of businesses according to ownership. The table on page 46 is taken from this source.

manager. Or the proprietor may turn his business into a Massachusetts trust. But at this place we merely wish to point out that a man can organize his business in several ways and still exercise control. If he selects the corporate form or the trust form he can avoid subjecting to the risks of his business venture property not definitely committed to the business.

It must be clear, therefore, that the individual proprietorship is distinctly a form of business organization. The fact that a person who does nothing about the legal form of organization will be deemed by the law to have chosen this form, does not render the sole proprietorship any the less a method of organizing. Here the income above the debts payable to creditors, the exclusive right to control the operations, and the entire risk are centered in the proprietor.

The general partnership. – If several persons engage jointly in business without making any special provision for the legal form of their organization, they will be held to constitute a general partnership. To be sure, they may, and usually do, make a contract orally or in writing setting up the partnership relation. But if they neglect this step, the law will imply a partnership.[3]

General agency in partnerships. – In the partnership, each partner is a general agent for the business. This simply means that each partner may make contracts that will bind the partnership, or the firm as it is sometimes called.

An example will make this clear. Jones, of the firm of Jones & Smith, buys a mahogany desk for the bookkeeper. Smith goes to another dealer and buys an oak desk. Both dealers can hold the firm to their contracts of purchase. Suppose Smith had agreed with Jones that he would not buy anything for the firm. The dealer who sold the oak desk may still insist upon the sale, unless, as in all agencies, he, the third party, knew that the power of the agent was limited.

The reader will realize that one should not enter into a partnership with a person whose judgment in making contracts is not good, or with one, who if he agrees to refrain from making contracts will forget or disregard his promise.

[3] For an example of a partnership agreement see C. W. Gerstenberg, "Materials of Corporation Finance," pages 1–3. For other forms relating to Partnership see S. Gordon, "Annotated Forms of Agreement," Chap. XVII.

Delectus personnae. – This formidable expression is merely the legal jargon for the right to select a partner that is implied in every partnership agreement. Because a partner is an agent, and because in law a partner cannot delegate his authority, it follows that a partner cannot transfer his interest to another person without his partner's consent. So, if a partner dies, goes insane, becomes bankrupt, or withdraws for any cause whatsoever, his executor, guardian, or trustee in bankruptcy does not take his place. In each of these cases the newcomer – the executor, guardian, or trustee – has the right only to make the remaining partners account for and pay over the cash value of the interest of the partner whom the newcomer represents.

Liability of partners. – The members of a general partnership are jointly and severally liable for the debts of the firm. By this we mean that the creditors may collect from the partners' several private estates if their joint or partnership property is insufficient to defray the debts. In the absence of a specific contract, partners share profits and losses equally, though it is customary where partners contribute different amounts of capital, to provide in the partnership contract that the profits and losses shall be distributed in the same proportion.

An illustration will serve to make clear a number of rules relating to partners' liabilities. *A, B,* and *C* are members of a partnership which has assets of $10,000 and owes respectively to *X, Y,* and *Z* $10,000, $20,000 and $30,000. To prevent any one creditor from seizing the $10,000 of assets, a receiver is appointed by a court of equity to wind up the partnership affairs. *A* owes $20,000 to his private creditors, and has assets worth $10,000. *B* owes $10,000 and has $20,000. *C* owes $20,000 and has $20,000. There is a rule of law, called marshalling of assets, which provides that in a case like this the partnership creditors have the first right to the partnership assets and private creditors have first right to the partners' individual properties. Hence, the $10,000 partnership assets will go to *X, Y,* and *Z; A's* $10,000 will go to his creditors; *B's* creditors will take $10,000 of his property, and the rest will go to *X, Y,* and *Z* under the rule of the joint and several liability of partners. *C's* creditors will take all his property. Since *B* will have paid $10,000 out of his own pocket to help satisfy the partnership creditors, he will have a "right of contribution" against *A* and *C;* that is, if their obligations are not wiped out by bankruptcy they will each owe him $3,333.33.

This division of losses would be followed as to *X, Y,* and *Z,* even if the partners had agreed that *B* should in no event be liable to outside creditors. *X, Y,* and *Z* would collect from *B,* but then *B* would have a claim of $5,000 against each of *A* and *B.* The point is that a person can not agree with another that a third person's rights shall be limited without that third person's consent. If *A, B,* and *C* wished to carry out their arrangement they should have formed a limited partnership and then, *X, Y,* and *Z* would have notice of *B's* limited liability and could guard the credit they extend in view of the known restriction on *B's* liabilities.

Division of profits and losses illustrated. – Partners, we saw, divide profits and losses equally. Suppose *A, B,* and *C* contributed respectively $30,000, $20,000, and $10,000 to a business in which they engaged without formal agreement. The firm is wound up and its assets of $60,000 are all that is left to pay $50,000 to creditors *X, Y* and *Z,* besides $10,000 advanced as a loan by *B,* and the obligations of the partnership to the partners.

According to the uniform partnership law, outside creditors must be paid off first, then debts to partners, then the capital, and finally profits, if any. Here there are losses which amount to the sum of all the debts and obligations, that is $120,000, less $60,000 of assets. This total loss of $60,000 must be divided equally. Therefore each partner will contribute $20,000 and will take out the amount of the obligation of the partnership for capital and any debts due from the partnership. *A* therefore will put in $20,000 and take out $30,000; that is, he will take out a net of $10,000. *B* will put in $20,000 and take out $10,000 for the debt and $20,000 for capital; that is, he will take out a net of $10,000. *C* will put in $20,000 and take out $10,000; that is, he will contribute a net of $10,000. In effect then, *C* will put in $10,000, and this with the $60,000 of partnership assets will yield $50,000 to *X, Y,* and *Z* and $10,000 net each to *A* and *B.*

The limited partnership. – About one hundred years ago some commissioners were sent from New York State to Louisiana to study the limited partnerships of the civil law, which in Louisiana takes the place of the common law prevalent in most English-speaking jurisdictions, to see if the device could not be introduced into the statutes of the Empire State.[4] The result was the Limited Partnership Law of New York, which has since been copied in England, in Canada, and in most American States. Since the limited partnership is not frequently used we shall describe it only briefly.

In the first place it must be organized just as the law prescribes. If this is not done a general instead of a limited partnership will result. The chief step in organization is the filing of the contract drawn according to law.[5] The limited or special partners are named; they are limited in their liability to the amounts they have agreed to put in. But their names must not appear in the official name of the partnership and they must not be given any voice in the business.

Since it is only by virtue of the statute that the liability of any of the partners may be limited, a substantial and even strict compliance with the statute is necessary to form this kind of organization. In one case where the statute required the cash contribution of special partners to be paid in before filing the certificate, and one of the special partners did not do this until after the certificate was filed, it was held that no limited partnership had been formed. The firm failed and all of the partners were held personally liable as general partners.

Another important rule to bear in mind is that as limited partnerships are creatures of the separate State statutes, outside of the State of its formation the organization will be treated as a general partnership and even special partners will be liable to creditors. If, therefore, a limited partnership does business in another State, it should first file a certificate and comply with the statutes of that State in order to limit the liability of its members.

The joint adventure. – The joint adventure, otherwise known as the "deal" or "syndicate," is very much like the partnership in point of law. The main differences are quite technical and relate

[4] F. M. Burdick, "The Law of Partnership," page 360.

[5] For example, see C. W. Gerstenberg, "Materials of Corporation Finance," pages 4–5, and S. Gordon, "Annotated Forms of Agreement," Form 334.

to the way in which actions are brought in court. In general effect, of course, the main difference is that while the partnership goes on indefinitely or for a limited time, the joint adventure is organized for a specific purpose and its duration is limited to the accomplishment or definite failure of that purpose. Usually all the business of a joint adventure is done in the name of a manager who is responsible to the participants.[6]

Joint stock companies. – The joint stock company is a form of partnership that was created to overcome some of the important disadvantages of the ordinary partnership. Like the partnership, each member of the joint stock company is individually and personally liable for the entire debts of the organization. But, unlike the ordinary partnership and like the corporation, the joint stock company has its capital divided into transferable shares represented by certificates. These may be sold by one person to another, enabling a partner to withdraw from the business without jeopardizing the life of the organization. These shares indicate the owner's right to participate in the control of the company – by voting – and in the profits of the business. In this respect, as well as in its form of control and management, it closely resembles the corporation.

Death, insanity, or bankruptcy of a member has no effect on the continued existence of the joint stock company. Nor has the withdrawal or transfer of membership. Each member is free to sell or pledge his shares. But even if he does this, he remains personally liable for the debts incurred while he was a shareholder. He has, however, no liability for any debts contracted after he disposed of his shares, nor before he acquired them.

Formation. – Joint stock companies are formed under a simple contract among the parties interested in the venture.[7] They do not require sanction of the State, nor must they pay any special organization or annual franchise taxes. Under the Federal income tax law, they are taxed the same as corporations. In New York, a joint stock company must file with the Secretary of State and

[6] For forms of joint adventures, see S. Gordon, "Annotated Forms of Agreement," pages 326–367.

[7] For a history of joint stock companies, see J. S. Davis, "Earlier History of American Corporations."

the county clerk a certificate stating its name, place of business, date of organization, number of shareholders, and names and addresses of officers. In New York the joint stock company must also pay an annual franchise tax corresponding to that imposed on corporations. In other States, however, the joint stock company is not so burdened. As a general rule, therefore, it may do business in any State in the union (except New York) without filing any certificates and without paying any organization or franchise taxes. In a Minnesota case, which would probably be considered good law in all parts of the Union, the highest State court said of a joint stock company, "The defendant not being a corporation, but a partnership, has the same right to do business in this State without its permission, and free from its control and visitorial power, as any other individual or partnership."[8] In this respect it enjoys a real advantage over the corporation, which invariably must file certificates and pay taxes in every State in which it does business.

Organization and management of joint stock company. – The articles of association and by-laws of the joint stock company define and regulate its organization and management in much the same manner as the certificate of incorporation and by-laws affect the corporate organization. Usually they provide that the management of the company shall be vested entirely in the hands of a small board of governors or directors,[9] periodically elected by the shareholders, as directors of a corporation are elected. Shareholders, unlike partners, are not general agents and cannot bind the association by their individual acts; the business is done for the company by officers and agents appointed and removed at the pleasure of the board of governors. The board also usually has the right to declare and pay such dividends from the earnings of the company as they deem expedient.

The joint stock company enjoys two advantages over the corporation: (1) it does not pay any organization taxes nor annual franchise taxes (except in New York), nor must it file with the State any certificate or annual reports usually required of

[8] State v. United States Express Co., 81 Minn. 87.

[9] For complete articles of association, see Articles of Pierce Fordyce Oil Association (share capital, $3,000,000), reprinted in C. W. Gerstenberg, "Materials of Corporation Finance," page 6.

corporations (except in New York); (2) moreover, the joint stock company may do business in any State outside the State of its formation (except in New York) without any formalities, while the corporation must usually file certificates and pay franchise taxes in those States in which it does business. The offsetting disadvantage of the joint stock company is the fact that each member is individually and personally liable for the entire debts of the company. In turn the member who may be held liable has the right of compelling the other members to contribute their shares of the loss.

Limiting the liability of members. – If the liability of members could be limited to the amount of their original capital contribution, the joint stock company would obviously be superior to the corporation. An attempt therefore has been made to do this by inserting a provision in the articles of association requiring the board of governors to stipulate against the personal liability of members in every contract made on behalf of the company. In the articles of the Pierce Fordyce Oil Association, for example, is found the following provision:

> "The Board of Governors shall have no power to bind the shareholders or members personally; and in every written contract or undertaking they shall enter into relating to the business of this Association, its property or any part thereof, reference shall be made to this agreement; and the person, firm or corporation so contracting with the Board of Governors shall look only to the funds and property legal and equitable of this Association for the payment of any debt, damage, judgment or decree or of any money that may become due and payable in any way by reason of the contract or undertaking, and neither the Board of Governors nor the shareholders or members present or future shall be personally liable therefor or for any debt incurred or engagement or contract made by said Board of Governors."

This provision will, of course, have no effect on parties dealing with the company unless it is called to their notice. In many jurisdictions it will have no effect unless the limitation of the members' liability is clearly and expressly stated in the contract. In at least one jurisdiction, New York, there is a grave question as to whether, even then, the members' liability would be limited. In Werner v. Beers, 23 Wend. (N. Y.) 102, the court apparently held that such a stipulation in a contract would limit the liability of the members of the association. But in a much more recent case, Hibbs v. Brown, 190 N. Y. 167, the question involved was whether a stipulation in bonds of a joint stock company – The Adams Express Company – against the personal liability of members made them non-negotiable. It was held it did not, three – the majority – of the judges so holding on the ground that such a stipulation was against public policy and therefore void. Thus, while in practically all other States such a provision would adequately protect the shareholders, in New York it probably would not. In no State, however, is there any method by which the liability of the members may be limited in case of the commission of a tort by the association. Of course, the question of the individual member's liability will never arise as long as the association remains solvent.

Limited partnership associations. – The statutes of Pennsylvania and Michigan permit the organization of limited partnership associations. These are created like corporations and in the State of their formation have most of the attributes of a corporation. A certificate of association must be filed with the Secretary of State and county clerk, and an organization tax must be paid. During its existence reports must be made and franchise taxes must be paid annually.

As in the corporation and the joint stock company, ownership is divided into shares, and the shareholders elect a board of directors or managers who conduct the business of the association. In Michigan the directors or managers are elected under the cumulative voting method.[10]

The limited partnership association also resembles the corporation and the joint stock company in the conduct of its affairs through officers and agents appointed and removed by the board of managers. It differs, however, from them in the fact that upon a transfer of its shares by an original owner, the purchaser must be elected to membership in the association before he has any rights therein. He may demand election to membership and if not granted, he may compel the association to pay him the value of

[10] See page 101.

his shares, agreed upon or determined by appraisers appointed by a court. The transfer of shares, however, does not affect the life of the association. Another peculiar provision of the laws of both Pennsylvania and Michigan affecting these associations is that which requires contracts involving over five hundred dollars to be signed by two of the managers. Unless the contract is so signed the association will be exempt from liability on it.

In the State of its organization the members of a limited partnership association are not personally liable for the association's debts. But the members will be held liable as general partners unless the organization strictly complies with the statutes authorizing the organization of limited partnership associations. Thus, in Pennsylvania, it was held that failure to include in the articles of association a detailed description of the property contributed as capital by the members, as required by the statute, rendered them liable as general partners.[11] Outside of the State of their organization, courts have been inclined to treat these associations as general partnerships. This form of organization, therefore, is suited only to a business to be entirely conducted in the State permitting its formation. Except for the smaller initial expense of organizing a limited partnership association, it has little, if any, advantage over the corporation. Of course, if the enterprise is to do business in several States, the corporation would be more useful.

[11] Sheble v. Strong, 128 Pa. St. 315.

MASSACHUSETTS TRUSTS[1]

Charles Gerstenberg

The Massachusetts trust. – This organization is known under various names, such as the business trust, or business association formed under deed of trust, the voluntary association formed under deed of trust, the common law trust, and the Massachusetts trust. As a modern business device it arose in Massachusetts where the law prohibited the organization of corporations whose purpose it was to own and deal in land. This suspicion of land holding corporations goes way back in English history to the Statute of Mortmain, 1279, the purpose of which was to deprive the monasteries of their land holdings. The basic idea of the suspicion is, that since a corporation has what is called continuous succession it may continue to increase in size until eventually it may become more powerful than the State itself.[2]

Since corporations could not be used for the purpose of assembling large sums of capital with which, for example, to build an expensive hotel, the lawyers adopted the trust principle. Basically this idea involves the separation of the ownership of property into two parts, the legal title being held in one person's hands (the trustee) for the benefit of other persons (beneficiaries or *cestuis que trustent* – the singular form of which is *cestui que trust*[3]) who hold the equitable title. The person who sets up such a device is called the creator or settlor and the device itself is called a trust. Simple examples of such trusts are provided when men (creators) draw wills leaving properties to trust companies (trustees) in trust for

1 [Chapter 5 of *Financial Organization and the Management of Business*, New York: Prentice-Hall, 1924. The long appendix to this chapter has been omitted here for technical reasons.]

2 For a very careful legal analysis of the nature of a Massachusetts trust, see *Shareholders in Business Trusts*, by Calvert Magruder, in 23 Columbia Law Review 421.

3 It is customary to speak of one *cestui* and of several *cestuis;* in pronouncing the latter word the final "s" is sounded.

their widows for the latters' lives (the widow is then called a life tenant) the estates upon the deaths of the widows to go out right to the testators' children (called remaindermen).

The management of property held in trust is in the hands of the trustee. He operates it if it is an operating property, he keeps it in repair, he brings legal actions to protect it, and if in its operation other persons are injured actions are brought against him alone. The *cestuis* are merely entitled to an accounting and to the income which such an accounting shows.

How the Massachusetts trust is created. – The Massachusetts trust is created through the drafting and execution of a deed of trust, which is merely a contract between the trustee and one or more persons acting as beneficiaries and who for this purpose represent not only themselves but such other persons as may thereafter, and from time to time, become interested in the trust, either by investing money in the trust, or by buying out, or in some other way receiving some other beneficiary's interest in it.[4] These interests in the trust are represented by certificates, frequently called certificates of stock, which in outward appearance simulate as far as possible the certificates of stock of a corporation. They may be listed and dealt in on the various stock exchanges. It is not uncommon for a trust to have several classes of common and preferred shares, and it is possible to have any division of income, risk, and control among the shareholders that may seem desirable. The trustees are not unlike directors of a corporation, who manage the property for the stockholders; the *cestuis que trustent,* or certificate holders of the trust, correspond to the stockholders in a corporation. The deed or declaration of trust, which is drawn up, describes the business of the association and the duties, rights, and liabilities of the trustees and shareholders. The deed usually provides that the trustees shall appoint and remove a president, vice-president, and other officers, agents, and employees to actively carry on the business of the trust. The trustees need not conduct the business in their own names; they may adopt a name for business purposes,[5] as for example, the Massachusetts Electric

[4] For an example, see C. W. Gerstenberg, "Materials of Corporation Finance," pages 11–20. The stockholders in that agreement, however, would be held liable as partners under rules explained later in this text.

[5] Rand v. Farquar, 226 Mass. 21.

Companies. In fact it is the general practice to specify a name in the deed of trust. Moreover, they usually have a common seal not unlike the seal of a corporation. Dividends are distributed by the trustees out of profits as determined by the deed of trust. As a rule, the indenture gives the trustees wide discretion in the matter of declaring dividends. A common provision governing dividends is that "the trustees may from time to time declare and pay dividends from the net income of the trust fund among the *cestuis que trustent;* and their decision as to the amount of dividends, and as to using there-for any portion of the surplus fund shall be final. They may set aside from time to time such portion of the net income as shall not be required for dividends for a surplus fund. Their decision as to what is income and what is capital shall be final." This provision gives the trustees the same authority over dividends as directors of a corporation usually have.

Duration of a trust. – For reasons that we need not go into here the laws of most States will not permit such a contract to be made for an unlimited time. In New York State and many other States the time cannot be longer than twenty-one years and nine months after the death of one or two persons named at the time the contract is made. To be sure, where a trust is limited in this way and the period expires the parties interested at that time can agree to another trust running for another maximum period.

Some examples of the Massachusetts trust. – The student may care to inquire further into some specific examples of these trusts. Well-known examples are: The Massachusetts Gas Companies, created in 1902. Its balance sheet for 1922 showed preferred and common stock issues of $25,000,000 each. This stock is listed on the Boston Stock Exchange. The Mackay Companies is a holding company, controlling a cable line and the "Postal Telegraph System." It has preferred stock of $50,000,000 and common stock amounting to $41,380,000. Its securities are listed on the New York Stock Exchange. The Chicago Elevated Railways, created in 1911, has $21,000,000 of funded debt, and $160,000 of preferred and $250,000 of common stock. Amoskeag Manufacturing Co., and Associated Simmons Hardware Cos. are two examples of industrial concerns using the trust form of organization. The former company was created in 1911 to replace a corporation organized in 1831.[6]

Comparison of trust with corporation. – Up to the present time only a few of the States have attempted to regulate these trusts. In Massachusetts the instrument or declaration of trust must be filed with the commissioner of corporations and with the clerk of every city or town in which the association does business.[7] The filing fees are nominal, and not nearly as large as the combined organization tax and filing fees paid by corporations. In 1916 Massachusetts also imposed an annual tax on dividends or shares in these associations. In New York since 1922 they must pay the same annual franchise tax as corporations. This tax is intended to offset to some ex tent the advantage the association enjoys in being free from an annual franchise tax which corporations must pay. There is some question about the constitutionality of this law, and a court decision is awaited with interest.[8]

Outside of Massachusetts, trusts need not pay any organization fees. It is customary, however, to file the trust deed in a public office and pay the filing fees, which are merely nominal. They are not required to file annual State reports, nor in most States must they pay any annual franchise taxes.[9]

Capitalization and organization of trust. – In some States the amount of preferred stock and bonds which a corporation may issue is limited to a portion of its common stock. The trust, however, labors under no such restriction. It is free to have as many classes of shares as it wishes; it may have any amount of preferred stock and any amount of bonds. In fact, its whole form of organization is much more flexible than the corporation, the range of possibil-

6 See "Works of Alexander Hamilton," Vol. VII, page 838, for form of an agreement drawn by Alexander Hamilton. (Sears, "Trust Estates as Business Companies," page 340.) See Credit Mobilier v. Commonwealth, 67 Pa. St. 233, for the trust agreement under which the famous Credit Mobilier operated.

7 Massachusetts General Laws, 1921, Chapter 182. To same effect, Oklahoma Laws, 1919, Chapter 16.

8 See opinion of the Justices, 196 Mass. 601, upholding a tax similar to the New York tax.

9 For a discussion of the Massachusetts trust under the Federal Tax Laws, see pages 149, *et seq*.

ities of form and organization being limited only by the desire and imagination of the organizers. It may have any number of trustees (most States require corporations to have three or more directors) the trustees need not be residents of the State of formation, and their meetings may be held in any State (usually the State statutes require one or more resident directors of a corporation and require their meetings to be held within the State of incorporation).

Permanency of management. – In a corporation, the management is subject to frequent change. Usually new directors must be elected each year. It is very frequently desirable, yes, in many cases essential, that the same management remain in control. For example, a minority interest may demand for their own protection that half of the board of directors be designated by them. This is partially accomplished in a corporation through a voting trust, of which we shall speak later. But a voting trust is legal only for a limited period of time – in New York ten years, and in Maryland five years, and in other States a reasonable period. In the case of the common law trust, however, the management may be permanent. Indeed if the stockholders of a Massachusetts trust wish to escape the liability of partners they must exercise no control, and they cannot, therefore, be given the power to elect the trustees periodically. Provision may be made, if desirable, for the selection of a new trustee by the certificate-holders or by a class of them in case of the death, withdrawal, or removal of a trustee. By classifying the trustees and by providing that a vacancy in a certain class of trustees shall be filled by the corresponding class of stockholders, the minority may be assured of permanent representation.

Conduct of business. – In many States corporations are forbidden to engage in certain activities. In a few States, for example, corporations may not deal in real estate, while in some they may not hold stock in other corporations. On the other hand, a trust may, like the individual or partnership, engage in any form of business.[10] The only limitation is that prescribed by the deed of trust which the

[10] In some States certain kinds of business are restricted to corporations, and these statutes have generally been upheld as means for enabling the State better to control business affected by a public interest. Banking and insurance are examples of such kinds of business. These statutes probably are as effective against business trusts as against other forms of organization. See W. M. Fletcher, "Cyclopedia of the Law of Private Corporations," pages 10517–8.

organizers themselves are free to prepare. Even where holding companies in corporate form are permitted, they are frequently subject to vigorous State regulation, particularly when the corporation is one which holds public utility securities. Trusts are free from such regulation; the inclination of State legislatures to regulate more severely public utility holding corporations will undoubtedly encourage the growth of trusts for this purpose. Another advantage of the trust is that it may do business in any State without any formalities. This right is guaranteed by the Constitution, which provides (Art. IV, Sec. 2) that "the Citizens of each State shall be entitled to all Privileges and Immunities of Citizens in the several States." Corporations, however, are not citizens within the meaning of this clause of the Constitution. They must invariably file certificates and pay franchise taxes and submit to regulation in each State in which they do business, as is more fully described hereafter.[11]

Liability of trustees. – A trustee in this form of association has much the same obligations to shareholders as a director of a corporation. In Hayes v. Hall, 188 Mass. 510, the court stated that "a trustee in the management of property held by him in trust shall not be permitted directly or indirectly to derive any personal advantage from its use or sale but must act solely for the interests of those beneficially interested." If he makes any profit he must account for it to the shareholders.

In managing trust property a trustee must use the judgment and care of a reasonably prudent man. If he fails to do so, he is liable for any resulting losses. Usually, however, the trust deed constituting a Massachusetts trust stipulates that the trustee shall be liable only for the result of his own gross or wilful negligence or bad faith. While this provision protects the trustee against loss because of failure to exercise what the law calls "the judgment of an ordinarily prudent man," it does not protect him if he uses the property of the trust for purposes other than those specified in the trust deed,[12] nor in cases where he shows "such reckless

[11] To the effect that a State cannot discriminate against trustees who are residents of other States, see State v. Cadigan, 73 Vermont 245, and State v. U.S. Express Co., 81 Minnesota 87.

[12] Digney v. Blanchard, 226 Mass. 335.

indifference to true interests of the trust as to amount to or partake of a wilful violation of duty."[13]

In dealing with outsiders, trustees are personally liable, unless they clearly indicate they are acting as trustees and that only the trust property is liable. In contracts with third parties, trustees usually stipulate that the "creditor shall look only to the funds and property of the trust for all payments, and not to the trustees or shareholders personally." This stipulation has been held valid.[14] Further than this, the trust deed itself usually provides that if the trustee shall ever become personally liable as trustee, not due to his acts in bad faith, he may be indemnified out of the trust property.

While in most States a director of a corporation is not entitled to any compensation unless the certificate of incorporation or by-laws so provide or unless the shareholders consent, trustees in a business trust are entitled to reasonable compensation for their services, unless there is a contrary provision in the deed of trust. Usually the trust instrument specifies what the compensation shall be.

Liability of cestuis. – It is well settled that the beneficiaries – the so-called shareholders – of the trust[15] are not personally liable for debts contracted or torts committed by the trustees. Creditors can look only to the trustees, or when the trust deed so provides, as indicated above, only to the trust property. While shareholders of a trust are not personally liable, members of a partnership are. It is very frequently an important and difficult problem to distinguish between a trust and a partnership. Stated very briefly, the problem in any given case is: does the trust deed under which a business trust is formed constitute merely a trust deed or does it really go further and constitute the interested persons members of a partnership?

In Massachusetts, where the law concerning trusts as business associations has been most fully developed, it has been held that provisions in a trust agreement giving the share holders power to remove the trustees without assigning any cause, and to appoint

[13] Warren v. Pazolt, 203 Mass. 328.

[14] Rand v. Farquar, 226 Mass. 91.

[15] The word "trust" is used here to indicate the ordinary relationship created when property is left to a trust company for named beneficiaries.

others to fill the vacancy, and to amend the declaration of trust, demonstrate that the association is a partnership and not a pure trust.[16] It appears then that if the shareholders have a right to control the trustees by the power to remove and elect trustees, or to elect them periodically, or if the shareholders have a right to manage the property themselves, the association will be considered a partnership, and the shareholders will be personally liable. On the other hand, if the trustees act as principals and are free from the control of certificate holders, a trust is created and the shareholders are not personally liable.[17] In the latter case, shareholders have only the right to "compel the trustee to account and to charge him with the consequences of dishonesty or neglect and cause his removal for the one offense or the other."[18] This includes the right of each shareholder to receive his share of the income of the trust in accordance with the trust deed and his share of the corpus of the trust when it comes to an end. In any event, even where the trust may be considered a partnership because of the control the shareholders may exercise over the trustees, the liability of the shareholders may usually be restricted by including in the trust deed and consistently observing a clause similar to the following:

> "Neither the trustees nor the *cestuis que trustent* (shareholders) shall ever be personally liable hereunder as partners or otherwise, but that for all debts the trustees shall be liable as such to the extent of the trust fund only. In all contracts or instruments creating liability, it shall be expressly stipulated by the trustees that the *cestuis que trustent* shall not be liable."

Anyone dealing with the association, even though it might otherwise be considered a partnership, who has notice of this provision[19] or who expressly agrees to be bound by this provision, has no right of action against either the trustees or shareholders personally. This provision, however, would not relieve the shareholders of personal liability (if the association

[16] Frost v. Thompson, 219 Mass. 360.

[17] Williams v. Milton, 215 Mass. 1.

[18] Wrightington, "Unincorporated Associations," page 48, and cases there cited.

[19] Bank of Topeka v. Eaton, 100 Fed. 8.

were held to be a partnership), in case of the commission of a tort by the trustees in managing the property, or if the trustees neglected to notify contract creditors and the latter had no information of the intention to limit liability to the amount of the trust estate. If the association were a pure trust, that is, if the shareholders did not control the trustees through the right of removal and election, then the share holders would be under no liability in any event – whether a clause limiting the liability of trustees and *cestuis* were included or not.[20]

Summary as to Massachusetts trusts. – The trust has most of the advantages of the corporation. Moreover, it is "more flexible, more economical, and more convenient than the corporation. Trustees can do business with more ease and rapidity than a board of directors. In particular (the trust) affords a convenient form of combining capital for the development and improvement of real estate," as the form of organization may be arranged to insure "a continuity of management and control that specially appeals to investors in real estate, and which cannot be secured by a corporation on account of the change of (directors) each year. Trustees are not changed as frequently as are directors of a corporation."[21]

Unless legislatures regulate these associations formed under deeds of trust in much the same way as they have regulated corporations, we may expect the formation of an increasingly large number of these voluntary associations for the conduct of business enterprises. As the voluntary association does not obtain a franchise or privilege of doing business from the State (such as the corporation must obtain) it will be much more difficult, if not impossible, for legislatures to regulate[22] and tax trusts to the same extent as they do corporations.

Disadvantages of the trust. – It must not be thought, however, that the trust is an ideal form of organization. The great difficulty

[20] See an excellent article by Calvert Magruder in 23 Columbia Law Review 423. It seems that Texas courts hold all business trusts the equivalent of partnerships as far as liability of interested persons is concerned.

[21] Report of Commissioners of Corporations in Massachusetts, January 17, 1912.

[22] The securities of business trusts are held to be subject to the control of Blue Sky Commissions. See Chapter XXI.

of the trust lies in the fact that the relationships which it creates are governed by the precedents of courts which are not uniform throughout the English-speaking jurisdictions. In fact, in many jurisdictions questions may arise that are entirely novel; what disposition the courts would make in an actual case brought before them is in doubt. Uncertainty of this kind "puzzles the will, and makes us rather bear those ills we have than fly to others that we know not of;" such uncertainty is so inimical to honest administration that many lawyers advise strongly in favor of the corporation. Taxes are less burdensome than confusion.

CAPITALIZATION[1]

Charles Gerstenberg

Original style of capitalization. – Partnerships and individual proprietorships do not have the problem of capitalization which arises in forms of organization issuing shares of ownership. Corporations, business trusts, and joint stock companies have the problem in very complicated form. Not only is there the question of the original amount of capitalization, but also the question of the kind of capitalization; then, too, as the company grows and needs more capital, the question is constantly before the managers: what form and what amount of securities shall be issued to those people from whom the new capital is obtained?

When a new business is being organized bonds ordinarily will not be used, though in the case of public utility companies and railways, in which large sums are used to acquire tangible property future earnings of which can be quite accurately foretold, bonds may be used in order to minimize annual charges. Purchasers of bonds buy safety and forego the expectation of large income. To be sure, bonds should never be used unless estimated earnings will give a factor of safety of at least 100 per cent; moreover, where bonds are used, the estimates of capital needed and the amount of funds actually raised should include a liberal amount to pay interest on the bonds during the period of construction. While industrial and mercantile companies should not undertake at the outset the burden of fixed charges, relatively small concerns usually reduce the amount of funds required from the general public by acquiring tangible properties subject to ordinary real estate mortgages.

If a new concern is to finance itself principally through the issue of stock, various forms of stock may be used to represent

[1] [Chapter 18 of *Financial Organization and the Management of Business*, New York: Prentice-Hall, 1924.]

the different interests of the owners. Generally the promoters will take the common stock, representing, as it were, the residual claim on earnings. The promoters show their faith by standing back in this way, and if the enterprise becomes very profitable, their foresight and faith will reap the reward they deserve. To outsiders, preferred stock may be offered. If the promoters wish to keep control they may make the preferred non-voting. If, to make the preferred stock attractive, the holders are given the right to participate in the earnings, the redemption feature may also be included to rid the company of the preferred stock when earnings become large and stable. To make the preferred saleable to those who insist upon some assurance of income, such features as the protection fund and cumulation of arrearages may be added. If earning capacity is doubtful, these contingent charges should not be included in the agreement made with the preferred stockholder, for while the right to cumulative dividends, for example, seems a very innocent provision, large accumulations of arrearages may become troublesome.

Selection of securities to vary control, income, and risk. – In describing the different forms of securities in preceding chapters, we pointed out their attributes and the circumstances under which securities with such attributes should be used. Here we may review briefly the principal forms of securities, arranging them as they serve the purpose of varying the control, the income, and the risk of the security holders. With such a catalogue of securities as this before him, the promoter of a new enterprise and the director of an expanding old enterprise should be able to make intelligent selection under varying circumstances.

I. Securities arranged in order as they restrict the right of control.

1. Non-voting stocks.
2. Bonds (their holders have the ultimate control of foreclosure).
3. Preferred stock and income bonds that are to vote if holders do not receive income.
4. Bonds convertible into stock.
5. Vetoing stocks.
6. Voting stocks.

II. Securities arranged in the order of potential claims to increasing amount of income.
1. Non-participating preferred stock.
2. Income bonds.
3. Ordinary bonds.
4. Bonds convertible into stock.
5. Profit-sharing or participating bonds.
6. Common stock.
7. Participating preferred stock.[2]

III. Securities arranged in the order of safety of principal.
1. Stocks not preferred as to assets.
2. Stocks preferred as to assets.
3. Sinking fund, redeemable stocks.
4. Debenture bonds.
5. Debentures to be protected by future mortgages, if and when executed.
6. Adjustment bonds.[3]
7. Junior mortgages.[4]
8. General refunding mortgages to take up prior liens.
9. Senior mortgages.

Nominal stock capitalization. –When a company is organized, how much stock should be issued? This problem arises in its most complicated form where a company is to take over operating properties, or is to issue its securities for property difficult to appraise, such as a mine or a patent.

[2] The effects of the cumulative feature and of the protective fund should be kept in mind.

[3] Adjustment bonds are usually secured by mortgages containing a "subordination clause," that is, a clause which provides that at any time in the future the company may issue bonds secured by a mortgage, whose lien will be superior to that of the adjustment issue.

[4] In placing mortgage bonds an important question is: what property secures them? Legal priority alone does not *fix* their status as safe or speculative securities. A bond with a sinking fund in addition to a mortgage may be considered safer than one without a sinking fund. So, too, a moderately termed bond may he considered safer than a long term bond, other things being equal for the company will always have to keep in mind the obligation of redeeming or refunding.

The question may be "dodged" by using stock without par value.

For public utilities and railways – companies enjoying monopolies against which the public must be protected by rate-making bodies – the nominal capitalization should equal the actual investment of the stockholders. If a public utility were thus capitalized, rates could be practically regulated by controlling dividends. If rates were so high as to yield more than a reasonable dividend on the stock, the excess could be kept in the company and used to extend the company's property and improve it – all to the advantage of the consuming public. To be sure, if this practice were permitted to be carried too far, one generation of consumers would pay the way for succeeding generations; moreover, the practice would open the way to unprofitable expansions.[5]

Industrial and mercantile concerns should capitalize on the basis that will make their securities sell at par. This is but another way of saying that they should capitalize on the basis of earning power. The most convincing argument, it seems to us, to justify this basis of capitalization, is that it recognizes the fundamental truth that a business is a profit-making entity and that it is worth what it will earn.[6]

Disadvantages of undercapitalization. – If stock is issued to an amount much in excess of capitalized earning power of a company, the company is said to be overcapitalized and the stock is said to be "watered." The disadvantages of overcapitalization are greater than those of undercapitalization, if for no other reason than because undercapitalization may easily be remedied by writing the intangible asset "goodwill" into the balance sheet and distributing the resulting surplus through a stock dividend. It is always wise to do this since the stock of a company that is undercapitalized will ordinarily not sell at its full value. Moreover, since the stock will sell well above par, it will be subject to wide fluctuations in value on the

[5] The question of valuing the stockholders' investment in public utilities is not touched upon in the text, for the author feels it is too large to be treated here even in outline. See R. H. Whitten, "Valuation of Public Service Corporations."

[6] Hartley Withers, in his "Stocks and Shares," repeats the story told by Boswell of Dr. Samuel Johnson's statement when asked to give his opinion of the real value of the Thrale brewery. Dr. Johnson's answer was, "We are not here to sell a parcel of boilers and vats, but the potentiality of growing rich beyond the dreams of avarice."

market.[7] Because undercapitalization makes a company appear to be making profits at an exceptionally high rate, competition will be encouraged, employees are likely to become disgruntled, customers may seek price reductions, and the public may be induced to invoke the regulatory powers of government. Perhaps it should be said in passing that undercapitalized companies operated at a disadvantage in this country during the years 1917 to 1921, when the Federal excess profits taxes were imposed. The possibility of another imposition of such a tax should be considered when intangible assets are being taken over by a corporation.[8]

[7] It hardly seems necessary to demonstrate this point when illustrations can be so easily obtained in the stock quotations of *The Commercial and Financial Chronicle* and in such newspapers as the *New York Times* and the *New York Evening Post* (Saturday edition), which give the annual range of securities sold on the New York Stock Exchange.

It will be noticed that most of the disadvantages of undercapitalization mentioned in the text apply to companies whose securities are listed on the stock exchanges. The properties of Henry Ford are so closely held that they are a law unto themselves. Probably his company represents the most extreme case of undercapitalization that can be found. According to the *Wall Street Journal,* at the end of 1923 the corporation had a capital stock of $17,264,500 on which the earnings for the year 1923 were estimated to be $158,000,000. If these earnings were capitalized at 7 per cent, the capitalization would amount to about $2,000,000,000.

[8] The theory of this tax was to place a burden on war profits. Profits above a certain rate on the investment were taxed at rates increasing with the increase of profits. Obviously it was to the advantage of a company to state its invested capital as high as possible in order to minimize the apparent rate of profits. To get at the rate of profits it was necessary to fix the investment.

"The invested capital of a corporation includes, generally speaking, (a) the cash paid in for stock, (b) the tangible property paid in for stock, (c) the surplus and undivided profits, and (d) the intangible property paid in for stock," with certain adjustments. (Internal Revenue Department Regulations 62, Section 831.) It would seem, therefore, that intangible property such as patents and goodwill, could not, under the old Excess Profits Tax Acts of 1917, 1918, and 1921, be included in invested capital unless paid for in stock. The following case, presented to the Treasury Department, illustrates the situation: *A* and *B*, who own most of the stock of a company, invented certain machinery for which patents were issued to them. The company paid the cost of the patents and used them as though it owned them, without compensation to the inventors. In 1916 the patents were put upon the books of the company at a certain value and a stock dividend declared. Even assuming that the patents were not formally assigned to the company until 1916, the Committee is clearly of the opinion that the patents were not specifically paid for by the issuance of stock, nor by any payment of cash. It is concluded, therefore, that the value at which the patents were placed upon the books of the company may not be included in its invested capital for war-profits and excess-profits tax, purposes. (Recommendation No. 9 of the Committee on Appeals and Review; Cumulative Bulletin, June, 1920, page 293.)

Disadvantages of overcapitalization. – The dangers of overcapitalization have been explained at great length by a number of economic writers.[9] Here we shall merely summarize these alleged dangers.[10]

I. Disadvantages to the corporation:
1. A company whose stock is watered and sells below par will have relatively poor credit standing.
2. Such a company will have difficulty in raising new capital funds. This disadvantage is not so important now that the use of stock without par value is permitted. A new issue of stock without par value has often proved a blessing to a company whose old shares sell below par.
3. Watered stock encourages payment of unearned dividends.
4. It also leads to neglect of depreciation and other reserves.
5. As a consequence of all the above faults unwieldy debts are likely to be incurred.
6. A large capitalization involves payment of a large organization tax; in some States the annual franchise tax is based on the amount of outstanding stock.

II. Disadvantages to the public:
1. Overcapitalization tends to raise the price and to reduce the quality of a company's products.
2. Undue pressure may be placed on the operating heads to keep down wages, and the appearance of small profits may give the company an advantage in the settlement of labor disputes.
3. The failure of overcapitalized concerns tends to precipitate panics and to injure classes of creditors.
4. Overcapitalization diverts funds from legitimate business into the hands of "stock jobbers."
5. It induces stock gambling.
6. It creates a bad ethical atmosphere in business.

[9] See R. T. Ely, "Outline of Economics," C. R. Van Hise, "Concentration and Control," Jenks and Clark, "The Trust Problem."

[10] We do not wish to imply that these dangers are not real. It has seemed more appropriate to the author to let his readers go to sources where the subject is treated more fully than we have space for here.

III. Disadvantages to stockholders:
1. Overcapitalization is usually accompanied by a certain amount of "rigging the market" when securities are first issued, and stockholders must suffer as true values are revealed in proven lack of earning power.
2. Low-valued stocks, such as result from overcapitalization, usually have relatively small value as collateral for loans.
3. Low-priced stocks are usually subject to much speculative manipulation. When a stockholder is most likely to need his stock for purposes of raising cash, either through sale or borrowing, it is likely to have an unreasonably low market value.
4. Stockholders of overcapitalized companies are likely to have to bear the great expense of corporate receiverships and reorganizations.

Is stock-watering ever justified? – Many commentators on corporation finance, especially theoretical economists, overlook the full significance of the distinction between present and prospective earning power as bases for corporate capitalization.

We may assume that *A* owns a mine the value of whose ore, according to reliable geological reports, is $10,000,000, and the estimated cost of extracting and marketing the ore, with all overhead expenses, is $1,000,000. If *A* turns the mine over to a corporation for all its capital stock, $2,000,000, and then returns $1,000,000 of the stock to the treasury for sale below par, has *A* confessed to overcapitalizing his company by his act of returning one-half the capital stock? His purpose has been to turn his potential "purchasing power" as it existed in the form of unextracted metal into active purchasing power by giving to others some inducement to supply the funds necessary to begin operations. The people who supply the funds take great risks: first, as to the accuracy of the geological reports; second, as to the possible occurrence of unusual and unforeseen difficulties in operation; and third, as to the continued integrity and ability of the managers. On this last point it may be observed that the original owners, to turn their property more quickly into active purchasing power, may sell out their holdings to persons of doubtful integrity and ability. A small purchaser of securities ordinarily has no guarantee that the majority interests will not change hands. Hence the risks are great and the person taking the risks will demand an offsetting advantage. This he gets in buying the treasury stock much below par. By taking treasury stock below par instead of unissued stock below par, the holder avoids complications with creditors. If the company prospers, the stock will rise in value and the original purchaser will receive the reward of his risk-taking.

In the same way stock issued for prospective earning power always affords a method of isolating the speculative element in an enterprise. Funds can be more readily raised through such a separation. In the first place, the speculative securities – common stock – may be sold to persons who are ready to assume the risks involved. If the proceeds of these shares go into the company, they form an "equity" behind the non-speculative securities – preferred shares or bonds – and the latter are therefore sold on better terms to the investing public, for the equity provides a sort of guarantee of safety – it "cushions" shrinkage in values due to one cause or another. If the proceeds go to the promoters and bankers, they prevent an equivalent amount from being taken from the proceeds of the sale of securities that are non-speculative in appearance – for the promoter and the banker must get compensation from some source, else they cannot "carry on." Finally, it may be urged that because the control usually rests in the speculative securities the holders of which get the last share in the earnings, the tendency must be to watch operations closely in order that the company may be made to yield the last dollar that will go to the speculative security holders.[11]

[11] The process of squeezing the water out of the United States Steel Corporation, which is a good illustration, is described, as follows, in A. Cotter, "Authentic History of The United States Steel Corporation," page 31: "Year by year the directors have voted large sums out of earnings for the building of new plants, the extension of old ones, until approximately $500,000,000 has been expended in this manner, thus providing adequate protection for the common stock and putting the company today beyond reach of criticism on the charge of over-capitalization."

The reader is referred to Hastings Lyon's little book on "Capitalization" for a more extended discussion of the points raised in the last paragraph of this section of the text.

EXPANSION[1]

Charles Gerstenberg

Capitalization of expansion. – Having examined the principles of initial capitalization, we are now ready to study the methods of capitalizing growth. To understand those methods we ought first to consider how and why growth takes place in a business concern. Indeed, before we can discuss how expansion can be financed we ought to examine the question: should the expansion take place at all?

These preliminary questions we shall consider in the next few sections.

How growth may take place. – The causes of growth may be listed and briefly described as follows:

1. Increasing the amount of the sales of the same product in the same market. – This may be done by putting on "greater sales pressure." For example, a sales force may be added to a business previously using mail order methods only. Or new sources of outlet may be sought. Instead of selling direct to the consumer, wholesalers, jobbers, and retailers may be enlisted. Or an advertising campaign may be started. Again, the increase may come from such an intangible thing as a change in price policy. In any event, the cause of the increase in sales may be and usually is directly traceable to some expedient that required funds. To the inexperienced, an increase in sales through the efforts of an enlarged sales force paid on a commission basis may seem to be an exception. Anybody who has had any experience with the hiring of salesmen, how ever, knows that the cost of hiring a salesman is likely to run from $500 to $1,000.

[1] [Chapter 19 of *Financial Organization and the Management of Business*, New York: Prentice-Hall, 1924.]

Even where the increase in business is entirely accidental, funds will be necessary to handle the business. New equipment will be needed for manufacturing and distributing, and a larger working capital will be involved. Moreover, it must be remembered, growth is the ordinary rule of life. Any business that is well-managed will grow with the normal growth of the country and funds will be needed from time to time. The table on page 284 shows the growth of a number of American corporations taken at random.

2. Expanding the market. – The expansion we have in mind here is likely to take the form of the establishment of branches. The amount of funds required will depend largely on the relations that are to be maintained between the branch and the home organization. The possibilities involved in such an event are described in books on marketing. If the branch is not in fact to be owned, but is to be a mere agency, funds may still be needed to aid the agency or to stock it with products.

3. Increasing the number of products. – Experience shows that in marketing new products old concerns enjoy certain ad vantages and suffer certain disadvantages. They have the advantage of experience and should not make mistakes. They also have the advantage of elasticity. To a certain extent new products can be added without disproportionately increasing the expenses in every department. On the other hand, frequently the new product is "everybody's business, and nobody's business," and because funds for expansion in this case come, as in most other cases, from the profits of the business, these funds so easily obtained are used carelessly.

The amount of funds needed for a new product, it also should be said, is often affected by the fact that the introduction of a new product is accompanied by the elimination of other, non-profitable products. While immediate funds may be needed, ultimately the amount of regular working capital required may be decreased.

4. Integration. – We pointed out earlier that new concerns frequently sell their products, and let others make them.[2] The time

[2] See pages 7–8.

TABLE No. 9

GROWTH OF CORPORATIONS SHOWN BY TOTAL ASSETS IN SUCCESSIVE YEARS

Company and Year of Organization	*In Year of Organization*	*1914*	*1915*	*1916*	*1917*	*1918*	*1919*	*1920*	*1921*	*1922*
United States Steel Corp. (1901)...	$1,647,443	$1,792,233	$1,848,542	$2,083,028	$2,449,550	$2,571,617	$2,365,882	$2,430,547	$2,339,105	$2,340,652
Bethlehem Steel Corp. (1904)...	43,858	106,378	145,780	220,737	381,542	391,006	357,236	389,770	366,422	436,880
General Electric Co. (1892).....	50,935	138,418	149,279	163,622	231,630	268,107	276,741	374,838	339,274	355,445
Westinghouse Electric & Mfg. Co. (1872).....	12,529[a]	82,672	76,427	82,433	127,543	164,714	184,893	159,734	206,265	167,070
American Locomotive Co. (1901)	57,209	73,425	80,872	86,620	84,106	91,545	93,176	92,032	85,630	87,770
Baldwin Locomotive Works (1911)	53,865	55,003	61,017	79,480	73,881	77,522	64,989	91,079	81,931	87,876
General Motors Corp. (1916)...	80,897	......	......	80,897	133,790	299,489	446,653	604,807	514,044	522,335
Studebaker Corp. (1911)	56,476	56,530	61,497	68,726	69,667	74,674	88,115	99,604	98,328	114,631

[a] This is the figure reported for 1892; earlier statistics not available.

may come when the concern will desire to manufacture its own product. Or it may wish to make not only the product, but the component parts of the product. Or it may wish to carry on its processes a step further. These two latter forms of expansion are known as integration. A leather concern that started out to buy timber lands to get its own tanning bark instead of buying tanning fluid, would be an example of the first form of integration. A printing house that added a bindery to its printing establishment would be an example of the second class. In either case, integration is likely to involve the form of expansion listed above as number three. For example, we have been told of a large printing house that started its own paper plant and then found that its own printing business could not take the entire product of the paper plant. The company, therefore, had to go out and sell paper, and this involved the raising of funds for the establishment of a marketing department for this part of the business.

5. *Betterments.* – A form of expansion that may be considered here, although it does not operate to increase sales but to reduce costs, is the substitution of modern machinery for obsolete machinery or for human labor. Assets of this kind are real additions to the wealth of the concern to the extent that they increase the profits of the company. The accounting principle which governs betterments, stated in general terms, is that the cost of the new asset is to be added to the capital of the company to the extent that the cost of the new assets exceeds the cost of the old assets. This points directly to the source from which assets of this kind should be financed. The cost of the old assets should be collected out of the earnings of those years during which the assets were used, and the excess amount only should call for a new source of funds.

6. *Buying out competitors.* – This is not the place to go into a full discussion of the effects of competition. We may however, venture a few observations. A strong concern, well founded and well operated, thrives on a certain amount of competition. Competition stimulates general interest in the product and serves to keep the concern "on its toes." Some times, however, the field is too narrow to support all the competitors. The stronger will likely buy out the weaker, or in effect do the same thing by making the competition more bitter until the weaker concerns

perish. Sometimes this process disorganizes the trade and is generally unsatisfactory. It may seem to cost more to buy out the weak competitor but in the long run it may prove profitable. Mr. Frank Munsey has on several occasions followed this practice in the newspaper field. It is said he paid $1,000,000 in cash for the *New York Globe* which he immediately practically dropped by combining it with *The Sun.*

7. *Consolidation.* – Expansion may take place by consolidation. Our own experience has shown us that when a stock arrangement is made, the results frequently prove more expensive than when a purchase for cash is made. Stock on such occasions is usually undervalued, and the stock offered to the smaller and weaker concerns proves an incubus that tends to dishearten the managers. If the concern is at all successful the managers soon realize that the holders of this stock are getting too much income for what they contributed. A fuller discussion of consolidation is given in Chapter XXIX. Here it is merely desirable to point out that at times consolidation should be looked upon as a form of expansion and should be treated as a problem to be solved on that basis.

To what extent should a concern expand? – Abraham Lincoln was once asked, "How long should a man's legs be?" The reader will recall Lincoln's famous answer: "Long enough to reach the ground." And so the first answer to the question, how big ought a concern be, is, as big as it can grow with increasing profits. The problem involves the two economic principles of large scale production and diminishing returns.[3] Books on economics will be found to contain a discussion of the law of diminishing returns; here we may simply point out that as businesses grow in size they need new co-ordinating forces, the cost of maintaining which, after a while, offsets the advantages of large scale production. In theory it works out this way: If a concern has one unit of product, *A,* and takes on a new unit, *B,* a co-ordinating system, *X,* must

[3] The advantages of large scale production will be found in Chapter XXVII. Professor J. M. Clark's "Studies in the Economics of Overhead Costs" was published while this book was in galley. The author regrets that he did not have the advantage of Professor Clark's research before this chapter was written. The reader who desires to pursue the subject treated in this chapter should read Professor Clark's book.

be built up. If a new product, *C*, is added, two new co-ordinating forces are required, *Y* and *Z*, *X* moving up to act as the co-ordinating force managing *Y* and *Z*. If another product, *D*, is added, the co-ordinating forces to be supplied will now, in abstract theory, number three, *L*, *M*, and *N*, and so on. The result up to this point is illustrated by the diagram on page 288.

The author's own observation leads him to believe that he cannot emphasize too strongly the need for caution in expansion. In the first place, if the step is unwisely taken the profits of many patient years of hard work may be wiped out in a few months. We could relate dozens of stories, uncomfortable to the actors, to illustrate our point. Business men can probably recall many examples of unwise expansion in their respective fields or those of their acquaintances. The outstanding difficulty of the problem is that when the suggestion to expand is made, all the psychological elements are in its favor: lure of profit, pride of power, fear of competitors' preemption of the field.[4]

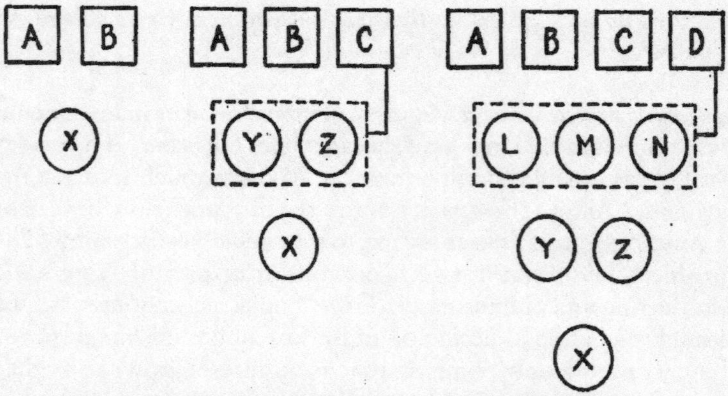

THEORETICAL INCREASE IN CO-ORDINATING OVERHEAD NECESSITATED BY ADDING A NEW PRODUCT

In every business there ought to be some conservative individual who will insist that the optimists "count ten" before urging expansion, and then further insist that the advisability of the

[4] For one who wishes to pursue this phase of the subject we can recommend W. Sombart, "The Quintessence of Capitalism."

TABLE No. 10
CAPITAL BUDGET

Department	Present Position			One Year Later			Two Years Later		
	A Capacity in Dollars of Sales	*B* Investment	*C* Ratio of A to B	*D* Sales	*E* Ratio of D to A	*F* Investment	*G* Sales	*H* Ratio of G to A	*I* Investment
Department No. 1	$ 100,000	$ 300,000	$33\frac{1}{3}$%	$ 75,000	75%	$ 300,000	$ 100,000	100%	$ 300,000
Department No. 2	150,000	375,000	40	100,000	$66\frac{1}{3}$	375,000	125,000	$83\frac{1}{3}$	375,000
Department No. 3	1,250,000	2,500,000	50	1,000,000	80	2,500,000	1,250,000	100	2,500,000
Department No. 4	350,000	350,000	100	300,000	$85\frac{5}{7}$	350,000	400,000	$114\frac{2}{7}$	**400,000**
Department No. 5	250,000	375,000	$66\frac{2}{3}$	250,000	100	375,000	300,000	120	**450,000**
Total	$2,100,000	$3,900,000		$1,725,000		$3,900,000	$2,175,000		**$4,025,000**

Department	Three Years Later			Four Years Later			Five Years Later		
	J Sales	*K* Ratio of J to A	*L* Investment	*M* Sales	*N* Ratio of M to A	*O* Investment	*P* Sales	*Q* Ratio of P to A	*R* Investment
Department No. 1	$ 125,000	125	**$ 375,000**	$ 150,000	150	**$ 450,000**	$ 175,000	175	**$ 525,000**
Department No. 2	150,000	100	375,000	175,000	$116\frac{2}{3}$	**437,500**	200,000	$133\frac{1}{3}$	**500,000**
Department No. 3	1,500,000	120	**3,000,000**	2,000,000	160	**4,000,000**	2,225,000	180	**4,500,000**
Department No. 4	500,000	$142\frac{6}{7}$	**500,000**	700,000	200	**700,000**	800,000	$228\frac{4}{7}$	**800,000**
Department No. 5	400,000	160	**600,000**	500,000	200	**750,000**	600,000	240	**900,000**
Total	$2,675,000		**$4,850,000**	$3,525,000		**$6,337,500**	$4,000,000		**$7,225,000**

proposed step be investigated in the way we have out lined in the first chapters of this book for a new concern.[5] Our experience is that business conferences on new products, or the establishment of branches, and the like questions, easily resolve themselves into a discussion of how can the thing be done. To discuss that question first is reasonable enough, because before deciding whether a step should be taken we must decide how it can be taken. But as the discussion veers over to this secondary question, the insidious assumption arises that the step *should* be taken and that the only question is, *how.*

Measuring amount of funds needed for expansion. – In general the same methods may be used for measuring the funds required for expansion as were already described for investigating a new project. In some lines of work quite definite relationships exist between the amount of gross income and the amount of investment. This relationship probably tends to exist in all cases where growth is homogeneous, as in the case of a gas company in which as new territory is served the entire plant tends to grow uniformly. In fact, in the whole public utility field, the rule that for each dollar of gross income the business will require five dollars of investment, tends to hold good. In a general way, therefore, the financial requirements of such concerns can be forecast from the tendency of growth of gross income.[6] In other cases the need for funds for growth must be determined from a study of past experience, from accurate studies of the needs arising from plans for projected expansion, from estimated increases in the business due not only to definite plans for expansion but to natural healthy growth, and from special studies carried on in connection with engineering plans for improving efficiency.

The table on page 290 was adapted from a form of capital budget used by one of the largest industrial companies in the United States. The same plan may be adapted to even the smallest retail store. The theory on which the table proceeds is that the ratio of capacity of output, expressed in dollars of sales, to the dollars of investment in the respective departments, will remain the same. In column *A* is placed the computed maximum output

[5] See diagram on page 292.

[6] See Chapters XXIII–IV–V. See also charts in Chapter XXI.

of each department with its present capacity, expressed in dollars of sales. In column *B* is placed the present investment in equipment and all assets pertaining to the department. In column *C* is the ratio of capacity to investment. In columns *D, G, J, M,* and *P* are placed the estimated sales for successive years, the estimates being derived from figures obtained from the various selling agencies and checked up in the main office. The amount of investment in each department will remain the same as the original investment till estimated sales catch up with present capacity. When the percentages in columns *E, H, K, N,* and Q exceed 100 (these are the ratios of future annual sales in the respective years to present capacity), then figures will be placed in the investment column at an amount proportioned to present investment, as the respective year's sales are to the present capacity. Thus in the third year, sales in department No. 1 will be 125 per cent of present capacity (column *K*); therefore, in that year the investment will be 125 per cent of the present investment, or $375,000 (column *L*). To indicate for each department years in which added investment will be needed, the figures in the investment column are printed in bold face whenever the investment of that year exceeds the investment of the previous year. In practice it is customary to underscore or draw a circle around the figure in red ink. The most important figure for the financial management is that given on the total line under the column of investment in each year. In planning ahead it is just as necessary to know how much is going to be needed ten years hence as to know how much will be needed in the next year. The limit of open-end mortgages and of stock authorizations can be properly set only when a long view ahead is taken.

Expansion determined by elasticity of personnel. – The extent to which expansion may be permitted depends on the elasticity of the present personnel. This is a question of management primarily, but if management fails, finance will be affected and our purpose here is merely to call attention to the fact that frequently products or markets are added that are really not profitable, for in the first reckoning it may have been assumed that the present force would be adequate. Gradually new appliances are added, new people are engaged, and capital costs and operating expenses mount up, finally requiring a financial revision.

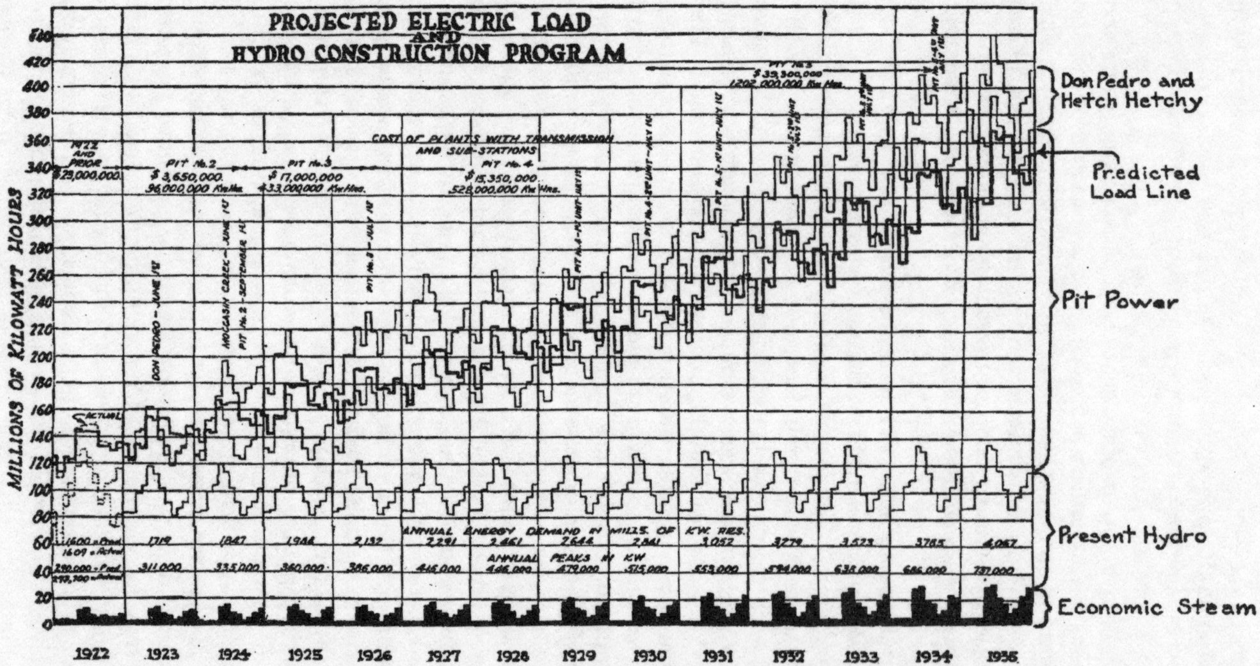

Diagram of the Equipment Budget to Show Its Relation to Output

Pit power refers to power development on the Pit River. Don Pedro and Hetch Hetchy also refer to hydro-electric plants. Economic steam refers to steam power used as auxiliary to hydro power. Notice in the years 1925, 27, 28, 29, 30, 31 and 35 how output meets equipment. (From *Pacific Service Magazine* of the Pacific Gas & Electric Co.)

Effect of expansion on working capital. – Expansion nearly always means an increase in working capital. The increase comes in two ways: first as a temporary increase to bear the burdens of getting the product started – this is equivalent to the demand by a new business for funds for "going concern value" – and then as a larger permanent amount of working capital to carry the increased business. This subject is developed at greater length in the chapter on working capital.[7]

Expanding an individual proprietorship or partnership. – How do individual proprietorships and partnerships finance expansion? The most obvious answer drawn from experience is, they don't; they incorporate and then expand. Certainly this statement is quite true when the business grows to require considerable outside funds. If sole proprietors take in partners they divide control; this may be avoided by incorporating and retaining an amount of stock that will insure control. If partnerships take in a great number of partners the result is likely to be confusion. Our observation has been that firms with large numbers of partners have developed by taking in important employees as partners in order to enlist their enthusiastic participation in the work of the business rather than by seeking to get their investment or the investment of rank outsiders.

Moreover, the growth of individual proprietorships and partnerships, even through reinvestment of profits, presents tax difficulties that the astute business man should seek to avoid. Partners are liable for Federal income taxes on all their earnings, whether withdrawn from the business or not. If the business is incorporated and the profits remain in the business for definite business purposes, the individual owners will not be taxed and the business itself will pay only 12 1/2 per cent.[8]

7 For a more complete discussion see Chapter IX. On account of the high rate of surtaxes on large incomes (see table, page 152), some business men have found it to their advantage to give shares in their business to persons entitled to a claim on their bounty, thus reducing the rate of tax on their own income, and reducing the aggregate tax on the entire income of the business. If this is done frankly, unequivocally, and irrevocably, the result will be an avoidance of taxes to which there can be no objection. See Bullen v. Wisconsin, 240 U. S. 625; Vol. III, American Federal Tax Reports, page 2,944.

8 See, for current information, Prentice-Hall Inheritance Tax Service.

But business men must also have regard to the now very important form of taxation known as inheritance taxes.[9] Practically every State of the Union imposes such taxes.[10] These are usually graduated, the rates increasing as the size of the inheritance increases, and as the relationship of the beneficiary becomes more distant.[11] Usually an inheritance tax is imposed on all inheritances wherever the property representing them is located,[12] by the State in which the decedent last resided, and taxes are also imposed by the States where the property is actually located. If, therefore, *A*, a member of the firm of *A* and *B* with property in every State of the Union that imposes inheritance taxes, except New York in which State *A* resides, should die, *A's* estate would be subject to double inheritance taxes.[13] If, however, the firm had incorporated in New York, that State alone could collect the tax, subject to the following exceptions: Some States would claim an inheritance tax if *A's* certificates were located within their jurisdiction, e. g. kept in a safe deposit vault located in the State; the remedy here is to keep the certificates in the State of residence. Other States claim the right to tax if the decedent owns stock in a corporation which has property within the State; in such cases the transfer agent of the corporation may insist upon the payment of the tax before making the transfer. If the firm were incorporated in some State other than New York, *A's* estate would have to pay the New York tax because of *A's* residence there, and would have to pay, under the inheritance tax laws of most jurisdictions, the inheritance tax on the transfer of shares in the State of incorporation.[14]

[9] In Wisconsin, to take an example where the rates are higher than in most States, inheritance taxes vary from 1 per cent to 40 per cent.

[10] The inheritance tax laws are constantly changing. At the present time the Federal government imposes an estate tax. An estate tax is one measured by the decedent's estate, whereas an inheritance tax is one measured by the size of the heir's inheritance.

[11] An exception is always made in the case of land. The State of residence cannot tax a transfer of land outside its jurisdiction, for the right to inherit land is derived solely from the State in which the land is located.

[12] For rules of the several States, see Prentice-Hall Inheritance Tax Service.

[13] Another tax on the value of the estate above $50,000 would be imposed by the Federal government.

[14] An example is the division of a bank's surplus account into "surplus" and "undivided profits," the former being equivalent to "appropriated surplus" and the latter to the ordinary surplus applicable to dividends in industrial and mercantile corporations. See chapter on dividend policies.

If, after considering these questions, a sole proprietor or partnership wishes to retain an unincorporated form of organization, (a business trust may be considered as an alternative), the means for raising funds are: (1) take in partners; (2) form a limited partnership and take in limited partners (this will effectually settle the question of control, since special partners have no voice in the business); (3) sell unnecessary business property; (4) increase the proprietor's investment by selling private investments; (5) borrow either with or with out security or mortgage. To a certain extent the principles expounded in respect to corporations will be applicable here and it seems unnecessary, therefore, to develop the subject further at this point, except to point out the importance of the personal element in sole proprietorships and partnerships when they seek to attract new capital. Since these concerns cannot count on the ordinary channels of investment for raising new fixed capital, but must count on the investments of individuals, personal relationships will have to be developed among people with means to contribute. The senior partner in one of the largest partnerships in the United States once said to the author, "Early in my life I discovered that it was just as easy to associate myself outside my business with men of means as with men without that power, and I made it a rule to seek out the acquaintance of big men and to maintain that acquaintance."

How corporations can raise new capital funds. – Corporations may increase their capital investments in the following ways:

1. Ploughing in surplus. This may be done by (a) simply increasing the surplus account as profits are made; (b) labeling a part of the surplus as an appropriated surplus;[15] (c) "distributing the surplus" through stock dividends.

It is generally said that American concerns tend to expand out of earnings, while English concerns expand out of the proceeds of the sale of securities. We shall show in the chapter on dividend policies the fallacy of the American practice of postponing a division of the profits earned each year. Here we may simply call attention to the fact that while financing expansion from the proceeds of the business is conservative, it frequently leads to unfair discrimination between owners of the business. In

[15] See pages 162–164.

partnerships this point is hardly well taken, for the proprietors, in the expected course of business, are to remain the owners. But in corporations, especially in the larger concerns, change of ownership is the normal thing, and it seems only proper that each "generation" should "pay its way" and that each "generation" should realize its own profits.

2. Selling unnecessary assets. Unprofitable and unused assets, it would seem, should always be disposed of, whether the company needs the funds or not. If they are not needed they may be invested in interest-bearing securities to serve as a working capital reserve.

3. Sale of stock.

4. Sale of bonds or notes.

5. Borrowing on ordinary real estate mortgages. For small concerns this form of borrowing may be a satisfactory expedient, though small property mortgages of this kind may prove troublesome, first, because such borrowing is usually for a short term, and secondly, because the underlying liens thus given may interfere with future general corporate mortgage borrowing.

Of the five sources of capital funds enumerated, only the third and fourth need occupy our attention here. In the next sections we shall discuss the principles that should govern the issuance of stocks and bonds during the expansion of a company.)

Keeping down the annual cost of capital. – Fundamentally, a business is run for the benefit of its owners. Capital for future expansion, therefore, should be raised by means that will keep down the annual cost of capital. Bonds are always best for this purpose, for the purchaser of bonds commutes size of income for safety of income. It must not be thought that reduction of annual cost of capital is the sole consideration; it would probably be better to say, other factors being favorable, this is the paramount consideration. Bonds, of course, should never be used where there is any danger that the interest cannot be met regularly.

Let us assume, to illustrate the principles set forth in the previous paragraph, that we are trying to decide, as did the stockholders of the United States Steel Corporation in 1902, whether we should retire 7 per cent preferred stock from the proceeds of 5 per cent bonds, that is, whether we should substitute 5 per cent bonds for 7 per cent stock. The answer to the problem is a paradoxical statement: if the company can surely pay annually the larger item – the 7 per cent dividends – then we ought to decide in favor of the smaller item – the 5 per cent interest; but if there is any danger that the company will not be able to pay the smaller item, then we ought to vote in favor of the larger item. We must have "safety first," but having that we must next try to keep down our costs – an apt illustration, this, of the old saying: "The curse of the poor is their poverty."

Keeping down annual costs of capital is not so important where new securities can be sold to old stockholders. If a company is earning 40 per cent on its stock, it will not wish to share these earnings with new investors; the high rate of earnings is probably a just reward to the old stockholders who took all the original risks of the business. If new stockholders are to be brought in now on a reasonable basis they ought to pay $400 or $500 a share for their stock. Or the company might write goodwill into its assets and declare a 300 per cent stock dividend to its old stockholders and then sell stock to outsiders at par. These expedients might be considered instead of the expedient of reducing annual cost by issuing bonds; they would hardly be as effective. But if the company could sell its stock to the old stockholders, each taking new shares in proportion to his holdings, the earning power would be kept "in the family" – there would be no dissipation of income among recent corners. It must be remembered, however, that even where the profits can be kept in the family, when a company has stable income and is successful, it can afford to take the risks of issuing bonds, for by "trading on the equity" the return on the owners' capital is magnified.[16]

Keeping control. – In the second place, new securities should not be issued to give away control. If stock is issued and all the old holders of stock participate in the new issue in proportion to their old holdings, relative control will not be affected. But the amount of new funds needed may be too large for the old holders to supply, or they may wish not to add so large an investment in one enterprise in which they already have large commitments. The use of bonds or stock without voting power will settle the problem. These expedients were used by Charles M. Schwab in 1917, in financing a total expansion of assets amounting to $160,000,000.[17]

[16] See page 276 for the list of securities representing degrees of control.

[17] See Chapter X.

Avoiding risk. – Enough has been said in the section above on "keeping down annual costs" and in the chapters on borrowing,[18] to indicate that risk must not be incurred where earnings are variable.

Where financing is being done through the issue of bonds under an open-end or limited open-end mortgage, the escrow or restriction clauses will probably take care of an undue assumption of risk.[19]

Where preferred stock is being used, the cumulative feature may be so worded as to provide that arrearages shall not begin to accumulate until some time after issue, that is, after the property obtained from the proceeds of the sale of the stock has had ample opportunity to get into operation.[20]

Keeping the best security till the last. – Managers of corporate financing operations must always think of the rainy days, of the emergencies. The general rule is to keep your best security or some of your best security till the last.[21] Un-issued bonds under a limited open-end issue are generally available in very large corporations and these may be made more attractive in times of great necessity by being deposited to secure short term notes.[22] Smaller companies can use ordinary real estate mortgages, or, if they have financed themselves in the past entirely on stock, may create a general corporate mortgage.

[18] See page 197 *et seq.*

[19] See page 124.

[20] We are not speaking here of emergencies in respect to working capital, but of emergencies that demand rush investments of capital funds. An example of what we have in mind is the funding of a large floating debt incurred during rapid expansion in a period of great general business prosperity, for example, the year 1919.

[21] See pages 234–236.

[22] The relation of the cycle of one industry to that of another is a very profitable study. If a business man can discover some line of industry, the ultimate periods of prosperity and depression in which precede the similar periods in his own industry by an approximately determined interval, he may lay his own plans on the basis of the changes in the correlative industry. See, for example, the relation of the industrial equipment business (machines and tools) to general industry as worked out theoretically by W. C. Mitchell in L. D. Edie, "The Stabilization of Business," pages 24–26.

The cycles of trade. – We may not, for lack of space, go into the question of business cycles at great length, but we must indicate, in a general way, the relation of economic movements to the financial problem of expansion and management.

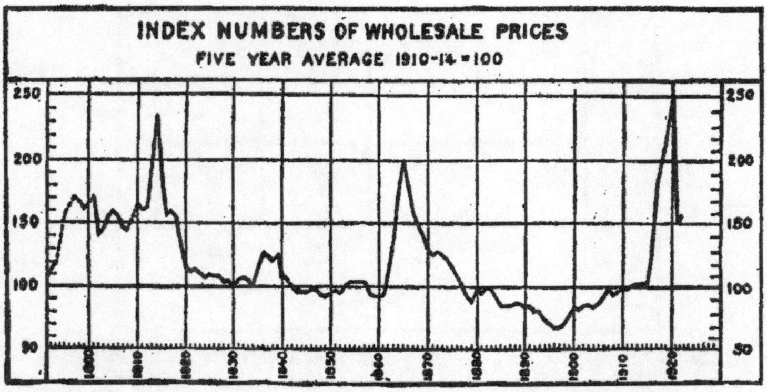

DIAGRAM SHOWING THE LONG TERM SWING OF COMMODITY PRICES. THE POST-NAPOLEONIC DROP IN PRICES LASTED FORTY YEARS; THE POST-CIVIL WAR DROP LASTED THIRTY-ONE YEARS

Economists recognize three distinct cycles:

1. The long swing of prices such as the movement downwards from the Civil War to 1896, and the movement up wards thereafter, shown in the preceding diagram.

2. The three to five year cycles of business activity, caused largely by alternating periods of under- and overproduction, and of expanding and contracting credit, shown below.

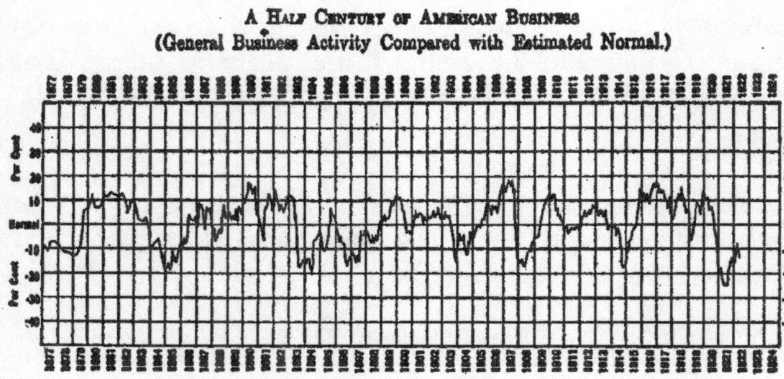

DIAGRAM SHOWING THE THREE TO FIVE YEAR CYCLES OF BUSINESS ACTIVITY

This diagram is a statistically treated combination of business factors, such as pig iron production, bank clearings, railroad traffic, etc., intended to show activity since 1877. The periods may be said to run from the bottom of one depression to the bottom of the next, as follows: 1879, 1885, 1888, 1891, 1894, 1896, 1900, 1903, 1908, 1911, 1914, 1919. (Diagram prepared by Statistical Department, American Telephone & Telegraph Co.)

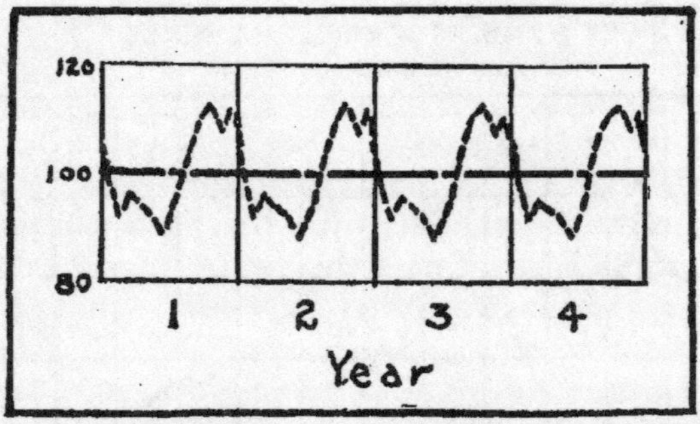

SEASONAL VARIATIONS IN DEMAND FOR AND SUPPLY OF FUNDS
INTEREST RATES ON 60-90 DAY COMMERCIAL PAPER

This is at once the average line for demand for funds and supply of funds through the year. Demand remaining the same, the line will fall as supply increases; supply remaining the same, the line will rise as demand increases. Diagram shows that the early spring normally is the best time to raise funds. (Diagram from Harvard Economic Service.)

3. The annual seasonal changes in the demand for and supply of funds caused chiefly by the regular recurrence of dividend and interest payments by large corporations and by the seasons and crop periods of planting and harvesting.

Besides these cycles the business man must learn to know the peculiarities of his own business and those of the special markets in which he enters either as buyer or seller. The problem here is not so much one of recurring cycles, but of alertness in recognizing conditions and the direction and probable duration of changes in conditions in the several lines of trade allied to the business man's own industry.[23]

What use may be made of the cycles. – From the standpoint of financial management, four distinct questions arise in connection with the cyclical movements of business:

[23] Borrowing by farmers from land banks of one kind or another will probably tend to break up somewhat the annual seasonal demands for funds caused by planting and harvesting.

1. Determination of buying and selling policies in relation to the need for funds.
2. Time at which funds ought to be raised.
3. Kinds of obligations to incur at different stages of the cycles.
4. Credit and collection policies.

Each of these we shall discuss briefly.

Buying and selling policies in relation to cycles. – Buying and selling policies cannot be said to be affected very directly by the long price movements. But in connection with trade activity cycles, the financial management must guard the company against undue expansion of inventories at the height of the active period; large inventories at such a time usually mean that the business is heavily in debt to material men and to the banks. When the reaction takes place, these obligations cannot be liquidated, for, in the first place, goods won't move at all, and then to get some money out of the inventories prices will have to be slashed and a loss taken. Likewise, when the period of depression is well on its way, goods should be bought to take advantage of the low prices of the period of stagnant business.

So, in selling, plans must be made for sales campaigns when business is in the trough of depression; when these plans are ready to be put into operation, general business activity will help the campaign along. If the plans are delayed, by the time the full effect of the campaign is to be obtained, general business may have made the turn into the period of depression and sales effort will be quite futile.

All this points to the fact that funds are needed for buying and selling operations at the end of the period of depression and in the early part of the rise in business activity.

At what time shall funds be raised? – But we are faced with the question: is it better to raise funds when they are needed or when they are easy to raise? Little doubt can be entertained of the wisdom of raising funds when they are easily obtained, provided suitable provision can be arranged for making them available when needed.

The best time to raise funds is when business is booming and people are optimistic. This is toward the end of the period of prosperity. But it is at that time that the wise executive will begin to put on the brakes. The wisest procedure is that which runs somewhat as follows: starting with the period of depression when the business is making plans for sales and laying up inventories, and if necessary planning and acquiring necessary equipment for the coming period of rising activity, we find interest rates low and funds plentiful in the banks. Moreover, prices are low, the construction business is dull, and contracts therefore can be made to advantage for equipment and construction. At this time the business man may borrow and buy on credit. Then as business booms, he may sell his securities at good prices and may pay off his loans. He is then in a strong position to weather the storm of rapidly falling business and may start the next cycle with the good credit standing on which this procedure is predicated.

Time of the year to raise funds. – Investment bankers are careful in timing the sale of securities. In the past the early spring has been the favorite time to sell corporate securities. Investors have received the first of the year interest and dividend payments; and since funds are not needed for agricultural purposes, they may be easily obtained from the banks to purchase and carry securities.[24] A careful program for the sale of securities will avoid an offering on or near the quarterly Federal tax dates.

[24] See the following books: D. F. Jordan, "Business Forecasting;" L. D. Edie, "The Stabilization of Business," F. Lavington, "The Trade Cycle," "Business Cycles and Unemployment," Report and Recommendations of a Committee of the President's Conference on Unemployment, W. C. Mitchell, "Business Cycles." Current information can be obtained from commercial services such as Babson's, Brookmire's, Standard Daily Trade Service, Alexander Hamilton Institute's Business Conditions Service, Harvard Economic Service. Letters published monthly by some of the large banks are worthwhile. The monthly bulletin of the Federal Reserve bank of the district in which a business is located should be read each month. Some of the larger banks publish excellent letters. See, for example, the publications of the National City Bank of New York and the Cleveland Trust Company. It is interesting to note that extremely practical use is being made of the relation of cyclical movements to speculative operations. A special news dispatch received by the author while this book was in galley form reads as follows: "Mr. J. Maynard Keynes, former economic adviser to Premier Lloyd George, (and author of the very well-known 'Economic Consequences of the Peace') has ventured into business. The principles upon which his company intends to act are thus set forth: 'It is now known that fluctuations in the relative values of long-dated and short-dated fixed interest securities and also of fixed interest securities generally and of ordinary shares are all affected by a periodic credit cycle. Changes in the short-period rate of interest affect the value of long-dated securities to a greater degree than should strictly be the case, with the result that considerable profits can be made by changing from

Business cycles as they affect kinds of securities. – At the beginning of a long period of price decline, such as we shall undoubtedly be in during the coming generation, the sale of high interest-bearing long term bonds would be the height of folly, for as time goes on the dollars of interest paid to the bondholders would constantly become more valuable – would buy more goods. At the time mentioned – the beginning of a long period of price decline – bonds should be made short term, or redeemable, or the company should sell stock. At the beginning of a long period of rising prices the company may well take advantage of the situation and sell long term low interest-bearing bonds.

If we consider now the shorter cycles of business activity we may be guided somewhat by what was said above, where it was suggested that at the end of the period of depression and at the beginning of a period of business activity money might be borrowed. If funds are to be raised through the sale of securities at that time, bonds or short term notes may be used. These may be refunded into stock as the business cycle brings profits and enables the company to increase the dividend rate. If the bonds are made convertible, this refunding will take place automatically through conversion of the bonds, since the increase in the dividend rate will enhance the market price of the stock and make it profitable for the security holders to exchange their bonds for stock.

Credit and collection policy in relation to cycle. – If one will compare the curve of business failures with the curve of business activity, he will discover that the general tendency of the failure curve is in the direction opposite to the curve of activity. In. a general way, then, credits ought to be granted in a more restricted fashion as the activity curve creeps upward. Moreover, since toward the end of each year there seems to be a seasonal increase in failures, in the early part of the year great effort should be

one class to another at the appropriate phases of the credit cycle. Similar periodic changes also take place in the relative values of money, on the one hand, and of goods and real property on the other.

So that here also the same principle of changing from one class to another at appropriate times can be applied. The company intends to move from one category of investment to another when it is deemed opportune, but not to adventure the funds of the company upon investments which would not be considered suitable for a prudently managed investment company.'"

made to collect old accounts; towards the end of the year it may be too late.

Progress of forecasting. – Business forecasting is still in its infancy. But much study is being given to the subject, and the business man is delinquent indeed who does not give serious consideration to the changes in business conditions as shown in statistical studies now currently available.[25]

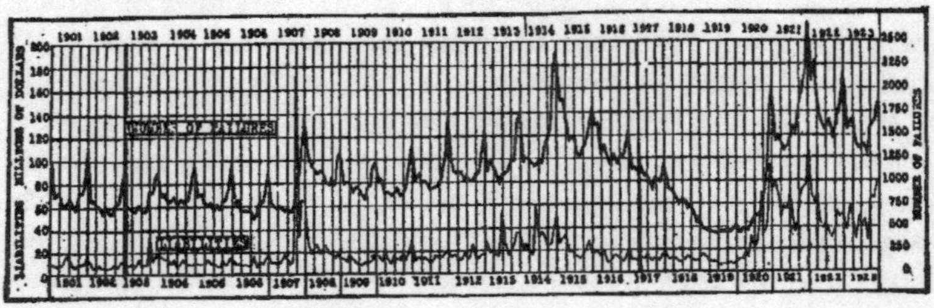

BUSINESS FAILURES AND LIABILITIES INVOLVED

Future financial needs should not be jeopardized. – The financial arrangement must always consider the probable effect of a present operation on future needs. For example, if only a comparatively small sum is needed today, a closed-end mortgage for that amount should not be given; the small under lying liens would embarrass the company later if it undertook to do some financing on a large scale. When a company is about to issue securities, and before it selects the form of securities to be issued, it ought to consider the effect of the proposed securities not only on the company and its credit at the moment of issue, but on the value of other securities, on the possibility of issuing other securities in the future, on the availability of future earnings for dividends to keep up the company's investment credit position,[26] and on the

[25] For example, if a company is relying largely on the sale of bonds under a limited open-end issue, it may be required by the escrow clauses to pay for a part of the cost of new property acquired in some way other than from the proceeds of the bonds. Unless the company is in a position to sell stock, it will have to use its earnings to supply the required "equity." Ploughing earnings into the property in this way prevents the payment of cash dividends, depresses the value of the company's stock, forces financing through the single channel of the bond issue, and makes the capitalization lop-sided with bonds. See C. W. Gerstenberg, "Materials of Corporation Finance," page 929.

[26] Bonds and preferred stock are usually made redeemable.

possibility of rearranging the financial structure of the company in the future.[27]

Simplicity of financial plan. – Other things being equal, a simple financial structure is to be desired because it is easy to manage. One class of stock and one issue of bonds under one mortgage make for a clear understanding on the part of investors of the rights they are buying when they take the company's securities. The soundness of this general principle will be sustained by an examination of the financial plans of companies of varying degrees of success in the same line of business.[28]

Extra features to give attractiveness. – The management of a company ought to know all the tools of financing before beginning a financial operation. Such features as the various forms of sinking funds, redemption and conversion features, accumulation of arrearages, guarantees, and the like, all described in previous pages, should be carefully considered before an issue of securities is determined upon. As has been repeatedly pointed out, most of these features affect in some way the control, income, or risk of the owner. The question in each case is: can an attractive feature be offered without unduly burdening the company, and if the feature is added, will the prospective purchasers' appreciation of the sacrifice be commensurate with the burden assumed? In a word, will the investor pay for what he gets?

Governmental control of capitalization. – Finally, the selection of corporate issues must depend on their relation to government action. Railroads and public utilities must get the consent of regulating commissions. In addition, the tax situation must always be one of the elements that will determine the form of securities – stocks or bonds – chosen for issuance.

[27] Compare, for example, the style of capitalization of a dozen railroads and of a dozen automobile companies.

CORPORATE VEHICLES: POST-WAR ENGINES OF FINANCE[1]

William Z. Ripley

The United States is not infrequently pictured to the world at large by travelers from abroad as a land of milk and honey, of material well-being where plumbing, radio sets, and Ford cars abound. Our achievements in the field of music, poetry, and philosophy are acknowledged; but there is not a due appreciation of the fact that our output in another domain of the imagination leads all the world. Chief Justice Marshall in the Dartmouth College case conceives of a corporation as "an artificial being, invisible, intangible, and existing only in contemplation of law." We turn out more of this particular transcendental product than all the rest of the universe put together. Our supremacy in the matter of wheat, hogs, cotton, and automobiles is matter of common knowledge; but the degree to which we have outstripped all creation in this particular line of politico-legal activity has not been adequately advertised.

Our annual crop of corporate charters – articles of association is another name for them – is not only the most bountiful of its kind on earth; the yield is a constantly accelerating one. This is due to the fact that there are forty-eight different sovereign commonwealths perpetrating these instruments, severally and independently, in America; whereas in the nations of Europe, even in the major industrial countries, there is but one such fountainhead. It is also true that the number of incorporations in some of these single states with us – not necessarily the larger or more important ones –exceeds that of such great industrial countries as the United Kingdom, France, or Germany. Thus does this forthputting of American corporations multiply itself geometrically. A few figures will fortify these bald assertions. In

[1] [Chapter 2 of *Main Street and Wall Street*, London: Brentano, 1927.]

the British Isles they are quite particular about the matter of registration of companies. In 1920, there were 79,541 such corporations enrolled with the Board of Trade. Our own little state of Delaware, all alone, prides itself upon a corporate progeny, all living, of approximately 70,000 members. During the year 1920 there were 11,011 new companies registered and 2541 stricken from the rolls in the United Kingdom, yielding a net increase of 8470 companies. Our own state of New York in the calendar year 1925 issued charters to 24,703 stock corporations – not including banks, insurance companies, and other non-business concerns. New Jersey, always active in this business, issued 5400 certificates of incorporation. Ohio and Illinois are typical of a group of states which sets on foot approximately 5000 companies a year apiece; and the tiny commonwealth of Delaware in 1925 was blessed with the addition of 5053 companies to its little family. None seem to have died. Massachusetts and Pennsylvania of late have averaged about 2000 new charters annually. States like Wisconsin produce in the neighborhood of 1500. West Virginia averages about 100 corporations per month. Even North Dakota, which we deem an agricultural bailiwick, contributed a modest quota of 206 during the year 1925. South Dakota did twice as well, with 398 new charters. Quite a few states view the matter so lightly that no figures whatsoever are available. Nevada printed a list for 1923 covering forty-one pages of type, indicating an output of about 900 charters. But Connecticut, through its secretary, advises us that it makes no tabulation of the matter, nor is it possible to furnish any statistics on the subject. It would be a long task to ascertain by count from our forty-eight secretaries of state just what the total annual output is. But one might upon this showing venture the guess that the number would be not less than 100,000 – roughly ten times the annual authorization of limited companies in the United Kingdom.

It is not only the present total of incorporations in the United States which is surprising; the rate of acceleration of this movement is equally disconcerting. Take New York, for instance, launching 24,703 new corporations in 1925. In 1900 the total was only about one-tenth of this number; it reached the figure of 10,000 annually in 1915, and of 15,000 annually about 1920. The last jump of 5000 took place in the twelvemonth just elapsed. Ohio has never been conspicuous in this particular line of business. It used to incorporate over 1000 concerns a year as far back as 1890. The annual product today is fivefold that figure. Massachusetts, an old industrial community, was launching from 200 to 500 corporations, annually, twenty-five years ago. The total for 1925 was almost five times as many. Bumper crops always occur, of course, in times of prosperity. The tide of incorporation rises and falls along with bank clearings, railroad tonnage, and the marriage rate. But there also is an interesting ebb and flow discernible in this current, arising, as will shortly appear, from the keen competition between the different commonwealths for pelf and prestige. New Jersey during the nineties and for a bit thereafter was so uniquely gracious in according permission to its corporate offspring to hold stock in other companies that it easily led the procession of the states. Now it has yielded place as to leadership to several others. Maine, by reason of its scandalous laxity, had its heyday during the orgy of corporation promotion about 1900. Today, owing to keen inter-state competition, it is enabled to charter only about one third as many new companies annually as before. Massachusetts was forced into the race in 1903. New York took a spurt ahead about 1912 through the in vention of the no-par stock device, and seems to have been able, thanks perhaps to its size and industrial pre-eminence, to have been able to maintain the leadership ever since. So it comes and goes. But the stream grows ever wider and deeper in its total flow. To its magnitude there seems to be no limit.

The fact is that the corporation in America is entirely supplanting such other forms of business organization as individual ownership or partnership. What used to be an exceptional device, confined to large enterprises, has now become the rule for all businesses, great and small. This increasing resort to the corporate device is demonstrated by the following table: –

	Percentage of industrial wage earners under corporate organization	Percentage value of all manufactured articles under corporate organization
1904	70.6	73.7
1909	75.6	79.0
1914	80.3	83.3
1919	86.5	87.7

This table gives the percentages at our various manufacturing censuses of wage earners and of production under the corporate form of organization. It clearly portrays the rapid rise of the device. The individual concern and the partnership are rapidly approaching the vanishing point. The total number of such hold-overs will of course always be considerable, but the convincing thing is the relative insignificance of these other forms of organization taken in the aggregate. In a rough estimate of 100,000 new incorporations in 1925, it is probable that nine tenths or more are for little concerns capitalized at less than $100,000 each. It is entirely characteristic of American conditions as a whole that the corporation should be steadily invading every branch of business down even to establishments of the smallest size; whereas in Europe to a much larger degree the limited company is still confined to enterprises of more than average magnitude.

The prevalence of the corporation in America is all the more significant in view of its history. In the British Isles, to be sure, the unpleasant experience of the people with their sovereigns had some effect for a time. Price, in his book *The English Patents of Monopoly*, characterizes the early promotion of corporations in England as "simply one of many shifty devices for raising money independent of parliamentary supplies." All down through the period from the accession of Elizabeth to the Civil War there was a succession of attempts to grant monopoly privileges for the conduct of various enterprises, always of course for cash. Now it was the starch makers of London, or again the manufacturers of playing cards, or it might be the silk weavers or the pin makers; all of them purchased their right to be and to do, for a price, with the express design of recovering the full amount with interest from the people at large. The protracted struggle for supremacy during the sixteenth and seventeenth centuries between Crown and Parliament could not but make an impression upon the atti tude of the people toward this particular engine of finance and management.

By way of contrast, historically, the corporation got into ill repute in the United States for quite another reason. It seems to have been very infrequent in the early days. Out of twenty-one business corporations within the United States before the adoption of the Constitution, only two were trading companies and one was a manufacturing concern. And for long thereafter this was not the normal form of organization except for a few businesses like banking, insurance, turnpikes, and bridges. Such corporations as were seemingly inherited from the old country were of the fraudulent sort, which were conducted not individually but as joint stock companies. A large proportion of the two hundred such concerns about 1720 were more or less off color, including, for example, those two mentioned by Williston, one a company to provide for "insurance and improvement of children's fortunes," and another for "making salt water fresh." Such exceptional forms of organization served as a screen behind which individuals might work their will, as in the field of mining, lotteries, and the like. New Jersey in 1791 issued a charter to the New Jersey Manufacturing Company, permitting it among other things to raise $10,000 by lottery each year in general aid of its other manufacturing business.

Coming on down into the nineteenth century one still discerns a strong flavor of public disapproval of the corporation as applied to private business, indicating that it was still an exceptional and to a considerable extent a distrusted business device. The first American work on political economy, published in 1820, has this to say upon the subject:

> Every moneyed corporation is *prima facie* injurious to the national wealth, and ought to be looked upon by those who have no money with jealousy and suspicion. They are, and ought to be, considered as artificial engines of power, contrived by the rich for the purpose of increasing their already too great ascendancy and calculated to destroy that natural equality among men which no government ought to lend its power in destroying. The tendency of such institutions is to cause a more unequal division of property and a greater inequality among men than would otherwise take place.

Twenty years later the governor of Massachusetts, within which commonwealth most of the existing corporations were then doing business, sent a stirring message to the Great and General Court, paying his respects to the corporation as follows: –

> These societies are one of the vices of our time. They encourage speculation and fraud, mobilize landed property, over turn matrimonial arrangements, escape publicity in the transfer of real property, diminish the sense of individual responsibility,

> create property in mortmain, prevent all penal remedies, are lacking in moral sense, and constitute finally a grave social peril by concentrating too much power in the hands of certain of our citizens.

This was the time, it will be recalled, of the creation of corporations, not under general law, but by special act of the legislature. The records show that a large proportion of the companies formed in this particular commonwealth during fifteen years preceding the Civil War were driven out of business by the courts. Of upward of 6000 new corporations created within five years, over 4000 had to be dissolved "mere fugitive organizations based upon credulity and to be plucked in transit," as Chandler in his *Express Trusts* puts it. For the neighboring state of New York thirty out of the forty-two companies chartered down to 1853 turned out to be frauds. It is stated that within a period of ten years five-sixths of them came to a bad end. No wonder that some of the states adopted the expedient contained in a Pennsylvania charter of 1866 for the New York California Vineyard Company. Under the terms of this instrument the corporation was empowered to do business anywhere "except in Pennsylvania," the land of its birth. Poor waifs indeed many of them were, thus laid upon the public doorstep, abandoned even by their governmental progenitors.

All this time, of course, there were a few sound corporations conducting business enterprises in the field of private industry. In such branches as cotton manufacture, for instance, soon after the industrial revolution it was necessary to assemble more capital than could customarily be provided by individuals or families. Yet even for these companies the capital stocks were usually owned by those who managed the enterprise. They were largely family concerns. Shares were but rarely bought and sold. Only six of them, and those the largest of the cotton mills, were dealt in publicly on the Boston Stock Exchange in 1830, although this number increased substantially within the succeeding generation. But it was not until the quarter century after 1860 that the practice of incorporation became sufficiently common to call for general laws upon the subject. Up to this time each corporation had been validated by a special charter, secured, perhaps, in too many cases through the liberal expenditure of money. But little by little the foundation was laid for the condition now confronting us – that of the corporation as the almost universally ccepted form of legal organization for the conduct of business enterprises of every size, shape, and hue.

A second outstanding peculiarity of the American situation is a product of the twofold nature of our governmental system. This it is, indeed, which with all its merits and advantages unquestionably casts a blight not only upon our corporations but upon a wide range of other economic and social activities. The province of the Federal Government being restricted mainly to external relations and to matters of interstate commerce, there remains to each of the forty-eight states a complete sovereignty in all of the other relations of life. Under early simple conditions, with both transportation and communication between the states difficult and expensive, it was imperative that each commonwealth should be more or less a law unto itself in most matters of daily living. The colonial period and the earlier years under the Federal Government were characterized by sharp conflicts over the retention of these local powers. Licenses and taxes were sought to be continued by domestic concerns against "foreigners" over the border. An odd instance of persistence of this provincial spirit is afforded by the laws of Rhode Island concerning imprisonment for debt – a survival of the Middle Ages. But how else can a tiny jurisdiction protect its merchants in this age of buying on the installment plan? Escape over the frontier is so very easy, bearing your part-paid parlor furniture or your radio set beyond the sheriff's reach. Little by little with improvement of highways, railroads, the telegraph and telephone, geographic barriers have broken down, until the United States as a whole has become, practically speaking, one great market. And, of course, along with the extension of markets has come a lessening of the barriers which set off the people of one state socially from their neighbors. So far has this progressed that it is the observation of European travelers in the United States that we are more nearly homogeneous in customs, manners, and ways of doing business over a vast area than are the little compact countries of Europe. For they are set off against one another not only by mountains and rivers, but also by reason of their differing political traditions, languages, and religions. From a social point of view our danger is that of too monotonous uniformity rather than of a jarring diversity in customs, manners, and mode of thought.

Nevertheless, problems of great moment have arisen in the United States because of the divergent and conflicting laws respecting all sorts of things among the forty-eight commonwealths. The need of uniformity has already brought about federal systems of banking, in matters of bankruptcy and similar concerns. Perhaps the three most pressing problems other than that of corporate legislation have to do with public finance, family law, and labor legislation – child labor in par ticular. In the field of public finance all sorts of conflicts in matters of taxation or of exemption therefrom arise. Certain states derive profit from constituting themselves – Florida, for example an asylum against the imposition of income taxes during life or of inherit ance taxes at death. Safety vaults may spring up apace and old people migrate in numbers to those places favored alike by Nature climatically and by man in respect of his exercise of the taxing power. In the domain of family relations, conflicting state legislation has also brought forth a multitude of inconveniences and of abuses. Massachusetts, maintaining a high standard for its marriage laws, found itself exposed to attack on the one side from Rhode Island and on the other from Vermont (at least until 1917), due to the laxity of the statutes in these two neighboring commonwealths. Brevity of residence, informality of registration or prior notice, laxity of parental control, in the little state of Vermont for many years made Bellows Falls a veritable Gretna Green for intending brides and grooms from Massachusetts. The Honeymoon Special train on the Boston and Maine Railroad got you there about noon, got you married, and safe home again, all in a jiffy. The common-law wedlock by handfasting, in New York, just over the western border, also attracted matrimonial candidates from Massachusetts, deterred by the formality of the statutes at home. Just now, because Delaware requires an interval of twenty-four hours after license, before marriage may take place, while in Maryland the wedding may occur at once, the marriage rate in Maryland is three times as high as it is over the border. Brooke County, the panhandle of West Virginia, is so inviting connubially because of its laws, that most of its weddings take place between citizens of Ohio or of Pennsylvania. Nebraska in 1922 amended its statutes, to require posting of a ten-day advance notice before issue of the license. As a result the state marriage rate dropped within two years from to only 3.1 per thousand. People simply sought and found their marital estate elsewhere. Or, had marriage been effected, how different were the requirements as respects divorce. South Carolina, at one extreme, per mitted no annulment for any cause whatsoever. Other states, from Rhode Island to Nevada, permitted divorce for almost any cause, up to a change in the direction of the wind or temperature. It has long been and still is futile to expect any substantial abatement of the divorce evil until a greater uniformity of state legislation in these matrimonial concerns may be brought about.

Precisely similar as respects inconvenience, friction, and abuse are the conditions among the states in the domain of labor legislation. The same corporation may own mills operating for a ten-hour day or longer, with women, young persons, and children of all ages working day and night, in the Southern states, and other mills situated in Massachusetts, constrained to operate only forty-eight hours a week, employing no persons under the age of fourteen years, with the prohibition of all labor of females or children at night. Even now there is a shocking contrariety of conditions as between Massachusetts and Rhode Island. One state accords the benefit of work men's compensation laws in cases of industrial accident; its neighbors may either be in the stage of employers' liability legislation or in a mediaeval condition characterized by no legislation at all. And, to cap the climax in this regard, we have the Federal Government, with a code quite its own, functioning over, in, and through all of these forty-eight states. The conflict of laws seems to reach a climax in this particular province of labor legislation. A railway employee may be alternating all day long at five- or ten-minute intervals between jurisdiction of the United States or of an individual state as respects compensation for accidents, hours of serv ice, or discipline. During those intervals when he is concerned with interstate business, he is subject to the laws of the United States. All the rest of the time he is merely a private citizen of an individual commonwealth.

Or take the longshoreman, engaged in one of the most dangerous callings known. The number of accidents in the loading and unloading of ships is appalling. These men, too, all day long are passing and repassing from state territory on the pier over to the jurisdiction of the Federal Government, in the maritime zone in which the vessel floats. If one happens to fall, to be struck, burned, or maimed on one side of an imaginary line, halfway up the gangplank, he is subject to one code of laws; but on the other side of that line his rights and liabilities are defined by those of an entirely different sort. Wherever one touches it, in all of these different human contacts one runs afoul of the complications arising from our dual American system of government.

The root of much of our trouble in maintaining decent standards of corporate practice arises, too, from the same multiplicity and overlapping of jurisdictions, exemplified in these other matters of daily living. The scandalous prostitution of the sovereign power of states, whether for purposes of public revenue or merely as utilized by de signing men for personal enrichment, may be illustrated by a few typical advertisements. *Collier's Weekly,* March 7, 1908, prints this one: –

> Incorporate in Arizona, costs less than elsewhere, advantages are worth thousands. Transact business anywhere. No tax in Arizona. No stock subscriptions required before incorporating. Any kind of stock may be issued and paid up in property, leases, or anything of value, and made nonassessable. No public statement and no books need be kept for public inspection anywhere. Stockholders exempt from liability if our form is used. The great incorporating business of Arizona was built up by President Stoddard while Secretary of Arizona. Resident agent for many thousand companies. All blanks, laws, by-laws, and particulars free. Companies incorporated same day we receive reasonable deposit on account and telegram stating name, capital, number of shares and names of first Directors. Incorporation better than partnership. Send for our latest revised pamphlet and learn the many and great ad vantages of having your business incorporated. Reference: Any bank in Arizona. Stoddard Incorporating Company, Box 3-7, Phoenix, Arizona.

That the business was still profitable thirteen years later appears from the following clipping from the *Scientific American:* –

> *Incorporate in Arizona*
> Complete in one day. Any capitalization, least cost, greatest advantages. Transact business anywhere. Laws, by-laws, and forms free. Stoddard Incorporating Co. Phoenix, Arizona.

Here is another from a Boston paper: –

> *This beats New 7ersey*
> Charters procured under South Dakota laws for a few dollars. Write for corporation laws, blanks, by-laws, and forms to Philip Laurence, late Asst. Sec. of State, Huron, Beadle Co., So. Dakota.

This, too, from a recent number of *System:* –

> *Charters – Delaware Best, Quickest, Cheapest,* most liberal. Nothing need be paid in. Do business and hold meetings anywhere. Free forms. Colonial Charter Company, Wilmington, Del.

One finds in the legal press, "The Corporation Laws of the State of Nevada offer the greatest inducements." Some years ago the secretary of state of South Dakota officially recommended the services of the South Dakota Corporation Charter Company. The president of this concern writes, "In nineteen cases out of twenty we are able to get the charter into the mails within ten hours after the application is received here."

The little state of Delaware has always been forward in this chartermongering business. The charges for service by the Delaware Registration Trust Company of Wilmington "for maintaining the principal office, acting as registered agent, exposing the sign, acting as custodian of the duplicate stock ledger, giving notice of stockholders' meetings, furnishing annual report blanks," and so forth, are $50 per year if the capital does not exceed $1,000,000; for upward of $1,000,000, $100 per year. "We can complete all details here within twenty-four hours of the receipt of the papers properly executed, remittance, etc." "To facilitate the business, save time and, if desired, to prevent publicity in obtaining your charter we will furnish the three incorporators from this office, who will attend to the filing of the original *certificate of incorporation,* the recording of the certified copy, and will then meet in our office and hold the *first meeting of incorporators* and elect or select directors who may meet in your city, elect officers, and proceed with the business of your company." In the *Daily Times-Star* for October 20, 1926, is this inviting bit: "Simple annual reports are necessary, *but they do not require disclosure of the corporation's financial affairs* [our italics]. Of all the company's books and records, only an original or duplicate stock ledger must be kept in Delaware." Such are the conditions under which may be launched upon a perpetual career, not alone in Delaware but in a considerable number of our other American commonwealths, legal creations which may, among other things, commit the following acts: Hold all of the meetings of its stockholders and directors anywhere under the sun; keep all of its original records and accounts at its principal office anywhere; issue all the bonds it desires without further authorization from the chartering state and even without tax thereon; put forth without limit capital stock for practically any sort of consideration, cash, no cash, property, real or imaginary, or services, actual or spurious; and all of this coupled with the privilege of non-liability on the part of the shareholders for any of the debts contracted by the corporation.

Standard American practice is further illustrated by what may be done in Maine. The Corporation Trust Company "maintains fully equipped offices for the organization and representation of business corporations in all the states." At Portland, conveniently situated opposite the Union Station, is a corporate hostelry, fully adequate to maintain the reputation of the state as a popular summer resort. According to the law, shareholders' meetings must be held and records must be kept at the "principal office" of the corporation within the commonwealth. There is just a trace of humor in the further clauses of the Corporation Trust Company's advertise ment: "It has spacious rooms for holding stockholders' meetings. Its facilities are adequate for handling meetings at which large numbers of proxies are presented."

A disgraceful misuse of the sovereign power of an American commonwealth, amounting in fact to a conspiracy against the citizens of foreign states, was brought to my attention some years ago in connection with the affairs of the Brazil Railway Company. This corporation was chartered in the state of Maine in 1906; and there upon embarked upon an extensive program of railroad construction and general promotion in Brazil, Uruguay, and Bolivia. Its magnitude is indicated by the capital shares, issued to the amount of $40,000,000, afterward raised to $60,000,000. Within six years its borrowings, over and above this, amounted to about $75,000,000. The most extraordinary thing about it was the charter. This instrument permitted the management, without approval of the shareholders, to dispose of the assets at any price; to purchase whatever property it might see fit, at any figure; to contract loans without let or hindrance; and to issue new securities also *ad lib*. Eighty-five different issues were finally placed in the various capital centres of Europe. The charter solemnly provided that the meetings of the shareholders should be held at the principal office in Maine. With equal solemnity, it proceeded to require that notices of these meetings must be given at the principal office in Maine, at least ten days in advance. And, just to make assurance doubly sure, it was further provided that unless the proxies were returned three days before the stated meeting, the treasurer should be authorized to cast the vote under the direction of the president of the corporation. That allowed exactly seven days for the notices of the meeting to reach the shareholders, all of whom were in Europe, and to return the proxies in time for their effective use. Was ever a fraud more patent upon the face of it? Little wonder that the whole affair resulted in a colossal smash – a tangle requiring the expert services of Mr. Cameron Forbes, late governor of the Philippine Islands, who was appointed receiver in 1914. At that time it was estimated that $12,000,000 of new money would be requisite for purposes of rehabilitation. The losses in this stupendous venture have, so far as I know, never even been estimated. As for the situation in general, the denunciation of Governor Fernald of Maine, in 1909, of the continued practice of receipt of large revenues from incorporation as "the price of prostitution" of the sovereign power of the commonwealth, is by no means exaggerated. Federal Judge Landis in a similar case summed up the matter not inaptly, when sentencing a broker to ten years' imprisonment for fraudulent promotion, "The state of Delaware would face indictment for licensing such corporations as the Pan Motor Company if I could summon a sovereign state into court."

The intensity of competition of state with state is peculiarly manifest in respect of the several novel practices which are shortly to be described somewhat more in detail. It is, bit by bit, from a timid proposal in a single venturesome state, that no-par stock has reached its present widespread acceptance; it is thus that the traditional right of shareholders to a prior participation in all new security issues has been, little by little, so grievously abridged; thus has it come about that the practice of legalizing new issues by a majority vote either of stock present or voting, or by a mere majority of the total number of shareholders, has crept in. The worst abuses of holding-company finance crept in, it may be, to get rid of an inconvenient accumulation of unpaid preferred dividends, or perhaps surreptitiously to appropriate an undisclosed surplus in some corporate treasury. Nor is there ever any security against the intrusion of some new kink at law. Virginia, perhaps, stands alone for the moment in the laxity of its statutes respecting liability of shareholders in the issue of new stock without par. Not only is there no par, but the mere issuance of a receipt of approval by the Corpora tions Commission operates to absolve the shares thus issued from any liability whatsoever subsequent thereto. There is a familiar story about the young man who was urged by his father to take a wife. The answer was, "Really you know, Father, I haven't the slightest objection in the world! But whose wife shall I take?" Such is the dilemma of the intending incorporator, confronted with the stock of attractive legal goods displayed upon the shelves of some of these merchandising states.

Much of this competition of state with state for corporate favor arises, of course, from the desire for public revenue. The income from fees and taxes is often very large. The state of New Jersey, in fact, was for many years able to subsist without much, if any, income from direct taxes upon private citizens or their property. At the present time, for states like Maryland or Wisconsin, an income approximating a quarter of a million dollars annually is obviously a matter of some importance. The fees and bonuses for a large state like Pennsylvania may constitute a substantial part of the total state revenue.

The general situation was well described by Federal Trade Commissioner Myers before the American Academy of Political Science in 1926 as follows: –

> Public opinion will not long tolerate a condition under which a few states vie with one another in creating corporations with unlimited capital and powers, without requirement that they engage in business in the states of their incorporation, and without provisions looking to the disclosure of their operations or accounts, to transact business and market their securities in other states. An effort has been made to justify these loose incorporation laws on the ground that they encourage the

> development of industry within the states; but the effort fails in view of the omission of any provision that the corporations shall conduct their operations in whole or in part within the states of their incorporation. The reference is irresistible that the incorporation of companies is solicited by these states because of the license fees and other revenue derived from the business. The creation of corporations has lost its dignity as an exercise of the sovereign prerogative for the furtherance of commerce and in the interest of the people of the state. What was once regarded as the conferring of a great privilege, to be limited and circumscribed by all necessary provisions for the protection of the public, has become a bargain sale, and states are advertising and competing for the business.

But it is the evidence of an unholy alliance between private profit and the exercise of this supposedly sovereign function which is at times the most debasing in its influence. The system tends to create a horde of shysters, ready to perpetrate any sort of corporate enormity, provided only that the fees are sufficiently ample. And attorneys, on their part, as one of them writes me, "pick their states of incorporation as you or I would pick out a department store at which to trade."

Another shameful angle to this business is that it tends to envelop our state legislative chambers in a noisome atmosphere of political honeyfugling, if not of downright corruption. A minor modification of a state statute may be worth large sums of money, because of its effect either upon plans in contemplation, or else as affording possible relief from the untoward results of acts already committed. And just because these amendments are seemingly so insignificant, they may be slipped through without arousing comment and perhaps almost entirely without notice. The temptation to spend money in what amounts to bribery, in order to attain such results, may upon occasion be very great. Nor need the immediate accountability for such corruption necessarily rest upon the corporations themselves. The system gives rise to a considerable body of irresponsible intermediaries – henchmen, lobbyists if you please – specialists in such branches of the law, hangers-on about the state capital. The great corporation merely whispers its need. Subservient agents hasten to bring about the desired result, and perhaps no questions are asked. Such were the corrupting influences in the old days of the railroads and of the liquor interests. Both of these are now happily nonexistent; the railroads withdrawn from politics for good, and the liquor interests having transferred their activities to the larger domain of political propaganda in general. Protective tariffs are still with us. And there yet remains in and about these legislative halls a murky atmosphere which is necessarily attendant upon corporate influence. In order to be specific, how ever, concrete illustrations are a propos. The New Jersey Act of March 28, 1902, which made provision for the so-called Steel Corporation Bond Conversion, was a piece of special legislation serviceable only for the commission of a proposed act. At Trenton also there was slipped through in the following year the notorious amendment of the New Jersey corporate code intended to relieve the directors of the American Malting Company from liability for the declaration of unearned dividends. This amendment was passed on the last day of the session by a bare majority of two votes in the House and one in the Senate. But it surreptitiously sought to vitiate the existing law by providing that directors should be liable to stockholders only in cases of willful or negligent violation of the statute. To be sure, the matter was finally settled out of court by the repayment of $340,000 in cash, and the restoration of $1,000,000 in common stock of the corporation. The statute apparently failed of its purpose; but the scandal of its enactment was not in the least lessened thereby. One might in the field of railroading adduce the further instance of the New York Act in 1900, so amending the law as just barely to admit the Harriman issue of Chicago and Alton bonds to the list of legal investments for savings banks.

So much for the stage setting. Now for the corporate actors. The next step in our analysis has to do with recent tendencies as revealed by the articles of association of some of our newer corporations. Obviously, however, they are not to be taken as typical of the mass. Rather are they samples selected more or less at random from the heap, although presumably because they are somewhat more brilliantly colored than the average. Their significance lies in the revelation of possibilities for the future, and particularly because for the most part they illustrate the steady encroachment of management upon the traditional rights of shareholders. Never mind if, as will doubtless be alleged, these novel charter provisions at law merely seem to be intended to bring the law into accord with existing facts. If the facts are wrong, it is then high time that we set about changing them. It is quite evident that an onslaught of such considerable proportions in the aggregate has already taken place as to call for serious consideration. Among these recent tendencies, the following are particularly to be noted: the limitation upon the right of shareholders to participate in future issues of securities; sole responsibility arrogated by management to issue new securities, if necessary having priority over those already existing; practically unrestrained authorization of managements to dispose of new shares upon any terms which they may think fit; power to sell the assets or to enter into new corporate relationships without let or hindrance; and, to complete the picture, an attempted exemption from liability on the part of directors and officers for results which may flow from a proprietary interest adverse to that of the corporation. These are the provisions which, taken as a whole, clear the ground for, and are now especially contributory to, the primary issue to be considered in the next chapter, namely the abrogation of the voting rights of shareholders, not alone in respect of these, but perhaps of all other matters appertaining to management and profit.

The right of shareholders in a corporation to participate to their advantage in all subsequent issues of shares by the company in which they have an investment has become traditional. It is of the very essence of corporate democracy that all members of the company shall stand upon an even footing one with another. Out of the exercise of this right has developed the modern practice of making provision for new capital by issues of stock at such a figure below the market price as shall yield a bonus to those who participate. This situation creates what are popularly known as stockholders' "rights."[2] They amount oftentimes to a substantial addition to the income of the shareholders in the case of prosperous concerns. The legal name for the advantage is that it is a preemptive right – a right, that is to say, to a first opportunity to buy new securities before that offer is extended to the general public. This preemptive right is almost as old as the privilege of limited liability, neither of them originating with the corporation but having developed out of experience with it as a convenient means for the attainment of certain objects. The objective of the

[2] For details of such transactions consult Ripley, *Railroads: Finance and Organization*, p. 267 *et seq.*

preemptive right is, of course, the provision of new capital by subscriptions drawn primarily from the partners in the enterprise, without disturbance of the existing ratios of investment and control. This traditional preemptive right has been of late put in serious jeopardy by a quite general practice which seems to have begun after 1919. At first it was embodied in new articles of association, merely as a matter of private contract. But it speedily developed into formal amendment of the corporation laws of Delaware, Maryland, and New Jersey dealing with the powers of boards of directors. The seriousness of the inroad upon the shareholder's rights has been but little appreciated by the world at large. So far has the movement progressed that even Massachusetts, one of the normally conservative states, had to come to it in 1920. The statutes themselves are ordinarily brief, providing perhaps merely that "such increased stock may in whole or in part be disposed of without being offered to the shareholder." The form which this innovation assumes in the charter itself is usually more elaborate, running something like this: –

> No holders of stock of the corporation, of whatever class, shall have any preferential or other right of subscription to any shares of stock of any class, or any securities convertible into shares of the stock of the corporation; nor any right of subscription to any thereof, other than such, if any, as the board of directors in its discretion may determine, and at such price as the board of directors may fix; and any shares or convertible securities which the board of directors may determine to offer for subscription to holders of stock may, as said board of directors shall determine, be offered to holders of any class or classes of stock at the time existing to the exclusion of holders of any or all other classes at the time existing.

Details vary, of course. Great Atlantic and Pacific Tea Company (Maryland), or National Dairy Products Company (Delaware), may be content merely to put an end to this right for preferred shareholders only. Pan-American Western Petroleum (Delaware) may limit the right upon approval by three fourths of the board of directors. Or, as in the case of General Baking Corporation (Maryland) or of the Standard Oil Company of California

(Delaware), not only have the stockholders no right to subscribe to additional shares of any class, but the board of directors can authorize the issue of new shares of any class, unlimited on account of the absence of par value and irrespective of any priority which there may be in the then existing nonvoting stock. Entirely similar disabilities are found among the recent charters of public utility companies, Eastern States Power Corporation (Maryland), Central and Southwest Utilities and International Power (Delaware), and National Electric Power (Maine), for example.

The argument in favor of this serious trespass upon the customary right of shareholders to a pro-rata subscription to all new issues of capital stock is a purely practical one. It originates naturally enough among the corporation lawyers, speaking on behalf of the banking, promoting, and management interests. This argument is in substance that corporations must of necessity, when committing themselves to a considerable program of construction or development, have assurance that the necessary funds therefor shall be presently available. The difficulty in practice is that the shareholders as a whole at best move slowly, and may never be positively depended upon to come forward with the necessary subscriptions. For shareholder bodies are sometimes fickle, affected by the general outlook, or, in particular, by rates for money and the competition of other investments. The actual yield of the new offering, therefore, it is alleged, may not be ascertained with certainty in advance. Under such circumstances there may have to be an underwriting of the proposed issue by outside bankers, which engage to take up all of the subscriptions which are not otherwise absorbed. This obligation, it is said, the bankers are loath to assume, first, because they do not know how large the balance unsubscribed may be; and, secondly, because the extent of this commitment may not be known for a considerable period – the time which is necessary in order to determine the shareholders' will. Because market conditions may materially change during the interval, the bankers are unwilling to shoulder an indeterminate risk without a considerably enhanced charge for the service. Sometimes, of course, this expense for underwriting, as in the case of acquisition of new property, may be avoided by issuing the stock directly in exchange therefor. Shareholders would naturally have no preemptive right under such circumstances. But in case of a prolonged construction program this plan is not feasible. Sometimes where there is a concentrated share ownership, the reluctance of the bankers is abated by the ease with which the general prospect may be foreseen after consultation with the dominant stockholders. But in many other cases, it is alleged, the provision of new funds by general shareholder subscription is apt to be slow, cumbersome, and expensive. And with thousands of very small stockholders, as under the modern development of customer ownership of public utilities, all such operations seem to be practically impossible. The fact, however, that the shareholder's interest in this matter is entirely eliminated without adequate compensation by the new device seems hardly to have been considered seriously by those who defend the innovation. The principal reason for concern in connection with it is due to the increasing complexity of the corporate structure nowadays. With the old simple financial set-ups, it is conceivable that internal tension between different classes of shareholders would not arise. But it is because of the extraordinary involution, of corporate structure and also of the increasing interplay of corporations with each other that one may seriously question whether this abolition of the preemptive right is a move in the right direction. It certainly is not, unless more carefully circumscribed than it appears to be at the present moment.

It seems to be clear, therefore, that the defense of the customary right of shareholders to participate on the basis of their holdings in all of the "juicy fruits," as one correspondent puts it, of new security issues, has never been more convincing than at this moment. Never has the danger been so great of an insidious undermining of the rights of the ill-represented main body of shareholders, by reason of the introduction of a number of new clauses in the charters of our corporations, great and small. At common law, the doctrine that the shareholder is entitled to maintain his full existing proportion of the stock of the company under all circumstances is derived from the fact that his relative voting power in the corporation will otherwise be diluted in the event of an issuance of more new shares. A second defense is that the shareholder, entitled by reason of his investment to a certain fraction of the company's earning power, will be subjected to a similar dilution of his right to participate in these earnings. It is argued that for modern large corporations these defenses have ceased to have validity, inasmuch as the shareholder who wishes to maintain his existing proportionate interest, either in voting power or as to earnings, may always have an open market in which he may buy enough new shares to bring up his proportion to its original figures. But this fails to meet the objection that if a considerable number of shareholders were thus compelled to go into the public market to buy enough shares to maintain their proportionate interest, they would probably have to pay an excessive price – a price at all events greater than would attach to the exercise of their preemptive right. In other words, the shareholder would be exposed to the danger of having part of his joint possession sold to others for an inadequate consideration. And this danger is a particularly imminent one, where, as we shall soon see, the management seeks to entrench itself legally by exemption from recovery of damages by the shareholder body. In any event, the invention of the no-par common stock, coupled with the various devices for disfranchising various groups of shareholders, especially as respects new issues of securities with special priorities, renders it a matter of prime importance that further abridgment of this customary right should be most critically reviewed.

The various other licenses created under present-day chartering practice, enabling managements to function in practical independence of the shareholding body, have already been enumerated. General Baking Corporation (Maryland, 1925) may be taken as a fair individual sample thereof. The corner stone is the issuance of no-par stock, not only the common shares, but in this instance the preferred shares as well. The stockholder's preemptive right to subscribe to additional shares of any class is abrogated. The voting shares may create any class of stock equal to or prior to the preferred shares. The directors can authorize the issue of shares of any class for any consideration, unlimited, of course, in this case on account of the absence of par value. The only moderation manifested seems to be in imposing some slight restraint upon the power of the directors to dispose of the assets of the corporation.

The foregoing provisions are of course extreme. But I have in mind the principal organization papers of another corporation which goes a step further toward the ultimate. For its Maryland charter also specifically disposes of any requirement "to accumulate any reserve or otherwise provide in advance for the payment of any sum to the holders of preference stock on liquidation, dissolution, or winding-up." Another section is so drawn as apparently to permit the board of directors to receive money or other property, credit any part of it to reserve or surplus regardless of whether it is in fact income or capital, and thereafter to distribute it without reservation as dividends or to charge off losses against it. Another permits the sale, lease, or exchange of all of the property and franchises without limitation as to terms, by a majority approval of the common stock voting shares "with or without a meeting or by vote at a meeting called for that purpose." Another section permits reincorporation or reorganization, coupled with the conveyance of all the assets to a new corporation. It will be said that the means authorized, namely by writing or proxy without a meeting, is the manner in which such things are usually brought to pass. But it is the sum total of these provisions, taken in connection with the one subsequently to be considered concerning relief from liability for directors on account of an adverse interest, which makes this particular charter the veritable consummation of a highly iniquitous tendency. The capsheaf perhaps of this at tempted arrogation of supreme power recites that in the event of the transfer of the assets as an entirety to a new corporation, "each holder of stock in the Corporation agrees forthwith to surrender for cancellation his certificate or certificates for stock of the Corporation, and to receive and accept in exchange therefor, as his full and final distributive share of the proceeds of such sale and conveyance ... a number of shares of the stock of the new company ... Such new company may, but need not, have all or any of the powers of the Corporation and the charter and by-laws of such new company may, but need not, contain all or any of the provisions con tained in the charter and by-laws of the Corporation." And all this, quite regardless of the fact that no court in its right senses – this dictum, by the way, from one who is no lawyer – would ever regard such a dragnet proviso as sustainable! The remarkable thing is that good lawyers should pander to the inordinate ambition of financiers by affixing their names as drafting counsel to such a document. It is difficult to conceive of another set of charter provisions, articles, and by-laws that go to such an extraordinary extent as do these in conferring arbitrary and absolutely uncontrolled power upon an inside group.

Illustrations abound of similar exceedingly broad grants of power to boards of directors for public utilities. Under the

Delaware charter of North American Light and Power Corporation it lies within the sole discretion of the management, represented by vote of the common stock only, to sell out all of the assets of the corporation. The same thing is true of the Interstate Power Company and of the National Electric Power Company, except that in the latter case the consent only of the Class B voting common stock is requisite. All of the preferred shareholders and of the nonvoting common shareholders are completely disfranchised so far as this vital matter is concerned.

An egregious malversation of the rights of shareholders and of the public generally is entailed in the device of so-called no-par capital stock. This expedient is handmaiden to a considerable shifty company in contributing to corporate obscuration and even to fraud. Without no-par stock some of the other innovations in corporate practice would lose much of their poignancy. By its aid a number of different elements contributory to a conspiracy against the interest of investors and of the public are welded together to form a substantial menace to sound corporate finance.

Ever since the introduction of limited liability – which, by the way, is not a congenital but only an acquired characteristic of corporations, the principle, in brief, which relieves the shareholder in an enterprise from any liability to his corporation beyond the amount of the actual investment – it has been customary to limit and define this liability by the imprint upon each share of stock of a stated par value. So universal was the practice that no one seems to have dreamed of its modification. And then about 1909 a committee of eminent attorneys, headed by Francis Lynde Stetson, persuaded the New York Bar Association to endorse the novel proposal to issue stock "without the dollar mark" – in other words, to represent it merely as "a certain aliquot part" of the net value of the enterprise. It would lead one astray to discuss whether or not this proposal stood in any definite relation to clearing up the wreckage created by the scandalous looting of the New York City Traction properties. That it proved serviceable in that connection in affording relief from troublesome litigation seems quite probable. The proposal had hard sledding at first. Passed by the New York Legislature, it was at first vetoed; and then in 1912 it was reënacted, to become law. Thereafter matters took the usual course. Maryland followed suit in 1916. The next year California, Delaware, and

Maine fell into line. By this time the landslide was in full motion. Virginia came next, followed in 1919 by Illinois, New Hampshire, Pennsylvania, and Ohio; until well-nigh forty states in the Union now permit the formation of corporations with shares of stock stripped of a stated par value. Adoption by business men has followed close upon the heels of statutory authorization; until at the present time, for common shares at least, no-par stock has become the rule rather than the exception, for public utilities as well as business concerns. The next step was the spread of authorization for the issuance of preferred shares without par value, this by Maryland in 1924. Delaware of course had to follow suit the next year or stand to lose business heavily. And so the matter goes. It is but the old, old story over again, traversing the same course of develop ment; and with practically the same states falling into line in the same order.

The reason for the original assertion of a par value was that it measured supposedly the capital which the shareholders had agreed to contribute to the enterprise.[3] Limited liability being the outstanding characteristic of the corporation, creditors were deserving of information as to the adequacy of the assets for satisfaction of their claims. Thus the corporation embarked upon its career with a certain stated investment, in theory at least. And creditors supposedly enjoyed two remedies; first, that stockholders, had they not paid in the full par, might be held personally liable for the balance; and, secondly, that directors might be held liable for any impairment of the capital fund by the declaration of unearned dividends. So much for the theory. As to the facts, a score of ways were invented for evasion of these liabilities. Shares might be issued in great excess in exchange for property or for services rendered, which were absurdly overvalued, this being perhaps the simplest and most direct means of evasion. Thus it turned out that stock watering – perhaps the most universally accepted of corporate sins in the eyes of the public – was not prevented by the statement of par value.

But there was downright inconvenience attaching to the use of par value. This was that it subsequently prevented what has well

[3] Two most illuminating papers are: on the economic side, *Quarterly Journal of Economics*, May 1924, and *Columbia Law Review*, May 1924, by Professor J.C. Bonbright; and, more technically at law, *Columbia Law Review*, January 1925, by A.A. Berle, Jr.

been called "flexible refinancing." For it was a universal statutory rule that, having once established a par value for capital shares, any issuance thereafter of more shares at less than this figure was unlawful – the reason, of course, being that it tended to dilute the worth of the securities first put out at the higher figure. So that here, too, corporations found themselves embarrassed when in need of further capital, being unable to raise moneys needed for development, in the event that the market price of the outstanding issues happened to be selling for less than $100, or what ever the stated par might be.

The entire campaign supporting the introduction of the new device of no-par stock consisted of presentation of its advantages, particularly the fact that the removal of the stated par value would permit new capital to be raised under all circumstances wherever existing market quotations might stand. And it was added, furthermore, that this possibility of financing by new stock issues tended equally to discourage the more dangerous resort to borrowings by the issue of bonds or short-time notes. All told, the device was appealing; it facilitated promotion, doing away with the disagreeable necessity of a contribution of stated amounts of money or of property; it loosened things up generally, and to that degree won its way to public acceptance. It was urged also that it tended to protect the investor against being deceived by false appearances. He was to contemplate a share of stock, not somehow as having inherently any definite value but as merely representing a fractional interest in the earnings and assets of the company. Thus – only vastly more in detail – were the advantages set forth. Some of us were skeptical from the start, perhaps over much so.[4] But since that time, as the wedge has little by little been driven home, it has become clear that the device is overflowing with possibilities of fraud and deception. All solid bench marks from which a financial history of any given enterprise may set forth are abolished, leaving in place thereof but constantly shifting sands. The possibilities of deception were perhaps never better exemplified than in the collapse of a promoter's dream in the failure of National Conduit and Cable in 1917. A long series of excesses in promotion, with escape from the liability which ought to attach thereto, is embodied in the records of our courts. The accountants are enabled to play

[4] Ripley, *Railroads: Finance and Organization,* 1915, p. 91.

ball with figures to an astounding degree. Our example from Dodge Brothers, Incorporated, on page 199 shows what may be done with so-called surplus. Another case, that of Di Georgio Fruit Corporation on page 196, demonstrates how readily true facts as to earnings may be concealed. Worst of all, as a menace to the public interest, is the issue of no-par shares in the field of public utilities. It is unquestionable that the scandalous stock watering which has placed the voting control of more than $1,500,000,000 of funds of the general public invested in public utilities in the hands of the common stockholders, who paid not a cent for their holdings, is directly traceable to misuse of this device.[5]

But, like most things on earth, human beings particularly, no-par stock is not altogether bad. It embodies a useful principle. It is indubitable that it affords relief from an undue inflexibility of financial set-up. Held within proper limits, it may confer this advantage, and yet be safeguarded against some of the evils which have just been set forth. The remedy is discoverable in the distinction between the laws on the subject in the two states of New York and California, and those of the two score or more other states which have legislated upon the subject. The state of New York having seen the light in 1923 put its house partially in order in this respect. It provided that whenever capital was represented by no-par shares that such stock nevertheless might have a stated value, that is to say that so and so many dollars of capital should be represented definitely by so and so many units of no-par capital stock. To be sure, New York still permitted true no-par shares to be emitted – shares, that is to say, which were not tagged with any fixed par value at issue. And for all of this second sort of no-par stock, the objections stated above as to let and license hold good. But as to the former sort the value of the consideration against which each piece of paper is put forth must be ex plicitly stated. For such stock there is a restoration of that old solid foundation which once prevailed for use of the accountants in starting their records. And the same thing is true for the lawyers, in their legitimate interest in protecting the public, by the assignment of a definite liability for a capital fund on the part of the promoters and the management. The corporation, however, while still required to start with a certain capital

[5] Cf. pp. 325, *et seq.*

fund, is in position to raise whatever additional capital is needed for growth. It may do this by the issuance of new shares at a stated figure but not necessarily the same as in the original forth-putting. The first issue might be at $100 per share, another at $33, and a third at $133. But always there should be a stated issue price, bringing to the corporate treasury that amount of new assets. Thus would "flexible refinancing" become a matter of fact and of record. This, then, is what ought to be done to clean up the situation.[6] New York and California ought to close out the present option which permits the issuance of true no-par stock. They should legitimatize only an issue with a stated par, permitting each lot, however, to stand upon its own feet as respects the issue price. And, the thirty or forty other states in the Union ought in the public interest to bring about the same result. For in so far as they fail to require a stated figure somewhere for each capital issue, the door hangs wide open for all sorts of financial jugglery. Nor, of course, can it be closed by the adoption of sound legislation by any two states, so long as the forty-odd others prefer for profit to pursue another course. Thus again are we brought face to face with this fundamental obstacle inherent in our governmental system.

There is a peculiar menace in the setting-off of a so-called initial surplus upon the creation of a corporation. This will be further developed in our chapter upon corporate publicity. But it should be noted in passing that the institution of no-par stock considerably widens the opportunity for resort to this unsafe distinction. The object of course of setting off at the outset a part of the capital contributed to form a corporation as initial surplus was to create the outward appearance of a fund dis tributable as dividends. The practice of stimulating markets by initiation of dividends upon small issues of preferred shares is a long-standing

[6] A section of the just proposed corporate code of Ohio, presented by a special committee of the State Bar Association, allows stock to be issued without par value: –

§ 13 (b) At any time or from time to time after organization, for such amount of consideration for each share (which amount shall be equal in respect of all the shares of the same class authorized to be issued at the same time) as may be fixed by the affirmative vote of the holders of a majority of the outstanding shares of the class to be issued, and like vote of the holders of shares of each class Junior thereto (regardless of limitations or restrictions on the voting power of any such classes) or by the board of directors when authorized by a like vote of the shareholders or by the articles.

one. The United States Steel Corporation, long before no-par stock was invented, started upon its career with a purely fictitious surplus of this kind amounting to $25,000,000. The misuse of the device in prospectuses which, among other things, mention the expectancy of shortly putting the new issue upon a dividend basis is nowadays frowned upon in conservative circles. No-par stock distinctly fends to enhance the danger of misrepresentation.

It has already been averred that no-par shares dovetail into all of the other iniquitous novelties at law which have been described, to constitute the groundwork for the culminating offense of all, disfranchisement of the public shareholder. In passing it may be well to drive this assertion home. Is it not obvious that the absolute and uncontrolled power afforded by these new charters to fix the price of each new issue of shares, independently of all the others, reduces the whole matter, as Berle puts it, "to the merest gamble on the integrity and judgment of the corporate officers and directors." Granted that these powers may not be so complete, actually, as the statutory language indicates, nevertheless proceedings in equity to correct a wrong once committed are wearisome, expensive, and time consuming. And there may be a limit to patience as well as to the resources of those who otherwise might have the courage to fight for their rights. For they must personally finance their campaigns, whereas the management is always in position to draw upon the corporate treasury. Again, is it not clear that all sorts of conflicts between different classes of shareholders in these complicated set-ups are certain to arise, enormously confused by rights of conversion of par into no-par, or no-par into par, back and forth every which way? Most of all is it not clear that this no-par device is utterly unsuited to all public-service companies wherein by all the principles of sound regulation the issue of securities ought not to exceed the actual amount of the investment? This must be true, for, were it ctherwise, there would be permitted the issuance of shares to represent goodwill, that is, shares which cost nothing but which merely represent capitalized earning power. It is a cardinal principle of sound public regulation that such capitalization of goodwill should not be. And inasmuch as the issuance of no-par shares cuts the ground from under any attempt to correlate closely the amount of the investment and a stated par value for the securities, it is clear that regulation and no-par shares are utterly incompatible one with another. A convincing demon stration of the difference between a no-par and a par value situation for public utilities is afforded by the recent financing of the Conowingo dam.[7] Most regrettable must it ever be that so much of the financing of our great public holding companies, as it will appear in the chapter on the subject, has been consummated without the healthful restraint which was imposed in this instance.

[7] Outlined on p. 325, *et seq.*

GIVING UP CONTROL: A BIRTHRIGHT FOR POTTAGE[1]

William Z. Ripley

Once upon a time, and it wasn't so long ago, either, – down in Boothbay, Maine, there were two brothers, John and James. Their last name was Doe. John, the elder, was quiet-eyed, slow-moving, and comfortable, tempera mentally. James was more jumpy, nimble-witted, ambitious to get on. One stayed on the farm; the other naturally gravitated to the city. In due season John's boy prepared to enter the academy at Damariscotta. Said his father: "Son, you're getting grown up. Suppose I die – you ought to have something all your own. I'm going to give you that best Jersey heifer. But you must remember to keep her well fed and healthy so that the milk will be pure. And keep her horns cut, in case she gets pernickety. Remember also that the fence in the northeast corner of the pasture is getting shaky. She might wander out on the highroad and upset somebody in a Ford. Because she's all yours, it's up to you to see that she behaves herself."

About the same time James, in the library of his city house, thus delivered himself to his son: "Now, Junior, before you go to college I want to give you my investment in the Boothbay Harbor Electric Light Company. This concern serves our old neighbors and friends, and I want you to feel a continuing interest in, and a responsibility for, our share in this local enterprise. If properly managed it should be a benefit to this community; and it will yield you an income to be applied to your education through the next few years. But you must never forget that you are partly responsible for this undertaking. Our family had a hand in starting it. That responsibility is an inseparable part of your ownership. I read something the other day, in an opinion by Justice Brandeis of the United States Supreme Court, which bears

[1] [Chapter 4 of *Main Street and Wall Street*, London: Brentano, 1927.]

this out: 'There is no such thing to my mind ... as an *innocent* stockholder. He may be innocent in fact, but socially he cannot be held innocent. He accepts the benefits of the system. It is his business and his obligation to see that those who represent him carry out a policy which is consistent with the public welfare.' He is right in that. This accountability for wealth underlies and justifies the whole institution of private property upon which the government of our great country is founded."

Thus did two men, good and true according to their several lights, recognize the public obligation that attaches to wealth. But how different were the results! The son of John, under the old simple conditions, continued to cherish, and in the community to stand sponsor for, his Jersey heifer. But with the son of James complications speedily developed. First of all, the Central Maine Power Company, heading up in Augusta, induced a majority of the stockholders in the local corporation, which, by the way, seems not to have been doing very well, to exchange their holdings for shares of the larger concern. There was nothing else for it but to follow along. Then a great consolidation was announced. It was headed by the Middle West Utilities Company, incorporated in Delaware, which took over the Central Maine Power Company and made it a part of an intermediate corporation, known as the New England Public Service Company, which through the Manchester Traction Light and Power Company and the National Light and Power Company (which latter itself owned the Twin State Power Company and the Vermont Hydro-Electric Company) covered all northern New England. Thus, by the close of 1923, the son of James had become a partner with 53,999 others in a joint investment of over $52,000,000 *in stocks alone*. The main office of the company had moved to Chicago (the annual meeting still being held in Delaware, however). The little New England corporation was now indissolubly bound up with five others in Illinois, three in Indiana, three in Kentucky, two in Oklahoma, one in Oklahoma and Texas, one in Missouri, one in Michigan, two in Nebraska, two in Virginia, one in Wisconsin, and one in Tennessee. This was the chain, constituted of many links, which made up the sole and tenuous connection between the son of James and his original electric light investment. It began to look indeed as if the days of the simple life and of direct responsibility of ownership were by way of passing in the field of public utilities in New England.

James and his son, thus lost in the shuffle of public utility corporations, turned to the field of private enterprise, in which, as they had been told, personal initiative still held sway, free from the deadening influence of governmental supervision. They perused the offerings of securities in the press by well-known and responsible firms. Might they not hope to acquire direct ownership in corporations which themselves managed the business? The first stumbling block was the holding corporation. They had become used to this complicated financial device in the large concerns like the United States Steel Corporation or the General Motors Company. They sought for less stupendous undertakings. One banking house offered gold notes which invited participation in the affairs, not of the Kaufmann Department Stores, Incorporated, "conducting the largest department-store business in the city of Pittsburgh," but only of a holding company, the Kaufmann Department Stores Securities Corporation, a finance or intermediate company. An other offering was of Stern Brothers, New York, "one of the oldest and best-known department stores in the United States," but "to ensure continuity of management and policy the common shares will be placed in a voting trust." Perhaps they sought an interest in the biggest hardware company in the United States. They found, however, that the Associated Simmons Hardware Companies merely controlled an immense business in St. Louis, deriving their status as a legal trust from Massachusetts. The DeForest Radio Company offering was yet otherwise eviscerated of all possible voting power by another kind of voting trust.

Coca-Cola sounded refreshing. A company chartered in Georgia turns Out some 25,000,000 gallons of a popular beverage, presumably at a profit. The stock is publicly listed and very widely held. But some 251,000 of its 500,000 shares were found to be lodged in the hands of a knot of insiders, incorporated as the Coca-Cola International Company. No shares of this corporation which held control were listed or available as a purchase to James or his son. Answering an advertisement of securities of the Associated Gas and Electric Company, they found that its business was really conducted at the office of the Associated Gas and Electric Securities Corporation – another finance company? From Armour and Company of Delaware, whose common stock was all owned by Armour and Company of Illinois, down to the latest offering of a dairy-products concern, every thing was tied up in this way. Hopeless indeed did it appear that any uninitiated public investor could understand, much less participate intelligently in, any of these affairs.

Nor was James wholly blameless for the loss of direct contact and responsibility between his son and his investment. For, finding himself getting on in years and being mindful of the mutability of human affairs, he might have taken out a charter as "James Doe, Ltd." – better, perhaps, than "Inc.," because carrying the suggestion, among other things, of a limited liability for inheritance taxes. His son and his wife, holding practically all of the stock in this immortal creation, no investments coming to them upon his death would cause a ripple in the Probate Courts. Or he might have put his possessions in a private trust, managing it himself as trustee during his lifetime, thereby splitting up the income and still further reducing taxes. Or the management of this "living trust" might have been turned over to a professional trust company. And any one of these agencies might in turn have purchased "Collateral Trustee Shares in the New England Investment Trust, Incorporated, the First National Bank of Boston, Trustee," or some similar investment concern, properly enough intended through diversification to spread the risk. And, finally, there was the life-insurance policy, based entirely upon investments to be handled by these great fiduciary corporations for him as agent, at the longest possible range.

What an amazing tangle this all makes of the theory that ownership of property and responsibility for its efficient, farsighted, and public-spirited management shall be linked the one to the other. Even the whole theory of business profits, so painstakingly evolved through years of academic ratiocination, goes by the board. All the managers, that is to say the operating men, are working on salary, their returns, except on the side, being largely independent of the net result of company operation year by year. The motive of self-interest may even have been thrown into the reverse, occasionally, so far as long-time upbuilding in contradistinction to quick turnover in corporate affairs is concerned. And what has become of the relation between labor and capital? What guaranty may possibly be given by the *real owners* to the working class that there shall not be taken from it an opportunity for future welfare and development as a result of these changes? The protracted struggle of the textile workers in 1926 at Passaic, New Jersey, has undoubtedly been prolonged by the absentee ownership and involved financial structure of some of the companies, the Botany Worsted Mills in particular. Veritably the institution of private property, underlying our whole civilization, is threatened at the root unless we take heed. The situation is not inaptly described by the colored candidate for the ministry, confronted by the request of the examining Board of Preachers to name some character in the Bible and then to relate all that he knew about it. "Ah thinks Ah 'll take Jezebel. Jezebel, she was a hussy, a-settin' up at a winder when David come down along th'u' Jerusalem. An' she hollered at 'im. An' he said, 'Ef I got a frien' up there, let him th'ow 'er down.' An' 'e had a frien' up there, an' 'e th'ow'd 'er down. An' David said, 'Let 'im th'ow 'er down again.' An' 'e th'ow'd 'er down again. An' David said, 'Let 'im th'ow 'er down, seventy times seven.' An' 'e th'ow'd 'er down seventy times seven. An' she busted into a thousand pieces. An' they gathered up the fragments that nothin' be lost. An' de question are: *Whose wife am she at de Reserrecshum?*" It is a query which might well be propounded at this time to several millions of our fellow citizens, in so far as they are part owners in the $70,000,000,000 capitalization of American corporations, according to the federal tax returns, in the year of our Lord 1923.

Thus far, however, the multiplication of these entanglements constitutes no innovation. They have been going on for a long time, insidiously undermining the principle of accountability. The individual and partnership forms of business organization disappeared in favor of the corporation even before the war. Well-nigh a thousand companies are now listed on the New York Stock Exchange alone – 163 railroads and 763 other corporations in 1924. But since the World War, and particularly in this heyday of prosperity, the facile initiating and legal minds have hit upon something better yet – and something, furthermore, which puts once and for all at rest the last vestige of power of participation of the owners of property in prudent and efficient management. The two twelvemonths, 1924-25, promise to go down in history – like the Year of the Plague, or the Year of the Big Wind – as the Years of the Split Common Stock and the Vanishing Stockholder.[2]

[2] W. H. S. Stevens's "Stockholders' Voting Rights and the Centralization of Voting Control" *(Quarterly Journal of Economics,* May 1926, pp. 352–392) is the most complete catalogue of the existing practice.

Since the days of old Blackstone the corporation, as we have seen, has been likened to a "little republic" set up for the accomplishment of some private purpose. And, the essence of full democracy being the exercise of the franchise, there appears to have been but little restriction of the voting rights of shareholders. For railroads this has always been true. Both the preferred and common shares of such companies have been commonly full voting issues. Apparently the practice of setting off preferred shareholders as nonvoting had not been invented when the great development of industrial combinations from 1898 to 1903 occurred, during which time approximately two hundred of our so-called trusts came upon the stage. The reason for this is obvious. Most of the individual concerns which went into such combinations as the Steel Corporation, the American Woolen Company, or the American Shipbuilding Company were in part acquired by inducing the owners of these concerns to accept preferred shares in payment for their interests. The amount of these particular issues was in those days adjusted to the tangible assets, leaving the common shares to represent the equity. The value of these common shares was thus made dependent upon successful management. But it was unlikely, therefore, that, having thus committed themselves to participation in the new enterprise by taking preferred stock, the former owners should have been willing to relinquish entirely their share in management. An occasional company – International Silver, for instance, or Federal Mining and Smelting, or Royal Baking Powder Company – somewhat restricted the franchise for its preferred shareholders; but not even as late as 1911-12, when the great merchandising companies made their appearance, does the full significance of this device seem to have been appreciated. And then, little by little, came the practice of setting off the preferred shareholders, depriving them of the right of participating in the election of management. Nor yet, thus far, was there any distinction introduced among various classes of the common shareholders.

The latest invention for prying people loose from their possessions now splits up these common shares. To be in the mode one has, let us call it, a "Class A participating" common stock, with a first lien on earnings after satisfaction of all prior claims of preferred stocks and bonds. This leaves a "Class B" common stock representing, according to circumstances, the cream, the scum, the froth, or the sediment of the business; for the full voting rights attach exclusively to these Class B common shares, none, or only a minority, of which are offered to the public at all. The appetite for the preferred shares may sometimes be whetted by a flavoring of the Class A common shares, but not of those which carry votes. "Dodge Brothers, Incorporated," is typical. A banking house buys up a private business for, it has been said, $146,000,000 or thereabouts. This sum, and more too, they recover – if the plan works out – by the sale to the public, for $160,000,000 of bonds and preferred stock at par and 1,500,000 *nonvoting* shares of Class A common stock. But not a single one of the 500,000 Class B voting (no-par) common shares is thus sold. The promoters have virtually paid themselves a handsome profit for the assumption of the entire directorial power, having mortgaged the property to the full amount of its original cost through outstanding bonds and preferred stock, including both assets and capitalized earning power. And the amazing thing is that this final deathblow to the exercise of voting rights by the general public has brought no voice of protest. Yet the plan bears every appearance of a bald and outrageous theft of the last tittle of responsibility for management of the actual owners by those who are setting up these latest financial erections. Isn't it the prettiest case ever known of having a cake and eating it too?

Perhaps the baldest case is of an artificial-silk concern, the Industrial Rayon Corporation, with 598,000 shares of nonvoting Class A stock distributed to the public with the reservation of the remaining 2000 out of 600,000 shares, as Class B stock, carrying exclusive voting rights. Or the invitation to participate in a well-known root-beer enterprise with 180,000 shares of Class A and Class B common shares with the concentration of control in 3872 "Management Shares." It savors rather of supererogation to add in the prospectus, "The management of the company will remain unchanged and continue in charge of the members of the Hires family." Or take, if you please, a well-known theatre enterprise, said to have over $20,000,000 in assets. There will be 4,000,000 shares – 3,900,000 Class A shares to be sold to you and me, and 100,000 Class B shares, in which will be vested exclusive control through voting rights. The Class A and Class B stock participate in dividends on exactly the same basis. But all of the power over management is stripped from one and conferred upon the other.

Universal Chain Theatres Corporation hits the bull's eye hard. First there is an issue of $4,000,000 of first preferred stock. This is followed by $2,000,000 of second preferred. Then come 199,000 shares of no-par common stock. Who is to run the concern? Why, the happy holders of "Management Stock," of course! This issue is created, defined, protected by reservations of all kinds, and exclusively reserved, without cost, by the people whose name it bears – The Management. The share of the public is simple. All it has to do is to put up the money. The Management does the rest.

Nor do these amazing arrangements set modest time limits for themselves. Voting trusts have been compelled to do so by the courts, their duration customarily being limited to ten years. One company, which proposed in 1926 to solicit public investment through the usual channels, arranged for so-called "Management Stock," a few hundred shares only. Voting rights for the public, invited to subscribe to Class A and Class B common shares, were to be equal all round, "except for the election of Directors at stockholders' meetings held on or before December 31, 1960." This particular charter then goes on to provide: "All shares of Management Stock shall be nonassignable and nontransferable, to the end that at no time shall any of the rights incident to the holding of shares of Management Stock in any manner be vested in or exercised by or on behalf of or for the benefit of any other than the three persons named above. Any attempt by any one of such three holders . . . in any manner to transfer or assign any legal or equitable right, title, or interest in respect thereof, or the death of any such holder of shares of Management Stock, shall *ipso facto* operate as a conversion of such shares into Class B Common Stock," and so forth. But hold! All is not lost. "On and after January 1, 1961 (or on and after any earlier date upon which all of the Management Stock shall have been converted), all shares of all classes of stock shall have equal voting rights on all questions." What a delightful plot to develop into a story like Frank Stockton's inimitable *The Wrong Box!* What fun to see how such a plan for control would ultimately work out in a quarter century or so!

There is no concealment about all this. It is perfectly open and above board. But who, we ask, under these circumstances has really given a hostage to fortune, to the public, or to the employees for honest and economic management of the business? The promoters stand to lose only the amount of their stake – a minus quantity in dollars in so far as the nonvoting shares have been made to cover not only the value of the tangible assets but the prospective capitalization of earnings. It is the public stockholders, the consumer and the wage earner, who stand to lose in event of misdirection. How can there be other than a whirlwind of abuse of power under such conditions?

Nor is it our great basic industries which are being swept by this plague. Most of the great combinations had their rise twenty-five years ago, with a minor outbreak in 1911-12. To-day it is neither the Steel Corporation nor the Harvester Trust nor the railroads which are following these newly beaten paths. Look at the newspaper offerings. The public is buying out the mail-order, chain, and department stores, foodstuff manufacturers, the makers of washing machines, refrigerators, confectionery, make-believe-silk stockings, toilet and beauty preparations, music, tags and napkins, phonograph records, pianos and radio outfits, theatres, our daily bread, our ice cream, root beer, cake, and even our homemade pies. At this rate every conceivable article of direct or indirect consumption will soon be more or less in the hands of the general public.

Most disconcerting is it when this latest financial development invades the field of public utilities, already sufficiently cluttered up with holding companies and trusts. The older and conservative companies are above criticism. But one takes exception to the offerings of the Southern Gas and Power Corporation, with an authorized note issue of $2,000,000 preferred stock $5,000,000, and Class A 250,000 shares, leaving the exclusive voting power, except in case of default in cumulative dividends, in 100,000 shares of "common stock, without par value." It is these last which are not offered to the public at all. This organization controls operating companies in thirty-seven communities, scattered over eight different states. Was there ever a clearer case in an essential public industry of what has been well defined by an expert as "one of the besetting sins of modern corporations ... the custom of trading on a thin equity, control resting in the hands of common stock holders, while the funds are supplied by the sale of preferred stocks and bonds"? Had this author written in 1925, he would have added "and even of a large number of common shares which have been stripped of voting power." Then he would have hit several nails squarely on the head with one rap of the hammer.

Much confusion nowadays doubtless results all along the line because of the necessary intermingling of entirely different functions which has accompanied the growth in the size of the business unit. Callings have become sufficiently specialized to constitute each a profession by itself. Bankers, on the one hand, have, sometimes perhaps against their will, sometimes by veritable force of it, been projected into the centre of an industrial situation. A business may have outgrown the financial capacity of the purely operating men. Indeed this happens whenever the business, whether it be New England Cotton Yarn, American Beaver Board Company, or the Goodyear Tire and Rubber Company, becomes overextended, as so many did in 1920. But the banker, thus assuming industrial responsibilities, has an entirely different perspective from the operating man. His attention tends to gravitate toward the marketing of securities, the course of quotations, and the like. He has an interest in dividends in their relation to market quotations rather than in their relation to mechanical processes. His shortcomings, standing alone, are as evident as are those of the operating staff. The operating people, on the other hand, are always calling for more money for amplification of facilities, without always perhaps having clearly in mind the possibility of earning a satisfactory return thereon. They want to see the wheels go round. The banker's query is first and foremost: How much will it cost and what will be the return?

This contrariety of interest, even under the best of circumstances, is apt to lead to strain and misunderstanding. On the other hand, it is equally awkward when operating men, by reason of the growth in magnitude of a business, find themselves overburdened with great problems in finance. The failure of Westinghouse in 1907 was distinctly due to the inability of a great engineer to envisage the financial future. The collapse of Rumeley Company eight years later is traceable to the same defect in personnel. The fact is that two distinct and yet interrelated activities dovetail into one another in great enterprises. And whenever either the banker on the one side or the operating man on the other seeks to go it alone there is like to be disaster. Each needs to lean upon the other. But inherently it is more often the banker, the financial man, who in the struggle for survival comes out on top. This it is which creates the situation wherein the power of the banker, springing at bottom from the use of the funds of all the people, is first applied to subjugation of the operating group; and then, to cap the climax, seeks to reduce the great body of the shareholders to subjection. This is the situation we find confronting the United States in 1925.

Nor is the situation peculiar to our own country. It springs from the overelaboration of the device of the stock corporation. An example in England is strikingly depicted by A. G. Gardiner in his *Portraits and Portents,* recently published. The pyramiding of control of the British press by Lord Rothermere, through majority ownership of the 700,000 shares of the Daily Mirror Newspapers, Limited, enables him to control a share and loan capital valued on the Stock Exchange at £24,000,000. The financial editor of the *Nation* thus describes it: "Lord Rothermere assumes a minimum of personal risk ... The public put up the big money and Lord Rothermere kept control." Thus is created "the master of the greatest machine of publicity the world has ever seen."

A technically correct and restrained description of the existing situation is this one by A. A. Berle, Jr.:[3] "The investment banking house is invariably in the centre of a web of economic interests, to which it renders a real service and from which it derives a real return, but which affords possibilities for profitable transactions not necessarily benefiting the controlled corporations. While the banker's action may be adequately regulated by a high sense of banking ethics which largely prevails among reputable houses, the law can hardly leave investors subject to the doubtful protection of private consciences."

From England there happens to come news of an apposite occurrence. It depicts a financial shipwreck, wherein it is impossible to fix the blame upon anybody in particular. British Controlled Oil Fields, Limited, has just collapsed, with a resultant loss of about two-thirds of the original capital, which amounted to £45,000,000. Everybody seems to disown responsibility for the debacle which took place in 1926. The voting trustees declare that their trust was created primarily to prevent the capture of control by foreign interests and that "the management of the company's affairs does not come within the ambit of their powers." The directorate, on the other hand, – which is now ousted, – apparently points to the real source of power as resident

[3] *Harvard Law Review,* April 1926.

in the trustees. And thus, while each puts the blame on the other, the shareholders foot the quite considerable bill.

A most engaging picture of the banker's function in industry is presented by one of the proponents of the modernist practices. Says De Roode:– "We cannot regard what I call organization capital in the same light that you regard investment capital ... Investment capital properly speaking looks for a return in the nature of interest; organization capital does not figure on interest, it figures on profit ... There is no need of pretending that it is not so. The people who put a big industry together want to sell it; they want to sell it at a profit ... They want to retain control because they are always left with some holdings in it."

Or again: "The economic value of nonvoting stock is that it effects economy in distribution and enables the investor to participate in industry more cheaply and hence more profitably ... A large amount of capital, for example, is necessary to finance the combination of a group of industries or enterprises. This capital will not go into such financing unless it obtains control. If to maintain such control this initial capital or a large part of it must be kept permanently in the enterprise, a higher price must be charged for that part of the capital which is sold to the public.

"Now this financing capital, or what we might call 'organization capital,' is frankly not content with the mere return obtainable from the industry. This capital is not looking for a return upon an investment; it wants profit ...

"If, on the other hand, therefore, the mechanism of nonvoting stock control may remain with the organizers and the greater part of their capital be quickly released, the price to the investor for participation can be .
much less than where control is dependent upon organization capital remaining permanently in the enterprise.

"In other words, this organization capital gets a quick and relatively small profit and, retaining control, moves on to the next enterprise." [Our italics.]

Was there ever drawn a more entrancing picture than this of the banker's function in industry? This busy "organization capital" bee, "with honied thigh," in Milton's words, buzzes from one flowery situation to another, extracting the precious nectar of control and just incidentally powdering the public with the preferred pollen.

There is of late another financial practice, also, which greatly accentuates this nullification of the ordinary share holder. This is the wide distribution of stock to employees and the consumers of the corporation's product, whether electric service, steel, or what not.[4] The effect in any event is bound to be cumulative with that of the insinuation of professional management power between ownership and operation.

Corporations have always been susceptible to control by concentration of voting power. Far less than half of the capital stock may be as effective for such control as possession of an actual majority. But it is elemental – requiring no proof – that, the larger the number of share holders, the more easily may a small concentrated block of minority shares exercise sway over all the rest. With a dozen owners, probably 51 per cent will be necessary for dominance. With 300,000 scattered holdings, a possible 15 or 20 per cent of the votes can never be over-matched at an election. In 1923 there were 250,000 new stockholders registered in the electric light and power companies alone. The total number of stockholders in all sorts of concerns has almost doubled since 1900, rising to an aggregate of 14,423,000 in 1923. These shareholders now possess over $70,000,000,000 worth of stock at par, on the showing of the federal income tax returns. Such possession used to be confined to the wealthy and the well-to-do class. Now it comprehends the small house holder and large numbers of wage earners. The former concentration of wealth is now yielding place to so wide a diffusion as to call for public recognition by way of legislation or oversight. But the important point to note is that the wider the diffusion of ownership the more readily does effective control run to the intermediaries. Financially, the matter is dangerous, for it tends to transform a contingent outstanding charge upon earnings into virtually fixed charges thereon. The cessation of dividends, either to employee holders or to consumers, is bound to be so productive of discontent and unrest that every nerve will be strained to the utmost, even over long, to prevent their cessation.

It is at just this point that some of the provisions at law, particularly those which abrogate the shareholder's rights to participate in new issues of securities, come into play. Such clauses, with devilish ingenuity, look sound enough above the water line; but

[4] For further details consult Chapter XI, *infra*.

they certainly will not stand examination in dry dock. For not only has the shareholder parted with every vestige of control of the enterprise represented by his investment, but now he makes a free gift of such rights as may accrue, resulting from future growth of the property. Heretofore it has been a fundamental rule in corporation law that there shall be no discrimination whatsoever between shareholders. Discrimination there may be between creditors and owners; but by this device even the common share holders are now set off, to the end that an inordinate share, if indeed not all, of the increment of profits in future shall attach to the holdings of those who are "in the know."

Why do stockholders submit to such indignity? The technique is simple, relying upon a fundamental attribute of human nature. Mr. Robert F. Herrick of Boston, in a frank address on holding companies, describing the manner in which the exchange of shares in one corporation for those of another may be brought about, thus puts it: "All the stockholders act like a flock of sheep. In the main they follow the lead of the directors, and if the details of carrying the plan through are so arranged that the stock in the new company has an apparent money value greater than the stock of the old company for which it is offered, the exchange once started takes place generally, and when a majority of the stock in the companies is exchanged, practically the consolidation is effected." There you have it in the words of an expert!

The docility of corporate shareholders permitting themselves to be honeyfugled or dragooned into exchanging securities of one corporation for another, is responsible for a considerable part of the loss of shareholders' rights of one kind or another nowadays. We are now in the midst of a veritable mania for such horse trades. This is what "Magpie" in the *Stock Exchange Gazette* of London has to say about it: –

> I understand that holders of Lago Oil and Transport will shortly be offered Pan-American B shares in the ratio of one for every three Lago shares held. Not long ago these Lago shares were given out in exchange for Lago Petroleum shares, which in their turn were distributed in exchange for British Equatorial Oil shares. I always have a feeling that the share holders are losing something when they are offered these exchanges, for I am quite sure that the Americans don't give any thing away;

> but if the majority accept, it is generally advisable to join with them, because it is awkward for the individual shareholder to be left with shares which have no market.

In the field of public utilities the hoodwinking of the shareholders out of the franchise is going on apace. Preferred stockholders in a company – Virginia Railway and Power, for instance – may have been entitled to six-per-cent dividends, noncumulative but possessed of voting power. The invitation to exchange for new seven per-cent cumulative preferred shares is too inviting to permit question as to whether the elimination of voting power is worth while or not. Possibly this abrogation of voting rights is essential to the building-up of an efficient combination. In this instance it looks as if it were.

Possibly also the charter provisions afford adequate protection to this particular issue. But the loss of the shareholder's right to vote is no less a fact. In another instance of one of these public utility companies the shareholders in the original company, incorporated in West Virginia, had the right of cumulative voting. But, having exchanged their stock for a Delaware corporation, they woke up to find themselves stripped of that rather valuable right. A somewhat similar elimination of the franchise by a rearrangement of subsidiaries in the American Light and Traction Company seems recently to have been thwarted by the resolute opposition of a minority which discovered the fact in time. And so it goes with these shareholder sheep. As long as an offer "looks good" they follow the leader, even though the circumstances as respects their rights may be "as dark as the inside of a cow," to borrow a phrase from the Kentucky mountaineers.

It will be objected that no real change is involved in these recent tendencies: that stockholders never did, and never will, exercise their voting rights. in fact the great trouble, oftentimes, is to secure enough proxies in widely owned corporations to validate the acts of their directors. But the fact remains that the power, even if rarely exercised, and then only under extreme provocation, was there; and every once in a blue moon some resolute individual or stockholder could rise in his place and organize a protective committee or dissenting group – and, if nothing else happened, at least there was a thorough ventilation of what sometimes proved to be a musty or unsafe tenement. Furthermore, one of the most encouraging things in life is the influence that can be wielded by an individual, acting almost single-handed and alone, to confront and often to overcome a corporate Goliath, provided he has the right on his side. My mind runs to the extermination of the Louisiana Lottery by a former colleague, Professor Homer Woodbridge: think of it – professor of heating and ventilation at the Massachusetts Institute of Technology! Or recall what Charles and Philip Cabot achieved in bringing about the elimination of the seven-day week and the twelve-hour day in the United States Steel Corporation! Or Lois Burnett Rantoul, undauntedly facing down every corporate influence in the Massachusetts Legislature, and bringing about the enactment of the first eight-hour-day law for women and children in the United States! Such things as these give one good heart, leading to the belief that the power of personality, alone, may win the most astonishing victories in the face of overwhelming odds. But all such achievement in this field of management of property is closed out forever once the people who own that property have allowed themselves to be utterly divorced from the exercise of their natural right to elect the directors and to influence, if not to determine, the corporate policy. For by such an abdication they give themselves over, body and soul – becoming mere wards, *non compos mentis,* so far as control over their own affairs is concerned. It is all so absurd, theoretically, that it seems incredible. Yet here are the facts!

But if the trend of corporation law and practice has been so consistently in the direction of diminishing rather than of accentuating the responsibility and accountability of the real property-owners, what is to be done about it? This, to my thinking, is a matter of vital concern to the successful functioning of our capitalistic system. For, at this particular juncture, the final deathblow to such accountability seems to be in the very act of delivery. Many suggestions have been made from time to time; some of them have already been successfully applied to our railroads. A few now bear upon our other public utilities. But absolutely nothing has yet been done to stem the current, much less to reverse it, as respects private business corporations. Something, to be sure, has been accomplished in the way of enforcement of liability for downright mismanagement or negligence, as against directors. But all such remedies, even when successfully invoked, – as for example on the New Haven Railroad, in the Old Dominion Copper suit, or in the well-known

American Grass Twine and American Malting Company proceedings about 1903, – are but cases of hanging the murderer after the innocent victim has expired. The reliance upon the courts, also, at best entails protracted and expensive litigation. Furthermore, too great an increase of such liability of directors, with the possible harassment of blackmailing or other proceedings, might readily enough make it impossible in future to secure the services of really able and responsible persons. Something may possibly be accomplished in this direction, but other and simpler remedies would seem to lie more nearly within reach.

Why not restrain the holding company? "Swat it!" says one public spokesman. I would do so; yet ever with a nice discernment. The fly – bluebottle, horse, domestic, or gad – is always a pest. Not so the finance corporation. It has its proper place and function in the scheme of things. But within that domain it should be rigidly confined. The very complexity of our form of government, involving relationships which transcend state boundaries, almost inevitably brings forth a litter of creations deriving their powers from the governments of the different commonwealths. This is a necessary outcome of the local demand for compliance with local needs. Piling of one corporation upon another also simplifies finance and management, augmenting credit and enabling largescale operation and the employment of higher-paid technicians. But it is also true that a large part of this complexity is the result of a deliberate intent to assume and concentrate power in the hands of an inner circle. The primary test of good faith is mathematical. When the Associated Merchants Company (of Connecticut) controlled, as it once did, the H. B. Claflin (dry goods) Company (of New Jersey), which in turn owned the operating H. B. Claflin and Company (in New York), by ownership of *45,001 out of 90,000* total shares, appearances are certainly against the arrangement; but when, as in the Continental or Purity Baking Corporations, recently set up, a bona fide attempt is made to secure *all* of the shares in the many operating concerns, the advantage and even the necessity of the plan are obvious.

Wade Ellis, the then attorney-general of Ohio, speaking twenty years ago, stated, in words which now seem prophetic, the case against the holding company: –

> "This is the most effective, the most invidious, and the cheapest of all combinations in restraint of trade. It is the most effective because, while agreements, and especially unlawful ones, may easily be broken, a transfer of the stock puts the bargain beyond the power of any conspirator to escape. It is the most invidious because, while it conceals all, it fears no exposure. It is the cheapest because it requires less money to buy a controlling interest in the stock of the competing companies than it does to buy their property, and yet the promoters have the use of the investment of all the minority holders in all the corporations brought under their control. In fact it generally requires no money at all, for the stock in the subsidiary companies is paid for in the stock of the holding company. Thus a vast industry is brought under the domination of manipulators whose circulating medium would not be a legal tender anywhere except on the stage."

I venture to suggest the possibility of drawing the line between the use of such a device to concentrate control in the hands of insiders, contrary to public policy, and the performance of its legitimate function in the field of business. What a dull and rigid life as human beings we should be compelled to lead, if our backbones were fashioned all in one piece. Even a corporation, to my thinking, may benefit from a proper amount of articulation. But it need not be a vaudeville contortionist, for all that!

What shall be said of the proposition that bondholders should be given voting rights, *pari passu* with the stock holders? One of the first acts of Governor Roosevelt of New York in 1900 was to appoint a special commission to draw up a model Companies Act. Section 61 of this proposed statute made it permissive to confer voting power upon debenture- and bond-holders "equal and equivalent to the stockholders." The corporate code of Delaware expressly provides for such a grant by articles of association. Most eminent legal talent supports this contention with reference to railroads. I have always believed it desirable and feasible whenever it is apparent that the real capital in the enterprise was provided through the sale of bonds, leaving the stock merely to represent real or anticipated capitalized earning power. Too often in the early days this used to be true of railroads. Many of them, however, have now waxed prosperous enough to fill out the measure of their financial clothes. The present situation among purely private corporations, in this instant wave of transformation, thoroughly supports the proposition that for many of these companies practically all of the real capital is advanced either by bondholders or by those who hold preferred stocks, which are in reality bonds. They are bonds in every vital respect, except that they have no foreclosure rights. But the preferred stocks have been bereft of all voting power, except and until the cessation of dividends. The amount of them issued, moreover, coupled with the Class A participating or nonvoting common stock, not unusually nowadays equals the full measure of material assets, plus capitalized present and prospective earning power. The proposition to enfranchise the bondholders, at least, is yet further fortified by the fact that the great life-insurance companies, which ordinarily confine their investments to bonds, have at their disposal expert financial talent of a high order, which might serve most acceptably upon the directorates of many of these companies – say, for example, public service corporations of the larger purely private business concerns.

The objection offered whenever I have advanced this proposition is that the bondholder is a "money lender" and that his intrusion into management "ignores the private property rights of the stockholder." Stockholders, forsooth! Who are they, indeed, in Dodge Brothers, Incorporated, where the only real stockholders – that is to say, those who have any power of direction – are bankers who have, for a handsome consideration to them selves, condescended to strip all the voting power from three quarters of the common shares – that portion alone which is sold to the public. Perhaps somebody will have the temerity to maintain that the remaining quarter – of Class B common shares, having "exclusive voting powers for all purposes," which the bankers retain for control as exclusively represents the real owners of the property. Tush! Everybody else is no more a stockholder, so far as management is concerned, than is the elevator boy or the apple woman on the corner.

Another pulmotor for the possible resuscitation of this moribund stockholders' responsibility is that of cumulative voting. For ten years past it has been my privilege to serve as a director of the Rock Island Railway, whose ancient charter, Section 9, permits each stockholder either to vote "for as many persons as there are directors to be elected, or to cumulate such shares and give one candidate as many votes as the number of directors, multiplied by the number of his shares of stock, shall equal, or distribute them on the same principle among as many candidates as he shall think fit." That proviso put a watchful minority at the switch, at least until such time as mutual confidence and friendly relations all round had cleared up the situation. Thus is the standard provided of at least a temporary two-party system, which conforms to the praiseworthy criterion set by the *Railway Age,* "that there should be someone continuously watching the detailed operation of the road in the interest of stockholders, other than the controlling interests, and in the interest of bond- and note-holders." Many of the great British banks, including the Bank of England and the London Westminster, graduate the voting power of shares, to prevent superdomination by the large stockholders. Granted that the proposal needs safeguarding, to prevent obstructive and hold-up tactics, it nevertheless embodies a principle worth consideration. We ought to be adopting the practice to-day, instead of splitting off the management shares from the main body of the capitalization.

The principle involved in cumulative voting is well stated in the original Michigan Corporation Law of 1885, reënacted in 1921. This provides that all shareholders shall have "the right to vote in person or by proxy, according to the number of shares of stock owned by him for as many persons as there may be directors to be elected, or to accumulate such shares and give one candidate as many votes as will equal the number of directors multiplied by the number of shares of his stock; or to distribute them on the same principle among as many candidates as he shall think fit." This particular statute has had a significant history. During the last forty years it has been repeatedly attacked, whittled down, actively debated, over and over again, the attack and defense being clearly distinguishable as springing, the one from the legal mind in direct employment of business interests, the other from the general sentiment that the law was fair and reasonable. Some ten other commonwealths, more or less, now permit corporate elections to be handled in this fashion. Pennsylvania even goes so far as to require that all elections under the Pennsylvania charter shall be so conducted. The principle was actively endorsed as far back as 1880 under an investigation made by the New York Chamber of Commerce. Governor Roosevelt's Commission in 1900 recommended the adoption generally. First-class corporate authority, however, both lay and legal, recognizes its validity for the purpose of tempering unduly autocratic management. And it is of interest that the device has been quite widely adopted in Europe; so-called "plural voting" shares being quite common both in France and in Germany. Yet curiously enough the object in these countries seems to have been to prevent seizure of control by foreign capital – a measure of protection against aggression rather than a re-enforcement of minority interests. Obviously the knife cuts both ways, but the right of cumulative voting would seem to make for a somewhat keener competition for first place and power than now, to that degree serving as a check upon inefficiency and as an incentive to meritorious performance. As a practical matter, however, it must be confessed that in states like Michigan, which have pottered with the practice for many years, little seems to have been accomplished. Yet all agree that, when factional strife develops, the device operates beneficially for the protection of the minority. It is agreed, furthermore, that the existence of the law prevents friction and has been of substantial and constructive value for that reason. It is said to operate like a policeman's club – "only occasionally used, but it serves a very useful purpose and while idle does no harm."

Inside control in practice often relies upon the voting rights attaching to floating stock in the market – that is to say, stock which is passing so rapidly from hand to hand that for convenience' sake it remains often for many years registered in the name of banking or brokerage houses. And in the case of non-dividend-paying corporations the proportion of such floating stock may be so great as, in and of itself, to carry control. And a system not unlike logrolling among Congressmen, under such circumstances, enables interchange and common under standing along the "Street" to perpetuate control by those who may not in fact have a dollar of actual stake in an enterprise. It has been proposed to disfranchise such floating stock. It might be serviceable to do so; but the practical difficulties in the way of carrying out such a plan seem to me insuperable.

The only thing that seems to keep the world going under the law of natural survival is that, whenever a pest develops, in the course of its spread it is almost certain to run into a parasite or an antidote which ultimately restrains or overcomes the epidemic. Such was the experience with the gypsy moth and the browntail moth in Massachusetts. Even the English sparrow seems at last to have met its match in the struggle for existence. So in this matter of control wrested from the natural owners, several agencies seem to be evolving which may in time automatically operate as important checks upon its spread. One of these is the device of the so-called investment trust, and to a lesser degree the advent of the new profession of investment counsel. As for these trusts, long current in England, the result of pooling by their means the investments of many people is, of course, not only to spread the risk but at the same time to render more nearly articulate the interest of the combined shareholders. While one hundred small stockholders in the Pennsylvania Railroad or the Steel Corporation might separately have no standing in court, if they consolidated their investments through taking shares in a trust set up for the purpose, they might in the aggregate win a foothold in corporate councils. If suitably developed under proper safeguards, these concentrated investments, handled by competent persons who devote their entire time and attention to the matter, might well participate in corporate government in an intelligent and entirely helpful way.

The professional investment trusts for profit are rapidly multiplying in numbers. Along with them are interesting developments exemplified in the creation at Columbia University of the so-called Faculty Investment Fund. This was set up in 1926. The purpose was to create a "mutual cooperative investment group." The advantages claimed are those of the service of investment counsel; greater spread of risk; a possibly enhanced income; and relief from the physical care of securities. Three competent trustees are empowered, for suitable compensation, to handle the business. There is obviously a heavy responsibility involved for all of these professional and nonprofessional agencies. For the professional ones there is danger that the trusts themselves will be subordinated to the interest of investment banking houses. I have in mind one such with a capital of five million dollars, representing the worth of securities which will be held for the public who participate. But in this particular trust the entire control rests in the hands of Class B stock holders. This voting management is constituted solely of partners in the banking house. Other details of the technique of this establishment clearly point to the conclusion that this is substantially a device for enabling bankers to borrow money from the public at a low rate of interest, in order to finance their syndicate underwriting operations in other directions. One must expect that such abnormalities will develop out of this movement. To keep the situation wholesome, there should be a rigid separation of these investment trusts from the business of promotion or of the marketing of securities. The lack of such separation is a very real danger. The possible menace to the purely cooperative mutual plan, as exemplified at Columbia, is of professional incompetence. The same possible defect attaches to another proposal of "The Inquiry": "the constitution of a so-called 'Christian bloc" – a permanent committee to scrutinize investments from the ethical point of view and to arrange proxies for members when any consider able number are interested in the same concern, wherever, in fact, anything other than a merely passive participation in management seems desirable. Doubtless a way will be found by which professional skill may be so combined with proper safeguards against abuse of the delegated power. Under such circumstances a really helpful and cooperative contribution might be anticipated on behalf of the real owners.

This present tendency to strip the public shareholders of their voting rights may be checked, either through re vision of our corporation laws, or by a vigorous attitude on the part of the courts. Direct action by the investing class, by boycotting all such offerings of securities, may give even more immediate results. But, in either or any event, no other safeguard against misuse of power by insiders is so likely to be effective as publicity.[5] Nothing kills bacteria like sunlight. A frank sharing of all proper information with the main body of the shareholders is basically right. It is also in the long run a matter of good business. It is absurd that, as has so frequently happened of late, corporate results of operation should be given to the real owners, not every month, not even twice a year, but only superficially in an abbreviated annual report. The stockholders are entitled to know the amount of gross business, the cost of conducting it, and especially the policy as respects depreciation and upkeep in full detail, in order that they may benefit by the intelligent judgment which competent experts will then speedily pass upon the real status as to net earnings. The United States Steel Corporation and the American Telephone Company are forthstanding examples of the

[5] Chapters VI and VII, *infra,* develop this in full detail.

value of such frank publicity, as a recommendation to the world at large of an investment; and any corporation which pursues the opposite course thereby invites and deserves distrust and suspicion. Yet it is unfortunately true that the policy of some of the chartermongering states – Delaware, West Virginia, and the rest – has been to discourage rather than to develop such full disclosure of the state of affairs. For private corporations, the present situation as concerns stockholders' rights to information is most unsatisfactory.

Our experience with railroads is significant in this connection. They still deserve and require a greater measure of liberality in the matter of rates than has yet been granted by the Interstate Commerce Commission. But, this step once taken, they will be at last well on the road to a safe and stabilized investment for the great body of the people. It is clear already that the best of them are slowly assuming their rightful place in this regard, forging steadily ahead through the turbulence of speculation in so many other forms of enterprise. For speculation germinates in and thrives upon mystery. It is indubitable that this stabilization, even though it is yet on a sub-normal plane, is largely the result of the complete publicity and standardization of railway accounts under federal supervision. Several million investors may well be content to leave the management of their railroad possessions in the hands of others, knowing that, quite apart from the regulation of rates, this standardized publicity permits a scientific check, month by month, upon policy and results. How different is this from the manner in which even some of our nation-wide private industrial corporations do business all over the United States, cloaked and hooded like the despicable Ku Klux Klan. The clause of the Roosevelt New York Companies Act of 1900 which, as a penalty for failure to render detailed and current reports of operation, proposed to disqualify directors, making them ineligible for election for the period of a year, may be impracticable. Yet there may be the germ of an idea in the suggestion.

A brief address upon this subject recently, before the American Academy of Political Science, seems to have hit the crazy bone of a certain type of self-appointed spokesman of the quasi-public companies. The mere suggestion of governmental supervision, as applicable to them, in lieu of the vanishing rights of stockholders, was characterized – rather breathlessly, it seemed to me – as an attack upon "all American business as honeycombed with dishonesty and greed; and all executive management as fraught with irresponsibility, indifference, and worse ... using the traditions of a great institution of learning to spread an exaggerated impression of American business – the kind of propaganda on which demagoguery and communism feed." Their soothing allegation that a beneficent economic revolution is occurring by reason of the widespread diffusion of corporate ownership is said to be "berated and rejected with a violence of invective and an indiscriminateness in denunciation that would make a Socialist orator blush for shame."[6] Fortunately I am privileged to introduce a witness in my own defense. The Committee on Public Securities of the Investment Bankers Association of America reported in 1923 as follows: "When administered with the broadest power, and in a judicial manner, state-wide regulation of public utilities has been conclusively proved, in the opinion of your committee, to afford the best guaranties which investors can have in this country for a maintenance of that integrity of investment *necessary for a ready flow of money into the business.*" [Our italics present the concern of all the people – owners and consumers alike – in the matter.] For further discussion on the point, we may refer our critics to this distinguished body.

What, then, is the present status of governmental supervision over public utility companies – other than railroads, telephones, and telegraphs – in the United States? The fact is that nearly all the commonwealths have regulatory bodies, most of them, however, having jurisdiction only over such matters as rates for water, gas, and electric light and power. The present situation, therefore, as respects these *operating* companies is quite reassuring. What concerns the future are the hierarchies of holding companies, superposed one upon another – the piling of Pelion upon Ossa to the seventh heaven. This is provocative of grave concern, for it is in the heights that the real sources of power find place. The experience of the little Boothbay Harbor company is entirely typical. But, to nail the conclusion, take the Pine Bluff, Arkansas, local operating concern. This is controlled by the Arkansas Light and Power Company, which is a part of

[6] The speaker is Henry M. Brundage, first vice-president of the Empire State Gas and Electric Association and vice-president of the Consolidated Gas Company of New York.

the Southern Light and Power Company of Delaware, also controlling the Mississippi Power and Light Company, the Louisiana Power Company, and the Louisiana Power and Light Company. And the whole congeries of them has been in turn acquired by the Southern Power and Light Company, this time incorporated in Maryland, which seems to be a part of the Electric Bond and Share Company of New York. Being the proud and happy possessor of some shares in this last-named corporation, I am thrilled with the sense of immediate participation in the local concerns of Pine Bluff, Arkansas! But that question has already been discussed from the point of view of the private owner. As concerns the public, it is self-evident that something besides superpower of electrical energy is entailed – and that is the growth of interstate corporations which are superpower systems of a different order. And for dealing with them we, as a people, have no machinery whatsoever.

Thus we are brought squarely to the perennial issue of federal versus state authority. Whatever is to be done about the affairs, either of private corporations dealing in the necessaries of life in more than any one state in the Union, or with, let us say, the Associated Gas and Electric Company, which supplies "electricity and/or gas and/or water, to over 300,000 consumers, serving a total population estimated at approximately 2,000,000 in more than 900 communities in New York, Pennsylvania, Maryland, Massachusetts, Connecticut, Vermont, New Hampshire, Maine, Kentucky, Tennessee, and the city of Manila," must evidently be done on a larger basis than a single commonwealth affords. (In passing we may note that this Associated Gas and Electric Company has $36,600,000 in bonds and almost 500,000 nonvoting shares outstanding with the public. Control is apparently vested in 300,000 Class B shares, no par value.) An experiment is just now being forced upon the three states of Pennsylvania, New Jersey, and New York, concerning the creation of a joint giant power commission, by the growth of these great industrial units. Necessary they probably are! Sound, for aught that I know to the contrary, they are! But when one of them sprawls over the map from Aroostook County, Maine, to the Philippine Islands, it is time to think what it means. And the contention that such concerns are already thoroughly controlled or supervised in the public interest, because forsooth each of their local operating companies is subject to existing state laws, would seem to be rather effectually disposed of. This is one of those rare cases where two and two do not make four, but something well over a dozen. It is inconceivable that joint giant power commissions should be set up by different groups of states, each group corresponding to the especial scope and extent of the particular corporation which it is intended to supervise. The answer, alas, seems to be always the same. If anything indeed needs doing, there is but one agency to which to turn – the exercise of the federal power.

There are already at Washington three agencies which may conceivably become involved in these matters under discussion. But the simple, the logical, the inescapable conclusion is that superstate public utility companies should be placed under the jurisdiction, either of the Interstate Commerce Commission, as the telephone and telegraph companies along with the railroads now stand, or else under an amplified power commission, similar to the one in the Department of the Interior which at present concerns itself with the licensing of water-power companies. Whether their rates need to be, or practically can be, thus regulated is another matter. But that their accounts ought to be formally standardized and made a matter of current public record is beyond all possible question.

What, then, about the private corporations, when direct responsibility for their management by the shareholders seems to be by way of evanescence? Whether this tendency be arrested or not, a greatly increased measure of publicity ought by all possible means to be stimulated. Standardized accounting for all private forms of business, already so successful in the case of railroads, telephones, and telegraphs, is probably hopeless of expectation. The variety of circumstance and the multifarious exigencies of each and every kind of business would present to any administrative agency a task transcending human power. And yet certain norms might well be set up by some such body as the Federal Trade Commission. To take a pressing instance: the present impasse, so far as bringing intelligent public opinion to bear upon the anthracite coal strike, might never occur again, were the recommendations of the Federal Coal Commission of 1922 respecting standardization of coal-mine accounts actually in force. The policy of what has been aptly termed "induced cost accounting" might well be elected as part of a general campaign of education by some federal body. Let us hope it will not be one possessed, as the present Federal Trade Commission seems to be, with a sole and apparently overwhelming disposition to commit hara-kiri!

A mighty and preeminently important duty is imposed upon the Federal Government by the general conditions respecting corporations which thus seem to be headed toward a climax. Whether the means for a restoration of responsibility shall be suggestively educational or strictly regulatory must depend upon circumstances. Perhaps we should revive the question of federal incorporation, so ably advocated by President Taft in his special message of 1911. This, or a federal license system whereby permission to engage in interstate commerce entails compliance with certain standards as to corporate structure and publicity, deserves attentive consideration. The report of the committee of the British Ministry of Reconstruction of 1911,[7] dealing more specifically with trade associations than with corporations, was a response to somewhat the same great need which is making itself felt at this time in the United States.

I would not conclude with the advocacy of any particular plan. The first duty is to face the fact that there is something the matter. For a remedy I am groping as yet, like a child in the dark. I am conscious that things are not right. The house is not falling down – no fear of that! But there are queer little noises about, as of rats in the wall, or of borers in the timbers. I believe that the trouble has to do with the growing dissociation of owner ship of property from responsibility for the manner In which it shall be put to use. And now is the time for action. It is not yet too late. Millions of our citizens made this first essay in thrift as a result of the great Liberty Loan campaigns during the war. It has been estimated that of the 14,400,000 stockholders in the United States no fewer than 3,400,000 were added within the three years following 1917. This betokens a great incursion into the field of investment by the common people – corporate possession being shared by those of moderate and small means with the wealthy class. The movement has been called "an economic revolution" –"the passing of ownership from Wall Street to Main Street." What would be the effect were these newcomers – consumers, employees, or others – to discover some day that

[7] This standard British Blue Book can be obtained through the British Library of Information, Whitehall Street, New York City.

ownership and control had parted company, each going its way as ships that pass in the night? Suppose that the ownership of many industrial plants, great and small, continues to reside all through the countryside, but that the lodgment of the power of direction has shifted to the great financial centres. We have had experience, to our sorrow, with the old sectional divisions between the East and the West. Is there no smouldering spark in this matter of corporate control, which may some day flare up as a political issue of the first order? I do not look to Sentinels of the Republic or to anti-syndicalist laws for the ultimate safeguarding of our institutions. Our security, in the last instance, must rest upon the ever-wider prevalence of what Lord Bacon held to be "clear and round dealing among men!" With that assured, we may quite confidently leave all the rest to take care of itself.